Oxford Dictionary of National Biography

Volume 60

Oxford Dictionary of National Biography

IN ASSOCIATION WITH
The British Academy

From the earliest times to the year 2000

Edited by
H. C. G. Matthew
and
Brian Harrison

Volume 60
Wolmark–Zuylestein

OXFORD
UNIVERSITY PRESS

OXFORD

UNIVERSITY PRESS

Great Clarendon Street, Oxford OX2 6DP

Oxford University Press is a department of the University of Oxford.
It furthers the University's objective of excellence in research, scholarship,
and education by publishing worldwide in

Oxford New York

Auckland Bangkok Buenos Aires Cape Town
Chennai Dar es Salaam Delhi Hong Kong Istanbul Karachi
Kolkata Kuala Lumpur Madrid Melbourne Mexico City Mumbai Nairobi
São Paulo Shanghai Taipei Tokyo Toronto

Oxford is a registered trade mark of Oxford University Press
in the UK and in certain other countries

Published in the United States
by Oxford University Press Inc., New York

© Oxford University Press 2004

Illustrations © individual copyright holders as listed in
'Picture credits', and reproduced with permission

Database right Oxford University Press (maker)

First published 2004

British Library Cataloguing in Publication Data
Data available

Library of Congress Cataloging in Publication Data
Data available: for details see volume 1, p. iv

ISBN 0-19-861410-1 (this volume)
ISBN 0-19-861411-X (set of sixty volumes)

Text captured by Alliance Phototypesetters, Pondicherry
Illustrations reproduced and archived by
Alliance Graphics Ltd, UK
Typeset in OUP Swift by Interactive Sciences Limited, Gloucester
Printed in Great Britain on acid-free paper by
Butler and Tanner Ltd,
Frome, Somerset

LIST OF ABBREVIATIONS

1 *General abbreviations*

AB	bachelor of arts
ABC	Australian Broadcasting Corporation
ABC TV	ABC Television
act.	active
A$	Australian dollar
AD	*anno domini*
AFC	Air Force Cross
AIDS	acquired immune deficiency syndrome
AK	Alaska
AL	Alabama
A level	advanced level [examination]
ALS	associate of the Linnean Society
AM	master of arts
AMICE	associate member of the Institution of Civil Engineers
ANZAC	Australian and New Zealand Army Corps
appx *pl.* appxs	appendix(es)
AR	Arkansas
ARA	associate of the Royal Academy
ARCA	associate of the Royal College of Art
ARCM	associate of the Royal College of Music
ARCO	associate of the Royal College of Organists
ARIBA	associate of the Royal Institute of British Architects
ARP	air-raid precautions
ARRC	associate of the Royal Red Cross
ARSA	associate of the Royal Scottish Academy
art.	article / item
ASC	Army Service Corps
Asch	Austrian Schilling
ASDIC	Antisubmarine Detection Investigation Committee
ATS	Auxiliary Territorial Service
ATV	Associated Television
Aug	August
AZ	Arizona
b.	born
BA	bachelor of arts
BA (Admin.)	bachelor of arts (administration)
BAFTA	British Academy of Film and Television Arts
BAO	bachelor of arts in obstetrics
bap.	baptized
BBC	British Broadcasting Corporation / Company
BC	before Christ
BCE	before the common (*or* Christian) era
BCE	bachelor of civil engineering
BCG	bacillus of Calmette and Guérin [inoculation against tuberculosis]
BCh	bachelor of surgery
BChir	bachelor of surgery
BCL	bachelor of civil law
BCnL	bachelor of canon law
BCom	bachelor of commerce
BD	bachelor of divinity
BEd	bachelor of education
BEng	bachelor of engineering
bk *pl.* bks	book(s)
BL	bachelor of law / letters / literature
BLitt	bachelor of letters
BM	bachelor of medicine
BMus	bachelor of music
BP	before present
BP	British Petroleum
Bros.	Brothers
BS	(1) bachelor of science; (2) bachelor of surgery; (3) British standard
BSc	bachelor of science
BSc (Econ.)	bachelor of science (economics)
BSc (Eng.)	bachelor of science (engineering)
bt	baronet
BTh	bachelor of theology
bur.	buried
C.	command [identifier for published parliamentary papers]
c.	*circa*
c.	*capitulum pl. capitula*: chapter(s)
CA	California
Cantab.	Cantabrigiensis
cap.	*capitulum pl. capitula*: chapter(s)
CB	companion of the Bath
CBE	commander of the Order of the British Empire
CBS	Columbia Broadcasting System
cc	cubic centimetres
C$	Canadian dollar
CD	compact disc
Cd	command [identifier for published parliamentary papers]
CE	Common (*or* Christian) Era
cent.	century
cf.	compare
CH	Companion of Honour
chap.	chapter
ChB	bachelor of surgery
CI	Imperial Order of the Crown of India
CIA	Central Intelligence Agency
CID	Criminal Investigation Department
CIE	companion of the Order of the Indian Empire
Cie	Compagnie
CLit	companion of literature
CM	master of surgery
cm	centimetre(s)

Cmd	command [identifier for published parliamentary papers]
CMG	companion of the Order of St Michael and St George
Cmnd	command [identifier for published parliamentary papers]
CO	Colorado
Co.	company
co.	county
col. *pl.* cols.	column(s)
Corp.	corporation
CSE	certificate of secondary education
CSI	companion of the Order of the Star of India
CT	Connecticut
CVO	commander of the Royal Victorian Order
cwt	hundredweight
$	(American) dollar
d.	(1) penny (pence); (2) died
DBE	dame commander of the Order of the British Empire
DCH	diploma in child health
DCh	doctor of surgery
DCL	doctor of civil law
DCnL	doctor of canon law
DCVO	dame commander of the Royal Victorian Order
DD	doctor of divinity
DE	Delaware
Dec	December
dem.	demolished
DEng	doctor of engineering
des.	destroyed
DFC	Distinguished Flying Cross
DipEd	diploma in education
DipPsych	diploma in psychiatry
diss.	dissertation
DL	deputy lieutenant
DLitt	doctor of letters
DLittCelt	doctor of Celtic letters
DM	(1) Deutschmark; (2) doctor of medicine; (3) doctor of musical arts
DMus	doctor of music
DNA	dioxyribonucleic acid
doc.	document
DOL	doctor of oriental learning
DPH	diploma in public health
DPhil	doctor of philosophy
DPM	diploma in psychological medicine
DSC	Distinguished Service Cross
DSc	doctor of science
DSc (Econ.)	doctor of science (economics)
DSc (Eng.)	doctor of science (engineering)
DSM	Distinguished Service Medal
DSO	companion of the Distinguished Service Order
DSocSc	doctor of social science
DTech	doctor of technology
DTh	doctor of theology
DTM	diploma in tropical medicine
DTMH	diploma in tropical medicine and hygiene
DU	doctor of the university
DUniv	doctor of the university
dwt	pennyweight
EC	European Community
ed. *pl.* eds.	edited / edited by / editor(s)
Edin.	Edinburgh
edn	edition
EEC	European Economic Community
EFTA	European Free Trade Association
EICS	East India Company Service
EMI	Electrical and Musical Industries (Ltd)
Eng.	English
enl.	enlarged
ENSA	Entertainments National Service Association
ep. *pl.* epp.	*epistola(e)*
ESP	extra-sensory perception
esp.	especially
esq.	esquire
est.	estimate / estimated
EU	European Union
ex	sold by (*lit.* out of)
excl.	excludes / excluding
exh.	exhibited
exh. cat.	exhibition catalogue
f. *pl.* ff.	following [pages]
FA	Football Association
FACP	fellow of the American College of Physicians
facs.	facsimile
FANY	First Aid Nursing Yeomanry
FBA	fellow of the British Academy
FBI	Federation of British Industries
FCS	fellow of the Chemical Society
Feb	February
FEng	fellow of the Fellowship of Engineering
FFCM	fellow of the Faculty of Community Medicine
FGS	fellow of the Geological Society
fig.	figure
FIMechE	fellow of the Institution of Mechanical Engineers
FL	Florida
fl.	*floruit*
FLS	fellow of the Linnean Society
FM	frequency modulation
fol. *pl.* fols.	folio(s)
Fr	French francs
Fr.	French
FRAeS	fellow of the Royal Aeronautical Society
FRAI	fellow of the Royal Anthropological Institute
FRAM	fellow of the Royal Academy of Music
FRAS	(1) fellow of the Royal Asiatic Society; (2) fellow of the Royal Astronomical Society
FRCM	fellow of the Royal College of Music
FRCO	fellow of the Royal College of Organists
FRCOG	fellow of the Royal College of Obstetricians and Gynaecologists
FRCP(C)	fellow of the Royal College of Physicians of Canada
FRCP (Edin.)	fellow of the Royal College of Physicians of Edinburgh
FRCP (Lond.)	fellow of the Royal College of Physicians of London
FRCPath	fellow of the Royal College of Pathologists
FRCPsych	fellow of the Royal College of Psychiatrists
FRCS	fellow of the Royal College of Surgeons
FRGS	fellow of the Royal Geographical Society
FRIBA	fellow of the Royal Institute of British Architects
FRICS	fellow of the Royal Institute of Chartered Surveyors
FRS	fellow of the Royal Society
FRSA	fellow of the Royal Society of Arts

FRSCM	fellow of the Royal School of Church Music		ISO	companion of the Imperial Service Order
FRSE	fellow of the Royal Society of Edinburgh		It.	Italian
FRSL	fellow of the Royal Society of Literature		ITA	Independent Television Authority
FSA	fellow of the Society of Antiquaries		ITV	Independent Television
ft	foot *pl.* feet		Jan	January
FTCL	fellow of Trinity College of Music, London		JP	justice of the peace
ft-lb per min.	foot-pounds per minute [unit of horsepower]		jun.	junior
FZS	fellow of the Zoological Society		KB	knight of the Order of the Bath
GA	Georgia		KBE	knight commander of the Order of the British Empire
GBE	knight or dame grand cross of the Order of the British Empire		KC	king's counsel
GCB	knight grand cross of the Order of the Bath		kcal	kilocalorie
GCE	general certificate of education		KCB	knight commander of the Order of the Bath
GCH	knight grand cross of the Royal Guelphic Order		KCH	knight commander of the Royal Guelphic Order
GCHQ	government communications headquarters		KCIE	knight commander of the Order of the Indian Empire
GCIE	knight grand commander of the Order of the Indian Empire		KCMG	knight commander of the Order of St Michael and St George
GCMG	knight or dame grand cross of the Order of St Michael and St George		KCSI	knight commander of the Order of the Star of India
GCSE	general certificate of secondary education		KCVO	knight commander of the Royal Victorian Order
GCSI	knight grand commander of the Order of the Star of India		keV	kilo-electron-volt
GCStJ	bailiff or dame grand cross of the order of St John of Jerusalem		KG	knight of the Order of the Garter
			KGB	[Soviet committee of state security]
GCVO	knight or dame grand cross of the Royal Victorian Order		KH	knight of the Royal Guelphic Order
GEC	General Electric Company		KLM	Koninklijke Luchtvaart Maatschappij (Royal Dutch Air Lines)
Ger.	German		km	kilometre(s)
GI	government (*or* general) issue		KP	knight of the Order of St Patrick
GMT	Greenwich mean time		KS	Kansas
GP	general practitioner		KT	knight of the Order of the Thistle
GPU	[Soviet special police unit]		kt	knight
GSO	general staff officer		KY	Kentucky
Heb.	Hebrew		£	pound(s) sterling
HEICS	Honourable East India Company Service		£E	Egyptian pound
HI	Hawaii		L	lira *pl.* lire
HIV	human immunodeficiency virus		l. *pl.* ll.	line(s)
HK$	Hong Kong dollar		LA	Lousiana
HM	his / her majesty('s)		LAA	light anti-aircraft
HMAS	his / her majesty's Australian ship		LAH	licentiate of the Apothecaries' Hall, Dublin
HMNZS	his / her majesty's New Zealand ship		Lat.	Latin
HMS	his / her majesty's ship		lb	pound(s), unit of weight
HMSO	His / Her Majesty's Stationery Office		LDS	licence in dental surgery
HMV	His Master's Voice		*lit.*	literally
Hon.	Honourable		LittB	bachelor of letters
hp	horsepower		LittD	doctor of letters
hr	hour(s)		LKQCPI	licentiate of the King and Queen's College of Physicians, Ireland
HRH	his / her royal highness		LLA	lady literate in arts
HTV	Harlech Television		LLB	bachelor of laws
IA	Iowa		LLD	doctor of laws
ibid.	*ibidem*: in the same place		LLM	master of laws
ICI	Imperial Chemical Industries (Ltd)		LM	licentiate in midwifery
ID	Idaho		LP	long-playing record
IL	Illinois		LRAM	licentiate of the Royal Academy of Music
illus.	illustration		LRCP	licentiate of the Royal College of Physicians
illustr.	illustrated		LRCPS (Glasgow)	licentiate of the Royal College of Physicians and Surgeons of Glasgow
IN	Indiana		LRCS	licentiate of the Royal College of Surgeons
in.	inch(es)		LSA	licentiate of the Society of Apothecaries
Inc.	Incorporated		LSD	lysergic acid diethylamide
incl.	includes / including		LVO	lieutenant of the Royal Victorian Order
IOU	I owe you		M. *pl.* MM.	Monsieur *pl.* Messieurs
IQ	intelligence quotient		m	metre(s)
Ir£	Irish pound			
IRA	Irish Republican Army			

m. *pl.* mm.	membrane(s)
MA	(1) Massachusetts; (2) master of arts
MAI	master of engineering
MB	bachelor of medicine
MBA	master of business administration
MBE	member of the Order of the British Empire
MC	Military Cross
MCC	Marylebone Cricket Club
MCh	master of surgery
MChir	master of surgery
MCom	master of commerce
MD	(1) doctor of medicine; (2) Maryland
MDMA	methylenedioxymethamphetamine
ME	Maine
MEd	master of education
MEng	master of engineering
MEP	member of the European parliament
MG	Morris Garages
MGM	Metro-Goldwyn-Mayer
Mgr	Monsignor
MI	(1) Michigan; (2) military intelligence
MI1c	[secret intelligence department]
MI5	[military intelligence department]
MI6	[secret intelligence department]
MI9	[secret escape service]
MICE	member of the Institution of Civil Engineers
MIEE	member of the Institution of Electrical Engineers
min.	minute(s)
Mk	mark
ML	(1) licentiate of medicine; (2) master of laws
MLitt	master of letters
Mlle	Mademoiselle
mm	millimetre(s)
Mme	Madame
MN	Minnesota
MO	Missouri
MOH	medical officer of health
MP	member of parliament
m.p.h.	miles per hour
MPhil	master of philosophy
MRCP	member of the Royal College of Physicians
MRCS	member of the Royal College of Surgeons
MRCVS	member of the Royal College of Veterinary Surgeons
MRIA	member of the Royal Irish Academy
MS	(1) master of science; (2) Mississippi
MS *pl.* MSS	manuscript(s)
MSc	master of science
MSc (Econ.)	master of science (economics)
MT	Montana
MusB	bachelor of music
MusBac	bachelor of music
MusD	doctor of music
MV	motor vessel
MVO	member of the Royal Victorian Order
n. *pl.* nn.	note(s)
NAAFI	Navy, Army, and Air Force Institutes
NASA	National Aeronautics and Space Administration
NATO	North Atlantic Treaty Organization
NBC	National Broadcasting Corporation
NC	North Carolina
NCO	non-commissioned officer
ND	North Dakota
n.d.	no date
NE	Nebraska
nem. con.	*nemine contradicente*: unanimously
new ser.	new series
NH	New Hampshire
NHS	National Health Service
NJ	New Jersey
NKVD	[Soviet people's commissariat for internal affairs]
NM	New Mexico
nm	nanometre(s)
no. *pl.* nos.	number(s)
Nov	November
n.p.	no place [of publication]
NS	new style
NV	Nevada
NY	New York
NZBS	New Zealand Broadcasting Service
OBE	officer of the Order of the British Empire
obit.	obituary
Oct	October
OCTU	officer cadets training unit
OECD	Organization for Economic Co-operation and Development
OEEC	Organization for European Economic Co-operation
OFM	order of Friars Minor [Franciscans]
OFMCap	Ordine Frati Minori Cappucini: member of the Capuchin order
OH	Ohio
OK	Oklahoma
O level	ordinary level [examination]
OM	Order of Merit
OP	order of Preachers [Dominicans]
op. *pl.* opp.	opus *pl.* opera
OPEC	Organization of Petroleum Exporting Countries
OR	Oregon
orig.	original
OS	old style
OSB	Order of St Benedict
OTC	Officers' Training Corps
OWS	Old Watercolour Society
Oxon.	Oxoniensis
p. *pl.* pp.	page(s)
PA	Pennsylvania
p.a.	per annum
para.	paragraph
PAYE	pay as you earn
pbk *pl.* pbks	paperback(s)
per.	[during the] period
PhD	doctor of philosophy
pl.	(1) plate(s); (2) plural
priv. coll.	private collection
pt *pl.* pts	part(s)
pubd	published
PVC	polyvinyl chloride
q. *pl.* qq.	(1) question(s); (2) quire(s)
QC	queen's counsel
R	rand
R.	Rex / Regina
r	recto
r.	reigned / ruled
RA	Royal Academy / Royal Academician

RAC	Royal Automobile Club		Skr	Swedish krona
RAF	Royal Air Force		Span.	Spanish
RAFVR	Royal Air Force Volunteer Reserve		SPCK	Society for Promoting Christian Knowledge
RAM	[member of the] Royal Academy of Music		SS	(1) Santissimi; (2) Schutzstaffel; (3) steam ship
RAMC	Royal Army Medical Corps		STB	bachelor of theology
RCA	Royal College of Art		STD	doctor of theology
RCNC	Royal Corps of Naval Constructors		STM	master of theology
RCOG	Royal College of Obstetricians and Gynaecologists		STP	doctor of theology
RDI	royal designer for industry		*supp.*	supposedly
RE	Royal Engineers		suppl. *pl.* suppls.	supplement(s)
repr. *pl.* reprs.	reprint(s) / reprinted		s.v.	*sub verbo* / *sub voce*: under the word / heading
repro.	reproduced		SY	steam yacht
rev.	revised / revised by / reviser / revision		TA	Territorial Army
Revd	Reverend		TASS	[Soviet news agency]
RHA	Royal Hibernian Academy		TB	tuberculosis (*lit.* tubercle bacillus)
RI	(1) Rhode Island; (2) Royal Institute of Painters in Water-Colours		TD	(1) *teachtaí dála* (member of the Dáil); (2) territorial decoration
RIBA	Royal Institute of British Architects		TN	Tennessee
RIN	Royal Indian Navy		TNT	trinitrotoluene
RM	Reichsmark		trans.	translated / translated by / translation / translator
RMS	Royal Mail steamer		TT	tourist trophy
RN	Royal Navy		TUC	Trades Union Congress
RNA	ribonucleic acid		TX	Texas
RNAS	Royal Naval Air Service		U-boat	*Unterseeboot*: submarine
RNR	Royal Naval Reserve		Ufa	Universum-Film AG
RNVR	Royal Naval Volunteer Reserve		UMIST	University of Manchester Institute of Science and Technology
RO	Record Office		UN	United Nations
r.p.m.	revolutions per minute		UNESCO	United Nations Educational, Scientific, and Cultural Organization
RRS	royal research ship			
Rs	rupees		UNICEF	United Nations International Children's Emergency Fund
RSA	(1) Royal Scottish Academician; (2) Royal Society of Arts			
RSPCA	Royal Society for the Prevention of Cruelty to Animals		unpubd	unpublished
			USS	United States ship
Rt Hon.	Right Honourable		UT	Utah
Rt Revd	Right Reverend		*v*	verso
RUC	Royal Ulster Constabulary		v.	versus
Russ.	Russian		VA	Virginia
RWS	Royal Watercolour Society		VAD	Voluntary Aid Detachment
S4C	Sianel Pedwar Cymru		VC	Victoria Cross
s.	shilling(s)		VE-day	victory in Europe day
s.a.	*sub anno*: under the year		Ven.	Venerable
SABC	South African Broadcasting Corporation		VJ-day	victory over Japan day
SAS	Special Air Service		vol. *pl.* vols.	volume(s)
SC	South Carolina		VT	Vermont
ScD	doctor of science		WA	Washington [state]
S$	Singapore dollar		WAAC	Women's Auxiliary Army Corps
SD	South Dakota		WAAF	Women's Auxiliary Air Force
sec.	second(s)		WEA	Workers' Educational Association
sel.	selected		WHO	World Health Organization
sen.	senior		WI	Wisconsin
Sept	September		WRAF	Women's Royal Air Force
ser.	series		WRNS	Women's Royal Naval Service
SHAPE	supreme headquarters allied powers, Europe		WV	West Virginia
SIDRO	Société Internationale d'Énergie Hydro-Électrique		WVS	Women's Voluntary Service
			WY	Wyoming
sig. *pl.* sigs.	signature(s)		¥	yen
sing.	singular		YMCA	Young Men's Christian Association
SIS	Secret Intelligence Service		YWCA	Young Women's Christian Association
SJ	Society of Jesus			

2 Institution abbreviations

All Souls Oxf.	All Souls College, Oxford	Garr. Club	Garrick Club, London
AM Oxf.	Ashmolean Museum, Oxford	Girton Cam.	Girton College, Cambridge
Balliol Oxf.	Balliol College, Oxford	GL	Guildhall Library, London
BBC WAC	BBC Written Archives Centre, Reading	Glos. RO	Gloucestershire Record Office, Gloucester
Beds. & Luton ARS	Bedfordshire and Luton Archives and Record Service, Bedford	Gon. & Caius Cam.	Gonville and Caius College, Cambridge
		Gov. Art Coll.	Government Art Collection
Berks. RO	Berkshire Record Office, Reading	GS Lond.	Geological Society of London
BFI	British Film Institute, London	Hants. RO	Hampshire Record Office, Winchester
BFI NFTVA	British Film Institute, London, National Film and Television Archive	Harris Man. Oxf.	Harris Manchester College, Oxford
		Harvard TC	Harvard Theatre Collection, Harvard University, Cambridge, Massachusetts, Nathan Marsh Pusey Library
BGS	British Geological Survey, Keyworth, Nottingham		
Birm. CA	Birmingham Central Library, Birmingham City Archives	Harvard U.	Harvard University, Cambridge, Massachusetts
		Harvard U., Houghton L.	Harvard University, Cambridge, Massachusetts, Houghton Library
Birm. CL	Birmingham Central Library		
BL	British Library, London	Herefs. RO	Herefordshire Record Office, Hereford
BL NSA	British Library, London, National Sound Archive	Herts. ALS	Hertfordshire Archives and Local Studies, Hertford
BL OIOC	British Library, London, Oriental and India Office Collections	Hist. Soc. Penn.	Historical Society of Pennsylvania, Philadelphia
BLPES	London School of Economics and Political Science, British Library of Political and Economic Science	HLRO	House of Lords Record Office, London
		Hult. Arch.	Hulton Archive, London and New York
		Hunt. L.	Huntington Library, San Marino, California
BM	British Museum, London	ICL	Imperial College, London
Bodl. Oxf.	Bodleian Library, Oxford	Inst. CE	Institution of Civil Engineers, London
Bodl. RH	Bodleian Library of Commonwealth and African Studies at Rhodes House, Oxford	Inst. EE	Institution of Electrical Engineers, London
		IWM	Imperial War Museum, London
Borth. Inst.	Borthwick Institute of Historical Research, University of York	IWM FVA	Imperial War Museum, London, Film and Video Archive
Boston PL	Boston Public Library, Massachusetts	IWM SA	Imperial War Museum, London, Sound Archive
Bristol RO	Bristol Record Office		
Bucks. RLSS	Buckinghamshire Records and Local Studies Service, Aylesbury	JRL	John Rylands University Library of Manchester
		King's AC Cam.	King's College Archives Centre, Cambridge
CAC Cam.	Churchill College, Cambridge, Churchill Archives Centre	King's Cam.	King's College, Cambridge
		King's Lond.	King's College, London
Cambs. AS	Cambridgeshire Archive Service	King's Lond., Liddell Hart C.	King's College, London, Liddell Hart Centre for Military Archives
CCC Cam.	Corpus Christi College, Cambridge		
CCC Oxf.	Corpus Christi College, Oxford	Lancs. RO	Lancashire Record Office, Preston
Ches. & Chester ALSS	Cheshire and Chester Archives and Local Studies Service	L. Cong.	Library of Congress, Washington, DC
		Leics. RO	Leicestershire, Leicester, and Rutland Record Office, Leicester
Christ Church Oxf.	Christ Church, Oxford		
Christies	Christies, London	Lincs. Arch.	Lincolnshire Archives, Lincoln
City Westm. AC	City of Westminster Archives Centre, London	Linn. Soc.	Linnean Society of London
CKS	Centre for Kentish Studies, Maidstone	LMA	London Metropolitan Archives
CLRO	Corporation of London Records Office	LPL	Lambeth Palace, London
Coll. Arms	College of Arms, London	Lpool RO	Liverpool Record Office and Local Studies Service
Col. U.	Columbia University, New York		
Cornwall RO	Cornwall Record Office, Truro	LUL	London University Library
Courtauld Inst.	Courtauld Institute of Art, London	Magd. Cam.	Magdalene College, Cambridge
CUL	Cambridge University Library	Magd. Oxf.	Magdalen College, Oxford
Cumbria AS	Cumbria Archive Service	Man. City Gall.	Manchester City Galleries
Derbys. RO	Derbyshire Record Office, Matlock	Man. CL	Manchester Central Library
Devon RO	Devon Record Office, Exeter	Mass. Hist. Soc.	Massachusetts Historical Society, Boston
Dorset RO	Dorset Record Office, Dorchester	Merton Oxf.	Merton College, Oxford
Duke U.	Duke University, Durham, North Carolina	MHS Oxf.	Museum of the History of Science, Oxford
Duke U., Perkins L.	Duke University, Durham, North Carolina, William R. Perkins Library	Mitchell L., Glas.	Mitchell Library, Glasgow
		Mitchell L., NSW	State Library of New South Wales, Sydney, Mitchell Library
Durham Cath. CL	Durham Cathedral, chapter library		
Durham RO	Durham Record Office	Morgan L.	Pierpont Morgan Library, New York
DWL	Dr Williams's Library, London	NA Canada	National Archives of Canada, Ottawa
Essex RO	Essex Record Office	NA Ire.	National Archives of Ireland, Dublin
E. Sussex RO	East Sussex Record Office, Lewes	NAM	National Army Museum, London
Eton	Eton College, Berkshire	NA Scot.	National Archives of Scotland, Edinburgh
FM Cam.	Fitzwilliam Museum, Cambridge	News Int. RO	News International Record Office, London
Folger	Folger Shakespeare Library, Washington, DC	NG Ire.	National Gallery of Ireland, Dublin

NG Scot.	National Gallery of Scotland, Edinburgh	Suffolk RO	Suffolk Record Office
NHM	Natural History Museum, London	Surrey HC	Surrey History Centre, Woking
NL Aus.	National Library of Australia, Canberra	TCD	Trinity College, Dublin
NL Ire.	National Library of Ireland, Dublin	Trinity Cam.	Trinity College, Cambridge
NL NZ	National Library of New Zealand, Wellington	U. Aberdeen	University of Aberdeen
NL NZ, Turnbull L.	National Library of New Zealand, Wellington, Alexander Turnbull Library	U. Birm.	University of Birmingham
		U. Birm. L.	University of Birmingham Library
NL Scot.	National Library of Scotland, Edinburgh	U. Cal.	University of California
NL Wales	National Library of Wales, Aberystwyth	U. Cam.	University of Cambridge
NMG Wales	National Museum and Gallery of Wales, Cardiff	UCL	University College, London
NMM	National Maritime Museum, London	U. Durham	University of Durham
Norfolk RO	Norfolk Record Office, Norwich	U. Durham L.	University of Durham Library
Northants. RO	Northamptonshire Record Office, Northampton	U. Edin.	University of Edinburgh
		U. Edin., New Coll.	University of Edinburgh, New College
Northumbd RO	Northumberland Record Office	U. Edin., New Coll. L.	University of Edinburgh, New College Library
Notts. Arch.	Nottinghamshire Archives, Nottingham		
NPG	National Portrait Gallery, London	U. Edin. L.	University of Edinburgh Library
NRA	National Archives, London, Historical Manuscripts Commission, National Register of Archives	U. Glas.	University of Glasgow
		U. Glas. L.	University of Glasgow Library
		U. Hull	University of Hull
Nuffield Oxf.	Nuffield College, Oxford	U. Hull, Brynmor Jones L.	University of Hull, Brynmor Jones Library
N. Yorks. CRO	North Yorkshire County Record Office, Northallerton		
		U. Leeds	University of Leeds
NYPL	New York Public Library	U. Leeds, Brotherton L.	University of Leeds, Brotherton Library
Oxf. UA	Oxford University Archives		
Oxf. U. Mus. NH	Oxford University Museum of Natural History	U. Lond.	University of London
Oxon. RO	Oxfordshire Record Office, Oxford	U. Lpool	University of Liverpool
Pembroke Cam.	Pembroke College, Cambridge	U. Lpool L.	University of Liverpool Library
PRO	National Archives, London, Public Record Office	U. Mich.	University of Michigan, Ann Arbor
		U. Mich., Clements L.	University of Michigan, Ann Arbor, William L. Clements Library
PRO NIre.	Public Record Office for Northern Ireland, Belfast		
		U. Newcastle	University of Newcastle upon Tyne
Pusey Oxf.	Pusey House, Oxford	U. Newcastle, Robinson L.	University of Newcastle upon Tyne, Robinson Library
RA	Royal Academy of Arts, London		
Ransom HRC	Harry Ransom Humanities Research Center, University of Texas, Austin	U. Nott.	University of Nottingham
		U. Nott. L.	University of Nottingham Library
RAS	Royal Astronomical Society, London	U. Oxf.	University of Oxford
RBG Kew	Royal Botanic Gardens, Kew, London	U. Reading	University of Reading
RCP Lond.	Royal College of Physicians of London	U. Reading L.	University of Reading Library
RCS Eng.	Royal College of Surgeons of England, London	U. St Andr.	University of St Andrews
RGS	Royal Geographical Society, London	U. St Andr. L.	University of St Andrews Library
RIBA	Royal Institute of British Architects, London	U. Southampton	University of Southampton
RIBA BAL	Royal Institute of British Architects, London, British Architectural Library	U. Southampton L.	University of Southampton Library
		U. Sussex	University of Sussex, Brighton
Royal Arch.	Royal Archives, Windsor Castle, Berkshire [by gracious permission of her majesty the queen]	U. Texas	University of Texas, Austin
		U. Wales	University of Wales
Royal Irish Acad.	Royal Irish Academy, Dublin	U. Warwick Mod. RC	University of Warwick, Coventry, Modern Records Centre
Royal Scot. Acad.	Royal Scottish Academy, Edinburgh		
RS	Royal Society, London	V&A	Victoria and Albert Museum, London
RSA	Royal Society of Arts, London	V&A NAL	Victoria and Albert Museum, London, National Art Library
RS Friends, Lond.	Religious Society of Friends, London		
St Ant. Oxf.	St Antony's College, Oxford	Warks. CRO	Warwickshire County Record Office, Warwick
St John Cam.	St John's College, Cambridge	Wellcome L.	Wellcome Library for the History and Understanding of Medicine, London
S. Antiquaries, Lond.	Society of Antiquaries of London		
		Westm. DA	Westminster Diocesan Archives, London
Sci. Mus.	Science Museum, London	Wilts. & Swindon RO	Wiltshire and Swindon Record Office, Trowbridge
Scot. NPG	Scottish National Portrait Gallery, Edinburgh		
Scott Polar RI	University of Cambridge, Scott Polar Research Institute	Worcs. RO	Worcestershire Record Office, Worcester
		W. Sussex RO	West Sussex Record Office, Chichester
Sheff. Arch.	Sheffield Archives	W. Yorks. AS	West Yorkshire Archive Service
Shrops. RRC	Shropshire Records and Research Centre, Shrewsbury	Yale U.	Yale University, New Haven, Connecticut
		Yale U., Beinecke L.	Yale University, New Haven, Connecticut, Beinecke Rare Book and Manuscript Library
SOAS	School of Oriental and African Studies, London		
Som. ARS	Somerset Archive and Record Service, Taunton	Yale U. CBA	Yale University, New Haven, Connecticut, Yale Center for British Art
Staffs. RO	Staffordshire Record Office, Stafford		

3 Bibliographic abbreviations

Adams, *Drama* — W. D. Adams, *A dictionary of the drama*, 1: *A–G* (1904); 2: *H–Z* (1956) [vol. 2 microfilm only]

AFM — J O'Donovan, ed. and trans., *Annala rioghachta Eireann / Annals of the kingdom of Ireland by the four masters*, 7 vols. (1848–51); 2nd edn (1856); 3rd edn (1990)

Allibone, *Dict.* — S. A. Allibone, *A critical dictionary of English literature and British and American authors*, 3 vols. (1859–71); suppl. by J. F. Kirk, 2 vols. (1891)

ANB — J. A. Garraty and M. C. Carnes, eds., *American national biography*, 24 vols. (1999)

Anderson, *Scot. nat.* — W. Anderson, *The Scottish nation, or, The surnames, families, literature, honours, and biographical history of the people of Scotland*, 3 vols. (1859–63)

Ann. mon. — H. R. Luard, ed., *Annales monastici*, 5 vols., Rolls Series, 36 (1864–9)

Ann. Ulster — S. Mac Airt and G. Mac Niocaill, eds., *Annals of Ulster (to AD 1131)* (1983)

APC — *Acts of the privy council of England*, new ser., 46 vols. (1890–1964)

APS — *The acts of the parliaments of Scotland*, 12 vols. in 13 (1814–75)

Arber, *Regs. Stationers* — F. Arber, ed., *A transcript of the registers of the Company of Stationers of London, 1554–1640 AD*, 5 vols. (1875–94)

ArchR — *Architectural Review*

ASC — D. Whitelock, D. C. Douglas, and S. I. Tucker, ed. and trans., *The Anglo-Saxon Chronicle: a revised translation* (1961)

AS chart. — P. H. Sawyer, *Anglo-Saxon charters: an annotated list and bibliography*, Royal Historical Society Guides and Handbooks (1968)

AusDB — D. Pike and others, eds., *Australian dictionary of biography*, 16 vols. (1966–2002)

Baker, *Serjeants* — J. H. Baker, *The order of serjeants at law*, SeldS, suppl. ser., 5 (1984)

Bale, *Cat.* — J. Bale, *Scriptorum illustrium Maioris Brytannie, quam nunc Angliam et Scotiam vocant: catalogus*, 2 vols. in 1 (Basel, 1557–9); facs. edn (1971)

Bale, *Index* — J. Bale, *Index Britanniae scriptorum*, ed. R. L. Poole and M. Bateson (1902); facs. edn (1990)

BBCS — *Bulletin of the Board of Celtic Studies*

BDMBR — J. O. Baylen and N. J. Gossman, eds., *Biographical dictionary of modern British radicals*, 3 vols. in 4 (1979–88)

Bede, *Hist. eccl.* — *Bede's Ecclesiastical history of the English people*, ed. and trans. B. Colgrave and R. A. B. Mynors, OMT (1969); repr. (1991)

Bénézit, *Dict.* — E. Bénézit, *Dictionnaire critique et documentaire des peintres, sculpteurs, dessinateurs et graveurs*, 3 vols. (Paris, 1911–23); new edn, 8 vols. (1948–66), repr. (1966); 3rd edn, rev. and enl., 10 vols. (1976); 4th edn, 14 vols. (1999)

BIHR — *Bulletin of the Institute of Historical Research*

Birch, *Seals* — W. de Birch, *Catalogue of seals in the department of manuscripts in the British Museum*, 6 vols. (1887–1900)

Bishop Burnet's History — *Bishop Burnet's History of his own time*, ed. M. J. Routh, 2nd edn, 6 vols. (1833)

Blackwood — *Blackwood's [Edinburgh] Magazine*, 328 vols. (1817–1980)

Blain, Clements & Grundy, *Feminist comp.* — V. Blain, P. Clements, and I. Grundy, eds., *The feminist companion to literature in English* (1990)

BL cat. — *The British Library general catalogue of printed books* [in 360 vols. with suppls., also CD-ROM and online]

BMJ — *British Medical Journal*

Boase & Courtney, *Bibl. Corn.* — G. C. Boase and W. P. Courtney, *Bibliotheca Cornubiensis: a catalogue of the writings … of Cornishmen*, 3 vols. (1874–82)

Boase, *Mod. Eng. biog.* — F. Boase, *Modern English biography: containing many thousand concise memoirs of persons who have died since the year 1850*, 6 vols. (privately printed, Truro, 1892–1921); repr. (1965)

Boswell, *Life* — *Boswell's Life of Johnson: together with Journal of a tour to the Hebrides and Johnson's Diary of a journey into north Wales*, ed. G. B. Hill, enl. edn, rev. L. F. Powell, 6 vols. (1934–50); 2nd edn (1964); repr. (1971)

Brown & Stratton, *Brit. mus.* — J. D. Brown and S. S. Stratton, *British musical biography* (1897)

Bryan, *Painters* — M. Bryan, *A biographical and critical dictionary of painters and engravers*, 2 vols. (1816); new edn, ed. G. Stanley (1849); new edn, ed. R. E. Graves and W. Armstrong, 2 vols. (1886–9); [4th edn], ed. G. C. Williamson, 5 vols. (1903–5) [various reprs.]

Burke, *Gen. GB* — J. Burke, *A genealogical and heraldic history of the commoners of Great Britain and Ireland*, 4 vols. (1833–8); new edn as *A genealogical and heraldic dictionary of the landed gentry of Great Britain and Ireland*, 3 vols. [1843–9] [many later edns]

Burke, *Gen. Ire.* — J. B. Burke, *A genealogical and heraldic history of the landed gentry of Ireland* (1899); 2nd edn (1904); 3rd edn (1912); 4th edn (1958); 5th edn as *Burke's Irish family records* (1976)

Burke, *Peerage* — J. Burke, *A general* [later edns *A genealogical*] *and heraldic dictionary of the peerage and baronetage of the United Kingdom* [later edns *the British empire*] (1829–)

Burney, *Hist. mus.* — C. Burney, *A general history of music, from the earliest ages to the present period*, 4 vols. (1776–89)

Burtchaell & Sadleir, *Alum. Dubl.* — G. D. Burtchaell and T. U. Sadleir, *Alumni Dublinenses: a register of the students, graduates, and provosts of Trinity College* (1924); [2nd edn], with suppl., in 2 pts (1935)

Calamy rev. — A. G. Matthews, *Calamy revised* (1934); repr. (1988)

CCI — *Calendar of confirmations and inventories granted and given up in the several commissariots of Scotland* (1876–)

CClR — *Calendar of the close rolls preserved in the Public Record Office*, 47 vols. (1892–1963)

CDS — J. Bain, ed., *Calendar of documents relating to Scotland*, 4 vols., PRO (1881–8); suppl. vol. 5, ed. G. G. Simpson and J. D. Galbraith [1986]

CEPR letters — W. H. Bliss, C. Johnson, and J. Twemlow, eds., *Calendar of entries in the papal registers relating to Great Britain and Ireland: papal letters* (1893–)

CGPLA — *Calendars of the grants of probate and letters of administration* [in 4 ser.: *England & Wales, Northern Ireland, Ireland*, and *Éire*]

Chambers, *Scots.* — R. Chambers, ed., *A biographical dictionary of eminent Scotsmen*, 4 vols. (1832–5)

Chancery records — chancery records pubd by the PRO

Chancery records (RC) — chancery records pubd by the Record Commissions

CIPM — *Calendar of inquisitions post mortem*, [20 vols.], PRO (1904–); also *Henry VII*, 3 vols. (1898–1955)

Clarendon, *Hist. rebellion* — E. Hyde, earl of Clarendon, *The history of the rebellion and civil wars in England*, 6 vols. (1888); repr. (1958) and (1992)

Cobbett, *Parl. hist.* — W. Cobbett and J. Wright, eds., *Cobbett's Parliamentary history of England*, 36 vols. (1806–1820)

Colvin, *Archs.* — H. Colvin, *A biographical dictionary of British architects, 1600–1840*, 3rd edn (1995)

Cooper, *Ath. Cantab.* — C. H. Cooper and T. Cooper, *Athenae Cantabrigienses*, 3 vols. (1858–1913); repr. (1967)

CPR — *Calendar of the patent rolls preserved in the Public Record Office* (1891–)

Crockford — *Crockford's Clerical Directory*

CS — Camden Society

CSP — *Calendar of state papers* [in 11 ser.: domestic, Scotland, Scottish series, Ireland, colonial, Commonwealth, foreign, Spain [at Simancas], Rome, Milan, and Venice]

CYS — Canterbury and York Society

DAB — *Dictionary of American biography*, 21 vols. (1928–36), repr. in 11 vols. (1964); 10 suppls. (1944–96)

DBB — D. J. Jeremy, ed., *Dictionary of business biography*, 5 vols. (1984–6)

DCB — G. W. Brown and others, *Dictionary of Canadian biography*, [14 vols.] (1966–)

Debrett's Peerage — *Debrett's Peerage* (1803–) [sometimes *Debrett's Illustrated peerage*]

Desmond, *Botanists* — R. Desmond, *Dictionary of British and Irish botanists and horticulturists* (1977); rev. edn (1994)

Dir. Brit. archs. — A. Felstead, J. Franklin, and L. Pinfield, eds., *Directory of British architects, 1834–1900* (1993); 2nd edn, ed. A. Brodie and others, 2 vols. (2001)

DLB — J. M. Bellamy and J. Saville, eds., *Dictionary of labour biography*, [10 vols.] (1972–)

DLitB — Dictionary of Literary Biography

DNB — *Dictionary of national biography*, 63 vols. (1885–1900), suppl., 3 vols. (1901); repr. in 22 vols. (1908–9); 10 further suppls. (1912–96); *Missing persons* (1993)

DNZB — W. H. Oliver and C. Orange, eds., *The dictionary of New Zealand biography*, 5 vols. (1990–2000)

DSAB — W. J. de Kock and others, eds., *Dictionary of South African biography*, 5 vols. (1968–87)

DSB — C. C. Gillispie and F. L. Holmes, eds., *Dictionary of scientific biography*, 16 vols. (1970–80); repr. in 8 vols. (1981); 2 vol. suppl. (1990)

DSBB — A. Slaven and S. Checkland, eds., *Dictionary of Scottish business biography, 1860–1960*, 2 vols. (1986–90)

DSCHT — N. M. de S. Cameron and others, eds., *Dictionary of Scottish church history and theology* (1993)

Dugdale, *Monasticon* — W. Dugdale, *Monasticon Anglicanum*, 3 vols. (1655–72); 2nd edn, 3 vols. (1661–82); new edn, ed. J. Caley, J. Ellis, and B. Bandinel, 6 vols. in 8 pts (1817–30); repr. (1846) and (1970)

DWB — J. E. Lloyd and others, eds., *Dictionary of Welsh biography down to 1940* (1959) [Eng. trans. of *Y bywgraffiadur Cymreig hyd 1940*, 2nd edn (1954)]

EdinR — *Edinburgh Review, or, Critical Journal*

EETS — Early English Text Society

Emden, *Cam.* — A. B. Emden, *A biographical register of the University of Cambridge to 1500* (1963)

Emden, *Oxf.* — A. B. Emden, *A biographical register of the University of Oxford to AD 1500*, 3 vols. (1957–9); also *A biographical register of the University of Oxford, AD 1501 to 1540* (1974)

EngHR — *English Historical Review*

Engraved Brit. ports. — F. M. O'Donoghue and H. M. Hake, *Catalogue of engraved British portraits preserved in the department of prints and drawings in the British Museum*, 6 vols. (1908–25)

ER — The English Reports, 178 vols. (1900–32)

ESTC — *English short title catalogue, 1475–1800* [CD-ROM and online]

Evelyn, *Diary* — *The diary of John Evelyn*, ed. E. S. De Beer, 6 vols. (1955); repr. (2000)

Farington, *Diary* — *The diary of Joseph Farington*, ed. K. Garlick and others, 17 vols. (1978–98)

Fasti Angl. (Hardy) — J. Le Neve, *Fasti ecclesiae Anglicanae*, ed. T. D. Hardy, 3 vols. (1854)

Fasti Angl., 1066–1300 — [J. Le Neve], *Fasti ecclesiae Anglicanae, 1066–1300*, ed. D. E. Greenway and J. S. Barrow, [8 vols.] (1968–)

Fasti Angl., 1300–1541 — [J. Le Neve], *Fasti ecclesiae Anglicanae, 1300–1541*, 12 vols. (1962–7)

Fasti Angl., 1541–1857 — [J. Le Neve], *Fasti ecclesiae Anglicanae, 1541–1857*, ed. J. M. Horn, D. M. Smith, and D. S. Bailey, [9 vols.] (1969–)

Fasti Scot. — H. Scott, *Fasti ecclesiae Scoticanae*, 3 vols. in 6 (1871); new edn, [11 vols.] (1915–)

FO List — *Foreign Office List*

Fortescue, *Brit. army* — J. W. Fortescue, *A history of the British army*, 13 vols. (1899–1930)

Foss, *Judges* — E. Foss, *The judges of England*, 9 vols. (1848–64); repr. (1966)

Foster, *Alum. Oxon.* — J. Foster, ed., *Alumni Oxonienses: the members of the University of Oxford, 1715–1886*, 4 vols. (1887–8); later edn (1891); also *Alumni Oxonienses … 1500–1714*, 4 vols. (1891–2); 8 vol. repr. (1968) and (2000)

Fuller, *Worthies* — T. Fuller, *The history of the worthies of England*, 4 pts (1662); new edn, 2 vols., ed. J. Nichols (1811); new edn, 3 vols., ed. P. A. Nuttall (1840); repr. (1965)

GEC, *Baronetage* — G. E. Cokayne, *Complete baronetage*, 6 vols. (1900–09); repr. (1983) [microprint]

GEC, *Peerage* — G. E. C. [G. E. Cokayne], *The complete peerage of England, Scotland, Ireland, Great Britain, and the United Kingdom*, 8 vols. (1887–98); new edn, ed. V. Gibbs and others, 14 vols. in 15 (1910–98); microprint repr. (1982) and (1987)

Genest, *Eng. stage* — J. Genest, *Some account of the English stage from the Restoration in 1660 to 1830*, 10 vols. (1832); repr. [New York, 1965]

Gillow, *Lit. biog. hist.* — J. Gillow, *A literary and biographical history or bibliographical dictionary of the English Catholics, from the breach with Rome, in 1534, to the present time*, 5 vols. [1885–1902]; repr. (1961); repr. with preface by C. Gillow (1999)

Gir. Camb. opera — *Giraldi Cambrensis opera*, ed. J. S. Brewer, J. F. Dimock, and G. F. Warner, 8 vols., Rolls Series, 21 (1861–91)

GJ — *Geographical Journal*

Gladstone, *Diaries* — *The Gladstone diaries: with cabinet minutes and prime-ministerial correspondence*, ed. M. R. D. Foot and H. C. G. Matthew, 14 vols. (1968–94)

GM — *Gentleman's Magazine*

Graves, *Artists* — A. Graves, ed., *A dictionary of artists who have exhibited works in the principal London exhibitions of oil paintings from 1760 to 1880* (1884); new edn (1895); 3rd edn (1901); facs. edn (1969); repr. [1970], (1973), and (1984)

Graves, *Brit. Inst.* — A. Graves, *The British Institution, 1806–1867: a complete dictionary of contributors and their work from the foundation of the institution* (1875); facs. edn (1908); repr. (1969)

Graves, *RA exhibitors* — A. Graves, *The Royal Academy of Arts: a complete dictionary of contributors and their work from its foundation in 1769 to 1904*, 8 vols. (1905–6); repr. in 4 vols. (1970) and (1972)

Graves, *Soc. Artists* — A. Graves, *The Society of Artists of Great Britain, 1760–1791, the Free Society of Artists, 1761–1783: a complete dictionary* (1907); facs. edn (1969)

Greaves & Zaller, *BDBR* — R. L. Greaves and R. Zaller, eds., *Biographical dictionary of British radicals in the seventeenth century*, 3 vols. (1982–4)

Grove, *Dict. mus.* — G. Grove, ed., *A dictionary of music and musicians*, 5 vols. (1878–90); 2nd edn, ed. J. A. Fuller Maitland (1904–10); 3rd edn, ed. H. C. Colles (1927); 4th edn with suppl. (1940); 5th edn, ed. E. Blom, 9 vols. (1954); suppl. (1961) [see also *New Grove*]

Hall, *Dramatic ports.* — L. A. Hall, *Catalogue of dramatic portraits in the theatre collection of the Harvard College library*, 4 vols. (1930–34)

Hansard — *Hansard's parliamentary debates*, ser. 1–5 (1803–)

Highfill, Burnim & Langhans, *BDA* — P. H. Highfill, K. A. Burnim, and E. A. Langhans, *A biographical dictionary of actors, actresses, musicians, dancers, managers, and other stage personnel in London, 1660–1800*, 16 vols. (1973–93)

Hist. U. Oxf. — T. H. Aston, ed., *The history of the University of Oxford*, 8 vols. (1984–2000) [1: *The early Oxford schools*, ed. J. I. Catto (1984); 2: *Late medieval Oxford*, ed. J. I. Catto and R. Evans (1992); 3: *The collegiate university*, ed. J. McConica (1986); 4: *Seventeenth-century Oxford*, ed. N. Tyacke (1997); 5: *The eighteenth century*, ed. L. S. Sutherland and L. G. Mitchell (1986); 6–7: *Nineteenth-century Oxford*, ed. M. G. Brock and M. C. Curthoys (1997–2000); 8: *The twentieth century*, ed. B. Harrison (2000)]

HJ — *Historical Journal*

HMC — Historical Manuscripts Commission

Holdsworth, *Eng. law* — W. S. Holdsworth, *A history of English law*, ed. A. L. Goodhart and H. L. Hanbury, 17 vols. (1903–72)

HoP, Commons — *The history of parliament: the House of Commons* [1386–1421, ed. J. S. Roskell, L. Clark, and C. Rawcliffe, 4 vols. (1992); 1509–1558, ed. S. T. Bindoff, 3 vols. (1982); 1558–1603, ed. P. W. Hasler, 3 vols. (1981); 1660–1690, ed. B. D. Henning, 3 vols. (1983); 1690–1715, ed. D. W. Hayton, E. Cruickshanks, and S. Handley, 5 vols. (2002); 1715–1754, ed. R. Sedgwick, 2 vols. (1970); 1754–1790, ed. L. Namier and J. Brooke, 3 vols. (1964), repr. (1985); 1790–1820, ed. R. G. Thorne, 5 vols. (1986); in draft (used with permission): 1422–1504, 1604–1629, 1640–1660, and 1820–1832]

IGI — *International Genealogical Index*, Church of Jesus Christ of the Latterday Saints

ILN — *Illustrated London News*

IMC — Irish Manuscripts Commission

Irving, *Scots.* — J. Irving, ed., *The book of Scotsmen eminent for achievements in arms and arts, church and state, law, legislation and literature, commerce, science, travel and philanthropy* (1881)

JCS — *Journal of the Chemical Society*

JHC — *Journals of the House of Commons*

JHL — *Journals of the House of Lords*

John of Worcester, *Chron.* — *The chronicle of John of Worcester*, ed. R. R. Darlington and P. McGurk, trans. J. Bray and P. McGurk, 3 vols., OMT (1995–) [vol. 1 forthcoming]

Keeler, *Long Parliament* — M. F. Keeler, *The Long Parliament, 1640–1641: a biographical study of its members* (1954)

Kelly, *Handbk* — *The upper ten thousand: an alphabetical list of all members of noble families*, 3 vols. (1875–7); continued as *Kelly's handbook of the upper ten thousand for 1878* [1879], 2 vols. (1878–9); continued as *Kelly's handbook to the titled, landed and official classes*, 94 vols. (1880–1973)

LondG — *London Gazette*

LP Henry VIII — J. S. Brewer, J. Gairdner, and R. H. Brodie, eds., *Letters and papers, foreign and domestic, of the reign of Henry VIII*, 23 vols. in 38 (1862–1932); repr. (1965)

Mallalieu, *Watercolour artists* — H. L. Mallalieu, *The dictionary of British watercolour artists up to 1820*, 3 vols. (1976–90); vol. 1, 2nd edn (1986)

Memoirs FRS — *Biographical Memoirs of Fellows of the Royal Society*

MGH — Monumenta Germaniae Historica

MT — *Musical Times*

Munk, *Roll* — W. Munk, *The roll of the Royal College of Physicians of London*, 2 vols. (1861); 2nd edn, 3 vols. (1878)

N&Q — *Notes and Queries*

New Grove — S. Sadie, ed., *The new Grove dictionary of music and musicians*, 20 vols. (1980); 2nd edn, 29 vols. (2001) [also online edn; see also Grove, *Dict. mus.*]

Nichols, *Illustrations* — J. Nichols and J. B. Nichols, *Illustrations of the literary history of the eighteenth century*, 8 vols. (1817–58)

Nichols, *Lit. anecdotes* — J. Nichols, *Literary anecdotes of the eighteenth century*, 9 vols. (1812–16); facs. edn (1966)

Obits. FRS — *Obituary Notices of Fellows of the Royal Society*

O'Byrne, *Naval biog. dict.* — W. R. O'Byrne, *A naval biographical dictionary* (1849); repr. (1990); [2nd edn], 2 vols. (1861)

OHS — Oxford Historical Society

Old Westminsters — *The record of Old Westminsters*, 1–2, ed. G. F. R. Barker and A. H. Stenning (1928); suppl. 1, ed. J. B. Whitmore and G. R. Y. Radcliffe [1938]; 3, ed. J. B. Whitmore, G. R. Y. Radcliffe, and D. C. Simpson (1963); suppl. 2, ed. F. E. Pagan (1978); 4, ed. F. E. Pagan and H. E. Pagan (1992)

OMT — Oxford Medieval Texts

Ordericus Vitalis, *Eccl. hist.* — *The ecclesiastical history of Orderic Vitalis*, ed. and trans. M. Chibnall, 6 vols., OMT (1969–80); repr. (1990)

Paris, *Chron.* — *Matthaei Parisiensis, monachi sancti Albani, chronica majora*, ed. H. R. Luard, Rolls Series, 7 vols. (1872–83)

Parl. papers — *Parliamentary papers* (1801–)

PBA — *Proceedings of the British Academy*

Pepys, *Diary*	*The diary of Samuel Pepys*, ed. R. Latham and W. Matthews, 11 vols. (1970–83); repr. (1995) and (2000)
Pevsner	N. Pevsner and others, Buildings of England series
PICE	*Proceedings of the Institution of Civil Engineers*
Pipe rolls	*The great roll of the pipe for . . .*, PRSoc. (1884–)
PRO	Public Record Office
PRS	*Proceedings of the Royal Society of London*
PRSoc.	Pipe Roll Society
PTRS	*Philosophical Transactions of the Royal Society*
QR	*Quarterly Review*
RC	Record Commissions
Redgrave, *Artists*	S. Redgrave, *A dictionary of artists of the English school* (1874); rev. edn (1878); repr. (1970)
Reg. Oxf.	C. W. Boase and A. Clark, eds., *Register of the University of Oxford*, 5 vols., OHS, 1, 10–12, 14 (1885–9)
Reg. PCS	J. H. Burton and others, eds., *The register of the privy council of Scotland*, 1st ser., 14 vols. (1877–98); 2nd ser., 8 vols. (1899–1908); 3rd ser., [16 vols.] (1908–70)
Reg. RAN	H. W. C. Davis and others, eds., *Regesta regum Anglo-Normannorum, 1066–1154*, 4 vols. (1913–69)
RIBA Journal	*Journal of the Royal Institute of British Architects* [later *RIBA Journal*]
RotP	J. Strachey, ed., *Rotuli parliamentorum ut et petitiones, et placita in parliamento*, 6 vols. (1767–77)
RotS	D. Macpherson, J. Caley, and W. Illingworth, eds., *Rotuli Scotiae in Turri Londinensi et in domo capitulari Westmonasteriensi asservati*, 2 vols., RC, 14 (1814–19)
RS	Record(s) Society
Rymer, *Foedera*	T. Rymer and R. Sanderson, eds., *Foedera, conventiones, literae et cuiuscunque generis acta publica inter reges Angliae et alios quosvis imperatores, reges, pontifices, principes, vel communitates*, 20 vols. (1704–35); 2nd edn, 20 vols. (1726–35); 3rd edn, 10 vols. (1739–45), facs. edn (1967); new edn, ed. A. Clarke, J. Caley, and F. Holbrooke, 4 vols., RC, 50 (1816–30)
Sainty, *Judges*	J. Sainty, ed., *The judges of England, 1272–1990*, SeldS, suppl. ser., 10 (1993)
Sainty, *King's counsel*	J. Sainty, ed., *A list of English law officers and king's counsel*, SeldS, suppl. ser., 7 (1987)
SCH	Studies in Church History
Scots peerage	J. B. Paul, ed. *The Scots peerage, founded on Wood's edition of Sir Robert Douglas's Peerage of Scotland, containing an historical and genealogical account of the nobility of that kingdom*, 9 vols. (1904–14)
SeldS	Selden Society
SHR	*Scottish Historical Review*
State trials	T. B. Howell and T. J. Howell, eds., *Cobbett's Complete collection of state trials*, 34 vols. (1809–28)
STC, 1475–1640	A. W. Pollard, G. R. Redgrave, and others, eds., *A short-title catalogue of . . . English books . . . 1475–1640* (1926); 2nd edn, ed. W. A. Jackson, F. S. Ferguson, and K. F. Pantzer, 3 vols. (1976–91) [see also Wing, *STC*]
STS	Scottish Text Society
SurtS	Surtees Society
Symeon of Durham, *Opera*	*Symeonis monachi opera omnia*, ed. T. Arnold, 2 vols., Rolls Series, 75 (1882–5); repr. (1965)
Tanner, *Bibl. Brit.-Hib.*	T. Tanner, *Bibliotheca Britannico-Hibernica*, ed. D. Wilkins (1748); repr. (1963)
Thieme & Becker, *Allgemeines Lexikon*	U. Thieme, F. Becker, and H. Vollmer, eds., *Allgemeines Lexikon der bildenden Künstler von der Antike bis zur Gegenwart*, 37 vols. (Leipzig, 1907–50); repr. (1961–5), (1983), and (1992)
Thurloe, *State papers*	*A collection of the state papers of John Thurloe*, ed. T. Birch, 7 vols. (1742)
TLS	*Times Literary Supplement*
Tout, *Admin. hist.*	T. F. Tout, *Chapters in the administrative history of mediaeval England: the wardrobe, the chamber, and the small seals*, 6 vols. (1920–33); repr. (1967)
TRHS	*Transactions of the Royal Historical Society*
VCH	H. A. Doubleday and others, eds., *The Victoria history of the counties of England*, [88 vols.] (1900–)
Venn, *Alum. Cant.*	J. Venn and J. A. Venn, *Alumni Cantabrigienses: a biographical list of all known students, graduates, and holders of office at the University of Cambridge, from the earliest times to 1900*, 10 vols. (1922–54); repr. in 2 vols. (1974–8)
Vertue, *Note books*	[G. Vertue], *Note books*, ed. K. Esdaile, earl of Ilchester, and H. M. Hake, 6 vols., Walpole Society, 18, 20, 22, 24, 26, 30 (1930–55)
VF	*Vanity Fair*
Walford, *County families*	E. Walford, *The county families of the United Kingdom, or, Royal manual of the titled and untitled aristocracy of Great Britain and Ireland* (1860)
Walker rev.	A. G. Matthews, *Walker revised: being a revision of John Walker's Sufferings of the clergy during the grand rebellion, 1642–60* (1948); repr. (1988)
Walpole, *Corr.*	*The Yale edition of Horace Walpole's correspondence*, ed. W. S. Lewis, 48 vols. (1937–83)
Ward, *Men of the reign*	T. H. Ward, ed., *Men of the reign: a biographical dictionary of eminent persons of British and colonial birth who have died during the reign of Queen Victoria* (1885); repr. (Graz, 1968)
Waterhouse, *18c painters*	E. Waterhouse, *The dictionary of 18th century painters in oils and crayons* (1981); repr. as *British 18th century painters in oils and crayons* (1991), vol. 2 of *Dictionary of British art*
Watt, *Bibl. Brit.*	R. Watt, *Bibliotheca Britannica, or, A general index to British and foreign literature*, 4 vols. (1824) [many reprs.]
Wellesley index	W. E. Houghton, ed., *The Wellesley index to Victorian periodicals, 1824–1900*, 5 vols. (1966–89); new edn (1999) [CD-ROM]
Wing, *STC*	D. Wing, ed., *Short-title catalogue of . . . English books . . . 1641–1700*, 3 vols. (1945–51); 2nd edn (1972–88); rev. and enl. edn, ed. J. J. Morrison, C. W. Nelson, and M. Seccombe, 4 vols. (1994–8) [see also *STC, 1475–1640*]
Wisden	*John Wisden's Cricketer's Almanack*
Wood, *Ath. Oxon.*	A. Wood, *Athenae Oxonienses . . . to which are added the Fasti*, 2 vols. (1691–2); 2nd edn (1721); new edn, 4 vols., ed. P. Bliss (1813–20); repr. (1967) and (1969)
Wood, *Vic. painters*	C. Wood, *Dictionary of Victorian painters* (1971); 2nd edn (1978); 3rd edn as *Victorian painters*, 2 vols. (1995), vol. 4 of *Dictionary of British art*
WW	*Who's who* (1849–)
WWBMP	M. Stenton and S. Lees, eds., *Who's who of British members of parliament*, 4 vols. (1976–81)
WWW	*Who was who* (1929–)

Wolmark, Alfred Aaron (1877–1961), painter and decorative artist, was born in Warsaw, Poland, on 28 December 1877, the eldest child in the family of four sons and one daughter of Levy and Gitel Wolmark. The Wolmarks, like many other central European Jewish families, were forced by continuous persecution to leave Poland; they emigrated to London during the 1880s—1883 has frequently been quoted but a date nearer 1888 seems more likely. The first extant document relating to Wolmark is his naturalization certificate, filled in by his father and sworn by him at the Worship Street police court in the East End of London on 1 January 1894. This document gives the family's residence as 65 Hanbury Street, Spitalfields; Wolmark's forename is given simply as Aaron, and it is probable that he adopted the English name of Alfred at a slightly later date. No record exists of his early education, which would have taken place within the Jewish community both in Warsaw and Spitalfields; clearly his aptitude for drawing was brought to the notice of the authorities, and he entered the Royal Academy Schools in 1895, where he studied for three years, winning a silver medal for figure drawing in December 1896.

While at the Royal Academy Schools, Wolmark was befriended by Anna Wilmersdoerffer, and it was through her influence that he received several portrait commissions; the financial assistance of the Wilmersdoerffer family also enabled him to return to Poland in 1903, where he executed several important works based on Jewish historical subjects, such as *Rabbi Ben Ezra*, inspired by Browning's poem. These subject paintings are strongly influenced in technique by his studies of Rembrandt, the only artist to whom he had a lifelong devotion, but in his more spontaneous works he was already beginning to lighten his palette. During the next few years his palette continued to lighten, but it was not until he saw the important exhibition 'Manet and the Post-Impressionists', organized by Roger Fry at the Grafton Galleries, London, during the winter of 1910–11, that the full impact of modern French painting was revealed to him.

On 11 July 1911 Wolmark married Bessie Leah Tapper, the daughter of Russo-Polish Jewish parents from the East End. (The couple had two sons and a daughter.) They set off for an extended honeymoon in Concarneau, where Wolmark painted many studies of Breton fisherfolk and harbour life. This series of paintings executed in bright flat areas of heavily applied pigment reduced his subject matter to its simplest form and led on to the geometric still lifes painted immediately after his return to London. He was at the height of his powers during the years from 1911 to 1915; in addition to painting he turned his hand to the decoration of pots, which he covered in strongly coloured aggressively geometric designs. Interior decoration, the theatre, and stained glass also occupied him at this time. His window for St Mary's Church, Slough (1915), was probably the most daring piece of modern glass in England at the time. Even the frames he designed for his paintings did not escape his decorative urge, being not only painted but, at times, covered with geometric collage of patterned wallpapers. His closest associate at this stage was Henri Gaudier-Brzeska, the French sculptor, who had settled in London. The Musée des Beaux-Arts, Orléans, acquired his portrait of Gaudier-Brzeska in 1957.

Wolmark despised bohemianism, and, although he liked to play the part of an artist, especially when frequenting the Café Royal in London, it was through the elaboration of his dress rather than its disregard that he wished people to be aware of his profession. There is a massive plaster head of Wolmark by Gaudier-Brzeska which captures his air of self-confidence, tinged with arrogance; the floppy bow-tie and flowing hair hint at the subject's dandified appearance. (Bronze casts are in the principal museums in Southampton, Liverpool, and Birmingham.) Passed as medically unfit for military service in 1915, he spent the war years in England. In 1919 he went to New York, where one of his brothers was living, and painted a series of cityscapes; these paintings were shown at the Kevorkian Galleries, New York, in 1920, and mark the last phase of his contribution to avant-garde British painting. During the ensuing decades he felt himself increasingly out of touch with the modern movement, and settled down to paint landscapes and figure subjects in a highly personal, expressionistic manner; he also did some teaching, not in art schools but rather in the manner of the old masters, taking pupils to work in his studio. In 1928 he held an exhibition at the Lefevre Gallery, London, of portrait drawings of well-known contemporaries, including Israel Zangwill (whose complete works he had illustrated for the Globe Publishing Company three years previously), Jerome K. Jerome, Ford Madox Ford, D. Y. Cameron, and G. K. Chesterton. During his life he held many exhibitions in London, New York, and Paris. An exhibition at the Leicester Galleries, London, in 1948 commemorated his seventieth birthday.

Wolmark died on 6 January 1961 at his home, 54 Colet Gardens, West Kensington, London. A memorial exhibition of his work was held at the Ben Uri Art Gallery, London, during September and October of that year; he had been one of the prime movers in the setting up of the Ben Uri Art Society in 1915, which did so much to foster artistic awareness among East End Jewry. Examples of his work are in the Tate collection and the National Portrait Gallery, London.   PEYTON SKIPWITH, *rev.*

Sources personal knowledge (1981) • private information (1981) • *CGPLA Eng. & Wales* (1961) • I. Grose, ed., *Alfred Wolmark, 1877–1961* [1985] [exhibition catalogue, The Belgrave Gallery, London, 7–29 Nov 1985] • *Alfred Wolmark, 1877–1961* [1975] [exhibition catalogue, Ferens Gallery, Hull] • *The Times* (7 Jan 1961)
Likenesses A. A. Wolmark, self-portrait, oils, 1911, Southampton Art Gallery • H. Gaudier-Brzeska, pencil drawings, *c.*1913, Southampton Art Gallery • H. Gaudier-Brzeska, plaster bust, 1913, Walker Art Gallery, Liverpool • A. A. Wolmark, self-portrait, ink drawing, 1926, NPG • H. Gaudier-Brzeska, bronze cast, Southampton Art Gallery • bronze cast, Liverpool Museum • bronze cast, Birmingham Museums and Art Gallery
Wealth at death £1806: probate, 14 July 1961, *CGPLA Eng. & Wales*

Wolpe, Berthold Ludwig (1905–1989), graphic artist and typographer, was born on 29 October 1905 in Offenbach am Main, Germany, the younger son and third child of Simon Wolpe, dentist, and his wife, Agathe Goldschmidt.

He was educated at a technical school (*Realschule*), as he was good even then at metalwork (through experience in his father's dental laboratory). He was expected to become an engineer, but in 1924 he went to Offenbach Art School and began his career. He worked under the great calligrapher Rudolf Koch, whose assistant he was from 1929 to 1934. Their association is celebrated in their book *Das ABC-Büchlein* (1934; English edition, 1976), an elegant little collection of roman and Gothic alphabets drawn by both men. He learned goldsmith work under Theodor Wende at Pforzheim Art School and taught in both Frankfurt and Offenbach from 1930 to 1933.

In 1932 Wolpe visited London and met Stanley Morison, who was interested in some bronze lettering of Wolpe's of which he had seen photographs. Morison asked Wolpe to design a printing type of capital letters in the same style for the Monotype Corporation. This was the birth of Albertus, first cut in 1934 and used in 1935, which quickly became the most widely used display face (that is, for advertising, not books) in Britain. Its apparent simplicity made it look easy to copy or reproduce photographically, and since there was no copyright in lettering it was 'stolen' by every signwriter in the country who had any taste. It appeared everywhere on buildings, shop fronts (such as Austin Reed), vans, paper bags, and posters, and if Wolpe had been paid a royalty for every time it was used (which he should have been) he would soon have become a rich man.

Wolpe, who was Jewish, settled in England in 1935, and from then until 1940 worked under Ernest Ingham at the Fanfare Press in St Martin's Lane, London. While there he was designing a lower-case for Albertus, issued in 1938, a new display face, Tempest, designed for Fanfare in 1935, a range of type ornaments for Fanfare published in his *A Book of Fanfare Ornaments* (with an introduction by James Laver) in 1939, a new text face, Pegasus, for the Monotype Corporation (cut only in 16 point) in 1937–40, and between 1935 and 1939 a series of innovative typographic yellow book jackets, printed by Fanfare, for Gollancz. He applied for naturalization in 1936, but it was not granted until 1947, and in 1940–41 he was interned in Camp Hay, New South Wales, Australia.

When Wolpe returned to Britain in 1941 he moved to the publishers Faber and Faber, in charge of jacket design, and remained there until his retirement in 1975. For Faber, Wolpe designed many books and more than 1500 jackets and covers. While working there he also taught lettering one day a week at Camberwell School of Arts and Crafts (1949–53) and at the Royal College of Art (1956–75), and, for about the last ten years of his life, he ran a unique lettering course at the City and Guilds of London School of Art. In 1966 he was invited to draw a new masthead for *The Times*, which was in use from 3 May 1966 to 20 September 1970.

Apart from his work as a designer (which included several other typefaces, distinguished emblems and devices, and lettering for permanent and ephemeral use) Wolpe was also an author and scholar of printing history and collector of any equipment or tools connected with writing, lettering, or measuring. He was vice-president of the Printing Historical Society in 1977. Among his books was *Renaissance Handwriting* (1960), written jointly with Alfred Fairbank. When living in Chelsea he found on a stall next door to his house a metal instrument thought by the stallholder to be something surgical, but which Wolpe had recognized as a pair of dividers, later established to be earlier than any in the British Museum. The bulging briefcase he used for carrying work to and from home was apt to be full of newly acquired treasures.

Whenever Wolpe rose to speak, for example at the Double Crown Club, of which he was an honorary member, or the Printing Historical Society, he always produced, with his diffident but entrancing smile, something wildly unexpected but totally apposite. He had a most striking head, with a big nose, which should have been drawn by Daumier or Dürer. It was in fact drawn by Charles Mozley in his little book *Wolperiana: an Illustrated Guide to Berthold Wolpe*, published by the Merrion Press for his friends in 1960. This book also contains one of the best photographs of him, taken outside Faber, by Frank Herrmann, who worked there. Wolpe was made a royal designer for industry in 1959 and appointed OBE in 1983. In 1981 he was Lyell reader in bibliography at Oxford University. The Society of Designer–Craftsmen made him an honorary fellow in 1984 and the Royal College of Art awarded him an honorary doctorate in 1968. He had retrospective exhibitions at the Victoria and Albert Museum (1980), the National Library of Scotland in Edinburgh (1982), and the Klingspor Museum in Offenbach (1983).

In November 1941 Wolpe made a most happy marriage with a sculptor, Margaret Leslie, daughter of Leslie Howard Smith, butcher, of Lewes, Sussex. They had two sons and two daughters. Wolpe's essential Jewishness was expressed in the closeness of his relationship with his family. He died in St Thomas's Hospital, London, after a heart attack, on 5 July 1989. RUARI McLEAN, *rev.*

Sources *Berthold Wolpe: a retrospective survey*, V&A (1980) · *The Independent* (6 July 1989) · *The Times* (8 July 1989) · personal knowledge (1996) · private information (1996)
Likenesses F. Herrmann, photograph · C. Mozley, drawing, repro. in C. Mozley, *Wolperiana: an illustrated guide to Berthold Wolpe* (1960)

Wolrich, Humphrey. *See* Woolrich, Humphrey (c.1633–1707).

Wolryche [Wolrich], **Sir Thomas**, **first baronet** (1598–1668), royalist army officer, was born at Worfield, Shropshire, and baptized there on 27 March 1598, the son and heir of Sir Francis Wolryche (d. 1614) of Dudmaston, in the parish of Quatt, Shropshire, and his wife, Margaret, daughter of Sir George Bromley of Hallon in Worfield, and his wife, Joan. With a pedigree allegedly traceable to 1279 the Wolryches were among the oldest families of Shropshire, their deed of grant reportedly among the oldest in England.

Thomas Wolryche, who matriculated from Trinity College, Cambridge, at Easter in 1614, studied geometry, history, and heraldry in particular, and was admitted to the Inner Temple on 11 October 1615. On his father's death he succeeded to the lordship of the Shropshire manors of Brompton, Presthope, and Hughley and to substantial estates near Much Wenlock, which town he represented in the parliaments of 1621, 1624, and 1625. In 1625 he married Ursula (*bap.* 1607), daughter of Thomas Ottley of Pitchford, Shropshire, and his wife, Mary, daughter of Roger Gifford MD, a former physician to Elizabeth I. On 27 August 1637 Richard Wolley, a former minister of Leighton, Shropshire, petitioned the king, claiming that Wolryche among others had enclosed all the common land at Leighton for private use, and that Wolryche had threatened him with violent words.

Wolryche was knighted at Whitehall on 22 July 1641, and was created baronet of Dudmaston on 4 August the same year. A deputy lieutenant, justice of the peace, and commander in the Shropshire trained bands, he sided with the royalists during the civil war. He was appointed a commissioner of array in 1642 and raised a royalist regiment at his own expense. By May 1643 he was commissioned colonel or lieutenant-colonel in his capacity as governor of Bridgnorth, which he was ordered to fortify and garrison by Lord Capel, royalist lieutenant-general of Shropshire, Cheshire, and north Wales.

Wolryche surrendered himself to parliament before December 1645, and was sequestered for delinquency. Petitioning to compound on 7 August 1646, he claimed that a Mr Pierpoint would confirm that he had been unable to present himself earlier. He declared a personal estate worth £300 and estate rents valued at £292 17s. per annum. On 11 March 1647 his fine was settled at £730 14s. He paid relatively promptly and on 3 November 1647 the committee for compounding ordered the Shropshire county committee to restore his tenants' cattle and return him full possession of his estates. The House of Commons issued an ordinance to grant him a pardon on 4 September 1648, and he was finally cleared of delinquency by the Lords on 6 October. However, on 19 April 1650 the county committee reported that Wolryche had deliberately undervalued his estates in his composition, and he remained in difficulties over this matter in 1652.

Wolryche returned to county government as a justice of the peace at the Restoration. He had twelve children and was succeeded as second baronet by his son Francis (*c.*1627–1688). He died on 4 July 1668 and was buried on 9 July at St Chad's, Shrewsbury. A monumental inscription commemorated him in the Wolryche mortuary chapel at St Andrew's Church, Quatt. He was survived by his wife, who proved his will on 7 November 1668.

ANDREW J. HOPPER

Sources GEC, *Baronetage* · M. A. E. Green, ed., *Calendar of the proceedings of the committee for compounding … 1643–1660*, 2, PRO (1890) · Venn, *Alum. Cant.*, 1/1 · P. R. Newman, *Royalist officers in England and Wales, 1642–1660: a biographical dictionary* (1981) · *DNB* · will, PRO, PROB 11/328, sig. 149, fols. 287r–287v · R. Tresswell and A. Vincent, *The visitation of Shropshire, taken in the year 1623*, ed. G. Grazebrook and J. P. Rylands, 2, Harleian Society, 29 (1889) · *CSP dom.*, 1637 · *JHC*, 6 (1648–51) · *JHL*, 10 (1647–8) · HoP, *Commons, 1660–90* · VCH *Shropshire*, vols. 3, 8–9 · Lord Hawkesbury, 'The family of Ottley of Pitchford', *Transactions of the Shropshire Archaeological and Natural History Society*, 2nd ser., 7 (1895), 361–80

Archives Shrops. RRC, family MSS, ref. 2922
Likenesses portrait; known to be at Dudmaston in 1900
Wealth at death £200 p.a. in annuities to sons; 2000 marks lump sum, plus £40 p.a. to daughters: will, PRO, PROB 11/328, sig. 149

Wolseley [Ouseley], **Sir Charles**, **second baronet, appointed Lord Wolseley under the protectorate** (1629/30–1714), politician, was born between September 1629 and April 1630, being aged sixteen at the time of his father's death on 21 September 1646 and thirty-three at the herald's visitation of Staffordshire on 4 April 1663. He was the eldest son of Sir Robert Wolseley, first baronet (1587–1646), government official and royalist army officer, and Mary (*b. c.*1608), daughter of Sir George Wroughton of Wilcot, Wiltshire. Wolseley was privately educated. His father, who fought for the king in the civil war, died in 1646 having already passed his estates of Morton and Wolseley in Staffordshire over to his son Charles in order to circumvent confiscation. The estates were, however, placed under sequestration but, owing to Sir Charles's youth, escaped the worst penalties and on 8 October 1647 a parliamentary ordinance discharged them subject to payment of £2500 to the committee for compounding. Wolseley restored his fortunes by marriage, on 12 May 1648, to the Hon. Anne (*b. c.*1630), youngest daughter of William *Fiennes, first Viscount Saye and Sele, a leading parliamentarian, who brought him a £3000 dowry. There were seven sons and ten daughters, the eldest son being Robert Wolseley [*see below*].

Assisted by Fiennes's influence in 1653 Wolseley was selected as MP for Oxford in the nominated assembly, being added to the council of state on 14 July and in September becoming JP for Oxfordshire and Staffordshire. Despite his youth he rocketed to prominence in national politics, and as early as 30 June 1653 was awarded Whitehall lodgings. An Independent, Wolseley was one of a few men in Cromwell's inner circle who advocated a greater degree of toleration in religion than Cromwell himself. Another was Bulstrode Whitelocke, with whom Wolseley soon established a friendship, being the first to advise him of his selection as ambassador to Sweden. After Whitelocke's departure Wolseley corresponded with him and appears to have written him a laudatory poem; while Whitelocke wrote that 'none was a more hearty friend to him and his business' (Longleat, Whitelocke MSS, vol. 14, p. 254v).

In parliament, on 12 July 1653, Wolseley was appointed to the committee to draft an explanation of its purpose and entreat public prayers for its work. On 24 August the council delegated him to move an addition of 500 to the military establishment in parliament. He was a teller on several occasions, including telling in favour of a committee to consider a replacement for chancery and against the sale of royal forests. Although not an active council member Wolseley was elected to the new council on 1 November 1653, mustering a respectable sixty-one votes. He played a crucial role on 12 December as one of the small group of Cromwellians who organized parliament's sudden dissolution. He declared 'he had lain a long time under the pressure of his own spirits, in sitting with those whose designs and ends were destructive to the Commonwealth', denounced the radicals' 'evil intents' in trying to curtail army pay, and declared that they 'lacked the spirit of justice' and 'intended to destroy the law and pull it up root and branch', 'to take away all property' (Spalding, 494–5). He signed the motion for parliament's resignation, writing to Whitelocke that most of his colleagues had 'grown so injurious to magistracy, property, and ministry that the safety of the whole would not admit them to sit longer' (Dec 1653, BL, Add. MS 32093).

Wolseley's speech made him the man of the moment, if unpopular with radicals, and on 16 December he joined Cromwell's council, with his brother-in-law Nathaniel *Fiennes, as its youngest member. He faced republican grumbles that he 'had done nought for the cause' (Oldys and Park, 3.477), and in 1656 John Hobart denounced him as one of those councillors who 'want hearts' (Bodl. Oxf., MS Tanner 52, fol. 159). Declaring privately that Cromwell's 'personal worth ... qualifies him for the greatest monarch in the world' (BL, Add. MS 32093, fol. 317), Wolseley served on a multiplicity of committees and was also active in the visitation of Oxford University in 1654 and in drawing up statutes for Durham College in 1656. He also sat on the commission to eject scandalous ministers and, representing Staffordshire in parliament in 1654 and from 1656 to his elevation to Cromwell's upper house in December 1657, he favoured leniency in the case of the Quaker James Nayler, who was accused of blasphemy. In January 1656 Whitelocke sought his help to avoid returning to Sweden. He also assisted with negotiations for a maritime treaty with the Dutch in 1656–7 and in drafting a declaration for the relief of persecuted Polish protestants in December 1657.

Wolseley predictably spoke in favour of the protector assuming the crown and securing a conservative constitutional settlement in 1657, arguing that 'the law knows not a Protector and requires no obedience from the people to him', which undermined civil obedience and encouraged pro-royalist juries. He begged Cromwell not to 'deny the nation their due' in the form of a king, bluntly reminding MPs objecting to Cromwell's illegalities that 'if the legislature had not sometimes been undertaken for another power than was parliamentary you had hardly sat here to make this settlement' (Diary of Thomas Burton, 2.40). But his principal role was as one of Cromwell's few confidants: Whitelocke recorded in May 1657 how Cromwell would sometimes have three or four hours' private discourse with himself, Wolseley, Lord Broghill, and William Pierrepoint and would be 'exceeding familiar w[i]th them' and 'their Councell was accepted & followed by him in most of his greatest affayres' (Diary of Bulstrode Whitelocke, 464).

Wolseley maintained influence after Cromwell's death as one of Richard Cromwell's senior advisers. After the officers' coup in April 1659 Sir Robert Howard secured his support for royalist plans. Elected in 1660 to the Convention Parliament for Staffordshire, he sued for a pardon successfully before 15 June 1660, supported by Lord Mordaunt, and was a commissioner for assessment in Staffordshire in 1661–3 and 1664–80. But Wolseley's religious

tolerance saw him at odds with resurgent Anglicanism, and he probably did not stand for election in 1661. Instead he concentrated his energies on extending his mansion at Wolseley and developing his park, gardens, and orchards there. His achievements were commended by his wife's niece, Celia *Fiennes, a frequent visitor. He put an equally sustained effort into writing in support of religious toleration. Whitelocke last met him at a conventicle in Greenwich in May 1667 where they heard John Owen preach, and his religious writings included Liberty of Conscience the Magistrates Interest, printed anonymously in 1668, in which he argued the magistrate's duty to protect all godly sects and 'endeavour in a Gospel-like way to see the Laws of Christ put into execution'. Wolseley resigned as JP in 1670 following the passage of the second Commontide Act. He denounced atheism in The Unreasonableness of Atheism Made Manifest in 1669 and The Reasonableness of Sustained Belief in 1672, condemning Thomas Hobbes's influence, and daringly supported divorce in The Case of Divorce and Remarriage Thereupon Discussed in 1672, prompted by the famous case of Lord Roos, who sought a divorce due to his wife's adultery.

An ally of the lord privy seal, Arthur Annesley, earl of Anglesey, Wolseley vehemently denied rumours in winter 1676–7 that he had encouraged Anglesey to stick by the 'Good Old Cause' and had assured him that most of the Staffordshire gentry would support him. During the exclusion crisis he showed 'great desire to be a Member', and unsuccessfully tried to stand for Stafford and, with Algernon Sidney's support, at Bramber. He also 'offered very bountifully' (HoP, Commons, 1660–90, 3.754) for nomination at Lichfield in 1681. In all three cases he stood down before the poll. During the Monmouth rebellion of 1685 he was imprisoned in Chester Castle as a potential sympathizer, but was released on royal orders. His importance as principal supporter of the Staffordshire dissenters led James II to woo him with a deputy lieutenancy and restore him as a JP in February 1688, and, having apparently 'declared himself right and ready to serve His Majesty in any capacity', he was nominated as court candidate for Woodstock in the abortive election plans of September. After the revolution, Wolseley lived in retirement, and died at his home on 9 October 1714. He was buried at Colwich church, Staffordshire. The baronetcy was inherited by his fourth but eldest surviving son, William, and the family retained the estate until the 1990s. In his twenties Wolseley had been on familiar terms with Cromwell, a leading political figure and force for political moderation; after 1660 his exclusion from politics drove him to seek, with some success, an outlet for his talents in landscape gardening and to join with other nonconformists in 'the literary campaign for liberty of conscience' (Worden, 229).

Robert Wolseley (1648/9–1697), eldest son of Sir Charles Wolseley, second baronet, matriculated at Trinity College, Oxford, on 26 July 1666 aged seventeen, entering Gray's Inn in 1667. A friend of John Wilmot, earl of Rochester, he wrote the laudatory introduction to

Rochester's posthumously published play, *Valentinian*, in 1685, declaring that 'true genius can enter into the hardest and dryest thing, enrich the most barren soil, and inform the meanest and most uncomely nature'. After killing William, son of Lord Wharton, in a duel following a 'poetical quarrel' in 1689, he reformed, and in February 1692 was appointed envoy to the elector of Bavaria, governor of the Netherlands, in Brussels. Taking leave of the king on 3 March he served until October 1696 and signed treaties with Hanover and Wolfenbuttel to hire new troops for William's campaign in 1694. He died unmarried some time after 6 April 1697.   TIMOTHY VENNING

Sources *The diary of Bulstrode Whitelocke, 1605–1675*, ed. R. Spalding, British Academy, Records of Social and Economic History, new ser., 13 (1990) · BL, Whitelocke papers, Add. MS 32093 · *JHL*, 8–10 (1645–8) · *JHC*, 7 (1651–9) · GEC, *Baronetage*, vol. 2 · Bodl. Oxf., MS Tanner 52 · [B. Whitelocke?], *Monarchy asserted to be the best, most ancient and legal form of government, in a conference held at Whitehall with Oliver, late protector, and a committee of parliament* (1660) · *CSP dom.*, 1652–60; 1676–7; 1687–9; 1691–3; 1696–7 · *Diary of Thomas Burton*, ed. J. T. Rutt, 4 vols. (1828) · Thurloe, *State papers* · G. J. Armytage and W. H. Rylands, eds., *Staffordshire pedigrees*, Harleian Society, 63 (1912) · G. D. Squibb, ed., *Wiltshire visitation pedigrees, 1623*, Harleian Society, 105–6 (1954) · C. H. Firth and R. S. Rait, eds., *Acts and ordinances of the interregnum, 1642–1660*, 2 (1911) · M. W. Helms and A. M. Mimardière, 'Wolseley, Sir Charles 2nd bt', HoP, *Commons, 1660–90* · *The memoirs of Edmund Ludlow*, ed. C. H. Firth, 2 vols. (1894), vol. 1 · Evelyn, *Diary* · R. Spalding, *Contemporaries of Bulstrode Whitelocke* (1990) · M. A. E. Green, ed., *Calendar of the proceedings of the committee for compounding … 1643–1660*, 2, PRO (1890) · B. Whitelocke, *Memorials of English affairs*, new edn, 4 vols. (1853) · W. Oldys and T. Park, eds., 'A second narrative of the late parliament (so called)', *Harleian Miscellany*, 10 vols. (1808–13), 3.470–89 · *The journeys of Celia Fiennes*, ed. C. Morris, rev. edn (1949) · B. Worden, 'Toleration and the Cromwellian protectorate', *Persecution and toleration*, ed. W. J. Sheils, SCH, 21 (1984), 199–233 · Longleat House, Wiltshire, Whitelocke MSS · Foster, *Alum. Oxon.* · J. Foster, *The register of admissions to Gray's Inn, 1521–1889, together with the register of marriages in Gray's Inn chapel, 1695–1754* (privately printed, London, 1889) · *Report on the manuscripts of his grace the duke of Buccleuch and Queensberry … preserved at Montagu House*, 3 vols. in 4, HMC, 45 (1899–1926), vol. 2 · W. A. Shaw, ed., *Calendar of treasury books*, 9–11, PRO (1931–5) · Burke, *Peerage* · V. de S. Pinto, *Enthusiast in wit: a portrait of John Wilmot, earl of Rochester, 1647–1680* (1962)
Archives BL, letters to William Blathwayt, Add. MS 34352 [Robert Wolseley] · BL, letters to Sir W. D. Colt, Add. MS 34096 [Robert Wolseley] · Bodl. Oxf., letters to Sir Robert Clayton · CKS, letters to Alexander Stanhope [Robert Wolseley]
Likenesses portraits; at Wolseley House, Staffordshire, in nineteenth century
Wealth at death *Journeys of Celia Fiennes*, ed. Morris; M. W. Helms and A. M. Mimardière, 'Wolseley, Sir Charles 2nd bt' · extensive property in Staffordshire, centred on Wolseley House; expensive landscaping of grounds and imports to garden; income est. £1000 p.a. in 1670s

Wolseley, Sir Charles, seventh baronet (1769–1846), politician, born on 20 July 1769 at Wolseley Hall, Staffordshire, was the son of Sir William Wolseley, sixth baronet (1740–1817), and his wife, Charlotte Chambers of Wimbledon. Sir Charles Wolseley (1629/30–1714) was his ancestor. Educated privately, in his late teens Wolseley embarked on a grand tour of the continent, during which he made contact with the revolutionary forces there (probably with the consent of his father, who was a keen reformer). He was present at the fall of the Bastille (14 July 1789), and implied in a speech delivered at Stockton on 28 June 1819 that he had participated in the assault. On 13 December 1794 he married Mary, daughter of Thomas Clifford of Tixall, Staffordshire. Following her death on 16 July 1811 he married, on 2 July 1812, Anne, daughter of Anthony Wright of Wealdside, Essex.

Wolseley appears to have made his first connection with the reform movement in England in 1811, when he signed a memorial in favour of parliamentary reform. The original list of members of the union of parliamentary reform (1812) contains his name, and he was one of the founders of the Hampden Club. He succeeded to the baronetcy on 5 August 1817, when the reform movement was becoming formidable, and identified himself with the more extreme section of radicals. His first appearance as one of the reformist leaders was as chairman of a great demonstration held at Sandy Brow, Stockport, in June 1819. At this time these demonstrations were used in order to make a show of electing popular representatives, and on 12 July that year the Birmingham reformers met at Newhall Hill. In his absence they elected Sir Charles as their 'legislatorial attorney', and empowered him to present their grievances to the House of Commons. Major John Cartwright (1740–1824) helped convey the resolution of the meeting to Wolseley Hall, where he and Sir Charles spent some days devising means for combating the repressive measures which the government had adopted. On 19 July Sir Charles was arrested for his speech at Stockport, taken to Knutsford, and freed on bail. While awaiting trial he assisted the victims of the Peterloo massacre: he supported some of their families, attended their trial, and became their surety. In April 1820 his own trial commenced at Chester. He and Joseph Harrison, a dissenting minister and schoolmaster, were charged with sedition and conspiracy, and were sentenced to eighteen months' imprisonment. Sir Charles was interned in king's bench, Abingdon. While in gaol he was elected on 16 January 1821, with eight others, including Jeremy Bentham and Sir Francis Burdett, to constitute a committee of Middlesex electors to promote reform, and his release was celebrated with a great demonstration.

Like the radicals generally, Wolseley supported Queen Caroline, and while in prison wrote letters on her behalf to *The Times* and to Lord Castlereagh. In one of them he offered to go to Como, where he said he was in 1817, and investigate the truth of the rumours regarding her conduct there.

Wolseley continued for some time to support the reformers, and when Hunt was released from Ilchester gaol in 1822 Sir Charles was one of his sureties. Gradually he withdrew from the forefront of political agitation, and from about 1826 he does not appear to have taken any public part in politics. He converted to Roman Catholicism, and was received into the Catholic church in October 1837. His second wife died on 24 October 1838. Wolseley died at Wolseley Hall, Staffordshire, on 3 October 1846. None of the children of his first marriage (two sons and one daughter) survived him. He was succeeded by Sir Charles Wolseley, eighth baronet (1813–1854), the eldest of the three sons and two daughters of his second marriage.

J. R. MacDonald, *rev.* Peter Spence

Sources GM, 2nd ser., 26 (1846), 536–7 · Gillow, *Lit. biog. hist.* · Burke, *Peerage* · *Annual Register* (1819) · *Annual Register* (1820) · G. Spencer, *Sermon on occasion of Sir C. Wolseley Bart making his profession of the Catholic faith* (1837) · *The Greville memoirs*, ed. H. Reeve, pt 1, vol. 2 (1874), 336

Wolseley, Frances Garnet, Viscountess Wolseley (1872–1936), gardener and author, was born on 15 September 1872 in Dublin, the only child of Sir Garnet Joseph *Wolseley (1833–1913), later Baron Wolseley of Cairo and Viscount Wolseley, commander-in-chief of the British army, and his wife, Louisa Erskine (1843–1920). She had the peripatetic childhood that befalls a soldier's daughter, with frequently changing homes in comfortable suburban villas, including The Limes, Mortlake, and Aylesford House, Wimbledon, and a consequently erratic private education. For her seventh Christmas she was taken to Cyprus, where her father was *en route* to the Anglo-Zulu War, while her tenth birthday was celebrated with the news of his victory at Tell al-Kebir—he sent her a visiting card found in Arabi Pasha's tent (having promised her the tip of the rebel's nose). In the spring of 1885 mother and daughter travelled to Cairo to join Lord Wolseley, and returned via Florence, Venice, and Paris.

Frances Wolseley was very much her father's daughter, resembling him in her short stature, smart dress, and brisk manner; she matured early into the role of tactful companion and chaperone to the sociable Lady Wolseley. Although she enjoyed her season as a débutante in 1891, privately she preferred a country life with horses and dogs. This became a reality in 1899, when the family settled at Trevor House, at Glynde in Sussex, and she was able to indulge her interest in gardening. Aiming to equip the daughters of middle-class families to earn their own livings, in 1902 she started courses in gardening and design for young women in the walled garden at Trevor House; by 1907 the Glynde College for Lady Gardeners was proving such a success that it had to be moved to a 5 acre teaching garden, with student accommodation, at Ragged Lands, just outside Glynde village. Frances Wolseley's two-year course set the highest standard and enjoyed the patronage of such distinguished gardeners as Gertrude Jekyll, Ellen Willmott, and William Robinson. In November 1909 the college students were featured in *Country Life* for their work building and planting the garden of the King Edward VII Sanatorium at Midhurst, which had been designed by Gertrude Jekyll.

While leaving the day-to-day work of the college in the care of graduates Elsa More and Mary Campion, Frances Wolseley pursued a wider campaign with her book *Gardening for Women* (1908), which suggested many ways in which women could help with the revival of the countryside economy and rural industries. She toured the country to inspect and publicize thriving enterprises in market

Frances Garnet Wolseley, Viscountess Wolseley (1872–1936), by Bassano, 1908

gardening, the horticultural colleges at Swanley and Studley, and other institutions running similar courses, and private gardens where women demonstrated responsible management. She also visited South Africa and Canada, showing particular interest in the Canadian women's institutes and their adoption in Britain. She was elected to the Worshipful Company of Gardeners of the City of London in 1913, and became Viscountess Wolseley upon the death of her father the same year.

From 1913 to 1921 Frances Wolseley lived with her mother at Massetts Place, near Lindfield: here she continued her campaign through articles and letters, culminating in her most important book, *Women on the Land* (1916), which explained the organization of smallholdings, market co-operatives, women's institutes, and gardening for schools. She also wrote *In a College Garden* (1916) to explain exactly the principles and practice of the Glynde College, which prospered until the death of the principal, Elsa More, just after the First World War. In 1919 *Gardens, their Form and Design* appeared, a radical analysis of the subject for that time, describing the role of the artist-gardener and setting out much of the theory for what was to be the new profession of landscape architecture a decade before the foundation of the Institute of Landscape Architects. After the death of her mother in 1920 Lady Wolseley moved to Culpepers, Ardingly, Sussex, and devoted her last years to local history research; she published *Some of the Smaller Manor Houses of Sussex* in 1925.

She died on 24 December 1936 at Culpepers and was buried at St Andrew's, Beddingham. In her will she left her collections of books and papers to Hove corporation, together with funds for the improvement of the library and the establishment of a Wolseley room; Hove Library special collections retain this material, as well as additional material relating to the life of her father.

JANE BROWN

Sources J. Brown, *Eminent gardeners* (1990) · *Sunday Times* (27 Dec 1936) · *Daily Telegraph* (28 Dec 1936) · *Morning Post* (28 Dec 1936) · Hove Central Library, Sussex, Wolseley collection, biographical file · J. H. Lehmann, *All Sir Garnet: a biography of Field-Marshal Lord Wolseley* (1964) · *The letters of Lord and Lady Wolseley, 1870–1911*, ed. G. Arthur (1922) · F. Wolseley, *Gardening for women* (1908) · F. Wolseley, *In a college garden* (1916) · GEC, *Peerage* · d. cert.
Archives Hove Central Library, Sussex, personal papers, corresp., diaries, commonplace books, etc.
Likenesses Bassano, photograph, 1908, NPG [*see illus.*] · photograph, repro. in Wolseley, *In a college garden*, frontispiece
Wealth at death £24,820 6s. 10d.: resworn probate, 22 Feb 1937, *CGPLA Eng. & Wales*

Wolseley, Garnet Joseph, first Viscount Wolseley (1833–1913), army officer, was born at Golden Bridge House, co. Dublin, on 4 June 1833, the eldest of seven children of Major Garnet Wolseley, 25th foot, and Frances Anne Smith.

An impecunious family Wolseley's father, who had sold his commission shortly after marriage, died when Wolseley was only seven years old, leaving the family in somewhat straitened circumstances. This was to become one key to Wolseley's later career, for he assumed the role of head of and principal provider for the family, supporting his mother and two of his three brothers, George and Fred. Eventually George rose to high military rank himself, but earlier in his career he frequently incurred debts which Wolseley covered. Fred pursued various unsuccessful business ventures in Australia, which were a drain on Wolseley's own finances, particularly in 1878 and 1893. Thus Wolseley's pursuit of financial reward from his services, such as the grants he received after the Asante and Egyptian expeditions, and his determination to ensure that his daughter would succeed to his peerage after his death, were connected with assumed family responsibilities and an intimate comprehension of the disadvantages of being impecunious. His mother could manage only a day school education for him in Dublin, and, eager to improve his opportunities of obtaining a commission, Wolseley worked in a surveyor's office, thus acquiring a knowledge of draughtsmanship and surveying.

Early military career Unable to afford a commission, Wolseley and his mother sought nomination from the commander-in-chief, Wellington, on the strength of his father's service. His mother's direct appeal was successful, and he was nominated to an ensigncy in the 12th foot on 12 March 1852. Wolseley later wrote that the first business of the young officer who wished to distinguish himself in his profession was to seek to get killed, and, in effect, this was the only means by which he could hope to advance while the system of purchase prevailed. In this

Garnet Joseph Wolseley, first Viscount Wolseley (1833–1913), by Paul Albert Besnard, 1880

sense, as Redvers Buller later noted, Wolseley was very much a self-made man. Wolseley inherited from his mother, a deeply religious Irish protestant, a profound belief in a destiny willed by God, which was to comfort him even in the darkest days of his failure to save Charles Gordon at Khartoum in 1885. Implicit fatalism allied to great courage was to bring Wolseley grievous wounds in his early career, but also that recognition he sought in his chosen profession. Ambition was to be another key to his future.

'Patriotic' assumptions and approach to public life Yet Wolseley also had immense pride in his country, which, like many other Anglo-Irish, he expressed solely in terms of love of England. He wrote in September 1882, 'To see England great is my highest aspiration, & that I might have a leading part in contributing to the attainment of that greatness, is my only real ambition' (Wolseley to his wife, 28 Sept 1882, Wolseley Collections, W/P 11/23). He despised foreigners and especially Irish nationalists, frequently alluding to the desirability of his filling some proconsular role in Ireland and, on at least one occasion, of putting himself at the head of the loyalists to resist the raising of a 'filthy green rag' (Maurice MSS, 2/2/18). The extremity of his patriotism was also apparent in his utter contempt for most party politicians. Wolseley despised the 'dirty dunghill sort of democratic wave … now passing over the world' (Wolseley to his wife, 24–7 Nov 1884, Wolseley Collections, W/P 13/31) and made little secret of his belief that party politics was the 'curse of modern England', as he expressed it in one public speech in April 1888. For Wolseley, the 'arch-traitor' Gladstone was to personify all that was wrong with the system, and his deep hatred for the 'canting old sinner' was only intensified by his attributing to Gladstone the blame for the peace concluded with the Boers after the death of his favourite, George Colley, at Majuba in 1881 and for the deaths of both Herbert Stewart, who had replaced Colley as his most favoured subordinate, and Gordon in the Sudan. Ironically, despite his Conservatism, he was regarded by his opponents within the army as a dangerous radical and by the Liberal leadership almost as a colleague.

However, Wolseley's tendency towards allegedly 'sinister caesarism' (Preston, 'Khartoum relief expedition', 97) has been exaggerated, for he always understood the restricted constitutional parameters within which the army existed and the requirements of his political masters; he wrote, for example, in August 1879 that the whole truth should not be told in dispatches for 'unpleasant truths that can be made use of by the opponents of the Government you are serving should be reserved for one's private correspondence with ministers' (Wolseley to his wife, 8–13 Aug 1879, Wolseley Collections, W/P 8/19). There was a cynicism in this. Moreover, while despising the press and war correspondents, he consciously used his public utterances and writing, as he put it in February 1878, 'to keep my name before the public' (Wolseley to his brother, 18 Feb 1878, Wolseley Collections, 163/iv). He always denied that he wrote for newspapers as opposed to periodicals, but much the same effect was achieved through the employment of many of his staff by the press on campaign and his promotion of official and semi-official campaign histories. On a personal level Wolseley could be charming, but this was not always the image conveyed, and Disraeli was to write to the queen on one occasion: 'It is quite true that Wolseley is an egotist and a braggart. So was Nelson ... Men of action when eminently successful in early life are generally boastful and full of themselves' (Beaconsfield to Victoria, 24 Aug 1879, Royal Archives, B61/34).

Soldiering, 1852–1861 Having secured his commission, Wolseley at once transferred to the 80th foot on 13 April 1852 in order to see active service in the Second Anglo-Burmese War. Within a few months of his arrival he distinguished himself in an assault on Myat Toon's stockade at Kyault Azein in March 1853, being so badly wounded in the left thigh that he would be troubled by the leg for the remainder of his life. Promoted to lieutenant in the 84th foot on 16 May 1853, he was invalided home and transferred to the 90th foot in Dublin on 24 February 1854. Promotion to captain followed on 26 January 1855 as a result of Wolseley's services in the Crimean War, and through his knowledge of surveying Wolseley was seconded to the engineers in the trenches before Sevastopol. There he met Charles George Gordon, who was to become one of his heroes; in turn, Wolseley would become one of only two men for whom Gordon prayed nightly. Wolseley was slightly wounded in the right thigh during one attack on the Quarries in June 1855, but on 30 August he was severely wounded by shellfire, suffering another wound to the right leg and losing the sight of his left eye.

On recovering Wolseley was appointed deputy assistant quartermaster-general in the Crimea on 8 November 1855 and served on as such until the end of hostilities in June 1856. He was recommended for a brevet majority but could not receive it until he had served for six years. Regimental service was resumed at Aldershot, and the 90th embarked for China in early 1857, only to be diverted to India through the outbreak of the mutiny. Wolseley participated in the advance for the first relief of Lucknow via Cawnpore. The 90th then remained at Lucknow until the second and final relief in February 1858. Wolseley was appointed deputy assistant quartermaster-general on Sir Hope Grant's staff on 1 April 1858, succeeding his future rival, Frederick Roberts, and campaigning with Hope Grant in Oudh. The brevet majority having been secured finally on 24 March 1858, Wolseley was rewarded for his further services with a brevet lieutenant-colonelcy on 26 April 1859. Hope Grant became Wolseley's first military patron and Wolseley remained on Grant's staff in the same capacity for the Second Opium War between March 1860 and March 1861, the campaign becoming the subject of his first book, the generally unremarkable *Narrative of the War with China in 1860* (1862). Promotion to an unattached majority had been received on 15 February 1861 and Wolseley received a majority in his regiment on 6 August 1861. In less than eight years Wolseley had risen, without purchase of his commissions, from ensign to brevet lieutenant-colonel at the age of only twenty-five, and had established a reputation for courage and judgement in action and as an able staff officer.

In Canada and marriage Granted a period of long leave on his return from China, Wolseley was suddenly ordered to Canada as a result of the *Trent* affair of November 1861 (when American officials boarded a British mail packet), taking up the appointment of assistant quartermaster-general at Montreal on 11 January 1862, a post he held until 31 March 1867. Like many other British officers in Canada, he took the opportunity of seeing something of the American Civil War, reaching the Confederacy and meeting both Robert E. Lee and 'Stonewall' Jackson in the aftermath of Lee's retreat from Maryland after Antietam. As indicated in 'A month's visit to the Confederate headquarters', an article largely reworked by his sister, Matilda, which Wolseley had published in *Blackwood's Magazine* in January 1863, he favoured British recognition of the South. In Lee, too, he found a heroic figure, rivalled only by Gordon. A later article, 'General Lee', published in *Macmillan's Magazine* in March 1887 has been described as a 'classic of Confederate literature' (Wolseley, *American Civil War*, 53). Wolseley also contributed a series of review articles on the war to the *North American Review* during 1889 and sketches of Nathan B. Forrest and William T. Sherman to the *United Service Magazine* in 1891–2, as well as encouraging G. F. R. Henderson to undertake his celebrated study of Jackson. However, his pro-Southern sympathies and hero-worship of Lee tended to detract from the analytical value of his work, and he was not the intellectual equal in this respect of either the commander-in-chief in Canada, Sir John Michel, or the adjutant-general of the Canadian militia, Sir Patrick MacDougall, both of whom were to become patrons of Wolseley during his Canadian service. Wolseley secured a brevet colonelcy on 5 June 1865, becoming deputy quartermaster-general on 1 October 1867 on Michel's recommendation and commanding first a cadet training school and then a camp of observation during the Fenian incursions.

Although by then retired from the Canadian command, Michel was also to recommend Wolseley to lead the Red River expedition in 1870. In the meantime, however, two other aspects of Wolseley's Canadian service were significant. First, Wolseley married Louisa Erskine (1843–1920) on his birthday, 4 June 1867, while on a short home leave. 'Loo' became an important prop to Wolseley, promoting his interests while he was overseas and serving as the recipient of the letters and journals he wrote as a safety valve. A woman of keen wit and shrewd observation, she was apt to accuse Wolseley of composing his letters with an eye on posterity. In turn, Wolseley was to accuse her of declining to assist his social and political duties on Cyprus—one of the few occasions when she accompanied him overseas—and feigning a lack of interest in his military career. She was also somewhat jealous of other women, such as the duchess of Edinburgh, who were friendly with her husband. None the less, the affection between the two throughout their marriage was clear and Wolseley felt keenly the separations on campaigns, his letters frequently addressed to his little porpoise, ratcatcher, periwinkle, whippersnapper, or similar endearments. Their only child, Frances Garnet *Wolseley, was born on 15 September 1872 and was to become a noted horticulturist.

Secondly, in 1869, and at the suggestion of Sir Richard Airey, the army's quartermaster-general, Wolseley added to his military reputation through the publication of his *Soldier's Pocket Book*. A practical manual of soldiering, which was to go through five editions, it was the only guide of its kind to military organization and tactics in the kind of small wars in which the army was increasingly involved. It was also the nearest that Wolseley would come to producing any substantial work of theory other than the paper on field manoeuvres submitted for the Wellington prize essay in 1872, which was placed second, and occasional articles in periodicals such as *Blackwood's Magazine*, *Macmillan's Magazine*, and the *Nineteenth Century*, which were written as often as not principally for money. The *Soldier's Pocket Book* demonstrated Wolseley's understanding of logistics and advertised his commitment to military reform. The former was particularly apposite, for on 5 April 1870 he was chosen by the new commander-in-chief in Canada, the Hon. James Lindsay, to lead the Red River expedition to overthrow a provisional government established by rebellious *métis* at Fort Garry, 600 miles beyond Lake Superior.

Some 1200 men had to be transported across a series of unnavigable portages through the wilderness of the Canadian north-west, with an imperative to complete the mission and return before the lakes froze. Wolseley took a minute interest in the organization of his force, which he formally took over on 10 May 1870, and reached Fort Garry on 24 August, only to find that the *métis* had fled. For his services Wolseley was created KCMG and CB, and was both praised by Lindsay and eulogized by G. L. Huyshe's semi-official campaign history. Wolseley was then brought home to take up the appointment of assistant adjutant-general in the discipline branch of the War Office on 1 May 1871.

The Second Asante War, 1873–1874 Wolseley did not play a leading role in the Cardwell reforms, as these were substantially completed before he returned to England. But he fully agreed with their aims, and particularly with short service and linked battalions, and he was quickly identified with the cause of reform within the War Office. He was selected by Cardwell in August 1873 to lead an expedition to punish Asante incursions into the Gold Coast protectorate by seizing their capital of Kumasi. Wolseley had been pressing for the appointment within the War Office, but his organizational and logistic ability was testified by the *Soldier's Pocket Book*, his achievements on the Red River, and his participation in the planning of the autumn manoeuvres in 1872. Moreover, he supported reform and this would be the first major expedition to test the Cardwell changes, although the recent re-organization had no immediate relevance to the actual conduct of colonial campaigning. Despite his reforming reputation, Wolseley at this time enjoyed the support of the army's commander-in-chief, the duke of Cambridge, who had already suggested his appointment as adjutant-general in India, only for the proposal to fall on Wolseley's lack of the required native language qualification.

Accordingly, Wolseley took up the appointment of governor of the Gold Coast with the temporary rank of major-general on 2 October 1873. As was the case in the Red River campaign, the difficulties were primarily climate and terrain, and he had to plan on the basis of using British troops for the minimum possible time. Indeed, three British battalions did not arrive until January 1874, by which time Wolseley's locally raised forces had compelled the Asante to withdraw across the Pra. He then advanced on Kumasi, defeating the Asante at Amoaful on 27 January and occupying their capital on 4 February. Having burned Kumasi, Wolseley was back at the coast by 19 February and had re-embarked his army eight days later. It was a model campaign, extensively reported by the press, and it established Wolseley as the 'Modern Major-General', memorably portrayed by George Grossmith in Gilbert and Sullivan's *Pirates of Penzance*. In addition, 'All Sir Garnet' became a cockney catchphrase. Wolseley was rewarded with the GCMG, KCB, a grant of £25,000, and major-general's rank on 1 April 1874. The honours came from the Conservatives, who had come into office during the campaign. Wolseley, whom Disraeli described as 'a little man, but with a good presence, and a bright blue eye, holds his head well, and has a lithe figure' (Monypenny & Buckle,

5.305), believed he would have been granted a peerage by the Liberals, and he turned down both the GCB and a baronetcy, believing the latter worthy only of 'common people'.

The Wolseley 'ring' The expedition also established the concept of the Asante or *Wolseley ring or gang, which was to arouse strong opinions among rival groups such as the traditionalists, ranged around Cambridge, and the 'Indians', who came to be identified primarily with Roberts. The struggle with the former tended to encompass reform issues such as short service and the latter principally the empire's strategic orientation. However, neither particular issues nor the positions assumed by individuals on them were necessarily constant, although the context of rivalry was invariably centred upon manoeuvring adherents into particular commands. Wolseley claimed that he always made a practice of noting down the names of able soldiers wherever he met them and that merit was his only criterion, and it was widely recognized that he had the knack of picking able men.

The selection of staff for the Red River campaign was dictated by those available in Canada and was essentially unplanned. Therefore Asante marked the effective beginning of the ring, although Redvers Buller, Hugh McCalmont, John McNeill, William Butler, and Huyshe had also been on the Red River expedition. In addition, Asante saw the adherence to Wolseley, among others, of Evelyn Wood, Colley, Frederick Maurice, Baker Russell, Henry Brackenbury, and George Greaves. Some were chosen fortuitously, while others such as Colley, Brackenbury, and Maurice, who had won the Wellington essay competition, were selected on intellectual reputation: Wolseley consistently encouraged the employment of Staff College graduates. He did not always have a free choice of staff as, for example, in 1879 in South Africa, when he inherited many of Lord Chelmsford's staff, or in Egypt in 1882, when the principal field commands were taken by those already designated to act in the autumn manoeuvres. He also found it politic on occasions to accept nominations by others such as Cambridge or the prince of Wales. Moreover in his later War Office appointments as adjutant-general, and even as commander-in-chief, Wolseley did not have exclusive control of the promotion system. Nevertheless, he was somewhat disingenuous in claiming that he always dropped failures or continually introduced fresh blood, and appointments were often a case of reshuffling the same cards, since he argued that he could rely instinctively on those familiar with his working methods and in whom he had full confidence.

This was not how Wolseley's opponents saw the 'mutual admiration society', and there was resentment on the part of those excluded from his well-publicized campaigns. There were undoubtedly victims of the ring, such as Sir John Glover in Asante and Sir Charles Wilson in the Sudan, but it was not as exclusive as often claimed and no worse in its practices than those of Cambridge or Roberts, and similar networks occurred in other areas of Victorian life. A more significant charge was that constant employment of the same officers failed to develop others, although this was the claim of those, such as Cambridge, who were most irked by Wolseley ignoring the claims of seniority. Yet Wolseley did arguably become something of a prisoner of the initial success of the ring, feeling it necessary to employ the same men lest his rejection of them reflect adversely on his earlier choice. His criticism of many of his followers increased over the years, although this was also a result of prominent subordinates growing in stature and seniority themselves. 'The Chief' was respected rather than liked, and he had associates rather than friends. Also, the deaths of the two men to whom he felt closest, Colley and Stewart, whom Wolseley had recruited to the ring in Zululand in 1879, affected him greatly. Wolseley never forgave Wood, for example, for obeying government instructions and making peace with the Boers after Colley's death, while Buller's apparent willingness to accept appointment as commander-in-chief ahead of Wolseley in 1895 was regarded as betrayal. What made increasing dissension and rivalry within the ring so destructive, notably during the Gordon relief expedition, was that Wolseley's command style was built upon individuals willingly fulfilling specific roles in a kind of orchestrated military collective. Moreover, Wolseley's capacity to manage affairs decreased in proportion to the growth in the scale of operations. Generally Wolseley was able to co-ordinate the diverse talents of his chosen subordinates in ways well suited to colonial campaigning, but in the last analysis improvisation was no substitute for a proper general staff.

Colonial soldiering, 1875–1882 Wolseley was a considerable political asset after Asante, and after a short spell back at the War Office as inspector-general of auxiliary forces from April 1874 to March 1875 he was sent out by the colonial secretary, Carnarvon, as high commissioner and general commanding to Natal, tasked with forwarding the cause of federation in southern Africa by pushing an amended constitution through the colonial assembly. Wolseley assumed his new position on 30 March, effecting the required administrative changes and returning to England in October to resume duty as inspector-general. He had grown sufficiently weary of the conservatism of the duke of Cambridge to contemplate retirement before his Natal appointment, while the duke himself was increasingly hostile to Wolseley's ambition to become commander-in-chief in India. Thus, while Wolseley regarded his next appointment on 25 November 1876, to membership of the Council of India at the India Office, as a possible stepping stone to the Indian command and found that his memoranda were taken far more seriously than at the War Office, Cambridge tended to welcome the opportunity to sideline him, and had earlier suggested Wolseley should be given the command in Canada.

Wolseley's claims for an active command could not be easily dismissed, however, and in February 1878 he was designated chief of staff to Lord Napier in the event of a British expeditionary force being sent to resist Russian control of the Dardanelles. He received promotion to lieutenant-general on 25 March 1878 and then on 22 July was appointed the first high commissioner and governor-general of Cyprus, intended as a *place d'armes* to counter Russian regional influence. Wolseley fretted that he thus missed the Second Anglo-Afghan War, where Colley, as the viceroy's private secretary, was pressing Wolseley's claims for field command. Similarly, it appeared that he would miss the Anglo-Zulu War, but after the disaster at Isandlwana and further mishaps suffered by Chelmsford, Wolseley was appointed governor and high commissioner in South Africa with the rank of local general on 23 June 1879. Before he could get to the front, however, Chelmsford secured victory over the Zulu at Ulundi and Wolseley's military role was confined to the pursuit and capture of the Zulu king, Cetshwayo, and the defeat of the Pedi chief, Sekukuni, in the Transvaal. Civil administration had few attractions for Wolseley, and in imposing the partition of Zululand and attempting to intimidate the Boers of the Transvaal into an acceptance of annexation he contributed to future difficulties in southern Africa. Once more expecting a peerage, which might further his claims to the Indian command, and once more returning to find a new government installed at home, Wolseley was offered only the GCB he had rejected six years previously. Wolseley also entertained some hopes of securing either the Bombay or Madras commands as a means of getting to India, where the commander-in-chief was due to retire in 1881. It was made clear, however, that he could not expect an Indian appointment, and on 1 July 1880 he became quartermaster-general at the War Office.

Reforming the army Wolseley was to continue as quartermaster-general until 31 March 1882 and then was adjutant-general at the War Office, albeit interrupted by the Egyptian and Sudan campaigns, until 30 September 1890. It was a period which was to throw him directly into opposition to Cambridge, who rightly sensed that it was he to whom Wolseley referred at a public dinner in June 1880 as one of 'those great boulders of prejudice and superstition who now impede the way' (Royal Archives, E25/96a). The duke feared that reform would undermine regimental tradition and the army's constitutional position, and held that long service was essential to discipline, and that drill and discipline was the primary route to military efficiency. Wolseley was hardly the dangerous radical portrayed by Cambridge and his cousin, the queen: he was to share Cambridge's opposition to the abolition of the post of commander-in-chief and its replacement with a continental-style chief of staff. Moreover, like Cambridge, he was to press for the expansion of the army, for a definitive statement of the army's priorities, and for politicians to accept their ultimate responsibility for national security policies determined on political and financial rather than military grounds.

However, Wolseley's reforming zeal and willingness to flout seniority in staff selection made him anathema to the duke and his circle. Particularly as adjutant-general, Wolseley oversaw modernization of the infantry drill book, the introduction of mounted infantry, improvement in campaign dress, greater tactical training, extension of the intelligence department, and the preparation of mobilization plans, the last two under the direction of

Henry Brackenbury. Wolseley also championed what might be regarded as an 'imperial school' as opposed to either a 'continental' or an 'Indian' school of strategic thought, placing the priority firmly on home defence and envisaging any likely war against Russia as being waged through amphibious operations at the peripheries such as the Baltic, Black Sea, or the Turkestan/Caspian area rather than across the north-west frontier. The 'Indian' view that any threat to India must be regarded as the empire's first priority did not command the support often implied. While Brackenbury was converted to the 'Indian' position after 1891, this did not challenge the prevailing orthodoxy within the War Office; the celebrated Stanhope memorandum of 1888, which virtually recapitulated Wolseley's strategic perceptions, held sway until Roberts became commander-in-chief. Even then, the triumph of the 'Indians' proved short-lived, as attention moved towards a German rather than a Russian enemy.

The duke and the queen disliked not only Wolseley's iconoclasm but also his apparent inability to refrain from public comment adverse to the duke. They blocked the attempt by Gladstone and his secretary of state for war, Childers, to make Wolseley a peer in March 1881, an elevation intended both to give the government military support for reform in the Lords and also to mollify Wolseley for his disappointment at the selection of Roberts to command in South Africa after Colley's death. Gladstone initially threatened to resign on the peerage issue but did not persist in this. However, Wolseley was offered the post of adjutant-general in December 1881 provided he guaranteed discretion in his public statements.

Egypt and the Sudan Wolseley's tenure as adjutant-general was twice interrupted by campaigns. On 20 July 1882 the cabinet decided to appoint him commander, with the temporary rank of general, of the expedition to suppress Arabi Pasha's nationalist revolt in Egypt: the cabinet minute read: 'Instructions to Wolseley: Put down Arabi and establish Khedive's power' (Gladstone, *Diaries*, 31 July 1882). He was formally appointed on 4 August, left England on 15 August, and after a feint at Alexandria, swiftly and secretly transferred his troops down the Suez Canal to Isma'iliyyah. A sharp action at Qassasin brought him up to Arabi's fortified lines at Tell al-Kebir and these were captured on 13 September. Arabi's army was routed and Cairo promptly occupied. Wolseley received promotion to full general on 18 November 1882, the thanks of parliament, and a grant of £30,000, and was created Baron Wolseley of Cairo and Wolseley, though he wanted a viscountcy. Cambridge and the queen, who had been gratified by Wolseley's employment of the duke of Connaught during the campaign, fully acknowledged Wolseley's able victory, but the duke thought it made him too powerful and suggested either a colonial governorship or the lord lieutenancy of Ireland.

Eighteen months after his return from Egypt, Wolseley saw Charles Gordon off to Khartoum and, as soon as the extent of the Mahdist revolt became evident, urged the necessity of a relief expedition. He did not prevail, and his belated appointment to command such an expedition on

1 September 1884 was from the first a forlorn hope, irrespective of the controversy that surrounded Wolseley's choice of following the Nile to Khartoum rather than advancing across the desert from Suakin to Berber, as was counselled by most other advisers to the government. Clearly, Wolseley was heavily influenced by the Red River experience and, indeed, Canadian voyageurs were brought over to handle the 800 special boats used on the Nile. The fall of Berber to the Mahdists in May 1884 and the subsequent difficulties in trying to push a railway out from Suakin tend to suggest the Nile route might have been the better, although this can never now be determined. The expedition was dogged by logistic delays, and, for the first time in his career, Wolseley's conduct of a campaign was limited by the government, which refused to allow him go any further forward than Korti. In any case he could not be everywhere, and, arguably, by maintaining such close control for so long he had hardly encouraged the development of initiative in his subordinates, now riven by mutual animosities. Wolseley was always regarded as a 'lucky' general and he himself was to remark that the 'sun of his luck' set when Stewart was fatally wounded before Methemmeh. Command of the desert column fell to Wilson, who wasted precious days before embarking on steamers for Khartoum. Wilson reached Khartoum two days too late, on 28 January 1885, but an earlier arrival might merely have hastened the Mahdist assault. Initially Gladstone's government appeared ready to avenge Gordon, but in April it was announced that there would be no further operations in the Sudan. Having reported on the situation at Suakin in May 1885, Wolseley supervised the withdrawal of his own force to Egypt. He returned to England an embittered man in July. It was small consolation to be created a knight of St Patrick and to be elevated to viscount on 19 August 1885 with succession to his daughter.

Commander-in-chief As the end of his term as adjutant-general approached there was talk of Wolseley finally going to India, but he firmly declined the possibility on the grounds not only that his daughter was coming out that season but also, and more significantly, because there no longer seemed any real possibility of war against Russia in central Asia. He now hoped for war against France and aimed to succeed Cambridge as commander-in-chief. Aldershot, Gibraltar, and even Australia had also been mentioned, but Wolseley took up the Irish command on 1 October 1890. With more leisure time than at the War Office he was able to indulge his tastes. He tended to dislike society functions yet enjoyed intelligent company, and he and Louisa always had a wide circle of literary and artistic acquaintances. He also contributed articles to periodicals, including a series on Napoleon for the *Pall Mall Magazine* in 1894, republished in book form as *The Decline and Fall of Napoleon* in the following year. He also began writing a much delayed long-term project, *The Life of John, First Duke of Marlborough*, of which two volumes were published in 1894. It remained uncompleted for, on 1 November 1895—he had been created a field marshal on 26 May

1894—Wolseley succeeded Cambridge as commander-in-chief.

His tenure was from the beginning overshadowed by the recommendations of the Hartington commission five years earlier that the post be abolished altogether and replaced by a continental-style chief of staff and a War Office council. Through the opposition of the queen, the duke, and leading Liberals, the proposal was buried, although an emasculated War Office council was established. Wolseley sometimes advocated a soldier as a continental-style minister of defence, but he did not wish his own perceived inheritance diminished. Indeed, he regarded a chief of staff as largely a device to create a role for Brackenbury, who had sat on the commission. As secretary of state after 1892, Campbell-Bannerman produced a modified version of the Hartington scheme, reducing the powers of the commander-in-chief, whose former departmental subordinates would now sit with him on an army board with direct and equal access to the secretary of state. Cambridge was finally eased out but it was Buller, who had succeeded Wolseley as adjutant-general, whom the Liberals intended to become commander-in-chief.

Buller, however, was not acceptable to the Salisbury administration, which suddenly came into office in June 1895, and Wolseley was offered the post. A complication was that the queen wanted her son, Connaught, to succeed her cousin, and at one stage during the incessant manoeuvring of that summer Wolseley had offered to waive his own claims in favour of Connaught and to go as ambassador to Berlin. When presented with a straight choice between Berlin and being commander-in-chief, however, he accepted the latter, with even further diminished powers as laid down in the order in council of 21 November 1895. Wolseley was to remark of his new position that he felt like the 'fifth wheel of a coach', and he strove unsuccessfully to restore what he regarded as the necessary authority of the commander-in-chief over the army's command and discipline. Wolseley's belief that Buller had betrayed him hardly helped the atmosphere within the War Office, and it was made more poisonous still by the new depths of mutual hostility between Wolseley and the politicians as represented by the new secretary of state, Lord Lansdowne, who had a firm preference for Roberts. Little was achieved beyond some increase in military establishments and the revival of the autumn manoeuvres in 1898, but by this time Wolseley's faculties were fading fast, for in 1897 he succumbed to an illness from which he never fully recovered and which badly impaired his memory.

Retirement and death Wolseley could certainly take pride in the efficiency and speed of the army's mobilization for the Second South African War in October 1899, and was equally justified in regarding the government as foolhardy in ignoring his advice to mobilize earlier. However, the deterioration in his relationship with Lansdowne had contributed to the lack of strategic direction at the beginning of the war, and the success of eventual mobilization paled beside the shock of the defeats of 'black week' in December. As a result, Roberts was sent out to supersede

Buller as commander-in-chief in South Africa without Wolseley being consulted. Wolseley was persuaded to remain at his post by the queen, finally retiring on 30 November 1900 to be succeeded—to his bitter regret—by Roberts. In many respects, therefore, his career ended unfulfilled, even if he had arguably laid the foundations for further professionalization of the army. Also, through no fault of his own, the Victorian army's 'only general' had never endured the supreme test of command in the field against an equal adversary.

In retirement Wolseley published, in 1903, two disappointing volumes of autobiography, *The Story of a Soldier's Life*, which took his account only as far as Asante. He was regimental colonel of the Royal Horse Guards from 29 March 1895 to 15 November 1907 and of the Royal Irish from 20 July 1898. He died at the Villa La Tourette at Menton in France on 25 March 1913 and was buried in St Paul's Cathedral, London six days later. His widow died on 10 April 1920 at Hampton Court and, after cremation at Golders Green, her ashes were placed in her husband's grave.

Assessment Wolseley's reputation was rapidly eclipsed not only through the greater prominence accorded Lord Roberts immediately prior to the First World War but also through the impact of that war itself on military and other historiography. Sir George Arthur produced in 1922 a bowdlerized and inaccurate edition of Wolseley's correspondence with Lady Wolseley, and two years later, co-operated with Maurice's son, also Frederick, in a biography. This attempted to portray Wolseley as the true architect of the army's ultimate victory in the 'great appeal to the arbitrament of the sword' (Maurice and Arthur, 342), which had eluded Wolseley in his own lifetime. The adulatory approach was largely repeated in the 1964 biography by Joseph Lehmann, *All Sir Garnet*, emanating from the 1960s revival of interest in the Victorian army. However, Wolseley was viewed with hostility by the Canadian historian Adrian Preston in editions of his campaign journals for South Africa (1971, 1973) and the Sudan (1967) and in articles over the next decade. Subsequently there has been another revival of interest in the period, and Wolseley has received a more scholarly appraisal which, while recognizing the complexities of his character, reasserted his reputation as the leading British soldier of his generation.   IAN F. W. BECKETT

Sources Hove Central Library, Sussex, Wolseley collections · PRO, Wolseley MSS, WO 147 · Royal Arch. · King's Lond., Liddell Hart C., Maurice MSS · J. H. Lehmann, *All Sir Garnet: a biography of Field-Marshal Lord Wolseley* (1964) · *The South African diaries of Sir Garnet Wolseley, 1875*, ed. A. Preston (1971) · *The South African journal of Sir Garnet Wolseley, 1879–1880*, ed. A. Preston (1973) · *In relief of Gordon: Lord Wolseley's campaign journal of the Khartoum relief expedition, 1884–1885*, ed. A. Preston (1967) · A. Preston, 'Wolseley, the Khartoum relief expedition and the defence of India', *Swords and covenants*, ed. A. Preston and P. Dennis (1976), 89–122 · A. Preston, 'Frustrated great gamesmanship: Sir Garnet Wolseley's plans for war against Russia, 1873–78', *International History Review*, 2 (1980), 239–65 · A. Preston, 'Sir Garnet Wolseley and the Cyprus expedition, 1878', *JSAHR*, 45/181 (1967), 4–16 · Viscount Wolseley [G. Wolseley], *The story of a soldier's life*, 2 vols. (1903) · F. Maurice and G. Arthur, *The life of Lord Wolseley* (1924) · G. Arthur, ed., *The letters of Lord and Lady Wolseley, 1870–1911* (1922) · G. Wolseley, *The American Civil War: an English view*, ed. J. Rawley (2002) [introduction by J. Rawley] · M. Pegram, *The Wolseley heritage: the story of Frances Viscountess Wolseley and her parents* (1939) · Gladstone, *Diaries* · C. Ballard, 'Sir Garnet Wolseley and John Dunn', *The Anglo-Zulu War: new perspectives*, ed. A. Duminy and C. Ballard (1981), 120–47 · I. Harvie, 'The Wolseley ring: a case study in the exercise of patronage in the late Victorian army', MA diss., Buckingham, 1993 · I. F. W. Beckett, 'Wolseley and the ring', *Soldiers of the Queen*, 69 (1992), 14–25 · I. F. W. Beckett, 'Edward Stanhope at the War Office, 1887–92', *Journal of Strategic Studies*, 5/2 (1982), 278–307 · I. F. W. Beckett, 'The Stanhope memorandum of 1888: a reinterpretation', *BIHR*, 57 (1984), 240–47 · H. Bailes, 'Patterns of thought in the late Victorian army', *Journal of Strategic Studies*, 4/1 (1981), 29–45 · H. Bailes, 'Technology and imperialism: a case study of the Victorian army in Africa', *Victorian Studies*, 24 (1980–81), 82–104 · B. J. Bond, 'The retirement of the duke of Cambridge', *Journal of the Royal United Service Institution*, 106 (1961), 544–53 · B. Bond, *The Victorian army and the Staff College, 1854–1914* (1972) · B. Bond, ed., *Victorian military campaigns* (1967) · E. M. Spiers, *The late Victorian army, 1868–1902* (1992) · W. S. Hamer, *The British army: civil–military relations, 1885–1905* (1970) · J. Luvaas, *The education of an army: British military thought, 1815–1940* (Chicago, IL, 1964) · 'Report of the commissioners appointed to inquire into the military preparations … connected with the war in South Africa: minutes of evidence', *Parl. papers* (1904), vol. 40, nos. 8704–9358, Cd 1790 [Wolseley's evidence, 27–8 Nov 1902] · W. F. Monypenny and G. E. Buckle, *The life of Benjamin Disraeli*, 5 (1920)

Archives BL, letter-book relating to Cyprus, Add. MS 41324 · BL, letters to Sir Henry Campbell-Bannerman, Add. MSS 41226–41233 · Cameronians (Scottish Rifles) Regimental Museum · Duke U., Perkins L., letters, XVIII-H · Hove Central Library, Sussex, corresp. and papers · Low Parks Museum, Hamilton, diaries · PRO, journals and papers, WO 147 | BL, corresp. with Sir Austen Layard, Add. MSS 39021–39026, 39131–39132 · BL, corresp. with Macmillans, Add. MS 55252 · BL, corresp. with G. D. Ramsay, Add. MS 46450 · BL OIOC, letters to Sir Owen Burne, MSS Eur. D 951 · Bodl. Oxf., letters to Doyle family · Bodl. Oxf., corresp. with Lord Kimberley · Bodl. RH, corresp. with Sir Geoffrey Lagden · CAC Cam., letters to W. T. Stead · Chatsworth House, Derbyshire, letters to Lord Hartington · Ches. & Chester ALSS, letters to Rhoda Broughton · CKS, letters to Edward Stanhope · CUL, corresp. with Sir John Glover · Devon RO, Buller MSS · Duke U., Wood MSS · Glos. RO, corresp. with Sir Michael Hicks Beach · King's AC Cam., letters to Oscar Browning · King's Lond., Liddell Hart C., corresp. with Sir Frederick Maurice · NA Scot., corresp. with earl of Airlie · NAM, letters to Lord Roberts · Natal Archives Depot, letters to Sir Henry Evelyn Wood · NL Scot., corresp. with Blackwoods · Norfolk RO, letters to Sir John Cowell · NRA, priv. coll., corresp. with Sir John Ewart · PRO, corresp. with Sir John Ardagh, 30/40 · PRO, Buller MSS, WO 132 · PRO, Carnarvon MSS, 30/6 · PRO, corresp. with Lord Cromer · PRO, letters to Lord Kitchener, PRO 30/7, WO 159 · Rhodes University, Grahamstown, South Africa, Cory Library for Historical Research, letters to Sir John Sprigg · Royal Arch. · Royal Artillery Institution, Woolwich, London, Brackenbury MSS · U. Durham L., corresp. with Sir Reginald Wingate · U. Leeds, Brotherton L., letters to Sir Edmund Gosse · University of Natal, Durban, Killie Campbell Africana Library, letter-book relating to South Africa · Warks. CRO, corresp. with Lady Anne Newdigate Newdegate · Wellcome L., letters to Sir Thomas Barlow

Likenesses lithograph, 1878, NPG · P. A. Besnard, oils, 1880, NPG [*see illus.*] · W. B. Wollen, portrait, 1881 (*The rescue of Private Andrews at the storming of the Motee Mohail, Lucknow*), Royal Marines · C. Sohn junior, oils, 1882, Royal Collection; on loan to Staff College, Camberley · J. E. Boehm, bronze cast of bust, 1883, NPG · Lady Butler, portrait, 1885 (*After the battle*; fragment), priv. coll. · F. Holl, oils, 1886, NG Ire.; related portrait, Hove Library, Sussex · wax figure, after 1894, Hove Library, Sussex · H. Schadow, oils, 1896, Gov. Art Coll. · H. D. Smith, oils, c.1905, Hove Library, Sussex · W. Strang, chalk drawing, 1908, NPG · Mrs A. Broom, photograph, 1911, NPG ·

W. G. John, bronze equestrian statue, 1918, Horse Guards Parade, London · Ape [C. Pellegrini], chromolithograph caricature, NPG; repro. in *VF* (18 April 1874) · Barraud, photograph, NPG; repro. in *Men and women of the Day* (1888) · attrib. J. E. Boehm, marble bust, Gov. Art Coll. · J. Brown, print (after H. T. Wells), NPG · W. & D. Downey, woodburytype, NPG; repro. in N. Downey and D. Downey, *The cabinet portrait gallery*, 3 (1892) · Lock & Whitfield, woodburytype, NPG; repro. in T. Cooper, *Men of mark: a gallery of contemporary portraits* (1876) · oils (after English School), Staff College, Camberley · photographs, NPG · print (after M. Menpes), NPG · prints, NPG · prints, Scottish United Services Museum, Edinburgh

Wolseley, Robert (1648/9–1697). *See under* Wolseley, Sir Charles, second baronet, appointed Lord Wolseley under the protectorate (1629/30–1714).

Wolseley, William (*c*.1640–1697), army officer, was the fifth son of Sir Robert Wolseley, first baronet (1587–1646), of Wolseley, Staffordshire, and his wife, Mary Wroughton (*b. c*.1608), daughter of Sir George Wroughton of Wilcot, Wiltshire. He was the younger brother of Sir Charles *Wolseley (1629/30–1714). In June 1667 he was appointed captain-lieutenant to the marquess of Worcester's newly raised foot regiment, disbanded a few months later when the treaty of Breda ended the Second Anglo-Dutch War. On 26 January 1673 he received a commission, again as captain-lieutenant, in Worcester's foot regiment raised in response to the Third Anglo-Dutch War and disbanded in 1674. On 1 April 1679 he was appointed to the same rank in an independent foot company in Chepstow Castle, again commanded by Worcester (afterwards duke of Beaufort) and was appointed captain in his foot regiment by a commission dated 20 June 1685. On 12 August 1688, when quartered at Scarborough, he came to prominent notice by causing his musketeers to toss Mayor Aislaby publicly in a blanket in retaliation for the mayor's caning in church of a clergyman who had refused to read the declaration of indulgence. The mayor complained of his treatment to James II in person, and Wolseley was summoned to appear before the council in London. 'The captain pleaded his majesty's gracious pardon, which was in the press, so was dismissed' (*Ellis Correspondence*). On 3 December 1688 Lord Montgomery, colonel of his regiment, and Lord Langdale of the same corps, both Roman Catholics, were seized in their beds at Hull by Captain Copley and the protestant officers of the garrison and kept in confinement. Wolseley now determined to join William of Orange, but his doing so was delayed by false rumours of massacres in various parts of the country.

Wolseley's force of character and protestant zeal were rewarded by William, who appointed him lieutenant-colonel of Sir John Hanmer's regiment, which in May 1689 accompanied Sir Percy Kirke to assist in relieving Londonderry. Wolseley's name appears as one of the council of war held by Kirke on his arrival in Lough Foyle. In June a deputation from Enniskillen, the other chief centre of protestant resistance in Ulster, sought support from Kirke. He responded by sending Wolseley and some other officers to take control of military operations in the Erne

William Wolseley (*c*.1640–1697), by Garret Morphey, 1692

valley. They were given arms and ammunition, and commissions to form the Enniskilleners into six regiments. Wolseley, who was to command in chief, was made colonel of the cavalry regiment; it initially consisted of twenty-five troops, reduced to twelve in 1690 and six in 1691, and was finally disbanded in 1698. His nephew Richard, ancestor of Sir Garnet Wolseley, was one of the troop commanders. The Enniskilleners were rough-riding countrymen whose uncouth appearance disturbed military professionals, but they proved effective soldiers. Their aggressive raiding parties had caused considerable trouble to the Jacobites, whose succession of attempts to suppress them had been unsuccessful. No sooner had Wolseley's party arrived at Enniskillen on 23 July than word came of yet another Jacobite attack on Crom Castle, the Enniskilleners' eastern stronghold on Lough Erne. He immediately led 2000 Enniskillen troops to its relief. An advance party drove back the Jacobite advance party under Anthony Hamilton, which had advanced west of Lisnaskea. Justin MacCarthy, the Jacobite commander, now raised the siege of Crom and took up a strong position on a hillside straddling the road to the south outside the village of Newtownbutler. The Enniskilleners were all for attack, and on 31 July, advancing to the 'very acceptable' cry of 'no popery' under Wolseley's leadership, they routed MacCarthy's force, which was said to number 5500. Wolseley reported more than 2000 dead, the capture of all the enemy's baggage and cannon, and 500 prisoners including the badly wounded MacCarthy. Many of the fleeing Jacobites were drowned or cut down in the surrounding wetlands. It was a striking victory which, coupled with the raising of the siege of Londonderry the same day, ended the Jacobite threat to Ulster.

Over the following winter Wolseley was involved in a series of clashes on the frontier between the two armies. He surprised and took Belturbet in December 1689 and on 12 February 1690 defeated the duke of Berwick in an engagement outside Cavan. He burnt the town but then withdrew, being unable, without artillery, to capture the castle. In May he captured Bellanacargy, but in the action was wounded in the scrotum, from which however he soon recovered. He commanded his regiment at the battle of the Boyne (1 July 1690), where it formed part of the cavalry force which William III led across the river at Drybridge. The Enniskilleners participated in the last serious fighting of the day in the vicinity of Donore church, suffering thirty casualties in a courageous charge against the Jacobites before becoming embroiled with the Dutch, whom they mistook for the enemy in the confusion. Wolseley participated in General Douglas's disorderly and unsuccessful expedition against Athlone, rejoining William for the unsuccessful siege of Limerick before returning to winter quarters in Ulster. He was present with his regiment at the dearly bought victory at Aughrim (12 July 1691). His services were rewarded in 1692 with his appointment as master-general of the ordnance in Ireland, at a salary of £500 p.a., in place of Lord Mountjoy. On 22 March 1693 he was made brigadier-general over all the horse, and in May 1696 was appointed one of the lords justices in Ireland and a privy councillor. He had received a three-year *custodiam* grant of extensive forfeited lands throughout Ireland, to the value of £1000, in 1695, renewed for a further three years in 1697. He died, unmarried, in December 1697. In 1700, under the Act of Resumption, his executors were obliged to forfeit an estate he had been granted in co. Westmeath.

CHARLES DALTON, rev. HARMAN MURTAGH

Sources C. Dalton, ed., *English army lists and commission registers, 1661–1714*, 1 (1892); 2 (1894); 3 (1896) • J. G. Simms, *Jacobite Ireland, 1685–91* (1969) • *Great news of a bloody fight in Newtown in Ireland* (1689) • A. Hamilton, *A true relation of the actions of the Inniskilling-men from their first taking up arms in December 1688* (1690) • W. McCarmick, *A further impartial account of the actions of the Inniskilling-men* (1691) • G. Story, *A true and impartial history of the most material occurrences in the kingdom of Ireland* (1691) • J. G. Simms, *The Williamite confiscation in Ireland, 1690–1703* (1956), 80–81 • G. Agar-Ellis, ed., *The Ellis correspondence: letters written during the years 1686, 1687, 1688, and addressed to John Ellis*, 2 vols. (1829), vol. 2, pp. 225–6 • J. L. J. Hughes, ed., *Patentee officers in Ireland, 1173–1826, including high sheriffs, 1661–1684 and 1761–1816*, IMC (1960), 141 • *CSP dom.*, 1692–8 • Burke, *Peerage* (1970), 2869
Likenesses G. Morphey, oils, 1692, priv. coll.; Sothebys, 13 Nov 1991, lot 26 [*see illus.*]
Wealth at death small estate in co. Westmeath, Ireland, *c*.1692, surrendered by executors under Act of Resumption, 1700: Simms, *The Williamite confiscation in Ireland*, 80–81

Wolseley, William (1756–1842), naval officer, was born on 15 March 1756 at Annapolis Royal in Nova Scotia, the son of Captain William Neville Wolseley, of the 47th regiment, then in garrison, and Anne, sister of Admiral Phillips Cosby. On his father's side William was descended from the Irish branch of the Staffordshire family of Wolseley. In 1764 the family returned to Ireland; and in 1769 William, who had been at school in Kilkenny, was entered on the cutter *Goodwill* at Waterford, commanded by his father's brother-in-law, Lieutenant John Buchanan. Two years later, when the *Goodwill* was paid off, Wolseley was sent by his uncle Phillips Cosby to a nautical school in Westminster, from which, after some months, he joined the *Portland*, going to Jamaica. He returned to England in the *Princess Amelia*, and in September 1773 joined the *Salisbury* (50 guns) with Commodore Edward Hughes, commander-in-chief in the East Indies. The *Salisbury* returned home at the end of 1777, and Wolseley, having passed his examination, was promoted (11 June 1778), to junior lieutenant of the *Duke*, one of the fleet with Augustus Keppel in July, though on 27 July she had fallen so far to leeward that she took no part in the action.

When the autumn cruise came to an end, Wolseley, at the suggestion of Sir Edward Hughes, going again as commander-in-chief in the East Indies, effected a transfer to the *Worcester*, one of his squadron. After some service against pirates in the Indian seas he commanded a company of the naval brigade at the reduction of Negapatam in October 1781, and again at the storming of Fort Ostenberg, Trincomalee, on 11 January 1782, when Wolseley was severely wounded in the chest and left for dead. After being found next day, he was carried on to the *Worcester* and shortly afterwards moved into the *Superb*, Hughes's flagship; in her he was present in the first four actions with the bailli de Suffren. After the last of these (3 September 1782) he was promoted commander of the fireship *Combustion* and on 14 September he was posted to the frigate *Coventry*, which on the night of 12 January 1783 ran in among the French fleet in Ganjam Roads, mistaking the ships for Indiamen, and was captured. Wolseley was civilly treated by Suffren, who sent him as a prisoner to Mauritius. Soon afterwards he was transferred to Bourbon, where he was detained until the announcement of peace. He then got a passage to St Helena in a French transport, and so home in an East Indiaman.

In 1786 Wolseley was appointed to the *Trusty*, fitting out at Portsmouth for the broad pennant of his uncle, Phillips Cosby. After a three-year commission in the Mediterranean, the *Trusty* went home and was paid off. In 1792 Wolseley was appointed to the frigate *Lowestoft* (32 guns), in which in early 1793 he was employed in convoy duty in St George's Channel. He was then sent out to join Lord Hood in the Mediterranean and was present at the occupation of Toulon. On 30 September, while detached under Commodore Linzee, he occupied the celebrated Mortella tower (the model for the British Martello towers) which, after being handed over to the Corsicans, was retaken by the French some three weeks later, and on 8 February 1794 beat off the *Fortitude* (74 guns), inflicting on her severe loss and damage. The tower was, however, shortly afterwards recaptured by a landing party under the command of Wolseley.

A few days later Wolseley was moved into the *Impérieuse*, which went home at the end of the year. He had hoped to be again appointed to her, but was disappointed and remained unemployed for the next five years. Towards the end of 1795 he married Jane (*d. c.*1840), daughter of John Moore of Clough House, co. Down; they had two sons and two daughters. His wife's great-grandfather, a Scottish officer, had served in Ireland under William III and obtained a grant of land. Wolseley now took a little place near Clough House, and lived there in retirement except during the rising of 1798, when he commanded a company of volunteers which took part in the 'battle' of Ballynahinch.

In February 1799 Wolseley was appointed to the *Terrible* (74 guns), one of the Channel Fleet under Lord Bridport, and after Lord St Vincent took command of the fleet in 1800 Wolseley spoke to him of the ill-disciplined nature of the Irish crew. In December 1800 he was moved into the *St George*, but, when that ship was selected as the flagship of Lord Nelson (February 1801), Wolseley was transferred to the *San Josef*, which was paid off on the signing of the peace of Amiens. Afterwards he commanded the sea fencibles of the Shannon district until his promotion to rear-admiral on 23 April 1804. He was then appointed to the command of the sea fencibles of all Ireland, from which he retired towards the end of 1805. He had no further employment, but was made vice-admiral on 25 October 1809 and admiral on 12 August 1819.

In the spring of 1842, the old wound received sixty years before at the storming of Fort Ostenberg re-opened. Surgery discovered and removed fragments of lead and cloth, but the wound would not heal. Wolseley died in London on 7 June 1842 having by then become senior admiral of the red.   J. K. LAUGHTON, *rev.* CHRISTOPHER DOORNE

Sources W. James, *The naval history of Great Britain, from the declaration of war by France in 1793 to the accession of George IV*, [7th edn], 6 vols. (1886), vols. 1–2 • J. Marshall, *Royal naval biography*, 1 (1823) • commission and warrant books, PRO, ADM 6/21 (1774–79); ADM 6/24 (1789–93); ADM 6/27–28 (1799–1804) • N. Tracy, ed., *The Naval Chronicle: the contemporary record of the Royal Navy at war*, 1 (1998) • *Steel's Original and Correct List of the Royal Navy* (1793–4) • *Steel's Original and Correct List of the Royal Navy* (1799) • *Steel's Original and Correct List of the Royal Navy* (1801) • W. L. Clowes, *The Royal Navy: a history from the earliest times to the present*, 7 vols. (1897–1903); repr. (1996–7), vol. 4 • *Private papers of George, second Earl Spencer*, ed. J. S. Corbett and H. W. Richmond, 3, Navy RS, 58 (1924), 339
Archives PRO NIre., copy of order book, as captain of HMS *Terrible*, corresp.

Wolseley ring (*act.* 1873–1890), military reformers, was a group of British army officers in the late nineteenth century who owed their high ranks to Sir Garnet Joseph *Wolseley (1833–1913). The ring developed owing to several factors: patronage was a way of Victorian life; promotion in the army was governed by seniority and not by selection; the Staff College did not turn out a sufficient number of staff officers; and Wolseley personally believed that he could select the best men.

The quality of senior officers during the Crimean War had not impressed Wolseley, and he began to keep 'a list of the best and ablest soldiers I knew' (Wolseley, *Story of a Soldier's Life*, 201). Wolseley's first experience of command was the 1870 Red River campaign. Then his choice of staff

officers was limited to those already serving in Canada. John McNeill, William Francis *Butler, Redvers Henry *Buller, and Hugh McCalmont all impressed him with their military knowledge and capacity for hard work and were earmarked for future use.

In 1873 Wolseley selected his staff for the Asante campaign, and it is the Second Anglo-Asante War that marks the real origin of the Wolseley ring. Apart from the officers listed above, he chose Henry *Brackenbury, John Frederick *Maurice, George Pomeroy Pomeroy-*Colley, Baker Creed *Russell, and Henry Evelyn *Wood to accompany him. Qualifications for membership of the ring included loyalty to the chief, intellect, bravery, and experience of war. Few new members joined the élite after this campaign: Herbert *Stewart was a notable exception.

Men from the ring accompanied Wolseley on the various tasks the government set him. These included civil appointments, such as in Natal in 1875 and in Cyprus in 1878. Foremost, though, was their staff work when on campaign. In 1879 Wolseley was appointed to replace Lord Chelmsford after the early disasters of the Anglo-Zulu War. He was joined in South Africa by Brackenbury, McCalmont, Russell, Maurice, and Colley. In Egypt in 1882 Wolseley accepted the services of lieutenant-generals Frederick Willis and Edward Bruce *Hamley as divisional commanders, but managed to find places on the staff for most of his ring.

The cohesion of the ring lasted until the expedition of 1884–5 to relieve Gordon in Khartoum, Wolseley's last experience of active-service command. He complained in a letter to his wife on 31 December 1884, 'they torture themselves with jealousy one of the other, and sometimes even in their dealings with me are inclined to kick over the traces'. Buller failed to ensure an adequate supply of coal to keep the steamers running. Butler proved incapable of working in a team, and Wood was so deaf that working with him was a strain on Wolseley's voice. Only Herbert Stewart earned praise, but he died from wounds in the campaign.

Wolseley's patronage extended to securing important appointments for his protégés while he himself served at the War Office. He collaborated with Wood to improve the training of the army. Maurice's intellect was encouraged and he became the 'pen of Wolseley' (Luvaas, 173–215). Yet loyalty to Wolseley did not always last. Wood was never totally forgiven for signing a peace treaty with the Boers in 1881 before the British defeat at Majuba and the death of Colley had been avenged. Brackenbury angered him by adopting the Indian viewpoint of the defence of India while serving there, in direct contradiction of his patron's opinions. He later served as director of ordnance when Wolseley was commander-in-chief. Buller equally was never totally forgiven for nearly being appointed commander-in-chief in 1895 instead of his patron, yet Wolseley did secure his appointment as commander of the First Army corps in the Second South African War.

The ring has been criticized because allegedly it did not bring the best men forward, its size was too limited, and it divided the late Victorian army. The argument that Wolseley's men were not as able as he supposed rests on the performances of Colley, Butler, and Buller in the graveyard of military reputations, South Africa. Colley disappointed his chief in the First South African War by attempting to take Majuba Hill with too few men and paid for his error with his life. Butler angered Wolseley by refusing to suggest provisions for the defence of Natal and Cape Colony when war with the Boers was imminent. Buller's poor strategic decisions during the war appalled Wolseley.

The commander-in-chief, the duke of Cambridge, had his own circle of officers whose careers he encouraged, yet he disputed Wolseley's right to select his own staff. He argued that 'no army could stand these sorts of preferences without entirely dampening the energies of senior officers', but Wolseley was unrepentant (Verner, 164). The duke objected to the list of staff officers selected for the autumn campaign in 1885 to retake Khartoum because he felt that more men should be given experience of staff work. Wolseley replied that many new men had been tried already and found wanting. He listed them with caustic comments: one colonel was 'not fit to be a corporal' (Wolseley to Cambridge, 4 April 1885, Cambridge MSS, Royal Archives, M858/47). Nor had the Marlborough House set surrounding the prince of Wales fared any better: Stanley Clarke was not recommended for a medal or promotion.

The argument that the Wolseley ring was a divisive factor in the Victorian army rests on its perceived competition with the Roberts ring based in India. This was more of a rivalry between the junior members of the rings, particularly Ian Hamilton, who upheld Roberts's reputation at every opportunity. There is little evidence of enmity between Wolseley and Roberts themselves other than their differences of opinion on the value of short service and their opposing ideas on Indian defence. The Wolseley ring and Roberts ring were just two among other circles formed around powerful men like the duke of Cambridge and the prince of Wales.

The Wolseley ring owed its existence and validity to the failure of the Staff College to supply an adequate number of staff officers and to the system of promotion by seniority. As the Staff College's reputation improved, Wolseley encouraged young protégés such as J. Adye and E. S. E. Childers to apply in order to gain the necessary theoretical knowledge of staff work. Similarly the establishment of a promotion board and the acceptance of selection as the method for future promotions at the end of the century meant that rings like Wolseley's should no longer have been necessary in the army. The effectiveness of the Wolseley ring is demonstrated by the fact that it ensured Wolseley's reputation as the foremost colonial commander in the late Victorian army.   HALIK KOCHANSKI

Sources Viscount Wolseley [G. Wolseley], *The story of a soldier's life*, 2 vols. (1903), vol. 2 · H. M. Kochanski, *Sir Garnet Wolseley: Victorian hero* (1999) · J. Luvaas, *The education of an army: British military thought, 1815–1940* (Chicago, IL, 1964) · W. Verner, *The military life of H.R.H. George, duke of Cambridge*, 2 vols. (1905) · *In relief of Gordon: Lord Wolseley's campaign journal of the Khartoum relief expedition, 1884–1885*, ed. A. Preston (1967) · *The South African diaries of Sir Garnet Wolseley, 1875*, ed. A. Preston (1971) · *The South African journal of Sir Garnet Wolseley, 1879–1880*, ed. A. Preston (1973) · I. Harvie, '"The Wolseley ring": a case-study in the exercise of patronage in the late Victorian army', MA diss., University of Buckingham, 1993 · E. M. Spiers, *The army and society, 1815–1914* (1980) · E. M. Spiers, *The late Victorian army, 1868–1902* (1992)
Archives Hove Central Library, Sussex, corresp. and papers | Devon RO, Buller MSS · PRO, Buller MSS · Royal Arch., Cambridge MSS

Wolsey, Thomas (1470/71–1530), royal minister, archbishop of York, and cardinal, was the son of Robert Wolsey of Ipswich (d. 1496), often described as a butcher but evidently also a grazier, and his wife, Joan Daundy (d. 1509). His modest beginnings later prompted biting satire from his many critics, and were not denied by his own biographer, his gentleman usher George *Cavendish, whose account of Wolsey's early days must largely have originated with the cardinal himself.

Early life Wolsey received his early education at Ipswich and proceeded to Oxford, where he graduated BA in 1486 from Magdalen, aged only fifteen (he was called the boy bachelor). When his father died Thomas was probably of canonical age to be ordained, but he was not made priest until 10 March 1498, in the parish church of St Peter at Marlborough by the bishop of Salisbury's suffragan. In 1497 he proceeded MA and was fourteenth fellow in a Magdalen list. At this point he was studying for a degree in theology, an odd choice if he had ambitions for an administrative career. In 1498 he was junior bursar and in 1499–1500 senior bursar, concerned as such with the college's great tower then under construction; his enemies claimed he took short cuts over the money. He was briefly master of Magdalen School and in 1500 dean of divinity. He probably resigned in 1502 but remained on good terms with the college, making gifts to it throughout his life.

Wolsey's first benefice came from the marquess of Dorset, whose sons he had taught. After an invitation to spend Christmas with the family he was instituted to the Somerset rectory of Limington on 10 October 1500, where according to Cavendish he antagonized Sir Amyas Paulet, a neighbouring landowner, who allegedly put him in the stocks. On 3 November 1501 he obtained a papal bull licensing him to hold more than one benefice and not to reside, and was collated to the vicarage of Lydd, Kent, in the following month. Although he did not begin to accumulate livings for some time, he later acquired Redgrave in Suffolk in 1506, and Great Torrington, Devon, in 1511. Seeking a higher position than parish priest, Wolsey entered the household of Henry Deane, archbishop of Canterbury, as one of his chaplains. When Deane died on 15 February 1503 Wolsey was his chief mourner and possibly executor. From 1503 to 1507 he served Sir Richard Nanfan, treasurer of Calais, who died on 7 January 1507 and for whom Wolsey acted as executor.

As a favour to Nanfan, according to Cavendish, Wolsey

Thomas Wolsey (1470/71–1530), by unknown artist, late
16th cent. [original, c.1520]

was given a post as a royal chaplain, in which he quickly attached himself to Richard Fox, bishop of Winchester, and Sir Thomas Lovell, as the men 'whome he thought to bere most rewle in the Councell and to be most in favour with the kyng' (Cavendish, 7). On their recommendation he was sent as an envoy to the emperor Maximilian in Flanders, and, according to the story he himself told Cavendish at the end of his life, amazed the king by completing his task, there and back, in three and a half days. In spring 1508 he was sent to Scotland. Reaching Edinburgh on 28 March, he complained that his business was already known to every goodwife. He saw James IV on 2 April but his mission was unsuccessful, as was his embassy to the Low Countries in October to negotiate the marriage of Henry VII to Margaret, the regent of the Netherlands. Nevertheless in February 1509 Henry rewarded him with the deanship of Lincoln Cathedral and the prebend of Welton Brinkhall. About this time Wolsey may have begun his liaison with the shadowy Mistress Lark (her first name may have been Joan); their relationship, along with the two children born of it, did much to fuel the accusations of lechery and fornication so widely levelled at him. He acknowledged and provided for the children, the son, Thomas *Wynter, being made successively archdeacon of Suffolk and of Norfolk when still under canonical age,

while the daughter, Dorothy, became a nun at Shaftesbury.

The rise to power Following Henry VIII's accession Wolsey became the new king's almoner in November 1509. Clearly he was rising in favour. The papal collector Polydore Vergil reports that he was pushed forward by the ageing Fox as a counter to Thomas Howard, earl of Surrey and later third duke of Norfolk, and also struck up a close alliance with the young king's favourite, Charles Brandon. However, Vergil loathed Wolsey, and also represents him as 'singing, laughing, dancing and playing with the young courtiers' (*Anglica historia*, 196n.), advising Henry to apply himself to studying good literature, and showing him the errors he had committed. Cavendish agrees that Wolsey recognized the young Henry's dislike of routine work, and describes him as 'puttyng the kyng in Comfort that he shall not nede to spare any tyme of his pleasure for any busynes that shold necessary happen in the Councell as long as he beyng there'. But there was more to Wolsey's assessment of Henry than that, and Cavendish also records, in an illuminating passage, how 'all his endevour was oonly to satisfie the kynges mynd knowyng rightwell that it was the very vayn and right Cours to bryng hyme to highe promocion', and how:

> he dayly attendyd uppon the kyng in the Court beyng in his especyall grace & favour who had than great sewte made unto hyme as Counsellours most comenly have that be in favour … In whome the kyng conceyved suche a lovyng fantzy especyally for that he was most earnest and Redyest among all the Councell to avaunce the kynges oonly wyll & pleasure without any respect to the Case The Kyng therfore perceyved hyme to be a mete Instrument for the accomplysshement of his devysed wyll & pleasure called hyme more nere unto hyme and estemed hyme so highly that his estymacion and favour put all other councellours owt of ther accustumed favour that they ware in byfore. (Cavendish, 11–12)

Wolsey's cultivation of the route to power brought him ecclesiastical as well as secular promotion. In February 1509 he became dean of Lincoln, and by June was dean of Hereford as well. In April 1510 he was made registrar of the Order of the Garter, and in the same month supplicated at Oxford for the degrees of BTh and DTh, both of which he took in June. A councillor no later than 1511, on 17 February in that year he became a canon of St George's, Windsor. By this time he lived in the house in St Bride's, Westminster (once Sir Richard Empson's), which Henry had given him. In January 1513 he was collated to the prebend of Bugthorpe in York Minster.

As Wolsey ceased to be Fox's protégé and rose in the young king's favour, a change in government ensued. The councillors who had remained from Henry VII had routinely countersigned royal documents in the early years of his son, but they now found the royal almoner becoming more and more a chief minister, and as such interposed between themselves and the monarch. In effect Wolsey managed the council for Henry. The measure both of his willingness to be solely the king's man and of his boundless energy and ability is his increasingly rapid promotion.

In February 1513 he became dean of York, and on 6 February 1514 bishop of Lincoln. He was consecrated on 26 March but held the diocese for only a few months. The death of Cardinal Bainbridge at Rome on 14 July 1514 left the archbishopric of York vacant and by 5 August Wolsey had been elected. He was made a cardinal on 10 September 1515. The red hat added to his magnificence, and also had symbolic value. But although his detractors suggested that this was the first step towards the papacy, Wolsey was never particularly successful at manipulating the papal curia and had many enemies there. In any case he must have known how difficult it would be for an outsider to rule a largely Italian curia.

Revenues A prominent minister could not function without an appropriate household, able to meet both his domestic and his public needs. When Wolsey was appointed a councillor the comparatively modest income he received from his existing benefices was clearly inadequate for all the clerks and other assistants he had to employ. The fact that he was bound to maintain a suitable team in his own household and at his own expense helps explain Wolsey's eagerness to gather money from any available source. By 1511 he may have had an annual income of approximately £1000 (equal to that of many peers), but this would probably still have been insufficient for his outgoings—and certainly for his tastes. Even the reward of bishoprics had associated expenses before the revenues could be enjoyed—Wolsey had to borrow £3400 from Italian bankers to meet his expenses in Rome in 1514.

In order to play the role that was expected of him Wolsey needed to accumulate funds and trustworthy servants rapidly. As soon as he became a bishop his household needs expanded again. Not only was he expected to have chaplains and musicians, and other ceremonial trappings, but he also needed suffragans and estate agents to handle his episcopal business. By now his household would have numbered about 160, and wages alone would probably have required £2000 per annum. The bishopric of Lincoln, although wealthy, would hardly produce all that was needed, and the small annuities granted him by people like Lady Margaret Pole, though evidence of his growing stature, added little to his income. The archbishopric of York in 1515 probably raised his net available income to over £5000, and the chancellorship in 1516 may have added another £2000 per annum. After 1517 he would in most years have received a substantial pension from France or the empire, while in 1518 he obtained the bishopric of Bath and Wells *in commendam*. It seems reasonable to estimate that by 1519 his yearly income was in the region of £9500, making him Henry's wealthiest subject.

Throughout the 1520s Wolsey's household continued to grow, as did his expenditure on building, plate and jewels, tapestries and clothing, creating the presence for which he was to be remembered. He reckoned that his expenses at Calais in 1521 amounted to £10,000, which Henry repaid by granting him St Albans Abbey *in commendam*, so adding at least £1000 to his yearly income. Exchanging Bath and Wells for Durham in 1523 must have brought in another £1000 per annum, and the exchange of Durham for Winchester in 1529 a few hundred pounds more. But it is only when his pensions from foreign rulers and the issues of his legatine jurisdiction are also taken into account that the estimate that just before his fall his annual revenues amounted to £30,000 becomes possible.

Taste and magnificence Wolsey did not wait for his finances to be assured before setting himself up as a prince of the church and a patron of the arts and education. In 1514 he began laying the foundations for what became a still larger household, many of whose members came from areas like Yorkshire in which he had personal interests, along with the heirs of noblemen, wards, and others who were to be given a good upbringing. Its size and expense—429 were taxed in 1524—were partly owing to its containing clerks and others on whom Wolsey depended for the conduct of business, but it certainly eclipsed that of any other subject. In his kitchens he employed seventy-three men and boys, and in his stables half as many as the king himself. Membership of Wolsey's household was much in demand, though he was not able to promote as many of his servants as might be expected. Offices in departments of state which were in the chancellor's gift were limited, while those in the king's gift were the object of intense competition in which Wolsey's support did not guarantee success. Men like Brian Tuke, Thomas Heneage, and Stephen Gardiner were well looked after, but many of his other lay servants were left in difficulties when he fell. On the other hand he was active in the exercise of ecclesiastical patronage, not only in his own dioceses but also in Worcester, which he managed on behalf of its absentee Italian incumbent.

Even given his lavish household and the expenses of office, Wolsey was increasingly able to spend on art, and particularly on architecture. What has been described as his building megalomania attracted considerable criticism. His personal enthusiasm is beyond question—for his college at Ipswich he even specified the quality of stone to be used; Cardinal College, Oxford, was to be comparable in magnificence only with King's College, Cambridge. His great house was Hampton Court (leased from 1515), but he also built at Bridewell, York Place (the forerunner of Whitehall), and at his country houses. The scale of his operations was eclipsed only by the king's, and as well as engaging in construction on his own behalf, Wolsey and his works organization were responsible for Henry's buildings too. Wolsey's buildings were traditional in ground plan, but he was certainly aware of the new style, and used it particularly in surface decoration, such as the Hampton Court terracotta emperors, and for special projects. One of these was his own tomb, whose sculptor, Benedetto da Rovezzano, was briefed to surpass Torrigiani's Westminster Abbey monument to Henry VII and Elizabeth of York; another was the various seals he had designed. The great silver crosses and pillars which always preceded Wolsey were also in the 'antique style', as was much of his massive collection of plate.

Wolsey was a patron of humanists and committed to the new learning (he himself wrote a grammar for his Ipswich college), although he only knew of Renaissance art as it was transmitted via the Netherlands. Flanders was also the source of his stained glass, where his investment rivalled and possibly eclipsed the best found anywhere else in England. Almost nothing of this pomp has survived, except among his tapestries, which he purchased on an enormous scale, again mainly from the Low Countries. Foreign ambassadors reported that he had sufficient to change the hangings weekly. Many represented sacred themes, but others were on classical subjects. As well as *objets d'art*, Wolsey's houses were full of music. At one time his household chapel was larger than the Chapel Royal, and even when it was reduced to a less competitive level, it was still recognized to be superior in performance. Whether this reflected personal taste or mere prestige is unclear, but Wolsey certainly maintained a number of composers in his entourage; the master of the choristers at Cardinal College was no less a figure than John Taverner.

While allowing Wolsey's evident personal interest in art and architecture, it must not be forgotten that this was more than a matter of individual taste. It exemplified the virtue of magnificence, which was a necessary attribute of any ruler or great minister. His reported response to Robert Barnes, who argued to his face that the gold on his crosses if sold would help many poor, makes the point precisely:

> Whether do you think it more necessary that I should have all this royalty, because I represent the king's majesty's person in all the high courts of this realm, to the terror and keeping down of all rebellious treasons, traitors, all the wicked and corrupt members of this commonwealth; or to be as simple as you would have us? (*Acts and Monuments*, 5.416–17)

If, to the outside world, he sometimes seemed to rival the king, in personal relations he was always careful to defer to Henry—hence his gift to him of his best singer. In many cases, actions that were condemned as instances of overweening pride—for instance, his meeting the emperor on horseback, and later sharing his stool in the cathedral at Bruges—can be seen rather as embodying the reverence demanded of one sovereign by another, when the latter's vicegerent was truly representative of his king. Similarly the pomp he employed as cardinal, and later as papal legate, celebrating divine office with pontifical rites while dukes and earls waited on him, can be defended as assertions of a distinct spiritual authority which existed alongside temporal power. Many of his contemporaries (and later commentators), however, have asserted Wolsey's private delight in emphasizing his superior status, particularly at the expense of the social élite.

Managing the church Absentee bishops were a common phenomenon in the English church and Wolsey evidently followed well-established paths in providing for his dioceses, although little can be said of this. Of Wolsey's handling of the church more generally, a great deal can and has been said, by contemporaries and subsequently, but with very little consensus. By itself the appointment as cardinal conferred no authority over the English hierarchy,

but after a long campaign promoted by Henry, the pope was told in 1518 that he could only send a legate to raise funds for a crusade, namely Cardinal Lorenzo Campeggi (or Campeggio), if Wolsey was given joint authority. Henry also squeezed the pope further by insisting that a third, rather than a quarter, of the money raised should come to the royal coffers. In August the two cardinals also had a bull permitting them to visit and reform religious houses. The legation should have lapsed with Campeggi's departure in 1519, and Wolsey had difficulty in obtaining an extension. Leo X was reluctant to override ordinary episcopal jurisdiction and often showed himself personally hostile to Wolsey, whose enemies put it about that his sole purpose was to raise money by bribes, just as the only effect of his legateship was to increase the pride of the clergy. Early in 1520 Henry thanked the pope for a three-year extension of his minister's legation, but told him that an indefinite one would enable the clergy to accept reform with greater alacrity. Only in January 1524, however, did Clement VII grant Wolsey legatine powers for life.

In the evaluation of Wolsey's legateship the principal problem is his motivation. To some it has appeared mere self-aggrandizement. His power now overrode that of all the English bishops and abbots. He could and did interfere in their affairs and fleeced them on every pretext. Another view is that he regarded his ecclesiastical authority as primarily a means of consolidating Henry's authority. A third possibility is that Wolsey saw the acquisition of authority as a way to reform. If this suggestion is correct, a further question is the degree of success he achieved. And if this was limited, was it because he was too busy or because he only paid lip-service to the need for ecclesiastical reform? Ironically, too, the legateship, which had only been obtained with Henry's sanction and encouragement, later proved the lever for Wolsey's fall, when he was indicted in 1529 for the offence of *praemunire*, illegally importing an alien jurisdiction into England.

The implications of Wolsey's joint position in church and state were, in the event, tested before his appointment as legate. The case of Richard Hunne, probably killed by the bishop of London's gaolers in December 1514 after his arrest for heresy, had aroused anti-clerical feeling in and around London. The preaching of Thomas Standish, a royal chaplain, in turn prompted ecclesiastical ire. A series of debates was held during 1515, at first at Blackfriars and finally before the king at Baynard's Castle. There Henry made his reservations concerning ecclesiastical autonomy quite clear. But first Wolsey knelt before Henry and offered the explanations and apologies of the clergy. He asked Henry to refer the matter to Rome but acquiesced in Henry's refusal, saying that:

> to his knowledge none of the clergy had ever meant to do anything in derogation of the king's prerogative and for his own part he owed his whole advancement solely to our lord the king; wherefore he said he would assent to nothing that would tend to annul or derogate from his royal authority for all the world. (Gwyn, *King's Cardinal*, 49)

On the other hand, very little of consequence resulted

from Hunne's Case, nor did it four years later when a dispute over rights of sanctuary came to a head. Henry once more asserted his authority over the church and blustered that he would strike down the abuse, but Wolsey, having again interceded for the church, was quietly able to preserve the great sanctuary of Westminster. These instances show the cardinal as the last great defender of the rights of the medieval church.

Wolsey had made substantial use of his legatine powers while he had them in 1519, ordering visitations of over sixty religious houses and cathedral chapters, and set up a court which superseded the ordinary episcopal courts in hearing testamentary cases. As he wrote to the pope, he sought to do 'some good in the Lord's vineyard' (Martène and Durand, 3.1289). It was doubtless in this spirit that he set about reforming the Augustinian canons by giving them new constitutions, and in March 1519 convened an assembly of bishops which issued legatine constitutions for the province of Canterbury, though little is known of their content. A. F. Pollard's argument that Wolsey projected a thorough reform of canon law, rather than just a reworking of existing episcopal constitutions, cannot be substantiated, but by 1522 a permanent legatine court was in existence, which seems to have been highly unpopular. Dr John Allen, whom Wolsey appointed its chancellor, was alleged by Vergil to have been recently convicted of perjury (in fact he had been convicted in Star Chamber of *praemunire* in 1518, before he became Wolsey's general commissary). Testamentary jurisdiction lay at the heart of episcopal resentment of Wolsey's legatine authority, and Vergil accordingly represents Allen's deputies as attending deathbeds like ghouls and harassing executors of wills. After some debate, however, Wolsey agreed to share his prerogative jurisdiction with Archbishop Warham and to give ordinary diocesan jurisdiction back to the bishops in return for a share in the profits.

Wolsey's legatine court had the advantage of being able to exercise jurisdiction over the many small peculiars and other exempt institutions. Thus in 1519 he conducted a visitation of Westminster Abbey, a highly privileged monastery. How far such activity represented a personal commitment to reform has been doubted. Wolsey's desire for and use of a legate's authority can also be interpreted as being born of a determination to control all the channels through which power flowed, and his reforming zeal is certainly belied by his virtually complete inactivity as a diocesan bishop. Yet Richard Fox wrote with enthusiasm about 'a more entire and whole reformation of the ecclesiastical hierarchy of the English people than I could have expected', and declared that Wolsey's skill in business, 'whether divine or human', would gain him 'true immortal honour from God and posterity' (*Letters of Richard Fox*, 115–16).

Learning and heresy What seems unquestionable is Wolsey's enthusiasm for education, as manifested in his college at Ipswich and Cardinal College at Oxford. He argued that education constituted the best way to reform the clergy, and that the diversion of resources from declining monasteries to vigorous educational foundations was essential to this end. Perhaps inevitably, given his own background, Oxford University was the principal beneficiary of his endeavours (in 1514 he declined the chancellorship of Cambridge). In 1518 he founded six lectureships in the humanities there at his own expense, and on 1 April 1523 he secured charters for his alma mater, confirming existing privileges and adding (modestly) to them. He seems also to have planned to draw up new statutes for the university. Above all, in January 1525 he began the construction of Cardinal College, an institution conceived and begun on the grandest scale—in April 1528 Thomas Cromwell reported that 'Every man thinks the like was never seen for largeness, beauty, sumptuous, curious and substantial building' (*LP Henry VIII*, 4/2, no. 4135). Wolsey intended to maintain existing studies but to add to them the essential elements of the new learning; hence his provision for daily lectures on Latin and Greek authors, and on philosophy. To help finance this grandiose scheme he later obtained papal bulls licensing the suppression of twenty-nine small religious houses, whose resources were to be diverted to his own educational establishments. Earlier attempts—at Tonbridge and Bayham priories in 1525, for instance—had met strong local opposition. Allegations that he had acted improperly were vigorously denied by Wolsey, however, who told Henry that it would be wrong to acquire anything *ex rapinis* for founding colleges that were intended for the king's honour, the advancement of learning, and the weal of his own soul.

Among the expressed purposes of Cardinal College was the combating of heresy. The condemnation of Luther in 1520 changed the parameters within which Wolsey had to work, and heresy became increasingly a factor in international politics. Henry and Wolsey presented themselves to Rome as vigorously anti-heretical, thereby helping Wolsey to secure a limited renewal of his legatine commission in January 1521. Soon afterwards he forbade the importation of heretical books, and a conference of theologians to consider the heresies followed. On 12 May he presided at a public burning of Lutheran books in St Paul's Churchyard in London. Although Wolsey was accused of leniency towards academic heretics, and even of accepting some of their criticisms, he was determined to prevent the circulation of heretical literature to the less educated. Early in 1525 he overrode papal objections to his proposed visitation of the house of the Observant friars at Greenwich (one greatly favoured by the Tudors)—Pope Clement had begged him to desist as the friars were important to the fight against the new heretics—but in 1526 he authorized a raid on the Hanseatic community in the London Steelyard, a move followed by more book burning and the recantation of Robert Barnes and other leading evangelicals. Wolsey also negotiated, though unsuccessfully, for the extradition from the Low Countries of the authors of heretical English books printed there, including William Tyndale.

By now, however, Wolsey had a rival for the king's ear in Anne Boleyn, in ecclesiastical matters as in others, as the troublesome business of election of an abbess of Wilton in 1528 demonstrated. Wolsey opposed the election of

Eleanor Carey (the sister of Anne's brother-in-law) on the grounds of her sexual misconduct, and though Henry subsequently withdrew his support for her, this did not stop his rebuking Wolsey for interfering in the election, underlining the royal displeasure by a none too veiled threat to the cardinal's colleges—'It is reported that the goods for building the same are not best acquired, and come from many religious houses unlawfully, "bearing the cloak of kindness towards the edifying of your College", which many cannot believe' (*LP Henry VIII*, 4/2, no. 4507). By now Wolsey was promoting a long-considered scheme to rationalize the diocesan map, creating a number of new bishoprics by converting existing large abbeys to cathedrals, but although in 1529 Campeggi came with a bull to this end, Wolsey was now in no position to employ either that or a bull issued on 30 April conferring wider powers to dissolve houses with under twelve inmates.

Foreign affairs, 1511–1518 Wolsey's first and arguably most important role in Henry's service lay in diplomacy. He was later seen as having been remarkably independent; at his fall he was accused of having declared war in January 1528 without the consent of king and council. In reality, Wolsey's apparent freedom represented a deliberate attempt to keep Henry clear of involvement in the deceptions of diplomacy, and claims that he intercepted and replied to letters addressed to the king without consulting him are inaccurate, for Henry saw Wolsey's letters before they were sent, and gave him instructions and advice. Henry, of course, also listened to Wolsey's advice, and historians are as divided over the cardinal's policies as they are over his attitude to the church. Was he purely an opportunist? Did he have a genuine wish to promote international peace? How far did he follow the interests of the pope, Christendom's true spiritual leader and the fount of Wolsey's ecclesiastical authority? Was his objective to exploit England's strategic position so as to make it more important than its resources justified and thereby put Henry on an equality with the emperor Charles V and François I of France? The diplomatic correspondence of the time, highly allusive, written in the awareness that it could fall into the wrong hands, and concerned with bluff and double bluff, makes it impossible to give firm answers to these questions.

Chief ministers, like ambassadors, existed to dissemble, to tell part of the truth misleadingly, to have at their fingertips lists of their country's grievances which could be proffered as appropriate. Wolsey, a master dissembler, expected others to dissemble. His outbursts of temper, his shared confidences with his audiences, and his arrogance all formed part of a performance which could be adapted to circumstances. The time he spent abroad, however, was strictly limited, and so his understanding of often fast-changing events, dependent as it was on agents and ambassadors, was not always either accurate or complete.

When Wolsey joined the royal council about 1511 its principal concern was Julius II's proposal for a holy league against France. Under Henry VII, England had avoided continental war. His son, by contrast, was spoiling for a fight, although his experienced commanders the Howards would have preferred to fight Scotland. What part Wolsey played in the conciliar debate about peace or war is uncertain, although it was later claimed that he persuaded Henry that the pope, as the fount of honour, should be supported. On 13 November 1511, however, an alliance of England, Spain, the pope, and Venice was finally agreed, and on 11 December Henry opted for war. To those who doubted the wisdom of English involvement in European conflict, and who, when the French king and the emperor were at war, 'thought it wisdom to sit still and let them alone', in the days of his dominance (according to Sir Thomas More) Wolsey would tell the fable of a country where a rain was foretold which would turn all whom it soaked into fools. Some wiseacres hid in caves, 'thinking afterwards to rule the fools, but the fools would have none of that, but would have the rule themselves. When the wise men saw this, they wished they had been in the rain too' (*LP Henry VIII*, 7, nos. 1113–14).

The cost of a policy of involvement and aggression, of venturing into the rain, did not become Wolsey's problem for another two years, although the campaign of 1512 gave him his first experience of the duties and pitfalls involved in organizing an army's commissariat. It also taught him some of the other hazards of war. Although he still had no formal office, he had conducted much of the previous correspondence with Ferdinand of Aragon, and the diplomat William Knight reported that Wolsey was considered to be the author of the conflict. Consequently he was blamed by many for the shambles that developed after Dorset's army landed in Spain on 7 June 1512, forcing the abandonment of the enterprise. But at court Wolsey was not made a scapegoat for England's military failure.

In 1513, following a shuffling of alliances, England sent another large army to France with Henry himself in command. Again, Wolsey managed the preparations, although John Stow's statement, that Wolsey was 'mete for policie and painfull travell, he being nothing scrupulous in any thing that the king would command him do … tooke upon him the whole charge of all the busines' (Stow, 836), exaggerates his responsibility. He was effectively quartermaster-general not war minister, and as such the linchpin of a fairly loose group instructed to organize both the troops and the supplies, with Henry himself taking an active part.

On 30 June Henry crossed the channel and Wolsey followed, commanding 200 men. On 16 August Henry enjoyed his first victories, defeating a French force near Thérouanne and capturing that town shortly afterwards. Tournai was taken on 24 September, and the next year Wolsey was made administrator of the diocese, although thanks to the limited area controlled by the English and to papal hostility, he was never able to enforce his claim to be bishop. However, as well as taking administrative steps to consolidate the English victory, and dealing with the domestic business concerning which Queen Katherine and others were now routinely writing to him, Wolsey was now also faced with the need for a diplomatic shift of front. Whatever his personal objectives, the guiding principle for English diplomacy at this time was to ensure that England, the least important of the three great Western monarchies, was not left isolated against a Valois–Habsburg alliance. Despite Henry's continuing preparations for another campaign and his negotiations with the Swiss, the emperor Maximilian and Ferdinand of Aragon now made peace with France, while the former also made peace with Leo X. The pope sent Henry a sword and cap of maintenance to persuade him to fall into line. But as anti-French feeling was widespread in England an accommodation was unlikely to be popular there.

Anne of Brittany's death on 9 January 1514 had made Louis XII of France an eligible widower. Wolsey proposed two sisters of Henry VIII, first Margaret, dowager queen of Scots, and then Mary (who was currently betrothed to Ferdinand's son Charles), to be Louis's new wife. Mary was chosen and the ensuing treaty of mutual support gave Henry an annuity of 100,000 crowns and the restoration of privileges. The English were to keep Tournai, and Louis undertook to prevent the duke of Albany, the French-born heir presumptive to the throne of Scotland, from leaving for that country. Wolsey then organized Mary's journey to France in October 1514. She was accompanied by Norfolk, whose willingness to concede French demands for the dismissal of her English servants caused her to complain bitterly of Wolsey's absence. The latter made efforts to moderate the blow. In any case the treaty was short-lived. The death of Louis on 10 January 1515 put François I on the French throne and left Mary an eligible widow. She secretly married Charles Brandon, duke of Suffolk, to Henry's fury. Mary appealed for help to Wolsey, who successfully mediated with Henry. He also eventually settled the issue of Mary's dowry with the French, albeit without satisfying anybody. François financed Albany's departure for Scotland, where he became governor of the realm, and himself set off for Italy, where he defeated the Swiss at Marignano on 14 September. Just four days earlier, increasingly in need of English support, Leo X had made Wolsey a cardinal.

Henry resented François's success, which also made Wolsey's ostensible policy of expelling the French from Italy impossible to achieve. Instead he and his king endeavoured to limit their expenditure on foreign affairs. On 22 May 1516 Wolsey wrote to Silvestro Gigli at Rome saying that, although the king was ready to invade France, all his councillors had opposed the plan, arguing that it would be better to postpone attack until England could overwhelm France single-handed. A series of diplomatic initiatives during 1516 and 1517 failed to prevent England's becoming isolated and cost at least £35,000 (Wolsey claimed £80,000). This was far less expensive than war, but still a sizeable percentage of Henry's income. Wolsey expressed amazement at what he saw as the dishonourable behaviour of the Habsburgs, and wrote so bitterly to the emperor that the ambassadors did not deliver the letter. As the king's principal adviser he was well aware that he would be blamed for the failure of his policies, and therefore behaved as if nothing had gone wrong, continuing instead to treat with all parties while denying that serious proposals were under consideration. In fact a secret anti-French league, including the pope, was again taking shape.

Polydore Vergil believed that at this time François was playing on Wolsey's ambition and greed in order to get his support. He also represented Wolsey as in turn playing on Henry:

> he brought out some small present or other, a beautifully fashioned dish for example or a jewel or ring … and while Henry was admiring it Wolsey would adroitly bring forward the project on which his mind was fixed … Henry praised Wolsey's diligence so highly that a few days later he said openly (and not by way of a joke) that Wolsey would rule not only himself but Francis as well. (*Anglica historia*, 247)

Despite an attack of the sweat in June 1517, which caused Wolsey's life to be despaired of, diplomacy went on. The ambassadors of the Archduke Charles (Maximilian's grandson) were lavishly entertained in England, and on 5 July a defensive league was finalized. Wolsey was able to attend the celebrations, but the fact that in August Henry wrote to him in his own hand, thanking him for his great pains and trusting that 'we shall dysapoynte oure enymys off theyre intendyd purpose' and advising him to take some recreation 'to the intente yow may the lenger endure to serve us' (*LP Henry VIII*, 2/1, ccxiv), suggests that his position may have been temporarily shaky. In September he went on pilgrimage to Walsingham.

Following the alliance with the Habsburgs the position of the French and the Scots remained unresolved. There was talk of war in February 1518, but then the birth of a dauphin on the 28th helped open the way for further negotiations with France. The resulting treaty of Universal Peace (also known as the treaty of London), signed on 2 October, was a personal triumph for Wolsey. It comprehended most of Europe's major and lesser powers, and also brought financial relief to England, both through the return of Tournai to France in return for 600,000 gold crowns and by the inclusion of Scotland in the peace on condition that she abstain from hostilities. The associated betrothal of Princess Mary to the dauphin François was celebrated with great ceremony by proxy on 5 October. The pope was dissatisfied with his own peripheral role but had been outmanoeuvred. Wolsey delivered an oration in praise of peace which was much acclaimed. The treaty's domestic consequences may have included a restructuring of the admiralty court, intended to provide redress for disputes arising from Anglo-French piracy—the grievances of merchants had previously done much to impede the progress of negotiations.

Royal minister From the end of 1515 Wolsey was also the king's principal minister in charge of domestic matters. When parliament opened on 3 November 1515 he still had no more secular authority than came from Henry's own favour to a councillor, even though he had a seat in the Lords and was the key agent in diplomatic negotiations. Two promotions marked his ascent to power. On 15 November his cardinal's hat arrived and was solemnly paraded through the streets of London, to be ceremonially bestowed on him two days later by Archbishop Warham in Westminster Abbey after a sermon by John Colet. Then when parliament was over Warham resigned as chancellor. Wolsey's patent to succeed him was issued on 21 December and on Christmas eve he took the oath of office. His stature was confirmed in February 1516 by his being chosen as one of the new-born Princess Mary's godfathers.

Vergil asserted that 'Wolsey, with his arrogance and ambition … claimed he could undertake himself almost all public duties' (*Anglica historia*, 231), and there is no doubt that other councillors resented the increasing concentration of power. At the end of May 1516 Thomas Alen reported 'great snarling' to the earl of Shrewsbury (*LP Henry VIII*, 2/1, no. 1959). Yet it would be wrong to imagine that the council was neglected. It still met regularly and frequently, and not all who attended were intimidated by the cardinal, if there is truth in the story that Thomas More, called a fool by Wolsey, responded 'But God be thanked the king our master hath but one fool on his council' (Foss, *Judges*, 5.212). The secret of Wolsey's authority was spelt out by Cavendish. Wolsey

> wold first make the kyng privye of all suche matters (as shold passe thoroughe ther handes) byfore he wold procede to the fynyssheng or determynyng of the same whos mynd & pleasure he wold fullfyll & folowe to the uttermost wherwith the kyng was wonderly pleased.   (Cavendish, 12)

The consequence was that the council became a forum where policy was more approved than decided. Everything, therefore, depended on a close collaboration between monarch and minister. During most of the year Wolsey visited Henry weekly for lengthy discussions. When the king went on his summer progress, communication was by letter, but from time to time the cardinal would attend in person; on foreign visits copious correspondence and regular messengers kept the king informed. Wolsey also made sure that Henry was attended by a small group of councillors to act as his eyes and ears, men like Richard Pace and Thomas More, and he changed them if there were signs that they were becoming too independent.

Wolsey's previous involvement in domestic affairs had been limited. Suggestions that he was behind improvements in the administration of the chamber's finances are unsupported, and he was not one of the temporary treasurers for the wars of 1512–13. At that date the experienced Sir Thomas Lovell was still the king's principal financial manager, while Henry himself, then and later, kept a closer eye on his own finances than is sometimes thought. Moreover the Howards kept a firm grip on the exchequer and its associated patronage—the second duke of Norfolk was lord treasurer from 1501 until 1522, when he resigned in favour of his son. On the whole, Wolsey's concern with finance was focused on raising the money the king needed, rather than on its bureaucratic administration, although he did cap the payments to the court via the groom of the stool and demand proper bookkeeping and audits. In 1516, however, he needed to clear the financial

accounts so as to enable the true state of the king's finances to be understood, and for that reason had the remaining business from the campaigns of 1513 finalized (there is no evidence in the surviving accounts that he was personally involved in this), since the delay in holding an audit had prevented the drawing up of a balance sheet. The contemporary historian Edward Hall, a persistent critic of Wolsey, typically presents this as far as possible to the cardinal's disadvantage, the process having been 'not to every mans contentacion, for some were found in arrerages and some saved themselfes by pollecy & brybowry, and waxed ryche, and some Innocents wer punished' (*Hall's Chronicle*, 585).

Wolsey was prominent again in the aftermath of the riots of 1 May 1517—'evil May day'—an outburst of xenophobia principally directed against foreign merchants by London apprentices. After a few exemplary hangings Queen Katherine begged for a pardon for the other offenders, which Henry granted, while Wolsey made an oration about clemency—the prisoners deserved death but a merciful ruler reprieved them. In August the minister made a pilgrimage to Walsingham, and on his return reported to Henry that the kingdom was in the greatest quiet and order. Then with the onset of autumn he resumed his usual activities and was active in pushing forward the enclosure inquiries that began in May that year, appointing friends and allies to the commissions so as to ensure that their momentum was maintained—as, indeed, it was. Domestic affairs, however, were dominated by disease. In January 1518 Wolsey imported continental ideas about quarantine in an attempt to combat plague, in the process risking unpopularity by trespassing on the authority of urban officialdom. He obtained the thanks of the physicians, however, when he arranged their incorporation and thereby gave them some much needed authority.

Wolsey's own authority at this time must have seemed unassailable. As chancellor it was his task to impress the French embassy which arrived at the end of September 1518 to propose the marriage of the new-born dauphin to Princess Mary. The ambassadors may have thought it would be easier to deal with the king without Wolsey and so entertained rumours that he would soon be dismissed. Instead Wolsey orchestrated continuous festivities and entertainments for them, involving them in formal ceremonies at St Paul's and providing a magnificent banquet at which the king appeared in disguise.

The reports of ambassadors impressed with Wolsey's authority have, however, led subsequent historians to overlook the political dimension to the cardinal's ministerial career. He could not take Henry's favour for granted, and from time to time others challenged his position. For example, he was under pressure from various quarters in 1515, 1516, and 1517. The attempt in 1519 to exclude from court a number of Henry's 'minions', younger courtiers who were beginning to dominate the privy chamber and hence the king's private life, has been attributed to him. If so, he was unable to keep them away permanently, for in the autumn they were recalled. The famous Eltham ordin-ances for the royal household, which Wolsey introduced in 1526, could be presented as a necessary part of a pro-gramme of financial retrenchment, but they also included a revision and reduction of the privy chamber staff which Wolsey drafted personally and which again reflected his nervousness of courtiers who had regular access to the king. Nor was he unhappy when fear of plague led Henry to abandon the normal court and keep moving from place to place with a small retinue. The Ven-etian ambassador could report how the king 'leaves every-thing in charge of Cardinal Wolsey, who keeps a great court and has comedies and tragedies performed' (CSP Ven-ice, 1520–26, 517).

Relations with the nobility For Henry VIII, as for all his pre-decessors, control of the nobility was essential for govern-ment, and Wolsey played a vital role in this. There was no royal hostility towards the nobility and the landed gentry. Indeed, the king depended on the authority they pos-sessed, but it had to be used in his service and at his behest, and Henry was always distrustful when an individ-ual who enjoyed a natural right to rule became forgetful of this requirement. Hence the letter which he wrote in his own hand to Wolsey, in an April when they were separ-ated by the sweat (it has been variously dated to 1518, 1519, and 1520), instructing him to 'make good watche on the duke off Suffolke, on the duke of Bukyngam, on my lord off Northe Omberland, on my lord off Darby, on my lord off Wylshere and on others whyche yow thynke suspecte' (LP Henry VIII, 3/1, no. 1).

Under Henry VII the nobility had been strictly con-trolled, but this had been relaxed in the reaction that fol-lowed his death. Wolsey's first use of his authority as chancellor was therefore to announce a more stringent monitoring of noble behaviour. On 2 May 1516 he made a speech in Star Chamber, on what he termed the new law of Star Chamber, whose burden was that those respon-sible for administering justice should not see themselves as being above the law. To any who asked 'Quis custodiet ipsos custodes?' ('Who judges the judges?'), he gave the answer, centralized royal authority. And to emphasize the point, on that same day the fifth earl of Northumberland was summoned into court for contempt of the council's jurisdiction in private suits, and was subsequently com-mitted to the Fleet. Wolsey also attempted to interfere in the marriage arrangements of the aristocracy, so funda-mental to their relations with one another. By 1518 discon-tent was evidently simmering among the nobility, and shadowy rumours of a plot against Wolsey circulated; the third duke of Buckingham, who had recently been given three months to take the necessary steps to reduce his own tenants to order, was reported to have complained that Wolsey would undo all noblemen if he could. In April that year Henry alluded darkly to 'great personages' and praised 'Wolsey's special regard for the surety of his per-son' (LP Henry VIII, 2/2, no. 4057). Wolsey too was given pro-tection. When Thomas Lucas, formerly Henry VII's solicitor-general, slandered the chancellor he was sent to the Tower.

Some time during 1519 Wolsey sent a 'Pryvie remembraunce' to Henry 'to put hymself in strength with his moost trusty servaunts in everie shire for the seurtie of his roiall person & succession' (BL, Cotton MS Titus B.i, fol. 192). The exemplary punishment in Star Chamber on 28 October of Sir William Bulmer, in a session at which the king presided, may have been a reflection of this suspi-cious policy—Bulmer had worn Buckingham's livery in the king's presence even though he was the king's sworn servant. But other measures reflect a genuine concern with justice, for instance the proceedings at the same time against Lord Edmund Howard and two other Surrey JPs for manipulating and intimidating the courts. The oaths taken by sheriffs and JPs at their swearing-in were revised in an attempt to prevent such abuses, and efforts were also made to reduce abuses of the traditional right of sanc-tuary.

It seems unlikely that such measures were seen as a threat to aristocratic interests, and there is no clear evi-dence that Wolsey, any more than the king, was hostile to the nobility as such, whatever his actions in individual cases. In general terms his policy towards the powerful can be described as one of offering carrots as well as sticks. He encouraged members of the gentry to become his cli-ents by holding out the prospect of desirable appoint-ments, and in the process established a network of dependants who could counteract disaffection in the localities. Viewed in this perspective, the words put into Wolsey's mouth when addressing the earl of Kildare, 'I wot well (my lord) that I am not the meetest at this boord to charge you with these treasons because it pleased some of your pufellows to report that I am a professed enimie to all nobilitie' (Holinshed, 6.281), seem to represent the per-ceptions of hindsight. The same is probably true of the duke of Norfolk's claim in 1546, when he was in the Tower, that Wolsey had spent fourteen years plotting his destruction, though the cardinal's bypassing the duke after he became treasurer in 1522 may well have aroused resentment, and Wolsey also fell out with the duke of Suf-folk, perhaps over the latter's French expedition of 1523. For as long as Wolsey had Henry's backing most nobles worked well enough with him, and some of them accepted his arbitration in their personal affairs. When John de Vere, fourteenth earl of Oxford, quarrelled with his mother—an issue that local JPs could hardly be expected to handle—it was Wolsey who tried to settle their differences. The earl of Worcester counted the car-dinal a good friend.

The most spectacular clash between the king's govern-ment and a nobleman, that involving the third duke of Buckingham, retains an element of mystery. The duke's royal blood (of which he was too aware for his own good), touchy personality, and penchant for wild talk were all likely to bring him under suspicion, even before it emerged that he had been speculating about what might happen should the king die. He was no friend to Wolsey, who had warned him to conduct himself more discreetly. Old suspicions and new provocations, it seems, sufficed to ruin the duke, who was summoned to London on 8 April

1521, charged and convicted of treason, and executed on 17 May. Nevertheless contemporaries attributed a major role to Wolsey. Robert Gilbert, the duke's chancellor, allegedly confessed that Buckingham accused Wolsey of practising necromancy to maintain the king's favour as well as of being Henry's bawd. Foreign ambassadors reported how Buckingham lost his head because he murmured against the cardinal's doings. Wolsey himself told the French ambassador that Buckingham's opposition to an alliance with France had been the cause of his beheading, but this cannot be taken as gospel.

Central and local government Whatever exactly precipitated Buckingham's fall, the duke's inability to defend himself may have helped Wolsey to advance central control over local government. In particular he turned his attention to improving royal control in areas where the monarch rarely appeared in person, and where immediate responses to local insubordination and misbehaviour were correspondingly desirable. This applied above all to the north of England and to Ireland. In Yorkshire, where he had long been archbishop, he restored the council of the north in 1525 under the nominal presidency of the duke of Richmond, and staffed it with servants and clients of his own, men like Thomas Magnus and John Uvedale; he also appointed them to commissions of the peace, at the expense of the local gentry. But York was too far south to be an effective centre for managing the Scottish borders, and the cardinal's success in those parts was limited. His being from 1523 bishop of Durham, a see with palatine powers and a major stronghold at Norham on the Anglo-Scottish middle march, gave him leverage there, but obedience could still be enforced only by those few resident lords who had the necessary resources, ability, and know-how to make them effective wardens. Indeed, Wolsey's efforts to control these men did more to weaken their authority than to advance that of the crown. It proved impossible to rule the east and middle marches without the participation of the earls of Northumberland, and Wolsey's symbolic shaming of the ageing Thomas, second Lord Dacre, in 1524–5, was no turning point in the development of the government of the region, still less a 'major triumph' (Guy, *Cardinal's Court*, 123); indeed, it had disastrous consequences thanks to the incapacity of Dacre's successor, the first earl of Cumberland.

Wolsey's policy in Ireland was equally ineffective, oscillating as it did between appointing outsiders with armies to serve as royal lieutenants (the earl of Surrey acted thus in 1520–22), which was costly, and attempts to promote other local magnates, notably Piers Butler, earl of Ormond, to counterbalance the almost viceregal power of the Geraldines, led by the ninth earl of Kildare. In 1524 he sent a three-man commission to settle disputes and reform government. It enjoyed a measure of success, but was not followed up. Little more effective was Wolsey's reestablishment in 1526 of a reorganized council in the marches of Wales, thanks to the incompetence of its first president, Bishop John Veysey of Exeter. Results only began to appear when Veysey was replaced by Rowland Lee in 1534.

Law and justice Fundamental to Wolsey's authority was his position as lord chancellor, an office whose eminence he underlined through the ceremonial he attached to it. His day during term time is well recorded. After hearing two masses and learning what noblemen, gentlemen, and others were waiting on him in his outer chambers, he emerged from his privy chamber in full cardinal's robes, having the great seal, his red hat, and two great silver crosses and two silver pillars (symbols of secular authority) borne before him. With many attendants, he rode on his mule, protected by footmen with pole-axes, to Westminster Hall. There he first consulted the judges in private, then went up to chancery, where he sat until 11 a.m., and thence to Star Chamber, 'where he spared nother highe nor lowe' (Cavendish, 24).

Wolsey's impact on the legal system constituted, in many ways, his most enduring achievement. This was somewhat strange, given his lack of training in canon and civil law—in contrast to his predecessors. John Stow later commented that 'It was a strange matter to see, a man not trayned up in the laws, to sit in the seate of judgement, to pronounce the lawe' (Stow, 845), and some of Wolsey's decisions drew criticisms at the time, though often from the losing party. Not that Wolsey showed any lack of confidence, and the story of one case suggests that he was erudite or perceptive enough to rebuke counsel for want of knowledge. Plaintiffs clamoured for him to hear their suits, and Sir Thomas More, the next chancellor, thought well of his predecessor's conduct in office.

In his own court of chancery Wolsey continued the positive but moderate approach taken by recent chancellors. Cases involving the title to land were regularly heard, although technically they should have been brought at common law, and the number of actions rose by a modest 8 per cent per annum. In the council, on the other hand, Wolsey was an innovator. The reduction in the time that councillors now devoted to policy allowed him to divert their attention to the sittings they held in Star Chamber to handle issues arising from the king's responsibility for law and justice. In theory they heard only cases not already provided for at common law, particularly any involving disorder, but Wolsey made clear his intention to offer justice generally. The Venetian ambassador observed that 'he favours the people exceedingly and especially the poor; hearing their suits and seeking to dispatch them instantly; he also makes the lawyers plead gratis for all paupers' (Brown, 2.314). This led to a surge of civil cases masquerading as allegations of riot or similar wrongdoing, brought in the hope that the authority of the royal council could give better justice than the increasingly hidebound common lawcourts. In consequence Star Chamber became clogged with business, and Wolsey had to set up first a series of temporary overflow tribunals, and then in 1519 he settled a permanent judicial committee which became the ancestor of the court of requests. Still the backlog continued to build, and attempts to delegate cases for settlement locally proved ineffective. In the end it was left to Wolsey's successors to give the court of Star Chamber adequate machinery. Nevertheless, as Sir Thomas Smith wrote, Star Chamber

> tooke great augmentation and authoritie at that time that Cardinall Wolsey Archbishop of Yorke was Chauncellor of Englande, who of some was thought to have first devised the Court, because that he after some intermission by negligence of time, augmented the authoritie of it.   (Guy, *Cardinal's Court*, 139)

Alongside private legal business Star Chamber took cases of a more political character. These were overwhelmingly brought by private complaint rather than official action, but still allowed Wolsey to deal with the powerful. In this he generally sought to discipline the offender rather than destroy him. Thus the Sacheverell–Grey dispute, which caused constant trouble in Leicestershire, resulted first in a summons for both Sir Richard Sacheverell and Thomas Grey, marquess of Dorset, to appear in Star Chamber, and then in their being ordered to stay away from the county courts where they had repeatedly clashed. Decisions of this kind might do little more than divert animosities into legal and non-violent channels, but even the usually critical Hall admitted that the cardinal's willingness to confront perjury, disorder, and interference with justice by the wealthy and powerful could be both meritorious and effective—'poore men lyved quyetly so that no man durst beare for fear of imprisonement; but he him selfe and his servantes, which were wer well punyshed therfore' (*Hall's Chronicle*, 585). This concern to enforce law and order remained one of Wolsey's priorities. Thus on 5 July 1526, despite pressing diplomatic business, he found time to assemble 110 JPs in Star Chamber, address them, and present them with detailed questions concerning the maintenance of justice in their localities.

Scurrilous innuendo was a common subtext where Wolsey's justice was concerned, for instance the rumour that he had imprisoned Sir John Stanley by way of a favour to his mistress's son-in-law. But his detractors may have had a point when they alleged that Wolsey exploited the actions brought into Star Chamber for personal and political ends. Thus although severity towards Sir Robert Sheffield (speaker of the House of Commons in 1512) could be justified by his indisputable involvement in felony, he had opposed Wolsey over Hunne's Case, and the petty humiliation heaped on Sir Robert (who died in the Tower in 1518) may imply a personal vindictiveness. Suspicions of this sort are certainly raised by the campaign against enclosure which Wolsey waged from 1517 until his fall. He began with a national inquiry to discover where and how much land had been enclosed and houses destroyed, and this led to at least 264 prosecutions for breaches of the Anti-Enclosure Acts of 1489 and 1514–15. A high percentage came to judgment, which may indicate the degree of pressure Wolsey brought to bear, and it has been suggested that he enjoyed a *frisson* of pleasure at the prosecution of nine peers, three bishops, and the rest who made up 'a roll-call of the possessing classes of the Midlands' (Scarisbrick, 'Cardinal Wolsey', 63). It should also be conceded,

however, that other of Wolsey's activities support the idea that he had a commitment to social justice and the common good, for instance his attempts to force market traders to observe the 'just price', or to purge London of vagrants and criminals, or the revaluations which he introduced in 1526 to protect the English currency.

Dealings with Habsburgs and Valois, 1519–1525 England's position following the signing of the treaty of Universal Peace on 21 October 1518 was less secure than it seemed. In particular little had been done to exploit the great victory at Flodden five years earlier, and neither Henry nor Wolsey showed much understanding either of Scottish politics or of the nature of society in the Anglo-Scottish borders. Opportunities for a long-term peace in the north were repeatedly missed, while François I used his influence with the duke of Albany to foment action against England. It did not make the situation in the north any less volatile that few English nobles were prepared to reside on the borders to act as march warden, or that those who did maintained a minimal peace by means that were wellnigh treasonable.

A potentially unstable situation was further undermined when the emperor Maximilian died on 12 January 1519. The princes of Europe intrigued for the imperial title, and Wolsey promised help to both Charles and François, but on 25 March he wrote to Rome suggesting that the pope's position would be compromised if either obtained the position. But when Leo X suggested that a third candidate would be preferable—a clear reference to Henry VIII—Wolsey pointed out to Henry the dangers of being an unsuccessful candidate and, reluctant to be the underbidder in a race in which the Habsburg Charles had a clear advantage, promised money only after the election, and responded sceptically to promises of votes in the next papal conclave.

Charles having been elected emperor on 18 June 1519, François turned to England for support, and especially to Wolsey, who he was informed was solely responsible for policy, making the cardinal his plenipotentiary for arranging a meeting with Henry to be held at Ardres. In conformity with the previous year's treaty, Wolsey and Henry continued their balancing act between the two great continental powers, and listened to both French and imperial offers. Late in May 1520 they entertained the emperor informally in England, and Wolsey refused offers of ecclesiastical revenues in Spain. Wolsey's success in reassuring the emperor was such that the Venetian ambassador described him as seven times more powerful than the pope. Indeed, much of that year was occupied with public demonstrations of the mutual goodwill of princes, largely orchestrated by Wolsey. On 29 May Charles re-embarked for Flanders and Henry crossed to Calais, moving to Guînes on 4 June. Once the English court had arrived in Calais, Wolsey went to meet François. A spectacular feat of organization, the celebrated Field of Cloth of Gold also saw the cardinal at his most magnificent, outshining most of the noblemen present as he provided feasts and managed protocol. But the surface glitter imperfectly concealed a further shift in political alliances, for when the festivities ended on 24 June Wolsey had not managed to reconcile François and Charles. Consequently Henry met Charles at Gravelines and escorted him to Calais, where a formal treaty was made on 14 July, committing the two rulers to maintaining existing relations. By the end of the year, however, there were proposals that Charles should marry Princess Mary, despite her betrothal to the French dauphin. Nevertheless Wolsey refused the emperor's attempts to persuade Henry to agree to declare war on the French immediately, advising his king to decline to be drawn into a Habsburg–Valois war, but rather to await a call for assistance from one of the combatants.

On 9 June 1521 a series of military set-backs led François to accept Wolsey's offer of arbitration with the emperor. Charles was persuaded to participate in negotiations by promises of later services. Possibly with the deception of both parties in mind, Wolsey crossed to Calais at the beginning of August 1521. It is a measure of the fluidity of the diplomatic situation that he should have carried with him a number of different commissions, empowering him variously to settle the differences between François and Charles, to negotiate peace with France, to form a confederation with the pope, the emperor, and the French king, and to conclude an alliance against France with the emperor. He also—illegally—took the great seal with him, allegedly to prevent Henry from sealing letters patent without his knowledge. Having presided at Calais over an unsuccessful conference between French and imperial ambassadors, on 16 August he arrived at Bruges with 1000 horsemen. Charles met him at the gates and embraced him. Ostensibly the honest broker between the continental giants, Wolsey was now negotiating an offensive alliance with Charles against France, and under a treaty concluded on 25 August committed England to declaring war in March 1523. Wolsey's own reward would be a pension of £1200 a year, ostensibly for relinquishing his claims to the bishopric of Tournai. Although King Henry alarmed Wolsey by speaking in warlike fashion of recovering his rightful inheritance, he also sent word on a number of occasions to say how satisfied he was with Wolsey's wisdom, which gained more than battles had.

At the end of 1522, however, foreign affairs took a turn that even the most astute diplomat could hardly control. On 1 December the imperial troops took Tournai. News came that Milan, too, had fallen to the imperial army and that Leo X had died on 1 December. Although both François and Charles had promised to promote Wolsey, the latter was reported by the Spanish ambassador to have claimed he would accept election only if Henry and the emperor thought he could be serviceable to them, and that 'your majesties, like father and son, shall dispose of that see, its authority and power, as if they were your own, and give laws to the rest of the world' (*LP Henry VIII*, 3/1.cxci). However, Wolsey doubted Charles's good faith in this and told the ambassador that if his master was in earnest he should order his troops to advance against Rome and command the cardinals to elect his nominee. When the conclave met, Henry's agents did their best but were handicapped by Wolsey's own statement that he

would not meddle with it. John Clerk asserted that Wolsey received as many as eight or nine votes at every scrutiny, but in the formal record Wolsey was registered as receiving seven votes in just one ballot. Eventually Charles's old tutor was elected as Adrian VI. François then took precautions against an Anglo-imperial alliance by sending Albany back to Scotland and providing him with French troops.

England formally declared war on France on 29 May 1522, and a forced loan was levied to finance hostilities. At the same time Charles made a further visit to England, leading to treaties on 19 June and 2 July which provided for concerted attacks on France. One English army raided Brittany before invading Picardy and another was sent to the Scottish borders. Wolsey and Henry kept tight control over the finances of war, and only Wolsey was empowered to sign warrants apart from Henry himself. However both men soon lost interest in sending further armies to France to assist Charles, who had reneged on all his promises. They were conscious of the danger from Scotland and the shortage of money, though Wolsey may also have been worried about the threat from the Yorkist pretender Richard de la Pole, whom François was aiding. The treason of Charles, duc de Bourbon, offered the prospect of an ally within France, but Wolsey doubted Bourbon's usefulness and determined only to help him if he acknowledged Henry as rightful king of France. Eventually, however, the possibilities offered by Bourbon's defection led to an agreement under which a 10,000 strong English army was to be sent to France under the duke of Suffolk, although it was late in the year. The council could not agree whether he should merely besiege Boulogne or go further, but ultimately a thrust deep into France was decided on. By 27 October Suffolk was at Montdidier, causing Wolsey to tell Henry VIII that 'ther shalbe never, or like opportunite geven hereafter for the atteynyng of Fraunce' (*State Papers, Henry VIII*, 1.143), but defeated by the weather, and with his army increasingly mutinous, the duke had to withdraw. For this he blamed Wolsey—after the latter's fall—claiming he had not sent reinforcements.

By now Wolsey had recommenced secret negotiations with the French. Matters were complicated by the death of Adrian VI on 14 September 1523. This time Wolsey seemed slightly more interested in the possibility of being elected pope, but, as before, Charles's position was crucial, and he favoured Giulio de' Medici. The emperor did write a letter on Wolsey's behalf, but then delayed the messenger. Although Clerk thought Wolsey might have a chance in what promised to be a bitter struggle, he noted that the people of Rome cried out against an absentee pope.

Meanwhile English policy made it necessary to keep up the appearance of friendship with Charles and the Low Countries. Henry talked of leading a new attack on France himself, and Wolsey made a speech to the people of London about French perfidy, while at the same time providing himself with an escape route by laying the blame for the war entirely on Charles's shoulders, and emphasizing the losses Henry had suffered. Publicly he claimed that Henry would treat only if the whole realm of France was surrendered, but he was careful to offer Charles expensive options which the emperor inevitably declined, leaving Wolsey free to pursue cheaper policies, for the issues of a subsidy and clerical aid were all spent. The principal imperial ambassadors and even Richard Pace, the cardinal's own man, blamed Wolsey for the course of events, often referring to his base nature and to bribery. But it was becoming increasingly difficult to maintain Henry's standing in Europe on the available resources. On 11 February 1525 letters of Louis de Praet, the imperial ambassador, came into English hands and were opened, to reveal that de Praet had written: 'I hope one day to see our master avenged for Wolsey is the main cause of all his misfortunes' (*LP Henry VIII*, 4/1, no. 1083). Wolsey summoned the ambassador before the council and charged him with untruth. Against this background of growing Anglo-imperial tension Charles's capture of François at Pavia on 24 February 1525 revolutionized the situation. Wolsey had assured Henry on 12 February that if the imperials won Henry would receive Charles's thanks for money recently sent, while if the French prevailed, 'yet, thanked be God, your affaires be, by your highe wisdome, in more assured and substancial trayne by such communications as be set furth with France apart, then others in owteward places wolde suppose' (*State Papers, Henry VIII*, 1.158). Yet although Henry was especially pleased that Richard de la Pole had been killed in the battle, and Wolsey sang high mass in St Paul's, the truth was that the cardinal had lost his leverage. On 26 March the emperor wrote to de Praet wondering what he might do to punish Wolsey.

Shortage of funds left Wolsey with few options. He encouraged the confederate Italian states to fight but refused to involve Henry in a distant war, arguing in a letter of 4 May that to do so would jeopardize the property of Englishmen in Charles's dominions as well as the money that the emperor owed Henry. To redress the balance of power he proposed Princess Mary as a new wife for François, Queen Claude having died in 1524, while pointing out that Henry had no need, secure as he was in a well-defended island, to make such an alliance. Henry's own proposals, both for a tripartite division of France between Charles, Bourbon, and himself, and for his own coronation as king of France, were rebuffed by the emperor. Instead Wolsey entered into negotiations with the French regent, Louise of Savoy, which culminated in the treaty of the More on 30 August 1525. Henry undertook to endeavour to secure the release of François, who in return promised to pay Henry 2 million écus at the rate of 100,000 per annum. Despite this, financial weakness kept England out of further continental wars, and although Wolsey helped to create the anti-imperial league formed at Cognac in May 1526, he had to restrict Henry's role to that of its protector.

Financial problems, 1525–1526 The financial considerations that caused England to ally herself with France at the expense of the Habsburgs in 1525 had long hampered her efforts in association with the latter. When war was imminent in 1522 Wolsey, appreciating the need for money and troops, organized a nationwide survey, the so-called 'general proscription', to obtain details of the available manpower, and also to assess the population's taxable wealth. Armed with the information provided, and reinforcing his efforts with an appeal to the nobility to protect their wealth and promote their honour by assisting the king, he was able to levy some £200,000 by two forced loans in 1522–3. But still more was needed, and it became apparent that adequate war finance required a parliament. On 29 April 1523 Wolsey sought a much larger grant from the Commons than ever before—a subsidy to be levied at the rate of 4s. in the pound on property as it had been reassessed a year earlier, to bring in perhaps £800,000. There can be little doubt that he was deliberately asking for more than he expected to get in order to settle graciously for a lower but still considerable sum, and he can hardly have been surprised when the Commons offered a lesser amount, even though he told them he would rather have his tongue pulled out with red-hot pincers than carry such a message to the king. In the event his strategy worked, for although there was much cantankerous debate the Commons finally granted four subsidies, which, however, eventually raised little more than the previous grants.

A year later the king's need for money in order to exploit the French defeat at Pavia saw commissioners sent out to demand a non-parliamentary tax based on the valuations of 1522 and called an 'amicable grant'. Coming so soon after the previous year's subsidy, at a time when the earlier forced loans had not yet been repaid, and being assessed at the penal level of between 25 and 33 per cent for the clergy and between 5 and 16 per cent for the laity, this demand was the last straw. In Hall's words:

> all people curssed the Cardinal and his coadherentes as subvertor of the Lawes and libertie of England. For thei said if men should geve their goodes by a Commission, then wer it worse than the taxes of Fraunce and so England should be bond and not free. (*Hall's Chronicle*, 696)

Discontent was widespread and dangerous, and full-scale revolt broke out in Suffolk and nearby. Whether the cardinal was wholly to blame is open to question—there is good reason to believe that Henry had been fully involved from the start. As Wolsey wrote to the dukes of Norfolk and Suffolk, 'it is the custom of the people, when anything miscontenteth them, to blame those that be near about the King' (*LP Henry VIII*, 4/1, no. 1318). Ten thousand protesters gathered at Lavenham, and although the two dukes managed to overawe them, the government had no option but to withdraw.

The retreat was covered by an adroit display of playacting. Wolsey stated that the levy had been discussed in council, where the judges, in particular, had declared it lawful. The king, however, agreed to spare his subjects, and Wolsey took responsibility for the unsuccessful project:

> because every man laieth the burden from hym, I am content to take it on me, and to endure the fame and noyes of the people for my goodwill towards the kyng, and comfort of you my lordes, and other the kynges counsailers.

He added, significantly, 'the eternall God knoweth all'

(*Hall's Chronicle*, 700). On 30 May 1525 he proclaimed the king's pardon to the rebels of Suffolk, and as they could not find sureties declared that 'I will be one because you be my countrey men, and my lorde of Norfolke will be another' (ibid., 702).

The king's Great Matter, 1527 At the opening of 1527 Wolsey seemed at the height of his power, underlined by the magnificent banquet that he offered to all the ambassadors and nobility, and at which Henry himself 'unexpectedly' turned up, to be entertained by a production of Plautus's *Menaechmi*, a masque, and dancing. By now, however, first the king's decision to divorce Katherine of Aragon, and then the rise of Anne Boleyn, were beginning to alter the political map. Wolsey certainly saw the pitfalls presented by these developments. In an attempt to pre-empt criticism he begged Henry that, whatever reports to the contrary he received concerning the cardinal's management of the business, he should 'conceive none opinion of me but that in this matter and in all other things that may touch your honor and surety I shall be as constant as any living creature' (*State Papers, Henry VIII*, 1.194). According to Cavendish, when Wolsey first heard about the king's plans, he knelt before Henry in his privy chamber for over an hour, trying to persuade him to reverse them. When he found the king immovable he hoped that a suitable princess could be found, for at first he knew nothing of Henry's plans to marry Anne.

The problems attendant upon Henry's Great Matter began increasingly to preoccupy the government. Nevertheless Wolsey continued to work for a European peace, hoping to mediate between the Habsburgs and their enemies. But his methods were sometimes counterproductive. In March he met with French envoys at Westminster to arrange the marriage of Mary either to François's son the duc d'Orléans or even to François himself. Claiming to be their only ally, Wolsey made exorbitant demands and said that if he advised Henry to abate them he would be thought a fool or a traitor and stand in danger of his life. He chopped and changed his proposals so often that the French ambassador described him as 'the most rascally beggar in the world and one who is wholly devoted to his master's interest' (*LP Henry VIII*, 4.cci). That master may have been less appreciative, for Henry was beginning to go behind Wolsey's back, telling the French ambassadors in April 1527 that he had things to communicate to François that the cardinal did not know. None the less a further Anglo-French treaty was concluded on the 30th.

His hand strengthened by having a continental ally, Wolsey now turned to the problem of the king's marriage, using his legatine authority to outrank the archbishop of Canterbury and begin preliminary and confidential inquiries into the validity of Henry's union with Katherine. On 17 May 1527 the king was summoned to appear before Wolsey in a secret tribunal, charged with cohabiting with his brother's wife. But despite all the precautions the Spanish ambassador knew of the scheme on the 18th. The fact that he attributed responsibility for it entirely to

Wolsey did not prevent his attempting to bribe the cardinal with a renewed promise of imperial assistance at the next papal vacancy. Nothing was achieved, and on 31 May proceedings came to an end. Within the next two days Wolsey knew of the sack of Rome and of the pope's becoming effectively the prisoner of Katherine's nephew Charles V. Realistically, he advised Henry that this meant that progress with the divorce would be set back. On 22 June, however, Henry informed Katherine of his intentions, and she managed to get a member of her household to alert Charles.

On 11 July Wolsey crossed the channel, dignified with the title of vicegerent. On his way to Dover, under an oath of secrecy, he had discussed the divorce with Archbishop Warham and John Fisher. The king's Great Matter apart, it was hardly the ideal time to be away from the king's side. Wolsey left at a time of domestic difficulties, with a growing threat from seditious preachers as well as more familiar problems with law and order, and when there were also court conspiracies against him, involving the Howards and the Boleyns. Once in France he proposed that, to counteract Charles's grip on Rome and on the pope, all the cardinals then at liberty should be convoked to Avignon, where they could declare themselves unconstrained by Clement's acts during his captivity. Alternatively Clement could delegate his authority totally to Wolsey, 'not for any auctorite ambicion, commodite private proufite or lucre but only for the avauncement of Your Grace's secrete affaire' (*State Papers, Henry VIII*, 1.278).

François provided flattering pageants for Wolsey, representing him as the 'cardinalis pacificus', though he knew the cardinal was hamstrung by the needs of the divorce. On 18 August an Anglo-French peace treaty was agreed at Amiens, but although Wolsey was reluctant to tarry in France for fear of losing his influence with the king, who was entertaining all the nobility most likely to want to undermine him, the ramifications of his foreign policy made it impossible for him to leave immediately. He learned that without consulting him Henry had sent agents to Rome, and feared this would be counterproductive, even though his own experienced diplomats had enjoyed little success. He reassured Henry of his devotion to his service, telling the king that every day separated from him felt like a year. But failure was not in Henry's vocabulary and, already impatient, he had begun to show Wolsey's letters to Norfolk and to Thomas Boleyn, Viscount Rochford—the father of Anne. When Wolsey finally returned to England at the end of September he found that he was obliged to have speech with Henry in Anne's presence.

Struggling to stay afloat, 1528 On the first day of the Michaelmas law term Wolsey made a speech in Star Chamber in which he tried to win popular support with promises that there would be no further taxes for wars in France, and railed against the emperor for the sack of Rome. Hall reports that men laughed: 'they knew that that he sayd was for his owne glory, and nothing should folowe as he sayd' (*Hall's Chronicle*, 733). The harvest failed in 1527, and famine and disease exacerbated the government's difficulties. The arrangements Wolsey subsequently made for a distribution of food, though equitable in principle, enraged those whose barns and storerooms were ransacked. War was declared on Charles on 22 January 1528. The move was unpopular with merchants and clothiers, and did not move the emperor on the divorce. On 13 February Wolsey again denounced Charles in Star Chamber, but according to Hall some people said softly 'that evil wil said never wel' (ibid., 744). The threat of an English descent on the Low Countries came to nothing. Margaret and Charles issued pamphlets directed at the English which upheld the imperial position. While one even attacked the king's divorce, all of them vilified Wolsey. The closing of Spanish and Flemish markets to English cloth was not fully effective but it combined with a worsening famine to produce a wave of unrest in March, especially in East Anglia and Kent; in May there were even allegations that a group of Kentish clothworkers had conspired to murder the cardinal. By early April Wolsey was making peace proposals to Charles V and Margaret.

Meanwhile the divorce had been stalled at the curia, where the pope's experts provided everything except what was needed, a decretal commission which would permit the case to be concluded in England. Wolsey warned Clement that if he did not co-operate the king would turn against the papacy and the Roman church, and that if he was himself dismissed because his legatine power had failed to secure the divorce, then papal power would also be diminished, but he was not believed. By 15 June Henry's agents had obtained the required commission, albeit with heavy restrictions on its use and even on its circulation, and on 25 July Cardinal Campeggi set out with it for London. Meanwhile in June the sweat had broken out in London, the law term was cancelled, and Wolsey left town for Hampton Court, where he once more carried on the business of the kingdom virtually alone. Henry urged him to avoid infection and sent him medical advice. Perhaps Wolsey caught the disease all the same, for on 5 July, apparently in expectation of death, he saw fit to assure the king that:

> if it shall fortune the same to be the last word that ever I shall speak or write unto your Highness, I dare boldly say and affirm your Grace hath had of me a most loving, true and faithful servant. (*LP Henry VIII*, 4/2, no. 4468)

Late in August the French ambassador found the cardinal in thoughtful mood, hoping for international peace and domestic reform, and declaring 'if this marriage took place, and an heir male came of it, that he would then retire, and serve God to the end of his days' (ibid., 4/2, no. 4649). He may have feared that once the divorce was settled, Anne Boleyn would destroy his influence.

Campeggi arrived in England on 9 October with the decretal commission. He read it once to Henry and Wolsey before hiding it. Henry's speech about the divorce to the notables on 8 November was poorly received and, faced with popular opposition, he hesitated; Anne had to stiffen his resolve. Suddenly the divorce seemed far away. Wolsey once more pressed Clement for an amplification of his commission, one granting the whole of the pope's ordinary and absolute jurisdiction, but Clement was now immovable. Efforts to persuade Katherine to retire to a monastery failed, and to make matters worse the papal chamberlain Francesco Campano arrived in England in January 1529 with secret orders that Campeggi should destroy the legatine commission and under no circumstances proceed to judgment. Nevertheless Wolsey remained to outward appearances as much in favour as ever. When the see of Winchester, the richest in England, became vacant in February, Henry granted it to him without a *congé d'élire*. In return he surrendered Durham to the king, who granted the revenues to Anne's father, Viscount Rochford. In February rumours of Clement's death raised the possibility of Wolsey's election as pope, which indeed might have solved all Henry's difficulties. But the story was false, and Clement continued to offer everything except what was needed.

His concentration on the divorce, abetted by some deceit on François's part, seems to have blinded Henry to the significance of the peace negotiations between Margaret of Austria and Louise of Savoy, although he wanted Wolsey to attend them in order to bid for French help with the divorce. He gave secret instructions to the duke of Suffolk to ask the French king if he believed the cardinal was forwarding that Great Matter, and received the equivocal suggestion that Henry should manage such an affair himself. At the same time the French ambassador reported on 22 May that Suffolk, Norfolk, and others were persuading the king that Wolsey had not done all that he might to promote a French alliance by advancing the proposed marriage of Princess Mary to the duc d'Orléans. By early June 1529 Henry seems to have been half convinced that the cardinal was failing him, and even Stephen Gardiner, who became Henry's secretary during that month, began to distance himself from his old patron.

Meanwhile the divorce proceedings continued, and finally both parties were summoned to appear on Friday 25 June. Wolsey asked the king: 'whether I have been the chief inventor and first mover of this matter with your majesty for I am greatly suspected of all men herein?' Henry said that he had rather been opposed to him. Vergil reports Katherine as accusing Wolsey 'of treachery, deceit, injustice and evil-doing in creating dissension … the bitterest enemy both of me and of law and justice' (*Anglica historia*, 331), to which Hall adds that she also accused him of tyranny, pride, vainglory, a voluptuous life, lechery, and malice to the emperor. She appealed to Rome and withdrew, and though proceedings continued they became bogged down in technicalities. Finally on 31 July Campeggi prorogued the court to 1 October, at which point Suffolk made his famous declaration that 'the olde saied sawe is true, that there was never Legate nor Cardinall, that did good in Englande' (*Hall's Chronicle*, 759); perhaps, as both Hall and Cavendish asserted, he spoke thus by the king's command. Meanwhile Clement had made peace with Charles on 29 June, and on 19 July he recalled the case to Rome. William Benet, the English envoy in Rome, insisted that this would lead to the ruin of the cardinal and the destruction of the English church, but Clement replied that no one foresaw the mischief more clearly than himself, and that he must follow his conscience.

Falling like Lucifer, 1528–1529 Increasingly made the scapegoat for the king's failure to obtain a divorce from Katherine, Wolsey was by this time deeply and increasingly unpopular. Hall records that a book containing thirty-four articles against the minister was given to the king after the failure of the Blackfriars court, wherein he 'evidently perceived the high pride and covetousnes of the Cardinall and … with what dissimulacion and clokyng he had handeled the kynges causes: how he with faire liyng woordes had blynded and defrauded the Kyng' (*Hall's Chronicle*, 759), but the king did not react. Without royal sanction Wolsey's critics on the council had to abandon their plan to arrest Wolsey without warning and seize and scrutinize all his papers. Even so, there were rumours on 30 July that there would soon be a great change and the extinction of Wolsey's authority. Anne Boleyn had now turned decisively against him, believing that he was trying to delay the divorce proceedings. Henry himself, likewise fixated on the divorce, had prevented the cardinal from attending the Franco-imperial negotiations at Cambrai. Wolsey offered further military support to France but in vain, for a peace treaty was signed on 3 August, so depriving him of the chance to use the threat of an Anglo-French alliance to put pressure on the emperor, and so on the pope. Nevertheless Wolsey continued to advise and meet Henry during August, particularly on difficulties in ratifying Cambrai. The minister wanted to exploit these in order to force greater French support, but Rochford and Gardiner persuaded the king that in order to further the divorce, maximum concessions needed to be made to France.

Wolsey reacted badly to the rejection of his advice, and the implication that he was cool on the divorce made the king unwilling to see him. On 19 September, however, he accompanied Campeggi to Grafton, Northamptonshire, for his fellow legate's formal leave-taking. There are important differences between the accounts of Henry's reunion with the cardinal provided by the latter's servant Thomas Alward and by Wolsey's biographer George Cavendish. For Cavendish the visit started in humiliation, with no lodgings being provided for Wolsey, and continued awkwardly, with Anne Boleyn doing her utmost to prevent any reconciliation between the king and his minister. But Alward, in a letter written just five days after the event, reported no remarkable differences from earlier meetings. Henry spoke amiably with Wolsey and Wolsey sat with the council before departing.

Nevertheless the pressure exerted on the king by Anne and her supporters, together with the simultaneous failure of his foreign policy and attempts to secure the king's divorce, combined to make Wolsey's position untenable. On Monday 3 and Wednesday 6 October the cardinal was in his place at the council table, and he presided in chancery on the 9th, but on that same day he was indicted for *praemunire* in king's bench. Implicit in the charge was the illegality of his legatine authority and of the courts held under it. On Monday 18th he surrendered the great seal, and next day the dukes of Norfolk and Suffolk and others came into Star Chamber and declared the causes of Wolsey's deprivation; they also replaced him as the king's chief councillors.

Wolsey's loss of office initiated a period of several months during which he fought to recover his position and the opponents and enemies who had united to bring him down endeavoured to prevent his recovery, both sides manoeuvring under the eyes of a king mindful of the cardinal's services and abilities. On 22 October Wolsey admitted that he had incurred the penalties of *praemunire* and surrendered all his property; an inventory of all his goods was made at once. Stow reported Wolsey as observing to Sir William Gascoigne, his treasurer:

> I would all the world knew that I have nothing but it is his [Henry's] of right, for by him, and of him I have received all that I have: therefore it is of convenience and reason, that I render unto His majestie the same againe with all my hart. (Stow, 920)

Du Bellay, writing on the same day, stated that Wolsey was offered the choice of answering to the king or to parliament and chose the former, observing that the allegations of peculation constituted no hanging matter, whereas he was accused of other offences, relating to his management of foreign policy, which would cost him his head. His being offered the alternative was a sign of favour to Wolsey and of the king's reluctance to destroy him completely. Nevertheless Du Bellay reported that:

> Wolsey has just been put out of his house, and all his goods taken into the King's hands. Besides the robberies of which they charge him, and the troubles occasioned by him between Christian princes, they accuse him of so many other things that he is quite undone. (*LP Henry VIII*, 4/3, no. 6019)

The endowments he had collected for his colleges at Oxford and Ipswich were declared forfeit to the crown, and he also lost York Place, albeit under protest.

Wolsey was ordered to Esher, and when he took to the water, with only one cross borne before him, people gathered on the banks, expecting to see him taken to the Tower. But at this moment of humiliation he received evidence of the king's merciful intentions, for at Putney he was overtaken by Henry Norris, the groom of the stool, who according to Cavendish brought him Henry's ring and a message telling him 'to be of good chere for he was as myche in his highenes favor as ever he was' (Cavendish, 102). Wolsey knelt in the mud to thank him for the joyful news, gave Norris his cross, and sent the king his fool (Patch Williams) as a gift. He and his household remained at Esher, in some confusion for want of furnishings, until on the night of 1–2 November Sir John Russell arrived, soaking wet, on a secret errand authenticated, again, by the king's ring. Russell may well have brought Wolsey the king's pardon; his mission certainly led to the arrival of 'plenty of howsshold stuff, vessell and plate And of all thynges necessary' (ibid., 112). Already at the end of October Du Bellay was reporting that 'it is not improbable that he may regain his authority' (*LP Henry VIII*, 4/3, no. 6030).

Nevertheless his adversaries continued to pursue Wolsey's ruin. The opening of parliament on 3 November saw Sir Thomas More, now lord chancellor, denounce 'the great wether which is of late fallen' (*Hall's Chronicle*, 764). The cardinal, said More, had now been been corrected, but his adversaries were not satisfied, and in an attempt to render him harmless recorded his faults in a set of forty-four articles (based on those drawn up for the proposed coup of June–July), which was presented to the king in the form of a petition on 1 December. The charges ranged from generalized allegations of accroachments on royal power, misuse of his power as legate and chancellor, and extortions from the clergy, both religious and secular, to minutely detailed accusations of wrongdoing in individual cases. Wolsey's signature on the document shows that in order to win security from further attack he was obliged to endorse them, a further humiliation which was also intended to disable him from restoration to his dignities and offices. But his submission had its reward, for when parliament adjourned on 17 December there had been no act of attainder and he was still archbishop of York. In curial eyes, moreover, and perhaps also his own, he was also still legate. Bishops could be tried for treason, but a papal legate might need to be handled more cautiously.

Last struggles and death, 1529–1530 Wolsey's enemies remained vigilant, determined to prevent his resurgence. In 1520 he had himself said that men never voluntarily surrender power, while in 1527, when the cardinal's position first began to look insecure, the imperial ambassador Mendoza judged that Wolsey was too able and powerful to be suffered to live in retirement or even in disgrace. This was probably how Norfolk, Suffolk, and Rochford saw the situation at the end of 1529, and according to Cavendish they combined to harass him: 'dayly they wold send hyme some thyng or do some thyng ayenst hyme wherin they thought that they myght geve hyme a cause of heveness or lamentacion' (Cavendish, 119). On about 17 December Wolsey wrote to Cromwell, who had remained faithful, pointing out that by his submission the king had received more than he would otherwise have had, and hoping for a settlement of his affairs.

Shortly afterwards Wolsey fell ill. He was, he told Cromwell, 'by the space of thre owers as one that shulde have dyde' (*LP Henry VIII*, 4/3, no. 6114). Henry sent his physician, Dr William Butts, and then a ring, and Anne Boleyn sent a token, and he recovered. Desperately anxious to stay near the court, he showered promises and pensions on his former supporters and on his enemies alike. He also tried to win Anne over, but was rebuffed; on 6 February 1530 Chapuys informed Charles V of an interview with Sir John Russell, who told how

> in consequence of some words he had spoken to the King in favour of the Cardinal the lady had been very angry and refused to speak with him. Norfolk told him of her displeasure, and that she was irritated against himself because he had not done as much against him [Wolsey] as much as he might. (ibid., 4/3, no. 6199)

When Norfolk asked Russell whether he thought the cardinal had any expectation of returning to favour, Russell told him that such was the cardinal's ambition and courage that he would not fail if he saw a favourable opportunity, and especially if the king should require his advice. The duke's response was to threaten to eat Wolsey alive. Forbidden to come within 7 miles of the court, the cardinal had moved to Richmond and stayed there until mid-Lent.

Meanwhile Henry continued to show himself lenient, sending Wolsey his furniture on 2 February, following this with a full pardon on the 12th, and on the 14th restoring him to the archbishopric of York, with all its possessions except York Place. On the 17th he entered into an indenture with Henry whereby he surrendered control of the see of Winchester and the abbacy of St Albans (leaving the possibility that they would be recovered), but in return received £6374 3s. 7½d. (£3000 in cash, the rest a quittance for money and goods already received) and a pension of 1000 marks. Such treatment was not what his adversaries had in mind for him, and at the beginning of March Norfolk told him through Cromwell to depart for York. He pleaded shortage of money and made other excuses, and did not leave for a month. In the interval he was visited by the French ambassador Passano, who found him 'so completely resigned and so armed with patience that there was hardly any need for me to advise such a course' (*CSP Spain*, 1529–30, 486).

Early in April Wolsey finally set off for his diocese. On the 10th, which was Palm Sunday, he reached Peterborough Abbey, where he stayed until Thursday in Easter week; he then continued north via Grantham and Newark, finally reaching his palace at Southwell on 5 June. Later in the summer he moved to Scroby, and finally at Michaelmas transferred to Cawood Castle, a few miles south of York. Everywhere he received visits from the local gentry, whose quarrels he worked to settle, and attended to his diocesan duties, not least by confirming hundreds of children. Although he himself wrote to the king in April complaining of his indebtedness, 'not knowing where to be succoured or relieved, but only at your Highness' most merciful and charitable hands' (*LP Henry VIII*, 4/3, no. 6344), at court it was reported that he rode so splendidly 'that some men thought he was of as good courage as in times past and wanted no impediment but lack of authority' (ibid., 4/3, no. 6335). In public he showed concern only for his colleges and for the possible effects of inquests into the lands of his archbishopric, but the lords of the council remained fearful that he would be recalled.

Some interpretations see him as still so ambitious that, as his enemies made out, he fell into treason. The case, as presented, says he entered negotiations with both the emperor and the French king, hoping above all to secure a papal order that Henry and Anne Boleyn should separate. This was to be supported by an interdict, which the cardinal expected would arouse such resentment, and ultimately resistance, against royal policy that he would himself become indispensable in dealing with it. This view of his own abilities was shared by the king. It must have alarmed Wolsey's enemies that Henry was reported as saying that in managing business the cardinal was a better man than any of them, and brought home to them how badly they needed to have him permanently removed. Whether the plot was Wolsey's or a fabrication of his enemies may be impossible to determine, resting as it does on diplomatic reports and suspect confessions, but it was sufficient finally to destroy him. Meanwhile he retained his honorific standing. On 13 July 1530 the cardinal's name stood second after Warham's in a list of ecclesiastical and lay magnates begging the pope to consent to the king's divorce.

About 23 October reports from Bologna of a papal brief prohibiting Henry's remarriage *pendente lite*, and ordering him to dismiss Anne Boleyn from court, had reached Henry; inevitably Wolsey was blamed. A few days earlier Thomas Arundel had written to Wolsey from London, reporting Norfolk's conviction that the cardinal was determined to recover his authority. Perhaps the fact that Wolsey planned to be enthroned as archbishop of York on 7 November and had summoned a convocation to meet at the same time gave colour to the duke's fears. But the decisive blow to Wolsey was most probably delivered by the French, whose fears of an Anglo-imperial *rapprochement* seem to have caused them to reveal (perhaps to Anne Boleyn) how the cardinal had been dealing with foreign powers. The king's response was swift. On 1 November William Walsh, a gentleman of the privy chamber, was sent from court to arrest Wolsey, and on the 4th he and the earl of Northumberland formally took him into custody at Cawood on a charge of high treason. Hall reports that Wolsey stood on his dignity as a cardinal-legate, but bowed to the royal authority represented by Walsh.

It was immediately apparent that there was now no hope for Wolsey. On 10 November Passano reported home how 'the King says he has intrigued against them, both in and out of the kingdom, and has told me where and how, and that one and perhaps more of his servants have discovered it, and accused him' (*LP Henry VIII*, 4/3, no. 6720). François denied knowing of any sedition or treachery on the part of the cardinal, but still felt able to declare that:

> he thought ever that so pompeos and ambysyous a harte, spronge out of so vyle a stocke wold once shewe forthe the basenes of his nature, and most comonlye against Him that hath raysed him from lowe degree to highe dignytye. (*State Papers, Henry VIII*, 7.213)

The story of Wolsey's last days is movingly reported by George Cavendish, who was in attendance on his master throughout. On 6 November, having taken an emotional farewell of his household, Wolsey set off south, going first to Pontefract and then to Doncaster. On the 8th he came to the earl of Shrewsbury's house at Sheffield Park, where he stayed until the 24th, troubled by grief and fear, and then increasingly by dysentery. Meanwhile on the 22nd Sir William Kingston had arrived with twenty-four men to convey Wolsey to the Tower, where Kingston was constable. The cardinal's sickness was now such that at first he could not travel, but on the 24th he rode to Hardwick Hall, and

next day to Nottingham. On the night of the 26th, barely able to stay astride his mule, he reached Leicester Abbey, responding to the monks who assembled to greet him with the words, 'Father abbott I ame come hether to leave my bones among you' (Cavendish, 174). When Kingston asked him about money missing from the inventory taken at Cawood, Wolsey replied that he had borrowed it to pay for his exequies and provide for his servants. Early on 29 November he ate a little chicken broth, but then recalled that as St Andrew's eve the day was a fast day, and ate no more. He made his confession, and then, according to Cavendish, uttered his famous lament, 'I se the matter ayenst me howe it is framed, But if I had served god as dylygently as I have don the kyng he wold not have geven me over in my grey heares' (ibid., 178–9). He also told Kingston to advise the king to repress the new Lutheran heresy, foreseeing disastrous consequences if it was allowed to spread. He had already swooned several times, and felt death upon him. After talking to Kingston he began to fall into a coma, and the abbot was called to give him the last rites. Wolsey died at 8 a.m.

What did Wolsey die from? The well-known portrait shows a man grossly overweight, but although he was frequently accused of greed, this usually meant avarice for possessions, and only Skelton accused him of gluttony. At first Wolsey had been a robustly healthy man, but as he aged he suffered from the stone (perhaps gallstones rather than kidney stones), jaundice, fevers, throat infections, and colic, and latterly from oedema (localized dropsy). His sickness grew worse after his fall, so that he lost his appetite and slept badly. He also suffered several times from the sweat. In the last two or three years of his life, moreover, he underwent several moments of near collapse, though skilled medical attention enabled him to recover from them. Adult onset diabetes seems a possible diagnosis. Even then easily identifiable, it was often linked to loosenesses of the bowels which were commonly termed 'dysentery'. Doctors knew at least some of the dietary measures which could help to control it. They also knew that failure to eat regularly was dangerous. Wolsey's refusal to eat after his arrest, and his subsequent dysentery and vomiting, are reported by the Venetian ambassador. For a man in such a condition a diabetic coma would be a likely consequence.

After Wolsey's death his body was laid out in his pontifical robes and the people of Leicester were admitted to see it, so that there could be no doubt of his death. He was then buried in Leicester Abbey church. The grandiose tomb he had commissioned from Benedetto da Rovezzano, unfinished when the cardinal died, was plundered by Henry for his own monument and has largely disappeared, except for the sarcophagus and base, which were moved to St Paul's Cathedral in 1808 to house the body of Lord Nelson.

Verdicts of posterity Wolsey's character and personality as they were recorded by contemporary writers present a portrait that is largely the work of his enemies, of men such as John Skelton, whose satirical pen has left an unforgettable image of overweening ambition, and the protestant exiles Jerome Barlow and William Roy, who represented Wolsey as an arrogant and lustful villain:

> Alas sens Englande fyrst began,
> Was never soche a tyrante theare.
> By his pryde and faulce treachery,
> Whoardom and baudy leachery,
> He hath bene so intollerable
> That poure commens with their wyves,
> In maner are weary of their lyves …
> (Barlowe and Roy, 80)

Particularly influential was William Tyndale's *The Practice of Prelates* (1530), which portrays Wolfsee, the wily wolf, as 'a man of lust and courage and bodily strength', and charges him with using necromancy to bewitch the king, with surrounding the king with spies, and with rising to greatness by being 'obsequious and serviceable and in all games and sports the first and next at hand and as a captain to courage others and a gay finder out of new pastimes, to obtain favour withal' (Tyndale, 307). Wolsey's desire for the papacy is underlined, in accordance with Tyndale's picture of him as a great traitor. Edward Hall in his chronicle (1547) is no less scathing, characterizing Wolsey as a deceiver, 'double both in speche and meanyng. He would promise muche and performe lytle; He was vicious of body and gave the clergie evil example. He hated sore the citie of London and feared it' (*Hall's Chronicle*, 774). Since Wolsey's connivance in Henry VIII's campaign for a divorce led Catholic writers, too, to vilify him as ultimately responsible for England's break with Rome, his reputation was from the first singularly free from hagiographical bias.

Literary conventions lay behind many of these images. Skelton, for instance, employs the accepted characteristics of the tyrant, seeking to ruin church, state, and people. In adopting this position Skelton was also writing to a political agenda, and he later wrote in favour of the cardinal. George Cavendish's *Life*, written under Mary but first published (in garbled form) in 1641, was fitted to another Renaissance template, that of dignity retained in adversity, when authority rightly and wisely used has been lost to the cynical manipulations of others. Cavendish's biography offers favourable interpretations of Wolsey's actions. Probably deliberately planned to counteract the hostile image of Wolsey presented by Hall (and perhaps also that of the no less prejudiced Polydore Vergil), it is the work of a man who from about 1522 was in Wolsey's household and could claim to have been present at scenes that would otherwise be lost to history. It may not be error-free but its literary devices produce a compelling image of Wolsey which leaves no doubt of his greatness, while remaining mindful of his humanity. Once it became available in an adequate edition, it did much to reshape perceptions of the cardinal. Until the early eighteenth century, however, those perceptions remained essentially hostile ones, derived from Hall and Vergil and reinforced by John Foxe. It was these that were transmitted by Holinshed's *Chronicles* to William Shakespeare's *Henry VIII*, and which made Wolsey a model of vaunting ambition and cynical statecraft. The pamphlet *Canterburies Dreame* of 1641 compares the cardinal with Archbishop William Laud (to the latter's disadvantage), and a century later Samuel Johnson, in *The Vanity of Human Wishes* (1749), probably had Sir Robert Walpole, another all-powerful minister, in mind when he recalled Wolsey's greatness and fall:

> To him the Church, the Realm, their Pow'rs consign,
> Thro' him the Rays of regal Bounty shine;
> Turn's by his Nod, the Stream of Honour flows,
> His Smile alone Security bestows …

until at last:

> Grief aids Disease, remember'd Folly stings,
> And his last Sighs reproach the Faith of Kings.
> (*Poems of Samuel Johnson*, 119–20)

By that time efforts were being made towards a more dispassionate approach. In 1724 Richard Fiddes believed his aim should be to do justice to Wolsey's injured memory, and accordingly stressed his better qualities: the cardinal's natural dignity of manners and aspect, his intention to found a society of canon and civil law, his concern for a reform of ecclesiastical mores, and his interest in religion. Joseph Grove in 1742 helped to rectify the balance by publishing hitherto unprinted correspondence. Appreciating that men can only be understood in the context of their own times, he compared Wolsey to Cardinal Ximenes de Cisneros, the minister of Ferdinand and Isabella, in order to identify and explain behaviour that would otherwise be incomprehensible or unacceptable to eighteenth-century readers. The known sources were re-examined, and early in the nineteenth century S. W. Singer at last brought out a worthy edition of Cavendish's *Life* (1815; 2nd edn, 1827).

The nineteenth-century biographies which built upon these and other advances in scholarship were heavily influenced both by a preoccupation with the concept of individual greatness and by a growing sense of Britain's imperial destiny, which in turn led to a rehabilitation of Wolsey the man and to a concentration on his foreign policy, the latter more easily examined as state archives were opened to the public. Already in 1812 John Galt, whose *Life and Administration of Cardinal Wolsey* went through several editions, summed him up as 'haughty, ambitious, masterly and magnificent, he felt himself formed for superiority and his conduct if not always judicious was uniformly great' (Galt, 239). J. A. Froude, whose *History of England from the Fall of Wolsey to the Death of Elizabeth*, 12 vols. (1856–70) started from Wolsey's overthrow, though he acknowledged Wolsey's remarkable qualities, was unable to escape his own strong anti-Catholic bias, and described the cardinal as 'a man who loved England well, but who loved Rome better' (1.114). But Mandell Creighton's *Cardinal Wolsey* (1888) elevated Wolsey above the merely 'average statesman [who] does from day to day the business which has to be done, takes affairs as he finds them and makes the best of them', arguing rather that he was able to 'frame a connected policy with clear and definite ends' (Creighton, 1).

As nationalism became ever more a creed, so Wolsey was increasingly reinterpreted as one of England's great statesmen. J. S. Brewer, after editing the volumes of the *Letters and Papers … of Henry VIII* that cover the period of Wolsey's dominance, praised his achievement as lord chancellor and judge, and regretted that 'No statesman of such eminence ever died less lamented' (*LP Henry VIII*, 4.dcxxxiii). As a man of faith, too, Wolsey's image was recast, E. L. Taunton in 1902 arguing that he was 'before everything, a Churchman and one with a keen sense of the realities of Religion' (Taunton, vii). In 1916, with Britain plunged into war, Ernest Law's book about Wolsey presented him on its title-page as England's first great war minister, one whose fixed and steady policy and fundamental principles might 'inspire and guide us now' (Law). But in the inter-war depression A. F. Pollard, whose biography of 1929 remained the standard authority for fifty years, saw Wolsey primarily as a cynically efficient administrator and power politician whose foreign policy was directed by the papacy. A bad loser and a born fighter, he was encumbered by clerical garments and spiritual professions for which he had no vocation. Historians of the second half of the twentieth century reverted to more modest profiles. G. R. Elton presented him as an essentially medieval chancellor, C. Haigh as a corrupt cardinal against whom 'no charge was too gross to be impossible' (Haigh, 394); J. J. Scarisbrick, more sympathetic, saw 'something lofty and great about him', without sparing his shortcomings (Scarisbrick, *Henry VIII*, 240). His most recent biographer, P. J. Gwyn (1990), has reversed Creighton's judgement, presenting Wolsey as a man with no higher objective than to carry on the government, pursuing policies formulated by Henry VIII.

The man and the minister Forming a judgement of Wolsey's character, his methods and objectives demands an appreciation of the context in which he operated and of its changing parameters. S. J. Gunn has developed Joseph Grove's comment on the European context by locating Wolsey as one of the distinctive breed of cardinal–ministers who served the rulers of early modern Europe. The comparison shows that he rose to high office faster and lasted longer than almost all the dozen or so others with whom he may be plausibly compared. Few had as wide a brief as he did, and few matched his overall achievements as a patron of culture and education. Yet although he conducted much of his life in public, the sheer breadth of the stage on which Wolsey habitually appeared, entailing contacts and a play of influence that extended across much of western Europe, often makes it hard to detect the thrust of his policy at any one moment. It is no easier to pin down the essence of his personality. Elements in his style of government are easily described—his theatricality, his blunt and colourful language, his use of threats and calculated outbursts of temper to achieve his ends— but ultimately he was a private man and his true thoughts are hidden.

Wolsey's contemporaries were unanimous that he relished and accumulated power. Giustiniani described him as 'the right reverend Cardinal, in all whom the whole power of the State is really lodged', and as the man 'who, for authority, may in point of fact be styled *ipse rex*'

(Brown, 1.139, 155). Erasmus saw him as omnipotent and described him as governing 'more really than the king himself', though he added that he was 'feared by all and loved by few if any' (*Opus epistolarum*, 8.322). Henry VIII himself in diplomatic communiqués sometimes reinforced this impression—writing to the pope in 1515 he asked Leo X to 'pay the same regard to what Wolsey shall say as if it proceeded from the lips of the King himself' (*LP Henry VIII*, 2/2, appx, no. 12). Nor can there be any doubt about either his immense capacity for work or his skills as a negotiator (though he may well have been unduly reluctant to delegate). Even his enemies praised his 'angel's tongue', his wit, and his judgement. But the principles that guided his actions are less clear. He was undeniably punctilious in his religious observances but, though the relationship of secular to ecclesiastical power was an inescapable crux for a churchman who was also the king's minister, it is by no means certain that he ever decided where his priorities should lie. Similarly he appears to have had a deep respect for the letter of the law, but his attitude to justice remains opaque. Cavendish represented Wolsey as saying after his fall, when Henry demanded the surrender of York Place by strict process of law, that a king should always 'have a respect to Concyence byfore the rigor of the comen lawe' (Cavendish, 118), but this was a rhetorical commonplace, and in any case his attempts at resistance were soon overborne. His concluding reminder to the king 'that there is bothe hevyn & hell' may have been just another trope (ibid., 119).

The lasting enigma of Wolsey's personality may be a sign that the dilemma he faced over a choice of moral imperatives was never resolved. Hence the wide differences in subsequent assessment, variously presenting him as a warmonger, a peacemaker, and a statesman; a religious reformer and a worldling hampered by clerical garb; an impartial judge and a corrupt taker of bribes. Although archival research from the late nineteenth century onwards has brought new material to light which has made it possible to amend or amplify current understanding of the affairs, both national and international, in which Wolsey was involved, little new has been discovered to help resolve either the ambiguities of his aims or the truth about the character of a fundamentally secret man who claimed to be in all things merely the king's servant. If it were possible to be sure of its sincerity, Wolsey's rebuke to the duke of Suffolk, after his secret marriage to the king's sister, that 'ye have failed to him which hath brought you up of low degree to be of this great honor' (*LP Henry VIII*, 2/1, xxvii–viii), could offer an insight into his own beliefs. But all that can be said for certain is that Wolsey was a man who displayed all the outward hallmarks of greatness, with failings in proportion to his aspirations and achievements.   SYBIL M. JACK

Sources J. D. Alsop, 'The structure of early Tudor finance, 1509–1558', *Revolution reassessed: revisions in the history of Tudor government and administration*, ed. C. Coleman and D. R. Starkey (1986), 135–62 · J. D. Alsop, 'The exchequer in late medieval government, 1485–1530', *Aspects of late medieval government and society: essays presented to J. R. Lander*, ed. J. G. Rowe (1987), 179–212 · S. Anglo, *Spectacle, pageantry and early Tudor policy* (1969) · *Authentick memoirs of life and*

… *actions of Cardinal Wolsey* (1731) • E. Auerbach, *Tudor artists* (1954) • J. Barlowe and W. Roy, *Rede me and be not wrothe*, ed. D. H. Parker (1992) • J. G. Bellamy, *Criminal law and society in late medieval and Tudor England* (1984) • G. W. Bernard, *The power of the early Tudor nobility* (1985) • G. W. Bernard, *War, taxation, and rebellion in early Tudor England* (1986) • HoP, *Commons, 1509–58* • J. R. Bloxam, *A register of the presidents, fellows … of Saint Mary Magdalen College*, 8 vols. (1853–85), vol. 3 • J. S. Brewer, *The reign of Henry VIII from his accession to the death of Wolsey*, ed. J. Gairdner, 2 vols. (1884) • S. Brigden, *London and the Reformation* (1989) • R. Brown, ed., *Four years at the court of Henry VIII* (1854) • H. Bullock, *Doctissimi viri H Bulloci oratio ad Thomam cardinalem, archiepiscopum Eboracensem* (1521); facs. edn by H. Bradshaw (1886) • W. Busch, *England under the Tudors*, 1, trans. A. M. Todd (1895) • *CSP Spain, 1529–30* • *CSP Venice, 1520–26* • *CEPR letters*, vols. 12, 13, 14 • T. W. Cameron, 'The early life of Thomas Wolsey', *EngHR*, 3 (1888), 458–77 • *Canterburie's dream* (1641) • S. J. Gunn and P. G. Lindley, eds., *Cardinal Wolsey: church, state and art* (1991) • J. S. Brewer and W. Bullen, eds., *Calendar of the Carew manuscripts, 1: 1515–1574*, PRO (1867) • G. Cavendish, *The life and death of Cardinal Wolsey*, ed. R. S. Sylvester, EETS, original ser., 243 (1959) • D. S. Chambers, *Cardinal Bainbridge in the court of Rome, 1509–1514* (1965) • D. S. Chambers, 'Cardinal Wolsey and the papal tiara', *BIHR*, 38 (1965), 20–30 • A. G. Chester, 'Robert Barnes and the burning of books', *Huntington Library Quarterly*, 14 (1950–51), 211–21 • A. G. Dickens, ed., *Clifford letters of the sixteenth century*, SurtS, 172 (1962) • *Collection of ordinances and regulations for the government of the royal household*, Society of Antiquaries (1790) • A. J. G. le Glay, ed., *Collection de documents inédits sur l'histoire de France*, 1st ser.: *Histoire politique* (1845), vol. 2 of *Négociations diplomatiques entre la France et l'Autriche* • M. Creighton, *Cardinal Wolsey* (1891) • C. G. Cruickshank, *Army royal: Henry VIII's invasion of France, 1513* (1969) • C. G. Cruickshank, *The English occupation of Tournai, 1513–19* (1971) • H. Ellis, ed., *Original letters illustrative of English history*, 1st ser., 3 vols. (1824); 2nd ser., 4 vols. (1827); 3rd ser., 4 vols. (1846) • S. G. Ellis, *Reform and revival: English government in Ireland, 1470–1534* (1986) • G. R. Elton, *Studies in Tudor and Stuart politics and government*, 2 vols. (1974) • *Emden, Oxf.*, 3.2077–80 • R. Fiddes, *The life of Cardinal Wolsey* (1724) • A. Fox and J. Guy, *Reassessing the Henrician age* (1986) • A. Fox, *Early Tudor literature: politics and the literary imagination* (1989) • J. Galt, *Life and administration of Cardinal Wolsey* (1812) • L. R. Gardiner, 'Further news of Cardinal Wolsey's end, November–December 1530', *BIHR*, 57 (1984), 99–107 • *The acts and monuments of John Foxe*, ed. J. Pratt, [new edn], 8 vols. (1877) • F. J Furnival and W. R. Murfill, eds., *Ballads from manuscripts*, 2 vols. (1868–73) • J. J. Goring, 'The riot at Bayham Abbey, June 1525', *Sussex Archaeological Collections*, 116 (1978), 1–10 • M. A. R. Graves, *The Tudor parliaments: crown, Lords and Commons, 1485–1603* (1985) • J. Grove, *History of the life and times of Cardinal Wolsey prime minister to Henry VIII*, 4 vols. (1742–4) • S. J. Gunn, *Charles Brandon, duke of Suffolk, c.1484–1545* (1988) • S. J. Gunn, 'The Act of Resumption of 1515', *Early Tudor England: proceedings of the 1987 Harlaxton symposium*, ed. D. T. Williams (1989), 87–106 • J. A. Guy, *The cardinal's court* (1977) • J. A. Guy, 'Wolsey, the council and the council courts', *EngHR*, 91 (1976), 481–505 • J. A. Guy, 'Wolsey and the parliament of 1523', *Law and government under the Tudors: essays presented to Sir Geoffrey Elton*, ed. C. Cross, D. Loades, and J. J. Scarisbrick (1988), 1–18 • P. J. Gwyn, *The king's cardinal: the rise and fall of Thomas Wolsey* (1990) • P. J. Gwyn, 'Wolsey's foreign policy: the conferences at Calais and Bruges reconsidered', *HJ*, 23 (1980), 755–72 • C. Haigh, 'Anticlericalism in the English Reformation', *History*, 68 (1983), 391–407 • E. Hall, *The union of the two noble and illustre famelies of York and Lancaster*, ed. H. Ellis (1809) • *Hall's chronicle*, ed. H. Ellis (1809) • B. Harris, *Edward Stafford, third duke of Buckingham, 1478–1521* (1986) • J. H. Harvey, 'The building works and architects of Cardinal Wolsey', *Journal of the British Archaeological Association*, 3rd ser., 8 (1943), 50–59 • P. Heath, 'The treason of Geoffrey Blythe, bishop of Coventry and Lichfield, 1503–31', *BIHR*, 42 (1969), 101–9 • Edward, Lord Herbert of Cherbury, *The life and reign of King Henry the Eighth* (1672) • R. Holinshed, *The chronicles of England, Scotland and Ireland*, 6 vols. (1807–8); facs. edn (New York, 1965) • E. W. Ives, *Anne Boleyn* (1986) • E. W. Ives, 'Crimes, sanctuary and royal authority under Henry VIII: the exemplary sufferings of the Savage family', *On the laws and customs of England: essays in honor of Samuel E. Thorne*, ed. M. S. Arnold, T. A. Green, S. A. Scully, and S. D. White (1981), 296–320 • M. E. James, *Society, politics and culture: studies in early modern England* (1986) • R. Knecht, *Francis I* (1984) • D. Knowles, '"The matter of Wilton" in 1528', *BIHR*, 31 (1958), 92–6 • D. Knowles [M. C. Knowles], *The religious orders in England*, 3 (1959) • E. Law, *England's first great war minister* (1916) • J. Le Grand, *Histoire du divorce de Henry VIII* (1688) • S. E. Lehmberg, *The Reformation parliament, 1529–36* (1970) • *LP Henry VIII*, vols. 1–7 • M. Levine, 'The fall of Edward duke of Buckingham', *Tudor men and institutions*, ed. A. J. Slavin (1972), 32–48 • E. Lodge, *Illustrations of British history*, 3 vols. (1791) • *Love letters of Henry VIII to Anne Boleyn* (1714) • W. D. Macray, *A register of the members of St Mary Magdalen College, Oxford*, 8 vols. (1894–1915) • E. Martène and U. Durand, *Veterum scriptorum et monumentorum historicum, dogmaticorum, moralium, amplissima collectio*, 9 vols. (1724–33), 4–33 • *Hist. U. Oxf. 3: Colleg. univ.*, (1986) • F. Metzger, 'The last phase of the medieval chancery', *Law-making and law-makers in British history*, ed. A. Harding (1980), 79–89 • H. Miller, *Henry VIII and the English nobility* (1986) • W. A. Pantin, ed., *Documents illustrating the activities of the general and provincial chapters of the English black monks*, 3, CS, 3rd ser., 54 (1937) • G. de C. Parmier, *The king's Great Matter* (1967) • A. F. Pollard, *Wolsey* (1929) • C. Rawcliffe, *The Staffords, earls of Stafford and dukes of Buckingham* (1978) • V. B. Redstone, 'Wulcy of Suffolk', *Suffolk Institute of Archaeology and Natural History*, 16 (1918), 71–89 • *Registrum Thome Wolsey cardinalis ecclesie Wintoniensis administratoris*, ed. H. Chitty, CYS, 32 (1926) • R. R. Reid, *The king's council in the north* (1921) • W. C. Richardson, *Tudor chamber administration* • J. Ridley, *The statesman and the fanatic: Thomas Wolsey and Sir Thomas More* (1982) • W. R. B. Robinson, 'Marcher lords of Wales, 1525–1531', *BBCS*, 26 (1974–6), 34–52 • F. Roth, *The English Austin friars* (1966) • J. G. Russell, *The Field of Cloth of Gold* (1969) • Rymer, *Foedera*, 1st edn, vols. 11–14 • Wilts. & Swindon RO, Salisbury episcopal register, Blythe, fol. 113 • J. J. Scarisbrick, *Henry VIII* (1968) • I. S. Leadam, ed., *Select cases before the king's council in the star chamber, commonly called the court of star chamber*, 2, SeldS, 25 (1911) • R. B. Smith, *Land and politics in the England of Henry VIII: the West Riding of Yorkshire* (1970) • D. R. Starkey, *The reign of Henry VIII* (1985) • *State papers published under … Henry VIII*, 11 vols. (1830–52) • A. Luders and others, eds., *Statutes of the realm*, 11 vols. in 12, RC (1810–28) • J. Stow, *The annales of England … untill this present yeere 1592* (1592) • R. Strong, *The National Portrait Gallery: Tudor and Stuart portraits* (1969) • R. S. Sylvester, 'Cavendish's *Life of Wolsey*: the artistry of a Tudor biographer', *Studies in Philology*, 57 (1960), 44–71 • E. L. Taunton, *Thomas Wolsey, legate and reformer* (1902) • M. J. Tucker, *The life of Thomas Howard* (1964) • W. Tyndale, *The practice of prelates* [1528], ed. H. Walker, Parker Society, 33 (1849) • *The Anglica historia of Polydore Vergil, AD 1485–1537*, ed. and trans. D. Hay, CS, 3rd ser., 74 (1950) • G. Walker, *John Skelton and the politics of the 1520s* (1988) • G. Walker, 'The "expulsion of the minions" of 1519 reconsidered', *HJ*, 32 (1989), 1–16 • R. Warnicke, *Anne Boleyn* • R. B. Wernham, *Before the Armada: the growth of English foreign policy, 1485–1588* (1966) • R. Whittington, *Libellus epigrammaton* (1519) • W. Wilkie, *The cardinal protectors of England* (1974) • D. Wilkins, *Concilia magnae Britanniae et Hiberniae*, 3 (1737) • W. W. Wooden, 'The art of partisan biography: George Cavendish's *Life of Wolsey*', *Renaissance and Reformation*, new ser., 1 (1977), 24–35 • C. Wriothesley, *A chronicle of England during the reigns of the Tudors from AD 1485 to 1559*, ed. W. D. Hamilton, 1, CS, new ser., 11 (1875) • Hunt. L., Ellesmere MSS 2652–2655 • BL, Stowe MSS 146–149 • BL, Harley MS 283 • BL, Cotton MSS Titus B. i, Vitellius C. i • BL, Sloane MS 1523 • *The letters of Richard Fox*, ed. P. S. Allen and H. M. Allen (1929) • Foss, *Judges*, vol. 5 • J. J. Scarisbrick, 'Cardinal Wolsey and the common weal', *Wealth and power in Tudor England: essays presented to S. T. Bindoff*, ed. E. W. Ives, R. J. Knecht, and J. J. Scarisbrick (1978), 45–67 • *The poems of Samuel Johnson*, ed. D. N. Smith and E. L. McAdam, 2nd edn (1974) • *Opus epistolarum Des. Erasmi Roterodami*, ed. P. S. Allen and others, 12 vols. (1906–58); repr. (1992) • *Reports of cases by John Caryll*, ed. J. H. Baker, 2 vols., SeldS, 115–16 (1999–2000)

Archives BL, corresp. and instructions to various ambassadors [copies] • PRO, letter book, PRO 30/5/1 | BL, Cotton MSS, political and diplomatic corresp. and papers • BL, Harley MSS, corresp. and papers

Likenesses oils, 1560–99 (original, c.1520), NPG [see illus.] • J. Faber senior, mezzotint (after H. Holbein the younger), BM, NPG • J. le Boucq (after type, c.1515–1520), Bibliothèque d'Arras, France • R. Sheppard, coloured line engraving (after H. Holbein the younger), BM, NPG • oils, second version, Christ Church Oxf. • watercolour, NPG

Wolsey, Thomas (d. 1610x12?), separatist leader, was ordained deacon on 6 June 1568 and priest on 1 April 1569 by Bishop John Parkhurst of Norwich. Nothing is known of his parents or his early life, or of his activities during the 1570s. About 1580 he became deeply involved in the emerging East Anglian separatist movement. He may have been a member of Robert Browne's and Robert Harrison's congregation, but this cannot be proven conclusively. However, between 1580 and 1582 he was jailed on two occasions for his religious beliefs. These periods of incarceration were difficult: by Harrison's account, he was thrust into 'lothsome prison houses' (Harrison, 43).

During this period Wolsey came into conflict with Edward Fenton, rector of Booton, Norfolk, not far from the town of Aylsham. Fenton was a radical nonconformist who had apparently considered separating from the established church, but eventually decided to remain within it. After several admonitions, Wolsey sent Fenton a letter severely rebuking him for his decision. Fenton replied by writing against both Wolsey and Harrison. Harrison then composed a letter defending both Wolsey (referred to only by his initials) and himself. It was printed eventually as the second portion of 'A treatise of the church and the kingdom of Christ'.

Wolsey appears to have remained behind in East Anglia when Browne, Harrison, and their followers departed for Middelburg in the spring or summer of 1582. In fact, according to Stephen Offwood, he seems to have spent much, if not all, of the rest of his life in gaol. Thetford assize records indicate that he and four other separatists were sentenced to death on 30 March 1584, but were later reprieved in prison. He was still confined at Thetford in July 1584, and at Norwich in July 1585. He was also listed as a prisoner in Norwich Castle in December 1595. When Offwood visited him in 1602, he was still a prisoner, but 'he had a keye for to lete in unto him [w]home he [w]ould and to goe out as he pleased at a back gate' (Offwood, 40).

In gaol or out, Wolsey converted sizable numbers of people to his views. Offwood records that 'he perverted many zealous professors, of which I knewe twentie', including Henry Barrow, the greatest of the Elizabethan separatists (Offwood, 40). After reading one of Robert Browne's books, Barrow visited Wolsey, who completed his conversion to separatism.

Wolsey's subsequent relationship with Barrow did not go smoothly. In the late 1580s and early 1590s, Wolsey was apparently beginning to adhere to several Jewish laws and practices, which Barrow condemned. Among other things, Wolsey maintained that it was unlawful for Christians to eat blood, things strangled, and meats offered to

idols. Barrow's death on 6 April 1593 seems to have ended the controversy, but it broke out again when Wolsey sent a letter to Francis Johnson's 'Ancient' separatist congregation at Amsterdam in 1602 reasserting these positions. Writing in the name of the whole church, Johnson and Henry Ainsworth replied on 7 December, rejecting Wolsey's opinions and threatening to discontinue their recognition of him as 'a Preacher of the kingdome of God' if he did not recant (Seasonable Treatise, 16).

Wolsey stands alongside Browne and Harrison as one of the founders of East Anglian separatism. He was one of its earliest exponents and one of its most effective spokesmen. Nevertheless, as Offwood observed, he was a 'harshe spirit', who rejected or excommunicated almost all of his followers at one time or another. After 1602 Wolsey's life is unknown, but Offwood claimed that he held his 'Jewishe errours' until his death (Offwood, 40). Since by Offwood's calculation his imprisonment lasted about thirty years, he probably died between about 1610 and 1612.

MICHAEL E. MOODY

Sources S. Offwood, An advertisement [1632], 40 • [F. Johnson and H. Ainsworth (?)], A seasonable treatise for this age (1657) • R. Harrison, 'A treatise of the church and the kingdom of Christ', The writings of Robert Harrison and Robert Browne, ed. A. Peel and L. Carlson (1953), 41–69 • bishop of Norwich, ordination registers, Norfolk RO, ORR/1, fols. 45r and 48r • [S. Timms], 'Popish and sectary recusants in Norfolk and Suffolk, 1595, no. 2', The East Anglian, 2 (1865), 177 • Norwich quarter session books, 1583–6, Norfolk RO, C/S 1/5, 66ar–66bv and 103a and 119r • A. Peel, The Brownists in Norwich and Norfolk about 1580 (1920)

Wolstenholme, Dean, the elder (1757–1837), animal painter, was born in Yorkshire. He was probably the son of Sir John Wolstenholme, baronet, and was descended from Sir John *Wolstenholme (1562–1639), who was one of the farmers of the customs in the reign of Charles I and left extensive property, including Nostell Priory, Yorkshire, to his son John, who received a baronetcy in 1664. Dean Wolstenholme spent most of his early life in Essex and Hertfordshire, where he lived successively at Cheshunt, Turnford, and Waltham Abbey. He was an enthusiastic sportsman who occasionally painted sporting subjects for pleasure; Sir Joshua Reynolds is said to have predicted that he would be a painter in earnest before he died. In 1793 he became involved in litigation over some property at Waltham, and after three unsuccessful chancery suits was left with few resources, so he adopted painting as a profession. On 18 January 1795, at St Olave, York, he married Mary Stabler, with whom he had a son, (Charles) Dean *Wolstenholme (1798–1883).

About 1800 Wolstenholme moved to London, and settled in East Street, Red Lion Square. In 1803 he exhibited his first picture, Coursing, at the Royal Academy. He is best known for his paintings of his favourite pastime—foxhunting—but also painted shooting scenes; portraits of hunters, cattle, sheep, and dogs; racecourses; and, in 1824, The Interior of the Riding School of the Light Horse Volunteers (which included several portraits). Many of his works were engraved; Fox-Hunting (exh. RA, 1804) for example was reproduced in aquatint by Thomas Sutherland, Reeve, and Bromley, and published by Ackermann. The

Epping Forest Stag Hunt (1811) is regarded as his masterpiece. After 1826 he painted little. He died in 1837, at the age of eighty, and was buried in St Pancras churchyard.

Wolstenholme 'was a man of remarkable physical strength; it is said that on one occasion he made a bet that he would carry two sacks of flour up a ladder, and won it' (Gilbey, 249). Of his hunting scenes—which remain popular, particularly in America—Walter Shaw Sparrow noted that 'they are vigorous, and show a liking for hilly land, and far horizons, and the charm and weight of trees' (Sparrow, 83). Although the work of the elder and younger Dean Wolstenholme is sometimes confused, Sparrow observed 'a depth in this primitive that I do not find in his son' (ibid.).   ERNEST CLARKE, *rev.* ANNETTE PEACH

Sources W. Gilbey, *Animal painters of England*, 3 vols. (1900–11), vol. 2, pp. 244–50 · W. S. Sparrow, *British sporting artists* (1922) · Graves, *RA exhibitors*, 8.329–30 · Redgrave, *Artists*, 458 · IGI
Likenesses D. Wolstenholme junior, portrait (after his rough sketch) · engraving (after D. Wolstenholme junior), repro. in Gilbey, *Animal painters*, facing p. 250

Wolstenholme, (Charles) Dean, the younger (1798–1883), sporting painter and engraver, was born on 21 April 1798 near Waltham Abbey, Essex, the eldest son of Dean *Wolstenholme (1757–1837), animal painter, and his wife, Mary Stabler. Dean Wolstenholme junior, as he was known, was first taught to paint by his father but the origin of his considerable engraving ability is lost. He lived for much of his life in London. With similar styles, there is confusion between father and son over the authorship of some paintings, but it is recorded that Wolstenholme junior exhibited thirteen paintings at the Royal Academy, the first being *Beach*, a bulldog bitch (1818); he also exhibited ten at the British Institution and thirteen at the Society (later Royal Society) of British Artists. Specializing in hunting and shooting scenes in Hertfordshire and Essex, he also painted some of the well-known London brewery yards in the 1820s. His best-known works were the *Death of Tom Moody* and the *Shade of Tom Moody*, which he also engraved. Inspired by Sir Walter Scott's novels, he turned to historical subjects, among which was the large (58 x 82 in.) *Queen Elizabeth Hunting the Hart in Enfield Chase*, exhibited at the British Institution in 1831 and the Royal Academy in 1846. In his earlier years he engraved his father's work, his own, and the work of others, and invented a colour printing process patented by Leighton Brothers. Later he regretted spending so much time engraving which 'had prevented him fully developing his powers as a painter' (*The Connoisseur*, 81).

Wolstenholme was a pigeon fancier who bred Almond Tumblers. He illustrated J. M. Eaton's *Treatise on the Art of Breeding and Managing Tame, Domesticated and Fancy Pigeons* (1852), and painted prize birds which were engraved life-size (fourteen of these prints are in the British Museum). In 1869 the Pigeon Franciers of England and Scotland gave him a testimonial in recognition of his 'skill [in breeding pigeons] and private character' (*Apollo*, 58). He died at Highgate, Middlesex, on 12 April 1883 and was buried in Highgate cemetery.   CHARLES LANE

Sources *DNB* · G. Paget, 'Charles Dean Wolstenholme junior, 1798–1883', *Apollo*, 44 (1946), 55–8 · R. Neville, 'Old-time sport from prints, books, and pictures', *The Connoisseur*, 9 (1904), 78–83 · S. Mitchell, *The dictionary of British equestrian artists* (1985) · Graves, *RA exhibitors* · Graves, *Brit. Inst.* · M. H. Grant, *A chronological history of the old English landscape painters*, 3 vols. (1926–47), vol. 2, pp. 316–17
Likenesses D. Wolstenholme, self-portrait, repro. in Paget, 'Charles Dean Wolstenholme junior', 55

Wolstenholme, Sir John (1562–1639), financier and merchant, of an old Derbyshire family, was the second son of John Wolstenholme, who moved to London in the reign of Edward VI and obtained a post in the customs. The son became one of the richest merchants in London and was knighted in 1617. The following year he acted as guarantor of a loan to James I. Wolstenholme took a prominent part in the extension of English commerce, in colonization, and in maritime discovery. In December 1600 he was one of the incorporators of the East India Company, and he later became one of the committees, or directors, of the company. He played an active role in the sustained efforts to discover a north-west passage. As such, he was one of those who fitted out the expeditions of Henry Hudson (d. 1611) (who named Cape Wolstenholme after him) in 1610, of Thomas Button in 1612, of Robert Bylot and William Baffin in 1615 (when his name was given to Wolstenholme Island and Wolstenholme Sound), and of Luke Fox in 1631. Together with Sir Thomas Smith (Smythe; 1558?–1625), he engaged Edward Wright (d. 1615) to give lectures on navigation.

Wolstenholme was deeply involved in the affairs of the Virginia Company, becoming a member of its council in 1609 and then engaging in a lengthy factional struggle for its control. In 1624 he was appointed a commissioner for winding up the company's affairs, and for several years afterwards he was a member of the king's council for Virginia. During the early 1630s he took a leading part in efforts to establish a new Virginia Company, and in 1631 he was a commissioner for the plantation of Virginia.

Wolstenholme also made a considerable mark as an office-holder and crown agent. In February 1619 he was a commissioner of the navy, but, following in the footsteps of his father, it was in customs administration that he exerted the greatest influence. He acted as one of the principals of the Great Farm of the Customs of 1621, before joining a rival syndicate in 1625. He was widely regarded as an expert on revenue matters, and in this capacity he acted as a royal adviser and served on several commissions on trade and related issues. Wolstenholme married Catherine Fanshawe, and had two sons and two daughters. He died on 25 November 1639 and was buried in Great Stanmore church.   J. K. LAUGHTON, *rev.* H. V. BOWEN

Sources *CSP col.*, vols. 1–4, 6, 8 · E. B. Sainsbury, ed., *A calendar of the court minutes … of the East India Company*, [1]: 1635–1639 (1907) · *CSP dom.*, 1603–40 · *APC*, 1615–31 · R. Ashton, *The crown and the money market, 1603–1640* (1960) · R. Brenner, *Merchants and revolution: commercial change, political conflict, and London's overseas traders, 1550–1653* (1993) · K. R. Andrews, *Trade, plunder and settlement: maritime enterprise and the genesis of the British empire, 1480–1630* (1984) · K. N. Chaudhuri, *The English East India Company: the study of an early English joint-stock company* (1965) · will, PRO, PROB 11/181, sig. 172

Likenesses N. Stone, tomb effigy, 1641, St John the Evangelist, Great Stanmore, Middlesex

Wolstenholme, Joseph (1829–1891), mathematician, was born on 30 September 1829 at Eccles, Lancashire, the son of Joseph Wolstenholme, a Methodist minister, and his wife, Elizabeth, *née* Clarke. Educated at Wesley College, Sheffield, he proceeded to St John's College, Cambridge, where he was admitted a pensioner on 1 July 1846. He was coached by Percival Frost and, having graduated third wrangler in 1850, obtained his MA in 1853. He was elected a fellow of his college on 29 March 1852. On 26 November 1852 he was elected to a fellowship at Christ's College, Cambridge, to which, under the college statutes, Lancashire men had a preferential claim. The same year he became an assistant tutor of Christ's. He served as an examiner for the mathematical tripos in 1854, 1856, 1863, and 1870, and as moderator in 1862, 1869, and 1870. He was awarded an ScD in 1883. In 1869 Wolstenholme vacated his fellowship upon his marriage to Thérèse Rosalia, daughter of Johann Kraus of Zürich. He remained in Cambridge as a private coach until his appointment in 1871 as first mathematical professor at the Royal Indian Engineering College, Coopers Hill.

Wolstenholme was joint author (with Percival Frost) of a *Treatise on Solid Geometry* (1863). He declined to be acknowledged as author in the second revised edition. He was also the author of *A Book of Mathematical Problems on Subjects Included in the Cambridge Course* (1867; enlarged 2nd edn, 1878; with corrections, 1893); *First Principles of the Differential and Integral Calculus* (1874), written for his students at Coopers Hill; and *Examples for Practice in the Use of Seven-Figure Logarithms* (1888). He published twenty-three mathematical papers, the majority concerned with questions of analytical geometry. Although mostly brief they are well regarded and demonstrate considerable skill and ingenuity. In 1862 he published an elementary result in number theory, which has become known as 'Wolstenholme's Theorem' despite having been anticipated by Edward Waring in 1782.

Although considered brilliant by his contemporaries, Wolstenholme's accomplishments were not widely recognized. He is best known for his book *Mathematical Problems*, of which the first edition (1891) contains 1628 and the second edition 2815 examples. About a hundred of the latter also appeared in the *Educational Times*. The original problems, many of which contain important results, encompassed almost all the mathematics subjects studied at Cambridge at the time and were designed specifically for students of the tripos. The book proved influential, providing a mainstay for several generations of undergraduates.

Wolstenholme had an encyclopaedic knowledge of English literature; at Cambridge he was renowned for reciting hundreds of lines of poetry while out walking. As an undergraduate he became friendly with Leslie Stephen. According to Stephen, Wolstenholme had gone to Coopers Hill because his 'Bohemian tastes and heterodox opinions had made a Cambridge career inadvisable' (Bell, 79). Stephen spoke unflatteringly about Wolstenholme's wife and every summer Wolstenholme went alone to stay with the Stephen family. Wolstenholme's home life was apparently so wretched that he 'consoled himself with mathematics and opium' (Bell, 79). It is generally agreed that Virginia Woolf, Stephen's daughter, based the character of Mr Augustus Carmichael in her novel *To the Lighthouse* (1927) on Wolstenholme.

At Coopers Hill, Wolstenholme settled into a routine of teaching but as time passed there was an increasing requirement for mathematics to be taught from a more practical perspective than the theoretical approach he espoused. In spite of formal requests to change, he refused to adapt and when he reached the age of sixty he was forced by the president of the college to retire. Wolstenholme died at his home, 13 Surrendale Place, Maida Vale, London, on 18 November 1891, leaving a widow and four sons. In 1893 a pension on the civil list was granted to his wife in recognition of his eminence as a mathematician and as a result of a petition signed by a number of members of the Cambridge University senate.

JUNE BARROW-GREEN

Sources *The Eagle*, 17 (1893), 67–8 · Venn, *Alum. Cant.* · F. W. Maitland, *The life and letters of Leslie Stephen* (1906), 48, 74 · L. Stephen, *Sir Leslie Stephen's mausoleum book*, ed. A. Bell (1977), 79 · R. Gow, 'Joseph Wolstenholme, Leslie Stephen and "To the lighthouse"', *Bulletin of the Irish Mathematical Society*, 34 (1995), 40–46 · *CGPLA Eng. & Wales* (1891) · d. cert.
Wealth at death £1659 7s. 7d.: probate, 18 Dec 1891, *CGPLA Eng. & Wales*

Wolverhampton. For this title name *see* Fowler, Henry Hartley, first Viscount Wolverhampton (1830–1911).

Wolverton. For this title name *see* Glyn, George Carr, first Baron Wolverton (1797–1873); Glyn, George Grenfell, second Baron Wolverton (1824–1887).

Wombwell, George (1777–1850), founder of a menagerie, was born on 24 December 1777 at Dudnor End, Essex, and from an early age took a keen interest in animals. His life was changed when he saw a pair of boa constrictors that had just been landed on the London docks. He bought them for, it is said, £75, and soon recovered this expenditure by exhibiting them. He established contacts with pilots who alerted him to ships bringing in unusual animals, and by 1805 he had established the nucleus of a menagerie.

At this time there were no zoological gardens, and the only permanent exhibitions of animals in London were a few at the Tower and a small collection at Exeter Change in the Strand. Pidcock and Polito had begun touring with animal exhibitions in the previous century, but Wombwell was soon to establish a travelling menagerie that eclipsed all rivals. He almost always attended Bartholomew fair, where his receipts could amount to £1700, but he also used market squares in provincial towns for his displays. His menagerie was conveyed in brightly painted wagons, which were drawn up into an open square on arrival. Elephants, giraffes, and camels would be picketed in the centre, and uniformed bandsmen played on an exterior platform to entice the crowds in. The price of

George Wombwell (1777–1850), by unknown engraver, pubd 1850

admission varied from 6 *d.* to 1 *s.* The animals exhibited in the early years included elephants, lions, tigers, leopards, panthers, hyenas, zebras, camels, jackals, apes, baboons, and monkeys. Among birds were a golden eagle, emus, cockatoos, and parakeets. Later a rhinoceros was added, with giraffes, a puma, a polar bear, black and brown bears, porcupines, a Brahman cow, and many more.

Wombwell was a master of publicity, and, in a less humane age, he exploited his animals to the full. His most notorious feat, which succeeded in arousing a public outcry, was to stage a fight between a lion and a pack of trained dogs, at Warwick in 1825. The original lion, Nero, was known as a gentle animal, and took no notice of the dogs, but when he was replaced with another lion, Wallace, and the dogs were introduced two at a time into the cage, they were immediately destroyed. Tickets for this event were priced from 1 to 5 guineas, and Wallace remained a popular object of interest for years. When Wombwell decided to miss Bartholomew fair one year and to remain in Newcastle, a rival advertised that he would have 'the only live elephant in the fair'. Wombwell

changed his plans and brought his show to London by a forced march within ten days, but his exhausted elephant died on arrival. However, Wombwell advertised 'the only dead elephant in the fair' and attracted even larger crowds.

As the number of animals in the menagerie grew, Wombwell split his show into two and then three separate menageries. He appeared at command performances at Windsor for both George IV and Queen Victoria. By 1843 there were sixteen wagons in the first of his shows, which remained popular despite—or perhaps because of—numerous accidents to members of the public and the death of Wombwell's niece Ellen *Blight, the 'Lion Queen', when an enraged tiger attacked and killed her in full view of spectators. George Wombwell died on 16 November 1850 in Northallerton, and was buried in Highgate cemetery, Middlesex, in a coffin made from the timbers of the *Royal George*, which had sunk off Spithead in 1782, and which Wombwell had begged from Prince Albert. His tomb is marked by a sculpted sleeping lion.

After Wombwell's death the different parts of the menagerie were placed in different hands. The original, number 1, was directed by his widow, Ann (*née* Morgan), until 1865, and then by her niece until it was sold in 1872. The number 2 menagerie was run by a niece, Mrs Edwards, and continued to expand until it was sold to E. H. Bostock about 1884. As Bostock and Wombwell's Menagerie, it continued to tour on a reduced scale until 1931, when the remaining animals were sold to London Zoo at Whipsnade. The third menagerie, under Wombwell's nephew George Wombwell, junior, flourished until 1855, when most of the animals died in an epidemic.

William Home, revolted by fights between the lion and the dogs, described Wombwell as 'undersized in mind, as well as in form, a weasen, sharp-faced man, with a skin reddened by more than natural spirits, and he speaks in a language that accords with his feelings and propositions'. On the other hand, despite the widespread modern revulsion against the exploitation of animals, before zoological gardens had been widely established, the touring menageries played a great part in educating the British public about the variety and wonder of the animal kingdom around the world. In this mixture of showmanship and instruction the Wombwell menageries played a great part. GEORGE SPEAIGHT

Sources E. H. Bostock, *Menageries, circuses and theatres* (1927) · T. Frost, *Circus life and circus celebrities* (1875) · H. Morley, *Memoirs of Bartholemew fair* (1859) · J. M. Turner, 'Wombwell's travelling menagerie: on the road 120 years' [unpublished] · H. Ritvo, *The animal estate: the English and other creatures in the Victorian age* (1987)
Likenesses J. Leighton, engraving, repro. in R. Chambers, ed., *Book of Days*, 2 (1864), 586 · engraving, NPG; repro. in *ILN* (7 Dec 1850) [see illus.]

Women agents on active service in France (*act.* 1942–1945) were trained in secrecy from the spring of 1942 to work abroad as agents of the Special Operations Executive (SOE), despite much opposition to the use of women in this field, because of a shortage of suitable men available for the work. Many women were already expert wireless operators, a skill essential for field agents who had to transmit regular requests for supplies from Britain, and they also made unobtrusive couriers, although many were young and often very attractive. SOE agents were not spies. Instead they were sent to conquered countries, where their task was to enable their 'organizer' and local resistance groups to carry out sabotage and later armed resistance to the forces of occupation.

Shortly after SOE's inception in July 1940 a chance encounter between the head of SOE and the commandant of the First Aid Nursing Yeomanry (FANY), later known as the Women's Transport Service, brought in about a third of FANY's numbers to join other civilians, servicemen, and servicewomen on SOE's many staffs, whose work embraced numerous countries. FANY now gave cover to, and produced, SOE's women agents, fifteen of whom came from the Women's Auxiliary Air Force (WAAF). Although it was a uniformed service, those in FANY were classed as civilians and could thus both travel abroad and carry arms, which were forbidden at that time to members of the women's forces. As General de Gaulle's own secret service, the Bureau Central de Renseignements et d'Action, was hostile to SOE, thirteen or more Frenchwomen (a few from the French Women's Army), some trained by SOE, worked in liaison with de Gaulle in what was known as the République Française (RF) section. The mainly British remainder were employed by F section, the French service independent of de Gaulle, which had its early headquarters in Baker Street, London. Of the nearly four hundred F section agents sent to France, more than fifty were women, although about ninety were trained for service there. A few other SOE sections also worked in France, mostly dealing with escape lines. The secret services of many other powers, both friendly and hostile, were also active in France.

SOE women agents came from all walks of society, from a princess born in the Kremlin to a shopgirl; their ages and characters were also highly various. However, they all had in common immense courage and intense patriotism. Usually their patriotism was for both Britain and France, as many had at least one French parent, spoke French fluently, or were familiar with France. The risks of their work were clearly explained in early selection interviews: they would have to work hard both by day and by night; life would be strenuous, lonely, and precarious, and they would always have to be alert to danger; if captured, they could face brutal interrogation, imprisonment, and probably death. Nevertheless, these women were willing to make this sacrifice and, secretly, few expected to return alive.

Chillingly, for the women of F section this expectation was all too often fulfilled. The figures tell their own story. All the women of RF section survived the war. Perhaps it was because they were more truly French, better protected in their own land, or perhaps because they arrived in 1944 only months before (or even after) the allied landings on D-day: even so, Alix D'Unienville was captured but escaped, and Marguerite Petitjean got away only by a whisker, the enemy hot on her heels, as she fled over the Pyrenees. The story of the F section women was very different. Of their number, at least twenty were imprisoned (one for only a day) and thirteen never returned. Of two others, working for SOE but not trained by it, Madame Wimille made an audacious escape, but Sonia Olschanesky [see below] ended in the crematorium at Natzweiler.

It is believed that it took between five and ten years to train a Russian agent. SOE could not afford to be so generous, and the longest training period given to a woman appears to have been about nine months for the training of a very few as wireless operators from scratch; the average was five to six months and, when agents were urgently needed, even less. Training usually took place at large, requisitioned country mansions, well away from prying eyes. Agents used to joke that SOE stood for 'Stately 'Omes of England'. For F section weaker entrants were sifted out at Wanborough Manor, where training in security, exercise, and methods was given. Then came survival and weapons training in Scotland, parachuting at Tatton Park, and various undercover courses in forgery, burglary, and other necessary activities at the finishing school in Beaulieu Abbey. Here new identities were created, and the women also faced gruelling evasion and interrogation tests. Wireless operators additionally were trained at Thame Park. The success of the training can be measured by the fact that, of all the women agents captured in action, none appear to have given away to the Germans any sensitive information.

Their training complete, the women agents were ready to be sent to France by felucca or submarine, to be landed by Lysander or Hudson aircraft, or to be dropped by parachute often from a Halifax (with other supplies), hoping that they would not be injured on arrival, met by a reception party of Germans (as sometimes happened), or find themselves stranded, lost, and alone in the dark with no contacts. In this, as in the skill and courage that they displayed throughout the difficulties and traumas of their careers in France, it is little wonder that many of these women agents won high awards. Three gained the George Cross (two posthumously).

The fiery Violette Reine Elizabeth *Szabo, née Bushell (1921–1945), reputed to be the best shot in SOE, a beautiful widow of twenty-three, parachuted twice into France as a courier. The first visit was short, to a network around Rouen which could not be revived. Three days after arriving in France for the second time in 1944, to assist the maquis in sabotage around Limoges, she and her two companions were caught in a German ambush. Her colleagues managed to get away, but, injuring her ankle, Szabo could not, and was captured. When interrogation could extract nothing from her, she was later imprisoned and eventually shot at the concentration camp at Ravensbrück on 5 February 1945. In addition to being appointed MBE and awarded the Croix de Guerre, she also received a posthumous George Cross.

Perhaps the best-known of the agents was a spirited thirty-year-old brunette, Odette Marie Céline Sansom, née Brailly (1912–1995) [see Hallowes, Odette Marie Céline], the

French-born wife of an Englishman. She landed near Cassis in November 1942 and became a courier to Peter Morland *Churchill (1909–1972). Later they were arrested by a German posing as a friend. Under torture Odette tried to exonerate Churchill. Finally, after a period of solitary confinement in Ravensbrück, she was released by the commandant, who believed her story that Churchill was the prime minister's relation and that she was Peter's wife (which she became in reality in 1947). She was awarded the George Cross and was appointed MBE and a chevalier of the Légion d'honneur, the only one of the three George Cross recipients to survive the war.

Princess Noor Inayat *Khan (1914–1944) was the third female SOE agent awarded the George Cross (she was also appointed MBE and awarded the Croix de Guerre). The least likely of British agents, of Indian and American parentage, at twenty-eight she was shy and unworldly. She had trained as a radio operator in the WAAF, and in the autumn of 1942 was approached by SOE, which was desperate for operators, whose survival rate was then only about six weeks before capture. Rushed through SOE training Khan found herself the only operator left in Paris following the destruction of the Prosper network in 1943. Refusing to save herself, she kept in constant touch with Britain. Finally betrayed, she was arrested, unfortunately with her wireless, messages, and codes intact. Twice she tried to escape; but she was imprisoned in chains in solitary confinement, and was finally shot at Dachau on 12 or 13 September 1944 with the word 'liberté' on her lips.

Two agents gained the George Medal. Both were couriers, and something more. Nancy Wake (b. 1912) was an energetic New Zealand-born Australian with a strong personality. She twice worked in France, initially from her home in Marseilles, where she was known to the resistance as White Mouse. After being captured and interrogated she was rescued from prison by her friends. Then, aged thirty-two, she parachuted back into France in April 1944, and became virtually the head of 7000 maquisards in the Corrèze, whom she led with verve and by example; she returned safely to Britain in September 1944. Known by her English name, 29-year-old Christine Granville was a Polish countess both by birth and marriage [see Gizycka, Countess Krystyna (1915–1952)], and was exceedingly beautiful, attractive, and tempestuous. Constantly on the move in the Vercors and elsewhere, she was an accomplished subversive agent who had many adventures. Finally, by a trick, she rescued her organizer from prison at Digne just before the allies arrived. She was also appointed MBE and chevalier of the Légion d'honneur, and was awarded the Croix de Guerre. She was murdered in London in 1952.

Given the American Distinguished Service Cross and created MBE, **Virginia Hall** (1906–1982), was an outstanding agent and one of three Americans who helped SOE. The others were Giliana Gerson, née Balmaceda, a Chilean by birth and an actress, who helped to run an escape line for a few months in 1941, and Elizabeth Devereux Reynolds (b. 1917), possessor of a fabulous memory, whose career as a courier was cut short by arrest but who was later released by the allies from her French prison. Virginia Hall, as unobtrusive as her unusual height and artificial foot (christened Cuthbert) allowed, went into France twice. She worked in Vichy in 1941, and later in Lyons, as a foreign correspondent to the Baltimore Sun, the New York Post, and fleetingly the Chicago Times; secretly, however, she was organizing many new SOE networks, until Gestapo suspicions forced her to escape over the Pyrenees in 1942. In 1944 she returned to France, to the Creuse and Haute Loire, having trained privately as a wireless operator, working for the American office of strategic services.

The sometimes colourful, but usually serious, secretive, and hardworking, **Yvonne Claire Rudellat** (1897–1945) was one of the first to go to France, in July 1942. An apparently frail grandmother of chameleon personality, she helped to create a network allied to the unfortunate Prosper network in Paris. Her success was instrumental in convincing SOE to continue using women agents in France. She was shot in the head in a car chase in June 1943, convinced the Gestapo of her loss of memory, but died, unrecognized, from typhus, about 24 April 1945 in Belsen after its liberation. She too was appointed MBE, and received the Croix de Guerre.

Of the eleven women agents who arrived in France down the short ladder of the Lysander aircraft, eight were captured, often within months of landing. Many of the arrivals were masterminded by Henri Déricourt, a very suspect agent. The Germans too, of course, may have found such landings more easily traceable. **Vera Eugenie Leigh** (1903–1944), still beautiful at forty, was one of these agents. She became a courier between Paris and the Yonne river, and was arrested in 1943. Another was the English-looking, intrepid 28-year-old **Diana Hope Rowden** (1915–1944), formerly in the WAAF, who was a courier in the Dijon area and was arrested at almost the same time. Leigh and Rowden went through the usual interrogation by Gestapo at the notorious Avenue Foch, and eventually in July 1944 they were moved to Natzweiler concentration camp. There they were joined by the gallant 24-year-old **Andrée Raymonde Borrel** (1919–1944), a French shopgirl, who had previously worked for the resistance before being parachuted back in 1942 to be a courier for Prosper in Paris and who had been arrested only a month before. A fourth in their number was **Sonia Olschanesky** (1923–1944), a French-born daughter of Russian parents, employed by SOE as a courier in contact with Paris, though she had not been trained by SOE. All four were detained in a cell together in Natzweiler after a hot afternoon in the train on 6 July 1944. That evening they were escorted one by one to the camp crematorium, where they were given a lethal injection of phenol and their bodies burnt. Both Borrel and Rowden were appointed MBE and awarded the Croix de Guerre, but Rowden's appointment as MBE, being posthumous, was later withdrawn.

Dachau concentration camp was the venue for an appointment with death for another four agents. **Yolande Elsa Maria Beekman** [née Unternährer] (1911–1944), sent as a wireless operator to St Quentin in 1943, a cheerful, reliable woman, was betrayed in her lodgings at a cafe. She had landed by Lysander, like the dreamy Noor Inayat Khan, whom she met at Dachau. Their companions at dawn on 12 or 13 September 1944 were the ebullient **Elaine Sophie Plewman** (1917–1944), sent by parachute to act as courier in Marseilles, and the modest **Madeleine Damerment** (1917–1944), intended for a courier, who had the ill luck to be captured by the Germans as soon as her parachute hit the ground. Following a night isolated in a windowless cell, the four women were taken to the sand-strewn crematorium yard at Dachau, where, kneeling hand in hand, two by two, they were shot neatly through the back of the head. All received the Croix de Guerre; Damerment was also appointed chevalier of the Légion d'honneur.

Lilian Verna Rolfe (1914–1945) was an imperturbable thirty-year-old woman who was set down by Lysander in April 1944 and destined for the area around Orléans. Three months later she was arrested by accident: the Germans were making a sweep of the area before evacuation, and discovered to their surprise that they had caught an SOE wireless operator. She was shot at Ravensbrück on 5 February 1945. She received the Croix de Guerre and was appointed MBE. Her fate at Ravensbrück was shared by the fiercely patriotic **Denise Madeleine Bloch** (1916–1945), of Jewish parentage. She also arrived by Lysander a few months before D-day in June 1944. She was to act as a wireless operator for a network around Nantes, with instructions to damage communications in this vital area. She was captured in a Gestapo raid at her lodging house, and was also shot at Ravensbrück. She was appointed chevalier of the Légion d'honneur. A shy doctor's wife, **Cecily Margot Lefort** [*née* MacKenzie] (1900–1945), landed by Lysander in June 1943 and was employed as a courier in south-eastern France. Captured and later imprisoned in Ravensbrück, she probably died in the nearby Judenlager extermination camp in February 1945. She received the Croix de Guerre. Eileen Nearne (b. c.1922), at twenty-two an energetic and resourceful wireless operator, already experienced in work at one of the SOE listening stations in Britain (where messages to and from agents were sent and received), went by Lysander to work in Paris. She was caught at her set and amazingly, even after torture, persuaded the Gestapo that she was just a little shopgirl who knew nothing. Nevertheless, she was sent to Ravensbrück and afterwards, while being moved, effected a miraculous escape and was rescued by the advancing Americans. She was appointed MBE and received the Croix de Guerre.

Three Lysander passengers survived without being captured. Two landed in early 1943. **Julienne Aisner** (1900–1947) was intended as a courier but was eventually to run a bar in Paris as part of an escape route. Customers causing grave suspicions decided her to return to Britain in haste in 1944. So too the discreet Francine Agazarian (b. 1913), a frantically busy courier for Prosper, returned in broken health three months after her arrival in Paris. The Mauritian Lise de Baissac (b. 1905) was very capable and had a cool head. She went to France twice. After arriving by parachute she single-handedly organized a network around Poitiers and helped nearby circuits in 1942–3. Recalled after the debacle of Prosper, she later returned by Lysander in 1944 and helped her organizer brother Claude de *Baissac in Normandy during and after D-day, finally meeting the advancing Americans in her FANY uniform. She was appointed to the Légion d'honneur and MBE, and received the Croix de Guerre. The Baissacs were joined in May 1944 by sweet-natured Philippa Latour (b. 1921), who parachuted in as their much-needed and overworked wireless operator; despite her dangerous work, she too survived unscathed, and received the Croix de Guerre and was appointed MBE. Two others who arrived in France by parachute were less fortunate. Yvonne Baseden (b. 1922) worked as an efficient wireless operator in the Jura mountain area until she was captured and finally sent to Ravensbrück. Having contracted tuberculosis, she was fortunately evacuated by the Red Cross early in 1945. She was appointed MBE and received the Croix de Guerre. Sadder still was the case of another wireless operator, the small, dark, pretty **Muriel Tamara Byck** (1918–1944), of Jewish family, who died suddenly of meningitis at Romorantin on 23 May 1944, six weeks after landing.

Most notable among those who survived was the redoubtable Pearl Witherington (b. 1914). Originally a courier in the Auvergne, she revived her ailing network after her organizer's capture, and eventually commanded an active maquis of over 3500 men. So effective were her 'modest capabilities' that a German army of 20,000 preferred to surrender to the Americans rather than fall into the hands of her maquis. In addition to appointment as MBE and chevalier of the Légion d'honneur, she received the Croix de Guerre. Another survivor was the unobtrusive, rock-steady **(Beatrice) Yvonne Cormeau** (1909–1997), who at thirty-three joined a network in Gascony as a wireless operator. Always on the move, she sent a record of 400 transmissions or more in thirteen months without a single miscode, and was always very careful of security. She was appointed MBE and chevalier of the Légion d'honneur, and was also awarded the Croix de Guerre. Marguerite Knight (b. 1920) was a keen and competent courier in the Yonne at a confused and dangerous time in her network, who managed to survive unharmed, as did Sonya Esmée Florence Butt (b. 1924), one of the youngest couriers; Butt's looks belied her talents, as she also became the weapons training officer for the maquis around Le Mans. Knight received the Croix de Guerre and was appointed MBE; Butt was also appointed MBE. The elusive 27-year-old **Jacqueline Nearne** (1916–1982), elder sister of Eileen (whose employment by SOE she opposed), went as courier to a huge south-western network in 1943 and had to be recalled fifteen months later, worn out by her constant travels. She received the Croix de Guerre, and was appointed MBE. Grey-haired **Marie-Thérèse Le Chene** (b. c.1887), by far the oldest woman agent, arrived to be courier to her husband in the vast area around Clermont-Ferrand in October 1942. She returned to Britain exhausted ten months later. Two agents escaped over the Pyrenees on foot: lively, fair-haired, blue-eyed Anne-Marie Walters

(1923–1998), daughter of the deputy secretary-general of the League of Nations, had been a courier in Gascony with a price on her head (she was appointed MBE); and Odette Willen (*b.* 1919), a part-trained wireless operator who found her network broken up almost before she had begun. Blanche Charlet (*b.* 1893) had a short career as a courier at Lyons before she was captured, and then achieved the almost impossible by escaping from her French prison; winter foiled her attempt to flee over the Pyrenees and she left by another route. **Mary Katherine Herbert** (1903–1983) was a courier in the Gironde and also spent some time in a French prison, where her quick wits and knowledge of Arabic talked her out of Gestapo suspicions. Afterwards she remained in hiding until the end of the war, having married Claude de Baissac.

Four other SOE agents were in post when the allies swept over their areas: Yvonne Fontaine (*b.* 1913), a careful courier, twice in France, latterly close to Paris; Madeleine Lavigne (*d.* 1945), a short-lived courier in Limoges; Ginette Jullian (*b.* 1917), a courier at Chartres; and Patricia Maureen (Paddy) O'Sullivan (1918–1994), a part-trained wireless operator in Limoges to a pair of Mauritian brothers, all careful of security. O'Sullivan was appointed MBE and received the Croix de Guerre. There may have been others, but they disappeared, unrecognized.

When the war was over, SOE was ordered to close down on 15 January 1946 (some records give 30 June 1946), and many records were destroyed or lost. After the organization's hasty demise, many questions remained unanswered. How had decoders dangerously ignored missing security checks on captured agents' wireless transmissions? Why had lives been put at risk by trusting known or suspected double agents? By what right had the Secret Intelligence Service withheld intelligence gained from Ultra, thus needlessly sacrificing many agents' lives? And there were other controversies. SOE's success in France is in dispute. Measured by the impact of battles in the field, it probably had infinitesimal success. Some of its sabotage work was ineffective and provoked much savage reprisal against French civilians. On the other hand, its handful of agents caused major disruption to the occupying forces, tying down or diverting much-needed police and soldiers, particularly directly before and after the north and south landings by the allies. It also gave hope, support, guidance, and supplies to the maquis and anti-German forces. Even General Eisenhower, the supreme allied commander, in a tribute to its efforts, stated that it 'played a very considerable part in our complete and final victory'.

For its individuals, when hostilities ceased, it was left to Vera Atkins, the briefing and conducting officer of F section, to take a year travelling through Europe to discover the fates of those agents who did not come back—most of whom she had known personally. It was through her efforts that the tragic details became known of those courageous ones who died. Both Britain and France owe a lasting debt of gratitude to the brave work of the SOE agents, and especially this small band of women, who hardened themselves to work and endure for between one and four years of German occupation, placing the freedom of their countries above their own, and whose survivors carried their nightmares with them for the rest of their lives.

BERYL E. ESCOTT

Sources M. R. D. Foot, *SOE in France: an account of the work of the British Special Operations Executive in France, 1940–1944* (1966) · R. Braddon, *Nancy Wake* (1956) · E. H. Cookridge, *Inside SOE* (1966) · E. H. Cookridge, *They came from the sky* (1965) · B. E. Escott, *Mission improbable* (1991) · N. Forward, *The white mouse* (Melbourne, 1987) · J. O. Fuller, *Madeleine, the story of Noor Inayat Khan* (1952) · R. Kramer, *Flames in the field* (1995) · S. King, *Jacqueline, pioneer heroine of the resistance* (1989) · E. Le Cheyne, *Watch for me by moonlight* (1973) · M. Masson, *Christine, search for Christine Granville* (1975) · R. J. Minney, *Carve her name with pride* (1956) · E. Nicolas, *Death be not proud* (1958) · M. Rossiter, *Women in the resistance* (1986) · J. Tickell, *Moon squadron* (1956) · K. Tickell, *Odette* (1949) · P. de Vomécourt, *Who lived to see the day: France in arms, 1940–1945* (1961) [on Muriel Byck] · A. M. Walters, *Moondrop to Gascony* (1946) · N. West, *Secret war* (1992) · B. Wynne, *No drums … no trumpets* (1961) · J. Gleeson, *They feared no evil* (1976) · L. Jones, *A quiet courage* (1990) · H. Bleicher, *Colonel Henri's story* (1954) · A. M. Webb, ed., *The Natzweiler trial* (1949) · Commonwealth War Graves Commission, www.cwgc.org [debt of honour register] · P. Cornioley, *Pauline: la vie d'un agent du SOE* (Paris, 1996) · B. Escott, *Twentieth century women of courage* (1999) · R. Miller, *Behind the lines* (2002) · M. Binney, *The women who lived for danger* (2002) · B. Escott, *The WAAF: a history of the women's auxiliary air force in World War Two* (2004)
Archives FILM IWM, 'Now it can be told'; 'School for danger', COI films
Likenesses photographs, Special Forces Club, London

Women artists in Ruskin's circle (*act.* 1850s–1900s) were bound by interlocking strands of affinity, and manifested in their lives and work the strong attraction and influence of the convictions of John *Ruskin (1819–1900). Ruskin's relationships with women with whom he could share, or on whom he could project, his artistic, religious, and social sensibilities were a defining force in his life. His most successful relationships were with women or girls who could feel to him like younger sisters, offering both emotional sustenance and a receptiveness to guidance. When the Coniston artist and anthologist of Ruskin's work, Susanna Beever [*see below*], by fourteen or so years his senior, suggested that she could be a sort of second mother to him, he replied that she was 'much more able to be my sister than mamma' (*Complete Works*, 37.102). Tensions indeed developed between him and his cousin Joan Severn, *née* Agnew, when she tried to take on the role of mother. Ruskin often liked to pretend that Susie Beever was still a little girl, calling her 'lassie'—a fiction which he played out with other mature women whom he none the less respected and admired. Although his tone could sometimes seem patronizing, he took women extremely seriously both as intellects and as forces for good, and urged them to take themselves seriously. In his encouragement and promotion of particular women artists, he could also elevate genres and qualities conventionally depreciated by association with feminine accomplishments. Those characteristics and aspirations to which he responded lay at the heart of how he viewed woman's redemptive role. This was a fundamental guiding principle. His expectation of individual women in this sense was high, and many recognized its significance and were affirmed by it. To record the lives of a group of these women is to recall the distinctiveness of this project and its widespread resonance in Victorian society.

Ruskin's acquaintance with women of artistic interests was extensive, but much more so was his female readership. These categories could merge through correspondence, as girls and women who had read Ruskin's writings, themselves often explicitly addressed to a female constituency, felt inspired to write to him. **Ada Charlotte Dundas** (b. 1864, d. after 1931), the daughter of Adam Alexander Duncan Dundas, a naval officer of Queensferry, near Linlithgow, and his wife, Charlotte Maria, née Hoope, can stand for many such: she wrote to Ruskin out of the blue at the age of fourteen and a half; he advised her on reading and on art, she asked him questions about religion, and he gave open and thoughtful responses which invested her questions with value. In February 1880 he wrote to her: 'If anything puzzles you that I can help you in always write, whether I can answer or not—it will be good for you to express the difficulty' (Bodl. Oxf., MS Eng. Lett. d. 138, fol. 19). They met for the first time nearly three years after she had first written, and only ever met intermittently (there was some anxiety in the family about her corresponding so freely with Ruskin). She spent a year in Dresden in 1881–2, and in 1885–6 translated the autobiography of the illustrator Ludwig Richter, to whose work Ruskin had first introduced her. Unhappy at home from 1882 until her marriage to John Julius Dodgshorn (1852/3–1931), in Queensferry on 5 July 1892, she commented later that her love for Ruskin and her interest in his work were all that had kept her going. An older woman, curiously of the same name, Adela (Ada) Dundas (1840–1887), the daughter of William Pitt Dundas, the registrar-general for Scotland, and his wife, Mary, née Strange, was one of many who sent her drawings to Ruskin for advice. In 1860 he arranged for her to be taught by his protégé William Ward, and in 1878 he included a study of fruit and leaf by her in the Ruskin Art Collection educational series. It is not clear when they first met. The girls at Winnington Hall School, run by Margaret Bell on Ruskinian principles, learned to draw by Ruskin's methods, and developed their confidence through engagement with his ideas. He continued to correspond with many of them after they had left the school. His conviction of his responsibility as an educator, seen so strongly in his correspondence, extended to his role both as a critic and as a patron and adviser to other patrons. In all these contexts, he gave particular attention to women.

Ruskin was ambiguous about the term 'artist', consistently denying its application to himself, and arguing that there was 'no real occasion for the gulph of separation between amateur and artist' (Sublime and Instructive, 8). His belief in the potentially transformative power of drawing, in training both the eye and the inner eye of conscience, gave a significance to the amateur who, through properly directed application, could transcend the unreflective professional. Women were pre-eminently such amateurs, and needed to recognize the significance with which they should invest that role. They should devote as much time and energy to practising drawing as they would to the piano. Sincerity was the keynote of quality in both the amateur and the professional.

Ruskin frequently pointed out that there had never been a great female artist. Yet he singled out for commendation the work of professional women artists, whose formation and practice lay at an angle to the accepted hierarchies of academic painting. One of the first professional women artists whom Ruskin publicly praised was Annie Feray *Mutrie (1826–1893) [see under Mutrie, Martha Darley], who, with her elder sister, Martha Darley *Mutrie, was a noted painter of flowers and fruit. Ruskin praised Annie Feray's paintings in his Royal Academy Notes of 1855, boosting the genre of flower painting when accomplished with such feeling for nature.

In the same year Ruskin first met Elizabeth *Siddal (1829–1862), who was presented to him by Dante Gabriel Rossetti. On seeing her work Ruskin offered to buy it all for £30, and subsequently offered her £150 p.a. on condition that she devote herself entirely to the fine arts, and that she place herself under the instruction of either William Holman Hunt or Rossetti. She aspired to be a professional artist, and was the only woman to exhibit at Russell Place in 1857, when Ruskin and Rossetti helped to mount her pictures. Her work was well received and her watercolours Clerk Saunders (FM Cam.) and May Margaret were later bought by Ruskin's American friend Charles Eliot Norton. Ruskin advised her to stop designing imaginary scenes and to concentrate on sketching from nature, while also offering to show her his collection of medieval manuscripts. Although she collaborated closely with Dante Gabriel Rossetti, in certain respects she worked to develop her own perspective, which was acknowledged and fostered by Ruskin.

At the same period, Ruskin found himself enmeshed in a correspondence with **Anna Elizabeth Blunden** (1829–1915). She was born on 22 December 1829 in St John's Square, London, the daughter of a bookbinder. Her parents in 1833 moved to Exeter, where they set up in business making artificial flowers and straw hats, and where Anna attended a Quaker school. She became a reasonably successful genre painter (she had given up her position as a governess and enrolled at art school after reading the first volumes of Modern Painters), and she fell obsessively in love with Ruskin. Hers was an extreme case of the admiration which Ruskin inspired in many women artists who had begun to read his work. After she had studied in London at James Mathews Leigh's General Practical School of Art at 79 Newman Street, her first picture, Love, was exhibited at the Royal Academy in 1854; another, of a seamstress gazing up to heaven, based on Thomas Hood's Song of the Shirt (engraved and reproduced in the Illustrated London News for July), was accepted by the Society of British Artists for their annual exhibition in Suffolk Street. Blunden exhibited annually in both places until 1867, by which time she was abroad. In 1855 she returned to Exeter, and from 1856 to 1867 she was based in a house in the cathedral close, where she and her sister Emily traded in Berlin wool. Intermittently she went to London, where she hoped for the chance to see Ruskin, and organized her work for exhibition. In 1866 she offered eight canvases for a Scottish exhibition, and in the same year her *Fairy Glen* was priced at £100. She set off in 1867 to study in Italy, and reached Rome early in the winter of 1868 after spending time in Düsseldorf and Switzerland. In 1872 she returned home on the death of her sister Emily in childbirth, and in December that year she married her widowed brother-in-law, Francis Richard Martino; the marriage was celebrated in Altona, near Hamburg, because it was within the prohibited degrees of affinity in Britain. Back in Britain, she settled in Birmingham, where Martino owned property and later founded the Martino Steel and Metal Company. Although socially isolated because of the circumstances of her marriage, Blunden continued to paint prolifically, regularly exhibiting at the Birmingham Society of Artists for nearly forty years. In 1874 her daughter, Violet Emily, was born. In later life she was recalled as cross-tempered and parsimonious. She died in Birmingham in December 1915. Her will, drawn up in 1906 and partly revised in 1913, instructed that her letters from Ruskin should be sold. The proceeds (together with those from the publication of her memoirs—provisionally entitled 'The romance of a life: the forbidden letters of John Ruskin'—which had not been accepted by a publisher in her lifetime) were to go towards building Park cemetery in Birmingham. The architect was to be 'one who has studied and admires Mr Ruskin's works' and who would follow the instructions of his chapter on Byzantine palaces in *The Stones of Venice* (*Sublime and Instructive*, 83).

Blunden had corresponded with Ruskin between 1855 and 1862. Having originally written to ask his opinion of her poetry, and having been told that she should not think of publishing it, she was undaunted and turned to trying to interest him in her career as a painter. Early in 1857 she sent him an oil painting (probably *The Daguerreotype*, exh. RA, 1857) and the studies for it. He criticized her lack of attention to detail and her sentimentality, urging her to spend time doing studies of ordinary objects—first a white handkerchief, then a coloured one with a simple pattern, then an apple, and only then part of a child's cheek. 'If you won't do this I can't much help you—but I should think that you would be able to please many people by your pretty feeling for expression, and talent for portraiture' (*Sublime and Instructive*, 91). This sense of her limitations—as of the genre in which she had thus far preferred to work—remained, and his last letter to her lamented her lack of taste, especially in the choice of subjects, which he attributed partly to want of education. Up to that point he had continued to advise her, even though he clearly found her irritating and embarrassing, especially after she had declared her infatuation with him. On 9 November 1858 he felt it necessary to respond robustly: 'I see nothing whatever in you that pleases me in the least' (ibid., 106). In 1859 he told her and had to remind her that she must only write to him in connection with her art. None the less she persisted, and clearly was capable of deriving encouragement from the slightest remark. A postscript commending a portion of landscape was taken out of all proportion by her as extravagant praise, and inclined her to develop this side of her work. Ruskin put her in touch with Octavia *Hill, who copied and drew for him, and in March 1860 he asked Anna Blunden to take on, as paid work, the copying of a watercolour by J. M. W. Turner at the South Kensington Museum. She subsequently did further copies in the National Gallery, and in 1861 a drawing to illustrate a lecture which Ruskin was giving on tree branching at the Royal Institution. She clearly managed to do this to his reasonable satisfaction, and at this point formed a small part of a minor industry of copyists working for Ruskin to produce copies, especially of Turner, for his own use, for teaching, and for his Guild of St George Museum, Sheffield. Others included **(Jane) Isabella Lee Jay** (1842/3–1919), who was probably already a professional copyist before Ruskin saw her work. In 1868 he praised her copies of Turner's paintings as the most accurate and beautiful he had yet seen. Her expressive copies were represented in the Guild of St George Museum alongside the more meticulous reproductions by William Ward. Ruskin felt that successful copies of great art were more instructive than original work by second-rate artists. Isabella Jay died on 20 July 1919 at 36 Queen's Road, Wimbledon, Surrey, at the age of seventy-seven.

The most successful woman high-art painter whom Ruskin admired was Elizabeth *Butler (1846–1933), whose *The 28th Regiment at Quatre Bras* (exh. RA, 1875; National Gallery of Victoria, Melbourne) he discussed in his *Academy Notes* for that year. Always fascinated by things military, he fixed on the vivid detail of battle—the fall of the cuirassier 'wrought through all the truth of its frantic passion with gradations of colour and shade which I have not seen the like since Turner's death' (*Complete Works*, 14.309). She seemed to be capable of a sincere engagement with the reality of the subject, to which he responded, calling the painting 'the first fine Pre-Raphaelite picture of battle we have had', and marvelling at it as 'Amazon's work' (ibid., 308). Despite this lavish praise, Ruskin did not pursue her work or focus on it publicly in the way that he did in the case of two of her contemporaries who had been fellow students of hers at the Female School of Art, South Kensington. Helen *Allingham (1848–1926) and Kate *Greenaway (1846–1901) both won Ruskin's admiration, especially for their depiction of children. About Helen Allingham's *Young Customers* (exh. 1875), an image of two children in a village toyshop, Ruskin enthused: 'a thing which I believe Gainsborough would have given one of his own pictures for—old-fashioned as red-tipped daisies are—and more precious than rubies' (ibid., 264).

One of the most striking features of Ruskin's Oxford Slade lectures of 1883, published as *The Art of England*, was his highlighting of women artists, both known and unknown. The fourth lecture, 'Fairy land', focused on Allingham and Greenaway, and was distinctive in its emphasis on the new responsibilities of art in the home in a period when techniques of reproduction had so greatly developed. Ruskin underlined the need to stimulate in the right way the imaginations of children, who were too often bombarded by crude sensationalism. At the same time he related true Christian art to the depiction of domestic art and particularly children. In this respect at least he saw his own age as one in which art had been revived: 'the radiance and innocence of reinstated infant divinity showered again amongst the flowers of English meadows by Mrs. Allingham and Kate Greenaway' (*Complete Works*, 33.340). Allingham's *Young Customers* was here referred to as 'a classic picture, which will have its place among the memorable things in the art of our time' (ibid., 341). He then introduced Kate Greenaway, citing the French critic Ernest Chesneau's praise of her, and showing some of her pencil sketches of fairies. Having criticized her for wasting her talents on producing ornamental borders for birthday books, he moved directly from commending her delicacy and revelatory power to an analogous focus on Turner. There could have been no higher compliment.

Kate Greenaway had read *Fors Clavigera* before coming into personal contact with Ruskin; she corresponded with him from 1880 and stayed with him at Brantwood. He constantly tried to encourage her to develop her drawing, feeling that it was so much more beautiful than the woodcut reproductions in her illustrated books, and wondered whether her 'proper work would be in glass painting—where your own touch, your own colour, would be safe for ever—seen, in sacred places, by multitudes' (*Complete Works*, 37.331). As he advised so many others, he urged both the study of thirteenth-century glass or manuscripts in the British Museum and drawing from nature: 'Now be a good girl and draw some flowers that won't look as if their leaves had been in curlpapers all night' (ibid., 453). She continued to send him drawings until his death, and, reinforced in her view by others, was not in fact deflected from her characteristic and popular style, which Ruskin appreciated, even if he constantly thought that it could be improved upon. On Christmas day 1881 he wrote to her about the significance of her work for children: 'I trust you may long be spared to do such lovely things, and be an element of the best happiness in every—English—household—that still has an English heart—as you are already in the simpler homes of Germany' (ibid., 383). He used several of her designs as head- or end-pieces for the last letters of *Fors Clavigera*; she designed dresses for the May queen festivities at Whitelands College, and produced four illustrations for a new edition of *Dame Wiggins of Lee* (1885).

In his first lecture in the Slade series Ruskin had already surprised his audience by turning from a discussion of Rossetti and Edward Burne-Jones to praise of two women artists, prefacing his comments with the statement: 'For a long time I used to say ... that, except in a graceful and minor way, women could not paint or draw. I am beginning, lately, to bow myself to the much more delightful conviction that nobody else can' (*Complete Works*, 33.280). Both of these women lived out Ruskin's principles of profound religious engagement with nature. One of them was the American Francesca Alexander (1837–1917), to whom Ruskin had been introduced in Florence in 1882.

She was at this point forty-five and had been a professional artist for twenty years, although Ruskin was to talk of her as if she were a young girl, and addressed her as 'lassie' and as his 'sweetest Sorel'. She had been brought up by her artist father in Ruskinian ways of looking at nature, and as a devout evangelical. At the age of seven she was said to have announced that she wanted to be an artist and to work for poor children. She collected stories and songs from the Tuscan peasantry, which she wrote and illustrated with figure drawings of the poor, many of whom gathered regularly in her studio, and whom she supported with the proceeds of sales of her work. For Ruskin her work—in both its form and its subject matter—embodied an ideal Christian and artistic simplicity and sincerity. He was to focus on this ideal in remembering—and transfiguring from its religious narrowness—the character of Rose La Touche. He bought and published Francesca Alexander's *The Story of Ida*, *Roadside Songs of Tuscany*, and *Christ's Folk in the Apennine*. In his third Slade lecture he read passages from her preface to the *Roadside Songs*, and showed some of her drawings; and in June 1883 he gave a drawing-room lecture in London at which he showed twenty of her drawings. The *Spectator* review, commending their excellence, saw them as exemplars of Ruskin's teaching.

The other woman discussed by Ruskin, **(Isabella) Lillias Trotter** (1853–1928), was completely unknown, and was not an artist by profession but a committed evangelical, at that point working for the YWCA in London. She was born on 14 July 1853 at Devonshire Place House, Marylebone, the seventh child of Alexander Trotter (1814–1866) of Dreghorn, Midlothian, a businessman, and the eldest of his second wife, Isabella Strange. She was educated at home in London by French and German governesses and was encouraged by her father in scientific and artistic pursuits; in the summer the family travelled on the continent. After the death of her father in 1866, she developed a new seriousness, and in the mid-1870s she attended with her mother evangelical conventions at Broadlands and Oxford; she sang in a choir during the Moody and Sankey revival of 1875. It was on a visit to Venice in October 1876 that she met Ruskin. Discovering that Ruskin was staying at the same hotel, her mother asked whether she could show him some of her daughter's watercolours. As Ruskin recounted in the Slade lecture: 'I saw there was extremely right-minded and careful work, almost totally without knowledge. I sent back a request that the young lady might be permitted to come out sketching with me.' He commented on her learning 'everything the instant that she was shown it—and ever so much more than she was taught', and went on to display her drawings of peasant life in Norway, commended for conveying the same attributes of Christian simplicity which Francesca Alexander was doing in Tuscany (*Complete Works*, 33.280–81). Her Norwegian notebooks were to form part of Ruskin's gift to the University of Oxford. She visited Brantwood regularly with her brother and sometimes her sister, and drew under Ruskin's encouragement. But in 1879 she was to decide that she could not commit herself to painting 'in the way he means, and continue still to "seek first the

Kingdom of God and His righteousness"' (Stewart, 19). She worked for the YWCA, took a Bible class at the Welbeck Institute, and began to hold meetings at her own home in Montagu Square for women in the business houses of Oxford and Regent streets. In 1886 she bought a nightclub to convert into a restaurant for such women; and she worked at night among prostitutes. She continued to paint and to send sketches to Ruskin, who felt, however, that her work was deteriorating:

> The power in these drawings is greater than ever—the capacity infinite in the things that none can teach; but the sense of colour is gradually getting debased under the conditions of your life ... Technically you are losing yourself for want of study of the great colour masters.   (ibid., 22–3)

In 1888 Trotter went to Algeria as a missionary, where she worked until her death, publishing Arabic translations of the gospels and organizing conferences for the missionaries of north Africa. At the same time she responded passionately both as an artist and as an evangelical to the landscape and colours of Algeria. Fascinated by the vivid sapphire blue of Kabylian berries growing deep under matted grass, she tried to paint them 'to show what God can do with the very feeblest ray; but the blue is an unattainable colour' (*Master of the Impossible*, 19). In 1926 she published a little story, *Focussed*, written for the YWCA, in which she used a similar image of a dandelion, catching a shaft of sun in a dark wood: from this she developed the metaphor of the lens to press the need for everyone to choose on what to focus and not to dissipate energy. Her aesthetic comments on detail and line, in Africa and on trips in Switzerland and north Italy, continued to show a strong Ruskinian sensibility. Until her death she sent watercolours of people, places, and plants—often in a bold and independent style—to him among others. She died in Algeria in May 1928.

Emily Mary Bibbens Warren (1869–1956) went the opposite way to Lillias Trotter in developing her career in response to Ruskin's advice. Born at 7 Bradninch Place, Exeter, on 20 October 1869, the fifth daughter of Matthew Henry Warren (c.1820–1879) and his wife, Mary, née Gifford, she found being the youngest child a struggle, and all her life was to feel held back by her family. This feeling seems in fact to have helped to nourish a forceful and independent character. At the age of five or six she wrote a letter (never posted) to Queen Victoria to request 'a change in the laws' after being punished for not keeping her shelf in the nursery cupboard tidy (McRae, 20). Painting early on became a means of expression. Emily's father, who had been part-owner of a fleet of ships carrying cod from Newfoundland to Europe and America, died bankrupt after being cheated by his partners. His widow and their daughters moved to London so that the elder ones could teach and help to support the family. Emily, as a ward-in-chancery, went to Malden Girls' School, where she was given scope to read what she wanted. She claimed to have read all Ruskin's works by the time she was fourteen. When she was only thirteen the visit of a medical missionary to the school captured her imagination. She was inspired at that point to write to Ruskin, enclosing a

drawing of a branch of heather, and expressing her interest in both art and medicine. He was clear in his response: 'you can't be a paintress and a lady doctor too, for you will soon come to think healing the far nobler and more divine art' (RF MS 96, Ruskin Library, University of Lancaster).

Emily Warren followed his advice and began taking night classes in art. She copied watercolours by Turner at the British Museum under Ruskin's instruction, studying the effects of light. Although she later noted that Ruskin had been disappointed in her appearance (she was a plain, large-faced woman with a stoop), more significantly in 1885 he observed: 'You have a perfect unsurpassable eye for colour' (McRae, 25). He commissioned her to hand-colour one or two impressions of Kate Greenaway's *Rosy Vale*, which illustrated the last letter of *Fors* in 1884. He paid her £30 for her first landscape, which enabled her to enrol in the architectural class of Bannister Fletcher. At the end of a year she qualified for a scholarship, which she could not take up because she needed to earn her living. In 1886 she began teaching English and art at Grey Coat School, where her sister Ada was headmistress. At the age of eighteen she graduated from the Royal College of Art. Meanwhile, Ruskin had obtained permission for her to sketch in the Natural History Museum, and over the next few years she took certificates in biology, botany, and geology at the College of Science, South Kensington, and continued her architectural studies. During the holidays she and her sister Louie visited cathedral cities in England and abroad. By the early years of the twentieth century she had become a popular watercolour painter, specializing in architectural subjects and landscapes. Queen Alexandra bought a view of an interior of St George's Chapel, Windsor (Royal Collection), in 1903. From about 1905 Warren was earning enough from her painting to give up teaching, and these years up to the First World War in some respects constituted her artistic heyday. Between 1910 and 1912, having re-read the thirty-nine volumes of Ruskin's complete works, she travelled round Italy, Switzerland, and England producing a hundred watercolours, of which forty-four were selected as illustrations to E. T. Cook's *Homes and Haunts of John Ruskin* (1912). In 1913 she was elected an associate of the Royal Society of British Artists (which was to elect her to a fellowship in 1939), and a member of the Society of Women Artists and the Aberdeen Society of Art. Also in 1913 two of her paintings were accepted and shown at the Royal Academy. She was a member of the British Water Colour Society and the Old Dudley Arts Society, as well as being an active committee member of the Society for the Preservation of Ancient Monuments, under whose aegis she produced a comprehensive record of famous buildings in London. She also lectured extensively to Ruskin societies.

In 1917 Emily Warren began a pair of oil paintings on a vast scale—11.5 feet by 6 feet—entitled *Canada's Tribute* (now in the Royal Military College, Kingston, Ontario), a depiction of the placing of Canadian regimental colours on Wolfe's monument in Westminster Abbey. This project was authorized by the London office of the Canadian war records, which urged her to portray all seventy-seven

commanders and fifty-two colours. All but two of the portraits were done from life. Warren went to Canada in 1919
to add the final details to these paintings and to organize
their sale. Unluckily the prime minister in 1920, Sir Robert
Borden, who had promised that the government would
buy them, fell ill before the sale could be transacted. The
paintings were being exhibited, draped with flags, in one
of the largest department stores in Ottawa to celebrate
the armistice. The context was inauspicious. Despite their
popularity with former servicemen, who protested vigorously, the director of the National Gallery in Ottawa
argued against their purchase on the ground that they
were old-fashioned and European. In fact, although Emily
Warren stayed in Canada (and held a Canadian passport
from 1929), she continued to be regarded as English,
which worked to the detriment of her artistic reputation
in a climate of rising nationalism and the search for a specifically Canadian modernism; she remained isolated
from the Canadian art establishment. Only in 1947, in the
context of another war, were the large canvases bought by
the state, after they had been exhibited in the parliament
building from 1941 (to 1948).

From 1919 to her death in 1956 Emily Warren spent
August to March in Canada, returning to England to paint
the spring flowers and to spend much of the summer
sketching there and on the continent. In both Europe and
Canada she obtained passes from railway companies in
return for publicity. She crossed Canada several times,
sketching, working on commissioned paintings, and giving lectures illustrated by lantern slides of her own paintings. She lectured for six seasons (1931–6) on architecture
at Columbia University. She was a member of the Ruskin
Centenary Council. She also raised money for the Red
Cross in Canada by demonstrating her gift of thought
transference, in which she maintained a serious interest.
Her last years became increasingly difficult, as her sisters
died in England, and travelling became more challenging
for her. Her finances caused continuous problems, but she
carried on working, showing indomitable energy into her
eighties. She died in her sleep on 28 June 1956 at Dun-
robin, and was buried at Springhill cemetery, Vernon,
near Ottawa. A devout Anglican, she had remained true to
her Ruskinian approach to landscape, and had produced a
large volume of work which continued to find a market,
although her interrelated religious and aesthetic convictions had fallen out of critical fashion.

The close relationship between artistic and religious or
philanthropic commitment, which came so naturally to
women inspired by Ruskin's writings, always had the
potential for causing tensions between him and other
women whose focus on art he felt was insufficiently concentrated. The tensions were most sharply felt in Ruskin's
relationship with Louisa *Beresford, marchioness of
Waterford (1818–1891), who found both inspiration and
frustration in Ruskin's writings:

There is a charm in Ruskin's writing that I find in no other,
though he often provokes me, and I sometimes disagree: but
he is right in saying all careless work is a proof of something

morally wrong: I am sure nothing truer was ever said.
(Hare, 3.257)

She saw herself as an amateur artist and did not exhibit in
professional galleries until the 1870s, although her work
had early on been admired by J. E. Millais and Rossetti.
When she did, it was with some success: at the Dudley Gallery exhibition of 1887 her name was printed as 'Mr
L. Waterford', prompting one critic to ask: 'Who is Mr.
Waterford, this new genius, reviving the glories of the
Venetian school?' (M. Joicey, *The Lady Waterford Hall and its
Murals*, 1938, 8). Yet she always saw her art, in Ruskinian
terms, as being part of her philanthropic and evangelical
mission, and she took very seriously her responsibilities
as a landowner. In writing to her from the 1850s Ruskin
spoke of himself as being as much an amateur as she was,
and went on to urge her to spend more time looking at
details in Venetian paintings in the National Gallery,
working between one and two hours a day on close drawing, taking pains. Initially he commended her philanthropic work by analogy with his own work for the Working Men's College, and he encouraged the idea of her decoration of Ford School. But from the mid-1860s,
particularly at moments when he himself was feeling
tired, depressed, or full of 'great spite … against religion',
he attacked her sharply and unfairly for being content to
be admired in fashionable drawing-rooms, and for not
having used her influence to reform artistic approaches.
He railed against her preoccupation with Ford, when she
could have been usefully copying crumbling Italian frescoes, and provoked an indignant response from her when
he wrote peevishly from Switzerland to say how terrible
the Cheviot country must be looking in November. She
protested at his inconsistency, affirming that its winter
colour was as beautiful as its summer, if one only opened
one's eyes to it. Despite intermittent discouragement and
diffidence, she continued to work hard on her mural project and to build up her exhibition material. Other artists
who recognized her quality, such as Rossetti and Watts,
were to comment on the fact that the circumstances of
her life had not permitted her to develop her artistic
potential to the full, but in fact in her own terms, which
were also in part Ruskin's, she constructed a coherent project for her life.

Ruskin sometimes combined trips to Ford with visiting
Pauline, Lady *Trevelyan, at Wallington, with whom he
developed a close friendship. She showed him her
sketches of plants, and discussed with him her purchases
of works by Turner, Rossetti, David Cox, and Leighton. She
reviewed his pamphlet *Pre-Raphaelitism* in *The Scotsman*,
and was a consistent enthusiast for Pre-Raphaelite artists.
Her botanical knowledge was considerable, and she drew
specific flowers for Ruskin, as well as procuring specimens. In 1853 he wrote to her from Glenfinlas about his
intention to send her leaves and flowers in dated envelopes so that she could give him their botanical names. A
lively, bright person, she was described by William Bell
Scott (who hated Ruskin) as 'intensely amusing and interesting to the men she liked'. He also observed, acutely,
that she was without vanity 'and very likely without the

passion of love' (*Autobiographical Notes*, 2.207), a characteristic that may have made her particularly attractive to Ruskin.

William Bell Scott attributed to the overpowering influence of Ruskin the fact that Lady Trevelyan had 'not risen above the Turner mania' (ibid., 2.5). Whenever possible, Ruskin certainly encouraged those with means to do so to emulate his role as a collector of Turner's work, and also to endorse his view of the Pre-Raphaelites. One of the most keen to follow his example, and to take his advice, was Ellen *Heaton (1816–1894). Energetic and blunt, she inserted herself—often tactlessly—into many artistic and cultural circles, and engaged in their philanthropic activities, distributing Honiton lace for Lady Trevelyan, for example. As a collector she was a shrewd businesswoman, and wanted to know on which artists to concentrate. Of contemporary artists, Ruskin urged her to commission Rossetti, Arthur Hughes, and J. W. Inchbold; she refused to buy Burne-Jones's work. She already supported Thomas Richmond's family. Often through Ruskin, she bought a large number of Turner's sketches and vignettes. Not infrequently he bought a few together, and, having made his own choice, passed on to her those in which he was less interested; they also arranged exchanges. She was generous in lending her pictures to friends and acquaintances: during the winters of 1857–8 and 1858–9, which she spent in Italy, she left her Turner sketches to Ruskin to enjoy. She also lent Rossetti drawings to Winnington Hall School to aid Ruskin's project of enhancing the girls' art education. She contributed to the construction and carving of the University Museum in Oxford, and, increasingly from the early 1860s, gave support to wider educational projects such as university extension.

Far from the metropolitan artistic world, but influential in disseminating Ruskin's artistic ideas to a wider constituency, was **Susanna** [Susan] **Beever** (1805–1893), who, with her elder sister **Mary Beever** (1802–1883), lived at The Thwaite, Coniston. They were the daughters of William Beever (d. 1831), a Manchester merchant, and his wife, Nanny, who died when the children were very young. William Beever first retired to Birdsgrove, near Ashbourne, Derbyshire, and then in 1827 settled in Coniston with five of his children, two of whom (Anne and John) died in 1858 and 1859 respectively, and a third (Margaret) in 1874. Henry, who had stayed in Manchester practising law, died in 1840. Both Susan and Mary were highly accomplished artists, whom Ruskin met in 1873, and in whose company he delighted. The sisters had become experts on local botany, collecting specimens, drawing and contributing to scientific works, and cultivating a beautiful garden full of flowers, fruit trees, and birds. Their help, and especially Susan's, was acknowledged repeatedly in publications on British flowering plants and on the flora of the Lake District. Ruskin described Mary as the more interested in business, policy, and progressive science, while he saw Susan as the more imaginative. They also cared for the poor and sick, and taught in the Sunday school; Susan published in 1852–3 tracts on ragged schools (printed by her brother John). In 1870 she published *A Book of Reference*

to *Remarkable Passages in Shakespeare*, which Ruskin kept by him. She was included in a list of the companions of the Guild of St George in 1876. It was a sign of Ruskin's trust in her judgement that he allowed her to make the selection from *Modern Painters* published as *Frondes agrestes* (1875). Of the many anthologies of his work, two of which were by women well known to him—Grace Allen (the daughter of his publisher) and Kate Stanley (chief governess at Whitelands College, which he supported)—this was the only one with which he was involved. In general suspicious of collections which took quotations out of context, and which he feared privileged style over the substance of his thought, he wrote to Susie Beever: 'I think … that your selection will just do for me what no other reader could have done, least of all I myself; keep together, that is to say, what may be right and true of those youthful thoughts' (*Complete Works*, 37.108). He recognized its didactic potential as a text to be read at home. He also encouraged the publication of a collection of his letters to Mary and Susan, as *Hortus inclusus*, in 1887. Ruskin saw the sisters as the embodiment of perfect womanhood, their characters shaped by the purity of the landscape in which they lived—an English Switzerland. The publication of his relationship with them was presented as an example of womanly influence, while also revealing to the public an attractively affectionate side of Ruskin, to be highlighted later by the editors of his *Works*. This was appropriate enough, in that Susie Beever was a friend in whom Ruskin found particular sympathy and wisdom. She died at The Thwaite on 29 October 1893, and he was later buried beside her in Coniston churchyard. The title *Hortus inclusus*, with its associations with the Virgin Mary, with cultivated nature and the symbolism of flowers, alluded to Ruskin's enduring preoccupations in an accessible form. It was his own last and most personal projection of his relationship with an artistic woman.

JANE GARNETT

Sources 'Women artists in Ruskin's circle', University of Lancaster, Ruskin Library [exhibition labels by Stephen Wildman, 1999] • *The complete works of John Ruskin*, ed. E. T. Cook and A. Wedderburn, 39 vols. (1903–12) • T. Hilton, *John Ruskin: the early years* (New Haven, 1985) • T. Hilton, *John Ruskin: the later years* (New Haven, 2000) • *Sublime and instructive: letters from John Ruskin to Louisa, marchioness of Waterford, Anna Blunden and Ellen Heaton*, ed. V. Surtees (1972) • *Reflections on friendship: John Ruskin's letters to Paulina Trevelyan, 1848–1866*, ed. V. Surtees (1979) • J. Ruskin and A. Dundas, correspondence, Bodl. Oxf., MS Eng. lett. d. 138 • F. Hays, *Women of the day: a biographical dictionary of notable contemporaries* (1885) • P. Usherwood and J. Spencer-Smith, *Lady Butler: battle artist, 1846–1933* (1987) • A. J. C. Hare, *The story of two noble lives*, 3 vols. (1893) • H. Neville, *Under a border tower* (1896) • M. Joicey, *The Lady Waterford Hall and its murals* (1983) • V. Akin Burd, ed., *The Winnington letters* (1969) • *The master of the impossible: sayings, for the most parts in parable, from the letters and journals of Lilias Trotter of Algiers*, ed. C. E. Padwick (1938) • I. R. G. Stewart, *The love that was stronger: Lilias Trotter of Algiers* (1958) • J. Marsh, *The legend of Elizabeth Siddal* (1989) • M. H. Spielmann, 'Francesca Alexander, and "The roadside songs of Tuscany"', *Magazine of Art*, 176 (June 1895) • *Autobiographical notes of the life of William Bell Scott*, ed. W. Minto, 2 vols. (1892) • D. S. Macleod, *Art and the Victorian middle class: money and the making of cultural identity* (1996) • P. St John, *Until the day breaks … the life and work of Lilias Trotter* (1990); repr. (1994) • C. McRae, *The light must be perfect: the life of Emily Warren*

(Toronto, 1982) • G. Chitty, '"Among my jewel friends": Ruskin and Ada Dundas', *Ruskin Programme Bulletin*, 27 (Oct 2001), 8–12 • J. Beever, *Practical fly-fishing founded on nature: a new edition with a memoir of the author by W. G. Collingwood* (1893) • d. cert. [Isabella Jay] • b. cert. [Lillias Trotter] • b. cert. [Emily Mary Bibbens Warren] • m. cert. [Ada Charlotte Dundas] • parish registers, General Register Office for Scotland, Edinburgh [birth and death extract for Adela (Ada) Dundas]

Archives University of Lancaster, Ruskin Library • University of Toronto, Thomas Fisher Rare Book Library, MSS letters, papers, drawings, sketchbook, photographs [Emily Mary Bibbens Warren] | Bodl. Oxf., letters to Ada Dundas, MS Eng. Lett. d. 138
Likenesses photograph, *c.*1858 (Anna Blunden), repro. in Surtees, ed., *Sublime and instructive*

Women in trade and industry in York (*act. c.*1300–*c.*1500) were enfranchised in some numbers as citizens in their own right, but there is no evidence that they were allowed any political voice. Equally, although the freedom of York was by the later middle ages a prerequisite for persons to set up shop and employ labour, it did not constitute a significant means of access to careers in commerce for women. Some women were enfranchised by right of patrimony—perhaps a reflection of their social status—others as petty retailers such as hucksters, chapwomen, and upholders. A handful occupied more significant niches, for example **Ellen Arnald** (*fl.* 1436), silkwoman; **Joan Caldecotes** (*fl.* 1417), vintner; **Margaret Lonsdale** (*fl.* 1317), mercer; and **Margaret Steyniour** (*fl.* 1388), spicer. A few of these women were widows, but the majority were spinsters, some of whom may later have married. Women normally became actively involved in running businesses upon marriage. The assistance of wives in the running of workshops is implicit in a founders' guild ordinance of *c.*1390, which permitted a named master an additional apprentice 'a cause qil nad nulle femme' ('because he had no wife'; Sellers, *York Memorandum Book*, 106). Women would have managed businesses in their own right only as widows.

It is hardly possible to trace the career of any individual woman from adolescence, through marriage, to widowhood. Women merchants and traders generally are comparatively inconspicuous in York records, and this is especially true of wives. By nature of the sources most women traders are only observed towards the end of their lives. But widows, though more evident, may only be noticed for a few years at a time. Freemen's widows would normally have continued to enjoy the franchise and so would not be separately registered. A crude estimate suggests that husbands and wives managed businesses together for a mean of twenty-one years, but that widows survived their husbands by a mean of only three years. It follows that only one business in eight was liable to be run by a widow, but since younger widows would often have remarried, and some older widows may have preferred to sell their businesses or hand them over to an adult son, the actual proportion would have been lower. The marital status of the women observed cannot always be certain: widows are sometimes distinguished as 'wife of', women identified as 'the daughter of' may sometimes have been already married, and married women appear not always

to have adopted their husband's name, though the latter is more true of the fourteenth century than later. Another difficulty is that names remained unstable into the fifteenth century. The **Colet Clathseller** (*fl.* 1376–1381) observed in the poll tax of 1377 was almost certainly identical with the Coleta Draper found in the poll-tax returns of 1381, but is also likely to have been the Coletta of Hopirton enfranchised as a clothseller in 1376. She is not readily noticed again, perhaps because she changed her name on marriage some time after 1381.

Despite these difficulties, there is considerable evidence of wives and widows engaging in trade and industry in York. One of those who continued to enjoy the franchise as a widow was **Margaret Burton** (*d.* 1488), a tanner who traded independently after the death of her husband John in 1479, and described herself as a citizen in her will of 1488, although she was not personally enrolled in the franchise register. **Isabel Nunhouse** (*fl.* 1441–1442), a weaver like her husband John (*d.* 1440), engaged in a craft that experienced recession earlier and more severely than most others, and she was obliged to have herself registered as a citizen in her own name in order to continue the business that she had formerly shared with her husband. Widows who traded for only a few years after their husbands' deaths also included **Nichola Irby** (*d.* 1395), who continued to trade as a merchant until her death only two years after that of her husband. The cogship *Anneys* of York which she left in her will may represent the completion of business left unfinished from her husband's estate. The brewer **Agnes** (*fl.* 1410) was noticed in a disputed marriage in 1410, the same year in which her first husband, Hugh Grantham, died. **Katherine Lam** (*d.* 1494), widowed in 1484, traded as a merchant for a few years until she handed on to her son Thomas in 1489.

Most conspicuous in the sources, however, are women such as **Katherine Lakensnyder** (*d.* 1394), named thus in the poll tax of 1377, though she is almost certainly the Katherine of Barneby noticed in the equivalent returns for 1381, whose husband died at least seventeen years before her. She was a widow of substance. Her household comprised eight servants according to the returns of 1377; six female servants were recorded four years later. By 1394 the household had shrunk to one male and two female servants. Her name may indicate an association with the cloth trade. But the number of women servants in her household, one of whom is named in the returns of 1381 as Emma Tapster—that is, barmaid—and her bequest of brewing utensils for her daughter Margaret, indicate that she was a brewer and may also have run a hostelry. At her death Katherine left the residue of her goods to her son Henry, but a life interest in her house to her servant William, which suggests that by this time her business interests may have been handled by a male employee, not by her son.

The case of **Alice Folston** (*fl. c.*1386–1395) illustrates how wives might be active partners in their husbands' crafts, or even effectively support themselves. In the aulnage accounts for 1394–5 Alice accounted for 6 ells of cloth. This probably indicates that she was a cloth trader rather than a weaver. She was by this date married to the trader Robert Lofthouse, who features more prominently in the same accounts. Though trading under their own names, the couple thus constituted a partnership. Alice had earlier been married to one Thomas Walshe (otherwise Lawles), a jeweller living in the poor suburb of St Maurice, with whom she had a number of children. Walshe seems not to have lived with her latterly, and had disappeared and was presumed dead, by about 1386. It may be, therefore, that Alice was forced to earn her own livelihood even within the lifetime of her first husband.

Cecily Yharom (*d.* 1396) is one of those who emerges into the record only towards the end of her life. By the time she made her will she was clearly a woman of some wealth. She had been married twice, first to Thomas Malton, possibly a cook, with whom she had two sons, both priests, and later to Henry Yharom, a draper. She is listed, though not by name, in the poll tax of 1377 with her first husband and a household of thirteen servants, the largest household recorded in the surviving returns. She was still living in the wealthy parish of St Martin, Coney Street, but was already widowed by the time of the third poll tax of 1381. She is here described as a brewer, but her household had shrunk to three women servants. It may be that she ran a hostelry.

The life of **Marion** [Mary] **Kent** (*d.* 1500), who died thirty-two years after her husband John, provides an example of a merchant's widow active in trade and the affairs of her guild at a period when other evidence suggests it was becoming harder for widows to retain these roles. Her relative youth and rank as the widow of a former mayor may explain her involvement in business activity, which she maintained until her son Henry was of sufficient age to take over the family business, perhaps from the late 1470s. By the time that she made her will in 1488, her household comprised only women servants. From her husband's death in 1468 until some time between 1473 and 1483 she traded in goods such as cloth, iron, dyestuffs, oil, and timber through the port of Hull. She supplied, *inter alia*, iron to York Minster and timber to the guild of Corpus Christi and was a member of the council of the mercers' guild in 1474–5. She managed various properties in York and the immediate region which had been bequeathed by her husband, and she is recorded as renting a messuage in Hertergate at an annual rent of 1 mark in 1468/9. Her association with a number of York guilds, including the prestigious guild of St Christopher and St George and the all-embracing guild of Corpus Christi, is evidence of her social rank, whereas her expenditure on temporary chantries, on clothing for poor men at her funeral, and her provision of 1*d.* dole, speaks of a conventional piety that was underpinned by a fair degree of wealth.

There is reason to believe that it became harder for women, especially the minority of wealthy and long-lived widows like Marion Kent or Katherine Lakensnyder, to continue in trade and industry from the middle of the fifteenth century. Economic recession within the city made it increasingly difficult for male apprentices to secure workshops and pressure was put on widows to give up workshops soon after their husbands' deaths, or to remarry.   P. J. P. GOLDBERG

Sources F. Collins, ed., *Register of the freemen of the city of York*, 1, SurtS, 96 (1897) · exchequer court probate register, Borth. Inst. · M. Sellers, ed., *York memorandum book*, 1, SurtS, 120 (1912) · R. B. Dobson, ed., *York city chamberlains' account rolls, 1396–1500*, SurtS, 192 (1980) · J. Lister, ed., *The early Yorkshire woollen trade*, Yorkshire Archaeological Society Record Ser., 64 (1928) · dean and chapter probate register, York Minster Library · [J. Raine], ed., *Testamenta Eboracensia*, 3, SurtS, 45 (1865) · W. Childs, ed., *The customs accounts of Hull, 1453–1490*, Yorkshire Archaeological Society Record Ser., 144 (1986) · J. I. Leggett, ed., 'The 1377 poll tax returns for the city of York', *Yorkshire Archaeological Journal*, 43 (1971) · J. N. Bartlett, ed., *The lay poll tax returns for the city of York in 1381* (1953) · H. C. Swanson, *Building craftsmen in late medieval York*, Borthwick Paper, 63 (1983) · H. C. Swanson, 'Craftsmen and industry in late medieval York', DPhil diss., University of York, 1980 · [M. Sellers], ed., *The York Mercers and Merchant Adventurers, 1356–1917*, SurtS, 129 (1918) · Ouse Bridge accounts, York City Archives · PRO, E 179
Archives York City Archives, Ouse Bridge accounts

Women medical practitioners in England (*act. c.*1200–*c.*1475)

Women medical practitioners in England (*act. c.*1200–*c.*1475) were a widespread, amorphous, and often maligned group, and one that is very difficult to define. Surgical texts written by men abound with disparaging references to 'the ladies': amateur healers who were accused of making their patients worse. Much of this is part of medieval anti-female satire, though it does imply a female threat to male hegemony. Since most medicine was practised part-time in the middle ages, medical practitioners may be mentioned in a wide variety of sources. The exclusion of women from the clerical and other professions, from municipal and legal offices, and from a prominent place in the life of guilds and confraternities—that is, from virtually every situation tending to throw up the right kinds of records—makes it especially difficult for the historian to identify women medical practitioners. Medical texts survive directed exclusively to women's problems, but they were usually excerpts from longer general practices written by men. Nevertheless, scattered sources suggest that many women healers were powerful, independent, and sought after for their skills: it was their very success that was sometimes seen as a threat to the practice of medicine by men.

It is clear that women provided most medical care in the home and within certain social groups. Linguistic evidence, however, is among that pointing to a wider participation on their part in the practice of both medicine and surgery. 'Leech' (Latin: *medicus*) was a common English word for any type of medical practitioner, including surgeons. It was in use in Old and Middle English, and appears in Anglo-Norman in the forms *le leche* and *la leche*. Both genders are found in Latin as well: *medicus* and *medica*. Similarly, Anglo-Norman preserves both genders for surgeon (although spellings vary greatly): *le cirurgien* and *la surgiene*. By contrast, the terms *physicus* and the rare *archiater*, both of which are characteristic of learned sources, are used only in the male gender, while *obstetrix* ('midwife') seems to have been applied only to women.

Excluded from the universities, which were in any case not much concerned with medicine as a curative art, women seem, like many of their male counterparts, to have learned their trade from others in the family. For instance, Thomas (*d. c.*1272/3), surgeon of London, mentioned in his will a son William and his daughters **Katherine** (*fl. c.*1272–*c.*1273) and Avice. In a quitclaim to some London tenements William and Katherine are both called surgeons, suggesting that at least two of Thomas's children had followed him into surgical practice. Two sisters and a brother practising medicine together at the beginning of the thirteenth century were **Solicita** (*fl. c.*1200), **Matilda** (*fl. c.*1200), and John, who lived in Hertfordshire. Solicita had a husband, William of Ford, while Matilda confirmed legal instruments with her own seal. John was called *medicus* while Solicita and Matilda were each *medica*. One example of a team of spousal practitioners is Thomas of Rasyn and his wife **Pernell of Rasyn** (*fl.* 1350), who practised together in Devon. They were pardoned for the death of one of their patients, whom they had been accused of killing 'through ignorance of their art' (*CPR*, 1348–50, 561).

Not every woman healer practised in association with a man. The court rolls of the manor of Hales in Worcestershire contain several mentions of a certain **Margery** (*fl.* 1300–1306), called 'Leech'. Margery's existence and vocation are known only from her involvement in several actions before the manorial court. She was three times fined for damage to the lord's land by allowing her cow to stray and by gathering nuts and firewood without permission. In 1302 she was thrown into a stream by Roger Ordrych. In 1232 **Matilda la Leche** (*fl.* 1232) of Wallingford, Berkshire, was assessed at 20*d.* for taxes. **Cecilia la Leche** (*fl. c.*1350) owned a tenement in Oxford that passed to Robert le Leche and then to his son Nicholas le Leche. The physician **Christiana** (*fl.* 1313) who received corn from the master of Jarrow Priory in 1313 was a woman. Dependence on men seems to have been the rule rather than the exception, however. One set of rules for the nuns of Syon stipulated that the infirmaress tend to the bodily needs of the sick according to the advice of male physicians called in from outside.

Little is yet known about whether women healers treated male patients, or were employed principally as gynaecologists. Prominent among the latter in the records is **Marjory Cobbe** (*fl.* 1469–1475), midwife to Edward IV's queen Elizabeth, who was granted, with her husband John, an annual pension of £10 in 1469, renewed six years later. There are, however, a few instances of women treating men. At Westminster Abbey a physician named **Joan** (*fl.* 1386–1389?) dispensed medicines to the monks in 1386-7 and a possibly identical Joan performed the same role in 1388-9: **Joan** (*fl.* 1407–1409), who provided medicines for two Westminster monks in three successive years, is probably distinct from these. In 1374-5 an unnamed woman, who was evidently a surgeon, was called into the Westminster Infirmary after others had failed, to treat a monk for a condition that was probably an ulcerated shin-bone. English drawings survive of women performing bloodletting on men, but whether these women were primarily healers or, like most medieval English medical practitioners, performed medical duties only part-time, is not clear.

But the most remarkable testimony to the existence, and to some extent acceptance, of women healers occurs in 1421, when the university physicians, anxious to see a regulated profession dominated by themselves, petitioned Henry V to confine medical practice to those who had been licensed by the universities. The petition asked that all of England's sheriffs assemble every medical practitioner in the realm at either Oxford or Cambridge, for 'trewe and streyte examinacion' (*RotP*, 4.130). Anyone, man or woman, who continued to practise without the licence of a university would be subject to a fine or imprisonment. Women, in common with others who were not clergy, were now to be offered legitimacy as medical practitioners. FAYE GETZ

Sources C. H. Talbot and E. A. Hammond, *The medical practitioners in medieval England: a biographical register* (1965) • F. Getz, 'Medical practitioners in medieval England', *Social History of Medicine*, 3 (1990), 245–83 • E. J. Kealey, 'England's earliest women doctors', *Journal of the History of Medicine and Allied Sciences*, 40 (1985), 473–7 • M. H. Green, 'Obstetrical and gynecological texts in Middle English', *Studies in the Age of Chaucer*, 14 (1992), 53–88 • P. M. Jones, *Medieval medical miniatures* (1984) • H. Kurath and S. M. Kuhn, eds., *Middle English dictionary*, [13 vols.] (1952–2001) • L. W. Stone and W. Rothwell, eds., *Anglo-Norman dictionary* (1985) • R. E. Latham, ed., *Dictionary of medieval Latin from British sources* (1975) • F. M. Getz, 'The faculty of medicine before 1500', *Hist. U. Oxf.* 2: *Late med. Oxf.*, 373–405 • E. Power, *Medieval English nunneries, c.1275–1535* (1922) • *RotP*, vol. 4 • *CPR*, 1348–50, 561 [Pernell of Rasyn]

Women traders and artisans in London (*act. c.***1200**–*c.***1500**) formed a significant group within the city's workforce at every social level. City custom allowed them considerable economic opportunities. No more than men are they commonly recorded before about 1250, but thereafter wills and the records alike of city government and of London's craft and trading associations bring their activities into ever sharper focus, in spite of the difficulties created by the instability of female surnames, resulting from migration and multiple marriages. The greater visibility of women in London's economic life in the later middle ages is not solely the result of the thickening of the records, however. The demographic decline which reduced the population of the city by half between 1300 and 1400 created an acute labour shortage which threw women more prominently into the trained labour force. So they are to be found not only at the poor and unskilled end of the labour market, but also training as apprentices, as independent artisans, managers of craft workshops, and heads of trading households.

Hucksters and prostitutes At the poorest end of the economic scale women were found in London selling a variety of goods, but particularly foods that they had grown or cooked themselves, or had bought in a city market, or from a wholesaler, and then sold on. Such women were known as hucksters, a word that appears about 1300 and which applied primarily, but not exclusively, to women. Hucksters appear in the mayor's court pursuing debtors or being pursued by their creditors. Most of them are only names, but **Joan Staunford** (*fl.* 1379), who leased one of the stalls at the Cheapside Cross, can be more precisely identified. She was a frutestere, a seller of fruit, with an eight-year-old son but, apparently, deserted by her husband. In October of the year in which his mother had leased the stall, young John had been bequeathed 40s. in the will of John Cornwaille, a currier. In order that she might receive the money on her son's behalf, in December 1379 the mayor and chamberlain entrusted Joan with the guardianship of John and the 40s., also providing two men to act as her sureties. Sixteen years later, when John would have been twenty-four, he came to court to seek his 40s. By this time his mother and one of her sureties were dead, so the court decided that the money should be levied from the tenements of the remaining surety. Hucksters were quite often in trouble in the mayor's court, not least when they engaged in the ubiquitous trade of selling second-hand clothing. Fourteen of the sixty-eight Londoners convicted in 1321 of selling clothes at the evening markets held at Cornhill and in Cheapside (contrary to civic regulation because it was too dark to examine the goods properly) were women.

Women hucksters were also sometimes convicted of deliberately practising to deceive the ignorant customer. **Alice Causton** (*fl.* 1364) used unsealed measures when she sold beer and thickened their bottoms with 1½ inches of pitch. She was condemned to stand in the thewe (a special pillory for women in which they were confined by the neck) and half the false measure was tied to the pillory beside her; the other half was to remain at the guildhall. Other women worked in London as prostitutes. Many of those involved in this trade must have been poor, but not all were. **Alison Boston** (*fl.* 1424) was prosecuted by the city authorities and convicted not for being a prostitute herself but for having taken on a girl as an apprentice whom she then hired out for 'immoral purposes'. She was condemned to the pillory, where she stood for an hour on three market days and was brought from prison to the pillory 'with pipes and minstralcy' to make her humiliation as public as possible. Displayed alongside her was a bill written in English to explain her offence, and this was carefully copied into the city's letter-book.

Female apprentices The city authorities may have been anxious to make a public example of Alison Boston because she had betrayed the trust and obligations required of the mistress of an apprentice. As early as 1276 girl apprentices were found in the city, but the surge in their numbers came in the century after 1350, when thirty-eight are recorded. It is remarkable, considering how few medieval apprentice indentures survive, that five of the thirteen from London concern girls. In these the girls were bound as apprentices to learn their craft for seven years on exactly the same terms as boys. **Eleanor Fyncham** (*fl.* 1447) was the daughter of Simon Fyncham, a prosperous parvenu gentleman from the Norfolk parish of Fincham, where he farmed 400 acres and contributed substantially to the building of the church tower; her brothers were 'parish gentry', London lawyers, and merchants. On 27 February 1447 Eleanor's brother John

Fyncham, 'gentleman', acted as her surety when she sealed (with her own seal) the indenture in which she bound herself to **Anne Rotheley** (*d.* 1496), 'throwester de serico' or silkwoman, the wife of the London goldsmith William Rotheley (*d.* 1469). The Rotheleys had several apprentices but do not appear always to have treated them well. Anne had been married before to another goldsmith, Richard Spencer (*d.* 1442x5), and in this marriage also had traded *sole* as a silk throwster and taken on apprentices. One of these, Joan Bosoun, the daughter of another goldsmith, sued Anne for failing to enrol her indentures at the guildhall within the first year of her term. William Rotheley served several times as warden between 1444 and 1465, but in 1468 he was fined by the Goldsmiths' court for having shut his 'mayde' (perhaps a reference to one of his wife's apprentices) out of his house at night, so that she had to borrow money to buy a night's lodging at the Pewter Pot. Such behaviour was thought to reflect badly on the Goldsmiths' fellowship and to be 'against all humanity', and Rotheley was fined 3s. 4d.

The city authorities repeatedly showed themselves concerned to ensure that apprentices were properly treated, and their indentures enrolled at the guildhall within the first year of their service. Such precautions were needed not least because girl apprentices might be very young. **Agnes Tickhill** (*fl.* 1410–1417), the daughter of the successful saddler William Tickhill, was placed as an apprentice with the wiredrawer William Celler for a term of fourteen years. This apprenticeship had been arranged by Thomasina March, a widow not free of the city who lived in Buckinghamshire. In 1417 William Tickhill, claiming that his daughter had been indentured without his knowledge or consent, complained that William Celler had left the city and had not taught Agnes his craft, nor had he enrolled her indentures at the guildhall. Agnes was now living with William Celler's wife, Joan, who claimed to be teaching her the craft of a cardmaker (for carding wool) for which she had been properly apprenticed the previous Christmas. Joan admitted that Agnes had originally been apprenticed under age, that Thomasina March had no authority over the girl, and that her indentures had not been enrolled at the beginning of her term. Having decided to examine Joan and Agnes separately, the court learnt that Agnes, who was still under age, had sealed the indentures at Christmas only because she was threatened with a beating, and that she would prefer to return to her father. She was therefore released from her indentures. If she was still under age (younger than fourteen) in 1417, then Agnes can have been only six or seven when first apprenticed to the Cellers in 1410.

Female servants Parents valued apprenticeship for their daughters because it provided girls with patrons and business contacts and secured for them status and authority within the working community. It was an investment for the future, raising the prospect of a 'better class' of husband (probably a citizen of London), while enabling the woman thus trained to keep herself either within, or following, her marriage. Many more girls, however, would have worked as servants for an annual wage. Such women might or might not have lived in their employers' house-holds, and their commitment would have been short-term, under arrangements rarely formalized in writing. Because the mayor and aldermen were not directly responsible for contracts between masters and servants, cases involving female servants rarely appear in the records of the city courts, but a few cases were brought by petition to the attention of the lord chancellor. Richard Swan (d. 1492), a prosperous London skinner, employed **Joan Chamberlain** (d. 1504?) as his servant on a one-year contract. She complained to the chancellor that Swan had tried to make her work for him beyond the agreed year by withholding 10s. of the wages due to her. Describing herself on this occasion as 'of London, gentilwoman' (PRO, C 1/61/377), she may have been the Joan Chamberlain, 'widow, citizen, brewer and freewoman' who drew up her will in 1504 (Sharpe, 2.644). If so, her stand against her employer earlier in her career suggests that she was a woman of mettle, just as her will attests her business suc-cess—it includes a bequest of £20 to be held in trust for the marriage of her niece, then acting as Joan's own servant.

Masters, too, might feel aggrieved. **Alice Shevyngton** (fl. late 15th cent.) had worked for William Gregory (prob-ably a skinner) for three years on annual contracts and received 16s. per annum. But although Gregory paid her wages regularly, in the fourth year Alice absented herself from his household for days and weeks at a time, 'pretend-ing herself to have connyng in the tretyng of sore ighen [eyes]' (PRO, C 1/66/264). To prevent her master from tak-ing action against her, Alice was herself suing him for debt, and such was her popularity in the community that Gregory doubted whether he would be able to secure a fair trial. It is not easy to understand why Gregory was so upset. He may have been old and ill, but he may also have resented Alice's independent stance. Servants might be of the same age as apprentices, but they could also be consid-erably older, and as such skilled, knowledgeable, married, and independent. Their relationship with their masters and mistresses was that of employer and employee, rather than that between a surrogate parent and child envisaged in apprentice indentures.

Femes soles It was unusual for women in medieval London to remain unmarried. A married woman could choose to trade as a feme sole independently of her husband and thus take on her own apprentices, run her own business, lease property, and sue and be sued for debt. But both hus-band and wife had to be free of the city. Both as wives and as widows women claimed to be freewomen of the city, with a status that carried privileges both within the city and further afield. The earliest reference to a widow iden-tifying herself thus occurs in the will of **Katherine Pole** (d. 1387), drawn up in July 1387, where she is described as a 'citizen and freewoman of the city of London' (Sharpe, 2.263). Katherine was the daughter of Richard Lacer, mer-cer and mayor of London, and had married a London citi-zen, John Pole. Both her father and her husband appear to have died in the plague year of 1361. Katherine, together with her sister Alice, was later in dispute with her father's executors about the administration of his estate, and she

may have asserted her status as a freewoman in her will in order to make more secure her bequest of a tenement to Elsyngspital at Cripplegate.

It may have been that women only really needed to trade as femes soles when they chose to follow crafts dif-ferent from those of their husbands, since if they followed the same craft it would have been difficult to distinguish the trade of one from that of the other. Many of the women who brewed as femes soles, for instance, were married to men who practised other crafts. Where a woman is found as a feme sole following the same craft as her husband it is usually as a widow who has taken over her husband's business. **Mary Lodewyk** (d. 1407), the widow of the London tallow-chandler Robert Lodewyk, who had died in 1406, described herself in her own will, drawn up in the following year, as libera of the city of Lon-don. To her apprentice Andrew she left the moulds for making white and green candles with other tools, and also a covered cup decorated with popinjays. She was also able to make substantial bequests to her sister and god-daughter, to her servants, to a range of individuals includ-ing 'Alice nedilwyfe' and 'Florence, a poor woman' (com-missary will, Guildhall MS 9171/2, fol. 98), and to anchor-ites.

Women who traded as femes soles are most visible when they were sued for debt. At the time that her hus-band Thomas (d. 1395) was serving as an alderman **Maud Ireland** (fl. 1380) traded as a feme sole and 'according to the usage of the city is bound to answer her own contracts' (CLRO, mayor's court files, 1/123); in January 1380 she was sued for a debt of £4 2s. 6d. owed to Bartholomew Beauvais for white silk bought for her by her servant Alice Waldene. **Margaret Houghton** (fl. 1441), whose husband, John, was the city's water bailiff between 1431 and 1444, traded sole as a shepster (a cutter of clothes, or dressmaker), and in 1441 was sued by the mercer William Thornhill, for 8s. owed for woollen cloth. But some women made a public statement of their sole status. On 15 November 1457 **Isa-belle Sayer** (d. 1473) came before the mayor and aldermen and said that she practised the art of a silkwoman and no other, and asked to be allowed to 'merchandise' without her husband, and to answer sole for her own contracts according to city custom. This was granted and entered as a record. Some time later Isabelle seems to have left the city and moved to West Bedfont in Stanwell, Middlesex, where she drew up her modest but self-sufficient will in 1473. She left the residue of her goods to her son William but made no mention of a husband. By her craft she had been able to maintain her independence and make bequests to the parish church, to various lights there, and to the fraternity of the Virgin.

Most of the women who appeared in the mayor's court to answer pleas of debt were probably doing business on quite a small scale. They may none the less have been able to read and write. There is good evidence that London women could write English, and doubtless read it also. **Joan Coggenhoe** (fl. 1423) was sufficiently skilled at writ-ing to be able to forge a deed, and was consequently con-demned to stand next to the pillory (not actually in it because she was too old), while a text of her forgery, together with an explanation of Joan's crime, was to be hung around her neck. There is a presumption in this case, as in that of the procuress Alison Boston, that those who saw these women in the pillory would be able to read the accounts of their offences that were displayed with them. And the groups that gathered round such ill doers in the market place would certainly have included women, at whom these deterrent accounts would have been particularly directed.

Business women and merchants In the case of other women, whose business dealings were substantial, the presumption of literacy is even stronger. **Agnes Ramsey** (*d.* in or after 1399), the daughter of the famous master mason William *Ramsey, and whose husband, Robert Huberd, was also a mason, ran her father's business after his death in 1349, and drew up a contract with Edward II's widow, Queen Isabella, for the construction of Edward's tomb in the London Greyfriars at a cost of over £100. Styled 'Domina Agnes Ramsey' in the accounts from 1377 of the fraternity of the Holy Trinity in the parish of St Botolph, Aldersgate (where her father's workshop and her own was situated), Agnes continued to collect her father's debts and to engage in property transactions until 1399. **Matilda Penne** (*d.* 1392/3) as the widow of a skinner ran her late husband William's business for twelve years after his death. From her shop in Wood Street she maintained contacts with other citizens engaged in the clothing trade, and there she trained her own apprentices and employed male servants (and also, perhaps, a female scrivener to keep the accounts). A woman of convinced piety, she based her religious life upon St Peter's Church, Wood Street, and it was there that she required to be buried. In her will, drawn up on 4 November 1392 and proved on 3 February 1393, Matilda remembered forty-three people, twenty men and twenty-three women, ranging from the wives of city aldermen to monks of Westminster Abbey to little-known neighbours. Disposing of cash bequests totalling between £60 and £70, and of valuable plate and furnishings, it is a document that testifies both to her independence and to her success in trading as 'a woman skinner, a shopkeeper and craftswoman in her own right' (Veale, 54).

The workshops of founders (who made brass pots as well as church bells) were quite often managed by women. Twice during the fifteenth century the notable bell foundry outside Aldgate was run by widows who added a distinctive lozenge to the mark of their late husbands to signify the change of management. One of these was **Joan Hill** (*d.* 1441), whose husband, Richard Hill, cast bells that still survive in churches in eleven counties, from Cornwall to Rutland. When he died in 1440 Joan took over the business, for instance entering into a contract with the parishioners of Faversham to cast five new bells for their church and to remake any bells found to be defective. In her own will, made less than a year later, Joan made bequests to four male apprentices, two female servants, six male servants, four further men whose tasks were not specified, a specialized 'bell-maker', a clerk, and the daughter of

another founder. She left her bell-making equipment to her daughter, another Joan, and the latter's husband, Henry Jordan, and clearly expected that they would carry on the business. **Joan Reynold** (*d.* 1483) was the widow of Robert Reynold, a master of the craft who had died in 1476. She continued to run the business for another six years and in her will made bequests of tools to named servants and apprentices. Whereas her husband gave a maser weighing 9 ounces to the Founders' Company, Joan gave a double cup with a handle 'over gilted' weighing twice as much. These and others like them were remarkable women, who made their mark in the commercial world of London and won respect within their social milieux.

Women in the companies and in public office The surviving records of the craft guilds and companies acknowledge the presence of women within the craft structure, but their role was not a formal one. Much of the evidence relates to women sharing in the religious, charitable, and social aspects of company life. The Skinners prayed for dead sisters as well as brothers of the craft, and the ordinances of many crafts and companies refer to sisters as well as brothers. Women who prospered through their links with the crafts remembered the latter in their wills. **Joan Bradbury** (*c.*1450–1530) married as her second husband the mercer Thomas Bradbury. It was probably with her encouragement that he started to become closely involved in the government of the city, culminating in his election as mayor in 1509. His death in office early in 1510 led to his widow's endowing a perpetual chantry for his soul (and also for that of her first husband, Thomas Bodley (*d.* 1492), a merchant tailor) in the church of St Stephen, Coleman Street. The Mercers' Company agreed to act as its trustees, and in return Joan gave her 'great house' in Cheapside for use as the company hall. A woman of strong personality and considerable managerial abilities, her charitable activities extended to the endowment of a grammar school at Walden, Essex, where her brother was vicar. But although it is clear that the social activities of the companies included women—the Mercers several times held their St Thomas's tide banquet in Joan Bradbury's house before it was finally conveyed to them—the participation of women in the craft and trade organization of London was not confined solely to their charitable and social functions. Many guilds acknowledged that it was desirable to encourage widows to continue to maintain the workshops or businesses of their dead husbands and to train their apprentices. It is apparent that tanners left the tools of their craft, and their stalls in the establishment known as the Tanner's Seld, to their widows almost always in trust for their children, or on condition that these widows married within the craft: they were guardians of a communal resource.

In the fifteenth century, when labour was scarce, crafts and trades recognized, albeit grudgingly, the presence of women workers within their guilds and companies. In this respect the Brewers' Company may, however, have been unusual; in the early fifteenth century a third of all brewers paying quarterage to the company were women. **Agnes Bugge** (*fl.* 1417–1430), the wife of the draper

Stephen Bugge, paid her dues independently to the Brewers' Company throughout the 1420s. When Stephen died in 1428-30 he bequeathed 'his' brewhouse to his widow, and in law it was undoubtedly his property, yet it is clear that it was she who had been the brewer while he was active as a draper. Agnes's success in her profession may be deduced from her response to the 'voluntary assessment' whereby in 1419/20 the brewers raised money to fund a dispute with the city authorities; at 20s. hers was the largest single contribution. Companies that recognized the existence of women workers over and above the wives and daughters sometimes specified in their ordinances were, nevertheless, apt to restrict their access to craft skills. If women sometimes flourished as traders and artisans, this owed much to their ability to create informal networks of female friends, servants, apprentices, daughters, dependants, and patrons, networks that supplemented the formal craft relationships. In the same way women very seldom held public office, in the sense of office in which they might have been placed in authority over a man. It was exceptional that in 1372 women were sworn alongside their husbands to supervise the dyeing of leather.

In 1422 the jurors of Queenhythe complained that the official measurer of oysters, John Ely, had farmed his office to women 'who know not [how to do it]; nor is it worship to this city that women should have such things in governance' (Thomas and Jones, 3.138-9). In spite of this attitude there were occasions when widows were allowed to carry on their husbands' official posts. **Katherine Bury** (*fl.* 1346-1348?), whose husband, Walter, had been the king's smith at the Tower, where he was succeeded by his son Andrew, was paid 8*d.* a day to 'keep up the king's forge in the Tower and carry on the work of the forge' while her son was away on the Crécy campaign (*CPR, 1345-8*, 131). She may well have been the Katherine *fabra* who in 1348 was paid for refurbishing the masons' tools at Westminster. Even more strikingly, **Alice Holford** (*d.* 1455) acted as bailiff of London Bridge for over twenty years after the death of her husband, Nicholas, 'citizen and textwriter', in 1434. The bailiff collected the tolls due from boats passing through the bridge and from carts crossing over it into London, a complicated task since the charges varied according to the goods and the person transporting them. In her will, drawn up in May 1455, Alice left a missal (which may have been the work of her late husband) for the chapel on the bridge, but only on condition that the master and bridgewards granted the house in which she had lived there to her son Nicholas, at the same rent (32s. per annum) that she had paid. The bridgewards were also to pay 5 marks to her executors. In a world in which masculine control was usually taken for granted, the firm, almost commanding, tone of Alice's will suggests a woman confident of her authority and bargaining power. CAROLINE M. BARRON

Sources CLRO, journals, vols. 1-6 • mayor's court file, CLRO, 1/123 • archdeaconry and commissary court wills, GL • PRO, chancery, early chancery proceedings, C 1/61/377; C 1/66/264 • R. W. Chambers and M. Daunt, eds., *A book of London English, 1384-1425*

(1931) • H. T. Riley, ed., *Memorials of London and London life in the XIIIth, XIVth, and XVth centuries* (1868) • R. R. Sharpe, ed., *Calendar of wills proved and enrolled in the court of husting, London, AD 1258 – AD 1688*, 2 vols. (1889-90) • R. R. Sharpe, ed., *Calendar of letter-books preserved in the archives of the corporation of the City of London*, [12 vols.] (1899-1912), vols. A-L • A. H. Thomas and P. E. Jones, eds., *Calendar of plea and memoranda rolls preserved among the archives of the corporation of the City of London at the Guildhall*, 6 vols. (1926-61) • *CPR, 1345-8* • C. M. Barron and A. F. Sutton, eds., *Medieval London widows, 1300-1500* (1994) • E. Veale, 'Mathilda Penne, skinner (*d.* 1392-3)', *Medieval London widows, 1300-1500*, ed. C. M. Barron and A. F. Sutton (1994), 47-54 • A. B. Beaven, ed., *The aldermen of the City of London, temp. Henry III-[1912]*, 2 vols. (1908-13) • J. Bennett, 'Women and men in the Brewers' Guild of London, c. 1420', *The salt of common life … essays presented to J. Ambrose Raftis*, ed. E. DeWindt (1995), 181-232 • J. Harvey and A. Oswald, *English mediaeval architects: a biographical dictionary down to 1550*, 2nd edn (1984) • M. J. Hettinger, 'Defining the servant: legal and extra-legal terms of employment in fifteenth-century England', *The work of work: servitude, slavery and labour in medieval England*, ed. A. J. Frantzen and D. Moffat (1994), 206-28 • P. Maddern, '"Best trusted friends": concepts and practices of friendship among the fifteenth-century Norfolk gentry', *England in the fifteenth century*, ed. N. Rogers (1994), 100-17 • T. Reddaway and L. Walker, *Early history of the Goldsmiths' Company* (1975) • S. L. Thrupp, *The merchant class of medieval London, 1300-1500*, pbk edn (1962)

Archives CLRO, journals, vols. 1-6 | PRO, C 1/61/377 [Joan Chamberlain]

Women's section of the Air Transport Auxiliary (*act. 1940-1945*)

was a civilian organization that came into existence, after several false starts, on 1 January 1940. Its members' male counterparts—experienced pilots who were ineligible for service with the RAF—had been employed very soon after the outbreak of war, initially using requisitioned Tiger Moths to transport mail, medical supplies, and civilian dignitaries, but before long ferrying the larger and more sophisticated aircraft being developed for the RAF from factory to airbase. But, while many women had participated in the flying craze of the 1930s or had in 1938 taken advantage of the government's Civil Air Guard scheme to learn to fly at subsidized rates, the question of whether they too should use this experience and knowledge in a wartime context was highly contentious. The editor of *The Aeroplane* was not alone in believing that 'the menace is the woman who thinks that she ought to be flying a high-speed bomber when she really has not the intelligence to scrub the floor of a hospital properly' (Curtis, 12).

That the women's section of the Air Transport Auxiliary (ATA) overcame this opposition so completely, growing to a strength of 166 pilots who between them flew every possible kind of aircraft except flying boats, under exactly the same conditions as their male counterparts, was due to the determination, skill, and persistence of some of the early members of the organization and in particular of their senior commander, Pauline *Gower (1910-1947). A highly experienced professional pilot, her position as the only female member of the committee on the control of flying (established in 1938 to examine the regulations governing flight) had afforded her a potentially useful introduction to some of the men who would shortly oversee the use of aircraft in war. When war was declared, therefore, on 3 September 1939, she lost little time in proposing that women should be able to join the newly formed ATA, and held out against opposition from senior figures in the Air Ministry until in November she secured authorization to recruit the first all-woman ferry pool, to be based at Hatfield. If the scope and terms of this fledgeling women's section were a disappointment—just eight women, who were restricted to flying Tiger Moths and were paid 20 per cent less than their male counterparts—then Gower was prepared to bide her time. Acutely aware, as were all the first recruits, that the slightest mistake risked stalling the expansion of the organization, her tact and judgement were impeccable, and through a series of patiently anticipated and perfectly timed interventions she succeeded in securing for her ever-growing pool of pilots a degree of formal equality of terms and conditions unmatched by any other wartime organization. In May 1940 she negotiated a small increase in numbers and the opportunity for the most experienced to take conversion courses to fly all types of non-operational aircraft. It was to be another year, however, before the most significant breakthrough—the agreement, in July 1941, that women should be allowed to fly operational planes—and by the end of the war they had flown everything from fighter planes such as the Spitfire to the huge Halifax and Lancaster four-engined bombers. Not only that, but from May 1943 they also received equal pay for their trouble.

All ATA pilots were required to fly without radio or other navigational aid bar visual contact with the ground, and ferry trips could routinely involve circumnavigating the balloon barrage around a heavily defended factory to deliver a plane hundreds of miles away to a new and often camouflaged airfield consisting of little more than a strip of grass. Furthermore, successful completion of a conversion course for a generic type of aircraft meant that they were required to fly, sight unseen, any model that came within that specification with no more introduction than that afforded by the ATA handling notes that every pilot carried and that listed the idiosyncrasies of the 140 different types of aircraft that they might be called upon to fly. In order to maximize time and available flying personnel each ferry pool's schedule of flights was drawn up and co-ordinated centrally by the operations officer and her team of ground crew, who sought to ensure not only that the maximum number of planes were successfully delivered to their destinations but that pilots were retrieved at the end of a day's ferrying by an ATA 'taxi' flight and delivered back to base.

The celebrated 'first eight', who joined the ATA on 1 January 1940, were all extremely experienced pre-war pilots and qualified flying instructors, and most were to become the backbone of the women's section. Youngest of the group was Joan *Hughes (1918–1993), who had become Britain's youngest qualified pilot at the age of seventeen and claimed that she would go without food and water rather than not fly. Having worked as an instructor for the Civil Air Guard she concentrated on instructing as the ATA expanded, but as well as being the only woman to instruct on all types of aircraft she clocked up an impressive ferrying tally and was one of only eleven

women to convert to four-engined bombers. Winifred (Winnie) Crossley, dashing and convivial, had worked for five years towing advertising banners and performing stunts with an air circus. Once in the ATA she broke important new ground when she was given the onerous and hugely significant task of being the first woman to fly an operational aircraft, and she too went on to convert successfully to four-engined bombers. Another four-engined bomber pilot was Marion *Wilberforce (1902–1995), who combined the flying necessary to complete that conversion with successful leadership as second in command and then commanding officer of the ferry pools at Hatfield and, later, Cosford. Rosemary Theresa *Du Cros, née Rees (1901–1994), a former ballet dancer, most closely resembled the stereotypical wealthy private pilot of the 1930s. She, too, successfully combined administrative authority, as second in command of Hamble ferry pool, with conversion to four-engined bombers. Margaret (Margie) *Fairweather (1901–1944) had over 1000 hours' flying experience, mostly gained touring Europe in her own plane, and was also instructing for the Civil Air Guard before the war. Quiet and self-effacing but an exceptionally able pilot, she too was one of the first to fly operational planes and later to convert to four-engined bombers. Tragically she was also the only one of the first eight not to survive the war when, on 4 August 1944, her plane suffered engine failure and she crash-landed.

Another early recruit was also one of the sixteen members of the ATA women's section who lost their lives during the war. This was Amy *Johnson (1903–1941), arguably Britain's most famous and most experienced female pilot, killed on 5 January 1941 when her plane crashed into the Thames. Notable among the third wave of recruits, who joined in June and July 1940, was Margaret Wyndham *Gore (1913–1993), who in 1938 had taken a part-time job in Smithfield market to finance flying lessons. Less experienced than most of the early arrivals, she was nevertheless a brilliant natural pilot who successfully converted to four-engined bombers, and as commanding officer of the women's pool at Hamble was a wise, calm, admirably efficient, and extremely popular leader.

The ATA flag was lowered for the last time on 30 November 1945. The pilots of the women's section had proved themselves faithful to the ATA motto, *Aetheris avidi* ('eager for the air'), but, as many were to find, neither their eagerness nor their experience was a passport to a career in aviation in the postwar climate. Pauline Gower, to whom the women's section of the ATA owed so much, tragically died giving birth to twin sons in 1947. That the members of the ATA women's section largely remain the forgotten pilots of the Second World War is no true reflection of her achievement or that of the remarkable organization that she led with such inspiration and force.

TESSA STONE

Sources L. Curtis, *Forgotten pilots* (1971) · M. Fahie, *A harvest of memories* (1995) · D. Barnato Walker, *Spreading my wings* (1994) · *The Times* (7 Aug 1944) · *The Times* (4 July 1947) · *The Times* (1 Sept 1993) · *The Times* (4 Sept 1993) · *The Times* (22 March 1994) · A. King, *Golden wings* (1956) · R. Du Cros, *ATA girl* (1983) · J. Moggridge, *Woman pilot*

(1957) • *WWW* • *DNB* • M. De Bunsen, *Mount up with wings* (1960) • V. Volkersz, *The sky and I* (1956)
Archives PRO, files, AVIA 27 • Royal Air Force Museum, Hendon, personnel files
Likenesses photographs, IWM

Womersley, John Ronald (1907–1958), mathematician, was born on 20 June 1907 in Worrall Street, Morely, Yorkshire, son of George William Womersley, grocer, and his wife, Ruth (formerly Gledhill). He was educated at Morely grammar school (1917–25) before going to Imperial College, London, where in 1928 he gained a first-class degree in mathematics. He spent two further years at Imperial, engaged on hydrodynamics research and gaining a diploma of Imperial College in 1930, then joined the British Cotton Industry Research Association at the Shirley Institute in Manchester to work on the application of mathematical methods to a range of textile problems. There Womersley became interested in the application of mathematical statistics to industrial problems and in statistical quality control. In 1936 he collaborated with D. R. Hartree to devise a method for solving partial differential equations suitable for application to the differential analyser which Hartree had built at Manchester University. This was Womersley's first introduction to large-scale computing machines.

In 1937 Womersley joined the armaments research department, Woolwich. As part of his work on internal ballistics he initiated a statistical analysis of cordite proof records which led to changes in charge adjustments made to certain weapons. During this time he built a small differential analyser for ballistics calculations which was destroyed during the war. In 1944 he joined the British Association mathematical tables committee, serving until 1948.

With the increase in mass production during the Second World War, and because of his interest in applying statistics to industrial problems, Womersley was asked in July 1942 to set up a Ministry of Supply advisory service on statistical quality control (later known as SR 17). By the end of the war this organization had a staff of approximately forty statisticians and did much to introduce sampling inspection methods to British industry.

Following his success at SR 17 Womersley was offered the post of first superintendent of the National Physical Laboratory (NPL) mathematics division at Teddington, Middlesex, in 1944. This division had two main roles: first to provide a mathematical service, a task similar to that performed by SR 17; and second to build an electronic computer, a task for which Womersley was perhaps less well qualified.

Before taking up his post at the NPL Womersley was given security clearance to travel to the United States to become one of the first overseas visitors to the ENIAC project and to hear about the first proposals to build an electronic stored program computer. He was also involved in one of the first international computer conferences, which took place in the United States in October 1945. Alan Turing joined the mathematics division and designed the ACE computer, but Womersley seems to

have failed to grasp the differences between Turing's radical ideas and the American proposals. Consequently the building of ACE was delayed and in 1947 Turing left the project. A prototype machine, the Pilot ACE, was operational by late 1950 (significantly behind the computers at Cambridge and Manchester) but by then Womersley had left the NPL.

In September 1950 Womersley accepted a post with BTM Ltd (a forerunner of ICL Ltd) and his appointment led to the development of the HEC range of machines based on the work of A. D. Booth at Birkbeck College, London. There is some dispute as to whether Womersley's appointment with BTM was successful and he left the company in 1954 to go back to mathematics. In that year Womersley worked with a team from St Bartholomew's Hospital on a mathematical investigation into blood flow in arteries which resulted in papers published in the *Journal of Physiology* (1954 and 1955) and in the *Philosophical Magazine* (1955). He continued this work when he took up a mathematical post in 1955 with the US Air Force at Wright Field, Dayton, Ohio.

Womersley was a tall, heavily built, and generally well liked man. He was always proud of his Yorkshire origins and never completely lost his accent despite living away from Yorkshire for all of his working life. He returned to Britain in 1957 for a serious operation from which he never fully recovered. He died at University Hospital, Columbus, Ohio, on 7 March 1958 leaving a widow, Jean (formerly Jordan), of whom nothing is known. The couple had three daughters, Barbara, Ruth, and Marion. Although not a brilliant mathematician, Womersley's real skill was his ability to foresee how mathematical techniques could be used to solve problems and to set up organizations to exploit those techniques. MARY CROARKEN

Sources F. Smithies, *Journal of the London Mathematical Society*, 34 (1959), 370–72 • *The Times* (19 March 1958), 13 • C. G. Darwin, *Nature*, 181 (1958), 1240 • personnel records, National Physical Laboratory, Teddington • M. G. Croarken, *Early scientific computing in Britain* (1990) • M. Campbell-Kelly, *ICL—a business and technical history* (1989) • private information (2004) • H. H. Goldstine, *The computer from Pascal to von Neumann* (1972) • G. A. Barnard and R. L. Plackett, 'Statistics in the United Kingdom, 1939–45', *A celebration of statistics*, ed. A. C. Atkinson and S. E. Fienberg (1985), 41–5 • d. cert.
Wealth at death apparently widow applied to British government for financial help after his death: private information (2004)

Womock [Womack], **Laurence** (d. 1686), bishop of St David's and religious controversialist, was the son of Laurence Womock (d. 1656), rector of North and South Lopham. The Womocks were a clerical dynasty. Arthur Womock was rector of the Lophams from 1578 to 1607 or 1608 when his son Laurence succeeded to these livings and simultaneously held the rectory of Fersfield. Laurence's son Arthur was rector of Fersfield from about 1642 to 1685. Laurence Womock contested his sequestration from the Lopham livings during the 1640s but had been replaced as minister there by 1654. His son, the younger Laurence, was admitted to Corpus Christi College, Cambridge, on 4 July 1629, matriculating on 15 December. He became a scholar on Sir Nicholas Bacon's foundation, graduated BA in 1632, was ordained deacon on 21 September 1634, and proceeded MA in 1639.

Although not ordained to the priesthood Womock seems to have acted for some time as chaplain to Lord Paget, and to have had an offer of a benefice in the west of England, where he acquired some fame by his preaching. He later claimed to have been the royalist chaplain at Hereford for the whole of the civil war and to have been plundered, sequestered, and imprisoned four times. Clement Barksdale, the Cotswold poet, addressed verses to him in his *Nympha libethris* (1651), headed 'after the taking of Hereford 1645', which allude to his powerful preaching and to 'a spice of prelacy' to which his enemies took exception (Barksdale, 9–10). The triers admitted him to the rectory of Icklingham, Suffolk, in 1654.

In the summer of 1660 Womock obtained the prebendal stall of Preston in Hereford Cathedral and, after petitioning for the office, on 8 September 1660 he was made archdeacon of Suffolk. On 22 September in the same year he was installed in the sixth prebendal stall at Ely. In 1661 the degree of DD was conferred upon him by royal letters and on 24 July 1662 he was ordained as a priest. In 1662 he was presented to the rectory of Horningsheath, near Bury St Edmunds, to which was added in 1663 the small Suffolk rectory of Boxford. He contributed £10 towards the purchase of an organ for his college chapel.

Womock married first, at Westly Bradford on 18 November 1668, a widow, Anne Aylmer of Bury. He married second, at St Bartholomew-the-Less, London, on 25 April 1670, Katherine Corbett of Norwich, spinster, aged forty. She survived her husband and was still living in October 1697. Womock's only known child was with Anne Aylmer, and his will refers to 'Anne my late daughter deceased', a daughter who, like her father, was buried in St Margaret's, Westminster (PRO, PROB 11/382, fol. 287v).

Although Womock was no doubt assiduous in his duties as minister and archdeacon—evidence survives of his eagerness to thwart presbyterian patrons from appointing semi-conforming incumbents—he made his way in the church through his dogged self-promotion and his relentlessly controversial writings. His first publication, in 1641, was a defence of set liturgies and this was a theme to which he returned in a series of tracts at the Restoration. In the last years of the interregnum he debated Arminianism and then the solemn league and covenant with Richard Baxter, Henry Hickman, and Zachary Crofton, and throughout the 1660s and 1670s published a steady stream of sermons and other works asserting the need for strict conformity and loyalty to the Anglican establishment. During the exclusion crisis Womock waded in to assert the rights of the church and in defence of the tory cause: he argued for the historical rights of bishops to sit in capital cases such as Danby's trial, he lambasted whig grand juries, and he heaped vituperation on Daniel Whitby who had dared to propose a measure of compromise with dissent. The zeal of his pamphlets recommended him to the tory commission for ecclesiastical promotions, and on 11 November 1683 he was consecrated as bishop of St David's in the archbishop's chapel at Lambeth, along with Francis Turner (to Rochester). On 3 January 1684 he resigned the archdeaconry of Suffolk to Godfrey King; he had resigned his Hereford prebend ten years earlier.

Womock, who does not appear to have gone into residence at St David's, died at his house in Westminster on 12 March 1686 and was buried in the north aisle of St Margaret's, Westminster, where a tablet upon a pillar commemorated him. His will, dated 18 February, was proved in March 1686. Womock had a fine collection of books and in his will instructed that they should go to his nephew's son (also Laurence Womock) if he should go to university. Otherwise the library was to be divided between his two nephews. His library was auctioned in Cambridge on 23 May 1687.   JOHN SPURR

Sources Venn, *Alum. Cant.*, 1/4.450 • W. Kennett, *A register and chronicle ecclesiastical and civil* (1728), 247, 451 • *Fasti Angl.* (Hardy) • *Calendar of the correspondence of Richard Baxter*, ed. N. H. Keeble and G. F. Nuttall, 2 (1991), letter 448 n. • R. A. Beddard, 'The commission for ecclesiastical promotions, 1681–4: an instrument of tory reaction', *HJ*, 10 (1967), 11–40, esp. 21–3 • *Walker rev.*, 275, 348 • *Hist. U. Oxf.* 4: *17th-cent. Oxf.* • C. Barksdale, *Nympha libethris* (1651), 9–10 • F. Blomefield and C. Parkin, *An essay towards a topographical history of the county of Norfolk*, [2nd edn], 11 vols. (1805–10), vol. 1, pp. 101, 236; vol. 3, pp. 654–5 • *Reliquiae Baxterianae, or, Mr Richard Baxter's narrative of the most memorable passages of his life and times*, ed. M. Sylvester, 1 vol. in 3 pts (1696) • B. Willis, *A survey of the cathedrals*, 3 vols. (1742), vol. 3, pp. 386–7 • Bodl. Oxf., MS Add. C 304 A, fol. 16 • Bodl. Oxf., MS Tanner 34, fols. 199, 226 • Bodl. Oxf., MS Tanner 36, fol. 88 • Bodl. Oxf., MS Tanner 37, fol. 225 • *Bibliotheca Womockiana* (1687) • PRO, PROB 11/382, quire 37, fols. 287r–288v • *DNB*
Archives Bodl. Oxf., corresp. | Suffolk RO, Bury St Edmunds, sermon notes

Wontner [*formerly* Smith]**, Arthur** (1875–1960), actor and theatre manager, was born in London on 21 January 1875, the eldest in the family of four sons and one daughter of Thomas Arthur Smith (1848–1920), partner in Wontner, Smith & Co., stocktakers in the City of London, and his wife, Emily Mary (1848–1923), daughter of Thomas Taylor Wontner, stocktaker. He was educated at the North London Collegiate School. His early life was regulated by strict discipline, his only contact with art being the family orchestra, to which each member contributed by playing a different instrument. His father intended him to follow his trade but, to his chagrin, his son chose to become an actor, supported by the odd pound from his mother. His father gave him nothing.

Giving up the family name (confirmed by deed poll in 1909), he called himself Arthur Wontner and started his career in the theatre in Ryde, Isle of Wight, on 18 April 1897, in *The Sorrows of Satan*. No manager or salary were recorded but he managed on his mother's contributions and joined Miss Sarah Thorne at the Theatre Royal, Margate, Kent, where he played thirty leading parts in eight months. He opened in London in 1898 in *The Three Musketeers*, and then toured for four years, adding fifty new parts to the first thirty. He was engaged by Herbert Beerbohm Tree to act in Australia, where he played in *The Eternal City* (1903–5), and he returned to London with 100 parts ready for performance. The first was *Raffles* (1906). He moved away from mere professionalism towards the art of a leading man in plays that required first-rate acting, performing in plays by Shakespeare, Oscar Wilde, H. G. Granville-Barker, Sir J. M. Barrie, and Ibsen. In 1929 Wontner went into management with Lady Mary Wyndham and then on his own. By his retirement in 1955 he had performed in over 200 plays. He also pursued a career in radio, television, and films, and he became famous in the role of Sherlock Holmes. His theatrical power emerges from the portrait by Alfred Cope at the Garrick Club of Wontner as Joseph Fouché in the Italian play *Napoleon*.

Wontner was twice married. In 1903 he married Rosecleer Alice Amelia Blanche Kingwell from Totnes, Devon, whom he met on the voyage to Australia. Her stage name was Rose Pendennis and she was the daughter of Henry Alfred Kingwell, who had an export business in New Zealand. They had two sons and one daughter. Rose died in 1943, and in 1947 he married Florence Eileen (*d.* 1970), daughter of Thomas Lainchbury, businessman. Wontner died on 10 July 1960 at his home, 177 Holland Park Avenue, London.   MARIUS GORING, *rev.*

Sources J. Parker, ed., *Who's who in the theatre*, 11th edn (1952) · *The Times* (12 July 1960) · personal knowledge (1993) · private information (1993) [H. Wontner] · Burke, *Gen. GB* (1969) · *CGPLA Eng. & Wales* (1960)
Archives SOUND BL NSA, performance recording
Likenesses A. Cope, portrait (as Joseph Fouché in *Napoleon*), Garr. Club
Wealth at death £21,763 12s. 10d.: probate, 7 Oct 1960, *CGPLA Eng. & Wales*

Wontner, Sir Hugh Walter Kingwell (1908–1992), hotelier, was born on 22 October 1908 at 62 Esmond Road, Acton, London, the elder son in the family of two sons and one daughter of Arthur *Wontner (1875–1960), actor and theatrical manager, and his first wife, Rosecleer Alice Amelia Blanche, *née* Kingwell (*d.* 1943), actress (her stage name was Rose Pendennis), daughter of Henry Alfred Kingwell, owner of an export business in New Zealand. He was born Hugh Walter Kingwell Wontner Smith, but the family dropped the name Smith by deed poll in 1909. He was educated at Oundle School, and went to France to learn French, working in the Hôtel Meurice in Paris, before joining the staff of the London chamber of commerce in 1927. In 1933 he was appointed general secretary of the Hotels and Restaurants Association of Great Britain, founded in 1910 by George Reeves-Smith, managing director of the Savoy Company, and chairman of the council of the association, and Wontner came into closer contact with him in 1936 when he became secretary of the London coronation accommodation committee, which was chaired by Reeves-Smith. On 4 January 1936 he married Catherine Irvin (*b.* 1911/12), only daughter of Thomas William Irvin, a lieutenant in the Gordon Highlanders who had died of wounds in France in 1916. They had two sons and one daughter.

In 1938 Reeves-Smith invited Wontner to join the Savoy Company as his assistant, and on his death in 1941 Wontner was appointed managing director of the Savoy. In 1948, after the death of the chairman, Rupert D'Oyly

Carte, the Savoy board elected Wontner chairman, a position he held until 1984, remaining managing director until 1979. He was elected life president in 1990.

Wontner took over the management of the Savoy Hotel at the height of the blitz: his office was destroyed by an exploding land-mine, and the hotel was damaged by bombs three times. Like all hoteliers in London, he faced the wartime problems of rationing, and the decline in the number of foreign visitors, but after the United States entered the war, the Savoy became popular with American officers and diplomats, and became a centre for American war correspondents. He became a spokesman for the catering trade in negotiations with government departments, and helped Lord Woolton, minister of food, to draw up the order imposing a 5s. limit on the price of a restaurant meal. In 1946 he was appointed chairman of a committee of the Ministry of Food to advise the government on the implications for the hotel and catering industries of the change from wartime rationing to peacetime conditions.

After the war Wontner was determined to restore the high standards of the Savoy, and of Claridge's and the Berkeley, the other hotels in the Savoy group, and put a lot of capital into repairing the war damage and improving and expanding the facilities. The Savoy became the scene of a number of lavish banquets, including that given by the Pilgrims of Great Britain to commemorate the unveiling of the statue of President Roosevelt in Grosvenor Square in April 1948, when the 900 guests included Princess Elizabeth and the duke of Edinburgh. In the same year George VI became the first British monarch to dine in a London hotel, and in 1953 on coronation day, 1400 guests attended the coronation ball. The Savoy bought the Connaught Hotel in 1956, and sold the Berkeley in the 1960s in order to build a new Berkeley Hotel, which opened in Knightsbridge in 1972. In 1970 Wontner added the Lancaster Hotel in Paris to the group.

Wontner was able to defeat at least three take-over bids. The first followed the attempt in 1953 by Charles Clore to buy the Savoy group: when his bid was rejected by the board, Clore sold his shares to the property developer Harold Samuel, who had his eye on the Berkeley Hotel, which occupied a valuable site in Piccadilly. Samuel was secretly buying large quantities of Savoy shares in preparation for a take-over bid, but this was thwarted by Wontner, who transferred control of the freehold of the Berkeley Hotel from the shareholders to the staff pension fund, until Samuel withdrew, and the freehold was transferred back to the Savoy. After this, Wontner devised a scheme to see off any future bids by changing the share structure: he created an issue of new 'B' shares carrying forty times as many votes as the old 'A' shares, and these new shares were acquired by the directors of the Savoy and their friends. After successfully fighting off a bid by Trafalgar House in the 1970s, Wontner fought a long battle in the 1980s to prevent Sir Charles Forte from buying the company. Forte wanted to expand the group of luxury hotels owned by Trusthouse Forte, and after his 1981 bid of £58 million was rejected he managed to acquire nearly 70 per cent of the shares, but only 42 per cent of the voting rights. Forte was infuriated by Wontner's refusal to negotiate: Wontner had 'a great gift for supercilious indifference' (Forte, 166).

Wontner's activities extended beyond the Savoy. He was one of those responsible for creating a new International Hotel Association in order to encourage the growth of tourism after the war, serving as president from 1961 to 1964, and he was also chairman of the British Hotels and Restaurants Association from 1957 to 1960. In 1938 he was invited to review the catering arrangements at Buckingham Palace, and was appointed a catering adviser to the royal household. He was appointed MVO by George VI in 1950, and in 1953 the queen revived the ancient title of clerk of the royal kitchens especially for him. He was appointed CVO in 1969 and knighted in 1972. He was also active in the politics of the City of London, and was elected alderman for Broad Street ward in 1963. For centuries Wontners had been masters of the Worshipful Company of Feltmakers, and he continued this tradition, serving as master from 1962 to 1963, and from 1973 to 1974. He was also a member of the Worshipful Company of Clockmakers, and master from 1975 to 1976. He was lord mayor of London from 1973 to 1974 (being appointed GBE in the latter year), and campaigned for the return from Hertfordshire of Sir Christopher Wren's Temple Bar, the original western gateway into the City; he established the Temple Bar Trust in 1976, which in 1984 became the owner of Temple Bar and thereafter negotiated its re-siting within Paternoster Square. As the son of an actor, and from 1937 a member of the Old Stagers, the oldest amateur dramatic society in the country, Wontner enjoyed his close involvement in the management of the Savoy Theatre as chairman and managing director from 1948 until his death, and after the theatre was destroyed by fire in 1990 he personally supervised its rebuilding.

Wontner was urbane, and a man of great charm, although seen by some as aloof. He spoke French fluently, collected antique clocks, and owned estates in the Chilterns and in Scotland. He died on 25 November 1992 at 8A Wellington Place, Westminster, London, following an acute pulmonary embolism; he was survived by his wife and their three children.   ANNE PIMLOTT BAKER

Sources S. Jackson, *The Savoy* (1964) · C. Forte, *The autobiography of Charles Forte* (1986) · P. Conterini, *The Savoy was my oyster* (1976) · I. Shenker, *The Savoy of London* (1988) · *The Times* (27 Nov 1992) · *Daily Telegraph* (27 Nov 1992) · *The Independent* (27 Nov 1992) · *The Guardian* (3 Dec 1992) · *WWW* · b. cert. · m. cert. · d. cert. · *CGPLA Eng. & Wales* (1993)
Likenesses group portrait, drawing, repro. in Shenker, *The Savoy of London*, 22 · photograph, repro. in Jackson, *The Savoy*, facing p. 177 · photograph, repro. in *The Times*
Wealth at death £2,683,424: probate, 6 May 1993, *CGPLA Eng. & Wales*

Wood, Abram (d. 1799), Gypsy patriarch, is a figure about whom information is meagre and mostly traditional. His surname is of English origin and it may be presumed that he migrated into Wales. His forename, like that of his wife, Sarah, is biblical, but his ancestry is completely obscure. However, a clear reference to Wood by name occurs in an interlude by Thomas Edwards (Twm o'r Nant), *Pleser a gofid* (1787), in which his 'cousin', Auntie Sal from the south, describes him as travelling 'Wales and England'.

A colourful description of Wood was left by his great-granddaughter Saiforella:

> Abram was very tall, not so very lusty, and middling thin. His complexion was very dark, with rosy cheeks. His face was round as an apple, and he had a double chin and a small mouth—very small for a man. He always rode on horseback, on a blood-horse, and would not sleep in the open, but in barns. He wore a three-cocked hat with gold lace, a silk coat with swallow tails—sometimes red, sometimes green, and sometimes black—and a waistcoat embroidered with green leaves. The buttons on the coat were half-crowns, those on the waistcoat shillings. His breeches were white, tied with silk ribbons, and there were bunches of ribbons at the knees. On his feet he wore pumps with silver buckles and silver spurs, and he wore two gold rings—only two—and a gold watch and chain. (Jarman and Jarman, *Y Sipsiwn Cymreig*, 65)

This idealized description of Abram Wood no doubt preserves family memories; yet it accords well with more generalized accounts of Gypsy chieftains arriving on the continent.

Abram Wood and his wife, Sarah, had three sons, Valentine, William, and Solomon, and a daughter, Damaris. From the three sons descended a numerous progeny known in Welsh as 'Teulu Abram Wood' ('the family of Abram Wood'): a name which rapidly became used for Gypsies in general in Wales, although other families also migrated into the country. Among his descendants were many colourful characters such as Alabaina, Sylvaina, Saiforella, and Ellen Ddu (Black Ellen), all celebrated practitioners of the arts of magic and fortune telling. A number of male descendants also took up the art of harp playing and included such well-known players of the instrument as John Roberts of Newtown (1816–1894) and Jeremiah Wood (c.1778–1867), who was family harpist to the Gogerddan family for fifty years. At least twenty-six harpists extending over six generations were descended from Abram Wood and it is probable that they preserved much traditional Welsh music which would otherwise have been lost. Black Ellen was notable among her own people as a teller of traditional folk tales and these were collected as narrated by her great-nephew Mathew Wood.

Abram Wood's first language was Romani and this was retained by many of his descendants down to the twentieth century, although it is now virtually lost. This speech was a pure and archaic form of Romani which was fully described by John *Sampson in his monumental grammar *The Dialect of the Gypsies of Wales* (1926). This also contains a large collection of sayings, aphorisms, names, and riddles attributed to the Woods.

Abram Wood's death on 12 November 1799 is recorded in the parish register of Llangelynnin, Merioneth, where he is described as: 'Abram Woods a travelling Egyptian.' His reputed grave in Llangelynnin churchyard has the later date of 1800.   ELDRA JARMAN

Sources *Journal of the Gypsy Lore Society* (1988–92) · *Journal of the Gypsy Lore Society* (1907–16) · *Journal of the Gypsy Lore Society* (1922) ·

J. Sampson, *Dialect of the Gypsies of Wales* (1926); repr. (1968) • E. Jarman and A. O. H. Jarman, *Y Sipsiwn Cymreig* (1979) • E. Jarman and A. O. H. Jarman, *The Welsh Gypsies: children of Abram Wood* (1991) • parish register (death), 12 Nov 1799, Llangelynnin, Merioneth, Wales • A. Sampson, *The scholar Gypsy: the quest for a family secret* (1997)

Archives U. Lpool

Wood, Alexander (1726–1807), surgeon, born on 24 June 1726 and baptized at Leith South, Edinburgh, six days later, was the son of Thomas Wood, a farmer in Restalrig, and his wife, Janet Lamb. He studied medicine at Edinburgh, and after taking his diploma settled at Musselburgh, where he practised successfully for a time. He then moved to Edinburgh, became a fellow of the College of Surgeons on 14 January 1756, and entered into partnership with John Rattray and Charles Congleton, to whose practice he subsequently succeeded. He possessed considerable ability as a surgeon, and was one of those whom Sir Walter Scott's parents consulted concerning his lameness.

Wood attained great celebrity in Edinburgh, where his philanthropy and kindness were proverbial. His character made him extremely popular with the townsfolk, and one night during a riot, when the mob, mistaking him for the provost, Sir James Stirling, were about to throw him over the north bridge, he saved himself by exclaiming 'I'm lang Sandy Wood; tak' me to a lamp and ye'll see'. Byron held him in high esteem, and in a fragment of a fifth canto of *Childe Harold*, which appeared in *Blackwood's Magazine* in May 1818, he wrote:

Alexander Wood (1726–1807), by George Watson

Oh! for an hour of him who knew no feud,
The octogenarian chief, the kind old Sandy Wood!

and spoke of him very warmly in a note to the stanza. Wood was also a friend of Robert Burns. They had first met at the C. K. Lodge of Freemasons and Burns later became a patient of Wood's. Wood, it was said, was

> a man after Burns's own heart—kind, quaint, fond of children and animals; he even resembled the poet so specifically, as to have had at one time a pet sheep, which like Burns's *Mailie*, 'trotted by him' through all the town on his professional visits. (Findlay, 28–9)

Wood married Veronica Chalmers. One of their sons, Sir Alexander Wood, was chief secretary at Malta, and a grandson, Alexander Wood, became a lord of session in 1842 with the title Lord Wood.

Wood died in Edinburgh on 12 May 1807. An epitaph was composed for him by Sir Alexander Boswell, and John Bell, who had been his pupil, dedicated to him the first volume of his *Anatomy*.   E. I. CARLYLE, *rev.* MICHAEL BEVAN

Sources W. Findlay, *Robert Burns and the medical profession* (1898) • 'Alexander Wood: surgeon and friend of Robert Burns', *Annals of Medical History*, new ser., 9 (1937), 193–4 [editorial] • J. G. Lockhart, *The life of Sir Walter Scott*, 1 (1902) • birth and bap. reg. Scot.

Likenesses D. Alison, oils, Scot. NPG • J. Kay, caricature, etching, BM • W. Maddocks, stipple (after Alison), Wellcome L. • G. Watson, portrait, Scot. NPG • G. Watson, portrait, Royal College of Surgeons, Edinburgh [*see illus.*] • portrait, repro. in J. Kay and J. Paterson, *Kay's Edinburgh portraits*, 1 (1885), following p. 115 • portrait, repro. in Findlay, *Robert Burns*

Wood, Alexander (1817–1884), physician, was born on 10 December 1817, in Cupar, Fife, the second son of James Wood (1785–1865), physician, and his cousin Mary (*d.* 1864), daughter of Alexander Wood of Grangehill, Fife. The family moved to Edinburgh's New Town in 1821, where Wood was educated at private schools until 1826, when he entered Edinburgh Academy. In 1832 he matriculated at Edinburgh University, studying both arts and medicine. He was twice elected president of the student Royal Medical Society. Wood graduated MD in 1839 and set up practice in the New Town where he was appointed physician to the Stockbridge and Royal Public dispensaries. On 15 June 1842 he married Rebecca Massey. In 1841 he had begun lecturing in the practice of medicine at the extramural medical school, but he failed to win appointment to the chair of medicine at Glasgow University in 1852 or the same post at Edinburgh in 1855.

A man of extraordinary energy Wood distinguished himself in a number of spheres. His main contribution to medicine was to develop the technique of administering drugs using hypodermic syringe. Wood became interested in the problem of relieving localized pain through James Young Simpson's experiments on anaesthesia. According to Wood's paper, 'A new method of treating neuralgia by subcutaneous injection', published in the *Edinburgh Medical and Surgical Journal* in 1855, early attempts to introduce drugs using an acupuncture needle failed. In 1853 Wood switched to using a syringe and treated a case of neuralgia by injecting morphia close to the site of the discomfort. Although Wood noted the subsequent deep sleep produced by the injection, he believed that his technique was of use only in the treatment of localized conditions. He did not recognize the potential of his method to deliver a variety of drugs to treat a wide range of generalized ailments—a potential worked out by Dr Charles Hunter in the early 1860s. Wood, a notoriously combative character, engaged in a priority dispute with Hunter over the discovery of the hypodermic method. In addition to this work Wood published on a variety of diseases, including rheumatism, skin disease, laryngitis, erisypelas, and scarlet fever.

Wood firmly embraced the new ideals of medicine which emerged in the mid-nineteenth century—of a unified, well educated, duly licensed body with an important role in all forms of public health. In 1849 he published *Rational Medicine*, promoting the soundly scientific nature of contemporary medicine for a popular audience. He also attacked unorthodox forms of medicine. *Homeopathy Unmasked* (1844) and *A Sequel to Homeopathy Unmasked* (1845) took a typically dismissive stance: homoeopathic laws were 'unscientific', the notion of dilution 'absurd' and homoeopathic remedies did not produce their claimed effects. *What is mesmerism* (1851), by contrast, was a careful and rational examination of the causes of the observed phenomena of hypnosis. Wood speculated that under a mesmeric trance the will and motor functions became uncoupled at some point between the brain and spinal cord.

Wood also took a prominent role in Scottish medical politics through his long and honourable connection with the Royal College of Physicians of Edinburgh. He was admitted as a fellow in 1840, served on its council from 1846, was elected secretary in 1850, and had the unusual honour of being immediately re-elected as its president, holding the post from 1858 to 1861. He also represented the college on the Scottish branch of the General Medical Council from 1858 to 1873. At this time the college was extremely active in all areas of medical politics. As a licensing body it was active in pursuing reform in medical registration and Wood played an important role in persuading the college to admit non-graduates to its licensing examinations. The college also lobbied on many other medical bills, and Wood took part in campaigns for legislation on lunacy, pharmacy, the registration of births and marriages, and sanitary reform. On several occasions he went to London to present the college's views directly to parliament. Wood was particularly active in planning a vaccination act for Scotland. He published *Vaccination as it is, was, and Ought to be* (1860) setting out a plan for legislation in Scotland, and led a deputation which successfully amended the bill to reflect the wishes of Scottish medical practitioners.

Wood also performed important public service in Edinburgh. Between 1846 and 1852 he was elected to the city's police commissioners, a body responsible not only for policing, but also cleaning, lighting, and generally keeping good order in the city, and served on several committees. In the 1870s he served as chairman of the Edinburgh Tramways Company. He chaired the acting committee of the Association for the Improvement of the Condition of the Poor, a charity which provided food and work for the unemployed. Wood was involved in the debates over a new poor law for Scotland in the 1840s, and published a lecture advocating the Scottish system of distributing outdoor relief over English workhouses as the best means of dealing with variations in the numbers of paupers during trade cycles.

This public work was fuelled by a strong personal faith. Wood was interested in religious debates from the 1820s and taught in Sunday schools from his student days. At the 1843 Disruption he joined the Free Church of Scotland and helped to found and run a local Free Church school. He edited the *Free Church Educational Journal* for part of its two-year existence. Wood suffered from angina and breathlessness for some years but it was increasing deafness which persuaded him to retire from practice in 1873. He died at his home, 12 Strathearn Place, Edinburgh, on 26 February 1884 after a short illness.

DEBORAH BRUNTON

Sources T. Brown, *Alexander Wood: a sketch of his life and work* (1886) · *Edinburgh Medical Journal*, 29 (1883–4), 973–6 · *BMJ* (1 March 1884), 442 · V. Berridge and G. Edwards, *Opium and the people* (1981), 139–40 · d. cert.
Archives Edinburgh City Archives, papers
Likenesses J. G. Watson, oils, 1861, Royal College of Physicians of Edinburgh · portraits, repro. in Brown, *Alexander Wood*

Wood, Sir Andrew (*d.* 1515), sea captain and merchant, served James III and James IV and, remarkably, was trusted by both kings. Wood first appears in royal records on 28 July 1477, already described as 'our lovet familiare serviture' Andrew Wood of Leith (Burnett, 8.450), receiving a nineteen-year lease of the lands and town of Largo in Fife. As a further reward for services to James III on land and sea during the Anglo-Scottish war of 1480–82, on 18 March 1483 Wood received a feu charter of Largo, a grant that makes it clear that, although he suffered losses, he also inflicted extensive damage on the English at sea.

Wood played an important role in the revolt of 1488, which cost James III his life, and in its troubled aftermath. Here information is available not only from official records, but also from Pitscottie's colourful late sixteenth-century chronicle, the accuracy of which has often been questioned. However, the gist of Pitscottie's narrative may be close to the truth, for he cites Wood among his sources—not a direct source, though Sir Andrew's son and namesake may have been, for he died only in 1579, the year in which Pitscottie completed his chronicle.

Wood remained loyal to James III throughout the uprising, commanding two royal ships, the *Yellow Carvel* and the *Flower*. These vessels were probably used to help the king to escape from Leith to Fife, and later Aberdeen, in March 1488, and to transport King James up the Forth in June. Subsequently it was believed—incorrectly—that Wood had picked up the fleeing king after the battle of Sauchieburn (11 June 1488); and there followed a confrontation at Leith between Wood and leaders of the new regime, men acting in the name of the adolescent James IV. The latter may have tried to organize an attack on Wood's ships, but his fellow mariners of Leith were disinclined to take the risk, and the outcome was a grudging acceptance of

Wood's ability to inflict damage on the new government. Their sense of the need to placate him probably explains the rapid confirmation of his 1483 feu charter of Largo, as early as 27 July 1488. Wood was perhaps the only prominent supporter of the late king who did not initially suffer for being on the wrong side in 1488.

Wood thereupon transferred his allegiance to the minority government of James IV—fortunately for the new regime, as the dramatic sea battle off the Fife coast between Wood and the English captain Stephen Bull, so colourfully described by Pitscottie (who probably turns one incident into two), probably occurred in 1489 or 1490, with Wood as the heroic victor. There was also the problem of pirates, in particular the Dane, Lutkyn Mere, whose ship was captured in the Forth in July 1489 (though whether Wood himself was involved is not known).

Wood was able to exact a high price for his services from a government that may have lacked the authority or power to constrain him. On 18 May 1491, in parliament, Wood was given retrospective approval for building operations that he had undertaken at Largo—the construction of houses and a fortalice, using English captives for the work; his feu charter of Largo was again confirmed, with additions; and it was stipulated that the confirmation would not be affected by any future royal revocations. For the first time, Wood's wife, Elizabeth Lundy, and his heirs, are associated with him in a royal grant.

If Wood's relationship with the minority government was at times an uneasy one, there can be no doubt as to his closeness to the adult James IV, who gradually assumed control of the kingdom in 1494–5. In 1494 Wood makes his first appearance in the records as Sir Andrew Wood, conveying Snowdon herald and other royal servants on embassy to Flanders; later in the year, Wood supplied sixty oars and 'estland' planks for the building of a royal rowbarge at Dumbarton; and on 18 February 1495 James IV granted his 'familiar knight' further Fife lands in the vicinity of Largo. Between 1497 and 1501 Sir Andrew was in charge of the rebuilding of Dunbar Castle, regarded as indefensible during the minority, but swiftly reconstructed on the orders of the adult James IV, with Wood installed as its keeper.

Wood's subsequent services to James IV, in spite of his being Fife-based, seem to have been concentrated in the west. In April and May 1504, together with James Hamilton, earl of Arran, Wood commanded the royal fleet sent from Dumbarton to lay siege to Cairn na Burgh Castle in the Treshnish Isles; and, according to Pitscottie, Arran and Wood were both involved in the 1513 war with England, with the latter sent by an indignant king to Ayr to relieve the tardy Arran of his command. The fleet, however, appears to have sailed without Wood. Two years later, in the summer or early autumn of 1515, Sir Andrew, after more than thirty years of service to the Scottish crown, died, probably at Largo, leaving two sons, Andrew (d. 1579) and John *Wood (d. 1570), from his marriage with Elizabeth, who also survived him.   NORMAN MACDOUGALL

Sources J. M. Thomson and others, eds., *Registrum magni sigilli regum Scotorum / The register of the great seal of Scotland*, 11 vols. (1882– 1914), vol. 2 · G. Burnett and others, eds., *The exchequer rolls of Scotland*, 8 (1885) · T. Dickson, ed., *Compota thesaurariorum regum Scotorum / Accounts of the lord high treasurer of Scotland*, 1 (1877) · *The historie and cronicles of Scotland … by Robert Lindesay of Pitscottie*, ed. A. J. G. Mackay, 1, STS, 42 (1899), 201–2, 211–16, 226–31, index · N. Macdougall, *James IV* (1989) · N. Macdougall, *James III: a political study* (1982) [index] · A. Spont, ed., *Letters and papers relating to the war with France, 1512–1513*, Navy RS, 10 (1897) [index] · R. L. Mackie, *King James IV of Scotland: a brief survey of his life and times* (1958), 63–5
Archives NA Scot., *R.M.S., E. R., T. A.*

Wood, Anne (1907–1998), singer and opera administrator, was born on 2 August 1907 at The Grange, Crawley, Sussex, a daughter of Percival Wood, JP for Sussex, and his wife, Eleanor. She was educated at St Mary's School, Calne, and studied singing with Elena Gerhardt, George Parker, and Eve de Reussy before joining the BBC Singers in 1934 at the same time as Peter Pears, who became her lifelong friend. The two lived for a while close to each other in London, and before the war often exchanged experiences and views, while sharing many musical encounters. During the war, as a fluent German speaker, she was employed by the Ministry of Economic Warfare to work on 'black' propaganda. By night she drove an ambulance. She was also employed by the Council for the Encouragement of Music and the Arts, later ENSA.

After the war Wood's singing career as a leading mezzo-soprano came to fruition. A resourceful interpreter of modern music, she sang in many premières, including that of Benjamin Britten's *Spring Symphony* at Amsterdam in 1950. She was also a noted recitalist and was fluent in the interpretation of oratorio.

Wood was one of the leading lights in the formation, in 1948, of the English Opera Group, working as an administrator alongside Britten, John Piper, and Eric Crozier, the last-named teaching her the ins and outs of operatic management, which stood her in good stead when she struck out on her own. On the basis of that experience, and to help young singers to tackle new scores, Wood formed the Opera Studio with the well-known soprano Joan Cross. Until then no such school existed in Britain. That was in 1949; by 1952 it had developed into the London Opera School, and in 1959 it became the National School of Opera, which gave stage experience and advice to many young artists, latterly on the stage at Morley College, London.

When it developed into a larger organization, the London Opera Centre, in 1964, under the aegis of Covent Garden, Wood and Cross, no longer in total control, decided to resign from what had been their own creation. Wood opted to change course and formed Phoenix Opera in 1965. It employed, in its small but productive way, many leading singers, producers, and designers, and—as a touring group—gave many deeply satisfying performances, a few of them, under Yehudi Menuhin's aegis, at the Bath Festival. In its ten-year existence it performed twelve operas, always well prepared and sung, in 66 different venues. In 1975 the Arts Council withdrew its grant, ironically just after the company had made a successful tour of Austria and Yugoslavia sponsored by the British Council, and gradually the company had to reduce its activities to vanishing point, much to Wood's chagrin.

In the 1980s Wood was a moving force in setting up a singing award in memory of Pears, but that enterprise also failed after a few years, because of a lack of funds. She continued, almost to the end of her life, encouraging young singers with her long-standing partner, Johanna Peters (*d.* 2000). Together, out of the limelight, they did a power of good for the development of singing talent.

Wood was a formidable character, with strong ideas on how opera should be organized and performed. She propounded them fearlessly, often in the teeth of opposition from the opera establishment. That did not endear her to the powers that be, and probably prevented her from achieving the eminence she undoubtedly deserved. She died in the Hospital of St John and St Elizabeth, Westminster, on 12 June 1998.   ALAN BLYTH

Sources *The Independent* (17 June 1998) · *The Guardian* (23 June 1998) · *The Times* (24 June 1998) · personal knowledge (2004) · private information (2004) · b. cert. · d. cert.
Likenesses photograph, repro. in *The Independent* · photograph, repro. in *The Guardian* · photograph, repro. in *The Times*

Wood, Anthony [Anthony à Wood] (**1632–1695**), antiquary, was born in the house known as Postmasters Hall, opposite Merton College, Oxford, on 17 December 1632, the fourth son of Thomas Wood (1581–1643) and his second wife, Mary Pettie (1602–1667). His father, who had been born in Islington, Middlesex, was a fairly wealthy man who had attended Broadgates Hall in Oxford, married well, and invested in property in Oxford; his second wife, Mary, came from a well-connected Oxfordshire family. Wood's education was disrupted by the civil war. Initially he was sent to New College School (1641–4), and then (June 1644 – September 1646) moved to the free school at Thame established by Lord Williams, where his master was William Burt. His days at Thame were enlivened by skirmishes between troops from the neighbouring garrisons of Oxford and Aylesbury. He matriculated at Merton College, with which his family had many associations, in May 1647, and was soon made a postmaster, but his progress through the college was slow, and he did not graduate BA until July 1652.

Oxford antiquary After his graduation Wood, or, as he styled himself, à Wood, remained in Oxford, devoting himself to the study of heraldry and of music, for he was becoming proficient on the violin; he also began to frequent the Bodleian Library. A book that made an early impression on him was William Burton's *The Description of Leicester Shire* (1622). His inclinations towards antiquarian research were strengthened by his discovery of William Dugdale's *Antiquities of Warwickshire* in 1656, just after its publication, as is evident from his *Life* of himself, constructed in the third person:

> My pen cannot enough describe, how A. Wood's tender affections and insatiable desire of knowledge were ravish'd and melted down by the reading of that book. What by musick and rare books that he found in the publick Library,

Anthony Wood (1632–1695), by Michael Burghers

his life at this time and after was a perfect Elysium.   (*Life and Times*, 1.209)

He experienced an eager desire to compile a similar volume for his own county, and began collecting monumental inscriptions in Oxford and around Oxfordshire to this end. His first appearance in print occurred at this time, when in 1656 he edited five sermons by his brother Edward Wood, a fellow of Merton, who had died of consumption in 1655.

Wood never had an official base in the university, even though he became over the years the incomparable historian of the place. It has been suggested that 'his notoriously peevish temper' prevented him from being elected a fellow of Merton (*DNB*). He possessed sufficient private means to pursue his researches, and in February 1660 he improved the upper story of the family house opposite

Merton, putting in a fireplace in one room and throwing out a window over the street in the other, so making himself a two-room hermitage where he conducted his studies for the rest of his life. In July 1660 he was given free access to the university archives so that he could, as he put it, 'advance his esurient genie in antiquities' (*Life and Times*, 1.326) and develop his plan of writing a detailed history of Oxford.

At this time Wood became familiar with the manuscript collections of an earlier Oxford antiquary, Brian Twyne, who had made copious excerpts from the muniments and registers of the university and colleges, the city archives, and those of the parish churches, and had assembled a wealth of information about Oxford from college libraries and other sources such as the Cotton Library and the record offices in London. With so much material at his disposal, Wood now began to project a broad scheme of research that would lead to three separate publications: on the history of the city of Oxford, including ecclesiastical antiquities; the annals of the university, with accounts of the official buildings and the programmes of study; and the antiquities of the colleges. This threefold scheme occupied him for much of the decade of the 1660s.

In this period Wood's life took on a settled routine. After the celebrations for the king's restoration in May 1660, he went back to his studies, pleased by the end of the Commonwealth and the return of Anglican church services. He attempted to participate in the fashion for natural philosophy in 1663, when he followed for a year a course in chemistry given by the German chemist and Rosicrucian Peter Stahl, but this encounter with modernism did not last long. The pattern of his days became quite regular: he worked in the mornings in his attic study or in libraries, and in the afternoons he would wander around town looking through the bookshops, and then walk out with a friend to one of the villages around Oxford to take a pot of ale in a country inn. His evenings were spent at musical gatherings or in common rooms or taverns. One can reconstruct his social life with some precision thanks to the minutely detailed accounts he kept of his expenditures.

Friends and family life In 1667 Wood began to go to London to work in the libraries there. He was given an introduction to William Dugdale by Thomas Barlow, his good friend who had been Bodley's librarian and was now the provost of Queen's College, and Dugdale arranged for him to meet Sir John Cotton and have access to the Cotton Library. In the same month, June 1667, Wood was given a letter of commendation to the old puritan activist William Prynne of Lincoln's Inn, who was now the keeper of the records in the Tower. Prynne took a liking to him, and took him to the Tower, where Wood found Dugdale working away, gathering material for the third volume of the *Monasticon* and for his *Baronage of England*. They dined together every day during Wood's London visit, with the result that an enduring friendship developed between them. In the next few years Anthony Wood derived much

satisfaction in furnishing Dugdale with additional documentation for the last volume of the *Monasticon* (1673), especially in relation to the priories and nunneries whose lands and assets were intended by Wolsey to be part of the endowment of Christ Church.

1667 saw another valuable antiquarian relationship established, for in August of this year John Aubrey sought out Wood to make his acquaintance. Aubrey had been a contemporary and friend of Wood's elder brother Edward at Trinity College, and imagined he would have much in common with Anthony. At first they got on well and Aubrey contributed much to Wood's biographical collections over the years.

Wood's mother, Mary, died at the end of February 1667, killed by an incompetent doctor, and his life was further unsettled in June 1669 by a quarrel with his brother Robert's wife, which resulted in his being 'dismist from his usual and constant diet, which for many years he had taken in the house where he was borne'. His health was affected by the change, and he began increasingly to suffer from deafness, 'the first and greatest misery of his life. It made him exceeding melancholy and more retir'd' (*Life and Times*, 2.163–4).

History of the university None the less, Wood's studies prospered. In October 1669 Dr John Fell, the dean of Christ Church, arranged for Wood's collections relating to the history of the university to be published by the university press where Fell was the dominant figure. Fell and the delegates offered good terms, with Fell willing to bear the costs of printing, and offering Wood £100 for his copy, and £50 for additional work in finalizing the manuscript. Fell wanted the book translated into Latin 'for the honour of the University in forreigne countries' (*Life and Times*, 2.172), a condition to which Wood agreed, the translation being carried out by Richard Peers of Christ Church and Richard Reeve of Magdalen College School. Fell also made a suggestion of considerable consequence for Wood, that he compile short biographies of authors and bishops who had attended the university; here was the genesis of *Athenae Oxonienses* and also of John Aubrey's *Brief Lives*, for Aubrey was willing to help Wood with this biographical work.

The *History* did much to enhance Wood's reputation in the university, and it brought him the honour of a meeting in February 1672 with the archbishop of Canterbury, Gilbert Sheldon, that great benefactor of the university. While the book was being printed, however, a good deal of wrangling went on between Wood and Fell, for Fell made numerous alterations to the text and to the translation. *Historia et antiquitates Univ. Oxon.* was eventually published in July 1674 in two volumes, very handsomely produced and dedicated to the king. The first volume contains the annals of the university, the second has accounts of university buildings and institutions, historical notices of the colleges and their famous men, and lists of university officers. Dr Fell rightly regarded the book as a notable memorial of Oxford's distinction, and distributed copies liberally at home and abroad, often with the addition of David Loggan's *Oxonia illustrata* that came out in 1675. Wood had wanted to use Loggan's views as illustrations to his book, but in the end Loggan's engravings were published as a separate volume. Wood was angry at the high-handed way in which Fell treated him, despite the dean's financial generosity, and upset by the Latin version of his history, so he was not in a contented frame of mind when the book was published. He set about rewriting the work in English for his own satisfaction; this English copy was the one that Wood usually cited in his diary notes, and it was eventually edited and published by John Gutch between 1792 and 1796. Gradually his pride in the book returned, and he liked hereafter to call himself 'the Historiographer of the University of Oxford'.

Collaborators and quarrels   Wood's close friends at this time included Thomas Barlow, Elias Ashmole, John Aubrey, William Dugdale, William Fulman, and Ralph Bathurst, the president of Trinity College. His friendships were, however, often destroyed by his spiteful nature. He fell out with Dr Bathurst, and was barred from frequenting Trinity College in 1673 because, as Bathurst told him, he 'never spoke well of any man' (*Life and Times*, 2.259). In the early 1670s, Wood was also developing friendships with several known Catholics, in particular Hugh Cressey, Francis Davenport (who was a priest under the name of Franciscus a Sancta Clara), and, most importantly, Ralph Sheldon, a Worcestershire gentleman who also had a manor at Weston in Warwickshire, who shared Wood's interest in books, heraldry, and antiquities, and who effectively became Wood's patron. Wood's association with men such as these led to the widespread belief that he himself had become a Catholic, but in his diaries he denies that this was ever the case. At the time of the Popish Plot when anti-Catholic feeling was running high, Wood came under suspicion and his rooms were searched by the vice-chancellor, but nothing incriminating was found.

After the publication of his *History*, Wood began to devote his energies to the compilation of a great biographical dictionary of Oxford writers, along the lines suggested by Dr Fell. Given the antiquity of the university, and the prodigious number of books written by its alumni, the task was immense. None the less, Wood possessed the industriousness and the perseverance required to see so ambitious a design through to completion. He certainly needed collaborators, and here John Aubrey proved invaluable, for his profuse acquaintance, so bewilderingly diverse, his insatiable curiosity, his imagination, and his inclination towards biography made him a most suitable partner in this enterprise. For about twenty-five years they met and corresponded, with Aubrey sending in his notes on authors for Wood to incorporate into his manuscript. Wood wanted details of Oxford writers, but he encouraged Aubrey to collect information about all manner of men, so that Aubrey would have material enough to make a volume of lives of the memorable men of the last century that would advance his own reputation. In the event, Wood benefited immensely from Aubrey's researches and from the lively style in which they were delivered, but Wood never acknowledged

Aubrey's help in his prefaces, nor did he assist Aubrey to get into print on his own account; and the only record he left of their relationship, other than private letters, were the sour and unappreciative remarks that he put into his *Life*. Here he remembered Aubrey only as 'a pretender to Antiquities' and as 'a shiftless person, roving and magotie-headed, and sometimes little better than crased' (*Life and Times*, 2.117). When some of the living subjects of *Athenae* began to complain about their biographies in the newly published book, Wood wrote to Aubrey blaming him for supplying information that had aroused the anger of numerous gentlemen against Wood, even though it was clear that Aubrey had advised Wood to use his judgement when editing his material for publication. Aubrey came to realize that he was being exploited, and, tolerant and generous-minded though his nature was, Wood's ingratitude finally provoked him to protest. In 1694, when Wood's book had been published, and Wood returned some of Aubrey's manuscripts in mutilated condition, Aubrey expostulated, 'I thought you so deare a friend that I might have entrusted my life in your hands and now your unkindness doth almost break my heart' (*Brief Lives*, 1.13).

The work of compiling the biographical register went on all through the 1680s. Wood chose to call the work *Athenae Oxonienses*, presumably because Oxford was a city so rich in authors that only Athens could equal her. He took the year 1500 as a starting point, and recorded for each figure a brief life and an account of the books he had written. Oxford men who had risen to be bishops were also included. The sources of his information were remarkably wide, for they included the books written by his subjects, the university registers and libraries, the London record offices, and cathedral archives. Enlarging the already vast scope of his design, he added what he called the *Fasti Oxonienses*, the academic annals that listed the officers of the university year by year, preferments, higher degrees awarded, and the incorporation at Oxford of graduates from Cambridge. This last inclusion means that Wood's book contains numerous entries for Cambridge authors, thus providing much information that is nowhere else recorded.

Financing this grand project was always going to be a problem. For many years Edward Sheldon, the translator and Ralph Sheldon's uncle, had promised to help with the costs of printing, but after Wood quarrelled with him his goodwill understandably diminished. Wood did, however, receive from Sheldon £30 in his lifetime, £40 in his will, and £50 in 1690 from his heir. The rest of the expenses were raised by the subscription method. Wood used a London stationer, Thomas Bennet, as his publisher, and the first volume of *Athenae Oxonienses* appeared in 1691, the second in 1692. If Wood failed to mention any of those scholars who had assisted him most, such as Aubrey or Andrew Allam of St Edmund Hall, he also chose to leave his own name off the title-page in both volumes. Fame was not the spur that drove him on, but the honour of the University of Oxford. The book was conventionally dedicated to the chancellor and vice-chancellor of the university. The reception was mixed, both admiring and critical, for many modern reputations had been assailed. Most troubling to Wood was the suit brought against him in the vice-chancellor's court at Oxford by Henry Hyde, second earl of Clarendon, for libel against his father Edward, the first earl, for Wood had printed matter that suggested that the lord chancellor had received money for offices at the Restoration. In July 1693 Wood was found guilty and expelled from the university; he was to pay the costs of the suit, and the offending pages of his book were to be publicly burnt.

Death and legacy Wood was much distressed by the verdict, but continued working on additions to the *Athenae*. In November 1695 he was recurringly sick, and on the 22nd his friend Arthur Charlett, the master of University College, ventured into the sanctum of his attic rooms, which few people ever entered, and convinced him that he was dying and should put his papers into order. The cause of his illness was 'a Total Suppression of Urine' (*Life and Times*, 3.497). On hearing of his malady, one of his old antagonists, Dr Robert South of Christ Church, unfeelingly told him, 'if thou canst not make water thou hadst better make earth' (*Life and Times*, abridged edn, 28). Wood gave his additional notes relating to *Athenae Oxonienses* to the young antiquary Thomas Tanner of All Souls, and his private papers to Tanner and Edward Bysshe of Wadham, and he willed all his books and manuscripts to the Ashmolean Museum (they were transferred to the Bodleian Library in 1858). Wood died at Postmasters Hall on 29 November 1695, and was buried the next day in Merton College chapel.

Among Wood's manuscripts were several significant compositions that were later published. His collections relating to the history and buildings of Oxford had been made during the years 1661 to 1666, but had never been worked up into a book. Some portions were published in 1773, but it was not until 1889–99 that a full edition of the *Survey of the Antiquities of the City of Oxford* was produced by Andrew Clark. This is a long, factual account of the city, street by street, building by building, excluding the colleges—quite the most detailed description of any town in the country at the time that it was written. Then there was the autobiography that traced his life up to 1672 and the rough diary notes that Wood kept from 1657 to 1695. Thomas Hearne printed the autobiography in 1730, and William Huddesford re-edited it with supplementary material in 1772. The autobiography and the diary notes were brought together in a magisterial edition by the indefatigable Andrew Clark under the title of *The Life and Times of Anthony Wood* (5 vols., 1891–1900).

Wood's writings have little pretence to literary merit. His style has the characteristics of the perpetual note-taker: dry, brusque, and factual. In addition, the censorious tone that often accompanies his personal memorials can give an acrimonious edge to his prose. His antiquarian works have no touches of the imagination, and yet, paradoxically, it is Wood's unaffected plainness that makes his private journals spring to life. He was to Restoration Oxford what Pepys was to Restoration London, although temperamentally the two men were poles apart. His biographical records in *Athenae Oxonienses* are indispensable, and without them, half the seventeenth-century entries in the *Dictionary of National Biography* could hardly have been written.   GRAHAM PARRY

Sources Wood, *Ath. Oxon.*, 1st edn • [W. Huddesford], ed., *The lives of those eminent antiquaries, John Leland, Thomas Hearne, and Anthony à Wood*, 2 vols. (1772) • A. Wood, *The history and antiquities of the University of Oxford*, ed. J. Gutch, 2 vols. in 3 pts (1792–6) • Wood, *Ath. Oxon.*, new edn • N. K. Kiessling, *The library of Anthony Wood* (2002) • A. Wood, *Survey of the antiquities of the city of Oxford*, ed. A. Clark, 3 vols., OHS, 15, 17, 37 (1889–99) • *The life and times of Anthony Wood*, ed. A. Clark, 5 vols., OHS, 19, 21, 26, 30, 40 (1891–1900) • *Brief lives, chiefly of contemporaries, set down by John Aubrey, between the years 1669 and 1696*, ed. A. Clark, 2 vols. (1898) • *The life and times of Anthony à Wood*, ed. A. Clark, abridged edn (1961) [with introduction by Ll. Powys] • A. Powell, *John Aubrey and his friends*, rev. edn (1963) • *DNB*

Archives BL, diary, Harley MS 5409 • Bodl. Oxf., corresp., diaries, and collections • Bodl. Oxf., corresp., journal, autobiography, and papers • Bodl. Oxf., historical notes • Bodl. Oxf., notebook, collections and papers • Bodl. Oxf., MS Rawl. B. 400a, B. 407a, b; MS Gough Oxon. 5 • University College, Oxford, corresp., notebooks, and papers | CCC Oxf., letters to William Fulman • Herefs. RO, letters between Wood, Thomas Blount, and other antiquaries [copies]

Likenesses Rose?, watercolour and wash drawing, 1677 (after bust), Bodl. Oxf. • M. Burghers, line engraving, *c*.1680, BM, NPG; repro. in Huddesford, ed., *Lives* • M. Burghers, mezzotint (after his earlier engraving), BM, NPG [*see illus.*] • pen, ink and wash drawing (after Rose), NPG

Wealth at death see will, repr. in Clark, ed., *The life and times of Anthony Wood*, vol. 3, pp. 502–4

Wood, Arthur Henry (1875–1953), conductor and composer, was born on 24 January 1875 in Cemetery Road, Heckmondwike, Yorkshire, the eldest child of George Henry Wood (*b*. 1850), tailor, and his wife, Henrietta Jackson Hepworth (*b. c*.1853/4). His father played in a local amateur orchestra as violinist, on which instrument Arthur initially followed him before settling on the flute and piccolo. In 1882 the family moved to Harrogate, where Wood received lessons from Arthur Brookes, a member of the municipal orchestra. He left school at the age of twelve, and at fourteen was organist of St Paul's Presbyterian Church, Harrogate. More particularly he became flautist, accompanist, and eventually assistant conductor of the municipal orchestra under J. Sidney Jones. He later recalled conducting four times per day, especially rueing the 7.30 a.m. band-calls designed to attract visitors to take the waters. At these he sometimes had to conduct in mittens, while the musicians played with their noses running. Later Wood joined the Bournemouth Municipal Orchestra under Dan Godfrey, and also had a spell in Llandudno.

It was Sidney Jones, the son of the Harrogate Municipal Orchestra's music director and composer of the musical play *The Geisha*, who brought Wood to London as music director for his comedy opera *My Lady Molly* at Terry's Theatre in 1903. About this time Wood married, and he and his wife, Ethel Louise, had a son and two daughters. Wood subsequently conducted at the Apollo Theatre in 1904 for André Messager's *Véronique* and in 1906 for the musical *The Dairymaids* by Paul Rubens and Frank E. Tours. The latter was the start of an association with the producer Robert Courtneidge that included Wood's appointment as the music director of the Shaftesbury Theatre from 1908 to 1916.

Wood's tenure as conductor at the Shaftesbury was notable especially for Lionel Monckton's and Howard Talbot's musical play *The Arcadians*. It was Wood who arranged the overture on Monckton's and Talbot's melodies that has often been used as a concert item. During this period he became recognized as one of the most accomplished and reliable of West End music directors, and he went on to fill the same position at the Gaiety (1917–21), the Prince of Wales's (1921–2, 1927–8), Daly's (1922–6, 1929–30), His Majesty's (1928–9), the Cambridge (1930–31), the Savoy (1931), the Coliseum (1932), and the Garrick (1934). During these years he also composed scores for several touring musical comedies and revues, including *Oh, Caesar!* (1916), *Petticoat Fair* (1919), *Fancy Fair* (1919), *Too Many Girls* (1919), *Archie* (1924), and *The Sheik of Shepherd's Bush* (1924). His tenure at Daly's during the 1920s covered the 1923 revival of *The Merry Widow* with Evelyn Laye, Derek Oldham, Carl Brisson, and George Graves. In 1925 Wood took the entire Daly's Theatre orchestra to the Opera House, Manchester, for the try-out of Oscar Straus's *Cleopatra*, but the orchestra pit flooded, and he conducted in evening dress and gumboots.

During the 1930s Wood conducted on tour—notably with Noël Coward's *Bitter-Sweet* (1931–2) and George Posford's *The Gay Hussar* (1933–4). In addition he became a frequent guest conductor for the BBC. Throughout his career he composed much finely crafted light orchestral music, of which *Three Old Dances* (1902) was an early example. As a composer for Boosey and Hawkes he produced works that particularly commemorated his native Yorkshire, as in *Three Dale Dances* (1917), *Three More Dale Dances* (1927), *Yorkshire Moors Suite*, *My Native Heath* (1925), *Yorkshire Rhapsody*, and *Barnsley Fair*. Besides other suites, such as *Three Mask Dances* (1927), his compositions ranged from a one-step, *You Can't Keep Still*, to a concertino for flute, published in a reduction for flute and piano in 1948. True to his north-country origins, he also composed marches for brass bands and became a respected adjudicator.

Of his light orchestral compositions the piece that gave Wood his greatest fame was the suite *My Native Heath*, which comprised four movements—'Knaresboro Status', 'Ilkley Tarn', 'Bolton Abbey', and 'Barwick Green'. The final movement, a portrayal of a maypole dance on the village green of Barwick in Elmet, east of Leeds, was adopted as the signature tune for the BBC radio series *The Archers*, a role it went on to fulfil into the twenty-first century.

Wood was a member of the Green Room and Savage clubs. He lived for many years at 20 Arlington Gardens, Chiswick, London, where he died on 18 January 1953, aged seventy-seven.   ANDREW LAMB

Sources J. Parker, ed., *Who's who in the theatre* (1930–51) · K. Gänzl, *The British musical theatre*, 2 vols. (1986) · K. Young, *Music's great days in the spas and watering places* (1968) · D. Forbes-Winslow, *Daly's: the biography of a theatre* (1944) · P. L. Scowcroft, *British light music* (1997) · b. cert. · d. cert. · census returns, 1881 · *BL cat.* · *CGPLA Eng. & Wales* (1953) · will
Likenesses photograph, repro. in Young, *Music's great days*
Wealth at death £4915 1s. 2d.: probate, 29 May 1953, *CGPLA Eng. & Wales*

Wood, Charles, first Viscount Halifax (1800–1885), politician, was born at Pontefract on 20 December 1800, the elder son of Sir Francis Lindley Wood, second baronet (*d.* 1846), of Hickleton Hall, near Doncaster, and his wife Anne, daughter of Samuel Buck, recorder of Leeds. His father had extensive business interests and added to estates comprising by his death 10,000 acres in the East and West Ridings of Yorkshire. From Eton College, Wood proceeded to Oriel College, Oxford, where he took firsts in classics and mathematics in 1821 (BA 1821, MA 1824). His tutor, Edward Hawkins, described him as the cleverest pupil he had ever had. At Oriel he formed lasting friendships with George Grey and Francis Baring (afterwards Lord Northbrook), who were to be his colleagues in the whig cabinet of 1846–52.

Political office and marriage After an interlude of travel, Wood entered parliament for Great Grimsby (9 June 1826) at a cost of £4000 and with the support of Lord Yarborough's interest. Three years later he married Lady Mary (1807–1884), daughter of Charles *Grey, second Earl Grey, with whom he had eight children. Returned for Wareham at the 1831 election (2 May), he was elected for the newly created constituency of Halifax the next year (14 December) and represented it until 1865, when he chose the less demanding seat at Ripon (12 July). Behind his enthusiasm for the Great Reform Bill lay a cool appreciation of its value as a 'substantial, anti-democratic, pro-property measure' (letter to his father, 1831; Lockhart, 1.17).

On the formation of the whig ministry in November 1830 Wood's father-in-law made him his private secretary and in 1832 (10 August) joint secretary to the Treasury, as chief whip. Under Melbourne he became secretary to the Admiralty (27 April 1835), resigning in sympathy with his brother-in-law, Lord Howick, when the latter fell out with the premier and Lord John Russell in September 1839. Wood succeeded to his father's baronetcy on 31 December 1846. Starting in that year, he held a series of offices, being sworn of the privy council on 6 July 1846. He was chancellor of the exchequer (6 July 1846 to February 1852); president of the Board of Control (30 December 1852 to February 1855) in the Aberdeen government; and then Palmerston's first lord of the Admiralty (13 March 1855 to February 1858). On 19 June 1856 he was made GCB for services in the Crimean War. He was secretary of state for India in subsequent Liberal administrations between 18 June 1859 and February 1866, when he retired following a hunting accident. Raised to the peerage as Viscount Halifax on 21 February 1866, he was brought back to be lord privy seal in Gladstone's first cabinet (6 July 1870 to February 1874) in recognition of his influence within the party.

A progressive whig Wood personified a cautiously progressive liberalism. Representing an industrial town for a generation, he responded to the decisive shifts of public opinion in his time: he was committed to repealing the corn laws by 1844, and when the next instalment of parliamentary reform arrived said, truthfully, that he was not 'in the least afraid of the working-classes' (Cowling, 89). His spell as chief whip was a formative experience. For more than half a century he worked to hold together the political broad church of old whigs, Liberals, and radicals; his affectionate nickname in a small circle, the 'Spider', alluded to this activity. A comprehensive liberalism, under aristocratic leadership, was the best security for good government as he understood it, safeguarding property and individual freedom in the face of an expanding electorate. His whip's approach to politics made him a timid chancellor, 'paralysed by ... surpluses' (Southgate, 139); he was a poor speaker. In 1848, when economy was in order, he succumbed to pressure against an increase in income tax; that year saw what were, in effect, three budgets. On the other hand, the Treasury's overall control of public expenditure was emerging during his chancellorship. His principled aversion to deficit finance made him a reluctant borrower, and he strove to limit the spending on famine relief in Ireland. Holding Irish landlords primarily responsible for the crisis, he objected to heavier calls upon the British taxpayer. Nor did he believe, at that time, that the direct intervention of government could do much to promote the structural changes needed in Irish society.

Secretary of state for India These convictions and prejudices were modified by Wood's having to rule India from Whitehall. In 1853 he saw through the extension of the East India Company's charter in a new India Act. He tried to adhere to the spirit of this final adaptation of the 'double government' of the subcontinent, dating from 1784, after its abolition in 1858. The rethinking and implementation of Indian policies after the upheavals of the mutiny compelled him to take a more active part in shaping them than any of his predecessors since the eighteenth century. The cotton lobby, whose expectations he disappointed by his insistence on protecting native interests, dubbed him Maharaja Wood. He was sardonic, in private, about free-trading Lancashire's importunity for fiscal concessions at the expense of the hard-pressed Indian revenue. The government of India, under Lord Canning, was more amenable to commercial pressure: but Wood disallowed Canning's original waste land resolutions of October 1861 as too favourable to the European purchaser, and summary in their treatment of possible native claims. Defending himself from criticism that he had wilfully ignored the cotton famine in Lancashire, he told J. T. Delane of *The Times* that 'nothing is so likely to create a combination against us, and a general discontent and rising as interference with their land' (Steele, 342). He had learned from the mistakes of British policy in Ireland: 'the ryots', he reminded Delane, 'are small people like the Irish tenantry' (ibid.). During the indigo disturbances of the early 1860s which set native cultivators against white planters in Bengal, he repeatedly declined to sanction changes in the law of contract to the permanent disadvantage of the ryot.

In other areas of policy, Wood's actions were less controversial. While he asserted his authority over the Council of India in London, as well as over viceroys, presidency governors, and their councillors, he took pride in getting his way by a process of consultation. India's finances were restored to health after the huge deficits incurred during the mutiny. At the same time he sought to appease critics in Manchester and elsewhere by emphasizing the scale of investment in railways and other public works begun when he was first responsible for India. In his prudent fashion, he addressed the problems of cultural and political change which were inseparable from economic development. His education dispatch of July 1854, which adopted many of the suggestions made by Dr Alexander Duff, is a landmark; the Indian universities it envisaged came into being in 1857. Before the mutiny he had introduced the 'competition wallah' into the covenanted civil service as an instrument of enlightened imperialism. Afterwards he hesitated over Canning's proposal to include Indians in his legislative council and in the councils of Madras and Bombay, and that of the lieutenant-governors of Bengal, but decided upon the experiment in the Indian Councils Act of 1861. It was the responsibility of the ruling race, he believed, to prepare Indians for self-government at some distant date (Moore, 253). The strongest secretary of state between 1858 and Indian independence, Wood exercised an important influence upon the evolution of British rule, confirming its liberal character at the higher levels, despite the heightening of racial antagonism in the mutiny.

Halifax lived to give qualified approval to the more pronounced liberalism of Lord Ripon's viceroyalty in the 1880s. Earlier, he condemned Lord Lytton's 'forward policy' on the north-west frontier, consistently with his view that the Indian empire was the stronger for avoidance of external conflicts. He died at Hickleton Hall on 8 August 1885, and was succeeded by his eldest son, Charles Lindley *Wood, the second viscount. DAVID STEELE

Sources J. G. Lockhart, *Charles Lindley, Viscount Halifax*, 2 vols. (1935–6) · D. Southgate, *The passing of the whigs, 1832–1886* (1962) · R. J. Moore, *Sir Charles Wood's Indian policy, 1853–1866* [1966] · E. D. Steele, *Palmerston and liberalism, 1855–1865* (1991) · R. D. Edwards and T. D. Williams, eds., *The great famine: studies in Irish history, 1845–1852* (1956) · Gladstone, *Diaries* · *The Greville memoirs, 1814–1860*, ed. L. Strachey and R. Fulford, 8 vols. (1938) · M. Cowling, *1867: Disraeli, Gladstone and revolution* (1967) · GEC, *Peerage*
Archives BL, corresp. and papers relating to Admiralty, Add. MSS 49531–49593 · BL OIOC · BL OIOC, corresp. and papers relating to India, MS Eur. F 78, MS Eur. D 557 · Borth. Inst., Hickleton MSS · Borth. Inst., corresp. and papers | Alnwick Castle, letters to Henry Drummond · BL, corresp. with Lord Aberdeen, Add. MSS 43197–43198 · BL, corresp. with W. E. Gladstone, Add. MSS 44184–44186 · BL, Halifax MSS · BL, corresp. with Lord Holland, Add. MS 51569 · BL, corresp. with Sir Robert Peel, Add. MSS 40503–40609 · BL, corresp. with Lord Ripon, Add. MSS 43529–43531 · BL OIOC, corresp. with Sir George Clarke, MS Eur. D 538 · BL OIOC, corresp. with Lord Elgin, MS Eur. F 83 · BL OIOC, corresp. with Lord Elphinstone, MSS Eur. F 87–89 · BL OIOC, Lawrence MSS · Bodl. Oxf., letters to Lord Clarendon · Bodl. Oxf., corresp. with Lord Kimberley · Bucks. RLSS, letters to Lord Cottesloe · Bucks. RLSS, letters to duke of Somerset · Glos. RO, letters to T. S. Estcourt · Heriot-Watt University, letters to William Gibson-Craig · Lambton Park, Chester-

le-Street, co. Durham, letters to earl of Durham · Lpool RO, letters to fourteenth earl of Derby · LUL, corresp. with Lord Overstone · Muncaster Castle, Cumbria, corresp. with Lord Seymour · NA Scot., letters to second Lord Panmure · NA Scot., corresp. with Richard Saunders-Dundas · NL Scot., Aberdeen MSS · NL Scot., letters to Edward Ellice · NL Scot., Gladstone MSS · NL Scot., corresp., mainly with Lord Rutherford · NMM, letters to Sir Alexander Milne · NRA, priv. coll., letters to duke of Argyll · PRO, letters to Lord Granville, PRO 30/29 · PRO, corresp. with Lord John Russell, PRO 30/22 · Staffs. RO, letters, and of his wife to Francis Meynell · Trinity Cam., letters to Lord Houghton · U. Durham L., corresp. with third Earl Grey; corresp. with Charles Grey · U. Durham L., letters to Viscount Ponsonby · U. Newcastle, Robinson L., letters to Sir Charles Trevelyan · U. Nott. L., corresp. with duke of Newcastle · U. Southampton L., corresp. with Lord Palmerston · W. Sussex RO, letters to duke of Richmond · W. Yorks. AS, Leeds, letters to Lord Canning · Wilts. & Swindon RO, corresp. with Sidney Herbert · Woburn Abbey, letters to duke of Bedford

Likenesses F. Bromley, group portrait, etching, pubd 1835 (*The reform banquet, 1832*; after B. R. Haydon), NPG · W. Walker, mezzotint, pubd 1856, BM, NPG · G. Richmond, oils, *c*.1873, Oriel College, Oxford; copy by A. de Brie, NPG · Ape [C. Pellegrini], chromolithograph caricature, repro. in *VF* (6 Aug 1870) · Caldesi, Blanford & Co., carte-de-visite, NPG · J. Doyle, drawings, BM · W. P. Frith, group portrait, oils (*The marriage of the prince of Wales, 1863*), Royal Collection · J. Gilbert, group portrait, pencil and wash (*The coalition ministry, 1854*), NPG · G. Hayter, group portrait, oils (*The House of Commons, 1833*), NPG · W. Holl, stipple (after G. Richmond), BM, NPG · J. Phillip, group portrait, oils (*The House of Commons, 1860*), Palace of Westminster, London · W. Walker & Sons, carte-de-visite, NPG

Wealth at death £55,478 7s. od.: probate, 2 Jan 1886, *CGPLA Eng. & Wales*

Wood, Charles (1866–1926), organist and university professor, was born on 15 June 1866 at 11 Vicar's Hill, Armagh, the third son and fifth child of fourteen children of Charles Wood (1833–1893), lay vicar of Armagh Cathedral and diocesan registrar of Armagh, and his wife, Jemima Taylor. A chorister at Armagh Cathedral, Wood was educated at the cathedral school and he studied harmony and counterpoint (1880–81) with Thomas Osborne Marks, the Armagh Cathedral organist. In 1883 he was awarded the Morley open scholarship in composition at the newly instituted Royal College of Music. At the Royal College of Music he studied composition with Hubert Parry and Charles Stanford, horn with Thomas Mann, piano with Frederic Cliffe and Franklin Taylor, and counterpoint with J. F. Bridge. Later he took lessons in composition exclusively from Stanford and in the organ as a co-second instrument. Wood remained at the Royal College of Music until 1889 owing to the continued renewal of his scholarship, even as a non-resident student, during which time he was appointed to teach harmony at the college (1888), and, with Stanford's encouragement, he won an organ scholarship to Selwyn College, Cambridge (also 1888). After five terms at Selwyn he migrated to Gonville and Caius where he was made a lecturer in harmony and counterpoint (1889) and elected organ scholar (officially becoming organist in 1891); later, in 1894, he became a fellow of the college. In 1897 he became university lecturer in harmony and counterpoint on the retirement of G. M. Garrett. At Cambridge, Wood took the degrees of BA and MusB in 1890 and those of MA and MusD in 1894. Besides

playing an active part as organist at Caius, he assisted Stanford as conductor of the Cambridge University Musical Society (1888–94) and he was bandmaster of the University Volunteers (1889–97). In addition to his work at the Royal College of Music he was an examiner for the Associated Board, which took him to Australia (1901–2), was a founder member and vice-president of the Irish Folk-Song Society (1904), and was president of the Musical Association (1924). In recognition of his contribution to British musical life he received the honorary LLD from Leeds University (1904) and an honorary DMus from Oxford (1924).

Wood's underlying desire (so his pupil Dent claimed) was to write for the stage and the concert room; his student works at the Royal College of Music—a string quartet (1885); a piano concerto (first performed under Stanford on 22 July 1886); a violin sonata (1886); a septet (1889); and an overture, *Much Ado about Nothing* (1889)—would appear to bear this out. However, whether through the exigencies of his life as a teacher or organist or by the demands of choral commissions, his subsequent instrumental output was restricted to one extended symphonic work, *Patrick Sarsfield: Symphonic Variations on an Irish Air* (1899), modelled on Parry's *Symphonic Variations*, and a series of highly assured string quartets (published with an introduction by Dent in 1929), which evince his natural classicism, a strong if conservative concept of form, and a thorough, idiomatic understanding of writing for strings. His works for the stage were similarly slender—two scores for the Cambridge Greek plays and two Dickens-inspired chamber operas—and a full-scale opera *Pat in Fairyland* (with J. Todhunter) was only sketched. Between 1885 and 1904 Wood produced a series of cantatas modelled essentially on those of his mentors, Parry and Stanford: *On Time* (Cambridge, 1898) found a powerful precedent in Parry's *Blest Pair of Sirens*, while *A Ballad of Dundee* (Leeds, 1904) looked to the narrative designs of Stanford's *Revenge* and *Voyage of Maeldune*. His most original choral work was his setting of Whitman's *Dirge for Two Veterans*, cast in the mould of a funeral march. The *Dirge* represented the zenith of his admiration for the poetry of Walt Whitman, an admiration that earlier had produced a number of fine songs, including 'Ethiopia Saluting the Colours' (1898). He also collaborated with Alfred Perceval Graves, not only in his earliest cantata, *Spring's Summons* (1885), but also in a series of publications of Irish folk-song arrangements that were very much in the manner and fashion of Stanford's collections.

Wood was subsequently best known, however, for his substantial contribution to Anglican church music. Though influenced by the symphonic aesthetic of Stanford's service settings, Wood was attracted more by archaic contrapuntal paradigms, which increasingly inform later works such as the evening service in F (*Collegium regale*, 1915) and the a cappella anthems 'Hail, gladdening light' (1919) and 'Tis the day of resurrection' (published 1927). A more intense antiquarianism, verging on the austere, is apparent in his two settings of the Nunc dimittis for R. R. Terry at Westminster Cathedral (both

1916), his communion service in the Phrygian mode (published 1923), and the *St Mark Passion* (1921), not to mention his utilization of metrical psalm tunes from Sternhold and Hopkins, the Genevan psalter, and plainchant. His interest in hymnody and carols (which produced *The Cowley Carol Book*, *The Cambridge Carol Book*, *An Italian Carol Book* and *Songs of Syon*) resulted from his close friendship with the scholar the Revd G. R. Woodward during the 1890s. Yet Wood was also capable of the most sumptuous romantic expression, as is evident in partsongs such as the canonic setting of 'Come, sleep' by Beaumont and Fletcher (published 1908) and Shelley's 'When winds that move not' (published 1913), as well as the two anthems for choir and organ, 'O Thou, the central orb' (published 1915) and 'Expectans expectavi' (1919).

On 17 March 1898 Wood married Charlotte Georgina (*b.* 1875/6), daughter of Captain Robert Wills-Sandford, Scots Greys, of Castlerea House, co. Roscommon. They had five children (two sons and three daughters), but the elder son, Patrick, was killed on active service in Italy with the RAF in 1918; the tragedy visibly affected Wood deeply. Owing largely to overwork and excessive travel, he was seriously ill with influenza in 1923 and he never fully recovered thereafter. After succeeding Stanford as professor of music at Cambridge in 1924, he held the position for only two years before dying from cancer in the Evelyn Nursing Home, Cambridge, on 12 July 1926. His wife survived him. He was buried in St Giles's cemetery on Huntingdon Road, Cambridge.   JEREMY DIBBLE

Sources I. Copley, *The music of Charles Wood* (1978) · E. J. Dent, *Notes for the festival booklet for the Armagh 'Wood' Festival* (1947) · *MT*, 67 (1926), 749 · E. J. Dent, *Introduction to eight string quartets by Charles Wood* (1929) · *DNB* · N. Temperley, ed., *Music in Britain: the romantic age, 1800–1914* (1981) · M. H. Nosek, 'Wood: a personal memoir', *MT*, 107 (1966), 492–3 · I. Copley, 'Charles Wood, 1886–1926', *MT*, 107 (1966), 489–92 · m. cert. · d. cert.
Archives CUL, MSS · Gon. & Caius Cam., collection · priv. coll., MSS · Royal College of Music, London, MSS
Likenesses photographs, Royal College of Music, London
Wealth at death £2920 2s. 3d.: probate, 24 Aug 1926, *CGPLA Eng. & Wales*

Wood, Charles Lindley, second Viscount Halifax (1839–1934), ecumenist, was born at the Admiralty in London on 7 June 1839, the second of the eight children and eldest son of Sir Charles *Wood, later first Viscount Halifax (1800–1885), Liberal politician, and his wife, Lady Mary (1807–1884), the fifth daughter of Charles Grey, second Earl Grey. He was privately educated until 1852, when he was sent to Eton College; from here he went in 1858 to Christ Church, Oxford, where he took a fourth in law and modern history in 1863.

As a child Charles, with his sister Emily, was invited to play with the royal children at Buckingham Palace, and the friendship formed with the prince of Wales, later Edward VII, proved to be lifelong. On the prince's marriage in 1862 Wood became groom of the bedchamber. He was expected to go into politics, like his father, and in the same year he became private secretary to his cousin, Sir George Grey, the home secretary, a post which he held

until 1864. He was subsequently offered a post in the government on at least two occasions, the last in 1886.

Although Wood had fallen under the influence of the Oxford Movement even before he went to university, it was there that he heard E. B. Pusey preach and began his friendship with H. P. Liddon, to whom he made his first confession about 1863. He did some work among the poor in London, in connection with the House of Charity, Soho, and in 1866 spent three months working among cholera victims in a temporary hospital in Bethnal Green, set up by Pusey and Priscilla Lydia Sellon. He even seriously considered joining the Society of St John the Evangelist when it was started, but R. M. Benson, the founder, told him he should serve God in the world. In 1868, to the initial regret of his father, he agreed to Pusey's request that he should be president of the English Church Union (ECU), an organization founded in 1860 to maintain the Catholic heritage of the Church of England, and to defend those who were under attack for their religious principles. He regarded this as his vocation in life: 'To see the Church of England, what it should be, and ultimately to see the reunion of Christendom, exhausts every possible ambition that I can picture to myself' (Lockhart, 1.145). He was president continuously until 1919, and again from 1927 until his death. Although his involvement in church politics made him feel obliged to resign from his position in the prince's household in 1877, he never regretted his decision. Indeed, on succeeding to his father's title as second Viscount Halifax of Monk Bretton in 1885, he affirmed it by changing the family motto to 'I like my choice'.

Wood proved to be an excellent chairman of the monthly meetings of the council of the ECU, holding together a group which included some forceful characters with divergent views, while putting his own arguments cogently and persuasively. He steered the ECU through a long series of controversies in the Church of England over doctrine and ritual, which became more bitter with the passing of the Public Worship Regulation Act in 1874 and the consequent imprisonment of several clergymen. Pusey praised him as 'the sense and moderation' of the council (H. P. Liddon, *Life of E. B. Pusey*, 4, 1898, 326). When he became a peer he took advantage of his right to speak in the Lords to defend the Catholic cause. It was in no small part due to Halifax that the bishops refused to allow any more prosecutions of ritualist clergy, and that the externals of Catholic worship were restored and tolerated in the Church of England.

Halifax had long shared Pusey's vision of the corporate reunion of the Church of England with Rome, based on mutual explanation of the Anglican and Roman formularies. Aided by the Abbé Fernand Portal, a Lazarist priest and theologian, with whom he formed a deep friendship after a chance meeting in Madeira in 1890, he initiated two dialogues. The first revolved round the question of the validity of Anglican orders, about which Portal wrote a pamphlet to stimulate interest in France. Halifax tried to rouse support for reunion on both sides of the channel. He introduced Portal to the two Anglican archbishops and made several speeches, including an important one in Bristol that he had printed and circulated. He visited both Archbishop E. W. Benson and the pope, Leo XIII, even drafting letters for each of them, although they refused to enter into direct correspondence, and, with Portal, he launched in 1895–6 the *Revue Anglo-Romaine*, a magazine dealing with the problems of reunion. The outcome was the establishment in Rome of a commission of Roman Catholic theologians and historians, whose conclusions led Leo XIII to issue his encyclical *Apostolicae curae* (1896) condemning Anglican orders as 'absolutely null and utterly void'. Halifax was deeply hurt but, convinced of the importance of the event, he collected all the relevant documents and correspondence and published them in 1912 under the title *Leo XIII and Anglican Orders*.

The second dialogue took place after a gap of twenty-five years. Halifax, then in his eighties, feeling that the 'Appeal to all Christians' of the 1920 Lambeth conference had created a more favourable climate, together with Portal, approached Cardinal Mercier, the Belgian primate, who was known to be sympathetic to the cause of reunion, with a view to discussing their differences. He succeeded in getting a letter of commendation from Archbishop Randall Davidson and this, together with the fact that the archbishop later nominated two additional theologians, Charles Gore and B. J. Kidd, to join the original two, W. H. Frere and Joseph Armitage Robinson, recruited by Halifax, gave the subsequent Malines Conversations a semi-official character. The first conversation in 1921 was based on a memorandum on the church and sacraments, drawn up by Halifax himself. The reluctance of the archbishop and the Vatican to be openly involved made the process very slow. Halifax worked tirelessly behind the scenes, writing letters to the press and to influential friends, and publishing a *Call to Reunion* in 1922, in order to help carry forward the talks. His increasing deafness, however, made it difficult for him to play an active part in the later conversations. After the pope put an end to them, following the deaths of Mercier and Portal, Halifax, ignoring the wishes of the archbishop of Canterbury and the new archbishop of Malines, published the separate but mutually agreed reports on the conversations by the Anglican and Roman Catholic participants in *The Conversations at Malines 1921–1925*, and his own *Notes on the Conversations at Malines* in 1928. Two years later, with a blatant disregard for the copyright laws, he published all the papers read at Malines, except one by Gore. Halifax was undoubtedly unrealistic about the possibilities of reunion at that time but, without what Gore called his 'so courageous a hopefulness' (Lockhart, 2.311), this first semi-official dialogue would never have taken place.

On 22 April 1869 Wood had married Lady Agnes Elizabeth Courtenay (1838–1919), only daughter of William Reginald *Courtenay, eleventh earl of Devon, and his wife, Elizabeth, daughter of Hugh Fortescue, first Earl Fortescue. It was a happy marriage which lasted fifty years. The couple had four sons, all but the youngest of whom died young, and two daughters. The fourth son was Edward Frederick Lindley *Wood, first earl of Halifax (1881–1959), viceroy of India and foreign secretary. Halifax enjoyed the life of a country gentleman, entertaining his friends and relations and hunting in Yorkshire, where he lived at Hickleton Hall, near Doncaster. He was 'a charming host and a whimsical companion', delighting in practical jokes, family games, and dressing up (Hodgson, 7). He died on 19 January 1934 at Hickleton, where he was buried four days later, one of his last achievements, the union of the ECU and the Anglo-Catholic Congress, having just been accomplished. A few years after his death, his son Edward published the ghost stories which he had collected throughout his life and loved to tell in *Lord Halifax's Ghost Book* (1936) and *Further Stories from Lord Halifax's Ghost Book* (1937).   PETER G. COBB

Sources J. G. Lockhart, *Charles Lindley, Viscount Halifax*, 2 vols. (1935–6) · Earl of Halifax [E. F. L. Wood], *Fulness of days* (1957) · R. Greenacre, *Lord Halifax* (1983) · G. B. Roberts, *The history of the English Church Union, 1859–1894* (1895) · B. C. Pawley and M. Pawley, *Rome and Canterbury through four centuries: a study of the relations between the church of Rome and the Anglican churches, 1530–1973* (1974) · S. Hodgson, *Lord Halifax* (1941) · GEC, *Peerage*

Archives Borth. Inst., corresp. and papers · LPL, corresp. and papers relating to Malines conversations · LPL, memorandum relating to negotiations with Leo XIII | BL, corresp. with W. E. Gladstone, Add. MS 44187 · BL, letters to Mary Gladstone, Add. MS 46243 · BL OIOC, corresp. with Sir Frederick Sykes, MS Eur. F 150 · BL OIOC, corresp. with Sir Harcourt Butler, MS Eur. F 116 · BL OIOC, corresp. with his son, first earl of Halifax, MS Eur. C 152 · Bodl. Oxf., corresp. with second earl of Selborne · Bodl. Oxf., corresp. with third earl of Selborne · Borth. Inst., corresp. with Walter Frere · Hants. RO, letters to Lady Louisa Fortescue · LPL, corresp. with A. C. Tait and related papers · LPL, corresp. with Athelstan Riley · LPL, corresp. with Edward Benson · LPL, corresp. with J. A. Robinson · LPL, corresp. with Thomas Alexander Lacey · Staffs. RO, letters to Francis Meynell · U. Durham L., letters to E. M. Copley · U. Durham L., letters to Henry George, third Earl Grey · U. Durham L., letters to Maria, Lady Grey · U. Leeds, Brotherton L., letters to Edmund Gosse · U. St Andr. L., corresp. with Wilfrid Ward · Westminster Abbey, letters to J. A. Robinson

Likenesses W. B. Richmond, drawing, 1880, Garrowby Hall, Yorkshire · W. Logsdail, oils, 1909, Hickleton Hall, Yorkshire · W. Logsdail, oils, 1909, estate office, Bugthorpe, Yorkshire · J. McLure Hamilton, oils, 1929, Garrowby Hall, Yorkshire · P. Evans, pencil drawing, NPG · S. P. Hall, pencil sketch, NPG · J. Russell & Sons, photograph, NPG · W. Stoneman, photograph, NPG · print, NPG

Wealth at death £81,079 7s. 5d.: probate, 18 July 1934, *CGPLA Eng. & Wales*

Wood, (John) Christopher [Kit] (1901–1930), painter, was born on 7 April 1901 probably in Knowsley, Lancashire, the first of the two children of Lucius Wood, a physician who practised on the earl of Derby's estate at Knowsley, and his wife, Clare Arthur. The family lived in Huyton until 1926, when they moved to Broad Chalke, Wiltshire. Christopher Wood was educated at Holmwood School, Freshfield preparatory school (1908–14), Marlborough College (1914–15), Malvern College (1918), and Liverpool school of architecture (1919–20). In 1915 an illness kept him at home for three years, leaving him with a permanent limp. He was apprenticed in 1920 to Thornley and Felix, dried fruit importers in London. He rented a room at 6 Oxford Terrace, Bayswater, and spent his spare time painting and socializing.

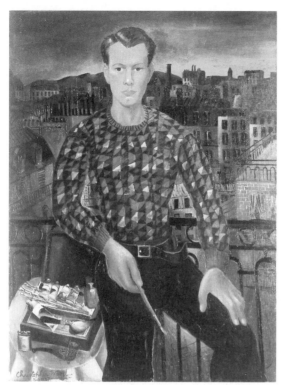

(John) Christopher [Kit] Wood (1901–1930), self-portrait, 1927

Through Robert Tritton, Wood met Alphonse Kahn, a wealthy homosexual art connoisseur and collector, and member of a banking family. Invited by Kahn, Wood arrived in Paris on 19 March 1921, to stay in his luxurious house at 41 avenue Bois de Boulogne. Kahn paid Wood's expenses and took him to museums, dealers, and studios. It was the start of a peripatetic life, usually based in his lovers' apartments, though Wood had a flat at 11 bis rue Balzac in 1921; rented rooms briefly in 1928 at 234 King's Road, Chelsea, London; then took a house nearby at 3 Minton Place, while maintaining a studio at 54 rue des Saints-Pères, Paris. He enrolled at the Académie Julian and later attended La Grande Chaumière.

In the early summer of 1921 Wood met Antonio de Gandarillas (b. 1887), a Chilean roving diplomat. Fourteen years older than Wood and married, though homosexual, Gandarillas lived a glamorous life partly financed by gambling. Their relationship lasted through Wood's life, surviving his affairs with Jeanne Bourgoint and, probably, Jean Cocteau; his plans to marry Meraud Guinness in 1927, frustrated by her parents' opposition; and his final liaison with a Russian emigrée, Frosca Munster, whom he met in 1928. His closest relationship was with his mother, the person whom he most wished to please and to whom he wrote thousands of letters. Wood was remote from his father, whom he identified with the middle-class banality of Huyton, which he loathed.

Insecure, compulsive, bisexual, and probably depressive, Wood craved both stability and the stimulus of emotional and physical excess. Gandarillas's chic social circle provided these conditions. Unwaveringly ambitious, Wood wrote to his mother in 1921 that he intended 'to try and be the greatest painter that has ever lived' (Ingleby, 59). He grasped at social status as a route to artistic success and, in return, charmed Parisian sophisticates with his handsome features, smart, conventional clothes, good manners, and astonishing naïvety, product of a secluded adolescence and a determinedly non-intellectual mindset. Yet the conflict between ambition and the life offered by Gandarillas became irreconcilable.

In 1922 Wood and Gandarillas established a pattern of leisurely travel interspersed with bouts of intense work. After touring the Netherlands they went to Monte Carlo, Nice, Marseilles, and north Africa, where Wood painted some unremarkable portraits and still lifes. He worked hard for two months in Taormina before visiting Malta, Greece, Constantinople, and Smyrna, a centre for drug distribution. It is not clear when he began to smoke opium though it was common practice in Gandarillas's circle. Both men were hospitalized with malaria in Smyrna; when they recovered they headed for Venice, northern Europe, then Gandarillas's house at 145 Cheyne Walk, Chelsea, London.

In 1923 Wood moved into Gandarillas's apartment at 60 avenue Montaigne, Paris, where they remained until early 1927 when they moved to a modern block at 6 rue des Marronniers. Financially and socially dependent, he benefited from Gandarillas's connections, which may have been how he met Picasso. Wood consistently avoided both artistic bohemia and fashionable society painters, aligning himself with modern, non-academic painting. In response to Picasso, whom he acknowledged as one of his primary models, he simplified his colour and imagery and began to draw statuesque nudes. Travelling with Gandarillas in the following year, Wood met Cocteau, whom he admired equally. In his own portrait drawings he adopted Cocteau's manner of drawing with a fluid line and almost no shading.

However, by the end of 1925 Wood wanted, he wrote, to make paintings 'full of English character' (Ingleby, 109). The opportunity came when he met Ben and Winifred Nicholson in the following year, initiating a relationship that was fundamental to his development. They introduced him to the Seven and Five Society, of which he was a member from 1927 to 1929. Wood spent March and April 1928 with them at Bankshead, Cumberland. Here, unable to smoke opium, to which he was addicted, he worked intensively. In flower paintings and pared-down landscape drawings, the trio arrived at a viable, modern alternative to French sophistication.

In August or September, during a day's visit to St Ives, Wood and Ben Nicholson encountered Alfred Wallis, whose untutored simplicity became a model for such paintings as Wood's *Porthmeor Beach* (oil, 1928), one of his first fully individual works. Often using house paint in emulation of Wallis, he painted solid, simplified forms in rich, natural colour. He had already recognized the centrality of a childlike vision to modern art, but though his painting was often compared to children's art, its deliberate simplicity masked its real sophistication. Wood's modernity was achieved through representations of the rural that identified it with a spiritual quality located in simplicity and changelessness.

In April 1929 Wood showed thirty-three paintings at Arthur Tooth & Sons, London, his one individual exhibition during his lifetime. That summer he worked first in Dieppe, painting fishing boats like *Boat in Harbour, Brittany* (oil on board, 1929; Tate collection) with meticulous attention to detail. Then, suffering severe financial problems caused by his worsening addiction, he moved to Douarnenez and Tréboul, where he was emotionally supported by the poet Max Jacob.

Towards the end of 1929 Boris Kochno invited Wood to design scenery and costumes for an episode in C. B. Cochrane's 1930 *Revue*, to be performed by the fashionable Ballets Russes. The theme was the human 'freaks' of the Luna Park circus. On 4 March 1930 Wood attended the well-received opening in Manchester. In May he showed with Ben Nicholson at the Galerie Barbazanges, in Paris. Ten paintings were bought by Lucy Wertheim, for whose London gallery Wood was to provide the opening exhibition in October. Under great pressure he returned to Tréboul, where he produced forty paintings in six weeks. Some were based on postcards; most depicted simple buildings, religious ceremonies, and light-hearted local events.

These are the paintings on which Wood's reputation depends. He received little critical recognition during his life, though the memorial exhibition of 1938 at the New Burlington Galleries, London, brought him considerable posthumous attention. He was then almost forgotten until the 1970s, when the first of several critical re-examinations of his work took place. Today he is acknowledged for playing an essential if limited role in establishing links between modernity, landscape, and concepts of the 'primitive'.

In Paris in July 1930 Wood made two somewhat surreal final paintings while stress steadily increased his addiction, led him further into debt, and made his behaviour ever less predictable. Deeply disturbed, he travelled to England on 19 August to finalize arrangements with Wertheim. Convinced that he was being followed and threatened, he diverged to the Isle of Wight. On 21 August he went to Salisbury, met his mother and sister Elizabeth (Betty), then jumped under the London-bound train at Salisbury station and was instantly killed. He was buried at All Saints' Church, Broad Chalke, on 23 August. Paintings by Wood are in many regional galleries, including Southampton Art Gallery; Laing Art Gallery, Newcastle upon Tyne; Whitworth Art Gallery, Manchester; and Manchester City Galleries. The Towner Art Gallery, Eastbourne, the Scottish National Gallery of Modern Art, Edinburgh, the Musée des Beaux-Arts, Quimper, and the Phillips Collection, Washington, DC, also hold examples of his work.   MARGARET GARLAKE

Sources R. Ingleby, *Christopher Wood: an English painter* (1995) · C. Harrison, 'The modern, the primitive, and the picturesque', in C. Harrison and M. Gardiner, *Alfred Wallis, Christopher Wood, Ben Nicholson* (1987) [exhibition catalogue, Pier Arts Centre, Stromness, 2–30 May 1987] · A. Cariou, M. Tooby, and F. Steel-Coquet, *Christopher Wood: a painter between two Cornwalls* (1996) [exhibition catalogue, Tate Gallery, St Ives, and Musée des Beaux-Arts, Quimper, 1997] · S. Faulks, *The fatal Englishman: three short lives*, pbk edn (1997) · E. Newton, *Christopher Wood, 1901–1930* (1959) · W. Mason, introduction, *Paintings and drawings by Christopher Wood* (1974) [exhibition catalogue, Kettle's Yard, Cambridge]
Archives Tate collection, corresp. and papers | Tate collection, letters to Doodie Reitlinger
Likenesses photograph, *c.*1920, Tate collection · photograph, *c.*1924, Tate collection · J. Cocteau, pencil drawing, 1925, Dartington Hall Trust, Totnes · C. Wood, self-portrait, oils, 1927, Kettle's Yard Gallery, Cambridge [*see illus.*] · photograph, 1929, Tate collection

Wood, Sir **David Edward** (1812–1894), army officer, son of Colonel Thomas Wood MP, of Littleton, Middlesex, and his wife, Lady Constance, daughter of Robert *Stewart, first marquess of Londonderry, was born on 6 January 1812. After passing through the Royal Military Academy at Woolwich, he obtained a commission as second lieutenant in the Royal Artillery on 18 December 1829. His further commissions were dated: lieutenant, 20 June 1831; second captain, 23 November 1841; first captain, 9 November 1846; lieutenant-colonel, 20 June 1854; brevet colonel, 18 October 1855; regimental colonel, 8 March 1860; major-general, 6 July 1867; colonel-commandant of the Royal Artillery, 8 June 1876; lieutenant-general, 26 November 1876; general, 1 October 1877.

After serving at various home stations, Wood went in 1842 to the Cape, where he took part in the campaign against the Boers, returning to England in 1843. He received the war medal. In 1855 he went to the Crimea, where he commanded the Royal Artillery of the 4th division at the battles of Balaklava and Inkerman, and in the siege of Sevastopol. He afterwards commanded the Royal Horse Artillery in the Crimea. He was mentioned in dispatches, and for his services was promoted brevet colonel, was made a companion in the Order of the Bath, military division, received the war medal with three clasps, and was permitted to accept and wear the Turkish medal, the insignia of the fourth class of the order of the Mejidiye, and that of the fourth class of the Légion d'honneur.

In October 1857 Wood arrived in India to assist in the suppression of the Indian mutiny, and commanded the field and horse artillery under Sir Colin Campbell, the commander-in-chief. He was prominent in the force under Brigadier-General W. Campbell on 5 January 1858 against the rebels at Mausiata, near Allahabad, when the mutineers were driven from their positions and followed up by horse artillery. He was brigadier-general commanding the field and horse artillery at the final siege of Lucknow, for his share in which he was mentioned in dispatches. He took part in various subsequent operations, and on his return to Britain in 1859 was made KCB, and received the Indian mutiny medal with clasp for Lucknow.

In 1864 and 1865 Wood commanded the Royal Artillery at Aldershot, and from 1869 to 1874 was general-commandant of Woolwich garrison. The grand cross in the Order of the Bath was bestowed on him in 1877. Wood married, in 1861, Lady Maria Isabella Liddell (d. 24 Aug 1883), daughter of Henry Thomas *Liddell, first earl of Ravensworth (1797–1878), and his wife, Isabella Horatia. They had no children. Wood died at his house, Park Lodge, Sunningdale, Berkshire, on 16 October 1894, and was buried at Littleton, Middlesex, on the 20th.

R. H. VETCH, rev. H. C. G. MATTHEW

Sources Army List • Hart's Army List • The Times (18 Oct 1894) • F. W. Stubbs, History of the … Bengal artillery (1877) • Burke, Peerage
Archives LMA, letters from Crimea
Wealth at death £5561 8s. 9d.: probate, 17 Nov 1894, CGPLA Eng. & Wales

Wood, Edgar (1860–1935), architect, was born on 17 May 1860 at Radclyffe Terrace, Middleton, Lancashire, the sixth of eight children of Thomas Broadbent Wood (1821–1909), a businessman and cotton mill owner, and his wife, Mary (1821–1871), daughter of John Sykes, a textile-card manufacturer of Lindley, Huddersfield, Yorkshire, and his wife, Charlotte. His father, a staunch Unitarian and Gladstonian Liberal, was active in public affairs as well as business. The family of his wife, Mary, shared similar business and cultural traditions at Lindley, Huddersfield, and the communities of both Middleton, where Wood lived for fifty-six years, and Lindley provided him with richly varied patronage. Little is known of Wood's early life, but in 1865 he survived a fever from which a brother and two sisters died. The family then moved to a spacious new house, Sunnybrow, Archer Park, Middleton. Mary Wood died in 1871, but on his father's remarriage Edgar gained a supportive stepmother in Jane Anne Haigh (1842–1903). He was educated at Queen Elizabeth's Grammar School, Middleton, then under the able headship of the Revd James Jelly.

As a boy, Wood wanted to be an artist, but his father insisted on a business career. Ultimately architecture provided a compromise. As an articled pupil of James Murgatroyd, Wood entered the large, commercial Manchester practice of Mills and Murgatroyd, which he found to be a suffocating experience. After qualifying by examination as an architect in 1885 he almost immediately set up practice, first in Middleton and later at Oldham and Manchester. His first public commission, a small shelter and drinking fountain (dem.) for Middleton's market place, was also his first to be illustrated in the British Architect (British Architect, 29, 1888, 135). Larger commissions followed and by 1893, with an office at 78 Cross Street, Manchester, Wood accepted G. A. E. (Bertie) Schwabe as his pupil. He remained for seventeen years, and from his recollections Wood's personal character emerges. He was described by Schwabe as a man 'who always gets his own way' and as 'always hounding some new ideal' (private information). He was of medium height with a healthy complexion and a full moustache; portraits express a hint of imperiousness. When Schwabe first joined him, Wood wore formal dress and top hat, following professional convention, but he soon decided that this was impractical for an architect and instead adopted tweeds and knickerbockers. This preference for rational informality in place of conventional propriety is characteristic of Wood, and in siting and planning his houses and schools salubrity held first priority.

Wood sought to practise architecture as an art. He designed, detailed, and supervised his work personally, and his only staff were Schwabe and an office boy. His methods were always direct: records of critical dates on progress and submissions, for example, were neat lists on key drawings. He was an inveterate traveller and his holidays were architectural tours to study and draw either at home or abroad. Vernacular architecture attracted him strongly and, significantly, his sketches extended to cubiform Arabic houses. However, he very seldom drew contemporary architecture but rather collected numerous photographs and cuttings illustrating modern and historic buildings. Wood was constantly searching for new means of expression. His early work shows the influence of the architect Alfred Waterhouse, but he was also attracted to the innovatory abstraction in the work of the Century Guild, founded in 1882, which advocated 'the unity of the arts'. This stance was adopted later by major arts and crafts societies, including the Northern Art Workers' Guild, inaugurated in 1896 in Manchester, with Wood as a leading member.

A gradual emancipation from conventional Victorian practice is reflected generally in Wood's early buildings, and his inclination to the avant-garde and radical reform is expressed in two Middleton works in particular. The stylistic influence of the Century Guild, with its exaggeratedly attenuated forms, represents the former and was pronounced in the Old Road Unitarian Chapel (1891–2; dem.), and in this building and his own home, Redcroft, Rochdale Road (1891–2), rich craftwork, architectural sculpture, and mural painting demonstrate reform through 'the unity of the arts'.

The influence of vernacular buildings appears in Wood's work from the mid-1890s. Initially some of his Lancashire buildings were over-rich in rural picturesqueness, but later he employed vernacular elements more rationally. These references were always faithful to their locality, as may be seen in the contrast between his Lancashire and Yorkshire buildings. The latter are far more severe in character than those in the Manchester region. Among them is Banney Royd, Edgerton, Huddersfield (1899–1901), Wood's largest and most widely published domestic commission. Paradoxically, within its gabled, traditional exterior it contains Wood's most inventive display of art nouveau detail. Technically the house is advanced and unusual because it employs cavity-wall construction.

By 1904 Wood was at the height of his professional career and many of his best-known commissions, such as Banney Royd, the Long Street Wesleyan Church at Middleton (1898–1901), Lindley Clock Tower (1899–1902), and the First Church of Christ, Scientist, Victoria Park, Manchester (1903–7), were either completed or in progress. Two of these, the clock tower and the First Church, precede expressionism in their wilful manipulation of architectural form and traditional materials. At this point, having carried expression in traditional building to its limits,

Wood turned to a new form of construction to which he had been introduced by **James Henry Sellers** (1861–1954), an architect and innovator.

Sellers came from the same locality as Wood but his background was entirely different. He was born on 1 November 1861 at Longholme, Hall Carr, Haslingden, Rossendale, Lancashire, the son of Thomas Sellers, a cotton-factory machinist, and his wife, Naomi Preston. He received only an elementary education and was architecturally self-educated. After commencing as an office boy to an Oldham architect he taught himself to draw and progressed to become an able assistant before becoming an architectural ghost in a succession of offices in northern cities. He was studious and had an extensive knowledge of architecture and its literature, but he found the experience of living in York to be a supreme revelation of Georgian design. His responsibilities included industrial projects, and he became familiar with reinforced concrete, then a new material. Sellers and Wood were both highly independent but agreed to an informal partnership whereby each partner was responsible for his own work. Nevertheless, projects and other architectural matters were fully discussed. In personality the two men were in striking contrast: Wood was flamboyant and imaginative, Sellers retiring, bookish, and analytical. Through the association Sellers found his professional freedom and Wood gained new technical and architectural insights.

Wood perceived that reinforced concrete offered possibilities for freer architectural expression and, after building several houses with unusual and attractive massing gained through combining flat- and pitched-roof construction, he produced an outstanding series of flat-roofed houses, of which the best-known is Upmeads, Newport Road, Stafford (1908). The design was shown at the Royal Academy but did not find favour; a leading critic described it as austere and fortress-like. Such comment left Wood undeterred. Simultaneously Sellers produced a small, masterly, classically simple, flat-roofed office building in King Street, Oldham (1906–8), for Dronsfield Brothers, engineers. The partners undertook a few projects jointly, the most important of which were two schools, at Durnford Street (dem.) and Elm Street, Middleton (1908–10). For their date they were remarkable in design, construction, and social provision; each had covered play areas and carefully selected planting.

Through his father's bequest, from 1909 Wood became financially independent and thereafter undertook no further large commissions, but in 1914 he designed a new house for his own use at 224 Hale Road, Hale, Cheshire. It closes this series of adventurous buildings with its flat roof related to concave plan forms. While planning to visit India, Wood entrusted the preparation of the working drawings to Sellers, although later he was actively involved in the detailing and decoration of the house. For some years he had used patterns of interlocking chevrons in the manner later common to art deco, and he made these the decorative theme of his house externally, internally, in the furniture, and in the garden. Their most striking use is on the front elevation, where a central panel of brightly coloured tiles rises above the similarly designed front door. Wood executed the interior patterning personally.

In the immediate post-war years Wood appears to have turned to painting and left the office to Sellers, who continued to practise until 1948, specializing in high-quality small industrial buildings, neo-Georgian domestic work, and the furniture for which he remains highly admired. Sellers married Sarah Mills (d. 1933), and died on 30 January 1954 at his home, Bollin Tower, Alderley Edge. He was cremated at Manchester crematorium.

After travelling widely in Italy, Wood decided about 1922 to settle at Porto Maurizio, Imperia, Liguria, where he rented part of a convent and devoted himself to painting, drawing, and travel. In 1932 on a nearby site he built a villa and created a garden, which he recorded in a fine pastel exhibited at the Royal Academy in 1934. By then drawing in pastel was his exclusive medium and he used it with great effect. In 1892 Wood had married Annie Maria Jelly (*bap.* 1859, *d.* 1936), daughter of his former headmaster. Annie Wood preferred life in England and did not share her husband's appreciation of Italy, and she made a new home with her family; the couple did not have any children. Wood engaged a series of housekeepers, and to the last of these he bequeathed the villa. He developed cardiac asthma after drawing at high altitude in the Italian Alps and died in his sleep at his home, Monte Calvario, Porto Maurizio, on 12 October 1935. He was buried in the English cemetery at Diano Marina, near Imperia.

Edgar Wood's work is significant not only for distinguished individual buildings but also in its totality. It is impressive for the constant creative search that led him to develop modern construction, to anticipate expressionist plasticity, art deco decoration, and cubic architectural forms twenty years in advance of their general adoption. He has been hailed as a pioneer of twentieth-century modernism and has been severally described as an art nouveau and arts and crafts architect, but he cuts across the contemporary stylistic categories. His modernism is that of a late Victorian who idealized nature and art but never technology, and was from first to last a radical individualist. A collection of his architectural drawings and sketches is in the Royal Institute of British Architects drawings collection, London, and examples of his colourful sketches and his furniture are represented in the Manchester City Art Galleries, and the Whitworth Art Gallery, Manchester, the Cecil Higgins Art Gallery, Bedford, and the Wolfsonian Museum, Miami Beach, Florida.   JOHN H. G. ARCHER

Sources J. H. G. Archer, 'Edgar Wood and the architecture of the arts and crafts and art nouveau movements in Britain', MA diss., University of Manchester, 1968 · J. H. G. Archer, 'Edgar Wood: a notable Manchester architect', *Transactions of the Lancashire and Cheshire Antiquarian Society*, 73–4 (1963–4), 152–87 · J. H. G. Archer, 'Edgar Wood and J. Henry Sellers: a decade of partnership and experiment', *Edwardian architecture and its origins*, ed. A. Service (1975), 372–84 · E. Wood, 'An architect's experiences in the development of design', *Builders' Journal and Architectural Record* (1900), 73–5 · L. Weaver, 'Upmeads, Stafford', *Small country houses of to-day*, 1 (1910), 202–7 · *Northern Art Workers' Guild exhibition* (1898) [exhibition catalogue, Manchester City Galleries] · *Partnership in style*

(1975) [exhibition catalogue, Manchester City Galleries] · *Birtles Hall, near Macclesfield, Cheshire* (1994) [sale catalogue, Sothebys, 4 May 1994] · personal knowledge (2004) · private information (2004) [Wood family, Sellers family, G. A. E. Schwabe] · b. certs. [Edgar Wood and James Henry Sellers] · d. cert. [James Henry Sellers]

Archives Middleton Library, Rochdale

Likenesses C. Jackson, photograph, *c*.1885, priv. coll. · F. W. Jackson, oils, 1891, repro. in Archer, 'Edgar Wood: a notable Manchester architect'; priv. coll. · H. B. Laycock, engraving, 1910 (James Henry Sellers), repro. in Archer, 'Edgar Wood and J. Henry Sellers'; priv. coll.

Wealth at death £42,991 11s. 5d.: administration, 22 July 1936, *CGPLA Eng. & Wales*

Wood, Edmund Burke (1820–1882), lawyer and politician in Canada, was born near Fort Erie, Upper Canada, on 13 February 1820, the fourth son of Samuel and Charlotte Wood. Of Irish-American descent, he was a low-churchman of the Church of England. He was educated in the Niagara region, and became a teacher after ruling out farming as a career following the loss of an arm. He graduated BA from Oberlin College, Ohio, in 1848, became a student-at-law, and was appointed clerk of the county court in Brant county in 1853, a post he resigned when called to the bar in 1854. He began a partnership in Brantford with Peter Long in 1854, but practised alone following its dissolution in 1860. An ambitious and versatile lawyer, Wood became solicitor of the Buffalo and Lake Huron Railway, cementing an alliance with railway interests and leading eventually to accusations of venality which marked most of his career. In 1855 he married Jane Augusta Marter of Brantford.

In 1863 Wood was elected as the Reform member for West Brant in the legislature of the united province of Canada, and he remained a supporter of John Sandfield Macdonald's government until the confederation of Canada in 1867. Elected in the first elections in 1867 to the Canadian House of Commons and the Ontario legislature, he sat in both houses until the abolition of dual representation in 1872. In 1867 he was appointed treasurer of Ontario in the provincial cabinet of John Sandfield Macdonald, where he was the leading Reform member of Macdonald's 'patent combination' coalition ministry of moderate Reformers and Conservatives. He earned a reputation as an able administrator, and concluded the financial arbitration between Ontario and Quebec. But, as a fractious colleague and strict defender of Ontario's economic interests, he found it difficult to adhere to party lines.

In 1871, following an inconclusive provincial election, Wood resigned from Macdonald's government and helped trigger the coalition's collapse; he rejoined the Reform or Liberal Party under the new provincial government of Edward Blake. His reputation in provincial politics irreparably damaged, he was not offered a post in the Blake administration in 1871 or its successor. He resigned from the provincial legislature in 1873 to seek a return to federal politics, and re-entered the House of Commons as a Liberal in a by-election in 1873 in West Durham, Ontario. Although his eloquence (which earned him the nickname 'Big Thunder') was crucial to toppling the Conservative

government later that year, he was not invited to join Alexander Mackenzie's Liberal administration. In 1874, his provincial and federal political careers over, he accepted the post of chief justice of Manitoba, having in 1872 been made queen's counsel and in 1873 bencher of the Law Society of Upper Canada.

Wood proved to be a controversial figure in Manitoba, presiding skilfully over a number of difficult trials but embroiling himself in many local disputes, including railway controversies and conflict-of-interest allegations. In 1881 a number of Manitoba lawyers and politicians petitioned for his removal. Before charges could be investigated, however, Wood, already incapacitated, collapsed after a stroke, and died in Winnipeg on 7 October 1882. He was survived by his wife, four sons, and two daughters. An individual of enormous abilities, Wood suffered from a headstrong and abrasive personality. He left few legacies, and his reputation for unscrupulousness compromised many of his achievements in building the professionalism of the bar in Manitoba.   DANIEL LIVERMORE

Sources R. St. G. Stubbs, 'Hon. Edmund Burke Wood', *Historical and Scientific Society of Manitoba, Papers*, 3rd ser., 13 (1958), 27–47 · I. R. D. Gibson and L. Gibson, *Substantial justice* (1972) · *Dominion Annual Register* (1882) · H. J. Morgan, ed., *The Canadian legal directory* (1878)

Archives Ontario Archives, Blake MSS · Queens University, Kingston, Ontario, Alexander Mackenzie MSS

Wood, Edward (1846–1930), building society manager, was born on 8 September 1846 at Baddesley Ensor, Warwickshire, the son of Edward Wood, a collier, later a colliery under-manager, and his wife, Eleanor, *née* Atkins. His father was illiterate in 1846 and could only make his mark when registering his son's birth.

Wood started work in the colliery's counting house and became its London agent when he was twenty-five. In September 1870 he married Elizabeth, the daughter of Robert Heuchan, a tea dealer; the couple had one son and three daughters. After moving to Battersea in 1871, Wood was active in local government as a Liberal and also became a prominent temperance campaigner.

The temperance cause was his lifetime passion, and this connection led to his election to the board of the Temperance Building Society in 1882. Founded in 1854, the Temperance flourished and in 1880 was the sixth largest building society. In 1887 the society's founder secretary died and Wood was appointed to replace him; he proved to be an able manager, paying meticulous attention to detail and keeping all aspects of the business under his close personal control.

In 1892 the collapse of the country's largest building society, the Liberator, faced all societies with a crisis, but especially the Temperance, since its investors were drawn from exactly the same nonconformist circles that had fuelled the Liberator's rapid growth. Wood acted swiftly and decisively. A letter sent to all members detailed the strength of the Temperance Society's balance sheet. Investors' fears were allayed by the waiving of the usual notice of one month for withdrawals; payment would be on demand. By 1896 the Temperance had resumed steady growth and by 1906 it was the largest society.

Early in his building society career Wood took a number of innovative steps. In 1895 he was one of the first managers to pay commission to builders developing estates for introducing borrowers to the building society. Assets reached a peak in 1909. Later the Temperance Society's relative position declined, especially after 1918. While other large societies had growing branch networks, the Temperance had none. Changes after 1918, such as mortgages for bigger proportions of the house price, for longer terms, and to less wealthy buyers, were seen as risking the huge reserves that the Temperance had built up, and it is clear that Wood's very conservative attitude to risk and delegation, although financially prudent, inhibited the long-term growth of the society. Wood had outside business interests as a board member (later chairman) of the Sceptre Assurance Company and the Artisans' General Dwelling Company, which owned more than 7000 houses.

In the aftermath of the collapse of the Liberator, Wood became more prominent in the National Association of Building Societies, whose executive committee he joined in 1887. He campaigned for increased powers for the registrar of building societies and for the annual publication of much detail from individual societies, especially concerning loans in arrears and properties in possession. The 1894 Building Societies Act largely reflected these views. Wood served as the association's chairman from 1903 to 1913, and continued on the executive until 1923. He ended London domination of the executive and made the association truly national. An excellent public speaker, he was adept in presenting statistical information. During his chairmanship government proposals increasingly impinged on building society territory, and Wood was a formidable leader of the association's delegations to ministers. He was a member of the 1908 royal commission on the Land Transfer Acts and was one of a group of financial specialists advising Lloyd George on the 1909 Finance Act.

An active figure in local government, Wood served as chairman of Battersea vestry and was its representative on the Wandsworth board of works. In 1886 he became Wandworth representative on the Metropolitan Board of Works—the forerunner of the London county council. He was prominent in the movement which achieved borough status for Battersea in 1888. He was a JP first for Surrey and then for London county, and was chairman of the Wandsworth bench from 1900 to 1926. Wood was a Wesleyan Methodist (a member of Bromwood Wesleyan Church, Clapham) and held high office in many temperance organizations: the Band of Hope, the United Kingdom Temperance Alliance, the Good Templars order, and the Temperance Orphanage (chairman, 1884–1930). In 1916 he published *The Nationalization of the Liquor Traffic*. He was a freemason and past master of a temperance lodge.

Wood died at his home, 58 Nightingale Lane, Clapham, London, on 20 September 1930, following a stroke at his diamond wedding celebration. He was cremated, and his ashes were interred at St Mary's Church cemetery, Battersea.   ESMOND J. CLEARY

Sources S. J. Price, *From queen to queen: the centenary story of the Temperance Permanent Building Society, 1854–1954* [1954] · S. J. Price, *Building societies: their origin and history* [1958] · *Building Societies Gazette* (Oct 1930) · E. J. Cleary, 'Wood, Edward', *DBB* · b. cert. · m. cert. · d. cert.
Likenesses photograph, repro. in Price, *From queen to queen* (1954), facing p. 45 · photograph; known to be at the Building Societies Association, London, in 1958
Wealth at death £48,848 11s. 0d.: probate, 8 Nov 1930, *CGPLA Eng. & Wales*

Wood, Edward Frederick Lindley, first earl of Halifax (1881–1959), politician and diplomat, was born on 16 April 1881 at Powderham Castle in Devon, the home of his maternal grandfather, the eleventh earl of Devon. He was the sixth child and fourth son of Charles Lindley *Wood (1839–1934), who later became the second Viscount Halifax, and his wife, Lady Agnes Elizabeth Courtenay (1838–1919). His great-grandfather was Earl Grey of the Reform Bill of 1832. The Woods had emerged from among the gentry of Yorkshire to become one of the great landowning houses of northern England, but with three elder brothers Edward seemed to have little prospect of inheriting his father's title. Between 1886 and 1890, however, each of his brothers fell victim to one of the Victorian child-killing diseases, leaving him heir to the family viscountcy. These bereavements help to explain the extraordinarily close bond which developed between Wood and his father, despite the latter's somewhat macabre sense of humour. The world into which he was born was dominated by religion and hunting, and these remained the great passions of Wood's life, notwithstanding his distinguished political career. In later life he was sometimes known as the Holy Fox, a play upon the title which he inherited. Wood's father had accepted the presidency of the English Church Union in 1868 at the age of twenty-nine and retained this position until 1919. Thereafter he devoted himself to the cause of the reunion of the Christian churches and provided a spiritual commitment from which his son never deviated. He was president of the union again from 1927 until his death in 1934; his influence upon his surviving son was immense.

Early career Wood was born with an atrophied left arm, but shrugged off its effects and learned as a child to shoot and ride to hounds. He went to St David's preparatory school in Reigate in September 1892 at the age of eleven. He was not at all happy there and he found Eton College, to which he transferred in September 1894, only marginally more congenial. Its emphasis on the classics and sports failed to arouse his enthusiasm. Only at Oxford did Wood's academic talents begin to blossom. He arrived at Christ Church, his father's old college, in October 1899. There he concentrated on his historical studies and took no part in the debates of the union. His reward was a first-class degree in modern history and election to a fellowship at All Souls in November 1903 which he held until

Edward Frederick Lindley Wood, first earl of Halifax (1881–1959), by Sir Oswald Birley, 1932

1910. As junior fellow, Wood's duties included the preparation of a mayonnaise sauce for Sunday dinner and decanting the college's vintage port, but he enjoyed the intellectual atmosphere and began an association which lasted for the rest of his life.

Upon the completion of his probationary year at All Souls Wood embarked upon an eighteenth-century-style grand tour with his Oxford friend Ludovic Heathcoat Amory. This took him to South Africa, India, Australia, and New Zealand and gave him the chance to study what became known as the dominions at a time of transition. Wood returned to England in 1905, but was not immediately tempted to enter politics at a difficult moment in the history of the Conservative Party. Instead, he returned to All Souls and devoted himself over the next two years to further academic study, which led to the publication of a short biography of John Keble. On 21 September 1909 he married Lady Dorothy Evelyn Augusta Onslow (1885–1976), daughter of the fourth earl of Onslow, who had held government office on four occasions and had also been governor-general of New Zealand. Lady Dorothy introduced a lightness and informality into her husband's life, which did something to lessen the natural aloofness for which Wood was already noted. It was a happy marriage, broken only by Wood's death fifty years later. The couple's first child, Anne, was born in July 1910, followed by a son,

Charles, in October 1912. Two further sons, Peter and Richard, were born in 1916 and 1920 respectively.

By the time of his marriage, Wood had decided to stand for parliament. Ripon was a natural Conservative seat, although the sitting tory member had, like so many of his colleagues, gone down to defeat in the Liberal landslide of 1906. With Conservative fortunes recovering, though not to the extent of producing a change of government, Wood was victorious in the general election of January 1910, securing a comfortable majority of more than 1000 over his Liberal opponent. Though he sat in the Commons until 1925, it was never his natural milieu, especially in the torrid atmosphere which characterized party politics in the years before the outbreak of the First World War. His own inclinations were towards reason, compromise, and conciliation, but these seemed to have little place in the parliamentary affairs of the day. He successfully defended his seat in the second general election of 1910—though with a reduced majority—but it was probably to his relief, as someone for whom the hustings offered little attraction, that this was the last occasion upon which Wood fought a contested parliamentary election. At the elections of 1918, 1922, 1923, and 1924 he was returned unopposed. Wood made little impact in the Commons before 1914. Over the Parliament Bill of 1911 he found himself, somewhat surprisingly, in the ditcher camp of outright resistance to the Liberal government's proposals, but he was more stirred by the bill to disestablish the Welsh church, which he opposed vigorously in debate.

The First World War and its aftermath As captain in the Queen's Own Yorkshire dragoons, a yeomanry regiment recruited around his home at Hickleton in the West Riding of Yorkshire, Wood found his fate largely determined for him with the outbreak of European war in August 1914. His parliamentary appearances were inevitably rare during this period, but he did on one occasion manage to urge the immediate introduction of conscription. His division was not involved at the front line until 1916. Somewhat to his surprise he was mentioned in dispatches in January 1917—'Heaven knows what for!'—and, believing that he would be more usefully employed in England, he was relieved to be offered the post of deputy director of the labour supply department in the Ministry of National Service. There he served from November 1917 until the end of 1918. Later in his career Wood became closely associated with policies designed to avoid war if this was at all possible. In the First World War, however, while initially showing some sympathy for Lord Lansdowne's call for a compromise settlement, he emerged among those Conservative hardliners who demanded all-out victory and a punitive peace with Germany, putting his name to the Lowther petition in April 1919 which encouraged Lloyd George to take up an intransigent position at the Paris conference.

In the post-war parliament Wood became a member of a small group of MPs which included Samuel Hoare, Philip Lloyd-Graeme, and Walter Elliot, whose aim was to espouse progressive policies. With his friend George Lloyd he produced a 100-page political pamphlet entitled *The*

Great Opportunity (1918), which argued that the Conservative Party should focus on the welfare of the community rather than the advantage of the individual. It also advocated a federal solution to the Irish question. Ireland, indeed, was one of Wood's main political interests at this time along with housing and agriculture. But his parliamentary career seemed likely to come to an early end when, in May 1920, he was offered and accepted the governor-generalship of South Africa. The offer, however, was withdrawn when it became clear that the South Africans expected someone of cabinet rank or a member of the royal family to fill this post. Soon afterwards Wood got his first foot on the ministerial ladder when appointed under-secretary for the colonies in April 1921. It was not an auspicious beginning, since the secretary of state, Winston Churchill, seemed reluctant at first even to meet his new assistant. Matters eventually improved, and in winter 1921–2 Wood toured the British West Indies in order to report to Churchill on the political and social situation there.

Like several others Wood's political prospects were transformed by the ending of Lloyd George's coalition government in October 1922. He had become increasingly disillusioned with the latter's premiership, attended a meeting of junior ministers on 16 October at which the extent of disquiet about the prime minister became apparent, and was among the majority who voted at the Carlton Club on 23 October that the Conservative Party should contest the next general election as an independent force. With many leading Conservatives remaining loyal to Lloyd George, Wood was elevated from the obscurity of junior office to the ranks of the cabinet as president of the Board of Education on 24 October 1922. His appointment did not arouse much excitement, though some saw his elevation as evidence of an improvement in the moral character of the administration. In the climate of post-war austerity education was not a position offering many opportunities for constructive action, and Wood inevitably regarded it as little more than a stepping stone to higher office. It was indicative of his priorities that he made sure that his ministerial schedule left time for two days' hunting each week. This first experience of cabinet government ended when Baldwin called a surprise general election in December 1923 on the question of tariffs, a decision about which Wood felt considerable misgivings.

After a brief interlude of Labour government, Wood returned to office as minister of agriculture on 6 November 1924. It was an appointment for which his landowning background equipped him well but, as was the case at education, it was not a post which then offered much scope for constructive initiatives. He was responsible for getting the agricultural returns and tithe bills through the House of Commons and found himself devoting far more of his time to his ministerial duties than at the Board of Education. But in October 1925 Wood was approached by the secretary of state for India, Lord Birkenhead, with the offer of the viceroyalty and governor-generalship in succession to Lord Reading, the Liberal lawyer. He had a family interest in India, as his paternal grandfather, Sir Charles Wood, had been the second holder of the secretaryship of state between 1859 and 1866. Nevertheless, his first inclination was to decline the offer on family grounds. With his sons of school age and, more importantly, with his 86-year-old father unlikely to survive a five-year viceroyalty, Wood was reluctant to leave Britain at this time. Only when his father recommended acceptance did he acquiesce. He now gave up his Commons seat, taking the title of Baron Irwin of Kirby Underdale, and left for India on 17 March 1926.

Viceroy of India In many ways Irwin was well fitted for his new post. He relished the pomp which was inseparable from it. Physically, he cut an impressive figure, and was an accomplished horseman. Six feet five inches tall, he easily gave an impression of aristocratic self-confidence which set him apart from lesser men. As a contemporary recorded: 'He has a magnificent head, and his tall figure and Cecilian stoop and sympathetic kindly eyes give more the impression of a Prince of the Church than a politician' (R. Bernays, *Naked Fakir*, 1931, 51). Yet at the same time he showed a sympathy for the Indian point of view unmatched by many of his predecessors. He also displayed considerable physical bravery in the face of more than one attempt to assassinate him during his time in the subcontinent. His viceroyalty was characterized by a patient commitment to ensuring that a contented India should remain inside the British Commonwealth for the foreseeable future. He set out to win Indian goodwill and co-operation, but could be firm when necessary, and stressed that it would be difficult to meet Indian wishes while Indians remained divided among themselves. In his first major speech as viceroy he appealed for an end to the endemic communal violence between Muslims and Hindus, and returned to this theme at intervals throughout his time in India. Towards terrorism he was uncompromising and, despite his Christian beliefs, felt no hesitation or remorse when signing death warrants which he considered justified.

Many of the parameters of Irwin's viceroyalty had already been drawn when he assumed the reins of office. An important provision of the Government of India Act of 1919, embodying the Montagu–Chelmsford reforms, had been that after an interval of ten years a commission should be appointed to inquire into the working of the new constitution and to advise on whether further reforms were needed. In the intervening period Indian national aspirations had grown apace, and Irwin fully accepted that eventual Indian self-government was inevitable and that Britain must steer the country in that direction in the medium-term future. Birkenhead decided to bring forward the appointment of the statutory commission, placing it under the chairmanship of Sir John Simon, but the fatal decision was that it should consist entirely of British members of parliament. Irwin, calculating that a mixed commission would have little chance of producing an agreed report and wrongly anticipating that Indians would, after suitable protest, fall into line with the British government's approach, had advised Birkenhead in this sense. It was the most fateful mistake of his viceroyalty, and one he came bitterly to regret. Once the composition of the commission was announced in November 1927, it became apparent that all the leading parties in India, including Congress, whose co-operation would be vital to any progress, would boycott Simon's mission. Irwin reassured Birkenhead that once Simon had arrived in India he would be able to win over moderate opinion, but the auguries were not good. In fact the Indian leaders treated the commission, which landed at Bombay on 3 February 1928, as if it had never arrived. Over the months which followed matters improved somewhat and Simon achieved some limited success, but his task was almost impossible, and Irwin became convinced that some new gesture would be necessary if real progress was to be made. Ironically, the viceroy's way ahead became easier following a change of government in Britain which saw Ramsay MacDonald form his second administration in June 1929, in which William Wedgwood Benn, a former Liberal, took the Indian portfolio.

Irwin arrived on leave in Britain on 13 July, bringing with him a suggested exchange of letters between Simon and the new prime minister. The idea was that Simon would propose a round-table conference to discuss the eventual findings of his commission. MacDonald would reply by agreeing to the conference while stating that the Montagu declaration of 1917 had contained an implicit commitment to the ultimate attainment by India of dominion status. The drafts were shown to Simon, who had serious misgivings about a round-table conference. On the question of dominion status, however, Irwin got the impression that Simon at this stage had no such objections. Simon's fellow commissioners took almost exactly the opposite view, with the result that the exchange of letters went ahead with the dominion status statement omitted. But Simon failed to convey his colleagues' strength of feeling against the proposed declaration. Their belief—which Simon soon came to share—was that such an announcement would cut the ground from beneath the commission's forthcoming report. Indeed, it is curious that Irwin, too, did not seem to understand this. Dominion status would inevitably become a minimum demand rather than a maximum goal. The viceroy went ahead, and in October made a public declaration that the British government viewed dominion status as the natural issue of India's constitutional progress.

This announcement had a dramatic impact in both Britain and India. Irwin's initiative was roundly denounced by much of the Conservative Party, even though he was only spelling out what had been implicit in British policy for more than a decade. His predecessor as viceroy, Lord Reading, joined in the condemnation while Simon also made his displeasure apparent. In India there was briefly renewed hope that British policy might yet satisfy national aspirations, but a conference in December 1929 between Irwin and Indian political leaders in New Delhi failed to produce agreement. Gandhi now withdrew to plan a campaign of civil disobedience with a view to securing complete independence from Britain. In a calculated gesture of defiance he walked for twenty-four days to the sea, where he picked up a handful of salt. This symbolic gesture broke a law which made it a punishable offence for Indians to own salt which had not been obtained through the government's monopoly. Irwin had little option but to order his arrest. He realized, however, that without Gandhi's co-operation there could be no real progress. George V had already opened the first round-table conference in November 1930, boycotted by Congress because of Gandhi's imprisonment. So in January 1931 the Indian leader was released, and on his initiative a series of eight meetings now took place between the viceroy and the mahatma. The contrast between the two men could hardly have been more stark, and Irwin never fully understood the Indian and his ways. As he once explained to his father,

> it was rather like talking to someone who had stepped off another planet on to this for a short visit of a fortnight and whose whole mental outlook was quite other to that which was regulating most of the affairs on the planet to which he had descended. (Birkenhead, 247)

But there developed a feeling of mutual respect in which the common strand of religious commitment and motivation was certainly important. Irwin showed a steely side to his character in these negotiations which led to the so-called Delhi pact of March 1931. Gandhi's concessions were substantial. Civil disobedience would be abandoned and Congress agreed to be represented at future sessions of the round-table conference.

Return to domestic politics Irwin returned to England at the end of his five-year appointment on 3 May 1931. Already appointed GCSI and GCIE in 1926, he now received a knighthood of the Garter, an order of which he was to become chancellor in 1943. The Labour government whose Indian policy he had served so well collapsed in August 1931, and Baldwin was keen to make use of his talents as one of the quota of Conservative ministers in the newly constituted National Government which replaced it. But Irwin declined the offer of the foreign secretaryship, preferring for the time being at least to return to his estates in Yorkshire. He was also concerned that this appointment would not go down well with the right wing of the Conservative Party who resented his attitude towards Indian self-government. Instead, he took advantage of his relative leisure to accept an invitation from Vincent Massey to travel to Canada to deliver the inaugural Massey lecture at Toronto University. But the Conservative leader was not to be denied: in June 1932, after the sudden death of Sir Donald Maclean, Irwin agreed with some genuine reluctance to return to his former position as president of the Board of Education. As in the 1920s, however, the prevailing economic climate offered little scope for policy initiatives. In any case Irwin's views on education were becoming dated. On a visit to Hickleton he announced, 'We want a school to train them up for servants and butlers' (Birkenhead, 326). Though this lay outside his strictly departmental responsibilities, he was also enlisted to help Samuel Hoare in preparing the government's largest single piece of legislation, the Government of India Bill, which finally worked its way onto the statute book in 1935. In the mean time Irwin succeeded Viscount Grey as chancellor of the University of Oxford in 1933 and, upon the death of his 94-year-old father in January 1934, became Viscount Halifax. When Baldwin and the ageing prime minister, Ramsay MacDonald, exchanged positions in June 1935, Halifax, with some feeling of relief, moved from education to the War Office. Though he was secretary of state for only a few months, this move marked the beginning of his close association with the foreign and diplomatic affairs of the decade which would dominate the remainder of his ministerial career. The experience quickly convinced him that the country was unprepared for war, though at the committee of imperial defence he challenged the assertion of the chiefs of staff that the country's paramount need was to step up the pace of rearmament. It was a weakness in his understanding of the international situation that he never fully grasped, until it was too late, the enormity of Hitler's capacity for evil. Like Neville Chamberlain, Halifax retained a misplaced confidence that negotiation and the application of human reason were the best ways to ameliorate the threatening European scene.

After the general election in November 1935 Halifax became lord privy seal and leader of the House of Lords. Then, when Neville Chamberlain became prime minister in May 1937, he was moved to be lord president of the council while still leading the Lords. In these non-departmental posts Halifax was free to range across the whole spectrum of government business, but both Baldwin and Chamberlain made especial use of his talents in the field of foreign affairs, where his interventions became increasingly important. During the cabinet discussion of the crisis created by the premature disclosure of the Hoare–Laval pact in December 1935 it was Halifax who warned that, if the foreign secretary was not dismissed, the situation might become so serious as to bring down the whole government. With Anthony Eden as foreign secretary Halifax was almost deputy foreign minister in the Lords, though this formal title was avoided probably out of sensitivity to Eden's position. In general the two men worked well together, though a legend later grew up surrounding the circumstances in which Halifax, as master of the Middleton hunt, accepted an invitation from the Reichsmarschall, Hermann Göring, to visit a hunting exhibition in Berlin in November 1937 and to shoot foxes in Pomerania. In later years this episode was presented, not least by Eden himself, as an illustration of Chamberlain's efforts to circumvent the Foreign Office in order to pursue his policy of appeasement in defiance of his professional advisers. In the circumstances Halifax was careful, after the Second World War, to place his own version of events on the record. According to this, Eden was himself instrumental in pressing Halifax to accept the invitation. The foreign secretary's later misgivings were partly the result of the promptings of his staff and partly a consequence of the way the visit was arranged, especially when it became clear that Halifax would be going to Berchtesgaden to meet Hitler. At this encounter,

where the English aristocrat nearly mistook the Führer for a footman, he failed to give any indication of British objections to German ambitions in Austria and Czechoslovakia. Indeed, he spoke of 'possible alterations in the European order which might be destined to come about with the passage of time'. In general, the visit did little to open his eyes to the true nature of the Nazi regime.

The foreign secretary and appeasement By February 1938 Eden's relations with Chamberlain had reached breaking point. Halifax warned the prime minister of the growing strains within the cabinet and, when the crisis came, did his best, but without success, to effect a reconciliation between the two men. Eden duly resigned on 20 February, exasperated above all by Chamberlain's increasing interference in the diplomatic arena and unwilling to make further concessions to Italy without corresponding gestures of good faith from Mussolini. Chamberlain appointed Halifax to the vacant ministry on 21 February. Despite criticism from the Labour Party and elsewhere that it was inappropriate to appoint a peer to so senior an office, he was the logical successor. He had emerged as one of Chamberlain's most trusted lieutenants and had been deeply involved in foreign affairs for the past two years.

Halifax's foreign secretaryship was the pivot of his career, and it remains the period upon which his historical reputation ultimately depends. Just as Eden did much to save his standing at the bar of history by his timely resignation, so Halifax did much to compromise his when he stepped into Eden's shoes. It was once usual to dismiss him as a mere cipher of his prime minister, one of the 'guilty men' collectively responsible for bringing Britain to the very brink of disaster in the summer of 1940 through the pursuit of the disastrous policy of appeasement. Chamberlain, as he testified in his private correspondence, certainly found Halifax a more congenial colleague than Eden—'I thank God for a steady unruffled Foreign Secretary' (Roberts, 102). Furthermore, Halifax's own memoirs did nothing to dispel the image that he was little more than a faithful subordinate, loyally carrying out the policies of his master in Downing Street. More recently, however, historians have used the documentary record to draw a more subtle picture, in which Halifax played a critical role in modifying Chamberlain's designs, emerging in the opinion of some as the dominant force in the making of British foreign policy by the spring of 1939. Halifax gave few indications of this independence of judgement during the early months of his foreign secretaryship. Indeed, he accepted the logic of Chamberlain's policies and had told the cabinet in December 1937 that

> in spite of all the efforts of the Foreign Secretary, the Prime Minister and others, we had arrived at a position which above all we had wished to avoid and in which we were faced with the possibility of three enemies at once. The conclusion which [Halifax] drew was … that this threw an immensely heavy burden on diplomacy and that we ought to get on good terms with Germany. (Roberts, 82)

Halifax had been in his new office just three weeks when Hitler incorporated Austria into the Reich. By this time Halifax was becoming more committed to a policy of rearmament, but the Anschluss left him under few illusions about the vulnerability of Czechoslovakia to the next initiative of Hitler's foreign policy. Indeed, he saw Britain's task in the summer of 1938 in terms of making the disagreeable task of forcing concessions on the Czechs as painless as possible.

Halifax's exclusion from Chamberlain's party on the latter's three visits to Germany in September 1938 seemed merely to confirm the ascendancy of the prime minister and the fact that Eden's replacement had removed the final brake upon the pursuit of Chamberlain's personal diplomacy. But it is now clear that it was Halifax, influenced by his permanent under-secretary, Sir Alexander Cadogan, who persuaded the cabinet to reject the terms which the prime minister brought back from his second meeting with Hitler at Godesberg. This brought the country to the brink of war, a situation averted only by Chamberlain's dramatic flight to the conference at Munich, which determined the dismemberment of Czechoslovakia on terms marginally more favourable than those put forward at Godesberg. More importantly, however, Chamberlain's authority had been successfully challenged. His ascendancy within the cabinet was never as strong again. Thus a growing appreciation of Halifax's weight within the government—and his position was always going to be strong, as Chamberlain could scarcely afford to lose a second foreign secretary—has helped to modify perceptions of the all-powerful position of the prime minister.

Halifax's mounting influence In the wake of Munich, Halifax urged Chamberlain not to use the popular mood of relief that war had been averted as an excuse to call a snap general election, but rather to seize the opportunity to broaden the basis of his government by the inclusion of Conservative critics such as Eden and Churchill and, if possible, Labour and Liberal opponents. Chamberlain took the first part of this advice but not the second. No general election was held, but the government remained essentially unchanged. It also fell to the foreign secretary to defend the settlement reached at Munich in the House of Lords on 3 October. He did so in more measured terms than had the prime minister in his notorious 'peace for our time' remark from the window of 10 Downing Street. Halifax argued that Munich was not a triumph but the lesser of evils, the best solution to an almost intolerable dilemma which offered no easy or entirely acceptable solution. In the weeks after Munich, Halifax was deeply affected by mounting evidence of Nazi barbarism, especially the anti-Jewish pogrom of 10 November, Kristallnacht. He now argued that a German expansion into eastern Europe would not help the cause of peace, but would simply draw the countries concerned into Germany's economic orbit. He advocated the use of British capital to lessen their dependence on Germany.

After accompanying Chamberlain on his visit to Rome in January 1939, Halifax seems to have been instrumental in bringing about a distinct change of emphasis in British policy that spring. As early as January he proposed that full staff talks should be held with the French with a view to preparing for a possible war with both Germany and Italy. The stiffening in Chamberlain's line after the Prague coup, evident in his Birmingham speech on 17 March, which culminated in the issuing of a guarantee of Polish independence at the end of the month, owed much to Halifax's influence. 'The Polish guarantee was his pet scheme and his favourite god-child', noted Henry Channon (R. R. James, ed., *Chips*, 1967, 209). Despite his natural reluctance to embrace the atheistic regime of Joseph Stalin, he was quicker than Chamberlain to appreciate that only an alliance with the Soviet Union could give military reality to the Polish guarantee. The ensuing negotiations with the Soviets were perhaps doomed to failure, but Halifax did little to instil a sense of urgency into the proceedings and has been criticized for not convincing the Russians of Britain's earnestness by leading the negotiating team in person. He was once again with Chamberlain in the crisis of September 1939 and as much as him the object of the cabinet revolt which put a stop to any further delay in the British declaration of war, which duly came on 3 September. He was at least adamant that there could be no further negotiations with Hitler while German troops remained on Polish soil.

Halifax remained foreign secretary in Chamberlain's reorganized war cabinet, though the role of diplomacy was inevitably transformed in the context of a European war. The main aim of his foreign policy was now to prevent the Soviet Union joining the ranks of Britain's military opponents. He favoured a cautious strategic approach, believing that the bombing of Germany at this stage of the conflict would merely provoke a retaliation which Britain was as yet ill-placed to resist. The fact that he alone among the four leading ministers who were regarded as the architects of appeasement—Chamberlain, Simon, Hoare, and himself—was not the object of vehement criticism in the crisis of May 1940 is striking. Indeed, there is evidence that many Labour leaders as well as the king and the majority of the Conservative Party would have preferred him to Churchill as Chamberlain's successor. As it was, it was Churchill who seized the initiative, welcoming a supreme challenge from which Halifax evidently drew back. Though the latter stressed the difficulties created by his position as a peer, there is little doubt that these could have been overcome had Halifax had the will to press his own claims. The crisis revealed inner self-doubts on the part of a man for whom political ambition had never been the most compelling motivation. A psychosomatic stomach-ache perhaps helped to confirm his misgivings. He may also have believed that he could, by remaining in his present position, exercise an influence over Churchill greater than he would have enjoyed as a prime minister with little grasp of military strategy. More importantly, Halifax's act of self-denial, by opening the way to Churchill's wartime premiership, was probably the most significant act of his long career.

Churchill's foreign secretary Though widely seen as a Chamberlain loyalist Halifax retained his position as foreign secretary in the new government. By now the war had reached a critical stage. Behind Churchill's rhetoric of unwavering resistance, the British government had to consider whether, with France collapsing and a German invasion perhaps imminent, the country could realistically hope to continue the struggle. Like many others, Halifax had serious doubts about Churchill's judgement and saw his own most important role as being to restrain the new prime minister's more romantic excesses. During the 'Phoney War' Halifax, confident that victory could be secured at a reasonable cost, had set his face against talk of a compromise peace. But as Britain faced the prospect of being left alone to confront Hitler's menace and with the fate of the army in doubt, he began to wonder whether the war could be won and to regard peace negotiations with the Nazis as a necessary development. Indeed, he believed that any peace terms which the Germans might offer would be more acceptable if Britain did not wait until her own position in the war had become absolutely desperate. Matters came to a head at meetings of the war cabinet on 26, 27, and 28 May, at which the debate became increasingly polarized between Churchill and Halifax. The latter argued that 'we had to face the fact that it was not so much now a question of imposing a complete defeat upon Germany, but of safeguarding the independence of our own Empire and if possible that of France' (Charmley, 403). At one point Halifax came near to resignation, an outcome which at that stage of the war might have been fatal to Churchill's government. But the prime minister successfully appealed over the head of his foreign secretary to the government's junior ministers. With their backing, and with Chamberlain now lining up behind him, Churchill was able to secure a majority in the war cabinet to thwart Halifax.

These events may well have sealed Halifax's ultimate fate. As the country survived the battle of Britain, Churchill's defiance seemed to have been justified—even though, on rational grounds, there had been much to be said for the foreign secretary's line that Britain should at least have investigated what peace terms were on offer. In the reshuffle which followed Chamberlain's final resignation from the government, Churchill tried hard to ease Halifax out of the Foreign Office. The latter was offered the lord presidency of the council, occupancy of 11 Downing Street, the leadership of the House of Lords, and a position which seemed to approximate to the deputy premiership. Halifax, however, preferred to stay where he was, although he did consent to resume the leadership of the Lords. Churchill was soon able to renew his efforts. When Lord Lothian, the popular and successful British ambassador in Washington, died suddenly in December, the prime minister invited Halifax to fill the vacancy. It was undoubtedly a post of great significance. Ultimate victory probably depended upon increasingly close American co-operation in the war effort, but Halifax was by no means a natural candidate for the post and it is difficult to escape the conclusion that Churchill was now determined to remove him from the higher reaches of the British government, even though the departing foreign secretary was assured that he could resume his place at the war cabinet table whenever he was on leave in London. Churchill's real motives are recorded in the diary of his private secretary. Halifax 'would never live down the reputation for appeasement which he and the F. O. had won themselves here. He had no future in this country' (J. Colville, *The Fringes of Power*, 1985, 321). Halifax's first reaction to Churchill's suggestion was one of horror. He and Lady Halifax tried desperately to persuade Eden, whom the prime minister had clearly pencilled in for the impending Foreign Office vacancy, to go in his stead. When, however, Churchill pressed the point, invoking the compelling dictates of duty in wartime, he had little alternative but to accept. The Halifaxes set sail in January 1941.

Ambassador in Washington An English aristocrat with a reputation for aloofness had few obvious qualifications for his new assignment in the most egalitarian of all societies. Though Roosevelt took the unusual step of welcoming the new ambassador in person as he stepped onto American soil, Halifax's first months in the United States were far from easy. He was guilty of a series of public relations disasters. He never really understood how the American government managed to function, once likening it to a disorderly day's rabbit-shooting. Gradually, however, he found his feet, aided by the tact of his cousin Angus McDonnell, who acted as a sort of stage manager for the new ambassador, and by his own readiness to throw himself tirelessly into his duties. From 1941 onwards Halifax became part of an increasingly professional propaganda effort in the United States. An incident in the autumn when he was pelted with rotten eggs and tomatoes by angry isolationists did his reputation much good in the longer term. His tours across the country brought him into contact with more ordinary American citizens than any of his predecessors had ever encountered. Halifax formed a good working relationship with the American president, while recognizing that he must necessarily take a back seat in the fostering of Anglo-American relations whenever Churchill was in the United States. He also won the confidence of the influential Harry Hopkins, Roosevelt's closest adviser. But Halifax's position was really transformed by America's entry into the war in December 1941 following the Japanese attack on Pearl Harbor. Thereafter he enjoyed a widespread popularity throughout the United States. It was a considerable act of transformation on Halifax's part, which allowed the man who had gloried in the imperial pomp of New Delhi to be seen eating a hot dog at a Baltimore ball game.

In March 1943, arguing that his most important work was now done, Halifax indicated to Eden that he would like to return home. He had been marked by family tragedy. In November 1942 he heard that his second son, Peter, had been killed in action in north Africa. Only two months later he learned that his youngest son, Richard, had been severely wounded. Halifax remained a somewhat reluctant ambassador over the following months. In May 1944 he was consoled by the news that Churchill had put his name forward for an earldom. In the event he was still in post when the war came to an end and he agreed to the request of the new Labour foreign secretary, Ernest

Bevin, that he should carry on until May 1946. This extension enabled him to play an important part in the negotiations led by Lord Keynes to secure an American loan after the abrupt termination of lend-lease, and he was still in the United States when Churchill delivered his celebrated iron curtain speech at Fulton, Missouri, of whose tone he was somewhat critical.

Final years On his return to Britain, Halifax was invited to join Churchill's shadow cabinet, but he declined the offer. He was now sixty-five, and in any case believed that his recent service under a Labour administration made his immediate return to the front rank of Conservative politics inappropriate. He preferred to go back to his Yorkshire estates, though he continued to play an active role in the House of Lords. One of his most telling interventions in the upper chamber came in a debate on a motion by Lord Templewood, the former Samuel Hoare, criticizing the decision of the Labour cabinet to hand over India to an Indian government by June 1948 at the latest 'without any provision for the protection of minorities or the discharge of their obligations'. In a measured speech which persuaded many wavering peers to support the government, Halifax concluded that he was not prepared to condemn what the government was doing unless he could honestly and confidently recommend a better solution, which he could not. One of his last important interventions in the Lords (11 December 1956) was to criticize the way in which Eden's government had mishandled the Suez crisis. He was particularly concerned about the damage done to Anglo-American relations.

Halifax's final years were characterized by a combination of honours, good works, leisure, and travel. He gave much time to the governing body of Eton, to the chancellorship of Oxford University, and to All Souls, of which he was an honorary fellow after 1934. Soon after his return from the United States he succeeded Lord Harewood as chancellor of the University of Sheffield and he derived considerable satisfaction from his appointment as high steward of Westminster. He received honorary degrees from more than a dozen British, Canadian, and American universities. As president of the Pilgrims he was able to renew his work for Anglo-American friendship and co-operation, and in 1947 he became chairman of the General Advisory Council of the BBC. He resumed his duties as master of the Middleton hunt, and devoted himself to his estates and the affairs of the local church. In July 1957 he was appointed grand master of the Order of St Michael and St George. He found time to write a slim volume of memoirs entitled *Fulness of Days*, published in 1957. It was an extremely reticent book which added little to the historical record. In particular he made few efforts to challenge what had by then become the orthodox view of appeasement as a short-sighted and mistaken policy. By the mid-1950s Halifax's health had begun to fail, though he lived long enough to celebrate his golden wedding anniversary on 21 September 1959. He also had the satisfaction of seeing his youngest son, Richard, who had been elected to parliament in 1950, secure junior office in 1955. He died at Garrowby Hall, Garrowby, Yorkshire, on 23 December 1959 after a heart attack, and was buried on 28 December in the churchyard at Kirby Underdale. His titles passed to his eldest son, Charles Ingram Courtenay Wood. His widow lived on until 1976.

Assessment Halifax's public career has three main component parts. He was a noteworthy viceroy of India, who played a key role in steering that country towards independence within the Commonwealth in the face of many siren voices of protest from within his own party. His period near the centre of power in the making of British foreign policy is now less roundly condemned than it once was. Though his background and character did not equip him to deal with the European dictators, he deserves some credit for abandoning, or at least for decisively modifying, the policy of appeasement. By March 1939 one prominent critic of the government's foreign policy had concluded that, thanks to Halifax's mounting influence, the government was 'now doing what we would wish' (Dutton, *Eden*, 135). After failing to become prime minister in May 1940, his role later that month in trying to persuade Winston Churchill of the need to consider a possible compromise peace shows not that he was a potential Quisling within the British cabinet, but rather that he was not taken in by the prime minister's sublime confidence in victory in the face of the weight of available evidence to the contrary. Exiled to the United States, he none the less made his most important contribution to public life, helping to lubricate the Anglo-American relationship which was often more fraught than early interpretations of the Churchill–Roosevelt partnership tended to suggest.

Halifax belonged to an age and a class for whom political affairs were never an all-consuming activity. 'It is well known', noted one contemporary in 1936, 'that Halifax is only too anxious to retire from public life as he invariably tells everyone that his one object is to give up politics and go back and live at his home' (Neville Chamberlain MSS, NC7/11/29/37, University of Birmingham). To a later generation his passion for the chase sits somewhat uncomfortably beside his deep spirituality. Indeed, he once admitted that

> it surely shows how deeply rooted we are in the elemental instinct that steeplechasing and clay pigeon shooting, in which the fact of killing is absent, does not make nearly such an appeal to us as hunting something for its life.
> (Birkenhead, 197)

But Halifax was not encumbered by any particular intellectual subtlety. He placed a strong faith in his own judgement and, having reached a decision, was not easily deflected from it. In each of the posts he occupied he exuded an old-fashioned aristocratic authority, accentuated by a speech impediment which prevented him pronouncing the letter 'r'. 'My withers are completely unwrung', he told John Wheeler-Bennett in response to criticism of the Munich settlement (ibid., 464). He was not an easy man to know. Most of those who met him were confronted by a form of professional charm which came easily to him, and with only a few close friends did he find it possible to relax his guard. Despite considerable inherited wealth he had a horror of waste and was extremely careful about money. R. A. Butler, who served as his junior minister at the Foreign Office, recalled an occasion at which an official brought in two cups of tea and four biscuits. Pushing aside the biscuits, Halifax insisted, 'Mr. Butler does not want these. Nor do I. Do not charge me' (Butler, 38). D. J. DUTTON

Sources A. Roberts, 'The Holy Fox': a biography of Lord Halifax (1991) · Earl of Birkenhead, Halifax: the life of Lord Halifax (1965) · Borth. Inst., Halifax MSS · A. Campbell-Johnson, Viscount Halifax (1941) · Earl of Halifax [E. F. L. Wood], Fulness of days (1957) · J. G. Lockhart, Viscount Halifax, 1839–85 (1935) · S. Gopal, The viceroyalty of Lord Irwin, 1926–1931 (1957) · J. Charmley, Churchill: the end of glory (1993) · R. A. Butler, The art of memory (1982), 30–44 · D. Dutton, Simon: a political biography of Sir John Simon (1992) · D. Dutton, Anthony Eden: a life and reputation (1997) · DNB · The Times (24 Dec 1959) · M. Cowling, The impact of Hitler: British politics and British policy, 1933–1940 (1975) · D. C. Watt, How war came (1989) · R. A. C. Parker, Chamberlain and appeasement: British policy and the coming of the Second World War (1993) · WW

Archives BL OIOC, corresp. and papers relating to India, MS Eur. C 152 · Borth. Inst., corresp. and papers · priv. coll., MSS · PRO, corresp., FO 800/309–328 | BL, corresp. with Lord Cecil, Add. MS 51084 · BL, letters to Albert Mansbridge, Add. MS 65253 · BL OIOC, corresp. with Lord Goschen, MS Eur. D 595 · BL OIOC, letters from Lord Hailey, MS Eur. E 220 · BL OIOC, corresp. with Sir Terence Keyes, MS Eur. F 131 · BL OIOC, letters from George Ambrose Lloyd, MS Eur. B 158 · BL OIOC, corresp. with earl of Lytton, MS Eur. F 160 · BL OIOC, corresp. with John Simon, MS Eur. F 77 · Bodl. Oxf., corresp. with L. G. Curtis · Bodl. Oxf., corresp. with H. A. L. Fisher · Bodl. Oxf., corresp. with Lord Monckton · Bodl. Oxf., corresp. with Gilbert Murray · Bodl. Oxf., corresp. with earl of Selborne · Bodl. Oxf., corresp. with Lord Simon · CAC Cam., corresp. with Lord Croft · CAC Cam., corresp. with M. P. A. Hankey · CAC Cam., corresp. with A. V. Hill · CAC Cam., corresp. with Sir Eric Phipps · CAC Cam., corresp. incl. speech notes with C. E. M. Roberts · CUL, Baldwin MSS · CUL, corresp. with Sir Samuel Hoare · CUL, corresp. with Lord and Lady Kennet · CUL, Templewood MSS · HLRO, letters to David Lloyd George · HLRO, letters to Lord Samuel · King's Lond., Liddell Hart C. · LPL, letters to Athelstan Riley · Lpool RO, corresp. with Lord Derby · NA Scot., corresp. with Lord Lothian · News Int. RO, letters to Geoffrey Dawson · NL Aus., corresp. with Lord Stonehaven · NRA, priv. coll., corresp. with William Wedgwood Benn · PRO, corresp. with Lord Chatfield, CAB 127/130 · PRO NIre., corresp. with Lord Dufferin · PRO NIre., letters to Lord Londonderry · RIBA BAL, corresp. with Goodhart-Rendel and Lewis, architects · Staffs. RO, letters to Francis Meynell · U. Birm., Chamberlain MSS · University of York, countess of Halifax MSS | FILM BFI NFTVA, documentary footage · BFI NFTVA, news footage | SOUND BL NSA, current affairs recordings

Likenesses W. Stoneman, photographs, 1923–48, NPG · photographs, 1926–c.1946, Hult. Arch. · J. Kramer, pastel drawing, 1931, Harrogate Corporation Art Gallery · photograph, 1931, NPG · S. Anderson, chalk drawing, 1932, NPG · O. Birley, oils, 1932, Viceroy's House, New Delhi · O. Birley, oils, 1932, priv. coll. [see illus.] · L. Edwards, group portrait, oils, c.1933, priv. coll. · E. Kennington, pastel drawing, 1940, IWM · O. Birley, oils, c.1947, All Souls Oxf. · L. Gowing, oils, c.1952, Christ Church Oxf. · C. Beaton, photograph, Gov. Art Coll. · C. Beaton, photograph, NPG · H. Coster, photographs, NPG

Wealth at death £338,800 10s. 8d.: probate save and except settled land, 31 March 1960, CGPLA Eng. & Wales · £12,481 6s. 4d.: probate limited to settled land, 2 Aug 1960, CGPLA Eng. & Wales

Wood [née **Price**], **Ellen** [known as **Mrs Henry Wood**] (1814–1887), writer and journal editor, was born on 17 January 1814 in Worcester, the eldest daughter of glove manufacturer Thomas Price and his wife, Elizabeth, daughter of Robert Evans of Grimley. Educated at home under the

Ellen Wood [Mrs Henry Wood] (1814–1887), by Sydney Hodges, 1873

influence of a father interested in music and classical scholarship and a mother who was active in Worcester Cathedral's work parties and social life, Ellen Price was noted for her retentive memory and active imagination. At the age of thirteen a spinal curvature became evident, and she was largely confined to bed for the next four years. As an adult, she was noticeably frail and under 5 feet tall, with a bent posture and a pretty oval face.

On 17 March 1836 Ellen Price was married at Whittington, near Worcester, to Henry Wood (1809/10–1866), who worked for a family-owned banking and shipping firm. The next twenty years were spent in France, primarily in Dauphiné; several children were born, of whom at least one died of scarlet fever. There were other difficulties as well. Ellen Wood's son Charles William Wood describes his father as a man 'possessing a mind a little wanting in ballast' (Wood, 50). Some unspecified event caused him to withdraw from business, and after a 'period of many trials and troubles' (ibid., 184), the Woods returned to England in 1856 and took a furnished house in Upper Norwood.

Perhaps in an effort to improve the family finances, Ellen Wood had been anonymously publishing short stories for several years. The first that has been identified appeared in the New Monthly Magazine (then edited by William Harrison Ainsworth) in February 1851. When Ainsworth took over Bentley's Miscellany in December 1854, her stories began to appear there as well. She produced her first novel, Danesbury House (1860), as the winning entry in a competition for which the Scottish Temperance League offered a prize of £100.

Thus, although Ellen Wood was 'unknown' when her first commercial novel became a surprise runaway best-seller, she already had some ten years' experience as a writer before the serial run of *East Lynne* began in the *New Monthly Magazine* in January 1860. Even with Ainsworth's recommendation, the publishers Chapman and Hall rejected the book (on the advice of their reader, George Meredith), as did Smith and Elder. Richard Bentley, however, accepted it, paid Ellen Wood £600 (far more than most beginners were offered), and ordered an initial print run of 2750 (500 was usual for a library novel). Published in three volumes in the autumn of 1861, *East Lynne* was well reviewed in the *Daily News*, the *Saturday Review*, and elsewhere. Most significant was a long notice in *The Times* for 25 January 1862. Written by Samuel Lucas (who edited *Once a Week* and knew how to recognize fiction with wide appeal), the review criticized *East Lynne* for a plot governed by coincidence and for outright errors in legal and political scenes. Yet for all of that, Lucas reported enthusiastically, the novel satisfies 'the indispensable requirement which is the rude test of the merits of any work of fiction … *East Lynne* is found by all its readers to be highly *entertaining*'.

East Lynne's extraordinary success stemmed from Wood's skill in interweaving two genres which became mainstays of popular fiction, the sentimental woman's novel and the sensation novel (forerunner of the detective story). The book takes up contemporary issues such as divorce, feminine individuality, sexuality, family rupture, and class tension; and although it provides no easy solutions, the repressions and conflicts and tears ultimately reaffirm an essentially moral view of the world. By the end of the century, Bentley had printed more than 400,000 copies of *East Lynne*, there were at least two dozen pirate editions in the United States, and plays based on Wood's story were regularly featured by touring stock companies throughout the English-speaking world.

In the seven years after *East Lynne*'s success, Wood published fifteen novels, often producing instalments of two at a time for magazine serialization. During 1862 and 1863, for example, *The Channings* and *Mrs. Halliburton's Troubles* were in *The Quiver* (a weekly paper which featured religious lessons and serial fiction), *A Life's Secret* appeared in *Leisure Hour* (also an inexpensive weekly, published by the Religious Tract Society), *Verner's Pride* came out in *Once a Week*, and *The Shadow of Ashlydat* was in the *New Monthly Magazine*. In addition to the moral fiction for family magazines, Wood also wrote sensational three-volume novels of rivalry, mystery, bigamy, and murder such as *Trevlyn Hold* (1864), *Elster's Folly* (1866), and *St. Martin's Eve* (1866).

By the time Henry Wood died in 1866, his widow could afford a substantial house in St John's Wood Park. In late 1867 she became editor and proprietor of *The Argosy*, a monthly magazine started by Alexander Strahan in 1865. From 1868 until 1873, the magazine's chief feature was an annual serial by Wood: *Anne Hereford* in 1868, *Roland Yorke* (1869), *Bessy Rane* (1870), *Dene Hollow* (1871), *Within the Maze* (1872), and *Master of Greylands* (1873). After 1873 her production slowed somewhat. Her son Charles Wood, who began

making signed contributions to *The Argosy* in 1876, eventually took over as business manager and became the magazine's editor and proprietor on her death.

Wood enlisted some other women contributors to *The Argosy* (Hesba Stretton, Julia Kavanagh, Christina Rossetti, Sarah Doudney, Rosa Nouchette Carey), but in the early years she may have written up to half of the contents of each issue. Among Wood's unsigned contributions were a series narrated by Johnny Ludlow, who tells stories about neighbours, friends, village characters, and incidents of Worcestershire life and, through the telling, reveals his own growth and character as well. Marked by lively humour, quiet pathos, and striking portraits of individuals in all walks of life, the Johnny Ludlow stories were often praised as superior to the work of sensationalists such as the editor of the magazine in which they appeared—which must have given Wood great pleasure when, in 1879, it finally became known that she had written them.

The enormous popularity of *East Lynne* damaged Wood's standing with the makers of literary reputations. By the end of the 1860s, intellectuals wrote condescendingly of the improbable plots, weak grammar, and dogmatic Christianity, the unmotivated evil of Wood's villains, and especially of the pathos, deathbeds, and tears. The appeal for ordinary readers, however, was based not only on Wood's skill at suspense and dramatic confrontation, but also on her careful attention to the physical details of daily life and on her use of material that exposed contemporary conflicts and ambiguities. The plot of *East Lynne*, for example, depends in part on the Matrimonial Causes Act of 1857. The hero of the piece, Carlyle, is morally justified in remarrying because he believes Isabel is dead, but if he had not divorced her beforehand, his marriage to Barbara would be invalid. In addition, the set pieces of moral preaching barely repress the emotional ambivalence in readers' response to Isabel's errors. Adeline Sergeant, writing in 1897, remarked that *East Lynne* owed 'half its popularity' to a 'reaction against inane and impossible goodness' (Sergeant, 181) as the only suitable characteristic for a heroine.

Wood's plots often reveal that marriage is unsatisfactory and that 'ideal' families harbour dark secrets. Many narrators speak with a woman's voice and appeal to women readers in a personal and conversational tone, calling on their sympathies to interpret the characters' motives. *The Channings* and its sequel, *Roland Yorke*, are family stories which describe thoughtless errors and even crimes committed by good-hearted but impulsive sons. *Mrs. Halliburton's Troubles* contrasts the struggles of an impoverished widow with a wealthy family's dishonesty and snobbery. *Trevlyn Hold* displays both bourgeois vigour and bourgeois values by allowing a sturdy, hard-working, thrifty yeoman to inherit the estate of a decaying aristocrat. In *St. Martin's Eve* the plot turns on the dangers of hereditary insanity in one family and inherited tendencies towards consumption in another.

St. Martin's Eve, like several other novels including *The Red Court Farm* (3 vols., 1868) and *Pomeroy Abbey* (3 vols.,

1878), was revised and expanded from materials Wood had used in short fiction during the 1850s. In *Mildred Arkell* (3 vols., 1865) she combined two separate sequences—one about David Dundyke and one concerning Mildred Arkell—which appeared in the *New Monthly Magazine* during 1854, rewriting the final incident to provide a happy ending (and to reveal that women willing to work as servants to support themselves are superior to the snobbish and the pseudo-genteel).

Light and extremely popular fiction often reflects the interests of mass readers and confirms their sense of the world. Wood's novels did not repeat the lurid anti-Catholicism of some essays and stories which she wrote immediately after the restoration of the Roman Catholic hierarchy. 'Seven Years in the Wedded Life of a Roman Catholic' in the *New Monthly Magazine* of February 1851, for example, had a wily priest, a submissive girl, a bereft mother, and eventually a suicide. Wood's most popular fiction used materials brought into currency during the 1860s by the rage for sensation fiction—inheritance, bigamy, murder, disguise, family conflict, shocks to decorum—combined with mild exposure of public institutions, up-to-the-minute details about railways and telegraph messages, and the tensions of a class system in transition.

Wood also responded with extraordinary skill to the demands of magazine serialization. The ten years' experience in writing short fiction perhaps taught her how to concentrate conflict and emotion in every instalment. To that she added a familiar tone that stimulated interaction with readers, characters sufficiently distinctive to be kept in mind over the months without degenerating into pure stereotypes, and enough overall suspense to keep buyers eager for issue after issue.

East Lynne is the only one of Wood's books to have remained generally available, and like some other extremely popular novels it has been used by late twentieth-century cultural scholars to provide evidence about nineteenth-century moral standards, women's roles, and ideologies of class and motherhood. There are other less recognized strengths in her work. Despite her reputation as a 'women's writer', several contemporaries praised her unusual ability to portray boys and businessmen. Ellen Wood's fiction provides a great deal of information about the domestic details of lower-middle-class life. The obituary in *The Spectator* noted her grasp of a world which had not previously appeared in English fiction:

> She could not describe a grand passion, or a great character, or a great deed; but she could embody for us the ordinary middle-class, unintellectual, half-disagreeable folk, of whom there are thousands round us, courting, fighting, stealing, giving, exactly as she has described them. (*The Spectator*, 255)

Wood's central talent may have been for short fiction. In more than one hundred stories narrated by Johnny Ludlow, which appeared in *The Argosy* from 1868 until her death, Wood quietly displayed the people and incidents of daily life. The accurate rendering of both Worcestershire dialect and young men's slang also showed her skill with voice and tone. Wood had first used a male persona as early as 1854 in 'Stray Letters from the East' which appeared in the *New Monthly Magazine* between July and December under the name Ensign Thomas Pepper. He appeared to be an irreverent young man who wrote amusingly different versions of his experiences in the Crimea depending on whether his letters were intended for a male friend, his guardian, or his girlfriend.

Wood was nearly fifty when she became a best-selling novelist. Her life as an author was hard-working and largely domestic. She was an orthodox churchwoman, a strong Conservative in politics, and a committed advocate of temperance (although not total abstinence), and her few literary friends were other earnest provincial women close to her own age, such as Mary Howitt and Anna Maria Hall. She always wore a black dress with an assortment of laces and scarves that somewhat concealed her deformed back. In later life she was troubled by bronchitis (complicated by the diminished lung capacity that was a consequence of spinal curvature). She died of heart failure at her home, 16 St John's Wood Park, on 10 February 1887 and was buried on 16 February in Highgate cemetery, after a funeral at St Stephen's Church, Avenue Road. She was survived by a daughter, Ellen Mary Wood, sons Henry, Charles, and Arthur, and at least one grandchild.

SALLY MITCHELL

Sources C. W. Wood, *Memorials of Mrs. Henry Wood* (1894) · A. Sergeant, 'Mrs. Henry Wood', in M. Oliphant and others, *Women novelists of Queen Victoria's reign* (1897), 174–92 · S. Lucas, 'East Lynne', *The Times* (25 Jan 1862) · *The Spectator* (19 Feb 1887) · *The Times* (11 Feb 1887) · M. Elwin, *Victorian wallflowers* (1934) · R. Bergauer, *Mrs. Henry Wood: Persönlichkeit und Werk* (1950) [incl. bibliography of Wood's pubns] · 'The popular novels of the year', *Fraser's Magazine*, 68 (1863), 253–69 · *DNB* · *IGI*
Likenesses S. Hodges, oils, 1873, Guildhall, Worcester [*see illus.*] · L. Stocks, stipple and line engraving (after R. Easton), BM; repro. in Wood, *Memorials*
Wealth at death £36,393 13s. 5d.: probate, 28 May 1887, *CGPLA Eng. & Wales*

Wood, Ethel Mary Reader. *See* Shakespear, Dame Ethel Mary Reader (1871–1946).

Wood, Sir (Henry) Evelyn (1838–1919), army officer, was born at Cressing, Essex, on 9 February 1838, the youngest son of the Revd Sir John Page *Wood, bt (1796–1866), rector of St Peter's, Cornhill, and vicar of Cressing [*see under* Wood, Sir Matthew, first baronet], and Emma Caroline Michell (1802–1879), daughter of Admiral Sampson Michell of Croft West, Cornwall. Wood's uncle was Lord Hatherley, and his sister Katharine (Kitty) [*see* Parnell, Katharine] married W. H. O'Shea and later C. S. Parnell.

Education and early career Wood attended Marlborough grammar school (1847–9) and Marlborough College (1849–52), leaving to enter the navy as a midshipman on 15 April 1852, after what he regarded as an unjust caning. In 1854 he was serving with HMS *Queen* off the Crimea and went ashore with the naval brigade. He was wounded while aide-de-camp to the brigade commander in the assault on

Sir (Henry) Evelyn Wood (1838–1919), by F. Spalding, c.1881

the Redan on 18 June 1855, having risen from a sickbed in order to participate in the attack. Upon recovering, he opted to transfer to the 13th light dragoons, in which he was commissioned on 7 September, and went back to the Crimea. After contracting typhoid and pneumonia in January 1856 he was nursed back to health by his mother, who travelled out to Scutari to do so. Having been promoted lieutenant on 1 February 1856 Wood returned to his regiment in Ireland, but transferred to the 17th lancers on 9 October 1857, embarking for India in 1858.

During the Indian mutiny, from May 1858 until October 1860, Wood served on operations in central India, acting as brigade major to a flying column between November 1858 and April 1859 and receiving the Victoria Cross for routing, with ten men, eighty mutineers at Sindhara on 29 December 1859. He was promoted captain on 16 April 1861 and received a brevet majority on 19 August 1862 for his mutiny services. Although he passed the entrance examination for the Staff College in 1862 Wood was unable to take up the appointment, as one of his seniors took precedence at a time when only one officer a year could attend from each cavalry regiment, and he exchanged as a captain into the 73rd foot on 21 October 1862. He was then able to attend the Staff College in 1863, and after passing out filled a number of staff appointments, as aide-de-camp to William Napier in Dublin from January 1865 to March 1866, and successively brigade major and deputy assistant adjutant-general at Aldershot from July 1866 to November 1871.

Marriage In the summer of 1867 he married the Hon. Mary Paulina Anne Southwell, a sister of the fourth Viscount Southwell and a Roman Catholic; they had three sons and three daughters. Wood was very close to his chief staff officer in South Africa in 1879, the Hon. Ronald Campbell, who was killed at Hlobane, but there is no real evidence to sustain allegations made in the early 1990s—largely in connection with his later role in promoting the career of Douglas Haig—that Wood was homosexual. Moreover, his wife's death in May 1891 was a severe blow to him, although their perceived mutual lack of some of the social graces had proved something of a handicap to Wood's career. Wolseley, for example, was to complain in October 1880 of the noise, poor food, and filth within the Wood household, while the duke of Cambridge opposed his appointment to the Aldershot command in November 1888 on the grounds that the Woods would make 'a very rough couple' (Cambridge to Ponsonby, 19 Nov 1888, Royal Archives, W10/82). Another important influence on Wood was his sister, the novelist Anna Steele, who allegedly wrote most of his speeches.

A burgeoning career Wood was promoted to an unattached majority on 22 June 1870 and then purchased a majority in the 90th light infantry on 28 October 1871. He was one of the last officers to so obtain promotion before the abolition of purchase, and he gained a brevet lieutenant-colonelcy on 19 January 1873 in consequence of the seniority achieved by his purchase. Having met Wolseley by chance in the War Office in May, while the former was planning the Asante expedition, and joked that his naval background would enable him to navigate west African waterways, Wood was summoned for special service on Wolseley's staff on 12 September 1873. In the Asante kingdom he raised and commanded African levies in the advance on Kumasi, and was slightly wounded at Amoaful on 30 January 1874. For his services he received a brevet colonelcy and the CB on 1 April 1874. His reputation now established as a member of the *Wolseley ring, he lectured on his Asante experiences at the Royal United Service Institution in June 1874. He served at Aldershot between September 1874 and February 1878, first as superintending officer of garrison instruction, then as assistant quartermaster-general. Wood also studied law and was called to the bar in 1874. In 1877 he was offered command of the Staff College, but declined, as he felt George Colley would be more suitable: but Colley also declined. However, Wood was chosen for special service in South Africa, where his name was soon to become familiar to the public in a way which would give him some independence from Wolseley's patronage.

In South Africa Wood joined the staff of Lieutenant-General Thesiger, later Lord Chelmsford, tasked with concluding the Cape Frontier War of 1877–8. Wood commanded a column with ability and resolution, and on 13 November 1878 he succeeded to the command of his former battalion, the 90th, which had arrived in South Africa in the previous January. The war had hardly ended when that against the Zulu began, and Wood was given command of Chelmsford's no. 4 column at Utrecht, in the Transvaal, intended to safeguard the left flank of the British invasion of Zululand. When Chelmsford's main force met disaster at Isandlwana on 22 January 1879 and the right flanking force became besieged at Eshowe, only Wood's column was free to maintain offensive operations, from a base established at Khambula. Wood and Redvers Buller, commanding the frontier light horse, relentlessly harried the local Zulu of the Qulusi clan to the extent that the main Zulu army was dispatched towards Khambula. Having chosen to raid the Qulusi mountain stronghold at Hlobane for cattle on 28 March, Wood and Buller were caught there by the advance of this impi. Buller suffered heavy casualties in the confused and rapid descent from the top of Hlobane while Wood, originally intending to act in support of Buller, had become involved in a firefight at the eastern foot of the plateau in which Campbell and Wood's political agent were killed. Wood tried to extricate the two bodies but had to bury them hastily under fire. Hlobane was a disaster, Wood losing ninety-four white dead and more than a hundred of his African levies. However, securely entrenched back at Khambula, Wood immediately redeemed himself by repulsing the Zulu on the following day with such heavy loss—probably more than 2000 dead compared with just eighteen dead among the defenders—that it proved the turning point of the war. For the second invasion of Zululand in May 1879 Wood was appointed local brigadier-general and his force redesignated the flying column, linking with the 2nd division for the final push on Ulundi. With the defeat of the Zulu, Wood and Buller both chose to return to England rather than join Wolseley, who had come out to supersede Chelmsford, in the final pursuit of Cetshwayo.

Wood returned to a hero's welcome, receiving the KCB but not the major-general's rank he thought his due, and for which Wolseley and the queen both pressed, since it would appear that Cambridge was determined to frustrate those associated with Wolseley from preferment in defiance of normal rules of seniority wherever possible. Wood made a considerable impression on the queen, who received him at Balmoral in September 1879, and to whom he was to address extraordinarily sycophantic letters in subsequent years. Wood's third daughter, born in 1881, was named Victoria Eugénie at the queen's wish. Compared with the reserved Buller, who accompanied him, Wood was 'wonderfully lively & hardly ceases talking, which no doubt came from his deafness & inability to hear any general conversation' (Victoria, 9 Sept 1879, Royal Archives, Z.388). The queen's private secretary, H. F. Ponsonby, feared Wood would be all too much for her but 'she hollered at him & he went off at all rates' (Ponsonby to his wife, 10 Sept 1879, Royal Archives, Ponsonby MSS, Add. A36 Box 18).

Character and habits It is not clear when Wood's deafness first occurred, but it was already pronounced by 1879 and became worse. Wood had two other abiding characteristics—vanity and hypochondria. It was often said that he

had his medal ribbons edged with a black border to accentuate their effect, while his 'curious jerky manner' (Lansdowne to Bigge, 15 July 1897, Royal Archives, W73/156) was attributed to what he himself admitted in his autobiography to be constitutional nervousness, despite his record of gallantry. He was, indeed, subject to frequent illnesses and somewhat accident-prone; his nose was once smashed by a giraffe he tried to ride at a private zoo in India.

In Africa again Having failed to secure promotion, Wood was given the brigade command at Belfast on 15 December 1879 and followed this with a similar post at Chatham on 12 January 1880, which he retained until January 1881, and which was broken by escorting the Empress Eugénie to Zululand in early 1880 to see the place where her son, the prince imperial, had been killed. Others in the party included Campbell's widow, and Wood took pains to erect suitable memorials to Campbell as well as others who had fallen at Hlobane and elsewhere. In January 1881 Wood agreed to go back to South Africa, initially only as 'staff colonel', to serve under Colley, to whom he was senior, against the Transvaal Boers. Given local rank as major-general, Wood pushed reinforcements up to Colley in Natal, and when Colley was killed at Majuba on 27 February, assumed command. Wood felt unable to resume the offensive until mid-March and was then directed by Gladstone's government to open negotiations. While obliged to arrange an armistice, Wood believed he would be able to defeat the Boers in renewed operations, and was condemned by many for not defying government instructions. Meanwhile Roberts was appointed to succeed Colley and, to the queen's dismay, Edward Newdigate was also named over Wood, although neither would reach South Africa before peace was concluded on 21 March 1881. In reaching agreement with the Boers, Wood had felt 'no discretion left to him, and that his only duty was to obey orders' (Wood to Victoria, 4 May 1881, Royal Archives, O40/144) although, when subsequently named as one of a royal commission for the settlement of the Transvaal, he did enter a dissenting opinion on boundaries and other issues. The queen was to sympathize with the unfavourable position in which Wood had been placed by governmental decisions beyond his control, but Wolseley never forgave him for not avenging Colley's death, and could not bear to have Wood near him. William Butler, who was to write Colley's biography, took a similar view.

Finally confirmed as major-general on 12 August 1881 and rewarded with the GCMG, Wood returned to Chatham in February 1882 after turning down the post of governor of Natal. He was selected to command the 4th brigade in Wolseley's Egyptian expedition in August 1882, but Wolseley kept him confined deliberately to occupation duties at Alexandria. After a short spell back at Chatham, he then accepted appointment as the first British sirdar (commander) of the newly reconstituted Egyptian army on 21 December 1882. Wood hoped to command the Gordon relief expedition but Wolseley was appointed in

September 1884, and Wood was again sidelined by his former patron to command the expedition's lines of communication. Wolseley believed Wood too desk-bound in this role, and tension also arose between Wood and Earle, commanding the river column. However, when Stewart was fatally wounded before Methemmeh in January 1885 and Buller sent forward to take command of the desert column, Wood replaced Buller as Wolseley's chief of staff. Wood's lack of organized working methods, such as mislaying telegrams he had stuffed in his pockets, proved an irritation to Wolseley, and Buller resumed his post in March. Wood had previously decided to resign the sirdarship, and went home in June 1885.

Later career and death Wood was appointed to the eastern district at Colchester on 1 April 1886 and, despite opposition from Cambridge, to the Aldershot command with the rank of local lieutenant-general on 1 January 1889, an arrangement necessitated by Wood being only tenth on the major-general's list. Both at Colchester and Aldershot he promoted more modern training, abolishing drill and ceremonies in favour of greater emphasis on field exercises, including night operations. He insisted, too, on better marksmanship among cavalrymen, while also promoting the cause of mounted infantry. Arguably, he proved one of the best trainers of troops in the army. He also did much to improve soldiers' conditions, supporting the reforms suggested by the Wantage commission in 1892, and later, as adjutant-general, he was to promote a series of early cinematic films to illustrate the soldier's life. Promotion to lieutenant-general came on 1 April 1890 and he received the GCB in the following year. He was considered for the chief command in India in 1892, although Henry Brackenbury believed his mind best suited to the narrower confines of Aldershot. The queen favoured Wood's appointment to India while Cambridge also favoured Wood going at least to Madras in order to enable the queen's son, the duke of Connaught, to get Aldershot. However, Wood became quartermaster-general at the War Office on 9 October 1893, reorganizing the arrangements for conveying troops overseas through new contracts with shipping companies and effecting more economical arrangements with railway companies.

Wood was promoted general on 26 March 1895 and on 1 October 1897 succeeded Buller as adjutant-general in the War Office, Wolseley supporting the appointment on military and public rather than personal grounds. With the changes that had taken place in the relative responsibilities of commander-in-chief and adjutant-general and their respective relationship to the secretary of state for war in 1895, Wood was now in an influential position, particularly as Wolseley and Lansdowne disliked each other and as Wolseley's health rapidly failed him. Wolseley was later to complain that he rarely saw his adjutant-general and had little knowledge of the papers that passed between Wood and Lansdowne, while, in testifying before the royal commission on the Second South African War, Wood indicated that he had not been privy to the intelligence reports sent to Wolseley. He also argued that he had

had little responsibility for the selection of field commanders and staffs for South Africa although the adjutant-general had considerable responsibility for mobilization. Yet Wood kept himself well informed: his distrust of Kitchener, for example, leading in 1898 to the selection of Major Douglas Haig as a special service officer specifically to report to him on operations in the Sudan. When Wolseley retired in November 1900 Wood became his acting successor until Roberts returned from South Africa, circumstances Wolseley's wife feared especially detrimental to her husband's interests. Significantly, Wood supplied information to Leo Amery whose *Times History of the War in South Africa* was especially critical of the commanders in South Africa. On 1 October 1901 Wood took command of the 2nd army corps with headquarters at Salisbury. He was created field marshal on 8 April 1903 and retired on 31 December 1904. In retirement he was regimental colonel of the Royal Horse Guards in succession to Wolseley in November 1907 and also constable of the Tower of London from February 1911.

Throughout his life Wood was a keen rider to hounds and a leading member of the Fishmongers' Company, of which he was prime warden in 1893. He contributed regularly to military periodicals and published a number of books including *The Crimea in 1854 and in 1894* (1895), *Cavalry in the Waterloo Campaign* (1896), and *Achievements of Cavalry* (1897); he edited two volumes of *British Battles on Land and Sea* (1915) and wrote autobiographical works—the two-volume *From Midshipman to Field Marshal* (1906) and *Winnowed Memories* (1918). He was a JP and, from 1897, a deputy lieutenant of Essex, but resigned from the chairmanship of the County Territorial Association in January 1914 in support of the campaign by Roberts for 'national service', since it was argued that the existence of the territorials prevented the introduction of compulsory service. In political terms, however, he was broadly Liberal and was approached on at least two occasions to stand for parliament in the Liberal cause, his brother, Page Wood, unsuccessfully contesting East Essex as an 'advanced' Liberal in 1880. Wood died of heart failure at Harlow, Essex, on 2 December 1919 and was buried in Aldershot military cemetery.

IAN F. W. BECKETT

Sources Hove Central Library, Sussex, Wolseley collections · Royal Arch. · PRO, Wolseley MSS, WO 147 · Devon RO, Buller papers · PRO, Buller MSS, WO 132 · E. Wood, *From midshipman to field marshal*, 2 vols. (1906) · E. Wood, *Winnowed memories* (1918) · J. H. Lehmann, *The First Boer War* (1972) · J. H. Lehmann, *All Sir Garnet: a biography of Field-Marshal Lord Wolseley* (1964) · B. Bond, ed., *Victorian military campaigns* (1967) · R. Lock, *Blood on the Painted Mountain: Zulu victory and defeat, Hlobane and Khambula, 1879* (1995) · *The frontier war journal of Major John Crealock*, ed. C. Hummel (1989) · J. P. C. Laband, ed., *Lord Chelmsford's Zululand campaign, 1878–1879* (1994) · P. Gon, *The road to Isandlwana* (1979) · *In relief of Gordon: Lord Wolseley's campaign journal of the Khartoum relief expedition, 1884–1885*, ed. A. Preston (1967) · *The South African journal of Sir Garnet Wolseley, 1879–1880*, ed. A. Preston (1973) · Gladstone, *Diaries* · private information (2004) · E. Wood, 'The Ashanti expedition of 1873–74', *JRUSI*, 18/78 (1874–5), 331–57 · C. de Groot, *Douglas Haig, 1861–1928* (1988) · D. Winter, *Haig's command* (1991) · 'Report of the commissioners appointed to inquire into the military preparations … connected with the war in South Africa: minutes of evidence', *Parl.*

papers (1904), 40.171–86, Cd 1790 [Wood's evidence of 29 Oct 1902] · Burke, *Peerage* · *Memoirs of Field-Marshal Lord Grenfell* (1925)
Archives Duke U., Perkins L., corresp. and papers · National Archives of South Africa, Pietermaritzburg, Natal Archives Depot, corresp. and papers · U. Durham L., corresp. and papers relating to Egypt · University of Natal, Durban, Killie Campbell Africana Library, corresp. and papers | Bodl. Oxf., corresp. with Lord Kimberley · Bodl. RH, corresp. with Sir Godfrey Lagden · CKS, letters to Edward Stanhope · Devon RO, Buller papers · HLRO, letters to Ralph Blumenfeld · Hove Central Library, Sussex, corresp. with Lord Wolseley · NAM, corresp. with Lord Chelmsford · NAM, letters to Earl Roberts · NRA, priv. coll., corresp. with N. M. Macleod · NRA, priv. coll., corresp. with Sir John Ewert · NRA, priv. coll., letters to Sir Norman Moore · PRO, Buller MSS, WO 132 · PRO, Wolseley MSS, WO 147 · Royal Arch. | F I L M BFI NFTVA, performance footage
Likenesses E. Wood, painting, 1852, repro. in Wood, *From midshipman to field marshal* · F. Spalding, photograph, *c.*1881, NPG [*see illus.*] · W. W. Ouless, oils, 1906, Fishmongers' Hall, London · O. Edis, photographs, 1914, NPG · F. Lion, lithograph, 1915, NPG · Barraud, photograph, NPG; repro. in *Men and Women of the Day*, 3 (1890) · Lock & Whitfield, woodburytype photograph, NPG; repro. in T. Cooper, *Men of mark: a gallery of contemporary portraits* (1883) · Maull & Fox, cabinet photograph, NPG · Spy [L. Ward], caricature, watercolour study, NPG; repro. in *VF* (15 Nov 1879) · E. Wood, sketches, repro. in Wood, *From midshipman to field marshal* · carte-de-visite, NPG · memorial, St Mary's Church, Old Harlow, Essex · memorial, St Paul's Cathedral, London · memorial, Marlborough College, Wiltshire · prints, NPG
Wealth at death £11,196 4*s.* 10*d.*: probate, 10 Feb 1920, *CGPLA Eng. & Wales*

Wood, Francis Derwent (1871–1926), sculptor, was born on 15 October 1871 at Eskin Place, Castlerigg, St John's, Keswick, Cumberland, fourth child of Alpheus Bayliss Wood, of Philadelphia, Pennsylvania, pencil mill manager (d. *c.*1908), and Ann Mary, daughter of John Hornby Maw, of Ironbridge, Shropshire (*c.*1830–1916). His parents were educated, artistic, and impoverished; Alpheus a capable watercolourist with an eye for antiques; Ann Mary, well read in Greek, Latin, and Hebrew, had been taught to paint by Ruskin. Francis Derwent Wood rejected their rigorous Christianity from an early age. The Woods moved to Switzerland in 1880. Frank was small for his age, nicknamed Le Microbe as a schoolboy at Collège Gaillard, Lausanne. He was soon fluent in three languages and was a passionate sketcher and fossil hunter. After he had spent two years at the *Kunstgewerbeschule* in Karlsruhe, Germany, where the family moved in 1885, in 1887 his mother wrote to Hamo Thornycroft seeking advice about her son's prospects as a sculptor. Impressed by the photographs she enclosed, Thornycroft became a lifelong mentor and friend of Derwent Wood (as he was often known).

Having returned to Shropshire in July 1887, Wood entered art school and worked as a modeller for the family firm of Maw & Co., tile manufacturers of Ironbridge, and later for the Coalbrookdale foundry. He enrolled at the National Art Training School in 1890 where he studied under Lantéri, winning a national scholarship. A year later he became paid assistant to Alphonse Legros at the Slade School of Fine Art. As a student at the Royal Academy Schools from 1894 he assisted Thomas Brock and, among many prizes, in 1895 won a gold medal and £200

travelling scholarship for *Daedalus and Icarus*, a work influenced by Alfred Gilbert (bronze, Bristol City Art Gallery; plaster, Russell-Cotes Art Gallery, Bournemouth). *Circe* was his first exhibit at the Royal Academy of 1895. The scholarship financed a year in Paris where, in his studio at 9 rue Falguière, Wood made sculpture that he successfully exhibited at the Salon. Among many artists he encountered, Wood particularly befriended Gauguin, whose paintings he greatly admired.

Between 1897 and 1900 Wood continued to assist Brock and was visiting director of modelling at Glasgow School of Art. Architectural commissions in Glasgow include figures of the arts for the Kelvingrove Gallery (*c.*1898). In London, Edwin Lutyens's Britannic House, Finsbury Circus, bears later architectural work (1921–5).

In 1900 Wood took the studio at 27 Glebe Place, Chelsea, and was elected a member of the Artworkers' Guild in 1901. He married Florence Mary Schmidt (1873–1969), a successful Australian soprano, on 25 March 1903 at St John's Church, Paddington. They lived until 1908 at 23 Clareville Grove, South Kensington, where their only son, Oliver, was born on 20 June 1904. In that year Wood became a founder member of the Society of British Sculptors. He was elected an associate of the Royal Academy in 1910 and Royal Academician in 1920. Increasing success enabled the purchase of the lease of 18 Carlyle Square in 1911. Friends including Augustus John, Walter Sickert, Ambrose McEvoy, George Lambert, and D. H. Lawrence joined them for lively musical evenings at which Florence sang and her 'darling François' played the flute.

Derwent Wood's numerous public monuments include *Sir Titus Salt*, Saltaire, Yorkshire (bronze, 1903), *General Wolfe*, Westerham, Kent (bronze, 1910), *Edward VII*, Rangoon (exh. RA, 1914), *William Pitt* (marble, exh. RA, 1918; Capitol, Washington, DC), and portraying a friend, *F. Henry Royce* (bronze, exh. RA, 1922; Derby). He also contributed the Australia Gate figures to Brock's Victoria memorial. Wood's portraits are remarkable for their modelling and character. *Henry James* (marble, exh. RA, 1914; Tate collection), *T. E. Lawrence* (bronze, exh. RA, 1920; Tate collection), and *Ambrose McEvoy* (bronze, exh. RA, 1915; NPG) are among many whose vigorous and animated features reveal the artist's greatest strength.

Wood joined up as an orderly in the Royal Army Medical Corps in 1915 and used his skills to develop a technique for masking facial disfigurements. He was commissioned in March 1916 on the strength of this distressing and vital work, and published his methods in *The Lancet* in 1917.

War memorials for Liverpool's cotton exchange, for Keswick (exh. RA, 1922), and for Ditchingham, Norfolk (bronze, exh. RA, 1920), were among those that dominated his tenure as professor of sculpture at the Royal College of Art from 1918 to 1923. The machine-gun corps memorial at Hyde Park, whose plinth is inscribed to the corps's 'Glorious heroes', is frequently criticized as an anodyne glorification of war (unveiled 1925, exh. RA, 1925, 1926). Wood intended the idealized David to represent the solitary machine-gunner, whose tragic role in the mechanized destruction of enemy hordes is revealed in the inscription

'Saul hath slain his thousands, but David his ten thousands'. He believed that if war memorials must be made, they should not evade the carnage of conflict. The monument teeters ambiguously between the glorification and the pathos of war.

Francis Derwent Wood was a prolific intellectual traditionalist whose influences ranged from the French Renaissance to Alfred Stevens, Gilbert, and Thornycroft. Rare stylistic experiments include *Penitent Thief* (bronze, 1918; Lady Lever Art Gallery, Port Sunlight) and *La Paimpolaise* (teak, beech, and tin, exh. RA, 1899). Typical of his classical realism are *Psyche* (bronze, exh. RA, 1908, 1919; Chantrey purchase 1919, Tate collection; bronze, 1920, Lady Lever Art Gallery, Port Sunlight) and *Atalanta* (exh. plaster RA, 1907, marble 1909; Manchester City Galleries). A bronze cast of *Atalanta*, erected in his memory by friends from the Chelsea Arts Club in 1929, was stolen from Chelsea Embankment in 1991.

A charming smile and frequent laughter leavened Derwent Wood's severe features. Modest in ordinary conversation, he could be argumentative and he voiced strong opinions about art. He abhorred capital punishment, had no time for Scotsmen, and was a generous employer whose assistants were well rewarded. He loved the Chelsea Arts Club, where he refuelled on cigarettes and legendary quantities of gin and bitters. He cut a flamboyant and dashing figure at the Chelsea Arts balls when he indulged his love of historic dress. He once appeared as Dante, whom he resembled. He was a member of the Garrick Club.

Wood sketched and painted on holidays in France with Henry Royce, and at Amberley, Sussex, with the Sickerts. Drawings, caricatures, and bold woodcuts occupied him during his final illness. After surgery for lung cancer, Francis Derwent Wood died on 19 February 1926 at 14 Henrietta Street, Westminster. A memorial service overflowing with mourners followed his burial on 23 February at Amberley church. Until it was stolen, one of his own sculptures marked his grave.   SARAH CRELLIN

Sources DNB • W. K. Parkes, *Sculpture of to-day* (1921) • private information (2004) • press cuttings collection, Tate collection, Tate collection • S. Beattie, *The New Sculpture* (1983) • A. Jarman and others, eds., *Royal Academy exhibitors, 1905–1970: a dictionary of artists and their work in the summer exhibitions of the Royal Academy of Arts*, 6 vols. (1973–82) • Graves, *RA exhibitors* • Leeds Museums and Galleries, archives, Henry Moore Institute • *CGPLA Eng. & Wales* (1926) • PRO, file WO 339/55999 [war record] • S. Crellin, 'Hollow men: Francis Derwent Wood's masks and memorials, 1915–1925', *Sculpture Journal*, 6 (2001), 75–88
Archives Bradford City Art Gallery • Tate collection, press cuttings collection
Likenesses G. W. Lambert, oils, 1906, NPG • G. C. Beresford, photographs, 1922, NPG • H. M. Bateman, caricature, Chelsea Arts Club, London
Wealth at death £10,155 1s. 9d.: probate, 7 May 1926, *CGPLA Eng. & Wales*

Wood, Sir George (1743–1824), judge, was born on 13 February 1743 at Royston, near Barnsley, the fourth child and first son of George Wood (1704–1781), vicar of Royston for nearly fifty years, and his wife, Jane (*c.*1709–1778), daughter of John Matson of Royston. Two other sons and three daughters survived infancy.

The living was a poor one, and George was articled to a local attorney named West in nearby Cawthorne. Much impressed with his aptitude and diligence, West urged that on completion of his articles Wood should study for the bar, and he entered at the Middle Temple on 16 November 1765. Deferring his call, he practised as a special pleader and quickly became an acknowledged master of that recondite art, who included among his pupils such future eminent lawyers as Edward Law (Lord Ellenborough) and Charles Abbott (Lord Tenterden).

Wood was called to the bar on 16 June 1775 and went the northern circuit. With his lack of oratorical skills he was better fitted for a junior than a leader—he never took silk—but he built a good practice and through the 1790s was regularly retained for the crown in a succession of notable trials for treason and sedition.

On 5 November 1796 Wood was elected MP for Haslemere, a pocket borough of the Lowthers', and dutifully followed the political line of his patrons. A silent supporter of the ministry until Pitt's resignation in 1801, he deserted Addington's administration in 1804, when Pitt withdrew his countenance from it, and resigned his seat at the Lowther family's behest in 1806, admitting that he could not give enough time to parliament.

On 28 May 1807 Wood accepted the exchequer barony vacated by Manners Sutton; he was accordingly made a serjeant at the same time, and was knighted soon afterwards. As his earlier career might have suggested, he proved a stern upholder of authority and the established order, and in the trial of John Drakard in 1811 for publishing a seditious libel he put forward a strikingly narrow view of the limits on the right to print criticism of the government:

> it is said that we have a right to discuss the acts of our legislature. That would be a large permission indeed. Is there, gentlemen, to be a power in the people to counteract the acts of the Parliament, and is the libeller to come and make the people dissatisfied with the government under which he lives? This is not to be permitted to any man, it is unconstitutional and seditious.   (*State trials*)

Henry Brougham, counsel for the defence, indignantly talked of moving for his impeachment. Despite his personal sympathies, however, he was scrupulous in insisting that the prosecution fully prove its case in criminal trials, and was generally regarded as a competent if rather laborious judge.

Much of the exchequer's business at this time was in tithe disputes, and Wood frequently dissented from the majority opinion. This stimulated him to a modest effort at law reform. He circulated a pamphlet (published after his death as *Observations on Tithes and Tithe Laws*, 1832) arguing that it should be made easier to plead long usage as evidence of a composition, and in 1817 persuaded J. H. Curwen to introduce a bill which he had drafted for this purpose. However, the bill was opposed by Sir William

Scott as inimical to the interests of the church, and was defeated in the Commons in 1818.

Wood married, but he and his wife, Sarah (1754/5–1839), did not have any children. He amassed a fortune from his practice said to be worth £300,000, and bought land in several parts of Yorkshire. Around 1813 he built a country house at Moor Grange in Holderness. He was unprepossessing in appearance, being very small and dark with unusually flat features. Both his accent and his blunt mode of expression marked him out as a Yorkshireman, and he was reputed amiable and amusing in private life.

Wood had become a bencher of his inn on 7 May 1802 and was reader in 1806. He was 'the father of the English bar' by the time that gout and old age led him to retire from the bench on 27 January 1823. He died at his house, 4 Bedford Square, London, probably on 7 July 1824, and was buried in the Temple Church. His wife lived until 18 December 1839, when the division of his estate among the families of his sisters and brother John was completed.

PATRICK POLDEN

Sources HoP, *Commons, 1790–1820*, 2.382–3; 4.641–2 · *GM*, 1st ser., 94/2 (1824), 177 · Foss, *Judges*, 9.53–4 · J. Foster, ed., *Pedigrees of the county families of Yorkshire*, 3 vols. (1874) · J. Hunter, *South Yorkshire: the history and topography of the deanery of Doncaster*, 2 (1831), 382, 396, 427 · H. A. C. Sturgess, ed., *Register of admissions to the Honourable Society of the Middle Temple, from the fifteenth century to the year 1944*, 1 (1949), 364 · G. Poulson, *History of Holderness*, 1 (1840), 259 · J. Campbell, *Lives of the lord chancellors*, 8 vols. (1845–69), vol. 6, pp. 387, 390; vol. 8, p. 279 · John, Lord Campbell, *The lives of the chief justices of England*, 3 (1857), 100–01, 270 · S. Romilly, *Memoirs of the life of Sir Samuel Romilly*, 3 (1840), 300, 333–4 · will, PRO, PROB 11/1693 · death duty registers, PRO, IR 26/1026 · I. R. Christie, *British non-elite MPs, 1715–1820* (1995), 93 · T. H. Ford, *Henry Brougham and his world* (1995) · *DNB* · London street directories · *IGI* · *State trials*, 31.535 · d. cert. [Sarah Wood] · private information (2004) [A. D. E. Lewis]
Likenesses T. Hodgetts, mezzotint, pubd 1819 (after J. Lonsdale), BM, NPG
Wealth at death £115,177 personal estate: PRO, death duty registers, IR 26/1026; will, PRO, PROB 11/1693 · approx. £300,000 total wealth: *GM*, 177

Wood, Sir George Adam (1767–1831), army officer, received his military training at the Royal Military Academy, Woolwich, and was commissioned second lieutenant, Royal Artillery, on 24 May 1781. His further commissions were: lieutenant, 15 May 1790; captain-lieutenant, 7 January 1795; captain, 3 December 1800; major, 24 July 1806; lieutenant-colonel, 1 February 1808; brevet colonel, 4 June 1814; regimental colonel, 11 May 1820; major-general, 27 May 1825. He served with the duke of York's army in Flanders in the campaigns of 1793 to 1795, taking part in the principal operations. Shortly after his return to England he went to the West Indies, and was present under Abercromby at the capture of St Lucia in May 1796, and of St Vincent in June of that year. In February 1797 he sailed with Abercromby's expedition from Martinique to the Gulf of Paria, and was at the capture of Trinidad on 17 February, and at the subsequent unsuccessful attempt on Puerto Rico.

Wood served with distinction in the Mediterranean from 1806 until 1808; he then went to Portugal, took part

in Sir John Moore's campaign, was at the battle of Corunna on 16 January 1809, and returned with the British army to England. In July he was in the expedition under the earl of Chatham to Walcheren, and was at the siege of Flushing and its capture on 14 August. He was knighted on 22 May 1812. He commanded the British artillery of the army under Sir Thomas Graham (afterwards Lord Lynedoch), which co-operated with the allies in the Netherlands and Flanders. He landed at Rotterdam in December 1813, and was at the siege of Antwerp in January 1814 and the action of Merxem on 13 January. He was at the unsuccessful assault on Bergen op Zoom on 8 March, and the subsequent blockade of that place and of Antwerp. For his services he received brevet promotion, and was made an aide-de-camp to the king.

In 1815 Wood commanded the Royal Artillery in the Waterloo campaign, in the battles of Quatre-Bras (16 June) and of Waterloo (18 June), in the march to Paris, and the operations against the fortresses of Maubeuge, Landrecies, Marienbourg, Philippeville, and Cambrai, and at the entry into Paris on 7 July. He was mentioned in dispatches, was made a CB, and received Russian, Dutch, and Austrian orders. In 1816 he was made a KH. He commanded the British artillery of the army of occupation in France until 1819, when he returned to England. He was appointed governor of Carlisle on 18 June 1825. He died in Cumberland on 22 April 1831.   R. H. VETCH, *rev.* JAMES LUNT

Sources war office records, PRO · *The dispatches of … the duke of Wellington … from 1799 to 1818*, ed. J. Gurwood, 2nd edn, enl., 8 vols. (1844–7) · royal artillery records, Royal Artillery Institution, Woolwich, London · F. Duncan, ed., *History of the royal regiment of artillery*, 1 (1872) · H. T. Siborne, ed., *Waterloo letters* (1891) · *GM*, 1st ser., 101/2 (1831) · J. Philippart, ed., *The royal military calendar*, 3 vols. (1815–16)
Likenesses S. Cole, oils, *c*.1815, NPG · H. W. Pickersgill, oils, *c*.1825, Royal Collection · oils, Royal Artillery Mess, Woolwich, London

Wood, George Arnold (1865–1928), historian, was born at Salford, Lancashire, on 7 June 1865, eldest son of George Stanley Wood (1840–1914), a cotton merchant, and Martha Pickering, *née* Alliott (1839/40–1871). He grew up in a nonconformist household that was strongly attached to the Liberal Party. He was educated at Mrs Hunt's school, Bowdon, Cheshire and then went to Bowdon College before going to Owens College, Manchester, in 1882. After graduating in 1885 he entered Balliol College, Oxford, gaining a BA with first-class honours in 1888 and an MA two years later. In October 1888 he enrolled in the Congregational Mansfield College, Oxford, but while at Balliol he had begun to lose his faith. He abandoned theology and in 1890 accepted the newly established Challis chair of history at the University of Sydney, thus becoming the first occupant of a history chair in Australia.

Wood reached Sydney in February 1891 and remained there for the next thirty-seven years. He alone taught history until 1916 when he was joined by a former student, J. F. Bruce. Life was arduous but pleasurable and stimulating, for the small university staff was composed mainly of Oxford and Cambridge graduates whose company proved congenial. Gregarious by nature and fond of sport and outdoor activities, Wood was also a devoted family man. On 27 December 1898 at Marrickville he married Eleanor Madeline Whitfeld (1876x8–1967), daughter of Edwin Whitfeld, former fellow of Trinity Hall, Cambridge, and currently a master at Sydney grammar school, and his wife, Eleanor Cooke. Wood's wife, a former student and first-class honours history graduate with wide intellectual interests, proved an ideal companion. The couple had three sons and a daughter and formed a close-knit family, from which Wood drew great strength.

Wood had attended Oxford University at a time when the study of history was being placed on a new footing by the regius professor, William Stubbs, a disciple of the German empirical school founded by von Ranke. Wood was deeply influenced by Stubbs and throughout insisted on the need for research to be based on original sources. Yet he also stressed that the writing of history was a creative process calling for the use of imaginative powers. He saw his subject as a moral force capable of influencing the present and providing direction for the future. Wood sought to develop in his students an appreciation of the 'noble and the good' and to instil them with those Liberal beliefs, particularly of a Gladstonian variety, which influenced his own outlook. Far from aiming at objectivity the historian must give full expression to his own personal feelings and political creed.

Such an approach strongly influenced Wood's writing and teaching. The burdens of office prevented him from publishing much and he produced only two books, *The Discovery of Australia* (1922) and the much slighter *Voyage of the Endeavour* (1925). A manuscript dealing with early New South Wales was not accepted, but chapters did appear in the journal of the Royal Australian Historical Society, to which he contributed other articles. He also completed a chapter on oceanic exploration for the Australian volume of the Cambridge History of the British Empire, but it did not appear. Wood's writings were original, stimulating, thoroughly researched, and sometimes, particularly in the case of his article on convicts, controversial. It was for his work as a teacher, however, that he was most noted. He established a warm relationship with his students, excited their curiosity, and widened their intellectual horizons. His lectures, neatly written and preserved among his papers, dealt with large issues and bore testimony to the strength of his belief in liberalism. He taught mostly British and European history from the middle ages, but he also developed an interest in British imperial history and made occasional incursions into the Australian past. This was a field that engrossed his attention after he became aware of the rich documentary sources through his association with two government-sponsored projects for the publication of the historical records, first of New South Wales, then of Australia. He encouraged postgraduate research in Australian history but thought the secondary literature inadequate for undergraduate purposes.

Wood saw his purpose as extending beyond the university into the broader community. As a professor he bore responsibilities for history in the secondary schools and he played a major role in determining the syllabus and setting, as well as examining, the two public examinations. He had well-developed ideas about how history should be taught in all levels at school and he worked hard to guide teachers. A great encourager, he involved himself in the work of the Royal Australian Historical Society and gave active assistance to a number of amateur writers. One of his first tasks after arriving in Sydney was to deliver a public inaugural lecture, 'The study of history', and thereafter he lectured regularly for community groups and the university's extension board. He was also active in the Workers' Educational Association from 1914 and displayed concern for the underprivileged. He had a strong interest in contemporary issues, served for a long time as a correspondent for the *Manchester Guardian*, and was a member of the New South Wales branch of both the Institute of International Affairs and the Institute of Pacific Relations.

On 14 October 1928 Wood committed suicide while undergoing treatment for shingles at a private hospital in Randwick, Sydney. His death was as tragic as his life was fruitful. A man whose courage was reflected in the way he withstood public opprobrium for opposing Britain's involvement in the Second South African War, he was noted for his integrity and high principle. Regarded with respect and affection by students and colleagues, he added fresh dimensions to Australian culture and contributed to the professionalization of history, laying the foundations for a strong history department at Sydney University. The Wood tradition was taken to Melbourne University by Wood's student and biographer, Professor R. M. Crawford, and it also influenced others who rose to literary, academic, and professional prominence.

BRIAN H. FLETCHER

Sources R. M. Crawford, '*A bit of a rebel': the life and work of George Arnold Wood* (1975) • B. H. Fletcher, 'Founding a tradition: G. A. Wood and J. F. Bruce, 1891–1930', *History at Sydney, 1891–1991: centenary reflections*, ed. B. Caine and others (1992) • B. H. Fletcher, 'George Arnold Wood and imperial history at the University of Sydney', *Royal Australian Historical Society Journal and Proceedings*, 79 (1993), 54–71 • B. H. Fletcher, *Australian history in New South Wales, 1888–1938* (1993) • B. H. Fletcher, 'History as a moral force: George Arnold Wood at Sydney University, 1891–1928', *The discovery of Australian history, 1890–1939*, ed. S. Macintyre and J. Thomas (1995) • J. A. Moses, 'The Christian basis of George Arnold Wood's historiographical assumptions', *St Mark's Review* (1991), 17–24 • J. A. Moses, *Prussian-German militarism, 1914–1918, in Australian perspective: the thought of George Arnold Wood* (1991)
Archives University of Sydney | Mitchell L., NSW, Angus MSS • Mitchell L., NSW, Ramily MSS • Mitchell L., NSW, Robertson MSS • Mitchell L., NSW, E. M. Wood MSS • NL Aus., Frederick Watson MSS

Wood, Haydn (1882–1959), composer, was born on 25 March 1882 at Slaithwaite in Yorkshire, the son of Clement Wood (1833–1886) and his wife, Sabra Sykes, who died in 1902. He was the youngest of twelve children, four of whom did not survive infancy. He was born into a musical family. His father having been captivated by a performance of Haydn's *Creation* shortly before his birth, Wood was named after that composer (but the name was pronounced to rhyme with maiden). When he was two his family moved to the Isle of Man, where he lived throughout his childhood. In a supportive family Haydn Wood received violin lessons from his older brother Harry and became a child prodigy. At twelve he was featured in solo recitals and at the island's holiday resort, Douglas. At fifteen he won a scholarship to the Royal College of Music, studying violin with Enrique Fernández Arbos and composition with Charles Villiers Stanford, whose traditionally minded approach consolidated Wood's own métier, which eventually brought him worldwide recognition as a composer of popular ballads and light classical orchestral music. At the opening of the Royal College of Music Concert Hall in 1901 the solo violinist was the nineteen-year-old Haydn Wood. Present were the great violinists Joseph Joachim and Pablo Sarasate, whose commendation helped decide him to go to Brussels for special training under César Thomson. As solo violinist he embarked on a world tour with soprano Mme Albani, with whom he was associated for eight years. Composition remained a driving force. In 1905 his 'Phantasy' string quartet came second in the competition for the prestigious Cobbett chamber music prize. His piano concerto received its first performance in London's Queen's Hall in 1913.

On 23 March 1909 Wood married the popular soprano (Clara) Dorothy Court (b. 1882/3), daughter of Thomas Court. This led to his writing lyrical romantic ballads, eventually numbering more than 200. His melodic gift and ability perfectly to marry his inspiration to the lyrics he astutely chose brought him enormous success, notably with 'Bird of Love Divine' (1912), 'Love's Garden of Roses' (1914), and 'A Brown Bird Singing' (1922). His most famous song, 'Roses of Picardy' (1916), was set at the request of his publisher, who had rejected its setting by another composer. Perfectly expressing the hope that rose above the anguish engendered by the horrors of the First World War, the song was an immediate hit. Over 3 million records and over 2 million song copies were sold and Wood's fortune was made.

Music for the stage came in 1915, when Wood contributed material for *Tina* at the Adelphi, followed in 1917 with the musical comedy *Cash on Delivery*. He also contributed to *Dear Love*, staged in 1929 at the Palace Theatre, London. He wrote *Lochinvar* and other major choral works, and several solo pieces for solo violin and other instruments.

Haydn Wood's numerous orchestral compositions, eagerly welcomed by the many light orchestras and ensembles flourishing in municipalities, theatres, cinemas, spas, and seaside resorts, ranged from unpretentious, tuneful miniatures such as *An Evening Song* (1923), many incorporated into suites such as *Paris* (1935), *Frescoes* (1936), and *Cities of Romance* (1937), to more extended pieces like *A May-Day Overture* (1918), and those founded on Manx folk tunes and dances such as the tone poem *Mannin Veen* (1932) and rhapsodies *A Manx Rhapsody* (1931) and *Mylechrane* (1946). His traditional style most effectively expressed itself in more serious symphonic works with his overture *Apollo* (1935), *Soliloquy* (1949), *Philharmonic Variations* for cello and orchestra, and in particular the violin concerto.

Wood was quiet and unassuming and his lifestyle in later years was increasingly retiring, though he did appear on the rostrum from time to time to conduct his own works. His music's popularity continued to the end of his life, and included a BBC Light Music Festival commission in 1954, *Gipsy Rhapsody*. His march *The Horse-Guards, Whitehall* from the suite *London Landmarks* (1946) was a signature tune for the popular BBC radio programme *Down your Way* over many years. His tuneful output continued into his seventies, including *Serenade to Youth* (1953) and the march *Lutine Ahoy* (1954). Having suffered from heart disease for some time, Wood died peacefully in a London nursing home, The Priory, Roehampton, on 11 March 1959, shortly before his seventy-seventh birthday. He was survived by his wife. They had no children.   ERNEST TOMLINSON

Sources A. Lamb, 'Wood, Haydn', *New Grove* • private information (2004) [Marjorie Koers, great-niece] • 'An interview with Haydn Wood', *c.*1944, priv. coll. • *The Times* (13 March 1959) • T. McDonald, disc notes, *British light music: Haydn Wood* (Marco Polo 8.223402, 1992) [CD booklet] • m. cert. • d. cert. • *CGPLA Eng. & Wales* (1959) • K. Gänzl, *The encyclopedia of the musical theatre*, 2 vols. (1994) **Archives** SOUND BL NSA, performance recordings **Likenesses** two photographs, 1936–54, Hult. Arch. **Wealth at death** £76,770 13s. 10d.: probate, 2 June 1959, *CGPLA Eng. & Wales*

Wood, Mrs Henry. *See* Wood, Ellen (1814–1887).

Wood, Henry Harvey (1903–1977), writer and a founder of the Edinburgh international festival, was born on 5 September 1903 in Edinburgh, the second of the three children of Henry Wood (d. 1934), paper maker, and his wife, Anne Cassidy. He was educated at the Royal High School in Edinburgh, the Edinburgh College of Art (where he won the draughtsmanship prize for his year and also exhibited work in the Royal Scottish Academy), and finally at Edinburgh University (where he was awarded the Elliott prize and the Vans Dunlop scholarship). In 1931 he graduated with first-class honours and was immediately engaged by the university as a lecturer in English literature. Here his scholarly lectures, delivered in dry, witty rhetoric with a suspicion of a lisp, were an inspiration to his students. On 6 July 1932 Harvey Wood married Lily Terry (b. 1907); they had a son and two daughters.

At the outbreak of war in 1939 Harvey Wood was turned down for active service for health reasons but was engaged briefly in intelligence work before being appointed in 1940 to establish a branch of the British Council in Scotland. Its purpose was to establish cultural contacts with, and outlets for, the allies of various nations stationed in Scotland during the war. The tides of war had washed up on British shores vast numbers of allied servicemen, including the remains of the Polish army and air force, who had made their way to Scotland. It was in Scotland too that a Norwegian brigade was created to take part in the liberation of Norway. In addition there were thousands of refugees, many of whom spoke little English. National centres were set up to provide English classes and entertainments for refugees, enabling them to escape from often uncomfortable lodgings. To this end the

Henry Harvey Wood (1903–1977), by Sir William George Gillies, 1922

British Council, in association with the allied governments in exile, founded the 'national houses' in Scotland (Scottish–Polish House, Scottish–Czechoslovak House, Scottish–French House, and the Scottish–American Centre), which were later replaced by Edinburgh International House.

Harvey Wood went even further and, enlisting the help of his friend the poet Edwin Muir, he brought a stream of poets, musicians, artists, and writers of many nationalities to Edinburgh, and the cultural programmes organized by the British Council in Scotland were considered greatly superior to those arranged elsewhere. One of its earliest undertakings was an exhibition in the National Gallery of Scotland of *The Art of our Allies*, in May 1941. A large section was contributed by Poles, whose commanders had released artists from military duties to complete their exhibits. The venture was described in *The Scotsman* (16 May 1941) as 'undoubtedly … one of the most interesting ever held in Scotland'. This was followed by exhibitions of Polish, Czech, French, Chinese, Greek, Dutch, and Norwegian art, for which British collectors lent generously, enabling displays of an unprecedented standard to be assembled. The quality of these exhibitions, and of the lunchtime concerts in the National Gallery, bore witness to the enormous enthusiasm and talent of Harvey Wood.

His experience in organizing cultural activities, and the local response to them, doubtless encouraged Harvey Wood to recommend to Rudolf Bing, who was planning a music festival in Britain, that Edinburgh had all the essential qualities for an international festival. He then lobbied influential local support and set up a meeting between Bing and the lord provost of Edinburgh, Sir John Falconer. Despite the enthusiastic support of the lord provost, the festival plan almost foundered on the rocks of apathy, civic obstruction, and local government politics, and Harvey Wood had to exercise determination, tact, and diplomacy to avert catastrophe and to steer the scheme into safe harbour. The result was the first Edinburgh international festival in 1947. Harvey Wood became the first chairman of the programme committee and a member of the executive council of the festival. It was he who persuaded the festival council to revive the 400-year-old Scottish morality play by Scotland's first known dramatist, Sir David Lyndsay of the Mount, *Ane Satyre of the Thrie Estaites*, which was the highlight of the second Edinburgh festival in 1948.

In 1950 Harvey Wood had to resign from active participation in the festival when appointed as the British Council's representative in France. In 1960 he took up a similar post in Italy after serving for several years as controller (education division), in London. He retired from the British Council in 1965 and returned to Edinburgh University. Among his published works are critical editions of *The Poems and Fables of Robert Henryson* (1933), which included previously unknown early texts, *The Plays of John Marston* (3 vols., 1934–9), a new edition of Alexander Montgomerie's *The Cherrie and the Slae* (1937), *Scottish Literature* (1952), *Two Scots Chaucerians* (1967), and *William MacTaggart* (1974). He was created an OBE in 1948.

Harvey Wood died of cancer at his home, 158 Coleherne Court, London, on 12 August 1977. His body was cremated five days later at Golders Green crematorium. His wife survived him.   EILEEN MILLER

Sources Edinburgh international festival archive, Edinburgh · *Harry Harvey Wood: the Edinburgh international festival and the British Council* (1997) · *Edinburgh festival: a review of the first ten years* (1956) · H. Harvey Wood, 'British Council in Scotland', *Edinburgh Evening News* (9 Nov 1950) · *The Scotsman* (15 Aug 1977) · D. Rintoul, 'Mr H. Harvey Wood, O.B.E.', *Schola Regia* [magazine of the Royal High School, Edinburgh] (c.1949) · W. M. Parker, 'A pillar of British Council: varied career of Mr Harvey Wood', *Edinburgh Evening News* (25 June 1951) · *The Scotsman* (16 May 1941) · G. Bruce, *Festival in the north: the story of the Edinburgh festival* (1975) · 'Mr Harvey Wood's post: British Council in France', *The Scotsman* (19 Aug 1950) · private information (2004) [Harriet Harvey Wood] · b. cert.
Archives priv. coll.
Likenesses W. G. Gillies, oils, 1922, Royal Scot. Acad. [*see illus.*] · A. Zylo, oils, c.1940, priv. coll. · H. Harvey Wood, self-portrait, pencil drawing, priv. coll. · portraits, priv. coll.
Wealth at death modest: private information

Wood, Sir Henry Joseph (1869–1944), conductor, was born in London on 3 March 1869. His father, identically named, was an optician and engineering model-maker residing and trading at 413A Oxford Street, London, and his mother, Martha, *née* Morris, was Welsh; he was their only child. Both parents were musical, Henry Wood senior being a keen amateur cellist and a solo tenor in the choir of St Sepulchre's, Holborn. Their son's early aptitude for music (he took with equal zeal to painting) was nurtured mainly from home, though he also took organ and piano lessons from E. M. Lott, the organist of St Sepulchre's.

Wood first won public notice as a fourteen-year-old organ recitalist in 1883. After taking private lessons in music theory from Ebenezer Prout, he entered the Royal Academy of Music (1886–8), where he acquired unusual skill as a piano accompanist for singers, playing for the great vocal teacher Manuel García. His principal studies were composition with Prout, organ with Charles Steggall, and piano with Walter Macfarren.

Wood's first ambition was to be a composer: several songs and other short pieces were published while he was

Sir Henry Joseph Wood (1869–1944), by Meredith Frampton, 1930

the symphonic component in such a way as to give the new series its distinction and its year-by-year renewal as a summer event (with occasional extensions to other seasons). By 1896 the dedication of Monday nights to Beethoven and Friday nights to Wagner was in place, with miscellaneous lighter music being played after the interval.

Minimal rehearsal time was allowed. Six concerts a week (from Monday to Saturday) were prepared in only three rehearsals of three hours each per week. Even with the economy of repeating favourite works several times during the season, and the inclusion of songs and other items without orchestra, acceptable standards could not have been achieved without the iron discipline which Wood developed—the rehearsal of each item rigorously pre-timed, and the players' parts copiously marked with precautionary instructions.

Wood's gifts, however, not merely as trainer but as interpreter, took him further. From January 1897 Newman made him the regular conductor of his most prestigious series at Queen's Hall, the Saturday afternoon symphony concerts, as also (from September of that year) of the shorter Sunday concerts and other events. The works of Wagner and of Tchaikovsky were recognized as among Wood's chief strengths. Queen Victoria chose selections from both when Wood and the orchestra were summoned to perform at Windsor Castle on 24 November 1898.

Concert innovator In Newman's London music festival of 1899, the Queen's Hall Orchestra under Wood was pitted against the Lamoureux Orchestra from Paris (Lamoureux, its conductor, was Wood's senior by thirty-five years) to public satisfaction. Wood pursued a parallel career as choral conductor which reached a peak with his appointment in 1902 to the triennial Sheffield music festival, where his later radical reinterpretations of such works as Handel's *Messiah* aroused both admiration and fury. Elgar and Delius were among the composers gratified by Wood's vivid interpretations of their recent choral works.

His 'sweeping, incisive, and picturesque' gestures and 'dark, wavy hair and full black beard' were noted by the American *Musical Courier* magazine when Wood appeared as one of the guest conductors of the New York Philharmonic Orchestra during its 1904 season. He was accompanied on this first transatlantic trip by his wife, the former Olga Hillman, *née* Mikhailov (1868–1909); Russian-born, she was divorced from her first British husband when she and Wood married on 10 July 1898. It was the happiest of marriages: a gifted soprano, she sang at Wood's concerts as Mrs Henry J. Wood, and it was as her piano accompanist that Wood made his earliest recordings in 1908–9. Her death in the latter year at the age of forty-one was one of the severest blows to him.

Wood's concert life had undergone a major change, Newman having been made bankrupt in 1902 in an ill-advised venture into theatrical management. Newman was nevertheless retained as adviser by Sir Edgar Speyer, a banker of German origin who took over the Queen's Hall Orchestra with lavish financial support. Wood's status was now enhanced as the conductor of new music by such

still at the academy, and three operettas were later (unsuccessfully) produced. But an advertisement of his talents in *The Stage* in June 1889 as 'pianist, composer and conductor' brought an engagement as musical director of Arthur Rousbey's touring opera company. A similar post followed with the more highly esteemed Carl Rosa Opera Company and then an appointment as assistant conductor in a London opera season presented at the Olympic Theatre by an Italian impresario, Lago. Wood's conducting of Tchaikovsky's *Eugene Onegin* (17 October 1892, London's first production of any Tchaikovsky opera) marked him out in his destined role.

The Promenade Concerts So, by self-discovery, Wood became the first British-born career conductor. He had observed the techniques of eminent visiting conductors, making Arthur Nikisch his idol and even imitating his appearance. He took only one further operatic engagement, conducting the London run of Stanford's *Shamus O'Brien* (1896). His place was to be on the concert platform, in particular that of the recently opened Queen's Hall (1893). Its manager, Robert Newman, engaged Wood at the age of twenty-six as conductor of the hall's first series of Promenade Concerts, opening on 10 August 1895. Financial support was provided by Dr George Cathcart, a musically minded throat specialist, who insisted on the adoption of the lower 'French pitch' in place of the prevalent higher pitch which caused singers such difficulties.

Initially, programming adhered to the model of earlier seasons of Promenade Concerts in London: the fare was mainly of lighter music, including ballads, with a cautious infusion of classics. Wood's double command over orchestral players and audiences, at a time of generally improved musical awareness, permitted an increase in composers as Debussy, Strauss, and Sibelius, and as the trainer of the orchestra which served those composers as guest conductors. Wood was likewise the pioneer of Mahler in Britain, giving the symphony no. 1 in 1903 and no. 4 in 1905. Audiences' occasional hostility he took in his stride, as when he gave the world première of Schoenberg's *Five Pieces for Orchestra* in 1912.

In 1904 Wood consolidated his command by ending the deputy system, which permitted a player to send a substitute if a more attractive engagement presented itself. In 1913 he became the first conductor to admit women to the general ranks of a major British orchestra. Newspaper reviews noted, as a novelty, his discouragement (by gesture) of applause intruding between the movements of a symphony or similar work. Equally innovatory was his gesture of motioning the orchestra to its feet to share in the applause for the conductor. At this time he began to conduct also for G. W. Brand Lane's concerts in Manchester.

Knighted in January 1911, Wood was reapproached in that year by the New York Philharmonic and offered the succession to Mahler as its titular conductor: he declined. In June 1911 he remarried; his bride, Muriel Ellen Greatrex (1882–1967), was a highly capable businesswoman to whom Wood happily left the burden of correspondence and legal matters. The couple resided (as Wood and his former wife had done) at 4 Elsworthy Road, Primrose Hill, in north London, with the addition from 1915 of a country retreat, Appletree Farm House, Chorleywood, Hertfordshire. There were two daughters of the marriage.

The New Queen's Hall and BBC Symphony Orchestras Wood successfully resisted pressure, at the beginning of the First World War, to ban German music. But Speyer, despite his British baronetcy, was driven out of Britain by anti-German feeling; Wood, to his discredit, made no protest. Fortunately the music-publishing firm of Chappell, already the hall's leaseholder, was willing to take over the Promenade Concerts and others under Wood's baton; his forces were now renamed the New Queen's Hall Orchestra. From 1915 he began to make orchestral recordings. In 1917 he declined the permanent conductorship of the Boston Symphony Orchestra, though he was to be a guest conductor in 1934.

At the Zürich festival in 1921, Nikisch and Bruno Walter were among Wood's fellow conductors. His success at the Hollywood Bowl in 1925 secured further summer engagements there in 1926 and 1934. Yet in comparison with that of Thomas Beecham, a conductor acclaimed equally in concerts and opera, Wood's star was paling and his British reputation becoming more narrowly focused on the annual Promenade Concerts and on his choral conducting. A grievous blow in 1927 was Chappell's abandonment, for financial reasons, not only of the Promenade Concerts but also of the year-round symphony concerts at Queen's Hall. The newly powerful BBC took over the Proms (the abbreviation had become general) and Wood as their conductor, but he no longer commanded an orchestra of his own.

Increasingly, Wood's artistic and financial fortunes came to depend on what share of concerts he might be allotted in the year-round season of the BBC Symphony Orchestra. The BBC chose Wood for important collaborations with Bartók (as pianist–composer) and Hindemith, and for the first performance in Britain (1930) of Mahler's symphony no. 8, the so-called 'Symphony of a Thousand'. But in the general repertory he had to compete against the availability not only of Adrian Boult as the orchestra's chief conductor but also of Beecham and such eminent foreign visitors as Bruno Walter, Willem Mengelberg, and Arturo Toscanini, in comparison with whom he was increasingly seen as a workhorse.

In 1929 Wood launched a hoax on an unsuspecting Proms public, fathering on one 'Paul Klenovsky' an arrangement for vast orchestral forces of Bach's toccata and fugue in D minor, originally for organ; only after five years of successful performances did Wood disclose his authorship. A quite different type of arrangement, his *Fantasia on British Sea Songs*, created for a Trafalgar day centenary concert in 1905, survived as a festive contribution to the last night of later seasons.

In 1923 Wood had taken on the conductorship of the senior orchestra at the Royal Academy of Music, giving its twice-weekly rehearsal dates priority in his diaries and retaining the post (to the great benefit of British orchestral playing) for some twenty years. With no less generosity and self-inconvenience he accepted the conductorship (1923–39) of the amateur Hull Philharmonic Orchestra, travelling thrice yearly to rehearse and conduct its concerts.

Private life Wood never ceased to give singing lessons, and in 1927–8 published a four-volume treatise, *The Gentle Art of Singing*. Among his early pupils had been a very young mezzo-soprano, Jessie Goldsack [**Lady Jessie Wood** (1882–1979)], to whom he gave an unusual number of concert engagements around 1900–02. (Born Jessie Amy Louise de Levante on 23 November 1882, she had adopted her mother's maiden name of Goldsack for professional purposes.) In 1902 she married, moved to Bowdon near Manchester, and almost completely withdrew from professional performance. After being widowed in 1933, she returned to London and, in the hope of resuming a career, recontacted Wood.

At a time of domestic strain between Wood and his wife, whose behaviour had become increasingly self-centred, the sympathetic personality of Jessie Linton (her married name) offered him refuge. He wrote to his wife in February 1935 announcing that he wished to set up home with his ex-pupil but to retain the conventional appearances of the existing marriage. Devastated, Lady Wood would consent neither to that nor to divorce. Accompanied by her elder daughter she sailed for Japan (her brother was British consul in Nagasaki) and afterwards indulged her passion for travel by visiting China, New Zealand, and elsewhere. She did not return to England until after Wood's death.

Through solicitors, a bitter legal dispute took place over the division of matrimonial assets, Wood accusing his wife of having cheated him in using his earnings to place substantial investments under her sole name. He could not prove, however, that she did so in bad faith, and the eventual settlement compelled him to give up Appletree Farm House to her. Apprehensive of further claims on his estate after his death, he also signed a statutory declaration (19 January 1938) charging his wife with constant cruelty and neglect throughout their marriage, a charge reinforced in a private document called *My Confession*, dated 4 February 1939.

The accusations were exaggerated, but latterly Wood's unkempt appearance on the conductor's rostrum had been noted, as was his new spruceness when Jessie Linton took over his life with solicitude for every private and professional detail. The problem of how they might assuage social proprieties while living as though man and wife was solved by Wood's solicitor Stanley Rubinstein. On 27 September 1938 Jessie Linton changed her name by deed poll to Lady Jessie Wood, Lady being a forename rather than a title. The conductor freely spoke of her as his wife—and inevitably, though in breach of protocol, she was often addressed as Lady Wood.

Most of Wood's friends—even Ethel Smyth, who at first had been violently critical of Wood's desertion of his wife—were won over by Jessie's charm and her utter devotion to Wood. She played a vital part in the renewed vigour which marked his last years. The year 1938, somewhat arbitrarily chosen as his fiftieth in the role of conductor, called forth nationwide celebrations, culminating in a concert at the Royal Albert Hall (5 October) at which Wood conducted a force of combined London choirs and orchestras. Vaughan Williams contributed to it (and dedicated to Wood) his *Serenade to Music*, for sixteen solo voices and orchestra. Proceeds from this and other celebratory events went to the charitable cause Wood chiefly cherished, the endowment of hospital beds for orchestral musicians.

Last years Under the conditions prevailing in the Second World War the BBC declined to organize the Promenade Concert seasons of 1940 and 1941, but, by collaborating with a private entrepreneur, Keith Douglas, Wood kept them going. His beloved Queen's Hall, however, was destroyed by German bombing on 10 May 1941 and the concerts of that year were moved to the Royal Albert Hall—and remained there when the BBC resumed them from 1942. The entry of the USSR into the war (June 1941) led to a new receptivity to Soviet music, and the BBC entrusted to Wood the first British performance (and indeed the first performance outside the USSR) of Shostakovich's symphony no. 7 (the 'Leningrad' symphony) in June 1942. His eagerness to give new works never dimmed.

Though in his seventies, Wood also travelled to provincial centres amid the difficult conditions of the blackout to conduct the London Symphony, the Hallé, and other orchestras—as much in order to help the orchestras survive as to gratify audiences. From 1943, however, his physical powers perceptibly diminished. In that summer's Promenade season he was compelled not only to share the conducting of certain concerts (as in the two previous seasons) but to withdraw entirely from others.

Wood's seventy-fifth birthday (3 March 1944) was marked by as much celebration as war permitted. A book of tributes had signatures of composers, conductors, and performers from the USA (including the exiled Bartók) as well as from Britain; a meeting of Soviet musicians saluted him in Moscow. The queen attended the concert given in Wood's honour by four London orchestras at the Royal Albert Hall on 25 March 1944, when Wood divided the programme with Boult and Basil Cameron. Proceeds went towards the building (which Wood always hoped for) of a new Queen's Hall, or a similar hall in central London.

Almost immediately after the 1944 Promenade season began at the Royal Albert Hall, new German aerial attacks with the V1 caused the BBC to terminate it. Instead, the BBC Symphony Orchestra performed from its Bedford base only those items which were to be broadcast. A performance of Beethoven's symphony no. 7 on 28 July 1944 was Wood's last. He became ill that night at his hotel in Bedford and died at Hitchin Hospital on 19 August. The death certificate stated the causes of death as '(1) coma; (2) uraemia; (3) arterio-sclerosis'.

Wood was cremated after a service at Hitchin parish church, and his ashes placed (by Lady Jessie Wood's decision) on 14 June 1945 at St Sepulchre's, Holborn, where he had learned the organ as a boy; a memorial window was designed by Gerald Smith in association with Frank Salisbury, who had painted Wood's official portrait (now in the National Portrait Gallery) in 1943. A bust by Donald Gilbert is displayed annually behind and above the orchestra during the Promenade season; it was given to the Royal Academy of Music with eight oil paintings by Wood on the condition that it should be thus displayed. At his death Wood left a modest £6460.

Reputation In May 1943 the BBC had accepted 'the exclusive right to use the title "the Henry Wood Promenade Concerts"' and after Wood's death (not before) began to use it; the series reached its centenary in 1995. To Wood's artistic energy, variety of taste, and avidity for new music is due the survival of those concerts not merely as a nightly summer entertainment but as a vital creative and educational force. His gargantuan capacity for work, the Proms forming only a sector of it, is further reflected in his unparalleled record of first performances (or first performances in Britain): at least 716 works by 356 composers.

Nevertheless it could be argued that Wood's peak as a conductor was reached in the decade before 1915. That was when, at the head of the orchestra which he had trained (and Speyer financed) to be the finest in London, he captured the most discriminating audiences with his strongly emotional performances of Wagner and Tchaikovsky as well as proving such a powerful advocate for the new music of Sibelius, Strauss, and Debussy. Later his work was perceived as too reliant on routine, and even his omnivorousness of taste showed up negatively against what the public saw as the virtue of specializing—as demonstrated in the repertories of Beecham or Bruno Walter.

No longer with his own orchestra to command, Wood became increasingly identified with the Proms almost to the exclusion of everything else, and the conditions of that seasonal engagement encouraged reliability above penetrative insights. The companies which issued his gramophone recordings directed them mainly to the popular end of the classical market, and the reappearance of some of his work on compact disc has not won him any significantly upgraded esteem as an individual interpreter. What he sustained to the end (through half a century of public prominence) were the qualities of energy and integrity. He was the supreme trainer of British orchestral players and the magnet of a popular adoration which was purely musical, his demeanour owing nothing to either exhibitionism or verbal asides. The failure in his last decades to consolidate a place in the pantheon of great interpreters does not topple his position as one of the most remarkable musicians Britain has ever produced.

Wood's autobiography, *My Life of Music*, vivacious in style but factually unreliable, appeared in 1938, his book *About Conducting* in 1945. Throughout his life he was a passionate amateur painter in oils: several of his paintings survive at the Royal Academy of Music along with his library of musical scores and other memorabilia. He had almost no other non-musical interests and very rarely read a newspaper. He became in 1906 a member of the Rationalist Press Association and was elected in 1937 an honorary associate of that body, but no explicit pronouncements of humanist (or any other) belief are known. His relations with fellow musicians usually remained formal, but many anecdotes survive of his considerateness towards his orchestral players and also of oddities of speech in rehearsal ('both sides of the orchestra aren't together'). His players nicknamed him Timber—more than a play on his name, since it seemed to represent his reliability too.

At the time of his seventy-fifth birthday celebrations in 1944 it was widely thought that Wood might be given a peerage or the OM; he received instead the less conspicuous distinction of Companion of Honour. He was made a member of the order of the crown of Belgium in 1920 and an officer of the French Légion d'honneur in 1926. He was awarded the Royal Philharmonic Society's gold medal in 1921, and became an honorary freeman of the Worshipful Company of Musicians in 1938. He received honorary doctorates from the universities of Manchester (1923), Oxford (1926), Birmingham (1927), Cambridge (1935), and London (1939). He became a fellow of the Royal Academy of Music in 1920 and of the Royal College of Music in 1923.

His wife, Lady (Muriel) Wood, died at Roehampton, London, on 21 May 1967. His unmarried companion Lady Jessie Wood, who continued indefatigably to promote his memory and wrote a valuable memoir, died at Seaford, Sussex, on 14 June 1979, aged ninety-six.

ARTHUR JACOBS

Sources A. Jacobs, *Henry J. Wood: maker of the proms*, rev. edn (1995) • R. Newmarch, *Henry J. Wood* (1905) • R. Newmarch, *A quarter of a century of promenade concerts at Queen's Hall* (1920) [and typed additional list] • B. Hall, *The proms and the men who made them* (1981) • R. Elkin, *Queen's Hall, 1893–1941* [1944] • D. Cox, *The Henry Wood proms* (1980) • J. Wood, *The last years of Henry J. Wood* (1954) • H. J. Wood, *About conducting* (1945) • H. J. Wood, *My life of music* (1938) • d. cert.

Archives BBC WAC • BL, corresp. and papers, Add. MSS 56419–56443, 56464–56466 • priv. colls. • Royal Academy of Music, London, scores and papers | BL, letters to Edward Speyer, Add. MS 42233 • Elgar Birthplace Museum, Broadheath, letters to Edward Elgar | SOUND Royal Academy of Music, London, recordings
Likenesses E. Kapp, sketches, 1929–44, Barber Institute of Fine Arts, Birmingham • M. Frampton, oils, 1930, Savage Club, London [*see illus.*] • F. Lion, oils, 1937, Savage Club, London • F. Man, photograph, 1938, NPG • H. E. Wiener, pencil drawing, 1938, NPG • W. Stoneman, photograph, 1940, NPG • F. O. Salisbury, oils, 1943, NPG; copy, Royal Academy of Music, London • H. Coster, photographs, NPG • A. Ellis, cabinet photograph, NPG • D. Gilbert, bronze bust, Royal Academy of Music, London • C. Harris, photograph, NPG • W. K. Haselden, ink drawing, NPG • C. P. Hawkes, ink and wash drawing, Royal College of Music, London • A. P. F. Ritchie, cigarette card, NPG • W. Rothenstein, drawing, NPG • G. Smith and F. Salisbury, memorial window, St Sepulchre's Church, Holborn, London • Spy [L. Ward], caricature, NPG; repro. in *VF* (17 April 1907) • drawings, repro. in Jacobs, *Henry J. Wood* • photographs, repro. in Jacobs, *Henry J. Wood* • photographs, priv. coll. • portrait (*Queen's Hall*), repro. in *VF* (1907)
Wealth at death £6460 2s. 10d.: probate, 29 Sept 1944, *CGPLA Eng. & Wales* • £60,972—Lady Jessie Wood: probate, 3 Sept 1979, *CGPLA Eng. & Wales*

Wood, Sir Henry Peart (1908–1994), educationist, was born on 30 November 1908 at 30 Ridley Street, Stanley, co. Durham, the son of Thomas Marshall Wood, a jeweller, and his wife, Marjery Eleanor, *née* Peart. The Woods were a Northumberland family connected with farming and shipbuilding. Henry Wood attended Morpeth grammar school and then studied physics at Durham University, graduating BSc in 1930 and MSc in 1934; he studied under Professor W. E. Curtis, sharing Curtis's interest in spectroscopy. On 30 March 1937 he married Isobel Mary Stamp (*b.* 1908/9), daughter of William Frederick Stamp, electrical engineer, of Carbis Bay, Cornwall. They had a son and two daughters.

In 1937 Wood became a lecturer in physics at Manchester University, his arrival coinciding with that of Patrick Blackett. It was a dynamic period in the history of the department and Wood's research interests dovetailed neatly with those of Blackett, who thought the young lecturer had the makings of a leading academic physicist. At Manchester, Wood also benefited from the comparatively small world of the Manchester senior common room to meet and learn from great Manchester personalities such as Sir Lewis Namier. With the outbreak of the Second World War he received a commission in the RAF and volunteered for active service. To his disappointment he was assigned instead to teaching the theory and physics of flight to pilots in training. Blackett had already noted his outstanding talents as a teacher and he earned the Manchester MEd in 1941. The nature of his commitment to his pupils may be inferred from his sadness at the high mortality among the pilots. In this period his interest in teaching was beginning to outweigh his interest in physics.

In 1944 Wood left Manchester to become principal lecturer in physics at Jordanhill College of Education in Glasgow. He rose rapidly, becoming vice-principal of the college in 1947 and principal in 1949. He was an unusual choice for the position, being a scientist and an Englishman, but he was a popular figure, respected both within the college and in the larger world of post-war education. He had the outsider's advantage of being able to see clearly the shortcomings and anachronisms of the college, of which there were many. Coming from the relatively democratic Manchester University he was shocked to discover the utter tyranny of heads of departments, the divide between graduates and non-graduates, and the abject silences that prevailed at department meetings. By nature a diplomat, he slowly instigated change, while taking advantage of a very dynamic period in educational policy to modernize the college.

Under Wood's direction the college revamped the diploma course, giving students greater choice and flexibility, started a special course for those wishing to teach in junior secondary schools, and offered training for teachers in further education. In 1963 the Glasgow School of Speech Therapy, long informally associated with the college, was brought under its auspices. He supported the training of teachers of physical education, a speciality for which Jordanhill became renowned. The number of students grew in the 1950s, and Wood pushed for a building programme to accommodate them. The increase in numbers, together with greater emphasis on research, put immense pressure on the library; a new library, opened in 1974, was named in Wood's honour.

Wood was anxious to improve morale and introduce democratic college government. He achieved the former by negotiating with the Scottish education department to suspend its annual inspection of the college. It must be said that he never achieved democratic governance—his own style was one of benevolent and enlightened autocracy. Although he did introduce consultation and discussion, he took final decisions himself. His authority was never challenged because the staff respected his judgement. Under his leadership Jordanhill retained a distinctive community ethos, despite its rapid growth.

Wood became an important figure in education nationwide, sitting on the Appleby, Wheatley, and Brunton committees, and advising developing countries on education. He was appointed CBE in 1960 and knighted in 1967. After his retirement as principal of Jordanhill in 1971 he remained active, serving as part-time lecturer at Glasgow University from 1972 to 1978 and assessor in education at Strathclyde University from 1978 to 1984. He received an honorary degree from Glasgow in 1972 and from Strathclyde in 1982. He died at the Western Infirmary, Glasgow, of respiratory arrest following a cerebral haemorrhage on 22 March 1994. He was survived by his wife and their three children.

Wood was a rather shy man, 'who never really sought the limelight', and who could appear aloof at short acquaintance (Harrison and Marker, 62). Nevertheless the warmth of his personality was evident to those who knew him. He was a better listener than talker, and 'never used two words when none would do' (ibid., 43). His views were always received with respect, for his perceptions and judgement were serious, intelligent, and always in the best interests not only of Jordanhill nor of Scotland, but of the world of which they formed a part.

ELIZABETH J. MORSE

Sources *The Independent* (1 April 1994) · M. M. Harrison and W. B. Marker, eds., *Teaching the teachers: the history of Jordanhill College of Education, 1828–1993* (1996) · WWW, 1991–5 · b. cert. · m. cert. · d. cert.
Archives University of Strathclyde, Glasgow, Jordanhill archives, MS notes on Jordanhill; notes on training of teachers in Scotland, unpublished [mimeo]
Likenesses photograph, repro. in Harrison and Marker, eds., *Teaching the teachers*, following p. 116 · photograph (in old age), repro. in *The Independent*
Wealth at death £55,614.21: confirmation, 16 June 1994, CCI

Wood, Sir Henry Trueman Wright (1845–1929), secretary of the Royal Society of Arts (1879–1917), was born on 13 November 1845 at 36 Bruton Street, Mayfair, Westminster, the eldest son of William Burton Perse Wood (d. 1852/3) and his wife, Emily Mary Roche, daughter of James Morris. He was a great-nephew of Sir Matthew *Wood and brother of Mrs Annie *Besant. He was educated at Harrow School and at Clare College, Cambridge, where he took a second class in the classical tripos in 1868. He remained at the university a further two years engaged in coaching and won the Le Bas prize for the best English essay on a subject of general literature in both 1869 and 1870. From 1870 he worked as a clerk at the Patent Office until 1872 when, on the recommendation of Sir Walter Besant, he was selected to edit the *Journal of the Society of Arts*. He was appointed assistant secretary of the society on 31 January 1876 and three years later, following the sudden death of Peter Le Neve Foster, was appointed on 3 March 1879 to succeed him as secretary, a post which he was to hold for thirty-eight years.

In addition to his work at the Society of Arts, Wood was involved in many other activities: he continued to work for the Patent Office on the abridgement of specifications; he assisted in the planning of technical education for the City and Guilds of London Institute; and he was secretary to section G (engineering) of the British Association from 1878 to 1884. As secretary of the Society of Arts he was also involved in the organization of many exhibitions, in particular the Health (1884), Inventions (1885), and Colonial (1886) exhibitions. He was largely responsible for the British sections of the Paris Exhibition of 1889 and the 1893 Chicago Exhibition. For his work on exhibitions he was knighted in 1890. He was a keen photographer and was president of the Royal Photographic Society in 1894–6, and served on the board of Kodak Ltd for many years.

As Trueman Wood he contributed fifteen articles to the earliest volumes of the *Dictionary of National Biography* published in 1885 and 1886 and a further eight in later volumes on persons of whom he had special knowledge. His major publications were *Industrial England in the Middle of the Eighteenth Century* (1910) and *A History of the Royal Society of Arts* (1913).

Sir Henry retired as secretary of the Royal Society of Arts (the prefix Royal had been granted in 1908) in September 1917 but he was elected a member of the council and served as chairman for the session 1919–20. His forty-five years' service to the society was commemorated by the institution of the annual Trueman Wood lectures and he was made a vice-president of the society.

On 7 October 1873 Trueman Wood married Mary Ann Oliver Mason, daughter of James Oliver Mason. They had a son and two daughters but Lady Wood died in 1907. Sir Henry was a freemason and a popular member of the Athenaeum and at one time chairman of its executive committee. In his youth he won a half-blue at Cambridge as an athlete and in later life took up golf and was captain of the Chorley Wood golf club. He had a wide circle of friends and although it was said that his tongue had a sharp edge on occasion he was also remembered for many acts of kindness. In his final years he resided at Waterside, Bourne End, Buckinghamshire, with his daughter and son-in-law; he died there on 7 January 1929. He was buried at Cookham church, Berkshire, on 9 January.

R. T. SMITH

Sources *Journal of the Royal Society of Arts*, 77 (1928–9), 228–30 · *The Times* (8 Jan 1929) · *The Engineer* (11 Jan 1929), 31 · *Engineering* (11 Jan 1929), 43–4 · D. Hudson and K. W. Luckhurst, *The Royal Society of Arts, 1754–1954* (1954) · *Journal of the Society of Arts*, 24 (1875–6), 177 · *Journal of the Society of Arts*, 27 (1878–9), 319 · *Journal of the Royal Society of Arts*, 65 (1916–17), 570–71 · *Journal of the Royal Society of Arts*, 67 (1918–19), 555 · b. cert. · m. cert. · d. cert.
Archives Salisbury and South Wiltshire Museum, letters to A. H. L. F. Pitt-Rivers · University of Sheffield Library, corresp. with William Hewins
Likenesses H. von Herkomer, oils, 1902, RSA
Wealth at death £47,210 15s. 8d.: probate, 9 Feb 1929, *CGPLA Eng. & Wales*

Wood, Herbert George (1879–1963), theologian and historian, was born on 2 September 1879 in London, the second of three children of the Revd John Roskruge Wood (d. 1923), minister of Upper Holloway Baptist Church, and his wife, Frances Anne Wren (d. 1886). His father was English, his mother was born in co. Tipperary, Ireland.

Although a small and sickly child who remained of diminutive stature, Wood showed promise as a student at the City of London School, which he credited with providing him the thorough grounding in classics he considered essential for any historian. In 1899, after a year reading Latin and logic in preparation for an external London degree, he went up to Jesus College, Cambridge, where in 1902 he attained a first class in the classical tripos. The next year he received his London degree, and he capped his academic achievements in 1904 by earning a first class in the Cambridge theological tripos. In that same year he was elected to a fellowship at Jesus College and to the presidency of the Cambridge Union.

Before taking up his Cambridge fellowship, H. G., as he came to be called, was invited to teach New Testament and early Christian theology at Woodbrooke College in Birmingham, a newly established Quaker theological settlement where Dr Rendel Harris, who had met Wood at Cambridge, was director of studies. During a brief stint at Woodbrooke, Wood fell in love with one of his students, Dorothea (Dora) Wallis (1883–1959), daughter of a prominent Scarborough Quaker family. They were married on 11 June 1907 while he was a tutor and lecturer in history at Jesus College; their first home was at St Luke's Lodge, Cambridge.

In summer 1910 Wood returned to Woodbrooke at a crucial juncture in the development of his own thought and in the evolution of British Quakerism. By 1910 the evangelical tone which had dominated Quakerism for most of the nineteenth century had been effectively replaced by a progressive, liberal theology espousing modern historical and scientific thought, while reasserting the early Quaker emphasis on the inward light of Christ and re-emphasizing Quakerism's historic but dormant peace testimony. Woodbrooke itself was a product of this so-called Quaker renaissance, and Wood generally embraced its main tenets. Thus, although he did not make a formal commitment to the Society of Friends until 1923, Quakerism became and remained the vital centre of his lifelong effort to affirm the historical validity and spiritual power of Christianity.

Herbert Wood thrived in Woodbrooke's seemingly placid but spiritually intense atmosphere. He believed that the college's mission was to produce spiritual leaders and teachers whose awareness of modern biblical scholarship would enhance their understanding of the simple and saving message of primitive Christianity grasped by George Fox and early Friends. The inward light, as Wood believed, was not only a reflection of that which was of God in every person but also an enlightening gift of the Holy Spirit illuminated by the cross of Christ. For him, Jesus's sacrifice was a demonstration of the burdens to be borne by all believers in witnessing their faith in a loving father. The cross would also prove central to Wood's pacifist vision.

Shortly after the outbreak of the First World War, ill health forced Rendel Harris to resign as Woodbrooke's director of studies, and Wood took up this position in addition to the wardenship he and Dora held from 1914 to 1918. The imposition of conscription in 1916 brought a grave crisis for Friends generally and for Wood personally. His own difficulty was resolved when he was granted status as a conscientious objector on the generous ground that his religious and educational work constituted alternative service of national importance; he later spent four months in France as a chaplain for the Friends' Ambulance Unit. Amid virulent public criticism of Friends' refusal to support the war and bitter internal controversies over the correct nature of Quaker war resistance, Wood's evolving sense of Christian pacifism began to take shape. In time, he came to believe that Quakers and other pacifists tended to underrate the power of evil and failed to understand that pacifism could not be based on political ideology, social theory, or an optimistic vision of human potential. Only by bearing one's allotted personal cross could one give true expression to the light and effective witness to the futility of war. Because this assertion of the peace testimony was at odds with the practical and humanistic thrust of many Quaker anti-war activists, Herbert Wood came to be considered 'unsound' on peace principles by some Friends.

During a quarter-century at Woodbrooke and after his

appointment, in 1940, to the first chair of theology at the University of Birmingham, Wood wrote extensively on the history of Christianity and Quaker theology, exerting enormous influence on two generations of Friends as well as a wider reading audience. This influence was reflected in an invitation in 1933 to become the first lay person and first Quaker to present the Hulsean lectures at Cambridge, later published as *Christianity and the Nature of History* (1937), and in the honorary doctorate of divinity conferred upon him by the University of St Andrews. Twenty years later, after publication of other notable historical and theological works, including *Christianity and Civilization* (1942), *Belief and Unbelief since 1850* (1954), and *Freedom and Necessity in History* (1957), the University of Birmingham awarded Wood his second honorary DD.

Herbert Wood remained active until his eightieth year, when he suffered the double blow of Dora's death and a severe stroke which left him unable to speak or write. He died in Bournville, Birmingham, on 9 March 1963 and was buried in Bournville. THOMAS C. KENNEDY

Sources R. C. Scott, *Herbert G. Wood: a memoir of his life and thought* (1967) · R. Davis, ed., *Woodbrooke, 1903–1953* (1953) · *The Friend* (15 March 1963), 299–303 · *Friends' Journal* (1 May 1963), 205–6 · M. Davie, *British Quaker theology since 1895* (1997) · I. Pickard, ed., *Memories of J. Rendel Harris* · CGPLA Eng. & Wales (1964)
Archives Woodbrooke Quaker Study Centre, Birmingham, papers
Likenesses photograph, repro. in *The Friend* · photograph, repro. in Davis, ed., *Woodbrooke*
Wealth at death £2512: probate, 17 Jan 1964, CGPLA Eng. & Wales

Wood, Herbert William (1837–1879), army officer, son of Lieutenant-Colonel Herbert William Wood (d. 5 June 1883) of the Madras native infantry, was born at Madras, India, on 17 July 1837. Educated at Cheltenham College, he joined Addiscombe College in February 1854, was commissioned as second lieutenant in the Madras engineers on 20 September 1855, and, after the standard course at Chatham, arrived at Madras on 26 October 1857. He was at once posted to the Saugor field division under Major-General Whitlock, and was present at the battles against mutineers at Jheegung on 10 April 1858, and at Kubrai, at Banda on 19 April, at the capture of Karwi on 6 June, the action in front of Chitrakut, the forcing of the Panghati Pass, and subsequent actions. He was promoted lieutenant on 27 August 1858, and continued to serve with the mobile column until March 1859.

After employment as executive engineer in the public works department in the North-Western Provinces, Wood was transferred to Madras in 1860. He was promoted captain on 15 January 1864. He served as field engineer in the Abyssinian expedition from January to June 1868, succeeding Captain Chrystie in charge of the works at Zoulla, and was thanked in dispatches. In December 1872 he was appointed to Vizagapatam, and on 24 August of the following year he was promoted major. He obtained three years' furlough and accompanied the Grand Duke Constantine's expedition, sent under the auspices of the Imperial Russian Geographical Society to examine the Amu Daria region. He published the results of his travels

in *The Shores of Lake Aral* (1876), which showed the difficulties with which the Russians contended in central Asia.

Wood returned to India in June 1876, but, after serving in the Madras presidency in poor health, he was seized with paralysis and died on 8 October 1879 at Chingleput, Madras. Wood was a fellow of the Royal Geographical Society and of the Royal and Imperial Russian Geographical societies, and a corresponding member of the Society of Geography of Geneva.

R. H. VETCH, rev. JAMES FALKNER

Sources Army List · *The Times* (5 Nov 1879) · *Hart's Army List* · *Royal Engineers Journal* (1879) · *East-India Register and Army List* (1857)
Likenesses photograph, c.1870, Army Museums, Ogilby Trust collection; version, NAM

Wood, James (c.1609–1664), Church of Scotland minister and college head, was born in St Andrews, the son of a local merchant. He was educated at the University of St Andrews, where he distinguished himself as 'a youth of great expectations and learning' (Wodrow, *Analecta*, 2.116). After graduating MA he served a term as a regent of the university. Originally a 'violent Arminian' (ibid.) and an episcopalian he became a presbyterian after meeting Alexander Henderson and, on his advice, reading David Calderwood's critique of English episcopacy, *Altare Damascenum*. He was ordained to Dunino, near St Andrews, in 1640. In 1644 he was elected professor of divinity at Marischal College, Aberdeen, and minister of Greyfriars kirk, but was not settled. The following year he was translated to the third charge (ecclesiastical history) at St Mary's, or the New College, St Andrews.

Wood was one of the commissioners sent by the kirk to meet with the exiled Charles II in negotiations in 1649 for the treaty of The Hague, and in 1650 for the treaty of Breda. At the latter he played an important role in the discussions which culminated in the king subscribing the covenants and returning to Scotland in June 1650. In the ensuing controversy between the kirk's radical and moderate parties Wood sided with the moderates in defending the king's sincerity and his royal prerogatives. Following the Cromwellian invasion of Scotland in the summer of 1650 he opposed the radicals' calls for the covenanting army to be purged in accordance with the acts of classes, and championed the moderates' plan to raise all fencible men to fight the invading enemy. Accordingly he condemned the radicals' western remonstrance and joined the commission of the general assembly in passing a series of public resolutions which paved the way for parliament's full repeal of the acts of classes. When the national kirk was irreparably divided between protesters and resolutioners during the 1651 general assembly he sided with the latter party and published a vigorous defence of the resolutioners' actions entitled *A vindication of the freedom & lawfulnes of the late generall assembly begun at St. Andrews and continued at Dundee* (1652).

Throughout the remainder of the 1650s Wood was one of the protesters' most outspoken critics. He also took a firm stand against the English regime's policy of religious toleration and published an extended refutation of Independency entitled *A Little Stone Pretended to be out of the*

Mountain, Tried and Found to be a Counterfeit (1654). In late 1656 he strongly advocated sending James Sharp to act as the resolutioners' agent in London, a decision which he lived to regret. Together with his colleague George Hutcheson he also wrote a detailed account of the resolutioners' struggle with the protesters for Sharp to distribute among the English presbyterians entitled *A true representation of the rise, progresse, and state of the present divisions in the Church of Scotland* (1657). In 1657, 'worn out' by the 'continuall vexations and contentions' he had with the principal of St Mary's, the protester Samuel Rutherford, he accepted the position of principal of St Salvator's College (*Letters and Journals of Robert Baillie*, 376). In early 1658 he was appointed by the resolutioners to draft a declaration outlining their terms for reunification with the protesters. It was published at Edinburgh under the provocative title *A declaration of the brethren who are for the established government and judicatories of this church*. Although ostensibly a plea for peace and unity in the national kirk it was, in fact, little more than an extended polemic against the protesters. It drew a forceful and lengthy reply from James Guthrie entitled *Protesters No Subverters and Presbyterie No Papacie* (1658), which Wood and Hutcheson answered point by point in *A Review and Examination of Protesters No Subverters* (1659).

Meanwhile, Wood's first wife, Catherine Carstairs (*b. c.*1620), had died, on 9 September 1658, and Wood married Anna Napier on 30 June 1659. When James Sharp conveyed the offer of a bishopric to him in the autumn of 1661 he promptly declined and soon after denounced Sharp to his face as the 'betrayer of the Church of Scotland' (Wodrow, *Analecta*, 3.87). At the behest of Sharp, now archbishop of St Andrews, he was removed from his post at St Salvator's by a special order of the privy council on 23 July 1663. After visiting him on his deathbed Sharp spread a rumour that Wood had professed himself 'indifferent to church government', believing it to be alterable at the pleasure of the magistrate. Although extremely weak, Wood dictated a testimony denying this and expressing his adherence to presbytery as 'the ordinance of God' (Wodrow, *History*, 1.404). He died two weeks later, on 15 March 1664, at St Andrews.   K. D. HOLFELDER

Sources R. Wodrow, *Analecta, or, Materials for a history of remarkable providences, mostly relating to Scotch ministers and Christians*, ed. [M. Leishman], 4 vols., Maitland Club, 60 (1842–3), vol. 1, pp. 29, 169; vol. 2, pp. 116–19; vol. 3, pp. 84–7 · R. Wodrow, *The history of the sufferings of the Church of Scotland from the Restoration to the revolution*, ed. R. Burns, 1 (1828), 403–6 · *Fasti Scot.*, new edn, 5.196; 7.411 · *The letters and journals of Robert Baillie*, ed. D. Laing, 3 (1842) · A. F. Mitchell and J. Christie, eds., *The records of the commissions of the general assemblies of the Church of Scotland*, 3 vols., Scottish History Society, 11, 25, 58 (1892–1909) · W. Stephen, ed., *Register of the consultations of the ministers of Edinburgh*, 2 vols., Scottish History Society, 3rd ser., 1, 16 (1921–30) · J. Buckroyd, *Church and state in Scotland, 1660–1681* (1980), 42 · D. C. Lachman, 'Wood, James', *DSCHT*
Archives NL Scot., letters and MSS

Wood, James [*called* General Wood] (**1672–1759**), nonconformist minister, son of James Wood (*bap.* 1639, *d.* 1694), nonconformist minister, and his wife, Anne Townley (*d.*

1724), was born at Atherton, Leigh parish, Lancashire. His grandfather, also James Wood (*d.* 1667), was ejected in 1662 from the perpetual curacy of Ashton in Makerfield, Winwick parish, Lancashire, though he continued to preach in the parish while resident in Thelwall, Cheshire. His father succeeded James Livesey as the perpetual curate of Atherton Chapel in 1657. He was silenced by the Act of Uniformity but continued to use the chapel (erected *c.*1645–8 and not consecrated) until he was imprisoned in 1670. He preached at Wharton Hall, Deane parish, seat of Robert Mort, and at his house in Chowbent before he recovered the use of Atherton Chapel about 1676.

Wood thus grew up in a parish with a strong puritan tradition, where the retention of the chapel of ease represented the autonomy of the protestant dissenters at the local level, their proprietary rights emphasizing their sense of unjust exclusion from the established church. He entered on 22 April 1691 Richard Frankland's academy at Rathmel, followed the year after by his brother Samuel. Both brothers were candidates for the ministry attending the general meeting of the Lancashire ministers held in Warrington on 9 April 1695. James began assisting his father and succeeded him at Atherton Chapel in 1695. He owes his fame to his raising a militia against the Jacobites in 1715. Urged on by Sir Henry Hoghton, a leading dissenter, in a letter of 11 November 1715, his local force joined Sir Charles Wills at the battle of Preston on 12 November 1715, where they were joined by other units raised by John Walker, the dissenting minister of Horwich, and John Turner, dissenting minister of Preston. Wood, who was dubbed General Wood, was assigned the defence of the ford over the Ribble between Penwortham and Preston. For his services he received a government annuity of £100. On 14 March 1717 he married Judith Brooksbank of Oxheys.

By about 1717 Wood's congregation numbered over 1000 hearers, who included fifty-three county voters, the third largest dissenting congregation in Lancashire after Manchester and Bolton. Despite their secure position in the industrializing parish of Leigh, their support for the Hanoverians and the parliamentary campaign of Sir Henry Hoghton, who began canvassing for re-election in 1720, probably lost them the chapel. 'Mad' Richard Atherton (1700–1726), son and heir of the last nonconformist lord of the manor, was a Jacobite. On coming of age in 1721 he demanded the surrender of Atherton Chapel, which was consecrated in 1723 by Thomas Wilson, bishop of Sodor and Man. During 1721–2 Wood ministered to his flock in a dwelling house in Hagg Fold. In 1722 a large meetinghouse was erected at Chowbent, in Atherton, Wood eventually devoting part of his pension to the cost. The endowments stayed with the original chapel; the communion table and plate endowed by Robert Mort in 1653 went with the protestant dissenters to the new chapel.

Wood attended both the Cheshire and the Lancashire provincial meetings of Congregational and Presbyterian ministers. He supposedly co-operated between about 1740 and 1750 with Josiah Owen in the policy of depriving the

Lancashire meeting of any function of religious supervision. Wood was personally popular but no preacher, fearing to make pulpit exchanges early in his career but opening his pulpit in later life to many of the liberal divines of his time. According to one of his congregants he remained a Calvinist, although his congregation by the time of his death had been persuaded towards the rationalist position by surrounding ministers and the influence of John Mort of Alderfold.

Wood died on 20 February 1759, a tablet to his memory being installed above the pulpit. Although the name Hannah (d. 17 Aug 1726) appears on a tombstone as his wife, evidence suggests she may have been his first wife and not a second wife. His son, James Wood, was educated for the ministry at Caleb Rotherham's academy at Kendal from 1749, matriculated at Glasgow in 1753, and acted as his father's assistant, but predeceased him.

ALEXANDER GORDON, rev. JONATHAN H. WESTAWAY

Sources J. J. Wright, *The story of the Chowbent Chapel, 1645–1721–1921* (1921) • J. Wood, letters to George Benson, Lancs. RO, Grundy papers • R. Lowe, *Extracts from a Lancashire diary, 1663–1678* (1876), 5, 8, 10, 13–17, 20, 22, 24, 26–8, 32, 35, 60 • A. Gordon, *Ancient days at Atherton: a sketch presented at the Chowbent Chapel bicentennial, 1921, and now offered by way of prelude to 'J. J. Wright's story of Chowbent Chapel'* (1921) • B. Nightingale, *Lancashire nonconformity*, 6 vols. [1890–93], vol. 1, p. 10; vol. 4, pp. 95–117 • F. Baker, *The life and times of the Rev. James Woods … called 'General' Woods … a discourse … at the Presbyterian chapel, Chowbent, Feb. 20th 1859* (1859) • 'Speech of Mr Valentine at the provincial meeting of dissenting ministers residing in Lancashire and Cheshire, held at Chowbent', *Monthly Repository*, 10 (1815), 451–2 • J. P. Rylands, 'The will of James Wood of Atherton, co. Lanc., Clerk. 1695', *Lancashire and Cheshire wills and inventories, 1563 to 1807, now preserved at Chester*, Chetham Society, new ser., 37 (1897), 60–61 • *Calamy rev.*, 540–41 • *The diary of James Clegg of Chapel en le Frith, 1708–1755*, ed. V. S. Doe, 3 vols., Derbyshire RS, 2–3, 5 (1978–81), 40, 55, 72, 85, 87, 464 • [H. Taylor], *Monthly Repository*, 21 (1826), 122 • *The manuscripts of Lord Kenyon*, HMC, 35 (1894), 464 [Benjamin Grosvenor to 'the Rev. Mr. Wood, in Chowbent', 18 Feb 1723, MS 1188] • parish register (baptisms), Chowbent, Newbent Chapel • parish register (burials), Chowbent, Newbent Chapel • J. Evans, 'List of dissenting congregations and ministers in England and Wales, 1715–1729', DWL, MS 38.4 • *DNB* • F. Nicholson and E. Axon, *The older nonconformity in Kendal* (1915) • J. H. Turner, T. Dickenson, and O. Heywood, eds., *The nonconformist register of baptisms, marriages, and deaths* (1881), 211

Archives Lancs. RO, letters to George Benson

Wood, James (1760–1839), mathematician and dean of Ely, was born on 14 December 1760 at Holcombe, Bury, Lancashire, the son of James Wood and his wife, both weavers. His father ran an evening school and taught his son the elements of arithmetic and algebra. Wood probably first attended Halmote House, the local school, then Bury grammar school, where he won its endowed exhibition to St John's College, Cambridge. He was admitted sizar on 14 January 1778 and subsequently won other scholarships. He graduated BA in 1782 as senior wrangler and first Smith's prizeman, was elected fellow of his college, and proceeded MA in 1785, BD in 1793, and DD in 1815.

While a tutor in 1789–1814, Wood published his *Principles of Mathematics and Natural Philosophy*, four volumes intended to prepare students for the tripos. *The Elements of Algebra* (1795) went through sixteen editions, the last in 1861; *The Principles of Mechanics* (1796) and *The Elements of Optics* (1798) also ran through several editions. The fourth volume, on astronomy, was contributed by Samuel Vince. Wood's equable temper and firm, courteous manner made him the ideal ruler of a college. He served as president (1802–15), master (1815–39), and vice-chancellor (1816–17) of St John's, where he lived for some sixty years. He was ordained deacon in 1785 and priest in 1787, and appointed dean of Ely in November 1820. He was instituted rector of Freshwater, Isle of Wight, in August 1823; this yielded an annuity of £200, and, apart from a visit during the summer, he left the parish in the hands of a curate.

Wood was a considerable benefactor to St John's during his lifetime. By his will he left his library to the college, which was also his residuary legatee. He died in the college on 23 April 1839 and was interred in its chapel.

C. W. SUTTON, rev. ANITA McCONNELL

Sources W. W. R. Ball, *A history of the study of mathematics at Cambridge* (1889), 111 • R. F. Scott, ed., *Admissions to the College of St John the Evangelist in the University of Cambridge*, 4: *July 1767 – July 1802* (1931), 568–70 • H. Dowsett, *Notes on Holcombe* (1901) • H. Dowsett, *Holcombe long ago* (1902) • *GM*, 2nd ser., 12 (1839), 201–3

Archives St John Cam., notebooks of lecture notes taken by others and collected by Wood; papers | BL, corresp. with Bishop Butler, Add. MSS 34583–34590

Likenesses R. Dighton, coloured etching, pubd 1809, BM, NPG • J. Jackson, oils, 1824, St John Cam. • E. H. Baily, marble monument, 1843, St John Cam.

Wood, Sir James Athol (1756–1829), naval officer, was the third son of Alexander Wood (1712–1778) of Burncroft, Perthshire, procurator fiscal of Perth, and Jean, daughter of Robert Ramsay of Banff. Following his two brothers Mark *Wood and George (d. 1824) he began his career in the service of the East India Company in 1772. He entered the navy in September 1774, serving as an able seaman in the *Hunter*. After promotion to master's mate he joined the *Barfleur* in July 1776 and moved to the *Princess Royal* in April 1777. He was given a temporary appointment as lieutenant in the *Asia*, then rejoined his former ship to go out to America. On 18 October 1778 he was made lieutenant in the *Renown* and was present at the attack on Charlestown in April 1780. In November 1781 he was appointed to the *Anson* (64 guns, Captain William Blair), and was present at the battle of the Saints on 12 April 1782. After the war Wood spent two years in France and then served on merchant ships in the East and West Indies.

In 1794 Wood was at Barbados and on the arrival of the fleet he offered his services to Sir John Jervis (later earl of St Vincent) who appointed him a lieutenant in the *Boyne*. After the capture of Martinique, Wood was put in charge of the prisoners and sent to France with the cartels, where in May the ships were seized and Wood was arrested and imprisoned. He was released on parole and shortly afterwards exchanged. On 7 July 1795 he was promoted to the command of the sloop *Favourite* and sailed to the West Indies, where he was ordered to blockade St Vincent and Grenada. He suggested the idea of an attack on Trinidad to Sir Hugh Christian, which was subsequently taken up by

Christian's successor, Rear-Admiral Henry Harvey. Trinidad was taken without loss on 18 February 1797. The Spanish burnt three of their ships of the line but a fourth, the *San Damaso* (74 guns), was captured. Wood was given command of the prize and ordered to England with a convoy. His promotion to post captain was confirmed on 27 March 1797.

In 1798 Wood was appointed to the *Garland* (28 guns) and sailed for the Indian Ocean. Off Madagascar on 26 July he sighted a French merchant ship at anchor near Fort Dauphine. As the *Garland* closed she struck a rock and sank before she could be run ashore. The merchant ship meanwhile had been run ashore and deserted by her crew. The entire crew of the *Garland* got safely ashore and salvaged some of their sails, guns, and provisions. Taking the merchant ship, Wood sailed with his men and remaining stores to the Cape, and then returned to England where on 15 December 1798 he and his officers were acquitted at the court martial for the loss of their ship.

In April 1802 Wood was appointed to the *Acasta* (40 guns), attached at the renewal of the war in 1803 to the fleet blockading Brest, where in company with the *Naiad* she was employed watching the Passage du Raz. On 3 December 1803 the *Acasta* after a chase of 45 hours captured the privateer *Aventure* (22 guns), with two prizes taken from the Jamaica convoy. In November 1804 the *Acasta* took a convoy to the West Indies. Wood arrived at Jamaica in February 1805 with orders for the recall of Admiral Thomas Duckworth and the appointment of Admiral James Richard Dacres. Duckworth decided to return home in the *Acasta* with a large quantity of goods and merchandise, including, it was alleged, 16 tons of mahogany and 120 lb of Spanish snuff. Duckworth superseded Wood and appointed his own captain, Richard Dalling Dunn, to the command of the *Acasta*, promising Wood the command of the *Hercule* (74 guns). However, Admiral Dacres had already determined that the *Hercule* would carry his flag and that he would appoint his own captain. Wood was therefore deprived of his command and pay as well as the substantial commission for the freight of treasure to which he would have been entitled had he remained in command of the *Acasta*. Furthermore Duckworth later declared that he would not 'cross the Atlantic in a ship commanded by a stranger', a comment Wood considered a scandalous libel (*Hansard 1*, 5.203–4).

Wood was forced to return to England as a passenger in his own ship and immediately called for a court martial on Duckworth. Wood accused him of tyranny and a breach of the eighteenth article of war forbidding the carriage of merchandise in ships of war, not realizing at the time that he had been reappointed to his command. The proceedings changed matters, and Wood was dismayed to find that the court martial found in favour of Duckworth, declaring the charge 'gross, scandalous, malicious, shameful, and highly subversive of discipline' (Laughton, 3.371). Wood's brother Mark, now the MP for Gatton, Surrey, called to have the proceedings of the court martial laid before the House of Commons but the motion was defeated. It was deemed that no advantage would arise to

the public by parliament interfering with the sentence of a court martial. Colonel Wood had declared before the house that the incident had nearly deprived his brother of his reason, a judgement confirmed by his subsequent behaviour.

Wood was appointed to the *Uranie* and then to the *Latona* (38 guns), cruising with the Channel Fleet off Brest. In a letter to Admiral John Markham, a friend of Duckworth who had spoken against Colonel Wood's motion, the earl of St Vincent wrote, 'Pray deliver me from Captain Athol Wood who is a very dangerous man, and I shrewdly suspect the diabolic report of the capture of the inshore squadron and my having been killed originated with him' (*Selections from the Correspondence of … Markham*, 55). Wood's unusual behaviour is further attested by a letter and a deposition made by the master of the *Latona* and addressed to Admiral Duckworth. This described how Wood had publicly called Duckworth a 'coward and a dirty rascal' and St Vincent a 'damned scoundrel'. The deposition related how Wood had grossly abused the master, used violent language, and shoved his fist in his face. Wood's usual mode of punishment for both officers and men was to 'work them up' by making them remain on deck during their watch below. One marine officer to whom he took a dislike was forced to visit all the sentries every few minutes, and it was not unusual for Wood to impose duties that could not be performed and then threaten the victim with a court martial. It was further alleged that Wood ordered a lieutenant to make false entries in the log concerning the *Latona's* master. It is clear from the deposition that Wood hounded the master and apparently anyone else he took against until they were rendered incapable of performing their duty or until they were pressed to be insubordinate (W. West to T. Duckworth, 24 Aug 1806, NMM, uncatalogued MS).

In 1806 Wood obtained, through his brother, the parliamentary seat of Gatton; however, being on active service, he never attended the Commons. The *Latona* was sent to the West Indies where, on 1 January 1807, a daring attack was made on the harbour of St Ann by a squadron of four frigates under the command of Captain Charles Brisbane. During the attack the *Latona* was warped alongside the Dutch *Kenau Hasselaar* (32 guns). Wood took possession of the frigate after it had been boarded by Brisbane and the crew of the *Arethusa*. Wood and the other captains received gold medals for the action. Wood moved to the *Captain* (74 guns) in December 1808 and was present at the attack on Martinique the following February. In July he took command of the *Neptune* and returned to England where he was knighted on 1 November 1809.

Wood was next appointed to the *Pompée* (74 guns) attached to the Channel Fleet. On 10 August 1812 she joined the *Diana* (38 guns) sailing 12 miles to leeward of a French squadron commanded by Vice-Admiral Allemand. When two British ships appeared to windward of the French, Allemand changed course, steering to cross the bows of the *Pompée* and *Diana*. Wood, not realizing until later that the ships to windward of the French were British, steered to avoid the French and during the night found himself pursued by two ships, one of which drew near enough to fire at him. After pumping 80 tons of water over the side, the *Pompée* eluded the French ships and the following day was joined by other ships of the Channel Fleet that had sighted but been unable to close with the French. An inquiry into the encounter was called for and the matter was referred to a court martial, during which Wood was admonished for not discovering the identity of the two British ships before steering away from the enemy. The verdict of the court was that Wood had formed an 'erroneous impression' and that his actions had not been motivated by 'any want of zeal'.

In November 1813 the *Pompée* joined Vice-Admiral Sir Edward Pellew off Toulon and Wood remained in the Mediterranean until November 1815. He was nominated a companion of the Bath on 4 June 1815 and promoted rear-admiral on 19 July 1821. In his retirement Wood lived at the Albany, London, where he kept a bed closet 'arranged to look like a ship's cabin' and was attended by a former steward of the *Latona*. He died, unmarried, at Hampstead in July 1829 and was the subject of a substantial obituary in the *Gentleman's Magazine* for August (*GM*, 177–9).

CLIVE WILKINSON

Sources DNB · R. G. Thorne, 'Wood, James Athol', HoP, *Commons, 1790–1820* · Hansard 1 (1812), 5.194–210 · W. James, *The naval history of Great Britain, from the declaration of war by France in 1793, to the accession of George IV*, [5th edn], 6 vols. (1859–60) · W. P. Gosset, *Lost ships of the Royal Navy* (1986) · *Letters and papers of Charles, Lord Barham*, ed. J. K. Laughton, 3 vols., Navy RS, 32, 38–9 (1907–11) · *Selections from the correspondence of Admiral John Markham*, ed. C. Markham, Navy RS, 28 (1904) · J. Leyland, ed., *Dispatches and letters relating to the blockade of Brest, 1803–1805*, 2 vols., Navy RS, 14, 21 (1899–1902) · *GM*, 1st ser., 99/2 (1829), 177–9
Archives NMM, lieutenant's journal, ADM/L/A138 · PRO, captain's journal, ADM 51/1399, 1449, 1485, 1971, 2601, 2664, 2665 | BL, Hardwicke papers, Add. MS 35899, fols. 88, 180
Likenesses H. R. Cook, engraving, 1810, NMM · H. R. Cook, stipple, pubd 1810, NPG

Wood, Sir John (d. 1484), administrator and speaker of the House of Commons, came of a family who originated in the rape of Chichester, but who also held lands elsewhere in west Sussex. He was the son and heir of another John Wood, who may have been clerk of estreats in the exchequer in the reign of Henry V. By 1444 the younger John Wood had begun what was to be a long, if intermittent, career in the exchequer. Over a forty-year period he held a number of important offices, including under-treasurer of the exchequer (1452–3 and 1480–83), keeper of the great wardrobe of the household (c.1458–1460), and treasurer of the exchequer (1483–4), and he was also sheriff of Surrey and Sussex (1475–6). As under-treasurer he acquired substantial profits from wool speculation in addition to the wages and fee of office. Wood was elected knight of the shire for Sussex (1449–50), and for Surrey (1460–61 and 1478), and the culmination of his political career came when he was chosen to be speaker of the Commons in January 1483, and was knighted at the dissolution of parliament. The shortness of the session during Wood's term as speaker was due to Edward IV's speedy success in obtaining a taxation grant, which had been his principal goal in summoning parliament. Wood may have been responsible for persuading the Commons to make the grant, so ensuring the brevity of his own speakership.

Like many who were politically active during the era of Yorkist–Lancastrian rivalry, Wood had to manoeuvre repeatedly owing to the shifting political allegiances of the day. He seems to have done so with adroitness; his success is evident in his appointments both to judicial and administrative commissions and as a JP for Surrey (1452–9, 1460–61, 1465–75, 1477–84) and for Sussex (1461–70, 1480–84). Conversely, set-backs such as his failure to be re-elected knight of the shire for Sussex in 1450, and his absence from significant office in the exchequer in the 1460s and 1470s, are probably attributable to changing political fortunes. His affairs in London required him to live nearby, and from 1455 he eschewed the traditional family connection with west Sussex for residence at East Molesey manor, in Surrey, near Kingston. He came into possession of this estate through what was probably his first marriage, to Elizabeth, daughter and coheir of John Mitchell, alderman and lord mayor of London, and widow of the former royal physician Thomas Morstede (d. 1450). Elizabeth died without issue in 1464, and Wood subsequently married Margery, daughter of Sir Roger Lewkenor of Trotton in Sussex, and sister of Sir Thomas Lewkenor, who served as sheriff of Sussex and Surrey (1473–4). This marriage was also without issue. Sir John Wood died on 20 August 1484; his second wife survived him.

MAX SATCHELL

Sources J. S. Roskell, 'Sir John Wood of Molesey', *Parliament and politics in late medieval England*, 3 (1983), 383–96 · J. S. Roskell, *The Commons and their speakers in English parliaments, 1376–1523* (1965)

Wood, John (d. 1570), administrator, was the second son of Sir Andrew *Wood (d. 1515) of Largo, Fife, and his wife, Elizabeth Lundy. Educated for the church, he graduated MA from St Leonard's College at the University of St Andrews in 1536 and was afterwards appointed vicar of Largo parish. The most important association in his life was with Lord James Stewart, later earl of Moray. It is unclear when this began, but Wood travelled to France with Lord James in the infant Queen Mary's party in July 1548. While there he supervised Lord James's education, before returning to Scotland by September 1549. Wood showed an early commitment to the Reformation in Scotland, and in September 1560 accompanied an embassy to London, where he delivered to Sir William Cecil a copy of John Knox's *History* as it had thus far been written. In December the first general assembly of the kirk identified him as one of those at St Andrews best qualified for preaching and ministering the sacraments. In the following April he went to the French court with Lord James to discuss with Queen Mary her return to Scotland. The English ambassador, Sir Nicholas Throckmorton, observed in him 'much virtue and sufficiency' and noting his adherence to the English interest recommended he receive a pension (*CSP for.*, 1561–2, 85). However, Wood's overriding loyalty was to his master rather than to the reformed church, as became apparent on Mary's return, when, following Lord James's lead, he refused to offer further assistance to the general assembly. Nevertheless his sympathies remained with the reformers, as he showed in 1563 when he angered the queen by pointedly failing to compliment her dancing and other courtly pursuits. On 9 December 1562 he was appointed a senator of the college of justice, taking the title of Tillydovie.

In 1565 political frustration caused Moray (as Lord James had become) to rebel against the crown. Wood was commanded to ward himself in Dumbarton Castle within six days, and on failing to do so was denounced a rebel. Moray dispatched him to London to seek assistance from the English crown, which was not forthcoming. The swift collapse of the uprising forced both men into exile and Wood was deprived of his judicial office. They were recalled to Scotland in March 1566 and Wood is recorded as sitting again as a lord of session in January 1568. When Moray returned to power as regent in 1568, Wood was appointed his secretary, in preference to the royal secretary Sir William Maitland of Lethington, who continued to act covertly in Mary's interest. Towards the end of May, Wood was sent to the English court to represent the regent's position to Queen Elizabeth and was sent translations of Mary's letters to present as evidence of the Scottish queen's guilt. Before Moray would participate in any English trial of Mary and her subjects, he needed to be certain that his half-sister would not be restored to the Scottish throne if she were found culpable of the murder of her husband, Lord Darnley. It appears that Cecil privately communicated the necessary assurance to Wood in London, and this stance was later confirmed in a letter from Elizabeth herself. Moray therefore joined Wood when the latter returned to England in September to attend the autumn conferences assembled at York and Westminster to investigate Mary's conduct. In order to protect Moray's reputation Wood pretended to be reluctant to present the indictment to the English council at Westminster, whereupon the bishop of Orkney snatched it from his hands.

Wood's final diplomatic mission to England was undertaken in June 1569, and during it the duke of Norfolk's intrigue with the captive queen was exposed. Before he set out Wood sought elevation to the bishopric of Moray; James Melville believed that he did so in order to be invested with a suitable dignity as an ambassador. He did not become a bishop, but when he returned to Scotland and reported to the privy council he received a vote of thanks for his services. In the autumn he accompanied Moray's expedition to the west march against lawbreakers in Liddesdale. When the countess of Moray received intelligence of the plot to assassinate her husband in Lithlithgow in January 1570, she sent Wood to warn him, but Moray disregarded the warning. The regent was killed on the 23rd, and Wood was himself murdered in Fife on 15 April 1570. His killers were at first thought to have come from Teviotdale, probably owing to the complicity of Sir Walter Scott of Buccleuch, but Arthur Forbes, son of the

laird of Rires, and Henry Forrest were eventually outlawed for the crime. George Buchanan thought that he was slain 'for nothing but for being a good servant to the crown and to the regent his master' (Buchanan, sig. D1r).

JOHN SIMMONS

Sources *CSP Scot.*, 1547–71 · *Reg. PCS*, 1st ser., vols. 1–2 · R. Pitcairn, ed., *Ancient criminal trials in Scotland*, 7 pts in 3, Bannatyne Club, 42 (1833) · *The works of John Knox*, ed. D. Laing, 6 vols., Wodrow Society, 12 (1846–64) · *Memoirs of his own life by Sir James Melville of Halhill*, ed. T. Thomson, Bannatyne Club, 18 (1827) · G. Buchanan, *Ane admonition direct to the trew lordis Mantenaris of the kingis graces authoritie* (1571) · *APS*, 1424–1592 · J. Bain, ed., *The border papers: calendar of letters and papers relating to the affairs of the borders of England and Scotland*, 2 vols. (1894–6) · *CSP for.*, 1558–71 · M. Lee, *James Stewart, earl of Moray* (1953)

Wood, John (*fl.* 1596), medical writer, was the author of *Practicae medicinae liber, vocatus amalgama, quo artificiosa methodo, et incredibili mortales sanandi studio, sine invidia, causæ, symptomata, et remediorum praesidia praecipuorum capitis morborum exponuntur: authore Iohanne Wood, generoso artis medicinae studioso, et professore* (1596); this was published in London, in quarto, by Humfrey Hooper. The treatise, which has neither preface nor dedication, is devoted entirely to diseases and disorders affecting the head. In 1602 the unsold copies of the work were reissued by John Bayly, with a new title-page in which the authorship was ascribed to D. Johnson. It has been supposed that Johnson was a pseudonym of Wood, but it is more probable that the authorship was falsely claimed by Johnson after Wood's death. E. I. CARLYLE, *rev.* ROGER HUTCHINS

Sources J. Wood, *Practicae medicinae* (1596) · BL, Egerton MS 2203

Wood, John (*bap.* 1704, *d.* 1754), architect and town planner, was born in Bath and baptized at St James's Church there on 26 August 1704, the son of George Wood, a local builder still working in Bath in 1727, of whom otherwise nothing is known (though he may have been connected with a John Wood who was buried at Swainswick, 3 miles north of the city, in 1697). Wood received a basic education 'in the English Tongue, in Writing and in Accounts' (Ison, 234) at the Blue Coat School, Bath, and was presumably instructed in building work by his father before establishing himself about 1721 as a joiner in the parish of St Anne's, Soho, London. During the next six years, in collaboration with several other craftsmen, he became a principal builder on the Cavendish–Harley estate, then being developed in the area north of Oxford Street, where from 1725 he probably lived. He took out building leases for the construction of about ten houses in the new streets and apparently acted as surveyor of the large house being built by James Brydges, first duke of Chandos, in Cavendish Square. While in London, Wood formed some connection with the architect and master builder Edward Shepherd, who was then engaged in the development of the Grosvenor estate south of Oxford Street, and through him may have come to know something of the work of Colen Campbell.

Also building in Cavendish Square was Lord Bingley, who employed Wood both in London and on his estate at Bramham in Yorkshire, where a new mansion house had recently been completed, and where Wood seems to have been given charge of laying out the grounds. His presence in Yorkshire gave rise to the erroneous belief that Wood was a Yorkshireman who went to Bath in 1727 only in response to a summons from the duke of Chandos. Chandos, who had suffered considerable discomfort in 1726 while staying in lodgings in Bath, decided in consequence to take leases on the site of the old St John's almshouse, with the intention of building superior lodging houses as a speculative investment. Wood, who by his own account had already, while in Yorkshire, conceived ambitious plans to develop sites in the city belonging to Dr Robert Gay and William Capell, twenty-third earl of Essex, became Chandos's architect in Bath. The outcome was inauspicious: a clutter of cramped and hence ill-lit houses (known as the Hospital of St John), in the internal layout and necessary engineering of which Wood proved himself so incompetent that he had to ask to be excused from providing water-closets in subsequent commissions. Yet their unadventurous exteriors set up a standard elevation which served as a formula for the large-scale development of the city over the ensuing century.

Probably early in 1727 Wood married Jane (or Jenny) Chivers (d. 1766), the daughter of one of Chandos's lodging housekeepers. They had three sons and at least three daughters. Only the eldest son, John [see below], followed his father's profession, the second becoming a clothier and the third dying young. Wood himself seems to have enjoyed indifferent health through much of his life: he suffered especially from asthma, which may have led to his early death and was doubtless in part responsible for his irascible temper and his tendency to score waspishly off potential rivals.

Wood convinced himself that 'Bath, like Alexandria, was founded for the capital Seat of a famous King' (Wood, 41); and his grandiose ambitions for the city involved at this stage its reinvention on what he saw as Roman lines, with a royal forum, a grand circus, and an imperial gymnasium. The corporation, however, dismissed his plans for rebuilding the old town as chimerical, and political uncertainty following the death of George I in 1727 caused Gay to back out of involvement in developments on his land. Wood thereupon took the bold step of leasing land from Gay on the edge of the city in order to create Queen Square as a speculative venture of his own. The presence of master builders among the sublessees, whose contracts provided that they could plan and decorate their own houses so long as they kept to Wood's own elevations, ensured that he himself did not have to bear responsibility for the planning or construction. But a new standard of formality in urban design for the city was established at a stroke. The north range—owing much to Colen Campbell, something to Shepherd's partially aborted scheme for Grosvenor Square, and perhaps also something to Henry Aldrich's Peckwater Quadrangle at Christ Church, Oxford—showed in particular how a range of ordinary town houses could be united 'so as to have the outside Appearance of one magnificent Structure' (ibid., 345). Wood himself lived at no. 9.

The success of this venture, completed in 1736 and confirmed by the building of a chapel, encouraged Wood to resurrect his megalomaniac plan for a vast 'forum' on the site of the abbey orchard. Of this, only the two long terraces of lodgings known as North and South Parade were completed, and these lost much of their intended palatial richness as a result of pressure to economize from lessees. Chief among these was the powerful businessman and quarry owner Ralph Allen, for whom in 1735 Wood began the large Palladian mansion of Prior Park, Bath. Its satisfactory completion was compromised by Wood's failure to accommodate his architectural ambitions to the mores of Allen's social life. Allen, offering cut-price stone from his own quarry, was, however, active in supporting Wood's successful campaign to be appointed architect for the new exchange in Bristol (1741–3). The appointment, together with that of several prominent craftsmen from Bath, gave rise to local resentment, and Wood failed to have his full scheme, centred on an Egyptian hall, accepted; but the principal elevation of the exchange, a tauter version of the Queen Square design, perfectly proportioned and enriched by Thomas Paty's superb carving, is arguably Wood's finest architectural composition and one of the most distinguished examples of English Palladianism. Its success led Bristol's great rival, Liverpool, to commission Wood in 1749 to design a combined exchange and town hall, a further development of the same scheme, the building of which was supervised by his eldest son; following a fire in 1795 it was much altered by James Wyatt and John Foster.

A more surprising commission had come in 1734 for a new nave for Llandaff Cathedral, Glamorgan, whose neglected fabric had been wrecked in storms. Wood knew nothing of medieval architecture and persuaded himself that surviving Norman fragments dated from a church supposed to have been built on the site as early as the second century, and hence fantasized its origins back via Roman, Greek, and Egyptian temples to Solomon's temple at Jerusalem. He therefore planned for Llandaff, within the simple groin-vaulted rectangle eventually built inside the medieval walls (by 1752 and demolished a century later), a pedimented baldachin which was to be a visual demonstration of the Judaic source of Roman architecture as set out in *The Origin of Building, or, The Plagiarism of the Heathens Detected*.

This book, printed in 1744, had followed closely on *An Essay towards a Description of Bath* (1742; revised and enlarged 1749), after which came *A Description of the Exchange of Bristol* (1745), *Choir Gaure Vulgarly called Stonehenge, Described, Restored and Explained* (1747), and a *Dissertation upon the Orders of Columns and their Appendages* (1751). Wood's bizarre and wildly unscholarly fantasies on the origins of classical architecture, expounded in these publications, had little influence on his contemporaries or successors. But it is possible that, without them, the dramatic townscape, the design of which occupied Wood's last years, would not have been conceived. The Romans were now bypassed, and Stonehenge (supposed by the first proponent of Palladian architecture in England,

Inigo Jones, to be of Roman origin), and more importantly the stone circles at Stanton Drew, near Bath, became for Wood druidic temples created directly from Solomonic sources on the orders of the mythical prince Bladud, whom he held to be the originator of Bath itself. The splendid Circus, at the summit of the steep climb of Gay Street from Queen Square, has—because of its continuous superimposed colonnades—been long likened to the Colosseum (in miniature) turned outside in; but it was never conceived as a container for violent physical entertainment, and may possibly represent a domestic fantasy somehow related to the prehistoric circles, to which it apparently makes close numerical allusions. The Circus, begun shortly before Wood's death and completed by his son, together with the linked geometry of Queen Square and the spectacular Royal Crescent which the younger Wood began in 1767, makes up what remains the most dramatically impressive piece of picturesque townscape in Georgian England.

Wood's fantastical speculations (with which freemasonry was entangled) are now only a part of the chronicles of self-delusion, but he has a twofold importance in the history of architecture and urban design: locally, in setting a model 'for the splendid monotony of Bath's standard streets and the sudden columned grandeur of its focal features' (Mowl and Earnshaw, 65)—a pattern for the rapid expansion which created regal Bath out of the huddled small town in which he was born and which was later imitated in Clifton; nationally, in breaking the mould of grid-iron layouts which was the staple of the early eighteenth-century development of London, and demonstrating the richness of picturesque effect which could result from mixing a variety of geometrical forms. Circuses did not become a popular architectural form—the only fully achieved successor to Wood's as a piece of townscape being the much later Park Circus in Glasgow—but crescents of various proportions and shapes flourished in towns large and small throughout the kingdom and are perhaps the most striking of all English contributions to formal town design.

Wood died in Bath on 23 May 1754 and was buried in the parish church of St Mary at Swainswick, Somerset. His will shows him to have made a considerable financial success of his speculations, though its conditions ultimately beggared his eldest son.

This son, another **John Wood** (*bap.* 1728, *d.* 1781), was born in Bath and baptized in Bath Abbey on 25 February 1728. He was evidently trained by his father and showed his competence early enough to oversee the building of Liverpool town hall from 1749 to 1754. In 1752 or early 1753 he married Elizabeth Brock (*d.* after 1807) of Bostock Hall, Cheshire; they had two sons and at least eight daughters, and they lived in Wood's later years at Eagle House, Batheaston.

Wood continued in Bath where his father had left off, though there is no evidence of his having shared the latter's historical fantasies. He completed the Circus and continued the layout of the immediate surrounding area, with its climaxes in the Royal Crescent (1767–75) and the New Assembly Rooms (1769–71). Possibly the positioning and semi-elliptical plan of the Royal Crescent had been settled before the elder Wood's death, but the architectural dress, in which a single giant order replaces the superimposed orders of the Circus, intervening surfaces that are left severely plain, and a centre without effective emphasis, belongs wholly to the onset of neo-classicism, of which the younger man was something of a pioneer. This is particularly evident in the severe Doric order of the Hot Bath (1775–8, now the Old Royal Bath) and in the noble but austere columned halls of the New Assembly Rooms, which nevertheless may owe something to the two-storey chapel, the one interior by his father that survives at Prior Park. At the same time the younger Wood introduced variations in fenestration to enliven plain street façades, which were much taken up by later Bath architects. Outside Bath his most noteworthy surviving work is Buckland House, Berkshire (1755–8, coarsely remodelled and enlarged in 1910), an extraordinary Anglicization of a pyramid-capped Palladian cuboid, its spare fenestration wonderfully at odds with the dark northern climate. Wood also tried his hand at castellated façades, for the General Infirmary at Salisbury, Wiltshire (1767–71), and Tregenna Castle, St Ives, Cornwall (1773–4)—half-hearted experiments in which, even if only on paper, he once again appears to have been foreshadowed by his father. Wood died at Eagle House, deeply in debt, on 16 June 1781 and was buried alongside his father in the chancel at St Mary's Church, Swainswick. ANDOR GOMME

Sources W. Ison, *The Georgian buildings of Bath*, 2nd edn (1980) · T. Mowl and B. Earnshaw, *John Wood: architect of obsession* (1988) [incl. bibliography] · Colvin, *Archs.* · J. Wood, *A description of Bath* (1749); 2nd edn (1769); repr. (1969) · C. H. Collins and M. I. Baker, *The life and circumstances of James Brydges, first duke of Chandos* (1949) · J. Summerson, 'John Wood and the English town-planning tradition', *Heavenly mansions and other essays on architecture* (1949), 87–110 · will, PRO, PROB 11/809, sig. 186

Archives Bramham Park, Yorkshire, estate maps · RA, sketches and notes relating to Bristol New Exchange | BL, Harley estate records, Add. MSS 18239–18240 · Hunt. L., Chandos letter-books

Likenesses group portrait, oils, *c.*1740, Bath Preservation Trust; repro. in Mowl and Earnshaw, *John Wood*

Wealth at death annuities of £150 to son John, £100 to daughter Jane (and £5000 on her marriage); £20 to son Thayer; plus £1500; £1000 to daughter Elizabeth; residual estate to wife and after her death to two surviving sons: will, PRO, PROB 11/809, sig. 186

Wood, John (*bap.* 1728, *d.* 1781). *See under* Wood, John (*bap.* 1704, *d.* 1754).

Wood, John (1788–1860), naval architect and shipbuilder, was born at Port Glasgow, Renfrewshire, on 10 October 1788, one of at least two sons of John Wood (*d.* 1811), a Port Glasgow shipbuilder. He followed his father into the business and his training included a spell of two years at the shipyard of John Brockbank (*d.* 1822) at Lancaster between 1806 and 1808. Lancaster was then in its brief heyday as a shipbuilding centre and Brockbank was an eminent builder from whom Wood doubtless learned much about naval architecture.

Wood returned to Port Glasgow and, on his father's death in 1811, took control of the yard with his brother

Charles (1790–1847). Their first contract, accepted before their father died, was for the hull of Henry Bell's pioneering steamship, the *Comet*. Thereafter they built further steamships of increasing size, including a towing steamboat, the *Tug* (1817), which gave its name to that class of vessel, and the *Talbot* (1818), which was the first steamer to ply between Dublin and Holyhead. In 1818 Wood experimented with screw propulsion, albeit hand-powered and without any immediate practical application. In 1822 the Woods built the *James Watt* (140 ft), which inaugurated a steamer service between Leith and London, a measure of how far steamers had come in the space of ten years.

The brothers diverged in their interests, with Charles travelling to Quebec where he experimented with two raft-ships, the *Columbus* and the *Baron Renfrew*. Designed in 1824 to bring timber across the Atlantic, they were both wrecked. He later returned to the Clyde and built at Bowling and at Dumbarton, as well as spending some time in the Netherlands. John Wood worked with both David Napier, who built engines for many of the earlier steamers, and Robert Napier, who was a great friend and admirer. When Samuel Cunard ordered four ships for the north Atlantic service, Robert Napier contracted John Wood to design and build the *Acadia* (1840), while Charles Wood built the *Caledonia* to the same design. John Wood also built the *Europa* for Cunard in 1845, but this was the last of his major contracts. He continued to build small wooden vessels, but more for recreation than business.

Although Wood had no interest in building in iron himself, in 1839 he had become a partner in the shipyard of John Reid & Co. (Reid was married to Wood's niece). It was on Wood's initiative that the yard undertook the building in iron of a floating church, later moored in Loch Sunart, which the Free Church of Scotland needed for congregations denied sites by hostile landowners. Wood also helped the Free Church of Scotland by providing the plans for a schooner, the *Breadalbane*, which was used to transport ministers to remote locations.

Awarded the silver medal of the Royal Scottish Society of Arts in 1814, Wood was likewise awarded the silver medal of the Royal Society of Edinburgh in 1844, for the invention of a self-registering tide-gauge. He was also an astronomer and a student of French. He was of a modest, retiring, and kindly disposition, entirely free of professional jealousy and endlessly generous with his time and knowledge to anyone who approached him. While recognizing the science that went into his construction, John Scott Russell considered him 'remarkable for the great refinement of his taste. He was a consummate artist in shipbuilding, and every line was as studied and beautiful as fine art could make it. John Wood was, in fact, a pattern shipbuilder' (Russell, 145). Wood died peacefully at his home in Port Glasgow on 22 December 1860.

LIONEL ALEXANDER RITCHIE

Sources *Glasgow Herald* (24 Dec 1860) · P. Gifford, *Men of the Clyde* (1995), 295–8 · J. S. Russell, 'On the late Mr John Wood and Mr Charles Wood, naval architects, of Port Glasgow', *Transactions of the Institution of Naval Architects*, 2 (1861), 141–8 · J. Napier, *Life of Robert Napier of West Shandon* (1904), 93–5 · D. D. Napier, *David Napier, engineer, 1790–1869: an autobiographical sketch with notes*, ed. D. Bell (1912) · W. F. Macarthur, *History of Port Glasgow* (1932) · *Shipbuilding and Shipping Record*, 65 (1945), 213 · J. Shields, *Clyde built: a history of shipbuilding on the River Clyde* (1949) · L. A. Ritchie, 'The floating church of Loch Sunart', *Records of the Scottish Church History Society*, 22 (1984–6), 159–73 · E. Kennerley, *The Brockbanks of Lancaster, the story of an 18th century shipbuilding firm* (1981)
Archives U. Glas. L., corresp. with James P. Napier
Likenesses portrait, priv. coll.; repro. in Shields, *Clyde built*, facing p. 117
Wealth at death £19,482 11s. 1d.: registration, 19 March 1861, NA Scot., SC58/42/27/252–260

Wood, John (1793–1871), worsted manufacturer and factory reformer, was the eldest child of John Wood (d. 1832), who, by 1800, was Bradford's leading manufacturer of such goods as combs and snuff-boxes in horn, ivory, and tortoiseshell at Roebuck Yard, Ivegate. At the age of fifteen he was apprenticed to Richard Smith, Bradford's largest spinner of worsted yarn. By 1812 he began business as a master spinner in a small steam-powered mill built for him by his father adjoining the tortoiseshell works at Goodmanend (Bridge Street), and by 1825 he extended the old mill with combing shops and wool warehouses, where he experimented with imported Australian wool. Employing 500 workers, Wood was the foremost master spinner in Bradford by 1828. About 1815 he married his first wife, the daughter of a Norwich mayor, and they lived at Southbrook Lodge in Horton. His wife died childless in 1826.

Wood played a significant peacemaking role in the great Bradford wool-combers' strike of 1825, a year when he also made his first vain efforts to persuade fellow mill owners of the benefit of a shorter working day, particularly for women and children. Wood's major claim to fame was his part in the launching of a movement for factory reform. In 1830 he was living alone at Horton Hall, where, on 28 September, he was visited by Richard Oastler, a prominent supporter of the campaign against black slavery. Oastler was told by Wood, 'You are very enthusiastic against slavery in the West Indies and I assure you there are cruelties daily practised in our mills on little children which if you know I am sure you would strive to prevent' (Ward, 35). That day Oastler pledged his support and so began the movement for factory reform.

In 1830 Wood appealed again to his fellow employers. In spite of his diffident and retiring nature, he was drawn into the agitation for reform. During 1831 short-time committees campaigned vigorously for reform and adopted Michael Sadler as their parliamentary champion. Wood is said personally to have donated £40,000 to Sadler's campaign for a ten-hour bill, aimed at reducing the excessive hours worked by children. At a public rally in 1831 he recruited to the cause the young Revd G. S. Bull, who was to become a leader of the movement and Wood's lifelong friend. Throughout 1832 Wood canvassed for Sadler at Westminster, and that year he attended a large Easter rally in York.

The 1832 commission on factory reform found Wood's Bradford mill exemplary, with children working eleven hours in a clean environment and receiving weekly medical inspections. Yet even here, despite Wood's opposition, children were beaten by overseers. In October 1832 Wood employed the Revd Matthew Balme as schoolmaster of a purpose-built school adjoining his mill. Financed by Wood from the legacy of £500,000 left to him on his father's death in 1832, this was the first-ever factory school, attended half-time by 500 children.

Wood became increasingly disenchanted with what, in his view, was the over-provocative campaign waged by Oastler and Sadler. Nevertheless he attended a mass rally in Manchester and accompanied Sadler for much of his triumphant tour of the northern factory districts in 1832. A year later he married Annie Elisabeth, the daughter of John Hardy MP, a self-made barrister and sympathetic industrialist and, like Wood, an Anglican tory. Sadler's failure at the 1832 elections convinced Wood of the need to offer the parliamentary leadership of the Ten Hours Movement to Lord Ashley, whose Factory Act of 1833 considerably improved children's working conditions but did not reduce the working day to ten hours. Wood's response was to lead by example at his own mill, where he introduced a ten-hour day without reducing wages. His mill became a beacon of good order, cleanliness, and moral decency and was visited and praised by politicians, clergy, and humanitarians alike.

By 1835 Wood looked towards retirement into the gentry and took into partnership his half-cousin William Walker, who continued Wood's business success and his humanitarian ideals. After that he was less active in business affairs but continued his Bradford philanthropy by building, at a personal expense of £15,000, St James's Church and school at Bowling. His appointment of his friend the Revd Bull to the incumbency did not please William Scoresby, Bradford's new vicar, who thwarted Wood at every turn in local Anglican matters and led him eventually to close the church.

Wood's disillusion with Oastler's fiery leadership of the factory reform movement finally led him to disown Oastler and break with the movement. Defeated and disillusioned in both political and church affairs, he decided to give up his manufacturing business and buy into the gentry at Thedden Grange and Shalden Manor, near Alton, Hampshire. He acquired a grant of arms, and his family line was assured with the births of three sons and three daughters. His oldest son, John Gathorne Wood (*b.* 17 July 1839), was the owner of 3092 acres in 1879. Wood finally sold his share of the business to Walker in 1854 and turned his back on Bradford for ever. He died at Thedden Grange on 28 February 1871 and was buried at Shalden church, Alton.   GARY FIRTH

Sources J. T. Ward, 'Two pioneers in industrial reform', *Journal of the Bradford Textile Society* (1964) · J. Clark, 'History and annals of Bradford', MS, 1840, Bradford Central Library · J. C. Gill, *The ten hours parson: Christian social action in the eighteen-thirties* (1959) · W. Cudworth, 'John Wood, millmaster and benefactor', *Bradford Observer Budget* (21 April 1906) · W. Hustwick, 'The Ten Hours Act', *Journal of the Bradford Textiles Society* (1958–9) · C. H. Driver, *Tory radical: the life of Richard Oastler* (1946) · d. cert. · *Hampshire Chronicle* (18 March 1871)

Archives Hants. RO
Likenesses photograph, repro. in Ward, 'Two pioneers' · photograph, repro. in G. Firth, ed., *Bradford as it was* (1978)
Wealth at death under £140,000: resworn probate, Aug 1871, *CGPLA Eng. & Wales*

Wood, John (1801–1870), history and portrait painter, son of an artist and drawing-master, was born in London on 29 June 1801. He studied in Henry Sass's academy and, from 1819, at the Royal Academy, where in 1825 he was awarded the gold medal for his painting *Joseph Expounding the Dreams of the Chief Butler and Baker*. The next year he exhibited *Psyche Wafted by the Zephyrs*, which was also well received. His early works were praised for displaying invention and design, and he gained a considerable, if short-lived, reputation. In 1834 he was awarded a substantial commission for the altarpiece of St James's Church, Bermondsey, London, and in 1836 received a prize at Manchester for his painting *Elizabeth in the Tower*. He continued to exhibit at the Royal Academy and British Institution until 1862 but his later works, largely scriptural subjects and portraits, suffered as a result of his failing health. Several of his works were engraved, including portraits of Sir Robert Peel and the antiquary John Britton (both National Portrait Gallery, London). Wood died at his home, 81 Upper Charlotte Street, Fitzroy Square, London, on 19 April 1870.

F. M. O'DONOGHUE, *rev.* SUZANNE FAGENCE COOPER

Sources *Art Journal*, 32 (1870), 204 · R. Parkinson, ed., *Catalogue of British oil paintings, 1820–1860* (1990), 305 [catalogue of V&A] · Redgrave, *Artists* · J. Johnson, ed., *Works exhibited at the Royal Society of British Artists, 1824–1893, and the New English Art Club, 1888–1917*, 2 vols. (1975) · Bryan, *Painters* (1903–5), 5.393 · Graves, *Brit. Inst.* · *CGPLA Eng. & Wales* (1870)

Archives BL, autobiography, Add. MSS 37159–37167 · Courtauld Inst., Witt Library | V&A, paintings collection
Wealth at death under £5000: probate, 19 May 1870, *CGPLA Eng. & Wales*

Wood, John (1811–1871), geographer, was educated at Perth Academy, then entered the East India Company's navy and rose to the rank of lieutenant. By 1835, after protracted negotiation and treaty making, the River Indus was opened for navigation. Aga Mohammed Rahim, a Persian merchant of Bombay, was the first to exploit this opportunity for commerce. He bought a steamship, the *Indus*, and, with the permission of the government, gave command of it to Wood. It departed in October 1835 and returned to Bombay in February 1836, leaving Wood upstream to investigate the tidal range and area of annual inundation. After completing his observations, Wood returned to Bombay.

Wood's experience led to his appointment in November 1836 as assistant to the mission to Afghanistan under Alexander Burnes. The mission had both commercial and military aims, and Wood was charged with gathering information about the Indus and the topography and mineral deposits of the surrounding area. His investigations culminated in his supposed discovery of the source of the Oxus on 19 February 1838. Burnes forwarded Wood's reports to the governor-general, commending him highly and noting the commercial benefits likely to flow from his work. It was understood that if open for trade, the river would also be an important military route. Wood, however, found himself out of sympathy with British policy towards Afghanistan and, feeling that he had in good faith given assurances to the Afghans which were subsequently broken, he resigned from the navy, with the rank of captain. His fame as a geographer, however, spread. His *Journey to the Source of the Oxus* (1841) was widely praised and he was awarded the patron's medal of the Royal Geographical Society in 1841.

Wood went to New Zealand, but returned dissatisfied. He acted as a trader from 1843 until, in 1849, Sir Charles Napier proposed that he should accompany him to the Punjab; but, to snub Napier, the court of directors of the East India Company refused to allow Wood to go. Disappointed, Wood went to Victoria, Australia, but returned to Europe in 1857. In 1858 he went to Sind to manage the Oriental Inland Steam Navigation Company. The company soon failed for lack of suitable ships, but Wood was appointed manager of the Indus steam flotilla in 1861, an operation which he ran efficiently and profitably until 1871. He died at his home, 6 Quadrant Road, Highbury, on 13 November 1871. His wife, Georgina, and their children survived him.

Wood is remembered as an early writer on a remote and strategically important region. A new edition of his *Journey* was edited by his son Alexander in 1872 and reprinted in 1976. Wood was careful to exclude from his book any mention that his journey had a clear military purpose and, although as early as 1896 George Curzon set out to prove that Wood's account of the source of the Oxus was mistaken, the book has remained popular as a travel narrative.   ELIZABETH BAIGENT

Sources A. Wood, preface, in J. Wood, *Journey to the source of the Oxus*, ed. [A. Wood], new edn (1872) · C. R. Markham, *The fifty years' work of the Royal Geographical Society* (1881) · *CGPLA Eng. & Wales* (1871) · Irving, *Scots.* · Boase, *Mod. Eng. biog.* · G. E. Wheeler, introduction, in J. Wood, *Journey to the source of the Oxus*, ed. [A. Wood] (1976), v–xiv · G. Curzon, *The Pamirs and the source of the Oxus* (1896) [repr. from the *GJ* (1896)]
Wealth at death under £2000: resworn probate, Feb 1872, *CGPLA Eng. & Wales* (1871)

Wood, John (1825–1891), surgeon, son of John Wood, woolstapler, and Sarah Wood, was born in Bradford on 12 October 1825. He was the youngest child of a large family, and his father could afford to give him only a very simple education at a local school, run by E. Capon. He was then articled to a solicitor, but he disliked the law and after suffering a severe injury to his hip, which resulted in permanent shortening and deformity, his interest turned to medicine. He went to work as a dispenser to Edwin Casson, then senior surgeon to the Bradford Infirmary. Here he learnt minor surgery, and was taught enough Latin to enable him to pass the preliminary examination at the Royal College of Surgeons. In October 1846 he entered the medical faculty of King's College, London, where his student career was marked by rapid success: he gained four college scholarships and two gold medals. In 1848 he passed the first MB examination at London University,

obtaining the second place in honours and the gold medal in anatomy and physiology, but he did not continue his university career.

Wood was admitted a member of the Royal College of Surgeons on 30 July 1849, and in the same year he became a licentiate of the Society of Apothecaries. He was appointed house surgeon at King's College Hospital for 1850, and in the following year he became one of the demonstrators of anatomy, under Richard Partridge. From 1850 to 1870 Wood almost lived in the dissecting rooms at King's College, though he was appointed assistant surgeon to King's College Hospital in 1856. When he succeeded to the office of full surgeon he resigned his demonstratorship of anatomy, and in 1871 he was offered the chair of professor of surgery at King's College. In 1877 he became a lecturer on clinical surgery jointly with Joseph Lister, and in 1889 he was appointed emeritus professor of clinical surgery.

Wood married twice: first, on 19 August 1858, to Mary Anne Ward, who died in childbirth the following year; and second, in 1862, to Emma, the widow of the Revd J. H. Knox and daughter of Thomas Ware. His second wife and children from both marriages survived him.

Wood held many important positions at the Royal College of Surgeons. Elected a fellow after examination on 11 May 1854, he was Jacksonian prizeman in 1861 for his essay on hernia; he was also examiner in anatomy and physiology from 1875 to 1880; examiner in surgery from 1879 to 1889 and in dental surgery from 1883 to 1888; a member of the council from 1879 to 1887 and vice-president in 1885; Hunterian professor in 1884–5; and Bradshaw lecturer in 1885. He was elected a fellow of the Royal Society in June 1871, and in the same year he became an honorary fellow of King's College, London. At various times he acted as an examiner for the universities of London and Cambridge. He was president of the metropolitan counties' branch of the British Medical Association, and he was an honorary fellow of the Swedish Medical Society.

Wood had 'a massive frame, a dark square face with piercing black eyes, and walked with a slight limp. His manner was abrupt and his voice harsh; he spoke with a broad Yorkshire accent' (Lyle, 215). He died at his home, 61 Wimpole Street, London, on 29 December 1891, and was buried in Kensal Green cemetery on 4 January 1892.

Wood has been described as one of the last English surgeons who owed their position to a thorough knowledge of anatomy; yet his mind was sufficiently open to the advantages of pathology to enable him to accept the teaching of his colleague Lord Lister. Wood's knowledge of anatomy enabled him to invent a somewhat complex method of operation for the cure of rupture, a method which the advance of aseptic surgery rendered obsolete. In plastic surgery he was an acknowledged master.

D'A. POWER, *rev.* KAYE BAGSHAW

Sources *The Lancet* (9 Jan 1892), 116–17 · *BMJ* (9 Jan 1892), 96–7 · V. G. Plarr, *Plarr's Lives of the fellows of the Royal College of Surgeons of England*, rev. D'A. Power, 2 vols. (1930) · H. Willoughby Lyle, *King's and some King's men* (1935) · private information (1900)

Likenesses C. B. Birch, group portrait, pencil drawing, c.1858, NPG · H. J. Brookes, group portrait, oils, 1894 (*Court of Examiners*), RCS Eng. · H. J. Brookes, group portrait, oils, 1894 (*Council of Royal College of Surgeons of England, 1884–85*), RCS Eng. · photograph; formerly in RCS Eng.

Wealth at death £30,585 9s. 9d.: probate, 2 Feb 1892, CGPLA Eng. & Wales

Wood, Mrs John. *See* Wood, Matilda Charlotte (*bap.* 1831, *d.* 1915).

Wood, John Bertram Musgrave- [*pseuds.* Jon, Emmwood] (1915–1999), cartoonist, was born on 22 February 1915 at 9 Grange View, Leeds, Yorkshire, the son of Gerald Musgrave Wood (*d.* 1939), a printer's art designer and painter of landscapes and maritime scenes, and his wife, Florence Hilda Johnson. He had two brothers, both of whom became painters, and a sister. Having been educated at Leeds Modern School he worked at first in his father's studio and then as a space salesman in an advertising agency, but left to study at Leeds College of Art. After only eighteen months he gave up his studies to serve on an ocean cruise liner (eventually becoming chief fruit steward), and began drawing caricatures of passengers. He returned to London in 1939, and with one of his brothers taught art for a short while in a number of Whitechapel's Jewish youth clubs. After the death of his father that year, he moved to Polperro, Cornwall, where his mother had set up an antiques business.

In September 1939 Musgrave-Wood enlisted as a PT instructor in the Duke of Cornwall's light infantry. He was later commissioned in the Sherwood Foresters, applied to be a commando, and was sent to New Delhi, India, in 1941. While there he volunteered to join General Orde Wingate's newly formed special force of long-range guerrillas—the Chindits—serving in Burma and China, and rose to become second-in-command of a battalion of Karen tribesmen in the Burma Rifles, with the rank of major. Demobilized in 1946, he returned to Cornwall and soon afterwards met Joan Mary Smith, *née* Cooke (1917/18–1999), a driver in the motorized transport corps, on a blind date in London; they were married within three weeks, on 17 June 1946. In the same year he and a fellow Chindit, Major Patrick Boyle, himself also a cartoonist and later thirteenth earl of Cork and Orrery, published a humorous book about their wartime experiences, *Jungle, Jungle, Little Chindit* (1946). In this book he signed his drawings Jon but he later changed his pseudonym to Emmwood (from M-Wood), to differentiate himself from another Jon, W. J. Philpin Jones (creator of the famous Eighth Army desert rat 'Two Types' characters).

By the time of his marriage Musgrave-Wood was living in Chelsea, London, and briefly studied portrait painting at Goldsmiths' College (c.1948), where a fellow student was art forger Tom Keating. During this period he also freelanced as a cartoonist for various publications, notably contributing colour caricatures of celebrities and social types drawn as birds ('Emmwood's Aviary') to the weekly *Tatler & Bystander*. In 1948 the magazine's theatre caricaturist Tom Titt (Jan Rosciszewksi) retired, and

Emmwood took over his job until 1954. He also drew television review illustrations for *Punch*, drew showbusiness illustrations for the *Sunday Express* (from 1953), and contributed to *Life* magazine. In 1955, for two years, he succeeded Arthur Horner as political cartoonist on the *Evening Standard*, and later was editor of the *Junior Express* newspaper, but left when the management wanted to turn it into a children's comic. In 1957 he joined the *Daily Mail*, as deputy to the paper's long-serving political cartoonist, Leslie Illingworth, and also drew illustrations for the *Mail*'s 'Diary' column. When Illingworth retired, in 1969, Emmwood took over his job, alternating his work at first with 'Trog' (Wally Fawkes) and then, when the paper merged with the *Daily Sketch* in 1971 and went tabloid, with the *Sketch*'s former cartoonist, Mac (Stan McMurtry). Emmwood retired in 1975 (being succeeded by Mac) and moved from his fifteenth-century cottage in Deal, Kent, to Provence, in France, to concentrate on his painting. He died in Vallabrix, near Uzes, Provence, on 30 August 1999, only a few months after his wife. They had had no children. He was buried in Vallabrix cemetery.

Emmwood was one of the founder members, in 1966, of the British Cartoonists' Association, and drawings by him were among those chosen for the National Portrait Gallery exhibition 'Drawn and Quartered: the World of the British Newspaper Cartoon, 1720–1970' in 1970. His work is held in such public collections as the Centre for the Study of Cartoons and Caricature at the University of Kent at Canterbury and the National Portrait Gallery.

Emmwood's cartoons were characterized by a clean line, and were usually drawn in pen, brush, and indian ink on board. He was a small, brisk, dapper man with a small neat moustache (in retirement he grew a full naval beard). He often wore a blazer and flannels, sported a bow tie or cravat, smoked a pipe, and 'looked like a nice gentleman farmer down from the Cotswolds' (*Daily Mail*). A lover of dogs (especially dachshunds, which frequently featured in his cartoons) and good wine, he was also a keen gardener and a sportsman who enjoyed cricket and tennis and was a much respected president of the Princes Golf Club, Sandwich, Kent.   MARK BRYANT

Sources private information (2004) [Melody Bourner] · M. Bryant, *Dictionary of twentieth-century British cartoonists and caricaturists* (2000) · M. Bryant and S. Heneage, eds., *Dictionary of British cartoonists and caricaturists, 1730–1980* (1994) · M. Bryant, 'Emmwood', *World encyclopedia of the press*, ed. D. Griffiths [forthcoming] · M. Bateman, *Funny way to earn a living* (1966) · M. Horn, ed., *World encyclopedia of cartoons* (1980) · *Daily Mail* (21–2 Sept 1999) · *The Independent* (24 Sept 1999) · *The Guardian* (24 Sept 1999)

Archives priv. coll., letters, photographs, cartoons, and paintings

Likenesses Fielding, photograph (aged five), priv. coll. · J. B. Musgrave-Wood, self-portrait, caricature, repro. in *Daily Mail* (22 Sept 1999) · J. B. Musgrave-Wood, self-portrait, caricature, repro. in Bateman, *Funny way*, 10 · J. B. Musgrave-Wood, self-portrait, caricature, repro. in *The Guardian* (24 Sept 1999) · Portman Press Bureau, photograph (at his wedding), priv. coll. · photograph, repro. in *Drawn and quartered: the world of the British newspaper cartoon* [exhibition catalogue, *Twentieth Century* magazine, 1970] · photograph, repro. in *The Guardian* · photographs, priv. coll.

Wood, John George (1827–1889), natural historian and microscopist, was born at 40 Howland Street, Fitzroy Square, London, on 21 July 1827, the eldest son of John Freeman Wood, surgeon, and his wife, Juliana Lisetta (*née* Arntz). A sickly child, he was initially educated at home; the family's move to Oxford in 1830 allowed him to lead an outdoor life and develop an interest in natural history. By 1838 he was considered sufficiently healthy to attend school, and was placed under his uncle, the Revd George Edward Gepp, at Ashbourne grammar school in Derbyshire. Wood matriculated from Merton College, Oxford, on 17 October 1844, and obtained the Jackson scholarship in the following year. He graduated BA in 1848, proceeding MA in 1851. For a time he worked under Henry Acland in the anatomical museum, but in 1852 was ordained deacon and became curate of the parish of St Thomas the Martyr, Oxford. In 1854 he was ordained priest, but resigned his Oxford curacy in the same year. In April 1856 he was appointed assistant chaplain to St Bartholomew's Hospital. In 1858 he was also appointed to a readership at Christ Church Greyfriars. On 15 February 1859 he married Jane Eleanor, fourth daughter of John Ellis of the Home Office; they had at least one son. Wood resigned his chaplaincy in 1862 and the readership in 1863 on account of ill health, and moved to Belvedere, near Woolwich. From about 1863 until 1873 he assisted in the work of the neighbouring parish of Erith, where he introduced choral services. Indeed, the efficiency of his choir led to his appointment as precentor of the Canterbury Diocesan Choral Union, whose annual festivals he conducted from 1869 to 1875. In December 1876 Wood moved from Belvedere, settling in 1878 in Upper Norwood.

From the early 1850s Wood was developing a career as a natural historian; his first book, *The Illustrated Natural History*, was published in 1851. Several more works had followed by 1856, when he began to give occasional lectures on natural history subjects. In 1879, having given a series of six lectures in Brixton, he resolved to take up lecturing as a second profession. With the assistance of George H. Robinson, manager of the book court at the Crystal Palace, 'sketch-lectures' were arranged for the winter months. These were delivered over ten seasons (1879–88), and took Wood throughout England and to America, where he delivered the Lowell lectures at Boston in 1883–4. Wood's lectures were noted for his blackboard illustrations, drawn in coloured pastels. He was a member of the Linnean Society from 1854 until 1877.

Wood wrote more than seventy books, some under the pseudonym George Forrest. The majority of them were on natural history, but he also published works on the history of the biblical period and English scenery, co-wrote books on athletics—such as *Athletic Sports and Manly Exercises* (1864)—and edited titles as diverse as Gilbert White's *Natural History of Selbourne* and the *Boy's Own Magazine*. His own natural history titles, such as *Our Garden Friends and Foes* (1863) and *Handy Natural History* (1886), were not rigorously scientific but were influential in popularizing the subject. His works on microscopy such as *Common Objects of the Microscope* (1861) and *Nature's Teaching* (1877) are still in

John George Wood (1827–1889), by unknown engraver, pubd 1889 (after Negretti & Zambra)

use by amateur microscopists who hold him in affection. As an obituarist observed:

> the man who had a thorough acquaintance with Mr Wood's works would become a kind of walking dictionary of useful information acquired through the study of literature far lighter than nine-tenths of the novels published these days. (*The Spectator*, 12 July 1890, 57)

Wood continued writing until shortly before his death, while on a lecturing tour, at Coventry on 3 March 1889. He was survived by his wife who received a civil-list pension in the following year.

B. B. WOODWARD, *rev.* PETER OSBORNE

Sources T. Wood, *The Rev. J. G. Wood* (1890) · Crockford (1889) · N. Crosland, *Rambles round my life: an autobiography*, 2nd edn (1898) · private information (1900) · private information (2004) [H. Series] · Boase, *Mod. Eng. biog.* · *CGPLA Eng. & Wales* (1889)

Archives LPL, corresp. and papers

Likenesses wood-engraving (after photograph by Negretti & Zambra), BM, NPG; repro. in *ILN* (16 March 1889) [*see illus.*]

Wealth at death £794 17*s.* 7*d.*: probate, 29 March 1889, *CGPLA Eng. & Wales*

Wood, John Muir (1805–1892), music publisher and writer, was born on 31 July 1805 in Edinburgh, the elder son of Andrew Wood, a music publisher, and his wife, Jacobina Ferrier. His father was a partner in the firm of Muir, Wood & Co. (later Wood & Co.). Wood was educated in Edinburgh, and then studied music there with Frédéric Kalkbrenner. He went to Paris for two years to study with Johann Peter Pixis, and from there to Vienna for two years with Czerny. In 1828 he returned to Edinburgh to teach music and then spent several years in London.

In 1848 Wood and his half-brother, George, set up a branch of the family firm in Buchanan Street, Glasgow, and Wood moved to Glasgow, to manage the business. On 22 January 1851 he married Helen Kemlo Stephen; they had three sons and five daughters.

In 1849, in collaboration with George Farquhar Graham, Wood brought out a collection of the *Songs of Scotland*, in three volumes, published by Wood & Co. in Edinburgh. Wood collected much of the material, and added detailed notes. The airs were harmonized by Edinburgh musicians, including Thomas Molleson Mudie, Finlay Dun, John

John Muir Wood (1805–1892), self-portrait [holding a photographic printing frame]

Thomas Surenne, and Graham. It was reissued in 1884, with additional historical notes, as *The Popular Songs and Melodies of Scotland*. From 1876 from to 1878 Wood edited and published the *Scottish Monthly Musical Times*. He contributed the articles 'Scottish music', 'The Coronach', 'The Scotch snap', and 'The Skene manuscript' to the first edition of Grove's *Dictionary of Music and Musicians*.

Wood played a leading part in Scottish musical life. While visiting Frankfurt am Main, he stayed with the Polish violinist Karol Lipiński, and learned to speak Polish. In 1848 he was able to manage a Scottish tour for Chopin, whom he had met there. He arranged concerts by well-known performers, and organized a visit to Glasgow by the Hallé Orchestra under Sir Charles Hallé.

Wood died at Armadale, Cove, Dunbartonshire, on 25 June 1892, and was buried in Glasgow necropolis. He was survived by his wife.

GEORGE STRONACH, *rev.* ANNE PIMLOTT BAKER

Sources *New Grove* • C. Humphries and W. C. Smith, *Music publishing in the British Isles, from the beginning until the middle of the nineteenth century: a dictionary of engravers, printers, publishers, and music sellers*, 2nd edn (1970) • H. G. Farmer, *A history of music in Scotland* (1947) • *Musical Herald* (Aug 1892) • *Glasgow Herald* (28 June 1892) • *N&Q*, 8th ser., 2 (1892), 40 • private information (1900)

Archives NRA, priv. coll., corresp. relating to musical education in Paris and Vienna

Likenesses J. M. Wood, self-portrait, photograph, Scot. NPG [*see illus.*] • photograph, repro. in *Musical Herald*

Wealth at death £1956 3s. 10d.: confirmation, 27 Oct 1892, CCI • £462 8s. 4d.: additional estate, 16 Dec 1892, CCI

Wood, Sir John Page, second baronet (1796–1866). *See under* Wood, Sir Matthew, first baronet (1768–1843).

Wood, John Philp (1762–1838), civil servant and antiquary, was born at King's Cramond, Edinburghshire, on 9 March 1762, the son of John Wood (d. 1792), the seventh son of Jasper Wood of Warriston, and of Isobel, the daughter of John Philp of Greenlaw. He was deaf—'scopulis surdior Icari' (deafer than the rocks of Icarus) in his own phrase—from early youth if not from birth. Though he was able to communicate orally, his speech was not distinct. Sir Walter Scott described meeting 'Honest John Wood, my old friend' on 28 June 1830, adding, 'I only regret I cannot understand him, as he has a very powerful memory and much curious information' (*Journal*, 603).

This disability was not an insurmountable disadvantage in the two activities which dominated Wood's life. The first of these was the excise. He entered the Excise Office in 1778, and in 1810 rose to the position of auditor of excise in Scotland. He took office as a highly skilled accountant with a detailed knowledge of the excise, and turned with vigour to rooting out its inefficiency and corruption.

The last annual accounts to have been audited—and very inaccurately—were those for 1799–1800. Wood, who, contrary to precedent, carried out his duties personally, took his responsibility to the barons of exchequer very seriously. He recognized his duty to audit the activities of the commissioners of excise, and he fearlessly exposed their idleness, errors, double accounting, and excessive travel claims. This earned him the continuing opposition of the commissioners, notably of James Sedgwick their chairman, who in 1811 complained of Wood that, 'from the natural defects to which he is unfortunately subject, he ought never to have been appointed Auditor' (NL Scot., MS 3106). But Wood quickly brought the audit up to date, and when he retired on a pension of £500 in October 1832, after fifty-four years of exemplary public service, the office was highly efficient. His final duty, carried out correctly but much against his will, was to prepare the excise for transfer to London.

Wood's other main activity, the one by which he is most remembered, is his antiquarian writing. His *Peerage of Scotland* (1813), founded on the work of Sir Robert Douglas, remains a standard work of reference at the end of the twentieth century, and his *Memoirs of the Life of John Law* (1824) is an important contribution to banking history. He wrote on historical subjects for the *Gentleman's Magazine*, and assisted John Nichols in the compilation of the Scottish part of his *Progresses of James I*. But his most famous work was *The Antient and Modern State of the Parish of Cramond* (1794), 'one of the most exact and elegant topographical works ever published' (*GM*, April 1795, 319).

The *Statistical Account* of Scotland, published by Sir John Sinclair from 1791, is recognized as being based on the form of parish history envisaged by Wood. Though his book on Cramond was not published until a large part of Sinclair's compilation had appeared, its existence was known, its use was acknowledged by the minister of Cramond in his account of the parish, and Wood himself, writing to the antiquary George Paton in November 1789 (NL Scot., Adv. MS 29.3.8), described the form such an account should take: 'Brevity was my great aim … it being done solely with a view to form a plan in which others being done, complete county histories might … be formed.'

Little is known of Wood's private life; he married, on 2 July 1803, Marion (1779–1856), the daughter of John Cadell of Cockenzie and the sister of Robert Cadell, Scott's publisher, with whom he had three sons and four daughters. He may have been responsible for the move of Braidwood's deaf school (where, probably he had been educated himself) to the old excise office in 1814. He died at his home, 8 South Charlotte Street, Edinburgh, on 25 October 1838, and was buried in St Cuthbert's churchyard.   PATRICK CADELL

Sources J. P. Wood, *The antient and modern state of the parish of Cramond* (1794) · *GM*, 1st ser., 65 (1795), 319 · *GM*, 2nd ser., 11 (1839), 323 · *The journal of Sir Walter Scott*, ed. W. E. K. Anderson (1972) · J. H. Stevenson, *The Cadells of Banton, Grange, Tranent and Cockenzie* (1890) · parish register (baptism), Cramond, 9 March 1762 · tombstone, St Cuthbert's churchyard, Edinburgh
Archives Edinburgh Central Reference Library, memorials of various families, etc. · NL Scot., corresp. and papers | NL Scot., Paton MSS · NL Scot., annotated copy of *A view of the political state of Scotland*
Wealth at death £5013 11s. 9d.: inventory, 1839, Scotland · £29 8s. 8d.: additional inventory, 1839, Scotland

Wood, John Turtle (1821–1890), archaeologist, was born on 13 February 1821 in Hackney, Middlesex, the only child of John Wood (*b.* 1779), from a Shropshire landowning family, and his wife, Elizabeth Turtle. He was educated privately and at Rossall School, and went on to study architecture under a tutor at Cambridge. In 1850 he was studying in Venice. After his return to Britain he was articled to H. E. Kendall, and practised as an architect in London, at Victoria Square, Grosvenor Place. In 1853 he designed a house in Oatlands Park for J. T. Darke. In the same year he married his first cousin Henrietta Elizabeth (1830/31–1906), daughter of Samuel Wood.

In 1858 Wood accepted an appointment as architect to the Smyrna and Aidin Railway in western Turkey, designing stations on that line. But his great ambition was to discover the remains of the famous temple of Artemis (or Diana) at Ephesus, south of Smyrna, which had completely disappeared from sight in the middle ages.

Accordingly, in 1863 Wood resigned his appointment and began his search. The British Museum agreed to get him a permit and to give him a grant, in return for any antiquities he might discover. In 1867, while excavating in the ancient theatre at Ephesus, he found an inscription in Greek referring to some gold and silver statuettes, which, on festive days, were carried from the temple to the theatre by way of the Magnesian gate. If he could find this gate, he reckoned that there would be a paved road leading to the temple. Late in 1867 he found the gate and the road. Following its course, on 2 May 1869, he found the wall of the temple enclosure. He now bought the site on

behalf of the British Museum and set out to find the temple. He found it on the last day of 1869 under nearly 20 feet of sand. The excavation was far from easy. The ground was waterlogged, necessitating constant pumping, so that progress was very slow; but by April 1874 the job was considered done. The temple was a sad ruin, but Wood managed to recover a quantity of very broken sculptures and architectural features, which he sent back to Britain.

In 1874 Wood returned to Britain. For eleven years, loyally assisted by his wife, he had worked under almost intolerable conditions. He suffered constantly from fever; he was frequently threatened by bandits and once nearly murdered; he was injured several times; he endured hot summers and cold winters and periodical earthquakes. In 1875 he gave four lectures on his discoveries at the Royal Institution, and 1877 saw the publication of his book *Discoveries at Ephesus*; a second book, *Discoveries on the Site of Ancient Ephesus*, published posthumously in 1890, added little to the earlier work. He returned briefly to Ephesus in 1883, without, however, achieving any significant results. In addition to his architectural and archaeological activities, he was also an accomplished artist, and frequently exhibited at the Royal Academy.

Wood was elected a fellow of the Society of Antiquaries in 1875, a fellow of the Royal Institute of British Architects (RIBA) in 1874, and an honorary fellow of the RIBA in 1878. In 1875 the British government awarded him a pension of £200 per annum in recognition of his discoveries at Ephesus. He had one son, who died aged thirty-two in 1889. This domestic tragedy probably hastened his own death from heart disease on 25 March 1890, at home at 66 Marine Parade, Worthing, Sussex.   R. A. HIGGINS, *rev.*

Sources W. Papworth, *Journal of Proceedings of the Royal Institute of British Architects*, new ser., 6 (1889–90), 275–6 · *TLS* (13 March 1937) · Boase, *Mod. Eng. biog.*
Likenesses L. S. Canziani, oils, 1937, BM
Wealth at death £1437 11s. 2d.: probate, 30 April 1890, CGPLA Eng. & Wales

Wood, John Warrington (1839–1886), sculptor, was born on 9 September 1839 in Warrington, Lancashire, the eldest of the five children of James Wood (*bap.* 1819, *d.* 1880/81), road surveyor for Warrington, and his wife, Charlotte Gibson (*bap.* 1817, *d.* in or after 1887), daughter of a local farmer, Thomas Gibson. His father was known locally as the Lancashire Braidwood (after the London firefighter) for his deeds as voluntary fire brigade superintendent. Despite the wishes of his parents, John Wood followed his father's early occupation as a stonemason and was apprenticed to a local one (*c.*1855–*c.*1863). His first important work was on the Manchester and Liverpool District Bank in Warrington. From 1858, in the evenings, he attended the new Warrington School of Art (Warrington Collegiate Institute), which had been founded in 1857. He received four local medals, a gold medal in 1858, and a national medallion awarded by the Department of Science and Art, South Kensington, London, in 1862. An ideal work, *Spring*, was shown in the exhibition of students' work in 1862 and preceded a commission from the MP Gilbert Greenall in 1863. By 1865 Wood was in Rome, and he added Warrington to his name, probably to avoid confusion with other sculptors. While in Rome he married, on 21 December 1872, Ann Lilias Hamilton, daughter of William Charles Stewart, Lord Hamilton, of Craighlaw, Wigtownshire, Scotland.

Wood's work, which is almost exclusively in marble, shows the influence of the expatriate sculptors Benjamin Spence and John Gibson. His style embraced Antonio Canova's classicism, yet his own taste was far more eclectic. As he said, 'I would far rather be on the side of Phidias than Bernini, but what I am striving hard to do is to arrive at the happy medium' (Wilmot, 140). He worked from his studio in Rome at piazza Trinità dei Monti 7, gaining a reputation for his portrait busts and religious sculpture; his most distinguished sitter, apart from Queen Victoria (work incomplete), was Austen Henry Layard, ambassador to Madrid (National Gallery, London). He executed over sixty portrait busts, mainly of dignitaries from the north-west of England, many of which are in Warrington Museum and Art Gallery, as are *Rachel* (exh. RA, 1868), *Nestlings* (exh. RA, 1871), *Elijah* (1872), and *Beatrice Cenci* (date unknown). Many works remain in the north-west. Wood's consistent patron was the brewer Andrew Barclay Walker, subscriber to the Warrington School of Art and founder of the Walker Art Gallery in Liverpool. He purchased Wood's *Eve* in 1871 for his Warrington country house, Bewsey New Hall.

Wood's ideal sculpture was mainly religious and attempted to strike a balance between realism and idealism. He began with single female subjects and mainly used them until 1875, when he produced his first group, *Sisters of Bethany* (Birmingham Museum and Art Gallery), which was highly acclaimed in the *Art Journal* of 1875 (and there reproduced in engraving) and exhibited at the Royal Academy in 1879. *Ruth and Naomi*, his last traced work (exh. RA, 1884; National Museums and Galleries on Merseyside), was stylistically similar and was described by the *Warrington Guardian* as his 'masterpiece' (21 March 1883). These two female groups were the sculptor's most original pieces. Several copies of each were sold and the designs stood apart from the eclectic nature of his other work.

Wood's most impressive work, *St Michael Overcoming Satan*, a subject from Milton's *Paradise Lost*, was commissioned in 1871 with £1000 raised by subscription from the people of Warrington. Fourteen buffaloes and two Campagna oxen hauled the marble to his studio in Rome, causing deep furrows which remained in the street for years. This memorable scene was recorded in a fine watercolour by Enrico Coleman, *Oxen Drawing a Block of Marble to the Studio of John Warrington Wood in Rome* (1872, National Museums and Galleries on Merseyside). In 1875 *St Michael* was exhibited at the Royal Academy, then taken to the new art gallery in the Warrington Museum which was 'designed for the purpose of receiving Mr Wood's group' (*Warrington Advertiser*, 6 Oct 1877; Wood was invited to make a speech at the gallery's opening in 1877). Also in 1875 Wood was commissioned by Walker to carve sculpture for the Walker Art Gallery. His *Raphael* and *Michelangelo* flanked the main entrance, a female personification of Liverpool surmounted the portico, and four reliefs commemorating

events from Liverpool's history decorated the external walls. The gallery opening was delayed by a year to accommodate Wood's sculpture, for which Walker incurred heavy expenses.

Wood enjoyed enormous commercial success. He noted that: 'All my works sold, and I had nothing left in my studio, even in the early part of the season' (Wilmot). By 1874 he had purchased in Rome the magnificent Villa Campana, near the church of San Giovanni in Laterano, which was the former home of the infamous art collector Pietro Campana. The villa became an attraction for artists, who were welcomed by Wood, known for his extraordinary personal charm. A friend commented that 'he seemed to carry sunshine all the day long' (ibid.). Wood's work sold well for a combination of reasons. His sculpture was technically accomplished and stylistically safe, and it satisfied a flourishing market for religious groups and portrait busts. Walker's early patronage earned Wood an immediate reputation in the north-west of England, and this was enhanced by Royal Academy submissions (twenty-seven works between 1868 and 1884). Election to the Accademia Nazionale di San Luca, and his famous studio with its 'open house' policy and the sculptor's willingness to communicate his work, made Wood's sculpture readily accessible to an international audience. His reputation was sustained by regular visits to London (he had a residence at 78 Sloane Street) and the north-west and constant press attention until his death in 1886.

In 1877 Wood was awarded the highest honour for an artist in Rome: election to the Guild of St Luke, though British critics later complained that 'his sympathies were with the followers of Canova, the inheritors of the decaying tradition of Classical Greece. A marked revival of the art of sculpture took place in his lifetime. But he played no part' (Wilmot). When he died suddenly at his apartments in the Lion Hotel in Bridge Street, Warrington, on 26 December 1886 at the age of forty-seven, after catching a chill (which, owing to a heart condition, was fatal), 'his Roman workmen, who adored him, wept like children' (Wilmot). Before he died his property in Rome had been sold and 'This together with what he had previously earned by his profession made him in a pecuniary sense independent of his chisel' (*The Examiner*, 1 Jan 1887). He was buried in Warrington cemetery on 29 December; his tombstone reads: 'His faith and work were bells of one accord' (Tennyson).   CHERRY ELIZABETH GRAY

Sources M. J. Taylor, 'Between Phidias and Bernini: the life and work of John Warrington Wood, 1839–1886', postgraduate diss., University of Manchester, 1984 · artists' files, Warrington Museum and Art Gallery · photographs, pamphlets, cuttings, etc., NL Wales · T. Wilmot, 'John Warrington Wood, sculptor', *Magazine of Art*, 14 (1890–91), 136–40 · 'Opening of the new gallery', *Warrington Advertiser* (6 Oct 1877) · 'Death of Mr J. Warrington Wood', *The Examiner* [Warrington] (1 Jan 1887) · E. Morris and J. Larson, *Liverpool renewed: John Warrington Wood's statue of Liverpool on the Walker Art Gallery and its replacement* (1997) [foreword by R. Foster, National Museums and Galleries on Merseyside] · journals of Lady Layard, vol. 1, BL, Add. MS 46158, fol. 63*v* · C. Owen, *Dawn* [Warrington], 6 (1906), 67–8 · Borough of Warrington, proceedings of the council, 1886–7, 9.83 · Borough of Warrington, proceedings of the council,

1887–8, 10.182, 194, 198 · J. J. Phelps, 'The Boydell effigy at Grappenhall', *Transactions of the Lancashire and Cheshire Antiquarian Society*, 44 (1927), 8–16 · census returns for Warrington districts, 1861, 1871 · Burke, *Gen. GB* (1898) · d. cert. · *Warrington Guardian* (21 March 1883) · indexes of baptisms and marriages, 1837–46, Warrington parish church of St Elphin · *The exhibition of the Royal Academy* (1868–74) [exhibition catalogues]

Archives Warrington Museum and Art Gallery, artists' files

Likenesses T. Birtles, photograph, Warrington Library, Broadside, 920 Wood. J. 4 · T. Webster and T. Birtles, two photographs (probably albumen prints), Warrington Museum and Art Gallery · photograph (after drawing), Warrington Library, Broadside, 920 Wood. J. 4

Wealth at death £386 5s. 11d.—effects in England: administration, 7 Dec 1887, *CGPLA Eng. & Wales*

Wood, Kenneth Maynard (1916–1997), electrical manufacturer, was born on 4 October 1916 in Lewisham, London, the elder son and second child in the family of two sons and three daughters of Frederick Cavendish Wood (d. 1929), who ran a company in Hatton Garden, London, dealing in silver goods, and his wife, Agnes, daughter of Charles Riley Maynard, the founder of Maynards, the confectionery manufacturers, famous for their wine gums. Against his mother's wishes he left Bromley county school at fourteen to go to sea, signing on for four years as a cadet on SS *Hartlepool*, bound for South America. Once back in England in 1934 he enrolled in evening classes in electrical engineering, mechanical drawing, and accountancy, taking various daytime jobs before working in a radio repair shop in London. He and a partner founded their own company, Dickson and Wood, in 1937, installing and repairing radios and televisions, but at the outbreak of the Second World War he sold the company and joined the RAF. He was transferred to the research department of Stanhope Engineering Company, at their request, to become their design engineer, and spent the war designing electronic equipment, including radar simulators for the navy, and simulators for rear-gunners for the RAF. On 26 August 1939 he married Mary Bull (b. 1915/16), daughter of Alfred Harold Hitchcock Bull, civil servant. There were no children of the marriage, which ended in divorce. On 22 April 1944 Wood married, second, Laurie Marion McKinlay (b. 1919/20), daughter of Michael McKinlay, commercial artist. They had two sons and two daughters.

In 1947, with a wartime colleague, Roger Laurence, Wood set up Woodlau Industries in a small workshop at 79 Goldsmith Road, Woking, Surrey. As managing director he launched his first product, the A100 Turnover toaster, based on a 1930s GEC model. His next idea was to make a food mixer. Again, this was not a new idea: a number of food mixers had appeared in the United States and on the continent in the 1930s. Wood put the A200 mixer, designed on the lines of the Sunbeam mixer, on the market in 1948, and it was soon being produced at the rate of 100 a month. After he moved to a factory in Hipley Street, Old Woking, he was able to turn out 575 mixers a week. At this point Laurence left the company, which was renamed the Kenwood Manufacturing Company in 1949. Wood felt he could improve on the design of the mixer, and after taking apart and analysing various rival models he designed the first Kenwood Chef, which was launched at the Ideal Home Exhibition in 1950. It was an instant success. The Kenwood Chef was more than just a food mixer: it had attachments which enabled it to liquidize, grind coffee, mince meat, extract juice, peel potatoes, fill sausages, whisk eggs, or slice beans. The early advertisements claimed that with a Kenwood Chef in the kitchen, 'you just plan the menus and then hand over the work to your Chef' (1956). One factor in Wood's success was the conviction that to sell a product he had to make people want to buy it. To this end he trained demonstrators to take the Kenwood Chef into department stores and electricity board showrooms, and also into school domestic science departments, in the hope that when the pupils got married they would ask for a Kenwood Chef as a wedding present. In an article in *Good Housekeeping* (March 1958) on kitchen time-saving devices for working brides, the biggest present of all was a Kenwood Chef.

Wood extended his range to other domestic appliances, introducing the Kenmix blender (1951), the electric knife-sharpener (1952), the Steam-O-Matic steam iron (1954), and the rotisserie, with an eye-level grill (1958). Targeting the kitchen jobs that caused the most work or which were the most unpleasant, in 1958 the company acquired Dishmaster, maker of dishwashing machines and garbage disposal units, and launched a new, fully automatic Dishmaster in 1959, anticipating the day when the dishwasher would be as essential a kitchen appliance as the refrigerator or the washing machine.

In 1958 Wood decided it was time to break into the commercial appliance market, and he arranged a merger with Peerless and Ericsson, manufacturers of equipment for commercial and institutional kitchens. Peerless and Ericsson, a public company, took over Kenwood, dropping their own name and adopting that of Kenwood Manufacturing Company. Wood remained managing director and became deputy chairman of the new public company. He travelled extensively to promote Kenwood products, and by 1959 exports accounted for 65 per cent of the company's output, with subsidiaries in Canada, Australia, New Zealand, and several European countries.

In the early 1960s the company suffered a severe setback when it tried to move into the refrigerator and home freezer market, lured by the hot summer of 1959, at the same time as the expensive move to a new purpose-built factory in Havant and the closure of the Woking factory. It cost the company £200,000 to withdraw from the refrigerator market but by 1964 recovery was underway. However, when Thorn Electrical Industries made a hostile takeover bid of £9.3 million, nearly doubling the price of the shares on the stock exchange, shortly after the company's twenty-first birthday celebrations in 1968, Wood agreed to the offer, and, heartbroken, he resigned from the board.

Wood was managing director of Dawson-Keith Holdings, an electrical power-plant manufacturer, from 1972 to 1980. He developed new business ventures, including the Forest Mere health farm at Liphook, Hampshire, and a 350 acre golf course in the grounds of his house. His second marriage having ended in divorce, Wood married Patricia Rose on 15 September 1978. She had three sons from her previous marriage. In 1993 Wood was listed by *Business Age* as one of the 500 richest individuals in Britain, worth £24.5 million. He died at his home, Dellwood Cottage, Wheatsheaf Enclosure, Liphook, Hampshire, on 19 October 1997, and was cremated at Guildford crematorium on 24 October. He was survived by his third wife, the two sons and two daughters of his second marriage, and the three stepsons of his third marriage. A model of the Kenwood Chef is on permanent display in the Science Museum in London.   ANNE PIMLOTT BAKER

Sources Sci. Mus., Kenneth Wood archive · H. Miller, *The way of enterprise: a study of the origins, problems, and achievements in the growth of post-war British firms* (1963) · *Daily Telegraph* (21 Oct 1997) · *The Times* (22 Oct 1997) · *The Guardian* (23 Oct 1997) · *The Independent* (24 Oct 1997) · *Business Age*, 36 (autumn 1993) · *WWW* · m. certs. · d. cert. · private information (2004) [stepson] · *WW*

Archives Sci. Mus., MSS

Likenesses photograph, 1950–51, Sci. Mus., Kenneth Wood archive; repro. in *Daily Telegraph* · photograph, repro. in *The Times* · photograph, repro. in *The Guardian* · photograph, repro. in *The Independent*

Wealth at death £911,202: probate, 11 Feb 1998, *CGPLA Eng. & Wales*

Wood, Sir (Howard) Kingsley (1881–1943), politician, was born on 19 August 1881 in West Sculcoates, Hull, the eldest of the three children of the Revd Arthur Wood, a Wesleyan Methodist minister, and his wife, Harriett Siddons Howard (who was related to Sarah Siddons). He was educated at the Central Foundation Boys' School, Cowper Street, London, a Methodist institution, near Wesley's Chapel in the City Road, Finsbury, where his father was minister for nine years. Wood himself later became a prominent Methodist and served for many years as treasurer at the chapel.

Solicitor, Conservative MP, and the Ministry of Health Wood was articled to a solicitor and qualified in 1903, having taken honours in his law finals and won the prestigious John Mackrell prize. In 1905 he married Agnes Lilian (*d.* 1955), daughter of Henry Frederick Fawcett, an artist; there were no children. Wood set up his own City practice—which subsequently became Kingsley Wood, Williams, Murphy, and Ross—specializing in industrial insurance law. As representative of the industrial insurance companies, he negotiated concessions in their favour from Lloyd George in the discussions leading to the National Insurance Act of 1911. He was chairman of the London Old Age Pension Authority in 1915 and chairman of the London Insurance Committee from 1917 to 1918. He was also a member of the National Insurance Advisory Committee from 1911 to 1919. From 1916 to 1919 he was chairman of the Faculty of Insurance, and served as its president in 1920, 1922, and 1923.

Wood was elected to the London county council in 1911 as Municipal Reform member for Woolwich, and served on committees on old-age pensions, housing, and insurance. In 1917 he presented a memorial to the government's food controller recommending that all bread should be sold by weight. However, it was in 1918 that he made his mark on national politics by organizing a

Sir (Howard) Kingsley Wood (1881–1943), by Walter Stoneman, *c*.1941

memorial proposing the establishment of a ministry of health. The prime minister, Lloyd George, adopted the proposal, and Wood was knighted in the same year. At the general election of 1918 he was elected as Conservative MP for West Woolwich, a seat which he held until his death, and became parliamentary private secretary to successive ministers of health, Christopher Addison (1919–21) and Sir Alfred Mond (1921–2), both Coalition Liberals. Wood voted against the break-up of the coalition in 1922 and, although he agreed to follow Bonar Law after the Carlton Club meeting, he also said that he was prepared to co-operate 'with men actuated by similar views of an anti-Socialist and constitutionalist nature' (Kinnear, 148). He did not hold office under Law but he served Neville Chamberlain, the Conservative minister of health, as parliamentary secretary from 11 November 1924 to 4 June 1929, forming long-lasting political links with him. One important measure sponsored by Wood was the Summer Time Bill of 1924, and he worked closely with Chamberlain on local government reform. Wood's growing reputation in government circles was reflected in his appointment as a civil commissioner during the general strike of 1926, and as a privy councillor in 1928.

Postmaster-general and minister of health Wood enhanced his reputation with his party by his effectiveness in opposition, following Labour's victory in the general election of 1929. In October 1930 he was elected first chairman of the executive committee of the National Union of Conservative and Unionist Associations, and in that position (which he held until 1932) he co-operated closely with Neville Chamberlain, who was then party chairman. When the National Government was formed under Ramsay MacDonald in 1931 the number of posts available for Conservatives was at first limited, and Wood had to be content with being appointed parliamentary secretary to the president of the Board of Education, Sir Donald Maclean, a Liberal, on 3 September. However, following the general election of that year, Wood achieved ministerial rank on 10 November 1931 when he became postmaster-general, in charge of the General Post Office (GPO), which was then a government department.

The Post Office had been much criticized for some years, especially on account of its telephone service. Wood appointed a committee on Post Office reform in 1932, and implemented its recommendations. These included the appointment in 1934 of a director-general—almost analogous to a managing director—in place of the secretary to the Post Office; the position had been filled by civil servants not noted for their commercial enterprise. Wood's own approach to the Post Office was very much that of a businessman. He established a new relationship with the Treasury whereby, instead of the whole of the Post Office's profits for a year being handed over to the chancellor, as hitherto, a fixed annual contribution was to be made to the exchequer and any surplus profit was to be used to improve the Post Office's services. Wood expanded the telephone service by improving efficiency, lowering charges, and making skilful use of publicity. The film unit and library of the Empire Marketing Board were taken over in 1933, and, as the GPO film unit, achieved a reputation for making documentaries of high quality. Wood's success in making the Post Office a source of pride rather than embarrassment for the government led to his entering the cabinet, at Chamberlain's suggestion, on 20 December 1933.

As postmaster-general Wood was the minister responsible for broadcasting, and he found himself at odds with Sir John Reith, the director-general of the BBC, over the renewal of the BBC's charter, which at the beginning of 1934 had only three more years to run. Reith felt that Wood had given the BBC insufficient protection from pressure from the cabinet to stop a broadcast in 1932 by a former German U-boat captain; Reith wanted a senior cabinet minister, such as the lord president (Baldwin), to be responsible for the BBC, rather than the postmaster-general, to ensure that the BBC's views would be adequately represented. Wood, for his part, was less inclined than his predecessors to agree with the director-general on every question, and Reith's diaries contain a number of uncomplimentary remarks about him. For example, Reith noted that it was 'utterly damnable that the BBC should be made the political catspaw of a little bounder like K.W.' (*Reith Diaries*, 110).

Wood's gifts as an organizer and publicist led to his being appointed chairman of the National Government propaganda committee in 1935, with responsibility for preparing for the forthcoming general election. When Baldwin became prime minister on 7 June 1935 Wood was put in charge of the Ministry of Health, which at that time was responsible for housing as well as the health services in England and Wales. Once more Wood's energy served the government well: the slum clearance programme was pursued with energy, and overcrowding was greatly reduced. There was also a marked improvement in maternal mortality, mainly due to the discovery of antibiotics able to counteract septicaemia, but also because a full-time, salaried midwifery service was created under the Midwives Act of 1936. Shortly after the government embarked upon a rearmament programme in 1936, Sir Thomas Inskip, the minister for co-ordination of defence, told the cabinet that a shortage of building labour threatened to cause delays; Wood said that the Ministry of Health would be prepared to slow down house-building to prevent a rise in prices. On the other hand, he told the cabinet that there was evidence of physical deterioration in the population of some of the special areas and asked that some of the factories which were to be built in connection with rearmament should be located in communities with high unemployment (cabinet minutes, 29 July and 14 Oct 1936, Cabinet Office papers, ser. 23, vol. 85).

Minister of air Wood's standing in his party was recognized in February 1938 when he was unanimously elected grand master of the Primrose League in succession to Baldwin, who had held the office since 1925. By 1938 there was growing discontent in parliament and the aircraft industry with the Air Ministry on account of its failure to maintain parity with the German air force. The secretary of state for air, Viscount Swinton, sat in the House of Lords, and when the air estimates were debated in March, Chamberlain, who had succeeded Baldwin as prime minister, had to defend the Air Ministry from demands for an inquiry into its administration. It was clear that this situation could not continue, and on 16 May Wood was appointed to be Swinton's successor. The new secretary of state had no previous experience of a defence department, but he had shown himself to be a capable minister and he could be relied on to represent the government effectively in the Commons.

The cabinet had approved a new programme, known as Scheme L, for the expansion of the air force in April, when it had authorized the Air Ministry to accept as many aircraft as the British aircraft industry could produce—up to a maximum of 12,000 machines in the next two years. Finance was made freely available; it was in 1938 that the Air Ministry overtook the Admiralty as the major spender among the defence departments. But there were many technical problems to be overcome, and in August, on the eve of the Munich crisis, deliveries of aircraft in Britain were no higher than they had been in May. A more ambitious programme, known as Scheme M, was proposed by the Air Ministry after Munich, but Wood accepted the Treasury's argument that, if Scheme M were revised to concentrate more on fighters and to go slowly on bombers, the strain on the economy would be alleviated. Fighter production in 1939 was three-and-a-half times greater than in 1938, while bomber production was two-and-a-half times greater; overall, the gap between British and German aircraft production had been closed by the time war broke out.

Relations with the aircraft industry were not much easier under Wood than they had been under Swinton, partly because of the Air Ministry's repeated requests for modifications to types in production, but also because of Wood's need to respond to parliamentary criticism of the industry's profits. In 1939 the Air Ministry calculated that if its existing agreement with the Society of British Aircraft Constructors on pricing of contracts was not modified, the average rate of profit on private invested capital would be 21 per cent, whereas the official view was that the maximum should be 15 per cent. In March, Wood announced that the agreement was to be modified, with the effect that the industry agreed to forgo a third of its forecast profits for the year. Despite these difficulties, he appears to have established good personal relations with Sir Charles Bruce-Gardner, the chairman of the Society of British Aircraft Constructors, who served on the secretary of state for air's Industrial Advisory Panel and the Air Council's Committee on Supply.

Chancellor of the exchequer: war finance By the spring of 1940 Wood felt exhausted by his efforts, and on 3 April he changed places with the lord privy seal, Sir Samuel Hoare, and had a brief period as a cabinet minister without departmental responsibility. However, British defeats in Norway later that month led to a debate in the House of Commons on 8 and 9 May, at the end of which the government majority decreased heavily. It fell to Wood, as a candid friend, as well as a senior member of the Conservative Party, to tell Chamberlain that resignation was inevitable. He also advised Churchill not to give way to pressure from those who wanted Lord Halifax to succeed Chamberlain. It is not possible to know if Wood's advice was decisive, but it certainly helped to produce the change of government on 10 May. Two days later, Wood was appointed to be chancellor of the exchequer. The new prime minister, Churchill, was by no means universally popular in the Conservative Party, and was doubtless glad to have the support of someone known to be a friend of Chamberlain.

Wood did not enjoy as prominent a position in the government as is normal for a chancellor of the exchequer. He was not at first a member of the war cabinet, although he was frequently in attendance at its meetings. He became a full member on 3 October 1940, but he was again excluded from its membership in a major reshuffle on 19 February 1942. As someone who had supported appeasement—he was believed to have advised calling a general election after Munich to take advantage of Chamberlain's popularity at the time—Wood was never likely to be close to Churchill. Indeed, he was treated with condescension by a number of Churchill's close associates, including Beaverbrook and Brendan Bracken (Colville, 232). However, the fundamental reason why the chancellor was not prominent in the war cabinet was that under Churchill the Treasury ceased to be the central department of government. Financial budgeting was replaced by the allocation of physical resources, especially manpower, as the means of establishing priorities in defence programmes. Non-military aspects of policy, including economic policy, were co-ordinated by a cabinet committee presided over by the lord president of the council: initially Chamberlain, subsequently Sir John Anderson, and then Clement Attlee. The Treasury's main jobs were to finance the war with as little inflation as possible, to conduct external financial policy so as to secure overseas supplies on the best possible terms, and to take part in planning for the post-war period.

Wood was no financial expert, but his capacity for hard work and his willingness to seek and act upon the best advice available were useful characteristics in a chancellor. At the beginning of July he set up a new consultative council to advise him, and was fortunate in securing the services of the economist John Maynard Keynes and of Lord Catto, a future governor of the Bank of England, as members. His first budget, on 23 July, was criticized, both at the time and subsequently by the official historian of financial policy, on the grounds that his proposals would not prevent an inflationary expansion of the government's short-term debt (Sayers, 56–7). In fact the extra taxation that Wood imposed was rather more than Keynes estimated at the time to be necessary to curb inflation. The standard rate of taxation was increased from 7s. 6d. to 8s. 6d., which, with a top rate of surtax of 9s. 6d. in the pound, gave a top marginal tax rate of 18s. in the pound. A new fiscal instrument, purchase tax, was introduced on articles regarded as luxuries or near-luxuries. In deference to the Labour members of Churchill's coalition, excess profits tax, which had been fixed at 60 per cent in September 1939, was raised to 100 per cent, despite advice from Treasury officials that such a rate would deny businessmen the incentive to economize on resources or take risks with new investment.

Subsequently Wood was won over to Keynes's conception of using national income accounting to estimate the additional revenue that must be raised if there was to be no inflation, rather than (as hitherto) confining the budget to central government revenue and expenditure. A white paper, *An analysis of the sources of war finance and an estimate of the national income and expenditure in 1938 and 1940*, was published in January 1941 and Wood's budget of 7 April 1941 was described by Keynes as 'a revolution in public finance' (*Collected Writings*, 22.354). There were still political limits on how far theory could be applied. Keynes thought that national income analysis showed that upwards of £300 million should be raised in additional taxation but, confronted by Churchill's hostility to what he considered to be severe tax proposals, Wood decided to aim at £250 million. The standard rate of income tax was raised to 10s. in the pound, giving a top marginal rate of 19s. 6d. in the pound, while income and personal allowances were reduced, greatly increasing the number of people liable to income tax. The extension of direct taxation was made politically more acceptable by the adoption of another of Keynes's ideas, post-war credits, so that part of the tax was a form of forced saving. In theory the post-war credits could be repaid to prevent a post-war slump, such as had occurred after the First World War, but in the event inflationary pressure after 1945 made repayments an inconvenient obligation for chancellors.

Also under Wood there began in 1940 the compulsory deduction of income tax at source from wages and salaries. He died on the morning of the day on which he was due to announce the scheme devised in 1943 for PAYE (pay as you earn), whereby tax liability was to be calculated on current, not past, earnings. His innovation was of lasting benefit to future chancellors. Wood's budgets in 1942 and 1943 followed the same lines as his budget of 1941, and overall he raised a significantly higher proportion of war finance through taxation rather than borrowing than his predecessors had done in the First World War.

Wood also sought to moderate wage claims by adopting a policy of subsidizing rationed goods that were within the cost-of-living index, while imposing heavy taxes on goods outside it. In his budget of 1941 he committed the government to stabilizing the index at its existing level, while warning that if wage rates continued to rise, the government would have to abandon this policy. The policy proved to be expensive, the cost of subsidies rising from £70 million in 1940 to £190 million in 1943, but it was thought justified from the industrial relations viewpoint, and was discontinued only gradually after the war.

Wood's period as chancellor saw Britain's external financial position greatly weakened, as gold and foreign exchange reserves were used, and overseas investments sold, to pay for essential imports, while industrial output was shifted from exports to war production. So when the Beveridge report was published at the beginning of December 1942, advocating a comprehensive scheme of social insurance, Wood warned the cabinet against taking on commitments that might exceed the country's resources. He pointed out that after the war it would be necessary to give priority first to maintaining defence forces sufficient to avoid a repetition of the events of 1914 and 1939, and then to reconstructing Britain's economy and export trade. He assumed that there would have to be cuts in tax rates, both to stimulate enterprise and to meet the expectations of the electorate. Beveridge's scheme of social insurance was only one of several reconstruction plans, and there were other pressing claims to financial assistance, such as those of housing, education, electricity, agriculture, forestry, and colonial development; Wood called upon the cabinet to determine priorities ('The financial aspects of the social security plan', memorandum by the chancellor of the exchequer, 11 Jan 1942, Cabinet Office papers, ser. 65, vol. 33). In that respect he was acting as an orthodox chancellor, but he faced a critical and restive House of Commons when, in an emotional debate on 17 February 1943, he emphasized the prevailing financial uncertainty and the need for caution in implementing the Beveridge plan (*Hansard 5C*, cols. 1825–38).

Although the coalition government had declared that it had accepted the principles of the plan, Wood's speech tended to spread doubt about whether the Conservatives were as committed to them as Labour was.

Wood overcame considerable handicaps to rise as far as he did in politics. His modest, nonconformist background was very different from that of traditional Conservative leaders, but was useful at a time when the Conservatives were seeking to attract nonconformists who had previously supported the Liberal Party; for example, in the 1920s Wood organized nonconformist Unionist League luncheons at which Conservative leaders would speak. He was a far from imposing personality: short, plump, and bespectacled. One experienced observer described him as an 'appalling speaker' (Colville, 47); his voice was thin and high, and he often delivered speeches from manuscript notes. On the other hand, he was respected because he was efficient, and was generally liked because he was genial. His successes as a minister can be attributed to his thoroughness, energy, shrewd judgement, and willingness to listen to advice. He inspired loyalty among his staff, and could be relied upon to take whatever decision was necessary and to maintain it, both in cabinet, where his influence was considerable, and in parliament, where he was normally adept at handling criticism. He succeeded Chamberlain as chairman of the Conservative Research Department in 1940, and he was very much missed by the party after his death. He died suddenly at his home in London, 12 Buckingham Palace Mansions, Westminster, on 21 September 1943.   G. C. PEDEN

Sources DNB • *The Times* (22 Sept 1943) • R. Jenkins, *The chancellors* (1998), 393–400 • cabinet minutes, PRO, cabinet office papers, ser. 23, vols. 77–100 • war cabinet minutes, PRO, cabinet office papers, ser. 65, vols. 1–28, 32–5 • budget committee papers, PRO, treasury papers, ser. 171, files 355–6, 360, 363 • secretary of state's private office papers, PRO, Air Ministry papers, ser. 19, vols. 25, 26, 35, 36, 556 • *Hansard 5C* • R. Hawtrey, 'Financial history of the war', PRO, treasury papers, ser. 208, vol. 204 [unpublished] • R. S. Sayers, *Financial policy, 1939–1945* (1956) • J. Colville, *The fringes of power: Downing Street diaries, 1939–1955* (1985) • M. Gilbert, *Winston S. Churchill, 6: Finest hour, 1939–1941* (1983), 300, 308–9 • *The collected writings of John Maynard Keynes*, ed. D. Moggridge and E. Johnson, 22 (1978), 212–15, 353–4 • W. J. Braithwaite, *Lloyd George's ambulance wagon*, ed. H. Bunbury (1957), 96, 168, 211–13 • J. C. W. Reith, *Into the wind* (1949) • *The Reith diaries*, ed. C. Stuart (1975) • J. Ramsden, *The age of Balfour and Baldwin, 1902–1940* (1978) • J. Ramsden, *The age of Churchill and Eden, 1940–1957* (1995) • M. Kinnear, *The fall of Lloyd George* (1973) • M. Cowling, *The impact of labour, 1920–1924: the beginning of modern British politics* (1971)

Archives PRO, corresp. and Air Ministry papers, AIR ser. 19 vols. 25–72, 566 | BLPES, corresp. with Hugh Dalton • Bodl. Oxf., corresp. with Viscount Addison • HLRO, corresp. with Lord Beaverbrook | FILM BFI NFTVA, 'The Rt Hon. Sir Howard Kingsley Wood, MP, postmaster-general', 1963 • BFI NFTVA, documentary footage • BFI NFTVA, news footage • IWM FVA, actuality footage • IWM FVA, news footage

Likenesses W. Stoneman, five photographs, 1921–c.1941, NPG [see illus.] • A. T. Nowell, oils, 1928; formerly in possession of the firm Kingsley Wood, Williams, Murphy, and Ross • photographs, 1936–43, Hult. Arch. • H. Coster, photographs, 1938, NPG

Wealth at death £63,981 9s. 3d.: probate, 20 June 1944, CGPLA Eng. & Wales

Wood, Lady Jessie (1882–1979). *See under* Wood, Sir Henry Joseph (1869–1944).

Wood, Sir Mark, first baronet (1750–1829), army officer and engineer, was born on 16 March 1750, the eldest of five sons and one daughter of Alexander Wood (1712–1778), procurator-fiscal, of Burncroft, Perthshire, and his wife, Jean Ramsay, of Banff. Under the aegis of Sir Archibald Campbell of Inveraray, he became an East India Company cadet and sailed for India on the *Bute* on 6 March 1770; he reached Madras on 14 August 1770. On 17 July 1772, ten days after becoming an ensign, he transferred to the corps of engineers with whom he had been doing duty. Ill health led him to return to Britain in the spring of 1778; he had no intention of going back to India. On 24 January 1779 he was promoted captain and two months later instructed by the secret committee of the East India Company to carry dispatches to India via Egypt. A journal that he was enjoined to write describes his three-month journey to Madras.

From Madras, Wood sailed to Calcutta, where, between 1780 and 1785, he oversaw the ongoing task of surveying the Hooghly River. In 1786 he was appointed surveyor-general of Bengal whereupon he sent to residents and soldiers stationed across India sections of Rennell's map with instructions to explore the countryside, record geographical features, and fill in any blank areas. In Calcutta, on 17 May 1786, Wood married Rachael Dashwood (d. 1802), a daughter of Robert Dashwood of Vellow Wood, Somerset, and Mary Sweeting, and whose brother was doing military service in India. The couple had four children, Alexander (who died aged fifteen by falling from a horse while on military exercise), Mark, Eliza-Georgina, and Rachael. Appointed chief engineer of Bengal in 1788, Wood took his seat on Bengal's military board and set about the maintenance of the recently completed works of Fort William. Until prompted by ill health to leave India for good in 1793, he rarely left Calcutta. He returned to Britain a nabob and with the rumoured £200,000 that he had accumulated in India, he purchased Piercefield estate, Monmouthshire, and shares in the East India Company. As Wood's company salary never exceeded £3700 per annum it appears likely that he acquired his fortune by working privately as an architect and investing in commerce. When presented at court in 1795 he gave George III an expensive ivory model of Fort William.

Wood's election to the Commons in 1794 was encouraged and facilitated by William Pitt and Henry Dundas. He voted with the ministry and, although 'not in the practice of writing long letters' (letter to D. Scott, 15 Aug 1796, BL OIOC, HMS 728, fol. 503), was sometimes consulted by Dundas about Indian affairs. In particular, he represented to Pitt and Dundas the strategic and commercial importance of Malta and, having suggested that the government purchase the island from the knights of St John, he accurately predicted that once the continental powers made peace France would occupy Egypt and threaten British India.

In 1800 Wood acquired his own electoral interest, selling Piercefield and purchasing for £90,000 Gatton Park, Surrey, a pocket borough encompassing 2000 acres where seven electors voted in two MPs. In the Commons he continued to support the ministry, and although he voted in favour of the treaty of Amiens, his dislike of the treaty's (unfulfilled) requirement that Malta be relinquished led to the publication in 1803 of both his earlier letters to Pitt and Dundas and his 1779 travel journal as *The Importance of Malta Considered*. Thereafter he sought position, including the governorships of the Cape, Madras, and Malta, posts to which Dundas did not think him equal; and in 1805 he made an unsuccessful claim for the Roxburghe succession. None the less in recognition of his status as head of an ancient house, the Woods of Largo, and for supporting Portland's administration, on 3 October 1808 he obtained a baronetcy.

The would-be courtier never won the patronage that he sought and Wood retired from the Commons in 1818. After a short illness he died, on 6 February 1829, at his London home, 66 Pall Mall. His niece remembered him as 'the kindest and most affectionate' (Montague, 42) of her many uncles and recalled how in the weeks before his death he took to Bible reading. He was buried on 13 February at Gatton church, Surrey, and was succeeded in his baronetcy by his son, Mark Wood (1794–1837).

BRENDAN CARNDUFF

Sources Mrs Montagu [F. M. Montagu], *Memorials of the family of Wood of Largo* (privately printed, London, 1863) · M. Wood, *The importance of Malta considered in the years 1796 and 1798; and also remarks, which occurred during a journey from England to India, through Egypt, in the year 1779* (1803) · E. W. Brayley, J. Britton, and E. W. Brayley, jun., *A topographical history of Surrey*, 4 (1844) · J. W. Anderson and R. G. Thorne, 'Wood, Mark', HoP, *Commons* · R. G. Thorne, 'Dashwood, James', HoP, *Commons* · GM, 1st ser., 99/1 (1829), 276 · C. E. Buckland, *Dictionary of Indian biography* (1906) · DNB · E. Ingram, *Commitment to empire* (1981) · P. J. Marshall, *East Indian fortunes: the British in Bengal in the eighteenth century* (1976) · *The Faringdon diary*, ed. J. Greig, 2 (1923) · V. C. P. Hodson, *List of officers of the Bengal army, 1758–1834*, 4 vols. (1927–47) · J. Philippart, *East India military calendar*, 1 (1823) · Burke, *Peerage* · biographical index, BL OIOC

Archives BL, Liverpool MSS, Add. MSS 38256, 38261, 38323, 38368 · BL, Anderson MSS, Add. MSS 45430, 45434 · BL OIOC · NA Scot., Melville MSS, GD 51 · NL Scot., Melville MSS

Likenesses J. Comerford, miniature, 1802, repro. in Sothebys catalogue (28 July 1975)

Wood, Marshall (d. 1882). *See under* Wood, Shakspere (1827–1886).

Wood, Mary Anne Everett. *See* Green, Mary Anne Everett (1818–1895).

Wood, Mary Hay (1868–1934), educationist and college head, was born at 267 Camden Road, Holloway, London, on 17 April 1868, the fifth daughter of Arthur John Wood (1821–1896), barrister and secretary to the statute law revision commission, and his wife, Elizabeth Nisbet Nicolson. Educated at North London Collegiate School (1875–86) under Frances Buss, she was the ablest in a family of high achievers and later one of North London Collegiate's most distinguished old pupils. An 1886 Goldsmith's scholar at

Girton College, where her elder sister, Emily Elizabeth Wood, had been a student, Mary Wood gained a lower second in the 1889 classical tripos and the Gibson prize in 1895. In 1905 she completed a London MA thesis, *Plato's Psychology and its Bearing on the Development of the Will*, published in New York in 1907, when she was also awarded a DLitt from Trinity College, Dublin. A love of classics remained paramount throughout her life, and in 1929 she was invited to address the Psychological Congress at Yale on Plato.

Between 1890 and 1891 Mary Wood taught at Blair Lodge School for Boys, Stirlingshire, then returned to North London Collegiate as visiting classics mistress, also teaching part-time at the Clergy Orphans' School in St John's Wood. By 1892 she was at North London Collegiate full time, revered as an outstanding member of staff. In 1904 she became lecturer in pedagogy at St Mary's College, Paddington. Subsequently head of St Mary's training department and later vice-principal, she was an inspirational and charismatic teacher.

In 1908 Mary Wood was appointed principal of the Cambridge Training College for Women, in Wollaston Road, which, although small and financially insecure, had acquired a high reputation since its foundation in 1885 as the first residential training college for women secondary teachers. She was a wise and patient negotiator, seeking to improve opportunities for women in the profession, campaigning for more graduate trainees, and highlighting the need for secondary teacher training. Faced with the continual problem of securing sufficient secondary school placements for teaching practice, Mary Wood defended the college's use of private preparatory schools as unavoidable. This followed criticisms in a 1928 report by HM inspectorate that staff in these establishments had poor academic qualifications. A highly successful administrator, she also found time to lecture and hold personal supervisions. Under her guidance the student intake steadily increased after the First World War. The term 'post-graduate' was added to the college title and its standing was consolidated and enhanced, bringing it into the front rank of teacher training institutions.

Mary Wood retained a large circle of friends and associates. Deeply religious, she was renowned for her scholarship, good advice, and skilful management, her warmth, her unstinting praise for colleagues, and her tremendous capacity for enjoyment. She was an ideal model for prospective teachers to emulate, with no greater tribute to her success than the excellent relationship she enjoyed with her staff. She was a founder, and first chair in 1920, of the Hillcroft College for Working Women, remaining actively involved until her death. A manager of Harrow Road School (1905–8), she was also governor of the Frances Mary Buss and Church Education Corporation schools, and twice president of the Cambridge branch of the British Federation of University Women. She was much involved in the city's activities in Cambridge, particularly those concerning women. A small figure who cycled everywhere fast, physically she changed little over the years; her voice and laughter remained infectious and unmistakable, her handwriting impetuous.

In June 1933 Mary Wood retired from Cambridge and planned to use her £120 retirement gift to travel to India, but in December 1933 discovered she had cancer. Characteristically, she donated the money to the college loan fund for needy students. Mary Wood died on 1 June 1934 at her home, 17 Oval Road, Regent's Park, London, and a memorial service was held at St Mary's, Lancaster Gate, in December. Subsequently the Wood memorial lectures were established in her honour.   JANET SHEPHERD

Sources Principal's reports, Cambridge Training College for Women, 1908–32, Hughes Hall, Cambridge · Annual Reports of Council for the Cambridge Training College for Women, 1908–33, Hughes Hall, Cambridge · Board of Education, returns and corresp., Cambridge Training College for Women, 1908–28, Hughes Hall, Cambridge · *The Times* (4 June 1934) · newsletters, Cambridge Training College for Women Old Students' Gild, 1932–4, Hughes Hall, Cambridge · *Girton Review*, Michaelmas term (1934) · *North London Collegiate School Magazine* (1934) · M. Bottrall, *Hughes Hall, 1885–1985* (1985) · P. Searby, *The training of teachers in Cambridge University: the first sixty years, 1879–1939* (1982) · *The training of women teachers for secondary schools: a series of statements from institutions concerned*, Board of Education (1912) · K. T. Butler and H. I. McMorran, eds., *Girton College register, 1869–1946* (1948) · b. cert. · d. cert.
Archives Hughes Hall, Cambridge
Likenesses R. Sell, crayon drawing, 1994 (after photograph), Hughes Hall, Cambridge · photograph, repro. in *Cambridge Training College for Women Old Students' Gild Newsletter* (1934)
Wealth at death £4633 9s. 9d.: probate, 28 July 1934, CGPLA Eng. & Wales

Wood [*née* Vining], **Matilda Charlotte** [*known as* Mrs John Wood] (*bap.* **1831**, *d.* **1915**), actress and theatre manager, was baptized on 28 November 1831 at St Peter's Church, Liverpool, the second daughter of the actors Henry Vining and Amelia Vining, *née* Quantrell (1803/4–1874) [*see* Vining family]. Despite going on the stage when she was ten, Matilda Vining, whose 'forte was low comedy' (*ILN*, 28 Feb 1885), came to prominence in England only in the late 1860s after gaining a reputation in America, principally in burlesque, and reached the height of her success in the 1880s in farces by Pinero. Her first stage appearance was in 1841 in Brighton. Shortly afterwards she joined a company playing in Southampton, where, on 25 March 1848, she married an actor, John William Wood (*d.* 1863), the son of John Wood, a silversmith; both declared that they were 'of full age'. She thereafter was known as Mrs John Wood. In October 1849 the couple joined John Knowles's company at Manchester Theatre Royal, where Mrs Wood's cousin George J. Vining (1824–1875) was already engaged and where they came to be regarded as the leading comedians. While Mrs Wood played principally 'pert waiting women or the heroines of extravaganzas' (*Manchester Guardian*, 10 May 1853), she also sang, and she exhibited a rare 'sweetness and pathos' when appearing as Ophelia to George Vandenhoff's Hamlet in May 1853 (ibid.).

In August 1854 the Woods sailed for America. Mrs John Wood won immediate acclaim when she appeared in Boston, under Thomas Barry's management, on 11 September 1854, as Gertrude in Planché's *The Loan of a Lover*. She also

Matilda Charlotte Wood (*bap.* 1831, *d.* 1915), by Barraud, pubd 1889

played at Wallack's Theatre, New York, in California, and in New Orleans. Her first experience of management was at the American Theatre, San Francisco, in 1859. Her husband, from whom she had separated, died in May 1863. Again undertaking management she reopened Laura Keene's theatre in New York on 8 October 1863 as the Olympic. Among other roles she played Jenny Leatherlungs in the burlesque *Jenny Lind at Last*. Her management lasted three years.

Mrs Wood's London début was on 12 November 1866 at the Princess's Theatre, then managed by George Vining, as Miss Miggs in a dramatization of Dickens's novel *Barnaby Rudge*. Here, too, she created the part of Pocahontas in *La Belle Sauvage*. After a further visit to America she leased the St James's Theatre, London, which had been closed for ten months, and opened it on 16 October 1869 with *She Stoops to Conquer*. A month later *La Belle Sauvage* began its 197-night run; there were successful productions also of John Poole's *Paul Pry*, *Fernande* (in which Fanny Brough made her London début), *Anne Bracegirdle*, and *Jenny Lind at Last*.

In 1872 Mrs Wood sub-let the St James's and went again to America, but returned to London a year later to appear at the Queen's Theatre on 15 November 1873 as Philippa Chester in Charles Reade's *The Wandering Heir*, at the opening of the Criterion Theatre on 21 March 1874 in the title role in H. J. Byron's *The American Lady*, and at the Gaiety as Mistress Page in *The Merry Wives of Windsor*. After a further

spell of management at the St James's she played in 1879–81 at the Haymarket and Criterion theatres, then appeared in central roles in a number of plays by Pinero at the Royal Court. When the Royal Court was rebuilt in 1888 she undertook the management herself, although she leased the theatre in partnership with Arthur Chudleigh. It opened on 24 September, when Mrs Wood's daughter Florence (whose father was 'Stephen Fiske, gentleman') played the title part in *Hermine*. Among the successes of Mrs Wood's nine-year management were Pinero's *The Cabinet Minister* and the farces *Aunt Jack* and *The Volcano* by Ralph Lumley (1865–1900), who married Florence in 1890.

Mrs Wood refused ever to give an interview, believing that 'artists should be silent off stage' (*The Sketch*, 10 Oct 1894). On stage, however 'her intelligence and experience made the most of a strong natural humour' (*The Times*, 13 Jan 1915). A pen portrait of her in 1874, which praised her as the 'Queen of comedy and song', commented: 'To a piquant chic peculiarly French and derived doubtless from the Quantrells—her ancestors upon the mother's side—she adds a frank-hearted humour … [She is] a female Charles Mathews' (*ILN*, 1874).

Mrs Wood's final years on the stage were spent principally in minor comic roles at the Theatre Royal, Drury Lane. In 1905 she played the part of Margaret Neilson for 105 performances there in Hall Caine's *The Prodigal Son*. Her last appearance was at the Ellen Terry jubilee celebration matinée, again at Drury Lane, on 12 June 1906, with Gertrude Kingston (1866–1937) and Genevieve Ward (1838–1922) as 'seats on the bench' in Gilbert and Sullivan's *Trial by Jury*. She died on 11 January 1915 at her home, Dilkoosha, Spencer Road, Birchington, Kent, and was buried on 16 January at the parish church.

C. M. P. TAYLOR

Sources J. Parker, ed., *Who's who in the theatre* (1912) • C. E. Pascoe, ed., *The dramatic list*, 2nd edn (1880) • W. Macqueen-Pope, *St James's: theatre of distinction* (1958) • *Thanet Times* (15 Jan 1915) • *The Times* (14 Jan 1915) • *Margate, Ramsgate and Isle of Thanet Gazette* (16 Jan 1915) • 'Mrs John Wood', *ILN* (1874) [undated cutting in file at Theatre Museum, London] • 'Mrs John Wood', *The Sketch* (10 Oct 1894) • playbills from the Theatre Royal, Manchester, 1849–54, Man. CL, Arts Library • file on Mrs Wood, Theatre Museum, London [includes numerous cuttings of reviews] • files for the Court Theatre, London, 1880s and 1890s, Theatre Museum, London • Hall, *Dramatic ports.* • W. Archer, *The theatrical 'World' of 1895* (1896) • T. A. Brown, *History of the American stage* (1870) • m. cert. • m. cert. [Ralph Robert Lumley to Florence Fiske, 5 July 1890, St Paul's, Knightsbridge, London] • IGI • d. cert.

Archives Theatre Museum, London, file

Likenesses Hanley, portrait, 1855 • portrait, 1858 (with Mr Wood), Harvard TC • Barraud, photograph, pubd 1889, NPG [*see illus.*] • eleven portraits, Harvard TC • photograph, repro. in 'Mrs John Wood', *The Sketch*

Wealth at death £19,700 9s. 4d.: probate, 22 Feb 1915, CGPLA Eng. & Wales

Wood, Sir Matthew, first baronet (1768–1843), druggist and politician, was born at Tiverton on 2 June 1768, the eldest of the ten children of William Wood (1738–1809), serge maker, and his wife, Catherine, *née* Cluse (*d.* 1798). Matthew, who was brought up as a dissenter, received a brief education at Blundell's Grammar School at Tiverton, but was soon obliged to assist his ailing father. At the age of fourteen he was apprenticed to his first cousin, Mr Newton, a chemist and druggist of Fore Street, Exeter, and five years later took employment as traveller for an Exeter wholesale druggist. Early in 1790 he moved to London to travel for Crawley and Adcock of Bishopsgate, and about two years later joined a new partnership set up by Adcock and others in Devonshire Square. This arrangement was short-lived and at its dissolution he set up a similar business for himself in Cross Street, in the rather poor district of Clerkenwell. In 1796 he married Maria (c.1770–1848), daughter of John Page, surgeon and apothecary, of Woodbridge, Suffolk. They raised three sons: John (later Sir John) Page Wood [see below], William Page *Wood (later lord chancellor and Baron Hatherley), and Western Wood [see below]; and two daughters: Maria, who married Edwin Maddy of Matson House, Gloucestershire, and Catherine, who married Charles Stephens of Earley Court, Reading.

From 1801 Matthew Wood was based at Falcon Square, Cripplegate, where in 1802 he invested £2000 in a patent to produce a colouring matter for beer. Also in 1802 Wood became by redemption a freeman and liveryman of the Fishmongers' Company and he was elected to the common council for the ward of Cripplegate Without. In 1804 he entered a partnership with Colonel Edward Wigan, trading as hop merchants in Southwark. When he retired from business in 1842 his son Western succeeded to his father's share, the firm being thereafter known as Wood, Field, and Hanbury. In 1807, while Wood was staying with his brother in Ireland, the incumbent Cripplegate alderman died. Wood was subsequently elected, and in 1809 he was chosen as one of the two sheriffs of London and Middlesex. In this office it befell him to execute the speaker's warrant for the arrest of Sir Francis Burdett, with whose political views he sympathized.

Wood was lord mayor of London in the troublesome period of 1815–16, and in 1816 had to calm one of the most serious outbursts against government repression. A huge public meeting at Spa Fields got out of hand and the crowd streamed into the City. Wood sympathized with their demands, but did his civic duty, confronting them by the Royal Exchange, where he persuaded them to disperse. The new city barge, built in 1816, was named the *Maria Wood* after his daughter. He achieved the rare distinction of being re-elected lord mayor in 1816–17, although the government was so hostile towards him that no ministers attended either of his mayoral banquets. During his second year of office Wood saved three Irishmen, allegedly victims of a police conspiracy, from execution, receiving the public thanks of the corporation of Dublin. He took a leading part in many city improvements, and gained popularity for the way in which he promoted resistance to repressive government measures and for his campaign against the London underworld. He laid the foundation of a new debtors' prison in Whitecross Street, and encouraged the construction of the new London Bridge and formation of the Post Office. In 1817 Wood was elected MP for the City of London and held the seat until his death,

though in 1826 he came bottom of the list of elected candidates, having declared in favour of Catholic emancipation. He was a consistent radical and a strenuous supporter of all whig ministries.

Wood was one of the chief friends and counsellors of Queen Caroline. When George IV came to the throne in 1820 he initiated divorce proceedings against his long-estranged wife, but she determined to return to England to fight the divorce and take her place as queen. Wood and his son William went to France to meet her and escorted her back to a triumphant entry into London on 6 June 1820, where she became the focus of popular radical sentiment. The king was obliged to seek a parliamentary divorce, through his tory ministers: this and popular perception of Caroline as a wronged woman led to the curious phenomenon of a radical movement in support of a member of the royal family. William acted as his father's interpreter when they went to Italy to gather evidence to rebut the accusations which had been laid against Caroline; she resided first at Wood's house in South Audley Street and he was one of the corporation that presented her with an address of sympathy on 16 June. He and the then lord mayor went to greet her at Temple Bar on 29 November, when she attended St Paul's to give thanks for the failure of the proceedings against her. Wood's many detractors considered that he was simply taking advantage of the publicity surrounding Caroline's actions in order to further his own radical ambitions; certainly she cared little for his political views and when she moved to Brandenburg House, in Hammersmith, no longer needed him as a champion. His actions on her behalf had, however, attracted the attention of Elizabeth, the maiden sister of an unrelated James Wood, banker, of Gloucester, to whom Matthew Wood was later introduced. Elizabeth left him at her death, about 1823, a house in Gloucester, and on the banker's death in 1836 the residue of his property was shared among his four executors, Matthew Wood being one. The will was disputed but maintained, and Wood received over £100,000, including the estate of Hatherley in Gloucestershire.

Wood was also a member of the committee administering the finances of the duke of Kent on behalf of his creditors, and he urged the duke and duchess to return to England for the birth of their child, with the result that the future Queen Victoria was born on English rather than foreign soil. When as queen she dined at the Guildhall on 9 November 1837 it was announced that the first title which she conferred would be a baronetcy for Matthew Wood, a gift understood to have been bestowed through personal friendship.

Wood was chief among the six Fishmongers who from August 1832 presided over the revival of Fishmongers' Hall and other Fishmongers' properties affected by construction of the new London Bridge. He was later chairman of the House of Commons committee on metropolitan improvements. In 1834 a group of radical MPs formed the Westminster Club in a house belonging to him at 34 Great George Street. This was the forerunner of the Reform Club.

Wood died at the residence of his son-in-law, Matson House, near Gloucester, on 26 September 1843, and was buried in a vault in Hatherley churchyard on 30 September. His widow died at Ramsgate on 2 July 1848.

Wood's eldest son, **Sir John Page Wood**, second baronet (1796–1866), was born at Woodbridge, Suffolk, on 25 August 1796. He was educated at Winchester College and graduated LLB from Trinity College, Cambridge, in 1821. He took his freedom in the Fishmongers' Company in 1818, and on 16 February 1820 married Emma Caroline (1802–1879), who had been born in Lisbon in 1802, the youngest daughter of Sampson Michell of Croft West, Kanwyn, Cornwall, an admiral in the Portuguese service. They raised a large family of five sons, the youngest being General Sir Evelyn *Wood, and six daughters, one of whom was Katharine *Parnell (Kitty O'Shea). Lady Wood was an accomplished artist and the author of many novels. In June 1821 Wood was ordained deacon, having in 1820 entered the service of Queen Caroline as her chaplain and private secretary; he was present at her death on 7 August 1821, afterwards escorting her body to Brunswick for burial.

From 1821 to 1843 Wood was chaplain to the duke of Sussex. The corporation of London appointed him to the rectory of St Peter's, Cornhill, in 1824, and in 1833 he was instituted to the vicarage of Cressing in Essex. He made his home at Rivenhall Place, and became very popular in north Essex where he was recognized as a whig champion and a strong Liberal supporter. An able, eloquent speaker, he was for twenty-five years chairman of the Braintree board of guardians and for twenty-two years chairman of the Witham magistrates' bench. In this role he dealt effectively in 1848 with the notorious 'Coggeshall gang' of thirteen burglars who so terrified their victims that none was prepared to testify against them; consequently the evidence was extremely vague, and Sir John was the only magistrate willing to commit them for trial. Even he feared the outcome if they were freed, and was relieved that they were duly found guilty and sentenced. He died at his son-in-law's house, Belhus, Aveley, near Romford, on 21 February 1866 and was buried at Cressing. His widow died at Belhus on 15 December 1879.

Western Wood (1804–1863), Sir Matthew Wood's third son, was born on 4 January 1804 at Falcon Square, in the City of London. On 16 June 1829 he married Sarah Letitia (d. 1870), youngest daughter of John Morris, a former Bombay civil servant. He was in partnership with his father as a hop merchant, the firm trading as Wood, Field, and Wood of Mark Lane, and on his father's retirement in 1842 obtained his share. He, too, was a freeman of the Fishmongers' Company. From 29 July 1861 until his death he was MP for the City of London, and for many years sat as a magistrate for Kent. He died at North Cray Place, Kent, on 17 May 1863.   ANITA McCONNELL

Sources E. A. Smith, *A queen on trial: the affair of Queen Caroline* (1993) • V. Hope, *My lord mayor* (1989), 136–8 • J. J. Baddeley, *The aldermen of Cripplegate ward* (1900) • G. W. Thornbury and E. Walford, *Old and new London: a narrative of its history, its people, and its places*, 6 vols. (1873–8), vol. 3, pp. 279–309, 318–20, 326 • C. Welch and P. Norman, *Modern history of the City of London* (1896) • B. B. Orridge, *Some account of the citizens of London and their rulers, from 1060 to 1867* (1867) • J. Nightingale, *Memoirs … of Queen Caroline* (1820) • *GM*, 2nd ser., 20 (1843), 541–4 • *GM*, 2nd ser., 30 (1848), 221 [death notice of Maria Wood] • *GM*, 3rd ser., 14 (1863), 810 [Western Wood] • *GM*, 4th ser., 1 (1866), 456, 585–7 [John Page Wood] • P. Metcalf, *The halls of the Fishmongers' Company* (1977), 118 • T. W. Lacqueux, 'The Queen Caroline affair: politics as art in the reign of George IV', *Journal of Modern History*, 54 (1982), 417–66 • d. cert. • d. cert. [John Page Wood] • d. cert. [Western Wood]

Likenesses R. Dighton, caricature, etching, 1819, NPG • R. Dighton, etchings, pubd 1819, BM, NPG • possibly T. Lane, line engraving, pubd 1821, BM, NPG • A. W. Devis, oils, NPG • R. Dighton, etching (after his earlier work), NPG • G. Hayter, group portrait, oils (*The Trial of Queen Caroline, 1820*), NPG • caricature, etching, NPG • cartoons, repro. in Lacqueux, 'The Queen Caroline affair'

Wealth at death under £6000—John Page Wood: probate, 1866, *CGPLA Eng. & Wales* • under £120,000—Western Wood: will with three codicils, 8 Aug 1863, *CGPLA Eng. & Wales*

Wood, Nicholas (1795–1865), civil and mining engineer, was born at the farm of Daniel at Sourmires in the parish of Ryton, co. Durham, on 24 April 1795, the son of Nicholas Wood, tenant farmer. He was of a delicate constitution in early life, and lived with his uncle at Hallgarth, near Winlaton. As a pupil at the village school in Crawcrook, his abilities were so marked as to attract the attention of his father's landlord, Sir Thomas Liddell (later first Baron Ravensworth). It was to Liddell's collieries in Killingworth, Northumberland, that Wood was sent in April 1811 to learn the business of a viewer or colliery manager.

George Stephenson was also at Killingworth at that time. He was fourteen years older than Wood, and the two were soon drawn into a lasting friendship by their common interests and ambitions. It was a tribute to Stephenson's opinion of him that his son Robert was apprenticed to Wood from 1819 to 1821 at Killingworth. Wood assisted Stephenson in the development of his safety lamp, which was first tested in 1815. He was closely associated with Stephenson in his experiments with steam locomotives, and in 1821 accompanied him to Darlington, where they met Edward Pease and discussed the projected Stockton–Darlington railway line.

As a result of his experience and observations Wood was able to publish in 1825 *A Practical Treatise on Rail-Roads, and Interior Communication in General*, a classic work of early railway literature, in which he discussed the various types of 'motive power' then in use: self-acting planes, fixed steam-engine planes, horses, and locomotive steam engines. The work appeared in three subsequent editions, in 1831, 1832, and 1838, considerably enlarged and brought up to date. In 1827 Wood's reputation in railway matters was such that he was invited to give evidence before committees of both houses of parliament on the Liverpool and Manchester Railway Bill. In 1829 he was one of the three judges for the Rainhill locomotive trials on the Liverpool and Manchester Railway, won by the Stephensons' *Rocket*. In 1845 he joined the 'battle of the gauges', taking sides with the Stephensons and the 'narrow-gauge' lobby.

Wood's knowledge of coal mining and the geology of

the north of England coalfields was such that his assistance was frequently called upon by mine owners and speculators, and he acquired interests in a number of mines in the area. Until 1844 he lived at Killingworth, but he then moved to Hetton Hall, co. Durham, and assumed the management of the collieries belonging to the Hetton Coal Company, in which he was a partner. He took a prominent part in official investigations of the coal industry, most notably with regard to safety. He reported to the select committee on accidents in 1835 that using men instead of children would, in many cases, mean that collieries could not be worked at a profit. He contributed to improvements in underground haulage technology, and was involved in the discussions leading to the Mines Inspection Act of 1851. In 1855 he examined all the candidates for the new mining inspectorate.

Wood was elected the first president of the North of England Institute of Mining Engineers (to which he subsequently read many papers) on its formation at Newcastle in 1852. He became a member of the institutions of Civil Engineers (1829) and Mechanical Engineers (1858), and a fellow of the Geological Society (1843) and the Royal Society (1864). Critical of the Royal School of Mines and its failure to link theory with mining practice, he attempted to establish a college of his own in the north-east in the 1850s, 'for the improvement and teaching of mining science, especially as applicable to coal mines' (C. Knight, *The English Cyclopaedia*, 1856). This unfortunately failed because of lack of financial support. Wood's most prominent characteristics were plain, practical good sense, perseverance in his pursuits, thoroughness in his investigations, and an equanimity of temper. Wood married Maria Forster, daughter of Collingwood Forster Lindsay of Alnwick, clerk to the magistrates of Northumberland. He and his wife had four sons and three daughters; but Wood was a widower some years before his own death on 19 December 1865 at 49 Sussex Gardens, Hyde Park, London. He was buried in the churchyard at Hetton.

RONALD M. BIRSE, rev.

Sources T. Doubleday, 'Memoir of the late Nicholas Wood, esq', *Transactions of the North of England Institute of Mining Engineers*, 15 (1866), 49–59 · *PICE*, 31 (1870–71), 236–8 · *The Engineer* (22 Dec 1865), 415 · *The Engineer* (12 Jan 1866), 37 · *PRS*, 16 (1867–8), lxi–lxiii · R. Church, *The history of the British coal industry, 1830–1931* (1986) · R. Welford, *Men of mark 'twixt Tyne and Tweed*, 3 vols. (1895) · Boase, *Mod. Eng. biog.* · 'Select committee on accidents in mines', *Parl. papers* (1835), vol. 5, no. 603

Archives GS Lond., maps · Northumbd RO, Newcastle upon Tyne, papers | National Railway Museum, York, report on Great Western Railway

Wealth at death under £400,000: probate, 19 Feb 1866, *CGPLA Eng. & Wales*

Wood, Paul Hamilton (1907–1962), cardiologist, was born on 16 August 1907 at Coonoor, India, the second son of Richard Boardman Wood, civil servant, and Geraldine, daughter of Alfred Tomson, land agent. After his early education at Yardley Court, Tonbridge, Kent, Wood's father retired to Tasmania and Wood continued his education at Launceston College, Tasmania (1920–24), and Trinity College, University of Melbourne (1924–31). He

excelled at sports but seems not to have displayed any outstanding academic ability at that time; a contemporary described him as 'busy … in the cultivation of friendships and the enjoyment of life' (*Medical Journal of Australia*, 683–4). Certainly he needed two attempts to complete his final examinations before qualifying MB, BS, in 1931, and he subsequently failed to obtain a house appointment in Melbourne. He served as house physician and house surgeon at Christchurch Hospital, New Zealand, between 1931 and 1932.

In 1933 Wood returned to England, obtained a house-physician post at the Brompton Hospital in London, and passed the examination for membership of the Royal College of Physicians. He had still not shown himself to be in any way out of the ordinary and was uncertain about his next move. On 29 December 1934 he married Elizabeth (Betty) Josephine, daughter of John Guthrie, senior surgeon at the Christchurch Hospital, New Zealand; they had two sons and a daughter. About the same time Wood contemplated applying for an appointment at the National Hospital for Nervous Diseases. No such appointment was available but he met a fellow Australian who was resident medical officer at the National Heart Hospital and was looking for a *locum tenens*. Wood took the job and began a rise to eminence in cardiology for which only the hackneyed adjective 'meteoric' seems appropriate. In 1935 he was invited by Francis Fraser to be one of his assistants, with full clinical and teaching duties, at the newly founded postgraduate medical school at Hammersmith Hospital, and in 1937 he was appointed physician to outpatients at the National Heart Hospital. At the outbreak of the Second World War, Wood was given charge of an Emergency Medical Service unit at Mill Hill for the investigation and treatment of effort syndrome; he proved, for the first time, that this was a psychosomatic disorder. In 1940 he was awarded his MD by Melbourne University and in the same year he was elected fellow of the Royal College of Physicians, where he was Goulstonian lecturer in 1941 and Croonian lecturer in 1958. He became consultant cardiologist at the Hammersmith postgraduate medical school in 1941. In 1942 Wood joined the Royal Army Medical Corps. He served in north Africa and Italy, reaching the rank of brigadier, and in 1946 he was appointed OBE.

After the war Wood returned to the Hammersmith as physician and senior lecturer, but he gave up this appointment in 1948, owing to increased responsibilities at the National Heart Hospital—he had become dean and director of its newly formed Institute of Cardiology in 1947. He was also appointed cardiologist at the Brompton Hospital and it was at these two institutions that he spent the remainder of his career; he also maintained a private consultant practice.

By the late 1940s Wood was already held in high regard by his peers but it was the publication of his book *Diseases of the Heart and Circulation* (1950) which established his international reputation. Many other publications followed, mostly on those types of heart disease which could be treated surgically. He lectured throughout the world but it was at bedside teaching sessions that his unusual gifts of perception, analysis, and exposition were most prominently displayed. His ability to determine the exact nature of a patient's symptoms, by close questioning together with the sharpness of his eyes, the sensitivity of his fingers, and the acuity of his hearing, meant that he could acquire the maximum information from an encounter with a patient. These skills, together with an unusually rapid speed of thought and the ability to present his findings in precise and lucid English, were the basis of his reputation as a teacher. He was particularly noted for his ability to relate clinical findings to data obtained by investigations such as cardiac catheterization. To be able to interpret, in terms of disordered physiology, what could be seen, felt, or heard on examination was a skill which many learnt from Wood. Supreme at the bedside, he was never an experimentalist and his only weakness was his lack of formal training in physiology, which he himself lamented. Certainly some of his accounts of pathophysiology, outside his own particular field, verged on the simplistic.

Physically Wood was short, with a rather ascetic appearance but with what was described as an 'impish' sense of humour. In debate he was forthright and he was certainly not always a comfortable colleague; he could make provocative, or even mischievous, interventions in discussions. Delighting in, and perhaps a little vain of, his speed of thought, with which he could appraise a new concept or demolish a weak argument, he could give offence to some who were struggling to keep up with him. Yet any tension was often dissolved by laughter and he was also described as having a warm, endearing personality.

Such little time as Wood had for relaxation he devoted to his home and garden, and he could apply his mind to a garden catalogue as assiduously as to a case history. Fishing near his country house, Fair Lady Lodge, West Runton, Norfolk, was another leisure pursuit. A cigarette smoker before the medical profession was fully aware of its hazards, he succumbed to a smoking-related disease. He had a heart attack while at work and made it clear that, if he were to suffer a cardiac arrest, resuscitation was not to be attempted. Wood died in the Middlesex Hospital, London, on 13 July 1962, survived by his wife and children. A memorial service was held at All Souls, Langham Place, London, on 30 July.   PETER R. FLEMING

Sources M. Campbell, 'Paul Wood', *British Heart Journal*, 24 (1962), 661–6 · E. G. Dimond, ed., 'Paul Wood revisited', *American Journal of Cardiology*, 30 (1972), 121–96 [with bibliography] · Munk, *Roll* · M. Campbell, 'The National Heart Hospital, 1857–1957', *British Heart Journal*, 20 (1958), 137–9 · *Medical Journal of Australia*, 2 (1962), 683–4 · *BMJ* (28 July 1962), 262–4 · *The Lancet* (28 July 1962), 205–6 · *American Heart Journal*, 66 (1963), 577–8 · private information (2004) · *WWW* · *Medical Directory* (1962) · m. cert.
Archives Royal Brompton Hospital, London, clinical case notes · Wellcome L., corresp., personalia, papers relating to lecture tours | FILM priv. coll., videotape about Wood
Likenesses photograph, repro. in Campbell, 'Paul Wood' · photographs, repro. in Dimond, ed., 'Paul Wood revisited'
Wealth at death £51,161 4s.: probate, 8 Nov 1962, CGPLA Eng. & Wales

Wood, Robert (1621/2–1685), mathematician, born at Peper Harow, near Godalming in Surrey, was the son of Robert Wood (d. 1661), rector of Peper Harow. He was educated at Eton College, and was taught mathematics by William Oughtred at Aldbury, Surrey. He matriculated from New Inn Hall, Oxford, on 3 July 1640 and obtained one of the Eton postmasterships at Merton College in 1642. He graduated BA on 18 March 1647, and MA on 14 July 1649, and, 'being both godly and every way able' (Green, 252), was elected a fellow of Lincoln College, by order of the parliamentary visitors, on 19 September 1650, in the place of Thankfull Owen, who had been appointed president of St John's College. Wood also became a member of the Experimental Philosophy Club, and later attended the meetings of James Harrington's Rota Club.

After studying physic for six years, Wood was licensed to practise by convocation on 10 April 1656. His main interest, however, appears to have been in economic problems. During the winter of 1655–6 he wrote the tract *Ten to One*, in which he argued that economic benefits would follow if the monetary system was decimalized. In 1656 Wood was sent to Ireland by Henry Cromwell, possibly as a result of the interest caused by *Ten to One*. Along with his friend William Petty and others he developed an interest in the factors causing Ireland's monetary crisis. Wood himself got into a debate with William Potter on the nature of bullion; Wood believed that it had an intrinsic value, while Potter took the view that, like any other commodity, it had no inherent value. Wood's interest in the political economy of Ireland extended beyond its monetary system. During his time there he worked on agricultural matters, specifically clover husbandry, and on the history of trades. He also had some involvement in Henry Cromwell's plans to establish a college in Dublin, and visited Oxford in 1657 carrying Cromwell's request for the loan of Oxford's statutes which were intended to be used as a model for the university in Dublin.

On his return to England, Wood was appointed professor of mathematics at Durham College, founded by Oliver Cromwell in 1657; however, he does not appear to have taken up the post. On the Restoration he was dismissed from his fellowship at Lincoln College and returned to Ireland, where he became chancellor of the diocese of Meath. He purchased an estate in Ireland, which he later sold in order to buy one at Shenfield in Essex. On his return to England he became mathematical master at Christ's Hospital, but after some years he resigned and returned to Ireland, where he was made a commissioner of the revenue, and finally accountant-general. He held this office until his death, in Dublin, on 9 April 1685. He was buried in St Michael's Church, Dublin. He had married a Miss Adams; they had three daughters.

Wood, who was elected a fellow of the Royal Society on 6 April 1681, also wrote *A new al-moon-ac for ever, or, A rectified account of time* (1680), and *The times mended, or, A rectified account of time by a new luni-solar year: the true way to number our days* (1681). In these works, which were dedicated to the Order of the Garter, and sometimes accompanied by a single folio sheet entitled 'Novus annus luni-solaris', he proposed that the first day of the month should always be within a day of the change of the moon, while by a system of compensations the length of the year should be kept within a week of the period of rotation round the sun. Wood translated the greater part of Oughtred's *Clavis mathematica* into English (1652). He published two papers in the *Philosophical Transactions* in 1681.

E. I. CARLYLE, rev. MICHAEL BEVAN

Sources A. Wood, *The history and antiquities of the University of Oxford*, ed. J. Gutch, 2 vols. in 3 pts (1792–6) • Wood, *Ath. Oxon.* • Foster, *Alum. Oxon.* • O. Manning and W. Bray, *The history and antiquities of the county of Surrey*, 2 (1809), 38; 3 (1814) • P. Morant, *The history and antiquities of the county of Essex*, 2 vols. (1768) • V. Green, *The commonwealth of Lincoln College, 1427–1977* (1979), 251–5 • C. Webster, *The great instauration: science, medicine and reform, 1626–1660* (1975), 416–20, 449–54
Archives University of Sheffield Library, letters and papers | BL, corresp. with Sir William Petty

Wood, Robert (1716/17–1771), traveller and classical scholar, was probably born in the manse at Summerhill, co. Meath, where his father, Alexander James Wood (1683–1747), who came from Dunmurry, co. Antrim, was the Presbyterian minister. Few details are known of Wood's early life and education. Robert Adam suggested something of his background: 'For his Birth is Irish, His Education is part Scotch and his improvements he made in Holland, in France and Italy' (NA Scot., GD 18/4785). Elsewhere Adam refers to Wood as 'a surgeon lad at Glasgow' (Fleming, 248). What is known for certain is that Wood was a third-year student at the University of Glasgow in 1732. By 1736 he was a member of the Middle Temple, and in July 1738 he was recorded at the University of Padua. Around that period he was probably working as a 'travelling tutor' and, according to Horace Walpole, was 'an excellent classic scholar' (Walpole, *Memoirs*, 289).

In October 1741 Wood was in Paris. In 1742 he visited Venice, Constantinople, Mitylene, and Scio. On 5 February 1743 he sailed from Latakia in Syria for Damietta in Egypt. By January 1745 he had been in Rome for some time acting as private secretary to an Irishman, Joseph Leeson (later first earl of Milltown). In October of that year Leeson had contact with a knowledgeable connoisseur and collector, John Bouverie, whose future, along with that of his friend James Dawkins, was to become entwined with Wood's.

Wood had known Bouverie and Dawkins from previous travels in France and Italy. During 1749 they probably planned a tour of the eastern Mediterranean and invited Wood to join them. Their particular interest lay in ancient architecture. Wood had already seen most of the ancient sites they intended to visit and considered his future companions well suited to the enterprise. They spent the winter of 1749–50 in Rome preparing for the expedition. Giovanni Battista Borra, a Piedmontese architect, was engaged as draughtsman. As Wood wrote, they chartered the *Matilda* from London and had her equipped with 'a library, consisting chiefly of all the Greek historians and poets, some books of antiquities, and the best voyage writers' (Wood, *The Ruins of Palmyra*, 'To the reader'). On 5 May 1750 they departed from Naples on a voyage during which they 'visited most of the islands of the Archipelago, part

of Greece in Europe; the Asiatic and European coasts of the Hellespont, Propontis, and Bosphorus, as far as the Black-sea, most of the inland parts of Asia Minor, Syria, Phoenicia, Palestine and Egypt' (ibid.). During their travels Wood revisited the area of the Troad and, delighting in 'poetic geography', they 'spent a fortnight with great pleasure in making a map of the Scamandrian plain with Homer in our hands' (ibid.). His interest in the Homeric question had begun in his youth and resulted in his influential *Essay on the Original Genius and Writings of Homer with a Comparative View of the Ancient and Present State of the Troade* (published posthumously in 1775). The *Essay* evolved from a letter to Dawkins (c.1755) and had been published privately in 1767 and in 1769. Wood's most influential contribution was his argument in favour of the historical accuracy of Homer's works and his observation that the landscape and customs recorded in the epics were still to be observed in their original settings. This he considered testified to the poet's genius in capturing both. He argued strongly in favour of the now generally accepted theory that Homer's works were part of an oral tradition. The *Essay*, which appeared in German (1773), was enthusiastically reviewed by Heine. Other editions appeared in French, Italian, and Spanish, and the work was pirated in Dublin.

After their adventures in the Troad the expedition continued and reached Guzel Hissar where Bouverie, who served as its archaeologist, died on 19 September 1750. The depleted party continued. They eventually arrived in Egypt on 4 November 1750 where nearly six weeks were spent measuring the pyramids and drawing plans which it was hoped to publish at a later date. They set out for Athens by ship, were blown off course, and arrived at Haifa. By 23 February 1751 they had arrived in Damascus. On 6 March they left for Palmyra, having hired a troop of horse to guard the expedition, and arrived on 14 March. During the five clear days they spent there (according to Dawkins's diary, the official record of the expedition, now in the Joint Library of the Hellenic and Roman Societies) they measured and drew plans of the ancient buildings and recorded details of inscriptions in the city. The drawings are now in the Mellon Centre of British Art, Yale University; private collections; the drawings collection of the Royal Institute of British Architects; and the Joint Library of the Hellenic and Roman Societies. The party then set out for Baalbek, ancient Heliopolis, where between 24 and 29 March again they measured, drew, made plans of the classical buildings, and recorded inscriptions. By May 1751 they were in Athens with James 'Athenian' Stuart and Nicholas Revett. On 7 June they left for England where they arrived in the autumn.

The expedition to the Near East resulted in two books written by Wood which stand at the beginning of a tradition to which other writers on archaeology in the second half of the eighteenth century would aspire: *The Ruins of Palmyra, otherwise Tedmor in the Desart* (1753), and *The Ruins of Balbec, otherwise Heliopolis in Coelosyria* (1757). Wood's working practices followed the example of Antoine

Desgodetz's *Les édifices antiques de Rome* (1682). In each work Wood presented a series of accurate drawings and measured plans of classical buildings from the two almost forgotten cities. He allowed the reader to reach his own conclusions as to the merit of the architecture. Horace Walpole wrote:

> But of all the works that distinguish this age, none perhaps excell those beautiful editions of Balbec and Palmyra … The modest descriptions prefixed are standards of writing: The exact measure of what should and should not be said, and of what was necessary to be known.   (Walpole, *Anecdotes*, 1.xiv)

The books were popular. *Palmyra* appeared in French editions in 1753, 1819, and 1829, and *Balbec* in 1757. A combined edition of the two works appeared in English in 1827. The works brought previously unknown remains to public attention and had a profound effect on classical taste in England. Their influence was reflected in the work of contemporary architects notably in the famous ceilings by Robert Adam at Osterley and Syon. Wood's reputation as a scholar was established. He was elected a member of the Society of Dilettanti in 1763 and became the main force behind the society's archaeological programme. He drew up its instructions for Richard Chandler's expedition to Asia Minor. It has also been suggested that he was the author of the text of Thomas Major's *Ruins of Paestum* (1768).

By March 1753 Wood was in Paris with Francis Egerton, third duke of Bridgewater, at the beginning of a grand tour through France and Italy during which the seeds of his future political career may have been sown. While he was in Rome, Wood's circle included Robert Adam, the abbé Peter Grant, and the Scottish artist Allan Ramsay (who painted his portrait in 1755—as did Anton Raphael Mengs). An expedition to Sicily was mooted in May 1755. By 1756 Wood had returned to London and was working on the *Essay* and *Balbec*. However, as he wrote later, his attention was to become fixed 'upon objects of so very different a nature, that it became necessary to lay Homer aside, and reserve the further consideration of my subject for times of more leisure' (preface to the *Essay*). The interruption was caused by his appointment by William Pitt the elder as under-secretary of state. He held office under Pitt and his successors until 1763. From March 1761 until his death in 1771 he sat for the duke of Bridgewater's borough of Brackley in Northamptonshire. When Pitt resigned in October 1761 Wood remained in office under Lord Egremont.

In 1761 Wood's work involved him in the preliminaries of the peace of Paris. However, his political career is best known for his illegal seizure of the papers of John Wilkes, who later brought a successful action for trespass against him. From 1764 to January 1766 Wood held the office of groom porter in the royal household. In January 1768 he became under-secretary to Lord Weymouth, at first at the northern, and later at the southern department, where he remained until December 1770. As Weymouth's dissolute lifestyle led 'to the total neglect of the affairs of his office, the business was managed as much as it could be, by Mr

Wood, his under-secretary' (Walpole, *Memoirs*, 3.97). During this period Wood fell under suspicion of directing foreign policy towards his own ends and profiting from the sales of stock at seemingly appropriate moments. Walpole reported in 1769 that Wood 'was vehemently accused of bending the bow of war towards the butt of his interest' during an altercation with France (ibid., 4.3). A similar situation arose during the Falklands Islands dispute in 1770. Weymouth left office in December 1770 and was followed by Wood.

Of Wood's character Robert Adam wrote from Rome to his sister Betty on 24 August 1755:

> we are at a vast loss for the want of Mr Wood, whose character is one of the most perfect among the Human Race. He is of universal learning possess'd of all Languages and having travelled all over the World to the best of purposes, has fund of stories serious and diverting which adapts him to all Capacities as a Learned, or as a Jovial Companion. He is intimate with all great people and all Nations and esteemed by those of his own, I mean of England.   (NA Scot., GD 18/4785)

However, in December 1769, when it was rumoured that Lord Gower might be appointed lord lieutenant of Ireland and that Wood might be appointed his secretary, a number of Irish gentlemen objected on the grounds of 'his mean birth and his public and private character' (*Eighth Report*, HMC, 191).

By the time of his death on 9 September 1771, at the age of fifty-four, in the house he had bought from the father of Edward Gibbon at Limegrove, Putney, Wood had much improved on the material circumstances into which he had been born. He was buried on 15 September in a new vault designed by Joseph Wilton in the west part of the new burial-ground in Upper Richmond Road, Putney. His origins were perhaps somewhat aggrandized in the epitaph on his tomb which was composed by Walpole and Wood's widow, Ann (1732–1803), daughter of Thomas Skottowe of Ayton, Yorkshire, with whom he had had at least three children (Robert, Thomas, and Elizabeth). Of his death Walpole wrote: 'On the 12th [*sic*] September died, after a very short indisposition, Mr. Robert Wood, a man whose character was much brighter in the literary than in the political world' (Walpole, *Memoirs*, 4.229). Wood's son Thomas and wife, Ann, were interred in the same vault.

D. M. WHITE

Sources Joint Library of the Hellenic and Roman Societies, Senate House, London, Wood MSS, esp. MSS 1–6, 7, 8, 10–11, 12, 18, 18a, and 23 · R. Wood, *An essay on the original genius and writings of Homer with a comparative view of the ancient and present state of the Troade* (1775) · R. Wood, *The ruins of Palmyra, otherwise Tedmor in the desert* (1753) · H. Walpole, *Memoirs of the reign of King George the Third*, ed. G. F. R. Barker, 4 vols. (1894) · H. Walpole, *Anecdotes of painting in England: with some account of the principal artists*, ed. R. N. Wornum, new edn, 3 vols. (1849); repr. (1876); repr. in 4 vols. (New York, 1969) · Walpole, *Corr.* · W. I. Addison, ed., *The matriculation albums of the University of Glasgow from 1728 to 1858* (1913) · E. Morpurgo, 'English physicians *doctorati*—at the University of Padua', *Proceedings of the Royal Society of Medicine*, 20 (1926–7), 1369–80 · HoP, *Commons, 1754–90* · J. Fleming, *Robert Adam and his circle in Edinburgh and Rome* (1962); repr. (1978) · R. Adam, letter to his sister, 24 Aug 1775, NA Scot., GD 18/4785 · archives, Presbyterian Historical Society of Ireland, Belfast · E. Harris and N. Savage, *British architectural books and* writers, 1556–1785 (1990) · will, PRO, PROB 11/971, sig. 393 [R. Wood] · will, PRO, PROB 11/1402, sig. 1015 [A. Wood] · C. A. Hutton, 'The travels of Palmyra Wood in 1750–51', *Journal of the Hellenic Society*, 47 (1927) · T. J. B. Spencer, 'Robert Wood and the problem of Troy in the eighteenth century', *Journal of the Warburg and Courtauld Institutes*, 20 (1957), 75–105 · Rose of Kilravock MSS, GD NA Scot., 125/23/10 · *The parish register of Great Ayton*, Yorkshire Parish Register Society, 90 (1931), 45, 88 · *Report on manuscripts in various collections*, 8 vols., HMC, 55 (1901–14), vol. 6, p. 264 [William Knox] · J. Ingamells, ed., *A dictionary of British and Irish travellers in Italy, 1701–1800* (1997) · *Eighth report*, 1, HMC, 7 (1907–9), 191 · J. Harris, trans., *Catalogue of the drawings collection of the Royal Institute of British Architects: Inigo Jones and John Webb* (1972) · J. A. Butterworth, 'The Wood collection', *Journal of Hellenic Studies*, 106 (1986), 147–54 · O. Zoller, *Der Architekt und der Ingenieur Giovanni Battista Borra (1713–1770)* (Bamberg, [1996])

Archives RIBA, drawings · U. Lond., Institute of Classical Studies, diaries and notebooks, drawings | BL, corresp. with duke of Newcastle, Add. MSS 32872–32936 · BL, letters to duke of Bridgewater, Egerton MS 2697 · PRO, letters to first earl of Chatham, 30/8

Likenesses G. Hamilton, oils, c.1749 (study for his group portrait), priv. coll. · A. R. Mengs, oils, 1755, Bridgewater gallery · A. Ramsay, oils, 1755, NPG · G. Hamilton, group portrait, oils, 1758 (*James Dawkins and Robert Wood Esqrs. first discovering sight of Palmyra*), NG Scot. · P. W. Tomkins, stipple and line engraving, 1819 (after A. R. Mengs, 1755), BM, NG Ire.; repro. in W. Y. Ottley, *Engravings of … the marquis of Stafford's collection of pictures in London* (1818) · J. Hall, group portrait, engraving (after G. Hamilton, 1758), NPG · engraving (*The meeting of Wood and Dawkins with Stuart and Revett at the monument of Philopappos*), repro. in J. Stuart and N. Revett, *The antiquities of Athens*, 3 (1794)

Wood, Robert Henry (1903–1979), broadcasting engineer, was born on 27 October 1903 at 21 Dale Road, Buxton, Derbyshire, the only son and younger of the two children of Robert Henry Wood, journalist on the *Buxton Advertiser*, and his wife, Elizabeth Stonier. When the family moved to Sheffield in 1917, Wood left school, taking up an electrical engineering apprenticeship at Cammell Laird, the Sheffield steelworks. He also attended evening classes at Sheffield University, leading to an associateship in electrical engineering. He built himself a wireless receiver in 1921 in order to listen to the earliest experimental broadcasts from the Marconi station at Writtle and the Metropolitan Vickers station at Trafford Park, and he began to write to the engineers at these stations, reporting on reception in his area. After finishing his apprenticeship he was promoted to power station assistant, but when the BBC was formed at the end of 1922 he wrote to Peter Eckersley, newly appointed chief engineer of the BBC, and in July 1923 was offered a job as assistant engineer at 2ZY, the BBC station in Manchester. He was promoted to chief engineer in February 1924.

At Manchester, Wood was a pioneer in outside broadcasting. The first outside broadcasts were from a cinema, where an orchestra played during the interval between the silent films into a microphone, and the music was relayed by telephone to the studio. He also set up live broadcasts of the Hallé Orchestra playing in the Free Trade Hall, and moved further afield to broadcast the choirs performing at the Morecambe Music Festival in 1924. Other successful outside broadcasts included the unveiling of the Manchester war memorial, and he also relayed programmes from Manchester to other BBC stations. In addition to his engineering responsibilities, Wood sometimes read the news or, as Uncle Bob, read a story on *Children's Hour*. He also gave evening lectures at Liverpool University and Manchester College of Technology. In 1925 Wood left to take up a position in charge of the transmitter at 5XX, the BBC experimental station at Chelmsford, and in summer 1925 he moved to the newly formed outside broadcasts department of the BBC in London. On 11 February 1926 he married Barbara (b. c.1904), daughter of W. Scott, who ran a fruit and fish business in Bangor, co. Down; they had one son and one daughter.

Early outside broadcast assignments included Stanley Baldwin's broadcast from Downing Street during the general strike in 1926—the first broadcast by a British prime minister—and for *Children's Hour* a 'fish supper' broadcast from the aquarium at London Zoo, an underwater broadcast of sea perch eating crabs. In 1927 Wood arranged the transmission of the first live coverage of a rugby match from Twickenham, the first live commentary on the Grand National, the first live broadcast of the Oxford–Cambridge boat race, and the unveiling of the memorial arch at the Menin Gate in Ypres, and began the 'seaside nights' from resorts such as Margate. He remained with the outside broadcasts department in London for the rest of his career, and was promoted to engineer in charge in 1935.

The first royal event for which Wood had responsibility was the wedding of the duke of Kent to Princess Marina in November 1934. Once Sir John Reith, director-general of the BBC, had permission to do this broadcast, Wood spent two months pacing out Westminster Abbey, working out where to place the microphones and how to balance the sound effects and the commentary, as the broadcast had to be done in the control room, out of sight. The success of this broadcast paved the way for the future, and Wood was in charge of the engineering arrangements for the sound broadcasting of every important royal occasion from then onwards, including the funeral of George V in 1936, when it was decided to cover the funeral without any commentary, conveying the whole event by pure sound: the gun salutes, the tolling bells, the sound of the gun carriage carrying the coffin up to Windsor Castle. Wood managed the coronation of George VI in 1937, a 7½ hour broadcast, with thirty-two microphones placed in Westminster Abbey, the wedding of Princess Elizabeth in 1947, the funeral of George VI in 1952, and the coronation of Elizabeth II on 2 June 1953, the most complex broadcasting operation in the history of the BBC. Wood also installed equipment in Windsor Castle in readiness for the abdication announcement by Edward VIII on 11 December 1936. He developed a close relationship with the royal family, especially George VI, and spent every Christmas day from 1935 until 1959 at Sandringham organizing the live Christmas broadcasts. These included George VI's last broadcast, in 1951, which Wood recorded in advance, converting what took a whole afternoon into a four-minute broadcast for Christmas day. He was made MVO by George VI in 1946, in recognition of his service to the royal family.

Wood became an expert on cathedrals, and built up a complete set of cathedral plans with notes on the acoustics to help in planning cathedral broadcasts, including George V's jubilee service in St Paul's Cathedral. In 1936 Wood was part of the BBC team of nine on the maiden voyage of the *Queen Mary* to New York. He installed microphone points all over the ship, and was responsible for fifty-six live broadcasts during the crossing, which were relayed all over the British empire, Europe, and North America. With the coming of television in 1936, Wood took on the additional responsibility for television outside broadcasts, enjoying the new technical challenge, but television was suspended from 1939 to 1946. He spent the Second World War in London, and was in charge of all Churchill's wartime broadcasts. Important occasions handled by Wood after the war included the 1948 Olympic games, and the Festival of Britain in 1951. The broadcasting arrangements for Churchill's funeral in 1965 were prepared by him in 1961.

Wood never lost his interest in technical innovations, and in 1947 designed the first parabolic microphone reflector, which enhanced the pick-up of very remote sound effects. But he felt increasingly under-appreciated by the BBC. His rank of engineer in charge was a lowly one in the BBC hierarchy, and was correspondingly poorly paid. After he resigned in 1964, he suffered a severe mental breakdown. He published his autobiography, *A World in your Ear*, shortly before his death in June 1979 while on holiday in Portugal.   ANNE PIMLOTT BAKER

Sources R. H. Wood, *A world in your ear: the broadcasting of an era, 1923–64* (1979) · BBC WAC · E. L. E. Pawley, *BBC engineering, 1922–1972* (1972) · *The year that made the day*, BBC [n.d., 1954?] · P. Scannell and D. Cardiff, *A social history of British broadcasting*, [1] (1991) · *Daily Telegraph* (25 June 1979) · b. cert.
Archives BBC WAC
Likenesses photograph, 1949, BBC WAC · photograph, repro. in Scannell and Cardiff, *Social History* · photographs, BBC WAC

Wood, Sir Robert Stanford (1886–1963), civil servant and educationist, was born in Islington, London, on 5 July 1886, the younger son of the Revd John Roskruge Wood, Baptist minister, and his wife, Frances Ann Wren. He was educated at the City of London School and at Jesus College, Cambridge, where in 1908 he obtained first-class honours in part one of the classical tripos and, the following year, second-class honours in part two of the historical tripos. After two years of teaching, mainly at Nottingham High School for Boys, and of serving as a scout commissioner, Wood joined the Board of Education in 1911 as an inspector of schools. In 1922 he married Iris Cecilie, daughter of Frederick Arnsby, piano manufacturer, with whom he had a daughter. During the inter-war years Wood rose through the ranks of the civil service to be principal private secretary to the president of the board, Lord Eustace Percy (1926–8), director of establishments (1928–36), and principal assistant secretary for technical education (1936–40).

In 1938 Wood was seconded for special service with Sir John Anderson (later Viscount Waverley), then lord privy seal and later home secretary, working on matters relating to home security in the event of war. In 1940 he returned to the Board of Education as deputy secretary (Maurice Holmes being secretary), an appointment which he held for six years. When almost all the board's staff moved to Bournemouth during the blitz, Wood remained in London to provide support to the president, Herwald Ramsbotham. In October 1940 he joined an informal committee of senior Board of Education officials which discussed plans for educational reconstruction. They produced a pamphlet, *Education after the War* (1941), widely referred to as the 'green book', which was circulated among educational bodies. Wood contributed an important paper, 'Partnership in education', which contended that the board should reassert itself in relation to local education authorities and should take the lead in forming policy. His note to the committee of 20 November 1940 contained 'most of the more important changes in the school system which were to be made after 1944' (Gosden, 242). It proposed the raising of the school-leaving age to fifteen and the replacement of the existing distinction between elementary and grammar schools with a new, age-based division between primary schools (catering for five- to eleven-year-olds) and a tripartite system of secondary schools for those aged over eleven.

From July 1941 R. A. Butler, Ramsbotham's successor as president, worked closely with Wood, who was made KBE in that year. Butler was anxious to support his senior civil servants' proposals for educational reform, and he consulted Wood on technical education and the relations between schools and industry. Wood played a key role in determining the membership and terms of reference for Sir Arnold McNair's wartime inquiry into teacher training and for Sir Cyril Norwood's committee on the secondary school curriculum and examinations. During the first part of 1943 much of Wood's time was consumed by developing ideas and drafting proposals on further education that featured in the white paper *Educational Reconstruction*, and which subsequently formed an important part of the 1944 Education Act. Wood also chaired an office committee on the post-war emergency recruitment and training of teachers and, over the winter of 1943–4, was the principal speaker at a series of Board of Education conferences intended to justify the controversial introduction of the one-year teacher training scheme. Some of those who attended these meetings were sceptical about his assurances that emergency-trained teachers could expect professional parity with colleagues trained for two years in permanent colleges and graduate teachers emerging from universities. The experience of operating the scheme tended to confirm these doubts, but Wood's achievement in developing an initiative that produced 35,000 additional teachers between 1945 and 1951 was nevertheless considerable.

By the terms of the 1944 act, the board became the Ministry of Education and, upon the retirement of Sir Maurice Holmes in 1945, it was widely expected that Wood would become permanent secretary. This did not happen, possibly because of objections from Ellen Wilkinson, the

Labour minister of education. Disappointed, Wood departed from the ministry in 1946 to succeed Kenneth Vickers as principal of Southampton University College. Having over many years become acquainted with some of the college's strengths, ambitions, and constraints, especially in the areas of technical education and teacher training, he was well qualified to lead the drive for university status, a task that was accomplished within five years.

Wood made the acquisition of new buildings and equipment a priority, although the building programme had to be carried through not only in the face of the usual post-war difficulties but in a town which also needed to replace the port, the thousands of houses, and the industrial buildings destroyed during the war. He continued his predecessor's policy of providing halls of residence for students, one of the main objects of his principalship being that the university should be a body of scholars leading a communal life. During his six years at Southampton, student numbers almost doubled, considerable funds were raised for development, and close contact was established with the educational authorities of both Southampton and Hampshire. A major development was the establishment of an institute of education with a circle of affiliated training colleges. In conjunction with Lillian Penson, vice-chancellor of London University (for whose external degrees Southampton students were then prepared), he developed the idea of a 'special relationship' with the University of London, which culminated in 1952 in the granting of a full university charter to Southampton. Wood became Southampton's first vice-chancellor but he retired on grounds of age at the end of the session.

Wood was made an honorary fellow of Jesus College, Cambridge, in 1952, and was also an honorary member of the Goldsmiths' Company of London. In 1955 he visited Palestine and Iraq to lecture on British universities for the British Council. He died at his home, 104 Iverna Court, London, on 18 May 1963.   DAVID CROOK

Sources DNB · I. Lawrence, *Power and politics at the department of education and science* (1992) · D. Crook, 'The reconstruction of teacher education and training, 1941–54, with particular reference to the McNair committee', PhD diss., U. Wales, Swansea, 1997 · M. Barber, *The making of the 1944 Education Act* (1994) · P. H. J. H. Gosden, *Education in the Second World War: a study in policy and administration* (1976) · A. T. Patterson, *The University of Southampton: a centenary history of the evolution and development of the University of Southampton, 1862–1962* (1962) · *CGPLA Eng. & Wales* (1963)
Archives BL, corresp. with Albert Mansbridge, Add. MSS 65196, 65253 · Bodl. Oxf., letters to O. G. S. Crawford
Likenesses C. Rogers, portrait, U. Southampton
Wealth at death £8943 6s. 7d.: probate, 6 Aug 1963, *CGPLA Eng. & Wales*

Wood, Sancton (1815–1886), architect and surveyor, was born in April 1815 at Hackney, Middlesex, the youngest of six children and the only son of John Wood and his wife, Harriet Russell, who was a member of the Smirke family of Wigton, Cumberland. His father was a member of an old and prosperous Cumberland family, who moved to London to pursue a business in cotton goods. Sancton took his forename from his uncle Philip Sancton, a successful London merchant, who had married his father's sister. He first entered a small private school in Devon, and then moved to a school at Hazelwood, Birmingham, run by T. W. Hill whose son Sir Rowland Hill (1795–1879) was author of the penny postal system. The school was run 'To leave as much as possible, all power in the hands of the boys themselves' (M. D. Hill, *Public Education*, 1822), a philosophy that failed to stimulate young Sancton Wood into serious study. Nevertheless his interest in drawing and family influence gained him a pupillage in the office of his cousin Sir Robert Smirke RA (1780–1867), followed by employment with Sydney Smirke RA (1798–1877). His contemporaries recalled his quiet retiring nature, sometimes excitable, but always courteous. He married c.1844, and he and his wife, Elizabeth Sarah (1813/14–1875), had two sons, Herbert (b. 1845) and William Winder (b. 1846). His wife and both sons predeceased him.

Wood's impeccable classical training in architecture and presentation, learned in Smirke's office, gained him early recognition. In 1837 he designed one of London's first railway termini, at Shoreditch for the Eastern Counties Railway. Budget restraint limited the scope of work, but success in competitions followed, beginning with a £100 prize for Ipswich station. Then in 1845 he headed a field of sixty-five competitors for the design of Kingsbridge terminus and company offices, Dublin (now known as Heuston station). The magnificent two-storey office block, nine bays wide by five bays deep, is dominated by attached Corinthian columns between the first-floor pedimented windows. The enclosing single-storey wing walls to the platforms are linked to the office block by an intervening domed turret at each corner. In 1846 he won the £100 prize for Blackburn station. Links with Irish railways led to further work for the Great Southern and Western, between Dublin and Cork, and the Limerick Junction line. He also designed the stand at the Curragh racecourse. Other railway commissions included stations on the Rugby and Stamford line (1846), and Syston and Peterborough route (1847).

Wood was elected an associate of the Royal Institute of British Architects in 1841, an associate of the Institution of Civil Engineers in 1848, and an associate of the Institution of Surveyors, also in 1848. Commercial buildings, schools, churches, and estate development, principally in the London area, were credited to him. These included the Queen's Assurance Company office (1852) at the southwest corner of King Street and Gresham Street; the Lime Grove estate, Putney; Hackney town hall (1864); and terrace houses, Lancaster Gate (1857). Interest in surveying led to his appointment as district surveyor for Putney and Roehampton, followed by a similar appointment at St Luke's, Chelsea (from 1866). He was a member of the examining board for district surveyors.

In 1850 Wood, his wife, and their two sons moved to 11 Putney Hill, London, a detached house of his own design where Wood died on 18 April 1886. He was buried six days later in the same grave as his wife and sons, at Putney Lower Common cemetery. His probate records his estate valued at £15,470.   OLIVER F. J. CARTER

Sources *The Builder*, 50 (1886), 761 · *The Builder*, 50 (1886), 795–6 · *PICE*, 86 (1885–6), 376–9 · *Dir. Brit. archs.* · A. K. Placzek, ed., *Macmillan encyclopedia of architects*, 4 vols. (1982) · H. R. Hitchcock, *Early Victorian architecture in Britain*, 2 vols. (1954) · d. cert. · *CGPLA Eng. & Wales* (1886)
Archives RIBA
Wealth at death £15,470 16s.: resworn probate, Jan 1887, *CGPLA Eng. & Wales* (1886)

Wood, Searles Valentine, the elder (1798–1880), geologist, was born on 14 February 1798 (St Valentine's day, hence his middle name), the son of John Wood, a solicitor, of Woodbridge, Suffolk, and his wife, Mary Ann, daughter of Simon Baker of Ipswich. He was brought up in Woodbridge until 1811, when he became a midshipman on the *Thames*, part of the East India Company's mercantile fleet. In 1821 he married Elizabeth (1791/2–1860), the only daughter of Thomas Taylor of London, a solicitor. The couple had one son, Searles Valentine *Wood the younger (1830–1884), who also became a geologist.

In 1826 Wood retired from the service of the East India Company after failing to obtain the command of a ship, and devoted himself to palaeontological studies. He travelled for a time, then settled at Hasketon, near Woodbridge, where he became a partner in a bank with his father, and gave much of his attention to the crag pits of East Anglia. However, he also collected extensively from the Hampshire Tertiaries, and the French Eocene mollusca.

About 1835, owing to ill health, Wood retired from business. Change and rest cured him, and he then settled in London, where he joined the London Clay Club. In 1837 Wood was introduced to Charles Lyell, with whom he was associated in the study of the Tertiary formations. In May 1838 Wood was appointed curator of the Geological Society's museum, but again ill health forced him to retire after a number of months. In 1844–5 he lived in France for the sake of his son's education, and on returning to Suffolk he lived at Martlesham, near Woodbridge.

While still young Wood began to study the East Anglian crag, at a time when fossils were much more easily obtained, with the result that during his long life he formed a splendid collection. Wood, who had already published 'Catalogue of crag shells' in the *Annals and Magazine of Natural History* (1840–42), was reported to have been urged by Lyell to embark on a description of the crag mollusca. The first part of this series focused on the univalves, and was published by the Palaeontographical Society (1848). In 1850, 1853, and 1855, Wood published the parts of his descriptions on the crag bivalves.

When he lived in London, Wood had agreed to divide the workload on the description of the mollusca of the English Tertiary formations with his friend Frederick Edwards. Of these formations, divided into the older Tertiaries, and the newer Tertiaries, or crags, Wood chose to study the latter group and Edwards the former. However, Wood completed his share of the work and came to the aid of Edwards by undertaking *A Monograph of the Eocene Bivalves of England* (1861–77), which was printed by the Palaeontographical Society (founded 1847). Wood also

issued a supplement to his *Crag mollusca* (3 vols.) in the society's volumes in 1871 and 1873. A second supplement followed in 1879. On completion of his work on the molluscan remains, Wood presented his then unrivalled collection to the British Museum (Natural History). He was also author of about ten separate papers on geological subjects.

Wood was elected FGS in 1839, and received the Wollaston medal in 1860. He was also a treasurer of the Palaeontographical Society and a member of various other societies, both English and foreign. Although he had wide interests in natural history, his efforts were concentrated on one specific topic, for as he stated, 'I was born in sight of one crag pit and shall probably be buried in sight of another'. He died at Martlesham, after a few days' illness, on 26 October 1880, and was buried in the churchyard at Melton, near Woodbridge, in view of the crag. He was survived by his only son.   YOLANDA FOOTE

Sources *Nature*, 23 (1880–81), 40–41 · *The Athenaeum* (6 Nov 1880), 611 · R. Etheridge, *Quarterly Journal of the Geological Society*, 37 (1881), 37–9 · *Quarterly Journal of the Geological Society*, 16 (1860), 35 · *Geological Magazine*, new ser., 2nd decade, 7 (1880), 575–6 · H. B. Woodward, *The history of the Geological Society of London* (1907) · *DNB*
Archives Linn. Soc., papers · NHM, drawings and notes · Norwich Castle Museum, corresp. and papers | U. Edin. L., letters to Sir Charles Lyell
Wealth at death under £2000: probate, 6 Nov 1880, *CGPLA Eng. & Wales*

Wood, Searles Valentine, the younger (1830–1884), geologist, was born on 4 February 1830 at Hasketon, near Woodbridge, Suffolk, the only child of Searles Valentine *Wood the elder (1798–1880), geologist and banker, and Elizabeth (1791/2–1860), only daughter of Thomas Taylor, solicitor, of London. He was educated at King's College School, London (1839–43), and in France (1844–5), and admitted a solicitor in 1851. Two years later, on 1 October 1853, he married Elizabeth (1827?–1912), daughter of John Gayler. They had no children.

As early as 1843 Wood was working with his father on the highly fossiliferous Eocene deposits at Hordle cliff, Hampshire. He was subsequently the sole or joint author of nearly sixty papers, and was a great pioneer in the study of glacial deposits, especially in East Anglia. In 1864 he was elected a fellow of the Geological Society and produced the first map of the glacial deposits of eight counties at a time when the government geological survey ignored these strata.

Following the death of a business partner Wood was able to retire in 1865, which allowed him to devote more time to a thorough study of the glacial beds of Suffolk and Essex. Together with his friend F. W. Harmer, who covered Norfolk, he compiled an important memoir and map, published by the Palaeontographical Society in 1871, which formed part of his father's monograph on crag mollusca. Wood also studied the glacial deposits of Lincolnshire and Yorkshire, publishing a detailed memoir and map in 1868.

Wood was most diligent in his research. He spent many weeks at his Brentwood home in 1871 processing more than two tons of sand, full of shell fragments, from a glacial deposit near Yarmouth, to obtain seventy species of mollusca, some of which were new types. As a result he was able to prove this bed was older than a similar one in Lancashire previously considered contemporaneous. The Geological Society published in 1880 and 1882 his exhaustive memoir on the Newer Pliocene period in England. Although an invalid for the last ten years of his life, he worked to within a few days of his death, often lying down, breaking lumps of clay for hours each day, searching for fossils. His major work on the Pliocene deposits at St Erth, Penzance, Cornwall, appeared posthumously.

Wood was always ready to help other workers and to share his extensive knowledge and ideas. Although he was always careful and conscientious in his work, and no one doubted his patience and industry, shortly after his death some of his writings were described as being 'rather difficult to follow, and somewhat tedious to read' (Woodward, 237) and 'complicated and absolutely bewildering' (Whitaker, 364). He died at home in Beacon Hill House, Martlesham, near Woodbridge, on 14 December 1884 as a result of diabetes apoplexy and was buried near his father at Melton on 20 December. W. H. GEORGE

Sources Geological Magazine, new ser., 3rd decade, 2 (1885), 138–42 · T. G. Bonney, Quarterly Journal of the Geological Society, 41 (1885), 40–41 · Nature, 31 (1884–5), 318–19 · C. Reid, The Pliocene deposits of Britain (1890) · H. B. Woodward, The history of the Geological Society of London (1907) · W. Whitaker, The geology of London, 1 (1889) · parish register (baptism), Hasketon, Suffolk, 14 Feb 1830 · m. cert. · d. cert. · parish register (burial), Melton, Suffolk, 20 Dec 1884
Archives BGS, notebooks and papers · GS Lond., maps and papers · NHM | BGS, letters to Frederic Harmer · U. Edin. L., corresp. with Sir Charles Lyell
Wealth at death £28,956 17s. 9d.: probate, 11 May 1885, CGPLA Eng. & Wales

Wood, Shakspere (1827–1886), sculptor, was born in Manchester on 13 November 1827, the son of Hamilton Wood of the firm of Wood, Rowell & Co., smallware manufacturers, of Manchester, and Sarah Anne, daughter of Charles Bennett of Newton Grange. On the breakup of the Manchester business the Wood family moved to London, where the father was connected with the Wood Carving Company until about 1846. Shakspere received a part of his education as a sculptor in the schools of the Royal Academy, and about 1851 he visited Rome for purposes of further study. Little is known about his artistic activities until 1868–71, during which period he sent five sculptures to London for exhibition at the Royal Academy. Of these, four, Miss Anstey, J. Hatchell, J. C. Tebbetts, and H. MacCormac, were portraits and one, Elaine, an ideal piece. The Scottish National Portrait Gallery in Edinburgh has in its collections two portrait medallions by Wood, one of the phrenologist George Combe, the other of Thomas De Quincey.

Upon settling in Rome, Wood took a keen interest in the objects of art and antiquity in and around the ancient city. In later years these interests came to predominate over his activity as a sculptor. In 1869 he published The Vatican Museum of Sculpture: a Lecture Delivered before the British Archæological Society of Rome. In 1872 his catalogue of sculptures in the Museo Capitolino was published, followed in 1875 by The New Curiosum urbis: a Guide to Ancient and Modern Rome. He also gave erudite lectures for English visitors, and contributed to The Times, becoming in time a regular correspondent. Shakspere Wood died in Rome in early February 1886, leaving a widow and children.

His brother **Marshall Wood** (d. 1882), sculptor, exhibited twenty-four works at the Royal Academy between 1854 and 1875, and two at the British Institution. At the academy in 1854 he showed a medallion of Robert Browning and a bust of Miss Helen Grey. In 1864 he was represented at the academy by portrait busts in marble of the prince of Wales and the princess of Wales, as well as other marble busts. He designed statues of Queen Victoria for Melbourne, Sydney, Calcutta, Montreal, and Ottawa, and of Richard Cobden for St Ann's Square, Manchester. He resided at 17 Osnaburgh Street, Regent's Park, London, and shortly before his death at 12 Powis Square, Brighton, Sussex, where he died on 16 July 1882, leaving a widow, Fanny Helen Wood.

ALBERT NICHOLSON, rev. CHRISTOPHER WHITEHEAD

Sources M. H. Grant, A dictionary of British sculptors from the XIIIth century to the XXth century (1953), 272 · Graves, RA exhibitors, vol. 4 · The Athenaeum (6 Feb 1886), 208 · Bénézit, Dict., 3rd edn, 10.790 · Thieme & Becker, Allgemeines Lexikon · CGPLA Eng. & Wales (1882) [Marshall Wood] · The Times (11 Feb 1886) · The Year's Art (1887), 230 · The Portfolio, 17 (1886), 64
Wealth at death £4643 13s. 4d.—Marshall Wood: probate, 21 Dec 1882, CGPLA Eng. & Wales

Wood, Sydney Herbert (1884–1958), civil servant, was born on 3 March 1884 at The Retreat, New Southgate, East Barnet, Hertfordshire, the son of James London Wood, lime and cement merchant, and his wife, Maria Colvin. He was educated at University College, London, where he took an honours degree in chemistry and then pursued research in the laboratory of the eminent physical chemist Sir William Ramsay. From 1908 he was warden of University College Hall at Ealing but in 1910 his growing interest in education led to appointment in the Board of Education, where he remained, apart from serving in the First World War, when he was awarded the Military Cross. On 27 July 1911 he married Frances Chick (b. 1884/5) of Branscombe, Devon, daughter of Samuel Chick, lace merchant. After her death he married, on 10 April 1922, Phyllis Hope Taunton (b. 1895/6) of Downton, Wiltshire, daughter of Major Henry Percy Taunton. There were one daughter from the first marriage and two sons from the second.

Between the wars the recognition of Wood's ability and understanding of various educational issues led to his being chosen as secretary to the committee on university education in London (1924) and subsequently as secretary to the royal commission on Durham University (1934). He served as principal private secretary to three successive presidents of the Board of Education—Lord Eustace Percy, Sir Charles Trevelyan, and Hastings Lees-Smith. In 1936, along with William Abbott from technical branch, he went to India at the request of its government to prepare the Report on Vocational and General Education in India (1937).

In 1938 Wood was promoted to principal assistant secretary heading the teacher training branch. There were about eighty mostly small training colleges, the majority provided by the churches, offering courses of up to two years. Shortage of finance and Treasury economies had made it impossible to improve the colleges, attract better staff, or lengthen the courses beyond two years. Public pressure in wartime for the reconstruction of the education system enabled Wood to persuade R. A. Butler to appoint the committee on the supply, recruitment, and training of teachers in 1942, with Sir Arnold McNair, vice-chancellor of Liverpool University, as chairman. Wood was himself both a member and the secretary, an unusual arrangement which enabled him to make a unique contribution. He was determined to raise standards by involving the universities in teacher training. 'It would be disastrous if one were to pass the universities by in this matter' (Wood to Savage, 31 May 1943, PRO, ED 86/94). He advocated a system of university-based schools of education which would include the colleges and this became scheme A in the committee's report. The committee itself had been divided, and the chairman, fearing that universities would become unbalanced by the sheer number of trainee teachers, proposed a series of regional training councils as scheme B. Universities found it difficult to agree a common position, in spite of much discussion which continued after the election of 1945 when Ellen Wilkinson became minister. Finally scheme A, by now described as university institutes of education, was broadly accepted and was destined to last for thirty years, achieving enormous changes in teacher training. Before these reforms came about Wood was also largely responsible for the emergency teacher training scheme by which thousands were trained in shortened courses to meet the immediate desperate shortage at the end of the war.

During the war years Wood made a vital contribution to the outstanding group of civil servants who planned the Education Act of 1944 and the post-war reconstruction of the system. Butler later wrote 'it was S. H. Wood who kept us on the progressive path' (Butler, 93). As a member of the group who met during the winter of 1940–41 Wood prepared papers for colleagues which summarized progress made and outlined solutions to problems. On crucial issues such as secondary education for all and external examinations, it was the papers he drafted towards the end of 1940 which embodied the ministry's post-war policies. One paper proposed an end to fees in all maintained secondary schools, and selection at eleven for grammar and modern schools, with further movement at thirteen to technical schools when appropriate. Abolition of fees would remove one obstacle to equality of esteem, but a more difficult problem was the 'chit' or school certificate since modern schools would be lacking in esteem if their pupils left without one. Either all schools or no schools should provide some sort of certificate. Such thoughts lay behind the ministry's initial attempts in the post-war years to abolish external examinations before the age of eighteen. Opposition from schools, parents, and local education authorities eventually led to Wood's other solution—of certificates for pupils in all types of secondary

school: the general certificate of education (GCE), introduced in 1951 to replace the school certificate and higher school certificate, then the certificate of secondary education (CSE) in 1965, thus widening the coverage greatly.

Wood, who was appointed CB in 1943, retired in 1945. He had a high moral sense coupled with a shrewd pragmatism, along with a very strong belief in the value of education. These firm values combined with a sense of the practical to shape the arguments in the decisive papers he wrote for the permanent assistant secretaries' group on refashioning the post-war school system. Thus in 1942 he did much to create German Educational Reconstruction, remaining chairman until 1952. This fruitfully drew together educators and exchanged students between the two countries. He continued with his active interest in youth work until his death and served as joint secretary of the Association of Girls Clubs and Mixed Clubs. He died of a dissecting aneurysm of the arch of the aorta on 4 March 1958 at his home, 14 Hillcroft Crescent, Ealing, Middlesex. He was survived by his second wife.   PETER GOSDEN

Sources *The Times* (5–15 March 1958) · *Education* (21 March 1958) · P. H. J. Gosden, *Education in the Second World War: a study in policy and administration* (1976), 110, 124, 148, 230, 243–9, 255, 275, 306, 374, 389, 423–4 · Baron Butler of Saffron Walden [R. A. Butler], *The art of the possible: the memoirs of Lord Butler* (1971), 93 · b. cert. · m. cert. [Frances Chick] · m. cert. [Phyllis Hope Taunton] · d. cert.
Archives PRO, former board of education files, papers, ED/46, ED/86, ED/136
Wealth at death £4548 12s. 1d.: probate, 26 Aug 1958, *CGPLA Eng. & Wales*

Wood, Thomas (d. 1577), soldier and religious activist, may have been of either Leicestershire or Yorkshire origin. Until 1960 he was known only as one of the four Englishmen who founded the protestant exile community in Frankfurt am Main on 27 June 1554 and as an elder of the later English congregation at Geneva. He has also been identified tentatively (though undoubtedly incorrectly) by Christina Garrett as the mercer of that name who had some association with John Knox in 1553. The publication by Patrick Collinson in 1960 of the copies Wood's son Ambrose made of 'my father Captaine Thomas Wood his lettres to certaine noble personages and other his good freinds' ('Letters of Thomas Wood' in *Godly People*, 83) not only brought him out of the shadows, but also transformed our understanding of Elizabethan history.

Collinson discovered most of the biographical details now available, but it is possible to supply further information about Wood's military career. Although he may have attended Cambridge University, Wood is first publicly encountered as a man-at-arms of the garrison of Boulogne, jousting to celebrate the accession of Edward VI on 24 February 1547. In 1548 he was serving as a junior officer with the Boulogne horse in Scotland. On 17 July he was taken prisoner in an ambush at Linton Bridge, Haddingtonshire, and not released until the end of 1549. In 1551 he went to Ireland to negotiate a lease of former monastic property granted him for his arrears of pay. At Cork in April he met an old acquaintance from Boulogne, the new lord deputy, Sir James Croft, who employed him as a confidential messenger with the privy council until December

1552. On 19 July 1552 (styled 'the king's servant') Wood was granted a lease in reversion of Tintern Abbey, co. Wexford.

Nothing is known about Wood's earlier association with the other three founders of the Frankfurt community, except that one, William Williams, the assay-master of the Dublin mint, was married to his sister Jane by June 1554. Nor are Wood's precise motives for going into exile known, but he was accompanied by his wife, Anne, and possibly some of his children. He ultimately left two sons (Thomas and Ambrose) and five daughters, one of whom, Debora, was born in Frankfurt. Wood was one of the signatories of the congregation's invitation to John Knox to become its pastor, which raises the question of whether he had made Knox's acquaintance while serving on the borders. He was also a member of the faction that, under the leadership of William Whittingham, followed Knox to Geneva, where he and his family arrived in October 1555. In December 1557 he was elected an elder of the English congregation.

By 9 March 1560 Wood was back in England. He then wrote to Lord Robert Dudley, later earl of Leicester, about an inspection carried out at Portsmouth, evidence both of his resumption of military service and of his association with the Dudleys, which had certainly begun earlier. He reached the high point of his military career two years later when he served under Dudley's brother Ambrose, earl of Warwick, as clerk of the council and captain of a company in the garrison of Newhaven (as the English called Le Havre) between October 1562 and July 1563. In August 1563 Sir William Cecil nominated Wood as clerk of the council in a proposed appointment of Warwick as lord deputy of Ireland, but this was never implemented. In 1568 Wood was styled of 'Tottenham, Midd. Esq.' and two years later as 'the queen's servant'. Since the manor of Tottenham was an established perquisite of servants of the household, Wood may have held a minor post in the latter. In 1570 he leased the manor of Groby, Leicestershire, from the crown, where he resided until his death. He served as a Leicestershire JP and was closely associated, both socially and financially, with the third earl of Huntingdon, Leicester and Warwick's brother-in-law. By mid-1576 he was seriously ill and he died at Groby at some point during the spring of 1577. Wood made his will on 16 July 1576 and it was proved on 3 May 1577. He was survived by a widow named Agnes, who was still alive in 1598, but whether she was a second wife, or Agnes a variant of Anne, is unclear.

The letters copied by Ambrose Wood are both the central source for his father's life after 1563 and, as Collinson appreciated, among the most important records of Elizabethan lay puritanism. The most significant are an exchange with Cecil over the suppression of a puritan exercise in London in 1566, one to Whittingham of 15 February 1574, and—the most dramatic—an exchange with Leicester and Warwick in the late summer of 1576. They reveal much about Wood's religious allegiances and his responses to the major issues of the day, but—as always—they raise possibly more questions than they answer.

The letter to Whittingham includes the important recollection concerning the Book of Common Prayer that 'yow were the first that made me and many others mislike with the said boke' ('Letters of Thomas Wood' in *Godly People*, 89). It is not clear whether this took place at Frankfurt or Geneva, but it could imply that Wood returned to England in 1559 a committed presbyterian. He certainly kept the records of the English congregation at Geneva (at least until he left). The combination of his strong antiepiscopal views in the 1570s and his firsthand knowledge of the events of the exile has led Collinson to suggest that he rather than Whittingham was the author or compiler of the famous and controversial account of the Frankfurt community, *A Brieff Discours off the Troubles Begonne at Franckford* [1575]. On the other hand, if read in sequence his letters reveal his increasing hostility to the episcopate following the 'persecution' of ministers who refused to wear the surplice, then those who refused to subscribe to the prayer book in 1571, and finally the suppression of exercises. This might imply an initial willingness to accept the Elizabethan church settlement that diminished over time in response to the church's treatment of nonconformity.

The correspondence with Warwick and Leicester was a consequence of Wood's illness in the summer of 1576. Wood had attended the great festivities at Kenilworth in 1575 and had spoken briefly to Leicester then. Had he been fit to travel in 1576, he would (he admitted) have preferred to see Leicester personally rather than to write. The surviving letters are eight in number: an initial letter to Leicester and a covering note to Warwick, both dated 4 August; an answer from Warwick on the 16th; one from Leicester on the 19th; a further letter from Wood to Warwick on the 20th; Wood's answers to Warwick's and Leicester's letters (both dated 7 September); and a final undated letter from Wood to both earls in early 1577. The subject of this exchange was an admonition from Wood that Leicester was being blamed for the dissolution of the exercise at Southam in eastern Warwickshire earlier in the summer. Wood also wanted to warn Leicester of 'verie common brutes verie dishonorable and ungodly' about him ('Letters of Thomas Wood' in *Godly People*, 92), but only by word of mouth (he had tried to do so at Kenilworth but could not find the opportunity). It has been assumed that these were related to Leicester's private life.

Leicester denied any responsibility for the Southam dissolution and claimed he had learned of it only when Elizabeth, who had her own sources, complained to him of 'disorders' there. But as important as the content of the exchange is its style. What has struck most commentators is the combination of both Wood's boldness in criticizing Leicester and Leicester's willingness to defend both his conduct and his commitment to religion at length in his answer of 19 August. Wood appreciated that his initial admonition to Leicester was 'plaine, and peradventure may be thought to plaine' ('Letters of Thomas Wood' in *Godly People*, 92), and sent it to Warwick unsealed for him to read and then deliver to his brother personally.

Yet the real significance of this exchange is that it was

not unique. Wood's correspondence with Cecil in 1566 had been a similar 'friendly admonition' (as Cecil termed it) that Cecil was being blamed for the suppression of the St Antholin's exercise. Nor is the exchange between Wood and Leicester the only example of puritan criticism sent directly to Leicester and long defences by Leicester of his conduct. Leicester's willingness to tolerate and respond to the apparently constant carping and admonishing, however irritating it may have been—'I stand on the topp of the hill, where I knowe the smallest slipp semeth a fall', as he wrote to Wood on 19 August ('Letters of Thomas Wood' in *Godly People*, 96)—was a key aspect to his role as 'patron-general' of Elizabethan puritans. It also accounts for the political influence of Elizabethan lay puritanism. Wood's Genevan loyalties were strong, but they should not obscure the fact that his public career in the crown's service placed him at the heart of the Elizabethan protestant establishment. What characterized that establishment was the very openness of the dialogue between men of Wood's rank and independence of mind and his nominal superiors, Cecil, Leicester, and Warwick.

SIMON ADAMS

Sources 'Letters of Thomas Wood, puritan, 1566–1577', ed. P. Collinson, *BIHR*, special suppl., 5 (1960) [whole issue]; repr. in P. Collinson, *Godly people: essays on English protestantism and puritanism* (1983), 45–107 • P. Collinson, 'The authorship of *A brieff discours off the troubles begonne at Franckford*', *Journal of Ecclesiastical History*, 9 (1958), 188–208; repr. in P. Collinson, *Godly people: essays on English protestantism and puritanism* (1983), 191–212 • P. Collinson, *The Elizabethan puritan movement* (1967) • S. Adams, 'The Dudley clientèle, 1553–1563', *The Tudor nobility*, ed. G. W. Bernard (1992), 241–65 • S. Adams, 'A godly peer? Leicester and the puritans', *History Today*, 40/1 (1990), 14–19 • [W. Whittingham?], *A brieff discours off the troubles begonne at Franckford* (1575) • [W. Whittingham?], *A brief discourse of the troubles at Frankfort*, ed. E. Arber (1908) • C. H. Garrett, *The Marian exiles: a study in the origins of Elizabethan puritanism* (1938); repr. (1966), 343 • *CSP for.*, 1547–53; 1562–3 • *CSP Scot.*, 1547–63, 293, 297, 303, 350 • *APC*, 1547–50, 361 • *CPR*, 1569–72, 68 • J. Morrin, ed., *Calendar of the patent and close rolls of chancery in Ireland, of the reigns of Henry VIII, Edward VI, Mary, and Elizabeth*, 1 (1861), 254 • Hatfield House, Hertfordshire, Cecil papers, 154, art. 2 • bond and receipts between Huntingdon and Wood, 1568–70, Hunt. L., Hastings papers, financial (HAF), box 4 • bond of Agnes Wood, 1598, Hunt. L., Hastings papers, financial (HAF), box 5 • Wood to Sir William Cecil, 24 April 1551, PRO, secretaries of state: state papers Ireland, Edward VI, SP 61/3/48–9 • Wood to Lord Robert Dudley, 9 March 1560, Longleat House, Wiltshire, Dudley MS I, fol. 120 • will, PRO, PROB 11/59, sig. 16

Archives Herts. ALS, commonplace book, Gorhambury MS B/VIII/143 | Hunt. L., Hastings papers financial (HAF), bond and receipts between Wood and Huntingdon • Longleat House, Wiltshire, letter to Lord Robert Dudley, 9 March 1560, Dudley MS I, fol. 120 • PRO, letter to Sir William Cecil, 24 April 1551, SP 61/3/48–9 • PRO, letters to Cecil, 3 Aug 1561, SP 12/19/9 • PRO, letters from Le Havre (Newhaven), 1562–3, SP 70/45–59

Wealth at death see will, PRO, PROB 11/59, sig. 16

Wood, Thomas (1607–1692), bishop of Lichfield and Coventry, was born in Hackney, Middlesex, on 22 July 1607, the third son of Thomas Wood (d. 1649), clerk of the spicery to James I, and his wife, Susan Cranmer (d. 1650). A scholar at Westminster School, he was a student at Christ Church, Oxford, from 1627, graduated BA on 27 April 1631, and proceeded MA on 24 April 1634. The following year he became rector of Whickham-on-Tyne, co. Durham, but he

seems to have spent little time there, his only recorded activity as rector being the baptism of one Grace Clavering in 1636. A chaplain to the king, in 1641–4 he was occupying the November turn. He proceeded BD at Oxford on 15 May 1641, and DD on 13 March 1642.

In 1645 the committee for compounding noted that neither Wood nor his curate, Pescote, had taken the covenant. Ejected from his rectory for scandal on 4 June 1651, he later claimed that the cause was his being a royal chaplain; the ejection was confirmed on 12 June 1655 and a successor, Cuthbert Stote, was admitted four months later. For at least some of this decade Wood lived abroad on family money.

After the Restoration, Wood regained Whickham by order of the House of Lords on 18 June 1660. He also became a canon of Durham that year and for a while was fairly assiduous in his residence in the area. In 1666 he married the same Grace Clavering he had previously baptized: the daughter of Sir James Clavering of Axwell Park, Newcastle, she belonged to one of the leading local families. Three years earlier, while retaining his prebend at Durham, he had become dean of Lichfield; there he was both neglectful of his duties and at odds with his bishop, John Hacket. The quarrel escalated to the point where Hacket deprived Wood of all say in the restoration of Lichfield Cathedral and, when he remained obdurate, excommunicated him publicly. Wood retaliated in 1668 by getting the court of arches to excommunicate the bishop. Archbishop Gilbert Sheldon privately sympathized with Hacket over his difficulties with his 'most untractable and filthy natured dean' (Spurr, 192), but concerned that public dissension would only provide ammunition for nonconformists and others disposed to criticize the church, intervened to effect a *modus vivendi*. In 1669 Wood became particularly assiduous in his Durham duties.

Following the death of Bishop Hacket on 28 October 1670 and after much backstairs negotiation, Wood's elder brother Sir Henry obtained the bishopric for him through the influence of Barbara Villiers, duchess of Cleveland, whose daughter Mary was about to marry Sir Henry's son. Wood was enthroned in 1671, but continued his previous behaviour. Scandalized by his neglect of duty, Sheldon was thinking of suspending him but died in 1677 before this could be effected. Archbishop William Sancroft finally suspended him in July 1684, but only after priming Bishop Francis Turner of Rochester to put the case tactfully at court and to establish that 'the King and Duke abandon the bishop as sordid and refractory' (Spurr, 191). The suspension remained in force until Wood was brought to submission in 1687. Wood had excused himself from residing in his diocese on the grounds that he had no house in which he could dispense episcopal hospitality; Sancroft handed the sequestrated income to the dean, Lancelot Addison, with a commission to erect such a house. The splendid result is the only episcopal residence in Europe known to have been built as a punishment of the resident, but though Wood was forced to accept it, he succeeded in avoiding residing there.

Wood died at Astrop Wells, Northamptonshire, on 18

April 1692 and was buried at Ufford, Suffolk, four days later. In his will he remembered only his college and his family homes, after making provision for his wife, there being no children. He left money to found an almshouse for ten old women in Hackney, and another for ten old men at Ufford, and a sum of £200 for the poor of Hackney, as well as a sum of £3000 for the use of the junior masters of Christ Church and a further estate of £200 p.a. in Norfolk for their maintenance.   B. S. BENEDIKZ

Sources Bodl. Oxf., MSS Tanner · chapter records, Durham, 1660–92, Durham RO · parish register, Whickham, 1538–1671, Durham RO · Lichfield chapter and episcopal records, 1663–92, Lichfield RO · Wood, *Ath. Oxon.*, new edn · Wood, *Ath. Oxon.: Fasti* (1820) · *Walker rev.*, 144 · J. Spurr, *The Restoration Church of England, 1646–1689* (1991) · H. E. Savage, *Reconstruction after the Commonwealth* (1918) · H. E. Savage, *The last quarter of the 17th century* (1932) · N. Sykes, *From Sheldon to Secker* (1961) · Foster, *Alum. Oxon.*, 1500–1714, vol. 3 · Venn, *Alum. Cant.*, 1/4 · T. C. Noble, *Biographical notice of Bishop Thomas Wood* (privately printed, 1882) · Hackney borough archives, Hackney, London N1 5SQ, Hackney Archives Department · W. Stubbs, *Registrum Sacrum Anglicanum*, 2nd edn (1897) · parish register, Hackney, 22 July 1607 [baptism]
Archives Bodl. Oxf., corresp.
Likenesses P. Lely, oils, Christ Church Oxf.; copy, bishop's palace, Lichfield

Wood, Thomas (1661–1722), lawyer and jurist, was born on 20 September 1661 at Oxford, in the parish of St John Baptist, the eldest son of Robert Wood (1630–1686) of Oxford and his wife, Mary (1638–1686), daughter of Thomas Drope (*d.* 1644), vicar of Cumnor in Berkshire, and niece of Francis *Drope. His most famous relative was his uncle Anthony *Wood. Wood became a scholar of Winchester College in 1675, and matriculated from St Alban Hall, Oxford, on 7 June 1678. On 24 August 1679 he was elected a fellow of New College, Oxford, where he graduated BCL on 6 April 1687 and DCL in 1703. On 31 May 1692 he was called to the bar at Gray's Inn, *ex gratia*, through the influence of his relative Chief Justice Holt.

As a young scholar at Oxford, Wood published a number of literary works, and gained a reputation as a controversialist. In 1692 Wood's uncle, Anthony Wood, was sued by Henry Hyde, second earl of Clarendon, in the vice-chancellor's court in Oxford for a libel against Clarendon's father. Wood served as his proctor in this case. Wood also authored several works in defence of his uncle including *A vindication of the historiographer of the University of Oxford and his works from the reproaches of the bishop of Salisbury* (1693) and *An appendix to the life of the right reverend father in God Seth Ward, lord bishop of Salisbury*, which was published anonymously (1697).

In 1704 Wood decided to abandon the hectic life of a practising lawyer and retreat to the country. In pursuance of this he took orders, married that year Jane Baker or Barker, and from 17 March 1704 until his death held the rectorship of Hardwick in Buckinghamshire, a benefice that had been in the gift of New College since 1660. He retained his connection with the university as he was assessor of the vice-chancellor's court between 1706 and 1708. It was from Hardwick that he wrote his best-remembered works, a short treatise on the need for legal education at the universities and two treatises designed to

Thomas Wood (1661–1722), by Michael Vandergucht, pubd 1724

provide systematic introductions to both the common and the civil laws. Wood's greatest accomplishment as a scholar and jurist was his attempt in these books to introduce a systematic element to the study of the two laws and to urge the extension of legal education beyond the confines of the inns of court to the universities, for those who might use the law but not as lawyers. In his *Some Thoughts Concerning the Study of the Laws of England in the Two Universities*, published in 1708, Wood made a strong plea for the inclusion of the common law into the curriculum at Oxford and Cambridge, from which it was then excluded. He argued (much as Blackstone would after him) that a knowledge of the common law was necessary for the English gentry and merchant classes both if the gentry were to fulfil its duty as magistrates and legislators, and because the common law was, as he put it, 'twisted and interwoven almost into all manner of Discourse and Business' (pp. 6–7). Wood also recognized, however, that the treatises and reports that made up the bulk of the materials studied at the inns of court would not be suitable for the students he envisaged studying at the universities. These were far too complex and non-systematic for anything but professional study at the inns. Thus, he published his *An Institute of the Laws of England, or, The Laws of England in their Natural Order* (1720), designed to provide a systematic treatment of the common law. These works on common law followed his *New Institute of the Imperial or Civil Law* (1704). The three works together provided both the philosophical grounds for teaching the law to non-lawyers at the universities and the texts by which to accomplish this goal. In fact, Wood's *Institute* proved to be popular not only among university students seeking a general introduction to law, but also among students at the inns of court who were always eager for systematic texts that could assist them in mastering the legal complexities with which they were faced.

The *Institute of the Laws of England* went through ten editions between 1720 and 1772; the *New Institute of the Imperial or Civil Law* went through four editions between 1704 and 1730. Both works shared a common approach, that of imposing a system and method upon difficult and often contradictory materials so as to render them suitable for a university course for those who would learn the law in its broad outlines, not for professional use but as a subject of general study to enable them better to bear the burdens of citizenship, as Wood had advised in his *Some Thoughts Concerning the Study of the Law in the Two Universities*. The *Institute of the Laws of England* was based, in some degree, upon earlier writings of Sir Henry Finch. By the beginning of the eighteenth century, much of the material included in Finch's work, such as the real actions, was irrelevant to lawyers and students. Wood's *Institute* was not only a well-written summary of the law, it was up to date and also included more original material, although later editions of the work included Wood's translation of the first chapters of *Les loix civiles dans leur ordre naturel*, by Jean Domat (*d.* 1696), a translation that Wood had first published separately in 1705 under the title *A Treatise on the First Principles of the Laws in General*. There can be little doubt that the systematic nature of Wood's treatise owed something to Domat, but Wood's work was also quite original. Both volumes were popular not only in Great Britain but also in North America and are found in a number of early American lawyers' and judges' libraries.

The quality of Wood's juristic scholarship has been the subject of some controversy. Thomas Hearne, a contemporary, dismissed Wood as 'a dabbler' (*Remarks*, 2.121). Blackstone, in many ways Wood's successor, was more positive about his achievement: 'upon the whole, his work is undoubtedly a valuable performance; and great are the obligations of the student to him' (Blackstone, vi). When seen as the link between Finch and Blackstone in the efforts to bring the common law into some systematic organization, Wood's works may be fairly and positively evaluated. The fact that he applied this same methodology to the civil law demonstrates the breadth of his learning.

Although Wood had a doctorate in civil law, modern scholars agree that 'he recognized the fact that the study of English law was more important to the student' (Holdsworth, *Eng. law*, 12.419). Nevertheless, his *New Institute of the Imperial or Civil Law* marked a milestone in English juristic writing. Wood's was one of the first English civilian treatises designed not simply for English civil lawyers but also for common lawyers and others with a general interest in law and jurisprudence. The *New Institute* is a work of comparative law and is designed to point out to readers not only a civilian rule, but also its common law analogue. By adopting this comparative approach, Wood hoped to teach students that English common law had borrowed over the centuries from civil and canon law. Although one of the most important juristic writers of the early eighteenth century, Wood has never been accorded the fame he deserves, nor has he been the subject of a full biography. He died at Hardwick on 12 July 1722.   M. H. HOEFLICH

Sources *DNB* · W. Blackstone, *An analysis of the laws of England*, 3rd edn (1758), vi · Holdsworth, *Eng. law*, 12.418–27 · D. R. Coquillette, *The civilian writers of Doctors' Commons, London* (1988), 198–203 · R. B. Robinson, 'The two institutes of Thomas Wood: a study in eighteenth-century legal scholarship', *American Journal of Legal History*, 35 (1991), 432–58 · P. Stein, 'Continental influences on English legal thought, 1600–1900', *The character and influence of the Roman civil law: historical essays* (1988), 215–18 · A. Watson, 'Justinian's *Institutes* and some English counterparts', *Studies in Justinian's Institutes: in memory of J. A. C. Thomas*, ed. P. G. Stein and A. D. E. Lewis (1983), 185–6 · C. E. Mallet, *A history of the University of Oxford*, 3 vols. (1924–7), vol. 2, pp. 459–560 · H. Johnson, *Imported eighteenth-century law treatises in American libraries, 1700–1799* (1978), 56–7 · *Remarks and collections of Thomas Hearne*, ed. C. E. Doble and others, 2, OHS, 7 (1886), 121 · A. W. B. Simpson, ed., *Biographical dictionary of the common law* (1984), 548–9 · J. L. Barton, 'Legal studies', *Hist. U. Oxf.* 5: *18th-cent. Oxf.*, 593–606
Likenesses M. Vandergucht, line engraving, BM, NPG; repro. in T. Wood, *An institute of the laws of England* (1724) [*see illus.*] · portrait, New College, Oxford

Wood, Thomas (1892–1950), composer, was born on 28 November 1892 at Chorley, Lancashire, the only child of Thomas Wood, a master mariner, and his wife, Hannah Lee. As a child he accompanied his father on many voyages and he always regarded this experience as an education of the most effective kind. It was supplemented, in his case, however, by other schooling, both general and musical; and Wood had already completed an external degree in music at Oxford before he arrived there in 1913 to work for the degree of BA which he obtained in 1918. In 1916 he migrated from Christ Church to Exeter College, with which he was to be associated for the rest of his life, and in 1917 his studies were interrupted by a period at the Admiralty. After the war, at the Royal College of Music, he studied under the direction of Sir Charles Stanford, to whom Wood's music owes much. He became DMus in 1920.

Wood spent a short time as director of music at Tonbridge School. On 2 July 1924 he married St Osyth Mahala (*b.* 1886/7), daughter of Thomas Eustace-Smith. The same year he returned to Exeter College as lecturer (he held the post until 1927) and there began the compositions for which he soon became known. During the next thirty years he produced a series of works, both choral and orchestral, of which the most successful were *Forty Singing Seamen* (1925), *A Seaman's Overture* (1927), *Daniel and the Lions* (1938), *Chanticleer* (1947), and *The Rainbow* (1951). Wood's achievements were made despite eyesight so poor as to be near blindness.

Apart from music the prevailing passions of Wood's life were the sea, foreign travel, and the British empire. For the empire he had a romantic idealist's love. He undertook extensive journeys, sometimes for musical activities, sometimes for personal interests, and at least once (1944) for the government. These journeys provided material for a number of books of which *Cobbers* (1934) was widely acclaimed as a penetrating account of the Australian scene and character. Wood's music was naturally influenced by these interests. English life, in the country or at sea, and the ways of ordinary men and women are the constant themes to which its sturdy plain-spoken individuality is well suited. After 1945, having come to feel that his wide interests were dissipating his talent, Wood prepared to devote himself wholly to musical composition. His sudden and untimely death on 19 November 1950, at his home, Parsonage Hall, Bures, Suffolk, frustrated an intention upon which his friends had based high hopes. He had been elected an honorary fellow of his college, and had been made a member of the Arts Council, in the previous year.   THOMAS ARMSTRONG, *rev.*

Sources T. Wood, *True Thomas* (1936) · private information (1959) · personal knowledge (1959) · d. cert. · m. cert. · *New Grove* · *CGPLA Eng. & Wales* (1951)
Archives BL, corresp. with Society of Authors, Add. MS 56851
Wealth at death £118,868 17s. 1d.: probate, 12 April 1951, *CGPLA Eng. & Wales*

Wood, Thomas McKinnon (1855–1927), politician, was born on 26 January 1855 at 22 Leslie Street, Stepney, London, son of Hugh Wood, merchant and shipowner in, successively, Kirkwall, Leith, and the Minories, London, and his second wife, Jessie, daughter of the Revd Thomas McKinnon, of Sauchieburn, Kincardineshire. He was educated at the Brewers' Company grammar school, Mill Hill School, and University College, London, where he matriculated in June 1872. In a distinguished undergraduate career he gained first place in the faculty of arts and the university exhibition in English. He studied political economy under L. H. Courtney and the philosophy of mind under G. C. Robertson. He graduated in 1875 with honours in logic and moral philosophy, and worked briefly on the ninth edition of the *Encyclopaedia Britannica*, covering subjects ranging from 'Casuistry' to 'Cromwell, Thomas'. He returned to London in 1878, when his father became blind, to join the family firm as a partner. The Wood family were active members of the King's Weigh House Congregational Chapel, where Wood met and married in 1883 Isabella, sister of the minister Alexander Sandison.

Wood's political career began with his election to the second London county council (LCC) in 1892, standing as a 'Progressive' (the municipal label of London Liberalism) for Central Hackney. Wood won for Progressivism a seat which had returned two Conservatives to the first council in 1889 and would return a Conservative to Westminster until 1906. He soon joined the Progressive inner circle, securing election to the party committee in February 1894, and his prominence within the majority group secured a succession of influential council positions. He chaired, at various times, the parliamentary, local government, water, and general purposes committees, and the

council itself in 1898–9. He became leader of the Progressive Party in April 1897, retaining this position until he entered the government in April 1908. Election to parliament in 1906 had already prompted his retirement as an elected councillor at the end of the last progressive LCC in March 1907, but he was elected an alderman of the seventh council and remained on the LCC until March 1909.

Wood was an effective local politician, presiding over the Progressives' two most remarkable landslide victories in 1901 and 1904, when radical Liberalism captured some of London's safest Conservative suburbs. He was not, however, an innovator in policy. He joined the council after the main objectives of Progressive municipal policy—the public ownership of water and other public utilities, the taxation of London's ground landlords, fair wages for council employees, and the extension of direct labour operations—had been defined, and he added little to the programme himself. The views articulated in such occasional statements as his address on 'Ideals of citizenship' at the 1904 Congregational Union Conference ('private enterprise necessarily and properly has to look first to the question of profit; a municipal government can do a great many things aiming not at profit but at the general benefit of the community') reflected standard progressive views. He was a typical urban radical of his day, subscribing equally to the progressive social programme and the traditional Liberal causes of free trade and Irish home rule. An offer from Harold Harmsworth, the future press baron Lord Rothermere, in 1901 to support the Progressives in return for the 'elimination of Home Rule and the acceptance of a policy of sane and unaggressive imperialism' held little appeal to Wood or most of his party. Indeed, Wood's greatest problems as party leader arose over the traditional Liberal concern of denominational education, when the Education (London) Act of 1903 established the LCC as the capital's education authority, implementing a measure detested by most nonconformists. Though a Congregationalist himself, Wood saw education as a social rather than a denominational issue, but his determination to operate the act disturbed some nonconformist progressives and ensured his vilification by militant dissent outside the council.

After three unsuccessful attempts, at East Islington (1895), St Rollox, Glasgow (1900), and Orkney and Shetland (1902), Wood entered parliament as Liberal member for St Rollox in 1906—one of five LCC Progressives to be returned. St Rollox was a largely working-class seat containing railway and other engineering works, and Wood's background in social politics helped him not merely to win the constituency in the Liberal landslide of 1906, but to retain until 1918 a seat which had previously returned a new member at every election since its creation. In his 1906 campaign he emphasized unemployment and old age pensions and indicated his support for universal suffrage, the payment of MPs, and the Labour Party's Trades Disputes Bill. At Westminster, though, he proved to be 'very nearly a silent member of the House of Commons—except when London measures were under discussion'.

Wood's ministerial career was undistinguished. He was appointed parliamentary secretary to the Board of Education by Asquith in April 1908, apparently to alleviate nonconformist misgivings over that year's abortive Education Bill. His handling of the education issue at the LCC made him a questionable choice for this task, but he had little opportunity to make further enemies before he was appointed under-secretary of state at the Foreign Office, in October 1908, ostensibly to enhance that department's commercial expertise. In October 1911 he became financial secretary to the Treasury, convincing himself that he would 'have more power than three fourths of the Cabinet', though T. P. O'Connor remembered him as doing his work there 'without any great distinction'. Despite an unimpressive ministerial record he was a convenient choice to succeed Lord Pentland as Scottish secretary, thus entering the cabinet, in February 1912. In this post he steered various measures through parliament, including the Mental Deficiency (Scotland) Act of 1913 and the Temperance (Scotland) Act of 1913; though not a teetotaller, he supported temperance and with the latter measure he became the only British politician to pass a local option bill into law. He also introduced measures necessary for Scottish wartime organization with skill and tact. In July 1916 he was again appointed financial secretary to the Treasury, remaining in the cabinet as chancellor of the duchy of Lancaster, but his ministerial career ended with the collapse of the first wartime coalition in December 1916, when he fell victim to the reconstruction of the government. The 1918 'coupon election' brought predictable humiliation to Wood, as to other Asquithians, when, after a campaign devoted largely to attacks upon Lloyd George, he lost his deposit at St Rollox, gaining only 8 per cent of the vote. He made one attempt to return to parliament in 1922, when he was defeated in his former LCC constituency of Central Hackney.

Wood served as deputy lieutenant for the county of London in 1899; he declined a knighthood in 1907, but was sworn a privy councillor in 1911. He became a life governor of University College, London, and received an honorary LLD from St Andrews University in 1899.

Wood's London addresses during his LCC years were, successively, Brookfield House, Highgate, and Portland Place. He acquired a house at Crowborough in Sussex in the 1900s. He had six sons and two daughters, four sons and one daughter surviving him. He died at 24 Queen's Gate, South Kensington, London, on 26 March 1927, two weeks after his wife. 'His nature had no expansiveness', O'Connor recalled, 'It was essentially dry, uninspired and uninspiring'. Another obituarist noted 'a certain brusqueness which unnecessarily alienated some of his political friends', suggesting that 'the cavalier way in which he sometimes treated opponents did not tend to smooth his political path'.   JOHN DAVIS

Sources Bodl. Oxf., MSS McKinnon Wood · T. P. O'Connor, *Daily Telegraph* (28 March 1927) · M. J. M. H., *University College Magazine* (June 1927) · *The Times* (28 March 1927) · *Morning Post* (28 March 1927) · A. G. Gardiner, *John Benn and the progressive movement* (1925) · minutes of the progressive party, London county council, 1889–1900, LMA · CGPLA Eng. & Wales (1927)
Archives Bodl. Oxf., corresp. and papers | U. Newcastle, corresp. with Walter Runciman
Likenesses L. Watts, oils, 1899, Guildhall Art Gallery, London
Wealth at death £130,372 2s. 3d.: probate, 13 July 1927, CGPLA Eng. & Wales

Wood, Wendy. *See* Meacham, Gwendoline Emily (1892–1981).

Wood, Western (1804–1863). *See under* Wood, Sir Matthew, first baronet (1768–1843).

Wood, William (*c*.1490–1537), prior of Bridlington, was, as an Augustinian canon, ordained subdeacon at York on 5 April 1511 and deacon on 19 February 1513. He became prior of his house on the resignation of William Brownefleet in June 1531, and for a brief time occupied the place in East Riding society traditionally assigned to the head of this wealthy monastery, in 1532 serving with the abbot of Meaux, Sir John Constable, and other gentlemen on a commission for fishgarths and weirs. In the same year he received a bequest from a Scarborough chaplain for forgotten tithes.

All too soon, however, events at Westminster intruded upon Wood's customary activities. In October 1535 he refused to accede to Cromwell's suggestion that the crown had founded the priory, maintaining that their founder had been 'Lord Water Gauntt' (Walter de Gant), whose body lay in the priory choir. At their visitation in the autumn of 1535 Cromwell's commissioners uncovered three cases of immorality among the canons, but made no allegations against the prior. Afterwards Wood sent the priory's charters to Cromwell, as instructed, together with an annuity, begging him to favour the house.

During the Pilgrimage of Grace, Bridlington had the ill fortune to be situated near Beverley, its starting point in Yorkshire, and the prior sent under duress, as he subsequently claimed, eleven men to help in the rising, providing each man with 20s. in his purse. Wood also gave Robert Aske 20 marks and the rebels in Holderness £4. He later dispatched four horsemen to the siege of Scarborough. He further compounded his offences by offering hospitality in the priory to the York Dominican friar, Dr John Pickering, who wrote there to encourage the commons his verses beginning 'O faithful people of the boreal region'. In the aftermath of the rising Wood was charged with being a principal procurer of the first insurrection and a great mover in the second. Found guilty of treason he was executed at Tyburn on 26 May 1537, together with the abbot of Jervaulx and the quondam abbot of Fountains. As a consequence of the prior's attainder Bridlington Priory, with all its possessions, was forfeited to the crown.

CLAIRE CROSS

Sources Borth. Inst., abp. reg. 26, fols. 112r, 122r · Borth. Inst., *sede vac.* reg. 5A, fols. 642r–643r · Borth. Inst., prob. reg. 11, pt 1, fol. 54v · *LP Henry VIII*, 5, no. 725; 9, nos. 670, 1173; 10, nos. 501, 998; 12/1, nos. 369, 1019, 1020(ii), 1172, 1285; 14/1, no. 867 · state papers domestic, Henry VIII, PRO, SP 1/102, fol. 90r · C. Cross and N. Vickers, eds.,

Monks, friars and nuns in sixteenth century Yorkshire, Yorkshire Archaeological Society, 150 (1995) • *VCH Yorkshire*, vol. 3 • G. W. O. Woodward, *The dissolution of the monasteries* (1966)

Wood, William (*fl.* 1629–1635), writer on America, is of unknown parentage. The dedication of his 1634 tract *New Englands Prospect* to Sir William Armyne suggests Lincolnshire roots, and its secular tone implies that Wood was not a puritan. He was first noted upon arrival in Massachusetts in 1629, roughly a year before the influx of immigrants under John Winthrop led to the founding of Boston and the colony's rapid rise in population and prominence. Wood probably lived initially at Salem, the principal English settlement before 1630, and may have moved to Saugus by 1631 when a William Woods took the Massachusetts freeman's oath (Shurtleff, 1.366).

Soon after his return to England in the summer of 1633 Wood composed his tract *New Englands prospect: a true, lively, and experimentall description of that part of America, commonly called New England*. It was entered in the London Stationers' register in July 1634, printed by Thomas Cotes, and sold at John Bellamie's shop in Cornhill. In September 1634 the Massachusetts government voted its 'thankefullnes' to 'Mr. Wood' as a benefactor of the colony (Shurtleff, 1.128). Wood apparently remained in London while Bellamie prepared a second edition of the book in 1635, which incorporated corrections and minor additions; a third edition (1639) had almost no changes.

New Englands Prospect filled an important niche. The first half describes south-eastern New England's topography, climate, and soil, and its flora and fauna. In all categories, Wood emphasized differences with England, especially the animals not found there—for example, black bears, moose, porcupines, wildcats, beavers, white-headed eagles, hummingbirds, and lobsters as big as 20 pounds. Underlying Wood's descriptions is praise for New England's bounty and beneficence. Even the region's admittedly 'evil' creatures are not serious threats to habitation: wolves are abundant but never hurt humans, horses, or cows; rattlesnakes are poisonous but not fatal if the antidote is used; mosquitoes are a nuisance but no more than in parts of England. The first half of Wood's book concludes with descriptions of the English settlements in Massachusetts (identified on the frontispiece map) and advice to prospective migrants on the appropriate food, tools, and other provisions to bring along. Part 1 is emphatically promotional.

In recent times Wood's book has been valued primarily for part 2, a diverse ethnography of south-eastern New England Native Americans. Despite its ethnocentricity, broad generalizations, and omissions, *New Englands Prospect* insightfully describes the location and size of each major Native American group and, more extensively, their physical characteristics, their clothing and ornaments, their customs in cooking and eating, their hospitality, and their hardiness. Wood is less perceptive about matters that require a deeper familiarity with Native American culture—religion, government, and warfare—but is rare among early English observers in his attention to native sports (games of chance, athletic contests), marriage and burial customs, and, controversially, native men's treatment of women. Wood concludes his book with 'a small Nomenclator' of eastern Algonquian words and phrases, from which he hopes readers 'may reape delight, if they can get no profit' (Wood, 1634, 84). *New Englands Prospect*'s sprightly style, some of it in whimsical poetry, and concise summaries of New England's natural history and native inhabitants continue to provide literary delight and intellectual profit.

Wood may have migrated permanently to New England in late 1635 or 1636. Several men named William Wood lived in Massachusetts in the mid-1630s and after, although none is identified in surviving documents as the author of *New Englands Prospect*. Perhaps the book had little appeal for neighbours who already knew first-hand about New England and its natives, although Wood earned encomiums in contemporaneous writings by Thomas Morton, Judocus Hondy, and the anonymous author of a pamphlet on Maryland. The date of his death is unknown.

ALDEN T. VAUGHAN

Sources W. Wood, *New Englands prospect* (1634) • W. Wood, *New England's prospect*, ed. A. T. Vaughan (1977) [incl. introduction] • N. B. Shurtleff, ed., *Records of the governor and company of the Massachusetts Bay in New England*, 5 vols. in 6 (1853–4) • K. B. Murdock, 'Wood, William', *DAB* • J. Walker, 'Wood, William', *American writers before 1800*, ed. J. A. Levernier and D. R. Wilmes (1983), vol. 3, pp. 1653–4

Wood, Sir William (1608/9–1691), toxophilite, was for many years marshal of the Society of Finsbury Archers, who held their meetings in Finsbury Fields. He was probably knighted by Charles II. In 1676 the society adopted the additional title of Queen Catherine's Archers and purchased, by subscription, a large and elaborately chased silver shield. This is known as the Catherine of Braganza Shield and has been attributed to John Cooques, the king's silversmith. It was entrusted to Sir William, as marshal, and subsequently was held by each succeeding captain of the Easter target until it passed to the Royal Toxophilite Society in 1781. The shield was mounted in a small cabinet, the insides of the doors of which carry portraits of Sir William Wood, painted on oak. He is portrayed in his official costume and has mustachios and a flowing beard.

A keen promoter of archery, Wood was the author of *The Bowman's Glory, or, Archery Revived*, published in 1682, with a second edition in 1691. He dedicated the book to Charles II. It has a prefatory poem 'In Praise of Archery', the texts of patents concerning archery issued by Henry VIII, James I, and Charles I, and descriptions of parades of archers. It includes 'A remembrance of the worthy show and shooting of the duke of Shoreditch' in 1583, which was reprinted in T. Roberts's *English Bowman* of 1801. The mock title of duke of Shoreditch had been bestowed by Henry VIII on an archer named Barlow. Wood died on 4 September 1691 at the age of eighty-two, and was buried on 10 September at St James's, Clerkenwell. A memorial tablet was placed on the outside of the church. Following the rebuilding of the church, in 1791 the Royal Toxophilite Society moved the tablet inside the building.

BERTHA PORTER, *rev.* STEPHEN PORTER

Sources *A history of the Royal Toxophilite Society* (1867) · E. G. Heath, introduction, in W. Wood, *The bowman's glory, or, Archery revived*, facs. edn (1969)
Likenesses R. Clamp, stipple, BM, NPG; repro. in F. G. Waldron and others, *The biographical mirrour*, 2 vols. (1795–8) · portraits on oak cabinet, Royal Toxophilite Society, Buckinghamshire

Wood, William (1671–1730), ironmaster, was born at Wolverhampton, Staffordshire, on 31 July 1671, the second son of Francis Wood (1647–1721) and Mary Grainger (*b.* 1642, *d.* after 1721). Nothing is known of his early life before his marriage on 22 February 1690 to Margaret (*b.* 1671), daughter of Richard Molineux of Willenhall, Staffordshire, a family made prosperous by the export of locks to the New World and in the linen trade in Dublin. Wood lived in the Deanery House, the largest house in Wolverhampton, and served as churchwarden and trustee of the Wolverhampton Blue Coat School. Between 1692 and 1707 eleven of their children were baptized at St Peter's Church, Wolverhampton. The next four children were not recorded in the St Peter's register and the family were living in London by 1720.

Wood was buying best iron from the Foleys in 1693–4. In 1703 the earl of Bradford bought the manor and town of Wolverhampton, and through his patronage Wood obtained the lucrative post of receiver-general of the land tax for Shropshire. In 1710 he was a shareholder in the Royal Africa Company and a friend and correspondent of Henry Morice, governor of the Bank of England. He became the leading figure in a company supplying iron and steel to London, an enterprise which prospered especially during the embargo on Swedish iron between 1717 and 1719. The partnership comprised three midland and three London ironmasters. He was in partnership also with his brother Richard Wood in ironworks at Tern, Shropshire, and with Thomas Harvey at Ruabon, Denbighshire. From 1720 Wood plunged into ever more ambitious enterprises. He formed a partnership to supply copper coins to the Royal Mint and in 1720 entered into an agreement with the Mines Royal Company and the Company of Mineral and Battery Works to supply calamine and brass and other metals in thirty-nine of the fifty-two counties of England and Wales in which the company still claimed rights of pre-emption. He proposed to set up a public company, though advised that this was in breach of the recently enacted Bubble Act, but in the same month the South Sea company collapsed and with it many other companies. Wood's company had ceased trading by July 1721, with losses of £26,675.

Wood nevertheless obtained in July 1722 a patent to supply halfpence and farthings for use in Ireland, during ten years, to the value of £108,000. At the same time he obtained the patent to supply coins to the American colonies, and he was exporting coins in 1722 and the earlier part of 1723. Minting of the Irish coins began in January 1723, in Phoenix Street, Westminster, and they were conveyed to Bristol for shipment to Ireland. Although the workmanship was good the brass content was low, and the measure involved a tax upon the country of between £6000 and £7000 a year. The imposition of English coinage in Ireland, and the lack of consultation, alienated Irish opinion at all levels of society, and opposition was voiced in the addresses of the Irish houses of parliament in September 1723. Wood published an injudicious reply. The wildest accusations were circulated, alleging bribery, mismanagement, deliberate fraud, and the destabilization of the Irish economy. It was in the context of a flood of pamphlets and broadsides that Jonathan Swift, dean of Dublin and tory polemical writer, published the first of his twopenny tracts called *Letter to the Shopkeepers Tradesmen Farmers and Common People of Ireland by M. B. Drapier.* This was followed by six more pamphlets, of which the last purported to be *A True Account of the Solemn Procession to the Gallows at the Execution of William Wood.* They conferred notoriety on Wood but were primarily a political attack on Walpole and the whigs and part of a much wider opposition campaign. Walpole's ministry was divided and its power threatened and the constitutional status of Ireland called into question. Nevertheless it was three years before Walpole gave way, and Wood's patent was not withdrawn until August 1725. In 1730 Wood was awarded a pension of £3000 a year in compensation for his losses in the affair.

Wood's next project was on an even larger scale. In 1728 he undertook to supply 10,000 tons of malleable iron to the Mines Royal Company and the Company of Mineral and Battery Works annually at the low price of £10 a ton. He intended to produce this huge quantity by a process, patented the previous year by his son Francis, to smelt iron with coal, rather than charcoal as was customary. A new works was built on Frizington Common near Whitehaven and a contract was agreed with Lord Lowther for the purchase of coal. After a year of great expense only a small quantity of poor-quality iron was made; Lord Lowther and other members of the board became disillusioned and sought to dissociate themselves from the enterprise. By this time Wood had received considerable supplies of money and the board refused to supply any more until iron was produced in the quality and quantity specified in the contract.

In December 1729 Wood announced that he was setting up yet another company, this time consisting of himself, two of his sons, and Kingsmill Eyre, and he petitioned the privy council to grant a charter under the name of the Governors and Company of Ironmasters of Great Britain with a subscribed capital of £1 million. There followed six months of vigorous lobbying of the privy council by Wood and two groups of opponents, the Mines Royal on the one hand, and on the other a party led by one Thomas Tomkyns (the holder of an earlier patent to smelt iron with coal). For a second time Wood was the subject of a virulent press campaign, but this one lacked the acerbity of Swift's prose. It consisted mainly of advertisements, vulgar diatribes in verse, and name-calling in the popular press. The privy council examined the application for incorporation on 4 August 1730, but Wood had died a few days earlier on 2 August. In his will, drawn up in 1729, Wood described himself as of Hampstead in the county of Middlesex and was said then to be living at Killigrew Court, in Scotland Yard, off Whitehall, in Westminster. He was buried at Wolverhampton on 6 August 1730. His sons Francis, Charles, and John were burdened with his debts but recovered their position, and each made important contributions to the development of the iron industry in the next generation.   M. B. ROWLANDS

Sources private information (2004) · J. M. Treadwell, 'William Wood and the Company of Ironmasters of Great Britain', *Business History*, 16 (1974), 97–112 · A. Goodwin, 'Wood's halfpence', *EngHR*, 51 (1936), 647–74 · M. Flinn, 'William Wood and the coke-smelting process', *Transactions* [Newcomen Society], 34 (1961–2), 55–71 · J. F. Ede, *History of Wednesbury* (1962), 30 · W. K. V. Gale, *The Black Country iron industry* (1966), 56 · G. Morton and N. Mutton, 'The transition to Cort's puddling process', *Journal of the Iron and Steel Institute*, 205 (1967), 723 · P. Riden, *A gazetteer of charcoal-fired blast furnaces in Great Britain in use since 1660* (1987) · J. H. Plumb, *Sir Robert Walpole*, 2 vols. (1956–60) · *Swift's Drapier's letters*, ed. H. Davies (1936) · R. A. Mott, 'Coalbrookdale: the early years', *Transactions of the Shropshire Archaeological Society*, 56 (1957–60), 82–93 · J. M. Treadwell, 'Swift, William Wood, and the factual basis of satire', *Journal of British Studies*, 15/2 (1975–6), 76–91 · J. M. Treadwell, 'William Wood of Jamaica: a colonial mercantilist of the 18th century', *Journal of Caribbean History*, 8 (1976), 42–64

Archives BL, Add. Ch 70568 · BL, Add. MS 22675 · BL, Add. MS 36138 · CUL, Companies of Mines Royal and Mineral and Battery Works, MS 54/9/1/ · PRO, E 112/104/64 · PRO, E 112/1281/20 · PRO, E 127/36/11 · PRO, PC 1/4/106/40–53 · PRO, Privy Council register · PRO, T 1/196/29 · PRO, T 22/2/17 · Wolverhampton Charity School Board · *Calendar of treasury papers*, 1714–19 | BL, papers relating to Royal Mines Company of Jamaica

Wood, William (1745–1808), Unitarian minister and botanist, was born on 29 May 1745 at Collingtree, near Northampton, the son of Benjamin Wood, a member of Philip Doddridge's congregation at Castle Hill, Northampton. He received his grammar school education at the school conducted by the Revd Stephen Addington at Market Harborough, Leicestershire, before, in 1761, at the age of sixteen, studying for the nonconformist ministry at the academy conducted by the Revd Dr David Jennings in Wellclose Square, London. On the death of the doctrinally orthodox Jennings in 1762 the academy removed to Hoxton, which with Samuel Morton Savage, Andrew Kippis, and Abraham Rees as tutors became the main place of education for rational dissenters in London. Wood preached his first sermon at Debenham, Suffolk, on 6 July 1766. Until he was chosen minister at Stamford, Lincolnshire, in September 1767 he preached to the principal congregations in London, including that of Dr Richard Price at Newington Green, who became a friend. He was ordained with Abraham Rees, his former tutor, at the meeting-house in St Thomas, Southwark. In November 1770 he moved to Ipswich, as assistant to the Revd T. Scott. Shortly afterwards he received an invitation to Old Meeting, Birmingham, which he declined. In 1772, at the age of twenty-six, he was invited to succeed Joseph Priestley at Leeds on the joint recommendation of Price and Priestley. He preached as a candidate on 10 January 1773 and began

his ministry on 30 May; he remained there until his death nearly thirty-five years later. His first sermon, on the reciprocal duties of minister and congregation, was afterwards published. Wood early in life had relinquished the Calvinist principles which he had inherited, and was an anti-Trinitarian by the time of his appointment at Leeds, but like most rational dissenters he did not preach on doctrinal matters from the pulpit. On 29 September 1780 Wood married Louisa Ann (1758–1806), second daughter of George Oates of Low-Hall, near Leeds, 'a family of great wealth at Leeds' (Hunter, 'Biographical notices'). They had three sons and one daughter.

At Leeds, Wood soon developed an interest in natural history as a result of the country rides he undertook for his health. His particular interest was botany, in which he gained some reputation. He was responsible for the natural history section of the *Annual Review*, and contributed botanical articles to Abraham Rees's *Cyclopaedia*, completing the entries for B and C before his death. He also contributed many entries for James Sowerby's *English Botany* (1790–99), which bears the name of its illustrator rather than Wood's friend and fellow Unitarian Sir James Edward Smith, the first president of the Linnean Society, who prepared the text. Wood was elected a fellow of the society in June 1791. He also assisted William Withering in the second edition of his *Botanical Arrangements of the Vegetables in Great Britain* (1787–92). His other publications were principally sermons, but included a liturgy, his *Form of Prayers* (1801), for the use of his congregation compiled from the services of the dissenters in Liverpool and Shrewsbury and of the Church of England. He published funeral sermons for William Turner senior of Wakefield (1794), Newcome Cappe of York (1804), and Joseph Priestley (1805), a sermon, *Commencement of the Nineteenth Century* (1801), and another for the charity schools attached to Old Meeting and New Meeting, Birmingham, which he considered his best sermon. He was actively engaged in the application to parliament for the repeal of the Test and Corporation Acts, and chaired the public meeting of the protestant nonconformist ministers of the West Riding held in Leeds on 24 April 1789. He was a country delegate to the London committee for repeal of the Test and Corporation Acts in early 1790. He published *Christian duty of cultivating a spirit of universal benevolence amidst the present unhappy national hostilities* (1781), two sermons delivered to mark the centenary of the revolution of 1688 (1788), and another on the day of thanksgiving for the restoration of peace (1802).

Wood had a crucial part in preventing the dissolution of Manchester Academy following the resignation of George Walker as theological tutor. 'By his advice, principally', it was removed to York, where the new theological tutor, Charles Wellbeloved, was minister (Wellbeloved, 94). As visitor to the college Wood gave Wellbeloved much encouragement during the early period at York. His eldest son, George William Wood, MP for South Lancashire (1832), a prominent Manchester manufacturer and a leading Unitarian layman of the early nineteenth century, was also to give invaluable support to Wellbeloved as college treasurer. Wood died in Leeds on 1 April 1808, from 'inflammation of the bowels' (Cappe, 230) and was buried four days later in Mill Hill Chapel yard, Leeds.

DAVID L. WYKES

Sources C. Wellbeloved, *Memoirs of the life and writings of the late Rev. W. Wood, F.L.S. and minister of the protestant dissenting chapel at Mill-Hill, in Leeds, to which are subjoined, an address, delivered at his interment, on Tuesday, April 5; a sermon, on occasion of his death, preached on Sunday, April 10, 1808* (1809) · C. Cappe, 'Biography: memoir of the late Rev. William Wood, of Leeds', *Monthly Repository*, 3 (1808), 229–34 [see also list of publications, p. 398] · [C. Cappe], *GM*, 1st ser., 78 (1808), 945 [unsigned memoir] · T. Jervis, 'Memoir of the Rev. William Wood', *Athenaeum: a Magazine of Literary and Miscellaneous Information*, 3 (1808), 480–87 · A. Rees and others, *The cyclopaedia, or, Universal dictionary of arts, sciences, and literature*, 45 vols. (1819–20), vol. 38 · R. V. Taylor, ed., *The biographia Leodiensis, or, Biographical sketches of the worthies of Leeds* (1865) · J. Britten and G. S. Boulger, eds., *A biographical index of British and Irish botanists* (1893) · J. Hunter, *Familiae minorum gentium*, ed. J. W. Clay, 1, Harleian Society, 37 (1894), 267 · J. E. Smith, J. Sowerby, and others, *English botany*, 36 vols. (1790–1814) · J. Hunter, 'Biographical notices of some of my contemporaries who have gained some celebrity', BL, Add. MS 36527, fol. 53r · minutes of proceedings of the committee of the Manchester Academy, 1786–1810, Harris Man. Oxf., MSS M.N.C. Misc. 65 · T. W. Davis, ed., *Committees for the repeal of the Test and Corporation Acts: minutes, 1786–90 and 1827–8*, London RS, 14 (1978), 49–50, 52 · B. Smith, ed., *Truth, liberty, religion: essays celebrating two hundred years of Manchester College* (1986)

Archives Harris Man. Oxf., corresp.

Likenesses H. Liversedge, oils, 1830 (after G. K. Ralph), Harris Man. Oxf. · silhouette, repro. in Wellbeloved, *Memoirs*, frontispiece

Wealth at death limited income: Wellbeloved, *Memoirs*, 105

Wood, William (1774–1857), conchologist and bookseller, born in Kendal, Westmorland, was possibly the son of Jonathan Wood and baptized on 2 February 1774 at Cockermouth, Cumberland. He studied medicine at St Bartholomew's Hospital, London, under John Abernethy, and first practised as a surgeon at Wingham, near Canterbury. Increasingly, however, his interests turned to natural history. He was elected a fellow of the Linnean Society on 20 March 1798, his proposers stating that 'amongst the various pursuits after knowledge [he had] made that of natural history his study'; by this time he was living in London at North Audley Street, though still practising medicine. Wood was especially interested in conchology, his growing fascination demonstrated by a paper, 'Observations on the hinges of British bivalve shells', read to the Linnean Society on 6 January 1801. His three-volume *Zoogeography, or, The Beauties of Nature Displayed* (1807), illustrated by William Daniell, was followed by *General Conchology* (1815), two works that established his status as a natural historian; he was elected a fellow of the Royal Society in 1812. His edition of Georges Buffon's *Natural History*, with a life of the author, was published in the same year.

From about 1815 Wood gave up medicine and established himself as a bookseller in the Strand, dealing mainly in books on natural history, and according to William Swainson he was 'the most learned bookseller in London for works connected with natural history'. Wood's new career allowed him to devote himself to natural history, and to make links with other naturalists. His most important publication was the *Index testaceologicus, or, A*

Catalogue of Shells, British and Foreign (editions in 1818, 1825, and 1828, with a supplement in 1828, and a revised edition, *An Illustrated Catalogue of British and Foreign Shells*, by Sylvanus Hanley, in 1856); it was illustrated with miniature figures of the species drawn from original specimens in a number of private collections, including those of Henry Constantine Jennings (1731–1819), John Mawe (1764–1829), J. E. Gray (1800–1875), and the distinguished botanical artist James Sowerby (1757–1822) and his son G. B. Sowerby (1788–1854). In his circular seeking subscribers for this work, Wood stated that the engravings would be produced by 'Mr Sowerby', but in the 1828 edition he noted that 'all the plates, (with the exception of the first six by … the late Mr. Sowerby) have been executed under the immediate inspection of the Author'. Swainson, however, stated that 'Mr. Wood jun.' was responsible for them. Against the general trend to favour J. B. Lamarck's system of classification, Wood adhered strictly to the Linnaean system, and the *General Conchology* and the *Index testaceologicus* became among the best-known of the popular books of the first quarter of the nineteenth century which still appeared in Linnaean guise, despite the fact that the system's flaws had been recognized by most competent conchologists. With some reluctance Wood acknowledged the advances made by Lamarck by providing a table in the third edition (1828) of the *Index testaceologicus* which equated the Linnaean and Lamarckian genera. Hanley's 1856 revision further remedied the inconvenience of seeking the species of a Lamarckian genus in plates adapted for the Linnaean system.

Wood's other major works were *Illustrations of the Linnean Genera of Insects* (1821), *Catalogue … of the Best Works on Natural History* (1824–32), *Index entomologicus, or, A complete illustrated catalogue … of the lepidopterous insects of Great Britain* ([1833–]1839, 3rd edn 1854), and *A Complete Illustration of the British Fresh-Water Fishes* (1842?–1843); these volumes illustrate Wood's interest in all aspects of natural history and his role as a popularizer of the subject. Wood, who was married, ceased his career in the book trade in 1840 when he moved to Ruislip in Middlesex. He died from bronchitis on 28 May 1857, at Ruislip, leaving a son, William.

PETER DAVIS

Sources W. Swainson, *Taxidermy: bibliography and biography* (1840) · S. P. Dance, *A history of shell collecting*, rev. edn (1986) · membership records, records of meetings, and collections, Linn. Soc. · W. Wood, introduction, *Index testaceologicus, or, A catalogue of shells, British and foreign*, 2nd edn (1828) · W. Wood, introduction, *Index testaceologicus, or, A catalogue of shells, British and foreign*, 2nd edn, suppl. (1828) · *IGI* · d. cert. · *DNB*

Archives Linn. Soc.

Wood, William Page, Baron Hatherley (1801–1881), lord chancellor, was born at his parents' home in Falcon Square, London, on 29 November 1801, the second son and fourth child of Sir Matthew *Wood, first baronet (1768–1843), hop merchant and sometime lord mayor of London, and his wife, Maria Page (c.1770–1848). Most of his early childhood was spent with his maternal grandmother at Woodbridge in Suffolk, where for a time he attended the free school. From 1809 to 1812 he was at Dr Lindsay's school at Bow in Essex, and in September 1812 he started at Winchester College where he remained until 1818 when, as a senior prefect, he was expelled for his involvement in a school protest against a master who had used corporal punishment on prefects. His expulsion did not hold him back in any way from pursuing further education, and he went for two years to Geneva, where he was placed in the charge of Duvillard, professor of *belles-lettres*, and attended university lectures. Through his father he was introduced to many politicians both in England and in Paris (1817). At the Auditoire in Geneva he learned French, Italian, and mathematics, and mixed with the university students. In 1820 he returned to England as an escort for Queen Caroline, who enjoyed his support and loyalty during her later court case. Indeed, Wood even collected evidence in Italy on her behalf.

By the time Wood entered Trinity College, Cambridge, in October 1820, he was much more mature, cultivated, and better informed than most undergraduates of his years, but his university years were hampered by ill health. In 1821 he won the second college declamation prize with an essay defending the revolution of 1688, and in 1822 was elected to a scholarship; but he came out only twenty-fourth wrangler in January 1824, and had to withdraw from the final classical examination altogether. In October 1824 he was only narrowly elected to a fellowship, since he was imagined by some to hold his father's radical opinions, and his prize essay of 1821 had not been forgotten.

On 1 March 1824, through the help of Brougham and Denman, Wood entered Lincoln's Inn where he read law in the chamber of Roupell. After studying conveyancing under John Tyrrell in 1826, he was called to the bar on 27 November 1827, and started practice at 3 Old Square, Lincoln's Inn. He soon found clients, and his first speech in court was delivered before the House of Lords in *Westmeath* v. *Westmeath*. He did much railway work before parliamentary committees from 1828 to 1841, as well as in the chancery courts, and it was out of one of his cases that the clause afterwards known as the 'Wharncliffe clause' originated. In 1841 he gave up parliamentary work, and his chancery practice immediately increased. He became a queen's counsel in February 1845.

Wood's father had inherited a large fortune, and his own savings from professional earnings were enough to make him independent of practice. As early as 1829 he was earning £1000 a year, and had become engaged to Charlotte (1804–1878), the daughter of Major Edward Moore. They were married on 5 January 1830, and lived in Dean's Yard, Westminster, until 1844; they had no children. As a queen's counsel Wood attached himself to the court of Vice-Chancellor Sir James Wigram.

Wood was a strong high-churchman and an advanced Liberal, and, entering parliament for Oxford in 1847, spoke principally on ecclesiastical topics, such as church rates, the ecclesiastical commission, the Deceased Wife's Sister Bill, and the admission of Jews to parliament. In 1850 he chaired a committee on the oaths question and moved that Baron Rothschild, who was Jewish, should be

allowed to take up his parliamentary seat. He also spoke and voted in favour of the ballot and household suffrage and against the game laws. In May 1849 he accepted from Lord Campbell, chancellor of the duchy, the vice-chancellorship of the county palatine of Lancaster, then a sinecure worth £600 a year, but only on condition that his court should be reformed and be made an actual working tribunal. An act was accordingly passed for this purpose, and he held the office for two years.

In 1851 Wood was a member of the commission on the court of chancery, and prepared several bills, all of which were ultimately passed, which aimed to improve chancery procedure. In the same year he was appointed solicitor-general in Lord John Russell's administration and was knighted. A vice-chancellorship was offered to him shortly afterwards, which he was inclined to accept, as the strain of office, particularly during the passing of the Ecclesiastical Titles Bill, which he heartily supported, took a heavy toll on his health. However, at Lord John Russell's request he refused the offer and held on.

The government fell in February 1852, but in December, when forming his administration, Lord Aberdeen offered Wood a choice between the solicitor-generalship and the vice-chancellorship (vacated by Sir George James Turner, on his appointment as lord justice). Wood accepted the vice-chancellorship and was sworn in before the beginning of the Hilary term 1853. For the next fifteen years he was an active chancery judge. His normal practice, which he only departed from once, was to deliver oral judgments only, because his eyesight was poor and he felt that a written judgment would cause unnecessary delay. Lord Campbell, when lord chancellor, criticized this approach in his appeal judgment in *Burch* v. *Bright*; however, the other vice-chancellors and the master of the rolls united in protesting against such indirect lecturing of a chancery judge. Wood then received an apology from Campbell.

In addition to his judicial work Wood was constantly engaged in commissions on various legal and ecclesiastical topics including questions concerning cathedrals, divorce, legal education, consolidation of statute law, and the University of Cambridge commission. He was also one of the arbitrators in the dispute between the estranged queen and the king of Hanover over the rights of possession of the Hanover crown jewels. He became a lord justice of appeal in February 1868, and was appointed lord chancellor in Gladstone's administration of December 1868.

Wood's selection was somewhat unexpected but, at a time when the disestablishment of the Irish church was being prepared, his two great characteristics of sound legal learning and earnest churchmanship made him eminently suited for the position. He was created Baron Hatherley of Hatherley in the county of Gloucestershire.

During his tenure as lord chancellor, Hatherley took an effective part in the Irish church debates, although he was not a particularly eloquent speaker. He passed the Bankruptcy Act of 1869—a measure afterwards deemed defective because it encouraged costly bankruptcy proceedings and did not adequately protect assets from being dissipated—and the Judicial Committee Act of 1871. He did not pass his judicature bill. Disappointed and nearly blind, he resigned in 1872. He died on 10 July 1881 at his home, 3 Great George Street, Westminster. He was buried in the churchyard of Great Bealings, Suffolk, five days later. The peerage became extinct on Hatherley's death. Sir Evelyn *Wood was his nephew and Katharine *Parnell his niece.

As a lawyer Hatherley was learned and industrious and he made a good and efficient judge. His decisions were rarely appealed and even more rarely reversed. Outside the law he had many activities and interests. As a young man he translated the *Novum organum* for Basil Montagu's edition of the works of Francis Bacon, and through Montagu he came to know a literary circle which included Coleridge, Carlyle, and Irving. His schoolfellow Dean Hook remained a friend all his life. A deeply pious man, from 1834 onwards Wood was a member of the committee of the National Society, and from 1836 to 1877 was a Sunday school teacher in his own parish of St Margaret's, Westminster.

Lord Westbury once described him as a mere bundle of virtues without a redeeming vice. Tolerant as well as devout, he supported the bill for the admission of Jews into parliament and disapproved of any religion-based political disability.

J. A. HAMILTON, *rev.* SINÉAD AGNEW

Sources Venn, *Alum. Cant.* · L. G. Pine, *The new extinct peerage, 1884–1971: containing extinct, abeyant, dormant, and suspended peerages with genealogies and arms* (1972), 144 · W. R. W. Stephens, ed., *A memoir of the right hon. William Page, Baron Hatherley*, 1 (1883), 5–7 · W. P. Baildon, ed., *The records of the Honorable Society of Lincoln's Inn: admissions*, 2 (1896), 106 · J. B. Atlay, *The Victorian chancellors*, 2 (1908), 337–70 · *The Times* (12 July 1881) · *St James's Magazine*, new ser., 4 (1869–70), 763–71 · E. Kilmurray, *Dictionary of British portraiture*, 3 (1981)
Archives BL, corresp. with W. E. Gladstone, Add. MS 44205 · Bodl. Oxf., letters to Lord Kimberley · LPL, corresp. with Lord Selborne · LPL, letters to A. C. Tait · NL Ire., letters to Lord O'Hagan · NRA, priv. coll., letters to Cecil and W. F. Hook · PRO, corresp. with second Earl Granville, PRO 30/29
Likenesses G. Richmond, oils, 1872, NPG · Ape [C. Pellegrini], caricature, chromolithograph, NPG; repro. in *VF* (28 Nov 1885) · L. C. Dickinson, group portrait, oils (*Gladstone's cabinet of 1868*), NPG · W. Holl, stipple (after G. Richmond; Grillion's Club series), BM · Lock & Whitfield, woodburytype photograph, NPG; repro. in T. Cooper, *Men of mark: a gallery of contemporary portraits* (1878) · H. T. Wells, group portrait, oils (*The lord chancellor's procession, 1868*), Gov. Art Coll. · lithograph, NPG · photograph, NPG
Wealth at death £105,247 1s. 5d.: resworn probate, Jan 1883, CGPLA Eng. & Wales (1881)

Woodall, Sir Corbet (1841–1916), gas engineer, was born on 27 August 1841 at Liverpool, the youngest of the three sons of William Woodall, manager of Liverpool gasworks, and his wife, Martha Basson. After education at the Crescent School, Liverpool (run by Congregationalists), he followed his brothers into the gas industry; he became the most notable of a dynasty of gas engineers stretching over four generations. After a couple of years gaining experience under his eldest brother, William *Woodall, at Burslem in the Potteries, Corbet moved to London in 1859 to work at Woolwich under Robert Morton, one of the leading gas engineers of the day.

When he was twenty-four Woodall was appointed engineer and manager of the small Stockton-on-Tees municipal gas works; he was one of many young men given major responsibilities in the rapidly expanding industry. There he was responsible for rebuilding the works on a substantially larger scale. Woodall's talents were quickly recognized and he began to act as a consultant to other gas undertakings in the north-east. After four years he returned to London as engineer and manager of the large Vauxhall gasworks of the Phoenix Company, where he could again combine his duties with private consultancy. His reputation as an engineer grew rapidly. He was interested not only in the making of gas but also its utilization. When electric lighting first threatened the gas lighting market in the late 1870s, he worked closely with a lighting manufacturer, William Sugg, to improve standards of street lighting. Their technical changes and designs were particularly successful and were widely adopted both in Britain and overseas. Woodall presented many technical papers to the Institution of Gas Engineers, of which he was elected president in 1877–8, 1897–8, and 1912–13; he was also an active member of the Institution of Civil Engineers and the Institution of Mechanical Engineers. When the Phoenix was taken over in 1880 by the neighbouring South Metropolitan Gas Company under Sir George Livesey, Woodall's near contemporary, his consultancy practice was so well established that he was able to devote himself to it full-time.

Woodall soon became recognized as one of the world's leading gas engineers, and he travelled widely abroad. As well as inspecting gasworks and advising on improved methods of gas making, he was in great demand to represent companies, giving evidence before parliamentary committees and acting as valuer or arbitrator in proceedings between companies. In 1889 he visited the USA on behalf of the Gas Light and Coke Company to advise on the practicability of new gas-making methods as an alternative to the traditional coal carbonization process used in Britain. In 1897 Woodall was invited to join the court of Gas Light and Coke; he also became a director of a number of other British and foreign gas companies.

In 1865 Woodall married Anne, daughter of W. H. Whiteman of Craydon; they had five daughters and five sons, four of whom entered the gas industry. Henry went into partnership in his father's consultancy and also became a director of the Gas Light and Coke Company. Harold was an engineer at Bournemouth and, in partnership with Arthur Duckham, developed the use of vertical retorts for gas making in Britain in place of the traditional horizontal retorts. Their contracting firm, Woodall–Duckham, became internationally known.

For some years before Woodall became a director of Gas Light and Coke, the company, which operated largely north of the Thames, had been in fierce rivalry with South Metropolitan, which supplied gas in south London. Although Gas Light and Coke had been the first gas company established in Britain (in 1812), South Metropolitan under Livesey was more technically advanced and better managed, and could therefore sell its gas much more cheaply. This caused considerable public unease, but with Woodall's guidance and great practical and managerial experience, the rehabilitation of the Gas Light and Coke Company began. Woodall's influence in technical matters was complemented in commercial matters by David Milne-Watson. On the death in 1906 of the governor of the company, Sir William Makins, Woodall was appointed to succeed him as head of what had become the largest gas company in the world.

As a young engineer, Woodall defended existing patterns of labour relations against nascent trade unionism. In later life he became convinced of the advantages of the partnership between managers and employees so enthusiastically promoted by his friend Livesey. When Woodall became governor of Gas Light and Coke he introduced 'co-partnership' to the company and, following his lead, it was adopted by far more companies after Livesey's death than during the latter's lifetime. Woodall was also instrumental in developing various training schemes for employees. He helped to form a Territorial Army battalion largely composed of employees, of which he was honorary colonel. In 1912 he received the honorary degree of DSc from the University of Leeds. In the following year, he was knighted for services to the gas industry. A Liberal in politics, he was active only at a local level, whereas his brother William was MP for Stoke-on-Trent (1880–85), and Hanley (1885–1900). He was appointed a JP for Bromley, Kent, in 1911. He was a committed Congregationalist and a generous supporter of charities.

In 1914 Woodall began to suffer from heart problems and spent much time in the south of France; but he never fully recovered, and died at Phyllis Court, Torquay, on 17 May 1916. Survived by his wife, he left estate valued at £97,442 11s. 9d. In a fitting tribute, his successor as governor of the Gas Light and Coke Company, David Milne-Watson, argued that he 'would have made a great statesman, a great lawyer or a great diplomatist' (DBB). Along with Sir George Livesey, he was one of the leading gas engineers of the time.   FRANCIS GOODALL

Sources D. Matthews, 'Woodall, Sir Corbet', DBB · Gas World (20 May 1916) · F. Goodall, 'The British gas appliance industry, 1875–1939', PhD diss., U. Lond., 1992 · T. I. Williams, *A history of the British gas industry* (1981) · S. Everard, *The history of the Gas Light and Coke Company, 1812–1949* (1949) · WWBMP · WWW
Archives LMA, archives of Gas Light and Coke Company · LMA, archives of Phoenix Company · LMA, archives of South Metropolitan Company
Likenesses portrait, repro. in Matthews, 'Woodall, Sir Corbet'
Wealth at death £97,442 11s. 9d.: probate, 19 Aug 1916, CGPLA Eng. & Wales

Woodall, John (1570–1643), surgeon, was probably born at Castle Street, Warwick, the eldest son of Richard Woodall (d. 1598), landowner and small farmer, and his wife, Mary, daughter of Peirse Ithell of north Wales. Woodall began his professional career as a surgeon in Lord Willoughby's regiment which took part in the Normandy campaign against the Catholic League from 1589 to 1590. He then spent eight years in Poland and at Stade, a Hanseatic port near Hamburg, where he was surgeon to the English merchants and occasionally interpreted in German for

John Woodall (1570–1643), by George Glover, pubd 1639

English ambassadors. After travelling to the Netherlands and other European countries he returned to London and became free of the Barber–Surgeons' Company by apprenticeship on 24 March 1601, as well as a freeman of the City of London. On 18 December 1603 he married the widow Sarah Stavely, *née* Henchpole (d. 1641); they lived in Wood Street, Cheapside. The following year he accompanied an embassy sent to negotiate business in Poland. A dispute over the considerable property left by his father at Warwick to Woodall's youngest brother was resolved by the latter's death in 1607.

Woodall (calling himself Udall initially) played a full role in the activities of the Barber–Surgeons' Company for nearly half his life. Warden of its yeomanry in 1609, he leased the company's Moorgate property between 1609 and 1611, served as anatomy steward from 1610 to at least 1612 and anatomy master from 1612 to at least 1613, was elected to the court of assistants in 1619, and rose from lower warden (1626), middle warden (1627), and upper warden (1628—but he did not serve) to master in 1632. In addition he trained many apprentices, frequently acted as auditor, elector, and examiner, and participated in the work of at least twenty committees (1620–41). The most important of these dealt with a parliamentary bill against the College of Physicians (1620 and 1621); others concerned surgery students' lectures (1635–6), and building a new anatomy theatre, great parlour, and library (1636–8). The anatomy theatre, designed by Inigo Jones in 1636, was modelled on the famous one at Padua and was not demolished until 1784. It carried a plaque which commemorated Woodall's generosity in providing the cedarwood for its seats and the wainscotting. Woodall also held the post of surgeon to two London hospitals—Thomas Sutton's at the

Charterhouse (1614–27) and St Bartholomew's (1616–43)—and was associated with Christ's Hospital (1642 and earlier).

In 1613 Woodall was appointed the first surgeon-general of the East India Company, probably recommended by Sir Thomas Smyth, its governor and his patron. Responsible for selecting surgeons, treating injured workmen at the company's small dockside hospital at Blackwall (Poplar), and supplying ships with surgeons' chests, he published in 1617 *The Surgions Mate, or, A Treatise … of the Surgions Chest*, the first good medical textbook of its kind in English, chiefly written for young sea surgeons. The instruments and medicines for a surgeon's chest, with their uses, are clearly described, followed by sections on acute surgical problems, potentially lethal medical conditions, a discourse on scurvy, and a treatise about alchemy and chemical medicines. Woodall's is also the earliest comprehensive clinical account of scurvy to prescribe lemon juice for its prevention and cure. Between 1626 and 1628 the Barber-Surgeons were authorized to supply surgeons' chests for the navy, merchant marine, and the army, which prompted Woodall to publish in 1628 his *Viaticum, the Path-Way to the Surgeons Chest*; specializing in the treatment of gunshot wounds it was mainly designed to instruct young surgeons with the English troops who attempted to relieve Huguenots blockaded in the Atlantic port of La Rochelle. This short work and Woodall's *Treatise … of … the Plague* and a *Treatise of Gangrene and Sphacelos* were incorporated with separate title-pages in a revised and extended edition of *The Surgeons Mate, or, Military and Domestique Surgery* in 1639. Dedicated to Charles I, it contains an equestrian portrait of Woodall engraved by William Marshall and a fine plate illustrating Woodall's own invented hand trephine, safely used for cutting holes in skulls for the next three centuries. His detailed description of the amputation of sphacelos, or dead tissue, at the upper limit of established gangrene, enabling him to save more than a hundred lives, was long accepted as a standard work on the subject. A discourse on venereal disease and a dispensatory of medicines, promised in the epilogue to his *Surgions Mate* in 1617, never materialized.

Woodall, often compelled to practise plague cures abroad in order to earn a living, remained at his London posts during the several visitations between 1603 and 1638, despite contracting the bubonic plague twice. At the end of his plague treatise there is a full account of his *aurum vitae* nostrum, or 'Cordiall Powder made of Gold', supported by copies of certified cures performed gratis with it at Northampton and Westminster during the 1637–8 outbreak. (A separate and extremely rare version of the treatise appeared in 1642 under the title *The Cure of the Plague by an Antidote Called aurum vitae*.) In or before 1612 he had presented the Barber-Surgeons' Company with a table and a picture of Paracelsus. *The Surgions Mate* also reflects his keen interest in both theoretical and practical Paracelsian iatrochemistry and chemical medicines. A 78-page section on alchemy, written for novice ship surgeons in the 1617 edition, is expanded in the second with an extra 12-page essay entitled 'Certain fragments concerning chirurgerie and alchymie', supplemented by an excellent table of alchemical symbols and a glossary of alchemical terms. In January 1625 Woodall was briefly imprisoned in the Fleet prison for bringing a legal action against Sir Thomas Merry, executor to John Pountis (in turn, executor to the magus John Dee); Merry had left his London house in Woodall's custody before making a final voyage to Virginia. Many years later Elias Ashmole acquired several of Dee's rare manuscript books and papers, found in the secret drawer to a chest belonging to Woodall, who also knew Dee's son Arthur, the alchemical writer.

Woodall invested large sums of money as a shareholder in the East India, Virginia, and Somers Island companies. Although the extent of his participation in the East India Company's first joint-stock venture in 1612 is not clear, he held at least a thousand shares in its second stock of 1620. By 1609, the year in which the Virginia Company obtained its charter, with Sir Thomas Smyth as its first treasurer, he was already shipping medical, surgical, and other provisions, later followed by cattle, to the colony's plantations. In 1623 he was appointed to a committee for importing tobacco, the company's main source of profit; he himself imported Virginia tobacco to England from about 1621 to 1634. After protracted legal proceedings (1626–34), he secured his option of purchasing the Virginia estate, worth £1000, of Sir Thomas Argall, a former deputy governor, and was again imprisoned in the Fleet during March 1635. In 1613 he owned a prosperous plantation in Bermuda, and when the island was incorporated as the Somers Island Company two years later he became a charter member, also importing Bermudan tobacco into England.

Woodall probably died at his house in Broad Street, St Benet Fink, on 28 August 1643, some two years after his wife, bequeathing substantial real estate assets to three sons and a daughter. He was buried at St Benet Fink, London, on 31 August. A forceful and often controversial character, he left an indelible imprint on the naval medical service through his books and his administrative ability—as Keevil writes, in *Medicine and the Navy* (1.224), 'The history of such men as John Woodall is the history of this service'.　　　　　　JOHN H. APPLEBY

Sources G. Keynes, 'John Woodall, surgeon, his place in medical history', *Journal of the Royal College of Physicians of London*, 2 (1968), 15–33 · J. H. Appleby, 'New light on John Woodall, surgeon and adventurer', *Medical History*, 25 (1981), 251–68 · Barber-Surgeons' Company minute books, GL, MSS 5257/3–5 · J. J. Keevil and others, *Medicine and the navy, 1200–1900*, 1: *1200–1649* (1957) · J. Kirkup, introduction, in J. Woodall, *The surgions mate*, ed. J. Kirkup (1978) · A. G. Debus, 'John Woodall, Paracelsian surgeon', *Ambix*, 10 (1962), 108–18 · Woodall family deeds, Warks. CRO, MSS CR 1886/5527, 5533A–B · J. Dobson and R. M. Walker, *Barbers and barber-surgeons of London* (1979) · *APC*, 1626, 1628–1629 · *Elias Ashmole (1617–1692): his autobiographical and historical notes*, ed. C. H. Josten, 5 vols. (1966 [i.e. 1967]), vol. 1, pp. 184–6 · parish register (burial), London, St Benet Fink, 9 Sept 1641, 31 Aug 1643 · will, PRO, PROB 10/639 · *CSP col.*

Archives GL, Barber-Surgeons' Company minute books

Likenesses G. Glover, line engraving, BM, NPG, Wellcome L.; repro. in J. Woodall, *The surgeons mate* (1639), title-page [*see illus.*]

Wealth at death considerable property in the City of London and at Stratford Bow: will, 1643, PRO, PROB 10/639

Woodall, Mary (1901–1988), museum director and art historian, was born at 13 Embankment Gardens, Chelsea, on 6 March 1901, the eldest child in the family of three daughters and one son of Henry Woodall, chairman of the British Gas Light and Coke Company, and his wife, Bertha Nettlefold. She was educated at Cheltenham Ladies' College and at Somerville College, Oxford, where she read history. Her family home, Yotes Court, Mereworth, Kent, was not far from Shoreham where Franklin White, a member of the staff of the Slade School of Fine Art, ran a school of art. Here her interest in the visual arts was aroused, and she went on to become a student at the Slade herself. This led to an interest in the drawings of Gainsborough and she was made a PhD for her work on this subject at the Courtauld Institute of Art, publishing *Gainsborough's Landscape Drawings* in 1939. She had a natural gift for administration and during the Second World War—somewhat to her surprise—she found herself a regional administrator for the WVS (later the WRVS) (1938–42), and then a temporary principal in the Ministry of Health and the Ministry of Supply (1942–5).

Immediately after the war Mary Woodall was appointed keeper of art at the City of Birmingham Museum and Art Gallery, where Trenchard Cox was director. It was a most happy partnership, and appropriate in another way: through her mother she had family connections with Birmingham, a city where she felt very much at home. In the post-war years the Birmingham Art Gallery flourished as never before. Both Woodall and Cox were well-known figures in the London art world, and through these links and their energetic sense of purpose they were able to attract much publicity to the gallery through donations and exhibitions. In 1947 she organized an exhibition anticipating the centenary in the following year of the formation of the Pre-Raphaelite Brotherhood, and in 1948 a pioneer exhibition of the work of Richard Wilson. One of her most important acquisitions was the early Degas *An Italian Peasant Woman*. She succeeded Cox as director in 1956 and on her retirement in 1964 became for ten years London adviser to the Felton Trust, Melbourne. She was appointed CBE in 1959 and received the honorary degree of DLitt from the University of Birmingham in 1965; in 1966–76, she was a trustee of the National Gallery. She was also the first woman president of the Museums Association (1962), and a fellow of University College, London.

Mary Woodall had great style: she hung the galleries at Birmingham with the sure eye of an artist and frequently had the walls redecorated by the workshop staff, mixing the colours herself. As a lecturer she could hold her audience as few art historians can, explaining in a patrician voice but with a practitioner's experience the techniques employed in the paintings and drawings she described. Her strong personality earned her the affectionate nickname in Birmingham of Mighty Mary. She published *Thomas Gainsborough: his Life and Work* in 1949 and edited the letters of Gainsborough in 1961; the latter, in a revised edition published in 1963, remains a key text for Gainsborough scholars.

Mary Woodall died, unmarried, on 31 March 1988, at The Close, a nursing home at Burcot near the village of Clifton Hampden, Oxfordshire, where she had lived for some years in retirement, and where her ashes were buried after cremation.   KENNETH GARLICK

Sources *The Times* (6 April 1988) · personal knowledge (2004) · private information (2004) [City of Birmingham Museums and Art Gallery] · *WWW*, 1981–90 · b. cert. · d. cert.
Likenesses M. Evans, pencil drawing, Birmingham Museum and Art Gallery
Wealth at death £195,420: probate, 5 Aug 1988, *CGPLA Eng. & Wales*

Woodall, William (1832–1901), politician, elder son of William Woodall of Shrewsbury and his wife, Martha Basson, was born in Shrewsbury on 15 March 1832 and educated at the Crescent Schools, Liverpool. He entered the business at Burslem of James Macintyre, china manufacturer, whose daughter Evelyn (*d.* 1870) he married in 1862; they had no children. On Macintyre's death in 1870 he became senior partner in the firm. He was also chairman of the Sneyd Colliery Company.

Woodall was active in local affairs, devoting himself especially to the cause of technical education. He was chairman of the Burslem school board (1870–80), of the Wedgwood Institute there, and of the North Staffordshire Society for Promotion of the Welfare of the Deaf and Dumb. He sat on royal commissions on technical education (1881–4) and the care of the blind and deaf mutes (1886–9). In September 1897 he accompanied Sir Philip Magnus and others to Germany to study technical instruction methods there.

Woodall was Liberal MP for the borough of Stoke-on-Trent, 1880–86, and was first representative of Hanley from 1885 to 1900. He was a strong supporter of home rule, disestablishment, and local veto, as well as of the extension of the franchise.

In 1884 Woodall succeeded Hugh Mason (MP for Ashton under Lyne) as leader of the women's suffrage group in the Commons, and introduced (10 June) an amendment to the Representation of the People Bill to provide that 'words having reference to the right of voting at parliamentary elections, importing the masculine gender, include women'. As chairman of the Central Committee for Women's Suffrage (established in 1872), he headed a memorial from 110 members to Gladstone, but the prime minister resisted the amendment as likely to imperil the bill. The division was taken on 12 June 1884, when 135 voted with Woodall and 271 against. In obedience to a strong party whip, 104 Liberal supporters of the women's cause voted with the majority: had they voted according to their convictions the amendment would have been carried by 72 votes instead of being lost by 136. On 19 November Woodall brought in a bill granting the vote to single women on the same terms as men, but the second reading was four times adjourned and it never reached a division. Under Gladstone's short third administration of 1886 Woodall was surveyor-general of the ordnance. He revived a bill for women's suffrage in July 1887, and after further delays he reintroduced it in April 1889 and again in 1891. He accepted office as financial secretary to the War Office (August 1892 to June 1895) in Gladstone's fourth government.

Woodall presented to Burslem a large wing to the Wedgwood Institute and free library, besides founding the Woodall Liberal Club there and bequeathing a collection of valuable pictures to the art gallery. He wrote for various magazines and reviews, republishing some articles in *Paris after Two Sieges* (1872). He was a chevalier of the Légion d'honneur. He died at the house of his nephew-in-law, Dr Woodhouse, 2 South Parade, Llandudno, on 8 April 1901. The Woodall Memorial Congregational chapel at Burslem was built in 1906.

CHARLOTTE FELL-SMITH, *rev.* H. C. G. MATTHEW

Sources The Times (9 April 1901) · H. Blackburn, *Women's suffrage: a record of the women's suffrage movement in the British Isles* (1902) · Gladstone, *Diaries* · private information (1912) · P. Magnus, *Educational aims and efforts* (1910) · *CGPLA Eng. & Wales* (1901)
Archives BL, Gladstone MSS
Likenesses W. H. Bartlett, group portrait, oils, c.1891 (*A Saturday Night at the Savage Club*), Savage Club, London · B. Stone, photograph, 1897, NPG · W. M. Palin, oils; formerly in Wedgwood Institute, Burslem, 1912 · Spy [L. Ward], caricature, watercolour study, NPG; repro. in *VF* (15 Oct 1896)
Wealth at death £3155 17s. 7d.: probate, 2 July 1901, *CGPLA Eng. & Wales*

Woodard, Nathaniel (1811–1891), founder of the Woodard schools, was born on 21 March 1811, the ninth of twelve children of John Woodard (1769–1840), a gentleman farmer of Basildon Hall, Essex, and his wife, Mary (1773–1836), daughter of Daniell Silley of Southampton. Rather the odd one out among his siblings, he seems to have been deeply influenced by the piety and devotion of his mother, who recorded that the young Nathaniel had visions. At the age of nineteen he went through a spiritual crisis and on 20 November 1830 entered a written 'covenant with my God, which I swear to keep by His grace' (Lancing College Archives, Woodard correspondence).

Woodard's education was at home with his mother, and not until 1831 did he persuade his father to let him study with the rector of Boughton in Norfolk, with a view to the priesthood. At the end of 1832 he took a job as tutor in the family of Mr Leicester, a Cambridge man, who encouraged him in his religious aspirations. In 1833 Woodard enquired about ordination without a degree, but this was refused. However, thanks to a sudden windfall from relatives, he was able to enter his name for Magdalen Hall, Oxford, in July 1834, the same year that he became engaged to Elizabeth Harriet Brill (1807–1873), also from Essex. His residence at the university coincided with the early years of the Oxford Movement, which was to be an important influence on his future career.

Woodard married on 24 March 1836 and three of his eight children were born over the next three years. His family responsibilities interrupted his studies, but he eventually graduated BA in 1840 and proceeded to his MA much later, in 1866. Ordained deacon by the bishop of London, C. J. Blomfield, on 6 June 1841, and given sole

charge, as curate, of St Bartholomew's, Bethnal Green, he set to work immediately to raise money to finish the church and equip a school. Though diffident and self-effacing in many ways he had a personal magnetism which drew people to him, and within two years William Cotton, director of the Bank of England, A. J. Beresford Hope, MP for Cambridge, Henry Tritton, a partner in Barclay's Bank, and the judge Sir John Patteson were among his many friends and supporters. Determined to convert the 'trades class' of the area, Woodard soon filled his church. In May 1843, possibly influenced by Manning, he preached a sermon commending the use of confession and absolution as provided for in the Book of Common Prayer. This offended a member of the congregation who made a complaint to the bishop, leading to a protracted correspondence between Blomfield and Woodard, and widespread comment in the national press.

After resigning from his post under pressure at the end of 1843, Woodard was appointed curate to St James's Church at a neighbouring parish, Clapton. After this difficult period (the bishop was soon to become one of his most faithful supporters) he emerged 'from the wilderness' and came in 1846 'to the promised land'—as curate to St Mary's Church, New Shoreham, on the Sussex coast, where the Tractarian vicar of the coeval parishes of Old and New Shoreham was the Revd William Wheeler. The busy port with an agricultural hinterland provided Woodard with his cause. He wondered why church and harbour said so little to each other, and felt that Shoreham's ignorance was a reflection of the national state of mind, particularly among the middle classes, and so he began what was to become his life's work, to provide a sound and inexpensive Christian education for England's neglected middle classes.

On 11 January 1847 Woodard opened in his vicarage a small day school for boys, St Mary's Grammar School, under the mastership of Revd C. H. Christie, a graduate of Queen's College, Oxford. Woodard made himself responsible for the religious instruction and another master taught elementary subjects, navigation, land surveying, and book-keeping, which particularly addressed the needs of this maritime and agricultural parish. He felt strongly that 'Education without religion is, in itself, a pure evil' (Otter, 121) and 'Good education is the best ... the only kind of preaching that is available for children' (ibid., 240). On 1 March 1848 he circulated *A Plea for the Middle Classes*, one of the most influential of the pamphlets with which he bombarded the nation until a few years before his death. Read and taken up by W. E. Gladstone, Robert Cecil, marquess of Salisbury, the earl of Shrewsbury, Henry Tritton, and other influential friends, his idea of filling England with Church of England schools run by dedicated, ordained masters on low salaries took hold.

Woodard gradually leased properties around St Mary's Church, Shoreham, opening Shoreham Grammar School and Collegiate Institution, for boarders, on 1 August 1848. It soon became known as St Nicolas' Grammar School and Collegiate Institution, after the patron saint of Old Shoreham church. Woodard was the non-teaching provost (which role he was to retain). He established two further schools in the area, St John's School (1849) and St Saviour's (1858); it seemed as if the entire vicinity was turned over to middle-class schooling. St George's Military and Engineering School, which he opened at Leyton, Essex, in 1851 for boys wishing to enter those professions, was a rare failure, existing only until 1855. St Mary's day school closed in 1853, the remaining pupils transferring to the boarding-school, which then became the College of SS Mary and Nicolas, catering for the upper middle classes—sons of clergymen, professional men, and gentlemen of limited means. St John's moved out of Shoreham in 1850 and became Hurstpierpoint College, with the Revd Edward Clarke Lowe (1823–1912) as headmaster. This school catered for the middle classes—sons of tradesmen, farmers, and clerks. In 1870 St Saviour's moved to Ardingly, in the heart of agricultural Sussex, taking sons of farmers, mechanics, small shopkeepers, and clerks—the lower middle classes. The schools, therefore, conformed to the tripartite social classification set out in Woodard's 1848 *Plea* and adopted by the Taunton commission's report on endowed schools nearly two decades later.

Woodard battled against detractors of his scheme, who from time to time raised fears of Roman Catholicism, though he never contemplated going over to Rome and would not allow advanced ritual in his school chapels. After rumours put about by a disgruntled former master, Revd John William Hewett (1824–1886), founder of Bloxham School, that Woodard encouraged the practice of auricular confession, Dr H. F. Carter founded New Shoreham protestant grammar school nearby in 1852, in response to concerns of some local residents about 'Romanizing tendencies … in this neighbourhood' (Baker and Barnett, 6). The actual practice in Woodard's schools was set out soon after the foundation of 1848. Although the headmasters and masters were in holy orders, responsibility for the spiritual and moral supervision of the boys was placed in the hands of a chaplain, trained by residence in the founder's own household. The chaplain would be exempt from the authority of the headmaster and would regularly interview the boys at stated intervals, and, if necessary, hear their confessions, though the latter would be optional. A subsequent inquiry by the official visitor of Woodard's schools, the bishop of Chichester, revealed that nothing had been done which was not fully in accordance with the provision of the prayer book. Accusations of 'confession and absolution', however, recurred. In 1857 Revd John Goring of Wiston, a landed gentleman in deacon's orders, published a correspondence alleging that confession was compulsory at St John's School. Woodard fought back against Goring in a pamphlet in which he admitted one or two boys had 'sought the benefit of absolution', but said this was the usual practice and that the initiative had been taken by the boys concerned (Handford, *Lancing College*, 21). On 22 November 1861 Woodard was again in trouble, at a major fund-raising meeting in Oxford attended by Gladstone and the future Lord Salisbury. Handbills by the anti-Puseyite controversialist C. P. Golightly were distributed alleging that confession was encouraged at both Lancing and Hurst-pierpoint and that the pupils were given crucifixes.

In 1855 Woodard paid lip-service to the idea of education for girls, helping his friend Miss Mary Anne Rooper, the headmistress of St Michael's School, founded at Hove in 1844, to settle on a new site in Bognor. The school was conveyed to the trustees of St Nicolas' College in 1864. It closed (as St Michael's Burton Park, Petworth) in 1994. Woodard himself was uncertain whether girls really benefited from a public school education. Boys were heading for the world and public life, but he doubted whether the same destiny awaited girls; but for E. C. Lowe's intervention, and his strong friendship with Miss Rooper, he would probably have done nothing for female education at all. Lowe approved of university education for women, and was keen for girls to be educated. In 1875 Woodard considered 'It is no part of our duty to teach girls … If others can do it better, let them.' In 1880 he felt that 'so slippery are women that we must watch our own progress before we promise more', and his private 1884 remark 'After all, we all know what women are for' would not have endeared him to many of that sex (Otter, 274). His reference to 'These fancy schools set up for girls are more fitted for show than solid and practical use' (Heeney, 108) perhaps sums up his true feelings on the subject.

Woodard resigned his New Shoreham curacy in 1850 to concentrate on his educational schemes, and made Brighton his family home until 1862, when he settled at Martyn Lodge, Henfield, Sussex, where he lived until his death. In 1852 he purchased Birvill's (Burwells) and Malthouse farms on the South Downs in the neighbouring parish of Lancing. They came with 226 acres and provided the site for Woodard's Society of SS Mary and Nicolas. Building of the new school, later known as the College of St Nicolas, Lancing, and in due course Lancing College, began in 1854, and during 1857–8 the pupils gradually moved up the hill from Shoreham. Numbers grew under the headmastership of Robert Sanderson (1828–1913) and by 1871 there were over 100 boys, with more than 300 at Hurstpierpoint and over 350 at Ardingly. Woodard believed that 'No system of education would be perfect which did not provide for the cultivation of the taste of the pupils through the agency of the highest examples of architecture' (Handford, *Nathanael Woodard*, 14). A supporter of the Gothic revival, his architectural legacy to the nation is Lancing chapel, the fourth tallest ecclesiastical building in England, conceived in early French Gothic style. Begun in 1868 and known locally as the cathedral of the Downs, it was not completed in Woodard's lifetime. He purchased stone quarries at Scaynes Hill and a chalkpit at Steyning, utilized the local flint, and excavated chalk from the school farmland to provide all the building materials cheaply. In 1882, feeling the weight of his work and his years, he ordered the east end of the half-finished chapel to be built to its full height, saying 'now should a niggardly generation arise and decide that it is too costly to build to the height I desire, then my work will have to be pulled down' (Handford, *Lancing College*, 27). Richard Cromwell Carpenter, as college architect, and his son

Richard Herbert Carpenter, with partner William Slater, who completed the chapel designs, produced this masterpiece, which was dedicated in 1911. Woodard's third son, Billy, with no professional training whatsoever, oversaw the construction of the building. Completion of the west end began in 1957 and the rose window was dedicated in 1978.

In forty years Woodard raised an estimated half a million pounds for his schools by the force of his personality and the exertion of his pen (about 15,000 items of his correspondence and pamphlets survive). As a fund-raiser and administrator he was rather more successful than the other contemporary founder of middle-class schools, J. L. Brereton. Many supporters covenanted annual sums, while fund-raising luncheons were held when each guest, expected to contribute money on the day, was also given a subscription form. Financial assistance came from former pupils, in particular Henry Martin Gibbs (1850–1928), who donated thousands of pounds to the building of Lancing College and its chapel. In November 1869 Woodard published a letter to the marquess of Salisbury entitled *The Scheme of Education of St Nicolas College*, proposing five centres of education for the nation, in the east, west, north, south, and the midlands, each to support a provost, twelve senior fellows (eight of these in holy orders), and twelve non-resident fellows (including some clergymen) elected from local gentlemen. In his lifetime Woodard founded eleven schools and acquired others. Before his death the southern division comprised Lancing, Hurstpierpoint, Ardingly, and St Michael's. All Saint's, Bloxham, was presented to the Society in 1896. The midlands division, established in 1873, had St Chad's, Denstone, St Oswald's, Ellesmere, and St Cuthbert's, Worksop, together with St Anne's and St Mary's at Abbots Bromley. The western division had King's College, Taunton. The northern and eastern divisions were started with acquired schools.

In March 1870, on Gladstone's recommendation, Woodard was appointed canon residentiary of Manchester and in June the same year Oxford awarded him an honorary DCL. He became subdean of Manchester Cathedral in 1881 and subsequently took on a parochial charge at Salford. On several occasions he had refused to have his portrait painted, saying that it was his work that should be remembered. He was tricked into having a photograph taken at the Oxford ceremony, and the only known portrait was painted from this likeness after his death and shows a calm, thoughtful man with a hint of humour about the mouth. He was father of seven sons (two died in infancy) and one daughter; his wife, Elizabeth, died in 1873. His mental powers declined in his last few years. On 8 January 1890 he married Dorothy Louisa Porritt, fifty-five years his junior, the daughter of Benjamin Porritt, a schoolmaster. Woodard died at his home, Martyn Lodge, on 25 April 1891 and was buried at Lancing College chapel five days later. The founder's chantry, designed by Temple Lushington Moore and modified by his son Richard Temple Moore, contains a recumbent bronze effigy by P. Bryant Baker (1916) which has 1810 incorrectly inscribed as his year of birth.

Woodard created what was, by the end of the twentieth century, the largest educational body in England apart from the state, comprising twenty-four schools administered by the Woodard Corporation under its five divisional bodies, Lancing being head of the southern division. There are also two associated and fourteen affiliated schools, three of the latter overseas, in Malawi, USA, and Australia.   JANET PENNINGTON

Sources Woodard correspondence, 1830–91, Lancing College · B. Heeney, *Mission to the middle classes: the Woodard schools, 1848–1891* (1969) · B. Handford, *Lancing College: history and memoirs* (1986) · B. Handford, *Nathanael [sic] Woodard*, rev. edn (1989) · M. C. Buck, 'Leyton', *Lancing College Magazine*, 76/6 (June 1987), 35–8 · J. W. Hunwicke, 'Beati Mundo Corde', *Lancing College Magazine*, 76/7 (Jan 1988), 27–32 · J. W. Hunwicke, 'Lancing's lost chaplain and the crisis of 1851', *Lancing College Magazine*, 76/8 (June 1988), 34–8 · J. W. Hunwicke, 'Lancing's lost chaplain and the crisis of 1851', *Lancing College Magazine*, 76/9 (Jan 1989), 28–31 [pt 2] · J. W. Hunwicke, 'Lancing's lost chaplain and the crisis of 1851', *Lancing College Magazine*, 76/10 (June 1989), 31–8 [pt 3] · M. C. Buck, 'Woodard's grand plan', *Lancing College Magazine*, 77/1 (Jan 1990), 22–4 · M. C. Buck, 'The appointment of Robert Sanderson', *Lancing College Magazine*, 77/2 (June 1990), 67–9 · J. Pennington, 'Ivan the Terrible v. Woodard the Determined?', *Lancing College Magazine*, 78/5 (spring 1995), 62–3 · The *Kalendars* of the Woodard Corporation, London, 1850–1996/7 · J. Otter, *Nathaniel Woodard: a memoir of his life* (1925) · Canon Woodard supplement, *Lancing College Magazine*, 84 (June 1891) · K. E. Kirk, *The story of the Woodard schools*, rev. edn (1952) · J. Elliott, 'Lancing College chapel: a question of attribution', *Architectural History*, 39 (1996), 114–23 · R. J. Tomlinson, *Lancing College chapel*, rev. edn (1992) · N. G. Baker and S. M. Barnett, *The history of Shoreham College* (1991) · m. cert., 1890 · d. cert.
Archives Hatfield House, Hertfordshire, Salisbury MSS · Lancing College, corresp. and papers · LPL · Woodard Corporation, 1 The Sanctuary, Westminster, London · Woodard Schools (Southern Division) Ltd, Nile Street, Nile House, Brighton | BL, corresp. with W. E. Gladstone, Add. MSS 44365–44450 · Bloxham School, corresp. with P. R. Egerton · W. Sussex RO, letters to duke of Richmond
Likenesses coloured photograph on glass, 1870 · Clayton, stained glass window, c.1896, Lancing chapel · P. B. Baker, bronze effigy, 1916, Lancing chapel · C. Webb, four stained glass windows, c.1949, Chichester Cathedral · C. G. Anderson, oils (after photograph, 1870), Lancing College, Sussex
Wealth at death £1096 12s. 8d.: probate, 30 June 1891, CGPLA Eng. & Wales

Woodbridge, Benjamin (1622–1684), nonconformist minister, was the son of John Woodbridge (1582–1637), rector of Stanton Fitzwarren, Wiltshire, and Sarah (1593–1663), daughter of Robert *Parker (c.1564–1614), the puritan whose scruples about the liturgy and vestments of the Church of England led him to write *De politeia ecclesiastica Christi* (1616). On 9 November 1638 he matriculated from Magdalen Hall, Oxford, but before graduating he left in 1639 for New England, where his elder brother, John [see below], had preceded him by five years. Resuming his studies at Harvard College, Woodbridge became the first graduate of the class of 1642. Upon returning to England he re-entered Magdalen Hall, and on 16 November 1648 proceeded MA. By this time, according to Cotton Mather, he had already established his reputation as 'an Eminent Herald of Heaven at *Salisbury*', and on 18 May 1648 succeeded William Twisse, former prolocutor of the Westminster assembly, as rector of Newbury, Berkshire.

Although his ministry was not without controversies, according to Edmund Calamy, before Woodbridge 'left them there was scarce a Family in the Town, where was not repeating, Praying, Reading, and Singing of Psalms in it'. Woodbridge was one of the Berkshire clerical assistants for the ejection of scandalous ministers in 1654, a Cromwellian reforming endeavour to purge the church of incompetent ministers.

Woodbridge's publications during this period help to reveal the controversies that surrounded his ministry and his own theological and ecclesiological convictions. In 1648 he published, under the pseudonym Filodexter Transilvanus, *Church-members set in joynt, or, A discovery of the unwarrantable and disorderly practice of private Christians, in usurping the peculiar office and work of Christ's pastours, namely publick preaching*. This was an attack on the anti-clerical attitude pervading the years of the revolutionary period, manifested, in this case, in a treatise entitled *Preaching without Ordination* (1647). *Church-Members Set in Joynt* was republished in 1656 and 1657. In 1652 Woodbridge was tangled up in a controversy over justification with William Eyre, curate of St Thomas's, Salisbury. By April 1652 Eyre had been preaching justification before faith from his pulpit in Salisbury, which both Thomas Warren, rector of Houghton, Hampshire, and Woodbridge refuted in lecture sermons in successive weeks as leaning dangerously towards antinomianism. Woodbridge's sermon was published as *Justification by Faith* (1652; repr. 1653); Eyre's full-scale defence of his view appeared in *Vindiciae justificationis gratuitae* (1654), which was subsequently answered by Woodbridge's *The Method of Grace in the Justification of Sinners*. Richard Baxter, in his *Right Method for a Settled Peace of Conscience* (1653), praised Woodbridge's *Justification by Faith*:

> There is a very Judicious Man, Mr. *Benjamin Woodbridge* of *Newbury* hath written so excellently well against this Errour, and in so small room, being but one sermon, that I would advise all private Christians to get one of them, and perused it, as one of the best, easiest, cheapest Preservatives against the contagion of this part of Antinomianism.

At the Restoration, Woodbridge was made one of Charles II's chaplains-in-ordinary and in 1661 he was chosen as one of the puritan commissioners at the Savoy Conference. In the same year he published *Moses and Aaron, or, The Rights of Church and State*, written by his uncle James Noyes, of Newbury, Massachusetts. Having refused the canonry of Windsor in 1662, Woodbridge was silenced by the Act of Uniformity on 24 August of the same year. His resolution to preach privately after his ejection from Newbury was thwarted by frequent disturbance and incarceration. In October 1665 he consented to take holy orders from the bishop of Salisbury at Oxford. However, being reproached for the inconsistency of his nonconformist principles, he resumed his nonconformist ministry in Newbury. After Charles II issued the indulgence of religion on 15 March 1672, Woodbridge was granted permission as a presbyterian to preach publicly in the market place in Newbury. When the Popish Plot erupted in 1678, he mustered courage to preach publicly each Sunday at

Highclere in Hampshire. After retiring to Englefield, Berkshire, subsequent to the discovery of the 'Presbyterian Plot' in June 1683 Woodbridge's health soon deteriorated; he died at Newbury on 1 November 1684 and was buried on 4 November at the parish church there. He was survived by his wife, Mary, of whom nothing further is known.

Benjamin's elder brother, **John Woodbridge** (1613–1695), local politician and minister in America, was born at Stanton Fitzwarren. He was preparing for the ministry at Oxford University but, owing to his refusal of the oath of conformity, was driven out without a degree. In the spring of 1634 he emigrated to New England, where he settled in Newbury, Massachusetts, and in 1639 married Mercy (1621–1691), daughter of governor Thomas Dudley; the couple had eleven children. He was the first town clerk of Newbury (1636–8), a selectman (1636), and also deputy to the general court (1637–8, 1640–41). Turning to a different calling, he left his role of civil magistrate to become a minister, receiving his ordination on 24 October 1645 as pastor of the church at Andover, Massachusetts, a post in which he remained until his return to England in 1647. Upon his return he was made chaplain to the parliamentary leaders who treated with Charles I in the Isle of Wight in 1648. In 1650 Woodbridge was appointed rector of Barford St Martin, Wiltshire, and he was also an assistant to the Wiltshire committee in 1657. Ejected from his parish after the Act of Uniformity in 1662, he returned to New England in 1663, and soon became assistant to his aged uncle Thomas Parker, minister of the church in Newbury. Through the machinations of a faction within the parish, Woodbridge was accused of abusing ecclesiastical discipline and subsequently gave up his post, once again returning to his initial call of a civil magistrate. He devoted much energy to ameliorate the financial situation of New England and published in March 1682 *Severals Relating to the Fund*, a pioneering work on currency and banking. He died in Newbury on 17 March 1695.

PAUL C-H LIM

Sources Filodexter Transilvanus [B. Woodbridge], *Church-members set in joynt* (1648) · B. Woodbridge, *Justification by faith* (1652; repr. (1653) · B. Woodbridge, *The method of grace in the justification of sinners* (1656) · Wood, *Ath. Oxon.*, new edn, 4.158 · J. L. Sibley, *Biographical sketches of Harvard graduates*, 1: 1642–1658 (Cambridge, MA, 1873), 20–27 · Calamy rev. · R. Baxter, *Right method for a settled peace of conscience* (1653) · C. Mather, *Magnalia Christi Americana*, 7 bks in 1 vol. (1702) · W. Money, *A history of Newbury* (1972), 152–7 · *CSP dom.*, 1653–4, 44, 201; 1657–8, 29; 1662–3, 63; 1664–5, 16 · *JHL*, 10 (1647–8), 78 · BL, Add. MS 28694, fols. 74–5 · PRO, SP 29/43/68 · *VCH Berkshire*, 4.143 · J. Woodbridge, *Severals relating to the fund* (1682) [John Woodbridge] · *DAB* [John Woodbridge] · will, PRO, PROB 11/379, fols. 397v–398r · Foster, *Alum. Oxon.*, 1500–1714 [John Woodbridge]
Wealth at death see will, PRO, PROB 11/379, fols. 397v–398r

Woodbridge, John (1613–1695). *See under* Woodbridge, Benjamin (1622–1684).

Woodburn, Arthur (1890–1978), politician, was born on 25 October 1890 in Edinburgh, the youngest among the eight children of Matthew Woodburn (d. c.1899), a brassfounder, and his wife, Janet, née Brown. He was given an education typical of the Edinburgh 'labour aristocracy' at Bruntsfield and Boroughmuir schools. While still at school he took a number of jobs, including work in his father's small foundry. He left Boroughmuir at fourteen and worked for a short time in the offices of the Free Church, though his own affiliation was to the United Free Church. He gained experience as a publicist while working on matters arising from the complex lawsuit between the two churches over the title to church properties. He later moved to the offices of Miller's London Road foundry in Edinburgh, and spent over twenty-five years of his career in engineering and foundry administration, specializing in costing and foreign contracts, in which he was aided by a good knowledge of German, French, Italian, and Spanish. Woodburn developed his language skills at evening classes at Heriot-Watt College, which he attended for twelve years after leaving school. He also studied commerce and accountancy, and later attended classes in economics at the extra-mural department of Edinburgh University, under the tuition of William Graham, president of the Board of Trade in the Labour government from 1929 to 1931.

Parallel to this Woodburn developed as a classic 'ethical socialist' member of the Independent Labour Party (ILP), which he joined in 1916. Like many members of the ILP he took a very critical pacifist stand towards the First World War, though in the early days of the conflict he was willing, and even eager, to fight. Kidney trouble and the need to support his mother kept him from enlisting, and by 1916 he opposed the war and had joined the No-Conscription Union. He declared his intention not to fight, even though he was occupationally exempt, and when he addressed public meetings against conscription he was arrested, court-martialled, and imprisoned, at one stage being incarcerated in the Tower of London. Long periods were spent in solitary confinement. After his release in summer 1919 he returned to work at the London Road foundry, where his employers had been broadly supportive of his opposition to the war. In that year he married Barbara Halliday, a teacher, the daughter of Francis Halliday, a rubber worker. A Labour Party activist herself, she was one of the first women members of Edinburgh town council, on which she served for many years, and was the city Labour Party's educational expert. There were no children from the marriage.

After the war Woodburn became associated with the labour college movement, although not with the communist and Scottish nationalist variant on it that was associated with John Maclean. He lectured on history, economics, and finance for the Edinburgh branch of the Scottish Labour College, of which he became honorary secretary in 1925. In 1937 he became president of the National Council of Labour Colleges. Like many other Scottish socialists and nationalists he was intrigued by Major C. H. Douglas's social-credit theories, and a mixture of these and 'counter-cyclical' public investment, along Keynesian

lines, featured in his evidence to the Macmillan committee on banking in 1930. He wrote widely on financial matters, and his An Outline of Finance (1931) went to four editions. He favoured state planning and regulation, and a visit to Stalin's Russia in 1932 convinced him that this was the 'land of hope' (Knox, 286). He was even willing to dismiss as propaganda the reports of the Moscow show trials, although his belief in the Soviet Union, as well as in state planning itself, began to fade after the Second World War.

In 1929 Woodburn contested South Edinburgh at the general election, and in 1931 Leith, both without success. In 1932, not long after his return from Russia, he was appointed full-time secretary to the Scottish council of the Labour Party. This was an exceptionally difficult position, as the débâcle of 1931 meant that Labour held only seven Scottish seats. The disaffiliation of the ILP during Woodburn's first year in office removed four of these members, as well as much of the individual membership and the property of the party, and he had more or less to set up a new organization from scratch. His task was complicated by the dominance of the Unionist right, which returned forty-five members out of seventy-four on 42 per cent of the vote in 1935, ably and not unprogressively led by the likes of Walter Elliot and Robert Boothby, and overwhelmingly supported by the Scottish press.

In 1934 Woodburn was a candidate for the general secretaryship of the Labour Party but was narrowly beaten (thirteen votes to eleven) by James Middleton. Woodburn persisted with expanding the Scottish council's membership and control, for which he had the precedent of his friend William Elger's modernization of the Scottish Trades Union Congress after 1924. Hostile to the popular front touted by the communists and to the indiscipline of former ILP 'loyalists' in the Scottish Socialist Party, which stood in relation to the Labour Party as the ILP had done prior to disaffiliation, he became a relentless disciplinarian. In 1939, dogged by a lawsuit oddly similar to the Free Church case, the Scottish Socialist Party went under, leaving the Scottish council with a tolerable organization and growing membership. At a by-election in October 1939 Woodburn was elected member for East Stirling and Clackmannanshire, against opposition from Transport House; he won by nearly 15,000 votes in a straight fight against a pacifist candidate, and represented the seat until he retired in 1970.

Woodburn had abandoned his pacifism, and during the war years served as parliamentary private secretary to Tom Johnston, secretary of state for Scotland from 1941 to 1945. As one of the Labour Party's finance spokesmen he sat on the select committee on national expenditure (1939) and chaired the subcommittee on finance and establishments from 1939 to 1945. He reached the Labour front bench in 1943, and between 1945 and 1947 in the Attlee government was joint parliamentary secretary to the Ministry of Supply and Aircraft Production (Ministry of Supply from 1946). On 7 October 1947 he succeeded Joseph Westwood as secretary of state for Scotland, with a seat in cabinet. Westwood had been reckoned a weak minister who suffered from Whitehall's desire to recover powers that had leaked to Scotland during the powerful wartime administration of Tom Johnston. Woodburn was less dismissive of his predecessor, but his passage was little easier.

Woodburn's main administrative concerns were the integration of Labour's nationalization and welfare legislation into the Scottish administrative structure; securing action on highland problems; and boosting a flagging housing programme, which was partly overcome by the industrialized production of pre-fabricated houses ('prefabs') at former aircraft factories. But a persistent political problem turned out to be the revival of Scottish nationalism. This stemmed from a split in the Scottish National Party in 1942, involving the secession of the followers of John MacCormick, party secretary. MacCormick's covenant movement got as many as 2 million signatures for a home-rule declaration, and demanded dominion status for Scotland. In part this was a regrouping of Scottish Liberals, once the country's major party and in the doldrums since the early 1920s. But it also drew on concern with over-centralization which the Conservatives themselves helped to fan, and Churchill mischievously denied that Scotland should be forced into the serfdom of socialism as the result of a vote in Westminster.

In his first electoral contest in 1929 Woodburn had favoured home rule but he was now bitterly hostile, a view shared by most members of his party. A white paper of January 1948 proposed minor measures of administrative devolution, plus a Scottish economic council which was supposed to act as a quasi-representative forum. It was dismissed by most of Scottish public opinion. Woodburn did nothing to calm matters by seizing on a rhetorical flourish of MacCormick's to accuse him of advocating violence. MacCormick was an eloquent speaker given to dramatic gestures, the most effective of which was the theft of the Stone of Scone from Westminster Abbey on Christmas day 1950, but his commitment to non-violence was unyielding. In the reshuffle after the general election of 1950 Attlee offered Woodburn a sideways move to the Ministry of Fuel and Power. Woodburn viewed this as a criticism of his Scottish policy, and quit the cabinet in February 1950, being succeeded by Hector McNeil, member for Greenock and previously a high-flier at the Foreign Office. McNeil was equally hostile to devolution, but not as thin-skinned about it, and had killed off the Scottish economic council before Labour lost power.

Woodburn remained on the back benches for a further twenty years. 'Solid, slow and deliberate in speech, yet not without a definite personal charm' (*The Times*, 3 June 1978), not to speak of a rare command of languages and unmistakable eyebrows, he settled down as a model House of Commons man and was on the select committee on procedure from 1956 to 1968. He was active in the British Inter-Parliamentary Union, visiting numerous countries in Europe and South America, and led the first Westminster delegation to the *Bundestag*. Unusually among Scottish Labour members Woodburn was always an enthusiast for the Common Market. After retirement he continued his international involvement and was elected in 1971 joint president of the British section of the Council of European Municipalities. He was a motorist into extreme old age, and his death in Edinburgh on 1 June 1978 was hastened by an accident while driving to visit his dying wife in hospital.   CHRISTOPHER HARVIE

Sources autobiography, NL Scot. • *DLB* • W. Knox, *Scottish labour leaders, 1918–1939* (1987) • *WWW* • *The Labour who's who* (1927) • *WWBMP* • *The Times* (3 June 1978), 16g–h • I. Donnachie, C. Harvie, and I. S. Wood, *Forward! Labour politics in Scotland, 1888–1988* (1989) • G. Pottinger, *The secretaries of state for Scotland, 1926–1976: fifty years of the Scottish office* (1979) • M. Fry, *Patronage and principle: a political history of modern Scotland* (1986) • L. Paterson, *The autonomy of modern Scotland* (1994) • S. Macintyre, *Little Moscows* (1980) • D. Milne, *The Scottish office and other Scottish government departments* (1957) • A. K. Cairncross, ed., *The Scottish economy: a statistical account of Scottish life by members of the staff of Glasgow University* (1954) • C. Harvie and M. Russell, *1946: the people's story* (1986) • *Labour and the wartime coalition: from the diaries of James Chuter Ede, 1941–1945*, ed. K. Jefferys (1987) • J. Margach, *The anatomy of power* (1979) • J. Mitchell, *Strategies for self-government: the campaign for a Scottish parliament* (1996) • G. Walker, *Thomas Johnston* (1988) • *CCI* (1978)

Archives NA Scot., minutes and papers relating to the national expenditure select committee's sub-committee on finance and establishments • NL Scot., corresp. and papers, including MS autobiography • NL Scot., corresp. and papers relating to bill for common European language • PRO, private office papers as parliamentary secretary, Ministry of Supply, AVIA 9

Likenesses F. Man, group portrait, photograph, 1943 (*Letter reading*), Hult. Arch.

Wealth at death £26,698.88: confirmation, 31 July 1978, *CCI*

Woodbury, Walter Bentley (1834–1885), photographer and inventor of the woodburytype process, was born at Manchester on 26 June 1834, the eldest of five children of John Taylor Woodbury (*d.* 1842) and his wife, Ellen Bentley. The death of Woodbury's father left his mother to look after a shop and her younger children while he was brought up by his maternal grandfather, Walter Bentley, a naturalist and friend of Audubon and Waterlow, and related to Thomas Bentley (1731–1780), partner to Joseph Wedgwood. Woodbury received a scientific education and in 1849 was taken as a pupil by a civil engineer in a Manchester patent office; in addition he taught himself photography. Three years later he sailed to Australia intending to make for the goldfields, but was employed in a multitude of jobs, as a cook, driver, surveyor's labourer, builder, and paperhanger, before obtaining a post as a draughtsman in the Melbourne waterworks; at the same time (1854–7) he practised as a photographer in Melbourne. The earliest panorama taken in Australia was an eight-section view of Melbourne taken by Woodbury in 1854, in which year he received the medal of photographers in the Australian dependencies.

Woodbury sailed to Java, where he set up his studio in 1857–8, counting the sultan among his sitters. Back in London his photographs were published by Negretti and Zambra. He was again in Java in 1860–64, and it was probably during this time that he married a local inhabitant, Marie, who survived him with several children. Back in England in 1864 Woodbury launched into his most inventive period, taking out more than thirty patents in Britain and abroad between 1863 and 1885, mostly for photo-mechanical printing, but also for improvements in optical and photographical apparatus.

The first woodburytype, a mechanically printed image, was produced in 1864. Earlier that year Joseph Wilson Swan had patented a carbon print and, shortly after Woodbury, he patented a similar form of mechanical reproduction of these images. Woodbury then offered Swan half his patent rights, proposing a partnership, but Swan declined. The method was laborious: from the carbon print a gelatine relief was shaped, a sheet of lead was then forced against the gelatine in a hydraulic press, generating the printing plate. At that time the prints were unique in having true continuous halftones and they were virtually indistinguishable from actual photographs. They could not be printed directly on book pages and did require mounting; nevertheless they were cheaper than handmade prints.

The artistic quality of woodburytypes enabled Woodbury to sell the French rights to Goupil & Co. of Paris in 1867 for £6000, the British rights to Disderi & Co. in 1868, and the American rights to John Carbutt of Philadelphia in 1870. From 1872 woodburytypes illustrated *The Picture Gallery of British Artists*, a monthly art journal, likewise *The Theatre* from 1878 to 1890, and were widely adopted for book illustration. But like many inventors Woodbury spent all his money on experiments. He was friendly with other photographic pioneers and contributed to the *English Mechanic* and *Science at Home*.

Woodbury seems to have led a somewhat vagrant existence, judging from the addresses given on his patent applications: at Fulham in 1870; Penge, near Croydon, in 1871; Greenhithe, Kent, in 1872; and Java House, Norwood Junction, Surrey, in 1879 and 1883. By 1885 he was so impoverished that a group of photographers started a subscription to enable him to develop his stannotype process, a simplified form of the woodburytype. For Woodbury it was too late. He arrived at Margate on 4 September 1885 with some of his children, and was found dead in his bed the following day. An inquest disclosed that he had been in the habit of taking laudanum, but the coroner found no evidence of an overdose. He was buried on 12 September at Abney Park cemetery, Hackney, London.

ANITA MCCONNELL

Sources H. Gernsheim and A. Gernsheim, *The history of photography* (1955), 276–9 · A. Davies and P. Stanbury, *The mechanical eye in Australia* (1985), 22, 26, 256 · W. J. Harrison, *History of photography* (1888), 112, 135 · *Photographic News* (11 Sept 1885) · M. Auer and M. Auer, *Encyclopédie internationale des photographes de 1839 à nos jours* (1985) · *CGPLA Eng. & Wales* (1885) · *DNB* · parish register (baptism), Manchester Cathedral, 12 Sept 1834
Archives National Museum of Photography, Film and Television, Bradford, Royal Photographic Society collection, photographic collection
Likenesses portrait, repro. in Harrison, *History of photography*, 135 · portrait, repro. in *Photographic News*
Wealth at death £240: administration, 22 Oct 1885, *CGPLA Eng. & Wales*

Woodcock [*née* Williams], **Elizabeth** (*bap.* 1756, *d.* 1799), survivor, was baptized on 12 December 1756 at Impington,

5 miles north of Cambridge, the daughter of William Williams and his wife, Elizabeth (*née* Veal). A resident of Impington throughout her life, she married there, on 30 January 1785, a farmer, John Sockling (*d.* 1794), and, following his death, on 31 March 1796, Daniel Woodcock (*d.* 1800), also a farmer. Woodcock is remembered for an ordeal which began on the evening of 2 February 1799 as she rode home from Cambridge during a heavy snowfall. Her horse, Tinker, shied, causing her to dismount, and then bolted across the fields. She chased him until overcome with fatigue, whereupon she sheltered under a hedge and fell asleep. Within an hour she had been enclosed by drifting snow, which formed a cave around her. Unable to rise because of frostbite in her legs, she waved her handkerchief on a stick through a hole in the cavern. Her attempts to attract attention proved unsuccessful until on 10 February her signal was spotted by a farmer, Joseph Muncey. With the help of others, including her husband, Woodcock was removed and taken to her house in Impington, now identified as 83 Station Road. Attended by a local surgeon, Thomas Verney Okes, she was thought to have some chance of survival, although the following weeks saw her suffer from fits, fainting, and the loss of her toes from frostbite. During her convalescence Woodcock attracted a number of sightseers whom, it was claimed, finally brought about her death on 11 July by providing her with excessive amounts of alcohol. She was buried in Impington parish churchyard. Woodcock's ordeal was recounted in several pamphlets, including Okes's *An Account of the Providential Preservation of Elizabeth Woodcock* (1799), which passed through three editions in three months as well as being reprinted in the *Gentleman's Magazine* on her death. Okes attributed her survival to a calm disposition and to modern medical practices for dealing with victims of hypothermia and starvation recently discussed by the Humane Society. Woodcock was survived by her husband, who died in the following year and was buried on 8 November 1800. In 1849 an obelisk was erected near Impington on the site of the snow cave, and on 27 April 1981 a plaque was unveiled at her Station Road residence.

ROBERT HALLIDAY

Sources T. V. Okes, *An account of the providential preservation of Elizabeth Woodcock, who survived a confinement under the snow of nearly eight days and nights* (1799); repr. with corrections in *GM*, 1st ser., 69 (1799), 711–15 · *A full, true and clear account of Elizabeth Woodcock of the parish of Impington near Cambridge who was buried under a vast drift of snow for eight days and eight nights* (1799) · E. Porter, *Cambridge customs and folklore* (1969) · *Cambridge Chronicle and Journal* (9 Feb–30 July 1799) · *Cambridge Chronicle* (23 Jan 1869) · W. Hone, *The Everyday Book and Table Book*, 2 vols. (1826) · parish registers, Impington, Cambs. AS
Likenesses J. Marshall, print, pubd 1799, Cambridge Central Library, Lion Yard, Cambridgeshire collection · J. Baldrey, drawing, Cambridge Central Library, Lion Yard, Cambridgeshire collection; repro. in Porter, *Cambridgeshire customs and folklore* · woodcut (after drawing by J. Baldrey), Cambridge Central Library, Lion Yard, Cambridgeshire collection; repro. in Hone, *Every-day Book*
Wealth at death seemingly not great as profits from books about her used to support Elizabeth and family

Woodcock, George (1904–1979), trade unionist, was born on 20 October 1904 at Bamber Bridge, in Walton-le-Dale,

George Woodcock (1904–1979), by Walter Bird, 1967

Lancashire, the second in the family of four sons and one daughter of Peter Woodcock, a cotton weaver and loom overlooker (a form of junior foreman), and his wife, Ann Baxendale. The family were devout Catholics, and he started his schooling at Brownedge Roman Catholic elementary school. At the age of twelve he became a 'half-timer', which meant that during one week he would work in the cotton mill from 6 a.m. to 1 p.m. and then attend school in the afternoon, and during the following week he would go to school in the morning and then work in the mill until 5.30 p.m. At thirteen he took up full-time employment as a cotton weaver, first looking after two looms and then graduating to three; at the age of fourteen he had four looms, the maximum allowed. Bamber Bridge, near to Preston, then had six cotton mills, two foundries, and a population of 4000. It was the centre of young Woodcock's universe and he never ceased to recall his early days in the cotton mill.

At that early stage Woodcock had two ambitions: initially he wanted to become a carpenter; but a second, more dominant objective was to become a professional footballer. His father and three uncles had played for Blackburn Rovers, and his own aim was to play for Preston North End, the team he followed for the rest of his life. He had already started his footballing apprenticeship playing for Brownedge in the local Catholic League. He spent most of his free time training, keeping a strict diet and devoting himself to keeping fit. Subsequently his doctors came to believe that these physical exertions may have contributed to his long and serious illness in his later teens which

ended his career as a cotton weaver as well as his hopes as a footballer. That illness changed the entire course of Woodcock's life.

At the age of eighteen Woodcock fell victim to tubercular adenitis—a tubercular infection of the glands which affected his lungs, heart, and bowel system. Woodcock was bed-bound for seven months in his fight to recover health. During that time he effectively re-educated himself by reading voraciously classical literature, history, and political economy. He emerged from that long illness with a profound desire to continue his education and immerse himself in political life. In 1924 he became a minor official of the Bamber Bridge and District Weavers' Union, and was active in the Independent Labour Party and, later, the Labour Party. At the 1929 general election he was an election agent for the Labour Party. But increasingly he was drawn more towards trade union work and won a TUC scholarship to Ruskin College, Oxford, in 1929. It was immediately evident to his Ruskin tutors that they had an exceptional talent on their hands, and in 1931 he won an extramural scholarship which took him to New College, Oxford, where he was much influenced by his tutor, R. H. S. Crossman. Years later Woodcock, ever conscious of his working-class background, remarked of his Oxford experience:

> It was a very good thing for me to go to the ancient seat of learning. There I found people who let me have my head, who checked me and also argued with me but never ignored or rejected my assertions outright. (*Free Labour World*, Feb 1963)

He went on to take a first in philosophy, politics, and economics in 1933, and won the Jessie Theresa Rowden senior scholarship, which enabled him to do postgraduate work at Manchester University. In 1933, while still a student, he married Laura Mary, daughter of Francis McKernan, an engine fitter, of Horwich, Lancashire. She shared his devout Catholicism. They had a son and a daughter.

In 1936, after two years in the civil service as an assistant commissioner for national savings, Woodcock joined the TUC as head of the research and economic department. He was recruited by the then general secretary, Walter Citrine, whose support, guidance, and advice was important, for Woodcock's distinction—as the TUC's first university-trained intellectual—was not regarded as an advantage by many of the traditional trade union leaders in the 1930s. Another, perhaps unexpected, helping hand came from Ernest Bevin, the transport union leader, who, though never an easy ally of any intellectual, also befriended the young Woodcock. Both Citrine and Bevin, in their quite different styles, encouraged Woodcock towards the ideas of John Maynard Keynes. Keynes's concept of a managed, modified capitalism caught Woodcock's imagination so powerfully that he remained a disciple for the rest of his life. At the heart of his political attitude there always remained a central focus—the need to maintain full employment and the obligation of trade unions to adjust their entire economic and industrial strategy to achieving that fundamental aim.

The wartime discussions about the nature of post-war

Britain in which Woodcock became involved—working closely with Citrine and in touch with Bevin at the wartime Ministry of Labour—also shaped his thinking. Already forming in his mind was the concept of a strong working relationship between the state and the trade unions to ensure a strategy that would establish and preserve full employment. When Citrine left the TUC in 1946 to join the National Coal Board, Sir Vincent Tewson became TUC general secretary, and Woodcock was appointed his second in command, as assistant general secretary, in 1947. Thus began one of the most difficult, and often deeply frustrating, periods of Woodcock's career, for the two men simply could not establish a close relationship. For thirteen years Woodcock brooded on opportunities lost to develop and foster the ideas which, he was convinced, could help the trade union movement to meet the tremendous challenges of the post-war years. By the time he succeeded Tewson, in July 1960, Woodcock was nearly fifty-six, impatient, inwardly angry, but still eager to seize the initiative to try to make up for what he regarded as the 'lost years of opportunity'. His nine years as TUC general secretary were indeed remarkable, arguably the most important post-war years for the TUC. Yet a number of his admirers believed Woodcock came to the job five years too late.

From the moment he took over the reins of office at Congress House Woodcock began building links with government. It was not an easy time. The 1960–62 period of the Macmillan government was punctuated with considerable industrial strife and economic difficulties—the railways, docks, postal services, and car and engineering industries were all involved in widespread disruption. The pressure was on the trade union leadership; and there were great changes in the Labour Party, with Harold Wilson taking over the leadership after the death of Hugh Gaitskell. At the 1962 Trades Union Congress Woodcock took the initiative on trade union reform. In a memorable speech he challenged the congress to answer the question 'What are we here for?' The whole focus of his challenge was to force the unions to reorganize and modernize themselves. And in that same year, against strong opposition and still greater scepticism, he persuaded the TUC general council to accept Macmillan's invitation to join in the newly created National Economic Development Council (Neddy). Both internally and externally Woodcock had begun a revolution in trade union thinking. He put a great deal of faith, and hope, in taking the unions into this relationship with the state in which government, industry, and the unions would have the opportunity to establish an instrument of national planning. The trade-off for the unions—he hoped—would be a firm guarantee of continuing full employment, even if that involved the unions sacrificing some of their independence in wage bargaining as well as curbing unofficial disputes. It was a bold gamble which Woodcock then carried into the years of the Labour government under Harold Wilson. 'We have left Trafalgar Square', he told the 1963 congress as he opened his offensive in favour of some form of incomes

policy and pleaded with the unions to remould their attitudes by recognizing they were now part of a broad consensus in a new relationship with state power and able to influence events. It was the opening shot in what was to become his main *cause célèbre* during the Wilson government period.

Woodcock was convinced that the future of trade unionism lay in that direction, and that it should be brought about not by new legislation (he was committed to the voluntary principle) but by dialogue across the tables of Whitehall, with each side pursuing a common objective for the 'social good' while preserving its own independence of democratic action. This was the key to his philosophy. It hinged, essentially, on a degree of self—and corporate—discipline which, in the end, was to prove its downfall.

Yet in the glow of Wilson's 1964 election victory, albeit with a narrow majority, Woodcock established a link with George Brown's new Department of Economic Affairs, which led to some dramatic, if temporary, achievements. The TUC became a virtual part of the department, involved deeply in discussing the ill-fated national plan and the tri-partite declaration of intent at the end of 1964 which launched a combined operation involving government, employers, and unions in a campaign for national economic recovery. Woodcock himself turned down a hint from Wilson that he might even join the government (Frank Cousins, the transport union leader, had already joined the cabinet as minister of technology). But Woodcock dismissed the idea; his primary aim was to stay with the TUC and steer the unions toward his goal.

Incomes policy became the centrepiece of the Wilson–Brown industrial policy in the years between 1964 and 1969. Woodcock was not averse to this, but consistently warned the government against putting too much pressure on the unions. Challenge them—yes, he argued; force the unions to confront the social and economic problems of the age—of course, that was essential. But, he warned ministers, do not be surprised if the unions cannot deliver. He lectured ministers that the unions were, by nature, defensive animals not normally given to creative involvement with government; it would be up to government to put them under pressure. He agreed with Wilson's proposal in 1965 to establish a royal commission on the trade unions under Lord Donovan, but insisted that employers' organizations should be coupled within the remit. He also pressed the prime minister to appoint him to the Donovan commission, which Wilson did.

When the commission reported, in 1968, one of its proposals was to create a commission on industrial relations (CIR) to help direct the reorganization of the unions and the modernization of industrial relations. Harold Wilson appointed Woodcock its first chairman in 1969, and in the summer of that year Woodcock retired from the TUC to help establish the CIR. Two years later he resigned that chair when the Heath government introduced its Industrial Relations Act under which the role of the CIR was changed. Woodcock could not accept that new remit.

Harold Wilson, after losing the 1970 election to Edward

Heath, wanted Woodcock to accept a life peerage; he declined. In later years he probably regretted that decision, though he took no action about it. That would have been out of character. He was appointed CBE in 1953 and sworn of the privy council in 1967.

George Woodcock was the outstanding intellect of the TUC armoury in the post-war years. Yet his objectives, so often brilliantly set out in lectures, writings, speeches, and private conversations, were frequently inadequately understood by many union leaders. This was partly due to Woodcock's own intellectual arrogance—though he never postured or offered false gods; it was much more a natural impatience with all but those of his admirers— and they were numerous—who did see in him and his ideas a way ahead for trade unionism in the modern state. His vision was unquestioned even by his critics; but his practical application was another matter.

Woodcock predicted the Thatcher years in an uncanny way. He saw the dangers of a return to mass unemployment unless the unions committed themselves to a different agenda. In a paper delivered to the British Association a few years before his death Woodcock warned: 'If this country were to return to the industrial instability and the heavy unemployment of pre-war days, that would certainly not improve the ability of the trade unions collectively to secure greater social justice and fairness for their members' (DNB). He was a natural raconteur. As TUC general secretary he encouraged a small, select number of journalists and writers to gather around him, and in them he would confide his hopes and his frustrations. His George Robey eyebrows were like a theatrical overhang on his unchanging soft Lancashire burr, which sometimes descended into a whisper, captivating smaller, intimate audiences while oft-times puzzling larger ones. Here was the philosopher king of trade unionism.

Woodcock had honorary degrees from Sussex (1963), Oxford (1964), Aston (1967), Manchester (1968), Kent (1968), Lancaster (1970), and London (1970). He became a freeman of the City of London in 1965. During his TUC years he lived in Epsom, Surrey, where his wife was a magistrate and, in turn, councillor, alderman, and mayor of Epsom. She was the first woman to be made a freeman of Epsom. George Woodcock died at Epsom District Hospital on 30 October 1979.   GEOFFREY GOODMAN

Sources DNB · *The Times* (19 Nov 1979) · *The Guardian* (31 Oct 1979) · *Daily Telegraph* (31 Oct 1979) · *The Observer* (4 Nov 1979) · *Catholic Herald* (9 Nov 1979) · R. Taylor, *The trade union question in British politics* (1993) · D. Barnes and E. Reid, *Governments and trade unions* (1980) · G. Goodman, *The awkward warrior: Frank Cousins, his life and times*, 2nd edn (1984) · A. Horne, *Macmillan*, 2: *1957–1986* (1989) · H. Wilson, *The labour government, 1964–1970: a personal record* (1971) · *TUC Congress Reports* (1960–69) · private information (2004) · personal knowledge (2004)
Archives U. Warwick Mod. RC, papers | FILM BFI NFTVA, *This week*, 9 Sept 1965 · BFI NFTVA, current affairs footage | SOUND BL NSA, current affairs recordings · BL NSA, recorded talks
Likenesses group photograph, 1946 (*Trade unionists*), Hult. Arch. · W. Bird, photograph, 1967, NPG [*see illus.*]

Woodcock, George (1912–1995), writer and journal editor, was born at Grace Hospital, Winnipeg, Manitoba, on 8 May 1912, the only child of (Samuel) Arthur Woodcock (d. 1926), railway clerk, and his wife, Margaret Gertrude, née Lewis (d. 1940). His parents had moved to Canada a few years previously in search of a better life, and his father at one point worked as a silver prospector, but they returned to England when George was only a few months old. There, partly through family connections, his father obtained a post with Great Western Railways. He was educated at Sir William Borlase's School in Marlow, Buckinghamshire, where his parents lived. He was unable to go on to university because of family poverty following his father's early death, and for eleven years (from 1929 to 1940) he too worked as a railway clerk for Great Western Railways in London. At the same time he began to make his name as a writer in small circulation magazines and he joined the literary bohemia of pre-war London; he also became involved in left-wing politics, moving from socialism to pacifism and also to anarchism.

During the Second World War Woodcock was a conscientious objector and worked on the land. At the same time he made his name as an editor, producing sixteen issues of his own magazine, *Now*, from 1940 to 1947. From 1942 he worked with the Freedom Press, the main British publisher of anarchist material, producing many articles and several pamphlets. In 1945, when three of the editors of its paper *War Commentary* were imprisoned for anti-war activity, he helped to keep the paper going while they were in prison and he founded the Freedom Defence Committee on behalf of dissenters who were too unpopular for anyone else. From 1943 he lived with Ingeborg Hedwig Elisabeth Roskelly, an artist, daughter of Otto Linzer, a ministry of finance inspector in Germany, and wife of Frederick Roskelly, an English journalist. She had left Germany in 1936. Following a divorce in which Woodcock was named as co-respondent, he and Ingeborg married on 20 January 1949.

After the war Woodcock began to produce successful general books, and he was on the verge of becoming an established author in England when in 1949 he returned with his wife to Canada. He spent the rest of his life there, though he frequently visited Britain and had most of his later books published in London. He and Ingeborg settled in British Columbia and had a hard struggle at first; he earned initially a precarious and eventually a prosperous living as a writer and broadcaster. From 1954 to 1956 he taught English at the University of Washington (until excluded from the United States because of his political views). He then taught English at the University of British Columbia from 1956 to 1963, becoming associate professor. Thereafter he preferred independent to academic status, though he retained a connection with the University of British Columbia and from 1966 to 1967 was a full-time lecturer in Asian studies. He became a leading advocate of and authority on Canadian literature, and was the founding editor of the prestigious academic quarterly *Canadian Literature* from 1959 to 1977. He and his wife spent much time travelling all over the world; they were also involved in relief work in India and Tibet, and established a fund for impoverished writers in Canada. In later years Woodcock developed a keen interest in Tibetan Buddhism, and on several occasions met the Dalai Lama.

Woodcock was the author or editor of well over 150 books over a period of sixty years. He produced biographical studies of H. W. Bates (1969), Aphra Behn (1948), Gabriel Dumont (1975), Mahatma Gandhi (1972), William Godwin (1948), Aldous Huxley (1972), Peter Kropotkin (1950), Wyndham Lewis (1971), Malcolm Lowry (1971), Hugh MacLellan (1969), Thomas Merton (1978), George Orwell (1966), P. J. Proudhon (1956), Herbert Read (1972), Mordecai Richler (1971), and Oscar Wilde (1950). He produced several works of literary criticism and edited several political and literary classics. He also produced many books of travel and anthropology, and on history and politics, several collections of essays, and entries in many reference books. Above all he wrote two standard books, *Anarchism: a History of Libertarian Ideas and Movements* (1962) and *Canada and the Canadians* (1970). The former became one of the most widely read and influential studies of the subject, and appeared in many editions and translations. He later added, as a companion volume, the anthology *Anarchist Reader* (1977). The two books established his permanent reputation, though they were both the object of much controversy. Towards the end of his life he provided the introductions for a new collection of the main writings of Peter Kropotkin in eleven volumes. However, he thought of himself primarily as a poet, and his poems were published over a period of sixty-two years and collected in several volumes. Towards the end of his life he produced three volumes of readable but unreliable autobiography—*Letter to the Past* (1982), *Beyond the Blue Mountains* (1987), and *Walking through the Valley* (1994)—and he became the subject of several studies himself.

Woodcock received many honours and awards, and was elected a fellow of the Royal Society of Canada in 1968 and a fellow of the Royal Geographical Society in 1971. He refused the honours offered by governments, preferring the respect of his peers. After suffering from heart disease for nearly thirty years, he died at his home, 6429 McCleery Street, Vancouver, on 28 January 1995. His wife survived him.   NICOLAS WALTER

Sources G. Woodcock, *Letter to the past* (1982) · G. Woodcock, *Beyond the Blue Mountains* (1987) · G. Woodcock, *Walking through the valley* (1994) · D. Fetherling, *The gentle anarchist: a life of George Woodcock* (1998) · *The Independent* (13 Feb 1995) · *Daily Telegraph* (20 Feb 1995) · N. Walter, 'George Woodcock (1912–1995)', *Freedom* (25 Feb 1995) · *WWW* · m. cert.
Archives Queen's University, Kingston, Ontario | Internationaal Instituut voor Sociale Geschiedenis, Amsterdam, corresp. with Boris V. Velensky · University of Toronto, Thomas Fisher Rare Book Library, Douglas Fetherling MSS
Likenesses photograph, repro. in *The Independent* · photographs, repro. in Fetherling, *Gentle anarchist*, frontispiece and following p. 108

Woodcock [*alias* Farington], **John** [*name in religion* Martin of St Felix] (**1603–1646**), Franciscan friar and martyr, was born in the parish of Leyland, Lancashire, in 1603. He was the elder son of Thomas Woodcock and his wife, Dorothy

(*née* Farington or Anderton), and a relative of the Woodcock family of Woodcock Hall, Clayton-le-Woods, Lancashire. Brought up within the Church of England, in his late teens he converted to Roman Catholicism (his mother's religion). This angered his father, and John went to live with Mr Anderton (probably his grandfather) of Clayton-le-Woods. In 1628 he went to the Jesuit college at St Omer, Southern Netherlands, and in 1629 to the English College, Rome; as a student he was described as a youth who afforded a remarkable example of the mildest disposition. Preferring to enter a strict religious order, he did not complete his studies in Rome, and instead began his noviciate with the Capuchin monks at the Convent of St Honoré in Paris. After a few months he was dismissed as being unsuitable for a variety of reasons: these included his difficulty to learn French and poor health. Unsettled, in 1630 he approached the recently established English Franciscan convent of St Bonaventure at Douai, Southern Netherlands, and then the Irish Franciscan foundation in Rome, eventually returning to Douai, where, in 1631, he was received and clothed with the Franciscan habit. Following ordination as a Roman Catholic priest, he went first to be a chaplain in the household of an Englishman, Mr Sheldon, in Arras, Southern Netherlands, and then from November 1639 to April 1640 as chaplain to the English Franciscan nuns at Nieuport, Southern Netherlands. In 1637 he had expressed a wish to be sent on the English mission, and in 1643 he again requested his superiors that he should be sent to England. In spite of his history of poor health, this time permission was granted. He landed at Newcastle upon Tyne and by August 1644 he was in his native part of Lancashire. According to tradition he was about to celebrate mass at the house of Mr Burgess of Woodend, Clayton-le-Woods, when the house was raided by pursuivants. Woodcock escaped but was arrested the following morning at nearby Bamber Bridge and taken as a prisoner to Lancaster Castle. Because of the civil war no assize courts were held until August 1646, when he was at last brought to trial. Although he was given the opportunity by the judge to plead guilty to the lesser charge of being a Roman Catholic, he refused to deny that he was a Franciscan and a Roman Catholic priest, and received the inevitable death penalty for treason. He was hanged at Lancaster Castle the following day, 7 August 1646.

Woodcock was beatified by Pope John Paul II in 1987 and so given the title Blessed. A relic of his arm bone is kept at the convent of the Poor Clares, Arundel, Sussex. Another relic (a piece of cloth) is treasured at Ladywell Shrine, near Preston, along with the altar and vestments that, by tradition, he used at Mr Burgess's house.   M. PANIKKAR

Sources *DNB* · Angelus à Sancto Francisco [R. Mason], *Certamen seraphicum provinciae Angliae pro sancta Dei ecclesia* (1649) · A. Kenny, ed., *The responsa scholarum of the English College, Rome*, 2, Catholic RS, 55 (1963), 412–13 · W. Kelly, ed., *Liber ruber venerabilis collegii Anglorum de urbe*, 1, Catholic RS, 37 (1940), 220 · C. Dodd [H. Tootell], *The church history of England, from the year 1500, to the year 1688*, 3 (1742), 109 · R. Challoner, *Memoirs of missionary priests*, ed. J. H. Pollen, rev. edn (1924), 484–5 · G. Oliver, *Collections illustrating the history of the Catholic religion in the counties of Cornwall, Devon, Dorset, Somerset, Wilts, and Gloucester* (1857), 563 · Father Thaddeus [F. Hermans],

The Franciscans in England, 1600–1850 (1898), 323–4 · P. Daly, 'John Woodcock OFM', *The Venerabile*, 29/1 (1987), 46–8 · H. Foley, ed., *Records of the English province of the Society of Jesus*, 6 (1880), 32 · J. Swarbrick, *The story of the old missionary altar* (privately printed, 1988)
Likenesses engraving, repro. in Mason, *Certamen seraphicum*, facing p. 149

Woodcroft, Bennet (1803–1879), engineer and Patent Office administrator, was born on 29 December 1803 at Heaton Norris, Lancashire, the son of John Woodcroft. Both his parents came from Sheffield, but about 1800 John Woodcroft had established himself as a merchant and manufacturer of silk and muslin in business at Manchester and Salford. He accumulated a large fortune which was subsequently dissipated by speculation in railway shares. Woodcroft was apprenticed to a silk weaver at Failsworth, near Manchester, and subsequently sought to educate himself by studying chemistry under John Dalton.

A talented inventor in the diverse fields of textile printing and machinery, and propulsion, Woodcroft made his first successful patent application in 1827 for a method of printing yarn before weaving—a process of great commercial value. He joined his father in partnership about 1828, but they fell out over the profits of Woodcroft's inventions and parted company before 1840. Meanwhile Woodcroft's other patents were that of 1838 for improved tappets for looms—his most successful invention—and a series of increasing pitch screw propellers, patented in 1832, 1844, and 1851. He was one of several inventors working to improve propellers, as marine engines came into use in naval vessels, who were persuaded to pool their claims upon the Admiralty; Woodcroft was a witness at the hearings and shared in the £20,000 parliamentary reward. The other patents brought him little financial return, as they were often illicitly operated without payment.

While at Manchester Woodcroft joined the Manchester Literary and Philosophical Society, and he developed friendships with the leading engineers of the town, including Joseph Whitworth, James Nasmyth, Richard Roberts, Eaton Hodgkinson, and Richard Fairbairn. About 1843 he set up as a consulting engineer and patent agent, moving in 1846 to London, where he was in the same business at Furnival's Inn, Holborn. He was appointed, in April 1847, professor of machinery at University College, London, but he found teaching uncongenial and its demands incompatible with his other interests, and resigned in June 1851. He was more at home in the Society of Arts, to which he was elected in 1845, where he took an active role in its administration and particularly in its exhibitions programme.

When the Patent Law Amendment Act was passed in 1852 Woodcroft was appointed assistant to the commissioner of patents, responsible for specifications. This position brought him into close contact with Prince Albert, who, following the success of the Great Exhibition of 1851, was encouraging manufacturers to take advantage of the new patent law to improve their designs and products. As a consulting engineer Woodcroft realized that the major obstacle to a modern patent system was the difficulty of seeing earlier specifications and the lack of indexes. In the space of five years he published 14,359 specifications granted between 1617 and 1852, together with indexes, which the commissioners bought from him for £1000. He also prepared classified abridgements and various ancillary technical documents. Copies were presented to more than a hundred free public libraries as well as to many foreign and colonial libraries, and were freely on sale.

During this period a dispute arose between Woodcroft and Leonard Edmunds, the clerk of patents, with mutual accusations of deceit concerning Woodcroft's payment of fees to those who prepared the abstracts and indexes. Woodcroft's brother Zenas Woodcroft, a printer of velvets living at Bennet Grange, near Sheffield, had assisted with the abstracts, but died in 1863. After a lengthy hearing Woodcroft was absolved of any financial misdeeds.

To assist in dealing with the patents, Woodcroft amassed, largely at his own expense, numerous technical books, which he handed over to form the nucleus of the Patent Office library, opened to the public in 1855 and later incorporated in the British Library. He collected portraits of inventors and, perhaps inspired by collections held in the United States patent office, gathered models of inventions from the Society of Arts and elsewhere. He also rescued from oblivion in Edinburgh the first marine engine, that invented by William Symington. These historic items went in 1857 to the new South Kensington Museum and were later transferred to the Science Museum.

Woodcroft resigned from the Society of Arts in 1858; he was elected a fellow of the Royal Society in 1859. In 1866 he married Agnes Bertha Sawyer (1833/4–1903) at St John's, Hampstead; there were no children. Woodcroft retired on 31 March 1876 and died at his home, 30 Redcliffe Gardens, South Kensington, London, on 7 February 1879; he was buried at Brompton cemetery. ANITA MCCONNELL

Sources J. Hewish, *The indefatigable Mr Woodcroft* (1979) · R. B. Prosser, *The Engineer*, 47 (1879), 118–19 · *Engineering* (14 Feb 1879), 140 · *PRS*, 29 (1879), xxxii · *The Times* (14 Feb 1879), 8 · *Manchester Guardian* (11 Feb 1879) · *Journal of the Society of Arts*, 27 (1878–9), 295 · *The Times* (22 Jan 1866), 5c–d · CGPLA Eng. & Wales (1879) · J. Hewish, *Rooms near Chancery Lane: the patent office under the commissioners, 1852–1883* (2000)
Archives Sci. Mus., letters relating to attempts to acquire specimens of Bell's Reaper for Patent Office Museum | Bolton Archive Service, corresp. relating to Samuel Crompton
Likenesses miniature on ivory, NPG
Wealth at death under £12,000: probate, 19 Feb 1879, CGPLA Eng. & Wales

Woodd, Basil (1760–1831), hymn writer, was born at Richmond, Surrey, on 5 August 1760, the only son of Basil Woodd (1730–1760) of that town, and his wife, Hannah (d. 12 Nov 1784), daughter of William Price of Richmond. He was educated by Thomas Clarke, rector of Chesham Bois in Buckinghamshire, and matriculated from Trinity College, Oxford, on 7 May 1778, graduating BA in February 1782 and MA in 1785. On 16 March 1783 he was ordained deacon, and in 1784 priest. On 10 August 1784 he was chosen lecturer of St Peter's, Cornhill, a post which he retained until 1808. In February 1785 he was appointed morning preacher at Bentinck Chapel, Marylebone, and soon after entering on his duties established evening preaching, an innovation which at first provoked opposition and afterwards imitation. He was able to purchase the lease of Bentinck in 1793, since it was a proprietary chapel. On 5 April 1808 he was instituted rector of Drayton Beauchamp, Buckinghamshire.

Woodd exerted himself successfully in establishing schools. Under his superintendence at least 3000 children passed through the schools connected with Bentinck Chapel. He was an active member of many religious societies, including the Society for Promoting Christian Knowledge, the Church Missionary Society, and the British and Foreign Bible Society. During his lifetime he published devotional works, a metrical psalter, and some original hymns, a few of which came into general use; the most notable of these was 'Hail, thou source of every blessing'. Woodd was twice married: first, on 8 February 1785, to Ann (d. 23 April 1791), daughter of Colonel Wood, and, second, on 3 July 1792, to Sophia Sarah (d. 15 Aug 1829), daughter of William Jupp of Wandsworth, an architect. With his first wife he had a son, Basil Owen (d. 1811), and two daughters, Anne Louisa (d. 1824) and Anna Sophia (d. 1817); with his second wife he had two sons and a daughter. Woodd died at Paddington Green, Middlesex, on 12 April 1831.

E. I. CARLYLE, rev. LEON LITVACK

Sources [H. Woodd], *Genealogical, heraldic, and other records … of the family of Woodd*, 2nd edn (1886) · *A family record, or, Memoirs of the late Rev. Basil Woodd* (1834) · J. Julian, ed., *A dictionary of hymnology*, rev. edn (1907)

Likenesses R. W. Sievier, stipple, pubd 1817 (after miniature by J. Barry), BM, NPG · portrait, repro. in *A family record*

Wooddeson, Richard (*bap.* **1704**, *d.* **1774**). *See under* Wooddeson, Richard (*bap.* 1745, *d.* 1822).

Wooddeson, Richard (*bap.* **1745**, *d.* **1822**), jurist, was baptized at Kingston upon Thames on 15 March 1745, the only son of Richard Wooddeson [*see below*] and his wife, Jane Style. After attending Kingston Free School, where his father was master, he matriculated at Pembroke College, Oxford, on 29 May 1759 before being elected to a demyship at Magdalen College the same year. He graduated BA in 1763 and MA in 1765. He was admitted a student of the Middle Temple on 3 March 1763 and was called to the bar on 24 November 1769. He was elected a fellow of his college in 1772, a position he held until his death. In 1766 he was elected to a Vinerian scholarship in the common law. In July 1773 he was appointed a deputy lecturer to the Vinerian professor, Robert Chambers, who was allowed to continue to hold the chair for up to three years while absent as a puisne judge in Calcutta. Wooddeson was elected a Vinerian fellow in 1776 and university lecturer in moral philosophy in March 1777. With the prospect of Chambers's resignation, Wooddeson saw himself as the 'natural Candidate', as 'Mr. Viner in his will ordains that the Professors shall be elected from among those who are or have been on his foundation' (BL, Add. MS 34414, fol. 17). None the less, when the contest came in April 1777 he

only just won against Giles Rooke by five votes. He held the chair until 1793.

In 1783 Wooddeson published *Elements of Jurisprudence*, which comprised the six introductory lectures to his Vinerian course, and which set out his vision of the nature of law. Although Wooddeson began with a discussion of the law of nature, and commented that civil laws which manifestly contradicted natural law could in conscience be disobeyed, he argued that it would be dangerous to apply the principle in practice, for if the validity of legislation were to be decided by subjects, 'government and subordination cease' (*Elements of Jurisprudence*, 48). For Wooddeson there were no bounds which could be set to legislative authority, save that it could not transfer its authority to another body. In his view, all government was founded in consent, albeit a consent manifested more by acquiescence and usage than any positive contract. Progressive experience, he felt, formed a constitution, with fundamental rules emerging and developing as a kind of cement holding the nation together. More controversially Wooddeson argued that such consent was not subsequently revocable, 'at the will even of all the subjects of the state, for that would be making a part of the community equal in power to the whole originally, and superior to the rulers thereof after their establishment' (*Elements of Jurisprudence*, 22). These views sparked a debate in the *Monthly Review* early in 1784.

The main body of Wooddeson's lectures was published in 1792–3 as *A Systematical View of the Laws of England*. Wooddeson stated here that his aim was not to repeat what William Blackstone had said, but only to supplement it, though he did aim to provide a basic groundwork for students. Writing after Mansfield, Wooddeson was able to devote more time in his work to modern developments in commercial law and equity than Blackstone. At the same time his work was less accessible and interesting to the general reader. He freely acknowledged the difficulty of acquiring legal learning, commenting that when English law was spoken of as the perfection of reason, all that was meant was 'the conformity of the law to the rational judgment of such enquirers as are well versed in the knowledge of it' (*Elements of Jurisprudence*, 101). His lectures were thus filled with more antiquarian learning and legal citation than Blackstone's. While it did not achieve the standing of the work of his predecessor, a second edition of his lectures (entitled *Lectures on the Law of England*) was brought out by William Rosser Williams in 1834.

In 1799 Wooddeson published *A Brief Vindication of the Rights of the British Legislature*, in answer to John Reeves's *Thoughts on the English Government*, which had criticized Wooddeson's *Elements* for treating the legislature as primary, and the executive as only secondary. While he argued that Reeves's notion that the king alone legislated was monstrous, the tone of the work was one of scholarly refutation, rather than polemic. In fact, Wooddeson was a bankruptcy commissioner on the same list as Reeves, and left him £50 in his will. Wooddeson also made a collection for a work on tithes, but owing to ill health he gave his notes to Samuel Toller, who published *A Treatise of the Law of Tithes* in part based on them in 1808.

Wooddeson acted for many years as counsel for the University of Oxford, as well as practising in king's bench and on the Oxford circuit. However, his main practice was as an equity draftsman, and as a commissioner of bankrupts. On 6 September 1808, while Wooddeson was in Margate, his house at 65 Chancery Lane caught fire while his servants were at Bartholomew fair and burnt down, entirely destroying his valuable library. He never married, and died on 29 October 1822 at his house at 12 New Boswell Court, Lincoln's Inn Fields. He was buried on 5 November in the benchers' vault in Temple Church. In his will he left £300 to the Clarendon Press, and £400 to Magdalen College, as well as leaving legacies to his fellow commissioners in bankruptcy. Magdalen also retained manuscripts of his verses.

His father, **Richard Wooddeson** (*bap.* 1704, *d.* 1774), was baptized at Findon in Sussex on 21 January 1704, the eldest son of Richard Wooddeson (*b. c.*1669), vicar of Findon, and his wife, Dorothy, possibly the Dorothy Hemming who married Richard Wooddeson at St Martin-in-the-Fields, Westminster, on 9 April 1703. He was a chorister at Magdalen College, Oxford, from 1712 to 1722, and a clerk from 1722 to 1725, matriculating from Magdalen College on 20 March 1719, and graduating BA in 1722, and MA in 1725. From 1725 to 1728 he filled the office of chaplain, and soon afterwards became a school assistant at Reading. In 1732 or 1733 he became master of the free school at Kingston, where he remained until 1772, when he retired to Chelsea owing to ill health. Wooddeson had a great reputation as a schoolmaster, counting among his students Edward Lovibond, George Steevens, George Keate, Edward Gibbon, William Hayley, Francis Maseres, George Hardinge, and Gilbert Wakefield. He married Jane Style on 17 November 1735, and they had two daughters, as well as a son. He died in Westminster on 15 February 1774.

MICHAEL LOBBAN

Sources H. G. Hanbury, *The Vinerian chair and legal education* (1958) · D. Lieberman, *The province of legislation determined: legal theory in eighteenth-century Britain* (1989) · M. Lobban, *The common law and English jurisprudence, 1760–1850* (1991) · T. M. Curley, *Sir Robert Chambers: law, literature, and empire in the age of Johnson* (1998) · D. Lemmings, *Professors of the law* (2000) · *GM*, 1st ser., 92/2 (1822), 648 · *GM*, 1st ser., 78 (1808), 845 · Foster, *Alum. Oxon.* · H. A. C. Sturgess, ed., *Register of admissions to the Honourable Society of the Middle Temple, from the fifteenth century to the year 1944*, 1 (1949), 359 · PRO, PROB 11/1664, sig. 619 · IGI · DNB · Browne's General Law List (1797) · Clarke's New Law List (1820)

Woodfall, George (1767–1844), printer, was baptized at St Faith's under St Paul's, London, on 17 July 1767, the son of Henry Sampson *Woodfall (1739–1805), printer and newspaper editor, and his wife, Elizabeth. Nothing is known of his education or his marriage, but Woodfall was his father's partner in the printing office at Ivy Lane, Paternoster Row, London, until December 1793. In that year Henry Sampson retired following a fire at the business. George Woodfall became known as a typographer of considerable ability. A copy of the Bible issued from his press in 1804 was said to contain only one error.

In 1812 Woodfall moved to 22 Paternoster Row and published the work for which he is best known and upon which he prided himself: an edition of the letters of Junius in three volumes. The study of these letters and the speculation about their supposed author occupied many scholars and commentators in the nineteenth century. Woodfall's father was the proprietor of the *Public Advertiser*, which published the *Letters of Junius* between January 1769 and January 1772. These anonymous letters were specifically written to discredit the ministry of the duke of Grafton and to reinstate the Chatham ministry, which had collapsed following the ill health of Chatham in October 1768. The anonymity of the letters prompted much effort in trying to trace the author, generally regarded to have been Sir Philip Francis, although over forty-five other names were proposed, including Edmund Burke and John Wilkes. The letters caused such a storm of indignation that in 1770 the government prosecuted Henry Sampson Woodfall for seditious libel for having printed them. The printer won the case, however, and always denied knowledge of the author's identity. His son spent several years in compiling the three-volume collection, for which John Mason Good wrote a preliminary essay and provided explanatory notes. Among George Woodfall's papers in the British Museum is a detailed review of John Jacques's *Junius and his Works* (1843), in which Woodfall argues against the notion that Francis either did or could have written the letters with that signature. Many of the Junius letters in manuscript, which Henry Sampson preserved, passed to George, who printed the hitherto unpublished ones and added facsimiles of the handwriting.

George Woodfall also played an important part in the introduction of steam printing by helping to finance, along with the printer Richard Taylor, Koenig's work on his steam-driven printing press from 1809 to 1814. In 1817 Woodfall moved his premises to Angel Court, Snow Hill. Dibdin styled him 'the laborious and high-spirited typographical artist to whom we are indebted for the quarto reprints of our "Old Chronicles" and for the reprint of "Hakluyt's Voyages"' (*Bibliographical Decameron*, 2.406). When Queen Victoria dined at Guildhall on 9 November 1837 she was presented with a quarto volume 'beautifully printed and illustrated by Mr George Woodfall', containing the words of the music sung at the event. Only two copies were produced, one of which was deposited in the city archives.

Woodfall's eminence as a printer was recognized by his contemporaries. He was active in the Association of London Master-Printers, taking a vigorous part in negotiations with their craftsmen and holding many senior positions, including that of chairman. In 1812 he was elected a stock-keeper of the Stationers' Company, in 1825 a member of the court of assistants, and in 1833–4 master of the company. He was re-elected stock-keeper in 1836, and in 1841 was elected master for the second time. He became a fellow of the Society of Antiquaries in 1823 and of the Royal Society of Literature in 1824. He served on the general committee of the Royal Literary Fund from 1820 to 1828, and on his resignation was elected to the council, an office he filled until his death except for the period between March 1835 and March 1838 when he was treasurer to the corporation. He was also a commissioner for the lieutenancy of the City of London. Woodfall carried on his business by himself until 1840 when his eldest son, Henry Dick Woodfall, became his partner.

George Woodfall died on 22 December 1844 at his house in Dean's Yard, Westminster. He left his manuscript correspondence, including that relating to the Junius letters, to his son, from whom they passed, through Joseph Parkes, to the British Museum.

W. F. RAE, rev. A. P. WOOLRICH

Sources Woodfall MSS, BM, Add. MSS 27774–27788 · *Annual Register* (1844) · C. Timperley, *Dictionary of printers and printing* (1839) · *Literary Gazette* (1844) · private information (2004) · [S. Morison and others], *The history of The Times*, 1 (1935) · [S. Morison], *Printing the Times since 1785* (1953) · M. Sessions, *The Federation of Master Printers: how it began* (1950) · F. Cordasco, *Junius bibliography* (1949); with suppl. (1953); (1957) · HMSO, *Abridgements of specifications relating to printing* (1859); repr. (1969) · IGI
Archives BL, MSS, Add. MSS 27774–27788

Woodfall, Henry Sampson (1739–1805), printer and newspaper editor, was born in London at the Rose and Crown inn in Little Britain on 21 June 1739, the eldest son of Henry Woodfall (1713–1769), printer, and his wife, Mary Sampson. Woodfall came from a famous eighteenth-century printing family. His grandfather, Henry Woodfall (c.1686–1747), had been apprenticed to the printer John Darby (d. 1730) of Bartholomew Close in 1701. In later life he 'carried on a considerable business and reputation' (Nichols, *Lit. anecdotes*, 1.300). Henry Sampson Woodfall's father was printer of the *Public Advertiser* in Paternoster Row, and master of the Stationers' Company in 1766, while at his death in 1769 he was a common councilman of many years' standing. Henry Sampson Woodfall's uncle, George, was a bookseller, based in Charing Cross, and his brother was William *Woodfall (bap. 1745, d. 1803), printer of the *Morning Chronicle* and famous for his parliamentary reporting.

According to one account, Henry Sampson Woodfall was taught Greek by his grandfather Henry Woodfall. By the age of five he was so good at reading Homer that Alexander Pope gave him half a crown as a reward for his skill. Woodfall was sent to school at Twickenham and made such progress in classics that when he moved to St Paul's School in 1751, at the age of eleven, he was qualified to join the seventh form. However, his juvenile looks were supposed to have condemned him to the fifth form instead. Upon leaving school in 1754 he was apprenticed to his father, who by 1758 had entrusted him with printing and editing the *Public Advertiser*.

Henry Sampson Woodfall was a freeman in the Stationers' Company from 1760, and operated from printing premises at the corner of Ivy Lane and Paternoster Row from 1761 until his retirement in 1793. Upon his father's death in 1769, he appears to have inherited shares in the paper. In the following year he was also listed as a partner in the *London Packet*. By this time he was married (his wife's name was Elizabeth) and they already had at least one child,

George *Woodfall (1767–1844), their son. Like his father and grandfather, George became a master printer and was master of the Stationers' Company in 1833–4 and 1841. At some point Henry Sampson Woodfall had another son, Henry, and a daughter, Elisabeth.

The *Public Advertiser* was a successful paper under Woodfall's command. Contemporary accounts claimed that the paper sold between 3000 and 4500 copies a day in 1779 (D'Archenholz, 42). Surviving accounts for the paper between 1766 and 1771 suggest more modest sales: from as low as 1500 in 1766, to about 3800 in 1770 and 1771, when the publication of letters by the anonymous political commentator Junius considerably boosted sales. In 1770 Woodfall was tried for libel, along with others, for publishing Junius's 'Letter to the king'. The result of the trial on 13 June 1770 was a verdict of 'printing and publishing only', which was tantamount to an acquittal. The continued publication of Junius's letters in the *Public Advertiser* supposedly made Woodfall a good deal of money, not just from increased sales of his newspaper, but also from the publication of editions of the letters. However, Woodfall may have seen his association with Junius as a mixed blessing. John Taylor recorded that when, at a dinner party in Woodfall's later years, it was suggested that Junius was dead, Woodfall replied: 'I hope and trust he is not dead, as I think he would have left me a legacy; for, though I derived much honour from his preference, I suffered much by the freedom of his pen' (Taylor, 2.253).

Woodfall's relationship with the anonymous author of these letters became the source of much conjecture during his lifetime, since some believed he knew the author's identity, a charge which Woodfall always denied. Surviving letters to Woodfall reveal that he was trusted with the identity of many of the other anonymous authors in his paper. Correspondents included the earl of Sandwich, Horace Walpole, Lord George Gordon, John Horne Tooke, and John Wilkes. He was also said to be on good terms with Garrick, Colman, Smollett, Goldsmith, and 'other wits of the day' (Nichols, *Lit. anecdotes*, 1.302). Despite his involvement with Junius, Woodfall liked to dissociate himself from the more scurrilous sections of the newspaper press. His paper was politically moderate, and published articles espousing a wide variety of views. In 1776 he described the outspoken and rival editor, the Revd Henry Bate, as 'beneath every thing but contempt' (BL, Add. MS 36593, fol. 128). According to Nichols, Woodfall was immune to the sort of corruption which editors such as Bate engaged in. 'With regard to the line of conduct he had adopted respecting his paper,' Nichols argued, 'in a pecuniary point of view, it was always most scrupulously honourable and correct; and, though frequently offered money to suppress certain articles of intelligence, not pleasant to the particular individual, yet never could he be prevailed upon to forgo what he deemed to be his duty to the publick' (Nichols, *Lit. anecdotes*, 1.301). Taylor described him as a man of 'firmness, public spirit, and inflexible integrity' (Taylor, 2.252).

In 1772 Woodfall was supposed to have refused an offer to succeed his father to the common council, saying that his duty was 'to *record* great actions, not to *perform* them' (Nichols, *Lit. anecdotes*, 1.301). But his claim not to want such promotion was probably disingenuous. In 1786 he confided to Wilkes that he wished to obtain the position of clerk 'of any public office' (BL, Add. MS 30873, fol. 29). Perhaps one of the reasons he failed to achieve his aim was that Woodfall was the subject of several prosecutions, all connected to his involvement in the *Public Advertiser*. In addition to the prosecution over Junius's writing, he appeared before the House of Commons for a libel on the speaker on 14 February 1774. Two days later Fox moved for him to be indicted for a libel on the constitution, and he was convicted and sentenced to three months' imprisonment in July. An action for libel by the earl of Chatham in 1776 failed owing to a legal technicality, and in 1779 Woodfall was prosecuted at the court of the king's bench for printing and publishing a handbill supporting Admiral Keppel. He was fined and sentenced to twelve months in Newgate. Despite his confinement, he appears not to have suffered too greatly, and detailed accounts for the food and wine he consumed during his time in prison still survive. In 1784 he was tried for a libel on Edmund Burke, who claimed damages of £5000 but was awarded only £100. In later years Woodfall was reported to have boasted 'that he had been *fined* by the House of Lords; *confined* by the court of the king's bench, and indicted at the Old Bailey' (Nichols, *Lit. anecdotes*, 1.301).

Woodfall disposed of his interest in the *Public Advertiser* in November 1793, and retired from business in the following month when his offices burnt down. The newspaper lasted only two more years after he ceased to run it. His involvement with the print trade did not entirely cease, as he was master of the Stationers' Company in 1797. From his retirement until his death he lived in Chelsea, London, where he died on 12 December 1805. He was buried in the churchyard there, although his tombstone was subsequently moved to make room for the Philip Miller obelisk. In his will Woodfall left his estate to his children. It included 'all sum or sums of money in the Government funds or India Companys funds and all my furniture plate silver china and all the rest and residue of my personal estate'.   HANNAH BARKER

Sources GM, 1st ser., 75 (1805) · I. Maxted, *The London book trades, 1775–1800: a topographical guide* (privately printed, Exeter, 1980) · misc. letters of H. S. Woodfall, BL, Add. MS 27780 · J. Taylor, *Records of my life*, 2 vols. (1832) · Nichols, *Lit. anecdotes* · C. H. Timperley, *A dictionary of printers and printing* (1839) · M. D'Archenholz, *A picture of England* (1791) · will, PRO, PROB 11/879 · accounts of *Public Advertiser*, 1765–71, BL, Add. MS 38169 · minutes of *London Packet*, BL, Add. MS 38729, fols. 165–6 · *The miscellaneous works of Hugh Boyd, the author of the 'Letters of Junius'*, ed. L. D. Campbell, 2 vols. (1800)
Archives BL, corresp. and papers, Add. MSS 27778–27780, 27774–27776 · BL, papers relating to proceedings in parliament against him, Add. MSS 27778, 41065
Wealth at death wealthy: will, PRO, PROB 11/879

Woodfall, William (*bap.* **1745**, *d.* **1803**), journalist and newspaper editor, was baptized at St Botolph, Aldersgate, London, on 7 February 1745, the second son of the printer Henry Woodfall (1713–1769) and his wife, Mary Sampson.

William Woodfall (*bap.* 1745, *d.* 1803), by Thomas Beach, 1782

Woodfall followed his father into the print trade and was apprenticed to the bookseller Richard Baldwin before joining his father at his newspaper, the *Public Advertiser*. For a brief period Woodfall seems to have had theatrical aspirations, and in the late 1760s travelled as an actor to Scotland, where he married a woman named Elen. The offspring from this marriage included Sophia and William, who became a novelist and actress and barrister and legal author respectively. After his father's death in 1769, Woodfall gave up his hopes of an acting career. While his elder brother, Henry Sampson *Woodfall (1739–1805), took over the *Advertiser*, he became editor of the *London Packet* in 1772, leaving it in 1774 to run the *Morning Chronicle*. He still retained some links with the theatre as a critic, and notably offended the actors Garrick and John Henderson with his reviews.

Woodfall became celebrated in his day for his parliamentary reporting, and played an important part in making parliamentary proceedings more public. According to James Grant:

> To great physical powers of endurance, and intellectual acquirements of no common kind, he united a memory almost incredible for its capacity of retention … so marvellously retentive was his recollection, that he has been known to write sixteen columns of speeches without having taken a single note to assist his memory.   (Grant, 1.199)

This famed ability earned him the nickname Memory Woodfall, and when he travelled to Dublin in 1784 to report the parliamentary debates there, his celebrity was such that crowds followed him in the streets because of his supposed 'supernatural powers' (GM, 792).

However, not all of Woodfall's contemporaries were

convinced. James Stephen, who worked as a parliamentary reporter in early 1780s, claimed that Woodfall:

> published debates with greater fullness and greater accuracy, too, than the use of shorthand notes has since produced, and the memory which was supposed to be his sole resource was naturally a subject of admiration and wonder. But we his contemporary fellow labourers well knew the advantages he possessed, and which reduced the apparently preternatural talent to intelligible tho' certainly more than ordinary dimensions. Being absolute master of his own paper, and being inclined from vanity or mistaken self-interest to sacrifice all other considerations to its reputation for Parliamentary reports, he used to publish the day after an important or long debate in either House several hours later than any other Morning paper, and never sent his Paper to press, or went himself to bed on such occasions till he had read all the other reports and supplied from them as far as he thought fit the omissions of his own. (*Memoirs*, 1.293)

It is also clear that Woodfall pestered politicians for copies of their speeches. On 9 December 1780, for example, Woodfall wrote to William Adam complaining that he had been promised a copy of Sir Hugh Palliser's speech on Admiral Keppel's court martial by 'a friend of Sir Hugh' who 'called upon me on Monday evening while I was scribbling' (Woodfall to Adam, 14 Dec 1780, Blair Adam MS; Aspinall, 333). It seems Woodfall's badgering was rewarded, for a detailed version of the speech finally appeared in the *Chronicle* four days later. In another letter, dated 24 February 1784, Woodfall wrote to Adam concerning an important debate on the removal of the coalition by the king: 'Can you help me by loosely throwing upon paper any points you recollect to be strongly put which have not appeared or have not been given in the papers already?' (ibid., 444), he asked. This plea also seems to have succeeded.

The *Morning Chronicle* was self-consciously neutral in its politics. However, like most other newspapermen of his generation, Woodfall was still sued for libel at several points in his career: most notably by the government in 1779 after he had congratulated Admiral Keppel on his acquittal from a court martial. For this offence Woodfall received a twelve-month prison sentence. In 1789 Woodfall sold his interest in the *Morning Chronicle* and set up an evening paper, *The Diary*, which lasted only until August 1793. At this point Woodfall appears to have retired from business. Ten years later he died in Queen Street, London, where he had lived, on 1 August 1803, after a week's illness, and was buried in St Margaret's churchyard, Westminster. He left £650 to his wife and possessions which indicated a comfortable lifestyle, including sets of prints, china, plate, books, and mahogany furniture.

HANNAH BARKER

Sources J. Grant, *The newspaper press: its origin, progress, and present position*, 3 vols. (1871–2) · *GM*, 1st ser., 73 (1803), 792 · *The memoirs of James Stephen, written by himself for the use of his children*, ed. M. M. Bevington (1954) · A. Aspinall, *Politics and the press, c.1780–1850* (1949) · J. Taylor, *Records of my life*, 2 vols. (1832) · H. Barker, *Newspapers, politics and public opinion in late eighteenth-century England* (1998) · I. Maxted, *The London book trades, 1775–1800: a topographical guide* (privately printed, Exeter, 1980) · A. Andrews, *The history of British journalism*, 2 vols. (1859) · C. Pebody, *English journalism and the men who have made it* (1882) · H. R. Fox Bourne, *English newspapers: chapters in the history of journalism*, 2 vols. (1887) · F. K. Hunt, *The fourth estate: contributions towards a history of newspapers, and of the liberty of the press*, 2 vols. (1850) · will, PRO, PROB 11/1398, sig. 744 · *IGI*

Likenesses T. Beach, oils, 1782, NPG [*see illus.*] · R. Dighton, etching, pubd 1792, NPG · stipple, pubd 1797, NPG; repro. in *An impartial report of the debates in the two houses of parliament in the year 1797*, 3 vols. (1797)

Wealth at death approx. £1000: will, PRO, PROB 11/1398, sig. 744

Woodford, Sir Alexander George (1782–1870), army officer, was the elder son of Lieutenant-Colonel John Woodford (d. 1800), and his second wife, Lady Susan (d. 1814), eldest daughter of Cosmo George Gordon, third duke of Gordon, and widow of John Fane, ninth earl of Westmorland. Lord William Gordon and Lord George *Gordon were his mother's brothers. Major-General Sir John George *Woodford was his younger brother. His father, John Woodford, was for some time in the Grenadier Guards. He served under General James Wolfe, and later took an active part in the volunteer movement of the day. He became lieutenant-colonel of the 6th fencible infantry (the Gordon regiment). During the Gordon riots, which his uncle led, he was the first officer to order the soldiers to fire on the rioters after the attack on Lord Mansfield's house.

Alexander Woodford was born at 30 Welbeck Street, London, on 15 June 1782. He went to Winchester College as a commoner in 1794, and in 1799 to the Royal Military Academy, Woolwich. His age placed him in the centre of the cohort which rose during the Napoleonic wars and went on to run the Victorian army. He obtained a commission as ensign in the 9th foot on 6 December 1794. His further commissions were dated: lieutenant, 15 July 1795; captain, 11 December 1799; regimental captain Coldstream Guards and lieutenant-colonel, 8 March 1810; colonel, 4 June 1814; regimental second major, 25 July 1814; regimental first major, 18 January 1820; regimental lieutenant-colonel, 25 July 1821; major-general, 27 May 1825; lieutenant-general, 28 June 1838; colonel of the 40th, or 2nd Somersetshire, regiment of foot, 25 April 1842; general, 20 June 1854; transferred to the colonelcy of the Scots Fusilier Guards, 15 December 1861; field marshal, 1 January 1868.

Woodford was promoted lieutenant in an independent corps and was brought into the 22nd foot on 8 September 1795, but placed on half pay the following year, as he was too young to serve. He was again brought into the 9th foot as captain-lieutenant of the newly raised battalion in 1799. He served with this regiment in the expedition to The Helder in September 1799, and was severely wounded on the 19th at the battle of Bergen. He was brought into the Coldstream Guards on 20 December 1799. In 1803 he was appointed aide-de-camp to Major-General Sir James Ochoncar Forbes. He rejoined his regiment to serve at the investment and bombardment of Copenhagen in 1807. He again joined the staff of Lord Forbes in Sicily and the Mediterranean as aide-de-camp from March 1808 to June 1810. From duty in London he joined his company at Isla de León for the siege of Cadiz in 1811, commanded the light battalion of the brigade of guards at the siege and capture on 19 January 1812 of Ciudad Rodrigo, at the siege and capture on 6 April of Badajoz, at the battle of Salamanca on 22 July, at the occupation of Madrid and the capture on 14 August of the Retiro, at the siege of Burgos in September and October, and in the retreat from that place. He commanded the 1st battalion of the Coldstream Guards during the battles of 1813 and 1814, including Vitoria and Nivelle. He was appointed aide-de-camp to the prince regent on 4 June 1841 for his service in the field, and aide-de-camp to the king on the prince's accession to the throne. He commanded the 2nd battalion of the Coldstream Guards at the battles of Quatre Bras on 16 and of Waterloo on 18 June 1815, at the storm of Cambrai on 24 June, at the entry into Paris on 7 July, and during the occupation of France.

For his services Woodford was frequently mentioned in dispatches, and received the gold medal with two clasps for the battles of Salamanca, Vitoria, and the Nive, the silver medal with two clasps for Ciudad Rodrigo and Nivelle, and the Waterloo medal. He was made a companion in the Order of the Bath, military division, and was permitted to accept and wear the insignia of knighthood of the Austrian order of Maria Theresa and of the fourth class of St George of Russia.

Woodford was lieutenant-governor and commanded the infantry brigade at Malta from 1825 until he was transferred in a like capacity in 1827 to Corfu. He was made KCB on 13 September 1831, and KCMG on 30 June 1832, in which year he was appointed to the command of the forces in the Ionian Islands, and acted temporarily as high commissioner. He was appointed lieutenant-governor of Gibraltar on 28 February 1835, and governor and commander-in-chief on 1 September 1836, a position he occupied for seven years. The grand cross in the Order of the Bath, military division, was bestowed upon him on 7 April 1852. He became lieutenant-governor of Chelsea Hospital on 25 September 1856, and succeeded to the governorship on 3 August 1868 on the death of Sir Edward Blakeney.

Woodford married, in 1820, Charlotte Mary Ann (d. 21 April 1870), daughter of Charles Henry Fraser, British minister at Hamburg. One of the six lancet windows in the north transept of Westminster Abbey was filled with stained glass by Woodford in memory of his second son, Lieutenant-Colonel Charles John Woodford (1823–1857) of the rifle brigade, who was killed while leading a charge at Cawnpore during the Indian mutiny in 1857. Woodford died at the governor's residence, Chelsea Hospital, on 26 August 1870, and was buried at Kensal Green cemetery on 1 September.   R. H. VETCH, *rev.* H. C. G. MATTHEW

Sources *Army List* · *Hart's Army List* · *The Times* (27 Aug 1870) · *The Times* (2 Sept 1870) · J. F. Crosthwaite, *Brief memoir of Major-Gen. Sir John Geo. Woodford* (1881) · R. Cannon, ed., *Historical record of the ninth, or the east Norfolk regiment of foot* (1848) · W. Siborne, *History of the Waterloo campaign* (1848) · W. F. P. Napier, *History of the war in the Peninsula and in the south of France*, 6 vols. (1828–40) · *ILN* (10 Sept 1870), 283
Archives Warks. CRO, corresp. and papers | NL Scot., corresp. with Sir George Brown

Likenesses M. & N. Hanhart, lithograph (after photograph by unknown artist), NPG
Wealth at death under £14,000: probate, 20 Oct 1870, *CGPLA Eng. & Wales*

Woodford, James Russell (1820–1885), bishop of Ely, was born on 30 April 1820 at Henley-on-Thames, Oxfordshire, the only son of James Russell Woodford, hop merchant, of Borough High Street, Southwark, and his wife, Frances, daughter of Robert Appleton of Henley. After attending Merchant Taylors' School (1828–38) he was Parkins exhibitioner at Pembroke College, Cambridge, in 1838, and graduated BA in 1842 and MA in 1845. He was ordained deacon in the diocese of Bristol and Gloucester in 1843, as curate of St John's, Bristol, and second master of Bishop's College, Bristol. The Conservative, low-church editor of the *Bristol Times*, Joseph Leech, noted of one of Woodford's sermons as a curate, 'In his language there was the utmost Anglican purity, evidencing, though not displaying, the scholar' (Leech, 37). He was ordained priest in 1845 by the bishop of Exeter, and was presented by James Monk, bishop of Gloucester, to the perpetual curacy of St Saviour's, Coalpit Heath, Gloucestershire, a mining district near Bristol 'proverbial for vice and irreligion' (Thompson, 44).

As a protégé of Archdeacon Thomas Thorp of Bristol, the president of the Cambridge Camden Society, Woodford became secretary of the Bristol and West of England Architectural Society in 1842. At Coalpit Heath he commissioned William Butterfield to build a church and parsonage, the architect's first such commission. In 1847 he became the first incumbent of St Mark's, Lower Easton, Bristol, also in Monk's gift, where he built a new church and established a model Tractarian liturgy, with chanted services and a surpliced choir. In 1855 he was presented by Monk to the vicarage of Kempsford, Gloucestershire, where he commissioned G. E. Street to restore the church.

Woodford was appointed an examining chaplain to Samuel Wilberforce, bishop of Oxford, in 1863, who spoke highly of his preaching. He remained close to Wilberforce, and through him knew W. E. Gladstone. In 1867 he became an honorary canon of Christ Church, Oxford. He was a select preacher at Cambridge in 1864, 1867, and 1873, and a chaplain to the queen in 1872. In 1868 he was elected vicar of Leeds. At Leeds parish church he introduced moderate high-church liturgical practices and was a pioneer of parish missions. Like his predecessors he used his patronage as vicar to appoint high-churchmen to Leeds parishes. In spite of his churchmanship he was respected and trusted by the evangelical Bishop Bickersteth of Ripon. Wilberforce thought that Leeds working men had taken him to their hearts.

In October 1873 Gladstone nominated Woodford as bishop of Ely. He was consecrated in Westminster Abbey in December 1873. At Ely he encouraged his clergy and parishes to undertake the restoration and extension of churches, and set up a diocesan fund to assist poorer parishes to do this. He was concerned to improve the quality of the clergy and ordained only graduates. He was among

James Russell Woodford (1820–1885), by Lock & Whitfield, pubd 1880

the first bishops to recognize the 'preliminary examination of candidates for holy orders', which established a common standard of theological competence for ordination candidates. In 1876, on the initiative of Harvey Goodwin, the former dean, and following the example of other high-church bishops, Woodford established a theological college attached to the cathedral in Ely to train graduates for ordination. He was one of a group of bishops who elevated the office of teacher into a minor order of the church. He had an uneasy relationship with nonconformists, and following the Burials Act of 1880, permitting nonconformist ministers to conduct burial services in parish churchyards, along with bishops Wordsworth and Magee he decided not to consecrate any more churchyards or parts of cemeteries.

In 1852 Woodford published Hymns Arranged for the Sundays and Holy Days of the Church of England (2nd edn, 1855). He was invited to join the committee which subsequently published Hymns Ancient and Modern in 1861, but he resigned, objecting to the proposed translations of Latin hymns from the Sarum Breviary as 'laboured renderings, without flow' (W. K. Lowther Clarke, A Hundred Years of 'Hymns Ancient and Modern', 1960, 24–5). He subsequently disagreed sharply with the compilers of Hymns Ancient and Modern over alterations, without his sanction, of his translation of Latin hymns. In 1863, with H. W. Beadon, he published The Parish Hymn Book (2nd edn, 1873), and in 1868, with Earl Nelson and E. A. Dayman, The Sarum Hymnal (2nd edn, 1870).

Woodford published seven collections of sermons and three visitation charges, as well as The Church Past and Present, being Four Lectures on Church History (1852) and Christ's Teaching and Influence on the World (1880). He edited The Tracts for the Christian Seasons (3rd ser., 1864) and Samuel Wilberforce's Sermons Preached on Various Occasions (1877). Woodford died, unmarried, at Ely, on 24 October 1885 and was buried in Ely Cathedral. St Aidan's, Roundhay, Leeds, where his mitre is preserved, was built as a memorial to him.

W. M. JACOB

Sources DNB · Boase, Mod. Eng. biog. · Venn, Alum. Cant. · P. G. Cobb, The Oxford Movement in nineteenth-century Bristol (1988), 9–11 · N. Yates, Leeds and the Oxford Movement, Thoresby Society, 55 (1975), 18–20, 57, 227 · J. Leech, Rural rides of the Bristol churchgoer, ed. A. Sutton (1982), 37 · P. Thompson, William Butterfield (1971), 44 · F. W. B. Bullock, A history of training for the ministry of the Church of England (1955) · P. T. Marsh, The Victorian church in decline: Archbishop Tait and the Church of England, 1868–1882 (1969), 121, 124, 261 · O. Chadwick, The Victorian church, 2 (1970), 259, 337, 383, 448 · R. G. Wilberforce, Life of the right reverend Samuel Wilberforce … with selections from his diaries and correspondence, 3 (1882), 23, 359, 401 · A. Haig, The Victorian clergy (1984), 203 · J. Julian, ed., A dictionary of hymnology (1892) · [H. M. Luckock], ed., In piam memoriam: Jacobi Russell episcopi Eliensis noni quinqagesimi (1885) [incl. notices, records, and sermons, repr. from The Guardian]

Archives BL, letters to W. E. Gladstone, Add. MSS 44439–44487 · Bodl. Oxf., letters to Samuel Wilberforce · CUL, letters to Sir George Stokes · Durham Cath. CL, letters to J. B. Lightfoot · LPL, corresp. with A. C. Tait

Likenesses W. B. Gardner, wood-engraving (after photograph by Russell & Sons), NPG; repro. in ILN (30 Aug 1873) · Lock & Whitfield, woodburytype photograph, NPG; repro. in T. Cooper, Men of mark: a gallery of contemporary portraits (1880) [see illus.] · portrait, repro. in ILN (31 Oct 1885), 444

Woodford, Sir John George (1785–1879), army officer, born on 28 February 1785 at Chartham deanery, near Canterbury, was second son of Lieutenant-Colonel John Woodford (d. 1800), and his second wife, Lady Susan (d. 1814), eldest daughter of Cosmo George Gordon, third duke of Gordon, and widow of John Fane, ninth earl of Westmorland. He was the younger brother of Sir Alexander George *Woodford. Educated at Harrow School under Joseph Drury, he was sent in 1800 to Brunswick to learn his military duties under the duke of Brunswick, whose wife, the Princess Augusta, sister of George III, showed him much kindness. In May 1800 the duke of Gloucester gave him a commission as ensign in the 1st regiment of guards, but arranged that he should remain to complete his year's training in Brunswick. On his return to England he attracted the notice of the duke of Queensberry ('Old Q'), who took him to Windsor to present him to the king, and made him a present of a fine horse. When the duke died in 1810 he left Woodford, though in no way related to him, £10,000. Woodford joined his regiment in 1801, but it was not until 1807 that he saw active service, when both he and his elder brother, Alexander, were at the siege of Copenhagen. In the following year he went to the Peninsula with the expedition under Sir David Baird, which joined the British forces under Sir John Moore. Woodford was deputy assistant quartermaster-general and aide-de-camp to Sir John Moore, and at dusk was wounded in the heel in the battle of Corunna by, it is said, the last shot fired. After eighteen months' convalescence he rejoined the army which, under Wellington, had just crossed the Ebro, and resumed his deputy assistant quartermaster-generalship. He was present at the battles of Nivelle, Nive, Orthez, and Toulouse, for which engagements he received a cross. In the final engagement at Toulouse on 10 April 1814 Woodford, serving under Sir Henry Clinton (1771–1829) in the 6th division, took a distinguished part.

In September Woodford was back in London, and with the legacy left him by 'Old Q', which had been paid in 1813, he purchased his captaincy in the 1st regiment of the Grenadier Guards (equivalent in rank and pay to that of lieutenant-colonel of infantry in the line). On the unexpected return of Napoleon in 1815 he joined Wellington's army, serving as assistant quartermaster-general to the 4th division under Lieutenant-General Sir Charles Colville. Woodford was at Wellington's headquarters on 18 June, with battle imminent; the duke ordered him to stay and act as aide-de-camp. He continued to serve under General Colville in the march to Paris, and assisted in the occupation of Cambrai. On the break-up of the army in Paris he returned to London, but in 1818 was appointed to the command of the army of occupation until the final evacuation of France in October of that year. He took advantage of his position to survey the field of the battle of Agincourt and its vicinity. Discoveries of considerable antiquarian and historic interest resulted.

In 1821 Woodford was given the command of the 3rd battalion of the Grenadier Guards at Dublin, and finally he was posted to it as colonel on 23 November 1823. He carried out various reforms in military discipline. He would not allow flogging in the battalion under his command, and on 26 May 1830, on his own responsibility, published the order 'The punishment called "standing under arms" is abolished'. Though Woodford's action annoyed the duke of Wellington, the punishment was never restored. The regimental orders of the Grenadier Guards from 1830 to 1835 are full of evidence of his attempts to improve the conditions of a soldier's life. On 18 May 1835 Woodford gave evidence to the commissioners for inquiry into the system of military punishments in the army. He published that year *Remarks on military flogging: its causes and effects, with some considerations on the propriety of its entire abolition*. Woodford, among other reforms, recommended recreation for soldiers in barracks, the teaching of useful trades to soldiers, and the establishment of regimental libraries. His command of the household troops brought him into contact with the king, William IV, who presented him with the Royal Guelphic Order of knighthood, but his reforming zeal, particularly an attempt to introduce a more comfortable uniform, greatly annoyed the king. Woodford was not wholly alone in advocating reform from within the army, but his high and central position gave him an important role in countering Wellington's persistent opposition. Woodford lived to see Gladstone's abolition of the purchase of commissions, and a number of lesser reforms which he had advocated, such as the ending of the wearing of the extremely uncomfortable stock (or starched neck-cloth).

In 1834, by the will of his aunt, Lady William Gordon,

Woodford inherited an estate on the western bank of Derwent Water, with Waterend House, erected by Lord William. He decided to retire there, and he issued on 10 January 1837 his last regimental order, was promoted to the rank of major-general, and retired from the service in October 1841. He had been made CB in 1815 and KCB in 1838. As a consistent advocate of abolition of purchase, he sold his commission to the government for £4500, half its market value. A good linguist, of scholarly tastes, he subsequently devoted much of his time to antiquarian research. Though he continued to live much like a soldier in camp, he surrounded himself with rare books and curiosities. After moving to Lake Viek Villa, Keswick, he died there on 22 March 1879.

ALBERT NICHOLSON, *rev.* H. C. G. MATTHEW

Sources J. F. Crosthwaite, *Brief memoir of Major-Gen. Sir John Geo. Woodford* (1881) · *Hart's Army List* · Boase, *Mod. Eng. biog.*
Archives Keswick Museum and Art Gallery, corresp., papers, and notebook · Warks. CRO, letters and papers | U. Southampton L., letters to first duke of Wellington
Likenesses photograph, repro. in Crosthwaite, *Brief memoir*
Wealth at death under £800: administration with will, 10 Jan 1880, *CGPLA Eng. & Wales*

Woodford [Woodforde], **Robert** (1606–1654), lawyer and diarist, was born on 3 April 1606 at Old, Northamptonshire, the son of Robert Woodford (1562–1636) and Jane Dexter. He was educated at nearby Brixworth School and became a provincial attorney. His marriage to Hannah Hancs or Haunch (1617–1699) of All Hallows, London Wall, on 22 January 1635, brought them fourteen children, the most prominent being Samuel *Woodford FRS (1636–1700), through whom Woodford was the progenitor of a dynasty of diarists culminating in his great-great-grandson James *Woodforde (1740–1803). In 1636 Woodford was elected steward of Northampton by the good offices of his lawyer patron, John Reading. The following year he began keeping a diary, which is the only significant source for the life and opinions of this obscure man.

The document fascinatingly illustrates the reality of a person struggling to live the sort of godly life enjoined by puritan ministers. The underlying world view was a sharply polarized one based on Calvinist experimental predestinarianism according to which the individual could detect the signs of election in himself and achieve assurance of salvation. Woodford's conversion predated the diary; he was now concerned to leave his carnal self behind and establish a spiritual identity as one of the godly in contradistinction to the ungodly adherents of Satan. Overt avoidance of the ungodly, which was the ideal, would have rendered normal life impossible, so Woodford usually attempted to avoid their sins—telling jokes, gambling, or over-indulgence in alcohol and tobacco—but was not always successful. The obverse of the coin was a love for things spiritual. Woodford was part of a community centred on the parish of All Saints, Northampton, and its vicar, Thomas Ball, who ensured that the town was a lively preaching centre. Ball and Andrew Perne led official activity but also a host of extra-curricular observances binding the community of saints together. By means of these spiritual comforts and prayer, the sabbath, and the sacraments, he achieved mixed success in preventing anxiety about worldly problems, particularly his family's health and impecuniosity, from undermining his faith. He did not achieve a settled assurance by the end of the diary but neither did he descend into the despair suffered by other godly writers.

The diary is also an excellent study of opposition to the personal rule of Charles I which, in the absence of parliaments, was extremely hazardous. The divisive analysis of English politics associated with John Pym and the leaders of parliamentary opposition to the crown in the 1620s had by 1637 achieved a wider acceptance. The perception was of an absolutist papist plot to subvert England's laws and true religion. In Woodford's view the immediate threat was that posed to a Calvinist orthodoxy by heretical churchmen who sought to overthrow the prevailing word-centred piety of the church and replace it with ecclesiological innovations—such as east-end altars—and doctrinal Arminianism, while stigmatizing the orthodox godly as subversive puritans. He went further than most writers in expressing doubts concerning Charles's complicity, repeatedly praying for the king's conversion and portraying him as incapable of distinguishing true religion from error. While national figures like Archbishop William Laud and Bishop Matthew Wren were identified as leaders of the conspiracy, Woodford's ire was reserved for the clergy who enforced the altar policy in his own parish, Robert Sibthorpe and Samuel Clarke. The latter was especially vilified for attempting to ban the Sunday afternoon sermon. Secular policies contrary to the subject's liberties, especially the prerogative tax of ship money, were attributed to the same anti-Christian influence: he personally witnessed the judges' verdict in Hampden's case. The climax of the conspiracy came with the bishops' wars, and by August 1640 he was ready to see an end to episcopacy.

Lacking powerful allies Woodford never felt confident enough to translate ideological opposition into open resistance. However, his support for the Long Parliament's condemnation of the policies of the personal rule was zealous. The diary lapsed in 1641 but it is easy to imagine how the Irish rising would have provided final confirmation of the operation of the conspiracy leaving him susceptible to the parliamentarian persuasion of the grand remonstrance. Very little is known about Woodford's remaining years; he continued in office into the interregnum and rose to become under-sheriff of Northamptonshire in 1653. He died on 15 November the following year. J. FIELDING

Sources A. J. Fielding, 'Opposition to the personal rule of Charles I: the diary of Robert Woodford, 1637–41', *HJ*, 31 (1988), 769–88 • R. Woodford, 'Diary, 1637–41', New College, Oxford, MS 9502 • New College, Oxford, MS 9494, fols. 11r–13v • D. H. Woodforde, ed., *Woodforde papers and diaries* (1932) [genealogical chart] • A. J. Fielding, 'Conformists, puritans and the church courts: the diocese of Peterborough, 1603–1642', PhD diss., U. Birm., 1989, 180–92, 203–27, 235–64 • T. Webster, *Godly clergy in early Stuart England: the Caroline puritan movement, c.1620–1643* (1997), 52, 55, 76, 128, 217–20, 226, 259 • T. Webster, 'Writing to redundancy: approaches to spiritual journals and early modern spirituality', *HJ*, 39 (1996), 33–56 • PRO, PROB 6/31, fol. 59

Archives New College, Oxford, diary, MS 9502 | New College, Oxford, notes on his life by his son, Dr Samuel Woodford, MS 9494

Wealth at death see administration, PRO, PROB 6/31, fol. 59

Woodford [Woodforde], **Samuel** (1636–1700), poet, was born on Good Friday, 15 April 1636, in the parish of All Hallows, London Wall, London, the eldest of the fourteen children of Robert *Woodford (1606–1654), gentleman, of Northampton, and Hannah, née Hancs or Haunch (1617–1698), of London. From St Paul's School he went in 1653 to Trinity College, Oxford, but a year later, on 20 July 1654, he registered as a commoner at Wadham College, Oxford, funded by a legacy from his maternal grandfather (d. 1649). Of his time at Oxford he was later to say that 'coming pretty ripe from Paul's School, I was too good to learn, and was so proud as to think my self almost as good as my tutor', with the result that he followed his own inclinations in reading Roman historians and the classical poets and 'neglected other more serious studies' (Ferrell, 141). He nevertheless took his BA on 6 February 1657. As an undergraduate he played the viol and enjoyed musical evenings with a group which included Thomas Ken, and it is during these years that his earliest extant poems were written. Woodford first appeared in print as a contributor to *Naps upon Parnassus* (1658), a collection of 'Jovial … Verses' by 'some of the WITS of the Universities' (title-page) mocking the conceit, and burlesquing the poetry, of another Wadham student, Samuel Austin. Thomas Sprat and Thomas Flatman, Woodford's lifelong friends, were also contributors.

By Woodford's own account his profligate ways so ran him into debt that he 'could not stay with any credit in that town any longer where I owed £50' and so, 'not because I was so infinitely pleased with it' but as a last resort (Ferrell, 142), in 1658 he left Oxford to become a student at the Inner Temple, where he was a chamber-fellow of Flatman. In London, through Flatman, Woodford associated with Charles Cotton, Izaak Walton, and Alexander Brome, and he continued in what he himself characterized as the life of indolence and excess he had led at Oxford, though he acknowledges that his dissolute ways did not extend to 'swearing, drunkenness whoredom and such grievous sins' which he shunned as 'so vile and carrying their just punishments' (ibid., 143). He was also the friend of Charles Beale, husband of the painter Mary Beale, and they may in part have been responsible for the reformation in Woodford's way of life which is evident from the diary he began to keep in 1660, for in their home he had the opportunity to meet a number of divines of puritan and latitudinarian persuasion, including John Tillotson, afterwards archbishop of Canterbury, Vincent Alsop, William Bates, and Richard Baxter.

Through the Beales Woodford met their relative Alice Beale (d. 1664). Despite opposition from his maternal great-uncle Edmund Heighes (d. 1661) and his wife, they were married by Tillotson on 10 October 1661 at St

Christopher-le-Stocks, London. The couple lived with the Beales in Hind Court, Fleet Street, where their first child, Alice, was born in 1662. When in 1663 Woodford's aunt withdrew her objections to their marriage, they moved into the Heighes's family home at Binstead, Hampshire, which Woodford had inherited on his uncle's death. There, on 14 January 1664, Alice Beale died giving birth to their second child, Heighes. Following her death, Woodford moved back to Hind Court. In 1665–6 he was living in Albrook, Hampshire.

It was as a religious poet that in 1667 Woodford established his reputation with the publication of his *Paraphrase upon the Psalms of David*, dedicated to George Morley, bishop of Winchester. This was inspired by the version of Psalm 114 by Abraham Cowley, of whom Woodford was a great admirer. It was written in the main during Woodford's residence with the Beales in 1664, and completed at Albrook in March 1666. During its composition, Woodford had the benefit of advice from his 'very judicious friend' Thomas Sprat (*Paraphrase upon the Psalms of David*, sig. b4ᵛ). Like Sprat, he was a fellow of the Royal Society (elected in November 1664) and he mentions incidentally a plan to write a verse history of the first week of Creation utilizing the discoveries of the society (ibid., sig. c2). In a long preface he surveys the earlier versions of the psalms by George Buchanan, George Sandys, Henry King, and Sir Philip Sidney (made available to him in manuscript by John Wilkins). He justifies poetry as 'the Stile, and Language of Heaven', arguing that a 'man of an Harmonious soul (such as all true *Poets* are' will surpass scholars in communicating biblical truth (ibid., sigs. a2, a3ᵛ–a4). He declares it to be his aim to give 'the true sense and meaning of the Psalm, and in as easy and obvious terms as was possible, suiting them to the capacity of the meanest' (ibid., sig. c2). To this end he prefers 'expressions and phrases generally known' to 'obsolete, or fantastical words' and 'innovation' (ibid., sig. b4). He used the work of Henry Hammond as his guide to the biblical sense. Metrically he sometimes followed Cowley's 'Pindarick way', but for the historical psalms he used 'the Heroick (or five foot)' couplet, and for others a variety of stanzaic forms (ibid., sig. c2ᵛ). The *Paraphrase* was popular, and in 1678 it went into a revised second edition.

In 1667 Woodford married his second wife, Mary Norton of Binstead. On 14 January 1669 he was ordained by Morley, and in 1673 he was presented to the livings of Shalden and of Hartley-Malduit, Hampshire, where he continued as rector until his death. Woodford was installed as a prebendary of Chichester on 27 May 1676, awarded a Lambeth DD on 19 August 1674, and became a prebendary of Winchester 'by the favour of his great patron' Morley (Wood, *Ath. Oxon.*) on 8 November 1680. His *Paraphrase upon the canticles and some select hymns of the New and Old Testaments, with other occasional compositions in English verse* appeared in 1679, dedicated to William Sancroft, archbishop of Canterbury. Its preface is largely devoted to a sustained discussion of prosody. (The Huntington Library copy has manuscript revisions in Woodford's hand.) Woodford contributed a

prefatory poem to Walton's *Life of George Herbert* (1670), a poem paraphrasing 'The Song of Hezekiah' to Timothy Rogers's *Practical Discourses on Sickness and Recovery* (1691), and he composed a number of odes, sonnets, and occasional poems.

In May 1685 the Woodfords went to Winchester to stay for a period with their 'good and honoured friend' Thomas Ken, formerly Morley's chaplain and then bishop of Bath and Wells (Woodforde, 30). Woodford died at Winchester on 11 January 1700. All his sons attended Winchester and Wadham College. John, Heighes, and Robert (*d.* 1762) were each ordained in the established church. William (*d.* 1758) was a fellow of New College (1699–1712), censor of the Royal College of Physicians (1773), and regius professor of medicine at Oxford from 1730 until his death. A complete edition of Woodford's works was published in 1713.
N. H. KEEBLE

Sources L. A. Ferrell, 'An imperfect diary of a life: the 1662 diary of Samuel Woodforde', *Yale University Library Gazette*, 63 (1989), 137–44 • E. N. Hooker, 'The early poetical career of Samuel Woodforde', *Essays critical and historical dedicated to Lily B. Campbell* (New York, 1950), 87–107 • D. H. Woodforde, ed., *Woodforde papers*, 2nd edn (1932) [incl. excerpts from Mary Woodford's diary] • Wood, *Ath. Oxon.*, new edn, 4.730 • *Ninth report*, 2, HMC, 8 (1884) [prints Robert Woodford's diary in pt] • Foster, *Alum. Oxon.* • Wing, *STC*
Archives Bodl. Oxf., literary MSS, diary, and notes • William Clark Andrew Library, notebook • Yale U., Beinecke L., diary | Hants. RO, Hampshire collections [copies] • Yale U., Beinecke L., Hampshire collections
Likenesses T. Flatman, miniature, 1661, FM Cam.

Woodford, William [*called* Doctor Fortissimus] (*d.* in or after **1397**), Franciscan friar and theologian, possibly came from Woodford or Colchester, Essex; his father was a substantial patron of his (unidentified) parish church, the chancel of which he rebuilt with a bell-tower. Woodford joined the Friars Minor at the London convent about 1350, was there ordained subdeacon in 1351 and priest in 1357, and evidently received his initial training at its studium. He must have gone up to Oxford to read theology about 1367; he became a bachelor about 1371 and a doctor of theology in 1373; his lectures on Matthew are evidently those of his doctoral regency. He probably returned to London in 1374, and became lector at St Paul's; but his order's business took him to Cologne in 1375, perhaps on the way to the Zürich general chapter, and he lectured in Oxford in 1376 on the church endowments against the opinions of his contemporary John Wyclif (*d.* 1384). In 1383 he responded, probably in lectures at the London convent, to a request to expound the theology of the eucharist, which would also answer Wyclif's unorthodox doctrines. He was again in Oxford in 1389–90, defending the religious orders in four determinations; by then he was acting as vicar to the minister provincial, probably during a vacancy. He seems to have exercised financial responsibilities for the province; he was robbed of £40 travelling to Oxford. About 1392 he contributed a refutation of the ideas of the Lollard Walter Brut to the case for Brut's prosecution, but concentrated primarily on the defence of the Franciscans;

first in his *Responsiones*, a refutation of an anonymous Lollard pamphlet, and second in two works in defence of mendicancy, about 1395, against the magisterial case put against it in 1356 by Richard Fitzralph (*d.* 1360). By this time he had the privilege of private quarters at his London convent, and had some wider reputation: he was called on by Archbishop Thomas Arundel (*d.* 1414) to put the case against a *mélange* of Wyclif's ideas as expressed in the latter's *Trialogus*, which were condemned by convocation in February 1397. He was remembered at this time by his Carmelite pupil Thomas Netter (*d.* 1430) as a 'devoted master'. He died after Easter day (22 April) 1397, and was buried in the Greyfriars Church, London.

Woodford's controversial works arose from his primary concern with pastoral theology, and in particular with the issues that confronted a confessor. He was himself the confessor of a lady who may be identified as Elizabeth, successively countess and duchess of Norfolk, at whose castle at Framlingham he wrote several books, and whose penances included repairing bridges and other good works in Essex; her grant of 20 marks annually to the Minoresses without Aldgate, London, during his lifetime and a bequest to him from the countess's associate, Lady Bedingfield, attest his role in her circle. His lectures on Matthew were divided into questions largely on such moral issues as, is all lying evil? or what should move a man to mercy?, some specifically directed to confessors. As his meticulous references show, he was the heir to the mature pastoral tradition, lightened with persistent curiosity about natural history, of the Franciscans. Pastoral experience provided the resource for his rejection of Wyclif's ideas on ecclesiastical endowments on practical grounds, and for his comprehensive explanation of the eucharist. Surprisingly however he accepted much of Wyclif's philosophical strictures on transubstantiation, rejecting most of the scholastic explanations of what the subject of 'this', in the phrase 'this is my body' in the words of consecration, might be; he denied Wyclif's contention that the eucharistic formula was subject to the usual rules of logical analysis, seeing it as an incantation, and transubstantiation as a suspension of the natural order which God's absolute power alone could sustain. Comprehensible only by faith, eucharistic doctrine needed to be defined by the weight of traditional interpretation; the task of the theologian was not only logical analysis, but also critical definition of what previous doctors had determined.

Woodford's historical sense allowed him to develop, in his defence of endowments and religious orders, an appreciation of the legitimate variety of rules and traditions; in his *Determinationes* he traced monastic rules back to the first century, and placed the formation of the canon of scripture firmly into the historical context of the early church. In spite of recent controversy between friars and monks, therefore, he vindicated monasticism, and argued, in his *Defensorium mendicitatis* and *Responsiones*, from its common ground with the rule of St Francis that mendicancy was one of several permissible enrichments of the common life of Christians. This was far from the claim to a unique role in the pattern of salvation made by the Franciscan spirituals of a century earlier, but it allowed him to point to specific practical advantages that the coming of the friars had brought to the church. Woodford's works were widely read in the fifteenth century, surviving in Czech, German, Italian, and French copies and influencing Thomas Netter's *Doctrinale antiquitatum fidei* of 1425-30. His title of Doctor Fortissimus was conferred in a list of scholastic epithets from the University of Greifswald, at some date after the university's foundation in 1456.

Besides Woodford's extant works, library catalogues and his own citations mention his *Lectura sententiarum*, *De conformitate nostra ad opera Christi*, *De anchoritis et cenobitis*, *Contra negantes purgatorium*, *Quaestio de paupertate*, *Liber viginti unius argumentorum*, and an *Opus contra Armachanum*.

JEREMY CATTO

Sources W. Woodford, 'Postilla super Mattheaum', CUL, Add. MS 3571 · W. Woodford, 'De sacramento altaris, Determinationes', Bodl. Oxf., MS Bodley 703 · W. Woodford, 'Littera contra librum Walteri Brut', Bibliothèque Nationale, Paris, MS Lat. 3381, fols. 115–124v · W. Woodford, 'Defensorium mendicitatis, contra errores Armachani', Magd. Oxf., MS Lat. 75 · W. Woodford, 'Determinatio de civili dominio', ed. E. Doyle, *Archivium Franciscanum Historicum*, 66 (1973), 49–109 · W. Woodford, 'Responsiones', ed. E. Doyle, *Franciscan Studies*, 43 (1983), 121–87 · W. Woodford, 'De causis condempnacionis articulorum xviii damnatorum Johannis Wyclif', *Fasciculus rerum expetendarum*, ed. E. Brown (1690), 1.190–265 · L. Waddingus [L. Wadding], *Scriptores ordinis minorum*, [new edn] (1806) · M. R. James and A. H. Thompson, eds., *Catalogue of the library of Leicester Abbey*, 2 vols. (1937–41) · K. W. Humphreys, *The friars' libraries* (1990) · W. G. Searle, *Catalogue of the manuscripts of Queens' College, Cambridge* (1472), Cambridge Antiquarian RS, 2 (1864) · J. I. Catto, 'William Woodford OFM', DPhil diss., U. Oxf., 1969 · E. Doyle, 'William Woodford's *De dominio civili clericorum* against John Wyclif', *Archivum Franciscanum Historicum*, 66 (1973), 49–109, esp. 93–106 · E. Doyle, 'William Woodford on scripture and tradition', *Studia historico-ecclesiastica: Festgäbe L. G. Spätling* (1977), 481–504 · E. Doyle, 'William Woodford, and John Wyclif's *De religione*', *Speculum*, 52 (1977), 329–36 · Emden, *Oxf.*, 3.2081–2 · A. Hudson, *The premature reformation: Wycliffite texts and Lollard history* (1988), 46–9 · J. I. Catto, 'Wyclif and Wycliffism at Oxford, 1356–1430', *Hist. U. Oxf.* 2: *Late med. Oxf.*, 175–261 · memorial stone, Greyfriars' Church, London

Archives Bibliothèque Nationale, Paris, MS Lat. 3381, fols. 115–124v · Bodl. Oxf., Bodley MS 703 · CUL, Add. MS 3571 · Magd. Oxf., MS Lat. 75

Woodforde, Anna Maria (1757–1830). *See under* Woodforde, James (1740–1803).

Woodforde, James (1740–1803), diarist and Church of England clergyman, was born on 16 June 1740 at the parsonage, Ansford, Somerset, the sixth child in the family of four sons (one of whom died in childhood) and three daughters of the Revd Samuel Woodforde (1695–1771), rector of Ansford and vicar of the neighbouring parish of Castle Cary, and his wife, Jane Collins (*bap.* 1706, *d.* 1766). She belonged to a family domiciled in that part of Somerset for at least two centuries. The Woodfordes, on the other hand, came originally from Northamptonshire,

James Woodforde (1740–1803), by Samuel Woodforde, 1780s
[detail]

making the transition from small, open-field farmers to professional men in the seventeenth century; their association with the Anglican church was already three generations old when James was born.

After attending two preparatory schools Woodforde was admitted as a scholar on the foundation of Winchester College in 1752. In his final year, 1758, he was seventh on the roll 'ad Oxon' which regulated the transfer to the sister foundation of New College, Oxford. As his place there was not assured, he was provisionally enrolled at another college, Oriel, and his father apparently helped out with a little judicious bribery. On 21 July 1759 he was able to celebrate by writing the first line of a diary: 'Made a Scholar of New-College.' In 1763 he was ordained and graduated BA, proceeding MA in 1767, and BD in 1775.

For ten years after graduation Woodforde worked as a curate in Somerset, most of that time assisting his father. He never married but in his thirties was sufficiently attracted by Elizabeth, or Betsy, White, a relative through marriage, to make her a cautiously guarded proposal. When he returned to university in 1773 it was with the intention of claiming the first suitable benefice in the gift of New College to become vacant. But Betsy did not wait for this, and married a man far richer than himself. Woodforde's reaction reveals less sorrow or grief than a sort of irritated pique. 'She has behaved to me like a mere Jilt', he told his diary. Meanwhile he became sub-warden of his college, and a pro-proctor. Late in 1774 he was presented to the living of Weston Longville, Norfolk, a well-endowed

preferment worth some £400 a year. In April 1776 he resigned his fellowship and went to live there, residing in the parish for the rest of his life, a quiet existence interrupted only by journeys to see his relatives in the west, on average once every three years. He was a gregarious, hospitable man, and kind-hearted, although his charities represented only an inconsiderable fraction of his income, largely derived from tithe. He seems not to have possessed a markedly religious temperament, and most of his concerns were those he could share with lay people, although his closest friends were fellow clerics.

Woodforde was a very ordinary man. He read little, and his exclusively classical education left only the faintest impression on his mind. His one outstanding characteristic is that he wrote his diary, the work of a lifetime. After the first few weeks he settled down to making an entry each day, and kept this up for forty-three years. The diary was unknown until selections were published by Oxford University Press under the title *The Diary of a Country Parson* (5 vols., 1924–31). In this edition Woodforde was made into a semi-comic figure, acquiring a reputation he has never quite lost. Food and drink were given so much editorial prominence that an unwary reader might well be left with the impression that Woodforde produced little more than a chronicle of gluttony. Later work on the diary has shown that its great virtue lies in its value as primary source material for the social and domestic history of its era and, for the general reader, in the incomparably vivid picture of country life and manners. Woodforde's manner of writing—one hesitates to call it a style—is the opposite of the antithetical, heavily Latinized literary prose of its time. It is very plain, simple, and lucid, having more in common with the speech rhythms of its day than with the elaboration of fine writing.

Although Woodforde has much to say about trivial indispositions, he was a healthy man until well past fifty. In 1797 he was afflicted by a more serious disease, possibly a stroke, from the effects of which he never recovered, although he continued to write his diary every day. It ends with an incomplete entry for 17 October 1802, appropriately noting: 'Dinner to day rost Beef' (Winstanley). He died at the parsonage on 1 January 1803 and was buried on 5 January inside Weston Longville church, beneath the chancel.

Anna Maria [Nancy] **Woodforde** (1757–1830) was born on 8 March 1757 at Alhampton, Ditcheat, Somerset, the eldest child of the diarist's elder brother, Heighes Woodforde (1726–1789), and his wife, Anne Dorville (1734–1799). From 1780 she lived with her uncle and kept house for him. In general they got along very well together. He appreciated her gift for laughter, and even the tones of her voice must have sounded refreshingly different from the Norfolk accent. In the earlier years of her stay her letters home were lyrical about the kindness and generosity of her uncle, and his rescue of her from a poverty-stricken life. But years passed; the suitor she must have dreamed of never appeared, and she drifted into middle age; the relationship soured and her uncle took to calling her 'Miss

Woodforde' in the diary. She also was a diarist. In 1792 she acquired a large manuscript volume, and in that year produced a full diary, to demand comparison with that of her uncle. She lived on until her death on 6 January 1830 at her home in High Street, Castle Cary, and was buried on 13 January at Ansford.   R. L. WINSTANLEY

Sources J. Woodforde, diary, 1759–1802, Bodl. Oxf. · A. M. Woodforde, diary, Bodl. Oxf. · private information (2004) [family] · R. L. Winstanley, *Parson Woodforde: the life and times of a country parson* (1995) · *Parson Woodforde Society Quarterly Journal* (1968–98) · Foster, *Alum. Oxon.* · D. H. Woodforde, *Woodforde papers and diaries* (1990) · R. L. Winstanley, *James Woodforde: parson and diarist* (1996)
Archives Bodl. Oxf., diaries, family papers, and sermons · New College, Oxford, papers · Norfolk RO · priv. coll. · Som. ARS
Likenesses S. Woodforde, portrait, 1780–89; Christies, 2 Aug 1951, lot 129 [*see illus.*] · S. Woodforde, pastel or watercolour drawing, Weston Longville parish church, Norfolk
Wealth at death £437 cash from sale of effects: inventory · £250 personal debts

Woodforde, Samuel (1763–1817), painter, was born at Castle Cary, Somerset, on 29 March 1763, the second son of Heighes Woodforde (1726–1789), accountant, of Ansford, and his wife, Anne (1734–1799), daughter and heir of Ralph Dorville. He was a lineal descendant of the painter Samuel Woodford. At the age of fifteen he was patronized by the banker Henry Hoare (*d.* 1785) of Stourhead, Wiltshire, and later by succeeding members of Hoare's family. On 8 March 1782 he registered as a student at the Royal Academy Schools, and exhibited pictures in 1784.

In 1786 a gratuity of £100 per annum from Sir Richard Hoare, first baronet, enabled Woodforde to depart, on 25 February, for Italy. Arriving on 17 April, he stayed mainly in Rome, studying the works of Raphael and Michelangelo, and copying *The Family of Darius* by Paolo Veronese. Later he visited Venice, and Florence, from whence he departed for London in 1791 accompanied by the antiquary Sir Richard Colt Hoare. From 1792 until 1815 he exhibited constantly, showing portraits, scenes of Italian life, historical pictures, and subjects from literature. On 7 October 1815 he married at St Bride's, Fleet Street, London, Jane Gardner, who accompanied him that year to Italy.

Woodforde sent in all 133 pictures to the Royal Academy, and 39 to the British Institution. Several of his early works remain at Stourhead. He is also represented in the collections of the Royal Academy and the Victoria and Albert Museum, London, and the Huntington Library, San Marino, California. A group portrait, *The Bennett Family* (exh. Royal Academy, 1803) is now in the Tate collection. Many of his literary subjects were engraved, including the forest scene in *Titus Andronicus*, engraved by Anker Smith for the publishers John and Josiah Boydell's *Shakspeare* (1803). He also made designs engraved by James Heath and others for an edition of Shakespeare published by Longmans (1805–7).

Woodforde was elected an associate of the Royal Academy in 1800, becoming Royal Academician in 1807. Joseph Farington referred to a child fathered by Woodforde, towards whose upbringing he contributed 4s. per week,

and recorded that 'Woodforde had £12,000 in the 3 per cents, accumulated' (Farington, *Diary*, 14.5118). Woodforde died of fever at Ferrara, Italy, on 27 July 1817 leaving his wife a pension of £170 a year.

CAMPBELL DODGSON, rev. TINA FISKE

Sources *An exhibition of original diaries, letters, books … belonging to various members of the Woodforde family*, John and Edward Bumpus Ltd [1933] · Farington, *Diary*, vol. 14 · W. Drummond, *Samuel Woodforde, Royal Academician, 1763–1817* [n.d., 1989?] [exhibition catalogue, Kyburg Gallery, 25 April – 6 May 1989] · J. Ingamells, ed., *A dictionary of British and Irish travellers in Italy, 1701–1800* (1997) · W. Sandby, *The history of the Royal Academy of Arts*, 2 vols. (1862) · D. Foskett, *A dictionary of British miniature painters*, 2 vols. (1972) · B. Stewart and M. Cutten, *The dictionary of portrait painters in Britain up to 1920* (1997) · Waterhouse, *18c painters* · Graves, *RA exhibitors* · Graves, *Soc. Artists* · Redgrave, *Artists* · Bryan, *Painters* (1903–5) · IGI · S. C. Hutchison, 'The Royal Academy Schools, 1768–1830', *Walpole Society*, 38 (1960–62), 123–91, esp. 146
Archives Archives of the British Province of the Society of Jesus, London, Thorpe MSS · Bodl. Oxf., diary and family MSS of James Woodforde
Likenesses H. Howard, exh. RA 1813 · S. Woodforde, self-portrait, oils; known to be in possession of Messrs Tracy, Kent & Co., New York in 1955
Wealth at death £12,000 'in the 3 per cents, accumulated': Farington, *Diary*, 14.5118

Woodgate, Sir Edward Robert Prevost (1845–1900), army officer, born on 1 November 1845, was the second son of Henry Arthur Woodgate (1801–1874), rector of Belbroughton in Worcestershire, and his wife, Maria Bradford. He was educated at Radley College and Sandhurst, and joined the 4th King's Own Royal regiment on 7 April 1865. With it he served in the 1868 Abyssinian expedition, and was present at the action of Arogee Ravine and the capture of Magdala. He obtained his lieutenancy on 7 July 1869. He was next employed on special service in the Second Anglo-Asante war of 1873–4, and took part in the actions of Esaman, Ainsah, Abrakampa, and Faysunah, the battle of Amoaful, and the capture of Kumasi. He was twice mentioned in dispatches. After passing through the Staff College in 1877, he attained the rank of captain on 2 March 1878, and was selected for special employment in the Anglo-Zulu War of 1879. He was mentioned in dispatches for his work as staff officer with Sir Evelyn Wood's flying column in the Zulu campaign, was present at Kambole and Ulundi, and received a brevet majority on 29 November 1879.

From 1880 to 1885 Woodgate served as brigade major in the West Indies. In the autumn of 1885 he went to India as a regimental officer, returning in December 1889. In 1893 he was appointed to the command of the 1st battalion of the King's Own (Royal Lancaster) regiment, and on 26 June became lieutenant-colonel. On 24 May 1896 he was nominated CB, and on 26 June 1897 he received his colonelcy, obtaining the command of the fourth regimental district at Lancaster. In April 1898 he was sent to Sierra Leone to organize the new West African regiment. The new corps was almost immediately called on active service against Bai Burch and others who had rebelled on account of the hut tax. Woodgate successfully conducted the operations against the rebels, but in 1899 he was invalided home, and was placed in command of the seventeenth regimental district at Leicester.

On 13 November 1899, on the formation of the 5th division under Sir Charles Warren for service in South Africa, Woodgate was given command of the 11th or Lancashire brigade with the local rank of major-general. Arriving at Durban in Natal in December 1899 he crossed the Tugela with Warren at Wagon Drift on 16–17 January 1900. On the night of 23 January he occupied the heights of Spion Kop, but his arrangements for its defence were faulty. On the following day he was wounded by a shell splinter, and on 23 March he died at Mooi River from the effects of his wounds. A few weeks before his death he was nominated KCMG in recognition of his services in Sierra Leone.

E. I. CARLYLE, rev. JAMES FALKNER

Sources Army List · The Times (26 March 1900) · Hart's Army List · A. C. Doyle, The great Boer War (1900) · B. Burleigh, War in Natal (1900) · C. À Court Repington, Vestigia (1919) · T. Pakenham, The Boer War (1979) · Boase, Mod. Eng. biog. · WWW **Likenesses** Lafayette, photograph, c.1899, NAM · photographs, 1899, probably NAM, Transvaal War Album **Wealth at death** £5517 4s. 10d.: resworn probate, Dec 1900, CGPLA Eng. & Wales

Woodgate, Walter Bradford [pseud. Wat Bradwood] (1840–1920), oarsman and writer, was born at Belbroughton rectory, Worcestershire, on 20 September 1840, the eldest son of the Revd Henry Arthur Woodgate (1801–1874), rector of Belbroughton and canon of Worcester, and his wife, Maria, née Bradford. His younger brother was Major-General Sir Edward *Woodgate. He entered Radley College in 1850, matriculated at Brasenose College, Oxford, as a scholar in 1859, graduated in 1863, and was called to the bar (Inner Temple) in 1872.

For more than half a century Woodgate was the outstanding figure on the upper Thames. He rowed his first race in 1858 for Radley against Eton over the Henley course; he rowed his last race there in 1868. He was in the Oxford winning crew in the university boat races of 1862 and 1863, and won the university pairs three times and the sculls twice; at Henley he won the Grand Challenge Cup in 1865, the Stewards' Cup in 1862, the Diamond sculls in 1864, and the Goblets in 1861, 1862, 1863, 1866, and 1868. He also held the Wingfield sculls in 1862, 1864, and 1867. At Henley in 1868 Woodgate's Brasenose four in the Stewards' Cup jettisoned its cox immediately after the start and the crew was disqualified. Nevertheless, by 1874 his point had been accepted and all the fours events had become coxless. Fred Weatherly (1848–1929), the cox, could not swim but survived to write 'Danny Boy' and 'Roses of Picardy' among other ballads.

Woodgate was not only a great oarsman, but his knowledge of the sport was unsurpassed and it covered almost a century of rowing: he entered the rowing world soon enough to meet the giants of its early days (he had known Thomas Stainforth, the Oxford stroke in the first university boat race in 1829), and he was present at Henley regatta in 1920. His textbook, Oars and Sculls, and How to Use

Them (1875), remains a classic, as does his Boating (1888), with its wealth of historical detail.

The breadth and variety of Woodgate's interests are evident in his Reminiscences of an Old Sportsman (1909), in which he wrote not only about country life, steeplechasing, and school and college life (he was the founder of Vincent's Club at Oxford), but also about the parentage of James I, the Royal Geographical Society's conflicting motives in their search for Dr Livingstone, his own indirect share in Pasteur's researches, politics, and police morality (he never took the law too seriously). As a journalist he helped to launch Vanity Fair and Land and Water, was associated with the Pall Mall Gazette in its early days, and contributed to The Field for half a century. He also wrote a few novels under the pseudonym of Wat Bradwood, and in 1893 published A Modern Layman's Faith.

Woodgate was a man of unflinching rectitude, of decided opinions, but also of great kindliness, and he was an excellent raconteur. As a young man he was strikingly handsome; in later years his fine, stern face and stalwart figure made him a typical John Bull, an effect accentuated by a low-crowned top hat. He died on 1 November 1920, in his sister's house, Brantwood, Highfield Lane, Southampton, of a heart condition brought on by bronchial trouble. He never married.

H. C. WACE, rev. ERIC HALLADAY

Sources W. B. Woodgate, Reminiscences of an old sportsman (1909) · The Times (2 Nov 1920) · The Field (6 Nov 1920) · The Field (13 Nov 1920) · R. D. Burnell, Henley royal regatta (1989) · R. D. Burnell, Henley regatta: a history (1957) **Likenesses** F. C. Ricardo, photograph, repro. in Woodgate, Reminiscences **Wealth at death** £567 12s. 1d.: probate, 6 April 1921, CGPLA Eng. & Wales

Woodger, Joseph Henry (1894–1981), philosopher of biology and theoretical biologist, was born on 2 May 1894 at Euston Road, Great Yarmouth, Norfolk, the son of Nathan Lamble Woodger, a fish merchant, and his wife, Julia, née Thorne. He was educated at Felsted School, Essex, and then as a student of the embryologist J. P. Hill at University College, London, where he was awarded the college prize in zoology and the Derby research scholarship on graduation in 1914. With the outbreak of the First World War he enlisted in the Norfolk regiment and served in Mesopotamia, where he was mentioned in dispatches. His appointment as a protozoologist to the Royal Army Medical Corps central laboratory in Amara in November 1917 marked the beginning of a research career that produced a small number of papers in zoology and a corpus of work in the philosophy of biology. Following demobilization in 1919 Woodger was appointed assistant in zoology and comparative anatomy at University College, London. In 1921 he was promoted to senior assistant. On 29 March of that year he married Doris Eden Buckle (b. 1891/2), a medical student. She was the daughter of Major-General Christopher Reginald Buckle. In 1922 Woodger was appointed reader in biology at the Middlesex Hospital medical school. He remained there for thirty-eight years (except for a period of evacuation to Leeds during the Second World War), becoming professor in 1949 and emeritus professor in 1959.

A term of leave in Vienna in the spring of 1926 changed the direction of Woodger's career. Unable to undertake the transplantation experiments on earthworms that he had planned, Woodger spent his time in philosophical discussions with Hans Prizibram, members of Prizibram's department, and the Vienna circle. Philosophy of biology became his avocation as he threw himself into the prevailing dichotomies in biology: vitalism–mechanism, structure–function, and preformation–epigenesis. His first and most influential book, *Biological Principles: a Critical Study*, was published in 1929 and earned him a DSc. A lifelong study of how biological statements should be made and supported ensued. Woodger's primary concern was that the definitions and concepts in biology should be established with as much rigour as the observations and experiments supporting them. To that end he turned to mathematical logic to construct a language of biology, adopted the ideas of Karl Popper, and utilized the philosophical approach of Alfred North Whitehead and Bertrand Russell and of the mathematical logicians Jan Lukasiewicz and Alfred Tarski, whom he visited in Warsaw in 1935. (Woodger translated and collected many of Tarski's papers as *Logic, Semantics and Metamathematics*, published in 1956.)

Although Woodger continued laboratory work for a time he increasingly devoted his research to philosophy of biology and theoretical biology. He founded the Theoretical Biology Club, whose members (including Dorothy and Joseph Needham, C. H. Waddington, J. D. Bernal, and P. B. Medawar) first met in Oxford or Cambridge, then in a cottage on the Norfolk broads and, after the war, in London. In 1933, having taught himself German during his early years at the Middlesex, Woodger translated Ludwig von Bertalanffy's *Kritische Theorie der Formbildung* (1928) as *Modern Theories of Development* (von Bertalanffy was the father of general systems theory). Woodger's own work, *Axiomatic Methods in Biology*, followed in 1937. A Rockefeller Foundation scholarship enabled Woodger to visit the United States in 1938. Perhaps Woodger's most important development in theoretical biology was the concept of the *Bauplan*, or essential structural body plan of an organism, which he put forward in an essay entitled 'On biological transformations' in the *Festschrift* for D'Arcy Wentworth Thompson, published in 1945. (The *Bauplan* concept enjoyed something of a revival in the late 1990s.)

Woodger was Tarner lecturer at Trinity College, Cambridge, in 1949, publishing his lectures on language as a theoretical tool in 1952 as *Biology as Language*. His last publication, 'Biology and the axiomatic method', appeared in the *Annals of the New York Academy of Science* in 1962, twenty-five years after his influential book on the same topic. A volume of essays, prepared to mark his seventieth birthday (Gregg and Harris, 1964), contains a complete list of his publications. An anti-mechanist who rejected the chromosome theory, Woodger was steadfast in his belief that genes could not be identified with molecules. He maintained that fields could not be integrated with such hypothetical entities, only with laws of structural organization based on concepts such as the *Bauplan*. He persisted with the preformation–epigenesis dichotomy long after many others had abandoned it.

Woodger retired in 1959. He spent his final years in Epsom Downs, Surrey, where his recreations (as listed in *Who's Who*) included reading the Bible and Shakespeare, and viticulture. He died on 8 March 1981 at Cuddington Hospital, Cheam, Surrey. BRIAN K. HALL

Sources J. R. Gregg and F. T. C. Harris, eds., *Form and strategy in science: studies dedicated to Joseph Henry Woodger on the occasion of his seventieth birthday* (1964) • W. F. Floyd and F. T. C. Harris, 'Joseph Henry Woodger, curriculum vitae', *Form and strategy in science: studies dedicated to Joseph Henry Woodger on the occasion of his seventieth birthday*, ed. J. R. Gregg and F. T. C. Harris (1964), 1–6 • M. Woodger, 'Publications by Joseph Henry Woodger', *Form and strategy in science: studies dedicated to Joseph Henry Woodger on the occasion of his seventieth birthday*, ed. J. R. Gregg and F. T. C. Harris (1964), 473–6 • *The Times* (19 March 1981), 16f • N. Roll-Hansen, E. S. Russell, and J. H. Woodger, 'The failure of two twentieth-century opponents of mechanistic biology', *Journal of the History of Biology*, 17 (1982), 399–428 • B. K. Hall, *Evolutionary developmental biology*, 2nd edn (1998) • D. Hull, *The philosophy of the biological sciences* (1974) • J. Needham, *Order and life* (1936); repr. (1968) • T. A. Goudge, 'Woodger, Joseph Henry', *The encyclopaedia of philosophy*, ed. P. Edwards, 8 (1967), 346–7 • P. G. Abir-Am, 'The philosophical background to Joseph Needham's work in chemical embryology', *A conceptual history of modern embryology*, ed. S. F. Gilbert (1991), 159–80 • G. Webster and B. Goodwin, *Form and transformation: generative and relational principles in biology* (1996) • D. Haraway, *Crystals, fabrics and fields* (1976) • b. cert. • m. cert. • d. cert.

Archives UCL, papers

Likenesses J. H. Woodger, photograph, before 1964, priv. coll.; repro. in Gregg and Harris, eds., *Form and strategy in science*

Woodham, Mrs [*née* Spencer; *other married name* Smith] (*d.* 1803), singer and actress, was a prominent performer on the stage in both Dublin and London. She was born Miss Spencer (no information about her parentage or forenames is known); the birth date of 1743 given in the *Dictionary of National Biography* may be a few years too late. According to her obituary in the *Gentleman's Magazine*, she was a protégée of Thomas Augustine Arne, was a competitor to Charlotte Brent, and was known as 'Buck Spencer, being uncommonly elegant in her dress and person' (*GM*, 1st ser., 73, 1803, 889). According to Highfill, Burnim, and Langhans (*BDA*), Miss Spencer performed at the Smock Alley Theatre in Dublin between 1755 and 1757. Esther K. Sheldon's *Thomas Sheridan of Smock-Alley* states that she made her acting début playing Catherine in *Catherine and Petruchio* on 25 October 1756. By 1759 she had moved to London, where she appeared at Drury Lane as a singer in various productions, including *Harlequin's Invasion* and *Galligantus*. Between 1760 and 1765 she performed at Sadler's Wells.

The *Biographical Dictionary* notes that a Mrs Smith then appeared on the stage in Richmond, proposing that this was Miss Spencer after her marriage to Adam Smith (*d.* c.1778x80), an actor-musician, about 1765–6. Seemingly part of a travelling company, in 1767 she performed in Bristol and a year later appeared in Edinburgh. She continued to appear at Richmond at least until 1775, and may also have appeared at the Haymarket, but the Mrs Smith of the Haymarket may well have been another performer, as a Mrs Smith appears at Drury Lane and occasionally at Covent Garden or the Haymarket, from the 1758–9 season until 1776–7, sometimes as an actress, at other times as a singer. Later trips may have included performances in Worcester (as part of Roger Kemble's company in 1772), Liverpool and Cambridge (1776), and Derby (1777–8). She may also have sung at Marylebone Gardens, under Samuel Arnold, during this period. A daughter of Adam and Mrs Smith joined her parents in performing at Brighton in 1778; this may have been Hannah (d. 1843), who later married John Conway Philip *Astley [see under Astley, Philip]. A song published about 1780, 'Who can describe the pow'r of love', was credited to 'A. Smith' and was described as sung 'at Vauxhall in Birmingham by Mrs A. Smith, late Mrs. Woodham' (Highfill, Burnim & Langhans, BDA), suggesting that Adam Smith died at about this time and that Mrs Smith then married a Mr Woodham, whom she later divorced. She seems to have retired from the stage at about this time. After her daughter's marriage in 1800, she lived with her at Astley's Amphitheatre, Westminster Bridge Road, Lambeth, where she was killed in a fire which consumed the theatre on 2 September 1803. Apparently, she had a chance to escape, but returned to the fire to rescue the day's receipts and there was burnt to death.

Many of the details of Mrs Woodham's career overlap with those of another singer, **Mrs Woodman** (fl. 1768–1789), who performed at Edinburgh in 1768 and 1769. On 23 March 1769 at Edinburgh she played Polly in *The Beggar's Opera*, in the same performance as that in which the future Mrs Woodham played Dolly Trull. She performed at Covent Garden in 1771–2 but made little impression. She gave two benefit performances in September 1773 at Marylebone Gardens. An appeal for donations in the *Public Advertiser* (21 February 1775) reported that she was imprisoned for debt following the death of her schoolmaster husband two years before, leaving her five children to support; gifts from the public secured her release. From 1785 to 1789 she made many appearances at Astley's Amphitheatre, a fact that probably suggested to the *Monthly Mirror* (16, 1803, 214–16) that it was Mrs Woodman, not Mrs Woodham, who was killed in the 1803 fire.

MARK HUMPHREYS

Sources Highfill, Burnim & Langhans, BDA · DNB · E. K. Sheldon, *Thomas Sheridan of Smock-Alley: recording his life as actor and theater manager in both Dublin and London* (1967) · GM, 1st ser., 73 (1803), 889 · G. W. Stone, ed., *The London stage, 1660–1800*, pt 4: 1747–1776 (1962) · C. B. Hogan, ed., *The London stage, 1660–1800*, pt 5: 1776–1800 (1968)

Woodham, Adam. *See* Wodeham, Adam (c.1295–1358).

Woodham, Henry Annesley (1813–1875), journalist, was baptized on 1 September 1813 in the parish church of Newbury, Berkshire, where his father, Henry Edward Higmore Woodham, was a solicitor. His mother, Elizabeth Spooner Woodham (d. 1857), was the daughter of Thomas Lamb, a surgeon in Newbury. He was educated, like George Canning before him, at the Revd Charles Richards's school in Winchester, and at Cambridge, where he matriculated as

a pensioner of Trinity College on 20 October 1834. In February 1835 he migrated to Jesus College, and was elected a foundation scholar there at midsummer. Between 1837 and 1839 he twice won the members' prize for Latin orations, and in 1839 came fifth in the classical tripos. In December 1841 he was the first fellow of Jesus to be elected under the new college statutes. In 1843 he published an edition of Tertullian's *Apologeticus*, a competent rather than a distinguished performance, apparently intended for undergraduate use. His second and last avowed book appeared in 1846, *An Application of Heraldry to the Illustration of Various University and College Antiquities*, but his literary career was just beginning rather than ending, for in 1845 he became one of the university men whom the new editor of *The Times*, J. T. Delane, was recruiting to his staff. Woodham remained a leader writer for the paper until within nine months of his death.

Woodham was not the last *Times* journalist to combine academic and newspaper work, but he was decidedly one of the most idiosyncratic. He remained a fellow of Jesus until his marriage, on 28 November 1848, to Elizabeth Humfrey (d. 1851), daughter of Charles Humfrey, a banker, of Cambridge, and flatly refused to work in London or after 3 p.m. Delane was thus compelled to send up materials and suggestions for leading articles by the early train, while Woodham sent down his productions in the evening or on the next day. Like all Delane's writers he had to be ready to turn his hand to any subject, but perhaps it was not without point that the editor repeatedly set him to writing on railway accidents. Woodham wrote also on mesmerism, bank frauds, the income tax, pauper education, fire insurance, sewage, notable murders, and dozens of other topics. He had various specialisms: India, ironclad ships (perhaps oddly for a clergyman), and foreign affairs, especially after Henry Reeve withdrew from the paper in 1855. He did not always give satisfaction to his employers. Mowbray Morris, the manager of *The Times*, thought that he often wrote like a pedagogue, and Delane occasionally complained of Woodham's refusal to vary his routine, even in emergencies. But most of the time the editor was glad to have so dependable and copious a writer on his staff. Woodham's annual salary was £1200, and in return he wrote more than 200 articles a year, averaging 2000 words each. It is easy to see what Delane meant when he remarked in 1869 that 'Woodham is, as usual, writing all the paper himself' (Dasent, 2.244). Woodham's articles were less lively than his private letters: he took care to subdue himself to the *Times* style; but his contributions were marked by a good judgement and good humour, which were not always characteristic of the Thunderer's pronouncements. Among his most memorable achievements was his sympathetic article on Abraham Lincoln's death (published 29 April 1865). Another was a biography of the duke of Wellington, published in *The Times* on 15 and 16 September 1852 and issued in the same year, without the author's name, in book form. This biography has often been attributed to Samuel Phillips, and authorship of it appears to have been claimed by Henry Reeve. But it was almost certainly Woodham's work.

Woodham was a devoted Cambridge man, dismissing Oxford as 'that sink of port and prejudice' (*The Times* Archive, Delane MSS, 3/107). He was twice an unsuccessful candidate for the regius chair of history. In university politics he was a conservative liberal. His wife's death in 1851 made his college his sole refuge: in 1862 he was elected an honorary fellow, and delighted in being the only man since Cranmer to have become a fellow of Jesus twice. His collegiate feeling extended to *The Times*. He liked to lure Delane, Reeve, and (especially) Morris to Cambridge and to get them drunk in the combination room. He was something of a toper himself, and decidedly a gormandizer. Food is a recurring theme in his letters—pheasants, mangoes, mutton, lobster at Hunstanton, and turtle soup at Bristol ('rather too thick'). When Delane mismanaged an invitation to the lord mayor's banquet, so that Woodham got neither drink nor food, he never heard the last of it. But for all that Woodham was a serious man and a wise friend, with considerable insight into human nature. He advised his colleagues on everything from Delane's coat of arms to Morris's troubles with his unsatisfactory son.

The Times did not quite monopolize Woodham's energies. He was made LLD in 1849 and elected a fellow of the Society of Antiquaries in 1856. He contributed frequently to the *Edinburgh Review* between April 1848 and July 1850. He died at his home, 66 Hills Road, Cambridge, on 16 March 1875, and was buried beside his wife and mother at St Mary's Church, Reading. HUGH BROGAN

Sources group records, News Int. RO, *The Times* archive · *The Times* (1846–74) · [S. Morison and others], *The history of The Times*, 2 (1939), 65, 443, 594 · *Some men of 'The Times'* (1929) · A. I. Dasent, *John Thadeus Delane*, 2 vols. (1908) · Venn, *Alum. Cant.* · *Wellesley index* · Hants. RO · m. cert. · d. cert. · Jesus College, Cambridge, archives · Trinity Cam.

Archives News Int. RO, *The Times* archive

Wealth at death under £12,000: resworn probate, June 1876, *CGPLA Eng. & Wales* (1875)

Woodhead, Abraham (1609–1678), Roman Catholic controversialist, was born in Meltham in March 1609 and baptized in Almondbury, Yorkshire, on 2 April 1609, the son of John Woodhead of Thornhill, and his wife, an Armytage. He entered University College, Oxford, under the tuition of Jonas Radcliff, in 1624. He was junior Freyston scholar, graduated BA on 5 February 1629, proceeded MA on 10 November 1631, was senior Freyston scholar, and eventually a Skirlaw fellow on 27 April 1633. He took orders in St Giles' Church successively on 16 June and 22 September 1633. His abilities as a scholar and Latinist are shown by his oration on 17 April 1634 for the foundation stone of the west wing of University College. He spoke eloquently on the college benefactors, not neglecting to give King Alfred his due as founder, 'dum sororcula Cantabrigia nondum esset somniatus cerebri chimaera' ('when our little sister Cambridge, that fantasy of the brain, was not yet thought of'; Bodl. Oxf., MS Eng. misc. c 88, 51). ''Tis a very good speech', commented Thomas Hearne (*Remarks and Collections*, 10.366).

On 5 May 1641 Woodhead was elected proctor, and on 1 September 1642 he and Obadiah Walker were nominated delegates to defend the university before the Long Parliament, which he did ably. However, as war began he obtained permission from his college to travel abroad with a succession of pupils who joined him at intervals during these travels, Thomas Radcliffe, Thomas Culpeper, Thomas Strode, Thomas Harlakenden, and George Radcliff. Formal permission to travel was granted on 22 June 1645, but he had probably been away three years already. According to Wood and Hearne he got as far as Rome, though Berington denies this, and no record of him has been found in Rome.

Already by this time it appears that Woodhead was questioning his protestant beliefs through reading the lives of the saints as well as controversialists like Jewell and Harding. 'The pious fame of the most excellent Cardinal Boromeus, St Philip Nerius, the Holy Founder of the Oratory, St Francis Sales, Zaverius, St Teresa and others' seems already to have been an influence, for the newly canonized saints of the Catholic Reformation were widely talked about all over Europe (Yorkshire Archaeological Society, MS 45, p. 6). Certainly his conversion to Catholicism must have been stimulated during his travels abroad, even though he was probably not actually received into the church there.

By 1647 Woodhead's pupils were the young duke of Buckingham and his brother Lord Francis Villiers, who had been travelling in Florence and Rome since 1643. They returned to England together as the war ended, and the duke regained his estates on the plea of youth. Woodhead stayed with him briefly in York House, but when the duke and his brother joined the Surrey insurgents in 1648 he moved to Hadham Hall, Hertfordshire, as tutor to Lord Capel, where he remained for three or four years. The loss of his fellowship brought some hardship to Woodhead: having been absent from the college for some years he was struck from the list on 17 October 1648 for non-appearance. He was supported partly by Gilbert Sheldon, for he writes from Hadham to repay a debt and thank him for his 'great charity to me in my necessitys' (Bodl. Oxf., MS Eng. misc. c. 88, fol. 18). Later he received a pension of £60 per annum, but lost this on resigning his position with Lord Capel late in 1652. The resignation appears to have been prompted by disputations with Dr Ferns, Capel's chaplain, and probably marks the moment of Woodhead's conversion to Catholicism, though Capel achieved his majority in 1652 and might have been expected to dispense with a tutor in any case.

While at Hadham, Woodhead corresponded with Dr Wilby, a physician and 'an impatient man of violent temper' (Slusser, 421). Some shorthand letters survive from 1651–2 when Wilby was tending his dying wife in Fenchurch Street. The letters are pious and prolix, including questions on health and how to mend a watch. But they are mostly about faith and mental prayer, albeit obscured by coded allusions as well as the shorthand. They demonstrate Woodhead's great interest in the life and work of St Philip Neri. In one revealing letter he tells us something of how he came to the Catholic faith, though he is nervous of discovery, and afraid that Wilby, who was evidently on the point of being received, was tactless:

> You put me and my writings too in extreme hazard, & so my friend Mr Walker … For myself the first motion I receiv'd was from reading Sts lives & then St Austin by way of index, and examining Jewel and Harding, then I saw D. Cressy book in which something I liked, but his strange violence, as I then thought (from which violence and heat I pray God bless you) very much displeased me, & so did his inveighing against particular persons Calvin, Luther, and his speaking somthing prejudicial (me thought) to the scriptures … burne this when you have read it.   (Yorkshire Archaeological Society, MS 51, 21 Feb 1652)

Previous letters had appealed for the return of a book on St Philip. 'When can I have my P. Neri & my Carlo againe?' (Yorkshire Archaeological Society MS 51, 24 Jan 1652) and 'You must at leasure get me my Neri from Mr Henshaw' (ibid., 27 Jan 1652). Following Mrs Wilby's death (on 31 August) Woodhead writes to console his friend

> Devotion, Dr, Devotion is the only cure we have & surely your friends have attained to much perfection that do not admire P. Neri, but all abroad doe, & so do my great informers … Remember every day some houre or other to nourish it with reading some piece of P. Neri, Ignat. Xaverius or some other life of a St.   (ibid., 13 Oct 1652)

The book on St Philip was evidently his favourite recommended reading, for at the end of the correspondence he notes 'Mr Gunning. I intend to send him the next weeke St Carloe & if Mr Perkins hath done with it Ph. Nerii' (ibid., 7 Dec 1652). It may have been the saint's life, which Woodhead had translated, or the rules and maxims, published as *The Institutions of the Congregation of the Oratory* (1687).

Soon after his wife's death Wilby bought a house at Hoxton near London, and Woodhead moved in with him. The house was bequeathed to Woodhead on Wilby's death in 1668 and had already played an important part in English Catholic history, for it was here that the Gunpowder Plot was 'uncovered' by means of a mysterious letter. In company with Wilby, Woodhead disappeared from the public eye, and spent the rest of his life in an obscurity so profound that 'he was commonly called the Invisible Man by his Friends, on account of his extraordinary retired life' (Yorkshire Archaeological Society, MS 45, e). Others joined this 'pious obscurity' where he 'spent the rest of his days in doing Good, in contemplation and strict piety and in biding an eternal fairwell to secular interest, to worldly fame, to pleasure and now chiefly taken up in Contending for a blesid eternity, and not in educating Youth as Mr Wood by mistake asserts' (Yorkshire Archaeological Society, MS 43, 3). For thirty years or so there existed in Hoxton a religious community of scholars, devoting themselves to prayer and writing. They published some anonymously, or under a variety of initials; other writings were left in manuscript at Woodhead's death. It is not entirely fanciful to refer to this community as a sort of oratory, for they obviously lived a common life, but without vows or formal religious profession, devoted to prayer and study and consciously inspired by St Philip Neri. The *Institutions* may well have been translated in order to serve as a rule for the community—certainly no other rule of life is found among the Woodhead writings.

Other members of the community certainly included Wilby and Walker, and Edward Perkins, who was to become Woodhead's executor. There must have been more of Woodhead's generation as well as the younger ones who arrived after the Restoration, such as Francis Nicolson, Thomas Deane, Nathaniel Boyse, William Rogers, and Robert Vinter. Anthony Wood's belief that the community was a school may derive from the presence of these young men: it is most unlikely that the Hoxton recluses actually taught school. It is unclear whether any of them were priests; Woodhead himself was surely not.

Their literary productions include translations and original compositions. Slusser attributes twenty-nine works to Woodhead, published before or after his death. Many are controversial, notably the five volumes of *Antient Church Government* (four published in 1662, 1687, 1688, and 1736) and other writings on the magisterium, treatises on indulgences and confession, and replies to pamphlets by Stillingfleet. Others are of a purely spiritual nature: *Motives to Holy Living* (1688) and *A Compendious Discourse on the Eucharist* (1688). Important translations include the works of St Teresa of Avila, the *Life* and *Foundations* published in 1671, and the remainder in 1675. More significant perhaps were *The Holy Life of Philip Nerius*, printed in Paris in 1659, and *The Institution of the Congregation of the Oratory*, printed by Walker at Oxford in 1687. The latter is a translation of the rule of life of St Philip Neri's Oratory in Rome, followed by a detailed description of the oratory prayers, and rules for what would now be called the 'Little Oratory' or association of laymen gathered around the priests of the oratory. There follow a hundred *Memorable Sayings and Advices of St Philip Neri*. Another translation is *Pietas Romana et Parisiensis* (1687), which describes the oratory and its exercises in detail.

Anthony Wood sums up Woodhead's life and character thus:

> He was so wholly devoted to retirement, and the prosecutions of his several studies, that no worldly concerns shared any of his affections, only satisfying himself with bare necessities, and so far from coveting applause or preferment (tho' perhaps the compleatness of his learning and great worth might have given him as just and fair a claim to both as any other of his persuasion) that he used all endeavours to secure his beloved privacy, and conceal his name.   (Wood, *Ath. Oxon.*, 2.614)

Obviously Woodhead inspired enormous personal devotion and won the respect of all who spoke of him, whether protestant or Catholic. His protest against Hugh Cressy's 'violence and heat' is characteristic, for he himself wrote with extraordinary gentleness even when directly answering protestant attacks.

Woodhead was restored to his fellowship at University College in 1660, but stayed only briefly in Oxford, for he was accused of popery before the vice-chancellor, and so retired to Hoxton. He was to hold the fellowship until just before his death, with an annual income of £20. At intervals he contributed to the college building fund, returning £15 of his income in 1670. He finally resigned his fellowship on 23 April 1678, and after two months' illness died peacefully of consumption at Hoxton on 4 May. His will, made 8 June 1675, bequeaths an annuity to his family, and the residue of his Meltham estate to support the 'Minister of the Word of God that should be there settled, who should officiate at the Chapel of Meltham, and to his successors for ever' (Hughes, 72–4). Joseph Hughes stresses this to prove that Woodhead never left the Church of England, but it is certain that he was a Catholic. His estate in London was left to his executors Obadiah Walker, Edward Perkins, and Joseph Hatt: this included his manuscripts, many of which Walker was to publish, with the licence of James II. He was buried under a plain stone in St Pancras churchyard, inscribed, 'Elegi abjectus esse in domo Dei; et mansi in solitudine, non quaerens quod mihi utile est, sed quod multis' ('I have chosen to be an abject in the house of my God and I abode in the wilderness, not seeking that which is profitable to me but to many'; Wood, *Ath. Oxon.*, 2.618). Following a rumour that the body was incorrupt Cuthbert Constable obtained permission to bury his wife in the same grave in 1732, and erected the tomb which survives.   JEROME BERTRAM

Sources A. Woodhead, MSS, W. Yorks. AS, Leeds, Yorkshire Archaeological Society, MSS 43–59 • *Remarks and collections of Thomas Hearne*, ed. C. E. Doble and others, 11 vols., OHS, 2, 7, 13, 34, 42–3, 48, 50, 65, 67, 72 (1885–1921), vols. 1–2, 10–11 • S. Berington, 'A succinct account of Mr Woodhead's writings and life', in A. Woodhead, *Ancient church government, Part III* (1736) [preface] • Wood, *Ath. Oxon.*, 2nd edn • J. Hughes, *The history of the township of Meltham, near Huddersfield* edited by C. H. (1866) • M. Slusser, 'Abraham Woodhead (1608–78): some research notes, chiefly about his writings', *Recusant History*, 15 (1979–81), 406–22 • *Hist. U. Oxf. 4: 17th-cent. Oxf.* • T. Hearne, letters to Constable and A. Woodhead; speech at University College in 1634, transcribed 1914, Bodl. Oxf., MS Eng. misc. c. 88 • W. Smith of University College, Oxford, collections, S. Antiquaries, Lond., MS Smith 1–27 b • *DNB* • G. Anstruther, *The seminary priests*, 3 (1976) • G. T. Forrest, *The parish of St Leonard, Shoreditch*, ed. J. Bird, Survey of London, 8 (1922) • T. H. Clancy, *English Catholic books, 1641–1700: a bibliography*, rev. edn (1996) • tombstone, St Pancras, London

Archives BL, papers, Add. MS 43377 • W. Yorks. AS, Leeds, Yorkshire Archaeological Society, collections relating to him, MSS 43–59

Wealth at death sufficient property in Yorkshire to provide £5 annuity at least; books and MSS in London

Woodhead, Sir German Sims (1855–1921), pathologist and health campaigner, was born on 29 April 1855 at Woodland Mount, Huddersfield, the oldest son of Joseph Woodhead (1824–1913), newspaper owner and MP for Spen Valley, and Catherine, eldest daughter of James Booth Woodhead of Holmfirth. His parents were both from Yorkshire and Woodhead proudly retained his Huddersfield dialect. He was educated at Huddersfield College and Edinburgh University. He graduated MB CM in 1878 and MD three years later. He became house surgeon to John Chiene before continuing his studies in Berlin and Vienna.

On his return to Edinburgh, Woodhead was inspired to take up pathology by D. J. Hamilton and he then worked as assistant to W. Greenfield. In 1883 he published his textbook *Practical Pathology*, and by 1910 it had gone through four editions. It was through this volume, which was renowned for its illustrations and elegance, that Woodhead was known to generations of students. He was

among the earliest British exponents of bacteriology, a position evident in 1885 when he published, with A. W. Hare, *Pathological Mycology*. A companion to his other book, it anticipated the close links that evolved between pathology and bacteriology. Through the influence and patronage of Hamilton, Greenfield, and John Batty Tuke, Woodhead became a pioneer of laboratory medicine in Edinburgh, being a founder member of the Edinburgh Pathological Club in 1886 and the first superintendent of the research laboratory of the Royal College of Physicians of Edinburgh from 1887 to 1890. He was then chosen to be the first head of a similar agency in London, the laboratories of the conjoint board of the Royal College of Physicians and the Royal College of Surgeons.

Woodhead's leadership and organizational skills greatly facilitated the growth and use of laboratory medicine in London and beyond. The conjoint laboratories were used by leading metropolitan researchers in physiology, pathology, and bacteriology, and Woodhead himself was increasingly drawn into consultancy and service provision in such areas as water pollution, tuberculosis, animal diseases, and, most importantly, the production and testing of diphtheria antitoxin for the metropolis. In 1891 he published *Bacteria and their Products*, which introduced the new subject both to serious students and to the wider public. In the following year he used his own resources to found the *Journal of Pathology and Bacteriology*, which he edited for thirteen years.

After nine years in London, Woodhead was appointed to the chair of pathology at Cambridge in 1899. This had been a largely academic post without direct access to clinical and public-health work, in a department that lacked modern facilities. The early 1900s were devoted to building up the medical school and to establishing stronger links with hospitals, local authorities, and voluntary agencies. Woodhead's work at Cambridge typified his whole career. He did not try to prioritize fundamental research but concentrated instead on applied research and practical work. This allowed him to give full rein to his teaching, organizational, and political skills, which benefited so many students, medical scientists, and patients, and, indirectly, the public at large. He pioneered the provision of clinically oriented courses for medical students, including courses in the long vacation that drew students from London. In the 1900s the department attracted many outstanding researchers, including T. S. Pigge Strangeways, G. H. F. Nuttall, G. S. Graham Smith, and Louis Cobbett, and Woodhead and Nuttall together bought the land to establish a field laboratory. Woodhead also took a leading role in the development of the Pathological Society of Great Britain, on its foundation in 1906. The society had a largely provincial constituency and aimed to promote the cause of experimental work, as against the 'dead house' pathology that still dominated in many metropolitan medical schools. At his death Woodhead was president of the Pathological and Bacteriological Laboratory Assistants' Association, a group he had long supported in trying to introduce qualifications and improved conditions for laboratory technicians.

Woodhead also had a high national profile in public health. In the 1890s and 1900s he took a leading part in the royal commissions that investigated the threat which bovine tuberculosis posed to humans. After 1900 this activity regularly took him away from Cambridge, as he played a major part in the commission's laboratory investigations, drafted many of its voluminous reports, and was called upon to speak at many international conferences. During and after the First World War he joined with P. C. Varrier-Jones and the Cambridge After-Care Committee, to found the famous Papworth Village settlement for former tuberculosis patients, a project described in their jointly authored *Industrial Colonies and Village Settlements for the Consumptive* (1920). Papworth offered a solution to a problem that contemporaries had long worried about: the physical and moral effects on working-class patients of the prolonged rest that was an essential part of the sanatorium treatment for tuberculosis. The colony provided different grades of light work and outdoor labour with the aim of allowing patients progressively to regain their strength and to readjust to the routine and rigours of manual labour. Woodhead's Quaker background led him to be a teetotaller, and in the 1900s he became an active temperance campaigner, speaking to public and medical audiences on the latest research on the physical and moral effects of alcohol. He also served on the council of the Imperial Cancer Research Fund and many government committees.

As a student Woodhead had been an outstanding sportsman; he was a record holder in sprints, a rugby half-back, a keen follower of football, and a good golfer. He had joined the Volunteer Medical Staff Corps at Edinburgh, and continued in the Officers' Training Corps, medical unit, rising to the rank of major. At the outbreak of the First World War he joined the Territorial Force, serving in Cambridge before becoming officer in charge of the Irish command depot in Tipperary as brevet colonel. Later he served as inspector of laboratories and consultant to the War Office, in which capacity he pioneered the chlorination of water supplies. Woodhead was made KBE in 1919.

Woodhead married Harriett Elizabeth St Clair Erskine, second daughter of James Yates of Edinburgh, in 1881; there were no children. He suffered a serious illness in 1906 and never regained his former vigour, though he soldiered on with apparently little concern for the fragility of his condition. He died on 29 December 1921 at Aisthorpe Hall, Lincolnshire. Woodhead was held in great affection by his contemporaries and liked for his self-effacing manner and kindliness, though he was able to be forceful in appropriate circumstances. A strong Congregationalist, his life was said to epitomize the Christian ideals of selflessness, generosity, and goodness.

MICHAEL WORBOYS

Sources J. Ritchie, A. E. Boycott, and H. R. Dean, 'German Sims Woodhead', *Journal of Pathology and Bacteriology*, 25 (1922), 118–37 • *In memoriam Sir German Sims Woodhead, 1855–1921* (1923) [a collection of obit. notices collected by his wife] • *BMJ* (7 Jan 1922), 39–41, 81–2 • *The Lancet* (7 Jan 1922), 51 • R. Williamson, 'The early history of

the department of pathology at Cambridge', *Cambridge and its contribution to medicine* [Cambridge 1969], ed. A. Rook (1971), 119–38 • *WWW* • *WWBMP*, vol. 2 [Joseph Woodhead]
Likenesses Russell, photograph, repro. in Ritchie, Boycott, and Dean, 'Woodhead', following p. 120, pl. X, XI
Wealth at death £6579: *BMJ*, 251

Woodhead, Grace Eyre (1864–1936), philanthropist and mental health reformer, was born on 24 February 1864 at 12 Norfolk Terrace, Brighton, the tenth of eleven children (ten girls and one boy) of Major Henry Joseph Plumridge Woodhead (d. 1903), a navy agent, and his wife, Emily (d. 1912). Grace was educated at Brighton high school and went up to Oxford in 1883 with her younger sister Hilda (d. 1937) to study history at Lady Margaret Hall. The Woodhead sisters and other new entrants were photographed with Elizabeth Wordsworth, the first principal of the college. Grace left Oxford in 1885 without taking a degree and there are no records of her life from that date until 1898 when she began providing holiday homes, in the Heathfield area of Sussex, for underprivileged, 'physically and mentally defective' children from special schools in London. By 1900 a headquarters had been established in Brighton and the scheme was providing permanent residence for a number of individuals.

Grace was prompted to reassess her work when the Mental Deficiency Act was passed in 1913; it instructed local authorities to establish mental deficiency committees, to ascertain mentally deficient persons in their area, and to provide suitable accommodation and community supervision. However, the underlying aim of the act was compulsory institutionalization and segregation of the sexes. Meetings to discuss the formation of a society 'for boarding out mentally and physically defectives under family guardianship' were held in the autumn of 1913. Dr Helen Boyle, founder of the Lady Chichester Hospital for Women with Nervous Diseases, was present at these discussions. The Guardianship Society was formed, with Grace as the secretary, and a close working relationship began between the two women and their organizations. Boyle was on the society's provisional council, acted as a medical consultant, and represented the society on the committee of the Central Association for the Mentally Defective, which had also just formed with Evelyn Fox as the first honorary secretary. The Guardianship Society was unique and its aims were clearly defined. It would board out patients to carefully chosen families where minimum standards of accommodation were laid down, medical treatment was provided, assistance was given to obtain training and employment, and a friendly interest was taken in the patients' moral and material welfare. The ethos was to provide gentle care in a small-scale family environment. The individuals who were capable of training and work contributed to their own upkeep and received pocket money. Goods and vegetable produce were sold locally or at annual sales to provide the society with funds. The society was charitable but was not run entirely by volunteers. Grace Woodhead did not draw a salary but clerical staff, home visitors, and workshop trainers were paid. Funds were obtained from subscribers and local authorities paid quarterly levies and were charged on a weekly basis for each case; small grants were obtained from the Board of Control which had been set up under the 1913 act.

The society had reciprocal arrangements with Helen Boyle's hospital; potential hospital cases were boarded out on a temporary basis and borderline cases were sent from the society to the hospital for assessment. By 1921 the society was providing respite care. In January 1926 an out-patient clinic for early nervous disorders and after care was opened at the society's offices in Grand Parade, under G. H. Harper Smith of the Brighton Borough Asylum. Grace Woodhead assisted at the clinic. The Lady Chichester Hospital had an out-patient clinic for women only and Boyle's influence on the society can be seen in this innovative development.

In the early 1920s two farms, Dungates and Tubwell, were run by married couples to create a homely atmosphere for working boys. In 1929 the cost of living at Dungates was a guinea a week, which was much cheaper than other institutions. In 1930 Walsh Manor was purchased and was used to train boys in poultry keeping, the growing of animal feed, and vegetable cultivation. These farms were temporary homes for two or three years, after which the young men were placed in permanent positions with local farmers. By 1931 there were six mixed sex occupational centres in the Brighton area and the work had grown to a point where the corporation of Brighton housing subcommittee was complaining about the number of 'defectives' coming to live in the area. Grace Woodhead resisted pressure to restrict her work to the Brighton area and continued to provide community care and co-educational training for cases from all parts of Britain. All employees and volunteers were accountable to her, and she involved herself in every aspect of the work of her society, but she shunned publicity and public speaking.

Grace Eyre Woodhead remained unmarried and continued her work until the final months of her life. She died on 5 April 1936 in a nursing home at 12 Dyke Road, Brighton, with her sister Hilda by her bedside. She was buried on 8 April at the extramural cemetery, Woodvale, Brighton. Grace left £200 to the society. A reorganization of its administration began immediately after her death, an indication, perhaps, of Grace's control over the organization.

In 1988 it was renamed the Grace Eyre Foundation. The modern organization provides specialized services for adults with learning disabilities through a network of registered carers in the local community. It runs day centres and provides home support, placement services, and respite care. From 31 Avondale Road, Hove, it continues to promote the care in the community approach started in Brighton by Grace Eyre Woodhead.

LOUISE WESTWOOD

Sources E. Sussex RO, Grace Eyre Foundation archives, GUA · E. Sussex RO, Lady Chichester Hospital archives, HB · E. Sussex RO, East Sussex mental deficiency committee, C/C/11/50 · proceedings, housing subcommittee, E. Sussex RO, Corporation of Brighton, DB/B/27/4 · *Brighton Herald*, E. Sussex RO, DB/B/77/32, 17 [funeral] · K. Jones, *A history of mental health services* (1972), 205 · V. M. Brittain, *The women at Oxford: a fragment of history* (1960), 57 · C. Avent and H. Pipe, eds., *Lady Margaret register, 1879–1990* (1990) · d. cert.
Archives E. Sussex RO, Lady Chichester Hospital archives · E. Sussex RO, archives of the Grace Eyre Foundation · E. Sussex RO, East Sussex mental deficiency committee archives
Likenesses group photograph, Lady Margaret Hall, Oxford, 1884, Bodl. Oxf.
Wealth at death £3815 17s. 1d.: probate, 4 Aug 1936, CGPLA Eng. & Wales

Woodhouse [*née* Blackburn], **Barbara Kathleen Vera** (1910–1988), animal trainer and broadcaster, was born on 9 May 1910 at St Columba's College, Rathfarnham, co. Dublin, a boys' public school where her father, the Revd William Blackburn, was headmaster; her mother, Leilah Alice (*née* Masterman), was the daughter of an English banker active in tsarist St Petersburg. Later in life, Woodhouse claimed that her affinity with animals was initially the result of overhearing her mother ask of a friend 'Why can't Barbara be beautiful, like the other children?' Animals, she reflected, in contrast to fickle human beings, 'didn't seem to mind what I looked like' (*Daily Telegraph*). Her idyllic childhood in the Irish countryside, surrounded by pigs, rabbits, and other pets, was ended when she was nine by her father's sudden death from a heart attack. The family decamped to Sandfield, a house on the outskirts of Oxford, where Barbara trained her first ponies, and continued her education at the nearby Headington School. 'Every mistress had hated me [there]', she later recalled, 'because I always went to school smelling of horse' (Woodhouse, *Talking to Animals*, 27).

In 1926 Barbara Blackburn moved to Harper Adams Agricultural College at Newport in Shropshire, the only girl among those studying agriculture. She gained the second-highest marks at the end of the course, having meanwhile also taught herself to be an excellent car mechanic, and was offered a temporary job experimenting on 'Which foods tainted milk and why?' as part of a larger Ministry of Agriculture project. On completing this research—and, to her surprise, finding herself sacked by the ministry for presenting her (well-substantiated) conclusions nine months early—she returned to Oxford and, with the enterprise that characterized her entire life, immediately opened a riding school. She enhanced her horse-training skills during a period in the early 1930s managing a series of *estancias* in Argentina, where a chance meeting with a Guarani Indian provided her with an extremely valuable insight: 'he told me that horses always go up to each other and sniff each other's noses, ... and that he always did the same thing when he wished to tame a horse himself' (Woodhouse, *Talking to Animals*, 28). This formed the basis of an infallible horsebreaking technique, which is depicted in a delightful group of photographs, reproduced in her autobiography, showing her approach to a nervous pony (ibid., 64–5).

Barbara Blackburn's first marriage, to Allan George Mill, had ended in divorce by 1940; perhaps reflecting the view of divorce common at this time, she made no mention of the relationship in any of her books. Shortly after her return to England she met and married, on 5 August 1940,

Barbara Kathleen Vera Woodhouse (1910–1988), by unknown photographer, 1980

Michael Clayton Woodhouse (b. 1910/11), a recently qualified doctor, the son of Alfred Edward Clayton Woodhouse, a medical practitioner and dental surgeon. Her husband's wartime general practice in the Wiltshire town of Melksham allowed her to manage her first farm nearby, and when after the war he began a long hospital career in London (mainly as consultant in physical medicine at St Mary's Hospital, Paddington), she was able to exchange it for the first of a pair of farms—both called Campions—in the home counties. There, at Stoke Mandeville in Buckinghamshire, she returned to agricultural research: after discovering by chance that her cows' milk yield markedly increased when their backs were covered with horse rugs, she designed and made—on a sewing machine in the middle of the farmyard—waterproof winter rugs and rather more delicate cotton sheets for the cows to wear in summer. A letter to a farming paper reporting her discovery led to her first brush with the national press, as Pathé and television cameras and journalists from Europe and the USA descended on the farm.

After moving to the second Campions, at Croxley Green in Hertfordshire, in the late 1940s—and by this time with three small children, two daughters and a son—Barbara Woodhouse began slowly to develop these media connections in typically enterprising ways. Her residential dog-training courses led to a notable appearance in the second edition of *What's my Line?* (in which the panel failed to guess her occupation), and a regular spot as dog trainer on the Scottish television series *The Smokey Club* in the early 1950s. As well as this television work—which also included training a succession of old English sheepdogs for Dulux paint commercials—she became involved in the world of film, producing documentaries about her training centre and a short film for the Children's Film Foundation shot entirely in and around her home.

Woodhouse was rarely afraid to mix her work with her domestic life: her dogs also provided the inspiration for a series of children's books, the products of a kitchen-table publishing operation which lasted over thirty years and resulted in eight original works. The first, a picture book, *Jyntee, the Tale of a Dog with a Broken Tail* (1951), was initially, like many children's stories, written to amuse her own sick child. Her books were not exclusively animal-related: among them are a set of (sociologically fascinating) foreign-language phrase books covering the phrases that 'we most need, in daily contact with foreign "helps"' (*Talking in French/English*, 1961, 4).

Although these activities made her well known in several specialist areas, Woodhouse did not become a household name until the age of seventy, through her BBC television series *Training Dogs the Woodhouse Way*, for which she was named Pye Television and Screenwriters' Guild female personality of the year in 1981. Although she called the celebrity this brought her 'unexpected success' (Woodhouse, *Just Barbara*, 117), it had been prepared for and, perhaps, planned, for many years. She had been a frequent broadcaster for the BBC since being asked in 1951 to present a radio talk entitled 'The kind way to break horses', while her book *Dog Training my Way* (1954) had been accompanied with a gramophone recording of her voice commands for the owner to use. For over a decade she had been urging the BBC to consider a series on dog training, and the direct approach eventually worked. The first episode was broadcast in January 1980: Woodhouse was shown teaching a group of dogs and their owners—her attention being at least as much on recalcitrant people as on their disobedient pets—chosen from over 2700 applicants.

The purpose of the series was to help the dog owner to train the animal so that it gave of its best, and in this Woodhouse was extremely successful. That it appealed to a larger audience than she had envisaged and rapidly became something of a cult was a tribute to Woodhouse's ability to present on screen, utterly unaffected, her natural 'mixture of shabby grandeur in appearance and imperious command in voice' (Day-Lewis). She directed her instructions at both dogs and their owners, her command 'Walkies! WALKIES!' becoming a catchphrase which she heard for the rest of her life—shouted to her from buses, trains, and the cabs of lorries, and providing inexhaustible material for impressionists. Her television work continued until a severe stroke in 1985 left her barely able to walk or speak. Even so, with typical determination, she still managed to write (jointly with Charles Warlow) and publish a final book: *Stroke* (1987), offering coping strategies to fellow sufferers. After a second and more serious stroke she died, at Great Missenden in Buckinghamshire, on 9 July 1988.   STEPHEN FOLLOWS

Sources The Times (11 July 1988) · S. Day-Lewis, The Independent (11 July 1988) · Daily Telegraph (11 July 1988) · The Guardian (11 July 1988) · Sunday Times (10 July 1988) · C. James, Glued to the box (1983) · B. Woodhouse, Talking to animals (1954) · B. Woodhouse, Just Barbara (1981) · b. cert. · m. cert. [Michael Clayton Woodhouse] · CGPLA Eng. & Wales (1989)
Likenesses photographs, c.1948–1980, Hult. Arch. [see illus.] · photographs, repro. in Woodhouse, Talking to animals
Wealth at death £690,808: probate, 11 July 1989, CGPLA Eng. & Wales

Woodhouse, James (bap. 1735, d. 1820), poet, was baptized on 18 April 1735 at Rowley Regis, Staffordshire, the eldest son of Joseph and Mary Woodhouse, 'honest yeoman' freeholders who worked a small farm that had been in the family for over three hundred years (Life and Political Works, 1.1, 1.9). As a boy Woodhouse learned to read and write at school, but his formal education ended at the age of seven. He went on to learn the cordwainer's craft, married young (to a woman named Hannah, the 'Daphne' of his poems), and supported an ever-increasing family by plying his trade.

In 1759 circumstance brought the 'Poetical Shoemaker' to the attention of the poet William Shenstone, whose estate—The Leasowes—was but 2 miles from Woodhouse's cottage (GM). At that time Shenstone's elaborate park was open to the public, and Woodhouse often indulged both his passion for nature and his poetic imagination among its sylvan walks. Shenstone, however, was forced to close the park because of misuse. Debarred from those 'pensive shade[s]', Woodhouse applied to Shenstone for renewed access by addressing verses to him (Life and Political Works, 1.19). Shenstone was impressed with Woodhouse's natural poetic 'genius', but apparently did not provide direct economic support to the struggling poet (Letters, 461). Instead, according to Woodhouse, Shenstone opened his library, acted as editor, and recommended him to wealthy friends such as Lord Lyttleton and Edward Montagu. Shenstone also brought Woodhouse to the attention of Robert Dodsley and his brother James, who sent Woodhouse books and employed him to distribute magazines in the early 1760s (Correspondence, 433, 460). The Dodsley brothers not only published Shenstone's Works in Verse and Prose in 1762, which included a poem by Woodhouse, but also Woodhouse's first volume of poems. After Shenstone died in 1763, Robert Dodsley—perhaps seeing something of himself in the shoemaker-turned-poet—took over the subscription and executed the final product, Poems on Sundry Occasions (1764), which sold well. Woodhouse became then a figure in the London literary world; he dined with Samuel Johnson at Mrs Thrale's table, and incurred the doctor's famous advice to 'give nights and days … to the study of Addison' (Johnsonian Miscellanies, 1.233). A second edition of Woodhouse's poems, which included several new effusions, appeared in 1766 as Poems on Several Occasions, inscribed to Lord Lyttleton, though Elizabeth Montagu was principally responsible for bringing this subscription to fruition. 'I have laid the foundation for a large subscription for him next year when he is to publish a new edition of his works', she wrote to her sister, Sarah Scott, on 21 January 1765 (Montagu MS MO 5818).

The Montagus became Woodhouse's primary patrons over the next two decades, though Woodhouse would later characterize their patronage as a form of 'bondage' (Life and Political Works, 1.68). In late 1767 he was appointed land bailiff to the Montagus' Berkshire estate, Sandleford, where his duties included land and labour management. After a falling out with Mrs Montagu in 1778, Woodhouse removed his family to Rowley, where he resumed shoe-making and agricultural work. However, following a reconciliation in 1781, Woodhouse returned to Mrs Montagu's service as house steward to both Sandleford and the new Portman Square house in London. Woodhouse performed his duties diligently for seven years, but his increasingly evangelical Methodism caused rifts in the relationship, most notably inciting his self-righteous indignation for Montagu's upper-class ostentation. Finally, in 1788—'despis'd and spurn'd for christian zeal'—Woodhouse was expelled from Montagu's service (ibid., 2.24). Throughout this period, 'growing grey in servitude, and poorer under patronage' (ibid., 2.139), Woodhouse wrote little and published no poetry.

Freed from the chains of servitude, and with timely financial backing from James Dodsley, Woodhouse opened a bookseller's shop at 10 Lower Brook Street, Grosvenor Square, around 1788, and began the last stage of his poetic career. A new Poems on Several Occasions appeared that year, and Woodhouse wrote both Norbury Park and Love Letters to my Wife in Verse in 1789, though neither was published until 1803 and 1804 respectively. Throughout the 1790s Woodhouse was at work on his autobiographical 'novel in verse', The Life and Lucubrations of Crispinus Scriblerus (Life and Political Works, 1.8). The poem contains important biographical details, long didactic digressions of a religious and political nature, and an unflattering portrait of Mrs Montagu, whom Woodhouse characterizes as vain, hypocritical, and prideful. Fearing reprisal from living relatives of Mrs Montagu, Woodhouse published only the tamest excerpts anonymously in 1814 and 1816 (New Monthly Magazine; Monthly Review). The complete text finally appeared in 1896 in a two-volume edition of his collected works edited by a grandson, R. I. Woodhouse. A posthumous recollection of Woodhouse in his bookselling days, penned by a former customer, described the poet as 'tall, erect, venerable, almost patriarchal, in his appearance—in his black-velvet cap, from beneath which his grey locks descended upon his forehead, and on each side of his still fine face' (Blackwood, 753).

According to his grandson Woodhouse gave up the bookselling business 'some time before his death', which 'was hastened by being knocked down by the pole of a carriage whilst crossing Orchard and Oxford Streets' (Life and Political Works, 1.2). He died of the injuries he sustained from the accident, in February 1820 at his home in Euston Square. His administrative will shows that he had amassed an estate of £5000, which was bequeathed to his widow. He was buried in St George's Chapel ground, near Marble Arch, London.   WILLIAM J. CHRISTMAS

Sources *The life and political works of James Woodhouse*, ed. R. I. Woodhouse, 2 vols. (1896) • *GM*, 1st ser., 34 (1764), 289–90 • Hunt. L., Montagu MS MO 5818 • PRO, PROB 6/196, fol. 171*v* • 'Sorting my letters and papers', *Blackwood*, 26 (1829), 753–5 • *The letters of William Shenstone*, ed. D. Mallam [1939] • *The correspondence of Robert Dodsley, 1733–1764*, ed. J. E. Tierney (1988) • *Johnsonian miscellanies*, ed. G. B. Hill, 2 vols. (1897) • R. Southey, *The lives and works of the uneducated poets*, ed. J. S. Childers (1925) • *New Monthly Magazine*, 3 (1815), 152 • *Monthly Review*, new ser., 80 (1816), 216–17 • *DNB* • *IGI*
Archives BL • NL Wales, letters | Hunt. L., letters, mainly to Elizabeth Montagu
Likenesses line engraving, pubd 1765, NPG • H. Cook, line engraving, pubd 1818 (after W. Hobday), BM, NPG • Cook, engraving (after W. Hobday, 1816?), repro. in Woodhouse, ed., *Life*
Wealth at death £5000: administration, PRO, PROB 6/196, fol. 171*v*

Woodhouse, John (*c.*1627–1700), Presbyterian minister and tutor, was possibly a younger son of John Woodhouse of Wombourn, Staffordshire. He underwent a religious conversion at an early age and was considered 'so notedly Serious' at university 'as to be admitted into the Intimate Society of some of the Gravest Divines in that Place' (Williams, 100). He entered Trinity College, Cambridge, in 1655 as a fellow-commoner but did not matriculate. He then served for some years as a private chaplain to a family, engaging in private study and reflection. During this period he acquired the stock of learning he later used as a tutor. According to Calamy, Woodhouse was a ministerial candidate in Nottinghamshire when the Act of Uniformity came into force, and though not ejected he was silenced by the act. He was subsequently chaplain to Lady Grantham (*d.* 1667) of Ratcliffe upon Soar, the widow of Sir Thomas Grantham. On 26 November 1667 Woodhouse married Mary, the daughter of Major William Hubbert of Rearsby, Leicestershire, with whom he obtained a considerable estate following the death of her brother George Hubbert (1638–1684) without heirs. 'Upon this change in his Condition, he applied himself to Educate Young Men; and to preach more publickly and constantly' in northeast Leicestershire (Williams, 103). 'About the Vale of Beaver [Belvoir] he diffused saving Light, and was an Instrument in the Conversion of great Numbers' (ibid., 104). He was reported in 1669 preaching on Sundays to a conventicle of about fifty persons at Saxelbye, and to another at Rearsby to about 20 persons with the former vicar, William Grace. He does not appear to have taken out a licence to preach under Charles II's declaration of indulgence (1672). In October 1675, while living at Warnaby, Woodhouse was licensed by Archbishop Sheldon to teach grammar within the dioceses of Lincoln, Lichfield, and Hereford. He moved shortly afterwards to the manor house at Sheriffhales, Shropshire, where he established one of the earliest nonconformist academies. During the early 1680s Woodhouse was in trouble for his nonconformity. In November 1683 he was forced to move in the king's bench for a prohibition upon a *capias* excommunication. A year later he was arrested upon another *capias* and sent to Shrewsbury gaol. He was again gaoled in June 1685 with other nonconformist ministers at Chester Castle following Monmouth's rebellion.

Sheriffhales was one of the most important nonconformist academies in the period before toleration because of the numbers taught and the distinction of so many of the students in later life. Woodhouse is said some years to have had between forty and fifty students, and although the total number he educated is unknown it must have been substantial. He educated lay as well as ministerial students. They comprised 'many eminent persons who made a considerable figure in the world, not only as ministers, but as gentlemen and magistrates' (Hunter, 'Collectanea', fol. 54*r*). They included Robert Harley, the future earl of Oxford, and his brother Edward Harley, Henry St John, later Viscount Bolingbroke, and Thomas Foley, later Lord Foley. He also educated many of the ministers who served the second generation of dissent, notably Chewning Blackmore, John Newman, Benjamin Robinson, and Ferdinando Shaw. The Presbyterian Fund supported eighteen students and Woodhouse supported several poor students himself.

The full course was extensive, and in the case of students for the ministry probably lasted four years. All the students had lectures in logic, ethics, metaphysics, rhetoric, theology, geography, history, mathematics, natural philosophy, anatomy, and physics, with practical exercises in subjects such as land surveying and animal dissection. They also studied Greek and Hebrew. Lay students intended for the law were read a lecture on the subject once a week. Ministerial students had a special course of theological reading and had a weekly polemical lecture either on Wollebius's *Compendium theologiae* or Ames's *Medulla theologica*, both Calvinist works. The senior students practised drawing up skeletons or heads of sermons and praying in the family. Joshua Toulmin, who had access to Woodhouse's own papers in the early nineteenth century, provided an account of many of the textbooks used. Woodhouse had a number of assistants to help with the teaching, evidence of the number of students and range of subjects taught. The academy closed in 1697 as a result of Woodhouse's ill health, but he succeeded Samuel Annesley as minister of Little St Helen's, London, where he remained until his death in October 1700. He was buried at Rearsby parish church on 17 October. Woodhouse published a couple of funeral sermons together with *A Catalogue of Sins … a Suitable Preparation for … the Lord's Supper* (1699). He had 'a plain warm, familiar Way of Preaching' (Williams, 104). His eldest son, William (1669–1743), was minister to a small congregation at Rearsby. The second son, George, by his behaviour 'disabled me' from securing him anything (will). The third son, John, studied medicine at Leiden, graduated MD in 1700, and practised in London. There were also three daughters.

DAVID L. WYKES

Sources *Calamy rev.*, 544, 566–7 • A. Gordon, ed., *Freedom after ejection: a review (1690–1692) of presbyterian and congregational nonconformity in England and Wales* (1917), 88, 389 • J. Toulmin, *An historical view of the state of the protestant dissenters in England* (1814), 225–

30, 559–67 • D. Williams, *A funeral sermon … on the decease of the Reverend Mr John Woodhouse* (1701) • E. Calamy, ed., *An abridgement of Mr. Baxter's history of his life and times, with an account of the ministers, &c., who were ejected after the Restauration of King Charles II*, 2nd edn, 2 vols. (1713), vol. 1, p. 539 • E. Calamy, *A continuation of the account of the ministers … who were ejected and silenced after the Restoration in 1660*, 2 vols. (1727), vol. 2, p. 700 • R. Morrice, 'Entring book: being an historical register of occurrences from April an. 1677 to April 1691', DWL, Morrice MS 31 P, pp. 392, 443, 445, 472 • deeds etc. of the Woodhouse family of Rearsby, Leics. RO, DE 570, boxes 1 and 2 (4914–4915) • postnuptial settlement of John Woodhouse and Mary Hubbert, Staffs. RO, D369/C/411–2 • J. Hunter, 'Collectanea Hunteriana volume VIII being memoirs to serve for a history of protestant dissenters', BL, Add. MS 24442, fol. 54*r* • J. Hunter, *Familiae minorum gentium*, ed. J. W. Clay, 1, Harleian Society, 37 (1894), 26 • parish register, Saxelbye, Leicestershire, 26 Nov 1667, Leics. RO [marriage] • parish register, Rearsby, Leicestershire, 17 Oct 1700, Leics. RO [burial] • will, Leics. RO

Archives Leics. RO, family deeds, DE 570, boxes 1–3, 4914–4916 • priv. coll., family papers
Wealth at death wealthy; owned estates in Leicestershire, Shropshire, Staffordshire, and Worcestershire: will and deeds, Leics. RO

Woodhouse, Peter (*fl.* 1605), poet, was the author of *The Flea*, or, adopting the subsidiary title, 'Democritvs his Dreame, or, The Contention betweene the Elephant and the Flea'. The poem, which appeared in 1605, was printed for John Smethwick, whose shop was 'in St Dunstans Churchyard in Fleet Street, under the Diall'. Fifty reprints were produced in 1877 as part of Alexander B. Grosart's series *Occasional Issues of Unique or Very Rare Books*. Woodhouse was by no means destitute of merit as a poet, but *The Flea* is the only memorial of him that exists.

The 'contention' of the title concerns the elephant's assertion that he is king of the beasts, a claim that is challenged by the flea:

How long shall uncontrouled arrogance
Exalt itselfe? How long shall pride advance,
…
Who ever thought such insolence to finde,
In this huge lumpe of folly, this bace hinde?
(Woodhouse, 12–13)

Although Woodhouse asserts that his censures are directed at 'some kinde of faultes and not some faultie men' (ibid., 34), it none the less seems likely that the elephant, the flea, and the other actors in the tale were intended to refer to persons whom it might have been dangerous to satirize more openly. The poem is prefaced by an 'Epistle to the reader' and by some verses 'in laudem authoris' signed 'R. P., Gent.' In place of the traditional dedicatory epistle to a noble patron Woodhouse offers an 'Epistle Dedicatorie to the Giddie Multidude', a decision that he explains as follows: 'I not knowing any one whose name I might be so bolde with, as to shelter, for this substance-wanting shadowe, dedicate it to you all, so shall I be sure to offend none' (ibid., 3).

E. I. CARLYLE, *rev.* ELIZABETH GOLDRING

Sources P. Woodhouse, 'The flea (1605)', *Occasional issues of unique or very rare books*, ed. A. B. Grosart (1877), vol. 4

Woodhouse, Robert (1773–1827), mathematician, was born at Norwich on 28 April 1773, the son of Robert Woodhouse, a draper, and his wife, Judith, the daughter of the Lowestoft Unitarian minister, James Alderson. Having attended the grammar school at North Walsham, on 20 May 1790 Woodhouse was admitted to Gonville and Caius College, Cambridge, and matriculated in Michaelmas term, 1791. He took a BA as senior wrangler and first Smith's prizeman in 1795, and gained his MA and a fellowship at Caius in 1798. In 1803 he became a fellow of the Royal Society. His younger brother, John Thomas (1780–1845), was also a fellow of Caius.

The historical significance of Woodhouse's mathematics is a function of the backwardness of Cambridge mathematics at the turn into the nineteenth century. Most Cambridge mathematicians continued to labour within the confines of fluxions, a calculus of Newtonian notation and methodology resting upon geometric and physical imagery. By means of a more powerful and abstract calculus expressed in more comprehensive notation, continental mathematicians exhibited that the commitment to fluxions was anachronistic. However, this had little effect at Cambridge, since the primary purpose of a Cambridge education, the core of which was mathematics, was not to produce mathematicians but, rather, liberally educated gentlemen. Euclidean geometry, and Newtonian fluxions, mechanics, and astronomy, seemed best fit for this end, and most Cambridge dons perceived no need to change. Woodhouse did.

Initially Woodhouse focused his reforming efforts on pure mathematics and its foundations. His arguments are given in three articles in the *Philosophical Transactions of the Royal Society* (1801, 1802) and in a book, *The Principles of Analytical Calculation* (1803). He demanded that analysis in general and the calculus specifically be placed upon a purely algebraic footing free of geometric and physical encumbrances such as limits or infinitesimals. Moreover he argued that such mathematical entities as complex numbers (for instance the square root of minus one) and divergent series (a series having no single finite sum) were useful, indeed sometimes necessary, for achieving results. For this reason, and because he could not conceive of false premises leading to correct consequences, he objected to their being excluded from analysis.

To justify his contentions, Woodhouse turned to the French doyen of algebraic analysis, J. L. Lagrange. Lagrange had founded the calculus on the expansion of a function in a Taylor series in which the successive coefficients of the terms of the series directly provided the successive derivatives of the function. Finding fault with Lagrange for failing implicitly to avoid limits and for not showing algebraically that each function considered could be developed in a Taylor series, Woodhouse embraced formalism built upon his redefinition of the equal sign. In pure algebra, Woodhouse submitted, '=' did not signify arithmetical equality, but rather, the result of some operation. The analysts' programme, according to Woodhouse, was first to prove algebraically that a function had a Taylor series, then to 'extend' this form (for instance to the complex realm or beyond the radius of convergence), and then to manipulate the algebraic symbols to reach the desired end. Within this framework for algebra, Woodhouse insisted, numerical equality and, therefore, whether or not a series was convergent, were irrelevant. Only in applied mathematics did arithmetic equality become a concern.

Woodhouse's arguments in *The Principles*, aimed at mathematical virtuosi, were polemical and maladroit, mathematically and grammatically, and as a consequence the book had little immediate impact. However, his views and his notation—the differential, functional, and operator notation of the continent—were imbibed by younger and more bellicose members of the university who, in the second decade of the nineteenth century, stimulated adjustments which would bring Cambridge up to speed in the 1830s. Consequently, the conceptions explicated by Woodhouse became ingrained at Cambridge, thereby facilitating the creation of axiomatic algebra, the development of modern logic, and, correspondingly, the continued scepticism among Cambridge mathematicians toward the convergency considerations which came to dominate continental analysis.

Woodhouse also exercised a less dramatic but more immediate influence. He served as a moderator of the tripos six times between 1799 and 1808, and he turned his attention to astronomy, the apex of the Cambridge curriculum. In the *Philosophical Transactions* (1804), he reviewed current literature on elliptic integrals, a subject neglected at Cambridge but useful in astronomy. In 1809, using the continental notation with explanations in notes, he provided *A Treatise on Plane and Spherical Trigonometry*, a textbook treating trigonometry analytically. This was an improvement over the usual geometrically orientated Cambridge texts, especially if astronomy were to be treated analytically. In 1810, in *A Treatise on Isoperimetrical Problems and the Calculus of Variations*, a work which became influential both as history and as mathematics, he introduced at Cambridge the calculus of variations, a subject crucial to treating astronomy analytically. Finally, between 1812 and 1821, he published textbooks on astronomy which took the student from elementary practical astronomy through physical astronomy. For the physical astronomy, he severed relevant segments from Laplace's *Mécanique céleste*, the paragon of Newtonian mechanics treated analytically; at times, when employing simpler mathematics, he referenced Laplace's more sophisticated treatment. Woodhouse's publications had an impact: they were cited 147 times as aids for answering questions and solving problems in the tripos for the years 1801 to 1820. It is with justification then, that in 1819 a reviewer wrote that 'No man has done so much to improve the studies of Cambridge as Mr. Woodhouse' (*EdinR*, 42, 1819, 394).

In 1820 Woodhouse became Lucasian professor of mathematics; the chair was esteemed as that of Newton but brought a niggardly income. In 1822 he attained the more lucrative Plumian professorship of astronomy and experimental philosophy, and as Plumian professor he became the first superintendent of the newly built Cambridge University observatory. Endowed with a decent income, Woodhouse resigned his fellowship and, on 20 February 1823, married Harriet Wilkens, a Norwich architect's daughter, and the sister of the noted architect William Wilkens, sixth wrangler of 1800 and a fellow of Caius. She gave birth to a son, named Robert, in 1825. Two years later, on 23 December 1827, Woodhouse died at Cambridge. He was buried in Caius College chapel.

HARVEY W. BECHER

Sources H. Becher, 'Woodhouse, Babbage, Peacock, and modern algebra', *Historia Mathematica*, 7 (1980), 389–400 · H. Becher, 'William Whewell and Cambridge mathematics', *Historical Studies in the Physical Sciences*, 11 (1980–81), 1–48 · Venn, *Alum. Cant.* · N. Guicciardini, *The development of Newtonian calculus in Britain, 1700–1800* (1989) · E. Koppelman, 'The calculus of operations and the rise of abstract algebra', *Archive for History of Exact Sciences*, 8 (1971–2), 155–242 · H. Pycior, 'Internalism, externalism, and beyond: 19th-century British algebra', *Historia Mathematica*, 11 (1984), 424–41 · review of *Elementary treatise on astronomy*, *EdinR*, 31 (1818–19), 375–94

Woodhouse, Thomas (*d.* 1573), Jesuit and martyr, was a native of Lincoln. Ordained priest shortly before the death of Queen Mary in 1558 he was presented to a parsonage in Lincolnshire. In 1560 he resigned his living because of the religious changes and withdrew to Wales as a tutor in the household of an unnamed gentleman. This position he also abandoned soon afterwards for the same reasons. In early 1561 Sir William Cecil's discovery of a Catholic plot to overthrow the established church destroyed any chance that Elizabeth I would allow a papal nuncio to enter the kingdom. In the consequent crackdown Woodhouse was arrested while celebrating mass and committed, on 14 May 1561, as a 'pore priste', to the Fleet prison, where he lived on charity like other pauper prisoners (Pollen, 'Lists', 48).

In 1563, during a severe visitation of the plague in London, Tyrrell, warder of the Fleet prison, received royal permission to escort all those imprisoned for Catholicism to his house in Cambridgeshire. Believing Tyrrell to be a Catholic at heart Woodhouse admonished him thrice for eating meat in Lent. Woodhouse's threats that he would stay no longer under his roof unless Tyrell repented did not have the desired effect. So the priest escaped his house and fled back to the Fleet prison.

The keeper of the Fleet allowed Woodhouse to visit friends in London by day and granted him freedom of the prison. He celebrated mass daily in his cell, visited the sick, and strengthened the faith of Catholic prisoners. An unnamed fellow prisoner testified 'in God's cause he [Woodhouse] feared nothing, and always had a good desire to suffer for the Catholic faith' (Foley, 7/2, 1262). The same witness reported that Woodhouse devised a plan in 1571 to convince the privy council to accept his life in exchange for that of John Story. In a letter of 19 November 1572 he urged William Cecil, lord treasurer,

> to persuade the Lady Elizabeth (who for her own great disobedience is most justly deposed), to submit herself unto her spiritual Prince and Father, the Pope's Holiness, and, with all humility, to reconcile herself unto him, that she may be the child of salvation.   (BL, Lansdowne MS 99, fol. 1)

An irate Cecil summoned the priest three or four days later. During the interview Woodhouse refused to recognize any of Cecil's titles, asserting that the queen lacked authority to award them because of her deposition. Upon his return to the Fleet he was placed in chains. Woodhouse then wrote short exhortations on obedience to the pope and the true church, signed his name, tied them to stones, and threw them out the prison window. Many thought him mad.

In 1573 Woodhouse requested admission into the Society of Jesus via the Jesuit provincial in Paris, and he was accepted. At his arraignment at the Guildhall he denied the authority of his judges. Found guilty of high treason for refuting the queen's authority he was committed to Newgate. On 19 June 1573 he was executed at Tyburn. The first priest to suffer execution in Elizabeth's reign, Woodhouse was beatified as a Jesuit by Pope Leo XIII on 29 December 1886. Verses written in prison are in the Archivum Romanum Societatis Iesu.

THOMAS M. MCCOOG

Sources T. M. McCoog, *English and Welsh Jesuits, 1555–1650*, 2 vols., Catholic RS, 74–5 (1994–5) • T. M. McCoog, ed., *Monumenta Angliae*, 1–2 (1992) • H. Foley, ed., *Records of the English province of the Society of Jesus*, 7 vols. in 8 (1875–83) • *The Elizabethan Jesuits: Historia missionis Anglicanae Societatis Jesu (1660) of Henry More*, ed. and trans. F. Edwards (1981) • J. H. Pollen, 'The blessed Thomas Woodhouse', *Lives of the English martyrs declared blessed by Pope Leo XIII in 1886 and 1895*, ed. B. Camm, 1 (1904), 187–203 • J. H. Pollen, ed., 'Official lists of prisoners for religion during the reign of Queen Elizabeth', *Miscellanea, I*, Catholic RS, 1 (1905), 47–72
Archives Archives of the British Province of the Society of Jesus, London, MS Anglia I, 3 • Archivum Romanum Societatis Iesu, Rome
Likenesses engravings (after frescoes by Ciriniani), repro. in N. Circignano, *Ecclesiae Anglicanae Trophaea* (1584)

Woodhouse [*née* Bousher], **Vera Florence Annie**, Lady **Terrington** (*b.* **1889**, *d.* in or after **1956**), politician, was born on 11 January 1889 at 45 Hanover Gardens, Kennington, London, the daughter of Henry George Bousher and his wife, Anne Elizabeth, *née* Koster. She married first, on 13 March 1907, Guy Ivo Sebright, the only son of Sir Guy Thomas Sebright, twelfth baronet. In the previous year he had been divorced by his first wife, Mary Louise Blane. He died in 1912; there were no children. She afterwards married, on 8 May 1918, Harold James Selborne Woodhouse, second Baron Terrington (1877–1940), a solicitor and businessman, and it was as Lady Terrington that she came to public notice as a Liberal politician in the early 1920s.

Lady Terrington contested the Wycombe division of Buckinghamshire at the general election of 1922, in which she was one of only thirty-three women candidates. Of these only Lady Astor, for the Conservatives, and Margaret Wintringham, for the Liberals, succeeded, although Terrington came a highly creditable second in a three-cornered contest at Wycombe. The result encouraged her to continue to the next election, which came in December 1923 as a result of the Baldwin government's decision to seek an electoral mandate with which to enact tariff reform. The issue dominated the campaign, and at Wycombe Terrington was effective in exploiting housewives' fears that tariffs would lead to price increases. She overturned the previous year's Conservative majority of 4473 with a Liberal majority of 1682 and afterwards attributed her victory to the effect of the women's vote. The achievement was the more notable in that Terrington, unlike Astor and Wintringham, had not inherited the seat from her husband, and she entered the House of Commons with three other women who could claim this distinction: Margaret Bondfield, Susan Lawrence, and Dorothy Jewson.

The election of a total of eight women in 1923 was seen as something of a breakthrough by contemporaries, and led *The Times* to suggest that the prejudice of male voters against women candidates was disappearing. It is not clear if this was so at Wycombe, although Terrington was successful on a platform that was strong in the advocacy of women's rights. In this respect, not least, she provided a clear alternative to the Conservative candidate, Colonel W. B. du Pré, an avowed anti-feminist, and her victory was greeted with special delight among women's societies such as the Six Point Group. Not all feminists were enthusiastic. Margery Corbett Ashby, commenting to her mother on a conference of women MPs in January 1924, said Terrington

> was endlessly off the point. It is really amazing how she got in. She is very good looking and has a very kind heart and I think must have got in on past good works and future good intentions, but she is completely uneducated. (Corbett Ashby papers, priv. coll.)

Terrington made her maiden speech in the Commons in February 1924, when she seconded the motion to abolish the means test in the administration of old-age pensions. She was conscious of giving an emotional performance, which she attributed to the 'rather depressing' debate that had just taken place. She sought on this occasion for equality of opportunity between men and women, and the same motive led her to support the Guardianship of Infants Bill in April 1924, which aimed at equalizing the rights of both parents in respect of the guardianship and custody of children from marriage. Terrington paid tribute to the efforts of women's societies in promoting 'a measure long overdue', one that she believed signalled another step towards equality: 'Therefore, Hon. Members can quite see that it is a question of women, women, women! We have got to a certain phase in our national life, but we have not got all yet that we want' (*Hansard 5C*, 171, col. 2674). The following month, at a meeting of the National Women's Liberal Federation, she moved a resolution promoting women's rights on a broad front, and specifically calling for an equal franchise.

During her short time in parliament Terrington proved a conscientious member, and was especially active in opposing cruelty to animals. As she explained to the Commons in March 1924: 'The suffering of animals is one of the things that I, as a woman, take most dearly to heart' (*Hansard 5C*, 171, col. 901). Her targets included the inhumane trapping of rabbits and vermin; the export of 'worn-out horses' to the continent; stag-hunting; and even the 'broncho-busting' displays at Wembley which were part of the 1924 British Empire Exhibition. At a public meeting of the Animal Defence and Anti-Vivisection Society at the

Steinway Hall in London, in April 1924, she urged women to buy meat only from animals slaughtered in accordance with the humane methods prescribed by the society.

But Terrington was also a diligent constituency member, and canvassed on horseback in both her election campaigns. She advanced the interests of agriculture in her rural constituency by favouring credit facilities for farmers and co-operative farming schemes. She promoted, too, the provision of smallholdings and of rural housing in Buckinghamshire. Her advocacy of temperance reform with local option was probably less popular with her constituents, though no less necessary, she thought, for she could count seventeen public houses within a quarter of a mile of her house: 'It is not a nice thing to go along a street and get the smell of beer and other things in your nose every yard' (*The Times*, 29 May 1924). She was associated with many charitable causes in the region and trod new ground in becoming the first woman president of Marlow Football Club.

Tall, elegant, and attractive, Terrington gained unwanted publicity during the 1923 campaign over her avowed determination not to dress down for parliament if she were to be elected. On 3 December the *Daily Express* published an article headlined: 'The best dressed woman MP. Lady Terrington's aim if elected'. It was based on an interview that Terrington had naïvely given to a woman reporter from the paper, in which she was quoted as saying:

> I shall put on my ospreys and my fur coat and my pearls. I do not believe in a woman politician wearing a dull little frock with a Quaker collar, and keeping her nicest clothes for social appearances. It is all humbug. (*The Times*, 11, 12 Nov 1924)

Terrington later sued the paper for libel, arguing that the report made her seem 'an extravagant and frivolous woman … given to vulgar ostentation' (ibid.). She denied the quotations attributed to her, including any reference to a 'Quaker collar', thought to be an allusion to Lady Astor. But her action failed in November 1924 after a jury decided that the dress of women MPs was a subject of public interest, and that in any case the report had not injured her.

This judgment came shortly after Terrington had lost her seat at the 1924 general election. Her supporters had been confident that she would hold Wycombe with an increased majority, though the circumstances of the poll were by then much less favourable to Liberal fortunes. In a campaign polarized between right and left, support for the Conservatives dramatically increased, and Major-General Sir Alfred Knox took advantage of this to score a resounding victory at Wycombe with a majority of 8294. Terrington's vote had fallen by more than 2500, though she still managed a third of the total cast. The election halved the number of women in parliament.

In spring 1925 the Wycombe Liberals showed their continued faith in Terrington by again adopting her as their candidate. She was soon, though, to experience personal difficulties which effectively curtailed her political career. In May 1926 she began divorce proceedings against her husband following the disclosure of his adultery with a married woman; the divorce was made absolute later that year. Prior to this, her husband had run into serious financial difficulties and was imprisoned during 1928–32 for fraudulent conversion. Terrington later emigrated to Cape Province, in South Africa, and on 28 March 1949 she married Max W. Lensvelt of Johannesburg. She made no mark on the public life of her adopted country comparable to that she had made in England, where she enjoyed the distinction of having been among the vanguard of women parliamentarians. The date of her death has not been established; she ceased to be included in *Who's Who* after 1956.   MARK POTTLE

Sources WW · WWW · Burke, *Peerage* · WWBMP · *Hansard 5C* (1924), vols. 170–72; 174–5 · E. Vallance, *Women in the house: a study of women members of parliament* (1979) · P. Brookes, *Women at Westminster: an account of women in the British parliament, 1918–1966* (1967) · *The Times* (1–18 Nov 1921) · *The Times* (6 Feb 1923) · *The Times* (8 Dec 1923) · *The Times* (8 April 1924) · *The Times* (29 May 1924) · *The Times* (19 July 1924) · *The Times* (25 Oct 1924) · *The Times* (11–12 Nov 1924) · *The Times* (8 Dec 1926) · *The Times* (29 July 1927) · *The Times* (6 April 1949) · F. W. S. Craig, *British parliamentary election results, 1918–1949*, rev. edn (1977) · b. cert. · m. cert. [Guy Ivo Sebright]

Likenesses group portrait, photograph, 1923, repro. in Brookes, *Women at Westminster* · photograph, repro. in *The Times* (8 Dec 1923)

Woodhouse, Violet Kate Eglinton Gordon [*née* Violet Kate Eglinton Gwynne] (**1871–1948**), keyboard player, was born on 23 April 1871 at 97 Harley Street, St Marylebone, London, the second daughter and fourth of seven children of James Eglinton Anderson Gwynne (1832–1915), engineer, inventor, and landowner, and his wife, Mary Earle (1841–1923), known as May, daughter of William and Cornelia Purvis. Violet's musical gifts were inherited from her mother's side of the family. Her mother, herself a fine singer and an intimate of the great soprano Adelina Patti, fostered her prodigious talent from childhood. By sixteen she was among the most promising pupils of the country's leading piano teacher, the German émigré Oscar Beringer.

Violet was determined to be a full-time musician. Her authoritarian father was equally determined that she should not be a professional. The solution was a husband with the means to indulge her ambition. Her engagement in 1893 to Lord Gage, a rich Sussex neighbour, was, however, broken off after her mother explained the facts of life to her. Two years later Violet married John Gordon Woodhouse (1870–1951), the shy heir to Sicilian Marsala estates. It was mutually understood that the marriage would be childless, if by no means loveless.

Dissatisfied with the narrow range of the conventional turn-of-the-century repertory, Violet was fascinated by the lecture-recitals of Arnold Dolmetsch, whose early music revival was beginning to gain critical attention. Under Dolmetsch's guidance she gradually transferred her affections to the harpsichord and clavichord. Another important influence on her at this time was the Spanish cellist Agustín Rubio, an inspirational teacher and one of the many émigrés who contributed to London's importance as a cosmopolitan musical capital.

In 1899 the Hon. William Reginald Shute Barrington (1873–1960) fell in love with Violet and went to live with her and Gordon. Barrington was the love of Violet's life, although it was never clear how far their relationship was consummated. In 1933 Bill, as he was known, succeeded his father, becoming tenth Viscount Barrington. A gentle and handsome man, he was completely uninterested in music, but had a watercolourist's eye and created three beautiful gardens for her. As the reputation of her musical salon grew, so also did her reputation for unorthodox—some said scandalous—living. In 1901 the Hon. Denis Tollemache (1884–1942), soldier and musician, and Maxwell Labouchère (1871–1918), known as Max, barrister, wit, and intellectual, joined the household, creating a surprisingly harmonious *ménage à cinq*.

Nor was it men alone who were drawn to Violet. Her dark looks (attributable to her grandmother's secret descent from an Indonesian rani), her vivacity and natural intelligence, her resolution and generosity of spirit, allied with her artistic genius, attracted the devotion, sometimes the infatuation, of many women, including the composer Dame Ethel Smyth, the music critic Christabel Marshall, and the novelist Radclyffe Hall.

The shock of the First World War destroyed Violet's idyll. All her men except Gordon, who was unfit, went to the front. Barrington contracted dysentery in Mesopotamia. Tollemache was twice wounded and was later captured after being listed missing presumed dead. Labouchère was fatally wounded in 1918. Both Tollemache and Labouchère won decorations for valour.

The aftermath of war left Gordon financially diminished, and Violet was now obliged to turn professional. In 1923 she became the first performer to record (for HMV) on the harpsichord. In 1926, however, the finances of the household took an extraordinary turn for the better when Gordon's two spinster sisters were simultaneously murdered by their butler. They had intended to leave their fortune to a cousin, but their wills were unsigned. As next of kin, Gordon was the sole inheritor. With her independence thus restored, Violet reverted to playing in her own salon, an ambience perfectly suited to early music and her chosen instruments. For the remainder of her life, with the rarest exceptions, she played to private audiences at Nether Lypiatt Manor, her beautiful Carolean château above Stroud, in Gloucestershire. A period of mellow happiness was broken by the outbreak of the Second World War, in which Violet, with her love of German culture and her painful earlier memories of war, found herself quite unable to share in popular patriotic sentiments. Tollemache died in 1942. Violet died at 11 Mount Street, Mayfair, London, on 9 January 1948 and was buried in Folkington churchyard, Folkington, Sussex, on 14 January. Gordon Woodhouse and Barrington continued to live at Nether Lypiatt until their own deaths, in 1951 and 1960 respectively.

Originally known as a pianist, Violet became the foremost clavichord player of her day and, with Wanda Landowska, the foremost harpsichordist. On these instruments contemporary reviewers ranked her with Pablo Casals on the cello, Lionel Tertis on the viola, and Andrés Segovia on the guitar. Her magnetism evoked comparison to the powers of a magician. In the words of her *Times* obituary, 'the subtlety of her playing was infinite and her clarity perfection … when she began to play, one became … entangled in a golden web of purest sound' (Douglas-Home, 306).

Perfectionist, scholarly, and a mistress of stylish showmanship, Violet cast her spell over the most discerning observers, including Bernard Shaw, Frederick Delius, Ralph Vaughan Williams, the Sitwells, and the music critic K. S. Sorabji. Among the admiring visitors to her

Violet Kate Eglinton Gordon Woodhouse (1871–1948), by Herbert Lambert for Elliott & Fry, 1944 [with her piano teacher, Rubio]

salon were Lawrence of Arabia, T. S. Eliot, Wilfred Owen, Siegfried Sassoon, Pablo Picasso, Serge Diaghilev, Auguste Rodin, and the cream of Europe's musicians.

The most important part of Violet's legacy was her role in the revival of pre-Romantic music, especially of early music played on appropriate instruments. She shared with Sacheverell Sitwell credit for rediscovering Domenico Scarlatti and made extensive use of the Fitzwilliam virginal book (containing music by William Byrd, John Bull, and Giles Farnaby), a source then almost unknown to the music-going public, although recognized by scholars as representing the genesis of modern European keyboard music.

In 1996 most of Violet's extant recordings were collected into a CD under the Pearl imprint. In his foreword Richard Luckett noted her 'scrupulous fidelity to the texts', adding that she played Scarlatti straight at a time when Wanda Landowska was adding, subtracting, and modifying 'almost as though he was in competition with Stravinsky'. Luckett contrasted Landowska's 'metronomic' playing with Violet's 'no less virtuosic, but infinitely more relaxed' style. An unusual feature of her playing was her use of the accelerando, with the result that 'her *rubato* effects are produced by a return to the initial tempo, rather than by slowing it—at odds with modern performance practice but historically justifiable'.

Some of the works that Violet admired were not deemed commercial propositions for recording. But perhaps the biggest loss to posterity is that wartime restrictions on materials prevented her from fulfilling her plan to record the whole of Bach's *Das wohltemperierte Klavier*.

JESSICA DOUGLAS-HOME

Sources J. Douglas-Home, *Violet, the life and loves of Violet Gordon Woodhouse* (1996) · O. Sitwell, *Noble essences* (1950) · E. Smyth, *As time went on* (1936) · E. Smyth, *What happened next* (1940) · private information (2004) · *WWW* · R. Luckett, disc notes, *Great virtuosi of the harpsichord*, 3 (Pavillion Records Ltd, Pearl, 1996) [GEMM CD 9242] · b. cert. · *CGPLA Eng. & Wales* (1948)
Archives archives of Reresby Sitwell, Renishaw, Derbyshire · Helmingham Archives, Suffolk · priv. coll. | SOUND BL NSA, interview recording · BL NSA, performance recordings · discography, *Recorded Sound*, 41 (1971), 772ff
Likenesses A. Langdon Coburn, photograph, *c*.1913, Knights Mill, Quenington, Gloucestershire · R. Fry, oil sketch, 1922, priv. coll. · A. Dechaume, pastel drawing, *c*.1930, Knights Mill, Quenington, Gloucestershire · H. Lambert, three photographs, *c*.1940, Knights Mill, Quenington, Gloucestershire · H. Lambert & Fry, photograph, 1944, NPG [*see illus.*]
Wealth at death £26,234 18s. 3d.: probate, 13 Sept 1948, *CGPLA Eng. & Wales*

Woodhouse, Sir William (*b.* in or before **1517**, *d.* **1564**), naval commander and administrator, was the second son of John Woodhouse of Waxham in Norfolk and Alice, the daughter of William Croft of Thorpe Market. Sir Thomas Woodhouse was his elder brother. As William's first service was as escheator of Norfolk and Suffolk in 1538–9, he must by then have been twenty-one. Nothing is known of his upbringing or education, but from the fact that he was a younger son, took to the sea, and was subsequently a member of the St George's Company of Norwich, it may

be presumed that he was apprenticed to a Norwich merchant. In 1542 he commanded one of the king's ships against Scotland. In December 1543 he was in command of the *Primrose*, a 240 ton, middle-ranking warship, and in 1544 had been promoted to the 300 ton *Minion*. He was knighted at Leith by the earl of Hertford in May of that year, and by the early part of 1545 was admiral of the narrow seas under Viscount Lisle as lord admiral, flying his flag on the *Great Bark* of 500–600 tons. When the council for marine causes was established in 1546 he was appointed master of the naval ordnance, with a salary of 100 marks a year.

In May 1541 Woodhouse was granted various minor offices in and around King's Lynn, and was described as the king's servant. It is clear that he was building up a substantial landed estate around Hickling in his native county, by grants and preferential purchases of former ecclesiastical lands. He bought the priory of Igtham from its incumbent prior ahead of its dissolution in 1535, which is fair indication of the sharpness of his business sense, and received other substantial grants by purchase and exchange in 1542 and 1545. He also held the advowsons of several Norfolk churches. From 1546 to 1550 he was keeper of Queenborough Castle in Kent, and in December 1552 he became lieutenant of the admiralty, or viceadmiral, in succession to Sir Thomas Clere. He remained second in command of the navy for the remainder of his life. In the early part of Elizabeth's reign he was responsible for reorganizing and improving the system of 'shipkeeping', the provision of skeleton crews for ships laid up on a care and maintenance basis. He did not invent this idea, which had been in use since the early part of Henry VIII's reign, but after the loss of the ancient but imposing *Henry Grace à Dieu*, which was burnt at her moorings in 1553, it became obvious that security would have to be improved. He commanded the channel fleet when war broke out with France in 1557, and was at sea again in 1562, to clear the channel of pirates.

Woodhouse sat in the parliaments of 1545, 1547, and March 1553 for the borough of Great Yarmouth; as a burgess for Norwich in 1559; and as knight of the shire for Norfolk in 1558 and 1563. Rather surprisingly, he was not appointed to the commission of the peace until February 1554, but he served thereafter continuously until his death, being *custos rotulorum* from 1561. He was also a founder member of the Muscovy Company in 1555, a sign of his business links with London.

Woodhouse married twice. His first wife was Anne, daughter of Henry Repps of Thorpe Market. She had died by 1551 when he married Elizabeth, the daughter of Sir Philip Calthorpe, and widow of Sir Henry Parker. It looks very much as though his second marriage was a direct result of his improved wealth and status. According to the heraldic visitation of 1563, the children of his first marriage were Anne, Mary, Thomas, and Henry, and of his second Thomas, William, and Elizabeth, from which it may be deduced that the first Thomas did not survive infancy. He died on 22 November 1564, and was buried in Hickling church, where what is alleged to be his monument remains, although all the inscriptions are defaced. His brother, Sir Thomas, continued to occupy the family seat at Waxham, where he died in 1571, and his rather grander tomb (which does have an inscription) survives.

DAVID LOADES

Sources CPR, 1547–1601 · F. Blomefield and C. Parkin, An essay towards a topographical history of the county of Norfolk, [2nd edn], 11 vols. (1805–10) · W. Rye, ed., The visitacion of Norffolk … 1563 … 1613, Harleian Society, 32 (1891) · HoP, Commons, 1509–58, vol. 3 · T. Glasgow, 'Vice Admiral Woodhouse and ship keeping the Tudor navy', Mariner's Mirror, 63 (1977), 253–63 · A. Hansell Smith, Community and court: government and politics in Norfolk, 1558–1603 (1974) · PRO, SP 1; SP 10; SP 11; SP 12 · PRO, E 150 · PRO, C 66

Woodhouselee. For this title name see Tytler, Alexander Fraser, Lord Woodhouselee (1747–1813).

Woodington, William Frederick (1806–1893), sculptor and painter, was born at Sutton Coldfield, Warwickshire, on 10 February 1806. He moved to London in 1815, and about 1820 was apprenticed to Robert William Sievier, who was at that time practising engraving but who shortly afterwards turned to sculpture, as did Woodington also. Early in his career he also worked for William Croggan, the successor to the firm which manufactured the artificial Coade stone. In 1825 Woodington first exhibited at the Royal Academy, and until 1882 was a frequent contributor of portrait busts, and figures and reliefs of biblical, mythological, and poetical subjects. He also exhibited at the Society of British Artists (1825, 1828) and the British Institution (1827, 1830, 1832). To the Westminster Hall exhibition of 1844 he sent two sculptural groups, The Deluge and Milton Dictating to his Daughters. Four years later he produced statues of William, earl of Arundel, and Hubert, earl of Kent, for the House of Lords.

In 1850 Woodington executed the work for which he is best-known—the bronze relief of the Battle of the Nile on the plinth of Nelson's Column in Trafalgar Square. The following year he was appointed curator of the Royal Academy School of Sculpture. In 1856 he made a colossal bust of Sir Joseph Paxton, architect of the Crystal Palace, for the Crystal Palace building, which was then situated at Sydenham, Kent. He was awarded second prize in 1857 in the competition for the Wellington monument in St Paul's Cathedral. Later, in 1861, he executed two of the reliefs on the walls of the consistory chapel in which the winning monument, the work of Alfred Stevens, was temporarily placed. His other notable commissions for architectural sculpture include the statues of Columbus, Galileo, Drake, Cook, Raleigh, and Mercator, and the pediment sculpture Wisdom Sending Forth her Messengers to the Nations of the Earth, all executed in 1867 for the Liverpool exchange (dem. 1937; location of sculptures unknown), and Plato, Archimedes, and Justinian for the civil service commission buildings in Burlington Gardens, London.

Woodington also practised painting, and frequently exhibited pictures. In 1853 he sent to the academy The Angels Directing the Shepherds to Bethlehem, in 1854 Job; his Three Friends Condole him in Silence, and in 1855 an illustration to Dante, A Vessel under Conduct of an Angel. In 1876 he

was elected an ARA. Woodington died at his house at Brixton, London, on 24 December 1893 and was buried in Norwood cemetery, London.

F. M. O'DONOGHUE, rev. MARTIN BARNES

Sources R. Gunnis, Dictionary of British sculptors, 1660–1851 (1953), 441–2 · Art Journal, new ser., 14 (1894), 61 · The Athenaeum (30 Dec 1893), 922 · Daily Chronicle [London] (27 Dec 1893) · The Times (27 Dec 1893) · T. Cavanagh, Public sculpture of Liverpool (1997), 301–2, 342 · B. Read, Victorian sculpture (1982), 22, 84, 90, 120, 226 · J. A. Mackay, The dictionary of western sculptors in bronze (1977), 397 · Thieme & Becker, Allgemeines Lexikon, 36.246–7 · Graves, RA exhibitors, 8 (1906), 345–6
Likenesses R. & E. Taylor, wood-engraving, NPG; repro. in ILN (13 May 1876)

Woodland, Austin William (1914–1990), geologist and geological administrator, was born on 4 April 1914 at 11 Cadwallader Street, Mountain Ash, Glamorgan, the eldest son of William Austin Woodland (1875–1971), a carpenter in the local colliery, and his wife, Sarah Jane Butler (1880–1928), and the brother of Bertram. He won scholarships to the local grammar school, and the University College of Wales, Aberystwyth, where he obtained first-class honours in geology in 1934 and a PhD in 1937 for a study of the manganese-bearing rocks of Merioneth that remains a standard reference. After two years in university teaching Woodland obtained the post he had long coveted, when in 1939 he was selected for the London staff of the Geological Survey of Great Britain. On 28 December that year he married Nesta Ann Phillips (1914–1981), a schoolteacher, whom he had met in university. She was the daughter of Lewis Phillips, schoolmaster.

Woodland's first assignments were to detail water resources in eastern England and to help assess the ironstone deposits of Northamptonshire. These routine tasks yielded unexpected scientific advances particularly in Suffolk, where he greatly extended the then known limits of the Crag and deduced the former presence of subglacial streams. It was in 1945, however, when he started the resurvey of his native coalfield, that he began the work that established his reputation as probably the foremost field geologist of his generation. When the mines were nationalized he became the main geological adviser to the National Coal Board in south Wales. His meticulous surface surveys led to a revised classification of the succession and to a recognition of major thrusting along the southern margin of the coalfield. His underground studies, which were much more thorough and protracted than was then usual, enabled him to produce a detailed correlation of the highly variable coal seams, leading to a proposed coalfield-wide nomenclature that was quickly adopted by the industry.

Ironically, Woodland's very success as a scientist spelled the end of his personal research, for in 1957 he was appointed to the first of many increasingly responsible administrative posts. Initially he supervised small teams of geologists in eastern England while playing a large part in establishing a northern base for the survey at Leeds. He moved there in 1959, became head of the station in 1962, and quickly gained a new reputation as a stimulating motivator and forward-looking administrator. He controlled all official geological surveys in northern England and north Wales and also set up a team to work on the continental shelf when interest in off-shore hydrocarbons was in its infancy. Leeds became the repository for all North Sea confidential records, and the new unit forged an invaluable link between central government and the oil industry. In 1971 Woodland returned to South Kensington as deputy director of the Institute of Geological Sciences (IGS), which had brought together the home and overseas geological surveys. He took over much of the administration of some 1100 staff, and particularly delighted in visiting and helping teams across the world. Later he planned the IGS's new national headquarters at Keyworth, near Nottingham. He was appointed CBE in 1975 and in 1976 became director of the IGS, a post he held until his retirement in 1979.

Woodland's official duties were coupled with service to learned societies and to innumerable national and international committees. He was president of the Yorkshire Geological Society and of Section C of the British Association, vice-president of the Geological Society of London, and secretary-general of the International Congress of Carboniferous Stratigraphy. He led the UK representations to a UN subcommittee on the peaceful uses of the sea bed, acted as geological adviser to the Aberfan disaster tribunal, headed the British delegation on the International Geological Correlation Programme, and sat on the Commission of the International Geological Map of Europe and the British National Committee for Geology and Geophysics.

Woodland's formative years in economically depressed Glamorgan led him to enter public service determined to ensure that geology should have an effective input to the national economy. His findings and maps were always immediately available to industry and government; this was at the cost of his publications, which do scant justice to the value of his work. His later writings explore the frontier between geology and its practical uses, but his most influential thinking in these years lies buried in the confidential files of the organizations he served. His especial strengths lay always in fieldwork, and he felt restive and unfulfilled when administrative duties precluded contact with those still active in the field. His approach to work and, indeed, to his hobbies (which included philately, gardening, and golf) could verge on the obsessional—he used to lunch on the move on the Welsh hillsides—but was tempered by the humour and good sense of his wife. He retired to Cardiff in 1979, and after a quiet retirement away from the tedium of committees died of cancer at Sully Hospital, Penarth, on 9 November 1990. He was cremated at Cardiff crematorium on 19 November. He and his wife had two children, Professor Hugh Woodland, a biologist, and Dr Jane Šik, a geophysicist.

W. B. EVANS

Sources BGS, records of the British Geological Survey · personal knowledge (2004) · J. Stubblefield, *Annual Report* [Geological Society of London] (1991), 33–4 · private information (2004) [family] · W. B. Evans, 'Austin William Woodland (1914–1990)', *Proceedings of the Yorkshire Geological Society*, 48 (1991), 345–6 · CGPLA Eng. & Wales (1990) · b. cert. · m. cert. · d. cert.
Likenesses photograph, 1976, BGS
Wealth at death £174,146: probate, 1990

Woodley, George (*bap.* **1786**, *d.* **1846**), poet and Church of England clergyman, was born in Dartmouth, and baptized at Townstal church there on 3 April 1786. He was the son of Richard Woodley. Woodley was largely self-taught, and began writing poetry aged eleven, while serving on a British man-of-war. After several years at sea, he lived at Plymouth Dock and then in London, trying to make a living as a writer. His first anthology, *Mt. Edgcumbe, with The Shipwreck, and Miscellaneous Verses*, was published anonymously in 1804. In that year, too, he competed for the gold medal of the Royal Humane Society for the best essay on the means of preventing shipwreck. Through a change of dates on the part of the society the essay arrived after the distribution of the prizes, but he claimed to have anticipated the invention of George William Manby. His lack of recognition here, and from the many authorities he approached with his scheme, left him lastingly bitter. His address to Dr Hawes (*GM*, 1st ser., 77, 1807, 1051–2) is dated from Dover.

In late 1808, Woodley left London for health reasons, and soon afterwards settled at Truro as editor of the *Royal Cornwall Gazette*, the tory paper of the county. Here he wrote poetry and some music, and competed for prize essays on theological and social subjects. *The Churchyard and other Poems* (1808) was followed in 1812, while he was living at Park Street in Plymouth, by *Portugal Delivered*. In the postscript to this work, he commented 'I can sit down, if not with perfect resignation, yet with some sort of lethargic acquiescence, under the cloud which is permitted to overshadow me'. Several of his better-known works were published soon afterwards: *Redemption* (1816); *Cornubia* (1819); and his only work to run to two editions, *The Divinity of Christ Proved* (1819; 2nd edn, 1821), for which essay he also received a prize of £50 from the Society for Promoting Christian Knowledge. The *Gazetteer of the County of Cornwall*, published at Truro about 1817, has been attributed to Woodley.

About June 1820 Woodley was ordained by the bishop of Exeter, and went to the Isles of Scilly as a missionary of the Society for Promoting Christian Knowledge, earning £150 per annum, on the islands of St Martins and St Agnes. He was ordained priest by Bishop Carey in Exeter Cathedral on 15 July 1821. During his years at Scilly, he rebuilt the church on St Martins, and restored that on St Agnes. Probably also in this period, he married a Mary Fabian at Stoke Damerel, and they had one son, William Augustus. Woodley published a well regarded *View of the Present State of the Scilly Isles* in 1822.

In June 1842 Woodley retired with a gratuity of £100 and a life pension of £75 per annum. He was appointed on 12 February 1843 to the perpetual curacy of Martindale in Westmorland which he held until his death there on 24 December 1846. His wife died at Taunton in August 1856.

Their son was the proprietor of the *Somerset County Gazette* (Taunton) and other papers; he died in Bristol, on 11 March 1891, and was buried in St Mary's cemetery, Taunton.

W. P. COURTNEY, *rev.* JESSICA HININGS

Sources G. Woodley, *Portugal delivered* (1812) · *GM*, 2nd ser., 28 (1847), 144 · *GM*, 1st ser., 77 (1807), 1051–2 · Boase & Courtney, *Bibl. Corn.*, vol. 2 · *N&Q*, 3rd ser., 3 (1863), 399 · W. O. B. Allen, *Two hundred years: the history of the Society for Promoting Christian Knowledge, 1698–1898* (1898) · private information (1900) · admin, Westmorland, June, 1847, PROB 6/223, fol. 46
Archives BL, letters to Royal Literary Fund, Loan 96
Wealth at death see administration, PRO, PROB 6/223, fol. 46

Woodlock [*née* Mahony], **Ellen** [*name in religion* Hélène] (1811–1884), philanthropist, was born on 27 January 1811 in Cork, the daughter of a wealthy woollen merchant, Martin Mahony, and his wife, Mary Reynolds. The family were strong financial supporters of the newly emerging Roman Catholic religious communities of women during the early nineteenth century. It seems likely that Ellen was educated in France, as was her brother Francis *Mahony (1804–1866), who later became famous as a writer under the pseudonym Father Prout. Little is known of her early life or of her marriage in 1830 to Thomas Woodlock, which ended when she was widowed about 1834. The couple had one son, Timothy, born shortly after the death of Thomas.

It appears that Ellen Woodlock spent the years following her husband's death in France and played some role in establishing the congregation of Les Dames de Saint Louis in 1842. By 1843 she was herself living as a sister in its convent at Juilly, her name in religion being Sœur Hélène; her son was educated by the sisters in a school nearby. She returned to Cork on three occasions to recruit members for the newly formed congregation. By 1851, however, she had been dispensed from her vows: it appears that she was considered 'eccentric' by members of the community. She herself was no longer attracted to the teaching mission of the St Louis congregation and wished to engage in a more active form of philanthropy; her interest was primarily in the care of children.

On returning to Cork, Woodlock established an industrial school in the city in 1851. She became an important figure in the Irish industrial and reformatory school movement. In 1852 she moved to Dublin, where she became a close friend of the writer and philanthropist Sarah Atkinson (1823–1893), and organized St Joseph's Industrial Institute in 1856. Here she took girls from the workhouse and attempted to provide them with skills to earn an independent living. She was a close friend of John Lentaigne, then director of government prisons in Ireland, and was strongly supported by him in her attempts to encourage the spread of industrial and reformatory schools. In 1858 she was instrumental in bringing members of the St Louis congregation to Monaghan to open a reformatory school, and in 1861 she gave evidence before a House of Commons select committee on poor relief in Ireland, where she spoke of the need to have children removed from the contaminating influences of the workhouse. She also took part in the Social Science Congress

meeting held in Dublin in 1861, and with Sarah Atkinson spoke on the condition of children in the workhouses.

Together with other Catholic philanthropists Woodlock formed a children's hospital in Dublin in 1873; it was handed over to the Sisters of Charity in 1876 and was later known as Temple Street Children's Hospital. Woodlock was part of a small group of lay Catholic philanthropists who supported the work of convents through raising funds and initiating enterprises which were later given to the care of nuns. Her friendship with Charles Bianconi (1786–1875), the successful promoter of the Irish car system, for example, encouraged him to give £12,000 to the St Louis sisters in Monaghan to purchase buildings for their reformatory. Woodlock was also among the first group of lay Catholics to engage in workhouse visiting in the 1860s. She died after a short illness at the home of her son, 8 Sydney Place, Cork, on 13 July 1884, and was buried in St Joseph's cemetery in the city. MARIA LUDDY

Sources M. Russell, 'Mrs Ellen Woodlock, an admirable Irishwoman of the last century', *Irish Monthly*, 36 (1908), 171–6 · *Weekly Register* (26 July 1884) · M. Pauline, *God wills it! Centenary story of the Sisters of St Louis* (1959) · *DNB*
Archives Archives of the St Louis Convent, Monaghan

Woodman, Mrs (*fl.* 1768–1789). *See under* Woodham, Mrs (*d.* 1803).

Woodman, Richard (*c.*1525–1557), protestant martyr, was born at Buxted, Sussex. Little is known of his parents, except that they were not married and his father was still alive in 1557. By the beginning of Mary's reign he was a prosperous iron maker, living in the parish of Warbleton, Sussex, where he employed a hundred workers. At the beginning of 1554 Woodman publicly admonished the rector of Warbleton for backsliding from the protestant doctrines he had preached during Edward VI's reign, and was consequently arrested, not for heresy, but for a violation of a statute (1 Mary c. 3) forbidding the harassment of authorized preachers performing their duties. Woodman was brought before two quarter sessions and imprisoned after each, following his refusal to offer sureties for future good behaviour. A visit from George Day, bishop of Chichester, failed to dent Woodman's obduracy and, in June 1554, he was sent to Edmund Bonner, bishop of London. This was a move of dubious legality, as Bonner had no conceivable jurisdiction over Woodman; nevertheless Woodman was imprisoned in the king's bench until November 1555.

During this time Woodman seems to have been involved in the disputes over predestination which were raging among the protestant prisoners in the king's bench. In June 1555 he wrote a confession of faith in response to 'certayne slaunders risen up againste me for certayne opinions that I should hold'. The confession went on to proclaim Woodman's belief in the Trinity, to denounce the pope as Antichrist, praise the Edwardian homilies as 'godly and sounde doctrine', defend infant baptism, and attack the Anabaptists, while endorsing the teachings of Thomas Cranmer and other protestant luminaries on the sacrament (Gonville and Caius MS 218; the confession is dated 1552 which must be a scribal error). The most likely explanation for this statement of orthodoxy is that Woodman was accused by anti-predestinarian protestants of holding Catholic and Anabaptist views, and that he wrote the confession to deny such charges. This hypothesis is confirmed by the fact that Woodman's confession was signed by John Philpot, John Careless, William Tyms, and other leading predestinarian protestants. Woodman was undeniably associated with Philpot, writing to him after the latter's transfer from the king's bench to imprisonment in Bonner's London palace; the letter survives in Emmanuel College, Cambridge MS 260, (fol. 171r).

In November 1555 Woodman was himself incarcerated in Bonner's palace. When examined by the bishop he defended himself by pointing out that the rector of Warbleton had been married and thus officially deprived of his benefice. As the statute which Woodman was accused of violating specified that it was a crime to harass an authorized minister, technically Woodman had not broken the law. When Woodman produced thirty witnesses to swear to the rector's married status, the charges against him were dropped and he was released on 18 December 1555. Once free Woodman and two other prisoners released along with him tried unsuccessfully to reconcile the feuding protestant prisoners in the king's bench. Woodman then returned to Sussex where he became an itinerant lay preacher. He later denied allegations that he conducted baptisms and marriages, but he admitted to writing and distributing letters denouncing the Catholic clergy. Woodman's activities created a local uproar and warrants were issued for his arrest. He went into hiding and then fled overseas, but soon returned home, where further attempts were made to arrest him. He eluded his pursuers, however, until his brother, with whom he had had financial disagreements, informed the authorities when the fugitive returned home to visit his family.

Woodman was arrested at his home and held by Sir Edward Gage, the sheriff of Sussex, for three weeks. Woodman insisted that he be tried by his ordinary (as was required for cases of heresy by 2 Henry IV c. 15) and on 12 April 1557 he was sent to London. On 14 April he was examined by John Christopherson, the bishop-designate of Chichester, and was re-examined by him on 27 April, but Christopherson, perceiving that Woodman was unlikely to recant, refused to examine him formally. (Christopherson had not yet been consecrated as bishop, and until consecrated he could not condemn Woodman.) On 25 May Woodman was examined by John White, bishop of Winchester. Woodman, however, maintained that White had no authority to examine him as the bishop of Winchester was not his ordinary. On 15 June he was examined again by White, with Nicholas Harpsfield, the archdeacon of Canterbury, assisting, and Woodman again denying that White had any jurisdiction over him. The next day Woodman was once more brought before White and Harpsfield. Woodman again insisted that he could be tried only by his ordinary, but this time the authorities were ready for him.

Woodman was informed that Cardinal Reginald Pole had appointed Harpsfield to act as Woodman's ordinary. Woodman was condemned and subsequently burnt at Lewes, with nine other martyrs, on 22 June 1557. Foxe gave his age at death as 'thirty years and somewhat more' (Foxe, 1602). Woodman was married, and spoke of his wife many times, particularly in his account of his arrest in 1557, but gave no further details.

Woodman provides an excellent example of the pastoral authority which zealous lay people exercised in the Marian protestant communities. Sir Edward Gage told Woodman that all the heretics in Sussex 'hung on me, as people did in times past upon St Augustine or St Ambrose' (Foxe, 1578), while Woodman's letter to Mrs Roberts, printed by Foxe, reveals his role as a leader of the protestant congregations in east Sussex.

THOMAS S. FREEMAN

Sources J. Foxe, *The second volume of the ecclesiasticall history, conteyning the acts and monuments of martyrs*, 2nd edn (1570), 2171–96 · J. Foxe, *Actes and monuments* (1563), 1571–602 · Gon. & Caius Cam., MS 218, 28–41 · BL, Harley MS 425, fol. 104r–v · BL, Harley MS 425, fols. 104v–105r · Woodman, to John Philpot, Emmanuel College, Cambridge, MS 260, fol. 171r · M. T. Pearse, *Between known men and visible saints: a study in sixteenth-century English dissent* (1994), 78–9

Woodman, Richard (1784–1859), engraver and portrait painter, was born on 1 July 1784, the son of an obscure London stipple engraver of the same name who flourished between 1780 and 1810. He was educated at the Philological School, Marylebone, and was then apprenticed in 1799 to the stipple engraver Robert Mitchell Meadows; here he was taught colouring by a fellow pupil, the watercolourist James Holmes. After completing his apprenticeship he worked for Richard Westall, colouring reproductions of his watercolours, before taking up, about 1807, a brief post as superintendent of the engraving department at Wedgwood's factory at Etruria, Staffordshire. On his return to London he first made a living producing watercolour copies for fellow engravers and as a miniaturist. Later he established himself as a versatile reproductive engraver for the book trade, working on steel and copper plates, and in stipple, aquatint, and etching. In 1809 he married Anne, the daughter of the sculptor Charles Horwell.

The market for sporting scenes and portraits provided Woodman with a regular source of employment. He was a frequent contributor to the *Sporting Magazine*, and he produced a number of stipple portraits of sportsmen, such as the jockey *Samuel Chifney the Younger*, after Benjamin Marshall (1828). He also engraved traditional sporting views, including *The Earl of Derby's Stag Hounds*, after James Barenger (1823), as well as light-hearted scenes such as *Eight Representations of Shooting*, a set of hand-coloured aquatints published in 1813.

Woodman exhibited twelve works at the Royal Academy between 1820 and 1840, miniatures and small watercolour portraits, and this work increasingly engaged his attention. However, it was as a reproductive engraver of portraits that he primarily made his living. Following in the footsteps of his master, Woodman produced numerous small-scale stipples for the book trade, particularly of actors in parts, including many after Samuel De Wilde. He also engraved portraits of historical characters on steel for Wright's *Gallery of Engravings* (1844–6) and *The Imperial Dictionary* and more complex figure subjects, sometimes in line. He produced plates for *Knight's Pictorial Gallery of Arts* (2 vols., 1858–60) and was praised for his engraving after Rubens's *Judgment of Paris*.

Woodman was a founder member of the Artists' Annuity Fund in 1810 and served as president in 1838–9. He was survived at his death in London on 15 December 1859, precipitated by a fall outside the National Gallery, by four children, among them Charles Horwell Woodman (1823–1888) and Richard Horwell Woodman (*fl.* 1835–1868), who both followed their father's trade. Examples of Woodman's work are in the department of prints and drawings at the British Museum and the Victoria and Albert Museum, London. GREG SMITH

Sources B. Hunnisett, *An illustrated dictionary of British steel engravers*, new edn (1989), 163 · R. K. Engen, *Dictionary of Victorian engravers, print publishers and their works* (1979) · Graves, *RA exhibitors* · IGI · DNB · *The exhibition of the Royal Academy* [exhibition catalogues]

Woodroffe, Benjamin (1638–1711), college head, was born in Canditch Street in the parish of St Mary Magdalen, Oxford, in April 1638, the son of the Revd Timothy Woodroffe (1593/4–1677). His father gained preferment under the parliamentarian authorities, and was installed as vicar of Kingsland, Herefordshire, in 1648 in place of the ejected minister, William Hughes; he appears to have continued to hold the living after the Restoration. Benjamin Woodroffe was educated at Westminster School and matriculated at Christ Church, Oxford, on 23 July 1656. He graduated BA on 1 November 1659, proceeded MA on 17 June 1662, and was incorporated at Cambridge in 1664. From 1662 he was listed as a tutor at Christ Church. In early 1668 he was elected as a university proctor while a fellow of Balliol College, but his election was referred to the king and privy council, who remitted the case to the university, where convocation found against him.

From the beginning of his academic career Woodroffe showed an interest in the new science. In April 1663 he studied chemistry at Oxford under Peter Staehl of Strasbourg, along with Anthony Wood, John Locke, and John Wallis. He was admitted a fellow of the Royal Society in May 1668; he was expelled from the society for non-payment of fees, but reappeared on its lists between 1698 and 1702.

Woodroffe cultivated close contacts with James, duke of York (the future James II), who appointed him chaplain in 1669. He served with the duke in the engagement with the Dutch off Southwold on 28 May 1672, publishing a Latin poem commemorating the sea battle, 'Somnium navale', in 1673. His political connections saw him advance steadily up the church hierarchy. He became lecturer to the Temple in November 1672 and, through the duke's influence, was installed canon of Christ Church on 17 December of that year. On 14 January 1673 he was created BD and

DD, and later in the year was instituted vicar of Piddle Hinton in Dorset. He resigned this post in 1674 when he was made subdean of Christ Church and appointed chaplain to the king. By this time Woodroffe was a regular preacher in Oxford although, according to Humphrey Prideaux, his sermons were the subject of some mirth owing to his supposed practice of recycling material from one sermon to use in another. In 1675 he was appointed to the vicarage of Shrivenham, Berkshire, on the nomination of Sir Heneage Finch (later first earl of Nottingham), whose sons he had tutored at Christ Church. Prideaux claimed that he had got the living at the expense of the poor Oxford scholar Richard Peers, though the charge seems to be a case of academic sour grapes, as it appears that Prideaux had been in competition with Woodroffe to educate the Finch children.

Woodroffe's marriage on 16 November 1676 to Dorothy Stonehouse (*b. c.*1653) of Besselsleigh, Berkshire, who brought with her a reputed fortune of £3000, allowed him to move into a house in Knightsbridge, nearer to the court. His metropolitan connections were further reinforced by the acquisition of the living of St Bartholomew by the Exchange on 19 April 1676. He held this preferment, along with his canonries at Christ Church and at Lichfield (to which he was collated on 21 September 1678), until his death. He published loyal sermons to Charles II and to James II in 1685. From 1684 to 1687 he was president of Sion College, reflecting his prominence among London Anglican divines. In 1685 he was rumoured to be a possible candidate for the bishopric of Oxford, but this did not fall his way. None the less James II continued to favour him, nominating him as dean of Christ Church on 8 December 1688. However, Woodroffe was not installed and Henry Aldrich was appointed to the deanery in his stead.

In spite of his close links to James, Woodroffe appears to have conformed at the revolution of 1688. In 1690 he published *The Fall of Babylon* to attest to his loyalty and refute allegations that he was popishly inclined. The book, which he dedicated to William III, identified the Roman Catholic church as the Antichrist and predicted its downfall in 1696. Woodroffe claimed that he had written the work in 1686, reproducing two letters from that year, one from the printers rejecting the book, and another from him to James II, admonishing the king for his attachment to the Catholic faith. Given the continued favour shown to Woodroffe by James, and the cleric's own habit of forging correspondence, it seems unlikely that these letters were genuine. Woodroffe became closely allied with the whig party, gaining personal audiences with William III and later preaching sermons in praise of the duke of Marlborough.

Woodroffe's loyalty to the new regime was rewarded with his becoming principal of Gloucester Hall, Oxford, on 15 August 1692, though by this stage it was an institution in decay. Woodroffe promoted scientific learning at the hall, giving the future mineral-master general, Moses Stringer, a post as lecturer in chemistry there. As part of the regeneration of the hall, Woodroffe pursued the idea of attracting to it Greek students taken to England by advocates of reunion with the Orthodox church. In 1697 he began building a large house to be called the Greek College (later known derisively as 'Woodroffe's folly'). The cost of the college was mainly borne by Woodroffe himself, though he received some money from the crown. By February 1699 it had five Greek students, a total that afterwards rose to ten. However, two of the students ran away, claiming that a third of their number, Stephen Constantine, had whisked them off as part of a papal mission to convert them to Catholicism. (It is more likely that their flight was a result of the poor conditions at the college.)

As part of his efforts to regenerate Gloucester Hall Woodroffe had made an unsuccessful attempt in 1697 to have it incorporated by the university as a college. He renewed his efforts in 1698 with the news that the Worcestershire baronet Sir Thomas Cookes, prompted by the archbishop of Canterbury, John Tillotson, intended to make a bequest of £10,000 for the endowment of a college. Woodroffe quickly drew up charters and statutes for the projected Worcester College. As in his plans for the Greek college, provision was made in the curriculum for the study of mathematics, philosophy, anatomy, chemistry, and botany. Although the charter and statutes were approved in October and November of 1698 they were later shown to be legally invalid. Cookes broke off negotiations with Woodroffe, upset at a concession made to the duke of Ormond, then chancellor of the university, which granted him, not Cookes and his heirs, the sole right to appoint future provosts of the college. These problems allowed another interested college, Balliol, to enter the fray. A bitter dispute over Cookes's legacy ensued, exacerbated by the wider struggle over political supremacy in the university, with tories favouring Balliol's claims and whigs those of Gloucester Hall.

Both Woodroffe and John Baron, master of Balliol, preached sycophantic sermons to the trustees of Cookes's school at Feckenham, Worcestershire. Baron and his supporter John Ince urged that Sir Thomas should not endow a college located in such a 'viscious and scandalous neighbourhood' as that occupied by Gloucester Hall (*The Case of Gloucester Hall*, 8). Woodroffe in turn drew up charters for Worcester College which he falsely claimed had the approval of Cookes and bought land for the new college without the baronet's consent. In the end the efforts of both men proved counter-productive, Cookes at one point saying that he would rather the money went to a workhouse.

Although the issue of the appointment of provosts was finally settled in Cookes's favour the baronet never changed his will, and following his death in 1701 the endowment was administered by a board of trustees. Acting under the patronage of Tillotson and Lord Chancellor Somers, Woodroffe introduced a private bill to the Lords in February 1702 to sanction his statutes and charter and change the board of trustees to favour the hall. He lost this action, but the dispute over Cookes's endowment would continue until well after his death. Gloucester Hall finally became Worcester College in 1714, ironically as a result of the high tory influence of Lord Harcourt, who hoped to use the college as a means to increase his family's interest in the university.

Woodroffe's scientific interests were frequently linked to his, largely unsuccessful, commercial ventures. In 1702 he, Moses Stringer, and Captain John Poyntz produced a petition to form a company for the island of Tobago, although nothing seems to have come of this. It was probably his interest in chemistry which led Woodroffe to become the owner of a rock salt mine in Cheshire, an enterprise which soon became a financial burden to him. In 1705 and 1707 Stringer printed letters to Woodroffe to help promote his 'elixir renovans', a supposed cure for old age and gout. Despite their long-standing academic and commercial relationship Woodroffe was one of nine men fined in September 1710 for attempting to get Stringer ousted from his official posts.

Woodroffe ended his life heavily in debt. His second wife, Mary Marbury, was the sister and one of three coheirs of William and Richard Marbury. Woodroffe attempted to buy the £19,000 estate of Marbury in 1705 but could not complete the purchase, losing two actions over the estate in the House of Lords. He was in debt from the expenses he had incurred over the Greek college (some £2000 he claimed) and owed £600 in salt duties. One John Harrington claimed that Woodroffe had not paid him for work done in St Bartholomew. Woodroffe was incarcerated for a time in the Fleet prison and an attempt was made to sequestrate his canonry at Christ Church in April 1709, but the dean and chapter successfully disputed the court's jurisdiction.

Woodroffe died in London on 17 August 1711 and was buried two days later in his own vault in St Bartholomew's Church. There is a portrait of him in the provost's lodging at Worcester College. Woodroffe gathered little praise from his contemporaries, Prideaux describing him as a 'man of a maggoty [whimsical] brain, and a singular method of conduct from all mankind besides' (Daniel and Barker, 129), but he was respected for his learning in ancient and modern languages. Moreover, although his methods were often unorthodox, not to say deceitful, it was his persistence, vision, and careful cultivation of gentry contacts which, to a considerable degree, assured the creation of Worcester College.   EDWARD VALLANCE

Sources A. H. Barrett, 'Benjamin Woodroffe of the Greek college', *Oxoniensia*, 53 (1988), 317–37 • L. M. Sutherland, 'The foundation of Worcester College, Oxford', *Oxoniensia*, 44 (1979), 62–80 • C. H. Daniel and W. R. Barker, *Worcester College* (1900), 129–233 • J. H. Appleby, 'Moses Stringer (fl. 1695–1713), iatrochemist and mineral master general', *Ambix*, 34 (1987), 31–45 • *DNB* • *Letters of Humphrey Prideaux … to John Ellis*, ed. E. M. Thompson, CS, new ser., 15 (1875) • *Walker rev.* • M. Hunter, *The Royal Society and its fellows, 1660–1700: the morphology of an early scientific institution*, 2nd edn (1994), 271, no. 9 • C. J. S. Thompson, *The quacks of old London* (New York, 1993), 248–50 • J. Redington, ed., *Calendar of Treasury papers*, 3, PRO (1874), 42, 207–9, 362, 399, 407 • *The case of Gloucester Hall in Oxford* (1702) • *Hist. U. Oxf.*, vol. 4, pp. 270, 428n., 523; vol. 5 • W. B. Bannerman, ed., *The registers of St Martin Outwich, London*, Harleian Society, 32 (1905) • J. L. Chester and J. Foster, eds., *London marriage licences, 1521–1869* (1887) • will, U. Oxf., chancellor's court wills, vol. W–Y, Hyp/B/21 • complaints of John Harrington, Bodl. Oxf., MS Rawl. B. 381, fols. 59, 61 • Foster, *Alum. Oxon.*

Archives Balliol Oxf., Ince papers, corresp. relating to foundation of Worcester College, Oxford · Bodl. Oxf., material relating to his position at St Bartholomew's, MSS Rawl. · Hunt. L., letters to Hastings family · Worcester College, Oxford, letters to Hastings family, MS 209
Likenesses R. White, line engraving, 1700, BM; repro. in B. Woodroffe, *Examinis et examinantis* (1700) · oils, Worcester College, Oxford
Wealth at death heavily in debt: petitions to queen, *Calendar of treasury papers*; *JHL*; *DNB*; will, Oxf. UA, chancellor's court wills, vol. W–Y, Hyp/B/21

Woodroffe, Sir John George (1865–1936), judge and tantric scholar, was born on 15 December 1865, the eldest son of James Tisdall Woodroffe, a lawyer, and his wife, Florence Hume. After completing his schooling in Woburn Park School, Surrey, he studied at University College, Oxford, and was awarded a second-class degree in jurisprudence. In 1889 he was called to the bar at the Inner Temple.

Like his father, who had been the advocate-general of Bengal and legal member of the government of India, Woodroffe opted to serve in India and enrolled as an advocate in the Calcutta high court in 1890. His contribution to enriching legal knowledge in India was aptly acknowledged when Calcutta University elected him the Tagore law professor for 1896–7 and made him a fellow. The government of India appointed him as the standing counsel in 1902. He was elevated to the bench of the Calcutta high court in 1904, and he held the high office with distinction for the next eighteen years. In 1905 Woodroffe married Ellen Elizabeth, daughter of S. D. Grimson; they had a son and a daughter. In 1915 he became the chief justice of Bengal and was knighted. After retiring from the judicial service in 1923, he served as reader in Indian law for seven years at Oxford University.

Woodroffe wrote a number of authoritative legal texts on civil and criminal law. With the Indian jurist Ameer Ali he compiled *Law of Evidence Applicable to British India* (1898) and *Civil Procedure in British India: a Commentary on Act V of 1908* (1908). Based on S. L. Phipson's *Law of Evidence*, the former contained both explications of clauses of the Indian Evidence Act and commentaries on it. Sir John's *Criminal procedure in British India (being a commentary on Act V of 1898 as amended up to date)* (1926) was an impressive treatise on both procedural and substantive criminal law in British India. His Tagore law lectures, published as *The Law Relating to Receivers in British India* (1900) and *The Law Relating to Injunctions in British India* (1919), long remained standard reference works.

Like William Jones, Sir John had an abiding interest in promoting oriental learning. With an unusual mastery of Sanskrit he enriched the understanding of Hindu philosophy, especially the Shakta school of thought which believes in the worship of the divine power (Mahashakti) as the Great Mother Mahadevi of the universe. Many of his commentaries on Tantra, a branch of the Shakta philosophy, were published under the pseudonym Arthur Avalon. In *Shakti and Shakta: Essays and Addresses on the Shakta Tantrashastra* (1918) he demonstrated that Shaktaism was neither irrational nor obscurantist. Sir John claimed this

Sir John George Woodroffe (1865–1936), by Lafayette, 1928

work to be Shakta doctrine's first British account from an Indian standpoint. In *Mahamaya: the World as Power: Power as Consciousness* (1929) Sir John joined co-author Pramatha Natha Mukkhayopadhyay to show how the doctrine of Shakti offered an alternative conception of consciousness to western philosophy. He criticized the 'racial and credal bias' of those European scholars who used 'exaggerated' Christian notions of 'universal piety and morals' to characterize Hinduism as 'the most puerile, impure and bloody of any system of idolatry'. Instead, in *Principles of Tantra*, part 1, in *The Serpent Power* (1919), and in the commentaries for the Tantric Text Series, he underlined Tantra as 'the great Mantra and Sadhana Shastra (Scripture)' wherein lay the source of fundamental concepts concerning 'worship, images, initiation, yoga'. In his foreword to *The Tibetan Book of the Dead* (1927) Woodroffe explained the science of death in the context of Tibetan Mahyana Buddhism. His *The Garland of Letters* (1922) was an interesting collection of studies in Mantra-Shastra, a term commonly applied to Tantra-Shastra.

Sir John sought oriental knowledge to unravel the racial, religious, and political presuppositions that underlay Britain's cultural conquest of India. Like many orientalists he exposed the basic fallacies within European critique of Indian culture written from a 'rationalist' standpoint. He juxtaposed western materialism to Indian spiritualism, but was confident that the Indian spirit, shaped by ideas and instincts of thousands of years, would assert themselves. Not unnaturally, a work by Kathleen Taylor, *Sir John Woodroffe, Tantra and Bengal* (2001), has described Sir John in its subtitle as 'an Indian soul in a European body'. But it is doubtful if he could impress upon the English audience his positive impressions of Indian civilization; for 'most hearers found it difficult to follow him in the bewildering mazes of the subject' (*The Times*). However, Woodroffe's glorification of Indian spiritualism was itself a part of the colonial sociology of knowledge. His characterization of the Indian civilization as essentially spiritual and primarily Hindu (Woodroffe, xii) undermined both the material and eclectic aspects of Indian culture.

Sir John Woodroffe died on 16 January 1936 at the Villa Aurelia, boulevard du Tenas, Beausoleil, Alpes Maritimes, France. He was survived by his wife.

SUPARNA GOOPTU

Sources A. Avalon [J. G. Woodroffe], ed., *Principles of Tantra*, pt 1 (1914) • W. W. Evans-Wentz, *The Tibetan book of the dead* (1927) • *The Times* (18 Jan 1936) • J. Woodroffe, *Is India civilized? Essays on Indian culture* (1918) • *CGPLA Eng. & Wales* (1936) • d. cert. • K. Taylor, *Sir John Woodroffe, Tantra and Bengal: an Indian soul in a European body* (2001)
Archives BL OIOC, MS Eur. F 285 | CUL, corresp. with Lord Hardinge
Likenesses Lafayette, photograph, 1928, NPG [*see illus.*] • photograph, repro. in *The Times*
Wealth at death £6473 15s. 1d.: probate, 5 March 1936, *CGPLA Eng. & Wales*

Woodrooffe [*née* Cox], **Anne** (1766–1830), author, only child of John Cox of Harwich, was born on 14 July 1766. She married Nathaniel George Woodrooffe (1764/5–1851), a clergyman and graduate of St Edmund Hall, Oxford, on 27 July 1803 at Streatham. That same year they moved to Somerford Keynes, Wiltshire, where her husband held the living until his death on 30 October 1851. Emma Martha, who married, aged forty-five, in the February after her father's death, was the only one of their three children to survive infancy.

Anne Woodrooffe's religious poetry (new edn, 1855) was unremarkable, but, given its primary aim of conveying the Christian message, her prose fiction was remarkable in its day for the lightness of touch and technical skill with which incident and character were developed. *The History of Michael Kemp, the Happy Farmer's Lad* (1819) explored the practical trials of conscience faced by a sincere Christian boy, from a labouring background, trying to make his way in the world. Although the book was aimed at the classes from which the hero came, sermonizing authorial commentary is kept to a minimum: instead the reader is offered detailed accounts of specific situations in which consulting the Bible and one's conscience can resolve the daily dilemmas of attempting to lead a Christian life. The hero's total probity results in his rise to the rank of tenant farmer, and the sequel, *Michael the Married Man* (1827), reflects the economic and social problems that accompany this transition in class. The role of exemplary parish clergymen in offering both a model and encouragement is also stressed. The characterization of good-hearted but foolish mothers, largely through dialogue, owes something to Jane Austen, but is perfectly adapted to the appropriate social class.

Prompted by the success of her first work and 'encouraged by an Essex clergyman', Anne Woodrooffe wrote *Cottage Dialogues* (1821) 'to entertain and improve the Lower Classes, who form so numerous and valuable a portion of our *growing*, and (we may add) our *reading* population' (*Cottage Dialogues*, 1821, preface). As in her other work, the structure is episodic, and in this case mingles events from the church's and the agricultural year. As indicated by the title, the message is embedded in a form most closely resembling drama, where, after a passage of scene setting, dialogue, often in dialect form, predominates. Country songs are also recorded. A second edition (1856) offered an

extra four 'dialogues' exploring such practical problems as the need, when setting up a parish school, to establish the schoolmistress's authority with the pupils' parents: Anne's husband and Squire Foyle had set up a village school in 1804.

Anne Woodrooffe's next book, *Shades of character, or, Mental and moral delineations designed to promote the formation of the female character on the basis of Christian principle* (2 vols., 1824; 7th edn, 1855), also relied largely upon dialogue and a series of domestic incidents to remodel the *Pilgrim's Progress* to suit the moral concerns of upper-middle-class girls at school and in the wider world. This work was also the reflection of a practical concern: she established a finishing school for girls at the vicarage where the boarders were educated according to the principles outlined in her book, which was said to contain a self-portrait in the character of Mrs E. Groves, who shared her unselfish concern for her immediate circle and the poorest of the parishioners. The frontispiece engravings of the Woodrooffe residence and Somerford Keynes church may have served as an additional advertisement for the enterprise. The religious tenor of the establishment can be gauged by the decision of Bishop Daniel Wilson of Calcutta, a militant evangelical, to entrust his only daughter to her, possibly on his wife's death in 1827.

Anne Woodrooffe died at Somerford Keynes vicarage on 24 March 1830 after 'an illness of only three days'. She was buried in the churchyard at Somerford Keynes, and in 1836 her husband, her grateful former pupils, and their friends renewed the east window of the church in her memory.

ELISABETH JAY

Sources preface, A. Woodrooffe, *Shades of character, or, Mental and moral delineations designed to promote the formation of the female character on the basis of Christian principle*, 2 vols., 4th edn (1841) • S. M. Woodrooffe, *Pedigree of Woodrooffe, with memorials and notes* (1878) • *Bath and Cheltenham Gazette* (30 March 1830) • R. G. Gibbon, 'Parson Woodrooffe' [in possession of the churchwardens of Somerford Keynes] • *GM*, 1st ser., 100/1 (1830), 381 • *GM*, 2nd ser., 37 (1852), 102

Woodrow, Henry (1823–1876), educationist, born at Norwich on 31 July 1823, was the son of Henry Woodrow, solicitor, and his wife, who was apparently descended from the family of Temple of Stowe. He was educated at Eaton, near Norwich, before going to Rugby School in 1839, where he was one of the six pupils who had supper with Dr Arnold the evening before his death. He graduated BA from Gonville and Caius College, Cambridge, in 1846 as fourteenth wrangler, and was elected to a junior fellowship, which he held until 1854.

In 1848 Woodrow accepted the position of principal of the Martinière College at Calcutta and thus began his lifelong association with India. On 18 October 1854 he married Elizabeth, daughter of Cornelius Butler, surgeon, of Brentwood, Essex; they had no children. In the same year Woodrow was appointed secretary to the Bengal council of education, and also took charge of the government school book agency. At this time the system of education of Bengal was in a sorry state, and since the other members of the council had other official duties and could give it little time most of the work fell to the secretary's lot.

The number of government vernacular schools had declined rapidly, and in 1855 the government responded to this crisis by establishing a separate department, the Bengal educational service. Woodrow became inspector of schools for eastern Bengal. In this new capacity he sought to generate interest in Western education among the Indian élites. His efforts bore fruit: the number of schools in his district—which stretched from Calcutta to Chittagong and had a population of some 15 million—grew from sixteen in 1855 to 600 by 1861, and more than 5000 by 1876. Woodrow's scheme of 'circle schools', in which one trained teacher would visit a cluster of village schools, was effective in improving the standards of elementary education at a time when there were few teachers available. He also stressed the need for training in practical skills such as surveying, which he believed would help persuade Indians of the benefits of government education. During his inspection visits he installed sundials where clocks were unavailable, to instill in the students a sense of the importance of time. The secretary of state for India, Lord Stanley, who had been a schoolfellow of Woodrow's, acclaimed his work: his 1859 education dispatch contained extensive quotations from Woodrow's reports and offered unambiguous praise of the system he had introduced.

After thirteen years the lieutenant-governor, Sir George Campbell, decided that the pace of progress in education obviated the need for a special department, and in a special resolution of 30 September 1872 re-entrusted the administration of government schools to the district collectors, restricting the educational department to teaching and reporting. Woodrow disliked the change, but quietly accepted it. In 1873 he went on furlough for eighteen months, during which he visited Vienna, Brussels, and Bonn, to study their educational systems. While in England he acted as an examiner for the competitive examinations held by the civil service commissioners.

After his return to Calcutta in 1875 Woodrow attempted, with partial success, to persuade the University of Calcutta to replace its traditional emphasis on metaphysics with the study of the physical sciences. He himself delivered lectures on chemistry, electricity, and physical sciences, both in Calcutta and more widely in Bengal. His creation of the Star of India in electric lights to commemorate the visit to India of the prince of Wales, on 24 December 1875, proved a memorable event. Earlier in 1875 he had served for a month as principal of Presidency College, Calcutta, but in September he was asked to act as director of public instruction in Bengal, succeeding definitely to the post on the death of his predecessor in January 1876. It was a fitting recognition of his contribution to the promotion of the Western education which served as an effective instrument for exercising Western cultural hegemony in colonial India. Unfortunately for Woodrow, his tenure of the office was short; he died at Darjeeling on 11 October 1876, survived by his wife.

Woodrow published in 1862 an edited version of Macaulay's 1835 minute on education in India, for which he was publicly congratulated by Lord Canning. He also wrote a pamphlet entitled *On the expediency of the introduction of tests for physical training into the present system of competitive examination for the army, navy, and Indian Civil Service* (1875). His missionary zeal won him a considerable body of Indian admirers who raised a fund to institute a scholarship in his name at the University of Calcutta, and who commissioned a marble memorial bust by the sculptor Edwin Roscoe Mullins. British officials and Indian newspapers alike mourned his loss; the collector of Midnapore district celebrated him in the *Calcutta Review* (July 1876) as the 'Nestor of Education in Bengal'.

E. I. CARLYLE, *rev.* SURANJAN DAS

Sources H. Woodrow, *An Indian career: a memoir of the late Henry Woodrow, esq., director of public instruction, Bengal* (1878) · W. F. B. Laurie, *Sketches of some distinguished Anglo-Indians*, 2nd ser. (1888) · Boase, *Mod. Eng. biog.*, vol. 3 · *Journal of National Indian Association* (1887) · *Calcutta Gazette* (1876)
Likenesses tablet, 1879, Rugby School chapel · E. R. Mullins, marble bust, University of Calcutta · bust, Gon. & Caius Cam.
Wealth at death under £1000 effects in England: probate, 14 Aug 1877, *CGPLA Eng. & Wales*

Woodruff, (John) Douglas (1897–1978), journalist and wit, was born at Wimbledon on 8 May 1897, the second of three children and the younger son of Cumberland Woodruff, a barrister employed in the Public Record Office, and his wife, Emily Louisa, daughter of William Hewett, of Norton Fitzwarren Manor, Somerset. Although Cumberland Woodruff earned his living as keeper of the Chancery master's documents, his chief interest was in archaeology, which hobby earned him a fellowship of the Royal Society of Antiquaries and may have accounted in part for Douglas Woodruff's early absorption in history.

Both parents were of staunchly protestant stock, but Emily Woodruff became a Catholic five years after her marriage, and Douglas followed his widowed mother into the same church at the age of thirteen, being influenced, as he later said, by the writings of Robert Hugh Benson—among them *Come Rack, Come Rope* (1912). If so, it must be counted a signal achievement on the part of Benson (himself the son of an archbishop of Canterbury) although later influences—G. K. Chesterton, whose works Woodruff collected long before Chesterton's conversion, and Hilaire Belloc, who became a friend—may have been stronger on the grown man.

After education at St Augustine's, Ramsgate, and, for a year, at Downside School, Woodruff found himself, in 1916, rejected for military service on grounds of a weak heart. Instead he joined the foreign service, acting as vice-consul in Amsterdam in 1917–19, chiefly concerned with the repatriation of wounded soldiers and, later, prisoners of war.

It was not until 1920, at the age of twenty-three, that Woodruff took up his exhibition in modern history at New College, Oxford, where his qualities were soon recognized. Lothian prizeman in 1921, president of the union in 1922, the year in which he completed the shortened course in *literae humaniores*, he won a first in modern history in 1923. Among fellow undergraduates, who included such distinguished Catholic converts as Evelyn Waugh,

(John) Douglas
Woodruff (1897–
1978), by Howard
Coster, 1936

was the entire Catholic church which, in its more sophisticated manifestations, beat a path to his door in Evelyn Mansions, Victoria.

Woodruff interpreted the world to English Roman Catholics at the same time as he interpreted Roman Catholicism to the outside world. A close friend of Pope Paul VI before his elevation to the papacy, Woodruff knew every bishop, cardinal, and foreign prelate of the slightest intellectual eminence. His own politics inclined towards Conservatism—he was an early supporter of the rebel cause in Spain—and he found much to distress him in the postconciliar church. A further sorrow in his last years was to see *The Tablet*, now edited by another hand, embrace all the liberal Catholic causes which he found least congenial. He was deputy chairman of the publisher Burns and Oates (1948–62), director of Hollis and Carter (1948–62), chairman of Allied Circle (1947–62), and chairman of Associated Catholic Newspapers (1953–70). He was appointed CBE in 1962. In 1968 he was awarded the grand cross of the order of St Gregory the Great.

Woodruff left no great work of scholarship by which he might be remembered, apart from the corpus of his weekly journalism, although his study of a famous Victorian court case, *The Tichborne Claimant* (1957), is noteworthy. Four selections from his signed notebook in *The Tablet*, 'Talking at random', are unmistakable offspring of his learned and witty fourth leaders in *The Times*.

On 25 February 1933 Woodruff married Marie Immaculée Antoinette (Mia) Acton (1905–1994), eldest daughter of Richard Maximilian, the second Baron Acton, of the foreign service. Although there were no children from the marriage she filled his life with nephews and nieces so that, like Chesterton, he was constantly surrounded by younger people. She also dispensed the generous hospitality which was such a feature of his life at their large flat near Westminster Cathedral, and later at his country retreat, Marcham Priory, near Abingdon, Berkshire. When failing eyesight removed his greatest pleasure, she read to him, often through the night, so that he was still contributing witty articles to *The Tablet* until a short time before his death, which occurred at Marcham Priory on 9 March 1978.

Among Woodruff's published works were *Plato's American Republic* (1926), *The British Empire* (1929), *Plato's Britannia* (1930), *Charlemagne* (1934), *Great Tudors* (1935), *European Civilization: the Grand Tour* (1935), *The Story of the British Colonial Empire* (1939), *Talking at Random* (1941), *More Talking at Random* (1944), *Still Talking at Random* (1948), *Walrus Talk* (1954), *The Tichborne Claimant* (1957), *Church and State in History* (1962), *The Popes* (1964), and *The Life and Times of Alfred the Great* (1974).   AUBERON WAUGH, *rev.*

M. Christopher Hollis, and Harold Acton, he was already seen as a venerable figure, as much for his age and slow, portly carriage as for his enormous erudition and wit.

After Oxford, Woodruff undertook a debating tour of the English-speaking world, in the company of Malcolm MacDonald and Christopher Hollis. This produced his first written work, *Plato's American Republic* (1926), which, despite its gentle humour, was thought to have given much offence in the United States. The experience may have reinforced a disinclination to give unnecessary offence which already existed in his gentle nature, and which stood him in good stead in the choppy waters of Catholic journalism.

At about this time Woodruff lost a part of what little fortune he possessed in a scheme to reinstate mead as the national drink of England. It did not prosper. After a short spell in academic life at Sheffield University, Woodruff turned to journalism and in 1926 became colonial editor of *The Times* under the editorship of Geoffrey Dawson. He held the post for ten years and was chiefly remembered as the inventor of the humorous fourth leader, although Dawson later claimed credit for this. A collection of his fourth leaders, called *Light and Leading*, was later published anonymously by *The Times*.

In 1936 Woodruff accepted editorship of *The Tablet*, then a moribund Roman Catholic weekly. There, for the next thirty years, his talents found their fullest expression until, on his resignation in 1967, he could boast that *The Tablet* was required reading for any student of foreign affairs, being received in every British embassy abroad and most foreign embassies in London.

Woodruff's secret, apart from a formidable intellect and prodigious memory, was his unfailing interest in everything that happened. Nothing bored him. For thirty years readers of *The Tablet* were treated to a three-page unsigned weekly leading article which, in Woodruff's rolling English sentences, took them on a *tour d'horizon* of the whole domestic and foreign scene. His source of information

Sources *The Times* (11 March 1978) · M. Craig, ed., *Woodruff at random* (1978) · *The diaries of Evelyn Waugh*, ed. M. Davie (1976) · *The Tablet* (15 March 1978) · personal knowledge (1986)
Archives University of Notre Dame, Indiana, corresp. and papers | City Westm. AC, corresp. relating to Allied Circle
Likenesses H. Coster, photograph, 1936, NPG [*see illus.*] · S. Elwes, portrait, 1949, priv. coll.
Wealth at death £48,002: probate, 17 April 1978, *CGPLA Eng. & Wales*

Woodruff, Philip. *See* Mason, Philip (1906–1999).

Woods, Sir Albert William (1816–1904), herald, was born on 16 April 1816 at Hampstead, Middlesex, the youngest of four sons and the fifth of six children, all apparently illegitimate, mentioned in the will of Sir William Woods (1785–1842), Garter king of arms. He was the second son and third of the father's four children with Mary Ann Young; the two eldest sons were with Elizabeth Blake. Mary Ann Young, variously described as the daughter of a greengrocer in St Paul's Churchyard, a banner maker in the College of Arms, and Woods's cook–housekeeper, was the sole executrix of his will. The paternity of Sir William Woods is uncertain; there was a tradition that he was an illegitimate child of Charles Howard, eleventh duke of Norfolk and earl marshal (1746–1815), although he bore the arms matriculated in the Lyon Office, Edinburgh, in 1812 by George Woods of London, brother and heir of the comedian William Woods, of the Theatre Royal, Edinburgh. Sir Albert Woods also bore these arms until 22 December 1891, when a new grant reshuffled the charges in his father's arms. Nothing is known of his education, which was described by his son-in-law Sir Arthur Naylor Wollaston (1842–1922) as private. Sir Anthony Wagner in *Heralds of England* records that he dropped his aitches and that Edward Bellasis (1800–1873), serjeant-at-law, puzzled whether there really was an 'h' in herald after a visit to the College of Arms in 1869 (p. 516).

About 1832 Woods began working in his father's office, and on 27 June 1837 was appointed Fitzalan pursuivant-extraordinary, as such attending the coronation of Queen Victoria. On 2 August 1838 he was appointed Portcullis pursuivant, following his father's appointment as Garter king of arms on 23 July 1838. On 1 December 1838 he married—at St George's, Camberwell, on her twenty-first birthday—Caroline (1817–1911), daughter of Robert Cole, merchant, of Rotherfield, Sussex, with whom he had two children: William Francis Woods (1840–1870), the father of Albert William Woods (1865–1890), Rouge Dragon pursuivant in 1886, whose gambling led to bankruptcy in 1889; and Caroline Marianne (1844–1902), wife of Sir Arthur Naylor Wollaston and mother of Sir Gerald Woods Wollaston (1874–1957), Garter king of arms (1930–44). Woods was promoted Norfolk herald-extraordinary on 28 October 1841 and Lancaster herald on 9 November 1841, and held the latter post with that of gentleman usher of the scarlet rod of the Most Honourable Order of the Bath, with the annexed office of Brunswick herald, to which he was appointed on 24 November 1841. Following the reorganization of the order in 1857 and the abolition of those offices he was made registrar and secretary of the Order of the Bath, as embodied in the new statutes of the order dated 31 January 1859.

On 28 July 1842 Woods was appointed inspector of regimental colours, in succession to his father, who had died on 25 July. He was elected a fellow of the Society of Antiquaries of London on 25 March 1847. On 5 August 1869 he was appointed king of arms of the Order of St Michael and St George, and, on 2 November 1869, Garter king of arms, in succession to Sir Charles George Young. He was knighted on 11 November 1869, and was appointed registrar of the Order of the Star of India (instituted 23 February 1861), of the Order of the Indian Empire and of the Order of the Crown of India (both instituted 1 January 1878), and of the Royal Order of Victoria and Albert. As Lancaster herald and as Garter, Woods was in attendance on six investiture missions to foreign sovereigns. He was a knight of grace and director-general of ceremonies of the order of St John of Jerusalem in England, and also a prominent freemason, being grand director of ceremonies from 1860 until his death. He was appointed CB in 1887, KCMG on 21 May 1890, KCB on 22 June 1897, and GCVO on 30 June 1903.

Woods was determined that his grants should mark a definite period in heraldry and that no nineteenth-century grantee could expect a simple coat. Sir Anthony Wagner wrote that Woods 'was businesslike, energetic and possessed immense knowledge of ceremonial, precedence and the day to day business of his office' but added that he 'was not an historian or a scholar and his influence on heraldic design has been thought deplorable' (Wagner, *Heralds of England*, 516). A portrait of Woods in *The Genealogist* in 1892, when he was aged seventy-seven, referred to his working as hard as any man half his age, and to his courteous and able exercise of his duties. By 1897 he was very seriously ill, yet continued to assemble all paperwork for his many offices from his home at 69 St George's Road, Warwick Square, Pimlico, while Sir William Henry Weldon (1837–1919), then Norroy, acted as his deputy for ceremonial purposes and Sir Henry Farnham Burke (1859–1930), then Somerset herald, prepared the coronation of Edward VII, in 1901–2. The impact of Woods's increasing debility was all the greater because he had, in the words of one contemporary, 'obtained somehow or other a veto and authority in all heraldic matters which few if any earlier Garters ever had' (A. C. Fox-Davies, in *Genealogical Magazine*, 7.480–82). Fox-Davies knew of no evidence of 'delay or inattention' (ibid.) but in December 1903 a secretary employed by Woods found 150 grants of dignities in the Order of the Bath, signed by Queen Victoria, and a further 485, signed by Edward VII, which had not been sent to the intended recipients. In the same year Sir William Alexander Baillie-Hamilton (1844–1920), then officer of arms of the Order of St Michael and St George, lamented:

> a great deal of the business of several of the Orders is still nominally in the hands of a nonagenarian hermit concealed in St. George's Road, who is of course long past his work, and is nothing worse than an obstruction, but who clings tenaciously to his fees and his prerogatives. (Galloway, 154)

Woods died, of heart disease, at his home in Pimlico on 7 January 1904, and was buried at Norwood cemetery, London, on 11 January. Like his predecessors he had been appointed for life, and his refusal to retire led directly to the formation, on 1 April 1904, of the Central Chancery of the Orders of Knighthood, which took away from Garter and the other heralds the registration and secretarial work connected with most orders of chivalry.

THOMAS WOODCOCK

Sources A. Wagner, *Heralds of England: a history of the office and College of Arms* (1967), 514–18, 520–23, 525–7 · W. H. Godfrey, A. Wagner, and H. Stanford London, *The College of Arms, Queen Victoria Street* (1963), 68–9 · P. Galloway, *The order of St Michael and St George* (2000), 152–7 · P. G. Begent and H. Chesshyre, *The most noble Order of the Garter: 650 years* (1999), 130–31, 137–40, 246–51, 298–9 · *Genealogical Magazine*, 7 (1904), 477–82 · *The Genealogist*, new ser., 9 (1892–3), 241 · J. J. Howard and F. A. Crisp, eds., *Visitation of England and Wales*, 21 vols. (privately printed, London, 1893–1921), vol. 12, p. 148 · *College of Arms MS knights pedigrees*, 1.192 · *The Times* (21 Nov 1911) · A. R. Wagner, *The records and collections of the College of Arms* (1952), 51 · *Royal blue book* (1871) · *Ex Libris Journal*, 14 (1904), 1 · *DNB* · d. cert.
Archives Coll. Arms, ordinary of arms compiled by him with later additions | BL, letters to Philip Bliss, Add. MSS 34575–34580 · BL, letters to C. A. Buckler, Add. MSS 37123, 37146 · BL, corresp. with W. E. Gladstone, Add. MS 44351 · JRL, corresp. and notes relating to orders of knighthood · Man. CL, Manchester Archives and Local Studies, letters to William Langton
Likenesses C. F. Kell, lithograph, BM · portrait, repro. in *The Genealogist*, frontispiece · portrait, repro. in H. G. Strohl, *Heraldischer Atlas* (1899), pl. II, fig. 2 · portrait, repro. in *Genealogical Magazine*, 476 · portrait, repro. in Begent and Chesshyre, *Most noble order*, 130 · wood-engraving, NPG; repro. in *ILN* (8 May 1875)
Wealth at death £41,582 18s. 4d.: probate, resworn, 1904

Woods, Alice Augusta (1849–1941), educationist and college head, was born at Wood End, Walthamstow, Essex, on 6 August 1849, daughter of Samuel Woods, a stockbroker of Quaker origin, and his wife, Emma King. She was educated at home. In 1875 she became assistant mistress at Chelsea high school, run by the Girls' Public Day School Company, whose headmistress was her cousin, Mary Woods. This seems to have confirmed her intention to study and teach, for in 1877, aged twenty-eight, she went to Girton College, Cambridge, and in 1880 took a second class in the moral sciences tripos (MA, 1928). For two years she taught at St Leonard's School, St Andrews, under Miss Lumsden, its founder, and from 1882 to 1884 was head of the junior department of the Girls' High School, Clifton, where her cousin was now head. In 1884 she became headmistress of a co-educational school opened in Bedford Park, Chiswick, by the residents of this intellectual and artistic garden suburb in west London. Here for eight years she was able to develop her progressive ideas.

In 1892 Miss Woods was appointed principal of Maria Grey College, founded in 1878 by the Teachers' Training and Registration Society as the first college to prepare students professionally for secondary school teaching. It had migrated in 1892 to new premises in Brondesbury, in the north-west London area, comprising a purpose-built kindergarten, girls' secondary school, and training college all contained in one building. By then, however, the college faced keen competition from other training colleges, and it was difficult to attract enough students to balance the books. The college was kept afloat financially by subscribers and donors, and a grant from the Pfeiffer Trust. Miss Woods described these financial difficulties to the royal commission on secondary education, in October 1894, shortly after her appointment, pointing out that Maria Grey College needed fifty students to support a staff of principal and four lecturers. She argued for the national need for professional training, advocating that

students should have higher education before proceeding to two years training, where theory and practice should go hand in hand, and that such training should also be accepted in elementary schools, after some kind of probation. She also advocated the need for experiment, including co-education at student level, though she acknowledged that in secondary schools after fourteen years of age current problems of staffing made it difficult to keep boys.

At Maria Grey College, Miss Wood's regime was considered to be administratively casual but educationally adventurous, her main interest being to raise the level of the students' work. Already they came with good qualifications: in 1892 there were ten graduates from Cambridge and six from London. Progress in higher education enabled the staff at Brondesbury to be fully graduate, except for Miss Riach at the kindergarten department, and she was a highly successful and well-known exponent of the revived ideas of Froebel, and of Dewey and Montessori. When in 1900 the University of London set up a board of pedagogy to plan a course and examination, Miss Woods was involved from the beginning; she was recognized by the senate as a university teacher and examiner, and nominated to serve on the subcommittee to draw up a scheme of training for the new diploma in education. By this time she was well known in educational circles for her contributions to the study of moral education and the co-educational movement. She was a friend of Michael Sadler and John Adams, first professor of education at London University.

In 1892 Miss Woods was co-opted onto the Middlesex county council education committee. She realized that the college could benefit from the Technical Instruction Act of 1889 which enabled the county councils to raise money for specified aspects of education, and although an application for aid in 1893 was refused, the authority later aided entry to the kindergarten division and increased aid to £250 a year, providing ten free places for Middlesex students. After 1902, when the county became the local education authority with responsibility for secondary education, it was much more willing to aid a school which would supply scholarship places for girls. In 1908 the Board of Education recognized the college for grants under the new regulations for secondary training colleges. By the time of her retirement in 1913—'I want to do other things in education' (Lilley, 40)—Miss Woods left a college with a high reputation for educational innovation, which had at least survived financially, and was closely and profitably linked with both local and central educational systems.

Throughout these busy years Miss Woods wrote, lectured, and travelled widely to inspect educational developments and training methods. She was well known in the USA, where she made four study tours. Her visits to the Glenmore School of Culture in the Adirondacks are recorded in correspondence in the college archives. In 1903 she edited a collection of papers, published as *Co-Education*, 'a missionary book', as Sadler wrote in the introduction. It claimed that this practice was rapidly increasing and that practical questions were arising in which the sharing of experience would be helpful. In her contribution, entitled 'The dangers and difficulties of co-education', Miss Woods argued that these would be overcome by those who 'recognize one moral law for men and women'. She lists twenty-nine co-educational schools, including county secondary schools and such schools as the King Alfred School in Hampstead, of whose governing body she was an active member. In 1902 she published a novel, *Edges*.

In her retirement Miss Woods wrote *Advance in Education* (1919), *Educational Experiments in England* (1920), *George Meredith as Champion of Women and of Progressive Education* (1937), and numerous articles on educational subjects. She also wrote a most useful pamphlet, *On How to Grow Old* (n.d.). During the First World War, now living in rural Hertfordshire, she became supervisor of women's work on thirteen farms in Radlett parish, and toured around on a bicycle, also inquiring into cottagers who would be willing to plant seed potatoes, but she 'drew the line on pigs'. Retaining all the characteristics of the pioneer to the end, Alice Woods died at her home, 15 Crosspath, Radlett, Hertfordshire, on 7 January 1941.   MARGARET BRYANT

Sources K. T. Butler and H. I. McMorran, eds., *Girton College register, 1869–1946* (1948) · WWW · I. M. Lilley, *Maria Grey College* (1981) · Brunel University, Maria Grey College records · 'Royal commission on secondary education: report', *Parl. papers* (1895), vol. 43, C. 7862 · T. A. Greeves, *Bedford Park: the first garden suburb* (1975) · b. cert.
Archives Brunel University, Middlesex, Maria Grey College records
Likenesses photograph, repro. in Lilley, *Maria Grey College*, 46
Wealth at death £12,008: probate, 7 April 1941, *CGPLA Eng. & Wales*

Woods, Donald Devereux (1912–1964), microbiologist, was born at Ipswich on 16 February 1912, the elder son of Walter James Woods, builder and decorator of Ipswich, and his wife, Violet Mabel Cobb. Woods was educated at Northgate School, Ipswich, and became a scholar at Trinity Hall, Cambridge; he graduated in 1933 with first-class honours in parts one (1932) and two (1933) of the natural sciences tripos. He remained at Cambridge with a Beit memorial fellowship and took his PhD in 1937. From 1933 to 1939 he worked in association with Marjory Stephenson at Cambridge and under her influence became interested in the metabolic processes of bacteria. In 1939 he joined the Medical Research Council's unit for bacterial chemistry as a Halley-Stewart research fellow, working at the Middlesex Hospital, London. In the same year he married Alison Lillian, daughter of George William Halls, agricultural engineer; they had one daughter.

From 1940 to 1946 Woods was engaged in war work at the chemical defence research establishment at Porton Down, Wiltshire. At the end of that period he became reader in chemical microbiology in the biochemistry department of the University of Oxford under Professor Rudolph A. Peters, and in 1951 he became a fellow of Trinity College, Oxford. He was elected a fellow of the Royal Society in 1952. In 1955 he was appointed to the first chair in chemical microbiology in the United Kingdom—the Iveagh professorship, endowed by Arthur Guinness, Son & Co.

Woods's major impact on his branch of science was made in a paper (published in 1940) which was prepared when he was working in the unit directed by Paul Fildes at the Middlesex Hospital. At that time sulphonamide drugs had become established as the first really effective chemotherapeutic agents for use against bacterial infections. Fildes's group was concerned with the substances essential for the growth of pathogenic bacteria, and one of its lines of attack was to analyse animal and vegetable extracts for the essential components. Sulphanilamide was known to inhibit bacterial growth quantitatively and the inhibition was prevented, also quantitatively, by extracts of yeast and other organisms. Woods set out to discover the anti-sulphanilamide factor in yeast extracts and, within four months, he had shown that it was p-aminobenzoic acid. Woods had been trained at Cambridge as a biochemist and, recognizing the similarity of the chemical structures of p-aminobenzoic acid and sulphanilamide molecules, he suggested that the drug could be acting as an inhibitor of an enzyme bringing about some essential metabolism of p-aminobenzoic acid. The idea rapidly received support by the identification of p-aminobenzoic acid in various biological complexes and the demonstration that it formed part of the molecule of folic acid, a substance essential to the functioning of a variety of enzymes important in biosynthetic reactions.

This demonstration by Woods—that a chemical analogue of an 'essential metabolite' could become a useful drug—appeared to open up a direct approach to the rational development of chemotherapeutic agents by structural modification of other metabolites. Woods was unable to follow this approach himself since he was engaged, for the next six years, in war work. During this period others confirmed the accuracy of his predictions, though it was many years before any 'metabolite analogues' which were effective for the clinical treatment of infections were discovered—mainly because the nature of the selective action of sulphanilamide was not understood at this time and because the majority of analogues proved to be non-selective *in vivo*.

When Woods returned to academic life in 1946, p-aminobenzoic acid had been established as the biosynthetic precursor of folic acid and he devoted much of the rest of his research career to elucidating the nature and functions of folic acid in its various forms. During this time a series of young research workers worked under his guidance and many of these later became leading investigators in other laboratories and universities. Woods was a dedicated teacher and had a gift not only for exposition but also for enlisting and maintaining the interest of a large number of collaborators, young and old. In 1953 he delivered the first Marjory Stephenson memorial lecture to the Society for General Microbiology; this lecture provides a delightful account both of his work at that time and of his approach to the problems of chemical microbiology. Woods was invited to give the Leeuwenhoek lecture to the Royal Society in 1964, but he died in the Radcliffe Infirmary, Oxford, on 6 November 1964, before he could deliver it. His wife survived him.

E. F. GALE, *rev.*

Sources *Journal of General Microbiology*, 9 (1953) · E. F. Gale and P. Fildes, *Memoirs FRS*, 11 (1965), 203–19 · private information (1981) · personal knowledge (1981) · *CGPLA Eng. & Wales* (1964)
Archives Bodl. Oxf., papers | Wellcome L., corresp. with Henry McIlwain
Likenesses W. Stoneman, photograph, 1952, repro. in *Memoirs FRS*, 11 (1965)
Wealth at death £3120: administration, 18 Dec 1964, *CGPLA Eng. & Wales*

Woods, Edward (1814–1903), civil engineer, was born in London on 28 April 1814, the son of Samuel Woods, a merchant. After an education at private schools, he became in 1834 an assistant to John Dixon, recently appointed chief engineer of the Liverpool and Manchester Railway. Woods was placed in charge of the section between Liverpool and Newton-le-Willows, including the tunnel then under construction by William Mackenzie (1794–1851) between Lime Street and Edge Hill stations. In 1836 he succeeded Dixon as chief engineer. He married Mary Dent, daughter of Thomas Goodman of Birmingham on 5 October 1840. They had three sons and two daughters.

Despite the amalgamation of the Liverpool and Manchester Railway with the Grand Junction Railway in 1845, Woods remained, until the end of 1852, in charge of the works on the Liverpool and Manchester section. These included the construction of the Victoria Tunnel (completed 1848) between Edge Hill station and the docks, a large goods station adjoining Waterloo Dock, and a line between Patricroft and Clifton, opened in 1850. In 1853 he established himself in London as a consulting engineer.

Woods's work on the Liverpool and Manchester line enabled him to observe at first hand the strengths and weakness of this pioneer railway. He played a prominent part in various early experimental investigations into the working of railways. When Count de Pambour visited Britain in 1834, and again in 1836, Woods assisted him with his experiments into fuel consumption and locomotive performance. Pambour's work was widely reported, and translated into English (*A Practical Treatise on Locomotive Engines*, 2nd edn, 1840). Woods clearly profited from this experience, and was soon conducting his own experiments. In 1836 he made observations on the waste of fuel due to condensation in the long pipes conveying steam about a quarter of a mile to the winding-engines used for hauling trains through the Edge Hill Tunnel. He was a member of a committee, with Dr Dionysius Lardner, appointed by the British Association in 1837 to report on the resistance of railway trains, and presented a separate report (*British Association Report*, 1841, 247). In 1838 he presented to the Institution of Civil Engineers a paper (*Transactions*, 2.137–55) 'On certain forms of locomotive engines', which contained some of the earliest accurate details of the working of locomotives, and for which he

was awarded a Telford medal. The consumption of fuel in locomotives was the subject of a paper presented by him to the Liverpool Polytechnic Society in 1843 (*Weale's Quarterly Papers on Engineering*, 2/5, 1844), and of a contribution to a new edition of Thomas Tredgold's *The Steam Engine* in 1850.

In 1853 Woods carried out, with W. P. Marshall, experiments on the locomotives of the London and North Western Railway (LNWR), between London and Rugby, and their three reports to the railway company recommended weights and dimensions for various classes of engines. These were followed, in 1854, by a joint report on the relative merits of coal and coke as locomotive fuel. Woods's research provided an invaluable insight into early locomotive design and performance, and influenced many of his contemporaries.

The consultancy work undertaken by Woods was chiefly connected with the railways of South America, including the Central Argentine Railway, the Copiapo extension, Santiago and Valparaiso, and Coquimbo railways in Chile, and the Mollenda–Arequipa and Callao–Oroya lines in Peru. Many of these lines were built by the American contractor Henry Meiggs, with Woods acting as UK consultant. He was responsible not only for surveys and construction, but also for the design of rolling stock to meet the somewhat special conditions. His son Edward Harry assisted him in much of this work, and acted as resident engineer and manager on the Central Argentine Railway. Other engineering work included a wrought-iron pier, 2400 feet long, built on screw piles at Pisco on the coast of Peru, a quay wall built at Bilbao in 1877, and Montevideo waterworks.

In the 'battle of the gauges' he favoured the Irish gauge (5 feet 3 inches) or the Indian gauge (5 feet 6 inches). He regarded break of gauge as a mistake, and in 1872 opposed the introduction of a new gauge in Victoria, Australia. In 1877, as president of the mechanical science section of the British Association, he delivered an address on 'Adequate brake power for railway trains'. Elected a member of the Institution of Civil Engineers in 1846, he was president in 1886–7. In 1884 he was president of the Smeatonian Society of Civil Engineers.

Woods died at his residence, 45 Onslow Gardens, London, on 14 June 1903, and was buried at Chenies, Buckinghamshire on the 18th. Two of his sons, and both daughters, survived him.   W. F. SPEAR, *rev.* MIKE CHRIMES

Sources *PICE*, 153 (1902–3), 342–50 · *Engineering* (19 June 1903), 818–19 · *The Engineer* (19 June 1903), 625 · *The Times* (16 June 1903) · T. J. Donaghy, *Liverpool and Manchester railway operations, 1831–1845* (1972) · d. cert. · m. cert. · *CGPLA Eng. & Wales* (1903)
Archives Inst. CE, original communication and membership records · PRO, RAIL Records
Likenesses M. Porter, oils, 1898, Inst. CE · Maull & Fox, carte-de-visite, Inst. CE
Wealth at death £128,012 5s. 4d.: probate, 18 July 1903, *CGPLA Eng. & Wales*

Woods, Helen Emily. *See* Kavan, Anna (1901–1968).

Woods, Henry (1868–1952), palaeontologist, was born on 18 December 1868 at Cottenham, near Cambridge, the only child of Francis Woods, a farmer, and his second wife, Mary Ann Granger, daughter of a Haddenham farmer. His father died when he was two years old. He was educated at the village school and, following a move with his mother in 1880, at the higher grade school in Cambridge. Although he gained several prizes and a scholarship, he left in 1883 to start work, but continued to study in his spare time. On entering St John's College, Cambridge, in October 1887 he proved to be a brilliant student. He gained a first class in part one of the natural sciences tripos in 1889, and was elected a scholar; obtaining a first class in part two of the tripos, the following year, taking geology, he was awarded the Harkness scholarship for the best performance in the examination. He took his MA in 1894 and won the Sedgwick prize in 1895.

Woods joined the teaching staff of the department of geology, Cambridge University, in 1892, filling a new post of demonstrator in palaeobotany. In 1894 he also became demonstrator in palaeozoology, and in 1899 he was appointed to the first lectureship in palaeozoology—a post he held until his retirement in 1934. His connections with the department lasted almost to the end of his life, and he continued to act as librarian until past the age of eighty.

Prior to his official appointment Woods had been working on the palaeontological collections in the department (Bulman, 645), and had published *A Catalogue of Type Fossils in the Woodwardian Museum, Cambridge* in 1891. He devoted considerable time to the collections until a full-time curator was appointed (in the 1920s). Woods was also involved in planning the new Sedgwick Museum with Professor McKenny Hughes, and on its completion in 1904 became responsible for its arrangement. A zealous teacher, he produced the fundamental treatise *Palaeontology: Invertebrate* (1893) from his lecture notes; this textbook went through numerous editions until its concentration on basic morphological facts, reflecting Woods's cautious attitude to the philosophical and interpretative aspects of palaeontology, meant that it was superseded by more modern works.

In 1910 Woods married Ethel Gertrude Skeat (d. 1939), the third daughter of Walter William *Skeat, professor of Old English at Cambridge. In 1908 she was awarded the Murchison fund by the Geological Society in recognition of her various contributions to palaeontology. She and Woods had no children.

Woods's original contributions established him as one of the foremost invertebrate palaeontologists of his generation. His *Monograph of the Cretaceous Lamellibranchia of England* (1899–1913) was still a fundamental reference at the close of the twentieth century. His meticulous observations and clear morphological descriptions, combined with a thorough comparison of the relationship of contemporaneous taxa, and a high standard of illustration, have ensured its lasting importance. His equally precise *Monograph of the Fossil Macrurous Crustacea of England* (1925–31) deals with a less abundant group, but has an identical status in modern taxonomy. Woods published other significant descriptive monographs on Cretaceous Mollusca

from South Africa (1906, 1908), New Zealand (1917), and Northern Nigeria (1911), and one on Tertiary Mollusca from Peru (1922).

Woods was usually reluctant to indulge in speculative hypothesis, but one of his earlier papers on the supposed evolution of the Cretaceous bivalve *Inoceramus* had a major role in establishing the importance of the Inoceramidae during that period. His earlier analysis of the chalk rock fauna (1896–7) modified contemporary opinion on chalk deposition and compares with more recent palaeoecological interpretation. He must be regarded as unique in that, despite publishing many systematic descriptions, he only created a single taxon at supra-specific level, the bivalve sub-genus *Cucullaea* (*Dicranodonta*), in 1899.

Tall and spare, with a pronounced stoop in later life, Woods had a quiet, reserved manner, tempered by his kindly grey eyes. The only available portrait of him is a passport photograph, confirming both his liking for travel and his self-confessed, unsociable, shy disposition. Although not a dynamic personality, or an outstanding lecturer, he instilled a love of fossils into many of his students.

The Geological Society of London awarded Woods the Lyell fund (1898), the Lyell medal (1918), and the Wollaston medal (1940). He was elected FRS in 1916, was a member of the Geologists' Association for sixty years, and was made an honorary member of the Royal Society of New Zealand, and of the Yorkshire Philosophical Society, for his work on Cretaceous fossils. Owing to financial necessity, he became a most practised and efficient examiner for many of the principal examination authorities. He served on the councils of both the Palaeontographical and the Geological societies. But apart from his work, his only other interest was gardening.

After a short illness Woods died on 4 April 1952 at his home, The Homestead, Meldreth, Cambridgeshire, where he had lived since 1924. Precise and methodical to the end, he bequeathed the bulk of his estate to the Palaeontographical Society and the Geological Society.

R. J. CLEEVELY

Sources O. M. Bulman, *Obits. FRS*, 8 (1952–3), 645–55 · C. P. Castell, 'Henry Woods', *Proceedings of the Geologists' Association*, 64 (1953), 66–7 · *Proceedings of the Geological Society*, 54 (1898), xlvii [award of the Lyell fund] · *Proceedings of the Geological Society*, 74 (1918), xlvi–xlvii [award of the Lyell medal] · *Proceedings of the Geological Society*, 96 (1940), li–liii [award of the Wollaston medal] · *Proceedings of the Geological Society of London* (1952–3), cxliii–cxlv · R. J. Cleevely, *World palaeontological collections* (1983), 198 · *DNB* · *CGPLA Eng. & Wales* (1952)

Archives BGS · NHM, department of palaeontology · U. Cam., Sedgwick Museum of Earth Sciences | BGS, letters to Finlay Kitchin · NHM, department of palaeontology, corresp. with A. W. Rowe

Likenesses photograph, repro. in *Obits. FRS*

Wealth at death £14,280 8s. 1d.: probate, 29 May 1952, *CGPLA Eng. & Wales*

Woods, Sir John Harold Edmund (1895–1962), civil servant, was born in Kensington, London, on 20 April 1895, the elder son of John Henry Woods (1866–1944) and his wife, Annie Alker, both of whom came from Wigan. His father was a cherubic, scholarly man who had been a wrangler at Peterhouse, Cambridge, and a mathematical coach before seeking ordination (1905) and was subsequently vicar of St Mark's, South Shields, and rector of Glaston, Uppingham.

Woods was educated at Christ's Hospital, Horsham, Sussex, and after the First World War at Balliol College, Oxford. He won classical and other school prizes, was captain of rugger, cricket, and fives, and was reappointed captain of the school for a second year. In 1914 he won an exhibition to Balliol but went straight from school into the army as a lieutenant in the 22nd battalion, Royal Fusiliers. In 1916 he was severely wounded in the leg and was invalided out, although not until 1918. He surmounted his war wound sufficiently to go up to Balliol (1918–20) and to sit the civil service entry examination in July 1920, passing second and joining the Treasury. His wounds, however, remained throughout his life, involving him in forty-five surgical operations with long periods in hospital and a major daily task of cleaning and plugging the huge hole in his leg.

In spite of his wound, of which the stick he always carried was a reminder, Woods remained an exuberant personality and a very clubbable man. John Henry, as he was universally and affectionately known, was good company, with an abundance of stories and a keen sense of fun. He was able to play cricket with the help of a runner and to complete a full round of golf. He could also indulge his passion for listening to good music. In 1928 he had attended the Imperial Defence College and in 1929 he served as assistant private secretary to the prince of Wales. He married in 1930 Molly, daughter of Noah Henry Baker, who was senior clerk of works, police architect and surveyors' department, Scotland Yard. They had one son and one daughter and enjoyed a very happy and full married life.

When Woods rejoined the Treasury he was in charge in the 1930s of the provision of government finance for work-creation schemes and the building of the new Cunard ocean liners, and secretary of the Trade Facilities Act advisory committee. He was also much in contact with the accountancy profession to which the Treasury turned for guidance on the role of public funds to rescue industries in difficulties. The friendships he formed in the world of industrial finance were subsequently strengthened in the war years and after; and in the discharge of his various responsibilities his powers matured.

In 1931 Woods was appointed private secretary to Philip Snowden, chancellor of the exchequer and later lord privy seal, who remained one of his heroes for his courage and integrity. In 1936 he became principal private secretary to Neville Chamberlain as chancellor of the exchequer and then in 1937–40 to his successor, Sir John Simon. In normal circumstances he would have gone on to be head of a department but instead, with the country now at war, he was promoted to principal assistant secretary at the Treasury and put in charge of expenditure for the armed services—not a congenial job to one who had

served throughout the First World War. His most important tasks were to formulate government policy on the pricing of munitions, supplemented by evidence on contract procedures to the public accounts committee; and, after appointment in 1943 as permanent secretary of the Ministry of Production, to co-ordinate munitions production in alliance with the chief executive, Sir Robert Sinclair, an alliance that continued in the post-war period under Churchill's brief caretaker government, when the ministry was merged with the Board of Trade.

In 1945, when the Labour government took over and Cripps succeeded Oliver Lyttelton as president of the Board of Trade, Woods, who was knighted (KCB) in that year (GCB, 1949), continued as permanent secretary. Although he and Cripps seemed at opposite extremes in personality they collaborated successfully, with mutual respect and understanding. His service at the board continued through six strenuous post-war years that formed the apogee of his career. The staff of the board had grown from 2400 before the war to 15,000, with responsibilities ranging from the great diversity of controls introduced in wartime to the export drive aiming to increase the volume of exports from 30 per cent of the pre-war volume to 150 (or even 175) per cent. The burden of securing effective co-ordination between different areas of policy was a very heavy one, however much was delegated to senior staff, and was not made easier by his loss of an eye in an accident. There were also periods—for example, before devaluation in 1949—when Woods was on extended sick leave.

The pressure continued when Harold Wilson took over from Cripps in 1947. Woods was asked to take on new duties such as membership of the Economic Planning Board. It was a period dominated by controls, in which the conditions for their removal were hard to create. He gave much thought to the action that might be taken and to preparing Harold Wilson's bonfire of controls. It was at this time that he drew attention to the move to replace controls by some form of voluntary action which he christened 'voluntaryism', observing that it sounded like 'the occupational disease of a church organist' (*DNB*).

In 1950 Woods was appointed chairman of a Treasury organization committee charged with examining how the Treasury conducted its affairs and distributed its responsibilities. But by this time he was finding the pressure of work beyond his powers and decided to retire from the civil service. Early in 1951 he accepted an invitation from his friend Sir George Nelson to join the board of the English Electric Company as an executive director. He played an important part over the next decade in the expansion in the company's business overseas and developed a close association, on behalf of English Electric, with a number of other companies.

Released from the pressure of government work, Woods was able to take on duties to which he felt attracted. As a devout Christian he gave priority to service to the Church of England in membership of the church's central committees, particularly the central board of finance, and sought to provide additional help to arch-bishops. Throughout the 1950s he accepted one appointment after another; in 1952 he was elected president of the National Institute of Economic and Social Research, and accepted membership of the committee on the Churchill Falls development power scheme in Canada; in 1953 he joined the advisory committee of the Revolving Fund for Industry and the Waverley committee on atomic energy; in 1954 he took part in the inquiry into the administrative and disciplinary consequences of the Crichel Down affair, and in 1957–9 he served as a member of the Radcliffe committee on the working of the monetary system. In addition to this sequence of responsibilities he was a visiting fellow of Nuffield College, Oxford, a director of the Sadler's Wells Trust Ltd, a governor of the Administrative Staff College at Henley, and treasurer of the British School at Rome.

In 1962 Woods's long spell of ill health forced him into a wheelchair and put an end to his active life. Later in the year, on 2 December, he died at his home, Burchetts, Haywards Heath, Sussex. ALEC CAIRNCROSS

Sources DNB · *The Times* (3 Dec 1962) · WWW · I. Elliott, ed., *The Balliol College register, 1900–1950*, 3rd edn (privately printed, Oxford, 1953) · *CGPLA Eng. & Wales* (1963)
Archives NRA, papers
Likenesses W. Stoneman, photograph, 1948, NPG
Wealth at death £17,455 0s. 9d.: probate, 4 March 1963, *CGPLA Eng. & Wales*

Woods, Joseph (1776–1864), architect and botanist, was born at Stoke Newington on 24 August 1776, the second son of Joseph Woods, woollen draper, and his wife, Margaret, daughter of Samuel Hoare. Delicate health caused Woods to be removed from school when only thirteen or fourteen years old, and he was mainly self-taught, but became proficient in Latin, Greek, Hebrew, French, Italian, and modern Greek. At sixteen he was articled to a businessman at Dover; but, preferring architecture, he placed himself in the office of Daniel Asher Alexander. He obtained admission to the Royal Academy Schools in 1798 and afterwards began to practise, but, having no business capacity, was not very successful. He designed the London Commercial Sale Rooms, Mincing Lane (1811–12; dem.); but, a failure having resulted from his miscalculation of the strength of some iron trestles, he had to make good the loss. The building was demolished in 1812.

In 1806 Woods formed the London Architectural Society, of which he became the first president; and in 1808 he printed, but does not seem to have published, 'An essay on modern theories of taste'. Having been entrusted in 1816 with the editing of the remainder of *Antiquities of Athens* by J. Stuart and N. Revett, he issued the fourth volume of that work.

Woods had already devoted considerable attention to geology, and still more to botany: his 'Synopsis of the British species of *rosa*', the first of a series of papers devoted to the more difficult or 'critical' genera of flowering plants, appeared in *Transactions of the Linnean Society* (12, 1818). In April 1816 he had started on a continental tour through France, Italy, and Greece, the results of which

appeared in a paper, 'On the rocks of Attica', communicated to the Geological Society in 1824 (*Geological Transactions*, 1, 1824, 170–72), and in *Letters of an Architect from France, Italy, and Greece* (2 vols., 1828), illustrated by the author.

On his return to Britain in 1819, Woods took chambers in Furnival's Inn; but in 1833 he retired from his profession and settled at Lewes, Sussex, where he devoted himself mainly to botany. Between 1835 and 1856 he contributed botanical papers to the Linnean Society's *Transactions*, and *The Phytologist*. He made various excursions in Britain and abroad while engaged upon *The tourists' flora: a descriptive catalogue of the flowering plants and ferns of the British islands, France, Germany, Switzerland, Italy, and the Italian islands* (1850). Accounts of his excursions appeared in the *Companion to the 'Botanical Magazine'* in 1835 and 1836 and in *The Phytologist* (1844, 1850, 1851, 1855). His visit to the north of Spain in 1857 was recorded in 'Botany' in the *Journal of the Linnean Society* (2, 1858). He studied the genus *Salicornia*, partly in conjunction with Richard Kippist (1812–1882), also a native of Stoke Newington, who had assisted him with *The Tourists' Flora*. The last series to engage his attention were the *Rubi*, many of which he sketched. He also amused himself, when over eighty years of age, by finishing up some of his early architectural sketches as presents to his friends; and he was for many years an exceptionally brilliant chess player.

Woods died, unmarried, at his house at 8 Priory Crescent, Southover, Lewes, on 9 January 1864, and was buried in the Quaker burial-ground in the same town. He was a fellow of the Linnean Society, the Geological Society, and the Society of Antiquaries; and, in addition to fifteen papers with which he is credited in the Royal Society's *Catalogue of Scientific Papers* (19 vols., 1867–1925, 6.436), he contributed to J. E. Smith's *English Botany* (36 vols., 1790–1814) descriptions of several species that he had discovered which were new to Britain. His fellow botanist Robert Brown (1773–1858) gave the name *Woodsia* to a rare and beautiful genus of British ferns. Woods's herbarium of British plants was given by him to James Ebenezer Bicheno and was later donated to the Royal Institution, Swansea; his larger general collection became the property of Frederic Townsend of Honington, Warwickshire.
G. S. BOULGER, rev. SUSIE BARSON

Sources Boase, *Mod. Eng. biog.* · Colvin, *Archs.* · *The Builder*, 21 (1863), 112–13 · *The Builder*, 22 (1864), 56 · *Transactions of the Royal Institute of British Architects* (1863–4) · *CGPLA Eng. & Wales* (1864)
Archives GS Lond. · Linn. Soc., journals, notebooks, drawings, and papers · S. Antiquaries, Lond.
Likenesses J. Cotman, portrait, 1822, V&A; copy, Linn. Soc.
Wealth at death under £6000: probate, 15 April 1864, *CGPLA Eng. & Wales*

Woods, Julian Edmund Tenison (1832–1889), Roman Catholic priest and scientist, was born on 15 November 1832 at Milbank Cottage, West Street, Southwark, the sixth son of James Dominick Woods, barrister and journalist, and Henrietta Maria Saint-Eloy, second daughter of the Revd Joseph Tenison of Donoughmore, co. Wicklow, who was the great-grandson of Edward *Tenison, bishop of Ossory. Julian was educated chiefly at Kent House, a Roman Catholic school in London, and at Newington grammar school. Having moved on the fringe of the Tractarian movement, he then became a Roman Catholic and joined the Passionist order. In 1852, his health having failed, he went to France, where he continued his studies, first at Lyons and then at Hyères, attending Marist seminaries. In 1854 he returned to England but, finding himself unable to remain, accompanied Bishop R. W. Wilson to Tasmania to work under him. Disagreements with Wilson, however, soon led to Woods's moving to Adelaide, where he worked as a journalist. He then entered a Jesuit college and was ordained deacon on 18 December 1856, and priest on 4 January 1857. He subsequently became a missionary priest in the south-eastern district of South Australia, where he worked energetically for ten years, especially in the parish of Penola. There, in 1866, he founded, with Mother Mary McKillop, the Sisters of St Joseph of the Sacred Heart. Towards the end of that time Woods assumed the name of Tenison before his surname.

In 1867 Tenison Woods became vicar-general of the diocese and for four years was resident in Adelaide, but he left that post to become a travelling missionary under the archbishop of Sydney. In 1873 he was missionary priest in Queensland, duty of this kind being specially attractive to him because it afforded opportunities for pursuing his scientific studies. He was frequently in dispute with his superiors, wherever he was posted. He founded several religious publications and edited the *Southern Cross* (1867–9) and the *Chaplet and Southern Cross* from 1870. Between 1874 and 1876 he spent much time in Tasmania, compiling a census of the conchology and palaeontology of the island, which was published in the *Transactions* of the local Royal Society.

In the 1870s Tenison Woods travelled widely conducting missions. He was then invited to visit the Malay States to report on their mineral resources. He made an extensive tour of Malaya and the islands to its east, witnessing some of the eruptions of Krakatoa and visiting China and Japan. On his return to Australia in 1886 he was sent by the government of South Australia to report on the mines of the northern territory. There he contracted a fever, and after staying for some time at Brisbane arrived at Sydney in 1887. He continued his scientific work but the hardships of travel had undermined his constitution. He died, of paralysis, at Sydney on 7 October 1889 and was buried in the Roman Catholic cemetery of Waverley. A monument was erected over his grave by public subscription.

Tenison Woods was a man of wide culture, a musician, an artist, and something of a poet, who wrote a number of hymns (printed for private circulation) and a poem entitled 'The Sorrows of Mary' (1883). His conversational powers made him popular in society, and he was loved by those among whom he worked, for he lived most frugally that he might give largely. He also wrote *A History of the Discovery and Exploration of Australia* (2 vols., 1865), *The Fish and Fisheries of New South Wales* (1892), and letters in newspapers describing his travels, together with more than 150 papers on natural history, geology, and palaeontology. Most of these were printed in the publications of Australian and Tasmanian societies, but two were contributed to the Geological Society of London (in 1860 and 1865), of which Woods was elected a fellow in 1859. His reports for government departments on his geological surveys were substantial. He was elected president of the Linnean Society of New South Wales in 1880 and received the Clarke medal of the Royal Society of New South Wales in 1888.

T. G. BONNEY, *rev.* H. C. G. MATTHEW

Sources private information (1900) [C. M. Tenison] · *AusDB*
Wealth at death £609: *AusDB*

Woods [*née* Bradley], **Margaret Louisa** [Daisy] (1855–1945), poet and author, was born on 20 November 1855 in Lawrence Sherriff Street, Rugby, Warwickshire, the third of the seven children of Marian Jane Philpot (1837?–1910) and George Granville *Bradley (1821–1903), then a master at Rugby School. Her father became headmaster of Marlborough College when she was three, and master of University College, Oxford, when she was fourteen. Educated largely at home, Daisy, as she was called, early found pleasure in poetry and history. At Oxford she enjoyed the intellectual stimulation provided by such friends as Rhoda Broughton, Oscar Wilde, Mrs Humphry Ward, and Mark Pattison (enamoured of her cousin Meta). On 29 March 1879 she married the Revd Henry George Woods (1842–1915), fellow and later president of Trinity College, Oxford. In 1887 they had a house, named Foxcombe Hall, built on Boars Hill, near Oxford, one of the first in the area. They had three sons, and two distinguished grandsons, both of whom earned the MC in the Second World War: Oliver Woods (1911–1972), who became Commonwealth correspondent and historian of *The Times*; and Major-General Henry G. Woods of the British army, named commander of the Order of the Bath and made an OBE.

All four of Daisy's sisters became writers—Edith Marian (Mrs Nicholl, later Ellison), Mabel Charlotte (Lady Birchenough), Emily Tennyson (Mrs Alexander Murray Smith), and Rose Marian Bradley—as did one of her two brothers (Arthur Granville). A poet since childhood, Daisy became recognized as such outside the family in 1881, when the Revd Henry Daniel of Worcester College, Oxford, printed a verse by her alongside the work of established writers in *The Garland of Rachel*. In 1888 the Daniel Press printed her *Lyrics*, and thereafter commercial publishers accepted her poetry. Her volumes included the poetic dramas *Wild Justice* (1896) and *The Princess of Hanover* (1902), *Collected Poems* (1914), and *The Return, and other Poems* (1921). Not all critics shared Robert Bridges' appreciation of her innovative prosody.

Mrs Woods's career in fiction began in 1887 with a much admired pastoral tale, *A Village Tragedy*. Later novels treat circus people, events from English, French, and Spanish history, and literary figures (Swift and Wordsworth). Her most imaginative story, *The Invader* (1907), depicts an unexceptional woman student at Oxford who, after hypnotism, periodically finds her personality taken over by an uninhibited second self that eventually undermines her marriage and causes her death. A decade before the book appeared, Mrs Woods had been gratified by her husband's resignation from Trinity College, giving her health as the cause. They had sold Foxcombe Hall to the eighth earl of Berkeley in 1893, and their life in London, where her husband served as master of the Temple from 1904 until his death in 1915, better suited her literary aspirations.

Mrs Woods wrote on travelling in Spain, France, and South Africa; women's domestic and literary roles; the relation of verse to music and dance; and Victorian authors she had known, notably Tennyson and Matthew Arnold. Until the late 1930s she was active in the Royal Society of Literature. She died at her home, Vine Cottage, Witley Road, Thursley, Surrey, on 1 December 1945. Her funeral was held at St Michael and All Angels Church, Thursley, on 4 December, after which she was cremated; her ashes were interred on 6 December in her husband's grave at Holywell cemetery, Oxford.

MARTHA S. VOGELER

Sources *The Times* (3 Dec 1945), 7e–f · *The Times* (4 Dec 1945), 6f · *The Times* (5 Dec 1945), 7b · *The Times* (20 July 1915) · *WWW* · Bodl. Oxf., MSS Margaret L. Woods · M. L. Woods, 'Oxford in the "Seventies"', *The Fortnightly*, 150 (1941), 276–82 · M. L. Woods, 'Mrs Humphry Ward: a sketch from memory', *QR*, 234 (1920), 147–60 · S. P. Sherman, 'Margaret L. Woods', *The Nation* (7 May 1914), 523–5 · W. L. Courtney, 'Mrs Woods', *The feminine note in fiction* (1904) · M. S. Vogeler, 'Margaret L. Woods', *Late nineteenth- and early twentieth-century British women poets*, ed. W. B. Thesing, DLitB, 240 (2001) · b. cert. · m. cert. · d. cert. · CD-ROM (baptism), Family Records Centre, London · M. Bradley, diary, BL, Egerton MSS · private information (2004) [H. G. Woods]

Archives Bodl. Oxf., lectures and papers · NRA, corresp. and literary papers | BL, corresp. with Macmillans, Add. MS 54969 · BLPES, letters to Frederic Harrison · Bodl. Oxf., corresp. with H. A. L. Fisher · Ches. & Chester ALSS, letters to Rhoda Broughton · Harvard U., Houghton L., letters to Sir William Rothenstein · Royal Society of Literature, archives · Trinity College, Oxford, Henry George Woods MSS · Worcester College, Oxford, letters to C. H. O. Daniel

Likenesses J. M. Cameron, photograph, 1864, NPG; repro. in C. Ford, *The Cameron collection: an album of photographs by Julia Margaret Cameron, presented to Sir John Herschel* (1975) · photograph (with her family), Trinity College, Oxford

Wealth at death £6297 4s. 5d.: probate, 9 March 1946, CGPLA Eng. & Wales

Woods, Marianne (b. 1782/3). *See under* Pirie, Jane (b. 1783/4).

Woods, Richard (1715/16–1793), landscape designer, was born in 1715 or 1716, according to his obituary in the *Laity's Directory* (1793). His parentage and place of birth are unknown, and as a Roman Catholic his baptismal records may not have survived. The circumstances of his education are also unknown although he obviously received sufficient schooling to become a competent surveyor and draughtsman. He may have been born in Chertsey, Surrey, where he can first be positively identified, in 1751, as the purchaser of a small piece of copyhold land in Gogmore Lane. At this date he was already married to his first wife, Hannah. By 1761 he had an additional address, in Sidney's Alley, London (off Leicester Square), but by 1764 he had moved from Chertsey to London Stile, near Kew Bridge. In 1768, at the height of his career, he settled in Essex as the

tenant of North Ockendon Hall, a mansion with a farm of 250 acres, and his final move, following the death of Hannah in 1783, was to a relatively modest pair of cottages at Herongate, in Ingrave, Brentwood. Here he married Mary Gorst on 22 November 1783 and obtained the post of surveyor to the ninth Baron Petre, which he held until his death.

The first recorded, though probably not the earliest, of Woods's forty-odd known commissions was in 1758 at Buckland, Oxfordshire, where he laid out the park, provided plants, and probably designed the garden buildings. The following year he was working at Hartwell House, Buckinghamshire, designing a 'New Garden Greenhouse and Pinery'. In the 1760s his practice moved to Yorkshire, where his commissions included Cannon Hall, Cusworth, Bretton Hall, Goldsborough, Kirklees, and Harewood. By 1764 he was also working for Lord Arundell at Wardour Castle, potentially the most important commission of his career; he spent seven years laying out the park round James Paine's new mansion, as well as at Irnham, Lord Arundell's other property in Lincolnshire. At this stage it looked as though Woods's career might approach Lancelot Brown's in importance, as he was invited first to Lulworth Castle (1769), then to Wynnstay (1770) and to Brocket Hall (1770). Of these three only Brocket was a success, described by William Angus in *Seats of the Nobility* (1787) as having 'most picturesque and beautiful' grounds, with 'the Water and Out-grounds … laid out and disposed by Mr. Wood of Essex in the most luxuriant and masterly Manner' (text to plate 28).

As a Catholic, Woods undoubtedly enjoyed patronage from some of the great Catholic families that he might not otherwise have been given, but in the majority of his commissions his religion does not seem to have been relevant. At the beginning of his career it is likely that he was involved at Woburn Farm, created by a fellow Catholic, Philip Southcote, in the 1740s and very close to Woods's own property in Chertsey. The possibility of an association with Southcote is strengthened by the close connection between the Southcote and Petre families. By 1780 Woods's reputation no longer shone so brightly, and his later work was restricted mainly to small properties in Essex. The size of his estate at his death shows how his practice had dwindled.

Each eighteenth-century 'improver' had an individual style within the prevailing fashion for artificial naturalism, which was given its most successful form by Lancelot Brown. Woods tended towards more detail, more flowers, and more features in his layouts. His most successful commissions are on a relatively small scale (c.40–100 acres), and included Cannon Hall (1760) and Cusworth (1761) in Yorkshire and Wivenhoe (1776), Copford (1784), and Brizes (1788) in Essex. At all of these he created a harmonious and varied setting for the house, pleasing rather than grand. His best-documented work is at Cusworth, Doncaster, where he wrote a series of memoranda for the foreman in which every step is explained in the construction of the features considered necessary for a landscape park.

While his business was flourishing Woods is known to have used several foremen who supervised the progress of work on site. Obviously he also had a number of draughtsmen and surveyors, as the style of his plans and drawings varies from place to place. The drawings known to be in his own hand are not very polished.

As part of his repertory as a landscape designer, Woods produced plans and drawings for garden structures such as pavilions, temples, greenhouses, and bridges. These are either included on the 'plan for improvements' which accompanied many of his commissions, or presented as separate drawings, with plan and elevation. His skill as an architect appears limited, and a number of his ideas can be traced to pattern books. Those of his designs that were executed lack the elegance and sophistication of Brown's, but are nevertheless pleasing additions to the landscape setting.

Woods died at his home, New Cottage, Herongate, on 30 April 1793. He was buried in Ingrave, and his widow, Mary, was left as administrator of his estate, valued at less than £300.

With those of other eighteenth-century landscape designers, Woods's reputation was obliterated by the Victorians, who deplored the replacement of formal gardens with naturalistic parkland. However, in his lifetime he was highly regarded, and even the great Brown 'had the taste to admire and fortitude to applaud' the plantation at Wardour 'suggested by Mr Wood of Essex' (Richard Warner, *Excursions from Bath*, 1801, 150). Few of Woods's gardens survive in a state close to their original form: the delightful garden at Copford Hall is in reasonable condition, as is the park at Cannon Hall. Cusworth Hall, typical of Woods at his best, is emerging from a state of over-use and neglect; lottery funding has been allocated for its complete restoration.   FIONA COWELL

Sources F. Cowell, 'Richard Woods (?1716–93): a preliminary account [pt 1]', *Garden History*, 14 (1986), 85–119 • F. Cowell, 'Richard Woods (?1716–93): a preliminary account [pts 2–3]', *Garden History*, 15 (1987), 19–54, 115–35 • R. W. King, 'The *ferme ornée*: Philip Southcote and Woburn Farm', *Garden History*, 2/3 (1974), 27–60, 28a • H. Prince, *Parks in England* (1967) • *Laity's Directory* (1793) • allegiance roll of 1778, Essex RO, Q/RRo 1/43/1 • *Catalogue of household effects* (1783) [sale catalogue, Christies, North Ockendon Hall, Essex, 29 Sept 1783] • court books, Manor of Chertsey Beomond, 1740–53, Surrey HC, 97/9 • lease of North Ockendon Hall, 1 Oct 1768, Essex RO, D/DBe E15 • court book of the manor of Ingrave, Essex RO, D/DP M 1378, p. 4 • Ingrave parish registers: marriages, 1755–96, Essex RO, D/P 187/1/4 • payments to Woods as surveyor to Lord Petre, Essex RO, D/P/A90 • administration of Woods's estate, 2 June 1793, Essex RO, D/ABAc 24
Archives Essex RO, Chelmsford, letters | Berks. RO, Buckland, D/EWe • Bucks. RLSS, Hartwell House, D/LE • Calderdale District Archives, Kirklees, MSS • Cusworth Hall Museum • Doncaster Central Library, Doncaster Archives, DD/BW • Dorset RO, Weld MSS, Lulworth Castle • Essex RO, Colchester, Wivenhoe Hall, D/DHt • Essex RO, Colchester, Copford Hall, D/DU 161 • Essex RO, Brizes (assum), D/DRo P1 • Herts. ALS, Melbourne MSS • Leeds district archives, Battie-Wrightson MSS • Leeds district archives, Harewood MSS • LMA, acc. 262/43/188 • NL Wales, Wynnstay MSS • Sheffield Central Library, Spencer-Stanhope MSS • U. Leeds, Bretton Hall College, archives • Warks. CRO, CR 1998/box 57 • Wilts. & Swindon RO, Wardour Castle
Wealth at death under £300: administration, 2 June 1793, Essex RO, D/ABAc 24

Woods, Samuel (1846–1915), trade unionist and politician, was born on 10 May 1846, at Peasley Cross, St Helens, the son of Thomas Woods, a miner, and his wife, Margaret (*née* Rothwell), until 1840 also a mine worker. Woods's first introduction to mining was at the age of seven. He returned to school from the age of nine to thirteen, but then went back to the pits. He was an assiduous attender at night school, and this education was reinforced by his durable and strong commitment to the Baptist church. He was a lay preacher and a total abstainer. He married a miner's daughter, Sarah Lee, in 1867; they had twelve children.

Woods's fellow workers elected him to the post of checkweighman in 1875 and three years later he started to organize the miners in the St Helens and Haydock districts of the Lancashire coalfield. From 1881 he was a significant figure in the newly formed Lancashire and Cheshire Miners' Federation, becoming the first Lancashire president in 1884. When delegates from several coalfields met at Newport in 1889 and formed the Miners' Federation of Great Britain (MFGB), Woods became the new organization's vice-president.

Woods was a thorough advocate of the central policies of the MFGB—the eight-hour day by legislation, and the achievement of a system of mutual defence between coalfields on the wages question. He was heavily involved in the 1893 lock-out which strengthened the credibility of the MFGB: it led to government intervention and the establishment of a conciliation board.

In the 1892 general election, Woods was returned for the Ince division of Lancashire. He campaigned 'first and foremost as a Labour candidate' (*Wigan Observer*, 25 June 1892), but also acknowledged he was a 'Home Ruler and a Radical' (ibid., 30 June 1892) and welcomed Liberal Party support. His victory over the incumbent, a Conservative employer, was followed by a frustrating period at Westminster. He successfully moved the second reading of the miners' Eight Hours Bill in May 1893. The bill progressed no further. The miners members—all Liberals—were divided. Those within the MFGB, including Woods, were keen advocates; those from the still independent Northumberland and Durham unions were opposed.

Woods was defeated at the 1895 general election, but early in 1897 he returned to the Commons after a by-election victory in a very different constituency, Walthamstow. His victory was something of a surprise and he was subsequently defeated at the 1900 election. His position on the Second South African War was attacked by his Conservative opponent; he responded by acknowledging his opposition to the diplomacy that had preceded the war, but claimed he had subsequently backed the government's policy. This was the end of his parliamentary career. He was subsequently associated with the National Democratic League, a combination of radicals and labour leaders.

In 1894 Woods was elected secretary of the Trades Union Congress's parliamentary committee in a three-cornered

Samuel Woods (1846–1915), by unknown engraver, pubd 1897

Archives People's History Museum, Manchester, papers | National Union of Mineworkers offices, Sheffield, Miners' Federation of Great Britain records · NUM, Hilden Street, Leigh, Lancashire area offices, Miners' Federation of Great Britain records · NUM, Hilden Street, Leigh, Lancashire Area Offices, Lancashire and Cheshire Miners' Federation records
Likenesses woodcut, NPG; repro. in *The Graphic* (13 Feb 1897) [*see illus.*]
Wealth at death £235: probate, 7 Dec 1915, *CGPLA Eng. & Wales*

Woods, Samuel Moses James (1867–1931), cricketer, was born at Glenfield, near Sydney, Australia, on 4 April 1867, fourth son in the family of five sons and seven daughters of John Woods and his wife, Margaret. His parents came from co. Antrim and, after their marriage in 1853, decided to seek their fortune in Australia. John Woods prospered in business and settled in Sydney, where Sammy received his first education at Royston College and Sydney grammar school. He soon developed a passion for cricket: his most remarkable feat at school was to take seven wickets in seven balls.

Their father took Sammy Woods and a younger brother, Harris, to Britain in 1884, when Sammy was sixteen. He went to Silwood House School in Tunbridge Wells and on to Brighton College. There his all-round sporting prowess flowered from a base provided for him by a banker friend of his father's, Gilbert Burrington of Bridgwater, who became in effect Sammy's guardian. It is not clear how he got into Cambridge in 1888 for he was, notoriously, not at all bookish and had been turned down by Oxford. After four years' residence—'four of the jolliest years of my life' (Woods, 30)—he left the university without taking a degree (1891). But as an undergraduate at Jesus College he had an immediate impact on university cricket, winning four cricket blues and playing a decisive role in three Cambridge victories. He took thirty-six wickets at an average of less than 9 and Oxford scarcely managed an innings over 100 in any of the matches in which he played. While still an undergraduate he played three test matches for Australia against England (1888) and eight matches for the Gentlemen v. the Players. In 1891, playing for Cambridge, he took fourteen Surrey wickets for 11 runs each. His rugby football prowess was also outstanding; he was a Cambridge rugby blue 1888–90, and played thirteen times for England between 1890 and 1895, leading England to the triple crown as captain in 1895.

It is as a Somerset cricketer that Woods is now best remembered. Between 1886 and 1910 he played in 299 matches for the county. He, virtually alone, ensured first-class status for Somerset and led them through their difficult early years. He scored 12,637 runs for his county, took 556 wickets, and was a brilliant fielder. Many of his finest performances were against the best sides, notably Yorkshire, Surrey, and Sussex: in 1895 he scored 215 against Sussex in two and a half hours. He played three tests for England in South Africa in 1895–6, thus joining the small band of men who have played test cricket for more than one country. He toured abroad under Lord Hawke to America twice, South Africa, and the West Indies. One of the greatest amateur fast bowlers during cricket's 'golden age' at the turn of the twentieth century, with a deadly

contest. Woods's defeat of the incumbent, the Northumbrian Charles Fenwick, was that of an MFGB official over another miner who was a strong opponent of the Eight Hours Bill. His secretaryship covered the years when the Labour Representation Committee was formed and several trade unions affiliated to the new political organization. Initially the political significance of this development was unclear and Woods as a Liberal could accommodate to it without great difficulty. As secretary to the parliamentary committee, Woods was at first industrious and efficient, but from 1900 his health deteriorated and complaints grew about his performance. He retired in 1904 and that was almost the end of his public career. He continued as MFGB vice-president until 1909; in the later years this was an honorific appointment supported by the MFGB's Liberals as a means of blocking the socialist, Robert Smillie. Woods died at his home, 238 Wigan Road, Brynn Ashton, near Wigan, on 23 November 1915.

Woods played a significant part in constructing both the Lancashire Miners' Federation and the MFGB and was a thorough advocate of the latter's policies. His religious enthusiasm meant that he was a reassuring figure for those nonconformists who were concerned about 'Labour agitators' (*St Helens Newspaper and Advertiser*). By the late 1890s he was a respected figure in Liberal circles, but his links with the coalfield were increasingly tenuous. His record was perhaps overshadowed by the emergence and subsequent dominance of independent labour politics. William Brace, a miners' leader of the next generation, remembered him for 'his genial companionship and kindly ways … a dapper gentle kind of soul' (Arnot, 204).

DAVID HOWELL

Sources R. P. Arnot, *The miners: a history of the Miners' Federation of Great Britain*, 1: … *1889–1910* (1949) · H. A. Clegg, A. Fox, and A. F. Thompson, *A history of British trade unions since 1889*, 1 (1964) · R. Gregory, *The miners and British politics, 1906–1914* (1968) · T. Ashton, *Three big strikes in the coal industry* (1894?) · T. Scott, 'The Lancashire and Cheshire Miners' Federation, 1900–1914', PhD diss., York University, 1977 · J. Bellamy, 'Woods, Samuel', *DLB*, vol. 1 · *Wigan Observer* (25 June 1892) · *Wigan Observer* (30 June 1892) · *St Helens Newspaper and Advertiser* (3 Dec 1915) yorker and a deceptive slower delivery, he had career statistics of 1040 wickets (at 20.82) and 15,345 runs (at 23.42).

Woods was famous for his sportsmanship (he loathed draws and always went for a win), his courage, his cheerful manner, and, standing over 6 feet tall and weighing 13½ stone, his fine physique. Gilbert Jessop called him 'the personification of pluck and good fellowship' (Woods, 6). His inability to settle down to a gainful occupation which would support him as an amateur player caused Somerset to appoint him assistant secretary, at a salary of £200 a year, in 1898. His playing career was ended by arthritis in 1911. At the outbreak of the First World War he was in his forty-eighth year and had difficulty persuading the army to take him. Eventually a friend at headquarters got him a commission in the Somerset light infantry; later he was transferred to the 20th Devons and served in the labour corps. Somerset made him club secretary in 1920. Paperwork was not his forte and an outcry among the members following an increase in subscriptions to meet a deficit led to his resignation in 1923 to make way for a new secretary 'with a business-like head' (Roebuck, 141).

Gradually Woods's accumulated injuries began to afflict him. Arthritis was made worse by the heavy drinking he so much enjoyed. Having no real home, he took rooms in pubs and hotels in Taunton and reputedly drank a bottle of whisky a day to alleviate his pain. His conviviality was unimpaired, however, and his stock of anecdotes and capacity to entertain never ran dry. He was a familiar sight in the streets of Taunton chatting with friends and often surrounded by children. Robertson-Glasgow said that everyone loved Sammy 'for the whole world's manliness and generosity seemed to have gathered in his heart' (46 Not Out, 1948, 129). Yet he had very few close relationships and, though fond of female company, he never married. Early in 1931 a London specialist diagnosed inoperable cancer of the oesophagus. Woods died in Taunton on 30 April 1931 and was buried on 4 May in St Mary's cemetery, Taunton, within sight of his beloved Quantock hills. A superb sportsman, without swagger, Woods 'was just a big man child' (Roebuck, 38).   D. R. W. SILK

Sources C. Jiggens, *Sammy: the sporting life of S. M. J. Woods* (1997) · S. M. J. Woods, *My reminiscences* (1925) · P. Roebuck, *From Sammy to Jimmy: the official history of Somerset county cricket club* (1991) · R. A. Roberts, *Sixty years of Somerset cricket* (1952) · *Wisden* (1932) · Venn, *Alum. Cant.*

Likenesses Hawkins & Co., Brighton, photograph, repro. in C. W. Alcock, *Famous cricketers and cricket grounds* (1895) · caricature, repro. in *VF* (6 Aug 1892) · photograph, repro. in Woods, *My reminiscences*, frontispiece · photograph, repro. in Roebuck, *From Sammy to Jimmy*

Wealth at death £137 18s. 3d.: probate, 1931 · A£641 effects in Australia: resealed probate, 1932

Woods, Sir Wilfrid John Wentworth (1906–1975), naval officer, was born on 19 February 1906 at Genoa Villa, Netley Road, Southsea, the only child of Sir Wilfrid Wentworth Woods (1876–1947), colonial civil servant, and his wife, Ethel Maud Palmer (c.1875–1942). Woods went to Seabrook Lodge preparatory school at Hythe in Kent and was then accepted as a naval cadet at the age of thirteen,

Sir Wilfrid John Wentworth Woods (1906–1975), by Walter Bird, 1966

attending the Royal Naval College at Osborne and Dartmouth from 1919 to 1923. He joined submarines in 1927 and went as third hand to HMS *L19* on the China station where submarines happily practised their trade 10,000 miles removed from the heavy hand of head office. On 27 January 1930 he married Murray Auriol Ruth Inglis (1907/8–1956), daughter of Charles Stuart Inglis, retired Royal Navy paymaster. They had one son (who predeceased them) and a daughter. In 1957 he married Joan Bridget Constance Eden, an officer in the Women's Royal Naval Service.

Woods's first command was the modern submarine HMS *Seahorse* in 1935, and his next appointments also hinted at a bright future. At the outbreak of the Second World War he was staff operations officer for the 6th submarine flotilla at Blyth before taking his second submarine command *Triumph* to the 1st flotilla in the Mediterranean, arriving at Alexandria in December 1940. Woods enjoyed a busy year savaging axis supply vessels and warships, including damage to the cruiser *Belzano*, as well as landing or recovering military personnel and agents off enemy-occupied shores. In June 1941 he was awarded the DSO for engaging the Italian U-boat *Salpa* in a gun duel and then sinking her with a torpedo: his narrative concluded '… no survivors were seen. Dived when clear of oil patch. Hands to breakfast' (Woods MSS).

Woods was decorated with Yugoslavian and Greek orders in recognition of special operations, and a bar to the DSO was for 'daring, enterprise and devotion to duty'.

Important staff posts and commands followed promotion to commander in June 1941 and to captain four years later. In 1955 he was appointed flag officer, submarines, as a rear-admiral (CB in 1957). Then, as vice-admiral, he was deputy supreme allied commander, Atlantic, from 1958 to 1960 in Norfolk, Virginia, where he cemented Anglo-American ties. Tall, upright, and good looking, and endowed with exceptional physical and mental stamina, he personified the ideal British representative to NATO organizations. He was knighted in 1960. Warm relationships with NATO continued when he was commander-in-chief, Home Fleet, 1960–63, and in his final naval post as commander-in-chief, Portsmouth, 1963–5.

Woods was seldom known as Wilfrid, even when knighted, save on the most formal occasions: his nicknames Sammy, Sam, or, occasionally, Tod point to the affection in which he was held throughout a naval career spanning forty-six years from cadet to admiral. He was one of those rare men who rose steadily to the top of his profession while attracting neither envy nor calumny *en route*: he was kind, caring, and consistently loyal not only to the service but to those who served him. The reports on him by his superiors, as he progressed upwards, speak mainly of great ability, particularly in staff work—'the best chief of staff anybody could ever want', wrote the demanding Mountbatten, then commander-in-chief, Mediterranean, in October 1954 (Woods MSS)—but the brief (and often stereotyped) pen-portraits imply underlying qualities of determination, dependability, and honesty.

In retirement Woods was a deputy lord lieutenant for Hampshire and, for four years, a most successful chairman of the RNLI: he wiped out the latter's deficit of £400,000 and made possible a much expanded lifeboat-building programme. He died on 1 January 1975 at the Royal Victoria Hospital, Bournemouth.

RICHARD COMPTON-HALL

Sources personal knowledge (2004) · officers' histories, Royal Naval Submarine Museum, Gosport, Woods MSS, esp. file 1976/40 · letters (private) from Mountbatten of Burma to Woods, Royal Naval Submarine Museum, Gosport, Woods MSS · Ministry of Defence letter, 21 Sept 1965, Royal Naval Submarine Museum, Gosport, archival file 1977/92, N/N2/466/28/65A · private information (2004) · *CGPLA Eng. & Wales* (1975) · *WWW* · b. cert. · d. cert. · S. W. Roskill, *The war at sea, 1939–1945*, 3 vols. in 4 (1954–61) · m. cert.
Archives Royal Naval Submarine Museum, Gosport, officers' histories | FILM IWM FVA, actuality footage
Likenesses W. Bird, photograph, 1966, NPG [*see illus.*] · photographs, Royal Naval Submarine Museum, Gosport
Wealth at death £37,079: probate, 7 Aug 1975, *CGPLA Eng. & Wales*

Woodstock, Anne of. *See* Anne of Woodstock (*c*.1382–1438).

Woodsworth, James Shaver (1874–1942), Methodist minister and politician in Canada, was born on 29 July 1874 at Applewood, the farmstead of his mother's family, the Shavers, in Etobicoke township, near Toronto, Ontario, the eldest son of six children of the Revd James Woodsworth (1843–1918) and his wife, Esther Josephine Shaver. The Woodsworth family originated in Yorkshire. J. S.

James Shaver Woodsworth (1874–1942), by unknown photographer, 1921

Woodsworth's grandfather Richard Woodsworth had migrated to Upper Canada in 1830, settling in York, the colonial capital. He married Mary Ann Watson, of loyalist stock, whose family had migrated to Upper Canada from the United States after the Anglo-American War of 1812–14. The couple had twelve children of whom James, J. S.'s father, was the seventh. James married Esther, of German-Dutch descent, in 1868. The Shavers originated in 'High Germany', then moved, first to New York and then Pennsylvania, before coming north to Ancaster (near Hamilton), Ontario, and finally settling in Etobicoke, where Esther's parents, Peter and Esther, built Applewood. James Woodsworth began in business, but abandoned that career for the Methodist ministry. He first ministered in Ontario before moving his family west when, in 1886, he was appointed first superintendent of the Methodist missions in the north-west. That mission field, or parish as Methodists delighted in calling it, covered all of present-day western Canada, thus making James Woodsworth the most influential Methodist west of Toronto.

Methodist ministry and social gospel, 1891–1918 Little is known of J. S. Woodsworth's childhood years and early education. In 1891 he entered the Methodist-affiliated Wesley College, established only three years earlier in Winnipeg. By the turn of the century the college would be a leading advocate of social reform in the west, but in 1891 it was still a small struggling institution with only a handful of students and a skeleton staff. Woodsworth studied mental and moral sciences—a preparation for his lifelong concern with ethical questions. He was a moderate achiever academically, winning a bronze medal (second prize) in philosophy, but he particularly excelled socially, being voted 'senior stick' (president of the student body) in his final year, 1895–6. He took five years to complete his three-year BA course, chiefly because of his need to teach in school during his college years to finance his education.

Upon graduation Woodsworth spent two years as a probationer, or circuit-rider minister, in southern Manitoba in preparation for entering the ministry. He once commented that he had not chosen the ministry, he was born into it. In 1898 he entered Victoria University, the Methodist college affiliated with the University of Toronto, to pursue a BD degree, which he obtained in 1900. In his final year, he studied at Mansfield College, Oxford, although he never enrolled there, attending Edward Caird's lectures on philosophy at Balliol College and Andrew Fairbairn's on theology at Mansfield. He worked on a paper on 'Christian ethics' in which he came to the surprising, and disturbing, conclusion that morality and man's pursuit of goodness could exist and thrive apart from Christianity, or, to put it in another context, the good life could be lived in the secular realm through the application of universal humanitarian beliefs and moral values. He used the opportunity of being in Oxford to tour England and to assist in the Mansfield Settlement House in London's East End, where he observed firsthand the plight of the poor. In later life he claimed that this experience had drawn him towards social reform.

Woodsworth was ordained in August 1900 and his first ministerial charge was in Carrievale, Saskatchewan, followed by a year at Keewatin in north-western Ontario. In 1902 he moved to Winnipeg, where he was appointed associate minister at Winnipeg's fashionable Grace Church. Two years later, in 1904, he married Lucy Lilian Staples (b. 1874) of Bethany, near Lindsay, Ontario. She had been a fellow student at Victoria University, where she majored in moderns and history. They had six children.

From the beginning Woodsworth had doubts about his calling to the ministry, wanting instead to be a university professor (although he lacked the necessary academic qualifications) or a missionary. In 1902 he wrote the first of a series of letters of resignation from the church, but was dissuaded by friends and church affiliates from submitting it. In 1906 he left Grace Church when the opportunity came for him and his wife to accompany his father on a tour of Europe and the Middle East; he saw it as an opportunity to reassess the direction of his life. Upon his return in 1907 he tendered his resignation from the ministry, citing the need to 'be free to think and speak out my own thoughts, and live out my own life' (McNaught, 35). Church officials declined to accept his resignation, offering him instead the position of superintendent of Methodist missions in Winnipeg, and placing him in charge of All People's Mission located in the heart of Winnipeg's ethnic North End.

Out of his experiences Woodsworth wrote two books: *Strangers within our Gates* (1909), which dwelt on the diverse ethnic population in the city and the need to assist them in becoming Canadians; and *My Neighbour* (1911), a sociological study that addressed problems associated with modern cities. Latter-day critics have chastised him for his narrow British perspective and even racist attitudes towards native people and ethnic groups in these writings. Clearly Woodsworth worried about the negative impact on national unity and a Canadian identity of such large numbers of non-British immigrants who ended up in ethnic ghettos, making it difficult to assist them in being assimilated into Canadian society. He believed it to be the responsibility of churches and other reform-minded institutions to help in this process of assimilation and integration. In his concern for the downtrodden of society and in his appeal to churches to become more involved in social issues he was advocating beliefs associated with the 'social gospel'—a creedless movement in the protestant churches directed at establishing 'the kingdom of God on earth'.

In 1913 Woodsworth left All People's Mission to become first secretary of the Canadian Welfare League, founded by the Canadian Council of Charities and Corrections to deal with the many social problems arising from mass immigration. He published the league's handbook, *Studies in Rural Citizenship*, which served as a study guide and provided him with material for a series of lectures he gave to students of social work in Winnipeg, Toronto, and Montreal. Then, in 1916, he was appointed director of the newly created Bureau of Social Research, established by the three prairie provinces. Both positions reflected his conscious move away from the ministry and even the church and into social work, believing the latter to be a more effective means to bring about positive social change.

The First World War altered the direction of Woodsworth's life significantly. He believed in pacifism, and thus opposed the Methodist church's support of the Canadian war effort. He particularly objected to military conscription—forced service as he called it—and went public with his protest in a letter to the *Manitoba Free Press* in December 1916. The letter resulted in the closing of the Bureau of Social Research and the termination of his position as director. It also caused a break between him and the church, resulting in his resignation in 1918, claiming that 'the teachings and spirit of Jesus are absolutely irreconcilable with the advocacy of war' (McNaught, 84).

Socialist politician, 1919–1942 Woodsworth turned now to labour-related activities. He worked briefly as a longshoreman on the Vancouver docks, organized the Federated Labour Party of British Columbia, assisted Finnish settlers on the west coast in establishing a co-operative store, worked for the Non-Partisan League in Alberta, and toured western Canada, giving lectures on the labour movement. He was in Winnipeg at the height of the city's general strike in the spring of 1919, and addressed striking workers. When the editor of the *Western Labor News* was arrested for his attack on the business community and government officials for their treatment of the strikers, Woodsworth took over his position and espoused the same views, resulting in his arrest as well on charges of seditious libel. He was never brought to trial, but the charges were never formally withdrawn.

By 1920 Woodsworth believed in the need for workers to have a political voice in parliament. In the federal election of 1921 he ran for the Independent Labour Party in Winnipeg Centre. His win gave him the distinction of being the first socialist representative of the working class in the Canadian parliament, and began a twenty-one-year career as the MP for Winnipeg Centre. He aimed to create the Canadian equivalent of the British Labour Party. In parliament he co-operated with members of the newly elected Progressive Party, that represented the farming interests, to bring in legislation that would benefit workers and farmers. When a split occurred among the Progressives between those who wanted to co-operate with the Liberal government to bring in new legislation and those who opposed collaboration as undermining the principles that the party stood for, Woodsworth allied with the latter to form the 'Ginger Group' in 1924. This group, and especially Woodsworth, succeeded in pressuring the Liberal government to bring in Canada's first pension plan in 1927.

The Ginger Group formed the political nucleus of Canada's first socialist party, the Co-operative Commonwealth Federation (CCF), founded in 1932. At the party's first convention the delegates chose J. S. Woodsworth as party leader, a position he held until 1940. He also became honorary president of the League for Social Reconstruction, an association largely of academics and professionals modelled after the British Fabian Society, that drafted the CCF's first socialist platform, known as the Regina manifesto (since it was adopted at the party's second annual convention in Regina, Saskatchewan). The CCF did not fare well electorally under Woodsworth's leadership, winning only seven seats in the federal election of 1935 and eight seats in 1940, but the party did acquire the reputation of being 'the conscience of the House'. This honour was due in large part to Woodsworth's championing of the civil liberties of minorities. He defended the communists when they were threatened by deportation under section 98 of the criminal code, even though the CCF was at the time feuding with the communists over socialist ideology; he criticized the government for denying Dukhobors the right to vote under the Franchise Act; he assisted Asians who were being discriminated against in British Columbia; and he supported Jehovah's Witnesses and communists in Quebec when they were being denied the right of free speech and assembly under the province's notorious padlock law.

The Second World War caused a crisis of conscience for Woodsworth not unlike that experienced during the First. Again, he went on record as being opposed to Canada's involvement—the only member of parliament to do so. In his speech to parliament, justifying his position, he declared:

I rejoice that it is possible to say these things in a Canadian Parliament under British institutions. It would not be possible in Germany, I recognize that ... and I want to maintain the very essence of our British institutions of real liberty. I believe that the only way to do it is by an appeal to the moral forces which are still resident among our people, and not by another resort to brute force. (McNaught, 312)

The party caucus, however, disagreed with his position, believing Hitler to be a greater menace to British democratic values than fighting. When the party voted in parliament for Canadian involvement in the war effort, Woodsworth tendered his resignation as party president. But the CCF council declined it. He continued as leader until a series of strokes in early 1940 forced him to step down. The party created a new position of honorary president for him, while abolishing the position of president, replacing it with that of national chairman. Woodsworth died of a stroke in Vancouver on 21 March 1942 and was cremated there the following day; he was survived by his wife and six children. R. DOUGLAS FRANCIS

Sources A. Mills, *Fool for Christ: the political thought of J. S. Woodsworth* (1991) · K. McNaught, *A prophet in politics: a biography of J. S. Woodsworth* (1959) · M. D. Johnson, 'The crisis of faith and social Christianity: the ethical pilgrimage of James Shaver Woodsworth', *Victorian faith in crisis*, ed. R. J. Helmstadter and B. Lightman (1990), 343–79 · H. Gutkin and M. Gutkin, 'An idealist in the political arena: James Shaver Woodsworth', *Profiles in dissent* (1997), 251–99 · R. Cook, *The regenerators: social criticism in late Victorian English Canada* (1985), 213–23 · G. MacInnis, *J. S. Woodsworth: a man to remember* (1953) · F. H. Underhill, 'J. S. Woodsworth', *In search of Canadian liberalism* (1960) · O. Ziegler, *Woodsworth: social pioneer* (1934) · *Winnipeg Free Press* (23 March 1942), 5
Archives NA Canada, MSS
Likenesses photograph, 1921, NA Canada [*see illus.*]

Woodville [Wydeville], **Anthony**, **second Earl Rivers** (*c.*1440–1483), magnate, was the eldest son of Richard *Woodville, first Earl Rivers (*d.* 1469), administrator and soldier, and his wife, Jacquetta, widow of John of Lancaster, duke of Bedford. His mother's dower was held for life only. Since Woodville could inherit only his father's barony and three manors in Kent and Northamptonshire, there was some justification for the condescension towards him of the Yorkist earls in 1460. Woodville's prospects were substantially improved by his marriage, in the same year, as second husband to Elizabeth Scales, heir of Thomas *Scales, Lord Scales, who died in July 1460; he was summoned to parliament as Lord Scales from 1462. Although the marriage was childless and in law he was not entitled to even a life estate in Elizabeth's lands on her death, he resettled them in 1466, which enabled him to retain them after her death in 1473, to the loss of her heirs; he bequeathed them to his own brother Edward.

Although some lands were held by a dowager in 1436, when the Scales barony was valued for taxation at £376, it was clearly a modest estate. The centre was Middleton near Bishop's Lynn, which was sacked by adherents of Clarence and Warwick in 1469. Altogether there were fifteen manors in Norfolk, one in Cambridgeshire, and the advowsons of two priories and several parish churches. Woodville was rarely resident, even apparently in the 1460s. He exercised influence at the important port of Bishop's Lynn, but he was a second-rate figure even in East Anglia, where the dukes of Norfolk and Suffolk, the earl of Oxford, and Lord Howard counted for more.

Anthony Woodville, second Earl Rivers (c.1440–1483), manuscript illumination [kneeling, second from left]

By birth a minor member of the international nobility Woodville had inherited the military tastes of his father and grandfather and was indeed one of the military specialists at the Yorkist court. He was also something of a knight errant, interested in jousting, crusades, and pilgrimages. His military career apparently commenced at Sandwich in January 1460, when he and his father were preparing an attack to recover Calais from the Yorkist earls and were carried off from Sandwich to Calais by them instead. This was the occasion when Richard Neville, earl of Warwick, and the future Edward IV 'rated' him as a parvenu: his father had been a mere knight who had married a duchess (Jacquetta, duchess of Bedford) and his lineage was far inferior to their own. He was on the losing side at Towton in 1461, where he was wounded and at first reported killed. In 1468 he was appointed commander of a naval force to support Brittany against the French, which was forestalled by a Franco-Breton truce, and again in 1470, when he repulsed Warwick from Southampton, patrolled the channel, and even outpointed Warwick's squadron in the Seine. He was also appointed lieutenant of Calais in succession to Warwick. Wounded again at Barnet in April 1471 he remained at London, where he repulsed the assault led by Thomas Neville, the Bastard of Fauconberg. He aspired to fight the Moors in Portugal, took yet another relieving force to Brittany in 1472, served on Edward's invasion of France in 1475, and witnessed Charles the Bold's camp at Morat. He was one of the principal commanders in Gloucester's successful invasion of Scotland in 1482.

The pinnacle of Woodville's jousting was his celebrated tournament with the count of La Roche, the Bastard of Burgundy, in 1467, which was recorded both by the Burgundian chroniclers and by an English herald. In 1465, in accordance with chivalric protocol, he challenged the renowned knight Antoine, count of La Roche, natural son of Philippe, duke of Burgundy, and, following political delays, the tournament was held at Smithfield on 11 and 12 June 1467 before a splendid audience presided over by the king. On the first day, when they fought on horseback, the Bastard's horse was killed; on the second, when they fought with axes, Woodville held his own and the joust was declared drawn. Next year, at the marriage celebrations of Margaret of York, he broke eleven lances with Adolf of Cleves.

Woodville was also an ostentatiously religious man. At his death he was found to be wearing a hair shirt, which was hung up at Doncaster and became an object of devotion and pilgrimage. He accompanied the king on pilgrimage to Bury St Edmunds in 1469, and in 1471, thankful for victory, he went to Portugal to fight the Saracens. In 1473 he went on pilgrimage to Santiago de Compostela and in 1475 to Rome and other holy places in Italy. Although robbed on his return, his property was restored by the Venetian *signoria* out of deference to the king of England. Pope Sixtus IV apparently made him defender and director of papal causes in England. His will provided for the foundation of an almshouse at Rochester and for the endowment of an existing hermitage at Grafton. Caxton testifies to his devotion to works of piety and abhorrence of 'thabhominable and dampnable synnes which communely be now a dayes' (*Cordyal*, epilogue); his piety seems to have prompted Woodville's decision to translate *The Dictes and Sayings of the Philosophers* ('glorious fair myrrour to all good Christen peple to behold and understonde'), the 'wise and holsom' *Proverbs of Christine de Pisan*, and the *Cordyal*, which might better be called 'the four last thingis undoubtedly coming'. Each of these was printed by Caxton, the *Dictes* being the first book printed in England (facsimile edition, 1877). Caxton alludes also to other lost works, notably ballads against the seven deadly sins, but Woodville's only surviving verses are those on the fickleness of fortune that he wrote in his last days. He had visited Renaissance Italy and his literary tastes were approved by Renaissance humanists such as Dominic Mancini.

Like his father Woodville opposed the Yorkists in 1460–61, was allowed to submit in 1461 once the Lancastrian cause was irredeemably lost, and was recognized as Lord Scales. What transformed his career, like that of the whole family, was his sister's marriage to Edward IV in 1464. He secured the lordship of the Isle of Wight and constableship of Carisbrooke Castle by exchange for land in Essex with Sir Geoffrey Gate, and in 1467 the constableship of Portchester Castle by sale from the earl of Worcester. In 1466 he was elected knight of the Garter and the next year was granted the reversion when his father was created constable of England. The tournament with the Bastard of Burgundy was part of Edward's *rapprochement* with Burgundy, which was sealed by Margaret of York's wedding to Charles the Bold in 1468, in which Woodville played a full part. Already identified as an enemy by Warwick in 1468, Woodville was denounced in the earl's manifesto of 1469, but escaped both the Yorkist defeat at Edgcote and the death that befell his father and brother. Now Earl Rivers, he had good cause for the resentment that he reportedly later felt towards Clarence. The following spring he helped chase Warwick and Clarence into exile and accompanied Edward IV himself in flight in the autumn, returning early in 1471, when he played an important role in Edward's decisive victories.

At this point Woodville, Earl Rivers since 1469, could have become a front-rank political figure, but he chose instead to go on crusade. His preface to the *Dictes* states that his vicissitudes had prompted him to devote his life to God's service. Given that his political services were needed at home, this action understandably aroused Edward's ire, and his later pilgrimages also interfered with his political career. Perhaps for this reason he failed to secure the constableship of England of which he held the reversion, or reappointment to the captaincy of Calais. These were granted instead to Edward's brother Gloucester and chamberlain Hastings. He did become chief butler of England in 1473. When available Rivers was much in demand, as ambassador and on campaign in Brittany in 1472, and twice in 1473–4 on embassy to Burgundy. Following the death of his first wife in 1473, his second marriage became a pawn in the political game: in 1477 Edward IV promoted him as candidate for Mary of Burgundy, though he was but a 'petty earl and she the greatest heiress of her time' (Ross, 251). Late in 1478 a marriage was actually agreed with James III's sister Margaret of Scotland, to be celebrated at Nottingham in October 1479, but differences with Scotland meant that it did not materialize.

The second marriage Rivers did contract, about 1480, was to Mary Lewis, daughter of Sir Henry Lewis and Elizabeth Beaufort, the daughter of Edmund, duke of Somerset (*d.* 1455), and sister of the last two Beaufort dukes. Mary was her father's heir; more important, she was potentially coheir to the Beaufort dukes themselves. Self-interest was a motive for this marriage and Rivers was quite prepared to pursue speculative claims at the expense of others. Rivers had earlier laid dubious claim to some of Sir John Fastolf's estates; he had blackmailed Maud, Lady Willoughby, into surrendering part of her inheritance in return for immunity for her Lancastrian husband, Sir Gervase Clifton; in his last years, he was seeking immediate possession of the dower of Philippa, Lady Ros, for which he held the reversion and to the lands of the Warwick trust; and he ordered the righting of various wrongs in his will. The surviving papers of his agent, Andrew Dymmock, show Rivers to have been hard-headed and businesslike. His second marriage was also childless. His only offspring was his bastard daughter, Margaret, later wife of Sir Robert Poyntz. His heir was his brother Richard Woodville, third and last Earl Rivers, who died unmarried in 1491.

Late in his career Earl Rivers carved out a role of political importance for himself as mentor of Edward, prince of Wales, the future *Edward V. Rivers was one of the prince's afforced council appointed on 20 February 1473 to manage his estates in the principality of Wales, county of Chester, and duchy of Cornwall. Following the king's progress through the north midlands and marches of Wales in mid-1473, Prince Edward and his council were settled at Ludlow, Shropshire, to govern the marches. There was a president, a chancellor, and a fully staffed household. Rivers was tutor and governor, a role for which he was fitted by his kinship to the prince, and by his martial and literary interests. The young prince trusted the maternal kin around him and resisted their removal; Mancini indicates that the boy shared his uncle's literary interests. Since most councillors resided elsewhere and Rivers was the prince's uncle, in practice he and his Woodville relatives dominated the prince's affairs. It was Rivers's warrants that authorized payments, presentations, or moved other seals; it was he who made nominations to parliamentary seats; he was receiver of the duchy of Cornwall; and it was he who led large forces against Scotland in 1482 and towards London in April 1483. The prince's authority and resources enabled Rivers to make Wales into a power base; they extended this power by securing possession of Pembroke and sympathetic appointments to Welsh sees.

Rivers was thus strongly placed to influence developments following Edward IV's death on 9 April 1483 and the succession of his son as Edward V. Earl and prince were at Ludlow and set off at once for London. At the request of the king's uncle, the duke of Gloucester, he proceeded via Stony Stratford (near Rivers's own seat at Grafton Regis) in Northamptonshire, where he rendezvoused with Gloucester and Buckingham and spent a convivial evening. If there had been any truth in later reports of a feud between Gloucester and the Woodvilles, Rivers could have avoided the duke. His willingness in the previous month to nominate Gloucester to arbitrate a dispute indicates that they were on good terms and that Rivers did not perceive Gloucester as his enemy. He was thus easily arrested, as the duke seized possession of the king and dispersed his household, and was dispatched with his nephew, the queen's son Richard Grey, to prison at Gloucester's Yorkshire castle of Sheriff Hutton. Gloucester alleged that Rivers had intended force against him and asked the royal council to authorize his execution— unsuccessfully since, even if Rivers had plotted against Gloucester, it did not amount to treason. Once the usurpation had been decided, Rivers was subjected to a form of trial conducted by the earl of Northumberland, and was executed at Pontefract on 25 June 1483. Before his death he had composed his will, asking to be buried with Richard Grey at Pontefract. He died an exemplary death.

Earl Rivers was characterized by James Gairdner as the noblest and most accomplished of all Richard III's victims. This verdict accords not only with those of William Caxton, Sir Thomas More, and Philippe de Commines, and with John Rous's account of his end, which Gairdner knew, but also with the verdict of Dominic Mancini that has been discovered since. His political reputation has benefited from his literary interests and his suffering at the hands of Richard III. The discovery of some of his papers and the study of his role as Prince Edward's mentor provides some corrective and brings out even more of the complexity of his character.   MICHAEL HICKS

Sources S. Bentley, ed., *Excerpta historica* (1840) · J. R. Lander, *Crown and nobility, 1450–1509* (1976) · M. A. Hicks, *Richard III and his*

rivals: magnates and their motives in the Wars of the Roses (1991) • E. W. Ives, 'Andrew Dymmock and the papers of Anthony, Earl Rivers, 1482–3', *BIHR*, 41 (1968), 216–29 • C. Ross, *Edward IV* (1974) • R. Horrox, *Richard III, a study of service*, Cambridge Studies in Medieval Life and Thought, 4th ser., 11 (1989) • P. de Commynes, *Mémoires*, ed. J. Calmette and G. Durville, 3 vols. (Paris, 1924–5) • *The book named Cordyal*, ed. W. Caxton, trans. A. Woodville (1479) • Abu al-Wafa al-Mubashshir ibn Fatik, *The dictes and sayings of the philosophers*, ed. W. Caxton, trans. G. de Tignonville and A. Woodville (1477); facs. edn with preface by W. Blades (1877)
Archives BL, Add. MS 22718 | PRO, E 315/468
Likenesses manuscript illumination, LPL, MS 265, fol. 6r [*see illus.*]

Woodville, Katherine (1457/8–1497). *See under* Stafford, Henry, second duke of Buckingham (1455–1483).

Woodville, Lionel (*c.*1454–1484), bishop of Salisbury, was the third son of Sir Richard *Woodville, afterwards first Earl Rivers (*d.* 1469), and Jacquetta (*d.* 1472), widow of John, duke of Bedford (*d.* 1435). His date of birth is unknown but a grant to him by Pope Paul II (*r.* 1464–71), now lost but mentioned in another later dispensation, gave him the right to receive any benefice when he was over twelve years of age, and his first recorded benefice, a canonry at Lincoln, was conferred in 1466. This, along with his ordination as a priest in 1478, suggests that he was probably born between 1450 and 1455. As *Edward IV's brother-in-law, it is not surprising that he received a substantial number of wealthy benefices from the 1460s onwards, and was provided to the bishopric of Salisbury on 7 January 1482. The temporalities of the see were restored to him on 28 March. He was educated at Oxford, but the dates of his degrees are unknown. He was probably BCnL by 1478 and the university offered to confer the degree of doctor of canon law in the following year, when he was also appointed chancellor of the university, a position he held until the autumn of 1483, when he was replaced during the duke of Buckingham's rebellion.

Lionel Woodville did not play any significant part in the political crisis after Edward IV's death in 1483. Initially he probably remained in Oxford, for he was not among the prelates who were present at the king's funeral. At the beginning of June, however, he was in sanctuary at Westminster, with his sister Queen *Elizabeth, but then apparently came to terms with the new regime, for he was named to the commission of the peace in Dorset and Wiltshire after Richard III's accession, although he seems to have been absent from the coronation. On 22 September 1483 he issued letters from the duke of Buckingham's manor of Thornbury concerning the appropriation of a benefice, but it is uncertain if he was there voluntarily or if he had perhaps been committed to the duke's charge, like Bishop John Morton (*d.* 1500). He incurred the king's suspicion in some way at this time, for on the following day Richard ordered the forfeiture of his temporalities. The king's doubts were justified, because Woodville became involved in Buckingham's rebellion shortly afterwards, and had to take sanctuary at Beaulieu. (There is no evidence to support suggestions that he fled to Brittany to Henry Tudor.) He was attainted for his participation in the rising in the parliament of 1484. He died later that year,

although his date of death is unknown—he was still alive on 22 July, but must have died by 1 December, when licence was granted to the dean and chapter of Salisbury to elect a successor. A late seventeenth-century manuscript from Salisbury states that he was buried at Beaulieu.   JOHN A. F. THOMSON

Sources Emden, *Oxf.* • D. P. Wright, ed., *The register of Thomas Langton, bishop of Salisbury, 1485–93*, CYS, 74 (1985) • H. E. Salter, ed., *Registrum annalium collegii Mertonensis, 1483–1521*, OHS, 76 (1923) • J. A. F. Thomson, 'Bishop Lionel Woodville and Richard III', *BIHR*, 59 (1986), 130–35

Woodville, Richard (*d. c.*1441). *See under* Woodville, Richard, first Earl Rivers (*d.* 1469).

Woodville [Wydeville], **Richard**, first Earl Rivers (*d.* 1469), magnate, founded his fortunes on two remarkable marriages, one of which was to make him father-in-law of Edward IV. The Woodvilles were modest Northamptonshire gentry who failed in the male line on the death about 1435 of Thomas Woodville, esquire, whose heirs were two sisters rather than his half-brother, Richard, father of the future Earl Rivers. As a younger son, the elder **Richard Woodville** (*d. c.*1441) pursued a distinguished military and administrative career that became the model for future generations of the family. Allegedly brought up with Henry IV he was in the garrison of the king's son Thomas at Guînes in 1411, was captain on Henry V's campaigns of 1415 and 1417, and later served the regent, John, duke of Bedford. He was in English France almost continuously from 1417 to 1435 as captain and bailiff, as seneschal of Normandy (1420), chamberlain of the regent, and treasurer of finances (1423), lieutenant of Calais in 1427 and again in 1435, and councillor of France; he was employed in positions of trust in England in 1425 and 1436. Returning to England, where he already held the Mote estate at Maidstone and where his brother bequeathed him Grafton Regis, Northamptonshire, he was MP for Kent in 1433, constable of Rochester, and sheriff of Northamptonshire in 1437, before his death about 1441. He was never knighted and married his daughter no higher than the ranks of the Kentish gentry.

The younger Richard Woodville added only a little to his father's modest estates. He was on Northamptonshire commissions from 1441, JP for Northamptonshire from 1448, and for Kent from 1454. His military career followed the pattern of that of his father. A captain in 1429, he was retained in royal service in France (1433) and was a knight of the regent, Bedford, in 1435. He was at Gerberoi in 1435, served under William de la Pole, duke of Suffolk, in 1435–6, Somerset and Shrewsbury in 1439, and the duke of York in 1441–2, when he was made captain of Alençon and knight-banneret, and was among the escort bringing Margaret of Anjou, who was connected with his wife, to England in 1444. With such a background he was an obvious choice as seneschal of Gascony in 1450, as lieutenant of Calais in 1454–5, and to defend Kent against invasion by the Yorkist earls in 1459–60. But Woodville was never in command and was not notably successful: he apparently suffered capture at Gerberoi in 1435, he failed to reach

Gascony before its fall in 1453, and suffered humiliating capture at Sandwich in 1460. His joust against the Spaniard Pedro de Vasquez at Smithfield in 1440 anticipated the distinction in tourneying of his sons and grandson.

The elder Richard's Lancastrian connections account for the knighting of the younger Richard by Henry VI in 1426 and for his presence in 1435 at the regent's court, where he encountered Jacquetta of Luxembourg, duchess of Bedford (d. 1472), whom, following the duke's death in 1435, he had married secretly by 1437. For Jacquetta marriage to a mere knight was a shocking *mésalliance*, which was disapproved of both by her Luxembourg relatives and by Henry VI. Hence Woodville was fined £1000 for marrying her without licence and for possession of her dower. However, the match made Woodville's fortune. It made him kin to the house of Lancaster, to his wife's family, the Luxembourg counts of St Pol, and through them to international royalty and nobility, including Margaret of Anjou and the dukes of Burgundy. Jacquetta's dower greatly increased his income, presumably to at least 2000 marks, albeit only for her life, and enabled him to support a noble lifestyle and to marry his children into the lower nobility: thus his son Anthony *Woodville was married to Elizabeth, Lord Scales's heir, his daughter *Elizabeth to Sir John Grey, heir to Lady Ferrers of Groby, and another daughter, Jacquetta, to John, Lord Strange of Knockin. Woodville's royal connections were a further justification for his election as knight of the Garter in 1450 and his creation as a baron on 9 May 1448. His mysterious choice of title, Lord Rivers, and his addition of a griffin to his arms, which imply links with earlier barons that cannot be traced, suggest that he felt the need for a lineage separate from that of his wife: his dependence on her was disparaged by the Neville earls in 1460. Even with her lands and his barony, which raised him far above his birth and patrimony, his commands, offices, and status were decidedly of second rank. Without Jacquetta's dower his heir might have found it hard to support the dignity of a baron.

Rivers took part in the suppression of Cade's rebellion and was apparently considered as a possible constable of England. Indicted in Kent as a member of the court in 1451 and closely associated with successive Beaufort dukes of Somerset in the 1450s, he was employed abroad and thus escaped some of the major crises. Rivers was not retained as lieutenant of Calais by Richard Neville, earl of Warwick, after 1456 and from 1457 occurs frequently on commissions in Northamptonshire and Kent. In 1457 he became constable of Rochester. Following the flight of the Yorkist earls to Calais he was preparing an expedition against them at Sandwich when he was surprised and borne off there as a prisoner. He later fought on the Lancastrian side at Towton, but was allowed to submit to the new Yorkist regime on the grounds that the Lancastrian cause was irretrievably lost. Like other erstwhile Lancastrians, he was required to serve against the northern rebels. Not only did he escape attainder, but he was again employed on royal commissions and from 1463 on the royal council. That his influence remained limited emerges from his daughter Elizabeth's use not of him but

of the king's chamberlain to obtain access to Edward IV in pursuance of her suit for jointure from her late husband, Sir John Grey of Groby.

Elizabeth's secret marriage in 1464 to Edward IV was a second remarkably unequal and inappropriate match that greatly advanced the Woodvilles and especially Rivers himself. He and his family constituted a numerous addition to the royal kin: with Jacquetta he had fourteen or fifteen children, of whom five sons and six daughters achieved maturity; there were also Haute, Dyve, and other cousins. Edward IV felt himself obliged not only to provide for them all, but to do so extremely generously. Rivers himself was appointed treasurer of England on 4 March 1466, created Earl Rivers on 25 May 1466, and became constable of England on 24 August 1467. Altogether his royal offices brought him an income, admittedly for life only, of £1586 a year. Although already provided for, his elder children were not ignored; Lionel *Woodville ultimately became a bishop; John became prior of St John and married the dowager duchess of Norfolk; and Elizabeth's eldest son, Thomas Grey, married Anne Holland, heir of the duke of Exeter. Most striking of all were the matches arranged for Rivers's remaining daughters: between 1464 and 1467 Katherine *Woodville [see under Stafford, Henry] married Henry Stafford, duke of Buckingham, and Margaret, Anne, Mary, and Eleanor were married to Thomas, Lord Maltravers, William, Lord Bourchier, William Herbert, Lord Dunster, and Anthony Grey of Ruthin, the heirs respectively of the earls of Arundel, Essex, Pembroke, and Kent. These matches constitute one of the most remarkable series of arranged marriages in late medieval England. They were not merely incidental to Elizabeth's elevation as queen, but were actively promoted by Earl Rivers and the king. It was the king himself who broke an earlier agreement for Anne Holland's hand. He was the initiator of the contract between Pembroke and Rivers, in which Rivers agreed to put Pembroke's demands to the king and secure his compliance. Edward endowed both the Bourchier and Arundel matches directly. Not only were these marriages generally at royal expense, but in some instances Edward had to recover grants from others to patronize the Woodvilles. In Rivers's own case, the offices of treasurer and constable were surrendered by existing holders in return for inducements: the earl of Worcester actually sold the constableship, so that Edward could bestow it on Rivers.

Such rapid advancement in such a short time was bound to cause resentment; the Woodville marriages in particular thwarted the legitimate aspirations of others, especially those of the earl of Warwick for his daughters and male heir. Warwick and the Nevilles also found themselves superseded in influence at court, particularly after the dismissal of Archbishop Neville as chancellor in 1467. Their advancement also signalled a change in foreign policy, from pro-French to pro-Burgundian, which certainly the Crowland continuator saw as the main source of political division between Edward IV and the Nevilles. Jacquetta's Burgundian connections were a factor here: in 1467 her son Anthony had a celebrated joust with Antoine, count of La Roche, the Bastard of Burgundy, and in 1468 Edward IV's sister Margaret married the duke of Burgundy himself.

Hence in 1469 Earl Rivers was among the royal favourites whom Warwick, Archbishop Neville, and Clarence determined to destroy as the essential preliminary to their recovery of power. They supported a manifesto denouncing evil government and the king's upstart favourites supposedly issued by the Yorkshire rebel Robin of Redesdale, whose defeat of Pembroke's army at Edgcote (27 July) led to Warwick's capture of the king and hence of the government. Rivers was not at Edgcote, but he and his son Sir John Woodville were seized at Chepstow, taken to Kenilworth, and executed there on 12 August 1469. Charges of sorcery against the Duchess Jacquetta were withdrawn after Edward IV's recovery of power.   MICHAEL HICKS

Sources J. R. Lander, *Crown and nobility, 1450–1509* (1976) · M. A. Hicks, *Richard III and his rivals: magnates and their motives in the Wars of the Roses* (1991) · C. Ross, *Edward IV* (1974) · T. B. Pugh, 'The magnates, knights and gentry', *Fifteenth-century England, 1399–1509*, ed. S. B. Chrimes, C. D. Ross, and R. A. Griffiths (1972), 86–128

Wealth at death approx. £3000

Woodville, Richard Caton (1856–1927), military artist, the posthumous son of Richard Caton Woodville (1825–1855), an American genre painter of English descent, and his second wife, Antoinette Marie, *née* Schnitzler, a portrait painter (whose father, Anton Schnitzler, was German and whose mother was Russian), was born at 57 Stanhope Street, London, on 7 January 1856. Little is known of his early life: the main source, his *Random Recollections* (1914), is considered unreliable. His mother took him to St Petersburg, and he was educated in Russia and Germany. He studied art at the Royal Academy in Düsseldorf under Professor Evon Gebhardt, a religious painter, from 1876 to 1877, and may have worked in the Paris studio of J. L. Gérôme. He then travelled in the barbaric Balkans.

Back in London in 1877 Woodville offered a drawing to the *Illustrated London News* (*ILN*). Its proprietor, William Ingram, liked his work, and Woodville was employed by the *ILN* for almost his entire working life, though he also contributed to the *Boy's Own Paper*, *Black and White*, and other periodicals. He portrayed royalty and 'society', and provided illustrations to fiction. However, it was as a military and war artist that he was most employed and best-known. At his London studio he drew for the *ILN* dramatic, picturesque reconstructions of war scenes, based on imagination and sketches from special artists (precursors of news photographers, sent to draw wars and other newsworthy events), including Melton Prior and Frederic Villiers. He portrayed mostly British imperial wars, and especially heroic charges and last stands. He never experienced battle: in 1882 he reached Egypt after the fighting was over. He was also a successful painter, mostly of incidents from British wars, historical and recent, and from 1879 exhibited regularly at the Royal Academy. He received commissions from Queen Victoria—including *The Guards at Tel-el-Kebir* (exh. RA, 1884; Royal Collection) and *Gordon's memorial service at his ruined palace in Khartoum, the day after the battle of Omdurman* (exh. RA, 1899; Royal Collection)—and he was a member of the suite of Prince Albert Victor on the latter's 1889 visit to India. Woodville also had commissions from foreign royalty and Indian princes, and gained high prices.

Woodville's work was popular and was reproduced as prints, in histories, encyclopaedias, and school textbooks,

Richard Caton Woodville (1856–1927), by unknown photographer, pubd 1895

and on postcards and magic lantern slides, becoming for many their images of historical reality. The *ILN* called him 'an historian in pictorial form of the bravery which has made the English nation what it is' (*ILN*, 7 Dec 1895, suppl., 3). Although some criticized his work—one critic called it 'an artist's victory over many a British defeat' (Hogarth, 57)—it was also much praised. He was called 'the English Meissonier' (*The Times*, 18 Aug 1927, 12). Frederic Villiers claimed that he was the best British battle painter, and wrote that 'next to de Neuville and Verestchagin the greatest painter of war pictures is undoubtedly Mr. Caton Woodville … in his pictures is all the real dash and movement of war' (Villiers, 24). Van Gogh admired his depiction of Irish poor in the *ILN*. In 1882 he was elected to the Royal Institute of Painters in Water Colours, and Millais said he should be an RA. He received foreign honours, including the French Palmes académiques for his Napoleonic battle scenes, and his work was imitated by others. Reportedly, but for his adultery and divorce he would have received a knighthood. His work has since been attacked for inaccurate portrayal of uniforms and accoutrements.

On 4 October 1877 Woodville married Annie Elizabeth Hill (*b*. 1854/5), daughter of Rowland Hill, a licensed victualler; they had two sons. Following their divorce in 1893 he married Mrs Nellie Waddington, *née* Curtis, with whom he had one daughter. His second wife left and divorced him, and he latterly lived with Madeleine Adelaide Scott, who passed as his wife. He omitted his wives and children from *Who's Who* and *Random Recollections*.

Considered handsome, a dapper man-about-town with a waxed moustache and German accent, Woodville had expensive tastes, moved with a fast bohemian and sporting set, and enjoyed big-game hunting, pig-sticking, fishing, and, it is said, many extramarital affairs. From 1879 he was an officer in the Royal Berkshire yeomanry, the volunteer Royal Engineers, the Royal North Devon hussars, and, finally, the national reserve. He was an enthusiastic imperialist and eulogized British rule in India. He published articles on sport and travel, and in 1914 his lively, name-dropping, and allegedly mendacious memoirs, *Random Recollections*.

Woodville portrayed the First World War as he had earlier wars: with dramatic charges and heroic stands (later criticized by historians). In 1927 his last major painting, *Hallowe'en, 1914: Stand of the London Scottish on Messines Ridge, 31st Oct–1st Nov 1914* (1927, London Scottish Regimental Association), was hung in the Royal Academy and by royal command at Buckingham Palace. Madeleine Scott died, aged fifty, on 26 December 1926. Impoverished, ill, depressed, and believing himself 'a finished man' (*The Times*, 22 Aug 1927, 7), on 17 August 1927 Woodville shot himself in the head with his revolver in his studio attached to his residence, Flat B, Dudley Mansions, 29 Abbey Road, St John's Wood, London: the coroner's verdict was suicide while of unsound mind. He was buried at Kensal Green cemetery, London. He left only £10 (probate value). Paintings by him are in the Royal Collection, the Tate collection, the Walker Art Gallery, Liverpool, and

elsewhere. Probably more than any other artist, before 1914 Woodville shaped the British public's image of war, especially imperial war.   ROGER T. STEARN

Sources R. C. Woodville, *Random recollections* (1914) • *The Times* (18 Aug 1927), 12 • *The Times* (22 Aug 1927), 7 • 'R. Caton Woodville and his work', *ILN* (7 Dec 1895), suppl., pp. 1–3 • R. T. Stearn, 'Richard Caton Woodville, 1856–1927', *Soldiers of the Queen*, 97 (1999) • private information (2004) [A. C. Woodville and Paul Hogarth] • F. Villiers, *Peaceful personalities and warriors bold* (1907) • *Men and women of the time* (1899) • *WWW* • Graves, *RA exhibitors* • P. Harrington, *British artists and war: the face of battle in paintings and prints, 1700–1914* (1993) • J. M. MacKenzie, ed., *Imperialism and popular culture* (1986) • P. Hogarth, *The artist as reporter* (1967) • P. Hogarth, *The artist as reporter* (1986) • J. Turner, ed., *The dictionary of art*, 34 vols. (1996) • *The Connoisseur*, 79 (1927), 127–8 • R. Greenwall, *Artists and illustrators of the Anglo-Boer War* (1992) • J. W. M. Hichberger, *Images of the army: the military in British art, 1815–1914* (1988) • J. Canning, 'The military art of Richard Caton Woodville', *Military Illustrated*, 11 (Feb–March 1988), 24–8 • J. Canning, 'The military art of Richard Caton Woodville', *Military Illustrated*, 13 (June–July 1988), 37–9 • J. Keegan and J. Darracott, *The nature of war* (1981) • M. Barthorp, 'All that was left of them', *The War Correspondent: The Journal of the Crimean War Research Society* (July 1997), 22–3 • b. cert. • m. cert. • d. cert. • divorce cert.
Likenesses H. J. Leman, photograph, repro. in Woodville, *Random recollections*, frontispiece • photograph, repro. in 'R. Caton Woodville and his work', *ILN*, 1 [*see illus.*]
Wealth at death £10: administration, 27 Sept 1927, CGPLA Eng. & Wales

Woodville, William (1752–1805), physician and botanist, was born at Cockermouth in Cumberland, the fourth of the six children of William Woodville (1714–1758), and Jane Fearon (1723–1804). He came from a family of well-to-do Quakers, and was initially educated at a local grammar school. He began his medical training in 1767 with a short apprenticeship to William Birtwhistle, an apothecary. He later matriculated at Edinburgh University, graduating MD in 1775 with a thesis on irritable fibres. Woodville returned to Cumberland to practise in Papcastle, until a tragic incident in 1778 interrupted his career. One night he fired a gun through a window and killed a man who had been creating a disturbance in his garden. Although this was generally accepted as an accident, Woodville was disowned by his Quaker meeting and left the county to set up practice in Denbigh. By 1782 he had moved to London: there his career flourished. He was appointed physician to the Middlesex Dispensary, admitted as a licentiate of the Royal College of Physicians in August 1784, and became a member of the Physical Society at Guy's Hospital.

Woodville's medical career was distinguished by his contributions to the prevention of smallpox. In 1791 he was appointed physician to the London Smallpox and Inoculation Hospital at St Pancras, a charitable institution offering care to smallpox victims and free inoculation. Woodville became a staunch supporter of the procedure: in 1797 he published a pamphlet aimed at a popular audience, advocating inoculation. By this time he was also writing a major history of inoculation, probably intended as a triumphal history of the steady growth of the procedure, with an emphasis on the role of the hospital in encouraging inoculation and thus helping to control smallpox. The first of the projected two volumes of the *History of the Inoculation of the Smallpox* (1796) described inoculation techniques used in the Near East and the Far East, its introduction to Britain, and its gradual popularization up to 1770. However, history caught up with the project. In 1799 the second volume was announced as ready for the press but it never appeared, as the previous year Edward Jenner had announced his discovery of vaccination, which attracted considerable attention: although the older procedure was still widely used, the book would have lost much of its original purpose.

Woodville quickly switched his allegiance to vaccination and played an important role in establishing its merits. News of Jenner's discovery had aroused interest among medical men, but his source of vaccine had been lost and further experiments with the new procedure were therefore impossible. Woodville remedied this in January 1799, when he was told of an outbreak of cowpox in a London dairy. Having compared the lesions among the milkers with Jenner's illustration, Woodville took some fluid for use as vaccine at the Smallpox Hospital. The results of this action, the first large-scale trial of vaccination, were published as the *Report of a Series of Inoculations for the Variolae vaccinae or Cow Pox* (1799). Its case histories of two hundred vaccinations, most of which were subsequently tested by inoculation, did much to prove the efficacy of the new practice. However, the *Report* also cast the first doubts as to the merits of vaccination. Woodville noted that vaccination frequently produced smallpox-like eruptions which he believed might communicate smallpox. This undermined one of the principal advantages of the new practice over inoculation—patients did not have to be isolated. Woodville's observation sparked off a dispute between Woodville and Jenner. Jenner blamed Woodville's results on contaminated vaccine: Woodville responded with his *Observations on Cow-Pox* (1800) arguing that hybridization between cowpox and smallpox was impossible. Thereafter the dispute fizzled out, unresolved. Relations between the two pioneers were partially restored by mutual friends, particularly John Coakley Lettsom, but never became cordial, Jenner being suspicious of any potential rival to his authority as the leading expert on vaccination. Woodville continued to promote vaccination through his practice at the Smallpox Hospital, and later briefly held a post as vaccinator to the Royal Jennerian Society, a charity offering free vaccination. In 1800 he travelled to France to assist in the introduction of the procedure there.

Woodville had a deep interest in botany. He was elected to the Linnean Society in 1791, and maintained a botanic garden within the grounds of the Smallpox Hospital. Between 1790 and 1794 he published *Medical Botany*, a four-volume catalogue of plants, based on the pharmacopoeia of the royal colleges of physicians in London and Edinburgh. Each plant was described by both its botanical characteristics and its therapeutic uses, and illustrated with an engraving.

Woodville died on 26 March 1805 at the Smallpox Hospital, having been moved from his house in Ely Place, Holborn, at his special request. His cause of death is variously recorded as smallpox (which seems unlikely, given his constant exposure to infection), dropsy, and a chronic pulmonary complaint. Woodville received a Quaker funeral and was buried at Bunhill Fields on 4 April. His library was sold at Sothebys on 3 July 1805.   DEBORAH BRUNTON

Sources 'Dictionary of Quaker biography', RS Friends, Lond. [card index] · *GM*, 1st ser., 75 (1805), 387 · Munk, *Roll* · A. Highmore, *Pietas Londinensis* (1810) · R. B. Fisher, *Edward Jenner* (1991) · A. Rees and others, *The cyclopaedia, or, Universal dictionary of arts, sciences, and literature*, 45 vols. (1819–20), vol. 23 · matriculation records, U. Edin. L., special collections division, university archives · H. Lonsdale, *The worthies of Cumberland*, 6 (1875) · Pardshaw monthly meeting, Cumbria AS, Whitehaven · P. J. Wallis and R. V. Wallis, *Eighteenth century medics*, 2nd edn (1988) · Desmond, *Botanists*, rev. edn · *DNB*
Likenesses N. Branwhite, group portrait, stipple, pubd 1801 (*Institutors of the Medical Society of London*; after S. Medley), BM · L. F. Abbott, oils, RCP Lond. · A. Ansiaux, portrait, repro. in A. H. Driver, *Catalogue of engraved portraits in the Royal College of Physicians of London* (1952) · W. Bond, stipple (after L. F. Abbott), Wellcome L. · L. Perrot, portrait, repro. in A. H. Driver, *Catalogue of engraved portraits in the Royal College of Physicians of London* (1952) · Woolnoth, line engraving (after T. H. Shepherd), Wellcome L. · aquatint silhouette, Wellcome L.

Woodward, Sir Arthur Smith (1864–1944), palaeontologist, was born on 23 May 1864 at Macclesfield, Cheshire, the elder son of Edward Woodward, silk dyer, and his wife, Margaret Smith, whose maiden name he used as an additional surname. Both families had long been connected with the silk trade in Macclesfield. As a child Woodward collected wild flowers, beetles, and seaweeds; a fossil he was given while on holiday at Llandudno led to an interest in geology.

Woodward was educated at the King Edward VI Grammar School, Macclesfield, which awarded him a scholarship to Owens College, Manchester. There he was taught by, among others, William Boyd Dawkins, the archaeologist and geologist, who became his lifelong friend. In 1882, and before graduation, Woodward obtained a position in the geology department of the British Museum (Natural History), then newly transferred to South Kensington. He worked under the direction of William Davies, arranging the collections of fossil vertebrates for exhibition. The quality of the fishes in the collections of the earl of Enniskillen and Sir Philip Egerton, which the museum had just acquired, turned Woodward to the special study of fossil fishes. He attended the Swiney lectures given in the museum in 1883 by Ramsay Heatley Traquair, then the authority on the subject, and evening classes in comparative anatomy and general biology at King's College. At the suggestion of the keeper, the museum's trustees instructed Woodward to make a catalogue of all the fossil fishes in the department: he thus entered on his life-work, which was to make him the greatest palaeoichthyologist of his time.

The first of the four volumes of the *Catalogue of Fossil Fishes in the British Museum* appeared in 1889, the last in 1901. Nearly one hundred years later they were still in

Sir Arthur Smith Woodward (1864–1944), by Walter Stoneman, 1918

great demand. Although Woodward produced over six hundred publications, most of them papers in scientific journals, the catalogue was his *magnum opus*. A monument of meticulous accuracy and of intense research, it was the first application of evolutionary theory to the whole field. It became the mainspring of Woodward's multifarious activities: he acquired a speaking knowledge of several European languages; travelled widely in quest of new material, both in the field and in public and private collections; made contact with palaeontologists of many nationalities, and entertained them at home; and worked to enrich the collections further, until, by the wealth of its material, his department drew researchers from all parts of the world.

In 1892 Woodward became assistant keeper and in 1901 he succeeded to the keepership. By delegating the supervision of invertebrates to the assistant keeper he was able to concentrate his studies on vertebrates generally, and fossil fishes in particular. In 1894 he married Maud Leonora Ida (1874–1963), daughter of the geologist Harry Govier *Seeley; they had one son, who entered the colonial service and died in 1924, and one daughter.

Woodward received many honours. The Royal Society elected him a fellow in 1901 and awarded him a royal medal (1917); he served as president of a number of scientific societies and received several other medals, including the Lyell (1896) and Wollaston (1924) medals of the Geological Society, the prix Cuvier of the French Académie des Sciences (1918), and the Mary Clark Thompson

medal of the National Academy of Sciences, Washington (1942). He also held honorary doctorates from the universities of Glasgow, St Andrews, Tartu, and Athens. He was knighted in 1924.

Woodward's reputation as a distinguished and successful scientist has been marred, though his fame increased, since exposure of the Piltdown fraud in the 1950s. In 1912 Charles Dawson, a Sussex solicitor, showed Woodward fragments of a human skull said to have come from Pleistocene gravels at Piltdown, Sussex. Woodward joined Dawson in excavations at the site and together they found further hominoid fragments, worked flints, and other mammalian fossils. In 1913 Woodward described 'Piltdown man' as *Eoanthropus dawsoni*, and with Dawson, Teilhard de Chardin, and others he continued to work the Piltdown site. Dawson died in 1916; nothing was found at Piltdown thereafter by Woodward or anyone else. The known parts of Piltdown man—a braincase of human type associated with an apelike lower jaw—became increasingly anomalous in comparison with human fossils found subsequently, and during the 1950s all the Piltdown fossils were shown to have been faked and/or planted at the site. Piltdown man comprises parts of an unusually thick human braincase and of an orang-utan lower jaw, stained and modified in various ways.

Since the Piltdown fakes were uncovered in the 1950s, there have been repeated attempts to identify the forger. Dawson must have been involved; candidates proposed as his co-conspirator include Sir Arthur Conan Doyle, W. J. Sollas, M. A. C. Hinton, Teilhard de Chardin, and Sir Arthur Keith. Whereas the true culprits and their motives may never be identified with certainty, their victim or dupe was certainly Woodward. Between 1912 and his death, he published some twenty-five papers bearing on Piltdown, and his last work, dictated to his wife during his blindness and issued posthumously in 1948, was *The Earliest Englishman*, a book on Piltdown man. Whether the forger's motives were self-advancement or spite, Woodward was completely taken in; the acuity displayed in his work on fishes and other vertebrates deserted him.

Woodward was a strict disciplinarian, and has been described as a humourless martinet. Although perhaps not easily approachable, he could be very kind and considerate to his junior staff. During his forty-two years at the museum he was absent through sickness for only one half-day—with a broken arm. His outside interests were few and this perhaps made it difficult for him to understand the wider outlook of his colleagues, to whom his single-minded zeal and devotion to duty were nevertheless an inspiration. Yet he appreciated music, and, surprisingly, enjoyed taking his children to the pantomime.

Following his early retirement in 1924, Woodward never again entered the British Museum, but he continued to work and travel until blindness overtook him in his final years. Apparently he was piqued at having been passed over for the directorship in 1919. Woodward died at his home, Hill Place, Balcombe Road, Haywards Heath, Sussex, on 2 September 1944. He was buried in All Saints' churchyard, Lindfield, Sussex, on 8 September. His library of nearly 10,000 works was purchased by University College, London.   W. D. LANG, rev. COLIN PATTERSON

Sources C. F. Cooper, *Obits. FRS*, 5 (1945–8), 79–112 · C. J. Stubblefield, 'Memorial to Arthur Smith Woodward', *Proceedings volume of the Geological Society of America, 1945* (1946), 285–310 · E. I. White, 'Sir Arthur Smith Woodward', *Proceedings of the Linnean Society of London*, 156th session (1943–4), 238–42 · E. I. White, *Quarterly Journal of the Geological Society of London*, 101 (1945), xliii–xlvi · F. Spencer, *Piltdown: a scientific forgery* (1990) · F. Spencer, *The Piltdown papers, 1908–1955* (1990) · order of service, funeral

Archives NHM, corresp. and papers · UCL, corresp. | BL, corresp. with Macmillans, Add. MS 55224 · Elgin Museum, letters to George Gordon · NHM, corresp. among a collection of letters of naturalists belonging to Charles Davies Sherborn

Likenesses J. Cooke, group portrait, oils, *c.*1915 (*Group at the Royal College of Surgeons examining the Piltdown Skull, 1913*), GS Lond. · W. Stoneman, photograph, 1918, NPG [*see illus.*] · photograph, repro. in *Obits. FRS* · photograph, repro. in Stubblefield, 'Memorial' · photograph, repro. in *Geological Magazine*, new ser., decade 6, 2 (1915), pl. 1 · photographs, repro. in Spencer, *Piltdown* · photographs, repro. in Spencer, *Piltdown papers*

Wealth at death £17,446 13s. 10d.: probate, 23 Jan 1945, *CGPLA Eng. & Wales*

Woodward, Benjamin (1816–1861), architect, was born on 16 November 1816 at Tullamore, King's county, Ireland, the fifth of the seven surviving children of a peripatetic militia officer, Captain Charles Woodward (1781–1864), and his wife, Mary (*c.*1786–1824), daughter of Dr Edward Atkinson of Armagh and his wife, Mary Macartney. He may have been educated at Carrickmacross grammar school, co. Monaghan, where his two elder brothers had boarded. Captain Woodward, a younger son of Meath gentry, settled about 1833 in Dublin, where Benjamin was apprenticed to a civil engineer, William Stokes (1793–1864). Stokes was a nephew of the regius professor of medicine at Trinity College, Dublin, Dr Whitley Stokes, a friend and colleague of the architect's grand-uncle, the anatomist Dr James Macartney, also of Trinity College, Dublin. Following his training, Woodward remained with Stokes, who had left Dublin to construct roads and bridges for the grand juries, mainly in the Irish midlands. Woodward developed an interest in antiquities, studying such monuments as the Rock of Cashel and Holy Cross Abbey, co. Tipperary. His measured drawings of Holy Cross, made in 1844, survive in the Royal Irish Academy.

By 1842 Woodward was already known to the Cork architect Sir Thomas *Deane, whose practice he joined in 1846 to assist in the design of Queen's College (now University College, Cork). Woodward was probably employed for his knowledge of Gothic detailing but it became apparent that his natural talents lay in architectural design. The college, in the Perpendicular style, was partly modelled on Oxford examples, but was also influenced by the work of Gothic revival architects such as Francis Johnston and contemporaries such as A. W. N. Pugin and Philip and Philip Charles Hardwick. Their next building was the district lunatic asylum at Killarney, co. Kerry (1847–52). The Puginian elevations, in the Early English style, were probably Woodward's but the planning, which owes much to

Benjamin Woodward (1816–1861), attrib. Lewis Carroll (Charles Lutwidge Dodgson), 1850s

the writings of the physician and alienist Dr John Conolly of Hanwell, followed board of works practice.

In 1851 Sir Thomas Deane suffered a breakdown following the death of his wife. The firm was reorganized with his son Thomas Newenham *Deane and Woodward as new partners. In their unplaced Belgic–Gothic design for the Cork town hall competition of 1851–2 can be seen the origins of their best-known building, the University Museum at Oxford (1854–60). After the practice moved to Dublin in the spring of 1854, the recovered and newly remarried Sir Thomas decided to remain in Cork, effectively in semi-retirement. Although senior designer, Woodward was shy and taciturn by nature and preferred to leave the day-to-day running of the new office (situated in Upper Merrion Street) to the younger Deane. The move followed success in a limited competition in 1852–3 for the new museum building at Trinity College, Dublin. Woodward, who never married, probably resided with his father in Blackrock. From 1855 he also had an apartment–office in London. Suffering from tuberculosis, he was treated by Dr William Stokes (1804–1878), the son of Whitley Stokes and himself regius professor of medicine at Trinity College, Dublin. Stokes, the leader of a group of Dublin intellectuals, also brought him patronage.

The museum building's Venetian Cinquecento-style elevations and extensive use of naturalistic ornament (carved by the O'Shea brothers) were inspired by the writings of John Ruskin, while the floor plans were devised by the college architect, John McCurdy. Internally, columns of various marbles (a forerunner of the didactic scheme at the University Museum, Oxford) flanked the dramatic central stairhall, top-lit through glazed-brick domes. Ruskin praised the building, though he did not visit it during Woodward's lifetime.

Deane and Woodward won the competition for the University Museum, Oxford, in December 1854, when their Gothic design triumphed over a classical submission by E. M. Barry. The style was eclectic, Early English with Belgic touches, and, as later revised, Italian polychromy. Ruskin, a friend of the chief promoter, Henry Acland, regius professor of medicine at Oxford, seems to have influenced design improvements and later sponsored some of the carving, entrusted to the O'Sheas and their nephew Edward Whelan. He was unhappy with the Gothic wrought-iron and glass roof over the central court (executed by F. A. Skidmore of Coventry), probably because an alternative wood and masonry design was not proceeded with. The carving of monkeys (on the eve of publication of Darwin's *On the Origin of Species* in 1859) proved controversial, but ultimately it was expense that curtailed the sculpted decoration (in 1861, a year after the building opened). Through Ruskin, Woodward met Dante Gabriel Rossetti and other Pre-Raphaelite artists, whom he employed in decorating the interior of his Oxford Union building in 1857. One of those artists, John Hungerford Pollen, also decorated two of Woodward's Irish buildings, the reconstructed picture gallery (1859–62) at Kilkenny Castle, co. Kilkenny, and Clontra, Shankill, co. Dublin (1858–62). Woodward's other principal works included Dublin's Kildare Street Club (1858–61), the remodelling of the library at Trinity College, Dublin (1856–61), and the Crown Life Office, Blackfriars, London (1856–8; dem., 1866). An influential design for the government offices at Whitehall was placed third in the competition of 1856–7. He also designed a large number of private houses (mostly in Ireland) as well as several schools.

From 1858 (towards the end of the main contract on the University Museum, Oxford), declining health compelled Woodward to spend periods abroad. In December 1860 he left for the south of France, where he wintered on the Îles d'Hyères. On his return journey, on 15 May 1861, he suffered a fatal lung haemorrhage at the Hôtel de l'Univers, rue de Bourbon, Lyons; he was buried two days later in an unmarked grave in the city's cimetière de Loyasse. His friends, led by Stokes and Acland, attempted to publish a memoir, but failed to secure the support of the Deanes and instead commissioned a portrait medallion (from Alexander Munro), which they presented to the University Museum, Oxford. Woodward was described by Rossetti as 'handsome in a thoughtful but not ascetic way' (*Letters of Dante Gabriel Rossetti*, 2.407); his declining health is evident in the contrast between an early pastel drawing by S. Catterson Smith (Trinity College, Dublin) and later photographic portraits (including one by C. L. Dodgson).

FREDERICK O'DWYER

Sources F. O'Dwyer, *The architecture of Deane and Woodward* (1997) · E. Blau, *Ruskinian Gothic: the architecture of Deane and Woodward, 1845–61* (1982) · *Letters of Dante Gabriel Rossetti*, ed. O. Doughty and J. R. Wahl, 4 vols. (1965–7) · *The works of John Ruskin*, ed. E. T. Cook and A. Wedderburn, library edn, 39 vols. (1903–12) · H. W. Acland and J. Ruskin, *The Oxford museum*, rev. edn (1893) · F. O'Dwyer and J. Williams, 'Benjamin Woodward', *Victorian Dublin*, ed. T. Kennedy (1980), 38–63 · T. Garnham, *The Oxford museum* (1992) · W. Tuckwell, *Reminiscences of Oxford* (1900); repr. (1901) · R. Fox, 'The University Museum and Oxford science, 1850–1880', *Hist. U. Oxf. 6: 19th-cent. Oxf.*, 641–91 · A. Pollen, *John Hungerford Pollen, 1820–1902* (1912) · C. L. Eastlake, *A history of the Gothic revival* (1872) · J. Conolly, *The construction and government of lunatic asylums* (1847)

Archives Oxf. U. Mus. NH, letters, documents, and photographs concerning the construction of the University Museum · Oxf. UA, drawings, minute books, and corresp. concerning the University Museum | Bodl. Oxf., Acland MSS · U. Newcastle, Robinson L., letters to Sir Walter Trevelyan and Lady Trevelyan

Likenesses S. C. Smith, pastel drawing, c.1848, TCD · attrib. L. Carroll [C. L. Dodgson], photograph, 1850–59, NPG [*see illus.*] · L. Carroll [C. L. Dodgson], photograph, c.1860, Bodl. Oxf. · photograph, c.1860, Oxf. U. Mus. NH · A. Munro, marble medallion, Oxf. U. Mus. NH · photograph (as a child; after miniature, c.1826), priv. coll.

Woodward, Bernard Bolingbroke (1816–1869), librarian and author, was born in Norwich on 2 May 1816, the eldest son of Samuel *Woodward (1790–1838), geologist and antiquary, and his wife, Elizabeth (d. 1866), daughter of Bernard Bolingbroke of Norwich. Samuel Pickworth *Woodward, palaeontologist and botanist, was his younger brother. He was sent in March 1822 to the Grey Friars Priory, a private school in Norfolk kept by William Brooke, to whom on 29 September 1828 he was apprenticed for four years. On the expiration of this apprenticeship he worked for a time under his father's supervision, copying armorial bearings and other heraldic devices for Hudson Gurney. In his spare time he studied botany and other natural sciences, and kept copious notes, some of which were used by Hewett Cottrell Watson, the botanist.

In January 1834 Woodward became tutor at J. S. Buck's school at East Dereham, Norfolk. Late the following year he obtained a post in the banking house of Messrs Gurney at Great Yarmouth. Through the influence of friends at East Dereham he became strongly attracted to the Congregational ministry, and on coming of age left Yarmouth and went to study under W. Legge at Fakenham, Norfolk, and the Revd Mr Drane at Guestwick, Norfolk. In 1838 he entered as a student at the newly established Highbury College, Middlesex, where he graduated BA on 17 June 1841.

On 27 April 1843 Woodward was publicly recognized pastor of the independent church of Wortwell-with-Harleston in Norfolk. Also in 1843 he married Fanny Emma, ninth daughter of Thomas Teulon of Berkeley Street, London, the descendant of a Huguenot family. With her he had three daughters. He soon began to apply himself to writing and in this connection developed a friendship with John Childs, head of the printing firm at Bungay, Suffolk. For a while he was tutor to Childs's grandsons. At the end of 1848 he resigned his pastorate, intending to concentrate on writing, and moved to St John's Wood, London, in March 1849. After his first wife's death on 30 April 1850, he married, on 19 August 1851, Emma, seventh daughter of George Barham of Withersdale Hall, Suffolk. In November 1853 he moved to Bungay to be nearer to his friends the Childs, who were concerned in the production of his larger works, and whom he assisted in many of their undertakings. In 1857 he was elected a fellow of the Society of Antiquaries. In 1858 he returned to the neighbourhood of Hampstead.

On 2 July 1860 Woodward was appointed librarian in ordinary to the queen at Windsor Castle. There were eleven candidates for the post, including the librarian of the London Library and the secretary of the Society of Antiquaries. Woodward was recommended by W. B. Donne as being 'a good classical scholar and modern linguist. Knows Sanscrit [*sic*] and Persian; a well grounded geologist and chemist and wonderfully well versed in English Literature' (Royal Archives, PP Vic 4814, 1860). He came to the Royal Library at a time when great changes were taking place, mainly at the behest of the prince consort. He had to supervise the newly designed print room, the reorganization of the books, which had hitherto been only arranged by size, the reconstruction of parts of the library rooms to provide more space, the establishment of an archive room, and the storage of the miniatures, cameos, and gems. There was also cataloguing work on the collections; he produced an initial catalogue of the drawings by Nicolas Poussin in the Royal Collection, published in the *Fine Arts Quarterly Review*. He also assisted W. C. Ruland with a catalogue of the prince consort's Raphael collection. During the rearrangement and dismounting of some of the master drawings by Michelangelo and Raphael, he discovered other important drawings on the versos. He continued the prince consort's work on the acquisition of prints and photographs for the collection. He did much to realize the prince's wish 'to make the choicest drawings in the Royal Collection accessible at a cheap rate to students of Art' (Royal Archives, PP Vic 20688, 1865) by organizing photographic reproductions.

Woodward's busy work in the library was made difficult by his official residence being in London. His later years were also shadowed by ill health and by a disagreement with the keeper of the privy purse as to how library funds had been used. He was permitted to resume his former literary activities in order to repay money owed to the library. He was on friendly terms with some of Queen Victoria's children, particularly Prince Alfred, Prince Arthur, and Princess Louise; but he got on less well with some of his colleagues in the royal household.

Woodward wrote histories of Hampshire, Wales, and the United States, as well as elementary textbooks on English history, Christianity, and astronomy. He also published *Specimens of the Drawings of Ten Masters from the Royal Collection at Windsor Castle* (1870). His preface to this volume is dated 1 September 1869, just six weeks before his death. He had been planning books on Leonardo da Vinci and his drawings in the Royal Collection, and a calendar of the Stuart papers. He wrote many articles and reviews for the *Eclectic Review*, Sharpe's *London Magazine*, the *Gentleman's Magazine*, and other periodicals. He brought out an edition of James Barclay's *Complete Dictionary of the English Language*

(1851), for which he wrote numerous articles, especially in biography and geography. He edited S. Maunder's *Treasury of Knowledge* (1859), for which he wrote a 'compendious English grammar', besides rewriting much of the rest. He also founded and edited the *Fine Arts Quarterly Review*, which appeared from May 1863 to June 1867. The main reason for his founding the *Review* was, as stated by him, 'the almost entire absence of records' relating to the art collections in the Royal Library which 'deprived them of half of their worth and usefulness'. The *Review* was a 'means of addressing himself to the students of the history of art in every country' (*Fine Arts Quarterly Review*, 1, 1863, Preface) to obtain clues to the information he wanted.

Woodward died at his official residence, Royal Mews, Pimlico, on 12 October 1869 and was buried at Kensal Green.   B. B. WOODWARD, *rev.* OLIVER EVERETT

Sources Royal Arch. · W. L. R. Cates, *Norwich Penny Magazine* (1870), 24 · private information (1900)
Archives Linn. Soc., corresp. and papers relating to shells · NHM, natural history notes and diary · Norfolk RO, corresp. and papers · Suffolk RO, Ipswich, antiquarian notes relating to Bungay | National Gallery, London, letters to Ralph Nicholson Wornum · V&A NAL, letters to E. Viner
Wealth at death under £3000: resworn probate, Nov 1870, *CGPLA Eng. & Wales* (1869)

Woodward, George Murgatroyd (1760?–1809), caricaturist and author, was the son of William Woodward, who in 1796 was living at Stanton Hall, Stanton by Dale, Derbyshire, a house belonging to a Mr Thornhill, whom he probably served as steward.

Woodward, later known as Mustard George, grew up in a Derbyshire town, living with his father and, to judge by the evidence of his later writings, received a sound education. He took early to caricature, ridiculing his neighbours in Derbyshire; a folio of these drawings dated 1781 is in the Derby Local Studies Library, among a sizeable collection of his prints, drawings, and book illustrations. His caricatures having caused something of a local stir, he persuaded his father to let him seek his fortune in London.

Apart from two caricature prints dated 1785 designed by Woodward and published by him from 28 Cary Street, Lincoln's Inn, London, it was not until 1790 that he made an impact on the London scene. Thereafter his output was copious. The British Museum catalogues list 525 examples of his work from the next twenty years, published by Holland, Fores, Ackermann, and latterly Tegg, all leading printsellers. These prints, designed by Woodward, are etched by others—Rowlandson, who was his friend and drinking companion, Isaac Cruikshank, Roberts, and Williams. Woodward's original drawings are vigorous but crude, marked by heavy outlines and coarse colouring; his value lay in his humorous ideas.

Woodward's political prints and broadsides are orthodox in outlook, generally supporting the government and always ready to lambast the French. His forte was social humour, and in this area his reputation between 1807 and 1809 surpassed even that of Rowlandson. Lacking the serious purpose of a satirist and going beyond the ritual mockery of hypocrisy and affectation, he concentrated on jokes, which were often ribald. For his contemporaries, much of the attraction of his work lay in the captions, which relied heavily on wordplay and were sometimes couched in doggerel verse. He tended to choose his subjects from the middle and lower classes rather than high society and had a partiality for sailors. In Dorothy George's words, 'he was the inventor of the sailor ashore ... generous, reckless, pugnacious, tough but tender-hearted, simple-minded and shrewd—belonging to a race apart' (George, *English Political Caricature*, 1.174).

Woodward was a pioneer of the strip cartoon. Elaborating a method of Bunbury and F. G. Byron, he produced between 1794 and 1800 a number of single-sheet caricatures, with titles like 'The Effects of Flattery', that were variations on a theme arranged in rows, a device that was much exploited. He showed versatility too in designing book illustrations, borders, and screen decorations.

Of Woodward's books, the first and most celebrated was *Eccentric Excursions*, published in 1796 with 100 plates engraved by Isaac Cruikshank after his designs. Woodward's text describes an idiosyncratic ramble round the country and reveals an engaging personality. At least seven other books followed, all broadly humorous and without literary distinction, of which *An Olio of Good Breeding* (1801) is perhaps the best. Sets of Woodward's humorous plates were also published, and from 1807 to 1809 he was the principal illustrator of Tegg's *Caricature Magazine, or, Hudibrastic Mirror*.

Woodward, on the title-pages of books and on caricatures, was occasionally referred to as 'esquire', reflecting the fact that he was an untrained artist who did not etch his designs. However, an amateur status was no indication of a gentlemanly lifestyle. Henry Angelo, whose *Reminiscences* is the sole source of most biographical information on him, reported that Mustard George kept low company and drank immoderately. He died at the Brown Bear public house in Bow Street, London, in November 1809, of a dropsy according to Redgrave, and with a glass of brandy in his hand as Angelo has it. He was buried at the expense of the landlord.

In Angelo's opinion, if Woodward had learned to draw and been temperate in his habits he might have rivalled Hogarth. Certainly his collaboration with Rowlandson constituted a lively, if frivolous, commentary on the social scene. Dorothy George described him as 'original, prolific, varied, humorous and good-humoured', and few students of the subject would dispute her conclusion that his death was 'a loss to caricature' (George, *English Political Caricature*, 1.174). There are holdings of his work at the department of prints and drawings, British Museum, and at the Victoria and Albert Museum.   SIMON HENEAGE

Sources H. Angelo, *Reminiscences*, 2 (1830) · F. G. Stephens and M. D. George, eds., *Catalogue of political and personal satires preserved ... in the British Museum*, 6 (1938); 7 (1942); 8 (1947) · M. D. George, *English political caricature: a study of opinion and propaganda*, 2 vols. (1959) · A. M. Broadley, *Napoleon in caricature, 1795–1821*, 2 vols. (1911) · Redgrave, *Artists* · J. R. Abbey, *Life in England in aquatint and lithography, 1770–1860* (privately printed, London, 1953) · J. Grego, *Rowlandson the caricaturist*, 2 vols. (1880) · *GM*, 1st ser., 79 (1809), 1175 · D. Donald, *The age of caricature: satirical prints in the reign of George III* (1996) · T. Wright, *A history of caricature and grotesque in literature and art* (1865)

Likenesses T. Cheesman, stipple, 1805 (after A. Buck), BM, NPG; repro. in G. M. Woodward, *The fugitive and other literary works* (1805)

Wealth at death buried at expense of landlord of pub he died in: Redgrave, *Artists*

Woodward, Henry (1714–1777), actor and pantomimist, was born in Southwark, London, on 2 October 1714, the eldest son of a tallow chandler in Southwark, and was initially apprenticed in his father's trade. From 1724 to 1728 he attended Merchant Taylors' School, where he became noted for his quick wits. It is not certain how he obtained an introduction to John Rich, manager of Lincoln's Inn Fields Theatre, but by 1 January 1729 he had joined Rich's juvenile troupe, playing The Beggar, Filch, and Ben Budge in John Gay's *The Beggar's Opera*, and so recommended himself to the manager that the latter began instructing him in acting, dancing, and traditional *lazzi* associated with the role of Harlequin. From 1730 for six seasons Woodward's theatrical apprenticeship was undertaken largely at Henry Giffard's Goodman's Fields Theatre, interspersed with summertime work at various fairbooths—Henry Fielding's great booth at Southwark (1731), the Cherry Tree Garden (1732), and Bartholomew fair (1734)—as well as occasional appearances (1734) at the Haymarket Theatre.

With Giffard's company Woodward explored the repertory available to boys and young men, such as Donalbain in *Macbeth* and Telemachus in *Penelope* by Thomas Cooke and John Mottley, rising to Roderigo in *Othello*, Osric, and Tattle by 1735–6. More notably, after his appearance in *Harlequin's Contrivance* (21 April 1732) he began steadily to take on the role of Harlequin in pantomime, eventually from September 1734 assuming the sobriquet Lun, Jr. in honour of his training with Rich (previously and popularly known when impersonating Harlequin as Lun). For many years it was his habit to name himself 'Lun, Jr.' when appearing in the central role in pantomime, and to use Woodward only when in a straight acting part. As he worked in two separate fields, for much of his career he received two salaries. By the time Woodward went with Giffard's company to Lincoln's Inn Fields Theatre in 1736 he had established a firm reputation for excellence of his characterization in all styles of comedy and for virtuoso physical brio in pantomime. From the time he penned a prologue for his own benefit night on 5 May 1731, he also showed an aptitude for writing, especially satirical pieces critical of prevailing tastes in theatrical culture (in December 1736, for example, he was inspired by current gossip concerning the strife between Susannah Maria Cibber and Kitty Clive about which of them should assume the role of Polly Peacham to write *The Beggar's Pantomime, or, The Contending Columbines*). By the time he joined Drury Lane for the 1737 season, Woodward had married. The precise date is uncertain but may have been sometime in 1734, since Mrs Woodward's name appeared increasingly on the bills after that September for Goodman's Fields Theatre, most frequently as a dancer.

The four seasons Woodward spent at the patent house

Henry Woodward (1714–1777), by Sir Joshua Reynolds, 1759–62

were marred initially by rivalry with the prevailing Drury Lane Harlequin, William Phillips, which ended only with Phillips's departure in 1739. Over those four seasons Woodward extended his repertory by undertaking some fifty-five new roles, of which ten were developments of his Harlequin persona. Some idea of the sheer extent of his skill in comedy may be gleaned from a selection of these many parts: Witwoud in William Congreve's *The Way of the World*, Jeremy in Congreve's *Love for Love*, Sir Amorous La Foole in *The Silent Woman* (Ben Jonson's *Epicoene*), Kastril in Jonson's *The Alchemist*, Sparkish in William Wycherley's *The Country Wife*, Sir Joseph Wittol in Congreve's *The Old Bachelor*, and Shakespeare's Pistol, Silvius, and Sir Andrew Aguecheek. The range extends from high comedy to farce, comedy of manners to pastoral, low comedy to delicate ridicule. Appearances in tragedy were few and, with the exception of Octavius in *Julius Caesar*, tended to be in secondary roles calling for a degree of caricature, such as the Poet in *Timon of Athens*, or for earthy realism, such as the First Citizen in *Julius Caesar*. During the summers Woodward gravitated to the fairs, except for June and July 1739, when he appeared for a short season in Dublin. During the summer of 1741 he joined George Lee in managing a booth theatre at the Tottenham Court, Bartholomew and Southwark fairs. By 25 September 1741 Woodward was established at Covent Garden (appearing as Sir Joseph in *The Old Bachelor*), where he remained for the following six seasons. His reputation made possible extensive touring during the summers to reputable provincial establishments such as the Jacob's Wells Theatre in Bristol, to Ward's company at Oswestry, and to Richmond in Surrey.

The repertory at Covent Garden allowed Woodward to hone his comic skills further by essaying some forty-six new roles. His value as a performer is evident from his salary, which by 1746 amounted to £2 15*s*. a week. What continues to impress is the variety of styles and tones: Shakespeare's Touchstone, Parolles, Guiderius, and Lucio, Dashwell in *The London Cuckolds* by Edward Ravenscroft, Young Fashion in *The Relapse* by John Vanbrugh, Young Bellair in George Etherege's *The Man of Mode*, Flash in David Garrick's *Miss in her Teens*, and Jack Meggot in Benjamin Hoadly's *The Suspicious Husband*. A year-long interlude saw Woodward at Thomas Sheridan's invitation performing at the Smock Alley Theatre, Dublin—a period which is most notable for his writing and performing a satirical monologue, *Coffee*, designed to ridicule Samuel Foote's *Dish of Chocolate* at the rival venue in Capel Street. The inevitable competition between the performers which ensued was to be sustained over several years.

When Woodward returned to London in 1748 it was to act under Garrick's management at Drury Lane, where he remained for a decade, triumphing almost immediately with an impersonation of Mercutio (opposite Spranger Barry and Mrs Cibber as Romeo and Juliet) that was hailed as a masterpiece of acting. Building on his earlier successes in Jonsonian comedy, Woodward now added to his repertory in quick succession Ananias (1749–50), Face (1752–3), and Subtle (1755–6) in *The Alchemist* and Sir John Daw in *Epicoene*; but it was as Bobadil in *Every Man in his Humour* (1751–2) that he again struck gold, the seedy, down-at-heel braggart with the expansive imagination calling on all his expertise in low comedy, his verbal brilliance, and his capacity for subtlety of characterization in roles that might easily invite mannerism or caricature. Other notable roles over this period included Petruchio in Garrick's rewriting of *The Taming of the Shrew* opposite Kitty Clive (1756)—an unhappy pairing where, it is said, the knockabout often exceeded what was rehearsed— Razor in the first performances of Arthur Murphy's popular farce *The Upholsterer*, and, perhaps surprisingly, Shakespeare's Polonius, where doubtless Woodward took advantage of the opportunity the part offers for darkly comic invention.

In 1749 the rivalry with Samuel Foote flared up again when Foote at the Haymarket began mimicking Garrick and Woodward; Woodward responded by introducing satirical comments of his own devising into performances of the role in which he had been aped and then played to huge acclaim the satire on Foote he had invented in Ireland for his benefit on 18 March, which earned him £223. Woodward's attempt to cap this success by aping Foote in his role of Malagene in Thomas Otway's *Friendship in Fashion* turned sour when the audience, made up largely of Foote's claque, grew riotous and threatened the fabric of the theatre. Woodward was the butt of further unruly behaviour from spectators when he featured in *Harlequin Ranger* (1752), a pantomime in which Garrick satirized the rival management at Covent Garden for introducing circus-type artistes into their recent stagings.

That he had always been successful in his tours to Ireland may be the reason why Woodward in 1758 decided (despite the advice against the venture of both his wife and Garrick) to join Spranger Barry as joint manager of a new theatre in Dublin to rival Smock Alley. The Crow Street Theatre inevitably failed for want of a large enough audience in Dublin to sustain two venues; a second theatre they opened in Cork in 1761 did not recoup their resources, and by July 1762 the partnership was dissolved. It had cost Woodward his accumulated savings of £3000 and the loss of his high, guaranteed earnings while acting for Garrick. After returning to London in 1762, he was employed by John Beard at Covent Garden, where he stayed for eight seasons. Among some twenty-two new roles were numbered Sir John Brute in Vanbrugh's *The Provoked Wife* and Ogleby in Garrick's and George Colman the elder's *The Clandestine Marriage*, while he was the first to play Young Brumpton in Arthur Murphy's *The School for Guardians*, Careless in Colman's *The Oxonians in Town*, Lofty in Oliver Goldsmith's *The Good-Natured Man*, and Captain Ironsides in Richard Cumberland's *The Brothers*. He also starred in his own pantomime, *Harlequin's Jubilee* (1769–70), which scathingly mocked Garrick's Stratford festival. Altercations with a new management at Covent Garden caused Woodward to secede and join forces with his old rival Foote, who was touring a company to the Theatre Royal, Edinburgh, for the winter of 1770–71. After a brief season at Tate Wilkinson's theatre in York in April 1771, he returned for a summer season with Foote at the Haymarket before rejoining the Covent Garden company under Colman's management at a weekly salary of £16 10s., where he remained until his death. Of the nine new roles essayed in these last years, the most notable were the original Captain Absolute in Richard Brinsley Sheridan's *The Rivals* and Jodelett in his own rewriting of William Davenant's *The Man's the Master*. Woodward's last performance was as Stephano in *The Tempest* on 13 January 1777. He died, supposedly of kidney malfunction, at his home in Chapel Street, Grosvenor Place (a house admired for the elegance and luxury of its furnishings, library, and pictures), on 17 April, nursed by the actress George Anne *Bellamy (1731?–1788), who had been his companion, after the death of his wife, for over ten years. He was buried in St George's, Hanover Square, on 24 April 1777.

No greater discrepancy of temperament can be envisaged than that which seemingly prevailed between Woodward's known character offstage and the personae he projected when in role. He was typically cast as dissolute, cynical, rakish, flamboyant, rhetorical, lying, passionate, grotesque, airily irresponsible, brutish, or duplicitous, while in life he was a model of propriety. Rare for an actor in the period, no scandal or gossip attached to his name; satirists such as Foote attacked his artistry, not his morals; even his liaison with George Anne Bellamy attracted no attention (she described it as platonic, but her memoirs are not distinguished by their accuracy). He was quiet and taciturn, perhaps through shyness, and so was slow to develop friendships. That he deployed his considerable income somewhat frugally, the better to promote a developed connoisseurship, was learned by many only after his death, when Bellamy rapidly sold his effects at auction to realize her bequest (his valuables ran to 450 lots, comprising books, jewels, plate, brocades, drawings, and paintings). Such a disciplined temperament clearly relished the opportunity the stage afforded to pursue its antithesis. While Woodward was much admired for his versatility and his athleticism, it was generally agreed that he could overplay on occasion, overdo his grimacing and his inventions of comic business, particularly with an eye to pleasing admirers in the gallery. It is hardly surprising therefore that his finest roles were Mercutio and Bobadil, two characters who in themselves run to excess. Surviving portraits, mostly in role, by Joshua Reynolds, Samuel De Wilde, and James Roberts, show why Woodward was admired in his day as utterly protean in his shape-changing: the contrast between his swarthy, hang-dog Bobadil and his dapper, suavely knowing Mercutio as recorded by these artists implies much about his skill as an actor fully to *embody* a given role. These images suggest that he acted with his *whole* self: voice, features, physique, carriage, stance. From his lifelong skills as the finest of Harlequins he carried over into more conventional acting a rare proficiency in physicalized mime, giving his impersonations great immediacy. Verse tributes after his death stressed this feature of his performances, as if the *look* of a characterization was what etched it into a spectator's memory. In Woodward's ability to physicalize a comic text lay his claim to genius. RICHARD ALLEN CAVE

Sources Highfill, Burnim & Langhans, *BDA* · A. H. Scouten, ed., *The London stage, 1660–1800*, pt 3: *1729–1747* (1961) · G. W. Stone, ed., *The London stage, 1660–1800*, pt 4: *1747–1776* (1962) · C. B. Hogan, ed., *The London stage, 1660–1800*, pt 5: *1776–1800* (1968) · *The letters of David Garrick*, ed. D. M. Little and G. M. Kahrl, 3 vols. (1963) · G. W. Stone and G. M. Kahrl, *David Garrick: a critical biography* (1979) · C. Oman, *David Garrick* (1958) · *DNB* · Genest, *Eng. stage* · R. Hitchcock, *An historical view of the Irish stage*, 2 vols. (1788–94) · *Theatrical biography, or, Memoirs of the principal performers of the three Theatre Royals*, 2 vols. (1772) · T. Wilkinson, *The wandering patentee, or, A history of the Yorkshire theatres from 1770 to the present time*, 4 vols. (1795) · *An apology for the life of George Anne Bellamy, late of Covent Garden Theatre, written by herself*, 6 vols. (1785) · *Managers' Notebook* · W. C. Russell, *Representative actors* [1888] · J. Doran and R. W. Lowe, 'Their majesties' servants': annals of the English stage, rev. edn, 3 vols. (1888) · T. Davies, *Memoirs of the life of David Garrick*, 2 vols. (1780) · T. Davies, *Dramatic miscellanies*, new edn, 3 vols. (1785) · *The thespian dictionary, or, Dramatic biography of the present age*, 2nd edn (1805) · C. Churchill, *The Rosciad*, 5th edn (1761) · P. Fitzgerald, *The life of David Garrick* (1899) · *The reminiscences of Thomas Dibdin* (1834)

Likenesses engravings, pubd 1753–78 · J. Reynolds, oils, 1759–62, Petworth House, West Sussex [see illus.] · engraving, pubd 1767 · engraving, pubd 1773 · J. R. Smith, engraving, pubd 1774 (after B. Vandergucht) · B. Vandergucht, oils, exh. RA 1774, Yale U. CBA; version, Garr. Club · J. Roberts, watercolour on vellum, 1776, BM · J. Thornthwaite, engraving, 1776, repro. in J. Bell, *Bell's British theatre* (1776) · J. Basire, engraving (after Taylor), repro. in Lowndes, *New English theatre* (1776) · S. De Wilde, oils (after sketch by J. Zoffany), Garr. Club · S. De Wilde, watercolour drawing, Harvard TC · S. Freeman, engraving (after B. Vandergucht), repro. in *The cabinet* (1807) · J. Goldar, engraving (after Taylor), repro. in Lowndes, *New English theatre* (1776) · J. Goldar, engraving (after E. Edwards), repro. in Lowndes, *New English theatre* (1777) · R. Hancock, decoration on saucer, Man. City Gall. · R. Hancock, engraving (after engraving, pubd 1753) · F. Hayman, pencil drawing, FM Cam. · J. Macardell, mezzotint (after F. Hayman), BM, NG Ire., NPG · J. Roberts, water-colour on vellum (as Captain Brazen in *The recruiting officer*), BM · J. Roberts, watercolour on vellum (after B. Vandergucht), BM · Roberts, engraving (after Thornthwaite); Christies, 27 March 1793, lot 14 · J. Thornthwaite, engraving (after J. Roberts), repro. in J. Bell, *Bell's British theatre* (1776) · J. Watson, mezzotint (after J. Reynolds), BM, NPG · T. Worlidge, oils (as Brass in *The confederacy*), Garr. Club · Bow porcelain figures, priv. coll. · Bow porcelain figures, London Museum · engraving, repro. in *Town and Country Magazine* (Oct 1776) · engraving, repro. in *Hibernian Magazine* (June 1777) · engraving (after J. Roberts), repro. in J. Bell, ed., *Bell's edition of Shakespeare's plays* (1776); Christies, 27 March 1793, lot 40 · engraving, repro. in *Hibernian Magazine* (1772) · theatrical prints, BM, NPG

Wealth at death £700 invested in bank annuities and £619 eventually paid from estate to George Anne Bellamy: will, 20 Jan 1777; Edward Willett, *Letters addressed to Mrs. Bellamy* · valuable furnishings, collections of paintings and drawings, silver, etc.; sold at auction by Bellamy in 1777

Woodward, Herbert Hall (1847–1909), composer and clergyman, was born on 13 January 1847 at The Friars, near Liverpool, the fifth and youngest son of Robert Woodward (1801–1882) and his wife, Mary (d. 1891), the youngest daughter of William Hall, of Ryall's Court, Ripple, Worcestershire. His father, a Liverpool merchant, purchased the Arley Castle estate, near Bewdley, in 1852. Both his parents' families had long been settled in Worcestershire. After attending Radley College, Woodward matriculated at Corpus Christi College, Oxford, in 1862. At Radley he studied music under Dr E. G. Monk and at Oxford under the Revd Dr Leighton Hayne; he graduated BMus in 1866 and BA in 1867. He then spent eighteen months at Cuddesdon Theological College, and, being ordained deacon in 1870 and priest in 1871 in the diocese of Oxford, became curate and precentor of Wantage. There he remained for eleven years, working as assistant priest under William John Butler, afterwards dean of Lincoln. He composed his communion service in E♭, which appeared in many editions, for the church choir at Wantage.

In 1881 Woodward was appointed a minor canon of Worcester Cathedral, and in 1890 he became precentor, succeeding the Revd E. V. Hall. In the autumn of 1881 he composed the anthem 'The radiant morn', which first appeared in the *Musical Times* in June 1882 (pp. 329–33), and became 'one of the best-known modern anthems in English church music' (*MT*, 46, 1905, 724). He formed at Worcester a successful preparatory boarding-school for the choirboys, of which he was warden for twenty-eight years, from 1881 until his death. He had a great influence on the services at the cathedral, and raised the standard of worship to a high level. Other works he published include communion services in D (1885) and A (1897), and numerous anthems including 'The sun shall be no more thy light by day' (1887), 'Rejoice greatly' (1889), 'Behold, the days come, saith the Lord' (1895), 'The day thou gavest, Lord, is ended' (1896), and 'Comes, at times, a stillness as of even' (1908). A bachelor with private means, he was widely known for his generous philanthropy. He resided at College Yard, Worcester, but died at 45 Devonshire Street,

Portland Place, London, after an operation, on 25 May 1909. He was commemorated at Worcester by the Woodward memorial wing of the choir-school buildings.

J. C. HADDEN, *rev.* DAVID J. GOLBY

Sources 'Church and organ music', *MT*, 46 (1905), 724–5 · Dotted Crotchet, 'Worcester Cathedral', *MT*, 46 (1905), 705–14 · H. H. Woodward, 'The radiant morn', *MT*, 23 (1882), 329–33 · Brown & Stratton, *Brit. mus.* · Burke, *Gen. GB*
Likenesses T. Bennett & Sons, photograph, repro. in 'Church and organ music', *MT*, 724
Wealth at death £25,737 5s. 2d.: probate, 2 July 1909, *CGPLA Eng. & Wales*

Woodward, Hezekiah (1591/2–1675), educationist and divine, was born in Worcestershire, the youngest of nine children. Like most educational reformers, Woodward was critical of his own upbringing. According to the autobiographical details in his 'Of the child's portion' (1640), published in *A Sons Patrimony and a Daughters Portion* (1643), he was sent to a grammar school in his home county for six and a half years and 'trained up according to the *bad fashion* … of most Teachers, then and now' with too much rote learning (p. 10). He was then dispatched, 'before I was fitted', to Balliol College, Oxford, where he matriculated on 16 June 1610 aged eighteen; he graduated BA on 15 February 1612. He admired his college tutor ('the ablest among many, and most conscientious in his duty, and as skilfull to teach his Schollers theirs') but felt that he had been put to rhetoric and logic too soon and that the six years he eventually spent in Oxford had not equipped him to master thoroughly a body of knowledge (p. 11). A speech impediment made him despair of a career as a preacher or a lawyer. Thereafter, he wrote movingly about the tongue as 'man's glory' but a 'rod of pride' to the foolish; 'man hath made wilde creatures tame; but the tongue no man can tame' (pp. 43–4). His published writings frequently returned to questions of verbal honesty and integrity, the swearing of oaths, the restraint of common insults, and taking the name of God in vain. Resolved 'to digge or to begge' as he later expressed it in his *A Light to Grammar and All other Arts and Sciences* (1641), he went twice to the continent, apparently visiting the court of the elector palatine, Frederick V, at Heidelberg before eventually returning about 1619 to Aldermanbury, just outside London, where he opened a school.

Woodward's significance as an educationist has not been sufficiently recognized. He was an associate of Samuel Hartlib's from the year in which the latter arrived in London in 1628. Through Hartlib's circle he came to be an enthusiast for the ambitious reform of learning proposed by Francis Bacon, whom Woodward refers to in a letter to Hartlib of 5 August 1644 as 'Our great *Advancer* of Learning' and 'that great *Scholler*'. It was doubtless Hartlib's contact that enabled Woodward to know and appreciate the 'very exact method' developed by William Brookes 'whereby the tongue may be moulded and framed to a speedy attaining of three languages' (H. Woodward, *A Sons Patrimony*, pt 2, 162). Brookes's method was destined never to be given the patent he sought for it but another of Hartlib's acquaintants, Thomas Horne, schoolmaster at

Leicester, Tonbridge, and finally Eton College, collaborated with him and eventually published a version of it in his own blueprint for the reform of secondary education. It was through Hartlib too, no doubt, that Woodward was introduced to the educational writings of the Moravian Jan Amos Komenský (Comenius). Horne had, at Hartlib's encouragement, published in 1633 his English translation of Comenius's famous *Janua linguarum*, and the influence of Comenius's writings on Woodward was particularly evident in the latter's *A Light to Grammar and All other Arts and Sciences* and *A Gate to Science, Opened by a Natural Key*. It is probably no coincidence that these two works were published in 1641, the year when Hartlib's efforts to invite Comenius to London were finally successful. Five years later Comenius recalled Woodward as one of his English patrons who had shown a 'first benevolence' towards his 'Herculean' labours of educational reform (*Letters of Sir Cheney Culpeper*, ed. Braddick, 276–80). Woodward's educational writings, especially the second edition of his *A Sons Patrimony* (1643)—which a 'zealous well-wisher', perhaps Hartlib, had overseen through the press—had their impact on Milton's treatise *On Education* (1644). His conceit of schools as 'seed-plots' in which all, from the meanest to the greatest, needed to be taught to read 'the book of the creatures' and '*spell* nature' (Hartlib MSS, 34/1/5A–6B) made schoolmastering an honourable profession and Woodward an influence on those who sought to teach in innovative ways after the civil wars.

Woodward—who was, as Anthony Wood put it, 'always puritanically affected' (Wood, *Ath. Oxon.*)—was a committed parliamentarian. In *The Churches Thank-Offering to God her King and the Parliament*, an anonymous publication of late 1641, he wrote of the 'Marvelous Delivrance' wrought in England by the calling of the Long Parliament and its first session as a year of jubilee. The afflictions of the realm would turn out to be mercies, and the 'strange Overtures and turning of things upside downe' in the church were God destroying the final yoke of papal tyranny for good and bringing his people into the bond of covenant. In *The Kings Chronicle* (1643—the first section having been initially published in 1641), he pointedly searched the scriptural stories of the bad kings of Judah to 'posture a Kingdom', by which he meant provide a platform for the deliverance of the nation from destruction. He used the same metaphor in his *A Good Souldier* (1644) in which the people (God's 'peculiars'), having plucked down the high and lofty ones, are urged to 'bring the three Kingdomes into covenant with their God' and to begin with reform from within. 'Babylon is fallen, is fallen, is certainly fallen', but 'Till we have Pastours after Gods own heart, we cannot avouch God for our God; we cannot enter covenant with Him' (p. 55).

Some of Woodward's writings of this period may well have originated as sermons preached at St Mary Aldermanbury, where Edmund Calamy (the elder) had succeeded John Stoughton in 1639, and where Hartlib was no stranger. His populist leanings and his early inclinations to the Independents made Woodward a figure of some notoriety. In late 1644 he paid 55s. to a printer to publish

(anonymously and without any licence) his *Inquiries into the Causes of our Miseries*, addressed partly against William Prynne. Only two of its anticipated three sections were ever produced and the second was seized by order of parliament while in the press for having been published without permission. On account of the 'frequent printing of scandalous books by divers, as Hezekiah Woodward and John Milton', he was briefly arrested by order of the House of Lords and examined by two judges at the end of the year (*JHL*, 7.116). In August 1644 he had also written in his *A Short Letter*, a 'large but modest' reply to Hartlib's request for his comments on Thomas Edwards's *Anti-Apology*. In this pamphlet he lamented Edwards's lack of charity and aggressive advocacy of the presbyterian cause; 'I confesse I doe most unwillingly make mention of *Presbyterian* and *Independent*, I am perswaded all the *good* and *choice* men are for the *old-Way*, the *Way of CHRIST* and his Apostles'. Reforming the church meant, for Woodward, the difficult task of reforming ourselves and our public behaviour, and, according to Wood, it was only after the civil wars, 'when he saw the independents and other factious people to be dominant, he became one of them' (Wood, *Ath. Oxon.*). In due course being 'not unknown to Oliver [Cromwell]' he became his private chaplain 'or at least favourite' (ibid.).

By April 1650 Woodward had been given by Cromwell the vicarage of Bray, near Maidenhead. There he remained through the Commonwealth and protectorate, allowing church property to fall into ruin, refusing to accept tithes, holding prayer-meetings in the vicarage for 'a select congregation', and publishing treatises which prompted Thomas Hearne to describe him as 'that most abominable and Prophane Fanatick, Hezekiah Woodward' (*Remarks*, 239). He defended strict sabbath observance and argued against formal prayers and the teaching of the Lord's prayer to children. In *Infant Baptism, and the Fierst Query Thereupon* (1656), he questioned whether 'deboysed' (that is, 'debauched') parents had the right to have their children baptized (and he himself refused the sacraments and baptism to those of his parishioners who 'were not of his private church' according to Wood). He also provided in *A Church-Covenant Lawfull and Needfull* (1656) a model 'engagement' or 'Church-covenant' to which congregations such as his own might independently subscribe, each agreeing to 'take special care' of fellow seekers of the truth.

In 1660 Woodward left Bray voluntarily to escape ejection and went to live in Uxbridge, Middlesex. There his notoriety for absenting himself from church and preaching at the Three Swans inn, where he was 'frequented by the best of the Towne' (*Calamy rev.*), led to his being presented by the churchwardens there and fined 7s. 8d. in 1669. However, on 13 May 1672 he was licensed as a presbyterian minister. He died on 29 March 1675 and was buried in Eton chapel yard; he was survived by his wife, Frances, who was buried near him after she died on 30 August 1681. In his will, drawn up at Uxbridge on 22 February 1675, Woodward left small sums to several friends, including his landlady, Mary Biscoe. His copy of Chrysostome was meant for John *Oxenbridge (1608–1674), who had married his daughter Frances (d. 1659) but who, unknown to Woodward, had predeceased him, and six of his best English books went to their daughter Theodora. Another son-in-law, Daniel Henchman of Boston, Massachusetts, widower of Sarah, received property in Ireland. The executor was Mary Parsone, a creditor and family servant of twenty years' standing.   M. Greengrass

Sources H. Woodward, A sons patrimony and daughters portion: payable to them at all times, but best received in their first times, when they are young and tender (1643) · Wood, Ath. Oxon., new edn, 3.1034 · Calamy rev., 545 · H. Woodward, A light to grammar and all other arts and sciences (1641) · H. Woodward, A short letter modestly intreating a friends judgement upon Mr Edwards his booke, he calleth an anti-apologie (1644), esp. preface · H. Woodward, A church-covenant lawfull and needfull to be entred-into by all, that intend to walk in church-fellowship according to gospel-order (1656) · 'The letters of Sir Cheney Culpeper, 1641–1657', ed. M. J. Braddick, Camden miscellany, XXXIII, CS, 5th ser., 7 (1996), 105–402 · University of Sheffield, Hartlib MSS · JHL, 7 (1644–5), 116, 118 · Remarks and collections of Thomas Hearne, ed. C. E. Doble and others, 2, OHS, 7 (1886), 239 · LMA, AM/PBR/002/Hezekiah Woodward/1675/July
Archives BL, Add. MSS, letters | University of Sheffield, Hartlib MSS, letters
Wealth at death property in Ireland: Calamy rev., 545

Woodward, John (1665/1668–1728), physician, natural historian, and antiquary, was born on 1 May 1665, or possibly 1668, in a village (possibly Wirksworth) in Derbyshire; he may have been of a Gloucestershire family and his mother's maiden surname may have been Burdett. At sixteen he was apprenticed to a London linen draper, where he was discovered by Peter Barwick, physician to Charles II. Barwick took Woodward into his house and taught him his profession, helping him obtain the post of professor of physick at Gresham College in 1692.

Woodward had received a good classical education at a local grammar school and took a precocious interest in natural history of every kind, but especially in fossils. He collected his first geological specimen in a London gravel-pit in 1688, and his first fossil shell in the Cotswolds on 13 January 1690. In 1693 he became a fellow of the Royal Society, and in 1695 was created MD, first by Archbishop Tenison and then by Cambridge University. He soon gained a successful medical practice, which he recorded in the posthumously published *Select Cases* (1759), and which brought him loyal patients such as Sir Richard Steele. He was active in the Royal College of Physicians from 1698, became a fellow on 5 March 1703, and was censor in that year and again in 1714–15. Early in 1711 he gave the Goulstonian lectures, setting out his own theory of medicine with an emphasis on keeping the right balance of bilious salts in the stomach (summarized in BL, MS Sloane 2039, fols. 115–35v). He dissented from the views of doctors John Freind and Richard Mead on the treatment of smallpox, preferring vomiting to purging, and thus began a long pamphlet war which, after the publication of his *State of Physick* (1718), reportedly led to a sword fight with Mead. In fear of his life, Woodward is alleged to have said that he preferred to die by Mead's sword than by his medicine (his own account appeared in *The Freethinker* in 1719).

John Woodward (1665/1668–1728), by William Humphrey, pubd 1774

In general Woodward favoured experimental knowledge before the authority of the ancients, here as elsewhere, and took the modern side in the contemporary battle of the books. Although he suffered much satire his views were taken seriously by many, including the Swiss J. J. Scheuchzer, who translated his work into Latin (1720), and the great Dutch physician, Hermann Boerhaave, with whom he corresponded.

Woodward set to work on a new theory of the earth in which he hoped to explain the fossils he had been collecting as once living creatures destroyed by the biblical flood and preserved in the strata according to the order of their gravity, just as he believed Moses had described it in the Pentateuch. He had already begun lecturing on these things at Gresham College in 1693, and his *Essay toward a Natural History of the Earth* (1695) immediately embroiled him in a controversy which lasted for many years. His rivals, John Ray and Edward Llwyd, Martin Lister and Tancred Robinson, along with John Arbuthnot, all opposed him, but Woodward was ably defended by John Harris, John Morton, and others at home and abroad. He continued to gather together fossils from all over the world and to develop his own ideas in a work which was never completed. Among his many foreign donors, correspondents, and admirers were Cotton Mather in America and the philosopher Leibniz, whom Woodward backed surreptitiously in his quarrel with Newton. In 1712 he was attacked by the German Elias Camerarius, and replied with a Latin work (*Naturalis historia telluris*, 1714) that was subsequently turned into English by John Holloway (1726) with some supplementary matter and a long introduction describing Woodward's subsequent efforts. In it Woodward explained how the dissolution of the earth had occurred through a providential suspension of gravity during the flood. According to Holloway, Woodward had also written 'A representation of the state of mankind in the first age after the deluge' and some other tracts, since lost, on the Mosaic testimony, using the methods of modern anatomy and biology to substantiate the biblical account. He seems to have intended a vast synthesis in which his views on geology, medicine, and universal history were to be combined with an orthodox Christian theology.

Early on Woodward wrote out meticulous instructions for making observations and collections for natural history and antiquities in *Brief Instructions* (1696), which demonstrates the universality of his interests in collecting. The rules he subsequently developed for collection and curation of geological material by his collectors (implemented from about 1700 and detailed in his 1728 work, *Fossils of All Kinds*) remain hard to improve on. He was thus a real pioneer in the world of museology. Between 1704 and 1706 he employed John Hutchinson (1674–1737) to collect material for him throughout England and Wales—probably the first such professional activity in Britain. Woodward also left an essay on the 'art of assaying' in manuscript (BL, Add. MS 25095), and drew up a catalogue of his own 'fossils' (rocks, minerals, and true fossils), that was printed posthumously in two volumes as *An Attempt towards a Natural History of England* (1728–9). His helpful views on classification had already appeared in an article on fossils in Harris's *Lexicon technicum* (1704) but were enlarged in 1728 in his *Fossils of All Kinds Digested into a Method*. The fossils were left at his death, in their original cabinets, to Cambridge University, along with an endowed professorship, the first in Britain, both of which bequests are described in his will.

The Royal Society was Woodward's favourite arena. From 1694 he offered papers, contributed specimens, initiated new members, introduced foreigners, and participated in debates. In 1697 he read 'Some thoughts and experiments concerning vegetation', for which he has been credited as a founder of plant physiology and the discovery of 'transpiration'. For many years he fought there against his rival Sir Hans Sloane until he was expelled from the council in 1710 after insulting Sloane and refusing to apologize. He attempted an abortive coup which failed, and thereafter pretty much withdrew from active participation.

Woodward was also very active as an antiquary; he believed that the evidence of antiquities was like that of fossils and could be used to reconstruct the early history of the world and mankind. Here again he collected artefacts of all kinds, including Egyptian antiquities, about which he wrote in a tract published many years after his death in *Archaeologia* (1776). His museum was visited by many and described by Ralph Thoresby, William Nicolson, and John Strype, among others, as well as by the foreign tourist Zacharias Conrad von Uffenbach. He contributed a piece on some Roman urns and the ancient boundaries of the Roman city of London for John Strype's *Survey of London*, which was reprinted separately in 1713. The auction catalogue drawn up at Woodward's death by Robert Ainsworth shows the great range of his antiquarian collections and library. Among many ancient objects he assembled was an alleged Roman shield, which subsequently went to the British Museum, of which he was very proud. Its appearance caused a sensation; he had it engraved and solicited learned opinion from all over Europe, eventually eliciting a long Latin treatise by Henry Dodwell that was edited and published in 1713 by Thomas Hearne. (There is an incomplete file of his correspondence on the matter in BL, Add. MS 6127, and Bodl. Oxf., MS Gough misc. antiq. 10, as well as letters in Zürich, Copenhagen, The Hague, and elsewhere.) Doubts about the shield's authenticity were early expressed, but it was only long after his death that it was assigned confidently to the Renaissance.

Woodward's contentious nature and his personal ambition turned him into the butt of much contemporary satire, including the Scriblerian collaboration, *Three Hours after Marriage*, and the *Memoirs of Martinus Scriblerus*, where he appears as the quintessential virtuoso, with all the failings of an abstruse and impractical learning. Unfortunately, this caricature survived long after his very real contributions to contemporary learning. Although he was often wrong in his conclusions, which were usually premature, he was among the early exponents of modern scientific and historical method. Woodward died in his apartments at Gresham College on 25 April 1728 and was buried in Westminster Abbey on 1 May. Besides his collections of antiquities and natural history, he left a library of more than 4000 volumes, as well as many hundreds of prints and drawings. He never married and has been described as 'notoriously homosexual' (Porter, 340).

J. M. LEVINE

Sources V. A. Eyles, 'John Woodward FRS, FRCP, MD, 1665–1728', *Journal of the Society of the Bibliography of Natural History*, 5 (1968–71), 399–427 · R. Porter, 'John Woodward: a droll sort of philosopher', *Geological Magazine*, 116 (1979), 335–43 · D. Price, 'John Woodward and a surviving British geological collection from the early eighteenth century', *Journal of the History of Collections*, 1 (1989), 79–95 · J. M. Levine, *Dr Woodward's shield: history, science, and satire in Augustan England* (1977) · J. Ward, *The lives of the professors of Gresham College* (1740), 283–301 · V. A. Eyles, 'John Woodward, 1665–1728, physician and geologist', *Nature*, 206 (1965), 868–70 · M. Jahn, 'A bibliographical history of John Woodward's *An essay toward a natural history of the earth*', *Journal of the Society of the Bibliography of Natural History*, 6 (1971–4), 181–213 · R. W. Purcell and S. J. Gould, *Finders, keepers* (1992), 81–94 · S. Glover, *The history and gazetteer of the county of Derby*, ed. T. Noble, 2 vols. (1829–33) · J. L. Chester, ed., *The marriage, baptismal, and burial registers of the collegiate church or abbey of St Peter, Westminster*, Harleian Society, 10 (1876), 322 · *DNB* · private information (2004) · BL, Add. MS 25095

Archives BL, Add. MSS 6127, 6194, 6209–6210, 6271 · BL, discourses on metals, Add. MSS 25095–25096 · BL, Sloane MS 2039 · Bodl. Oxf., MS 18176 · CUL, corresp. and papers · CUL, notebook describing mines, fossils, etc. in Cornwall and elsewhere · U. Cam., Sedgwick Museum of Earth Sciences, papers · University of Bristol, corresp. | BL, letters to Hans Sloane, Sloane MSS 4037–4062 · Bodl. Oxf., letters to Thomas Hearne · Bodl. Oxf., letters to Edward Lhuyd · CUL, letters to John Strype · Kongelige Bibliotek,

Copenhagen, Sperling corresp. • NHM, letters to Sir Hans Sloane • Niedersachsischen Landesbibliothek, Leibniz corresp. • Zentralbibliothek, Zürich, Scheuchzer corresp.

Likenesses W. Humphrey, mezzotint, pubd 1774, AM Oxf., BM, NPG [*see illus.*] • oils (as older man), U. Cam., department of Geology • Wedgwood medallion (after S. Bevan), Wedgwood Museum, Stoke-on-Trent

Wealth at death fossils in original cabinets and endowed professorship to University of Cambridge

Woodward, Josiah (1657–1712), Church of England clergyman and moral reformer, was born on 13 February 1657 at Dursley, Gloucestershire, son of Joseph Woodward (*c.*1616–1662), the Presbyterian rector of Dursley, and his wife, Ann. He matriculated at St Edmund Hall, Oxford, on 14 March 1673; he took a BA in 1676, an MA in 1679, and BD and DD in 1699. The date and place of his ordination, along with his activities in the 1680s, remain to be established, but he may well have been serving in a clerical capacity somewhere in London. By 1689 he was minister at Poplar, Middlesex, where he was described by Foster as 'the East India Company's minister', and he appears to have held this living for the rest of his life (Foster, *Alum. Oxon.*, 4.1677). On 20 January 1691 he married, at St Mary Aldermanbury, Martha Nicholas of Stondon Massey, Essex; it is not known whether they had children. In 1711 he was appointed to the living of All Saints', Maidstone, Kent, and in the summer of 1712 he became rector and vicar of Newchurch in Romney Marsh, but died within weeks of his appointment.

Woodward was an effective publicist and prolific author in the cause of moral reformation. On 28 December 1696 he preached one of the earliest surviving sermons before the Society for the Reformation of Manners, and he was to be its first historian. He published *An Account of the Rise and Progress of the Religious Societies in the City of London*, which survives only in the 'second enlarged edition' of 1698 and in later editions, and *An Account of the Societies for the Reformation of Manners* (1699). Throughout the 1690s and 1700s he specialized in writing penny tracts, often anonymously. He sought to dissuade his readers from swearing, drunkenness, 'Sodom's vices', and 'wordly-mindedness'; he provided moral guidance to sailors, soldiers, the poor, and the young, and spiritual consolation to English captives enslaved abroad; he wrote catechisms and exhortations to sabbath observance. Many of these tracts were commissioned and distributed by the Society for the Propagation of Christian Knowledge (SPCK) and several were reissued and abridged throughout the eighteenth century; *The Seaman's Monitor* (1705), for example, had reached its fourteenth edition by 1799. Woodward was a corresponding member of the SPCK from 1699, and his personal contribution to the work of reformation is apparent from the SPCK minute books where he can be observed advising on the regulation of religious societies as well as preaching and publishing. His interest in education also led him to establish the Blue Coat School in Maidstone.

Woodward gave the Boyle lectures in 1710, which were published as *The Divine Original and Incomparable Excellency of the Christian Religion* (1711), and became enmeshed in several controversies. He attacked the French Prophets and defended the societies for the reformation of manners against Henry Sacheverell. In 1709 Woodward was also forced to refute the charges of Dr James Sharp, reader at St Dunstan and All Saints', Stepney, that he was a fellow traveller of dissent and occasional attender of conventicles. Woodward enjoyed good contacts with leaders of the church such as William Wake, but for all this he remains a shadowy figure whose personality and public role attracted less attention from contemporaries than might be expected. He died at Maidstone on 6 August 1712 'to the no little grief of the poor, especially of the boys and girls' of the Blue Coat School, according to the tombstone raised by 'his deeply sorrowing wife' over his grave in the chancel of All Saints', Maidstone (Cave-Browne, 130–32, 192–3).   JOHN SPURR

Sources Foster, *Alum. Oxon.* • *Calamy rev.* • parish register, Dursley, Glos. RO, P124 IN 1/2 • marriage settlement between Rev Josias Woodward of Poplar, Middlesex, and Martha Nicholas of Stondon Massey, Essex, Glos. RO, D247/18 • E. McClure, ed., *A chapter in English church history: being the minutes of the Society for Promoting Christian Knowledge for … 1698–1704* (1888) • J. Cave-Brown, *The history of the parish church of All Saints', Maidstone* [n.d.] • E. Hasted, *The history and topographical survey of the county of Kent*, 2nd edn, 12 vols. (1797–1801); facs. edn (1972), 344 • *IGI*

Woodward, Sir (Ernest) Llewellyn (1890–1971), historian, was born in Ealing, London, on 14 May 1890, the only son of George Ernest Woodward (1865–1939) and his first wife, Helen Thwaites. His maternal grandfather was descended from Huguenots, who had been cabinet-makers in Clerkenwell, London. His other forebears came from the west country and 'had concerned themselves from time immemorial with barns and cattle and small coasting ships' (Woodward, 15). His father was a middle-ranking civil servant in the naval ordnance department of the Admiralty and many of Woodward's early recollections were of Woolwich arsenal.

Woodward was educated at Merchant Taylors' School, London, winning a scholarship to Corpus Christi College, Oxford, in 1908. He completed his degree in 1911 with a second in *literae humaniores* (Greats) but it never really held his interest, and he proceeded to read modern history in which he took a first in 1913. St John's College awarded him a senior studentship and he went to study in Paris, where he lived in a community of eccentric priests and developed an affinity for French, and a distaste for German, modes of thought. His interest, at this time, was in the fall of the Roman empire, but in 1913 the second Baron Acton invited him to help in editing a collection of the letters between the first baron, the eminent historian, and J. J. Ignaz Döllinger, the leader of the German Old Catholics, who rejected the proclamation of papal infallibility at the first Vatican Council. For the first time Woodward became interested in nineteenth-century controversies. He had been raised in a moderate and humane form of Anglican evangelicalism but at Oxford he was attracted to Anglo-Catholicism (he lived for a time in Pusey House) and intended eventually to be ordained. Some later nicknamed him the Abbé. But his faith gradually faded—there was, as he said in his autobiography, 'no tempest'—and he became an agnostic (Woodward, 217).

The First World War cut across Woodward's career. In 1915–16 he served with an artillery brigade on the western front. Home on sick leave in 1916, he completed his first book, *Christianity and Nationalism in the Later Roman Empire*, in which he tried to bring together problems old and new by asking how far the struggle between orthodoxy and heresy was really a struggle between nationalities. He was posted to military intelligence in Salonika in 1917 and had the chance to explore the region, including Mount Athos, before being invalided home in 1918. He was then attached to the historical branch of the Foreign Office and employed to write a history of the Congress of Berlin (1878) as a briefing paper for the Paris peace conference. Before going to Salonika on 19 September 1917 he had married Florence Marie, the youngest daughter of Robert Stuart O'Loughlin, dean of Dromore.

On resuming civilian life, Woodward made a false start as a history master at Eton College, for which he found he had no talent, and returned thankfully to Oxford, at first as a lecturer at Keble College. In 1919 he won a fellowship by examination at All Souls, where he remained until 1944, becoming domestic bursar of the college in 1925. He combined this with a lectureship at New College from 1922 to 1939, which gave him the contact with undergraduates that he would have lacked at All Souls. He was active in many of the university controversies of the time, including that concerning the building of the New Bodleian Library, and he had an acute eye for the eccentricities of his fellow dons, which he retailed in *Short Journey* (1942).

In 1930 Woodward published a book of musings, *The Twelve-Winded Sky*, which angered more religiously minded dons and was denounced in a university sermon, but most of his writings related to the nineteenth century. His *Three Studies in European Conservatism* (1929) dealt with Metternich, Guizot, and the Catholic church, and he considered writing a biography of Guizot. But, despite this interest in conservatism, his own instincts were towards the liberal side. He still retained some faith in the idea of progress, and was dismayed by the pygmies who seemed in control of politics. He rather distrusted Germany and was so concerned in the early 1930s with trends in British foreign policy that he thought of standing for parliament. He then wrote his *Great Britain and the German Navy* (1935), which examined the naval race before the First World War, mainly through a detailed study of diplomatic documents. In his autobiography he commented wryly on the fact that 'as far as I know, no politician has ever read it', and 'a sharp and provocative pamphlet' would have been more effective (Woodward, 241–2). His researches had led him to doubt the reliability of *Die grosse Politik der europäischen Kabinette, 1871–1914*, the great German publication which then dominated diplomatic history. Not surprisingly, he was one of the first to realize the potential

menace of Hitler and in a letter to *The Times* on 27 March 1933 warned his countrymen.

In 1938 Woodward published his volume in the *Oxford History of England* series, *The Age of Reform, 1815–1870*. Like several books in the series, it was a remarkable piece of work. Although many of the details have been revised by later research, his breadth of interests enabled him to synthesize the political, economic, social, and intellectual strands in a way which has rarely been equalled. He had travelled widely in the 1930s, visiting Africa, North America, and Asia, and he contemplated writing a more general history of the British empire but, once again, war intervened.

Woodward was seconded for official work, first in political intelligence and then in the Foreign Office. At the Foreign Office he prepared a collection of diplomatic documents on Anglo-German relations, 1925–39. This led in 1944 to his being entrusted by the then foreign secretary, Anthony Eden, with editing the formidable volumes of *Documents on British Foreign Policy, 1919–1939* for publication, following the trail blazed by G. P. Gooch and H. W. V. Temperley in their *British Documents on the Origins of the War, 1898–1914*. Like them he insisted on editorial independence.

In 1944 Woodward became professor of international relations at Oxford with a fellowship at Balliol College, transferring in 1947 to become the first holder of the new chair of modern history, with a fellowship at Worcester College. His interest in expanding modern studies also brought him into association with Nuffield College. He was elected a member of the British Academy in 1946 and knighted in 1952.

Despite this growing academic recognition, Woodward was becoming restless in Oxford, a dissatisfaction perhaps compounded by his wife's increasing ill health. In 1951 he left for the United States, for a research professorship at the Institute for Advanced Study at Princeton. He remained in Princeton for ten years, although he returned to Britain annually and settled in Oxford on retiring in 1961, the year in which his wife died. He became a distinguished fellow of All Souls and an honorary fellow of Worcester and Corpus Christi colleges. He was allowed to build a house in Worcester College grounds (bequeathed to the college on his death) and lived there with his surviving sister. There had been no children of his marriage.

In his later years Woodward produced a number of books, including his *Great Britain and the War of 1914–1918* (1967), but his main project (apart from editing the *Documents on British Foreign Policy* series) was to write a multi-volume work, *British Foreign Policy in the Second World War*, based on unpublished documents in the Foreign and Cabinet offices. Official objections delayed the project. He published a précis in 1962 but only the first volume of the major work was published before his death, although he had virtually completed revising three of the remaining four volumes.

Woodward died in Oxford on 11 March 1971. Although earlier he and his wife had kept a hospitable house in Oxford, his friends thought him easier to get to know than to know well. He was a man of broad interests and complex character, who enjoyed life but set no great store by material possessions; a good man and a lively talker, he almost deliberately eschewed founding a 'school' of history, believing that 'a tutor ought to take the greatest care not to try to "convert" his pupils'.

R. B. Wernham, *rev.* Muriel E. Chamberlain

Sources R. Butler, *PBA*, 57 (1971), 497–511 · *The Times* (12 March 1971) · *The Times* (13 March 1971) · *The Times* (20 March 1971) · E. L. Woodward, *Short journey* (1942) · personal knowledge (1986) · *WW*
Archives Worcester College, Oxford, letters | Bodl. Oxf., corresp. with Sir Alfred Zimmern · CUL, corresp. with Sir Herbert Butterfield · U. Birm. L., corresp. with Lord Avon
Likenesses W. Stoneman, photograph, 1948, NPG; repro. in Butler, *PBA*, facing p. 497
Wealth at death £84,872: probate, 24 May 1971, *CGPLA Eng. & Wales*

Woodward, Richard (1726–1794), Church of Ireland bishop of Cloyne, was born in Grimsbury, near Bristol, and baptized at Oldland, Gloucestershire, in July 1726, the elder son of Francis Woodward (*d.* 1730) of Grimsbury and his second wife, Elizabeth Bird of Bristol. After her husband's death Elizabeth married Josiah Tucker, dean of Gloucester. Richard was educated by Tucker and matriculated from Wadham College, Oxford, on 21 October 1742; he graduated BCL on 16 October 1749 and DCL on 14 February 1759. Following his appointment as rector of Donnyatt, Somerset, he met Thomas Conolly of Castletown, co. Kildare, while travelling on the continent. Conolly, whose sister Caroline was the wife of John Hobart, second earl of Buckinghamshire, later lord lieutenant of Ireland (1777–80), persuaded Woodward to settle in Ireland, where, under his and the earl's patronage, advancement was certain.

On 6 October 1763 Woodward married Susanna (*d.* 1795), daughter of Richard Blake; they had five sons and one daughter, Mary, who in 1786 married Charles Brodrick, fourth son of the third Viscount Midleton, who, in turn, was bishop of Clonfert, bishop of Kilmore, and archbishop of Cashel. Woodward was installed as dean of Clogher on 31 January 1764, a preferment which he held until his appointment to the episcopal bench in 1781. He was awarded the degrees of BMus and DMus from Trinity College, Dublin, in 1768 and 1771 respectively. He was installed as chancellor of St Patrick's Cathedral, Dublin, on 4 July 1772 and held this position until 1778, when he exchanged it for the rectory of Louth in the archdiocese of Armagh. While dean of Clogher he took a keen interest in the provision of a state-sponsored workhouse system for the poor and took a primary role in the establishment of the Dublin House of Industry in 1769. In the previous year a pamphlet of his, which had called for 'national provision' for the poor, was very influential in the passing of the Poor Relief Act of 1772. As a member of the Incorporated Society for Promoting English Protestant Schools in Ireland he defended that society's charter schools against the damning strictures of the English prison reformer John Howard and Sir Jeremiah Fitzpatrick, inspector-general of prisons. He was also a firm supporter of the

various Catholic Relief Acts (1774–82), which removed many restrictions of the penal laws on Roman Catholics.

Woodward was appointed bishop of Cloyne on 3 February 1781 and consecrated at Christ Church, Dublin, the following day; also in that year he was awarded the degree of DD from Trinity College, Dublin. In 1787 the publication of his pamphlet *The Present State of the Church of Ireland*, which argued for the retention of the established status of that church, caused a sensation. It was written as a reaction to the provocative activities of the Rightboys, an agrarian movement in Munster and parts of south Leinster. The main demand of the Rightboys was a reduction in the level of tithes payable to the Church of Ireland clergy, in view of their additional financial obligations to the Roman Catholic clergy. The pamphlet ran to several editions, both in Dublin and London, and eventually developed into a paper war of over ninety publications between the defenders of the church establishment and their Roman Catholic and Presbyterian adversaries.

Woodward died on 12 May 1794 at Cloyne, where he was buried in St Colman's Cathedral. A monument was erected in the nave of the cathedral by his widow, who died on 11 May 1795.   J. Falvey

Sources J. S. Donnelly, 'The Rightboy movement, 1785–8', *Studia Hibernica*, 17–18 (1977–8), 120–202 · W. J. McCormack, *The Dublin paper war of 1786–1788* (1993) · J. Kelly, 'The genis of protestant ascendancy', *Parliament, politics and people*, ed. G. O'Brien (1989), 93–107 · J. Kelly, 'Eighteenth-century ascendancy', *Eighteenth-Century Ireland*, 5 (1990), 173–88 · J. Liechty, 'Irish evangelicanism, TCD and the mission of the Church of Ireland at the end of the eighteenth century', PhD diss., NUI, Maynooth, 1987 · *Report on the manuscripts of the marquess of Lothian*, HMC, 62 (1905) · J. Falvey, 'The Church of Ireland episcopate in the eighteenth century', MA diss., NUI, Cork, 1995 · J. O'Carroll, 'Contemporary attitudes towards the homeless poor, 1725–1775', *The gorgeous mask: Dublin, 1700–1850*, ed. D. Dickson (1987) · K. Milne, *The Irish charter schools, 1730–1830* (1997) · *DNB*
Archives NL Ire., Brodrick MSS · Norfolk RO, corresp. with earl of Buckinghamshire
Likenesses J. Horsburgh, oils, Wadham College, Oxford

Woodward, Samuel (1790–1838), geologist and antiquary, was born at Rose Lane, Norwich, on 2 October 1790, the only son of William Woodward (1762–1795), bombazine-weaver, and his wife, Elizabeth Springall. He had little schooling, being sent to work with a shawl-weaver before the age of seven. When he was eleven he entered the employment of Alderman John Herring, a textile manufacturer who encouraged and helped his self-education. From 1814 Woodward worked in the Norwich Union Fire Office until he was sacked for refusing to vote tory in 1820. On 24 July 1815 he married Elizabeth Pickworth Bolingbroke; the couple had two daughters and six sons, including the palaeontologist Samuel Pickworth *Woodward and the librarian and author Bernard Bolingbroke *Woodward. From 1820 until his death he worked as a clerk in Gurney's (later Barclays) Bank at Norwich where he received great help and encouragement from two partners, Hudson Gurney and Dawson Turner.

Woodward had developed early an interest in natural history, geology, and antiquities: from 1824 he corresponded widely on these topics, and his letters contain many observations and provide a useful picture of contemporary geological and antiquarian thought. He built up a collection of fossils and antiquities, partly by fieldwork and partly by gift and exchange. He was a skilful and accurate draughtsman, providing illustrations for his publications and as a record of fossils and antiquities in his own and other people's collections.

Most of Woodward's antiquarian papers were published in *Archaeologia*, having been communicated by Hudson Gurney to the Society of Antiquaries. The subjects included excavations at Wymondham Abbey and Roman remains in Norfolk. His geological publications included a *Synoptical Table* of British fossils (1830), the first attempt to list all known fossils. His belief in the then popular theory that many geological deposits were the result of the biblical flood influenced his discussion of strata in his *An Outline of the Geology of Norfolk* (1838) and publications in the *Philosophical Magazine*.

Woodward was only occasionally able to travel outside Norfolk (and then only because of assistance from Hudson Gurney) and he was at times aggrieved by the attitude of some of the more prominent geologists that provincial workers were unable to make original contributions. By 1835 he was ill with diabetes, but continued his studies until his death, at his home, Grove Cottage, Lakenham, Norwich, on 14 January 1838. He was buried at St Stephen's churchyard, Norwich. He was survived by his wife, who died in 1866.

Woodward's work as a bank clerk had left him relatively little free time to pursue his wide interests, but he left many unpublished notes and manuscripts. Two of these were published posthumously: *The Norfolk Topographer's Manual*, a catalogue of books and engravings, edited and augmented by W. C. Ewing and Dawson Turner (1842), and the *History and Antiquities of Norwich Castle* edited by B. B. Woodward (1847).

In 1872 he was styled 'the Father of Norfolk Geology' by his friend John Gunn, chiefly because of his work on the divisions of the Chalk and on local fossils. Although many of his geological and archaeological interpretations have been superseded, his observations and collections are still of value.   BARBARA GREEN

Sources H. B. Woodward, 'A memoir of Samuel Woodward', *Transactions of the Norfolk and Norwich Naturalists' Society*, 2 (1874–9), 563–93 [incl. bibliography] • H. B. Woodward, 'A geologist of a century ago: Samuel Woodward of Norwich, antiquary and geologist', *Geological Magazine*, new ser., 3rd decade, 8 (1891), 1–8 • Woodward correspondence, 1824–38, Norwich Castle Museum, Woodward MSS [11 vols.] • B. McWilliams, 'The place of early collectors in the development of geological studies in Norfolk', *Bulletin of the Geological Society of Norfolk*, 25 (1975), 3–14
Archives NHM, papers • Norwich Castle Museum, Norwich, corresp. | NL NZ, Turnbull L., letters to Gideon Algernon Mantell
Likenesses lithograph, 1833 • Miss Turner, lithograph, BM • H. B. Woodward, lithograph, repro. in Woodward, 'A geologist', frontispiece

Woodward, Samuel Pickworth (1821–1865), naturalist and palaeontologist, was born on 17 September 1821 in Briggs Lane, Norwich, the second son of Samuel *Woodward (1790–1838), bank clerk and notable amateur naturalist, and his wife, Elizabeth Bolingbroke (*d.* 1866). At the age of seven he was sent to Priory School, Grayfriars, Norwich, but completed his education at Lakenham following the family's move there in 1831. Encouraged by his father he studied the natural history of the local countryside. On leaving school in 1836 he was engaged by Dawson Turner (1775–1858) to work on his collection of dried plants and this stimulated in Woodward a lifelong interest in botany. In 1837 he briefly served as an usher at a Fakenham school, then as a clerk in a Norwich lawyer's office. On his father's death in 1838 he moved to London and catalogued the library of the banker Hudson Gurney (1775–1864), who then secured an appointment for him in the British Museum Library. In June 1839 he was appointed sub-curator to the Geological Society of London working under William Lonsdale (1794–1871), from whom he acquired the habits of scrupulous neatness and accuracy for which he was always renowned. While at the library Woodward's attention was directed to Mollusca by Edward Forbes (1815–1854) who served as curator and librarian (1842–4).

In 1845 Woodward was appointed professor of botany and natural history (including geology) at the newly established Royal Agricultural College at Cirencester, teaching the practical application of these sciences to farming. Due to financial problems the college had to reduce staff in 1847 and his post ended. He had married Elizabeth Teulon in 1845 on obtaining the post and, while at Cirencester, had also taken a prominent role in founding the Cotteswold Naturalists' Club.

On returning to London, Woodward's services were used by the Botanical Society and Professor Tennant, until his contact with Hudson Gurney led to an application for a vacancy in the natural history department of the British Museum. He became a first-class assistant in the department of geology and mineralogy in September 1848, responsible for the curation and display of fossil invertebrates. By devoting his leisure hours to the study of the Mollusca, Woodward was able to publish (1851, 1853, and 1856) *A Manual of Mollusca* in three parts. Its value and practical advice were widely acknowledged and Woodward became the recognized authority. Darwin considered that Woodward had 'done good service to the cause of science' in publishing it and felt he was deeply indebted for 'so much solid instruction' (*Correspondence*, 6.123).

However, Woodward's main contribution was in resolving the relationship of the unusual bivalves belonging to the extinct group Rudistae when establishing the structure of the Hippuritidae (1854). He also gave considerable attention to the Echinodermata and described the anomalous genus *Echinothuria* from a fossil species (1863).

Woodward was elected a member of the Botanical Society of London (1839); chosen as an associate of the Linnean Society (1841); elected a fellow of the Geological Society (1854); was awarded the balance of the Geological Society's Wollaston fund in 1854 and 1857 in recognition of his palaeontological labours; and in 1859 was made a member of the Geological Society's council for the remainder of his life. The University of Göttingen conferred the honorary degree of doctor of philosophy upon him in 1864. He was an examiner in geology for the University of London.

During his service to the Geological Society and the British Museum (Natural History), Woodward gave assistance to many eminent workers, considering that it was his duty to do so rather than to conduct investigations of his own. Unfortunately, he did not live to fulfil his own contribution on Cretaceous Mollusca for the monographs of the Palaeontographical Society; he was a chronic sufferer from asthma and the last twenty-seven years of his life were dogged by ill health, which restricted his activities and severely limited his own published output. However, he contributed papers to each of the major British geological journals and to natural history and zoological periodicals, and wrote articles for various encyclopaedias. He also reported the activities of the geological section of the British Association for *The Athenaeum* in 1841–56, and served as a critic and reviewer of scientific books for *The Critic* and other journals. His son, H. B. Woodward, felt that his father's articles for periodicals were 'the best memorial of a literary man' as 'Such fugitive pieces are usually more spontaneous and exhibit the writer's feelings … more truly' (Woodward, *Memoir*, 4). Woodward's Congregationalist religious convictions meant that it was impossible for him to accept Darwin's ideas on evolution. He remained a firm believer in the 'design of nature' and argued with conviction for 'the oneness of the scheme of Creation', but acknowledged 'collecting data is a serious matter!' (*Correspondence*, 6.125). This led Lyell to consider that Woodward was 'the best arguer I have met with against natural selection and variation' (*Life, Letters, and Journals*, 364). Other contentious issues were the origin of 'island faunas' and the question of the proportion of species to genera throughout time. Woodward recognized his own faults: 'I fear I am very slow—I seldom see the force of a joke in less than 48 hours—but I might come to some conclusion by … a fortnight hence' (*Correspondence*, 6.125).

The winter of 1864–5 aggravated Woodward's asthma and in the spring he remained at home on sick leave to recover his strength. Later, while on convalescence at Herne Bay, Kent, he ruptured an artery in the lungs through exertion on an expedition he could not resist. As a result he died on 11 July 1865, at the age of forty-three.

R. J. CLEEVELY

Sources H. B. Woodward, 'A memoir of Dr S. P. Woodward', *Transactions of the Norfolk and Norwich Naturalists' Society*, 3 (1879–84), 279–312 [incl. list of pubd papers] • W. J. Hamilton, *Quarterly Journal of the Geological Society*, 22 (1866), xxxiv–xxxvi • [H. B. Woodward], *Geological Magazine*, 2 (1865), 383–4 • 'Samuel P. Woodward', *Proceedings of the Linnean Society of London* (1865–6), lxxxvi–lxxxvii • E. Forbes, 'Proceeds of the Wollaston fund to Dr S. P. Woodward', *Quarterly Journal of the Geological Society*, 10 (1854), xxi–xxii • H. B. Woodward, 'Samuel P. Woodward, PhD, ALS', *The Naturalist*, 2 (1865–6), 155–6 • *Men of the time* (1884) • *The correspondence of Charles Darwin*, ed. F. Burkhardt and S. Smith, 6 (1990) • *Life, letters, and journals of Sir Charles Lyell*, ed. Mrs Lyell, 2 vols. (1881) • *CGPLA Eng. & Wales* (1865)

Archives American Philosophical Society, Philadelphia, corresp. • BGS, papers • Linn. Soc., notes and papers • Royal Agricultural College, Cirencester • U. Cam. | NL NZ, Turnbull L. • U. Edin. L., letters to Sir Charles Lyell
Likenesses Messrs Sawyer & Bird, autotype (after photograph, 1856), repro. in Woodward, 'Memoir', frontispiece
Wealth at death under £2000: probate, 8 Aug 1865, *CGPLA Eng. & Wales*

Woodward, Thomas (1801–1852), sporting and animal painter, was born on 5 July 1801 at Pershore, Worcestershire, the eighth of the ten children of Herbert Woodward (1759–1838), solicitor, and his wife, Elizabeth Dovey (d. 1831). At the age of about eighteen he began a year's study in London under the animal painter Abraham Cooper, initially emulating his style. Woodward first exhibited in 1821; over the next thirty years he showed over 160 paintings, chiefly at the Royal Academy and the British Institution. His work was usually noticed and sometimes praised by reviewers; seven works were engraved for the *Sporting Magazine*. A friendship with Edwin Landseer (a year his junior, but by the 1830s enjoying fame such as Woodward never achieved) reputedly led to occasional collaboration and more certainly to introductions to patrons such as William Wigram, master of the Puckeridge hounds, for whom Woodward painted several works, including *Portraits of Four Favourite Foxhounds of the Puckeridge Hunt* (exh. RA, 1845; ex-Christies 14 July 1989) and *Brood Mares and Foals* (exh. RA, 1848). In Woodward's finest sporting paintings, such as *Hunters and Grooms at Covertside* (also known as *A Meet of the Worcestershire Hunt at Woodcote Green*; exh. RA, 1834; priv. coll.), landscape plays an important part.

Like many other sporting and animal painters seeking to broaden their subject matter, Woodward tackled subjects from literature, such as *Mazeppa* (exh. RA, 1828), and from history, such as *The Battle of Worcester* (exh. RA, 1837; Worcester Art Gallery), but he displays greater sensitivity in genre subjects, often combining animals and young countryfolk, such as in *Runaway* (exh. British Institution, 1825) and *The Dead Lamb* (exh. RA, 1847; both priv. coll.). He worked in Wales in the 1830s, and regularly in Scotland from the mid-1840s, but he achieved his best work in his native Worcestershire, where he himself rode to hounds. Three examples of his work are in the Worcester Art Gallery and two in the Tate collection; two portraits of favourite horses, commissioned by Queen Victoria (in 1842) and Prince Albert (in 1844), are in the Royal Collection.

A self-portrait painted at the age of forty-two (priv. coll.) reveals a physically slight man, holding palette and brushes, with the sketch of a horse on his easel. An obituary notice in *Berrow's Worcester Journal* (11 November 1852) describes Woodward as 'of a quiet and it may be even too retiring a cast'; in fact, he was consumptive. He died, unmarried, at Worcester on 30 October 1852 and was buried on 4 November in Pershore Abbey, where a brass plaque commemorates him.

JUDY EGERTON

Sources C. W. Graham-Stewart, 'Thomas Woodward', 1989 [with occasional updated supplements; copies at Courtauld Inst., Witt Library; British Sporting Art Trust Library, Newmarket; Yale U. CBA] • *Berrow's Worcester Journal* (11 Nov 1852) • artist's MS account book, 1827–52, priv. coll. • Graves, *RA exhibitors* • Graves,

Brit. Inst. • B. Taylor, introduction, *A loan exhibition of the works of Thomas Woodward, 1801–1852* (1972) [exhibition catalogue, Spink & Son, London, 8–25 Feb 1972] • O. Millar, *The Victorian pictures in the collection of her majesty the queen*, 2 vols. (1992), vol. 1, p. 341; vol. 2, pp. 346–7 • Redgrave, *Artists* • *Art Journal*, 14 (1852), 375 • *GM*, 2nd ser., 38 (1852), 654 • b. cert. • d. cert. • Worcs. RO
Archives priv. coll.
Likenesses T. Woodward, self-portrait, oils, 1842, priv. coll. • T. Woodward, self-portrait, oils, Ardblair Castle, Perthshire; listed with Scot. NPG, Ardblair H.5088

Woodward, Thomas Jenkinson (1745–1820), botanist, born on 6 March 1745 at Huntingdon, was the only son of Benjamin Woodward (*d.* 1757) of Huntingdon, where his family had long been established. His parents died when he was quite young but he inherited from his father and from both grandfathers, and was in consequence well off. He was educated at Eton College from 1758 to 1762, then at Clare College, Cambridge, where he graduated LLB in 1769. Shortly afterwards he married Frances (*d.* 27 Nov 1833), the daughter and heir of Thomas Manning of Bungay, Suffolk. They had no children.

While living at Bungay Woodward was appointed a magistrate and deputy lieutenant for the county of Suffolk, and on his subsequent removal to Walcot House, Diss, Norfolk, to the same offices for that county. On the establishment of the volunteer system he became lieutenant-colonel of the Diss Volunteers. He was elected a fellow of the Linnean Society of London in 1789.

Woodward was devoted to botany, especially the English flora, and was described by Sir James Edward Smith as one of the best English botanists, whose skill and accuracy was only equalled by his liberality and zeal in the service of the science; it was in his honour that Smith named the fern genus *Woodwardia*. Woodward was joint author with Samuel Goodenough, bishop of Carlisle, of *Observations on the British Fuci* (1797), and contributed seven papers to the *Philosophical Transactions of the Royal Society* and the *Transactions of the Linnean Society* between 1784 and 1794, on fungi and algae. He also provided much information to Sir J. E. Smith for Smith and Sowerby's *English Botany*, to William Withering for the second edition of his *Systematic Arrangement of British Plants*, and to Thomas Martyn (1735–1825) for his edition of Philip Miller's *Gardeners' Dictionary*.

He died at his home at Diss on 28 January 1820 and was buried in the town.

B. B. WOODWARD, *rev.* ANITA MCCONNELL

Sources D. E. Allen, 'Discovery of the herbarium of T. J. Woodward', *Watsonia*, 14 (1982), 177–8 • *GM*, 1st ser., 90/1 (1820), 189, 280–81 • R. A. Austen-Leigh, ed., *The Eton College register, 1753–1790* (1921), 575–6 • will of Benjamin Woodward, PROB 11/829, sig. 106
Archives Linn. Soc., corresp. and papers | Linn. Soc., letters to Sir James Smith

Woodyer, Henry (1816–1896), architect, was born in Guildford, Surrey, in August 1816, the youngest of three children and the only son of Caleb Woodyer (1766–1849), a surgeon and accoucheur, and his wife, Mary Ann Eleanor, *née* Halsey (1788–1864). He was educated at Eton College (1829–35) and then at Merton College, Oxford (1835–8). After a brief period working in the office of William Butterfield, Woodyer set up in business on his own at 4 Adam Street in London's Adelphi. He married Frances Martha Bowles (1830–1852) on 5 August 1851; she died in childbirth on 21 June of the following year, leaving Woodyer and an infant daughter, Hester Fanny. Together father and daughter moved to Grafham Grange near Dunsfold in Surrey, and became constant companions for the next thirty-nine years.

The majority of Woodyer's clients were, like him, devout 'high' Anglicans. Many of his early commissions were from family friends and associates. Thereafter his clients were often his own friends, whom he had met at Eton and Oxford. He developed an image of self-confidence and stand-offishness, and, at Grafham, lived the life of a rather bohemian and mildly eccentric cultured country gentleman. He smoked fragrant cigars, carried his drawings in a rolled up umbrella, and wore a loose-fitting blue serge suit, a crimson tie, a soft black hat, and a long dark Inverness cloak. Though never rich, he enjoyed the pleasures of life, and for relaxation sailed his yacht—the *Queen Mab*—in the Mediterranean. His architecture is as distinctive as his image. Yet while his best designs are full of imaginative touches, his style is somehow neurotic. He was always keen to strike out, to exaggerate, to be idiosyncratic, especially in his use of narrow windows, extra-steep roofs, peculiar dormer windows, acute arches, and slightly odd proportions. Even the details of his designs have a tense, agitated quality, undue prominence being given to unimportant details, to nervy lines, and to spiky tracery. But there is also originality, especially in his spires, chancel screens, and mechanical font covers. Even his restorations are original, with distinctive touches in place of an emphasis on the copying of ancient work.

Woodyer's most notable designs are for the churches at Highnam in Gloucestershire (Holy Innocents, 1849–51), Christ Church in Reading (1861–2 and 1874–5), and the restoration of All Saints', Wokingham (1862–4). He was also responsible for designing buildings for a number of religious communities, including the House of Mercy at Bovey Tracey in Devon (1865–8), a similar establishment at Clewer (1854–82), the Community of All Hallows at Ditchingham in Norfolk (1859–64), St Peter's Convent at Horbury in the West Riding of Yorkshire (1862–4), and All Saints' Hospital at Eastbourne (1869–70). Beyond that his output was mainly connected with churches—new and restored—parsonages, and local schools, though he also designed Cranleigh School (1863–5)—the quadrangle and chapel in an asymmetrical form of Tudor—and was responsible for certain minor extensions and restorations at Eton (1857–60 and 1876–7). He also maintained a sizeable country house practice.

Woodyer's daughter married in 1891, and two years later he moved to Padworth Croft, near Reading. He died there of heart failure on 10 August 1896 and was buried four days later in Grafham churchyard.

JOHN ELLIOTT

Sources Council for the Care of Churches, Gordon Barnes MSS • J. Elliott and J. Pritchard, *Henry Woodyer: gentleman architect* (2002) • A. Quiney, 'Altogether a capital fellow and a serious fellow too: a brief account of the life and work of Henry Woodyer', *Architectural History*, 38 (1995), 192–219 • *The Times* (14 Aug 1896), 1 • biographical file, RIBA BAL · Foster, *Alum. Oxon.* · *Church Times* (4 Sept 1896) · Council for the Care of Churches, Basil Clarke MSS · *Reading Mercury* (22 Aug 1896) · C. L. Eastlake, *A history of the Gothic revival*, new edn, ed. J. M. Crook (1970), 328–32 · P. Thompson, *William Butterfield* (1971), 343–65 · H. Redfern, 'Some recollections of William Butterfield and Henry Woodyer', *Architect and Building News* (14 April 1944), 22 · *CGPLA Eng. & Wales* (1896) · d. cert. · IGI

Archives Council for the Care of Churches, London, corresp. and papers · RIBA | Council for the Care of Churches, London, Basil Clarke MSS

Wealth at death £805 7s. 2d.: probate, 22 Oct 1896, *CGPLA Eng. & Wales*

Woolavington. For this title name *see* Buchanan, James, Baron Woolavington (1849–1935).

Wooldridge, Harry Ellis (1845–1917), musician and artist, was born on 28 March 1845 in the parish of St Lawrence in Winchester, Hampshire, the son of Harry Wooldridge, stationer and publisher, and his wife, Emma Frances Jones. He was educated privately before starting work at Lloyd's, but in 1865 he enrolled in the Royal Academy Schools, London. A friendship with Edward Burne-Jones encouraged Pre-Raphaelite sympathies and he embarked on a wide-ranging career in art and design in the late 1860s and the 1870s. He exhibited paintings at the Royal Academy, which were always well hung and the first of which was purchased by Frederic Leighton. A cabinet which he had decorated was placed in the South Kensington (later the Victoria and Albert) Museum, and he undertook commissions—from G. F. Watts and T. G. Jackson, among others—to execute murals and to design stained glass. His large reredos at St Martin's Church, Brighton, and many of the windows manufactured by James Powell & Sons, in a Renaissance style, date from the 1870s. He also painted frescos in St John's Church, Hampstead, London.

Meanwhile, Wooldridge was also exploring old Italian music in the British Museum. An accomplished singer from an early age, he now became interested in contrapuntal music and was asked to edit and revise William Chappell's *Popular Music of the Olden Time* under the new title of *Old English Popular Music* (1893). He omitted any songs which did not exist in early printed sources, rejecting popular tunes based on oral tradition, and he substituted his own harmonizations for those of G. A. Macfarren, who had harmonized the tunes in the original edition.

On 18 June 1894 Wooldridge married Julia Mary Olding (b. 1850/51), daughter of Stephen Olding, banker; they had no children. He was appointed Slade professor of fine art at Oxford in 1895, and was twice re-elected to the post from which he retired in 1904. From Trinity College, as an honorary MA (1895), he taught in rounded periods of Caroline diction and rhythm. In his inaugural lectures he reviewed theories of art from Plato to Hegel. While accepting much of Hegel's analysis, he criticized his attribution of artistic developments to entirely moral and political causes, pointing out the importance of newly discovered materials and methods and their exploration within artistic communities as forces for change.

Wooldridge collaborated with his friend, the poet Robert Bridges, on the *Yattendon Hymnal* (1899), and he served on the committee for the revision of *Hymns Ancient and Modern* but retired after several meetings, dissatisfied with the quality of the work. There are church settings and compositions by him in *Musica antiquata* (1907–8, 1913): the combination of aesthetic sensibilities with scholarly knowledge here shown identifies the best of these simple four-part polyphonic settings with the workmanship of the original masters. For the Purcell Society he edited *Three Odes for St Cecilia's Day* (1899) and *Birthday Odes for Queen Mary* (1902). While at Oxford he was asked to contribute the first volume of the *Oxford History of Music*, for which he conducted much obscure research: his two volumes, *The Polyphonic Period* (1901 and 1905), traced the development of polyphonic music to the end of the sixteenth century.

Wooldridge had a well-formed and thickset frame, blue eyes, and a ruddy auburn beard trimmed like a Frenchman's. Punctilious in dress and manners, he was a good raconteur and mimic. Although generous and genial, he was notably intolerant of pretension, particularly of the artistic kind. His knowledge of Latin and Greek was poor, but he spoke French and Italian like a native and was extremely well read. Wooldridge died at his home, 90 Oakwood Court, Kensington, London, on 13 February 1917. He was survived by his wife.

ROBERT BRIDGES, *rev.* ANNE PIMLOTT BAKER

Sources F. W. Sternfeld, introduction, in W. Chappell, *The ballad literature and popular music of the olden time: a history of the ancient songs, ballads, and of the dance tunes of England* (1965), v–ix · H. C. Colles, 'Wooldridge, H(arry) E(llis)', *New Grove* · *WWW* · Graves, *RA exhibitors* · b. cert. · m. cert. · personal knowledge (1927) · *CGPLA Eng. & Wales* (1917)

Archives Bodl. Oxf., corresp. with Robert Bridges

Likenesses R. Fry, sketch

Wealth at death £553 5s. 3d.: probate, 27 April 1917, *CGPLA Eng. & Wales*

Wooldridge, Sidney William (1900–1963), geomorphologist and geographer, was born in Hornsey, north London, on 16 November 1900, younger son (there was also a daughter) of Lewis William Wooldridge, bank manager, and his wife, Helen Chadwick. His early childhood was spent in Cheam, Surrey, and his later schooling was at Glendale county school, Wood Green, London, where he enjoyed explorations in the countryside inspired by evening classes in geology. From 1918 he read geology at King's College, London, graduating with a first-class degree in 1921 and publishing his first paper that year. He began research in petrology, gaining his MSc in 1923 and DSc in 1927, but his research on the Tertiary and Pleistocene deposits on the North Downs and Chilterns showed an increasing interest in geomorphology. He became demonstrator (1922), assistant lecturer (1925), and lecturer (1927) at King's College, teaching on the combined geography and geology course which drew together human geographers at the London School of Economics (LSE) and geologists and geomorphologists at King's; the course became very influential in the 1930s in uniting human and physical sides of geography. In 1933 his increasing interest in geography made him one of three prime movers behind the foundation of the Institute of British

Sidney William Wooldridge (1900–1963), by unknown photographer

Geographers, a forum for professional academic geographers dissatisfied with the Royal Geographical Society's continuing emphasis on exploration and on research by amateur geographers. A personal link with the subject came in 1934 when he married Edith Mary Stephens, a geography student at King's and later a geography teacher.

Wooldridge worked mainly on the stratigraphy, structure, and morphological evolution of the London basin and the Weald. River development and denudation chronology were particular interests, and his method involved meticulous fieldwork and mapping to identify complex features such as river terraces and erosion surfaces. His work was inspired by the theories of W. M. Davies on cycles of landscape evolution, and bore fruit in a number of research papers, a successful textbook, and *Structure, Surface and Drainage of South-East England* (1939), a landmark in the development of geomorphology. With his co-author David Leslie Linton he was awarded the Royal Geographical Society's Murchison award in 1942. This followed other awards which provided funds for the fieldwork he considered of prime intellectual importance and whose social aspects he relished. In the 1930s he began to publish on human and historical geography, probably influenced by his King's colleague L. Dudley Stamp. Wooldridge's interest lay in relating early human settlement to physical features. Linton again co-authored several of his important papers in the field. The south-east and particularly the Weald proved fruitful ground for his theses that detailed elucidation of the physical landscape

was a prerequisite for understanding human settlement and land use, and that the geographer's goal was regional description grounded in physical geography with human geography following from it.

With the outbreak of the Second World War, King's College was evacuated to Bristol and, isolated from his colleagues of the LSE, Wooldridge became responsible for both physical and human geography, a development which completed his transformation from a geologist to a geographer. From 1944 to 1947 he was professor of geography at Birkbeck College, London, where he enjoyed teaching adults, but returned to King's in 1947 as its first professor of geography. Wooldridge served as president of the Institute of British Geographers (1949–50) and president of the geography section of the British Association meeting of 1950; he was on the council of the Royal Geographical Society (1947–51), and was chairman of the field studies council in 1952. These responsibilities, combined with a strenuous schedule of examining and lecturing at his own and other institutions, led to a stroke in 1954. Reluctant to relinquish any activity, he carried on after a brief respite, but the strain under which he worked led to more difficult relations with colleagues. None the less, honours continued to come his way: he was made CBE in 1954 in recognition of his work on the government's sand and gravel council; in 1957 he received the Victoria medal of the Royal Geographical Society; and in 1959 he was elected fellow of the Royal Society, one of the few geographers ever to be so honoured.

Wooldridge was a keen golfer and cricketer, a lay Congregationalist preacher until he converted to the Church of England late in life, and an enthusiast for amateur operetta. He died suddenly on 25 April 1963 at Halliday Hall, King's College, while on official college business.

The years following Wooldridge's death inevitably brought a re-evaluation of his work. Later laboratory techniques rendered his own, and his conclusions that followed therefrom, unacceptable, and later evidence on palaeo-environments made his assumptions look simplistic: but these developments he could not have foreseen and would have welcomed. More serious are criticisms of his reliance on Daviesian theory and consequent over-emphasis on form to the neglect of process (though he himself was aware of this shortcoming of the Daviesian method given the prevailing lack of knowledge about processes) and on the identification of stages in the evolution of both the physical and the human landscape. Thus, although reissued in 1955, by about 1970 *Structure, Surface and Drainage* had become a classic work, rather than a statement of current knowledge, and his method of regional description had been largely abandoned by geomorphologists. However, his role as a pioneer geomorphologist was incontrovertible, and his calls for a historical perspective in and regional focus to geographical enquiry continued to inspire those who sought to unify its physical and human aspects.   ELIZABETH BAIGENT

Sources W. C. V. Baldwin, 'Sidney William Wooldridge, 1900–1963', *Geographers: biobibliographical studies*, 8, ed. T. W. Freeman (1984), 141–9 · *The Times* (27 April 1963) · J. H. Taylor, *Memoirs FRS*, 10

(1964), 371–88 • D. L. Lindon, 'Professor S. W. Wooldridge', *GJ*, 129 (1963), 382–3 • J. C. Pugh, *Nature*, 198 (1963), 938–9 • P. J. Perry, 'S. W. Wooldridge: the geographer as humanist', *Transactions of the Institute of British Geographers*, new ser., 15 (1990), 227–31 • D. K. C. Jones, ed., *The shaping of southern England* (1980) • R. J. Chorley, R. P. Beckinsale, and A. J. Dunn, *The history of the study of landforms*, 2 vols. (1973)
Likenesses photograph, repro. in Taylor, *Memoirs FRS* [*see illus.*]
Wealth at death £2484 15s. 2d.: probate, 16 Sept 1963, *CGPLA Eng. & Wales*

Wooler, Thomas Jonathan (1786?–1853), journalist and radical, was born in Yorkshire. Apprenticed to a printer, he followed the printing trade during his early adult years. Wooler moved south as a young man and began associating with metropolitan radicals. He distinguished himself as a debater, taking on such formidable opponents as John Gale Jones at the British Forum. In 1808 he ran his own debating club, the Socratic Union, which met at the Mermaid tavern, Hackney. Wooler became closely associated with *The Reasoner* (1813–14), a literary magazine that published reports of debates held at the Globe and Mermaid taverns; he may have edited as well as published *The Reasoner* in 1814. In 1813 he also published the short-lived *Republican: A Weekly Historical Magazine*, in which he reprinted extracts from Paine's *Rights of Man*. He next published a theatrical journal, *The Stage* (1814–16), in which he attacked the prices and privileges of the patent theatres.

In late January 1817 Wooler published the first edition of the *Black Dwarf* (1817–24), one of the most influential radical journals of the post-war years. The journal's tone was satiric; its politics were those of radical constitutionalism. Wooler was a gifted writer known for his habit of directly typesetting his articles without first committing them to writing. Among his contributions to the journal were regular letters from the character named the Black Dwarf to various fictional correspondents. He was arrested in early May 1817 and faced two trials for seditious libel for two articles published in the third and tenth numbers of the *Dwarf*, the first entitled 'The right of petition' and the other 'The past—the present—and the future'. Wooler was tried at Guildhall before Justice Charles Abbott and two special juries on 5 June 1817. The attorney-general, Samuel Shepherd, led the prosecution. Wooler defended himself brilliantly, with advice from Charles Pearson, the young City radical. He was acquitted in the second trial and, although found guilty in the first, serious procedural errors regarding the status and delivery of the jury's verdict led to a decision on appeal for a new trial. However, the government chose not to bring Wooler to trial. Following his court cases Wooler campaigned successfully to reform the procedures for selecting special juries in London, publishing a pamphlet entitled *An Appeal to the Citizens of London Against the Alleged Lawful Mode of Packing Special Juries* (1817).

Wooler was mentioned as a parliamentary candidate in 1818, but withdrew from contests at both Coventry and Hull. Active in the campaign for parliamentary reform, he was arrested again in 1819 for his part at a large meeting held at New Hall Hill, Birmingham, on 12 July at which Sir Charles Wolseley was elected the 'legislatorial attorney'

for Birmingham. Wooler was tried, along with William Greathead Lewis, George Edmonds, Charles Maddocks, and Major John Cartwright, on 3 and 5 August 1820 at the Warwick assizes before Lord Chief Justice Richards and a special jury. On this occasion he was convicted, and despite an appeal to king's bench he was sentenced to fifteen months in Warwick gaol. Wooler continued to publish the *Black Dwarf*, which had a circulation of 12,000, with financial assistance from Major Cartwright until 1824. In late 1825 he again appeared before the court of king's bench, where he failed to win a rule to show cause in his petition against the benchers of Lincoln's Inn for having denied his application to enter chambers to study to become a barrister. He exposed the exclusive practices of the inns of court in his *Case between Lincoln's Inn, the Court of King's Bench and Mr. T. J. Wooler* (1826). Wooler gradually drifted out of radical politics, commenting after the passing of the 1832 Reform Bill that 'these damned Whigs have taken all the sedition out of my hands' (Griffiths, 609). Subsequently he worked as a legal advocate in the police courts. In 1845 he published a legal handbook entitled *Every Man his Own Attorney*, intended to enable readers to avoid the expenses of a lawyer. He also translated Guglielmo Paladini's *Progetto di un nuovo patto sociale per lo regno delle Due Sicilie* (4 vols., 1827) and assisted Francis Place in editing Jeremy Bentham's *Plan of Parliamentary Reform* (1818). Wooler died on 29 October 1853 at his home, 10 Carburton Street, Portland Road, London. He was married to a daughter of John Pratt of Kingsland and had a son.   JAMES EPSTEIN

Sources *GM*, 2nd ser., 40 (1853), 647–8 • *DNB* • *N&Q*, 3rd ser., 8 (1865), 295 • J. A. Epstein, *Radical expression: political language, ritual, and symbol in England, 1790–1850* (1994) • *A verbatim report of the two trials of Mr. T. J. Wooler … for alleged libels before Mr Justice Abbott, and a special jury* (1817) • D. Griffiths, ed., *The encyclopedia of the British press, 1422–1992* (1992) • R. Hendrix, 'Popular humour and the *Black Dwarf*', *Journal of British Studies*, 16/1 (1976–7), 108–28 • Boase, *Mod. Eng. biog.* • *A new biographical dictionary of 3000 cotemporary* [*sic*] *public characters, British and foreign, of all ranks and professions*, 2nd edn, 3 vols. in 6 pts (1825)
Likenesses etching, pubd 1817 (after C. Landseer), BM, NPG • G. Cruickshank, caricature, 1820, repro. in *British Museum Catalogue*, 13677 • S. Freeman, stipple (after T. Smith), BM, NPG • print, NPG

Woolf, Arthur (*bap.* 1766, *d.* 1837), mining engineer, was baptized at Camborne in Cornwall on 4 November 1766, the eldest son of Arthur Woolf, a carpenter at Dolcoath mine, and his wife, Jane Newton. He was apprenticed to a carpenter at Pool, near Camborne, and after the expiry of his indentures he went to London and entered the service of Joseph Bramah at Pimlico as a millwright.

On leaving Bramah's employment Woolf was engaged to erect a steam engine at a colliery near Newcastle upon Tyne, and in 1795 he became a master engineer. In the next year he assisted Jonathan Carter Hornblower to repair a fault in a two-cylinder engine which he had erected at Meux and Reid's Griffin Brewery, Clerkenwell. In consequence he was appointed resident engineer in the brewery, where he remained until October 1806. On 29 July 1803, while residing at Wood Street, Spa Fields, he took out a patent (no. 2726) for 'an improved apparatus for converting water and other liquids into vapour or steam for working steam engines'. Two boilers built according to his ideas were erected in 1803 in the Griffin Brewery. Woolf also proposed to turn his apparatus to heating 'water or other liquids employed in brewing, distilling, dying, bleaching, tanning', and other processes.

Woolf had long considered the possibility of increasing the efficiency of steam engines by driving with steam at a higher pressure than Watt was accustomed to use. Richard Trevithick had already shown the advantages of high-pressure engines, but the danger of explosion prevented him from developing the new departure thoroughly. Woolf ingeniously avoided most of the risks of accident by raising the temperature of the steam in the cylinder itself. In 1804 and 1805 he took out patents embodying his improvements (nos. 2772, 2863).

In 1808 Woolf became partner with an engineer named Edwards in a steam-engine factory at Lambeth, and while in this position he took out another patent (no. 3346) on 9 June 1810 for further 'improvements in the construction and working of steam engines'. His improvements, in fact, consisted of a revival of Hornblower's compound engine, which was rendered possible by the expiry of Watt's patent. Using steam of a fairly high pressure and cutting off the supply before the end of the stroke in the small cylinder, Woolf expanded the steam to several times its original volume. In engines of this type the steam passed directly from the first to the second cylinder, and in consequence the term 'Woolf engine' was applied to all compound engines which discharged steam directly from the high- to the low-pressure cylinder without the use of an intermediate receiver. This type of engine was more commonly adopted in France than in Britain.

Encouraged by his Cornish contacts, in 1811 Woolf dissolved his partnership and returned to Cornwall to devote himself to improving methods of mining. In 1813 he erected winding engines at West Wheal Fortune (St Hilary) and at Wheal Abraham mine. In 1813 and 1814 he erected steam stamps for crushing ore at Wheal Fanny, Redruth. About 1814 he introduced his compound engine into the mines for the purpose of pumping, erecting engines at Wheal Abraham and Wheal Vor in 1814 and 1815. In 1824 he erected engines at Wheal Busy, in 1825 at Wheal Alfred and Wheal Sparnon, and in 1827 at Consolidated Mines. From 1818 until May 1830 he was engineer at Consolidated Mines, and he was at various times consulting engineer to at least thirty Cornish mines. At Wheal Abraham he established an informal school which produced notable local engineers such as Richard Jenkyn (c.1790–c.1860), Matthew Loam (1794–1875), and Michael Loam (1797–1872). He also introduced improvements to Trevithick's 'Cornish' boiler design. His engines were, however, quickly superseded by Trevithick's high-pressure single-cylinder engine, which had the advantage of greater simplicity in construction. From about 1816 until 1833 he acted as superintendent of Harvey & Co.'s engine foundry at Hayle. He was also active as a civil engineer, and a notable construction was the swing-bridge he designed for the Penryn to Falmouth road. Woolf's first wife died in 1830, aged sixty-seven, and on 15 June 1832 he married Emblin Vincent. Woolf died at the Strand, Guernsey, on 26 October 1837.

E. I. CARLYLE, rev. PHILIP PAYTON

Sources T. R. Harris, Arthur Woolf: the Cornish engineer, 1766–1837 (1966) • Boase & Courtney, Bibl. Corn., 2.905–6 • S. Hocking, 'A brief sketch of the life and labour of Arthur Woolf, engineer', Report of the Miners' Association of Cornwall and Devon (1874–5), 8–22 • Philosophical Magazine, 17 (1803), 40–47 • Philosophical Magazine, 19 (1804), 133–7 • Philosophical Magazine (1805), 294–6, 316–20 • Philosophical Magazine, 23 (1806), 123–8, 335–45 • Philosophical Magazine, 26 (1806), 316–17 • Philosophical Magazine, 46 (1815), 43–4, 120–22 • Philosophical Magazine, 46 (1815), 295–7, 460–61 • Annual Report of the Royal Institution of Cornwall, 54 (1872), xlvii–xlix • J. A. Phillips and J. Darlington, Records of mining and metallurgy (1857) • E. Galloway, History of the steam engine, from its first invention to the present time (1826)

Woolf, Charles Moss (1879–1942), film producer and distributor, was born at 54 Russell Square, Bloomsbury, London, on 10 July 1879, the son of Jonas Woolf, a Jewish furrier, and his wife, Rosetta (Rose) Hyman. He had two brothers and seven sisters. After leaving school he began work in the family firm, John Woolf & Sons, a wholesale furrier's business in Aldersgate Street in the City of London. Woolf married Vera Birn, with whom he had a son, Sir John *Woolf (1913–1999). She died some time before 1919. In 1919 he married Gladys Esther, daughter of Moss Capua, a wholesale furrier; they had a son, James *Woolf (1920–1966) [see under Woolf, Sir John].

During the First World War, Woolf was involved with aircraft production, and when the war was over his interest in new technology continued. In February 1919 he set up the W and F Film Service with two of his brothers-in-law. He found that by importing French and German films and inserting English titles he could offer exhibitors an alternative to the American films which dominated the British market. However, having established a successful distribution company, he too turned to Hollywood and secured the rights to the early Tarzan films and Harold Lloyd's popular comedies. He also ventured into production, helping two young producers, Victor Saville and Michael Balcon, to set up their own company, Gainsborough, which was responsible for several successful films including Alfred Hitchcock's The Lodger (1926).

In 1927 W and F was bought out by Isidore Ostrer's conglomerate, the Gaumont-British Picture Corporation, and in August 1929 Woolf was appointed joint managing director in charge of the distribution side of the corporation. Gaumont-British already owned two distribution companies but in 1933, when rationalization led to the formation of a single company, Gaumont-British Distributors, it was Woolf and his W and F team which emerged as the dominant force. Nevertheless, in 1935, while the British film industry was enjoying a boom, Woolf was persuaded by the producer Max Schach to re-establish his independence. In October he launched General Film Distributors (GFD) with financial backing from the merchant banker Saemy Japhet and three powerful industrialists—J. Arthur Rank, Lord Luke of Pavenham, and Lord Portal of Laverstoke. Rank was already involved in Pinewood Studios and, with Portal and Pavenham, in the General Cinema Finance Corporation which in 1936 acquired a substantial share in the American company, Universal.

Initially, GFD throve on the films made by independent producers making use of the modern facilities of Pinewood Studios, but by 1937 the boom was over and many of the new companies collapsed. GFD weathered the storm by taking over the distribution of Universal's popular American films. Gaumont-British Distributors, by contrast, withered and died. Woolf's influence on J. Arthur Rank was considerable and he encouraged him to expand his interests by buying up the Gaumont-British cinema chain. At the end of 1941 Rank at last succeeded in this aim and, owing to the untimely death of Oscar Deutsch, he was also able to seize control of the more modern and dynamic Odeon circuit. GFD—the symbol of which was a man striking a gong—became the central core of the Rank Organisation and Woolf, as Rank's right-hand man, became the pre-eminent figure in the British film industry. His two sons, Sir John Woolf and James Woolf, followed their father into the film industry, their production companies Romulus and Remus Films being responsible for such highly successful films as *Room at the Top* (1959) and *Oliver!* (1968).

Sharp-tongued and outspoken, C. M. Woolf could be an intimidating figure, particularly for young producers and directors whose films needed to win his approval. His initial reaction to Hitchcock's *The Lodger*, for example, was that it was unshowable; but he was also dynamic, approachable, and willing to take risks, qualities which enabled him to make a substantial contribution to the British film industry. His Jewish background was clearly important, not least in the raising of finance, and must have eased his relations with Isidore Ostrer and Oscar Deutsch.

C. M. Woolf's career was cut short by his unexpected death on 31 December 1942 at University College Hospital, London, following an operation on a duodenal ulcer.

ROBERT MURPHY

Sources A. Wood, *Mr Rank: a study of J. Arthur Rank and British films* (1952) · G. Macnab, *J. Arthur Rank and the British film industry* (1993) · M. Balcon, *Michael Balcon presents … a lifetime of films* (1969) · R. Low, *The history of the British film*, 4: *1918–1929* (1971) · R. Low, *Film-making in 1930s Britain* (1985) · private information (2004) · H. Wilcox, *25,000 sunsets* (1967) · R. Murphy, 'Woolf, Charles Moss', *DBB* · b. cert. · d. cert.
Wealth at death £94,353 11s. 7d.: probate, 15 June 1943, *CGPLA Eng. & Wales*

Woolf, James (1920–1966). *See under* Woolf, Sir John (1913–1999).

Woolf, Sir John (1913–1999), film and television producer, was born on 15 March 1913 at 16 Bracknell Gardens, Hampstead, London, the son of Charles Moss *Woolf (1879–1942) and his first wife, Vera Birn. His half-brother **James Woolf** (1920–1966), film producer, was born on 2 March 1920, the son of Charles Moss Woolf and his second wife, Gladys Esther Capua. Their father, a master furrier at the

time of John's birth, made a fortune financing and distributing films after the First World War, and both John and James grew up with the film business.

After completing a cosmopolitan and multilingual education at the Institut Montana in Switzerland, John Woolf rose to become general sales manager of his father's company, General Film Distributors (GFD). On 24 September 1937 he married the film actress Dorothy Frances Vernon, formerly Long (*b.* 1915/16), daughter of Charles George Long. There were no children of the marriage, which ended in divorce. During the Second World War he served as staff captain in the 2nd army corps in Newmarket before joining the directorate of army cinematography in the War Office; he was assistant director from 1944 to 1945. His responsibilities included making films to apprise the American top brass of new inventions, for which he was awarded the bronze star. He ended the war with the rank of lieutenant-colonel. Afterwards he rejoined GFD, now part of the Rank empire, where among other deals, he obtained a $500,000 advance from the Theater Guild for the American rights to Laurence Olivier's *Henry V* (1944). On 4 September 1946 he married as his second wife the film actress Edana Doreen (*b.* 1920/21), daughter of Abe Rubinstein Romney, advertising contractor. Again there were no children of the marriage, which ended in divorce.

Unhappy with John Davis's plan to establish Eagle-Lion and take Rank's best films away from GFD, John Woolf decided in 1948 to set up independently with his younger brother James, who was working in America with the publicity department of Universal Films and towards whom he always felt very protective. John persuaded S. G. Warburg to back its new company Independent Film Distributors, which would distribute and advance the front money (i.e. the least risky 70 per cent) for several low-budget feature films. The balance would come from the newly formed National Film Finance Corporation (NFFC) and the producers themselves. As most of these first ventures were unsuccessful, the Woolfs established their own production company, Romulus Films, to produce pictures that would appeal to both British and American audiences. For their first projects, John sent James to Hollywood to find film-makers who were having difficulties with the House Un-American Activities Committee.

The first Romulus film, *Pandora and the Flying Dutchman* (1951) starring Ava Gardner and James Mason, for which the Woolfs and the NFFC put up all the non-American costs, was only a limited success. But the third picture, *The African Queen* (1952), was extremely popular. Co-produced with Sam Spiegel and directed by John Huston, it boasted Katharine Hepburn and an Oscar-winning performance by Humphrey Bogart. John Woolf only just managed to put his package together, however. He had to persuade the NFFC chairman, Lord Reith, to overrule the corporation's honorary adviser, Michael Balcon, who wanted it to star John McCallum and Googie Withers. Romulus produced two more films with Huston: *Moulin Rouge* and *Beat the Devil* (both 1953). The first, which Woolf suggested, won three Oscars including that for best colour photography. But despite its star cast, the second, which Woolf backed only to please Huston, was a commercial failure, although it later became a cult classic.

Smooth, moustached, and one of the shyest men in the film business, John Woolf generally made films from successful and well-received novels and plays. As he always had more than one eye on a film's potential financial success, he always set out to provide entertainment, not to put across any particular message. Thus his films had no recurrent theme, unless it were that of the determined individual, usually a man, who is at odds with his immediate milieu, be it the African jungle, middle-class Yorkshire, or Gaullist France.

Once he had bought the story rights, Woolf packaged the screenplay with internationally recognized stars and an established director. Although he often used American and continental European actors, he regularly employed British writers and directors. The one film on which he did not—*The Iron Petticoat* (1956), a sub-*Ninotchka* farce co-financed with MGM—turned out to be a commercial disaster. The screenplay by the American Ben Hecht had to be extensively rewritten to accommodate Bob Hope's fears that he would be upstaged by Katharine Hepburn. Woolf was a 'hands on' producer. Even with a good director, he maintained an office in the studio and visited the set daily to ensure that everything proceeded according to plan. He even knew how to handle Huston. When Huston told him he wanted the principal set for *Moulin Rouge* until the following Tuesday, Woolf simply said 'That's a pity. I'm striking the set after Saturday!' (*Daily Telegraph*).

Romulus also co-produced *The Galloping Major* (1951) with Monja Danischewsky and *Treasure Hunt* (1952) with Anatole de Grunwald. Its next two films, *Women of Twilight* (1952), which appeared in the USA as *Twilight Women*, and *Cosh Boy* (1953), which appeared in the USA as *The Slasher*, were both co-produced with Daniel Angel. They were the first two British pictures to which the British Board of Film Censors awarded its new X certificate. Even so, several local authorities still banned *Cosh Boy*. In a financially astute move, the Woolfs also inserted a new character, Jerry Nolan, into *Women of Twilight*. He was played by their first contract star, Laurence Harvey (Larushka Skikne). Later, attracted by her shy and unspoiled looks, Romulus also put Heather Sears under contract.

According to Bryan Forbes, James Woolf was a midwife for talent. He lived his life through others, mostly operating from hotel bedrooms. To enable him to participate more actively in production, John established a twin company, Remus Films, that would produce the Romulus package. *The Good Die Young* (1954), *Carrington VC* (1954), which appeared in the USA as *Court Martial*, and *I Am a Camera* (1955), which had to be heavily rewritten for the British Board of Film Censors, soon followed. Next came *Sailor Beware*, which appeared in the USA as *Panic in the Parlour*, *Dry Rot*, and *Three Men in a Boat* (all 1956). Many of these films starred Harvey, who, according to Terence Stamp, James Woolf considered to be his idealized *alter ego*.

On 12 July 1955 John Woolf married as his third wife, his second cousin Ann (*b.* 1930/31), daughter of Victor *Saville, film director. The couple, whose marriage was happy, had two sons. Also in 1955 Woolf invested nearly £1 million in four prestigious projects packaged by Sir Alexander Korda after the Conservative government had put British Lion into receivership: Carol Reed's *A Kid for Two Farthings* (1955), Zoltan Korda's *Storm over the Nile* (1955), Laurence Olivier's *Richard III* (1955), and David Lean's *Summer Madness* (1955), which appeared in the USA as *Summertime*. All four were a success, but it was the success of *A Kid for Two Farthings*, Wolf Mankowitz's fable about optimism among east London's Jewish traders, that persuaded the Woolfs to finance the production of another Mankowitz tale, *The Bespoke Overcoat* (1955). Directed by Jack Clayton, their regular associate producer, the film became an Oscar-winning short. The Woolfs' next two productions, *The Story of Esther Costello* (1957) and *The Silent Enemy* (1958), featured Sears and Harvey respectively. Even so, John Woolf still found time to commission smaller producers such as Roger Proudlock and Peter Rogers to make films of stories that he already owned. His biggest commercial misjudgement, however, was to turn down Rogers's proposal that he finance *Carry on Sergeant*, the first of the enormously successful *Carry on* series.

Room at the Top (1959), starring Harvey, Sears, and Simone Signoret, which the Woolfs asked Clayton to direct, was the first British X certificate film to be a critical success. It won six Oscar nominations and the awards for best actress and best-adapted screenplay. For British critics, Joe Lampton's class envy was the central issue of the film, whereas for their American counterparts it was the film's sexual honesty. Unfortunately the follow-up, *Life at the Top* (1965), which James Woolf co-produced, was less successful. After *The L-Shaped Room* (1962) and *The Pumpkin Eater* (1964), which he also co-produced, the Woolfs separated professionally and James went to Hollywood, where he co-produced *King Rat* (1965), written and directed by Bryan Forbes. He suddenly died there, aged only forty-six, on 30 May 1966.

John Woolf, as sole producer, paid £250,000 for the film rights of the hit musical *Oliver!* Columbia agreed to co-finance. Lionel Bart's Fagin, unlike Alec Guinness in David Lean's *Oliver Twist* (1948), was a lovable old rascal. Directed by Carol Reed and released in 1968, the film won six Oscars, including that for best picture. For his last two productions, Woolf turned to continental Europe. Taking advantage of the newly signed Anglo-French and Anglo-German co-production treaties, he filmed two Frederick Forsyth novels, *The Day of the Jackal* (1973) and *The Odessa File* (1974), under the direction of Fred Zinnemann and Ronald Neame respectively.

Woolf had begun a second career in 1958 as one of four co-founders of Anglia Television, which was awarded the ITV franchise for eastern England and became one of the leading suppliers of drama to the ITV network. Under his leadership, Anglia's drama department produced over 100 plays and two long-running series that were sold in over seventy countries: *Orson Welles' Great Mysteries* (1974–6), in which the eponymous actor introduced short stories by classic authors such as Wilkie Collins, Somerset Maugham, and O. Henry; and *Tales of the Unexpected* (1979–89), initially hosted by Roald Dahl, who introduced his own stories featuring stars such as John Gielgud, Julie Harris, and John Mills.

Woolf began a third career in 1968, when he bought British and American Film Holdings to house the profits from his film activities. He ran it first as an investment holding company and later as an investment trust. In twenty-five years the company grew nearly seventyfold, through astute investments first in other trusts and life assurance companies, and later in Lord Delfont's newly formed First Leisure Corporation. In 1975 Woolf was knighted. A connoisseur of Chinese jade, he lived for eleven years near Henley-on-Thames in a house designed by Frank Lloyd Wright. He later moved to Chelsea Harbour. He died from Crohn's disease and heart failure at his home, 24 Thames Quay, Chelsea Harbour, Fulham, London, on 28 June 1999. He was survived by his third wife, Ann, and a son, Jonathan, one son having predeceased him.   VINCENT PORTER

Sources B. McFarlane, ed., *An autobiography of British cinema* (1997) · B. Box, *Lifting the lid* (2000) · B. Forbes, *Notes for a life* (1974) · T. Stamp, *Double feature* (1989) · D. Gifford, *The British film catalogue, 1895–1985* (1986) · N. Sinyard, *Jack Clayton* (2000) · W. Hall, 'Ava can be ALL things to ALL men', *London Evening News* (19 Aug 1968) · S. Daneshku, 'Second feature bargain became the big picture', *Financial Times: Quarterly Review of Personal Finance* (21 Oct 1994), 17 · *The Times* (1 June 1966) [James Woolf] · *The Times* (30 June 1999) · *Daily Telegraph* (30 June 1999) · *The Guardian* (1 July 1999) · *The Independent* (1 July 1999) · *WWW* · private information (2004) [Jonathan C. Woolf] · b. cert. · m. certs. · d. cert.

Archives SOUND BFI, BECTU History Project, Sir John Woolf interviewed by Roy Fowler, 28 January 1992, tape 238

Likenesses photograph, 1969, repro. in *The Independent* · photograph, 1970, repro. in *Daily Telegraph* · photograph, repro. in *The Times* (30 June 1999) · photograph, repro. in *The Guardian*

Wealth at death £4,749,048—gross; £4,494,274—net: probate, 28 Feb 2000, *CGPLA Eng. & Wales*

Woolf, Leonard Sidney (1880–1969), author and publisher, was born on 25 November 1880 in Kensington, London, the third of ten children of Sidney Woolf QC (1844–1892) and his wife, Marie de Jongh (1848–1939). He was brought up in Reform Judaism, became an atheist in his teens, and remained sceptical about the religious temperament. Some of his earlier writing depicts anti-semitism, but Woolf maintained that it had no influence on his life. Woolf was eleven when his father died, leaving his family in financial difficulties. Fears of economic and social instability underlay Woolf's political convictions. His mother risked her small capital to educate her children, who then supported her. Woolf attended St Paul's School for five years as a scholar. He went to Trinity College, Cambridge, in 1899 on scholarships for five years, obtaining a first class in part one of the classical tripos (1902) but only a second in part two (1903). At Trinity, Woolf became friends with Saxon Sydney-Turner, Lytton Strachey, Clive Bell, and Thoby Stephen (son of Sir Leslie, brother of Virginia and Vanessa). Out of these friendships the Bloomsbury group developed.

Woolf's formative education at Cambridge took place

Leonard Sidney Woolf (1880–1969), by Vanessa Bell, 1940

largely through the Apostles, to which he was elected—the first Jew—in 1902. G. E. Moore was the dominant influence there, and to him Woolf owed his commitment to rationality, clarity, and common sense; Moore's concern with states of mind and his basic distinction in *Principia ethica* (1903) between instrumental and intrinsic value was incorporated into Woolf's political theory. Through the Apostles Woolf also came to know John Maynard Keynes, Roger Fry, Desmond MacCarthy, and E. M. Forster—all of whom became associated with the Bloomsbury group—as well as Bertrand Russell and Goldsworthy Lowes Dickinson, who influenced Woolf's political writings.

In 1904, partly because of his family's financial needs, Woolf joined the colonial civil service in Ceylon rather than becoming a schoolmaster or lawyer. He served for seven years, at Jaffna, Kandy, and finally, Hambantota where, as the youngest assistant government agent in the service, he administered 100,000 Sinhalese in a district of 1000 miles. There he continued what he later called his anti-imperialist education. Striving to improve the lives of the villagers with an efficiency that was at times ruthless, he became increasingly ambivalent about his government's mismanagement of jungle agriculture, the absurdity of one civilization imposing itself on another, and the hypocrisy of the British failure to prepare its colony for self-government. Returning on leave to England in 1911, Woolf began *The Village in the Jungle* (1913), a novel that movingly reflected these concerns. He became involved again in London with his Cambridge friends and relatives who now made up the Bloomsbury group: Virginia Stephen, her sister and brother-in-law, Vanessa and Clive

Bell, Vanessa's future partner, Duncan Grant, Strachey, Fry, Keynes, Forster, and the MacCarthys. Woolf's growing disillusionment with imperialism was one reason for his resignation from the civil service in 1912, but a more important motive was that he had fallen in love with Virginia Stephen (1882–1941) [see Woolf, (Adeline) Virginia].

With their marriage on 10 August 1912, Virginia took Leonard's family name and made it that of the most famous woman writer of her time. For literary history, Leonard became, in effect, Mr Virginia Woolf. He had recognized her genius before their marriage, but not the extent of her mental instability. For nearly thirty years one of Leonard's chief occupations was caring for Virginia. Without his vigilant love, her books would never have been written; he was her first reader, her editor, and her publisher. Though not a sexually active marriage, theirs was one of profound and enduring affection. In 1915 the Woolfs moved to Richmond for ten years, then returned to Bloomsbury; weekends and longer periods were spent in Sussex where in 1919 they bought Monk's House, a cottage in Rodmell, near Vanessa's family at Charleston. There with Virginia, Leonard wrote, gardened, bowled, cared for his dogs, and worked as parish clerk. The Woolfs were bombed out of Bloomsbury in 1940. After Virginia's suicide in 1941 Leonard continued to live alone at Monk's House and in London; he watched over Virginia's reputation, publishing five volumes of her uncollected essays, and editing a selection of her diaries. A late loving relationship of Leonard's with the artist Marjorie Tulip (Trekkie) Parsons (1902–1996) is revealed in their published letters.

Leonard Woolf's education as a socialist began with his return from Ceylon. After his autobiographical second novel, *The Wise Virgins* (1914), which satirized Bloomsbury and offended his family, Woolf turned to journalism for a livelihood. He became interested in the Women's Co-operative Guild through friendship with Margaret Llewelyn Davies, and joined the Fabian Society under the tutelage of Beatrice and Sidney Webb. Woolf wrote two books on consumer co-operative socialism, maintaining in them that economics should be organized according to the needs of consumers and that control of production is a means toward a civilized life rather than an end in itself, as both capitalists and Marxists thought. He had become, he wrote later, 'a socialist of a rather peculiar sort' (*Beginning Again*, 105).

With the First World War, Woolf's critiques of imperialism and capitalism coalesced into internationalism. An inherited tremor of his hands kept him from having to decide whether he was a conscientious objector. In 1916 he wrote two Fabian reports on international government, arguing that it could make war unlikely through the resolution of disputes, and showing how far international laws and organizations already existed without compromising state sovereignty. Woolf's reports became part of the basis for the League of Nations and then the United Nations.

During the First World War Woolf also became involved in editing the first of a series of periodicals; he eventually contributed towards editing *The Nation*, the *Political Quarterly* (which he co-founded in 1931), and the *New Statesman*. Even more important was the Hogarth Press, which Leonard and Virginia started in 1917. With no printing or publishing experience and no capital, the Woolfs created a remarkable enterprise that expressed their Bloomsbury values. Its initial purpose was to publish modernist writing that the Woolfs liked and that other publishers did not. They began by printing two of their own stories and then works by various writers including Katherine Mansfield and T. S. Eliot. They went on to publish work by many others including Forster, Fry, Keynes, Russell, Vita Sackville-West, Christopher Isherwood, Freud (the standard translation of his writings), and of course Virginia Woolf herself. The Hogarth Press was never a full-time activity for the Woolfs, but something they initially did as recreation from their writing. As the press grew and prospered it became a burden, and in 1938 Virginia sold her half-interest to John Lehmann, who remained Leonard's partner until their disagreements led Woolf to sell Lehmann's share to Chatto and Windus in 1946.

After the First World War, Woolf's anti-imperialism, socialism, and internationalism found expression in a number of books and pamphlets, the most important being *Empire and Commerce in Africa* (1920), which analysed the economic imperialism of African colonization. Woolf began to develop here the theory of political history that he expressed more fully in later books. The logic of history, he claimed, was to be found only in the beliefs, desires, and ideals of individuals' states of mind that made up what he called 'communal psychology'.

From 1919 to 1945 Woolf served as secretary to the Labour Party's advisory committees on international and imperial questions. He was literary editor of the *Nation and Athenaeum*, under Keynes's chairmanship, from 1923 to 1930, when the Woolfs' rising income enabled him to resign and write *After the Deluge: a Study of Communal Psychology*. The first volume (1931) surveyed the growth of democratic communal psychology in the eighteenth century; the second (1939) concentrated on 1830 to 1832. Woolf interrupted this work to write three shorter books in the 1930s on totalitarianism. In them he again advocated the need for socialist co-operation and international government, and he warned of the impending destruction of his civilization's values, which for Woolf were freedom, democracy, equality, justice, liberty, tolerance, and the love of beauty, art, and intellect. Woolf's insistence on these liberal (and Bloomsbury) values alienated socialist colleagues not yet disillusioned by Stalinism. The last volume of *After the Deluge*, retitled *Principia politica* (1953), became something of a political autobiography. Two more volumes were planned, but Woolf abandoned them after reviews criticizing his knowledge, methodology, and organization. He turned instead to direct autobiography and wrote the five volumes on which his reputation as a writer now mainly rests. *Sowing* (1960), *Growing* (1961), *Beginning Again* (1964), *Downhill All the Way* (1967), and *The Journey not the Arrival Matters* (1969) provide the most reliable description of the development and character of the

Bloomsbury group as well as an indispensable account of Virginia Woolf's life by the person who knew her best.

Leonard Woolf's own personality is revealed in his autobiographies with remarkable detachment and integrity; a fatalistic strain in them sometimes masks the considerable charm, dry humour, and deep feelings of the man. The high value he gave rationality renders his political analyses simplistic at times, yet he knew how little most people were guided by reason. Woolf's capacity for unremitting, efficient work made him hard on subordinates; he once calculated that his had done between 150,000 and 200,000 hours of wholly useless work. Futile as his political writing and committee work may have appeared to him, he was nevertheless right about the wrongs of imperialism and capitalism, the need for international organization, and the evils of fascist and communist totalitarianism. Leonard Woolf suffered a stroke and died at Monk's House on 14 August 1969. Following cremation, his ashes were buried there.   S. P. ROSENBAUM

(Adeline) Virginia Woolf (1882–1941), by George Charles Beresford, 1902

Sources L. Woolf, *Sowing* (1960); *Growing* (1961); *Beginning again* (1964); *Downhill all the way* (1967); *The journey not the arrival matters* (1969); published as Q. Bell, introduction, *An autobiography* (1980) · L. Woolf, *Letters*, ed. F. Spotts (1989) · L. Luedeking and M. Edmonds, *Leonard Woolf: a bibliography* (1992) · A. O. Bell and A. McNeillie, eds., *Virginia Woolf: diary*, 5 vols. (1977–84) · *The letters of Virginia Woolf*, ed. N. Nicolson, 6 vols. (1975–80) · Q. Bell, *Virginia Woolf: a biography*, 2 vols. (1972) · L. Woolf and T. Parsons, *Love letters, 1941–1968*, ed. J. Adamson (2000) · D. Wilson, *Leonard Woolf: a political biography* (1978) · G. Spater and I. Parsons, *A marriage of true minds: an intimate portrait of Leonard and Virginia Woolf* (1977) · J. H. Willis, *Leonard and Virginia Woolf as publishers: the Hogarth Press, 1917–1941* (1992) · J. H. Woolmer, *A checklist of the Hogarth Press, 1917–1946*, 2nd edn (1986) · S. P. Rosenbaum, *Victorian Bloomsbury* (1987) · S. P. Rosenbaum, *Edwardian Bloomsbury* (1994) · S. P. Rosenbaum, *Georgian Bloomsbury* [forthcoming] · S. S. Meyerowitz, *Leonard Woolf* (1982) · H. Lee, *Virginia Woolf* (1996) · M. Cole, 'Woolf, Leonard Sidney', *DLB*, vol. 5 · N. Rosenfeld, *Outsiders together: Virginia and Leonard Woolf* (2000) · *DNB* · *CGPLA Eng. & Wales* (1970)

Archives NYPL, Berg collection, corresp. and literary papers · U. Sussex, corresp., family papers, and literary MSS · U. Texas | BL, letters to John Lehmann, Add. MS 56234 · Hunt. L., letters to Saxon Sydney-Turner · King's AC Cam., letters to Julian Bell · King's AC Cam., letters to John Maynard Keynes and Lady Keynes · King's AC Cam., letters to G. H. W. Rylands · King's Cam., Charleston papers · U. Durham L., letters to William Plomer · U. Leeds, Brotherton L., letters to Norah Smallwood · U. Reading, Hogarth Press archives · U. Sussex, Monks House Papers | FILM BBC interview conducted by Malcolm Muggeridge, recorded March 1967 | SOUND BL NSA, 'Leonard Woolf', BBC Radio 3, 17 Feb 1970, P503R · BL NSA, performance recording

Likenesses V. Bell, double portrait, oils, 1912 (with Adrian Stephen), U. Hull · H. Lamb, oils, 1912, priv. coll. · V. Bell, oils, *c*.1938, NPG · G. Freund, colour print, 1939, NPG · V. Bell, oils, 1940, NPG [*see illus.*] · T. Parsons, oils, 1945, Monks House, Sussex · C. Hewer, bronze bust, 1968, NPG · photographs, repro. in Woolf, *Autobiography* · photographs, repro. in Spater and Parsons, *Marriage of true minds* · photographs, NPG

Wealth at death £157,732: administration, 1970 · £157,732—further grant: 1971

Woolf [née Stephen], (Adeline) Virginia (1882–1941),

writer and publisher, was born Adeline Virginia Stephen on 25 January 1882 at 22 Hyde Park Gate, London. She was the third child of Leslie *Stephen (1832–1904), a London man of letters and founding editor of the *Dictionary of National Biography*, and his second wife, Julia Prinsep Duckworth, *née* Jackson (1846–1895) [*see* Stephen, Julia Prinsep], whose soulful, large-eyed beauty had made her a frequent subject for the pioneering Victorian photographer Julia Margaret *Cameron, her great-aunt. The niece wrote Cameron's biography for the *Dictionary of National Biography*, and drew on her own nursing practice for her *Notes on Sickrooms* (1883). The Stephen forebears were evangelicals, part of the Clapham Sect around the reformer William *Wilberforce; Leslie Stephen was the son of Jane Catherine Venn (daughter of John *Venn [*see under* Venn, Henry], rector of Clapham) and Sir James *Stephen, the colonial under-secretary who framed the bill to abolish slavery in 1833. As lawyers, writers, and educators, the Stephens belonged to the professional élite—the intellectual aristocracy, so called—in nineteenth-century England. Julia Jackson grew up in a different set, that of the Pre-Raphaelite artists who gathered at Little Holland House in London. Though artists, including Holman Hunt, proposed to her, she chose to marry a polished gentleman, Herbert Duckworth. She was a grieving young widow with three children when she married Leslie Stephen and produced four more: the artist Vanessa *Bell (1879–1961), (Julius) Thoby Stephen (1880–1906), Virginia, and the psychoanalyst Adrian Stephen (1883–1948).

Childhood In spring 1882, just after Virginia's birth, Leslie Stephen was on one of his habitual tramps in Cornwall when, on an impulse, he rented Talland House outside St Ives. There was no furniture in the upstairs rooms nor did the cold water tap work, but there was a perfect view across the sea to Godrevy lighthouse. So each year from mid-July to mid-September, for the following ten years, the Stephen family moved to that large square house with its terraced gardens, divided by hedges of escallonia, descending the slope towards the sea. An entry in Virginia's diary for 22 March 1921 looks back to an ordinary summer day in August 1890, to the sound of the sea and the children in the garden, and concludes that all her life was 'built on that, permeated by that: how much so I could never explain'.

The rest of the year was spent in London, shut up at 22 Hyde Park Gate, in Kensington, a tall, narrow house, crammed with the ill-assorted offspring of different unions. The younger Stephens, as a close-knit group of gifted children, excluded Laura, the slower child of their father's first marriage to Minny Thackeray [see Stephen, Harriet Marian (1840–1875)]. When Laura showed signs of disturbance, she was detached from the family and put away for life in an asylum.

It was decided at an early age that Virginia was to be a writer. Writing absorbed her, she said, 'ever since I was a little creature, scribbling a story in the manner of Hawthorne on the green plush sofa in the drawing room at St. Ives while the grown-ups dined' (V. Woolf, *Diary*, 19 Dec 1938). At five she could write a letter in 'a most lovely hand' and tell her father a story every night. Later, after her elder brother, Thoby, went away to school, she, Vanessa, and Adrian devised a serial in the night nursery—as in the Brontë parsonage—a romance about the unsuspecting Dilke family next door who were made to discover gold under the nursery floor. At St Ives there was a different serial, a garden story about Beccage and Hollywinks, spirits of evil who lived on the rubbish heap and disappeared through a hole in the escallonia hedge.

Virginia's bookishness drew her closer to her father than his other children were. Her mother caught her, at nine, twisting a lock of her hair as she read, in imitation of Leslie Stephen. Throughout her life, she retained a fascination for 'that old wretch my father' (V. Woolf, *Letters*, 3 May 1927), though she often condemned him. During her adolescence he seemed a tyrant; then, as she grew older, she would dip into his letters and memoirs, and find a mirror image of herself, 'a fastidious delicate mind, educated & transparent' (*Diary*, 22 Dec 1940). The ambivalence was never resolved. Her father was forty-nine when she was born, and she and the other children of his second marriage saw an eminent Victorian with a great forehead and nose, a long grey beard, and heavy eyebrows, wisps of which lowered over his eyes. In colossal hiker's boots he would hop along before or behind the family party, swinging his stick, and humming 'like a stridulous grasshopper' (*Letters*, 10 Aug 1909).

Virginia's strongest memories from childhood were the idyll of St Ives, a basis for art, and at the other extreme, humiliation at the age of six when George Duckworth, her grown-up half-brother (the eldest son of her mother's first marriage), lifted her onto a ledge and explored her private parts—leaving her prey to sexual fear and initiating a lifelong resistance to certain forms of masculine authority.

There is a photograph of Julia Stephen reading with her four youngest children about 1894. Virginia's face is long, her bones thin and delicate, and her observant eyes are rounded at their lower edge like pears. The photograph breathes the stillness of the children's absorption. More than thirty years later Virginia Woolf created a similar scene in her most famous novel, *To the Lighthouse* (1927), based on childhood memory. As the mother, Mrs Ramsay, reads aloud she thinks that 'they were happier now than they would ever be again'. In actual life, domestic security exploded for Virginia at thirteen, when Mrs Stephen died unexpectedly, at forty-nine, on 5 May 1895. This was closely followed by the death of her half-sister and surrogate mother, Stella Duckworth Hills, while pregnant in 1897. Later, in an autobiographical fragment (among her essays of 1940, Berg collection, New York Public Library), Virginia pictured herself as she was at that time: an emergent creature struck by successive blows as she sat with wings still creased 'on the broken chrysalis'.

Breakdowns Further blows came. Leslie Stephen died in 1904, and then, too, Virginia's elder brother, Thoby, from typhoid, contracted on an expedition to Greece in 1906. That decade of deaths sealed off her childhood and divided it sharply from the rest of her life. Ghostly voices spoke to her with increasing urgency, perhaps more real than the people who lived by her side. When voices of the dead urged her to impossible things, they drove her mad but, controlled, they became the material of fiction, as in her treatment of Septimus Warren Smith, haunted by dead fellow soldiers of the First World War, in her novel *Mrs Dalloway*. He commits suicide after doctors prescribe a sanatorium.

In September 1897 there is the first record, in her *Early Journals*, of Virginia Stephen's wish to die: 'This diary is lengthening indeed', she wrote at the age of fifteen, 'but death would be shorter & less painful.' To go on she needed a rhinoceros skin—'and that one has not got!'

After the deaths of Mrs Stephen and Stella there was no controlling George Duckworth, who would prowl by night, and pounce. He was his sister's 'first lover' according to Virginia's memoir '22 Hyde Park Gate':

> creaking stealthily, the door [of her bedroom] opened; treading gingerly someone entered. 'Who?' I cried. 'Don't be frightened', George whispered. 'And don't turn on the light, oh beloved. Beloved—' and he flung himself on my bed, and took me in his arms. (*Moments of Being*)

Though he fondled his sister by night, by day he ridiculed her appearance and spoke of her as 'the poor goat'.

Shame and Victorian proprieties forbade mention of this. When she was twenty-two Virginia collapsed on 10 May 1904, two and a half months after her father's death. That summer she threw herself out of a window and was nursed back to health, within three months, by Stella's friend Violet Dickinson. She and Virginia developed a 'romantic friendship'. Miss Dickinson was thirty-nine, large (6 feet 2 inches), high-spirited, harum-scarum—the first and kindest of the strong women to whom Virginia looked for petting and cherishing. Violet, prescribing fresh air and friendship, was more successful than any later nurse.

During the 'black summer' of 1910 Virginia's mental health was again threatened, though to judge by her witty letters she was in no sense mad. In July and August she spent six weeks at a private nursing home, Burley, in Twickenham, which specialized in patients with nervous disorders. This was her first experience of a sanatorium, and she loathed it: the phoney religious atmosphere and the ugliness of an institution decorated in mottled green and red. Worse, she felt shut up with the tiniest of minds. In this the staff seemed indistinguishable from the patients. She told her sister that to escape, 'I shall soon have to jump out of a window.'

Despite Virginia's protests, her doctor, Sir George Savage, could think of nothing better than to send her back to Burley in 1913, when she sank into depression. This time she emerged suicidal. On 9 September 1913 she saw two new mind specialists, Dr Maurice Wright and the distinguished Sir Henry Head (overbearing and dangerously misguided in the view of Henry James who had consulted Head in 1912). Both doctors prescribed a return to the sanatorium. She went home, took an overdose of veronal, and nearly died. In October she was installed in George Duckworth's house near East Grinstead, Sussex, becoming once more the dependant of the man who, for her, epitomized sexual abuse and social power. A relapse followed in February 1915, when she lost control. Incoherent, sometimes screaming, she lapsed into a coma.

Whatever the diagnosis—it has been called acute neurasthenia or manic depression—Virginia's instability had some biochemical base which was not understood. She certainly had a genetic basis for mental suffering—her father was depressive and gloomy, her mother melancholic—yet aspects of her disturbance are open to explanation and, beyond that, even in 'madness' hers remained a rare mind. Two facts counter any glib diagnosis: first, in her own view breakdowns were connected with the position of women. Her feminist treatise *A Room of One's Own* speculates on the fate of Shakespeare's sister, a hypothetical woman born to write in the sixteenth century, who

> would have been so thwarted and pulled apart by contrary obligations to genius and womanhood that she would certainly have gone crazed, shot herself, or ended her days in some lonely cottage outside the village, half witch, half wizard, feared and mocked at.

The second counter-truth is that in 'the lava of madness' she found her subjects. 'It shoots out of one everything shaped, final, not in mere driblets, as sanity does' (*Letters*, 22 June 1930). She prolonged her apprenticeship that the volcanic matter might be cooled by an educated intellect. This was the result of a rigorous but unconventional training.

Education Virginia Stephen was educated at home. When she was six her father passed on her first letter to her godfather, adding that when he felt 'lazy' in the mornings he amused himself 'by reading lessons with the children instead of dictionarying' (*Letters*, 1.1). Between thirteen and fifteen Virginia had further lessons for two hours every morning (some Livy or Greek exercises) with her father in his study on the fourth floor of 22 Hyde Park Gate. It had a high ceiling of yellow-stained wood and three long windows which overlooked the roofs of Kensington. Along the walls were complete editions of English and French classics—twenty, thirty, or forty volumes—bound in red calf. Leslie Stephen lay in a rocking chair, somewhat like a cradle, with a board across its arms and on it a china inkstand. There he wrote his books and read, dropping books in a circle around him. In April 1897 he noted that Ginia was devouring books, almost faster than he liked—among them Lockhart's *Life of Sir Walter Scott*, Macaulay's *History*, and the two volumes of *Essays in Ecclesiastical Biography* by her grandfather Sir James Stephen.

Lessons were often preceded by walks with Leslie Stephen in Kensington Gardens. At such times he was simple and confiding. He had contempt for novelists who merely reflected workaday life with servile fidelity, and he taught Virginia to admire 'fountains of poetic interest' which Hawthorne could discover in a prosaic scene (L. Stephen, 'Nathaniel Hawthorne', *Hours in a Library*, 1, 1892, 169–98). His quick, terse judgments had a sure directional instinct like his hiker's steps, when he could do 40 miles a day; to be with him felt like an adventurous expedition. Though his silences might last from the Round Pond to Marble Arch, they were 'curiously full of meaning, as if he were thinking half-aloud about poetry and philosophy and people he had known', as she wrote in 'Leslie Stephen', an essay of 1932. He had once been a Cambridge don, and Virginia had the advantage, at fifteen, of daily supervisions which were all the better for their informality. In her essay on her father she recalls:

> To read what one liked because one liked it, never to pretend to admire what one did not—that was his only lesson in the art of reading. To write in the fewest possible words, as clearly as possible, exactly what one meant—that was his only lesson in the art of writing.

All the same, because he did not see how closely she approached his own high gifts, Virginia was wary, and did not show him some of her pieces, including 'A history of women'. For Leslie Stephen held contradictory attitudes to women's education. In theory, as he had written to his wife when courting her, he hated 'to see women's lives wasted simply because they have not been trained well enough to take an independent interest in any study' (1877, Berg collection, New York Public Library), but later, at one lunch, Virginia noticed how he snubbed his niece Katherine Stephen (who became principal of Newnham College, Cambridge) for presuming to be an intellectual.

At twenty Virginia went in for another 'orgy of reading' ('Hours in a library', 1916, in V. Woolf, *Essays*), including Hakluyt's *Voyages of the Elizabethan Seamen* which her father brought her from the London Library. At this stage she decided that, as there was no acceptable contemporary giant, she would stay with the classics 'and consort entirely with minds of the very first order'.

Leslie Stephen shaped Virginia's tastes, especially for biography. She picked up his reverential glow balanced by humour. He taught her to pit observed truth against established paradigms, and that if writing is to last it must have, for its backbone, some fierce attachment to an idea. But his deepest influence on his daughter's writing may lie in his unorthodox tramps. Virginia, too, was a walker. A year after her father's death she returned to his favourite ground in Cornwall, and in her Cornwall diary of 1905 lies the origin of her narrative experiments. As her fiction was to follow the uncharted paths of the mind's free movement, so this diary records how she would step aside from the highway at St Ives and trust to footpaths 'as thin as though trodden by rabbits', which led over hills and moor (V. Woolf, *Early Journals*). As though she were tracking a metaphor for her future work, she followed natural paths which ignored artificial boundaries. Padlocked gates and farm walls were deceptive barriers, for when she climbed over, the path would continue. By tramping literally in her father's footsteps, she came upon an exploratory plot that ignored the signposts of birth, marriage, and death in order to find those unlooked-for moments that shape our lives. As early as 1905, tracking her individual way across the gorse where there were only grey farms, she noted that 'for the walker who prefers the variety & incident of the open fields to the orthodox precision of the high road, there is no such ground for walking as this'. In his postscript to the *Dictionary of National Biography* Leslie Stephen had said he was impatient of the kind of research that seemed incapable of fruitful conclusions. The success of his daughter's novels was to depend on their conclusions, where she would justify the mind's keen ramble by a dramatic find.

Virginia was largely self-educated, and continued with a programme of reading throughout her life. Her only sustained formal study was in Greek. At fifteen she attended a few Greek classes at King's College in London, and at eighteen wrote to a cousin, Emma Vaughan, in June 1900: 'Greek … is my daily bread, and a keen delight to me.' In October that year she began private lessons with old Clara Pater, sister to Walter Pater, in an atmosphere of Persian cats and Morris wallpaper, but these lessons proved too undisciplined, and in 1902 Miss Pater was replaced by Janet Case, one of the first women to pass through Girton College, Cambridge, who gave Virginia the only systematic tuition she ever had and introduced her to the feminist cause.

Early writings: finding her subject George Duckworth tried to launch Virginia, with her sister Vanessa, in London society. It was a failure: at social events Virginia would know and speak to nobody all evening and would stand, crushed by the crowd, against a wall. On one occasion she managed to read Tennyson behind a curtain. Though she was to draw on London society in her works, notably in *Mrs Dalloway*, she was too intellectual and unconventional to feel at ease in such a set. Later, in another feminist treatise, *Three Guineas*, she characterized women as 'Outsiders'. It was her view that the 'Outsider' is latent in all women. In her essay 'Thoughts upon social success' (1903;

Early Journals) the society woman, encased in artifice, appears unreachable: the dinner bell striking eight calls her into existence. If approached by an authentic woman, 'she folds all her petals closely round her' (ibid.).

After her father's death in 1904 Virginia—together with Vanessa, Thoby, and Adrian—left the solid red brick of Kensington for the superb fadedness of Bloomsbury. In their new home at 46 Gordon Square, Vanessa dispensed with the red plush and wallpapers of Hyde Park Gate; instead she painted the walls white and allowed light to enter the tall, clean, rather cold rooms. The trees seemed to fountain from the centre of the square. For the sisters this meant freedom to put writing and painting first; to reinforce their conspiratorial bond at Hyde Park Gate with a shared artistic purpose; and to speak their minds as they shook off time-wasting activities such as going to balls, drawing on white gloves, making tea-table conversation (at which they were wonderfully adept) with important men.

Virginia's first story, 'Phyllis and Rosamond' (1906), feels its way into a mode of existence she and her sister had recently escaped: the lives of two society girls, daughters at home, two specimens of the many who 'cluster in the shade'. Here, in the unseen space of consciousness, the young writer found a prime subject for future work. It is no accident that her first published essay (for a women's supplement of a clerical journal called *The Guardian*) recounts a pilgrimage to Haworth parsonage, the Yorkshire home of the Brontës who, half a century before, had voiced the hidden trials of women.

At home Virginia Stephen played up to the family's caricature of her as mad genius and helpless, scatty dependant of her sister. She would expand on the agony of shopping for one forced to keep her underclothes pinned together by brooches. Yet she was professional and direct as a teacher from 1905 to 1907 at Morley College, a night school for workers in south London. It soon became obvious that the organizers preferred the safety of mediocrity. The principal, Mary Sheepshanks, suggested that Virginia might hold a little social evening or pass on a little English grammar, but she replied that the newly literate should not be fobbed off with sham learning. Virginia insisted on a proper course in English history, even though only three pupils came, and hoped to give them a foundation for further study rather than the unconnected fragments offered by the college curriculum.

As a writer, too, Virginia Stephen showed herself self-disciplined, professional, prolific, and courageous. In biographical reviews between 1908 and 1910 she developed a theory crucial to her development as a novelist. With Elizabeth I, with the traveller Lady Hester Stanhope, or the letter writer Jane Carlyle, she examined the hidden moments and obscure formative experiences in a life, rather than its more public actions. In her first novel, *The Voyage Out*, drafted between 1908 and 1912 and published in 1915, a would-be novelist called Terence Hewet expounds the challenge which the author had set for herself: 'I should like to write about Silence; the things people don't say. But the difficulty is immense.' The heroine,

Rachel Vinrace, is a silent creature who is surfacing throughout a voyage, and then dies before her shape is clear. In Rachel we have a new kind of heroine, easily defaced, therefore faceless, and, because we cannot *see* her, we can hear her breathe, and faintly, far off, pick up her elusive note. Rachel may be defined by sexual fear or by the other self she imagines as she looks overboard: the great white monsters of the lower waters who would explode if they came to the surface. The aim, though, is not just to stress a woman's vulnerability, but to suggest possibilities latent as yet in human nature. When Rachel and her aunt look out of the window at night into the dark garden of the foreign villa, they speak in broken sentences like people in their sleep. They barely break the night's silence: 'Very gentle their voices sounded, as if they fell through the waves of the sea.'

During the twentieth century it was customary to separate the pre-modern from the modernist author, but these advanced explorations of women's nature challenge any such methodological divide.

Bloomsbury and marriage In Gordon Square the two Stephen sisters brought together a group of innovative men whom Thoby had known in Cambridge: Leonard Sidney *Woolf (1880–1969), a stubborn, passionate man, alert to the ills of society and with the practical sense to combat them; the biographer Lytton Strachey; the art critic Clive Bell; the artists Roger Fry and Duncan Grant; the novelist E. M. Forster; and the economist John Maynard Keynes. The shock of Thoby's death in 1906 sealed his sisters' ties to his friends. Vanessa married Clive Bell in 1907, and the Stephens' 'Thursday evenings' continued at 29 Fitzroy Square, where Virginia and Adrian set up a separate home. This proved the beginning of the Bloomsbury group, afterwards called 'Old Bloomsbury' to distinguish it from its later adherents. Old Bloomsbury abjured the chattiness of society for speculative silence; granted agency to women; welcomed sexual freedom and homosexuality; and generally ridiculed the social, religious, and moral orthodoxies of the Victorians. This appeared avant-garde, especially to disapproving relatives of the unchaperoned Stephen sisters, and even more so when it was reported that Vanessa had managed to shake off all her upper clothing when she danced at a party in 1911, while Virginia had bathed naked in the river at Grantchester with the poet Rupert Brooke. Yet the group looked back to the reforming energy of Clapham, continued to uphold the rational humanism of Leslie Stephen's generation of Victorian agnostics, and reinforced the family piety of their forebears with their relish for recollections and memoirs.

The amusingly congenial Lytton Strachey came from the same upper middle-class intelligentsia as the Stephens. Strachey was an active homosexual, and after an abortive proposal from him in 1909 Virginia, at thirty, married Leonard Woolf on 10 August 1912 in St Pancras town hall. A few months earlier, in May, he had resigned from the colonial service after a six-and-a-half-year stint as civil servant in Ceylon, demonstrating his determination to marry Virginia. The pair embarked on a writing life in London and in Virginia's and Vanessa's rented retreat, Asheham House, at the foot of the South Downs in Sussex.

Virginia introduced Leonard to friends and relations as a penniless Jew. As a Jew, and also as a heterosexual male, he was alien; as Thoby's friend, he felt close. She was stimulated and a little put out by the severity of his judgments— 'I despise you forever', he might say if she wished to kick up her heels at a fashionable party given by Lady Ottoline Morrell. Leonard Woolf backed his wife's writing with an inflexible work routine, even on Sundays; he plucked out her 'thorns'; and he nursed her through periods of mental suffering. He was hurt by his wife's antisemitic remarks about his family, while he, for his part, was a bit obtuse to the inhibiting effects of sexual fear, and early on blamed his wife as a sexual failure—endorsed by Vanessa, who had suffered from Virginia's flirtation with Clive Bell and where an element of rivalry always interfused sisterly bonds. Leonard's accusation was repeated in his autobiographical novel *The Wise Virgins* (1914). But their correspondence reveals that 'the Woolves' developed their own dramas of intimacy, conducted in the private language of playful animals. This kind of lovemaking—in which a man lends himself to a woman's imaginative drama—is re-created in her greatest story, 'Lappin and Lapinova' (published in 1939, but begun as far back as 1919).

The adjustment to marriage, as well as fears for the publication of *The Voyage Out*, were the background to Virginia Woolf's breakdowns in 1913 and 1915. In 1915 Miss Thomas, director of Burley, announced that Virginia's mind was 'played out' and persuaded her family that her character had permanently deteriorated. But the doctors and nurses who believed there could be no full recovery were wrong. By November 1915 she was 'sane'. The twenty dark years were over, and the fertile stretch of her life began.

High priestess of modernism From 1915 until 1924 the Woolfs lived quietly at Hogarth House, Richmond. There, in 1917, they ordered a hand-printing machine and set up the Hogarth Press, at first as a hobby and with a view to publishing their own work. Soon, though, the Hogarth Press became a publishing phenomenon, putting out some of the most advanced writing of the day, including works by T. S. Eliot, Katherine Mansfield, E. M. Forster, Maynard Keynes, Gorki, Freud, Robert Graves, Edith Sitwell, and of course the Woolfs themselves. When they moved to 52 Tavistock Square in Bloomsbury in March 1924, they re-established their press in the basement.

At the time the press was established Virginia Woolf was writing her second novel, *Night and Day*, which revives the subject of her first, unpublished story, 'Phyllis and Rosamond': the undefined nature of women who 'cluster in the shade'. Katharine Hilbery is the granddaughter of an eminent Victorian poet. Her character is modelled on Vanessa: her silent stoicism and secret commitment to mathematics, an equivalent to Vanessa's painting and, like that, in conflict with a sense of responsibility as a daughter at home. Katharine is drawn into the contrasting lives of the new woman, the idealistic political worker

Mary Datchet, and of the abrasive solicitor Ralph Denham, rising out of a graceless suburban household which yet, as Katharine perceives, seethes with vigour. The Hilbery house is in Cheyne Walk, in the Chelsea area of London where George Eliot had lived and later Henry James. There art and prosperity mingle as a stable, pre-war civilization. But it has become too mannered, a milieu that cherishes the effete writer William Rodney, to whom Katharine almost automatically becomes engaged. Katharine's mute uneasiness questions the intellectual aristocracy. As her unease deepens into wordless futility, she is driven to reject the Strachey-like Rodney for the ungentlemanly but life-giving Denham. Biographically, the novel offers a rationale for the Woolf marriage, while it circles the unknown and unused potentialities of women in the context of their struggle for the vote, not granted until its year of publication, 1919.

The continuity with the Victorian novel led Katherine Mansfield to disparage *Night and Day* as old-fashioned. There was no novelty, Mansfield claimed: no attention to the war and no evidence of modernity. This remained the view through the twentieth century. It was not recognized that the ordeal of consciousness, as developed by George Eliot and Henry James, was Virginia Woolf's starting point for the novel of the future where, as she put it in 'The Mark on the Wall' (1917), her plan was to follow the mental track of 'modest mouse-coloured people … Those are the depths [novelists] will explore, those the phantoms they will pursue, leaving the description of reality more and more out of their stories.' She discards the pretensions of the great soul for a nondescript old woman in a third-class carriage or a housewife ordering the fish, and relocates the Romantic drama, the awakening to a moment of sublimity, in the domestic scene. This is the source of Virginia Woolf's continuing appeal for most readers: her repeated demonstration that the most humdrum domestic actions, knitting a brown stocking, or dishing out the *bœuf en daube*, or sewing a dress for a party, can stir moments of inward enlargement, just as a mark on the wall sends the writer's thoughts racing on different tracks, on the history of the house and its occupants or the question of death and after.

From 1919 Virginia Woolf shaped the modern novel. Her essays 'Modern novels' (1919) and 'Poetry, fiction and the future' (1927) introduce a principle that writers have no need of sensational events: any day can suffice. She rejects the narrative coherence of Victorian fiction in favour of 'an ordinary mind on an ordinary day', often several minds. Three short fictions, 'The Mark on the Wall' (1917), 'Kew Gardens' (1919), and 'An Unwritten Novel' (1920), were less stories than theoretical expositions of the new form of fiction that she had come upon, back in 1905, in the course of tramps in Cornwall. Her aim was to find in the 'moment of being' a climactic inward event, parallel to what her friend T. S. Eliot termed 'unattended moments' and what James Joyce termed 'epiphany'. Woolf and Eliot wished to cut through the voluminousness of nineteenth-century writing in order to identify 'the

moment of importance'. Both wished to cross the frontiers of consciousness where words fail. Virginia Woolf said that she had to crack through the paving stone and be enveloped in a mist. This was not mere cloudiness, as hostile critics assumed, but the first move to crack through the predictable façade of the traditional novel where every button on a gentleman's jacket is in place. The Victorians had trusted language to say just what they meant; the moderns found this impossible, and therefore communicated through symbols—the lighthouse or the waves—which require a reciprocal effort on the part of the reader. Virginia Woolf therefore gave fiction the depth of poetry.

Although she dismissed the shallow realism of her immediate predecessors H. G. Wells, John Galsworthy, and Arnold Bennett, it is significant that her criticism skirts George Eliot, founder of realism—for George Eliot had attended to 'the roar from the other side of silence' (*Middlemarch*, chap. 20). In this sense Virginia Woolf's modernism was not as new as it appeared. She also followed Henry James in her conviction that dramas of interior life were as momentous and dangerous as visible ones; and, like James, cultivated an inclusive view of truth as opposed to the reductive categories of standard thinking. Arguably, the most innovative element in her work was her challenge to the category *per se*.

Stung by Mansfield's view of her as old-fashioned, Virginia Woolf cultivated an up-to-date image with shorn hair, lipstick, and lifted chin, as seen in the jutting profile of her Man Ray portrait. Her post-war letters practised the modish tone of mocking hilarity as she watched Mrs Clifford's mouth 'open like an old leather bag' (*Diary*, 1.254). Her next novel was almost ostentatiously modern, a collage of broken impressions that makes up the portrait of a young man who died, as Thoby did, still unformed. All through *Jacob's Room* his would-be biographer talks directly to the reader: we two push ourselves forward—busy, agog, distractable—while our subject slips out of sight. The would-be biographer is vibrating 'at the mouth of the cavern of mystery, endowing Jacob Flanders with all sorts of qualities he had not at all … What remains is mostly a matter of guess work. Yet over him we hang vibrating.' The biographic obsession is comic in its futility. The deliberately fragmented narrative with its curt sentences, its gaps and tantalizing glimpses, compels us to share in the biographer's effort and failure.

A problem rose out of the haste for modernity: the book's treatment of the myriad people who glanced at Jacob but did not *see* him. Given their brash, instant visibility, they should hit the eye with the jolt of the crowded caricatures in Eliot's post-war poems or with the deflating humour of Katherine Mansfield, both of whom the Hogarth Press had published in 1918 and 1919 as samples of advanced writing. But the casual thrust of derision never quite brought out the best in Virginia Woolf. Her opinions became rash to the point of prejudice. She had neither Eliot's lethal strike nor the worldly-wise affections of Mansfield. She herself feared that *Jacob's Room* would come to appear 'sterile acrobatics' (*Diary*, 14 Feb 1922).

It was published in 1922, the same year as Eliot's *The Waste Land* and Joyce's *Ulysses*. Censorship had not allowed the Hogarth Press to publish *Ulysses*, but though Virginia Woolf disliked this novel (she spoke of an adolescent scratching his pimples), Joyce's expansion of consciousness flowing through the hours of the day surely influenced her next novel, *Mrs Dalloway* (1925), whose original title was 'The Hours'. Here she found her distinctive mode: her use of consciousness became more focused, more penetrating (digging out caves, she said, behind her characters).

Far from a floating self-indulgence suggested by the outworn phrase 'stream of consciousness' (associated with Virginia Woolf in the past), a 'framework of steel' (*To the Lighthouse*) provides the substructure of each novel. This may be seen in the bifurcation of *Mrs Dalloway*, which follows concurrently the minds of two people who never meet but whose lives do bear on each other, in the way of light/shadow, sanity/insanity, public/private. The shell-shocked Septimus Warren Smith represents the underside of consciousness which the ruling society of Westminster does not acknowledge.

To the Lighthouse (1927) experiments with the passage of time through a tripartite frame. The reader moves from the Victorian setting of the opening section to the post-war setting of the final section via the blind corridor of 'Time Passes'. The brutal impersonality of this bravura piece of writing takes us through the period of the First World War during which precious lives—Mrs Ramsay, her daughter dying in childbirth, her son killed at the front— are sidelined in square brackets, and the Ramsay house, representing civilization, almost rots away. Civilization is restored, first by the cleaner Mrs McNab, then by the artist Lily Briscoe who returns to complete her painting of Mrs Ramsay reading to her child; only, now, Mrs Ramsay must be distilled from memory—not the beauty a photograph might record, but what will endure: the unseen source of her life-giving power. The passage of time has shaped this woman as a wedge-shaped core of darkness. It is an abstraction, a modernist portrait.

On the publication day of this great novel, its author drooped under 'the damp cloud' of a review in the *Times Literary Supplement*, 'timid', 'doubting', a replica of its reviews of her previous two novels (*Diary*, 5 May 1927). Yet a month later she began to find herself 'almost an established figure ... They don't laugh at me any longer', she noted in her diary on 6 June. 'Possibly I shall be a celebrated writer.'

Virginia Woolf's most daring novel, *The Waves* (1931), has not yet had its due. Its 'framework of steel' invents a revolutionary treatment of the lifespan. Here the writer is at her furthest remove from the traditional biographic schema, the public highway from pedigree to grave. Not only are there no pedigrees in *The Waves*; there are no placing surnames and no society to speak of, for here she explores the genetic givens of existence, unfolding what is innate in human nature against the backdrop of what is permanent in nature: sun and sea. A writer called Bernard wishes, he tells his reader, 'to give you my life'. That life, like those of his five friends, is composed in each case around a defining phrase—'a limpet clinging to a rock' or 'the nymph of the fountain, always wet'—which gives a life its internal coherence. Compared with this, the set form of the lifespan—the chronology of birth, school, mating, death—is, says Bernard, 'a convenience, a lie' because it does not see, beneath the platform of public action, the half-finished sentences and half-discernible acts on which life turns. The diagram of the lifespan allows parallel lives to reach their apogee at any one of nine phases from childhood to old age.

Part of Virginia Woolf's greatness lay in her continuation of Henry James's aim to define the novel as a form of art. She fulfils its inherent flexibility when she blends the novel with other genres to create new forms: where *The Waves* is a poem–novel, *The Years* (1937) is an essay–novel, and *Between the Acts* (1941) a drama–novel. Her flair for experiment remained at the ready throughout her life: as she brought a great work to completion, she would see, on her horizon, another wave rising, far out.

Women and the lives of the obscure Virginia Woolf entered the political arena with *A Room of One's Own* (1929). It originated as two papers read to women undergraduates in the Arts Society at Newnham College and the ODTAA Society at Girton College, Cambridge, in October 1928. The aim was to establish a woman's tradition, recognizable through its distinct problems: the age-old confinement of women to the domestic sphere, the pressures of conformity to patriarchal ideas, and worst, the denial of income and privacy ('a woman must have money and a room of her own if she is to write'). A brief history of women's writing tries to prove that their works were deformed by inward strife—not convincingly when we are pressed to agree that *Jane Eyre* is flawed by its author's protest against the limitations imposed upon women. On the other hand, Virginia Woolf is brilliantly persuasive when she ridicules the power bias of male history narrowing in on war and kings with golden teapots on their heads. A counter-history waits in the wings: the untried potentialities of women, nurtured but unspoilt in women's colleges, who are not to be imitation men but are to think back 'through their mothers'. Virginia Woolf wants to retrieve rather than discard the traditions of womanhood, a position forecast in 1906 at the outset of her career with a historical story, 'The Journal of Mistress Joan Martyn', set during the fifteenth-century Wars of the Roses. It suggests that women excluded from historical record were the true makers of England as they passed their unnoticed code of preservation from mother to daughter, cultivating domestic order and the arts of peace, as opposed to militarized thugs who repeatedly destroyed it.

The second feminist treatise, *Three Guineas* (1938), was cooler than *A Room of One's Own*, addressing the 'Sir' who struts about in uniforms with medals and honorary degrees. Virginia Woolf's pacifism, in the run-up to the Second World War, evoked understandable opposition—

Leonard Woolf was lukewarm, and certain friends, Victoria (Vita) Sackville-*West and Maynard Keynes, sent her to Coventry—but her attack on war as a pastime of men in power has survived its ill-timed publication and has come to underpin the conviction that, far from withdrawing from politics, Virginia Woolf had a politics which looked beyond her age. She cast her vote against power itself; nor could she condone the adversarial sport of party politics because she cared too much for the fate of ordinary people.

What was timely in *Three Guineas* was its point that certain professions, like the church and diplomatic corps, were still closed to women. Where the 'woman question' in the nineteenth century was concerned largely with issues of the vote and education, Virginia Woolf became the leading spokeswoman for the dominant issue of the twentieth century: professional advance. Her support for the advancement of women co-existed with her readiness to love women. It was flirtatious rather than physical, and she remained evasive and ambivalent about her sexual identity, but she adored, romanced, mythologized, and wished to be petted by women, in particular the writer and gardener Vita Sackville-*West, where romance, from December 1925, was bound up with the amusement Virginia Woolf found in the aristocracy. According to Vita, they made love only twice, despite many opportunities (Vita Sackville-West to Harold Nicolson, 17 Aug 1926, Nicolson, 158–9). *Orlando: a Biography* (1928) celebrates Vita as a man-woman, switching gender to endorse the androgynous creative mind through the ages.

Though women throughout the world appropriated Virginia Woolf in these terms during the 1970s and 1980s (a time when her public image changed from that of precious aesthete to that of fighter for the cause), some lost sight of the longer-term issue that underpins her work from start to finish: the question of woman's nature and what it will contribute to civilization. This is the subject of 'The Mysterious Case of Miss V.' (1906), which reappears as a proposition in *The Voyage Out*: that it will take yet six generations for women to come into their own. For this reason the feminist Woolf has remained pertinent, increasingly a contemporary as her twentieth-century generation recedes further into the past. In a speech of 21 January 1931 before the London National Society for Women's Service (printed eventually with *The Pargiters*, 1977), she told a parable of a fisherwoman who unreels the rod of reason into the pool of consciousness—when the line races away to the depths of the pool, the fisherwoman reels it back. Reason comes to the surface panting with rage and disappointment, but the fisherwoman tells her that men are not ready to hear the facts about women's passions which she has retrieved. The question of woman's obliterated desire is restated in fictional terms in the honeymoon-and-after story 'Lappin and Lapinova'.

Virginia Woolf's commitment to unseen aspects of womanhood was bound up with an impulse to explore the lives of the obscure. She celebrated (and practised) marginal genres of diary and letters which were open to women. Her biographical theories broke the march of

verifiable fact as practised by her father in the 378 lives (amounting to 1000 pages) which he contributed to the *Dictionary of National Biography* from 1885 to 1901. On 3 December 1923 his daughter observed in her diary, 'I shouldn't have been so clever, but I should have been more stable, without that contribution to the history of England.' In a biographical dictionary, of course, subjects are chosen on the basis of public importance; Virginia Woolf inverts this in her essay 'The Art of Biography' (1939):

> The question now inevitably asks itself, whether the lives of great men only should be recorded. Is not anyone who has lived a life, and left a record of that life, worthy of biography—the failures as well as the successes, the humble as well as the illustrious? And what is greatness? And what is smallness?

So she chose to write on Selina Trimmer, who took up her duties as a governess in 1790; on Sara Coleridge, who edited the works of her father, the poet; on Flush, the spaniel who shared the sickroom of Elizabeth Barrett and accompanied her when she eloped with Browning; and on Harriette Wilson, who, as a courtesan (to, among others, the duke of Wellington), lived the life of an outcast, winding 'in and out among the bogs and precipices of the shadowy underworld'.

Virginia Woolf's biographical essays took up the challenge of the gaps in such lives—it might be said in all lives—which she approached by accepting that a measure of imaginative truth must co-exist with factual truth. The greater her work, the more completely it takes issue with her father's practice of biography as he edited the *Dictionary of National Biography* during the first ten years of her life. At the age of five Thoby had produced a box which he called his 'contradictionary box'. Asked the reason for its name, he said it was full of rubbish. Leslie Stephen had discerned gleams of satire. In a sense Virginia Woolf's whole *œuvre* was contra-dictionary: her lives of the obscure; the intractable absence of the biographic subject who cannot be deduced from his leavings in *Jacob's Room*; the unseen inward life of Mrs Ramsay, lit momentarily by the beam of the lighthouse; and invisible presences—the continuing presence of the dead, blurring the formal limits of the lifespan. All forecast possibilities for biography. 'The art of biography is still in its infancy', Virginia Woolf observed in the second draft of *The Waves*, 'or more accurately speaking, is yet to be born.'

Virginia Woolf did not venture to apply her theories to her one full-scale effort, *Roger Fry: a Biography* (1940), perhaps because she felt an obligation to the Fry family (who commissioned it) to present the kind of proper, discreet portrait they would expect. In the course of writing this book she groaned under the burden of fact, much as her father had done in the 1880s, locked by his own rulings to the 'drudgery' of 'Dryasdust' (*DNB*, 3.1029). Even so the daughter, like the father, did exercise the selectiveness that Virginia Woolf advocates in 'The Art of Biography': 'almost any biographer, if he respects facts, can give us much more than another fact to add to our collection. He can give us the creative fact; the fertile fact; the fact that suggests and engenders.'

A public voice In the last decade of Virginia Woolf's life she began to develop a public voice to counter the rant of political demagogues. She called the autumn of 1932 'a great season of liberation' as she resolved to speak out as a woman against the abuses of power (*Diary*, 31 Dec 1932). In this she was encouraged by a new friendship with an older, militant feminist, Dame Ethel Smyth, who had composed the music for the suffragettes' 'March of the Women' and conducted it with a toothbrush from a window in Holloway prison. While Virginia was enlivened by Ethel's directness, she did not welcome her demands for attention, nor as a lover, and resisted Ethel when she blamed Leonard for his wife's lack of religious sense: 'Lord! How I detest these savers up of merit', she wrote (*Letters*, 8 Aug 1934), 'my Jew has more religion in one toe-nail—more human love, in one hair.'

In 1932 Virginia Woolf began to write a series of feminist essays with an idea of alternating essays and fiction in a work which became a fictional chronicle of a family from the 1880s to the 1930s, emphasizing the fate of Victorian daughters of the author's generation. This was *The Years*. The discarded essays (collected posthumously as *The Pargiters*) were closely linked with the outspokenness of *Three Guineas*. In her defiant role as outsider, Virginia Woolf refused all honours: the Clark lectures at Cambridge for 1933; appointment as Companion of Honour in 1935; and honorary degrees from Manchester and Liverpool in 1933 and 1939. She would not allow herself to be used as a token woman. 'It is an utterly corrupt society', she wrote in her diary on 25 March 1933, '& I will take nothing that it can give me.'

A public voice requires an audience, and in her final novel, *Between the Acts*, Virginia Woolf turns away from the élite audience of her modernist novels to address a national audience, the grass roots of rural England, through a form of drama which became popular in the late thirties: the historical pageant. The novel is set in a country house in 1939 just before the outbreak of war, and the challenge of its pageant, as of local dramas going on between the acts, is the question of whether England's national treasure—its character and literature—can be retrieved from the past and sustained through the present threat of invasion.

The novel was written during the blitz. The Woolfs' London home at 37 Mecklenburgh Square, Bloomsbury, where they had moved with their press in 1939, was bombed in September 1940, and they retreated to a village existence in their country home, Monk's House, in Rodmell, Sussex. When Virginia Woolf went up to London she saw 'the desolate ruins of my old squares: gashed; dismantled; the old red bricks all white powder … Grey dirt & broken windows … all that completeness ravished' (*Diary*, 15 Jan 1941). It reinforced her fear that the treasures of the past would not survive. Her feeling for certain alleys and little courts between Chancery Lane and the City amounted to a passion, the closest she came to patriotism: the England of Chaucer, Shakespeare, Pepys, Samuel Johnson, and Dickens. As German bombers flew nightly over Rodmell, she shook free from war propaganda which attributed insane love of power to an occasional dictator. Reframing the old Clapham issue of slavery, she suggested that we are all enslaved, irrespective of nationality, by 'a subconscious Hitlerism in the hearts of men'. The word 'slavery' reverberates through her 'Thoughts on peace in an air raid' (1940): 'If we could free ourselves of slavery we should free men from tyranny.'

Rodmell is only 3 miles from Newhaven, where the German Ninth Army would have landed if operation Sea Lion had been carried out. The Woolfs could not know that both of them were already on Himmler's list for immediate arrest, but they were aware of the danger to a Jew and his wife. In 1940 Leonard devised two contingency plans for their joint suicide, though at this point Virginia hoped for ten years more and to finish her novel. But towards the end of the year and early in 1941 she lost confidence that she could reach a wider audience and began to think there was no cure for womanishness bred by manliness—'both so hateful' (*Letters*, 25 Jan 1941).

Just before 11.45 on the morning of Friday 28 March 1941 Virginia Woolf weighted her pocket with a large stone and drowned herself in the fast-running River Ouse near Monk's House. She was hearing voices and feared she was going mad, but there was no outward sign of derangement. Her suicide notes were written with rational civility and gratitude to her husband. After her body was recovered three weeks later, on 18 April, Leonard buried her ashes in Monk's House garden under one of the two elms with boughs interlaced which they had called Leonard and Virginia. The elms are no more; and the ashes are now under a replica of Stephen Tomlin's bust of Virginia Woolf in 1931 with long, stiffened face and owlish, in-turned eyes.

After-life Virginia Woolf left nine novels, nearly 4000 letters, about 400 essays (some attributions uncertain), and thirty volumes of her diary. With the rise of brutal regimes in the thirties, she began to appear too withdrawn, too fragile and precious, to critics from Wyndham Lewis to Queenie Leavis, who did not pick up her public voice. From the mid-1930s to the mid-1960s her reputation dropped. Her search for a wider public, set in motion in her last years, had seemed to founder in the whirlpools of her diffidence and the cross-currents of the Second World War. Yet her pacifism, unacceptable at the time, began to read convincingly twenty-five years later when Americans of the late 1960s rejected their warmongers in Vietnam, a mark of civilization as Virginia Woolf conceived it. Not surprisingly her wide popularity began then and there, reaching cult status with the publication of Quentin Bell's biography of his aunt in 1972. Nicholas Henderson, who was British ambassador to the United States, described how the celebrity-hunters of Washington 'prostrated themselves at Quentin's feet asking to be told "everything"' (*Mandarin: the Diaries of an Ambassador, 1969–1982*, 1994, 337). There followed a burst of posthumous publication from 1975 to 1985. The complete diary, a monument to its age, may come to be seen as the editing feat of the century, not only for its accuracy, but for the family and social detail which Anne Olivier Bell offers in her comprehensive notes. At the same time there were informed editions of the complete letters (in six volumes, edited by Vita's son, Nigel Nicolson), essays, various memoirs, drafts of her novels, and the complete shorter fiction. Her international reputation has continued to spread, stimulating other media. A CD of eighteen songs, *Woolf—a Portrait in Song* by Chappelle, Smith, and Taylor, celebrates a life too long perceived as tragic. In 2002 a ballet, *Orlando*, was put on by the Compagnie Buissonnière in São Paulo.

The experimental modernity of the early 1920s was the image Virginia Woolf imprinted on the public until, in the 1970s and 1980s, this image shifted to another partial truth: the feminist Virginia Woolf who advanced the struggle for women's rights. In the nineties Eileen Atkins gave a marvellously accurate one-woman performance as Virginia Woolf delivering *A Room of One's Own* in Cambridge. There was a *Bookmark* programme on BBC2, bringing together the life and work in November 1984, directed by Anna Benson Gyles. In the same year there was a dramatization of *To the Lighthouse* on television. Films of *Orlando* and *Mrs Dalloway* came out in 1993 and 1998 with Vanessa Redgrave in the latter role.

At the same time there has been a curious insistence on narrowing Virginia Woolf's life to the woes of insanity and suicide, particularly evident in biographical plays, from Edna O'Brien in the late 1970s to the film *The Hours* (2003). There has often been a similar bias in treatments of other women writers—the suicide of Sylvia Plath and the mental decline of Iris Murdoch, going back to the brooding tombstones in Mrs Gaskell's life of Charlotte Brontë. In each case the effect is to distance the work in order to dwell instead on the sufferings that bring greatness down. There has been a concurrent tendency to judge a woman by her flaws—Charlotte Brontë's failure to be a lady by nineteenth-century standards of passionlessness; Plath's excessive ambition by 1950s standards of femininity; and Virginia Woolf's self-confessed snobbery and anti-semitism, at present to the fore. It is not that genuine flaws should be ignored, but we need to be aware that flaws in men—say, Wordsworth's abandonment of the pregnant Annette Vallon or Dickens's unkindness to his wife or Tolstoy's crazed religiosity—are still perceived differently, and appear incidental to starry reputations.

For this and other reasons, the woman writing has remained somewhat elusive. As the queen of the Bloomsbury group and as a writer of letters, Virginia Woolf flaunted different colours according to her company. 'How queer', she acknowledged, 'to have so many selves' (*Diary*, 4 July 1935). The result was an abundance of legends in her lifetime and for three to four decades following her death. The batty image constructed by her family and her flights of fancy at Bloomsbury parties gave her a reputation for untrustworthiness which has influenced the popular view of her life; the myth of the frail lady authoress with her frigid body, a precious aesthete withdrawn from the world, is endlessly repeated. But she kept the hardworking professional out of sight. She had to 'be

private, secret, as anonymous and submerged as possible in order to write' (*Letters*, 17 Sept 1938).

In the shadow of legend was the 'restless searcher' (*Diary*, 27 Feb 1926). She liked to imagine a voyage of discovery or the fin of a submerged form lurking in the waves. 'Why is there not a discovery in life?' she went on. 'Something one can lay hands on & say—This is it?' Each afternoon, when she took long walks, London itself beckoned as an unexplored land. Crossing Russell Square, close to home, she sensed 'the infinite oddity of the human position', and felt, she said, 'my own strangeness, walking on the earth'.

LYNDALL GORDON

Sources *The definitive collected edition of the novels of Virginia Woolf* (London, Hogarth Press, 1990) [series in 9 vols., various eds.] · V. Woolf, *Moments of being: unpublished autobiographical writings*, ed. J. Schulkind (1976) · *The diary of Virginia Woolf*, ed. A. O. Bell and A. McNeillie, 5 vols. (1977–84) · *The letters of Virginia Woolf*, ed. N. Nicolson, 6 vols. (1975–80) · *A passionate apprentice: the early journals of Virginia Woolf*, ed. M. A. Leaska (1990) · *The essays of Virginia Woolf*, ed. A. McNeillie, 6 vols. (1986–) · *The complete shorter fiction of Virginia Woolf*, ed. S. Dick, 2nd edn (1989) · L. Woolf, *Autobiography*, 5 vols. (1960–69) · L. Gordon, *Virginia Woolf: a writer's life* (1984); rev. edn (2000) · J. R. Noble, *Recollections of Virginia Woolf* (1972) · S. P. Rosenbaum, *The Bloomsbury group: a collection of memoirs, commentary and criticism* (1975) · Q. Bell, *Virginia Woolf: a biography* (1972) · B. J. Kirkpatrick, *A bibliography of Virginia Woolf*, 3rd edn (1980) · R. Kennedy, *A boy at the Hogarth Press* (1972) · R. Majumdar and A. McLauren, eds., *Virginia Woolf: the critical heritage* (1975) · H. Lee, *Virginia Woolf* (1996) · N. Nicolson, ed., *Vita and Harold* (1992)
Archives BL, notebook, Add. MS 61837 · BL, memoir of her father · Girton Cam., papers · NRA, corresp. and literary papers · NYPL, Berg collection, literary MSS and notebooks · U. Sussex, corresp., family papers, and literary MSS · U. Sussex, corresp. and papers | BL, letters to S. S. Kotelianksy, Add. MS 48974 · BL, letters to John Lehmann, Add. MS 56234 · BL, corresp. with Society of Authors, Add. MS 63351 · Harvard U., Houghton L., corresp. with Theodora Bosanquet · King's AC Cam., corresp. with Roger Fry · King's AC Cam., letters to John Maynard Keynes · King's AC Cam., letters and postcards to G. H. W. Rylands · King's AC Cam., letters to W. J. H. Sprott · King's AC Cam., letters to Thoby Stephen · LUL, letters to Gladys Easdale · NYPL, Berg collection, letters from T. S. Eliot · UCL, letters to Arnold Bennett | FILM BBC TV *Bookmark* programme (Nov 1984), directed by Anna Benson Gyles (on life and work) · TV production of *To the Lighthouse* (c.1985) | SOUND 'Craftsmanship', broadcast in the series 'Words Fail Me', 29 April 1937, published in *The Listener* (5 May 1937)
Likenesses G. C. Beresford, photographs, 1902, NPG [*see illus.*] · photographs, *c.*1902–1933, Hult. Arch. · G. C. Beresford, double portrait, photograph, 1903 (with her father), NPG · F. Dodd, chalk drawing, 1908, NPG · V. Bell, portrait, *c.*1911–1912 · V. Bell, oils, 1912, NPG · R. Strachey, oils, 1920–29, NPG · W. Lewis, pencil, pen, and wash drawing, 1921, V&A · Lenare, photograph, 1926–9 · J. E. Blanche, oils, 1927?, Museum of Art, Rhode Island School of Design · S. Tomlin, lead cast of bust, 1931, NPG · Ramsey & Muspratt, two photographs, bromide print, 1932, NPG · B. Anrep, group portrait, mosaic, 1933 (*The awakening of the muses*), National Gallery, London · Man Ray, photograph, silver print, 1934, NPG · G. Freund, two colour prints, 1939, NPG · M. Beck, photograph, repro. in *Vogue* (1927)
Wealth at death £14,051 3s. 5d.: resworn probate, 19 Aug 1941, CGPLA Eng. & Wales

Woolhouse, John Thomas (1666–1734), oculist, was born at Halstead, Essex, son of Thomas Woolhouse, royal oculist and of the third generation, according to Woolhouse, to have followed that profession. Woolhouse was educated at Westminster School and matriculated in 1684 at

Trinity College, Cambridge, on a scholarship. He graduated in 1686/7 and then travelled throughout Europe to familiarize himself with the various methods of treating diseases of the eye. He started a practice in London, and served for a time as groom of the chamber to James II; however, according to one story he found that the smoke of the city brought on consumption, and he moved to Paris. Elsewhere it was said that he accompanied James into exile. Whatever drove him across the channel, he was working in Paris from before 1700 to about 1730.

In 1711 Woolhouse was living at the Hôtel Notre-Dame, rue St Benoist, where he served as surgeon to the Hospice des Quinze-Vingts. He had a large practice, and many students. Woolhouse was undoubtedly skilled, and originated the operation of iridectomy to restore sight in cases of occluded pupil, and he was the first to describe the complete and systematic extirpation of the lachrymeal sac when the duct was blocked. On the other hand, he argued forcefully against Lorenz Heister's correct teaching that cataract formed in the crystalline lens. Woolhouse had been writing to Hans Sloane, James Jurin, and others at the Royal Society since 1712, and in 1721 he was elected a fellow, being at that time oculist to the French king. He was also a member of the Royal Academy of Berlin and of the Institute of Sciences of Bologna.

Accusations of near or outright charlatanry have been levelled at Woolhouse, principally, it seems, on the grounds of one of his publications, *Expériences des différentes opérations manuelles et des guérisons spécifiques* (1711). This treatise, which was republished several times in later years, did not fulfil the claims of its title, but merely listed the operations without indicating how they were to be performed. Woolhouse wrote principally in French, with some of his minor works in Latin. He left unpublished two volumes on ophthalmology—one descriptive, the other on treatments with and without operation—and a collection of his lectures. Woolhouse's last dated letter from Paris was sent in 1730. His death on 15 January 1734 was noted in the *Gentleman's Magazine*, without giving any location. No will has been traced and it is not known if he had a wife and family.

ANITA MCCONNELL

Sources R. R. James, 'Woolhouse, 1666–1733/4', *British Journal of Ophthalmology*, 18 (1934), 193–217 · *GM*, 1st ser., 4 (1734), 50 · H. Haeser, *Lehrbuch der Geschichte der Medicin*, 2nd edn, 2 (Jena, 1865); repr. (Hildesheim, 1971), 705–6 · J. Hirschberg, *The history of ophthalmology*, trans. F. C. Blodi, 3 (1984), 25–34 · D. M. Albert and D. D. Edwards, eds., *The history of ophthalmology* (1996)
Archives BL, letters mainly to Sir Hans Sloane, Sloane MSS 4046–4067, *passim* · Hunt. L., letters to the Hastings family · Royal Society of Medicine, London, R. C. Sing lectures · RS, letters mainly to Dr Jurin

Wooll, John (*bap.* 1767, *d.* 1833), headmaster, the son of John Wooll of Winchester, gentleman, was baptized at St Thomas's, Winchester, on 18 May 1767. He was educated at Winchester College under Joseph Warton, being admitted as scholar in 1779. He matriculated from Balliol College, Oxford, on 17 January 1785, but migrated to New College, graduating BA in 1790, MA in 1794, and BD and DD in 1807. He obtained a scholarship at New College on 19 July 1786,

and held a fellowship there from 1788 to 1799, when he vacated it by marriage. While at Oxford he published a poem entitled *The King's House at Winchester*, about a building which was used for the accommodation of refugee clergy fleeing from the revolution in France.

Wooll was instituted in 1796 to the living of Wynslade, Hampshire, but exchanged it for the rectory of Blackford, Somerset, the value of the latter benefice being within the maximum amount of preferment held to be tenable with a fellowship. In 1799 he was appointed to the headmastership of Midhurst Free Grammar School, and raised the school to great efficiency, introducing the system of tuition in use at Winchester. In 1806 he published *Biographical Memoirs of Joseph Warton*, his old master at Winchester.

In 1807 Wooll was appointed headmaster of Rugby School, in succession to Dr Henry Ingles. He remained headmaster until 1828. Inevitably he was overshadowed by his famous successor, Thomas Arnold. Yet, for a period, Rugby under Wooll flourished: numbers exceeded 380 before 1818, making it second only to Eton in size. Wooll presided over the rebuilding of the school, including the addition of a chapel in 1820. One of his sermons, exemplifying for the benefit of his pupils, through the murder of William Weare in 1823, 'the dangerous and irresistible progress of habitual sin', passed through two editions in 1824. An able classical scholar, Wooll produced many distinguished pupils. T. L. Claughton (afterwards bishop of St Albans) and John Frederick Christie, fellow of Oriel College, were picked out as belonging to a 'very good batch of sixth-form men sent to Oxford by Dr Wooll' (Mozley, 1.145). His fault was reckoned to be an excessive recourse to flogging, though an obituarist noted, possibly in pointed contrast to Arnold, that he rarely had recourse to expulsion (*GM*, 1834). One former pupil recalled him as 'a good-natured, amiable, pompous little man' (McCrum, 15). Pupil numbers began to decline after 1818, falling to 123 by the end of 1827. After his resignation in 1828 Wooll settled in Worthing, Sussex, where he died on 23 November 1833. His wife, Mary, survived him. A monument (by Westmacott) to his memory was erected at the cost of his pupils in the school chapel at Rugby.

W. P. COURTNEY, rev. M. C. CURTHOYS

Sources *GM*, 2nd ser., 1 (1834), 227 · Foster, *Alum. Oxon.* · T. F. Kirby, *Winchester scholars: a list of the wardens, fellows, and scholars of … Winchester College* (1888) · M. McCrum, *Thomas Arnold, head master: a reassessment* (1989) · will, PRO, PROB 11/1825/798 · T. Mozley, *Reminiscences, chiefly of Oriel College and the Oxford Movement*, 2 vols. (1882)
Archives LPL, corresp. with Cadell & Davies
Likenesses C. Turner, mezzotint, pubd 1813 (after T. Lawrence), BM, NPG · T. Lawrence, portrait

Woollard, Frank George (1883–1957), developer of mass production, was born on 22 September 1883 in London, the son of George Woollard, general steward to a firm of private bankers, and his wife, Emily Constance, *née* Powell. He was educated at the City of London School and Goldsmiths and Birkbeck colleges. Between 1900 and 1905 he was apprenticed to Dugald Drummond with the London and South Western Railway (LSWR) at Eastleigh,

Hampshire. There he was exposed to two factors that would shape his future career: he was involved in the design of an early motorized vehicle, the Clarkson Steam Omnibus, and he also witnessed the introduction of a crude assembly line in 1904 to manufacture all steel coaches. The cycle time on this line was seven and one-third hours, a factor which encouraged Woollard later in his career to consider flow production techniques in the British automobile industry despite relatively short production runs.

About 1905 Woollard left LSWR to begin a career in the car industry. He worked for a number of years in the design office of Weigel Motors Ltd, which was well known for its car racing successes. In 1911 he married Catherine Elizabeth Richards, daughter of Henry Richards, engraver. They had a son who died in infancy and a daughter, Joan Elizabeth, who became a sculptor and painter. After a brief time with Medhurst and Brewer, consulting engineers, he became chief draughtsman with E. G. Wrigley & Co. in Birmingham, rising to director and chief engineer in 1917 and assistant managing engineer in 1918. During the First World War, he was responsible for the production of tank gearboxes, his first exposure to producing large numbers of standardized products. After the war, he supervised a contract to manufacture front and rear axles, and gearboxes for the Morris Cowley. Production was reorganized along flow lines to meet Morris's demands.

In 1923 Woollard left Wrigley to become director and general manager of the engine branch of Morris Motors Ltd. His first task was to reorganize the old Hotchkiss plant in Coventry. With the use of flow production assembly techniques, within a year output increased from 300 to 1200 engines per week. In early 1924 the machinery used to manufacture engine blocks, the heaviest and most complex component of an engine, was reorganized and placed in order according to the sequence of individual operations. Initially, the machines were linked with hand conveyors and workers manually pushed blocks between production stations. In late 1924 a bold step was taken towards automated production with the introduction of a hydraulic system which automatically moved blocks between stations, clamped them into fixtures, and sequenced the machines.

Woollard had appreciated that such a system offered advantages in the areas of planning and co-ordination, and in the control of labour, giving management more authority to set the pace of work. He believed that such control would be accepted by the workforce if it was accompanied by rising living standards. At the time, this was itself almost as radical a concept as the shift to automated production. Woollard's innovative use of automatic transfer machinery had to be abandoned because of failures in the electric, hydraulic, and pneumatic control mechanisms. However, he paved the way for Ford to implement a similar system in Detroit some twenty years later.

Woollard was a director of Morris Motors from 1926 to 1932, leaving the company in 1932 partly because of personal disagreements with Morris, who retained a firm control of company policy. He moved on to become managing director of Rudge-Whitworth Ltd (1932–6), director of Birmingham Aluminium Casting Company Ltd, and director of the Midland Motor Cylinder Company Ltd (1936–53), after which he retired. His inability to find employment with one of the major British vehicle companies may indicate how little his innovative methods were appreciated by the majority of entrepreneurs in control of the motor industry. He was active, and it would seem respected, within a number of professional associations. Having joined the Institution of Automobile Engineers (IAE) in 1915, he went on to become its president from 1945 to 1947. He arranged the IAE's merger with the Institution of Mechanical Engineers (IME) in 1947, becoming the first chairman of the automobile division of the IME. He was also a member of the Institution of Production Engineers, chairman of the executive committee of the Aluminium Development Association (1949–52), and chairman of the Zinc Alloy Die Casting Association (1952–6). He was a founding member of the British Institute of Management and a member of the American Society of Automotive Engineers.

In later life, Woollard became active in educating industrial administrators at the University of Birmingham and Birmingham College of Technology, where he was chairman of the industrial administration group (1951–7). He also returned to writing. His *Principles of Mass and Flow Production* (1954) extended the ideas originally presented in a series of papers in 1925. Based on his experiences at Morris Motors, it provides a rare insight into the question of mass production in the pre-1939 British context.

Woollard was known as kind, gifted, and philosophical, someone with a sense of humour, a twinkle in his eyes, and a sincere interest in the welfare of his colleagues and his students. He died of heart failure on 22 December 1957, in the Queen Elizabeth Hospital, Edgbaston, Birmingham.   WAYNE LEWCHUK

Sources F. G. Woollard, *Principles of mass and flow production* (1954) · F. G. Woollard, 'Some notes on British methods of continuous production', *Proceedings of the Institution of Automobile Engineers*, 19 (1924–5), 419–64, 886–9 · R. J. Overy, *William Morris, Viscount Nuffield* (1976) · K. Williams and others, *Cars: analysis, history, cases* (1994) · *The Times* (28 Dec 1957) · d. cert.
Likenesses photograph, c.1945, Institution of Mechanical Engineers, London
Wealth at death £36,950 8s. 7d.: probate, 26 March 1958, CGPLA Eng. & Wales

Woollcombe, Dame Jocelyn May (1898–1986), director of the Women's Royal Naval Service, was born on 9 May 1898 at 6 Yarborough Road, Southsea, Hampshire, the daughter of Lieutenant (later Admiral) Maurice Woollcombe (1868–1930) and his wife, Ella Margaret, daughter of Colonel Roberts. Educated at Moorfield School, Plymouth, and abroad, from 1916 to 1919 she worked as a clerk in the naval intelligence division of the Admiralty. The Women's Royal Naval Service (WRNS) was disbanded after

Dame Jocelyn May Woollcombe (1898–1986), by Vandyk, 1950

the First World War but was re-formed in 1939; Woollcombe then joined up, serving first as a chief officer, based at headquarters command, Plymouth, and afterwards at the Admiralty as superintendent (manning) in the chaotic early days of war. Rapid promotion raised her to deputy director in 1943, responsible for organizing the recruitment and training of WRNS ratings, 74,000 strong at their peak; for this she was appointed CBE in 1944. She helped to found the WRNS Benevolent Trust, which was granted a royal charter in 1949, during her period of chairmanship.

When hostilities ceased it was decided to maintain the WRNS as a permanent service. This conversion took place under Woollcombe's directorship from 1946 to 1950. In 1949 she was appointed aide-de-camp to the king, the first time that this honour had been conferred on a woman, and in 1950 she was made DBE. After retirement she presided over the Association of Wrens from 1960 to 1982.

Dame Jocelyn's interest in providing training for girls and women led her to voluntary work with the Girl Guides and the duke of Edinburgh's award for girls; she was also secretary of the Hungarian section of the British Council for Aid to Refugees from 1957 to 1958, was involved with the organization Freedom from Hunger, and was a governor of the Sister Trust (an organization concerned with providing accommodation for London University students) from 1956 to 1965. She listed drama as her recreation in *Who's Who*.

Dame Jocelyn died at her home, 2 Thorn Park, Plymouth, on 30 January 1986. Those who passed through the service during her years in command, and those with whom she subsequently met in various welfare organizations, remembered her with much affection. Serving Wrens provided a guard of honour for her funeral at St Gabriel's Church, Plymouth, where she was buried.

LESLEY THOMAS

Sources D. Stubbs, 'Dame Jocelyn Woollcombe, D.B.E.', *The Wren* (June 1986), 3–5 · V. S. Mason, *Britannia's daughters: the story of the WRNS* (1992) · *WWW* · *Annual Obituary* (1986), 78–9 · b. cert. · d. cert.
Likenesses Vandyk, photograph, 1950, NPG [*see illus.*]

Wooller, Wilfred (1912–1997), rugby player and cricketer, was born at Wentworth, Church Road, Rhos-on-Sea, Denbighshire, on 20 November 1912, the second of four children of Wilfred Wooller, a builder and contractor, and his wife, Ethel, *née* Johnson (d. 1924). His parents had moved to Wales from Eccles in Lancashire. He was educated at John Bright School, Llandudno, Rydal School, and Christ's College, Cambridge, where he graduated in 1936 with a third-class degree in archaeology and anthropology. Wooller shot to fame in 1933, when, still at school, he played rugby for Wales against England. He later wrote that he was 'masquerading as a schoolboy' (Arlott, 73) for he was twenty and 'should have been up at Cambridge, but for an inability to master Latin in my entrance exam' (ibid.). He had already played minor counties cricket for Denbighshire and senior club rugby for Sale. His début match was Wales's first win at England's Twickenham ground (in use since 1910). It introduced Wooller as one of the dominant figures of 1930s rugby, a dynamically unpredictable and individualistic three-quarter who combined size more normally associated with a forward—he was 6 feet 2 inches and 14 stone—with unusual speed and football skills. A powerful runner with 'a huge lengthening stride, he ran like a train' (Arlott, 71), feared by opponents for his high knee-action, he made a speciality of the kick-and-chase move. His skill in this was decisive in Wales's 13–12 win over New Zealand in 1935; he was twice deprived of a try by an unlucky bounce, but the ball fell on each occasion for his team-mate Richard Rees-Jones to score. He was an unusually prolific kicker of drop goals, at a time when they counted 4 points, as against 3 for a try.

After arriving at Cambridge as an international player, Wooller won three blues. On graduating in 1936 he moved to Cardiff to work in the coal industry and joined Cardiff Rugby Football Club. He played seventy-one matches for them, and scored thirty-six tries and thirty drop goals, and he was captain in 1938–9. He won eighteen Wales caps, the last three as captain in 1939, and scored 26 points, including six tries. He also won two cricket blues, played occasional county cricket for Glamorgan in 1938 and 1939, represented Wales at squash, and appeared in friendly matches for Cardiff City Football Club.

During the Second World War Wooller served in the 77th heavy anti-aircraft regiment, and reached the rank of lieutenant. He was captured in Java in 1942 and spent the remainder of the war as a prisoner of war. One of only 500 survivors from a group of more than 3000, he lost 3 stone in captivity. After returning to Wales he was employed in

Wilfred Wooller (1912–1997), by unknown photographer, 1955

wing views to his time as a prisoner of war and was a fervent supporter of sporting contact with apartheid-era South Africa. The Welsh journalist John Billot recalled him as 'mixing exceptional charm with often brutal arrogance' (*Western Mail*, 11 March 1997). In 1958 a botched attempt to displace him as captain of Glamorgan led to civil war in the club, which culminated in the resignation of most of the committee. He retired from playing, of his own choosing, in 1960 but continued as club secretary until his retirement in 1977. In 1991 he became president of the club.

Wooller also worked as a journalist, reporting rugby for the *News Chronicle* from 1946 until the paper's demise in 1960, then for the *Sunday Telegraph* from 1961 to 1988. From the 1960s he was also a cricket broadcaster and was the man at the microphone when Gary Sobers became the first man to hit six sixes in a first-class over, at Swansea in 1968. His 1971 book, *A History of County Cricket: Glamorgan*, had a strongly autobiographical flavour. He also, for many years, ran his own insurance business.

Wooller's first marriage, in 1941, to Gillian Windsor-Clive (1922–1961), was dissolved in 1946, and he married, secondly on 29 September 1948, Enid Mary James (*b.* 1924/5), optician, of Ogmore Vale, Glamorgan, the daughter of David William James, optician. His second marriage produced three sons and two daughters. He died in Llandough Hospital, Cardiff, on 10 March 1997 and was buried in Thornhill cemetery two days later. His second wife survived him.   HUW RICHARDS

Sources A. Hignell, *The skipper: a biography of Wilfred Wooller* (1994) · D. Foot, 'That bloody Wilf Wooller', *Beyond bat and ball* (1993), 17–36 · W. Wooller, *A history of county cricket: Glamorgan* (1971) · J. Arlott, ed., *Wickets, tries, and goals* (1949) · *Glamorgan County Cricket Club Yearbook*, 1998 · A. Hignell, *Who's who of Glamorgan CCC, 1888–1991* (1991) · D. E. Davies, *Cardiff rugby club, history and statistics, 1876–1975* (1976) · J. B. G. Thomas, *Great rugger players, 1900–1954* (1955) · D. Smith and G. Williams, *Fields of praise: the official history of the Welsh Rugby Union, 1881–1981* · A. Jones and T. Stevens, *Hooked on opening* (1984) · *Western Mail* [Cardiff] (11–12 March 1997) · *Daily Telegraph* (13 March 1997) · *The Independent* (12 March 1997) · *The Times* (12 March 1997) · E. H. D. Sewell, *Rugger: the man's game* (1950) · C. Westcott, 'Wilf Wooller', *Class of '59* (2000), 15–21 · b. cert. · m. certs.
Archives SOUND BL NSA, performance recording
Likenesses photograph, 1955, Empics Sports Photo Agency, Nottingham [*see illus.*]
Wealth at death under £180,000: administration with will, 29 Sept 1997, *CGPLA Eng. & Wales*

1946 by Glamorgan County Cricket Club as assistant secretary, and became secretary and captain in 1947. He retained the captaincy until 1960. He was a highly competent cricketer. As a batsman he scored a total of 13,593 runs at an average of 22.58. A fast-medium bowler who could move the ball both ways, he took 958 wickets at an average of 26.96. In 1955 he completed the 'double' of 1000 runs and 100 wickets. A fearless close-to-the-wicket fieldsman, he took 413 catches.

Wooller's greatest cricket skill was captaincy. He was an autocratic, abrasive leader who believed firmly in cricket's traditional division between amateur and professional. His combative aggression, more typical of Australian than British cricketers, led the Sussex player Alan Oakman to recall: 'Anything I had to do with Wilfred Wooller was confrontational—never malicious, but always attempting to wear you down mentally' (*Glamorgan County Cricket Club Yearbook*, 1998, 143). The journalist David Foot wrote that aggression was combined with 'a rare intuition, allied to a personal knowledge of the technique, and flaws, of the majority of batsmen' (Foot, 33). In 1948 he led Glamorgan, a first-class county since only 1921, to its first county championship. Success was founded on exceptional fielding. Wooller recalled 'We caught everything above the ground' (Foot, 31). While he never played test cricket, Wooller was asked about his availability to captain England's 1951–2 tour of India—he could not go—and was a test selector from 1955 to 1962. Always conscious of Glamorgan's role as 'a county serving a nation' (Jones, 171), he encouraged the development of young Welsh players.

Wooller's dominant personality polarized opinion. Jim Pressdee, a young Glamorgan player, entertained RAF hutmates by cursing 'that bloody Wilf Wooller' (Foot, 18) in his sleep. Wooller, who as 'a conversational monopolist had few equals' (Foot, 22), attributed his strongly right-

Woollett, William (1735–1785), printmaker, the eldest son of Philip Woollett (*bap.* 1705, *d.* 1784), victualler and innkeeper, and his wife, Ann Hinkley, was born in East Lane, Maidstone, Kent, on 15 August 1735. Showing an early enthusiasm for drawing (fourteen drawings by the twelve-year-old Woollett are in Maidstone Museum), he was apprenticed to the engraver John Tinney in the Goldsmiths' Company on 4 April 1750. He became a freeman of the company on 5 April 1758. There is a self-portrait of Woollett aged about twenty in Maidstone Museum: looking serious and determined, he holds a graver and a book

William Woollett (1735–1785), by Gilbert Stuart, exh. Incorporated Society of Artists 1783

labelled 'imitation'. According to his friend John Hall he was 'rather below the middle stature, and extremely simple and unpretending in manner and demeanour' (*Memoirs and Recollections of … Raimbach*, 15). By 1759 he was also studying at the St Martin's Lane Academy: that year he won a prize for a drawing awarded by the Society for the Encouragement of Arts, Manufactures, and Commerce for which only artists aged under twenty-four who were enrolled at the academy qualified. He married a woman named Hannah about 1762 and they took an attic apartment in Long's Court, St Martin's Lane, before moving in 1768 to a house nearby in Green Street. They had five children, all of whom died in infancy. After Hannah died about 1770, Woollett married Elizabeth (1746–1819), whose maiden name was probably Weston.

By now Woollett had won a reputation, chiefly as a draughtsman and secondarily as an engraver. His first signed prints were views of country houses and gardens, engraved from his own drawings and published by John Tinney. They are elegant and lucid and brought him a reputation for handling landscape that underpinned his subsequent career. Further drawings by Woollett of the palace and gardens at Kew and of Mereworth Castle were engraved by Mason, Canot, and Elliott. The direction of Woollett's career changed in 1760 when John Boydell first employed him to engrave a copy of a painting by Claude, and then proposed a subscription to publish four modern English landscapes. These were the paintings by George and John Smith that had won the prizes for landscape painting awarded by the Society for the Encouragement of Arts, Manufactures, and Commerce in 1760 and two paintings by Richard Wilson, one of which had been exhibited at the Society of Artists' first exhibition. Boydell aimed to demonstrate that modern English art could hold its own against admired continental models. Woollett was to engrave them all; he began with *Niobe* and alarmed Boydell by taking longer over the job than either of them had expected. The reason was that Woollett had decided to emulate the stormy seascapes engraved by the Frenchman Jean-Joseph Baléchou after Joseph Vernet. Baléchou had won the world's admiration with a new style of engraving employing dense tonal hatching superimposed on boldly etched outlines. Woollett's *Niobe* was similarly densely hatched and intricately worked, but even continental critics recognized it as a masterpiece. The print was widely credited, not least by its delighted publisher, with being instrumental in raising the reputation of English engraving to parity with French. It sparked a stirring notice in the *Critical Review* and a congratulatory poem by John Lockman in the *London Magazine*. The other three landscapes cemented Woollett's reputation as a master. Allan Ramsay invited him to engrave a portrait of the king.

On the strength of such distinguished work Woollett was elected a fellow of the Society of Artists upon its incorporation in 1765. He was a director in 1767–8 and from 1769 to 1777 and was secretary in 1770–71. When the Royal Academy gained the ascendancy over the society, Woollett's courtly connections provided an introduction to the academy but he refused to join as a mere associate, considering membership on such terms 'injurious to the profession, and degrading to the individual' (*Memoirs and Recollections of … Raimbach*, 19).

During the 1760s Woollett also engraved fine landscapes by George Smith and George Stubbs for the picture dealer and publisher Thomas Bradford and he began to publish, or to take a share in ventures, on his own account. Boydell, Bradford, and Woollett co-published a pair of paintings by Cornelis Dusart, and he shared the risk on a pair of Wilsons with Ryland and Bryer. Each of these prints represented months—sometimes years—of intense work for his studio and the completion of a plate was cause for celebration. Stories that on such occasions Woollett would let off a little cannon from his roof may be exaggerated, but Raimbach's report that he would line up his family on the landing for them all to give three cheers rings true. Woollett's was always a large family. In 1781 Elizabeth Woollett gave birth to twins for the fifth time. She had triplets once, but few of their children survived beyond infancy. Only Elizabeth, Anne, and George survived their father. Boarding apprentices and pupils supplemented the infants. When John Tinney died in 1762, his apprentice John Browne was turned over to Woollett and became Woollett's assistant. The pair exhibited in 1765–6 as Messrs Woollett and Browne. The Goldsmiths' Company holds records of three more apprentices: Thomas Morris from 1764, John Emes from 1778, and James Stow from 1783. To take Stow, Woollett was paid the exceptionally high premium of 200 guineas. But a number of others worked for Woollett as pupils or assistants. The watercolourist Thomas Hearne was trained by Woollett from 1765 to 1771, Benjamin Pouncy (who married Woollett's sister Ann) worked for him in the 1770s, as did William Ellis (son of Woollett's friend Joseph Ellis). The painter James Jefferys from Maidstone and Samuel Smith were also pupils in the early 1770s.

Letters show that Woollett took his pupils on summer sketching tours in Suffolk, staying with his patron Charles Davy at Henstead near Southwold. Davy was tutor to Sir George Beaumont, who was one of the party when Woollett visited with Hearne, Pouncy, and Smith in August and September 1771. Woollett also went sketching with William Parsons, the actor and amateur painter who was a neighbour in the 1760s and a close friend. He took pupils to visit another patron, the tobacco merchant and whig politician Samuel Athawes, who had houses near Maidstone and near Henley. Another friend was George Stubbs, who painted portraits of Woollett and of his dog. There is more fragmentary evidence of Woollett's continental acquaintance. He exchanged gifts of prints with Johann Georg Wille who worked in Paris and sent proof prints as presents to one of Wille's patrons, the baron de Joursanvault, a wine-maker from Volnay in Burgundy.

Few had much to say against Woollett, either as an engraver or as a man. An exception was William Blake, whose grossly unfair accusation that Woollett's best plates were etched unacknowledged by John Browne is repeated more often than it deserves. It was part of any senior pupil's training to etch the design on the master's plate but Woollett deviated from less generous studio practice to credit such contributions from assistants (though even he did not credit apprentices). Moreover, Woollett's prowess as a draftsman and etcher had been amply demonstrated—not least through Niobe—before Browne joined him. It is hard to escape the conclusion that Blake's view of Woollett was soured by the failure of Blake's own career as a reproductive engraver.

In 1772 Woollett began to engrave Benjamin West's painting The Death of General Wolfe and took a third share in the risk of publication with William Wynne Ryland and John Boydell. In November 1775, just before publication, he presented a proof impression to George III and was appointed engraver to the king. The print proved vastly profitable and led to a series of similar publications, including Woollett's Battle of La Hogue (1781). In 1782 Woollett moved to a new house, 1 North Street, off Charlotte Street, in what had become the most fashionable quarter for artists in London. As a top professional he petitioned for strengthened copyright law in 1777. Similarly, in 1783 with Francesco Bartolozzi and William Wynne Ryland he signed a voucher for William Hogarth's widow Jane, certifying that her husband's plates had not been retouched since his death.

At the height of his fame, on 23 May 1785, Woollett died at his home, 1 North Street. Raimbach recalled that he died 'from the effect of an accident, unskilfully treated by an ignorant pretender. John Hunter was called in, but too late' (Memoirs and Recollections of … Raimbach, 9). He was buried on 28 May in the churchyard of St Pancras, Pancras Road, and 'attended to the ground by a considerable number of his pupils and friends, whose concern for the death of so worthy and benevolent a man, was expressed in a manner which deeply affected even the vulgar who were present' (Morning Chronicle). He had not made as much money from his career as he would have done had he lived a decade longer. Nevertheless, his widow Elizabeth continued to publish and sell his prints and lived well enough by them until the revolutionary wars gradually strangled the international art trade. In 1813, a few years before her death, Elizabeth Woollett made over Woollett's plates to Hurst and Robinson in exchange for an annuity, but these publishers failed in 1825 and Woollett's daughter was reduced to appealing for charity. At the time of his death Woollett was widely considered to be Europe's best living engraver. When the greatest print connoisseur of the day, Carl Heinrich von Heinecken, had a frontispiece engraved for his Dictionnaire des artistes in 1778, Woollett was depicted as the latest in a series of the ten best engravers since Albrecht Dürer. His prints are represented in all major British and European collections.

TIMOTHY CLAYTON

Sources private information (2004) [D. Woollett] • parish register of St Martin-in-the-Fields, City Westm. AC • parish register, St Pancras, LMA • Woollett correspondence, BM, department of prints and drawings, collection of C. Lennox-Boyd • will, PRO, PROB 11/113, sig. 345 • Goldsmiths' binding books, Goldsmiths' Company, London, VII.134; VII.222; VIII.25; VIII.337; IX.69 • Morning Chronicle (31 May 1785) • L. A. Fagan, A catalogue raisonné of the engraved works of William Woollett (1885) • Memoirs and recollections of the late Abraham Raimbach, ed. M. T. S. Raimbach (1843) • Graves, Soc. Artists • T. Clayton, The English print, 1688–1802 (1997) • Farington, Diary, vols. 2–16 • A. Griffiths, 'Wille and Woollett', Print Quarterly, 11 (1994), 47–8 • D. Morris, Thomas Hearne and his landscape (1989) • papers of the Society of Artists, RA • Goldsmiths' Company records, Goldsmiths' Company, London • A register of the premiums and bounties given by the society instituted at London for the encouragement of arts, manufactures, and commerce from the original institution in the year 1754, to the year 1776 inclusive (1778) • GL, MS 11936, Sun Insurance policies 386728, 532981 • Critical Review, 12 (1761), 312–13 • London Magazine, 30 (1761), 701 • C. Lennox-Boyd, R. Dixon, and T. Clayton, George Stubbs: the complete engraved works (1989) • I. Bignamini, 'George Vertue, art historian, and art institutions in London, 1689–1768', Walpole Society, 54 (1988), 1–148

Archives RA, papers relating to Society of Artists

Likenesses W. Woollett, self-portrait, pencil, chalk, and wash drawing, c.1756, Maidstone Art Gallery, Kent • T. Hearne, pencil drawing, 1770, BM • G. Stubbs, oils, c.1770 • T. Hearne, pencil and wash drawing, 1771, priv. coll. • C. Davy?, red chalk drawing, c.1780, BM • G. Stuart, oils, exh. Incorporated Society of Artists 1783, Tate collection [see illus.] • J. K. Sherwin, line engraving, pubd 1784, BM, NPG • C. Watson, stipple, pubd 1785 (after G. Stuart), BM, NPG • F. Bartolozzi, engraving, 1794 (after T. Hearne, 1770) • W. Jefferys, pastel drawing, Maidstone Art Gallery, Kent • C. Watson, engraving (after G. Stuart) • W. Woollett, self-portrait, chalk drawing, BM

Woolley, Frank Edward (1887–1978), cricketer, was born on 27 May 1887 at Tonbridge, Kent, the fourth and youngest son (there were no daughters) of Charles William

Frank Edward Woolley (1887–1978), by unknown photographer, c.1930

Woolley, a motor engineer, of Tonbridge, and his wife, Louise Lewis, of Ashford.

At his birthplace young Kentish cricketers were schooled in the recently established Tonbridge nursery on the Angel ground and here Woolley, like most of his pre-First World War professional contemporaries, was coached to admirable effect by Captain William McCanlis. When his first chance came for Kent at Old Trafford in May 1906 he began by scoring 0, missing a catch, and taking one for 103. However, in the second innings he made 64, and, despite the wealth of talent available, by the end of the season he had secured his place in the side which for the first time won the championship for Kent. Woolley was tall, spare, and upright of stature, and he batted left-handed with a power of stroke and uninhibited freedom which over a playing career of thirty-three seasons (less the four years of war) won him a unique place in the annals of the game. There was no batsman of whom bowlers stood more in awe. He seemingly disdained them all, as an estimated rate of scoring throughout his career of 55 runs an hour (based on his longer innings) bears ample testimony. Yet when he did opt for defence his bat was rigidly straight and his head unerringly behind the line of the ball.

After the middle 1920s Kent asked less of Woolley as a bowler. Before the war, however, he was rated the best all-rounder in England, and on turning pitches his slow left-arm bowling delivered from his full height and with sharp finger-spin was often rated even more difficult than that of his friend with Kent and England, Colin (Charlie) Blythe, on whose method he had based his own.

Only Sir Jack Hobbs has exceeded Woolley's aggregate of 58,969 runs. He shares with W. G. Grace the record of having made 1000 runs twenty-eight times, in his case in successive seasons. Twelve of these times he reached 2000, and, in 1928, 3352. Only twenty-six bowlers have bettered his tally of 2068 wickets, and only Wilfred Rhodes can match his all-round record. No one approaches his 1017 catches, most of them taken at slip where his exceptional reach made them look, like everything else he did, deceptively easy. In his younger days he was adept anywhere, and he never lost the ability to throw flat, fast, and straight to the top of the stumps.

Massive though these figures are—and possible only in a strong, fit man dedicated to his profession—they are no adequate evidence of the measure of the enjoyment Woolley's cricket afforded. He was truly labelled the Pride of Kent, but in his last summer, 1938, at the age of fifty-one, the crowds rose to him all over England, and his reception at Lord's when, as captain of the Players, he came in to bat was as memorable to those present as Woolley's dignified acknowledgement. Standing at the crease with his bat in the 'order arms' position he raised his cap in all four directions, before taking guard. He then, in scoring 41, gave an object-lesson in playing the fastest bowling against Kenneth Farnes, whose great speed earned him an analysis of eight for 43 in this match.

The first of Woolley's 145 hundreds was made in his first match at his native Tonbridge in 1906, according to Wisden 'in about an hour and a half'. In his last match there thirty-two years later he took a hundred off Worcestershire before lunch. He made no fetish of three figures, however, and in fact was got out thirty-five times in the 90s.

As it happens, the two innings Woolley himself rated his best were those of 95 and 93 against Warwick Armstrong's victorious Australians at Lord's in 1921, when the fast bowlers J. M. Gregory and E. A. McDonald were at their peak. 'I never had to work so hard for my runs', he used to say when reminiscing. Since it is sometimes adduced from his test batting average of 36 that he was unduly vulnerable against the best bowling it is worth mentioning that, such was the strength of English batting, coupled with the value of his bowling, he never batted higher than no. 5 until he had played in eighteen of his sixty-four test matches. Before that he had been put in more often at no. 6, 7, or even 8. No opponent ever doubted his supreme quality, from Donald Bradman downwards.

Woolley married first in 1914 Sibyl Fordham, of Ashford, Kent; they had one son, Richard, killed in action at sea in 1940, and two daughters. After his first wife's death in 1962, he married in 1971 Martha Morse (née Wilson), of Akron, Ohio, widow of Major Sydney J. Morse, of the Royal Tank Corps. Woolley died on 18 October 1978 at their home in Chester, Nova Scotia. For years his widow made a pilgrimage on his birthday to Canterbury Cathedral, which had been the scene of his memorial service.

E. W. SWANTON

Sources F. Woolley, *The king of games* (1936) · *Early memoirs of Frank Woolley as told to Martha Woolley* (1976) · I. Peebles, *Woolley, the pride of Kent* (1969) · O. Warner, *Frank Woolley* (1952) · personal knowledge (2004)
Archives FILM BFI NFTVA, news footage · BFI NFTVA, sports footage
Likenesses photograph, *c.*1930, Popperfoto [*see illus.*] · photographs, repro. in Woolley, *King of games* · photographs, repro. in Peebles, *Woolley*

Woolley, Hannah. See Wolley, Hannah (*b.* 1622?, *d.* in or after 1674).

Woolley, John (1816–1866), educationist, was born in Petersfield in Hampshire on 28 February 1816. He was the second son of George Woolley, a surgeon in Petersfield, and his wife, Charlotte, daughter of William Gell of Lewes in Sussex. Joseph *Woolley was his younger brother. The family moved to London a few years after John's birth, and he was educated at the Western grammar school and at Brompton. In 1830 he entered London University (afterwards University College), where he won a first prize in logic and otherwise distinguished himself. He matriculated at Exeter College, Oxford, in 1832, and, after being elected to a scholarship, took a first in classics, graduating BA in 1836, MA in 1839, and DCL in 1844. In 1837 Woolley was elected to a Stowell Fellowship at University College, Oxford, and subsequently he became a tutorial fellow there. While at Oxford he formed a warm friendship with Arthur Penrhyn Stanley, then a fellow of University College. In 1840 he published an *Introduction to Logic* which was much used for some years and which attracted the notice of Sir William Hamilton (1788–1856). On Trinity Sunday 1840 he took holy orders.

In July 1842 Woolley married, at Frankfurt am Main, Mary Margaret Turner, daughter of Major William Turner of the 13th light dragoons. They had six surviving children. Emmeline, their eldest daughter, became a prominent musician in Sydney. In consequence of his marriage he forfeited his fellowship, and he became headmaster of King Edward VI's Grammar School, Hereford. In 1844 Woolley was elected the first headmaster of Rossall School. In this post he was not successful, for, though an able scholar, he was a poor disciplinarian. In 1849 he was appointed headmaster of Norwich grammar school.

In January 1852 Woolley was chosen principal of the newly formed Sydney University. He arrived in Australia in June, and delivered an inaugural speech at the opening of the university in October in the hall of the new Sydney grammar school. Besides being principal, he was professor of classics and logic in the university. He pressed for the new university to be a secular institution and one which would offer a liberal education to equip a future colonial governing class. He excluded professional training in law and medicine and the University of Sydney was criticized for the irrelevance and impracticality of its curriculum. Woolley was one of the original trustees of the Sydney grammar school, and spent much time and labour in organizing it. He was the first to propose the scheme, later established, for connecting the primary schools of New South Wales with the university by a system of public examinations. In addition to his role as an educationist, Woolley was an active freemason, being chaplain to lodges of the English and Scottish constitutions.

In 1865 Woolley visited England, and during his absence in 1866 he was elected president of the Sydney Mechanics' School of Arts, which he had revived in 1853. He drowned on his return voyage in the steamship *London*, which foundered in the Bay of Biscay on 11 January 1866. A public testimonial amounting to £2000 was collected in New South Wales and presented to his widow as a tribute to his services.

E. I. CARLYLE, *rev.* C. A. CREFFIELD

Sources AusDB · *British Controversialist*, 3rd ser., 16 (1866), 161–78 · J. H. Heaton, *Australian dictionary of dates and men of the time* (1879) · P. Mennell, *The dictionary of Australasian biography* (1892) · Ward, *Men of the reign*
Likenesses W. M. Tweedie, portrait, University of Sydney · portrait, St Paul's College, Sydney · portrait, repro. in St Vincent Beechey, *The rise and progress of Rossall School* (privately printed, London, 1894), 12
Wealth at death £500—in Australia: probate, 1866, Australia · under £3000—in England: probate, 1866

Woolley, Joseph (1817–1889), naval architect, was born at Petersfield, Hampshire, on 27 June 1817. He was the third son of George Woolley, surgeon, of Petersfield, and his wife, Charlotte, daughter of William Gell of Lewes, Sussex, and was the younger brother of John *Woolley. He was educated at Brompton grammar school; he matriculated in 1835 from St John's College, Cambridge, and in 1839 was elected a scholar, graduating BA as third wrangler in 1840, and MA in 1843. (He was incorporated MA at Oxford on 28 May 1856.) In 1840 he was elected a fellow and tutor of St John's College. Among his pupils was the astronomer John Couch Adams. He was ordained deacon in 1840 and priest in 1841.

On 14 July 1846 Woolley married Ann, daughter of Robert Hicks of Freshwater, Isle of Wight; she survived her husband. He relinquished his fellowship, and was ordained a curate in Norfolk. In the following year he was presented to the rectory of Crostwight, Norfolk, by Edward Stanley, bishop of Norwich. In 1848 he was appointed principal of the Central School of Mathematics and Naval Construction, newly founded by the Admiralty at Portsmouth Dockyard, and retained this post until the closure of the school in 1853. During this period he had under his tuition many well-known naval architects, including Edward James Reed and Nathaniel Barnaby.

Woolley's mathematical abilities and the interest which he took in applying his scientific knowledge to the solution of problems connected with ship design and construction enabled him to render valuable services to the science of naval architecture. While in the position of principal of the School of Naval Construction, he devoted his attention to advancing technical knowledge. In 1850 he published *The Elements of Descriptive Geometry*, intended as an introductory treatise on the application to shipbuilding of descriptive geometry. The second volume, however, though almost ready for press, never appeared owing to the closure of the school. On leaving his post at Portsmouth, Woolley was appointed Admiralty inspector of schools, and in 1858 he was nominated one of HM inspectors of schools.

In 1860 Woolley played a large part in the foundation of the Institution of Naval Architects, and he later assisted with it, and published papers in its *Transactions*. One of the earliest efforts of the institution was to press government to re-establish an advanced School of Naval Construction. In 1864 the Royal School of Naval Architecture and Marine Engineering was founded, and Woolley was appointed inspector-general and director of studies. He held this post until the school was merged into the Royal Naval College, Greenwich, in 1873.

In 1870 Woolley was asked by the Admiralty for his views on W. Froude's proposals for model testing. He had been a doubter but was now convinced and strongly supported Froude. Shortly after the loss of the *Captain* in 1870 he was nominated a member of Lord Dufferin's committee which was appointed to consider many contentious points concerning the design of warships. In 1874 and 1875 he was associated with E. J. Reed as editor of *Naval Science*, a quarterly magazine dedicated to promoting improvements in naval architecture and steam navigation.

Woolley remained a clergyman until 1873, when he took advantage of the Clerical Disabilities Relief Act (1870) to relinquish his orders. He lived at Kingston upon Thames, of which he was joint mayor (with Henry Shrubsole) in 1879. He died on 24 March 1889 at his residence, Afton House, Mount Harry Road, Sevenoaks, Kent.

E. I. CARLYLE, *rev.* DAVID K. BROWN

Sources 'Memoir of Dr Joseph Wooley', *Transactions of the Institution of Naval Architects*, 30 (1889), 463–5 · D. K. Brown, 'William Froude', PRO, ADM 116/137 · D. K. Brown, *A century of naval construction: the history of the Royal Corps of Naval Constructors, 1883–1983* (1983) · Boase, *Mod. Eng. biog.* · Venn, *Alum. Cant.* · private information (2004) · *CGPLA Eng. & Wales* (1889)
Wealth at death £1340 17s. 2d.: probate, 13 May 1889, *CGPLA Eng. & Wales*

Woolley, Sir (Charles) Leonard (1880–1960), archaeologist, was born at 13 Southwold Road, Upper Clapton, Hackney, London, on 17 April 1880, the third of eleven children (four boys and seven girls) of the Revd George Herbert Woolley, curate of St Matthew's, Upper Clapton, and his wife, Sarah Cathcart. Coming from a large family, he had to finance his education by scholarships for St John's, Leatherhead, and New College, Oxford, where he achieved a first in *literae humaniores* (1903) and a second in theology (1904). By his final year at university Woolley had abandoned his initial ambition of taking holy orders, settling instead on becoming a schoolmaster. When the warden of New College, W. A. Spooner, advised him to take up archaeology, Woolley acquiesced. After studying modern languages on the continent, he was in 1905 appointed assistant to Arthur Evans, keeper of the Ashmolean Museum. Woolley served his apprenticeship in field archaeology while excavating with D. Randall-MacIver in

Sir (Charles) Leonard Woolley (1880–1960), by Vaughan & Freeman

Wadi Halfa (Egyptian Nubia) in 1907–11; during this period he also conducted a brief excavation of Roman baths at Teano in Italy.

Woolley's first experience with the ancient Near East came at Carchemish (Syria), a project that D. G. Hogarth had organized for the British Museum. When the excavation director, R. Campbell Thompson, left the project after the first season (1911), Woolley accepted the position and directed the five remaining seasons of the project (1912–13, 1920). Working with T. E. Lawrence as his assistant, Woolley uncovered defensive works, temples, and palaces of neo-Hittite (9th–8th centuries BC) Carchemish; the sculptured orthostats that graced the buildings provided important documentation of neo-Hittite art. Woolley also recovered traces of earlier occupations, but circumstances prevented him from uncovering significant portions of these.

Woolley and Lawrence also collaborated in a survey of Wadi Araba south of the Dead Sea, their work bringing to completion the Palestine Exploration Fund's programme of mapping all the Holy Land. This work, published in 1915 as *The Wilderness of Zin* under both collaborators' names, produced information and experience that was later useful to Lawrence's war. With the outbreak of the First World War Woolley served as an intelligence officer posted to Cairo, attaining the rank of major before the Turks took him prisoner late in 1916 when his ship blew up in the eastern Mediterranean. During his internment Woolley entertained his fellow prisoners of war with written vignettes of his archaeological experiences in Italy, Egypt, and Syria; published in 1920 as *Dead Towns and Living Men*, these stories humorously depict the often difficult and sometimes dangerous conditions of archaeological work in Ottoman Near East. When the unsettled post-war conditions impeded further excavation at Carchemish, Woolley collaborated in 1921 with T. Eric Peet in excavations at Tell al-Amarna (briefly the capital of New Kingdom Egypt) on behalf of the Egypt Exploration Society.

After several seasons in Egypt Woolley began the work for which he is best remembered, his excavations at Ur in southern Iraq. R. Campbell Thompson (1918) and R. H. Hall (1918–19) had started excavations there on behalf of the British Museum, but this work fell into abeyance for lack of funds. When in 1922 the British Museum accepted the proposal by the University of Pennsylvania Museum of a joint venture at Ur, Woolley was named the expedition's director. He worked at Ur for twelve seasons between 1922 and 1934, assisted during many of those seasons by Katharine Keeling, who became his wife, and by Max Mallowan. He also completed the excavations at the nearby site of al-ʿUbayd that Hall had begun. Woolley revealed at Ur occupation beginning in the prehistoric ʿUbaid period and enduring into Hellenistic times, a span of four and a half millennia (roughly 4500–200 BC). His most enduring discoveries belong to the eight centuries between 2600 and 1750 BC, from the heyday of the Sumerian civilization to the time of Hammurabi.

Woolley first encountered the famous royal cemetery in autumn 1922 while extending Hall's work but elected to defer tackling it until the 1926–7 season in order to give himself time to master the technical difficulties of Mesopotamian excavations and to train a skilled workforce; few archaeologists would have had the patience to follow this intelligent course. Of the sixteen tombs that Woolley identified as royal, many contained stunning wealth, as did several other tombs that did not satisfy his criteria for royalty; among the thousands of burial objects are some of the great examples of Sumerian art. The royal tombs also contained as many as seventy-four other bodies, apparently retainers accompanying their master in death; this macabre touch stirred great popular interest. The royal tombs formed the initial (2600 BC) nucleus of a larger cemetery of several thousand poorer graves, the interments occurring over the next half-millennium. Although Woolley argued for the royalty of his sixteen burials, subsequent scholars have mulled over the nature of the cemetery without reaching firm conclusions.

The architectural gems of the city belonged to the Ur III (2100–2000 BC) period when Ur was the capital of a small empire, and to the early Old Babylonian (2000–1750 BC) period when the city fell into the hands of neighbouring princes. The first Ur III king built the religious centre of the city; his ziggurat, or stepped tower-like platform, has become an iconic image of Mesopotamian architecture. Later Mesopotamian kings periodically renovated the ziggurat and main temples, notably in the fourteenth century BC and sixth century BC. Woolley also uncovered several residential quarters of the Ur III and Old Babylonian periods; although less spectacular than some of his other results, their combination of architecture, private archives, burials, and other finds continues to be an invaluable resource for understanding the social and economic fabric of more ordinary life in ancient Mesopotamia.

A change in the antiquities laws of Iraq encouraged many Mesopotamian archaeologists to shift their attention to Syria after 1933, then under the French mandate. In 1937 Woolley initiated his third great excavation project in Hatay (a part of northern Syria transferred to Turkey in 1938). He chose Tell Atchana (ancient Alalakh) and the port at al-Mina to investigate connections between the Aegean world and the Near East, Hatay forming a corridor between the eastern Mediterranean coast and the interior; his team also excavated at two prehistoric mounds near Atchana during the project's seven seasons (1937–9, 1946–9). At Atchana Woolley found a sequence of palaces and temples belonging to the middle and late Bronze ages (2000–1200 BC). The walls of one palace had been decorated with frescoes in a style borrowed from Minoan art, an unanticipated result for Woolley's research. Their archives of cuneiform tablets make Alalakh levels VII (*c*.1700 BC) and IV (*c*.1450 BC) the most discussed portions of the sequence; the inscription carved on the statue of King Idrimi is still one of the few historical sources for the time around 1500 BC. The excavations at al-Mina revealed ten levels of structures that Woolley identified as warehouses associated with Greek pottery and other objects, a sequence that Woolley assigned to the eighth to fourth centuries BC. Although the al-Mina results are incompletely published, they remain a cornerstone of discussions about Greek commercial enterprise in the east.

At the request of the archaeological survey of India, Woolley visited the subcontinent in 1938 on an inspection tour, aiming to revive the moribund survey. He advised a focus on training, and recommended that Mortimer Wheeler be named director-general; this happened in 1944. During the Second World War Woolley served as lieutenant-colonel with a brief to safeguard European patrimony. He was knighted in 1935, and received numerous scholarly distinctions (honorary degrees from the universities of Dublin and St Andrews, and the Lucy Wharton Drexel (University Museum, 1955) and the Flinders Petrie (University of London, 1957) medals.

For much of his adult life Woolley split his year between Near Eastern fieldwork and London, where he turned his attention to writing and lecturing; in both worlds he was extraordinarily energetic. He was a hard but fair taskmaster in the field, and drove himself very hard—the workday began within half an hour of sunrise, and Woolley continued well past midnight in his office. He worked with two or three assistants, a small staff that supervised a workforce of up to 400 men ('the maximum consistent with proper supervision', in Woolley's words); such ratios of staff to workforce, although common at the time, can compromise the quality of excavation. As a result, Ur's contribution to Mesopotamian chronology remained secondary, and Atchana's history has attracted a prolonged, ongoing debate. But the extensive exposures of public and residential architecture that he achieved in his three major Near Eastern excavations would have been otherwise impossible, and the trade-off was worth while.

Woolley held the admirable view, commonly expressed but rarely honoured in the profession, that failure to publish archaeological excavations is criminal. His record on this score was exemplary, for in addition to presenting annual reports and public lectures about his results he also produced usually multi-volume final reports for each of his three major projects. *Carchemish* appeared in three volumes (vol. 1 by Hogarth, 1914; vol. 2 by Woolley, 1921; vol. 3 by Woolley and R. D. Barnett, 1953); the usefulness of these volumes is often marred by inadequacy in excavation techniques of the day. He completed the ten volumes of the Ur report (*Ur Excavations*) soon after the project's conclusion, several volumes appearing during the lifetime of the project although budgetary problems delayed publication, the last volume appearing in 1976. The Ur reports, so rich in detail, are Woolley's principal legacy to Near Eastern archaeology. The final report on Tell Atchana (*Alalakh: Excavations at Tell Atchana*, 1955) appeared just six years after the excavations there ended, although this volume did not match the excellent standard of the Ur reports.

Woolley also composed several interpretative studies, among them *The Sumerians* (1928), *The Development of Sumerian Art* (1935), and *Abraham* (1936). Of less enduring value by their very nature, these works were marred from the beginning by shortcomings of Woolley's intellectual attitudes. His was not an academic bent, and his scholarship emphasized fieldwork over library research. Only incompletely did he attend to contemporary research on early Mesopotamia, and this limited his understanding of Sumerian civilization and of Ur itself, thereby encouraging his ill-founded persuasion that civilization arose significantly earlier in Mesopotamia than in Egypt; he therefore endorsed a chronology significantly older than that accepted by scholarship in the 1930s and later. Despite his youthful decision against holy orders he greatly exercised his theological interests, notably at Ur in his eager identification of a silt deposit as evidence of Noah's flood; his search for traces of Abraham sometimes forced his interpretations into unlikely directions.

Woolley found time to write popularizing books as well. In addition to his general introduction to archaeology, *Digging up the Past* (1930), he presented his findings at Ur in *Ur of the Chaldees: a Record of Seven Years of Excavation* (1929; revised in 1954 to include all twelve excavation seasons). He also gave Tell Atchana a popular treatment in *A Forgotten Kingdom* (1953). In these writings Woolley explained his results and their implications to the reading public, to satisfy the intense curiosity that his Ur discoveries had

aroused and to encourage continued public support of ever more costly archaeological excavations. Here again he set a laudable standard that most archaeologists fail to meet. In these books, as well as in public lectures and in the tours he gave to the frequent visitors to his excavations, Woolley displayed both his gift for story-telling and showmanship, and his keen imagination that sometimes overcame scholarly sobriety.

Woolley married Katharine Elizabeth Keeling (1888–1945), the widow of Lieutenant-Colonel (Bertram E.) Francis Keeling, on 11 April 1927; she was the daughter of Carl Theodore Menke, of King's Norton, Worcestershire, a merchant of Prussian origin. Suffering persistent ill health but accompanying Woolley in his fieldwork none the less, Katharine Woolley was 'a daunting and powerful personality of whom even at this time it is difficult to speak fairly' (Mallowan, 36). The Woolleys were childless. Woolley died at 16 Fitzroy Square, St Pancras, London, on 20 February 1960, and was cremated at Golders Green, Middlesex, on the 24th. CHRISTOPHER EDENS

Sources *DNB* · M. E. L. Mallowan, *Mallowan's memoirs* (1977) · C. L. Woolley, *Ur of the Chaldees*, rev. R. Moorey (1982) · C. L. Woolley, *Dead towns and living men* (1920) · C. L. Woolley, *Carchemish II* (1921) · C. L. Woolley, *Ur excavations II: the royal cemetery* (1934) · C. L. Woolley, *A forgotten kingdom* (1953) · C. L. Woolley, *Alalakh: excavations at Tell Atchana* (1955) · C. L. Woolley, *The Sumerians* (1928) · H. F. V. Winstone, *Woolley of Ur: the life of Sir Leonard Woolley* (1990)
Archives BM, displays of excavated materials · University of Pennsylvania, Philadelphia, University Museum, displays of excavated materials | BL, corresp. with Sir Sydney Cockerell, Add. MS 52769 · Bodl. Oxf., corresp. with J. L. Myres · Palestine Exploration Fund, London, corresp. and papers relating to work for Palestine Exploration Fund · Rice University, Houston, Texas, Woodson Research Center, corresp. with Sir Julian Huxley | SOUND BL NSA, performance recording
Likenesses W. Stoneman, photograph, 1954, NPG · Vaughan & Freeman, photograph, Sci. Mus., Science and Society Picture Library [see illus.] · double portrait, photograph (with his wife, excavating at Ur), repro. in Woolley, *Ur excavations II* · negatives, BM · photographs, repro. in Winstone, *Woolley*
Wealth at death £11,833 12s.: probate, 5 Oct 1960, *CGPLA Eng. & Wales*

Woolley, Sir Richard van der Riet (1906–1986), astronomer, was born on 24 April 1906 in Weymouth, Dorset, the fourth of five children of Charles Edward Allen Woolley, paymaster rear-admiral in the Royal Navy, and his wife, Julia van der Riet, of Simonstown, Cape Colony. He went to Allhallows School, Honiton, Devon, from 1919 to 1921, when the family moved to Cape Town. He entered its university to study mathematics and physics, and by the age of nineteen he had the degrees of BSc (1924) and MSc (1925). Reverting to undergraduate status, in 1926 he entered Gonville and Caius College, Cambridge. He spent his first summer there with the scientific expedition led by H. G. (Gino) Watkins, exploring Edge Island, east of Spitsbergen. After graduating as a wrangler in the mathematical tripos (1928) he worked from 1928 to 1932 for his PhD under Sir Arthur Eddington, from 1929 to 1931 at Mount Wilson observatory, California, as a Commonwealth Fund fellow.

In 1933 Woolley became chief assistant to the astronomer royal, Harold Spencer Jones, at the Royal Observatory, Greenwich. Seeking more scope for initiatives of his own, he returned to Cambridge in 1937 as John Couch Adams astronomer. From 1939 to 1955 he was Commonwealth astronomer and director of Mount Stromlo observatory, Australia. In 1940 the Australian government converted the observatory into an optical munitions factory, with Woolley as director. So impressed were they by his unfolding personality and resourcefulness that they also made him head of the army inventions directorate. His resulting acquaintance with leaders in scientific and public life led him to play an influential part in the phenomenal post-war development of Australian science.

From 1956 to 1971, as eleventh astronomer royal and director of the Royal Greenwich Observatory (RGO) at Herstmonceaux, Sussex, Woolley initiated far-reaching developments in British astronomy. He had also general oversight of the Royal Observatory, Cape of Good Hope, from 1960, and in 1971 the British and South African governments concluded an agreement whereby it became the headquarters of a new South African astronomical observatory (SAAO). In December 1971 Woolley retired from the Royal Observatory, forthwith becoming director of SAAO. He retired in December 1976.

Woolley's career had a remarkable coherence. His aim was the discovery of the physical constitution of the universe and the way in which the known laws of physics determine its operation. Pursuing this aim on three different continents, he erected large telescopes and promoted the education and training of astronomers, thereby creating the environment in which modern observational astrophysics could flourish. He was honorary professor in the formative years of the Australian National University and became an active visiting professor at the University of Sussex and later the University of Cape Town. He created vacation courses at the RGO, where he won young scientists' interest by having them join in *doing* astronomy. He made Stromlo the leading observatory in the southern hemisphere and generated the concept of the Anglo-Australian telescope. His friendship with leaders of Australian science and government eventually led to its becoming a reality on Siding Spring Mountain. He strongly supported the construction there of the UK Schmidt telescope. At Herstmonceaux he activated construction of the Isaac Newton telescope. When it was inaugurated in 1967 it was the largest in Europe (it was later moved to La Palma).

Telescope building and other duties were never allowed to halt Woolley's own observational researches. He made important and pioneering studies of the passage of radiation through both stellar and terrestrial atmospheres, the temperature of the sun's corona, the statistical mechanics of star clusters, the Magellanic clouds, and the stars within seventy-five light-years of the sun. He was particularly concerned with determination of the kinematics and dynamics of the galaxy and the presence of 'dark matter' within it. The resurgence of British optical astronomy and the related developments in Australia and South Africa owe their inception to Woolley and the telescopes he started. He was himself neither a popularizer nor a proponent of revolutionary ideas, although he respected some who were.

From 1952 to 1958 Woolley was vice-president of the International Astronomical Union, and from 1963 to 1965 president; in 1971 he was gold medallist of the Royal Astronomical Society. He was elected a fellow of the Royal Society in 1953 and in 1956 an honorary fellow of Gonville and Caius College. He was master of the Worshipful Company of Clockmakers (1969) and had honorary degrees from Melbourne (1955), Uppsala (1956), Cape Town (1969), and Sussex (1970). He was appointed OBE (1953) and knighted in 1963.

Woolley was about 6 feet tall, with a fine presence; he had exceptional friendliness and charm and was an obvious leader. He was a man of open spaces, with an instinctive feeling for the countryside around him. On Stromlo he kept horses and rode a lot, and he enjoyed walking on Table Mountain. He was a talented pianist and liked country dancing and bell ringing. He played a whole range of ball games and encouraged others to participate.

In 1932 Woolley married Gwyneth Jane Margaret, daughter of Hugh Harries Meyler, of independent means. She enhanced his love of the arts and greatly supported him in entertaining guests. He was devastated by her unexpected death in 1979 in Sussex. His health suffered, but (Emily May) Patricia, widow of Ronald Marples, a Royal Air Force gunner missing over Malta, and daughter of John Mowley, mining engineer, helped him back to normality. She became his second wife in 1979 and they went to live in South Africa, where many visiting astronomers enjoyed their hospitality. Patricia died in 1985. At the end of that year he married Sheila, former wife of David George Gillham, professor of English at Cape Town University, and daughter of William Penry Hammett, shipping agent. Woolley had no children. He had a bad fall and died on 24 December 1986 at Somerset West, Cape Province, South Africa, where his home was at 4 Myrtle Street. He was survived by his wife.

WILLIAM McCREA and DONALD LYNDEN-BELL, rev.

Sources W. McCrea, *Memoirs FRS*, 34 (1988), 923–82 · personal knowledge (1996) · *WW*
Archives CUL, papers
Likenesses photographs, repro. in McCrea, *Memoirs FRS*, 922

Woolman, John (1720–1772), Quaker minister and antislavery campaigner, was born at Rancocas in Burlington county, New Jersey, on 19 October 1720. He was one of thirteen children of Samuel Woolman (1690–1750) and his wife, Elizabeth, *née* Burr (1695–1773). In 1678 his forebears settled in the Quaker colony of West Jersey, where his grandfather was a proprietor; Woolman's father was a farmer. His formal education was at a Quaker school near Mount Holly but early on Woolman was exposed to the large libraries of Philadelphia Friends. His *Journal* indicates his knowledge of a wide range of literature; aside from the expected Quaker classics there are references from mystic writings, including those of Jakob Boehme,

John Everard, William Law, and the *Imitation of Christ*, attributed to the Catholic Thomas à Kempis.

When he was twenty-one Woolman moved to Mount Holly, which was not far from his home. There he kept books for a shopkeeper. Later he also became an apprenticed tailor. An experience at the shop set the future course of his life. Since his father had taught him basic legal skills Woolman was asked by his employer to write a bill of sale for a female black slave. As he wrote in his *Journal*, he was compelled to tell his employer that he thought slave-keeping was 'a practice inconsistent with the Christian religion' (*Journal and Major Essays*, 33). The next time Woolman was asked to write another bill of sale he refused. Thus began his crusade against slavery: a slow but steady pricking of consciences within the Society of Friends that eventually would spark further moves for abolition in America.

Woolman's efforts were largely accomplished by religious journeys, and the first, in 1743, took him to points in New Jersey. By the end of the decade he had covered 4000 miles, often on foot. From Pennsylvania Woolman went into New England and also made his first southern journey into Maryland, Virginia, and North Carolina. Woolman's life as a Quaker spokesman began at the age of twenty-two, when he was first recorded a minister by Burlington monthly meeting. For seventeen years he was clerk of meeting, a representative to Philadelphia yearly meeting; for sixteen years he was also a member of the overseers of the press for yearly meeting.

On 18 October 1749 Woolman married Sarah Ellis (1721–1787), with whom he had two children, Mary and John; John lived only a month or two. Three years before his marriage, in 1746, Woolman was working independently as a tailor; gradually he had also developed a retail trade at Mount Holly. Because of his calling to speak against slavery he felt that the 'cumber' of business was beginning to stand in the way of what he demanded from himself:

a humble man with the blessing of the Lord might live on a little, and … where the heart was set on greatness, success in business did not satisfy the craving, but … in common with an increase of wealth the desire of wealth increased. (*Journal and Major Essays*, 35)

Throughout his life Woolman made a plea for the simple life: 'I had seen the happiness of humility and there was an earnest desire in me to enter deep into it' (*Journal and Major Essays*, 35). Coupled with his concern over slavery was his regard for the poor whom he encountered. Next to his journal Woolman's *A Plea for the Poor* (not published until 1793) has become his best-known work and for many years was used by the Fabian Society as one of its tracts. However, in his own day *Some Considerations on the Keeping of Negroes* (1754) proved the more influential. Thomas Drake writes:

No other antislavery document had hitherto received such extensive circulation in any language anywhere. It opened the way and set the pattern for pamphlets by Anthony Benezet on Africa and the slave trade, for pamphleting by John Wesley, Granville Sharpe and Thomas Clarkson in England and for antislavery pronouncements by Philadelphia Yearly Meeting. (Drake, 56)

It was at Philadelphia yearly meeting on 26 August 1758 that Woolman made an impassioned appeal for Friends to abolish the practice of holding slaves: 'In infinite Love and goodness He hath opened our understanding … concerning our duty toward this people; and it is not a time for delay' (*Journal and Major Essays*, 93). On that day the Quakers began the process by which they freed their slaves—the first large body so to do in America. Dean Willard Sperry of Harvard Divinity School says that if he 'were asked to date the birth of social conscience in its present-day form' he would place it at the time Woolman spoke at Philadelphia yearly meeting in 1758 (*Nexus*, 15, 1972, 36).

Woolman continued his journeys, turning his attention again to the south and to New England, where at Newport in 1760 he met with several economically powerful Quaker slaveholders, who in time would follow the example of their Philadelphia brethren. With other Quaker leaders Woolman also stood by the peace testimony in the conflict which became known as the French and Indian War (1754–63). He also championed the Native Americans, and in 1763 made an extraordinary journey to Wyalusing in Pennsylvania to be among them and to 'feel and understand their life and the spirit they live in; if haply I might receive some instruction from them, or they be in any degree helped forward by my following the leadings of Truth amongst them' (*Journal and Major Essays*, 127). Unlike others of his time Woolman saw that the Indians' plight was similar to the state of black slavery and that for both 'the seeds of great calamity and desolation are sown and growing fast on this continent' (ibid., 129).

Woolman expressed an eirenic attitude toward other religious groups that he encountered on his journeys. These included the Moravians, who operated the missionary community at Wyalusing. He was careful to note that 'the Indians, knowing that the Moravian[s] and I were of different religious Societies' desired 'no jarring or discord' in their meetings together (*Journal and Major Essays*, 132). As such he often worshipped with different religious groups and was never interested in proselytizing.

By 1761 Woolman had given up his successful retail merchandising business and had come to rely on tailoring and orchard tending as his gainful occupations. Like a few other Quakers—notably Benjamin Lay and Joshua Evans—he refused to use slave-grown products, including indigo dye. Eliminating dyed clothing presented a 'singularity' which created a stir among some Friends. Woolman's attire was an all-white apparition: 'white hat, coarse raw linen shirt, coat without cuffs, white yarn stockings, and shoes of uncured leather' (Sox, 100–01).

In May 1772, following his recovery from pleurisy, Woolman embarked on what would be his last journey. He decided to travel in steerage across the Atlantic to England rather than in cabin accommodation, remembering how his 'fellow creatures'—the black slaves—had made their passage from Africa. For a long time Woolman had desired to take his concern over slavery to England. He arrived in London in time for yearly meeting and at first his appearance caused him to be regarded as 'some itinerant enthusiast'. But once he spoke 'all obstruction was removed' and he made a powerful impression upon Friends (Cadbury, 45–6).

From London Woolman travelled north on foot as far as Westmorland and Yorkshire. Another concern of his was man's treatment of animals. In his youth he had claimed that to 'say we love God as unseen and at the same time exercise cruelty toward the least creature ... was a contradiction in itself' (*Journal and Major Essays*, 28). Woolman knew that the 'flying coaches' sometimes ran horses to death and he refused to use them. On foot he arrived at York in October 1772, unaware that he was suffering from smallpox. After attending all but one of the sessions of York quarterly meeting he was so ill that he had to be removed outside the city walls to Almery Garth, the home of Thomas and Sarah Priestman, where Esther Tuke nursed him until his death on 7 October 1772. Tuke wrote that he complained little and 'departed without struggle, sigh or groan' (*Journal and Essays*, 148–9). Woolman was buried on 9 October at the Quaker burial-ground at Bishophill in York.

Oddly Woolman probably has been more celebrated in England than in America. Writing in the heat of the 1960s civil-rights debate in America, Edwin Cady noted, 'for all the obvious intellectual culture of both, neither [Martin Luther] King nor [James] Baldwin seems aware of the existence of Woolman' (Cady, 164). However, the accolades for Woolman in England have been generous. Writing in the early nineteenth century Charles Lamb said that Woolman's *Journal* was 'the only American book' he had ever read twice, and Samuel Taylor Coleridge despaired of the man 'who could peruse the life of John Woolman without an amelioration of heart' (Sox, 2). G. M. Trevelyan wrote, 'we should be doing better than we are in the solution of the problems of our own day. Our modern conscience-prickers often are either too "clever" or too violent (than Woolman)' (Trevelyan, 48). For A. N. Whitehead the honour of making the first modern formulation of an explicit purpose to procure the abolition of slavery 'belongs to the Quakers, and in particular to that Apostle of Human Freedom, John Woolman' (Whitehead, 29).

Next to Francis of Assisi, Woolman has become probably the most quoted religious spokesperson for animal concern, and in recent times he has also attracted the interest of environmentalists. In his *Conversations on the True Harmony of Mankind* (composed in 1772 before he left for England but not published until 1837) he wrote, 'The produce of the earth is a gift from our gracious Creator to the inhabitants, and to impoverish the earth now to support outward greatness appears to be an injury to the succeeding age' (Reynolds, 134–5).   DAVID SOX

Sources *The journal and major essays of John Woolman*, ed. P. P. Moulton (1989) • *The journal and essays of John Woolman*, ed. A. Mott Gummere (1922) • H. J. Cadbury, *John Woolman in England: a documentary supplement* (1971) • E. H. Cady, *John Woolman* (1965) • R. Reynolds, *The wisdom of John Woolman* (1948) • D. Sox, *John Woolman: quintessential Quaker* (1999) • D. B. Shea, *Spiritual autobiography in early America* (1968) • T. E. Drake, *Quakers and slavery in America* (1950) • R. M. Jones, *The Quakers in the American colonies* (1911) • F. B. Tolles, *Quakers and the Atlantic culture* (1960) • J. Whitney, *John Woolman: Quaker* (1943) • A. N. Whitehead, *Adventures of ideas* (1933) • G. M. Trevelyan, *Clio, a muse, and other essays* (1913)
Archives Haverford College, Pennsylvania, Quaker collection, corresp. and MSS • Hist. Soc. Penn., corresp. and MSS • RS Friends, Lond., letters and other papers • RS Friends, Lond., material • Swarthmore College, Swarthmore, Pennsylvania, Friends Historical Library, corresp. and MSS

Woolmer, Alfred Joseph (1805–1892), literary and historical genre painter, was born on 20 December 1805. Nothing is known of his parents or about his education. Although his place of birth is usually identified as Exeter (a historic seat of the Woolmer family), census records list his birthplace as Chelsea, Middlesex. At the age of twenty-two he began contributing to exhibitions of the Royal Academy, the British Institution, and the recently formed Society of British Artists, to which he was elected a member in 1841. For the next decade this exceptionally prolific artist exhibited ten to sixteen pictures with the society each year, in addition to contributions elsewhere. These numbers halved from 1853 and declined to two or three a year from 1875. Nevertheless, his sixty-year career yielded a total of 355 works exhibited with the society, forty-five with the British Institution, and twelve at the Royal Academy.

Woolmer's paintings embody the concept of *ut pictura poesis*. Although he often illustrated specific incidents from favourite writers—chiefly Shakespeare, Byron, Milton, and Tennyson—he concentrated on evoking the mood of his literary and historical subjects. Suffused with a nebulous atmosphere suggestive of nostalgia and romance, his pictures rely on exotic costumes, quaint manners, and sumptuous settings to conjure the enchantments of imagined worlds. In formulating his rich, painterly style, he culled lessons from an eclectic array of past artists, some studied on the continent, others at old master exhibitions held annually in London. One such exhibition in the summer of 1832 provided the subject of an uncharacteristically realistic painting, *Interior of the British Institution* (Yale U. CBA). Woolmer offered self-conscious tributes to influential precursors in more fanciful paintings such as *Rembrandt's Studio* (ex Christies, London, 16 May 1962) and *Titian Contemplating Colour* (ex Lowndes Lodge Gallery, London, May 1968). He was best-known for sensuous, mildly erotic images of ladies at their *toilette* and for elegant courtship scenes set in light-dappled gardens and shady bowers. Although inspired by Antoine Watteau, such imagery also links him with the English vogue for romantic historical costume pieces initiated in the 1820s and 1830s. Woolmer scouted out striking scenic effects during sketching trips to Scotland, northern Wales, the Sussex coast, the Alps, Italy, and France. His predilections for rich impasto, the dissolution of form by light, and pyrotechnical meteorological phenomena generated a visionary style reminiscent of Turner or Samuel Palmer.

Conspicuous in both number and appearance, Woolmer's exhibition contributions were singled out for prominent critical notice during the 1850s and 1860s. Writers praised the splendour of his imaginative vision and technical facility but complained that he squandered his exceptional gifts by relying on splashy atmospheric effects to disguise cursory drawing and negligent finish. Many were perplexed by the lack of obvious meaning in his more enigmatic subjects. His copious output supports the charge of hasty work, but critical demands for clarity of subject and execution were inappropriate in view of his intentions. His rejection of narrative in favour of the evocation of mood, and his painterly concern with expressive brushwork and daring effects of light and colour, placed him at odds with contemporary art trends and help to explain his exclusion from official honours and monographic critical notice.

Woolmer changed residences frequently before moving in 1849 to Fortis Green, Finchley, Middlesex, where he remained until 1864. He then resided briefly in Holloway, finally settling at 9 Chester Road, New Highgate, from 1868 to 1875. Woolmer was married, though the identity of his wife is unknown, and the Miss Marion Woolmer who exhibited five pictures at the Society of British Artists was presumably his daughter. In 1875 Woolmer moved to 34 Dartmouth Park Avenue, Kentish Town, where he died on 19 April 1892, six years after exhibiting his last picture. In light of his productivity, he left a surprisingly meagre estate.   ROBYN ASLESON

Sources J. Johnson, ed., *Works exhibited at the Royal Society of British Artists, 1824–1893, and the New English Art Club, 1888–1917*, 2 vols. (1975) · 'Society of British Artists', *The Athenaeum* (31 March 1860), 448 · 'Suffolk Street Gallery', *Building News*, 7 (1861), 303–4, esp. 303 · 'Society of British Artists', *The Builder*, 21 (1863), 258 · 'Society of British Artists, Suffolk Street', *Art Journal*, 27 (1865), 132 · 'Fine Arts: Society of British Artists', *Building News*, 13 (1866), 215–16 · 'British Institution', *Art Journal*, 29 (1867), 85 · Graves, *RA exhibitors* · Graves, *Brit. Inst.* · Bénézit, *Dict.*, 3rd edn · d. cert. · census records, 1805 and 1881, London
Wealth at death £313 6s.: resworn probate, April 1893, *CGPLA Eng. & Wales* (1892)

Woolner, Thomas (1825–1892), sculptor, was born on 17 December 1825 at Hadleigh, Suffolk, the son of Thomas Woolner and his wife, Rebecca Leeks. After schooling locally and in London, where his family moved after his father joined the Post Office, he was indentured at the age of twelve to the painter Charles Behnes. On the latter's death in 1840 he joined Behnes's brother William, a talented portrait sculptor, who trained him well, particularly in carving, and gave him work when his apprenticeship finished. In 1842 he entered the Royal Academy Schools, and he first exhibited at the academy the following year, a group: *Eleonora [sic] Sucking the Poison from the Wound of Prince Edward* (1842). His *Death of Boadicea* sent in unsuccessfully in 1844 to the Westminster Hall competition for commissions for the new Palace of Westminster, attracted an enthusiastic press. *Puck* (plaster, exh. British Institution, 1847; Tate collection) and *Eros and Euphrosyne* (Wedgwood black basalt, exh. RA, 1848; priv. coll.), his earliest surviving pieces, are pictorial in approach, following the sculptural conventions of the time.

The event that set the course of Woolner's career occurred in 1847: he met his new studio neighbour, Dante

Thomas Woolner (1825–1892), by Dante Gabriel Rossetti, 1852

Gabriel Rossetti. The two of them, along with John Everett Millais and William Holman Hunt, joined the Cyclographic Society, a sketching club. This foursome, together with three other young artists, formed the Pre-Raphaelite brotherhood (PRB) in 1848—the major force in British art in the 1850s and early 1860s.

The character of Woolner's sculpture now changed. Hunt observed his 'burning ambition to do work of excelling truthfulness and strong poetic spirit'—central Pre-Raphaelite precepts (Hunt, 1.128). The bronze medallion profile portrait of Alfred Tennyson (1848–9; Usher Art Gallery, Lincoln), whom he had met through his friend the poet Coventry Patmore, brilliantly combines their tenets of precise realistic detail and intensity of feeling. He also applied the new principles wholeheartedly in the memorial *William Wordsworth* (1851; Grasmere church, Cumbria), where the profile head of the poet is flanked by minutely observed daffodils, crocuses, celandines, snowdrops, and violets. William Michael Rossetti regarded him as being (after his brother) the most forceful and entertaining member of the PRB—Woolner's poem 'Our Beautiful Lady' is the opening piece in the first issue of their short-lived journal *The Germ*, published in 1850.

His defeat by Frederick Thrupp in the competition for the national monument to Wordsworth for Westminster Abbey (model of the poet, Wordsworth Trust, Grasmere), together with his modest critical and financial success, persuaded Woolner in 1852 to try gold prospecting in Australia with Bernard Smith (1820–1885), a sculptor and friend of the PRB, and Edward Latrobe Bateman, the nephew of the governor of Victoria. His emigration inspired Ford Madox Brown's masterpiece *The Last of England* (Birmingham Museum and Art Gallery). Letters home give a vivid picture of a prospector's life and the countryside. Reckoning that his £50 of gold had cost him £80, Woolner abandoned prospecting in 1853 and returned to Melbourne to sculpt. He modelled numerous portrait medallions at £25 each, including one of William Charles Wentworth (1854; version Art Gallery of New South Wales, Sydney), the campaigner for self-government for New South Wales. Woolner tried—unsuccessfully—to secure the commission for a statue of him for Sydney University. Although busy, he found that his lack of an established record of public sculpture prevented him from obtaining the major commissions necessary to fulfil his ambitions, so he returned to England in 1854.

Woolner persuaded Tennyson—a lifelong friend, along with his wife Emily, and to whom he gave the stories for *Enoch Arden* and *Aylmer's Field*—to sit for a new portrait medallion (plaster version, 1856; Tate collection), which relaunched his career, and then for a bust (model completed about April 1856). The marble bust, finished in 1857, proved to be the turning point of Woolner's career, establishing him as an outstanding bust-maker of men; he rarely tackled women, perhaps recognizing the superiority in this field of Alexander Munro, another sculptor associated with the PRB. Breaking with the classical tradition, he devised an innovative design which set the pattern for most of his busts over the next fifteen years or so: the bust, with almost square-cut shoulders and bold, deep-channelled lines along the edge of the chest, is set on a distinctive oblong base. The naturalistic treatment of Tennyson's curly hair, his frown, and his tightly buttoned coat endows the bust with a brooding presence. Ruskin called it 'a triumph of Art' (letter from Woolner to Mrs Tennyson, 8 March 1857; Woolner, 131–2). Subscribers eventually bought it, and gave it to Tennyson's old Cambridge college, Trinity, which also owns Woolner's bust of the geologist *Adam Sedgwick* (1860) (with *Areolepsis Sedgwickii*, the fossil fish he discovered, appropriately carved on the base) and seated figures of the historian *Thomas Babington Macaulay* (1866) and *William Whewell* (1873), a master of Trinity. Cambridge also acquired Woolner's *Charles Darwin* (1869; botany department, University of Cambridge).

Oxford University, where the PRB had good contacts, gave Woolner his first public commission: a much admired limestone figure of Francis Bacon (1857, cost £70) for a series of great scientists for the Gothic revival University Museum, in whose building Ruskin was involved. Also in this museum is Woolner's Caen stone full-length commemorative figure of Prince Albert (1864) wearing contemporary dress, whose handling Hunt felt settled the vexed question of whether contemporary dress could be used successfully in sculpture. Through Hunt, Woolner met Thomas Combe, the university printer and patron of the PRB, who commissioned busts of himself (1863; AM Oxf.) and *Cardinal Newman* (1867; Keble College, Oxford). The university was also presented in 1866 with Woolner's masterly bust of W. E. Gladstone (AM Oxf.), its pedestal decorated with three reliefs illustrating Homer's *Iliad*, reflecting Gladstone's Homeric expertise. Mrs Gladstone felt the bust went to the core of her husband's personality.

Hunt also introduced Woolner in 1857 to his patron, Thomas Fairbairn from Manchester, who ordered a poignant group of his deaf and dumb children, *Constance and Arthur* (1862; priv. coll.). In it Woolner does not flinch from recording the expressionless faces of the children or from attempting to capture the gentle way they communicate in their silent world.

The success of *Bacon* brought Woolner further architectural commissions. His work for churches included designs for panels for the new pulpit at Llandaff Cathedral (c.1858; all except *Moses on Mount Sinai* destroyed during the Second World War), then being restored by John Prichard and John Pollard Seddon, and a marble reredos with a highly original windswept crucifixion for the church of the Evangelist, Liverpool (1876), designed by G. E. Street. His secular work varied in scale. The young Alfred Waterhouse involved him in an ambitious Gothic-style sculpture programme for the new assize courts at Manchester (1859–64, dem.; some figures survive in Manchester City Galleries). He provided four bronze panels illustrating acts of charity for J. T. Knowles's fountain (1872–3) in Wigton, Cumbria, erected by the philanthropist George Moore as a memorial to his wife.

Established as a portraitist, Woolner received few commissions for imaginative work. However, probably through William Bell Scott, a painter associated with the PRB, he met in 1856 Sir Walter Trevelyan and his wife, Emily, who gave him an outstanding one: *The Lord's Prayer, or, Civilization* (finished 1867) for their hall, decorated by Scott, at Wallington, Northumberland. The group shows a young mother teaching her naked, truculent son, who stands on a pedestal/altar decorated with reliefs illustrating the evils of paganism, to pray. The allegory—Christianity's civilizing influence—is typically PRB, as is the composition and handling, especially the complex twist of the mother's body and her elaborately designed dress, which recall Hunt's paintings.

The few commissions he received for ideal sculpture did not deter Woolner from experimentation. In the 1860s, like many British artists, he attempted to revitalize the old-fashioned neo-classical style and did so successfully by handling it in a more realistic manner. The energetic Achilles in the relief *Achilles Shouting from the Trenches*, from the Gladstone bust pedestal—a version of which he gave as his diploma piece to the Royal Academy—is typical of his approach. In his neo-classical-style relief of a Shakespearian subject, *Virgilia Bewailing the Banishment of Coriolanus* (marble, 1871; St Mary's College, Strawberry Hill, Twickenham), the despair of Virgilia is deepened by the telling gesture of her lifeless outstretched arm. His inventiveness never left him. In *The Housemaid* (bronze, 1892; Salters' Company, London), a life-size figure of a girl kneeling on a doorstep wringing out her cloth, he treats a common urban sight with dignity and without sentimentality, equalling the best depictions of the rural poor by the 'new' sculptors.

With growing critical and financial success, Woolner felt able to buy in 1861, for £1200, 29 Welbeck Street, London, which he initially shared with the critic F. T. Palgrave, and where he lived until his death. In 1864 he married Alice Gertrude Waugh—two of whose sisters married Hunt—with whom he had six children.

From the 1860s Woolner secured commissions for the public statues of the great that became a feature of many towns in England and the empire. An early commission, *John Robert Godley* (bronze, 1863–7; Christchurch, New Zealand), where the subject's cloak is over one arm, was much admired by Godley's friends for its lifelike quality. The dignified *David Sassoon* (1869; Bombay University) is different in character, calling to mind the meticulous paintings of Holy Land life by Hunt with its careful observation of Sassoon's Parsi robes and turban. To commemorate the centenary of the death of Captain Cook (unveiled 1879; Sydney), Woolner modelled a striking figure of him with upraised arm proclaiming his discovery of Australia, a pose that captures the wonder and delight the explorer felt at the moment of discovery. The restless seated figure of John Stuart Mill (1878; Thames Embankment, London) commemorating that explorer of new ideas, seems tormented by thought.

As well as commemorating the famous, Woolner carved a small number of church memorials, ranging in ambition from a modest tablet with a border of ivy and oak, *Mr and Mrs Bright* (after 1870; Unitarian church, Ullet Road, Liverpool), to the austere recumbent effigy *Bishop John Jackson* (1887; St Paul's Cathedral, London). His wall memorial to J. Coleridge Patterson, the first bishop of Melanesia (1875; Merton College Chapel, Oxford), typifies his concern to make a design appropriate to the deceased's life. Local flora surrounds the missionary's portrait medallion, and a corpse laid on a native boat is shown sailing past in the relief below. In contrast, a Rossetti 'stunner' angel with long flowing hair welcomes Mrs Ellen Peel into heaven on her memorial relief (c.1867; Wrexham parish church).

Of all the members of the PRB, Woolner's circle of friends was perhaps the most intellectual, including as it did Gladstone, Browning, Tennyson, and Carlyle and their spouses. His patrons tended to come from learned institutions or to be serious-minded, with artistic pretensions and social consciences; he himself taught at the London Working Men's College. As might be expected from a friend of so many poets, he wrote verse himself, of a high emotional charge. His published work includes *My Beautiful Lady* (1863; Bodl. Oxf., MS Eng. poete 58), which went through three editions, *Pygmalion* (1881), and *Silenus* (1884). Coventry Patmore was amazed by his early poetry. Elected an associate of the Royal Academy in 1871 and a Royal Academician in 1874, he was appointed professor of Sculpture at the academy in 1877, although he resigned five years later, having given no lecture. He died at his home in Welbeck Street on 7 October 1892 and was buried at St Mary's, Hendon.

Woolner was gregarious but could be difficult. W. M. Rossetti saw him as 'a genial personage, full of gusto for many things in life; a vigorous believer in himself and his performances' (*Family Letters*, 131). F. G. Stephens, who had known him for over forty years, wrote in his obituary that Woolner was:

> In every respect a man of energetic character and high aims … His uncompromising habit of calling a spade a spade and

his undeviating courage in denouncing shams, or what he considered such, not less than his outspoken contempt for trivialities, procured for Woolner not a few admirers, and it must be admitted at least an equal number of foes. (*The Athenaeum*, 15 Oct 1892, 522)

Rossetti and Millais's popular success has overshadowed Woolner's contribution to British art and his adherence, like that of Hunt, to those PRB principles that were quickly abandoned by the more famous pair. In sculpture, few contemporaries could equal his poetic works, and none could surpass his busts, which capture the brilliant intellects of some of the icons of the Victorian age. Borough Museums and Galleries, Ipswich, holds a collection of Woolner's sculpture.

TIMOTHY STEVENS

Sources A. Woolner, *Thomas Woolner, RA, sculptor and poet: his life in letters* (1917) • B. Read, *Victorian sculpture* (1982) • B. Read and J. Barnes, eds., *Pre-Raphaelite sculpture: nature and imagination in British sculpture, 1848–1914* (1990) • W. Holman Hunt, *Pre-Raphaelitism and the Pre-Raphaelite brotherhood* (1905–6) • F. G. Stephens, 'Thomas Woolner RA', *Art Journal*, 61 (1894), 80–86 • F. G. Stephens, *The Athenaeum* (15 Oct 1892), 522–30 • *Dante Gabriel Rossetti: his family letters*, ed. W. M. Rossetti (1895) • R. Trevelyan, 'Thomas Woolner: Pre-Raphaelite sculptor', *Apollo*, 107 (1978), 200–05 • *The diary of Ford Madox Brown*, ed. V. Surtees (1981) • *Autobiographical notes of the life of William Bell Scott*, ed. W. Minto, 2 vols. (1892) • C. Cunningham and P. Waterhouse, *Alfred Waterhouse, 1830–1905: biography of a practice* (1992) • CGPLA Eng. & Wales (1893)
Archives Bodl. Oxf., corresp. and papers • Henry Moore Institute, Leeds, Centre for the Study of Sculpture, diaries, photographs | AM Oxf., letters to Mrs Alfred Tennyson and Hallam Tennyson • BL, letters to W. E. Gladstone, Add. MSS 44401–44985 • BL, corresp. with Macmillans, Add. MS 55230 • Bodl. Oxf., letters to J. C. Horsley • Bodl. Oxf., letters to W. M. Rossetti • Bodl. Oxf., letters to F. G. Stephens • Bodl. Oxf., letters to J. L. Tupper and Annie Tupper • Co-operative Union, Holyoake House, Manchester, corresp. with G. J. Holyoake • Lincoln Central Library, Tennyson Research Centre, letters to Lady Tennyson and Hallam Tennyson • Mass. Hist. Soc., letters to Henry Adams • Mitchell L., NSW, letters to Sir Henry Parkes • RBG Kew, letters to J. D. Hooker • U. Leeds, Brotherton L., letters to E. Gosse • U. Newcastle, Robinson L., letters to Sir Walter Trevelyan and Lady Trevelyan
Likenesses D. G. Rossetti, pen and brown ink drawing, 1850, Birmingham Museum and Art Gallery • D. G. Rossetti, pencil drawing, 1852, NPG [*see illus.*] • J. M. Cameron, photograph, 1864, Gernsheim collection • E. Edwards, photograph, 1864, NPG • A. Legros, oils, 1874, Ipswich Borough Museums and Galleries • J. P. Mayall, photograph, c.1875, NPG • Lock & Whitfield, photograph, 1877, NPG; repro. in T. Cooper, *Men of mark: a gallery of contemporary portraits* (1877) • A. C. Gow, oils, 1883, Aberdeen Art Gallery • woodcut, 1883 (after T. B. Wirgman), BM • J. M. Johnstone, woodcut, 1891 (after photograph), BM • R. W. Robinson, photograph, 1891, NPG • cabinet photographs, NPG • photograph, repro. in L. Reeve, ed., *Portraits of men of eminence*; copy, NPG • photographs, cartes-de-visite, NPG
Wealth at death £65,766 19s. 3d.: administration, 7 Feb 1893, CGPLA Eng. & Wales

Woolrich [Wolrich], **Humphrey** (c.1633–1707), religious writer, was probably born at Newcastle under Lyme, Staffordshire, and he spent much of his life in that county, but little else is known of his background.

A Baptist in early life, Woolrich joined the Quakers soon after their rise because he felt that his former brethren had set up 'water instead of the name of the Lord, and the letter instead of the life' (Woolrich, *Declaration*, 25). As a

Quaker, Woolrich actually baptized a female convert in 1658 (contrary to the practice of the sect) and gave an account of this in *The Unlimited God* (1659), in which he related how the woman 'was moved of the Lord to desire me only to baptise her with water, and said, the spirit by which the Baptists are led, did not convince her' (Woolrich, *Unlimited God*, 2). He evidently felt it was better to agree to her request than reject it, for he left it to others to decide 'whether it is better to save life, or to destroy' (ibid.). His actions incurred criticism from some members of the Quaker movement, although he apparently received the support of George Fox.

In 1659 Woolrich was imprisoned in London for preaching and in the same year wrote *A Declaration to the Baptists*, largely an account of a dispute held at Withcock, Leicestershire, on 27 February 1659 at which Isabel Hacker, the wife of Colonel Francis Hacker, was present. At the end of 1660 Woolrich was imprisoned with John Pennyman and Thomas Coveney and together they penned the tract *Some grounds and reasons ... to manifest the unlawfulness of ... magistrates and others who commit men to prison, or fine them for not putting off the hat* (1660). About this time Sir Richard Browne, lord mayor of London in 1661 and a man hostile towards the Quakers, committed Woolrich to prison for keeping his hat on before him. It is possible that this and the former imprisonment were one and the same. During his confinement he again wrote a number of tracts including *To the King and both Houses of Parliament* [1661], concerning Quaker sufferings, in which he wrote,

> though our expectation be to the Lord for deliverance, yet we know right well, that the coming in of King Charles, and the assembling of you together by him, is not without his hand; and as we are freeborn Englishmen, we have just cause to expect much from you, that we should not lie in holes, prisons and dungeons as we have done, and be kept in slavery in the land of our nativity.   (p. 5)

In the same year he also wrote *One More Warning to the Baptists*, in response to the attacks on Quaker theology by Mathew Caffyn. He saw two further periods of incarceration during 1661, one at Staffordshire, where he was taken from a meeting, afterwards refusing the oath of allegiance, and the second time at Leicestershire.

On 2 December 1662 Woolrich arrived in Chester at the end of the assizes. The following Sunday he entered the cathedral during the anthem, and when the singing ceased attempted to speak, but was hastily removed and confined in the castle. In February 1682 he was fined £20 and sent to prison for offering prayers at the burial of a Quaker woman in her husband's garden at Keele, Staffordshire, the minister having threatened to arrest the corpse if Woolrich did not pay the fees.

Little is known of Woolrich's life beyond the 1680s. He wrote about twenty tracts during his lifetime. One of his later works, a broadside, concerned periwigs, which he criticized some 'ministering Friends' for wearing, adding, however, that his heart was 'tender' towards 'aged Friends, or any who, through weakness have lost their hair' (H. Woolrich, *A Brief Testimony Against Friends Wearing of Perriwigs*, 1708).

Prior to his death Woolrich suffered for two years from cancer of the mouth and was 'troubled with a great swelling in his face and mouth, which much deprived him of his speech' (Tomkins, 2.92). He died at the Friends' almshouses, Clerkenwell, on 31 August 1707 and was buried on 2 September.

CHARLOTTE FELL-SMITH, *rev.* CAROLINE L. LEACHMAN

Sources J. Besse, *A collection of the sufferings of the people called Quakers*, 1 (1753) · H. Woolrich, *A declaration to the Baptists* (1659) · H. Woolrich, *The unlimited God* (1659) · J. Tomkins, *Piety promoted*, rev. J. Kendal, 2 (1789) · J. Smith, ed., *A descriptive catalogue of Friends' books*, 2 (1867) · RS Friends, Lond., Quaker Digest Registers
Archives BL, 'This is a living testimony', Harley MSS 6813, fols. 88, 89, 91 · RS Friends, Lond., Portfolio MSS 6/29, 15/126

Woolrych, Humphry William (1795–1871), biographer and legal writer, was born at Southgate, Middlesex, on 24 September 1795, the son of Humphry Cornewall Woolrych (d. 1816), landowner of Croxley in Rickmansworth, Hertfordshire, and his wife, Elizabeth, elder daughter and coheir of William Bentley of Red Lion Square, London. He was descended from Sir Thomas Wolrich, first baronet, of Shropshire. He was educated at Eton College and matriculated from St Edmund Hall, Oxford, on 14 December 1816, but did not proceed to a degree. On 3 July 1817 at Abbots Langley, Hertfordshire, he married Penelope (d. 1876), youngest daughter of Francis Bradford of Great Westwood, Hertfordshire; they had three sons and four daughters.

Woolrych was admitted student at Lincoln's Inn on 24 November 1819, and called to the bar in 1821. In 1830 he was called *ad eundem* at the Inner Temple; he was admitted at Gray's Inn on 13 July 1847, and in 1855 he was created serjeant-at-law. He published three works on the post of serjeant-at-law, including *Lives of Eminent Serjeants-at-Law* (1869), and was a persistent advocate of the maintenance of the order. He published other biographical volumes, notably a life of Edward Coke and one of Judge Jeffreys. He was the author of numerous legal texts, some poetry, and a novel, *Our Island* (1832).

Woolrych lived at Croxley and at 9 Petersham Terrace, Kensington. He died at home in Kensington on 2 July 1871, and was buried in Rickmansworth cemetery.

W. P. COURTNEY, *rev.* ERIC METCALFE

Sources Foster, *Alum. Oxon.* · Burke, *Gen. GB* · *GM*, 1st ser., 63 (1793), 861 [marriage of Humphry Cornewall Woolrych] · *GM*, 1st ser., 86/1 (1816), 376 [obit. of Humphry Cornewall Woolrych] · W. P. Baildon, ed., *The records of the Honorable Society of Lincoln's Inn* [incl. *Admissions*, 2 vols. (1896), and *Black books*, 6 vols. (1897–2001)] · private information (1900)
Wealth at death under £14,000: probate, 15 July 1871, *CGPLA Eng. & Wales*

Woolston, Thomas (*bap.* 1668, *d.* 1733), religious controversialist, was baptized in November 1668 at St Sepulchre's, Northampton, the fourth of the six surviving children of Henry Woolston (d. 1694), currier, and his wife, Ann. A tanner in a town noted for the leather trade, his father served on the vestry of St Sepulchre and in local government. His younger brother Joseph (d. 1742) was a leather merchant and a churchwarden, like their father, and became mayor of Northampton. When their father died in 1694 he left £100 to his first son, Henry, £150 to Joseph, and one broad piece of gold 20s. to Thomas.

Apparently unsuited for trade, Woolston attended the Northampton Free School and then another school in nearby Daventry before admission to Sidney Sussex College, Cambridge, at sixteen. His tutor was James Johnson and his friends included Bardsey Fisher, Joseph Craven, and Richard Allin. His signatures in the *Liber gratiarum* of the university indicate that he graduated BA in 1689, MA in 1692, and BD in 1699. He had probably participated in the disputations required for these degrees, but his name does not appear on the honours lists. He was elected a foundation fellow of his college on 17 January 1691 and took holy orders soon afterwards. In 1693 he obtained recognition of his MA from Oxford.

Woolston soon began to read Origen and, ascribing to other church fathers his belief in the figurative, rather than the literal, significance of the events recorded in the Bible, he concluded that only a figurative exegesis of biblical texts could yield the ultimate truth of scripture. Thus he believed that the material events recorded in the Bible prefigured spiritual events. He drew a parallel, for instance, between Pharaoh drowning with his army in the Red Sea and the Roman emperor drowning with his empire in the sea of Christianity. His doctrine, which he aired in the English and Latin sermons required for the BD, shocked his listeners, yet they did not protest because they considered him a competent theologian.

Woolston published his English sermon in 1722 as *The Exact Fitness of the Time in which Christ was Manifested in the Flesh* and his Latin sermon in 1720 as the *Dissertatio de Ponti Pilati ad Tiberium epistola circa res Jesu Christi gestas* ('Dissertation on Pontius Pilate's letter to Tiberius about the acts of Jesus Christ'). He developed the subject of the latter in his 384-page *Old Apology for the Truth of the Christian Religion* (1705), printed in an edition of 750 copies by Cambridge University Press, on whose board of curators he sat. In this work he argued that, even though the letter supposedly by Pilate was spurious, Pilate would have sent such a letter and that it probably would have conveyed a request by Jesus that the Romans, who often adopted the gods of conquered nations, worship him. Although Woolston condemned both Pharaoh and the emperors for denying their subjects the right to embrace the true faith, he praised the kings of England for forcing theirs to embrace protestantism.

The angry reaction to this work drove Woolston to contemplate an 'exit out of this world [for] shame' (T. Woolston, *A Free Gift to the Clergy*, 1722, 5). His ideas seemed 'so wild' to his colleagues that a rumour slandered him with 'a disorder of mind' and, when he heard it, 'he grew really disordered and … was accordingly confined for a long time' (Whiston, 1.198). He would later admit to having had 'the misfortune of a distracted brain' and would pray God 'to continue me in that state of reason he has been … pleased to restore me to' (T. Woolston, *A Free Gift to the Clergy*, 50). After his release he wrote letters (now lost) to friends and famous people attributing the rumour of his madness to the inability of his enemies to refute his doctrine.

The pamphlets that Woolston published in London expressed his resentment of the clergy for their rejection of his figurative interpretation of scripture. Although he is aggressive and self-pitying in the first of his four pamphlets entitled *A Free Gift to the Clergy*, none of these writings suggests mental disorder. He answered his own four *Free Gifts* (1722–4) by his ironical *Ministry of the Letter Vindicated* (1724) and also answered his *Letters to the Reverend Dr. Bennet* (1720–21), in which he defended the Quakers, who he believed shared his figurative doctrine, with another pamphlet published in 1721. Although initially in vain, he had dedicated himself to provoking a controversy that would give him an opportunity to advocate his doctrine.

Woolston's confinement must have ended before 1720, when his *Dissertatio* appeared in London. Despite his absence, Sidney Sussex College continued to pay his biannual stipend to friends on his behalf from 1705 until 1724. Successive masters—first Bardsey Fisher, then Joseph Craven—maintained his fellowship, on the pretext of a bodily distemper, but he finally lost it by denying that he had one. Henceforth he lived on the sale of his pamphlets and a pension of £30 from Joseph. He invited the public to buy them from him in the City of London, at Bell Alley, Coleman Street, Moorgate, at first, and then next door below the Star in Aldermanbury. 'He defrayed all the expenses of [his] booksellers, printers and publishers' (Stackhouse, 23).

Unable to provoke a controversy, Woolston intervened in one already in progress. The deist Anthony Collins had challenged the clergy, in his *Discourse of the Grounds and Reasons of the Christian Religion* (1724), to prove that Jesus had accomplished Old Testament prophecy. On the pretext of arbitrating the dispute, Woolston attacked the literal interpretation of Jesus's miracles, in his *Moderator between an Infidel and an Apostate* (1725). He argued that the clergy had committed the apostasy of sacrificing the spirit for the letter. His assault on the literal significance of the resurrection and the virgin birth gave rise to the scandal he had been longing for. Apparently the bishop of London, Edmund Gibson, induced Charles Yorke, the attorney-general, to prosecute him for blasphemy and the court of king's bench convicted him but, before it could sentence him, the controversialist, William Whiston persuaded Yorke to withdraw the case because of the court's incompetence in theology.

Woolston acknowledged Whiston's generosity in his next work, the *Defence of the Miracle of the Thundering Legion* (1726), in which he apparently intended to refute the accusations of his enemies, who denied that he was a Christian. Unfortunately, his six *Discourses on the Miracles of our Saviour* (1727–9) had just the opposite effect. Each discourse began with an ironical dedication to one of the leading bishops of his day: Edmund Gibson, Edward Chandler, Richard Smalbroke, Francis Hare, Thomas Sherlock, and John Potter. At the start of each discourse he criticized the literal interpretation of miracles before providing a figurative interpretation that he attributed to the fathers. He relied on quotations, often spurious or altered, to substantiate his intention of restoring primitive Christianity, which he conflated with a synthesis of patristic theology. His interpretation identified four kinds of miracles which he then questioned: harmful miracles, such as Jesus withering the fig tree that bore no fruit out of season and converting water into wine for drinkers who had already drunk too much; innocuous miracles, as when Jesus divined the Samaritan woman's five husbands; healings, for example the cure of the woman with the issue of blood and the man born blind; and resurrections, of Jairus's daughter, the widow of Naim's son, and Lazarus, whose deaths he doubted. Although he accepted Jesus's own death, Woolston none the less suspected that his disciples had plied the guards with drink and stolen the body while they slept, and he argued that the resurrection was spiritual and not literal. He likewise interpreted the transfiguration as a parable prophesying a spiritual transfiguration which he had already discussed in his third and fourth *Free Gifts*. Here he related two voyages that he had made to heaven, where he had consulted Elijah and the church fathers on this transfiguration.

Evidently, Woolston was no deist, but rather a mystic, yet his sarcasm suggested that he was trying to destroy Christianity. His circumstantial affinity with deist writers such as Collins earned him an undeserved reputation for deism. The bishops to whom he had ironically dedicated his *Discourses* scornfully dismissed his professions of Christianity. More than sixty replies appeared in print, including two learned volumes by Richard Smalbroke, bishop of St David's. Archbishop Wake, Gibson, Smalbroke, and other clergymen urged the civil magistrate to prosecute him for blasphemy, which Gibson, in a pastoral letter, defined as a ludicrous or shameful treatment of religion.

Woolston's *Discourses* were selling in the thousands and the early *Discourses* ran to six editions. The *Sixth Discourse* appeared just two weeks before the jury of the king's bench found him guilty of blasphemy. The common law subsumed blasphemy under subversive libel, which it defined as language that tended to undermine the authority of church or state. Conviction depended on the effect of the language rather than the intention behind it and, in practice, on an assumption of public disapproval. The chief justice, therefore, only had to confirm such an assumption by the jury. Remanded to the king's bench prison in Southwark, Woolston waited five months for sentencing, which the judges kept postponing in an attempt to extract a promise from him that he would publish nothing further. Undeterred, he published Part 1 of the *Defence of his Discourses* (1729). The judges promptly sentenced him to a £25 fine for each of the first four *Discourses*, and a one-year prison term. To prevent further publication, they extended his imprisonment until he should agree to stop, and imposed security of £2000. He never yielded.

Woolston soon purchased the liberty of the rules so that he could live outside the overcrowded prison, and he was allowed to return to his old address in the City, where he continued to sell his pamphlets. After the second part of his *Defence* appeared in print in 1730 he published a portrait of himself engraved by Vandergucht after a painting by Dandridge (now lost). Offended by his presence in the Chapter Coffee House, the clergymen who frequented it soon succeeded in having him confined within the prison. Three weeks later, however, he left again to reside in Birdcage Alley in the nearby Mint.

Apparently a victim of the influenza epidemic that killed John Gay, Woolston died in Birdcage Alley in January 1733, and was buried in the churchyard of St George the Martyr in Southwark. His brother Joseph inherited his books and papers, which have since disappeared.

WILLIAM H. TRAPNELL

Sources [T. Stackhouse], *The life of Mr Woolston, with an impartial account of his writings* (1733) · H. Lemker, *Historische Nachricht von Thomas Woolstons Schiksal, Schriften und Streitigkeiten* (Leipzig, 1740) · W. Whiston, *Memoirs of the life and writings of Mr William Whiston: containing memoirs of several of his friends also*, 2nd edn, 2 vols. (1753), vol. 1 · W. H. Trapnell, *Thomas Woolston: madman and deist ?* (1994) · *Selections from the journals and papers of John Byrom, poet-diarist, short-hand writer, 1691–1763*, ed. H. Talon (1950), 1.i–ii · *Account of the trial of T. W.* (1729) · D. F. McKenzie, *Cambridge University Press, 1696–1712: a bibliographical study*, 2 vols. (1966) · Venn, *Alum. Cant.* · *DNB* · parish register (baptism), Northampton, St Sepulchre, Nov 1688 · parish register (burial), Southwark, St George the Martyr, Jan 1733 **Archives** BL, Add. MSS 35585, 35886, 36136, 5821 · CUL · CUL, Liber Gratiarum · Northants. RO, MS 22211 · Northants. RO, parish registers · PRO, state papers domestic · PRO, TS · PRO, probate court of Canterbury · Sidney Sussex College, Cambridge, account book, fellows' records, registers · Sidney Sussex College, Cambridge, Allin MSS · Southwark Local Studies Library, London, rates books **Likenesses** J. Vandergucht, line engraving (after B. Dandridge), BM, NPG **Wealth at death** very little; will, PRO

Woolton. For this title name *see* Marquis, Frederick James, first earl of Woolton (1883–1964).

Woolton, John (*c.*1537–1594), bishop of Exeter, was born near Whalley, Lancashire, the son of John Woolton of Wigan. Although his father was of humble origins, his mother was a younger daughter of John Nowell of Read Hall, Whalley, the brother of Alexander and Laurence Nowell, and it was to Alexander that the young John Woolton owed his education. On 26 October 1553, only weeks after the accession of Queen Mary, Woolton became a student at Brasenose College, Oxford, where Alexander Nowell was a fellow. He supplicated for the degree of BA on 26 April 1555, aged about eighteen. He was still at Brasenose in October, but soon afterwards fled abroad to join Nowell in exile, perhaps in Frankfurt. The two men probably returned to England in spring 1559.

In 1560 Woolton was ordained priest by Edmund Grindal, bishop of London, and later married the daughter of Protector Somerset's purveyor of household provisions. His first ecclesiastical preferment came in 1563, when he received the crown living of Spaxton, Somerset, and soon afterwards became chaplain to Gilbert Berkeley, bishop of Bath and Wells. In 1565 he became rector of Sampford Peverell, Devon, and a year later was collated to a prebend in Exeter Cathedral. By this time he had become known as a preacher, and in 1568 Sir Peter Carew and Sir John Chichester asked Grindal to intercede with Archbishop Matthew Parker to grant Woolton a licence for non-residence, so that he might preach more freely and without hindrance. Grindal duly petitioned Parker on 2 July, assuring the archbishop that Woolton would not neglect his cure if granted such dispensation because he was 'reported to be a man of very good conscience' (Nicholson, 299).

In 1570 Woolton was admitted to the rectory of Braunton, Devon, and admitted a canon residentiary of Exeter Cathedral. A series of preferments in Devon followed: the rectories of Farringdon (1571); Whimple (1572, at the presentation of Francis Russell, second earl of Bedford); and of Kenn (1573). At Oxford in 1574 he was dispensed from taking the degree of MA before proceeding BTh (which he did in 1579, at the same time proceeding DTh). He was appointed warden of Manchester collegiate church in 1575, and during the next two years published a series of six treatises on Christian life reflecting the school of theology associated with Grindal and his circle. Over sixty more such tracts remained unpublished at his death. During the 1570s he read a divinity lecture twice a week in Exeter Cathedral for four years and preached twice every Sunday. In the plague year of 1576 he conscientiously remained in Exeter to continue his preaching and to minister to the sick.

Following the death of Bishop William Bradbridge on 28 June 1578, the earl of Bedford urged William Cecil, Lord Burghley, to press for Woolton's appointment to the see of Exeter. He was elected on 2 July 1579 and consecrated on 2 August, retaining all his promotions except his canonry. Since Exeter was an impoverished see, worth only about £500 per annum, Woolton was allowed to hold two further livings *in commendam*: Lazant in Cornwall from 1584 and Haccombe in Devon from 1585. Following his installation he at once set about the primary visitation of his diocese, but due to ill health had to hand responsibility over to deputies. His visitation was similarly conducted by others, this time due to his wife's sickness. But Bedford's hopes that the new bishop should be a diligent and preaching divine were certainly fulfilled, and Woolton continued his practice of expounding scripture regularly on Sundays.

Woolton's episcopate was not without difficulties. He received a constant stream of directives from government, and had serious conflicts with radical protestants, notably Eusebius Pagit, presented to Kilkhampton in Cornwall in 1580. A long-standing puritan activist, Pagit allied himself with the local schoolmaster David Black, a Scottish presbyterian, in making his parish a centre of resistance to the established church. In 1584–5 the two men were cited before the high commission in London. Black backed down and eventually returned to Scotland, while Pagit was first suspended and then deprived, whereupon he counter-attacked against Woolton, accusing him of moral and ecclesiastical shortcomings which included nepotism, failing to visit his diocese, not hearing sermons, and refusing to discipline delinquent members of his own household. The bishop had to defend himself

before Archbishop Whitgift. Unsurprisingly, perhaps, Woolton's religious standpoint became steadily more conservative from about this time. It is said that when on 13 March 1594 he died at his palace in Exeter of asthma, from which he had suffered for some time, several nonconformist ministers were waiting in his consistory court anticipating deprivation. He was buried seven days later on the south side of his cathedral choir. A monumental inscription was placed in the south tower.

Woolton was survived by two sons, John and Matthew, and by five daughters, Margaret Barrett, Susan Goodwin, Mary Baber, Hester, and Alice. John, who had been a fellow of All Souls College, Oxford, was imprisoned for a while by his father for converting to Catholicism, but later returned to the Church of England, and in 1593 was licensed to practise medicine. Clearly now reconciled with his father, he was made the latter's residuary legatee and also his executor. Margaret's husband was Thomas Barrett, whom Woolton made archdeacon of Exeter and referred to in his will as a dear friend. Matthew, Hester, and Alice were unmarried, the girls still under twenty when their father died. Woolton left £100 to each of his three married daughters, 400 marks and silver plate worth £40 to Matthew, and £200 apiece to Hester and Alice. There were small bequests for three of his servants, but £50 to be distributed among the poor of Exeter and of the parishes of Kenn and Lazant. Known in his day as a good and diligent preacher, Woolton was also acknowledged to have been a well-learned and wise pastor of his flock.

KENNETH CARLETON

Sources Foster, *Alum. Oxon., 1500–1714*, 4.1669 · C. B. Heberden, ed., *Brasenose College register, 1509–1909* (1909) · G. Oliver, *Lives of the bishops of Exeter, and a history of the cathedral* (1861) · J. A. Vage, 'The diocese of Exeter, 1519–1641: a study of church government in the age of the Reformation', PhD diss., U. Cam., 1991 · F. O. White, *Lives of the Elizabethan bishops of the Elizabethan church* (1898) · W. Nicholson, ed., *The remains of Edmund Grindal*, Parker Society, 9 (1843) · Wood, *Ath. Oxon.*, new edn, 1.600–01 · A. L. Rowse, *Tudor Cornwall*, 2nd edn (1969) · P. Collinson, *The Elizabethan puritan movement* (1967) · will, PRO, PROB 11/83, sig. 37
Archives BL, Harleian MS 5827, fol. 50
Wealth at death pecuniary bequests of £1047; left silver plate valued at £40; two gold rings; unspecified residue: will, PRO, PROB 11/83, sig. 37

Wootton [*née* Adam], **Barbara Frances**, **Baroness Wootton of Abinger** (1897–1988), university professor, was born on 14 April 1897 in Cambridge, the only daughter and youngest of three children of James *Adam (1860–1907), tutor at Emmanuel College, Cambridge, and his wife, Adela Marion Kensington, classicist and a fellow of Girton. Her father had been born into the family of a farm worker in Aberdeenshire, whence he made his way by scholarship from village school to Cambridge University and a degree in classics.

Barbara herself was healthy, good-looking, and precocious. Her father died when she was ten and he only forty-seven. Her best schoolfriend died at school, and her brother Arthur in war. She was then widowed by war. Her husband, John Wesley (Jack) Wootton, a research student at Trinity College, Cambridge, and the son of Arthur

Barbara Frances Wootton, Baroness Wootton of Abinger (1897–1988), by Walter Bird, 1964

Wootton, from a nonconformist manufacturing family in Nottingham, was a friend of her elder brother Neil. They were married on 5 September 1917 and had thirty-six hours together before she saw him off to France at Victoria Station. He died of wounds on 11 October 1917 and in due course the War Office returned to her his blood-stained uniform. It is reasonable to speculate that the phobias and obsessions which plagued her had their origins in these adversities. Yet she herself remained resolutely pre-Freudian in her attitudes towards responsibility in the face of disaster. Utter self-reliance was her creed. 'We would do better', she thought, 'to encourage children from the earliest possible age, however wretched their backgrounds, to believe that they are, or at least soon will be, masters of their fates.'

Though Barbara prayed earnestly to be sent away to school like her brothers, she did not escape the home nursery until at thirteen she was allowed to enter the Perse High School for Girls in Cambridge as a day pupil. Her mother wanted her to study classics at Girton College, and she was dutifully successful in the entrance examinations, becoming a candidate for the first part of the tripos, even though her strong personal inclination was to abandon dead languages for Alfred Marshall and modern economics. As her final examinations approached she succumbed, apparently psychosomatically, to virulent tonsillitis. Her illness caused her to get an *aegrotat* degree (1918). Liberation from the well intentioned matriarchal dominion of her childhood began with part two of the tripos.

She put aside the Greek and Latin texts and turned to read economics with determined enthusiasm. She gained a first class in 1919. Yet, ironically, as a woman she was prevented from appending BA to her name.

After leaving Cambridge Wootton took up a research studentship at the London School of Economics. In 1920 Girton recalled her to a fellowship and the directorship of social studies in the college, and the board of economics invited her to lecture on economics and the state. The University of Cambridge at this time did not officially allow the admission of women and therefore could not license lectures by a non-member. Hubert Henderson intervened gallantly, offering himself as the advertised lecturer but on the understanding that the university would add in brackets that the lectures would be delivered by Mrs Wootton.

Wootton married again in 1935, her second husband being George Percival Wright, the son of Thomas Wright, of 29 Prothero Road, London. He was her colleague in adult education and London government, and was temporarily a cab driver. There was no permanent peace, for Wright turned out to be a 'natural polygamist', who kept a succession of 'secondary wives' round the corner, though making it clear to each that his loyalty to Barbara was paramount. She nursed him through a long illness until he died of cancer in 1964. There were no children of the marriage.

Wootton forsook not only the classics but also conventional scholarship and institutional religion. Her circumstances and her temperament gradually formed her into a rationalist, an agnostic, and a socialist—a method, a philosophy, and a commitment which lent steady consistency to a long professional and public life. Her rationalism evolved, no doubt, in part from sheer intellectual power but also from the experience of bereavement and the illogicality of a gifted woman's place in her society. Her agnosticism was nurtured by deep scepticism about the benevolence of any conceivable deity or principle of cosmic order in the First World War. Her socialism was rooted in the same experiences which convinced her that, given sympathy for others, critical reason was the only road to salvation on this earth.

Wootton worked for the research department of the Labour Party and the Trades Union Congress from 1922, as principal of Morley College from 1926, and as director of studies for tutorial classes at London University from 1927 until she took up a readership at Bedford College in 1944. In that year she was disappointed in a competition for the chair and headship of the department of social science at the London School of Economics, which went to T. H. Marshall. Within academe her preoccupation was always with practical problems. She was promoted to the rank of professor in 1948. She became an acknowledged expert in criminology, penology, and social work, writing many books on those subjects. Her *Social Science and Social Pathology* (with V. G. Seal and R. Chambers, 1959) remains a classic in the application of utilitarian philosophy and empirical sociology to the enlightened management of society. From 1952 to 1957 she was Nuffield research fellow at Bedford College.

Wootton became an outstandingly vigorous public figure. She was a governor of the BBC from 1950 to 1956 and served on four royal commissions (workmen's compensation, 1938–44; the press, 1947–9; the civil service, 1953–5; and the penal system, 1964–6). She was also chairman of the Countryside Commission (1968–70). Created a life peer in 1958, she was the first woman to sit on the woolsack in the House of Lords, as deputy speaker from 1967. Her ambivalence to the upper chamber surprised some democratic socialists. She recognized that it was 'totally indefensible in a democracy'. 'No one in his senses would invent the present house if it did not already exist … but … ancient monuments are not light-heartedly to be destroyed.' More generally she made the best of the institutions she found and was unwilling to see her country pay the price in misery to ordinary people that revolution along Stalinist lines would entail. She preferred to work piecemeal, and her service as a justice of the peace for London, to which she was appointed in 1926 at the age of twenty-nine, that is, before she was entitled as a woman to vote, is a long record of humane public effort. She held thirteen honorary doctorates and was made a CH in 1977. She died on 11 July 1988 at her house, Holmesdale Park, Coopers Hill Road, Nutfield, Surrey, admired by those who knew her, honoured by a Festschrift, and widely revered as a woman whose steadfast faith was in argument and persuasion towards a socialist commonwealth.

A. H. HALSEY, rev.

Sources *The Independent* (13 July 1988) · *The Times* (13 July 1988) · *Barbara Wootton: selected writings*, ed. P. Bean and V. G. Seal, 4 vols. (1993) · P. Bean and D. Whynes, eds., *Barbara Wootton: essays in her honour* (1986) · B. Wootton, *In a world I never made* (1967) · T. Morris, 'In memoriam: Barbara Wootton, 1897–1988', *British Journal of Sociology*, 40 (1989), 310–18 · personal knowledge (1996) · *CGPLA Eng. & Wales* (1988)

Archives BL, letters to Albert Mansbridge · Rice University, Houston, Texas, Woodson Research Center, corresp. with Sir Julian Huxley

Likenesses W. Bird, photograph, 1964, NPG [*see illus.*]

Wealth at death £396,833: probate, 15 Aug 1988, *CGPLA Eng. & Wales*

Wootton, John (1681/2–1764), landscape painter and sporting artist, was born in Snitterfield, Warwickshire, and may have been the John Wootton who was baptized on 13 June 1684 at Hampton Lucy, Warwickshire, the son of Thomas Wootten and his wife, Elizabeth. Of his early years, virtually nothing is known beyond his presumed service as a page to Anne Somerset, daughter of the first duke of Beaufort, who became countess of Coventry in 1691. Lady Anne's family connections probably launched Wootton's career, which began under the tutorship of the Dutch painter John Wyck, presumably at Mortlake, Surrey, in the late 1690s. On 8 April 1706 a licence was issued for Wootton to marry Elizabeth Walsh (*b.* 1679/80) at St Giles-in-the-Fields, Middlesex, or St Peter Paul's Wharf, London.

There is no trace of Wootton's youthful works such as those Horace Walpole saw at Shortgrove and at Audley

John Wootton (1681/2–1764), by Bernard (III) Lens, *c.*1720

End in Essex, and Joseph Farington noted at Antony House in Cornwall. Wootton's artistic reputation was well established by the second decade of the eighteenth century when he painted life-size portraits of horses for the duke of Rutland (*Bonny Black*, 1711, Belvoir Castle, Leicestershire) and the duke of Devonshire (*Scarr with his Trainer A. Scotman*, 1714, Chatsworth, Derbyshire). In 1714 Edward Harley, second earl of Oxford, became Wootton's most munificent patron. From that time Wootton received a steady demand for replications of his popular Newmarket set pieces of *The Warren Hill* and for variations on the formula he devised for the newly emergent English thoroughbred racehorse classically profiled against a decorous landscape, often accompanied by an exotic Arabian groom.

Wootton's contribution in moulding the English landscape painting tradition, though less appreciated than his innovations in the sporting genre, was considerable. As the first native artist to adapt the pastoral mode to the representation of English rural scenery, notably in *View from Box Hill* (1716, Welbeck Woodhouse, Nottinghamshire), he was a vital link between Dutch émigré artists in England in the late seventeenth century and English painters who came to prominence in the second half of the eighteenth. In the early 1720s he recast the classical landscape idiom of Gaspard Dughet and Claude Lorrain, making it relevant to the moral and aesthetic values of Englishmen of the Augustan age. Works which bear the didactic and ironic imprint of his literary landscape sensibility include *Classical Landscape with a Temple* (early 1730s, Mapledurham House, Oxfordshire), painted for Alexander Pope, and *Landscape with a Statue of Hercules* (c.1730–c.1735, Cornbury Park, Oxfordshire). The frequent suggestion that Wootton's dissemination of this classical idiom in England ensued from a trip he made to Italy sponsored by the third duke of Beaufort remains unsubstantiated and unlikely.

Although Wootton was an assiduous worker, he was also a convivial companion. In the company of his artist friends he was apt to 'draw nothing but corks' (Whitley, 1.78). His witty puns enlivened Harley's circle of virtuosi and literati. His satirical inclinations are evident in his frontispiece to James Bramston's *The Art of Politicks* (1729), in his illustrations to John Gay's *Fables* (1727), and in the mock-heroic form of his canine portraits. A glimpse of his congenial domestic life is offered in a family portrait by Gawen Hamilton (1736, priv. coll.) which depicts Wootton's second wife, Rebecca Rutty (c.1693–1748), whom he married in 1716 (probably on 27 February), his two surviving children, Henry (*b.* 1721, *d.* after 1767) and Elizabeth (1728–1767), and an elderly woman presumed to be his mother.

Wootton's 'great Vogue & favour with many persons of the greatest Quality' (Vertue, *Note books*, 3.34) may be credited to his acuity, accommodating manner, and extraordinary versatility. While his professional reputation was established with his paintings of the pedigree horses and hounds of titled patrons, his range expanded to tapestry-size hunting pieces (in the great halls at Badminton House, Gloucestershire; Althorp, Northamptonshire; and Longleat House, Wiltshire), vast representations of military sieges (*Battle of Lille* and *Battle of Tournay*, 1742, Royal Collection), topographical and classical landscapes, and sporting conversation pieces. When reliable portraiture was needed, he collaborated with various artists (including Kneller, Hogarth, Richardson, Hudson, and Jervas) who could render the likenesses he was either unable or unwilling to provide.

Wootton ceased painting about 1760 when artistic careers were increasingly advanced by public exhibitions rather than aristocratic patronage. Thereafter his reputation as a classical landscape painter was eclipsed by Richard Wilson and Thomas Gainsborough and, as a painter of horses, by George Stubbs. Wootton died at the end of October or beginning of November 1764 and was buried on 3 November in St Marylebone parish church, Middlesex.   ARLINE J. MEYER

Sources A. Meyer, 'The landscape paintings of John Wootton (1682–1764): painter of the Augustan age', PhD diss., Columbia University, 1982 · G. W. Kendall, 'John Wootton, life and a list of engravings after his pictures', *Walpole Society*, 21 (1932–3), 23–42 · A. Meyer, *John Wootton (1652–1764): landscape and sporting art in early Georgian England* (1984) [exhibition catalogue, Iveagh bequest, Kenwood, London] · Vertue, *Note books* · BL, Portland MSS, Loan 29/110 · letters to Lady Anne, countess of Coventry, Badminton House Archives, 503.1 · will, PRO, PROB 11/904, sig. 451 · *Anecdotes of painting in England, 1760–1795 … collected by Horace Walpole*, ed. F. W. Hilles and P. B. Daghlian (1937) · parish registers, Middlesex, St Marylebone, Nov 1728–June 1730, LMA · St Anne's parish, King's Square district, land tax and poor rate books, 1718?–June 1728, City Westm. AC · W. Gilbey, *Animal painters of England*, 3 vols. (1900–11) · O. Sitwell, 'The red folder—1', *Burlington Magazine*, 80 (1942), 84–90 · W. T. Whitley, *Artists and their friends in England, 1700–1799*, 2 vols. (1928); repr. (1968) · IGI · will, PRO, PROB 11/933, sig. 380 [Elizabeth Wootton] · *Daily Advertiser* [London] (27 Feb 1761) · parish records, 2/1717–2/1718 (new calendar), St Paul's Covent Garden · parish records, 11/1721?–7/1726, St Anne's, Soho

Archives Badminton House, Gloucestershire · BL, Portland MSS, loan 29/110 · Goodwood House, West Sussex

Likenesses J. Thornhill, drawing, c.1715–1717 (*The connoisseurs and Sir James Thornhill*), Art Institute of Chicago · group portrait, c.1717 (*A group of connoisseurs*), Beaverbrook Art Gallery, New Brunswick · Bernard (III) Lens, miniature, c.1720, priv. coll. [*see illus.*] · M. Dahl, oils, 1723 · J. Smibert, group portrait, c.1724 (*A group of virtuosi*) · G. Hamilton, group portrait, oils, 1735 (*A conversation of virtuosi … at the King Armes*), NPG · G. Hamilton, group portrait, oils, 1736 (*John Wootton and his family*), priv. coll. · H. Hysing, oils · T. Murray, oils · J. Wootton, self-portrait, chalk drawing, BM · C. F. Zinke, miniature

Wealth at death proceeds from sale of house and collection of paintings, prints, and drawings and of his own work; some securities: will, PRO, PROB 11/904, sig. 451

Worboise [*formerly* Worboys], **Emma Jane** [*known as* Mrs Etherington Guyton] (**1825–1887**), novelist, was born on 20 April 1825 in Legge Street, Birmingham, the eldest child of George Baddeley Worboys (1803?–1867), gun maker, and his wife, Maria Lane (*b.* 1807?, *d.* after 1887), whose father possessed property in Birmingham. Her family were Congregational, and she was a supporter of the church throughout her life. Little is known about her early life or education, but she attended a private boarding-school and between 1843 and 1854 may have worked as a governess. She appears to have early shown a talent for writing and by the time she was twenty had produced a large quantity of manuscripts, both prose and poetry. Her father's bankruptcy in 1843, at which time he was described as a 'toyman' (*Bristol Mercury*, 8), may well have contributed to her determination to make her own career as a writer. Her first book, published under Worboise, the altered spelling of her surname, was *Alice Cunningham* (1846). Between that date and the year of her death she completed some fifty domestic novels, most with a broad-church message, which were very popular and were often reprinted. *Overdale* (1867) was subtitled *The Story of a Pervert*, but the 'perversion' took the form of an attraction to Tractarianism, a common theme in her work. Her idol was Dr Thomas Arnold, headmaster of Rugby School, of whom she wrote a *Life* in 1859, which went into several editions. She contributed to the *Christian World* newspaper from 1857 and edited the monthly magazine the *Christian World Magazine and Family Visitor* from 1866 to 1885, in which latter publication most of her later works were first serialized. A quotation from Dr Arnold was prominently featured in every edition: 'I never wanted articles on religious subjects half so much as articles on common subjects, written with a decidedly religious tone'. The magazine survived her editorship by only two years. She was described by Marianne Farningham (Mary Anne Hearne), a novelist and colleague, as:

tall and of commanding presence, with a face that denoted strength and intelligence. She could be severe when severity was necessary, and sarcastic when sarcasm seemed the best weapon, but she could also be exceedingly kind and tender. As an editor she was a good deal less impatient than many editors are prone to be. (*Birmingham Mail*, 25 April 1925)

It was not until 1882 that Emma Jane Worboise first began to sign herself in the *Christian World Magazine and Family Visitor* as 'Mrs' Worboise. Although a contributor to the magazine in 1866 was called Ernest Etherington, no evidence has been found for the existence of a Mr Etherington Guyton, her supposed husband, who has been variously described as being of French descent and a Baptist minister. Certainly, from 1881 she was calling herself 'Mrs Etherington Guyton, widow'. This may have been a device to cloak her identity, perhaps related to the incipient alcoholism which brought about her retirement. She died from alcoholism at Wellington House, a sanatorium at Clevedon, Somerset, on 25 August 1887 and was buried in Clevedon cemetery on the 27th.   BRETT HARRISON

Sources *The Athenaeum* (10 Sept 1887), 343 · *Croydon Chronicle* (3 Sept 1887) · E. W. Neesham, 'A sometime Erdington authoress', *Erdington News* (18 Feb 1911) · *Birmingham Mail* (20 April 1925) · *Birmingham Mail* (25 April 1925) · 'Literary register', *Congregational Year Book* (1887) · *Christian World Magazine and Family Visitor* (1866–85) · census return for 9 Somerset Street, Kingsdown, Bristol, 1841, PRO, HO 107/377/13 · census return for 28 Legge Street, Birmingham, 1851, PRO, HO 107/2051–2059 · census return for 24 Lee Bank Road, Edgbaston, Birmingham, 1861, PRO, RG 9/2123/49 · census returns for Melrose, Caterham Valley, Surrey, 1881, PRO, RG 11/804/17 · *CGPLA Eng. & Wales* (1888) · R. H. Blackburn, 'Thorneycroft Hall: a rebuttal to *Jane Eyre*', *Brontë Society Transactions*, 85 (1975), 353–60 · *Bristol Mercury* (9 Sept 1843), 8 · *Felix Farley's Bristol Journal* (6 May 1843), 2 · *Felix Farley's Bristol Journal* (9 Sept 1843), 2 · d. cert. · parish register (baptism), Birmingham, St Mary's, Whittal Street, 1825 · registry, Clevedon cemetery, Clevedon, Somerset

Likenesses T. W. Hunt, stipple, NPG · steel-plate engraving, repro. in E. J. Worboise, *Thornycroft Hall*

Wealth at death £66 15s.: probate, 23 March 1888, *CGPLA Eng. & Wales*

Worboys, Sir Walter John (1900–1969),

chemical industrialist and design promoter, was born at Cottesloe, Western Australia, on 22 February 1900, the eldest child of Walter Worboys, engineer, and his wife, Amanda Urquhart. He was educated at Scotch College and the University of Western Australia where he graduated in chemistry and geology. He proceeded as a Rhodes scholar to Lincoln College, Oxford, where his supervisor was Nevil Sidgwick, and gained his DPhil in chemistry in 1925. He then joined Synthetic Ammonia and Nitrates Ltd, a subsidiary of Brunner, Mond & Co., as a research chemist at Billingham, and devoted himself to the production of synthetic nitrogen and fertilizers, then in an early stage of development.

On 22 March 1927 he married Ethelwyn Bessie (Betty), daughter of Henry Lavers, an Australian mining engineer; they had one son and one daughter.

Brunner Mond became one of the founder constituents of Imperial Chemical Industries, with which company Worboys remained until he retired as commercial director in 1959. During his later years with the chemical industry he carried a full share of its burdens. He was chairman of the Association of British Chemical Manufacturers in 1953–6 and president in 1957–9. He was a member of council of the Society of the Chemical Industry in 1955–8 and gold medallist in 1957, and became a fellow of the Royal Institute of Chemistry in that year.

Worboys's interest in industrial design, always active, was greatly stimulated by his service as chairman of ICI's plastics division from 1942 until 1948, when he became a director of the main company. Plastics lent themselves with equal facility to good or bad design; Worboys resolved to exploit the good and to discourage the bad, and he employed designers to serve both aims. He joined the Council of Industrial Design in 1947 and in 1953–60 was its chairman. The council, started by the Board of Trade in 1944 to encourage good design as a necessary feature of the post-war export drive, had never enjoyed an easy life, and in its early days had perhaps more critics than friends. There were those who felt that good design could best be determined by market forces, others who saw in any attempt to influence it the hand of government interference. When Worboys became chairman he decided, probably on the strength of his experience with the Festival of Britain of 1951 in which he took an active part, that if the council was to make its mark there was an overwhelming need for a permanent exhibition gallery in London. Such a project meant much greater government support; the fact that this support was provided on a pound-for-pound basis with industry was Worboys's special achievement and his success was due, not only to his enthusiasm and driving force, but also to his ability to convince Whitehall that under his guidance the council and its Design Centre (as the permanent exhibition was to be called) would develop on sound and productive lines.

In the event, the Design Centre went from strength to strength, impressively fulfilling the bold and original conception that manufacturers could be persuaded to pay for space in which the goods shown would be selected by another body. The formation of the Design Centre was a turning point in the fortunes of the Council of Industrial Design; in a world where much that is ugly is created daily, the work of the council has provided a steady influence for good. As Sir Gordon Russell, former director of the council and Worboys's close partner in its work, wrote: 'When the history of the revolt against ugliness comes to be written, it will be seen how important was the work of a very small group of top-ranking businessmen after the last war. Of these Walter Worboys was a natural leader' (*The Times*, 21 March 1969). Worboys's concern with industry, with design, and with the arts made a clear bond with the Royal Society of Arts; he became a fellow of the society in 1949, was awarded the bicentenary medal in 1956, and was elected a member of its council in 1961. In 1967 he became chairman of council, a post he held until his death.

Some ten years remained to Worboys after he left ICI, and into this period he compressed a new career. In 1960 he became chairman of British Tyre and Rubber Industries and started a much needed programme of modernization and reorganization, which contributed greatly to the subsequent growth and strength of the company. In 1965 the Westminster Bank, of which he was a director, persuaded him to accept the formidable responsibility of chairing the British Printing Corporation, whose affairs were then at a low ebb. He held both these posts until his death, and they constituted a heavy burden. During this period Worboys began to undertake new commitments in the educational field. Early in the 1950s he had become a governor of Radley College and in 1962 he became chairman of the governing council of Roedean School. Worboys also played a notable part in the university developments of the 1960s by serving as a member of the academic advisory committee for the University of East Anglia and as chairman of the corresponding body for Brunel University. He presided over the government committee on road traffic signs set up in 1961 with results which were appreciated by road users throughout the land.

In appearance Worboys always seemed active, fit, and alert. He was a man of distinction, endowed with the eye at once of the administrator, the artist, the scholar, and the man of affairs. To all his many activities he brought a sense of style. He set uncompromising standards, both of behaviour and performance. His manner could vary from warmth to severity, and his tolerance for the imperfect was limited, but at heart he was most kindly. He was essentially a man of his times. Justly described in the company's house journal as one of the architects of the modern ICI, he was equally at home in the City, in Whitehall, and in the arts. He accomplished much and the burden it placed on his daily life was cheerfully borne. He found his pleasures in his family, his work, in the arts, and in his country home, Norton Hall, Norton-on-Tees. His appointment as an honorary fellow of Lincoln College in 1957 gave him especial satisfaction. He was knighted in 1958 and received an honorary doctorate from Brunel University in 1967. Worboys died at his London home, Flat 8, 69 Onslow Square, Kensington, on 17 March 1969.

M. J. DEAN, rev.

Sources G. Russell, *Designer's trade: autobiography of Gordon Russell* (1968) • private information (1981) • personal knowledge (1981) • m. cert. • d. cert. • *The Times* (18 March 1969), 12h • *The Times* (25 March 1969), 12g • W. J. Reader, *Imperial Chemical Industries, a history*, 2 vols. (1970–75) • *WWW*
Likenesses A. Fleischman, bronze head; known to be in family possession in 1981
Wealth at death £63,064: probate, 4 July 1969, *CGPLA Eng. & Wales*

Worcester. For this title name *see* Waleran, count of Meulan and earl of Worcester (1104–1166); Percy, Thomas, earl of Worcester (*c*.1343–1403); Tiptoft, John, first earl of Worcester (1427–1470); Somerset, Charles, earl of Worcester (*c*.1460–1526); Somerset, William, third earl of Worcester (1526/7–1589); Somerset, Edward, fourth earl of Worcester (*c*.1550–1628); Somerset, Edward, second marquess of Worcester (*d*. 1667).

Worcester, Florence of (*d*. 1118). *See under* Worcester, John of (*fl*. 1095–1140).

Worcester, John of (*fl*. 1095–1140), Benedictine monk and chronicler, was very probably responsible for the work formerly attributed to Florence of Worcester [*see below*]. Orderic Vitalis (*d*. 1143) saw the monk John at Worcester at

work on a chronicle not later than 1124, and reports that Bishop Wulfstan (*d*. 1095) had asked him to continue the world chronicle of Marianus Scotus (*d*. 1082). Like Marianus's chronicle, John's is a world history extending from the beginning of humankind to 1140. He occasionally supplemented or corrected Marianus's account of world events, but the substantial English history (from 450 to 1140) that he grafted on to Marianus, and the respect that he showed for his sources, make his chronicle particularly valuable. The backbone of his annals was a translation of one or more versions of the Anglo-Saxon Chronicle, and John's differences from existing vernacular witnesses are therefore of significance. He had considerable recourse to Bede's *Historia ecclesiastica* for events down to 731, and John's extensive copying of Asser's *Vita Ælfredi* makes his text, as one of three surviving partial medieval witnesses to that life, of crucial importance in its reconstruction.

For much of the tenth and early eleventh centuries saints' lives—those of Dunstan by B, Adelard, and Osbern, of Oswald by Byrhtferth, and of Ælfheah by Osbern—fill in some of the gaps in the Anglo-Saxon Chronicle. And from the early eleventh century to the chronicle's conclusion in 1140 John's additional information is often of great interest, while after 1106 or so he departs increasingly from the one surviving version of the Anglo-Saxon Chronicle; and in these years, and in the later years of Henry I and the first five years of Stephen, he becomes an important contemporary source. John complemented the consular tables and lists of popes, with which Marianus had introduced his chronicle, with genealogies of English kings, brief and valuable narratives of the English kingdoms, and episcopal lists. Although it contains only occasional details about its compiler, his chronicle shows that John stayed at Winchcombe for some time (annals 1130, 1134); that he relied on the oral testimony of Grimbald, Henry I's physician, Bishop Henry de Blois, and the abbot of St Valéry-sur-Somme (annals 1130, 1134, 1137); that he witnessed the sack of Worcester in 1139; and that his accounts of the campaigns in the west in Stephen's reign seem based on personal knowledge. The interest in celestial phenomena, which is a notable feature of his work, seems confirmed by the appearance of his distinctive hand in the Worcester copy of the Tables of al-Khwarizmi in Adelard of Bath's translation (Bodl. Oxf., MS Auct. F.1.9.).

John's chronicle survives in five twelfth-century manuscript copies and in a single leaf from a sixth. The chief manuscript (Oxford, Corpus Christi College, MS 157) was a working copy which John himself extensively revised. He made marginal additions and rewrote some annals, he erased and rewrote the annals for 1128–31, and he continued the chronicle to its present imperfect end in 1140. The other four copies, which all depend directly or indirectly on the Corpus Christi manuscript, testify to two versions of the chronicle ending in 1131. The first version is represented by Dublin, Trinity College, MS 502, and LPL, MS 42, written at Coventry and Abingdon respectively, and the second by a Bury copy, Bodl. Oxf., MS Bodley 297.

Cambridge, Corpus Christi College, MS 92, which was probably begun at Abingdon and completed at Peterborough, is hybrid. The evolution of the text shows how John, during its compilation, kept in touch with contemporary history writing at Durham, Canterbury, and Malmesbury.

After he had revised and continued the Oxford Corpus Christi copy, John compiled and in part transcribed a self-styled *chronicula* (Dublin, Trinity College, MS 503), which was made up of much material extracted from Corpus, MS 157, and of added information from other sources. This *chronicula* was completed at Gloucester, where interpolations were added, and the history extended to 1141. The extant complete twelfth-century copies show that the full chronicle was copied at Bury, Abingdon, and Coventry, and that a copy was taken to Peterborough. It was very popular in the twelfth and thirteenth centuries and was taken over into many other chronicles and histories, in particular into those of Walter of Coventry and Roger of Howden. The earlier editions of the chronicle by Howard, Petrie, and Thorpe, did not take Oxford, Corpus Christi College, MS 157, as their basis, and the first edition to do so, that of Weaver, was confined to the annals from 1118 to 1140. A new edition is included in the Oxford Medieval Texts series.

Florence of Worcester (*d.* 1118), a monk at Worcester, is praised for his skill and industry in an obituary under the annal for 1118 in John of Worcester's chronicle. The view of the early editors that he was the author of the Worcester chronicle to 1117 or 1118, and that this was later continued by others, is no longer held for three reasons. The chronicle shows no differences in style before and after 1118; in its annals before that year it used Eadmer's *Historia novorum*, which was not completed until 1122; and John clearly had a decisive role in the making of the chronicle in its later stages. The eulogistic obituary suggested, however, that Florence had a part in the compilation of the chronicle, a role that must probably remain undetermined.   P. McGurk

Sources Florence of Worcester, *Chronicon ex chronicis, ab initio mundi usque ad annum Domini 1118 deductum*, ed. W. Howard (1592) · H. Petrie and J. Sharpe, *Monumenta historica Britannica* (1848), 522–642 · *The chronicle of John of Worcester, 1118–1140*, ed. J. R. H. Weaver (1908) · John of Worcester, *Chron.*, vol. 2 · M. Brett, 'John of Worcester and his contemporaries', *The writing of history in the middle ages: essays presented to Richard William Southern*, ed. R. H. C. Davis, J. M. Wallace-Hadrill, and others (1981), 101–26 · A. Gransden, *Historical writing in England*, 1 (1974), 143–8
Archives Bodl. Oxf., MS Bodley 297 · CCC Cam., MS 92 · CCC Oxf., MS 157 · LPL, MS 42 · TCD, MS 502 · TCD, MS 503

Worcester, Senatus of [called Senatus Bravonius] (*d.* **1207**), prior of Worcester and theologian, is of unknown birth; his unusual name and advanced theological training have been taken as evidence of foreign origin although his byname of Bravonius suggests rather that he was a native of the west of England. He was precentor at Worcester Abbey, a post that also included responsibility for the abbey library, by 1175, and chamberlain by 1186; he became prior in 1189, and remained so until 20 November 1196. His resignation, exactly a month after the consecration of John de Coutances as bishop of Worcester, may

have been connected with the election of the new bishop, as he indicates in a letter to Walter of Rouen that he pushed it through quickly and discreetly (it took place in Stratford upon Avon rather than Worcester), in defiance of direct instructions from Canterbury, and immediately 'proclaimed at the crossroads of Ascalon' (Bodl. Oxf., MS Rawl. G.168, fol. 222v; letter 6).

The description of Senatus in the Worcester annals as *magister et theologus* does not indicate that he was a teacher, as has been suggested (although his style of writing suggests an academic bent); *magister* indicates only his level of education, and may be linked with *theologus* to indicate that he was a theologian of some repute, at least locally. Roger of Gloucester (*d.* 1179), bishop of Worcester for much of Senatus's career, appointed him as his penitentiary or *archipresbiterum* and consulted him on one of the major theological and pastoral problems of the day, regarding absolution and indulgences; Senatus's answer, which is of considerable sophistication, focuses on the distinction between the internal and the external forum. The post of penitentiary also included preaching, and Senatus is known to have sent a collection of twenty-two sermons to Bishop Roger, although they have not been identified in modern times.

Senatus's other extant theological treatises in letter form are also works of some interest. His letter on the canonical hours to John Cumin, archbishop of Dublin, draws heavily on the work of Rupert of Deutz, while that on the canon of the mass to Master Alfred (possibly the prior of Cirencester) also appears to be an *enarratio* (an interpretation), although its source has not been traced. Senatus's letter to Master William of Tonbridge, a teacher in Oxford who had links with Worcester, draws upon a wide range of scholars including Anselm of Lucca and John of Stella to criticize as theologically suspect the *Sententiae* of Pierre de Poitiers, which William had been using as a textbook. Other extant works by Senatus include lives of two bishops of Worcester, St Oswald and St Wulfstan (the latter essentially an abbreviation of William of Malmesbury's version). The unfinished collection of seven of Senatus's letters in the Bodleian Library (Bodl. Oxf., MS Rawl. G.168) was probably organized by the prior himself (following a tradition of letter collections of other Worcester priors), and gives some interesting information. In his second letter to Alfred, Senatus refers to the great Bible sent to King Offa from Rome, and which was then kept at Worcester; a passage in this letter which has been taken to refer to another work by Senatus—a concordance of the gospels—is actually a (rather confusing) explanation of how to use Eusebius's tables of passages in the gospels. Other details can be gleaned from the two letters referring to Oxford: the letter to William of Tonbridge indicates that Pierre de Poitiers was being used in Oxford as early as the beginning of the thirteenth century, as William was an Oxford master, while Senatus's earlier letter to Clement, prior of Osney, describes Oxford as 'the city that lies close to you, in which there are many eloquent speakers and men who can weigh the words of the law'

(Bodl. Oxf., MS Rawl. G.168, fol. 29r; letter 4)—an interesting record of Oxford's reputation as an academic and legal centre at the end of the twelfth century. Senatus died in 1207, presumably at Worcester Abbey.

PETER DAMIAN-GRINT

Sources C. H. Turner, ed., *Early Worcester manuscripts: fragments of four books and a charter of the eighth century belonging to Worcester Cathedral* (1916), xlv–li · N. Karn, 'Monastic letter-writers in twelfth-century England', DPhil diss., U. Oxf., 2002 · M. G. Cheney, *Roger, bishop of Worcester, 1164–1179* (1980) · J. Greatrex, *Biographical register of the English cathedral priories of the province of Canterbury* (1997) · *Ann. mon.*, 4.355–564 · R. Sharpe, *A handlist of the Latin writers of Great Britain and Ireland before 1540* (1997) · R. R. Darlington, ed., *The cartulary of Worcester Cathedral Priory (register I)*, PRSoc., 76, new ser., 38 (1968) · P. Delhaye, 'Deux textes de Senatus de Worcester sur la pénitence', *Recherches de Théologie Ancienne et Médiévale*, 19 (1952), 203–24 · Senatus, *Vita sanctissimi Wulfstani confessoris atque pontificis*, in *The Vita Wulfstani of William of Malmesbury*, ed. R. R. Darlington, CS, 3rd ser., 40 (1928), 68–108 · Senatus, 'Vita S. Oswaldi archiepiscopi', *The historians of the church of York and its archbishops*, ed. J. Raine, 2, Rolls Series, 71 (1886), 60–97 · [H. Wharton], ed., *Anglia sacra*, 2 vols. (1691) · Bale, *Cat.* · R. W. Hunt, 'English learning in the late twelfth century', *TRHS*, 4th ser., 19 (1936), 19–42, esp. 29–42 · C. N. L. Brooke, 'The archdeacon and the Norman conquest', *Tradition and change: essays in honour of Marjorie Chibnall*, ed. D. E. Greenway, C. J. Hoddinott, and J. E. Sayers (1985), 1–19 · C. Franzen, *The tremulous hand of Worcester: a study of Old English in the thirteenth century* (1991)

Archives Bodl. Oxf., MS Rawl. G.168, fols. 197r–233 | CCC Cam., MS 48, fols. 199r–200r · LPL, MS 238, fols. 207r–214

Worcester [Botoner], **William** (1415–1480x85), topographer and author, was the son of William Worcester, whittawer of Bristol, and Elizabeth (*née* Botoner), and was born at his father's house in St James's Back in the northeast suburbs of the city. His mother was the daughter of a substantial local citizen whose family came from Coventry, and her son used her surname as well as his father's. He had an unspecified number of siblings who were dead by 1489, as well as a sister Joan still alive in that year. Worcester may have attended the grammar school of Robert Londe (*fl.* 1426–1462) above the New Gate of Bristol, since he mentions Londe twice in his writings, before going to study at Oxford about Easter term 1432. A manuscript of Pliny and Diodorus Siculus which he gave to Balliol College (Oxford, Balliol College, MS 124) contains an inscription (not by Worcester) identifying him as a former scholar of Hart Hall. This was either the hall in New College Lane (now Hertford College), favoured by west-of-England men, or the hall in Merton Street belonging to Balliol. Nothing is known of his university studies.

By 1438 Worcester had entered the service of Sir John Fastolf of Caister, Norfolk, a knight with extensive lands and interests in England and France, with whom he remained until Fastolf's death. Although usually described merely as a 'servant', Worcester filled various roles as a secretary and agent: writing letters, collecting evidence for lawsuits, and administering property. He went at least twice to northern France in the early 1440s on Fastolf's business. As the knight grew older, Worcester also ministered to his bodily needs. Fastolf was not a generous employer, and Worcester came to feel himself ill-rewarded. Writing about 1454 to John Paston (d. 1466), who had addressed him as Master Worcester, he asked

Paston to 'forget that name of mastership, for I am not amended by my master of a farthing in certainty, but … have 5s. yearly, all costs borne, to help pay for bonnets that I lose'. Worcester added, however, 'I write to make you laugh' (*Paston Letters*, ed. Davis, 2.101–2). Equally, his employment gave him the status of a gentleman retainer, contact with men of cultural interests, and sufficient means to get married. He later claimed that Fastolf, before he died, promised to bequeath him a livelihood 'according to his degree' (*Paston Letters*, ed. Gairdner, 1.507–9). This was to include the manor of Fairchilds in Hellesdon, Norfolk, worth 10 marks a year.

When Fastolf died in 1459, Worcester was one of his ten executors. The estate immediately became the subject of disagreements, since Paston (another executor) claimed that Fastolf had given him the chief role in administering and disposing of the property. Worcester disputed this. He seems to have felt a duty to see Fastolf's wishes fulfilled, particularly with regard to the foundation of a college of priests at Caister, and wished to secure his own promised bequest. The resulting quarrels among the executors caused Paston and his ally Thomas Howes (who was Worcester's uncle) to draw apart from Worcester, who joined Sir William Yelverton (d. 1472) in opposing them. Despite this, Worcester continued to see and correspond with members of the Paston family. He spent much of the 1460s winding up Fastolf's affairs and engaging in the resulting legal disputes. This was troublesome and costly to him, and at one point he and his wife were imprisoned for debt. Paston first demurred about recognizing Worcester's claim, and then offered compensation which was not forthcoming. Eventually, in 1470, the archbishop of Canterbury remitted the administration of Fastolf's estate to William Waynflete, bishop of Winchester (d. 1486), and in 1474 Waynflete agreed to pay Worcester £100 to continue recovering Fastolf's assets, together with a share of the proceeds. By this time Worcester had at last gained possession of the Fairchilds property and two tenements in Southwark.

Worcester once observed that he had little to do with women until he was thirty. His marriage was therefore delayed until at least 1445 and also arose within the Fastolf circle, his wife, Margaret, being the niece of Thomas Howes, another of Sir John's household officers and rector of Castle Combe, Wiltshire, which Worcester visited in his master's service. Margaret shared her husband's tribulations. In 1460 Worcester spoke of his distress about 'my poor wife, for the sorrow she taketh' when he was obliged to leave her on business (*Paston Letters*, ed. Gairdner, 1.504–5), but she lived to see his affairs stabilize and survived him. Their children are mentioned in 1460, but only one son is known by name: another William, who dedicated a work by his father to Richard III between 1483 and 1485. In 1470 Worcester considered living in Cambridge to save money, but by the later 1470s he seems to have settled in Pockthorpe, the north-eastern suburb of Norwich, not far from Hellesdon. He died at an unknown date between the autumn of 1480 and the summer of 1485; a document issued after his death calls him 'late of Pockthorpe by Norwich, gentleman' (*Paston Letters*, ed. Davis, 2.606–8).

Worcester figures in history as a participant in the affairs of Fastolf, Waynflete, and the Paston family, but his chief importance rests on his own cultural interests and writings. These, as with many late medieval authors, were executed part-time during a busy career. Fastolf patronized writers, and Worcester helped produce works for his master. He used to be regarded as the author of a volume of *Annals* of fifteenth-century history, but this is a composite work to which he contributed only a few notes. He helped to edit a chronicle in French of the Hundred Years' War, now known as Basset's chronicle (London, College of Arms, MS 9, fols. xxxi–lxvi), compiled for Fastolf by at least three other men in 1459, and he corrected Stephen Scrope's *The dicts and sayings of the philosophers*, a translation from French. His own writings included a lost and probably uncompleted life of Fastolf, *Acta domini Johannis Fastolf*, mentioned in 1460 and belonging to the uncommon genre of knightly biographies. He turned into English a French version of Cicero's *De senectute*, which he presented to Waynflete in 1473 without receiving reward (to his disappointment); this may be the text that Caxton printed in 1481. His most ambitious literary work was *The boke of noblesse*, apparently first written in 1451 and revised in 1472 and 1475. It urges the English king and nobility to cultivate warlike qualities, the better to govern the kingdom and to pursue the English claims in France.

Worcester's scholarly interests were many. In 1440 he compiled a table of 1022 fixed stars, and incorporated a symbol for Saturn into his signature. He owned and made notes from a number of medical treatises, and studied foreign languages. About 1458 a correspondent wrote to John Paston that:

> William hath gone to school to a Lombard called Karoll Giles to learn and to be read in poetry or else in French, for he hath been with the same Karoll every day two times or three and hath bought divers books of him.

The writer quoted Worcester as saying 'that he would be as glad and as fain of a good book of French or of poetry as my Master Fastolf would be to purchase a fair manor' (*Paston Letters*, ed. Davis, 2.175). He began the study of Greek under William Selling of Canterbury (d. 1494), and bought a volume from the library of his fellow Bristolian John Free (d. 1465), containing works by Euripides and Sophocles, but it lacks any annotations by him. He wrote out the Hebrew alphabet and made notes from a Hebrew psalter belonging to Peterhouse, Cambridge. Most of all, he engaged in English topographical and historical studies, stimulated perhaps by his travels and legal researches on Fastolf's behalf. Towards the end of his life Worcester made a number of journeys on his own account: partly to gather historical materials and partly for reasons of business, leisure, and spirituality. The longest of these, in the summer of 1478, took him from Norwich via London and Bristol on a pilgrimage to St Michael's Mount, Cornwall, with a diversion to Tintern Abbey in south Wales. In 1479 he visited London and Walsingham Priory, and in 1480 he travelled to Bristol via Oxford and Cirencester, as well as to Glastonbury and Wells.

During these journeys Worcester made notes (now known as his *Itineraries*) on a wide variety of topics: natural history (rivers, islands, and birds), buildings (churches, castles, and houses), religion (saints and festivals), and biography (obituary lists and anecdotes of famous people). He was interested in Atlantic exploration, the geography of Africa, and the Mediterranean. As well as pursuing his numerous interests, Worcester seems to have aimed at two specific projects. One was a history of the ancient families of East Anglia, for which he gathered at least 188 folios of notes, still extant when Sir Henry Spelman used them in the early seventeenth century. The other was a description of Bristol, the notes for which survive: an original scheme to describe in detail the topography of the city, including walls, streets, wharves, churches, cellars, and many other buildings, with measurements of widths and lengths, virtually making it possible to compose a map. Worcester was thus a pioneer of English historical scholarship, matched in his day only by his slightly younger contemporary John Rous of Warwick (d. 1492).

Friar John Brackley, no friend of Worcester, characterized his appearance about 1460 as that of 'a one-eyed man with black colouring and a swarthy face' (*Paston Letters*, ed. Davis, 2.211). He further insinuated that Worcester was Irish. In truth, Worcester was cultured and (as emerges from the letters by and about him) humorous and sociable. His notes reveal him talking freely with anyone, from a knight or abbot to a young smith or ferryman in Bristol. His impact as a scholar and writer, however, was not great in his own day or until long afterwards. His works on Fastolf and East Anglia did not survive, and although the manuscript of his *Itineraries* passed to Corpus Christi College, Cambridge, it was little known until it was edited in 1778. Some care is therefore still required if Worcester is to receive his due as an original and widely curious scholar.   NICHOLAS ORME

Sources *Itineraries [of] William Worcestre*, ed. J. H. Harvey, OMT (1969) · W. Worcester, *The topography of medieval Bristol*, ed. F. Neale, Bristol RS, 51 (2000) · J. G. Nichols, ed., *The boke of noblesse: addressed to King Edward the Fourth on his invasion of France in 1475*, Roxburghe Club (1860) · K. B. McFarlane, 'William Worcester: a preliminary survey', *Studies presented to Sir Hilary Jenkinson*, ed. J. C. Davies (1957), 196–221; repr. in K. B. McFarlane, *England in the fifteenth century: collected essays* (1981), 199–224 · *The Paston letters, 1422–1509 AD*, ed. J. Gairdner, new edn, 3 vols. (1872–5); repr. in 4 vols. (1910) · N. Davis, ed., *Paston letters and papers of the fifteenth century*, 2 vols. (1971–6) · Emden, *Oxf.*, 3.2086–7 · C. Richmond, *The Paston family in the fifteenth century: the first phase* (1990) · A. Gransden, *Historical writing in England*, 2 (1982) · T. D. Kendrick, *British antiquity* (1950)

Archives BL, Add. MSS 678, 5844, 28208, 27443–27444, 27450, 34888–34889, 38692, 39848, 43488 · BL, Cotton MS Julius F.vii, 18, 25, 38, 169 · BL, Royal MSS 18 B.xxii, 13 C.i, SI 4 · Bodl. Oxf., astronomical notebook · CCC Cam., 'Itineraries' · LPL, 'Boke of noblesse' | Coll. Arms, MS 9, fols. xxxi–lxvi

Worde, Wynkyn de (d. 1534/5), printer, appears in written documents only from 1479; his date of birth and family background are unknown. His name suggests he was born in a place named Wörth. The letters of denization granted in 1496 refer to him as 'de ducatu Lothoringie oriundo' (PRO, patent rolls, 20 April 1496, C 66/577–66/578), and though neither Woerth-sur-Sauer (Bas-Rhin, Alsace) nor Wörth am Rhein formed part of the duchy of Lorraine then, one or other is probably his birthplace. From Woerth he probably travelled up the Rhine to Cologne, and became Johannes Veldener's apprentice before joining William Caxton during his visit to Cologne (1471–2); he went with Caxton on his return to Bruges (1472) and subsequently accompanied him to Westminster (1475 or 1476). In his 1495 reprint Wynkyn refers to Caxton's printing of Bartolomaeus Anglicus's *De proprietatibus rerum* at Cologne about 1471 (an edition now attributed to Veldener), which suggests Wynkyn took part in its printing. If so, he may have been born about 1455. In various records Wynkyn is named as Winandus van Worden, John or Johannes Wynkyn or Wykyn, Wynkyn Vort, and even William Wykyn, though there seems no doubt that Wynkyn was his Christian name, and 'de Worde' indicates his family's origin.

Caxton never refers in his books to Wynkyn, though one may assume he worked in Caxton's printing shop until his death in 1492. A document of 1479 (Westminster Abbey Muniments, 17849) records the letting of two tenements in the sanctuary of Westminster Abbey to Wynkyn and his wife, Elizabeth, suggesting that Wynkyn had been in Westminster long enough and was sufficiently comfortable financially to marry this Englishwoman. Elizabeth had apparently lived there previously, and she may have been the widow or daughter of John Dardan, saddler, who rented one of these tenements before 1479. On Dardan's death Elizabeth and Wynkyn took out a new lease, but gave it up next year, perhaps because they lived elsewhere. The parish accounts of St Margaret, Westminster, show that Elizabeth and Wynkyn attended that church, rented a pew there, and were members of its fraternity of the Assumption until Elizabeth died, in 1498. They also record that in 1500 'Juliane de Worde' died and was buried inside the church. Wynkyn had remarried, for he rented a pew for his wife shortly after Elizabeth's death, and Juliana may have been that wife or a daughter.

Caxton's death early in 1492 changed Wynkyn's life. Caxton's will is not extant; although Caxton had a daughter, Wynkyn took over the business. The sacrist's rolls for Westminster Abbey indicate that from 1491/2 Wynkyn rented the shop by the chapter house, formerly rented by Caxton, at 10s. a year. He paid this rent until 1499. Wynkyn's edition of Walter Hilton's *Scala perfectionis* (1494) was 'sette in printe in William Caxtons hows' (colophon). Besides the premises formerly occupied by Caxton, Wynkyn rented rooms just outside the abbey from 1495/6 until 1499/1500. He began, after Caxton's death, by using Caxton's device, founts, and woodcuts. We know of five books printed in these first two years, some such as the *Golden Legend*, being reprints of Caxton's books, though with modified colophons. One volume, entitled *Here Begynneth the Lyf of Saint Katherin of Senis*, contained the life of St Katharine and the revelations of St Elizabeth of Hungary, and may have acted as a supplement to the *Golden Legend*. Two other books represent a new departure: the *Treatise of Love* is a translation of French devotional tracts, and the *Chastising of God's Children* is a guide for a woman religious by her spiritual adviser, printed from an earlier English adaptation of a Latin text with Carthusian links. Caxton had avoided spiritual and devotional material associated with religious houses. Although five books in two years represent a modest start to Wynkyn's business, Caxton himself printed only six texts in his three and a half years as a printer in Bruges. Perhaps Wynkyn was finding his feet and deciding how to develop the business. New developments characterize his work of 1494: an edition of *Speculum vitae Christi* is the first book to refer to Wynkyn by name as the printer; another text, *Scala perfectionis*, contains a verse explicit in rhyme royal stanzas. Many scholars denigrate Wynkyn's attainments by assuming he was unable to compose poetry, and claim that he employed Robert Copland to write these verses for him. But there is no evidence to support this view, and Wynkyn may be their author, for he is not known to have employed Copland until later. The explicit is followed by Wynkyn's own mark, which occurs here for the first time. Two books published in 1495 also have verse colophons: his reprints of Caxton's *Polychronicon* and *De proprietatibus rerum*. Both were requested by the mercer Roger Thorney, indicating that Wynkyn was in touch with Caxton's former colleagues. That year he also published *Lives of the Fathers*, which Caxton finished translating on the last day of his life, though why Wynkyn delayed its printing so long is unclear.

In 1500/01 Wynkyn left Westminster for London, where he settled at the sign of the Sun in Fleet Street in St Bride's parish. By 1509 he also had a shop at St Paul's Churchyard at the sign of Our Lady of Pity. The move reflects the importance of London as a publishing and mercantile centre, and a recognition that Wynkyn had embarked on a new publishing policy. He turned away from the courtly material favoured by Caxton, which had led him to settle at Westminster, to religious, popular, and educational books, which were better distributed from London. A base in London let him keep an eye on other printers with whom he alternately competed and entered into partnership. Printers and publishers then formed a close circle. Wynkyn worked, for example, with printers such as Richard Pynson, Julian Notary, and Peter Treveris, for they issued many texts co-operatively and exchanged woodcuts, borders, type, and probably text. Several printers started their careers as Wynkyn's apprentices. Robert Copland referred to him as his former master, and translated books for him and brought some to his attention. Henry Watson was another of his servants who translated books for him. In Wynkyn's will three other printers are identified as former servants: John Butler, James Gaver, and John Byddell; six servants included in the will may have been apprentices, and one servant is identified as a bookbinder. Wynkyn was happy to work with different people and, unlike Caxton, to acknowledge their contribution to his editions.

Features which formed part of Wynkyn's marketing

policy include the following. From the beginning he used woodcuts, despite their variable quality, to make his books attractive: his different editions contain over 1100. His editions also opened up new areas ignored by Caxton. One consists of religious and spiritual books, prompted possibly by his association with Lady Margaret Beaufort, Henry VII's mother. He printed *Scala perfectionis* for her as early as 1494, though unnamed people also recommended religious books at that time. Possibly through Margaret he established links with Syon House, a Bridgettine foundation, and published books from its library and distributed others to its nuns. He may have taken particular interest in his female clientele. He also published books by the monks of Syon, such as Richard Whitford. Through Margaret, whose printer he formally styled himself for the final months of her life in 1509, he published works by John Fisher and other bishops; these included Fisher's funeral sermon for Margaret. Margaret's household accounts contain numerous references to her purchase of books printed by Wynkyn, probably religious texts in the main. Much of this material was English in origin and authorship, like his abbreviated *Book of Margery Kempe*, though some was based on continental models. This type of material could create problems because of religious controversy and potential heresy. One of his books, William de Melton's *Sermo exhortationis*, was issued with the imprimatur of John Colet, dean of St Paul's. On 19 December 1525 Wynkyn was arraigned before the vicar-general at St Paul's Cathedral for printing the *Image of Love*, translated by John Gough and printed on 5 October 1525, of which sixty copies had been distributed among the nuns of Syon, and other copies sent to Oxford and Cambridge. Wynkyn acknowledged that he was present in October 1524 with other printers when all had been cautioned by the bishop of London about heretical material. The *Image of Love* was declared heretical, and Wynkyn was instructed to recover whatever copies he could and not to distribute any more. Otherwise he appears to have suffered little from this matter.

Educational texts, mainly by English writers, constituted another development in Wynkyn's publishing. He worked with individual grammarians, acting as their publisher. He published over 150 editions of grammatical works by Robert Whittington and over 75 editions of those by John Stanbridge, some of which were issued with other London printers. A third new area was English poetry by past and living writers, including both elevated and popular material. Over twenty editions of Lydgate's works were issued, along with fifteen popular romances, such as *Ipomydon*. Wynkyn published many contemporary poets—not only well-known ones, such as Stephen Hawes and John Skelton, but also minor poets, such as William Walter and Christopher Goodwin. He continued the Caxton tradition of printing prose romances translated from French, such as *Huon of Bordeaux*.

Given the quantity and diversity of the books he published, Wynkyn needed to establish a marketing network. In addition to his links with London printers and bookbinders, trading associations are indicated through his contacts with Hugo Goes, a York printer; John Scoler and Charles Kyrforth, Oxford stationers; Robert Woodward, a Bristol stationer; and Henry Jacobi, Henry Pepwell, and John Gough, London stationers, of whom the first also sold books in Oxford. John Tourner, a stationer, was a witness of Wynkyn's will. He had servants such as Robert Maas with Dutch names who may have formed part of his links with the Low Countries, and he was in contact with French printers. He had links with leather producers, probably through his own bookbinding activities. He also had a wide range of patrons, who requested books from him. Some are unnamed scholars; others are monks, such as Whitford, merchants, such as Thorney, or nobles, such as Margaret Beaufort.

Wynkyn died at some point between 5 June 1534, when he signed his will, and 19 January 1535, when it was proved. He has often been compared unfavourably with his master, Caxton. The former is presented as a mere artisan, but the latter as a scholar and man of letters. The evidence, however, suggests Wynkyn had vision and energy, and achieved success in his profession. His estate, for example, was valued at £201 11s. 1d. in 1523/4. In his will his household consisted of eight servants, and he left bequests to nine people who were publishers, stationers, or bookbinders, also referring to three members of the parish and two leather producers. Some of these owed him debts which were written off. The three witnesses were a stationer and two important merchants. Wynkyn asked to be buried before the altar of St Katharine in St Bride's. All of this suggests a rich and respected member of the parish and a well-connected entrepreneur, who traded in London and the provinces and had links abroad. He makes no reference to any surviving wife or children, and on his death John Byddell took over the business. Wynkyn's various qualities need emphasizing: after Caxton's death he had sufficient vision to embark on a new publishing policy; to imitate his former master might have led to financial ruin. He was personable enough to get on with patrons from many classes and to run a heterogeneous household. No evidence of his involvement in litigation has been found. He was willing to give his helpers the credit they deserved, and he did not ignore their contribution as Caxton did. He probably knew several languages, and there is no reason to underestimate his learning and acumen. Previous assessments fail to give him due credit for his achievements.   N. F. BLAKE

Sources N. F. Blake, 'Wynkyn de Worde: a review of his life and work', *Études de linguistique et de la littérature en l'honneur d'André Crépin*, ed. D. Buschinger and W. Spiewok (Greifswald, Germany, 1993), 21–40 • J. Moran, *Wynkyn de Worde: father of Fleet Street*, 2nd edn (1976) • H. M. Nixon, 'Caxton, his contemporaries and successors in the book trade from Westminster documents', *The Library*, 5th ser., 31 (1976), 305–26 • M. C. Erler, 'Wynkyn de Worde's will: legatees and bequests', *The Library*, 6th ser., 10 (1988), 107–21 • H. R. Plomer, *Wynkyn de Worde and his contemporaries from the death of Caxton to 1535* (1925) • H. S. Bennett, *English books and readers, 1475–1557: being a study in the history of the book trade from Caxton to the incorporation of the Stationers' Company* (1952) • N. F. Blake, 'Wynkyn de Worde: the early years', *Gutenberg Jahrbuch* (1971), 62–9 • N. F. Blake, 'Wynkyn de Worde: the later years', *Gutenberg Jahrbuch* (1972), 128–38 • A. S. G. Edwards and C. M. Meale, 'The marketing of printed books in late medieval English', *The Library*, 6th ser., 15 (1993), 95–124 · E. G. Duff, *The printers, stationers, and bookbinders of London and Westminster in the fifteenth century* (1899) · G. Bone, 'Extant manuscripts printed by W. de Worde with notes on the owner, Roger Thorney', *The Library*, 4th ser., 12 (1931–2), 284–306 · S. Powell, 'Lady Margaret Beaufort and her books', *The Library*, 6th ser., 20 (1998), 197–240 · St Margaret's churchwarden accounts, 1480–82, Westminster Abbey Muniments, bk A, pp. 182, 356, 391 · Westminster Abbey Muniments, 17849, 19741, 19754

Likenesses line engraving, BM, NPG · woodcut, BM, NPG

Wealth at death see tax assessment £201 11s. 1d., 1523/4

Wordie, Sir James Mann (1889–1962), polar explorer and scholar, was born on 26 April 1889 at Partick, Lanarkshire, the youngest son of John Wordie, carting contractor, and his wife, Jane Catherine Mathers Mann. He was a first cousin of Sir James Mann. He was educated at Glasgow Academy and Glasgow University, where he obtained his BSc with honours and distinction in geology in 1910. He went as an advanced student to St John's College, Cambridge, reading for part two of the natural sciences tripos (geology) and graduating in 1912. He then began research work in geology. In 1913 he won the Harkness scholarship in geology and in 1914 was appointed university demonstrator in petrology—an office he held until 1917 and again from 1919 to 1923. His work brought him into touch with geologists such as Frank Debenham and Raymond Priestley, returned from the second expedition of Captain Scott. These contacts strengthened an interest in Arctic and Antarctic exploration and scientific discovery, already awakened by reading books on travel and mountaineering in his father's library and by working with J. W. Gregory.

In 1914 Wordie joined the Antarctic expedition of Sir Ernest Shackleton as geologist and chief of the scientific staff, and so served under a distinguished explorer whom he always acknowledged as his master. The expedition proved arduous and perilous in the extreme. Wordie himself spent a year in *Endurance* drifting 'beset and sinking' in the Weddell Sea; a period of discomfort and danger at Ocean Camp; and a winter marooned on Elephant Island while Shackleton made his epic voyage to South Georgia for help. Wordie ably played his part in maintaining the morale of the expedition; and in spite of its failure to fulfil its exploratory intentions and in spite of the rigours he had undergone, he brought back important geological specimens and useful observations on oceanography and on the polar ice pack.

Wordie returned in 1917 to a country at war, joined the Royal Artillery, and saw service in France. On his demobilization, the polar regions called him back: in 1919 and again in 1920 he went to Spitsbergen as geologist and second-in-command of the Scottish Spitsbergen expedition under W. S. Bruce. In 1921 he won a fellowship at St John's College, Cambridge, and henceforward made the college, and Cambridge more generally, the base from which to set out on a long series of Arctic and Antarctic expeditions. He went to Jan Mayen and east Greenland in 1921, 1923, 1926, and 1929 (in the former he made the first

ascent of Beerenberg, for he was a dedicated mountaineer); to north-west Greenland, Ellesmere Island, and Baffin Island in 1934 and 1937. The Second World War ended further polar exploration, but throughout it (indeed, from 1923 to 1949) Wordie served on the *Discovery* committee of the Colonial Office which advised on the oceanographical work undertaken by *Discovery I* and *II*. From 1937 to 1955 he chaired the committee of management of the Scott Polar Research Institute in Cambridge of which he was a founder member.

The young explorer under Shackleton, the leader of expeditions which introduced many young men (notably Gino Watkins and Vivian Fuchs) to the polar world, had now become the elder statesman of Arctic and Antarctic exploration, whose advice was widely sought and always influential. During the war Wordie served for a time as director of the Cambridge sub-centre of the naval intelligence division. His knowledge of local conditions was invaluable to the planning of operation TABARIN, whose objective was the maintenance of British claims to Graham Land and adjacent territories. This grew into the Falkland Islands Dependencies Survey, whose advisory scientific committee sat under his chairmanship. So it was that in 1947 Wordie was in polar latitudes for the last time, visiting South Orkney and South Shetland as well as Graham Land. But in his role of elder statesman of polar exploration he remained influential, as deputy chairman advising Fuchs when the Trans-Antarctic Expedition was being planned and as chairman of the British national committee for the International Geophysical Year (1954–8). He was also chairman of the British Mountaineering Council (1953–6). He is commemorated by the Wordie Glacier in Graham Land and the Wordie Crag in Spitsbergen.

Closely bound up with Wordie's interests in polar exploration was his service to the Royal Geographical Society. He was a fellow from 1921 and became a member of the council in the following year. He was honorary secretary from 1934 to 1948, spanning the difficult war period. After a time as foreign secretary he was president of the society, from 1951 to 1954, and in that capacity he welcomed back the expedition under Sir John Hunt which made the first ascent of Mount Everest; he became the first chairman of the Mount Everest Foundation.

Wordie's third great absorbing interest was St John's College, Cambridge, to which he was devoted. After election to his fellowship in 1921 he was appointed a tutor in 1923. From 1921 until 1952 (with intermissions) he was director of studies in geography. In 1933 he became senior tutor, an office which he held with that of president from 1950 until (perhaps rather to his surprise) he was elected master in 1952. He held the mastership until 1959, when his health had already begun to fail. As a tutor Wordie showed himself, though shy, an excellent judge of men, and brought his remarkable memory to bear on them, their affairs, and their family connections with unfailing accuracy. His filing system seemed, too, to depend on memory, for his large table was littered with papers from which he never failed to extract the document required.

As an elder statesman and eventually master, his shrewdness and instinctively accurate judgement of people served the college well; and the college benefited also from the affection he generated in his pupils. As a committee man he was better at deciding on a line of action (usually the right one) than at justifying it in argument.

Wordie gained the Back grant of the Royal Geographical Society in 1920 and its founder's gold medal in 1933; the Bruce medal of the Royal Society of Edinburgh (1926); the gold medal of the Royal Scottish Geographical Society (1944); and the Daly medal of the American Geographical Society (1952). He received honorary degrees from the universities of Glasgow and Hull, was an honorary fellow of Trinity College, Dublin, and was a commander of the order of St Olaf of Norway. He was appointed CBE in 1947 and knighted in 1957.

On 21 March 1923 Wordie married Gertrude Mary (d. 1971), daughter of George Thompson Henderson; they had three sons and two daughters. He died in Cambridge on 16 January 1962.   B. H. FARMER, rev.

Sources 'Exploration's elder statesman', *New Scientist* (5 Dec 1957) • *The Times* (17 Jan 1962) • G. R. Crone, 'Sir James Mann Wordie', *GJ*, 128 (1962), 122–4 • *The Eagle*, 59 (1960–63), 317–19 • personal knowledge (1981) • Burke, *Peerage* (1959) • *CCI* (1962)
Archives NL Scot., corresp. and MSS | Scott Polar RI, letters to Hugh Mill | FILM BFI NFTVA, documentary footage • BFI NFTVA, home footage
Likenesses R. Moynihan, oils, 1954, St John Cam.
Wealth at death £21,037 12s. 3d.: confirmation, 18 May 1962, *CCI*

Wordie, William (1810–1874), carrier and contractor, was born on 23 March 1810 at Stirling, son of John Wordie (1783–1830), carrier, and Janet Stewart. William was locally educated and probably went from school into his father's modest cartage business in Stirling, running twice weekly between there and Glasgow. But by the late 1820s it had run into debt. John Wordie died suddenly on 30 June 1830, and left William to continue with half a dozen horses and carts, and many creditors. By 1837 he was paying these off by energetic pursuit of business, now offering a daily service to Glasgow. In that year he married, on 20 December, Janet (1814–1901), daughter of the farmer and landowner Peter Jeffrey of Throsk, on the Forth below Stirling. They had two sons and five daughters. In 1837 also he took John McArthur of Stirling into a partnership, which lasted until 1852.

By the late 1830s road carriers in Scotland faced competition. The pioneer Garnkirk and Glasgow Railway opened in 1831, and the Edinburgh and Glasgow gained their act in 1838, and opened in 1842. Road transport between major centres would suffer although the railways did not as yet consider substantial goods traffic. To gain it they needed a collection and distribution organization, and this William Wordie and a few others in Scotland offered, as Pickfords did in England. In 1842 Wordie contracted with the new Edinburgh and Glasgow Railway to collect and forward goods by rail, using not only his carts but his own railway wagons. Cartage depots were opened at the stations, the first of many.

Railway expansion in Scotland was rapid, especially by the Caledonian company, who in 1849 opened a line from Glasgow to near Falkirk, where a junction was made with the Scottish Central, who had built through to Stirling and Perth, opened in 1848. By 1850 the railway reached Aberdeen via Coupar Angus and Forfar. In 1849 William Wordie had opened an office in Glasgow, and, probably in 1852, moved his head office there from Stirling; he had a house in Glasgow by this time. Freed now from the McArthur partnership, Wordie & Co. rapidly expanded. The contract with the Caledonian had been won in 1851, and the Scottish Central and Aberdeen railways followed in 1854, so by the mid-1850s Wordie & Co. was carrying for the companies which made up the line between Glasgow and Aberdeen via Perth and Dundee. An agreement with Pickfords was made, for forwarding goods, which was to endure until nationalization in 1948, and in 1865–6 Wordies benefited by the Caledonian take-over of the companies forming the Aberdeen route. By this time William Wordie was moving further north. In 1860 he opened a depot in Inverness; he was already at Elgin, both now linked to Aberdeen by rail. In 1865 the Highland Railway was formed by amalgamation, and in 1868 Wordie & Co. gained their cartage work. A year later the company secured the cartage contract for the neighbouring Great North of Scotland Railway.

By the time of his sudden death on 9 October 1874 at his Garngabber estate near Lenzie, following a heart attack, William Wordie controlled a large business, some 700 horses, with stables and depots from Glasgow to Thurso. He was an important figure in Scottish transport, and, as the obituary in the *Glasgow Star* said, 'Mr Wordie had always a kindly word, and his little, quick, energetic figure will be missed from the platforms of our northern railways' (quoted in the *Glasgow Herald*, 10 Oct 1874). He was buried at Stirling new cemetery on 12 October. He was survived by his wife; and his sons, John and Peter, expanded further, over to Ireland and into England, until it was said, 'You'll find Wordie & Co. wherever you go'.

EDWARD PAGET-TOMLINSON

Sources E. Paget-Tomlinson, *The railway carriers* (1990) • S. Orr, 'Wordie, William', *DSBB* • W. Drysdale, *Old faces, old places and old stories of Stirling* (1898) • *Glasgow Herald* (10 Oct 1874) • *Stirling Observer* (15 Oct 1874) • *Stirling Journal* (16 Oct 1874)
Archives Central Regional Council Archives, Stirling • Mitchell L., Glas., Strathclyde regional archives
Likenesses photograph, c.1870, priv. coll.
Wealth at death £43,765 5s. 4d.: Orr, 'Wordie, William'

Wordsworth, Charles (1806–1892), Scottish Episcopal bishop of St Andrews, Dunkeld, and Dunblane, the second son of Christopher *Wordsworth (1774–1846), master of Trinity College, Cambridge, was nephew of William *Wordsworth, the poet, and elder brother of Christopher *Wordsworth (1807–1885), bishop of Lincoln.

Education and early years, 1806–1835 Charles was born at Lambeth on 22 August 1806, his father then being chaplain to Archbishop Manners-Sutton. His mother, Priscilla, née Lloyd, died in 1815 at the age of thirty-three, and Mrs Hoare, widow of the banker Samuel Hoare of Hampstead, and his sister, did much to supply a mother's place. At

Charles Wordsworth (1806–1892), by unknown photographer

Sevenoaks School, near his father's benefice of Sundridge, he began to show his taste for Latin verse and cricket. In 1820, when his brothers went to Winchester, Charles, having somewhat delicate health, was sent to the milder discipline of Harrow School, to which his friend and neighbour H. E. (later Cardinal) Manning was also sent. Other contemporaries were the two Merivales, Herman and Charles (later dean of Ely), and the two Trenches, Francis and Richard (later the archbishop of Dublin). Here his special tastes abundantly developed. Charles Merivale called him 'king of our cricket field', though his nervousness prevented him from making high scores in set matches. His name must, however, always be associated with the history of the game. He played in the first regular Eton and Harrow match in 1822, in the first Winchester and Harrow match in 1825, and he brought about the first Oxford and Cambridge match in 1827. He had also much to do with the first Oxford and Cambridge boat race in 1828. He played tennis at Oxford, and was an excellent skater until late in life. He did not take to golf, which he never played until he reached the age of eighty-four. He was brilliant as a classical scholar, and in writing Greek and Latin verses he became a poet. Latin-verse composition was his peculiar delight and solace to the end of his long life.

Wordsworth's Harrow successes were crowned by greater distinctions at Christ Church, Oxford, which he entered in 1825 as a commoner, Charles Thomas Longley and Thomas Vowler Short being his tutors. His Virgilian poem on Mexico, with which he won the chancellor's prize for Latin verse in 1827, led to his obtaining a studentship in 1827 from Dean Smith. He took his degree (first-class classics) in the spring of 1830, and then taught private pupils (colleges at that time providing little individual tuition), including James Hope (Scott), W. E. Gladstone, H. E. Manning, Francis Doyle, Walter Kerr Hamilton, Lord Lincoln (later fifth duke of Newcastle), Thomas Dyke-Acland, Charles Canning, and Francis Popham.

In September 1831 Charles went with William Wordsworth and Dora, his uncle and cousin, on their last visit to Sir Walter Scott at Abbotsford. From July 1833 to June 1834 he travelled as tutor to Lord Cantelupe in Germany, Denmark, Sweden, and Norway, returning by Greifswald and Berlin, where he learnt something of German university education, and became more or less acquainted with professors Schleiermacher, Neander, Böckh, Henning, Immanuel Bekker, and D. F. Strauss. He also visited Dresden and Leipzig. In the same summer he travelled in France with Roundell Palmer (later Lord Selborne). After Palmer's departure he met in Paris Charlotte (d. 1839), the orphan daughter of the Revd George Day of Earsham, near Bungay, to whom he became engaged to be married. On his return to Christ Church he was appointed to a public tutorship by Gaisford (dean in 1831), and was ordained deacon by Bishop Bagot of Oxford on 21 December 1834. He did not proceed to the priesthood until six years later, on 13 December 1840.

Teaching at Winchester, 1835–1846 At midsummer 1835 Wordsworth was elected second master of Winchester College. The mastership had never been held except by a Wykehamist. The office brought him an opportunity for the exercise of his special faculty of teaching as well as valuable experience of management, involving the internal control of the ancient college and its seventy scholars. He enjoyed there not only the intimate friendship of Warden Barter but close companionship with George Moberly, the headmaster (later bishop of Salisbury), and frequent meetings with John Keble at Hursley. Wordsworth's marriage to Charlotte Day followed on 29 December 1835 in Norwich Cathedral, and his married life was extremely happy. But his wife died after giving birth to her only child, a daughter (Charlotte Emmeline), on 10 May 1839. Her death was followed on 31 December 1839 by that of his elder brother John *Wordsworth [see under Wordsworth, Christopher (1774–1846)].

Wordsworth and Warden Barter (who initiated the sermons in chapel) were largely responsible for bringing about a new period in the religious life of England's oldest public school. Wordsworth's efforts were directed chiefly to revitalizing the traditional system of the place. He succeeded in instituting a set time for private prayer, and the chapel service was much improved, partly by the efforts of John Pyke Hullah. Wordsworth was orthodox but not narrow. He inherited from his father and his friends, such as Joshua Watson and Hugh James Rose, the traditions of the old high-church Anglicanism, to which he added much of the zeal of the Oxford Movement, while his Quaker connections gave him broader and more evangelical sympathies.

Wordsworth's Winchester life and its aspirations and successes are reflected in several books. His churchmanship was developed to its highest point in a sermon, *Evangelical Repentance* (1841; with large appendix, 1842). He published several volumes of sermons and addresses, as well as *The College of St Mary, Winton, near Winchester* (1848). His greatest success in scholarship was the production of a Greek grammar (*Graecae grammaticae rudimenta*), which for a long time was the chief Greek grammar in England. Among his scholastic methods was the learning of Latin prose (Cicero) by heart by every boy. He was an able translator, as his translations of the hymns of Ken and Keble, published in 1845, show.

At the beginning of 1846 Wordsworth resigned his post at Winchester, partly on account of his father's failing health (he died on 2 February 1846). In the spring he preached a farewell sermon and edited his addresses, published as *Christian Boyhood at a Public School* (1846) in two volumes.

Warden of Trinity College, 1846–1852 Shortly after delivering his farewell sermon Wordsworth accepted the offer made by his former pupil Gladstone of the wardenship of the new Episcopalian Trinity College then being founded at Glenalmond, Perthshire. The scheme for founding this college, which was to be a training college for ordination candidates and a public school for boys, was first broached by James Hope and Gladstone in 1841, and was encouraged by Dean Ramsay in Edinburgh. Much money was collected for it in England as well as among the Scottish gentry, and in September 1844 the site was chosen, being the gift of George Patton. The buildings, designed by Sir Gilbert Scott, were soon in progress, but it was not until 8 September 1846 that the first stone of the chapel was laid by Sir John Gladstone. On 28 October Wordsworth entered on a second marriage, with Katharine Mary (d. 23 April 1897), the eldest daughter of William Barter, rector of Burghclere, Hampshire, and niece of his friend the warden of Winchester. They had twelve children, five sons and seven daughters, of whom three sons and five daughters survived him.

When Trinity College opened in May 1847, Wordsworth began with fourteen boys, the first being the eighth marquess of Lothian; two others were sons of Bishop Ewing of Argyll. The divinity students came about a year later. Notwithstanding the difficulties attaching to such joint education, Wordsworth made it a success, and was aggrieved when the elder students were settled in Edinburgh in 1876. The school discipline was naturally much based on that of Winchester; the prefectorial system was instituted and school games encouraged. Even a school for servitors was established (1848), somewhat after the older model. The chapel, which was in great part Wordsworth's gift to the college (consecrated on 1 May 1851), was the centre of daily life. All students wore surplices, and all were taught to sing. The success was great and real. The Scottish office

for holy communion was used (by the bishop's desire) alternately with the English. *Three Sermons on Holy Communion* (1855) worthily embodies Wordsworth's teaching to his boys on this subject.

During his time at Glenalmond, Wordsworth gradually became interested in Scottish church questions. Unfortunately his interest took largely the form of criticism of the actions of Patrick Torry, bishop of St Andrews, Dunkeld, and Dunblane, his diocesan, and of Gladstone, the leading member of the college council. Bishop Torry's *Prayer Book* (1850) was the first book since 1637 purporting to be a complete and independent Scottish prayer book, and it gave offence to many. Wordsworth censured it in seven letters to *The Guardian* newspaper, and led the condemnation of it in the diocesan synod. His opposition to Gladstone was on the subject of the duty of church establishment, of which Wordsworth was always, as Gladstone had been, a staunch upholder. Wordsworth refused his vote to Gladstone, who became candidate for Oxford first in 1847, and in sermons and letters lost no opportunity of showing his opposition to Gladstone's views.

Bishop of St Andrews: disputed election and ecclesiastical differences, 1852–1863 Bishop Torry died on 3 October 1852. Wordsworth was one of the seventeen presbyters with whom the election of a successor lay. He and Bishop Eden of Moray were nominated for the vacancy. The electors (excluding himself) were exactly divided, eight against eight. The decisive voice was in his hands, and he was persuaded, in accordance with precedent, to vote for himself, in order to counteract what he regarded as the dangerous policy of his opponents. Owing to some informality the process had to be repeated, his rival on the second occasion being Dr T. G. Suther (later bishop of Aberdeen). On appeal to the bishops of the Scottish church, Wordsworth's election was upheld. He retained his wardenship with the bishopric until 1854. He left seventy boys in the college, and reported that there had been on average five divinity students each year.

Elected bishop of St Andrews, Dunkeld, and Dunblane on 30 November 1852, Wordsworth was consecrated at St Andrew's Church, Aberdeen, on 25 January 1853. The principles on which he acted in this office were mainly three: to prevent the capture of the Scottish Episcopal church by a narrow party, especially by a party made up of Englishmen and controlled from England; to convince the Scots of the value of episcopacy and episcopal ordinances; to make some concessions to presbyterians by which they might be conciliated, the main principle of episcopacy being saved (Wordsworth, *Episcopate* 37–9). Wordsworth was a strong believer in the duty of establishment of religion where it was possible and in the synodal system. He held different opinions on the place of the laity in church synods at different times, but ended by advocating their presence and right to vote (ibid., 194).

There was no episcopal residence, and Wordsworth, after leaving Glenalmond, moved from place to place before settling down finally at Perth, first at Pitcullen Bank (Easter 1856 to 1858) and then at the Feu House (1858 to October 1876). He was thus brought into close connection with the cathedral of St Ninian, a venture supported chiefly by two men who had little or no connection with the diocese (Lord Forbes and G. F. Boyle, afterwards earl of Glasgow), and run chiefly by high-churchmen from England. He felt it a costly experiment for a poorly endowed diocese, but in many respects he sympathized with it. His wise treatment of its affairs in his first synods conciliated his opponents. But when he came to live permanently in Perth, and tried to make St Ninian's his own church, a fundamental divergence between himself and Provost Fortescue and Precentor Humble showed itself.

Unfortunately the eucharistic controversy was introduced in an acute form into Scotland by Alexander Penrose Forbes, bishop of Brechin, in his 'primary charge', delivered in 1857. Not only was high doctrine taught, but it was taught *ex cathedra*, and with rigorous logic, as necessary truth, and scant regard was shown for the traditional teaching of the Scottish church. Agitation followed, and the storm was further intensified by the publication in January 1858 of *Six Sermons* by the Revd Cheyne of St John's, Aberdeen; Cheyne went further than Forbes, and put the same kind of doctrines in a more provocative and more nearly Roman form. Forbes's charge was censured in a pastoral letter drafted by Wordsworth (27 May 1858), in which all the six remaining bishops concurred. This was followed by the suspension of Cheyne by the bishop of Aberdeen on 5 August and by the issue of Wordsworth's very valuable 'Notes to assist towards a right judgment on the eucharistic controversy' (September 1858), with a 'Supplement' dated Advent. These 'Notes' were never published, but circulated privately, especially among the clergy. Cheyne was declared to be no longer a clergyman of the Episcopal church (9 November 1859). On 3 October 1859 proceedings were formally instituted against Bishop Forbes.

The same year saw an open breach between Wordsworth and the cathedral clergy. The points at issue were the attempt to reopen the cathedral school, the 'cathedral declaration' on the eucharist, and certain ritual matters. Wordsworth left the cathedral, and did not return to it except to perform some necessary episcopal acts, such as confirmation, for more than twelve years (1859–72). He did his best, however, to stave off proceedings in Bishop Forbes's case, and published anonymously *Proposals for Peace*. The trial took place in February and March 1860, and Wordsworth delivered an 'opinion' which had previously been approved by George Forbes, the bishop's brother. The court unanimously censured and admonished Bishop Forbes, but with the least possible severity. Cheyne later on tendered some explanations, and was restored in 1863. Wordsworth's attitude in the controversy was one of reserve, working for united action, and refraining from public demonstrations on his own part.

Reunion proposals and further controversy, 1863–1882 The restoration of peace and the simultaneous revival experienced by the episcopal and presbyterian communions gave an opening for that reunion work which Wordsworth had deeply at heart. His powerful synodal and other

addresses in these years brought the question well forward, and at one time an important conference was in prospect. His most popular contribution was a sermon, 'Euodias and Syntyche', preached in 1867 (published 1869). The foundation of a school chapel at Perth in 1866, of which the bishop was practically incumbent, was a relief to him after his disappointments with the cathedral. An important and successful conference of clergy and laity was held at Perth in 1868, and the bishop had hopes of getting the question of the admission of laymen to church synods sympathetically treated by the general synod. By the friendly generosity of Bishop W. K. Hamilton a sum of some £200 a year was added to his income from 1866 to 1871, when he obtained a fellowship at Winchester, a matter of great comfort to him.

But, with these exceptions, the years that remained at Perth were a period of depression. Provost Fortescue resigned in 1871, and in his place Wordsworth appointed John Burton, who soon came under the influence of Precentor Humble. The struggles of 1859 were repeated in 1872 over the 'Perth nunnery' and alleged breaches of faith in regard to ritual. Wordsworth's charge in this year led to an indictment of the bishop by Humble before the episcopal synod, which was unanimously dismissed on 27 March 1873. After various negotiations with the chapter, the bishop in April 1874 announced his intention of resigning. But he took no steps to make it effective. He then established a *modus vivendi* with Burton, but he was never easy in his relations with the chapter as long as he remained at Perth. Humble's death on 7 February 1876 removed the chief actor in these disputes.

During this period Wordsworth published *On Shakespeare's Knowledge and Use of the Bible* (1864; 3rd edn 1880). In 1866 his Greek grammar was adopted by the headmasters of England. In 1870 he became one of the New Testament revisers, but before the revision was completed in 1881 he expressed his reasons for differing from the action of the majority, who, he thought, made far too many changes. In 1872 he published an important volume, *Outlines of the Christian Ministry*, which was supplemented in 1879 by *Remarks on Dr Lightfoot's Essay*.

In October 1876 Wordsworth left Perth for St Andrews. He first resided at The Hall (hitherto a hall for episcopalian students attending the university), which he called Bishop's Hall or Bishopshall; it later became St Leonard's Girls' School. In 1887 he moved to a smaller house on the Scores, which he called Kilrymont, the former name of St Andrews. St Andrews brought him opportunities of once again influencing young men, and introduced him into the congenial literary society formed by the professors of the university. Most of these were presbyterians, and this revived his hopefulness in reunion work. The new efforts may be dated from his sermon at the consecration of Edinburgh Cathedral on 30 October 1879. In the spring of 1884 the bishop received the honorary degree of DD from the universities of St Andrews and Edinburgh, and began a practice of occasionally preaching in presbyterian churches in connection with academic functions, especially in the college church at St Andrews, where he preached about once a year until 1888.

In May 1884 Wordsworth published an article in the *Scottish Church Review* entitled 'Union or separation', which suggested reunion, with optional Episcopal ordination for presbyterians. The alarm excited by this proposal led to his being denied his proper place at the Seabury commemoration at Aberdeen in October 1884. His charge of September 1885, *The Case of Non-Episcopal Ordination Fairly Considered*, is in the same line. The fullest and most logical expression of the scheme is given in a letter to Archbishop Benson in preparation for the Lambeth conference, dated 24 May 1888, and entitled *Ecclesiastical Union between England and Scotland*, his most important publication on the subject.

Later years, death, and reputation, 1882–1892   Wordsworth's relations with his own cathedral began to improve after the move to St Andrews, and from 1882 onwards he held his synods again there. In 1885 Provost Burton died, and the Revd Rorison of Forfar accepted the offer of his position. The cathedral now became a thoroughly diocesan institution. From 1886 to 1890 some £8000 was spent on it. The chapter house, with Wordsworth's library presented by his sons, is his memorial. Wordsworth was severely ill in the winter of 1890–91, but he delivered one more important charge, that on Old Testament criticism, in October 1891, and saw the appearance and rapid success of the first volume of his autobiographical *Annals* (1891). His charge of 1892 was delivered in his absence by the dean. Wordsworth died at St Andrews on 5 December 1892; he was buried in the cathedral yard, and a memorial tablet was erected.

Wordsworth left his own communion in a much higher position in public opinion than when he first came to the country, and this change was in part due to his courage, persistent energy, and ability. In appearance he was tall and handsome, with a strong and prepossessing countenance, set off by brown curly hair and brightened by a winning smile. He had a taste and a talent for friendship, and numbered among his firmest friends bishops W. K. Hamilton and T. L. Claughton, and Roundell Palmer, Lord Selborne. In disposition he was generous, and free in expense. He was very accurate and orderly, even in trifles, and expected others to be so. His character, as well as his experience as a teacher, made him critical, and he could be occasionally severe, and he was therefore sometimes misjudged. He was on the one hand impulsive and eager, and on the other sensitive and subject to fits of depression; on the whole he was sanguine and resolute, and gifted with much perseverance and consistency. He published frequently and on a variety of subjects, with works on Scottish religious history in 1861 and 1881, an edition of Shakespeare's historical plays (3 vols., 1883), further Latin translations, and numerous pamphlets; there is a bibliography of his works in his biography by his nephew John Wordsworth.

JOHN WORDSWORTH, *rev.* H. C. G. MATTHEW

Sources J. Wordsworth, *The episcopate of Charles Wordsworth, bishop of St Andrews* (1899) · C. Wordsworth, *Annals of my early life, 1806–*

1846: with occasional compositions in Latin and English verse, ed. W. E. Hodgson, 2 vols. (1891–3) · G. St Quentin, *The history of Glenalmond* (1956) · Gladstone, *Diaries*
Archives LPL, corresp. · NL Scot., sermons, corresp., and papers · Wordsworth Trust, Dove Cottage, Grasmere, corresp. | BL, corresp. with W. E. Gladstone, Add. MS 44346 · LPL, corresp. with Lord Selborne · NL Scot., letters to J. S. Blackie · NL Scot., letters to J. R. Hope–Scott · University of Dundee, corresp. with Alexander Forbes
Likenesses G. Richmond, portrait, 1840; formerly in the headmaster's house at Winchester College, 1900 · W. Walker, stipple, pubd 1848 (after G. Richmond), BM · H. T. Munns, portrait, 1882 · G. Horsburgh, oils, 1893; formerly in the possession of Mr W. B. Wordsworth, 1900 · W. L. Colls, engraving (after H. T. Munns, 1882), repro. in Wordsworth, *Episcopate of Charles Wordsworth* · T. Rodger, carte-de-visite, NPG · engraving (after G. Richmond), Winchester College, Hampshire · photograph, NPG [see illus.] · wood-engraving (after photograph), BM; repro. in *ILN* (10 Dec 1892)
Wealth at death £21,011 9s. 7d.: confirmation, 24 Feb 1893, *CCI*

Wordsworth, Christopher (1774–1846), college head, was born at Cockermouth in Cumberland on 9 June 1774. He was the youngest son of John Wordsworth (1741–1783), agent to Sir James Lowther, and his wife, Ann, *née* Cookson (1747–1778), and the youngest brother of William *Wordsworth. His mother died in 1778, and his father in 1783, after which time two uncles, Richard Wordsworth and Christopher Crackanthorpe, supplied the place of guardians. Having attended the grammar school at Hawkshead, he matriculated as a pensioner at Trinity College, Cambridge, in 1792. He proceeded BA in 1796 as tenth wrangler, and in 1798 was elected a fellow of Trinity. Extracts from a diary kept by him at Cambridge between 1793 and 1801 were published by his grandson Christopher (Wordsworth, *Social Life at the English Universities*, 587–99), and give details of an enterprising and energetic academic and cultural life. In 1799 he proceeded MA and in 1810 DD by royal mandate.

While Charles Manners-Sutton, first Viscount Canterbury, had been an undergraduate at Trinity College (1798–1802), Wordsworth had served as his private tutor, and by this means became acquainted with his father, the bishop of Norwich, who in 1805 became archbishop of Canterbury. A steady flow of patronage resulted. In 1804 Wordsworth became rector of Ashby-with-Oby and Thinne, Norfolk, a preferment which enabled him to marry, on 6 October 1804, Priscilla (*d.* 1815), eldest daughter of Charles *Lloyd, the Quaker banker and philanthropist of Birmingham, and sister of Charles Lloyd, the poet. In 1805 he was made domestic chaplain to the new archbishop. In 1806 he became rector of Woodchurch in Kent, advancing in 1808 to the deanery and rectory of Bocking, Essex, to which Monks-Eleigh, Suffolk, was added in 1812. These preferments were exchanged in 1816 for St Mary's, Lambeth, where Wordsworth was a vigorous supporter of church extension, and Sundridge in Kent, where the family of Henry Edward Manning were prominent parishioners. When Charles Manners-Sutton became speaker of the House of Commons in 1817, Wordsworth became his chaplain.

By this time Wordsworth had gained a considerable

reputation as a scholar and as an able apologist for the Church of England. His *Six letters to Granville Sharp, esq., respecting his 'Remarks on the uses of the definitive article in the Greek text of the New Testament'* (1802) earned the respect of the great critic Richard Porson, and his industriousness as an editor resulted in the publication of *Ecclesiastical Biography* (6 vols., 1809, 1818), in which selected lives were presented in chronological order so as to illustrate the history of the Church of England from the Reformation to the revolution of 1688. In 1810 he published *Reasons for Declining to Become a Subscriber to the British and Foreign Bible Society*, and in 1811 he was instrumental, with his close friend Joshua Watson, in setting up the National Society to provide education in accordance with the principles of the Church of England. Throughout his life Wordsworth remained firmly convinced of the advantages of a national structure of religious provision, a subject that provided the matter for his last published work, *The Leaven to Leaven the Whole Lump, or, Duties Individual and National* (1845), in which he continued to call for heavy state funding for a programme of school and church building.

Yet, though a high-churchman of the old school, Wordsworth was awake to the danger of laying too much stress upon the church as a mere 'establishment'. Similarly, he was capable of appreciating the good in other Christian traditions, a fact exemplified by his continuing cordial relations with his wife's Quaker relatives, by his praise for the private use made by continental clergy of the Roman Catholic breviary, and by his deliberate inclusion of works by Richard Baxter, in his *Christian Institutes* (4 vols., 1837), a work of otherwise impeccable Anglican orthodoxy. Such eirenic instincts, combined with a firm grasp of the authentic traditions of the Church of England, greatly influenced his response to the rise of the Oxford Movement. Although sympathetic in its early days to the efforts of men such as William Palmer and Hugh James Rose, and one of the first of 7000 clergy to sign the address to the archbishop of Canterbury in February 1834, Wordsworth soon became suspicious of what he detected as a 'spirit of Anti-Anglican Novelty' in the movement, and his initially high opinion of John Henry Newman was finally destroyed in 1841 by the publication of Tract 90. Thereafter, Wordsworth's attitude was unrelentingly hostile. In 1842 he criticized Edward Pusey and John Keble for failing to check their less judicious followers, and in 1843 he welcomed the publication by his son Christopher *Wordsworth of *Theophilus Anglicanus, or, Instructions for the young student, concerning the church, and the Anglican branch of it*, mainly on the grounds that 'nothing [was] more likely to arrest the progress of the evils threatened to us from Newman and Newmanism'.

In politics Wordsworth was a conservative. His promotion to the mastership of Trinity following the death of William Lort Mansel on 27 June 1820 was at the hands of Lord Liverpool, who acted on the recommendation of Archbishop Manners-Sutton. Wordsworth retained the post until 1841, and, although latterly in weakened health, he delayed his resignation until Sir Robert Peel had returned to office in 1841 in order to be sure that William Whewell would succeed him. At the time of his appointment in 1820 Wordsworth exchanged his preferment at Lambeth and Sundridge for the living of Buxted-with-Uckfield in Sussex. Having been away from Cambridge for sixteen years, he made an energetic return, serving as vice-chancellor in 1820–21 and again in 1826–7. During his first tenure of the office he granted a licence to the Union Debating Society, which had been previously forbidden, and made proposals for a public examination, in classics and divinity, which was seen as an important step towards the establishment of the classical tripos in 1822. At Trinity he moved immediately to provide more accommodation for undergraduates, overcoming considerable opposition from some of the fellows. The New Court, designed by William Wilkins, anticipated similar enterprises elsewhere in Cambridge, notably at King's, St John's, and Corpus Christi. It provided the college with an extra 200 rooms and was occupied in Michaelmas 1825. Wordsworth also sought to encourage undergraduates by instituting personal prizes for Latin verse composition. During his mastership a permanent fund was created for the augmentation of poorer college livings, and for the building of adequate parsonage houses.

Wordsworth's commitment to Trinity was evident in 1822, when, on the death of Thomas Fanshaw Middleton, he was said to have declined the offer of the bishopric of Calcutta, and on another unspecified occasion, when he refused the deanery of Peterborough. Elsewhere, his achievements as master contradict the claim that he was not a successful appointment. As a widower, his wife having died in 1815, with no female relatives to supply that place in his household, it was inevitable that the style of his mastership should be more secluded than many might have wished, but some at least, like Miss Fenwick in 1839, appreciated his manner: 'a gentle but dignified old Abbot he might have been, and learned in all the learning of the olden time' (Wordsworth, *Annals*, 299–300). The resentment of some undergraduates, who objected when Wordsworth sought to enforce better observance of college rules, particularly in the matter of chapel attendance, can hardly be regarded as surprising, any more than his clash in 1834 with Connop Thirlwall over the questions of compulsory chapel and the admission of dissenters to degrees. Indeed, Wordsworth's inflexibility on such matters can be seen as consistent with his high sense of the responsibilities of his post, an understanding that he expounded with great clarity and force in a pamphlet *The Ecclesiastical Commission and the Universities* (1837), a spirited justification of the existing state of relations between the universities and the church in which he warned against the 'too liberal … use of the compasses and the scissars, to the neglect … of higher, more vital, and more venerable matters' (pp. 33–4).

Apart from the works mentioned above, Wordsworth was also author of *Sermons on Various Subjects* (2 vols., 1814), and of a series of works published between 1824 and 1828 asserting the right of Charles I to be regarded as the author of the Eikon basilike. William Grant Broughton,

Henry Hallam, John Lingard, and Henry John Todd contributed to the resulting controversy.

Wordsworth had three sons: John [see below], Charles *Wordsworth, and Christopher Wordsworth. Following his resignation from the mastership of Trinity, he retired to his living at Buxted, where he died on 2 February 1846.

His eldest son, **John Wordsworth** (1805–1839), classical scholar, born at Lambeth on 1 July 1805, was educated first at a school at Woodford, Essex, kept by Dr Holt Okes, and then at Winchester College (1819–23). In October 1824 he went up to Trinity College, Cambridge, where he was elected to a scholarship and won the Porson prize in 1826. Although distaste for mathematics disqualified him from classical honours when he proceeded BA in 1828, he secured election to a fellowship at Trinity in 1830, proceeding MA in 1831. Between 1830 and 1833 he resided in Cambridge, and contributed a notable review of James Scholefeld's *Aeschylus* to the first number of the *Philological Museum*. In 1833 he made a long visit, by way of France and Switzerland, to Italy, where he collated the Medicean manuscript of Aeschylus at Florence with a view to a new edition. Some of this work was used by John Conington in his edition of the *Choëphoroe* (1857). On returning to Cambridge he took up the duties of an assistant tutor at Trinity, giving lectures that were noted for their diligence and erudition. He also began work on an edition of Dr Bentley's *Correspondence* which was later completed by his brother Christopher, and made large collections for a classical dictionary.

In 1837 Wordsworth was ordained deacon and priest by the bishop of Ely, but his health began to fail, and he was obliged to resign his lectureship and to withdraw as a candidate for the headmastership of King Edward's School, Birmingham. He remained in Cambridge, where he died, unmarried, on 31 December 1839; he was buried on 6 January 1840 in the antechapel of Trinity College, where a monument was erected to his memory by subscription, with a bust executed by Weekes under Chantrey's supervision.   RICHARD SHARP

Sources DNB · C. Wordsworth, *Annals of my early life, 1806–1846: with occasional compositions in Latin and English verse*, ed. W. E. Hodgson, 2 vols. (1891–3) · E. Churton, ed., *Memoir of Joshua Watson*, 2 vols. (1861) · P. B. Nockles, *The Oxford Movement in context: Anglican high churchmanship, 1760–1857* (1994) · C. Wordsworth, *Social life at the English universities in the eighteenth century* (1874), 587–99 · J. Mackintosh, *Works*, 1 (1854), 508–42 · *GM*, 2nd ser., 25 (1846), 320–22 · *GM*, 2nd ser., 13 (1840), 436–7 · *The correspondence of Richard Bentley*, ed. C. Wordsworth, 2 vols. (1842), vol. 1, pp. xvi–xix

Archives BL, corresp. and papers, Add. MSS 46136–46138 · LPL, corresp. and papers, MSS 1822, 1824, 2149, 2150 · Trinity Cam., corresp., journals, and papers · Wordsworth Trust, Dove Cottage, Grasmere, corresp. | BL, corresp. with Sir Robert Peel, Add. MSS 40490–40551 · Harrow School, corresp. and papers as headmaster of Harrow School · Trinity Cam., letters to W. Whewell

Likenesses oils, in or before 1841, Trinity Cam. · H. Weekes, marble bust (John Wordsworth), Trinity Cam.

Wordsworth, Christopher (1807–1885), bishop of Lincoln, born at Lambeth Palace on 30 October 1807, was the third and youngest son of Christopher *Wordsworth (1774–1846), master of Trinity College, Cambridge, from 1820, and his wife, Priscilla (1781–1815), daughter of

Charles Lloyd, a Quaker and banker of Bingley Hall, Birmingham. John *Wordsworth (1805–1839) [see under Wordsworth, Christopher], fellow of Trinity, and Charles *Wordsworth (1806–1892), bishop of St Andrews, were his elder brothers. At the time of his birth, his father was chaplain to the archbishop of Canterbury, Charles Manners-Sutton (1755–1828). At Winchester College, between 1820 and 1825, Christopher's prodigious intellectual gifts became apparent; he also distinguished himself as an athlete, excelling at football, fives, and cricket, where, as a member of the first eleven, he caught out for a duck Henry Manning, who was playing for Harrow, an event he often recounted. In cross-country running he was the only boy in the school who could cover 9 miles in an hour, mainly uphill on the outward journey.

Wordsworth entered Trinity College, Cambridge, in 1826; a host of college and university prizes followed. In 1830 he graduated senior classic in the classical tripos and fourteenth senior optime in the mathematical tripos; he won the first chancellor's medal for classical studies and was immediately elected a fellow of Trinity and subsequently an assistant college tutor. His distinction in classical languages was such that he was later singled out to translate into Greek and Latin messages from the English episcopate to leaders of foreign churches. He began to travel in Italy and Greece and made his mark in the field of inscriptions and exploration: in 1832 he went to Paestum and to Pompeii, where he was the first to decipher the graffiti. In Sicily he developed an interest in Theocritus, the subject of later writing in 1844. During a prolonged visit to Greece and the Ionian Islands he made a conjecture as to the site of Dodona which was later corroborated. He was the first Englishman to be presented to King Otho. Passing over the heights of Mount Parnes in deep snow, he and his party were attacked by brigands; Wordsworth was injured in the shoulder by a stiletto, but managed to escape capture. Two books of a pictorial and descriptive kind on *Greece* (1839) and *Athens and Attica* (1836) followed his return. Wordsworth married on 6 December 1838 Susanna Frere (1811–1884), second daughter of George Frere, a solicitor of Twyford House, Bishop's Stortford, originally a Norfolk family. His wife's self-effacing, calm, and dependable nature was a considerable asset, and brought stability and happiness. There were seven children: two sons, both of whom entered the ministry, John *Wordsworth (1843–1911), later bishop of Salisbury, and Charles, and five daughters, the eldest of whom, Elizabeth *Wordsworth (1840–1932), became the first principal of Lady Margaret Hall, Oxford.

In 1835 Wordsworth was ordained priest by Bishop Hugh Percy of Carlisle. Like his father he remained constant to the high-churchmanship of the seventeenth- and eighteenth-century tradition, rather than that of the Tractarians. He was appointed public orator at Cambridge in 1836 and, in the same year, headmaster of Harrow School. Harrow proved a difficult assignment. Wordsworth tightened up the discipline, which had become lax, and took a personal interest in raising the academic standards of the boys' work on an individual basis. His overall management of the school revealed tendencies which continued to influence his ministry. The number of pupils dropped sharply until there were scarcely more than sixty-four boys, a decline for which he was largely responsible, as to sacrifice principle for expediency was not in his nature. Local feeling was aroused by the cessation of the boys' attendance at the parish church and the building of a school chapel, while pupils found long sermons on the nature of the church and the duties of membership (published under the title *Theophilus Anglicanus* in 1844) hard to digest. Wordsworth refused to take boarders personally into the headmaster's house; he consigned them into the care of John William Colenso (1814–1883) who, as house tutor, designed a method of central heating which caused the house to burst into flames on the day after installation. The Wordsworths' first child was consequently born in other accommodation. Expulsion for misdemeanours was frequent, and included a monitor, cousin of William Gladstone. Wordsworth's refusal to accept as foundationers local boys whose parents were not in financial need brought matters to a head: he resorted to litigation, also a practice he was to repeat. On 16 March 1844 the governors requested his resignation; he declined to comply until another appointment came to hand. His failure to secure the regius professorship of divinity at Cambridge in 1843 (repeated in 1850) was a heavy disappointment. Eventually Sir Robert Peel, an old Harrovian, solved the impasse; Wordsworth was offered a canonry at Westminster, to which he moved in December 1844.

From the calmer base of a house in Little Cloister at the abbey, Wordsworth soon applied himself energetically within his new surroundings. During his periods of residence he preached twice every Sunday sermons which, though considered inordinately long, were well received and subsequently published. He helped to found the Westminster Spiritual Aid Fund (with a contribution from the queen and Prince Albert) to build churches, schools, and parsonages and to endow clergy in the area; he set up a scheme for the training of nurses for the sick and poor and for ladies to visit in the Westminster Hospital. In 1848 he preached nine sermons on the Apocalypse, later printed, as Hulsean lecturer at Cambridge. His uncle the poet died in April 1850; Christopher became his literary executor and published *Memorials of William Wordsworth* (1851) in two volumes. In the same year he added responsibility for the parish of Stanford in the Vale with Goosey in the Oxford diocese—the gift of the dean and chapter—to his Westminster canonry. He held both in plurality from 1850 to 1868, moving his family regularly from one to the other. At Stanford, in addition to his pastoral work, he worked on his most considerable literary achievement, a commentary on the entire Bible (New Testament, 1860; Old Testament, 1870), in which his aim was to reconcile the interpretation of scripture with recent advances of science. A significant study on *St Hippolytus and the Church of Rome* was published in 1853, and in 1862 *The Holy Year*, a series of hymns, some of which long remained in use. In Westminster he championed the cause of the Society for

the Revival of Convocation; after its accomplishment in 1852, he became an active member of the lower house as representative of the chapter and spoke often. In 1865 he became archdeacon of Westminster. A strong opponent of *Essays and Reviews* (1860), he contributed to the *Replies to the 'Essays and Reviews'* (1862), with a preface by the bishop of Oxford, Samuel Wilberforce (1805–1873). In particular he attacked Benjamin Jowett (1817–1893) with considerable force for failing to account for patristic interpretation of the scriptures. Wordsworth attributed to the Church of England a special mission to bring about reunion at home and reform abroad. He made several tours to investigate the religious situation in France and Italy, followed by reports of a critical nature. His thirteen letters to the editor for English religious affairs of the French periodical *L'Univers*, published as *Letters to M. Gondon … on the Destructive Character of the Church of Rome* (1847), were not the only writings in which he made such views known. His sympathy for the Greek church inclined him towards membership of the Eastern Church Association, founded in 1853 by John Mason Neale, and his activity within the Anglo-Continental Society led to the publication of letters between members and its secretary, Canon Frederick Meyrick. In 1867 and again in 1878, at the time of the Lambeth conferences, he made translations of the resolutions into Greek, Latin, and modern Greek; in addition he was the author of the *Responsio Anglicana*, in October 1868, an answer to a papal letter of September the same year. His championship of the Old Catholics after their break from Rome in 1870 belongs to his period as a bishop.

A vacancy in the see of Lincoln was created in 1868 with the move to London of Bishop John Jackson. Disraeli's offer of a bishopric on account of his 'confidence in your abilities, your learning and shining example' (Overton and Wordsworth, 203) Wordsworth at first refused, thinking himself too old at sixty-one. His close friend Edward White Benson (1829–1896) persuaded him to change his mind, and the letter to the prime minister was rescued from a pillar box. He was consecrated on 24 February 1869. His period of episcopacy amounted to less than one-third of his ministry and did not include many of his accomplishments, but in spite of his doubts he brought to his diocese a good deal of his customary energy, and showed that he had not abandoned his capacity to meet controversy head-on and take unpopular decisions. The attitudes which he had adopted all his life he continued to hold with remarkable consistency: a high doctrine of the nature of the church, a dislike of pluralism, an ordered view of administration, and a tendency to believe that the problems faced by the early fathers were still current and could be met by patristic example. First, he sought assistance in his large diocese: a petition to the queen for a suffragan bishop of Nottingham was successful in 1870 with the appointment of the former archdeacon Henry Mackenzie. The division of the diocese by the creation of the see of Southwell was achieved in 1884. His diocesan synod of 1871 was the first for several generations; annual diocesan conferences were held subsequently. He did not flinch from going to law when he refused to institute prospective incumbents of whom he did not approve, or to oppose secular authority on various pieces of legislation in which he did not feel sufficient consideration had been given to the church, such as the Public Worship Regulation Bill of 1874 and the Burials Bill of 1880 to allow secular use of churchyards. It was commented that he was influenced by the line taken by St Ambrose against the emperor in the fourth century in regard to state interference in ecclesiastical matters.

Similar convictions governed Wordsworth's attitude towards public education. *Discourses on Education* had appeared in 1844, and two published sermons in 1851. In July 1870 he opposed Forster's bill in the House of Lords; the legislation, he considered, would lead to 'a race of godless teachers and infidel scholars' (*Hansard 3*, 1170). In his diocese, as part of his own programme of educational reform, fifty-nine new church schools were built and seventy-nine improved; St Paul's College for mission work was founded and the ancient chancellor's school (*cancellarii scolae*) revived as Lincoln Theological College. Relationships with Wesleyan Methodists were less successful: he was out of sympathy with dissenters because he considered they threatened the unity of the church, and his attempts to heal the schism between denominations were not found acceptable. He grew close to the Old Catholics on the continent, who found in him a learned figure who supported their views, and the establishment of a base of understanding owed much to his influence; it included a paper in favour of clerical marriage. Wordsworth attended the Old Catholic Congress in Cologne in September 1872 and made what Gladstone thought a 'John Bullish' speech. A second visit was paid to the congress of 1875 in Bonn.

Throughout his life Wordsworth remained wiry and lightly built; his contemporaries continued to comment on his quickness of movement and he was a graceful skater into old age. His appearance also remained remarkably unaltered: his complexion was dark; his long, straight hair drawn across a broad brow; two deep creases stretched down on either side of his nose; his grey eyes made rapid darting movements from side to side. This inherent physical energy was matched by constant mental activity. A retentive memory and ability to remain absorbed led to a literary output that was enormous and did not flag. But there was a price to be paid: his family wrote of his highly susceptible nervous system, neuralgia, and depression; he could be short-tempered under stress. Following the death of his wife in October 1884 Wordsworth's health deteriorated rapidly, and he died at Harewood, Yorkshire, on 21 March 1885. After a funeral in Lincoln Cathedral he was buried on 25 March at Riseholme, the village where he had lived throughout his episcopate.

MARGARET PAWLEY

Sources J. Overton and E. Wordsworth, *Christopher Wordsworth, bishop of Lincoln, 1807–1885* (1888) · A. C. Benson, *The leaves of the tree: studies in biography* (1911) · E. Wordsworth, *Glimpses of the past* (1912) · Harrow School, archives · G. Battiscombe, *Reluctant pioneer: a life of Elizabeth Wordsworth* (1978) · C. B. Moss, *The Old Catholic movement, its origins and history* (1948) · F. Meyrick, *Correspondence between members of the Anglo-Continental Society and oriental churchmen* (1874) · *Hansard 3* (1870), 201.1170 · Gladstone, *Diaries*
Archives BL, corresp. and papers incl. family corresp., Add. MSS 46136–46138 · Harrow School, Middlesex, corresp. and papers as headmaster at Harrow School · Lincs. Arch., corresp. and papers · Lincs. Arch., notes relating to missionary subjects · LPL, corresp. and papers · LPL, papers mainly relating to Anglo–Continental Society · Trinity Cam., diary · U. Birm. L., letters · Wordsworth Library, Dove Cottage, Grasmere, corresp. and papers relating to his *Memoirs of William Wordsworth* (1851) | BL, corresp. with Sir Robert Peel, Add. MSS 40511–40597, *passim* · BL, corresp. with W. E. Gladstone, Add. MS 44364 · Keble College, Oxford, letters to John Keble · LPL, corresp. with A. C. Tait · Trinity Cam., letters to William Whewell · U. Lpool L., Radcliffe Library, Christopher Wordsworth MSS
Likenesses W. Walker, stipple, pubd 1848 (after G. Richmond), BM · G. Richmond, crayon drawing, 1853; formerly in possession of the Wordsworth family, 1900 · J. Mansell, crayon drawing, 1869–85; formerly in possession of the Wordsworth family, 1900 · E. R. Taylor, oils, 1869–85; formerly in possession of the Wordsworth family, 1900 · E. Long, oils, 1878, Old Palace, Lincoln · Elliott & Fry, photograph, 1884, repro. in Overton and Wordsworth, *Christopher Wordsworth*, frontispiece · Miller, bust; formerly in possession of the Wordsworth family, 1900 · T. Rodger, carte-de-visite, NPG · photograph, NPG · wood-engraving (after photograph), BM; repro. in *ILN* (10 Dec 1892)
Wealth at death £89,750 4s. 7d.: resworn probate, Oct 1885, CGPLA Eng. & Wales

Wordsworth, Dorothy (1771–1855), writer, was born on 25 December 1771 in Cockermouth, Cumberland, the third among the five children and the only daughter of John Wordsworth (1741–1783), attorney, of Cockermouth, and his wife, Ann (1747–1778), daughter of William Cookson, linen draper, of Penrith. She was the sister of William *Wordsworth (1770–1850) and Christopher *Wordsworth (1774–1846). She was educated at a boarding-school in Hipperholme, near Halifax, and then at a day school in the same town. But personal circumstances were much more important than formal education in shaping her life and disposition. Her mother died in 1778, her father in 1783, and she grew up, happily or otherwise, with a succession of relatives at Halifax, Penrith, and Forncett rectory, near Norwich, home of her uncle William Cookson. There she helped with parish work and ran a Sunday school under the eye of Cookson's college friend William Wilberforce, whom she met again at Rydal many years later. When her uncle was installed as a canon of Windsor (1792), she went to stay there with the family. It was her sole introduction to fashionable society. She was eventually reunited with William at Windy Brow, Keswick, in 1794, and thereafter she devoted her life to looking after him, reviving his poetic powers and love of nature after his withdrawal from the French Revolution. 'She, in the midst of all, preserved me still / a Poet', Wordsworth later recalled in *The Prelude* (1805 edn, x.919–20). In 1795, with the help of a legacy from Raisley Calvert, they set up house together at Racedown Lodge, Dorset. Two years later they moved to Alfoxden House on the Quantock Hills in Somerset, in order to be near Coleridge at Nether Stowey, and there she

Dorothy
Wordsworth
(1771–1855), by
unknown artist,
c.1806

met Charles Lamb and William Hazlitt. Her taste in land-scape (like 'a perfect electrometer', according to Coleridge) is revealed for the first time in her 'Alfoxden journal' (1798), where the interplay between her impersonal records of the sights and sounds of nature and the poems of Wordsworth and Coleridge is already apparent. It was the first fruit of the creative partnership between brother and sister which is celebrated at the climax of Wordsworth's 'Tintern Abbey' during their tour of the Wye.

Dorothy Wordsworth's hopes for their return to the Lake District were finally realized 'home at Grasmere' in 1799, in the workaday setting of Dove Cottage, where they were soon joined by the Coleridges, Robert Southey and his wife, and later Thomas De Quincey. After William's marriage to Mary Hutchinson in 1802, Dorothy remained an indispensable member of his household, enduring the death of the 'sailor brother' John in the wreck of the *Abergavenny* (1805), and the loss of her investment in its cargo, which deprived her of financial independence. Further troubles followed, including the breach with Coleridge in 1810 while the family was living at Allan Bank, and in 1812 the death of two of William's children after the move to the rectory, while the parents were absent. But amid the vicissitudes of family life, Dorothy stayed true to her deepest instincts, proving that her role as transcriber of his poems, housekeeper, and devoted aunt to his children was not incompatible with her own imaginative life. The 'Grasmere journal' (1800–03) mingles William's poetry with the comings and goings of a rural society, joining the sublime to the matter-of-fact, and reveals her intense response to the seasonal appearances of nature, and the life of beggars and wayfarers on the open road whose circumstances were unchanging. She always directs attention away from herself to her surroundings. Her human sympathies are perhaps best reflected in her narrative of the deaths of George and Sarah Green in a snowstorm, written to raise money for the orphans (1808, published 1928).

When the family moved to Rydal Mount (1813), Dorothy's pursuits remained largely unchanged, and she shared her brother's growing circle of friends and visitors.

She cultivated lasting friendships through her correspondence, which mirrors the conditions under which the lake poets worked; her natural and unaffected letters, which reveal her personality more directly than her *Journals*, played an indispensable part in holding the wider Wordsworth circle together. Particularly dear to her were her schoolfriend Jane Pollard, who married John Marshall, the Leeds industrialist, and Catherine Clarkson, wife of the abolitionist Thomas Clarkson, of Playford Hall, Ipswich. She stayed with both families from time to time. A later friend was Henry Crabb Robinson, whose Rydal diaries chart the course of her physical and mental decline. The generosity of spirit that invariably shines through her letters seemed to mark all her human contacts.

The *Journals* describe many of Dorothy Wordsworth's travels. A winter at Hamburg and Goslar in Germany (1798–9), an excursion to Calais during the peace of Amiens to visit Annette Vallon and William's 'French' daughter Caroline in 1802, and in 1820 a continental tour to Switzerland and the Italian lakes after the Napoleonic wars, comprised her journeys abroad with her brother. She visited Scotland twice, in 1803 and 1822, the first time in his and Coleridge's company, when they passed some days with Sir Walter Scott. Her 'Recollections' of the tour, which form her most ambitious piece of writing, are best read alongside William's 'Memorials' of the same journey. She also visited the Isle of Man on her own in 1828. But she was happiest among her 'Hutchinson' relatives in the Welsh border country; at Coleorton, the estate of Sir George Beaumont in Leicestershire in 1806–7 and thereafter, where she returned to keep house for her nephew John Wordsworth, at Whitwick rectory (1828–9); or with Christopher at Cambridge, where she held her own in academic society. Her tastes were easily satisfied, and a walk under the stars, an excursion over the fells, or a coach ride by moonlight furnished her mind with unforgettable impressions. As De Quincey wrote, 'She was content to be ignorant of many things, but what she knew and had really mastered lay where it could not be disturbed—in the temple of her own most fervid heart' (De Quincey, 239).

Dorothy Wordsworth found fulfilment in ways which elude precise analysis. Onlookers were impressed by the vivid presence of the poet's 'exquisite' sister, as Coleridge called her, but she had few views or wishes of her own, being content to follow her brother's lead in literary, political, and religious matters. Her few poems are unremarkable, though William thought five of them good enough to be included in his own volumes. But in her *Journals*, unpublished in her lifetime and unknown outside her own circle, she found a unique outlet for her genius without competing with the writers who surrounded her. She had no desire to set herself up as an author, and seemed relieved when Samuel Rogers failed to secure publication of her Scottish 'Recollections'. 'I have not those powers which Coleridge thinks I have', she protested to Lady Beaumont, 'My only merits are my devotedness to those I love, and I hope a charity towards all mankind.' (*Letters of William and Dorothy Wordsworth*, 1.525).

In 1835, after several years of illness, Dorothy Wordsworth succumbed to a form of pre-senile dementia with only rare moments of remission, during which she resumed her journal; for the last two decades of her life she was confined to the house and terrace of Rydal Mount. No likeness of Dorothy Wordsworth in her prime has survived. Neither the early silhouette at Dove Cottage nor the much later portrait at Rydal Mount (1833) gives any hint of the 'wild eyes' and impulsive nature glimpsed by De Quincey, or the paradox which her personal appearance had originally presented to Coleridge: 'if you expected to see a pretty woman, you would think her ordinary—if you expected to find an ordinary woman, you would think her pretty!' (*Collected Letters*, ed. Griggs, 1.330). She died on 25 January 1855 in the care of her sister-in-law, surviving William by five years, and was buried beside him in Grasmere churchyard on 31 January.

Dorothy Wordsworth's life was comparatively uneventful and she never married, finding her true self in devotion to others and in the 'appropriate form' of her *Journals* and letters. No other observer was so close to Wordsworth and Samuel Taylor Coleridge during their most productive years together at Alfoxden and Grasmere; and no one else had such an eye for the landscapes which inspired them, or could provide them with living materials for poetry out of her own observations. Coleridge is reported to have said that they were three persons, but one soul.

Although De Quincey believed that Dorothy Wordsworth was worthy of a biographical memoir in her own right, she was largely overshadowed by her more famous brother. A separate account of her own achievements, and of her intangible contribution to William's visionary world seemed almost impossible, and she was not accorded her own entry in the *Dictionary of National Biography*. It was only after her *Journals* and *Letters* were progressively published in complete editions in the twentieth century that she was taken seriously as a woman writer and as a notable figure in the English Romantic movement. In the later twentieth century feminist critics opened up new lines of enquiry into her work, but in the longer term it seems unlikely that any one approach will fully explain the elusive nature of her genius, or the fascination it continues to exert on her readers.

ALAN G. HILL

Sources *Journals of Dorothy Wordsworth*, ed. E. de Selincourt (1941) · *Letters of William and Dorothy Wordsworth*, ed. A. G. Hill, 2nd edn (1967–93) · *Collected letters of Samuel Taylor Coleridge*, ed. E. L. Griggs, 6 vols. (1956–71) · T. De Quincey, 'Literary and Lake reminiscences', *Works*, ed. D. Masson, 2 (1896–7) · *Henry Crabb Robinson on books and their writers*, ed. E. J. Morley (1938) · R. Gittings and J. Manton, *Dorothy Wordsworth* (1985) · Wordsworth literary MSS, Grasmere · D. Wordsworth, *The Grasmere journals*, ed. P. Woof (1991) · *George and Sarah Green, a narrative, by Dorothy Wordsworth*, ed. E. de Selincourt (1928)

Archives Cornell University, Ithaca, New York · Wordsworth Trust, Dove Cottage, Grasmere, corresp., diaries, and papers | BL, corresp. with Catherine Clarkson, Add. MSS 36997, 41186 · BL, letters to John Wordsworth, Add. MS 46136 · U. Edin. L., letters to Mary Laing and David Laing

Likenesses painted silhouette, *c*.1806, Wordsworth Trust, Dove Cottage, Grasmere, Cumbria [*see illus.*] · S. Crosthwaite, oils, 1833, Rydal Mount, Cumbria · J. Harden, pencil sketch, 1842, Abbot Hall Art Gallery, Kendal, Cumbria

Wordsworth, Dame Elizabeth [*pseud.* Grant Lloyd] (1840–1932), college head, was born on 22 June 1840 at Harrow on the Hill, Middlesex, the eldest of the seven children of Christopher *Wordsworth (1807–1885), headmaster of Harrow School, from 1844 canon of Westminster, and from 1868 bishop of Lincoln, and his wife, Susanna Hatley Frere (1811–1884). In 1844 the family moved to 4 Little Cloister, in the precincts of Westminster Abbey, and from 1851 until Elizabeth was twenty-eight they usually spent four months of each year in Westminster and eight in Stanford in the Vale, in Berkshire, where her father held a living. She was educated at home, apart from one rather fruitless year at a boarding-school in Brighton when she was seventeen. Her father, intelligent governesses, and her own wide reading provided a substantial but uneven academic education. She learned almost no mathematics or science, but studied Latin, history, modern languages, English literature, drawing, and singing, and taught herself Greek from her younger brother John *Wordsworth's school books in order to read the New Testament and Homer. Christian faith shaped her upbringing profoundly, and throughout her life she treasured the liturgy, devotion, and traditions of high-church Anglicanism. Her piety was straightforward, scholarly, and practical, rooted in detailed study of the Bible and theology, but also in humdrum parish work in rural Stanford. Westminster, meanwhile, gave access to clerical and academic society in London, to galleries, and the theatre. From the age of thirteen she also travelled extensively in Europe with her family, and continued to do so with relatives and friends all her life.

Elizabeth was intelligent, witty, and unusually well read in several languages. Her father relied on her as a research assistant for an ambitious Bible commentary, and then as his secretary when he was appointed bishop and the family moved to Riseholme Palace near Lincoln. She never queried the convention by which her brothers John and Christopher were sent to Winchester College and then Oxford and Cambridge respectively, while she, as a girl, was educated informally at home. But when the headship of an Oxford hall of residence for women students was proposed to her in 1878 she accepted, and her father approved, although her brother John, then a fellow of Brasenose College, Oxford, saw no need for such an initiative.

During the ten years between the move to Riseholme and Elizabeth Wordsworth's appointment as founding principal of Lady Margaret Hall, her range of friendships and academic interests widened, and she became a writer. From 1868 she experienced a particularly close relationship with Edward White Benson, headmaster at Wellington College and examining chaplain to her father at Lincoln, and his wife, Minnie. The Wordsworth and Benson families saw a good deal of one another, but Edward Benson and Elizabeth became especially intimate friends,

Dame Elizabeth Wordsworth (1840–1932), by Sir James Jebusa Shannon, 1891

passionately sharing intellectual and ecclesiastical interests in long conversations and letters. Her friendship with Edward Benson was expansive and personally engaging in a way that was not repeated with any other man. By the mid-1870s the intensity of communication had abated, while her friendship with the Benson family as a whole continued.

In 1870 Elizabeth met the novelist Charlotte Mary Yonge in Oxford and they became lifelong friends. Elizabeth herself published a first novel, *Thornwell Abbas*, in 1876 under the pseudonym Grant Lloyd, followed by a second, *Ebb and Flow*, in 1883. From the early 1870s she also wrote poems, plays, stories, essays, and devotional pieces, as well as co-authoring a biography of her father in 1888. She acquired the reputation of a minor poet. She often stayed with her brother John and his wife in Oxford, and became a regular and popular participant in Oxford dinner parties. She attended lecture courses by the historian Robert Laing in the series given from 1873 onwards by Oxford dons for women, and wrote essays for Laing which he thought outstanding. Whether socially or through these lectures, she met many of the men and women who were determined to provide a university education for women in Oxford, including Edward Talbot, founding warden of Keble College, and his wife, Lavinia. She was not herself part of this pioneering group; her own energies were concentrated on her family, her writing, and her father's work in Lincoln.

In November 1878 Elizabeth Wordsworth accepted Edward Talbot's invitation to become principal of a residential hall for women that a committee of high-church Anglicans was establishing in Oxford. Her interest in

higher education for women owed nothing to feminist principle, and everything to her conviction that well-educated women would be better wives and mothers and more useful members of the Church of England and of English society. She proposed that the new hall be named after Lady Margaret Beaufort, mother of Henry VII and a patron of the arts and learning, whom she described as a gentlewoman, a scholar, and a saint. She wanted her students to be all three.

Lady Margaret Hall (LMH) accepted its first students in 1879, and Elizabeth remained its principal until her retirement in 1909. She was small, brisk, confident, and outspoken, and she brought to the new venture her characteristic generosity of mind and informality. Although her ideal was a family-sized community, plans for expansion were drawn up almost immediately, and she was impatient to see them implemented. The first new building to be added to the original Victorian villa was designed by Basil Champneys and completed in 1884. One of the four buildings by Reginald Blomfield that established the central form and classical style of the college was opened in 1896 and, at the insistence of the LMH council, bore her name, with the second following in 1910, the year after her retirement. Student numbers rose from nine in 1879 to fifty-nine in 1909. The individual students rather than the institution were always her main interest. She enjoyed their company, and encouraged them to walk, row, play tennis and hockey, and to ride bicycles when these appeared, seeing no need to impose further restrictions beyond the already strict conventions of the period. She expected them to be lively as well as hard-working. The students in turn found her inspiring, entertaining, and idiosyncratic. They listened to her Bible studies on Sunday evenings, acted in her annual plays, met the many visitors who called to see her, monitored her odd taste in headwear, and enjoyed having such a learned and notable, if sometimes disconcerting, character as their principal. Some of them were also deeply disappointed by her lack of interest in feminist causes, including the suffrage, and irritated by her conventional views on a woman's main role as wife and mother. She was none the less clear-sighted about the need of many women to be financially and emotionally self-reliant, and was determined to equip them to make their way independently.

In 1886, a year after Bishop Wordsworth died, Elizabeth unexpectedly inherited £600 from his estate, and decided to found St Hugh's Hall in his memory, for women students who could not afford the fees at LMH. This personal initiative was a great success; the hall later became St Hugh's College, Oxford. Meanwhile she continued to be a generous benefactor of LMH, giving or loaning money on several occasions for its development. Elizabeth Wordsworth, founder of one hall for women and founding principal of another, none the less managed to keep a low profile in the controversy in the 1890s over whether to admit women to the BA degree. She eventually argued for it, even though the LMH council opposed it, but she did not have very strong views on the matter. She was adamant, however, that a proposal being discussed at the same time, to introduce a non-resident diploma for women, would undermine the existing halls, and she opposed her council's support for it. An initiative that gained her full approval and active commitment was the opening of the Lady Margaret Hall Settlement in Lambeth in 1897, with its obvious practical commitment to those in need.

In 1900 Elizabeth Wordsworth gave up her house in Lincoln to live all year round in Oxford, first at Gunfield House, next door to LMH, and then, after retirement, at 12 Rawlinson Road. She received an honorary MA from Oxford University in 1921, one year after degrees were opened to women. She was elected an honorary fellow of Lady Margaret Hall and of St Hugh's in 1926. In the jubilee year of LMH, 1928, she received the honorary degree of DCL from Oxford University and was made a DBE. She died at her home in Rawlinson Road on 30 November 1932, and was buried on 5 December in Wolvercote cemetery, the most unselfconscious yet the most influential pioneer of women's university education that Oxford had known.

FRANCES LANNON

Sources E. Wordsworth, *Glimpses of the past* (1912) • *Brown Book* (July 1933) [Wordsworth memorial issue] • G. Bailey, ed., *Lady Margaret Hall* (1923) • Lady Margaret Hall, Wordsworth MSS • *Annual Reports*, minutes, and records, Lady Margaret Hall, Oxford • *Annual Reports*, St Hugh's College, Oxford • *St Hugh's College Chronicle* (1932–3) • J. Overton and E. Wordsworth, *Christopher Wordsworth, bishop of Lincoln, 1807–1885* (1888) • G. Battiscombe, *Reluctant pioneer: a life of Elizabeth Wordsworth* (1978) • *DNB* • *Oxford Times* (9 Dec 1932)
Archives Lady Margaret Hall, Oxford, papers
Likenesses J. J. Shannon, oils, 1891, Lady Margaret Hall, Oxford [*see illus.*] • A. G. Walker, chalk drawing, *c.*1909, Lady Margaret Hall, Oxford • T. Binney Gibbs, pencil drawing, 1922, Lady Margaret Hall, Oxford • photographs, Lady Margaret Hall, Oxford • two photographs, NPG
Wealth at death £15,848 8*s.* 0*d.*: resworn probate, 14 Jan 1933, *CGPLA Eng. & Wales*

Wordsworth, John (1805–1839). *See under* Wordsworth, Christopher (1774–1846).

Wordsworth, John (1843–1911), bishop of Salisbury, eldest son of Christopher *Wordsworth (1807–1885), and his wife, Susanna Hatley, daughter of George Frere, was born on 21 September 1843 at Harrow School, where his father was then headmaster; Christopher Wordsworth was later bishop of Lincoln, and was the nephew of the poet William Wordsworth. John's brother, the younger Christopher Wordsworth, was sometime fellow of Peterhouse, Cambridge. His sister Elizabeth *Wordsworth was the first principal of Lady Margaret Hall, Oxford; another sister, Susan (*d.* 1912), was the first head of the Southwark Diocesan Society of Grey Ladies. John Wordsworth was taught first by a Mrs Wallace at Brighton, and then at Ipswich; he went to Winchester College as a pensioner, and in October 1861 became a scholar of New College, Oxford. He gained a first-class mark in classical moderations, though not in his finals, and took a second in *literae humaniores* in 1865, when he was awarded his BA. He won the Latin essay prize in 1866 and the Craven scholarship in 1867, and he proceeded to an MA in 1868.

After a year as assistant master at Wellington College under Edward White Benson, afterwards archbishop of Canterbury, Wordsworth was elected in 1867 to a fellowship at Brasenose College, Oxford. He was ordained deacon (1867) and priest (1869) by Bishop Wilberforce of Oxford, and became chaplain of Brasenose College. In 1870 he was appointed as examining chaplain and was collated to a prebend in Lincoln Cathedral by his father, who had just been made bishop of Lincoln. In the same year he married Susan Esther Coxe (*d.* 1894); they had a son and a daughter.

Although Wordsworth was initially interested in divinity, his work at Brasenose was mainly classical. In 1874 he published *Fragments and Specimens of Early Latin*, a standard text for many years, though its philology dated quickly. The publication gave him the reputation of being one of the best Latin scholars in Oxford, however, and he soon applied himself to biblical study. In 1878 Oxford University Press accepted a proposal from him for the publication of a critical edition of the Vulgate New Testament which would attempt to recapture the exact words of St Jerome. He began to collect his material, engaging assistants to collate western-European manuscripts, and examining earlier collations (such as those of Richard Bentley and John Walker). They purchased unused material of Constantin Tischendorf and searched the works of the patristic writers for quotations. Wordsworth fulfilled all the requirements of palaeographical, grammatical, historical, and exegetical knowledge, and his notes and indices were known for their erudition.

As a preliminary to the substantive publication, certain important manuscripts were from 1883 onwards printed in full in *Old Latin Biblical Texts*. In this task Wordsworth was helped by William Sanday and some other scholars, later including the Revd Henry Julian White, professor of New Testament studies in King's College, London. The four gospels were printed in 1889 (St Matthew), 1891 (St Mark), 1892 (St Luke), and 1895 (St John). An *Epilogus* of discussions and results followed in 1898, the whole forming a quarto volume of over 800 pages. The Acts appeared in 1905. White continued the work after Wordsworth's death, with the assistance of the Revd George Mallows Youngman. Before his death Wordsworth published a minor edition of the whole Vulgate New Testament, which appeared in 1912. Although he grew less involved in the work in his latter years, he retained full knowledge of every detail and gave the final decision on doubtful questions.

Meanwhile Wordsworth had gained high office at Oxford and in the Church of England. In 1877 J. B. Mozley, regius professor of divinity, chose him as his deputy, and he served as deputy professor for two years. The lectures he wrote during that time formed the basis for the Bampton lectures of 1881. Entitled 'The one religion', they provided a comparison of Christianity with other great religions. Wordsworth was neither an orientalist nor a philosopher; but the Bampton lectures show his strong interest in missionary work. He was among the founders of the Oxford Missionary Association of Graduates, and of St Stephen's House, which was designed to prepare members of the university for mission life. In 1883 he was elected as the first incumbent of a newly founded Oriel professorship of the interpretation of scripture. The post carried with it the sinecure of the canonry of Rochester, where Wordsworth threw himself into the work both of the church and of the cathedral. Two years later he was nominated to the see of Salisbury in succession to George Moberly. He was consecrated bishop on 28 October 1885, and was made DD at Oxford in the same year. Thereafter, his duties as bishop had to take precedence over his literary work (apart from the Vulgate).

Succeeding to a well-administered diocese, without the problem of an increasing population, Wordsworth was able to devote much of his time to the general policy of the church. He developed his knowledge of ecclesiastical law. He was fearless in risking litigation and became the first to exercise the power under the Pluralities Act Amendment Act (1898), under which a bishop could, at the expense of an incompetent priest, appoint a new curate to his neglected parish. He also revived the canonical right of examining and rejecting, on the score of insufficient learning, the presentee to a benefice. His diocesan work in the field of education involved efforts to maintain elementary church schools. He also founded and endowed the Bishop's School at Salisbury for the secondary co-education of boys and girls, a progressive step at the time. Wordsworth's influence inside the Church of England was especially powerful. He was close to Archbishop Benson, and his assistance proved indispensable to Benson's successors. He was one of the assessors in the bishop of Lincoln's case in 1889–90, and he studied the relevant law and history in order to give a reasoned judgment.

Wordsworth believed in the ideal of a unified church. However, although in practice a tolerant man, he had inherited much of his father's antipathy towards Rome, and he was firmly of the view that the differences between Catholicism and the Church of England were wide. He acknowledged the intellectual and scholarly strength of the Roman Catholic scholars, but lost no opportunity to assert his church's claims to antiquity or superiority. He watched the growth of the Old Catholics in Austria and was always alert to signs of internal revolt in the Roman Catholic church. Wordsworth saw the churches' only hope of unity as lying in a general recognition of episcopacy. It was through this commonly held understanding that he felt drawn to the Orthodox Swedish and Moravian churches; and he was energetic in the negotiation of terms of possible association. His last work, the Hale lectures, delivered at Chicago in 1910, and published in England in 1911, on the national church of Sweden, was inspired by this motive. Although composed in ill health, it was a substantial and original contribution to religious history and was translated into Swedish.

In his De successione episcoporum in ecclesia Anglicana (1890) and De validitate ordinum Anglicanorum (1894), he attempted to refute what he saw as the scruples of the Jansenist Church of Holland. He continued the correspondence throughout his life, though his hopes were never fully realized.

Wordsworth also made some efforts to continue the attempts of his uncle, Charles Wordsworth, to draw together the episcopal and presbyterian churches of Scotland. His elaborate history of his uncle's episcopate, published in 1899, and his later researches, such as his Ordination Problems (1909) and Unity and Fellowship (1910), were concerned with examining precedents for the absorption of apparently imperfect fringe religious societies into approved and recognized religious groups. In addition he wrote much on practical ministry, drawing inspiration from history; he published Holy Communion (1910) and Ministry of Grace (1901, 1902). The latter is a history of the Christian ministry. Wordsworth remained conservative in his attitudes towards criticism of the Bible, where history showed institutions and scripture to be authoritative.

In his preaching Wordsworth showed himself equally sure of his ground, both scripturally and historically. He spoke impressively and often with originality. He read widely on the local and national history of his diocese and kept abreast of current affairs. Though he was an accomplished critic and writer of Latin, he was not greatly interested in style in English literature, but he admired the moral tones of his great-uncle's poetry. He was made honorary LLD of Dublin in 1890, of Cambridge in 1908, and honorary DD of Bern in 1892. In 1905 he was elected a fellow of the British Academy. Wordsworth's first wife, Susan, died in 1894; and in 1896 he married Mary Anne Frances William, with whom he had four sons and two daughters.

Wordsworth died suddenly at the bishop's palace, Salisbury, on 16 August 1911. He was buried on 19 August at Britford, near Salisbury. His wife survived him. Bishop Wordsworth is memorable for his contributions to theological studies and for his efforts in trying to unite different churches on the basis of episcopacy. A memorial and choir stalls were also erected in his honour in Salisbury Cathedral.   E. W. WATSON, rev. SINÉAD AGNEW

Sources The Times (17 Aug 1911), 9 · The Times (21 Aug 1911), 9 · Salisbury Diocesan Gazette (Sept–Dec 1911), 183, 203, 223 · W. Sanday, 'John Wordsworth, bishop of Salisbury, 1885–1911', PBA, [5] (1911–12), 530–48 · Men and women of the time (1899) · CGPLA Eng. & Wales (1911) · A. T. C. Pratt, ed., People of the period: being a collection of the biographies of upwards of six thousand living celebrities, 2 vols. (1897), 398 · Journal of Theological Studies, 13 (1911–12), 201 · Allibone, Dict. · E. Kilmurray, Dictionary of British portraiture, 3 (1981) · M. Pawley and B. C. Pawley, Rome and Canterbury through four centuries: a study of the relations between the church of Rome and the Anglican churches, 1530–1973, 2nd edn (1981)

Archives Christ Church Oxf., corresp. · King's Lond., college archives, sermons · LPL, corresp. and papers, papers, corresp., corresp and papers relating to Anglo-Continental Society, etc., corresp. relating to Jerusalem and East Missions Fund · St Ant. Oxf., Middle East Centre, corresp. and papers relating to Jerusalem and East Mission Fund · Wilts. & Swindon RO, letter-book | Bodl. Oxf., corresp. with Lord Kimberley · Dorset RO, corresp. with the Williams family · LPL, corresp. with Archbishop Benson · LPL, corresp. with Temple

Likenesses S. P. Hall, group portrait, watercolour, 1902 (The Bench of Bishops, 1902), NPG · G. Reid, oils, 1905, bishop's palace, Salisbury; reduced copy by E. S. Carlos, 1906, Brasenose College, Oxford · Rotary Photo, photograph on postcard, NPG · photograph, NPG

Wealth at death £33,455 9s. 8d.: probate, 18 Sept 1911, CGPLA Eng. & Wales

Wordsworth, William (1770–1850), poet, was born in Cockermouth, Cumberland, on 7 April 1770, the second of the five children of John Wordsworth (1741–1783) and his wife, Ann Cookson (1747–1778). The other children were Richard (1768–1816), who became a lawyer; Dorothy *Wordsworth (1771–1855); John (1772–1805), East India Company sea captain; and Christopher *Wordsworth (1774–1846), clergyman and scholar, who became master of Trinity College, Cambridge. The imposing house in which they were born signalled the professional status of their father, who served Sir James Lowther (from 1794 first earl of Lonsdale) in many functions, but primarily in legal and electoral matters. He was also bailiff and recorder of Cockermouth, posts he owed directly to the Lowther interest.

Childhood and schooling William and Dorothy spent long periods of their early childhood with their Cookson grandparents in Penrith, where William attended Ann Birkett's dame-school, but in 1778 brother and sister were split up. On the death of their mother in March, Dorothy was dispatched to relatives in Halifax, and William was enrolled, in May 1779, together with his brother Richard, at the grammar school at Hawkshead in Furness, north Lancashire. William and Dorothy did not see each other again for nine years, a separation which had enormous significance for the lives of both.

John Wordsworth senior died on 30 December 1783. William had not been happy at Penrith, and now his already strained relations with his relatives worsened. At his death John Wordsworth was owed large sums of money from his employer, but Sir James contumaciously declined to honour the debt (after his death in 1802 they were acknowledged by his successor and finally settled in 1804), and the Wordsworth children found themselves reliant upon the goodwill of their guardians, their uncles Richard Wordsworth of Whitehaven and Christopher Crackanthorpe Cookson. Wordsworth, by his own account a child of 'stiff, moody, and violent temper', resented every slight as a reminder of his dependent status (*Memoirs of William Worsworth*, 1.9).

Wordsworth's memories of schooldays, however, were ones of great happiness. In his autobiographical poem *The Prelude* he records his gratitude that he grew up 'fostered alike by beauty and by fear'. The poem's opening books recall boating on Windermere and Coniston, skating, bird-nesting, nutting, walking on the fells, and riding to Furness Abbey, experiences which the mature poet recognized as having furnished his mind with imagery of the natural world. Very late in life he reiterated his hostility to an overemphasis on book-learning for children, remarking that his views were those of 'one who spent half of his boyhood in running wild among the Mountains' (letter of 16 Dec 1845; *Letters*, 7.733).

Schooldays in Hawkshead also nourished Wordsworth's literary imagination in a variety of ways. He was boarded out with Ann Tyson, and he drank in the stories about the neighbourhood told by his deeply loved surrogate mother. He watched and listened to the working people of

William Wordsworth (1770–1850), by Benjamin Robert Haydon, 1842

Hawkshead—shepherds, quarrymen, saddlers, blacksmiths, wallers, pedlars, and vagrants—and the concern of much of his later poetry for 'humble and rustic life' had its origins in what he learned. And he read. At his father's urging he had already memorized passages of Shakespeare, Spenser, and Milton, and from his father's library he had gone through the whole of Fielding, some Swift, *Don Quixote*, and *Gil Blas*. Now, encouraged especially by one of his headmasters, William Taylor, Wordsworth added to the school's instruction in Latin and Greek a personal exploration of eighteenth-century English poetry, up to the latest publications (Wu, vol. 1 gives the fullest account). He began writing himself, and in the year he left school (1787) his first published poem appeared in the *European Magazine* under the pseudonym Axiologus, a sonnet entitled 'On Seeing Miss Helen Maria Williams Weep at a Tale of Distress'. By this date he had also written hundreds of lines towards a never finished evocation of the Hawkshead region, *The Vale of Esthwaite*.

In the summer of 1787 Wordsworth was briefly reunited with Dorothy, who had returned for what proved an unhappy stay at Penrith. In October he left the Lake District for the first time in his life, for Cambridge.

Cambridge and the Alps, 1787–1790 When Wordsworth took up residence at St John's College in late October 1787 the auguries were good. Hawkshead School had prepared him so well in mathematics and the classics that he judged himself a year ahead of other freshmen. A fellowship reserved for men from Cumberland was held by his uncle William Cookson, and as he expected preferment shortly there was hope that the nephew might follow him into it. Cookson was an intimate friend of William Wilberforce; John Robinson, MP for Harwich and a cousin of Wordsworth's father, was a powerful figure with the ear of the king, and indicated that he would be watching Wordsworth's career with interest. Hawkshead friends, such as Robert Greenwood at Trinity, John Millar at Jesus, John Fleming at Christ's, Fletcher Raincock at Pembroke, and many others, were an antidote to loneliness.

Wordsworth none the less failed to capitalize on any of these advantages. In college examinations in December 1787 he was placed in the first class, and the following June in the second class. Thereafter, however, he did not fulfil the college examination requirements for a man reading for honours, and in the final university examination of January 1791 graduated without honours.

Reviewing his Cambridge years in *The Prelude*, Wordsworth later touched on many factors which might have contributed to his failure to make the best of his opportunity—principled dislike of competitive examinations; irritations such as compulsory chapel attendance; a sense that the academic community was moribund; the temptations of sociability. His most telling judgement, though, is simply:

> I was not for that hour
> Nor for that place.
> (*The Prelude*, 1805, 3.80-81)

His subsequent behaviour indicated how strongly he resented the pressure upon him to distinguish himself at Cambridge in the expected way that would lead to professional advancement.

As an undergraduate Wordsworth took Italian lessons from Agostino Isola, who introduced him to Tasso and Ariosto, and he composed a substantial loco-descriptive poem, *An Evening Walk*. During the long vacation of 1788 he returned to Hawkshead, and in Penrith spent time with Dorothy and with Mary Hutchinson (1770-1859), whom he later married, and although the evidence is inconclusive, it seems that he went back to Hawkshead for much of the following summer vacation too. For the summer of 1790, however, what Wordsworth planned was so reckless that he kept it secret from all his family, even his sister: a walking tour across revolutionary France to the Alps.

Wordsworth's companion was Robert Jones, a Welshman who remained a lifelong friend. They crossed from Dover to Calais on 13 July 1790, the eve of the anniversary of the fall of the Bastille, but mountain country was their destination, not Paris. By late September, with £20 apiece, they had travelled nearly 3000 miles, more than 2000 of them on foot. Jones later recalled: 'We were early risers in 1790 and generally walked 12 or 15 miles before breakfast' (letter of 23 Feb 1821; Reed, 1.98). Having arrived in Lyons, travelling partly by boat along the Saône, they visited the monastery of the Grande Chartreuse on 4-5 August and then proceeded to Lake Geneva and on to the vale of Chamonix. They crossed the Alps at the Simplon Pass and by 19 August were at Lake Maggiore. Lake Lugano and Lake Como were included before a circuitous route took them via Lucerne to Lake Constance. They visited the Rhine falls

at Schaffhausen on 8 September before returning to Lucerne and then to Basel. A journey down the Rhine by boat to Cologne was followed by a rapid return home by about 11 October via Aix-la-Chapelle (now Aachen) and Ostend.

Wordsworth, declaring himself a 'perfect Enthusiast in [his] admiration of Nature in all her various forms' (*Letters*, 1.35), recorded his immediate responses in a long letter to Dorothy of 6 and 16 September 1790, and he drew on them poetically for *Descriptive Sketches* (1793) and book 6 of *The Prelude*, written in 1804. What he dwells on most in the latter account is the way in which he and Jones were cheated of their eagerly awaited experience of the sublime by discovering that by mischance they had actually crossed the Alps without being conscious of it. When Wordsworth retraced his steps in 1820 he made a point of discovering again the path that had misled them in 1790.

Once back, Wordsworth returned to Cambridge and then went on to Forncett, near Norwich, the living of his uncle William Cookson, where Dorothy was currently staying. Brother and sister relived every step of the European tour before Wordsworth left for Cambridge to complete his degree. At the end of January 1791 he moved to London.

London, 1791, and France Lodging near Cheapside, Wordsworth revelled in the spectacles of the city, as he did on every visit to London until late in life. He attended parliamentary debates and may well have been present on 6 May 1791 at the momentous rupture of Burke and Fox over the significance of the French Revolution. He also witnessed the activities of those excluded from formal politics. Through Samuel Nicholson, a member of the Society for Constitutional Information, Wordsworth was introduced to the world of dissenting radicalism. Listening to Joseph Fawcett preach at the Old Jewry meeting-house and encountering or hearing about such prominent activists as John Jebb, John Frost, Horne Tooke, and Joseph Johnson marked the beginning of Wordsworth's political awakening.

From London, Wordsworth went late in May to Wales, to stay with Robert Jones at his family's home at Plas-yn-Llan, Denbighshire. Another joint walking tour included the climbing of Snowdon, recorded in the final book of *The Prelude*. To Wordsworth's relatives, however, such activities were no answer to the pressing question of what he was to do with his life now that he had his degree. John Robinson offered to secure him a curacy, but Wordsworth wriggled out of any immediate commitment. William Cookson suggested that further study, of oriental languages, might be sensible for one destined surely to become a clergyman or tutor. What Wordsworth settled on was a return to France. Ostensibly he was going to perfect his command of the language; in reality he was in flight from his relatives' expectations and their conception of an appropriate career.

Wordsworth arrived in Paris on 30 November 1791. He behaved as a tourist, ticking off the famous sites and pocketing a fragment of the Bastille as a souvenir. He attended meetings of the Jacobin Club and got to know Brissot. But he had never intended to stay long, and on 5 December he left for Orléans. Here the course of Wordsworth's life changed irrevocably. Visiting her brother in Wordsworth's lodgings was Marie-Anne (Annette) Vallon (1766–1841), a 25-year-old, ardent anti-revolutionary from Blois. He fell in love with her, and in the spring of 1792 he followed the now pregnant Annette back home.

At Blois, Wordsworth's nascent radicalism was quickened by contact with members of the society 'Les Amis de la Constitution' and above all by his friendship with Captain Michel de Beaupuy, to whose altruistic zeal for the revolutionary cause book 9 of *The Prelude* pays feeling tribute. But nothing at Blois, at a time of accelerating political and social crisis, could help Wordsworth to acquire what he needed most: an income to support Annette and their unborn child. He had to return home. After a spell in Orléans, where Annette had been moved to conceal her pregnancy, Wordsworth went on 29 October to Paris. The city was in the grip of terror after the September massacres, but for six weeks he lingered, absorbed by the power struggles unleashed by Louvet's failed attempt to curb Robespierre. He returned to London at about the time when his daughter, Anne-Caroline, always known as Caroline, was born, 15 December 1792.

London to Racedown, 1793–1795 Wordsworth's situation on his return to London was desperate, and rapidly grew worse. The years 1793 to 1795 were the most unsettled and troubled of his life. From February 1793 the outbreak of war with France put Annette and Caroline out of reach. The tolerance of John Robinson and William Cookson had run out: even the curacy was no longer on offer. Wordsworth had no money, no home, nor any immediate prospects. He was, moreover, completely out of sympathy with the prevailing national mood. The polemic he wrote but wisely did not publish at that time—*A Letter to the Bishop of Llandaff*, a full-blooded republican's testament—reveals how complete his disaffection was. What he did hasten to publish were his poems *An Evening Walk* and *Descriptive Sketches*, but though they attracted some notice they did not materially help him in his plight.

During the summer a projected tour of the west country with a Hawkshead friend, William Calvert, came to an abrupt end with a carriage accident and Wordsworth once again headed on foot for Robert Jones's home. His route took in Salisbury Plain, which provided material for a stridently radical poem, 'Salisbury Plain', and the Wye, which he later recalled in the opening lines of 'Tintern Abbey'. Fragmentary evidence suggests that late in September, Wordsworth recklessly returned to France to see Annette. Kenneth Johnston in *The Hidden Wordsworth* (1998) argues the case for this most fully, but it remains uncertain whether Wordsworth did hazard his life in this way.

In 1794 Wordsworth was reunited with Dorothy in the north of England. For part of the time they stayed at Windy Brow, a Calvert family farmhouse at Keswick, where Wordsworth substantially added to *An Evening Walk*. Towards the end of the year it was agreed that Wordsworth would accompany Calvert's consumptive brother, Raisley, to Portugal, but Raisley died early in January 1795. He left Wordsworth £900, 'from a confidence on his part',

Wordsworth later maintained, 'that I had powers and attainments which might be of use to mankind' (*c*.23 Feb 1805; *Letters*, 1.546).

Back in the south by February 1795, Wordsworth associated with the élite of London radicalism: William Frend, Thomas Holcroft, William Godwin, James Losh, George Dyer, and others less well known. In a series of letters the previous year to William Mathews, a Cambridge friend, Wordsworth had laid out his political principles as one 'of that odious class of men called democrats' (23 May 1794; *Letters*, 1.119). They allied him closely with those who sought radical reform but recoiled from the violence of revolution, whose effects were now convulsing France. It is unclear, however, how active Wordsworth was in radical politics. His brother Richard was moved to urge him to 'be cautious in writing or expressing [his] political opinions' (ibid., 1.121), a sensible warning, given that just by associating with the likes of Holcroft, Wordsworth made himself a marked man; but did he do anything more than debate and follow the pamphlet wars of the day?

Wordsworth's confession of principles to Mathews stems from a scheme of theirs to establish a journal of philosophical radicalism to be called *The Philanthropist*. That scheme seems to have foundered, but a journal called *The Philanthropist* did appear from March 1795 to January 1796, and Johnston (*The Hidden Wordsworth*, 1998) has argued forcefully that Wordsworth was deeply involved in it and that his withdrawal to the country in the summer of 1795 was a prudent retreat before the increasing pressure of government surveillance of all radical activity. The evidence, however, is inconclusive.

Wordsworth did withdraw from London, and the fact that he had a place to which he could withdraw came about, like the Calvert legacy, from the fortunate chance of another rapidly ripened friendship. Through Francis Wrangham, with whom he was collaborating on a Juvenalian satire, and Basil Montagu, Wordsworth met John and Azariah Pinney, sons of a wealthy Bristol merchant and plantation owner. They offered him rent-free occupancy of one of their father's properties, Racedown Lodge in Dorset. Dorothy Wordsworth was to join her brother and together, for £50 a year, they would look after Montagu's little son, also Basil, whose mother had recently died. Invited by John Pinney senior, Wordsworth stayed in Bristol *en route* for Racedown, and here he met for the first time the bookseller Joseph Cottle, Robert Southey, and Samuel Taylor Coleridge. By late September 1795 Wordsworth and Dorothy had settled into Pinney's substantial house: they never lived apart again.

Racedown and Alfoxden, 1795–1798 In the late spring of 1797 Dorothy Wordsworth reported that her brother was 'as chearful as any body can be … the life of the whole house' (19 March [1797]; *Letters*, 1.181), and there is no doubt that overall their time at Racedown was happy. The house had an excellent library. There were frequent visitors, and a six-month stay by Mary Hutchinson greatly added to their contentment. They walked, and for the first time Wordsworth laboured seriously in the garden. Both enjoyed bringing up little Basil, teaching him nothing but what his curiosity demanded and making it their 'grand study', Dorothy wrote, 'to make him *happy*' (19 March [1797]; ibid., 1.180).

Domestic ease, though, was not untroubled. Generous but unwise loans to Montagu and one of his friends meant that the Wordsworths grew very short of money: 'carrots cabbages turnips and other esculent vegetables … the produce of my garden' sustained them, Wordsworth declared (letter of *c*.25 Feb 1797; *Letters*, 1.178). There was the question of Annette and Caroline. The widening of the war seemed certain to ensure that Wordsworth would be able to do nothing about them for some time to come. And there was the question of his future. Compared with his industrious brother Richard, for example, Wordsworth, it seemed to his relatives, was still squandering youthful years, directionless.

In reality the Racedown period was the threshold to Wordsworth's discovery of his characteristic poetic voice and themes. Ideological excess and militarism in France forced Wordsworth (and many others) to sift the beliefs and ideals that had drawn them to the French social experiment. The zealotry of debate and pamphlet warfare, Wordsworth's diet over previous months, came to seem to him to be a damaging commitment to the local and transient in politics and no route either towards understanding human beings or alleviating their sufferings. Most important of all, Wordsworth came to the conviction that the kind of rationalism exemplified by Godwin was sterile. The Racedown period was not a sudden crisis. Wordsworth did not abruptly abandon the opinions he had espoused in *A Letter to the Bishop of Llandaff*, but rather he subjected all of them to re-examination.

The result, Wordsworth's own kind of poetic radicalism, was not manifest for another year at least, but the poetry he composed now was its necessary prelude. 'Salisbury Plain' was transformed into *Adventures on Salisbury Plain*, in which interlocking stories of human wretchedness dramatize most of what in the earlier poem is rendered in hortatory declamation, the conviction that in war it is invariably the poor who suffer most. His next work, *The Borderers*, though clearly contemporary in the range of its concerns, leaves the war-torn eighteenth century for the lawless world of the border country in the thirteenth. A blank verse tragedy, *The Borderers* explores the human lust for power, the evil potentialities of rationalism untempered by love or domestic pieties, and the nature of guilt.

Adventures on Salisbury Plain impressed Charles Lamb, whom Wordsworth first met at this time, and Coleridge, but negotiations to publish it with Cottle lapsed, and it did not appear until 1842, and then in a greatly revised form called *Guilt and Sorrow*. *The Borderers* was likewise hidden until the same year, when it too appeared in revised form, having been declared unactable by the Covent Garden management in 1797. Neither work, therefore, though exhibiting considerable poetic and intellectual powers and being of the greatest importance to Wordsworth's poetic development, did anything to promote him into visibility.

What did, and in the near future, was Wordsworth's fresh encounter with Coleridge, one of 'the two Beings', he later declared, 'to whom my intellect is most indebted' (W. Wordsworth to William Rowan Hamilton, 25 June 1832; *Letters*, 5.536). Letters had followed their meeting in 1795, but intimacy began only in March 1797 when Wordsworth called on Coleridge in Nether Stowey. In June, Coleridge repaid the call, and the two poets eagerly read their recent work to each other. Enchanted by their new friend, William and Dorothy went on 2 July to Nether Stowey. They had, in fact, left Racedown for good.

Alfoxden to Grasmere, 1797-1799 Through the good offices of Thomas Poole, a wealthy tanner and farmer from Nether Stowey with radical leanings, the Wordsworths secured for £23 a year the tenancy of Alfoxden House, a mansion with nine bedrooms and three parlours. Here they were visited by many acquaintances such as Thelwall and Lamb, and by a new one, William Hazlitt, who recorded his impressions in *My First Acquaintance with Poets*. Wordsworth's attachment to Lamb deepened over a lifetime, but the friendship with Hazlitt faltered and eventually soured. The Wordsworths delighted in Alfoxden's beautiful situation amid the Quantocks, but what mattered most was that it was only 3 miles from Nether Stowey. Over the next year intimacy between them and Coleridge deepened on repeated walks between their homes and rambles to the neighbouring coast and Exmoor. On one excursion in November 1797, while at Watchet, the two poets planned out 'The Ancient Mariner', hoping to sell it to defray expenses.

When Coleridge first visited Racedown, Wordsworth read him his most recent composition, 'The Ruined Cottage' (revised for book 1 of *The Excursion*, published in 1814), whose blank verse, it is generally agreed, speaks for the first time with Wordsworth's mature voice. At Alfoxden the poem's structure was considerably altered to frame the story of one woman's suffering and death within the commentary of a wise pedlar, whose philosophic utterances about loss and the kinds of natural compensation available to man set out the themes that were to dominate much of Wordsworth's greatest poetry. Convinced that his friend was uniquely gifted to combine philosophy and poetry, Coleridge urged him to write a comprehensive work on 'Nature, Man, and Society', and by March 1798 Wordsworth was enthusiastically broadcasting its title. It was to be called *The Recluse*, and so ambitious was it that Wordsworth declared, 'I know not any thing which will not come within the scope of my plan' (letter of 6 March [1798]; *Letters*, 1.212).

The project was not to advance at Alfoxden, for barely were the Wordsworths settled in before they knew they had to leave. In August 1797 gossip about the new tenants at Alfoxden, their strange ramblings, and their hospitality to such a notorious radical as John Thelwall had been passed on to the Home Office. An agent, James Walsh, was dispatched and soon reported that Alfoxden housed not French infiltrators but disaffected Englishmen, whose names were already known to the authorities. Though Poole vouched for their probity to Alfoxden's owner, the

Wordsworths were informed that their lease would not be renewed.

Coleridge planned a visit to Germany, and the Wordsworths wanted to join him. Newly funded by an annuity from the Wedgwoods, Coleridge could afford it. The Wordsworths could not, and it was in their financial need that one of the most famous volumes of English poetry had its birth. In *Biographia literaria* (1817) Coleridge spoke of the 'plan' of *Lyrical Ballads*, but it is clear that there was no plan as he describes it. The most promising scheme to raise money was that Cottle should publish Wordsworth's recent longer works—'The Ruined Cottage', *Adventures on Salisbury Plain*, *The Borderers*, and *Peter Bell*—but for unknown reasons it lapsed. What took its place was a hastily constructed volume, whose authors insisted on remaining anonymous, which consisted largely of lyric poems Wordsworth had composed over the spring and early summer of 1798, some of his earlier unpublished pieces, and a few poems by Coleridge, including 'The Ancient Mariner'. 'Tintern Abbey' was added at the last moment after a tour of the Wye area undertaken after the Wordsworths had left Alfoxden on 25 June 1798. *Lyrical Ballads, with a Few Other Poems* was published on 4 October 1798, by which time its authors were in Germany.

They went first to Hamburg. During their stay Wordsworth and Coleridge met Klopstock, but thereafter they split up. Coleridge, seeking intellectual community, eventually settled in Göttingen; the Wordsworths went to Goslar. Unable to speak the language fluently and restricted by an unusually severe winter and their tight funds, the Wordsworths gained little personally from their German sojourn. Poetically, however, Wordsworth took a momentous step. In a notebook used by his sister for German language exercises, he began to compose blank verse about his own boyhood experiences at Hawkshead. They became the first version of his autobiographical testament, what is for many his most impressive poem, *The Prelude*.

The Wordsworths returned to England at the end of April 1799 to stay at the Hutchinson family farm at Sockburn-on-Tees. A visit to the Lake District, on which he was accompanied at various times by his brother John, Coleridge, and Cottle, confirmed Wordsworth in the conviction that it was here that he wanted to settle. In November he negotiated the tenancy of a cottage he had seen at Town End, Grasmere, and late in the afternoon on 20 December 1799, after an extraordinarily arduous journey from Sockburn, mostly on foot along half-frozen roads, Wordsworth and Dorothy moved into the cottage, their home for the next eight years.

Grasmere, 1800–1806 One of the earliest poems Wordsworth wrote at the cottage, later named and now always known as Dove Cottage, was called 'Home at Grasmere'. The title is revealing. The dwelling house at Town End was the first home of Wordsworth's adult life, and Grasmere was where he chose to put down roots. Here he began family life with Mary Hutchinson, his wife from 1802, and here he composed most of the poetry on which his fame rests. Life at Dove Cottage was a continual struggle, whose daily victories against lack of space, limited food, testing weather, and chronic ill health from damp are chronicled in Dorothy Wordsworth's *Grasmere Journals*. But creating a home satisfied Wordsworth profoundly, even the labour once more in the garden, and the vale itself, the people as well as the landscape, memorialized in poems such as 'Michael' and in the lyrics 'Poems on the Naming of Places', was an inexhaustible quarry for his imagination.

In the summer of 1800 Coleridge moved with his family into Greta Hall, Keswick, where Southey joined him with his family in 1803. Lamb was lured away from London for a visit to the Lakes and Grasmere in 1802. But Wordsworth also made two new friends now who were to matter to him in different ways until they died. One was the 'great and amiable man' Sir Walter Scott (note to 'Yarrow Revisited', *The Fenwick Notes of William Wordsworth*, ed. J. Curtis, 1993, 47). The other was Sir George Beaumont, who, with characteristic generosity, marked the beginning of their acquaintance by giving Wordsworth a parcel of land at Applethwaite, near Keswick.

Wordsworth and Mary Hutchinson had been moving towards marriage, and two events in 1802 made it possible. The first was the recognition by the earl of Lonsdale's successor, Sir William Lowther, that the Wordsworth family claim on the estate would be met. The second was the realization that the brief respite in the war offered by the treaty of Amiens gave Wordsworth the opportunity to settle matters in France. He was not in a position financially to settle money on Annette, and no evidence has survived that he did so in the coming years (though he was to make an annual allowance to Caroline later). But he seized this unlooked-for opportunity to see his French family. He and Dorothy stayed a month in Calais with Annette and Caroline, now nine years old.

Wordsworth and Mary Hutchinson were married from the farmhouse of her brother Thomas at Gallow Hill, near Scarborough, in Brompton church on 4 October 1802, and on the same day they and Dorothy began the journey back to Grasmere.

Wordsworth's marriage became the bedrock of his life. His attachment to Mary was passionate. Shelley's characterization of Wordsworth as 'a solemn and unsexual man' (*Peter Bell the Third*) has stuck, but the second epithet at least is wide of the mark. Letters between Mary and William from 1810 and 1812 that surfaced only in 1977 read like avowals at the beginning of a love affair rather than after nearly ten years of marriage. At Grasmere and subsequently at Rydal, Wordsworth very consciously built the kind of domestic security his own early life had lacked. His sister continued to live with them. To Mary, as she said in old age, Dorothy was 'my chosen companion through life' (*The Letters of Mary Wordsworth, 1800–1855*, ed. M. E. Burton, 1958, xxi), and in due course Mary's own sister, Sara Hutchinson, was added as a permanent member of the domestic circle at Town End.

The first child of William and Mary Wordsworth, John, was born on 18 June 1803. Dorothy, usually called Dora, followed on 16 August 1804. Thomas was born on 15 June

1806, Catherine on 5 September 1808, and the last child, William, on 12 May 1810.

In August and September 1803 Wordsworth, Dorothy, and Coleridge made a tour of Scotland, whose diverse rewards, beginning at the grave of Burns and ending with the company of Scott, are described in full in Dorothy Wordsworth's *Recollections of a Tour Made in Scotland, A.D. 1803*. Two weeks into the tour, however, Coleridge and the Wordsworths split up, and the division indicates what was happening to their relationship. Coleridge was miserably in love with Sara Hutchinson, whom he had known since November 1799; he was chronically ill and slipping into drug addiction. Mrs Coleridge understandably blamed the Wordsworths for succouring her husband on his frequent visits to Grasmere. The Wordsworths loved Coleridge but thought his feelings for Sara were selfish and his treatment of his wife lamentable. With such discord the creative harmony of Alfoxden could not be restored, and it was with sad acknowledgement of the fact that the Dove Cottage family said farewell to Coleridge early in 1804, as he began his journey to the Mediterranean in search of sunshine and health. They did not see him again for over two years.

Much greater pain afflicted them in the following year. On 5 February 1805 John Wordsworth, now captain of an East Indiaman, the *Earl of Abergavenny*, was drowned in the wreck of his ship off Portland Bill. Wordsworth and Dorothy had not seen him since 29 September 1800, when they had waved him off down the path to Patterdale where it leaves Grisedale Tarn. The family at Town End were inconsolable. What his brother's death meant to him is revealed in part by one of Wordsworth's most moving poems, written the following year, 'Elegiac Stanzas, Suggested by a Picture of Peele Castle, in a Storm, Painted by Sir George Beaumont'.

Writings, 1798–1807 A second edition of *Lyrical Ballads*, dated 1800, was issued by Longman and Rees late in March 1801. Now in two volumes, the collection decisively announced Wordsworth's arrival: his name was on the title-page; the majority of the poems were his; 'The Ancient Mariner' was moved so that it no longer opened volume 1. Many of the new poems reflect what Grasmere had come to mean to Wordsworth. The series 'Poems on the Naming of Places' links the poet and members of his family to particular localities. 'Michael' and 'The Brothers' revivify the pastoral by dwelling on the fortitude and dignity with which the Lake District's inhabitants face the hardships of their life.

That such lowly people are especially worthy of poetic attention is one of the main propositions of the substantial essay which prefaces the collection. The brief prose 'Advertisement' to the first edition of *Lyrical Ballads* (1798) had introduced the poems as 'experiments … written chiefly with a view to ascertain how far the language of conversation of the middle and lower classes of society is adapted to the purposes of poetic pleasure', but the preface of 1800 extends the topic very boldly. The lives, customs, and language of 'low and rustic life' are the focus, it claims, because here the 'primary laws of our nature' can be discerned most clearly in their operation, untainted by the superficialities of a metropolitan society.

The preface's other most important claim is that these are designedly poems of sentiment, differing from the common run of such poems in that here 'the feeling therein developed gives importance to the action and situation and not the action and situation to the feeling'. Numerous causes, Wordsworth maintains, are combining at the present time to degrade public taste. By dwelling upon the 'great and simple affections of our nature' the poems in *Lyrical Ballads* are to serve as an educative counterbalance.

Implicit in this proposition is a high claim for the power of poetry to foster human betterment. Major additions to the preface for the third edition of *Lyrical Ballads* (1802) amplify it, as Wordsworth identifies the true poet as one who 'rejoices more than other men in the spirit of life that is in him' and celebrates poetry as a cultural power and as the 'breath and finer spirit of all knowledge'.

The preface established publicly the major concerns of Wordsworth's poetry and identified this previously barely known poet as a writer with a mission. Only close friends knew on what else he was engaged during these years. By the end of 1800 Wordsworth had fashioned his autobiographical blank verse into a poem in two parts addressed to Coleridge. It declares itself a harbinger of *The Recluse*, but when progress on that project faltered, Wordsworth returned to the history of his own poetic evolution. As he chronicled his life up to 1798 Wordsworth re-examined his political, religious, and aesthetic convictions and expanded the poem's scope so majestically that when it was completed in 1805 it had grown from two to thirteen books. It is Wordsworth's masterpiece, but as it was conceived throughout as a prelude to a greater work, *The Recluse*, so long as Wordsworth remained committed to the project for the philosophical poem, the autobiographical one had to remain unpublished. It was Wordsworth's widow and executors in 1850 who called it *The Prelude*. In Wordsworth's lifetime it was always known as 'The Poem to Coleridge' or 'Growth of a Poet's Mind'.

To the Grasmere years also belong most of Wordsworth's finest lyrics—poems such as 'To the Cuckoo' and 'To a Butterfly'; memorials of the tour of Scotland, such as 'Yarrow Unvisited' and 'The Solitary Reaper'; political sonnets such as 'Great men have been among us' and 'To Toussaint L'Ouverture'; other sonnets no less famous such as 'The world is too much with us' and 'Composed upon Westminster Bridge'. In 1804 Wordsworth completed his greatest ode, 'There was a time', after 1815 entitled 'Ode: Intimations of Immortality from Recollections of Early Childhood'. Brought together for publication in 1807 as *Poems, in Two Volumes*, this varied, original collection ought to have been a triumph. It was a disaster. The sonnets and the odes affronted no aesthetic codes, but the lyrics certainly did. In the 1802 preface to *Lyrical Ballads*, Wordsworth had declared that the 'objects of the Poet's thoughts are every where', and these poems explored that conviction in a manner which even Coleridge thought exhibited a 'daring Humbleness of Language & Versifica-tion' and a startling 'adherence to matter of fact, even to prolixity' (*Collected Letters*, ed. Griggs, 2.830). They were too daring by far for Francis Jeffrey. His merciless anatomy of the volumes in the *Edinburgh Review* for December 1807 was only the most thoroughgoing of the many onslaughts which, while generally conceding merit to the sonnets, castigated the bulk of the lyrics as puerile trash.

From Dove Cottage to Rydal Mount The years 1806 to 1813 were the most troubled of Wordsworth's married life. He was worried about money, about how to provide a decent home for his growing family, about the disintegration of his relationship with Coleridge, and about his future as a poet.

Over the winter of 1806–7 the family decamped to a farmhouse owned by Sir George Beaumont near his new house at Coleorton, Leicestershire, where Wordsworth energetically oversaw the laying-out of the winter garden. Coleridge joined them, but it was an uneasy reunion. The Wordsworths thought him 'utterly changed' (Dorothy Wordsworth, letter, 6 Nov 1806; *Letters*, 1.86); Coleridge began to torment himself with the conviction (quite unfounded) that Wordsworth had become Sara Hutchin-son's lover.

In May 1808 the Wordsworths moved to Allan Bank, to the west of Grasmere village, a house spacious enough for Coleridge to join them in September and for his sons, now at school in Ambleside, to stay at weekends. Thomas De Quincey too became one of the circle before taking over the tenancy of Dove Cottage in February 1809. At Allan Bank, to everyone's surprise, Coleridge laboured heroic-ally over every aspect—writing, printing, distribution—of the production of a weekly paper, *The Friend*, which ran from June 1809 to March 1810.

Allan Bank was fraught with personal tensions. The Wordsworths felt that Coleridge, clearly still dependent on drugs, was abusing Sara Hutchinson's compassion and generosity—she was amanuensis for much of the produc-tion of *The Friend*—and neglecting his own family respon-sibilities. Coleridge believed that the Wordsworths were becoming selfishly introverted and he contrasted their increasing coldness to him with the warmth of their wel-come to the newcomer, De Quincey. Shortly after Cole-ridge left for London in October 1810 the mixture of resentment, anger, and suspicion bubbled over.

The catalyst was Basil Montagu, who was travelling south with Coleridge. *En route* Montagu declared that Wordsworth had cautioned him against taking Coleridge in, as he was a 'rotten drunkard' and an 'absolute nuis-ance'. Coleridge was stunned that his dearest friend should have become his 'bitterest Calumniator' (letter of 24 April [1812]; *Collected Letters*, ed. Griggs, 3.389) and broke off all communication with Grasmere. When the Words-worths eventually learned of Coleridge's suffering, Wordsworth stiffly refused to justify himself against what he maintained was a false accusation. At length, in April 1812, Wordsworth and Coleridge were brought into con-tact in London, largely through the mediation of Henry Crabb Robinson, and a reconciliation was patched

together. The two poets continued friends, and after Cole-ridge's death in 1834 Wordsworth reportedly called him 'the most *wonderful* man that he had ever known' (reported by R. P. Graves in *Memoirs of William Wordsworth*, 2.288), but the creative intimacy born at Alfoxden was extinguished for good after Allan Bank.

In May 1811 the Wordsworths moved into the disused rectory opposite Grasmere church. Here two of the child-ren died within months of each other—Catherine of con-vulsions on 4 June and Thomas of measles on 1 December 1812. At Catherine's death both parents were away, Words-worth in London and Mary at her brother-in-law's in Rad-norshire, and neither was at her burial. Grief and self-reproach threatened to pitch Mary into permanent decline, and Wordsworth recognized that it was impera-tive to get her away from a house which was only yards away from the children's graves. In May 1813 the family moved to Rydal Mount, a house on rising ground just south of Grasmere, owned by Lady le Fleming of Rydal Hall. It did not disappoint. Allan Bank had been intoler-ably smoky; the rectory was dangerously ill-drained. Rydal Mount was commodious, with a fine view over the head of Windermere, and it became the Wordsworths' permanent home.

At the same time financial worries eased. They had become so acute that Wordsworth had been forced to beg for help from Lord Lonsdale. A generous promise of £100 a year was transformed in April 1813 into the more easily acceptable offer of an official position, that of distributor of stamps for Westmorland and the Penrith area of Cum-berland. Wordsworth hoped to make £400 a year, but in practice the distributorship, despite his conscientious attention to the duties of the office, brought in much less. Wordsworth's son William later deputized for him until 1842, when he took over the distributorship on his father's retirement.

From July to September 1814 Wordsworth, Mary, and Sara Hutchinson, joined for part of the time by John Wordsworth, toured Scotland as far north as Inverness. In Edinburgh they met Robert Gillies, who was to become a staunch admirer, and James Hogg, the Ettrick Shepherd, who guided them on a visit to the Yarrow. When they arrived at Abbotsford, Scott was absent, but they were warmly received by his wife and daughter.

Wordsworth's improved finances also enabled him to do something for his daughter Caroline. On her marriage in 1816, Wordsworth offered Caroline £30 a year, an arrangement that lasted for almost twenty years. In 1835, feeling that age was overtaking him and that his financial position was likely to worsen, Wordsworth concluded the payments with a generous capital settlement of £400.

Writings, 1807–1815 What new writing Wordsworth pub-lished between moving into Allan Bank and leaving for Rydal Mount was entirely prose. Outraged by the diplo-matic trading which allowed the defeated French army to evacuate Portugal in 1808, Wordsworth became unexpect-edly absorbed for a year in composing a vehement denun-ciation of national conduct, *The Convention of Cintra*, pub-lished in May 1809. For *The Friend* he contributed an essay on education, called *A Reply to 'Mathetes'* in reply to a letter from John Wilson ('Christopher North'), and three 'Essays upon Epitaphs', only one of which appeared before Coleridge's periodical collapsed. The essays have come to be regarded as some of Wordsworth's profoundest meditations on language as an agency in human community. What later became Wordsworth's most famous and best-selling prose, however—his *Guide to the Lakes*—appeared first anonymously. Over 1809–10 he composed the letter-press to accompany forty-eight engravings issued by a former acquaintance, Joseph Wilkinson, as *Select Views in Cumberland, Westmoreland, and Lancashire* (1810). In 1820 he reclaimed his own work, publishing it as an annexe to a volume of new poems, *The River Duddon*, and in 1822 it achieved a separate identity at last as *A Description of the Scenery of the Lakes in the North of England*.

Wordsworth's most urgently felt compulsion, however, was to counter the failure of *Poems, in Two Volumes* by affirming to himself, and ultimately to the public, his poetic vocation. In 1807 he composed *The White Doe of Rylstone*, a historical narrative. Despite the urgings of his family that money was desperately needed, however, Wordsworth broke off negotiations for its publication. Further work on the first book of *The Recluse*, 'Home at Grasmere', concluded the poem, but not in a fashion which pointed to any development of a larger structure. It remained unpublished until 1888. Other work towards the philosophical poem, though, did engage him. Revising 'The Ruined Cottage' to stand as the opening to a new quasi-dramatic narrative and incorporating throughout meditative blank verse dating back to Alfoxden with fresh composition, Wordsworth eventually completed a poem in nine books, *The Excursion*.

Published in 1814 as an elegant and costly quarto, *The Excursion* announced to the world for the first time its author's larger ambitions. The title-page declared the poem to be only a 'portion' of *The Recluse*, and a preface explained what that work was ultimately to consist of, namely three poems 'containing views of Man, Nature, and Society'. The preface also divulged the existence of the autobiographical poem and printed a lengthy passage of eloquent but difficult blank verse as a 'Prospectus' to the whole of the design of *The Recluse*.

In the following year Wordsworth followed this major publication with another: two handsome volumes entitled *Poems … Including Lyrical Ballads, and the Miscellaneous Pieces of the Author*, in effect Wordsworth's first collected works. The contents were grouped under non-chronological classifications of the poet's own devising, which he employed with variations for the rest of his life, and were buttressed by a preface and a supplementary essay in which Wordsworth expounded his matured views on poetry and its elements. In 1815 also *The White Doe of Rylstone* appeared in expensive quarto form.

Coleridge was disappointed in *The Excursion*, and the revelation in his letter of 30 May 1815 of just how different had been the two poets' conception of *The Recluse* almost certainly blocked Wordsworth from any further serious work towards the philosophic poem. Nor was Francis Jeffrey won over. The *Edinburgh Review* (no. 24, November 1814) carried his most sustained and considered attack on the chief of 'the Lakers', which opened unforgettably with 'This will never do'. To Percy Bysshe and Mary Shelley, *The Excursion* demonstrated that Wordsworth had become 'a slave' (*Journals of Mary Shelley*, 1, ed. P. R. Feldman and D. Scott-Kilvert, 1987, 25). To Byron everything about the poem—its opulent format, the dedication to Lord Lonsdale, its metaphysical pretensions—indicated that its author had become a social and intellectual lackey. The influence of *The Excursion* on Shelley, however, was not inconsiderable, and Keats deemed it one of the 'three things to rejoice at in this Age' (letter of 10 Jan 1818; *The Letters of John Keats, 1814–1821*, ed. H. E. Rollins, 2 vols., 1958, 1.203). Slowly the positive assessment of Wordsworth's achievement took hold. For years his remained a coterie reputation, but after 1815 it grew steadily.

Travel and revision, 1815–1832 London was always a lure for Wordsworth, and in 1817 an extended autumn visit was enjoyed so energetically that after a month Sara Hutchinson was hoping 'we shall go out in the evenings no more' (*Letters of Sara Hutchinson*, ed. K. Coburn, 1954, 114). One evening has become famous as Benjamin Robert Haydon's 'immortal dinner'. On 28 December, Haydon, who had already brought Keats and Wordsworth together on an earlier occasion, was host in his painting-room to a party at which Charles Lamb became tipsy, and Wordsworth is said to have hesitated to join in a toast proposed by Keats, 'Newton's health and confusion to mathematics'.

Foreign travel was always a greater lure still, and in this period, with money less of a worry than it had been, Wordsworth yielded to it. In the summer of 1820 he returned to the Alps and traced exactly the ground he had walked with Robert Jones. Dorothy Wordsworth recorded in her *Journal of a Tour of the Continent, 1820* how deeply her brother was moved when he identified the track that had misled him on the Simplon Pass thirty years before. Their return route took them to Paris, and here Mary Wordsworth met Annette Vallon and Wordsworth was reunited with his daughter. Henry Crabb Robinson, who had joined the party at Lucerne, thought it 'indelicate' that Caroline always called Wordsworth 'Father' (*Henry Crabb Robinson*, 1.248).

In 1823 Wordsworth and Mary toured Belgium and the Netherlands; in the following year it was north Wales. 1828 saw Wordsworth, his daughter Dora, and Coleridge on a tour of Belgium, the Netherlands, and the Rhineland. In 1829 Wordsworth pursued a demanding itinerary in Ireland for five weeks.

The tour that meant most to him in this period after the Alpine excursion of 1820, however, took place in 1831. Summoned by the ailing Sir Walter Scott to visit before he left for Italy, Wordsworth and Dora made Abbotsford the starting point for a full Scottish tour. In Scott's company they revisited the Yarrow, and with high emotion the two men bade each other farewell. Wordsworth and Dora then followed the route of earlier Scottish excursions, and the

61-year-old was so much invigorated that he often walked 20 miles a day.

Dora was glad that their activity took her father's mind off the progress of the Reform Bill, and she had reason to be grateful, for the poet had been settling into tiresome gloom for over a decade. After the defeat of Napoleon, Wordsworth was alert to any sign that his countrymen had not learned the lessons to be drawn from the French politics of the previous twenty-five years. In practice this meant that he became increasingly partisan. In the Westmorland election of 1818 he campaigned tirelessly to ensure victory for Lord Lonsdale's candidates, convinced that the contender, Henry Brougham, was little better than a Jacobin. He was unsympathetic to radicals such as Cobbett and Hone, not because he thought the conduct of public affairs beyond reproach—far from it—but because he believed that activities such as theirs could only stir up unrest from below and dissolve national unity. Wordsworth strongly opposed Catholic emancipation in 1829 and the Reform Bill of 1832. Both measures weighed on him so heavily that friends and his family became alarmed for his health.

In a moment of depression Wordsworth told Haydon in 1831, 'The Muse has forsaken me' (23 April [1831]; *Letters*, 5.378). This was not quite true, but his finest work was behind him. In 1819 Wordsworth published revised versions of poems written much earlier, *Peter Bell* and *The Waggoner*, and in 1820 a sonnet sequence, *The River Duddon*, with other recent compositions, which was enthusiastically received. A sonnet sequence history of the Anglican church, *Ecclesiastical Sketches*, followed in 1822, and in the same year *Memorials of a Tour on the Continent, 1820*. Two other publishing events were more significant for Wordsworth's reputation. The first was the reissuing of *The Excursion* in a more portable format in 1820. What became a favourite poem for Victorian readers was issued separately many times until late in the century. The second was Wordsworth's work in 1820 on a four-volume set of collected works, which he oversaw with meticulous attention to organization and revision of texts. Collections were issued in 1827, 1832, 1836, 1845, and 1849–50, with reprints in many other years. For all save the last of these major new editions, each of which folded new poems into the existing classifications, Wordsworth scrutinized every line with an eye to revision, in the belief that his corpus was a self-referential and still developing whole.

Later writings In 1835 Wordsworth collected his recent work in the volume *Yarrow Revisited*. The finest poems in it are retrospective and elegiac—'On the Departure of Sir Walter Scott from Abbotsford, for Naples', 'Musings near Aquapendente', and 'Extempore Effusion upon the Death of James Hogg'. In the latter poem Wordsworth mourns the passing of Hogg, Scott, Coleridge, Lamb, and others in verse as powerful in its economy as any he had ever written. But the volume is not wholly backward-looking. 'The Warning' is a Jeremiad about the state of contemporary society, a theme returned to in a prose postscript to the whole volume. Here, however, the more attractively humane Wordsworth is to the fore, notably in the condemnation of the spirit inspiring the new poor law of 1834.

The success of *Yarrow Revisited*, attested by second and third editions in 1836 and 1839, emboldened Wordsworth to gamble on changing publishers. Longmans were abandoned for Edward Moxon, whose reverence for Wordsworth allied to his attentiveness in details of business endeared him to the Wordsworth circle. Moxon accompanied the poet to Paris in 1837, visited him at Rydal Mount, and was his host in London.

Moxon published Wordsworth's next collected edition in 1836. One of the many revisions in it was especially significant: the title-page of *The Excursion* no longer carried the legend 'a Portion of the Recluse'. Over the years admirers had somewhat tactlessly asked Wordsworth when *The Recluse* would be completed and the poet sporadically maintained the fiction that he was preparing himself for further composition, but by 1836 he had in fact recognized what he told Ticknor a couple of years later, that 'he had undertaken something beyond his powers to accomplish' (*The Life, Letters, and Journals of George Ticknor*, 2, ed. G. S. Hillard, 1876, 167).

That his poetic career was drawing to a close was also acknowledged in the labour Wordsworth expended on thorough revision of the autobiographical poem. Charging his family to publish it after his death, Wordsworth scrutinized every line for the preparation of a new manuscript fair copy.

Wordsworth's final discrete volume of poems also engaged with the distant past. *Poems, Chiefly of Early and Late Years* (1842) contained recent work, but its chief interest was that it included 'Guilt and Sorrow, or, Incidents upon Salisbury Plain' and his drama *The Borderers*, both having lain in manuscript since the late 1790s. Wordsworth had always vehemently opposed chronological presentation of his work. The classification system elaborated over the sequence of his collected editions had been intended to avoid what he described as the 'very worst' way of displaying a poet's corpus (27 April 1826; *Letters*, 4.444). Now, however, in an introductory note which conceded the claim of 'literary biography', Wordsworth underscored the historical interest of what he was disclosing, as he located the origins of 'Guilt and Sorrow' in 1793 and the beginning of the war with France. What he did not reveal was that though the note recalls the poet's state of mind in that period, the poems had been substantially revised and, in the case of 'Guilt and Sorrow' especially, their radicalism muted.

Wordsworth concluded the setting of his poetic affairs in order. In 1843, at the urging of his beloved friend Isabella Fenwick, Wordsworth composed extensive notes about the whole of his life's work, upon which all editors and biographers have drawn, and in 1847 he dictated memoranda about his early life for his nephew Christopher to use after his death in whatever form of biographical notice might seem appropriate. They and the 'Fenwick notes' were used in Christopher Wordsworth's two-volume *Memoirs of William Wordsworth* (1851). In 1845

Wordsworth oversaw the publication of a handsome single-volume edition of his collected works. The text was, as usual, subjected throughout to revision, but the most significant was that to *The Excursion*, in which the language of Christian doctrine was more explicitly introduced. Revision, however, what the poet's family called 'tinkering', was not quite over. New readings in the last collection in six volumes in 1849–50 established the text of his corpus in this, the last authorized edition of the poet's lifetime.

Personal characteristics Wordsworth was tall for his day and proud of it. His passport of 1837 and Haydon, who measured him for a portrait sitting in 1842, put his height at 5 feet 9½ inches. Regular walking until advanced old age kept him spare, and though he was troubled by the usual infirmities of age, Wordsworth's only serious medical worry was for his eyes, which frequently became so inflamed that he feared he would go blind. In later life he regularly wore a shade or tinted glasses.

Comments about Wordsworth in his prime tend to emphasize his robust directness, practicality, and seriousness, and there are many witnesses who also found him, as Charles Greville did in 1831, 'very cheerful, merry, courteous, and talkative' (25 Feb 1831; *The Greville Memoirs: a New Edition*, ed. H. Reeve, 8 vols., 1888). During his middle years, however, Wordsworth often left an unappealing impression on those who did not know him intimately. Deeply wounded by professional failure, he became prickly and egotistical. Keats was not the only one who found him domineering. From the 1820s Wordsworth sank into such an utterly disproportionate gloom about the state of the country that eventually even his family remonstrated with him. In the late 1830s, though his disapproval of social and political developments remained strong, he seems to have mellowed personally.

Numerous portraits capture Wordsworth across the whole of his poetic life from *Lyrical Ballads* to the laureateship. Wordsworth in 1798 was drawn by Robert Hancock; the pencil and chalk portrait is now in the National Portrait Gallery. Portraits by Richard Carruthers, now in the Wordsworth Museum, Grasmere, and Benjamin Robert Haydon, now in the National Portrait Gallery, present differing images of Wordsworth in 1817 and 1818. The Carruthers oil was judged a strong likeness by the Wordsworth circle, but it was the pencil and chalk Haydon, familiarly known at Rydal as 'the Brigand', that was judged to have caught some of the fire of the reckless youth who had earlier walked across revolutionary France. Mary Wordsworth could not bear to part with it. Henry William Pickersgill painted Wordsworth in 1832–3 for St John's College, Cambridge, and again in 1840 (painting now in the Wordsworth Museum, Grasmere). The finest image of the poet in late life is certainly Haydon's *Wordsworth on Helvellyn* (1842), now in the National Portrait Gallery.

Friendships Wordsworth is popularly associated with solitude. One of his most famous poems speaks of 'the bliss of solitude' ('I wandered lonely as a cloud'). In *The Prelude* he remarks that in childhood he was taught to feel

> perhaps too much,
> The self-sufficing power of Solitude.
> (*The Prelude*, 1805, 2.77–8)

The Recluse was so named because it was to embody the views of one 'living in retirement'. But though he drew on resources nurtured in solitude, Wordsworth was not in the ordinary sense of the word a solitary man.

Wordsworth's friends and acquaintances were very numerous. The extant correspondence indicates their range, but the volumes of letters do not include many people, such as friends from school and college days, to whom Wordsworth is known from other evidence to have remained attached. To list all their names here would be neither possible nor useful. Some account of Wordsworth's friendships with more famous figures, however, will suggest how fully engaged he was in the contemporary literary, the artistic, and to some extent the political milieu.

In the 1790s Wordsworth met many of the most important radicals such as John Thelwall and William Godwin. The friendship of Sir George Beaumont introduced him in his middle years to London circles of arts and politics, where he encountered Joseph Farington, David Wilkie, James Northcote, John Constable, Samuel Rogers, Charles James Fox, and others. The diaries of Benjamin Robert Haydon record the course of his volatile friendship with the poet. At Henry Taylor's breakfast salon Wordsworth was introduced to John Stuart Mill. William Charles Macready became a disciple, as did John Kenyon. Through the Cambridge connections of his brother Christopher Wordsworth made the acquaintance of churchmen and academics, such as William Whewell and Hugh Rose. Charles Blomfield, bishop of London, became a fast friend. In 1837 Thomas Talfourd solicited Wordsworth's aid in promoting a copyright bill, partly because of the range of connections he would be able to lobby. Wordsworth's friendship with Lord Lonsdale put him on the guest list of many of the Lake District's leading families, but in his later years the circle there he valued most was a small one that included Eliza Fletcher, of Lancrigg, Grasmere, the Arnolds, and Isabella Fenwick. With Harriet Martineau in Ambleside, Wordsworth could never get on.

Wordsworth told the young Thomas De Quincey:

> My friendship is not in my power to give: this is a gift which no man can make, it is not in our power: a sound and healthy friendship is the growth of time and circumstance, it will spring up and thrive like a wildflower when these favour, and when they do not it is in vain to look for it. (29 July 1803; *Letters*, 1.400)

A small number of people stand out as those whose friendship meant a great deal to Wordsworth, irrespective of how often they met. Of Sir Walter Scott, Wordsworth said simply, 'I love that Man' ([30 July 1830]; ibid., 5.310). Robert Southey did not endear himself to Wordsworth when they were both young, but over the years Wordsworth came to value Southey's steadiness and courage in adversity. At his death, though not invited by Southey's divided family, Wordsworth made his way through driving rain to his funeral. Charles Lamb, his preference for London streets over the Lake District mountains notwithstanding, had a special place in Wordsworth's affections from their first meeting in 1796. Wordsworth's friendship with Sir George Beaumont began with an act of patronage—the gift in 1803 of a parcel of land, mentioned above—but it was sustained until the latter's death in 1827 by mutual interests and high personal regard. William Rowan Hamilton, who conquered Wordsworth at once in 1827, seemed with Coleridge to be one of 'the two most wonderful men' he had ever met (R. P. Graves, *Life of Sir William Rowan Hamilton*, 3 vols., 1882–9, 1.269). It is not likely that Wordsworth ever called Henry Crabb Robinson wonderful, but in his later years he came to depend upon his steadfast, unostentatious support. In 1842 Wordsworth dedicated 'Memorials of a Tour in Italy' to Crabb Robinson,

> For the kindnesses that never ceased to flow,
> And prompt self-sacrifice to which I owe
> Far more than any heart but mine can know.

The most important relationships of Wordsworth's life, other than that with his wife, were those with Dorothy Wordsworth and Coleridge. In 'Home at Grasmere' Wordsworth pays beautiful tribute to what his sister meant to him:

> Where'er my footsteps turned,
> Her Voice was like a hidden Bird that sang;
> The thought of her was like a flash of light
> Or an unseen companionship, a breath
> Of fragrance independent of the wind.

Dorothy Wordsworth's Grasmere journals record a degree of intimacy and passion between brother and sister which alarmed Wordsworth's first scholarly biographer, William Knight, and which continues to discomfit many readers. Dorothy shared the poet's passion for walking and for observation of natural phenomena, and some of Wordsworth's verse draws on his sister's journal entries.

One of the early bonds between Wordsworth and Coleridge was that the latter was completely enthralled by Wordsworth's 'exquisite Sister' ([*c.*3 July 1797]; *Collected Letters*, ed. Griggs, 1.330). Wordsworth was awed by Coleridge's intellect, by his range of reading, and by the creative fertility of his thought. Wordsworth's hesitant but emerging faith in his own powers in the late 1790s was greatly strengthened by Coleridge's conviction that his friend was destined to be the greatest philosophical poet in the language. The interplay of their poetry and aesthetic theorizing was subtle and energetic. *The Prelude* is addressed to Coleridge; its concluding lines embrace him; its chronicle ends with the summer of 1798, when Wordsworth and Coleridge had 'wantoned in wild Poesy', rightly, for that was when both poets were happiest, in a creative intimacy they were never to recapture. For the misery of the slow disintegration of their friendship Wordsworth found large compensation in the contentment of his marriage, but Coleridge had no such recourse, and the conviction that Wordsworth had turned against

him remained one of the 'griping and grasping Sorrows' of his life (8 Oct 1822; *Collected Letters*, ed. Griggs, 5.249).

Final years, 1833–1850 As Wordsworth entered old age he remained physically vigorous; he climbed Helvellyn for the last time when he was seventy. In 1833 he visited the Isle of Man and then Scotland, memorializing the latter tour in a series of sonnets. One of his busiest London visits ever occupied two months in 1836, and the following year Wordsworth and Crabb Robinson travelled through France to Italy, seeing Rome, Florence, Milan, and Venice, before returning through Germany and Belgium. Though he lamented that he was too old to use his experiences in fitting poetry, Wordsworth none the less composed one final travel sequence, 'Memorials of a Tour in Italy'. In 1841 he returned to the west country and revisited places such as Alfoxden, made precious by association with Coleridge and *Lyrical Ballads*.

Wordsworth's fame continued to grow. In 1838 he was awarded an honorary degree by Durham University, and in the following year he received one from Oxford at a ceremony in which he was eulogized by John Keble and applauded by a packed audience in the Sheldonian Theatre, including Matthew Arnold and Arthur Hugh Clough. The honorand presented the Newdigate prize for poetry to the twenty-year-old John Ruskin. Before the ceremony Wordsworth was entertained by John Henry Newman, among others. After the death of Robert Southey in 1843, Wordsworth was offered the post of poet laureate. After declining initially on the grounds of age, he accepted when Sir Robert Peel insisted that it was the queen's particular wish and that nothing would be required of him. On 25 April 1845 Victoria's laureate knelt before her, wearing court dress borrowed from Samuel Rogers and encumbered by Sir Humphry Davy's sword.

Wordsworth's fame drew hundreds of visitors to Rydal Mount, whose names were mostly recorded in the Rydal Mount visitors' book, now in the Wordsworth Library, Grasmere. Notable among them were John Stuart Mill, John Kenyon (on behalf of Elizabeth Barrett), the radical poet Thomas Cooper, Dr Thomas Arnold, Alfred Tennyson, and Aubrey de Vere, and Americans such as George Ticknor, William Ellery Channing, Orville Dewey, Charles Sumner, Ralph Waldo Emerson, and Henry Reed, who edited Wordsworth's poetry for the American readership. In the Lake District circle of which he was the acknowledged ornament, Wordsworth also met Elizabeth Gaskell, William Rathbone Greg, Harriet Martineau, and many other notable figures. In the early 1840s Wordsworth was courted by Frederick William Faber, who took every opportunity to foster the view that Wordsworth was truly the laureate of the Oxford Movement.

The years of Wordsworth's greatest fame, however, were also a time of much personal grief. In 1833 Dorothy Wordsworth was taken seriously ill, and in the coming years she fell prey to a form of Alzheimer's disease. She was nursed at Rydal Mount until her death in 1855, and at the very end of Wordsworth's life Mary Wordsworth remarked that the one thing that continued to give him pleasure was ministering to the 'dear, dear Sister' of 'Tintern Abbey' (reported by Henry Crabb Robinson, 15 Jan [1849]; *Correspondence of Henry Crabb Robinson*, 2.685). The death of Sara Hutchinson, a mainstay of the Rydal Mount household, in June 1835 followed closely on that of Coleridge on 25 July 1834 and that of Charles Lamb on 27 December 1834. Wordsworth's surviving brother, Christopher, master of Trinity College, Cambridge, died in 1846 (Richard had died in 1816). The most deeply felt loss was that of Dora on 9 July 1847, and Wordsworth's grief was intensified by self-reproach. Passionately devoted to his daughter, Wordsworth had done all he could to prevent her marriage in 1841 to Edward Quillinan, a widower thirteen years her senior with two daughters, and in the years before Dora's death he had never fully accepted her choice of husband.

By the time of Hartley Coleridge's death on 6 January 1849 Wordsworth was waiting for his own. At Hartley's burial in Grasmere churchyard, Wordsworth pointed out to the sexton where his own and Mary's graves were to be, saying that Hartley would have wished to lie near to them. Having taken pleurisy from recklessly walking out in frosty weather, Wordsworth died at Rydal Mount on 23 April 1850 and was buried in the churchyard at St Oswald's, Grasmere, four days later. Dorothy Wordsworth died on 25 January 1855; Mary Wordsworth died on 17 January 1859. They too were buried in the churchyard at St Oswald's. *The Prelude* was rushed through the press, appearing just three months after Wordsworth's death.

Aftermath After Wordsworth's death funds were raised by public subscription for memorials: a profile medallion by Thomas Woolner in Grasmere church; a memorial window, paid for in large part by American contributions, in Gilbert Scott's new church in Ambleside; and a statute by Frederick Thrupp in Westminster Abbey.

For many years Wordsworth's heirs effectively controlled the image of the poet that was to be transmitted to posterity, not least through policing the copyright vested in the last authorized edition of 1849–50 and in all unpublished writings. The biography by the high-church bishop of Lincoln, Christopher Wordsworth, *Memoirs of William Wordsworth* (1851), smoothed over Wordsworth's radicalism, omitted (against the author's wishes, it should in fairness be added) all mention of Annette Vallon, and emphasized the poet's adherence to the Church of England. Moxon & Co. continued to issue the only definitive editions, with the result, for example, that *The Prelude*, which other publishers could not touch until it came out of copyright until 1892, was less widely known than its importance warranted. Wordsworth's prose was collected by Alexander Grosart in 1876, and towards the end of the copyright term William Knight, professor of moral philosophy at St Andrews, was allowed to produce the first ever scholarly edition of the poetry and a biography, eleven volumes in all, between 1882 and 1889. Late in his research Knight almost certainly worked out the secret of Wordsworth's illegitimate daughter, but with Wordsworth's surviving son, William, still alive, he did not disclose it. The story was revealed by George McLean Harper in *William Wordsworth* (1916).

By the time of his death Wordsworth was an acknowledged classic and there was no swing of the pendulum against him. Critical writing, however, was meagre, and obeisance little more than routine until serious critical reassessments by Richard Holt Hutton, Aubrey de Vere, John Campbell Shairp, Walter Pater, Leslie Stephen, Stopford Brooke, and Edward Caird returned Wordsworth to prominence from the 1870s. Much was made of the spiritual elements of the poetry. Wordsworth was claimed as a kindred spirit by Christians from Quakers to Roman Catholics. Leslie Stephen spoke for non-Christians when he extolled Wordsworth's ethics as capable of systematic exposition. In one of the century's most famous tributes to Wordsworth's healing power, John Stuart Mill recorded in his *Autobiography* (1873) how at a crisis in his life, when emotional and intellectual aridity threatened his sanity, immersion in Wordsworth's poems had helped to save him: 'they seemed to be the very culture of the feelings which I was in quest of' (J. S. Mill, *Autobiography and Literary Essays*, ed. J. M. Robson and J. Stillinger, 1981, 150). The most influential essay, however, played down ethics and philosophy. In his introduction to his selection of Wordsworth's poetry published in 1879 Matthew Arnold made two declarations that immediately became critical commonplaces, namely that all Wordsworth's greatest work was written before 1810 and that there was too much of it, making selection vital if the poet's influence was to survive. His third point sparked a debate which has continued into the twenty-first century. In reverencing the 'philosophy', Arnold claimed, Wordsworth's disciples were honouring the weakness, not the strength, of his poetry.

Despite grumbling about 'Wordsworthians', Arnold served as president of the Wordsworth Society in 1882–3. The society, whose most active member was William Knight, existed from 1880 to 1886. In 1890 Dove Cottage was bought and made over to a body of trustees which included Stopford Brooke, William Knight, and Hardwicke Drummond Rawnsley. In addition to Dove Cottage, the Wordsworth Trust now maintains in Grasmere a museum and a library in which the bulk of the poet's extant manuscripts are preserved.

The most important scholarly event after Knight's edition was the appearance of Ernest De Selincourt's parallel text of the first and last completed versions of *The Prelude* in 1926. In the notes and textual apparatus to this edition and to the five-volume edition of Wordsworth's complete poetical works which De Selincourt inaugurated in 1941 (completed by Helen Darbishire in 1949), the editors revealed the existence of a large number of manuscripts and of early versions of poems unknown to scholars. Since 1975 the Cornell Wordsworth Series, under its general editor Stephen Parrish, has been presenting them in their entirety. It is largely thanks to successive editorial uncoverings that the Wordsworth studied in schools and universities at the beginning of the twenty-first century is substantially different from the Wordsworth delineated in the *Dictionary of National Biography*.

The poet From 'The Idiot Boy' (1798) to the Fenwick note to *An Evening Walk* (1843) Wordsworth consistently dated his 'strong indentures' to 'the muses' from his fourteenth year. In fact, despite the accomplishment of his early work, Wordsworth's career was not wholly settled until 1798, the year that saw the summer of *Lyrical Ballads* and the beginnings of *The Recluse*. Thereafter he pursued his vocation unwaveringly. The preface to *Lyrical Ballads* (1800 and 1802) formulates his most eloquent defence of the poet and of poetry as the most philosophic of all writing, but throughout his letters appear observations such as this declaration to Lady Beaumont: 'To be incapable of a feeling of Poetry in my sense of the word is to be without love of human nature and reverence for God' (21 May 1807; *Letters*, 2.146).

Many of Wordsworth's lyrics derive their charm from an appearance of spontaneity. This, coupled with selective quotation from the preface to *Lyrical Ballads* about poetry as 'spontaneous overflow of powerful feelings' and the fact that in her journal Dorothy Wordsworth does frequently record her brother composing out of doors, gave currency to an image of Wordsworth as a poet at his most creative when extemporizing to the fields. Arnold's remark in the introduction to his selection that Wordsworth had no style, that it was as if nature held the pencil, prolonged its life. But it was always a misapprehension, for, whatever the origins of any particular composition may have been, Wordsworth was meticulous about his craft. Admonishing William Rowan Hamilton to pay more attention to 'Workmanship' in his own verses, Wordsworth insisted that:

the materials upon which [the logical faculty] is exercised in Poetry are so subtle, so plastic, so complex, [that] the application of it requires an adroitness which can proceed from nothing but practice, a discernment, which emotion is so far from bestowing that at first it is ever in the way of it. (24 Sept 1827; *Letters*, 4.546)

What Wordsworth praised in Shelley was his 'workmanship of style' (A. B. Grosart, *The Prose Works of William Wordsworth*, 3 vols., 1876, 3.463).

Drafts, revised drafts, and fair-copy manuscripts survive as fascinating remains from Wordsworth's struggles in composition, but all his printed texts constitute further evidence, for what was unusually strong in him was the conviction that a poem was not finished, nor finished with, when it was published. For each successive collection of his work he revised his poems, line by line, including punctuation. So compulsive was the urge to repossess a published poem that he began revising *Lyrical Ballads* (1800) in one of the first copies he received from the printer. The labours of revision often brought on illness and invariably made Wordsworth irritable and difficult. At sixty-seven he begged his wife's forgiveness for his 'ungovernable' impatience during a particularly trying period of revision ([5 July 1837]; *Letters*, 6.424).

Continual revision was entailed in part by Wordsworth's conviction that his large and varied corpus was one growing and unified whole. Introducing the *Recluse* project in 1814, Wordsworth saw it as resembling a Gothic church, adding that his minor pieces,

when they shall be properly arranged, will be found by the attentive Reader, to have such connection with the main Work as may give them claim to be likened to the little cells, oratories, and sepulchral recesses, ordinarily included in those edifices.

This organic view of his work is reflected in the classification system he devised to present his collected poems from 1815 onwards, for it obscured or concealed both dates of composition and the groupings of the poems on first publication.

Addressing Benjamin Robert Haydon, Wordsworth begins a sonnet, 'High is our calling, Friend!'. In many such utterances, notably in Wordsworth's letter to John Wilson of 7 June 1802, the 'calling' is identified as that of the teacher. 'Every great Poet is a Teacher', Wordsworth declared to Beaumont, 'I wish either to be considered as a Teacher, or as nothing' ([February 1808]; *Letters*, 2.195). His conception, however, of how poetry could teach was flexible and generous and it encompassed every genre, but fundamental to it all was a concern to honour the primary human affections and the essentials of human experience. Assessing his own achievement in late life, Wordsworth quoted aptly from one of his earliest poems, 'The Old Cumberland Beggar', when he observed to Crabb Robinson: 'If my writings are to last, it will I myself believe, be mainly owing to this characteristic. They will please for the single cause, "That we have all of us one human heart!"' ([*c*.27 April 1835]; ibid., 6.44).

STEPHEN GILL

Sources *The letters of William and Dorothy Wordsworth*, ed. C. L. Shaver, M. Moorman, and A. G. Hill, 8 vols. (1967–93) · S. Gill, *William Wordsworth: a life* (1989) · M. Moorman, *William Wordsworth: a biography*, *The early years, 1770–1803* (1957); *The later years, 1803–1850* (1965) · T. W. Thompson, *Wordsworth's Hawkshead*, ed. R. S. Woof (1970) · M. L. Reed, *Wordsworth: the chronology of the early years, 1770–1799* (1967); *The middle years, 1800–1815* (1975) · E. Legouis, *William Wordsworth and Annette Vallon* (1922) · K. Johnston, *The hidden Wordsworth* (1998) · N. Roe, *Wordsworth and Coleridge: the radical years* (1988) · *Collected letters of Samuel Taylor Coleridge*, ed. E. L. Griggs, 6 vols. (1956–71) · D. Wordsworth, *The Grasmere journals*, ed. P. Woof (1991) · B. R. Schneider, *Wordsworth's Cambridge education* (1957) · S. Gill, *Wordsworth and the Victorians* (1998) · *The correspondence of Henry Crabb Robinson with the Wordsworth circle*, ed. E. J. Morley, 2 vols. (1927) · *Henry Crabb Robinson on books and their writers*, ed. E. J. Morley, 3 vols. (1938) · F. Blanshard, *Portraits of Wordsworth* (1959) · R. Gittings and J. Manton, *Dorothy Wordsworth* (1985) · D. Wu, *Wordsworth's reading, 1770–1815*, 2 vols. (1993–5) · R. Holmes, *Coleridge: early visions* (1989) · R. Holmes, *Coleridge: darker reflections* (1998) · C. Wordsworth, *Memoirs of William Wordsworth* (1851) · E. Quillinan, diary, Wordsworth Trust, Dove Cottage, Grasmere

Archives BL, music book, Add. MS 54194 · Cornell University, Ithaca, New York, corresp. and papers · Harvard U., Houghton L., letters and MSS · Hunt. L., corresp. and papers · Indiana University, Bloomington, Lilly Library, corresp. · Morgan L., letters from him and his sister · NL Scot., letters · Royal Arch. · St John Cam., papers · Wordsworth Trust, Dove Cottage, Grasmere, corresp., literary MSS, and papers · Yale U., Beinecke L., papers | BL, letters to Sir John Taylor Coleridge, Add. MS 47553 · BL, letters to Barron Field, Add MS 41325 [extracts] · BL, corresp. with W. E. Gladstone, Add. MSS 44356–44527 · BL, corresp. with Sir William Hamilton, RP 307 [copies] · BL, Longman MS · BL, letters to William Mathews,

Add. MS 46136 · BL, letters to Thomas Poole, Add. MS 35344 · BL, letters to Edward Quillinan, Ashley MSS 4641, A 4642 · BL, letters to Daniel Stuart, Add. MS 34046 · BL, letters to his brother Christopher Wordsworth and his nephew John Wordsworth, Add. MS 46136 · Bodl. Oxf., letters to Sir Henry Taylor · CKS, letters to Lord Stanhope · Cumbria AS, Carlisle, letters to earl of Lonsdale and Lord Lowther · Mirehouse, Cumbria, corresp. with John Spedding · NL Scot., letters to J. G. Lockhart · NL Scot., letters to Sir Walter Scott · priv. coll., letters to Hook family and MS poem · UCL, letters to Samuel Rogers · V&A NAL, letters to Joseph Cottle and W. S. Landor · V&A NAL, corresp. with Alexander Dyce

Likenesses R. Hancock, pencil and chalk drawing, 1798, NPG · W. Shuter, oils, 1798, Cornell University, Ithaca, New York · B. R. Haydon, life mask, 1815, St John Cam.; cast, NPG · R. Carruthers, oils, 1817, Wordsworth Trust, Dove Cottage, Grasmere; replica, Municipal Art Gallery, East London, South Africa · B. R. Haydon, pencil and chalk drawing, 1818, NPG · H. H. Meyer, stipple, pubd 1819 (after R. Carruthers), BM, NPG · F. Chantrey, marble bust, 1820, Indiana University, Bloomington · W. Boxall, oils, 1831, NPG · H. W. Pickersgill, chalk drawing, 1832, St John Cam. · H. W. Pickersgill, oils, 1832, St John Cam. · M. Gillies, miniature, 1839, Wordsworth Trust, Dove Cottage, Grasmere · H. W. Pickersgill, portrait, 1840, Wordsworth Trust, Dove Cottage, Grasmere · B. R. Haydon, oils, 1842, NPG [see illus.] · B. R. Haydon, chalk and pencil drawing, 1843, Wordsworth Trust, Dove Cottage, Grasmere · B. R. Haydon, oils, 1843 (unfinished), Wordsworth Trust, Dove Cottage, Grasmere · S. Crosthwaite, oils, 1844, Wordsworth Trust, Dove Cottage, Grasmere · H. Inman, oils, 1844, University of Pennsylvania, Philadelphia · T. Faed, group portrait, oils, 1849 (*Sir Walter Scott and his friends at Abbotsford*), Scot. NPG · F. Chantrey, pencil drawing, NPG · H. W. Pickersgill, oils (replica), NPG · R. Roffe, stipple (after W. Boxall), NPG · J. Stephanoff, group portrait, watercolour drawing (*The trial of queen Caroline, 1820*), Palace of Westminster, London · F. Thrupp, marble statue, Westminster Abbey · stipple (after R. Hancock), BM, NPG

Wealth at death see will, 1847, PRO, PROB 11/2114, fol. 52

Worgan, John (*bap.* 1724, *d.* 1790), organist and composer, was baptized on 2 November 1724 at St Botolph without Bishopsgate, London, the second surviving son of John Worgan (1689/90–1741), carpenter, and his wife, Mary, who died some time after 1753. He received his first musical instruction from his elder brother, James, who was also an organist and composer. He later studied with Thomas Roseingrave (1688–1766) and Francesco Geminiani (1687–1762) while they were in London. Worgan came to share Roseingrave's enthusiasm for the keyboard sonatas of Domenico Scarlatti and he acquired the Albero manuscript containing forty-four of Scarlatti's sonatas (BL, Add. MS 31553), from which he published two collections of twelve sonatas each in 1752 and 1771. In 1748 Worgan obtained the MusB degree at Cambridge and proceeded to MusD in 1775.

Worgan was an outstanding organist, his first post being obtained in 1743 at St Katharine Cree. On 14 September 1749 he added St Andrew Undershaft, and on his brother's death in the spring of 1753 he resigned from St Katharine's to succeed him at St Botolph, Aldgate. He is known to have been organist at St John's Chapel, Bedford Row, in 1762. Also in 1753 he succeeded his brother as organist at Vauxhall Gardens, and on 1 September he married Sarah Maclean, whom he divorced in 1768. They had at least six children: John (*bap.* 15 June 1755); George Bouchir (*bap.* 3 May 1757); Charlotte Sophia (*bap.* 2 Sept 1761); James (*bap.* 27 Nov 1762); Mary (*bap.* 8 Jan 1764); and Joseph (*bap.* 18 April 1768), all baptized at St Andrew's, Holborn. His second wife, Eleanor, died on 11 January 1777. They had at least one child, Thomas Danvers Worgan, who was baptized on 27 March 1773 at St Marylebone. On 12 June 1779 he married Martha Cooke, widow. He was at Vauxhall until 1761, and again from 1770 to 1774, and it was there that Worgan's organ playing first brought him fame. Burney remarked:

> by constant practice he became a very masterly and learned fughist on the organ, and as a concerto player a rival of Stanley … His organ playing, though more in the style of Handel than of any other school, is indeed masterly, in a way quite his own.   (Burney, *Hist. mus.*)

Worgan's other duty at Vauxhall was to compose songs for the spring and summer evening entertainments. His thirteen published collections of Vauxhall songs, duets, and cantatas reveal him as a competent exponent of the pastoral vocal style. He was quick to compose patriotic songs and no fewer than five celebrate the successes of British arms in 1759. For the national thanksgiving called for 29 November he composed an anthem, 'We will rejoice in thy salvation', which he had printed and sent to cathedrals and chapels.

Worgan's published output in other forms was small, principally *Six Sonatas for Harpsichord* (1769), *Pieces for the Harpsichord, Composed … for Forming the Hands of Young Pupils* (1780), and *A New Concerto for the Harpsichord* (1785). Other works in manuscript are to be found in the British Library and in the Bodleian at Oxford. Interest in his two performed oratorios was not sustained. *Hannah*, with words by Christopher Smart, was performed once at the King's Theatre on 30 April 1766, and *Manasseh* was performed for the benefit of the Lock Hospital on 30 April 1766 and 13 May 1767.

For many years Worgan suffered from the stone, and he underwent an operation but died soon afterwards, on 24 August 1790, at his home, 22 Gower Street. His funeral took place at St Andrew Undershaft on 31 August, during which the organ was played by one of his pupils, Charles Wesley. He was buried in the church, and was survived by his third wife and his daughter Charlotte Sophia, who had married Sir William *Parsons (*d.* 1817).

ROBERT J. BRUCE

Sources 'Memoir of the life and works of John Worgan, MusD', *Quarterly Musical Magazine and Review*, 5 (1823), 113–34 · Burney, *Hist. mus.*, 4.587–668 · [J. S. Sainsbury], ed., *A dictionary of musicians*, 2 vols. (1824) · *New Grove* · D. Dawe, *Organists of the City of London, 1666–1850* (1983), 157–9 · Highfill, Burnim & Langhans, *BDA*, 16.273–4 · R. Newton, 'The English cult of Domenico Scarlatti', *Music and Letters*, 20 (1939), 138–56

Archives BL, Add. MSS 29386, 31670, 31693, 31808, 37522, 38488 · Ely Cathedral | Bodl. Oxf., Tenbury MSS

Wealth at death see will, cited Dawe, *Organists of the City of London*

Workman, Herbert Brook (1862–1951), Methodist minister and college head, was born in Peckham, London, on 2 November 1862, son of John Sansom Workman, a Welseyan Methodist minister, and his wife, Mary Brook. Educated at Kingswood School, London, of which his younger brother, W. P. Workman, was later headmaster

(1889–1918), he took a London BA (1884) and MA (1885) from Owens College, Manchester, and prepared at Didsbury College for the Methodist ministry. He married in 1891 Ethel Mary, daughter of Alban Gardner Buller, solicitor, of Birmingham; they had two sons and one daughter.

Workman had a notable spell of fifteen years as a circuit minister before serving as principal of Westminster Training College in 1903–30. After the long regime of the redoubtable J. H. Rigg the college needed a new, tough broom. Workman brought to the task not only his own growing reputation as a scholar, with a flair for picking colleagues and pupils of coming eminence, but great gifts of shrewdness and administrative prescience. He raised the college to a new eminence, and his concentration on training teachers at Westminster and at the sister college of Southlands stood his church in valuable stead at a time of crisis in its educational policy when numbers of Methodist day schools were closing. From 1919 until his retirement in 1940 he held the important office of secretary of the Methodist education committee. The most notable of his achievements was the consolidation of a ring of Methodist residential schools, to which, through his efforts, there were notable additions. He was a member of the senate of the University of London, which awarded him the degree of DLitt (1907).

Workman was the first distinguished church historian to come from the Methodist church, and perhaps the first protestant and nonconformist scholar to show sensitive sympathy with the medieval church. It is true that his first historical writings, begun as a circuit minister, treated the elements of dissent within medieval Christendom. The small volumes *The Church of the West in the Middle Ages* (2 vols., 1898–1900) and *The Dawn of the Reformation* (2 vols., 1901–2) have long been superseded, but are remarkable for the care and accuracy with which their author had studied a great range of authorities and sought the truth among the primary documents. These studies found their climax in the sympathetic portrayal of John Hus, to which his *Letters of John Hus* (1904) formed a useful epilogue. There followed studies in the early church, *Persecution in the Early Church* (1906) and *The Evolution of the Monastic Ideal* (1913), which showed his flair for colourful and interesting narrative material. His *Christian Thought to the Reformation* (1911) is in contrast disappointing and not very perceptive. His great work, however, was his massive study *John Wyclif* (2 vols., 1926). Workman was preparing a further volume to cover the history of later Lollardy at the time of his death. Probably his best single writing was his classic essay, published as *The Place of Methodism in the Catholic Church* (1921), originally written for the *New History of Methodism* (2 vols., 1909), of which he was one of the editors. There his evangelical convictions and his wide catholic sympathies enabled him to set the evangelical revival against the long perspective of the Christian past. The worth of his studies was recognized by the University of Aberdeen, which awarded him the degree of DD in 1914. Workman died at his home, 29 Vineyard Hill Road, Wimbledon, on 26 August 1951. He was survived by his wife.   E. G. RUPP, *rev.*

Sources *The Times* (27 Aug 1951) · *Who's who in Methodism* (1933) · private information (1971) · personal knowledge (1971) · *CGPLA Eng. & Wales* (1951)
Wealth at death £2891 4s. 4d.: probate, 24 Oct 1951, *CGPLA Eng. & Wales*

Worlidge, John (d. 1693), writer on agriculture, of Petersfield, Hampshire, was said to have been at one time woodward to the earl of Pembroke, whose lands ran in this area. Worlidge was a popular and influential writer on husbandry and rural crafts, his books generally appearing under the name J. W. Gent. His treatise *Systema agriculturae, or, The Mystery of Husbandry Discovered* (1669) was the first systematic and comprehensive treatment of arable and livestock husbandry. It displayed Worlidge's familiarity with earlier authors on these subjects, to which he had made worthwhile additions, and it went through five editions before being supplanted by the numerous agricultural reference books of the eighteenth century. The section on cider was subsequently expanded and published as *Vinetum Britannicum, or, A Treatise of Cider* in 1676, dedicated to Elias Ashmole, with later editions. Worlidge's *Systema horti-culturae, or, The Art of Gardening* was published in 1677, also with later editions. In it Worlidge stressed the benefits of cultivating vegetables and fruit, both to the gentry who made greater profit from their land, and to the populace whose diet was thereby improved. *Apiarum, or, A Discourse of Bees*, a very important aspect of fruit growing and originally contained within the *Vinetum*, was published separately in 1676. Worlidge was a correspondent of John Houghton (1645–1705), writer on trade and industry, who in 1681 published two contributions from 'the ingenious Mr John Worlidge of Petersfield', on the improvement of land by growing parsley, and on improving and fining cider.

Worlidge died in 1693, leaving in his will, proved on 8 August 1693, bequests to his wife, Grace, and his children, Edward, Martha, Grace, and John, of whom nothing more is known. His books were expanded, presumably by other hands, and reissued after his death. It is now considered unlikely that he was the author of the *Dictionarum rusticum, urbanicum, et botanicum* (1704), sometimes attributed to him.   ERNEST CLARKE, *rev.* ANITA McCONNELL

Sources S. Felton, *On the portraits of English authors on gardening*, 2nd edn (1830), 28–31 · J. Thirsk, 'Agricultural innovations and their diffusion', *The agrarian history of England and Wales*, ed. J. Thirsk, 5/2 (1985), 533–89 · G. E. Fussell, *The old English farming books: 1523–1730* (1947), vol. 1 of *The old English farming books* (1947–91), 95–6 · will, proved, 8 Aug 1693

Worlidge, Thomas (1700–1766), portrait painter and etcher, was born in Peterborough, the son of Richard Worlidge, a lawyer. By the early 1740s he had settled into a working life divided between London and Bath. He received his earliest artistic training from the Genoese émigré Alessandro Grimaldi (whose daughter, Arabella, became his first wife) and from the engraver Louis-Philippe Boitard. His enthusiasm for the work of Rembrandt, which was shared by a number of influential artists and collectors in mid-eighteenth-century England, was the dominant force in his life and work.

Thomas Worlidge (1700–1766), self-portrait, 1754

Although Worlidge consistently styled himself 'painter' and probably always earned his living by portraiture, few paintings by him are now known. A signed portrait of an unidentified man dated 1755 (Victoria Art Gallery, Bath) shows him to have been solidly competent if rather old-fashioned in his handling of oils. The painter James Carmichael was apprenticed to him in 1753.

Worlidge's imitations of Rembrandt in etching and drypoint were judged by George Vertue to have 'succeeded very well', and they sold quickly and remained popular after his death (Vertue, *Note Books*, 3.159). Sir Edward Astley, briefly the owner of Arthur Pond's famous collection of Rembrandt prints, appears to have been his major patron, and Worlidge's etching of 1762, *Sir Edward Astley as Jan Six*, after Rembrandt, a double tribute to Astley, shows him in the guise of Rembrandt's great patron. His most ambitious and extraordinary print was his depiction of the ceremony in the Sheldonian Theatre for the installation of the earl of Westmorland as chancellor of Oxford University in 1759. For this the artist invited subscriptions at the relatively high price of 1 guinea, by advertising in London, Oxford, and Bath. People wishing to have themselves depicted in the scene could be included on payment of 2 guineas. Worlidge could also produce highly polished reproductive work, as is shown by his illustrations of a foetus for William Hunter's *Anatomia uteri humani gravidi tabulis illustrata* (1774). The largest collection of his prints is in the Peterborough City Museum and Art Gallery, Cambridgeshire. Charles Dack, an honorary curator of that museum, made a valiant attempt to catalogue the artist's work in his *Sketch of the Life of Thomas Worlidge, Etcher and Painter* (1907).

While he always kept a London address, generally in the Covent Garden area, and moved into Thomas Hudson's old house in Great Queen Street in 1763, Worlidge visited Bath almost every year. Like Gainsborough, he came to a captive fashionable clientele during the winter social season. A small full-length portrait drawing of Beau Nash, Bath's master of ceremonies, dated 1736 (Royal Collection), suggests an early association with the town, and his marriage on 12 June 1743 to Mary Wickstead (or Wicksteed; *d.* 1790) of Bath, a needlework artist, cemented the link. They had nine children, some of whom were baptized in London and others in Bath. The Wickstead family operated a profitable 'machine' for the production of engraved stone seals and a famous toy shop which retailed Worlidge's prints as well as seals and luxury goods in general. The Wicksteads were intimately involved with Worlidge's last major project, his *Select Collection of Drawings from Curious Antique Gems … Etched after the Manner of Rembrandt*, published in a collected form in 1768 after the artist's death, which occurred on 23 September 1766 at his home, The Vineyard, Hammersmith Road, Hammersmith, Middlesex. He was buried in St Paul's churchyard, Hammersmith. Worlidge's jaunty Rembrandtesque etched *Self-Portrait* of 1754 is inserted as a frontispiece to some editions of the *Gems*.   SUSAN SLOMAN

Sources C. Dack, *Sketch of the life of Thomas Worlidge, etcher and painter, with a catalogue of his works* (1907) · C. White, D. Alexander, and E. D'Oench, *Rembrandt in eighteenth century England* (1983) [exhibition catalogue, Yale U. CBA] · R. Sharp, 'The Oxford installation of 1759', *Oxoniensia*, 56 (1991), 145–53 · Stacey Grimaldi's miscellaneous writings, ed. A. B. Grimaldi, 4 (1884), 638–40 · T. Worlidge, *A select collection of drawings from curious antique gems: most of them in the possession of the nobility and gentry of this kingdom, etched after the manner of Rembrandt* (1768) · C. W. King, *Antique gems and rings*, 2 vols. (1872), vol. 1, p. 469 · T. Dodd, 'Memorials of engravers in Great Britain, 1550–1800', BL, Add. MS 33407, fols. 185–200 · *Bath Advertiser* (21 April 1759) · *Bath Journal* (16 Sept 1754) · apprenticeship records, PRO, IR 17 · *The compleat drawing master* (1763) · T. Fawcett, *The Bagatelle and King James's Palace: two Lyncombe pleasure gardens* (with notes on Lyncombe spa and Wicksteed's machine (privately printed, Bath, [n.d.]) · Bath Abbey; baptismal records (transcripts) St Thomas à Becket, Widcombe, parish records (microfiche), Bath RO · IGI

Likenesses T. Worlidge, self-portrait, etching, 1754, Victoria Art Gallery, Bath · T. Worlidge, self-portrait, etching and drypoint, 1754, BM [*see illus.*]

Worlock, Derek John Harford (1920–1996), Roman Catholic archbishop of Liverpool, was born at 7F Grove End Road, St John's Wood, London, on 4 February 1920, the second of three children of Captain Harford Worlock (1883–1956), journalist, civil servant, and Conservative Party agent, and his wife, Dora Dennis Hoblyn (1881–1953), daughter of Charles Dennis Hoblyn, of Newlyn, Cornwall, a London stockbroker. His paternal grandfather was Thomas Worlock, civil servant; his mother was an organizer for the women's suffrage movement. His parents both became Catholics in July 1913, prior to their marriage in 1914. He was baptized on 12 February 1920, with his twin sister, in the family house, the ceremony being registered at Our Lady's Catholic Church, St John's Wood, on 27

Derek John Harford Worlock (1920–1996), by Paul Woodward, 1989

March. He first attended Priory House preparatory school in Swiss Cottage (1926) and then Oakland House preparatory school in Blackheath (1927). In 1929 the family moved to Winchester, as his father, who had fought at the battle of the Somme, became Conservative Party agent for that constituency. There he attended Winton House School until 1934, when he was accepted in Douglass House, at St Edmund's College, Ware, Hertfordshire, as a junior candidate for the priesthood for the diocese of Westminster. From an early age he had shown determination to be a Catholic priest and in this was encouraged by his parents. After studies of philosophy and theology he was ordained to the priesthood in Westminster Cathedral by Archbishop Bernard William Griffin on 3 June 1944, three days before D-day. During his student days he was captain of Douglass House and of the college rugby team, the writer and producer of plays, senior warden responsible for air-raid and fire precautions, and an industrious student. At one point his ordination was in question because of ill health, which also prevented him from pursuing further studies at Cambridge University.

Early ministry and Vatican II After ordination Worlock's first appointment, in July 1944, was as a curate in the parish of Our Lady of Victories, Kensington, where he was engaged in ministering to victims of the war bombing. In July 1945 he was appointed under-secretary to Archbishop Griffin and thereby involved in much contact and negotiation with the newly formed Labour government, especially in matters of health, welfare, and education. In 1947 he became first secretary to Cardinal Griffin and, in August 1949, was made a monsignor at the age of twenty-nine. He accompanied Cardinal Griffin on trips to Europe, Canada, and the United States, which were aimed at the social and spiritual rebuilding taking place in the post-war period. From the early 1950s he had virtual responsibility for the administration of the diocese, because of Griffin's ill health. After the death of Cardinal Griffin on 20 August 1956, Worlock became secretary to the new archbishop, William Godfrey, in December 1956. As a former papal diplomat, Godfrey enjoyed good contacts in the Holy See, and personal friendship with Pope John XXIII. When in 1958 the pope announced the holding of the Second Vatican Council, Cardinal Godfrey was made a member of the central preparatory commission. For Worlock this meant numerous journeys to Rome, in support of the cardinal, who at that time was recovering from a cancer operation. By the time of the opening of the Second Vatican Council in October 1962, Worlock was well known in Rome and given advisory and administrative tasks in support of the bishops from England and Wales attending the council.

On 20 January 1963 Cardinal Godfrey died. John Carmel Heenan was appointed to succeed him that September. During the second session of the council, in the autumn of 1963, Worlock continued his work as an adviser (or *peritus*), but on his return to London his nineteen years' work in Archbishop's House, Westminster, came to an end. In March 1964 he was appointed parish priest of St Mary and St Michael, Commercial Road, east London. There he combined pastoral duties and innovations with his continuing involvement in the work of the council. He attended the third and fourth sessions of the council during the autumns of 1964 and 1965, helping to draft sections of the council documents, particularly the decree on the apostolate of the laity (*Apostolicam actuositatem*) and the pastoral constitution on the church in the world of today (*Gaudium et spes*). At this time he first made the acquaintance of many leading bishops and theologians from around the world, including Karol Wojtyla, the future Pope John Paul II. He also kept frank and detailed diaries of the events of the Second Vatican Council. In 1965 he published *English Bishops at the Council*, an uncontroversial account of aspects of the work of the council.

Bishop of Portsmouth In the course of the final session of the Second Vatican Council, on 18 October 1965, Worlock was appointed sixth bishop of Portsmouth, at the age of forty-five. With the ending of the council on 7 December, he was able to return to England and take up these new duties, with episcopal ordination on 21 December. During his ten years as bishop of Portsmouth, he worked endlessly to implement the conclusions of the council in all aspects of the life of the church, its liturgy, education, social mission, in relation to other Christian churches, and in relation to public and political life. Some of his thoughts about this reform were expressed in a book, *Give Me Your Hand* (1977). During this time he was appointed episcopal secretary of the bishops' conference of England and Wales. As president of the laity council for England and Wales, and as a member of the pontifical council for the laity, he promoted the responsibilities and roles of the Catholic laity. He also became a regular member of the international synod of bishops, a body newly established by the council, which met every few years. He was elected to this task by the bishops' conference of England and Wales.

Archbishop of Liverpool On 7 February 1976 Worlock was appointed to succeed Archbishop George Andrew Beck as the tenth archbishop of Liverpool, at the same time as Abbot Hume of Ampleforth was appointed archbishop of Westminster. Derek Worlock took up his new appointment on 16 March, and thus became responsible for one of the largest Catholic dioceses. He was, shortly afterwards, elected vice-president of the bishops' conference which led to the enduring and fruitful partnership between himself and Cardinal Hume. Although different in temperament and talent, with Hume intuitive and charismatic, and Worlock methodical and far-sighted, this partnership gave particular character to Catholic life in England for twenty years.

Worlock's arrival in Liverpool also established the partnership he enjoyed with Bishop David Sheppard, the Anglican bishop of Liverpool. Throughout the next twenty years they worked closely together on all major issues of concern to the city and their church communities. Often in partnership with the leader of the free churches, they gave a new profile to the Christian presence and gospel in the north-west of England. Together they published two books about their ministry in Liverpool: *Better Together* (1988) and *With Christ in the Wilderness* (1990). Together they were able to welcome Elizabeth II on her silver jubilee visit to Liverpool in the summer of 1977, including her attendance at services in both the Anglican and Catholic cathedrals.

In 1979 Worlock went to Latin America in order to visit some of his priests who were working there. On his return he established the Liverpool archdiocesan missionary project (LAMP) which ensured that the resources of the archdiocese were shared with the poorest parts of the church in Latin America. His skills as a diplomat and organizer were crucial in two major Catholic initiatives at that time. In 1980 the national pastoral congress was held in Liverpool. This major gathering undertook a review of Catholic life and put forward recommendations for the future. Worlock was essential in its planning, execution, and follow-up. He also played a central role in the visit of Pope John Paul II to Britain in May 1982, the first ever visit a pope had made to Britain. With the outbreak of the conflict in the Falklands, the visit came under threat of cancellation, but Worlock played a crucial role in ensuring that it went ahead. The visit of the pope to Liverpool was remembered as a turning point in relationships between the churches in these islands.

In response to the Toxteth riots of 1981, Worlock became more directly involved in the public life of Liverpool. He took significant steps, at some personal risk, to foster better relationships between the local community and the police, and worked hard for the establishment of the Liverpool 8 law centre. During these years, the well-established church leaders group was involved in a number of important industrial disputes in and around Merseyside, always with the intention of effecting reconciliation between conflicting parties. Worlock and Sheppard were also members of the Merseyside enterprise forum, and, after the successful international garden festival held in Liverpool in 1984, they took the initiative of establishing the Michaelmas group, a forum for up to twenty leaders of industry and enterprise at which ways of revitalizing the city could be explored. At this time Liverpool politics were dominated by the Militant Tendency group, and all Worlock's political skill was required in his attempts, with Sheppard, to foster understanding between the city and central government. In the autumn of 1984 he also took steps to see if there was any scope for further discussion when the national miners' strike had become deadlocked. Although his efforts were not successful, and open to misinterpretation, they were typical of his determination to apply his vision of Christian reconciliation to the most complex of social problems. He also took particular interest in housing issues, sustaining detailed and challenging dialogue with successive government ministers.

In May 1985 a major disturbance at the Heysel football stadium in Brussels before a match between Liverpool and Juventus caused the death and injury of many people from Turin. Worlock and Sheppard took a major role not only in bringing consolation to many but also in attempting to repair the damaged relationships. They went to Turin with a delegation of Liverpool city councillors, and Worlock celebrated a mass of reconciliation in the cathedral of Turin. A further tragedy occurred on 15 April 1989 at the Hillsborough Stadium, Sheffield, in which ninety-six Liverpool supporters died. At the mass held the following evening in the Catholic Metropolitan Cathedral, attended by almost 8000 people, Worlock exercised a unique ministry to a city in a moment of shock and horror.

Throughout the period after the Second Vatican Council, Worlock also sought to promote better understanding and greater visible unity between the Christian churches, through his tireless work for the establishment of the Council of Churches for Britain and Ireland. The inaugural ceremonies for that new council took place in the two cathedrals of Liverpool in 1989. Earlier, he had worked with the six Merseyside church leaders to establish a covenant to unity, entitled 'Called to partnership', signed on 26 May 1985 in the Anglican cathedral. Growing out of this, the Merseyside and region churches ecumenical assembly (MARCEA) was established as a forum for ensuring Christian partnership wherever possible. From 1973 until 1994 he attended the annual meetings of the national conference of priests of England and Wales. Appointed to this task by his fellow bishops shortly after its establishment, he guided and defended the conference through many difficulties. In this he demonstrated characteristic dedication and loyalty to the priests, courage and astuteness in the advice he gave, and willingness to see through a task once undertaken.

In July 1992 Worlock was first diagnosed as suffering from cancer. Intensive treatment gave him sufficient remission to continue a public ministry. In January 1995 he and Sheppard were made freemen of the city of Liverpool, a rare honour. In July 1995 he undertook his last public engagement: characteristically the ordination of a young man to the priesthood. In the new year's honours list of 1996 he was made a Companion of Honour, but was unable to travel to receive the award. He died at Lourdes Hospital, Mossley Hill, Liverpool, on 8 February 1996, and was buried in the Metropolitan Cathedral, Liverpool, on 15 February 1996.   VINCENT NICHOLS

Sources J. Furnival and A. Knowles, *Archbishop Derek Worlock: his personal journey* (1998) • *The Times* (9 Feb 1996) • *The Independent* (9 Feb 1996) • *The Guardian* (9 Feb 1996) • personal knowledge (2004) • private information (2004)
Archives Liverpool Roman Catholic Cathedral | curial offices, Liverpool, diocesan papers
Likenesses Coleman, portrait, *c.*1970, bishop's house, Portsmouth • P. Woodward, photograph, 1989, NPG [*see illus.*] • H. Elwess, portrait, *c.*1992, priv. coll. • G. Thompson, portrait, St Joseph's College, Upholland, Lancashire • photograph, repro. in *The Times* • photograph, repro. in *The Guardian* • photograph, repro. in *The Independent*
Wealth at death under £145,000: probate, 22 Feb 1996, *CGPLA Eng. & Wales*

Wormald, Francis (1904–1972), palaeographer and art historian, was born at Dewsbury Mill in the West Riding of Yorkshire on 1 June 1904, shortly after his twin brother, John; their twin sisters, Ellen and Ann, were born in 1909. Their parents were Thomas Marmaduke Wormald JP (*d.* 1939), chairman of Wormalds and Walker, blanket manufacturers, of Dewsbury Mill, and Frances Mary Walker-Brook (*d.* 1920), whose family owned a woollen mill in Huddersfield. The boys were born in the mill house attached to their father's factory, but the family later moved to Field Head, a Georgian house at Mirfield. Thomas Wormald did not like his children to make friends outside the family, and they had to devise their own amusements, most of which were contrived by Francis. The only outdoor game for which he cared was croquet, which he played with pitiless proficiency all his life. Taken on a shooting expedition with his father for the first time, he was said to have bagged a snipe with his first cartridge and a brace of pheasants with the next two, but he refused to go shooting again because it hurt his hands, in which he had a slight abnormality. He liked collecting things, a lifelong passion pursued with taste and discrimination, and would scour local cottages for pieces of porcelain and trawl the Huddersfield bookshops for bargains. When he was about seven years old he was taken to the British Museum, and upon seeing the illuminated manuscripts on exhibition he decided on the spot that he would join the museum's manuscripts department.

The move to Mirfield brought Wormald into contact with a formative influence in his intellectual and religious life. Opposite the gates of Field Head was Hall Croft, home

to the society which became the Community of the Resurrection, presided over by Walter Howard Frere, the liturgiologist. Mrs Wormald entertained the community regularly, though Mr Wormald disliked their socialistic leanings—they had even dined Keir Hardie—and their Anglo-Catholicism, about which Wormald and his father had many arguments. Frere ignited his interest in liturgical matters, already well developed by the time he went to Eton College, and his profound and lifelong Anglo-Catholic faith owed much to Frere's example.

Wormald's education began with a governess from Huddersfield and continued at Stanmore Park preparatory school. In 1918 he was sent with his brother to Eton, where he was nicknamed Tea-tray because of his fondness for what was on it. His Eton career was not distinguished scholastically, but he went up to Magdalene College, Cambridge, in 1922 and took a second class in the history tripos in 1925 (he proceeded LittD in 1950). At Cambridge he acquired the nickname Auntie and a reputation as a theatrical performer, especially as a talented comedian. After graduation he worked for a time in the Pepys Library at Magdalene.

In 1927 Wormald fulfilled his boyhood ambition by obtaining appointment as an assistant keeper in the department of manuscripts at the British Museum. However, his main interests—illuminations and liturgies—were respectively the provinces of his senior colleagues Eric Millar and A. J. Collins, and he was put to cataloguing miscellaneous papers for the *Catalogue of Additions to the Manuscripts*. He learned Portuguese to cope with some sixteenth- and seventeenth-century papers on India. He continued, however, to pursue his interests through private study and contacts with academic friends outside the museum.

After Mirfield and Howard Frere, the second transforming influence in Wormald's life was the migration from Hamburg to London in January 1934 of the Warburg Institute, with its galaxy of great names in the study of European art and culture, notably Fritz Saxl, Rudolf Wittkower, Hugo Buchthal, Ernst Gombrich, and Otto Pacht. Wormald was soon on terms of scholarly intimacy with all of them; he taught classes at the Warburg, and with Roger Hinks did much to establish the institute's distinguished place in the London academic scene. It was Wormald's genius to marry the European academic tradition of these learned and inspiring teachers with his distinctively English and down-to-earth approach to art-historical and iconographic studies. His observation was acute and his prose style spare, direct, and quite free from art-historical jargon. He wrote more than sixty books and articles on illuminations, iconography, liturgy, and calendars, and contributed about 100 book reviews to the *Burlington Magazine* and the *Times Literary Supplement*, many of which were weighty contributions to knowledge in their own right. His major publications were *English Benedictine Kalendars before AD 1100* and *English Benedictine Kalendars after AD 1100* (Henry Bradshaw Society, vols. 72, 1934; 77, 1939; and 81, 1946), *English Drawings of the Tenth and Eleventh Centuries* (1952), *The Benedictional of St Ethelwold* (1959), and

The Winchester Psalter (1973). He also published important works in collaboration with other scholars, notably (with Hugo Buchthal) *Miniature Painting in the Latin Kingdom of Jerusalem* (1957) and (with C. E. Wright) *The English Library before 1700* (1958).

On 19 July 1935 Wormald married his cousin Honoria Mary Rosamund Yeo (1898–1991), daughter of Gerald Yeo, a barrister, of Emsworth, Hampshire, and Margaret Leighton; she was then reading medicine at University College, London, and had just taken her first MB. A medical examination for life insurance revealed that Wormald had Bright's disease; he was given a few months to live, but the disease subsided, though it eventually returned to kill him. Very few of his friends knew of this, and the Wormalds simply decided to ignore it. They lived in Wormald's flat in Mecklenburgh Square until 1941, when they moved to Dolphin Square. Wormald spent the war years in the Ministry of Home Security, where his duties included making civil defence training films. He also did firewatching duty at St Paul's Cathedral.

With the resumption of his duties in the manuscripts department after the war, Wormald rapidly consolidated his academic reputation and was regarded as the heir apparent to the then keeper, A. J. Collins. In 1950, however, at the urging of Sir Harold Idris Bell, the former keeper of manuscripts, he accepted the newly established chair of palaeography at King's College, London; a post he took up rather reluctantly, feeling, as he put it, like a cloistered monk obliged to become a bishop. He led a busy life of research, teaching, travel to foreign libraries, and service on numerous university committees, including the board of studies in palaeography, of which he was chairman 1951–62, and the committee of management of the Warburg Institute. With the University of London librarian, Jack Pafford, he established the library's palaeography room, the finest in the world devoted to its subject. His palaeography classes at the Institute of Historical Research could be an alarming experience. He would distribute photographs of apparently indecipherable scripts to the class, and require each victim in turn to read his text aloud. Any prompting by others would infuriate him; he had a sharp tongue when provoked, but his essential kindness ensured no lasting hurt to those who felt it. He would patiently get a student to tease out the words of the vilest Late Roman Cursive by himself, letter by letter; 'What do you see?', 'What does it look like?', he would say again and again, until the right answer was forthcoming. He had the gift of showing students that they knew more than they thought.

In 1960 Wormald was appointed director of the Institute of Historical Research in succession to Sir Goronwy Edwards. His regime was like a blast of fresh air. New decorations, curtains, furnishings, and pictures swept away the institute's post-war institutional drabness, and its social life was developed with receptions and other diversions for students and staff. The Wormalds had a genius for hospitality, which they did not confine to the institute. They delighted in the company of young people, and they often entertained students in their Warwick Square flat,

which was surmounted by Honoria's cherished roof-garden. They were both superb cooks, and dinner *chez* Wormald was always a memorable occasion. Francis was fond of life's pleasures, but Yorkshire canniness governed what he spent on them. At conferences abroad he would always sniff out a restaurant offering the best food at the cheapest price. His enjoyment of life was reflected in his benignly Pickwickian appearance: medium height, comfortably rotund in later years, and with round steel spectacles on a broad, friendly face.

Wormald's conscientiousness and common sense made him much in demand for committees. His portfolio included the Royal Commission on Historical Monuments, the National Monuments Record Committee, the Advisory Council on Public Records, the Advisory Council on the Export of Works of Art, the advisory committee of the Victoria and Albert Museum, the council of the British School at Rome, the executive committee of the Friends of the National Libraries, the councils of the British Academy (of which he was elected fellow in 1948), the Royal Historical Society, the Henry Bradshaw Society, the Canterbury and York Society, the Walpole Society, the British Records Association, and the Royal Archaeological Institute. He was vice-president of the Society of Antiquaries (1956–60), director (1964–6), and president (1965–70), and he was an ornament of the Cocked Hats, its dining club. In 1967 he was the society's statutory nominee as a trustee of the British Museum. He was elected to the Roxburghe Club in 1953 and the Society of Dilettanti in 1966. He was made honorary keeper of manuscripts at the Fitzwilliam Museum, Cambridge, in 1950.

Among Wormald's other honours were fellowships of Magdalene College, Cambridge (1961), and King's College, London (1964), and he was also honorary fellow for life of the Pierpont Morgan Library. He was made *membre adhérent* of the Société des Bollandistes in 1960. The University of York bestowed an honorary doctorate on him in 1969 and the University of Cambridge offered him a doctorate of laws in 1972, but he died before he could receive it. Official recognition of his services to palaeography came with his appointment as CBE in 1969. He retired as director of the Institute of Historical Research in 1968 and gave his last anniversary address to the Society of Antiquaries on 23 April 1970. Soon afterwards symptoms of his old illness returned and in September 1970 he was treated for kidney failure at St Thomas's Hospital. He was discharged and was able to complete his last book, *The Winchester Psalter*, posthumously published in 1973. He returned to St Thomas's in December 1971, but was discharged for Christmas. He returned again on 10 January 1972 and died early the next day. His funeral and cremation were private. At a service of thanksgiving for his life at his parish church, St Stephen's, Rochester Row, on 20 January 1972, the archbishop of Canterbury, a friend from Cambridge days, gave the blessing. Honoria died at Aldsworth, Sussex, on 26 November 1991.

Wormald's small but choice collection of manuscripts (some of which were kept in a drawer with his shirts) was divided after his death between the Fitzwilliam Museum, the British Library, the Bodleian and University of London libraries, and private beneficiaries. His fine library of about 1800 books, and the extensive remains of his incoming correspondence, formed the nucleus of the Wormald Library in the Centre for Medieval Studies, King's Manor, University of York. His collection of about 1000 offprints went to the Warburg Institute. The Society of Antiquaries owns a portrait of him as president by Hermione Hammond.   MICHAEL BORRIE

Sources T. J. Brown, 'Francis Wormald', *PBA*, 61 (1975), 523–60 · personal knowledge (2004) · *CGPLA Eng. & Wales* (1972)
Archives BL, medieval MSS, Add. MSS 57528–57534 · Bodl. Oxf., MSS · LUL, collection of deeds · LUL, corresp., notebooks, and papers · LUL, MSS · S. Antiquaries, Lond., descriptions of heraldic MSS · University of York, corresp. with scholars (interleaved with his library) | BL, corresp. with Sir Sydney Cockerell, Add. MS 52769 · priv. coll., MSS · U. Reading L., letters to Sir Frank and Lady Stenton, notes relating to the Bayeux Tapestry
Likenesses H. Hammond, oils (as president of the Society of Antiquaries of London), S. Antiquaries, Lond.
Wealth at death £179,721: probate, 29 March 1972, *CGPLA Eng. & Wales*

Wormald, Thomas (1802–1873), surgeon, son of John Wormald, a partner in Child's Bank, and Fanny, his wife, was born at Pentonville, London, in January 1802. He was educated at Batley grammar school, Yorkshire, and afterwards by William Heald, vicar of Birstal, who had once practised as a surgeon apothecary in Wakefield. Wormald returned to London in 1818, and was apprenticed to John Abernethy, surgeon to St Bartholomew's Hospital. Abernethy employed Wormald to make preparations for his lectures, to teach the junior students, and to assist Edward Stanley (1793–1862), the demonstrator of anatomy in the medical school, in preserving specimens for the pathological museum. Despite his workload Wormald found time during his apprenticeship to undertake further study on the continent.

Wormald was admitted a member of the Royal College of Surgeons of England in March 1824. Abernethy, who was at this time considering resigning his anatomy lectureship, made arrangements for Wormald to become the demonstrator of anatomy in place of Stanley, who was to be promoted to the lectureship, but in fact Frederic Carpenter Skey was elected demonstrator. In October 1824 Wormald was nominated house surgeon to William Lawrence, then newly appointed surgeon to St Bartholomew's Hospital. In 1826 Wormald was appointed jointly with Skey to give the anatomical demonstrations at Barts, and from 1828 to 1843 he was sole demonstrator. In September 1828 Wormald married Frances Meacock; they had eight children.

Wormald was elected assistant surgeon to St Bartholomew's on 13 February 1838, but it was not until 1861 that he became full surgeon at the hospital. He reached retirement age in 1867, and hospital regulations compelled him to resign his post there. He was then appointed consulting surgeon, and retired to his country house in Hertfordshire.

Wormald was also surgeon at the Foundling Hospital from 1843 to 1864, and his services were appreciated

enough for him to be chosen a governor in 1847. At the Royal College of Surgeons he held all the important offices. Elected a fellow in 1843, he was a member of the council from 1849 to 1867; Hunterian orator in 1857; examiner from 1858 to 1868; and chairman of the midwifery board in 1864. He was a vice-president in 1863–4, and he was elected president in 1865.

Wormald died at Gomersal, in Yorkshire, during a visit, on 28 December 1873, and was buried in Highgate cemetery in London.

Wormald was the last of the apprentices of John Abernethy, and his death broke the last link which connected St Bartholomew's Hospital with Hunterian surgery. Contemporaries viewed him as an excellent teacher of surgical anatomy, who had an original lecture style and an inexhaustible sense of humour. As a surgeon, he was seen as a perfect assistant. In 1838 Wormald published (with A. M. McWhinnie) *A Series of Anatomical Sketches and Diagrams with Descriptions and References*. Reissued in 1843, these sketches were seen at the time as one of the best series of anatomical plates issued for the use of students.

D'A. POWER, *rev.* JEFFREY S. REZNICK

Sources St *Bartholomew's Hospital Reports*, 10 (1874), xxiii–xliii · T. Wormald, *The Hunterian oration: delivered at the Royal College of Surgeons … 1857* (1858) · V. G. Plarr, *Plarr's Lives of the fellows of the Royal College of Surgeons of England*, rev. D'A. Power, 2 vols. (1930) · private information (1900) · *CGPLA Eng. & Wales* (1874)
Likenesses Disderi & Co. Ltd, photograph, 1896?, Wellcome L.
Wealth at death under £45,000: probate, 24 Jan 1874, *CGPLA Eng. & Wales*

Wormall, Arthur (1900–1964), biochemist, was born on 17 January 1900 in Leeds, the second child in the family of two sons and two daughters of James William Wormall, a printer and lithographer, and his wife, Ann Phillis. He entered the boys' modern school, Leeds, and at seventeen was awarded a senior city scholarship to Leeds University, where he read for the honours BSc degree in chemistry under Professor J. B. Cohen. He served in the university Officers' Training Corps and joined the Royal Air Force in 1918. The end of the First World War in November allowed him to resume his degree course without any serious delay and to become engaged at the same time in his first research problem. He was also able to take up a junior appointment as demonstrator in biochemistry in the department of physiology and biochemistry at Leeds. Wormall remained at Leeds University for the next fourteen years and became lecturer (1926) and senior lecturer (1933). He was awarded the degree of DSc in 1930. Wormall married Eva Jackson in 1925; they had two daughters. In June 1928 he was elected to a Rockefeller medical research fellowship and chose to work for about a year with Karl Landsteiner at the Rockefeller Institute in New York and then at the Marine Biological Station, Woods Hole, Massachusetts.

After his return to England, Wormall accepted an appointment from the Colonial Office to visit Uganda to investigate some special aspects of sleeping sickness. He returned to Leeds on completing this assignment and became involved in an exacting teaching load in the physiology department. Nevertheless it was at this time that Wormall made several valuable contributions to the clarification of the nature of serum complement in terms of chemistry of the reactive components and this work stimulated many of the numerous investigations by others on this subject. He enjoyed an increasing reputation as an able investigator in immunochemistry. During this period at Leeds he also became especially interested in the action of mustard gas (di-2-chloroethyl sulphide) and related vesicants on tissue constituents.

In 1936 Wormall was appointed the first professor of biochemistry at St Bartholomew's Hospital Medical College, London, where he spent much time launching a new department; he remained professor of biochemistry at the medical school for the rest of his life. As early as 1936 Wormall considered the possibility of using isotopic tracers and was a pioneer worker on this important aspect of immunochemistry. With the outbreak of the Second World War in 1939 Wormall moved his department from London to the Sir William Dunn Institute of Biochemistry at Cambridge. Difficulties resulting from this move, and the heavy academic responsibilities both in London and Cambridge, considerably reduced the amount of his research; but at the war's end Wormall and his colleagues returned to London and resumed the task of developing the use of radioactive tracers in immunological investigations.

At the time of Wormall's return, the development in London University of a BSc (special honours) degree course, together with an extensive reorganization of his own department of biochemistry, occupied much of his time and he frequently regretted the amount of his energy that had to be given to these and other activities rather than to research. There can be no doubt, however, about the excellent advice he gave to the board of governors and college council—in particular that concerning the purchase of land for future expansion of St Bartholomew's Hospital. In 1949 Wormall and G. E. Francis organized a course on the use of stable isotopes in biological investigations. It was the first of its kind in the United Kingdom, proved a great success, and continued annually for fifteen years. In 1952 Wormall was invited by the University of São Paulo, Brazil, to organize the first Latin-American course in radioisotopes and his success was recognized in 1953 by the conferment on him of a doctorate *honoris causa*.

Although always busy, Wormall was never too occupied to help others. In spite of failing health and long periods in hospital, he remained cheerful and full of hope. In December 1955 he suffered a cerebral thrombosis which kept him away from his work for nearly a year. After a brief return to the department he had a further stroke in April 1962 and from then on he was completely paralysed until he died in St Bartholomew's Hospital on 9 May 1964.

As a Yorkshireman and therefore a cricketer, Wormall was probably as pleased by his election to the MCC as he was by his election to the Royal Society, both in 1956.

W. T. J. MORGAN, rev.

Sources W. T. J. Morgan and G. E. Francis, *Memoirs FRS*, 12 (1966), 543–64 · *WWW*
Wealth at death £901: administration with will, 29 June 1964, *CGPLA Eng. & Wales*

Wormell, Richard (1838–1914), mathematics writer and teacher, was born on 17 September 1838 at Humberstone Gate, in Leicester, the eldest son of Robert Wormell, a slater, and his wife, Mary *née* Joyce. Nothing is known of his social circumstances and early education except that the journals of the mathematician Thomas Archer Hirst refer to him as a former mason and bricklayer. In his early twenties Wormell moved to London to become a pupil teacher at the Borough Road Normal College, Southwark, where his interest in geometry was consolidated. In 1865, while teaching at an elementary school in Westminster, he gained the external BA degree of the University of London. At this time he lodged with the mother of William Barrett, who was then assisting John Tyndall at the Royal Institution. Barrett's conversations fired Wormell's scientific interests and inspired him to develop a mathematical theorem concerning Foucault's pendulum. Barrett took the proof to Tyndall, who showed it to his friend, Hirst. Impressed, Hirst became Wormell's patron, encouraging him to take the London MA degree in mathematics, for which he obtained top marks and a gold medal in 1866. In the same year Wormell was appointed mathematics instructor and deputy headmaster of the new Central Foundation School in Finsbury, whose establishment was being funded by city banks, merchants, and guilds to prepare 'scholars for the practical way of life'. No Latin was taught, and because the curriculum emphasized science, technology, commerce, and languages, the teaching of mathematics was particularly central. Undeterred by heavy teaching responsibilities, Wormell gained an external BSc degree in 1868. In the same year, when the foundation stone for the school's permanent building in Cowper Street was laid, Wormell's teaching was publicly commended. In 1868 he also published textbooks on plane geometry and arithmetic, the first of his twenty-five textbooks. These books were all characterized by their child-centred, Pestalozzian approach. In teaching geometry, for example, its applications had to be studied alongside logical demonstrations which, controversially, avoided the Euclidean order of proof.

In 1870 Wormell married Dora Gildon Guy, only daughter of J. Guy of Twickenham; they had five sons and three daughters. Wormell spent 1873 with Hirst teaching mathematics at the Royal Naval College, Greenwich, only to return to the Cowper Street School as the unanimous choice for the vacant headmastership in 1874. During his tenure, which lasted until his retirement in 1900, he was very active as an educationist. He was a founding member of the reforming Association for the Improvement of Geometrical Teaching in 1871; he was a council member of the College of Preceptors from 1875, its president in 1905–8, and the editor of its *Educational Times* from 1883 to 1893. He was one of only two headteachers to serve on the Bryce royal commission on secondary education in 1894–5, and was president of the Headmasters' Association in 1895–6.

In 1875 Wormell persuaded J. P. Gassiot to endow his school with workshops and laboratories for teaching mechanical and electrical engineering. Evening classes conducted at the Cowper Street School helped inspire T. H. Huxley's report on technical education for the City and Guilds Institute in 1877. In November 1879, what was to become the City and Guilds' Finsbury Technical College was launched in the school's workshops by H. E. Armstrong and W. E. Ayrton. To Wormell's intense disappointment, however, it was the electrician S. P. Thompson who was made principal of Finsbury College in 1885.

After his retirement in 1900, Wormell lived at Roydon in Essex, where he died at his home, The Grange, on 6 January 1914. His wife survived him.   W. H. BROCK

Sources WWW · *Educational Times* (2 Feb 1914), 66–7 · T. A. Hirst, journals, Royal Institution of Great Britain, London · M. E. Bryant, *The London experience of secondary education* (1986) · W. Brock, 'Who were they? Richard Wormell (1838–1914)', *School Science Review*, 81 (June 2000), 93–7 · b. cert. · CGPLA Eng. & Wales (1914)
Archives GL, City and Guilds archives
Likenesses portrait, c.1899, Central Foundation School, London; repro. in *Educational Times* (1 Aug 1899), 317
Wealth at death £5358 9s. 8d.: probate, 4 May 1914, CGPLA Eng. & Wales

Worms, Henry De, first Baron Pirbright (1840–1903), politician, was born on 20 October 1840, the youngest child of Baron Solomon Benedict De Worms (1801–1882) and his wife, Henrietta, eldest daughter of Samuel Moses Samuel. Solomon De Worms was descended from a wealthy Frankfurt Jewish family, which had settled in London in the early nineteenth century; Solomon's mother was a sister of Nathan Meyer Rothschild, the first of the Rothschild family to settle in England. Solomon and his brothers were the owners of extensive tea plantations in Ceylon; in 1871 Solomon was made a baron of the Austrian empire, and in 1874 Queen Victoria gave him and his descendants permission to use the title in England, in recognition of his work in Ceylon.

De Worms was educated at King's College, London, of which he became a fellow in 1873, and at the Inner Temple; he was called to the bar in 1863, practising at the Kent sessions. Subsequently, however, he gave up the law to assist in the management of his father's business, which he did until its dissolution in 1879. His interests had already turned in a political direction. Through his friendship with the Austrian ambassador in London, Count von Beust, he had in 1867 obtained an introduction to Benjamin Disraeli; the following year he stood as Conservative candidate at Sandwich, thus becoming the first professing Jew to stand for election to parliament in the Conservative interest—a feat which earned him a great deal of Jewish communal disapprobation at the time, since the Conservatives had earlier opposed the abolition of Jewish disabilities. Ironically, however, the Sandwich election was marked by some blatantly antisemitic propaganda emanating from the Liberal side; in the event De Worms was unsuccessful, and did not stand at the general election of 1874 which brought Disraeli to power—and which saw the return of the obscure Nottingham coal owner, Saul Isaac, as the first professing Jewish Conservative MP. In

Henry De Worms, first Baron Pirbright (1840–1903), by Bassano, 1895

1880, however, De Worms was returned for Greenwich, and from 1885 to his elevation to the peerage a decade later he sat for the East Toxteth division of Liverpool.

De Worms's knowledge of the international commodity market was prodigious, and earned him a place in Lord Salisbury's first administration (1885–6) as parliamentary secretary to the Board of Trade. In the second Salisbury government (1886–92) he held office first at the Board of Trade and then, from 1888, as under-secretary of state for the colonies. In 1887 he had been elected president of the international conference on sugar bounties, and the following year toured a number of European capitals urging the abolition of the bounty system; to his great regret the British parliament refused to ratify the convention in which the conference had resulted.

De Worms was a man of many talents—a fine speaker, an accomplished pugilist—but also had a reputation as a bore ('Baron de Bookworms'). A fellow of the Royal Society, he was the author of a treatise on *The Earth and its Magnetism* (1862) as well as of studies of *The Austro-Hungarian Empire* (1870) and *England's Policy in the East* (1877). From an early age he had been brought up to expect to take an active part in Jewish communal affairs. He held the posts of treasurer (1872) and vice-president (1880–82) of the United Synagogue in London, and from 1872 to 1886 served as president of the Anglo-Jewish Association, which practically conducted the foreign policy of Anglo-Jewry at this period. In 1886, however, his daughter, Alice, married out of the faith; worse still, he saw fit to attend her church wedding. This led to his being forced to resign the presidency of the Anglo-Jewish Association, and seems to have planted the seeds of a gradual estrangement from his fellow Jews and from their faith. De Worms, though not a strictly observant Jew, had identified himself very closely with the Jewish world. In parliament he had taken up the causes of the oppressed Jewries of Romania and Russia. Chief Rabbi Hermann Adler's wife, Henrietta, was his second cousin, both his own wives were Jewish, and it is clear that he had originally intended for himself a Jewish burial. However, he grew increasingly bitter at his exclusion from the inner circle of the Anglo-Jewish gentry, and his failure to be included (1901) in the list of those Jewish leaders who were deputed to congratulate Edward VII on his accession to the throne may have been the final straw. When he died, in 1903, he left instructions that he was to be buried in a Christian cemetery.

On 5 May 1864 De Worms married Fanny, eldest daughter of Baron von Todesco, of Vienna, with whom he had three daughters and from whom he obtained a divorce in 1886; on 25 January 1887 he married Sarah Barnett (d. 1914), the only daughter of Sir Benjamin Samuel Phillips, and his wife, Rachel. De Worms died at 42 Grosvenor Place, London, on 9 January 1903, and was buried in the churchyard of Wyke St Mark, near Guildford, Surrey; as he left no male heir, his title became extinct.

GEOFFREY ALDERMAN

Sources C. Bermant, *The cousinhood: the Anglo-Jewish gentry* (1971) · C. Roth, ed., *Encyclopaedia Judaica*, 16 vols. (Jerusalem, 1971–2) · A. Allfrey, *Edward VII and his Jewish court* (1991) · G. Alderman, *The Jewish community in British politics* (1983) · DNB · A. Newman, *The united synagogue, 1870–1970* (1977) · GEC, *Peerage* · *Jewish Chronicle* (16 Jan 1903)

Archives UCL, Gaster MSS

Likenesses Bassano, photograph, 1895, NPG [*see illus.*] · B. Stone, photograph, 1897, NPG · Ape [C. Pellegrini], caricature, chromolithograph, NPG; repro. in *VF* (22 May 1880), 292–3 · Brown, Barnes & Bell, photograph, NPG; repro. in *Our conservative and unionist statesmen* (1899), 6 · L. Fildes, portrait, priv. coll. · L. Mayer, oils, Gov. Art Coll. · Russell & Sons, photograph, NPG; repro. in *Our conservative and unionist statesmen* (1896), 1

Wealth at death £368,905 10s. 11d.: resworn probate, 1903, CGPLA Eng. & Wales

Wornum, George Grey (1888–1957), architect, was born on 17 April 1888 at 6 College Terrace, London, the eldest son and second of eight children of George Porter Wornum, a doctor of medicine, and his wife, Edith Howard. His paternal grandfather was Ralph Nicholson *Wornum, keeper of the National Gallery. He was educated at Bradfield College from 1902 and at the Slade School of Art from 1905 to 1906, having inherited from his father an artistic flair and a love of making things. In 1906 he was articled to his uncle the architect Ralph Selden Wornum; during his pupillage he attended evening classes at the Architectural Association, where he won the silver medal and travelling studentship in 1909. In 1910 he set up on his own in independent practice; his first commission was a studio for his cousin Hugh G. Rivière in St John's Wood. As jobs were scarce, he also worked for Herbert Batsford as a book illustrator and editor of a series of volumes on English and French architecture and craftsmanship of the seventeenth and eighteenth centuries.

During the First World War, Wornum served in the Artists' Rifles and Durham light infantry and was badly wounded in 1916, when he suffered leg injuries and the loss of his right eye. In 1919 he resumed his career, in partnership with Philip D. Hepworth. By 1920 Louis De Soissons was associated with them and after Hepworth left the firm in 1921, De Soissons and Wornum practised, sometimes together and sometimes apart, from Blue Ball Yard in St James's until 1930; their joint works included several of the Earl Haig memorial homes, and some influential flats for middle-class tenants on moderate incomes at Larkhall Rise, Clapham. During this period in the 1920s he maintained his associations with the Architectural Association and visited Sweden several times; he also became a close friend of the architect Eric Mendelsohn and his wife, Luise. On 11 June 1923 he married Miriam Alice Gerstle (1898–1989) of San Francisco, a talented artist and decorator; they had a son, Michael, and two daughters, Jennifer and Brigit. He was elected president of the Architectural Association for the year 1930–31, a role he carried out with style and vitality, always believing that the social side of his profession was important.

From 1930 Wornum practised independently from 39 Devonshire Street, Westminster, and this decade also saw his major works. His winning competition design in 1932, chosen from 284 entries, for a new headquarters building of the Royal Institute of British Architects (RIBA) at 66 Portland Place, earned him national recognition. Although the exterior of the building was criticized at the time in relation to the existing Georgian character of Portland Place, the outstanding merit of the design was the transparency of its interior and the imaginative handling of the staircase levels. His wife, Miriam, was responsible for much of the colour designing and textiles throughout the building. The quality and craftsmanship of its applied decoration and sculpture, carried out by a comparatively unknown group of younger artists, make it the most interesting period piece of contemporary art of the inter-war period in London.

The decorative interiors at the RIBA led to the commission to decorate the first-class accommodation of the RMS *Queen Elizabeth*, begun in 1938 and completed in 1945. In 1936 Wornum was one of three architects appointed to organize the coronation decorations in London: he himself was responsible for the scheme of the processional route in Westminster. Another celebrated work of a different kind was the central cleansing and transport depot of the City of Westminster in Gatliff Road, Westminster (1936), awarded the RIBA bronze medal in 1938. His later work also included successfully replanning Parliament Square in Westminster in 1949–50. Wornum's health declined in the 1940s as a long-term result of his war injuries, and he spent much time in the Bahamas and California.

Wornum was tall and fair, with a characteristic limp and a dark monocle worn on a broad ribbon; his unusual charm of manner, and his vitality, made him popular with clients and colleagues. He was elected a fellow of the RIBA in 1923 and was awarded the RIBA gold medal in 1952. He died in New York on 11 June 1957, and was named CBE in the birthday honours list published two days after his death. In his work he was essentially a progressive traditionalist and his reputation was based largely on his decorative ability. MARGARET RICHARDSON

Sources G. G. Wornum and M. Wornum, 'Grey matter', RIBA BAL, MSS collection, Ref WO G/1 [typescript] [2 vols; vol. 1: autobiography by G. Wornum; vol. 2: biography by M. Wornum] · fellows' nomination form, 1923, RIBA BAL, MSS collection · M. Richardson, 66 Portland Place: the London headquarters of the Royal Institute of British Architects (1984) · RIBA Journal, 59 (1951–2), 78, 162–5 [RIBA gold medal] · The Builder, 183 (1952), 738–9, 774–5 [RIBA gold medal] · RIBA Journal, 64 (1956–7), 439 · The Times (14 June 1957) · The Builder, 192 (1957), 1115 · J. Lever, ed., Catalogue of the drawings collection of the Royal Institute of British Artists, 18: T–Z (1984), 263–9 · m. cert.
Archives RIBA BAL, MSS collection, Grey matter typescript
Likenesses photographs, 1933–4, RIBA · C. Wheeler, bronze bust, RIBA · portrait photographs, RIBA
Wealth at death £5088 1s.: probate, 16 Jan 1958, CGPLA Eng. & Wales

Wornum, Ralph Nicholson (1812–1877), art critic and gallery keeper, the eldest son of Robert Wornum (1786–1852) and Catherine Nicholson (1784–1856), was born at Thornton, near Norham, Northumberland, on 29 December 1812. His father was a well-known pianoforte maker of Store Street, Bedford Square, and principally known as the inventor of the universally used upright action for the pianoforte. Having studied at University College, London, in 1832, Ralph Wornum was to have read for the bar, but he soon abandoned the law, turning to art as his profession. He attended Henry Sass's academy for three months and then received twelve lessons in painting from George Reinagle. Inspired by the writings of Johan Heinrich Fuseli and encouraged by Professor George Long, editor of the Penny Cyclopedia, he went abroad in 1834, spending the following six years familiarizing himself with the galleries, museums, and churches of Munich, Dresden, Rome, Venice, Florence, and Paris.

It was during these formative years that it became clear to Wornum that his work as an artist would take second place to his writing. During this time he drafted his Outline of a General History of Painting amongst the Ancients (1847), which was re-published as Epochs of Painting; it was widely adopted as a textbook by art schools. At the close of 1839 he settled in London as a portrait painter, but did not seem at ease in this role or to enjoy much recognition: a portrait offered for exhibition at the Royal Academy in 1841 was rejected.

Wornum gradually achieved recognition as an important contributor to art journals, encyclopaedias, and biographical dictionaries. From 1840 he contributed to the Penny Cyclopedia and in 1841 he wrote the article on pictura for Smith's Dictionary of Greek and Roman Antiquities. In 1846 he began working for the Art Journal and, having drawn attention to the shortcomings of the National Gallery catalogues then in circulation, was authorized by Sir Robert Peel to compile an official catalogue. He travelled to the Netherlands and Belgium that year to prepare the catalogue which was published the following year, and which, according to the Art Journal, served 'as a model for all similar publications' (Art Journal, 1878, 75). In 1848 Wornum was appointed lecturer on art to the government schools of design, that same year producing his work Essay upon the Schools of Design in France. In 1852 he visited art schools in Paris and Lyon and was appointed librarian and keeper of casts to the schools of design. In 1851 he was awarded the prize of a hundred guineas offered by the Art Journal for the best essay on the subject 'The Exhibition of 1851 as a lesson in taste'.

In December 1854 Wornum succeeded General Thwaites as keeper of the National Gallery and secretary to the trustees, upon the recommendation of Sir Charles Eastlake. His appointment was taken as an augury of reform in the administration of the gallery. Wornum's 'whole time and knowledge were now secured for the public' (GM, 2nd ser., 43, 1855, 168), and the salary of the post was raised to £750 a year. In March 1856 a Treasury minute reconstituted the administration of the gallery: the keeper was to reside within the gallery to ensure the safe custody of the collection and to compile a complete catalogue of works that might be suitable for inclusion in the national collection. Wornum was also responsible for hanging the paintings and supervising their cleaning. However, it was to the Turner collection that he devoted most of his energies.

In 1860–61 Wornum was instrumental in returning the Turner collection, which had been banished first to Marlborough House, and then to South Kensington, to its place in the National Gallery, in accordance with the terms of the artist's bequest. During 1861 he edited, in a sumptuous folio, The Turner Gallery forming a series of sixty engravings. In the introduction to The Turner Gallery, Wornum pleaded eloquently for an enlargement of the Trafalgar Square galleries which were quite inadequate to display the 725 pictures then belonging to the nation. He also deprecated the separation of the pictures by British from those by foreign artists. Wornum served the gallery for twenty-two years and supported three distinguished directors: Sir Charles Eastlake, Sir William Boxall, and Sir Frederic Burton. These years were a period when the gallery made many important acquisitions. While the directors were touring Europe, Wornum remained at the gallery ensuring that the pictures were displayed and catalogued while maintaining a practical administration characterized by efficiency and careful record keeping.

In 1867 Wornum published his major work on Hans Holbein, Some Account of the Life and Works of Hans Holbein, Painter of Augsburg, with Numerous Illustrations. This biographical and critical work (dedicated 'To my friend, John Ruskin') included a valuable catalogue of portraits and drawings by Holbein at Windsor. It was here that Wornum insisted correctly on the credentials of the Basel version of the Holbein Virgin and child (The Meier Madonna) as against the world-famous Dresden copy which Eastlake (among others) had accepted. This was Wornum's great triumph as a connoisseur. He also wrote a pamphlet on The Meier Madonna which was published by the Arundel Society in 1871.

Wornum had strong religious beliefs. He and other family members were members of the New Church of Emanuel Swedenborg, though as a non-separatist he remained in communion with the Church of England. He was an active supporter of the Swedenborg Society and helped draw up the laws and regulations of the Swedenborg Association in 1845, established in order to publish the scientific works of Swedenborg. He debated with the Revd John Hyde of Manchester, James John Garth Wilkinson, and other Swedenborgians the authority of the writings of St Paul, and published a tract on this with the title *Saul of Tarsus, or, Paul and Swedenborg* (1877).

Wornum was married twice: first on 14 January 1843, to Elizabeth Selden (1823–1860) of Virginia, stepdaughter of George Long, prompting William Bell Scott to comment that 'Ralph Nicholson Wornum was a Hercules in muscular development, and he married one of the most perfectly formed and most beautiful women in London' (*Autobiographical Notes*, 156). On 1 August 1861, after her death, he married his first cousin Harriet Agnes Nicholson (*b.* 1821, *d.* after 1900). He had fourteen children in all. By all accounts he was of average height and powerful build, with a large head and, in later years, a long white beard. He was affectionately known as Old Snowball. He died at his residence, 20 Belsize Square, South Hampstead, on 15 December 1877 of hemiplegia, asthma, and emphysema, leaving a widow and a large family.

THOMAS SECCOMBE, *rev.* DAVID CARTER

Sources National Gallery, London, archives, Wornum MSS · D. Robertson, *Sir Charles Eastlake and the Victorian art world* (1978) · J. Rowlands, *The paintings of Hans Holbein the younger* (1985) · *Art Journal*, 40 (1878), 75 · Redgrave, *Artists* · *Autobiographical notes of the life of William Bell Scott: and notices of his artistic and poetic circle of friends, 1830 to 1882*, ed. W. Minto, 2 vols. (1892) · m. certs. · d. cert.
Archives National Gallery, London, corresp. and papers incl. journals, sketches, and family papers · National Gallery, London, National Gallery records | LUL, letters to the Society for the Diffusion of Useful Knowledge
Likenesses R. Wornum, self-portrait, 1867, National Gallery, London · R. Wornum, self-portrait, oils, 1873, National Gallery, London · photographs, 1873, National Gallery, London · wood-engraving, pubd 1878 (after photograph), NPG; repro. in *ILN* (5 Jan 1878)
Wealth at death under £1500: probate, 28 March 1878, *CGPLA Eng. & Wales*

Worrell, Sir Frank Mortimer Maglinne (1924–1967), cricketer, was born at Bridgetown, Barbados, on 1 August 1924, the son of Athelston Worrell, a ship's steward. He was educated at Combermere School, where he was coached by the former test cricketer Derrick Sealy. He first played for the island as a slow left-arm bowler at the age of seventeen, while still at school, but his batting, in which he was right-handed, developed so rapidly that in 1942–3 he scored his first century in first-class cricket, 188 against Trinidad at Port of Spain, and in the following season he played what proved to be the highest innings of his career: 308 not out in an unbroken partnership of 502 with J. D. Goddard, again against Trinidad. This was a world record for the fourth wicket until Worrell and C. L. Walcott surpassed it two seasons later with an unbroken 574, yet again against Trinidad, when Worrell made 255 not out.

Sir Frank Mortimer Maglinne Worrell (1924–1967), by unknown photographer, 1963

In 1947 Worrell left Barbados for Jamaica after failing to get a job at home. In Jamaica he got employment as a clerk, joined Kensington cricket club, and also played football. His international career began against the MCC tourists in 1947–8. He made 294 in three tests, and his 131 not out at Georgetown was the first of his nine test centuries. In 1948 he began a long and happy association with Radcliffe in the central Lancashire league: his aggregate of 1694 (average 112.80) in 1951 was a record for the competition. Between 1948 and 1959 (not every year), he compiled 9103 runs (average 77.14) in league cricket for Radcliffe and later for Norton. While in Radcliffe, he married on 28 May 1948 a fellow Barbadian, Velda Elaine Brewster (*b.* 1922/3), daughter of Mervyn Brewster, photographer. She and their daughter Lana survived him. With an eye to the future, Worrell took his BA (Admin.) in 1959 at Manchester University.

With many international players taking part, the northern leagues were a stern academy of cricket and Worrell gained valuable experience of English conditions. He learned to play on wickets of varying pace, and he quickened his bowling, relying now on swerve rather than spin. Thus he was well equipped to take his place in the West Indies touring team to England in 1950, which after losing the first test won the remaining three and became the first West Indies team to win a rubber in England. With his lithe elegance, perfect timing, and exquisite footwork, he was one of the celebrated trio—Everton Weekes and Clyde Walcott were the others—of outstanding batsmen in this talented side. He headed the test averages with 539 runs at 89.83, and on the tour he made 1775 at 68.26, with six centuries, as well as taking thirty-nine wickets. His 261 at Nottingham was then the highest individual score for either country in tests against each other in England, while his stand of 283 for the fourth wicket with Weekes was the highest test partnership for the West Indies in any part of the world. It was beaten by himself and Garfield Sobers when they put on 399 against England at Barbados in 1960.

In Australia in 1951–2 the West Indies could not repeat their English success. Worrell, with only 337 in ten test innings, was not the only batsman to be unhappy against the Australians' pace on hard pitches and their use of the short, fast bumper, although he made 108 at Melbourne, batting almost one-handed after an injury. With the disappointment of their high expectations the side's morale collapsed, there was frequent dissension, and they lost four of the five tests. But it was Worrell's most successful series as a bowler; his seventeen wickets at 19.35 included six for 38 at Adelaide in the only test the West Indies won. Home series against India, England, and Australia were, by his own standards, not years of abundance, although he made 237 against India at Kingston in 1953. When the West Indies came to England in 1957, he easily headed the tour averages with 1470 runs at 58.80, and his four centuries included a masterly 191 not out in the third test at Nottingham, when he batted right through the innings. He also took seven wickets for 70 in the fourth test at Leeds. But the tour was a disappointment for the team, whose confidence characteristically disintegrated after the first test slipped from their grasp when they had seemed certain to win it. They were then beaten three times by an innings.

Because of injuries Worrell captained the side in the last four matches of the tour, and he showed qualities of leadership which led, after various internal struggles, to his appointment as captain in Australia in 1960–61. The post had been offered to him twice before but Worrell had rejected it to enable him to complete his studies at Manchester University. His acceptance, in the end, came at a time when the newly independent territories in the Caribbean were looking for black leaders in all walks of life. A remarkable series began with the first tie in the history of test cricket, and although the West Indies eventually lost by two matches to one, the result would have been reversed if two vital decisions had not gone against them. Although personally Worrell had only a moderate tour, his side fulfilled his promise that they would bring back to cricket the spirit of adventure. On their departure Worrell's men received a send-off 'normally reserved for Royalty and national heroes' (*Wisden*, 1962, 832). The Worrell trophy was instituted to commemorate the Brisbane tie. In the following year, 1961–2, he led the West Indies to a 5–0 victory over India.

Worrell fought his last campaign when he led the West

Indies in England in 1963. This was another eventful rubber which the West Indies won 3–1 after a dramatic drawn game at Lord's. Worrell did not do much with the bat, but his 74 not out in 95 minutes at Manchester, with fifteen fours, recalled the player he had been in his vintage years. At the end of the tour he announced his retirement, but he managed the side that defeated the visiting Australians in 1965 and made the West Indies unofficial world champions. In his career he made 15,025 runs at 54.24, with 39 centuries, and took 349 wickets at 28.98. In 51 tests, 25 against England, he made 3860 at 49.48 and took 69 wickets at 38.72.

But although in his prime Worrell was a great batsman, correct yet uninhibited, with a free swing whose delicacy concealed its power, statistics do not measure his contribution to the game. It was he who disciplined the West Indies into an organized force in international cricket. The political, cultural, and ethnic differences of the scattered Caribbean islands had made earlier teams unpredictable and at times almost uncontrollable. Their resolution was easily weakened by disappointment, and insular rivalries had a divisive effect. But under a relaxed and easy manner Worrell inspired his players with his own strength of character and breadth of outlook. His firmness, which at times could be ruthless, prevented the psychological deterioration which had weakened earlier touring sides, and he welded a team of talented but erratic and temperamental players into the finest in the world. In so doing he raised the status and self-respect of black cricketers.

Worrell was a lover of England and a true federalist—in the sense that he believed in the West Indies and did not allow himself to be involved in insular jealousies. He was knighted in 1964. In 1961 he was appointed warden of Irvine Hall, at Mona, near Kingston, in the University College of the West Indies. He described himself, in a BBC interview two years later, as '*in loco parentis* to students, an administrator responsible for moral welfare and discipline, a personal adviser' (Tennant, 75). He was also heavily involved in planning sports facilities. He found time to play cricket with an underprivileged boys' club called Boys Town.

In 1962 Worrell was nominated by the prime minister of Jamaica, Sir Alexander Bustamante, to a seat in the country's upper house—the senate. But, beyond two speeches, he contributed little in his two years before leaving Jamaica in 1964 to become dean of students and warden of two halls in that part of the university which was based in Trinidad. The post was similar to that in Jamaica but with more responsibility. He took a strong line on discipline and exercised 'enormous moral authority' (Tennant, 88). There was still some cricket—with five first-class matches in England in 1964—and opportunities to lecture abroad. It was on a visit to India, at the request of the government, that he felt unwell. The University of Punjab had given him an honorary doctorate of laws in February 1967. Five weeks later, on 13 March 1967, he died in the university hospital at Kingston of leukaemia; he was buried in Barbados, where he had bought land for his eventual retirement.

The Times declared Worrell would be 'remembered as much for his leadership as for his play' (*The Times*, 14 March 1967). His funeral and burial in Barbados were followed by a memorial service in Westminster Abbey, London, the first ever held there for a sportsman. In his memory a fund was set up to benefit young people, in education and in sport, throughout the Commonwealth.

M. M. REESE, *rev.* GERALD M. D. HOWAT

Sources C. Nicole, *West Indian cricket* (1957) · C. L. R. James, *Beyond a boundary* (1963) · *Wisden* (1968) · I. Tennant, *Frank Worrell: a biography* (1987) · E. Eytle, *Frank Worrell* (1963) · F. Worrell, *Cricket punch* (1959) · M. Manley, *A history of West Indies cricket* (1990) · m. cert.
Likenesses photographs, 1950–63, Hult. Arch. [*see illus.*] · photograph, *c.*1967, repro. in Tennant, *Frank Worrell*, 91 · photograph, repro. in Worrell, *Cricket punch*, 20

Worsdale, James (*c.*1692–1767), portrait painter and rake, was the son of a poor colour grinder. He was engaged as a servant to Sir Godfrey Kneller, and subsequently became his apprentice and copyist, but was dismissed for surreptitiously marrying Lady Kneller's niece. In later times he claimed to be the natural son of Sir Godfrey.

Though critics have questioned his artistic ability, Worsdale obtained a considerable amount of patronage as a portrait painter, and was appointed master painter to the Board of Ordnance about 1744. (Twenty years later his will of 8 October 1764 named thirty-eight fellow gentlemen of the ordnance, to whom he left bequests of between 2 guineas and £10.) His success was due mainly to his amusing conversation, conviviality, and clever singing and acting. He painted royal portraits, possibly after Kneller, for the nisi prius court, Chester, 1733. His portraits of Princess Louisa, Princess Mary, Sir John Ligonier (1756), William, duke of Devonshire (1738), Richard 'Beau' Nash, Thomas Southerne (1734), and other persons of mark were engraved by John Brooks, Gerhard Bockman, John Faber junior, and John Simon.

In Ireland, Worsdale was befriended by Lord Blayney and Lawrence Parsons, first earl of Rosse, with whom he founded the Hell Fire Club in Dublin in 1735. His group portrait of five of its members, painted for Henry Barry, fourth Lord Sankey, is now in the National Gallery of Ireland, Dublin. He also was active in forming and painting the Limerick Hell Fire Club. His portrait (1746–50) of William Stanhope, first earl of Harrington, lord lieutenant of Ireland, is in the National Portrait Gallery, London.

Worsdale was associated with the stage in London and Dublin. In Ireland he acted with the Smock Alley company from 1737 to 1740, but his only known role was on 18 April 1740 as Lady Scardale in *The Assembly*, a farce ascribed to him. In 1741 he was appointed deputy master of revels. He acted with the Aungier Street company from 1740 to 1744, playing, among other roles, the queen in *The Queen of Spain, or, Farinelli in Madrid* (1744, possibly by James Ayres) and Manly in *Cure for a Scold* (1735), two more plays attributed to him. The latter was a ballad opera or farce taken from the *Taming of the Shrew*. In 1752, at Drury Lane in London, he acted the part of Lady Pentweazle in Samuel

Foote's comedy *Taste*, and was given the author's third night's profits. Appropriately, the play ridiculed the high prices people of fashion were prepared to pay for antiquities, leaving contemporary native artists 'totally neglected or despised' (Cooke, 65).

Worsdale was professedly the author of a number of songs, plays, and operas, including *The Extravagant Justice* and *Gasconado the Great* (1759), but these seem to have been chiefly the work of others—needy writers whom he exploited. Laetitia Pilkington, who was one of these, described him in her *Memoirs* in extremely uncomplimentary and accusatory terms. Vertue referred to him as a 'little cringing creature', 5 feet tall or shorter, and asserted that he pushed himself into notoriety solely by his artful ways and 'barefacd mountebank lyes' (Vertue, *Note Books*, 3.59). Worsdale died in his lodgings at the house of Mrs Lloyd, Blackheath, Kent, on 10 June 1767, and was buried at St Paul's, Covent Garden. He had numerous romantic liaisons and left bequests to at least five illegitimate children. In leaving to one Dr Arne his 'honesty of heart' and to his wife, Celia Arne, 'most inhumanly treated by the said Dr Arne … 20 pounds for her whole and sole use Independent of her Cruel and Unworthy husband' (PRO, PROB 11/930), Worsdale's bequest is illustrative both of his generosity, also apparent in his other many bequests, and of the sanguine nature of his personality.

F. M. O'DONOGHUE, *rev.* ARIANNE BURNETTE

Sources Highfill, Burnim & Langhans, *BDA* · A. Crookshank and the Knight of Glin [D. Fitzgerald], *The painters of Ireland, c.1660–1920* (1978) · W. G. Strickland, *A dictionary of Irish artists*, 2 (1913) · J. C. Smith, *British mezzotinto portraits*, 4 vols. in 5 (1878–84) · Vertue, *Note books*, vol. 3 · L. C. Jones, *The clubs of the Georgian rakes* (1942) · W. Cooke, *Memoirs of Samuel Foote*, 3 vols. (1805) · Waterhouse, *18c painters* · L. Pilkington, *Memoirs of Laetitia Pilkington*, ed. A. C. Elias, 2 vols. (1997) · H. Walpole, *Anecdotes of painting in England: with some account of the principal artists*, ed. R. N. Wornum, new edn, 1 (1849); repr. (1862) · D. E. Baker, *Biographia dramatica, or, A companion to the playhouse*, rev. I. Reed, new edn, rev. S. Jones, 3 vols. in 4 (1812) · Genest, *Eng. stage*, vol. 3 · will, PRO, PROB 11/930, fols. 73r–76r · Redgrave, *Artists* · Lord Killanin, *Sir Godfrey Kneller and his times, 1646–1723* (1948)
Archives University of Cincinnati, material collected by W. J. Lawrence
Likenesses W. Dickinson, mezzotint impressions, pubd 1769 (after R. E. Pine), BM, NG Ire., NPG
Wealth at death £2235 in money; plus freehold in Cambridgeshire: will, PRO, PROB 11/930, fols. 73r–76r

Worsdale, John (*b.* 1766, *d.* in or after 1828), astrologer, was born on 2 December 1766 in Fulbeck, near Grantham, Lincolnshire. After working as a parish clerk there, he studied mathematics (and probably astrology) under Nathaniel Tingle of Helpringham, near Sleaford, in 1778. He was writing and practising astrology in Spanby, near Falkingham, by 1796; then in Donington Northope, near Boston; and finally, by 1819, in Lincoln 'near the Cathedral' (J. Worsdale, *Celestial Philosophy*, 1828, title page), where he remained until his death.

Worsdale was one of a flourishing community of astrologers and astronomers, throughout the eighteenth and early nineteenth centuries, in Lincolnshire, Leicestershire, and Rutland. He wrote several books defending and explicating his subject: *Genethliacal Astrology* (1796, 1798); *A Collection of Remarkable Nativities* (1799); *The Nativity of Napoleon Bonaparte* (1805); *Astronomy and Elementary Philosophy* (1819); and *Celestial Philosophy* (1828). These were not, however, general or indiscriminate defences. His particular astrology was rigorously purist and highly technical, in the tradition of earlier astrologers such as John Partridge, who still took their mandate from Ptolemy and adhered to a combination of Aristotelian astronomical principles and precise mathematical procedures. As such, he was unforgiving of the 'wretched compilations of borrowed and stolen trash' (*Genethliacal Astronomy*, vii) of magical-populist astrologers such as his contemporaries Thomas White and Ebenezer Sibly. At the same time he was equally hostile to the attempts of some of his predecessors, such as John Gadbury, to reform astrology along contemporary scientific lines, which he regarded as ignorant meddling with tradition.

By the time of his death, Worsdale had won some recognition for his efforts from the tiny but disputatious metropolitan astrological community. There can be no doubt, however, that he was obliged to make his living as a judicial astrologer whose services were in demand for astral advice regarding urgent or intractable personal problems. This must have been grating for him, as most of his clients, although probably not all, came from the common people of Lincolnshire whom he despised as 'the Vulgar and Illiterate', hopelessly unfit to understand 'the Sydereal Mysteries' (Worsdale, dedication). He constantly plundered his casebooks for his favourite proof of astrology as such, and of the particular techniques he used. This involved the 'apheta' or 'hyleg'—namely a precise prediction of someone's death, followed by its remorseless and usually violent fulfilment. Since the occurrence and timing of death is factually indisputable, this was a customary astrological course of action though Worsdale seems to have taken it to unusual lengths.

The plebeians on whom Worsdale looked down took an appropriate (if unintended) posthumous revenge. As 'the Lincolnshire wiseman or astronomer' (Penny, 8–9), his name lived on into the early twentieth century in popular folklore. Accompanied by a familiar spirit such as a blackbird or black cat, his uncanny prescience was plainly intimated to be magical, if not diabolical.

In politics, Worsdale was a whig; he predicted, from the map of its founding, that America would 'establish FREEDOM and LIBERTY in every part of the habitable Globe' (*Astronomy and Elementary Philosophy*, 47). In religion, although he lashed 'Infidels, Deists, and Atheists' as well as 'deceitful Popish priests' (ibid., 39), God seems to have been reserved for First Cause, while occasionally authorizing comets as 'awful warnings' of 'DIVINE VENGEANCE' (ibid., 50, 53). However, his main interest is as the last representative of any national prominence of a particular astrological tradition in Britain, embodying a defiantly elitist and pre-modern Aristotelian rationalism and naturalism. His last recorded work, the foreword to his *Celestial Philosophy*, is dated 11 October 1828; it is not known when he died.   PATRICK CURRY

Sources J. Worsdale, *The nativity of Napoleon Bonaparte* (1805) · E. Howe, *Urania's children* (1967), 26–8 · P. Curry, *Prophecy and power: astrology in early modern England* (1989), 132–4 · J. A. Penny, *Folklore round Horncastle* (1915)

Worsdell family (*per. c.*1800–1910), coach and carriage builders and engineers, originated with **Thomas Clarke Worsdell** (1788–1862), born on 3 December 1788 at Hayes, near Bromley in Kent. He was the son of Thomas Clarke Worsdell (1748–1826), a market gardener in Kent, later an innkeeper, then agent for the Hand in Hand insurance company, and his wife, Elizabeth Carter (*b.* 1750). About 1800 the family moved to London where Thomas Clarke senior found employment at a coaching inn. On leaving school young Thomas was apprenticed to coach-builders Howe and Shanks of Little Queen Street, Long Acre, London. In 1807 he married Elizabeth Taylor (1784–1863) in London, but other details of his early life are scarce. About 1812 he moved to north Lancashire where he continued to work as a coach-builder. By 1816 he had joined the Society of Friends, and in time all five Worsdells became Friends, and this had a marked effect on their private and public lives. In 1827 Thomas was able to establish a coach-building business with his son Nathaniel in Liverpool, which soon achieved a high reputation for the quality of its work. Through Quaker influence he was introduced to George Stephenson and with him planned the first carriages for the Liverpool and Manchester Railway (L&MR). In 1828 Thomas became superintendent of coaching for the L&MR, and at his Crown Street works he built large numbers of coaches, as well as tenders for the *Rocket* and other locomotives, and a variety of goods wagons. Stephenson called him 'the best coach builder I ever knew'. In January 1837 he left England to take up the post of locomotive, carriage, and wagon superintendent on the Leipzig and Dresden Railway, returning about four years later as carriage inspector successively at Manchester, Euston, and Hull, where he was joined by his son George. He retired from railway work in 1847 and settled at Nantwich near Crewe, where he developed his lifelong interest in homoeopathic medicine, treating both people and animals with, it was said, considerable success. He died on 18 April 1862 at his home, 7 Welch Row in Nantwich, his wife surviving him by less than a year. They were both buried at the Friends' meeting-house, Nantwich.

Thomas's eldest son, **Nathaniel Worsdell** (1809–1886), was born on 10 October 1809 in London. He attended school in Knutsford, Cheshire, to the age of thirteen, and was apprenticed to Jonathan Dunn, coach-builder in Lancaster, in 1823. On 3 October 1833 he married Mary Wilson (1811–1869) of Bentham near Lancaster, and Nathaniel remained at the Crown Street works when the rest of the family moved to Leipzig in 1837. The carriage of mail on the railways began at a very early date, and Nathaniel built some mail vans in 1838 which incorporated his own patented device for the automatic picking up and setting down of mailbags in transit. The Post Office was very interested but would not agree to his asking price (£3500, subsequently reduced to £1500) for the right to use his patent, and it soon introduced a device of its own which was a clear infringement. As a Quaker, however, Nathaniel would not pursue the matter in the courts and he never received any compensation from the Post Office. In 1843 he moved as carriage and wagon superintendent to the new Grand Junction Railway works at Crewe where he remained until he retired in 1880. He was involved in many of the charitable and educational activities of the growing railway community and also served as a Liberal on the local council. He died on 24 July 1886 at his home, Southlea, 8 Chetwynd Road, Oxton, Birkenhead, Cheshire, a much respected man, strict but just, and ever mindful of his employees' welfare. His wife, Mary, had predeceased him; both were buried at the Quaker burial-ground at Briggflatts near Sedbergh in Yorkshire.

George Worsdell (1821–1912) was Thomas's youngest child, born on 21 May 1821 at Preston, Lancashire, and on leaving school near Blackburn he trained under his father at the Crown Street works before moving with him in 1837 to Leipzig. He returned to England the following year and by 1845 had decided to set up his own business manufacturing railway equipment. Within six years his Dallam Forge at Warrington in Lancashire had been awarded a gold medal at the Great Exhibition of 1851 'for excellence of iron and of railway plant'. In the same year, on 27 March, he married Jane (1820/21–1903), the youngest daughter of Edward Bolton, a prominent local Quaker. Within a few years, however, both he and the Dallam Forge suffered serious setbacks: his health broke down in 1857 when the business failed and he was declared bankrupt, but he made a good recovery until forced again by ill health to retire in 1872 at the age of fifty-one. Relieved of stress, he lived to the age of ninety-one, and died on 1 December 1912 at his home, 70 Brookfield Terrace, Lancaster. Under new management from 1865 the Dallam Forge again prospered, and eventually it became in 1930 part of the Lancashire Steel Company, remaining in production until July 1980.

(Thomas) William Worsdell (1838–1916), Nathaniel's eldest son, was born on 14 January 1838 at 17 Laurel Street, Liverpool. He attended Quaker schools in Yorkshire and Hampshire, then about 1855 went as an apprentice to the Birmingham engineering works of his uncle Thomas Worsdell (1818–1893), another of Thomas Clarke's sons. He became manager of the works in 1861 but fell out with his uncle and emigrated to the United States soon after his marriage, on 29 June 1865, to Mary Ann Batt (1844–1918) at Yealand Conyers in Lancashire. He worked on the Pennsylvania railroad until 1871 when he returned to England as works manager under Francis William Webb at the London and North Western Railway's (L&NWR) Crewe works. After ten years in that post he was appointed locomotive superintendent of the Great Eastern Railway, leaving after four years for the same position, at twice the salary, with the larger and more prosperous North Eastern Railway (NER) at Gateshead. A strong advocate of compound cylinder locomotives, six of the fifteen classes he designed for the NER were of this type. Like all the Quaker Worsdells he was held in awe by his workforce but in spite of his imposing physique he did not enjoy good health and he

resigned in 1890, to be succeeded by his brother Wilson. He joined the Institution of Mechanical Engineers in 1864, serving as a member of council in 1886–92. He had built a house, Stonycroft, at Arnside in Westmorland, as a holiday home and lived there during a very active retirement until his death there on 28 June 1916. His wife survived him by two years and they were both buried at the Friends' meeting-house in Yealand Conyers.

Wilson Worsdell (1850–1920), the second youngest of Nathaniel's sons, was born on 7 September 1850 at Monks Coppenhall, near Crewe. He attended the Friends' school at Ackworth from 1860 to 1866, and the following year joined his brother William in the Pennsylvania Railway's workshops at Altoona. They both returned to Crewe in 1871, and Wilson worked with the L&NWR there and later at Chester, where he was in charge of the locomotive sheds from 1877. On 1 June 1882 he married Mary Elizabeth (1856–1945), daughter of George Bradford, a linen draper, at St John's Church, Hanley, Staffordshire. In 1883 he moved to the NER at Gateshead as assistant mechanical engineer, finding himself again under his elder brother when William was appointed locomotive superintendent in 1885. William's early retirement in 1890 allowed Wilson to step into his shoes much earlier than he could have anticipated, and for the next twenty years he was in charge of locomotive building for the NER at Gateshead and Darlington. During that time he produced more than twenty different types of steam locomotive, and rebuilt some of those designed by his brother William to improve their performance. The brothers' engines played a notable part in the celebrated railway races to Edinburgh and Aberdeen in the 1880s and 1890s, sustaining average speeds hardly bettered by steam locomotives since. Wilson was also responsible in 1903–4 for the north Tyneside third rail suburban electrification scheme, one of the first in Britain. He served as a member of council of the Institution of Mechanical Engineers and as a JP. He took a keen interest in the welfare of his staff and workers, and was both liked and respected by all. He retired at the end of May 1910 and died suddenly on 13 April 1920 at his home, The Glebe, South Ascot, Sunninghill, Berkshire. He was buried at All Souls' churchyard, South Ascot.

RONALD M. BIRSE

Sources G. Hill, *The Worsdells: a Quaker engineering dynasty* (1991) [incl. bibliography, portraits, illustrations, appxs, and genealogy] · J. Marshall, *A biographical dictionary of railway engineers* (1978), 242–5 · d. cert. [Thomas Clark Worsdell] · d. cert. [Nathaniel Worsdell] · m. cert. [George Worsdell] · d. cert. [George Worsdell] · d. cert. [Thomas William Worsdell] · d. cert. [Wilson Worsdell] · *CGPLA Eng. & Wales* (1886) · *CGPLA Eng. & Wales* (1912) · *CGPLA Eng. & Wales* (1916) · *CGPLA Eng. & Wales* (1920)

Likenesses C. Bragger, portrait, 1880 (Nathaniel Worsdell) · J. H. Campbell, oils, 1890 (Thomas William Worsdell) · photographs, repro. in Hill, *The Worsdells*

Wealth at death £12,091 1s. 4d.—Nathaniel Worsdell: resworn probate, Dec 1886, *CGPLA Eng. & Wales* · £2643 15s.—George Worsdell: resworn probate, 27 Dec 1912, *CGPLA Eng. & Wales* · £67,346 18s. 10d.—Thomas William Worsdell: probate, 5 Oct 1916, *CGPLA Eng. & Wales* · £11,103 4s. 7d.—Wilson Worsdell: probate, 29 July 1920, *CGPLA Eng. & Wales*

Worsdell, George (1821–1912). *See under* Worsdell family (*per. c.*1800–1910).

Worsdell, Nathaniel (1809–1886). *See under* Worsdell family (*per. c.*1800–1910).

Worsdell, Thomas Clarke (1788–1862). *See under* Worsdell family (*per. c.*1800–1910).

Worsdell, (Thomas) William (1838–1916). *See under* Worsdell family (*per. c.*1800–1910).

Worsdell, Wilson (1850–1920). *See under* Worsdell family (*per. c.*1800–1910).

Worsley, Benjamin (1617/18–1677), physician and projector, was the eldest son of Francis Worsley of Kenton, Warwickshire, and his wife, Mary, daughter of Shipman Hopkins of Coventry. He was probably brought up in London. The only certain detail concerning his formal education is his admission as a pensioner at Trinity College, Dublin, in 1643 at the late age of twenty-five. He claimed to possess a degree from Trinity College. He entered public service under Thomas Wentworth, first earl of Strafford, lord lieutenant of Ireland, and was in 1643 surgeon-general in the army in Ireland.

Worsley's career as a projector began in 1646 when his scheme for the manufacture of saltpetre attracted attention, primarily on account of its value for gunpowder production. He capitalized on this opportunity by making the saltpetre project the centrepiece of a programme for revitalization of the British economy and the development of an integrated manufacturing and trading system embracing an expanding colonial empire. He published little, but elaborations of his proposals for the exploitation of technical innovation and the regulation of trade are found in abundance in such archives as the Hartlib papers and Shaftesbury papers, and his views were seriously regarded, even though his reputation suffered as a result of a bitter controversy with William Petty.

At first Worsley was ahead of Petty. In 1646 his saltpetre scheme impressed the young Robert Boyle and brought patronage from Boyle and his sister, Lady Ranelagh. Worsley was the prime mover in the Invisible College established at this time—a group of intellectuals exchanging ideas by correspondence, motivated by utopian aspirations, and particularly engaged in promoting science and technology. This agency brought him into association with Samuel Hartlib. Worsley was reappointed surgeon-general to the army in Ireland in 1647, but seems not to have taken up the post. Between 1647 and 1649 he was based in the Netherlands, where he acted as a major source of intelligence on economic and scientific affairs. In 1649 his hopes revolved around a scheme for developing the economy of Virginia. With the promise of a situation in America he returned to England and his efforts contributed to the council of state's decision to establish a council of trade, presided over by Sir Henry Vane the younger, a patron of Worsley's. The council's main achievement was the 1651 Navigation Act, of which Worsley claimed to have been 'the first sollicitour'. He also wrote at this time *The Advocate* (1652), in defence of the act, and a related economic tract, *Free Ports* (1652).

Renewed prospects opened up for preferment in Ireland. Between 1651 and 1653 Worsley served as secretary to the commissioners in Ireland and commissioner-general for the revenue, and then, having failed to be selected to join the embassy to Sweden, he returned to Ireland as surveyor-general of forfeited estates. He remained in this post until 1658, but the real work was undertaken by Petty, for whom Worsley developed a deep jealousy. Petty responded with venom in his history of what became known as the 'down survey'. Having failed as surveyor-general, Worsley made an unsuccessful attempt in 1659 to secure the Post Office farm surrendered by John Thurloe. His tenuous hold on office was reduced to his positions as justice of the peace in Queen's county and commissary-general of musters. In 1656 he married Lucy, daughter of William Cary of Dartmouth, Devon.

After the Restoration, Worsley, who was living in Tuthill Fields, was inhibited from his more radical schemes for social and religious reform. He played no part in the newly founded Royal Society or the College of Physicians, although at this time he began to describe himself as an MD. He concentrated on economic issues, especially on American colonial affairs. Repeating the pattern of 1650, in 1660 he was involved in the establishment of the council of trade. He continued to write on general policy questions, but he also tried to turn his knowledge to profit. For instance, in 1666 he was granted a licence for the cultivation of senna in the plantations. The continuing strength of his reputation is witnessed by his involvement between 1668 and 1673 in the revival of the committees involved with trade and plantations. After serving as a commissioner of trade between 1668 and 1669, he was appointed assistant secretary of the council of foreign plantations in 1670, and in September 1672 he was promoted to the post of secretary and treasurer of the council of trade and foreign plantations, under the presidency of his patron Anthony Ashley Cooper, first earl of Shaftesbury. He resigned on account of the Test Act in September 1673, being succeeded by John Locke. A catalogue of his fine library was published in 1678, revealing a huge collection of nonconformist, and especially Socinian, religious literature. Worsley died in 1677.   CHARLES WEBSTER, *rev.*

Sources C. M. Andrews, *British committees, commissions, and councils of trade and plantations, 1622–1675* (Baltimore, MD, 1908) · K. H. D. Haley, *The first earl of Shaftesbury* (1968) · W. Petty, *The history of the survey of Ireland: commonly called the down survey, AD 1655–6*, ed. T. A. Larcom (1851) · G. H. Turnbull, *Hartlib, Dury and Comenius: gleanings from Hartlib's papers* (1947) · C. Webster, *The great instauration: science, medicine and reform, 1626–1660* (1975) · J. B. Whitmore, 'Dr Worsley being dead', *N&Q*, 185 (1943), 123–8 · Bodl. Oxf., Clarendon MSS · PRO, Shaftesbury MSS, 30/24 · Sheffield University, Hartlib MSS · T. C. Barnard, *Cromwellian Ireland: English government and reform in Ireland, 1649–1660* (1975) · J. C. Sainty, ed., *Officials of the board of trade, 1660–1870* (1974) · M. Greengrass, M. Leslie, and T. Raylor, eds., *Samuel Hartlib and universal reformation: studies in intellectual communication* (1994)

Worsley, Charles (1622–1656), parliamentarian army officer and major-general, was born in Manchester on 24

Charles Worsley (1622–1656), by unknown artist

June 1622 and baptized six days later in Manchester collegiate church, the eldest son of Ralph Worsley (1592–1669) of Platt, in Rusholme, near Manchester, and his wife, Isabel Worsley (d. 1627), daughter of Edward Massey of Manchester and widow of Alexander Ford of Wigan. Ralph Worsley was a successful merchant who prospered enough to buy up the Platt estate in 1625, adding it to lands which the family already owned in Rusholme; he died able to style himself gentleman while still active in the putting out of yarn and selling of cloth. He was a committed supporter of parliament in the civil war and was on the parliamentarian subcommittee of accounts sitting at Manchester in May 1648.

Charles Worsley fought for parliament in Lancashire during the first civil war, rising to the rank of captain. During the mid- and late-1640s he made money by informing on Lancashire royalists who had concealed parts of their estates from the parliamentarian sequestrators. He also purchased sequestered lands in Lancashire. On 18 September 1644 he married Mary Booth, the daughter of John Booth of Manchester, in Didsbury chapel; they had one son, Ralph, and two daughters, Sarah and Martha. A third daughter was born two months premature, and barely survived twelve hours; her mother followed her into the grave a week later, on 1 April 1649.

In 1650 Worsley was appointed commander of a new regiment of foot soldiers raised for Oliver Cromwell in Lancashire, and was given the rank of lieutenant-colonel. He was with Cromwell in Scotland in 1650, and the following year was involved in operations in the north-west of

England against James Stanley, seventh earl of Derby, though he did not take part in any of the decisive battles fought by the New Model Army during the early 1650s. On 6 October 1652 he married his second wife, Dorothy Kenyon (d. 1693), daughter of Roger Kenyon of Whalley in Lancashire. They had three children, only one of whom, a son, Charles (baptized by the Independent minister Thomas Jollie in July 1653), survived childhood.

In late 1652 Worsley's regiment was stationed at St James's Palace in Westminster (and seems to have continued there until at least August 1654, when another child was born there). In April 1653 Worsley commanded the detachment of musketeers which entered the House of Commons at Cromwell's forcible closure of the Rump Parliament. He helped Thomas Harrison turn Algernon Sidney out of his place, and took charge of the key to the Commons and the mace, which remained in his house for several months. In 1653 he wrote a strongly millenarian preface to the writings of the London presbyterian minister Christopher Goad, *Refreshing Drops and Scorching Vials*. In 1654 Worsley was elected to the first protectorate parliament as MP for the new seat of Manchester.

In the summer of 1655 Worsley was responsible for guarding a number of royalists, including Sir Ralph Verney, who had been secured in the aftermath of the risings in March of that year, and in the autumn of 1655 he was appointed one of Cromwell's major-generals. In August he had been given command of the militia troops in Staffordshire, Worcestershire, and Derbyshire, but in October his association was changed to Lancashire, Staffordshire, and Cheshire. He began to act as major-general in early November 1655 and over the next eight months displayed what John Morrill has called 'exceptional zeal and thoroughness' in the work of reformation (Morrill, 277). A staunch puritan himself, he made the main thrust of his work as a major-general a concerted attempt to bring about a godly moral reformation within his association. In early November he told Cromwell's secretary of state, John Thurloe, that he had been encouraging the 'best of people' within the towns of his area 'to be puttinge in execution the laws against drunkennesse, sweringe, profaining the Lord's Day, and other wickednesses', and had found that 'God hath already put into his people a prayinge sperit for this great and goode worke' (Bodl. Oxf., MS Rawl. A 32, fols. 373–6). He had in fact written to a number of Independent congregations of his association inviting them to send him a list of their reform aspirations and their grievances against their ungodly neighbours. One response from 'the Church of Christ meeting at Altham' in Lancashire exhorted him to establish a magistracy of 'just men fearing God and hating covetousness' and to purge the local ministry of 'profane and heretical ministers who fill most pulpits in the country' (*Notebook of … Thomas Jolley*, 127–8); it also encouraged him to punish drunkards and sabbath-breakers, suppress alehouses, and take action against non-attendance at church.

Worsley needed little encouragement in these matters, and within a few weeks he was reporting good success against drunkards and profaners, 'for some towns have made proclamation and take a very strick course and make diligent search every night for such'. He was clearly very pleased with this progress and remarked: 'I cannot but admire at the freenesse of good people of severall judgements to promote this work' (Bodl. Oxf., MS Rawl. A 32, fols. 871–4). By December he reported that so many transgressors had been arrested that the gaols of his association were almost full. During the early months of 1656 the commissioners for securing the peace of the Commonwealth in Lancashire and Cheshire ordered the closure of as many as 200 unlicensed alehouses in the Blackburn area and a similar number in and around Chester. The Cheshire commissioners also continued to secure large numbers of 'suspicious idle and lewd persons', and imprisoned along with them 'several persons' who had flouted the 1653 civil marriage act by marrying in religious ceremonies. Worsley commented of all this work: 'Those things give matter of rejoicing to the good, and is a terror to the bad' (Bodl. Oxf., MS Rawl. A 35, fols. 104–5).

In December 1655 Worsley told Thurloe that he was 'extreamly trobled' by the activities of Quakers in the north-west. He informed him that there were large numbers of them in his counties and that they 'troble the markets and get into private houses up and down in every towne and draw people after them'. He made clear he was taking action against them, but on several occasions requested further direction from the government. (Bodl. Oxf., MS Rawl. A 33, fols. 369–72, 515–18, 571–4).

The relentless pressure for moral reformation in the north-west was sustained into the early summer of 1656, but the effort ultimately proved too much for Worsley himself. In mid-May he reported to Thurloe that he was not feeling well and that he intended to 'take physic at home' (Bodl. Oxf., MS Rawl. A 38, fols. 357–8). A few days later, however, he was summoned to London along with his fellow major-generals to take part in a series of meetings with Cromwell. In early June his condition worsened and he died on 12 June 1656. His funeral, which was attended by all the other major-generals, took place the following day. He was accorded full military honours and laid to rest in Henry VII's chapel in Westminster Abbey; through oversight his body was not disinterred at the Restoration. When his will was read to him just before his death he asked that an estate belonging to the royalist Sir Cyril Trafford, which he had bought from the sequestrators, should be returned to the exchequer as he 'would not for all the world wrong the Commonwealth' (PRO, SP 18/130/129). His widow was given an allowance of £100 a year and her dead husband's salary for a further year. In 1659 she remarried, her new husband being Waldive Lagoe, who had been Worsley's lieutenant-colonel and had inherited his regiment. Worsley was succeeded as major-general by Tobias Bridge.

CHRISTOPHER DURSTON

Sources Thurloe state papers, Bodl. Oxf., MS Rawl. A · interregnum state papers, PRO, SP 18–28 · J. S. Morrill, *Cheshire, 1630–1660: county government and society during the English revolution* (1974), 276–87 · J. Booker, *The history of the ancient chapel of Birch, in Manchester*

parish, Chetham Society, 47 (1859), 24–49 · C. H. Firth and G. Davies, *The regimental history of Cromwell's army*, 2 vols. (1940) · *DNB* · F. P. Verney and M. M. Verney, *Memoirs of the Verney family*, 4 vols. (1892–4) · *The notebook of the Rev. Thomas Jolley*, ed. H. Fishwick, Chetham Society, new ser., 33 (1895), 127–8 · I. Gentles, 'The new model officer corps, 1647: a collective portrait', *Social History*, 22 (1997), 142–3 · C. Goad, *Refreshing drops and scorching vials* (1653), second preface · K. Wrightson, 'The puritan reformation of manners with special reference to the counties of Lancashire and Essex', PhD diss., U. Cam., 1974 · Greaves & Zaller, *BDBR*, 3.343

Archives Man. CL, Manchester Archives and Local Studies, family and estate papers | Bodl. Oxf., MSS Rawl., Thurloe state MSS A

Likenesses G. Scharf, pen-and-ink drawing, 1859, NPG · J. B. Hunt, engraving, repro. in Booker, *History of the ancient chapel of Birch*, facing p. 50 · oils, Platt Hall, Manchester [*see illus.*]

Worsley, Edward (1604/5–1676), Jesuit, who was born in Lancashire, is said to have been an Oxford student and a protestant minister, but his name does not occur in the records of that university. He entered the Society of Jesus on 7 September 1626. Having repeated his studies at the college of Liège (1628–34) he was made professor of logic, metaphysics, scripture, and theology. He was professed of the four vows on 29 September 1641 and from 1651 to 1655 was a missioner in the London district. He was declared rector of the college at Liège on 31 October 1658. In 1662 he was acting as English procurator and missioner at the Jesuit professed house, Antwerp.

Worsley was the author of a number of works, mostly of controversy, published under the initials E. W. His 1665 *Truth Will Out* was a response to Jeremy Taylor's *Dissuasive from Popery*. Five of his works were published by Michael Cnobbaert of Antwerp, beginning with *Protestancy without Principles, or, Sectaries Unhappy Fall from Infallibility to Fancy* (1668), a work which informs the theological understanding of John Dryden's *The Hind and the Panther*. Worsley's work included 'A few notes upon Mr. Poole's appendix against captain Everard', referring to the former parliamentarian army officer and Catholic convert Robert Everard, the main text being partly directed against the work of the future bishop, Edward Stillingfleet. Stillingfleet was also challenged in Worsley's next three works, *Reason and Religion, or, The Certain Rule of Faith Whereby the Infallibility of the Roman Catholick Church is Asserted* (1672), a work strongly influenced by John Sergeant; *The Infallibility of the Roman Catholick Church and her Miracles Defended* (2 vols., 1674), in the second volume of which the author maintains the miraculous translation of the house of Loreto; and *A Discourse of Miracles Wrought in the Roman Catholick Church* (1676). His *Anti-Goliath, or, An epistle to Mr [Daniel] Brevint, Containing Some Reflections Upon his Saul and Samuel at Endor* (1678) was published posthumously, Worsley having died at the professed house, Antwerp, on 2 September 1676, aged seventy-one. He was 'regarded by his own community and by externs as an oracle alike of talent, industry, learning, and prudence' (Foley, 4.597).

THOMPSON COOPER, *rev.* PAUL ARBLASTER

Sources *DNB* · H. Foley, ed., *Records of the English province of the Society of Jesus*, 4 (1878), 597–8; 7 (1882–3), 863 · T. M. McCoog, *English and Welsh Jesuits, 1555–1650*, 2, Catholic RS, 75 (1995), 338 · C. Dodd [H. Tootell], *The church history of England, from the year 1500, to the year*

1688, 3 (1742), 314 • T. H. Clancy, *English Catholic books, 1641–1700: a bibliography* [1974], 108–9, 141 • A. F. Allison and D. M. Rogers, eds., *The contemporary printed literature of the English Counter-Reformation between 1558 and 1640*, 2 (1994), 167 • T. H. Clancy, *A literary history of the English Jesuits: a century of books, 1615–1714* (1996) • V. M. Hamm, 'Dryden's *The hind and the panther*', *Publications of the Modern Language Association of America*, 83 (1968), 400–15

Worsley, Sir Henry (1768–1841), army officer in the East India Company, born on 20 January 1768 at Appuldurcombe, Isle of Wight, was the second son of Francis Worsley (*c*.1729–1808), rector of Chale, Isle of Wight, and his wife, Anne, third daughter of Henry Roberts of Standen, Isle of Wight. In June 1780 he embarked for Bengal as an infantry cadet, and in January 1781 he landed in Madras to take part in the defence of Fort St George, which was besieged by Haidar Ali. He arrived in Bengal in April, was promoted ensign and lieutenant in the course of the year, and joined the 2nd European regiment at Cawnpore. In 1782 he served with the 30th regiment of Sepoys in capturing Chet Singh's forts in the neighbourhood of Benares. In the following year he was appointed adjutant, and served with the 1st battalion of his regiment against insurgents in the Kaimur hills. In 1785 the regiment was disbanded because of the general peace, and Worsley was appointed to the 8th regiment of Sepoys. Early in 1789 he embarked with a detachment of volunteer Sepoys for service in Sumatra. On their return in December the officers and men received the special thanks of Lord Cornwallis.

Towards the close of 1791 Worsley volunteered for service in the Anglo-Mysore War, and was appointed to the 7th battalion of Bengal Sepoys. He took part with the centre column in the night attack on Tipu's fortified camp under the walls of Seringapatam on 6 February 1792, and in the subsequent operations against that town. In the following year he was reappointed to the 32nd battalion, and by the regulations of 1796–7 he was posted to the 1st native infantry, receiving the brevet rank of captain. During a visit to Europe he was promoted captain-lieutenant and captain on 1 November 1798, and was posted as captain to the 15th native infantry, which he joined in 1801. At the close of the year and during 1802 he was employed in command of part of the 1st battalion in tranquillizing the districts ceded by the nawab of Oudh. On 4 September 1803 he fought at Aligarh, and on 11 September he commanded his battalion at the battle of Delhi. On 10 October he again commanded his battalion in the attack made on the enemy's infantry and guns under the walls of Agra, when he received the thanks of the commander-in-chief, Lord Lake, in general orders. He also led it at the battle of Laswari on 1 November. In 1804 he joined the 21st native infantry, and on 21 September was promoted major. In command of a detachment he cleared the Doab of Holkar's troops, which had overrun it after Monson's reverse, and occupied the city of Mathura, where he was employed in protecting the communication of Lake's army. Without specialist assistance he constructed a bridge of boats over the Jumna at Mathura, which proved of great use to the British force. Lake highly appreciated

Worsley's services, and obtained for him the post of deputy adjutant-general. Early in 1806 he succeeded to the office of adjutant-general with the rank of lieutenant-colonel.

On 29 November 1809 Worsley attained the regimental rank of lieutenant-colonel, but in the beginning of 1810 ill health compelled him to resign his office, and in 1811 he went to Europe on furlough. In 1813 he accepted the post of principal private secretary to the governor-general, Francis Rawdon Hastings, second earl of Moira. His health compelled him to resign almost immediately, but in 1818 he returned to India, and Moira at once appointed him military secretary. In a few months his health again obliged him to resign; he joined his unit in the vain hope of restoring his health by active service. In 1819 he returned finally to Europe. On 12 August he was promoted brevet colonel, and in August 1822 colonel with the command of a regiment. He became major-general on 24 August 1830. On 4 June 1815 he was made a CB, on 26 September 1831 KCB, and on 16 February 1838 GCB. In 1837 he gave £1000 to the Royal Asiatic Society, in recognition of which they placed his bust in their house. His wife was Sarah Hastings (probably a relative of the marquess of Hastings), with whom he had one daughter, Elizabeth. He died at Shide, Isle of Wight, on 19 January 1841, and was buried at Chale.

Worsley has frequently been confused with **Henry Worsley** (1783–1820), army officer, born in February 1783, who was the third son of James S. Edward Worsley (1748–1798), rector of Gatcombe, Isle of Wight, and his wife, Ann Hayles. In the autumn of 1799 he obtained an ensigncy in the 6th foot, and accompanied the expedition to the Netherlands under the duke of York. In 1800 he received a lieutenancy in the 52nd foot. In 1802 the 2nd battalion became the 96th foot, to which Worsley was posted. In 1804 he obtained a company, and in 1805 went to America with Sir Eyre Coote (1762–1824?). In 1809 he joined the 85th and took part in the expedition to the Scheldt under John Pitt, second earl of Chatham. In 1811 he went to the Peninsula, and was at the battle of Fuentes d'Oñoro and the siege of Badajoz. Shortly afterwards he was promoted major in the 4th garrison battalion, then at Guernsey, but, obtaining his transfer to the 34th regiment in 1812, he returned to Spain and served in the advance on Madrid and the retreat from Salamanca. After the battle of Vitoria in 1813 he was recommended for promotion, received the rank of lieutenant-colonel, and served in the conflicts in the Pyrenees, gaining the thanks of Lord Hill. In 1816 he went to India, but was forced shortly afterwards by ill health to return to Europe. He was appointed captain of Yarmouth Castle in the Isle of Wight, and a CB. He died, unmarried, after three years' extreme ill health resulting from his service in unhealthy areas, at Newport, Isle of Wight, on 13 May 1820, and was buried at Kingston, Isle of Wight. Accounts of his services, confused with those of Sir Henry Worsley, appeared in *GM* (1841), Ward's *Men of the Reign*, and *La biographie universelle*.

E. I. CARLYLE, *rev.* ROGER T. STEARN

Sources private information (1900) [Mr C. Francis Worsley] · J. Philippart, *East India military calendar*, 3 vols. (1823–6), vols. 1, 3 · W. Berry, *County genealogies: pedigrees of the families of the county of Hants* (1833) · Dodwell [E. Dodwell] and Miles [J. S. Miles], eds., *Alphabetical list of the officers of the Indian army: with the dates of their respective promotion, retirement, resignation, or death … from the year 1760 to the year … 1837* (1838) · P. Moon, *The British conquest and dominion of India* (1989) · V. C. P. Hodson, *List of officers of the Bengal army, 1758–1834*, 4 (1947) · A. Harfield, *British & Indian armies in the East Indies, 1685–1935* (1984) · T. A. Heathcote, *The military in British India: the development of British land forces in south Asia, 1600–1947* (1995) · R. Muir, *Britain and the defeat of Napoleon, 1807–1815* (1996) · Foster, *Alum. Oxon.*, 1715–1886 · *GM*, 1st ser., 93 (1823)
Archives BL OIOC, letters to Sir Richard Jones, MSS Eur. C 234

Worsley, Henry (1783–1820). *See under* Worsley, Sir Henry (1768–1841).

Worsley, Israel (1768–1836), Unitarian minister, was born at Hertford. His grandfather John Worsley (*d.* 1767) was for fifty years a successful schoolmaster at Hertford and author of grammatical tables (1736) and of an able translation of the New Testament, published posthumously by subscription in 1770 and edited by Matthew Bradshaw and the author's son Samuel Worsley (*d.* 1800). Israel Worsley's father, John Worsley (*d.* 1807), had continued the school at Hertford for thirty years with less success, being too easy a disciplinarian; he published a Latin grammar (1771). Israel Worsley entered Daventry Academy in 1786 under Thomas Belsham, who was responsible for his adoption of Unitarian views. In December 1790 a committee of merchants at Dunkirk (where there was no English service) engaged Worsley as their minister. The services were conducted apparently with a *Book of Common Prayer Compiled for the Use of the English Church at Dunkirk … with a Collection of Psalms* (1791); this volume is reprinted in *Fragmenta liturgica* (1848, vol. 6) by Peter Hall (1803–1849), who seems to have been unaware that it is itself a reprint of the 'reformed' prayer book of Theophilus Lindsey. How long this experiment lasted is not certain. Worsley established a school at Dunkirk. After the outbreak of war in 1793 he retreated to England, but returned after the peace of Amiens in 1802. He was arrested on the resumption of hostilities in 1803 and ultimately escaped with difficulty through Holland.

From 1806 to 1813 Worsley ministered at Lincoln, and from 1813 to February 1831 at Plymouth, where he established a fellowship fund and a chapel library. He left Plymouth with his family for Paris, intending to stay for six months only, but he was persuaded to open in June a place for Unitarian worship, eventually settled in the rue Provence. In January 1832 he formed a French Unitarian association for the circulation of tracts. The cholera epidemic of March 1832 dispersed his congregation—largely English, American, and German residents—but he kept his chapel open until June 1833. On his return to England he again ministered at Lincoln in 1833–6.

Besides sermons, tracts, and school books, Worsley published an *Account of the State of France … and the Treatment of the English* (1806); a *Memoir of Jacob Brettell* (1810); *Observations on … Changes in the Presbyterian Societies of England* (1816), valuable for Unitarian history; *Lectures on … Nonconformity* (1823, 2nd edn 1825); and *View of the American Indians … the Descendants of the Ten Tribes of Israel* (1828). Worsley died at Le Havre on 3 September 1836. His son William (1796–1881) studied at the University of Glasgow (BA, 1816) and at Manchester College, York, in 1816–19; he was Unitarian minister at Thorne (1819–22), Hull (1822–5), and Gainsborough (1825–75).

ALEXANDER GORDON, *rev.* R. K. WEBB

Sources F. Kenworthy, 'A Unitarian chapel in Paris', *Transactions of the Unitarian Historical Society*, 6/3 (1935–8), 205–8 · *Christian Reformer, or, New Evangelical Miscellany*, 19 (1833), 269, 308, 369 · *Christian Reformer, or, Unitarian Magazine and Review*, 3 (1836), 824 · T. Belsham, 'A list of students educated at the academy at Daventry [pt 3]', *Monthly Repository*, 17 (1822), 284–7, esp. 286 · W. Urwick, *Nonconformity in Hertfordshire* (1884), 514 · J. Murch, *A history of the Presbyterian and General Baptist churches in the west of England* (1835), 505 · *Unitarian Almanac* (1882), 24 · [J. Watkins and F. Shoberl], *A biographical dictionary of the living authors of Great Britain and Ireland* (1816) · *Memoir of the Rev. John Kenrick* (1854), 13
Archives DWL, student essays
Wealth at death under £300: Lincoln 3/503, death duty registers

Worsley, Philip Stanhope (1835–1866), poet, was born at Greenwich, Kent, on 12 August 1835, the son of Charles Worsley (1783–1854), rector of Finchley, Middlesex, a member of the family of the Worsleys of Gatcombe, Isle of Wight, and his wife, Madeline Maria le Geyt. After attending Sir Roger Cholmeley's School, Highgate, Middlesex, he was admitted to a scholarship at Corpus Christi College, Oxford, on 28 May 1853 and graduated BA and MA in 1861. He was awarded the Newdigate prize for his poem 'The Temple of Janus' in 1857 and was a fellow of his college from 1863 to 1866.

Worsley's health interfered with the pursuit of any profession, and he devoted himself chiefly to studies of the classics and poetry. His version of the *Odyssey* in Spenserian stanzas was published in 1861 and reissued in 1868 and 1877, and his translation of the first twelve books of the *Iliad* in the same metre appeared in 1865. His original poems, first published as *Poems and Translations* in 1863 and reprinted in 1875, demonstrate that his skill was interpretation rather than invention. His Spenserian translation of the *Odyssey* and the first half of the *Iliad* (it was later completed by John Conington), however, was a unique achievement. No version diverging so widely from the form of the original can become the standard version; Worsley's effort was nevertheless a useful test of the power and resources of the English language, and as such it was praised by Matthew Arnold.

On 8 May 1866 Worsley died, unmarried, at Freshwater, Isle of Wight, after a long illness which terminated in tuberculosis.

RICHARD GARNETT, *rev.* MEGAN A. STEPHAN

Sources S. Austin, *The Athenaeum* (19 May 1866), 670 · *GM*, 4th ser., 1 (1866), 925 · Foster, *Alum. Oxon.* · Allibone, *Dict.* · S. J. Kunitz and H. Haycraft, eds., *British authors of the nineteenth century* (1936), 672 · private information (1900) · *IGI*
Archives NL Scot., corresp. with Blackwoods and poems

Worsley, Sir Richard, seventh baronet (1751–1805), antiquary and politician, was born on 13 February 1751, the son of Sir Thomas Worsley, sixth baronet (1726–1768), of

Appuldurcombe, Isle of Wight, and his wife, Elizabeth (1731–1800), daughter of John Boyle, fifth earl of Cork and Orrery and Henrietta, his first wife. He was educated at Winchester College, spent nearly two years with his parents in Naples (1765–7), and matriculated at Corpus Christi College, Oxford, on 9 April 1768, succeeding his father in the baronetcy on 23 September. He did not take a degree but completed his education with a European tour in 1769–70; Gibbon's friend D'Eyverdun was his tutor. It gave him a lifelong scholarly interest in art and antiquities.

Worsley also had political ambitions. He entered the House of Commons for Newport, Isle of Wight, at the 1774 general election, a seat where he shared the electoral interest with the Holmes family and the government. Worsley was a reliable supporter of the North administration, anxious for office. He was appointed one of the clerks comptrollers of the board of green cloth in 1777, and was comptroller of the king's household 1779–82. He was sworn of the privy council on 9 February 1780, and was governor of the Isle of Wight 1780–82. These were compensation for his failure to win a seat at the Hampshire by-election of December 1779 which left him £6000 out of pocket. Worsley lost all his offices when the North administration fell in 1782.

Worsley's political career was badly damaged by the very public collapse of his marriage. On 20 September 1775 he had married Seymour Dorothy, the younger daughter and coheir of Sir John Fleming, first baronet (d. 1763), of Brompton Park, Middlesex, and his wife, Lady (Jane) Fleming (d. 1811), and had with her a son, Robert Edwin (who died young), and a daughter. Though the marriage brought Worsley over £70,000, the couple soon fell out. Lady Worsley's numerous affairs (twenty-seven lovers were rumoured) became notorious. On 22 February 1782 Worsley brought an action for criminal conversation with his wife against George M. Bissett, an officer in the Hampshire militia and a neighbour on the island. The jury found for the plaintiff but, on the ground of Worsley's connivance, awarded him only 1s. damages, not the £20,000 claimed. He subsequently entered into articles of separation with his wife in 1788.

Worsley gave up his seat at Newport in 1784 having already quitted England for the continent. In 1783–4 he was in Spain, Portugal, and France and, having wintered in Rome, he left the city in February 1785 for an extensive journey in the Levant, accompanied by Willey Reveley as his draughtsman. He reached Athens in May 1785, then travelled extensively in the Greek interior, going on to Rhodes, Cairo, and Constantinople. In 1786 he made an excursion to Sigeum and Troy, and also visited the Crimea. He returned to Rome in 1787, and went home during 1788. During his travels Worsley made a remarkable collection of statues, reliefs, and gems, which he arranged at his house at Appuldurcombe. It included the most important collection of Greek marbles yet seen in England. In 1798 he issued the first part (dated 1794) of the 'Museum Worsleianum', a sumptuous illustrated description of his collection. The cost of part one, exclusive of binding, was

a staggering £2,887 4s. Part two came out in 1802 and his *Catalogue Raisonné of the Principal Paintings at Appuldurcombe* was privately printed in 1804. It indicates a sensitive, informed man of taste, as much interested in the history and provenance of a work as in its aesthetic qualities. Failure in marriage had redoubled his ardour as a collector.

Worsley returned to the Commons in 1790 as MP for Newtown, Isle of Wight, and tried to secure another public office (as early as 1785 he had hoped for the post of British envoy to the Porte). Having vacated his seat for the young George Canning in June 1793, Worsley was made British envoy to the Venetian republic, arriving in February 1794. He bent his efforts to prevent the French minister from taking advantage of the republic's neutrality, while resuming his collection of *objets d'art*, buying at depressed wartime prices. Worsley returned home on the eve of Venice's extinction as an independent state in 1797 with a £600 annuity from the crown for his services. Resuming his seat for Newtown (where he had been re-elected in 1796 in his absence), he eventually left the Commons on Pitt's resignation in February 1801.

Worsley's last few years were spent 'in a state of seclusion' (*GM*, 781) mainly at Sea Cottage (later known as Marine Villa), near St Lawrence, in the Undercliff of the Isle of Wight, with a Mrs Sarah Smith, his mistress from *c.*1788 until his death. He had constructed this property in the early 1790s and later embellished the grounds with small classical temples and employed a French *viticulteur* in an unsuccessful attempt to plant a vineyard. Ill health prevented his taking part in the defence of the island against the threatened Napoleonic invasion, but he continued to collect paintings and sculpture. Dealers fuelled his acquisitive instincts and he could rarely resist the urge to buy. As a result the estate was encumbered with debts when he died of apoplexy at Appuldurcombe on 8 August 1805. He was buried in Godshill parish church. Worsley was succeeded in the baronetcy by his fourth cousin, Henry Worsley-Holmes, while Appuldurcombe passed to his niece, Henrietta Anna Maria Charlotte, daughter of the Hon. John Bridgeman Simpson, who in 1806 married the Hon. Charles Anderson-Pelham, later first earl of Yarborough. Worsley's widow, who regularly used the style of Lady Fleming after her separation, married John Lewis Cuchet (he subsequently used the name Fleming) on 12 September 1805 at Farnham, her £70,000 jointure having reverted to her on Worsley's death.

Worsley was one of the most important collectors of his generation, particularly after divorce had ruined his reputation. His political skills were modest, and his abrasive, somewhat self-important character also limited his influence. Antiquarian studies were always an important refuge. His father and grandfather had begun work on a *History of the Isle of Wight* and Worsley brought it to completion, albeit with unacknowledged contributions from the Newport attorney Richard Clarke. It was published in 1781 after four years' labour and was well received, Worsley having been elected both FSA and FRS in 1778 on its strength. He found it satisfying work, gathering materials patiently and searching the sources with some expertise.

Modern opinion considers it 'well researched, organized, and written, and handsomely produced' (Hicks, 166). Worsley's ancestral sensitivities combined well with his aesthetic ones to complete the building of his family seat at Appuldurcombe and effect other estate improvements, including the landscaping of the grounds by Capability Brown.   NIGEL ASTON

Sources *GM*, 1st ser., 75 (1805), 781, 874–5 · GEC, *Baronetage*, 1.67; 5.127 · E. B. James, 'The Worsleys of the Isle of Wight', *Letters archaeological and historical relating to the Isle of Wight* (1896), 1.481 · HoP, *Commons, 1754–90*, 3.659 · HoP, *Commons, 1790–1820*, 5.650–51 · *Memoirs of Sir Finical Whimsy and his lady* (1782) · Walpole, *Corr.*, 25.227–8, 245 · M. A. Hicks, 'Hampshire and the Isle of Wight', *English county histories: a guide*, ed. C. Currie and C. Lewis (1994), 165–75, esp. 166 · T. Barber, *Picturesque illustrations of the Isle of Wight* (1834) · V. Batsford, *Historic parks and gardens of the Isle of Wight* (1989) · L. Boynton, *Appuldurcombe House* (1986) · L. Boynton, 'The Marine Villa', *The Georgian villa*, ed. D. Arnold (1996), 118–29 · K. Pomian, *Collectors and curiosities* (1990) · *Archivists' Report* [Lincolnshire Archives Committee], 15 (1963–4), 15–20 · J. Ingamells, ed., *A dictionary of British and Irish travellers in Italy, 1701–1800* (1997), 1018–19 · private information (2004) [B. Ford]

Archives BL, family corresp. and papers, Add. MS 46501, fols. 71–120 · Isle of Wight RO, Newport, corresp. and papers, MS JER/WA/38/1, 2, 4 · Lincs. Arch., corresp. and papers, Worsley MSS 13–55 | BL, letters to Francis Drake, Add. MS 46825, fols. 64, 82 · BL, letters to Dr Farr, Add. MS 37060 · BL, letters to duke of Leeds, Add. MS 27915 · Bodl. Oxf., corresp. with John Charles Brooke · Lincs. Arch., corresp. and papers, Bradford MSS 1/1–1/11, 2/2/2–2/2/9, 2/4/1–2/4/54 · NL Scot., corresp. with Robert Liston · NMM, letters to Lord Minto

Likenesses J. Reynolds, portrait, *c*.1780 · G. Engleheart, miniature, 1800, V&A · A. Cardon, stipple, BM, NPG

Wealth at death wealthy, but estate encumbered with debts

Worsley, Thomas (1711–1778), architect and equestrian, was born, probably in London, on 15 July 1711, the eldest of nine children of Thomas Worsley (1686–1751) of Hovingham, Yorkshire, landowner and MP, and his first wife, Mary (*d.* 1728), daughter of Sir Thomas Frankland and his wife, Elizabeth. From an early age Worsley was passionate about women, architecture, and horses, specifically *haute école*. He was educated at Eton College (1725–8) and then at the Swiss Riding Academy in Geneva (*c*.1732–1735) before travelling extensively in Europe in 1735–7, 1738, and 1739–40. On his last trip he formed a liaison with Lady Walpole, estranged wife of Sir Robert Walpole, later second earl of Orford. When in Florence he also favoured Madame Suares, famed for her 'extreme beauty' (Walpole, 23.306). In 1748 he ran off with his stepsister's maid Elizabeth Lister (*c*.1728–1809), daughter of a poor clergyman and 'a mighty pretty girl' (Newby Hall MS 2833/90), with whom he had a daughter that year. They had eleven children but did not marry until 1757.

After succeeding his father in 1751, Worsley spent the rest of his life rebuilding Hovingham Hall to his own designs on the model of Andrea Palladio's interpretation of an ancient Roman town house. Handsome vaulted stables for his stud lay at the centre of the house (with state apartments above them); the house is, uniquely, approached through a riding-house. Apart from perhaps two other stables and a riding-house, Worsley is not

known to have designed any other executed buildings, although he advised his friends. His architectural drawings are of remarkably high quality for an amateur.

Worsley was an equerry-in-ordinary to George II from 1742 to 1760. In 1760 his old Eton schoolfriend the third earl of Bute (also a keen horseman and amateur architect) was appointed prime minister. Thanks to Bute, Worsley held the office of surveyor-general of the office of works from 1760 to 1778 and sat as MP for the Treasury seat of Orford from 1761 to 1768. From 1768 to 1774 he sat as MP for Callington, through the influence of his former lover Lady Orford. Worsley proved a conscientious head of the office of works but did not enjoy his time in the House of Commons; there is no record of his ever having spoken. As surveyor-general, Worsley was close to George III, another architectural and equestrian enthusiast, and may have provided the design for the riding-house when Buckingham House was rebuilt. As a reward the monarch gave him Giambologna's great sculptural group *Samson and the Philistine*, now in the Victoria and Albert Museum. In 1757 Worsley was left a substantial collection of paintings and the lease of a valuable estate at Islip in Oxfordshire by Edmund Charles Blomberg. This, together with his surveyor-general's salary, allowed him to build extensively, create a fine collection of books and virtu, and consolidate his estate, at the same time paying off his father's debts and leaving his accounts in surplus.

Worsley mixed a peculiar ability to engender deep friendship and love from a close circle of friends and certain members of his family with a talent for provoking irritation and anger in others: one sister described him as 'dark and secret' (Newby Hall MS 2827/22). He confessed that there were very few friends whom he preferred to his horses. He cannot have been easy to get on with: in his latter years he suffered severely from the stone, which made him petulant. He was also distressed by the early deaths of his children, seven of whom predeceased him. In 1774 he was devastated by the death of his eldest son, Thomas: 'The bribe to life is gone, health and my eldest son, who I saw all virtue and goodness' (BL, Add. MS 41135). His eldest surviving son, Edward, was declared a lunatic in 1815. Worsley died on 13 December 1778 at Hovingham Hall, according to Horace Walpole 'à la romaine: he had such dreadful internal complaints that he determined to starve himself and for the last four days tasted precisely nothing' (Walpole, 24.428). He was buried on 22 December 1778 at Hovingham, Yorkshire.   GILES WORSLEY

Sources G. Worsley, 'Thomas Worsley: an eighteenth century amateur architect', BA diss., U. Oxf., 1982 · H. M. Colvin and others, eds., *The history of the king's works*, 5 (1976) · Hovingham Hall, Yorkshire, Worsley MSS · Mount Stuart Trust, Isle of Bute, Bute MSS · HoP, *Commons* · Walpole, *Corr.*, 17.249, 286–7; 21.460; 24.428; 43.241, 276 · W. Yorks. AS, Leeds, Newby Hall papers · PRO, records of the office of works · BL, Add. MS 41135

Archives Hovingham Hall, Yorkshire · NRA, priv. coll., papers as surveyor-general | BL, corresp. with first earl of Liverpool, Add. MSS 38202–38204, 38304, 38469, 41135 · Mount Stuart, Rothesay, Bute MSS · N. Yorks. CRO · PRO, records of the office of works · RIBA, Chambers MSS · W. Yorks. AS, Leeds, Newby Hall MSS

Worsley, William (*c*.1435–1499), dean of St Paul's, was reputedly the son of Robert Worsley of Booths, in the parish of Eccles, Lancashire, and an unknown mother. A kinsman of the Booths of Barton in the same parish, he enjoyed the early patronage of William Booth (*d.* 1464), successively bishop of Lichfield and archbishop of York. Worsley first appears as a commoner at Winchester College in 1442. He doubtless owed his place there to William Booth, who already had influential connections at court, and who as bishop of Lichfield collated him to his first benefice, a canonry and prebend in Lichfield, in 1449. When Booth was translated to the see of York in 1452, Worsley continued to enjoy his patronage; he vacated his canonry at Lichfield, and instead acquired canonries and prebends at Southwell, Nottinghamshire, in March 1453, and at York itself in July 1457. In 1460, probably at the earliest possible age, that of twenty-four, he was ordained to the priesthood at York, and in August 1464 he witnessed Archbishop Booth's will at Southwell.

Throughout this time Worsley was pursuing an education. Following the Wykehamist path to Oxford for his first degree, he transferred to Cambridge by December 1459 to study canon and civil law, seemingly in the wake of Laurence Booth (*d.* 1480), his patron's youngest brother, who was chancellor of Cambridge in 1457–8. In 1462 Worsley obtained a dispensation from lecturing further for the degree of BCnL. By 1468 he had a doctorate in civil law, possibly from a foreign university. In that year he received papal dispensation to hold in plurality canonries and prebends in Southwell, York, and London, all of which he had obtained while under the lawful age, and also the rectory of Eakring, Nottinghamshire.

On 28 September 1476 Worsley became archdeacon of Nottingham, consolidating his position in the chapter at York. The promotion followed on Laurence Booth's election as archbishop of York in the same year, but should probably not be construed as nepotism. Indeed, Worsley appears to have been well regarded in ecclesiastical circles, for on 22 January 1479 he was elected dean by the chapter in London. He held this dignity until his death in 1499, and was remembered in the city as 'a famous doctor and preacher' (Fabyan, 685). Between February 1493 and December 1496 he was also archdeacon of Taunton in the diocese of Bath and Wells.

Worsley avoided involvement in the political crises of 1483 and 1485, but in 1494 he was among a group of notable churchmen and members of Henry VII's household, who included the steward Lord Fitzwalter and, later, the chamberlain Sir William Stanley, to be arrested on charges of treasonable correspondence with the Yorkist pretender Perkin Warbeck. The grounds for the charges against Worsley remain obscure. In November 1494 he was tried and attainted of high treason, but saved from execution (unlike Stanley) by his cloth. On 6 June in the following year, however, after paying a heavy fine, he was pardoned and reinstated 'in name and blood'. He made his will on 12 February 1499, and died on 14 August. He was buried in St Paul's Cathedral. MICHAEL J. BENNETT

Sources Emden, *Cam.* • Emden, *Oxf.* • 'Register of William Bothe, archbishop of York, 1452–64', Borth. Inst., Reg. 20 • register of Thomas Kempe, bishop of London, 1450–89, GL, MS 9531/7 • accounts of Dean Worsley's steward, 1479–97, GL, MS 25166 • *CEPR letters*, vols. 12–17 • *Chancery records* • [J. Raine], ed., *Testamenta Eboracensia*, 4, SurtS, 53 (1869), 155–7 • R. Fabyan, *The new chronicles of England and France*, ed. H. Ellis, new edn (1811) • *VCH Lancashire* • W. Dugdale, *The history of St Paul's Cathedral in London*, new edn, ed. H. Ellis (1818) • C. N. L. Brooke, 'The earliest times to 1485', *A history of St Paul's Cathedral and the men associated with it*, ed. W. R. Matthews and W. M. Atkins (1957) • I. Arthurson, *The Perkin Warbeck conspiracy, 1491–1499* (1994)
Likenesses effigy, St Paul's Cathedral, London
Wealth at death little wealth: Raine, ed., *Testamenta*

Worth, Adam [*alias* Henry J. Raymond] (*c*.1844–1902), criminal and art thief, was born in eastern Germany to Jewish parents, who emigrated to Cambridge, Massachusetts, when he was a young child. Worth, who had no formal education, enlisted in the Union army in 1861 at the outset of the American Civil War. His first recorded crime was that of 'bounty jumping', the practice of deserting from one regiment and then signing up with another to obtain whatever bounty was on offer, which he refined to new levels by faking his own death at the second battle of Bull Run before re-enlisting under an assumed name.

At the end of the war Worth settled in New York and began his criminal apprenticeship as a pickpocket. With the patronage of the notorious fence Fredericka 'Marm' Mandelbaum, he soon rose to prominence in the New York underworld, achieving distinction as a bank robber, forger, and gambler, and earning the nickname Little Adam, a sobriquet reflecting his small stature and large criminal pretensions. In November 1869, in partnership with 'Piano' Charley Bullard, a talented pianist and safebreaker, Worth tunnelled through the wall of the Boylston National Bank in Boston and extracted from the bank safe an estimated $200,000 in cash and securities. Pursued by the Pinkerton Detective Agency, the pair fled to England, where they met and formed an unlikely *ménage à trois* with Kitty Flynn (*c*.1850–1894), an attractive and ambitious Irish barmaid. Worth adopted the alias Henry J. Raymond, in ironic tribute to the highly respectable and recently deceased editor of the *New York Times*. After some years running an illegal gambling parlour in Paris, the trio settled in London, where Worth gradually built up an international criminal industry, of which he was the controller, banker, and principal beneficiary.

The detective William Pinkerton described Worth in a posthumous pamphlet (*Adam Worth, alias 'Little Adam'*, 1904) as 'the most inventive and daring criminal of modern times', but he also noted that, in contrast to the vast majority of Victorian villains, Little Adam deplored violence, eschewed alcohol (at least initially), and displayed extraordinary loyalty to his associates and minions. Worth's earnings from forgery, robbery, and fraud enabled him to live the life (and adopt the views and even the accent) of a wealthy English Victorian gentleman, with an apartment in Piccadilly, a substantial mansion in Clapham, a string of racehorses, and a steam yacht. Kitty Flynn had two children attributed to Bullard (whom she had married) but who were widely believed to have been fathered by Worth between about 1869 and 1876. After Kitty Flynn left both men to marry a Cuban sugar millionaire, Worth married Louise Bohljahn about 1886, with whom he had two more children.

Worth's most famous crime was carried out in 1876, when he broke into the Mayfair premises of Thomas Agnew & Sons, art dealers, and stole Thomas Gainsborough's portrait of Georgiana, duchess of Devonshire, which had been sold two weeks earlier for 10,100 guineas, then the highest price ever paid for a portrait at auction. He had initially intended to use the painting as ransom to extract an associate from Newgate prison. The plan came to nothing and instead, for romantic reasons that remain partly mysterious, he kept the portrait for the next twenty-four years, having designed a false-bottomed trunk in which to transport it. Worth himself described his relationship with the painting as an 'elopement'.

The criminal network established by Worth, who would eventually become Sir Arthur Conan Doyle's model for the evil Professor Moriarty in the Sherlock Holmes stories, continued to expand profitably until 1892, when he was arrested in the course of a rash attempt to rob a mail carriage in the Belgian city of Liège. Worth was exposed, ruined, and sentenced to seven years' hard labour in the Prison de Louvain. His wife, hitherto ignorant of his real character, was placed in a lunatic asylum soon after hearing of his fate. Scotland Yard had learned, through informers, that Worth was the thief of the Gainsborough painting (which had been hidden in a warehouse before his disastrous attempted robbery in Liège), but all efforts to persuade him to surrender the painting, even when offered his liberty in exchange, were flatly rejected.

Worth obtained early release for good behaviour, but emerged from prison in poor health and broken in spirit. He soon contacted Pinkerton, his erstwhile adversary, and declared that he intended to return 'the Lady', less out of contrition than through a desire to provide for his two children. Protracted negotiations followed, at the culmination of which art dealer Morland Agnew travelled to a Chicago hotel and was presented with the portrait by an elderly bellboy widely believed to have been Worth himself, in disguise. Within hours of the painting's return to Britain it was purchased by the American millionaire J. Pierpont Morgan. Worth, who was by then drinking heavily, followed the portrait back to Britain. On 8 January 1902, four days after Morgan took possession of the masterpiece, Worth died at his residence at 2 Park Village East, in Camden, London; he was buried two days later, under the alias Henry J. Raymond, in an unmarked grave in Highgate cemetery.   BEN MACINTYRE

Sources B. Macintyre, *The Napoleon of crime: the life and times of Adam Worth, the real Moriarty* (1997) • *Adam Worth, alias 'Little Adam': the theft and recovery of Gainsborough's 'Duchess of Devonshire'* (privately printed by Pinkerton's Detectives, 1904) • D. Horan, *The Pinkertons: the detective dynasty that made history* (1967) • S. Lyons, *Why crime does not pay* (1913) • B. P. Eldridge and W. B. Watts, *Our rival, the rascal* (1893) • T. Byrnes, *Professional criminals of America* (1895) • F. Morn, *The eye that never sleeps* (1982) • C. Kingston, *Remarkable rogues* (1921) • C. M. Stevens, *Famous crimes and criminals* (1907) • A. Cunningham, *Pictures in the collection of J. P. Morgan* (1929) • M. Estrow, *The art stealers* (1960) • B. Masters, *Georgiana, duchess of Devonshire* (1982) • Adam Worth, Bullard, Shinburn files, Pinkerton Detective Agency, Encino, California • duchess of Devonshire file, T. Agnew & Sons Archives, Bond Street, London • Georgiana, duchess of Devonshire file, Chatsworth House, Derbyshire • d. cert.

Archives Chatsworth House, Derbyshire, Georgiana, duchess of Devonshire file • Pinkerton Detective Agency, Encino, California, archive, Adam Worth, Bullard, Shinburn files • T. Agnews and Sons Archives, Bond Street, London, duchess of Devonshire file

Likenesses photograph, 1892, Pinkerton Detective Agency, Encino, California, archive

Worth, Charles Frederick (1825–1895), couturier, was born on 13 October 1825 at Wake House, North Street, Bourne, Lincolnshire, the youngest son of William Worth, solicitor, and his wife, Mary Anne Quincey. After the failure of his father's business in 1836, Worth was first apprenticed to a printer in Bourne, but after a year left for London to train as a shop assistant at Swan and Edgar, drapers of Regent Street. From 1845 his education continued at Lewis and Allenby, silk mercers of Regent Street, where having acquired the skills of bookkeeping, stock ordering, and customer service, Worth expanded his knowledge of continental textiles and fashion. On the completion of his apprenticeship he left London at the end of 1845 to find employment in Paris.

During 1846 Worth was engaged as a selling clerk with Gagelin-Opigez & Cie, one of the most developed of European fashion houses, specializing in shawls, embroidered fabrics, dressmaking supplies, and some ready-made articles. By the mid-1850s Worth progressed to designing dresses for the firm. A white silk court train embroidered in gold and already displaying the characteristic attention to luxurious appearance and innovative form that distinguished Worth's mature work, was exhibited at the 1855 Universal Exhibition, where it was awarded a first-class medal.

In 1851 Worth married Marie Augustine Vernet (1825–1898), a mannequin at Gagelin. By 1856 they had two sons, Gaston Lucien and Jean Phillipe, and compelled by a lack of recognition at Gagelin and the need to support a growing family, Worth set up a trading partnership with Otto Gustave Bobergh at 7 rue de la Paix in 1857. By 1869 Worth and Bobergh had established a prestigious client list including the Empress Eugénie of France, the queen of Sweden, and Pauline, Princess von Metternich. The firm's style was characterized by extravagant combinations of floating tulle and richly coloured taffetas and velvets that reflected both Worth's and Bobergh's interest in historical dress alongside an investment in technical virtuosity. Marie Worth played a central role in the business, acting as saleswoman and model and introducing many new customers. Worth recognized the importance of image in sustaining the élite identity of the company, ensuring that both the decoration of the firm's headquarters and his own personal bearing conformed to customer expectations of elegance, opulence, and artistic inspiration.

The Franco-Prussian War of 1870–71 marked a shift in the fortunes of the business. The rue de la Paix house was temporarily converted into a hospital and trading came to a halt during the siege of Paris. However, British and American clients provided alternative sources of revenue and Worth directed his attention towards encouraging a struggling French silk industry. Bobergh dissolved the partnership and returned to his native Sweden in the winter of 1870, but Worth re-opened in 1871 and increasingly drew his sons into the firm while retaining ultimate control over artistic direction. By the late 1880s, having survived the effects of war and succeeding economic depressions, Worth had established the features associated with the modern couture house. These included biannual presentations of seasonal collections, the display of new lines on living models, the branding of exclusive designs with the couturier's name, the franchising of toiles, paper patterns, and fashion plates, and the fostering of the myth of male 'style dictator'.

Worth's business enjoyed its most successful years during the 1890s, when its products reached an international market and corresponded directly with the tastes of rich plutocratic consumers. Offices were established in London and Biarritz and by the turn of the century yearly turnover was placed at about 5 million francs. Much of this success must be attributed to the personal drive and charisma of Worth himself, who combined astute presentation skills with a clear flair for the process of fashion design. His sons ensured that creative flamboyance was married to sound business sense.

Worth died of pneumonia at his château near Suresnes, just outside Paris, on 10 March 1895, and was buried there according to the rites of the Church of England.

CHRISTOPHER BREWARD

Sources D. de Marly, *Worth: father of haute couture* (1980) · E. Coleman, *The opulent era: fashions of Worth, Doucet and Pingat* (1989) · J. P. Worth, *A century of fashion* (1928)
Likenesses F. Nadar, photograph, 1892, Nadar Archive, Paris · Friand, oils, Worth Parfums, Paris

Worth, Edward (*c.*1620–1669), Church of Ireland bishop of Killaloe, was born in co. Cork of unknown parents and background. In 1638 he was elected to one of the scholarships reserved for natives of Ireland at Trinity College, Dublin. In 1645 he was appointed dean of Cork. As the protestants of the district divided between supporters of Charles I and of the Westminster parliament, Worth gravitated to the latter. Late in 1649, after Cromwell had landed in Ireland, he joined Broghill in negotiations which resulted in a section of the Munster protestants accepting the authority of the recently created English Commonwealth.

Worth seems to have remained in south Munster during the early 1650s, at Ringrone outside Kinsale, the living of which he had held formerly and perhaps still served unofficially. In November 1654 Lord Cork heard him preach publicly. Shortly afterwards Worth attested that Cork did not clandestinely use the proscribed Book of Common Prayer. He was also master of St Stephen's Hospital in Cork. He re-emerged in 1653 as a champion of doctrinal orthodoxy when he tried to refute, first by preaching and then in print, the ideas of the Baptists which had recently been introduced into Cork. A wish to check the spread of heterodox opinions (including those of the Quakers) drew Worth deeper into public activity. Under the government of Lord Deputy Fleetwood, religious novelties were tolerated and even promoted. However, the arrival of Henry Cromwell to replace Fleetwood in 1655 inaugurated a more conservative approach to religious questions: an approach congenial to Worth. Early in 1655 he had tried to hinder a petition circulating in co. Cork which requested that Fleetwood continue as Irish lord deputy. Within co. Cork he organized an association of ministers, modelled after that which Richard Baxter had created in England. The aim was to vet the learning and opinions of would-be ministers before they were ordained. By this device, it was hoped to impose better discipline on the church of the area and offer a model for the rest of Ireland.

Winning Henry Cromwell's approval, Worth grew in importance. Already in the spring of 1655 he had been inserted into panels which were to decide on the competence and orthodoxy of various aspirant ministers. In 1656 he first accepted a modest salary (£60 p.a.) from the state as one of its authorized preachers, at Kinsale. In 1656 he joined with other 'classical Presbyterian ministers' around Cork to establish a weekly lecture from which the sectaries were excluded. By December 1657 he had been added to the panel in Dublin which adjudicated the qualifications of all aspiring preachers in Ireland. In 1658 Worth travelled to England where he met others—notably at Oxford and Cambridge—who shared his aims of reviving a parochial and tithe-supported ministry. Above all, he and his followers insisted on the need for ordination, and planned, through the association, to oversee the process by guaranteeing minimum standards. Only then, it was argued, would the conversion of the Irish Catholics proceed apace.

Worth's influence reached its zenith while Henry Cromwell governed in Dublin. A convention of ministers, summoned to Dublin in 1658, attempted to hammer out a formula which would restore greater order to the fragmented protestant churches in Ireland. During the meeting, Worth preached at St Werburgh's Church in the shadow of Dublin Castle. His congregation included many of the governors of Ireland. No national agreement resulted from the gathering. Worth's schemes had been resisted by Samuel Winter, provost of Trinity College and leader of the religious Independents. Winter also advocated associations of the clergy, but with divergent emphases. After radicals replaced Cromwell in the summer of 1659, Worth lay low. However, he maintained contact with the like-minded in Scotland and England, such as Richard Baxter. Early in 1660, when a coup brought more conservative elements to the fore in Ireland, Worth went to London. There he enquired after suitable recruits to minister in Ireland. In addition, he may have positioned himself the better to secure his own and the Irish church's future in the impending restoration. Certainly he was among those consulted shortly after Charles II's return about how best to settle the church. Worth advocated, but fruitlessly, a version of the moderated episcopacy previously championed by Archbishop Ussher.

Worth returned to Ireland where, early in 1661, he was consecrated bishop of Killaloe. This appointment testified to Worth's pliancy, happy enough to return to the church in which he had originally been ordained. But it also told of the need of the Church of Ireland to attract some of those who had collaborated with the Cromwellians. The diocese of Killaloe was impoverished by the extensive lay impropriation of livings. Worth strove to recover some of its alienated wealth, but antagonized the powerful, such as the O'Briens, earls of Thomond, who held much church property. During the 1660s Worth acted as a conduit between the Irish episcopate and Archbishop Sheldon of Canterbury. He died unmarried on 2 August 1669 while in Hackney in Middlesex, and was buried that month at St Mildred's, Bread Street, London. Worth had inherited modest property. During his career he amassed more. He bequeathed money to maintain poor scholars at St Stephen's Hospital in Cork and at Trinity College, Dublin.

TOBY BARNARD

Sources *The whole works of Sir James Ware concerning Ireland*, ed. and trans. W. Harris, 1 (1739), 597 · *The Clarke papers*, ed. C. H. Firth, 3, CS, new ser., 61 (1899), 77–80 · BL, Lansdowne MS 823, fols. 79, 87, 91 · BL, Sloane MS 4274, fol. 176 · St J. D. Seymour, 'Family papers belonging to the Purcells of Loughmoe, co. Tipperary', *Journal of the North Munster Antiquarian Society*, 3 (1913), 203 · E. Worth to H. Cromwell, 6 June 1660, Cambs. AS, Huntingdon, 731 dd Bush/145 · E. Worth, letter to Lord Broghill, [n.d., 1655?], Harvard U., Houghton L., Orrery papers, MS 218 22F · E. Worth, *The servant doing and the Lord blessing: a sermon at the funeral of … Richard Pepys* [1659] · E. Worth, *Scripture evidence for the baptizing the infants of covenanters* [1653] · *The agreement and resolution of severall associated ministers in the county of Corke for the ordaining of ministers* (1657) · R. Scrope and T. Monkhouse, eds., *State papers collected by Edward, earl of Clarendon*, 3 vols. (1767–86), vol. 2, p. 501 · Worth's notebook on the revenues of the see of Killaloe, Representative Church Body Library, Dublin, MS D 14/1 · H. Cotton, *Fasti ecclesiae Hibernicae*, 5 vols. (1847–60), vol. 1, p. 195; vol. 4, p. 403 · R. Dunlop, *Ireland under the Commonwealth*, 2 vols. (1913) · Thurloe, *State papers*, 5.353 · M. Boyle, letter to G. Sheldon, [18 March 1664–18 March 1665], Bodl. Oxf., MS Add. C. 306 · St J. D. Seymour, *The puritans in Ireland, 1647–1661* (1912) · T. C. Barnard, *Cromwellian Ireland* (1975) · Burtchaell & Sadleir, *Alum. Dubl.*, 895

Archives Representative Church Body Library, Dublin, notebook, MS D 14/1 | BL, letters to H. Cromwell, Lansdowne MS 823

Worth, Richard Nicholls (1837–1896), journalist and antiquary, the eldest son of Richard Worth, a builder of Devonport, and his wife, Eliza (*b.* 1812), daughter of Richard Nicholls, was born on 19 July 1837 at Devonport. On 22 March 1860 he married Lydia Amelia, daughter of Richard Davies of the dockyard, Devonport, at Stoke Damerel. They had one son and one daughter.

Worth was apprenticed in 1851 at the *Devonport and Plymouth Telegraph*, and became a member of the staff in 1858. In 1863 he joined the *Western Morning News*, where he remained until 1865. In 1866 he moved to Newcastle upon Tyne to be editor of the *Northern Daily Express* but, finding the climate disagreeable, he rejoined the staff of the *Western Morning News* in 1867. In 1877 he joined the firm of Brendon & Son, printers and publishers, in Plymouth, receiving a testimonial of plate by public subscription in Devon

and Cornwall for his services as a journalist. He remained in the printing and publishing business until his death, though he continued to contribute occasionally, not only to the local press but also to *Nature*, *The Academy*, and other periodicals.

Worth devoted all his spare time to researching the history and geology of the west of England, and published about 140 papers between 1869 and his death, in the proceedings of local societies. Some of his scientific papers appeared in the *Quarterly Journal of the Geological Society* of London, of which society he became a fellow in 1875. He produced calendars of the records of Tavistock (1887) and Plymouth (1893), a bibliography of Plymouth, Devonport, and Stonehouse under the title *Three Towns bibliotheca* (1871) as well as *A History of the Town and Borough of Devonport* (1870), *A History of Plymouth* (1871; 2nd edn, 1873; 3rd edn, 1890), and *A History of Devonshire* (1886). He also wrote the text of Stanford's tourist guides for several counties. He was twice president of the Plymouth Association, and in 1891 of the Devonshire Association.

Worth died suddenly at Shaugh Prior, where he was temporarily resident, on 3 July 1896, and was buried in the village churchyard. His son Richard Hansford Worth (1868–1950) was educated at Plymouth high school and became a civil engineer. He was a founding member of the Marine Biological Association and his many painstaking studies of Dartmoor were collected and published as *Worth's Dartmoor* (1953; new edn, 1967).

T. G. BONNEY, *rev.* IAN MAXTED

Sources H. Hicks, *Quarterly Journal of the Geological Society*, 53 (1897), lxii · R. H. Worth, *Report and Transactions of the Devonshire Association*, 28 (1896), 52–7 · *Annual Report and Transactions of the Plymouth Institution and Devon and Cornwall Natural History Society*, 12 (1895–6), 215–18 · Boase & Courtney, *Bibl. Corn.*, 2.907 · G. C. Boase, *Collectanea Cornubiensia: a collection of biographical and topographical notes relating to the county of Cornwall* (1890) · private information (1900) · *Report and Transactions of the Devonshire Association*, 83 (1951), 17–21 [obit. of Richard Hansford Worth] · E. N. M. Phillips, 'Richard Hansford Worth: a personal tribute', *Dartmoor Magazine*, 5 (1986), 14 · *CGPLA Eng. & Wales* (1896)

Likenesses Lane, oils, 1873; known to be in family possession in 1900

Wealth at death £1847 1s. 6d.: probate, 26 Aug 1896, *CGPLA Eng. & Wales*

Worth, William (*bap.* 1677, *d.* 1742), Church of England clergyman and classical scholar, was born at Penryn, Cornwall, and baptized at St Gluvias, its parish church, on 20 February 1677. He was the second son of William Worth (1634/5–1690), merchant of Penryn and Jane, *née* Pennalerick. He matriculated from Queen's College, Oxford, on 14 March 1692, but moved to St Edmund Hall, where he graduated BA (17 October 1695) and MA (4 July 1698). In 1702, on the nomination of Archbishop Thomas Tenison, he was elected a fellow of All Souls, Oxford. Three years later he became the chaplain to the bishop of Worcester, and on 14 December of that year he was collated to the archdeaconry of Worcester. He proceeded BD in 1705 and DD in 1719. The £5 annual salary he received for this archdeaconry was greater than that of any preferment tenable with his fellowship at All Souls. On 7 January 1707 the warden of the college declared that the fellowship was vacant. Worth appealed to Thomas Tenison against the warden's action, but on 12 June 1707 renounced the appeal and lost his fellowship, though he retained the archdeaconry which he held for the rest of his life. Bishop William Fleetwood was led to publish his *Chronicon preciosum* on the occasion of this dispute.

On 17 February 1716 Worth was appointed to the third canonry at Worcester Cathedral. From 16 July 1707 he held the rectory of Halford in Warwickshire, until 9 April 1713 when he was collated to the rectory of Alvechurch, and on 11 July of that year to the rectory of Northfield, both in Worcestershire; he enjoyed both these benefices, with his canonry and archdeaconry, until his death.

In 1700 at Oxford, Worth edited *Tatiani oratio ad Graecos: Hermiae irrisio gentilium philosophorum*, with his own annotations and those of many previous scholars; according to Hearne 'most of the notes, with the dedication and preface, were written by Dr. Mill' (*Remarks*, 1.40). Worth's notes to the tract of Hermias were included in the edition by Johann Christoph Dommerich, which was printed at Halle in 1764. He greatly assisted Browne Willis in his account of Worcester Cathedral (in *A Survey of the Cathedrals*, 1740, vi), and extracts from his collections on Worcestershire are embodied in Treadwell Russell Nash's history of that county. Edward Dechair in his edition of the *Legatio pro Christianis* (1706) of Athenagoras was much indebted to Worth for various readings in manuscripts. A letter from Worth to John Potter, afterwards archbishop of Canterbury, on the death of the biblical scholar John Mill is printed in the *Gentleman's Magazine* (1801, 2.587) and in Henry John Todd's *Memoirs of the Life of Brian Walton* (1821, 1.79–81). Worth was married to a Miss Price and their only daughter, Mary, married on 3 March 1740 William Winsmore, mayor of Worcester. Worth died on 7 August 1742 and was buried in Worcester Cathedral on 11 August.

W. P. COURTNEY, *rev.* PHILIP CARTER

Sources *Remarks and collections of Thomas Hearne*, ed. C. E. Doble and others, 11 vols., OHS, 2, 7, 13, 34, 42–3, 48, 50, 65, 67, 72 (1885–1921), vol. 1, pp. 40, 43, 131, 167, 172–3, 270, 289, 307, 316; vol. 2, pp. 28, 65–6, 75; vol. 4, p. 430 • Foster, *Alum. Oxon.* • V. Green, *The history and antiquities of the city and suburbs of Worcester*, 2 vols. (1796) • Boase & Courtney, *Bibl. Corn.* • G. C. Boase, *Collectanea Cornubiensia: a collection of biographical and topographical notes relating to the county of Cornwall* (1890) • *Fasti Angl., 1541–1857*, [Ely] • PRO, PROB 11/722, fol. 320r–v [will] • *GM*, 1st ser., 10 (1740), 147 • IGI

Worthington family (*per.* 1849–1963), architects, came to prominence with **Thomas Worthington** (1826–1909), who was born on 11 April 1826 at Crescent Parade, Salford, Lancashire, the fourth of six sons of Thomas Worthington (1779–1842), a merchant of Manchester, and his second wife, Susanna (1792–1869), the daughter of Samuel Barton, a tallow chandler of Hackney. Thomas's twin sister died in infancy and a son of his father by a previous marriage died in 1827. The family were Unitarians and members of the historic Cross Street Chapel, Manchester. Thomas Worthington senior owned a warehouse in High Street, Manchester, then the spine of the city's cotton

trade. His death in 1842 left the family impoverished, but Susanna owned property and maintained the family in a smaller house in Cheetham Hill, Manchester. Thomas was educated at the Unitarian school of Dr John R. Beard in Higher Broughton, Salford. At the age of fourteen he was articled for seven years to Henry Bowman and began to 'grind at the drill and routine of an Architect's training' (T. Worthington, 'Memories', 10). The Gothic style championed by A. W. N. Pugin was then at its height, and Bowman, a scholarly architect, published two books of carefully measured and drawn architectural plates: *Specimens of Ecclesiastical Architecture* (1846) and, with J. S. Crowther, *Churches of the Middle Ages* (1853). Worthington joined Bowman in 'church hunting' and also assisted in the preparation of plates. In 1844 he won the Royal Society of Arts gold medal for a finely drawn design of a Gothic chancel, and two years later the silver medal essay prize of the Institute of Architects. He was introduced to William Tite, an architect practising on a national scale, who offered him 'a berth'. On completing his articles, Worthington joined Tite's office. For some months he worked from Carlisle on railway projects until a financial crash halted investment and his employment.

In February 1848 Worthington set out with a Mancunian friend, Henry Darbishire, on a tour of the continent with the aim of seeing Rome and the colourful architecture of northern Italy, then attracting popular attention. Sketching *en route* (Worthington was a talented watercolour painter), in mid-March they reached Rome, where, apart from a walking tour to Assisi and Perugia, they remained until late May. Worthington then continued alone to Naples and Paestum before returning north to the cities of Tuscany. He arrived home in October with a first-hand knowledge of Italian Gothic and Renaissance architecture which he had recorded in sketchbooks and to which he later referred when in practice. In his memoirs, written fifty years later, Worthington summarized the diary and notes kept during his tour.

Tite advised Worthington to establish his own practice in Manchester and, after gaining experience of quantity surveying, in 1849 he opened an office in King Street, a prime location in the city. He received commissions for houses in developing residential areas and submitted a design in the competition for a building to house the Great Exhibition of 1851. Though unsuccessful, his entry was noticed by the architectural commissioners and he was appointed secretary to the Manchester local committee for the exhibition; he declined a London appointment, astutely choosing to represent the interests of exhibitors from Lancashire and Yorkshire.

By 1850 the need to improve the living conditions of the poor was widely recognized. Through his Unitarian inheritance, Worthington actively participated in voluntary societies promoting reform. Foremost was the Manchester Statistical Society, national in the range of its inquiries and the first of its kind in the country. Worthington contributed to its investigations and published two papers in its annual transactions. Housing reform was most conspicuous among his social interests; his first Statistical

Society paper was on 'Homes for the poor' (*Transactions*, 1860–61), and in 1866, by invitation of Lord Shaftesbury, he lectured on housing to the Social Sciences Association, then meeting in Manchester. His appointment as architect to a charitable body two years later enabled him to realize his ideas. When abroad he had noticed the widespread use of urban tenements, and this and the improved health produced by model housing schemes in London led him to propose multi-storey blocks combining improved facilities with a more humane character. On a congested Salford site he built two four-storey blocks with adequately ventilated dwellings of varied size, each including a scullery, rubbish chute, and WC compartment. Although built economically, and a notable improvement on other contemporary models, Worthington's more generous example was not followed, but in other fields he proved more influential. As architect to a company founded to provide public laundries, baths, and swimming pools in needy areas of Manchester and Salford, between 1855 and 1860 he completed three projects, each meeting different functions and incorporating improvements progressively. These were typologically important and became influential through the technical press. Copies of drawings were purchased for use abroad.

Less innovative conceptually but of wider significance was Worthington's work on hospital design. From 1858 Florence Nightingale's *Notes on Hospitals* promoted a vigorous campaign to improve hospital design, mainly by introducing the pavilion principle, which reduced cross-infection by locating airy wards in isolated, cross-ventilated, widely spaced parallel blocks. In Manchester this principle was strongly supported by the Statistical Society, and when in 1862 the building of a new hospital was proposed for the Chorlton Union at Withington, Worthington was entrusted with the design. It contained 480 beds in five three-storey blocks and closely followed the new principles. In 1865 the design was published, and a letter of 23 July 1865 from Miss Nightingale comments that, if the estimated costs were achieved, the hospital would 'set up a model to the whole country' (Pass, 91). Worthington presented a paper on the project to the Statistical Society (*Transactions*, 1866–7), and as a pamphlet the design was circulated to all boards of guardians and to centres in Europe and the colonies. Miss Nightingale's forecast was fulfilled and Worthington's reputation was established.

Worthington's general practice expanded simultaneously with the social projects. In 1862 he was invited to prepare designs for a 'receptacle' in which to house and display a newly commissioned commemorative statue of Prince Albert. His design, a richly decorated Italian Gothic ciborium, received royal approval and preceded G. G. Scott's similar memorial designed for Kensington Gardens, London. Early in 1863 the newly created space was named Albert Square, and the memorial, placed at its centre, became the focal point of the emerging prime civic space of the city.

A pronounced Italian influence is evident in much of Worthington's architecture. In 1858 he made a second Italian tour concentrating on the Veneto, the inspiration of which is reflected in the handsome memorial hall (which commemorated the deposition of dissenting clergy in 1662), completed in 1866, also in Albert Square. Stylistically, Worthington was a versatile pluralist, equally at ease with the Renaissance palazzo mode as with Venetian Gothic. He also had a flair for English Gothic, which he used in his designs for a number of Unitarian chapels in the Manchester area. A fine, soaring example is Brookfield Unitarian Chapel, Gorton (1871). For his last major commission, Manchester College, Oxford, Worthington looked back to the Perpendicular style he had studied as a pupil. Uncharacteristically, it is ill-suited to its context, but in central Manchester he used the eclectic high Victorian Gothic vocabulary skilfully, and in his police and magistrates' courts in Minshull Street (1868–72) he produced a masterpiece of urban design.

On 10 April 1863 Worthington had married Elizabeth Ann Scott (1835–1870) of Stourbridge, Worcestershire, and he later built Fieldhead, a house where they lived at Crumpsall, a suburb of north Manchester. Four children, including Percy Scott Worthington [*see below*], were born there, and in 1869 the family moved to Broomfield, Alderley Edge, an attractive house that Worthington had designed in 1847. Elizabeth died shortly after the birth of their fifth child, a son. On 10 October 1873 Worthington married Edith Emma Swanwick (1847–1942), the 26-year-old daughter of a friend. The family increased by six more children, the youngest of whom was Hubert Worthington [*see below*].

Worthington served as president of the Manchester Society of Architects in 1875, as vice-president of the Royal Institute of British Architects (RIBA) from 1885 to 1889, and as president of the Royal Manchester Institution; in 1881–2 he led the negotiations for the transfer of its fine building and modest art collection to Manchester corporation with the proviso that the corporation would spend £2000 annually for twenty-five years on expanding the art collection. Manchester gained a distinguished art gallery, and the funding laid the foundation of the modern collection.

From 1895 Worthington largely withdrew from the practice and in 1906 his connection was formally dissolved. His interest in architecture remained undimmed and his son Hubert recalled that when he was an architectural student his father could hardly be stopped from taking a hand in his entries for student competitions. Just over 6 feet tall, he had 'a noble head and figure with his snowy white hair and beard and his fresh complexion' (J. H. Worthington, 8). Thomas Worthington died peacefully at Broomfield on 9 November 1909 and was buried in the graveyard of the Unitarian chapel at Dean Row, Wilmslow, where the family had worshipped.

Sir Percy Scott Worthington (1864–1939), architect, the eldest son of Thomas and Elizabeth Worthington, was born on 31 January 1864 at Green Bank, Bennett Road (then described as 'Polygon'), Crumpsall. In 1878 he went to Clifton College, Bristol, where he proved himself to be a good sportsman and scholar. He entered Corpus Christi College, Oxford, in 1883 to read classics, and graduated in 1887. Following architectural studies under his father, he spent a period in the office of John McVicar Anderson in London; he also attended the Royal Academy Schools and University College, London, where he was awarded the Donaldson medal. A sketching tour through the Balkans to Athens and Istanbul followed. Writing on the construction of five famous domes, in 1889 he won the silver medal essay prize of the Royal Institute of British Architects, and in 1890 he qualified as an architect by examination. In 1880 Thomas Worthington had made his chief assistant John Elgood a partner in his firm, which was then styled Worthington and Elgood. In 1891 Percy Worthington became a partner, and following Elgood's death in 1893 the firm became Thomas Worthington & Son. On 3 July 1895 at the Presbyterian meeting-house, Hale, Altrincham, Cheshire, Percy Worthington married Lucy Juliet (1866–1956), the daughter of Charles Henry Wolff. They lived modestly, first in a converted cottage at Styal, Wilmslow, and from 1922 at Gorsey Brow, Mobberley, a house he designed. They had one son, Thomas Shirley Scott Worthington (1900–1981), who became a partner in the practice in 1945, and a daughter.

Percy Worthington shared the interest of his generation in vernacular buildings and the revival of arts and crafts. Good examples of the latter include the richly detailed Ullet Road Unitarian Church, Sefton Park, Liverpool (1896–1902), and the first phase of Ashburne Hall, Fallowfield, Manchester (1909–31), a women's hall of residence. From about 1904 Worthington turned to the current revival of classicism, using its vocabulary with assured inventiveness, as is illustrated in Manchester by the Union Bank, London Road (1910–11), and the office of Liverpool and London Globe Insurance, Albert Square (1915–19), and by many neo-Georgian houses in Cheshire, among which the remodelled Kerfield House, Ollerton (1912), is notable. On some of his major commissions, such as the faculty of arts building, Manchester University (1911–19), and the masonic temple, Bridge Street, Manchester (1923–9), which despite its extremely compact form is surprisingly spacious and grand internally, he embraced full neo-classicism using giant orders and highly formal planning, quietly integrating and exploiting the new technology of steel and reinforced concrete with apparent ease. These two commissions were the principal works cited when Worthington received the RIBA gold medal in 1930. Towards the end of his career he worked in a quieter form of classicism, best seen in Manchester grammar school (1928–31), produced in collaboration with Francis Jones (1864–1975).

In a professional life of almost fifty years Worthington was responsible for more than a hundred projects—domestic, educational, ecclesiastical, and medical—and won many of his major commissions in competition. He maintained a consistently high standard of design and craftsmanship, and his work on hospitals was described by his obituarist and confrère W. G. Newton as pioneering.

From 1919 his half-brother Hubert was active in the practice, but it appears that generally each was responsible for his own projects.

In 1919 Manchester University conferred the degree of doctor of letters upon Worthington and in 1935 he was knighted. Like his father, he had given generous support to many of Manchester's institutions, and in 1903–4 he had been instrumental in the creation of a school of architecture in the university. He served on the Royal Fine Arts Commission and was vice-president of the RIBA. Percy Worthington died at his home on 15 July 1939 and was cremated three days later. There is a memorial to him in Mobberley churchyard. He was described by Newton as modest, unhurried, meditative, and possessed of 'a critical judgement, perhaps over-acute, and at all times an obstinacy not to be satisfied with anything less than the best, as he saw it' (DNB).

Sir (John) Hubert Worthington (1886–1963), architect, the youngest son of Thomas Worthington and his second wife, Edith, was born on 4 July 1886 at Chorley, Alderley Edge, Cheshire. He was educated at Sedbergh School (1900–05) and then at the school of architecture, Manchester University. During this period he visited Rome and returned full of enthusiasm for the Italian Renaissance, especially the work of Peruzzi. He was also inspired by the work and personality of Edward Lutyens and, after being articled to his half-brother Percy, from 1912 he spent two years in Lutyens's office. During the First World War, when a captain in the Manchester regiment, Worthington was severely wounded on 1 July 1916 in the offensive on the Somme, but he survived overnight in a shell hole and was rescued the following day. His subsequent army duties were educational, but the Manchester regiment remained a part of his life. He was mentioned in dispatches.

Worthington returned to architectural practice in 1919, when he joined Percy in the family firm. Twenty-two years his senior, Percy Worthington was then engaged on his major works. Hubert proposed opening a London office and was keen to extend the firm's patronage, but his early commissions were small and in the north. In 1923 he was appointed professor at the Royal College of Art, London, a post he held for five years. In addition to his enthusiasm for the Italian Renaissance and the work of Lutyens, he had as his architectural bible Geoffrey Scott's The Architecture of Humanism (1914). Early commissions included the war memorial cloister at Sedbergh (1922–4) and the dining-hall and staff wing at Rossall School (1926–8), both Renaissance-inspired designs. The arcaded cloister at Sedbergh is cut into a hillside and supports a terrace facing the grandeur of a Pennine landscape. In contrast, the building at Rossall is enclosed. The large, expressive dining-hall and flanking clock tower are reminiscent of an Italian basilica and campanile. The studied quiet of Sedbergh and the exuberance of Rossall are equally characteristic of Worthington's personality. Simultaneously he carried out many smaller schemes in the Greater Manchester area; particularly notable are his gateway and lodge to Ashburne Hall (c.1926), where the handsome set of gates, a *tour de force* of wrought ironwork, provides a fine flourish to the setting.

In 1929 Worthington was appointed Slade lecturer in architecture at Oxford University, and four years later he designed a new wing to the university's Radcliffe Science Library (1933–4), the first of many commissions he executed for the university and its colleges. Most were for new buildings, such as the forestry and botany building, but he also carried out internal restoration and refurbishment of the Radcliffe Camera in 1939 and the Bodleian Library in 1955. As a designer Worthington aimed to create a personal style based largely on traditional building. Probably Lutyens was the role model, but Sir Herbert Baker's Rhodes House in Oxford provided a precedent in the modern use of squared limestone rubble in small blocks with ashlar dressings. Worthington adapted this mode for almost all his Oxford commissions and combined it with idiosyncratically detailed door casings and window heads. His buildings have weathered handsomely, but the mannerisms have detracted from his reputation. His library interiors are notably successful, the most distinctive being that at New College (1939). Notable exceptions to the usual pattern of his Oxford designs are the neo-Georgian Lincoln House in Turl Street (1939) and the dolphin gate to Trinity College (1947–8) on St Giles'.

On 20 October 1928 Worthington married, at Holy Trinity Church, Sloane Street, Chelsea, (Sophie) Joan (b. 1905), the daughter of Sidney Marshall Banham, a physician; they had three children. Following Percy Worthington's death in 1939 Hubert became the principal of the firm, and in 1941 he was joined in the practice by his wife. Though unqualified professionally, she had studied architecture at the Royal College of Art during his professorship. A gifted draughtswoman, one of her roles was to prepare exhibition drawings. The Second World War reduced the range of the practice but brought industrial work and the care of damaged historic buildings, and in 1943 Worthington was appointed by the Imperial War Graves Commission as principal architect for Egypt and north Africa. The work, which lasted until the 1950s, included the selection of sites and the design and supervision of the various cemeteries and memorials to the missing, among them one at Valletta, Malta, to missing airmen. Economy favoured large cemeteries, but Worthington insisted that sites should be located close to the battlefields and given their familiar names. They extend from Alexandria to Tunisia. Worthington adopted simple means of expression with low buildings, occasionally shallow-domed, screen walls, and pergolas. The largest cemetery is at El Alamein, where there are more than 7000 graves. The architectural design relies on stark, simple geometry. One of the most attractive cemeteries is Knightsbridge, close to the Egyptian border, where the sloping site is terraced and the headstones follow the stepped formation.

Worthington's major rebuilding commission was the inns of court, London, where the intricate and historic area occupied by the Middle and Inner temples had been so heavily devastated that not only repair but reconstruction was required. This work was shared with Sir Edward Maufe and T. W. Sutcliffe. Some of the repairs and remodellings are historic reconstructions, but the larger replacements reflect the styles of their respective designers. Their outstanding achievement was the retention and re-creation of an intimate historic environment. More personal to Worthington was his work at Manchester Cathedral, where he succeeded Percy as architect in 1938. He was called out early on 23 December 1940 after a heavy air raid. The north-east corner had been demolished and the blast had left the famous choir stalls of c.1510 precariously balanced against each other across the chancel. Worthington immediately organized a team of skilled craftsmen to secure the stalls and collect the oak fragments, relating them where possible to individual stalls. In their repaired state the war damage is almost indiscernible. The repair of the general fabric was not completed until 1955, and Worthington and his wife visited the site daily when in Manchester.

Worthington served as vice-president of the RIBA in 1943–5 and was a member of the Royal Fine Arts Commission from 1945 to 1950. He received a knighthood in 1949, but the honour he prized above all was his membership of the Royal Academy, where he was elected an associate in 1945 and an Academician in 1955. In his later years he was regarded as representative of the pre-war establishment with outmoded architectural ideas, but in practice he showed a flexible awareness of contemporary design. It is evident in the development plan he prepared in 1951 for Manchester College of Science and Technology which was adopted and has been largely realized.

Tall and broad, with a colourful personality, Worthington was a conspicuous figure. He was open, direct, businesslike, quick to respond but unpretentious. The family home at Alderley Edge was modest, architecturally informal, comfortable, and quietly reflective of a lifelong interest in the arts. Worthington died at Manchester Royal Infirmary on 26 July 1963 and was cremated. He is commemorated in the chapel of the Manchester regiment in Manchester Cathedral, where the east window was donated by his friends from the regiment, and a plaque records his devoted service to the cathedral.

JOHN H. G. ARCHER

Sources personal knowledge (2004) · private information (2004) · T. Worthington, 'Memories', c.1897–1898, priv. coll. · J. H. Worthington, 'Notes on father', 1963, priv. coll. · T. Worthington, 'Some further remarks on the homes of the poor, and the means of improving their condition', *Transactions of the Manchester Statistical Society* (1860–61), 92–114 · T. Worthington, 'Some account of the pavilion hospital recently erected at the Chorlton Union Workhouse, Withington, near Manchester', *Transactions of the Manchester Statistical Society* (1866–7), 17–32 · A. J. Pass, *Thomas Worthington: Victorian architecture and social purpose* (1988) · J. Taylor, *The architect and the pavilion hospital: dialogue and design creativity in England, 1850–1914* (1997) · T. S. Ashton, *Economic and social investigation in Manchester, 1833–1933* (1934); 2nd edn (1977) · *Transactions of the Manchester Statistical Society* (1858–63) · P. Longworth, *The unending vigil: a history of the Commonwealth War Graves Commission, 1917–1984*, 2nd edn (1985), 178–211 · 'The royal gold medal, presentation to Mr Percy Scott Worthington', *RIBA Journal*, 37 (1929–30), 359–68 · P. Ogden, 'Thomas Worthington', *RIBA Journal*, 17 (1909–10), 223–4 · W. G. Newton, 'Percy Scott Worthington', *RIBA Journal*, 46 (1938–9), 950–52 · E. Maufe, 'John Hubert Worthington', *RIBA Journal*, 70 (1963),

223–4 · d. cert. [Thomas Worthington] · *CGPLA Eng. & Wales* (1910) · b. cert. [Percy Scott Worthington] · m. cert. [Percy Scott Worthington] · d. cert. [Percy Scott Worthington] · *CGPLA Eng. & Wales* (1939) · b. cert. [John Hubert Worthington] · m. cert. [John Hubert Worthington] · d. cert. [John Hubert Worthington]

Archives Commonwealth War Graves Commission, Maidenhead, report of a tour of North Africa made for Imperial War Graves Commission [John Hubert Worthington] · Commonwealth War Graves Commission, Maidenhead, personnel file [John Hubert Worthington] · JRL, corresp., professional and family papers [John Hubert Worthington]

Likenesses W. Dring, pastel drawing, *c.*1960 (John Hubert Worthington) · photograph (Percy Scott Worthington), repro. in 'The royal gold medal', *RIBA Journal* · photograph (John Hubert Worthington), repro. in Maufe, 'John Hubert Worthington' · photographs (Thomas Worthington), repro. in Pass, *Thomas Worthington*

Wealth at death Thomas Worthington: probate, no value given, 1910 · £45,013 8*s.* 3*d.*—Percy Scott Worthington: probate, 1 Sept 1939, *CGPLA Eng. & Wales*

Worthington, Sir (John) Hubert (1886–1963). *See under* Worthington family (*per.* 1849–1963).

Worthington, Hugh (1752–1813), dissenting minister, was born at Leicester on 21 June 1752, the second of four sons of Hugh Worthington (1712–1797), dissenting minister, and his wife, Gratia, daughter of Benjamin Andrews Atkinson (*d.* 1765), Presbyterian minister in London. The elder Hugh Worthington was born near Stockport on 11 June 1712, the son of John Worthington (*d.* 1757), a tanner. Having graduated MA from the University of Glasgow in 1735, he ministered at Leek, Staffordshire (1735–8), at Newington Green (1738–41, when he was also librarian of Dr Williams's Library), and at Great Meeting, Leicester, from 1743 until his death on 29 October 1797.

Having been educated by his father, the younger Hugh studied at Daventry Academy under Caleb Ashworth from 1768 to 1773. Visiting London at Christmas 1773 he made such an impression while preaching at the old Presbyterian congregation at Salters' Hall that he was invited to become assistant to the minister, Francis Spilsbury the younger. He thereupon resigned the post of classical tutor at Daventry, which had been offered him on completion of his course, and began as afternoon preacher at Salters' Hall on 1 January 1774; having succeeded to the pastorate on Spilsbury's death he was ordained on 15 May 1782. In 1785 he was elected a trustee of Dr Williams's foundations and the next year he was one of a committee of nine to establish a new college in London, soon settled at Hackney, where he lectured on classics and logic until his resignation in 1789. On 25 July 1782 he married Susanna (*d.* 1806), eldest daughter of Samuel Statham (1685–1779), minister at Loughborough; two daughters died in infancy.

Within the religious variety of the mid-eighteenth century the rational dissenters, as they came to call themselves by the early nineteenth century, formed a continuum, with scant regard for denominational boundaries, that ran from their Anglican allies (the latitudinarians) to those who, with Joseph Priestley, insisted on the simple humanity of Christ and who often maintained the Priestleyan doctrine of philosophical necessity. Worthington's position lay in the middle—anti-

Trinitarian and anti-Calvinist but holding to the Arian belief that Christ, though divine, was a creature of God the Father and subordinate to him. In 1789, with other like-minded ministers, Worthington projected a conference to stem the rapid progress of Unitarianism (or Socinianism, as its enemies usually referred to it), but the inability of the conferees to agree on the question of inspiration led to its awkward collapse.

Some historians, perhaps too impressed by Victorian and evangelical pulpit styles, have readily accounted for a perceived decline in eighteenth-century dissent by invoking the 'Arian blight', a charge not easily maintained against Worthington. His preaching was distinctly idiosyncratic. His voice was 'hard and dry, pungent and caustic' ('The late Mr Worthington's sermons', 29); his sermons (as with most of his fellow preachers, on moral rather than theological topics) were scarcely correctly composed, by contemporary standards, and were read until an extempore peroration. But he commanded attention by his 'upright posture, his piercing eye, his bold and decisive tone, his pointed finger, the interest he gave to what he delivered', despite (so this Unitarian critic recalled) 'the entire nothingness of what he often said' ('Observations on preaching', 91). His powerful prayers, recalled an obituarist, and 'those short extemporaneous effusions in which … he poured forth the fulness of his spirit … penetrated to the very hearts of his hearers' (*Monthly Repository*, Aug 1813, 546), making him to the end of his life an inspiration to younger and often theologically more radical ministers. A list of his publications appears in the memoir in the *Christian Moderator* for 1 October 1826.

Worthington had long suffered from pulmonary weakness and asthma, and in the summer of 1813 he retreated to Worthing in the hope of recovery but he died there, of a haemorrhage in the lungs, on 26 July. His funeral service at Salters' Hall was conducted by Thomas Taylor, minister of the Presbyterian congregation in Little Carter Lane and one of the last surviving pupils of Philip Doddridge. His burial was in the cemetery at Bunhill Fields on 6 August.

ALEXANDER GORDON, *rev.* R. K. WEBB

Sources [J. Joyce], 'Memoir of the late Rev. Hugh Worthington', *Monthly Repository*, 8 (1813), 563–75 · *Monthly Repository*, 8 (1813), 545–50 · V. R. X. [J. Kitcat], 'Memoir of the late Rev. Hugh Worthington', *Christian Moderator*, 6 (1 Oct 1826), 184–90 · 'Observations on preaching, preachers, and academical institutions', *Monthly Repository*, 12 (1817), 90–91, esp. 91 · 'The late Mr Worthington's sermons', *Christian Reformer, or, New Evangelical Miscellany*, 9 (1823), 28–32 · 'Autumnal' [H. Worthington the younger], 'Memoirs of the late Rev. Hugh Worthington [the elder]', *Protestant Dissenter's Magazine*, 3 (1797), 401–8 · C. Surman, index, DWL · A. H. Thomas, *A history of Great Meeting, Leicester* (1908) · *GM*, 1st ser., 52 (1782), 357

Archives DWL, student essays | DWL, letters to Mrs Hayes and Miss Hayes

Likenesses Harding, line engraving (after W. Read), BM

Worthington, John (*bap.* 1618, *d.* 1671), Church of England clergyman, translator, and editor of philosophical works, was baptized at Manchester collegiate church on 8 February 1618, one of at least five children of the draper Roger Worthington (*d.* 1649) and his wife, Katherine Heywood (*d.*

1651). Educated at Manchester grammar school, he was admitted as a sizar at Emmanuel College, Cambridge, on 31 March 1632, studying under Benjamin *Whichcote and Richard Clarke successively. He graduated BA in 1635 and proceeded MA in 1639, later proceeding BD (1646) and DD (1655). As a student, he was particularly noted for his proficiency in Latin, Greek, and Hebrew. He was appointed lecturer for a year in 1641, made a fellow at Emmanuel on 4 April 1642, and ordained in June 1646. The following October he was made a university preacher. On 14 November 1650 he became master of Jesus College, an office he occupied alongside those of rector at Horton, Buckinghamshire (April 1653–May 1654), and Fen Ditton, Cambridgeshire (from November 1654).

Worthington married his erstwhile tutor's niece, the seventeen-year-old Mary Whichcote (1640–1667), on 13 October 1657. They had five children: Mary, who died at the age of just under three months in January 1659, Damaris (b. 1661), John (1663–1737), Anne (b. 1665), and a second Mary (1667–1674). Three weeks after his marriage, and still not yet forty, Worthington was elected vice-chancellor of Cambridge, but found this a 'burdensome office' of which he was glad to be relieved when John Bond was elected in his place the following November (Diary and Correspondence, 1.118).

While a student, Worthington established lasting friendships with the Cambridge Platonists Henry More and Ralph Cudworth, and by 1653 at least was corresponding regularly with the Anglo-German intelligencer Samuel Hartlib. His correspondence with these figures, especially that with Hartlib, supplies perhaps his best claim to be remembered. Besides much information about scholarly activities and publications at Cambridge, it features informed and often entertaining comment on everything from the prospects for the conversion of the Jews to the possibility of good angels having beards. Worthington also acted as a sensitive and impartial mediator in a brewing row between More and Cudworth in early 1665, when the latter took it into his head that his hitherto faithful friend More was trying to upstage him by publishing his *Enchiridion ethicum* (1667) just as Cudworth was himself planning a *Natural Ethics* (which he never in fact published).

In 1660, at the Restoration, Worthington was removed from his mastership to permit the reinstatement of Richard Sterne, Archbishop Laud's erstwhile chaplain, who had been ejected from the post in 1644 for his zealous royalism. Worthington yielded his office with singularly good grace, ordering a banquet and concert in honour of his replacement, before retiring to Fen Ditton on 3 November 1660 to devote himself to his pastoral duties and to 'books, and the service of ingenuous scholars wherein I am capable' (Diary and Correspondence, 2/1.117). Sterne had already been earmarked for the bishopric of Carlisle, which he took up the following month, and Worthington had hopes of regaining the post, but the appointment went instead to John Pearson. Worthington was tutor to his wife's cousin Paul Whichcote, who came to live with the family, for just over a year before Whichcote entered Cambridge

at Easter 1662. In July that year Worthington began on his edition of the works of the eschatologist Joseph Mede, making frequent 'tedious and lonesome journeys' to London to consult material for it (ibid., 2/1.134): during these visits he lodged at Gresham College in the rooms of the former physic professor Jonathan Goddard.

In August 1662 Worthington subscribed to the Act of Uniformity. On 27 May following he transferred to the living of Barking and Needham in Suffolk (on the ejection of John Fairfax, who had refused to subscribe but was as gracious to Worthington as he had been to Sterne). From this date he also held the sinecure of Moulton All Saints in Norfolk. Lack of access to libraries and fellow scholars was a great sorrow to him in Barking, and he resigned the living on 8 May 1665 for that of St Benet Fink in London. He insisted on remaining in London and attending his parishioners after plague broke out that year, but when in September 1666 the great fire destroyed almost the entire parish, including Worthington's house and church, he accepted the invitation of William Brereton to be preacher at Holmes Chapel, Cheshire. While there, he arranged the papers of their late mutual friend Hartlib, which Brereton had bought, into the somewhat *ad hoc* series of bundles in which they were eventually rediscovered in 1933. Brereton had apparently held out hopes of an adequate living and involvement in a 'design of Christian societies' such as Hartlib had so eagerly promoted (Diary and Correspondence, 2/1.228). Worthington almost immediately realized, however, that Brereton was in no financial position to fulfil either promise, and the same December he accepted the living of Ingoldsby, Lincolnshire, which Henry More had procured for him. It was not until the following April, however, that he finished moving his family and goods from Cheshire. To the Ingoldsby rectorship was added, two years later, the prebend of Asgarby.

Ingoldsby proved no more congenial than had Barking or Holmes Chapel, and Worthington continued to complain of his isolation from scholars and books and the unhealthy atmosphere of his new home, and to cast around for employment somewhere better suited to his temperament and constitution. On 8 August 1667 Mary Worthington died, six days after and presumably as a result of the birth of their fifth child. As is touchingly apparent in the letters to, from, and about her, the marriage had been an exceptionally happy one, and Worthington never reconciled himself to this loss.

On 6 August 1669 Worthington's pleas for a more suitable post were finally rewarded with that of 'lecturer' (that is, assistant preacher) at the parish church of Hackney in Middlesex, where he and his remaining family then moved. Archbishop Gilbert Sheldon also promised him a return to the rectorship of the rebuilt St Benet Fink, but Worthington died before this plan could be realized.

Worthington's diligent and self-effacing nature suited him admirably to the tasks of translator and editor. He revised the translation of Thomas à Kempis's *De imitatione Christi*, his version appearing in 1654 as *The Christian's Pattern*. He was also editor of the *Select Discourses* (1660) of the

Cambridge Platonist John Smith (another pupil of Whichcote), and of the complete works of Joseph Mede (dated 1664, that is, early 1665: Worthington also oversaw the second edition of 1672, though he did not live to see it published). The latter, a monumental task, was undoubtedly the scholarly achievement of which he was proudest. No commentary on the book of Revelation since Mede's *Clavis Apocalyptica* (1627), he considered, 'hath brought forth to the world what hath been much observable, but what has been lighted at his flame' (*Diary and Correspondence*, 2/1.69). No works of his own composition, apart from the prefaces to these editions, were published during his lifetime, though a number appeared after his death, drawn from manuscripts left to his son. Most are collations of his sermons and none begins to attempt the intellectual rigour and complexity of the works he edited. Directed to an unlearned public (though he could not resist throwing in the odd Greek quotation), they are homely and decidedly repetitious attacks on sectarianism and dogmatism. Irrelevant doctrinal quibbles, he repeatedly insists, merely provide a smokescreen behind which Satan can bring in far more pernicious errors. Their spirit (and most of their content) is well summarized in one line of a letter to Hartlib:

> If the Christian religion were but once freed from all those unworthy dogmata which have clogg'd and encumber'd it, then would the beauty, healthfulness, and vigour of it be discover'd; and it would be fitted for better entertainment in the world, and a quicker passage through the nations of the earth. (*Diary and Correspondence*, 1.242)

Worthington was no philosopher and would not have dreamed of describing himself as one. His correspondence with More and Cudworth does not engage in any detail with their ideas. His contribution to the Cambridge Platonist movement lay rather in his editorial labours on Smith and Mede, and his consistent support for and encouragement of his friends' work. His son later described him as an Arminian, but he himself would surely have objected to being placed in any doctrinal pigeonhole narrower than that of protestantism. Privately as well as publicly, he refused to be drawn on contentious issues. Even Hartlib—himself no dogmatist—chided him gently for considering it no more than 'probable' that the pope was Antichrist (*Diary and Correspondence*, 1.81). His favourite recreation was music, and he was an accomplished singer and viol player.

Worthington died at Hackney on 26 November 1671, of 'a sort of Pleurisy' according to a rather vague contemporary account (*Diary and Correspondence*, 2/2.380), leaving an estate worth some £3000 to be held in trust for his four surviving children. He was buried four days later in the chancel of Hackney parish church. JOHN T. YOUNG

Sources The diary and correspondence of Dr John Worthington, ed. J. Crossley and R. C. Christie, 2 vols. in 3, Chetham Society, 13, 36, 114 (1847–86) · R. C. Christie, A bibliography of the works written and edited by Dr John Worthington, Chetham Society, new ser., 13 (1888) · The Hartlib papers, ed. J. Crawford and others, 2nd edn (2002) [CD-ROM] · A. Gray and F. Brittain, A history of Jesus College, Cambridge, rev. 2nd edn (1960), 85–9 · J. Ward, The lives of the professors of Gresham College (1740), 271 · Venn, Alum. Cant.

Archives BL, corresp., Add. MSS 4634, 4476, 4223, 6194, 6271, 6299, 32498 · CUL, corresp. and papers
Wealth at death approx. £3000; incl. value of land and goods: will, 15 Sept 1670, proved 23 Sept 1671; *Diary and correspondence*, ed. Crossley and Christie, 2.2, 367–71

Worthington, Sir Percy Scott (1864–1939). *See under* Worthington family (*per.* 1849–1963).

Worthington, Thomas (*c.*1548–1626), Roman Catholic priest and biblical scholar, was born at Blainscough Hall, near Wigan, Lancashire, son of Richard Worthington and Dorothy Charnock, of Charnock, Lancashire. Privately educated, he attended Brasenose College, Oxford, between about 1566 and 1570 and received a BA degree. He entered the English College, Douai, on 15 February 1573, when Gregory Martin was dean and professor of scripture, and later became one of his assistants in translating the Vulgate Bible. In 1577, after his BTh graduation at Douai University and ordination at Cambrai, he lectured in theology at the college.

In 1579 Worthington returned to England for ministry and managed to escape capture for four years until Richard Topcliffe arrested him at Islington and put him in close confinement in the Tower of London. He was not indicted. Instead, in a royal warrant of 15 January 1585 he was listed among twenty priests sentenced to be banished to France, and he reached Rheims in the spring. During his absence Gregory Martin had completed his English version of the Bible, and a New Testament appeared with annotations by Richard Bristow. Worthington lectured on scripture at Rheims, where the English College was in exile, for two years and began his commentary on the Old Testament. In 1587 William Allen sent him to Deventer as a military chaplain but by May 1588 he had enrolled in the university at Trier to complete his doctorate in theology. He returned to Rheims to be vice-president of the college and lecture for a year on moral theology but in July 1591, after resigning his offices, he moved to Brussels, presumably to continue his work on Martin's text. At Louvain, Thomas Stapleton was the professor of scripture, whose lectures Worthington would later edit for publication. A new text of the Vulgate had appeared by order of Sixtus V and Allen was in Rome, at the request of Clement VIII, with the editors preparing more emendations. After William Rainolds and Allen died in 1594, Worthington, as the sole survivor among Martin's original assistants, took up the task of a final version. He was out of touch with the college at this time, since in 1596, in his letter about the students at the English College in Rome, he wrote several errors about the current regime at Douai under Richard Barret.

Nevertheless, Worthington was appointed by Cardinal Cajetano, at the recommendation of president Barret and the faculty of the college, to become president of Douai College in July 1599. He would be notable for his literary achievement, but he failed to impose overdue reforms demanded at two visitations of Douai in 1599 and 1612. In his first year he produced four books at Antwerp: two containing thirty-four *Orationes academicae* edited for his friend Thomas Stapleton, and the Latin and English texts of his own *The Rosarie of Our Ladie*. In 1608 he had printed at Arras two volumes by Richard Bristow called *Motiva*, which presented twenty-five 'motives' from scripture and tradition for membership in the church. His most important work was the two volumes of *The Holie Bible Faithfully Translated into English*, printed at Douai separately in 1609 and 1610. In an unsigned preface he explained that his delay came from a lack of money: 'al proceded … of one general cause, our poore estate in banishment' (sig. 2). His style was eirenical: 'we speake to you al … whether you be of contrarie opinions in faith … or professe with us the same' (sig. 4v). His comments were so extensive that when the first volume reached the book of Job, 'for avoiding prolixitie … we have for most part contracted our Annotations into the margen' (p. 1110). In a book totalling more than 2300 pages in two quarto volumes Worthington had edited the finest example of collaboration in the college's history.

In 1601 Worthington published his first polemical book, *A Relation of Sixtene Martyrs*, in which the recent executions of laity and priests in England were narrated while adding two 'declarations'. In the first he insisted that they suffered only for religion and not for treason as charged; in the second he argued that the 'Secular priestes agree with the Jesuites' (pp. 57–63), citing the praise of Cardinal Allen for them and accusing their 'adversaries' of ambition. Worthington's esteem for the English Jesuits led to misrepresentations about his policies in complaints to Rome. However, the correspondence of Thomas Fitzherbert during 1608–10, as an observer in Rome, later provided documentation to clear his name. Clearly Worthington's attention was focused on books concerned with scripture or polemics and not on the needs of the college, so that there was relief on all sides as Matthew Kellison became president and Worthington was invited to the papal court in 1613. There he received a pension and an appointment to the Congregation of the Index, but after two years he sought leave to return to England.

In 1615 Worthington entered into a controversy with the Church of England theologian John White about the marks of the true church in his *Whyte Dyed Black*. His return angered Archbishop Abbot, who commented that the pope had made Worthington 'a Monsignor and a Protonotary Apostolike to please the doting foole with a bable' (*Downshire MSS*, 5.532). In 1616 Worthington visited Nottinghamshire and Derbyshire as archdeacon of the clergy and tried to found a sodality for priests and laity. He then began writing a manual based on scripture, *An Anker of Christian Doctrine*, in four parts, which stirred up controversy by 1622 and was placed, along with the Douai Bibles, on John Gee's list of popish books available for sale in London in 1624. Following the lead of three nephews, John (*d.* 1652), Lawrence (*d.* 1635), and Peter (*d.* 1613), who had become Jesuits earlier, he was also admitted to the society by the provincial in London. He died during his first year as a novice in 1626, while on a visit to Biddulph Hall, Staffordshire. His importance at Douai was largely as lecturer,

writer, and the final editor of a bible which in its time was a milestone for the survival of the Catholic community in England.   A. J. LOOMIE

Sources *Letters of Thomas Fitzherbert, 1608–1610*, ed. L. Hicks, Catholic RS, 41 (1948) • *Letters of William Allen and Richard Barret, 1572–1598*, ed. P. Renold, Catholic RS, 58 (1967) • A. F. Allison and D. M. Rogers, eds., *The contemporary printed literature of the English Counter-Reformation between 1558 and 1640*, 2 vols. (1989–94) • P. Milward, *Religious controversies of the Jacobean age* (1978) • H. Foley, ed., *Records of the English province of the Society of Jesus*, 7 vols. in 8 (1875–83) • P. Guilday, *The English Catholic refugees on the continent, 1558–1795* (1914) • J. H. Pollen, ed., *Unpublished documents relating to the English martyrs*, 1, Catholic RS, 5 (1908) • T. M. McCoog, *English and Welsh Jesuits, 1555–1650*, 2, Catholic RS, 75 (1995) • T. H. B. M. Harmsen, *John Gee's Foot out of the snare (1624)* (1992) • *Report on the manuscripts of the marquis of Downshire*, 6 vols. in 7, HMC, 75 (1924–95), vol. 5 • D. M. Rogers, ed., facsimiles of Worthington's books, English Recusant Library, 265, 266 [Douai Bible] • *DNB*

Worthington, Thomas (1671–1754), prior of Bornhem, was born on 23 November 1671, the fourth son of Thomas Worthington (*d.* 1708) of Blainsco in the parish of Standish, near Wigan, Lancashire, and his wife, Jane, eldest daughter of John Plompton of Plompton, Yorkshire. He entered the English Dominican Priory at Bornhem, near Antwerp, on 27 November 1691, and made his vows there on 2 December 1692. He was then sent to study at the English Dominican house of St John and Paul on the Coelian Hill in Rome. He was ordained priest there in 1695. In the same year the Roman priory was surrendered by the provincial authorities in favour of a new foundation in Louvain. Worthington, together with Thomas Dryden (Sir Erasmus Dryden, bt), the son of the poet John Dryden, made the official surrender to the Holy See.

Worthington subsequently moved with other members of the Roman community to the College of St Thomas Aquinas at Louvain, where he became a lector in sacred theology on 19 August 1704. On 10 March 1705 he was elected prior of Bornhem and was re-elected on 12 March 1708. In April of the same year he was appointed prior provincial of the English province by the master of the order. In August 1708 the death of his father brought him back to England, where he remained for some years, installing himself first in London but then moving to Croxteth in Lancashire in 1713, a year after ceasing his first term as provincial. In 1717 he was once more elected prior of Bornhem and took office in January 1718, being re-elected in 1721 and 1725. In 1719 he had been created a master of sacred theology by the master of the order. On 4 January 1726 he was reappointed by the master as provincial, and in 1727 accompanied Dominic Williams, now vicar apostolic of the northern district, to England, where he acted as his chaplain, to the disquiet of the secular clergy, until 1729. In 1730 he became chaplain and resident priest on the mission of Middleton Hall, the house in the parish of Rothwell, near Leeds, of Ralph Brandling. In an important initiative, he was responsible for obtaining permission to reinstate provincial chapters in England. The first provincial chapter to meet in England since the Reformation subsequently assembled at the house of Mr Besley in Panton Street, Haymarket, London, on 20 April 1730. On this occasion Father Ambrose Burgis was elected provincial. Worthington served as provincial for a third time from 1742 to 1746, but remained in residence at Middleton Hall. In 1750 he was elected prior of Bornhem for a sixth time but was excused by the master of the order on the grounds of age. Age notwithstanding, his brethren elected him provincial once more on 26 September 1750 and he died, aged eighty-three, on 25 February 1754, in the fourth year of his provincialate at Middleton Hall. He was buried on 26 February at Rothwell, near Leeds.

Worthington published *An Introduction to the Catholic Faith, by an English Dominican* (1709). He also produced a number of scriptural works as well as compiling historical works relating to the English Dominican province. He also wrote a personal memoir of Dominic Williams, which is a valuable source of information on the life and work of an eighteenth-century English vicar apostolic.

ALLAN WHITE

Sources Blackfriars, London, Dominican archives, profession register • W. Gumbley, *Obituary notices of the English Dominicans from 1555 to 1952* (1955), 65–6 • R. Palmer, 'Under the penal laws', pt 1, *Merry England*, 67 (Nov 1888), 25–41 • R. Palmer, 'Under the penal laws', pt 2, *Merry England*, 68 (Dec 1888), 135–54
Archives Blackfriars, London, Dominican archives • George Square, Edinburgh, Dominican archives

Worthington, Thomas (1826–1909). *See under* Worthington family (*per.* 1849–1963).

Worthington, William (1703–1778), Church of England clergyman and religious writer, son of Thomas Worthington of Aberhafesb, Montgomeryshire, was educated at Oswestry School. He matriculated from Jesus College, Oxford, on 9 May 1722, aged eighteen, and graduated BA on 22 February 1726. He then became usher in the school at Oswestry. In 1742 he gained an MA from St John's College, Cambridge, and in 1738 he was awarded the degrees of BD and DD at Oxford. He came under the patronage of Francis Hare, bishop of St Asaph, who presented him in 1729 to the vicarage of Llanyblodwell, Shropshire, and in 1748 moved him to Llanrhaeadr, Denbighshire. Hare also gave him the sinecure rectory of Darowen, Montgomeryshire, in 1737, and Archbishop Drummond, to whom Worthington had been chaplain for several years, presented him in 1768 to a stall in the cathedral of York. Worthington also held the living of Easthyn (Hope) in Flintshire from 1751 until his death.

Worthington disagreed with William Warburton's interpretation of the book of Job and published a dissertation on Job with *An Essay on … Man's Redemption* (1743). He gave the Robert Boyle lectures for 1766–8, and these appeared in print as *The Evidence of Christianity* (1769). He published a response to the dissenting Hugh Farmer's *Essay on Demoniacks* (1775) in 1777 and another rejoinder in 1779. Worthington also published on various other theological matters. He was very interested in missionary work abroad and left legacies to the SPCK and to other protestant missionary societies in his will. He died at Llanrhaeadr on 6 October 1778.

THOMPSON COOPER, rev. EMMA MAJOR

Sources Venn, *Alum. Cant.* • Foster, *Alum. Oxon.* • *GM*, 1st ser., 48 (1778), 493 • will, PRO, PROB 11/1050, fols. 288–90 • Nichols, *Lit. anecdotes*, 7.477 • ESTC • Watt, *Bibl. Brit.* • J. Cooke, *The preachers' assistant* (1783) • R. Williams, *Enwogion Cymru: a biographical dictionary of eminent Welshmen* (1852), 544 • J. Lamb, *The rhetoric of suffering* (1995)
Wealth at death £1000; plus large collection of books (2000): will, PRO, PROB 11/1050, sig. 83

Worthington, William (1723–1800), brewer, was born at Orton on the Hill, Leicestershire, the fourth child of William Worthington (1687–1742), yeoman farmer, and his wife, Elizabeth. In 1744, on reaching his majority, Worthington moved to Burton upon Trent to work as a cooper in Joseph Smith's small brewery situated on the west side of the High Street. Burton was already famous as a brewing centre, noted for the exceptional qualities of its water which produced a fine-quality, strong ale able to withstand long and arduous journeys. By the 1750s, a modest but growing export trade with the Baltic States, via the Trent Navigation and Hull, was well established.

It was this lucrative, but risky export trade which attracted Worthington to brewing, and in 1760, having raised a mortgage of £320, he purchased the brewery from Smith's successor, Richard Commings. The following year he extended the property, adding a tunhouse and second brewhouse. In 1760 he also married a widow, Ann Tarratt; they had two sons. Worthington's wife is thought to have provided the finance for his first export of ale to the Baltic and, eighteen months later, when nothing further had been heard of the shipment, to buy out his partner's share in the venture. Her confidence was rewarded: the proceeds were to exceed all expectations and establish the brewery, later to become one of the best-known of all British breweries, on a sound footing.

The few surviving letter-books reveal the difficult and speculative nature of the export trade. Yet Worthington's business flourished; it is difficult to trace its growth with accuracy, but by the 1780s the brewery probably had an annual output approaching 1500 barrels, much on a par with that of Worthington's two great rivals, Benjamin Wilson and Michael Bass (Owen, *Industry in Burton*, 56). Like them, William was as much merchant as brewer. While brewing formed the heart of his enterprise, consignments of ale, sent mainly to Danzig and St Petersburg, were frequently bartered for iron bars, staves, and wood. Indeed, by the 1780s, Worthington with his younger son, Thomas, was listed among Burton's leading timber merchants.

Worthington's two sons, William (1764–1825) and Thomas (1766–1805), followed him into the business, their marriage in 1791 to the two daughters of Henry Evans, a wealthy Burton brewer, greatly enhancing the prospects of the brewery. The previous year Evans had purchased on behalf of his daughters the brewery built and worked by John Walker Wilson, situated opposite Worthington's business. On their marriage, the brewery passed into Worthington hands. By the time of Worthington's death in 1800, Worthington & Co. ranked among the biggest provincial breweries; eighty years later, Alfred Barnard noted that it was the 'largest pale ale brewery in the hands of a single family' (Barnard, 1.411). Besides the brewery, Worthington left his sons and widow substantial property in Burton, farms at Hartshorne and Gresley, and a considerable fortune.   CHRISTINE CLARK

Sources C. C. Owen, *The development of industry in Burton-upon-Trent* (1978) · C. C. Owen, 'The greatest brewery in the world': a history of Bass, Ratcliff & Gretton, Derbyshire RS, 29 (1992) · A. Barnard, *The noted breweries of Great Britain and Ireland*, 1 (1889), 409–48 · *Licensed Victuallers' Gazette and Hotel Courier* (2 Jan 1875), 13–19

Wortley, Charles Beilby Stuart-, Baron Stuart of Wortley (1851–1926). *See under* Wortley, James Archibald Stuart-, first Baron Wharncliffe (1776–1845).

Wortley, Edward James Montagu-Stuart- (1857–1934), army officer, was born on 31 July 1857, the second son of Francis Dudley Montagu-Stuart-Wortley (1829–1893) and his wife, Maria Elizabeth, *née* Martin (d. 26 Sept 1891), the eldest daughter of William Bennet Martin of Worsborough Hall, Yorkshire. As the grandson of John, second baron Wharncliffe (1801–1855), he was heir presumptive to the earldom. The family was known for its wealth, and sporting and social rather than political influence.

After Eton (1866–70), Stuart-Wortley joined the army via the militia, and was gazetted to the King's Royal Rifle Corps (ensign, October 1877; lieutenant, March 1880). He first experienced action with the Kurram field force in the Second Anglo-Afghan war in 1879, and was mentioned in dispatches. He also served in the ill-fated Transvaal campaign of 1881. In 1882 he was military secretary to General Valentine Baker in Egypt, then aide-de-camp to Sir Evelyn Wood, and fought at Tell al-Kebir (13 September 1882). He served on Wolseley's Gordon relief expedition (1884–5) and was involved in the final dash for Khartoum in the vain attempt to save General Gordon.

In 1886 Stuart-Wortley entered staff college by nomination and after graduation was posted to Malta, where he served three years as an infantry brigade major (captain, March 1886). On 5 February 1891, while serving in Malta, he married Violet Hunter, daughter of James Alexander Guthrie of Craigie, Dundee. They had two daughters and a son.

Created CMG in 1896, Stuart-Wortley returned to Egypt to serve on the staff of the sirdar, Francis, Lord Grenfell. He served in Kitchener's reconquest of the Sudan, and at the battle of Omdurman (2 September 1898) for his spirited and successful command of 'friendly' irregulars, Stuart-Wortley was awarded the DSO. Almost immediately he was appointed assistant adjutant general to Sir Redvers Buller and served on his staff during the South African campaign until the relief of Ladysmith (28 February 1900) when he was given command of the 2nd battalion, King's Royal Rifle Corps.

Unusually for an officer of comparatively junior rank (major, brevet lieutenant-colonel) Stuart-Wortley was in 1901 appointed military attaché in Paris. This reflected not only his successful army career but also his wealth and social and diplomatic acumen. The new king, Edward VII, who, like his mother, took a particular interest in military matters, wrote encouraging the new attaché 'to devote all

his good will to maintaining the most cordial relations with the French Army' (Rennell Rodd, p. 298). Edward's personal gratification with Stuart-Wortley's conduct in the successful negotiations for the Anglo-French entente was expressed by his creation as MVO in 1903. In 1906 Stuart-Wortley was made an officer of the Légion d'honneur and appointed CB. He was given the substantive rank of colonel and in April 1908 command of the 10th infantry brigade.

In the autumn of 1908, at the height of an anti-German campaign in the British navalist press, Stuart-Wortley published in the *Daily Telegraph* an 'interview' with the Kaiser. This, his only incursion into popular journalism, unwittingly earned Stuart-Wortley notoriety. (The choice of the *Telegraph* was significant because, unlike the rest of the Unionist press, it treated stories on Germany and its Kaiser with restraint, even sympathy.) In December 1907, after completing an official visit to Britain, the Kaiser was for a fortnight Stuart-Wortley's private guest at his New Forest mansion, Highcliffe Castle, Christchurch, Hampshire. Stuart-Wortley had been impressed by Wilhelm's frequent and apparently heartfelt expressions of amity and respect for all things British. Stuart-Wortley supposed that if the public could be made aware of the Kaiser's true opinions, this would improve Anglo-German relations. He had proposed that the Kaiser give an interview to the journalist W. T. Stead, but Wilhelm refused. Stuart-Wortley believed he might overcome the Kaiser's aversion if he rather than a professional journalist conducted the interview, and his friend Harry Lawson, son of the *Telegraph*'s owner, encouraged this idea. Stuart-Wortley wrote down, as best he could recall, Wilhelm's conversations with him at Highcliffe, to which he added observations the Kaiser had made to him in September at the German army manoeuvres at Saarbrücken. All was dictated to J. B. Firth, a *Daily Telegraph* journalist, and his transcript was submitted to the Kaiser for approval.

The text was not carefully examined by German officials before it was approved, with only minor alterations. When it was published in the *Daily Telegraph* on 28 October 1908, the interview did not create the hoped-for impression. The Kaiser's frequent interventions in diplomatic affairs, by speech or letter, not uncommonly created unintended crises. On this occasion the Kaiser's mixture of naïve, boastful, and sometimes false assertions so carefully collected by Stuart-Wortley, in Germany and Britain alike, prompted embarrassment, amusement, and outrage. The anti-German scare in parliament and the press was exacerbated, while Stuart-Wortley's chagrin was only partly assuaged by the Kaiser's award of the Prussian Red Eagle and Star, second class.

A year after being promoted major-general in March 1913, Stuart-Wortley was given command of the North Midland territorial division. In March 1915 this was the first complete territorial division to cross to France, and in May it was retitled the 46th (North Midland) division. It served on the western front, held a dangerous part of the Ypres salient with heavy casualties, and in October, during the battle of Loos, attacked the Hohenzollern redoubt, again with heavy losses.

In 1916, as part of 7 corps in General Sir Edmund Allenby's Third Army, the 46th division was ordered to attack the village of Gommecourt on the extreme left (north) of the front as a diversion to the main Somme offensive, to capture the salient, and then to meet counter-attacks and inflict heavy casualties. On 1 July, after an inadequate artillery bombardment, 46th division met uncut wire and heavy fire, and their attack failed, with heavy casualties. Immediately after the battle Allenby ordered a court of inquiry into the handling of 46th division, which first sat on 4 July. Before it had completed its investigations, on the morning of 5 July, Stuart-Wortley was relieved of his command and ordered back to England, the first general to lose his command in the battle of the Somme. Most agreed that he was a poor commander. Brigadier-General Frank Lyon (chief staff officer, 7 corps) wrote that he was 'a worn-out man, who never visited his front line and was incapable of inspiring any enthusiasm' (Middlebrook, 284). According to Sir James Edmonds, he was sacked not so much for his Gommecourt failure, but because Haig was jealous of his correspondence with the king. His dismissal seems to have been the result of a combination of his poor reputation, the desire for a scapegoat, and Haig's dislike.

Later in 1916 Stuart-Wortley was sent to Ireland to command the 65th division. This command grew heavier, more thankless, and harassing. He left Ireland in March 1918, received no further wartime employment, and retired in July 1919. Indulging his love of sport and travel, he enjoyed an energetic retirement. He died in Tangier, Morocco, on 19 March 1934.

Stuart-Wortley, known by his friends as Eddie, reportedly enjoyed widespread popularity, both at court and in the mess and servants' hall. His army career, begun with such bright promise, faded disappointingly. Like other gallant, late-Victorian army officers brought up in quite other traditions, he apparently found life after the Second South African War less congenial in the reformed, more professional British army.　　　A. J. A. MORRIS

Sources *Daily Telegraph* (28 Oct 1908) · Montagu-Stuart-Wortley papers, Bodl. Oxf., MS Eng. hist. D. 256 · *The diary of Edward Goschen, 1900–1914*, ed. C. H. D. Howard, CS, 4th ser., 25 (1980) · Prince von Bulow, *Memoirs, 1903–1909* (1931) · Kaiser Wilhelm II, *My memoirs, 1878–1918* (1922) · M. Balfour, *The Kaiser and his times* (1975) · A. J. A. Morris, *The scaremongers: the advocacy of war and rearmament, 1896–1914* (1984) · *WWW, 1929–40* · Burke, *Peerage* · *The Times* (20 March 1934) · J. R. Rodd, *Social and diplomatic memories*, 2 (1923) · *Hart's Army List* (1893) · T. Travers, *The killing ground* (1990) · *The Eton register*, 3 (privately printed, Eton, 1906) · M. Middlebrook, *The first day on the Somme, 1 July 1916* (1971); repr. (1984) · J. M. Bourne, *Britain and the great war 1914–1918* (1994) · Lord Burnham [E. F. L. Burnham], *Peterborough Court: the story of the Daily Telegraph* (1955) · P. Dennis, *The Territorial Army, 1906–1940*, Royal Historical Society Studies in History, 51 (1987) · I. F. W. Beckett, *The amateur military tradition, 1558–1945* (1991)

Archives Bodl. Oxf., MS Eng. hist. D. 256 | U. Durham, Wingate MSS, corresp. with Sir Reginald Wingate

Wortley, Lady Emmeline Charlotte Elizabeth Stuart-

[*née* Lady Emmeline Charlotte Elizabeth Manners] (1806–1855), poet and travel writer, was born on 2 May 1806, the

Lady Emmeline Charlotte Elizabeth Stuart-Wortley (1806–1855), by Frederick Christian Lewis senior (after Sir Francis Grant, 1837)

second daughter of John Henry Manners, fifth duke of Rutland (1778–1857), and Lady Elizabeth Howard (d. 1825), fifth daughter of Frederick *Howard, fifth earl of Carlisle (1748–1825). On 17 February 1831 Lady Emmeline married the Hon. Charles James Stuart-Wortley (1802–1844), second son of James Archibald Stuart-*Wortley, first Baron Wharncliffe (1776–1845); they had three children: Archibald Henry Plantagenet (1832–1890), Adelbert William John (d. 1844), and Victoria Alexandrina [see Welby, Victoria Alexandrina Maria Louisa], who married Sir William Earle Welby-Gregory on 4 July 1863.

Lady Emmeline's earliest poems appeared in *Blackwood's Magazine* and in *Poems* (1833), and for the next eleven years she published a volume of verse annually. Some poems were written as a result of her travels, for example *Travelling Sketches in Rhyme* (1835), *Impressions of Italy, and other Poems* (1837), and *Sonnets* (1839), written chiefly during a tour through Holland, Germany, Italy, Turkey, and Hungary (1839). In 1837 and 1840 Lady Emmeline edited the popular annual *The Keepsake*, for which she wrote many poems. Among the contributors was Tennyson, who in *The Keepsake* for 1837 published his poem 'St Agnes' (afterwards republished under the title of 'St Agnes' Eve' in the volume of 1842). Lady Emmeline's associates also included the countess of Blessington, Theodore Hook, Richard Monckton Milnes, Caroline Norton, and Mary Shelley.

From the time of Lady Emmeline's European wedding journey, she became an avid traveller, at first touring for enjoyment, but with her itineraries becoming 'increasingly punishing' (Robinson, 122) after the death of her husband and youngest son in 1844. In 1849–50 she visited America with her daughter and published *Travels in the United States* (1851) and *Sketches of Travel in America* (1853). During this trip, she and the twelve-year-old Victoria did not confine themselves to the eastern United States, but made their way to Mexico, across Panama, and into Peru. Victoria also wrote about these travels: *A Young Traveller's Journal of a Tour in North and South America During the Year 1850* was published in 1852. Lady Emmeline's last published book of travel, *A Visit to Portugal and Madeira*, appeared in 1854, although an account of a journey to Spain, *The Sweet South*, was printed posthumously for private circulation in 1856. Although Lady Emmeline was a fairly prolific poet and travel writer the quality of her work is not generally of a high standard.

While riding in the neighbourhood of Jerusalem on 1 May 1855 Lady Emmeline was kicked by a mule and fractured her leg. She was not in good health at the time, yet persisted in journeying without a guide from Beirut to Aleppo, and returned by an unfrequented road across Lebanon. Afflicted with dysentery and sunstroke, she died at Beirut on 30 October 1855.

ELIZABETH LEE, *rev.* GILL GREGORY

Sources J. Robinson, ed., *Wayward women: a guide to women travellers* (1990) • E. M. E. Cust, *Wanderers: episodes from the travels of Lady Emmeline Stuart-Wortley and her daughter Victoria, 1849–1855* (1928) [with preface by Sir Ronald Storrs] • J. Shattock, *The Oxford guide to British women writers* (1993) • Burke, *Peerage* • *GM*, 2nd ser., 45 (1856), 183 • Allibone, *Dict.*

Archives NRA, priv. coll., family corresp.

Likenesses F. Grant, oils, Belvoir Castle, Leicestershire • F. C. Lewis senior, engraving (after F. Grant, 1837), NPG [*see illus.*]

Wortley, Sir Francis, first baronet (1591–1652), poet and royalist army officer, was from an ancient Yorkshire family, the son of Sir Richard Wortley (*d.* 1603) and Elizabeth (*d.* 1642?), daughter of Edward Boughton of Cawston, Warwickshire. He matriculated from Magdalen College, Oxford, on 17 February 1609, was knighted on 15 January 1610, and created a baronet on 29 June 1615. A gentleman of the privy chamber to James I, he was MP for East Retford, Nottinghamshire, in the parliaments of 1625 and 1626. He mortgaged mills and coalmines in the Barnsley area. He was admitted to Gray's Inn on 1 August 1624, and in 1636 was awarded an MA degree at Cambridge. His literary friends included Ben Jonson—he contributed to *Jonsonus virbius* (1638)—and Sir William Dugdale. He married, first, Grace (*d.* 1615), the daughter of Sir William Brouckner of Melksham, Wiltshire, with whom he had one son and one daughter, and, second, Hester, daughter of George Smithies, alderman of London, and widow of Christopher Eyre; she predeceased him.

Wortley 'was a tall, proper man, with grey hair' (Jackson, 1.281). His life exemplified the family motto 'amicitas volo, inimicitas sperno', which he disingenuously translated as 'I study my friends, and scorne my causelesse enemies' (F. Wortley, *Characters and Elegies*, 1646, sig. A4v). On 31 May 1625, outside Westminster Hall, he jostled and insulted Sir Thomas Savile. Savile accused Wortley, 'This is your old trickes to gett the advantage of doing the first

wrong, and then to goe garded with your fencers' (*Hodgkin MSS*, 286), and he retaliated by kicking Wortley. They drew swords, and Wortley wounded his opponent and forced him to retire, but Sir Thomas's footman cut a slash in Wortley's face from the eye to the chin of his right cheek. 'A little page of Sir Francis Wortley' (ibid.) drew off the footman with his master's rapier and a general mêlée ensued. The cause of their quarrel, which began two years earlier at York, is unknown. In September 1639 Wortley was visited at Wortley Hall by John Taylor, the 'water poet', who gave an account of an excursion to Wortley's hunting lodge at Wharncliffe.

In September 1640 Wortley told the king that he had brought 100 gentlemen volunteers to serve him against the Scottish covenanters, 'and the king asking what armour they brought he told him good hearts and good swords' (*CSP dom.*, 1640–41, 62): Wortley helped the prince of Wales put on his first sword. He was one of the organizers of the petition of the Yorkshire gentry of 22 April 1642, that urged the king to arm himself by seizing the Hull magazine before it was shipped to London. At York on 2 May he addressed a large company in the court of the Old Deanery: 'he drew out his sword and waved over his head and cried, "For the king, for the king"' (Snow and Young, 259). He had gone to York at the head of a troop of horse, selected from a review of the county's cavalry, which grew to about 140 by the end of May. At this time, according to one informed opinion, 'divide Yorkshire into an 100 parts, Sir Francis Wortley and the rest of his party were able to command 90' (ibid., 264). There was a move in the Lords to impeach Wortley of high treason and he gained a reputation as a 'prime and pernicious royalist' (Newman, 422). He is reported to have garrisoned Wortley Hall with 150 dragoons. In October 1642 his men killed a Mr Rellisone, a defender of Bakewell House, Warwickshire, who had been armed only with a bow and arrows. The next month he crossed and plundered the Staffordshire moorlands at the head of a troop of horse before occupying Stafford, where the mayor won over the townspeople by distributing free beer. By the end of January 1643 Wortley was established in a fortified Stafford, and was raising cavalry with money lent by the townspeople.

On 3 June 1644 Wortley was captured by Sir Thomas Fairfax's men at the taking of Walton House, near Wakefield, and on 22 August he was committed to the Tower. In 1646 he published his *Characters and Elegies*, described as 'a salad to more solid dishes' should it meet with a favourable reception (sig. A4). The characters are moralizing essays, rather than witty satires, and the elegies fulfil his definition of poetry as metrical prose. In June 1646 he petitioned to be released from the Tower, claiming that he needed to go to the spa at Tonbridge to restore his health. Although the petition was supported by Fairfax, it was unsuccessful. On 19 August 1647 the king sent the prisoners in the Tower a pair of fat bucks for a feast. Wortley celebrated the gift with *A loyall song of the royall feast, kept by the prisoners in the Towre in August last, with the names titles and character of every prisoner* (1647). In the same year he published *Mercurius Britannicus his Welcome to Hell*, in which he threatens the life of Marchamont Nedham. According to information received by the authorities in July 1650, Wortley and his son-in-law, Sir Henry Griffith of Burton Agnes, sent John Gohogan, an officer under the late king, to Charles II at The Hague to give intelligence against the government. The king is said to have 'thanked them for their good will, and promised them abundant rewards if his designs prospered' (Green, 1376–7). In April 1649 and again in August 1650 Wortley was allowed to compound for his estate, but on 30 September 1650 his entire estate was seized. According to Anthony Wood, he was at some point released from the Tower and 'lived in the White Friars near Fleet Street in London' where he died (Wood, *Ath. Oxon.*, 3.392), but it has not been possible to corroborate this claim. In his will, dated 9 September 1652 and proved on 13 September, he asked to be buried at Windsor with his father.   IAN WILLIAM McLELLAN

Sources J. Hunter, *South Yorkshire: the history and topography of the deanery of Doncaster*, 2 vols. (1828–31) • P. R. Newman, *Royalist officers in England and Wales, 1642–1660: a biographical dictionary* (1981) • C. Jackson, ed., *Yorkshire diaries and autobiographies*, [1], SurtS, 65 (1877) • R. Hutton, *The royalist war effort, 1642–1646* (1982) • *The manuscripts of J. Eliot Hodgkin … of Richmond, Surrey*, HMC, 39 (1897), 285–8 • M. A. E. Green, ed., *Calendar of the proceedings of the committee for compounding … 1643–1660*, 5 vols., PRO (1889–92) • A. Steele Young and V. F. Snow, eds., *The private journals of the Long Parliament*, 2: 7 *March to 1 June 1642* (1987) • GEC, *Baronetage* • Wood, *Ath. Oxon.*, new edn • J. Taylor, *Part of this summer's travels, or, News from Hell, Hull, and Halifax* (1640), 24–5 • J. Eales, *Puritans and roundheads: the Harleys of Brampton Bryan and the outbreak of the English civil war* (1990) • A. Fletcher, *The outbreak of the English civil war* (1981) • J. Vicars, *Magnalia Dei Anglicana, or, England's parliamentary chronicle*, 3 (1646), 147 • J. Nalson, *An impartial collection of the great affairs of state*, 1 (1682), 502
Likenesses A. Hertochs, line engraving, BM, NPG • oils, Tower of London
Wealth at death bequeathed £150 for the poor at Tankersly and Wortley; plus £50 for making a vault at Wortley: Jackson, ed., *Yorkshire diaries*, 1.281

Wortley, James Archibald Stuart- [*formerly* James Archibald Stuart-Wortley-Mackenzie], **first Baron Wharncliffe** (1776–1845), politician, was born on 6 October 1776, the second but eldest surviving son of James Archibald Stuart (1747–1818), lieutenant-colonel of the 92nd regiment of foot, and Margaret, daughter of Sir David Conyngham, bt, of Milncraig, Ayrshire. John *Stuart, third earl of Bute, was his grandfather, and John, first marquess of Bute, his uncle. His father's mother (the countess of Bute) was Mary, only daughter of Edward and Lady Mary Wortley *Montagu; she had been created a peeress on 3 April 1761 as Baroness Mountstuart. In 1794 the father succeeded on her death to her Wortley estates in Yorkshire and Cornwall, and took the name of Wortley on 17 January 1795. In 1803 he took the additional name of Mackenzie on succeeding to the Scottish property of his uncle, James Stuart Mackenzie of Rosehaugh.

The army, marriage, and early political career The younger James Archibald, who eventually dropped the last surname of Mackenzie, was educated at Charterhouse (1789–90). He entered the army in November 1790 as an ensign in the 48th foot. In the following May he transferred into the

7th Royal Fusiliers, and on 4 May 1793 obtained a company in the 72nd highlanders. He served in Canada from 1792 to 1794 and at the Cape from 1795 to 1797. On 10 May 1796 he became lieutenant-colonel, and on 1 December colonel of the 12th foot. In 1797 he was sent to the Cape with dispatches from George, Lord Macartney, and on 27 December purchased a company in the 1st foot guards. He left the army at the peace of 1801. On 30 March 1799 he married Lady Elizabeth Caroline Mary, daughter of John Creighton, first earl of Erne (1738?–1828), and his second wife, Mary Caroline (d. 1842). Lady Granville said of her that 'She has all the charm of intelligence without the tax of *esprit*' (GEC, *Peerage*). The marriage associated him with Lord Liverpool and his supporters.

In 1802 Stuart-Wortley succeeded his father in the House of Commons as MP for the family borough of Bossiney, which he continued to represent until his father's death in 1818. Although he was not a prominent MP, he gained a reputation for independence of view. On 21 May 1812, in the aftermath of Spencer Perceval's assassination, he moved a resolution on his own initiative for an address to the prince regent, calling for 'a stronger and more efficient administration'. The motion, seconded by Lord Milton, was carried against ministers by a majority of four (*Hansard 1*, 23, 21 May 1812, 249–84). Next day ministers resigned, and Lord Wellesley was commissioned to form a government. Negotiations with the whigs having come to nothing, and Stuart-Wortley having failed in a secret attempt to bring Liverpool and George Canning together, on 11 June he moved a second motion, deploring the failure and ridiculing the whigs; it was eventually negatived without a division.

Henceforth Stuart-Wortley acted with the moderate tories as an independent supporter of the Liverpool ministry. He was encouraged to stand for Yorkshire where his estates lay, but after taking soundings did not press his claim. He continued to take a minor part in politics, deprecating harsh treatment of the princess of Wales in 1814, advocating retrenchment in the army in 1816, and voting that year with the opposition against the creation of new governmental offices.

In 1818 Stuart-Wortley was returned unopposed for Yorkshire. His colleague as MP was Lord Milton (afterwards Earl Fitzwilliam). Stuart-Wortley at once found himself involved in fiscal policy, supporting retrenchment and moderate tariff reform, and presenting merchants' petitions. He played in important role in preventing riots in Yorkshire in 1819, but he opposed parliamentary reform. On the other hand, he proposed a property tax to relieve the poor from the burden of taxation. In May 1820 he declared against further protection to agriculture, holding that the distress of that interest bore no proportion to that of manufactures (*Hansard 2*, 1, May 1820, 116, 117).

In questions of foreign policy Stuart-Wortley shared the views of Canning. On 21 June 1821 he moved for copies of the circular issued by the members of the Holy Alliance at Laibach, stigmatizing their proceedings as dangerous to the liberties of both England and Europe. The motion was negatived by 113 to 59 (*Hansard* 2, 5, 21 June 1821, 1254–60). In April 1823 he defended the ministerial policy of neutrality between France and Spain, and moved and carried an amendment to a motion condemning it. He also acted with the liberal sections of both parties in supporting Catholic emancipation, to which he had announced himself a convert as early as 1812, and on 28 May 1823 he seconded Lord Nugent's motion for leave to bring in a bill to assimilate the position of English and Irish Roman Catholics. But his attitude to the question lost him his seat in 1826.

Stuart-Wortley's position towards economic questions probably also unfavourably affected his relations with some of his constituents. In February 1823 he had supported both by speech and vote Whitmore's bill to amend the corn laws. On 7 July 1823, in opposing the Reciprocity of Duties Bill, he gave his opinion that it would be impossible to retain for any considerable time the protection given to agricultural produce (*Hansard* 2, 9, 7 July 1823, 1439).

In 1824 Stuart-Wortley brought in a bill to amend the game laws. Its object was twofold: to abolish the system by which the right to kill game was vested in a class and to make it depend on the ownership of the soil, and to diminish the temptations to poaching by legalizing the sale of game. The bill was often reintroduced in succeeding years, and it was not until 1832 that a measure which embodied its main provisions became law.

Wharncliffe and the Reform Bill On 12 July 1826, having been defeated in his Yorkshire constituency, Stuart-Wortley was created Baron Wharncliffe of Wortley. He abandoned his earlier hostility to parliamentary reform and in 1831, after carrying an amendment raising the voting qualification at Leeds, he took charge of the Grampound Disfranchisement Bill, the object of which was to transfer its representation to that town. When the House of Lords proposed instead to give additional members to the county of York, Wharncliffe advised the abandonment of the measure. On 28 March 1831, by moving for statistics of population and representation, he initiated the first general discussion of the reform question in the House of Lords. While making an able and hostile analysis of the government bill, he declared his conviction that no body of men outside parliament would back resistance to a moderate measure (*Hansard* 3, 3, 28 March 1831, 983 et seq.). On the rejection of the first Reform Bill in committee of the House of Commons, on 22 April 1831 he moved an address to the king praying him to refrain from using his prerogative of proroguing or dissolving parliament. As Lord Brougham was replying, the king was announced, and, after a scene of great confusion, the prorogation took place. When on 3 October that year the second Reform Bill came up for second reading in the upper house, Wharncliffe moved that it be read a second time six months hence. He objected that the proposed ten-pound franchise was a bogus one, that the measure was designed to delude the landed interest, and he took exception to its populational basis. He refrained, however, from any defence of nomination boroughs. After a brilliant debate the second reading was defeated by 199 to 158. Two days later Wharncliffe presented petitions against the measure from bankers and merchants of London, and maintained that the opinion of the capital was opposed to the bill. But he had lost confidence in the possibility of successful resistance. In an interview with 'Radical Jones' [*see* Jones, Leslie Grove], he was impressed by his prediction of the dangers which would follow the rejection of the Reform Bill. Within a month of the defeat of the measure Wharncliffe and Harrowby were approached by the whig government through their sons in the Commons (Wharncliffe's son John was MP for Bossiney). After a meeting of the two fathers and sons at Harrowby's house in Staffordshire, a memorandum was drawn up as a basis for negotiation. The memorandum was shown to the cabinet and approved. But many tories declined to accept Wharncliffe's compromise. The City of London refused its adhesion, and Lord Grey broke off the negotiations. Grey sent the king Wharncliffe's memorandum, and William IV expressed regret at the failure of negotiations, but thought what had passed was calculated to be useful. On 11 December a further meeting between Wharncliffe, Harrowby, and Chandos on the one side, and Grey, Brougham, and Althorp on the other, proved equally fruitless. Nevertheless, in January 1832, Wharncliffe advised the tories to support the second reading of the new bill and afterwards modify it in committee. He impressed on Wellington the danger of coming into collision with crown, Commons, and people in a useless struggle. His remonstrance failed to move the duke, and Wharncliffe determined to act independently of him. In two interviews with William IV (on 12 January and in early February), he assured the king that as he and his friends were determined to support the second reading there was no need of a creation of peers. On 27 March Wharncliffe and Harrowby made their first public declaration of their intention to support the bill, Wharncliffe being, according to Greville, 'very short and rather embarrassed'. On 9 April their support secured for the second reading a majority of nine.

Wharncliffe felt acutely his separation from the tory party, and on 7 May voted for Lyndhurst's amendment postponing the disfranchising clauses, by which the progress of the bill was again delayed. His position was now very difficult (*Croker Papers*, 2.174); he had offended both his own party and the whigs. Grey resigned on the carrying of Lyndhurst's amendment, and Wellington, when seeking to form a government, was advised by Lyndhurst not only to offer office to Wharncliffe's son, but to consider well before he decided not to include Wharncliffe himself. The whigs soon resumed office, and the bill was proceeded with. On 24 May Wharncliffe moved an amendment to prevent persons voting for counties in respect of property situated in boroughs, and said he was not reconciled to the bill, which went further than the occasion required. The following day he proposed that the ten-pound qualification should be based on the assessment for poor rate (*Hansard* 3, 13, 24 May 1832, 19, 111, et seq.). He abstained from voting on the third reading, but signed the two protests drawn up by Lord Melros (ibid., 377–8). Anxious to regain the favour of his party, Wharncliffe in 1833 sent Wellington a sketch of a proposed policy in the new parliament, with which the duke concurred.

Later political career   In February 1834 Greville described Wharncliffe as 'very dismal about the prospects of the country'. On 13 December of the same year Wharncliffe was invited by Peel to join his first ministry, notwithstanding the lukewarmness of his recent opposition to the Irish Tithe Bill. He accepted the office of lord privy seal after receiving an assurance that the policy of the new ministry would be liberal in character. In January 1835 he acted as one of the committee to arrange the Church Reform Bill. In April he retired with his colleagues, and remained in opposition during the next six years. During these years Wharncliffe found time to edit the letters and works of his ancestor, Lady Mary Wortley Montagu. His edition appeared in five volumes in 1837, and superseded Dallaway's. It was reissued in 1861 and 1893.

When Peel returned to office in the autumn of 1841, Wharncliffe became lord president of the council. His return to tory favour was marked by his appointment as lord lieutenant of Yorkshire in 1841. As lord president, he was, according to Greville, fair, liberal, and firm. 'He really, too, does the business himsel.f' On the other hand, he was not so successful as leader in the upper house. He was too liberal in education matters for the high-church party, and did not have sufficient weight in cabinet to enforce the execution of his views. He took part against Peel in the cabinet discussions which preceded his change of policy on the subject of the corn laws, though Peel expected Wharncliffe would ultimately come round. However, on 19 December 1845 he died unexpectedly, of 'gout and apoplexy' (GEC, *Peerage*) at Wharncliffe House, Curzon Street, London. Greville, who knew him well, said no man ever died with fewer enemies. Wharncliffe was an important representative of moderate tory opinion. He offered the party a way out of its difficulties in 1830–32 which brought him enduring hostility from the party, the more staunchly held the more the need for moderate reform became recognized. His role in preventing the need for the creation of peers preserved the powers of the Lords unchanged for the rest of the century; for the tories, at least, this was a priceless service.

Wharncliffe's children   Wharncliffe and his wife had three sons and one daughter, Caroline, who married the Hon. John Chetwynd Talbot.

The eldest son, **John Stuart-Wortley**, second Baron Wharncliffe (1801–1855), born at Egham, Surrey, on 23 April 1801, graduated BA from Christ Church, Oxford, in 1822, with a first class in mathematics and a second in classics. He represented Bossiney from 1823 to 1832, Perth burghs in 1830, and the West Riding of Yorkshire from 1841 until his succession to the peerage. He acted with the Huskissonian party until appointed secretary to the Board of Control on 16 February 1830 in the last tory ministry before the Reform Bill. He shared his father's views on the reform question. He was an unsuccessful candidate for Forfarshire in 1835, and twice failed to obtain election for the West Riding of Yorkshire, but in 1841 won a great triumph for his party in that constituency. He was an enlightened agriculturist and a cultivated man. He was elected FRS in 1829. Besides publishing pamphlets on the abolition of the Irish viceroyalty, on the institution of tribunals of commerce, and a letter to Philip Pusey on drainage in the *Journal of the Agricultural Society*, he was author of *A brief inquiry into the true award of an equitable adjustment between the nation and its creditors* (1833), and translator and editor of Guizot's *Memoirs of George Monk* (1838). He died of consumption at Wortley Hall, near Sheffield, on 22 October 1855, and was buried at Wortley. With his wife, Georgiana, third daughter of Dudley *Ryder, first earl of Harrowby, he had three sons and two daughters. The eldest son, Edward Montagu Granville Stuart-Wortley, born on 15 December 1827, was on 15 January 1876 created earl of Wharncliffe and Viscount Carlton; he died on 13 May 1899.

The first Lord Wharncliffe's youngest son, **James Archibald Stuart-Wortley** (1805–1881), was born in St James's Square, London, on 3 July 1805. He graduated BA from Christ Church, Oxford, in 1826, and was soon after elected fellow of Merton. He was called to the bar from the Inner Temple in 1831, and took silk ten years later. In 1844 he became counsel to the Bank of England, and in the following year was appointed solicitor-general to the queen dowager and attorney-general to the duchy of Lancaster. In 1846 he was sworn of the privy council, and was judge-advocate-general during the last months of Peel's second administration. In 1851 he became recorder of London, and was solicitor-general under Lord Palmerston in 1857. From 1835 to 1837 he represented Halifax as a Conservative and from 1842 to 1859 sat for Buteshire (after 1846 as a Peelite). Stuart-Wortley married, in 1846, the Hon. Jane Lawley [see Wortley, Jane Stuart- (1820–1900)], only daughter of Paul Beilby Thompson, first Baron Wenlock. Despite the assistance of various Peelites, including William Ewart Gladstone, she was unable to prevent the onset of severe bouts of depression which effectively ended his public career. He died at Bolton House, Grantham, on 22 August 1881. His second son, **Charles Beilby Stuart-Wortley**, Baron Stuart of Wortley (1851–1926), lawyer and politician, became a QC and was tory MP for Sheffield. He was under-secretary for the Home Office in 1885 and again from 1886 to 1892; he was created Baron Stuart of Wortley in 1917. He was an urbane man with wide intellectual interests. His first wife was Beatrice (Bice) Trollope (1853–1881), daughter of the writers Thomas Adolphus *Trollope, and his wife, Theodosia *Trollope, and niece of the novelist Anthony *Trollope. She died in childbirth the year after they married. His second wife was Caroline, daughter of Sir John *Millais.

G. LE G. NORGATE, *rev.* H. C. G. MATTHEW

Sources D. G. Henry, 'Stuart (afterwards Stuart Wortley Mackenzie), Hon. James Archibald', HoP, *Commons, 1790–1820*, 5.308–9 · M. Brock, *The Great Reform Act* (1973) · *The Greville memoirs, 1814–1860*, ed. L. Strachey and R. Fulford, 8 vols. (1938) · GM, 2nd ser., 25 (1846), 202–4 · GM, 2nd ser., 44 (1855), 643 · GEC, *Peerage* · *The Croker* *papers: the correspondence and diaries of … John Wilson Croker*, ed. L. J. Jennings, 3 vols. (1884) · *Dod's Peerage* (1881) · Gladstone, *Diaries* · N. Gash, *Sir Robert Peel: the life of Sir Robert Peel after 1830* (1972) · N. Gash, *Mr Secretary Peel: the life of Sir Robert Peel to 1830* (1961) · A. Aspinall, ed., *Three early nineteenth-century diaries* (1952) [extracts from Le Marchant, E. J. Littleton, Baron Hatherton, and E. Law, earl of Ellenborough]

Archives Sheff. Arch., corresp. and papers | BL, corresp. with Sir Robert Peel, Add. MSS 40369–40580 · BLPES, corresp. with Sir Joshua Jebb · Harrowby Manuscript Trust, Sandon Hall, Staffordshire, letters to Lord Harrowby · Lpool RO, letters to Lord Stanley · NRA, priv. coll., letters to earl of Haddington · U. Southampton L., letters to first duke of Wellington

Likenesses attrib. I. Cruikshank, group portrait, pencil and wash caricature, *c.*1835 (*Members of the House of Lords*), NPG · J. Doyle, pen and chalk caricature, BM · F. Grant, portrait; known to be in family possession in 1898 · F. Holl, engraving (after portrait by H. P. Briggs) · H. T. Ryall, stipple (after portrait by H. P. Briggs), BM; repro. in H. T. Ryall, *Portraits of eminent conservatives and statesmen* (1836–46)

Wealth at death £8394 17*s.* 9*d.*—James Archibald Stuart-Wortley: probate, 1881

Wortley, James Archibald Stuart- (1805–1881). *See under* Wortley, James Archibald Stuart-, first Baron Wharncliffe (1776–1845).

Wortley, Jane Stuart- [*née* Jane Thompson] (1820–1900), philanthropist, was born at York on 5 December 1820, the only daughter of Paul Beilby Thompson (1784–1852) and his wife, Caroline Neville (*d.* 1868), daughter of Richard, second Baron Braybrooke. In 1839 Paul Beilby Thompson was raised to the peerage as Baron Wenlock and took the name of Lawley before that of Thompson. His children took Lawley as their sole surname. Jane Lawley spent her youth at the family home, Escrick, an estate near York, where she developed her passion for horses and was taught the philanthropic skills that prepared her for her later career in public life. On 6 May 1846 she married James Archibald Stuart-*Wortley (1805–1881) [*see under* Wortley, James Archibald Stuart-], the third son of James Archibald Stuart-*Wortley, first Baron Wharncliffe (1776–1845). Their children included Charles Beilby Stuart-*Wortley [*see under* Wortley, James Archibald Stuart-]. Her husband, a Peelite, became privy councillor and judge-advocate-general. He was member for the Isle of Bute and in 1851 was appointed recorder of London.

In 1852 Jane Stuart-Wortley inherited a considerable fortune from her father. This inheritance, together with the political positions her husband acquired (he became solicitor-general in 1857), ensured that the couple led a socially prominent life among London's political luminaries, including the Gladstones and Sidney Herbert. Jane Stuart-Wortley was not a political partisan, and preferred what one biographer has called 'a passive assumption that no wrong-doing could or ought to be possible' (How, 137–8). The London phase of her life lasted until 1858, when her husband was forced to resign all political offices after falling off his horse and suffering a spinal injury. The financial implications of James Stuart-Wortley's accident were compounded by poor investments; the family (which by now included several daughters) was forced to sell its London home and move to Upper Sheen House

near Mortlake, where Jane devoted a considerable amount of time to caring for her invalid husband. By 1869 James's condition worsened, and the family moved back to London.

The Stuart-Wortley daughters were now old enough to help care for their father; with her own domestic nursing responsibilities alleviated, Jane was able to launch her philanthropic career by working among the unfortunates in London's East End. She was in many ways a 'typical' benevolent Victorian, promoting the poor's self-elevation and improvement and supporting the work of various working men's clubs, district visitors, and garden schemes, such as the one developed by a Mr Vatcher at the back of the London Hospital in Stepney. Here, a decrepit piece of land owned by the Brewers' Company was transformed into an oasis of ferns and greenery, with a pool for waterfowl and a summer house and aviary for the pleasure of the human visitors. 'It is most satisfactory', Stuart-Wortley remarked in an article for *Nineteenth Century*, 'to observe the poor men and women sitting resting there, quietly reading or watching the waterfowl' (Stuart-Wortley, 'The East End', 368). She believed that women from the upper classes, such as herself, had a special philanthropic role to play: 'to raise the others by every possible influence that can affect them religiously, socially, or physically' (ibid., 372). She was also involved in the Female Emigration Society, where she sat alongside Mrs Sidney Herbert and Mrs Kinnaird on the ladies committee, and later moved on to the British Women's Emigration Society. In 1893 she contributed an essay on emigration to Baroness Burdett-Coutts's book *Woman's Mission*, in which she made clear her commitment to provide the colonies with the labour of Britain's 'surplus' population and to help those disadvantaged by poverty or by being orphaned to start a new life.

Stuart-Wortley's work among London's poor impressed upon her their need for adequate medical care, and with this in mind she set about providing a district nurse for the poor in the parish of Christ Church, Watney Street. She followed the development of the East London Nursing Association, founded in 1868, and in 1875 joined the committee and eventually became the association's treasurer: 'No better woman's work [than nursing the poor in their own homes] can well be devised than this' (Stuart-Wortley, 'The East End', 369).

Stuart-Wortley eventually developed cataracts, which curtailed somewhat activities such as reading, but which did not stop her from playing the piano nor writing speeches on various topics, including nursing, by using a typewriter. Progressive blindness also had little impact upon her involvement in benevolent causes. Her husband died in 1881, at which time she moved to Clarges Street, London, where she continued to plough her philanthropic impulses into good works. These activities, however, were brought to an abrupt, although by no means permanent, halt in 1895 when she suffered a serious bout of influenza. This illness precipitated a move from London to Ripley in Surrey, close to the home of one of her daughters, Mary Caroline Milbanke, countess of Lovelace.

In Ripley, Stuart-Wortley involved herself in community affairs; she became a school manager and started a district nursing scheme for Ripley and the surrounding area. Her lifelong interest in colonial and imperial matters found an outlet in the Second South African War; her son-in-law General Neville Gerald Lyttelton served at the front. Rather than seeing the conflict as a disaster, Stuart-Wortley believed that it would make Britain 'greater than ever' (How, 148). In December 1899 she caught influenza, and this time she did not recover. She died on 4 February 1900 at Ripley House, Ripley. LORI WILLIAMSON

Sources J. Stuart-Wortley, 'Emigration', *Woman's mission: a series of congress papers on the philanthropic work of women*, ed. Baroness Burdett-Coutts [A. G. Burdett-Coutts] (1893), 87–91 · J. Stuart-Wortley, 'On nursing', *Woman's mission: a series of congress papers on the philanthropic work of women*, ed. Baroness Burdett-Coutts [A. G. Burdett-Coutts] (1893), 216–23 · J. Stuart-Wortley, 'The East End as represented by Mr Besant', *Nineteenth Century*, 22 (1887), 361–77 · F. D. How, *Noble women of our time* (1901) · d. cert. · m. cert. · Burke, *Peerage* (1889)
Likenesses photograph, repro. in How, *Noble women*
Wealth at death £10,948 15s. 4d.: resworn probate, Oct 1900, CGPLA Eng. & Wales

Wortley, John Stuart-, second Baron Wharncliffe (1801–1855). *See under* Wortley, James Archibald Stuart-, first Baron Wharncliffe (1776–1845).

Wostenholm, George (1800–1876), cutlery manufacturer, was born on 31 January 1800 in Sheffield into the fourth generation of a family of cutlers. His father and great-grandfather, both named George Wolstenholme (a name that was shortened to facilitate its inclusion on knives), had built up the business from 1745, and by the early nineteenth century it was based at the Rockingham works in Sheffield.

Apprenticed to his father, Wostenholm was admitted as a freeman of the local craft guild, the Cutlers' Company, in 1826 and was granted the trade mark he was to make world-famous: I*XL. A contemporary was to describe him as 'masterful, keen, energetic, and far-sighted', a man 'whose whole thought and ideas—apart from realising a fortune—seemed to be centred in achieving in his cutlery the legend of his trade mark, I*XL' (H. Coward, *Reminiscences*, 1919, 40). His success was attained by close attention to quality and by exploiting the American market.

Father and son built up George Wostenholm & Son, though in 1830 there was a brief partnership with William Stenton, who initiated the firm's American trade. The USA was Sheffield's best market for cutlery in the early nineteenth century: about one half of the total exports of the British manufactured steel industry went to America until the mid-1830s. George Wostenholm, who took control of the firm on the death of his father on 31 December 1833, seized the opportunities this offered with alacrity. He made thirty visits to the USA after 1831, a New York office was opened, and the I*XL mark was established as far west as San Francisco. For Wostenholm it was the ideal market: with an expanding frontier there was an enormous demand for pocket knives, ranch knives, and weapons. Wostenholm was quick to identify the American fashion

for daggers and Bowie knives in the 1840s and 1850s and became the leading maker. The result was that the firm's trade became almost exclusively American and expanded dramatically.

Wostenholms became the fastest growing cutlery firm in Sheffield, and in 1848 its owner acquired a large Sheffield factory, which he named appropriately the Washington works. It was not a factory in the modern, mechanized sense, as cutlery was mostly handmade, and Wostenholm relied, as did every other Sheffield maker, on outworkers; but the Washington works did achieve some economies of scale and was regarded as a sign of a new era. By 1850 between 300 and 400 workers were employed at the Washington works, not far behind local rivals Joseph Rodgers & Sons, which had over 500 at its Norfolk works.

Wostenholm declined various public offices, including that of master cutler (though he eventually agreed to serve in 1856), preferring to pursue his business interests instead. He was, however, a JP and had a few interests outside his firm, one of which was the chairmanship of Truswell's Brewery Company Ltd. His most important non-cutlery activity was as a property developer, buying up land in the Sheffield suburb of Sharrow and laying out his Kenwood estate there along the lines of the townscapes he had admired in America.

Wostenholm was married three times: first to Mary Hobson (d. 1853); second in August 1855 to Frances Crookes, the daughter of a London merchant, who died ten years later; and finally to Eliza M. Rundle (d. 1886), the daughter of W. Rundle of Stockport. However, Wostenholm had no children.

Wostenholm was active until the end, though he sold out to his business associates in 1875, when Wostenholms became a limited liability company with a paid-up capital of £43,400 and over 500 workers. He died on 18 August 1876 at his home, Kenwood House, Sheffield, leaving a fortune of £250,000, and was buried at All Saints' parish church, Ecclesall.

Although Rodgers was the dominant Sheffield cutlery firm in the nineteenth century, George Wostenholm was arguably the most dynamic and successful individual cutlery manufacturer. His death marked the end of an era, for by the late 1870s the decline of the American trade and the advent of mechanization were beginning to erode the firm's trade. Unable to adapt to mass production, Wostenholms went into a slow decline and finally closed in 1983, its fate mirroring the decline of the Sheffield industry. GEOFFREY TWEEDALE

Sources G. Tweedale, *The Sheffield Knife book* (1996) · G. Tweedale, *Sheffield steel and America: a century of commercial and technological interdependence, 1830–1930* (1987) · G. Tweedale, 'Strategies for decline: George Wostenholm & Son and the Sheffield cutlery industry', *Transactions of the Hunter Archaeological Society*, 17 (1993), 43–56 · G. Tweedale, 'Wostenholm, George', *DBB* · Nether Edge Neighbourhood Group, Local History Section, *They lived at Sharrow and Nether Edge: a miscellany* (Sheffield, 1988) · H. Bexfield, *A short history of Sheffield cutlery and the house of Wostenholm* (1945) · W. R. Williamson, *I*XL means I excel: a short history of the I*XL Bowie knife* (1974) · W. Odom, *Hallamshire worthies* (1926) · J. H. Stainton, *The* *making of Sheffield, 1865–1914* (1924) · *Sheffield and Rotherham Independent* (19 Aug 1876) · d. cert. · tombstone, All Saints' parish church, Ecclesall

Archives Sheffield Central Library, business records of George Wostenholm & Son

Likenesses photographs, Sheffield Central Library

Wealth at death £250,000: probate, 11 Nov 1876, *CGPLA Eng. & Wales*

Wotton. For this title name *see* individual entries under Wotton; *see also* Kirkhoven, Charles Henry, Baron Wotton and earl of Bellamont (1643–1682/3) [*see under* Stanhope, Katherine, *suo jure* countess of Chesterfield, and Lady Stanhope (*bap.* 1609, *d.* 1667)].

Wotton, Anthony (*bap.* 1561?, *d.* 1626), Church of England clergyman and religious controversialist, was born in London, and possibly baptized on 17 October 1561 at St Mary-le-Bow, probably the son of the puritan lecturer Anthony Wotton, a colleague of William Charke and Stephen Egerton. After studying at Eton College, Wotton was admitted to King's College, Cambridge, on 1 October 1579, where he studied with William Temple. He graduated BA in 1584, proceeded MA in 1587 and BD in 1594, and was a fellow at King's until 1597. Impressed by Wotton's disputation with John Overall in 1594, Robert Devereux, earl of Essex, appointed him as his chaplain. Following William Whitaker's death in December 1595, Wotton competed unsuccessfully with Overall for the regius professorship of divinity, although his lecture on James 2: 24 was well received. In early March 1596 he was appointed professor of divinity at Gresham College, London, a position he resigned upon his marriage, on 27 October 1598, to Sybell, daughter of William Brisley of Isleworth, Middlesex. Hugo Gray succeeded him at Gresham.

While at Gresham, Wotton preached in London churches, and after resigning he accepted the lectureship at Allhallows, Barking, which he retained until his death. His affiliation with Essex almost got him into serious trouble, for the earl sent for him during the rebellion of 1601, but the summons arrived too late. Although Wotton refused to read the official denunciation of Essex from his pulpit, he expressed displeasure with the insurrection. For praying that James I's eyes might be divinely opened, he was briefly suspended by Bishop Richard Bancroft in 1604, but he was untroubled by the ecclesiastical courts during his years at Allhallows.

In 1600 Wotton wrote a substantive critique of Thomas Wright's *Certaine Articles or Forcible Reasons* (1600), an attack on protestantism, but he delayed publication when Essex rebelled. Troubled by the reprinting of Wright's book, at the urging of friends he published *An Answere to a Popish Pamphlet* (1605), in which he insisted that differences among protestant conformists and nonconformists involved ceremonies, not substantive matters. He then came to the defence of William Perkins, who had been attacked by William Bishop in *A Reformation of a Catholike Deformed* (1604); Wotton's *A Defence of M. Perkins Booke, called 'A Reformed Catholike'* (1606 [1607]) supported Perkins's views on such subjects as original sin, justification by grace alone, and the possibility of acquiring assurance of

salvation. Responding to yet another Catholic work, John Percy's *A Treatise of Faith*, Wotton, in *A Trial of the Romish Clergies Title to the Church* (1608), denounced Catholicism as the church of Antichrist, stressed the role of scripture as the sole rule of faith, identified justification as a crucial issue dividing Catholics and protestants, and argued that protestant doctrines could be traced back to the early church, the break in ministerial succession notwithstanding. Wotton's familiarity with patristic literature and Greek is manifest in his *Sermons upon a Part of the First Chap. of … John* (1609).

From 1611 Wotton came under attack from a fellow protestant, George Walker, shortly to become rector of St John the Evangelist, London. After reading such Dutch theologians as Arminius and Junius, Walker saw an affinity with the heretics Servetus and Socinus, and he concluded that Wotton, too, was espousing Socinianism. When Wotton refused to meet with him, he denounced Wotton from the pulpit. The two eventually agreed to a debate before ministerial colleagues, including Lewis Bayly, John Downham, Thomas Gataker, and William Gouge, all of whom concluded that Wotton was not a heretic. Walker refused to accept their judgment, Wotton continued to disseminate his views in manuscripts, and William Bradshaw published *A Treatise of Justification* [1615] in an attempt to end the dispute. Although Walker wrote a critique of Wotton's manuscripts, the archbishop of Canterbury's chaplain refused to license it for publication.

In the meantime Percy published *A Reply Made unto Mr. Anthony Wotton and Mr. John White* (1612), charging Wotton with 'grosse *untruthes*' (p. 10), deliberate misrepresentation, and inaccurate use of the church fathers. He also issued a new edition of *A Treatise of Faith* (1614) with marginal notes attacking Wotton. The latter resumed his attacks on Catholicism in two works published in 1624; the first, *De reconciliatione peccatoris*, was published in Basel after printers in Leiden and Amsterdam rejected it because of its reputedly Socinian views, according to Walker. In fact, Wotton believed this book cleared him from charges of Socinianism. The second work, *Runne from Rome*, included a critique of Cardinal Robert Bellarmine and was intended to give protestants substantive grounds for their repudiation of Catholicism. The publication of *De reconciliatione* prompted Walker to renew charges against Wotton. The latter's response was published posthumously by his son, Samuel, as *Mr. Anthony Wotton's Defence* (1641), with a preface and postscript by Gataker, who also wrote *An Answere to Mr George Walkers Vindication* (1642). Accusing Gataker of having 'raked up Mr. *Wottons* rotten body of errours out of his grave' (p. 32), Walker supplied his own version of the controversy in *A True Relation* (1642).

Wotton also turned his attention to Richard Mountague, charging him with espousing Catholic and Arminian tenets in *A Gagg for the New Gospel?* (1624) and *Appello Caesarem* (1625). Wotton's critique, *A Dangerous Plot Discovered* (1626), which he dedicated to parliament, listed eighteen Catholic and two Arminian tenets which he professed to have found in Mountague, including assertions that the church of Rome is the true church, that 'the Church representative' cannot err (p. 11), that grace is resistible, and that believers can permanently fall from grace. Contrary to Mountague's claim, he insisted that predestination was not a novel doctrine. He also wrote epistles for Peter Ramus's *The Art of Logick* (1626), which he had commissioned his son to translate. Wotton died on Tower Hill on 11 December 1626. His eldest son, Anthony (b. 1599), died young; Samuel (1600–1681) was rector of West Wretham, Norfolk; Robert (d. 1661) was rector of Gatesthorpe (Gasthorpe), Norfolk, and Tuddenham St Mary, Suffolk; and John (b. c.1609) was a fellow of King's College, Cambridge. RICHARD L. GREAVES

Sources J. Ward, *The lives of the professors of Gresham College* (1740) · Venn, *Alum. Cant.*, 1/4.466–7 · *CSP dom.*, 1598–1601, 558–60; 1601–3, 26 · P. S. Seaver, *The puritan lectureships: the politics of religious dissent, 1560–1662* (1970) · P. Collinson, *The Elizabethan puritan movement* (1967) · G. Walker, *A true relation of the chiefe passages betweene Mr. Anthony Wotton, and Mr. George Walker* (1642) · P. Lake, *The boxmaker's revenge: 'orthodoxy', 'heterodoxy' and the politics of the parish in early Stuart London* (2001) · T. Fuller and J. Nichols, *The history of the University of Cambridge, and of Waltham Abbey*, new edn (1840) · A. Milton, *Catholic and Reformed: the Roman and protestant churches in English protestant thought, 1600–1640* (1995) · D. D. Wallace, *Puritans and predestination: grace in English protestant theology, 1525–1695* (1982) · DNB · *Calendar of the correspondence of Richard Baxter*, ed. N. H. Keeble and G. F. Nuttall, 1 (1991), 50, 58, 191 · IGI
Archives BL, Add. MS 6194, fols. 281–2 · BL, Add. MS 6209, fol. 87 · GL, MS 9234/6, fol. 43r

Wotton, Sir Edward (1489?–1551), administrator, was the elder son of Sir Robert Wotton of Boughton Malherbe, Kent (c.1463–1524), and his wife, Anne Belknap. Nicholas *Wotton, a career diplomat who became dean of Canterbury, was his younger brother. The Wottons had been prominent members of the Kent gentry since the early fifteenth century, when Nicholas Wotton, a leading London merchant, bought property in the county and consolidated his position there by marriage. Sir Robert was prominent in the government of Kent, where he was sheriff in 1499, and was also employed at Calais, as master porter and later comptroller. Nothing is known of Edward Wotton's early life, but he was clearly a man of some education; the Welsh chronicler Ellis Gruffudd, who was for many years a soldier in the Calais garrison, described Wotton as both learned and religious, with a keen interest in the scriptures, and in 1538 a correspondent of Heinrich Bullinger's reported how Wotton had received a book of Bullinger's and was making good progress with it.

Much of Wotton's public life was devoted to responsibilities inherited with his position as a member of Kent's ruling élite. First recorded as a JP in July 1524, he was repeatedly reselected thereafter. He was regularly nominated to commissions of oyer and terminer, and was twice chosen sheriff of the county, in 1529 and 1535. Knighted by 22 April 1528, during that year he was among the gentry who peaceably quelled demonstrations by unemployed clothworkers, and twenty years later again adopted conciliatory tactics to help defuse a tense situation, this time when dissatisfaction with the policies of Protector Somerset led to vociferous protests throughout much of Kent. Never especially prominent at court, Wotton none the less

took part in several of the more spectacular ceremonies of Henry VIII's reign. He accompanied Henry and Anne Boleyn to Calais for their meeting with the French king in October, attended Anne's coronation in 1533 as a knight servitor, was present at the baptism of Prince Edward in 1537, and travelled to Calais in December 1539 to greet Anne of Cleves.

It was presumably his long service in local government that led to Wotton's appointment as treasurer of Calais on 24 November 1540, after he had been sent to the pale in July. His promotion served a dual purpose. It reflected the crown's determination to overhaul administration there, largely in accordance with recommendations made by Sir William Fitzwilliam's commission in 1535. And it also met the need for a highly competent administrator at Calais to oversee the large-scale refortification of the town begun in the late 1530s. Between 1539 and 1542 about £1000 a month was being spent on building work, with over 1100 men being employed at Rysbank Fort in April and May 1541. For much of this time Wotton had overall responsibility for the receipt and disbursement of wages, the purchase of building materials, and the administration of the construction budget.

Wotton remained treasurer of Calais until his death. Although works at Rysbank wound down from mid-1542, they continued elsewhere in the pale. But they were no longer Wotton's principal concern. As a leading member of the council of Calais and the chief financial officer there, from 1542 his energies were mainly devoted to preparations, and payments, for war with France. Between June and October 1544 he and his colleagues had to facilitate the landing and the re-embarkation of the two armies, comprising more than 25,000 men, dispatched by Henry against Boulogne and Montreuil. He was also personally responsible for providing the pioneers needed for the sieges of the two towns, and was criticized by the duke of Suffolk, the general commanding at Boulogne, for failing to supply the numbers required. Then when most of the English soldiers had returned home, Wotton played an important role in mustering and paying the thousands of Italian, German, and Spanish mercenaries who were employed to defend Boulogne and Calais against French counter-attack. Practically every day he and his fellow councillors had to cope with the disorders which arose at Calais from there being so many 'depraved, brutish foreign soldiers from all nations' garrisoned within the town (Gruffudd, 14). No doubt it was his detailed knowledge of the area which in 1546 caused Wotton to become involved in the negotiations to settle the boundaries of the English territory within the Boulonnais which followed that year's Anglo-French peace treaty.

Wotton's work as a trustworthy and dedicated crown official, and possibly also his evangelical sympathies, provides the best explanation for his inclusion among the eighteen executors appointed by Henry VIII in his will of 30 December 1546 to advise the young Edward VI. But although he retained his position on the privy council after its reorganization by Protector Somerset on 12 March

1547, Wotton's continued employment at Calais necessarily limited his involvement in Somerset's government, and he is not known to have attended a council meeting before 23 February 1548. In March he signed the council's letter ordering the administration of the eucharist in one kind only, but although he was employed as a commissioner in England in summer 1548, he did not attend another council meeting until that of 17 January 1549 which ordered the arrest of the protector's brother, Thomas Seymour, Baron Seymour of Sudeley. No doubt he was often engaged abroad. His experience of handling large sums of money probably accounts for Sir William Paget's urging Somerset in spring 1549 'to appoint Sir Edward Wotton (if he be able to lie at london as I thincke he be aswell as at his house) and Sir Walter Myldemaye to assyste for the money matters', in a programme which Paget envisaged as raising 'all … the money theye can possible, and make what shifte theye can to devise for more' (Hoak, 183, 185). But there is no evidence that this advice was acted on, and although Wotton became a member of the council's standing committee for Calais and Boulogne in autumn 1549 he made infrequent appearances at meetings of the council itself—thirteen in October–November 1549, when he gave tacit support to the coup against Somerset, six in November–December 1550.

Wotton retained his place on the privy council under the new government formed by John Dudley, successively earl of Warwick and duke of Northumberland, but continued to devote himself mainly to his duties at Calais. He died on 8 November 1551 and was buried at Boughton Malherbe. He had married twice. His first wife, Dorothy, daughter of Sir Robert Rede, died in September 1529, after which he married Ursula, daughter of Sir Robert Dymoke of Scrivelsby, Lincolnshire, and widow of Sir John Rudston. She predeceased him. His heir was his elder son, **Thomas Wotton** (*b.* in or before 1521, *d.* 1587). Educated at Lincoln's Inn, Thomas was MP for the Cornish borough of West Looe in 1547, and the fact that in 1554 he was sent to the Fleet 'for obstinate standing in matters of religion' shows that he had adopted his father's evangelicalism (HoP, *Commons, 1509–58*, 3.659). It was a position he maintained throughout his life. In the 1560s he supported Archbishop Matthew Parker's measures against radical puritans and Catholic recusants, but clearly sympathized with the former, since he became a patron of Edward Dering, and in 1584 was one of the leaders of the Kentish gentry in their resistance to Archbishop John Whitgift's drive for ecclesiastical conformity.

Unlike his father, Thomas Wotton played little part in national affairs, devoting his energies to the administration of his home county. Sheriff of Kent in 1558–9 and 1578–9, he was a JP, and of the quorum, from the accession of Elizabeth until his death. Some time after 1567 he erected the tomb in Canterbury Cathedral of his uncle Dean Nicholas Wotton, who had made him his heir, and was thus responsible for the execution, and perhaps also the design, of what has been described as 'stylistically one of the most precocious tombs of the period' (Eustace, 513).

His standing in Kentish society is underlined by his receiving the dedication in 1576 of the *Perambulation of Kent* by William Lambarde, whose patron he had been. In 1573 Wotton entertained Queen Elizabeth at Boughton; she offered him a knighthood, but he declined. He died on 11 January 1587, three days after drawing up his will, in which he left £400 to his wife, Eleanor, daughter of William Finch of The Moat, Kent, and widow of Robert Morton. She was his second wife, his first having been Elizabeth, daughter of the Sir John Rudston whose widow had been Wotton's own stepmother. His heir Edward *Wotton, later first Baron Wotton (1548–1628), was the second but oldest surviving son of Thomas Wotton's first marriage. The diplomat and writer Sir Henry *Wotton (1568–1639) was Edward's half-brother. Their father was buried in Boughton church. LUKE MACMAHON

Sources LP Henry VIII, vols. 1–21 · T. Benolt and R. Cooke, The visitations of Kent taken in the years 1530–1 … and 1574, ed. W. B. Bannerman, 1, Harleian Society, 74 (1923) · M. St C. Byrne, ed., The Lisle letters, 6 vols. (1981) · J. G. Nichols, ed., The chronicle of Calais, CS, 35 (1846) · D. Loades, The reign of King Edward VI (1994) · D. I. Grummitt, 'Calais, 1485–1547: a study in early Tudor politics and government', PhD diss., U. Lond., 1997 · B. Ficaro, 'Nicolas Wotton, dean and diplomat', PhD diss., University of Kent, 1981 · H. M. Colvin and others, eds., The history of the king's works, 3 (1975) · HoP, Commons, 1509–58, 3.659–60 · E. Gruffudd, 'Calais and Boulogne, 1543–1550', trans. M. B. Davis · A. R. Maddison, ed., Lincolnshire pedigrees, 4 vols., Harleian Society, 50–52, 55 (1902–6) · D. E. Hoak, The king's council in the reign of Edward VI (1976) · P. Collinson, The Elizabethan puritan movement (1967) · K. Eustace, 'Post Reformation monuments', A history of Canterbury Cathedral, ed. J. Collinson, N. Ramsay, and M. Sparkes (1995), 511–52

Wotton, Edward (1492–1555), physician and naturalist, born in the parish of St Mary the Virgin, Oxford, was the son of Richard Wotton, senior bedel of theology of the university, and his wife, Margaret. He was educated at Magdalen College School and became a chorister at Magdalen College in 1503. In 1506 he was elected demy, and on 9 February 1514 graduated BA; he was elected fellow of Magdalen in 1516, and in 1520 was accused of conspiring with other fellows to elect certain undergraduates to scholarships. Soon afterwards he became first reader in Greek at Corpus Christi College, just founded by Richard Fox, bishop of Winchester, though he was not definitely appointed until 2 January 1524, and retained his rooms at Magdalen. In a letter to Wotton, Bishop Fox, said that he had heard of Wotton's talents from the president of Corpus Christi and regretted that the statutes of Magdalen did not permit him to make Wotton fellow of Corpus. He made him, however, *socio compar*, and gave him leave to travel in Italy for three or five years from 1 May next, 'to improve his learning, and chiefly to learn Greek'. Wotton spent most of his time at Padua, where he graduated MD, being incorporated at Oxford in that degree on 16 May 1526. It is claimed that during his time in Italy Wotton played a part in preparing the first edition of Galen's complete works in their original Greek, which were published at Venice in 1525.

Wotton was admitted a fellow of the College of Physicians on 8 February 1528, was consiliarius in 1531, 1547, and 1549, elect in 1531, censor in 1552, 1553, and 1555, and president in 1541, 1542, and 1543. He does not appear, as is often stated, to have been physician to Henry VIII, but he served the duke of Norfolk and Margaret Pole, countess of Salisbury in that capacity, receiving from her an annuity of 60 shillings, and corresponded with her son Reginald, afterwards Cardinal Pole.

Wotton was the first English physician to make a systematic study of natural history, and he acquired a European reputation by his *De differentiis animalium libri decem*. The book was dedicated to Edward VI, and published at Paris in 1552 under the direction of Sir John Mason, Edward VI's ambassador to France, who had persuaded Wotton finally to allow it to be printed. The copy in the British Library, a fine folio, is probably unsurpassed in its typographical excellence by any contemporary work. *De differentiis* was the product of many years of accumulating material from learned authors, in the pattern of earlier sixteenth-century compendia. Its books follow an Aristotelian order: the first three are on the characteristics of animals in general; the next six begin with man, then quadrupeds, and so on down to squids, crustaceans, and molluscs. They form an astonishing mosaic of material, but suggest that no original observations of the animals were made by Wotton. The naturalist Conrad Gesner, of Zürich, who had commenced the publication of his *Historia animalium* in 1551, mentions Wotton's work in the 'Enumeratio authorum' prefixed to his fourth book (Zürich, 1558), and remarks that, while Wotton teaches nothing new, his book deserves to be read and praised as a complete and clearly written digest of previous works on the subject. However, Gesner delivered a harsher verdict in the annotations he made in a copy of Wotton's book acquired by the Library of the Wellcome Institute in London.

Wotton also collected materials for the history of insects, which were published in Thomas Moffet's *Insectorum sive minimorum animalium theatrum olim ab Edoardo Wottono, Conrado Gesnero, Thomaque Pennio inchoatum, tandem Tho. Moufeti* (1634).

Wotton died on 5 October 1555, and was buried in St Alban, Wood Street, Cheapside, London, where also was buried his wife Katharine, who died on 4 December 1558. Their son Henry graduated BM from Christ Church, Oxford, in 1562, and DM in 1567, was proctor in 1556, and, like his father, Greek reader at Corpus; he was admitted a candidate of the College of Physicians on 12 May 1564, and fellow on 18 January 1572, and was censor in 1581 and 1582.   A. F. POLLARD, *rev.* PATRICK WALLIS

Sources Foster, *Alum. Oxon.* · Munk, *Roll* · Wood, *Ath. Oxon.* · W. D. Macray, *A register of the members of St Mary Magdalen College, Oxford*, 8 vols. (1894–1915) · F. D. Hoeniger and J. F. M. Hoeniger, *The development of natural history in Tudor England* (Charlottesville, VA, [1969]) · C. E. Raven, *English naturalists from Neckam to Ray: a study of the making of the modern world* (1947) · R. Fox to Wotton, BL, Lansdowne MS 989, fol. 129 · *CSP Venice* · *The diary of Henry Machyn, citizen and merchant-taylor of London, from AD 1550 to AD 1563*, ed. J. G. Nichols, CS, 42 (1848) · J. Aikin, *Biographical memoirs of medicine in Great Britain: from the revival of literature to the time of Harvey* (1780) · *The visitation of London, anno Domini 1633, 1634, and 1635, made by Sir Henry St George,* 2, ed. J. J. Howard, Harleian Society, 17 (1883) · V. Nutton, 'Conrad Gesner and the English naturalists', *Medical History*, 29 (1985), 93–7

Likenesses W. Rogers, line engraving, NPG · engraving, repro. in T. Moffet, *Insectorum sive minimorum animalium theatrum* (1634), frontispiece

Wotton, Edward, first Baron Wotton (1548–1628), diplomat and administrator, was born at Boughton Manor, Boughton Malherbe, Kent, the second but first surviving son among the six sons and three daughters of Thomas *Wotton (*b.* in or before 1521, *d.* 1587) [*see under* Wotton, Sir Edward], administrator, of Boughton Manor, Kent, and his first wife, Elizabeth (*d.* 1564), daughter of Sir John Rudston of London and his wife. Sir Henry *Wotton (1568–1639) was his half-brother. The Wottons were among the leading gentry families of Kent.

Education and early life Privately educated, Wotton travelled on the continent and lived for several years in Naples with the result that, according to the Spanish ambassador, Bernardino de Mendoza, he became skilled in Italian, Spanish, and French. After his return to England he married, on 1 September 1575, Hester (*d.* 1592), illegitimate daughter of Sir William *Pickering of Oswaldkirk, Yorkshire, and his mistress. They had at least three sons and two daughters, including Pickering (*d.* 1605), Thomas Wotton, second Baron Wotton of Marley (1587–1630), and Philippa (*d.* 1626).

In February 1577 Wotton accompanied Philip Sidney to Prague to greet the newly elected emperor Rudolf II, and on their return the two men also brought Elizabeth I's compliments to Louis VI Simmern, elector palatine, and William the Silent, prince of Orange. Soon afterwards, in September, 'young Mr. Wotton and other gentlemen that are languaged' were sent by Sir Francis Walsingham, principal secretary, to escort to London Charles Philippe de Croye, marquis d'Havré, a councillor of state in Brussels, who went to England for talks on the Dutch crisis with the queen. Wotton's experience led in 1579 to his appointment as special envoy to Portugal, where he presented the queen's compliments to Henrique II on his accession to the throne. Since he needed only ten days for this ceremonial visit, he told Walsingham that he hoped he 'will accept good will in lieu of good service'. He then appraised the five contenders who might succeed Henrique, and noted that Philip II was first, although he saw two hindrances: 'the great and deep-rooted hatred' between the Portuguese and the Castilians and, second, the mounting resentment in England and France and among the princes of Italy at another addition to Spain's greatness (*CSP for.*, 1579–80, 45–8). He subsequently went to the court of Philip at Segovia to offer Elizabeth's greetings.

Late in 1584 Wotton was elected to parliament as knight of the shire for Kent, where during the session of spring 1585 he served on two committees and was eligible for its vital subsidy committee. In June he was named special ambassador to Scotland, where on the queen's behalf he proposed to James VI a defensive league with an initial grant of £4000 and a pledge of £4000 yearly. He also tried to persuade the young king to marry a protestant princess and advised against the influence of his chancellor, James

Edward Wotton, first Baron Wotton (1548–1628), by unknown artist

Hamilton, third earl of Arran. Although James expressed gratitude to Elizabeth on 27 June for 'so honourable and so wise a gentleman, so well affected to amity and so well thought of by you, as Edward Wotton, your ambassador' (*Salisbury MSS*, 13.268), by the end of August the king had proved a stubborn negotiator. He insisted upon a larger subsidy and an English peerage, both of which Elizabeth was unlikely to grant. He also declined to discuss his marriage and, on the advice of the French ambassador, postponed his approval of an alliance. However, James did agree to an alliance in 1586, a year after a disappointed Wotton returned to London. Wotton faced further involvement in Scottish affairs in September 1586, when he was sent as special ambassador to Paris to present to Henri III copies of the evidence for the complicity of Mary, queen of Scots, in the Babington plot. A year after his return, on 3 January 1588, he was admitted to Gray's Inn, and finally in 1589 he received his first court appointment, as a gentleman of the privy chamber.

Domestic service: disappointment and reward Following the death of Walsingham in April 1590, by the connivance of William Cecil, Baron Burghley, lord treasurer, the duties of the 'acting secretary of state' were taken over by his son, Sir Robert Cecil. Wotton's hope of gaining the secretaryship was renewed when, on 31 August 1591, it was known at court that 'the queen had given it out and the parties, Sir Edward Stafford and Mr. Wotton, were ready to be sworn at Nonsuch' to be the secretaries (*CSP dom.*, *1590–95*, 97). However, Burghley intervened again, to deny

Wotton the office. Once more, in 1592, after Wotton had received a knighthood the previous year, his expectations were again raised when Robert Beale, the former personal secretary to Walsingham, wrote a detailed treatise entitled 'Instructions for a Principall Secretarie … for Sir Edward Wotton' (Read, 1.423–42), but, for the last time, Burghley prevented his appointment. Hester Wotton died on 8 May 1592 and was buried at Boughton Manor four days later. Wotton served as JP and member of the quorum for Kent after 1593 and was sheriff of Kent in 1594–5. When Sir Robert Cecil obtained the office of secretary permanently in July 1596, Wotton bore no grudge over the victory, for his career benefited by their mutual friendship, as he pointedly reminded Cecil in 1599: 'For myself I esteem it a great part of my earthly happiness to be well thought of by you' (*Salisbury MSS*, 9.430); and he certainly did not lack for appointments. In August 1599, because of 'news increasing dayly of the Spaniards coming', he became 'the Treasurer of the Army of London's' recruits, as they assembled at Tilbury (*Letters of John Chamberlain*, 1.80). In February 1601, in reaction to the coup staged by Robert Devereux, earl of Essex, he joined the committee entrusted with the disposition of troops for the defence of London. Afterwards he examined witnesses for 'seditious words' in the earl's speeches (*Salisbury MSS*, 11.58, 66). In that year he was also among five nominated courtiers who 'flatly refused or avoyded' the onerous post of ambassador in France. (*Letters of John Chamberlain*, 1.122). Finally Wotton's years of service were rewarded by two major appointments. On 22 December 1602 he was sworn of the privy council and made comptroller of the household, where he was responsible for services 'below stairs', such as supplies, food, and transport.

The following year proved to be equally auspicious, for it was noted that during Christmas 'the court hath flourist more than ordinarie', since 'the new controller hath put new life into yt by his example, being allwayes freshly attired and for the most part all in white, *cap a pied*' (*Letters of John Chamberlain*, 1.180). On 13 May 1603 James VI and I created Wotton Baron Wotton, of Marley. Wotton successfully sought the hand of Margaret (1581–1659), daughter of Philip Wharton, third Baron Wharton, and his first wife, Frances, in marriage; he was more than thirty years older than her. The marriage was held in September. In November, Wotton was appointed with several other peers to the commission to preside in Winchester at the trials of Sir Walter Ralegh, Henry Brooke, eleventh Baron Cobham, and others involved in the notorious Main plot, to find evidence that they were planning the king's death in order to put Arabella Stuart on the throne. As a prominent landowner, Wotton was appointed lord lieutenant of Kent in April 1604, a position he retained for sixteen years.

Elder statesman Because of his skill in Spanish, Wotton was asked to escort Juan de Velasco, duke of Frias and constable of Castille, in August 1604, when he came in the name of Philip III to ratify the treaty of peace with Spain.

After he had appraised this grandee he wrote from Canterbury to Cecil that he was 'a very grave gentleman, courteous enough, his behaviour void of vanity, no tedious complimenter and in a word, to my thinking, his cariage not unlike yours' (*Salisbury MSS*, 16.208). He later accompanied the constable back to Dover and their cordial relationship endured, for in Spain in October 1605 the constable led a party of nobles to the funeral of Pickering Wotton, Wotton's eldest son, who died in Valladolid as a Catholic after his conversion by the Jesuit Richard Walpole.

In appreciation of his services James granted Wotton the leases of two manors in Denbighshire in May 1605, and shortly afterwards he and Cecil were executors of the large estate of George Clifford, third earl of Cumberland. Their names were also linked by Antoine le Fevre de la Boderie, the French ambassador, after the death of Thomas Sackville, Baron Buckhurst and earl of Dorset, the lord treasurer, in May 1608, for he believed that Cecil would succeed Buckhurst and Wotton become secretary of state. When Cecil remained secretary and also became lord treasurer, la Boderie retained his good opinion of Wotton: 'he is an upright man, among the more courteous and well-mannered here … he speaks French and Italian very well and shows good judgement, but he is thought to be a little Spanish' (la Boderie, 3.253).

It was once again his experience in languages that led to Wotton's final diplomatic mission in July 1610 as ambassador-extraordinary to Paris. He was instructed to bring James's condolences to Marie de' Medici on the death of Henri IV, to congratulate the young Louis XIII on his accession, and to witness the oath of Marie de' Medici, as regent, to a defensive league recently negotiated with France. This time he complained to Sir Thomas Edmondes that his entourage was too large: 'the number will be between 50 and 60 persones whereof there are some 7 or 8 knights and gentlemen of account', but he found 'no small comfort in this employment falling upon me so unseasonably in my ould age' that Edmondes was ready in Paris to assist him (BL, Stowe MS 171, fol. 316r). From there an informant wrote to William Trumbull in Brussels that Wotton had been given a jewel worth 4500 crowns, when he took his leave of the young French king, 'having given the Queen and everyone great satisfaction' (*Downshire MSS*, 2.362, 371).

After the final prorogation of his first parliament in 1610, James was reported to be planning to bring more privy councillors into the House of Commons when the next one was convened. Consequently it was expected, according to George Calvert, that a peer such as Wotton would resign as comptroller, 'he retiring himself into the country with his young lady and contenting himself with the quality of a counceller at large' (BL, Stowe MS 172, fol. 28r); however, Wotton refused to resign without a substantial fee. In the meantime the profits from his various offices increased his fortune, so that he was able to purchase from Cecil in May 1612 the manor of Canterbury Park for £12,000. After Cecil's death Wotton was chosen as one of six commissioners of the treasury to serve in the interim until Sir Thomas Egerton was appointed a year later. In March 1614, when James granted a charter to the Company for the Export of Dyed and Dressed Cloths, Wotton was named one of its twenty-two commissioners. Of greater financial advantage was his appointment as treasurer of the household, following his resignation of the comptrollership in November 1616. Although he held this office for little more than a year, there were at least two valuable awards during his tenure. He received warrants to the exchequer and the court of wards for a share in the profits of the 'arrears of alienations' for certain regnal years of Elizabeth, since by his means 'the detention of the duties was made known to the king' (*CSP dom.*, 1611–18, 418) and in 1617 he received a grant of all concealed wardships since 1588. In January 1618 Chamberlain observed that Wotton, 'growing weary of waiting at court', had agreed to resign his office of treasurer for £5000 to his friend from Paris, Edmondes (*Letters of John Chamberlain*, 2.125). However he retained his appointments as lord lieutenant of Kent, which included a right to the shipwrecks on that coast, as a privy councillor, and, since March 1617, as one of the commission for Spanish affairs, who advised the king on the negotiations of Prince Charles's marriage.

The final years Since he had the opportunity to live in greater privacy in London and Boughton Manor, with fewer days of attendance at court, Wotton began to practise his personal belief as a Catholic, a step that he had wished to take since 1610. On 22 April 1618, according to a letter to Philip from Diego Sarmiento de Acuña, count of Gondomar, Fray Diego de la Fuente, the chaplain of the embassy, received into the Roman Catholic church 'a Privy Councillor of the highest rank and ability', providing him with 'confession, mass and holy communion', for he had never before practised these rites (Archivo general de Simancas, estado, 2598, fol. 38r). While the ambassador withheld the name of the convert as a precaution, Philip already knew his identity from Alonso de Velasco, his predecessor. In a letter written eight years earlier to Philip on 3 August 1610, Velasco related that Wotton had come to the embassy and revealed that he was 'a Catholic in private' ('Catolico en secreto'). He begged him tearfully to secure from Paul V 'a sealed document' ('bulla'), stating that he could be absolved at the time of his death. In effect he would not be expected to make public his renunciation of the established church by avoiding its services. He said that if he was known to be a Catholic it would put at risk his offices, wife, children, and estates, and so he urged Velasco to appeal to Philip to write to his ambassador in Rome on his behalf (ibid., 2587, fol. 108r). Accordingly, on 19 November, Philip wrote to the count of Castro, his ambassador in Rome, asking him to bring to the pope an enclosed autographed petition 'on behalf of a person for whom I have a very high regard' (ibid., 1862, unfoliated) but advised secrecy. After a long wait, Philip was pleased to learn from Castro by 11 April 1612 'that his Holiness had granted the document sought on behalf of Baron Wotton', which would be given to him by Velasco at a convenient time (ibid., 1863, unfoliated). It was a difficult time for English recusants, as Gondomar had learned after his first arrival in May 1614. In private conversations with Queen Anne, Henry Howard, earl of Northampton, and Wotton about how to improve the lot of English Catholics with the strict enforcement of the penal laws, he concluded that nothing could be done at present. Wotton's partial retirement early in 1618 enabled him to follow certain other Catholic gentry who sheltered at times itinerant priests in their manor houses in Kent. For six years his recusancy went unnoticed. In May 1620 he resigned the lord lieutenancy of Kent at the request of George Villiers, duke of Buckingham, who wished to give it to Ludovick Stuart, second duke of Lennox, but in its place he was added to the commission for ecclesiastical causes. He continued to attend the privy council as needed, to serve as JP, and even to appoint to certain benefices in the established church.

However, early in 1624 there was a radical change. Wotton was summoned to the Maidstone assizes on a charge of recusancy, for until then his age—seventy-six years—and 'a protracted illness of twelve years' had excused his attendance at the parish of Boughton Manor (Loomie). To the surprise of the JPs, Wotton admitted that he was indeed a Catholic and was relieved to say it openly, and concluded by reminding them of his previous and current services to the crown. No doubt out of respect for his long service and high standing, the assizes demurred from passing judgment. On 20 May 1624 George Abbot, archbishop of Canterbury, presented to the House of Lords a petition from the Commons against Catholics in public office. Among those named was Wotton: 'for he and his wife do forbear the church and are justly suspected to affect the Roman Religion' (Loomie, 343), but the Lords deferred further action at that time. After Charles I came to the throne, Wotton was one of seven peers ordered not to take the oath as privy councillors in April 1625, 'and so are discharged of the Counsaile' (Letters of John Chamberlain, 2.609). For the first two parliaments of 1625 and 1626 Wotton was excused by ill health, but he gave his proxy each time to the influential lord chamberlain, William Herbert, earl of Pembroke. He died at Boughton Malherbe on 4 May 1628, aged eighty, and was buried in the same church at Boughton Malherbe, that, on a plea of illness, he had avoided for twelve years. His private Catholic practice was ignored until the furore arose in 1633, when his widow, who had retired to Canterbury, arranged, without consulting church authorities, to move the baptismal font in the church at Boughton Manor closer to the baron's tomb. Below it a stone was inscribed: 'To her beloved husband, Lord Edward Wotton, Baron of Marley, a Catholic. His grieving wife, Lady Margaret Wotton, daughter of Lord Wharton of Wharton, a Catholic'. For her disruption of the church's interior, as well as her recusancy, the widow was fined £500 by the court of high commission.   A. J. LOOMIE

Sources HoP, *Commons, 1558–1603* • A. J. Loomie, 'A Jacobean crypto-Catholic: Lord Wotton', *Catholic Historical Review*, 53 (1967), 328–45 • GEC, *Peerage* • G. M. Bell, *A handlist of British diplomatic representatives, 1509–1688*, Royal Historical Society Guides and Handbooks, 16 (1990) • *CSP dom., 1590–95; 1597–1601; 1603–10; 1611–23* • *The letters of John Chamberlain*, ed. N. E. McClure, 2 vols. (1939) • *Calendar of the manuscripts of the most hon. the marquis of Salisbury*, 24 vols., HMC, 9 (1883–1976), vols. 9, 11, 13, 16 • *Report on the manuscripts of the marquis of Downshire*, 6 vols. in 7, HMC, 75 (1924–95), vols. 2, 4 • unbound vols., Archivo General de Simancas, sección de estado, legajos 1862, 1863, 2587, 2598 • C. Read, *Mr Secretary Walsingham and the policy of Queen Elizabeth*, 3 vols. (1925) • BL, Stowe MSS 171, 172 • *CSP for., 1579–80* • A. L. de la Boderie, *Ambassades de monsieur de la Boderie en Angleterre … (1606–1611)*, ed. P. D. Burtin, 4 vols. (1750), vol. 3

Archives PRO, state papers domestic, letters | Hunt. L., letters to Temple family • PRO, state papers foreign • PRO, state papers Scotland

Likenesses portrait, priv. coll. [*see illus.*]

Wotton, Sir Henry (1568–1639), diplomat and writer, was born at Boughton Hall, Kent, the second and only surviving son of an estate manager, Thomas *Wotton (*b.* in or before 1521, *d.* 1587) [*see under* Wotton, Sir Edward], and his second wife, Eleanor Morton, daughter of Sir William Finch of Eastwell, Kent; Edward *Wotton (1548–1628), from 1603 Baron Wotton of Marley, was his half-brother.

Education and travel, 1584–1604 After being educated privately Wotton attended Winchester College before matriculating at New College, Oxford, on 5 June 1584. He moved, in October 1584, to Hart Hall, where he studied civil law under Alberico Gentili and met one of his lifelong friends, John Donne. In 1586 he moved to Queen's College, where he studied natural philosophy before graduating BA on 8 June 1588.

In October 1589, supported in part by a legacy from his deceased father, Wotton travelled for the first time on the continent as both student and tourist. After visiting cities in north Germany he attended lectures in law at Heidelberg for six months and also sought to master the language: 'I dare boldly to say that before I visit Italy there is no German that shall not take me for a German' (Smith, 1.238). In 1590 he visited Bavaria and Austria before he arrived in Vienna, where he was pleased to lodge in the house of a protestant, Dr Hugo Blotius, who was master of the library of the emperor, Rudolf II. Again he attended the lectures of members of the law faculty, whom he found 'all marvelously devout Papists', but 'that troubles me not' (ibid., 1.240). In late August 1591 he headed for Italy, where he visited the cities famous during the Renaissance. After his first tour of Rome he commented to Edward, Lord Zouche: 'in my opinion … her delights on earth are sweet and her judgements in heaven heavy' (ibid., 1.274). While living in Florence for eleven months he described it to Zouche in 1592 as 'a paradise inhabited by devils' (ibid., 1.281). He also confided 'I have received instruction to remain in Tuscany, not far from the Great Duke's court … I wait to whom I shall be addressed' (ibid., 1.287), which implied that he could be reporting to a courtier in London.

In June 1593 Wotton arrived in Geneva, where he lodged for over a year in the house of Isaac Casaubon, the eminent classical scholar, under whose tutelage he read Greek authors and improved his French. Before starting

Sir Henry Wotton (1568–1639), by unknown artist

his return to England in August 1594 Wotton completed an essay entitled 'The state of Christendom', which, although not printed until 1657, reflected his personal view of life across the channel after five years. Because of the current Anglo-Spanish war his deepest grievance was that he did not hear enough 'in praise of my countrey and in disgrace of Spain' (Wotton, *State of Christendom*, 3). 'Chief Actors' in his 'tragical discourse' were

> the mighty monarch of Spain, the merciful queen of England, the unfortunate Don Antonio of Portugal [d. 1594], the valiant king of France [Henri IV], the imperious prelate of Rome [Clement VIII], the sleeping and secure states of Germany, the politique and grave senate of Venice and the weak but wise princes of Italy.   (ibid., 4)

There followed sixty-three discourses which stressed his devotion to Queen Elizabeth and his disdain of Philip II, 'the terror of princes', and illustrated his acquaintance with classical authors.

Late in 1594 Wotton became one of the secretaries of the earl of Essex, to whom he offered the reports by his network of informants with whom he then corresponded. Since they wrote from Siena, Florence, Geneva, Heidelberg, Basel, Vienna, Prague, Utrecht, and The Hague, Wotton's services were valuable. Similarly, being fluent in German, on Essex's behalf he twice visited the margrave of Baden while he was in London. In spring 1596 Wotton, as a secretary of Essex, and John Donne, as a 'gentleman volunteer', joined the fleet led by Charles Howard of Effingham. The role of the two friends was minimal, but the costly expedition to Cadiz resulted in 'nothing more substantial than a couple of captured galleons, a sacked city and three dozen self-incinerated merchant vessels' (Wernham, 112). Wotton and Donne sailed again with

Essex in the summer of 1597 to the Azores, where it was hoped that a Spanish treasure fleet would be captured. Since that fleet had already anchored in a fortified harbour on Terceira it proved to be a grave risk to attempt any assault, so the squadron returned to England with little to show the critics of Essex at court. This time John Donne sent to Wotton a graceful verse letter advising him to be 'thine owne home and in thy selfe dwell', with his faith: 'free from German schismes, and lightnesse of France, and faire Italies faithlessnesse'. To this Wotton replied with verses on the theme that 'the mind is its owne place' (Bald, 120). In April 1599 he accompanied Essex to Dublin, from where he wrote to Donne with a firm loyalty to the earl: 'for our wars, I can only say we have a good cause and the worthiest gentleman of the world to lead it' (Smith, 1.309). The high point of Wotton's service in Ireland was as one of two negotiators with the earl of Tyrone, in which capacity he drafted articles of peace according to Essex's instructions. However, after he returned to London he learned of Elizabeth's severe displeasure at Essex's other decisions and at these articles.

Accordingly Wotton prudently left the household of Essex, and late in 1600 went on another tour of the continent with his nephew, Pickering Wotton, oldest son of his half-brother, Edward. After witnessing the festivities for the marriage of Henri IV in Paris they travelled to Florence, where they met Sir Anthony Sherley, who was related to the family of Henry Wotton's mother. Here Wotton was presented to Ferdinand I, grand duke of Tuscany, who later asked him to go on a secret mission to James VI of Scotland to inform him that the duke had learned of a plot to poison him and to carry a box of antidotes prepared by Ferdinand's personal physicians. Leaving his nephew in the care of friends, Wotton left in May 1601 disguised as an Italian merchant, Ottavio Baldi. As James had known the threats of the Ruthven raiders in 1583 and of the Gowrie conspiracy in 1600 the unexpected arrival of 'Ottavio Baldi' was welcomed at Dunfermline. According to Izaak Walton's account in the preface to *Reliquiae Wottonianae*, Wotton 'whispers to the king in his owne language that he was an Englishman, beseeching him for a more private conference … and that he might be concealed during his stay in that nation, which was promised' (Walton, sig. B4–C). Wotton stayed under the protection of a grateful king during the winter and, after a difficult journey through the empire, arrived in Florence in May 1602.

Following the death of Queen Elizabeth, Wotton wrote to Secretary Cecil from Venice in May 1603 that he was grateful to learn from his brother Edward that Cecil had a 'good and gracious conceit' of him and that he felt encouraged 'to carry towards your honourable person the same unfeigned zeal and devotion with my brother's' (Smith, 1.318). He admitted his former loyalty to Cecil's rival but insisted that he had no part in Essex's rebellion and now offered his 'perpetual fidelity and devotion'. His pledge was accepted for, on 5 December 1603, the Venetian ambassador was told of Wotton's appointment, since King James had known him in Scotland to be a 'discreet and prudent gentleman' (*CSP Venice, 1603–7*, 190). Although his appointment was made on 26 December 1603 he did not reach London until April 1604. To add further dignity to this first 'lieger', or resident, ambassador to Venice since 1550 James conferred a knighthood on him on 8 July. John Donne, though pleased at this promotion, was saddened at the prospect of his absence in his poem: 'Fortune … spies that I beare so well her tyranny, that she thinks nothing else so fit for mee' (Bald, 146).

First embassies to Venice and Savoy, 1604–1612 After hiring a small palace at Canareggio near the Grand Canal, Wotton was gratified by his ceremonial reception by the doge, Marino Grimani, and his *collegio*, or council, of twenty-five senators. They listened to his oration in Italian in praise of the republic's history, which avoided any mention of the grievances of English merchants. For his first year his duties were hardly a burden, but he soon became engrossed in the famous quarrel between Pope Paul V, elected in May 1605, and the new doge, Leonardo Donà, elected in January 1606. Tensions already existed between Rome and Venice, due to laws passed during Grimani's regime, that 'could not be justified by any papal concessions'; they were, in fact, an interference with the existing law as it had grown up in the course of more than a thousand years' (von Pastor, 25.117ff.). When negotiations broke down in Rome, Paul V imposed an interdict on the republic and excommunicated the doge, expecting vainly to force a change in policy. Instead Donà, 'a devotedly religious man, governed by a stern sense of duty … secure in his own conscience' (Lane, 397), threatened severe punishment of all who obeyed the decree and publicly attended mass daily at St Mark's.

Wotton was pleased at such a resolute challenge to the pope and particularly at the writings of Paolo Sarpi, the official theologian of the republic. Without consulting Cecil he urged the doge to join a defensive league against the pope that he presumed would include James I, Henri IV, and some protestant Swiss cantons. However, Donà showed no interest and reminded him that 'Venice was determined to maintain its faith' (*CSP Venice, 1603–7*, 348–9). Even then, on 22 September 1606, Wotton made another offer of English forces against the pope, but was cautioned by Cecil to secure the precise terms first from King James. It was not until April 1607 that Cardinal de Joyeuse, in the name of Henri IV, created a face-saving solution by telling each side 'that the other had yielded more than it really had' (Lane, 398). By this date Wotton was planning with his chaplain how to open up the republic to protestant books and preachers. He praised Sarpi in his letters and sent his portrait to Cecil, now earl of Salisbury, in September 1607, so that James might 'behold a sound protestant as yet in the habit of a friar' (Smith, 1.399). His zeal for this cause peaked in April 1608, when he wrote a long report to James describing Sarpi's plan to advance the religious reform of the entire Veneto.

Wotton's unconcealed disbelief at the end of the quarrel of Donà and the pope annoyed Salisbury, who commented to Thomas Lake in April 1609 that Wotton 'still writes doubtfully of the composition between Rome and Venice … I always embraced a contrary opinion' (*CSP dom., 1603–25*, 516). Another sign of Wotton's continued misunderstanding of Donà's view of the pope occurred in August 1609 when, in a public audience, he presented to him a copy of King James's book: *A Pre-Monition to All … Monarchs*. Since it was already known in Italy that in several passages James compared the pope to the Antichrist of the book of Revelation, Donà accepted it but then locked it in his private archive and forbade its sale in the Veneto. Unaware that Donà was offended, Wotton, without permission, resigned as ambassador, claiming that his king had been insulted. At once Donà sent a special ambassador to assure James of the republic's continued goodwill, but only weeks later was Wotton aware that he had exceeded his instructions. On 6 August 1610 Wotton wrote to Salisbury to secure his recall: 'for no doubt the maxim is good, that no season or weather can be ill to go homewards' (Smith, 1.494), and the name of a successor, Sir Dudley Carleton, was duly announced. At his farewell audience on 7 December 1610 Wotton received a gold chain; Donà, praising his service, commented ironically that, 'Although there was in your house another religion, yet both you and all your suite have acted so prudently and circumspectly' (*CSP Venice, 1610–13*, 90).

During March and April 1612 Wotton journeyed as an ambassador-extraordinary to Savoy with detailed orders from Salisbury. He was to assure Prince Charles Emmanuel of James's strong friendship despite his refusal of a dual marriage treaty proposed by the count of Cartignana in February 1611. He had sought a match between Prince Henry, the heir of James I, and the Infanta Maria of Savoy, and between Princess Elizabeth and Victor Amadeus, heir to Charles Emmanuel. On the king's behalf Wotton had to state that 'the Prince oure sonn' was 'advanced to so much rypeness of age and judgement' that the choice of a consort was to be his own (*Salisbury MSS*, 21.344–5). In November 1611, the count had returned to suggest again the match of Princess Elizabeth with Victor Amadeus but was politely refused, since the discussions of her betrothal to the elector palatine were well advanced. Accordingly, Wotton's mission to Turin was largely a ceremonial renewal of friendship, for which his fluency in Italian was well suited. However, before his departure on 15 June 1612, after a cordial reception by Charles Emmanuel, Wotton had earnestly on his own initiative tried to promote a defensive alliance of Savoy with England, but he failed to arouse support at that court.

After his return Wotton faced the wrath of King James, who was embarrassed by the published attack of Kaspar Schoppe, or Scioppius (d. 1649), on James's new book, an apologia for his oath of allegiance. This Catholic polemicist revealed that in August 1604, during a visit to Augsburg, Wotton had written in a friend's commonplace book in Latin: 'H. W.: *Legatus est vir bonus peregre missus ad mentiendum rei publicae causa*'. If this had remained in the original English as: 'An ambassador is an honest man sent to lie [reside] abroad for the good of his country', the pun in the verb 'to lie' would have been amusing. In a Latin version this *double entendre* disappeared entirely, so that for many weeks Wotton faced the king's anger, who had warned 'yt was no jesting matter' (*Letters of John Chamberlain*, 1.385).

To recover the king's favour Wotton wrote an apology in Latin, which he sent to a friend in Heidelberg, who had it printed and distributed in the empire. To console himself in the midst of such misfortunes he was inspired to write one of his better-known poems, known as 'The Happy Life', which began: 'How happy is he born and taught, that serveth not another's will' (Smith, 1.129–30). He made progress in earning James's good graces by his forceful speech in the House of Commons on 21 May 1614. Here he defended strongly the king's right to levy impositions as a hereditary, not an elected monarch:

> Elective kings could not impose, because they received their thrones by the will of the people and were dependent on them … In Spain the king could impose in Castile, where he was hereditary monarch, but not in Aragon, where he was elected. (Moir, 114–15)

He was seconded in this debate by another diplomat, Ralph Winwood, but later in June, during a new debate on taxes, the house heard him use 'some indiscreet and undecent language' against another MP, so that he 'was cried downe and in great daunger to be called to the barre, but scaped yt narrowly' (*Letters of John Chamberlain*, 1.538).

Embassy to The Hague, 1614–1615 The Addled Parliament was barely dissolved when James selected Wotton to be ambassador-extraordinary to the Dutch republic to protect English interests during the negotiations over the impasse over the strategic Cleve and Jülich territories on the border of the empire. He made an initial blunder by angering Maurice of Nassau, when, following his stubborn insistence that Marquess Spinola did not plan to attack Wesel, in the duchy of Cleve, it was left without a garrison and was swiftly captured. In October 1614 Sir Edward Cecil complained to William Trumbull: 'They lay the blaem upon Sir H. Wotton … throughe an opinion had that Spinola would not attempt yt' (*Downshire MSS*, 5.44). Wotton began to salvage his reputation by his joint efforts with the ambassadors of France and Spain in drafting the treaty of Xanten, which divided the governance of the disputed region to the satisfaction of both claimants. For over six months he continued to be involved in new diplomatic problems, for in May 1615 he told his friend in Paris, Sir Thomas Edmondes, that he had been involved in four different treaties. In the first he had collaborated with Du Maurier, the French ambassador, in 'the sequestration' of Jülich and, in the second, he was concerned with the implementation of agreements reached at Xanten for the 'provisional possession of the two pretendants' for Cleve and Jülich. His third negotiation was not yet completed, for it was a plan to have a defensive alliance 'between the United Princes' (protestant princes of the empire), and the United Provinces. His fourth was a partial settlement of several trade disagreements between England and the Dutch republic 'which hath exceeded the other three in both length and difficulty' (ibid., 5.210). In September 1615 Wotton left The Hague with a gift from the states general of the United Provinces of 6500 livres, for which he was grateful since he was still in debt from the expenses of his previous diplomatic posts.

Later embassies in Venice, 1616 and 1621 When notified in August 1615 of his second appointment to Venice, Wotton commented with a typical classical allusion that his fortune resembled Plutarch's image of the Meander: 'the onley river of the worlde that after manye wyndinges and wandringes retourneth againe into his oune headd' (*Downshire MSS*, 5.317). His journey was unhurried, as a year later he had reached only as far as the court of the elector palatine, whom he vainly tried to persuade, along with other protestant princes, to have closer relations with Venice. When he visited Savoy for the same reason he also met a cold response. After arriving in Venice in July 1616 his letters revealed a period of discouragement abetted by poor health and financial debt. A fire which damaged half of his residence in January 1618 only made matters worse. However, his many complaints were reduced once the numerous regulations governing commerce between Venice and England were placed in charge of a special consul. Furthermore, King James gave leave to the republic to hire English ships and volunteers to curb the attacks of pirates on Venetian galleys in the Adriatic.

Wotton's reputation in London suffered once again after July 1617, when he sponsored an Italian adventurer, Tommaso Cerronio by name, without proper scrutiny in advance. Cerronio, claiming to be the superior of the Jesuit residence of Santo Fidele in Milan, assured him by letter that he had heard details of a plot to kill King James and Prince Charles. Immediately, without any investigation, Wotton sent his secretary from Venice to Milan with funds to escort Cerronio to London, where he was questioned by Archbishop George Abbot and Secretary Sir Ralph Winwood. They reported that his plot was 'so senseless and so sleveless a tale' that they were surprised 'at a man of learning traveling so far to tell it' (*CSP dom.*, 1611–18, 485). In London, Chamberlain wrote that the plot 'was not all worth the whistling, being certain strange chimeraes and far fetched ymaginations' (*Letters of John Chamberlain*, 2.101). There was no comment from James, but early in 1619 Wotton was recalled to London.

During his return journey to England, Wotton again visited the court of the elector palatine, Frederick V, and his wife, Princess Elizabeth. After his arrival home he wrote his famous lyrical poem in honour of Elizabeth: 'You meaner beauties of the Night, that poorly satisfy our eyes' (Smith, 1.170–71). Meanwhile, shortly after that visit, in August 1619, Frederick made his ill-advised decision to accept the title of king of Bohemia, without King James's approval and despite the stronger Habsburg claim, thus precipitating the turmoil of the Thirty Years' War. In answer to the pleas of Elizabeth, James chose the experienced Wotton to be his ambassador-extraordinary to the princes who might be helpful to Frederick. He then resumed his post in Venice for the third time. When Wotton arrived in Strasbourg in August 1620 Archduke Leopold welcomed him and expressed his desire to retain James's friendship. However, he accused the elector of intrigues in Bohemia against his brother, the emperor, and with the Turks over Hungary. By the time Wotton finally reached Vienna to see Emperor Ferdinand II the battle of White Mountain of 8 November 1620 had been won by the Habsburg forces and Frederick had been forced to flee Bohemia.

After a hazardous journey across the alps, in March 1621, Wotton's embassy in Venice also began inauspiciously. His ceremonial first audience with the doge, Antonio Priuli, was not, in his private opinion, accompanied by the large escort of senators appropriate to his status. After a furious protest later to the doge he decided to absent himself from the latter's presence for nine months, although he continued to send reports to London from Venice. In December 1621 he expressed dismay at a recent success of Spanish forces in the Valtelline: 'being now able to walk (while they keep a foot in the Lower Palatinat) from Milan to Dunkercke upon their own inheretances and purchases' (Smith, 2.221). His relations with the doge remained cold, for when, in May 1622, he begged for help for the elector palatine's weak military force led by Count Mansfeld, he was given a donation so small that he described it as 'naked bones without flesh' (ibid., 2.238).

Meanwhile, Wotton was disturbed to learn that Marc-Antonio de Dominis had left England and returned to Italy. This former archbishop and primate of Dalmatia had renounced his Catholic allegiance in 1616 and had been given funds by Wotton to go to England as a person 'of singular gravity and knowledge' (Smith, 2.100). King James honoured him by the positions of dean of Windsor and master of the Savoy and he had written a treatise against papal authority. However, six years later he was in Rome to appeal to the new pope, Gregory XV, for reconciliation. Angry at this desertion Wotton commented: 'Who can hinder Rome to lie and flatter themselves with their own fictions' (ibid., 2.240). Another crisis faced him shortly afterwards, when the palace of the countess of Arundel, Aletheia Howard, who was living currently on the Grand Canal, was falsely reported by a witness in the public trial of Antonio Foscarini to be the place where he had betrayed state secrets. Foscarini had been formerly the Venetian ambassador to England from 1611 to 1615 and knew the countess and several of her guests. However, after Wotton related this bizarre testimony to the countess he blundered by counselling her to remain outside the city of Venice until he advised her return. Furious at this testimony, and his advice as well, the countess insisted that he accompany her officially as ambassador to the doge at once. In the presence of the doge and other witnesses the countess insisted upon her innocence and demanded that the doge give her a written statement that there never was evidence against her, which the doge wisely decided to grant.

Artistic interests Wotton's flawed handling of the countess of Arundel's reputation and his inability to regain the confidence of an influential person of her rank did not enhance his chances for a new appointment at court after his return to London in late 1623. He turned away from Venetian politics to indulge his deep admiration for Italian art.

Wotton's *Elements of Architecture Collected … from the Best Authors & Examples*, a short book printed in 1624, undoubtedly reflected his accumulated insights during two decades in Italy. Among his contemporaries architecture was not yet a profession, but it was a frequent topic of discussion among his gentry friends, wealthy enough to plan the design of a country house, or its interior. In 1608 Wotton, aware that Salisbury was decorating Hatfield House, sent him from Venice a portrait of the Doge Leonardo Donà, describing it as 'done truly and naturally, but roughly *alla Venetiana*, and therefore to be set at some good distance from the sight' (Smith, 1.419). In his preface to *Elements*, he wrote: 'Architecture can want no commendation where there are noble men or noble minds'. In the first paragraph of part 2 he observed: 'Everyman's proper mansion … is the theatre of his Hospitality … the seate of Selfe-fruition … the comfortablest part of his owne life'. He did not dwell upon the famous landmarks of the Veneto, for his purpose was to praise the elegant simplicity of Andrea Palladio's work and the magisterial advice of Vitruvius. Accordingly, he limited himself to explaining the four principles which they approved as norms for architecture. These were harmony, proportion, proper decor, and 'the useful casting of all rooms for office, entertainment or pleasure'. His text, also reprinted by Izaak Walton, was known to later readers, such as John Evelyn and Christopher Wren.

Provost of Eton College, 1624–1639 In the spring of 1624 Wotton's financial needs were considerable, largely because of James's inability to pay his diplomats on time. Having decided to seek the provostship of Eton for the final stage of his career, Wotton had to follow the typical path of crown patronage. He had already shown deference to the duke of Buckingham by sending artistic works from Italy, and had two valuable reversions to use as a gift to the courtiers who would influence James's choice. In 1611 Wotton had received the reversion of a vacancy in the six clerks' places in the chancery, which he handed over to Sir William Beecher, clerk of the privy council, in exchange for his prior claim to the provostship. In April 1624 Wotton resigned into Buckingham's hands the reversion to the mastership of the rolls, which was said to be worth £5000. This bargaining led to his choice as provost by the king on 19 July 1624.

Since his duties did not preclude his attendance at Westminster, Wotton planned to return to the House of Commons in 1625. At first he was defeated as the candidate for Canterbury on 6 May 1625, but later at Sandwich he won the election by opposing Sir Edwin Sandys. However, he was not as prominent as in 1614, for a severe outbreak of plague delayed the sessions and he kept silent during the debates in the Commons which disapproved the concessions to Catholics required by the marriage treaty of Henrietta Maria. In 1627 Wotton was ordained a deacon of the established church, and assured King Charles: 'so far am I from aiming at any high flight … that there I intend to rest' (Smith, 2.304). Afterwards he composed three hymns: 'On the Birth of Prince Charles' (1630), 'A Translation of Psalm 104' (1633), and, during a severe illness in

1637, 'A Hymn to my God'. In 1638 he completed two short meditations: one on chapter 22 of Genesis and the other on Christmas day. In 1633, as a salute to the king on his return from his coronation in Edinburgh, he published a Latin panegyric *Ad regem e Scotia reducem*.

Two of Wotton's distinguished literary friends had already died. His cousin Francis Bacon passed away in 1626, but the family ties continued since Wotton's niece Philippa had married Bacon's nephew Edmund, with whom he continued to correspond. In 1631 John Donne, his close friend of more than forty years, also died. In 1638 he was visited by John Milton, who left with him a copy of his *Comus*, that enchanted Wotton, for he wrote to him: 'I should much commend the tragical part if the lyrical did not ravish me with a certain Dorique [pastoral] delicacy in your songs and odes, whereunto I must plainly confess to have seen nothing parallel in our language' (Smith, 2.381). He then went on to give advice on Milton's future travels in Italy. By far his most cherished friend during his last years was Izaak Walton (*d.* 1683), who wrote the first biography of Wotton as a preface to an edition of his collected works, the *Reliquiae Wottonianae* (1651). Twenty-five years younger than Wotton, Walton paid tribute to his nobility of mind in executing his duties as ambassador and noted the honour and trust bestowed upon him. However, Walton was criticized for passing over 'the large amount of correspondence which reveal a different person', for he merely composed 'the story of a gentleman told in a gentlemanly manner' (Novarr, 194). Walton once again presented this idealized portrait in his more famous *Compleat Angler* (1653), in which he advised his readers: 'I do easily believe that peace and patience, and a calm content, did cohabit in the cheerful heart of Sir Henry Wotton' (Walton, *Compleat Angler*, 37).

On 12 March 1635 Wotton was arrested in St Martin's Lane, London, by bailiffs of Westminster for a debt of £300, and was confined to his lodgings until payment. After Secretary Sir Francis Windebank informed King Charles of this arrest it was learned on 28 March that 'the king has discharged the 300 l. for which Sir Henry Wotton was arrested, and has ordered him a royal protection against his creditors until the 3000 l. due him from the king has been discharged' (*Hastings MSS*, 2.78).

A severe illness prompted Wotton, on 1 October 1637, to draw up his will, in which he arranged that his few possessions would be distributed in a fitting manner. His most notable gift was to King Charles, who received four portraits 'of those dukes of Venice in whose time I was there employed' (Smith, 1.215–19) and also his collection of the papers of Sir Nicholas Throckmorton, who had been an ambassador to Scotland and France under Queen Elizabeth. Other paintings, rare objects, and important works in his library went to selected courtiers and friends. By other statements in the document his executors would be able to claim enough money from the royal treasury to pay his debts. A most unusual request he made at this time was the Latin epitaph he desired to be placed on his tomb in Eton College chapel: 'Here lies the first author of this sentence: "The Itch of Disputation will prove the Scab of

the Church". Inquire his name elsewhere.' Wotton died at the college, after a 'feverish distemper', in early December 1639.

A talent for languages played a major role in his career from the outset. Not only was he noted among the students of Eton for his frequent apt selections from Latin and Greek authors while provost, but his lengthy tours and studies on the continent gave him a facility in Italian, German, and French, which was a compelling motive for his appointments as both extraordinary and ordinary ambassador. He incurred considerable debts by his missions to the princes of the empire, Emperor Rudolf II and his brother Archduke Leopold, the Dutch republic, Savoy, and the Venetian republic for three tours of duty. His travels and diplomatic activities can be traced in more than five hundred surviving letters, in which his polished style also displays far more of his unpredictable character. Talented and witty, his eccentric actions and clear prejudices probably hindered his rise to higher office at court, for which he had ambitions.

A. J. LOOMIE

Sources L. P. Smith, *The life and letters of Sir Henry Wotton*, 2 vols. (1907); repr. (1966) · *CSP Venice, 1603–25* · *CSP dom., 1603–25* · I. Walton, preface, in H. Wotton, *Reliquiae Wottonianae*, 4th edn (1685) · *The letters of John Chamberlain*, ed. N. E. McClure, 2 vols. (1939) · *Report on the manuscripts of the marquis of Downshire*, 6 vols. in 7, HMC, 75 (1924–95), vol. 5 · *Report on the manuscripts of the late Reginald Rawdon Hastings*, 4 vols., HMC, 78 (1928–47), vol. 2 · *Calendar of the manuscripts of the most hon. the marquis of Salisbury*, 5, HMC, 9 (1894); 21 (1970) · H. Wotton, *The state of Christendom* (1657) · R. C. Bald, *John Donne: a life*, ed. W. Milgate (1970) · F. C. Lane, *Venice: a maritime republic* (1973) · R. B. Wernham, *The return of the armadas: the last years of the Elizabethan war against Spain, 1595–1603* (1994) · Ludwig Freiherr von Pastor, *The history of the popes*, ed. and trans. E. Graf, 25 (1937) · T. L. Moir, *The Addled Parliament of 1614* (1958) · D. Novarr, *The making of Walton's 'Lives'* (1958) · G. M. Bell, *A handlist of British diplomatic representatives, 1509–1688*, Royal Historical Society Guides and Handbooks, 16 (1990) · I. Walton, *The compleat angler, or, The contemplative man's recreation* (1653)

Archives BL, corresp. and papers, Harley MSS · Leics. RO, commonplace book · NRA, corresp., dispatches, literary MSS | BL, letters to Sir Thomas Edmondes, Stowe MSS 168–175, *passim*

Likenesses C. Johnson, oils, 1620, Bodl. Oxf. · P. Lombart, line engraving, pubd 1654, NPG · line engraving, 1657, BM, NPG; repro. in Wotton, *State of Christendom* (1657) · line engraving, BM, NPG · oils, NPG · oils, Eton [*see illus.*] · oils, second version (of Eton portrait), NPG

Wealth at death impoverished; owed £3000 by the crown; arrears of salary: *Hastings MSS*, HMC, 2.78; will; Smith, *Life and letters*, 1.215–19

Wotton, Nicholas (*c.*1497–1567), diplomat and dean of Canterbury and York, was the fourth child and second son of Sir Robert Wotton of Boughton Malherbe, Kent (*c.*1463–1524), administrator, and his wife, Anne, daughter of Sir Henry Belknap. Sir Edward *Wotton (1489?–1551) was his elder brother. Sir Robert was a local administrator (sheriff in 1499 and JP) and full-time crown official in Calais until his death in 1524. Nicholas's sister Margaret was married to Thomas Grey, marquess of Dorset, and his sister Mary to Sir Henry Guildford. While Nicholas's elder brother, Edward, followed his father into crown service and Calais administration, Nicholas was sent to university. Although there is no surviving record, Thomas Fuller claimed he

Nicholas Wotton (c.1497–1567), by unknown artist

was at Oxford (c.1515–20), where he probably acquired a doctorate in both canon and civil law.

Early life and early career Wotton took clerical orders, and was presented to the rectory of Boughton Malherbe by his father in December 1517. In 1518 he was collated to the nearby vicarage of Sutton Valence by William Warham, archbishop of Canterbury. There is no evidence that he actually served either of these churches, and the details of his early career are vague. It is likely that he remained at Oxford until the end of the decade, then participated in the circle of humanist scholars at Canterbury, and made his first trip to the continent. He returned to England with Jean Luis Vives, whom he accompanied to Oxford in 1523. Wotton was again in Italy in the mid-1520s, spent some time in Perugia, and was admitted a brother of the hospital of St Thomas in Rome where he witnessed the imperial sack of the city in 1527. He returned to England in 1528 and was appointed official principal of the bishop of London. By this time Nicholas's brother Edward was a leading Kent magistrate; he served as sheriff of Kent in 1529 and 1535. According to Lord Herbert of Cherbury, Nicholas attended the first legatine divorce hearings in 1529 and soon after undertook his first diplomatic mission. In June 1530 he joined Edward Fox in the attempt to win favourable verdicts from French universities on Henry's right to a divorce. In that year he exchanged Sutton Valence for the rectory of Ivychurch, also in Warham's gift. He continued his legal career in London, and in 1536 attended the convocation, and acted as a proctor for Anne Boleyn in the divorce proceedings brought by the king. He was listed as one of the authors of *The Institution of a Christian Man* (the

Bishops' Book) in 1537, and the following year was made a royal chaplain and appointed commissary of faculties, an office he continued to exercise by deputies until at least 1549.

Henrician diplomat After a decade as an ecclesiastical lawyer, Wotton began his career as a diplomat properly in 1539. Four years after Henry VIII's renunciation of papal supremacy England was politically isolated in Europe, and faced the combined onslaught of France and the emperor. Thomas Cromwell's response was to seek alliances with the German protestant states. In March 1539 Wotton was one of a three-man delegation sent to Cleves, to negotiate a marriage between Henry VIII and one of the duke's sisters, and to establish a defensive league with the German princes. Following the arrival in London of a Cleves delegation to negotiate the marriage treaty Wotton was left as resident ambassador in Cleves. That summer Wotton's services were rewarded with another ecclesiastical sinecure, the archdeaconry of Gloucester, to which he was admitted in 1540. In the wake of the marriage treaty with Cleves (October 1539), the king offered Wotton a bishopric. He declined, and in November privately wrote to his friend Anthony Bellasis, 'if it be possible yet, assay as far as you may to convey this bishopric from me' (*LP Henry VIII*, 14/2, 501). Wotton was one of the English party that accompanied Anne of Cleves to England in December 1539, and he returned to Cleves as resident in 1540, where he attempted, unsuccessfully, to discourage the duke from restoring good relations with the emperor and with France, and had to inform the duke of the annulment of the king's marriage to Anne of Cleves. He was not recalled until June 1541.

Although his mission to Germany had been unsuccessful, he was rewarded with further ecclesiastical promotions, most notably as dean of the newly erected secular chapter of Canterbury in April 1541 (with a salary of £300 p.a.), and reappointed archdeacon of Gloucester, when it became a bishopric in 1541. Between June 1541 and March 1543 Wotton was at home, either in London or Canterbury, but little or nothing is known of his activities. He attended a convocation early in 1542, but seems to have taken no part in the developing conspiracy of Canterbury canons and local gentry against Archbishop Thomas Cranmer, known as the 'prebendaries' plot', of 1543. When the political crisis came to a head in summer 1543, Wotton was abroad. He and Sir Thomas Seymour were sent as ambassadors to Mary, Charles V's sister and regent of the Netherlands, following an Anglo-imperial alliance in February 1543. Wotton participated in negotiations that led to open war between both powers and France, and in November 1543 was transferred to the imperial court as ambassador to the emperor. In June 1544 he was joined by William Paget in negotiations leading to the joint Anglo-imperial invasion of France that summer. About the same time Wotton was rewarded with yet another sinecure, the deanery of York. During the summer Wotton accompanied Charles V's forces, while Henry VIII invaded northern France and eventually took Boulogne. Notwithstanding

Wotton's diplomatic efforts the emperor signed a separate peace in September, leaving England alone at war with France. Further high-powered delegations, including Bishop Stephen Gardiner and Edward Seymour, earl of Hertford, in November 1544, and William Paget in March 1545, were sent to help Wotton convince the emperor to renew war against France; all failed. Finally, in August 1545, Wotton was recalled and replaced by Bishop Thomas Thirlby of Westminster.

Wotton was ill during the next gap between diplomatic missions, but was soon appointed to the delegation (led by the earl of Hertford and John Dudley, Viscount Lisle) sent to negotiate peace with France in April 1546. Before leaving Wotton was made a privy councillor (7 April). The negotiations quickly led to a treaty (June 1546), by which England was to retain Boulogne until 1554. Wotton was appointed resident ambassador to France, a post he took up in July 1546 and retained uninterruptedly for three years. Henry VIII named him (as well as his brother, Sir Edward) among the sixteen executors of his will, but Wotton remained abroad and took no part in the political intrigues that resulted in the appointment of Hertford as protector of the young king and leader of the council. Although he helped negotiate a defensive league with France in March 1547, the death of François I and the rise of the Guise party at the court of Henri II ensured that long-term amity between the two countries was impossible, a diagnosis that Wotton offered the privy council as early as April 1547. A sense that war was always imminent pervades a letter from Wotton to his friend George Brooke, Lord Cobham, in which Wotton assured Cobham that if there was a breach between England and France, Wotton would look after his sons who were in Paris. There were many grounds for conflict between England and France, especially over Boulogne and French influence in Scotland. By summer 1549, with Somerset's government in disarray and popular rebellions in England, France attacked Boulogne. Wotton was recalled in September, and quickly joined the councillors who organized the coup against Protector Somerset in October. Wotton was rewarded with one of the two posts of secretary of state, in place of Sir Thomas Smith, who was seen as a Somerset partisan. The new government rapidly made peace with France, and Wotton was replaced as secretary by William Cecil in September 1550. During 1549–51 Wotton and Sir William Petre served as an informal 'foreign relations committee' of the council, and Wotton attended regularly. Just three weeks after he gave up the secretary's post he was rewarded with a dispensation from the Henrician statute which prohibited clergy from taking lands in lease and from buying and selling merchandise.

The 1550s: France and Scotland Wotton was perceived as a crown official rather than an ecclesiastic, despite his position as dean of both Canterbury and York. Yet in January 1551 he was appointed to the general heresy commission; in February 1552 to the commission to rewrite English ecclesiastical law; and in October 1552 to another heresy commission for the south-east of England, as the privy council became concerned with sectarian protestant heresy. In April 1551 Wotton was dispatched to Germany to replace Sir Richard Morison, whose explicit protestantism irritated Charles V. Wotton defended the English government's right to insist on its subjects' religious conformity, without provoking the emperor. But Wotton was recalled in August, and was present for the trial of Protector Somerset in October. He undertook a variety of council business for eighteen months, including dealing with the Flemish settlement at Glastonbury and with the Hanse merchants of the Steelyard. In autumn 1552 he took part in negotiations with the French ambassador and paid a rare visit to Canterbury during the king's summer progress.

In April 1553 Wotton and Sir Thomas Chaloner were sent to France to offer English mediation between France and the emperor, then at war. Wotton was therefore abroad during Edward VI's final illness and Northumberland's plot to deprive Mary of the throne. When the dust settled, Wotton was appointed resident ambassador in France by Queen Mary (August 1553), who may have seen Wotton as more acceptable in religion than most English diplomats. He remained as ambassador until war erupted in 1557. He had to break the news of Mary's proposed marriage to Philip II of Spain in 1554, and spent much of his embassy trying to counter French support for English protestant exiles like the Dudleys, Carews, and Staffords. Wotton's position was made more difficult by the involvement of a number of his own relatives in Sir Thomas Wyatt's rebellion in 1554, for whose pardon he successfully pleaded in letters home. He was also involved in attempts to initiate peace talks between France and Spain, but was seen as too pro-imperial to be a mediator. The stronger pressure from Philip of Spain was drawing England into conflict with France. Following Mary's declaration of war in June 1557, Wotton returned home. During the interval between the arrest of Archbishop Cranmer in 1553 and the installation of Cardinal Pole as archbishop in 1556, Wotton apparently took no active role in religious affairs in Canterbury diocese, although he was moved to protest about possible changes in the statutes governing the dean and chapter proposed by the canons in his absence, which might diminish the dean's authority. The diocese was in practice administered by two officials whose appetite for religious persecution was greater than Wotton's: Nicholas Harpsfield and Richard Thornden.

Following the French capture of Calais, Wotton was on the peace delegation led by the earl of Arundel and Bishop Thirlby in September 1558. The protracted negotiations—involving England, France, Spain, and Scotland—were interrupted only briefly by Mary's death in November. The English demand for the restitution of Calais was a sticking point, but after Spain agreed a separate peace with France in February 1559, Wotton and the English government accepted the reality that Calais could not be recovered short of war, and agreed a face-saving compromise in which France retained Calais. The treaty of Cateau Cambrésis was signed in April and Wotton returned home to report to a new sovereign. He was sent out to France again in May to receive the French ratification of the treaty, but not reappointed as ambassador. De Feria, the Spanish ambassador in London, felt that Wotton would become an important councillor of Queen Elizabeth, possibly being appointed archbishop. But there is no evidence that the new regime considered him for any important post. His religious conservatism—demonstrated in a paper he prepared for Elizabeth, 'Discourse on Scotland' (April 1560), in which he suggested nothing stronger than that the English should demand of France and Mary of Guise that protestants in Scotland be permitted to practise their religion 'quietly'—was out of step with the times. Nevertheless, Wotton was sent with Cecil and Sir Ralph Sadler to negotiate with Mary of Guise and French commissioners over the French military presence in Scotland, and the consequences of the establishment of protestantism by the Scottish lords. Meetings were held at Newcastle upon Tyne, Berwick, and eventually Edinburgh. Cecil complained about having to do all the work, 'for Mr Wotton, though very wise, loves quietness'. A treaty of Edinburgh, which side-stepped many of the contested issues but achieved the withdrawal of French troops, was signed in July 1560.

The final years During the next five years Wotton's public activities were confined to the domestic arena. As an elder statesman on the privy council, he concentrated on commercial and legal matters, although he was again frequently assigned to deal with foreign ambassadors. In 1561 he took part in negotiations to renew the commercial accords between England and the Hanseatic League, and negotiated the erection of a corporation to work the mines of England. He also served on a number of legal commissions, and was (along with several Kent gentry, including his nephew Thomas *Wotton of Boughton Malherbe [see under Wotton, Sir Edward]) on the commission to study the endowment and repair of Rochester Bridge in 1561. Perhaps significantly, when trouble broke out between England and France in 1562–3, Wotton was not asked to join the peace negotiations. It is also suggestive of Wotton's ambiguous position in Elizabeth's government that he did not attend the convocation of 1563. Nevertheless, in spite of his advanced age, Wotton was sent abroad (with Viscount Montagu and Walter Haddon) in March 1565 to settle the trade dispute between England and the Netherlands. The negotiations were protracted but fruitless. By June 1566 Wotton was already in poor health, and he finally returned to London in October. He died there on 26 January 1567 and was buried in Canterbury Cathedral.

Wotton was one of the most long-serving, and probably the last, of the great early Tudor clerical diplomats. The church provided them with an education, as it supplied the state with sinecure offices to reward its servants. Wotton was exceptional in his tenure of the deaneries of Canterbury and York, but there was never any pretence on his part of spiritual commitment or leadership. As his most recent biographer generously pointed out, 'Wotton spent much of his career distancing himself from the clergy and clerical affairs' (Ficaro, 271). Thomas Fuller was more severe: 'He was a doctor of both laws, and some will

say of both gospels … he never overstrained his conscience, such was his oily compliance in all alterations' (T. Fuller, *The Church-History of Britain*, 1655, bk 9, section 2). The only ecclesiastical matter that did command his attention was his patronage as dean of Canterbury; he attended some cathedral chapters in the 1560s. A number of letters, especially from the early 1560s, show him making appointments to church livings and chapter offices, leasing rectories and estates, and granting scholarships to the King's School. Wotton was at pains to gratify powerful friends and relations: Sir Robert Dudley in 1560 over the office of steward of the liberties of the dean and chapter; and Cecil in 1562 over the lease of chapter lands. As well as being an accomplished linguist, Wotton was an avid student of antiquities. He borrowed manuscript books from the cathedral library, and he figures among the speakers in John Twyne's *De rebus Albionicis*; two volumes of his own notes on historical and genealogical topics survive in the British Library. He left no will. The only extant contemporary image of Wotton is the sculpted effigy on his elaborate tomb in Trinity chapel, Canterbury Cathedral, erected by his nephew and heir, Thomas Wotton.

MICHAEL ZELL

Sources *DNB* · B. Ficaro, 'Nicholas Wotton: dean and diplomat', PhD diss., University of Kent, 1981 · D. M. Loades, *Two Tudor conspiracies* (1965); 2nd edn (1992) · D. M. Loades, *The reign of Mary Tudor: politics, government and religion in England, 1553–1558*, 1st edn (1979); 2nd edn (1991) · D. S. Chambers, ed., *The faculty office registers, 1534–59* (1966) · *CPR, 1547–58* · Canterbury Cathedral, archives and library, Canterbury letters; cathedral act book, 1561–8; Christ Church letters · dean and chapter accounts, 1541–76, Canterbury Cathedral, archives and library, MA 40 · tombstone, Boughton Malherbe church, Kent · Fuller, *Worthies* (1662), 2.77–8 · BL, Hartley MS 6064, fol. 83 [funeral description] · J. Dart, *The history and antiquities of the cathedral church of Canterbury* (1726), 86
Archives BL, Add. MS 38692 | BL, MS Harl. 902
Likenesses effigy, Canterbury Cathedral, Trinity chapel · oils, Canterbury Cathedral, deanery [see illus.]

Wotton, Thomas (*b.* in or before **1521**, *d.* **1587**). *See under* Wotton, Sir Edward (1489?–1551).

Wotton, Thomas (*c.*1695–1766), bookseller and genealogist, probably born in London, was the son of Matthew Wotton (*b.* in or before 1661), bookseller, whose shop was at the Three Daggers and Queen's Head, near St Dunstan-in-the-West, Fleet Street. Matthew was the son of a grocer, Thomas Wotton, from Bewdley, Worcestershire, and was described by John Dunton as 'a very courteous, obliging man' of the highest character, whose trade 'lay much among the lawyers' (*Life and Errors*, 1.210). Thomas was apprenticed to his father and was freed by patrimony on 4 February 1723. He continued the family business, and was warden of the Stationers' Company in 1754 and its master in 1757.

Wotton made his mark by publishing historical works, including an edition of John Rushworth's *Historical Collections* and editions of John Selden and Francis Bacon. In 1727 he edited and printed *The English Baronets*, an account in three volumes of all baronets alive at that date. The work was dedicated to the antiquary Holland Egerton (*c.*1689–1730), of Heaton, Lancashire, who had succeeded his father, Sir John Egerton, third baronet, of Wrinehill, Staffordshire, and Farthinghoe, Northamptonshire, in 1725. Wotton was assisted in its compilation by William Holman, of Halstead, Essex, and Thornhaugh Gurdon, of Norfolk, both of whom placed their collections at his disposal, and also by Arthur Collins, who had published an incomplete baronetage, in two volumes, in 1720. A revised and enlarged edition of Wotton's work appeared in 1741 in four octavo volumes (the third volume being in two parts, usually bound separately). For this edition Wotton made use of the voluminous collections of Peter Le Neve, Norroy king of arms from 1704 to 1729.

Wotton retired to his country house, Point Pleasant, Kingston upon Thames, Surrey, where he died on 1 April 1766. He died intestate, and letters of administration were granted to his widow, Frances Maria Wotton. She too died intestate, in 1773, when letters of administration were granted to her daughter and only child, Frances, wife of John Thomas, who also obtained a further grant of her father's property left unadministered by her mother.

In 1771 a new, abridged edition of *The Baronetage of England* (usually known as Kimber's Baronetage) was published by Edward Kimber and Richard Johnson. Kimber died while the work was still in progress and it was Johnson who penned a very fulsome tribute to Wotton in the preface. Of Wotton he wrote:

> (that indefatigable Labourer in the golden mines of Antiquity, whose Avenues were rendered almost inaccessible by the destructive Hand of Time, and the cruel Ravages of barbarous Nations) has cleared the Paths, which lead to the Perfection of this intricate Science. Neither the great Difficulties attending to Genealogical Enquiries, (in which so many Centuries were to be traced, and the Thread to guide them generally so slender, and, sometimes broken,) nor the Impossibility of persuading some Families to give the least Assistance, were able to deter him from this very difficult Pursuit.

DAVID WILLIAMSON

Sources DNB · GEC, *Baronetage* · E. Kimber and R. Johnson, eds., *The baronetage of England*, 3 vols. (1771) · administration, PRO, PROB 6/142, fol. 115v; PROB 6/148, fol. 98r · Frances Maria Wotton, administration, PRO, PROB 6/148, fol. 95v · D. F. McKenzie, ed., *Stationers' Company apprentices*, [3]: 1701–1800 (1978) · H. R. Plomer and others, *Dictionaries of the printers and booksellers who were at work in England, Scotland and Ireland, 1557–1775* (1977) · *The life and errors of John Dunton, late citizen of London*, 2 vols. (1818)
Archives BL, letters, notes, and pedigrees relating to *Baronetage* and grangerized version of print edition · Essex RO, Chelmsford, letters to William Holman

Wotton, William (1666–1727), linguist and theologian, was born on 13 August 1666 at Wrentham, Suffolk, the second son of Henry Wotton, rector of Wrentham, and his wife, Sarah. William had an extraordinary memory and was a prodigious natural linguist who could read Latin, Greek, and Hebrew verses when aged five. He was educated by his father, who described these remarkable abilities in *An Essay on the Education of Children* (written in 1672, published in 1753). He was admitted pensioner at St Catharine's College, Cambridge, on 20 April 1676, aged nine. He matriculated and graduated BA at the same time in 1680, having acquired Arabic, Syriac, and Chaldee and a

knowledge of logic, philosophy, mathematics, geography, chronology, and history. Evelyn described him as 'so universally and solidly learned at eleven years of age, that he was looked on as a miracle' (*Diary of John Evelyn*, 2.135). In 1679 Wotton was invited to London by Gilbert Burnet, later bishop of Salisbury, and introduced to learned society. Francis Turner procured for him a fellowship of St John's College, Cambridge, whence he proceeded MA in 1683 and BD in 1691. He was elected a fellow of the Royal Society in 1687 and ordained at Salisbury on 22 December 1689. In 1691 he was presented with the sinecure vicarage of Llandrillo-yn-Rhos, Caernarvonshire, by William Lloyd, bishop of St Asaph, and became chaplain to Daniel Finch, earl of Nottingham, and tutor to his family. Finch appointed him rector of Middleton Keynes, Buckinghamshire, in 1693, and Wotton resigned his fellowship and moved to this parish. About 1696 he married Anne (*c*.1671–1719), daughter of William Hammond of Canterbury. They had one daughter, Anne (*bap.* 1700, *d.* 1783), who married the antiquary William *Clarke (1695–1771).

Wotton published *A New History of Ecclesiastical Writers* (13 vols., 1692–9), an annotated translation of the work by Louis Dupin, and began compiling a biography of Robert Boyle at the suggestion of Burnet and with the help of Evelyn. This was advertised in the *London Gazette* in 1699, but was never completed, although surviving fragments display a remarkably modern approach to the writing of biography.

In 1694 Wotton published *Reflections upon Ancient and Modern Learning*, a reasoned analysis of the merits of the ancients and moderns in different branches of literature and learning, and a defence of the Royal Society. Taking the side of the moderns, he was answering William Temple's *Essay on Ancient and Modern Learning* and the works of Charles Perrault. It was 'one of the first historical accounts of the growth of scientific ideas' (Hunter, xxxvi) and 'of all the works in the controversy … was easily the most complete and the most judicious' (Levine, 34). A second edition in 1697 included Richard Bentley's *Dissertation on Phalaris*. The following year Thomas Rymer published *An Essay Concerning Critical and Curious Learning* in support of Wotton's views, giving rise to further pamphlet exchanges. Jonathan Swift satirized Wotton in *The Tale of a Tub* and *The Battle of the Books* (both published in 1704, although written earlier). This initiated a third edition of Wotton's *Reflections* in 1705, containing a defence of his work together with his *Observations upon 'The Tale of a Tub'*. In 1710 Edmund Curll published *A Complete Key to 'The Tale of a Tub'*, including 'An examination of Mr Wotton's Observations'.

Wotton took part in early debates upon the origins of life. In 1695 he contributed an abstract of Agostino Scilla's work on marine fossils *De corporibus marinis lapidescentibus* to the *Philosophical Transactions*, and in 1697 he wrote a 'Vindication' of the work, which was published in John Arbuthnot's *Examination of Dr Woodward's Account of the Deluge*. He likewise became involved in an exchange of open letters between John Harris and the naturalist Tancred Robinson during 1697. Soon afterwards he undertook, at the suggestion of Burnet, a *History of Rome from the Death of Antonius*, which was published in 1701 and dedicated to the bishop. In return Burnet presented Wotton in 1705 with the prebendary of Grantham Australis in Salisbury Cathedral, which he held until his death. Prior to this Wotton supplemented his stipend by teaching wealthy students, including Browne Willis from nearby Whaddon Hall. He was also said to be the translator of *A New Ecclesiastical History of the Sixteenth Century*, published in 1703.

In 1704 Wotton joined the attacks on the deists John Toland and Matthew Tindal with *A Letter to Eusebia; Occasioned by Mr Toland's Letters to Serena* and *The Rights of the Clergy in the Christian Church Asserted* (1706), which was a rebuttal of Tindal's *The Rights of the Christian Church Asserted*. Tindal responded in 1707 and 1708, and Wotton subsequently published a vindication of his work. He was also attacked by John Le Clerc in 1711.

In 1707 Wotton was awarded a Lambeth degree of doctor of divinity by the archbishop of Canterbury, Thomas Tenison, and in 1708 he published a useful conspectus of George Hickes's massive *Thesaurus*, with Hickes's approval and incorporating his footnotes. Other minor works from Wotton's period at Middleton Keynes included *The Case of the Present Convocation Considered* (1711); *Reflections on the Present Posture of Affairs* (1712), which was attacked by the nonjuror Charles Leslie; *Observations on the State of the Nation* (1713), and *A Vindication of the Earl of Nottingham* (1714). Several of his publications were either anonymous or used the initials M. N., derived from the last letters of his names. However, *Bart'lemy Fair, or, An Enquiry after Wits* (1709), 'by Mr. Wotton', is usually now attributed to Mary Astell.

Wotton's conduct at Middleton Keynes scandalized the neighbourhood, 'having no regard to common decency in respect to Wine and Women' (Levine, 404). In 1714 he was forced to move to Carmarthen, perhaps to avoid his creditors or else to avoid prosecution for sexual misconduct. He remained in Wales until about 1722, living under the pseudonym of Dr Edwards, becoming fluent in Welsh, and commenced a transcription and translation of the *Cyfreithjeu Hywel Dda* (as *Laws of Hywel Dda*), assisted by Moses Williams. He also drew up detailed descriptions of the dilapidated cathedrals of St David's and Llandaff at the request of Browne Willis. These were published, with other materials under Willis's name, in 1717 and 1718, and caused local controversy, owing to Wotton's outspoken comments about the neglected cathedral fabrics and misuse of their finances. Similar surveys of St Asaph and Bangor followed in 1720 and 1721. *A Discourse Concerning the Profusion of Languages at Babel* appeared, poorly translated into Latin, without his knowledge, in *Oratio Dominica* (1715), edited by John Chamberlayne; Wooton's English version was published in 1730. This work introduced the concept of an Indo-European proto-language by relating Icelandic, the Romance languages, and Greek, predating by more than seventy years Sir William Jones's famous lecture comparing Sanskrit with the classical languages. He also suggested the technique of glottochronology (calculating the rate of change of language by comparing ancient texts of known date with modern forms). Other works from his period at Carmarthen included *Miscellaneous Discourses Relating to the Traditions and Usages of the Scribes and Pharisees* (1718) and *The Omniscience of the Son of God* (1719). After returning to England he preached a sermon in Welsh before the British Society in London in 1722. He wrote an account of Thomas Stanley, published in Scevole de Sainte-Marthe's *Elogia Gallorum* (1722), and a description of the 'Caernarvon record' from the Harleian manuscripts, in *Bibliotheca litteraria* (1723).

Wotton died on 13 February 1727 and was buried at Buxted in Sussex. Subsequently several of his works were published by his son-in-law, including the unfinished *Laws of Hywel Dda* (1730) and *Advice to a Young Student*, which was reprinted several times as *Some Thoughts Concerning a Proper Method of Studying Divinity*. Thomas Birch wrote a life of Wotton (BL Add. MS 4224, fols. 148r–167v), which was the basis of later biographical accounts. There are conflicting accounts of Wotton's character. Boyle considered him 'modest and decent' (Nichols, 51), others talked of his 'humanity and friendliness of temper' (Chalmers, 32.310), while Hearne considered him 'a great Talker & Braggadocio, but of little judgment in any one particular science' (*Remarks*, 1.47). According to William Cole, his morals 'were as bad as his facts were excellent' (Levine, 404), and Nichols coyly referred to his exceptionable behaviour and conduct, 'particularly with regard to the fairer sex' (Nichols, 52). Browne Willis described his friend and mentor as 'a very debauch'd Man, & that by his folly he is like to be undone' (*Remarks*, 3.236). The flaws in his character may explain why his considerable achievements in a range of disciplines are not better known.   DAVID STOKER

Sources *British biography … from Wickliff to the present day*, 10 vols. (1773–80) · A. Chalmers, ed., *The general biographical dictionary*, new edn, 32 (1817), 306–11 · J. M. Levine, *The battle of the books: history and literature in the Augustan age* (1991) · M. L. Spieckermann, *William Wottons 'Reflections upon ancient and modern learning' im Kontext der englischen 'Querelle des anciens et modernes'* (Frankfurt, 1981) · M. Hunter, *Robert Boyle by himself and his friends with a fragment of William Wotton's lost 'Life of Boyle'* (1994) · A. R. Hall, 'William Wotton and the history of science', *Archives Internationales d'Histoire des Sciences*, 9 (1949), 1047–62 · *The diary of John Evelyn*, ed. W. Bray, new edn, 2 vols. (1907) · D. Stoker, 'Surveying decrepit Welsh cathedrals: the publication of Browne Willis's accounts of St David's and Llandaff', *Y Llyfr yng Nghymru* [*Welsh Book Studies*], 3 (2000), 7–32 · J. Nichols, *Anecdotes, biographical and literary of the late Mr. William Bowyer, printer* (privately printed, London, 1778) · H. Wotton, *An essay on the education of children in the first rudiments of learning, together with a narrative of what knowledge William Wotton, a child six years of age, had attained unto* (1753) · *Remarks and collections of Thomas Hearne*, ed. C. E. Doble and others, 11 vols., OHS, 2, 7, 13, 34, 42–3, 48, 50, 65, 67, 72 (1885–1921) · DWB · DNB · Venn, *Alum. Cant.* · R. Blench and M. Spriggs, eds., *Artefacts, languages and texts* (1999), vol. 3 of *Archaeology and language* (1997–9), 6–9

Archives Bodl. Oxf., letters | BL, MS life of Wotton, Add. MS 4224, fols. 148r–167v

Wealth at death poor; Nichols, *Lit. anecdotes*, says that he had not a grain of economy

Woty, William (*bap.* 1732, *d.* 1791), poet and literary editor, the son of Elizabeth and William Woty, was baptized at Alton, Hampshire, on 20 October 1732. Although little is known about his early years several poems indicate that he enjoyed a happy childhood in Hampshire. In 'An Elegy on the Death of a Late Deceased Schoolmaster, Near Alton in Hampshire', he writes, without naming the schoolmaster:

> A Parent always held my first esteem …
> You, as my Tutor was the next I lov'd;
> 'Twas yours to rear me with a father's care.
> (W. Woty, *The Shrubs of Parnassus*, 1760, 9)

After apparently receiving a good education he moved to London and began work as a law clerk, probably at Lincoln's Inn. There he found ample material for the poems that he soon began contributing to periodicals. In 'The Discontented Lawyer's Clerk' he comments on the work done 'all for eighteen-pence a day', adding the footnote: 'Half a guinea a week being reckoned a prodigious sum for a Clerk who works only ten hours a day, and is obliged to appear like a Gentleman' (ibid., 147). Describing legal attire, he writes:

> The ceremonial *tye* of barrister
> Loquacious, boasting its redundant locks
> I laugh to scorn.
> ('The Chimney Corner', *The Poetical Works of Mr. William Woty*, 1770, 2.120)

Woty published his first collection with the title, *The Shrubs of Parnassus, Consisting of a Variety of Poetical Essays, Moral and Comic, by J. Copywell, of Lincoln's Inn, Esq.* (1760). Next, under his own name, came *The Blossoms of Helicon* (1763). During this period he also co-edited, with Francis Fawkes, *The Poetical Calendar, Intended as a Supplement to Dodsley's Collection* (12 vols., 1763) and *The Poetical Magazine, or, The Muses' Monthly Companion* (1 volume only, January–June 1764). About 1767 he accepted employment with Washington, Earl Ferrers, 'as secretary and advisor in his law transactions' (*GM*, 1791, 379). He continued to write verse and to publish individual works in addition to the two-volume *Poetical Works* of 1770. Samuel Johnson, James Boswell, Tobias Smollett, and David Garrick are listed among the names of the many subscribers to the first collections, and Woty apparently had a strong interest in the London theatre. *Shrubs* includes two prologues written for performances at the Theatre Royal, Covent Garden, and one written for the Theatre Royal, Drury Lane; also 'Verses on Mr Smart's *Benefit*' and 'Verses addressed to Mr Murphy, on his tragedy called the *Orphan of China*'. Later Woty published *The Stage: a Poetical Epistle to a Friend* (1780) and two short dramatic pieces: *The Country Gentlemen, or, The Choice Spirits* (1786) and *The Ambitious Widow: a Comic Entertainment* (1789). The latter mixes conventional satire of lawyers and physicians with ridicule of the latest fashion in women's caps; *Country Gentlemen* combines criticism of arranged marriages with ridicule of poets who 'don't mind sacrificing Sense to Sound'.

Much of Woty's verse is satirical, although his collections include works in such traditional forms as the ode, epistle, and elegy. Some of his best work demonstrates close observation of the habits and customs of Londoners, as in 'White Conduit House', a description of the Sunday crowds at a popular tea-garden, published in the *Gentleman's Magazine* (1st ser., 30, 1760, 242). He frequently alludes to Alexander Pope or quotes from his poems, as, for example, in 'Verses Written at Donnington Park in Leicester-Shire', where he writes:

> could the Poet from the tomb arise,
> And on this rural Eden feast his eyes; …
> Then Donnington, in his immortal lays,
> As first in merit, would be first in praise:
> Her broader shades his polish'd verse would grace,
> And Windsor mourn to hold a second place.
> (*Poetical Works*, 1.140–41)

In 1758 a pirated copy of Woty's *The Spouting Club* was published as by Richard Lewis. Other individually published poems include *The Muse's Advice: Addressed to the Poets of the Age* (1761); *Campanalogia: a Poem in Praise of Ringing* (1761); *The Female Advocate* (1770, 1771); *Church Langton* (1771); *Particular Providence* (1774); *The Estate-Orators: a Town Eclogue* (1774); *The Graces: a Poetical Epistle from a Gentleman to his Son* (1774); and *The Patent* (1776).

Before his death in 1778 Earl Ferrers ensured Woty's future independence by making arrangements for him to receive an annuity of £150 (*GM*, 1791, 379). Woty then published his last collections: *Poems on Several Occasions* (1780); *Fugitive and Original Poems* (1786); and *Poetical Amusements* (1789). Woty died in Leicestershire (possibly at Lutterworth) on 5 March 1791. The writer of his obituary in the *Gentleman's Magazine* states that Woty 'was a true *bon vivant*; but by a too great indulgence of his passion for conviviality and society he unfortunately injured his constitution' (ibid.). JOYCE FULLARD

Sources *GM*, 1st ser., 61 (1791), 285, 379 · *Two burlesques of Lord Chesterfield's letters*, ed. S. L. Gulick (Los Angeles, CA, 1960) · *N&Q*, 4th ser., 2 (1868), 372, 479, 498 · D. E. Baker, *Biographia dramatica, or, A companion to the playhouse*, rev. I. Reed, new edn, rev. S. Jones, 1/2 (1812), 760; 2 (1812), 24, 135 · J. Nichols, *The history and antiquities of the county of Leicester*, 3 (1800–04); repr. (1971), 917, 1142 · *GM*, 1st ser., 30 (1760), 242, 534 · *Monthly Review*, 25 (1761), 479 · *IGI*
Wealth at death at time of death presumably still receiving annuity of £150 willed to him by Earl Ferrers: *GM*

Woulfe, Peter (1727?–1803), chemist and mineralogist, was born in Ireland of unknown parentage. He studied chemistry with G. F. Rouelle, demonstrator at the Jardin du Roi in Paris, having acquired chemical and mineralogical knowledge through travel in France, Germany, Hungary, and Bohemia. He was a good linguist, skilled in French, German, Italian, Latin, and Greek. After settling in London, Woulfe carried out chemical experiments in the laboratory of John Stuart, earl of Bute. He first lived in Clerkenwell, but in 1771 he acquired chambers in Barnard's Inn (no. 2, second floor) on the south side of Holborn. The register of admission described him as 'gentleman', and he seems never to have been short of money. Woulfe spent his winters in London and his summers in Paris, where he knew many of the chemical community. His absence from London may have saved him when Barnard's Inn was badly damaged by fire during the No Popery riots in June 1780, especially as some have believed, on slender evidence, that Woulfe was a Catholic.

Woulfe is remembered chiefly for the compound distillation apparatus which he described in 1767. This arrangement of a retort with flasks and tubulated receivers had been used by J. R. Glauber a century earlier, but Woulfe improved it by introducing water into the flasks. He was thus able to prepare saturated solutions of soluble gases, and to wash out soluble impurities from insoluble gases. However, his 1767 paper in *Philosophical Transactions of the Royal Society* does not show the square-shouldered vessel with two or three necks which was later known as Woulfe's bottle. This vessel was described by Lavoisier in his textbook of 1789; the middle neck was fitted with a safety tube to guard against a build-up of pressure. The safety tube is usually attributed to J. J. Welter, but Lavoisier gave the credit to his colleague J. H. Hassenfratz of the École des Mines.

Woulfe's arrangement made the laboratory a safer place, for he described the distillation of nitric acid without any escape into the room of those fumes 'which have such an effect on the lungs of the operator as frequently to make him spit blood' (*Philosophical Transactions of the Royal Society*, 57.517–34). A large earthenware version of Woulfe's bottle was employed in the early chemical industry to trap noxious fumes. Other significant chemical contributions by Woulfe include the preparation of picric acid from indigo, and the investigation of tin (IV) sulphide (mosaic gold). His alleged discovery of elemental tin in Cornwall was probably the remains of early smelting.

The London scientific community held Woulfe in high esteem. He was elected FRS in 1767, awarded the society's Copley medal in 1768, and delivered the first Bakerian lecture in 1776. Joseph Priestley acknowledged that Woulfe had assisted him with suggestions and the gift of apparatus. Accounts of Woulfe's eccentricity stem largely from anecdotes quoted by W. T. Brande, professor of chemistry at the Royal Institution. Woulfe breakfasted at four in the morning, and friends invited to the meal were instructed to use a secret code of knocks on the door. His rooms were so cluttered with apparatus and specimens that Dr Babington claimed that he put down his hat and was unable to find it again.

The passage in the 1767 paper which Brande quoted as evidence for Woulfe's belief in alchemy merely shows him to have been a phlogistonist; at that date there was little alternative. As the new antiphlogistic chemistry emerged from France, Woulfe acquired most of the literature of the chemical revolution.

Woulfe believed that a trip to Edinburgh and back by stagecoach would cure minor ailments. In the first half of 1803 he died from a pulmonary infection arising from a chill which he caught on such a journey. By his own choice he died alone at Barnard's Inn, without medical attention. He was buried in St Pancras churchyard, now built over.

ALEC CAMPBELL

Sources *Torbern Bengman's foreign correspondence*, ed. G. Carlid and J. Nordström, 1 (1965), 357 • P. Woulfe, 'Experiments on the distillation of acids, volatile alkalies, etc.', *PTRS*, 57 (1767), 517–34 • Woulfe sale (1803) [library sale, Sothebys, June 1803] • W. A. Campbell, 'Peter Woulfe and his bottle', *Chemistry and Industry* (31 Aug 1957), 1182–3 • J. R. Partington, *A history of chemistry*, 3 (1962) • H. B. Wheatley and P. Cunningham, *London past and present*, 3 vols. (1891), vol. 3, p. 21 • G. W. Thornbury and E. Walford, *Old and new London: a narrative of its history, its people, and its places*, 6 vols. (1873–8), vol. 2, p. 574 • W. T. Brande, *A manual of chemistry*, 2nd edn, 1 (1821), 26 • A. L. Lavoisier, *Traité élémentaire de chimie* (1789), 450 • J. Priestley, *Observations and experiments*, 1, 87 • J. Timbs, 'Middle Row, Holborn', *GM*, 4th ser., 5 (1868), 183–8, esp. 187

Wealth at death see Partington, *History of chemistry*

Woulfe, Stephen (1787–1840), judge, was born in co. Clare, Ireland, the second son of Stephen Woulfe, of Tiermaclane, Ennis, co. Clare, and his wife, Honora, the daughter of Michael McNamara of Dublin and sister of Admiral James McNamara and Colonel John McNamara of Llangoed Castle in Brecon. The Woulfes of Tiermaclane had settled in Limerick as early as the fifteenth century, and they remained Roman Catholics throughout the Reformation and penal years. Woulfe was educated by the Jesuits at Stonyhurst College, Lancashire, where Richard Lalor Sheil, Nicholas Ball, and Sir Thomas Wyse were his contemporaries. He was one of the earliest Roman Catholic students to gain admission to Trinity College, Dublin, where he matriculated on 7 November 1808. He was called to the Irish bar in Trinity term, 1814. At some point he married Frances, daughter of Roger Hamill of Dowth Hall, co. Meath; they had two children.

Woulfe was said to have been a good advocate and an effective speaker. He took an active part in Irish politics, engaging in agitation for Roman Catholic emancipation and marking himself out by withstanding the so-called tyranny of Daniel O'Connell. His opposition to O'Connell was mainly over the question of the securities which were demanded as a corollary of Catholic emancipation. Unlike O'Connell, Woulfe was quite ready to accept the right of the British crown to veto the nomination of Catholic bishops, and in 1816 he published a tract in defence of the veto; this was also the substance of a speech which he delivered at Limerick during the Lent assizes of 1816. On 6 May 1829 he followed O'Connell in subscribing the address to the king on the subject of Catholic relief.

Woulfe's moderate views on the question of Catholic emancipation recommended him to William Plunket, who, upon his appointment as lord chancellor of Ireland in 1830, gave him the lucrative post of crown counsel for Munster. Woulfe was then appointed third serjeant on 23 May 1834 and, having entered parliament as a whig member for the city of Cashel in September 1835, he was made solicitor-general for Ireland on 10 November 1836. He retained his seat in parliament until July 1838 but mainly because of poor health did not become prominent as a debater. He was appointed attorney-general for Ireland on 3 February 1837, and on 11 July 1838, in succession to Henry Joy (1767–1838), he was made chief baron of the Irish exchequer. He was the first Roman Catholic to hold the post and accepted the honour with some reluctance, but in the end he felt he had made the right decision. Indeed he refused to resign in favour of O'Connell, when placed under pressure to do so.

Woulfe was said to have been careless in his dress and awkward and angular in his movements, but to have been very effective as a speaker. An amateurish lawyer of the old school, he was not claimed to have been learned in the law, but rather to have been shrewd and observant. He was credited with the saying that 'property has its duties as well as its rights' (D. O. Madden, *Ireland and its Rulers*, 2 1844, 299). An old Irish Catholic *par excellence*, he had been partly educated at St Patrick's College, Maynooth, and trod a middle ground on the issue of emancipation, being neither a repeater of O'Connell's ilk nor a Castle liberal. Treading this moderate line proved difficult, and so between 1829 and 1835 he virtually seceded from politics altogether.

Woulfe died at Baden-Baden in Germany on 2 July 1840, leaving his widow, Frances, their son, Stephen Roland, who succeeded his uncle Peter Woulfe in 1865 in the estate of Tiermaclane, and their daughter, Mary, who in 1847 married Sir Justin Sheil KCB.

THOMAS SECCOMBE, *rev.* SINÉAD AGNEW

Sources Burke, *Gen. Ire.* (1899) · J. Hutchinson, ed., *A catalogue of notable Middle Templars: with brief biographical notices* (1902), 266 · Burtchaell & Sadleir, *Alum. Dubl.*, 2nd edn · R. B. Mosse, *The parliamentary guide* (1837), 233 · W. M. Torrens, *Memoirs of William Lamb, second Viscount Melbourne*, new edn (1890), 418, 428, 454 · *GM*, 2nd ser., 14 (1840), 676 · *The Times* (10 July 1840) · *The Times* (13 July 1840) · R. L. Sheil, *Sketches, legal and political*, ed. M. W. Savage, 2 (1855), 107, 119

Likenesses S. C. Smith, print (after M. Cregan), King's Inns, Dublin

Wragge, William Lindley [Clement] (1852–1922), meteorologist, was born on 18 September 1852 at New Road, Stourbridge, Worcestershire, the only child of Clement Ingleby Wragge, solicitor, and his wife, Anna Maria, formerly Downing; although it was not his baptismal name, he was commonly known by his father's forename Clement. He was orphaned in early childhood. Wragge was educated at Uttoxeter grammar school, Staffordshire, and articled to a London solicitor. He developed an interest in many scientific disciplines, including meteorology, geology, and astronomy and travelled widely overseas, keeping comprehensive journals recording his observations. In 1876 he joined the surveyor-general's department at Adelaide, Australia, and took part in two field expeditions. Probably during this time he married Leonora Thornton (*b. c.*1855), who had been born near Adelaide, according to the 1881 census return. They had a son, Clement Lionel Egerton, born in 1880.

In 1878 Wragge returned to England and, living at Farley, near Cheadle, Staffordshire, presented his collection of ethnography, geology, and natural history to Stafford to establish a museum. He was a fellow of the Royal Geographical Society and in November 1879 was elected a fellow of the British Meteorological Society. He investigated local variations in climate, setting up three meteorological stations at heights ranging from 350 feet to 1216 feet above sea level. Observations at the highest station (Beacon Stoop) involved a daily climb by Wragge of 400 feet, a minor task by comparison with his later exploits on Ben Nevis. In 1877 David Milne Home, chairman of the Council of the Scottish Meteorological Society had proposed the setting up of a meteorological observatory on

Ben Nevis (4406 feet), the highest mountain in Britain. In January 1881, while attempts to obtain government funding were continuing, Wragge offered to make daily ascents during the summer, if the society would provide instruments to be read simultaneously at the summit and near sea level in Fort William. This offer was accepted and from 1 June to mid-October 1881 Wragge, occasionally relieved by an assistant, made the daily climb, often in appalling weather conditions. His subsequent bedraggled appearance led to his nickname of 'Inclement Wragge'. The Fort William observations were made by his wife. Wragge was awarded a gold medal by the society in March 1882 for the meticulously recorded observations. During the summer of 1882, with the help of two assistants, he carried out a more ambitious programme with additional observations at intermediate stations. However, in September 1883 the directors of the permanent observatory, which was built following a public appeal, appointed R. T. Omond rather than Wragge as its superintendent.

Disappointed, Wragge returned to South Australia, where, in 1884, he started observations at Walkerville and on Mount Lofty. In 1886 he founded the Meteorological Society of Australasia. He produced a report on Queensland's weather service and in January 1887 was appointed the Queensland meteorological observer. He expanded the observation network, issued forecasts and carried out research into tropical revolving storms in the south-west Pacific. He was a devotee of map meteorology and gave classical, biblical, or personal names to individual weather systems. He represented Queensland at the Munich Meteorological Congress in 1891. Not content with limiting his operations to Queensland, the completion of the Noumea–Queensland cable in 1893 brought New Caledonia into his network and he also established weather stations in Tasmania (Mount Wellington and Hobart) and in New South Wales (Mount Kosciusko and Merimbula). In 1898 Wragge published an *Australasian Weather Guide and Almanac for 1898*. He antagonized his colonial counterparts by issuing forecasts for the whole of Australia from the 'Chief Weather Bureau, Brisbane' and quarrelled with the premier Sir Robert Philp. In 1902, apparently owing to Queensland government expenditure cuts, the weather bureau at Brisbane was closed and Wragge's post abolished, but in a short-lived weekly publication entitled *Wragge: a Meteorological, Geographical and Popular Scientific Gazette of the Southern Hemisphere* (1902) he announced that he would undertake the functions of a central weather bureau for Australia as a private venture, but with an annual subsidy of £1000 from the governments of Queensland, New South Wales, and Tasmania. However, when the Commonwealth Meteorological Bureau was finally established in 1907 H. A. Hunt was appointed as the commonwealth meteorologist, and Wragge, deeply disappointed, went to Auckland, New Zealand, where he built an observatory. On a return visit to Queensland in 1913 he failed to find support for a centre for tropical cyclone research.

Wragge was a tall, thin man of great energy and ambition, a fitness enthusiast and an ardent conservationist.

He turned to theosophy early and took up yoga and the occult in later life. His flaming red hair gave a clue to his temperament and 'in the professional field he was his own worst enemy' (*AusDB*), having the unfortunate ability to antagonize his colleagues and political masters. None the less, he had a major influence on the development of Australian meteorology. While on a lecture tour Wragge suffered a stroke; he returned to his home at Walata, Birkenhead, New Zealand, where he died on 10 December 1922. He was buried nearby in the cemetery of the church of Our Father. He was survived by his wife and son.

MARJORY G. ROY

Sources 'Wragge, Clement Lindley', *AusDB*, 12.576–7 · C. A. Woolrough, 'Report to Charles Greaves Esq on the meteorological system of Ben Nevis', Edinburgh meteorological office, Scottish meteorological archives · *Quarterly Journal of the Royal Meteorological Society*, 49 (1923), 140 · 'Correspondence and notes', *Quarterly Journal of the Royal Meteorological Society*, 5–36 (1879–1910) · 'Donations received during the year', *Quarterly Journal of the Royal Meteorological Society*, 5–36 (1879–1910) · *Symons Monthly Meteorological Magazine*, 14–38 (1879–1903) [occasional reports] · 'Reports of the council to the general meeting of the Scottish Meteorological Society', *Journal of the Scottish Meteorological Society*, 5–7 (1877–84) · minute book of the council of the Scottish Meteorological Society, 1881, Edinburgh Meteorological Office, Scottish Meteorological archives · minute book of the directors of the Ben Nevis Observatory, 1883, Edinburgh Meteorological Office, Scottish Meteorological archives · observation books of Ben Nevis data, 1881–2, Edinburgh Meteorological Office, Scottish Meteorological archives · 'Meteorological work in north Staffordshire: a visit to Mr C. L. Wragge's stations', *Staffordshire Sentinel* (4 Sept 1880) · *Auckland Star* (11 Dec 1922), 7b · census returns for Farley, Staffordshire, 1881 · b. cert. · b. cert. [Clement Lionel Egerton Wragge]

Archives Edinburgh meteorological office, Scottish meteorological archives, observation books

Likenesses photograph, Edinburgh meteorological office, Scottish meteorological archives

Wrangham, Francis (1769–1842), writer and Church of England clergyman, was born on 11 June 1769, the only son of George Wrangham (1742–1791), a farmer who worked the Raysthorpe farm near Malton in Yorkshire. Wrangham was educated from 1776 by clergymen in Yorkshire before spending two years at Hull grammar school, leaving in 1786.

College years Wrangham matriculated from Magdalene College, Cambridge, in October 1786. In Trinity term of his first academic year he won Sir William Browne's gold medal for Greek and Latin epigrams; he later included these in his first book of poems (printed 1795, published 1802). In October 1787, at the invitation of Dr Joseph Jowett, a fellow and principal tutor of Trinity Hall, Wrangham migrated from Magdalene to Trinity Hall. He was elected a minor scholar and graduated BA in January 1790 as third wrangler in the mathematical tripos, second Smith's prizeman, and winner of the chancellor's medal for classical studies. Wrangham declined a lucrative post to stay at Trinity Hall as a tutor, fully expecting to be elected to the next fellowship that fell vacant. On 22 March 1793 Wrangham proceeded MA, and the following July, with high recommendations from his tutors at Trinity Hall, was ordained.

In August a divinity fellowship fell vacant, but despite

Francis Wrangham (1769–1842), by James Thomson (after John Jackson)

Wrangham's qualifications, John Vickers of Queens' College was elected, although he was technically ineligible because he already held a remunerative ecclesiastical position. Vickers was well connected, while Wrangham was thought too radical in politics and socially inferior. There was also the suggestion that Jowett of Trinity Hall took umbrage at the following epigram reportedly by Wrangham:

THIS *little* garden *little* Jowett made,
And fenc'd it with a *little* palisade:
A *little* taste hath *little* Doctor Jowett
This *little* garden doth a *little* shew it.
(Sadleir, *Wrangham*, 55)

Wrangham, in his account of his 'Academical Life', denied having written it, but it was apparently enough to prejudice Jowett against him. The lord chancellor upheld the decision on Wrangham's appeal, but its injustice was widely recognized.

Wrangham's politics did not help him. He was detected as the author of the radical farce *Reform: a Farce, Modernised from Aristophanes*, published in 1792 under the name of 'S. Foot Jr'. Based on this and other gossip, rumours spread in his college that he was a Jacobin sympathizer (a difficult position to be in at this time when many in England feared that French radicalism might seep across the channel). Although his early biographers play down Wrangham's republicanism as a youthful episode, this propensity in Wrangham, both early and late, is undeniable, even if later in his career he recognized the utility of cultivating the friendship of political conservatives in high places (as with Sir Egerton Brydges) or diplomatically styling himself a 'Whig to a *very moderate* degree' (as he did in a letter of 15 February 1819 to Wordsworth; Sadleir, *Wrangham*, 13).

Literary and church career After his failure to be elected to the fellowship Wrangham left Trinity Hall for Trinity College, supporting himself thereafter by tutoring, and also obtained a curacy in Cobham, Surrey, in 1794, which he gladly left when, late in 1795, Humphrey Osbaldeston presented him to the rectory of Hunmanby-with-Folkton, near Scarborough, at £600 p.a. Early in 1796, at the age of twenty-seven, Wrangham moved into the Hunmanby rectory and remained rector for the rest of his life in addition to his later preferments.

On 7 April 1799, at Bridlington, Wrangham married Agnes (*c*.1779–1800), the youngest of the five daughters of Colonel Ralph Creyke of Marton in Yorkshire. She died in childbirth on 9 March 1800, but her baby daughter, Agnes, survived to marry William Wilberforce's son Robert Isaac Wilberforce. On 2 July 1801 Wrangham married Dorothy (*d*. 1860), second of the two daughters of the Revd Digby Cayley of Yorkshire. Dorothy claimed descent from Edward I and Eleanor of Castile, and brought in a welcome £700 p.a. Wrangham and his second wife had three daughters and two sons: Philadelphia, George, Digby, Anne, and Lucy, born in approximately 1802, 1804, 1805, 1807, and 1810, respectively. A progressive in educational philosophy (he was an advocate of the system of Joseph Lancaster), Wrangham delighted in educating his children, including his daughters. Letters and remembrances attest to his fatherly devotion, and he even dedicated to his children a poem for their enjoyment, 'The Quadrupeds' Feast'.

Wrangham was prolific as a writer, translator, and editor. He wrote epigrams, prospectuses, poetry in English, French, and Latin, drama, sermons, political and didactic pamphlets, letters of instruction to his clergy, history, theology, and biography. For some time after he left Cambridge he continued to enter poems for the university's Seaton prize, winning this in 1794 with 'The Restoration of the Jews', in 1800 with 'The Holy Land', in 1811 with 'Sufferings of the Primitive Martyrs', and in 1812 with 'Joseph Made Known to his Brethren', all of which were later published. Even a rejected poem of 1795, 'The Destruction of Babylon', was included, at the request of the judges, along with the 1794 and 1800 winning poems, in the *Musae Seatonianae* of 1808.

Wrangham's first book of poems, intended for publication in 1795, but probably not published until 1802, is especially noteworthy because it contained a translation of one of his Latin poems by Coleridge, and one from the French by Wordsworth. Wordsworth sent Wrangham some imitations of Juvenal in November 1795, but their planned joint book of satirical poems never materialized. Wrangham published many other books of poetry, including *The Raising of Jaïrus' Daughter* (1804); *A Poem on the Restoration of Learning in the East* (1805); *Death of Saul and Jonathan* (1813); *Poetical Sketches of Scarborough* (compiled by James Green and to which Wrangham was a contributor) (1813);

Poems (1814); *The Quadrupeds' Feast* (1830); and various other collected or selected poetical works.

Wrangham's work for his parishioners included championing charity schools in the early 1800s; disseminating plans for a dispensary for the poor; establishing a free parish library at Hunmanby; instituting and overseeing a cow insurance scheme; and advocating a savings bank, the last two designed to bring some financial security to his poorer parishioners. As archdeacon, he required the clergy in his charge to fill in questionnaires to aid the consistent application of the religious instruction and social benefits he prescribed for their congregations.

Wrangham's advocacy of education for his parishioners fits with the political outlook he had been cultivating since his Cambridge days. In a letter of 3 December 1808 Wordsworth wrote confidentially to Wrangham that he was composing his radical 'Convention of Cintra' essay (later suppressed). In the same year, when Leigh Hunt and his brother John were about to be prosecuted for sedition for their attacks on the prince regent in *The Examiner*, Wrangham wrote to Hunt praising *The Examiner* and distributed prospectuses for the paper. Wrangham was also an early champion of Catholic emancipation (a position with which Wordsworth disagreed in a letter to Wrangham of 3 December 1808) though he later acknowledged that it was probably this more than anything else which checked his advancement in the church.

Nevertheless, Wrangham did advance in the church, in part, perhaps, because, however liberal his secular politics were, his theological views were fairly orthodox. He argued in print against deists, dissenters, and Unitarians, and for missions abroad. From 1814 to 1834 Wrangham was examining chaplain to Edward Venables-Vernon, later Edward Harcourt, archbishop of York, and through this patronage served a succession of preferments. He was elevated to the archdeaconry of Cleveland on 28 June 1820 and allowed to exchange the living of Folkton for that of Thorpe Bassett. On 12 December 1823 he was collated to the prebendal stall of Ampleforth in York Cathedral and on 9 April 1825 to the fourth prebend at Chester Cathedral. The latter carried with it the right of institution to the rectory of Dodleston in Cheshire, to which benefice Wrangham succeeded on 3 December 1827, resigning that of Thorpe Bassett to his son. On 2 October 1828 he surrendered the archdeaconry of Cleveland for that of the East Riding. Harcourt once said to Sydney Smith, a dear friend of Wrangham, that he considered Wrangham an 'ornament to [his] diocese', and for sometime thereafter, he retained the nickname 'Ornament Wrangham'. Wrangham was elected fellow of the Royal Society on 15 November 1804.

Wrangham also made translations from ancient Greek, Latin, French, and Italian. His translations of classical authors as well as modern authors include *A Few Sonnets Attempted from Petrarch in Early Life* (1817), which was dedicated to Byron; *The Lyrics of Horace* (1821; 2nd edn, 1832?); a translation of Virgil's *Eclogues* (1830); and *Homerics* (1834), which contains translations of *Iliad*, book 3, and *Odyssey*, book 5. Sermons, theological dissertations, and didactic and hortatory pamphlets make up the bulk of his publications. In addition to all of these, he was a contributor to J. Nichols's *Literary Anecdotes*, *Blackwood's Magazine*, the *Gentleman's Magazine*, and the *Classical Journal*, and he contributed many other articles and poems to periodicals and anthologies. He was also a prolific editor of both ancient and modern authors. He numbered among his correspondents Wordsworth, Byron, Leigh Hunt, Sir Walter Scott, Samuel Parr, Sir Egerton Brydges, and Mary Russell Mitford. Several books in Trinity College, Cambridge, and the British Library contain his marginalia. A complete and accurate bibliography of Wrangham's writings has not yet been compiled, owing, in part, to the fact that he delighted in reissuing many of his voluminous writings in privately printed new editions of small runs in varying formats, many of which, scarce then, are scarcer now.

Book collecting and final years But perhaps the greatest passion of Wrangham's life was book collecting. He was a member of the Bannatyne and Roxburghe clubs and undertook some editing work for the latter. He was not particularly interested in antiquarian books as such, nor were typography or beauty of design his principal concern. Instead, in addition to books that interested him for their subject matter or author (he was a voracious reader), he collected rare books—the rarer, the more obscure, the more limited the run, the more difficult to obtain, the better. Oddly enough for one not particularly interested in design, he also collected books printed on coloured paper. His correspondence with Egerton Brydges exhibits his anxiety lest he fail to secure volumes in very limited runs from the Lee Priory or other presses with which Brydges had connections. He regularly corresponded with antiquarian books dealers in London, enquiring about availability and prices. His library included books on theology, ecclesiastical history, classical scholarship, French and Italian literature, and a range of ephemera. He had bibliographies, compilations, and anthologies such as Brydges and Dibdin as well as single volumes and sets issued by the Roxburghe and Bannatyne clubs. Although he had a few incunabula, and volumes of important sixteenth- or seventeenth-century editions of Malory, Shakespeare, and Milton, he declined to collect books simply because they were sought after. Wrangham's contribution to later bibliographers was a function of his mania for rarity, for he rescued from oblivion many titles unknown except through his collection.

Wrangham estimated in a letter to Wordsworth of 15 February 1819 that he owned at least '14,000 volumes and about as many Tracts collected in about one tenth of the number of volumes—most of them scarce—and several (I doubt not) unique' (Sadleir, *Wrangham*, 15). He had so many books that he was eventually forced to build an additional wing onto his vicarage at Hunmanby. He also relocated several thousand to his house in Chester, whence he retired after he resigned as archdeacon in 1840. He donated most of his pamphlets (about 10,000, bound in about 1000 volumes, described in a MS catalogue) to Trinity College in 1842, and the remainder of his books was auctioned in London by Leigh Sotheby in 1843, in two sales, one in July (2669 lots) and one in November–December (3089 lots). Two catalogues of the contents of his library were issued during his life: *A Bibliographical and Descriptive Tour of Scarborough* (1824), by John Cole, and *The English Portion of the Library of the Ven. Francis Wrangham* (1826), executed by Wrangham himself.

Wrangham has been described as a devoted family man, a benevolent and courteous chaplain, an elegant speaker, and a man of polished manners. Though serious about his vocation, Wrangham had a keen sense of humour. Arriving one Sunday at the church of Old Cottam, he was told by a farmer's wife that a turkey hen occupied the pulpit, brooding over her eggs. Wrangham immediately told the congregation of this development and gave over preaching for that Sunday, saying, 'I don't suppose the few people gathered here will mind not having a sermon to-day' (Sadleir, 'Supplement', 428). Sydney Smith enjoyed teasing the archdeacon, and, calling on Wrangham's vast storehouse of knowledge, said to him, 'I am sorry to give you trouble, but to apologize to you for asking information is as it were to beg pardon of a cow for milking, or the pump for taking water of it' (Avendaño). Wrangham, who suffered from paralysis for a few years before his death, died at Chester on 27 December 1842 and was buried in the lady chapel of Chester Cathedral.

DAVID KALOUSTIAN

Sources M. Sadleir, *Archdeacon Francis Wrangham, 1769–1842*, Bibliographical Society (1937) · M. Sadleir, 'Archdeacon Francis Wrangham: a supplement', *The Library*, 19 (1939), 422–61 · *DNB* · A. Bell, 'Portrait of a bibliophile XX: Archdeacon Francis Wrangham, 1769–1842', *Book Collector*, 25 (winter 1976), 514–26 · H. Gunning, *Reminiscences of the university, town, and county of Cambridge from the year 1780*, 2 vols. (1854) · M. de Avendaño, 'Family tree of Oswald Wrangham', www.geocities.com/Athens/Forum/3937/wrangham notes.html#337, 15 Dec 2001 · E. Brydges, *Recollections of foreign travel, on life, literature, and self-knowledge*, 2 vols. (1825) · T. F. Dibdin, *Reminiscences of a literary life*, 2 vols. (1836) · J. Conington, *Miscellaneous writings*, 2 vols. (1872) · J. H. Overton, *The English church from the accession of George I to the end of the eighteenth century* (1906) · W. Jerdan, *National portrait gallery of illustrious and eminent personages of the nineteenth century*, 5 vols. (1830–34) · *Fasti Angl.*, 1541–1857

Archives U. Edin. L., commonplace book · BL, collection of works and MS autobiography | BL, letters to Sir Egerton Brydges, RP 2194 · BL, letters to John Martin, Add. MSS 37065–37967 · Bodl. Oxf., letters to Edmund Henry Barker · Bodl. Oxf., letters to T. F. Dibdin · CUL, letters, mostly to Basil Montagu · Denbighshire RO, corresp. with Sir John Lowther · Man. CL, Manchester Archives and Local Studies, letters to John Fry · NL Scot., corresp. with Blackwoods and poems · NL Scot., letters to J. G. Lockhart · Sheff. Arch., letters to James Montgomery · TCD, letters to R. P. Graves · U. Edin. L., letters to David Laing · W. Yorks. AS, Leeds, Yorkshire Archaeological Society, letters to William Radcliffe

Likenesses R. Hicks, stipple (after J. Jackson), BM, NPG; repro. in Jerdan, *National portrait gallery* · J. Thomson, stipple (after J. Jackson), NPG [*see illus.*] · E. Westooy, miniature, Trinity Cam. · engraving, repro. in Sadleir, *Archdeacon Francis Wrangham* · engraving, repro. in F. Wrangham, *Scraps* (1816) · stipple, BM, NPG

Wratislaw, Albert Henry (1821–1892), headmaster and Czech scholar, was born on 5 November 1821 (often wrongly given as 1822) at Rugby, Warwickshire, the eldest son of William Ferdinand Wratislaw (1788–1853), a solicitor, and his wife, Charlotte Anne, *née* Keele (d. 1863). He was educated at Rugby School during the headship of

Thomas Arnold, from August 1829 (when he was seven). He left at the age of fifteen; intending to join the legal profession, he was articled to his father. Before completing the term of his articles, however, he changed his mind in favour of the church and entered the University of Cambridge, matriculating at Michaelmas 1840 from Trinity College. On 28 April 1842 he migrated as a pensioner to Christ's College and was admitted there as scholar on 29 October. He graduated BA in 1844, being placed in the first class in classics and the second class in mathematics. On 17 April 1844 he was admitted a fellow of Christ's and commenced MA in 1847. His appointment in August 1850 as headmaster of Felsted School, Essex, led to the revival along Rugbeian lines of what had become a moribund institution.

Wratislaw was of Czech ancestry: his grandfather Marc Mari Emanuel Wratislaw emigrated to England in 1770 or 1771, settled in Rugby, and died in 1796. Family tradition had it that they were descended from the Bohemian counts Vratislav z Mitrovic. Wratislaw, whose father's efforts to establish his noble ancestry remained inconclusive, began to take an interest in Czech while still at Christ's. From July to October 1849 he travelled in Bohemia and quickly attained a considerable proficiency in the Czech language. He met Václav Hanka, librarian of the National Museum, and joined the Czech literary society Matice Česká. An astonishingly swift result of this visit was his 1849 anthology of translations of Czech verse, *Lyra Czecho-slovanská* ('The Czecho-Slavonic lyre'). From then on he visited Bohemia regularly. His Czech interests, strengthened by reverence for the Czech protestant past, were focused on the early period. He translated for a multilingual edition, published by Václav Hanka in Prague in 1852, a complete version of the poems in the ostensibly medieval Dvůr Králové (Queen's Court) manuscript, which Hanka claimed to have discovered, but which was later exposed as a forgery. Wratislaw also had these translations published in Cambridge as *The Queen's Court Manuscript* (1852).

On 28 December 1852 at High Wycombe, Wratislaw married Frances Gertrude Helm (b. 1830/31), second daughter of the Revd Joseph Charles Helm. They went on to have nine children. In 1855 Wratislaw became headmaster of King Edward VI Grammar School, Bury St Edmunds, and he was one of the thirteen present at the meeting at Uppingham in December 1869 that marked the birth of the Headmasters' Conference. His wife died in June 1868, and on 4 July 1871 he married Emily Snape Shelford (b. 1832/3), daughter of the Revd William H. Shelford. With her he had four more children. In April and May 1877 Wratislaw gave four lectures at Oxford on the Ilchester Foundation which were published as *The Native Literature of Bohemia in the Fourteenth Century* (1878). For many years he corresponded in Czech with the historian František Palacký and other Czech luminaries. Wratislaw published many books and articles on Czech subjects, but his greatest single original contribution to literary scholarship was his discovery in the library of Trinity College, Cambridge, in December 1874 of a unique manuscript of the fourteenth-century rhymed Dalimil chronicle. In 1879 he retired from the headmastership, and became vicar of the parish of Manorbier, Pembrokeshire, where he arrived at Easter that year. In May he was elected a corresponding member of the Královská Česká spoleČnost nauk (Royal Scientific Society of Bohemia). His *John Hus: the Commencement of Resistance to Papal Authority on the Part of the Inferior Clergy* (1882) showed conclusively that his familiarity with the language and original sources enabled him to write on Czech literature and history with an authority unequalled in Britain; but he lacked the expertise to see through the Dvůr Králové forgeries and continued to the end to believe that they were genuine.

A man of wide interests, whose publications extend far beyond Czech studies into aspects of theology, education, university reform, and the classics, Wratislaw was also a keen entomologist and botanist. Though his achievements as a headmaster are beyond doubt, assessments of him as a disciplinarian are strangely at variance. He was 'a Broad Churchman, and a Liberal in an orthodox and Conservative neighbourhood' (Statham, 114). The inscription said once to have been visible in Bury St Edmunds Cathedral on a monument erected 'by 54 of his old boys, in honour of a great master, a kind teacher and an eminent scholar' (Venn, *Alum. Cant.*) can no longer be traced.

Towards the end of 1884 the sight in Wratislaw's left eye began to fail and he started to suffer from arthritis. By the end of 1885 he had to hand over his parish duties and in 1886 he lost the sight of his left eye completely. On 14 January 1888 he returned to his native Rugby, but moved again in December that year to 90 Manor Road, Stoke Newington, London. In 1889 he retired to Southsea, Hampshire, where he died of cerebral disease and apoplexy on 3 November 1892, aged seventy, at his home, Graythwaite, Alhambra Road. His wife, Emily, died on 3 June 1908, aged seventy-five.

GERALD STONE

Sources J. D. Naughton, 'The reception in nineteenth-century England of Czech literature and of the Czech literary revival', PhD diss., U. Cam., 1977 · J. Peile, *Biographical register of Christ's College, 1505–1905, and of the earlier foundation, God's House, 1448–1505*, ed. [J. A. Venn], 2 vols. (1910–13) · G. H. Statham, 'Reminiscences of a septuagenarian', 1913, Suffolk RO, Bury St Edmunds [property of M. P. Statham] [quoted in Naughton] · Venn, *Alum. Cant.* · A. C. Percival, *Very superior men* (1973) · M. R. Craze, *A history of Felsted School, 1564–1947* (1955) · R. W. Elliott, *The story of King Edward VI School, Bury St Edmunds* (1963) · *CGPLA Eng. & Wales* (1892) · b. cert. · m. certs. · d. cert.

Archives Literární archiv Památníku národního písemnictví, Prague, Pozůstalost J. Jirečka

Likenesses portrait, repro. in *Světozor* (2 Aug 1867), 32 · portrait, repro. in *Světozor* (14 Aug 1879), 385

Wealth at death £1086 4s. 10d.: probate, 30 Nov 1892, *CGPLA Eng. & Wales*

Wratislaw, Theodore William Graf (1871–1933), poet and civil servant, was born on 27 April 1871 in Rugby, Warwickshire, the son of Theodore Marc Wratislaw (1831–1919), solicitor, and Sarah Townsend. Educated at Rugby School from 1885 to 1888, he went into his father's office but loved poetry rather than the law, though in 1893 he passed his solicitors' finals. He published two slim volumes at his own expense in Rugby in 1892 and moved to

London to mix (uncommittedly) in the 'Uranian' circle centring on the *Artist and Journal of Home Culture*. *Caprices* (1893), with dedicatees such as Charles Kains Jackson, Lord Alfred Douglas, Oscar Wilde, and Gleeson White, and poems such as 'To a Sicilian Boy' (replaced at proof on the objection of a journalist), associates his name with decadent ideals, but three years later the 120 copies of the edition had not sold out.

Wratislaw returned to his father's office but continued to contribute to the *Yellow Book* and *The Savoy*, and published *Orchids* in 1896, again in a limited edition. In 1895 he entered the estates office at Somerset House, London, where he did what he described in a 1914 letter as 'penal servitude' until December 1930 (unpubd letter, 3 March 1914). On 20 September 1899 he married Sara Caroline Ester Harris (*b.* 1875/6), daughter of Elias Harris, a stock-and sharebroker from Cape Town, Cape Colony. Sara died on 22 September 1901, and on 9 April 1908 he married Theodora Russell (*b.* 1875/6), a widow, the daughter of Robert Percival Banks, the former vicar of Drumbeg, Sutherland. They divorced in 1913, and on 19 May 1915 he married Ada Ross (1884/5–1942), daughter of Thomas Philip Ross, an insurance manager. The daughter of his first marriage, Isolde Eleanor Josephine Wratislaw (1901–1984), worked in the consular service in Italy, ending her career as British consul-general in Palermo and Milan.

Wratislaw lived long enough to see his inclusion by A. J. A. Symons in *An Anthology of 'Nineties Verse* (1928). Perhaps too close in style and subject to Arthur Symons to achieve a truly independent voice, he has remained an essential component of the picture of 1890s poetry. His yearning for literature remained until his death, at his home, York Lodge, Ashley Road, Walton-on-Thames, Surrey, on 13 September 1933. A correspondent in *The Times* of 18 September 1933 commented that 'the beautiful voice that lent added grace to his poems is silent as the night'.   R. K. R. Thornton

Sources K. Beckson, 'Introduction', in T. Wratislaw, *Oscar Wilde: a memoir* (1979) · M. S. Turpin, 'The Wratislaws of Rugby', *Rugby: further aspects of the past* (1977) · R. K. R. Thornton and I. Small, 'Introduction', in T. Wratislaw, *'Caprices' 1893 with 'Orchids' 1896* (1994) · J. Gawsworth, ed., *Selected poems of Theodore Wratislaw* (1935) · S. M. Ellis, 'A poet of the nineties: Theodore Wratislaw', *Mainly Victorian* (1924) · *The Times* (18 Sept 1933) · b. cert. · m. certs. · d. cert. · private information (2004) [family, friends]
Archives Princeton University, New Jersey, corresp. with John Gawsworth · U. Cal., Los Angeles, corresp. with Stewart M. Ellis
Likenesses photograph, 1902? (with daughter Isolde Eleanor Josephine), NPG · photograph, repro. in Wratislaw, *Oscar Wilde*
Wealth at death £1988 17s. 3d.: probate, 2 Nov 1933, CGPLA Eng. & Wales

Wraxall, Sir Frederic Charles Lascelles, third baronet (1828–1865), writer, was born at Boulogne, France, on 2 January 1828, the eldest son of Charles Edward Wraxall (1792–1854), lieutenant in the Royal Artillery, and Ellen Cecilia, daughter of John Madden of Richmond, Surrey. His grandfather was Sir Nathaniel William *Wraxall, first baronet (1751–1831). He was educated at Shrewsbury School (where he was Dyke scholar), and matriculated from St Mary Hall, Oxford, on 26 May 1842, but left the university without graduating.

From 1846 Wraxall spent the greater part of his life on the continent. On 18 May 1853 he married Mary Anne (*d.* 1882), daughter of J. Herring. In 1855 he served for nine months at Kerch in the Crimea as first-class assistant commissary, with the rank of captain, in the Turkish contingent. His experiences during this period are recounted in his *Camp Life: Passages from the Story of a Contingent*, published in 1860. Throughout his life he continued to be interested in military matters. In 1856 he issued *A Handbook to the Naval and Military Resources of European Nations*; in 1859 *The Armies of the Great Powers*; and in 1864 *Military Sketches*, which was chiefly concerned with the French army and its leaders. In 1858 Wraxall managed the *Naval and Military Gazette*, and from January 1860 to March 1861 *The Welcome Guest*. He sent frequent contributions to the *St James Magazine* and other periodicals. In 1860 he edited for private circulation the Persian and Indian dispatches of Sir James Outram. In May 1863 he succeeded his uncle, Sir William Lascelles Wraxall, as third baronet.

Wraxall was well versed in modern history, more particularly that of France and Germany during the eighteenth and nineteenth centuries. His most important historical work was *The Life and Times of Caroline Matilda, Queen of Denmark and Norway* (3 vols., 1864). He claimed to have shown by original research the worthlessness of the evidence on which the queen was divorced after the Struensee affair, and in the third volume of this work published for the first time the letter protesting her innocence which the queen had written to her brother, George III of England, just before her death. He obtained through the duchess of Augustenburg a copy of the original in the Hanoverian archives, and through Sir Augustus Paget was afforded access to the privy archives of Copenhagen, though the English Foreign Office remained closed to him. He was also a skilled translator, publishing the authorized English translation of Victor Hugo's *Les misérables* in 1862 (reissued in 1864 and 1879), in addition to many other works from the French and German.

In addition to his more serious literary endeavours Wraxall also published several entertaining novels, including *Wild Oats: a Tale* (1858), *The Fife and Drum, or, Would be a Soldier* (1862), *Married in Haste: a Story of Everyday Life* (1863), and *Golden Hair: a Tale of the Pilgrim Fathers* (1864). He also produced *Remarkable Adventures and Unrevealed Mysteries* (2 vols., 1863), containing articles on Struensee, Königsmark, D'Acon, Cagliostro, Clootz, and other adventurers, and *Criminal Celebrities, a Collection of Memorable Trials* (1861).

Wraxall died in Vienna on 11 June 1865. As his marriage had been childless, the baronetcy passed successively to his younger brothers, Sir Horatio Henry Wraxall, fourth baronet (*d.* 1882), and Sir Morville Nathaniel Wraxall, fifth baronet (1834–1902).

      G. Le G. Norgate, *rev.* Megan A. Stephan

Sources Burke, *Peerage* (1980), 2879 · *Men of the time* (1862), 805 · Walford, *County families* (1865) · Foster, *Alum. Oxon.* · *The Athenaeum* (17 June 1865), 815 · *ILN* (24 June 1865), 590 · Allibone, *Dict.* · S. J.

Kunitz and H. Haycraft, eds., *British authors of the nineteenth century* (1936), 673
Archives BL, business transactions with Richard Bentley · NL Scot., letters to Blackwoods

Wraxall, Sir Nathaniel William, first baronet (1751–1831), traveller and memoirist, was born on 8 April 1751 in Queen's Square, Bristol, the only son (there were four daughters) of Nathaniel Wraxall (1725–1781), a merchant of that city, and Anne (*d.* 1800), daughter of William Thornhill and great-niece of Sir James Thornhill, the painter. He claimed descent from an ancient family of Wraxall, a village 6 miles west of Bristol, but there is no proof of this connection.

After receiving some sort of education in Bristol, he was sent to Bombay in 1769 with the East India Company, and was appointed judge-advocate and paymaster of the forces in the Gujarat expedition, and that against Baroche in 1771. For reasons that remain unclear, he abandoned this career in 1772 and returned to England, and seems to have decided to become a professional travel writer. During 1774–5 he travelled extensively in Europe, especially Portugal and Scandinavia, moving (at what must have been some considerable expense) in diplomatic and royal circles, garnering numerous anecdotes which later found their way into his published travelogues and the *Historical Memoirs* (published in 1815). During 1774 he became involved with those of the Danish nobility who were campaigning for the return from exile in Germany of Queen Caroline Matilda, sister of George III. Wraxall had an interview with Caroline Matilda in her Hanoverian retreat at Celle in September 1774 and became devoted to her cause, carrying messages between her and George III. He gave some £500 of his own money towards reinstating her on the Danish throne; unfortunately, Caroline Matilda died on 11 May 1775. Thereafter Wraxall wrote several times to George III, asking to be reimbursed: these requests remained unanswered for five years, until Wraxall became an MP in 1780, at which point he received 1000 guineas from Lord North, no doubt to ensure his loyalty in the House of Commons.

In 1775 Wraxall published *Cursory Remarks Made in a Tour through some of the Northern Parts of Europe*, dedicated to Viscount Clare in gratitude for his patronage. Wraxall's travelogue is elegantly written, and its Scandinavian and Russian itinerary was novel and therefore of great interest to the reading public (it rapidly went through four editions); although the *Gentleman's Magazine* (1st ser., January 1776, 24) wished that he could 'be prevailed on to strike out all mention of every woman that he would have us believe reigned the sovereign of his affections for an hour'. The narrative is self-consciously chivalric and testifies to Wraxall's lifelong interest in tales of intrigue and distress, although Queen Caroline Matilda's predicament does not figure in the text, presumably in the interests of diplomacy. He presents himself as a citizen of the world, observing that 'I have always found the great and good to be of no country' (Wraxall, *Cursory Remarks*, 32), and boasts that 'danger and fatigue have no terrors for me, when knowledge is the reward of my endeavors' (ibid., 268).

Samuel Johnson wrote to Hester Thrale (22 May 1775) that 'Wraxal is too fond of words, but you may read him' (*Letters of Samuel Johnson*, 2.209–10).

Wraxall continued to travel around Europe during the late 1770s, visiting Germany and Italy in 1778–9. In 1780 he returned to England and became member of parliament for Hindon (Wiltshire), through the influence of Lord George Germain, a lifelong ally. His maiden speech, on 25 January 1781 in the midst of the rupture with Holland, urged the ministry to cultivate the emperor Joseph as a European ally. In the same year Horace Walpole complained that Wraxall was 'popping into every spot where he can make himself talked of, by talking of himself; but I hear he will come to an untimely beginning in the House of Commons' (Walpole, 29.104). In fact Wraxall sat in the House of Commons for fourteen years, representing Ludgershall in 1784 and Wallingford (Berkshire) in 1790. In 1794 he resigned his seat at the request of Francis Sykes, the proprietor of the borough of Wallingford, and accepted the stewardship of the Chiltern Hundreds. Although he does not seem to have played a significant parliamentary role, Wraxall's pretentious rhetorical style in the house was satirized in the ninth of the 'Probationary odes for the laureateship' in *The Rolliad* (1795), which also makes fun of his boastful, adventuring spirit:

> I burn! I burn! I glow! I glow!
> With antique and with modern lore!
> I rush from Bosphorus to Po—
> To Nilus from the Nore
> (p. 315)

Nevertheless the government seems to have taken advantage of his experience, appointing him to a secret committee to inquire into the causes of the war in the Carnatic in 1781, during which the territories of England's ally, the nabob of Arcot, were devastated by Haidar Ali. Subsequently, in conjunction with John Macpherson, later governor-general of Bengal, and his relative James 'Ossian' Macpherson, Wraxall acted as an agent (or *vakeel*) for the nabob of Arcot, who was petitioning to have his debts wiped out by the British government. He also took it upon himself to send news overland to India of the 1783 peace, which arrived six weeks in advance of the tardy official communication.

On 30 March 1789 Wraxall married Jane Lascelles, daughter of Peter Lascelles of Knights in Hertfordshire. They had two sons, William Lascelles (*b.* 5 Sept 1791) and Charles Edward (*b.* 9 Aug 1792). Between the late 1770s and 1815 Wraxall published several more works of travel narrative and historical anecdote, including *Memoirs of the kings of France of the race of Valois: interspersed with interesting anecdotes, to which is added, A tour through the western, southern, and interior provinces of France* (2 vols., 1777), which was translated into French in 1784, and saw several English editions; *Memoirs of the Courts of Berlin, Dresden, Warsaw, and Vienna* (2 vols., 1779); and an uncompleted *History of France, from the Accession of Henry III to the Death of Louis XIV* (3 vols., 1795; 6 vols., 1814). In 1787 he published (anonymously, although his authorship was widely known) a polemical pamphlet entitled *A Short Review of the Political State of Great-*

Britain, which celebrates the continuing popularity of George III despite 'the abyss of ruin into which a long train of unfortunate councils has plunged the empire' (p. 4), laments the misdirected brilliance of Fox and the 'departed greatness' (p. 43) of Lord North, defends Warren Hastings, and calls upon the prince of Wales to cast off his train of 'obscure and unprincipled individuals', not to mention his Roman Catholic mistress, in the national interest. The pamphlet provoked several responses, both hostile and supportive, and the prince of Wales himself is said to have threatened the publisher, Debrett, with a prosecution for libel.

These works may be seen as rehearsals for the publication which was to bring Wraxall great fame and notoriety in 1815: the *Historical Memoirs of my Own Time, from 1772 to 1784* (2 vols.). The first part of the narrative is a collection of anecdotes gathered during his European travels, including some grisly tales of aristocratic murder allegedly told to Wraxall by Lady Hamilton; but it was the second and more substantial section which generated public interest and critical outrage. Here Wraxall describes in fascinating, often scurrilous detail the political world and the London social scene, commenting on everything from hairstyles and costume to the conduct of the American war. He was a supporter until 1783 of Lord North; but he relates how Fox's India Bill of that year prompted him to abandon the coalition party (even though North had promised him a seat at the board of greencloth) and throw his weight behind Pitt, to whom he remained generally loyal, and who arranged for his election as member for Ludgershall in 1784. However, with the exception of George III, neither friend nor foe of Wraxall's escaped having their character and physiognomy delineated for the amusement of his readers. The *Historical Memoirs* were a great popular success: the first edition of 1000 copies (at 26s. per copy) sold out in five weeks. However, printing of a second was interrupted when Wraxall found himself accused of libel by the former Russian ambassador in London, Count Vorontsov, for suggesting in the *Memoirs* that the count had related how Catherine the Great had been responsible for the death of the German princess of Württemburg. Wraxall was found guilty, and sentenced to six months' imprisonment and a fine of £500. The count's diplomatic character having been cleared by the verdict, he kindly campaigned for the reduction of Wraxall's punishment, so that he only served three months in the king's bench, in 'two airy, spacious apartments' where he was shown 'every possible indulgence and attention' by the marshal (N. Wraxall, *Posthumous Memoirs of his Own Time*, 3 vols., 1836, 1.ix). Once released, Wraxall quickly expunged the offending passages and brought out a second edition, in June 1816, of the *Historical Memoirs*, which sold out by August. A third edition in 1818 contained various additions, and refutations of his critics. During the later years of his life he continued to write his frank and often malicious memoirs, but was careful this time to ensure that they would be published only posthumously; he had been 'instructed by experience in the legal dangers and penalties that attend the premature disclosure of historical truth' (ibid., 1.v). For all his high-minded rhetoric Wraxall seems to have enjoyed the furore wrought by the earlier *Memoirs*, recalling that: 'Never, I believe, did any literary work procure for its authour a more numerous list of powerful and inveterate enemies' (ibid., 1.ix). One notable exception was Sir George Osborn, former equerry to George III, who wrote to Wraxall in 1816: 'I personally know nine parts out of ten of your anecdotes to be perfectly correct' (ibid., 1.xi). And Hester Thrale found them so interesting that she made numerous marginal annotations. However, the literary journals of the day were unanimous in their disapproval, the *Quarterly Review* denouncing the *Historical Memoirs* as 'pompous gossip and inflated trash' (April 1815, 213), the *British Critic* attacking their 'outrageous and unnecessary indecency' (July 1815, 24), and the *Edinburgh Review* condemning their 'union of nastiness and obscenity' (June 1815, 190) while nevertheless printing lengthy excerpts. It was in the *Edinburgh Review* that an epigram probably penned by George Colman the younger, and subsequently much misquoted, was first printed:

> Men, measures, seasons, scenes, and facts all
> Misquoting, misstating,
> Misplacing, misdating,
> Here lies Sir Nathaniel Wraxall!

By the time of *Posthumous Memoirs*, and no doubt partly because Wraxall was dead and therefore now incorrigible, the reviews had come to acknowledge that his anecdotes contain much that is true and interesting: *Blackwood's Edinburgh Magazine* compared him to Boswell, and commended his 'dexterous mind' and grasp of 'the *important* idea' (July 1836, 63); and the *Gentleman's Magazine* declared that the *Posthumous Memoirs* 'will not be considered as one of the ephemeral productions of the day, but … will be consulted by those who wish to obtain information relative to one of the most eventful and interesting periods of English history' (*GM*, 2nd ser., 5, 1836, 123). The *London and Westminster Review* described Wraxall's last work as a 'parliamentary epic' (January 1837, 495), and indeed both sets of his memoirs may be viewed as such, presenting vivid and intimate accounts of the American crisis, the illness of George III, the trial of Warren Hastings, debates in the House of Commons, Georgiana, duchess of Devonshire, and the colourful careers and characters of Fox, Pitt, Sheridan, and Burke, of whom Wraxall writes:

> He always reminded me of the image which Nebuchadnezzar sees in his dream, recorded by the prophet Daniel; 'whose brightness was excellent,' and whose 'head was of fine gold;' but whose 'feet were part of iron and part of clay'. (*Posthumous Memoirs*, 2.89)

In both sets of memoirs there are also amusing recollections of London literary celebrities, to whom Wraxall frequently pays backhanded compliments: of Hester Chapone, for instance, he recalls that 'a most repulsive exterior concealed very superior attainments' (*Historical Memoirs*, 1.111). He seems also to have dabbled in literary editorial work, planning in 1802 to publish some of the Dorset papers, which were erroneously suspected to contain some letters by Shakespeare, and going through the papers of James Macpherson in 1805 (albeit primarily as a source for his own memoirs). In 1799 the prince regent, clearly unaware that it was Wraxall who had written the 1787 pamphlet attack on himself, appointed him his 'future historiographer'; and in 1813 he was created a baronet at the regent's request. Little is known of his later years. He died on 7 November 1831 at Dover, on his way to Naples, and was buried in St James's Church at Dover.

KATHERINE TURNER

Sources GM, 1st ser., 102/1 (1832), 268–70 • *Debrett's Peerage* (1828) • *The historical and the posthumous memoirs of Sir Nathaniel William Wraxall, 1772–1784*, ed. H. B. Wheatley, 5 vols. (1884) • N. W. Wraxall, *Historical memoirs of my own time*, ed. R. Askham (1904) • C. F. L. Wraxall, *Life and times of her majesty Caroline Matilda, queen of Denmark and Norway*, 3 vols. (1864) • N. Wraxall, *Cursory remarks made in a tour through some of the northern parts of Europe* (1775) • *The letters of Samuel Johnson*, ed. B. Redford, 2–3 (1992) • *Autobiography, letters and literary remains of Mrs Piozzi*, ed. A. Hayward, 2 vols. (1861) • Walpole, *Corr.*, vol. 29 • *The Rolliad: probationary odes for the laureateship* (1795) • J. Prior, *Life of Edmond Malone, editor of Shakespeare* (1860) • *The correspondence of King George the Third with Lord North from 1768 to 1783*, ed. W. B. Donne, 2 vols. (1867) • *DNB*
Archives BL, political memoirs, e.g. MSS 2141–2144 • NL Scot., diary of Scottish tour • Yale U., Beinecke L., reminiscences, anecdotes, travel journals | BL OIOC, letters to Paul Benfield, MS Eur. C 307 • NL Ire., letters to Lord and Lady Glandore • PRO, letters to William Pitt, PRO 30/8
Likenesses T. Cheesman, stipple (after J. Wright), BM, NPG; repro. in Cadell and Davies, *Contemporary portraits* (1813) • R. Cooper, stipple (after J. Jackson), BM, NPG; repro. in N. W. Wraxall, *Historical memoirs of my own time* (1815)

Wray, Sir Cecil, thirteenth baronet (1734–1805), politician, was born on 3 September 1734, the only surviving son of Sir John Wray, twelfth baronet (1689–1752), landowner, of Sleningford, in the West Riding of Yorkshire, and Frances (1700–1770), daughter and eventual heir of Fairfax Norcliffe of Langton, Yorkshire, and Mary Hesketh. He was educated at Westminster School from 1745 and Trinity College, Cambridge, from 1749. Having succeeded to the baronetcy at his father's death, on 26 January 1752, Wray came into possession of large estates in Lincolnshire, Yorkshire, and Norfolk. He had a brief military career as a cornet in the 1st dragoons, from December 1755, but retired two years later. Thereafter his military ambitions were confined to the local sphere as a captain of militia, and later of yeomanry, in Lincolnshire. He married Esther Summer (1736/7–1825) in or before 1760, when he moved from his town house in Lincoln to a newly built Gothic fantasy some 10 miles distant, which was called Summer Castle, after his wife's maiden name, though it was more commonly known as Fillingham Castle. Wray possessed insufficient influence to stand for parliament in his own county but with the support of Lord Lincoln, later second duke of Newcastle, he successfully contested East Retford in 1768 and retained the seat for the duration of two parliaments.

Wray possessed 'no superior talents', according to the diarist Nathaniel Wraxall, but was 'independent in mind as well as fortune' (*Historical and Posthumous Memoirs*, 3.80). A member of the Bill of Rights Society, he voted in general with the opposition and gave conspicuous support to John Wilkes in 1769 over the Middlesex election case; he even tried, albeit unsuccessfully, to raise a pro-Wilkes petition in Lincolnshire. On 27 March 1775 he spoke against the government's American policy, stopping short of an outright denial of the theoretical right of taxation, while declaring it to be unjust for that power to be exercised without 'opening the trade of the whole world to America … a measure which no one could wish to see adopted' (Almon, 1.391). He also spoke in favour of the repeal of the Declaratory Act on 6 April 1778. Wray believed himself naturally suited to the role of independent critic of government: 'I have not', he stated a few years later, 'been in a habit of making ministers; my life has been spent in pulling them down' (Debrett, 9.352).

Wray gave up his parliamentary seat in 1780, having forfeited his patron's support, and does not appear to have stood elsewhere until invited to contest Westminster in 1782 at a by-election caused by Admiral Rodney's elevation to the peerage. This request was delivered by Charles James Fox, the holder of the other Westminster seat, and at the behest of the Westminster Association for parliamentary reform. Wray's credentials as a reformer had been demonstrated by support for John Cartwright in the late 1770s and by joining Christopher Wyvill's Yorkshire Association in 1780. He was initially reluctant to stand, not least because of the expense involved, but consented after receiving reassurances that the Westminster Association would cover his costs. He was returned without opposition on 12 June 1782. He soon parted political company with Fox, as he strongly disapproved of the latter's new alliance with the former premier Lord North. He spoke out against their combined attack on Lord Shelburne's peace preliminaries, on 21 February 1783, accusing North of gross mismanagement as prime minister and blaming him for involving the country in 'the cursed American war, the cause of all our ruin' (Debrett, 9.352). Under no circumstances, therefore, could Wray bring himself to support the Fox–North ministry that was formed in the wake of Shelburne's defeat. He continued to pursue an independent line, voting with Fox and Pitt in favour of parliamentary reform in May 1783. In June he made the outlandish suggestion that the land tax should be raised, arguing that this would be preferable to the government's receipts tax. It was only proper, in his opinion, that the landed gentry, who had so conspicuously and ruinously supported the American war, should now face up to the costs rather than trying to shift the burden onto the middling sort via iniquitous new taxes. Wray's reforming zeal was also evident in his presentation of a Quaker petition for the abolition of slavery on 17 June. In a speech on 4 December he bitterly condemned the East India Bill as a 'most violent, arbitrary, and unprincipled measure' (ibid., 12.333). This conspicuous defection by Fox's fellow member for Westminster contributed to the groundswell of hostile extra-parliamentary opinion towards the coalition. After the king's dismissal of the Fox–North ministry Wray rallied to the support of Pitt, who reciprocated by spending some £9000 on Wray's campaign at the general election of 1784, on a joint ticket with Admiral Lord Hood.

At the notorious Westminster election of 1784 the poll was kept open for forty days, the maximum period permitted, and the election resolved itself into a battle between Fox and Wray for the second seat, since Hood as a popular naval hero soon established a commanding lead. The contest was closely followed in the press and accompanied by vitriolic caricatures. Wray's camp made scurrilous attacks on the duchess of Devonshire, showing her as an aristocratic strumpet who traded kisses and favours for the votes of butchers and other menial tradesmen. The partisans of Fox countered by portraying in their squibs massed ranks of serving girls protesting against another of Wray's eccentric taxation schemes. Wray had proposed to levy taxes on the employers of maidservants, and this plan was misrepresented as a direct tax on the servants themselves, who were shown striking him with their brooms and denouncing him as a niggardly brute. Also unpopular was Wray's proposal to reform Chelsea Hospital, whereby more funds would be devoted to pensions and some residential restrictions removed. This was misrepresented as a mean-hearted attempt to starve poor old soldiers, who were shown in the popular prints as auxiliary troops to the maidservants and attacking Wray with their crutches. Further insults came when the polls were finally closed on 17 May, Fox having defeated Wray by a mere 236 votes (6234 to 5998), and Wray was caricatured in 'The Westminster deserter drum'd out of the regiment'.

At Wray's insistence a parliamentary scrutiny of the Westminster poll was ordered, an action which Pitt initially supported in the hope of deepening the already considerable embarrassments of the opposition. But this investigation was allowed to lapse on 3 March 1785, when the minister failed to carry a procedural point and decided not to contest the motion for the bailiff to make the return. Wray played no further significant part in politics and is not known to have attempted a return to parliament. He died, with no surviving children, at Summer Castle on 10 January 1805 and was buried at Fillingham church. The baronetcy passed to his first cousin William Ullithorne Wray but the Sleningford estate was entailed to his nephew Thomas, second son of John Dalton (1726–1811), who had married Wray's sister Isabella (d. 1780).

DAVID WILKINSON

Sources M. M. Drummond, 'Wray, Sir Cecil', HoP, Commons, 1754–90 · C. Dalton, History of the Wrays of Glentworth, 1523–1852, 2 vols. (1880) · The historical and the posthumous memoirs of Sir Nathaniel William Wraxall, 1772–1784, ed. H. B. Wheatley, 5 vols. (1884) · J. Almon, ed., The parliamentary register, or, History of the proceedings and debates of the House of Commons, 17 vols. (1775–80) · J. Debrett, ed., The parliamentary register, or, History of the proceedings and debates of the House of Commons, 45 vols. (1781–96) · F. G. Stephens and M. D. George, eds., Catalogue of political and personal satires preserved … in the British Museum, 6 (1938) · DNB · GEC, Baronetage
Archives N. Yorks. CRO, corresp. with Christopher Wyvill, ZFW
Likenesses line engraving, pubd 1784, NPG · Opie, portrait; in possession of Miss Dalton, Staindrop, c.1900 · J. Reynolds, portrait; last known location Sleningford, near Ripon, Yorkshire · caricatures, BM · miniature; in possession of Miss Dalton, Staindrop, c.1900 · portrait, Langton · portrait, Fillingham Castle, Lincolnshire

Wray, Sir Christopher (c.1522–1592), judge, was born in the parish of Bedale, Yorkshire, third son of Thomas Wray (d. c.1540), seneschal in 1535 of Coverham Abbey, Yorkshire, and his wife, Joan (d. 1562), daughter and coheir of Robert Jackson of Gatenby, Yorkshire. The story that Wray was 'the natural son of Sir Christopher Wray, Vicar of Hornby, by a wench in a belfry' (Campbell, 1.200) is clearly false. It is said that he was educated at Buckingham (Magdalene) College, Cambridge, of which he was a benefactor; but there is no evidence for his membership of the college, he did not himself refer to any such association, and in 1580 he apparently knew very little about Magdalene.

Marriage and early career Wray was admitted to Lincoln's Inn on 6 February 1545, and called to the bar in 1550. In 1553 he was MP for Boroughbridge, Yorkshire, holding the seat in all Mary's parliaments. In 1558 he became a bencher of his inn, and from January 1559 until 1563 was steward of Wetherby, Yorkshire. But his future lay in Lincolnshire: by January 1559 he was 'of Glentworth' in Lincolnshire, having married Anne (d. 1593), daughter of Nicholas Girlington of Normanby, Yorkshire, and widow of Robert Brocklesby (d. 1557) of Glentworth. They had two surviving daughters: Frances, who married first Sir George St Paul, and second Robert *Rich, earl of Warwick; and Isabel [see Darcy, Isabel], who married first Godfrey Foljambe, second Sir William Bowes, and third John, Lord Darcy of Aston. Their son William, MP for Great Grimsby and for Lincolnshire, and sheriff of Lincolnshire in 1594, was created baronet in November 1611.

Wray built a house at Glentworth, the queen assisting him with profits from the coinage. He was a justice of the peace for Lindsey, Lincolnshire, from 1559, for Kesteven, Lincolnshire, from 1562, and for Holland, Lincolnshire, from 1569, and also, among others, for Middlesex, Norfolk, and the North Riding of Yorkshire. Wray's growing association with Lincolnshire was marked in the late 1550s by his retainer, with Robert Mounson, as counsel to the corporation of Lincoln. By 1562 Wray was of counsel to Henry Neville, earl of Westmorland, and sufficiently prominent a lawyer that the chancery plaintiff in Brend v. Hyldrache (1562) had to be assigned counsel by the court as none would act voluntarily, for 'the matter in question toucheth Mr Wray of Lincoln's Inn' (Monro, 340). He was appointed autumn reader in Lincoln's Inn for 1562, although in the event did not read until Lent 1563, and in 1565 appeared for the plaintiffs in Sharington v. Strotton, a leading case on contract. He missed Elizabeth's first parliament, but in 1563 was member for Great Grimsby, Lincolnshire, a seat earlier under the control of the earls of Westmorland, where Sir Francis Ayscough had demanded his election, telling the borough that it would please the earl. A commissioner of sewers in Lincolnshire in 1564, he was elected treasurer of Lincoln's Inn in 1565. In parliament he was a committee of an Informers Bill in 1566, and in the same year was appointed to confer with the Lords concerning the succession.

Sir Christopher Wray (c.1522–1592), after unknown artist, 1582

Serjeant-at-law and speaker Wray was created serjeant-at-law in April 1567, giving his second reading as serjeant-elect in the Lent vacation of that year. Rapid promotion followed: he became queen's serjeant on 18 June 1567, and in Michaelmas term argued the case of *Mines* for the crown, subsequently advising the Company of Mineral and Battery Works on the implications of the decision. Eligible as a serjeant for assize commissions, from 1567 until 1570 he rode the home circuit with Mr Justice Southcote, and in June 1570 became second justice at Lancaster, being replaced in 1575 by Mr Justice Mounson. Licensed in May 1570 to take the assizes in his native county, in the summer of that year he rode the northern circuit with Mr Justice Harpur, dealing with the northern insurgents of 1569 at the York, Carlisle, and Durham assizes. He received the submission of the rebels in the West Riding of Yorkshire, including those of his brother Thomas, and John Gower, son of his sister Anne, for whose pardon Henry Radcliffe, earl of Sussex, to whom Wray was to be executor, wrote to Sir William Cecil in June 1570, pointing to his relationship to Wray 'whom, I think, her Majesty favours' (*CSP dom.*, addenda, 1566–79, 300).

In 1571 Wray was MP for Ludgershall, Wiltshire, the seat perhaps found for him as speaker designate, though his election may have been helped by the Wiltshire landowner Richard Kingsmill, a fellow member of Lincoln's Inn. Wray was presented to the queen as speaker on 4 April 1571; his oration on religion, authority, and laws expounded her majesty's absolute power in matters spiritual or ecclesiastical, touched on the necessity of treasure in maintaining authority, and commended her majesty for giving free course to her laws. Though an experienced parliament man, Wray proved a weak chairman: he soon lost the initiative and was unable to contain the puritan campaign to reform religion, which brought an early dissolution at the end of May 1571. Wray was not an MP again, but he acted as an assistant in the Lords, advising on bills and receiving petitions. In June 1571 the University of Cambridge thanked him for assisting the passage of the statute 13 Eliz. c. 29, confirming the university's privileges.

Judge and benefactor On 14 May 1572 Wray was appointed a justice of the court of queen's bench, and soon sat as a commissioner at the trial for treason of John Hall and Francis Rolston. But promotion came rapidly: he was knighted on 6 November 1574, and on 8 November appointed chief justice of the court of queen's bench. Promotion brought a move to the sought-after Norfolk circuit, which he rode from 1575 until his death. In 1575 he was a commissioner to inquire into ecclesiastical offences in the diocese of Lincoln. On 23 April 1577 he was in a special commission to visit the University of Oxford, and in November 1577 reported to the privy council on recusants in the inns of chancery. He set bounds to the jurisdiction of the ecclesiastical commissioners, prohibiting the commissioners in Lancashire in a charity case, and defended his action in 1581 in a letter to William Chaderton, bishop of Chester, pointing out that the matter belonged to the common law and that the judges could not delay granting justice at the behest of the commissioners. Wray himself was appointed a commissioner in 1589. He was equally stern in his treatment of nonconformist puritans, in 1576 finding 'great disorder for religion' in Suffolk and Norfolk (*Salisbury MSS*, 2.136) and begging Lord Burghley to issue an ecclesiastical commission, and in 1591 he agreed that the puritan Cartwright and his followers, refusing the oath before the ecclesiastical commissioners, should be brought into Star Chamber.

In 1579 Wray became *custos rotulorum* for Huntingdonshire, and presided at the trial of John Stubbe for disseminating an attack on the Alençon marriage, interpreting a Marian statute to apply to the case in hand, though his colleague Mr Justice Mounson, who questioned the legality of Stubbe's sentence, was briefly imprisoned and obliged to resign his seat on the common pleas bench. In 1581 Wray presided over the prosecution for treason in the king's bench of the Jesuit Edmund Campion and his associates, which was closely followed by contempt proceedings in Star Chamber against Lord Vaux and others for refusing to swear that they had not harboured Campion. In the same year he was joined on the Norfolk circuit by Edmund Anderson, serjeant-at-law, shortly to become chief justice of the common pleas, who in supporting the anti-puritan campaign of Edmund Freake, bishop of Norwich, did not conceal his hatred for all types of nonconformity. For the next four years Wray and Anderson effected a sustained repression of puritan preachers, undermining the authority of the local magistrates and provoking a rebuke from the council in 1582.

In 1583 Wray was in the commission under which John Somervyle and others were convicted of an attempt to assassinate the queen, and in February 1585 was in the commission under which William Parry was convicted of treason. In the same year he presided in Star Chamber over the inquest upon the suicide in the Tower of Henry Percy, earl of Northumberland, and in February 1586 was in the commission that convicted of treason William Shelley, a conspirator with Northumberland in the Throckmorton plot. The trial for treason of Anthony Babington and his associates followed in September 1586, Wray again being among the commissioners, as he was at Fotheringhay in October 1586 for the trial of Mary, queen of Scots. At the subsequent trial in Star Chamber of Secretary Davison for dispatching Mary's death warrant, Wray acted as lord privy seal in place of Sir Thomas Bromley, who was ill, observing that Davison had meant well, but that what he had done 'was *bonum*, but not *bene*' (*State trials*, 1.1239). Wray was again in the commission when Philip Howard, earl of Arundel, was tried for treason before the Lords in April 1589. His last state trial was that of Sir John Perrot for treason in April 1592.

Wray left a lasting mark upon local administration by assembling the judges in 1590 to reform the wording of the commission of the peace. He left a lasting mark also in Cambridge: in 1580 he sent for Degory Nicholls, master of Magdalene College, and finding 'the number of Fellows to be but few, & the number of Scholarships to be none ... seemed somewhat to pity our poverty' (CUL, MS Mm.2.22, p. 235). He contributed to the cost of gates in 1585, and in 1587 entered into an indenture reciting his payment for building work which completed the college's street-front, and regulating his provision from the rectory of Grainthorpe, Lincolnshire, for two fellows and seven scholars, to be drawn almost exclusively from Lincolnshire. His wife, Anne, founded two further scholarships in 1591, and Wray endowed a third fellowship in his will. Gifts followed from Godfrey Foljambe, first husband of Wray's daughter Isabel, and from Wray's daughter Frances, countess of Warwick. Magdalene was not yet rich, but without the Wray benefactions might not have survived.

A self-made man Choice, it was said, in his friend, his wife, his book, his secret, and his expression and garb, Wray was a self-made man, an able and ambitious lawyer whose rise was celebrated in his generous Lincolnshire benefactions, and was not to be hampered by obscure birth. Nor was it to be hampered by religion. Certified as 'indifferent' in religion in 1564, he had married into a Catholic family, and was probably of Catholic inclination: in 1565, with William Lovelace and the staunchly Catholic Edmund Plowden, he acted for the deprived bishop of London, Edmund Bonner, at his trial for refusing the oath of supremacy; years later, presiding at the trial of the Jesuit Edmund Campion and seeing Plowden (whose religion had perhaps denied him judicial office) in the crowd, Wray sent a note asking him to withdraw. Indifference never shook Wray's reliability: his were safe hands, if lacking political courage. A learned judge, who may have compiled law reports, he had a reputation for decency and judicial impartiality, and was, said Coke, 'a most reverend Judge, of profound and judicial knowledge, accompanied

with a ready and singular capacity, grave and sensible elocution, and continual and admirable patience' (3 Co. Rep. 26a). There was little patience, however, for counsel who affected the latest styles of dress, nor, perhaps, for those who were under-prepared: Wray alone of the utter barristers of Lincoln's Inn escaped a fine in 1553 for not being ready to moot, and he alone of the serjeants created in April 1567 had a ring for the lord admiral, Edward Clinton, unusually present at the ceremony in the common pleas, though Wray was perhaps forewarned: Lord Clinton had interests in Grimsby, and Wray had been a feoffee to uses in his son's marriage settlement. Among Wray's friends were Thomas Cony of Bassingthorpe, Lincolnshire, in whose house he had a room set apart; John, Lord Lumley, a well-known Catholic sympathizer; and Edwin Sandys, archbishop of York. His most constant opponent was the protestant zealot Richard Topcliffe, with whom he was embroiled in litigation over a lease of the prebend of Corringham and Stow, Lincolnshire.

Wray died at Glentworth on 7 May 1592 and was buried in the chancel of Glentworth church, where there is an elaborate monument. In addition to his legacy to Magdalene, he provided by will for the school of Kirton in Lindsey, Lincolnshire, and for the inmates of his almshouse at Glentworth. He had also built the sessions house at Spital in the Street, Lincolnshire.

Sir Drury Wray, ninth baronet (1633–1710), was born in Lincolnshire on 29 July 1633, third son of Sir Christopher *Wray (d. 1646) of Ashby, Lincolnshire, grandson of the chief justice, and his wife, Albinia (d. 1660), daughter and coheir of Edward Cecil, Viscount Wimbledon. About 1657 he married Anne Casey (d. 22 April 1697), daughter and heir of Thomas Casey of Rathcannon Castle, co. Limerick. They had two surviving sons, both of whom died without issue after succeeding to the baronetcy, and seven daughters. A commissioner to execute the poll money ordinances of 1660 and 1661, Wray received grants of land in the counties of Limerick and Tipperary in 1674, and was sheriff of Limerick in 1685. He succeeded his great-nephew, Sir Baptist Wray, as ninth baronet about 1689. A captain in 1690 in the Jacobite Sutherland's horse, he fought at the battle of the Boyne, and was attainted in 1691, forfeiting his lands, though his son Christopher was allowed a reversion in fee of lands in Cork and Limerick after his father's death. Wray left Ireland after his attainder, but later returned, and died on 30 October 1710, to be buried in the church of Clonlara, co. Limerick. His younger son, Sir Cecil Wray, acquired the Glentworth estate, which passed, on his death without issue, to Sir John Wray of Sleningford, Yorkshire, grandson of Wray's younger brother Cecil.   N. G. JONES

Sources HoP, *Commons, 1558–1603* · C. Dalton, *History of the Wrays of Glentworth, 1523–1852*, 2 vols. (1880) [incl. transcripts of will and letters] · Cooper, *Ath. Cantab.*, vol. 2 · G. O. Wray, 'Family and pedigree of Wray', *The Genealogist*, 4 (1880), 278–85 · will, 6 Jan 1591/6 Jan 1592, PRO, PROB 11/79, sig. 47 · A. R. Maddison, ed., *Lincolnshire pedigrees*, 4, Harleian Society, 55 (1906) · J. Raine, ed., *Wills and inventories from the registry of the archdeaconry of Richmond*, SurtS, 26 (1853) · W. P. Baildon, ed., *The records of the Honorable Society of Lincoln's Inn: admissions*, 1 (1896), 55 · W. P. Baildon, ed., *The records of the*

Honorable Society of Lincoln's Inn: the black books, 1 (1897), esp. 293–353 · CPR, 1558–75 · CSP dom., 1547–80; addenda, 1580–1625; 1581–90 · APC, 1558–88, 1590, 1596–7 · J. S. Cockburn, A history of English assizes, 1558–1714 (1972), 50, 91, 165, 196–209, 264–7, 293 · State trials, 1.1049–1249 · S. D'Ewes, ed., The journals of all the parliaments during the reign of Queen Elizabeth, both of the House of Lords and House of Commons (1682) · Baker, Serjeants · P. Cunich and others, A history of Magdalene College, Cambridge, 1428–1988 (1994) · R. Willis, The architectural history of the University of Cambridge, and of the colleges of Cambridge and Eton, ed. J. W. Clark, 2 (1886) · J. E. Neale, Elizabeth I and her parliaments, 1: 1559–1581 (1953) · Calendar of the manuscripts of the most hon. the marquis of Salisbury, 2, HMC, 9 (1888) · John, Lord Campbell, The lives of the chief justices of England, 1 (1849) · C. Monro, Acta cancellariae (1847) · Camden miscellany, IX, CS, new ser., 53 (1895), 27 · J. H. Thomas, ed., The third part of the reports of Sir Edward Coke (1826), 26a [3 Co Rep]

Archives BL, Lansdowne MS 1084, fols. 38r–42v

Likenesses portrait, 1582; formerly in possession of Cecil Wray, 1791 · effigy on monument, c.1592, St Michael's, Glentworth, Lincolnshire · engraving (after portrait, 1582), repro. in Dalton, History, vol. 1, frontispiece · oils (after portrait, 1582), NPG [see illus.] · portrait (after portrait, 1582), Magd. Cam. · portrait; known to be at Fillingham Castle, Lincolnshire, in 1900 · portrait; known to be at Sleningford Park, Yorkshire, in 1900

Wealth at death bulk to wife: will, PRO, PROB 11/79, sig. 47

Wray, Sir Christopher (bap. **1601**, d. **1646**), politician, was baptized on 14 May 1601 at Glentworth, Lincolnshire, the eldest son of Sir William Wray, first baronet (1555–1617), and his second wife, Frances (1576–c.1637), widow of Sir Nicholas Clifford of Bobbing, Kent, and daughter of Sir William Drury of Hawsted House, Suffolk. On his father's death, Wray's elder half-brother, Sir John Wray, succeeded to the baronetcy while Wray inherited the estates at Ashby, near Grimsby. On 3 August 1623 he married Albinia (c.1605–1660), daughter of Edward Cecil, Viscount Wimbledon, and soon after he was knighted, at Theobalds on 12 November. He was MP for Grimsby in 1628, and in 1630 he defended the rights of the commoners of the Isle of Axholme, disputing the crown's legal right to improve the fenland. In 1636 he successfully resisted ship money, allegedly remarking that he would not pay 'if it was but a groat' (Dalton, 1.222). He attended to the legal business of Grimsby's corporation and was returned as its MP again in 1640.

Part of a powerful kinship network of Lincolnshire's parliamentary gentry, he was on the committee that presented the grand remonstrance to the king on 1 December 1641, and was appointed a deputy lieutenant to Lord Willoughby of Parham, parliament's lord lieutenant of Lincolnshire. He implemented parliament's militia ordinance in the county in June 1642 and arrested local royalists. He was commissioned as captain of a troop of horse which he led into Yorkshire on 21 October to join his kinsman John Hotham. His troop was extremely active there. One royalist wrote that they were the 'only means our miseries were brought to this height' (Portland MSS, 1.68–9). On 9 November Wray marched north from Wetherby with John Hotham in a failed attempt to prevent the royalist army crossing the Tees into Yorkshire, and his troop fought in engagements at Piercebridge, Tadcaster, and Sherburn. On 17 December the committee at Lincoln requested his return to Lincolnshire, but he was still

included on the royalists' list of Yorkshire traitors on 17 January 1643. Hotham rejoined him in Lincolnshire in April 1643, but they were defeated soon after at Ancaster Heath on 11 April. By then Hotham was in secret correspondence with the royalists, promising that Willoughby, Wray, and others would lay down their arms in exchange for royal pardon. On 5 May, Wray had to write to parliament to defend himself from charges of not fully prosecuting the war. As Willoughby lost control of the county to the royalists in 1643, Wray defended him vehemently in the House of Commons, while Wray's son and nephews assaulted a parliamentarian colonel for speaking out against him.

Wray became a supporter of the presbyterian faction in parliament, and acted as teller for those in favour of displacing army officers who would not take the solemn league and covenant. In February 1645 he was appointed to a committee investigating ways of repaying MPs who had suffered heavy losses in parliament's service, and on 18 April he was named as a commissioner of the admiralty. In October he secured the election of his son William as his fellow MP for Grimsby, removing the rival candidate, Colonel Edward King, by having him sent to London to answer unsubstantiated charges of slandering two Lincolnshire MPs. From 5 December 1645 Wray briefly served as a commissioner resident with the Scots forces besieging Newark. He returned to London in January 1646, where he died on 6 February. He was buried a week later at St Giles-in-the-Fields. ANDREW J. HOPPER

Sources C. Dalton, History of the Wrays of Glentworth, 1523–1852, 2 vols. (1880) · JHC, 1 (1547–1628) · C. Holmes, Seventeenth-century Lincolnshire, History of Lincolnshire, 7 (1980) · C. Holmes, 'Colonel King and Lincolnshire politics, 1642–1646', HJ, 16 (1973), 451–84 · The manuscripts of his grace the duke of Portland, 10 vols., HMC, 29 (1891–1931), vol. 1 · J. W. F. Hill, Tudor and Stuart Lincoln (1956) · E. Gillett, A history of Grimsby (1970) · U. Hull, Brynmor Jones L., Hotham papers, DDHO/1/13 · DNB · Commonwealth exchequer papers, PRO, SP 28/2A/77 · GEC, Peerage, new edn, vol. 12/2 · Keeler, Long Parliament, 400

Archives BL, Lansdowne MS 878, fol. 22 · PRO, Commonwealth exchequer papers, SP 28/2A/77; SP 28/299/837, 849 · U. Hull, Hotham MSS, DDHO/1/13

Wealth at death over £5600—personal estate; manors of Ashby, Bastings, and Butterwick; estates in Uxford and Binbrooke: will, proved 27 March 1646, PRO, PROB 11/195, sig. 36; abstract in Dalton, History of the Wrays

Wray, Daniel (1701–1783), antiquary, born on 28 November 1701 in the parish of St Botolph, Aldersgate, London, was the youngest child of Sir Daniel Wray (d. 1719), a soap-boiler living in Little Britain, London, and his second wife, Elizabeth. His father was knighted on 24 March 1708, while high sheriff of Essex, where he owned an estate near Ingatestone. At the age of thirteen Wray went to Charterhouse School as a day scholar. In 1718 he matriculated from Queens' College, Cambridge, where he graduated BA in 1722, and proceeded MA in 1728. Between 1722 and 1728 he made a prolonged visit to Italy in the company of James Douglas, later fourteenth earl of Morton. On 13 March 1729 he was admitted a fellow of the Royal Society, and on 18 June 1731 he was incorporated at Oxford. He lived mainly at Cambridge until his election as a fellow of the Society of Antiquaries in January 1741, when he became a more frequent resident of London, lodging at the house of Arthur Pond, the painter and engraver. He subsequently moved to lodgings at Richmond, Surrey. He and Pond, together with George Knapton, John Dyer, and others, founded the Roman Club in London.

After marriage to Mary Darell, the daughter of Robert Darell of Richmond, Wray and his wife lived in Covent Garden, Soho, and Richmond. In 1755 he became vice-president of the Society of Antiquaries and on 18 June 1765 was appointed one of the trustees of the British Museum. He was a devoted antiquary and collector of rare books but, although he wrote much, he published little during his lifetime except for three papers on classical antiquities in the first two volumes of *Archaeologia*. Wray's friendship with Philip Yorke, later second earl of Hard-wicke, began in 1737. In 1741 Philip and his brother Charles Yorke brought out the first volume of the *Athenian Letters*, to which Wray contributed under the signature W. In 1745 Philip Yorke appointed Wray his deputy teller of the exchequer, an office he held until 1782. Among Wray's many literary friends were Henry Coventry, William Heberden the elder, William Warburton, Conyers Middleton, and Nicholas Hardinge. Wray was a source of encouragement to many of his younger contemporaries, and among those who considered themselves especially indebted to him were Francis Wollaston, George Hard-inge, and William Heberden the younger.

Wray died on 29 December 1783, and was buried in the family vault in the church of St Botolph, Aldersgate, where there is a tablet to his memory. His widow, who presented his library to Charterhouse, together with a copy of Dance's portrait of Wray, died on 19 March 1803. After his death George Hardinge compiled a memoir to accompany a collection of Wray's verses and correspondence, which he published in 1817 in the first volume of *Literary Illustrations* with a dedication to Philip Yorke, third earl of Hard-wicke. Fifty copies of the memoir were printed separately for private distribution. Two sonnets to Wray by Thomas Edwards (1699–1757) appear in later editions of his *Canons of Criticism*. A sonnet by Richard Roderick printed in Robert Dodsley's *Collection of Poems* (1775) and in *Elegant Extracts*, edited by Vicesimus Knox, was also thought by Hardinge to be addressed to Wray. In 1830 James Falconar published *The Secret Revealed*, in which he made out a plausible case for the identification of Wray with Junius, although doubt was later cast on his evidence for this claim.   E. I. CARLYLE, *rev.* J. A. MARCHAND

Sources Nichols, *Illustrations*, 1.1–168, 826–30; 2.87, 100, 126, 130; 3.43; 4.524–37; 8.406 • *GM*, 1st ser., 54 (1784), 4, 72 • *GM*, 1st ser., 73 (1803), 60 • Nichols, *Lit. anecdotes*, 2.441–2, 712; 7.716; 8.525; 9.445, 609 • Venn, *Alum. Cant.* • Foster, *Alum. Oxon.* • A. Chalmers, ed., *The general biographical dictionary*, new edn, 32 vols. (1812–17) • H. B. Wheatley and P. Cunningham, *London past and present*, 3 vols. (1891), vol. 1, p. 226 • T. Thomson, *History of the Royal Society from its institution to the end of the eighteenth century* (1812), appx 38 • O. Manning and W. Bray, *The history and antiquities of the county of Surrey*, 3 (1814), 127 • *IGI* • J. Ingamells, ed., *A dictionary of British and Irish travellers in Italy, 1701–1800* (1997), 1020–21

Archives BL, letters to Lord Hardwicke, Add. MSS 35401–35402 • BL, letters to Thomas Birch, Add. MSS 4322, 4475 • Bodl. Oxf., corresp. with Thomas Edwards • Bodl. Oxf., letters to Samuel Pegge

Likenesses E. Pozzo, bronze sculpture, 1726 • N. Dance, oils, 1769?, Queens' College, Cambridge • J. Powell, portrait, 1785 (after N. Dance), NPG • N. Holland, portrait, Queens' College, Cambridge • B. Longmate, aquatint (after silhouette by M. Wray), BM, NPG; repro. in Nichols, *Illustrations* • H. Meyer, engraving (after N. Dance), repro. in Nichols, *Illustrations*, vol. 1, frontispiece • bronze (after bronze sculpture by E. Pozzo), repro. in Nichols, *Illustrations*

Wealth at death £5000; plus old South Sea annuities

Wray, Sir Drury, ninth baronet (1633–1710). *See under* Wray, Sir Christopher (*c.*1522–1592).

Wray, Sir John, second baronet (*bap.* 1586, *d.* 1655), politician, was baptized on 27 November 1586 at Louth, Lincolnshire. He was the eldest surviving son of Sir William Wray (*d.* 1617) of Ashby and Glentworth in the same county, and of his first wife, Lucy (*d.* 1600), daughter of Sir Edward Montagu of Boughton, Northamptonshire. The Wrays had moved to Lincolnshire from Yorkshire in the mid-sixteenth century, and quickly established themselves as one of their adopted county's wealthiest and most godly families. Wray's father built up a considerable estate around his principal residence at Ashby, and sat for the nearby borough of Grimsby in 1584 and 1604, and for Lincolnshire in 1601. Wray was admitted to Sidney Sussex College, Cambridge, in June 1600 and to Lincoln's Inn on 4 May 1603; he finished his education with a three-year tour of the continent. By his marriage to Griselda (*d.* 1654), the only daughter of Sir Hugh Bethell of Ellerton, Yorkshire, on 7 September 1607, he acquired £2000 and two manors. Wray and his wife had twelve children, of whom four sons and three daughters survived him. He was knighted in September 1612 and succeeded to his father's baronetcy in August 1617.

Wray was returned for Grimsby on his father's interest in 1614, but when Sir William died the Ashby estate, and with it the family's interest at Grimsby, was inherited by Wray's half-brother, Sir Christopher *Wray. Sir John established his seat at Wharton, near Glentworth, and continued his father's patronage of puritan ministers, among them the future Westminster assembly divine Thomas Coleman. Wray's 'more than ordinarie zeale for holinesse and religion' (R. Bernard, *A Ready Way to Good Works*, [1635], 87) was possibly a factor in his return for Lincolnshire in 1625. Although appointed a forced loan commissioner the following year, he refused to pay the levy and was imprisoned in the Gatehouse prison, Westminster, for eight months. He was returned for Lincolnshire to the 1628 parliament, where he spoke against the duke of Buckingham. During the personal rule he criticized the crown-sponsored scheme for draining the Isle of Axholme, and in 1636 was removed from the Lindsey commission of the peace for refusing to pay ship money. His friendship with Archbishop Laud's *bête noire*, Bishop John

Williams of Lincoln, would also have done little to endear him to the crown.

Wray's standing as one of Lincolnshire's foremost landowners and 'patriots' was confirmed on 30 March 1640, when he was elected for the county to the Short Parliament. He was a critic of the perceived abuses of the personal rule, denouncing ship money and Laudian innovations in religion, and implying that the crown's seizure of Lincolnshire's militia arms for use against the Scots was illegal. He scorned the king's offer to give up ship money in return for twelve subsidies as an attempt 'to buy ship money and purchase war [with the Scots]' (*Diary of Sir Thomas Aston*, 131). Several of his speeches in the Short Parliament evince a genuine desire for closer ties between England and Scotland, at least in terms of religion.

Wray was returned for Lincolnshire again on 12 October 1640, and from his speeches—nine of which were published in 1641—it seems that his main preoccupation in the Long Parliament was church reform. He expressed the hope that MPs' 'constant resolutions will be to settell religion in his [*sic*] splendor and purity by pulling Dagon from the altar' (*Eight Occasionall Speeches*, 2). The only way to preserve the protestant religion, he argued, was 'to lay the axe to the root, to unloose the long and deep fangs of superstition and popery' by a 'thorough reformation' (ibid., 4). But although often described as a presbyterian, he made it clear that it was not his intention to overthrow the government of the church by bishops 'in the plurall, but to limit and qualifie it in some particulars' (ibid., 6). In other words, he was against prelacy, not the office of bishop. Indeed, he declared that 'I love some of them so well, am so charitable to the rest, that I wish rather their reformation than their ruine' (ibid.). There are signs that his attitude towards the bishops may have hardened during the course of 1641. Thus on 8 February 1641 he moved that the root and branch petition be referred to a committee, and on 27 May he presented a petition from Lincolnshire 'for the abolishing of the government of archbishopps, bishopp[s], & ther subordinate officers' (BL, Harley MS 163, fol. 237), which served as a prelude to Sir Edward Dering's introduction of a bill for abolishing episcopacy. Wray supported this bill on the grounds that the house had 'indeavoured by all meanes possible to reforme the episcopacy government, but could not, & now this bill is as a vomitt to them' (BL, Harley MS 477, fol. 108). On 13 November, in his last recorded speech on further reformation, he argued that unless the bishops could justify their 'spirituall primacy over the ministers of Christ' from scripture, then the king was within his rights 'utterly to abolish all lordly primacy' (*An Occasionall Speech*, 5). Yet here again, his problem with episcopacy was not the office of bishop but rather its tendency to degenerate into prelacy. Like many of England's leading puritan ministers during the early 1640s he may well have favoured the retention of bishops as diocesan co-ordinators within a system of church government that lay somewhere between 'primitive' episcopacy and Scottish-style presbyterianism.

Although not fully committed to classical presbyterianism, there can be no doubting Wray's concern to promote a closer union between England and Scotland. He supported the terms of the 1641 treaty with the Scots, arguing that nothing should be allowed to divide the English from 'them who worship but one God, and serve but one master with us' (*Eight Occasionall Speeches*, 8). 'Think of it [i.e. the treaty] what you will', he told the house, 'their subsistance is ours, we live or die, rise or fall, together' (ibid.). He was a leading promoter of parliament's protestation of May 1641, which he conceived of in very Scottish terms as a covenant with 'God and the king':

> first, binding our selves by a parliamentary and nationall oath (not a Straffordian, nor a prelaticall one) to preserve our religion entire and pure, without the least compound of superstition, or idolatry: next, to defend the defender of the faith, his royal person, crowne, and dignity, and maintaine our soveraigne in his glory and splendor, which can never be ecclipsed, if the ballance of justice goe right, and his lawes be duly executed. (*Eight Occasionall Speeches*, 12)

In May 1642 Wray was appointed a parliamentary commissioner for Lincolnshire, and spent most of the summer helping Lord Willoughby of Parham wrest control of the county's trained bands from the king's party. He had returned to Westminster by mid-September, when he pledged to bring in money and plate for advancing the earl of Essex's army. He subsequently received numerous committee appointments for maintaining parliament's forces, sequestering delinquents, and for raising money to prosecute the war effort. He apparently supported Pym's policy of a Scottish alliance, and certainly had little sympathy for those MPs and peers whose distaste for bringing in the Scots led them to abandon the house in the summer of 1643. Nevertheless, his continued patronage of the Erastian presbyterian Thomas Coleman suggests that he remained unconvinced by the Scots' arguments for *jure divino* presbyterianism.

Wray was granted leave of absence by the Commons in May 1646, and thereafter seems to have abandoned his seat entirely. He was not among those MPs excluded at Pride's Purge, but there is no evidence that he served the Rump in any capacity. He died towards the end of 1655, and was buried at Glentworth on 31 December. His estate included at least seven Lincolnshire manors and four advowsons, and before his death he was able to settle lands worth £2500 a year on his eldest son, John Wray, who represented Lincolnshire in the 1654 parliament.

DAVID SCOTT

Sources 'Wray, Sir John', HoP, *Commons, 1640–60* [draft] · *Eight occasionall speeches made in the House of Commons … by Sir John Wray* (1641) · *An occasionall speech made to the House of Commons … by Sir John Wray* (1641) · C. Dalton, *History of the Wrays of Glentworth, 1523–1852*, 2 vols. (1880) · *JHC*, 2–7 (1640–59) · *JHL*, 4–9 (1628–47) · C. Holmes, *Seventeenth-century Lincolnshire*, History of Lincolnshire, 7 (1980) · *The Short Parliament (1640) diary of Sir Thomas Aston*, ed. J. D. Maltby, CS, 4th ser., 35 (1988) · *The journal of Sir Simonds D'Ewes from the beginning of the Long Parliament to the opening of the trial of the earl of Strafford*, ed. W. Notestein (1923) · C. Russell, *The fall of the British monarchies, 1637–1642* (1991) · J. T. Cliffe, *The puritan gentry: the great puritan families of early Stuart England* (1984) · J. W. F. Hill, *Tudor and Stuart Lincoln* (1956) · inquisition post mortem, PRO, C 142/386/87 ·

chancery: entry books of decrees and orders, 1656, PRO, C33/208, fol. 3v

Wealth at death estate valued at at least £2500 p.a.: PRO, C33/208, fol. 3v

Wray, John. *See* Ray, John (1627–1705).

Wren, Christopher (1589–1658), dean of Windsor, was born in the city of London on 17 September 1589, the younger son of a mercer, Francis Wren (1553–1624). Like his elder brother, Matthew *Wren (1585–1667), later bishop of Ely, Christopher was admitted as a scholar at Merchant Taylors' School (9 February 1601) but unlike him he went to Oxford. He was elected a Sir Thomas White scholar at St John's College in 1605 and matriculated in October 1608; he graduated BA in June 1609 and proceeded MA in 1613. As a graduate he wrote a successful Latin drama, *Physiponomachia*, based on a passage from Ovid's *Metamorphoses*, which he dedicated to his college's president, John Buckeridge. In April 1619 he and Brian Duppa of All Souls were appointed to serve as proctors. On 21 June 1620 he defended his BD and a week later he was granted a licence to preach. He became a household chaplain to Bishop Lancelot Andrewes, a close friend of Buckeridge and formerly master of Matthew Wren's Cambridge college. Andrewes himself was also an old boy of Merchant Taylors' School and in 1620 he appointed the younger Wren to be rector of Fonthill Bishop in Wiltshire. There Christopher married in 1620 or 1621, Mary Cox, the daughter of Robert Cox of Fonthill Abbey; they had three children. Christopher Wren remained rector until 1639 and in 1623 he became rector also of the neighbouring parish of East Knoyle. It was there that he and his family lived—Wren's second son, Christopher *Wren (1632–1723), the future architect, was born in the village.

In 1628, while Wren was appointed a chaplain to the king, his brother Matthew, already master of Peterhouse, Cambridge, became dean of Wolverhampton and of Windsor and register of the Order of the Garter. When Matthew resigned his offices on becoming bishop of Hereford in 1634, Christopher was not elected despite having been the front runner, but did succeed to all his other positions, being admitted to the deanery at Windsor on 4 April 1635. Later in life Wren took great pleasure in pointing out that his family had been associated with Windsor since before the Reformation since one Geoffrey Wren had held the seventh stall there under Henry VII. Like his brother before him Dean Wren was assiduous in attending to chapter business, even transferring two chapter meetings, in October 1636 and in 1638, to the deanery when recurrent ill health prevented him leaving his home. He followed his brother's 1628 initiative in insisting upon order and decency in the life of the chapel, complaining to the king in 1637 of 'promiscuous and undecent sitting in, and filling the stalles in the Choyre by weomen and people of meane qualitie' (Windsor Castle, chapter acts, VI. B 2, fol. 138r), against which the king provided for reordering the chapel.

As dean Wren had oversight of the worship for the Garter knights whenever they were at Windsor, and as register of the Garter, an office traditionally linked with the deanery, he took a serious interest in the history of the order and in record keeping. He delighted Charles I by establishing that Henry VII had been entitled 'defender of the faith', 'long before the Pope's pretended Donation' of 1521 (Wren, *Parentalia*, 143).

Wren was also an architect and as well as designing country houses he was asked by Charles to provide an estimate (15 May 1635) for a building for the queen at Windsor, to include banqueting rooms and galleries for her lord chamberlain. Nothing came of this £13,000 project. At East Knoyle, on the other hand, Wren used the profits from his deanery to undertake the redecoration of the chancel. In 1639 he employed a Dorset man, Robert Brockway, to undertake the work that he designed and supervised himself. This plasterwork included a sanctuary roof with cherubim and angels. On the walls there were anagrammatic Latin mottoes and pargetting: Jacob's dream, the ascension, the sacrifice of Isaac, and a portrait of the donor himself, kneeling as a supplicant lamenting with the psalmist that he is yet far off and wingless, unable to reach the highest heavens (Psalm 55).

In November 1638 Wren was presented to the living of Great Haseley in Oxfordshire by the unanimous vote of the Windsor chapter, but he had little enjoyment in the living, and by Easter 1641 sought to exchange it with Christopher Potter, the dean of Worcester. At the outbreak of the civil war he took care to safeguard the registers of the Order of the Garter, hiding them with the order's silver, beneath the floor of the treasury. This precaution paid off when the castle was first ransacked in 1642 but three years later a more determined search found them. Although Wren successfully petitioned for the return of the documents of the order, the 1637 altar silver, made by Christian van Vianen, and other treasures were never returned. The deanery itself was sacked on 21 September 1642, allegedly by parliamentary order, although both houses denied this, and as well as personal papers Wren's collection of gift silver, from the king, the elector palatine, and other knights of the Garter, was taken. At the time all that was returned to him was his harpsichord, valued at 10s.

In 1645 Wren compounded as a delinquent after an initial charge, despite a royal order on 12 December 1644 for his protection. His creative decoration at East Knoyle was censured before the Faulstone commission meeting at Longford Castle in May 1647. He moved to Bletchingdon in Oxfordshire, where his son-in-law William Holder was incumbent, and died at the vicarage there on 29 May 1658. He was survived by his wife.

NICHOLAS W. S. CRANFIELD

Sources C. Wren, *Parentalia, or, Memoirs of the family of Wrens* (1750) • E. Ashmole, *The institution, laws and ceremonies of the most noble order of the Garter* (1672) • C. Wren, *Physiponomachia acted, 1609–1611*, ed. H.-J. Weckermann (1981) • Foster, *Alum. Oxon.* • Mrs E. P. Hart, ed., *Merchant Taylors' School register, 1561–1934*, 2 vols. (1936) • C. J. Robinson, ed., *A register of the scholars admitted into Merchant Taylors' School, from AD 1562 to 1874*, 2 vols. (1882–3) • chapter acts, Windsor Castle, VI.B.2 • S. Bond, ed., *The chapter acts of the dean and canons* *of Windsor: 1430, 1523–1672* (1966) • A. Claydon, *A guide to East Knoyle church* (1996) • A. Tinniswood, *His invention so fertile: a life of Christopher Wren* (2001)

Archives Windsor Castle, Windsor, official MSS, Windsor chapter acts books

Likenesses R. Brockway, plasterwork effigy, 1639, St Mary the Virgin Church, East Knoyle • G. Vandergucht, line engraving (after portrait, LPL), BM, NPG; repro. in Wren, *Parentalia* • portrait

Wren, Sir Christopher (1632–1723), architect, mathematician, and astronomer, was born at East Knoyle, Wiltshire, on 20 October 1632, the only surviving son of Christopher *Wren DD (1589–1658), at that time rector of East Knoyle and later dean of Windsor, and his wife, Mary, the daughter of Richard Cox of Fonthill, Wiltshire. His paternal grandfather, Francis Wren (1553–1624), was a London mercer, but the family came from Durham and, they believed, originally from Denmark. A previous child, born on 22 November 1631 and baptized Christopher, had died the same day; John Aubrey's confusion of the two persisted occasionally into late twentieth-century literature. The surviving copy of the parish register is misleading, but Dr Wren's copy of Christoph Helwig's *Theatrum historicum* (1618; NL Wales) contains his accurate family record even to the hour of birth.

Early life and education As a child Wren 'seem'd consumptive' (Wren, 346)—the kind of sickly child who survives into robust old age. He was first taught at home by a private tutor, the Revd William Shepheard, and by his father, a man of scholarly aspirations and wide interests including natural philosophy, mathematics, and architecture. After Dr Wren's appointment as dean of Windsor in March 1635 his family spent part of each year there, but about 1639 he engaged a plasterer to embellish the chancel walls of East Knoyle church with plaster reliefs and pietistic inscriptions. This work survives, but of the 'very strong roof' he made at Knoyle neither the location nor the survival is known.

The Laudian high Anglicanism which brought Dr Wren preferment in 1635 was to become an embarrassment. He was more fortunate than his elder brother Matthew *Wren (1585–1667), bishop of Ely, imprisoned for twenty years, but in the autumn of 1642 parliamentary soldiers searched the Windsor deanery, seizing the treasury of the Order of the Garter of which the dean was registrar, and many personal effects. He took refuge at Knoyle and, while it supported the king, at Bristol.

Little is known about Wren's schooling. According to Aubrey, Sir Christopher determined to give his son the public education he himself had not received. The story that he was at Westminster School from 1641 to 1646 is unsubstantiated; *Parentalia* places him there 'for some short time' before going to Oxford (in 1650). According to *Parentalia* he was 'initiated' in the principles of mathematics by Dr William Holder, who became rector of Bletchingdon, Oxfordshire, in 1642 and married Wren's elder sister Susan the following year. Although, according to Aubrey, in adulthood he was no great reader, Wren received a thorough grounding in Latin; he also learned to draw. Some youthful exercises are preserved or recorded (though few

Sir Christopher Wren (1632–1723), by Edward Pierce, *c*.1673

are datable); his earliest talents were for Latin composition and for devising graphic and other visual aids. In his tenth year he wrote a new year greeting for his father in Latin prose and verse, directed *E musaeo meo*, while from his early teens two projects survive for hand-signing alphabets for deaf people. One is titled (in Greek) *Cheirologia*, suggesting a prompt response to the proposition in William Bulwer's *Chirologia* (1644), only taken up in print in 1661 by George Dalgarno. Instructing deaf people was a preoccupation of Holder, and the mutual interest suggests that he may have contributed to Wren's education even before his marriage, as well as after 1646 when the Wren family, finally evicted from Knoyle, lodged with the Holders at Bletchingdon; Dean Wren remained there until his death on 29 May 1658. Work of this period included a design for a 'pneumatic engine' or air pump (later perfected by Robert Boyle), a pasteboard star calendar, a *sciotericon* to plot equal hours from a sundial, a device for writing in the dark, a recording weather clock, and a pasteboard calculator for the orbit of the moon. Bletchingdon is not far from Oxford, and it was probably through Holder that Wren met there Sir Charles Scarburgh. He assisted Scarburgh in his anatomical studies, and in a letter of 1647 Wren acknowledged his gratitude to the physician not only for his teaching but also, in a recent unspecified illness, for saving his life. Before 1648 he was making pasteboard models to illustrate Scarburgh's lectures on muscular action, and translating into Latin, at Scarburgh's suggestion, William Oughtred's tract on dialling or gnomonics, for a new Latin edition (1652) of Oughtred's *Clavis mathematicae*. Already a common thread appears in Wren's interests: mechanics, anatomy, and applied mathematics, and the preference for practical results and visual demonstrations that would lead him to architecture.

Wren entered Wadham College, Oxford, on 25 June 1650. His choice was probably influenced, through Holder and Scarburgh, by Wadham's strength in mathematics and natural science under the wardenship of John Wilkins, appointed the previous year after a term as chaplain to Charles Louis, elector palatine. (As a child, Wren had met the elector when he was a visitor to the Windsor deanery, but he did not meet Wilkins then as Wilkins was not yet in the elector's service.) At Wadham, Wren's formal education was conventional; his informal studies were at least as important. The curriculum was still based on the study of Aristotle and the discipline of the Latin language, and it is anachronistic to imagine that he received scientific training in the modern sense. But as a gentleman commoner he could dine at the fellows' table, and Wilkins was host to the circle of distinguished scholars, of varied though moderate political persuasion who, soon after the Restoration, formed jointly with a similar group in London the nucleus of the Royal Society. Original and sometimes brilliant practical workers, experimental philosophers in the mould publicized earlier in the century by Francis Bacon and later by Thomas Sprat, Wilkins's circle included at various times the mathematicians Seth Ward, John Wallis, and Robert Wood, the experimenters Boyle and Robert Hooke, the physicians Jonathan Goddard and Thomas Willis, and the astronomer Lawrence Rooke.

Scientific work in Oxford and London Wren graduated BA on 18 March 1651 and MA on 14 December 1653. As an undergraduate he designed a box-beehive and a practical hygrometer, and contributed twenty lines of florid and allusive verse to a collection celebrating William Petty's resuscitation of a hanged Oxford woman (R. Watkins, ed., *Newes from the Dead*, Oxford, 1651). Election to a fellowship at All Souls on 3 November 1653 ensured the continuation of his research, although he was often in London. John Evelyn visited him in Oxford in July 1654 noting—as did others—his close collaboration with Wilkins, who shared and fostered his interest in mechanical devices and demonstrations. With Wilkins's encouragement he developed an instrument for writing two copies of a document at once, and drew from the image in a microscope; he also caught Wilkins's enthusiasm for telescopes, and after 1654 interest in computational astronomy ceded to optical. In 1655 they built an 80 foot instrument for observing the whole face of the moon.

Early in his fellowship Wren developed a perspectograph or scenographic apparatus, in which, by a movable sight linked to a pen, a view could be traced on paper; later, in 1663, he showed this device to the Royal Society, and prototypes were built. By 1657 he had persuaded Boyle to test Descartes's hypothesis that atmospheric pressure varied, like the tides, with lunar influence—this was before Newton's law of gravitation. Boyle's experiments disproved the hypothesis and led to the advance of the barometer from a philosophical curiosity to a useful instrument. Wren's anatomical studies included dissections of fish and other creatures, and experiments about 1656 with intravenous injection into animals. Incorporating earlier observations and using newly improved optics, he studied the appearance and phases of Saturn sufficiently to draft a monograph on the subject, but promptly abandoned it when he received advance news of Christiaan Huygens's hypothesis (*Systema Saturnium*, 1659). Wren continued to divide his time between Oxford and London, as he would do well into the 1660s. On 7 August 1657 he was appointed to the chair of astronomy at Gresham College in the City of London, apparently on the recommendation of Wilkins to Oliver Cromwell, whose widowed sister Wilkins had recently married. Cromwell intervened personally in the appointment, Rooke, the current holder, being assigned the chair of geometry to accommodate him. Gresham was noted for mathematical study, especially applied mathematics (including navigation, which Wren was required to teach). He subsequently lectured on light, Saturn, and Johannes Kepler, and on dioptrics, the nascent science of lenses named by Kepler and amplified by Descartes.

The Gresham lecture Wren's inaugural lecture of August 1657 survives in disparate Latin and English versions (printed in Ward and *Parentalia* respectively); it is the only account of his view of the sciences. Both versions are carefully composed. His tributes to the founder, Sir Thomas Gresham, to previous professors, to the City, and to the muse of astronomy are gracious, well turned, and apt; Wren enumerated, with examples familiar to an educated audience, the practical applications and benefits of his discipline, especially to trade and industry. The most important passages, however, give a more personal and individual view of the 'new philosophy', its invention, its foundations, and its heroic figures. This, Wren claimed, had liberated all the sciences from the intellectual constraints of ancient Greek and Roman thought, but astronomy was particularly firmly supported: on the one hand by the absolute authority of mathematical truth, on the other hand by the new disciplines of magnetics, initiated by William Gilbert, and dioptrics. Mathematical demonstrations:

> being built upon the impregnable Foundations of Geometry and Arithmetick, are the only Truths, that can sink into the Mind of Man, void of all Uncertainty; and all other Discourses participate more or less of truth, according as their Subjects are more or less capable of Mathematical Demonstration. (Wren, 200–01)

Indeed for Wren logic was but a branch of mathematics, and to the latter he awarded the Aristotelian title of *organon organōn*, or instrument of instruments. Wren understood the earlier reference to Aristotle in the title of Bacon's *Novum organum* (1620) and Bacon's vision of a new science founded on inductive reasoning from observation and experiment. However, although by the mid-seventeenth century it was commonplace both to acknowledge Bacon and to disown Aristotle, Wren did neither, not even mentioning Bacon. The 'new science' was not attributable solely to Bacon, its herald rather than its inventor. Mathematics is deductive, one reason why Bacon, the advocate of induction, neglected it; moreover, mathematics in general and geometry in particular involve intuitive as well as logical thought, and here

Wren's position is explicitly distinct from Bacon's. He praises Copernicus, Kepler, Galileo, and Descartes, but calls Gilbert the 'Father of the new Philosophy' in preference to Descartes, 'but a Builder upon his [Gilbert's] Experiments' (Wren, 204). He ranks the physiologist William Harvey equally with Gilbert, noting that both are English and adding a reference to 'the useful Invention of Logarithms … wholy a British Art' (ibid., 206). He also repudiates the occult science of his time, in which several of his colleagues showed more than a passing interest. He condemns 'the ungrounded Fancies of … astrological Medicasters' (*pseudomedici* and 'quack astrologers'; ibid., 202). Little weight, therefore, can be placed on his occasional interest in strange phenomena (he once cured a sickness by eating dates after dreaming of them) or from his attendance at the Oxford chemistry classes of the hermetist Peter Staehl; most of his circle did likewise.

Growing reputation Wren was in contact with Parisian scholars by 1658, when Blaise Pascal challenged the mathematicians of Europe with two problems concerning differential curves. The first was the calculation of line, area, and other quantities of a cycloid—the arc traced by a point on the circumference of a travelling wheel. The second was to derive, from given dimensions, the length of a chord across an ellipse. Wren partly solved both problems, which were germane to the understanding of planetary orbits. However, in the first he substituted simpler values than those specified, and in both he offered not the numerical solutions required but geometrical constructions from which they could be derived. In counterchallenge he re-presented a problem of Kepler's concerning ellipses. Pascal commended his work but withheld the prizes, as Wren had not satisfied the conditions. He was still working in London and Oxford; in 1659 he was a bursar of All Souls, and designed and set up the sundial, carved by William Byrd, on the south wall of the chapel—reset in 1877 on the Codrington Library (H. Colvin and J. S. G. Simmons, *All Souls*, 1989, 70–71).

A list in *Parentalia* of Wren's inventions before 1660 includes devices for surveying, musical and acoustical instruments, developments in fishing, underwater construction and submarine navigation, and experiments in printmaking; he experimented with, but did not invent, the mezzotint technique, which Prince Rupert demonstrated to the Royal Society in 1661. Wren found it prudent to stay in Oxford when, in the anarchy after the resignation of Richard Cromwell, Commonwealth troops occupied Gresham College (in October 1659, not a year earlier as often assumed). Life at Gresham returned to normal with the Restoration, but within a year Wren had resigned his chair: on 5 February 1661 he was elected to the Savilian chair of astronomy at Oxford in succession to Seth Ward. On 12 September he received a DCL. The Restoration brought other changes. Wren's uncle Matthew was released from the Tower and his cousin the younger Matthew received a court appointment. The Wadham and Gresham circles became the nucleus of the Royal Society, inaugurated at a meeting after Christopher's Gresham lecture on 28 November 1660; thereafter he helped to draw up the society's royal charter. Charles II's initial enthusiasm for the new science stemmed not only from natural curiosity—his salad days had perforce been curtailed by affairs of state—but also from the political function he envisaged for the society in mending ideological bridges, uniting minds of diverse faction in the common cause of a single nation.

Wren came particularly to the king's notice through the Royal Society and his use of optics. In May 1661 the society forwarded a royal command to accomplish two projects he had begun, based on optics. From telescopic observations he was modelling a relief globe of the moon, as big as a human head; he was also the first Englishman to make microscopical drawings of minute creatures. Neither project survives, though both were completed; the drawings of insects hanging at Whitehall in 1688 probably perished in the fire of 1698. In the autumn of 1661 Wren assigned his microscopy to Robert Hooke, who in *Micrographia* (1665) acknowledged him as its originator. At the same time Wren was approached by his cousin Matthew with a royal commission, as 'one of the best Geometricians in Europe', to direct the refortification of Tangier, ceded by Portugal as part of the queen's dowry. Wren excused himself on grounds of health, and a military engineer was subsequently engaged.

However, before the end of 1661 Wren was unofficially advising on the repair of old St Paul's Cathedral after two decades of neglect and distress, and this assignment took temporary precedence over his duties as Savilian professor. But in 1662 he lectured on spheres, on the date of Easter (*De paschate*, not on Pascal as often stated), and on navigation—appropriate topics when mathematics was increasingly seen as the key to all scientific knowledge. Later Oxford lectures are unrecorded, but Royal Society and other sources show the drift of his studies in the next three years: graphite for lubricating timepieces; a mechanical corn drill; a self-regulating weather clock recording temperature and wind direction; an egg incubator; a demonstration model of an eye—based on that of a horse—as proposed by Descartes with a translucent retina. He also worked on a theory of elastic impact from the collision of balls suspended by threads, on respiration and the vital principle of air (a subject not fathomed until the discovery of oxygen over a century later), and on tracking the comets of 1664–5, then believed to travel in a straight line. In collaboration with Thomas Willis he made drawings from dissections, beautiful in themselves and remarkably accurate and informative, including those of the brain engraved for Willis's *Cerebri anatome* (1664). In 1664 he was incorporated MA at Cambridge.

First steps to architecture It was not unusual for the well-educated to take up architecture as a gentlemanly activity, widely accepted in theory as a branch of applied mathematics; this is implicit in the writings of Vitruvius and explicit in such sixteenth-century authors as John Dee and Leonard Digges. Wren's father was a keen and erudite observer of buildings. Oxford saw much fine building throughout the first half of the seventeenth century, and Wren's own college, Wadham, was a paragon of Jacobean modernity (1610–13). He arrived at Gresham with a far from casual eye, having in Oxford absorbed intuitively the fundamentals of architectural design. He was also familiar with Vitruvius's *De architectura*; *Parentalia* mentions among his pre-1660 work 'new designs tending to strength, convenience and beauty in building', confirming knowledge of Vitruvius's tripartite formula. It remained only for him to realize that architecture could be the supreme demonstration of the truths he had championed in his Gresham lecture.

The Tangier invitation may have arisen from Charles II's casual opportunism in matching people to tasks; however, Wren was already on the way to architectural practice. The reward offered was certainly significant—the reversion of the surveyorship of the royal works on the death of Sir John Denham (1615–1669). Denham's appointment had been opportunistic, service to the king in exile counting for more than familiarity with building. On the other hand, by 1661 Wren's architectural interests were evident to his associates and would not have escaped an observer as shrewd as Charles. In later years Wren complained to his son that Charles had done him a disservice in making him an architect, and that he would have made a better living in medicine. Nevertheless he must have known that the king's judgement and his own compliance had been right. By the early 1660s he had mastered architecture and understood it thoroughly. Several colleagues might have taken it up as a set of rules and formulas for design, but he alone—and to a lesser extent Hooke—possessed, understood, and exploited the combination of reason and intuition, experience and imagination essential to what we call genius.

This is the setting for Wren's only foreign journey, to Paris and the Île-de-France; he left London in late June 1665 and did not return until early March 1666. He incidentally avoided most of the plague, but he had made plans months earlier; his motives reflect his range of interests. His name was known and respected in Paris, and for a distinguished member of the Royal Society, armed with useful introductions, the strengthening of foreign correspondence would have been sufficient reason to travel. Another was more cogent—first-hand study of contemporary European architecture. He was already designing and supervising buildings, and although records of his journey are sparse—primarily one long letter from Wren himself—the two figures he expressly wished to meet, and undoubtedly met, were the French architect François Mansart and the Italian sculptor and architect G. L. Bernini, who arrived in Paris from Rome at the request of Louis XIV on 2 June 1665. On his return Wren wrote of 'daily conference with the best Artists', French and Italian, and first-hand study of modern design and construction cannot have attracted him less than the prospect of meeting scientific colleagues.

Early architectural commissions By 1663 Wren was confident enough, and well enough known to close associates, to put theory into practice with two commissions. In 1663 his uncle Matthew gave Pembroke College, Cambridge, a new chapel, a modest building whose interior (extended

in 1880 by George Gilbert Scott) is conventional, with classically inspired plasterwork and joinery of a high standard. It was consecrated in Wren's absence on 21 September 1665, but he was certainly in overall charge of the work. The exterior required a street front without a portal, access being from the court, and Wren made a novel adaptation of a small Roman temple front from Serlio's *Architettura*.

Wren's understanding of structures and of the classical language of architecture, his empirical and innovative attitude to prototypes, and his regard for the particulars of his brief were all manifested in a more substantial work, the Sheldonian Theatre, Oxford, proposed and ultimately paid for by Archbishop Gilbert Sheldon, formerly warden of All Souls. Contemporaries associated this building with the Royal Society, to whom Wren showed a wooden model (now lost) of his design on 29 April 1663. That design, always said (through a misreading of *Parentalia*, p. 335) to have derived from the theatre of Marcellus in Rome, was apparently intended not only for the academic ceremonies but also for both anatomy demonstrations and the staging of plays. Site work began the following spring, and on 26 July 1664 the foundation stone was laid for a different design. The theatre's U-shaped plan recalls a Roman theatre less than does Robert Streater's illusionist ceiling depicting the canvas *velarium* pulled back to reveal a sky full of allegorical figures. There is no stage, and the big high windows, raked seating, and unobscured vision proper to an anatomy theatre make an ideal setting for the real spectacle of academic ceremonial. These features were the core of Wren's brief, and although contemporaries recognized his use of Renaissance architectural language as more advanced than elsewhere in Oxford, function was his guiding principle in a building for which there was no typical precedent to follow. His restriction of the classical orders outside to the entrance front thus stemmed from scepticism of received ideas rather than from ignorance or inexperience. To span the interior without intermediate pillars he devised a system of modified king-post trusses connected by bolts and scarf joints, widely believed by contemporaries to reflect the latest mechanical theories but actually derived from traditional roof carpentry. The theatre was inaugurated on 9–10 July 1669; Evelyn, who attended, recorded the ceremonies in his diary. Both the public spaces and the hidden ones under the seating galleries were also used by the university press, and for many years after the construction of Nicholas Hawksmoor's Clarendon building (1712–13) books still bore the imprint 'At the Theatre'.

The Savilian professor's talents were noticed by colleagues. In 1664 he designed a chapel screen for All Souls (rebuilt and transformed by Sir James Thornhill, 1716); this was followed by screens at St John's (*c*.1670, des. 1848) and Merton (1671–3, partly reinstated 1960)—three different and skilful classical insertions into Gothic interiors. Trinity College built to his design a detached range of rooms in the garden (1665–8); the core of this remains, with later additions. A similar range at the Queen's College (1671–4) survives in essence. At Emmanuel College,

Cambridge, the new chapel and cloister range was conceived by William Sancroft, briefly master before becoming dean of St Paul's. With Sancroft in London and Wren either there or in Oxford, progress was at first slow. Building began in 1668 according to a wooden model, and although the structure was finished in 1673 (date on façade) the furnishing delayed the consecration until September 1677. The cloister closes the back of the first court, with a gallery above and the west end wall of the chapel (based on the earlier one at Pembroke) forming the centrepiece. Wren again followed the spirit rather than the letter of classical design, producing an original solution where neither the nature of the site nor the repertory of antiquity offered an obvious precedent.

An established architectural career Wren might never have been more than the first of a line of Oxford scholars with architectural interests, but for two circumstances: the great fire of London and his appointment as surveyor-general of the king's works. The fire changed the problem of St Paul's from practical repair and ideal fantasy to complete rebuilding over thirty-five years; it also caused the replacement of many of the City's parish churches. Although he had assistants in both, St Paul's is Wren's cathedral and its lesser neighbours will always be known as the Wren churches.

His appointment as surveyor of the king's works on 29 March 1669 gave Wren status, command of the largest building organization in the country, and creative opportunities limited solely—if strictly—by the exchequer. Because of a recent reform his surveyorship was at the monarch's pleasure and not for life, but he was retained for almost four decades. He is often stated to have become Denham's deputy in 1661 (an error at least as old as Horace Walpole's *Anecdotes of Painting in England*, 1762–71), but he did so only during the last weeks of Denham's life. However, Charles II had engaged him privately in 1664 to make a design for rebuilding Whitehall Palace. The king sketched the design for Evelyn, but the only official records are a bill for a wooden model and a corresponding drawing in Wren's hand. This episode left no doubt of Wren's ability, and the 1669 appointment confirmed a process which had begun in 1661. Wren received an official house in Scotland Yard, where he lived and worked until 1718. On 7 December 1669 he married, at the Temple Church, Faith (1636–1675), the daughter of Sir Thomas Coghill; as her family home was Bletchingdon they had probably known each other for some years.

Wren never abandoned his scientific interests, and although he attended fewer Royal Society meetings he often spoke. During the later 1660s and early 1670s he addressed the society on topics including the mechanics of muscular action, the physiology of flies, and an improved friction brake for winding gear. In December 1668 he produced his theory, or 'law of nature', of the collision of bodies, which he had formulated several years earlier. In June 1669 he demonstrated a machine for grinding aspherical lenses; optical theory showed that these would gain better performance from the limited range of glass types available, but the practical problems were not overcome until the advent of computer-controlled machines in the late twentieth century. As vice-president of the society in 1678–80 he attended regularly; in January 1681 he was elected president when Boyle declined the office, and he served for two years with energy and distinction.

The Royal Society was also identified with Wren's plan for rebuilding London immediately after the great fire, for the problems of crowding, traffic, smoke, and hygiene in a largely medieval city had exercised fellows in the early 1660s. Within a fortnight several plans were made; Wren's promptness reflects his capacity for rapid thought. An ideal plan and a document for discussion, the failure to implement it has been lamented ever since, but its completely new street pattern would have taken too long, and cost too much, when the revival of trade and commerce depended on the utmost speed. His real part in the rebuilding was less spectacular. As the most distinguished of the surveyors chosen by crown and City soon after the fire to deal with practical problems, he helped frame the 1667 and 1670 London Building Acts, whose precautionary regulations transformed the fabric of the City; the most significant was the prohibition of timber construction. As royal surveyor his first task was the new custom house in Thames Street (1669–71, rebuilt 1718). With an eye to recent Dutch commercial architecture he made a warehouse resemble a royal palace—appropriately for a building representing the crown within a city jealous of its independence. The case of Temple Bar (1670–72) is similar. To compel the City to rebuild its ceremonial western entrance, the king arranged for the money to be provided, his surveyor naturally producing the design. Wren's authorship is not documented, but his son claimed to have his original design, and once again its form is without precedent in city gateways. Temple Bar was re-erected at Theobalds Park, Hertfordshire, in 1878, and scheduled in 1997 for reconstruction in Paternoster Square, near St Paul's. Otherwise Wren's creativity was severely limited by the state of the economy. The fire affected the whole nation, and work on the new Greenwich Palace designed by John Webb had been abandoned. Most of Wren's alterations to Hampton Court in the 1670s were swept away by William and Mary, while the constant additions at Whitehall, where rebuilding was also deferred, perished in the fires of 1691 and 1698. His principal work was administrative, but any doubt of his fitness, although relatively inexperienced, to rebuild the churches and cathedral would have been forestalled by his official position.

The City churches A cathedral was so large and costly that neither its commencement nor its completion could be hurried, but on 17 May 1670 Wren took charge of a small office, modelled on the office of works, under the commissioners for rebuilding the churches. He was responsible for about fifty new churches in place of the eighty-six destroyed or severely damaged in the fire; the total remains inexact because, where a church only needed repairs, his office merely handled the payments, funded by a tax on all coal coming into London. Moreover, St Clement Danes (a rebuilding) and St Anne's, Soho, and St James's, Piccadilly (new parishes), are in Westminster and unconnected with the fire but are usually included. Wren's friends among the clergy were aware of new, mainly foreign, ideas about new types of building for protestant liturgy, but post-Reformation England was well provided with churches, even if many were run down. In the few seventeenth-century buildings new ideas had seldom been taken up, and the fire offered the opportunity of building specifically for the liturgy of the 1662 Book of Common Prayer and at the same time for proclaiming the reformed faith in a modern—classical—style of architecture.

Four decades later another building programme opened. Wren wrote a paper of advice for the Fifty New Churches Commission (1711) expounding his ideas in the light of experience, and exemplifying many of them by the paragon of St James's, Piccadilly. This was an 'auditory', of basilican plan but on similar principles to the Sheldonian Theatre. All should be able to see and hear clearly both the preacher in the pulpit and the celebrant at the communion table, which should be decorously but not dramatically emphasized. Internal supports are few and slender. Large clear-glass windows give ample light, and galleries on three sides increase the accommodation. Wren's larger churches, on open sites, fit this general pattern though no two are identical. Other sites were far from ideal—small, irregular, cramped by secular neighbours. Some smaller churches are simple halls, rectangular or nearly rectangular (St Edmund the King, Lombard Street); often old foundations were reused at the expense of geometrical purity. Others have a single side aisle, sometimes with a gallery (St Margaret, Lothbury). Difficult sites spurred Wren's inventiveness: two churches were polygonal with oval domes of timber and plaster (St Benet Fink, Threadneedle Street, des.). Four others had round domes (for example St Mary Abchurch) and another four derive from a Byzantine type known to Wren by repute and used in the protestant Netherlands; in this, the arms of a Greek cross are defined within a square by four large columns (as in St Martin Ludgate). One of the finest churches, the most complex spatially and the purest geometrically, is St Stephen Walbrook, in which a dome coincides with the centre of a short Latin cross contained within a rectangle.

Building began in 1670–71 with fifteen churches; the rest followed, in batches or singly, until 1686, and most were completed by 1690 except for the elegant steeples that gave the city skyline its character until the early twentieth century. Most of these were added to finished towers in the twenty years after the renewal of the coal tax in 1697. Renaissance architects had consistently sought to adapt the steeple, a Gothic form, to the less emphatically vertical language of classicism. Wren completed one big London steeple, at St Mary-le-Bow, in 1680, providing not only an exemplar for the next two centuries but also a sample of what, when funds allowed, could be achieved in London.

One mind may invent many variations on a theme, but their execution would overburden even an architect otherwise uncommitted. Wren relied not only on administrators and draughtsmen but also on other designers. By 1670 Hooke had taken up architecture, and in the main building campaign of the 1670s and 1680s was effectively in charge of several churches and was certainly a designer rather than a mere draughtsman. His diary from 1672 to 1680 shows them working so closely together, if not always harmoniously, that Hooke must be seen as Wren's associate. While an autograph Wren drawing may establish his sole authorship of a design, the evidence of Hooke's drawings is not in itself conclusive; Hooke's elevation for St Edmund the King, Lombard Street, bears Wren's initials as a mark of approval. Stylistic arguments are of limited value, even when not coloured by modern aesthetic criteria or the assumption that Wren was the better, more meticulous, or more 'advanced' partner. Nicholas Hawksmoor rose through the churches office from 1684 to 1701 and was designing by the early 1690s, but his creative share is elusive; his drawings for the lantern spire of St Augustine by St Paul, Watling Street, do not correspond to the building, and the last Wren steeples (St Vedast, St Stephen Walbrook) are very different from Hawksmoor's first designs under the 1711 New Churches Act. Similar doubt surrounds the contribution of William Dickinson in the office from 1691 onwards. Fittings and furniture of the churches were outside the commission's responsibility, paid for by individual parishes and designed by the executant craftsmen.

Wren's churches well suited the liturgy and the society of their time; this is evidenced by their influence on English religious architecture of the eighteenth and nineteenth centuries. But by about 1840 many were in poor repair and increasingly unsuited to changes in taste and liturgy. Moreover, as the City of London became a place only of work, not of residence, churches became redundant and their sites more valuable than their fabrics. The ecclesiological movement led to refurbishment: high box pews were removed, stalls were introduced for robed choirs before the altar, and stained glass was inserted. The progressive damage of these changes was exceeded by the effects of the Second World War, after which only half the churches were left and almost half of those had to be virtually rebuilt, often with further liturgical and decorative changes. Thus St Bride's, Fleet Street, was reseated as a sumptuous collegiate chapel, and the least altered survivors have, like St Peter Cornhill, largely Victorian interiors. The concept of 'a Wren church' has changed profoundly since his time, but the remaining examples are among the best-known and most popular of his works.

St Paul's Cathedral, 1666–1674 St Paul's has always been the touchstone of Wren's reputation. His association with it spans his whole architectural career, including the thirty-six years between the start of the new building in 1675 and the declaration by parliament of its completion in 1711. His first advice to the king in the autumn of 1661 was no doubt in consultation with the dean, John Barwick. Besides restoring services and repairing the Commonwealth damage and desecration, they envisaged completing the programme begun thirty years earlier by Inigo

Jones for Charles I but abandoned in 1642 after the external recasing of the nave and transepts and the construction of a colossal western portico. A royal commission was opened on 18 April 1663; the surveyor, Denham, was a member; Wren was not, but was consulted. Among the clergy the driving force would be William Sancroft, dean after Barwick, from late 1664 to 1677. Subscriptions were invited and some work was done, but the fabric was obviously decrepit; the central tower, robbed of its wooden spire by lightning in 1567, was hazardous. Sancroft's second year in office was overshadowed by the plague, but on 1 May 1666 Wren, fresh from Paris, made a radical proposal, to replace the old crossing with four massive piers carrying a lofty dome, as 'an Ornament to His Majestie's most excellent Reign, to the Church of England, and to the great Citie' (Bolton and Hendry, 13.17). Within days he was preparing 'lines not discourses', and on 5 August he told Sancroft his drawings were finished; they extended Jones's 'trew latine' recasing to the interior of the Norman nave. At a site meeting on 27 August his design had a mixed reception, but Evelyn noted the cupola, 'a forme of Church-building not as yet known in England, but of wonderful grace' (*Diary*, 1955, 3.449). For Wren the dome would be the most enduring legacy of his travels; a week later the old building was in flames.

On 26 February 1667 Wren reported on the feasibility of a temporary church in the ruins; on 15 January 1668 a makeshift choir and 'auditory' were ordered in the west end. Preparations began, but Wren was scarcely surprised at Sancroft's letter of 25 April: 'What you whispered in my Ear … is now come to pass. Our Work at the West-end … is fallen about our Ears' (Bolton and Hendry, 13.46). By July 1668 the commission had requested a new design for 'a Quire, at least' (ibid., 23), the king had ordered the demolition of the old choir and crossing, and Sancroft told Wren to 'take it for granted, that Money will be had' (ibid., 49).

Wren now envisaged a cruciform church on the scale and orientation of the old one; the surviving plan (Wren drawings, All Souls College, Oxford, II.42) retains the traditional long nave of medieval cathedrals, with a large dome at the crossing and a re-creation of Jones's portico. The detailing is classical: 'trew latine'. Progress was slow; appointed surveyor of repairs in succession to Denham on 30 July 1669, Wren could make no confident forecasts while funding was hypothetical and the site covered by ruins and rubble. After trying gunpowder to bring down large masses, he settled for a safer battering ram on the ancient Roman pattern.

The situation was considerably clearer by April 1670, when the distribution of coal tax revenue was extended to include St Paul's; Wren had, in anticipation, made a new design. Part of a wooden model survives at St Paul's, showing a galleried 'auditory' prefiguring St James's, Piccadilly, but twice as long and having, instead of side aisles under the galleries, arcades closed to the interior and open to the churchyard. Contemporary evidence of the missing part of the model is inadequate, but it certainly comprised a large and distinct western vestibule facing Ludgate Hill, which made the whole 'capable of any grand ceremony'

(Wren, 282) and rose into a dome. This satisfied both the liturgical requirements and Wren's insistence on a noble modern city landmark; smaller and more compact than the old church, it reconciled parsimony with grandeur. The response was equivocal; some saw it as too novel and some as unimpressive. Not for the first or the last time, Wren wiped the slate clean. 'The generality', wrote his son, 'were for grandeur' (ibid.), and in March 1672 Wren was paid for drawings identifiably of an enormous domed Greek cross—basically a central mass carried on eight arches and ringed by an ambulatory. This costly and liturgically impractical late example of the ideal Renaissance centrally planned church would have set London to rival Paris or Rome; in November 1672 it received royal approval and a second model was ordered. But Wren constantly outpaced his paymasters, and within weeks he redesigned the whole building, adding a smaller domed western vestibule and a giant portico. On 12 November 1673 a new commission was opened; construction of the Great Model, still at St Paul's, was authorized as a record, and Wren was formally appointed surveyor to build the new cathedral rather than repair the old. Two days later he was knighted at Whitehall.

On 21 February 1674 Hooke walked through the Great Model; even undecorated, this object 6.3 metres long said more than drawings could about Wren's design. With a king prevaricating on the doorstep of Rome, the popish associations of a design so obviously emulating St Peter's were patent to those clergy desiring a traditional 'cathedral form'; moreover, it had an economic drawback. Medieval cathedrals were built in stages, starting with the choir or eastern arm, but a structure reducible to a dome with its supports must be erected—and funded—to completion before it was usable. Wren was confined to a 'cathedral form', albeit one closer to recent French basilican churches than to native Gothic prototypes: however, the warrant design, so called from the royal warrant of 14 May 1675 attached to the drawings (Wren drawings, All Souls College, Oxford, II.9–14), is not the design on which work began only a few weeks later.

The building of St Paul's Bureaucracy moves slowly, and from subsequent events it is clear that Wren both overhauled the Great Model even before its completion and also reworked the warrant design while the drawings awaited approval at Whitehall. This extraordinary conduct can only be understood in the knowledge that he had the confidence of Sancroft and of the king. The warrant design was the first to rest on an adequate brief: a traditional Latin cross plan, external elevations and portico re-creating Jones's, and the internal dome and exterior landmark now accepted as essential. But according to *Parentalia* Wren resolved to make no more models, which wasted time and aroused contention, nor to 'publickly expose his drawings' (Wren, 283). He also secured the king's privy licence for 'variations, rather ornamental than essential' (ibid.). The dome centre had been set out on site for the Great Model in the summer of 1673, and there was no formal foundation ceremony. Contemporaries record that an unidentified 'first stone' was placed in the footings on or about 21 June 1675; a month later the masons' contracts were completed and mains water supplied. Surviving preparatory drawings show Wren stretching to the limit the king's licence in a radical revision of the warrant design. This process occupied months before building started; when the design was complete it was, except for changes in detailing, final up to the roof-line. The drawings were known to very few; simple part-models and templates were used to guide the workmen. So effective was the secrecy that for years the London printmakers could offer only fictitious images of the new building, unaware that almost every dimension of the warrant design was changed and almost every feature of the exterior. The basilican elevation was replaced by two full storeys, rising clear of all other buildings more like a palace than a church, with a massive construction of thick walls and hidden flying buttresses to support adequately, both structurally and visually, a larger dome than proposed before the fire. Building proceeded from east to west, although for statical reasons all the crossing piers were carried on equally.

By 1694 the choir was ready for fitting; the first service was held there on 2 December 1697. By 1700 the body of the church was complete and the cylindrical base of the dome was rising. Engravings authorized in 1702 show a dome different both from that proposed in 1675 and from that finalized in 1704 when the western towers also were redesigned. There were financial as well as artistic reasons for the delay. Only the renewal of the coal tax in 1697 assured the worthy completion of the building, and with it the skyline that would dominate the City until the twentieth century; the pure geometry of the dome deliberately contrasts with the complex western towers and the dozens of elaborate stone or leaded church steeples of which the last were finished in 1717. The last stone of the lantern was placed on 26 October 1708 by Wren's son Christopher, and by the end of the year the gilded ball and cross were in place.

The top of the cross is 111.5 metres above street level, only a few metres higher than the pre-fire design. Indeed most of the significant levels are very similar between Wren's first and last designs, but the last is much larger in diameter and in bulk and far more complex in structure. The inner dome, of brick, springs from a tapering drum containing large windows that flood in light, and terminates in an eye through which the inside of the lantern is visible. The outer dome, 16 metres higher and of lead-covered wood, provides a landmark visible from far and near without making the inside disproportionately lofty. This structure is carried by a brick cone springing from the same level as the inner dome and carrying the tall stone lantern that stabilizes the whole structure; the cone is invisible inside and outside. Both structurally and visually, Wren's dome is without identifiable precedent, but not surprisingly it has always been a source of wonder and an inspiration to many later architects.

The cathedral was declared complete in 1711, and Wren was paid the half of his salary that, in the misguided hope of accelerating progress, parliament had withheld for fourteen years. He did not attend the building commission after 1710; now in his late seventies, he faced accusations of condoning fraud and irregularity. Just as in earlier life he had been reluctant to offer full proof of the self-evident, he later cut corners in administration. Nothing was proved, but against his wishes the commission engaged Thornhill to paint the inner dome in false perspective, and finally in 1717 authorized a balustrade around the roof-line. This diluted the hard edge Wren had intended for his cathedral, and elicited the apt parthian comment that 'ladies think nothing well without an edging' (Bolton and Hendry, 16.131).

St Paul's is Wren's masterpiece; nevertheless it has always received adverse criticism, much of it for not fitting the critic's idea of a post-medieval protestant cathedral. History has inevitably brought change. Especially since the Second World War building heights have risen, and the cathedral no longer stands proud of its neighbours. Yet open planning has given better views of the building as a whole than Wren ever expected, designing for a constricted site virtually rebuilt before work started, on the building lines of a medieval city such as Rouen or Florence. Within, Wren had minimized the apparent length of the nave, turning the western bays into a broad assembly area and obscuring the west–east vista by a wooden organ screen between the dome area and the choir. Until well into the nineteenth century all services were held in the choir and the rest of the building was unseated; thereafter urban expansion and the vogue for theatrical sermons led to the removal of the screen, the division of the organ, and the effect of a single continuous space amply seated. The persistent desire of artists to embellish Wren's white light-filled interior finally resulted, at the end of the nineteenth century, in the mosaic treatment of the choir vaults and successive attempts to provide a grander setting for the altar.

Secular work of the 1670s During the 1670s Wren received significant secular commissions which manifest both the maturity and the variety of his architecture and the sensitivity of his response to diverse briefs; two of these works also involved Hooke. The Monument commemorating the great fire, erected on Fish Street Hill near its source, was funded from the coal tax (1671–6). It is a colossal column, a concept consciously indebted to Roman models; several projects survive from different hands, including Hooke's. Wren was certainly in control of the final design, which is not Hooke's—an orthodox fluted Doric column, probably modelled on the smaller one erected in Paris a century earlier for Catherine de' Medici. For the apex Wren proposed a colossal statue of Charles II, but the king preferred the striking symbol of a flaming urn in gilt bronze to the imperial associations of a statue.

Hooke also worked on the Royal Observatory on the hill above the palace (and later Royal Naval Hospital) at Greenwich. It was built rapidly in 1675–6 for John Flamsteed, the astronomer royal, to make a new star map in the hope of solving the problem of longitude in navigation. Half a century later the problem was solved with John Harrison's clock, but the observatory site, chosen by Wren, gave the world Greenwich mean time and the zero meridian. The site offered height and clear air away from London, and the firm base of Duke Humphrey's Tower, a derelict fort; construction was therefore directed not by the king's works but by the Board of Ordnance. It was a rural building designed to a low budget, little more than the £500 offered by the king. It recalls the conceits—and the specifically English 'Renaissance' style—of Elizabeth's reign. The lead-capped turrets answer those of the Tower, the headquarters of the Ordnance a few miles upriver, and the tall windows of the great octagonal room accommodated long telescope tubes—at least until the equipment outgrew the room and its floor proved shakier than the foundation below. Although much of the management was Hooke's, it is simplistic to imagine that Wren, personally engaged by the king, relinquished control of a design he had many reasons to foster.

The library of Trinity College, Cambridge, was entirely in Wren's hands although directed from London. It is his most elegant building and the grandest library in Cambridge. His drawings and an accompanying letter (Wren drawings, All Souls College, Oxford, I.44–7) illuminate his design in exceptional detail. It is a traditional European collegiate library—a long upper room above a cloister walk—but it is much more. Wren's colleague Isaac Barrow, master of Trinity, having failed to interest his university in a 'theatre' or Senate House like Sheldon's in Oxford, with an added library, decided to improve his own college, whose library had suffered a serious fire. A new site was available: the open river end of Nevile's Court, whose sides comprised ranges of lodgings with ground-level arcades. There was space for a magnificent building that would attract gifts of books and money, and Wren's first proposal was for a free-standing circular domed reading room shelved around the perimeter wall—an idea before its time, and only practicable on the scale of Sir Anthony Panizzi's British Museum Library.

The preferred solution appeared more conventional, continuing the old cloister walk and upper-floor level across the opening. However, in most respects the new building differs from its neighbours. It is larger in scale and visually distinct on both sides. Decoration is sparing and scrupulously classical. But while the court front is open and articulated by arches and half-columns, the back is closed, astylar, and entirely rectilinear, exemplifying Wren's opinion in one of his tracts that things not visible together need not correspond. This also applies to the interior, even less predictable from without than the Sheldonian or the first model for St Paul's. In fact, like the executed dome of the cathedral, Trinity Library consists of disparate exterior and interior linked by an unseen common structure. The cloister walk is low, limited by the continuous floor level overhead, and the library interior is twice as high, allowing a zone for bookcases with a range of tall windows above it; yet the external elevations appear to be two equal storeys. The discrepancy is resolved by a remarkable integrated and consistent physical structure. With a logic worthy of twentieth-century frame building, a regular system of supports rises from foundations through piers to transverse beams and book-stacks and to windows and roof trusses. This powerful hidden geometry conditions visible and sensible experience of the building; it dictates where the bookcases stand and is expressed even in the compartmented ceiling Wren intended, added only in 1850–51. Wren's letter to Barrow explains his choice of flooring for quietness and comfort, considerations as important as his conscious imitation in the cloister walk of the Greek *stoa* and his rejection of an exterior giant order of pillars as over-scale. Other features were hidden until repair works revealed them in the 1920s: inverted arches in the foundations, complex floor beams carrying the book-stacks, and iron tie-rods within them. The span of Wren's career saw changes in English architecture comparable to almost three centuries in Renaissance Italy, and in this development Trinity Library is closest to the High Renaissance of Donato Bramante and Jacopo Sansovino.

Domestic and public life Wren's domestic life is best documented in the 1670s, partly because the major portion (1672–80) of Hooke's diary records—albeit briefly—their frequent conversations. These concerned not only the new churches and cathedral but many other matters. This period also encompassed most of Wren's married life. Gilbert, the first child of Wren and Faith, was baptized on 26 October 1672 and buried on 23 March 1674; their second, Christopher [*see below*], was born on 18 February 1675. Faith died on 3 September 1675, of smallpox. On 24 February 1677 Wren married Jane (1639?–1680), the daughter of William, second Baron Fitzwilliam of Lifford, at the Chapel Royal (probably Whitehall), of which Wren's brother-in-law Holder was subdean. The private ceremony may have been precipitate; it surprised Hooke, and a daughter, Jane, was baptized on 13 November. William was born on 16 June 1679. His mother died on 4 October 1680, leaving the architect with three small children; their ties remained close, so it is reasonable to suppose that they were brought up at Scotland Yard. Until 1687, when her husband left the Chapel Royal, Wren's sister Susan Holder was a neighbour; their own mother had died early, she had helped to bring up Christopher, and now she probably helped with his children. Another member of the household throughout the 1680s was the young Nicholas Hawksmoor, Wren's personal assistant and most talented informal pupil.

Wren never went abroad after 1666, and in 1698 he advised his son Christopher against going on aimlessly from France to Italy. The king's business took him on occasion to Dover, Newmarket, Hampton Court, Windsor, Portland, Winchester, and elsewhere, but he preferred clients and even artificers to visit him in London, within reach of most of his work. From Scotland Yard he could reach St Paul's in under half an hour on foot—less by river—and there is no good evidence that he ever lived elsewhere. He would go to the City several times a week, reserving Saturdays for St Paul's; in Paris he had noted with approval the weekly inspections of the Louvre works by Colbert, the king's superintendent of buildings. An account of the younger Christopher is appended. Jane died unmarried on 29 December 1702 and was buried at St Paul's; according to her monument there, she was talented in letters and music, lived at home, and was greatly mourned. William was disabled; in 1698 his father called him 'poor Billy … lost to me and to the world' (Bolton and Hendry, 19.119), but he lived until 15 March 1738, his father's will having provided for his care.

'Architecture has its political use' (Wren, 351), Wren wrote, and he seems to have considered himself a public architect. Although his priorities were his buildings and his family, he occasionally engaged energetically in other areas. Between 1679 and 1683 he sat on the committee of the Hudson's Bay Company, in which he had bought stock. His family's politics appear to have been conservative, just as their religion was orthodox. He nevertheless stood for parliament several times, failing election for Cambridge University in March 1667 and for Oxford in January 1674. In James II's parliament he represented Plympton St Maurice, Devon, from 1685 to July 1687 and was active in committee work; his motive in this instance was probably to secure continued funding for St Paul's. In 1689–90 he was twice elected for New Windsor, but both elections were overturned. From late in 1701 until the death of William III the following March he represented Melcombe Regis.

Wren's opinion was also sought on monetary reform. In 1695 he reported, with others, on the coinage (Ming-Hsun Li, *The Great Recoinage of 1696 to 1699*, London, 1963, appx 1). His shrewd assessment of the problems included cogent and practical arguments for a new standard coin divided centesimally, an idea proposed by Robert Wood in the 1650s.

Royal works of the 1680s By historical accident all Wren's large secular commissions date from after 1680. At the age of fifty his personal development, as was that of English architecture, was ready for a monumental but humane architecture, in which the scale of individual parts related both to the whole and to the people who used them. Wren's first essay, the Chelsea Hospital, does not entirely satisfy the eye in this respect, but met its brief with such distinction and success that even in the twenty-first century it fulfils its original function, albeit with the benefit of modern standards of comfort and hygiene. The project stemmed from concern for the veterans of civil war armies and the new regiments instituted by Charles II. Most of the funding came from subscriptions and from a levy on soldiers' pay. Wren asked no fee for his design, the main bulk of which was built by 1685, with extensions under James II and William III. However, on completion in 1693 a gratuity acknowledged his responsibility for the work.

Chelsea offered the standards of light and ventilation recently set by Hooke's Bethlem Hospital; it also deliberately emulated—more in concept than design—the Invalides of Louis XIV, plans of which reached Whitehall in 1678. Both king and architect recognized the 'political use' and propaganda value of the building, not only to house several hundred pensioned soldiers but also to display the magnanimity of the king. The wards at Chelsea are partitioned to give individual privacy while keeping the camaraderie of regimental life; here, as in any domestic building, the standard door and window are the units of scale. But the size of the central court, a rectangle of some 70 metres, and the building's symbolism, warrant the giant columns and pilasters in the centre of each elevation. In places the two scales come into conflict; Wren, who habitually stated rather than argued a case, must have been satisfied with this.

The new palace begun in 1683 at Winchester, the ancient capital of England, was similar in scale and prestige. Winchester was near the coast and far from the eye of Westminster, and the narrowing sequence of courts imitates that of Versailles, still being enlarged for Louis XIV. Both king and surveyor understood the ironic compliment to Louis; Charles received secret subsidies from the latter in return for promises, subsequently broken. Work stopped on Charles's death in 1685; ultimately converted into barracks, the building was gutted in 1894 and replaced by a historicist pastiche. Imperfect images of the original suffice to show that, with time, Wren had absorbed the impact of Bernini's project for the Louvre, drawings of which, in 1665, he 'would have given my skin for' (Wren, 262): a flat balustraded skyline replaced the pitched roofs and dormers he had used at Chelsea, and a square mansard dome was to crown the porticoed centre.

King Charles's reconstruction of the state rooms at Windsor Castle was notable for the integration of architecture, sculpture, and illusionist painting, a style long identified by scholars as a hallmark of the European baroque and the favourite of absolutist rulers. These works were in the hands of a separate comptroller, Hugh May, and were virtually complete when, on May's death in February 1684, Wren assumed his post and seems to have persuaded the Treasury that May's Whitehall comptrollership was superfluous, until the appointment by William and Mary of William Talman in May 1689. His first commission in this genre was therefore the new Roman Catholic chapel at Whitehall Palace, part of a new range ordered by James II soon after his accession. The interior, fulsomely described by Evelyn upon its opening in December 1686, was burnt down in January 1698 with most of the palace, including the highly decorated riverside apartments and the terrace Wren began in 1688 for Mary of Modena and finished for Mary II.

Commissions under William and Mary Wren's only palace to be both completed and preserved is therefore Hampton Court. In 1687 he had feared for his post under James II's policy of appointing Roman Catholics, but he survived both this and the revolution of 1688. William and Mary visited Hampton Court within days of their accession in February 1689 and found it old-fashioned but attractive. A new home nearer London was also necessary, since William refused to live in damp and smoke-ridden Whitehall. By midsummer, work was in progress on partly rebuilding Hampton Court, and the sovereigns had bought a Jacobean mansion near Kensington village from the earl of Nottingham. Wren was in charge both of Hampton Court and of transforming Nottingham House into Kensington Palace. Both works were, like Chelsea and Winchester, brick built with stone dressings, not from Dutch taste—in an Anglophile monarch—but from economy, the shortage of masons and Portland stone during the building of St Paul's, and—not least—the king's desire for speed, which led William to take some responsibility for a fall of masonry at Kensington; after a more serious accident at Hampton Court, he supported Wren against efforts by the new comptroller, Talman, to discredit him.

Between February and June 1689 Wren drew several designs for Hampton Court, reducing a vast palace, retaining only the Tudor great hall, to new south and east ranges housing the king's and queen's apartments and suggesting to the traveller from London a square block rivalling the centre of Versailles. This compromise preserved the extensive Tudor kitchens and other service buildings, and the new structure was finished when Mary died at the end of 1694. Work then ceased until the peace of Ryswick (September 1697) released William from the European wars. The exterior of Hampton Court has been faulted by purists misinterpreting Wren's empirical skill in providing the essentials of a modern palace with speed and economy. He was now master of large-scale civil architecture, and both the richness of colour, texture, and imagery and the convincing illusion of a great four-storey block almost 100 metres square show the continuing attraction of Versailles. During his last year William held court at rural Hampton in emulation of the French palace. With the loss of Whitehall and most of Stuart Windsor, Hampton Court has the only surviving state suites of the period; however, Wren's designs of 1694 were discarded, and Talman was probably responsible for the interiors of the King's Side; the Queen's Side was finished for Queen Anne.

At Kensington between 1689 and 1696 Wren, assisted by Hawksmoor as clerk of works, rebuilt much of the house, inserting state rooms and adding service ranges. By 1718, when George I commissioned further state rooms replacing the core of the old house, Wren was virtually powerless in the works. Three centuries later Kensington Palace is still a suburban mansion set in extensive gardens. Wren's greatest secular work would have been an entirely new Whitehall, but as imaginative artefacts his large drawings for two alternative projects (now at All Souls, Oxford) have a place in his work analogous to the Great Model. The fire of 1691 destroyed the south end of the riverside range, but on 4 January 1698 a more serious fire reduced the rambling Tudor palace and the many seventeenth-century additions to rubble and ashes; little remained beyond the buildings facing St James's Park and Inigo Jones's Banqueting House, whose protection Wren had ordered at all costs. His new designs gave prominence to the latter; besides its intrinsic merits it was remembered—if not always honoured—as the execution place of Charles I. Wren must have made his designs very soon after the fire: King William saw status but no use in a palace there, and his deferment to parliament of financial provision effectively ended the project. The dream of a great metropolitan palace of linked courts had been sustained by impecunious monarchs and their surveyors since Charles I and Jones; Wren succeeded in managing such large and complex masses, using both giant and smaller columns, and varied rhythms, scales, and textures. The larger components offered strong relief and richness of shadow; the progression through the courts would have been as exciting as the sheer size of individual units. With an idiosyncratic freedom of vocabulary born of long experience, Wren's Whitehall would have stood comparison with contemporary continental palaces, occupying the place in civil architecture he had foreseen for his cathedral in religious.

The Royal Naval Hospital, Greenwich Wren's response to a challenge is nowhere better seen than in his last major building, the Royal Naval Hospital at Greenwich. The sea victory of La Hogue (1692) cost serious casualties, a number of whom were accommodated in the abandoned palace begun for Charles II by John Webb in 1664. The philanthropic concerns underlying Chelsea turned to the navy, and Wren was among those who in 1693 discussed a permanent institution on this site. The sovereigns' grant of the site in October 1694 stemmed from Queen Mary's particular interest and her desire for greater magnificence than Chelsea's. Wren again gave his services free; however, Hawksmoor was paid as his personal clerk from 1696, thereafter as clerk of works, and, in 1705, as Wren's deputy. Work began in 1696 on completing and converting Webb's building, with a service range behind it. Wren made several designs before producing his final one early in 1698. His brief was constrained by the extent and nature of the site, bounded on the north by the Thames and on the west by the area around Webb's building. In the park to the south lay Inigo Jones's Queen's House. Webb had envisaged a large court open to the river, its sides formed by his original building on the west and a duplicate on the east; the axis of the court was in line with the Queen's House, but he proposed to block it with a third building with a domed centrepiece. Wren explored this theme, although he already knew that this axis was excluded from the royal gift and could not be built upon. Seen from the river, the customary approach, Greenwich is thus a building without a middle, but Wren exploited this defect by treating the whole like a classical landscape, with tall domed vestibules framing the house and the hill behind it. In the foreground he duplicated Webb's building as originally intended, and in the middle distance the domes mark the nearer and inner corners of courtyards containing hall, chapel, and ward blocks. The proscribed land is framed by receding colonnades, a form which, he observed, could extend to any length without disproportion. The appearance of the observatory several degrees off the axis—a flaw to eighteenth-century eyes—picturesquely softens the formal symmetry of the newer buildings.

After brief euphoria funds failed, and the hospital took almost a century to complete. Wren's vision was realized as far as the setting and layout and almost everything visible on the main axis are concerned; elsewhere other and later designers contributed. Almost from the start Hawksmoor had a free hand in the courts behind the colonnades, and the western one (1698–1704) is largely his, including the detailing of the great hall painted by Thornhill. Neither Wren nor Hawksmoor designed the later eastern court, including the chapel. The hospital was in use until 1869 and reopened four years later as the Royal Naval College. In 1997, as the buildings were transferred to civilian education, the outstanding character and beauty of Greenwich, including Wren's hospital, were recognized by designation as a UNESCO world heritage site.

Wren and Gothic: domestic work In 1713 Wren wrote a surveyor's report on Westminster Abbey. Although medieval architecture, subsumed in the seventeenth century under the name Gothic, was generally disparaged in the prevailing Renaissance aesthetic, the royal architect was inevitably involved in the care of historic buildings. In churches and the universities the tradition of the pointed arch had not quite died out when the fashion for conscious medievalism began that led to the Gothic revival. Wren was prepared to admire in private ancient buildings disparaged by his public taste. In an earlier report on Salisbury Cathedral (1668) he commended the structural audacity—rather than skill—of the medieval builder, but also appreciated the beauty of its illumination and the simplicity of its window tracery. Even before the fire he meant to modernize St Paul's. The Westminster report, however, is clear that repairing or completing Gothic buildings requires a historically sympathetic eye. In 1698 he succeeded Hooke as surveyor of a Westminster with its west front and towers still unfinished and the crossing unmarked externally. His part in the long-term building programme was largely by delegation to William Dickinson; the completion of the west end was due to Hawksmoor in the 1730s. The 1713 report illustrates Wren's theoretical position. He had been obliged in some of the City churches 'to deviate from a better style'; the obvious but controversial example is St Mary Aldermary (1679–82), which was funded from a private bequest. Some old materials were used, but archaeology has established that it is not the simple reconstruction of a Tudor building it appears to be. The unique plaster fan vaults have more in common with archaistic seventeenth-century vaults in Oxford (as in Brasenose College chapel, 1659) than with Tudor ones. In the same years and style Wren designed Tom Tower, the belfry completing the gateway to Christ Church, Oxford.

Wren had no connection with the popular concept of the 'Wren house', a rectangular gentry house with a hipped roof invented before the civil war and fashionable beyond the seventeenth century. There is substantial evidence for his authorship of two plain but elegant houses, designed for Whitehall colleagues and successive Treasury ministers: Tring Manor, Hertfordshire, for Henry Guy, and Winslow Hall, Buckinghamshire, for William Lowndes. In both the interior disposition is unusual but logical. Tring (c.1687–90) was remodelled in the 1870s, but the carcase survives, including the dramatic arrangement of stair hall and two-storey great room along the middle of the house. Roger North, who knew architect and client,

attests Wren's authorship. Winslow (1699–1702) is little altered, a three-storey double pile with matching end staircases and a spine-wall containing the chimney flues. Wren was also engaged by the duchess of Marlborough to design Marlborough House, Pall Mall (1709–11, attic storeys added 1861–3). He indeed carried responsibility for this, but Colen Campbell ascribes the design to his son, 'Christopher Wren, Esq.' (*Vitruvius Britannicus*, 1, 1715, 5).

Wren's last years The duchess had her plain brick house, but she dismissed Wren with the interior unfinished. Handwriting suggests a serious illness early in 1711; he recovered, but his immediate circle must have been anxious to conceal his condition in the face of mounting criticism of his competence and his taste. Nevertheless both Wrens were appointed to the Fifty New Churches Commission of October 1711, and Sir Christopher was an active member during the first months when the commission was framing its programme. The new commission of December 1715 included no architects. His comprehensive letter of advice to his colleagues (already mentioned) draws on his own experience with the City churches.

Other attacks followed. In 1712 the *Letter Concerning Design* of Anthony Ashley Cooper, third earl of Shaftesbury, circulated in manuscript. Proposing a new British style of architecture (generally interpreted as neo-Palladianism), Shaftesbury censured Wren's cathedral, his taste, and his long-standing control of the royal works. In 1715 the surveyorship was put into commission, leaving Wren in nominal charge of a board of works. On 26 April 1718, on the pretext of failing powers, he was dismissed in favour of the incompetent William Benson. He left Scotland Yard for the Old Court House on Hampton Court Green, the official residence of which he had obtained a personal lease in 1708. In 1714 he had claimed to the Royal Society—prematurely—to have solved the longitude problem; the treatise he promised is lost. Wren died on 25 February 1723 at his son's house in St James's Street, Westminster, after 'catching a cold' (Ward, 106); the attribution of this to a winter visit to St Paul's is apocryphal. He was buried on 5 March in the cathedral crypt, beneath a simple black marble floor slab. An inscribed wall-tablet nearby ends with the words *Si monumentum requiris, circumspice* ('If you seek his monument, look around you').

By either temperament or experience Wren was, according to his son, a 'Christian stoic'. Physically slight and sparing of words, he impressed all who met him; the most revealing portrait is the marble bust by Edward Pierce of c.1673 (Ashmolean Museum).

Writings and theory Besides official and personal letters, Wren's surviving writings comprise occasional reports, his Gresham lecture, and five incomplete 'tracts' on the theory and history of architecture. These (reprinted by Soo, 1998) were transcribed by his son; with his church reports they provide the principal evidence of his view of architecture. The tracts, probably dating from early in his architectural career, may represent lectures or drafts connected with the early Royal Society's publication programme. Wren's theory is empirical, embracing both the certainties of natural (geometrical) law proclaimed in the Gresham lecture and the accidents of the world of experience. While he discovered in architecture the grandest of geometrical demonstrations, he acknowledged the customary and arbitrary elements of the observer's experience. If we experience his cathedral as geometry made real, that was his intention, but it has no numerical basis. For Wren the authority of the classical orders and Vitruvius's *De architectura* was no more absolute than that of the Latin or Greek classics; nothing should be accepted on the mere word of the ancients, and every design should derive from first principles. Thus Wren might use an earlier building as an exemplar but would in no sense copy it, and more of his detail is invented than derived. Especially at St Paul's he developed drawing as a method of design research, but he recognized that drawings, models, and buildings appear differently to the eye.

Conclusion: Wren's achievement and reputation If Wren had died in the great plague he would have merited a few columns in the *Oxford Dictionary of National Biography*. Oughtred had called him at sixteen 'a youth of absolutely marvellous talent' (Wren, 184), and Evelyn, at twenty-two, a 'miracle of a youth' (Evelyn, *Diary*, 3.106). In 1662 Isaac Barrow described him as 'once a prodigy of a boy; now, a miracle of a man, nay, even something divine' (Wren, 346). Three years later, in the preface to *Micrographia*, Hooke wrote that 'Since the time of Archimedes, there scarce ever met in one man, in so great a perfection, such a Mechanical Hand, and so Philosophical a Mind.' Among several references to Wren in his *Principia* (1687), Newton not only called him 'one of the foremost geometers of this age' but acknowledged his prior formulation of the inverse-square law for the force governing the motion of the planets. The fullest tribute to his early achievement is that of Thomas Sprat. Sprat, in a unique exception to his own rule, named Wren among fellows of the society, because many of his discoveries had gone unrecorded and some 'he did only start and design … since carry'd to perfection by the Industry of other hands'. Sprat continued, 'It is not Flattery but honesty, to give him his just praise; who is so far from usurping the fame of other men, that he indeavours with all care to conceal his own' (*History of the Royal Society*, 1667, 317–18). By all accounts Wren's opinions and his habitually well-chosen words were valued. At the Royal Society on 21 June 1665 the subject of human flight was discussed, a topic of particular interest in the light of John Wilkins's recent speculations about flight both within and beyond our atmosphere (*Discovery of a New World*, 1640 edn). The meeting was concerned with the former, but Wren's comment showed his grasp of the mechanics involved and forestalled further speculation: 'a man would be able so often to move his wings, as he could with double his own weight on his back ascend a pair of stairs built at an angle of 45 degrees' (T. Birch, *History of the Royal Society*, 1776, 2.59).

Nevertheless contemporaries observed Wren's brilliance rather than his practical achievement. Even among the originals who founded the Royal Society, Wren was exceptional. He was younger than most; he published little. He did not adopt and monopolize one specialism; he discarded any problem he knew how to solve, and his attention span was short. Contemporaries complained that he valued the neatness of a solution above the presentation of proofs, claiming that the truth, once stated, was self-evident. Like his fellows he subscribed to Bacon's principle of the utility of the sciences, but he was not the archetypal Baconian that Sprat, the Royal Society's apologist, made him out to be. In his Gresham lecture and in his practical work he took a different course. While his motto, *Numero, pondere et mensura*, does not preclude scepticism, it looks towards the certainties of divine order, founded in the truths of number. His experimental work was by turns optical, mechanical, and physiological; it tended always towards highly visible results—lenses and optical images, machines, models, and dissections. Accumulations of statistical or observational data bored him. He relinquished the microscope, and his use of the telescope became occasional. As in the case of Pascal, he preferred geometrical, visual, and intuitive solutions for mathematical problems.

Wren was of his time, and any but the narrowest definition of English baroque must include him; there are many parallels between his later work and that of Hardouin-Mansart, Carlo Fontana, and J. L. von Hildebrandt on the continent. As the architect of St Paul's and the City churches, Wren is England's most famous architect, but he has never fitted a stereotype. Criticisms of St Paul's have always been so diverse as to cancel each other; like all masterworks it changed perceptions of its genre. This was recognized in the praise (*Analysis of Beauty*, 1753) of William Hogarth, who shared not only Wren's respect for nature and empiricism in art but also his mingled understanding and distrust of the arts of France. Horace Walpole's praise is tempered by the observation that he had 'great ability, rather than taste' (Walpole, *Anecdotes of Painting in England*, 1849, 2.181). *Parentalia*'s emphasis on taste is deliberate; Wren, whose contemporaries were Bunyan, Dryden, and Pepys, was a Restoration, not a Georgian, figure. His genius has been seen in versatility, desire to succeed, survival to complete his cathedral. His English prose reflects the justness rather than the complexity of his school Latin. In architecture, perhaps as early as 1663, he reformulated for himself and the next generation classical 'Vitruvian' principles of architecture, as an empirical system of which his writings reveal only fragments but which informs all his designs. He fostered talent where he found it—Hawksmoor is the outstanding example, following his teaching rather than his style—but the idiosyncrasy of his colleagues and the popularity of a new Palladian architecture based on rules of taste precluded the development of a 'Wren school'.

Wren's first biographer was not his son but the slightly younger John Ward (1740); James Elmes's centenary biography relies heavily on both Ward and *Parentalia*, and does justice to the scientific work, as did F. C. Penrose in the *Dictionary of National Biography*. At the close of the nineteenth century, the century of revivals, Wren was due for imitation, and the term 'Wrenaissance' was coined. A by-product of this interest was the establishment of the Wren Society, whose unique twenty-volume series published hundreds of drawings, documents, and other records of him and his associates. His science was neglected, but in 1937 John Summerson's essay *The Tyranny of Intellect* extended the mould formed by Sprat to present him as an artist hampered by the logic of a scientific mind. The deficiencies of this view have since become evident, and we can now see that Wren's brilliance lay in the unique breadth, depth, diversity, and consistency of his mind.

Christopher Wren (1675–1747), the eldest surviving son of Sir Christopher Wren and Faith Coghill, was born at Scotland Yard, London, on 18 February 1675. From Eton College he went, in 1691, to Pembroke College, Cambridge, but left in 1693 without graduating; in 1693 he was elected FRS. In 1698 he was in France with the younger Edward Strong; it is uncertain whether, against paternal advice, he continued with the stonemason to Italy. In autumn 1705 he was in the Netherlands, where he bought a number of books. On 5 December 1702 he was appointed clerk engrosser and chief clerk in the office of works, a fiscal post he retained until September 1716, when he was dismissed in Lord Halifax's reorganization. There is contemporary evidence that he was responsible for Marlborough House, Pall Mall (1709–11); his father was believed to be training him to succeed him as surveyor-general, but there is no record of any other architectural practice.

On 14 May 1706 Wren married Mary (d. 1712), the daughter of the court jeweller Philip Musard, at St James Garlickhythe. Their son Christopher was born on 5 January 1711. Another son, Charles, was born on 10 December 1711 but did not live. Mary Wren died a year later and was buried at St Martin-in-the-Fields on 16 December 1712. In 1713 Wren presented a statue of Prince George to the town of New Windsor to adorn the market hall (court house); he represented the borough in parliament from 1713 to 1715, when his re-election was disqualified as irregular. In August 1713 his father had bought for him the Elizabethan house (since rebuilt) and estate of Wroxall, Warwickshire, from Constance, the daughter of Sir Thomas Middleton and the widow of Sir Roger Burgoyne. On 8 November 1715 he married Lady Burgoyne; a son, Stephen, was born on 14 May 1722.

Wren also lived in St James's Street, Westminster, where his father died in 1723; thereafter he took over his father's lease of the Court House, Hampton Court. Soon after Sir Christopher's death Wren began to commission large engravings of his father's work, but met unspecified difficulties; those randomly completed were published as a set in 1749. He had begun to compile *Parentalia* by 1719, copying many documents but apparently making scant use of his father's reminiscences. By the early 1740s he was in poor health; the latest manuscript (Royal Society) is dated 1741, but he was unable to see it to press. This was done in 1750 by his son Stephen and Joseph Ames FRS

FSA. According to Stephen's introduction he was learned, pious, a good antiquarian, and loved for his 'communicative disposition'. He was a serious collector of ancient coins; his catalogue *Nummarum antiquarum sylloge* (1708) was dedicated to the Royal Society. He died on 24 August 1747 and was buried at Wroxall.   KERRY DOWNES

Sources C. Wren, *Parentalia, or, Memoirs of the family of the Wrens* (1750) [facs. edn 1965] · A. T. Bolton and H. D. Hendry, eds., *The Wren Society*, 20 vols. (1924–43) · K. Downes, *The architecture of Wren*, 2nd edn (1988) · *The diary of Robert Hooke … 1672–1680*, ed. H. W. Robinson and W. Adams (1935) · B. Little, *Sir Christopher Wren: a historical biography* (1975) · J. Summerson, *Sir Christopher Wren* (1953) · J. Ward, *The lives of the professors of Gresham College* (1740) · J. Elmes, *Memoirs of the life and works of Sir Christopher Wren* (1823) · H. M. Colvin and others, eds., *The history of the king's works*, 5 (1976) · A. N. L. Munby, ed., *Sale catalogues of libraries of eminent persons*, 4, ed. D. J. Watkin (1972), 1–43 · J. Summerson, 'The mind of Wren', *Heavenly mansions and other essays on architecture* (1949), 51–86 · J. A. Bennett, *The mathematical science of Christopher Wren* (1982) · M. Hunter, 'The making of Christopher Wren', *London Journal*, 16 (1991), 101–16 · K. Downes, *Sir Christopher Wren: the design of St Paul's* (1988) · K. Downes, *Sir Christopher Wren: an exhibition* (1982) [exhibition catalogue, Whitechapel Art Gallery, London, 9 July – 26 Sept 1982] · *Aubrey's Brief lives*, ed. O. L. Dick (1949) · A. F. E. Poley, *St Paul's Cathedral measured, drawn and described*, 2nd edn (1932) · M. Feingold, 'The humanities', *Hist. U. Oxf. 4: 17th-cent. Oxf.*, 211–358 · M. Feingold, 'The mathematical sciences and new philosophies', *Hist. U. Oxf. 4: 17th-cent. Oxf.*, 359–448 · J. Summerson, 'The penultimate design for St Paul's', *Burlington Magazine*, 103 (1961), 83–9 · K. Downes, 'Sir Christopher Wren, Edward Woodroffe, J. H. Mansart and architectural history', *Architectural History*, 37 (1994), 37–67 · J. A. Bennett, 'Christopher Wren: the natural causes of beauty', *Architectural History*, 15 (1972), 5–22 · J. A. Bennett, 'A study of *Parentalia*', *Annals of Science*, 30 (1973), 129–47 · P. Jeffery, *The City churches of Sir Christopher Wren* (1996) · L. M. Soo, *Wren's 'tracts' on architecture and other writings* (1998) · D. McKitterick, ed., *The making of the Wren Library, Trinity College, Cambridge* (1995) · T. F. Reddaway, *The rebuilding of London after the great fire* (1940) · J. Bold, *Greenwich: an architectural history of the Royal Hospital for Seamen and the Queen's House* (2000) · M. Hunter, *Science and society in Restoration England* (1981) · R. G. Frank, *Harvey and the Oxford physiologists* (1980) · L. Weaver, *Sir Christopher Wren* (1923)

Archives All Souls Oxf., drawings and papers · BL, report on design for the Monument, Add. MS 18898 · BL, papers, Sloane MS 3323 · LUL, proposal for the recoinage · Middle Temple, London, MSS · RIBA BAL, accounts and papers · RS, papers · Warks. CRO, papers relating to Hungerford market · Wilts. & Swindon RO, plan of proposal to rebuild London after great fire, with sketches of Royal Hospital and Greenwich | GL, accounts and papers relating to London · LPL, reports on churches in Cripplegate and Lower Wapping · Notts. Arch., accounts as surveyor of the king's works · Warks. CRO, letters relating to building of Arbury stables

Likenesses E. Pierce, marble bust, c.1673, AM Oxf. [see illus.] · attrib. J. Closterman, oils, c.1695, RS · J. Faber the younger, mezzotint, c.1710 (after unknown painting, Christopher Wren (1675–1747)), BM, NPG; repro. in Wren, *Parentalia* (1750), frontispiece · attrib. G. Gibbons, boxwood medallion, c.1710, RIBA · D. Le Marchand, ivory medallion, c.1710 (Christopher Wren (1675–1747)); priv. coll. · G. Kneller, oils, 1711, NPG · D. Le Marchand, ivory medallion, c.1720, NPG · D. Le Marchand, ivory medallion, c.1723, BM · J. Cheere, bust, c.1750, All Souls Oxf. · G. C. Gaab, copper medal, 1783, BM · T. Holloway, line engraving, pubd 1798 (after G. Kneller), BM, NPG · W. Wilson, medal, 1846, NPG · E. Kirkhall, line engraving (after J. Closterman, c.1695), BM · J. Smith, mezzotint (after G. Kneller), BM, NPG · A. Verrio, G. Kneller, and J. Thornhill, oils, Sheldonian Theatre, Oxford · plaster death mask, All Souls Oxf. · portrait, All Souls Oxf.

Wren, Christopher (1675–1747). *See under* Wren, Sir Christopher (1632–1723).

Wren, Matthew (1585–1667), bishop of Ely, was born in the parish of St Peter Westcheap, London, on 23 December 1585 and was baptized on 2 January 1586, the son of Francis Wren (1553–1624), a mercer, and his wife, probably Susan Widgington; his grandfather Cuthbert Wren (*d.* 1558), from Monk's Kirby, Warwickshire, was of Danish stock. In June 1595 he was admitted as one of five scholars, alongside William Juxon, at the Merchant Taylors' School, where his brother Christopher *Wren (1589–1658) joined him in February 1601. In June that year he was admitted as a Greek scholar at Pembroke College, Cambridge, where an old Taylorian, Lancelot Andrewes, was master. He graduated BA in 1605, was elected a fellow on 5 November that year, and proceeded MA on 2 July 1608 (incorporated ten days later at Oxford). He became successively junior (1610) and senior treasurer (1611) of the college, an appropriate background for a later bursar (1621–4).

Career to 1625 Wren was ordained deacon on 20 January 1611 and priest on 10 February. In 1615 he proceeded BD, became one of the household chaplains of Andrewes, now bishop of Ely, and on 21 May was appointed to the rectory of Teversham, near Cambridge. In 1616 he became president of Pembroke, where the following year he instituted a fund-raising campaign to restore and augment the library holdings. His exhaustive benefactors' list of books names more than eighty donors, among them the bishop of Ely, Nicholas Felton, Jerome Beale, Walter Balcanquhall, Henry Isaacson, Ralph Brownrigg, Mark Frank, Littledon Osbaldeston, William Quarles, and Edmund Lacy. Under Andrewes's close supervision he also compiled a list of estate papers for the not insubstantial college patrimony, built up by Andrewes between 1589 and 1606.

Before 1621 Wren had become one of the forty-eight chaplains-in-ordinary serving James VI and I, in a December turn, having, it is said, impressed the king in 1616 in a Cambridge disputation with John Preston over whether dogs can make syllogisms. On 27 January 1623 he was chosen, probably by Andrewes, as one of the three chaplains, regarded as 'men altogether free from the suspition of being Puritans' (D'Ewes, 128), who were to attend on the prince of Wales on his ill-fated jaunt to Madrid in pursuit of the Spanish match. In the end only Wren and Leonard Mawe, master of Peterhouse, travelled to Spain. Wren reported back on the constancy and steadfastness of the prince's adherence to protestantism although at the time contemporaries at home expressed reservations and were puzzled at the intimacy the chaplains may or may not have had with their royal master. With the failure of the expedition, Wren returned to England and was debriefed at Winchester House by Andrewes, Richard Neile, bishop of Durham, and William Laud, then bishop of St David's. It is said that Andrewes forewarned that Wren would live to see that day when Charles would 'be put to it upon thy Head and his Crown' to defend the Church of England

Matthew Wren (1585–1667), by unknown artist, before 1628 [copy]

(Wren, 45–6). Wren himself revealingly observed that 'for upholding the doctrine and discipline and right estate of the church' he had more confidence in Prince Charles than in his father (Bodl. Oxf., MS Rawl. D 392). In the meantime, Wren did not lack reward for his efforts: on 10 November 1623 he was granted a prebendal stall at Winchester by Bishop Andrewes and on 7 May he received the royal living of Bingham, Nottinghamshire, for which he later resigned his fellowship at Pembroke (8 November 1624).

Master of Peterhouse and dean of Windsor, 1625–1635 Early in the new reign, on 26 July 1625, Wren was made master of Peterhouse, in succession to Leonard Mawe. His regime there is characterized by the same methodical attention to detail and regard for history and precedents as he had shown at Pembroke. He produced an inventory for the treasury of the medieval college 'by his care and personal pains', and a chronologically arranged list of all the library collection, which was maintained until 1649. His more immediate task was the building of a new college chapel. Letters were sent out to potential subscribers in March 1628: the former master Mawe himself gave £300. The building was consecrated by Francis White, bishop of Ely, on 17 March 1632, the only college chapel to be built in Cambridge in the early Stuart era. It provided for the beauty of holiness with a railed-in altar at the east end beneath a decorated sanctuary roof. Altar cloths of velvet, satin, and taffeta richly embroidered in silver and gold thread work, and decorated with sacred monograms, were among the chapel treasures later hidden away from the parliamentary visitors.

As head of house, Wren was also closely involved in university politics, taking an active role in attempts to counteract the impact of the Synod of Dort and canvassing for the appointment of the duke of Buckingham as chancellor in the summer of 1626. In the wake of the publication of Richard Mountague's *Appello Caesarem* (1625), Samuel Ward, the Lady Margaret professor of divinity, had undertaken to attack Arminianism, in both the university commencement of that year and in a university sermon in January 1626, later printed as *Gratia discriminans*. Wren is thought to be the author of a point-by-point manuscript refutation of the sermon text (Bodl. Oxf., MS Rawl. 150), which shows his own wide knowledge of Dutch Arminian writings and his command of patristic theology. Ward was not readily silenced and continued teaching a Calvinist reading of the irresistibility of God's grace in his Cambridge lectures throughout 1627 and 1628 while Wren's *A Sermon Preached before the Kings Majestie* (1627) furthered the controversy.

On 24 July 1628 Wren was installed as dean of Windsor, by royal mandate of 8 July, following the death of Henry Beaumont. By virtue of this office he became also dean of Wolverhampton and, from 1635, register of the Garter. Wren assiduously attended chapter meetings at Windsor. Except when he was vice-chancellor of Cambridge and accompanying the king to Scotland, his only prolonged absences were in the spring and early summer of 1632 and in January, May, and November 1634. He kept the annals of the order in the exemplary manner of his archival work for his Cambridge colleges (the *Liber rubeus*) and had the statutes of the order Englished (BL, Add. MS 6334). He did not apparently attempt to alter the internal furbishment of St George's Chapel; necessary controls over seating and precedence were left to his successor. Three weeks after becoming dean, on 17 August 1628, at Sproughton, near Ipswich, Wren married Elizabeth (1604–1646), daughter of Thomas Cutler and widow of Robert Brownrigg, who was nearly twenty years his junior; they had about fourteen children.

In May 1633 Wren accompanied Charles I into Scotland for the king's long-overdue Edinburgh coronation. At their return he may have helped Charles draft demands to be made to the dean of the Chapel Royal in Scotland for the better ordering of services and adoption of the rites of the English church or, as he put it in a letter to Bishop James Wedderburn of Dunblane on 8 October, 'till some course may be taken for making one that may fit the custom and constitution of that church' (NL Scot., Wodrow MS LXVI, fol. 19). On 20 October 1633 Wren was made clerk of the closet, for which he was given special leave by the Windsor chapter, under Thomas Horne as acting dean. On 14 May 1634 he was chosen as a governor of Sutton's Hospital, the Charterhouse. The fact that the death in 1626 of his patron Lancelot Andrewes had not halted his climb to higher preferment may suggest the king's continuing gratitude to him since the visit to Madrid in 1623. On 5 December 1634 Wren was elected bishop of Hereford and he resigned the mastership of Peterhouse on 22 January 1635 before he received royal assent for this appointment

(27 February). His consecration at Lambeth was delayed until 8 March 1635 because of building work in the chapel. Later that month his younger brother, Christopher, was admitted to the deanery at Windsor in his place by royal mandate.

Bishop of Hereford, of Norwich, and of Ely, 1635–1640 Although Wren was at Hereford less than eight months, he was not idle in the summer of 1635: he visited the diocese and reformed the statutes of the cathedral church. In this he built on Lindsell's short-lived attempt the previous year to examine worship as well as fabric. Both sets of articles expand Lindsell's; the diocesan articles are based on his 1633 Peterborough articles of enquiry, which derived from Bishop Overall's influential visitation of 1619. With insight Wren asked in his *Articles of Visitation* (1635, art. 7, 5) 'how long have the said popish or puritanicall recusants obstinately abstained, either from divine service, or from the communion? Whether of any long time, or of late only?' That year, when Charles issued instructions that communion tables should be railed in at the east end of churches, Wren, who was reckoned to have the king's ear, was thought to be one of the prime movers.

On 10 November Wren was elected to the vast bishopric of Norwich. Here, despite also being appointed on 7 March 1636 dean of the Chapel Royal, he was equally zealous, lamenting that some churches were open to the elements or engulfed 'within the sea', as at Eccles (Bodl. Oxf., MS Tanner 68, fol. 209), and harrying patrons including the treasurer of the navy, Sir William Russell, for neglect. He inherited a diocese within which a large number of migrant protestants lived and worked. Insisting upon conformity necessarily drove many towards puritanism or into continental exile, although such migrations were not new, could owe much to the transitory labour patterns of kersey cloth workers, and probably peaked in the first year of his successor, Richard Mountague. Wren's primary visitation articles of 1636 both reveal his determination and appear to confirm his role in promoting the altar policy the previous year. Article three insisted that:

> the communion table in every church do always stand close under wall of the chancell, the ends therof north and south, unlesse the ordinary give particular direction otherwise. And that the raile be made before it (according to the archbishops late iniunctions) reachinge crosse from the north wall to the south wall, neere one yard in hight, and so thicke with pillars, that doggs may not get in

although at his trial he later denied that he had ever tried to enforce this alleged innovation in his own diocese. Although this was the arrangement he had earlier made at Peterhouse he permitted the tables to be moved out of the rails for communion at both Yarmouth and Lavenham.

In August that year Wren reminded the dean of Norwich of the need to reform cathedral worship:

> Holy dayes not to be neglected in any part … the stoole at south end of the table to be removed, & clothes decently put on, Rubbish in the galleries to be removed … Sick to be prayed for, When, What prayers, all by singing. (Bodl. Oxf., MS Rawl. C 368, fol. 3r)

The following spring he ensured that the assize court sermon be properly appointed and that the preacher 'say the

2nd service *in habitu*, & pray not, but as is appointed' (ibid., fol. 6*r*). John Hassall, the dean, had once also been one of the household chaplains to the king's more Calvinist-minded sister and was unsympathetic to his bishop's demands.

Such specific and seemingly intrusive questions in Wren's visitation occasioned wider concern. The Norwich aldermen, by no means a united body, set out to proceed against their new bishop, troubled not only by the complexity of the articles themselves—132 in all, six questions for each—but especially by the changes concerning the administration of the communion. These demanded that communion be received from holy tables that had been railed about. On Wren's side the support of Alderman John Anguish (who had until recently been mayor and a collector of ship money) and other civic worthies was to be decisive, although little could protect Wren from the invective of William Prynne's penmanship. Writing under the pseudonym of Matthew White, in *Newes from Ipswich* Prynne protested over a jurisdictional case in the town; he had a ready audience and three editions of his attack circulated widely. A more local difficulty arose in that at Norwich the bishop was allowed to conduct a visitation only once every seven years. Concerned that his reforms would lose their effect under the four archdeacons whom he had inherited Wren devised a unique solution. He appointed fifty-nine commissioners, armed with his orders, to inspect and report offenders to him. These included Edmund Duncon, Dr Thomas Lushington, Edmund Mapletoft, and John Quarles.

On 20 March 1638 Wren was elected bishop of Ely. When he came to leave Norwich he reported to the king that a diocese of 1200 parishes was unworkable and he proposed that Suffolk form a second bishopric, with a cathedral either at Sudbury or at Bury St Edmunds, thereby reviving earlier plans of Henry VIII. His Ely visitation articles replicated those of Norwich, showing Wren's determination to harry puritanism and to ensure conformity, a policy which aligned him closely with Charles I and William Laud, archbishop of Canterbury since 1633. There can be little doubt as to why the lord chamberlain appointed him on 6 March 1640 to preach at the opening session of the Short Parliament in April. According to Laud he was to preach again before parliament on 27 December 1640 but by then both Laud and Wren were under parliamentary censure.

Imprisonment in the Tower In the first six weeks of the Long Parliament, Wren was criticized and on 19 December, the day following the impeachment of Archbishop Laud, he and Bishop Pierce were each bound over for £10,000 to appear daily. A committee of the House of Commons considered his case as a result of depositions lodged against him in July 1641 by counties, including Cambridgeshire. Nine articles of impeachment were drafted and on 5 July the Commons agreed that Wren was unfit for office in the church and Commonwealth. He prepared to answer Sir Thomas Widdrington's attack of 20 July, but proceedings were not taken against him until later in the year. On 30 December he was sent to the Tower with other

bishops. In prison he preached on Psalm 50, verse 23, on 13 February 1642. Subsequent to his release on 6 May, he appealed to parliament in *Bishop Wren's Petition* (1642) but after his palace at Ely was ransacked on 30 August he was again committed to the Tower where he remained for nearly eighteen years.

Within a few years Wren lost his wife, who died on 8 December 1646. While in the Tower he maintained the legal jurisdiction of his diocese as best he could through his chancellor, at least until 1645. In 1652 and 1653 he was canvassed by Gilbert Sheldon for ways in which the vestigial Church of England would be best maintained with bishops. Sheldon expected much more of 'his Lordship's wisdom, courage, and goodness, than from any other; and if I should say, from all the rest of his Order', a high regard not shared by many (Barwick, 538–9). He was among those bishops consulted by Edward Hyde in 1655 about the maintenance of the episcopate, an order threatened increasingly by age and illness. He had disdained Oliver Cromwell's 'terms projected for his enlargement' as 'an abject submission to his detestable tyranny' (Wren, *Parentalia*, 34) and was finally released only on 15 March 1660, following which he took lodgings in London. As one of 'your poor outcaste bishops' (Bodl. Oxf., MS Carte 30, fol. 613) Wren formally greeted Charles II on 4 May but he seems not to have enjoyed much confidence from the new king, who boycotted the service of thanksgiving that Wren had arranged at Westminster Abbey on 29 May 1660. Later he bluntly reminded Charles II that he well knew the cost of royal service: 'Sir, I know my way to the Tower' (Wren, 30).

Final years and death With John Cosin, Wren was closely involved in the redrafting of the prayer book for convocation in 1661 and chaired meetings for its revision at his London palace. He wrote that he was well aware that 'not one of five hundred is so perfect in it as to observe alterations' and that significant changes could be made to the liturgy without criticism as those 'who are likeliest to pry into it, do know themselves to have been the causers of it' (letter cited in Jacobson, 45). But the wholesale 'Laudian' revision of the prayer book, by which, as William Sancroft noted, 'the Bishops at Ely House ordered all in the old method' (Parker, ccxxii), was later abandoned, except in notable changes in the ordinal. It seems that the bishops sought a deliberately more moderate policy of accommodation with puritan sensitivities. Wren was not among the bishops who on 24 February 1662 presented the book in its final state to the council for approval.

Wren returned at once to the administration of his diocese. In his visitation of 1662 the articles follow his of 1638 and are the only Restoration articles still to recommend the east end railed altar. In 1663, by virtue of being visitor of the college, he appointed his son-in-law Joseph Beaumont to be master of Peterhouse against the fellows' choice of Isaac Barrow, one of their own number. He also set about providing a new chapel at Pembroke on land reclaimed from a long-term lease to St Thomas Hostel, buying out a Lancastrian lease (1471) for the remaining forty years. This mausoleum chapel was designed by his nephew Christopher *Wren (1632–1723) and cost him £3658 rather than the £5000 recorded in the family history. A model for it survives at Pembroke College. It was consecrated on Wren's name day in 1665.

At his death at Ely House in Holborn on 24 April 1667, Wren's 'body was conveyed to Cambridge by the heralds with all decent pomp and ceremonye' (Wren, 34) and was buried in Pembroke College chapel on 11 May. The elaborate funeral was devised for him by his friend William Dugdale, the Garter knight. Surprisingly the chief mourner was his second son, Thomas Wren, who had graduated MD in 1660 and become archdeacon of Ely under his father in 1663; the master of Trinity, John Pearson, preached the Latin eulogy, later published as *Oratio ad exsequias Matthaei Wren*. He drew attention to the silver mitre and crosier that lay on the coffin, a practice revived at the Restoration and first reported by John Evelyn at the funeral of Bishop Nicholas Monk of Hereford (20 December 1661). 'Adspicite sacras infulas vobis quasi in Lycaeo ante oculos positas, cogitate haec episcopatus insignia tanquam tropaea ad Athenas reducta' ('Look at these sacred items laid out before your eyes as if they were in the Lyceum; think on these badges of episcopacy like trophies brought back to Athens'; Pearson, 2.86).

At his death Wren was immensely wealthy. He settled £2500 each on his four surviving daughters and charged his four sons to protect and oversee their interests. He left his library and papers to Archdeacon Thomas and his son-in-law Dr Beaumont and provided that his works be published by agreement with a committee of seven divines. The strictures of this prevented any of his writings being issued. Little of what he wrote and collated in the Tower that had not already been published in a collection by his first son (*Increpatio BarJesu*, 1660) can be judged as more than *florilegia*.   NICHOLAS W. S. CRANFIELD

Sources J. Pearson, 'Oratio ad exsequias', *The minor theological works of John Pearson*, ed. E. Churton, 2 vols. (1844) · C. Wren, ed., *Parentalia* (1750) · Peterhouse, Cambridge, register and chapel box 9 · will, Pembroke Cam., college MS Kζ · Pembroke Cam., Hardwick MSS G3, G4, G5 · Windsor Castle, chapter acts register, VI B.2 · Mrs E. P. Hart, ed., *Merchant Taylors' School register, 1561–1934*, 2 vols. (1936) · Bodl. Oxf., MSS Rawl. C. 368, D. 392 · Bodl. Oxf., MS Tanner 68 · Bodl. Oxf., MS Carte 30 · BL, Add. MSS 4224; 6334; 6469 · BL, Egerton MS 1048 · NL Scot., Wodrow MS 46 · LPL, MS 943; Laud's registers I–II · *The diary of Sir Simonds D'Ewes*, ed. E. Bourcier (Paris, 1974) · dean and chapter act book, Norfolk RO, 24/2 · PRO, LC 5/134 · P. Barwick, *The life of John Barwick* (1724) · J. Parker, *An introduction to the successive revisions of the Book of Common Prayer* (1877) · W. Jacobson, *Fragmentary illustrations* (1874) · IGI · *The diary of Samuel Newton, alderman of Cambridge (1662–1717)*, ed. J. E. Foster, Cambridge Antiquarian RS, 23 (1890), 18–20

Archives Bodl. Oxf., corresp. · CUL, abstracts by him relating to Norwich and Ely cathedrals · Peterhouse, Cambridge, MS, *Hoi Anamērychismoi* · Peterhouse, Cambridge, register, chapel box 9 | Pembroke Cam., commonplace books and list of benefactors to the library · St George's Chapel, Windsor, collation of Garter statutes

Likenesses oils, before 1628 (copy), Pembroke Cam. [*see illus.*] · G. Vandergucht, line engraving (after oil painting, Pembroke Cam.), BM, NPG; repro. in Wren, ed., *Parentalia*

Wealth at death immensely wealthy; bequests of at least £10,000: will, Pembroke Cam., college MS Kζ

Wren, Matthew (1629–1672), political writer and politician, was born at Peterhouse, Cambridge, on 20 August 1629, and baptized on 30 August at Little St Mary's, Cambridge, the first surviving son of Matthew *Wren (1585–1667), master of Peterhouse and bishop of Ely, and his wife, Elizabeth (1604–1646), widow of Robert Brownrigg of Sproughton, Suffolk, and daughter of Thomas Cutler of Ipswich. He matriculated from Peterhouse in 1642, but the civil wars interrupted his studies. With his father imprisoned Wren seems to have spent the war and its aftermath in Oxford. By 1656 he was part of the intellectual circle of John Wilkins, the master of Wadham College and the future bishop of Chester. It was Wilkins who directed Wren's attention to the work of James Harrington. In return Wren dedicated to Wilkins both the anonymous *Considerations upon Mr. Harrington's Commonwealth of Oceana* (1657) and its sequel, the acknowledged *Monarchy Asserted: in Vindication of the Consideration upon Mr. Harrington's Oceana* (1659). Both were trenchant critiques of Harrington which received much praise from royalist supporters such as Bishop Brian Duppa, who wrote that 'his wit is clear and sprightly, and doth so smoothly deal with his curly-headed adversary' (*Correspondence of … Duppa and … Isham*, 142). Wren's only other published work was *Increpatio Barjesu* (1660).

Following the Restoration Wren's royalist credentials ensured his appointment in May 1660 as secretary to Edward Hyde, first earl of Clarendon and lord chancellor. He was probably a founder member of the Royal Society in November 1660, serving on the council in 1662–3 and 1666. He was elected to parliament for Mitchell, Cornwall, at the 1661 election. He was created MA from Oxford on 9 September 1661. In the House of Commons he was part of Clarendon's interest and was appointed to many parliamentary committees. Wren also evinced an interest in several trading ventures, being named in the charters of the Company of Royal Adventurers trading to Africa and the Royal Fishing Company, and later still the Royal African Company. Andrew Marvell portrayed him as an agent of Clarendon's corrupt regime:

> gross bodies, grosser minds, and grossest cheats;
> And bloated Wren conducts them to their seats.
> (*Poems and Letters*, 1.151–2)

Wren survived the fall of Clarendon on 30 August 1667, succeeding Sir William Coventry (on Clarendon's recommendation) as secretary to the duke of York at the beginning of September. Henceforth he was one of York's political dependants. His new post brought Wren into close contact with naval affairs and Samuel Pepys, who initially thought him lacking in Coventry's drive to master business. In September 1668 Wren complained to Pepys of the corruption of the court, the high expenditure, and the impossibility of earning a sufficient income without compromising his honour. He was active in the Commons on naval business and behind the scenes as a mediator between York and such figures as the duke of Buckingham.

Although an indifferent seaman Wren accompanied

York and the fleet to sea in the spring of 1672. He was wounded at the battle of Sole Bay on 6 June 1672, died at Greenwich on the 14th, and was buried in Pembroke College chapel, Cambridge. Wren had drawn up his will on 19 May in anticipation of the impending battle with the Dutch, and being unmarried he left a named estate to each of his three brothers and instructed that a fourth be sold to pay his debts and his sister's unpaid portion of £2500.

STUART HANDLEY

Sources E. Cruickshanks and B. D. Henning, 'Wren, Matthew', HoP, Commons, 1660–90, 3.762–3 • The Genealogist, new ser., 6 (1890), 168–71 • Venn, Alum. Cant. • Pepys, Diary, vols. 5–9 • M. Hunter, The Royal Society and its fellows, 1660–1700: the morphology of an early scientific institution (1982), 164–5 • The political works of James Harrington, ed. J. G. A. Pocock (1977) • The poems and letters of Andrew Marvell, ed. H. Margoliouth, rev. P. Legouis, 3rd edn, 2 vols. (1971), vol. 1, pp. 151–2 • The correspondence of Bishop Brian Duppa and Sir Justinian Isham, 1650–1660, ed. G. Isham, Northamptonshire RS, 17 (1951), 142 • will, PRO, PROB 11/341, sig. 1 • CSP dom., 1672, p. 163 • The life of Edward, earl of Clarendon … written by himself, new edn, 3 vols. (1827), vol. 3, pp. 292–3 • B. J. Shapiro, John Wilkins, 1614–1672: an intellectual biography (1969) • J. A. W. Gunn, Politics and the public interest (1969), 104–7 • P. Seaward, The Cavalier Parliament and the reconstruction of the old regime, 1661–1667 (1988) • DNB

Wren, Percival Christopher (1875–1941), novelist, was born on 1 November 1875 at 37 Warwick Street, Deptford, London, the son of John Wilkins Wren, schoolmaster, and his wife, Ellen, née Sasbury. Reliable reference works such as The Oxford Companion to English Literature state that he was born in 1885 in Devon. In this they have been deliberately misled. In other contexts Wren is described as a sailor, an explorer, a trooper in a British cavalry regiment, and a recruit to the French Foreign Legion. There appears to be no credible evidence for any of these suggestions. It seems that Wren fabricated this misinformation, and, as an alternative, concealed important facts about his personal affairs; for example, few details are available about his family, although a marriage certificate has been found which shows that he married Alice Lucie Shovélier (b. 1870/71) on 23 December 1899. At this time he was still signing himself as Percy, but at some stage he changed his name to Percival, and later added Christopher.

There appears to be no reliable evidence to explain Wren's motives for falsifying his past, but by adding his assumed middle name he perhaps hoped to indicate a genealogical relationship to Sir Christopher Wren (1632–1723); or he may simply have enjoyed hoodwinking the public about his background. Whatever his reasons, when Wren applied to join the Indian educational service (IES), to which he was appointed in 1903, he was forced to reveal his real date and place of birth; he also gave the information that he was educated at West Kent School, studied as a non-collegiate student at Oxford, and graduated BA in 1898. From then until 1903 he worked as a schoolmaster. From 1903 to 1910 he was headmaster of Karachi high school, and in 1904–6 he was also educational inspector for Sind. In 1910 he became assistant to the director of public instruction in Bombay, and after a period of war service, from December 1914 to October 1915, he took up his last post in the IES as principal of Elphinstone high school, Bombay; he retired in November 1917.

Wren did not limit his activities to teaching. Between 1910 and 1912 he published four textbooks, including one on teaching English, one as a guide to the theory and practice of education, and one entitled Indian School Organization (1911). These books reveal at least one aspect of his character: he was not lacking in self-assurance. For instance, in the preface to Indian School Organization he explained: 'It is hoped that this book may be found useful … by teachers in general and headmasters in particular and may prove suggestive to Indian educationalists whose experience happens to be less varied than that of the author'. During the First World War Wren suffered a period of ill health. His war service as a captain in the Indian army reserve of officers, infantry branch, was interrupted by sick leave from February to October 1915; and in Bombay in 1917 he had another period of nine months' sick leave before retiring from the IES.

Wren's first novel, Dew and Mildew, set in India, was published in 1912. Between that year and 1941, the year of his death, he published over thirty more novels. The most popular were those with a setting based on the French Foreign Legion, the earliest of which, The Wages of Virtue, appeared in 1916, and his most notable success, Beau Geste, in 1924. The latter was filmed three times, in 1926, 1929, and 1966, and was televised by the BBC in 1984. It was remarkable for its clever opening. While travelling from Kano to Lagos, an officer of the French army recounts to a British member of the Nigerian civil service the mysterious circumstances in which, going to the relief of a desert fort, manned by legionnaires, surrounded by rebel Tuaregs, he reaches his objective only to find no sign of a battle or siege, but a fort defended by corpses.

Two other of Wren's novels were filmed: Beau Sabreur (1926) in 1928 and Beau Ideal (1928) in 1931. Wren's last novel, Odd—but even so, was published in 1941. He died at Moor Court, Amberley, near Stroud, Gloucestershire, on 22 November 1941. He was survived by his wife, Isabel, who was probably his second wife, and a stepson, R. A. Graham-Smith, of Marbleton rectory, Heathfield, Sussex; he may have had other children, but efforts to trace them have failed.

H. F. OXBURY

Sources private information (2004) [U. Oxf.] • BL OIOC, IOR V/12/304 • The Times (24 Nov 1941) • b. cert. • m. cert. [Alice Lucie Shovélier] • d. cert. • CGPLA Eng. & Wales (1942)
Archives JRL, corresp. with Basil Dean • U. Reading L., corresp. with publishers
Wealth at death £1597 3s. 10d.: probate, 10 Feb 1942, CGPLA Eng. & Wales

Wrenbury. For this title name see Buckley, Henry Burton, first Baron Wrenbury (1845–1935).

Wrench, Benjamin (1776x81–1843), actor, was born in London, where his father held a lucrative position in the exchequer; his grandfather was Sir Benjamin Wrench MD (1664/5–1747) of Norwich. His father died before the boy reached his seventh year, and, having declined a proffered living and a commission in the army offered by General Tryon, a relative, Wrench adopted the stage as a profession. He made his first appearance at Stamford in Lincolnshire, and was coached by Mrs Robinson Taylor, the manager of the Nottingham circuit, whom he married. He then joined in York the company of Tate Wilkinson, and went on to Edinburgh, where he successfully played Othello, Gossamer in *Laugh when you can*, Job Thornberry in *John Bull*, and Jeremy Diddler in *Raising the Wind*.

When R. W. Elliston left Bath in 1804 he was replaced by Wrench, who made his début in January 1805 as Gossamer and as Walter in *Children in the Wood*. Young Rapid in *A Cure for the Heartache*, Doricourt in *The Belle's Stratagem*, Rolando in *The Honeymoon*, and Jaffier in *Venice Preserv'd* followed during the season, which was the last in the old Bath Theatre. In the new house Wrench opened in October 1805 as Percy in *The Castle Spectre*. During the season he played Archer in *The Beaux' Stratagem*, Orlando, and Belcour in Richard Cumberland's *The West Indian*. He then returned to York, and while there received an offer from Drury Lane, where he appeared, with the company then temporarily occupying the Lyceum, as 'Wrench from Bath and York', playing in October 1809 Belcour in *The West Indian* and Tristram Fickle in *The Weathercock*. He was also seen as the first Henry Torringham in James Cobb's *Sudden Arrivals* (1809) and as Edward Lacey in *Riches*, adapted by Sir James Bland Burges from Philip Massinger's *The City Madam*. Wrench remained at Drury Lane until 1815, adding to his repertory such parts as Dick in *The Heir-at-Law*, Gratiano in *The Merchant of Venice*, and Count Basset in *The Provoked Husband*. He played a few original characters in obscure plays by Masters, Millingen, Leigh, and other forgotten playwrights, among which may be named Gaspar in *The Kiss*, taken by Clarke from *The Spanish Curate* of Beaumont and Fletcher (1811). Wrench left Drury Lane in 1815, and divided his time between the Lyceum and the provinces—Birmingham, Bristol, Dublin, and other large towns. In 1820, as Captain Somerville in *Capers at Canterbury*, he made his first appearance at the Adelphi, where he had perhaps his greatest success, in November 1821, as Corinthian Tom in W. T. Moncrieff's *Tom and Jerry, or, Life in London*. In October 1826 Wrench appeared for the first time at Covent Garden, playing Rover in John O'Keefe's *Wild Oats*, followed by a large number of varying parts. He also had a great success at the Lyceum in *He Lies Like Truth*, and was at that house when (16 February 1830) it was burnt to the ground. In 1834, in the rebuilt theatre, Wrench and Robert Keeley made a great hit in John Oxenford's *I and my Double*. In the same year at the Haymarket, Wrench was the first Caleb Chizzler in *But However* by Henry Mayhew and Henry Baylis. In 1840 he was at the Olympic. His last engagement was at the Haymarket. Wrench's marriage had become unhappy. He drank, and left his wife in financial difficulty. On 24 November 1843 he died of asthma at his lodgings at 2 Pickett Place, London.

As an actor, Wrench was a good comedian but he never reached the first rank. In the provinces he played a large round of comic characters, including Charles Surface, Dr Pangloss, Captain Absolute, and many others. He was of medium height, light complexioned, with high shoulders and flat features.

JOSEPH KNIGHT, rev. NILANJANA BANERJI

Sources *The biography of the British stage, being correct narratives of the lives of all the principal actors and actresses* (1824) • *Actors by Daylight*, 1 (1838) • *Oxberry's Dramatic Biography*, 4/57 (1826) • W. Donaldson, *Recollections of an actor* (1865) • Hall, *Dramatic ports.* • Genest, *Eng. stage* • *Dramatic and Musical Review* (Nov 1843) • [J. Roach], *Authentic memoirs of the green-room* [1814] • T. S. Munden, *Memoirs of Joseph Shepherd Munden* (1844) • *The theatrical looker-on* (1823) • GM, 2nd ser., 21 (1844), 438 • d. cert.
Likenesses De Wilde, portrait (as Sir Freeman in *Free and easy*), Garr. Club; repro. in *Oxberry's Dramatic Biography* • Sharpe, portrait (as Wing in *Amateurs and actors*), Garr. Club; repro. in *Oxberry's Dramatic Biography* • portrait, repro. in W. Oxberry, *New English drama* (1818) • portrait, repro. in *Theatrical Inquisitor* (1814) • portrait, repro. in *Oxberry's Dramatic Biography* • portrait, repro. in *Actors by Daylight* (4 Aug 1838) • prints, Harvard TC

Wrench, Sir (John) Evelyn Leslie (1882–1966), promoter of the British empire and author, was born at Brookeborough, co. Fermanagh, Ireland, on 29 October 1882, the younger son of Frederick Stringer Wrench (1849–1926) of Killacoona, co. Dublin, an Irish land commissioner, and his wife, Charlotte Mary (d. 1935), daughter of Sir Alan Edward Bellingham, third baronet, of Castle Bellingham, co. Louth. His older brother, F. A. C. Wrench, a sublieutenant in the Central India horse, died of malaria in 1903. He had two sisters, Mary and Winifride.

Wrench was educated at Summer Fields School, Oxford (1893–6), and at Eton College (1896–9), where he excelled at modern languages but fell behind in other subjects. His schooling was frequently interrupted by injury or ill health, and after one such episode, in March 1899, his parents withdrew him from Eton in order to allow him to travel on the continent. Discarding an earlier vocation to become a missionary, Wrench determined on a diplomatic career, and, after travelling through Russia and Turkey with his family, he spent eight months in Germany perfecting his knowledge of the German language. While there, however, he hit upon the idea of emulating the German production of picture postcards. On his return to England at the age of seventeen he founded the Wrench Series. Old Etonian contacts were useful in obtaining permission to set up stalls at royal and public buildings, but the success of Wrench's business owed a great deal to his own skills as a salesman and organizer. At one point Wrench was employing 100 staff and had a turnover in excess of £5000 a month. Wrench himself was catapulted into the public eye as a fine example of a young British entrepreneur. Over-rapid expansion proved his undoing, however, as too much capital was locked up in stands and stock. The banks foreclosed early in 1904, and Wrench was forced to sell his business for a nominal amount. Wrench's failure was a personal blow, but it was one from which he was able to learn. Thereafter, his enthusiasm was always tempered by perseverance and a certain stoicism.

One of those who had been impressed by Wrench's entrepreneurial abilities was Alfred Harmsworth, Lord

Sir (John) Evelyn Leslie Wrench (1882–1966), by Lafayette, 1930

Northcliffe. In July 1904 he invited Wrench to join his staff as a private secretary. Wrench agreed, and for the next eight years he acted as Northcliffe's assistant and trouble-shooter, serving variously as editor of the overseas edition of the *Daily Mail*, editor of the *Weekly Dispatch*, managing director of the Paris *Daily Mail*, and export and sales manager of the Amalgamated Press.

As a young student in Germany in 1900 Wrench had been much affected by the continental reaction to Britain's difficulties during the Second South African War. His imperial enthusiasm was reawakened during a visit to Canada in 1906, when he stayed with Lord Grey, who showed him Cecil Rhodes's political will and testament. This kindled in Wrench the idea of an 'empire crusade', modelled on the German Navy League, to harness support for the empire in Britain and its overseas dominions. Wrench's sense of mission was strengthened during the 1909 Imperial Press Conference, and in 1910, with Northcliffe's encouragement, he launched the Overseas Club with an article in the *Daily Mail*. Wrench at first combined the organization of the club with newspaper work, but he soon found that he had to fight the impression that it was merely a publicity stunt for the overseas *Daily Mail*. Turning down Northcliffe's offer to make him editor-in-chief of periodicals and a director of the Amalgamated Press, Wrench resigned his newspaper posts in 1912 in order to devote himself fully to his imperial mission.

The Overseas Club (renamed the Overseas League following its amalgamation with the Patriotic League of Britons Overseas in 1918) enjoyed a rapid success. Wrench

described it as 'a kind of "Grown-up Boy Scouts"' (Wrench, *Uphill*, 266). Branches of the club—many of them founded by Wrench during an empire tour in 1912–13—were regularly supplied with speakers and suggestions as to activities by the central office, and, from 1915, with the journal *Overseas*, edited by Wrench. During the First World War the club raised more than £1 million towards providing tobacco and other 'comforts' for the troops.

Wrench joined the Royal Flying Corps as a second lieutenant on 23 March 1917 and was immediately posted to Scotland to oversee recruiting work. During this time he was involved in attempts to found an Irish Unity League, to promote the idea of a united Ireland within the British empire. A brief visit to Ireland soon convinced him that the scheme was not worth pursuing. In June 1917 he joined the staff of the Air Board, and in December he was promoted major and appointed principal private secretary to the air minister, Lord Rothermere. Following the latter's resignation in April 1918 Wrench joined the Ministry of Information, where he was given overall control of the British empire section, reporting directly to Sir Roderick Jones and Lord Beaverbrook. He was created CMG for his war services in 1917.

During the war Wrench conceived the idea of a new organization to promote friendship and co-operation between the British empire and the United States, which he saw as vital to the stability of the post-war international order. With the help of Walter Hines Page, the American ambassador, and Sir George Perley, the Canadian high commissioner, he launched the English-Speaking Union at a dinner in London on 28 June 1918, presided over by Lord Balfour. Like the Overseas Club, the English-Speaking Union prospered rapidly, promoting exchanges, travelling fellowships, lectures, and social events, and from January 1919 publishing the journal *Landmark*, again edited by Wrench. Absorbing the Atlantic Union (founded by Sir Walter Besant in 1897) in February 1919, the English-Speaking Union attracted members from throughout Britain and the self-governing dominions, and Wrench was closely involved in setting up a sister society, the English-Speaking Union of the United States, with William H. Taft as its first president, in May 1920.

Throughout the inter-war years Wrench devoted much of his time to the affairs of the Overseas League and the English-Speaking Union. In addition, he became a contributor to *The Spectator* in 1922, joined the board the following year, bought a controlling interest from St Loe Strachey in 1925, and served as editor from 1925 to 1932. He later sold his controlling interest to Ian Gilmour, but he remained chairman of the board for the rest of his life. For his various public services Wrench was knighted in 1932.

In 1929 Wrench founded a third society, the All Peoples Association, with the aim of promoting international amity in general and Anglo-German understanding in particular. The rise of Nazism made the work of the association increasingly difficult, and Wrench found himself (unfairly) branded as a pro-Nazi. In 1936 he reluctantly decided to close the association. The publication of his book *I Loved Germany* in 1940—attempting to distinguish between Nazism and the traditional characteristics of the German people—was widely criticized by contemporaries.

On 18 May 1937 Wrench married his first cousin, Hylda Henrietta (1879–1955), daughter of Sir Victor Alexander Brooke, third baronet, sister of Sir Alan Brooke (later Viscount Alanbrooke), and widow of Sir Frederick Des Voeux, seventh baronet. Hylda was an enthusiastic supporter of Wrench's many causes, serving as chairwoman of the Overseas League's Soldiers and Sailors Fund from 1914 to 1918 (receiving the CBE in 1918) and as the league's honorary controller from 1918 to 1940. After their marriage she was an invaluable collaborator as well as companion. Her death was a great blow. They had no children.

In August 1940 Wrench and his wife set out on a lecture tour of Canada, the United States, New Zealand, and Australia, putting the case for a vigorous war effort. Returning via Singapore, they were stranded in India, where they stayed until April 1944. While there, they busied themselves organizing social functions and welfare work for American servicemen and civilians. In May 1942 the viceroy, Lord Linlithgow, appointed Wrench American relations officer with the government of India. Wrench's main task in this post was to organize meetings for American journalists with representatives of the Muslims, the untouchables, the princely states, and others opposed to Congress policies. He later considered that his efforts had gone a long way towards moderating the pro-Congress line of the American press.

After the war Wrench devoted himself increasingly to writing. Particularly noteworthy were his three biographies, *Francis Yeats-Brown* (1948), *Geoffrey Dawson and our Times* (1955), and *Alfred, Lord Milner: the Man of No Illusions* (1958). All three were based on personal acquaintance as well as access to the private papers of his subjects.

In 1958 Wrench was involved in the foundation of yet another society, the Anglo-Kin Society, which aimed to encourage genealogical and topographical research in Britain for the benefit of the descendants of British settlers overseas. He was president of the Dickens Fellowship from 1961 to 1964, and was for many years senior trustee of the Cecil Rhodes Memorial Museum Foundation at Bishop's Stortford, Hertfordshire. On the occasion of the Overseas League's golden jubilee in 1960 (when it was given the title Royal) Wrench was advanced to KCMG. His work for Anglo-American understanding was recognized by the award of the Benjamin Franklin medal by the Royal Society of Arts in 1964. He also received honorary degrees from the universities of Bristol and St Andrews.

Contemporaries remembered Wrench as ascetic-looking, graceful, and charming, with an infectious enthusiasm and boundless energy. He was not an original thinker, but he wrote fluently and engagingly. His main talent was for organizing people. His first loyalty was to the empire, but, like his hero Lord Milner and his friends Lionel Curtis and Philip Kerr (Lord Lothian), he conceived of the empire as a free association of peoples, co-operating to promote self-government and international stability. He was a firm supporter of Indian constitutional reform while editor of *The Spectator* and, despite his lifelong concern to promote friendship between peoples of British descent, he condemned racism in any form. Again like Curtis and Kerr, he found it easy to transfer his enthusiasm from the idea of imperial unity to that of eventual world unity, whether through federation or some other means.

Wrench died at his home, the Mill House, Marlow, Buckinghamshire, on 11 November 1966. He was buried at All Saints' Church, Marlow, on 15 November, and a memorial service was held in St Paul's Cathedral on 9 December.

ALEX MAY

Sources DNB · *The Times* (12 Nov 1966) · *The Times* (16 Nov 1966) · *The Times* (17 Nov 1966) · *The Times* (18 Nov 1966) · W. V. Griffin, *Sir Evelyn Wrench and his continuing vision of international relations during 40 years* (1950) · E. Wrench, *Uphill: the first stage in a strenuous life* (1934) · E. Wrench, *Struggle, 1914–1920* (1935) · E. Wrench, *I loved Germany* (1940) · E. Wrench, *Immortal years, 1937–1944* (1945) · WWW, 1961–70 · Burke, *Peerage*
Archives BL, Add. MSS 39541–39597 · BL, corresp. and diaries, Add. MSS 59541–59597 · BL, Milestones, a collection of newspaper cuttings, invitation cards, photographs, and other material, LR 402 el | BL, corresp. with Lord Northcliffe, Add. MSS 62222–62223 · Bodl. Oxf., corresp. with L. G. Curtis · Bodl. Oxf., letters to Geoffrey Dawson and family with related papers · Bodl. RH, corresp. with Lord Lugard · HLRO, corresp. with Lord Beaverbrook · PRO NIre., corresp. with Edward Carson, D 1507
Likenesses O. Birley, oils, 1921, Royal Overseas League, Park Place, London · Lafayette, photograph, 1930, NPG [*see illus.*] · W. Stoneman, photograph, 1945, NPG · W. Stoneman, photograph, 1955, NPG · M. L. Williams, oils, English-Speaking Union, London · photograph, repro. in Wrench, *Struggle* · photograph, repro. in *The Times* (12 Nov 1966) · photographs, BL, Milestones, LR 402 el · photographs, English-Speaking Union, London · plaster bust, English-Speaking Union, London
Wealth at death £69,494: probate, 21 Dec 1966, CGPLA Eng. & Wales

Wrenn, Ralph (*d.* 1692), naval officer, was a relative of Matthew Wren, secretary to James, duke of York, and it was probably Matthew Wren who arranged for him to go to sea in the *Drake* in 1667. He served as captain of the *Hopewell* fireship from 18 April to 17 November 1672 and of the *Rose* dogger from 8 March 1673. His able performance at the battle of the Texel on 11 August 1673 saw Prince Rupert and William Coleman recommend him for promotion, and he served as first lieutenant of the *Reserve* from 22 March 1676 to 19 June 1677 and then as captain of the *Spragge* fireship from 20 July 1677 to 14 July 1679. Further recommendation from Sir Thomas Allin saw his promotion on 5 November 1679 as lieutenant to Morgan Kempthorne in the *Kingfisher*, part of Arthur Herbert's Mediterranean Fleet. When Kempthorne was killed as the *Kingfisher* engaged seven Algerine pirates on 22–3 May 1681, Wrenn took command and beat off the enemy, winning recommendation to Charles II and, on 9 August, command of the *Nonsuch*. Back in England in August, he returned to the Mediterranean after being made captain of the *Centurion* on 23 May 1682. He was still there when consulted by George Legge, Lord Dartmouth, about destroying the mole at Tangier in the summer of 1683. Dartmouth sent him to Lisbon, where he persuaded merchants to let him carry their goods back to England; he stuffed his ship full of merchandise, earning a stiff rebuke from Pepys for such private trading.

By April 1687 Wrenn was begging Pepys for renewed employment, for 'I was never in a worse [condition] than I am in at this time: for I am almost brought to a morsel of bread' through the extravagance of his wife, Elinor. He had paid out more than 'I am willing the world should know and am strongly perplexed with her creditors several 20 and 30l debts and if I have not some employment must either leave my country or go to a prison' (MS Rawl. A 189, fol. 191). He was appointed on 26 July 1687 to command the *Mary Rose*, serving in the West Indies until June 1688, and in September 1688 was appointed to the *Greenwich* which served with Dartmouth when William of Orange invaded England in November. On 26 February 1689 he informed the navy board that over one hundred seamen who had been turned over from the *Mary Rose* to the *Greenwich* had gone to London to complain to a Commons committee that he had mistreated them badly and not paid their wages for service in the former ship. He was discharged on 16 March 1689, but on 13 February appointed captain of the *Coronation* hired ship, returning to the West Indies until November. In June 1691 he was awarded command of the 48 gun *Norwich*, and in October was ordered back to the West Indies as commodore. He arrived at Barbados on 16 January 1692 with seven warships and a fireship. Learning of a large French presence, he dispatched two of his fourth rates and the fireship to Jamaica and hired two stout merchant ships to strengthen his force. He set out to attack one French division but, returning to Barbados, learned that their whole fleet had gone to Jamaica. He set off thither on 17 February and four days later sighted the French fleet of eighteen ships, plus six or seven fireships and tenders, off Desirade. Thus heavily outnumbered he withdrew, but was attacked by the French the following morning; after four hours of fighting he managed to withdraw in good order, without losing a ship, and returned to Barbados. He died there on 26 March 1692 from fever and was buried the same day at Bridgetown, his fleet firing their guns and 'their colours half mast high'.

Wrenn's inventory, dated 24 November 1692, states that most of his goods were seized in lieu of rent, but that he had wages due, and some goods at Barbados; his widow, and executrix, was granted a pension of £100 per annum. Opinions on Wrenn were varied—Pepys was highly critical of his illicit trading, and Admiral Edward Russell pronounced him 'good for nothing' in 1691 (Russell, Rich MS xd 451 (98)). Yet his final staunch action against superior odds was pronounced 'the bravest action performed in the West Indies during the war' (T. Lediard, *The Naval History of England ... from the Norman Conquest ... to the Conclusion of 1734*, 1735, 655).

J. K. LAUGHTON, *rev.* PETER LE FEVRE

Sources *CSP dom.*, 1667–8, 295 · recommendations for promotion, captain's list, 1637–9, no. 43, captain's list, 1679–84, no. 8, PRO, ADM 6/428 · PRO, ADM 106/358, fols. 434–5 · letters to navy board, PRO, ADM 106/394, fol. 280 · letters and warrants, 1681–3, PRO, ADM 2/1750, p. 68 · journal 8 (*Antelope* master's log), PRO, ADM 52/2 · journal 4 (*Mordaunt* master's log), PRO, ADM 52/68 · journal 2 (*Greenwich*, Lieutenant George Pomeroy), PRO, ADM 52/40 · PRO, ADM 8/1, fol. 216v · Bodl. Oxf., MSS Rawl. A. 189, fol. 191; A. 234, fol. 3v · Henry Capel, letter-book, 1673–80, BL, Add. MS 60386 · will, 7 Oct 1691, PRO, PROB 11/412, fols. 165r–165v · inventory, 24 Nov 1692, PRO, PROB 5/1124 · E. Russell, 'Characters of captains, Nov. 1691', Folger, Rich MS xd 451 (98) · D. Hepper, *British warship losses in the age of sail, 1650–1859* (1994) · *The Tangier papers of Samuel Pepys*, ed. E. Chappell, Navy RS, 73 (1935), 143, 241 · A. Bryant, *Samuel Pepys: the saviour of the navy* (1969), 92 · W. A. Shaw, ed., *Calendar of treasury books*, 21, PRO (1952), 65
Archives PRO, admiralty papers
Wealth at death see inventory, 24 Nov 1692, PRO, PROB 5/1124; will, PRO, PROB 11/412, fols. 165r–165v

Wrey, Sir Bourchier, fourth baronet (*c.*1653–1696), politician, was the first son of Sir Chichester Wrey, third baronet (*c.*1628–1668), and his wife, Lady Anne (1628–1662), daughter and coheir of Edward Bourchier, fourth earl of Bath, and widow of James Cranfield, second earl of Middlesex. His father's marriage saw the family seat shift from Trebigh in Cornwall to Tawstock in Devon. On 23 April 1661 Bourchier was made KB, an honour he was reputed to owe to Lady Bath.

Wrey's father was a soldier and politician, and Wrey followed in his footsteps. He was commissioned a lieutenant in his father's Admiralty regiment on 6 July 1666 and was raised to captain on 15 May 1668. He served in the French army under the duke of Monmouth at Maastricht in 1676. Wrey was returned to parliament for Liskeard at a by-election held on 18 February 1678. He was not active in the parliament, and did not stand again at the election of February 1679. He was promoted major in the Admiralty regiment on 31 January 1680. He was a supporter of the court, being added to the Cornish bench in February 1680, and he was one of the promoters of a loyal address from Devon in September 1681. On 3 May 1681 he married Florence Rolle, who is thought to have outlived him. He had left the army by 1 May 1683, when a commission was signed for his replacement. He was active in securing the surrender to the crown of Barnstaple's charter, being named a freeman in the new charter in November 1684, and being sworn on 28 March 1685. He was also named a freeman in the new charter issued for Liskeard. He was elected to the new parliament on 7 April 1685, this time for Devon, his brother, Chichester Wrey, taking the Liskeard seat. Following the outbreak of Monmouth's rebellion, Wrey raised a volunteer troop of horse.

Wrey was an opponent of James II's religious policies, returning the standard negative replies when tendered the 'three questions'. However, he was still expected to be returned for Liskeard in the parliament James II was planning for later in 1688. Wrey was one of the Devon Tories who joined Prince William of Orange at Exeter in November 1688, and he lent the prince £500. He was duly returned for Liskeard in the elections to the convention on 14 January 1689. He voted against the motion that the crown was vacant in February 1689, and in May was repaid the £500 he had lent the prince.

Wrey was again returned to parliament in 1690. He fought a duel on 4 February 1692 with the Hon. Thomas Bulkeley, MP for Beaumaris, with Sir William Williams acting as his second. Although Wrey's sword was broken, he was not injured. In June 1694 Wrey quarrelled with another MP, James Praed, while riding in a calash in Falmouth, which resulted in Wrey's being 'run through the body, but supposed not mortal' (Luttrell, 3.322). A few days later he was reported dead, but this proved to be a false report. It seems unlikely that Wrey ever fully recovered from his wound. He made his will on 16 August 1694, with a codicil two days later, but he was still able to secure his election to parliament at the election held in October 1695. In the new parliament he signed the association.

Wrey died on 28 July 1696 and was buried at Tawstock on 13 August. He bequeathed £1000 to his brother, Chichester, and £500 to each of his younger sons in addition to the settlement already made. He laid down precise instructions for the education of his heir, and ordered his younger sons to be bred up as physicians, lawyers, or merchants. His daughters he left to the 'sole care and circumspection' of his wife.

Wrey's heir, Sir Bourchier Wrey (1682/3–1726), fifth baronet, inherited a life interest in the Welsh estates of Sir William Williams which brought him many years of expensive litigation. He married, on 28 February 1708, his cousin Diana (b. 1683), daughter of John Rolle, of Stevenstone, Devon, and widow of John Spark MP. He was buried on 12 November 1726. Sir Bourchier's son and heir, also **Sir Bourchier Wrey**, sixth baronet (1714/15–1784), was educated at Winchester College (1727–31) and at New College, Oxford, from where he matriculated on 21 October 1732, aged seventeen. He then spent three years on a grand tour through Italy, Germany, and the Netherlands, where he was remembered by Sir Horace Mann as 'too wise and solemn for anybody then' (Walpole, Corr., 19.238). In 1742 he became a member of the Society of Dilettanti, and the same year his cousin Henry Rolle described him to the duke of Newcastle as 'one who has a great interest in his county' (Matthews). The political crisis in February 1746 took him to London, his having been spurred into action by Lady Orford.

When his cousin Henry Rolle was created a peer Wrey succeeded him in his Barnstaple parliamentary seat at a by-election on 20 January 1748. He soon came into conflict with the lord lieutenant of Devon, the second earl of Orford, and was criticized as having been bred a Jacobite from his cradle. On 10 July 1749 he married Mary (1723/4–1751), daughter of John Edwards of Highgate, Middlesex. In 1752 Wrey went to the Baltic ports of Bremen, Hamburg, and Lübeck as a delegate of the 'society for carrying on the herring fishery', on a mission to improve the conditions of British fishermen. In parliament in 1753 he opposed the earl of Hardwicke's marriage bill. Wrey did not stand again at the 1754 election, withdrawing before the poll at Exeter. On 1 May 1755 he married Ellen (d. 1813),

daughter of John Thresher of Bradford, Wiltshire. They had two sons. He rebuilt the pier at Ilfracombe in 1761. Wrey died on 13 April 1784 and was buried at Tawstock on the 22nd; he was succeeded by his son Sir Bourchier Wrey, seventh baronet.   STUART HANDLEY

Sources J. P. Ferris, 'Wrey, Sir Bourchier', HoP, Commons, 1660–90 · GEC, Baronetage · will, PRO, PROB 11/438, sig. 132, fols. 343r–345r · C. Dalton, ed., English army lists and commission registers, 1661–1714, 1 (1892), 69, 98 · N. Luttrell, A brief historical relation of state affairs from September 1678 to April 1714, 6 vols. (1857), vol. 1, p. 122; vol. 2, p. 351; vol. 3, pp. 322, 324 · J. L. Vivian, ed., The visitations of Cornwall, comprising the herald's visitations of 1530, 1573, and 1620 (1887), 564–5 · J. R. Chanter and T. Wainwright, Reprint of the Barnstaple records, 1 (1900), 74, 82, 232 · CSP dom., Jan–July 1683, 224; 1695, 260 · S. R. Matthews, 'Wrey, Sir Bourchier', HoP, Commons, 1715–54, 2.558 · Walpole, Corr., 19.224, 238 · H. Chitty, Winchester long rolls, 1723–1812 (1904), 11–21 · L. Cust and S. Colvin, History of the Society of Dilettanti (1898), 218, 251
Likenesses G. Knapton, portrait, 1744, repro. in Cust and Colvin, History, 218
Wealth at death see will, PRO, PROB 11/438, sig. 132, fols. 343r–345r

Wrey, Sir Bourchier, sixth baronet (1714/15–1784). See under Wrey, Sir Bourchier, fourth baronet (c.1653–1696).

Wright, Abraham (1611–1690), Church of England clergyman and author, was born in Black Swan Alley, Thames Street, London, on 23 December 1611, the son of Richard Wright, a London silk dyer. He was baptized at St James Garlickhythe, London, six days later. He attended the Mercers' Chapel school in Cheapside under Dr Nicholas Grey, later master of Charterhouse and of Eton College, transferring to Merchant Taylors' School in 1626. He was elected scholar of St John's College, Oxford, on 11 June 1629, and matriculated on 13 November after taking the requisite oaths and signing the articles of religion. He came to the notice of the president of the college, William Juxon, shortly to be bishop of London and later archbishop of Canterbury, and in 1632 was elected fellow of St John's, where he was reputed 'an exact master of the Latin tongue, even to the nicest criticism' (Wood, Ath. Oxon., 4.275). Wright graduated BA on 16 May 1633 and proceeded MA on 22 April 1637.

On the visit of Charles I to St John's College on 30 August 1636 to celebrate the opening of William Laud's new quadrangle, Wright delivered the speech welcoming the king; after dinner Love's Hospital, a play by George Wild, was performed before the king and queen by Wild, Wright, and other members of St John's; as Laud recalled, the drama was 'merry, and without offence, and so gave a great deal of content' (Works, 5.153). Wright himself earned a reputation as a playwright: his comedy, The Reformation, is known to have been acted at St John's, but the text has not survived. He was also a poet, some of his English verse being printed in Flos Britannicus (1636) and Horti Caroli rosa altera (1640). On 27 September 1637 Wright was ordained deacon by Francis White, bishop of Ely, in the chapel of Ely House in Holborn, London. In the same year Wright published at Oxford a collection of epigrams by 120 continental authors, Delitias delitiarum. Following his ordination as priest on 22 December 1639 at Christ Church, Oxford, he gave many sermons at St Mary's, Oxford, and at St Paul's, London. During the civil war Wright preached before Charles I at Oxford, and in January 1644 addressed the MPs gathered there to attend the king. In 1643 he married Jane (*bap.* 1623, *d.* 1645), daughter of James Stone of Yarnton, Oxfordshire. At Yarnton was born their eldest son, James *Wright (*bap.* 1644, *d.* 1716/17), called to the bar of the Middle Temple in 1675 and the author of *The History and Antiquities of Rutland* (1684–7).

In August 1645 Wright was presented by Juxon to the vicarage of Oakham, Rutland; he was instituted, but refused to take the covenant and was not inducted to the living. He returned to Oxford, but was expelled from his fellowship by the parliamentary commission. Wright travelled to London, where he lived until, after the execution of the king in early 1649, he was appointed tutor to the son of Sir James Grime or Graham at Peckham, Surrey. Here, he 'read the common prayer on all Sundays and holy days, and on principal feasts he preached and administered the sacraments' (Wood, *Ath. Oxon.*, 4.276). In 1655 he returned to the City, and was elected by the parishioners minister of St Olave, Silver Street, London. He did not formally take up the rectorship 'because he would avoid oaths and obligations' (ibid.), but an arrangement was made to pay him its income. By these means Wright was able to minister at the parish for four years, according to the rites of the Church of England. In 1656 he published *Five Sermons*, in which each sermon was in a different style. The purpose of this exercise, as the preface to the reader explained, was to show the inferiority of the lay preachers who then abounded, for there was 'a vaste difference betweene shop-board breeding and the universities'. The theme was continued in his book *Parnassus Biceps* (1656), a miscellany of ninety-four poems of the time of James I and Charles I, including six of his own poems, which recalled those halcyon days 'when the buttery and kitchin would speak Latine, though not preach, and the very irrational turnspits had so much knowing modesty as not to dare to come into a chappel or to mount any pulpits but their own' (preface, sig. A2v). Wright was forced to leave St Olave's shortly after the presentation of William Nokes on 11 February 1659. As one of the most prominent cavalier ministers he aroused the suspicions of the authorities, and 'was more than once examined for keeping intelligence with the loyal party' (Wood, *Ath. Oxon.*, 4.276).

After the Restoration Wright was asked to become chaplain to the king's sister, Elizabeth of Bohemia, but he declined, returning in October 1660 to the rectory of Oakham. He was 'no favourer of sectaries and their conventicles, and therefore not belov'd by the dissenters of his parish, which was always full of them' (Wood, *Ath. Oxon.*, 4.276). In *A Practical Commentary on the Pentateuch* (1661) Wright directed his prefatory remarks to chief justices. In the light of the sad experience of schism in biblical times, he argued, a general council of the church should be held as the only means to 'prevent the ruin of our own miserably divided church'. After this, however, he lived for many years in quiet rural obscurity. At some point he married Jane Wait. Their son Richard was born in 1666/7, and a daughter Jane was born in 1677. In 1682 he acquired the manor of Manton, Rutland, settling it upon 'that sonne of mine that shall be first married to one who shall be worth to him on the day of his marriage seven hundred pounds or more' in land or cash, a dispensation which may recall the parable of the prodigal son (will, PRO, PROB 11/399, sig. 82). He died on 9 May 1690 and was buried in Oakham church.

STEPHEN WRIGHT

Sources Wood, *Ath. Oxon.*, new edn, 4.275–8 • H. Wilson, *History of Merchant Taylors' School* (1812) • *Hist. U. Oxf.* 4: 17th-cent. Oxf. • C. J. Robinson, ed., *A register of the scholars admitted into Merchant Taylors' School, from AD 1562 to 1874*, 2 vols. (1882–3) • *Walker rev.* • *The works of the most reverend father in God, William Laud*, 5, ed. J. Bliss (1853) • J. Wright, *History and antiquities of Rutland* (1684–7); repr. (1973) • *IGI* • will, PRO, PROB 11/399, sig. 82 • H. I. Longden, *Northamptonshire and Rutland clergy from 1500*, ed. P. I. King and others, 16 vols. in 6, Northamptonshire RS (1938–52), vol. 15, p. 205 • J. Walker, *An attempt towards recovering an account of the numbers and sufferings of the clergy of the Church of England*, 2 pts in 1 (1714) • A. Wright, *Parnassus biceps*, ed. P. Beal (1990)
Archives Bodl. Oxf., papers • Bodl. Oxf., sermons

Wright, Sir Almroth Edward (1861–1947), medical scientist, was born at Middleton Tyas, near Richmond, Yorkshire, on 10 August 1861, the second son of the Revd Charles Henry Hamilton *Wright (1836–1909), an eminent Hebraist and militant protestant, and his wife, Ebba Johanna Dorothea, daughter of Nils Wilhelm Almroth, governor of the royal mint, Stockholm. Sir C. T. H. *Wright, librarian to the London Library, was a younger brother. Wright was educated privately by his parents and tutors and then at the Royal Academical Institution, Belfast. At the age of seventeen he entered Trinity College, Dublin, and took his degree in modern literature in 1882, and his medical degree a year later. With travelling scholarships he spent a year in Germany studying under J. F. Cohnheim, C. Weigert, and C. F. W. Ludwig, three of the leading figures of the day in pathology and physiological chemistry. On his return to London he read law for a time and later took a clerkship at the Admiralty, which he said allowed him more than enough time to spend on medical research at the Brown Institution. In 1887 he moved to his first full-time post, as temporary demonstrator of pathology at Cambridge. He then moved to Sydney for two years and returned to England, via a further term in Germany, to work at the newly opened conjoint laboratories of the two royal colleges. Not every late nineteenth-century medical research scientist followed such a hectic schedule, but almost all had to improvise careers from short-term and often part-time appointments. In 1889 Wright married Jane Georgina Wilson (*d.* 1926), daughter of Robert Mackay Wilson JP, of Coolcarrigan, co. Kildare; they had two sons and one daughter.

In his first permanent post, that of professor of pathology at the army medical school at Netley, Hampshire, between 1892 and 1902, Wright changed the curriculum from its traditional emphasis on morbid anatomy towards

Sir Almroth Edward Wright (1861–1947), by Sir Gerald Kelly, 1933

the new areas of patho-physiology, bacteriology, and immunology, and, more significantly, he established a highly successful and productive research group. During these years he, and the group that became known as 'Wright's Men', explored many lines of research, but the most notable was the development, testing, and introduction of anti-typhoid inoculation. He also served on the Indian plague commission in 1898–9. Following various disputes with the army authorities, not least their reluctance to adopt his vaccine, Wright left the army medical school in 1902 to take up the appointment of pathologist at St Mary's Hospital, London, where he transformed a small department into one of Britain's leading medical research laboratories and in time an independent research institute. Wright retained his association with St Mary's until 1946.

During the first decade of the twentieth century, Wright's main work was the development and promotion of his system of vaccine therapy. This novel use for vaccines, which had previously been thought able only to prevent infections, was based on new ideas concerning the operation of the human immune system and complex laboratory methods for preparing vaccines and monitoring their effects. There was a considerable vogue for vaccine therapy in the 1900s which increased the demands for clinical laboratories in hospitals and general practice. Wright's work at this time had a broader significance, for it became the flagship of a project to recast medicine so that the laboratory replaced the clinic as the source and arbiter of medical knowledge. Wright challenged clinicians with his vision of future physicians who were reliant on the laboratory for diagnosis, prognosis, and therapies. Wright's department attracted patients seeking cures for chronic infections, and many of its staff were able to develop large private practices. Medical scientists from around the world came to see the system, and the department attracted support from the Parke Davis Company, who marketed its products. St Mary's made beds available for clinical research, the first such facility in Britain. However, the unalloyed success of vaccine therapy was transient and after 1910 its value was viewed with increasing scepticism, with many clinicians only too pleased to see laboratory medicine damaged and Wright's own professional standing dented.

However, Wright's interests and work had already moved on. In 1911 he went to South Africa to study pneumonia among the African workers in the Rand goldmines, and after failing with vaccine therapy he resorted to trials with a system of preventive inoculation similar to that developed for typhoid fever. On his return to England, Wright abandoned his large private practice and devoted himself to full-time research. He was appointed director of the bacteriological department of the newly founded Medical Research Committee (later Council) in 1913, but the outbreak of the First World War meant that he never took up the post. Instead he went to France as a temporary colonel in the Army Medical Service and set up a laboratory in the casino at Boulogne, where he worked on new methods to control wound infections. His ideas and methods were once again controversial, not least because he questioned the value of antiseptic surgery and promoted a complex alternative of saline treatments. The value of his methods was severely tested, largely because of the aggressive way in which it was promoted and the polemical exchanges that Wright was drawn into. None the less, he received three awards for his wartime researches—the Leconte prize of the Paris Académie des Sciences in 1915, the Buchanan gold medal of the Royal Society in 1917, and the first gold medal of the Royal Society of Medicine in 1920. After the war Wright returned to St Mary's and for a further twenty-five years continued to work on the problems of immunization, in particular the changes induced in the blood in response to vaccination by bacterial products. The continuing commercial success of vaccine therapy and Wright's connections were the basis for the conversion of his laboratories in 1930 into an Institute of Pathology and Research, which later became the Wright–Fleming Institute. Throughout the fifty years he was active in medical research, Wright was continually devising new and ingenious techniques. Many of these were described in his work *Techniques of the Teat and Capillary Glass Tube* (1912).

Wright's labours were not confined to medical science. The operations of the human mind were never far from his thoughts, and he strove incessantly to build up what he called a system of logic that would lead to truth. The greater part of his writing on this theme survived in manuscript and was published posthumously under the title *Alethetropic Logic* (1953) under the direction of his grandson Dr G. J. Romanes. Wright also published *The Unexpurgated Case Against Woman Suffrage* in 1913. The book, which expanded upon his notorious letter to *The Times* (28 March 1912), argued that women were physically, intellectually, and morally inferior to men, so that to concede them the suffrage would be harmful to the state. It drew a forceful response from Beatrice Webb in the *New Statesman* (1 Nov 1913).

Wright was knighted in 1906, and appointed CB in 1915 and KBE in 1919. He was elected FRS in 1906. He became a corresponding member of the Institut de France and was an officer of the order of the crown of Belgium, and a member of the order of St Sava, Serbia. He received the freedom of the city of Belfast in 1912 and was made an honorary fellow of Trinity College, Dublin, in 1931. He received honorary degrees from the universities of Dublin, Edinburgh, Belfast, Leeds, Paris, and Buenos Aires. He died on 30 April 1947 at his home, Southernwood, Farnham Common, Buckinghamshire, where his ashes were later scattered.

Wright is now principally remembered as the model for the bombastic Sir Colenso Ridgeon in George Bernard Shaw's *The Doctor's Dilemma* and for his outspoken opposition to women's suffrage. Yet in the early decades of the twentieth century he was perhaps the leading medical scientist of his generation and was even styled as the British Pasteur. However, the verdict on his medical work became very mixed. The development of anti-typhoid inoculation has been widely regarded as a pioneering innovation in the development of preventive vaccines made of killed bacteria, and it undoubtedly saved many lives. Against this, a jaundiced view is now taken of his system of vaccine therapy, his methods of wound treatment, and the ideas on immunity that he elaborated in the 1920s and 1930s. The gap between the trajectory of his early career and his final standing as a medical eccentric should not obscure the fact that 'The Celtic Siren' was a crucial figure in twentieth-century British medicine.

MICHAEL WORBOYS

Sources R. Colebrook, *Almroth Wright: provocative doctor and thinker* (1954) · Z. Cope, *Almroth Wright: founder of modern vaccine-therapy* (1966) · *The Times* (1 May 1947), 7 · *The Lancet* (10 May 1947) · *BMJ* (10 May 1947), 657–60 · R. T. Mummery, *Nature*, 159 (1947), 731–2 · B. Harrison, *Separate spheres: the opposition to women's suffrage in Britain* (1978) · DNB

Archives BL, annotated notebook of experiments, Add. MS 56138 · Medical Research Council, London, corresp. and papers · RS · St Mary's Hospital, London, MSS · TCD, corresp. and papers · Wellcome L., corresp. and papers | BL, George Bernard Shaw MSS · California Institute of Technology, corresp. with G. E. Hale · Society for Psychical Research, London, corresp. with Sir Oliver Lodge · TCD, letters to John Joly

Likenesses F. Dodd, charcoal drawing, 1932, NPG · G. Kelly, oils, 1933, St Mary's Hospital, London, Wright–Fleming Institute [*see illus.*] · D. Gilbert, bronze bust, *c.*1935, St Mary's Hospital, London · photographs, St Mary's Hospital, London, Wright–Fleming Institute

Wealth at death £48,280 15*s.* 7*d.*: probate, 20 Aug 1947, CGPLA Eng. & Wales

Wright, Basil Charles (1907–1987), maker of documentary films and author, was born on 12 June 1907 in Sutton, Surrey, the only son (there were also younger twin sisters) of Major Lawrence Wright TD and his wife, Gladys Marsden, and was brought up in a comfortably well-off middle-class family. He was educated at Sherborne School and entered Corpus Christi College, Cambridge, as a Mawson scholar in 1926 to read classics. He took a first in part one

of the classical tripos (1928) and a third in part two of economics (1929), having already decided while an undergraduate that he would become either a poet, dramatist, or film-maker.

A double chance—Wright had happened to attend the première of *Drifters*, directed by John Grierson, the first 'documentary' film in the particular British definition of the genre (which struck him as 'the sort of film I wanted to make'), and Grierson happened to have seen an amateur film of his while looking for an editor to work in his film unit at the Empire Marketing Board—determined that he would become a film-maker and a documentarist. He was one of the first to join the small band of documentarists being gathered together at the board, and he remained throughout his professional life one of the most devoted, unquestioning, and faithful members of the British documentary movement and a follower of its mercurial and magnetic leader, John Grierson. He followed Grierson to the General Post Office film unit in 1933; he resigned when Grierson was pushed out in 1937, and co-founded the Realist Film Unit, an independent commissioning and production unit for sponsored productions. In 1936 he co-directed, with Harry Watt, *Night Mail*.

Wright joined the Film Centre in 1939 as executive producer, a post he retained until 1944. During this time of war (the golden age of the documentary with, for once, ample resources available), although by nature a personal film-maker, he worked tirelessly and selflessly as producer, administrator, and adviser to no fewer than thirty-six films, which were directed by others. His creative contribution to many of these was substantial, including to some of the classics, such as *Diary for Timothy* (1946).

Wright finished the war as producer in charge of the Crown Film Unit (1945) and adviser to the director-general of the Ministry of Information. This should have provided him with the means for resuming his creative career, but he responded unhesitatingly to Grierson's call to join him at International Realist in New York. This was an abortive attempt by Grierson to restart his own production career after leaving Canada in the wake of revelations by Igor Gouzenko about Soviet infiltration. Wright then followed Grierson to UNESCO and devoted his energies again primarily to paperwork.

Wright's creative career restarted in 1953, although he sensed that he was now too old. Only six more films followed before his swansong, *A Place for Gold*, in 1960. He devoted the remaining twenty-seven years of his life to studying, writing, and teaching about film, trying to keep alive the ideals of the Griersonian documentary. He taught at the University of Southern California (1962–8), was senior lecturer in film history at the National Film School (1971–3), and was visiting professor at other institutions such as Temple University, Philadelphia (1977), and Houston University (1978). He also taught film-making in developing countries, and held many honorific positions, including those of governor of the British Film Institute (1953) and fellow of the British Film Academy (1955).

Wright's most influential and important film, in some

ways never quite matched later, came early in his career. *Song of Ceylon* (1936), which won the gold medal and prix du gouvernement at Brussels, put the British documentary movement on the map, showing that film could be an art form, the first time the British film was recognized in that way. Of his other films, *Children at School* (1938) and *The Immortal Land* (1959, for which he was awarded the Council of Europe award) are perhaps the most representative of his special poetic and aesthetic gifts, as well as his technical mastery of the craft of documentary film-making. In 1936 he was awarded the gold cross of the royal order of King George I of Greece.

As a film-maker Wright's contribution to the development of the documentary lies essentially in bringing to it an aesthetic sensitivity. He was widely recognized as the 'poet of the documentary movement'. However, the insistence of Grierson on public service and his strident, if not always consistent, opposition to his documentarists' being 'aestheticky' and personal prevented those poetic shoots from their full flowering. As the critic David Thomson fairly remarked, Wright's work at its best was sensitive, graceful, and pictorial, but it was also without dynamic personality or heart.

As a writer Wright contributed greatly to the critical and theoretical debates essential to the development of the documentary movement, especially during the Second World War, when through the pages of the *Documentary Newsletter* he took over part of the role of the intellectual leader of the documentary movement while Grierson was in Canada. He was film critic of *The Spectator* and *Sight and Sound* in the late 1940s. He published two books, *The Use of the Film* (1948) and *The Long View* (1974), the latter one of the classic histories of the cinema from an aesthetic perspective.

Basil Wright had an attractive personality, at once cultured, scholarly, and sensitive, and yet efficiently practical and with a quiet sense of humour. His lifelong recreational interests were opera, ballet, and gardening. In appearance he was of medium height, with a lightly built, trim body and regular features, his scholarly appearance emphasized by dark-rimmed spectacles. He never married and lived for the latter half of his life with a long-time companion, Kassim Bin Said, at Little Adam Farm, Frieth, Henley-on-Thames, Oxfordshire. He died on 14 October 1987 at Little Adam Farm, of bronchopneumonia and cerebral atrophy.   NICHOLAS PRONAY, *rev.*

Sources *The Times* (15 Oct 1987) · *The Independent* (16 Oct 1987) · D. Thomson, *A biographical dictionary of the cinema* (1975, [1976]) · G. R. Levin, *Documentary explorations* (1971) · personal knowledge (1996) · private information (1996) **Archives** University of Stirling, corresp. with John Grierson **Likenesses** photograph, repro. in *The Independent* **Wealth at death** £457,166: probate, 2 Feb 1988, *CGPLA Eng. & Wales*

Wright, Sir (William) Charles, second baronet (1876–1950), ironmaster and steelmaker, was born at Legge Lane, Lady Wood, Birmingham, on 13 January 1876, the only son of Sir John Roper Wright (1843–1926), engineer and first baronet, and his first wife, Jane Eliza, daughter of Charles Wilson, a master mechanical engineer of Birmingham. Wright was educated privately and had begun to study for his army entrance examination when, in 1893, he decided to join his father in the steelmaking business of Wright, Butler & Co. Ltd. He at once applied himself zealously to learning the business, passing through all the production departments of the company's works in Glamorgan and Monmouthshire. During this time, in 1898, he married Maud, the daughter of Isaac Butler, one of his father's business associates and JP, of Pant-teg, Monmouthshire.

In 1902 Wright, Butler & Co. Ltd merged with companies controlled by Alfred *Baldwin (1841–1908) to form Baldwins Ltd. By 1903 Wright had become a director of Baldwins, and following the acquisition of the mothballed Port Talbot steelworks in 1906, he became manager of the Port Talbot Steel Company Ltd, where production of steel commenced in January 1907. When Alfred Baldwin died in 1908, Wright's father moved up from managing director to chairman of Baldwins, and Wright took over as managing director. This elevation within the company, and the increased responsibilities he acquired, pushed him into the forefront of the iron and steel industry and the public life of south Wales. He became a JP for Glamorgan and, in 1912, high sheriff of the county.

Wright also maintained links with the army. In 1900 he had become an honorary captain and, in 1907, lieutenant-colonel commanding the Glamorgan Royal Field (Reserve) Artillery. In 1909 he became honorary colonel and joined the general reserve of officers, continuing in this position until 1931. Despite his military connections, Wright's major contribution during the First World War was not on active duty in the front line, but helping to control iron and steel production. On 22 June 1915 he was appointed to the Ministry of Munitions to supervise the supply and distribution of steel, but he left on 16 February 1916 to undertake military duties, among which was a special mission to Italy in connection with the supply of sheet steel for the Italian army. On 2 January 1917 he returned to the ministry as deputy director and subsequently became controller of iron and steel production on 20 August 1917. For his services during the First World War he was appointed CB in 1918 and KBE in 1920; he was also made an officer of the Légion d'honneur (France) and a knight commander of the order of the Crown of Italy.

In 1925 Wright succeeded his father as chairman of Baldwins Ltd, and was at the forefront of the rationalization process in south Wales. Most notable was the merger of the heavy steel interests of Baldwins and Guest, Keen, and Nettlefolds Ltd in 1930. Wright became chairman and managing director of the new company, the British (Guest Keen Baldwins) Iron and Steel Company Ltd (GKB). His prominent position within the steel industry was reflected in his election as president of the Iron and Steel Institute (1931–3) and as president of the British Iron and Steel Federation (1937–8). He joined the iron and steel control, Ministry of Supply, on its formation in 1939, as deputy controller, and succeeded Sir Andrew Duncan as controller in January 1940. He resigned on account of illness towards the end of 1942, but resumed the post for a few months in 1943, when his successor was likewise indisposed. For his services he was promoted GBE in 1943.

At the end of that same year Wright resigned as managing director of GKB, subsequently resigning as company chairman in 1947. In part linked to his age and state of health, these decisions were also a consequence of further reorganization of the iron and steel industry in south Wales. As one of the architects of these and earlier changes Wright felt it was time to leave subsequent developments in the hands of younger men. He had played his part in the merger between Baldwins and Richard Thomas & Co. Ltd in 1944–5, to form Richard Thomas and Baldwins Ltd (RTB), and that, on 1 May 1947, between GKB, John Lysaght, RTB, and Llanelly Associated Tinplate Companies, to form the Steel Company of Wales Ltd. Wright ultimately severed his links with the industry on 31 March 1949, resigning as a director of GKB some seventeen months before his death, at his home, Englemere Hill, Ascot, Berkshire, on 14 August 1950 from cancer. Without issue, the baronetcy to which he had succeeded in 1926, on the death of his father, became extinct.

A tall man with a fine presence, Wright displayed generosity, kindness, and consideration for others; but he was a hard worker and a born leader who expected, and obtained, co-operation from others. A man of action, to whom order and method came naturally, when there was work to be done he tackled it eagerly and gave quick decisions with a sure touch. While his father was acknowledged as an engineer, and is noted for his association with William Siemens in the development of the open-hearth process of steelmaking at the Landore works in south Wales, Wright is best remembered as an organizer. Although he made frequent overseas trips to keep abreast of modern technological developments, his strength was in establishing strong managerial teams, and fostering cordial relationships with key customers and politicians.

J. B. NEILSON, rev. TREVOR BOYNS

Sources G. M. Holmes, 'Wright, Sir William Charles', DBB · Western Mail [Cardiff] (16 Aug 1950) · WWW · private information (1959) · b. cert. · d. cert.
Likenesses O. Birley, oils, 1944, British Steel Corporation, Irthlingborough · O. Birley, portrait, priv. coll.; copy, formerly in British Iron and Steel Federation, Steel House, London, 1959
Wealth at death £270,323 1s. 7d.: probate, 22 Sept 1950, CGPLA Eng. & Wales

Wright, Charles Henry Hamilton (1836–1909), Hebraist and theologian, was born at Dublin on 9 March 1836, the second son of the ten children of Edward Wright, barrister of Floraville, Donnybrook, co. Dublin, and his wife, Charlotte, daughter of Joseph Wright of Beech Hill, Donnybrook. Edward Perceval *Wright was his eldest brother. Wright was educated privately, and entered Trinity College, Dublin, on 1 July 1852. As an undergraduate he actively engaged in religious controversy and propaganda for the protestant side, and in 1853 he wrote his first work, *Coming Events, or, Glimpses of the Future*, as well as an anonymous attack on Roman Catholicism, *The Pope the Antichrist*. He became interested for a time in Celtic philology, publishing *A Grammar of the Modern Irish Language* (1855), but soon turned to theology and oriental languages, which remained his lifelong interest. In 1856 he won the primate's Hebrew premium, and he graduated BA with a first class in the divinity testimonium examination in 1857. He was awarded the Arabic prize in 1859, and proceeded MA in the same year, BD in 1873, and DD in 1879. He became PhD at Leipzig in 1875.

Wright was ordained to the curacy of Middleton-Tyas, Yorkshire, in 1859, but though an earnest preacher he was unsuited to ordinary parochial work. On 23 June 1859 he married Ebba, daughter of Professor Nils Wilhelm Almroth, governor of the royal mint in Stockholm. They had at least five sons, including Sir Almroth Edward *Wright (1861–1947), pathologist; Charles Theodore Hagberg *Wright (1862–1940), librarian; and Eric Blackwood Wright (1860–1940), colonial judge. He was appointed in 1863 to the English chaplaincy at Dresden, where he became acquainted with F. J. Delitzsch and other German biblical scholars and became a member of the German Oriental Society. His trenchant protestantism made him popular with some of the English residents but it offended members of the high-church party, who successfully petitioned A. C. Tait, bishop of London, to appoint an additional chaplain. In 1868 Wright became chaplain of Trinity Church at Boulogne in France, where he served not only British seamen but also German prisoners of the Franco-Prussian War, 1870–71. Thanks to his efforts the English church was repaired.

After returning to Ireland, Wright served successively as incumbent of St Mary's, Belfast (1874–85), and of Bethesda Church, Dublin (1885–91). In 1891 he accepted the benefice of St John's, Liverpool; he retired in 1898. In 1878 Wright was elected Bampton lecturer; his lectures 'Zechariah and his prophecies' were published in 1879. In Dublin in 1880–81 he delivered the Donellan lectures, entitled 'The book of Ecclesiastes in relation to modern criticism'; these were published in 1883. He was also Grinfield lecturer in Oxford, on the Septuagint, in 1893, and also from 1895 to 1897. In addition he acted as examiner in Hebrew for the universities of Oxford, London, Manchester, and Wales.

One of the last great militant protestants, Wright devoted himself with conspicuous ability to the cause of the Protestant Reformation Society, of which he was clerical superintendent from 1898 to 1907. His prolific writings against Roman Catholicism were published in pamphlet form and also in *A Protestant Dictionary* (1904), of which he was joint editor. While his abilities were recognized even by his opponents, his personality created barriers. He was never rewarded with a more leisured clerical office and died at his London house, 90 Bolingbroke Grove, Wandsworth Common, on 22 March 1909.

Wright's numerous biblical works included several Hebrew texts of books of the Old Testament, with notes, and some exegetical studies. His theology was mainly conservative, though he could accept an allegorical rather than a critical reading of the text at some points. His biblical works were not widely read. After his death a tablet was erected in St Mary's Church, Dublin, which described him, *inter alia*, as 'a knight of the North Star of Sweden'.

G. S. WOODS, rev. JOANNA HAWKE

Sources *The Times* (24 March 1909) · *The Guardian* (31 March 1909) · C. H. H. Wright, *Sunbeams on my path*, 2nd edn (1900) · private information (1912) [C. T. Hagberg Wright] · private information (2004) [Mr Alan Bell, London Library] · P. Schaff and S. M. Jackson, *Encyclopedia of living divines and Christian workers of all denominations in Europe and America: being a supplement to Schaff-Herzog encyclopedia of religious knowledge* (1887) · *CGPLA Eng. & Wales* (1909)
Archives LPL, corresp. with A. C. Tait and related papers
Wealth at death £2925 14s. 4d.: Irish probate sealed in England, 21 July 1909, *CGPLA Eng. & Wales*

Wright, Sir Charles Theodore Hagberg (1862–1940), librarian, was born at Middleton Tyas, near Richmond, Yorkshire, on 17 November 1862, the third of the five sons of Charles Henry Hamilton *Wright (1836–1909), an Anglican clergyman and theological scholar, and his wife, Ebba Johanna Dorothea, daughter of Nils Wilhelm Almroth, governor of the royal mint, Stockholm. Sir Almroth Edward *Wright, the bacteriologist, was an elder brother. He was educated at the Royal Academical Institution, Belfast, before following in his family tradition at Trinity College, Dublin, where he graduated BA (1885), and later proceeded LLB (1888) and LLD (1899). After his first-class degree in Greek and Latin he continued his education abroad, spending in 1888 almost a year in St Petersburg, where he lived in a professorial family and achieved fluency in Russian. Developing an antipathy to the all-apparent oppressiveness of imperial rule, he was discreetly sympathetic to nihilist aspirations. He travelled also in France, Germany, Romania, and his maternal Sweden, acquiring an unusually wide range of linguistic skills.

In 1890 Wright became an assistant librarian of the National Library of Ireland, and in 1893 he was appointed (from among 253 applicants) secretary and librarian of the London Library, where he continued in office for forty-seven years. The independent subscription library, founded in 1841, had outgrown its converted household premises in St James's Square. Complete rebuilding was urgently necessary, and the library's catalogues were inadequate for its growing stock. Wright had limited professional experience but boundless energy. The freehold buildings were reconstructed from 1896 at a cost of £20,000, and opened in December 1898. Adjoining properties were acquired, providing space for extensions in 1922 and 1934. During his period of office the stock of books grew from 167,000 to 475,000 and the membership from 2293 to 4400.

Even more importantly, Wright set to work on recataloguing the entire library, working long hours, and by 1903 had produced the large first volume (revised in 1913–14) of the author catalogue. Two supplements followed during his librarianship, with a third (covering the accessions of 1928–50) eventually appearing in 1953. Accompanied by four volumes of subject indexes (1909–

55), this thorough, succinct, and consistent set of catalogues met the library's own needs and provided a valuable general reference tool which retains its value as a bibliographical guide. Wright, who also devised the library's unusual but serviceable classification, was from 1905 helped in his cataloguing work by his assistant (and later successor) C. J. Purnell, but the credit for its conception and execution is his alone. The subject catalogue office was adorned by a prominent notice: 'No guessing, no thinking. Accuracy, accuracy, accuracy!'

Wright was a successful fund-raiser for building projects and for a staff superannuation fund. He was an energetic publicist for the library, which he described in a notable article as 'The soul's dispensary' (*Nineteenth Century*, March 1922, and separately reprinted). Autocratic to, but respected by, his staff, he was—with his black velvet jacket and heavy moustaches—a familiar figure to members. His reputation grew even in his last years, when his involvement in library administration lessened. He received a knighthood in the new year's honours of 1934.

Wright's enthusiasm for Russian literature showed itself in the growth of the library's strong collection of foreign literature, and in his frequent essays in literary periodicals. A Tolstoyan who edited two volumes of the master's uncollected stories, he drew on his wide range of British literary contacts to organize (and present) a congratulatory address on Tolstoy's eightieth birthday in 1908. The 1917 revolution elicited Wright's guarded optimism but by the time of his final visit to Russia in 1928 any idealism it had shown had expired. During the First World War Wright had been much involved with the organization of Red Cross libraries for the sick and wounded, and in translation work and lecturing. On 20 February 1919 he married Constance Metcalfe (*b*. 1863/4), daughter of Horace Lockwood, of Nunwood, Yorkshire, and widow of Tyrrell Lewis; there were no children.

Wright held on to the librarianship to be in office for the library's centenary in 1941, but died at 6 Westbourne Street, Lancaster Gate, on 7 March 1940, and was buried at Paddington new cemetery on 11 March following. His wife survived him. Two large albums of his occasional writings, collected by a female admirer, in 1912 and later, are held by the London Library.

ALAN BELL

Sources *The Times* (8 March 1940) · S. Gillam, 'Hagberg Wright and the London Library', *Library History*, 1 (1967), 24–7 · J. Wells, *Rude words* (1991) · *CGPLA Eng. & Wales* (1940) · m. cert.
Archives London Library, C. Honora Blandford's collection
Likenesses W. Orpen, oils, 1917, London Library
Wealth at death £20,242 14s. 3d.: probate, 9 May 1940, *CGPLA Eng. & Wales*

Wright, Christian Edington Guthrie (1844–1907), founder of the Edinburgh School of Cookery, was born on 19 April 1844 in Glasgow, the only child of Harry Guthrie Wright, manager of the Glasgow and South-Western Railway Company. Her mother died following her birth, and father and daughter eventually settled in Edinburgh in the early 1860s, living for most of their lives at 2 Lansdowne Crescent. Educated at a private boarding-school, she attended extramural classes at Edinburgh University

Christian Edington Guthrie Wright (1844–1907), by unknown photographer [detail]

and became a founder member of the influential Ladies' Edinburgh Debating Society. She was honorary treasurer of the Edinburgh Association for the University Education of Women.

In 1875 Guthrie Wright took the lead in the successful establishment of the Edinburgh School of Cookery. Her efforts to set up the school were in keeping with the methods advocated by the National Union for Improving the Education of Women of all Classes. The union's president, Princess Louise, became the principal patron of the school.

Guthrie Wright personally undertook training at the National Training School of Cookery, South Kensington, which she attended in the summer of 1875 in the company of the Edinburgh school's first lecturer, Isobel Middleton. On their return, the school's opening lecture took place on 9 November before an audience of more than a thousand women. The school developed rapidly. Initially it delivered public lectures on cooking and household health on a peripatetic basis. Most of the lectures formed a regular series in Edinburgh, but over the next few years public lectures were also delivered in other centres, literally from the Shetlands to the Channel Islands. Guthrie Wright and her colleagues (notably Louisa Stevenson) encouraged the development of other schools of cookery, for example in Glasgow and Dundee, and also in various English cities including Newcastle. From 1880 to 1890 the Edinburgh school operated a branch in Manchester and provided public classes for women all over the north of England. The branch operated profitably throughout the decade, but always on the understanding that the Edinburgh school would withdraw if local leaders were willing to take over. This duly happened in 1890, the Manchester school going on to develop as the Elizabeth Gaskell College (ultimately a constituent part of Manchester Metropolitan University).

In 1879 Guthrie Wright published an influential *School Cookery Book*, in the compilation of which she was assisted by Sir Thomas Dyke Acland and two distinguished medical doctors. This book exemplified her determination to have cookery introduced into the curriculum for girls attending ordinary school board schools and to have the subject widely disseminated among working-class women. She was opposed by many members of school boards, typically men concerned about costs, but also some women who did not wish girls to have their attention diverted into 'female' subjects.

Initially Guthrie Wright worked closely with many of the English leaders of the movement for domestic education. Edith Nicolls of the National Training School in London, Fanny Calder of the Liverpool School of Cookery, and Grace Paterson of the Glasgow School of Cookery seem to have been particular associates. In October 1876 the schools of Edinburgh, Liverpool, Leeds, and Glasgow combined to form the Northern Union of Training Schools of Cookery, the object being to establish cookery teaching qualifications of an agreed standard. In Guthrie Wright's opinion, however, some of the schools did not achieve the required quality of training and, to avoid risking the Edinburgh school's growing reputation, it was withdrawn from the union in 1878.

In 1887 Guthrie Wright assisted in the foundation of Queen Victoria's Jubilee Institute for Nurses (district nurses intended to care for the poor in their own homes) and became the honorary treasurer of the Scottish council of the institute. In the following decade she succeeded in raising £20,000 to train and locate nurses in many parts of Scotland and was credited with the successful establishment of the institute.

The Edinburgh School of Cookery eventually developed at Atholl Crescent, where it offered residential courses as well as public lectures. In the early twentieth century the teaching of domestic subjects was seen as a way of tackling the problem of high infant mortality rates. At the time of her death the Scottish education department was preparing to implement Guthrie Wright's proposals for the compulsory instruction of schoolgirls in cooking, health, and hygiene, the teaching to be delivered by trained, qualified staff. In 1930 the Edinburgh School of Cookery became the Edinburgh College of Domestic Science and in 1972 it assumed its modern title, Queen Margaret College.

Politically a Liberal and a friend of the fifth earl of Rosebery, Guthrie Wright was a devout Episcopalian. She was unmarried. She died at her home, 2 Lansdowne Crescent, Edinburgh, on 24 February 1907, bequeathing some of her property to St Mary's Cathedral, from where her funeral four days later took place 'amid every manifestation of the respect and esteem in which she was held by the citizens of Edinburgh and the public generally' (*The Scotsman*, 1 March 1907). TOM BEGG

Sources T. Begg, *The excellent women: the origins and history of Queen Margaret College* (1994) • S. E. S. Mair, 'An appreciation of Christian Edington Guthrie Wright', *The Edinburgh School of Cookery Magazine* (April 1925), 21–3 • L. M. Rae, *Ladies in debate, being a history of the Ladies' Edinburgh Debating Society, 1865–1935* (1936) • M. E. Baly, *A history of the Queen's Nursing Institute* (1987) • *The Scotsman* (28 April 1875) • *The Scotsman* (19 Oct 1875) • *The Scotsman* (10 Nov 1875) • *The Scotsman* (16 Nov 1875) • *The Scotsman* (28 Sept 1876) • *The Scotsman* (30 Sept 1876) • *The Scotsman* (25 Feb 1907) • *The Scotsman* (1 March

1907) · *The Scotsman* (1875–1907) · *Edinburgh Courant* (1875–1907) [reports and articles of various dates] · *The Edinburgh Daily Review* (1875–1907) [reports and articles of various dates]

Archives Queen Margaret College, Edinburgh

Likenesses photograph, Queen Margaret College, Edinburgh [*see illus.*]

Wealth at death £13,743 14s. 11d.: Scottish confirmation, 16 April 1907, CCI

Wright, Christopher (1570?–1605). *See under* Wright, John (*bap.* 1568, *d.* 1605).

Wright, Edward (*bap.* **1561**, *d.* **1615**), mathematician and cartographer, a younger son of Henry and Margaret Wright, was born in Garveston, Norfolk, and was baptized there on 8 October 1561. Perhaps, like his elder brother Thomas (*d.* 1579), he was educated at school in Hardingham before matriculating as a sizar at Gonville and Caius College, Cambridge, on 8 December 1576. His father was already deceased when Thomas was admitted a pensioner at Caius in April 1574. Edward proceeded BA in 1580–81, then remained as a scholar until proceeding MA in 1584. He was a fellow of the college from 1587 to 1596, having married on 8 August 1595 Ursula Warren (*d.* 1625); their son Samuel (1596–1616) was admitted as a sizar at Caius in 1612. Little more is known of his family.

As a student at Cambridge, Wright was a near contemporary of Robert Devereux, the adolescent earl of Essex; if not at Cambridge then later, Wright became close to the earl, for the latter was meeting with him over his studies even in the weeks before his rebellion, in 1600–01. Other contemporaries at Cambridge included Henry Briggs and Christopher Heydon (another friend of the earl's), with whom Wright shared intellectual interests and studies.

In 1589, while still a fellow of his Cambridge college, Wright temporarily forsook the life of a scholar, and with dispensations from the crown and college, he shipped, as Captain Edward Carelesse, on a boat of a fleet commanded by George, earl of Cumberland, on a raiding voyage to the Azores, confiscating 'lawful' prizes from the French, Portuguese, and Spanish there and *en route*. The account of this expedition, referring to Wright in the third person, is appended to his treatise *Certaine Errors of Navigation* (1599) and is presumed to have been written by him. In the same sentence in which Wright introduces himself, he says that he was captain of the *Hope* in Sir Francis Drake's West Indian voyage of 1585–6, which evacuated Sir Walter Ralegh's Virginia colony and took the settlers back to England. Wright probably had ample opportunity on the return voyage to make the acquaintance of and to discuss navigational mathematics with Thomas Harriot, one of the colonists and his near contemporary. The Azores expedition was successful in its accumulation of captured goods and ships, but the return voyage, which ran short of fresh water, was harrowing. There is no evidence of Wright's ever having put to sea again.

Wright resumed his Cambridge fellowship and resigned it in 1596, having evidently already moved to London before then, for he was there making observations of the sun with his fellow Norfolk native Christopher Heydon in 1594–7. (Heydon, although a patron of astronomers,

seems not to have provided Wright with financial support.) In London he became a lecturer in mathematics for the education of the merchant seamen and completed *Certaine Errors of Navigation*. The impetus for Wright's publication of the first edition of *Certaine Errors* came from his outrage at two apparent cases of plagiarism. A well-regarded navigator, Abraham Kendall, died at sea (1596) in possession of a manuscript copy of Wright's work, and this text, retrieved and brought to London, was taken to be Kendall's own, until it was passed to Wright for his review. At roughly the same time the cartographer Jodocus Hondius (1563–1612), who was deeply chagrined upon the discovery of his borrowing, used Wright's methods without acknowledgement in one of his maps. The exact nature of Wright's London employment is somewhat uncertain until some years had elapsed; certainly by 1614, but perhaps as early as 1612, his services as a lecturer in navigation were funded by the East India Company, at £50 a year. He was also employed as a tutor to Prince Henry, to whom he dedicated the second edition of *Certaine Errors* in 1610 and, but for the prince's death in 1612, would have been his librarian. Upon the prince's death Wright, described as 'a very poor man', was left £30 8s. He was employed by Sir Hugh Myddleton as a surveyor for the New River project of bringing water to London, and, similarly, he prepared a plan to show how to bring water from Uxbridge for the use of the royal household.

In his first years in London, Wright evidently developed a close working relationship with William Gilbert (1544–1603), to whose *De magnete* (1600) he not only wrote the preface, but also (as a near contemporary writer, Mark Ridley, asserts) for which he anonymously composed chapter 12 of book 4, describing a method of determining the magnetic variation by reference to astronomical observations. He was a practical man, and designed astronomical instruments, even if he did not make them himself. His *Description and Use of the Sphære* (1613), about a kind of armillary sphere, can be read as a guide to the use of a kind of instrument, but it was specifically written as the manual for the use of one instance of it, the one built for Prince Henry.

But it is upon his work on the mathematics of navigation that Wright's fame chiefly rested, and the most famous project, within this body of work, was the further development of the map projection created by Mercator in his map of 1569. This work proceeded more or less in parallel with the mathematical explorations of Thomas Harriot in the 1590s, and the first fruits appeared in print, with acknowledgement, in Thomas Blundeville's *M. Blundevile his Exercises, Containing Sixe Treatises*, in 1594. Hakluyt, in the 1599–1600 edition of *Principal Navigations*, issued the first world map built on the Mercator projection to be published in England; it was the work of Wright. This seems to be the map alluded to by Shakespeare in *Twelfth Night* (III. ii): 'He does smile his face into more lines than is in the new map, with the augmentation of the Indies'. Wright's development of the Mercator projection (which is often visualized as the projection of a sphere from its centre onto the interior surface of an enclosing cylinder) was the numerical solution, in the absence of the integral calculus, of the following problem: to increase the distance apart of parallels of latitude in proportion to the exaggeration arising from the assumption that, for any given difference in longitude, they are equally long. Harriot had a contemporaneous solution of the problem. Wright's chart of the Azores, which accompanies his account of the voyage, is the first usable published chart to be based on this rigorous application of the Mercator projection.

Like other practical mathematicians of his time, Wright immediately took up John Napier's new invention, logarithms, upon Napier's first publication, and he translated this work, *Mirifici logarithmorum canonis descriptio* (1614), into English as *A Description of the Admirable Table of Logarithmes* (1616), which contained tables extended by Wright and additional information by Henry Briggs. It was this book upon which he was working at his death, in London, in late November 1615. The work was then completed by his son Samuel and, upon the latter's death, seen through the press by Briggs. (A nineteenth-century claim that this book contains the first example of the decimal point is clearly incorrect.) Wright was buried on 2 December at St Dionis Backchurch.   A. J. APT

Sources D. W. Waters, *The art of navigation in England in Elizabethan and early Stuart times*, 2nd edn (1978) · R. Strong, *Henry, prince of Wales and England's lost Renaissance* (1986) · J. V. Pepper, 'Harriot's earlier work on mathematical navigation: theory and practice', *Thomas Harriot: Renaissance scientist*, ed. J. Shirley (1974) · M. Feingold, *The mathematicians' apprenticeship: science, universities and society in England, 1560–1640* (1984) · P. J. Wallis, 'Wright, Edward', *DSB* · A. J. Apt, 'The reception of Kepler's astronomy in England: 1596–1650', DPhil diss., U. Oxf., 1982 · parish register, London, St Michael Cornhill, 8 Aug 1595, GL [marriage] · parish register, London, St Dionis Backchurch, 2 Dec 1615, GL [burial]
Archives BL, papers, Sloane MS 651 · TCD, observations, MSS 3, 387, 396

Wright, Edward Perceval (1834–1910), naturalist, was born on 27 December 1834 at Dublin, the eldest son of Edward Wright, barrister, of Floraville, Donnybrook, and his wife, Charlotte, daughter of Joseph Wright of Beech Hill, Donnybrook. Charles Henry Hamilton *Wright was his younger brother. Edward was educated at home, and began to study natural history under Professor George James Allman before he entered Trinity College, Dublin, at the end of 1852. He graduated BA in 1857 and proceeded MA in 1859, taking an MA *ad eundem* at Oxford. Wright continued his medical studies and graduated MD in 1862; he then visited the medical schools of Berlin, Vienna, and Paris to study ophthalmology.

Although he wished to practise ophthalmic surgery, Wright spent almost his entire career within the University of Dublin. In 1857 he was appointed curator of the university museum and, the following year, lecturer in zoology, a not very exacting post which he held for ten years. While holding this position Wright simultaneously continued his medical studies and lectured in botany at the medical school of Dr Steevens's Hospital, Dublin. In 1865 and 1866, at the university, he also acted as deputy to the ailing professor of botany, William Henry Harvey (1811–1866).

By 1866 Wright seems to have abandoned ideas of becoming an ophthalmic surgeon. In 1867 he paid a six-month visit to the Seychelles and, although his collecting apparatus was lost by shipwreck on the way out, he brought back an important collection of plants and animals. He spent the spring of 1868 in Sicily and the autumn of the same year in dredging off the coast of Portugal. In 1869 Wright was appointed professor of botany in the University of Dublin, succeeding Professor Alexander Dickson (1836–1887) who had resigned the chair in 1868 to move to Glasgow. After a little while the university also appointed Wright as keeper of the herbarium.

Wright was a fluent, thorough, and conscientious teacher. He was 'a man of unspeculative mind' (McDowell and Webb, 242) so, while he devoted most of his energies to the arrangement of the herbarium, he did not use the collections for taxonomic studies. He spent many vacations on the continent of Europe, when evidently he collected specimens for the herbarium, and was lamed for life in a carriage accident in Switzerland. In 1872 he married Emily Shaw, second daughter of Colonel Ponsonby Shaw. The couple had no children.

Wright was a prolific author in zoology and botany. His principal research lay in marine zoology and an early indication of this was his participation in the meetings of the British Association for the Advancement of Science; at Leeds in 1858, he, in conjunction with Joseph Reay Greene, presented a report on the marine fauna of the south and west coasts of Ireland.

In 1854, while an undergraduate, Wright founded the quarterly *Natural History Review* which he edited until 1866. His earliest papers, published in this journal, illustrate his diverse interests; they deal with rare Irish birds, fungi parasitic upon insects, the collecting of molluscs, and a disease of the minnow. In subsequent papers Wright covered topics as varied as native filmy ferns and the flora of the Aran Islands in Galway Bay, Irish sea anemones, sponges, and sea slugs (nudibranchs). With Alexander Henry Haliday (1806–1870), Wright described the troglodyte animals of the Mitchelstown caves, co. Kilkenny, Ireland, where they discovered three blind species including the springtail *Lipura wrightii*. With Dr Theophil Studer he reported on the corals (*Alcyonaria*) of the *Challenger* expedition. In conjunction with Thomas Henry Huxley, Wright described the fossil Amphibia in the Kilkenny (Jarrow) coal measures. His books included English editions of Figuier's *Ocean World* (1872) and *Mammalia* (1875). While pursuing ophthalmological studies, Wright translated from F. C. Donders's *The Pathogeny of Squint* (1864), and in 1865 published a paper entitled 'A modification of Liebreich's ophthalmoscope'.

Wright was an energetic supporter of Dublin's scientific societies; he served, at various times, as secretary to the Dublin University Zoological and Botanical Association and to the Royal Geological Society of Ireland. He was a member of the Dublin Microscopical Club, the first president of the Dublin Naturalists' Field Club (1886–7), and, because he took a keen interest in archaeology, president of the Royal Society of Antiquaries of Ireland (1900–02).

He became a member of the Royal Irish Academy in 1857, and, having been elected to its council in 1870, was secretary from 1874 to 1877, and from 1883 to 1899, carefully supervising the publications. In 1883 he was awarded the Cunningham gold medal.

After his wife's death in 1886 Wright moved into rooms in Trinity College, close to the herbarium. Owing to heart disease, he resigned as professor of botany in 1904, but continued with his post as keeper of the herbarium. He died of bronchitis at Trinity College on 2 March 1910, and was buried at Mount Jerome cemetery, Dublin.

E. CHARLES NELSON

Sources E. P. Wright, 'The herbarium of Trinity College, a retrospect', *Notes from the Botanical School of Trinity College, Dublin*, 1 (1896), 1–14 · R. B. McDowell and D. A. Webb, *Trinity College, Dublin, 1592–1952: an academic history* (1982) · D. A. Webb, 'The herbarium of Trinity College, Dublin: its history and contents', *Botanical Journal of the Linnean Society*, 106 (1991), 295–327 · R. Ll. Praeger, *The natural history of Ireland* (1950) · R. L. Praeger, *Some Irish naturalists: a biographical note-book* (1949) · G. Sharkey, ed., *Reflections and recollections: 100 years of the Dublin Naturalists Field Club* (1986) · DNB · CGPLA Eng. & Wales (1910)
Archives National Museum of Ireland, Dublin, zoological specimens · RBG Kew · TCD, botanical specimens | ICL, corresp. Thomas Huxley · NHM, letters to Albert Gunther relating to zoological record
Likenesses photograph, repro. in *Irish Naturalist*, 19 (1910), 61–3
Wealth at death £5848 15s. 3d.: probate, 15 April 1910, CGPLA Ire. · £293 4s. 5d.: Irish probate sealed in London, 27 April 1910, CGPLA Eng. & Wales

Wright, Edward Richard (1813–1859), actor, was in trade in his early life, and became a resident of London and a member of the Skinners' Company. In September 1832, after acting at Margate John Reeve's part of Marmaduke Magog in Buckstone's *The Wreck Ashore*, he was seen in London, in 1834, at the Queen's Theatre. His reception there was not very encouraging, but he became quite successful in the provinces. He spent some time on the stage in Birmingham and Bristol, then moved to the St James's Theatre in London, built and opened by John Braham, and on the first night (29 September 1837) made his earliest recognized appearance as a comedian, as Splash in *The Young Widow* and Fitzcloddy in a farce called *Methinks I See my Father*. His reception was favourable. In March 1838 he was the original Wigler in Selby's *Valet de Sham*; later he was the first Simmons in Haynes Bayly's *The Spitalfields Weaver*. In December 1838 at the Adelphi, with which his fame is principally associated, and where he was destined to remain for nearly twenty years, Wright was the first Daffodil Primrose, a valet in Stirling's *Grace Darling, or, The Wreck at Sea*, and in October 1839 the first Shotbolt in Buckstone's *Jack Sheppard*. During one year he visited the Princess's; then, returning to the Adelphi, remained there, with the exception of visits of a few days or weeks to the Strand, the Standard, or other houses, until the year of his death. His constant associates were Paul Bedford and, in his later years, Sarah Woolgar (Mrs Alfred Mellon).

At the Adelphi, Wright made his first conspicuous success, in 1842, as Tittlebat Titmouse in Peake's adaptation of Warren's *Ten Thousand a Year*. In September 1843 he was with Bedford and Oxberry at the Strand, where he appeared in *Bombastes furioso* and *The Three Graces*, but in November was back at the Adelphi, and in February 1844 was Bob Cratchit in Stirling's adaptation of *A Christmas Carol* and Richard in a burlesque of *Richard III*. He also played at the Princess's in a farce called *Wilful Murder* and in a burlesque by à Becket of *Aladdin*, and was seen at the Strand.

After a long absence, due to illness, following his performance at Easter 1845 in Buckstone's *Poor Jack*, Wright reappeared at the Adelphi on 1 September 1845 as Barbillon in Stirling's *Clarisse, or, The Merchant's Daughter*, and proceeded to take many roles, that of Paul Pry being one of his most popular representations. Occasionally he was also seen in female parts, such as that of Venus in the burlesque *The Judgment of Paris*. Other roles in which his name appears include Alderman Cute in *The Chimes*, by Mark Lemon and à Becket, and Chatterton Chopkins in *This House to be Let*, a skit on the sale of Shakespeare's house. In 1852 he was at the Princess's; from there he migrated in turn to the Lyceum, the Haymarket, Sadler's Wells, and the provinces, but was once more at the Adelphi in 1855. His most popular success, which has always since been associated with his name, was his Master Grinnidge, the travelling showman in Buckstone's *The Green Bushes*. Scarcely less admired was his John Grumley in *Domestic Economy*. He was excellent, too, in *Slasher and Crasher*, as Blaise in Buckstone's *Victorine*, as Medea in Mark Lemon's burlesque of the same name, as Watchful Waxend in *My Poll and my Partner*, and several parts in which he replaced John Reeve. At the last performance at the old Adelphi (2 June 1858) he played Mr Osnaburg in *Welcome, Little Stranger*. Soon after the opening of the new house, in 1859, he appeared for a few nights, but at the end of March his engagement finished, and he was not seen again on the stage. Towards the close of that year he took refuge from ill health, domestic and financial worries, and legal proceedings at Boulogne, where he died on 21 December 1859. He was buried in Brompton cemetery. He was survived by his wife, Rose Olivia Wright, who died on 25 August 1888, at the age of sixty-two.

In his best days Wright was an excellent low comedian; W. C. Macready pronounced him the best he had seen. He took unpardonable liberties with a public that laughed at, pardoned, petted, and spoiled him, and he often did not know his part and resorted to gagging. On occasion he could be indescribably and repulsively coarse. Some of his performances had remarkable breadth of humour. He inherited the method and traditions of Reeve and to some extent those of Liston. At his death many of his characters came into the hands of John Lawrence Toole.

JOSEPH KNIGHT, rev. NILANJANA BANERJI

Sources *The Era* (25 Dec 1859) · *The life and reminiscences of E. L. Blanchard, with notes from the diary of Wm. Blanchard*, ed. C. W. Scott and C. Howard, 2 vols. (1891) · *Era Almanack and Annual* (1889) · Hall, *Dramatic ports.* · B. N. Webster, ed., *The acting national drama*, 1 (1837) · E. H. Yates, *Edmund Yates: his recollections and experiences*, 4th edn (1885) · G. L. M. Strauss, *Reminiscences of an old bohemian*, new edn (1883) · R. B. Peake, *Ten thousand a year* (1883) · *The Dramatic and Musical Review* (1842–9) · 'Memoir of Mr Wright', *Theatrical Times* (5 Dec 1846), 225–6

Likenesses R. Kemp, chromolithograph (as Splash in Rodwell's *The Young Widow*), NPG · lithograph (after unknown artist), NPG · portrait, repro. in Cumberland, *Minor theatre* (1844) · portrait, repro. in 'Memoir of Mr Wright', *Theatrical Times* · portrait, repro. in *Thespian Times* (3 June 1857) · portrait, repro. in *ILN* (14 Jan 1860) · prints, Harvard TC

Wealth at death under £100: probate, 21 July 1860, CGPLA Eng. & Wales

Wright, Elsie (1901–1988). *See under* Griffiths, Frances (1907–1986).

Wright, Fortunatus (*d.* 1757), merchant and privateer, was the second son of John Wright (*d.* 1717), a Liverpool ship-owner and merchant. It is highly likely that Fortunatus served his apprenticeship with his father. Some confirmation of this early seafaring background may be taken from William Hutchinson's *Treatise on Practical Seamanship* (1777) in which he describes himself as a mariner and speaks with some pride of having served under Fortunatus Wright. In November 1730 Wright married his first wife, Martha Painter, at St Hilary's Church, Wallasey, Cheshire; the couple had four daughters. This marriage appears to have ended within several years. By early 1738 Wright had begun a relationship with Mary (*d.* after 1757), the daughter of William Bulkeley, a landowner at Bryn-ddu on Anglesey. William's diary records the arrival (17 March 1738) of Wright, described as a brewer and distiller from Liverpool, to ask for permission to marry his daughter. This took place in Dublin on 22 March and the first of their four daughters and two sons was born early in 1739.

In 1741 Wright left Liverpool alone and went to Italy, possibly as a result of his involvement in a costly lawsuit with the Turkey Company over the detention by one of his ships of a vessel in which the company had an interest. Equally, it may be that this incident was confused in early memoirs with a later one involving the Porte. Wright arrived in Lucca in June 1742 in a blaze of publicity. Taking firearms into Lucca was forbidden, yet Wright not only refused to surrender his pistols but defied the authorities in an aggressive way. He was expelled and moved to Leghorn. Horace Mann, the British representative in Florence, became involved and provided much detail of the incident in his letters to England.

With the outbreak of war with France in 1744 the British merchants in Leghorn suffered from the depredations of French privateers and paid Wright to fit out his brigantine *Fame* as a privateer. Hutchinson, in his *Treatise*, describes Wright's manner of working which gave him significant success. According to the *Gentleman's Magazine* for December 1746, the '*Fame* had taken sixteen French ships in the Levant worth £400,000.' As the war continued Fortunatus Wright became the focus of several notable incidents. On 19 December 1746 the *Fame* captured a French barque carrying the servants and baggage of the prince of Campo Florida and sent it into Leghorn. Curiously the French ship had a *laissez-passer* from George II. The capture caused a dispute between Wright and Burrington Goldsworthy, the English consul in Leghorn, who ordered him to free the ship. Wright refused and Mann suggested the case should

be put to the naval commander-in-chief in the Mediterranean, who found against Wright.

Another incident which contributed to Wright's notoriety concerned a complaint from the Ottoman empire that Turkish goods in French ships had been made prizes by British privateers. Despite pressure from Goldsworthy, Wright refused to surrender the money obtained from a particular prize, the French ship *Hermione*. The Turkey Company intervened and obtained a ruling from the government that Turkish property could not be taken as prize, even from French ships. An instruction to this effect, dated 30 March 1747, was sent to the Mediterranean. Wright acknowledged this but claimed it could not be applied retrospectively and again refused to repay the money from the prize. He was arrested by the Tuscan authorities on 11 December 1747 and spent six months in prison before, on 10 January 1748, Vienna ordered that he be handed into the custody of the British consul. Before an opportunity occurred to send him home Wright was released on Admiralty bail. The suit against him dragged on for two more years and was apparently resolved in a general settlement with the Porte. Wright remained in Leghorn with the reputation ascribed to him by Hutchinson of 'that great but unfortunate hero'.

Wright's talent for controversy was again evident in 1756 when, on the declaration of war, he immediately became the focus for a diplomatic and naval incident which, in its seriousness, seemed likely to ruin the merchant trade out of Leghorn and to threaten the already delicate relationship between England and Tuscany. Having established a reputation as a successful privateer in the previous war, Wright now set about building a suitable vessel to his own design to renew his privateering activities in the hostilities reopened in the Mediterranean. According to Mann, Wright was well aware of the restrictions in force in Leghorn with regard to the armament and size of crew permitted on ships sailing from the port, restrictions aimed principally at the British. He apparently negotiated with the port authorities on this matter and requested that his ship, the *St George*, be inspected by the captain of the port to certify that it complied with the regulations. Mann claimed that when Wright sailed on 26 July with four British merchant ships bound for England in his convoy, the governor recognized that he had complied with the various restrictions.

Some four leagues out of Leghorn, Wright and his convoy were attacked by a well-armed French xebec, specially fitted out by the merchants of Marseilles to oppose Wright. The xebec expected little resistance from the *St George* which, according to intelligence from Leghorn, was lightly armed. In fact, as soon as she was outside Tuscan jurisdiction, the merchant ships, by prior arrangement, had transferred guns and men to the *St George*, making her into the formidable vessel that Wright intended. The result was that Wright resisted the xebec with great vigour, aggressively beating off two attempts at boarding. Wright pursued the xebec but, on the appearance of another French ship, abandoned the chase and returned to Leghorn with the merchant ships. The ships were arrested but Wright refused to obey the orders of the port captain and, as Mann described, he was accused of offending the neutrality of the port of Leghorn and abusing the Tuscan flag.

In correspondence with Henry Fox, Horace Mann enclosed copies of an extensive exchange of letters between himself and the Tuscan authorities, including Pandolfini, who maintained that the governor of the port had concluded that he had been deceived by Wright and that the 'remonstrances which the French minister and consul had made put the government under a necessity to enquire into the affair to be sure the laws of neutrality had not been offended as claimed by the French' (Hardwicke papers, BL, Add. MS 35481, fol. 47).

While the diplomatic wrangle unfolded the master of the brig *Industry*, lying at Leghorn, joined Edward Hawke in his flagship *Ramillies* off Toulon on 16 September, having left Leghorn in a small longboat with ten men. The master carried dispatches from Sir Horace Mann and from Mr Dicks, the consul in Leghorn, which described 'the great hardships our trade in that port labours under' (NMM, ADM 1/383). Appraised of the situation, Hawke immediately dispatched Sir William Burnaby in the *Jersey*, with *Isis* under command, to bring the British ships to Gibraltar and at the same time to remonstrate with the Tuscan authorities on their unjustifiable treatment of British subjects. The presence of the British naval ships allowed the convoy to sail from Leghorn on 23 September 1756.

The *St George* resumed her privateering activities and shortly put into Malta where French influence was strong enough to prevent Wright getting any stores and provisions or even taking on board some English seamen who had been put on shore by French privateers. Finally Wright was obliged to put to sea on 22 October without them. After that he took several prizes which were sent into Cagliari. On 22 January 1757 Mann wrote to William Pitt that the Leghorn government, recognizing that their actions had ruined the trade of the port, had given permission for Wright to send his prizes there and that he had written to Wright to that effect. Whether Wright ever got this letter is unknown. It was reported in a Liverpool newspaper on 19 May 1757 that the *St George* had been destroyed in a storm on 16 March, and on 2 July 1757 Mann wrote conclusively of Wright 'It is feared by some circumstances and by his not having been heard of for some months, that he foundered at sea' (BL, Add. MS 35481) and added a commendation of Wright's activities at the request of the British merchant community.

It is probable that Wright came from a good social background for his daughter, Philippa, from his second marriage, married Charles, grandson of John Evelyn of Wotton. Charles Evelyn's daughter, Susanna, married John Ellsworthy Fortunatus Wright who served as a naval lieutenant in the American War of Independence, retiring from service in 1783. He then became master of St George's Dock, Liverpool, and was accidentally killed in 1798.   KENNETH BREEN

Sources BL, Hardwicke papers, Add. MS 35481 [for letters from Sir Horace Mann] · Hawke's Mediterranean dispatches, PRO, ADM 1/383 · W. Hutchinson, *A treatise on practical seamanship* (1777) · R. Beatson, *Naval and military memoirs of Great Britain*, 2nd edn, 6 vols. (1804) · *GM*, 1st ser., 16 (1746) · G. Williams, *History of the Liverpool privateers and letters of marque* (1897) · A. C. Wardle, 'The early history of the Liverpool privateers', *Transactions of the Historic Society of Lancashire and Cheshire*, 93 (1941), 69–97 · B. D. Roberts, *Mr Bulkeley and the pirate* (1936)

Wright [*married name* D'Arusmont], **Frances** (1795–1852), social reformer and promoter of women's rights, was born at Dundee on 6 September 1795, the daughter of James Wright (*d.* 1797), linen merchant, and Camilla Campbell (*d.* 1797). Her father was a wealthy man of independent means and strong liberal feeling, who had circulated Paine's *Rights of Man* and French political writings in his native town. But before the age of two and a half she had lost both her parents and, with a sister Camilla and a brother Richard (who died at the age of fifteen), she was brought up in London by a succession of maternal relatives of conservative opinions. When she was twenty-one she and Camilla went to live with James Mylne, a great-uncle who taught moral philosophy at Glasgow College. In this new environment she read widely. Self-educated, reflective, and enjoying both the friendship of cultured and intellectual women and the complete devotion of her younger sister, she worked her own way to her father's political opinions and conceived an abstract love for the United States of America, which seemed to embody those liberal ideals which she found lacking in England, where the climate was against reform. She became fascinated by Botta's history of the American revolution, which described the infant republic as realizing the ideas of Greece and Rome.

In the summer of 1818, the 22-year-old Frances decided to make the thirty-day voyage to America with Camilla, with the intention of sending back to Robina Craig Millar, a distant relative and a kind of substitute mother, a series of letters 'that would serve as the basis for a book'. She was already an author of sorts, having written *Altorf*, a play focusing on the struggle of the Swiss against Austrian tyranny, which was published in 1819, and *A Few Days in Athens*, a kind of utopian treatise on Epicurean philosophy, which was published in 1822. The sisters landed in September 1818 in New York, and Frances made important connections with the help of the letters of introduction she had brought with her. *Altorf* was successfully staged at the Park Theatre in New York and brought her to the attention of notables such as Thomas Jefferson, and she was introduced to the family of John Garnett, a cultured and intellectual émigré, with whose daughters, Harriet and Julia, Frances formed a deep friendship. It was at this time that she became intellectually aware of and deeply troubled by the flaw in her beloved America—the disgrace of slavery.

Two years later, in May 1820, Frances returned to England after a residence in New York and stays in Philadelphia, New Jersey, Washington, DC, and Montreal. Back home, she wrote and published *Views of society and manners in America—in a series of letters from that country to a friend in England, during the years 1818, 1819, 1820* (1821; reprinted

1963), an enthusiastic and rambling travel account of her impressions of America and its institutions and practices, both political and social. She found the New World fundamentally a positive place, advanced far beyond the Old in terms of justice and freedom for all, and her book is a tribute to her idealized view of America's democratic society, with its politically astute citizens, and relatively more emancipated women. 'What country before', she asked in her book, 'was ever rid of so many evils?' (p. 83). The book, one of the first narratives from a tourist's point of view, brought her widespread attention.

After Frances returned to Europe she made the acquaintance of two notable and powerful older men: Jeremy Bentham and the marquis de Lafayette. With the first she strengthened her own innate ability to look critically at institutions. The second became an intimate friend and a major influence in her life. In September 1821 she made an extended visit to Lafayette's estate, La Grange, outside Paris. The marquis de Lafayette was 'the Hero of Two Worlds', a symbol of the liberty she wanted to bring to all the world. To Lafayette she developed an extreme devotion which ultimately became destructive, alienated his family, and brought scandal to her own person. The 26-year-old Frances became so devoted to the 64-year-old widower as to suggest marrying him or being adopted as his daughter; wiser than she, he refused both offers. Nevertheless, the friendship deepened, as she embarked on assembling materials for a life of the general.

In 1824 Frances and Camilla followed Lafayette to the United States. During this visit, in 1825, Frances began to focus more closely on the slavery issue. She had written a pamphlet called 'A plan for the gradual abolition of slavery in the United States without danger of loss to the citizens of the South'. She had visited Robert Owen, a successful textile manufacturer and freethinking socialist, who had just purchased Harmony, Indiana, for his own utopian experiments, and she conceived the idea for an experimental community like his, but one which would organize slaves instead of utopian colonists. Both of them wanted to establish the theory that character could be moulded by environment. But New Harmony's community had excluded black people. Frances Wright now yoked Owen's theories to ideas of emancipation. In December 1825 she purchased a large tract of land (640 acres) on the Wolf River in Tennessee and established Nashoba (the Chickasaw name for 'wolf'), a 'colony' of slaves who, to gain their freedom from her, would work out their purchase price in five years, during which time they would be given a basic education. In this preliminary stage of her struggle to solve racial issues in America, she envisioned eventually creating a biracial society in which the two races would live, separate but equal.

Frances Wright moved quickly to put her vision into practice and bought ten slaves (six men and four women). Eventually there were about thirty slaves, half of them children, working on as much as 1800 acres. Hard, punishing work began, clearing the land and building cabins. She hired people to help and even tried to convince the genteel Garnett sisters to join her. Her dramatic self-promoting idealism ran high at first: she described her life thus to Mary Shelley: 'I have made the hard earth my bed, the saddle of my horse my pillow, and have staked my life and fortune on an experiment having in view moral liberty and human improvement' (*Letters of Mary Wollstonecraft Shelley*, 2.172–5). However, problems developed which would result in the failure of her grand experiment. Inspired by Owen's 'Declaration of mental independence', she began a crusade against the marriage tie, an idea which brought her into direct opposition with the religious revivalism then sweeping the country, the so-called second 'great awakening'. Even more dangerously, she had conceived ideas about the appropriateness of miscegenation and the potential equality of black and white people, and about the evils of organized religion and private property.

There were even more fundamental problems at Nashoba. The land was second-rate and the climate very unhealthy. Anticipated financial support did not come, and the southern planters remained uninterested in either the principles or the economics of Frances Wright's experiment. Even her great model, New Harmony, was collapsing under labour and administrative problems. Arduous trips on horseback to and from New Harmony, and the fever-ridden climate, contributed to the serious weakening of her health. She turned Nashoba over to ten trustees, including Lafayette, Robert Owen, and one of Owen's sons, Robert Dale. In 1827 she returned to Europe with Robert Dale Owen to recuperate and left behind at Nashoba Camilla, who dreaded the Atlantic crossing. She hoped during this visit to recruit more freethinking liberals like herself. As she wrote to a potential recruit:

> I have devoted my time and fortune to laying the foundation of a society where affection shall form the only marriage, kind feelings and kind action the only religion, respect for the feelings and liberties of others the only restraint, and union of interest the bond of peace and security. (Woloch, 156)

That summer one of the Nashoba trustees, an eccentric Scottish overseer named James Richardson, published an article in *The Genius of Universal Emancipation* which revealed that miscegenation and sexual intercourse without marriage were openly accepted at Nashoba. Indeed, he himself had just formed a liaison with the teenage daughter of Mademoiselle Lalotte, a mixed-race schoolteacher from New Orleans, with several children. The scandal resulting from this publicity fatally damaged Frances Wright's cause. She was already having difficulty enlisting further European recruits: Mary Wollstonecraft Shelley, for one, declined, but declared Frances Wright to be 'the most wonderful and interesting woman I ever saw' (*Letters of Mary Wollstonecraft Shelley*, 2.13). Mrs Frances Trollope (1779–1863), however, was interested, prompted by her family's severe financial problems and the imminent break-up of her English home at Harrow. She also found appealing the idea of placing one of her sons in the school at Nashoba. She sailed with Frances Wright for Nashoba, taking three of her children and the French artist Auguste

Hervieu, who also would work in the school there. However, when she arrived (in December 1827) and saw the situation, she left within ten days, sailing for Cincinnati, where she would eventually settle and write her own travel book on America, *Domestic Manners of the Americans* (1832; reprinted 1949).

Nashoba was in desperate straits. Frances Wright finally had to accept its lack of potential to end the institution of slavery in America, or even to be a successful community of co-operative labour. The slaves had been judged indolent and flogging had been reintroduced. Clearly, it was time to move on. In her own words: 'Cooperation … has well nigh killed us all' (Eckhardt, 165). In 1830 she was to take the slaves (by then eighteen adults and sixteen children) to Haiti. With the end of Nashoba ended also the practical side of Frances Wright's idealism. She had lost half her fortune as well as her popular status in American society. Nevertheless, she remained undaunted and turned to a new area of social service. This time she would not work on utopian experiments in isolated areas of the country, but turned to writing and lecturing in the major cities of the east and midwest to promote her ideals. Still she continued to be obsessed with America as a land of unlimited possibilities. In June 1828 she joined Robert Dale Owen in New Harmony as co-editor of the *New Harmony Gazette*, renamed the *Free Enquirer*, which pledged a devotion 'to free, unbiased, and universal inquiry'.

Characteristically Frances Wright had now entered another area of new ground for women. With *Views of Society in America* she had written the first serious book by a woman about America. With the Nashoba experiment she had been the first woman to implement a plan of utopian living. Now she would be the first woman since colonial times to edit a general circulation American paper. Next, at her own expense, she planned an extensive lecture tour, and became the first woman to embark upon a series of public lectures before mixed audiences in America. In these public appearances she broke all the conventions of female decorum, dressing in a tunic and trousers, and wearing her hair cropped. As Frances Trollope wrote:

> That a lady of fortune, family, and education, whose youth had been passed in the most refined circles of private life, should present herself to the people as a public lecturer, would naturally excite surprise anywhere … but in America where women are guarded by a sevenfold shield of habitual insignificance it has caused an effect which can hardly be described. (Trollope, *Domestic Manners of the Americans*, 67–9)

Others were more harsh, and denounced her as a monster and a harlot. She was even attacked by the feminist Catherine Beecher:

> There she stands with brazen front and brawny arms, attacking the safeguards of all that is venerable and sacred in religion, all that is safe and wise in law, all that is pure and lovely in domestic virtue … I cannot conceive any thing in the shape of a woman, more intolerably offensive and disgusting. (Eckhardt, 250)

In her writings and in her public appearances Frances Wright never ceased to attack what were for her the great evils of American and European life: the corrupting power of wealth, the divisiveness and waste of organized religion, and the many abuses suffered by women (the legal disabilities of married women, the attitudes towards birth control, and the restrictions inherent in the pervasive 'cult of true womanhood'). While none of her remedies ever took root (state boarding-schools; the so-called 'guardianship system', which would separate children from parents; the abolition of private property and family life in general), she was nevertheless an important early voice on women's issues. Women reformers such as Elizabeth Cady Stanton and Susan B. Anthony read her work and were inspired by her courage, and thus her ideas later found more practical and substantive form in the work of other women writers and reformers.

By 1829 Frances Wright was back in New York, where she formed another pseudo-commune of free enquirers, in a former Baptist church that they later called the Hall of Science. There she sponsored lectures, debates, schooling in secularism, and a bookstore selling the works of Thomas Paine and Mary Wollstonecraft. She became influential in the working-class political movement in New York city. In July 1830 she sailed for Europe once again and settled in Paris. Between 1833 and 1836 she delivered numerous lectures on social questions, especially slavery and female suffrage. Then at the age of thirty-five, and in contradiction of her stated principles, she married Guillaume Sylvan Phiquepal-D'Arusmont (*b.* 1811), a French physician and educational reformer sixteen years her junior, whom she had met at New Harmony, and with whom she had already had a daughter. Subsequently they had a second daughter, who died before she was three months old and whose birth date was given to the elder child, Frances Sylva, a lie that was maintained to give her legitimacy. Frances Wright had an erratic relationship with both her husband and Sylva, and eventually separated from her husband. She divorced him in 1850 in Tennessee, and in 1851 in Ohio, but he retained custody of Sylva. Frances Wright's devotion to causes and abstract principles separated or alienated her in the end from all the major friendships and relationships of her life, including those with Lafayette, Robert Dale Owen, the Garnetts, and Mrs Trollope.

While Frances was away in Europe, the Hall of Science and the *Free Enquirer* failed. In the last decade or so of her life she was based in America (ultimately in Cincinnati), although she made several more Atlantic crossings, mostly for personal and financial reasons. She continued to lecture; railed at the banking system and at working conditions in New England factories; and began to develop the argument that a colony for black people should be established outside the United States. Her last published work was *England the Civilizer: her History Developed in its Principles* (1848), another utopian vision for a peaceful world, published anonymously, though its authorship was well known. Its central premise was that the world had been made the worse through the abuses of male power. The problem with governments was that they had been dominated by men who elevated force as a positive element. Women, instead, stressed 'the conservation, care, and happiness of the species' (Eckhardt, 279).

She also wrote her memoirs. She died in relative obscurity on 13 December 1852 in Cincinnati, at the age of fifty-seven, from complications following a fall on the ice the previous winter. She was buried in Spring Grove cemetery, Cincinnati. Her daughter later became a devout Episcopalian and opponent of women's suffrage.

As a practical reformer Frances Wright was a failure. But the goals which she enumerated for black people and for women were pursued by subsequent generations of reformers and eventually entered the mainstream of American social life. An erratic but brilliant social theorist, she identified crucial social issues years before society was able to address them. Although many of her own projects ultimately failed, and she endured social opprobrium, she left a considerable legacy to society in the realm of ideas.

HELEN HEINEMAN

Sources C. M. Eckhardt, *Fanny Wright: rebel in America* (1984) · E. T. James, J. W. James, and P. S. Boyer, eds., *Notable American women, 1607–1950: a biographical dictionary* (1971) · N. Woloch, *Women and the American experience* (1984) · M. A. Travis, 'Frances Wright: the other woman of early American feminism', *Women's Studies* (June 1993), 1–5 · W. R. Waterman, *Frances Wright* (1967) · *The letters of Mary Wollstonecraft Shelley*, ed. B. T. Bennett, 3 vols. (1980–88)
Archives L. Cong., papers · New Harmony Workingmen's Institute, New Harmony, Indiana, papers | Cincinnati Historical Society, Gholson-Kittredge MSS · Co-operative Union, Holyoake House, Manchester, letters to George Holyoake · Cornell University, Ithaca, New York, Theresa Wolfson MSS · Duke U., Percy Bysshe Shelley papers, letters · Harvard U., letters to Julia Garnett and Harriet Garnett · University of Chicago, Lafayette papers, letters · University of Illinois, Robert Owen papers, letters
Likenesses A. Hervieu?, portrait, L. Cong. · Nogel & Weingartner, engraving, Smithsonian Institution, Washington, DC · portrait, priv. coll.; repro. in H. Heineman, *Mrs. Trollope: the triumphant feminine in the nineteenth century* (1979), fig. 3

Wright, Francis Beresford (1806–1873), iron manufacturer, was born on 21 December 1806, probably in Derbyshire, the second son in the family of three sons and four daughters of John Wright (1758–1840) of Lenton Hall, Nottinghamshire, ironmaster, and his wife, Elizabeth. His father was co-founder of the iron manufacturing Butterley Company, and his mother was the daughter of another co-founder, Francis Beresford of Osmaston, near Ashbourne.

Little is known of Wright's early years, but in 1830, on the retirement of his father, he became the senior partner in Butterley, which he dominated for the next forty-three years. He applied himself to business with intense seriousness of purpose. 'Ad rem' was his family's motto. On 12 August 1830 Wright married Selina, daughter of Sir Henry FitzHerbert, baronet, of Tissington Hall, Derbyshire. They had five sons and six daughters.

The company prospered under Wright's direction, and by the time of his death Butterley was the biggest industrial concern in Derbyshire and one of the greatest in the country. The company had been valued in 1830 at £30,000; by 1858 its capital stood at £436,000. The original coal and iron concerns of Butterley were expanded, and engineering work was undertaken for the railways. The company constructed Vauxhall Bridge over the Thames, the railway bridge at Trent Junction, and the railway viaduct over the

Derwent. Perhaps Wright's success is best symbolized by the construction in 1869 of the roof of St Pancras Station, a 240 foot tied arch of cast iron, weighing 9000 tons, with no intermediate structure, probably then the largest single span of its kind in the world.

The outward sign of Wright's success was the building of a great country house, Osmaston Manor, outside Ashbourne, in 1846–9. Measuring 333 feet by 192 feet, it had stables for seventeen horses, rooms for twenty servants, a brewhouse, a bakehouse, and a central tower standing 150 feet high. It was said to be the first house since Roman times to have central heating: over 3 miles of piping were used but there was no chimney in the house itself. A hydraulic lift ran up the mansion's four storeys. It was the showpiece of the county. A parapet round the clock bore the significant words 'Work while it is Day'.

Wright was a high-minded evangelist who made Butterley into a model employer. The company organized a sick fund for its workers and built, at Ironville, a school for about two hundred of their children. Among Wright's many charitable actions was the building of the church of St Martin at Osmaston (because he disapproved of the high-church tendencies of the parish church) and the founding of Trent College in 1866, one of whose houses was named after Wright. A chapel there was built in his memory in 1875. His puritanical streak led him as lord mayor to attempt to ban the 'demoralizing pleasure fair' in Ashbourne and to outlaw Shrovetide football.

Francis Wright was a magistrate, high sheriff of Nottinghamshire (1842), a fine horseman, and a lover and planter of trees. He died on 24 February 1873 at Osmaston Manor and was buried in Osmaston parish church.

ROBERT PEARCE, *rev.*

Sources R. H. Mottram and C. Coote, *Through five generations: the history of the Butterley Company* (privately printed, 1949) · R. Christian, *Butterley Brick* (privately printed, 1990) · P. Riden, *The Butterley Company, 1790–1830* (1990) · private information (1993) · d. cert. · R. Pearce, *Francis Beresford Wright* (1998)
Likenesses portrait, repro. in R. Pearce, *Francis Beresford Wright* (1998), pl. 4
Wealth at death under £1,400,000: resworn probate, June 1874, CGPLA Eng. & Wales (1873)

Wright, George Newenham (1794/5–1877), writer and Church of England clergyman, was the son of John Thomas Wright MD, and was probably born in Dublin. He matriculated from Trinity College, Dublin, in 1809, was a scholar in 1812, and graduated BA in 1814 and MA in 1817. He took holy orders in 1818, and, after holding several curacies in Ireland, became rector of St Mary Woolnoth, London, and later master of Tewkesbury grammar school. He died of 'natural decay', at the age of eighty-two, on 24 March 1877 at 4 Pierrepont Street, Bath, where he lived with his son the Revd William Wright, the sole executor of his will. Nothing is known of his wife or the rest of his family.

From the 1820s to the 1840s Wright published many minor works on subjects ranging from the Greek language to biography and philosophy. The bulk, however, were topographical works including several on Ireland, two of which have illustrations by George Petrie. None was of lasting importance.

D. J. O'DONOGHUE, *rev.* ELIZABETH BAIGENT

Sources Allibone, *Dict.* · *BL cat.* · d. cert. · *CGPLA Eng. & Wales* (1878) · Foster, *Alum. Oxon.*
Wealth at death under £4000: probate, 9 April 1878, *CGPLA Eng. & Wales*

Wright [*née* Lowenfeld], **Helena Rosa** (1887–1982), family planning practitioner and sex therapist, was born in Tulse Hill Road, Brixton, London, on 17 September 1887, the elder daughter of Heinz (later Henry) Lowenfeld (1859–1931), a Polish-Jewish immigrant to Britain, who became a successful entrepreneur and theatre manager, and his wife, Alice Evens (*c.*1863–1930), daughter of a naval captain. Her sister was Margaret *Lowenfeld (1890–1973), later a distinguished child psychiatrist. The family soon moved to Lowndes Square, Knightsbridge, London, where they enjoyed a luxurious lifestyle.

Helena's parents were divorced in 1902 and the two girls initially lived with their mother, though continuing to visit Chrzanow, the Lowenfeld estate in Polish Austria. In girlhood Helena travelled widely within Europe, the Near East, and North America. Her mother's remarriage caused considerable tensions between them and led to a rapprochement between Helena and her father: she later took over the management of his businesses when he was caught on the continent by the outbreak of war in 1914.

At the age of six Helena stated that it was her ambition to become a doctor. Educated at the Froebel Educational Institute, West Kensington, London, then by governesses, and at Princess Helena College and High School for Girls, Ealing, London, her scholastic career was not remarkable until she went to Cheltenham Ladies' College from 1901 to 1907, whence she proceeded to the London School of Medicine for Women and the Royal Free Hospital in 1908. Her father bargained that if she gave the London season a year's try, he would withdraw his objections to her chosen career; she did so, but gladly returned to medicine.

Helena was active in the London Inter-Faculty Christian Union and the Student Christian Movement, and in 1910 became a student volunteer for the mission field. She qualified MRCS and LRCP in 1914 following an initial failure through disagreeing with the examiner, and obtained the MB, BS (London) the following year. After house surgeon posts in London at the Hampstead General Hospital and the Hospital for Sick Children, Great Ormond Street, she sought work in a military hospital. As a civilian junior surgeon at the Bethnal Green Hospital she met Henry Wardel Snarey Wright (whom she rechristened Peter) of the Royal Army Medical Corps, who became her husband on 17 August 1917. He too was a student volunteer planning to go to China. Neither was a proselytizing evangelist, but both were primarily concerned with medical practice and education: Helena had been baptized and confirmed in the Church of England but lacked sectarian enthusiasm.

Neither had any prior sexual experience and their difficulties in achieving mutual adjustment had a major

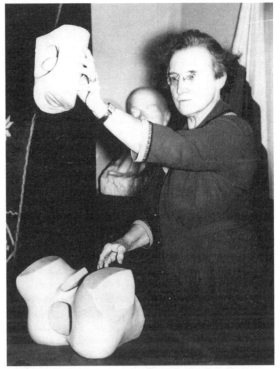

Helena Rosa Wright (1887–1982), by unknown photographer, 1957 [lecturing to midwives in Warsaw]

impact on Wright's later theories. She became pregnant almost at once and their eldest son, Henry Beric, was born on 17 June 1918 (they had another three sons but never the longed for daughter). Shortly afterwards the Wrights made the acquaintance of Marie Stopes, who had just published *Married Love*. Helena Wright read Stopes's contraceptive handbook, *Wise Parenthood*, in manuscript and 'took out all the nonsense'. In 1922 they went to Shandong Christian University, Jinan, under the auspices of the Society for the Propagation of the Gospel, Wright insisting on having her own recognized job. Their joint salary was subsidized by Henry Lowenfeld and Helena Wright's mother.

Following a furlough in London during 1927, they were unable to return to China due to the volatile political situation there. Wright therefore set up in private gynaecological practice and became involved in the already vigorous birth control movement. In 1930 she addressed the 1930 Lambeth conference of the Church of England: her almost hypnotic confidence in her own opinions persuaded the bishops to give modified approval to the use of contraceptives within marriage. Wright was active in the National Birth Control Association (co-ordinating the work of the existing birth control organizations) from its inception in 1930. As chief medical officer at North Kensington Women's Welfare Centre, London (a post she held for thirty years), she initiated training programmes for doctors and other health professionals.

In private practice Wright additionally evolved an early and pioneering form of sex therapy, on lines which can be deduced from *The Sex Factor in Marriage* (1930). These ideas were extended, but not modified, in *More about the Sex Factor in Marriage* (1947). Although still of her time in envisaging men as initiators, Wright argued the necessity for, and possibility of, women taking responsibility for their own arousal and satisfaction. Exhorting them to will themselves into wanting to feel sexual pleasure, she advocated their familiarizing themselves by sight and touch with their genital organs. She emphasized the importance of clitoral stimulation, regarding the clitoral orgasm not as a dangerous diversion on the road to what, following Freud, was considered to be the full and mature vaginal version, but a necessary gateway towards that end.

During the Second World War the War Office ignored Wright's concerns about contraceptive instruction for servicewomen. In 1948 she was involved with the Cheltenham Congress on Population, leading to the establishment of the International Planned Parenthood Federation (IPPF) in 1952. This initiated a new range of international activities, both as treasurer, later chairman, of the IPPF medical committee, and on educational forays to India, Japan, and Poland. On these she was accompanied by 'Dr Wright's daughter', a life-size flesh-coloured plastic model of the female pelvis and thighs, for demonstrations, of her own design; 'mirth in the Patent Office' meant that it was never patented.

While in principle objecting to abortion as a failure of birth control, Wright arranged abortions prior to the 1967 act, and publicly stated her views, despite being subjected to a police enquiry in 1947. She also arranged the adoption of unwanted illegitimate babies. Her rather cavalier attitude to the legislation concerning such third-party adoptions brought her into conflict with local authorities and adoption agencies, and she was prosecuted in 1968. Pleading guilty, she received an absolute discharge.

Although committed to the cause of women, and seeing women doctors in family planning clinics as ideally mother figures, Wright addressed her patients very much as a doctor, and was not perceived by either patients or associates as particularly feminine: indeed many found her intimidating. She had strong convictions about the desirability of premarital experience and extramarital relationships, and these were stated explicitly in her final published work, *Sex and Society: a New Code of Sexual Behaviour* (1968). Wright had several long-standing relationships, including one with the architect Oliver *Hill, whom she had known since childhood, and another with the historian (Kenneth) Bruce *McFarlane, who became an accepted member of the family, but these never endangered her marriage. Wright was described as short and rather stocky, with bright eyes behind pince-nez, and unconcerned about dress. Her determined and dominating character was much remarked upon, but so was her considerable warmth and sympathy.

Although superannuated from her appointment at North Kensington in 1960 Wright continued to teach at the Walworth Women's Welfare Centre and the Marie Stopes Memorial Clinic. She provided contraceptive advice to women prisoners in Holloway, and was also involved in drama for male prisoners in Wormwood Scrubs. In 1972 (aged eighty-five) she cut down her working week to three days and in 1975 passed on her practice, having seen 20,000 patients, exclusive of clinic practice.

Wright was interested in astrology, the paranormal, spiritual healing, and extra-sensory perception, the last being one of her few points of contact with her sister. Her hobbies included painting, and she travelled widely both professionally and for pleasure until an advanced age. Predeceased by her sister, husband, and second son, Christopher, she died on 21 March 1982 in the Royal Free Hospital, London (where to her gratification her granddaughter was a medical student), after an operation for gallstones.

LESLEY A. HALL

Sources B. Evans, *Freedom to choose: the life and work of Dr Helena Wright, pioneer of contraception* (1984) · *Medical Directory* (1962) · *CGPLA Eng. & Wales* (1982)
Archives Wellcome L., papers | BL, corresp. with Marie Stopes, Add. MS 58567 · Magd. Oxf., corresp. with K. B. McFarlane · Wellcome L., Barbara Evans and Family Planning Association archives | SOUND BBC WAC
Likenesses photograph, 1957, Wellcome L. [*see illus.*] · photographs, Wellcome L., Family Planning Association archives · photographs, repro. in Evans, *Freedom to choose*
Wealth at death £26,908: probate, 25 May 1982, *CGPLA Eng. & Wales*

Wright, Ichabod Charles (1795–1871), translator, was born on 11 April 1795 at Mapperley Hall, Nottinghamshire, the eldest of the three sons and ten daughters of Ichabod Wright (1767–1862), banker and freeman of Nottingham, and Harriet Maria (d. 1843), daughter of Benjamin Day of Yarmouth and Norwich. His grandfather Ichabod Wright (1700–1777) was originally an ironmonger of Nottingham, but in 1761 founded the bank in Long Row there.

Wright was educated at Eton College (1808–14) and at Christ Church, Oxford, matriculating on 22 April 1814. He graduated BA (with second-class honours) in 1817 and MA in 1820, and held an open fellowship at Magdalen from 1819 to 1825. On 21 December 1825 he married Theodosia (1806–1895), daughter of Thomas Denman, first Lord Denman. That same year he became joint manager of the bank at Nottingham and devoted his best energies to his business and to the theory of banking, about which he published a number of pamphlets.

Between 1830 and 1840, however, Wright gave his leisure to the study of Italian literature, producing a metrical translation of the *Divina commedia*. It was published originally in three instalments, dedicated respectively to Lord Brougham, Archbishop Howley, and Lord Denman, 'all ardent admirers of Dante' (the translator further acknowledged special encouragement and help from Panizzi and from Count Marioni). The first instalment, *The Inferno of Dante Translated into English Rhyme: with an Introduction and Notes* (1833 and 1841), was commended by *The Athenaeum* for its exactitude and *The Edinburgh* entreated Wright to proceed; but the rival *Quarterly*, 'with every disposition to encourage any gentleman in an elegant pursuit', conceived it to be its duty to ask 'how far (Cary's volumes being in every collection) it was worth Mr. Wright's while to undertake a new version of Dante'. What little advantage, the reviewer concluded, Wright might have gained as to manner was counterbalanced by losses on the side of matter (*QR*, July 1833, 449). *The Purgatorio, Translated into English Rhyme* (1836 and 1840) was, however, generally thought to have increased Wright's reputation, and it was followed in 1840 by *The Paradise*.

The three portions were published together in 1845 as *The Vision and Life of Dante*, and reissued in Bohn's Illustrated Library (1854 and 1861), with thirty-four illustrations on steel after Flaxman. Wright's version, which derived much benefit from the commentary (1826) of Gabriele Rossetti, is generally admitted to be accurate and scholarly, although he adopts the six-line stanza in preference to the *terza rima* of the original.

After an interval of nineteen years Wright issued the first part of his *The Iliad of Homer, Translated into English Blank Verse* (1859, 1864). The blank verse was good without being striking, and Matthew Arnold wrote in his lectures *On Translating Homer* (1861) that Wright's version, repeating in the main the merits and defects of Cowper's version, as Sotheby's repeated those of Pope's version, lacked, 'I must be forgiven for saying so, any proper reason for existing' (Arnold, *Homer*, 42). This drew from the translator *A letter to the dean of Canterbury on the Homeric lectures of Matthew Arnold, esq., professor of poetry in the University of Oxford* (1864). Wright poked fun, not unsuccessfully, at the professor of poetry's *ex cathedra* English hexameters, and this reflection on the chair of poetry at the ancient university elicited from Arnold (in the preface to *Essays in Criticism*, vi–xv) his notable apostrophe to Oxford, 'adorable dreamer', and his appeal to Wright to pardon a vivacity doomed to be silenced in the imminent future by the 'magnificent roaring of the young lions of the "Daily Telegraph"'.

In addition to his versions of Dante and Homer, by which alone he is remembered, Wright published *A Selection of Psalms in Verse* (1867), *Thoughts on the Currency* (1841), *The Evils of the Currency* (1847, 6th edn 1855), an exposition of Sir Robert Peel's Bank Charter Act of 1844, and *The War and our Resources* (1855). His poems were printed privately in 1873.

While Wright's two-rhyme version of Dante's *terza rima* was little read after the end of the nineteenth century, in his own time his translation of the *Commedia* was undoubtedly influential. It led to a number of later attempts to render Dante's triple rhyme in English, and it helped to establish the principle of literality in translation practice.

Ichabod Charles Wright died on 14 October 1871 at Heathfield Hall, Burwash, Sussex, the residence of his eldest son. THOMAS SECCOMBE, rev. ALISON MILBANK

Sources M. Arnold, *Essays in criticism* (1865) · M. Arnold, *On translating Homer: three lectures given at Oxford*, new edn (1905) · G. F. Cunningham, *The divine comedy in English: a critical bibliography*, 1 (1965) · *QR*, 49 (1833) · V. J. de Sua, *Dante into English* (1964) · I. C. Wright, *Dante, translated into English verse*, rev. edn (1866) · *The Times* (18 Oct 1871) · *The Times* (23 Oct 1871) · Ward, *Men of the reign* · Burke, *Gen. GB* (1965) · Walford, *County families* (1871) · BL cat. · *National union catalog*, Library of Congress · P. Toynbee, *Dante in English literature*, 2 (1909) · J. P. Briscoe, *A Nottingham translator of Dante and Homer* (1901) · Foster, *Alum. Oxon., 1715–1886* · d. cert.

Archives U. Leeds, Brotherton L., corresp.

Likenesses C. Turner, mezzotint (after E. U. Eddis), BM, NPG · ink drawing, Castle Art Gallery, Nottingham

Wealth at death under £20,000: probate, 23 Nov 1871, *CGPLA Eng. & Wales*

Wright, James (*bap.* **1644**, *d.* **1716/17**), antiquary and author, was probably born at Yarnton, Oxfordshire, where he was baptized on 12 May 1644, the eldest son of Abraham *Wright (1611–1690), clergyman and author, and his wife, Jane (*bap.* 1623, *d.* 1645), daughter of James Stone. He did not study at any university but became a student of New Inn, London, in 1667, migrating on 14 November 1670 to the Middle Temple, by which society he was called to the bar on 14 May 1675.

Living and working as a lawyer in London, Wright loved country diversions and regularly visited his father at Oakham, Rutland, as well as the village of Manton, of which he acquired the manor in 1683. Wright was an engaging man of letters: a translator, a poet whose conventional poetry had genuine charm, an antiquary, an essayist, and a historian of the Jacobean and Caroline stage. He possessed valuable manuscripts, being 'perhaps one of the first collectors of Old Plays since [William] Cartwright' (Warton, 601). Unfortunately, most of his collections were consumed in the fire of the Middle Temple of 1678. Among them was a sixteenth-century transcript of John Leland's 'Itinerary' made before the original manuscript was damaged (*Remarks*, 2.227).

Wright published most of his writings anonymously. He refused to send Anthony Wood a list of his works for the *Athenae Oxonienses*, regarding him as 'an injudicious Writer' (S. G. W.). Yet about 1710 Wright entrusted Thomas Hearne with a list of his publications, as appears from a manuscript entry by Hearne, dated 1719, in Richard Rawlinson's copy of Wright's *Poem … on the … Ruins in St Paul's Cathedral*. According to Hearne, Wright translated *Sales epigrammatum: being the Choycest Distichs of Martials Fourteen Books of Epigrams* (1663). This volume, possibly compiled by his father, was dedicated to his lifelong friend Sir William Bromley (1664–1732), tory speaker of the House of Commons and secretary of state, by 'James Wright M. Arts'. However, as Wright had no degree, this ascription remains puzzling. Wright is also credited with translations of *Thyestes: a Tragedy Translated out of Seneca* (1674), and a guidebook, *A New Description of Paris* (1687).

Wright's first original work described St Paul's after the great fire: *A Poem, being an Essay on the Present Ruins in St Paul's Cathedral* (1668). Poems on Wren's rebuilding of the cathedral were published later: *Three Poems* (1697) and *Phoenix Paulina* (1709). Wright became one of England's pioneer county historians with his main antiquarian work, *The History and Antiquities of the County of Rutland* (1684). In the preface, he thanked the royalist Sir Wingfield Bodenham of Ryhall for the use of his collections and mentioned the encouragement he had received from the antiquary William Dugdale. Nine pages of *Additions* appeared in 1687, and *Farther Additions, with a View of Burley-*

on-the-Hill (eight pages, in verse) in 1714. Wright's only political publication followed soon after his *Rutland*, namely *A Compendious View of the Late Tumults and Troubles in this Kingdom* (1685), a succinct account of the Popish Plot. In addition to his own work, Wright prepared an epitome in English of Dugdale's *Monasticon Anglicanum* (1693), dedicated to Sir William Bromley.

Wright was a versatile writer with a special interest in the theatre. 'During the fluctuations of government, and afterwards', wrote Thomas Warton, 'he was attached to the principles of monarchy in their most extensive comprehension; and from this circumstance he might have also derived a predilection for the theatre, which he had seen suppressed by the republicans' (Warton, 603). His father's royalism and taste for drama may also have influenced him. His interest was first revealed in such pieces as *Country Conversations … Chiefly of the Modern Comedies* (1694). It was followed by *Historia histrionica: an Historical Account of the English Stage* (1699). This account was, by William Warburton's advice, incorporated as a preface in Robert Dodsley's *Select Collection of Old Plays*, vol. 11 (1744). It assumes the form of a dialogue between Lovewit and Truman, an old cavalier, who discourses amiably upon playhouses and actors (such as John Lowin, Thomas Pollard, Joseph Taylor, and Ellyaerdt Swanston) of the period before the civil war. The work has been republished regularly and is considered to be well-informed (Bentley, 5.53).

Wright was a moderate tory. Hearne recorded that he had converted to Catholicism, being told 'that he continued always so from his first turning, which was I hear in K. Charles IInd's time'. In 1717 Hearne added that 'at the beginning of the Revolution he would have been a Preacher, had he not declined the Oaths, & lay under Suspicion of being a Catholick' (*Remarks*, 4.252, 6.70). This information is not confirmed by other sources. Wright never married and he died in his chambers in the Middle Temple in late December 1716 or early January 1717; the cause of his death is unknown.   THEODOR HARMSEN

Sources J. Simmons, 'James Wright', *English county historians*, ed. J. Simmons (1978), 44–55 · J. Wright, *The history and antiquities of the county of Rutland* (1684); repr. (1973) · *Remarks and collections of Thomas Hearne*, ed. C. E. Doble and others, 11 vols., OHS, 2, 7, 13, 34, 42–3, 48, 50, 65, 67, 72 (1885–1921) · T. Warton, ed., *Poems upon several occasions, English, Italian, and Latin, with translations* (1785), 601–4 · S. G. W. [S. G. Wright], 'A critic of Anthony Wood', *Bodleian Quarterly Record*, 7 (1932–4), 176–8 · G. E. Bentley, *The Jacobean and Caroline stage*, 7 vols. (1941–68), vols. 2, 5–6 · PRO, PROB 11/555, fol. 74–5 · Yarnton parish register, Oxfordshire county archives · Bodl. Oxf., MSS Rawl. letters 12, 18 · Wright–T. Hearne correspondence, 1709–12, Bodl. Oxf., MSS Rawl. D. 1166, D. 1170 · Bodl. Oxf., MSS Tanner 26, fol. 41; 456, fol. 36 · C. T. Martin, ed., *Minutes of parliament of the Middle Temple*, 4 vols. (1904–5) · H. A. C. Sturgess, ed., *Register of admissions to the Honourable Society of the Middle Temple, from the fifteenth century to the year 1944*, 3 vols. (1949) · Wood, *Ath. Oxon.*, new edn, 2.844; 4.269, 278 · VCH *Rutland*, 2.5–27, 79 · C. Phythian-Adams, 'Leicestershire and Rutland', *English county histories: a guide*, ed. C. R. J. Currie and C. P. Lewis (1994), 228–45 · *A catalogue of the library of … James Wright … and an eminent physician, lately deceas'd* (1719) [sale catalogue, Woodwards, 13 May 1719] · T. Tanner, *Notitia monastica, or, A short history of the religious houses in England and Wales* (1695) · E. Solly, 'St. Paul's Cathedral', *N&Q*, 6th ser., 10 (1884), 36 · 'Wright, Abraham', *The general biographical dictionary*, ed. A. Chalmers, new edn (1812–17) · Mrs B. Stapleton, *Three Oxfordshire parishes: a history of Kidlington, Yarnton and Begbroke*, OHS, 24 (1893) · Allibone, *Dict.* · W. C. Hazlitt, 'Stipendable lachrymae', *N&Q*, 3rd ser., 2 (1862), 469

Archives BL, notes of cases and other legal matters, Add. MSS 22609–22610 · BL, *History of Rutland*, Add. MSS 46378A, 46382A · BL, Add. MS 29569, fol. 346 · Bodl. Oxf., comments on Anthony Wood's *Athenae Oxonienses*, miscellaneous collections of Abraham Wright, MS Eng. misc. e. 82, fols. 43–9 | BL, Abraham Wright's commonplace book, Add. MS 22608 [with, on folio 1, James Wright's signature] · Bodl. Oxf., corresp. with T. Hearne, MSS Rawl. Lett. 12, Lett. 18; MSS Rawl. D. 1166, D. 1170 · Bodl. Oxf., letters to A. Wood, MSS Tanner 26, fol. 41; 456, fol. 36 [Wood to Wright, see Clark, ed., *Wood's life and times*, vol. 3, p. 350]

Wealth at death see will, PRO, PROB 11/555, fols. 74–5; *Remarks and collections*, ed. Doble and others

Wright, Sir James, first baronet (1716–1785), colonial governor, was born on 8 May 1716, the fourth son of Robert Wright, lawyer, and Isabella Pitts, who lived on Russell Street, Bloomsbury, London. About 1730 the family moved to Charlestown, South Carolina, where Robert Wright served as chief justice of the colony. James studied law and in 1739 acted as the colony's attorney-general. In 1741 he furthered his education at Gray's Inn in London. He married Sarah Maidman (d. 1763) of Charlestown in February 1742. They had eight children: James, Alexander, Mary, Charles, Ann, Isabella, Elizabeth, and Charlotte. Wright continued to serve in an acting capacity until 29 May 1747, when his appointment as attorney-general was made official. He was back in London in 1757 as South Carolina's agent to parliament. On 13 May 1760, while in London, he was appointed lieutenant-governor of Georgia to replace the ailing Henry Ellis, Georgia's second royal governor. Upon Ellis's resignation Wright assumed the governorship in April 1761.

The French and Indian War was in its last phase when Wright reached Georgia in November 1760. He benefited from Ellis's astute management of government and adroit American Indian diplomacy. Wright presided over the 1763 American Indian congress at Augusta, attended by three other southern governors and some 900 American Indians, and secured a treaty opening the land between the Savannah and Ogeechee rivers for settlement. The treaty of Paris in the same year extended Georgia's boundaries south to the St Marys River and west to the Mississippi River. By prohibiting colonial settlement west of the Appalachian mountains, the royal proclamation of 1763 funnelled frontiers people into the Georgia backcountry. The lawless element among the newcomers, referred to as 'Crackers' by Governor Wright, soon trespassed on American Indian territory across the Ogeechee boundary. Wright secured a new treaty in 1773, at which time the 1763 proclamation line had been effectively abandoned, that opened additional land in north-western Georgia and behind the coastal counties. These acquisitions help explain Wright's popularity in the backcountry, even as merchants in the more heavily populated low country protested against parliamentary taxation of internal American trade.

The protests began in 1765 following the imposition of

Sir James Wright, first baronet (1716–1785), attrib. Andrea Soldi

the Stamp Act. Georgia was the only colony of the thirteen which later rebelled in which stamps were effectively sold. In the wake of the Stamp Act, an opposition party gained strength in the Georgia Commons house of assembly. At the same time a divisive issue concerned four southern parishes created out of the territory ceded to Georgia by the treaty of Paris of 1763. In the general discussion about taxation and representation it occurred to the house that the new parishes were in fact taxed, but had no representatives in the assembly. Wright agreed to issue writs of election, but insisted on waiting for approval from London. In 1770 the impatient house refused to pass a tax bill because the four parishes were still not represented. Thereupon Wright dissolved the assembly. The belated arrival of official permission ended this controversy, but new issues arose. The 1771 Commons house elected Noble Wimberly Jones its speaker. Because Jones had been a leader of the opposition to British taxation, Wright disapproved the election. The house passed a resolution to the effect that Wright's action constituted a subversion of the rights of the people. Wright dissolved the assembly again and then left for England, where on 5 December 1772 he was awarded a baronetcy for faithful service. James Habersham, as acting governor in Georgia, inherited the quarrel with the Commons regarding the election of speaker.

In London, Wright secured approval of the pending 1773 cession of American Indian land, and most Georgians welcomed his return in February 1773. Dissatisfaction over the surrender of their hunting lands as a result of the treaty of Augusta in June 1773, and anger at the encroaching Georgians, caused young warriors of the Creek nation to attack outlying settlements in the winter of 1773–4. The revolutionary movement was stilled as Georgians looked to Wright in the crisis. The governor persuaded the other southern governors to impose a ban on trade with the hostile American Indians, who relied heavily on British manufactured guns and ammunition. The strategy brought the headmen of the Creek to Savannah to plead for a resumption of trade. It was a critical moment for Wright and for Georgia. If he sided with the settlers and demanded more land west of the Ogeechee River, he would anger the powerful merchants who depended upon American Indian trade and feared losing the trade to Mobile and Pensacola in British West Florida. Wright decided not to ask for land in his October treaty with the Creek and merely reopened trade in return for their promise to punish their guilty people, and as a result he lost his support in the backcountry. Land-hungry settlers viewed the royal government as an obstacle to their ambitions. Leaders from the western parishes proceeded to form an alliance with the low-country radicals.

A provincial congress met on 18 January 1775, and elected delegates to the Second Continental Congress in Philadelphia, but because Georgians remained divided, the delegates declined to attend. News of the opening battles of the American War of Independence at Lexington and Concord reached Georgia on 10 May 1775 and accelerated the revolutionary movement. Georgia's second provincial congress, meeting in Savannah on 5 July 1775, adopted the continental association banning trade with Britain, set up local committees to enforce it, and appointed a council of safety as its executive agency. Wright asked to be allowed to return to England, acknowledging that he had lost control of the colony. When British ships appeared in the Savannah River in January 1776, Wright was placed under house arrest by the revolutionary council of safety. He managed to escape to the *Scarborough* and return to England. In London, Wright joined the exiled governor of South Carolina, Lord William Campbell, in a lobbying effort for a military campaign in the south. They argued that thousands of loyal persons in the interior waited only for the presence of British troops to declare for the king. When the war in the north reached a stalemate, the British ministry decided to try the southern strategy. A British army under Lieutenant-Colonel Archibald Campbell landed below Savannah on 28 December 1778, quickly overwhelmed that city's defences, and then marched to Augusta to liberate the backcountry. The expected pro-British American Indians did not materialize, and patriot reinforcements forced Campbell to retire from Augusta after a two-week occupation. A British victory at Briar Creek below Augusta on 3 March 1779 meant that royal government could be re-established in coastal Georgia. Thus Georgia became the only one of the thirteen rebellious colonies to be restored to British rule.

Governor Wright resumed his post on 14 June 1779 and convened a royal assembly. In September the sudden arrival off the Georgia coast of a massive French force allied to the American patriots, and commanded by Charles Henri, Count D'Estaing, threatened the restored government. General Benjamin Lincoln's revolutionary army joined the French in a siege of Savannah. The much smaller British contingent in Savannah, commanded by General Augustine Prevost, withstood the siege and turned back the allied 'grand assault' on the British lines on 9 October 1779. The Polish volunteer Count Casimir Pulaski was killed in this assault. A British army under General Henry Clinton took advantage of the victory by landing on the coast near Savannah, and forcing the surrender of Charlestown on 12 May 1780, and for a time it seemed that both Georgia and South Carolina would be restored to British rule. Governor Wright warned the ministry against leaving the two provinces defenceless when Charles, second Earl Cornwallis, marched his army into North Carolina and Virginia. Wright's fears were realized when, instead of following Cornwallis, the American general Nathanael Greene decided to take the isolated British outposts in the south. Troops under Lieutenant-Colonel ('Light-horse Harry') Lee recaptured Augusta in June 1780, and General Anthony Wayne besieged Savannah. Despite Wright's protests, the British military decided to surrender Savannah in July 1782. Governor Wright, once more an exile, departed with the troops on 10 July 1782.

In London, Wright headed a commission charged with ascertaining compensation for property losses by loyalists. He estimated his own losses at £33,000 sterling, but received in return only an annual pension of £500. He died at his home in Fludyer Street, Westminster, on 20 November 1785, and was buried in the north cloister of Westminster Abbey on 28 November. In his will he named his sons James and Alexander his executors, together with his friends William Knox and Archibald Hamilton. James succeeded him as baronet.

Wright's importance lies in his effective administration of Georgia during his twenty-two-year tenure in office. Georgians gradually learned to govern themselves. The white population increased from an estimated 5000 in 1752 to 50,000 in 1776. There were only a few blacks in Georgia at the beginning of the royal period: by 1776 the number had increased to about 18,000. For better and for worse Governor Wright set the example for Georgia's rising gentry in the acquisition of lands and slaves for rice and indigo production. He accumulated eleven plantations worked by 523 slaves. By the time of the American War of Independence plantation slavery was securely established in Georgia.   EDWARD J. CASHIN

Sources K. Coleman, 'James Wright', *Georgians in profile: historical essays in honour of Ellis Merton Coulter*, ed. H. Montgomery (1958), 40–60 • K. Coleman, *Colonial Georgia: a history* (1976) • A. D. Candler and others, eds., *The colonial records of the state of Georgia*, 26 vols. in 28 (1904–16); ongoing, with some vols. rev. (1970–) • E. J. Cashin, 'Sowing the wind: Governor Wright and the Georgia backcountry on the eve of the revolution', *Forty years of diversity: essays on colonial Georgia*, ed. H. H. Jackson and P. Spalding (1984), 183–97 • B. Wood, *Slavery in colonial Georgia, 1730–1775* (Athens, Georgia, 1984) • *DNB* • K. Coleman and C. S. Gurr, eds., *Dictionary of Georgia biography*, 2 vols. (Athens, GA, 1983)

Archives Duke U., Perkins L., papers • Georgia Historical Society, Savannah, letter-book and papers • PRO, corresp., 30/55 | Staffs. RO, Dartmouth papers, reports to Lord Dartmouth • U. Mich., Clements L., American Series, corresp. with General Thomas Gage
Likenesses attrib. A. Soldi, oils; Sothebys, 10 June 1953, lot 91 [*see illus.*]
Wealth at death claimed losses of £33,000 because of the American war; principal asset was £500 pension in compensation: Coleman, 'James Wright'; will, PRO, PROB 11/1141, sig. 254

Wright, Sir James, first baronet (*bap.* 1717, *d.* 1804), diplomatist and art collector, was baptized on 18 January 1717, probably in Coventry, the son of Thomas Wright of Coventry and his wife, Mary, daughter of Sir John Huband. He attended Mr Legiat's school in Warwick, Winchester College (1730–34), and Trinity College, Cambridge, whence he matriculated in 1735. In December 1754 Wright married Catherine Stapleton (1732/3–1802), who had inherited £30,000 from her father, Sir William Stapleton, fourth baronet, of Greys Court in Oxfordshire.

Soon after their marriage the Wrights went on a long European tour. By December 1758 they were in Venice, where Catherine gave birth to a stillborn child, then travelled in Italy for the next eighteen months. In Venice they gained the friendship of Lady Mary Wortley Montagu, who introduced them to her daughter and son-in-law, Lord and Lady Bute. Wright's ensuing friendship with Bute lasted until 1778 when he and Dr Anthony Addington tried to effect a political alliance between Bute and Chatham. After returning to England, they visited Bath in the autumn of 1760 and then settled in London. They became friendly with the king and queen and in 1762 Wright was appointed a groom of the bedchamber, a post he held for many years. He was knighted on 3 July 1766 on his appointment as British minister to Venice. He and his wife arrived in Venice on 13 September, and were welcomed by the British in Venice. Sir Lucas Pepys wrote of 'Our Minister at Venice, Sir James Wright, Nephew to Lord Northington; who is as obliging and good-natured as his wife is well-bred and agreeable' (Gaussen, 1.355). Wright's embassy seems to have been characterized by connoisseurship and ill health rather than by any diplomatic distinction. He had started amassing his art collection on his previous visit to Venice and added to it works by Venetian artists and by early Renaissance painters, including Ghirlandaio. Wright returned to England to recuperate in August 1769 and resumed his post in Venice two years later. He was created a baronet on 12 October 1772 and was relieved of his embassy in September 1774, over a year since he had returned to England once again.

Wright owned properties in London, Essex, Devon, and Hampshire and he established a 'patent artificial slate manufactory' near his Ray House estate in Essex. After acquiring the original patent in 1778 he added a 'process' from Venice, that was intended to make the slate noxious to all vermin, as he described in one of his pamphlets on the subject. The manufactory was successful for some years, both in England and abroad.

The illness of their only son, George (1770–1810), occasioned the Wrights' last tour of Italy. In 1790 Lady Wright left for Venice with George, accompanied by the artist Maria Cosway and Maria's brother George Hadfield. Sir James followed later with their two adopted daughters and George's tutor. A keen gardener as well as collector, Wright bought plants, antiques, and art on this tour, and commissioned other works of art, including Hadfield's Praeneste watercolours. He was a perceptive patron; his architects included the Adam brothers for Ray House and Philip Norris and John Papworth for Ray Lodge, built for his son in 1796–7, and he commissioned family portraits from Matthew William Peters, Robert Fagan, Joshua Reynolds, and Johann Zoffany.

Little is known of the Wrights after they returned from Italy in 1793. They lived in Bath for some years before Lady Wright's death on or about 6 January 1802; Sir James died at their son's house in Bathford on 8 March 1804. George Wright, who had married Rebecca Maclane, of Berkshire, in 1796 and had a daughter, Ruperta (b. 1799), sold most of his inheritance after his father's will was proved on 17 March 1804. His father's artificial slate business and his stone pipe-cutting in Ireland failed under George's management. JULIA KING

Sources J. King, 'An ambassador's house in Essex', *Georgian Group Journal*, 7 (1997), 117–29 · [W. Combe], *An heroic epistle to Sir James Wright* [n.d.], 12–13 · A. C. C. Gaussen, *A later Pepys: the correspondence of Sir William Weller Pepys … master in chancery, 1758–1825*, 1 (1904), 1.335, 354n., 355 · sale catalogues, Christies (8–12 June 1804) · Sir John Soane's Museum, London, Adam volumes, 22/273; 41/80–95; 10/159 · W. L. Speirs, 'Topographical index to the collection of Adam drawings', in A. T. Bolton, *The architecture of Robert and James Adam* (1922), 1–92, 26, 92 · D. Lysons, *The environs of London*, 4 (1796), 275, n. 22, 287; suppl., 365 · *The complete letters of Lady Mary Wortley Montagu*, ed. R. Halsband, 3 (1967), 202, 215–16, 239–40, 259 · D. B. Horn, *British diplomatic representatives, 1689–1789* (1932), 85 · *VCH Essex*, 2.417; 6.342 · Venn, *Alum. Cant.*, 1/4.473 · GM, 1st ser., 74 (1804), 284 · J. Ingamells, ed., *A dictionary of British and Irish travellers in Italy, 1701–1800* (1997), 1022 · will, PRO, PROB 11/1406, sig. 222
Likenesses M. W. Peters, group portrait (with family) · J. Reynolds, double portrait (with Lady Wright) · J. Zoffany, double portrait (with Lady Wright)

Wright, John (*bap.* 1568, *d.* 1605), conspirator, was a grandson of John Wright of Ploughland Hall, Yorkshire, who had been seneschal to Henry VIII. His father, Robert (*d.* 1594), married as his second wife Ursula Rudston, daughter of Nicholas and Jane Rudston of Hayton. Their two sons, John and **Christopher Wright** (1570?–1605), were both members of the group of Catholic gentlemen who sought a Spanish invasion of England in the last years of Elizabeth's reign, and who later were conspirators in the Gunpowder Plot. A sister of John and Christopher, Martha, married Thomas Percy, another gunpowder conspirator.

John Wright was baptized at Welwick, Yorkshire, on 16 January 1568. The Jesuit Oswald Tesimond, who may have been at school with him, describes Wright as courageous and an excellent swordsman, blessed with a 'good physique and sound constitution. Rather on the tall side, his features were pleasing. He was somewhat taciturn in manner, but very loyal to his friends, even if his friends were few' (Edwards, 63–4). Like Guy Fawkes, he and his brother were educated at St Peter's School, York. As notorious

recusants, both were placed under arrest during the queen's illness in 1596, along with their future co-conspirators Robert Catesby and Francis Tresham, and the same men were imprisoned for their part in the Essex rebellion in February 1601. All this suggests principled resistance to the regime and its religion of long standing, but according to another Jesuit, John Gerard, John became a Catholic only in 1601, in the traumatic aftermath of treason and imprisonment. He now proved himself 'staid and of good sober carriage', and his house at Twigmore, Lincolnshire, was noted as a resort for missionary priests (Morris, 59). Certainly, his fatal friendship for Catesby never faltered. During Elizabeth's last illness in March 1603 the brothers were once again imprisoned, along with their charismatic cousin and other like-minded associates, on the grounds of state security, William Camden describing them all contemptuously as men 'hunger-starved for innovation' (Smith, 347–8).

Early in 1604 Catesby told Wright and Thomas Winter of his plans to destroy king and parliament. There is little sign of doubt or scruple thereafter. Basing himself and his family at Lapworth, in Warwickshire, John was an active and committed member of the conspiracy's inner ring, visiting his colleagues and stabling horses at Lapworth in the months before November 1605. He fled London with Catesby upon the discovery of the treason, flinging off his cloak to ride faster, and participated in the poorly supported 'midlands rebellion' which followed. The remnants of the rebel force made a stand at Holbeach, Stephen Littleton's house in Staffordshire, but by then they had lost the will to fight, and when Sir Richard Walsh, the sheriff of Worcestershire, attacked the house on the morning of 8 November there was little resistance. Catesby, Percy, and both brothers Wright were mortally wounded, three of them, it seems, the victims of one marksman, John Street of Worcester. The dying men were stripped of their clothing and neglected by the sheriff's men, or at least by the 'baser sort' among them (Hatfield MS 113/4).

Christopher Wright had fled London in the company of Thomas Percy early on the morning of 5 November. Unlike his brother in appearance—taller, fuller of face, with fairer hair (Morris, 70)—but equally trustworthy, he had been recruited to the plot early in 1605, essentially as an extra pair of hands: the conspirators were then trying, without much success, to dig a mine under the foundations of the House of Lords (Hatfield MS 113/54). Earlier, however, it appears that he had been sent by Catesby to Spain in March 1603 to establish whether Philip III's regime would continue to support their co-religionists in England after the death of Elizabeth. It may be that he travelled to Madrid under the alias Anthony Dutton, or else the part played by the mysterious Dutton was, under interrogation, later attributed to the dead Christopher Wright by the surviving conspirators, Fawkes and Thomas Winter.

John and Christopher Wright were both married. Their wives, Dorothy and Margaret, were subsequently arrested in Warwickshire and brought to London for examination.

John and Dorothy Wright had children: a daughter, eight or nine years old in 1605, is mentioned in PRO, SP 14/216/52.

MARK NICHOLLS

Sources PRO, SP 14/16, 216 · Salisbury (Cecil) MSS, Hatfield House MSS 113/4, 113/54, 112/91 [Thomas Winter's confessions respecting Gunpowder Plot and 'Spanish treason'] · M. Nicholls, *Investigating Gunpowder Plot* (1991) · *The condition of Catholics under James I: Father Gerard's narrative of the Gunpowder Plot*, ed. J. Morris (1871) · *The Gunpowder Plot: the narrative of Oswald Tesimond alias Greenway*, ed. and trans. F. Edwards (1973) · A. J. Loomie, 'Guy Fawkes in Spain: the "Spanish treason" in Spanish documents', *BIHR*, special suppl., 9 (1971) [whole issue] · A. J. Loomie, ed., *Spain and the Jacobean Catholics*, 1, Catholic RS, 64 (1973) · T. Smith, ed., *V Cl Camdeni et illustrium virorum ad G Camdenum epistolae* (1691) · G. Poulson, *The history and antiquities of the seigniory of Holderness*, 2 (1841), 516 · *DNB*
Likenesses C. van de Passe, group portrait, line engraving (*Gunpowder Plot conspirators*, 1605), NPG

Wright, John (1770/71–1844), publisher and editor, was born in Norwich, the son of a clerk to a manufacturing house. After an apprenticeship to his uncle, J. Roper, a silk mercer, he found employment in London as foreman or superintendent in Thomas Hookham's rooms (presumably his literary assembly and circulating library) in Bond Street. By 1797 Wright was established as bookseller and publisher at 169 Piccadilly, where for George Canning and John Hookham Frere, among others—including perhaps prime minister William Pitt—and editor William Gifford, he published the *Anti-Jacobin, or, Weekly Examiner*, an anti-whig journal full of witty, satirical poetry aimed at pro-revolutionary sympathizers, appearing on Mondays between 20 November 1797 and 9 July 1798. Acquiring the adjoining premises at 168 Piccadilly, contributors had easy access to their publisher and reputedly consorted to pen their poetry (the story may originate with William Upcott, then Wright's amanuensis). Wright's shop gained notoriety in August 1800 as the scene of a fracas in which John Wolcot (Peter Pindar) attempted to cane his nemesis William Gifford.

Wright may be the 'John Wright Jr.' licensed in April 1790 to sell state lottery tickets at 168 Piccadilly (Hill, 88 n. 1). He should not be confused, however, with the printer John Wright (c.1769–1807).

Wright's reputation as a tory bookseller and propagandist had reached America, where the expatriate William Cobbett secured Wright's services as his London agent and publisher. Upon their arrival in London in 1800, the Cobbett family temporarily lodged with Wright. The *Anti-Jacobin* was not financially successful, and Wright subsequently lost government patronage when he aimed to publish *Poetry of the Anti-Jacobin* in a de luxe edition illustrated by caricaturist James Gillray. Frere feared the publication would 'put money into the pockets of our two rascally Josias and damn us in the eyes of posterity' (Hill, 92), and Canning paid Gillray to abandon the project. By March 1802 Wright was bankrupt. Committed briefly to Fleet prison, he was released on terms that placed him in debt to Cobbett, who welcomed Wright into his home at 15 Duke Street, Westminster, and employed him to superintend the production of *Cobbett's Weekly Political Register* (1802) and to edit other landmark serial publications (with

title changes): *Cobbett's Parliamentary Debates* (1804); *Cobbett's Parliamentary History of England* (1806); and *Cobbett's Complete Collection of State Trials* (1890; chief editor, Thomas Bayly Howell). Cobbett called Wright 'one of the cleverest men in England. He is a good scholar, writes well, has great good taste' (Spater, 1.170). When the Cobbetts moved to Botley, Hampshire, Wright took lodgings over a tailor's establishment at 5 Panton Square, becoming Cobbett's man in London, 'the poor devil who now corrects Cobbett's bad English, edits his Parliamentary History, brushes his coat, puffs him in the coffee-houses and debating-shops, and does all his other dirty work' (*The Satirist*; quoted in Smith, 2.110n.). Wright received no formal salary although he was assigned by verbal agreement two-thirds of the profits on the *Debates* and half on the *Parliamentary History* and the *State Trials*.

Cobbett's imprisonment in 1810 forced a financial reckoning, which exposed mutual negligence and mismanagement based on bill discounting and advances secured on non-existent profits (only the *Political Register* made money), and proving Cobbett's prophetic reference (28 October 1808) to 'us whose accounts the devil himself would never unravel' (Green, 356). These circumstances and subsequent arbitration spawned a bitter and lasting enmity, culminating in two lawsuits against Cobbett for libel: *Wright v. Clement* (against Cobbett's publisher; 10 December 1819) and *Wright v. Cobbett* (11 December 1820). In a savage attack Cobbett had abused Wright in the *Register* for exposing his attempted negotiations with government in 1810 to suppress the *Political Register* and for releasing during the Westminster election of 1818 a letter from 1808 injurious to Henry Hunt. Cobbett alleged that he had discovered Wright falsifying his accounts and described graphically 'the big round drops of sweat that in a cold winter's day rolled down the caitiff's forehead'. Wright obtained £500 damages against William Innell Clement, the bookseller, for publishing the libel, and £1000 damages against Cobbett.

Wright continued to edit the *Parliamentary Debates* for Thomas Curson Hansard (who sided with Wright and removed Cobbett's name from the title-page), and to maintain his connections with members of parliament. In 1826 one such friend, Richard Bateson Robson, baited then unleashed Wright on a crusade against the water supplied to the city of Westminster by the Grand Junction Water Works Company, of which Robson was a director and former chairman. In a pamphlet, *The Dolphin, or, Grand Junction Nuisance* (March 1827), and monograph, *The Water Question* (January 1828; also published in *The Times*), Wright denounced the water supplied by the company's 'dolphin' (a circular wooden structure over a suction device at the mouth of the great Ranelagh common sewer near Chelsea Hospital, which pumped its contents to an onshore steam engine) as 'a fluid saturated with the impurities of fifty thousand houses—a dilute solution of animal and vegetable substances in a state of putrefaction—alike offensive to the sight, disgusting to the imagination, and destructive to health' (*The Dolphin*, 61; quoted in Stern, 31). Testimonials of a dozen physicians and chemists were secured against the partisan defences of Sir Gilbert Blane and Dr Richard Reece. At a public meeting in April 1827 the cause was championed by Sir Francis Burdett and Lord Wharncliff, whose motions in parliament prompted a royal commission of inquiry and ultimately the appointment of engineer Thomas Telford to investigate alternative water sources.

While *The Times* (25 August 1828) reminded the public of its debt to Mr Wright, Mr Hansard waited for his copy. Wright was often late in supplying Hansard, according to their agreement, transcripts of a given day's debate within fifteen days. Hansard eventually refused payment, and Wright sued for 'work and labour' (*The Times*, 7 June 1830). Wright's work was meticulous, if delayed, sometimes because members of parliament corrected their speeches, and sessions were long (one extra Saturday session on the Catholic question occupied 160 pages). The case was an uncomfortable one, best settled out of court. The verdict was entered for Wright subject to a reference to William Selwyn, who, in November, awarded in Hansard's favour (*The Times*, 4 Dec 1830).

So ended Wright's long association—more than a quarter of a century—with the parliamentary debates. The firms of John Murray and Richard Bentley employed him as literary editor for editions of Lord Byron, George Crabbe, Boswell's *Life of Johnson*, and, in 1840, the first complete edition of Horace Walpole's letters. But parliamentary politics was his forte. In 1815 he had edited the speeches of Charles James Fox, and in 1831, after his break with Hansard, the speeches of the recently deceased William Huskisson (the prefatory 'life' contributed by Edward Leeves). This edition, financed at his own expense, was not successful. He also assisted the editors of *The Letters of William Pitt, Earl of Chatham*.

No longer directly involved with contemporary parliamentary matters, Wright turned to the parliamentary past, specifically the thirteenth ('unrecorded') parliament of 10 May 1768 – 13 June 1774, the only record of which survived in the shorthand notes of Sir Henry Cavendish. Wright's fifteen-year search for these notes ended in January 1839 when he found them among the British Museum Egerton manuscripts. His ability to extract and publish within six months *Debates of the House of Commons in the year 1774 on the bill for making more effectual provision for the government of the province of Quebec* suggests his long familiarity with the shorthand system of Thomas Gurney. With the encouragement and financial assistance of his former legal counsel Lord Brougham and his friend Hudson Gurney, Wright was able to transcribe notes up to 27 March 1771 (2 vols., 1841–3) before his death on 25 February 1844 at 26 Osnaburgh Street, Regent's Park. He was buried in St Marylebone parish church.   PAGE LIFE

Sources DNB · *Literary Gazette*, 1416 (9 March 1844), 162–3 · I. Maxted, *The London book trades, 1775–1800: a preliminary checklist of members* (1977) · D. Hill, *Mr. Gillray, the caricaturist: a biography* (1965) · G. Spater, *William Cobbett: the poor man's friend*, 2 vols. (1982) · W. M. Stern, 'J. Wright, pamphleteer on London water supply', *Guildhall Miscellany*, 1/2 (Feb 1953), 31–4 · J. Wright, *The water question: memoir addressed to the commissioners appointed by his majesty in pursuance of the addresses of both houses of parliament to inquire into

the state of the supply of water to the metropolis* (1828) · J. Wright, *Report of the action, Wright v. Clement, for certain libels published in Cobbett's political register; tried in the court of king's bench at Westminster, on Friday, the 10th of December, 1819, before Lord Chief Justice Abbot, and a special jury* (1819) · 'Wright v. Cobbett', *The Times* (12 Dec 1820) · 'Wright v. Hansard', *The Times* (7 June 1830); (4 Dec 1830) · *The Times* (29 March 1802) · *The Times* (25 Aug 1828) · P. W. Gaines, 'Two letters written by William Cobbett from America', *Yale University Library Gazette*, 48 (July 1973), 44–55 · D. Green, *Great Cobbett: the noblest agitator* (1983) · E. Smith, *William Cobbett: a biography*, 2 vols. (1878) · L. Melville [Lewis Saul Benjamin], *The life and letters of William Cobbett in England & America, based on hitherto unpublished family papers*, 2 vols. (1913)

Archives BL, letters to J. Backhouse, Sir R. Peel, E. Leeves *re* William Huskisson papers, Add. MS 38758, fols. 256, 263, 265–7, 271, 273 · BL, letters, etc. to publisher R. Bentley, Add. MS 46613, fol. 187; 46614, fol. 194; 46650, fol. 136 · BL, corresp. with William Cobbett, Add. MSS 22906–22907 · BL, corresp. with William Cobbett, and papers *re* lawsuit, Add. MS 31126 · BL, letters to J. Gillray, Add. MS 27337, fols. 89, 91 · BL, letters to third Lord Hardwicke, Add. MS 35650, fol. 221; 35651, fol. 95 · BL, letters to Thomas James Mathias, Add. MS 22976, fols. 139–40, 152 · BL, letters to Sir R. Peel, Add. MS 40373, fol. 210; 40386, fol. 1; 40507, fol. 271 · BL, letters to W. Windham, Add. MS 37888, fols. 19, 46 · Bodl. Oxf., corresp. with W. Cobbett, MS 25447, fols. 44–49v · GL, corresp. and papers relating to London's water supply ['Papers of J. Wright, pamphleteer, on the supply of water in the metropolis, incl. correspondence, handbills, extracts from newspapers, parliamentary memoirs and miscellaneous documents, 1818–1831'] · LMA, records of the Grand Junction Water Works Co., Acc. 2558/GJ

Wright, John (1805–*c*.1846), weaver and poet, was born on 1 September 1805 in the parish of Sorn, Ayrshire, the son of James Wright of Galston, coal-driver, and Grizzle Taylor (*d.* 1842). John, the fourth of seven children, grew up in Galston, where at the age of seven he was removed from school to assist his father. He was remembered as a wayward youth, fighting with his playmates and fleeing half naked into the countryside after his parents had locked up his clothing in a vain attempt to keep him at home. Wright's Sunday school education was furthered by George Brown, the weaver to whom he was apprenticed at thirteen. Brown possessed a small library and hosted literary meetings in his home. Wright read with avidity and composed a tragedy entitled 'Mahomet, or, The Hegira' before learning to form his letters.

At the age of sixteen Wright fell in love with a young woman who married another, either put off by his passion for the muse, as he suggests, or perhaps by his erratic behaviour. This episode became the basis for *The Retrospect*, the long poem Wright began in 1824. Loosely modelled on James Beattie's *The Minstrel* and Byron's *Childe Harold*, it describes Wright's happy childhood and anguished initiation into poetry. He suffered from a mental disorder his memoirist describes as 'monomania', perhaps manic depression. *The Retrospect* does battle with the private demons of frustrated love and ambition in a fantastic and wildly discontinuous *mélange* of description, declamation, and narrative. Wright had attempted to cure his madness by winter bathing in the River Burnawn: kelpies and threatening waters figure in the poem, along with Edom O'Gordon, the witch of Endor, and much Ayrshire scenery and legend. While Wright imitates promiscuously, James

Hogg was certainly an influence. With the encouragement and assistance of John Struthers and Dugald Moore, Glasgow poets of equally humble backgrounds, Wright travelled to Edinburgh to seek a publisher. After much tribulation he was able to raise a subscription with the aid of John Wilson and Henry Glassford Bell. *The Retrospect, or, Youthful Scenes, with other Poems and Songs* was published in 1830 to glowing notices in the *Monthly Review*, *Blackwood's*, and the *Quarterly Review*. After Wright had gathered further subscriptions during a tour of Scotland, *The Retrospect* achieved a second edition in 1833.

In the meantime the poet plied his trade at Cambuslang, near Glasgow, where, about 1831, he married Margaret Chalmers, granddaughter of the parish schoolmaster. They had two children before the poet took to drink and abandoned his family, about 1835, in what he described as a 'Byronic separation'. Wright continued to compose while labouring at his loom, but his literary career was essentially over. In an attempt to set the poet and his family to rights his *Whole Poetical Works* were republished by friends in 1843 with an anonymous memoir and a much-abridged version of *The Retrospect*. About 1846 a Galston acquaintance discovered John Wright lying drunk and unconscious in the streets of Glasgow; he was carried to the infirmary where he died of a fever the next day. He was buried in the town's necropolis.

DAVID HILL RADCLIFFE

Sources J. Paterson, *The contemporaries of Burns and the more recent poets of Ayrshire* (1840) • memoir, J. Wright, *Whole poetical works* (1843) • C. Rogers, *The modern Scottish minstrel, or, The songs of Scotland of the past half-century*, 6 vols. (1855–7) • *DNB* • D. McAllister, ed., *Poets and poetry of the covenant* (1894)
Likenesses oils, repro. in Wright, *Whole poetical works*

Wright, John Buckland (1897–1954), illustrator, was born John Wright on 3 December 1897 at Redroofs, in Dunedin, New Zealand, the second of three children of John Wright (*d.* 1901) and his wife, Florence Octavia Greenwood. He changed his name some time before 1945. His father died in a work-related accident in 1901, and in 1905 his mother left New Zealand for Europe, taking the family with her. John was sent to a preparatory school in Switzerland, and after the family moved to England in 1908 he first attended Clifton College in Bristol and then spent five years at Rugby School. His mother had married Lawrence Pepys-Cockerel in 1908, and John was thereafter effectively brought up by his maternal grandparents.

Having been refused for active service during the First World War because he suffered from a stammer, Buckland Wright joined the Scottish ambulance division attached to the French army and was awarded the Croix de Guerre for gallantry in rescuing French civilians from burning buildings. After the war he attended Oxford University, where he graduated with a BA in history in 1920, and then went to the Bartlett school of architecture, University of London, graduating in 1922. He rejected a junior partnership in the architectural firm of Adam, Holden, and Pearson, having been entranced by the idea of becoming an engraver through the study of engraving tools at the Victoria and Albert Museum in London, and from reading

Gordon Craig's *Woodcuts and some Words* (1924). He left for continental Europe to study as an artist, and in 1925 settled in Brussels. There he met and became engaged to Mary Bell Anderson, a young Canadian musician. He taught himself wood-engraving, and in 1927 was elected a member of the Xylographes Belges and helped found La Société de la Gravure Originale Belge. After exhibiting in Belgium, he met A. A. M. Stols, the director of the Halcyon Press, who commissioned him to illustrate a series of books beginning with *The Sonnets of John Keats* (1930). In the spring of 1929 he moved to Paris, where he and Mary Anderson were married on 30 December.

Buckland Wright's first one-man exhibition was held in Brussels in November 1930, and through further exhibitions, reviews of his work, and the growing number of books he illustrated his reputation grew quickly. In 1933 he accepted a commission from Joseph Ishill of the Oriel Press, New Jersey, and then joined Stanley Hayter's famous studio, Atelier 17, which drew to Paris artists from all around the world. There he met and worked with such artists as Picasso, Matisse, and the British engraver Anthony Gross, and he began to experiment with many different techniques, such as drypoint, mezzotint, and aquatint, producing a large number of copper prints. Many prints from this period, up until the end of the Second World War, were non-representational. For example, two of his 1935 engravings of Leda and the swan are composed of swirling abstract lines, as is *Nymphe Surprise No. 1*, while his *Composition No. 8: the Model No. II* shows a curvaceous model in the studio standing before a canvas on which the artist has produced an abstract painting of the same figure. In the same year he was producing representational and erotic impressions of nymphs for *Cupid's Pastime*, a book he was to print at his own expense under the imprint JBW Editions. A very large proportion of the engravings produced throughout Buckland Wright's career depict partly clad or nude female figures, and show the engraver's delight in—perhaps even obsession with—the lines and curves of a woman's body.

In 1934 Buckland Wright became a member of the Society of Wood Engravers, based in London, and he exhibited regularly with them until his death. In 1935 he met Christopher Sandford of the Golden Cockerel Press, with whom he established a close working relationship and subsequent friendship which lasted for eighteen years. He illustrated seventeen books for the press, the first of which, *Love Night* by Powys Mathers (1936), contained fifteen of his wood-engravings. This was a great success and was perhaps the turning point in his career, introducing his work to collectors in Britain and elsewhere.

In 1936 Buckland Wright was appointed co-director of Atelier 17, and he continued to teach there until the beginning of the Second World War. At the outbreak of war the Buckland Wrights left Paris for London, where John worked in a camouflage unit and then as a press censor in the Ministry of Information and at Reuters, while Mary held a position at the Supreme Headquarters Allied Expeditionary Force. John continued to engrave and to exhibit throughout the war, and in 1940 he was chosen to represent Britain at the Venice Biennale. The work of the Golden Cockerel Press was inevitably curtailed, but its *Hymn to Proserpine* (1944) contained eight of his engravings, and *Endymion* was published soon after the war, in 1947. Many regard the fifty-eight engravings that Buckland Wright produced for *Endymion* as his finest. The illustrations feature ever-present erotic female figures set among highly decorative trees and foliage, which recall the designs of the art nouveau period.

A first child, Christopher, was born in 1945, followed by Richard in 1947, and a daughter, Mary, in 1949. In 1948 Buckland Wright received the first of a number of important commissions from the Folio Society, the first being to illustrate Homer's *Odyssey*, and he also began teaching at the Anglo-French Art Centre and the Camberwell School of Arts and Crafts in London. He produced coloured engravings for *Salmacis and Hermaphroditus*, published by the Golden Cockerel Press in 1951, and he used the scraperboard technique for illustrations that he contributed to the *London Magazine*. In 1952 he was appointed to the Slade School of Fine Art to organize the etching class, and in 1953 he published his book *Etching and Engraving: Techniques and the Modern Trend*, which continued to be in use as a student textbook at the beginning of the twenty-first century. In 1954 he produced many separate etchings, provided the Folio Society with ten aquatints for its edition of *The Decameron*, and began discussions with Stanley Hayter about the establishment of a branch of the Atelier 17 in London. Later that year he contracted a viral infection, and after a short illness he died unexpectedly from a heart attack, on 27 September 1954 at University College Hospital, London. He was survived by his wife.

ALAN HORNE

Sources C. Buckland Wright, ed., *The engravings of John Buckland Wright* (1990) • A. Reid, *A check-list of the book illustrations of John Buckland Wright* (1968) • D. Chambers and C. Sandford, *Cock-a-hoop: a bibliography of the Golden Cockerel Press, 1949–1961* (1976) • C. Sandford and O. Rutter, *Pertelote: a bibliography of the Golden Cockerel Press, October 1936–April 1943* (1943) • C. Sandford, *Cockalorum: a bibliography of the Golden Cockerel Press, June 1943–December 1948* (1950) • R. Gainsborough, 'The wood-engravings of John Buckland Wright', *Image*, 4 (1950), 49–62 • R. Cave, ed., '"A restrained but full-blooded eroticism": letters from John Buckland Wright to Christopher Sandford, 1937–1939', *Matrix*, 9 (winter 1988), 55–75 • www.uflib.ufl. edu/spec/rarebook/buckland/wright.htm, 6 April 2000 • J. Selborne, *British wood-engraved book illustration, 1900–1940* (1998) • *CGPLA Eng. & Wales* (1955)

Archives BL • Rijksmuseum, Amsterdam • V&A | University of Florida, Joseph Ishill collection

Wealth at death £2337 5s. 11d.: probate, 1955, *CGPLA Eng. & Wales*

Wright, John Masey (1777–1866), watercolour painter, was born on 14 October 1777 in Pleasant Row, Penton Place, Pentonville, London. The son of an organ builder, the infant Wright had a remarkable ear for music and astonished listeners by his extempore playing. He was apprenticed to another organ builder but he was dismissed for making sketches on the organ pipes. Subsequently he worked for Broadwood, as a piano tuner, before turning to art as a career. So far as is known Wright's only training as an artist was received from Thomas Stothard, who befriended him when he was about sixteen; he never painted from living models.

At the age of thirty-three, Wright married a Miss Meadows and went to live in Bishop's Walk, Lambeth, which was then a theatrical quarter; here he shared a house with the Scottish painter John H. (or Jock) Wilson. Through Wilson, Wright came to know Thomas and Henry Aston Barker, the sons of Robert Barker, who was the originator of panoramic exhibitions. Wright worked for Henry Barker for seven years at the Strand Panorama, where he exhibited life-size battle scenes from the Napoleonic wars; his panorama of Waterloo was said to have made Barker's fortune. (Two of Wright's oil paintings, the *Battle of the Pyrenees* and the *Battle of Vittoria*, were acquired by the third duke of Wellington, in 1899, for Stratfield Saye House.) At one time he was employed simultaneously by the Barkers, at £8 a week, and as a scene painter by His Majesty's Theatre, for another £6. Wright was also employed as a drawing-master in various country houses: Lady Craven, the marquess of Lansdowne, and Earl de Grey were among his patrons.

Between 1812 and 1818 Wright exhibited nine pictures at the Royal Academy before his election in 1824 to the Society of Painters in Water Colours. In all he exhibited 134 drawings with the society and 29 at Suffolk Street; he worked in both watercolours and oils. Although he described himself as a portrait painter in the 1851 census most of his known work was inspired by literary sources, in particular the works of Shakespeare and Oliver Goldsmith, with whom Wright seems to have felt a particular affinity. His style and subject matter seem very derivative of Thomas Stothard, but Wright's work has a particular delicacy of colouring and it retains its own charm. In 1843 *The Scrutiny in Don Quixote's Library, by the Curate and Barber* won a prize of £20 from the Art Union of London. Wright's pictures were usually priced for a few guineas although one of his drawings was on sale at 85 guineas in 1846. The Victoria and Albert Museum has seven of his watercolours, none of which is signed.

Simultaneously Wright was producing illustrations for such annuals as *Literary Souvenir* and *Amulet*, and also for editions of Shakespeare, Scott, Burns, and other writers. His love of literature was such that his son recalled how, during an illness, he broke out in his sleep reciting long passages from Shakespeare.

A kindly, generous man, Wright 'could never keep money in his pockets but gave away liberally and always had some little pensioners' (Royal Watercolour Society MSS, J105/16). In later years he suffered considerable hardship and both the Royal Academy—following an approach by Samuel Palmer—and the Society of Painters in Water Colours assisted him financially. Penury, however, obliged Wright to work until the end of his life. In a letter of 26 November 1861, at the age of eighty-four, he wrote that he was sending in pictures to the winter exhibition of the society despite a violent cough 'that tears me almost to death' and chronic constipation: 'So I am in what you might call a pretty pickle' (Royal Watercolour Society MSS, J105/10). But Wright's work had long been out of fashion and seemed anachronistic, given that it lacked the realism and intensity favoured by contemporary taste; Roget comments that his paintings 'were little heeded by the many, and when he passed away were scarcely missed' (Roget, 2.204).

A self-portrait in the Castle Museum, Nottingham, and a photograph of Wright in the archives of the Royal Watercolour Society show a benign, white-haired, and bearded old man. After having lived at many addresses in London he died on 13 May 1866 at his last home, Box Cottage, Twickenham Common. He left four daughters and a son, who was nearly blind. In 1876 this son applied to the Artists' General Benevolent Institution, stating that his father had been unable to leave provision for his family except in the form of his pictures, which had already been sold. Contemporary documents spell his middle name 'Masey'; 'Massey' appears in Samuel Redgrave's *Dictionary of Artists of the English School* (1878), the form which has frequently been followed in later references.

SIMON FENWICK

Sources J. L. Roget, *A history of the 'Old Water-Colour' Society*, 2 vols. (1891) · Bankside Gallery, London, Royal Watercolour Society MSS · J. J. Jenkins, *Art Review* (Feb 1867) · F. G. Burnett, 'John Massey Wright', *Old Water-Colour Society's Club*, 54 (1979), 42–7 · census returns for St Pancras, 1841, 1851
Archives Bankside Gallery, London, Royal Watercolour Society MSS
Likenesses photograph, c.1865, Bankside Gallery, London · J. M. Wright, self-portrait, Castle Museum, Nottingham

Wright, John Michael (*bap.* 1617, *d.* 1694), painter, was baptized as Mighell Wryghtt in St Bride's, Fleet Street, London, on 25 May 1617. His father was James Wright, later described as a tailor and citizen of London. Little is known of Wright's early life, and the accounts of the principal informants—Bainbrigge Buckeridge, Thomas Hearne, and George Vertue—tend to be contradictory. However, two consistent themes are lent credibility by later events in his life: a Scottish connection and an adherence to what Hearne calls 'the Romish religion'.

The first unambiguous Scottish link was the nineteen-year-old Wright's apprenticeship to the Scottish portrait painter George Jamesone in Edinburgh on 6 April 1636. The reasons for this quite unusual step may have been familial or even religious, but two other factors may have played a part: plague was rampant in London at the time, and Jamesone had by this date established a not inconsiderable reputation. The apprenticeship was entered into for five years, but the increasing political turmoil may have shortened its duration (Jamesone was imprisoned during the latter half of 1639). In these years Wright is likely to have lodged in his master's premises, which were in a tenement on the north side of the High Street, near the Netherbow Gate. There is no evidence of independent work by Wright at this time, but his earliest known painting, a little portrait of Robert Bruce, second earl of Elgin and Ailesbury, painted in Rome in the early 1640s (priv. coll.), is modest and still quite provincial.

It is possible that it was during this Scottish sojourn that Wright met, or even married, the wife who was described some thirty years later as being 'related to the most noble and distinguished families of Scotland'. The identity of this wife, to whom he was certainly married by 1656, and with whom he had at least one child, a son called Thomas, remains a mystery.

Wright probably arrived in Rome during 1642, when, in the company of a scholar of Scottish descent, James Alban Gibbes, a Mr Wright signed the pilgrim book of the English College. There are no details of his further training as a painter while in Rome, but his repertory of skills and his knowledge must have increased enormously, so much so that in 1648 he became a member of the Academy of St Luke (where he was designated *inglese*). Other foreign members at this time included painters of such supreme quality as Nicolas Poussin and Velázquez. On 10 February of the same year Wright was also elected a member of the Congregazione dei Virtuosi, having been proposed by a Pietro Ferreri. This was a charitable organization concerned with promoting religion by means of the arts. It also organized an annual exhibition in the Pantheon, where Wright must have measured himself against the best painters working in the city.

During his more than ten years in Rome, Wright built up a substantial collection of books, prints, and drawings (including some attributed to Raphael, Correggio, and Titian) and acquired some forty paintings, perhaps as a dealer as much as a collector. It is interesting that in his list of Wright's graphic art, Richard Symonds, amateur and royalist, is careful to designate Wright as *Scotus*. Wright also became what Hearne termed 'a bare antiquarie' (which might suggest a dealer whose knowledge lacked profundity) and 'very well versed in the Latin tongue … and a great master of Italian and French' (*Reliquiae*, 344).

It was presumably accomplishments of this sort that led during the early 1650s to Wright's undertaking antiquarian duties for Archduke Leopold William of Austria, currently governor of the Spanish Netherlands. Although the published sources refer to this phase in Wright's life, it is documented only by a passport, issued to 'Juan Miguel Rita, pintor Ingles', enabling him to travel to England to purchase paintings, medals, and antiquities. The passport, dated 22 May 1655, is signed by Leopold at Brussels, so Wright was probably there at this time. It is also the earliest evidence that Wright had taken the additional Christian name of John, presumably to mark his commitment to Roman Catholicism.

If Wright went to England on behalf of the archduke shortly afterwards, this is not recorded. However, he did enter the country, through Dover, on 9 April 1656, and three days later had taken lodgings in London with a Mrs Johnson in Weld Street in the parish of St Giles. According to his registration he had left his family in Italy, where he shortly intended to return. It is also noted that he had practised painting in France and 'other parts'—presumably the Netherlands. Since leaving Scotland, therefore, he had furnished himself with a variety of experience far wider than that of any other painter working in Britain during the second half of the seventeenth century.

Wright did not return to Italy, and was in due course joined by his family in Cromwellian England. It was soon evident that, despite his Catholicism, he was able to operate on both sides of the political divide. In 1658 he painted a small, allegorical portrait of the protector's daughter, Mrs Elizabeth Claypole (NPG), while in the following year he painted Colonel John Russell (Ham House, Surrey), who was active in the 'Sealed Knot' conspiracy to restore the monarchy. The latter is perhaps his masterpiece, the kind of painting that allowed John Evelyn to describe him as 'the famous Painter Mr Write' (Evelyn, 3.113). The signatures on these paintings continue Wright's use of his two Christian names, but he was not always consistent in this.

During the 1660s Wright appears to have had financial problems—he seems never to have been a good businessman—for he was granted the royal privilege of disposing of his collection of old master paintings by means of a lottery. Fourteen of these paintings were in the event acquired by the king. Two public events significantly affected Wright's career at this stage: the plague of 1665 and the great fire of London in 1666. The plague brought normal life to a halt, and Wright sought work in the country, something he was always willing to consider. It was at this time that he painted at least three members of the Arundell of Wardour family. The aftermath of the fire brought Wright a singular benefit. In 1670 he won a commission from the aldermen of the City to paint twenty-two full-length portraits of the judges who had unravelled the many disputes over property boundaries caused by the devastation of the fire. These portraits were seen hanging in the Guildhall in 1673 by John Evelyn, who attested that they were good likenesses, though he now thought less of Wright as an artist. Their condition deteriorated disastrously over the years, and only two remain in the Guildhall Art Gallery and Library. The remainder have been dispersed or destroyed.

After the restoration of Charles II in 1660 Wright had received some royal patronage—notably to paint an allegorical ceiling for the king's bedchamber in Whitehall Palace (Nottingham Castle Museum)—but he was not granted a royal office, which he must have desired. The position of king's painter during the 1660s was the preserve of Sir Peter Lely. However, in 1673 Wright was granted the office of picture drawer in ordinary and thereafter frequently signed his paintings, rather grandiloquently, Pictor Regius. One of the earliest to be signed in this way was a group portrait from 1673 of Sir Robert Vyner and his wife with two of their children (NPG). Compositionally it is close to Lely, but it has none of that painter's suave glamour, which must have been far more in accord with courtly taste. Samuel Pepys, immediately after an appreciative visit to Lely's studio, remarked: 'Thence to Wright's the painter's: but Lord, the difference that is between their two works' (Pepys, 3.113). Pepys, however, was not a good judge of painting. Wright's portrait has a plain and sympathetic realism, and contains a carefully observed, atmospheric landscape which was unusual in English painting at this time.

Wright's evident concern with his social status was marked by a curious episode in 1676. On 3 March someone signing herself Marie L[ady] of Hermistan, and evidently a Catholic, dispatched a letter from London to Cosimo (III) de' Medici, grand duke of Tuscany, pleading that he should attempt to persuade the king to grant Wright a baronetcy. Wright, with the miniaturist Samuel Cooper, had met Cosimo when he visited London in 1669; and Cosimo had subsequently called on Wright at his studio, where he commissioned a portrait of the duke of Albemarle. Wright may also by this time have painted his state portrait of Charles II (Royal Collection), so that the time for such a plea might have seemed ripe. Nothing, however, materialized. The identity of the writer, whose letter contains the only known reference to Wright's wife, remains obscure.

As harassment of Catholics again intensified, Wright spent more time working in the country. His six family portraits for Sir Walter Bagot of Blithfield in Staffordshire occasioned a series of letters from Wright to his patron, written in 1676 and 1677, which give much information about his prices and methods as well as conveying a strong impression of Wright's personality, which must have been lively and engaging.

The following year, 1678, brought the public hysteria generated by Titus Oates's Popish Plot, and Wright removed himself to Dublin, where, still calling himself Pictor Regius, he painted the rather French-looking portrait *The Ladies Catherine and Charlotte Talbot* (NG Ire.). Here he also painted his two famous full-lengths of Celtic chieftains in exotic costume, the *Sir Neil O'Neill* (Tate Collection) and the *Lord Mungo Murray* (Scot. NPG).

The accession in 1685 of Charles II's brother James, an avowed Catholic, brought Wright's last great chance of significant royal favour. Hearne reports that the new king had 'a particular fondness for him' and that this led to Wright's appointment as steward to the earl of Castlemaine, who was sent out to Rome on an embassy to the pope, Innocent XI, at the beginning of 1686. The embassy had a number of specific tasks, but was mainly intended to follow precedent and to demonstrate that England could become a major player on the Catholic side in the conflicts of continental Europe: the conversion of England was to be seen as a possibility. Wright's knowledge of Rome, and of the Italian language, must have played a part in this appointment. His precise role seems to have been to co-ordinate the production of a number of elaborately carved coaches and all the attendant costumes and decorations that made up the vast procession which eventually made its way to an audience with the pope in January 1687. He also oversaw the great banquet for more than 1000 guests, the tables replete with intricate sugar sculptures, which followed in the Palazzo Doria Pamphilij. The banqueting room bore at its head a large state portrait, which an engraving depicts as having precisely the same form as Wright's earlier state portrait of Charles II.

The pope, however, was unimpressed, having no desire to see the *status quo* in England upset. While still in Rome, Wright published an illustrated account of the embassy in

Italian, dedicated to the duchess of Modena. Shortly after his return to England in October 1687, he published an English version, dedicated this time to the duchess's daughter, Queen Mary.

With the revolution of 1688 and the expulsion of the king, Wright's career was virtually at an end. He now suffered relative poverty, although he remained in good spirits until early in 1694, when his health deteriorated. He made his will in March, leaving his house in the parish of St Paul's to his niece Katherine Vaux. His pictures, drawings, prints, and books he left to his nephew Michael Wright, also a painter. However, a codicil declared that his books should be sold on behalf of his son, Thomas, who was still abroad. These books were auctioned at Wright's house in James Street ('over against Hart Street end') on 4 June. Death was not long delayed, and on 1 August the burial of John Michael Wright, the name he had fashioned for himself, was recorded at St Martin-in-the-Fields.

The account of Wright's funeral by Thomas Hearne describes the painter as he was in his prime: 'He was of middle stature, free and open, and innocently merry in his conversation … of great plainness and simplicity, and of a very easy temper' (*Reliquiae*, 346).

DUNCAN THOMSON

Sources S. Stevenson and D. Thomson, *John Michael Wright: the king's painter* (1982) [exhibition catalogue, Scottish National Portrait Gallery, Edinburgh] · C. H. C. Baker, *Lely and the Stuart portrait painters: a study of English portraiture before and after van Dyck*, 2 vols. (1912) · E. Waterhouse, *Painting in Britain, 1530–1790*, 4th edn (1978) · [B. Buckeridge], 'An essay towards an English school of painting', in R. de Piles, *The art of painting, with the lives and characters of above 300 of the most eminent painters*, 3rd edn (1754), 354–439 · *Reliquiae Hearnianae: the remains of Thomas Hearne*, ed. P. Bliss, 2nd edn, 3 (1869) · Vertue, *Note books*, vol. 1 · Evelyn, *Diary* · Pepys, *Diary*, vols. 3, 6–7 · M. Wright, *An account of his excellence Roger earl of Castlemaine's embassy, from his sacred majesty James the IId … to his holiness Innocent XI* (1688) · J. P. Ferris, 'The return of Michael Wright', *Burlington Magazine*, 124 (1982), 150–53 · W. J. Smith, 'Letters from Michael Wright', *Burlington Magazine*, 95 (1953), 233–6 · J. L. Howgego, 'The Guildhall fire judges', *Guildhall Miscellany* (Feb 1953), 20–30 · J. Fenlon, 'John Michael Wright's "Highland laird" identified', *Burlington Magazine*, 130 (1988), 767–9 · A. J. Loomie, 'John Michael Wright's visit to London in the summer of 1655', *Burlington Magazine*, 129 (1987), 721 · parish register, St Martin-in-the-Fields, Westminster, London [burial] · will, GL, M/MIC/224, 27 March 1694 · parish register, St Bride's, Fleet Street, GL, MS 6536 [baptism] · K. Gibson, '"Best belov'd of kings": the iconography of King Charles II', PhD diss., Courtauld Inst., 1997, vol. 1, p. 128

Archives BL, Egerton MS 1635, fol. 75 · GL, M/MIC/224 | Archivio di Stato, Florence, Medici papers, filza 1085, carta 362 · Bodl. Oxf., MSS Rawl., Series A, vol. 26, fol. 101 · NL Wales, Bachymbyd letters, 299, 303, 304, 313, 316, 329

Wealth at death left house in parish of St Paul's, London; large collection of pictures, drawings, prints, and books: will, GL, M/MIC/224, 27 March 1694

Wright, John Wesley (1769–1805), naval officer, son of James Wright of a Lancashire family, a captain in the army, was born at Cork on 14 June 1769. While very young he went with his father and the family to Minorca, where he learned music and French, in both of which he excelled. Presumably he also learned Spanish. Early in 1781 he was entered on the *Brilliant* with Roger Curtis, and was for the next two years at Gibraltar during the siege. In 1783, when the *Brilliant* was paid off, Wright was sent to a school at Wandsworth, Surrey, where he remained two years. He was then employed for some time in a merchant's office in the City, and—apparently in 1788—was sent on an 'important commission' to St Petersburg. He remained in Russia for the next five years, visiting Moscow and other places, and acquiring a thorough knowledge of the language. He was introduced to Sir Sidney Smith, and at his request joined the *Diamond* in spring 1794 with the rating of midshipman, and apparently serving as captain's clerk; he seems to have described himself as the 'secretary' of his friend. After nearly two years on the coast of France, he was with Smith on the night of 18–19 April 1796, when he was taken prisoner. His confidential relations with Smith secured him the particular attentions of the French government; he was sent with Smith to Paris, was confined in the Temple as a close prisoner, was repeatedly examined as to Smith's plans, and finally escaped with Smith in May 1798. Wright then joined the *Tigre*, apparently as acting lieutenant, for his commission was not confirmed until 29 March 1800. He continued with Smith throughout the commission at Acre and on the coast of Egypt until promoted, on 7 May 1802, to the sloop *Cynthia*, which he took to England.

On the renewal of the war Wright was appointed to the brig *Vincejo*, in which for the next year he was employed on the coast of France. On the morning of 8 May 1804 he was blown into Quiberon Bay, and was off the mouth of the Vilaine, when the wind died away. Some seventeen gunboats came out of the river, and surrounded the brig, which the calm rendered almost defenceless against such odds; after being pounded for two hours, the brig was compelled to surrender. Wright was sent to Paris and again kept a close prisoner in the Temple. He was repeatedly interrogated as to whether he had landed some royalist agents: Georges, Pichegru, Rivière, and others were named. Wright refused to answer despite many threats of ill treatment. After being so detained for nearly eighteen months it was announced that he had committed suicide on the night of 27 October 1805. It was immediately said in England that if he was dead he had been murdered; and, in fact, so little was the story believed by the authorities that his name was not removed from the navy list until the autumn of 1807.

Wright's linguistic abilities and intimate connection with Smith made him an obvious spy suspect. After the restoration of the French monarchy, Sir Sidney Smith and others made unofficial inquiries in Paris which seemed to prove that Wright was murdered. However, their evidence was unreliable. The only statement of any value was that his letters were in good and determined spirit, and no cause for great depression was shown. Possibly he died of natural causes, maybe a heart attack, and the French authorities announced suicide to denigrate him. Possibly he died from torture or violent interrogation.

J. K. LAUGHTON, *rev.* ANDREW LAMBERT

Sources P. Shankland, *Beware of heroes: Admiral Sir Sidney Smith's war against Napoleon* (1975) · 'Biographical memoir of John Westley [*sic*] Wright', *Naval Chronicle*, 34 (1815), 1–30, 89–117, 177–208, 265–

88, 353–76, 441–56 [later instalments spell 'Wesley' correctly] · *Naval Chronicle*, 35 (1816), 441–56; 36 (1816), 1–20, 89–112, 177–205, 265–86 · *Annual Register* (1805), pt 1, pp. 6, 118, 427 · T. Pocock, *A lust for glory* (1996)

Likenesses T. Blood, stipple, 1815, BM, NPG; repro. in *Naval Chronicle* · G. Calleja, engraving, repro. in Shankland, *Beware of heroes*, 174

Wright, John William (1802–1848),

watercolour painter, was born in London, the son of John Wright (*c*.1745–1820) and his wife, Priscilla Edwards, *née* Guise (*d*. 1802), both miniaturists. After his mother's death his father remarried. When Wright was ten he was sent to school at Loughborough House, Brixton, Surrey, but was soon removed because of his delicate health and was educated at home. He was taught to paint by the portrait painter Thomas Phillips until 1820. He may have been the John William Wright who was admitted to the Royal Academy Schools in 1822, apparently aged seventeen. At first he supported himself by teaching, and by painting portraits in oils. Between 1823 and 1846 he exhibited thirty-nine pictures at the Royal Academy, mainly portraits.

In 1831 Wright was elected an associate of the Old Watercolour Society and from then on devoted himself to painting in watercolours. He exhibited there frequently, including many theatrical subjects—especially scenes from Shakespeare's plays—and sentimental pictures with titles such as *There's Nothing Half so Sweet as Love's Young Dream*. He became a full member in 1842 and was appointed secretary in 1844. He also exhibited at the Society of British Artists in Suffolk Street from 1824 to 1835. From 1832 he painted images of women for annuals such as *The Keepsake*, the *Literary Souvenir*, *Heath's Book of Beauty*, *Fisher's Drawing-Room Scrap Book*, and *The Female Characters of Shakespeare*. His portraits of Lord Tenterden, Bishop Gray, and Bishop Marsh were engraved for *Fisher's National Portrait Gallery of Illustrious and Eminent Personages*. Wright died on 14 January 1848 at his home in Great Marlborough Street, London. He was survived by his wife and two children.

ANNE PIMLOTT BAKER

Sources *GM*, 2nd ser., 29 (1848), 554 · Mallalieu, *Watercolour artists*, vols. 1–2 · Wood, *Vic. painters*, 3rd edn · S. C. Hutchison, 'The Royal Academy Schools, 1768–1830', *Walpole Society*, 38 (1960–62), 123–91 · J. Johnson, ed., *Works exhibited at the Royal Society of British Artists, 1824–1893, and the New English Art Club, 1888–1917*, 2 vols. (1975) · Graves, *RA exhibitors* · Bryan, *Painters* (1903–5) · H. Blättel, *International dictionary miniature painters / Internationales Lexikon Miniatur-Maler* (1992) · *DNB*

Wealth at death left widow and children in straitened circumstances: *GM*

Wright, Joseph, of Derby (1734–1797),

painter, was born at 28 Irongate, Derby, on 3 September 1734, the third of the five children of John Wright (1697–1767), attorney, and his wife, Hannah Brookes (1700–1764).

Background, training, and early works Born into a professional family solidly established in Derby, Wright was educated at Derby grammar school, teaching himself to draw by copying prints. In 1751, probably shortly after his seventeenth birthday, Wright began two years' training

Joseph Wright of Derby (1734–1797), self-portrait, *c*.1785

under Thomas Hudson, then the most highly reputed portraitist in London. A large group of studies for heads, hands, and costume details (110 sheets, Derby Art Gallery), evidently assembled by Wright from his own and other students' work, including drawings from Allan Ramsay's studio, throws valuable light on workshop training in this period.

Wright returned to Derby in 1753, and during the next few years painted small Hudsonesque portraits in and around that town. Rarely self-confident, and at this stage well aware that he needed further instruction, he re-entered Hudson's studio in 1756 for a further fifteen months, forming a lasting friendship with his fellow pupil John Hamilton Mortimer.

Wright was content to make Derby his principal base throughout his career. While most of his contemporaries believed that reputations could be made only in the metropolis, Wright chose chiefly to live and work among his family and friends. His career demonstrates that he did not lose by this. As a portrait painter he received abundant commissions from midlands sitters, and his understanding of the society that bred them gave his portraits an individuality lacking in much fashionable metropolitan portraiture. The midlands in Wright's day were alert to scientific enquiry. Wright's name is often linked with the Lunar Society of Birmingham, that small group of scientists, philosophers, and industrialists who from about 1764–5 met monthly (on the Monday nearest to the full moon) to discuss the practical application of scientific knowledge. Wright did not belong to it, for as Nicolson notes he was 'not in the remotest sense a professional philosopher or man of science' (Nicolson, *Joseph Wright of Derby*, 1.131); but in Derby he was well placed, especially through his

'Lunatick' friends John Whitehurst and Dr Erasmus Darwin, to 'draw from the mainstream of this transforming current of ideas' (Egerton, 15).

From 1765 Wright exhibited in London, annually at the Society of Artists, 1765–76, then less regularly from 1778 to 1794 at the Royal Academy. Wright also exhibited in 1778 and 1783 at the Free Society of Artists, and in 1784 and 1787 at the Society for Promoting the Arts in Liverpool. The label Wright of Derby was first bestowed on him by the *Gazetteer*'s exhibition reviewer of 1768 (quoted more fully below). In an age when it would have been improper to use artists' Christian names, it was necessary to differentiate between the work of two 'Mr Wrights'—Joseph Wright, who began exhibiting in 1765, and Richard Wright, of Liverpool, an exhibitor since 1762. Bestowed for convenience, the label Wright of Derby has stuck to this day. There is no reason to suppose that Wright himself resented it; but with time it carried unjustified connotations of provincialism which tended to diminish his reputation.

1760–1773: early portraiture and first decade of exhibited works Wright's début as an independent artist is in a sense marked by the commencement *c*.1760 of the account book (MSS, NPG archives) in which he recorded most of the commissions received throughout his career. Known to be incomplete, imprecisely dated, and somewhat randomly arranged, Wright's account book nevertheless provides valuable documentation of his work and his patrons, as well as including some illuminating memoranda. Portraiture was to be the mainstay of Wright's career; but he developed an unusually wide range of subjects, many drawn from literature and imagination, eventually finding his greatest pleasure in landscape painting.

Wright's commissions during the early 1760s were mostly for small portraits of sitters in Derby and east midlands towns (Newark, Lincoln, Boston, Retford, and Doncaster). A robust example from *c*.1760 is *William Brooke*, several times mayor of Doncaster, bulking large in brown velvet and painted on a confident scale (127 x 101.6 cm; Doncaster Museum and Art Gallery). While owing something to Hudson prototypes, this already shows that power of candid observation which is characteristic of almost all Wright's portraiture; he rarely flatters. Some of his most sympathetic portraits of the early 1760s are of children (for example, of the Wilmot and Rastall children, in different private collections), depicted with almost solemn directness; older girls in pearls and Hudsonesque finery tend to look plain under his gaze. Wright's most conspicuous early success was with six sharply individual portraits of young men in the uniform of the Markeaton hunt; these were displayed in Derby town hall *c*.1762–3 (they are now in various collections in England and the USA). In painting these portraits—six variations on a theme—Wright learnt to concentrate on what chiefly interested him, which was the play of light and shade over faces, garments, and still-life objects.

Candlelight pictures Wright first exhibited in London in 1765, at the Society of Artists. During the next decade over half the thirty-five or so works he showed there were 'candlelights', in which the source of light—a candle, sometimes a lamp, later fire from a forge—was usually concealed but could be observed to throw powerful shadows over faces, stuffs, and objects, altering perceptions of colour itself as objects receded from light. Many of Wright's smaller candlelight pictures combine dramatic effects with fairly prosaic subject matter, as in *Two Girls Dressing a Kitten by Candlelight* (Kenwood House, London), or in pictures of girls reading letters or boys blowing bladders.

In four candlelights of the 1760s Wright devised more original and elevated subjects. *Three Persons Viewing the 'Gladiator' by Candlelight* (the first work he exhibited, in 1765; priv. coll.) depicts three men, including Wright himself seen in profile, studying a small version of the Borghese *Gladiator*. Absorption in study also infuses the reverentially solemn *Academy by Lamplight*, in which boys learn to draw from the antique (exhibited 1769; Yale U. CBA). Two large candlelights above all made Wright's name in the 1760s. These were *A philosopher giving that lecture on the orrery, in which a lamp is put in the place of the sun* (exh. 1766; Derby Art Gallery) and *An Experiment on a Bird in the Air Pump* (exh. 1768; National Gallery, London). When *An Experiment on a Bird in the Air Pump* was exhibited in 1768, the *Gazetteer*'s reviewer singled out Wright's handling of candlelight as evidence that 'Mr. Wright, of Derby, is a very great and uncommon genius in a peculiar way' (23 May 1768).

An Experiment on a Bird in the Air Pump has become the best-known of all Wright's works, largely because of the compelling image of the lecturer who holds the power of life or death over a white bird in the receiver of his air pump. *The Orrery*, which is concerned with remoter laws governing the movements of the heavens, is no less fine (and includes a portrait of Wright's friend the cartographer Peter Perez Burdett, taking notes). In both pictures Wright depicts people of his own times, of both sexes and various ages, listening and watching intently as scientific knowledge (of a kind not in itself new in the 1760s, but new to ordinary people) is imparted to them. Detailed observation of apparatus—the elliptical brass curves of the orrery, the pistons which can exhaust air from the haunted glass receiver of the air pump—is combined with the sympathetic portrayal of a wide range of audience reactions: children in awe, or fear; some grown-ups eager to learn, but not all likely to comprehend; some blasé; others evidently preferring conversation to instruction. Candlelight heightens the tension and solemnity in each scene. Both subjects were engraved in mezzotint, *The Orrery* by William Pether in 1768 and *The Air Pump* by Valentine Green in 1769, which helped to spread Wright's fame.

What inspired Wright's candlelights? The greatest candlelight pictures had been painted over a century earlier, by masters of the Utrecht school such as Honthorst and Terbrugghen; but few examples had reached England by the 1760s, and Wright did not go abroad until 1773. He may have seen Godfried Schalcken's *Boy Blowing on a Fire-brand* (then at Althorp, now NG Scot.) or, more likely, William Shipley's copy of it (then in London, now Museum and Art Gallery, Maidstone). Some of Wright's English contemporaries, notably Henry Robert Morland, painted candlelights of 'fancy' subjects, and George Romney portrayed his brother in *Boy with a Candle* in 1761 (Abbot Hall Art Gallery, Kendal). Nicolson showed that Wright borrowed ideas for his candlelights from the two series of mezzotint *Heads* by Thomas Frye, published in 1760 and 1761–2 (Nicolson, *Joseph Wright of Derby*, 1.42–4); but these were in monochrome. Frye's mezzotints influenced the very beautiful chiaroscuro effects that Wright achieved in drawing with black and white chalk on paper, as in *Study of a Young Girl with Feathers in her Hair* (priv. coll.) or *Study of a Boy Reading* (Sothebys, 30 November 2000). But Wright's greatest candlelight paintings are primarily the products of his own imagination, based on observation of people of his own time.

Liverpool: portraits and industrial subjects Wright spent almost three years (from late 1768 to the autumn of 1771) in Liverpool, probably with the encouragement of P. P. Burdett, who (having himself moved from Derby to Liverpool) became in 1769 first president of the newly founded Liverpool Society of Arts. Wright's portraits of these years include two remarkable double portraits of friends, each revealing Wright's ability candidly to assess compatibility in married couples. *Peter Perez Burdett and his First Wife, Hannah* (1765; Narodni Gallery, Prague) portrays an ill-matched pair: Burdett restlessly perched, his telescope alluding to his profession as cartographer, while his wife looms large but vacuously beside him in her finery. *Mr and Mrs Thomas Coltman* (exh. 1771?; National Gallery, London) are by contrast in harmony with each other and with the countryside in which they move.

In Liverpool Wright's attention was divided. To increase income, he worked hard at portraiture, emerging as a realistic portraitist of members of Liverpool's prosperous middle class, exemplified in such portraits as *Fleetwood Hesketh* (1769; Walker Art Gallery, Liverpool), *'Mrs' Sarah Clayton*, a businesswoman in her own right (Fitchburg Art Museum, Massachusetts), *Thomas Staniforth*, a slave trader (1769; Tate collection), and the hard-headed *Mrs John Ashton* (1769; FM Cam.). Such portraits have an uningratiating realism far removed from the 'polite' portraiture of his contemporaries.

Portraiture did not distract Wright from continuing to invent subjects deploying candlelight and other (sometimes multiple) sources of light. Notes headed 'Night Pieces' (in his account book, c.1770) record ideas for the picture that took shape as *A Blacksmith's Shop*. In this, a white-hot iron bar on the blacksmith's anvil provides the principal source 'from whence the light must proceed'. Candlelight illuminates minor details, while outside a full moon (a recurring motif in Wright's work) contributes distantly dramatic light. *The Blacksmith's Shop*, exhibited in 1771 (Yale U. CBA), was purchased by Lord Melbourne while it was still on Wright's easel; an admirer commissioned a closely similar version (Derby Art Gallery). A different *Blacksmith's Shop, Viewed from without*, also exhibited in 1771 but untraced since 1810, is now known only from William Pether's mezzotint engraving, entitled *A Farrier's Shop*, published in 1771. Two 'night pieces' of iron forges followed. The *Blacksmiths' Shops* had depicted centuries-old methods of work; but Wright's iron forges, though installed in old buildings, depict the new technology of tilt hammers driven by water power. *An Iron Forge*, exhibited in 1772, was purchased by Lord Palmerston (Tate collection). *An Iron Forge Viewed from without*, exhibited in 1773, was purchased by agents for the collection of Catherine the Great, empress of Russia (it remains in the State Hermitage Museum, St Petersburg).

The fact that there were eager purchasers for Wright's *Blacksmiths' Shops* and *Iron Forges* indicates a likely demand for further industrial subjects; but Wright at this stage showed no inclination to supply it. Instead he turned to literature, almost perversely selecting subjects with scope for exotic or archaic dress. Some of his more recondite subject pictures of the late 1760s and early 1770s failed to sell in his lifetime; these included *A Philosopher by Lamp Light* (exh. 1769; Derby Art Gallery); *The alchymist, in search of the philosopher's stone, discovers phosphorus, and prays for the successful conclusion of his operation, as was the custom of the ancient chymical astrologers* (a Gothic work of imagination; exh. 1771; Derby Art Gallery); and *The Old Man and Death* (from Aesop's *Fables*; exh. 1774; Wadsworth Atheneum, Hartford, Connecticut). Throughout his career Wright showed no inclination to paint pictures for their potential popularity, instead painting pictures of his own choice. These included such diverse subjects as *The Earthstopper on the Banks of the Derwent* (exh. 1773; Derby Art Gallery), in which a hunt servant is depicted by night with his lantern, stopping up foxes' earths before the morning's hunt; and *Miravan Breaking Open the Tomb of his Ancestors* (exh. 1772; Derby Art Gallery), based on Gilbert Cooper's narrative of a Persian tale of sacrilege in search of gold.

In a self-portrait of perhaps c.1772–3 (priv. coll.), Wright portrays himself in turban and 'Persian' dress similar to those he had used for *Miravan*. In the Rembrandtesque tradition, it is unmistakably the portrait of an artist, dedicated (at an age approaching forty) to his art, and confronting the spectator as he might confront a sitter, with a porte-crayon in his hand. The most confident of all his self-portraits, it may have been painted in anticipation of his only journey abroad, to Italy.

Italy and Bath On 28 July 1773 Wright married Ann (or Hannah) Swift (1749–1790); the daughter of a leadminer, she was later described by Wright's niece Hannah as 'a person in an inferior situation of life' (MS memoir of Wright, c.1850, Local Studies Library, Derby). On 1 November 1773, with his wife, his pupil Richard Hurlestone (*fl.* 1763–1780), and the painter John Downman, Wright embarked for Italy, on his only journey abroad.

In his fortieth year, Wright was older than most artists who went to Italy to study ('He has come late to this school,' Father Thorpe observed in a letter of 3 September

1774 to Lord Arundell; Nicolson, *Joseph Wright of Derby*, 1.9); but he threw himself wholeheartedly into drawing antique sculpture and the ruins of Rome, reporting to his sister Nancy that his attention was 'continually engaged with the amazing and stupendous remains of antiquity' (letter of 22 May 1774; Bemrose, 32–3). Greatly admiring Michelangelo, he drew constantly in the Sistine Chapel. Many of Wright's Roman drawings are in the Derby Art Gallery collection (see Fraser). Two sketchbooks used in Rome are in the collection of the Metropolitan Museum of Art, New York, and another is in the British Museum; together they include subjects ranging from the antique to studies of living figures in the Roman streets, landscape, and skies.

In Italy, Wright found two subjects which for him were open-air candlelights on a very grand scale: *The Eruption of Vesuvius* and the annual *Fireworks Display* or *Girandola in Rome*. 'The one [is] the greatest effect of Nature the other of Art that I suppose can be,' he wrote to his brother Richard (letter of 15 January 1776, Derby Public Library). Wright watched the Girandola from viewpoints close enough to make many drawings. On a visit to Naples in October–November 1774 he could not witness a full eruption of Vesuvius (the last had occurred in 1766–7), but he observed outpourings of red-hot lava and copious smoke. For more sensational effects, he derived ideas from the principal painter of Vesuvius, his near-contemporary Pierre-Jacques Volaire (1729–*c*.1802). Wright was to paint Vesuvius and the Girandola repeatedly, often as pendants, and with varying effects. The grandest and most sombre of his Vesuvius–Girandola pendants, painted 1778–9, were purchased for Catherine the Great of Russia (the *Vesuvius* is in the Pushkin State Museum of Fine Arts, Moscow; the *Girandola* is in the State Hermitage Museum, St Petersburg). Wright's extravagantly lurid *Vesuvius in Eruption, with a View over the Islands in the Bay of Naples* (*c*.1776–80; Tate collection) may first have been in the collection of that other Vesuvius enthusiast the bishop of Derry (and, from 1779, fourth earl of Bristol).

In the Gulf of Salerno, Wright found a new subject in two deeply fissured sea-washed caverns or 'grottoes'. First he made meticulously detailed finished drawings of them (Georgian House, Edinburgh). Later they prompted him to invent mysterious subjects, such as *A Grotto by the Sea-Side in the Kingdom of Naples, with Banditti; a Sunset* (exh. 1778; Boston Museum of Fine Arts, Massachusetts) and *A Grotto in the Gulf of Salernum, with the Figure of Julia, Banished from Rome* (exh. 1780; priv. coll.), eventually adapting one of the grottoes for Prospero's cell in a scene from *The Tempest* for John Boydell's Shakspeare Gallery (exh. 1789; untraced, engraved by Robert Thew, 1800).

Apart from his visit to Naples, almost all Wright's time in Italy was spent in and around Rome, where his daughter, Anna Romana, was born in August 1774. Free from the demands of portraiture, Wright found a new interest in landscape. John Downman, who travelled to (and probably from) Italy with the Wrights, proved a stimulating sketching companion. The beauty of the Roman Campagna took Wright almost by surprise. In a letter of 22 May

1774 to his sister Nancy (Derby Public Library) he wrote: 'The natural scenes are beautiful and uncommon, with an atmosphere so pure and clear, that objects twenty miles distant seem not half the way'. A large collection of Wright's landscape drawings from 1773–5 is in the collection of Derby Art Gallery. *Fire at a Villa Seen by Moonlight*, a small work in oil on paper (Agnew Etherington Art Centre, Queen's University, Kingston, Canada), is probably one of the few Roman views that he painted on the spot. Most of Wright's Italian landscapes were painted ten or fifteen years later, some from sketches but mostly from recollection.

Wright left Rome on 10 June 1775, making a fairly speedy journey northwards, with only a fortnight in Florence and one week in Venice ('When one has seen Rome, other places suffer by comparison,' he noted in his journal; Bemrose, 39). After nearly two years abroad, he was back in Derby by 26 September 1775.

On 4 November 1775 Wright moved to Bath, hoping for the success that Gainsborough had enjoyed there; but by 15 January 1776 he reported that he had 'not had one Portrait bespoke' (letter to his sister Nancy; Nicolson, *Joseph Wright of Derby*, 1.13). The lack of commissions enabled him to complete the first of his Vesuvius and Girandola paintings, sent in from Bath to the Society of Artists in 1776. When Bath society eventually yielded a commission, it proved exasperating: the duchess of Cumberland's 'order of a full length dwindled to a head only', confirming Wright's opinion that 'the great people are so fantastical and whimmy, they create a world of trouble' (MS letter to Richard Wright, 9 Feb 1776, priv. coll.). The arrival of John Milnes of Wakefield, cotton manufacturer, was welcome. Wright had begun his portrait in Derby, and now completed it in Bath (Musée du Louvre). Milnes became one of Wright's greatest patrons. Otherwise, working in Bath had proved vexatious and unprofitable. By June 1777 Wright was back in Derby.

Portraits and literary subjects Many of Wright's portraits of the 1780s and early 1790s seem to reflect his pleasure at being back among congenial sitters. His portrait of John Whitehurst FRS, horologer, geologist, and formerly Wright's near-neighbour in Derby (*c*.1782–3; priv. coll.), reflects both the sitter's keen intellect and Wright's reverence for him. About 1792–3 he painted the most striking of several portraits of Dr Erasmus Darwin, wielding a quill (priv. coll.). Erasmus Darwin had moved in 1783 from Lichfield to Derby, adding (to greater distinctions) the role of being Wright's physician. The candour and sympathy of Wright's conversation pieces of sitters whom he knew and liked are revealed in *Revd D'Ewes Coke, his Wife Hannah and Daniel Parker Coke* (*c*.1781–2; Derby Art Gallery) and in *Revd Thomas Gisborne and his Wife Mary*, sitting under a green umbrella (1786; Yale U. CBA). Wright's portrait of Sir Brooke Boothby, seventh baronet, a minor poet (1781; Tate collection), belongs to a more meditative world. Immaculately dressed, Boothby reclines full-length in a darkening glade, one hand on a volume lettered 'Rousseau', an allusion to the manuscript of the *Dialogues* entrusted to him by

Rousseau himself (in 1776), and published by Boothby at his own expense the year before he sat to Wright.

In the 1780s Wright drew on a wide variety of literary sources for subjects of a tender and affecting kind. Sterne had already inspired his *Captive* and *Maria*, and Dr Beattie his *Edwin*. Wright found an equally affecting subject in *The Lady from Milton's 'Comus'* (exh. 1785; Walker Art Gallery, Liverpool). A contemporary source (J. Adair, *The History of the American Indians*, 1775) inspired *The Widow of an Indian Chief Watching the Arms of her Deceased Husband* (exh. 1785; Derby Art Gallery). From Homer's *Odyssey* (in Pope's translation) he took the subject of *Penelope Unravelling her Web, by Lamp-Light* (exh. 1785; J. Paul Getty Museum, Malibu). Wright discussed many of his subjects with the poet William Hayley, especially *The Corinthian Maid* (exh. 1785; National Gallery of Art, Washington); painted for Josiah Wedgwood, this included a glowing potter's furnace in the background. Wright's painting *The Dead Soldier* (prostrate beside his mourning wife and infant child; from the Revd John Langhorne, *The Country Justice*, 1774) reduced Hayley and many others to tears. Wright repeated the subject several times (a good example, signed and dated 1789, Nicolson, no. 240, is in the M. H. de Young Memorial Museum of Fine Arts, San Francisco).

One-man exhibition, 1785 In 1783 Wright quarrelled with the Royal Academy. Having exhibited there annually from 1778 to 1782 he was elected an associate in 1781; but when his name came up for election as a Royal Academician in February 1783, some failure in communication (still puzzling) resulted in his being passed over in favour of the far less able Edmund Garvey. Wright took umbrage. Offered full membership when a vacancy occurred the following year, he declined, and requested that his name be removed from the list of associates. Almost immediately he began planning a gesture of defiance—a one-man exhibition, staged in 1785 at Mr Robins the auctioneer's rooms in Covent Garden.

Wright's selection of twenty-five pictures for this indicates the range of subjects for which he wished to be known. He included only three portraits; by contrast, he showed nine literary subjects of an affecting kind, including *The Lady from Milton's 'Comus'*, *The Indian Widow*, and *Penelope Unravelling her Web* (all noted above), *Julia in a Cavern by Moonlight* (priv. coll.), and two *Hero and Leander* subjects, now untraced. *A Distant View of Vesuvius*, two views of Dovedale (*Morning* and *Evening*), and *A Wood Scene, Moonlight* (not all now identifiable) represented other aspects of his work. The most sensational exhibit was the large *View of Gibraltar During the Destruction of the Spanish Floating Batteries, 13 September 1782*, bought by his patron John Milnes (but long untraced). The exhibition was highly praised by reviewers, the *General Evening Post* for 12–14 April 1785 declaring that 'it is universally acknowledged by artists and amateurs to be the noblest spectacle of the kind ever shewn in this kingdom'. Wright waited until 1788 before exhibiting further work at the Royal Academy. He did not seek membership again.

Last years From the mid-1780s Wright found increasing pleasure in landscape painting, beginning with recollections of classic Italian scenes such as *Lake Nemi* and *Lake Albano*, each painted many times and infused with Wright's reverence for Claude and Richard Wilson. But from about 1790 he began to see landscape through his own eyes. *An Italian Landscape* dated 1790 (National Gallery of Art, Washington) is painted in an entirely individual manner, with patterns of flat colour thinly painted in mauves, greens, russets, and greys. Wright found Derbyshire landscapes as paintable as those of Italy, and demonstrated as much with 'companion' views of San Cosimato and Dovedale (Trustees of the Kedleston Estate Trust, Kedleston Hall, Derbyshire; versions exist). Wright's sheer skill with paint contributes drama to *Landscape with Figures and a Tilted Cart: Matlock High Tor in the Distance* (c.1790; Southampton City Art Gallery), in which Matlock high tor is seen to be almost incandescent in a glow of light. Some scenes are lit by moonlight, others by dramatic effects of fire; but most need no such added sensation. Landscapes of his last years, such as *Landscape with a Rainbow*, 1794, and *Rydal Water*, 1795 (both Derby Art Gallery), reveal powers of enrapt observation, free from conventions of the picturesque. Similar qualities, allied to an almost elegiac feeling imparted by still water, sunset, and receding hills, are evident in *Ullswater* (Wordsworth Trust, Grasmere), probably painted in 1795 after two tours of the Lakes (1793 and 1794).

'I know not how it is, tho' I am ingaged in portraits … I find myself continually stealing off, and getting to Landscapes', Wright wrote to his patron John Leigh Philips (MS letter, 31 Dec 1792, Derby Public Library). But portraiture was his chief source of income, and he could not escape it. From about 1789 new sitters in the shape of midlands industrialists were eager to sit to him—and for portraits generally on a much larger scale than those commissioned by the Derbyshire middle classes. About 1780 Wright had painted *Francis Hurt* (priv. coll.), owner of lead mines, with a lump of iron ore beside him, and on a conventional 127 x 101.6 cm (50 x 40 in.) scale. Wright's portrait of Richard Arkwright, painted some ten years later, c.1789–90, was on a very large scale (241.3 x 152.4 cm; 95¼ x 60 in.; priv. coll., on loan to Derby Art Gallery); it included Arkwright's attribute, a set of spinning rollers (not certainly his invention, though they made his fortune). Wright's portrait of Samuel Oldknow (c.1790–92; Leeds City Art Galleries), the biggest manufacturer of fine muslins in the country (resting his arm on a bolt of fine muslin), was on a similarly large scale.

About 1782–3 Wright had painted a view, *Arkwright's Cotton Mills by Night* (priv. coll.), with little points of candle-light showing from every window of the many-storeyed buildings. The view was neither commissioned nor purchased by Arkwright. Wright's own reaction to this eruption of the factory system into the Derbyshire countryside is not easy to conjecture. F. D. Klingender considered that Wright's picture, showing the mills emerging from a bank of clouds, was 'a romantic view' (*Art and the Industrial Revolution*, rev. edn, 1968, 61). All one can safely say is that

Wright's is not an urgent view. Arkwright's mills (built at Cromford, 1771 and 1776) had been operational for many years before Wright painted them. Possibly the painting chiefly reflects Wright's continuing interest in 'night pieces'. Living in the midlands, he may have become resigned to such aspects of 'progress' as the factory system. A companion *View of Cromford Bridge* and a small picture, *Arkwright's Cotton Mills by Day*, are untraced, but from an old photograph of the latter (repr. Nicolson, *Joseph Wright of Derby*, fig. 331) it appears to be a fairly prosaic picture.

By 1786 Joseph and Ann Wright had five children (one had died in infancy). His niece Hannah recalled that he was indulgent to his children: 'there was not any part of the house in which they might not play, and they could even whip tops in the room where the pictures were arranged all round, and upon the floor' (MS memoir, *c*.1850, Derby Local Studies Library). This suggests that Wright (like Turner, at a later date) may have kept a room with pictures 'arranged all round' for visitors and prospective purchasers to inspect. More widely, Wright's reputation was sustained at home and abroad by the increasing number of engravings of his work; in all, forty-five of his works were engraved (they are catalogued and discussed by Clayton, in Egerton).

Wright painted many self-portraits from *c*.1758 to 1793 (some now lost, including the self-portrait shown in his one-man exhibition of 1785, purchased by Josiah Wedgwood). Among them are a smouldering *Self Portrait in a Black Feathered Hat*, *c*.1767–70 (charcoal, heightened with white; Derby Museum and Art Gallery); a recently rediscovered self-portrait in a broad-brimmed hat (*c*.1780–82; Yale U. CBA); and a self-portrait of *c*.1785 (NPG) in which the gaze seems troubled. Wright seems rarely to have been in robust health, and appears to have suffered from about 1767 from recurring periods of depression, in which he found it impossible to work. He found some consolation through his love of music. He played the flute, having been taught by 'Tacet' (Bemrose, 9), presumably Joseph Tacet, and took part in weekly musical evenings in Derby. When, on his visit to the Lakes in 1794, he wanted to describe 'the most stupendous scenes I ever beheld', it was music that inspired a comparison: 'They are to the eye what Handels Choruses are to the ear' (letter to Richard Wright, 23 Aug 1794; priv. coll.).

Ann Wright died on 17 August 1790. Wright had been treated by Dr Erasmus Darwin for some years for asthma, and latterly for dropsy. He died at his home, 26 Queen Street, Derby, on 29 August 1797, and was buried in St Alkmund's Church, Derby. The most comprehensive collection of his works is in Derby Art Gallery. His work is also well represented in the Yale Center for British Art, New Haven, Connecticut, the Walker Art Gallery, Liverpool, and the Tate collection. JUDY EGERTON

Sources B. Nicolson, *Joseph Wright of Derby: painter of light*, 2 vols. (1968) • W. Bemrose, *The life and works of Joseph Wright, commonly called 'Wright of Derby'* (1885) • J. Egerton, *Wright of Derby* (1990) [incl. D. Fraser, 'Joseph Wright and the Lunar Society', 15–24; T. Clayton, 'The engraving and pubn of prints of Joseph Wright's paintings', 25–9; T. Clayton, 'A catalogue of the engraved works of Joseph Wright of Derby', 231–58; R. Jones, 'Wright of Derby's techniques of painting', 263–71; P. Mitchell, 'Wright's picture frames', 273–88; exhibition catalogue, London; Grand Palais, Paris; and Metropolitan Museum of Art, New York, 7 Feb – 2 Dec 1990] • D. Fraser, *Wright in Italy* (1987) [exhibition catalogue, Gainsborough's House, Suffolk, 8 Aug – 20 Sept 1987] • J. Wallis, *Joseph Wright of Derby* (1997) [incl. catalogue of drawings held by Derby Museum and Art Gallery; exhibition catalogue, Derby Art Museum and Art Gallery] • R. Rosenblum, 'Wright of Derby: Gothick realist', *Art News* [USA], 59/1 (March 1960), 24–7, 54 • B. Nicolson, 'Addenda to Wright of Derby', *Apollo*, 88 (1968), suppl. *Notes on British art*, 12, pp. 1–4 • B. Nicolson, 'Wright of Derby: addenda and corrigenda', *Burlington Magazine*, 130 (1988), 745–58 • W. Busch, *Joseph Wright of Derby: Das Experiment mit der Luftpumpe: eine heilige Allianz zwischen Wissenschaft und Religion* (Frankfurt am Main, 1986) • D. H. Solkin, *Painting for money: the visual arts and the public sphere in eighteenth-century England* (1993), 214–46 • will, PRO, PROB 11/1298, fols. 316r–316v

Archives Derby Central Library, corresp. and papers • NPG, account books • priv. coll., letters, various | Keele University, corresp. with Josiah Wedgwood

Likenesses J. Wright, self-portrait, oils, *c*.1753–1754, Derby Museum and Art Gallery • J. Wright, self-portrait, pencil drawing, *c*.1758, FM Cam. • J. Wright, self-portrait, black and white chalks on paper, *c*.1765, Derby Museum and Art Gallery • J. Wright, self-portrait, charcoal drawing, *c*.1767–1770, Derby Museum and Art Gallery • J. Wright, self-portrait?, oils, *c*.1770, Derby Museum and Art Gallery • J. Wright, self-portrait, oils, *c*.1772–1773, priv. coll. • J. Wright, self-portrait, oils, *c*.1780–1782, Yale U. CBA • J. Wright, self-portrait, oils, *c*.1785, NPG [*see illus.*] • J. Ward, mezzotint, pubd 1807 (after J. Wright), BM, NPG • J. Wright, group portrait, oils (*A Philosopher giving a lecture on the Orrery*), Derby Museum and Art Gallery • J. Wright, self-portrait, oils, National Gallery of Canada, Ottawa

Wright, Joseph (1756/7–1793). *See under* Wright, Patience Lovell (1725–1786).

Wright, Joseph (1855–1930), philologist and dialectologist, was born on 31 October 1855 at Park Hill, Thackley, in the township of Idle, near Bradford, the son of Dufton Wright (1817/18–1866), a woollen cloth weaver and quarryman, and his wife, Sarah Ann Atkinson. His place of birth explained his later whimsical comment: 'I've been an idle man all my life, and shall remain an idle man till I die' (Wright, 1). Nothing, however, could have been further from the truth, for Joseph Wright, largely self-educated, was a man of phenomenal vigour and assiduity. In this he contrasted with his cheerful but shiftless father and took after his energetic mother, who worked hard to bring up four children in the poverty-stricken life of their small one-roomed cottage. For a short period she even had to go with her family into Clayton workhouse, where Joseph, aged five, like Oliver Twist, asked for more bread, and got it—this being an early indication of his enterprising spirit.

Early life and education Sarah Ann, a lifelong Methodist who attended the Primitive Methodist Chapel at Windhill, had a crucial influence on her son. She gave him the example of dignity in the face of hardship, especially after her husband's death in 1866 at forty-eight, and inspired in him a desire to better himself. In later life when he had achieved academic fame she would speak with pride of 'Ahr Jooa' (our Joe), and once, when he was showing her All

Souls College at Oxford, she remarked of this fine building: 'Ee, but it 'ould mak a grand Co-op!', thus illustrating how Joseph Wright was always able to keep in touch with his working-class roots in dialect-speaking Yorkshire (Wright, 2).

Joseph Wright started to bring a little extra income into the family by getting a job at the age of six, working as a donkey-boy at Woodend quarry, Windhill, not far from his home in Thackley. He worked from 7 a.m. until 5 p.m. leading a donkey-cart containing quarrymen's tools, which he took to the smithy to be sharpened or repaired. In the following year, 1862, when he was seven, he managed to get an indoor job at Salt's, the famous mill in the model village built by Titus Salt further along the River Aire at Saltaire. Here the boy worked as a 'doffer' in the spinning department, removing full bobbins and replacing them with empty ones, for which he was soon being paid 3s. 6d. a week. Like other boys of his age he worked as a 'half-timer', attending for a while the school provided by Titus Salt. This was the only formal schooling he ever received, and here he learnt little more than arithmetic, and was not taught to read or write.

At the age of thirteen Joseph moved to Stephen Wildman's mill at Bingley, where he worked first as a doffer, then as a wool-sorter, earning between £1 and 30s. a week, the extra wages being vital to his mother after her husband's death. It was at this mill that the turning point came. During the Franco-Prussian War of 1870, when Joseph had to depend on a few literate workmates for news read aloud from the papers, he became determined to learn to read and write. This was accomplished, at the age of fifteen, with his only two books, the Bible and *The Pilgrim's Progress*, and with help from a reasonably educated workmate, Alfred Brook.

Joseph now started attending night school, first paying 6d. a week and avidly reading the fortnightly instalments of *Cassell's Popular Educator*. At a night school in Windhill, under John Murgatroyd, he embarked on French, followed by German and Latin. At the mechanics' institute in Bradford he studied arithmetic, geometry, and algebra. The first certificate he received was in 1875, signed by Isaac Pitman. He had gained proficiency in shorthand by taking down sermons heard at his mother's Methodist chapel, where he regularly attended morning and evening services. He also attended the Sunday school, where he organized a lending library, and was also in great demand at the popular 'penny-readings', when he recited dialect poems such as those by John Hartley.

By running his own night school at home, charging local lads 2d. a week, Wright supplemented his income: he eventually saved £40, which he spent in 1876 on a journey to Germany during a temporary closure of the mill. He walked all the way from Antwerp to Heidelberg, where at the university he studied German and maths for eleven weeks of a fourteen-week term, at which point his money ran out. On his return to England he managed to secure a post as a teacher at Springfield School, Bradford, and at the same time studied at the Yorkshire College of Science (later Leeds University). In 1879 he became a resident master at the Wesleyan Grove School, Wrexham, went to Roubaix for a while to improve his French, and finally taught at Margate.

In the spring of 1882, having passed the intermediate exam of a London BA degree, Wright returned to Heidelberg, intending to study mathematics. He was, however, encouraged by Professor Hermann Osthoff, aware of his outstanding gift for languages, to devote all his time to comparative philology. Managing to support himself by

Joseph Wright (1855–1930), by unknown photographer

teaching mathematics, he obtained a PhD degree three years later with a three-part oral exam and a thesis entitled 'The qualitative and quantitative changes in the Indo-Germanic vowel system in Greek'. His exceptional talent while still a student led Karl Brugmann, a prominent member of the *Junggrammatiker*, to invite him to produce an English translation of his *Grundriss der vergleichenden Grammatik der indo-germanischen Sprachen*, which was published in 1888. So Joseph Wright became part of the late nineteenth-century expansion of historical linguistics, parallel to a similar rapid growth in the physical sciences.

Academic career and publications In 1886 Wright moved to the University of Leipzig, where he studied phonetics, German literature, and Lithuanian. He also worked for Julius Groos, the Heidelberg publisher, supervising the issue of thirty books. In the following year he moved to London, and in 1888 was invited by Professor Max Müller to Oxford, where he was appointed lecturer to the Association for the Higher Education of Women, teaching Gothic, Anglo-Saxon and Old German. He was also appointed deputy lecturer in German at the Taylor Institution, where he prepared primers in Old High German, Middle High German, and Gothic, published by the Clarendon Press, and later became honorary secretary to the institution's curators. That he still remained close to his Yorkshire roots is shown by the publication in 1892, almost entirely in phonetics, of his *Grammar of the Dialect of Windhill in the West Riding of Yorkshire*. Academic colleagues were said to have at first regarded this as a leg-pull, but he now began to give serious attention to all English dialects, starting the work that was to be his lasting memorial.

Wright's one ambition was to produce a comprehensive *English Dialect Dictionary*. The project had already been started by Professor W. W. Skeat on behalf of the English Dialect Society, founded in 1873. When Wright was appointed deputy professor of comparative philology at Oxford in 1891, Skeat was only too pleased to hand over to him the material already accumulated: an estimated million slips of paper, weighing a ton. Wright, having decided that at least a further million slips would be needed, set about organizing more than a thousand helpers in committees in various parts of the country, their task being to collect words and phrases in local dialect. Of particular interest is the committee in Bradford, Yorkshire, where he had appealed for help to a meeting at the technical college in November 1894. When the members of the Bradford committee had completed their work in 1897, having contributed 35,000 items, they decided that, rather than disband, they would form the Yorkshire Dialect Society (now the oldest of its kind in the world). Dr Wright, who became one of the society's first vice-presidents, was especially pleased, as the English Dialect Society had ceased to function during the previous year.

In 1901 Wright was appointed professor of comparative philology as successor to Max Müller. In the ongoing laborious task of supervising publication of the dictionary he testified to the inspiration and support provided by his wife, Elizabeth Mary (1863/4–1957), daughter of Frederick Simcox Lea. They had first met when she attended his lectures at Oxford. Elizabeth did most of the secretarial work for the dictionary, which included sending out countless letters and 50,000 prospectuses. They celebrated their engagement on the day the first volume appeared, in July 1896, and they married on 6 October. Their attachment was truly romantic and their marriage especially happy in the home built by Joseph at Oxford (subsequently demolished, though the name he gave to the house, Thackley, was preserved in the name of the block of flats on the site). Contemporaries described them as 'the happiest couple in Oxford', but they had nevertheless experienced great sorrow through the loss of both their son and daughter in early childhood.

Achievements The six substantial volumes of the *English Dialect Dictionary* 'of all dialect words still in use, or known to be in use during the last two hundred years' (preface) were finally published in 1905—but at Professor Wright's own expense, as he could find no publisher willing to take the financial risk. The estimated personal cost of £25,000 was as little compared with the monumental task of preparing some 5000 pages containing 100,000 headwords with half a million quotations. No wonder he said of the dictionary that it was 'the one thing I wish to be remembered by'. This also applied to *The English Dialect Grammar*, which he considered an essential philological introduction to the dictionary, published with the final volume in 1905. Although a modern approach would favour a basis of systematic dialect surveys, with etymology for every item, there can be no doubt that Joseph Wright's colossal undertaking will always hold a unique place on the reference shelves. In the words of a Yorkshire Dialect Society resolution welcoming its appearance: 'It is undoubtedly the final English Dialect Dictionary, as the materials from which it is composed are fast disappearing' (Halliday, 16).

Joseph Wright did not rest on the laurels of his lexicography. He continued to give his vigorous and methodical lectures, and to contribute to the life of Oxford, in particular playing a major part in organizing the university's first real school of modern languages, recruiting staff, creating libraries, and doubling the number of language students between 1905 and 1914. He also worked hard for the school of English, serving on the committee and organizing in 1913 one of the first courses for foreign students of English. His great love of clear and thorough teaching was expressed not only in his lectures but in a series of books written especially for students, including a *Historical German Grammar* (1907), an *Old English Grammar* (1908), a *Grammar of the Gothic Language* (1910), and a *Comparative Grammar of the Greek Language* (1912). He then revised his *Middle High German Primer* (1917), and published introductory grammars in Old English and Middle English in 1923 and his *Elementary Historical New English Grammar* in 1924.

Joseph Wright's status as scholar and pioneer was recognized by his election as a fellow of the British Academy on 25 June 1904, and by the award of honorary degrees from the universities of Durham, Aberdeen, Leeds, Dublin, and

Oxford, as well as his honorary membership of the Royal Flemish Academy, the Utrecht Society, the Royal Society of Letters of Lund, and the Modern Language Association of America. His prodigious output continued into old age, when he claimed he could still work fifty or sixty hours a week without feeling tired. It is not surprising that soon after arriving in Oxford a scholar who owed so much to German universities should have gained election to 'the Club': the small group of dons who wanted more prominence for research and the professoriate by comparison with college-based undergraduate teaching. Wright was still forthrightly aligning with this position in his full and detailed evidence to the Asquith commission on Oxford and Cambridge (1919–22), and could have made few friends with his claim that 'far too many of the administrative affairs of the University are in the hands of men whose minds have lost their elasticity' (Bodl. Oxf., Asquith Commission papers, box 1, MS Γογ Oxon b 104, fol. 235). His last years were saddened by the university's controversial failure in 1928 to accept his bequest of £10,000 for extending the Taylor Institution. At the age of seventy-four he succumbed to pneumonia, and died at his Oxford home, Thackley, 119 Banbury Road, on 27 February 1930. He was buried at Oxford.

Those who knew Joseph Wright testified to the personal charm of this bearded, bespectacled, pipe-smoking Yorkshireman, who presided with his wife over regular Sunday tea parties for friends and Oxford students, offering them his 'birthday cake', home-made fruit cake baked every week. In 1925 Sir Michael Sadler described him as 'a good Yorkshireman—hearty, simple, unaffected, affectionate, vigorous, undismayed, and one of the great scholars of the age' (Gunner, 16). The impressive thing about Joseph Wright was not only that he rose to this scholarly eminence from ragged illiteracy, but that he never allowed academic interests to obscure his origins, and enjoyed nothing better than to be able to use his native Yorkshire speech, which, like all dialects, he regarded as an authentic language, with every right to be taken seriously.

ARNOLD KELLETT

Sources E. M. Wright, *The life of Joseph Wright*, 2 vols. (1932) • C. Firth, 'Joseph Wright, 1855–1930', *PBA*, 18 (1932) • W. J. Halliday, 'The Yorkshire Dialect Society, 1897–1947', *Transactions of the Yorkshire Dialect Society*, 7 (1947) • G. E. Gunner, 'Joseph and Elizabeth Mary Wright', *Transactions of the Yorkshire Dialect Society*, 15 (1985) • F. Austin Hyde, 'Yorkshire remembers Dr. Joseph Wright', *The Dalesman* (Oct 1955) • C. Firth, *Modern languages at Oxford* (1929) • *DNB* • *CGPLA Eng. & Wales* (1930) • Bodl. Oxf., Asquith Commission papers, box 1, MS Γογ Oxon b 104 • b. cert. • m. cert. • d. cert.
Archives U. Oxf., letters, photographs, etc. | BL, letters to W. A. Copinger, Add. MS 62551 • Bodl. Oxf., corresp. relating to *English dialect dictionary* • Bodl. Oxf., papers relating to *English dialect dictionary* • JRL, letters to John Howard Nodal relating to English Dialect Society
Likenesses E. Moore, portrait, U. Oxf., Taylor Institution; copy, U. Leeds • photograph, *Telegraph and Argus*, Bradford • photograph, NPG [*see illus.*] • photographs, repro. in Wright, *Life of Joseph Wright*, vol. 1, facing p. 32, facing p. 36; vol. 2, facing p. 388
Wealth at death £24,666 7s. 7d.: probate, 1930, *CGPLA Eng. & Wales*

Wright, Laurence (1590–1657), physician, was the third son of John Wright (*d.* 1644), of Wright's Bridge, near Romford, Essex, and his second wife, Bennet, daughter of Laurence Blaseby, a London merchant. He matriculated as a pensioner of Emmanuel College, Cambridge, on 24 March 1606 and proceeded BA in 1610. He enrolled as a medical student at Leiden on 22 August 1612 and graduated MA at Cambridge in the following year. In 1618 he was incorporated MD at Padua, having been consiliarius there in 1615–16. Wright subsequently pursued a medical career and was admitted a candidate of the College of Physicians, London, on 22 December 1618. He was elected a fellow on 22 December 1622, and thereafter held numerous posts in the college, including those of censor (1628 and 1639) and consiliarius (1647, 1650–57). As an elect of the college from 1642 until his death in 1657, Wright was an active attender of meetings at the college throughout the troubled years of the civil war and interregnum, and was almost certainly rewarded for his loyalty to the new regime by being appointed physician-in-ordinary to Oliver Cromwell. In 1651 he attended on Cromwell in Scotland and was frequently consulted by the Cromwellian council of state in medical matters. In 1656 he was consulted by the parliamentary committee on the proposed Edinburgh College of Physicians, and in 1657 he was ordered to examine the Quaker James Naylor, prior to his trial before parliament. Undoubtedly, Wright's elevation to such a position of authority and trust in the new regime was facilitated by the fact that he shared Cromwell's religious outlook and was one of the staunchest defenders of Independency, or Congregationalism, in professional medical circles in mid-seventeenth-century London. He also held a long-standing association with the Charterhouse Hospital in London, acting as physician from 1624 to 1643, and being chosen as its governor on 21 March 1652.

In terms of his medical practice and outlook Wright would appear to have been highly conservative. A die-hard Galenist, he seems to have possessed little sympathy for the progressive or reformist leanings of some of his medical colleagues. He was also active in upholding the monopolistic powers of the college against all interlopers, a role which became increasingly arduous in London in the years immediately following the breakdown of royal authority in 1642. Something of the flavour of Wright's uncompromising and intransigent temperament can be seen in the observation of the president of the college in 1634: in adjudicating a professional dispute between Wright and John Clark, he warned Wright 'not to be forward in Censuring other men', a trait 'to which he is ever apt' (Annals, 3.332).

Wright married Mary Duke (*d.* 1698), the daughter of John Duke (*d.* 1629), physician, of Foulton Hall, Ramsey, and Colchester, Essex; they had two sons, Henry and Laurence. Duke's mother-in-law, Anne (*née* Snelling), was first cousin to John Winthrop the elder, a tie of kinship which Wright exploited to establish close personal, religious, and financial bonds with the puritan Winthrops. In December 1628 Wright cured John Winthrop the elder of a dangerous fever, and thereafter the London physician corresponded frequently with his famous kinsman, acting for much of the 1630s and 1640s as one of Winthrop's financial and business advisers in London. These letters are also of interest in shedding important light on Wright's religious position. In 1647, for example, he made clear his distaste for presbyterianism, when he confessed to having opposed its principles 'before it was owned in this kingdome many yeers' (*Winthrop Papers*, 5.138). Apparently conditions were much more to his liking in the 1650s, when he attempted to persuade, among others, John Davenport, the founder of New Haven, to return to his native England.

Wright possessed property at Henham and Havering in Essex and was patron of the living of the former in 1654. Undoubtedly a wealthy man, he died from 'a quartan ague' (Munk) on 3 October 1657; he was buried in the church of South Weald, Essex. His wife survived him. Wright's son, Henry (*c*.1637–1664) was also a loyal servant of the protectorate, who through his father's patronage was added to the trade committee of the council of state on 5 February 1656, and was made a baronet by Cromwell on 10 April 1658 (confirmed 11 June 1660). On more than one occasion Laurence Wright tried to marry his son into the aristocracy. In 1656 he attempted unsuccessfully to broker a marriage with the royalist Ishams of Northamptonshire. Henry did eventually achieve his father's goal, however, when in 1658 he married Anne (*d*. 1708), the daughter of the moderate Presbyterian and parliamentarian John Crew, who in 1661 was created Baron Crew of Steane. Henry Wright also served as MP for Harwich from 1660 until his death on 5 February 1664.

PETER ELMER

Sources Venn, *Alum. Cant.* · Munk, *Roll* · *The Winthrop papers*, ed. W. C. Ford and others, 6 vols. (1929–92) · annals, RCP Lond., 3.294, 332 · Isham papers, Northants. RO, 353, 395 · *CSP dom.*, 1651–2; 1654–8 · HoP, *Commons* · R. W. Innes Smith, *English-speaking students of medicine at the University of Leyden* (1932)

Wright, Lawrence (*d*. 1713), naval officer, is first mentioned as lieutenant of the *Baltimore* in 1665. In 1666 he was in the *Royal Charles*, flagship of George Monck, first duke of Albemarle, in the Four Days' Battle and in the St James's day fight. In 1667 he was a lieutenant in the *Constant Warwick* and in the following year served successively in the *Old James*, the *Victory*, and the first-rate *Royal Sovereign*. In 1670 he was assigned to the *Newcastle* in the squadron under Vice-Admiral Sir Edward Sprague in the Mediterranean. Following his return to England with that squadron in 1672 he was successively and briefly appointed first lieutenant in the yacht *Mary* and the *Prince*, before taking post as a captain in the *Nonsuch*.

In the autumn of 1673 Wright was in the squadron in the western approaches to the channel. During October the king noted critically that the *Nonsuch* remained in Plymouth with another vessel, when the commander-in-chief and the rest of the squadron were on station. The king demanded an explanation and Samuel Pepys immediately sent orders 'to hasten' the *Nonsuch* in her preparations for sea (Tanner, 1.88). In December Wright was again ordered to cruise in the Soundings, and after a short

period on station Pepys repeatedly urged him in January 1673 'to lose no time in refitting and getting to sea' with 'despatch' (ibid., 1.199, 200, 222, 226, 228, 231, 261). After experiencing various difficulties and delays caused by the ship's condition and the crew, who wanted their wages paid, the *Nonsuch* visited Tangier and Cadiz, before eventually being paid off in October 1674.

At a meeting of the Admiralty commission in the robes chamber in the presence of the king on 14 November it was reported that Wright, along with eight other captains, had been guilty of transgressing the lord admiral's instructions by bringing home merchandise in his ship. The king ordered that they would not face a court martial provided that their wages were stopped until they paid to the Chatham chest the value they received for carrying the cargo.

Having done this, Wright was commissioned on 28 January 1676 to command the *Phoenix*. In April he sailed from Woolwich, calling to pick up passengers and gunpowder at Portsmouth, bound for Jamaica. In September Samuel Pepys was obliged to apologize for Wright's treatment of Lady Russell, one of the passengers. Pepys remarked 'not that either the perfection of a courtship is to be looked for from a tarpauling, or the fulness of accommodation from so small a ship as the *Phoenix*, pestered as she must be for so long a voyage', but 'in this case, both might have been bettered' (Tanner, 3.271).

Shortly after her arrival Lord Vaughan, the governor of Jamaica, reported that the *Phoenix* was leaky and of little use. Although it meant that there would be no English warship in the West Indies, Vaughan ordered her to return to England, where she arrived in August 1677. In January 1678 Wright was posted to the *Antelope*, where he remained for three months until 27 March, when he was appointed second captain in the *Royal Charles*. On 30 November he was ordered to command the *Unicorn*, guardship at Chatham. Six months later he moved to the *Reserve*, where in June 1679 he received orders as commander-in-chief of the convoy to the Newfoundland fishery.

From 1682 to 1685 he commanded the yacht *Mary* in the last years of the reign of Charles II. Shortly after taking up this command he was also ordered to command the fireship *John & Alexander* during July 1682 and, in the following month, the *Golden Horse*, which had recently been brought back after having been captured in the Mediterranean during the previous year. James II renewed his commission to command the *Mary* in April 1685 and he remained in command of the royal yacht until March 1687, when he was moved into the *Foresight*, in which he carried Christopher Monck, second duke of Albemarle, to Jamaica. Albemarle died in October 1688 after just over a year as governor. Wright, having in July 1687 shifted command to the *Assistance*, returned to England with Albemarle's widow and remains. He arrived at the end of May 1689. In June 1689 he took command of the *Exeter* for ten days, and then moved to the *Dunkirk* for the next three months. In the following October he was appointed to the 60-gun ship *Mary* as commodore and commander-in-chief of an expedition to the West Indies, with orders to fly the union flag at the main, and with instructions 'to act according to the directions of General Codrington in all things relating to the land service', and 'in enterprizes at sea to act as should be advised by the governor and councils of war, when he had opportunity of consulting them' (Admiralty minute, 6 Feb 1690). He was, 'when it was necessary, to spare as many seamen as he could with regard to the safety of the ships', and he was not 'to send any ship from the squadron until the governor and council were informed of it and satisfied that the service did not require their immediate attendance'. To enable Wright to carry out these instructions the king, in council, also appointed him a member of the councils of both Barbados and the Leeward Islands.

After facing continual difficulties in obtaining provisions and making preparations for sea, a total of sixty-nine warships and merchantmen sailed from Plymouth Sound on 9 March 1690, and after a stormy passage reached Barbados on 11 May, with the ships' companies very sickly. Colonel James Kendall, the new governor of Barbados, sailed in the *Mary* with Wright and reported to secretary of state Lord Nottingham that Wright had assured him 'that since his going to sea, he had not known so much wind nor shipt so much water'. Graphically describing the worst part of the storm, Kendall wrote:

> I should not do justice to our admiral, Lawrence Wright, if I did not assure your Lordship that no man living could behave himself with more prudence, courage, and conduct then he has done … there is a general complaint through the whole fleet of these tarpaulins and if our ship had been lost the chief cause would have been for want of good …
> (Hattendorf, 222–3)

Although Kendall attempted to hurry Wright's departure, it was not until mid-June that Wright could go on to Antigua and join Codrington, who combined the two functions of governor of the Leeward Islands and commander-in-chief of the land forces. It was resolved to attack St Kitts by sea and land. This was done, and St Kitts was reduced with but little loss. St Eustatius also was taken possession of, and in August the squadron went to Barbados for the hurricane months. In October Wright rejoined Codrington at St Kitts and it was resolved to attack Guadeloupe, but while preparations were being made, Wright received orders from home to return to England. He accordingly went to Barbados, which he reached on 30 December. The want of stores and provisions delayed him there, and before he was ready to sail counter orders reached him, directing him to remain and co-operate with Codrington. But, in accordance with previous orders, he had sent two ships to Jamaica and two others had sailed for England in charge of convoy. Those that he had with him were in a very bad state, leaking, and with their lower masts sprung. In order to strengthen his squadron as much as possible, he hired six armed merchant ships into the service; but it was the middle of February before he could put to sea, and when he at last joined Codrington at St Kitts, a serious quarrel between the two threatened to put a stop to all further operations.

The quarrel sprang out of the ill-defined relations of the two men, their personality differences, and the probable confusion in the minds of both between the governor and the general, who was, in fact, only a colonel in the army. It is likely that Wright saw the distinction as marked in his instructions more clearly than Codrington did; but the quarrel seems to have been very bitter on both sides. However, after some delays, Wright and Codrington agreed to take the neighbouring island of Marie Galante, as a logical preliminary to attacking the larger island of Guadeloupe, 16 miles away. As with the previous successful joint operations at St Kitts and St Eustatius, the land forces were put ashore at a distance from the fortifications and they successfully seized them without serious opposition from the land side, while Wright's squadron maintained control of the sea approaches. Several weeks later, after additional troops arrived, those on Marie Galante were re-embarked. Following their earlier procedures, the joint forces of Codrington and Wright proceeded to the south-east side of Guadeloupe and began a march across the island to attack the two fortifications at Basse-Terre. French forces intercepted them *en route*, but the English troops drove them back and proceeded to the city of Basse-Terre, which the English burnt. Wright's ships were brought up to bombard the fortifications, but due to wind and current conditions they could not maintain position. To resolve this difficulty Wright and Codrington attempted to establish batteries ashore with guns from the ships. While this work was in progress, they received a sighting report that eleven French warships under Ducasse were approaching. Wright put to sea and chased the French, but as his ships were foul and some of them jury-rigged, the enemy easily outsailed him. Finding pursuit useless, he recalled his ships and returned to Guadeloupe, when it was resolved to give up the attack, avowedly at least, in consequence of great sickness among the ships' companies and the troops, though it is possible that Wright, and certainly Codrington, realized that the appearance of the French squadron threatened the absolute command of the sea which was a primary condition of success. The squadron returned to Barbados, where Wright himself was struck down by the sickness, and on the urgent advice of the medical men turned the command over to the senior captain, Robert Arthur, on 28 June 1691 and took a passage to England.

Writing to London, Codrington accused Wright of 'cowardice and falseness' (*Finch MSS*, 3.83–5), suggesting that he was a traitor who sympathized with the French. In the West Indies party feeling ran extremely high, with most of the officials, as military men, taking the side of Codrington and attributing the failure at Guadeloupe to Wright. The merchants, too, whose trade had been severely scourged by the enemy's privateers while the English ships, by the governor's orders, were kept together to support the attacks on the French islands, attributed their losses to Wright's carelessness, if not treachery, and clamoured for his punishment. Numerous accusations followed him to England, and he was formally charged 'with mismanagement, disaffection to the service, breach of instructions, and other misdemeanours' (*CSP col.*, 13.484–99). In July 1691 he was ordered home in custody, but this order was changed pending receipt of sworn charges. Wright reported in September from Kinsale that his illness had forced him to land in Ireland and he was proceeding to London as soon as he was well enough to travel. A warrant for his arrest on suspicion of high treason was issued on 22 September and he was eventually brought to London. On 20 May 1693 the joint admirals presided at a court martial, which, after 'duly examining the witnesses upon oath', after 'mature deliberation upon the whole matter', and 'in consideration that Mr. Hutcheson, late secretary to the governor, was the chief prosecutor, and in regard of the many differences that did appear to have happened betwixt the governor and Captain Wright', was of the opinion that 'the prosecution was not grounded on any zeal or regard to their majesties' service, but the result of particular resentments', that it was 'in a great measure a malicious prosecution', and resolved that Wright was 'not guilty of the charge laid against him'. The influence of the accusers was, however, so strong that the sentence of the court was virtually set aside, and Wright had no further employment until, after the accession of Anne, he was appointed on 14 May 1702 commissioner of the navy at Kinsale. During the War of the Spanish Succession Kinsale was the smallest of the navy's dockyards. Due to the shoal at the harbour entrance it could only handle ships that were fourth rates or smaller, but its strategic location, repair facilities, and victualling and store depots made it very important to smaller warships protecting trade in the western approaches. When the dockyard was closed at the end of hostilities Wright was moved to the Navy Board as extra commissioner on 8 May 1713. It was only for a few months, for he died in London on 27 November 1713. In Wright's will, written in June 1711, he left to his daughter Roberta all his 'houses, leases, lands, tenements, and goods', from which he also provided an income of £60 p.a. to his wife, Mary, and £30 p.a. to his sister, Susannah Mills.   J. K. LAUGHTON, rev. JOHN B. HATTENDORF

Sources J. R. Tanner, ed., *A descriptive catalogue of the naval manuscripts in the Pepysian Library at Magdalene College, Cambridge*, 4 vols., Navy RS, 26–7, 36, 57 (1903–23) • NMM, Sergison MSS, SER/136 • *CSP dom.*, 1676–7; 1686–7; 1689–92; 1695; 1701–4 • *CSP col.*, vols. 9–13, esp. 1676–7, 1679, 1687–92 • Pitcairn-Jones, 'Ship histories', NMM [card file] • J. Burchett, *Memoirs of transactions at sea during the war with France* (1703) • J. B. Hattendorf and others, eds., *British naval documents, 1204–1960*, Navy RS, 131 (1993) • PRO, ADM MS 6 • J. M. Collinge, *Navy Board officials, 1660–1832* (1978) • *Report on the manuscripts of Allan George Finch*, 5 vols., HMC, 71 (1913–2003), vol. 3 • PRO, PROB 11/537, fols. 246v–247r

Wright, Lawrence [*pseud.* Horatio Nicholls] (**1888–1964**), songwriter and music publisher, was born on 15 February 1888 at 23 Upper Conduit Street, Leicester, the second son of Charles Wright, music teacher and shopkeeper, and his wife, Ellen. He was taught piano, violin, mandolin, guitar, and banjo by his father. When he left St George's School, Leicester, in 1900, he worked at first for Wilsons printers before joining a seaside concert party in Eastbourne at the age of fourteen. He acquired his own music stall at Leicester Market Hall when he was eighteen, having already begun composing songs under the name Horatio Nicholls. He also opened a music shop at 29 Lower Conduit Street

but, after having had enormous success with his publication of the sheet music of 'Don't go down the mine, Daddy' by William Geddes and Robert Donnelly, and being ambitious to develop his business, he decided to move to London. In 1912, in order to begin plugging his songs at music-halls, he rented the basement of 8 Denmark Street in Soho. He was soon to be instrumental in turning Denmark Street into the UK's answer to New York's Tin Pan Alley. He did, in fact, become known as the Daddy of Tin Pan Alley, even though he started up some twenty years after the Manhattan publishing houses.

Wright's first big success as a songwriter was 'Blue eyes', written just before the outbreak of the First World War. When war came, he enlisted and served in the Royal Naval Air Service. One of the best-known trench songs, 'Are we down-hearted—no', was written by Wright and Worton David in their barracks. While serving in the war, he also composed the tune of 'When God gave you to me'. After the war he returned to music publishing, setting up business at Wright House, 19 Denmark Street; within a few years, he was able to advertise that the Lawrence Wright Music Company had the largest orchestral subscription club in the world. For a while he employed Ray Noble (who became famous directing the New Mayfair Orchestra in recordings featuring Al Bowlly) as a staff arranger for his firm.

Wright founded the music magazine the *Melody Maker* in January 1926, largely to promote his own printed music catalogue. The cover of the first issue was illustrated with a photograph purporting to be of Horatio Nicholls, who was described within its pages as 'one of the finest and most popular composers of lighter music, not only in England, but throughout the world'. The *Melody Maker* only began to extend its jazz interests in the 1930s when it was taken over by the Oldham Press. However, besides owning the copyright to many hit songs, Wright had been astute enough to buy up the British and Commonwealth publication rights to music by distinguished jazz musicians such as Duke Ellington, Fats Waller, and Hoagy Carmichael. As a result, jazz standards like 'Mood Indigo', 'Ain't Misbehavin'', and 'Stardust' were to be found in his list. He also sought out material on the continent: he heard Jacob Gade's tango 'Jealousy' in France and asked Winifred May (better-known by her pseudonym Patience Strong) to write a lyric.

Using the *nom de plume* Horatio Nicholls, Wright was prolific as a songwriter. His output includes such well-known songs as 'That old-fashioned mother of mine' of 1919 (words by Worton David), 'Shepherd of the hills' of 1927 (words by Edgar Leslie), and, perhaps best-known of all, 'Among my souvenirs' (words again by Leslie), which was not only hugely popular when written in 1927, but again when revived by Hoagy Carmichael in the film *The Best Years of our Lives* (1946) and when recorded by Connie Francis in 1959. 'Among my souvenirs' is unusual in being a 34-bar melody falling into phrases of 8+8+9+9 bars. The typical Wright song is a standard 32-bar two-step waltz or foxtrot with regular phrasing.

From his youth on, Wright had written topical songs

and songs in celebration of national events ranging from the coronation of George V (the march 'Long may he reign') to the achievements of the air pilot Amy Johnson (the song 'Amy' composed with Jack Hylton to words by Joe Gilbert in 1930). In the 1920s he developed a passion for composing exotic music, such as his waltz 'Allah' (1922) and the songs 'Sahara' and 'Araby' (the words to both by Jean Frederick). To publicize the sheet music of 'Sahara' he paid some glamorous young women to ride camels around Piccadilly Circus, London. This was but one of his many remarkable publicity stunts; others included dropping sheet music from an aeroplane, and using the transatlantic telephone to plug a song. In addition to songs, he published Wright Tutors for piano, accordion, guitar, banjo, and mandolin, and in 1929 he produced a booklet entitled *How to Write a Successful Song*, in which he suggested that a lack of knowledge of music need be no impediment to this.

In 1943, Wright suffered a serious stroke and spent fourteen weeks in University College Hospital, London. Another stroke, in 1952, left him unable to use his right hand, and necessitated the use of a stick when walking. However, he continued to produce his variety entertainment *On with the Show*, which had been given annually since 1924 on Blackpool's north pier and was to survive until 1956. His first singing booth was opened in Blackpool: it was a place where people could hear singers and a pianist perform music from his catalogue. He opened similar booths in other holiday resorts such as Llandudno. In 1961 the BBC broadcast his life story (entitled 'Among my Souvenirs') and, in 1962, he received an Ivor Novello award for outstanding services to British popular and light music.

Wright fell and suffered a leg fracture at his Blackpool home, 13 Carlin Gate, and was taken to Victoria Hospital where he died suddenly on Saturday 16 May 1964. He had lived a stormy personal life, which included three divorces, but at his bedside in hospital was Lillian Jackson, a Liverpool singer and pianist who had been his close friend for twenty-five years. His body was received in the Actors' Chapel of the parish church of St Stephen on the Cliffs prior to cremation at Carlton crematorium, Blackpool, on 22 May. He remained the owner of Wright House in Denmark Street at the time of his death and left £366,000 in his will. The Beatles' company, Northern Songs, bought up the entire Wright catalogue for £812,500 in 1969. In 1984 he was celebrated posthumously in an album of music (published by ATV Music, London) containing one hundred songs that appeared in the Lawrence Wright catalogue from the twenties to the fifties.

DEREK B. SCOTT

Sources *Daily Telegraph* (18 May 1964) • *The Guardian* (18 May 1964) • *Manchester Evening News and Chronicle* (18 May 1964) • *The Times* (18 May 1964) • C. Larkin, ed., *The Guinness encyclopedia of popular music*, 4 vols. (1992) • L. Osborne and D. McCamley, eds., *100 great songs: ATV Music presents Lawrence Wright* (1984) • sheet music of 'Allah' (1922) and 'Araby' (1924) • *West Lancashire Evening Gazette* (27 Oct 1960) • *West Lancashire Evening Gazette* (18 May 1964) • *West Lancashire Evening Gazette* (22 May 1964) • *West Lancashire Evening Gazette* (22 May 1980) • *Blackpool Gazette and Herald* (22 May 1964) • *Blackpool Gazette and Herald* (30 Oct 1964) • L. Wright, *Souvenirs for a century* (1988) • d. cert. • E. Rogers and M. Henessy, *Tin Pan Alley* (1964) **Archives** Blackpool Central Library, collection **Wealth at death** £366,297: probate, 22 Oct 1964, *CGPLA Eng. & Wales*

Wright, Leonard (*d.* in or after 1591), religious controversialist and moralist, may have been the son of William Wright of Bassingbourn, Cambridgeshire, who attended schools in Bassingbourn and Walkern, Hertfordshire, matriculated as a pensioner at St John's College, Cambridge at Michaelmas 1572, and migrated to Gonville and Caius College on 9 June 1574, aged eighteen. There is evidence from his pamphlets that in his youth he was a gentleman able to indulge his recreational interests and that he could have attended university. In 1589 he joined the episcopal counter-attack on the Martin Marprelate tracts, in pamphlets which liberally quote scriptural and classical sources (including the early church fathers).

In his first sally, *A Summons for Sleepers* (March 1589), Wright wrote that Martin and his followers sought 'to marre the Prelate, the auncient grave Pastors, reverend Fathers, and chiefe pillers of our Church', and he compared them to Jack Straw's 'notable and presumpteous crue' (sig. [-]1r–v). Wright equated the Martinists with the Anabaptists of Münster in their 'hipocriticall puritie, churlish sterne countenance, … [and] privie conventicles' (p. 22), as well as their rebellion and rejection of infant baptism. In *The Hunting of Antichrist* (1589) Wright lambasted the new crowd of schismatics who, like 'the theevish cur, … privily in corners (and where they dare in open place)' undermined Elizabeth I's church and government (sig. D1r) and whose allies in Scotland had made the clergy there 'bare and beggerly' (sig. E2r). The writer or writers of the Marprelate pamphlets responded no less caustically. They described him as 'wringle-faced Wright' (*The Protestation of Martin Marprelat*, 31) and satirically suggested that 'Sir Leonard Wright' was a minor attendant in Archbishop Whitgift's household whose task was to 'leade him by the arms' and 'carry his ba[u]ble' (*The Just Censure and Reproof of Martin Junior*, sig. C2v). The use of 'Sir' could mean they thought he was a clergyman, but there is no indication that he ever held a benefice.

Besides sniping at the Martinists and defending the Elizabethan bishops and clergy, Wright denounced usurers, covetous landlords, corrupt officials and lawyers, and 'newe fashions' such as 'great monstrous ruffes' and doublets so deeply slashed that their wearers' 'guts were ready to fall out' (L. Wright, *Summons*, 1589, 31). *Summons* had seven editions, the last in 1637, and the first (1591) of two editions of *The Pilgrimage to Paradise* was dedicated to Baron St John of Bletso (whose chaplain, Tobie Bland, also attracted scorn from the Martinists). Wright's *A Display of Dutie* (1589), of which there were four more editions by 1621 and which is dedicated to the 'most valiant, and famous, Thomas Candish Esquier' (sig. A2r), contains moralistic essays; advice on diet, exercise, and marriage; and curiosities such as an encomium to baldness—'few men lyving untill full age, beccommeth not balde: and the best natures sonest' (p. 38). It is not known when Wright died. A William Wright, perhaps his brother, sold a manor in Bassingbourn parish in 1599.   J. SEARS MCGEE

Sources L. H. Carlson, *Martin Marprelate, gentleman: Master Job Throkmorton laid open in his colors* (1981) · Venn, *Alum. Cant.* · *The Marprelate tracts, 1588, 1589*, facs. edn (1967) · *The Marprelate tracts, 1588–1589*, ed. W. Pierce (1911) · W. Pierce, *An historical introduction to the Marprelate tracts* (1908) · L. Wright, *The hunting of Antichrist* (1589) · *VCH Cambridgeshire and the Isle of Ely*, vol. 8

Wright, Lucy Olivia (1845–1896), philanthropist, was born on 3 November 1845 at Foulksrath Castle, co. Kilkenny, Ireland, the eighth of the nine children of Thomas Wright (*d.* 1854), agent to Lord Carrick, and his wife, formerly a Miss Ball (*d.* 1869), who came from an old Dublin and Drogheda family with Huguenot links. She had seven brothers and a sister; her younger brother, William, to whom she was close, became a clergyman. Mrs Wright was a religious and philanthropic woman who gave her children a Christian upbringing. Lucy Wright gained both her religious convictions and her musical taste from her mother, and her good looks, wit, and humour from her father.

After Thomas Wright's death, his widow and her family moved firstly to Palmerstown, near Kilkenny city, in 1856, then to Blackrock, near Dublin, in 1863, during which time Lucy Wright went to school at Rhyl in north Wales. Her elder and only sister had married a cousin, the Revd Arthur Wright, who was vicar of St Anne's, Birkenhead; in 1868 Lucy and her mother went to live with them. After Mrs Wright's death nearly a year later, Lucy Wright remained with her sister and brother-in-law and moved with them to Tilston, Cheshire, at Christmas 1869. It was here that she began Sunday school teaching and other parish work.

Lucy Wright first became interested in the Girls' Friendly Society while staying with a former school friend in north Wales in 1878, at which time a branch was being started in the St Asaph diocese. The society had been founded in 1875 by Mary Elizabeth Townsend 'To unite for the Glory of God in one Fellowship of Prayer and Service the Girls and Women of the Empire, to uphold Purity in Thought, Word and Deed'. Membership consisted of middle- and upper-class associates, paying at least 2*s.* 6*d.* a year, who were members of the Church of England, and working-class members of 'virtuous character', paying at least 6*d.* a year, with no religious restriction. In June 1879 Lucy Wright attended the branch secretaries' conference at King's College, London, and at the end of the year she became secretary of the council on probation. The title was changed to secretary of the society in October 1880. Although the society had been founded in 1875 it was not until May 1880 that the constitution was finally passed, and the next decade was to be a time of considerable expansion, with the formation of diocesan councils, councils for Gibraltar and northern and central Europe, and branches and similar societies in Scotland, Ireland, and America. Lucy Wright was closely involved in all this activity, besides attending the meetings of the central committees, arranging conferences, and other secretarial duties.

During her sixteen years in office the membership increased from 52,000 to over 200,000. She worked closely with Mrs Townsend, who remained the president, and a lasting friendship was forged.

At first Lucy Wright travelled around the country on society business, but increasing frailty confined her to the London office, where she welcomed all. Towards the end of 1895 her health deteriorated and she went to Bordighera in Italy as the guest of Mr and Mrs Townsend, who owned a villa there. She became much worse during February 1896, and one of her nieces went to stay with her. She died there quite suddenly on 26 March 1896 and was buried in the cemetery at Bordighera.

Lucy Wright was not only a very efficient central secretary, but also a very popular one. Townsend, in her obituary in the *Girls' Quarterly*, dwelt on her attractive personality: 'Everything interested her; no one ever enjoyed the society of friends, or the opportunities of culture that London life affords, or the relaxation of a holiday more than she did, and her own bright manner and winning personality made her attractive to all …. She was always such good company, so full of fun and so susceptible to the real joy of humour'. She emphasized the personal, rather than the administrative, success of Lucy Wright's work: 'To welcome all, to listen to all, to solve problems, to sympathise with the trials of workers, to encourage the fainthearted, to receive confidences while betraying none, to interpret people to each other in the best way, to inspire others to go forward while keeping herself in the background, this was her true sphere of personal work'. The weekly church newspaper *The Guardian* concluded its tribute by noting that 'Few women have been personally known to so large a circle; few certainly have been more beloved'.   VALERIE BONHAM

Sources M. E. Townsend, 'Lucy Olivia Wright: a sketch from life', *Girls' Quarterly* (July 1896), 51–5 · *The Times* (15 April 1896) · *Friendly Leaves* (May 1896) · *The Guardian* (15 April 1896) · *Girls' Friendly Society Associates Journal and Advertiser* (May 1896)
Archives Girls' Friendly Society, London, archives
Likenesses engraving, repro. in Townsend, 'Lucy Olivia Wright'
Wealth at death £1272 13*s.* 1*d.*: probate, 26 May 1896, *CGPLA Eng. & Wales*

Wright, Sir Martin (1692/3–1767), judge, was the eldest son of William Wright, a barrister, and his second wife, Dorothy Finch. He was born into a legal family: his father was recorder of Oxford, a judge in Wales, and a bencher of the Inner Temple, serving as treasurer of the inn in 1719; his brother John also became a barrister of the Inner Temple. In 1709, at the age of sixteen, he matriculated from Exeter College, Oxford, and in November of the same year was admitted to his father's inn, where he was called to the bar in 1718. Wright married Elizabeth, daughter and coheir of Hugh Willoughby MD, of Barton Stacy, Hampshire; and they had two sons and two daughters. Their marriage settlement was dated 2 December 1719.

Wright achieved public notice in 1730 by the publication of his *Introduction to the Law of Tenures*, and three years later he was created serjeant-at-law. In 1738 he obtained an appointment as one of the king's serjeants, and the following year became a baron of the exchequer. Hardwicke had recommended Giles Eyre, a fellow king's serjeant, whom Walpole rejected as a tory, but had also suggested Wright as 'a very thorough Whig and a good lawyer' (Lemmings, 277). Mr Baron Abney wrote in his notebook that the appointment so disappointed Eyre that it hastened his death (Abney's reports, MS IHR 976). Wright remained in the court of exchequer for but one year, from November 1739 until November 1740, when he was translated to the king's bench. In company with other judges he was knighted in 1745, on the occasion of the loyal address after the Jacobite rising. He reported cases throughout his judgeship of the king's bench; the manuscript was bequeathed to the Inner Temple, where it remains, in fourteen volumes; there are also some of his exchequer reports in manuscript, preserved in a copy taken by Thomas Parker (and now in the Lilly Library, Bloomington, Indiana). On 6 February 1755 he surrendered his patent on grounds of ill health, and was granted a pension which was renewed by George III in 1761. He nevertheless lived another twelve years after retirement, dying at Fulham on 26 September 1767.　　　　J. H. BAKER

Sources Foster, *Alum. Oxon.* · Baker, *Serjeants* · Sainty, *King's counsel* · Sainty, *Judges* · Foss, *Judges* · Inner Temple Library, London, Petyt MS 509 · Sir Thomas Abney's reports, U. Lond., MS IHR 976 · BL, Add. MS 36131, fol. 247 · BL, Hardwicke correspondence, Add. MS 35596, fol. 246 · W. Musgrave, *Obituary prior to 1800*, ed. G. J. Armytage, 1, Harleian Society, 44 (1899) · will of Sir Martin Wright, PRO, PROB 11/933, fols. 117v–121r · D. Lemmings, *Professors of the law* (2000), 277 · *DNB*

Archives Indiana University, Bloomington, Lilly Library, MS books · Inner Temple, London, MS books

Likenesses oils, Inner Temple, London

Wright [née Wesley], **Mehetabel** [Hetty] (1697–1750), poet, was born in Epworth, Lincolnshire, the seventh of nineteen surviving children of Samuel *Wesley (*bap.* 1662, *d.* 1735), rector of Epworth and Wroot, and his wife, Susanna Annesley (1669–1742) [*see* Wesley, Susanna]. Her brothers John *Wesley and Charles *Wesley founded the Methodist movement. Hetty, as she was known throughout her life, was strikingly intelligent, and was given the same education as her brothers. She was said to be able to read the Greek Testament at the age of eight.

Hetty grew into a young woman of 'mirth, good humour and keen wit. She indulged this disposition so much, that it was said to have given great uneasiness to her parents' (Clarke, 2.284). By her mid-twenties she had apparently received several offers of marriage; she formed one strong attachment, but her father opposed this match to 'an unprincipled lawyer'. In 1725 she eloped on at least two occasions, and eventually returned home several months pregnant. Her despairing parents forced her to marry William Wright, a plumber and glazier of Louth, Lincolnshire, at Haxey, on 13 October 1725. She moved to Louth with her sister Molly as companion. Her husband, doubtless attracted to the marriage by the offer of a dowry to set up his own business, was a good tradesman but 'a man utterly unsuited to her in mind, education, manners' (Clarke, 2.287). Her daughter was born on 18 February

1726, but died in December. Several other children all died in infancy, these deaths attributed by Hetty to the lead works which formed part of her husband's business.

Family disputes continued. In August 1726 Hetty's brother John caused offence in one of his early sermons by criticizing their father's treatment of her. Her attitude to her father remained impenitent, and he spoke of having disowned her. In 1727 she set up a school, but this failed, and in January 1728 Hetty and her husband were settled in London, where he established a successful business in Frith Street, Soho.

By 1729 Hetty had re-established correspondence with her father, and from 1743 she became increasingly influenced by John's religious views. This increased following a visit to the Wesley family at Bristol to recuperate after a serious illness in 1744.

According to Clarke, the family historian, 'she had a naturally fine poetic genius, which, though common to the whole family, shone forth in her with peculiar splendour' (Clarke, 2.285). Hetty's poems display real quality, ranging from memorial verses to acerbic lines on her wretched marriage. She writes movingly on her grief at the death of a child. The poems appeared sporadically in magazines, and were not collected until the nineteenth century. A visitor recalled Hetty towards the end of her life as 'an elegant woman, with great refinement of manners; and had the traces of beauty in her countenance, with the appearances of being broken-hearted' (Clarke, 2.298). She died on 21 March 1750.　　　WILLIAM R. JONES

Sources A. Clarke, *Memoirs of the Wesley family*, 2nd edn, 2 vols. (1836) · R. Lonsdale, ed., *Eighteenth-century women poets: an Oxford anthology* (1989) · *The journal of the Rev. John Wesley*, ed. N. Curnock and others, 8 vols. (1909–16) · J. Todd, ed., *A dictionary of British and American women writers, 1660–1800* (1984)

Wright, Sir Nathan (1654–1721), lawyer, was born on 10 February 1654 at Thurcaston, Leicestershire, the second but eldest surviving child of Ezekiel Wright (*bap.* 1604, *d.* 1668), rector of Thurcaston and a former fellow of Emmanuel College, Cambridge, and his wife, Dorothy (*bap.* 1626, *d.* 1691), the second child of John Oneby of Hinckley, Leicestershire, and his wife, Emmet. Wright entered Emmanuel College, Cambridge, on 15 April 1670, was admitted to the Inner Temple on 2 February 1671, and was called to the bar on 29 November 1677. He married (licence 4 July 1676) Elizabeth (1654–1705), daughter of George Ashby of Quenby, Leicestershire, and his wife, Mary. They had seven sons and four daughters.

In 1680 Wright was chosen recorder of Leicester. With the surrender of Leicester's charter in 1684 he was replaced by the earl of Huntingdon, who appointed Wright deputy recorder in an effort to placate local opinion. Wright became deputy recorder of Nottingham in April 1688 and later that year again became recorder of Leicester after its charter was restored.

Wright served as a junior counsel to the crown in the trial of the seven bishops who had refused to co-operate with James II's religious policies (1688). He was called to the bench on 21 April 1692 and took the oath of serjeant-at-law six days later. During the rest of the decade he represented several prominent clients, including the new East India Company (1698), the archbishop of Canterbury on his right to deprive Bishop Watson of St David's (1699), and the duke of Norfolk on the bill enabling him to divorce his wife (1700). Together with Sir Bartholomew Shower, Wright was chosen to arbitrate in a dispute between London tradesmen and gentlemen farmers. Their decision was published on 10 June 1697. Wright also represented the crown on several occasions and, in December 1696, was counsel in the House of Lords for the bill of attainder against Sir John Fenwick. Vernon says Wright 'managed this cause with great applause' (James, 1.132), especially as his co-counsel Pratt became too ill to participate. Wright was shortly thereafter rewarded with a knighthood and made king's serjeant.

Wright was named lord keeper on 21 May 1700. He was not the first choice and his appointment disappointed some. Sir Christopher Musgrave commented, 'Is it not ominous to chuse a Lord Keeper from the Gravel Pits?', a reference to Wright's place of residence (*Portland MSS*, 3.620). Wright himself, just recovering from a serious illness, accepted with some reluctance and seems to have regarded the appointment as only short-term. On the accession of Queen Anne, he offered his resignation, which the queen refused.

Wright was twice (1700 and 1701) named one of the lords justices to govern England while William III was out of the country. He was also one of the commissioners in 1702 to negotiate an Anglo-Scottish union and spoke strongly in favour of union. In early 1705 he became embroiled in the Aylesbury election dispute between the two houses of parliament when he granted writs of habeas corpus to two of the counsel committed by the Commons, provoking a protest from the lower house and a response to that protest from the upper.

Before becoming lord keeper Wright had not been very active in partisan politics, allowing some to see him as a whig and others as a tory. However, in 1701 he was one of those on the privy council advising William III against dissolving the tory parliament, and by Anne's reign he was described by Marlborough as a 'violent party man' (Snyder, 1.376). He particularly angered the whigs by his regulation of the commissions of peace, removing over 600 justices, including the whig leader Sir John Somers, and appointing a substantial number of new justices of the peace, usually on the recommendation of tory MPs and local gentry. The whigs in the House of Lords subjected Wright to vehement criticism in early 1704 and the house formally requested a review of the composition of the commissions of peace. Wright made some changes, but they did not satisfy the whig-dominated upper house, which criticized him again the following year. Lord Treasurer Godolphin, viewing Wright as a political liability, sought his dismissal and the election of a more whiggish parliament sealed his fate. He was dismissed as lord keeper on 6 October 1705 and replaced by William Cowper five days later.

Wright's wife died later that month and he retired to his principal estate at Caldecote, Warwickshire. He subsequently participated little in law or politics, though he was appointed justice of the peace for Leicestershire in 1712 and travelled to Leicester in 1715 to support the tory candidates in a controversial parliamentary election.

Macky described Wright as 'a plain man, both in person and conversation, of middle stature' with 'a fat broad face much marked with the small-pox' (*Memoirs of the Secret Services*, 50). Both Bishop Gilbert Burnet and Sarah, duchess of Marlborough, claimed that Wright was disdained by members of both parties and modern historians agree that he enjoyed little political influence or support. An able common lawyer, he came to the lord keepership without any real experience in equity and consequently proceeded cautiously, often consulting other judges. But while he was slow and set few precedents, he was perceived as fair and only one of his rulings was overturned by the House of Lords.

Wright prospered as a lawyer and judge. As early as 1684 he was described as worth £500 per annum 'and rising' (Greaves, 389) and by the early eighteenth century he was able to spend close to £50,000 to purchase various estates in Leicestershire and Warwickshire, including Caldecote which he bought in 1702. He also secured for his eldest son, George, the lucrative office of clerk of the crown in chancery, as well as lesser posts for other relatives.

Wright died at Caldecote on 4 August 1721 and was buried in the parish church on 15 August. A few years later his body was moved to Gayhurst, Buckinghamshire, the principal estate of his son George, where there are marble statues to both Wright and his son.

ROBERT J. FRANKLE

Sources J. Nichols, *The history and antiquities of the county of Leicester*, 4 vols. (1795–1815) · L. K. J. Glassey, *Politics and the appointment of justices of the peace, 1675–1720* (1979) · R. W. Greaves, 'The earl of Huntingdon and the Leicester charter of 1684', *Huntington Library Quarterly*, 15 (1951–2), 371–91 · N. Luttrell, *A brief historical relation of state affairs from September 1678 to April 1714*, 6 vols. (1857) · Foss, *Judges* · J. Campbell, *Lives of the lord chancellors*, 8 vols. (1845–69) · Holdsworth, *Eng. law*, vol. 6 · G. Holmes, *Augustan England* (1982) · Burke, *Gen. GB* (1836) · *Letters illustrative of the reign of William III from 1696 to 1708 addressed to the duke of Shrewsbury by James Vernon*, ed. G. P. R. James, 3 vols. (1841) · *The Marlborough–Godolphin correspondence*, ed. H. L. Snyder, 1 (1975) · *Memoirs of the secret services of John Macky*, ed. J. M. Grey, Roxburghe Club (1895) · *The manuscripts of his grace the duke of Portland*, 10 vols., HMC, 29 (1891–1931) · Le Neve's *Pedigrees of the knights*, ed. G. W. Marshall, Harleian Society, 8 (1873), 457 · *DNB* · parish register, Thurcaston, Leicestershire, 10 Feb 1654 [birth] · parish register, Dennington, Suffolk, 8 Oct 1604 [baptism] · C. E. Botwright, ed., transcript of the register of baptisms, marriages, and burials of the parish of Dennington, Suffolk, Church of Jesus Christ of the Latter Day Saints, Salt Lake City, Utah [microfilm] · parish register, Ashby Magna, Leicestershire, 22 Oct 1626 [baptism] · parish register, Caldecote, Warwickshire, 15 Aug 1721 [burial] · F. A. Inderwick and R. A. Roberts, eds., *A calendar of the Inner Temple records*, 3 (1901), 119 · J. L. Chester and J. Foster, eds., *London marriage licences, 1521–1869* (1887), 1514 · W. Musgrave, *Obituary prior to 1800*, ed. G. J. Armytage, 6 vols., Harleian Society, 44–9 (1899–1901), 6.329 · W. A. Shaw, ed., *Calendar of treasury books*, 15, PRO (1933), 442

Archives Leicester Museum MSS, account book · Leics. RO, notebook | BL, Caryll Papers, Add. MS 28277
Likenesses R. White, portrait, 1700, repro. in Nichols, *History and antiquities* · R. White, line engraving, *c.*1728, BM · marble statue, *c.*1728, Gayhurst church, Buckinghamshire · oils, Inner Temple, London · oils; on loan to Royal Courts of Justice, London

Wright, Sir Norman Charles (1900–1970), agricultural and nutritional scientist, was born in Reading on 19 February 1900, the second son of the Revd Francis Henry Wright, registrar of the University of Reading, and his second wife, Agnes Mary Dunkley. He was educated at Christ Church choir school, Oxford. From University College, Reading, he gained a scholarship to Christ Church, Oxford, where he obtained a fourth class in chemistry and physiology in 1922. As a Ministry of Agriculture research scholar at Gonville and Caius College, Cambridge, he obtained a PhD in 1925. He proceeded to an Oxford DSc in 1937. At both universities he won a college oar, which could be seen on the walls of his homes. From 1924 to 1926 he was a research assistant at the National Institute for Research in Dairying at Shinfield, Reading; the next two years were spent as a Commonwealth Fund fellow in the United States—first at Cornell University, New York, and later, in the US Department of Agriculture in Washington, DC.

On his return to Britain in 1928 Wright was appointed physiologist to the newly established Hannah Dairy Research Institute, Ayr, and two years later, at the early age of thirty, became its first director. While at Hannah, in 1928, Wright married Janet Robison Ledingham, eldest daughter of Dr John Rennie of Aberdeen University. They had one daughter, Mary Elizabeth. In 1936–7 Wright advised the Imperial Council of Agricultural Research in India on the development of the Indian beef and dairy industries. In 1945 he was special adviser to the government of Ceylon. In 1944–5 he was a member of the Anglo-American Scientific Mission to the Middle East Supply Centre and in 1946 was British member of the first United Nations Food and Agriculture Organization (FAO) mission to Greece. In 1947 Wright succeeded Sir Jack C. Drummond as chief scientific adviser to the Ministry of Food; later he became chief scientific adviser (food) of the merged Ministry of Agriculture, Fisheries and Food, a post which he held until he was invited to become deputy director-general of the FAO, based in Rome, in 1959.

Wright was a meticulous worker and an excellent chairman. He chaired the Food Standards Committee from 1947 to 1959 and the National Food Survey Committee from 1948 to 1959. In those functions he developed an extensive knowledge of agricultural and food sciences, nutrition, and social and economic sciences. He also chaired or served on many other committees and councils, including the Agricultural Research Council (1950–55) and the Colonial Research Council (1950–54). He was successively chairman, vice-chairman, and a member of the committee for colonial agricultural animal health and forestry research from 1946 to 1959. He was chairman of the FAO programme committee in Rome from 1953 to 1959.

Wright stayed with the FAO at their headquarters in Rome until 1963 when he returned to London and became for five years secretary of the British Association for the Advancement of Science. He was the first honorary president of the British Dietetic Association (from 1963 to 1969) and addressed the association on food and the future. He became a member of the UN advisory committee on the application of science and technology to development in 1964 and of the council of the British Nutrition Foundation and of the Nestlé Foundation in 1967, holding all three appointments until his death. Wright was appointed CB in 1955, knighted in 1963, and received the honorary degree of LLD from the University of Leeds in 1967.

Wright was wise and kind, with a keen sense of humour. He was severely red–green colour blind and in spite of an apparently strong physique he suffered much from spinal trouble. His chief recreations were travel and photography. Many of his photographs were added to the pictorial archives of the Royal Borough of Kensington. He also enjoyed playing the piano. He died on 16 July 1970 at his home, 65 Addison Road, Kensington, London. He was survived by his wife.

D. F. HOLLINGSWORTH, rev. V. M. QUIRKE

Sources *The Times* (18 July 1970) · *Bulletin of the Ministry of Agriculture, Fisheries and Food* (May 1957) · personal knowledge (1981) · *CGPLA Eng. & Wales* (1971)
Archives Bodl. Oxf., corresp. and papers relating to British Association · U. Reading L., papers and notes
Wealth at death £14,836: probate, 1971, *CGPLA Eng. & Wales*

Wright, Patience Lovell [*née* Patience Lovell] (1725–1786), wax modeller, was born at Oyster Bay, Long Island, America, the fifth daughter of John Lovell (*d.* 1762) and his wife, Patience Townsend. Her father, a Quaker farmer and miller, moved his family in 1729 to Bordentown, New Jersey, where Patience was educated at home in the 'Arts of the Dairy, of Agriculture, and every Branch of such useful and Pastoral Knowledge' (Sellers, *Patience Wright*, 14). She left home to live in Philadelphia from 1745 to 1748, which some biographers interpret as an early rebellious act (taking their lead from Philip Thicknesse's account). On her return to Bordentown, on 20 March 1748 she married a wealthy Quaker, Joseph Wright (*d.* 1769), a cooper, with whom she had four children—Elizabeth, Joseph, Phoebe, and Sarah. When widowed in 1769 she set up business in Philadelphia with her sister Rachel Wells, creating a waxworks exhibition that achieved popular success touring centres such as Boston. In 1771 a catastrophic fire destroyed her exhibits at Queen Street, New York, where she was then living, and this may have prompted her move to London in 1772. Here she set up a similarly successful business making wax portraits of leading society and political figures, notably her countryman Benjamin Franklin, with whom she developed a close and lasting friendship. The production of these *bustos* was a theatrical event, where she would model the wax under her apron, keeping it warm on her lap, and then produce the finished portrait miraculously to the visitor. This is recorded in the etching of her that appeared with an article about her in 1775 in the *London Magazine*, where she was described as the 'Promethean Modeller'. Her fiery temperament and her striking appearance added to her notoriety as a 'crazy-pated genius' (Thicknesse, 1.226). As in Philadelphia, she staged an exhibition of famous figures from history and the present day at her Pall Mall showrooms, a form of public entertainment that continued to be popular, as exemplified by Madame Tussaud's exhibition in the nineteenth century. Her wax effigy of the earl of Chatham (wax and wood, life-size, 1775; Westminster Abbey, London), a different genre of waxwork, is one of the very few surviving examples of her work. (Sellers's biography provides a catalogue of her works as far as it can be assembled.)

Wright's popular success, recorded by Philip Thicknesse who observed her at Bath, was assured after she made portraits of George III and Queen Charlotte, with whom she seems to have had direct and informal contact. However, her political sympathies were not those of the British establishment, and her staunch republican views became increasingly evident and socially difficult as the American War of Independence progressed. Various machinations in aiding sympathizers to the American cause later earned her a reputation as a spy. The portrait of her by her son Joseph Wright [*see below*], shown at the Royal Academy exhibition in 1780, in which she is depicted with modelled heads of Charles I and her busts of the king and queen, has been interpreted as an indicator of her political standpoint. She lived in various locations in London, notably Cockspur Street, Haymarket (which was a meeting place for artists, especially Benjamin West and John Hoppner, who married her daughter Phoebe), and Chudleigh Court, Pall Mall. In 1781 she decided to move to Paris, *en route* for America, largely prompted it seems by her and her family's increasingly difficult position caused by her frequent and voluble espousal of the American cause. In Paris, based at the Hotel de York, she continued her political machinations, with Franklin as the focus for her schemes, while continuing to develop her technique as a wax modeller, her activities there being recorded by Elkanah Watson, a fellow American. However, she returned to London after the end of the war rather than following her original plan to resettle in her homeland. It was in London that she died, on 25 February 1786, after a fall following one of her frequent visits to the American ambassador, John Adams.

Joseph Wright (1756/7–1793) was born in Bordentown, New Jersey, on 16 July 1756 according to his sisters' account, or 1757 according to the register of the Royal Academy Schools, where his age was given on entry on 8 April 1775 as '17 16th last July' (Hutchison, 141). After receiving lessons in art from his mother, Wright entered the Academy of Philadelphia in 1769 and remained there until 1772, when he and two of his four sisters accompanied their widowed mother to England. Following his studies at the Royal Academy Schools, where he gained a silver medal in 1778 and remained until 1781, and with the assistance of Benjamin West, Wright became a portrait painter. At about the time he exhibited a portrait of his mother at the Royal Academy he also painted a portrait of the prince

of Wales (later George IV). But the controversy that arose from the pro-American sentiments evident in his portrait of his mother meant that he never again exhibited at the Royal Academy. After producing a satirical engraving, *Yankee Doodle, or, The American Satan*, he travelled to Paris, where his mother was modelling wax portraits. While there he executed a portrait of Benjamin Franklin based on that produced by J. S. Duplessis. His acquaintance with Franklin enabled him to raise the status of his variant portrait beyond that of a copy.

In 1782 Joseph Wright returned to America, where he practised both portrait painting and wax modelling in Philadelphia. George Washington sat to him several times, the first of which was in 1783 at Rocky Hill, New Jersey. Of this small portrait Wright began a replica for Thomas Jefferson, but he only had time to paint the head before Jefferson left for Paris in 1784; the work was completed by John Trumbull in Paris in 1786. That year Wright moved to New York, where he was successful as a portrait painter. Examples of his work from this period are in the National Museum of American History, Washington, DC; in the New York Society Library; and with the New York Historical Society.

After the United States capital moved back from New York to Philadelphia in 1790 Wright was engaged in work for the US mint. While he held no official appointment, letters by Washington and Jefferson indicate that his commissions amounted to a *de facto* appointment. During this period Wright took on a pupil, William Rush, who became a noted sculptor. Wright died on 13 September 1793 in Philadelphia during an epidemic of yellow fever, a few days after his wife, Sarah Vandervoort, the daughter of his landlady in New York, whom he had married on 5 December 1789. His last work, uncompleted at his death, was a portrait of his family (Pennsylvania Academy of the Fine Arts). Though described by his sister Phoebe Hoppner as 'inclined … to be idle', and by Washington as 'a little lazy', Wright is noted to have been 'an artist of considerable talent held in high regard by his contemporaries' (Meschutt).   ALISON YARRINGTON

Sources C. C. Sellers, *Patience Wright: American artist and spy in George III's London* (Middletown, 1976) · C. Streifer Rubenstein, *American women sculptors* (Boston, 1990), 13–23 · *DAB* · E. J. Pyke, *A biographical dictionary of wax modellers* (1973) · G. C. Groce and D. H. Wallace, *The New York Historical Society's dictionary of artists in America, 1564–1860* (1957), 705 · C. C. Sellers, *Benjamin Franklin in portraiture* (1962), 426–8 · D. Meschutt, 'Wright, Joseph', *ANB* · S. C. Hutchison, 'The Royal Academy Schools, 1768–1830', *Walpole Society*, 38 (1960–62), 123–91, esp. 141 · P. Thicknesse, *Memoirs and anecdotes of Philip Thicknesse*, 3 vols. (privately printed, London, 1788–91), vol. 1, p. 226

Likenesses line engraving, 1775, BM, NPG; repro. in *London Magazine* (1775) · J. Downman, drawing, 1777, BM · attrib. J. Hoppner, oils, *c*.1781–1783 (*The Sybil*); on loan to Boston Athenaeum

Wright, Peter (1603–1651), Jesuit, was born at Slipton, Northamptonshire, of poor parents who were zealous Catholics. His father died when Wright was young, leaving his mother to bring up a large family. He sought work and was engaged for ten years as a clerk in the office of a lawyer. About 1627 he enlisted in the English army in the

67, 294, 386 • P. Wright, *R. P. Petri Writi ... mors quem ob fidem passus est Londini XXIX Maii MDCLI* (Antwerp, [1651])

Archives 114 Mount Street, London, Stonyhurst Anglia MSS, vols. 5, 7 • Stonyhurst College, Lancashire, Stonyhurst College MSS, sermons
Likenesses C. Galle, engraving, repro. in Wright, *Writi* • C. Galle, line engravings, BM, NPG [*see illus.*] • engraving, repro. in Betts, *Blessed Peter Wright*, 156 • engraving, repro. in Oliver, *Collections*, facing p. 211

Wright, Peter Maurice (1916–1995), Security Service officer and author, was born at 26 Cromwell Road, Chesterfield, Derbyshire, on 9 August 1916: it was said that he arrived prematurely because of shock to his mother, Lous Dorothy, *née* Norburn, caused by a nearby Zeppelin raid. His father, (George) Maurice Wright (who became chief scientist at Marconi), had served in MI6 during the First World War, enabling Wright to claim that 'the thread of secret intelligence work had run through the family through four and a half decades'. He was a sickly child. He had a terrible stammer, suffered from rickets, and wore leg irons almost into his teens. Brought up in Chelmsford, Essex, he attended Bishop's Stortford school until 1931, and then worked for a while as a farm labourer in Scotland before joining the School of Rural Economy at Oxford in 1938. On 16 September 1938 he married Lois Elizabeth Foster-Melliar (*b.* 1914/15), with whom he had two daughters and a son.

Although he lacked any formal qualifications, Wright worked for the Admiralty research laboratory during the Second World War. At its end he sat entry exams for the scientific civil service, passing out joint first. For four years he was a principal scientific officer at the services research laboratory and in 1950, at the height of the cold war, he began working as an adviser for the Security Service (MI5), joining the service full-time in 1955. On his appointment Dick White, the head of MI5, told him, 'I'm not sure we need an animal like you in the Security Service' (Wright, 29), but they shared a bond, both having been educated at Bishop's Stortford school. Told from the start that his late entry would deny him any of the agency's directorships, he quickly came to regard most of his colleagues as snobbish: they in turn regarded him with undisguised contempt as a technician, and not as a gentleman. At MI5 he was highly proficient in developing microphones and bugging devices, and many of his ideas were shared with the American CIA.

Technically proficient, Wright became obsessed with the belief that the KGB was infiltrating British institutions. Among the conspiracy theories he supported was the idea that the Labour leader Hugh Gaitskell had been killed by the KGB, a notion put forward by CIA chief of counter-intelligence James Jesus Angleton. With like-minded MI5 officers Wright became convinced that senior figures in the intelligence world, in politics, and in the trade unions were Soviet agents. After Kim Philby's defection in 1963 following a tip-off, Wright became convinced that the KGB had penetrated the higher reaches of the intelligence agencies. In 1964 he became chairman of a joint MI5/MI6 committee, codenamed Fluency, appointed to find the traitor and investigate the whole history of

Peter Wright (1603–1651), by Cornelis Galle

Netherlands. He soon left and after studying for two years with the Flemish Jesuits at Ghent he entered the society in the English province at Watten in 1629. After his philosophical and theological course at Liège he was ordained priest about 1636. He was appointed first to the staff of the English College at St Omer as prefect in charge of discipline; then in 1642 he became a camp commissioner, or military chaplain, to the English and Irish forces at Ghent. In 1643 he was sent to the English mission to the Oxford and Northampton district and in 1646 to London. It was during these years that he was chaplain to Sir Henry Gage, civil war governor of Oxford, and attended him at his death from wounds received at a skirmish at Abingdon. He then acted as chaplain to the marquess of Winchester in London, at whose house he was arrested on 2 February 1651. Committed to Newgate, he was tried for high treason under the statute of 27 Eliz., c 2 of 1585 for being a priest in England. He was condemned to death and was hanged, drawn, and quartered at Tyburn on 19 May 1651. His remains were preserved by the English Jesuits at St Omer but were lost at the French Revolution. Wright was beatified on 15 December 1929.

THOMPSON COOPER, *rev.* GEOFFREY HOLT

Sources H. Foley, ed., *Records of the English province of the Society of Jesus*, 2 (1875), 606–64; 7 (1882–3), 870 • R. Challoner, *Memoirs of missionary priests*, ed. J. H. Pollen, rev. edn (1924), 499–504 • T. M. McCoog, *English and Welsh Jesuits, 1555–1650*, 2, Catholic RS, 75 (1995), 340 • C. Dodd [H. Tootell], *The church history of England, from the year 1500, to the year 1688*, 3 (1742), 114 • *Florus Anglo-Bavaricus* (Liège, 1685), 84–6 • M. Tanner, *Societas Jesu usque ad sanguinis et vitae profusionem militans* (Prague, 1675), 141–6 • records and catalogues, British province of the Society of Jesus, 114 Mount Street, London • G. Oliver, *Collections towards illustrating the biography of the Scotch, English and Irish members, SJ* (1838), 211 • J. R. Betts, *Blessed Peter Wright ... his life and times* (1997) • H. Chadwick, *St Omers to Stonyhurst* (1962),

Peter Maurice Wright (1916–1995), by Stuart Nicol

Soviet penetration of Britain. Given his head, Wright began to seek evidence. He became convinced that Sir Roger Hollis, then head of MI5, was a double agent. The evidence was circumstantial, but to a conspiracy theorist it was enough. His sights were also focused on Labour prime minister Harold Wilson, who he believed to be a Soviet agent. The 'Wilson plot' resulted in break-ins, leaks, dirty tricks, and false stories planted in the press to discredit the Labour government. None the less when Wright retired in 1976, Harold Wilson was again prime minister.

Peter Wright parted company with MI5 in a rancorous mood, believing that he had been cheated out of much of his pension entitlement. He settled in Tasmania, where he bred horses. He returned to Britain at the request of Victor Rothschild, who asked him to help dispel rumours that he was a Soviet agent. Wright agreed, and the result was Chapman Pincher's *Their Trade is Treachery* (1981), which carried the allegations that Hollis (now dead) had been a traitor. When Wright's role in supplying information for the book became known, journalists besieged him. As a result he agreed to break the Official Secrets Act and write his own memoirs. Although appallingly edited, the ghost-written work was published as *Spycatcher* in Australia in 1987; it was an immediate best-seller, its appeal enhanced by the ban on the work in the United Kingdom, under the Official Secrets Act, and made Wright very wealthy.

The Conservative government had determined to prevent publication of Wright's book wherever they could, and began an action in the Australian courts. They famously sent cabinet secretary Sir Robert Armstrong to give evidence. His admission that the government had been 'economical with the truth' when dealing with the Chapman Pincher book brought mockery on the government case. The sight of the frail Wright in his wide-brimmed hat and dark coat entering court compounded the impression of an overweening government seeking to inhibit free speech, and the whole episode slipped into farce. The matter ended in a House of Lords judgment allowing publication in Britain, and in the longer term the Wright case became an important step in opening up British intelligence to public scrutiny. Wright went on to publish *The Encyclopaedia of Espionage* in 1991, which had little impact. By this stage of his life he had become increasingly reclusive, suffering from diabetes and heart trouble; a year before his death in Tasmania on 27 April 1995, he was diagnosed as having Alzheimer's disease.

When the furore over *Spycatcher* died down, the prevailing tendency was to dismiss the substance of Wright's allegations as the product of the over active imagination of a bitter man. His belief that Hollis was a KGB mole is generally not accepted, and Wright himself admitted that his account of the extent of the plot to discredit Wilson was overstated. But the more general portrait he painted of an 'inefficient, infiltrated and unaccountable security service' (Neil) rang true. The implications of the *Spycatcher* affair were thus wide-ranging, both in terms of the enhanced public scrutiny of the security services, and in terms of the limits to which British governments can go to prevent free speech in the interests of national security: in 1991 the European Court of Human Rights ruled that the British government had contravened the law in trying to prevent Wright's book from being published.

PETER MARTLAND

Sources P. Wright, *Spycatcher* (1987) · *The Times* (28 April 1995) · *The Independent* (28 April 1995) · T. Bower, *The perfect English spy* (1995) · *The Guardian* (27–8 April 1995) · *Daily Telegraph* (28 April 1995) · A. Neil, 'The spy who revealed the rot in the core of Britain', *Sunday Times* (30 April 1995) · b. cert. · m. cert.
Likenesses S. Nicol, photograph, News International Syndication, London [*see illus.*] · photograph, repro. in *The Independent*

Wright, Phoebe (1710s?–1778), embroiderer and designer, may have been, according to evidence from her will, the sister of Benjamin Holmes, hosier and glover of Bishopsgate Street Without in Spitalfields, London, and of Joseph Holmes, silk and gauze weaver of Milk Street, off Cheapside, who was married at Christ Church, Spitalfields, in 1742. The will, made after Phoebe separated from her husband, about whom nothing is known apart from his surname, Wright, is undated but it must have been made before the birth of her niece Nancy Wilton in 1752 as she is not mentioned in it. That Phoebe Wright was already a woman of substance at the time is evident from her reference to her mahogany chairs and dining table and a steel grate, all of which, plus the bed she used herself, she left to her brother Benjamin. That her maiden name was Holmes is further suggested by the bequest of 'my best drawing table' to her niece, and presumably namesake, Phoebe Holmes.

In the *Universal Dictionary of Trade and Commerce* by Malachy Postlethwayt, first published in London in 1751, Phoebe Wright is mentioned, among a number of English designers of woven silks who came to the fore about 1744, as having 'eminently distinguished herself by the correctness and elegancy of her drawing and her colouring' (Postlethwayt, 1.736). No designs on paper by her are known, but at Wardour Castle, Wiltshire, is preserved a set of church vestments embroidered in Rome in 1777 for the eighth Baron Arundell of Wardour after designs by her. That on the chasuble incorporates trailing stems with flower sprigs very close to those on contemporary silks. Phoebe Wright was also a professional embroiderer. The earliest reference to her, in a letter of 29 November 1742 from Mary Pendarves, later Delany, to her sister, states that the finest clothes at court on the birthday of the prince of Wales were 'Lady Caroline Lenox's, gold and colours on white, embroidered by Mrs Wright' (*Autobiography … Mrs Delany*, 3.250). It was most unusual for the two skills to be combined in a single person, professional embroiderers generally having to rely on professional artists or pattern drawers for their designs.

Phoebe Wright lived on Great Newport Street in Soho, still quite a fashionable district in her day as well as being the home of various artists and engravers, including Sir Joshua Reynolds (1725–1793), a neighbour on Great Newport Street from 1753 to 1760. While Phoebe Wright would doubtless have trained apprentices in the usual way of an embroiderer she was singled out for royal patronage by Queen Charlotte, who, probably from the late 1760s onwards, made her a yearly grant of £500 to enable her to run a school for training indigent girls of good family in embroidery. Six pupils aged fifteen were admitted at any one time and their training appears to have lasted for two to three years.

In 1770 Phoebe Wright exhibited 'A specimen of needlework now executing for her Majesty' at the Royal Incorporated Society of Artists of Great Britain. This was part of the largest project undertaken by the embroidery school in her day, namely the hangings for a state bed at Windsor Castle and matching covers for two armchairs and eight stools. This embroidery, which is still extant though now at Hampton Court and applied to a new ground, is described in *The Windsor Guide* of 1783 as featuring 'a variety of the most curious flowers, the colours of which are beautiful, and disposed with the greatest accuracy and judgement' (p. 14). The design was by Phoebe Wright herself, while the embroidery was in coloured silks with a little chenille, in accordance with the fashion of the day. She lived to see the completion of the bed but not its installation at Windsor, as she died suddenly at Great Newport Street in November 1778; she was buried at St Anne's, Soho. Her school was taken over by her niece Nancy, whom she had also trained and who had married Joseph Pawsey in 1774, but from the time of her death onwards, while it continued to execute many royal commissions, it had to rely for its designs on the flower painter Mary Moser. It remained in existence, though no longer in London, until Queen Charlotte died, and eventually it came to be associated solely with Nancy Pawsey, Phoebe Wright's name having been forgotten.

As a gifted and independent woman Phoebe Wright was on dining-out terms with such contemporaries as the bluestocking Elizabeth Montagu and Thomas Bentley, the business partner of Josiah Wedgwood. Her designs and embroideries, which seem to have included some of the embroidered pictures popular in her day, were treasured after her death by admirers such as Margaret Cavendish Bentinck, duchess of Portland, and Jemima, Marchioness Grey, who wrote on 23 November 1778: 'She is a great loss indeed to an Art which she has brought to an amazing degree of Perfection and with a sense of taste unknown before' (Phillips, 93).   PATRICIA WARDLE

Sources M. Phillips, 'Queen Charlotte's bed', *Connoisseur Yearbook* (1961), 93 · O. Hedley, *Queen Charlotte* (1975) · *James Beattie's London diary, 1773*, ed. R. S. Walker (1946) · P. Thornton, 'The royal state bed', *The Connoisseur*, 195 (1977), 136–47 · *The autobiography and correspondence of Mary Granville, Mrs Delany*, ed. Lady Llanover, 1st ser., 3 vols. (1861); 2nd ser., 3 vols. (1862) · M. Postlethwayt, *The universal dictionary of trade and commerce*, 2 vols. (1751–5) · *A catalogue of the pictures, sculptures, models, designs in architecture, drawings, prints*, Royal Incorporated Society of Artists of Great Britain (1770) [exhibition catalogue, Spring-Garden, London, 16 April 1770] · *The Windsor guide* (1783) · will, PRO, PROB 11/1131 · P. Johnstone, *High fashion in the church* (2000), 107, pl. 22b

Wright, Richard (*c.*1720–*c.*1775), marine painter, was born in Liverpool and brought up as a ship and house painter. He was probably the Richard Wright baptized on 4 April 1723 at St Nicholas, Liverpool, the son of Edward Wright. An entirely self-taught artist, he was in practice in Liverpool by 1746 and first appeared as an exhibitor in London in 1760, and between that date and 1773 exhibited twenty-five works with the Incorporated Society of Artists and one with the Free Society of Artists. His wife, Louisa, was also a painter and exhibited still lifes, mainly of fruit, at the Society of Artists between 1770 and 1777. They had three children: Edward, a landscape painter, who was baptized on 10 April 1746 at St Nicholas, Liverpool; Nancy, born on 29 May 1748 and baptized on 24 June at St Nicholas, and who exhibited landscapes at the Society of Artists in 1772 and 1773; and Elizabeth, born on 25 March 1751 and baptized on 26 April, also at the same church. Like her brother and sister she too was a painter and exhibited landscapes at the Society of Artists between 1773 and 1776.

Wright was a man of rough manners and warm temper, and during his membership of the Incorporated Society he took an active lead among those discontented with its affairs. His exhibited pictures included *A Storm with a Shipwreck*; *Sunset, a Fresh Breeze*; *A Fresh Gale*; and *River with Boats … Moonlight*. In 1764 a premium was offered by the Society of Arts for the best marine picture; he won this, as was the case with similar prizes given by the society in 1766 and 1768. Waterhouse recorded that 'he painted the marine view in the background of Reynolds's *Duchess of Ancaster*' (Waterhouse, 430). His most notable work, *The Fishery* (Walker Art Gallery, Liverpool; version in Yale U. CBA), is a sea piece of 'good quality with dramatic lighting' (Archibald, 235) for which he obtained a premium of 50 guineas in 1764; from it William Woollett engraved a fine plate. No doubt owing to the excellence of the engraver's work, a copy of this was published in France, on which the name of Vernet is affixed as painter. On the royal yacht *Fubbs* which conveyed Princess Charlotte of Mecklenburg-Strelitz to England to marry George III, Wright made several pictures of the storms encountered on the return journey to Harwich. His picture, *The Royal Yacht Bringing Queen Charlotte to England in a Storm* (*c.*1761), is in the Royal Collection. Wright died about 1775; he was survived by his wife.   ALBERT NICHOLSON, *rev.* ANNETTE PEACH

Sources IGI · E. H. H. Archibald, *Dictionary of sea painters* (1980) · Waterhouse, *18c painters*

Wright, Richard (1764–1836), General Baptist minister, eldest son and second child of six, was born at Blakeney,

Norfolk, on 7 February 1764 and baptized there the following day. His father, Richard Wright, was a labourer; his mother, Anne (d. 1810), claimed cousinship with Sir John Fenn (1739–1794). A relative sent him to school, and would have done more for him had his parents not become dissenters. He went briefly into domestic service as a footboy, and then was apprenticed to a shopkeeper. In 1780 he joined the Independent church at Guestwick under John Sykes (d. 1824) and began village preaching on week nights, an irregularity for which he was excommunicated. The Wesleyan Methodists opened their pulpits to him, but he did not join their ranks.

For a short time Wright ministered to a newly formed General Baptist congregation at Norwich. Here he made the acquaintance of Samuel Fisher, who had been dismissed on a morals charge from the ministry of St Mary's Particular Baptist Church, Norwich, and had joined the Sabellian Particular Baptists, founded by John Johnson (d. 1791). Fisher ministered for periods of six months alternately at a chapel of this connection in Deadman's Lane, Wisbech, Cambridgeshire, and a chapel erected in 1778 by his friends in Pottergate Street, Norwich; Wright was engaged to alternate with Fisher at both places. The arrangement was soon broken, and Wright gave his whole time to Wisbech. His views rapidly changed; he carried his congregation with him from Calvinism to Unitarianism. After they had been disowned by the Sabellian Particular Baptists, he arranged their admission to the General Baptist assembly. His influence extended to the General Baptist congregation at Lutton, Lincolnshire, which had become Universalist in 1790; through this connection, in 1797 he met William Vidler, to whose periodical, the *Universalist's Miscellany*, he contributed in the last half of 1797 a series of letters (reprinted later that year in Edinburgh). The two men exchanged visits, and by 1802 Wright had made Vidler a Unitarian. At this time he wrote much on Universalism.

Wright began to travel as an itinerant preacher, and in 1806 the Unitarian Fund was established in London, with Wright as the first travelling missionary, making his journeys mostly on foot. He was more effective in private than as a preacher, but his debating skill and temper were alike admirable: a small man, he was said to have mounted the table at a public dinner in 1810 to make a rousing speech. In 1810 he resigned his charge at Wisbech to devote himself entirely to itinerant work. His travels extended through most parts of England and Wales, and in Scotland as far as Aberdeen.

In 1819 the Unitarian Fund brought Wright to London to superintend the organization of local preachers. In September 1822 he became minister of a Baptist congregation at Trowbridge, Wiltshire, which he brought into the General Baptist assembly. In 1827 he moved to a small congregation at Kirkstead, Lincolnshire.

Among Wright's very numerous publications, most of them often reprinted, were: *An Abridgment of Five Discourses … on Universal Restoration* (1798); *The Anti-Satisfactionist* (1805), against the sacrificial doctrine of atonement; *An Apology for Dr Michael Servetus* (1806); *An Essay on the Existence of the Devil* (1810); *Essay on the Universal Restoration* (1816); *Essay on a Future Life* (1819); *The Resurrection of the Dead* (1820); *Christ Crucified* (1822); and *Review of the Missionary Life and Labours … by himself* (1824). He left an autobiography, which was not published.

Wright died at Kirkstead on 16 September 1836, and was buried on 21 September. His first wife had died on 6 June 1828; he left a widow and three daughters. Wright's brother, Francis Brown Wright (d. 1837), was a printer and lay preacher in Liverpool, author of *History of Religious Persecutions* (1816), and editor of the *Christian Reflector* (1822–7), a Unitarian monthly. Another brother, John Wright (d. 1828), a lay preacher in Liverpool and the subject of an abortive prosecution for blasphemy for a sermon delivered on 1 April 1817, emigrated to Georgetown, near Washington in the United States. Richard Wright's grandson, John Wright (1824–1900), was minister at Bury, Lancashire, and for a time after its founding in 1861 one of the editors of the *Unitarian Herald* newspaper.

ALEXANDER GORDON, *rev.* R. K. WEBB

Sources [F. B. Wright], 'Memoir of the late Rev. Richard Wright', *Christian Reformer, or, Unitarian Magazine and Review*, 3 (1836), 750–53, 834–8 · J. Gordon, 'George Harris: a memoir', *Christian Reformer, or, Unitarian Magazine and Review*, new ser., 16 (1860), 261–73, esp. 264 · parish register, Blakeney, Norfolk, 8 Feb 1764 [baptism]
Archives Harris Man. Oxf., notebooks, sermons, and papers

Wright, Sir Robert (c.1549–1608x10), tutor, represents a notable example of social mobility in Elizabethan England. 'Meanly born' as the son of a Shrewsbury shoemaker, Peter Wright, and grandson of a husbandman, Wright rose by education and patronage to 'good estate and quality' (Bruce, 20–21). Known to have been a pupil at Shrewsbury School in 1562, he became a protégé of the headmaster Thomas Ashton, following in his footsteps to Trinity College, Cambridge, and into service with the Devereux family. He graduated BA in 1570–71, and MA in 1574, and became a fellow of Trinity in 1573. During 1576 Wright became 'scolemaster' to Robert Devereux, son and heir to Walter, first earl of Essex. This appointment was clearly arranged by Ashton, who sought both to promote Wright and to relieve himself of the task. Wright's instruction of Robert Devereux continued after the latter succeeded as second earl of Essex in September 1576. When Essex was sent to Trinity College as a royal ward in May 1577, Wright became his tutor there, winning an increase in pay to £20 p.a. He also took charge of the young earl's personal expenditure. When Essex left Cambridge in 1581, Wright remained with him and became his steward when the earl set up his own household in 1587. During the following eight years he was involved in many legal transactions on behalf of Essex, usually in company with Gelly Meyrick and the earl's solicitor Thomas Crompton.

At Christmas 1588 Wright married Dorothy, *née* Walwyn, the widow of a rich gentleman pensioner, John Farnham. Essex had almost certainly helped to secure Wright this valuable match. He also ensured Wright's return as MP for Tamworth in 1588–9 and for Shrewsbury in 1593. Wright received a further reward for his service to the earl in 1595 when he became clerk of the queen's stables, an office which Essex controlled as master of the horse. Essex may also have been responsible for Wright's brother Richard winning the common packership of the city of London with royal support at the end of 1594, allowing him to resign as clerk of the Merchant Taylors' Company in January 1595. There is little evidence about Wright's relationship with Essex in the late 1590s. If he is the 'Mr Wright' who rebuffed William Temple early on the morning of Essex's rising of 8 February 1601 (PRO, SP 12/278/57) he had distanced himself from his former master by the time of the earl's final fall. Despite this, he protested his 'unspotted love' for Essex in his will and bequeathed the basin and ewer which he had received as a wedding gift from Essex to the earl's son.

Wright apparently remained as clerk of the royal stables until his death, being knighted at Richmond on 17 May 1605. Although his sister Lucy had married a Shrewsbury neighbour, Wright and his brother established themselves among the families involved in royal service and the great livery companies of London. In 1597 Wright's stepdaughter Dorothy Farnham married George Wright of Richmond, the Oxford-educated son of a London vintner. Wright's brother Richard had already married George Wright's sister Rebecca. George Wright (knighted in 1604) ultimately succeeded Wright as clerk of the royal stables, while Richard Wright became master of the Merchant Taylors' Company in 1611 and used his brother's contacts at court to ensure that his sons won the reversion to his city packership. Wright himself had no children and left the bulk of his estate to his widow, who died in 1638. He bequeathed his books to his brother's sons and money to his sister's children, as well as maps to George Wright and two church leases to his brother Richard. Another £150 was earmarked for the poor of Richmond parish. Wright undoubtedly shared the Calvinism exhibited by his brother and son-in-law, but his nephew Peter Studley (a son of his sister Lucy) later emerged as a staunch anti-puritan. The place, date, and cause of Wright's death remain uncertain. His will was made in 1608 and proved on 27 March 1610.   PAUL E. J. HAMMER

Sources Longleat House, Wiltshire, Devereux MSS 1–5 · *Calendar of the manuscripts of the most hon. the marquis of Salisbury*, 24 vols., HMC, 9 (1883–1976) · BL, Lansdowne MSS 25–30 · PRO, SP 12, 14, 15 · will, PRO, PROB 11/115, fols. 206r–207r · G. W. Fisher, *Annals of Shrewsbury School*, rev. J. S. Hill (1899) · Venn, *Alum. Cant.*, 1/1–4 · PRO, C54, C66 · BL, Add. MS 5750 · J. L. Chester and G. J. Armytage, eds., *Allegations for marriage licences issued by the bishop of London*, 2 vols., Harleian Society, 25–6 (1887) · J. C. C. Smith, ed., *The parish registers of Richmond, Surrey*, 2 vols. (1903–5), vol. 1 · *Liber famelicus of Sir James Whitelocke, a judge of the court of king's bench in the reigns of James I and Charles I*, ed. J. Bruce, CS, old ser., 70 (1858) · HoP, *Commons, 1558–1603* · W. A. Leighton, *Early chronicles of Shrewsbury, 1372–1603* (1880) · T. Newton, *Illustrium aliquot Anglorum encomia* (1589), 124 · W. A. Shaw, *The knights of England*, 2 vols. (1906) · P. E. J. Hammer, *The polarisation of Elizabethan politics: the political career of Robert Devereux, 2nd earl of Essex, 1585–1597* (1999)

Archives BL, letters and accounts relating to Essex's time at Cambridge, Lansdowne MSS 25, 30

Wealth at death substantial; probably several thousand pounds; bulk of estate to widow: will, PRO, PROB 11/115, fols. 206r–207r

Wright, Robert (*c.*1550–1624), Church of England clergyman, was the son of John Wright of Wright's Bridge, Kelvedon Hatch, Essex. He matriculated pensioner from Christ's College, Cambridge, in June 1565, graduating BA (first in the *ordo*) in 1569 and proceeding MA in 1572. In 1574 he quitted Cambridge to follow Thomas Cartwright to Heidelberg University, where, with three Christ's contemporaries, he matriculated on 31 January 1575. After the death of the elector palatine Friedrich III in October 1576, Heidelberg's Calvinist regime temporarily collapsed and Wright returned to England. Although unordained, he began a career of itinerant preaching in godly households, including those of Lord St John of Bletso, Lord Grey of Wilton, and John Butler of Thoby Priory, Essex, later MP for Maldon.

By Christmas 1579 Wright had reached Rochford Hall, Essex, secondary seat of Robert, second Lord Rich. In what has been widely seen as an early exercise in congregationalism, Rich requested his household to accept Wright as their teacher and, in effect, chaplain. In the following months he duly organized religious services and catechized the household, in the process antagonizing the local clergy by drawing attention to their inadequacies.

After Rich's death in February 1581 Wright went abroad, where he was ordained by 'Villiers and other ministers of Antwerp' (BL, Lansdowne MS 109/3). He returned to Rochford by the summer and married John Butler's daughter, Jane (*c.*1550–*c.*1623); their first child was born in February 1582. In September 1581 the third Lord Rich and his bastard uncle Richard visited John Aylmer, bishop of London, to solicit a preaching licence for Wright. When Aylmer refused without assurances of Wright's conformity and knowledge of his orders, Richard Rich physically assaulted him. This incident led directly to a trial before the high commissioners on 7 November 1581, as a result of which Wright, Richard Rich, and the preacher William Dyke were imprisoned for their activities. Their case engaged the sympathy of Lord Burghley, and in September 1582 Aylmer was obliged to agree to Wright's release in return for his 'good allowance' of English orders and the prayer book (BL, Lansdowne MS 36/19).

Wright was probably a founder member, with George Gifford, of the secret clerical conference known to posterity as the Braintree classis, which probably first met in 1582. Settling after his release in Frierning, Essex, he alleged to Aylmer's episcopal visitors in July 1583 that he held Archbishop Grindal's preaching licence. Aylmer does not appear to have pursued him until the autumn of 1584, when he was suspended. Meanwhile, on the eve of the 1584 parliament he, John Huckle, and Gifford were selected for a 'general' conference, and in February 1585 he and Gifford were the Braintree delegates to the 'national synod', which met in London during the final parliamentary session.

On 16 November 1584 Wright covenanted with the Ipswich authorities to become assistant town preacher to Robert Norton from Michaelmas 1585 at a salary of £50. In the event the quarrel between Norton and his then assistant, William Negus, led to the resignation of both in 1585, and Wright took sole charge of preaching duties. He was formally elected town preacher on 8 September 1586 on a yearly contract, renewable at the pleasure of the town and himself.

Wright remained one of the leaders of the conference movement. In 1589, in one of his more hare-brained outbursts, Martin Marprelate drew attention to certain Martinists in East Anglia, including Wright, who were 'all very seditious men' (*The Just Censure and Reproofe of Martin Junior*, sig. A4v). Like Norton before him, Wright seems to have quarrelled with the town authorities over his acceptance of a benefice, and early in 1590 he abruptly left Ipswich to succeed William Fulke as rector of the nearby crown living of Dennington, remaining there for the rest of his life.

In 1621 Wright erected a memorial to Fulke in Dennington church in which he described himself as 'sacrae theologiae professor'. His own memorial inscription records that he and Jane raised eight children past infancy and that 'he spent his younger days in the Study of Divinity at Sundry Universities, at home and in foreign countries'. Wright was buried at Dennington church beside Jane on 7 April 1624, in his seventy-fourth year. His legacy to the parish was later expanded into the Dennington Charity Estate by his second son, Nathan. His fourth son, Ezekiel, rector of Thurcaston, Leicestershire, was the father of Sir Nathan Wright, lord keeper of the great seal. A genealogical table of his sons' descendants was compiled by the antiquary John Nichols. BRETT USHER

Sources *The just censure and reproofe of Martin junior* (1589) • J. Peile, *Biographical register of Christ's College, 1505–1905, and of the earlier foundation, God's House, 1448–1505*, ed. [J. A. Venn], 2 vols. (1910–13) • G. Toepke, ed., *Die Matrikel der Universität Heidelberg*, 1–2 (Heidelberg, 1884) • J. Hasler, 'Butler, John II', HoP, *Commons, 1558–1603*, 1.519–20 • P. Collinson, *The Elizabethan puritan movement* (1967) • BL, Lansdowne MSS 33, 36, 109 • T. E. Key, 'Monumental inscriptions in Dennington church', *Proceedings of the Suffolk Institute of Archaeology and Natural History*, 8 (1892–4), 77–9 • N. Bacon, *The annalls of Ipswche*, ed. W. H. Richardson (1884) • R. G. Usher, ed., *The presbyterian movement in the reign of Queen Elizabeth, as illustrated by the minute book of the Dedham classis, 1582–1589*, CS, 3rd ser., 8 (1905) • J. Nichols, *The history and antiquities of the county of Leicester*, 4 vols. (1795–1815)
Archives BL, Lansdowne MSS

Wright, Robert (1560–1643), bishop of Coventry and Lichfield, was born in St Albans, Hertfordshire. He matriculated from Trinity College, Oxford, on 11 November 1574, aged fourteen, and that year was elected a scholar. He graduated BA on 13 June 1580, became a college fellow in the following year, and proceeded MA on 7 July 1584, BD on 6 April 1592, and DD in July 1597. In 1596 he edited a book of Latin elegies, *Funebria*, dedicated to the memory of Sir Henry Unton. Between 1589 and 1619 he accumulated a string of country benefices which he seldom visited: he was rector of Woodford in Essex from 1589 to 1619; of St John the Evangelist, London, from 1589 to 1590; of St Katharine Coleman, London, from 1591; of Brixton Deverell, Wiltshire, from 1596; and of Hayes in Middlesex from 1601. He became vicar of Sonning in Berkshire in June 1604, and from December 1601 until 1632 was a canon residentiary and treasurer of Wells Cathedral. In 1619 he added the living of Rattingdon in Essex to his other acquisitions. Although not licensed to preach until 1605, Wright also served as a chaplain to Queen Elizabeth and James I, a role in which he appears to have enjoyed a somewhat mixed reputation. In March 1610 Sir Dudley Carleton described him as the 'worst' of the Oxford preachers who had recently achieved prominence at the court.

In April 1613 Wright was chosen by Dorothy Wadham as the first warden of the newly established Wadham College, Oxford. He obtained a royal dispensation to allow him to marry, despite the requirement in the college statutes that the warden should remain celibate. It was perhaps for this reason that he came into dispute with Dorothy Wadham and was forced to resign his post after only three months. It is not clear exactly when he married, and his wife's name is unknown. Subsequently he withdrew to his residence at Sonning, where his son Calvert was baptized in 1620. He was elected on 28 January 1623 and consecrated on 23 March bishop of Bristol, where his efficient management of the episcopal estates (while retaining his treasurership at Wells) caught the eye of William Laud. As bishop of London, Laud later recommended Wright's translation to the see of Coventry and Lichfield in 1632.

Wright's historical reputation has been decidedly mixed. In the earliest account of his life Anthony Wood depicted his worldliness and devotion to his own interests over those of the church. While it has been suggested that Wright was a zealous advocate of ecclesiastical reform, the evidence from his episcopal career suggests that he was, indeed, an avaricious and sometimes negligent administrator, though he was prepared to introduce reforming policies in areas where they did not provoke strong resistance. It appears that he supported the religious initiatives of Charles I and Archbishop Laud but implemented them with pragmatism and caution.

In 1636 Wright was rebuked by Laud for despoiling the episcopal estates of Eccleshall in Staffordshire. He was subsequently criticized for his repeated failure to submit annual accounts of the state of his diocese, and when he did send a report on the see in 1638 it was concerned mainly with the terms of the leasehold on his residence at Lichfield. But despite his preoccupation with such worldly matters, Wright presided over the implementation of Laudian policies. Unlike his predecessor Thomas Morton, he insisted on the controversial practice of bowing at the name of Jesus in the articles of his first visitation in 1633. After 1635 there was an increase in the number of lay people presented to the bishop's court for 'gadding' to hear sermons outside their own parishes, and a similar trend was evident in the treatment of clergy and parishioners who refused to conform to prayer book services. It appears that Wright also promoted the renovation of parish churches in line with national policies. Surviving churchwardens' accounts suggest that the great majority of parishes in the diocese acquired altar rails before 1638. Several parishes were visited by episcopal inspectors in the late 1630s to check that alterations and repairs had been carried out.

The pragmatic side of Wright's nature is exemplified in his dealings with Shrewsbury and Coventry. In 1633 he became involved in a bizarre dispute arising from a Shropshire axe murder. The curate of St Chad's in Shrewsbury, Peter Studley, was apparently encouraged by the bishop to compose an aggressively anti-puritan account of the atrocity, which was eventually published as *The Looking-Glasse of Schisme* (1634). Studley's book provoked outrage in the local godly community by suggesting that the murder was inspired by the principles of 'puritan' religion. The bishop's support for Studley was limited, however. When the curate reported the godly divine Samuel Fisher for being a 'factious minister' Wright decided not to suspend him, since this action would have offended Fisher's influential supporters in the town. The bishop's willingness to compromise was illustrated again in 1637 when he apparently overruled his chancellor, Charles Twysden, over the placing of communion tables in the parish churches in Coventry. Twysden had caused the tables to be moved into the chancels of both churches and surrounded by rails. Following an appeal from the town corporation, which fiercely opposed the alteration, Wright ruled that the table in St Michael's could be moved into the nave at the time of the eucharist and returned to the chancel for the rest of the week. While such measures allowed Wright to maintain friendly relations with local interest groups they also diluted the impact of Laudian policies in the diocese.

Perhaps the best example of the limitations of Wright's episcopate was his treatment of lectureships. In 1633 he informed Laud that he had begun to suppress 'seditious' preaching in his see, but it appears that this early initiative was not maintained. Wright's reluctance to offend town corporations and influential members of the gentry meant that he allowed lectureships to flourish in places such as Birmingham, Coventry, and Nuneaton throughout the 1630s. Contemporary accounts suggest that these provided platforms for godly clergy, including nonconforming divines such as Humphrey Fenn and Tristram Diamond, and attracted large audiences despite the new restrictions on gadding to sermons. Wright's failure in this area suggests that he was a 'severe disappointment' (Hughes, 86) to his superiors.

Wright's response to the political events of 1640 to 1642 was characteristically pragmatic. It appears that he initially supported Laud and his allies but backed down when his own position came under serious threat. In May 1640 he supported the highly contentious new canons which were introduced by the convocation. He joined with eleven other bishops in December 1641 to petition the king against their exclusion from the House of Lords, and against the alleged intimidation of those bishops who had attempted to attend its sessions. This action led to his arrest, along with the other petitioners, and imprisonment in the Tower pending impeachment for treason. In February 1642 Wright defended his actions and pleaded for clemency in a speech to parliament, published as *A Speech Spoken in the House of Commons* [1642]. This denied that he had played any part in framing or circulating the petition, and claimed that he had offered his signature only when it was 'suddenly' presented to him. He apologized for this rash action and expressed his desire to 'regain the esteem and reputation which I was long in getting, and long enjoyed, but lost in a moment'. He appealed to the knights of his diocese 'for their testimony and knowledge of my courses amongst them', and entreated the house to allow him to return to his see. This request was granted and he returned to his episcopal residence at Eccleshall Hall in Staffordshire. The mansion was garrisoned for the king at the outbreak of the civil war and besieged by Sir William Brereton in 1643. The house was under siege when the bishop died in August 1643. Soon after, the royal garrison evacuated, taking his body with them, but they abandoned it near the drawbridge in the rush to escape parliamentary forces. Wright was survived by his son Calvert, who had graduated from Wadham College, Oxford, in February 1637. He squandered his father's inheritance and died a debtor in the king's bench prison, Southwark, in 1666.   D. J. OLDRIDGE

Sources D. Oldridge, *Religion and society in early Stuart England* (1998) · A. Hughes, *Politics, society and civil war in Warwickshire, 1620–1660* (1987) · Wood, *Ath. Oxon.*, new edn · *Harleian Miscellany*, 6 (1745) · W. Laud, *The history of the troubles and tryal*, ed. H. Wharton (1695) · K. Fincham, ed., *Visitation articles and injunctions of the early Stuart church*, 2 (1998), 56–74 [incl. Wright's visitation articles, 1631, 1633, 1637] · P. Studley, *The looking-glasse of schisme* (1634) · R. More, *A true relation of the murders committed in the parish of Clun* (1641) · J. Davies, *The Caroline captivity of the church: Charles I and the remoulding of Anglicanism, 1625–1641* (1992) · *Hist. U. Oxf.* 4: *17th-cent. Oxf.*, 191 · Foster, *Alum. Oxon.* · *Fasti Angl., 1541–1857*, [Bath and Wells], 15 · *Fasti Angl., 1541–1857*, [Bristol], 10 · T. Malbon and E. Burghall, *Memorials of the civil war in Cheshire and the adjacent counties*, ed. J. Hall, Lancashire and Cheshire RS, 19 (1889), 73–4

Archives Lichfield Joint RO, visitation comperta, B/V/1/53–66 · Staffs. RO, churchwardens' accounts · Warks. CRO, churchwardens' accounts

Likenesses oils, c.1632, Trinity College, Oxford; version, Wadham College, Oxford

Wright, Sir Robert (c.1634–1689), judge, was the son of Jermyn Wright (c.1608–1681) of Wangford, Suffolk, and his wife, Anne (b. 1608), daughter of Richard Bachcroft (or Butchcroft) of Bexwell, Norfolk. He was descended from a family long seated at Kelverstone, Norfolk. Wright was educated at the free school at Thetford and at Bury St Edmunds grammar school. He entered Gonville and Caius College, Cambridge, on 1 April 1651 (his namesake entered Peterhouse), and Lincoln's Inn on 14 June 1654. He was called to the bar on 25 June 1661. He had married, some time before 1660, Dorothy (d. 1662), daughter and heir of Thomas Moore of Wiggenhall, St German, Norfolk. This brought him an estate 4 miles from King's Lynn, valued at £1000 p.a. She died in 1662. Wright continued to practise on the Norfolk circuit, being described by Roger North (1653–1734) as 'a comely person, airy and flourishing both in his habits and way of living', although

> he was so poor a lawyer that he could not give his opinion on a written case, but used to bring such cases as came to him to his friend, Mr [Francis] North, [who] wrote the opinion on a

Sir Robert Wright (*c*.1634–1689), by Robert White (after John Riley, 1687)

paper, and the lawyer copied and signed under the case as if it had been his own.   (North, 1.324)

At some unknown date after 1662, but before 22 September 1665, Wright married, as his second wife, Susan (*b*. 1633, *d*. in or before 1681), daughter of Matthew *Wren, bishop of Ely. This increased his legal practice, but 'his voluptuous unthinking course of life' led him into debt. Wright mortgaged his estate to Francis North for £1500 and raised £500 more from Sir Walter Plumer by pledging that it was free from encumbrances. On 10 April 1668 Wright was returned to parliament in a by-election held at King's Lynn. The following year he was named as counsel for the navy, and in 1673 was named by Samuel Pepys as someone who could vouch for his protestantism. In parliament Wright was a supporter of the court and perceived as a potential speaker in debates. The leader of the opposition, the earl of Shaftesbury, described him as 'doubly vile' in one assessment of the Cavalier Parliament. He was appointed counsel for Cambridge University in 1678. On 31 October 1678 information was relayed to the House of Commons that Edmund Coleman, the duke of York's secretary, had visited Wright's lodgings shortly before his arrest. A search of Wright's chambers revealed no incriminating evidence and Wright was able to secure a resolution clearing him of involvement in the Popish Plot. He did, however, stand as a surety for Coleman and subsequently petitioned for part of his estate as compensation. Although he applied to King's Lynn corporation for support, Wright did not stand at the election of February 1679. In 1679 he became deputy recorder of Cambridge. Wright's support for the court saw him knighted on 15 May 1680 and made a king's serjeant on the 17th. He also became a serjeant-at-law, his patrons being his future father-in-law, Scroggs, and the earl of Yarmouth, the leader of the Norfolk tories. On 24 April 1681 he married Anne, daughter of Sir William *Scroggs of South Weald, Essex, the lord chief justice (1678–81). Also in April Wright was made chief justice of Brecon, presumably with the backing of Scroggs and Jeffreys.

On 30 October 1684 Wright was appointed a baron of the exchequer on Jeffreys' recommendation (although if his own later testimony can be believed, the future earl of Ailesbury was responsible), in spite of Lord Keeper North's opposition. In February 1685 Wright became recorder of Cambridge. He attached himself to Jeffreys, reputedly entertaining his superior judge with mimicry. Wright was reappointed on the accession of James II, and he accompanied Jeffreys into the west country in the wake of the Monmouth rebellion. Upon his return James II transferred Wright to king's bench on 10 October 1685. In 1686 he gave his opinion in favour of the dispensing power, when the judges discussed the case of *Godden* v. *Hales*. His support for James II's prerogative powers saw him promoted to be chief justice of common pleas on 13 April 1687, but on 21 April he exchanged offices with Sir Edward Herbert, chief justice of king's bench, again because of his malleability to royal wishes, this time over the declaration of martial law in the army in time of peace. Ailesbury, for one, felt that he had been overpromoted, but 'the prevailing party carried it for him', and that 'he behaved himself with modesty, and for want of talent his head turned round, and he had the misfortune to displease both sides' (*Memoirs of … Ailesbury*, 1.171). Interestingly, he was dispensed from taking the oaths in 1687 which may suggest that his malleability extended to a change of religion, but there is little evidence that he actually took this step.

In 1687 Wright sat in judgment on the earl of Devonshire, fining him £30,000 for striking Colonel Thomas Colepeper while in the royal presence, an action he described as 'next door to pulling the king off his throne'. Having been named to the commission for ecclesiastical causes in 1686, in October 1687 Wright was sent to Oxford to visit Magdalen College. Subsequently, all but three of the fellows were expelled for resisting the royal authority, and declared incapable of holding any ecclesiastical preferment. John Hough, the fellows' choice as president of the college, protested against the proceedings, only to be told by Wright that he would uphold his majesty's authority while he had breath left in his body, and bound him over to appear in king's bench for breaking the peace.

On 29 June 1688 Wright presided over the trial of the seven bishops. It seems that the show of public support for the bishops, particularly among the peerage, unsettled Wright. Although he declared the petition a libel, other judges disagreed and brought the dispensing power in suspending ecclesiastical laws into question. With the bench divided the bishops were acquitted, and Wright probably retained his place only because of the want of a successor. Following his landing in December 1688 the prince of Orange caused two impeachments of high treason against Jeffreys and Wright to be printed at Exeter. Wright was accused, among other offences, of taking bribes 'to that degree of corruption as is a shame to any court of justice', of ejecting the fellows of Magdalen College without trial, and of turning out Lenthall and his officer from the king's bench without trial. He was also attacked over his conduct of the Devonshire trial and his support for the dispensing power. Wright continued to sit in court until the flight of James II and then went into hiding. On 10 January 1689 he wrote to the earl of Danby defending his actions: 'I never advised any of those fatal counsels, nor assisted any other ways than as one unwillingly gotten into a round is pressed along by the force of it, against his own inclinations', and pledging his assistance 'in the establishment of the Protestant religion' (BL, Add. MS 28053, fol. 382). Wright was discovered in the Old Bailey on 13 February and brought before the lord mayor of London, who committed him to Newgate. On 6 May he was brought before the Lords to answer for his action in the case of the earl of Devonshire when his overruling the earl's plea of privilege and committing him to prison was declared a manifest breach of the privilege of parliament. Wright was returned to Newgate, where he died of fever on 18 May 1689. On 18 June it was decided to except his name from the Bill of Indemnity, but his name does not occur in the final act. His son, Robert, emigrated to South Carolina, where he became chief justice.

STUART HANDLEY

Robert Alderson Wright, Baron Wright (1869–1964), by Sir Gerald Kelly, exh. RA 1952

Sources HoP, *Commons, 1660–90*, 3.766–8 • Sainty, *Judges*, 12, 34, 50, 126 • Baker, *Serjeants*, 447, 545 • Venn, *Alum. Cant.* • G. W. Keeton, *Lord Chancellor Jeffreys and the Stuart cause* (1965), 112–3, 327, 427–9, 434 • *Seventh report*, HMC, 6 (1879), 420 • N. Luttrell, *A brief historical relation of state affairs from September 1678 to April 1714*, 1 (1857), 416–17, 444, 469, 502, 530, 536, 554 • Foss, *Judges*, 7.280–84 • R. North, *The lives of … Francis North … Dudley North … and … John North*, ed. A. Jessopp, 1 (1890), 324–6 • F. Hargrave, ed., *A complete collection of state-trials*, 4th edn, 11 vols. (1776–81), 11.1353–72; 12.26–112, 183–524 • *Miscellanea Genealogica et Heraldica*, ser. 5, vol. 3, 73 • *The Genealogist*, new ser. 6, 171 • J. Miller, *Popery and politics in England, 1660–1688* (1973), 221 • *DNB*

Likenesses J. Riley, 1687 • R. White, line engraving (after J. Riley, 1687), BM, NPG [*see illus.*]

Wright, Robert Alderson, **Baron Wright** (1869–1964), judge, was born on 15 October 1869 at South Shields, co. Durham, the son of John Wright, marine superintendent, and his wife, Elizabeth Middleton, daughter of John Carr, of Shields. Little is known about Wright's background, but he lived with his mother until she died. Sources refer to him as being educated privately but it is not known what he did in his late teens and early twenties, although at one point he was a schoolmaster. At the age of twenty-four he went up to Trinity College, Cambridge, where he gained a first class in both parts of the classical tripos in 1895–6 and part two of the moral sciences tripos in 1897. In 1899 he won a prize fellowship at Trinity, which paid him £200 a year for six years and enabled him to be called to the bar in 1900, at the ripe age, for those days, of thirty-

one. After the death of his mother Wright married in 1928 Marjory Avis Bullows (*d.* 1980), an accomplished horsewoman and master of the Tedworth hounds. They had no children.

In understanding Wright there are a number of influences to consider. It is almost certain that he had absorbed a good sense of commercial practice from his father and his early years of work. Second, his pupillage was at the commercial bar and he entered the chambers of Thomas Scrutton who was the leader of the commercial bar, which had been reinvigorated by the establishment of the commercial court (or list) in the 1890s. Although not an easy man, Scrutton was a superb commercial lawyer. He was also, for a practitioner, remarkably thoughtful on the issue of the public role of the courts, and he was concerned about how the law approached social issues. Wright's exposure to such social issues was further enhanced by his appointment as lecturer in industrial law at the newly founded London School of Economics. By the time he reached his thirties, therefore, Wright, in comparison with his peers, had been more exposed to academic law, the interaction of law and social policy, and the role of law in commercial life.

Despite these advantages—if such they were—Wright's practice developed slowly, even by the slow standards of the commercial bar in those days. After ten years at the bar his practice was so modest that he considered becoming a full-time academic. It was, however, a time when Europe was gearing up for war, and suddenly shipping cases boomed. Within one year, Wright's practice went from £300 per annum to £3000 per annum. His career was launched. When war broke out in 1914 he was already forty-five, and so entitled to remain at the bar, rather than enlist. The First World War was especially lucrative for the commercial bar. Wright became an expert in war risk insurance and was in constant demand. By 1917 he had taken silk.

Wright was no flamboyant advocate at a time when that was thought to be an asset. He was seen as primarily a presenter of facts and arguer of law. If prolix, he was persuasive, and his success grew. In 1925, at the age of fifty-six, he was appointed a judge of the King's Bench Division of the High Court and given the customary knighthood. He might have remained there or joined Scrutton in the Court of Appeal, had it not been for the lord chancellorship of Lord Sankey. Sankey was attempting to raise the quality of the judiciary, and particularly that in the final appeal court, the House of Lords. The late twenties had been a period of the retirement of the high tory law lords Atkinson, Carson, and Sumner, and the Liberal Shaw. Lord Cave (1924–8) and Lord Hailsham (1928–9), the Conservative lord chancellors, began depoliticization. In a remarkable move, Sankey (lord chancellor, 1929–35) completed the professionalization process in 1932 by translating Wright directly from the King's Bench Division to the House of Lords, without the intervening step of the Court of Appeal. Wright remained a lord of appeal in ordinary (a law lord) until 1947, although he agreed to serve as the presiding judge of the Court of Appeal (the master of the rolls) from 1935 to 1937.

Wright was one of the few significant British appeal judges of the twentieth century. To understand his contribution, however, one has to realize that legal fashions change, and for two decades after his retirement Wright's style of judging and his broad progressive approach to law were out of fashion. At the bar in the fifties and sixties it was said 'cite Wright, but follow Atkin' (the latter being Lord Atkin of Aberdovey). This trend was consolidated by Lord Jowitt (Labour lord chancellor, 1945–51) and by Lord Simonds (Conservative lord chancellor, 1951–4). They used their formalistic approach to law to attempt to downplay the work of Wright. Thus, for many years, Wright lived in the shadow of Atkin although, in the last twenty-five years, with the return of a more progressive and purposive approach to law, the importance of Wright as a remarkable appeal judge has been appreciated.

In some areas it is true that Wright was overshadowed by Atkin. Wright did not deliver judgments (speeches) as famous as that of Atkin's in *Donoghue* v. *Stevenson* (1932). Yet Wright was responsible for providing the system of assessing damages in the new tort of negligence: 'The law cannot take account of everything that follows a wrongful act' (*The Liesbosch* v. *The Edison*, 1933), while at the same time underlining that the new tort was indeed totally separate from contract:

> Now that the forms of action have been abolished and it is recognised that negligence is an independent tort, it is not necessary to consider if the duty is to be based on contract or whether it is based simply on the relationship between the parties. (*Lindsey County Council* v. *Marshall*, 1936)

Wright's greatest contribution in tort, however, reflected his interest in protecting working men. He greatly restructured the nineteenth-century doctrine of common employment, while insisting that employers were under a duty to provide a safe system of work, independent of any liability under the Workmen's Compensation Acts:

> What is all important is to adapt the standard of what is negligent to the facts, and to give due regard to the actual conditions under which men work in a factory or mine, at the long hours and the fatigue, to the slackening of attention which naturally comes from constant repetition of the same operation, to the noise and confusion in which the man works, to his preoccupation in what he is actually doing at the cost perhaps of some inattention to his own safety. (*Wilsons and Clyde Coal Company* v. *English*, 1937)

It was, however, in the area of contract and commercial law that, not surprisingly, Wright came into his own. He advanced the position, so alien to the formalists, that it was unreasonable to expect to develop principles of contract which applied to all factual situations (*Luxor (Eastborne) Ltd* v. *Cooper*, 1940). He pioneered a more flexible approach to the interpretation of contract: 'the duty of the court is to construe such documents fairly and broadly, without being too astute or subtle in finding defects' (*Hillas & Co.* v. *Arcos*, 1932). His linking of commercial law and practice covered such areas as misrepresentation (*Spense* v. *Crawford*, 1939) but, perhaps most significantly, the principles of frustration of contract, so essential for a period of international tension and conflict. His approach could not have been more flexible:

> in ascertaining the meaning of the contract and its application to the actual occurrences, the court has to decide not what the parties actually intended, but what as reasonable men they should have intended. The court personifies for this purpose the reasonable man. (*Joseph Constantine SS Line Ltd* v. *Imperial Smelting Corp.*, 1941)

It was this commercial and reasonable approach to contract law that so offended the high priests of formalism in the late forties and fifties.

In no area was Wright more underestimated than in public law. Civil libertarians have tended to look down on him because he was in the majority in *Liversidge* v. *Anderson* (1941), while Atkin dissented over the suspension of habeas corpus. Wright's explanation, however, was that the Birkett committee (advising the home secretary on cases of detention under the emergency powers) provided a more effective protection than the courts, and he was perhaps right. Certainly his broad approach to statutory interpretation made him a better constitutional lawyer than his peers. In the disastrous decision of the judicial committee of the privy council in *Attorney-General for Canada* v. *Attorney-General for Ontario* (1937), where a panel chaired by Lord Atkin struck down the Canadian New Deal, including the federal social security system and the minimum wage, as he later admitted, Wright dissented. (At that time dissents could not be recorded publicly.) The dissent was appropriate; Atkin's decision led to Canada's decision to abandon appeals to London. Wright made it clear that he was of the same mind as Sankey that a constitution had to be treated as a 'living tree', while Atkin's 'watertight compartments' were alien to him. It was no doubt this same innate political sense that led Wright to take the law out of efforts to browbeat unions through the tort of conspiracy in *Crofter Hand Woven Harris Tweed Co. v. Veitch* (1942).

Wright's approach to law was complemented by his other public duties. During the 1930s he chaired Lord Sankey's Law Revision Committee. His work signified a new approach to law reform. In 1945 he became chair of the United Nations War Crimes Commission, charged with collecting the material for the Nuremberg trials. In 1946 he was treasurer of the Inner Temple. In 1947 he retired as a law lord, and in 1948 was made GCMG. He returned to his house in the Savernake Forest in Wiltshire, at Durley, where he maintained a rigorous schedule of riding until, at the age of ninety, he was injured in a car accident. He died at his home, Durley House, Burbage, Wiltshire, on 27 June 1964.   ROBERT STEVENS

Sources R. Stevens, *Law and politics: the House of Lords as a judicial body, 1800–1976* (1978) · *DNB* · A. L. Goodhart, 'Lord Wright, 1869–1964', *PBA*, 51 (1965), 429–37 · A. L. Goodhart, 'Lord Macmillan and Lord Wright', *Law Quarterly Review*, 63 (1947), 259 · private information (2004) · personal knowledge (2004) · *CGPLA Eng. & Wales* (1964) · *WWW*
Archives Bodl. Oxf., papers and letters to A. L. Goodhart, MSS Eng. c. 2891, 3113
Likenesses W. Stoneman, photograph, 1936, NPG · G. Kelly, oils, exh. RA 1952, Inner Temple, London [*see illus.*] · photograph, repro. in Goodhart, 'Lord Wright, 1869–1964'
Wealth at death £84,746: probate, 8 Sept 1964, *CGPLA Eng. & Wales*

Wright, **Sir Robert Samuel** (1839–1904), judge and jurist, born at Litton rectory, Litton, Somerset, on 20 January 1839, was the eldest son of the Revd Henry Edward Wright, rector of Litton, and his wife, a daughter of the Revd Edward Edgell. He was educated at King's School, Bruton, Somerset, before matriculating in 1856 at Balliol College, Oxford, where he was awarded a scholarship in 1857. One of Benjamin Jowett's favourite pupils (and subsequently his close and lifelong friend) he had a brilliant university career. He gained first classes in classical moderations (1859) and in *literae humaniores* (1860). He won university prizes for his Latin verse (1859), English essay (1861), and historical essay (1862). In 1861 he was Craven scholar. He was a fellow of Oriel from 1861 to 1880 and an honorary fellow there in 1882. The influence of Balliol and Balliol graduates may be detected at almost every stage of Wright's life, and there was a certain appropriateness in death having come to the college's most famous master while staying with his former pupil.

Wright's sights were set on the law. He became a student of the Inner Temple in London in November 1861 and, after proceeding BCL in 1863, he was called to the bar in June 1865. But he did not immediately abandon the classics: he remained in Oxford until 1865, teaching privately and examining for the university. He edited *A Golden Treasury of Ancient Greek Poetry* (1866) and, with J. E. L. Shadwell, *A Golden Treasury of Greek Prose* (1870). During this period he also helped with Colonial Office inquiries into hospitals and lunatic asylums, in 1863–4, and prisons, in 1864–7, and with the Taunton commission's inquiry in 1864–6

into the need for secondary schools in towns without endowed grammar schools.

Wright's work (and his Balliol connections) led in 1870 to his appointment as secretary to the royal commission on the truck system, whose report (1871, C.326) he had a large hand in writing. It also led to the Colonial Office inviting him to draft a criminal code for Jamaica (1877, C.1893) that might also serve as a model for other colonies. His on-the-spot investigations into evasions of the 1833 Truck Act by colliery owners and other employers reinforced his radical instincts (which revealed themselves also in his support for university education for women), making him a strong supporter of the trades union and land nationalization movements, while his code work led him to think hard about the principles underlying the criminal law. His elegant, lucid, and concise essay, *The Law of Criminal Conspiracies and Agreements* (1873), for a century the classical text, reflects both concerns: it was this branch of the law that was then chiefly being deployed against organized labour.

Although well-regarded and formally approved, the code—and its accompanying code of criminal procedure, also drafted by Wright—was never brought into force in Jamaica. Indeed, despite its status in the 1880s and 1890s as a model code for the colonies, it was brought into force in only four other Caribbean colonies and, across the Atlantic, in the Gold Coast (in 1892). After all the controversy surrounding the contemporary English scheme for codification based on Sir James Fitzjames Stephen's draft code of 1878, it seems to have been thought inadvisable that a colony with so blemished a recent legal history should get too far ahead of the mother country. Yet Wright's code was, in several respects, rather better than Stephen's. It was more detailed, leaving less to 'the common law', providing more definitions (especially of fault terms), and dealing more fully with the general principles governing all the individual offences. It was also more liberal in such matters as murder, attempted suicide, abortion, and sedition, and it gave wider discretion to the jury in cases of insanity. The procedure code included forward-looking provisions for a public prosecutor, for the defendant to be examined by the court, and for majority verdicts by juries, and it gave rights of appeal to both prosecution and defence.

Wright's attention was next directed, by Earl Cairns and the newly established statute law committee, to English criminal law, but his 'Report on the consolidation [and simplification] of the criminal statutes' (*Parl. papers*, 1877–8, HL, 178) was, like the Jamaican codes, lost in the codification debacle. Wright had, meanwhile, been building up a substantial practice, as much advisory as forensic, in London and on the northern circuit, and had attained sufficient standing to conduct the official inquiries into several colliery disasters. Appointment (by Sir Henry James) as junior counsel to the Treasury ('the attorney-general's devil') followed in 1883, and Wright prosecuted in that year's Fenian trials. He also appeared in the Dilke divorce case of 1886.

An attorney-general's 'devil' himself needs a 'devil's

services. They were initially provided for Wright by H. H. Asquith, the future prime minister (and a Balliol graduate), who remembered Wright's eccentric but regular habits as a bachelor living and working in the Temple, rising early, walking to the Reform Club for his breakfast and his dinner, and, when not in court, spending all day in chambers 'with a tall hat on his head and a briar pipe in his mouth. He was an indefatigable worker and smoker', little interested in social life, though 'fond of country sports, especially shooting' (Asquith, 1.82–3). His interest in the theory of the law continued, and with Sir Frederick Pollock he published *An Essay on Possession in the Common Law* (1883), 'a composite, not a joint, work', Wright dealing with the concept in the criminal law. Like his essay *Conspiracies* it remains authoritative. *An Outline of Local Government and Local Taxation*, written with Henry Hobhouse, followed in 1884 and reached an eighth edition in 1937.

Wright stood for parliament as a Liberal, unsuccessfully, for Norwich in 1884 and for Stepney in 1886. Lord Coleridge, the chief justice, and Mr Justice Bowen (both Balliol graduates), were nevertheless able to persuade the Conservative Lord Chancellor Halsbury to appoint him (on 11 December 1890) a judge in the Queen's Bench Division where there was, they said, 'a great need for a strong man … not only a lawyer, but a man of force of mind and character'. They considered Wright 'probably the ablest man at the Bar, except four or five men at the very head who do not practically count for this place, a scholar, a man of distinction' (Heuston, 44). Their expectations may not have been wholly fulfilled. Wright discomforted counsel by his 'abrupt speech and angular and peppery manner' (Asquith, 1.82–3), to which, as well as great kindness and generosity, Asquith also attested (and *Vanity Fair*, on 27 June 1891, added the charge of 'being as full of superciliousness as a good Radical should be'); however, Wright's summings-up in criminal cases were famously favourable to defendants and his sentences notably lenient. (Poachers of his own game were always proceeded against civilly, in the county court, not criminally.) Yet his reputation as a lawyer is such that his best-known decision, in the case of *Wilkinson* v. *Downton* (1897), concerning liability in tort for the consequences of a practical joke that went disastrously, but unforeseeably, wrong, has always been taken to be correct, irreconcilable though it is with any known legal principle. And the House of Lords twice preferred his views to those of the Court of Appeal: in the case of *Compania de Mocambique* v. *B.S.A. Co.* (1893) and in the significant case of *Allen* v. *Flood* (1898), in which the legality of trade combination was at issue and where he was also in a minority among the Queen's Bench judges. He would have been better suited to the Court of Appeal, but there were few vacancies before his early death.

Wright married in 1891, only after reaching the bench. His wife, Merriel Mabel Emily Chermside, was the daughter of a clergyman, Richard Seymour Chermside, prebendary of Salisbury. Of their two sons, one died in infancy; the other, Michael Robert (1901–1976), followed his father to Balliol, and fulfilled a diplomatic career as British ambassador to Norway. Wright had bought a country estate, Headley Park, Hampshire, in the year of his marriage. The home farm at Headley was said to have been run as 'a small republic with [Wright] as permanent president. Seated under a tree, he would invite the opinion of his labourers, and decide upon the course to be pursued in greater or less accordance with the sentiments of the meeting' (*DNB*, 1912). On one occasion an employee who was guilty of dishonesty accepted a short term of imprisonment in an outhouse, as an alternative to prosecution.

Wright's radicalism made him resist knighthood for a long time, but he was finally knighted in 1891. He died on 13 August 1904 after surgery and several months' illness. He had asked that there should be no memorial, and was buried at Headley in a plain coffin which, at his request, was brought into the church in a luggage cart.

P. R. GLAZEBROOK

Sources M. L. Friedland, 'R. S. Wright's model criminal code', *Oxford Journal of Legal Studies*, 1 (1981), 307–46 • M. L. Friedland, *A century of criminal justice* (1984), 1–45 [Wright's model criminal code] • H. H. Asquith, *Memories and reflections, 1852–1927*, ed. A. Mackintosh, 2 vols. (1928), vol. 1 • R. F. V. Heuston, *Lives of the lord chancellors, 1885–1940* (1964) • *DNB* • E. H. Coleridge, *Life and correspondence of John Duke, Lord Coleridge*, 2 (1904) • C. Biron, *Without prejudice: impressions of life and law* (1936) • *The Times* (15 Aug 1904) • *CGPLA Eng. & Wales* (1904)

Archives Castle Howard, York, letters to Rosalind, countess of Carlisle

Likenesses Spy [L. Ward], caricature, repro. in *VF* (27 June 1891) • Stuff [Wright], caricature, chromolithograph, NPG; repro. in *VF* (27 June 1891)

Wealth at death £39,863 9s. 11d.: probate, 5 Oct 1904, *CGPLA Eng. & Wales*

Wright, Ronald William Vernon Selby (1908–1995), Church of Scotland minister, was born on 12 June 1908 in Glasgow, the eldest son in the family of four children of Vernon O. Wright (1879–1942), organist, formerly an officer in the Argyll and Sutherland Highlanders and later an insurance inspector, and his wife, Anna Gilberta Selby, daughter of Major R. E. Selby. He was educated at Edinburgh Academy and Melville College and at Edinburgh University, where he was deeply influenced by Alfred Edward Taylor, the professor of moral philosophy. He then studied theology at New College, Edinburgh, where he was taught by Hugh Ross Mackintosh, to whom he became deeply attached. During his student years in Edinburgh, 1929–36, he was an officer cadet in the Royal Scots, student assistant at St Giles's Cathedral, and warden of St Giles's boys' club. He was a close friend of George MacLeod, who founded the Iona community, but he never became a member.

After being assistant minister of St Mungo's Cathedral in Glasgow for one year, Selby Wright was called back to Edinburgh in 1937 to become the minister of the Canongate Kirk, the church of the palace of Holyroodhouse and Edinburgh Castle, where he was to serve for the next forty years. There he continued his student work among the boys from the deprived back streets of the Royal Mile, and re-established the Canongate boys' club, which he was to run for fifty years. Although he was unusually tolerant with young people, his standards were unchangeably high. He was strict on discipline and expected the highest level of honesty and integrity from both old and young alike. The old Canongate Kirk, like much of the lower end of the Royal Mile, was in a very run-down condition, but through Selby Wright's untiring efforts, especially after the war, it was restored to something like its former glory. At the same time he set about recovering the historic worship of the church in line with John Knox's Book of Common Order, giving the sacraments a central place in the life of the parish, and provided the congregation with an enriched liturgy.

Commissioned as a Territorial Army chaplain in 1939, Selby Wright was called up with the outbreak of war and was sent on active service as the padre with the 9th (Highland) battalion, the Royal Scots, to France. There he experienced the disastrous plight of the British expeditionary force, and after some appalling experiences at St Valéry managed to escape from the German army on one of the last little ships to leave the beaches of Dunkirk. In June 1941 he was persuaded by Melville Dinwiddie, the BBC Scottish controller, and James Welch, the director of religious broadcasting at the BBC, to become a regular broadcaster on the radio. At first Selby Wright was reluctant to leave his battalion but he was soon regularly broadcasting to the country and to the forces in particular, and he soon became widely known and loved as 'the radio padre'. The whole venture was heralded as an astonishing success. Most notable was his ability to talk in a direct conversational style which gave inspiration, encouragement, and hope throughout the dark days of the war. In 1942 he became senior chaplain of the 52nd (Lowland) division and travelled to the Middle East and around the Mediterranean, continuing his radio ministry from transit camps in Italy. In 1943 he published *Let's ask the padre*, the fruit of what he taught and learned in his many hours leading 'padre's hours', and talking with young servicemen and -women. In November 1943, in his eagerness to be with fighting troops, he was posted to the 10th Indian division as senior chaplain. He saw service in Italy, Austria, and Germany. Throughout his life he maintained close contact with the military. From 1941 to 1976 he was editor of the quarterly *Scottish Forces Magazine*.

After the war the kirk and manse of the Canongate were the base from which Selby Wright called for creative reconstruction, not only in the parish and in the old town but through a fresh appreciation of the spiritual, ecclesiological, and literary heritage of Scotland, in which he was steeped. All his many publications, like his Canongate sermons and school addresses, were illuminated with brilliant allusions which reflected unusually wide reading and literary foraging in his extensive library. It was in line with his reverence for the tradition of the Church of Scotland that he devoted considerable attention to renewing the character and form of divine service in the Canongate Kirk. He drew upon the theological and liturgical insights of the universal kirk, but in such a way as to blend together historic reformed and classical liturgical traditions of worship. It was characteristic of him that his concern for the renewal of church worship was not divorced from the life and people in the parish and indeed in Edinburgh as a whole. His ceaseless pressure for reconstruction in Edinburgh brought him into wider civil activities. He served as a justice of the peace from 1963, as a member of the Edinburgh education committee from 1960 to 1970, and as chairman of Edinburgh and Leith Old People's Welfare Council from 1956 to 1969. He was always jealous of the kirk's connection with the state as the established church in Scotland, and accepted appointment by Edward Heath, the prime minister, to the Douglas-Home constitutional committee, which he felt he must serve as a parish minister. He successfully made friends and built bridges across the social divide, and looked upon all men as equal in the sight of God.

In 1961, in commemoration of his twenty-five years in the Canongate, Selby Wright was appointed by the queen as one of her extra chaplains in Scotland. Two years later he became her chaplain and served the royal family until 1978. It was said that 'he was one of Her Majesty's favourite preachers' (*The Independent*). He was also chaplain to the queen's bodyguard for Scotland, the Royal Company of Archers (1973–93), and he was appointed chaplain to the Merchant Company of Edinburgh in 1973. Just before his sixty-fifth birthday he was called to be moderator of the general assembly of the Church of Scotland, from 1972 to 1973. His moderatorial visits took him to India, where he encountered at first hand the horror of the slums of Calcutta and Old Delhi. He did much to strengthen and quicken the link between the overseas work of the Church of Scotland and the church in south India. At home he made a point of maintaining contact with the Roman Catholic church, not only through his friendship with Cardinal Gordon Joseph Gray, but also in his official visitation of various Roman institutions, such as St Augustine's secondary school in Edinburgh when he was moderator, and Sancta Maria Abbey at Nunraw.

Selby Wright loved the company of others yet he remained unmarried. Always interesting in conversation, he never missed an opportunity to drop names or give a commentary on the activity and movements of the great and the good. He was at all times generous in his judgements of others, with a discreet but sharp sense of humour. He was highly regarded by many, but never lost touch with the needs of the common man. He never tired of the company of young people. He made a point of understanding their needs, temptations, worries, and fears, and of finding simple direct answers to moral and spiritual problems. That was what gave rise to his successful series of little books entitled *Asking them Questions*. He was a frequent visitor and popular preacher at many public schools and held a number of honorary chaplaincies. Rarely has a minister of the kirk been so widely and happily acclaimed by church and state, crown and university. He was made an honorary doctor of divinity by Edinburgh University in 1956 and was appointed CVO in 1968. He had the cross of St Mark conferred on him by the patriarch of Alexandria when the latter visited the general assembly in 1970. He was remembered for his unfailing kindness to others, his unflagging concern for the needy, especially for the disadvantaged young of the Canongate, for his Christian ministry to poor and rich alike in times of peace and war, for his joyful godliness, for his selfless Christian ministry, and for his utterly impeccable moral character and purity of life. He was in every sense a man of the people but above all else he was a man of God. He died peacefully on 24 October 1995, seated in his armchair at his home, the Queen's House, 36 Moray Place, Edinburgh. His ashes were buried in the churchyard of the Canongate Kirk after cremation on 28 October; a memorial service was held on 6 December 1995.

DAVID GEORGE COULTER

Sources R. S. Wright, *Another home* (1980) · T. F. Torrance, *Year Book of the Royal Society of Edinburgh* (1996–7), 153–6 · D. G. Coulter, 'The Church of Scotland chaplains of World War Two', PhD diss., U. Edin., 1997 · *The Scotsman* (25 Oct 1995) · *The Independent* (26 Oct 1995) · *The Times* (26 Oct 1995) · WWW, 1991–5 · personal knowledge (2004)

Archives NL Scot., corresp. and diary; corresp. and papers, acc. 11296 | BBC WAC, corresp. with Lord Reith | SOUND New College, Edinburgh, taped interviews

Likenesses L. Boden, pencil drawing, 1951, Scot. NPG · D. Banner, pencil and chalk drawing, 1958, Scot. NPG · oils, Museum of the Royal Army Chaplain's Department, Amport House, Andover · photograph, Museum of the Royal Army Chaplain's Department, Amport House, Andover · photograph, Church of Scotland, Edinburgh · photograph, repro. in *The Times* · photograph, repro. in *The Independent*

Wealth at death £115,111.13: confirmation, 4 Dec 1995, CCI

Wright, Samuel (1683–1746), Presbyterian minister, was born at Retford, Nottinghamshire, on 30 January 1683, the son of James Wright (1651–1694) and his wife, Elinor or Eleanor Cotton (d. 1695). His father was educated at Lincoln College, Oxford (BA 1669), and Magdalene College, Cambridge (MA 1673), but became a nonconformist through the influence of his future father-in-law, William *Cotton (d. 1675) [see under Cotton family], a wealthy ironmaster of Wortley, near Sheffield, and preached at Attercliffe, near Sheffield, and Retford. His paternal grandfather, John Wright (d. 1685), was ordained on 13 August 1645 by the presbyterians to the chapelry of Billinge, Wigan, and was nominated a member of the fourth presbyterian classis of Lancashire on 2 October 1646. Ejected at the Restoration, he preached at Prescot from 1672.

Orphaned when he was about eleven years old, Wright suffered a further loss when his younger sister died a year later; much affected by these deaths, he often had 'strong and terrifying visions' as a child (Hughes, 37). He was brought up by his mother's relatives, who sent him to boarding-schools at Attercliffe and Darton, near Wakefield. In 1699 he entered Timothy Jollie's nonconformist academy at Attercliffe and in 1704 left to become chaplain to his uncle Cotton at Haigh, Lancashire. On Cotton's death, he went to live with another uncle, Thomas Cotton (1653–1730), who was Presbyterian minister at Dyott Street, Bloomsbury. For a time Wright was chaplain to Lady Susannah Lort (née Holles) at Turnham Green and preached the Sunday evening lecture at Dyott Street. In 1705 he became assistant to Benjamin Grosvenor at

Crosby Street Presbyterian Chapel, and the following year he undertook in addition a Sunday evening lecture at St Thomas's Chapel, Southwark, in conjunction with Harman Hood. On the death in January 1708 of Matthew Sylvester, Wright accepted the charge of the congregation, which had dwindled to 'a handful of people', at Meeting House Court, Knightrider Street, Blackfriars, where he was ordained on 15 April. His ministry was very successful, not least because of his striking preaching style, which won praise from Thomas Herring, later archbishop of Canterbury; according to his memorialist, 'people flocked in crowds to hear him, as doves to the windows' (Hughes, 40). In addition, Wright's communion services were remarkable for their fervour, and he was a sedulous pastor. The meeting-house was twice enlarged and had the honour of being wrecked by the Sacheverell mob in 1710. From 1718 Wright was assisted by Thomas Newman, and a new meeting-house was built for him in Carter Lane, Doctors' Commons, which opened on 7 December 1734.

On 6 April 1710, at St Katharine by the Tower, Wright married his predecessor's widow, Elizabeth Sylvester, née Hughes (bap. 1670), the daughter of Obadiah Hughes (bap. 1639, d. 1705) and his first wife, Elizabeth (d. 1672). They had one daughter, probably Elizabeth, who was baptized at St Katharine's on 4 October 1713. Although an orthodox Calvinist, Wright took the side of the non-subscribers at the Salters' Hall conference of 1719, probably influenced by Grosvenor. His defence of religious liberty led him to contribute to the whig *Occasional Papers* (1716–18), which were also known as the Bagweell papers, from the initials of the contributors' names. Wright's popularity remained high. As well as being a Sunday lecturer at Little St Helen's, in 1724 he was chosen as one of the merchants' lecturers at Salters' Hall and elected a trustee of Dr Williams's foundations.

Wright published more than forty works, principally sermons on topics of practical divinity, and was highly praised by Philip Doddridge 'for his great simplicity, and awful solemnity' (Wilson, 2.146). He was rather forbidding in his manner and was satirized in the mid-1730s by the anonymous versifier of 'Lines on London dissenting ministers of a former day':

> Behold how papal Wright with lordly pride
> Directs his haughty eye to either side,
> Gives forth his doctrine with imperious nod,
> And fraught with pride addresses e'en his God.
> (N&Q, 1st ser., 1, 1849–50, 454)

He contributed to the commentary on the New Testament started by Matthew Henry, writing on the epistle of James. On 1 May 1729 Edinburgh University awarded him the degree of DD by diploma; a portrait of him in his doctor's gown hangs in Dr Williams's Library in London. In 1732–3 he had a sermon debate with Thomas Mole (d. 1780) on the foundation of moral virtue, which Wright could trace no further than to the divine will.

After a long illness Wright died on 3 April 1746 and was buried in the south aisle of Stoke Newington church. Funeral sermons were preached by his wife's nephew

Obadiah Hughes (1695–1751), and by John Milner of Peckham; Hughes also composed the Latin inscription on his tomb. ALEXANDER GORDON, *rev.* S. J. SKEDD

Sources O. Hughes, *Simeon's prayer, for leave to die, considered and improved. A sermon occasioned by the death of S. Wright* (1746) • J. Toulmin, 'A sketch of the life, character, and writings of the Rev. Samuel Wright', *Protestant Dissenter's Magazine*, 5 (1798), 321 • A. Gordon, ed., *Freedom after ejection: a review (1690–1692) of presbyterian and congregational nonconformity in England and Wales* (1917), 391 • *Calamy rev.* • W. Wilson, *The history and antiquities of the dissenting churches and meeting houses in London, Westminster and Southwark*, 4 vols. (1808–14) • Venn, *Alum. Cant.* • Foster, *Alum. Oxon.* • *IGI*
Likenesses oils, DWL

Wright, Stephen (*d.* 1780), architect, may have been born in Oxburgh, Norfolk, to the poor of which village he left £20 in his will, and he appears to have begun his professional life as a clerk or assistant to William Kent. He was probably the 'Stephen' referred to in letters from Kent to Richard Boyle, third earl of Burlington, in 1738–9; he received a legacy of £50 under Kent's will, dated 1748; and the following year he was in possession of some of Kent's drawings. In 1746 he was appointed to a post in the office of works, as clerk of the works at Hampton Court, presumably through the influence of Burlington; and his subsequent career was based on that institution and the patronage of one leading public figure, Thomas Pelham-Holles, first duke of Newcastle.

How and when Wright's link with Newcastle was established is not clear—it may have been through his employment to complete the London house which Kent had designed for the duke's brother Henry Pelham (1695–1754), after Kent's death in 1748—but there is plentiful evidence of the connection. In 1758, four years after he had added the clerkship of Richmond New Park Lodge to that he held at Hampton Court, when the comptroller of the works, Thomas Ripley, was dying, he wrote to Newcastle to apply for his post; and although in the event the preferment went to Henry Flitcroft, it was by Newcastle's 'immediate appointment' that Wright was promoted to the posts of master mason and deputy surveyor vacated by the latter. Equally, the greater part of the work in his small private practice came from the duke and his successor. Newcastle employed him at Claremont, Surrey (1752), and as chancellor of Cambridge University secured his employment to design the university library (1754–8); while for the second duke he worked at Clumber House, Nottinghamshire (1768–78; dem.), and designed the bridge in Newark in the same county (1775). The Cambridge library, his most important work, is an accomplished Palladian composition in the manner of William Kent, while in his additions to Milton Hall, Berkshire (1764–72), he provided some attractive interiors in the Kentian Gothic style.

'An honest and worthy man', in the words of his office of works colleague Kenton Couse, he died after 'a lingering tho' not very painful illness' (*History of the King's Works*, 5.89) on 28th September 1780. He was buried in the churchyard at Hampton, Middlesex.   PETER LEACH

Sources Colvin, *Archs.* • J. Gwilt, ed., *An encyclopaedia of architecture*, 2nd edn (1851); rev. edn, rev. W. Papworth (1867); new edn (1881); new edn (1888) • H. M. Colvin and others, eds., *The history of the king's works*, 5 (1976) • will, PRO, PROB 11/1070, sig. 498

Wright, Sydney Fowler (1874–1965), writer, was born on 6 January 1874 at Holly Street in the midlands town of Smethwick, the son of Stephen Wright (1841–1936), an accountant and Baptist lay preacher, and Emily Gertrude Fowler (1843–1882). He attended King Edward's School, Birmingham, but left at an unusually early age in order to complete his own education. He followed his father into the profession of accountancy and married Julia Ellen (Nellie) Ashbarry (1866–1918) on 5 January 1895; they had six children before she died in 1918. Fowler Wright's early literary work was mostly lyric poetry; he was one of the founders of the Empire Poetry League in 1917, and he edited its journal, *Poetry* (later retitled *Poetry and the Play*), until 1932. His first publication was a series of excerpts from a lifelong project to render the entirety of Arthurian legend into verse, *Scenes from the Morte d'Arthur* (1919), published under the pseudonym Alan Seymour. He married Anastasia Gertrude (Truda) Hancock (1897–1956) on 25 October 1920, subsequently adding a further four children to his family.

Although Fowler Wright wrote his first novel, the disaster story *Deluge*, in 1920, it was not published until 1927, when he issued it under his own imprint, having earlier published *The Amphibians* (1925) under the Empire Poetry League's Merton Press imprint. *Deluge* was unexpectedly successful, and became a best-seller when it was reprinted in the USA in advance of a Hollywood film version which was released in 1933. He then became a full-time writer, producing numerous novels under his own name as well as abundant crime fiction under the name Sydney Fowler. *The Amphibians*, a phantasmagorical Wellsian romance of the far future heavily influenced by Dante—a translation of whose *Divine Comedy* was another of Fowler Wright's major projects—was reprinted along with a sequel as *The World Below* (1929) but a projected third volume was never written. The same fate befell the story projected to complete the story begun in *Deluge* and continued in *Dawn* (1929). Another trilogy, of prehistoric fantasies, begun with *Dream, or, The Simian Maid* (1931) was completed, although the original publisher rejected *Vengeance of Gwa*, which appeared in 1935 under the name Anthony Wingrave, and *Spiders' War* did not appear until 1954, and then only in America. A trilogy of future war novels, begun with *Prelude in Prague* (1935; revised for publication in America as *The War of 1938*) and continued in *Four Days War* (1936) and *Megiddo's Ridge* (1937), also required more than one publisher.

This record of interrupted and miscarried projects bears testimony to the fact that Fowler Wright's celebrity was very brief; he was so comprehensively deserted by fame after 1931 that the two works he considered to be his masterpieces—his 332,000-word *Song of Arthur* (which had to be rewritten in its entirety when the first manuscript was lost in the blitz) and a long historical novel called *Cortés* or *For God and Spain*—were never published in his lifetime.

Both were made available, however—along with everything else the author published and his other previously unpublished works—on a pioneering world wide web page established in the mid-1990s by his family for that purpose, which offered the first opportunity to gauge the full extent of his ambition and achievement.

Fowler Wright remains best-known as a writer of vivid Wellsian scientific romance, in which field he produced *The Island of Captain Sparrow* (1928), *Power* (1933), the startling dystopia *The Adventure of Wyndham Smith* (1938), and the graphic short stories collected in *The New Gods Lead* (1932; expanded in 1949 as *The Throne of Saturn* and further expanded in 1996 as *S. Fowler Wright's Short Stories*) in addition to the works already cited. He also produced several notable historical novels in addition to *Cortés*, including *Elfwin* (1930), *David* (1934), and *The Siege of Malta* (1942), the last-named completing a fragment by Walter Scott, a biography of whom he had written in 1932. His later crime novels are mostly dispirited pot-boilers, although *Three Witnesses*, published in 1935, was also made into a film that year. The best of his works in this genre, including *The Case of Anne Bickerton* (1930) and *The Hanging of Constance Hillier* (1931), exhibit a rapt fascination with strong female characters also seen in many of his scientific romances. His semi-autobiographical novel *Seven Thousand in Israel* (1931) casts further light on his preoccupation with such contemporary issues as automation, birth control, and the erosion of privacy. His extrapolation of these preoccupations into hypothetical futures and pasts typically embraces a Rousseauesque celebration of freedom modified by voluntary social contracts and the nobility of heroic individual struggles within challenging environments; he was an outspoken opponent of the 'new gods' of his era, which he named as Comfort and Cowardice.

In 1940 Fowler Wright was employed by Hatchard's bookshop in London to edit its trade paper *Books of Today*. He subsequently reprinted some of his better-known works under the Books of Today imprint, as well as his second story collection, *The Witchfinder* (1946). His productivity declined markedly after the Second World War, and after the death of his second wife in 1956 he moved between the various homes of several of his children until he died on 25 February 1965 in Midhurst, Sussex; he was buried at St Mary's Church, Rattle Road, Eastbourne.

BRIAN STABLEFORD

Sources B. Stableford, 'Against the new gods: the speculative fiction of S. Fowler Wright', *Foundation*, 29 (Nov 1983) · J. E. C. Macfarlane, 'Sydney Fowler Wright: founder of the Empire Poetry League', *S. Fowler Wright's short stories* (1996), 198–213 [speech delivered 3 Dec 1958] · B. Stableford, *Scientific romance in Britain, 1890–1950* (1985) · 'The works of Sydney Fowler Wright, 1874–1965', www.sfw.org [incl. Wright's short stories and supplementary information] · private information (2004) [family]

Likenesses photograph, repro. in S. Fowler Wright, *Short stories* (1996), cover

Wright, Thomas (*c.*1561–1623), Roman Catholic priest and religious controversialist, was born on 6 November in a year variously given as 1560, 1561, and 1562, at York, the son of John Wright, an apothecary. His was a strongly recusant family that gave two sons, himself and his younger brother, William *Wright, to the Society of Jesus; his uncle, a learned Marian priest, whose name may have been Thomas, is sometimes confused with him. He left York in 1577 for the English College, Douai, and the following year, when the college moved to Rheims for safety, he proceeded to the newly founded English College, Rome. Despite his oath to go on the English mission he insisted on entering the Society of Jesus, which had as yet no mission in England; his desire was granted on 3 February 1580. After four years' study of theology at Milan he was ordained priest on 20 September 1586. During the next few years he taught at Jesuit colleges in Genoa, Milan, and Rome before being sent in 1594 to the English College, Valladolid, as prefect of studies.

Wherever he went Wright seems to have fomented trouble, partly owing to his insistence on returning to England against the judgement of his superiors, and partly owing to certain 'extravagant propositions' of his that had come to the attention of the Jesuit-general Claudio Acquaviva, for which he was even in danger of dismissal from the society. The nature of these propositions appears in a Latin tract attributed to 'Wright a priest' found among the papers of Lord Burghley, recommending the granting of toleration to English Catholics in return for their support of the English government against King Philip of Spain and even the pope in case of invasion. It was no doubt thanks to this tract and its recommendations that Wright was able to return to England in 1595 under the protection of the earl of Essex, though this led to his dismissal from the Society of Jesus 'with regret on either side'. On reaching London he approached Essex's secretary, Anthony Bacon, and so came to meet the earl, whom he supplied with useful intelligence concerning Philip's plans to invade England again in 1596.

For a time Wright moved in the Essex circle. But owing to indiscreet remarks against the Anglicans made on the occasion of a return home to York he was confined to the house of the dean of Westminster. There he met the Anglican poet and divine William Alabaster and so became a means of the other's conversion to Rome. For this he was transferred to stricter confinement at the gatehouse. During his imprisonment Wright composed two books on the blessed sacrament, one on 'the real presence' and the other on 'the disposition or garnishment of the soule', published in 1596. He was also working on a more substantial book, *The Passions of the Mind*, which he mentions as just completed in a letter of 17 October 1598 to Anthony Bacon. Published in 1600, this book had many reprints and was used by Robert Burton in his *Anatomy of Melancholy*.

After escaping from prison in February 1600 Wright published his most notorious work of controversy, *Certaine Articles or Forcible Reasons*, to refute what he called 'the palpable absurdities, and most notorious and intricate errors of the Protestants religion'. Described by William Waad in a letter to Sir Robert Cecil as 'the most railing pamphlet against religion that ever was set forth'

(Rogers, 266), it elicited heated replies from three protestant authors, William Barlow, Edward Bulkeley, and Anthony Wotton. Wright was recaptured on 13 June 1600, imprisoned in the Tower, and interrogated about his dealings with Essex, being the obvious link between the earl and the English Catholics. But when the Essex rebellion occurred in February 1601 Wright turned against his former patron in his disillusionment.

Removed to the Clink, Wright allied himself with the party of appellant priests. On the accession of James I in 1603 he was banished with forty other priests, but he was back again in London by August, convinced of the imminence of toleration. After the Gunpowder Plot of 1605 he urged patriotic Catholics not only to take the newly devised oath of allegiance but also, as a further proof of loyalty, to attend Anglican churches if only for the sermon. He is described by the Jesuit Robert North as the leader of those 'pastors and spiritual guides' whose lax teaching has made 'whole counties and shires run headlong without struggle into the heretics' churches' (Foley, 4.284). His Jesuit brother was sent to London to lead the opposition to him and issued a tract on the subject, only to find himself confronted with an opposite tract by Thomas; neither tract has survived. From Rome, Robert Parsons published a reply in Latin in 1607, but without mentioning Wright in particular.

Expelled from England in 1610 with other priests, Wright supported the proposal of founding a college of controversy against the heretics, which was realized in 1611 with the college of Arras, though he himself never became a fellow. He worked among English, Scottish, and Irish soldiers at Antwerp, and in July 1613 was the protagonist at four conferences on matters of controversy with the English diplomat Sir Thomas Roe at Spa in Germany. These conferences were published in 1614 as *Quatuor colloquia*, where he is described as doctor and professor of theology, as well as theologian to the apostolic nuncio at Cologne. When William Bishop was appointed vicar apostolic for English Catholics in 1623 Wright was chosen by him as one of his nineteen canons for the renewal of the Catholic hierarchy, but he died that year.

PETER MILWARD

Sources R. V. Caro, 'William Alabaster', *Recusant History*, 19 (1988–9), 62–79 • T. A. Stroud, 'Father Thomas Wright: a test case for toleration', *Biographical Studies*, 1 (1951–2), 189–219 • D. M. Rogers, 'A bibliography of the published works of Thomas Wright (c.1561–1623)', *Biographical Studies*, 1 (1951–2), 262–74 • C. Dodd [H. Tootell], *The church history of England, from the year 1500, to the year 1688*, 2 (1739), 91 • H. Foley, ed., *Records of the English province of the Society of Jesus*, 4 (1878), 284 • P. Milward, *Religious controversies of the Elizabethan age* (1977), 146–7 • P. Milward, *Religious controversies of the Jacobean age* (1978), 139–40 • T. M. McCoog, *English and Welsh Jesuits, 1555–1650*, 2 vols., Catholic RS, 74–5 (1994–5) • 'Wright, William (1563–1639)', *DNB*

Wright, Thomas (1711–1786), astronomer and landscape gardener, was born on 22 September 1711 at Pegg's Poole House, Byers Green, co. Durham, the third son of John and Margaret Wright. His father was a yeoman and carpenter who had a smallholding. He was educated at home, and then probably (1724?) at King James's School, Bishop Auckland, in which town Thomas Munday taught him mathematics instead of language, because of a speech impediment. From 1725 to 1729 he was apprenticed to Bryan Stobart, a clock- and watchmaker in the town. Wright's father, anxious that he was too studious, is said to have burnt his books. In 1730 he took a course probably at Dr Theophilus Pickering's Free School in Gateshead, on mathematics and navigation; that summer he went to London, where he spent time with the respected instrument makers Thomas Heath and Jeremiah Sisson. He also visited Amsterdam. Having returned aged twenty to Sunderland he set up a school to teach navigation, and sold instruments.

In 1733 Daniel Newcome, rector of Sunderland, invited Wright to stay, and introduced him to Richard Lumley, of Lumley Castle, the second earl of Scarbrough. Through Lumley the Admiralty approved the publication in 1734 of Wright's *Clavis pannautici*, which described the pannauticon, a paper instrument dedicated to George II. A natural teacher, Wright gave lectures in London in 1734 on astronomy, and proposed lectures in Durham. He devoted time to astronomical calculations of dubious accuracy. In 1735 he was an unsuccessful candidate for election to the Royal Society. In 1742 he published his teaching aid *Clavis coelestis*, an enormous engraved diagram (6 ft x 4 ft) of the heavens and theories of their arrangement, with an accompanying description and discussion in quarto. In the same year he was offered the professorship of navigation at the Imperial Academy at St Petersburg, at £300 p.a., but asked for £500 and the negotiations fell through. In 1750 he published the book for which he is most famous, *An Original Theory of the Universe*. This has an impressive subscribers' list, including Lord Anson and the dukes of Beaufort, Bedford, Norfolk, and Portland; it is richly embellished with engravings, some spectacularly on a dark ground, and fragments of poetry. The text is rhetorical, sometimes to the point of opacity.

Wright ponders the question of why we see the Milky Way as we do, and concludes that the stars must be arranged in a disc or grindstone, or a spherical shell like the rind of an enormous orange. The sun is in the middle of this layer, so that when we look in the plane of the disc or shell we see a multitude of stars, the Milky Way, whereas at right angles to it there are very few. The grindstone plate is well known; the shell one, a vast orange with the eye of God at its centre, less so. The book did not attract the attention of astronomers, but Immanuel Kant saw—and perhaps creatively misunderstood—a review of it in a German publication.

It was only in the nineteenth century, after the work of William Herschel, that the spiral shape of the galaxy became accepted, and Wright with his grindstone was seen as a precursor. William Whiston's writings were a major influence on Wright, who once believed that each system in the universe had its own gravitational and spiritual centre, sometimes shown as divine eyes, and that stars were all equal in size (so that fainter ones were farther away) and had planets like the sun. Later in life, in *Second or Singular Thoughts* (not published until 1968), he changed his opinion, putting the sun in the centre of the universe, with the stars as volcanoes erupting comets downwards from a solid outer shell; the location of heaven and hell, rather than simply astronomical theory, was always important to him.

Wright visited Ireland in 1746–7, by which time Lumley's patronage had made him well known in aristocratic circles. He was living on the fringes of high society, surveying estates, planning at least fifteen gardens (in a style similar to that of William Kent) and grottoes, and giving tuition (particularly to ladies) in mathematics and astronomy. He was nearly a year in Ireland, and on his return published in 1748 *Louthiana*, a volume illustrated with engravings describing the antiquities and curiosities of co. Louth; a second volume was planned, but never published. In 1755 and 1758 Wright published two volumes of *Universal Architecture*, the first containing six designs for arbours, and the second grottoes; a third, on alcoves, was never published. He also designed buildings, such as the deer shelter in Auckland Park for the bishop of Durham, and improvements to buildings, such as pinnacles or 'minarets' for Durham Cathedral.

In 1755–6 Wright bought from his brother, for £20, the house in Byers Green where he had been born, rebuilt it in Roman style, and retired there in 1763 to finish his studies, now that his wealthy patrons were dying off. About 1778 Wright wrote a description of the house, which was published posthumously in *The Gentleman's Magazine* in 1793; the house was demolished in 1967. He erected a Gothic tower at Middleston for an observatory, but did not live to complete it.

Wright died at his home on 22 February 1786, and three days later was buried at St Andrew's churchyard, South Church, Bishop Auckland. His will was dated 12 July 1780, and his heir was his 'dear natural daughter' Elizabeth, aged twenty-two when he died. She died in 1788 and was buried beside her father; her mother's identity is not known, but she is believed to have lived with Wright and to have survived Elizabeth. Wright's life provides a good example of how a scientifically minded man could make his way in the eighteenth century through appropriate patronage and in a range of activities.

DAVID KNIGHT

Sources M. Tooley, *Thomas Wright of Durham: exhibition guide* (1993) · T. Wright, *Clavis coelestis* (1742) · M. Hoskin, introduction, in T. Wright, *An original theory or new hypothesis of the universe, 1750*, ed. M. Hoskin (1971) · T. Wright, *An original theory of the universe* (1750) · M. A. Hoskin, preface, in T. Wright, *Clavis coelestis* (1742); repr. (1967) · T. Wright, *Second or singular thoughts upon the theory of the universe*, ed. M. Hoskin (1968) · T. Wright, *Arbours and grottos*, ed. E. Harris (1979) · *DSB* · 'A sketch of the character of Mr Thomas Wright', *GM*, 1st ser., 63 (1793), 9–12, 126–7, 213–16 · E. Hughes, 'The early journal of Thomas Wright of Durham', *Annals of Science*, 7 (1951), 1–24 · will, 13 June 1788, U. Durham L. [Elizabeth Wright] · will, 12 July 1780, U. Durham L.
Archives BL, autobiography and notes relating to Druidian, Roman, Saxon, and Irish antiquities, Add. MSS 15627–15628, 33771 · Central Library, Newcastle upon Tyne · RS, papers read to Royal Society · Tyne and Wear Archives Service, Newcastle upon Tyne, papers · U. Durham L., papers relating to astronomy, cosmology, and meteorology | Col. U., Avery Architectural and Fine Arts Library · V&A, sketchbooks [see Tooley, 7]
Likenesses T. Frye, mezzotint, 1737, BM, NPG · line engraving, c.1750, BM, NPG; repro. in 'Sketch of the character of Mr Thomas Wright', *GM* · G. Allen and P. Fourdinier, engraving, repro. in Wright, *Clavis coelestis* (1742), facing title page
Wealth at death will, 12 July 1780, U. Durham L. · daughter's possessions under £100: will, 13 June 1788, U. Durham L.

Wright, Thomas (1789–1875), prison visitor, was born in Manchester, of a Scottish father and Manchester mother, on 20 September 1789. He had two sisters, one of whom died young and one outlived him. Wright was educated at a Wesleyan Sunday school and was apprenticed at the age of fifteen to the Manchester iron foundry of Ormerod. He remained there all his working life to 1852, starting at 5 a.m. and finishing at 6 p.m. every day, and was promoted to foreman in 1841, with a wage of £3 10s. per week. Brought up a Wesleyan Methodist, he spurned religion as a young adult. In 1817 he was reconverted to Christianity after experiencing a sudden and profound despair at his own sinfulness, and joined the Independent chapel on Grosvenor Street, Piccadilly, Manchester. He was a deacon there from 1825 until his death. In 1838 he obtained permission from the visiting justices to visit Salford New Bailey House of Correction, a short-sentence prison holding on average 600–700 prisoners of both sexes, serving less than six months, from the courts of Manchester, Bolton, and Salford. Wright spent his evenings and every Sunday afternoon in the prison, initially receiving considerable support from the Revd C. F. Bagshawe, the prison chaplain.

Wright's theories on the causes of crime may be deduced from his letters and from his evidence to the two select committees of parliament on criminal and destitute youth and on regulation of public houses in 1852 and 1854 respectively. He believed that descent into crime was progressive: poor parental care (especially from mothers) resulted in cold, abusive, drunken, and comfortless homes, from which children were sent out to beg or steal. As the children grew they received a grossly defective moral and general education. Subsequently, young people found themselves in an environment where there were few employment opportunities and in vicious and criminogenic neighbourhoods. Drawn into theatres, public houses, and music- and dance-halls, and often living in squalid, overcrowded lodging-houses, they quickly became addicted to gambling, alcohol, and promiscuity. Weekend pleasure-seeking meant that they did not hear the word of God on Sundays and ultimately, to feed their addictions, they became criminals. Inevitably this resulted in committal to prison and, once branded a prisoner, all shunned them on release except other criminals: they had either to starve or return to crime.

Wright's solutions to these problems were practical and sometimes drastic. He believed that young people at risk needed to be removed from the criminogenic environment either to refuges or penitentiaries, both institutions

Thomas Wright (1789–1875), by George Frederic Watts, c.1850–51

offering basic education, training for work, and moral discipline. He was therefore closely connected with the Manchester Boys' Refuge and Manchester Female Penitentiary, as well as the Redhill Reformatory, Surrey, for boys and Bristol Reformatory for girls (both pioneering new institutions working with young offenders); he referred young offenders or young people at risk to these establishments. He was also a strong advocate for compulsory education and supported the ragged schools of Manchester and Salford.

It was, however, prison visiting for which Wright gained fame. On his second visit to Salford New Bailey he engaged a prisoner in conversation, and on his release Wright stood surety for the man with an employer. Following the success of this venture he set up a network of potential employers, including his own, and befriended men in the prison who were recommended to him by the governor and the chaplain. Without condescension, he approached them with a warm-hearted and sincere Christian message of hope. Free of denominational bigotry, Wright merely expected that those who asked his help should attend a religious service of their own choosing each week. Frequently he laid out his own money as a guarantee with an employer, and where he could not find work he gave money or goods, such as clothing, so that the former prisoner could survive until employment was found. He helped many hundreds of prisoners, a few of whom he assisted to emigrate to Australia or America. Although Wright was unostentatious his work was publicized by the prison inspector, Captain William J. Williams, who

noted that his practical, sincere, and kindly manner inspired wide respect among prisoners. Williams attributed this respect to the prisoners' belief that Wright cared as much for them as for himself. After several years of encountering Wright in action, he concluded that he was one of only two effective prison visitors of the day, the other being Sarah Martin (1791–1843) of Great Yarmouth.

Wright subsequently visited prisoners in Liverpool, Scotland, and London; he also visited many offenders under sentence of death in northern prisons in order to comfort them just before their execution and to accompany them to the gallows. This feature of his work inspired Charles Mercier's portrait of him in 1869 entitled *The Condemned Cell*. It was widely reported that Wright had been offered a Home Office salary to widen the scope of his work, but that he turned the offer down because he believed that this would damage his reputation for disinterestedness among prisoners. Be that as it may, following a campaign by the Salford bench and publicization of his work in Charles Dickens's *Household Words*, a public subscription of £3248, including a £100 donation from the royal family, was raised in 1852. This enabled Wright to give up thirteen hours a day at work (with around four hours' sleep a night after his prison visiting) and concentrate entirely on philanthropy.

Thomas Wright married twice and was father to nineteen children; his first wife died in March 1828 and his second in January 1862. He himself died at his home, 3 Sidney Street, Chorlton upon Medlock, Manchester, on 14 April 1875 and was buried in the cemetery of Birch in Rusholme church. He exemplified the enterprise of moral reformation and reclamatory intervention which dominated ideology and policy relating to prisoners in Britain between 1835 and 1860, and he was duly eulogized as a humble labourer in that part of God's vineyard. However, he was more than a 'reach me down' figure to justify current policy: he won deep respect from people of all classes, and that severe judge of human character and philanthropic intention, the seventh earl of Shaftesbury, referred to Wright as 'that good man' who set 'standards for the great of this earth to measure themselves by' (Hodder, 2.376–7).

BILL FORSYTHE

Sources I. McDermid, *Life of Thomas Wright* (1876) · W. Tallack, *Penological and preventive principles* (1889) · F. Hill, *Crime: the amount, causes and remedies* (1853) · 'Inspectors of prisons … northern and eastern district', *Parl. papers* (1845–50) [reports 10–16] · 'Select committee on criminal and destitute juveniles', *Parl. papers* (1852), vol. 7, no. 515 · 'Select committee on the regulation of public houses', *Parl. papers* (1854), 14.231, no. 367 · E. Hodder, *The life and work of the seventh earl of Shaftesbury*, 3 vols. (1886) · C. Dickens, 'An unpaid servant of the state', *Household Words* (6 March 1852), 553–5 · *The Graphic* (8 May 1875), 450 · L. Radzinowicz and R. Hood, *A history of English criminal law and its administration from 1750*, rev. edn, 5: *The emergence of penal policy in Victorian and Edwardian England* (1990) · d. cert.

Likenesses G. F. Watts, chalk drawing, c.1850–1851, NPG [*see illus.*] · J. D. Watson, portrait, 1853, Strangeways Prison, Manchester · C. Mercier, portrait, 1869, London corporation · photograph, repro. in McDermid, *Life*

Wealth at death under £1000: probate, 10 June 1875, *CGPLA Eng. & Wales*

Wright, Thomas (1792–1849), engraver and portrait painter, was born at Birmingham on 2 March 1792, the son of William Wright and his wife, Mary, and was baptized at St Martin's, Birmingham, on 29 May 1792. After serving an apprenticeship with Henry Meyer he worked as an assistant to William Thomas Fry, for whom he engraved the popular plate of Princess Charlotte and Prince Leopold in a box at Covent Garden Theatre, after George Dawe. About 1817 he began to practise independently as a stipple engraver and also executed portraits in pencil and miniature. Wright became much associated with Dawe, and undertook the portraits for *Essex, Suffolk and Norfolk Characters* (1820) after Dawe and Abraham Wivell. In 1822 he followed Dawe to St Petersburg to engrave his gallery of portraits of Russian generals; there he also executed a fine plate of the emperor Alexander, and another of the Empress Alexandra with her children, both after Dawe. He was rewarded with diamond rings from the royal family and a gold medal from the king of Prussia.

Wright returned to England in 1826 and married Dawe's sister. During the next four years he was employed on the plates to Mrs Anna Jameson's *The Beauties of the Court of King Charles II* (1831–3), which constitute his best work, and also on some of the plates, after Holbein, Walker, and Van Dyck, to the folio edition of Edmund Lodge's *Portraits of Illustrious Personages of Great Britain* (12 vols., 1823–34; 2nd edn, 1835). In 1830 he again went to Russia, and remained for fifteen years, working under the patronage of the court. There he brought out a series of portraits entitled *Les contemporains russes*, drawn and engraved by himself and published in St Petersburg. On finally leaving St Petersburg he presented a complete collection of impressions from his plates, numbering about 300, to the Hermitage Gallery (later the Hermitage Museum). Wright died, after a long illness, at his home in George Street, Hanover Square, London, on 30 March 1849. He was a member of the academies of St Petersburg, Florence, and Stockholm.

F. M. O'DONOGHUE, rev. JOANNA DESMOND

Sources B. Hunnisett, *An illustrated dictionary of British steel engravers*, new edn (1989) · R. K. Engen, *Dictionary of Victorian engravers, print publishers and their works* (1979) · *Engraved Brit. ports.* · Printsellers' Association, *Index of painters and engravers* (1894) · print catalogue, V&A · Redgrave, *Artists* · *The Athenaeum* (16 June 1849), 626 · IGI

Wright, Thomas (1809–1884), physician and palaeontologist, was born on 10 November 1809 at Paisley, Renfrewshire, the son of Thomas Wright and his wife, Barbara (*née* Jarvis). He received his early education at the local grammar school in Paisley, after which he was apprenticed to his brother-in-law, a surgeon in that town. When his relative moved to Ayrshire, Wright's medical studies were temporarily halted, and he was persuaded by a friend to enter the manufacturing industry. However, such a career did not suit him and he ultimately rejoined his brother-in-law, and resumed medical studies. Subsequently he became a student at the Royal College of Surgeons in Dublin, under the guidance of the surgeon Abraham Colles (1773–1843) and the anatomist Arthur Jacob (1790–1874).

Wright developed a predilection for anatomy and a talent for dissection. Finding the working conditions agreeable, he next entered the Ledwich school of anatomy, medicine, and surgery, Peter Street, Dublin, where he became assistant demonstrator. Although offered a demonstratorship at the same institute, he became seriously ill with abscesses and blood poisoning caused by a dissecting wound, and was unable to accept the post.

On recovering his health Wright qualified as MRCS in 1832, and shortly afterwards settled at Cheltenham. On 8 November 1832 at Lapworth, Warwick, he married Elizabeth, daughter of Captain Vincent May. He acquired a large practice at Cheltenham, became medical officer for Cheltenham and surrounding districts, and was for many years surgeon to the Cheltenham General Hospital and Dispensary. On 20 April 1846 he married, second, Mary (d. 1878), the youngest daughter of Sir Robert Tristram Ricketts (1772–1842), baronet, of The Elms, Cheltenham. In the same year Wright graduated MD at St Andrews University.

Wright's enthusiasm for scientific studies never flagged. At first he was engrossed in delicate microscopic work, but owing to the strain on his eyesight, he instead became devoted to palaeontology and gradually formed a collection of Jurassic fossils which was rich in Cephalopods, and was perhaps unequalled at the time for sea urchins and starfish. Notwithstanding his many occupations, he found time to be an active member, and vicepresident, of the Cotteswold Field Club, president of the Literary and Philosophical Association of Cheltenham, an enthusiastic advocate of science as a branch of education, and a frequent lecturer on scientific topics throughout the west and south-west of England.

Wright's vacations were devoted to travel both in Britain and in continental Europe, in order to enlarge his knowledge, especially of Jurassic rocks and fossils. He was the author of about thirty-two papers on geological subjects; seven of them were published in the *Quarterly Journal of the Geological Society*, but one of the most valuable, on the correlation between Jurassic rocks of the Côte d'Or, Gloucestershire, and Wiltshire, appeared in the *Proceedings* of the Cotteswold Club. Yet more important were his *Monograph on the British Fossil Echinodermata from the Oolitic Formations* (1855–80), and *Monograph on the British Fossil Echinodermata from the Cretaceous Formations* (1864–1908), which were both printed for the Palaeontographical Society. In 1878 he began a *Monograph on the Lias Ammonites of the British Islands*, which was completed after his death and issued in 1878–86.

Wright was elected FRSE in 1855, FGS in 1859 (receiving the Wollaston medal in 1878), and FRS in 1879. He was president of the geological section of the British Association meeting in 1875 (at Bristol), and also received honorary distinctions from various British and foreign societies. He died on 17 November 1884 at his home, 4 St Margaret's Terrace, Cheltenham. He was survived by a son, Thomas Lawrence Wright, and two daughters; the elder daughter married a geologist, Edward Bestbridge Wethered, and the younger daughter married Canon Charles Byron Wilcox, vicar of Christ Church, Birmingham. Wright's fossil collection was purchased for an American museum.

YOLANDA FOOTE

Sources *Midland Medical Miscellany* (1 Nov 1883) · T. G. Bonney, *Quarterly Journal of the Geological Society*, 41 (1885), 39–40 · *Geological Magazine*, new ser., 3rd decade, 2 (1885), 93–6 · A. Boyle and F. Bennet, eds., *The Royal Society of Edinburgh: 100 medical fellows elected 1841–1882* (1983), vol. 4 of *Scotland's cultural heritage* (1981–4) · Burke, *Peerage* (1889) · *London and Provincial Medical Directory* (1867) · J. Leyland, ed., *Contemporary medical men and their professional work: biographies of leading physicians … from the 'Provincial Medical Journal'*, 2 vols. (1888) · *Nature*, 31 (1884–5), 103–4 · *DNB* · *CGPLA Eng. & Wales* (1884) · bap. reg. Scot.
Archives NHM, corresp. with Sir Richard Owen and William Clift · U. Edin. L., letters to Sir Archibald Geikie
Likenesses photograph, repro. in Leyland, ed., *Contemporary medical men*
Wealth at death £25,183 14s. 4d. in UK: probate, 8 Dec 1884, *CGPLA Eng. & Wales*

Wright, Thomas (1810–1877), historian and antiquary, was born at Tenbury, Worcestershire, on 23 April 1810, the son of Thomas Wright. His father's family came from near Bradford. His paternal grandfather, Thomas Wright, a Wesleyan Methodist, was the author of a satirical poem, 'A Modern Familiar Religious Conversation' (1778); he also left a manuscript autobiography which was published by his grandson in 1864. His father, one of a large family, was apprenticed as a bookseller and printer, but sought work outside Yorkshire and settled at Ludlow, Shropshire. He wrote a guide to the town, *The History and Antiquities of Ludlow* (1822; 2nd edn, 1826). Thomas was the younger of two brothers; his brother, William Airey, who was the elder by ten years, became a printer.

Education and early topographical interests Wright was educated at the King Edward Grammar School in Ludlow under a Mr Hind. While still a schoolboy, he completed volume 5 of T. Allen's *History and Antiquities of London* (1827). His evident and precocious literary abilities caused Mr Hutchings of Broad Street, Ludlow, to pay for him to go to Trinity College, Cambridge, as a sizar in 1830. He graduated BA in 1834 and proceeded MA in 1837. He was placed under William Whewell, but the major influence on his later life was J. M. Kemble, who introduced him to Old English: Wright's permanent interest in vernacular sources stems from this period. However, while he was in Cambridge much of his time must have been spent expanding and revising Philip Morant's *History and Topography of the County of Essex* (1836). His lifelong associate J. O. Halliwell (later Halliwell-Phillipps) was also a Trinity man, but when he took up residence in Michaelmas term 1837, Wright had probably already moved to London. However, Halliwell certainly received support from Wright in the formation of the Cambridge Antiquarian Society in 1839–40. Wright clearly retained an interest in the history of his university after he had left Cambridge, and in 1840 published, with M. Prickett, an edition of Thomas Fuller's *History of the University*. He also published *Ancient Laws of the Fifteenth Century for King's College* (1850)

Thomas Wright (1810–1877), by D. J. Pound, pubd 1859 (after Maull & Polyblank)

with James Heywood, and *Cambridge University Transactions During the Puritan Controversies* (1854).

From about 1837 until his death Wright lived in London, residing for thirty or so years at 14 Sydney Street, Brompton. In his early years there, he met Francisque Michel and François Guizot. The former arranged for a French edition (1836) of his work on the state of Anglo-Saxon studies before the English edition; Wright also wrote an introduction to Michel's edition of an Anglo-Norman poem on the conquest of Ireland. It was through Michel, perhaps, that he met Minette Eliza, a Frenchwoman some years his junior, who became his wife; they had no children.

Antiquarian and literary societies Wright was much involved in forming and joining new antiquarian and literary societies. He was secretary of the Camden Society at its formation in 1838, and secretary and treasurer of the Percy Society, and he edited *The Chester Plays* (1843–7) for the Shakespeare Society and Gaimar's *Anglo-Norman Metrical Chronicle* (1850) for the Caxton Society. The Historical Society of Science, for which he edited *Popular Treatises on Science Written in the Middle Ages* (1841) and *The Archaeologist and the Journal of Antiquarian Science* (1841–2), both co-operative projects with Halliwell, had a very short life. He joined the Ethnological Society in 1853, became secretary in 1857, joint secretary in 1860, and vice-president in 1869. Wright was elected to the Society of Antiquaries in 1837, and became a corresponding member of the Académie des Inscriptions et Belles-Lettres in 1842. The nomination paper for his election to the Antiquaries shows that it was initiated by T. Crofton Croker, the Irish folklorist, and supported by Sir Frederic Madden and Joseph Hunter, both outstanding medievalists, and Edgar Taylor, another folklorist: Wright was evidently well regarded then as both folklorist and medievalist.

Wright's chief writings Wright's subsequent publications certainly seemed to support this reputation. His interest in Old English, Middle English, and Anglo-Norman texts continued in the 1840s and 1850s—evidenced in editions of *Early Mysteries* (1838), *The Owl and the Nightingale* (1842), Langland's *Piers Ploughman* (1842), and Chaucer's *Canterbury Tales* (1848)—as too did his wider linguistic concerns. In 1852 he published a *Dictionary of Obsolete and Provincial English*, and in 1852–6 a *Universal Pronouncing Dictionary* in five volumes. He also tried his hand at biography: the *Biographia Britannica literaria* (1842–6), of which only two volumes were published (Saxon and Norman), is one of Wright's more useful works. He also published the *Autobiography of Joseph Lister* (1842), translated Reinhold Pauli's *Life of Alfred* (1852), and edited volumes 2 to 12 of the *New General Biographical Dictionary*, edited by H. J. Rose (1848). His interest in folklore, sorcery, and legend was exhibited in publications such as *Proceedings Against Dame Kyteler Prosecuted for Sorcery* (1843), *St Patrick's Purgatory* (1844), *Narratives of Sorcery and Magic* (1854), and his edition of T. C. Croker's *Fairy Legends and Traditions of the South of Ireland* (1862). He also published *Early Christianity in Arabia: a Historical Essay* (1855), a work that had original Arabic and Hebrew references and was, according to Wright, unaltered from pre-Cambridge days. In 1848 it was followed by *Early Travels in Palestine*, still a useful work, and in 1854 a revised edition of Marsden's *Marco Polo* appeared. More mainstream historical works included illustrated three-volume histories of *Scotland* (1852–5), *Ireland* (1854), and *France* (1856–8), all clearly written with an eye to the American market. He also edited two volumes of letters from Queen Elizabeth's reign (1838), *Three Chapters of Letters Relating to the Suppression of the Monasteries* (1843), the *Chronicle of Peter Langtoft* (1866), and the *Churchwardens' Accounts of the Town of Ludlow* (1869). His translation of Giraldus Cambrensis ran to several editions, and among other works his edition of Neckham's *De naturis rerum* (1863) is of interest. His most colourful work was the Anglo-Norman text with all the heraldry in colour for *The Siege of Caerlaverock, 1300* (1863). *A History of Domestic Manners and Sentiments in England During the Middle Ages* (1862) was Wright's most significant work of medieval history. Containing 319 illustrations by F. W. Fairholt, fairly freely redrawn from contemporary manuscripts, it was a pioneering work and is still worth consulting. The text drew heavily on the vernacular literature with which Wright was familiar and gives a vivid insight into medieval life. It later appeared in an enlarged edition, with a different title, *Homes of other Days* (1871). The main criticism of the work is that it did not link up with the studies of surviving domestic architecture being made at Oxford by J. H. Parker.

Changing interests By the 1860s, however, Wright's preoccupations were evolving. His changing interests may be demonstrated by contrasting his two-volume works (mostly published lectures), *Essays on subjects connected with the literature, popular superstitions, and history of England in the middle ages* (1846) and *Essays on archaeological subjects, and on various questions connected with the history of art, science, and literature in the middle ages* (1861). In the earlier publication, the linguistic origins of his studies, his interest in Old and Middle English and Anglo-Norman, are evident; from 'Dr Grimm's mythology' derived his interest in legend, folklore, and sorcery, exemplified in the second volume of the essays, in which Robin Hood and Hereward the Wake feature. By 1861 the archaeology of Roman Britain, barrows, Anglo-Saxon cemeteries, and other related subjects were of equal or greater interest to him.

These new concerns were early expressed in the work by which Wright became best known to his contemporaries. *The Celt, the Roman, and the Saxon: a history of the early inhabitants of Britain, down to the conversion of the Anglo-Saxons* (1852; later editions 1861, 1875, 1885) was a standard work until the end of the nineteenth century. Owing to his rejection of the three-age system, Wright started with Caesar's invasions and put the prehistoric remains, on which he was well informed, in chapter 2. Chapters 3 to 13 deal with Roman Britain by topics and are based on first-hand knowledge; they perhaps had rather more influence on later students than is sometimes admitted. The last two chapters on pagan Saxon cemeteries show a growing interest in this subject. He had no doubt learnt a great deal from Charles Roach Smith's London collections. From 1859 he was involved with the excavations at Wroxeter, which inspired his last major work, *Uriconium* (1872).

Archaeological interests and later writings There had been excavations at the Roman town of Wroxeter, near Shrewsbury, since the time of Thomas Telford, but the identification of the colonnade on the east side of the forum by Sir Henry Dryden made better orientation possible. This led to a suggestion by the local MP that further work should be done by Wright. This started in 1859, but had to be suspended for lack of funds and was not resumed for some years. Wright's main achievement was to identify the baths south of the old work and their connection with the 'basilica' or palaestra to the north. This is the area now exposed to public view, and although interpretation of the periods has greatly altered, credit must be given to Wright for identifying the buildings in this area.

Wright also exhibited other new interests later in life. An early interest in ballads, carols, and political songs, which had produced such publications as *Commonwealth Ballads* (1841), *Songs and Ballads of the Reign of Philip and Mary* (1860), and *Political Poems and Songs from Edward III to Richard III* (1858), was succeeded by growing fascination with satire and its visual form, caricature. His publications in this area included *Satirical Poets of the Twelfth Century* (2 vols., 1872), *Caricature History of the Georges* (2nd edn, 1868), *History of Caricature and Grotesque in Literature and Art* (1865), and *The Works of James Gillray* (1875). Once again, he had the good fortune to have the services of Fairholt to illustrate his work. A curious late work of Wright which deserves mention was his *Womankind in Western Europe, from the Earliest Times to the Seventeenth Century* (1869), which has aroused interest among modern feminists and was reprinted in New York in 1987. It clearly derives from *A History of Domestic Manners*, where the drawings of women from manuscripts are frequent. Although, like John Stuart Mill, Wright had no doubt about the equality of the sexes, his idealization of medieval women and the lapse thereafter is not wholly to modern taste.

Money, reputation, and death The volume of Wright's publications was formidable, although some of it can hardly be described as more than hack work. He neither enjoyed inherited wealth nor held any post that offered a full salary: he had to live by his writing and by any help that a patron could offer. Fortunately, he enjoyed the valuable patronage of Joseph Mayer of Liverpool, many of his letters to whom survive in the British Library. Much of his enormous output is attributable to the necessity of earning a livelihood. On 19 June 1865 he was granted a pension of £65 per annum from the civil list 'as an author who has contributed much to English literary and political history'; this was increased by £35 in 1872 'in recognition of his literary merits'. The pension terminated with Wright's death in 1877, but when Gladstone replaced Disraeli in office it was restored to his widow.

According to Roach Smith, Wright did seek employment (a letter of 5 May 1860 at the Society of Antiquaries shows that he wanted the secretaryship), but temperamentally he does not seem to have been a very employable person. His ability to support himself by his literary work was in marked contrast to other antiquaries, but the labours involved seem to have had harmful consequences. According to Roach Smith, who knew him well, he often had to work almost continuously through the day and much of the night to fulfil his tasks, and contemporaries attributed his mental collapse in later life to overwork. As serious, too, was the poor quality of much of his work; his textual work was justly criticized as 'swarm[ing] with errors of transcription' (*Quarterly Review*, March 1848, 319).

Wright's main relief from this relentless drudgery was trips into the country, alone or with two or three men friends. He often revisited his boyhood area on the Welsh border, and published *Wanderings of an Antiquary* (1854), *Ludlow Sketches* (1867), and a guidebook to *Ludlow Castle and Church* (1869; 18th edn, 1929). These excursions were not aimless but directed principally towards Roman remains; his published work showed that he had visited nearly all the visible Roman remains in the country. Although quite a frequent visitor to Paris, he does not seem to have travelled in France, perhaps because unlike many of his contemporaries he had virtually no interest in Gothic architecture, possibly due to a nonconformist dislike of the Roman Catholic church. Of the dissolution of the monasteries, he remarked that it was 'the greatest blessing conferred by Providence upon the country since the first introduction of Christianity' (*Three Chapters of Letters Relating to the Suppression of Monasteries*, CS, 26, 1843, v).

Although he had many friends who were prehistorians, Wright was isolated from the great change in outlook on the origins of mankind that came about in the middle of the nineteenth century, or rather he resisted it. His emphatic rejection of the Danish three-age system or the great antiquity of man generally accepted after 1859 has provoked discussion among modern scholars. He frequently referred to the matter in his writings and devoted a whole lecture to the subject: 'On the early history of Leeds in Yorkshire and on some questions of prehistoric archaeology agitated at the present time' (1864). He found repugnant the notion of humanity evolving from a lower state, and required some act of creation. He had virtually to deny the existence of a prehistoric period, and so Bronze Age swords had to be contemporaneous with the Romans. The absurdity of his position would have been more serious had he not confined his attention largely to the Roman period and the middle ages.

Perhaps Wright's naivety had its most dramatic exposure at the creation of the British Archaeological Association in 1843. Roach Smith and Wright had decided to found this association, which was inaugurated at a congress held at Canterbury in 1844. Wright prepared *The Archaeological Album, or, Museum of National Antiquities* (1845). The jejune nature of the work was bound to antagonize the more serious-minded, particularly the architectural historians such as Robert Willis. Heaping obloquy on Wright, a large part of the association, led by Albert Way, seceded from it and set up an institute of their own. The two bodies still exist today.

Much of Wright's work has been entirely superseded but it is still a matter for surprise how often the only thing written on a subject is what Wright wrote or transcribed, and it is usually unwise to ignore his work, however carelessly done. His scholarship has been described as broad rather than deep: he was a disseminator of knowledge rather than a great advancer of it. An intellectual rather than a stolid antiquary, he was admired more by his French than his English contemporaries, and often found himself out of step with colleagues who could not understand his way of thinking. His main contribution was to demonstrate the value of vernacular literature in understanding the everyday life and beliefs of people in the middle ages. This is not to overlook his work, now quite superseded, at Wroxeter and on Roman Britain.

The contrast between the fame and apparent success of Wright in middle life with the abject misery and poverty of his last years proved a considerable shock to his friends and colleagues, and the failure to assist his distress provoked mutual recriminations and a long-lived controversy. Wright's letters to Joseph Mayer show a marked deterioration from 1872 as dementia (possibly Alzheimer's disease) began to take a hold. Roach Smith, who visited Wright in September 1875, wrote to Mayer, horrified by what he had found. Many of the books and much of the furniture had been sold and Wright could only totter from one room to the other, unaware of where he was. 'I believe that his life may terminate at any time suddenly', Roach Smith thought, because of untreated diabetes. His wife was 'blind or nearly so' (Roach Smith to Mayer, BL, Add. MS 33347, fols. 256–257). The pension of £100 and £60 from Halliwell-Phillipps, together with gifts from Mayer, meant that it was not really starvation that was the hazard but the health of the couple, who were clearly quite incapable of looking after themselves. Roach Smith said that Wright had not been able to earn any money from writing for two or three years, a fair indication of how dependent upon this his budget had been. Roach Smith tried to raise money from societies and it was this that led to his well-known strictures on the Society of Antiquaries.

Wright died at 282 King's Road, Chelsea, on 23 December 1877 and was buried in Brompton cemetery on 29 December in the same 'compartment' as his mother, Hannah, buried in 1854, and his elder brother, William, buried in October 1859. His wife, Minette, was also buried there on 13 April 1883.   MICHAEL WELMAN THOMPSON

Sources E. A. Fitch, 'Historians of Essex, 8: Thomas Wright', *Essex Review*, 9 (1900), 65–71 · C. Roach Smith, *Collectanea Antiqua*, 7 (1880), 244–66 · C. R. Smith, *Retrospections, social and archaeological*, 1 (1883), 71–84, 293–5 · N. C. Hultin, Introduction, in T. Wright, *Womankind*, reprint (1987) · R. M. Dorson, *The British folklorists: a history* (1968), 66–74 · P. Levine, *The amateur and the professional: antiquarians, historians and archaeologists in Victorian England* (1986) · *The Athenaeum* (29 Dec 1877) · *The Academy* (29 Dec 1877), 594–5 · letters to Joseph Mayer, Charles Roach Smith, and Sir Frederic Madden, BL, Add. MSS 33346–33347, MSS Egerton 2841–2848 · Venn, *Alum. Cant.* · parish register (burial) Brompton, London, 29/12/1877

Archives Royal Society of Literature | BL, letters to Joseph Mayer, letters to Sir Frederic Madden, letters to Charles Roach Smith, Add. MSS 33346–33347; Egerton MSS 2841–2848 · Bodl. Oxf., corresp. with Sir Thomas Phillipps · CUL, letters to the Royal Society of Literature · Herts. ALS, letters to Lord Lytton · JRL, letters to E. A. Freeman · U. Edin. L., corresp. with James Halliwell-Phillipps · U. Edin. L., letters to David Laing · Yale U., Beinecke L., letters to T. J. Pettigrew

Likenesses J. Durham, marble bust, 1850, Society of Artists · D. J. Pound, stipple and line engraving, pubd 1859 (after photograph by Maull & Polyblank), NPG [*see illus.*] · G. G. Fontana, marble bust, 1869, Walker Art Gallery, Liverpool · G. G. Fontana, plaster model, Walker Art Gallery, Liverpool · wood-engraving (after photograph by C. Watkins), NPG; repro. in *ILN* (12 Jan 1878)

Wright, Vincent (1937–1999), historian and political scientist, was born at 31 Quay Street, Whitehaven, Cumberland, on 6 August 1937, the son of Walter Hogarth Wright (d. 1953), a coalminer, and his wife, Mary Teresa Kinsella (d. 1997). He attended Whitehaven grammar school, but at sixteen left to join the treasurer's department of Burnley corporation. While there he studied part-time for A levels, then did national service in the Royal Navy (1955–7), and subsequently enrolled for the BSc (Econ) at the London School of Economics and Political Science (LSE), where he gained a modest finals result in 1960. Despite that, William Pickles, the leading specialist on French politics at the LSE, encouraged him to go to France to begin doctoral work and in 1965 he gained a London PhD with a thesis on the politics of the *département* of the Basses-Pyrénées between 1848 and 1870. By this route he became absorbed in the administrative and political history of nineteenth-century France and a pioneer in using both official and private French archival sources for this period. His book *Le conseil d'état sous le Second Empire* (1972) was the first of two distinguished contributions to French administrative history which established his reputation in that field. The second, derived from his doctoral thesis, was *Les préfets du Second Empire* (1973, jointly with Bernard Le Clère) and dealt with the role and character of the prefectoral corps in the mid-nineteenth century. His concentration on France at this stage in his life was confirmed by the appearance of *The Government and Politics of France* (1978), an elegantly written textbook which, as three subsequent editions demonstrated, was long-lasting and popular. This book, though it continued to reflect a keen sense of the influence of earlier history, also marked a shift of focus to problems of government and politics in the contemporary world.

After some early experience at the University of Bordeaux, Wright really began his academic career in 1965 with a lecturership in politics at the University of Newcastle. He moved in 1970 back to the LSE, where he became successively senior lecturer and reader (1974). Then in 1977 he was elected to an official fellowship in politics at Nuffield College, Oxford, where he remained until his death. Though it is doubtful whether he found Nuffield College a particularly congenial intellectual milieu, his appointment there was ideally suited to his temperament and scholarly interests. It gave him complete freedom to pursue his steadily widening research interests, to write as much and as often as he wished, and to devote himself wholeheartedly to building up the many intellectual contacts and friendships that he formed not only in France, but in other western European countries too, especially Italy and Spain. This wide knowledge of people and places admirably complemented his historical sensitivity and contributed much to the fluency and perceptiveness of his many contributions to comparative political analysis. From the early 1980s onwards as editor, contributor, and collaborator he initiated and steered through to publication a wide range of books dealing with such matters as the governance of the evolving European Community, the role of the state in contemporary industrial societies, the problems of public policy making in complex societies, regionalism, and the relations between politics and administration. Alongside this substantial output he continued to produce many articles testifying to his mastery of French political and administrative history. Foremost among the preoccupations of his life from 1977 until the end was the joint editorship of *West European Politics*, a stimulating and widely read journal launched by Wright and his colleague at the LSE Gordon Smith, early in 1978. The high standards maintained by this journal owed much to Wright's talents as a stern yet sympathetic editor.

Vincent Wright had a keen sense of humour and brought some of the attributes of an impresario to his academic endeavours, especially in his later years. He had outstanding talent in persuading friends and colleagues to write chapters for books on themes which he thought important, to join in research projects, to take part in conferences or seminars, or to advise one of his graduate students. For though Wright had no formal teaching duties at Oxford he enjoyed organizing seminars (to which he made incisive contributions) and was a devoted super-visor of research students. In the wake of his many academic links in western Europe he became a familiar figure at conferences and colloquia, adviser to several new academic institutions, and the holder of visiting professorships in several universities as well as at the European University Institute in Florence. Academic honours came to him from several quarters and in 1995 he was elected a fellow of the British Academy. But Wright often reacted to such signs of public recognition with a touch of self-mockery. At heart he remained a very private person who greatly valued the company of his friends and gained most intellectual pleasure from exploring the archives of France. Here he could be sure of finding yet more evidence of that inescapable quirkiness of human behaviour which, so he firmly believed, sets limits to the generalizations of the discipline he formally pursued. For it was French history to which he was really dedicated—so much so, that, even when struck down by a painful cancer, he devoted his remaining energies to completing books on freemasonry in provincial France towards the end of the Second Empire and on the *préfets* appointed by Gambetta at the beginning of the Third Republic. He had collected archival material on these topics over many years, often with the help of his partner for thirty-three years, Dr Basil Smith, who sustained him during his final illness. Wright died at Sobell House, the John Radcliffe Hospital, Oxford, on 8 July 1999, and was cremated in Oxford, on 13 July.

NEVIL JOHNSON

Sources *The Independent* (14 July 1999) · *The Guardian* (21 July 1999) · J. Hayward, 'The incomparable comparatist: Vincent Wright', *West European Politics*, 22/4 (1999) · S. Cassese, 'In memory of Vincent Wright', *International Review of of Administrative Science*, 65 (1999), 467–71 · *WW* (1999) · record of memorial meeting, 16 Oct 1999, Nuffield Oxf. · V. Wright, 'The path to hesitant comparison', *Comparative European politics: the story of a profession*, ed. H. Daalder (1997)
Likenesses photograph, Nuffield Oxf.
Wealth at death £154,466: probate, 1999, *CGPLA Eng. & Wales*

Wright, Waller Rodwell (1774/5–1826), civil servant and writer, was the son of Matthias Wright, of Bury St Edmunds. Wright attended school at Bury St Edmunds, and from there went to Trinity College, Cambridge, matriculating in Michaelmas term 1792. It appears that he took no degree, as he was admitted to Lincoln's Inn on 23 November 1793, and called to the bar on 7 February 1800. He then became British consul-general for the republic of the Seven Islands (Ionian Islands), serving from 1800 to 1804. On his return to England he became recorder for Bury St Edmunds and on 16 November 1805 married Mary Ann Bokenham. Thereafter he was president of the court of appeals at Malta. Wright's library at Zante was rifled by the French in 1804, and the materials which he had collected for a work on the Greek islands were scattered or destroyed. His reminiscences took the form of *Horae Ionicae: a poem descriptive of the Ionian Islands and part of the adjacent coast of Greece* (1809). Byron praised this poem in his *English Bards and Scotch Reviewers* (1809); it is throughout the work of an ardent disciple of Pope, and there are some charming lines among its heroic couplets. A 'Postscript'

contains a few remarks on the modern Greek spoken in the Ionian Islands. To the third edition of 1816 Wright appended two odes and *Orestes, a Tragedy: from the Italian of Count Vittor Alfieri*. This latter work was in blank verse, for which Wright showed little aptitude. One of the odes, on the duke of Gloucester's installation as chancellor at Cambridge, had been printed in 1811 and forwarded in September by R. C. Dallas to Byron, who wrote: 'It is evidently the production of a man of taste, and a poet, though I should not be willing to say it was fully equal to what might be expected from the author of *Horae Ionicae*'. Wright was good friends with Dallas, who gave him the manuscript of *Childe Harold* to read. 'It was probably Wright who convinced the timid Dallas that *Childe Harold* had great possibilities of popular success' (Marchand, 279). Wright died in Valletta, Malta, in 1826.

THOMAS SECCOMBE, rev. REBECCA MILLS

Sources will, PROB 11/1722, fols. 184–5 · *The works of Lord Byron*, ed. W. E. Henley, [1] (1897), 374 · *Life, letters, and journals of Lord Byron*, ed. T. Moore (1838), 136 · Watt, *Bibl. Brit.*, 2.986r · W. R. Wright, *Horae Ionicae: a poem descriptive of the Ionian Islands and part of the adjacent coast of Greece* (1809) · [J. Watkins and F. Shoberl], *A biographical dictionary of the living authors of Great Britain and Ireland* (1816) · *Monthly Review*, new ser., 60 (1809), 98–101 · Venn, *Alum. Cant.* · W. P. Baildon, ed., *The records of the Honorable Society of Lincoln's Inn: the black books*, 4 (1902); repr. (1991) · L. A. Marchand, *Byron: a biography*, 3 vols. (1957) · *IGI*
Likenesses C. Knight, stipple, pubd 1813 (after E. Scott), BM, NPG
Wealth at death see will, PRO, PROB 11/1722, fols. 184–5

Wright, Whitaker (1845–1904), speculator, was born on 9 February 1845, and spoke with a Northumbrian burr, but his early circumstances are unknown. At the age of twenty-one he went to the United States as an assayer, and in the late 1870s participated in the mining boom at Leadville in Colorado before acquiring a mine in New Mexico. Several speculative fortunes were made and lost by him at this time. He next moved east, becoming chairman of the Philadelphia mining exchange and a member of the New York stock exchange. The failure of the Gunnison Iron and Coal Company exposed him to heavy losses, and he returned to England in 1889.

In the 1890s Wright's fortunes recovered when he established himself as a company promoter specializing in overseas mining ventures. The times were propitious for a man of his experience. He could talk plausibly of mining camps, and understood the vulnerabilities of the speculative investor. He weighed 16 stone, with a massive head and neck, and his solidity inspired confidence. During 1896 he floated Lake View Consols with capital of £250,000, and formed other companies to exploit mines in Western Australia. In 1897 he consolidated his interests in a new combination called the London and Globe Finance Corporation with himself as managing director and the marquess of Dufferin and Ava as chairman. This corporation's promotion work was very profitable: typically, it acquired the Ivanhoe mine at Kalgoorlie from a small colonial company capitalized at £50,000 and refloated it in London with capital of £1 million. In 1897 Wright launched the British America Corporation with

Whitaker Wright (1845–1904), by Harry Furniss

capital of £1.5 million to acquire mining interests in British Columbia and the Yukon. This company and London and Globe became jointly interested in floating mining companies, rigging the markets in their shares, and juggling their finances.

Wright bought for £250,000 the estate of Lea Park near Godalming in Surrey. He installed an observatory, a theatre, a velodrome, a private hospital, and stabling for fifty horses. With a touch of megalomania he constantly devised new effects in architecture and landscaping: hills which obstructed views were levelled, and armies of labourers employed in lake-building. He was fond of billiards, which he played in a saloon constructed of glass beneath the wide sheets of water in his grounds. The drawing-room of his sumptuous London house in Park Lane was a replica of the Cabinet des Rois of Louis XV. He kept a yawl at Cowes with the suggestive name of *Sybarita*. 'Everything was swagger,' according to *Blackwood's Magazine*, 'the whole thing was a gorgeous vulgarity—a magnificent burlesque of business.'

There were many danger signals: the Baker Street and Waterloo Railway, which was one of London and Globe's promotions, consumed £600,000; but speculators in their cupidity were convinced that they could get clear before the inevitable collapse. During 1899 London and Globe made large profits as Lake View shares rose from £9 to £28 following the discovery of a rich patch of ore. When a reaction set in, based on the knowledge that this rich find was exhausted, Wright determined to support the share price. The results were disastrous, and on 28 December 1900 London and Globe announced its insolvency. This disaster bankrupted members of the stock exchange, liquidated many of London and Globe's allied companies, and ruined countless numbers of Wright's infatuated dupes. The subsequent investigations of the official receiver disclosed that Wright's empire had rested on fraudulent accounts and balance sheets concealing deficits. Dividends paid by London and Globe had not been earned, but were provided by money pillaged from Wright's other companies.

Although there was strong political pressure for Wright's prosecution, it was at the instigation of a creditor that in March 1903 a warrant was issued for his arrest. He had sailed four days earlier for New York, where he was arrested. After resisting extradition for some months by every legal artifice, he returned to England in August. At his trial, beginning on 11 January 1904, prosecuting counsel showed that capital of £5 million had been lost in two years, not a penny of which had reached his shareholders, while additional debts of about £3 million had been accumulated. On 26 January 1904 he was convicted on all counts, and sentenced to the maximum of seven years' penal servitude. Immediately after sentence at the central law courts in London, he went to a consulting room with his solicitor, Sir George Lewis, to whom he handed his watch saying, 'I will not need this where I am going' (*DLB*). He then swallowed cyanide and died within a few minutes. He was buried with pomp in Witley churchyard, near Godalming, on 30 January 1904.

Wright left a widow, Anna Edith, together with a son and two daughters. He was the basis of Mr Ponderevo in the novel *Tono-Bungay* by H. G. Wells (1909).

RICHARD DAVENPORT-HINES

Sources PRO NIre., Dufferin and Ava MSS • 'Whitaker Wright Finance', *Blackwood*, 175 (1904), 397–409 • 'Whitaker Wright's sentence', *The Economist* (30 Jan 1904), 165–6 • W. R. Lawson, 'Stock jobbing companies', *National Review*, 36 (1900–01), 869–81 • H. Furniss, *Some Victorian people* (1924) • A. Vallance, *Very private enterprise* (1955) • G. E. Morrison, diary, 5 Dec 1902, Mitchell L., NSW • H. G. Nicolson, *Helen's tower* (1937) • S. F. van Oss, 'The Westralian mining "boom"', *Nineteenth Century*, 40 (1896), 711–20 • *Financial Times* (27 Jan 1904) • *The Times* (12 Jan–1 Feb 1904) • *ILN* (30 Jan 1904) • B. Jones, *Follies and grottoes* (1974), 199–201

Archives Northern Ireland RO, first marquess of Dufferin and Ava MSS

Likenesses H. Furniss, caricature, pen-and-ink sketch, NPG [*see illus.*] • photograph, repro. in *Review of Reviews*, 28 (1903) • sketch, repro. in Furniss, *Some Victorian people*

Wealth at death £148,200: probate, 11 July 1904, *CGPLA Eng. & Wales*

Wright, William (1563–1639), Jesuit, son of John Wright, an apothecary of York, was born there in February 1563. His elder brother, Thomas *Wright, was a Roman Catholic priest dismissed from the Society of Jesus. Wright was educated in York until an uncle, an unnamed Roman Catholic priest, sent him in June 1581 to the English College then in Rheims. On 27 August he left for Rome and he was admitted into the English College there on 18 October 1581. He joined the Society of Jesus the following 8 December. Having completed his noviceship in 1583 he studied philosophy at the Roman College until he was sent to the Austrian province on 7 September 1585 for reasons of health. In Vienna he completed his theological studies and was ordained about 1591. He remained there as a lecturer in philosophy and as prefect of the sodality until 1597. He then moved to the Jesuit college in Graz to lecture in philosophy and theology and to continue his own studies. He was awarded a DD at Graz about 1600. On 23 June 1602 he was professed of the four vows at Graz.

In September 1605 Wright asked to be sent on the English mission. Permission was granted in late 1606 and he entered England in the entourage of Count François Vaudemont. He resided at Hengrave Hall, Suffolk, the seat of the Gage family. Betrayed by a spy a few months after his arrival, and accused of being the superior of Jesuits in England, Wright was imprisoned in the Tower of London but after four days was transferred to the White Lion. Richard Bancroft, archbishop of Canterbury, and the ex-Jesuit Sir Christopher Perkins (or Parkins) examined him at Lambeth on 7 July 1607. To them he summarized his Jesuit career and denied being the Jesuit superior. In subsequent meetings Bancroft, Thomas Morton, whose kindness Wright praised, and other Anglican divines debated with the Jesuit theological matters, including the recent oath of allegiance. In these disputations Wright undermined the religious convictions of two protestant ministers. One, later committed to prison for religious reasons, periodically screamed out: 'O Mr. Wright, from an English cleric, Lord deliver us!' (Foley, 2.283). Aided by friends Wright escaped from prison about 16 September to an undisclosed location in the east midlands, a region known in Jesuit catalogues as the Leicestershire mission and later as the residence of St Anne which embraced the counties of Leicester, Derby, Rutland, and sections of Nottingham. By 1609 Wright was Jesuit spiritual prefect of a group of Catholics that centred on Elizabeth Manners, countess of Rutland and daughter of Sir Philip Sidney, and, except for much of 1630 when he was on the continent for reasons of health, he remained in the east midlands for the rest of his life.

A skilled theologian, Wright participated in many early Stuart theological controversies. Unlike his brother Thomas, he opposed the oath of allegiance and he translated two treatises by Martin Becanus SJ against it and its defenders—*The Confutation of Tortura Torti* (1610) and *The English Jarre* (1612). The seventeenth-century Jesuit historian Daniello Bartoli attributed to Wright a major role 'in establishing the truth of the impossibility of taking the oath of supremacy with a safe conscience, contrary to the opinion and exhortations of the Archpriest [George] Blackwell' (Foley, 2.285). Wright also contributed *A Discovery of Certaine Notorious Shifts* (1614) and *A Treatise of the Church* (1616) to a dispute initiated by John White, chaplain to James I, over the nature and identity of the true church. On a related theme Wright translated works by Leonard Lessius SJ regarding the possibility of salvation outside the Roman church, as *A controversy, in which is examined, whether every man may be saved in his owne faith and religion?* (1614) and *A Consultation what Faith and Religion is Best to be Imbraced* (1618). His *A Brief Treatise* (1623), dedicated to 'an honourable person', Mary Villiers, countess of Buckingham, argued that salvation could only be found in the Roman church. *A Brief Treatise* and *An Epistle Dedicated to an Honourable Person* (1622) were Wright's contributions to the last major theological battle between Roman Catholics and Anglicans during the reign of James I: the struggle for the soul of the countess of Buckingham, mother of the all-powerful duke of Buckingham, which climaxed in the famous conferences in 1622 between John Percy (alias Fisher the Jesuit) and William Laud, then bishop of St David's.

From its foundation in 1621 until 1633, Wright was superior of the residence of St Anne. He remained a consultor until his death and besides his more priestly ministries taught grammar to children, probably at the small Jesuit school in Stanley Grange, 6 miles from Derby. He died on 18 January 1639. The eighteenth-century Catholic historian Charles Dodd, not noted for pro-Jesuit sympathies, praised Wright: 'He was equally esteemed for his learning and humility. For, although he was a doctor of divinity, yet he willingly submitted to the drudgery of teaching children their rudiments' (Dodd, 2.136).

THOMAS M. McCOOG

Sources H. Foley, ed., *Records of the English province of the Society of Jesus*, 7 vols. in 8 (1875–83), vol. 2, pp. 275–86; vol. 7/2, pp. 871–4, 10003–4 · T. M. McCoog, ed., *Monumenta Angliae*, 1–2 (1992) · T. M. McCoog, *English and Welsh Jesuits, 1555–1650*, 2 vols., Catholic RS, 74–5 (1994–5) · A. F. Allison and D. M. Rogers, eds., *The contemporary printed literature of the English Counter-Reformation between 1558 and 1640*, 2 vols. (1989–94) · Archivum Romanum Societatis Iesu, Rome · C. Dodd [H. Tootell], *The church history of England, from the year 1500, to the year 1688*, 3 vols. (1737–42) · P. Milward, *Religious controversies of the Jacobean age* (1978) · T. F. Knox and others, eds., *The first and second diaries of the English College, Douay* (1878)

Wright, William (1735–1819), military physician and naturalist, was born in March 1735, at Crieff, Perthshire, Scotland, the second of two sons by his father's second marriage. He remained close throughout his life to his brother James who was two years older. Wright, it appears, came from a humble background and his father's occupation is unknown. After early schooling at a grammar school in Crieff he was apprenticed to a local surgeon, George Dennistoun, in Falkirk. In 1756 he attended lectures at Edinburgh medical school, but did not take a degree. In the summer of 1757 he made a voyage to Greenland, although the purpose of the voyage and his role in it are not known.

Wright began his medical career in 1758 when he joined the navy as surgeon's second mate. Late in 1759 he was promoted to surgeon's first mate. In 1760 his ship sailed as part of a squadron under Rodney for the West Indies. He remained in service in the West Indies until the end of the Seven Years' War (1763), serving both on board ship and in shore-based hospitals in Martinique and elsewhere in the eastern Caribbean. This wartime service provided his first exposure to the ravages of diseases on non-immune British troops. It also exposed him for the first time to the institution of slavery within the island colonies of the empire. After five and a half years in the navy, he returned to Britain in September 1763 and was paid off.

With the war over, Wright charted a new course. First he improved on his qualifications. He obtained the qualification of surgeon (an improvement on surgeon's first mate), by submitting himself for examination at Surgeons' Hall,

London, although there was no chance of a naval posting. A friend's father, Dr Simson, who was professor at St Andrews University, obtained for him an MD without the need to attend the university. It is likely he would have paid a fee for this degree. Armed with these qualifications, he embarked for Jamaica in early 1764, to seek a position as a physician. Despite his abilities and experience he was forced to accept a position as assistant to a Dr Gray at Savanna-la-Mer. Wright's luck changed when an old friend from his time at Edinburgh University, Thomas Steel, offered him a partnership in a medical practice at Hampden estate, Trelawney, Jamaica, owned by James Stirling. The practice was responsible for the medical care of 1200 slaves and also the local free population. This practice gave him experience of the diseases of the black slave population of Jamaica. His later writings on yaws, a disease particularly identified with black slaves by eighteenth-century medicine, may be traced to these years. He remained in Jamaica for thirteen years until 1777. During these years he became financially successful by investing the income from his medical practice in slaves and land. In mid-1765 he and Thomas Steel owned four slaves, in 1767 fifteen slaves, by 1771 thirty-three slaves. When their joint property was finally sold following the death of Thomas Steel in 1784, the income gained was sufficient to allow Wright 'immunity from application to professional employments' (*Memoir of the Late William Wright*, 75). He was appointed surgeon-general of Jamaica in 1774.

Wright's first resident stay in Jamaica (1764–77) also marked the beginning of his career as a naturalist. By late 1768 the University of Edinburgh had established a museum of natural history and was seeking specimens from collectors. Wright became a collector of Jamaican plants for John Hope and Dr Ramsay, both professors of the University of Edinburgh. Seeing botanical investigation as a route to gentility that his practice as a doctor to slaves could not provide, he pursued his avocational interest with intensity. He made large collections of exotic dried plants, often with hoped-for medical applications. He began a correspondence with Sir Joseph Banks who, as *de facto* director of the botanic gardens at Kew and a leading figure in the Royal Society, was an enormously influential patron within the eighteenth-century scientific community. He also started to publish. Two of his papers on medically useful plants were read to the Royal Society in April and May 1777, while he was still in Jamaica. One was on his discovery of a Jamaican species of Cinchona (*Cinchona jamaicensis*). It is and was an effective febrifuge, and is the basis of modern anti-malarial drugs. In August 1777 Wright left Jamaica, whether intending a permanent or temporary return to Britain is not known. During a visit of several months from October 1777 to January 1778, he was introduced into London's leading scientific circles, meeting Sir Joseph Banks for the first time, and the then president of the Royal Society, John Pringle. In March 1778 he was elected a fellow of the Royal Society on the basis of his two papers.

The warm welcome Wright received within metropolitan scientific circles and his acceptance into the Royal Society as a significant contributor to botanical knowledge marked a turning point. He was never to give up the role of botanical collector and naturalist because it allowed him a vocation as a gentleman of science with social rewards that matched, and at times exceeded, those of his career as a physician. His single most important scientific and professional relationship was perhaps that with Sir Joseph Banks. Banks eased his acceptance into the Royal Society and remained the patron though he was the younger man. Wright's last known letter to Banks (in 1807) indicates that the connection between them endured over three decades, perhaps longer. At many times over this period Wright offered Caribbean plant specimens (and sometimes seeds) to Banks. Some went to the Royal Botanic Gardens at Kew, others entered Banks's private herbarium and are now to be found in the Natural History Museum herbarium in London.

Wright's return to Britain proved not to be permanent. At the invitation of Banks he accepted the post of regimental surgeon to the Jamaica regiment under General Rainsford. In the summer of 1780 he sailed with his regiment but his ship was captured and he was taken prisoner of war for three months. He returned to England at the end of 1780. About this time, in a letter to his brother James (12 October 1781), he describes himself as 'destined to be myself a wanderer over the face of the earth' (*Memoir of the Late William Wright*, 64). He reached Jamaica on a second attempt, this time as regimental surgeon to the 99th foot. This second stay in Jamaica lasted from 1782 to 1785. Wright's gifts of plants to Sir Joseph Banks from this period in Jamaica have been noted by Everard Home, a correspondent of Banks. It is thus likely Wright was acting as a semi-official collector for Banks during this period.

Wright returned to Britain in September 1785, spending several months in London before moving to Edinburgh where he had decided to settle. He was now in possession of a secure private income from the sale of his property in Jamaica, ready to involve himself in the scientific societies and gentlemanly culture of a burgeoning mercantile city. In 1788 he was elected a fellow of the Royal Society of Edinburgh, a member of the Society of Natural History of Edinburgh, and a member of the Royal Physical Society of Edinburgh. He was also active in the affairs of the Royal College of Physicians of Edinburgh, having been elected earlier in 1782. He was a political conservative, sharing with many of his class a horror of the French Revolution and the British radical sympathizers of the revolution. As was to be expected from someone whose income was derived from the labour of slaves, he believed the parliamentary campaign to abolish the slave trade, if successful, would damage British commerce. Soon after May 1792, he gave evidence as a witness to the parliamentary committee for the abolition of the slave trade, evidence which almost certainly favoured continuing the trade.

Though Wright was comfortable in Edinburgh, he felt unsatisfied and under-recognized. When offered a military posting to the West Indies with an expeditionary force commanded by Sir Ralph Abercrombie, he accepted. The offer of a posting quickly ran into trouble when it was opposed by the army medical board and the physician-general Sir Lucas Pepys, on the grounds of a rule restricting appointments to licentiates of the Royal College of Physicians of London. This objection which affected many other physicians at the time, particularly graduates of Scottish universities, was overruled by Abercrombie and the secretary of war. Wright became physician to the army and director of military hospitals in Barbados from April 1796 until April 1798. This was his fourth visit to the West Indies. During this two-year period, when his duties permitted, he took time away from hospital to make collections of Windward Island plants, including those of Barbados. He returned to Britain in June 1798.

Wright's service in Barbados finally brought him the recognition he desired. The post had been offered because of his expertise in tropical diseases and he had carried out his task creditably. He was now a very senior figure almost at the peak of professional success. In 1801 he was elected to the Royal Medical Society, and in the same year was elected president of the Royal College of Physicians of Edinburgh, serving until 1803. Wright was close to other important physicians of the time, including James Currie and Maxwell Garthshore. He continued his activities as a botanical collector and naturalist. His Caribbean plant specimens became part of the collections of many important British naturalists. Among this group were Richard Pulteney, Jonathan Stokes, and Aylmer Lambert. His exchange of botanical information with Sir Joseph Banks (president of the Royal Society from 1778 to 1820) also continued. In 1807 he became an associate of the Linnean Society. In 1808 Wright, who was a Neptunist in geology, became a founder member and vice-president of the Wernerian Natural History Society. Before his death, he began to receive some recognition from British naturalists: in 1811 a Fucus plant was named after him by Dawson Turner.

In his character Wright was said to suffer from 'a certain diffidence in manner in the presence of strangers, which, in his case, may be said to have been constitutional' (*Memoir of the Late William Wright*, 45–6). He appears to have suffered no moral anxiety about slavery. His career illustrates well the upward mobility afforded by empire that was possible for men from humble backgrounds in the eighteenth century. He achieved eminence and distinction, but this was mainly through energetic practical activity. His writings consisted of a number of individual papers; he wrote no monograph-length work on either tropical disease or Caribbean flora. The *Memoir of the Late William Wright* (1828) includes eighteen papers by Wright on botany and tropical medicine. Additionally, Wright undertook, together with others, the preparation of a second edition of James Grainger's *An Essay on the More Common West India Diseases* (1764). In addition to adding a preface (in the form of an advertisement), he corrected some mistakes, added practical notes and observations, and an index giving Linnaean identities to the flora and fauna described by Grainger. He viewed Grainger's book as a model work on diseases of black slave populations, and on proposals for managing slaves. Based on his Barbados experience (1796–8), Wright drew up a widely circulated report on the diseases common among British troops in the West Indies, reproduced in *Memoir of the Late William Wright*.

In his medical career he was particularly identified with the use of cold baths for fevers. Although 'The desire of posthumous distinction … was indeed his ruling passion' (*Memoir of the Late William Wright*, 162), he did not achieve it. On balance, though an eminent physician, he was a minor player in late eighteenth-century natural history, a foot soldier of science. His heritage to the present may be seen through the survival of plants he collected in a number of herbaria, including the Natural History Museum in London, the Royal Botanic Garden in Edinburgh, and the Liverpool Museum. He never married, but adopted his nephew James whom he trained for the medical profession. Wright died in Edinburgh on 19 September 1819 of an influenza or catarrhal fever, and was buried in the west ground at Greyfriars, Edinburgh, on 23 September.

Norris D. Saakwa-Mante

Sources *Memoir of the late William Wright, M.D.* (1828) • *The Banks letters*, ed. W. R. Dawson (1958), 248, 418, 532, 767, 798, 799, 882 • R. P. Stearns, 'Colonial fellows of the Royal Society of London, 1661–1788', *Osiris*, 8 (1948), 73–121, esp. 116–17 • 'The Jamaica portrait gallery', *Journal of the Institute of Jamaica*, 2/2 (1895), 183 • *The history of the collections contained in the natural history departments of the British Museum*, British Museum, 1 (1904), 84 • H. S. Miller, 'The herbarium of Aylmer Bourke Lambert: notes on its acquisition, dispersal, and present whereabouts', *Taxon*, 19 (1970), 489–656, esp. 545–6 • W. Fawcett, 'William Wright, a Jamaican botanist (1735–1819)', *Journal of Botany, British and Foreign*, 60 (1922), 330–34 • J. Britten and G. S. Boulger, 'Jonathan Stokes and his *Commentaries*', *Journal of Botany, British and Foreign*, 52 (1914), 299–306, 317–23, 302–3, 319, 323 • F. A. Stafleu and R. S. Cowan, 'William Wright', *Taxonomic literature: a selective guide*, 7, Regnum Vegetabile, 116 (1988) [incl. bibliography on Wright] • Desmond, *Botanists*, rev. edn, 160 [incl. bibliography on Wright] • P. Manson-Bahr, 'Scottish pioneers in tropical medicine', *Edinburgh Medical Journal*, 3rd ser., 55 (1948), 220–31, esp. 221 • W. S. Craig, *History of the Royal College of Physicians of Edinburgh* (1976), 1076 • Nichols, *Illustrations*, 3.781 [letter of Richard Pulteney to William Wright] • parish register (burial) 23 Sept 1819, Edinburgh

Archives Liverpool Central Library • Liverpool Museum, plant specimens • NHM • NHM, plant specimens • Royal Botanic Garden, Edinburgh, plant specimens • U. Oxf., department of plant sciences, plant specimens | NHM, Brown MSS

Likenesses J. Rogers, stipple, 1823 (after R. E. Drummond), Wellcome L. • W. H. Lizars, engraving (after miniature by J. Caldwell), repro. in *Memoir*

Wright, William (1773–1860), ear surgeon, born at Dartford in Kent on 28 May 1773, was the son of William and Margaret Wright. He was trained by John Cunningham Saunders probably at St Thomas's Hospital, London. He does not appear to have obtained any medical diploma or licence.

Wright began his professional career in 1796, in Bristol. Here he probably became acquainted with those doctors and scientists interested in the medical use of gases; the Pneumatic Institute formally opened in 1798 under Humphry Davy. Wright himself experimented with the application of certain vapours into the ear. He then discovered that inhalation of ether or nitrous oxide vapour suppressed the coughing elicited when probing an inflamed and sensitive ear canal. In 1820 he attended an elderly patient whose chronic cough was so bad that he could not keep his head still enough for Wright to treat his ear. On the second visit the patient was made to inhale the vapour of warmed ether; his cough ceased, and Wright was able to carry out his treatment. This identification of a problem and its solution by means of the ether appears to have been one of the earliest records of administration of an anaesthetic, though Wright did not claim this honour at the time or in later years when anaesthesia became commonplace.

Also at Bristol, a Miss Anna Thatcher came under Wright's care. She was almost deaf and mute, but his method of treatment was so successful that in a year she could repeat words, and in 1817 she had a long audience and conversation with Queen Charlotte, who thereupon appointed Wright her surgeon-aurist-in-ordinary. He moved to London and soon acquired a large and fashionable practice. He began to attend the duke of Wellington in 1823, and remained one of his medical attendants until the duke's death.

Wright campaigned against the use of mercury in the treatment of ear disease, and in 1825 he published three issues of a journal, *The Aurist*. He also wrote books dealing with the treatment of deafness and advising deaf persons how to manage their handicap. Wright died on 21 March 1860 at his home, 4 Duke Street, St James's Square, London.   D'A. POWER, *rev.* ANITA McCONNELL

Sources *Medical Times and Gazette* (31 March 1860), 328 · private information (1900) · N. Weir, *Otolaryngology: an illustrated history* (1990), 71–2 · N. A. Bergman, 'William Wright, aurist: nineteenth century pneumatic practitioner and a discoverer of anesthesia', *Annals of Otology, Rhinology and Laryngology*, 103 (1994), 483–6 · d. cert.

Wright, William (1830–1889), Semitist, son of Captain Alexander Wright (*d.* 1854) of the East India Company's service, was born in northern India on 17 January 1830. He had a sister and a younger brother. His mother (*d.* 1857) was a daughter of Daniel Anthony Overbeck, the last Dutch governor of Bengal, and, knowing Persian and several other languages, encouraged her son in his philological pursuits. His school and first university education was at St Andrews, where he graduated in 1849. He then spent a year at the University of Halle, studying Semitic languages with Professor Emil Rödiger, and gaining at the same time a knowledge of Persian, Turkish, and Sanskrit. Rödiger always spoke of Wright as his best pupil.

At the University of Leiden (1851–3) Wright devoted himself to the study of Arabic manuscripts, under the guidance of Reinhart Dozy. There he identified a number of important works of Arabic literature and philology which he subsequently edited and published, the first being the *Travels* of Ibn Jubayr (1852), which earned him an honorary doctorate from Leiden in 1853, at the age of twenty-three. He then returned to Scotland, where he continued editorial work on al-Maqqari's *Analectes* (1855–61), on Muslim Spain, in collaboration with Dozy. He subsequently held

successively the chair of Arabic at University College, London (1855–6), and at Trinity College, Dublin (1856–61). In 1859 he married Emily, daughter of John Littledale. There were no children of the marriage. During this period he made frequent extended visits to the Bodleian Library at Oxford to study and transcribe manuscripts, but was rejected for the posts of under-librarian in 1857 and Laudian professor of Arabic in 1861, through the personal intervention of Dr E. B. Pusey, who suspected him of heretical opinions. Instead he was appointed in 1861 as an assistant (later assistant keeper) in the department of manuscripts at the British Museum, in order to catalogue the great collection of Syriac manuscripts. While there, he continued to work on Arabic texts, completing his exemplary edition of the *Kamil* of al-Mubarrad (1864–92), as well as editing and publishing a number of Syriac biblical, apocryphal, and literary texts. He also compiled a catalogue of the museum's Ethiopic manuscripts (1877), extending his interest in Semitic palaeography and epigraphy to the publication of noteworthy facsimiles for the Palaeographical Society (Oriental Series, 1875–83) and other texts.

In 1870 Wright was appointed as Sir Thomas Adams's professor of Arabic in the University of Cambridge, a post he held until his death. As a teacher he had a lasting influence both on colleagues and on a succession of distinguished pupils. Cambridge University Library also benefited both from his active role in acquiring a fine collection of early Indian and Tibetan manuscripts from Nepal, through his brother, Dr Daniel Wright (1833–1902), and from his catalogue of its Syriac manuscripts (1901). He was held in great esteem by his fellow scholars abroad, and was awarded membership of the Institut de France, and of the Imperial Academy of St Petersburg, among other distinctions.

Wright was one of the most active and eminent Semitic scholars of his day, contributing extensively to major works by his contemporaries, such as Dozy, Payne Smith, and Neubauer, as well as to the Revised Version of the English Bible. His achievements across the whole field can be seen in his ground-breaking *Lectures on the Comparative Grammar of the Semitic Languages* (1890). But he is known to posterity chiefly for three works which are still widely consulted: his *Grammar of the Arabic Language* (1859 and later edns), his *Catalogue of the Syriac Manuscripts in the British Museum* (1870–72), and his *Short History of Syriac Literature* (originally in *Encyclopaedia Britannica*, then in book form, 1894).

Wright was at times a severe critic of fellow scholars, but he enjoyed a reputation for kindliness and loyal friendship. Politically he was a Conservative, being an opponent of Gladstonian Liberalism, and of Irish home rule in particular. A late photograph reveals a nervous and delicate countenance; he suffered from frail health throughout his life, and died from the effects of pernicious anaemia at the age of fifty-nine on 22 May 1889 at his home, St Andrews, Station Road, Cambridge. He was buried in Scotland at St Andrews; his wife survived him.

G. J. ROPER

Sources A. Marx, 'William Wright's letters to Moritz Stein-schneider', *Occident and Orient … Gaster anniversary volume*, ed. B. Schindler (1936), 424–38 · 'Attestations in favour of William Wright LL.D., 1844–61', CUL, Add. MS 4498 · M.-J. de Goeje, 'William Wright', *Journal Asiatique*, 8th ser., 13 (1889), 522–9 · T. Nöldeke, 'William Wright', *Deutsche Rundschau*, 60 (1889), 306–8 · *Journal of the Royal Asiatic Society of Great Britain and Ireland*, new ser., 21 (1889), 708–13 · *The Academy*, 35 (1889), 378 · J. Fück, *Die arabischen Studien in Europa bis in den Anfang des 20. Jahrhunderts* (Leipzig, 1955) · A. J. Arberry, *The Cambridge school of Arabic* (1948) · E. G. Browne, *A year amongst the Persians*, 3rd edn (1950) · A. Dalby, 'A dictionary of oriental collections in Cambridge University Library', *Transactions of the Cambridge Bibliographical Society*, 9 (1986–90), 248–80 · D. McKitterick, *Cambridge University Library, a history: the eighteenth and nineteenth centuries* (1986) · J. W. Goodison, *Catalogue of Cambridge portraits* (1955) · personal knowledge (1900) [*DNB*] · private information (1900) · m. cert. · *CGPLA Eng. & Wales* (1889)
Archives CUL, testimonials
Likenesses Elliott & Fry, photograph, *c*.1880, CUL, Cambridge Antiquarian Society H176 · J. Hutchinson, marble bust, 1890, FM Cam.
Wealth at death £1200 14*s*. 4*d*.: resworn probate, July 1889, *CGPLA Eng. & Wales*

Wright, William (1837–1899), missionary and author, born on 15 January 1837 at Finnards, near Rathfriland, in co. Down, Ireland, was the youngest child of William Wright, a north of Ireland farmer, and his wife, formerly Miss Niblock. He was educated at a small country school, and supplemented the deficiencies of his instructors by a miscellaneous course of reading. Possessed of unusual ability, he decided to prepare himself for the civil service, and, after passing a few months at the Royal Belfast Academical Institution, he matriculated at Queen's College in 1858. A visit to Belfast by Charles Haddon Spurgeon convinced Wright to become a missionary, and on leaving Queen's College he studied theology at the assembly's college and at Geneva. About 1865 he went to Damascus as missionary to the Jews.

During the ten years that Wright spent in the East he acquired a knowledge of Arabic, studied the customs and topography of Palestine, and made expeditions in Syria and northern Arabia. His *Account of Palmyra and Zenobia, with Travels and Adventures in Bashan and the Desert*, though not published until 1895, was largely written during the journeys which it describes. While in the East he acted as special correspondent to the *Pall Mall Gazette*. At Damascus he made the acquaintance of Edward Henry Palmer and of Sir Richard Burton. For Burton he had a high regard, and published an appreciative sketch of his character in October 1891 in the first number of *The Bookman*, under the signature Salih.

On returning to England, Wright succeeded Robert Baker Girdlestone as editorial superintendent of the British and Foreign Bible Society in June 1876. This post he retained until his death. During his tenure of office 150 new versions of the whole or parts of the Bible passed through his hands, and all the great vernacular versions of India, China, and other countries underwent revision. He published several works on the Bible, including an edition, *Bible Helps* (1896). In 1882 he received an honorary DD from Glasgow University.

Wright's literary labours were not limited by his official

duties. While in Syria he made casts of the Hamath inscriptions, and from further investigations came to the conclusion that they were Hittite remains and that a Hittite empire had at one time existed in Asia Minor and northern Syria. In 1884 he published *The Empire of the Hittites*, with a conjectural decipherment of Hittite inscriptions by Archibald Henry Sayce, who had come to similar conclusions. A second edition of the book appeared in 1886, and Wright contributed the article 'Hittites' to *Chambers's Encyclopaedia* in 1895. In 1893 he published *The Brontës in Ireland*, which reached a third edition within a year.

Wright was twice married; his last years were saddened by the long illness and death of his eldest son, W. D. Wright, a minister of the Presbyterian Church of England. He died on 31 July 1899 at his home, Woolsthorpe, 10 The Avenue, Upper Norwood, London, and was buried on 4 August in Norwood cemetery. He left a widow, Sophia Colyer Wright, three sons, and four daughters.

E. I. CARLYLE, *rev.* H. C. G. MATTHEW

Sources *Bible Society Monthly Report* (Sept–Oct 1899) · *The Presbyterian* (10 Aug 1899) · *British Weekly* (3 Aug 1899) · *The Times* (2 Aug 1899) · *Missionary Herald of the Presbyterian Church of Ireland* (2 Oct 1899) · *CGPLA Eng. & Wales* (1899)
Likenesses portrait, repro. in *Missionary Herald of the Presbyterian Church of Ireland*
Wealth at death £10,752 1*s*. 2*d*.: probate, 29 Aug 1899, *CGPLA Eng. & Wales*

Wright, William Aldis (1831–1914), literary and biblical scholar, was born at Beccles, Suffolk, on 1 August 1831, the second son of George Wright (1789–1873), Baptist minister there, and his second wife, Elizabeth Higham, sister of Thomas Higham (1795–1844), the engraver. After education at the Northgate House Academy and from 1847 at the Fauconberge Grammar School, Beccles, he was admitted in 1849 to Trinity College, Cambridge, as a sub-sizar, and was nineteenth wrangler in 1854. He taught in a school at Wimbledon in 1855, returned to Cambridge, and, on the removal of the religious tests, graduated BA in 1858 and MA in 1861.

Wright's first publication was an essay on Herrick in the *Oxford and Cambridge Magazine* for September 1856. He found regular employment on William Smith's *Dictionary of the Bible* (1860–63) and made his name as a scholar by his contributions to it, by his 1862 edition of Bacon's *Essays*, and by the part which he played with Henry Bradshaw in the exposure of the falsehoods of Constantine Simonides (*The Guardian*, 3 Sept 1862, 26 Jan and 11 Nov 1863). In 1863 he was appointed librarian of Trinity College at Cambridge. His election to a fellowship, delayed by disagreements over his status as a nonconformist, occurred only in 1878. He was senior bursar from June 1870 (when he resigned the librarianship) to December 1895, and vice-master from February 1888 until his death. Although one of the great figures in the university, and frequently a valuable ally for the university library, he took no part latterly in university politics: he neither taught nor lectured. Few undergraduates ventured to speak to him, and even the younger fellows of his college were kept at a distance

William Aldis Wright (1831–1914), by Albert George Dew Smith, 1894

by the austere precision of his manner. His old-fashioned courtesy made him a genial host, but his circle of chosen friends was small.

Wright's edition (Golden Treasury series) of Bacon's *Essays* foreshadowed his later work in the accuracy of its text and the concise learning of its notes. He insisted on keeping the old spelling and punctuation, and was the first to point out emphatically that editors of early printed texts must expect variations in different copies of the same issue. He had used ten copies of the text which he reprinted, and found that some of the sheets were in three states, anticipating later editorial methods. He showed that the older punctuation was 'rhetorical and not grammatical' in a memorandum (unpublished), 'On the use of the comma in the annexed book' (that is, the copy of the prayer book annexed to the Act of Uniformity of 1662), which he presented in 1894 to the Oxford and Cambridge university presses.

In 1863, after the publication of the first volume of the *Cambridge Shakespeare*, Wright succeeded John Glover as joint editor with William George Clark, and brought out the remaining eight volumes from 1863 to 1866. He was solely responsible for the second edition (1891–3), which remains the great monument to his industry and accuracy. However, he was not responsible for its plan. In conversation he admitted the disadvantages of a modernized text and said that an editor who knows his business is better without a colleague. While the *Cambridge Shakespeare* was in progress he edited with Clark the *Globe Shakespeare* (1864; rev. 1904); and when it was complete they edited,

between 1868 and 1872, *The Merchant of Venice*, *Richard II*, *Macbeth*, and *Hamlet* in the Clarendon Press series. Thereafter Wright carried on the series alone and added thirteen plays between 1874 (*The Tempest*) and 1897 (*1 Henry IV*). Besides presenting a mass of new material he was the first editor to give due attention to the Elizabethan usage of words, and the value of this series has been acknowledged by many later editors. It was in his nature to be silent about poetic beauty and dramatic genius; but learning, accuracy, and common sense combined to make him one of Britain's greatest Shakespearian scholars.

In 1864 Wright undertook to collaborate with John Earle and Henry Bradshaw on an edition of Chaucer which ultimately became the *Oxford Chaucer*, edited by Walter William Skeat; but he retired in 1870, partly under the pressure of new duties. In 1867 he printed privately *The Clerk's Tale* from MS Dd. 4.24 in the Cambridge University Library. His other publications during the busy years of his librarianship were an abridgement of the *Dictionary of the Bible*, called the *Concise Dictionary* (1865); *The Bible Word-Book*, begun by Jonathan Eastwood (1866; 2nd edn 1884); the Clarendon Press edition (1869) of *Bacon's Advancement of Learning*; and the Roxburghe Club edition (1869) of Guillaume de Deguileville's *Pilgrimage of the Lyf of the Manhode*. In 1868 he edited with William George Clark and John Eyton Bickersteth Mayor the first number of the *Journal of Philology*, and he continued as its editor until 1913.

In 1870, when Wright became bursar of his college, he also became secretary to the Old Testament Revision Company. He missed only one of its 794 meetings from June 1870 to May 1885. His work on Smith's *Dictionary of the Bible* had made him highly proficient in Hebrew, a study which he had begun as a schoolboy and which he continued under the guidance of S. M. Schiller-Szinessy; but he had the rarer qualification of knowing sixteenth-century English. None of the revisers could have had greater respect than he had for the English of Coverdale, and he is understood to have been largely responsible for the conservatism of the revision. (His official papers, showing every stage of the revision, are now in Cambridge University Library.) While engaged on the revision he also edited *Generydes* for the Early English Text Society (1873–8) and contributed to Smith's *Dictionary of Christian Antiquities* (1875–80) and *Dictionary of Christian Biography* (1877–87). In 1887 he completed for the Rolls Series his edition of the *Metrical Chronicle of Robert of Gloucester*, which he had been forced to put aside in 1870.

From 1889 to 1903 Wright edited, as literary executor, the writings of his friend Edward FitzGerald, with whom he first became acquainted in 1868 as a result of shared interest in dialect. He worked on this project while maintaining, until 1895, his demanding position as bursar, yet he was able also to do an exacting revision of the *Cambridge Shakespeare* and edit separate plays, as well as a *Facsimile of the Milton MS. in the Library of Trinity College, Cambridge* (1899). He brought out FitzGerald's *Letters and Literary Remains* in three volumes in 1889, and published the *Letters* by themselves, with additions (Eversley series) in 1894, the aim of the collection being 'to let FitzGerald tell the story of his own life'. *Letters to Fanny Kemble* followed in 1895, *Miscellanies* (Golden Treasury series) in 1900, and *More Letters* in 1901. All were combined in the final edition of FitzGerald's *Letters and Literary Remains* (7 vols., 1902–3). Wright took care never to come between the author and the reader, but his notes are informative none the less. In all respects he provided an example of how a contemporary ought to be edited.

Until his first serious illness, two years before his death, Wright had unwearying energy. His work after the age of seventy continued to show the same wide range; in quality it never varied. For Cambridge University Press (of which he was a syndic from 1872 to 1910) he edited *Milton's Poems with Critical Notes* (1903), the *English Works of Roger Ascham* (1904), and the Authorized Version of the Bible as printed in the original two issues (5 vols., 1909). In 1905 he brought out the third edition of Bishop Westcott's *History of the Bible* (undertaken at Westcott's request in 1901) and (with S. A. Hirsch) a *Commentary on the Book of Job from a Hebrew MS. in the Cambridge University Library*. Then he turned to Anglo-Norman and presented the Roxburghe Club with an edition (1909) of the long-lost Trinity College MS of *Femina*. For his last work he fittingly chose an edition of six English translations of the Psalms from Tyndale to the Revised Version, and produced his *Hexaplar English Psalter* in 1911, at the age of eighty. In the same year he contributed to the second Lord Tennyson's *Tennyson and his Friends* an account of James Spedding. Since 1871 he had been engaged on an edition of Burton's *Anatomy of Melancholy*, and had succeeded in tracing all but a few of the quotations. Before his death he distributed many of his books among the Cambridge libraries. By his will he left £5000 to the University Library and £5000 to the library of his college, as well as a valuable collection of early printed books and over 150 Hebrew manuscripts.

The amount of Wright's work is the more remarkable considering that he suffered from writer's cramp and had to learn to use his left hand. However, he allowed nothing to interfere with his methodical habits, and he faced all his tasks with an iron will. As an editor he felt it his duty to present his material in such a way that it would speak for itself. He distrusted theories and intuitions, and all the short cuts which cleverness is tempted to adopt. 'Ignorance and conceit', he said, 'are the fruitful parents of conjectural emendation', and he would quote the rabbinical saying, 'Teach thy lips to say "I do not know"'. He never forgot that he was the servant rather than the master of his material, and consistently, throughout a career of over fifty years, was the most impersonal of the great editors. A superficial reader may find his work dry, and may even think of him as a mere scholiast, but all those who are editors have continually found that Wright has taken account of facts which others have failed to see. He received the honorary degrees of LLD at Edinburgh (1879), DCL at Oxford (1886), and LittD at Dublin (1895). His one mistake was over the Squire Papers, forgeries of correspondence by Oliver Cromwell (*The Academy*, 11 April and 2 May 1885; *English Historical Review*, April 1886); FitzGerald had believed in their authenticity, and for once Wright's judgement was misled by friendship. Generous in lending his books, in conversation, as in his writings, he might seem to be incapable of any display of sentiment, but the friends who were permitted to get behind his somewhat rigid sincerity found a warm heart and great depth of feeling. He died, unmarried, on 19 May 1914 in the Cambridge rooms he had occupied since 1865, and was buried in St Giles's cemetery in Cambridge.

D. N. SMITH, rev. DAVID MCKITTERICK

Sources *The Times* (20 May 1914) · *Morning Post* (20 May 1914) · *Cambridge Review* (27 May 1914) · *Journal of Philology* (1914), 299–304 · S. K. Bland, *Memorials of George Wright* (1875) · G. W. Prothero, *A memoir of Henry Bradshaw* (1888) · *Life and letters of Alexander Macmillan*, ed. C. L. Graves (1910) · *The Trinity Magazine* [magazine of Trinity College, Cambridge] (June 1914), 149–50 · *The letters of Edward FitzGerald*, ed. A. M. Terhune and A. B. Terhune, 4 vols. (1980) · D. A. Winstanley, *Later Victorian Cambridge* (1947) · personal knowledge (1927) · private information (1927) · *CGPLA Eng. & Wales* (1914) · d. cert.
Archives CUL | BL, letters to George Grove, Add. MSS 35222–35223 · BL, letters to W. C. Hazlitt, Add. MSS 38899–38913 · BL, corresp. with Macmillans, Add. MS 55015 · U. Edin. L., special collections division, corresp. with James Halliwell-Phillipps · U. Leeds, Brotherton L., letters to Sir Edmund Gosse
Likenesses W. W. Ouless, oils, 1887, Trinity Cam. · A. G. Dew Smith, photograph, 1894, NPG [*see illus.*] · W. Strang, chalk drawing, 1910, FM Cam. · photographs, Trinity Cam.
Wealth at death £75,060 6s. 3d.: probate, 15 Sept 1914, *CGPLA Eng. & Wales*

Wright, William Ambrose [Billy] (1924–1994), footballer, was born on 6 February 1924 at 33 Belmont Road, Ironbridge, Shropshire, the elder of two sons of Thomas Wright, iron-moulder, and his wife, Annie, née Thompson. His father, a good amateur footballer, and his mother, a keen fan, kindled an interest in the game, further stimulated at Madeley senior school, where his teacher Norman Simpson picked him for the school team despite his diminutive stature. Simpson was also instrumental in encouraging Wright to join the ground staff at Wolverhampton Wanderers in 1938. The club intended to release him in 1939 because of his size, but he was so upset that it rescinded the decision, and he made his first team début at outside-right during a wartime match in 1939. With the exception of a season at Leicester City in 1940–41, when war-related disruption prevented Wolves from playing, and his wartime service as a physical training instructor (he ended the war as a corporal in the Shropshire light infantry), he remained with the club until his retirement in August 1959. He had by then played 490 Football League games. For most of his career he was a right-half, but in 1954 injuries to colleagues, first in the England side and then at club level, saw him forced to convert to centre-half. Although only 5 feet 8 inches tall, unusually small for a player in this position, his footballing intelligence, allied with considerable jumping power, more than compensated and he became an extremely accomplished player in his new role. On 27 July 1958 he married Jocelyn Victoria Barbara Carey (b. 1923/4), known as Joy Beverley, pop singer, the eldest of the three Beverley Sisters and daughter of George Arthur Chinery, actor (one half of the singing comedy duo Coram and Mills). She had one son by a

William Ambrose [Billy] **Wright (1924–1994)**, by Terry Fincher, 1955

previous marriage, and had two daughters, Vicky and Babette, with Wright; they, with their cousin Sasha, formed another singing trio, the Little Foxes, in the 1980s.

Wright became captain of Wolves in 1947, and led them to victory in the 1949 FA cup final and to Football League championships in 1954, 1958, and 1959. He won the footballer of the year award in 1952 and, at a time when the reputation of English football was under threat following heavy defeats for the national side against Hungary in 1953 and 1954, Wright's standing and that of his club were greatly enhanced by Wolves' victories over leading Russian and Hungarian club sides Spartak Moscow and Honved in 1954. Over 20,000 people came to see his final match, a pre-season training game on 8 August 1959 between the Wolves first team and their reserve side.

Wright's England career began in a 'victory' match against Belgium in 1946, and he made his first appearance in an official international in a 7–2 defeat of Northern Ireland in September 1946. He became England captain in 1948 and, apart from a brief spell out of favour in 1951, was a virtually automatic choice until his retirement, with the England team, 'for years now … built around him' as *The Times* noted in 1959 (*The Times*, 6 April 1959). He became the first England player to be capped 100 times, when selected against Scotland in April 1959, and eventually played in 105 international matches, captaining the side on 90 occasions. On his retirement he joined the Football Association and took charge of the England youth and under-23 teams. He was widely expected to take over from his close

friend Walter Winterbottom as manager of the English national side and his decision to join Arsenal as manager in 1962 surprised many. The club was passing through a long spell of mediocrity and Wright was unable to alter the pattern. Although he did much to develop the club's youth policy, thus nurturing several of the players responsible for reviving the club's fortunes in the early 1970s, he failed to motivate the senior players. The fans lost patience, and when only 4544 of them—the club's lowest ever first division home crowd—turned up to a match in May 1966, his fate was settled. Several days later he was sacked. Wright had already been a presenter on the television programme *Junior Sportsview*, and he left football to build a new and highly successful career in television administration. He was head of sport and outside broadcasts for ATV from 1966 to 1981 and then controller of sport for Central Television from 1982 to 1985. After a period as a television consultant, he finally retired in 1989.

Most observers acknowledged that Wright was not blessed with exceptional natural footballing gifts; his ball skills in particular were quite modest. However, he was an expert and fierce tackler, and he possessed remarkable powers of anticipation; it was above all this ability to 'read' the game that made him such an effective player. He was, moreover, an excellent leader, who captained essentially through example and quiet exhortation, although perhaps the slightly retiring temperament this suggests militated against his being a successful manager. He had a very equable temperament, reflected in an unblemished disciplinary record during his career, and seems to have been genuinely liked and respected within the game. As well as being one of the most successful players of his generation, he personified and perhaps helped engineer a key transitional period in the social and cultural status of the professional footballer. Earlier in his career, he still very much typified the footballer as working-class youngster close to his roots: he learned of his appointment as England captain, for example, from his bus conductor as he travelled back to his lodgings in Tettenhall. Increasingly, however, he prefigured the new genre of football star that was to emerge in the 1960s. No fewer than five autobiographies appeared under his name between 1950 and 1962, and his photograph appeared frequently outside the back pages of the press. Wright's public profile was given a distinctive twist by his marriage to Joy Beverley: despite attempts to keep the ceremony secret, several thousand people and a large number of journalists descended on Poole register office to witness it, and the (at that stage) rather unusual union between the worlds of pop music and professional football became a major and continuing news story. The greater trappings of stardom that awaited later generations eluded him, however, partly because he played his entire career under the maximum-wage system, but also because, for all its achievements, Wolverhampton Wanderers was a somewhat unfashionable club. Wright certainly eschewed controversy, and his autobiographical output suggests an individual aware of his achievements, but very much at ease within the footballing establishment, and a devoted family man with few vices beyond an enjoyment of golf. Both his talent and his glamorous but unthreatening image made him a suitable CBE, as he was made for his services to football in 1959.

Wright died of cancer at his home, 26 Farnham Close, Friern Barnet, London, on 3 September 1994, and was survived by his wife, two daughters, and stepson. His death was especially mourned in Wolverhampton, and over 3000 people watched his cortège leave the Molineux football ground—where a grandstand had recently been named after him—on its way to Wolverhampton crematorium, on 12 September. The extensive and affectionate obituaries that he received in the national media certainly reflected Wright's popularity within the game, but also a degree of nostalgia for an earlier period when football was perceived to have been a less complex and less commercial affair. Similar forces were at work when a collection of his football memorabilia was sold by Christies for £116,759 in 1996. Such responses should not disguise the fact that Wright played a quiet but important part in shaping the image of the modern football star.

DAVE RUSSELL

Sources W. Wright and B. Butler, *One hundred caps and all that* (1962) • *The Independent* (5 Sept 1994) • *The Independent* (21 Nov 1996) • *The Times* (5 Sept 1994) • *The Times* (13 Sept 1994) • *Daily Mirror* (28 July 1958) • *Daily Express* (6 April 1959) • P. Soar and M. Tyler, *Arsenal: official history* (1989) • *WWW*, 1991–5 • b. cert. • m. cert. • d. cert.
Likenesses photographs, 1948–80, Hult. Arch. • T. Fincher, photograph, 1955, Hult. Arch. [*see illus.*] • photograph, repro. in *The Times* (3 Sept 1994) • photograph, repro. in *The Independent* (5 Sept 1994) • photographs, repro. in B. Wright, *Captain of England* (1950) • photographs, repro. in B. Wright, *Billy Wright's football scrapbook* (1951) • photographs, repro. in Wright and Butler, *One hundred caps*
Wealth at death under £125,000: administration, 6 Oct 1994, *CGPLA Eng. & Wales*

Wright, William Valentine (*bap.* 1826, *d.* 1877), soap manufacturer and wholesale druggist, was baptized on 26 February 1826 at St Peter and St Paul's parish church, Aldeburgh, Suffolk, the son of William Wright, builder and carpenter, and his wife, Susannah. His middle name suggests that he was born on 14 February.

Following apprenticeship to the drug trade with Messrs Grimwade, Ridley & Co. of Ipswich, he went to London and was an assistant at the pharmacy of John Bell & Co. in Oxford Street. He remained there until 1848, when he obtained a partnership with an elderly druggist, James Curtis, in the latter's premises at 11 Old Fish Street Hill. On 6 March 1849, at Wivenhoe parish church, Essex, Wright married Elizabeth Mustard, a young woman of his own age born in nearby Great Bentley. The couple had nine children, five daughters and four sons, and by 1871 the family was living at Alde House, Thornton Road, Clapham, together with a niece, a cook, and a maid. James Curtis retired soon after Wright's marriage, and Wright continued alone until 1860, when he was joined by G. B. Francis, a former assistant with him at Bells.

Wright lived at just the right time to take advantage of the burgeoning soap industry of the nineteenth century, which had grown in response to the demands of an expanding population. The smoke and grime of industrial towns made soap for their inhabitants a necessity, instead of a luxury, as it had earlier been. And as the standard of living of city dwellers rose from 1860, a huge potential market for soap was created, first among the middle classes, then among the industrial workers.

Wright did more than simply make soap. By this time he was making and selling a liquid coal-tar solution, calling it Wright's Liquor Carbonis Detergens. He marketed a product that not only cleaned, as all soaps did, but also cleansed: this soap could be used not simply for washing but also for treating the skin. Doctors noted its antiseptic properties, especially in treating skin diseases, and it quickly became a standard remedy. Wright sought to bring it to a wider public, and eventually succeeded in incorporating it in a soap base. Thus, about 1866, Wright's Coal Tar Soap was born. Meanwhile in 1863 the City of London corporation had purchased Wright's premises for road improvements. Using the compensation money for disturbance, Wright moved the business in 1867 to new premises in Southwark.

Wright met an untimely death when travelling with his son Charles in Dundee. Inflammation in the face developed into erysipelas, and on 17 September 1877 he died at the Royal Hotel, Nethergate, Dundee, aged fifty-two. He was survived by his wife who retained her interest in the business until she sold it in 1892. Although Wright pioneered the manufacture of coal-tar soap, it was left to his son, William Valentine jun., to take over the business after his death and actively promote the new product. It did not really become popular outside medical circles until 1892, however, when the firm made radical changes in the methods of manufacturing soap and adopted a milling process in place of the former melting method.

ADRIAN ROOM

Sources 'Jubilaeus carbonis detergentis', *Chemist and Druggist* (26 July 1913), 135–6 • parish records (baptism), 26 Feb 1826, St Peter and St Paul's parish church, Aldeburgh, Suffolk • m. cert. • d. cert.
Likenesses photograph, *c.*1877, repro. in *Chemist and Druggist* (15 Dec 1877) • photograph, repro. in 'Jubilaeus carbonis detergentis'
Wealth at death under £45,000: probate, 1 Oct 1877, *CGPLA Eng. & Wales*

Wrightslands. For this title name *see* Craig, Sir Lewis, of Riccarton, Lord Wrightslands (1569–1622).

Wrinch [*married names* Nicholson, Glaser], **Dorothy Maud** (1894–1976), mathematician and theoretical biologist, was born on 13 September 1894 in Rosario, Argentina, the elder daughter of Hugh Edward Hart Wrinch, mechanical engineer, and his wife, Ada Minnie Souter. Growing up in Surbiton, Surrey, she attended Surbiton high school and from there went to Girton College, Cambridge, on a scholarship in 1913. She studied mathematics and moral sciences (mathematics tripos, part one, second class, 1914; part two, first class, 1916). She also played on Girton tennis teams and was active in college debates and in the Mathematical Club (of which she was president in 1916). In her fourth year of studies she concentrated on symbolic logic and attended Bertrand Russell's lectures (moral sciences tripos, part two, second class, 1917); she remained at Girton as a research scholar in the year 1917/18. In 1921 she was awarded a London DSc. For a time she kept close working and social contacts with Russell, and while he was in prison for his anti-war activities she supplied him with books and news.

Wrinch was appointed to a mathematics lectureship at University College, London, in 1918, but two years later returned to Girton as a Yarrow research fellow. In 1922 she married mathematical physicist John William *Nicholson (1881–1955), then a fellow of Balliol College, Oxford, and with his help obtained a tutorship at Lady Margaret Hall, Oxford. Over the next sixteen years she held various research fellowships and lectureships or tutorships at the Oxford women's colleges. Her marriage, badly strained by Nicholson's deteriorating mental state, was dissolved in 1938. One daughter, Pamela, was born in 1927.

Dorothy Wrinch's early work was in mathematics, pure and applied, logic, and philosophy. Among her forty-two publications appearing between 1919 and 1929 were studies in classical analysis, classical mechanics, and mathematical physics (including work with her father and with her husband), papers in mathematical logic in the tradition of Whitehead and Russell, and joint studies with Harold Jeffreys on the theory of scientific method. In 1929 she received an Oxford DSc, the first awarded to a woman. She was an active member of the mathematics subsection of the British Association and for a number of years served on the International Commission on the Teaching of Mathematics.

By the late 1920s Wrinch's academic interests were expanding. A brief excursion into sociology resulted in her short book *Retreat from Parenthood* (1930, published under the pseudonym Jean Ayling). Reflecting her strong feminist outlook the work presented a broad plan of social reorganization to make child rearing more compatible with professional life. Her interests soon settled on biological questions, however, particularly the challenges in the new field of theoretical biology, where, she felt, the application of mathematical techniques would be critical for advances.

In 1932, having already familiarized herself with the basic principles of biology and chemistry by attending courses in Vienna and Paris, Wrinch became a founding member of the Biotheoretical Gathering. Among the particular interests of this group of Cambridge biochemists and crystallographers was the structure of proteins and chromosomes; the possibility of linear sequences of amino acids or nucleic acids being involved in the genetic process was already being considered. In her first publications in the field (1934, 1936) she proposed possible models for chromosomes at the molecular level; although she was working from the incorrect picture of the overall structure then commonly held, she made the valuable suggestion that chromosome specificity was linked to the specific sequencing of constituent groups in the chain structure. With help from her friend, Oxford chemist and crystallographer Dorothy Crowfoot, she went on to consider the problem of the structure of globular proteins and here produced one of the most elegant hypotheses among the early attempts to find a basic plan in these giant molecules. Following an initial proposal that the chains of linked amino acids that constitute proteins could polymerize to form a mosaic sheet network to which she gave the name 'cyclol', she suggested (1937) that the sheets would fold into series of closed geometric figures, such as octahedra, built of definite, computable numbers of amino acid residues. The theory provided an attractive explanation for many recent observations on proteins, and when it was demonstrated (1937) that, by an extraordinary coincidence, the number of amino acid residues in egg albumen was consistent with her model, she considered her proposal strikingly verified.

Dorothy Wrinch's work was of great interest to chemists and biologists at the 1938 Cold Spring Harbor Symposium on proteins; her tremendous enthusiasm contributed much to its favourable reception. Considerable controversy soon followed, however, with eminent scientists, including Nobel prizewinner Irwin Langmuir, taking sides. At times Dorothy Wrinch felt unfairly treated by some in the chemical community; her arguments with chemist Linus Pauling were particularly heated. However, in the years after the Second World War chemical and crystallographic evidence gradually proved that proteins do not have the cyclol structure. Nevertheless, Dorothy Wrinch's bold hypothesis, presented at a time when experimental evidence was sparse, was valuable in that it triggered widespread interest in proteins; further, her detailed and explicitly geometrical argument powerfully stressed the idea that complex protein structures had to be considered in terms of detailed molecular architecture. Her methodology was pioneering.

With the coming of the Second World War, Wrinch had moved to the United States, partly for her daughter's safety. After a year as a visiting fellow in the chemistry department at Johns Hopkins University, Baltimore, she obtained in 1941 a visiting professorship at three small Massachusetts colleges, Amherst, Smith, and Mount Holyoke. Her appointment was arranged largely by Otto Charles Glaser (1880–1951), chairman of the biology department and vice-president of Amherst College, whom she married on 20 August 1941. From 1942, for almost three decades, she held research positions at Smith, where she supervised a few graduate students, conducted seminars, and continued her studies—further work on protein structure and the development and application to proteins of techniques for interpreting X-ray patterns of complicated molecular structures.

Despite the handicaps of losing her close contact with Dorothy Crowfoot, generally increasing intellectual isolation, and gradual reduction of research funding, Wrinch continued to publish at an impressive rate, often bringing out seven or eight papers a year. Her monograph *Fourier Transforms and Structure Factors* (1946) remained in use for decades, and she made important contributions to extending methods of analysis of the sets of points which in X-ray diffraction patterns represent crystal structure. For a time she was a consultant to John von Neumann at the Institute for Advanced Study in Princeton in his pioneering work on the development of computers, the analysis of complex protein X-ray data being considered a major application. In the summers she lectured at the Marine Biological Laboratory, Wood's Hole, Massachusetts, an institution with which Otto Glaser was closely connected and where she had many friends. The main focus of her work, however, was the presentation and defence of her cyclol theory; she doggedly ignored the accumulating evidence against it. Her two books, *Chemical Aspects of the Structure of Small Peptides* (1960) and *Chemical Aspects of Polypeptide Chain Structure and the Cyclol Theory* (1965), presented the history of protein chemistry as she saw it.

A controversial figure in early research in molecular biology, bright, ambitious, hardworking, and adventurous, Dorothy Wrinch was for much of her life a restless outsider, something of an exile in her American environment, who took up difficult problems in a field in which she, a mathematician by training, had insufficient background. Possessing a sharp wit and a dynamic, forceful personality, she was not always easy to get along with. Nevertheless, she was also an attractive woman and an inspired teacher who set high standards. After Otto Glaser's death she lived on the Smith College campus, moving to Wood's Hole, Massachusetts, on her retirement in 1971. She died in Falmouth Hospital, Falmouth, Massachusetts, of pneumonia, on 11 February 1976 and was cremated two days later at Forest Hills crematory, Boston. Her ashes were taken to Wood's Hole.

MARY R. S. CREESE

Sources P. G. Abir-Am, 'Synergy or clash: disciplinary and marital strategies in the career of mathematical biologist Dorothy Wrinch', *Uneasy careers and intimate lives: women in science, 1789–1979*, ed. P. G. Abir-Am and D. Outram (1987), 239–80 • P. Laszlo, 'Dorothy Wrinch: the mystique of cyclol theory or the story of a mistaken scientific theory', *Molecular correlates of biological concepts* (1986), vol. 34A of *Comprehensive biochemistry*, chap. 13 • D. Crowfoot Hodgkin and H. Jeffreys, *Nature*, 260 (1976), 564 • M. Senechal, ed., *Structures of matter and patterns in science, inspired by the life and work of Dorothy Wrinch, 1894–1976: proceedings of a symposium* [Smith College, Northampton, MA 1977] (1980) • M. M. Julian, 'Women in crystallography', *Women of science: righting the record*, ed. G. Kass-Simon and P. Farnes (1990), 335–77 • M. M. Julian, 'Dorothy Wrinch and a search for the structure of proteins', *Journal of Chemical Education*, 61 (1984), 890–92 • d. cert. [from Registry of Vital Records and Statistics, Commonwealth of Massachusetts, Boston, Massachusetts] • *The Times* (8 March 1976) • M. Senechal, 'A prophet without honor. Dorothy Wrinch, scientist, 1894–1976', *Smith Alumnae Quarterly* (April 1977), 18–23 • Smith College, Northampton, Massachusetts, Archives • Girton Cam. • *WW* • A. G. Debus and others, eds., *World who's who in science* (1968) • *Who was who in America*, 6 (1976) • 'Glaser, Otto Charles', *American men of science*, ed. J. Cattell, 10th edn (1960) • C. W. Carey, 'Wrinch, Dorothy Maud', *ANB*, 24.68–71 • private information (2004) [Lady Jeffreys] • d. cert.

Archives Smith College, Northampton, Massachusetts, Sophia Smith collection, papers, notes, corresp., molecular models, etc. | Lady Margaret Hall, Oxford, Wrinch-Nicholson archives • U. Sussex, letters to J. G. Crowther

Likenesses C. H. Waddington, photograph, 1933, repro. in Abir-Am, 'Synergy or clash', following p. 240 • photograph, 1935, repro. in Abir-Am, 'Synergy or clash', following p. 260 • photographs, Smith College, Northampton, Massachusetts • photographs, Smith College, Northampton, Massachusetts; repro. in Senechal, ed., *Structures of matter and patterns in science*

Wriothesley, Charles (1508–1562), herald and chronicler, was born on 8 May 1508 into a heraldic dynasty founded by his grandfather John *Writhe, Garter king of arms. A younger son of Sir Thomas *Wriothesley (d. 1534), also Garter, and his first wife, Jane Hall (d. after 1510), he was also the nephew of William Wriothesley, York herald. He was born in London, and from around 1511 lived at Garter House, a mansion built by his father in Barbican Street in Cripplegate ward, as a material embodiment of the family's rise to prominence. Perhaps because a training in civil law was useful to heralds, his father sent him to Cambridge. A tax roll of 1522 records both his presence and that of his cousin Thomas Wriothesley, the future lord chancellor, among the *scholastici* of Trinity Hall, Cambridge, the civil lawyers' college. A London tax roll of the same date improbably assesses the fourteen-year-old 'Charles Wreothesle' of 'St Giles's without Crepulgate' for a loan at £38 6s. 8d. in lands and fees and £40 in goods, but this almost certainly refers to a levy upon his father as master of Garter House, and merely serves to show that Charles was still legally resident there (*LP Henry VIII* 3/2, no. 2486).

Two years later, in October 1524, the death of a senior herald, followed by the promotion of a pursuivant, gave the Wriothesleys an opportunity to extend their dynasty into a third generation. Although only sixteen, Charles was appointed Rouge Croix pursuivant, filling the vacancy left by Thomas Wall's promotion to Windsor herald. His appointment, at an annual salary of £10, was formalized by patent on 29 May 1525. About this time he may also have entered the service of Thomas Audley, later Baron Audley, whom he repeatedly refers to as his 'lorde and master' in his *Chronicle*. Perhaps under the influence of Audley, who had recently come down from Cambridge to become autumn reader at the Inner Temple, Charles resumed his interrupted legal training. In 1529 he became a gentleman of Gray's Inn.

The early 1530s marked the zenith of Wriothesley's career as a herald. He attended the creation of Anne Boleyn as marquess of Pembroke in 1532, and then her coronation the following year. His master Audley succeeded Sir Thomas More as lord chancellor in 1533, and his own father's death on 24 November 1534 initiated a series of promotions in the College of Arms—Thomas Wall to Garter the day following, himself to Windsor a month later—which must have seemed to portend even greater future advancement. It seems to have been his promotion to major heraldic dignity, coinciding as it did with the drama of the new queen's succession, which inspired Wriothesley to begin his *Chronicle*; the first event that he records in extensive detail is the coronation of Anne Boleyn. Conceiving of his narrative not just as a personal document, but also as a record of the dynasty he served as perceived from the viewpoint of the city of London, he chose to begin his history with the accession of Henry VII, a decision that left him with a considerable chronological gap to fill. He therefore prefaced his own narration with material drawn from the *Chronicle* of Richard Arnold, a relative of the Wriothesleys (Arnold's sister was John Writhe's second wife). He mostly copied Arnold's work verbatim, sometimes paraphrasing and occasionally adding details, until shortly before that work ended in 1520. He then eked out the next thirteen years with accounts of important events as he remembered them or as he gleaned them from other chronicles, until he reached 1533, at which point his work becomes more detailed, personal, and circumstantial. Always conscious of his position as a herald and member of the king's household, Wriothesley strove to create a chronicle at once loyal and carefully observant. The events he describes are almost always seen from the point of view of a well-connected London citizen, albeit one inhabiting the margins of royal power. Wriothesley records the progress of the Reformation, for instance, as it was debated in sermons at Paul's Cross and dramatized in executions at Smithfield and Tyburn. Only occasionally is he allowed in to witness a coronation. Particularly in the earlier portions of his *Chronicle*, he endeavours to present a sympathetic account of Henry VIII's religious reforms. Thus he approvingly describes the execution of Friar Forrest as that of 'a false traitor to his Praynce, an heretiacke, and a seditious person to the Kinges leighe people', and delights that the obdurate heretic was burned along with a wooden idol which the 'people of North Walles honored as a sainct' (Wriothesley, 1.80).

However interesting his *Chronicle*, Wriothesley's work as a herald seems to have been undistinguished, and he plainly did not prosper. When Thomas Wall died in 1536, after only two years' tenure as Garter, Wriothesley found himself overlooked for the promotion to his father's and grandfather's office. His patron Audley died in 1544, and even the succession of his cousin Thomas, now Baron Wriothesley, to the lord chancellorship does not seem to have improved his prospects. In that same year Charles Wriothesley was appointed to attend on the middle ward of the king's army during Henry VIII's expedition against France, and he accordingly describes both the capture of Boulogne and the consequent rejoicing in London in his *Chronicle*. His cousin's disgrace and fall in 1547 may well have doomed his chances of further advancement, for when Christopher Barker died in 1550 Wriothesley was again passed over for promotion to Garter. In the latter year he was remembered in the will of his cousin, who had died as earl of Southampton, with a bequest of £20. His name appears in the charter of 1554 whereby King Philip and Queen Mary established the heralds and their successors as a corporation with perpetual succession and granted them the house called Derby Place in which to keep safe their records and rolls and all things touching their faculty.

Some time after his father's death Wriothesley left Garter House and took up lodgings in the house of Sampson Camden, a painter–stainer who was father of the future scholar and herald William Camden. He may have married twice; a manuscript pedigree in the College of Arms says that his wife was the daughter of a Mr Mallory, but in narrating the suppression of Barking Abbey in 1539 Wriothesley himself mentions 'Alis my wife that now is', a phrase that suggests that she may have been a second wife (Wriothesley, 1.198). When he died at his lodgings in Camden's house on 25 January 1562, however, there was no mention made of a wife or children in his funeral certificate. His fellow heralds paid for a splendid funeral. He was buried not in St Giles Cripplegate, along with all the other members of his family, but in the middle aisle of St Sepulchre's, Holborn. He left no will, and the great library of books that he had inherited from his father was sold after his death, many of its contents to Sir Gilbert Dethick and his son William, the founders of a new heraldic dynasty. Wriothesley's *Chronicle*, which survives only in a transcript made early in the seventeenth century for the third earl of Southampton, was edited in two volumes for the Camden Society by W. D. Hamilton (1875–7).

GORDON KIPLING

Sources J. Anstis, ed., *The register of the most noble order of the Garter*, 2 vols. (1724) • R. Arnold, *The customs of London, otherwise called Arnold's chronicle*, ed. F. Douce (1811) • L. Campbell and F. Steer, *A catalogue of manuscripts in the College of Arms collections*, 1 (1988) • J. P. Collier, ed., *Trevelyan papers prior to A.D. 1558*, CS, 67 (1857) • J. Foster, *The register of admissions to Gray's Inn, 1521–1889, together with the register of marriages in Gray's Inn chapel, 1695–1754* (privately printed, London, 1889) • W. H. Godfrey, A. Wagner, and H. Stanford London, *The College of Arms, Queen Victoria Street* (1963) • *LP Henry VIII*, vols. 1–21 • *The diary of Henry Machyn, citizen and merchant-taylor of London, from AD 1550 to AD 1563*, ed. J. G. Nichols, CS, 42 (1848) • *DNB* • Rymer, *Foedera*, 1st edn, vol. 15 • J. Stow, *The survey of London*, ed. H. B. Wheatley (1912) • A. R. Wagner, *The records and collections of the College of Arms* (1952) • C. Wriothesley, *A chronicle of England during the reigns of the Tudors from AD 1485 to 1559*, ed. W. D. Hamilton, 2 vols., CS, new ser., 11, 20 (1875–7) [incl. funeral certificate]

Wriothesley, Henry, second earl of Southampton (*bap.* 1545, *d.* 1581), magnate, was baptized on 24 April 1545 at St Andrew's, Holborn, the third and only surviving son of Thomas *Wriothesley, first earl of Southampton and first Baron Wriothesley (1505–1550), lord chancellor, and his wife, Jane (*d.* 1574), daughter and heir of William Cheney of Chesham Bois, Buckinghamshire, and his wife, Emma. Henry Wriothesley's godparents were Henry VIII, Princess Mary, Charles Brandon, first duke of Suffolk, and Henry Fitzalan, twelfth earl of Arundel. Thomas Wriothesley was elevated to a barony on 1 January 1544, was lord chancellor from 1544 to 1547, and was promoted to the earldom of Southampton on 16 February 1547; but he fell from power and was dismissed from office on 6 March 1547. Despite his disgrace, Southampton was one of the greatest noblemen in Hampshire, with an annual landed income of at least £1466 13s. 4d. in the late 1540s. He died on 30 July 1550, when his heir was still a minor. His widow's dower was £466 13s. 4d.

The wardship of the second earl of Southampton was granted to William Herbert, first earl of Pembroke, on 14 December 1550. Southampton remained with his mother and was privately educated and brought up a Catholic. Little is known about his youth or education but he was certainly taught French. His wardship passed to Sir William More of Loseley, Surrey, in 1560. Southampton married into one of the leading Catholic families of Sussex. His wife was Mary (b. in or before 1552, d. 1607), daughter of Anthony *Browne, first Viscount Montagu (1528–1592), and his first wife, Jane; the marriage took place at Montagu House in London on 19 February 1566. The couple had two sons, including Henry *Wriothesley, third earl of Southampton (1573–1624), the courtier and patron of Shakespeare, and a daughter, Mary Wriothesley (c.1567–1607). Southampton was admitted to Lincoln's Inn on 19 March 1566. He entertained Elizabeth I at Titchfield Place, Hampshire, in 1569 and probably spent most of his time looking after his six residences and managing his estates. His landed income was between £2000 and £3000 in the 1560s and he lived in a grand way, maintaining a large and lavish household.

Southampton was arrested on 18 June 1570 for intriguing with the Spanish ambassador, Guerau de Spes, and for suspected complicity in the contemplated marriage of Thomas Howard, fourth duke of Norfolk, to Mary, queen of Scots. He was placed under house arrest with More at Loseley from July to November 1570. Examined on 31 October 1571 for suspicion of having consulted with John Leslie, bishop-elect of Ross, as to whether he might conscientiously obey Elizabeth after the bull of excommunication, *Regnans in excelsis*, Southampton denied the allegations, but was confined to the Tower of London until 1 May 1573. During his imprisonment he was allowed to visit his father-in-law and to spend time at Montagu's seat at Cowdray Park, Sussex. Back in favour, Southampton was appointed JP for Hampshire on 12 July 1574. The dowager countess died on 15 September. The earl and countess of Southampton did not live in complete marital harmony, and their divisions caused a falling out between Montagu and his son-in-law. The countess, who was 'put away, suspected of incontinency' (*Miscellanea*, 2.183), loyally made excuses for her husband to her father, who was angry that Southampton had 'barred [her] his bord and presence' (GEC, *Peerage*, 12/1.127, n. c). Southampton expressly stated in his will of 29 June 1581 that his daughter should be brought up by either his sister, Katherine Cornwallis, or his aunt, Lawrence, insisting that she 'be not in howse with her Mother' (PRO, PROB 11/65, sig. 45). He died on 4 October 1581 at Itchel in the parish of Crondall, Hampshire, aged thirty-six, and was buried on 30 November at Titchfield, after a lavish funeral, costing over £138. Southampton also ordered that up to £1000 be spent to create a monument there for his parents and himself out of alabaster, known as the Titchfield monument. His will, proved on 7 February 1583, provides ample evidence of his Catholic friendships and religious convictions. He did not make specific provisions for his widow, only that she should not try to possess Dogmersfield, Hampshire, which was to be allotted to his heir, who inherited lands worth £1097 6s. per annum. The dowager countess married twice after his death: her second husband was Sir

Thomas Heneage and her third Sir William Hervey. Her will, dated 22 April 1607 and proved on 14 November, instructed that she be buried with Southampton at Titchfield.   J. G. ELZINGA

Sources GEC, *Peerage* · DNB · C. C. Stopes, *The life of Henry, third earl of Southampton, Shakespeare's patron* (1922) · G. Gibbons, *The political career of Thomas Wriothesley, first earl of Southampton, 1505–1550: Henry VIII's last chancellor* (2001) · CSP Spain, 1538–44 · JHL, vol. 1 · C. Wriothesley, *A chronicle of England during the reigns of the Tudors from AD 1485 to 1559*, ed. W. D. Hamilton, 2 vols., CS, new ser., 11, 20 (1875–7) · APC, 1571–5, 102, 130, 267 · *Miscellanea, II*, Catholic RS, 2 (1906) · CSP dom., 1547–1601 · will, PRO, PROB 11/65, sig. 45
Archives Hants. RO, personal, official, family, and estate papers, MS 5M53 · PRO, papers, SP 7 | BL, Add. MSS 25114, fols. 333–46; 28023, fol. 8 · BL, Harley MSS 282, 283 · BL, Lansdowne MSS 2, arts. 8, 9; 16, arts. 22, 23; 17, art. 14 · BL, Stowe MS 141, fol. 78 · Bodl. Oxf., MS Ashmole 836, fols. 395, 427 · Northants. RO, collection of letters of William Paget
Likenesses G. Johnson, tomb effigy, c.1594, St Peter's Church, Titchfield, Hampshire · H. Enworth, portrait · L. van Heere, portrait, Bridgewater House
Wealth at death approx. £3000(?): will, PRO, PROB 11/65, sig. 45

Wriothesley, Henry, third earl of Southampton (1573–1624)

Wriothesley, Henry, **third earl of Southampton** (1573–1624), courtier and literary patron, was born at Cowdray House near Midhurst in Sussex on 6 October 1573. He was the third child and only surviving son of Henry *Wriothesley, second earl of Southampton (bap. 1545, d. 1581), and his wife, Mary Browne (b. in or before 1552, d. 1607), daughter of the first Viscount Montague. His parents had a stormy marriage, and when the boy was six they separated, largely because the father—a fervent Catholic who had spent eighteen months confined in the Tower of London—accused his young wife of adultery with a commoner named Donesame. In a long, rambling, somewhat incoherent letter to her father, the countess claimed that as for 'donesame his coming hither' for a secret tryst at the family's Dogmersfield estate, this could 'never' be proved (Akrigg, 14), but her husband was obdurate, unforgiving, and convinced of his own rightness. Serving as a go-between for his difficult parents, the young Henry Wriothesley carried a letter from the countess to his father, after which he was forbidden to see his mother.

The angry second earl, according to Father Foley, went briefly to prison again for his Catholic practices in consequence of the anti-recusancy act of 16 January 1581 (Foley, 3.659). That ordeal worsened his already uncertain health, and two days before his son's eighth birthday, the father died: thus on 4 October 1581 the boy became third earl of Southampton. The troubled state of his parents' marriage, the boy's enforced separation from his mother, and no doubt what he had heard said about her, contributed to Southampton's early distrust of women, and for years he was to turn primarily to men for stimulus or affection. He did not come to be on easy terms with his mother, who remained a widow during nearly all of his minority; but on 2 May 1594 she married Sir Thomas Heneage, vice-chamberlain of the royal household, who died within a year, and in 1598 she took as a third husband a man younger than herself, Sir William Hervey, who had seen army service in the Lowlands and is sometimes thought to be the 'Mr W. H.' in Thomas Thorpe's dedication to *Shake-*

Henry Wriothesley, third earl of Southampton (1573–1624), by unknown artist

Speares Sonnets (1609). Southampton's mother died in November 1607.

Formal training Upon his father's death Southampton became a royal ward. For the time being or until his maturity, his landed property was held in trust by Lord Howard of Effingham, and custody of the young earl along with power to arrange his marriage fell to his guardian, Lord Burghley, who besides being the queen's powerful lord treasurer was also master of the wards. Despite his administrative life, Burghley maintained with the help of expert tutors, at his Cecil House in London's Strand, a brilliant educational establishment for young noblemen: it has been called 'the best school for statesmen in Elizabethan England' (Hurstfield, 255). Here Southampton received a sound training in Latin, history, and literature, and heard something about government, politics, and modern Europe. Book-loving, full of wise sayings, and pleased to dine with his wards, Burghley must have contributed to Southampton's love of literature. One advantage of being at Cecil House was that the young earl had a chance to meet others destined to rise to power in affairs of the state, including perhaps his future hero, the earl of Essex, who, at fifteen or sixteen, may have visited from his residence in Wales.

At the age of twelve in the autumn of 1585, Southampton was admitted to St John's College, Cambridge, where as a young nobleman he merited special attention and help. Early in the next year the college acquired a new, scholarly master, Dr William Whitaker, a man of mildly puritan sympathies, but St John's was chiefly run by Whitaker's assistant, John Alvey, a keen-minded puritan. The

protestant training which Southampton received at Cecil House and at Cambridge firmly offset the Catholic atmosphere he had known in his father's home. At St John's there were lectures on topics such as Greek, arithmetic, geometry, or cosmography, and many students read both modern and ancient history; but much of Southampton's education focused on theology, ethics, and the oral and written presentation of arguments. In the summer Burghley kept up the argumentative emphasis by giving him Latin themes to write. Two of these survive, and although neither is very logical, Southampton lets his heart speak for him. The first theme, written in June 1586, replies to the topic, 'The arduous studies of youth are agreeable relaxations in old age'. The essayist believes that old age is 'often' wretched, but that 'young men may, with justice, relax their minds and give themselves up to enjoyment'. He quotes Cicero on youth's need for more freedom and on the wisdom of letting desire and passion sometimes 'triumph over reason' (BL, Lansdowne MS 50, fol. 51). Whatever Burghley felt about that, he knew the earl would have complex estates to manage and might benefit from legal training. By the time Southampton, at sixteen, had his MA degree at Cambridge in 1589, he was admitted at Gray's Inn. Burghley hardly wished him to neglect language and literature, and in any case the earl preferred the arts. Southampton soon had in his 'pay and patronage' John Florio, as a hot-tempered, gifted Italian tutor. According to Florio, the earl acquired such skill with Italian that he had no need to travel abroad to polish his mastery of the tongue, and Florio's Italian–English dictionary later includes the earl as one of its three dedicatees. The inns of court were filled with a good many idle, fashionable young men concerned with dancing, fencing, or the theatre, rather than with legal statutes; and the comely earl hardly had much time for the law himself. Significantly, he can be traced at Gray's Inn at a holiday time when skits, satires, and plays were performed, but there is little sign that he acquired much technical knowledge of litigation.

Sexuality and early reputation In 1589 Burghley noted the birthdays of the royal wards and observed that the earl was approaching a marriageable age. For Southampton, he had a bride ready. Burghley decided to marry him to his own granddaughter, Lady Elizabeth Vere, who at nineteen had lost her mother, Anne, and appeared to be neglected by her father, the earl of Oxford. Such an alliance with a famous, staunchly protestant family might have cleared Southampton of a papist taint. His mother was guilty of Catholic indiscretions, most of them minor, as when she tried to clear an 'olde poor woman', charged it seems with recusancy (Folger, MS L. b. 338); and his father's link with a regicidal plot had led to the Tower. Yet despite pressure by July 1590, the earl refused to be wed, though Burghley found allies for the wedding plan in the earl's mother and grandfather. In resisting his guardian, the earl incurred more than Burghley's mere displeasure, since the law held that if a ward would not marry at his lord's request, on coming of age he must pay him what anyone would have given for the marriage. Southampton thus faced paying an enormous fine, said to be £5000, on turning twenty-one in October 1594. Living on a moderate allowance, he had begun to show a plucky, defiant spirit.

Also he had begun to attract many admirers. Southampton made of himself an exhibit, and his image survives in more contemporary portraits than anyone else's but the queen's. As a young man he was strikingly attractive, with nearly feminine features, bright blue eyes, and a soft, alluring gaze to match his sweetly toned voice. He was to show off his lightly built, slender form with costly, clinging fabrics such as a white silk doublet, and strike poses with his dancing hat-feathers, his purple garters, and his long auburn hair with one tress falling to the breast. Was he homosexual or bisexual? Those terms were then unknown, and Southampton's sexual proclivities are difficult to discover. A Tudor male was not thought of as being unalterably defined by his sexual preferences, even if he had a male lover or a 'Ganymede'. William Reynolds, a less than reliable witness who expected to be believed, wrote later that when in Ireland, Southampton slept in a tent with his brother officer, Piers Edmondes, and 'the earle Sowthamton would cole and huge [embrace and hug] him in his armes and play wantonly w[ith] him' (BL, MS M/485/41). Among the earl's closest friends were the brothers Sir Charles and Sir Henry Danvers, neither of whom married; and Thomas Nashe complimented Southampton, somewhat ambiguously, in the dedication of *The Unfortunate Traveller* in 1594: 'A dere lover and cherisher you are, as well of the lovers of Poets, as of Poets themselves'. Yet the earl did not remain a bachelor. In the mid-1590s Southampton became involved with one of the queen's maids of honour, the demure Elizabeth Vernon, daughter of John Vernon of Hodnet, Shropshire, and a cousin of Robert Devereux, second earl of Essex. Born on 11 January 1573, she was a few months older than Southampton who for a while broke off their relationship, but married her hastily in August 1598.

Just before he turned twenty-one the young Cambridge graduate had the appeal of an androgynous icon and a potentially great patron. Sir Philip Sidney's death in 1586 had left room for a new inspirer, a symbol of high attainment in art and war. Southampton was manly enough to hope to fight in battle, but attractive enough to elicit delicate verses. Noting his attendance with the queen at Oxford, John Sanford in a Latin poem claimed that no one present was more comely, 'though his mouth yet blooms with tender down' (*Apollinis et musarum euktika eidyllia*, 1592). In the same year a poem of fifteen pages in Latin entitled *Narcissus*, by his guardian's secretary John Clapham, was dedicated to the young earl. A group of writers loyal to Essex and Southampton formed around them, and by the time Gervase Markham and Barnabe Barnes, in new sonnets, had praised Southampton's bright eyes and lovely voice, he had attracted the greatest poet of all.

Shakespeare's patron Just when and how the earl first met Shakespeare are not clear, but they had acquaintances in common. Southampton attended the royal court with the younger Fulke Greville, whose father at Stratford had known a board of aldermen which included the dramatist's father. Young Fulke Greville could have put the earl

in touch with Shakespeare, but it is just as possible that keen, *au courant* playgoers at Gray's Inn did. Except for small respites, bubonic plague kept London's theatres shut for almost two years starting in mid-1592, and it was in this period that Shakespeare sought the help of a fashionable patron. Ironically, Southampton had little but enthusiasm to offer any poet. He hardly had funds to spare; he lived on a fixed allowance and faced paying a gigantic fine to Burghley, plus another vast sum to get his estates out of wardship. After he turned twenty-one in 1594, his need for money became desperate. In November of that year, he leased out part of Southampton House, and a few years later had to sell off five of his manors, including Portsea and Bighton.

Shakespeare's use of the earl as a patron was of brief duration. His dedicatory letter printed in *Venus and Adonis* (soon after 18 April 1593) suggests that he barely knows the nineteen-year-old earl: 'I know not how I shall offend in dedicating' the present work, Shakespeare admits, though he hopes to offer 'some graver labour'. The graver labour was probably *The Rape of Lucrece* (printed in spring 1594), and despite the formality and hyperbole in his new letter to Southampton, prefacing the volume, Shakespeare's tone is more intimate and confident than the year before. His love for his patron is 'without end', he declares; and he adds, 'What I have done is yours, what I have to doe is yours'.

However, that pledge of loyalty was superseded by events. By the summer of 1594 Shakespeare had joined the Chamberlain's Men, a stable, lasting troupe which held his loyalty and saved him from needing the support of the earl's name or patronage. The myth that Southampton gave him £1000 is unfounded, and it is only a conjecture that Shakespeare was entertained at the earl's Titchfield estate where he perhaps found the name 'Gobbo' (for Shylock's servant) among local parishioners' names. Shakespeare was not ungrateful for the privilege of dedicating *Venus and Adonis* and *Lucrece* to a nobleman. His respect for the Essex-and-Southampton faction appears in his only clear, specific allusion to a contemporary, extra-dramatic event, when the Chorus in *Henry V* (v.0.29–35) refers to Essex's possibly victorious return from Ireland in 1599. Still later, Shakespeare agreed to devise an *impresa* for Southampton's close friend the sixth earl of Rutland.

Southampton may be involved in Shakespeare's sonnets, but a too-close connection is often supposed to exist between Tudor poets and patrons. In 1594 Shakespeare was casting off his allegiance to the earl; but there is no real likelihood that he traduced him by drawing his portrait as the fickle, treacherous Young Man of the sonnets, who is implicitly 'lascivious' (sonnet 95), 'sensual' to a 'fault' or to his 'shame' (sonnets 34, 35), and ridden with vices. The naïve notion that Southampton was Shakespeare's weak, lustful Young Man was first argued in 1817, when older sonnet conventions were often forgotten, and Tudor lyrics were mistakenly interpreted in the light of Romantic or Wordsworthian criteria such as directness, candour, and reportorial fidelity. Shakespeare mocked 'wailful sonnets' as early as *Two Gentlemen of Verona*

(III.ii.69); he played exuberantly on the name 'Will' in sonnets 135, 136, and 143, and had a wide, sophisticated knowledge of artful disguisings, games, and tricks of sonneteers of the early 1590s (Honan, 181–90). His sonnets were meant to elicit expert appreciation, but they are not literal reports, and though profoundly exploratory they do not sketch 'real' characters, scenes, or experiences as candidly as modern sonnets may. The Dark Lady is a composite portrait, which takes details from Sidney's seventh sonnet in *Astrophil and Stella* (1591), and no one has shown incontrovertibly that Shakespeare's sonnet-characters had real models. Moreover, he had no need to risk his career, damage a company, or mortify a patron or the patron's friends by presuming to write intimately of the sexual habits of an earl. It is not clear that Southampton received any of these lyrics, and the few private friends who knew manuscript versions of some of them by 1598 were writers such as Francis Meres and Michael Drayton. The references to 'love' and 'duty' in the letter in *The Rape of Lucrece* have echoes in sonnet 26; but in his prose address and in that sonnet alike, Shakespeare draws on the commonplace literary language of courtly love. There is no sign that sonnet 26 was meant for Southampton, and its 'idiomatic overlap with the prose address is too slight to be in itself significant' (Kerrigan, 207).

Nevertheless, Southampton's comeliness and physical grace must have impressed Shakespeare, who received some 'warrant' of the earl's approval of *Venus and Adonis* as this is acknowledged in the dedicatory letter in *Lucrece*. Shakespeare may well have drawn upon his feelings for the earl without presuming to delineate him, but he cannot have intruded often in Southampton's set, or some notice of this would have survived; there is no sign that he mixed with the literati, or even with poets at the fringes of the earl's set such as Barnes, Markham, or Drayton. In all probability, Shakespeare's meetings with his patron were few. In urging a young man of high estate to marry, sonnets 1–17 seem to fit the earl's predicament in opposing Burghley's marriage plan. But these seventeen sonnets are artistic variations upon a theme, and in defying the conventions of courtly love they were meant to be admired, not to affect behaviour. It is unlikely that they were designed to brainwash Southampton into marrying, and one cannot be certain that the earl saw them. There are parallels between the earl's military career and the brief, fictive one of Bertram in *All's Well that Ends Well*, but the main outlines of Bertram's career come from Shakespeare's literary sources. The sonnet that is most likely to bear upon the earl is no. 107, if it relates to King James's accession and responds to his order, of 5 April 1603, to release Southampton from prison: 'Now with the drops of this most balmy time', wrote Shakespeare, 'my love looks fresh'. That he recalls his patron in 'my love looks fresh' is slightly strengthened by the fact that other verse-congratulations on Southampton's release from custody in 1603 were offered by Samuel Daniel and John Davies of Hereford.

Shakespeare's sonnets differ from those of other Tudor sonneteers partly in an indefiniteness, or in an unresolved attitude to half-truths, lies, and self-deceptions in human relationships which his lyrics explore, and the earl offered him, at best, a hypothetical object of a poet's 'love', or an ideal to be tested. In his later-written sonnets, he may take as much from his acquaintance with another elegant patron, William Herbert, third earl of Pembroke, but, again, without necessarily using him as a model or assuming intimacy with the feelings of a living nobleman. There is no reason to think that either patron would have recognized himself in the volume of Shakespeare's sonnets printed by Thorpe in 1609.

Public and private life, 1595–1603 At twenty, Southampton was mentioned for nomination as a knight of the Garter, and although he was not chosen, the mention was a high compliment. Two years later, on 17 November 1595, he distinguished himself in the lists set up in Queen Elizabeth's presence in honour of the thirty-seventh anniversary of her accession, and was likened by George Peele, in his account of the scene in his 'Anglorum feriae', to Bevis of Southampton, an ancient model of chivalry. Nashe penned for either the young earl or Lord Strange a bawdy poem entitled 'The Choise of Valentines', which opens and closes with a sonnet to 'Lord S.'. Yearning for a military career, the earl was honoured in 1595 by a sonnet in which Gervase Markham inscribed to him a patriotic poem on Sir Richard Grenville's fight off the Azores. In 1596 Southampton finally proved himself as a volunteer with his friend Essex in the military and naval expedition to Cadiz. The next year he again accompanied Essex on the expedition to the Azores.

These experiences developed in him a martial ardour which improved his position, but on his return to court in January 1598 he gave some proof of an impetuous temper. One evening in that month Sir Walter Ralegh with Southampton and a courtier named Parker were playing at primero in the presence chamber, but when Ambrose Willoughby, an esquire of the body, requested them to desist on the monarch's withdrawal to her bedchamber, Southampton struck Willoughby, and during a scuffle the esquire pulled off some of the earl's auburn locks. Next morning the queen thanked Willoughby for what he did. Later, in 1598, Southampton accepted a place in the suite of the queen's secretary, Sir Robert Cecil, who was going on an embassy to Paris. It was while in Paris that he learned that Elizabeth Vernon was pregnant, and hurrying home he secretly married her. Observers at court had thought Southampton too fantastic and volatile to take a wife, but his volatility was offset by a capacity for loyalty, and the marriage was a happy and enduring one. His wife bore him three daughters named Penelope (b. 1598), Anne, and Elizabeth, as well as two sons, James (b. 1605), and Thomas *Wriothesley (1608–1667), who because of his brother's early death in 1624 succeeded to the family estates. Angry to learn that her maid of honour had been seduced and secretly wed, the queen in 1598 committed the bride to one of the least unpleasant lodgings in the Fleet, where Southampton was ordered to join her on his return from France. He and his wife were soon released from gaol, but he never recovered Elizabeth's favour.

Seeking employment in war, Southampton set out for Ireland in March 1599 with his friend Essex, the lord deputy, who nominated him general of the horse, though the queen refused to confirm this appointment. The young earl fought well in minor skirmishes, but by the autumn he was back idling in London where, with the fifth earl of Rutland, he saw 'plays every day' (Collins, 2.132). A real tragedy was then at hand. When Essex was committed to custody after his return from Ireland, Southampton was drawn into a conspiracy whereby Essex and his friends aimed to recover by violence their influence at court. In July 1600 Southampton revisited Ireland in a futile attempt to recruit the lord deputy, Lord Mountjoy, for Essex's cause. On Thursday 5 February 1601 several friends of Essex persuaded actors at the Globe theatre to revive for the following Saturday a play that was probably Shakespeare's *Richard II* so as to incite the London public by presenting on stage the deposition of a king. On Sunday 8 February, a day after the performance, the rising failed completely. Arrested and sent to the Tower, Southampton was brought to trial with Essex on a capital charge of treason at Westminster Hall. Both defendants were condemned to death, but thanks to Sir Robert Cecil's argument that the younger earl was weakly led astray by his love of Essex, his own sentence was commuted to life imprisonment. Essex was beheaded on 25 February, and Southampton, stripped of his earldom, spent over two years in prison.

Later life, 1603–1624 Essex had been James's sworn ally, and one of the king's first acts on his accession to the crown of England was to set Southampton free in April 1603 and so enable him to resume his place at court. It was then that Samuel Daniel and John Davies offered congratulations on the earl's release in verse. On 2 July 1603 he was made KG. He was recreated earl of Southampton in the same month, and on 18 April 1604 was fully restored to his former rights by an act of parliament. The king not only appointed Southampton captain of the Isle of Wight and Carisbrooke Castle, as well as bailiff of royal manors on the island, but granted him the manors of Romsey in Hampshire, Compton Magna in Somerset, and Dunmow in Essex. He became one of the two lord lieutenants of Hampshire on 10 April 1604, and commissioner for the union with England on 10 May. The new queen showed him special favour. In 1603 he entertained her at Southampton House, where Shakespeare's players acted *Love's Labour's Lost* in her presence. The earl was a steward at the magnificent entertainment given at Whitehall on 19 August 1604 in honour of the signing of a treaty of peace with Spain, and twice danced a coranto with the queen.

But Southampton's impetuosity had not diminished. In July 1603, in the presence chamber, when the queen expressed astonishment that so many great men had done so little for themselves on the day of Essex's uprising, Southampton said that their opponents falsely had made the attempt look like a treasonous attack on Queen Elizabeth's person. Had it not been for that, he added, Essex's opponents would not have dared to put down the revolt. Lord Grey, an old enemy of Southampton and an opposer

of Essex, was standing by, and, imagining himself aimed at, retorted that the daring of Essex's opponents was not inferior to that of his friends. Southampton gave the interlocutor the lie direct, and was afterwards ordered to the Tower for infringing the peace of the palace. Although he did not wholly forfeit the good opinion of the king, and only occasionally fell into royal disfavour, Southampton was distrusted by James's chief minister, Lord Salisbury, and henceforth found it hard to obtain anything but ornamental offices.

Partly for that reason, Southampton devoted his leisure and ample wealth to organizing colonial enterprise. He helped to equip Weymouth's expedition to Virginia in 1605, and became a member of the Virginia Company's council in 1609. He was admitted a member of the East India Company in the same year. In April 1610 he helped to dispatch Henry Hudson to seek the north-west passage, and he was an incorporator both of the North-West Passage Company in 1612 and of the Somers Island Company in 1615. He was chosen treasurer of the Virginia Company on 28 June 1620, and retained office until the company's charter was declared void on 16 June 1624. Southampton exhibited skill as well as unexpected tact in the company's troubled final months, since he kept the good favour of the king and shareholders alike. On 19 November 1623 the company granted him twenty shares of land in the colony in recognition of his 'singular wisdome', care, industry, and 'unquestionable integritie' (Wriothesley papers, 312). The map of Virginia commemorates his labours as a colonial pioneer. Southampton hundred was named in his honour (17 November 1620), and the city of Hampton and its adjacent harbour of Hampton Roads took their name from what was originally known as the Southampton River.

In domestic politics, Southampton was less successful. In April 1610 he quarrelled absurdly and violently with the earl of Montgomery at tennis. On 4 June 1610, at Prince Henry's creation as prince of Wales, Southampton acted as the prince's carver, to the pleasure of the king. Later he accompanied James I on a long visit to Scotland in 1617, and the king acknowledged his attentions by nominating him eventually as a privy councillor. He was sworn on 19 April 1619, but in the next few years he quarrelled with Buckingham, almost to the point of a fist fight in the House of Lords. On 3 May 1621 he not only supported a proposal to degrade Sir Francis Bacon but foolishly asserted that he ought to be banished. On 16 June Southampton was arrested and confined to the house of John Williams, the lord keeper and dean of Westminster, on the charge of mischievous intrigues with members of the Commons. He was released a month later and ordered to repair to his own seat of Titchfield in the custody of Sir William Parkhurst, but only relieved from Parkhurst's restraint on 1 September.

Southampton was slow to acknowledge his real sympathies in religion. After his father died, he was head of one of the great Catholic families, but his protestantism became apparent when he married. Although engagingly spontaneous, he could be evasive and secretive. In youth he was self-indulgent, and it was partly because he spent so much on clothes, pleasures, and pastimes that he was strapped for funds until about 1597. His fondness for the theatre and for military service did not abate, and even in 1614 he had gone out as a volunteer to engage in the war in Cleves. Numerous works were dedicated to him, and over a dozen portraits of him survive. Having inherited an estate valued at £1097 6s. per annum, Southampton sold off some holdings, but acquired property after 1603, invested in the East India Company, and left an estate probably worth well over £1500 per annum at his death.

Last days and his significance In 1624 Southampton with his elder son, James, took command of a troop of English volunteers who meant to assist the Dutch in their campaign against Spain. After landing in the Low Countries, father and son were both attacked by fever. Young James died at Rosendael. The exhausted, grieving earl accompanied his son's body to Bergen-op-Zoom, but there, on 10 November 1624, he himself died 'of a Lethargy', perhaps a heart attack (Akrigg, 174). He was survived by his wife, who was still alive in November 1655. Father and son were buried in the chancel of the church of Titchfield, Hampshire, on 28 December.

Opinions of Southampton have changed considerably in time. Gervase Markham offered a brief biography of him in a work entitled *Honour in his Perfection* (1624). Nathan Drake's *Shakspeare and his Times* (1817) supplied the first full argument for Southampton's identity with the hero of Shakespeare's sonnets. Absurd speculations about Shakespeare's relations with his patron reached a peak in the 1930s, but have been countered by G. P. V. Akrigg's first sixteen chapters in *Shakespeare and the Earl of Southampton* (1968) and also by later researches into historical contexts and the Tudor sonnet vogue. Southampton is accurately seen as a key, early promoter of colonizing in Virginia, and a man whose passion for books and literature, which brought him into contact with Shakespeare, never diminished. Before King James's accession Southampton was seldom in a position to offer large sums of money or other tangible gifts to writers, though he aspired to be a significant patron of letters, and after his prospects improved he helped the universities. Thanks to his generosity, Oxford's new Bodleian Library in 1605 was able to buy over 400 books and manuscripts, including forty-eight texts in Spanish and a copy of the first edition of Cervantes' *Don Quixote* (Ungerer, 17). In late life the earl presented books and illuminated manuscripts worth £360 to furnish a new library at St John's College, Cambridge. Until his death, and even after it, he was the object of literary eulogies. Shakespeare, Drayton, Daniel, and others were indebted to his personal charm, talk, encouragement, or reputation in the 1590s. In early manhood, he symbolized artistic beauty and high aspiration for many Elizabethans, and helped to inspire some of their greatest lyric poetry.

PARK HONAN

Sources G. P. V. Akrigg, *Shakespeare and the earl of Southampton* (1968) · Hants. RO, Wriothesley papers, MS 5M53 · *DNB* · J. Hurstfield, *The queen's wards* (1958) · *CSP dom.*, 1547–1625 · W. Shakespeare, *The sonnets and 'A lover's complaint'*, ed. J. Kerrigan (1986) · P. Honan, *Shakespeare: a life* (1998) · A. L. Rowse, *Shakespeare's Southampton: patron of Virginia* (1965) · G. Ungerer, 'The earl of Southampton's donation to the Bodleian in 1605 and its Spanish books', *Bodleian Library Record*, 16 (1997), 17–41 · V. Traub and T. Braunschneider, 'Recent studies in homoeroticism', *English Literary Renaissance*, 30 (2000), 284–329 · A. Bray, *Homosexuality in Renaissance England* (1995) · BL, MS M/485/41 · BL, Lansdowne MS 50, fol. 51 · H. Sydney and others, *Letters and memorials of state*, ed. A. Collins, 2 (1746), 132 · H. Foley, ed., *Records of the English province of the Society of Jesus*, 3 (1878), 659 · Folger, MS L. b. 338 · T. Nashe, *The unfortunate traveller* (1594) · J. Sanford, *Apollinis et musarum euktika eidyllia* (1592)

Archives BL, MS M/485/41 · Hants. RO, corresp. and papers, 5M53 · Hunt. L., MS HA 13684 · U. Nott. L., corresp. | BL, Harley MSS 570, 7000 · BL, Lansdowne MSS 16, 37, 43, 50, 107, 627 · Hatfield House, Hertfordshire, Cecil MSS, vols. 100–03, 164, 170

Likenesses N. Hilliard, oil miniature, 1594, FM Cam. · oils, c.1600, priv. coll., on loan to NPG; repro. in Rowse, *Shakespeare's Southampton*, facing p. 133 · oils, c.1610–1615, priv. coll. · S. de Passe, line engraving, 1617, BM · D. Mytens, oils, c.1618, Althorp, Northamptonshire; version, NPG · I. Oliver, oil miniature, c.1620; formerly owned by collector at Hamburg · P. van Somer, oils, before 1621, Shakespeare Memorial Gallery, Stratford upon Avon; repro. in Rowse, *Shakespeare's Southampton*, facing p. 296 · attrib. M. van Miereveldt, oils, priv. coll. · attrib. M. van Miereveldt, oils, Hardwick Hall, Derbyshire · P. Oliver, oil miniature; formerly owned by J. Whitehead · P. Oliver, oil miniature; formerly owned by F. Cook · oils, Buccleuch estates, Selkirk [*see illus.*] · oils, St John Cam. · oils; formerly owned by W. Digby

Wealth at death over £1500 p.a.; inherited lands est. £1097 6s. 0d. in 1582; spent lavishly and had many encumbrances; sold off five manors; later acquired at least three more; invested in East India Company; wealthy enough to finance expedition before death: Akrigg, *Shakespeare and the earl of Southampton*, 19–22, 38–9, 58–9, 69, 73, 165, and 175 n. 2

Wriothesley, Sir John. *See* Writhe, John (d. 1504).

Wriothesley [*formerly* Writhe], **Sir Thomas** (d. 1534), herald, was born at 'Colatford', Wiltshire, the elder son and second of four children of John *Writhe, Garter king of arms (d. 1504), and his first wife, Barbara (d. 1480/1483), daughter of John or Januarius (Janvier) Castlecombe or Dunstanville. Colatford has not been identified, but was either near Castle Combe or, more probably, Cricklade, with which the family was already associated and where Wriothesley lived later.

In 1489 Wriothesley was made Wallingford pursuivant in the private service of Prince Arthur and continued as such under Prince Henry; in 1491 he accompanied his father to Brittany. On 26 January 1505 he was appointed Garter king of arms, over the heads of all the royal heralds-in-ordinary, at the suit of his father's old friend Roger Machado, Clarenceux king of arms. It was now that he became dissatisfied with his original surname of Writhe, and eventually settled on the grander one of Wriothesley, which he applied retrospectively to his ancestors. His brother William, York herald and father of Thomas Wriothesley, first earl of Southampton, joined him in this change [*see* Wriothesley, Thomas (1505–1550)].

As Garter, Wriothesley helped organize and took part in most of the great domestic ceremonies of the reign—the funeral of Henry VII, the coronation of Henry VIII, the Westminster tournament of 1511, the funeral of the young Prince Henry soon after, the creation of the king's illegitimate son as Henry Fitzroy, duke of Richmond, in 1525, the creation of Anne Boleyn as marchioness of Pembroke in 1532, and her coronation in 1533. In 1529 he gave evidence at the divorce proceedings of Katherine of Aragon. In 1513 he went on the Thérouanne expedition, and in 1514 he accompanied Princess Mary to France for her marriage to Louis XII. He was present at the Field of Cloth of Gold in 1520, and can be identified in the picture at Hampton Court. He took the Order of the Garter to Archduke Ferdinand of Austria in 1523, when he was knighted, and to François I in 1527.

Wriothesley appears to have been licensed under the privy seal or signet to carry out visitations (though no such 'proto-visitation' has survived) and entered into private agreements with his fellow kings of arms to grant arms and conduct funerals in their provinces. In London (where he was assessed at £40 for the forced loan of 1522) he lived at first in Red Cross Street, Cripplegate, and later built Garter House in nearby Barbican Street, whose chapel is mentioned by John Stow and can be seen in Wyngaerde's panorama of London. Garter House was not only a valuable base for the heralds in the years before their second charter, but was also where Wriothesley (himself able to paint and draw) maintained his workshop or studio. The latter's output was considerable, and includes large parts of a great armory and ordinary of all English arms. Several of its choicest manuscript productions—the Westminster tournament roll, the parliament roll of 1512, the additions to his father's 'Garter book', and his own 'Prince Arthur's book'—include representations of Wriothesley. But if he was always keen to promote his office, person, and dynasty in the favourable Henrician climate, this should not detract from his achievement. His collections are an essential link between the heraldry of the middle ages and that of the later College of Arms, while his drawings of monuments anticipate the work of later Tudor heralds. J. H. Round's aspersions on Wriothesley as a genealogist are unfounded; he continued his father's work of codification, and a number of his pedigrees are longer than the first visitation ones. The modern rectilinear form of pedigree is first found in his manuscripts.

A later Garter has called Wriothesley's Gartership 'active, prosperous and in many ways distinguished' (Wagner, *Heralds of England*, 147). His hopes of permanently asserting the primacy of his office over the other kings of arms were dashed in 1530, however, when Thomas Benolt, Clarenceux king of arms, following an audience before the king, managed to obtain a commission under the great seal to carry out visitations which expressly forbade interference by any other herald. Thenceforward Garters played no part in the visitation process.

Wriothesley's first wife, whom he married before 1500, was Jane (*d.* after 1510), daughter of William Hall of Salisbury; he had ten children with Jane, their only surviving son being Charles *Wriothesley, Windsor herald, and the chronicler. His second wife was Anne (*d.* before 1525), widow of Robert Warcop and previously of Richard Goldesborough, and daughter of Sir William Ingleby of

Ripley, Yorkshire, with whom he had a daughter who died in infancy. He may also have had a third wife, another Anne. 'Worn out with age' (Anstis, 2.393), Wriothesley died, probably in London, on 24 November 1534, and was presumably buried with his family in St Giles Cripplegate. No will of his has been found. His library may have stayed intact until the death of his son Charles in 1562; after that it was probably dispersed. Manuscripts of his are now to be found in the College of Arms, the British Library, and elsewhere.   ROBERT YORKE

Sources A. Wagner, *Heralds of England: a history of the office and College of Arms* (1967) · A. R. Wagner, *Heralds and heraldry in the middle ages*, 2nd edn (1956) · A. Payne, 'Sir Thomas Wriothesley and his heraldic artists', *Illuminating the book … essays in honour of Janet Backhouse*, ed. M. P. Brown and S. McKendrick (1998), 143–62 · M. Noble, *A history of the College of Arms* (1805), 81–6, 108–10 · J. Anstis, ed., *The register of the most noble order of the Garter*, 2 vols. (1724), vol. 1, pp. 367–73, vol. 2, p. 393 · officers of arms, Coll. Arms, vol. 1, fols. 217–22 · W. H. Godfrey, A. Wagner, and H. Stanford London, *The College of Arms, Queen Victoria Street* (1963), 41–5 · A. R. Wagner, 'Additions and corrections to "A catalogue of English mediaeval rolls of arms"', *Rolls of arms: Henry III*, Harleian Society, 113–14 (1967), 257–9 · A. R. Wagner, *English genealogy*, 2nd edn (1972) · A. R. Wagner, *The records and collections of the College of Arms* (1952) · BL, Harley roll MS, P. 4 · pedigrees Wryothsley, Coll. Arms · BL, Harley MS 4900, fols. 41v–42 · BL, Cotton MS Claudius C.iii
Archives BL, heraldic collections, MSS Add. 5530, 45131–45133, 46354, and 62541, Egerton 3713, Harley 1074 (?), 1417, 1499, and 4900, Harley roll P. 4, Loan 90 (part) · Bodl. Oxf., MS Ashmole 1113 · S. Antiquaries, Lond., heraldic collections, MSS 443 and 476 · Trinity Cam., MS 0.3.59 | Coll. Arms, commonplace book, heraldic MSS; Everard Green Roll; Garter stalls *temp.* Henry VII and Henry VIII; pedigrees Wryothsley; Westminster tournament roll, MSS A.18, I.2, L.6 (?), 8a, 9, 10 and 12b, M.3, 7, 9 *bis*, 14 *bis*, 16 *bis* and 17; Vincent 152–3, 187 (?) and 199 (part); muniment room 6/41–2, 9/60
Likenesses Wriothesley studio, painting on vellum, *c.*1511, Coll. Arms, MS Westminster tournament roll, memb. 8; repro. in Wagner, *Heralds of England*, 152–3 · Wriothesley studio, painting on vellum, *c.*1512, Trinity Cam., MS 0.3.59; repro. in Wagner, *Heralds of England*, 156–7 · Wriothesley studio, line drawing on vellum, *c.*1517–1523, BL, Harley roll P. 4, memb. 1; repro. in Payne, 'Sir Thomas Wriothesley and his heraldic artists', 142 · oils, *c.*1520, Royal Collection · Wriothesley studio, painting on vellum, after 1523, Coll. Arms, MS Vincent 152, fol. 178; repro. in Payne, 'Sir Thomas Wriothesley and his heraldic artists', 27 · Wriothesley studio, painting on vellum, BL, Loan MS 90, fol. 15; repro. in Payne, 'Sir Thomas Wriothesley and his heraldic artists', 147

Wriothesley, Thomas, first earl of Southampton (1505–1550), administrator, was the grandson of John *Writhe, Garter king of arms, nephew of Sir Thomas *Wriothesley, his successor, and cousin of Charles *Wriothesley, who became Windsor herald. His father, William, like his brother Thomas, adopted Wriothesley as the family name. William, York herald, married Agnes, daughter of James Drayton of London, and they had four children. Thomas, the eldest son, was born on 21 December 1505, his sisters, Elizabeth and Anne (who married Thomas Knight of Hook in Hampshire), in 1507 and 1508, and his brother, Edward, in 1509. It was a sign of the family's rising status and fortunes that Edward Stafford, third duke of Buckingham, and Henry Percy, fifth earl of Northumberland, were godfathers at Edward's baptism.

Education, and early career in government Thomas Wriothesley was first educated at St Paul's School, London,

Thomas Wriothesley, first earl of Southampton (1505–1550), by Hans Holbein the younger, 1538?

where his contemporaries included John Leland and William Paget. About 1522 he proceeded to Trinity Hall, Cambridge, where his fellow students again included Paget, while his teacher in civil law was Stephen Gardiner. All three had leading roles in one of Plautus's comedies, and the red-haired Wriothesley, noted for his looks, was praised for his performance. Leland, who appears to have been his friend from childhood, later wrote a tribute to his qualities of mind, integrity, and handsome appearance. Wriothesley did not, however, proceed to a degree, but instead pursued a career at the court of Henry VIII. In 1524, when only nineteen, he became a client of Thomas Cromwell, whom he styled his master and from that date many documents are in his handwriting. In 1529–30 he was clerk to Edmund Peckham, cofferer of the household; in 1530 he was king's messenger; and before 4 May 1530 he was appointed joint clerk of the signet under Stephen Gardiner, who was now the king's secretary. He remained in that post for a decade and during that time he also continued to serve Cromwell. Wriothesley carried out a wide range of administrative business and became known as an effective middleman. At the same time he began to experience the material benefits of office, for example the reversion of the office of bailiff in Warwick and Snitterfield, and an annuity of £5 from St Mary's, York.

In December 1532 Wriothesley was sent to Brussels with dispatches, and in the following October royal service took him to Marseilles. From there he complained to Cromwell that his 'apparel, and play sometimes, whereat he is unhappy, have cost him above 50 crowns' (*LP Henry VIII*, 6, no. 1306). It is probable, albeit uncertain, that these missions concerned Henry VIII's 'great matter', the annulment of his marriage to Katherine of Aragon. His services in this and in the dissolution of the monasteries gained Wriothesley the favour of the king, while at the same time Cromwell came to appreciate his intelligence, diligence, and managerial skills. Sometimes he was employed in politically sensitive matters, such as the examination of Lord Thomas Howard's love affair with Lady Margaret Douglas, or the destruction of St Swithin's shrine and the removal of all relics and treasure at Bishop Gardiner's cathedral in Winchester. He was also constantly busy as an administrator during the 1530s, not only as chief clerk of the signet but also as Cromwell's private secretary and his representative at the privy seal. He was 'manifestly the most successful civil servant of his day, in a way the head—not officially of course—of the civil service in the later 1530s' (Elton, 312).

King's servant By 1533 Wriothesley had married Jane (*d.* 1574), daughter and heir of William Cheney of Chesham Bois, Buckinghamshire, and Emma, daughter of Thomas Walwyn of Much Marcle, Herefordshire. She was also connected, presumably by parental marriage, to Stephen Gardiner and his private secretary and nephew, Germayne Gardiner, who was her half-brother. She died on 15 September 1574 and was buried at Titchfield. Thomas and Jane had three sons: William, who died in August 1537; Anthony, who died an infant *c.*1542; and Henry *Wriothesley (*bap.* 1545, *d.* 1581), the only surviving son and successor. They also had five daughters: Elizabeth, Mary, Katherine, Anne, and Mabel. In 1534 Wriothesley was admitted to Gray's Inn, while in 1536 he was appointed engraver of the Tower mint (29 May) and constable (with Lord Sandys) of Donnington Castle (21 July). When the Pilgrimage of Grace erupted during that year, he attended Henry VIII at Windsor throughout the crisis, transmitting the king's fund-raising instructions to Cromwell. In October 1537 he informed Gardiner and Lord William Howard of Queen Jane Seymour's death and attended Prince Edward's baptism. Wriothesley the bureaucrat had also become the courtier. As such he enjoyed the material rewards which resulted from loyal service and royal favour. Between 1537 and 1547 he acquired, chiefly through royal grant, former monastic manors and religious houses in eight counties, as well as three houses and a manor in London. The nucleus of his estates was in Hampshire: Quarr Abbey on the Isle of Wight (granted in 1537); the eleven manors and 5000 acres of Titchfield Abbey (1537); Beaulieu Abbey (1538); and Micheldever Manor, purchased from the king in 1544. Wriothesley made Titchfield the centre of his domain and transformed the buildings into a residence befitting the rising bureaucrat and courtier. Leland wrote that 'Mr Wriothesley hath buildid a right stately house embatelid, and having a goodely gate, and a conducte castelid in the midle of the court of it' (*Itinerary*, 1.281). Yet even as he sought wealth and status he was not insensitive to others' needs. When his agent, John Craford, advised him that many local inhabitants were sanctuary men in Beaulieu Abbey he allowed them to remain there for life.

In contrast to the self-assured advancement of his career and fortunes Wriothesley had an ambiguous and potentially dangerous relationship with Stephen Gardiner, bishop of Winchester. On the one hand they had a range of connections which were conducive to a positive, co-operative relationship: their time at university and afterwards his admission to Gardiner's household; his wife's kinship with the Gardiners; the friendship between Wriothesley and the bishop's nephew Germayne, who addressed him as his 'good loving brother' (*LP Henry VIII*, 12/1, no. 1209); and the two men's common service to the king. The bishop was increasingly alienated, however, by Wriothesley's apparent enthusiasm for reform, especially by his opposition to superstitious practices and their exploitation. This was given practical expression when he destroyed the shrine of St Swithin: 'which done we intend both at Hyde and St Mary's to sweep away all the rotten bones that be called relics' (*LP Henry VIII*, 13/2, no. 401). He was outspoken in his anti-clericalism and particularly critical of bishops' temporal powers. During Gardiner's embassy in France in 1538 Wriothesley provided Cromwell with intimate inside information about the bishop's household in order to discredit him. In July 1538 he came face to face with the returning bishop on the London–Dover road. It was an awkward meeting, during which Gardiner was excessively courteous. With 'no more than a beck and a good morrow with Germain' Wriothesley went on his way as Henry's ambassador to the regent of the Netherlands. His mission was a vain attempt to negotiate marriages between his royal master and the duchess of Milan and between Princess Mary and Don Luis of Portugal. When he returned to England in March 1539, just in time to prevent the regent from forcibly detaining him, he learned of his election to the House of Commons as a knight of the shire for Hampshire, achieved by Cromwell's direct electoral intervention in what Gardiner regarded as his parliamentary domain.

Royal secretary and chancellor   On 6 January 1540, a month after Wriothesley had been sent to Hertford to secure the consent of Princess Mary to her prospective marriage with Philip of Bavaria, Henry married Anne of Cleves. His distaste for his new bride was so great that Wriothesley pleaded with Cromwell, 'For Godde's sake, devyse for the relefe of the King; for if he remain in this gref and trouble, we shal al one day smart for it' (Strype, 1/2, appx 462). He was deeply involved in proceedings to that end, giving evidence of the king's distaste and of his consequent non-consummation of the marriage. He was also sent with the duke of Suffolk and the earl of Southampton to advise Anne that the king intended to terminate the marriage and to obtain her consent to this. In April 1540 the insecure Cromwell secured the appointment of Wriothesley and Ralph Sadler as joint principal secretaries to the king. The warrant of appointment dispensed with the statutory requirement of 31 Hen. VIII c. 10, that the principal secretary was to sit in the House of Lords, as both men 'may do the King service in the Nether House "where they now have places"' (*LP Henry VIII*, 15, no. 437). Wriothesley was also appointed to the privy council (which he regularly attended) and, when Cromwell was created earl of Essex on 18 April that year, the two secretaries were knighted. On 1 August Wriothesley was also appointed commissioner to take and receive recognizances within the verge of the king's household.

The fall of Cromwell in June 1540 resulted in a prolonged period of political instability. The clients and supporters of the dead minister at once came under threat from a conservative resurgence. Although Wriothesley rapidly distanced himself from his former employer he was subjected to examination. He was even accused by Walter Chandler of slander against the king and of unjust retention of some manors near Winchester. However, the charge was judged malicious, and in December 1540 Chandler was compelled to apologize to Wriothesley before the privy council. Nevertheless Wriothesley moved to come to terms with the political changes. Richard Morison later wrote of him that 'he was an earnest follower of whatsoever he took in hand, and very seldom did miss where either wit or travail were able to bring his purpose to pass' (*CSP for.*, 1547–53, no. 491). So the secretary secured his position now by a rapprochement with Gardiner. On 26 July 1540 the revival of his fortunes was marked by the royal grant in fee of the 'great mansion' within the Austin Friars, London. His revived relationship with Gardiner also proved to be lucrative: for example, in October 1542 a grant of the mastership of the game in Fareham Manor and annuities worth £86, because of the bishop's 'great love and singular affection' for Wriothesley (Redworth, 180). This continued generosity, supposedly conditional upon the secretary's willingness to act against heretics, later aroused the jealousy of William Paget.

Political life at Henry's court remained full of rumour, uncertain, and even hazardous. Nevertheless, the later Henrician years were a time of advancement for Wriothesley, who enjoyed growing influence and royal favour. Only when the king met Wriothesley and Norfolk secretly and went with them to an all night privy council meeting at Southwark Palace did he accept the truth about Queen Catherine Howard. Wriothesley and Southampton searched the duchess of Norfolk's Lambeth house for evidence; the secretary examined and extracted confessions from her music teacher Henry Manox and the courtier Francis Dereham; and finally, on 13 November 1541, he went to Queen Catherine at Hampton Court and 'declared certeine offences that she had done in misusing … wherefore he there discharged all her household' (Wriothesley, 1.130–31). In the following weeks he was prominent in examination of the duchess of Norfolk and her household.

During the final years of Henry VIII's reign Wriothesley was active and wide-ranging in his service to the king. On 29 January 1543 he became joint chamberlain of the exchequer. In 1542–4 he worked closely with the imperial ambassador Eustace Chapuys, to revive an Anglo-Habsburg alliance against France; in February 1543 Chapuys, Gardiner, Wriothesley, and Bishop Thomas Thirlby of Westminster concluded such an alliance, and

Wriothesley also frequently acted as intermediary, messenger, and informant between king and emperor. In October 1543 Henry commissioned the same three Englishmen to negotiate a league with Charles V, one that resulted in a joint invasion of France a year later. On 26 June 1544 Wriothesley also joined Suffolk and Paget to sign a treaty with the fourth earl of Lennox, in which the latter undertook to work for an English victory in Scotland. On 9 July he was named as one of Queen Katherine Parr's regency council during the king's absence in France, after he had briefly acted as treasurer of the wars (January–April 1544). Before and afterwards he was burdened with a number of fund-raising responsibilities, including administration of a London loan (1542), the 1545 subsidy collection, commissions of array for six southern counties (1545), and the victualling of Calais in July 1546. The strain had become evident by October 1545, when he lamented to Paget that he did not know 'howe we shall possibly shift for thre monethes folowing' (*State Papers Published under … Henry the Eighth*, 11 vols., 1830–52, 1.839–40).

Henry VIII showed his confidence in Wriothesley when the chancellor, Baron Audley, who was seriously ill delivered up the great seal on 21 April 1544. Next day Wriothesley was authorized to exercise the office, and on 3 May, after Audley's death, he became lord chancellor. He continued to be heavily involved in administrative and financial business, however, and so, on 17 October 1544, a commission was granted to Sir Robert Southwell, master of the rolls, and three masters of chancery 'to hear and determine matters in Chancery in place of Lord Chancellor Wriothesley, who is occupied in the King's affairs' (*LP Henry VIII*, 19/2, no. 527 (24)). He accumulated offices and with them more responsibilities: the constableship of castles at Southampton (from 7 July 1541), Christchurch (20 February 1541), and Portchester (28 October 1542); JP for Hampshire from 1538; the stewardship of Christchurch and Ringwood, Hampshire, from 20 February 1541, and of the forfeited lands of Margaret, countess of Salisbury, from October 1542; and joint clerk of the crown and attorney of king's bench (from 1542, with Thomas White). He also continued to sit in parliament. He was re-elected for Hampshire in 1542, and during the first session Henry VIII required him to report on a Lords' debate on Ireland.

As lord chancellor, Wriothesley summoned parliament in 1545, opened it, and presided over the upper house. He also secured a private act confirming his exchange of lands with the bishop of Salisbury and the earl of Hertford. In the second session (January 1547) he was one of those authorized to sign acts in the absence of the dying king. The late Henrician years, between 1540 and 1547, marked the peak of Wriothesley's career and reputation. He was praised by the king and also by Chapuys, who in 1542 described him as one of 'the two people who enjoy nowadays most authority and have the most influence and credit with the king', the official 'who enjoys most credit' with Henry, and the man 'who nowadays … almost governs everything here' (*CSP Spain*, 1538–42, no. 244; 1542–

3, nos. 14, 74, 85). He also acted as an intermediary, forwarding ambassadorial requests to the king and delivering royal messages to Chapuys, as they worked to revive the old alliance against France. His wide-ranging services and the consequent respect and favour in which he was held brought their due rewards. These ranged from a £100 annuity in 1544 to thirty-five ex-monastic manors in Hampshire and five other southern counties, granted in 1544–6. On 1 January 1544 he was elevated to the peerage as Baron Wriothesley of Titchfield; he was elected a knight of the Garter on 23 April 1545; and on the following day his son was baptized Henry with the king standing godfather.

Conservative champion Wriothesley's prominence in government meant that he was actively employed in enforcing the conservative religious policy of Henry's final years. Rich, Bonner, Wriothesley, and especially Gardiner were prominent among the royal servants, some of them rigorous Catholic conformists, who sought to expose and punish not only individual evangelicals but also their support networks of friends, followers, patrons, and protectors, especially in the court. Whether or not Henry was actively responsible for the persecution or simply susceptible to Gardiner, who at Windsor in 1543 complained that heresy had crept into every corner of the court and even into Henry's privy chamber, he certainly authorized or allowed a search for reformers. Wriothesley was prominent in the business. In 1543 he examined the musician John Marbeck before the privy council; in 1546 he extracted from Dr Edward Crome the names of confederates at court, in London, and the countryside. In the same year he arrested George Blagge of Henry's privy chamber, tried him at the Guildhall, and sentenced him to death by burning. When the king learned of this he was 'sore offended' and ordered Wriothesley 'to draw out his pardon himself' (*Acts and Monuments*, 5.564). As lord chancellor he frequently sentenced reformers to the pillory and other penalties in Star Chamber.

Wriothesley did not restrict his activity to protestants. In 1545 he publicly punished a Catholic priest for counterfeiting a miracle; another stood at the Cheapside pillory and was burnt in both cheeks for a false accusation. Nevertheless the most notorious example of Wriothesley's harshness concerned a protestant heretic, Anne Askew. She was summoned by him in May 1546 and examined in order to expose her connections with Queen Katherine Parr, the duchess of Suffolk, and the countess of Hertford. Her stubbornness led to her imprisonment in the Tower, where she was racked. According to Foxe, using what he claimed was Anne's own account, her continued obstinacy prompted Wriothesley and Rich 'to rack me with their own hands, till I was nigh dead' (*Acts and Monuments*, 5.547). To have racked a woman who should have been protected by law, both because she was a gentlewoman and because she had already been condemned, 'without some signal from the king' would have been very dangerous, especially as the chance of keeping it secret 'would have been slim', and it has been argued that acting thus would have been 'too great a risk for Wriothesley to take, even for an opportunity to remove potential rivals … such as Hertford' (Redworth, 236, n. 22). Nevertheless the balance of probabilities is that Wriothesley did do as Anne claimed, a sign of his desperation for political advantage which was also potentially disastrous for his future. He was present at Anne Askew's execution on 16 July 1546, having also attended when Crome recanted in a sermon preached on 27 June.

Anne Askew was executed as the decline of Henry VIII's health was causing politicians increasingly to prepare themselves for the next reign. Wriothesley's exact religious position is seldom clear, and may well have been subordinated to his temporal aspirations. Askew herself demanded of him 'how long he would halt on both sides?' (*Acts and Monuments*, 5.544). An ambitious trimmer, he acted against her in 1546 at a time when the tide was flowing against religious reform, in order to expose her evangelical religious associates among the wives of powerful men and potential rivals at court. These included friends and servants of Queen Katherine, who frequently urged religious reform on Henry. On one occasion in 1546 he lost patience and gave Gardiner and Wriothesley leave to draw up charges against her which he actually signed. According to Foxe, whose account reflects protestant opinions of Wriothesley and his accomplices, this was a plot engineered by Gardiner to remove the reform-minded queen. The attempt to bring down Katherine and her household was also designed to pre-empt the return from France of John Dudley and Edward Seymour. They, too, were inclined to religious reform and they were also Henry's favoured military commanders. Wriothesley was closely involved in the proceedings against the queen and it was he who came with a body of armed men to arrest her and three of her ladies as they walked with the king in the garden. But Katherine had persuaded the king that she was no heretic, and now Henry angrily rebuffed the chancellor, calling him knave, beast, and fool, and drove him away.

When Seymour and Dudley returned the conservative cause was lost, and Wriothesley began to switch sides. He performed his last major service to King Henry in the proceedings against the Howards, who were leading figures among the religious conservatives. He assisted Henry in drawing up the accusations against the earl of Surrey, detained the earl in his house for several days, examined him, and drafted the charges and a list of interrogatories. He was also one of the commissioners at his trial on 13 January 1547. He also witnessed the written confession of Surrey's father, the third duke of Norfolk, and headed the commission which notified parliament of the royal assent to the bills of attainder against the two men. He was naturally active in proceedings against the Howards as Henry's dutiful lord chancellor. It is clear, however, that he was also distancing himself from the other conservatives, led by Gardiner, as they too fell from favour in 1546–7. Gardiner was excluded from the court and the king's will and he was infrequently called to the privy council. The fact that Wriothesley arranged Surrey's humiliating street walk to the Tower is a confirmation of his well-timed political

shift. However, it should be said that he was usually willing to act harshly, even brutally, in the king's service. In January 1545, for example, he sentenced Alderman Richard Rede to be sent on military service against the Scots, to punish him for failing to contribute to a benevolence.

Fall from power On 31 January 1547 the tearful lord chancellor announced the king's death to parliament. Nevertheless Wriothesley was an immediate beneficiary of his demise. Henry's will named him one of sixteen executors and privy councillors and the recipient of £500. Paget's deposition as to the late king's intentions included an earldom and, on 16 February, he was duly created earl of Southampton with an annual allowance of £20. On 5 February he was appointed chief commissioner of claims for the coronation of Edward VI, at which he bore the sword of state on the 20th. Yet only a fortnight later, on 6 March, the great seal was taken from him, he was confined to his home at Ely Place, and he had to give a recognizance of £4000. Although he remained a privy councillor he was excluded from the council board. His ostensible offence was abuse of authority. Presumably because he expected to be preoccupied with government business, on 18 February he had sealed and issued a commission to four civilians to hear and determine all causes entered into chancery. This relieved him of many legal duties. '[D]ivers studentes of the Commen Lawes' petitioned the government that this had diverted business from the common law courts to chancery insomuch 'as very fewe matters be now depending at the Comen Lawes' and that, in other ways too, the chancellor was prejudicing the common law (*APC*, 1547–50, 48–50). Southampton's commission was referred to the judges and the king's law officers. They found him guilty of issuing a commission without a warrant or consultation with the other executors. Furthermore he had 'menassed divers of the said lerned men and others' (ibid., 56). Abuse of his authority, however, was only the pretext for his fall. His commission of 1547 was no different from that of 1544; he had the authority, like his predecessor, to issue such commissions; and there exist copies of Edward VI's authorization of the lord chancellor's warrant to make such commissions.

The chief cause of Southampton's fall was his animosity to Edward Seymour, formerly earl of Hertford, and now duke of Somerset, and his opposition to the office of protector. As he later told Charles V's ambassador, François van der Delft, his troubles were the result of Somerset's long-time enmity towards him and of his own refusal to 'consent to any innovations in the matter of government beyond the provisions of the will' (*CSP Spain*, 1547–9, 91–2, 100–01, 106). On 31 January 1547, three days after Henry VIII's death, the late king's executors made Somerset lord protector, in accordance with the authority bestowed on them by his will. He was, however, required to abide by majority decisions, which strictly limited his power. Southampton opposed any change which would reinforce Somerset's authority or freedom of action and, so long as he held the great seal, no further change was possible. It was a group of senior government lawyers who solved Somerset's problems. Led by Baron Rich and Sir John

Baker they brought to light what was merely a technical error in the commission to the civilians issued by Southampton, and exploited it to secure his dismissal as chancellor. When he surrendered the great seal it was promptly used to give legal authority to a patent issued by the young King Edward VI, which not only made Somerset protector of the realm and governor of the royal person, but also invested him with the power to choose the privy council and to control its business.

Southampton's fall neutralized a possible political rival to Somerset, who was also his personal enemy. Southampton's bold, sometimes harsh actions, and his outspoken manner (which included past criticisms of Somerset) were arguably also the responses of a loyal, dedicated royal servant. But he was also undeniably ambitious, and fully capable of alienating others, for instance by his conduct in religious affairs. He also resisted proposed reforms which would have expanded the court of augmentations' jurisdiction and so harm the interests of chancery, especially the fees received by its officials. In 1547 a bill to create a new court of augmentations was placed in his charge, but it did not proceed, thereby thwarting its promoters. When Henry died Wriothesley was isolated. He was also vulnerable because, according to Paget, he was arrogant and, in Richard Grafton's words, he was guilty of 'overmuch repugnyng to the rest in matters of Counsaile' (Grafton, 2.499–500). When Southampton fell, however, he submitted to his sentence, publicly acknowledging it to be a just one. He was released on 29 June 1547, his fine was remitted, and by 17 January 1549 he had resumed his place at the council board. He regularly attended parliament in 1547 (thirty-three of thirty-five sittings) and 1548–9 (sixty-one of seventy-three), and he was active in both sessions. In particular he resisted protestant religious innovation, though not, perhaps, as energetically as he might have done, for on 20 February 1549 the imperial ambassador reported that 'the ex-Chancellor lost his constancy in the end and agreed to everything' (*CSP Spain, 1547–9*, 345).

Defeat and death   Although Southampton's political fortunes revived he bore a continuing grudge against the protector as the man responsible for his fall. However, when Thomas, Baron Seymour of Sudeley, conspired to overthrow his brother Somerset and assumed that Southampton would assist him, the earl advised him not to intrigue and raise faction. '[F]or my parte thank God of yt, when I was at the worst rather than I wolde have consented in my harte to any faction or partie tumult. If I had had a thousande lives I woulde have lost them all ... than attempt yt' (PRO, SP 10/6, no. 15). Southampton was sufficiently astute to realize that to ally himself with the protector's brother would be disastrous. When the doomed Thomas Seymour was imprisoned Southampton was a member of the joint parliamentary committee which interrogated him in February 1549.

Nevertheless Southampton was active in conciliar moves against the protector in October 1549. By then he had moved back to the leadership of a group of religious conservatives, including the twelfth earl of Arundel.

Although Warwick and the evangelicals shared with the conservatives an immediate common objective, to topple the protector, the alliance was an unnatural one. It was, however, in the short term a successful one, and once the protector had been removed Southampton enjoyed a brief period of prominence, during which he was appointed to attend upon Edward VI. 'Wriothesley ... is lodged ... next to the king. Every man repaireth to Wriothesley honoureth Wriothesley, sueth unto Wriothesley ... and all thinges be done by his advise' (Ponet, sig. Iiii–iiiv). Warwick, however, feared a Catholic coup, intended to make Mary regent, and with good reason, because by December 1549 Southampton and Arundel sought not only Somerset's destruction but his own too. Warwick knew it, and said as much. At a council meeting in January 1550 he put his hand on his sword and told Southampton: 'my lord you seeke his bloude and he that seeketh his bloude would have myne also' (Hoak, 256). By 14 January 1550 Southampton and the earl of Arundel had been expelled from the court and placed under house arrest, while their associates, such as the fifth earl of Shrewsbury and Sir Richard Southwell, were removed from the centre of government.

Southampton now ceased to attend council meetings and in February he was removed from the council list. He was also seriously ill. Although his condition improved in March he was reported to be 'desiring to ... be under the earth rather than upon it' (*CSP Spain, 1550–52*, 47), and on 28 June he was allowed for reasons of health to retire to Titchfield. He was too ill to travel, however, and on 30 July 1550 he died at his London home, Lincoln House in Holborn, which he had obtained by exchange with Warwick. According to Ponet, 'fearing least he should come to some open shamfull ende, he either poisoned himself, or pyned awaye for thought' (Ponet, sig. Iiiiv). The fact that he was repeatedly ill of a quartan fever suggests that he may have been a consumptive, possibly the cause of death. He was buried in St Andrew's Church, Holborn, on 3 August, but his body was later removed to Titchfield. His will, dated 21 July 1550, was proved on 14 May 1551. Apart from the usual bequests to family, servants, and friends he gave gilt cups to 'my verie good Lordes therles of Warwick and Arundell'. And 'for a remembrance of my duetie toward my sovereigne Lorde, and for the great benefites that I have receaved of his most noble father of famouse memorie', he granted Edward VI the income from fourteen manors and other lands in five counties during his son's minority (PRO, PROB 11/34, fols. 97v–98).

Assessment   In 1551 Sir Richard Morison wrote that 'I was afraid of a tempest all the while Wriothesley was able to raise any ... I never was able to persuade myself that Wriothesley could be great, but the King's Majesty must be in greatest danger' (*CSP for., 1547–53*, no. 491). Some had a very different opinion. Leland praised his intellect, character, and probity. He certainly had high ambitions, and as he realized them so he assumed the airs and graces of a new member of the élite. By 1545 he was licensed to retain 140 men in his livery, and whenever he appeared in public he was preceded by his gentlemen and followed by his yeomen clad in velvet and gold chains. He rebuilt Titchfield as a residence fit for a king to visit, which Henry VIII did on 31 July 1545. According to Foxe, whose portrayal was later accepted by Burnet, Lodge, Strype, and others, Wriothesley was a careerist who was also variously a zealous papist, a Romanist, even leader of a popish party, and certainly a Catholic. His acceptance of the royal supremacy and his enthusiastic destruction of shrines, tombs, and relics make it impossible to be so certain. Indeed his sharp criticisms of bishops, the religious formula adopted in his will, his patronage of reformers such as Richard Taverner and Robert Talbot, the choice of John Hooper to preach at his funeral, and the fact that his children's teacher landed in trouble for heresy, all suggest that Wriothesley had some protestant sympathies. His true religious convictions were masked, however, by his social and political conservatism, the precariousness of court politics, and especially by the devoted loyal service of an obedient royal servant.

Wriothesley helped to implement royal religious policies, whether they were in a Catholic or a protestant direction. He profited from the dissolution of the monasteries, but he also drafted a paper on ways in which monastic wealth could be used to establish new hospitals, build highways, and maintain the army. He was respected as a lord chancellor who protected royal interests and rule of law. His dicta were repeated: that while force awed, justice governed the world; and that every man who sold justice sold the king's majesty. He was respected for other qualities too. Roger Ascham addressed him as a great patron of both literature and the University of Cambridge, while Leland referred to him as a friend to the muses, and in 1537 his servant John Huttoft gave 'immortal thanks for your goodness' (*LP Henry VIII*, 12/2, no. 546). Yet he was at the same time unbending and even cruel to those who opposed or offended royal wishes. He could also be without scruple—in 1547, immediately after Henry VIII's death, he, Warwick, Arundel, and Baron Russell all reduced their tax assessments.

MICHAEL A. R. GRAVES

Sources *LP Henry VIII*, vols. 4–21 · *CSP Spain*, 1538–52 · *CSP for.*, 1547–53 · A. J. Slavin, 'The fall of Lord Chancellor Wriothesley: a study in the politics of stability', *Albion*, 7/3 (1975), 265–86 · will, PRO, PROB 11/34, sig. 13, fols. 96v–98v · J. Strype, *Ecclesiastical memorials*, 3 vols. (1822) · A. J. Slavin, 'Lord Chancellor Wriothesley and reform of augmentations: new light on an old court', *Tudor men and institutions*, ed. A. J. Slavin (1972) · J. Ponet, *A short treatise of politike power* (1556) [in *Theatrum orbis terrarum* (1972)] · GEC, *Peerage*, new edn · *VCH Hampshire and the Isle of Wight*, vols. 2–5 · *Calendar of the manuscripts of the most hon. the marquis of Salisbury*, 1, HMC, 9 (1883) · *APC*, 1542–54 · *Select works of John Bale*, ed. H. Christmas, Parker Society, 37 (1849) · G. Redworth, *In defence of the Catholic church: the life of Stephen Gardiner* (1990) · BL, Add., Harley and Stowe MSS · DNB · A. L. Rowse, 'Thomas Wriothesley, first earl of Southampton', *Huntington Library Quarterly*, 28 (1964–5), 105–29 · HoP, *Commons, 1509–58*, 3.663–6 · C. Wriothesley, *A chronicle of England during the reigns of the Tudors from AD 1485 to 1559*, ed. W. D. Hamilton, 2 vols., CS, new ser., 11, 20 (1875–7) · *The itinerary of John Leland in or about the years 1535–1543*, ed. L. Toulmin Smith, 5 vols. (1906–10); repr. with introduction by T. Kendrick (1964), vol. 1 · *Literary remains of King Edward the Sixth*, ed. J. G. Nichols, 2 vols., Roxburghe

Club, 75 (1857) · *CSP dom.*, 1547–80 · M. A. R. Graves, 'The Tudor House of Lords in the reigns of Edward VI and Mary I', PhD diss., Otago University, 1974 · J. J. Scarisbrick, *Henry VIII* (1970) · G. R. Elton, *Tudor revolution in government* (1953) · H. Ellis, ed., *Original letters illustrative of English history*, 1st ser., 2 (1824); 2nd ser., 2 (1827) · *The acts and monuments of John Foxe*, ed. J. Pratt, [new edn], 8 vols. in 16 (1853–70) · S. Brigden, *New worlds, lost worlds: the rule of the Tudors, 1485–1603* (2001) · R. Grafton, *Chronicle or history of England, 1189–1558*, 2 vols. (1809) · D. E. Hoak, *The king's council in the reign of Edward VI* (1976) · E. W. Ives, 'Henry VIII's will—a forensic conundrum', *HJ*, 35 (1992), 779–804 · E. W. Ives, 'Henry VIII's will: the protectorate provisions of 1546–7', *HJ*, 37 (1994), 901–14 · state papers domestic, Edward VI, PRO, SP 10/6 · R. W. Goulding, 'Wriothesley portraits', *Walpole Society*, 8 (1920), 17–94

Archives BL, political corresp., Add. MSS 32647–32652, *passim* · Hants. RO, personal, official, and estate papers · PRO, Wriothesley papers, SP 7 | BL, Harley MSS, corresp. · PRO, SP 1

Likenesses H. Holbein, miniature, 1538, Metropolitan Museum of Art, New York · H. Holbein the younger, chalk drawing, 1538?, Louvre, Paris [*see illus.*] · group portrait, oil on panel, *c.*1570 (*Edward VI and the pope*), NPG · oils (after type by H. Holbein the younger, 1538), Woburn Abbey, Bedfordshire · portrait, Beaulieu

Wealth at death considerable: PRO, PROB 11/34, sig. 13, fols. 96v–98v

Wriothesley, Thomas, fourth earl of Southampton (1608–1667), politician, was born at Little Shelford in Cambridgeshire on 10 March 1608, the second but only surviving son of Henry *Wriothesley, third earl of Southampton (1573–1624), and Elizabeth Vernon (*b.* 1573, *d.* in or after 1655). He was educated at Eton College (1613–19) and St John's College, Cambridge (1625–6). Southampton spent most of the later 1620s and early 1630s in France and the Low Countries. On 18 August 1634 he married his first wife, Rachel de Beaujeu (1603–1640), eldest daughter of Daniel de Massüe, seigneur de Ruvigny, and widow of Elysée de Beaujeu, at Charenton in France. They moved to England shortly afterwards and, before Rachel's death in childbirth on 16 February 1640, they had two sons (Charles and Henry, who died young), and three daughters (Magdalen, who died an infant, Elizabeth, and Rachel [*see* Russell, Rachel, Lady Russell]).

Relations with Charles I Following his return to England, Southampton found himself in debt after an unwise bet at Newmarket and began selling timber on his main estates at Titchfield in Hampshire. Charles I took advantage of this to buy 1000 of Southampton's best oak trees for shipbuilding at a reduced price of £2294 10s. Southampton then became one of the most notable victims of Charles's attempts to revive ancient claims to royal forest. In October 1635 a forest court chaired by the earl of Holland at Winchester challenged Southampton's title to the greater part of his estate at Beaulieu in the New Forest. Charles claimed that the lands were royal forest, which would have had the effect of reducing the rents paid to Southampton from £2500 to £500 per annum. By exploiting this legal technicality Charles forced him to beg for the restitution of lands that were rightfully his, but Southampton petitioned for relief and Charles relented in July 1636.

Southampton's bitterness against the king may well help to explain why he insisted in the Short Parliament that discussion of grievances should precede supply. Hyde later wrote that by 1640 Southampton 'had never had any

Thomas Wriothesley, fourth earl of Southampton (1608–1667), by Sir Peter Lely, c.1661

conversation in the Court, nor obligation to it; on the contrary he had undergone some hardness from it'. He had 'a particular prejudice' against Strafford, but became alarmed 'as he saw the ways of reverence and duty towards the King declined' (Clarendon, *Hist. rebellion*, 2.530). These attitudes were closely associated with 'a perfect detestation of all the Presbyterian principles'. Southampton was 'a man of great and exemplary virtue and piety' who 'strictly observed the devotions prescribed by the Church of England' and was 'averse and irreconcileable to the sedition and rebellion of the Scots' (*Life of … Clarendon*, 3.238).

It seems that this attachment to the crown and the church ultimately overcame Southampton's bitterness at the way that Charles I had treated him: on 3 May 1641 he was one of only two peers (the other was Lord Robartes) who refused to assent to John Pym's protestation following the revelation of the first army plot; Southampton voted against Strafford's attainder, and on 3 June was appointed lord lieutenant of Hampshire; at the beginning of November, Charles asked Nicholas 'to thanke Southampton in my name, for stopping the Bill against the Bishops' (*Diary of John Evelyn*, 4.114); and by the middle of that month Henrietta Maria regarded Southampton's proxy as vitally important in the mobilization of the king's supporters within the upper house. Southampton was sworn a gentleman of the bedchamber on 30 December, and was appointed a privy councillor on 3 January 1642. He was given leave by both the king and the Lords to leave Westminster in February, but initially chose to remain there, on 5 March entering his protest against the militia ordinance. He obtained leave to go to York on 17

March and had arrived there by the twenty-seventh. It is possible that he was back in London about 24 April when he married his second wife, Elizabeth Leigh (1620?–1658), eldest daughter of Francis *Leigh, Lord Dunsmore (created earl of Chichester in 1644), and his second wife, Audrey Boteler. They had four daughters, only one of whom, Elizabeth, survived youth.

Promoting peace Although Southampton was among those who in June 1642 engaged to provide the king with forces, throughout the civil wars he remained deeply committed to seeking an accommodation with the houses. Immediately after the king raised his standard Southampton advised him that a message to parliament 'might do good, and could do no harm' (Clarendon, *Hist. rebellion*, 2.300). Charles eventually agreed to send Southampton—together with Edward Sackville, earl of Dorset, Sir John Colepeper, and Sir William Uvedale—to inform the houses of his 'constant and earnest care to preserve the public peace' (ibid., 2.304). However, when he entered the Lords, Southampton was ordered to withdraw from the house, to pass the message to the gentleman usher, and then to leave London immediately.

Southampton nevertheless persisted in promoting peace talks. He was one of the king's commissioners at the treaty of Oxford (February–April 1643). Then, in December 1644, he and the duke of Richmond acted as the king's messengers to the houses, requesting the appointment of commissioners which led to the treaty of Uxbridge (January–February 1645), although the talks again proved abortive. Later that year, when the prince of Wales was sent to the west country with his own council, Southampton expressed a particular wish to remain with the king and continued to urge him to bring the war to an end. In April 1646 he was involved in a further attempt to reach agreement with the parliamentarian army at Woodstock, and on 20 June he was one of the privy councillors who signed the Oxford articles of capitulation; the city formally surrendered four days later.

Before Southampton left Oxford he received a rebuke from Prince Rupert which led to a quarrel in which the prince sent him a challenge. However, friends of both parties intervened and the threatened duel never took place. In October 1647, Southampton was one of a small circle of royalist peers whom the king summoned to Hampton Court to advise him. The following month, during his flight from Hampton Court, the king visited Southampton at Titchfield, and the earl briefly followed him to the Isle of Wight. Towards the end of March 1648, Viscount Saye and Sele and several Commons allies—including Sir John Evelyn, William Pierrepont, and possibly Oliver Cromwell—attempted a personal approach to Charles I. They tried to enlist Southampton's help, but he refused to become implicated in such a contravention of the vote of no addresses. In the end he informed them bluntly:

> my lords, I must tell you that I shall as a sworne privy
> councillor to his Ma[jes]tie give him such advise as is best
> and safest for him, but my lords you shall not heare nor be
> privy to what I say. (Bodl. Oxf., MS Clarendon 31, fol. 54v)

Southampton was among the peers permitted to attend

the king on the Isle of Wight during the treaty of New-port, and he was also one of those who were with Charles during his trial. Following the king's execution, he obtained leave to stay in the palace of Whitehall, where it is said that he witnessed Cromwell approach Charles's corpse, consider 'it attentively for some time', and then mutter the words 'cruel necessity' (J. Spence, *Observations, Anecdotes, and Characters of Books and Men*, ed. J. M. Osborn, 1, 1966, 244). Finally, Southampton attended the king's funeral at Windsor on 8 February.

Parliament's treatment of Southampton's estates was relatively lenient. In November 1645 the committee for the advance of money had assessed him at £6000, although there is no evidence that this sum was ever paid. In the autumn of 1646 he begged to compound under the Oxford articles and was assessed at the rate of one-tenth, or the value of two years' income from his estates, and on 26 November his fine was set at £6466. In the autumn of 1648 the Commons confirmed his composition fine and ordered him to be pardoned for his delinquency and the sequestration to be taken off his estates. There is, how-ever, no evidence that this fine was ever paid, and there-after the committee for compounding apparently ceased to pursue him.

After Charles I's execution After the king's execution Southampton lived in retirement in Hampshire. Although the council of state kept an eye on him, his political activ-ities were extremely limited throughout the 1650s. He was deeply loyal to Charles II and in October 1651, during the king's flight after the battle of Worcester, he sent word from Titchfield that he had a ship ready for Charles. The king had already secured a boat to take him to France but he 'ever acknowledged the obligation with great kind-ness, he being the only person of that condition who had the courage to solicit such a danger' (Clarendon, *Hist. rebel-lion*, 5.211). After the king's escape Southampton 'had still a confidence of His Majesty's restoration' (*Life of … Claren-don*, 3.237). Yet Clarendon thought the earl 'of a nature very much inclined to melancholic' (Clarendon, *Hist. rebel-lion*, 2.529) and Southampton apparently believed that there was little chance of overthrowing the republic in the immediate future. His advice to Charles was always 'to sit still, and expect a reasonable revolution, without mak-ing any unadvised attempt', and he 'industriously declined any conversation or commerce with any who were known to correspond with the King' (*Life of … Claren-don*, 1.338–9).

Southampton declined to recognize the republican regime, and was not among those royalists known to have taken the engagement. According to Clarendon, Crom-well 'courted' the earl, but Southampton:

> could never be persuaded so much as to see him; and when Cromwell was in the New Forest, and resolved one day to visit him, he being informed of it or suspecting it, removed to another house he had at such a distance as exempted him from that visitation. (*Life of … Clarendon*, 1.338)

There were occasional exceptions to Southampton's general quietism, most notably in November 1655 when he refused to give Major-General Kelsey particulars of his

estate to permit assessment for the decimation tax, and as a consequence was briefly imprisoned in the Tower. He claimed that the decimation tax violated the Oxford art-icles, under which he had surrendered and compounded for his estates, and also the Rump Parliament's Act of General Pardon and Oblivion (February 1652). As under Charles I, he strongly defended legal propriety and chal-lenged any policies that he perceived as breaches of the rule of law.

Southampton was released from the Tower by the end of 1655, and from then until the Restoration he lived very quietly, avoiding any involvement in royalist conspir-acies. Southampton's second wife died late in 1658, and the following year, on 7 May, he married his third wife, Frances, *née* Seymour (*c*.1620–1680/81), widow of Richard Molyneux, second Viscount Molyneux of Maryborough (*d.* 1654), and daughter of the marquess of Hertford. He remained on very friendly terms with Hyde, and corres-ponded regularly with him throughout the interregnum. In June 1659 Hyde assured John, Viscount Mordaunt, that he would find Southampton 'one of the most excellent persons living. Of great affection to the King; of great honor; and of an understanding superior to most men' (*Abergavenny MSS*, 204). Hyde greatly valued Southamp-ton's advice and regularly asked for his opinions; their close friendship, together with the king's favour, explains Southampton's appointment to high office at the Restor-ation.

Service to Charles II On his arrival at Canterbury on 27 May 1660 Charles II appointed Southampton to the privy coun-cil and created him a knight of the Garter. On 8 September he was appointed lord treasurer, an office which he held until his death. Throughout these years Southampton was keen to strike a balance between avoiding a vindictive settlement while at the same time ensuring that the restored monarchy was financially secure and not dependent upon parliament. Ludlow praised his magna-nimity for insisting in August 1661 that those exempted from the general pardon be given fourteen days to save themselves. Six months later Southampton opposed the excessive use of force to suppress Venner's rising in terms which were wholly consistent with the attitudes he had evinced earlier in his career:

> They had [he said] felt the effects of a military government, though sober and religious, in Cromwell's army: he believed vicious and dissolute troops would be much worse: the King would grow fond of them, and they would quickly become insolent and ungovernable: and then such men as he was must be only instruments to serve their ends. (*Burnet's History*, 1.280)

He begged Clarendon to avoid anything that smacked of arbitrary rule and to preserve lawful, constitutional gov-ernment; Clarendon, whose own commitment to the rule of law was deep, was won over by these arguments. South-ampton consistently opposed the creation of a standing army, partly on grounds of cost, but also because he dis-liked any hint of authoritarian government.

A similar magnanimity characterized Southampton's

attitudes towards the church. Burnet praised his commitment to 'moderating matters both with relation to the government of the Church and the worship and ceremonies' (*Burnet's History*, 1.316). Southampton sought to make the church as comprehensive as possible, and hoped that at least the more moderate presbyterians could be encompassed within it. He was one of the peers who tried to soften the terms of the Act of Uniformity, although their efforts were only partially successful. There is some evidence that his stance did not endear him to some members of the Restoration episcopate. Equally, he wanted such comprehension to be established by statutory means and, like Clarendon, he strongly resisted the king's attempts in 1662–3 to introduce a bill that would have enabled him to issue dispensations from the Act of Uniformity. Both Southampton and Clarendon 'were very warm against it, and used many arguments to dissuade the King from prosecuting it' (*Life of … Clarendon*, 2.344); both actively opposed the bill when it came before the Lords and helped to ensure that it was dropped. According to Clarendon, Southampton even expressed the view that the Indulgence Bill was 'unfit to be received … being a design against the Protestant religion, and in favour of the papists' (ibid., 2.345). Southampton regarded such use of royal prerogative powers as unacceptable, and clearly remained profoundly attached to a vision of royal powers tempered by the rule of law. Indeed, Burnet later claimed that Southampton blamed 'all the errors' of Charles II's reign on his 'coming in without conditions' (*Burnet's History*, 1.162), and even criticized his friend Clarendon for giving so favourable an impression of the king in 1660 that such conditions were not deemed necessary.

The hallmarks of Southampton's conduct as lord treasurer were caution, conscientiousness, and incorruptibility. Burnet wrote that 'he was an incorrupt man, and during seven years management of the Treasury he made but an ordinary fortune out of it' (*Burnet's History*, 1.171). Southampton refused to derive personal benefit from the office, and reached an agreement with the king whereby he received a fixed annual salary of £8000. He lamented that his own example of restraint was not followed by the king and many of his other courtiers: he made a number of urgent representations to Charles, especially in 1663–5, warning him that 'the revenue is the centre of all your business' (BL, Harleian MS 1223, fol. 202), but his calls for a policy of retrenchment were of only limited effect. According to Clarendon, in 1662 Southampton suggested the sale of Dunkirk as a way of boosting income, and in 1665 he strongly resisted the approaching war against the Dutch Republic, conscious that this would only disrupt trade, diminish customs revenues, and drain the exchequer.

Disillusionment and final years By the mid-1660s Southampton's disillusionment with the spendthrift king, together with deteriorating health, led him to withdraw more and more from active public work. In 1664 Lord Arlington, Baron Ashley, and Sir William Coventry asked the king to remove Southampton, complaining that he was delegating all his work to his secretary, Sir Philip Warwick. Although Clarendon successfully headed off this appeal, during the autumn of 1665 there was a further proposal, this time backed by James, duke of York, to replace Southampton with a commission. From then until his death rumours of the lord treasurer's replacement continued to circulate regularly.

These attacks took place against a background of worsening illness, and towards the end of 1666 Southampton fell gravely ill. After his death a large stone was discovered in his bladder, and one kidney was also found to be much enlarged. Southampton had never been robust—Sir Edward Walker wrote of his 'infirm body' (Bodl. Oxf., MS Ashmole 1110, fol. 170)—and after bearing the very painful illness with great bravery he died at his London home, Southampton House, on 16 May 1667 and was buried at Titchfield on 18 June. Clarendon mourned his friend and colleague, and summed him up as 'a person of extraordinary parts, of faculties very discerning and a judgment very profound'; and 'a man of great and exemplary virtue and piety' (*Life of … Clarendon*, 3.229, 238).

DAVID L. SMITH

Sources Clarendon, *Hist. rebellion* • *The life of Edward, earl of Clarendon … written by himself*, new edn, 3 vols. (1827) • Bodl. Oxf., Clarendon MSS • PRO, state papers domestic, Charles I, SP 16 • PRO, state papers domestic, interregnum, SP 18 • PRO, committee for sequestrations MSS, SP 20 • PRO, committee for compounding MSS, SP 23 • JHL, 3–11 (1620–66) • *Diary of John Evelyn*, ed. W. Bray, new edn, ed. H. B. Wheatley, 4 vols. (1906) • GEC, *Peerage*, new edn • *The Nicholas papers*, ed. G. F. Warner, 1, CS, new ser., 40 (1886) • *The Nicholas papers*, ed. G. F. Warner, 2, CS, new ser., 50 (1892) • *The Nicholas papers*, ed. G. F. Warner, 3, CS, new ser., 57 (1897) • *The Nicholas papers*, ed. G. F. Warner, 4, CS, 3rd ser., 31 (1920) • D. L. Smith, *Constitutional royalism and the search for settlement, c. 1640–1649* (1994) • BL, Sloane MS 1116 • BL, Add. MS 12514 • *Burnet's History of my own time*, ed. O. Airy, new edn, 2 vols. (1897–1900); suppl., ed. H. C. Foxcroft (1902) • *The manuscripts of the marquess of Abergavenny, Lord Braye*, G. F. Luttrell, HMC, 15 (1887)

Archives Hants. RO, personal, official, family, and estate papers | Leics. RO, corresp. with earl of Winchilsea

Likenesses S. Cooper, miniature, 1661, Woburn Abbey, Bedfordshire • P. Lely, portrait, *c*.1661; Christies, 8 July 1998, lot 29 [*see illus.*] • T. Simon, silver medal bust, 1664, NPG; repro. in E. Hawkins, *Medallic illustrations of the history of Great Britain and Ireland*, 2 vols. (1885), pl. XXI • P. Lely, portrait, Woburn Abbey, Bedfordshire • oils (after P. Lely, *c*.1661), NPG • portrait, Welbeck Abbey, Nottinghamshire

Wealth at death £3233 p.a. in 1646: PRO, committee for compounding MSS, SP 23/3, 307

Writer, Clement (*d.* 1659×62), religious controversialist, was one of three known surviving children of unidentified parents. Given his prolonged association with Worcestershire it is possible that he descended from the county. He claimed to have received little formal education, and never married. He first appears in 1627 in conjunction with Captain Edward Spring and an unspecified debt of £8. The state papers indicate that pecuniary difficulties and related litigation dogged him for much of his remaining life. In 1631 an adversary, John Racster, requested Sir Dudley Carleton, secretary of state, to use his influence on his behalf with Sir Nathaniel Brent, judge of the prerogative court, against Writer. In protracted litigation against his uncle, George Worfield, Writer petitioned unsuccessfully for compensation for seven years' remuneration and expenses incurred in conducting Worfield's lawsuits, later claiming that Lord Keeper Sir Thomas Coventry had unjustly decreed against him to the extent of £1500. In 1640 he sought redress against Coventry from what he called 'the grand committee of the courts of justice' (Writer, *Case*, 1), but the committee was dissolved before his case could be considered. In 1646 his complaint was heard by the Commons committee for petitions, and a subcommittee was appointed to deal with the matter, but the committee itself was suspended before it could receive a report. Frustrated by this succession of disappointments, Writer published *The Sad Case of Clement Writer* (1646) in his defence, arguing that the failure to hear his case in 1640 was a miscarriage of justice that had denied him the opportunity to present his evidence; copies were distributed to MPs. In 1652 Thomas Fowle, solicitor for the Commonwealth, referred his case against Coventry to the Worcester committee for sequestration, but the dissolution of parliament once again prevented the matter from being resolved. Writer ultimately petitioned Cromwell, and the council of state delegated the case to yet another committee in October 1656. It is not known if he ever obtained redress.

Legal problems notwithstanding, Writer was actively involved in the affairs of the day. He was in business as a clothier in Worcester, where he owned property, during the 1630s, and by the early 1640s was trading in London and living in Blackwell Hall. Although he had rejected presbyterianism for Independency about 1638 after reading the works of John Robinson, he became a prominent member of Thomas Lambe's London General Baptist congregation. In 1641 he accompanied Lambe on an evangelistic mission in Gloucestershire, and his name appears in association with other known General Baptists. On the outbreak of civil war he enlisted horse for the support of the parliamentary army; he himself took up arms, but by 1645 had seemingly returned to civilian life when he attended meetings concerning the issue of religious toleration between the sects, the Independents, and the presbyterians.

Repeated attempts to determine precisely Writer's religious sympathies have proved difficult, and he remains elusive. Contemporaries were provoked by his departure from theological orthodoxy and reacted accordingly. Thomas Edwards, with some spleen, called him an 'Anti-scripturist', 'arch-heretique', 'fearfull apostate', even an 'atheist' (Edwards, 1.27), a depiction which has persisted in some modern historiography. Richard Baxter also thought he was both 'apostate' and 'infidel' (*Reliquiae Baxterianae*, 1.116), and in 1655 published *The Unreasonableness of Infidelity* with Writer in mind. However, these assessments by more moderate figures were obviously polemically motivated, and neither Edwards's early view of 1646 or Baxter's later judgement should be taken as the last word. More recently Writer has been portrayed as a General Baptist, a Seeker, even a Leveller, the latter on account of his acquaintance with William Walwyn, who

has also been designated a Seeker. The truth probably lies somewhere here, with the term 'Seeker'. Baxter believed that this was Writer's own estimation of his position, although after two meetings and correspondence, Baxter himself remained uncertain. Writer's defection from presbyterianism, his antipathy to ceremony and dissatisfaction with all organized churches, including ultimately those of the General Baptists, and his enquiring mind and emphasis on the Spirit's immediacy were all marks of a Seeker outlook. He could probably be accommodated in the last of Baxter's six categories of Seeker, those who had 'over-grown the Scripture, Ministry and Ordinances' (McGregor and Reay, 126).

Writer's publications reveal his matured thought. He is said to have contributed to Richard Overton's *Mans Mortalitie* (1644), a provocative work which denied the immortality of the soul, a position which his own works subsequently substantiated. Mortalism is thus added to the long list of heresies of which Writer was suspected, the most serious being his liberal view of scripture and the nature of revelation. He was concerned over textual variations of the Bible, questioned Moses' authorship of the Pentateuch, recognized the Bible's openness to conflicting interpretation, and contended that the history of the canon raised difficult questions about inspiration. In the eyes of many this amounted to an attack on biblical infallibility. Such views would not have been approved by most General Baptists and this suggests that by the later 1640s he had moved away from the sect's theological position. Writer's doubts were raised in *The jus divinum of presbyterie* (1st edn, 1646) and *Fides divina: the ground of true faith asserted* (1655), and some of them were discussed at meetings with Baxter in 1653 and 1657. Writer maintained that Baxter had misrepresented him in *The Unreasonableness of Infidelity*, and eventually replied to his charges in 1658 in his *An Apologetical Narration, or, A Just and Necessary Vindication of Clement Writer*.

Writer's questions, however, substantial though they were, do not provide grounds for dismissing him as an 'anti-scripturist'. Despite his reservations, he did not reject outright the authority of scripture. Rather he believed that doctrine was necessary and should be based on 'Scripture and weight of sound reason' (Writer, *Jus divinum*, 1646, 18). The *Jus divinum* itself attempts to demonstrate 'by Scripture' the nature of true ministry, and both it and *Fides divina* repeatedly call on scripture for support. The *Apologetical Narration* displays a thorough knowledge of the biblical text and relies heavily upon it, identifying its author with radical contemporary eschatology. Writer's apparent ambivalence may be explained in part by his insistence on the Spirit's enlightenment. He commended Samuel How's *The Sufficiencie of the Spirit's Teaching without Human Learning* (1st edn, 1639), and insisted that scripture must be interpreted in light of the Spirit's primacy in the believer's personal experience. Thus he suspected learning, the religious establishment, particularly presbyterianism, and a formally trained ministry in which the individual call is not evidently endorsed by the Spirit: 'For the Ministry of the Gospel is a divine office, so it must necessarily be derived from a divine power, and bring with it suitable evidence' (Writer, *Jus divinum*, 1646, 53). This opposition to ecclesiastical structures and those who maintained them, in addition to his bold criticisms of the Bible, explains the antagonism he received from those who regarded themselves as defenders of orthodoxy. He was, in fact, far more typical of the radical sectarian and Seeker mentality than Edwards or Baxter, and others, have been prepared to allow.

By his will dated 2 August 1659 (proved in 1662), it appears that at the time of Writer's death he was comfortably placed with assets valued at several hundred pounds, including several houses, two mills, and adjoining lands in the city and county of Worcester. Most of his assets were distributed in small bequests to relatives and friends, notably to the children of his brother, Thomas Writer, and to various cousins, with a bequest of £20 to his friend William Walwyn. The will also made provision for sundry debtors, mostly tenants, to be excused their obligations and for the poor of Worcester and other adjoining localities to receive some relief, evidence perhaps that one Seeker, at least, had discovered the essence of true religion, a generous spirit. BRYAN W. BALL

Sources *CSP dom.*, 1627–9; 1631–3; 1635–6; 1656–7 • T. Edwards, *Gangraena, or, A catalogue and discovery of many of the errours, heresies, blasphemies and pernicious practices of the sectaries of this time*, 3 vols. in 1 (1646) • *Reliquiae Baxterianae, or, Mr Richard Baxter's narrative of the most memorable passages of his life and times*, ed. M. Sylvester, 1 vol. in 3 pts (1696) • C. Hill, *The world turned upside down: radical ideas during the English revolution* (1972); repr. (1975) • *DNB* • *Calendar of the correspondence of Richard Baxter*, ed. N. H. Keeble and G. F. Nuttall, 1 (1991), 1638–60 • C. Writer, *The sad case of Clement Writer* (1646) • [C. Writer], *An apologetical narration, or, A just and necessary vindication of Clement Writer, against a four-fold charge laid on him by Richard Baxter* (1658) • 'Writer, Clement', Greaves & Zaller, *BDBR*, 3.344–5 • D. Masson, *The life of Milton*, 3 (1873) • K. Lindley, *Popular politics and religion in civil war London* (1997) • will, PRO, PROB 11/307, sig. 30 • J. F. McGregor, 'Seekers and Ranters', *Radical religion in the English revolution*, ed. J. F. McGregor and B. Reay (1984), 121–40

Wealth at death assets valued at several hundred pounds, incl. several houses, two mills, and adjoining lands in and around Worcester: will, PRO, PROB 11/307, sig. 30

Writhe, John (*d.* 1504), herald, was probably the son of William Writhe, who represented the borough of Cricklade in the parliament of 1450–51 and was receiver to John Beaufort, duke of Somerset, and of Agnes, daughter of John Gibbes. After his death he was incorrectly named Wriothesley.

It is doubtful that Writhe was ever Antelope or Rouge Croix pursuivant under Henry V, as has been claimed, but by February 1474 he was certainly Falcon herald. On 25 January 1477 Edward IV made him Norroy king of arms and on 6 July 1478 promoted him to Garter king of arms. Writhe officiated at Edward's funeral in April 1483 and at Richard III's coronation the following July. Richard confirmed his appointment as Garter on 30 November 1483, though Writhe appears to have resigned from office for reasons unknown in January 1485. As Garter he took part in the coronation of Henry VII who reappointed him on 13 February 1486 with back pay to the date of Bosworth.

Writhe was the first Garter of the College of Arms,

incorporated in March 1484, but, contrary to popular belief, the college did not take its arms from Writhe. As Falcon and Garter he was employed on numerous diplomatic missions to Scotland and the continent, and at least once to Ireland. In July 1494 he was even threatened with imprisonment for denouncing in the streets of Malines Perkin Warbeck's claim to the English throne. An experienced armorist, Writhe collected and compiled many important armorial and genealogical manuscripts. His magnificent 'Garter book' must have entailed considerable historical research and contains many pedigrees, which he very probably wrote. In 1498 Henry VII granted him and Roger Machado, Clarenceux king of arms, a joint licence to make visitations.

Writhe may have lived in Red Cross Street, adjoining Barbican House in London. He was a citizen and draper of the city. He died in 1504 between 25 March (the date of his will) and 30 April (when it was proved) and was buried in St Giles Cripplegate. His son Thomas [*see* Wriothesley, Sir Thomas], who succeeded him as Garter and changed the family name to Wriothesley, styled him Sir John but there is no proof that he was knighted. He married first Barbara (*d.* 1480/1483), daughter and heir of John or Januarius (Janvier) Dunstanville (or Castlecombe), with whom he had the aforementioned Thomas (father of Charles *Wriothesley, Windsor herald), William, York herald (the father of Thomas *Wriothesley, first earl of Southampton), and two daughters, the elder of whom possibly married John Mynne, York herald. He married second Eleanor, daughter of Thomas and sister and heir of Richard Arnold, with whom he had a son and three daughters, and third Anne Mynne (possibly a relative of John Mynne, York herald), with whom he had two daughters. ADRIAN AILES

Sources J. Anstis, ed., *The register of the most noble order of the Garter*, 2 vols. (1724) • W. H. Godfrey, A. Wagner, and H. Stanford London, *The College of Arms, Queen Victoria Street* (1963) • A. Wagner, *Heralds of England: a history of the office and College of Arms* (1967) • M. Noble, *A history of the College of Arms* (1805) • A. R. Wagner, *A catalogue of English mediaeval rolls of arms*, Harleian Society, 100 (1950) • L. Campbell and F. Steer, *A catalogue of manuscripts in the College of Arms collections*, 1 (1988) • C. Wriothesley, *A chronicle of England during the reigns of the Tudors from AD 1485 to 1559*, ed. W. D. Hamilton, 1, CS, new ser., 11 (1875) • *Chancery records* • B. W. Greenfield, 'The Wriothesley tomb in Titchfield church', *Hants. Field Club, papers and proceedings* (1889), 65–82 • A. F. Sutton and P. W. Hammond, eds., *The coronation of Richard III: the extant documents* (New York, 1984) • J. Gairdner, *History of the life and reign of Richard the Third*, rev. edn (1898) • will, PRO, PROB 11/14 fols. 71–71v

Archives BL, Buccleuch MSS, Wrythe Garter book • BL, Add. MS 46354 • Coll. Arms, MS M10 | BL, Add. MS 37687E • Coll. Arms, MS L8a • Coll. Arms, Vincent MS 92, fols. 727–730, 744–746v • priv. coll., 'Wagner's roll' • V&A, MS L4362-1948 [pressmark PC 5/3]

Likenesses portrait, Coll. Arms; repro. in Prince Arthur's Book, 1524–1534?, Vincent MS 152, fol. 178

Wealth at death lands in Wiltshire, Chichester, and Middlesex; library and various gifts: will, PRO, PROB 11/14, fols. 71–71v

Wrixon-Becher. For this title name *see* O'Neill, Elizabeth [Elizabeth Wrixon-Becher, Lady Wrixon-Becher] (1791–1872).

Wroe, John (1782–1863), founder of the Christian Israelites, was the eldest son of Joseph Roe (or Wroe), who was probably the man who married Susannah Fernley in 1778. John was born in the Wroe farmstead in Rooley Lane, Bowling, Bradford, Yorkshire, on 19 September 1782, and baptized in Bradford parish church on 8 December. His name was sometimes Latinized to Joannes Roes by his followers. His education was minimal and to the end of his life he had difficulty in reading. His father, with whom he worked from an early age, was a farmer, a worsted manufacturer, and a collier. John claimed that he was badly treated as a child and that his hunchback was the consequence of having to carry 'a window stone to the second floor'.

Dissatisfied with the drudgery and dependence, Wroe eventually (about 1810) set up on his own in the farming and wool-combing business. On 22 April 1816 he married Mary (d. 1853), a daughter of Benjamin Appleby of Farnley Mills, near Leeds. Later that year he developed manic symptoms and planned to shoot his brother Joseph, who he felt had tricked him. Troubled with debts, he became feverish in 1819 and on his recovery started to read his Bible. Later in the year he began to have cataleptic trances during which he saw visions. Some of his neighbours began to regard him as a prophet and from 12 November, when Abraham Holmes was the first scribe, they began to write down Wroe's descriptions of his visions. His wife was more sceptical and had his head shaved on 1 February 1820, but to little effect. He now became associated with the followers of Joanna Southcott and particularly with their leader in the north of England, George Turner, though Wroe did not join the society, as he was led by his visions to seek to become a Jew. He walked to the synagogue at Liverpool where he was rebuffed by the rabbi, and then, with a similar intention, walked to London where, he claimed, he gave some of his visions and a letter of encouragement to Queen Caroline, who was returning from her trial on 30 August 1820.

Some Southcottians were impressed by the fulfilment of certain of Wroe's predictions, and a year after Turner's death in September 1821 several of the committees of the Southcottian societies recognized him as Turner's successor. Adopting a lone and charismatic identity, he now left his wife and three children and set out on a series of tours, first to the northern meetings of the movement but then, unexpectedly, in 1823, with another Southcottian, William Lees, to Spain, France, and the Habsburg empire as far as Milan, leaving messages in synagogues and churches. On his return to England in December 1823 he acquired a following among some of the Southcottians in Kent, but the most positive welcome given to him was in Lancashire, Cheshire, and the West Riding of Yorkshire. He himself returned to live in Bradford for a while, but he established his headquarters in Ashton under Lyne and later had a fine mansion there, on the banks of the River Tame, provided by some of his wealthier admirers.

The cohesion of his following was strengthened by a rapidly growing body of regulations and ritual which Wroe issued, usually based on the Pentateuch. Males were expected to let their beards grow and to wear a uniform consisting of a dark, broad-brimmed hat, a long, claret-coloured coat, and a silk waistcoat. Everyday conduct, from their vegetarian diet and abstinence from alcohol and tobacco to strict sabbath observance, marked out the Christian Israelites as a special community, who were divided by their leader into twelve tribes. In April 1824 Wroe was publicly circumcised and from then on the rite was required of his followers, causing an outcry in September 1824 when an infant died from the operation. Other important ceremonies in the life of the community were the baptisms or public cleansings which took place in the waters of the rivers Medlock (in Ashton) or Aire (in Bradford), with large crowds in attendance, and which were a form of public penance. Wroe himself was evidently a turbulent and impulsive character, giving way at different times to sexual self-indulgence. His remorse at these lapses is probably reflected in his insistence on being rebaptized on several occasions.

What attracted people to Wroe is not immediately apparent. He was physically unimpressive and his manners and lifestyle were not prepossessing. He would disappear and wander in the fields for days at a time eating only nuts and wild berries. He was far from eloquent—let alone literate—and his clothes and person were unkempt, but 'a certain John-the-Baptist-like roughness was not out of place in a true prophet' (Harrison, 140). Equally significantly he had influential and wealthy followers, such as the textile producers William and Edward Lees and the mine owner Samuel Swire, who later became mayor of Ashton. Another wealthy supporter, John Stanley, spent £9500 on the construction of the community's sumptuously furnished 'sanctuary' in Church Street, Ashton, which was opened on 25 December 1825. The unpopularity of Anglicanism and the restraints which a few years earlier had been imposed by landowners on the building of nonconformist chapels in this area, together with the social disruption of emergent industrialism, were other factors which contributed to Wroe's success. The community soon developed a colourful ritual and an elaborate hierarchy of priests and Levites serving under a high priest anointed with seven oils, but Wroe was not part of it. His role was that of a prophet. 'He stood or sat in his ordinary clothing in the outer court in the gallery. With his hat on his head, and his iron rod in his hand, he addressed the people from time to time' (ibid., 147).

In 1827 the Bradford magistrates acquitted Wroe on a charge of sexual misconduct with Martha Whitley, his twelve-year-old servant-girl, but in October 1830 further accusations were made—this time in the context of his own community—when three young women of the congregation confessed to sexual misbehaviour with him. Although the proceedings against him ended in a somewhat dubious acquittal, several of his followers now abandoned him, including the highly articulate and educated James Elishama Smith, whose account of Wroe is valuable as it is critical and yet surprisingly respectful. Smith, who was well aware of Wroe's shortcomings, describes him as a tyrant who was dreaded by his followers. 'But though they feared him, they confessed that his law was good, and made them better men' (Smith, 1.269). Even after his departure from the region Wroe retained a distinctive following in Ashton, where his adherents were popularly known as Joannas. At a later date both G. F. Muntz and Friedrich Engels were mistaken for his followers because of their beards.

In the face of considerable popular hostility, Wroe withdrew from Ashton in some style, on Easter Monday 1831, and soon made his new headquarters in Wrenthorpe near Wakefield. In 1842 his house was burgled and, as a result of false evidence, three innocent people were transported, though they were released five years later on the discovery of the real culprits. His wife, whom he had left long before, died on 16 May 1853. Wroe himself continued to travel widely, but whereas he had previously confined his journeys to the British Isles and continental Europe he now preached further afield. He paid four visits to North America, where he established a following, one of whom was Daniel Milton (formerly surnamed Trickey), who later established himself as Wroe's successor in Wakefield. In Australia, which he also visited four times, 'handsome Israelite sanctuaries arose in Sydney, Melbourne, Adelaide and elsewhere' (Balleine, 92). His English mansion, Melbourne House, near Wakefield, was provided by some of his Australian admirers and was dedicated in 1857 in the presence of followers from a variety of countries. On a final journey to Australia in 1862 he dislocated his shoulder. He died suddenly on 5 February 1863 at Collingwood, Melbourne. No portrait of him exists, as any such representation was regarded as a breach of the Decalogue. On his death his followers, who had expected his mansion to be left to them, were disappointed to find that it had been made over to members of Wroe's family.

TIMOTHY C. F. STUNT

Sources *The life and journal of John Wroe*, 2 vols. (1859–61) • J. F. C. Harrison, *The second coming: popular millenarianism, 1780–1850* (1979), 138–52 • J. E. Smith, *The coming man*, 2 vols. (1873) • G. R. Balleine, 'John Wroe, Judaizer', *Past finding out: the tragic story of Joanna Southcott and her successors* (1956), 83–93 • *AusDB* • W. Scruton, *Pen and pencil pictures of old Bradford* (1889) • W. Cudworth, *Histories of Bolton and Bowling (townships of Bradford) historically and topographically treated* (1892) • parish records (baptism), Bradford parish church, 8 Dec 1782 • *DNB*
Archives Tameside Archive Service, Stalybridge, copies of his sermons with related papers
Wealth at death under £2000: probate, 7 March 1864, *CGPLA Eng. & Wales*

Wroe, Richard (1641–1718), Church of England clergyman, the son of Richard Wroe (d. 1673), yeoman, and his wife, Grace (d. 1680), was born at Radcliffe, Lancashire, on 21 August 1641 and baptized there on 5 September. He was educated at Bury grammar school and Jesus College, Cambridge. Entered as a pensioner on 19 June 1658 and a scholar from 19 January 1660, he graduated BA in 1662 and was elected fellow on 23 July 1662. He proceeded MA in 1665, BD in 1672, and DD in 1686, and was incorporated MA of Oxford University in May 1669.

John Pearson, master of Jesus College in 1660–62 and later bishop of Chester (1673–86), greatly promoted Wroe's career. Ordained deacon on 14 June 1663 and priest on 12 March 1666, Wroe became vicar of Whittlesford,

Cambridgeshire, on 18 May 1671. He resigned this and his fellowship in 1674 when he moved back to the north-west. Having obtained in 1672 through the influence of Lord Delamere (afterwards earl of Warrington) a royal mandate for the next presentation, he was admitted to a fellowship of the college at Manchester on 9 March 1675. Bishop Pearson appointed him his domestic chaplain, presented him to the vicarage of Bowdon, Cheshire, on 24 June 1674, and on 15 March 1679 to a prebend in Chester Cathedral. He was curate of Wigan from 1679 to 1681. Wroe became warden of Manchester College, with Pearson's support and against some competition, being installed on 2 March 1684 and resigning Bowdon by November 1684. On 8 November 1684 he became vicar of Garstang, Lancashire, until replacing this benefice by the rectory of West Kirby, Cheshire, on 5 November 1696. On the death of Bishop Stratford of Chester in 1707, a friend suggested that Wroe should attempt to be his successor while continuing to be warden of Manchester College, but without effect.

William Hulme appointed Wroe one of the first trustees of the Hulmeian benefaction along with other whig churchmen, by his will in 1691. As rural dean of Manchester from 1695 Wroe rendered great assistance to Bishop Gastrell in the compilation of his 'Notitia Cestriensis', the bishop's compilation on the history and present state of his diocese and its parishes. He also investigated small benefices for augmentation from Queen Anne's Bounty. He acted as visitor of Manchester grammar school and feoffee of Chetham's Hospital and Library, supplying information on them for Bishop Edmund Gibson's translation of William Camden's *Britannia* (1695). He was a student of natural philosophy, experimenting on mercury, keeping a weather diary, and corresponding with his former pupil John Flamsteed.

Wroe married three times: first to Elizabeth, who died on 30 July 1689; second, on 22 June 1693, to Ann Radcliffe, *née* Eyre, who died the following January; and third, on 3 March 1698, to Dorothy Kenyon (d. 1729), daughter of Roger Kenyon of Peel. With Dorothy he had four sons, three of whom predeceased him.

During his wardenship Wroe had great influence in Manchester due to his high personal character, earnest piety, and persuasive eloquence, which earned him the titles of 'silver-tongued' and 'the Lancashire Chrysostom' (Clayton, 74). While zealously upholding the Church of England against Roman Catholics and dissenters, he escaped the ferocious party warfare endured by his successor Samuel Peploe, and was friendly with the presbyterian Henry Newcome and the nonjuror John Byrom. He evidently steered a judicious course through the political and religious conflicts of his time. Though preaching a sermon (not among the five he published) on 5 February 1687 which favoured James II and which pleased his diocesan Thomas Cartwright (a committed supporter of royal policies), Wroe has had the reputation of being a faithful whig. He encouraged his patron, the earl of Warrington, in opposition to the Stuarts. His correspondence with the tory Kenyons, before and after they became his in-laws, shows his interventions in local elections. As a JP for

Lancashire, Wroe provoked the criticism, 'Shepherd, attend to your flock and leave the huntsmen to look after the hounds' (Raines, 152). Wroe died at Deansgate, Manchester, on 1 January 1718 and was buried in the choir of the collegiate church five days later.

C. W. SUTTON, *rev.* HENRY D. RACK

Sources J. Clayton, 'Richard Wroe', *Transactions of the Lancashire and Cheshire Antiquarian Society*, 37 (1919), 67–90 • F. R. Raines, *The rectors of Manchester, and the wardens of the collegiate church of that town*, ed. [J. E. Bailey], 2 vols., Chetham Society, new ser., 5–6 (1885), 148–57 • [J. E. Bailey], 'Silver-tongued Wroe', *Palatine Note-Book*, 2 (1882), 1–7 • [J. E. Bailey], 'The sermons of Warden Wroe, 1682–1704', *Palatine Note-Book*, 2 (1882), 33–7 • *The manuscripts of Lord Kenyon*, HMC, 35 (1894), 229, 280, 282, 355, 378, 401, 413–15, 440, 451–3 • S. Hibbert and W. R. Whatton, *History of the foundations in Manchester of Christ's College, Chetham's Hospital and the free grammar school*, 4 vols. (1828–48), vol. 2, pp. 20–55 • H. Fishwick, *The history of the parish of Garstang in the county of Lancaster*, 2, Chetham Society, 105 (1879), 182–5

Likenesses Geikie of Edinburgh, engraving, pubd *c*.1824 (after Indian ink drawing) • W. Ford of Manchester, lithograph (after Indian ink drawing) • Indian ink drawing, priv. coll.; repro. in Bailey, 'Silver-tongued Wroe', 1; formerly at Plumpton Hall, 1919 • portrait; formerly in possession of Lord Kenyon, Peel Hall, Bolton, 1882

Wealth at death miscellaneous legacies of about £60; £1000 from income of estates to wife; residue to son; in 1697 income as warden was £166 13*s.* 4*d.*: will, Clayton, 'Richard Wroe'

Wrong, George Mackinnon (1860–1948), historian of Canada, was a descendant of English and Scottish families whose efforts to recreate British rural gentry in the unfavourable environments of Barbados, New York, New Brunswick, or Upper Canada petered out just after his birth, on 25 June 1860, at his grandfather's pioneer farm at Grovesend, Upper Canada, near Lake Erie. His bookish, fanciful father, Gilbert Wrong, his mother, Christian Mackinnon, and their many dependants moved a few miles eastward to Vienna, a village which was dwindling (with the forest industries) but possessed a good grammar school, where Wrong received his early education. He then worked for a time in a bookstore in Toronto, where he also converted from Methodism to evangelical Anglicanism.

At the age of nineteen Wrong enrolled in theology at the newly incorporated Wycliffe College, a low-church divinity school, and in 1880 in the arts course at University College in Toronto. By 1883 his energies and abilities had enabled him concurrently to complete his studies in divinity and to graduate with first-class honours in mental and moral philosophy. Although he entered holy orders and occasionally thereafter served and preached, he never held a parish but followed his scholarly bent as lecturer in ecclesiastical history and liturgics at Wycliffe and by vacation study in England and on the continent. He was actively involved in charity and social work, serving on the founding committee of the Toronto Mission Union and raising funds for various social Christian projects. In 1886 he married Sophia Hume (*d.* 1931), the daughter of (Dominick) Edward Blake, formerly prime minister of Ontario.

When Sir Daniel Wilson, president of Toronto University and professor of English literature and history at University College, died in 1892, Wrong applied for the chair, but was made lecturer only. Two years later he became the first professor of history at the University of Toronto. This appointment was attributed by some to nepotism by Wrong's father-in-law, who was chancellor of the university. A professor who made the charge in the press was dismissed, and his removal provoked a 'students' strike' in which W. L. Mackenzie King and Hamar Greenwood took a leading part. This and other university matters were investigated by royal commission in 1895, but Wrong was cleared of the accusation.

Wrong's chosen role was to prod Canadians into realization and emulation of the new historical scholarship of Germany, Great Britain, and the United States by founding the *Review of Historical Publications Relating to Canada*, which from 1897 to 1919 (and from 1920 as part of the quarterly *Canadian Historical Review*) annually listed or reviewed exactly every discoverable cogent item and made it unwise to publish uncritical history. Wrong managed to combine extensive study, writing, editorial work, public and academic responsibilities, and social activity in Canada, Great Britain, and the United States, perhaps because he rose daily at 5 a.m. Between 1894 and his retirement in 1927 he secured the recognition of history as a distinct discipline and created a separate department at Toronto, drawing heavily on Oxford for personnel and teaching methods.

More than any other person of his day, Wrong made English-speaking Canadians aware of sound history, an achievement which was signalized by honours at home and abroad. Shortly after 1900 he and others whom he had influenced directly or indirectly began to furnish good, readable textbooks of British and Canadian history which secured recognition in the primary and secondary schools. Co-operative scholarship provided higher education and serious readers with large series of biographical and historical monographs which incorporated the best available scholarship. Wrong's editorial assistance to the Canadian publisher Robert Glasgow in the *Chronicles of Canada* (32 vols., 1914–16) laid the foundations for Glasgow's later *Chronicles of America* (50 vols., 1918–21), to which Wrong contributed *The Conquest of New France* (1918) and *Washington and his Comrades in Arms* (1921). In 1905 he played a leading role in founding the Champlain Society, whose admirable editions of original or rare historical materials reflected his editorial hand for at least twenty years. He used his retirement after 1927 for writing some long-planned books until health and eyesight began to fail him about 1940. In particular *The Rise and Fall of New France* (2 vols., 1928) and *Canada and the American Revolution* (1935) are very attractive examples of his style. *A Canadian Manor and its Seigneurs* (1908), a charming product of research into the records of Murray Bay, was reprinted in 1926.

Wrong's publications were, however, rarely based on archival research, and he was critical of excessive specialization. He was particularly influenced by Lord Acton, from whom he drew the conclusion that, although the historian must be as impartial as possible, it was also his duty to draw moral judgements from the past that could be applied to the present. His studies of Canadian history focused on two major themes. A committed imperialist and one of the founders in 1909 of the Canadian branch of the Round Table, Wrong was concerned to document Canada's significance in the evolution of the Commonwealth. His other fascination was English–French relations in Canada. He drew heavily on Francis Parkman's work, but he did not share Parkman's disdain for the *ancien régime* in New France. None the less, in retrospect, there is little in Wrong's work that was original. That on French Canada was frequently patronizing and only slightly altered the standard interpretation of New France as an essentially conservative and backward society. As Carl Berger points out, even *Canada and the American Revolution*—perhaps Wrong's best-known work—'was anachronistic and derivative as a piece of historical scholarship' (Berger, 46). None of it is much read today.

Wrong's marriage to his first wife provided him with access to the Canadian social élite, and their children formed an unusual Anglo-Canadian group. Margaret Christian (1887–1948) became a leader in African education; Edward Murray (1889–1928) was fellow and tutor of Magdalen College, Oxford; Harold Verschoyle (1891–1916) was killed in action; Humphrey Hume (1894–1954), after teaching history at the University of Toronto, entered the Canadian department of external affairs in 1927 and subsequently held its highest posts at home and abroad; and Agnes Honoria (b. 1903) married C. H. A. Armstrong, QC, of Toronto. In 1933, following his first wife's death, Wrong married Elizabeth Burgwynne. She survived him when he died, about midnight, on 28 June 1948 in Toronto.

J. B. Brebner, rev. Phillip Buckner

Sources G. M. Wrong, *Chronicle of a family* (1938) [privately circulated] · W. S. Wallace, 'The life and work of George M. Wrong', *Canadian Historical Review* (Sept 1948) · C. Martin, 'Professor G. M. Wrong and history in Canada', *Essays in Canadian history presented to George Mackinnon Wrong*, ed. R. Flenley (1939) · personal knowledge (1959) · private information (1959) · C. Berger, *The writing of Canadian history: aspects of English–Canadian historical writing, 1900–1970* (1976)
Likenesses L. Swann, portrait, priv. coll. · E. Wyly Grier, portrait, University of Toronto

Wroth, Sir Henry (1604/5–1671). *See under* Wroth, Sir Robert (c.1539–1606).

Wroth [*née* Sidney], **Lady Mary** (1587?–1651/1653), author, was born on 18 October, probably in 1587, the eldest daughter and eldest surviving of eleven children of Robert *Sidney, first earl of Leicester and Viscount Lisle of Penshurst (1563–1626), poet and governor of Flushing, and Barbara *Sidney, *née* Gamage (c.1559–1621), a wealthy Welsh heiress and first cousin to Sir Walter Ralegh. Mary was niece to Sir Philip *Sidney and to Mary *Herbert, countess of Pembroke, for whom she was apparently named. She spent her girlhood at Penshurst, Baynard's Castle in London, and other estates owned by the Sidneys and the Herberts, with several extended stays at Wilton to visit her aunt Mary Herbert. She travelled with her

mother at least three times to Flushing. A letter from Robert Sidney suggests his special fondness, as he directs his wife to 'make much of little Mall' (*De L'Isle and Dudley MSS*, 2.100). According to reports to Robert Sidney by his steward Rowland Whyte, Lady Sidney took care that her children were 'well taught, and brought up in learning and qualities fit for their birth and condition', and Mary was particularly 'forward in learning, writing, and other excercises she is put to, as dawncing and the virginals' (ibid., 2.424, 176). Mary danced before Queen Elizabeth on a royal visit to Penshurst and again at court in 1602, to be 'much comended by her Majestie' (ibid., 2.618–19). A likeness of her as a girl appears in a group portrait of Lady Sidney and her children painted by Marcus Gheeraerts the younger in 1596, now on display at Penshurst. Josephine Roberts has tentatively identified Mary as the girl with an archlute in another Penshurst portrait; she and her mother may also be the subjects of a smaller painting at Penshurst (Roberts, introduction, *Poems*, 7).

Marriage and early widowhood On 27 September 1604 Mary married Sir Robert Wroth (c.1576–1614), who as eldest son of Sir Robert *Wroth (c.1539–1606) acquired the leasehold to Loughton Hall and the estate of Durrants in Enfield on his father's death in 1606. Beginning with difficulties over her father's payment of her dowry, various indications suggest that this marriage was not initially happy. In a letter to his wife in October 1604, Sidney relates a conversation with a discontented Sir Robert Wroth, who 'protests that hee cannot take any exceptions to his wife nor her cariage towards him' (*De L'Isle and Dudley MSS*, 3.140), and Ben Jonson later noted that 'my Lady wroth is unworthily maried on a Jealous husband' (*Ben Jonson*, 1.142). Near the end of his life, however, Wroth's will praised his 'deere and loving wife' for her 'sincere love, loyaltie, virtuous conversation, and behaviour' towards him (PRO, PROB 11/123/60).

The couple apparently had very different tastes. Robert Wroth was an avid huntsman, and a shared enthusiasm for the sport brought King James and his entourage to his estates several times during his marriage. The king stayed at Loughton Hall for two nights on a progress in July 1605. In 1606 Sir Robert assumed his father's offices of forester of Linton Walk, Waltham Forest, and keeper of Woodford Walk in Essex, where he was charged with protecting game and leading royal hunts. In 1605 Mary Wroth, along with several gentlewomen, young countesses, and Queen Anne, danced in *The Masque of Blackness*, designed by Ben Jonson and Inigo Jones, and then the *Masque of Beauty* (1608), in which her gracefulness was praised by an onlooker. In his *Conversations with Drummond* Jonson also refers to casting Wroth in his pastoral play, the *May Lord* (*Ben Jonson*, 1.143). These literary contacts developed into a friendship; Ben Jonson dedicated his play *The Alchemist* (1610) to Mary Wroth, as well as addressing to her two epigrams (*Ben Jonson*, 8.66–8) and a sonnet, in which he claimed that copying out her sonnets made him 'a better lover, and much better Poet' (*Ben Jonson*, 8.182). During her marriage, Mary Wroth was also praised by such writers as William Drummond, George Chapman, John Davies of

Hereford, George Wither, and Joshua Sylvester, some of whom refer to her literary activities as writer and patron. Shortly before 17 February 1614 Wroth gave birth to a son James 'after much longing' (*Letters of John Chamberlain*, 1.512). About a month later, on 14 March 1614, Robert Wroth died of gangrene 'in pudendis' leaving his estate burdened with a £23,000 debt. The subsequent death of her young son on 5 July 1616 left Mary Wroth with even more debt, for on the death of Robert Wroth's heir much of the remaining estate became the property of Robert's uncle John Wroth.

Evidence exists that at some time during her widowhood Mary Wroth gave birth to two children, apparently through a romantic involvement with her cousin William *Herbert, third earl of Pembroke (1580–1630). Described by Clarendon as 'immoderately given up to women' (Clarendon, *Hist. rebellion*, 1.73), Herbert's name was linked with various women before and after his marriage on 4 November 1604 to Lady Mary Talbot, daughter to the seventh earl of Shrewsbury. In 'Herbertorum Prosapia', a seventeenth-century manuscript compilation of the history of the Herbert family held at the Cardiff Library, a cousin of the earl of Pembroke named Sir Thomas Herbert records the earl's paternity of Wroth's two children:

> He had two naturall children by the Lady Mary Wroth the Earle of Leicesters Daughter, William who was a Captain under Sir Hen Herbert, Collonell under Grave Maurice, and dyed unmarried and Catherine the wife of Mr. Lovel neare Oxford.

Edward, Lord Herbert of Cherbury, was the author of a poem whose title alludes to Mary Wroth's child by the earl: 'A merry rime sent to the Lady *Wroth* upon the birth of my L. of *Pembroke's* child, born in the spring' (E. Herbert, *Occasional Verses*, 1665, 42). A letter from John Leeke to Sir Edmund Verney in 1640 refers to a 'curtuous and kinde letter' from his 'owld mistress, the Lady Mary Wroth', with news that 'by my Lord of Pembroke's good mediation the Kinge hath given hir sonne a brave livinge in Ireland' (*Seventh Report*, HMC, 434b–435); by 1640 this title of lord of Pembroke was held by Philip Herbert, rather than by his brother William, who had died in 1630. According to Thomas Herbert's report, Wroth's son later fought in the English civil war on the royalist side under Prince Maurice, nephew to Charles I. Less is known of Katherine, but something may be deduced from a will by one Judith Fox, dated 12 March 1636; naming her 'noble and best friend' Mary Wroth as her executor, Judith Fox bequeathed £10 to 'the honourable Master William Harbert' (PRO, PROB 11/174). As Roberts has argued, the terms of this will suggest that Katherine was born at some time after 1619 (Roberts, introduction, *Urania*, lxxv). In 1636 Katherine was apparently not yet seventeen, for Fox requests that if Wroth dies before Fox's will is to be executed, the responsibility should then fall to 'my deere friend Mistress Katherine Herbert her heire or Assigner and theis six men above named to bee her guardians' (PRO, PROB 11/174).

Urania Mary Wroth's alleged relationship with William Herbert and her children born from that union assume literary significance in the dense topicality of *The Countess of Montgomery's Urania*, the first extant romance written by an Englishwoman. Named for her relative and neighbour Susan Vere, wife of Philip Herbert, then earl of Montgomery, the complete *Urania* consists of a folio published in 1621 and an unpublished manuscript continuation in the author's holograph, currently in the collections of the Newberry Library, Chicago. The diffuse plot of the *Urania*, filled with hundreds of characters, is loosely organized around the narrative of Pamphilia's constant love for the unfaithful Amphilanthus. Pamphilia writes poetry expressing her love, and she confides in her friend Urania. She also assumes her uncle's throne to become queen of Pamphilia. Involved in various enchantments, she rescues her friend Urania from the Tower of Love; together the friends are later confined in a magical theatre. She suffers from the infidelities of Amphilanthus, whom she believes she sees imprisoned in a burning hell of deceit.

In the manuscript continuation Pamphilia and Amphilanthus exchange vows before five witnesses in a *de praesenti* marriage. Amphilanthus then marries, but does not consummate his marriage, with the daughter of the king of Slavonia, while Pamphilia marries Rodomandro, king of Tartaria. Moving into the narratives of the next generation, the manuscript continuation introduces a mysterious young knight, Fair Designe, named for the cipher on his armour, and the text hints strongly that Amphilanthus is his unknown father.

Josephine Roberts has observed that in the *Urania*, Wroth seems to 'narrate herself in the conditional or subjunctive mode, as she could have, should have, or might have been' (Roberts, 'Knott', 126). For this reason events such as the *de praesenti* marriage between Pamphilia and Amphilanthus may not correspond to any actual occurrences. Moreover, one-to-one correspondences sometimes break down; and often situations or events become refracted into numerous narratives, so that not only Pamphilia, but Bellamira and Lindamira as well, resemble Wroth in some details of her personal life. Still, most scholars would agree that the autobiographical references of this plot are inescapable. Anagrams of the names of her husband, father, and siblings point to topical referents within the text.

In a contemporary and extremely critical poem, 'To Pamphilia from the Father-in-Law of Seralius', Lord Denny, baron of Waltham, treats the character Pamphilia as a direct referent to Mary Wroth. His assumption seems warranted, for Wroth composed a spirited reply, 'Railing Rimes Returned upon the Author'. The first-cousin kinship between Pamphilia and Amphilanthus suggests a topical connection between Amphilanthus and Wroth's first cousin William Herbert. As a further cue, in the manuscript continuation Amphilanthus recites a poem of his own composition, 'Had I loved butt att that rate', which can be dependably ascribed to William Herbert (Roberts, introduction, *Poems*, 44). In this context, Fair Designe would seem to allude to Mary Wroth's son William.

While many topical referents have been lost to modern

readers, the *Urania*'s scandalous topicality aroused strong responses at the time. In his poem Lord Denny strenuously objected to Wroth's sensationalist representation of an incident apparently occurring in his own family, in a narrative in which a husband, Sirelius, intervenes to save his wife's life from her father, who accuses her of adultery. The *Urania* represented other scandals as well, including perhaps the sexual relationship between John Carr, earl of Somerset, and Sir Thomas Overbury. John Chamberlain describes a contemporary perception of Wroth as taking 'great libertie or rather licence to traduce whom she please, and thincks she daunces in a net' (*Letters of John Chamberlain*, 2.427). On 15 December 1621, apparently in response to public outrage, Mary Wroth requested the duke of Buckingham to procure a warrant from the king to enable her to gather in any books that had already been sold because of the 'strang constructions which are made of my booke', that were 'as farr from my meaning as is possible' (Bodl. Oxf., MS Add. D.111, fol. 173r–v). The truth of her claim in this letter that she had never intended publication of the *Urania* is difficult to ascertain. Entered in the Stationers' register on 13 July 1621 by publishers John Marriott and John Grismand, the *Urania* lacked the usual prefatory materials, such as commendations by friends and an author's dedication or letter to readers. These were apparently expected but never arrived, for sig. B, which begins the text, directly follows an elaborately drawn frontispiece engraved by Simon van de Passe. While variants indicate a large number of stop-press corrections, there is no evidence for authorial reading of proofs. Wroth did take an interest in the printed folio, however, for a copy now owned by Dr Charlotte Kohler contains extensive corrections in Wroth's hand.

While both the published folio and the manuscript continuation of the *Urania* show the influence of Sir Philip Sidney's *The Countess of Pembroke's Arcadia* in, for example, their mid-sentence endings, few critics agree with Sidney Lee that the *Urania* is a 'close imitation' of her uncle's romance (*DNB*). Roberts has convincingly argued for Wroth's use of other works, such as Spenser's *Faerie Queene* and the *Amadis de Gaule*, as well as of various political, social, and personal contexts (Roberts, introduction, *Urania*, xxviii–xxix). As the *Urania*'s topical allusions suggest, these extra-literary influences played a vital role. Described by Schleiner as a 'coded combination of reportage, gossip, and witty commentary' (L. Schleiner, *Tudor and Stuart Women Writers*, 1994, 157), the *Urania* demonstrates 'a new engagement with the minutiae of contemporary life' (P. Salzman, *English Prose Fiction, 1558–1700*, 1985, 141). With the importance of such figures as William Herbert, earl of Pembroke, in the Jacobean court, such minutiae hold political as well as personal significance.

Once inciting such critics as Sidney Lee to judge its narratives as 'tedious' as well as 'extraordinarily long-winded and awkward' (*DNB*), the diffuse aesthetic of the *Urania* has become increasingly valued as a strength. Freely adapting a traditional romance form to accommodate the experience and perceptions of a Jacobean woman, the

Urania has proven itself as a valuable text for feminist readings of early modern society. The increasing seriousness of scholarly attention to the *Urania* is due in part to the recent accessibility of the 1621 folio with Roberts's 1995 edition and with the edition of the manuscript continuation, begun by Roberts and completed after her death by Janel Mueller and Suzanne Gossett.

Sonnets and 'Love's Victory' Wroth was also the first known Englishwoman to write a sonnet sequence. As Jonson's claim to copy or to 'exscribe' one of her sonnets indicates, these poems were first circulated in manuscript among her private friends. Her sequence 'Pamphilia to Amphilanthus' exists in two different arrangements: a holograph manuscript of 117 sonnets and songs now held at the Folger Shakespeare Library, Washington, DC, and a version composed of 103 sonnets and songs originally appended to the folio of the *Urania* published in 1621. Continuing the theme of Pamphilia's constant love for Amphilanthus, the sequence opens with a dream vision in which Venus, accompanied on her chariot by Cupid, places a lover's burning heart in Pamphilia's breast. In its lyric complaints of longing and unrequited love, this sequence recalls an older literary fashion developed around Petrarch's *Canzoniere* which Wroth, however, transforms in her inversion of the genders of poet and beloved. Following the example of her uncle Philip Sidney and her father, Wroth includes a corona of sonnets, with the first line of each sonnet linked to the last line of the previous one. Beginning and ending with the line 'In this strang labourinth how shall I turne?', Wroth's corona achieves a moving evocation of psychic entrapment. Characterized by a melancholy tone, the sequence includes frequent apostrophes to such personified figures as Night, Sleep, Time, Stars, and Love. Notable individual lyrics include 'Like to the Indians, scorched with the sunne', recalling her role in Jonson's *Masque of Blackness*, and 'Faulce hope which feeds butt to destroy', which develops an image of miscarriage. The last sonnet, 'My muse now happy, lay thy self to rest', leaves the 'discource of Venus, and her sunn' to 'young beeginers'.

First edited in 1988 by M. G. Brennan, Mary Wroth's 'Love's Victory' exists in two holograph manuscripts, a complete version at Penshurst Place and an incomplete version at the Huntington Library, California. This tragicomedy in five acts was identified as written by Wroth by Peter J. Croft, who recognized her hand in the Penshurst manuscript. 'Love's Victory' explores four very different forms of love, each demonstrating the power of Venus and her son Cupid, through the relationships of four couples: Philisses and Musella, who love virtuously; Lissius and Simeana, who struggle with pride and jealousy; Silvesta, who loves a Forester but chooses to remain chaste; and an earthy Rustic and Dalina, who enjoy sensuous pleasures and especially lust. The strong resemblance of this plot, with its eight characters, to an episode in the manuscript continuation of the *Urania* suggests that it represented Wroth's attempt to treat similar material in two genres. The play seems to have been written for amateur acting of the kind performed in private houses as represented in two entertainments in the manuscript continuation of the *Urania*. While there is no record of any performance of 'Love's Victory', it may have been acted in the house of Sir Edward Dering. A relative of Mary Wroth by marriage, Dering owned a version of 'Love's Victory' in his extensive collection of plays, and sometimes gathered friends and relatives to perform plays at his house in Kent.

In addition to her extensive literary activities, Wroth maintained several close friendships in her widowhood, among them that with Susan Vere, countess of Montgomery, her neighbour and relative by marriage. Wroth visited her Sidney relatives at Penshurst, where she informed Lady Anne Clifford of 'a great deal of news from beyond the sea' (*Diaries of Lady Anne Clifford*, 61). Rumours circulated of a prospective marriage with Henry de Vere, eighteenth earl of Oxford. Wroth entertained Dudley Carleton, ambassador to The Hague, at her residence at Loughton about 1619, and her correspondence refers to some 'rude lines' she had presented to him (*CSP dom.*, *1619–23*, 40). In 1619 she walked in the official funeral procession at Queen Anne's death.

Much of Mary Wroth's widowhood was, however, occupied with her substantial debt. She sued for various protections against collection of debts in 1623, 1624, 1627, and 1628. In 1623 and 1624 she wrote letters addressed from Loughton, and a reference in 1630 describes Loughton as 'nowe in the occupaccion of the Lady Wroth' (chancery forest roll, no. 153, 21 Sept 1630). In 1643 she was living in Woodford, where she paid taxes in 1646 and 1648; and in 1645 she was also listed as owning property in East Wickham (parish book of Woodford, 26 April 1646, 8 Jan 1648, cited in Roberts, introduction, *Poems*, 39–40; *CSP dom.*, *addenda*, *1625–69*, 675). Beyond these references, little is known of the last decades of her life. A note in a chancery deposition of 1668 states that she died in 1651 or 1653 (*Chancery Proceedings before 1714*, 110, Whittington, PRO C10, 110/89, cited in Roberts, introduction, *Poems*, 40). The cause and place of her death are unknown.

MARY ELLEN LAMB

Sources *Report on the manuscripts of Lord De L'Isle and Dudley*, 6 vols., HMC, 77 (1925–66) • *The letters of John Chamberlain*, ed. N. E. McClure, 2 vols. (1939) • *Ben Jonson*, ed. C. H. Herford, P. Simpson, and E. M. Simpson, 11 vols. (1925–52) • J. Nichols, *The progresses, processions, and magnificent festivities of King James I, his royal consort, family and court*, 4 vols. (1828) • J. Roberts, introduction, in M. Wroth, *The first part of the countess of Montgomery's Urania* (1995) • J. Roberts, introduction, *The poems of Lady Mary Wroth* (1983) • W. R. Fisher, *The forest of Essex* (1887) • W. C. Waller, 'An extinct county family: Wroth of Loughton Hall', *Transactions of the Essex Archaeological Society*, new ser., 8 (1900–03), 145–81, esp. 156–80 • *CSP dom.*, *1603–25* • *Letters and epigrams of Sir John Harington*, ed. N. E. McClure (1930) • *The diaries of Lady Anne Clifford*, ed. D. J. H. Clifford (1990) • Clarendon, *Hist. rebellion* • *Seventh report*, HMC, 6 (1879) • T. Herbert, 'Herbertorum Prosapia', Cardiff Central Library, Phillipps MS 5.7, p. 92 • M. Brennan, introduction, in M. Wroth, *Love's victory: the Penshurst manuscript* (1988) • J. Roberts, 'The knott never to bee untide: the controversy regarding marriage in Mary Wroth's *Urania*', *Reading Mary Wroth*, ed. N. Miller and G. Waller (1991), 109–32 • J. Orrell, 'Antimo Galli's description of *A masque of beauty*', *Huntington Library Quarterly*, 43 (1979–80), 13–23
Archives Bodl. Oxf., holograph MS of letter to duke of Buckingham, Add. MS D.111, fol. 173r–v
Likenesses M. Gheeraerts the younger, group portrait, oils, 1596, Penshurst Place, Kent • attrib. J. de Critz senior, oils, c.1620, Penshurst Place, Kent • M. Gheeraerts the younger, oils, c.1620, Penshurst Place, Kent

Wroth, (Charles) Peter (1929–1991), civil engineer and soil mechanic, was born on 2 June 1929 at Alndyke, Russells Crescent, Horley, Surrey, the son of Charles Wroth, physician, and his wife, Violet Beynon Jenour. He was educated at Marlborough College and, after national service in the Royal Artillery, went to Emmanuel College, Cambridge, where he read mathematics and mechanical sciences.

After a brief spell of teaching at Felsted School, Wroth returned to Cambridge, as a research student, in 1954. He married on 11 December of that year Mary Parlane Weller (1927–1988), daughter of Christopher Harold Weller, a minister of religion. His Cambridge supervisor was the charismatic Ken Roscoe, who was building up a group working in soil mechanics, a branch of civil engineering. Roscoe's group was bringing a new scientific rigour to the subject, and Wroth's doctoral research, which involved both laboratory tests and theory, was central to this programme. On completing his research he joined the civil engineering consultants G. Maunsell & Partners, where he worked on the design and construction of the innovative pre-stressed concrete flyover at Hammersmith, in west London. He returned to Cambridge as a lecturer in 1961 and soon became a fellow of Churchill College. As tutor for advanced students at Churchill he had responsibility for graduates there, a role he clearly relished. The following years were busy with teaching and research, and with family life, which now included twin daughters, Rachel and Helen, and two sons, Richard and Christopher.

The book that Wroth co-authored with Andrew Schofield, *Critical State Soil Mechanics* (1968), represented a fundamental change in the approach to the subject, one that many readers found hard to grasp. Gradually, however, the ideas became established, and now form the core understanding of how soils behave as engineering materials. Much of this acceptance was due to Wroth's clear exposition of the subject in lectures and courses. His lecturing style was a model of precision, often supported by multi-coloured diagrams neatly drawn on the overhead projector during his talk.

In 1970 Roscoe died in a car crash, and Wroth stepped in to lead the soil mechanics group. The professorship, however, went to his friend and rival Schofield, who was at that time at Manchester. With Wroth and Schofield both at the peak of their careers the Cambridge soil mechanics group went from strength to strength, carrying out first-class experimental and theoretical work. It was at this time that Wroth developed the 'self-boring pressuremeter', an ingenious device for measuring the properties of soils. One of its attractions for him was that it offered scope for elegant analyses that could be used to convert measured data to useful soil properties. He travelled widely, taking his sabbatical leave at Cornell and Duke universities in the USA, and establishing links with a number of groups worldwide, especially in Australia.

In 1979 Wroth moved to Oxford University, as professor of engineering science and fellow of Brasenose College. For the next ten years, as head of the department of engineering science, he developed it as a broad-based engineering school. During his tenure the department expanded enormously in terms of buildings, staff, and students. At the same time he built up a substantial research group in soil mechanics and played a central role in the geotechnical community in the UK and internationally, as chairman of the British Geotechnical Society, editor of the academic journal *Géotechnique*, and, in 1984, as the Rankine lecturer. Although a busy man he was particularly generous with the support that he gave to his students and junior colleagues, whom he encouraged to develop their own careers by participating at conferences and meeting the leading academics in the field. He was a talented sportsman; at hockey he was a Cambridge blue, and he went on to captain Wales for several seasons. He had played for the Cambridge second cricket eleven, and enjoyed his golf. He had a lifelong enthusiasm for the more esoteric sport of real tennis, no doubt because it offered an intellectual as well as a physical challenge.

Following the protracted illness and death from cancer of his wife, Mary, in 1988, Wroth married on 8 July 1989 Rachel Anne (b. 1943), daughter of the retired professor Denis King Britton and herself a fellow of St Catharine's College, Cambridge. The following year they spent principally on sabbatical leave in Australia and New Zealand. During this time Wroth was elected master of Emmanuel, his old undergraduate college. He took up the mastership in Michaelmas term 1990, but his return to Cambridge was all too brief. He became unwell in mid-December, suffering from myeloma. The cancer developed very rapidly, and he died at Addenbrooke's Hospital, Cambridge, on 3 February 1991. His wife survived him.   GUY HOULSBY

Sources *The Times* (5 Feb 1991) · *Daily Telegraph* (7 Feb 1991) · *The Guardian* (5 Feb 1991) · *Emmanuel College Cambridge Magazine*, 22 (1989–90), 4–9 · G. Milligan, *The Independent* (6 Feb 1991) · *Oxford Today* (1991?) · *International Society for Soil Mechanics and Foundation Engineering News*, 18/2 (April 1991) · *WWW* · *People of today* (1991), 2022 · personal knowledge (2004) · b. cert. · m. certs. · d. cert.
Likenesses photographs, U. Oxf., department of engineering science · photographs, Emmanuel College, Cambridge

Wroth, Sir Robert (c.1539–1606), landowner and politician, was the first of seven sons of Sir Thomas *Wroth (1518?–1573), courtier, of Durants, Enfield, Middlesex, and his wife, Mary (d. in or after 1573), third daughter of Richard *Rich, first Baron Rich (1496/7–1567), lord chancellor of England, and his wife, Elizabeth. His brothers included Richard (d. 1596), Thomas (d. 1610), and John Wroth (d. in or after 1616). Sir Thomas Wroth was one of the four principal gentlemen of the privy chamber to Edward VI and the family was closely tied to the protestant regime, forcing it to flee first to Italy in 1554 and then the following year to Strasbourg. Wroth returned to England in 1559 but preferred to live quietly on his estates until his death on 9 October 1573.

Robert Wroth matriculated *impubes* as a pensioner from St John's College, Cambridge, on 29 September 1552, and was admitted to Gray's Inn in 1559. He was a JP for Middlesex from about 1573 and of the quorum for Middlesex and for Essex from about 1579. He married Susan (d. in or after 1606), daughter and heir of John Stonard (d. 1579), of Loughton, Essex, by 1576. The couple had at least four sons, including: Robert Wroth (c.1576–1614), who married Mary *Wroth, *née* Sidney (1587?–1651/1653), the author, in 1604; and Henry Wroth (c.1578–1652×6), whose second son was Sir Henry Wroth [see below]. Stonard transferred the lease of his Loughton estate to Wroth in 1578 for £1100 and it became Wroth's principal residence. His wife and he inherited Stonard's property in 1579. In 1602 Wroth tried unsuccessfully to purchase Loughton from the duchy of Lancaster, promising that he would repair it for Elizabeth I to visit. She never did, but James I visited Wroth there in August 1605, staying for three nights.

In August 1579 Wroth received a life grant of the keepership of Chingford Walk, the New Lodge, and other offices in Waltham Forest, Essex, and was subsequently made riding forester (1597) and walker of the forest (1603). He was sheriff of Essex from 1587 to 1588. He was also one of the men chosen to muster and train the militia in Middlesex during preparations against the Spanish Armada in 1588, and continued to carry out military duties during the 1590s. Wroth was knighted in 1597. He was elected to parliament for St Albans in 1563, Bossiney in 1571, and Middlesex in 1572, 1584, 1586, 1589, 1593, 1597, 1601, and 1604. He was an extremely active MP, sitting on many committees, initially for local affairs but then of national importance, including one on the liberties and privileges of the House of Commons (28 May 1571), speaking with growing confidence on a broad range of interests and managing the passage of a wide variety of bills. In February and March 1587 he supported increased taxes to pay for the war with Spain, was a moderate voice in heated debates over, for example, James Morice's bills and the reintroduction of the 1581 anti-Catholic bill in February and March 1593, and participated vigorously during the debate on the monopolies in November 1601. He has been called one of the 'chief architects' of the Elizabethan poor law, but also supported private bills for more personal interests. He was a moderate but firm protestant, and assisted Richard Rogers, a contentious reformed preacher, to regain a lectureship from which he had been suspended for refusing to subscribe to the articles of 1583 of John Whitgift, archbishop of Canterbury.

Wroth entertained often at Loughton, tempting visitors, in particular his friend Sir Michael Hicks, secretary to William Cecil, Baron Burghley, with hunting parties and promises of oyster feasts. Hicks and Wroth shared a love of hunting and devotion to puritanism, and Hicks often visited Loughton. During the 1604 parliament Wroth spoke out against wardship, purveyance and monopolies, and the Catholic penal statutes on 23 March. However, he was a client from 1598 to 1606 of Robert Cecil, first earl of Salisbury, the principal secretary, making the issue of his motives in parliament during these years more complicated. He probably acted with Salisbury's agreement as part of a government programme to remove aspects of fiscal feudalism in return for parliamentary taxation. Wroth died on 27 January 1606 and was buried at Enfield the following day. His funeral service took place on 3 March.

Sir Henry Wroth (1604/5–1671), royalist army officer, was born in 1604 or 1605, the second son of Henry Wroth (c.1578–1652x6), landowner, and his wife, Jane (d. 1653), daughter of Sir Thomas Harris of Maldon, Essex. His father was a gentleman pensioner to James I and his elder brother, John Wroth (d. in or after 1660), inherited Loughton, while he inherited Durants. Henry Wroth is reputed to have been a staunch royalist who followed Charles I to Oxford. The king knighted him at Hereford on 15 or 16 September 1645. Little is known about his life during the interregnum but Thomas Fuller claimed he signed the royalist declaration in May 1660 and was to be made a knight of the Royal Oak after the Restoration. By 1653, Wroth married Anne (1632–1677), daughter of William Maynard, first Baron Maynard of Wicklow, and his second wife, Anne. The couple's second daughter, Jane (bap. 1659, d. 1703), was a maid of honour to Mary, princess of Orange, and married William Frederick van *Nassau van Zuylestein, later first earl of Rochford.

Wroth's strengths lay in military and local affairs: commissions were issued in the 1660s for his troop and in July 1666 he was involved in impressing men for military service. In 1664 he escorted Colonel John Hutchinson from the Tower of London on his transfer to Sandown Castle, Kent, and on finding him unable to ride, hired a guard to take him by water. On 23 October 1667 Thomas Armstrong took command of Wroth's former troop. Wroth was also trusted with special local affairs: in 1664, he examined a man regarding a muster of 'old Oliver's boys' at Ely, and in June 1666 Frances Manley advised Henry Bennet, first earl of Arlington, to alert him regarding rebels hiding in Enfield Chase. The following year Wroth, as JP for Middlesex, took information on a possible secret meeting in Enfield.

Wroth was a patron of the noted church historian Fuller, who became his friend while perpetual curate of Waltham Abbey. Fuller dedicated part of his church history to Wroth, due to Sir Thomas Wroth's association with Edward VI, and flight from England in the cause of English protestantism. Fuller mentions the sable wings added to the Wroth coat of arms as an allusion to that flight. Wroth's arms are displayed, along with those of other patrons and contributors, at the front of Fuller's *Pisgah-Sight of Palestine* (1650). Wroth died at home on 22 September 1671, and was buried at Enfield on the 26th.   L. L. FORD

Sources CPR, 1558–82 • CSP dom., 1625–49; 1660–85 • T. Fuller, *The church history of Britain*, ed. J. S. Brewer, new edn, 6 vols. (1845), vol. 4, pp. 213–14, 228 • GEC, *Peerage* • *Report on the manuscripts of his grace the duke of Buccleuch and Queensberry … preserved at Montagu House*, 3 vols. in 4, HMC, 45 (1899–1926), vol. 3, pp. 80–82 • HoP, *Commons, 1558–1603*, 3.658–65 • W. Hunt, 'The puritan moment: the coming of revolution in an English county', MA diss., U. Cam., 1993, 66, 79–80, 104, 255 • J. C. Jeaffreson and W. J. Hardy, eds., *Middlesex county records*, 6 vols., Middlesex County RS (1886–92), 2.148, 206–7 • A. G. R. Smith, *Servant of the Cecils: the life of Sir Michael Hickes, 1543–1612* (1977) • N. Tyacke, 'Wroth, Cecil and the parliamentary session of 1604', BIHR, 50 (1977), 120–25 • Venn, *Alum. Cant.* • *VCH Middlesex*, 2.41 • W. C. Waller, 'An extinct county family: Wroth of Loughton Hall', *Transactions of the Essex Archaeological Society*, new ser., 8 (1900–03), 145–81

Wroth, Sir Thomas (1518?–1573), courtier and landowner, was the son of Robert Wroth (1488/9–1535), a wealthy landowner in the home counties and Somerset who served as attorney-general of the duchy of Lancaster from 1531 until his death, and his wife, Jane, daughter of Sir Thomas Haute of Kent and widow of Thomas Goodere of Hadley, Hertfordshire. Their seat at Durants in Enfield, Middlesex, had been in the hands of the Wroths since the fifteenth century.

Since Thomas Wroth was not yet of age at the time of his father's death his wardship was held by the king; in 1536 it was granted to Thomas Cromwell, who had been a friend of his father. After a proposed marriage to a daughter of Sir Brian Tuke failed to materialize Cromwell sold his ward's marriage to Sir Richard Rich for 300 marks, and in 1538 Wroth wed Rich's third daughter, Mary. Their large family came to include seven sons and seven daughters. Thomas was educated at St John's College, Cambridge, which he left without a degree, and Gray's Inn, which he entered in 1536. He was granted livery of his lands in 1540, and Rich was instrumental in securing for him additional properties, including the manor of Highbury, forfeited by Cromwell at his fall, and lands in Hertfordshire and Middlesex which had belonged to dissolved monasteries. In 1542 he was named bailiff of the manor of Ware, Hertfordshire, which had belonged to Margaret Pole, countess of Salisbury, before her attainder. In 1545 he was listed as providing 100 men to serve in Henry VIII's military campaign against France.

Wroth's involvement in government affairs reached its peak under Edward VI. He had been one of the prince's gentleman ushers since 1541. At the time of Edward's accession he was knighted and named a gentleman of the privy chamber, and following Protector Somerset's fall in 1549 he was designated one of the four principal gentleman of the chamber, two of whom were to be in attendance at all times. His colleagues were Sir Edward Rogers, Sir Thomas Darcy, and Sir Andrew Dudley, all experienced military men; the group was later enlarged to include Sir Henry Sidney and Sir Henry Neville. These companions were charged with 'the singular care' of the king and were rewarded with a stipend of £100 a year (APC, 1547–50, 344–5). Wroth had been a member of the parliament of 1545, sitting for Middlesex, and he also sat in Edward's parliaments of 1547 and 1553. In autumn 1547 he was sent to the Scottish borders to congratulate Somerset on his victory at Pinkie, and two years later he was appointed standard-bearer during the minority of Sir Anthony Browne. He was a member of the important commission which recommended a reorganization of financial administration, implemented in part under Mary Tudor, and was named to commissions for the recovery of crown debts and the enforcement of penal laws. He served with Sir

William Paget as joint lord lieutenant of Middlesex from 1551 to 1553. In 1552 he was granted a lease of Sion House, the great former nunnery, and was one of the adventurers in a trading voyage to Morocco. A riot which occurred at Enfield in the summer of 1548 was evidently directed against Wroth's property there, but it was settled when it was discovered that the issues in dispute had already been resolved by a decree of the duchy of Lancaster. Four of the rioters were briefly committed to prison, and six more were bound over to be of good behaviour. In November 1551 he attended a disputation on the nature of the eucharist, held at Sir William Cecil's home prior to the introduction of the prayer book of 1552.

Wroth was with Edward VI when the young king died. A committed evangelical—it has been plausibly suggested that he owed his appointments at court to Archbishop Cranmer's influence—he had signed the letters patent devising the crown to Lady Jane Grey, but like a number of his fellow courtiers he joined in proclaiming Princess Mary as queen once her accession became inevitable. Nevertheless he was sent to the Tower late in July 1553, but he was not detained long and was included in the general pardon issued in October. But having been charged with complicity in the rising of Henry Grey, duke of Suffolk, early in 1554, he fled overseas, living at first in Italy and after 1555 among the Marian exiles at Strasbourg. In 1556 he succeeded in evading a messenger sent from England to recall him.

Upon hearing of Elizabeth's accession Wroth returned to England. He was again elected to the Commons in the parliaments of 1559 and 1563 as one of the knights of the shire for Middlesex. He was one of the commissioners sent to visit the dioceses of Ely and Norwich in 1559. In 1562 he was named to a special commission to consult with the lord deputy of Ireland on the government of that realm; after some delay he spent the period between February and August 1564 in Dublin. In 1569 he was a commissioner for musters in Middlesex, and in 1571 he helped to inventory the fourth duke of Norfolk's goods in the Charterhouse. Despite these services he did not achieve the prominence in Elizabethan government that he and some other exiles seem to have expected. His primary role was now that of country gentleman and landowner rather than courtier. While an exile in Strasbourg he had made friends with Edmund Grindal, whom in 1570 he entertained at Durants. Later that year he was appointed to a commission to investigate dilapidations at York, where Grindal had just become archbishop.

Wroth's long will was signed on 5 October 1573 (PRO, PROB 11/57, fols. 124v–129r). Its protestant preamble declares his desire to 'enjoye the benefites of Christes Death', and his confidence that 'myne evill Deedes which Deserved hell' will be 'washed awaie by his blessed blound shedding'. His eldest son, Robert *Wroth, was granted several manors in Essex, including Chigwell, but his wife, Mary, was to enjoy the bulk of his property, as well as the estate at Enfield, for the remainder of her life. Provision was made for all his children, including his younger sons, Richard, Thomas (d. 1610), later father of Thomas *Wroth

(1584–1672), Edward, John, Gerson, and Peter; his married daughters, Mabel, wife of Richard Hardres, Judith, wife of Robert Burgoyne, and Winifred, wife of Thomas Goddard; and his unmarried daughters, Elizabeth, Anne, Marie, and Frances. There was also a bequest to his sister Anne, wife of Sir George Penruddock. Wroth's son Edward, who was bound apprentice to a London mercer, was to receive £300 'to gett his Lyvinge by marchyndize'. Lands in Middlesex, Essex, Somerset, and Hertfordshire are mentioned, as is a London house in Warwick Lane, held from the dean and chapter of St Paul's. There are also references to a silver ewer and basin which had belonged to Wroth's father and a 'gilt boll pinked with a Cover' that King Edward had given him. Unusually detailed provisions for the execution of the will reveal Wroth's legal and administrative background. Wroth died on 9 October 1573, presumably at his home of Durants; his will provided that he should be interred at the place of his death according to the judgement of his executors, but 'without all sumptuousnes' of heraldry or black mourning dress.

STANFORD LEHMBERG

Sources LP Henry VIII, vols. 9–21 · HoP, Commons, 1509–58, 3.666–8 · HoP, Commons, 1558–1603, 3.664–5 · will, PRO, PROB 11/57, fols. 124v–129r · The chronicle and political papers of King Edward VI, ed. W. K. Jordan (1966) · C. H. Garrett, The Marian exiles: a study in the origins of Elizabethan puritanism (1938) · APC, 1547–1580 · W. K. Jordan, Edward VI, 1: The young king (1968) · W. K. Jordan, Edward VI, 2: The threshold of power (1970) · P. Mirant, The history and antiquities of the county of Essex, 2 vols. (1763–8) · inquisition post mortem, PRO, C 142/171/97 · DNB · P. Collinson, Archbishop Grindal, 1519–1583: the struggle for a reformed church (1979)
Wealth at death substantial; manors: will, PRO, PROB 11/57, sig. 16

Wroth [Wrothe], **Sir Thomas** (1584–1672), politician, was born in London and baptized at St Stephen, Coleman Street, on 5 May 1584. He was the eldest son of Thomas Wroth (d. 1610), a wealthy Kent lawyer of the Inner Temple, and his wife, Joan, daughter of Thomas Bulmer of London, and grandson of Sir Thomas *Wroth (1518?–1573). Although he matriculated as a commoner of Gloucester Hall, Oxford, in 1600 he was later described as a scholar of Broadgates Hall (afterwards Pembroke College). After leaving Oxford without a degree he entered the Inner Temple in November 1606 with his brother, Peter (d. 1644). After inheriting a large fortune from his father in 1610 he purchased the Somerset estates of his insolvent cousin, Sir Robert Wroth, and established his family seat at Petherton Park (1614). He was knighted on 14 October 1613 and entered parliament in 1628 as member for Bridgwater, which he also represented in the Long Parliament (1640–48), the Rump Parliament (1648–53), the second protectorate parliament (1656–8), Richard Cromwell's parliament (1658–9), and the Convention Parliament (1660). In Somerset he was appointed justice of the peace (1636), deputy lieutenant (1639), sheriff (1639–40, a post which excluded him from sitting in the Short Parliament), and recorder of Bridgwater. His marriage to Margaret (d. 1635), daughter of Richard Rich (d. 1598) of Leighs in Essex, produced no children.

Largely through the influence of his brother-in-law Sir

Nathaniel *Rich, the colonial pioneer, Wroth became involved in colonial enterprise as a subscriber to the Virginia Company in 1609. He was subsequently a prominent supporter of the Warwick group within the company (1621–4), which opposed Sir Edwin Sandys. Appointed member of the Council for New England (3 November 1620), Wroth was later made a commissioner for the government of the Bermudas (25 June 1653). During the first part of his career he enjoyed writing as a leisure activity. His publications include *The Destruction of Troy, or, The Acts of Aeneas* (dedicated to Sir Robert Sidney, 1620), *Abortive of an Idle Hour, or, A Centurie of Epigrams* (1620), and an account of the life of his wife (1635). He also maintained a lucrative practice at the bar, which provided the means to support his increasingly active role in politics.

By 1640 the government was growing suspicious of Wroth's activities in Somerset and his puritan beliefs, especially after they had intercepted a highly critical letter from him on the state of the church, which seemed to hint at armed resistance. It was endorsed 'a dangerous or seditious letter' (*CSP dom.*, 1635, 377–8). As sheriff he courageously warned the council of mass opposition to the collection and payment of ship money (1639–40), only to be censured for speaking frankly 'to prepare an excuse for doing nothing … [rather] than to perform your duty' (Barnes, 239). In spite of his diligent efforts he managed to collect only £200 out of the £8000 demanded, including £95 from his own pocket. Conscientious in his responsibilities he was one of only three deputy lieutenants in Somerset to work hard in recruiting men for the 1640 northern expedition against the Scots and in pacifying the mutinous troops.

When the Long Parliament assembled Wroth quickly identified with the opposition to the king and was nominated to present the Commons with a petition from Somerset. This condemned a perceived plot to subvert English liberties and vowed to defend parliament if necessary with the sword (25 February 1642). In the summer of that year he assisted Alexander Popham in executing the militia ordinance within Somerset, was appointed a member of the county committee, and busied himself in raising and training forces in the west of the county. He served successfully in the early months of the war in the earl of Stamford's regiment in Devon (December 1642 – January 1643), although he and other local commanders failed in their attempts to defend Taunton against the advance of the marquess of Hertford's army (June 1643). After the recapture of Somerset by parliament in the summer of 1645 Wroth joined Colonel John Pyne's radical war party faction, which dominated the county committee. Although Wroth was appointed a presbyterian elder for the Bridgwater and Dunster classis in Somerset (1648), he allied himself politically both locally and in parliament with the Independents.

On 3 January 1648 Wroth, in an outrageous speech, seconded Sir Arthur Hesilrige's motion on the vote of no addresses by demanding that the king should be impeached and deposed. 'From devils and kings good Lord deliver us … I desire any government rather than that of

kings' (Underdown, *Diary*, 155). Nicknamed 'Wrath' by his enemies, he later supported Pride's Purge (6 December 1648), took the dissent from the vote permitting further negotiations with the king (perhaps on 20 December), and was one of the judges appointed to try the king. However, he attended only one session of the court (15 January) and did not sign the death warrant. For although he was in favour of major constitutional change he inwardly preferred the idea of deposition to that of execution. More moderate than many of the radicals in parliament, he firmly resisted any attempts to cause social disruption— hence the readiness with which he and Pyne raised volunteers in Somerset to suppress a local Leveller rising in the spring of 1649. By September the council of state had appointed him to be one of twenty-one militia commissioners for the county under Colonel John Disbrowe.

Unlike Pyne, however, Wroth was also intolerant of the Quakers for their practice of civil disobedience. Incensed by the disorder provoked during James Nayler's progress through Somerset in the autumn of 1656 he took a prominent part in the subsequent debate on Nayler in the Commons (December 1656). On one occasion he tried to pre-empt their decision by assuming the death penalty: 'Seeing Nayler must die,' he said, 'I desire to know what manner of death it must be' (*Diary of Thomas Burton*, 1.53). A few days later he screamed: 'Slit his tongue, or bore it, and brand him with the letter B' (*Diary of Thomas Burton*, 1.153).

By 1659 civilian radicals like Wroth, who had supported the action of the military in 1648, had become disillusioned by the endless intrusion of a costly army in political affairs and were supporting the call for lower taxes and a return to legal forms of government. In the debate on the militia (4 March 1659), Wroth commented sharply: 'It is said the soldiers have ventured their lives. They were well paid for it. I had a sword once [in the civil war]. I never had a penny for it. It cost me £10,000' (*Diary of Thomas Burton*, 4.17). After the Restoration his petition for pardon (May 1661) was granted and he lived quietly in retirement on his estates at Petherton Park, where he died, aged eighty-eight, on 11 July 1672. A purchaser of church lands, it is estimated that he had enjoyed an income of between £500 and £1000 per annum by 1648. In his will (proved on 24 August 1673), he left his estates to his great-nephew, Sir John Wroth.   JOHN WROUGHTON

Sources T. G. Barnes, *Somerset, 1625–1640: a county's government during the personal rule* (1961) · W. W. MacDonald, 'Wroth, Sir Thomas', Greaves & Zaller, *BDBR*, 3.346 · D. Underdown, *Pride's Purge: politics in the puritan revolution* (1971) · D. Underdown, *Somerset in the civil war and interregnum* (1973) · *DNB* · B. Worden, *The Rump Parliament, 1648–1653* (1974) · D. Underdown, 'The parliamentary diary of John Boys, 1647–8', *BIHR*, 39 (1966), 141–64 · *Diary of Thomas Burton*, ed. J. T. Rutt, 4 vols. (1828), vols. 1–4 · N. Tyacke, *The fortunes of English puritanism, 1603–1640* (1990) · M. Noble, *The lives of the English regicides*, 2 (1798) · *CSP dom.*, 1635; 1660–61

Wroth, Warwick William (1858–1911), numismatist, was born on 24 August 1858 at Clerkenwell, London, the eldest son in the family of four sons and four daughters of Warwick Reed Wroth (1825–1867), vicar from 1854 to his death of St Philip's, Clerkenwell, and author of *Sermons, Chiefly*

Mystical (ed. E. Vaux, 1869). His mother, Warwick Reed's second wife, was Sophia, youngest daughter of Thomas Brooks, of Ealing, Middlesex.

Wroth was educated at the King's School, Canterbury (1867–76), where he was a king's scholar and where he received a sound classical training. He joined the staff of the British Museum as a second-class assistant in the department of coins and medals on 22 July 1878. He was promoted to first-class assistant on 2 August 1887 and became assistant keeper (deputy to the keeper) on 27 July 1906. Promotion being almost invariably by seniority, Wroth was then in line for the keepership, but according to G. F. Hill he was unwilling to accept the restrictions attached to the post, such as residence in the museum. During his career he mainly devoted his energies to a study of Greek coins, and achieved a high reputation both in the UK and on the continent by his continuation of the catalogues of Greek coins at the museum.

Wroth's first four volumes were compiled under the supervision of R. S. Poole and dealt with coins of eastern Greece, beginning with those of *Crete and the Aegean Islands* (1886), and continuing with those of *Pontus Paphlagonia, Bithynia and the Kingdom of Bosporus* (1889); *Mysia* (1892); and *Troas, Aeolis and Lesbos* (1894). His two subsequent volumes, *Galatia, Cappadocia and Syria* (1899) and *Parthia* (1903), were produced by Wroth alone. He then worked on Byzantine coinage, producing *Imperial Byzantine Coins* (2 vols., 1908) and the coins of the *Vandals, Ostrogoths and Lombards and of the Empires of Thessalonica, Nicaea and Trebizond* (1911). Before his death he returned to Greek coinage, and was preparing to catalogue the coins of Philip II and Alexander III, and the later kings of Macedon and Thrace. He also worked on the Roman, medieval, and English series of coins and the collection of medals, developing a wide general knowledge of the museum's collections.

Between 1882 and 1907 Wroth also contributed to the *Journal of Hellenic Studies*, the *Numismatic Chronicle*, the *Athenaeum*, and the *Classical Review*. He co-operated with Barclay Head in 1911 in a new edition of Head's *Historia Numorum* (1887). Wroth also contributed memoirs of numismatists, medallists, coin engravers, and others to the *Dictionary of National Biography* from its inception in 1885 until his death. He is said to have had 'a remarkable memory and a genuine artistic taste' (Hill and Allan, 107). While he is now regarded as an extremely competent cataloguer, he is not considered to have been a great scholar. His work tended to attract such contemporary comments as 'exact', 'scientific', and 'orderly'. He is described as 'being of a somewhat retiring disposition' (Hill and Allan, 108) and 'in consequence little known except to those who came into contact with him in his official capacity' (ibid.). He was, however, 'courteous but genial' (ibid.) to museum visitors. His spare time was spent 'extending his acquaintance with old London' (ibid.), on which he was an authority, especially as regards the eighteenth century. He owned a good collection of prints of London. With his brother Arthur Edgar Wroth he published in 1896 *The London Pleasure Gardens of the Eighteenth Century*, which embodied many years' research. This was supplemented by a paper on 'Tickets of Vauxhall gardens' (*Numismatic Chronicle*, 3rd ser., 1898, 73–92) and by *Cremorne and the Later London Gardens* (1907). He had a wide knowledge of English literature. He was elected FSA on 7 March 1889 but had little involvement in the affairs of learned societies.

Wroth did not marry. He died unexpectedly on 24 or 26 September 1911 at Charing Cross Hospital, London, after an operation for peritonitis and was buried on 30 September 1911 after a funeral service at St Andrew's, West Kensington. W. B. OWEN, *rev.* M. L. CAYGILL

Sources G. F. Hill and J. Allan, *Numismatic Chronicle*, 4th ser., 12 (1912), 107–110 [incl. bibliography] • BM • private information (2004) • *The Times* (29 Sept 1911) • G. F. Hill, 'Autobiographical fragment', *The Medal*, 12 (1988), 37–48 • register, 1859–1931, King's School, Canterbury • *The Athenaeum* (30 Sept 1911), 397 • Venn, *Alum. Cant.* • d. cert.

Archives BM, department of coins and medals, unpublished works on medals and 17th-century tokens

Likenesses photograph, BM, department of coins and medals

Wealth at death £4153 10s. 5d.: resworn probate, 14 Oct 1911, CGPLA Eng. & Wales

Wroth, William (1575/6–1638x41), nonconformist minister, was probably born in Monmouthshire. Whether he belonged to the family of that name at Llandeilo Bertholau or at Llangattock-juxta-Usk, or indeed at Abergavenny, where successive generations of William Wroth were prominent townsmen in the reign of Elizabeth I, cannot now be established. He was admitted to New Inn Hall, Oxford, on 27 November 1590, aged fourteen, and graduated BA from Christ Church on 18 February 1596. He proceeded MA from Jesus College on 26 June 1605.

It is not certain when Wroth took up the living of Llanfaches, in his native county. Contradictory evidence survives for both 1611 and 1617 as the date of his appointment, but he must have been at Llanfaches by the latter date. He also held the living of Llanfihangel Rogiet from 1613, and there was little to suggest in his early career that he was to challenge the order of things in the Church of England. His patrons at Llanfaches were two gentlemen called Sir Edward Lewis, successive heads of the Glamorgan family from Y Fan, near Caerphilly, a family which has also been linked with the career of William Erbery, a Church of England clergyman who later developed distinctly antinomian views. It has been suggested that Wroth's conversion took place in 1620 and was a spectacular one, from career clergyman to firebrand preacher, but there is no evidence for the theory. What is certain is that by October 1635 he was sufficiently out of step with the established church hierarchy to be brought before the court of high commission with William Erbery, perhaps for opposing the Book of Sports. His case was protracted, but he had probably left his living by April 1638.

By then Wroth must have set about turning the nucleus of his congregation at Llanfaches into a separate church, along the lines of the 'New England way', although no purpose-built chapel building was erected under his auspices. In November 1639 the London minister Henry Jessey was sent by his congregation to assist 'old Mr Wroth' (*Life and Death of Mr. Henry Jessey*, 9) and the ministers Walter Cradock and Henry Walter in 'gathering and constituting' (ibid.) the Llanfaches church, which was quite broad in its theological scope, and should not be identified exclusively with any particular sect to emerge in the country later. Jessey's own assessment of the significance of the Llanfaches church to Wales, or at least southeast Wales, was that it was 'like Antioch the mother church in that gentile country' (ibid.), and thus it has been regarded by historians of Welsh nonconformity subsequently. Wroth was also active in succouring the separatist church at Broadmead, Bristol, and encouraged the exchange of preachers between Llanfaches and Broadmead. On his visits to Bristol, where he stayed for extended periods, Wroth taught the children of the congregation the following verse:

> Thy sin, thy end, the death of Christ,
> The eternal pangs of hell;
> The day of doom, the joys of heaven:
> These six remember well.
> (Underhill, 27)

Wroth made his will in September 1638. He left 3 acres of land in Magor in a trust, the profits of which were to benefit twelve of the poorest people in Llanfaches. All his other estate was left to Henry Walter, his colleague in the Llanfaches church, and among the signatories of the will was Richard Blinman, 'minister of God's Word' (NL Wales, LL 1641/40), who had emigrated to New England by February 1640. In a premonition of the civil war Wroth hoped 'he might never hear a drum beat' (Underhill, 29) and died before 12 April 1641, when his will was proved at Llandaff.

STEPHEN K. ROBERTS

Sources T. Richards, 'Eglwys Llanfaches', *Transactions of the Honourable Society of Cymmrodorion* (1941), 150–84 · *Life and death of Mr Henry Jessey* (1671) · *DWB* · E. B. Underhill, ed., *The records of the Church of Christ, meeting in Broadmead, Bristol, 1640–1687*, Hanserd Knollys Society (1847) · Foster, *Alum. Oxon.* · J. Jones, ed., *Monmouthshire wills proved in the prerogative court of Canterbury, 1560–1601* (1997) · *CSP dom.*, 1635–6
Wealth at death no value given; three acres of land: Jones, ed., *Monmouthshire wills*; NL Wales, LL 1641/40

Wrotham, William of (d. **1217/18**), administrator, was of obscure origin and parentage, though his father, Godwin, held land in Shipbourne, Kent, near Wrotham, and was perhaps a tenant of the archbishops of Canterbury. In 1194, though still at this point a layman, William became a canon of Wells and was granted the prebend of St Decuman, Watchet. In 1204 he is first styled archdeacon of Taunton. He may have owed his rise in royal service through association with Geoffrey fitz Peter, earl of Essex, who granted him the manor of Sutton-at-Hone, Kent, in 1197. This was later intended for the foundation of a hospital, but eventually became a preceptory of the knights hospitaller. From 1194 he accounted, on Geoffrey's behalf, for the vill of Lydford, Devon. In 1197 Wrotham was given the chief forestership of Somerset (which he granted to his brother, Richard, as his deputy in 1207) and this brought him lands accounted at one knight's fee. According to the late thirteenth-century hundred rolls, Henry II had given him the stewardship of Exmoor, as well as that of the park of North Petherton, Somerset, where he gradually accumulated a considerable estate. In 1198–9 he was

joint sheriff of Devon and Cornwall and served as a royal justice in 1198–9, and as a justice in the bench and exchequer in 1209–10.

Wrotham was first involved in the administration of the royal stannaries (tin mines) in 1197; the following year Archbishop Hubert Walter (d. 1205) placed them under Wrotham's overall control, a post he held (except for a brief interlude in 1200) until 1215. His reorganization of their administrative and financial procedures greatly increased royal revenue: in the first year they accounted to the exchequer for over £1100. In 1202 Wrotham became one of the keepers of the fifteenth on merchants, perhaps appointed because of his mercantile experience in the stannaries. Three years later he and his fellow keeper, Reginald of Cornhill (d. 1210), were placed in charge of the assize of money and operated the mints of London and Canterbury. He was appointed keeper of the temporalities of the vacant see of Winchester at the end of 1204, and the following year performed the same office (in conjunction with Cornhill) for Bath and Glastonbury abbeys. Between 1206 and 1209 he also accounted for the revenues of Whitby Abbey and periodically farmed the town's tallage.

But Wrotham's main activities lay in the administration of the royal fleet, in which he played an increasing role from 1205, by when he was one of the keepers of the fleet along the south coast, and also oversaw naval expenditure during John's abortive invasion of France. The following year he had general control of the naval expedition to Poitou and command of the fleet of the Cinque Ports. Thereafter he had, until 1215, effective charge of John's naval affairs, with his headquarters perhaps at Portsmouth, then being developed as the major royal dockyard. In 1214 he co-operated with Peter des Roches (d. 1238) in founding the God's House Hospital in that town.

Such service brought its rewards in lands, offices, and cash revenues. In addition to his earlier ecclesiastical preferment, in 1207 Wrotham was given the churches of Warden in Sheppey and East Malling, and the keepership of the royal forest in Cornwall and Devon. King John gave him escheated lands in Dartford and Sutton-at-Hone, and in 1208 he received two tenements in Westminster and the revenues from some escheated lands in Gloucestershire, while in 1214 he was given a prebend in the collegiate royal chapel of Hastings and purchased more property in Westminster.

But in the autumn of 1215 this zealous functionary, named by Roger of Wendover as one of John's 'evil advisers' who supported the king during the interdict, joined the baronial rebellion. Wrotham was consequently deprived of his naval command, and obliged to surrender his custody of the forest of Somerset and Lydford Castle. By the summer of 1217, however, he had returned to the royalist cause and regained his lands in the south-west, but he was dead by 16 February 1218 when John Marshall received the wardship of Richard of Wrotham, William's nephew and heir, the son of William's brother, Richard.

BRIAN GOLDING

Sources F. W. Brooks, 'William de Wrotham and the office of keeper of the king's ports and galleys', *EngHR*, 40 (1925), 570–79 · W. R. Powell, 'The administration of the navy and the stannaries, 1189–1216', *EngHR*, 71 (1956), 176–88 · S. Painter, *The reign of King John* (1949) · *Chancery records* · *Pipe rolls* · F. Palgrave, ed., *Rotuli curiae regis: rolls and records of the court held before the king's justiciars or justices*, 2 vols., RC, 27 (1835) · N. Vincent, *Peter des Roches: an alien in English politics, 1205–38*, Cambridge Studies in Medieval Life and Thought, 4th ser., 31 (1996) · [W. Illingworth], ed., *Rotuli hundredorum temp. Hen. III et Edw. I*, 2 vols., RC (1812–18) · T. D. Hardy, ed., *Rotuli litterarum clausarum*, RC, 1 (1833), 352b

Wrottesley, Sir Frederic John (1880–1948), judge, was born on 20 March 1880 in Hampstead, London, the third son of the Revd Francis John Wrottesley (1848–1922), then a curate in Hampstead and later vicar of Denstone, Staffordshire, a great-nephew of the first Baron Wrottesley, and his wife, Agnes Mabel Stilwell (d. 1917), daughter of Frederic John Freeland. He was a kinsman of George Wrottesley. Educated at Tonbridge School and at Lincoln College, Oxford, where he was a classical scholar, Wrottesley gave to both institutions a wholehearted devotion then and later. He obtained a second class in classical moderations in 1901 and a third in *literae humaniores* in 1903, and was called to the bar by the Inner Temple in 1907. He won rapid success in the charmed circle of the parliamentary bar, but his career was interrupted by the First World War when he was commissioned in the Royal Field Artillery, serving in France, attaining the rank of major, and being mentioned in dispatches. On 26 November 1915 he married Marion Cecil (d. 1955), daughter of Lieutenant-Colonel William Patterson of the Duke of Cornwall's light infantry; they had no children.

Wrottesley became a KC in 1926 and in 1930 was made recorder of Wolverhampton. In 1931 he was chairman of the gas legislation committee appointed by the Board of Trade to inquire into the working of the basic price system for gas companies, and in 1936 he conducted an inquiry into the marketing of sugar beet. His experience of the parliamentary bar familiarized him closely with many matters of local government. He was a good friend to the teachers of law and much interested in his subject from the academic angle, and he was no stranger to legal authorship: his works *The Examination of Witnesses in Court* (1910) and *Letters to a Young Barrister* (1930) won golden opinions from the profession.

It was on the bench that Wrottesley's career came to its full maturity. He was appointed a judge of the King's Bench Division and knighted in 1937. Despite his learning and common sense, some doubted whether one who had practised exclusively in the parliamentary bar would acquit himself well when confronted with problems of ordinary criminal and civil law. Such fears were groundless. At the very outset of his judicial career a supreme test awaited him in the shape of a case involving that very difficult piece of legislation, the Truck Act of 1831, and incidentally also a matter connected with the statute of limitation then in force. The case was *Pratt v. Cook* (1938). His judgment on the point of the operation of the Truck Act was reversed by a divided Court of Appeal which was, however, unanimous in approving his view on the period

of limitation. Then in 1940 his entire judgment was restored by the House of Lords. This achievement set the seal on his judicial reputation, and he was ever afterwards regarded as a learned, careful, and just judge—possessed of that undefinable quality, the true judicial temperament.

Wrottesley's success on the civil side inspired professional optimism about his success on the criminal side; nor was it disappointed. His lack of previous experience of crime and criminals seemed to constitute no bar to his understanding of the problems involved. He took the trouble to study criminology, together with the history and practice of the prison system, and to get acquainted with those concerned in the daily administration of the multiplicity of matters affecting punishment and probation. By characteristic efforts he acquired a profound knowledge of the ramifications of criminal law itself, and rapidly took his place in the foremost rank of criminal judges. Perhaps the most interesting of his decisions, from a legal point of view, was *R. v. Jarmain* (1946), where he applied what might be called the doctrine of 'follow through'. It was in a sense an extension of the doctrine of constructive crime, whereby a person who causes the death of another person in the course of committing a crime involving violence is guilty of murder; for here the crime, theft, had been committed after the death. Wrottesley, delivering the judgment of the court of criminal appeal affirming Jarmain's conviction for murder, ruled that a person who uses violent measures in the commission of a crime does so at his own risk, and is guilty of murder even though the death of the victim were caused by inadvertence and were interposed, in point of time, between the attempt at the felony and its ultimate consummation.

In a leading case which he tried Wrottesley held that evidence of strikingly similar facts could be put before the jury provided that the evidence was more probative than prejudicial—for example, a multiplicity or series of charges of strikingly similar criminal homosexual acts could be tried together. His ruling was upheld by the Court of Appeal (*R. v. Sims*, 1946).

In 1947 Wrottesley was raised to the Court of Appeal and sworn of the privy council, a promotion which gave rise to widespread satisfaction. But he was destined to enjoy only a short tenure for in 1948 growing ill health forced his resignation. He had, however, occupied it long enough to complete what many would regard as the crowning achievements of his career in the fields of equity and constitutional law, for he was a member of the court which prepared the elaborate judgment in *Re Diplock* (1948). Trustees of a will had, in obedience to its provisions, distributed the testator's property among charities. This action turned out to have been premature, since one of the next of kin succeeded in convincing the House of Lords that the will did not create a valid charitable bequest. The Court of Appeal in a long and learned judgment held that the next of kin were entitled to recover from the recipients the money thus wrongly paid away. In *R. v. Chancellor of St. Edmundsbury and Ipswich Diocese* (1948),

Wrottesley read the judgment of the court, which laid down that while the King's Bench Division can issue an order for prohibition, it cannot issue an order for *certiorari* to an ecclesiastical court.

Wrottesley was a bencher of his inn, master of the Skinners' Company (1940–41), and an honorary fellow of Lincoln College, Oxford, which was always one of the main interests of his life, and which he was always more than ready to help with his wise advice. He was the most prudent of counsellors and the truest of friends. He died on 14 November 1948 at his home, Manor Farm, Newnham, near Basingstoke, Hampshire.

H. G. HANBURY, *rev.* ALEC SAMUELS

Sources personal knowledge (1959) · Burke, *Peerage* (1939) · *WWW*
Likenesses W. Stoneman, photograph, 1938, NPG · M. Grixoni, oils; in possession of family, 1959 · E. Kennington, pastel drawing, Skinners' Hall, London
Wealth at death £70,699 9s. 9d.: probate, 1949, *CGPLA Eng. & Wales*

Wrottesley, George (1827–1909), army officer and antiquary, born at 5 Powys Place, London, on 15 June 1827, was the third son of John *Wrottesley, second Baron Wrottesley (1798–1867), a landowner and astronomer, and Sophia Elizabeth (*d.* 1880), third daughter of Thomas Giffard of Chillington Hall, Staffordshire. He was educated at the Blackheath proprietary school. After entering the Royal Military Academy, Woolwich, in 1842, he obtained a commission in the Royal Engineers in 1845. He was ordered almost immediately to Ireland to assist with famine relief work, and in 1847 was transferred to Gibraltar, where he remained until 1849. In 1852 he joined the Ordnance Survey. He took part in the Crimean War, and sailed for the Dardanelles on survey work in January 1854. On the 7th of the same month he had married Margaret Anne, daughter of Sir John Fox *Burgoyne. With Sir John, he went on a mission to the Turkish general Omar Pasha. He afterwards became aide-de-camp to General T. B. Tylden, the officer commanding Royal Engineers in Turkey, and in this capacity he accompanied Lord Raglan to Varna. He was engaged at Varna on plans and reports on the Turkish lines of retreat from the Danube, when he was struck down by dysentery and fever, which later caused complete deafness. In October 1854 he was invalided home and promoted to captain. On Sir John Burgoyne's return from the Crimea to the War Office in 1855 as inspector-general of fortifications, Wrottesley was appointed his aide-de-camp, and he stayed with the field marshal, acting continually as his secretary on commissions and confidential adviser until Burgoyne's retirement in 1868. He was secretary of the defence committee of the War Office from 1856 to 1860; secretary of the committee on the influence of rifled artillery on works of defence in 1859; and secretary of the committee on the storage of gun powder in magazines in 1865. In 1863, being then a major, he presided over the committee on army signalling which introduced the use of Morse code. He was made lieutenant-colonel in 1868, and on Burgoyne's retirement took over the command of the engineers at Shorncliffe. In 1872 he

commanded at Greenwich, and in 1875 became officer commanding Royal Engineers at Woolwich, before retiring from the army in 1881 with the honorary rank of major-general.

Wrottesley collected and edited *The Military Opinions of General Sir J. F. Burgoyne* in 1859 and published *The Life and Correspondence of Field Marshal Sir J. Burgoyne, Bart.* (2 vols.) in 1873. But his principal literary interest lay in the history of his ancestral county, Staffordshire, and, more especially, in the genealogies of its principal landed families. He was active in the campaign that led to the establishment in 1872 of the William Salt Library at Stafford to house the antiquarian collections of William Salt. In 1879 he founded with Robert William Eyton and others the William Salt Archaeological Society, now the Staffordshire Record Society; its principal aim was 'the editing and printing of original documents relating to the county of Stafford'. Wrottesley was honorary secretary from 1879 until his death. He contributed prolifically to the society's volumes, its Collections for a History of Staffordshire. Five of his contributions, including full-scale histories of the families of Bagot, Giffard, Okeover, and Wrottesley, were republished separately. In his *Pedigrees from the Plea Rolls* (1905) he reprinted material he had previously published in *The Genealogist* and *The Reliquary and Antiquary*.

Wrottesley was one of the founders of the modern school of genealogy, basing family histories firmly on record evidence, exploding long-held genealogical myths, and using the legal and financial records of central government systematically to explore genealogical and political connections and personal motives unmentioned by narrative sources. John Horace Round, a great admirer and correspondent of Wrottesley, whom he remembered fondly as 'the Nestor of genealogists', said of him in an obituary notice 'no genealogist, perhaps, could claim with better reason that he placed truth foremost'. Wrottesley had, too, that other virtue of the new school, the ability to use family history and political history to illustrate each other. After Wrottesley's first wife died childless on 3 May 1883 he married, on 21 February 1889, Nina Margaret, daughter of John William Philips of Heybridge, Staffordshire. Wrottesley died at his home, 75 Cadogan Gardens, London, on 4 March 1909, and was buried in the Wrottesley vault in Tettenhall church, Staffordshire, on 8 March. His second wife, who survived him, was also childless.

J. C. WEDGWOOD, *rev.* D. A. JOHNSON

Sources G. Wrottesley, 'A history of the family of Wrottesley of Wrottesley, co. Stafford', *Collections for a history of Staffordshire*, William Salt Archaeological Society, new ser., 6/2 (1903), 383–4 · M. W. Greenslade, *The Staffordshire historians*, Staffordshire RS, 4th ser., 11 (1982), 136–50 · J. C. Wedgwood, *The Genealogist*, new ser., 26 (1909–10), 40–44 · J. H. Round, 'Mr Horace Round's review of General Wrottesley's work as an archaeologist', *Collections for a history of Staffordshire*, William Salt Archaeological Society, new ser., 12 (1909) · 'Memoir of the Major-General the Honourable George Wrottesley', *Collections for a history of Staffordshire*, William Salt Archaeological Society, new ser., 12 (1909) · *Collections for a history of Staffordshire*, William Salt Archaeological Society, new ser., 3 (1900), frontispiece [portrait] · private information (1912) · Wrottesley notes and correspondence, William Salt Library, Stafford ·

Staffordshire Advertiser (6 March 1909), 5 · *Staffordshire Advertiser* (13 March 1909), 3
Archives William Salt Library, Stafford | Bodl. Oxf., corresp. and papers relating to Norman family of Toeni · LUL, letters to J. H. Round · W. Sussex RO, corresp. with Oswald Barron
Likenesses photograph, repro. in *Collections for a history of Staffordshire*, frontispiece
Wealth at death £2394 6*s.* 4*d.*: resworn probate, 27 May 1909, CGPLA Eng. & Wales

Wrottesley, John, first Baron Wrottesley (1771–1841). *See under* Wrottesley, John, second Baron Wrottesley (1798–1867).

Wrottesley, John, second Baron Wrottesley (1798–1867), landowner and astronomer, was born at Wrottesley Hall, Tettenhall, Staffordshire, on 5 August 1798.

His father, **John Wrottesley**, first Baron Wrottesley (1771–1841), politician, born on 25 October 1771, was the eldest son of Major-General Sir John Wrottesley, eighth baronet (1744–1787), and his wife, Frances (*d.* 1828), the daughter of William Courtenay, first Viscount Courtenay (*d.* 1762). He was a descendant of Sir Walter Wrottesley. On 31 January 1782 he entered Westminster School, but was later expelled for leading a rebellion. He trained for a military career at de Pignerolle's academy at Angers and served in the Netherlands and France during the revolutionary war as an officer in the 13th lancers, but retired disillusioned after the disastrous Flanders campaign.

On 2 March 1799 Wrottesley was returned to parliament for Lichfield as a whig. He was re-elected in 1802, but in 1806 retired before the poll. On 23 July 1823 he was returned for Staffordshire, and after the passage of the Reform Act in 1832 he continued to sit for the southern division of the county; he was defeated at the poll in 1837. On 11 July 1838 he was advanced to the House of Lords with the title of Baron Wrottesley of Wrottesley. He was a good practical farmer, and his lands at Wrottesley were furnished with the latest improvements in agricultural machinery. While in parliament he procured the exemption of draining tiles from duty. He died at Wrottesley on 16 March 1841, and was buried in the ancestral vault at Tettenhall church on 24 March.

Wrottesley's first marriage, on 23 January 1795, to Caroline, the eldest daughter of Charles Bennet, fourth earl of Tankerville, brought five sons and three daughters. She died on 7 March 1818, and he married, secondly, on 19 May 1819, Julia (*d.* 29 Sept 1860), the daughter of John Conyers of Copt Hall, Essex, and the widow of Captain John Astley Bennet RN, the brother of Wrottesley's first wife. There were no children of this union.

Wrottesley's eldest son, John, was admitted to Westminster School on 22 January 1810. He left in 1814, matriculated from Christ Church, Oxford, on 15 May 1816, and graduated BA in 1819 and MA in 1823. He entered Lincoln's Inn on 19 November 1819 and was called to the bar in 1823. On 28 July 1821 he married Sophia Elizabeth (*d.* 13 January 1880), the third daughter of Thomas Giffard of Chillington in Staffordshire; they had five sons and two daughters. Wrottesley joined the committee of the Society for the Diffusion of Useful Knowledge, of which he continued a member until his death. While practising as an equity lawyer he settled at Blackheath, where between 1829 and 1831 he built and fitted up an astronomical observatory. Assisted by John Hartnup, he concentrated on observing the positions of certain fixed stars of the sixth and seventh magnitudes. He took ten observations of each star, a task which occupied him from 9 May 1831 to 1 July 1835, and the finished *Catalogue of the Right Ascensions of 1318 Stars* was presented to the Royal Astronomical Society in 1836. Wrottesley was a founder member of the society, its secretary from 1831 to 1841, and its president from 1841 to 1843. The society printed the *Catalogue* in its *Memoirs* in 1838, and presented Wrottesley with its gold medal on 8 February 1839. On 29 April 1841 he was elected a fellow of the Royal Society.

After his father's death in 1841, Wrottesley erected an observatory at Wrottesley Hall and provided it with a fine equatorial of 129 inches focal length by Dollond, with a 7¾ inch lens. In 1842 and 1854 his two supplementary catalogues of stars were published in the Royal Astronomical Society's *Memoirs*.

Wrottesley served on several royal commissions of a scientific nature. He was one of the original poor-law commissioners, and published, in conjunction with Charles Hay Cameron and John Welsford Cowell, *Two Reports on the Poor Laws* (1834). In 1853 he called attention in the House of Lords to the collections of meteorological observations and discoveries being published by Lieutenant Matthew Fontaine Maury of the US Navy, and advocated a similar policy of encouraging merchant captains to keep records of winds and currents during their voyages—a project which was later adopted by the Board of Trade.

In November 1854 Wrottesley succeeded William Parsons, third earl of Rosse, as president of the Royal Society, a post which he resigned in 1857. In 1860 he was elected president of the British Association, and on 2 July he received the degree of DCL from the University of Oxford. Besides the catalogues already mentioned, Wrottesley contributed other astronomical papers to the *Memoirs* and *Monthly Notices* of the Royal Astronomical Society, and to the Royal Society, as well as a treatise on navigation for the Library of Useful Knowledge (1829) and *Thoughts on Government* (1860). He died at Wrottesley Hall on 27 October 1867. His two youngest sons—Henry (1829–1852) and Cameron (1834–1854)—were killed in action. He was succeeded by his eldest son, Arthur, third Baron Wrottesley (1824–1910), while his third son, George *Wrottesley, had distinguished careers as a soldier and antiquary.

E. I. CARLYLE, rev. ANITA McCONNELL

Sources *Monthly Notices of the Royal Astronomical Society*, 28 (1867–8), 64–8 · *PRS*, 16 (1867–8), lxiii–lxiv · *GM*, 4th ser., 4 (1867), 820 · *ILN* (9 Nov 1867) · HoP, *Commons* · *GM*, 2nd ser., 15 (1841), 650–51 · W. Pitt, *A topographical history of Staffordshire* (1817) · *Journal for the History of Astronomy*, 17/4 (1986) [*The Greenwich list of observatories*, ed. D. Howse], esp. 66, 83 · Foster, *Alum. Oxon.* · W. P. Baildon, ed., *The records of the Honorable Society of Lincoln's Inn: admissions*, 2 (1896), 85 · *The Greville memoirs*, ed. H. Reeve, new edn, 3 (1888), 9, 13 · d. cert.

Archives CUL, letters to Sir George Stokes · RS, corresp. with Sir John Herschel · UCL, letters to Society for the Diffusion of Useful Knowledge
Likenesses engraving, repro. in *ILN*
Wealth at death under £20,000: probate, 9 Dec 1867, *CGPLA Eng. & Wales*

Wrottesley, Sir Walter (*c*.1430–1473), soldier and administrator, was the eldest son of Hugh Wrottesley of Wrottesley, and of Thomasine, heir of the Greslies of Drakelow. Although descended from well-established south Staffordshire gentry, Wrottesley never occupied the estates, which were held in jointure, in his own right—the longevity of his parents precluded this. But his political activity quickly extended beyond the patrimonial base. By the 1460s he was spending increasing amounts of time in London, partly as a result of property acquired through his marriage about 1456 to Jane, formerly the wife of John Vyncent and the daughter and heir of William Baron of Reading, one of the tellers of the exchequer. At the same time Wrottesley was increasingly drawn into the orbit of the houses of York and Neville.

Wrottesley's father, Hugh, supported Richard, duke of York (*d.* 1460), in his confrontation with Henry VI at Dartford in 1452, and in 1459 Richard Neville, earl of Warwick (*d.* 1471), appointed Walter his deputy as sheriff of Worcestershire. Following the Yorkist victory at Northampton on 10 July 1460 Walter became sheriff of Staffordshire, while his brother Henry took the office in Worcestershire. In January 1462, with Edward IV firmly enthroned, Walter, now addressed as king's knight, was rewarded with lands in Staffordshire and Dorset forfeited by James Butler, earl of Wiltshire (*d.* 1461). Although it was once believed that Wrottesley was a retainer of Edward IV who switched allegiance to Warwick, successful gentry regularly had several patrons and, until Warwick's rebellion in 1470, the two affiliations would not have been mutually exclusive.

By November 1464 Wrottesley was of Warwick's council, and in June 1468 he was appointed chamberlain of the exchequer, the earl's office by hereditary right. This deepening association implicated him in the Lincolnshire rising of February 1470, and the confiscation of his lands was ordered in the following April. During the readeption of Henry VI (1470–71) Wrottesley was appointed sheriff in Warwick's lordships in Glamorgan and replaced Lord Wenlock as Warwick's deputy as captain of Calais. At about the time of Warwick's defeat and death at Barnet on 14 April 1471, but before the news reached Calais, Wrottesley dispatched 300 men to assist Thomas Neville, the Bastard of Fauconberg, in raising Kent in the name of Henry VI and marching on London. Margaret of Anjou's defeat at Tewkesbury on 4 May, followed by Fauconberg's retreat, ended all hope of resistance to Edward IV and, by early June, Lord Hastings had invested Calais from the sea. The formidable defences and the prospect of French intervention encouraged negotiations, which finally brought surrender in return for pardons under the great seal issued on 6 August.

Wrottesley died on 10 April 1473 and was buried in the church of the Greyfriars, London. He had had with Jane Baron four sons and five daughters. The eldest son, Richard, inherited the Staffordshire estates, while the second son, William, succeeded to his mother's Berkshire property. Jane was still living in 1478, by when she had married Sir Richard Darell. ANTHONY GROSS

Sources G. Wrottesley, 'A history of the family of Wrottesley of Wrottesley, co. Stafford', *Collections for a history of Staffordshire*, William Salt Archaeological Society, new ser., 6/2 (1903) · *Chancery records* · CLRO, Husting rolls · PRO, exchequer accounts various, E 10 411/13, E 10 412/2 [Edward IV, household accounts] · J. Stow, *A survey of London*, rev. edn (1603); repr. with introduction by C. L. Kingsford as *A survey of London*, 2 vols. (1908); repr. with addns (1971) · J. Caley and J. Bayley, eds., *Calendarium inquisitionum post mortem sive escaetarum*, 4, RC (1828)
Archives priv. coll., Huntbach MSS

Wroughton, Richard [*real name* Richard Rotten] (1748–1822), actor and theatre manager, was born in Bath. His parentage and exact date of birth are unknown, although he was reported to be the son of a Colonel Rotten and the brother of a major in the 11th light dragoons. *The Secret History of the Green Rooms* (1790) records that he trained as a surgeon in Bath; other contemporary accounts allude to a young milliner who nursed him through severe illness and accompanied him to London. On 15 January 1769, still under the name Richard Rotten, he married Joanna Townley, a milliner, at Bath Abbey; however, about this time he began to use the name Wroughton. His first stage appearance was on 24 October 1768 at Covent Garden, as Zaphna in James Miller's *Mahomet*. This début (under the sobriquet 'A Young Gentleman') was followed that season by eight more roles, some of them fairly substantial for a relative newcomer, including Malcolm in *Macbeth*, Richmond in *Richard III*, and the title role in George Lillo's *George Barnwell*. Wroughton remained at Covent Garden for fifteen seasons, taking on a comprehensive range of leading and supporting roles, and quickly developed a penchant for 'young tragic heroes and men of fashion: rakes, beaux, and leads in sentimental comedy' (*BDA*). By 1786 he had successfully persuaded George Colman, the manager of Covent Garden, into raising his salary from £3 to £12 per week—a figure bettered only by Charles Macklin and the manager W. T. Lewis. In addition Wroughton's fortunes were boosted by his acquisition, in 1784, of a part share in Sadler's Wells, which he also managed.

Throughout the 1780s and 1790s Wroughton made a living as an actor and manager, at first at Covent Garden and, after a violent quarrel with Lewis, from 1787 onwards at Drury Lane. During this period he performed more than 200 leading and supporting roles (including Romeo in *Romeo and Juliet*, the Bastard in *King John*, Edgar in *King Lear*, Jaques in *As You Like It*, and, most successfully, Ford in *The Merry Wives of Windsor*). He was popular with audiences but not with the critics, and earned the scorn of Francis Gentleman in *The Dramatic Censor* (1770):

> Mr WROUGHTON has of late been most cruelly obtruded upon the public … cruelly for himself and the audience … Messrs. CAUTHERLY and WROUGHTON are pretty equal competitors for the palm of insipidity; to say which is worst would puzzle the acutest criticism, and imagination is almost at a loss to conceive the wretchedness of either.

In another piece of criticism (*The Theatres*, 1772) Gentleman described Wroughton as a 'theatrical weed' with a 'vacant face'. Eventually the consensus emerged that Wroughton was a competent and an industrious actor, rather than an inspired performer, who was able to work well enough within his limitations; in 1790 *The Secret History of the Green Rooms* concluded that 'his voice was hoarse, his face was round and inexpressive, and he was slightly knock-knee'd, yet he counterbalanced these defects by a spirited natural enunciation, an agreeable prepossessing smile, and an easy deportment' (*BDA*).

After a brief attempt at retirement in Bath between 1798 and 1800, Wroughton returned to London to resume work as an actor–manager at Drury Lane, although by 1802 he had become embroiled in a legal dispute with the proprietors over unpaid salary arrears (which amounted to £210 by the end of 1808). Relations with the Drury Lane management were further soured when he joined with a group of other actors to petition George III to set up a third patent theatre in London. The plan came to nothing, and despite Wroughton's perceived disloyalty he continued to be engaged by Drury Lane until the end of the 1814–15 season. In 1815 he retired from the stage; that year also saw the publication of his adaptation of Shakespeare's *Richard II*, a play which, on account of the political sensitivity of its subject matter, had rarely been seen during the eighteenth century. Accentuating the tragedy of the king as an isolated heroic figure by some judicious editing and interpolation of lines from *Richard III*, *Troilus and Cressida*, *Antony and Cleopatra*, *Henry VI*, *Titus Andronicus*, and *King Lear*, Wroughton fashioned the play into what proved to be a remarkably durable vehicle for Edmund Kean, who took the title role (it was performed until 1828 and was taken to New York in 1820 and 1826). It is not known when his first wife died; however, on 2 February 1811 he married Elizabeth Thomas at St Marylebone. Wroughton died at his house in Howland Street, Fitzroy Square, on 7 February 1822, leaving his considerable fortune (including five shares in the Basingstoke Canal) to his widow. He was buried on 14 February at St George's, Bloomsbury.

ROBERT SHAUGHNESSY

Sources Highfill, Burnim & Langhans, *BDA* · will, PRO, PROB 11/1654, sig. 115 · [J. Haslewood], *The secret history of the green rooms: containing authentic and entertaining memoirs of the actors and actresses in the three theatres royal*, 2 vols. (1790) · F. Gentleman, *The dramatic censor, or, Critical companion*, 2 vols. (1770)
Archives Harvard TC
Likenesses T. Cook, engraving, 1776, BM; repro. in J. Bell, *Bell's British theatre* · J. Golder, engraving, 1777, Harvard TC; repro. in *New English theatre* · R. Laurie, mezzotint, pubd 1779 (after R. Dighton), BM, NPG · S. De Wilde, watercolour drawing, 1815, Garr. Club · J. Roberts, drawing (as Edward in Shirley's *Edward the Black Prince*), BM · theatrical prints, BM, NPG
Wealth at death see will, PRO, PROB 11/1654, sig. 115

Wulfhelm (*d.* 941), archbishop of Canterbury, succeeded Athelm as bishop of Wells when Athelm was promoted to Canterbury in 923; and on the death of Athelm in 926, he succeeded him in the primacy. The following year Wulfhelm went to Rome to receive his pallium from the pope, thereby setting a precedent which all future archbishops of the middle ages were expected to follow. Any such previous journey had been undertaken by archbishops not as a matter of course but only in response to pressing circumstances, as was the case, for example, with Wigheard and Berhtwald.

In the laws of King Æthelstan (924–39)—for example, the code issued at Grately in Hampshire—Æthelstan speaks of having had the counsel of Wulfhelm; and Wulfhelm, alone among the king's witan who were present, is mentioned by name. Whether Wulfhelm also helped in the actual drafting of any of Æthelstan's legislation cannot be ascertained, but to judge by his regular attendance at royal councils there seems to be no doubt of the importance of his role as right-hand man to the king. Æthelstan's gifts to Canterbury of two richly illuminated gospel books may be taken as recognition of this relationship between king and archbishop. One of the books is of Irish provenance; the other came from Lotharingia or Germany and may in the first instance have been a gift to the king, made during negotiations for the marriage in 929 between Edith, the king's sister, and the future Otto I. These marriage negotiations also explain the appearance of Wulfhelm in the confraternity books of a number of German monasteries. Further evidence of Wulfhelm's connections with the continent is provided by the entry in the Lotharingian/German gospel book of a poem written in Carolingian minuscule, a precocious example of this script in England; a likely explanation would be the presence in Wulfhelm's household of a continental scribe. Wulfhelm died on 12 February 941.

HENRIETTA LEYSER

Sources N. Brooks, *The early history of the church of Canterbury: Christ Church from 597 to 1066* (1984) · D. N. Dumville, *English Caroline script and monastic history* (1993)

Wulfhere (*d.* 675), king of the Mercians, was the son of King *Penda and perhaps of Penda's queen, Cynewise. After Penda's defeat and death at the battle of the 'Winwæd' in 655, the Mercian kingdom was occupied by Oswiu of Northumbria for three years. During this time Wulfhere, who was still a youth, was kept hidden by three Mercian ealdormen, Immin, Eafa, and Eadberht. In 658 these three raised a rebellion against Oswiu, drove the Northumbrian ruler's men out of Mercia, and established Wulfhere as king (Bede, *Hist. eccl.*, 3.24). He seems quickly to have re-established, and even extended, his father's supremacy in southern England. The core of his kingdom was Mercia itself, with Middle Anglia (the area of the east midlands between Mercia and East Anglia) and Lindsey (modern Lincolnshire); during his reign a series of bishops were appointed with authority over this huge area, Jaruman, Ceadda (Chad), and Winfrith (ibid., 4.3). It may have been in Wulfhere's reign that London first came under Mercian control; certainly he was in a position in 666 to sell the bishopric of London to Wine, former bishop of the West Saxons (ibid., 3.7). The East Saxon rulers Sigehere and Sæbbi were subject to him, and when a part of the East Saxon kingdom reverted to paganism in the 660s Wulfhere sent Bishop Jaruman to retrieve the situation (ibid., 3.30).

But Wulfhere's domination also penetrated south of the Thames. In the early 670s a local ruler of Surrey named Frithuwold made a generous donation to the monastery at Chertsey, which was shortly afterwards confirmed by Wulfhere during a ceremony at a royal vill at Thame, in what is now Buckinghamshire (*AS chart.*, S 1165). This episode not only indicates that Frithuwold acknowledged Wulfhere's overlordship, but also provides evidence that the Mercian king was gaining control over territory which had formerly been under Kentish influence: for Chertsey had been founded by the Kentish king Ecgberht. Wulfhere also clashed with the West Saxons, the other major kingdom south of the Thames. The Anglo-Saxon Chronicle notes that in 661 he harried Ashdown (an old name for the Berkshire Downs), part of the disputed upper Thames region which was at that stage under West Saxon domination. He probably managed to conquer the area, or at least seriously to challenge West Saxon authority there, for the West Saxon see at Dorchester-on-Thames seems to have been abandoned at about this time. He also subdued the Isle of Wight and the Jutish territory of the Meonware (the people living around the River Meon, that is, in the extreme south-east of modern Hampshire and perhaps also in the western extremity of modern Sussex), and bestowed these two provinces upon his godson Æthelwealh, king of the South Saxons (Bede, *Hist. eccl.*, 4.13). Æthelwealh's wife was a sister of the rulers of the Hwicce, a west midlands tribe which seems to have been at this point under Mercian domination, and he himself had accepted Christianity as a result of Wulfhere's persuasion; it seems very likely that the South Saxon ruler acknowledged Wulfhere's overlordship.

Apparently supreme in the south, Wulfhere was tempted to follow his father's example and to challenge the Northumbrian kings. Probably in 674 he led a coalition of southern armies northwards, with the intention of forcing the Northumbrians to pay him tribute. He was defeated and put to flight by the Northumbrian king Ecgfrith. As a consequence Lindsey was detached from the Mercian realm and briefly became part of the Northumbrian kingdom; and it seems that Wulfhere may have been forced to pay tribute to Ecgfrith. Shortly afterwards Wulfhere died, and was succeeded by his brother *Æthelred, who regained Lindsey for the Mercians. Bede puts Wulfhere's death in 675, and attributes to him a reign of seventeen years (Bede, *Hist. eccl.*, 4.24). Some modern scholars, influenced in part by differing accounts of the length of Æthelred's reign, have adjusted Bede's dates so that Wulfhere's death falls in 674; but the grounds for this are not entirely convincing, and a good case can be made that Bede's dating should be respected.

Unlike his notorious father, Wulfhere seems to have been a Christian and a stout supporter of the church. It was during his reign that an episcopal structure was set up in the Mercian kingdom, and he would appear to have been involved in the appointment of bishops. He took an interest in the ecclesiastical affairs of his subordinate kingdoms, playing an important role in steering the East Saxons back from paganism and apparently promoting the conversion of the South Saxon ruler. To Bishop Ceadda he made a generous donation of 50 hides at Barrow, in what is now Lincolnshire, for the construction of a monastery (Bede, *Hist. eccl.*, 4.3). A lost charter from Worcester, of uncertain authenticity, recorded a grant by Wulfhere to an Abbot Colman of another 50 hides at Hanbury, in modern Worcestershire, which was the site of another early monastery (*AS chart.*, S 1822). There is a less specific reference to grants of land for minster foundation to Wilfrid of Northumbria, whom Wulfhere invited to Mercia to carry out episcopal duties. The Mercian ruler was remembered at the fenland monastery at Medeshamstede (later refounded as St Peter's Abbey, Peterborough) as a significant benefactor, perhaps with some justification. Another later tradition, of uncertain credibility, attributes to Wulfhere and Æthelred the foundation of a minster, most probably at Castor in Northamptonshire, for their sister Cyneburh, widow of Alchfrith of Northumbria; it has been suggested that Wulfhere may indeed have founded a string of minsters on the edges of his kingdom for other alleged sisters and female relatives, including houses at Bicester and Aylesbury.

Wulfhere's best-known wife is Eormenhild, daughter of King *Eorcenberht of Kent; they had a daughter, *Werburh, who was to be venerated as a saint at Chester. Eormenhild was believed to have ended her life at Ely, the monastery founded by her aunt Æthelthryth. Another hagiographical source claims that Wulfhere was married to Eadburh, apparently a kinswoman of the rulers of the Hwicce, who went on to become abbess of the monastery at Gloucester. It is possible that Wulfhere repudiated one of these women (most probably Eadburh) in order to marry the other. He is known to have had one son, *Coenred, who became king of the Mercians in succession to his uncle in 704. It is possible that he had a second son, named Berhtwald, who is mentioned as a nephew of Wulfhere's brother and successor, Æthelred.   S. E. KELLY

Sources Bede, *Hist. eccl.*, 3.7, 24, 30; 4.3, 12–13; 5.24 • *ASC*, s.a. 661 • E. Stephanus, *The life of Bishop Wilfrid*, ed. and trans. B. Colgrave (1927), 30, 42, 80, 106 • *AS chart.*, S 68, 1165, 1782, 1822 • S. Wood, 'Bede's Northumbrian dates again', *EngHR*, 98 (1983), 280–96 • D. P. Kirby, 'Bede and Northumbrian chronology', *EngHR*, 78 (1963), 514–27 • P. H. Blair, 'The *Moore memoranda* on Northumbrian history', *The early cultures of north-west Europe: H. M. Chadwick memorial studies*, ed. C. Fox and B. Dickins (1950), 245–57 • P. Sims-Williams, *Religion and literature in western England, 600–800* (1990), 58, 105–7, 122–4 • J. Blair, 'Frithuwold's kingdom and the origins of Surrey', *The origins of Anglo-Saxon kingdoms*, ed. S. Bassett (1989), 97–107 • J. Blair, *Anglo-Saxon Oxfordshire* (1994), 56–61 • D. W. Rollason, *The Mildrith legend: a study in early medieval hagiography in England* (1982), 13, 33, 80–82, 84, 87, 116 • S. Keynes, *The councils of Clofesho* (1994), 33–4

Wulfhild [St Wulfhild] (*d.* after 996), abbess of Barking and Horton, was the daughter of a nobleman called Wulfhelm. As a girl she was sent to the nunnery of Wilton to be educated and while there attracted the interest of King *Edgar (943/4–975). At this time she does not seem to have taken vows as a nun, but had made a personal commitment so that she was not inclined to respond positively to the king's proposals. When her aunt Wenflæd arranged a meeting for them on her estate at Wherwell (Hampshire) Wulfhild feigned illness so that she could retire from the feast and eventually made her escape through a drainage channel. Cornered by the king in the cloisters of Wilton, she fled to the church for sanctuary leaving the king clutching the sleeve of her gown. Finally discouraged, Edgar proposed a union with her cousin *Wulfthryth instead. Wulfhild was compensated for her ordeal by being made abbess of the nunneries of Barking (Essex) and Horton (Dorset). Her eleventh-century biographer Goscelin drew parallels between her sufferings and those of virgin martyrs like Thecla and Agatha. He emphasized her renunciation of marriage and earthly pomp as one of the justifications of her subsequent sainthood, though he also added instances of virtues such as humility and charity. After an unspecified number of years as abbess of Barking, Wulfhild was expelled from there through the machinations of Ælfthryth, the third wife of King Edgar, though the exact circumstances are not explained. Wulfhild retained her position as abbess of Horton and appears as such in the list of distinguished women in the *Liber vitae* of New Minster, Winchester. At Barking she was regarded as the legitimate abbess, and after twenty years she was allowed to return, reputedly after St Æthelburh, the first abbess of Barking, appeared to rebuke Ælfthryth for her actions. Wulfhild continued as abbess of Barking for another seven years until she died, as she predicted, on 9 September, the eve of the commemoration of the translation of St Æthelwold. The exact year is not known, but it must have been after 996, when the translation of Æthelwold occurred. Wulfhild died in London, where she had gone for safety because of viking attacks, but her body was taken back to Barking for burial in the church.

Miracles attributed to Wulfhild began to be performed at both Barking and Horton; in one, which emphasized her dual control, a blind and paralysed woman was given back her sight at Horton, but had to crawl to Barking to regain the use of her legs. The translation of Wulfhild's body and official recognition of her saintly status was made thirty years after her death by her successor Leofflæd. One of the nuns, Wulfrunna (Judith), who had been educated by Wulfhild and played a major part in organizing her translation and publicizing the cult, was Goscelin's main informant. Although at Barking Wulfhild was ranked alongside its seventh-century saints, Æthelburh and Hildelith, her cult never seems to have achieved a wider popularity. BARBARA YORKE

Sources 'La vie de Sainte Wulfhilde par Goscelin de Cantorbéry', ed. M. Esposito, *Analecta Bollandiana*, 32 (1913), 10–26 • S. Millinger, 'Humility and power: Anglo-Saxon nuns in Anglo-Norman hagiography', *Medieval religious women*, ed. J. A. Nichols and L. T. Shank, 1 (1984), 115–29 • B. A. E. Yorke, 'The legitimacy of St Edith', *Haskins Society Journal*, 11 (2003), 97–113 • M. A. O'Donovan, ed., *Charters of Sherborne*, Anglo-Saxon Charters, 3 (1988) • S. Keynes, ed., *The Liber vitae of the New Minster and Hyde Abbey, Winchester* (Copenhagen, 1996)

Wulford, Ralph. *See* Wilford, Ralph (c.1479–1499).

Wulfred (d. 832), archbishop of Canterbury, presided over the reforming synod held at Chelsea in 816, led the English episcopate in a prolonged campaign against lay lordship of monasteries, and also reformed his own cathedral community and enlarged its endowment.

Background and reform of cathedral community Wulfred's pontificate is surprisingly well documented, thanks to a substantial series of authentic Canterbury charters, to the professions of faith made by bishops-elect, and to the coins issued in his name, as well as to the canons of the Synod of Chelsea. Nothing is known of his early career before the year 803 when he attended a synod at 'Clofesho' as archdeacon in the following of Archbishop Æthelheard. The unusual elevation of a member of the Christ Church *familia* (community) to the archbishopric in 805 may show that Alcuin's advice to Archbishop Æthelheard some eight years previously, that the community should be reformed so that they would be able to elect one of their own number as pontiff, had been heeded. Although Wulfred had later acquired substantial estates 'of his own right' in Kent (Birch, no. 332; *AS chart.*, S 1264), his family roots seem to have been Middle Saxon rather than Kentish. His kinsman, Werhard, had his patrimony at Hayes (in modern Middlesex), where both Wulfred himself and the *praefectus* Werenberht also owned property. There are other hints of a connection with a long-established noble family whose names begin with the letter W and whose landed power lay in the vicinity of Harrow, Hayes, and Twickenham. If that is so, then the elevation of Wulfred to the archiepiscopate was a sign of the Mercian dominance of the church of Canterbury in the early part of the reign of King Cenwulf (r. 796–821). Wulfred attended the synod of 'Acleah' on 26 July 805 as 'archbishop elect' and the reckoning of his pontifical years in later charters suggests that his consecration must have taken place in or after October of that year.

Fundamental to Wulfred's work was the reform of his own cathedral community at Christ Church along lines comparable with those pioneered at Metz by Bishop Chrodegang and which the emperor Louis the Pious and Benedict of Aniane were to attempt to impose on all Frankish cathedrals between 813 and 816. Already in a charter dated between 808 and 813, Wulfred announced that he had 'revived the holy monastery of the church of Canterbury by renewing, restoring and rebuilding it' (Birch, no. 342; *AS chart.*, S 1265); he insisted that the community should maintain the office at the canonical hours, should eat in the communal refectory, and sleep in the dormitory, and that property owned by individual brethren had to be bequeathed to the community. Subsequently the archbishop made grants of land to the community which were conditional upon the maintenance of this reformed regime. Wulfred's reform represents an attempt to return to the monastic ideals that Pope Gregory I had recommended for Augustine's clergy. In referring to the 'priests and deacons' of Christ Church as being subject to 'the rule of the life of monastic discipline' (Birch, no. 342; *AS chart.*, S 1265) Wulfred was, however, retaining traditional terminology rather than using the new language of the Carolingian reforms which described the clergy of cathedral or collegiate churches as 'canons' subject to a 'canonical' rule.

Political difficulties and territorial acquisitions From the start of his pontificate Wulfred encountered political problems. On the coins minted at Canterbury in his name, a bust of a metropolitan bishop, based on papal models, was introduced and the name of the Mercian king was dropped and replaced by that of the moneyer. These changes may reflect archiepiscopal assertiveness. Certainly by the year 808 there had been a prolonged breach with the Mercian king, Cenwulf, for in that year Pope Leo III referred in a letter to Charlemagne to the fact that Cenwulf 'had not yet made peace with his archbishop' (Haddan & Stubbs, 3.563). Good relations with Cenwulf were restored between 809 and 814, but were then disrupted between 815 and 821 by the bitter struggle to remove lay control of monastic or 'minster' churches. Thereafter rapid changes in the Mercian royal succession and, from 825–7, the subjection of Kent to West Saxon rule hindered any lasting resolution of the minster dispute and limited the influence of a Mercian archbishop of Canterbury.

Despite these difficult circumstances, Wulfred followed a vigorous territorial policy, both in the acquisition of estates for his own use and in reorganizing and extending the properties of his cathedral community of Christ Church. He spent a personal fortune of at least 17,720 silver pennies on the purchase of estates in Kent and in what is now Middlesex and he disposed of more distant properties in the Thames valley or further afield. Thus he accumulated adjacent estates which could be administered as large single manors. Many of the great medieval manors of the archbishops and of the monks of Canterbury (Bishopsbourne, Eastry, Lympne, Graveney, Otford, and Petham in Kent and Harrow in Middlesex) can be shown to have taken their definitive form in his time. He also insisted that grants made to Christ Church were inalienable permanent gifts (so long as the community maintained the reformed life that he had established for them), but was careful to insist that he himself had full powers of disposal over those estates that he had accumulated for his own use. The distinction was important. Some of Wulfred's own properties do indeed seem to have passed into the permanent endowment of the archbishops of Canterbury. But although Wulfred's own will has not survived, he is known to have used the bulk of his own estates to enrich his kinsman, the priest Werhard, a member of the Christ Church community who can be shown to have risen very rapidly until he became 'priest-abbot' by the mid-830s. It also seems probable that two other senior members of the Christ Church community in the first two decades of the ninth century, Wulfhard and Wernoth, were members of Wulfred's kin. For more than forty years, from his own emergence as archdeacon by the year 803 until Werhard's last appearance as priest-abbot in 845, Wulfred's nepotism would seem to have ensured that his own family was the dominant group in the cathedral community.

Decline in Latin learning Under Wulfred's leadership Christ Church developed a scriptorium distinguished by a highly calligraphic version of the insular cursive minuscule script, used both for formal charters and for important books. Astonishingly, however, this high point in the history of insular script coincided with appalling standards of Latin grammar and orthography. Indeed, two charters, of the years 822 and 823, which can plausibly be attributed to the hand of Wulfred himself, are replete with false agreements and with spellings affected by his vernacular pronunciation. Trained by such an archbishop, several of the cathedral clergy could compose (utilizing earlier models) formal professions of faith for bishops-elect to present to the archbishop at the time of their consecration. Doubtless they also could comprehend the routine services and familiar passages of the scriptures; but few, if any, of them had sufficient command of grammar to be able to compose in Latin for new needs. With standards of Latin so low in the metropolitan church, there was a serious danger that educational decline would threaten the routine pastoral work of the church.

Dispute over control of minsters; and death Concern for pastoral standards in the province of Canterbury lay behind the major dispute of Wulfred's pontificate. For more than a century leading English churchmen had insisted that monasteries or minster-churches should not fall under the hereditary control of royal or local noble families to the detriment both of their monastic discipline and of the pastoral care of their extensive *parochiae* (parishes). In 803, indeed, Wulfred had attended the synod of 'Clofesho' which had forbidden minster communities to choose laymen as lords and had required them to observe monastic discipline. In 814 he travelled to Rome, accompanied by Wigbert, bishop of Sherborne, returning the following year with Pope Leo III's blessing. The unstated purpose of this visit may have been to gain advance papal support for the reforms adopted in 816 at Wulfred's Synod of Chelsea. The decrees of this synod, probably composed by Wulfred himself, assert canonical tradition, the unity of the Southumbrian episcopate, and the rights and powers of the English bishops acting in synod. Particularly notable are the emphasis (c.4) on the duty of bishops to appoint the heads of monastic houses in their diocese with the consent of the communities and the prohibition (c.8) of lay lordship of monastic houses while authorizing bishops to secure the property of communities threatened with impoverishment by the rapacity of laymen.

In overriding traditional canonical restrictions on episcopal interference in monastic elections and property, the synod set the stage for a major clash of church and state. Within a year Wulfred was embroiled in a bitterly fought test case with Cenwulf over the Kentish minsters of Reculver and Minster in Thanet. In the course of a long struggle (816–21) the king used his influence at Rome and at the court of the emperor, Louis the Pious, to secure the archbishop's suspension from office and to acquire papal privileges confirming his rights over the monasteries he had inherited or acquired. The archbishop produced forged charters attributed to kings Wihtred of Kent (696–716) and Æthelbald of Mercia (742) (S 22, 90) which purported to grant control of monastic elections and property to the archbishop; he may also have responded to his suspension by deposing the king. Certainly the moneyers of the Canterbury mint at this time preferred to produce anonymous coins, bearing the royal or the archiepiscopal busts but omitting their names. Shortly before his death in 821, Cenwulf imposed a settlement whereby the archbishop retained the lordship of Reculver and Minster but at the massive cost of ceding to the king an estate of 300 hides (perhaps at Eynsham, Oxfordshire) and a fine of £120, the wergeld (blood-price) of a king. In Canterbury eyes this solution was not respected by the king's sister, Cwenthryth, who was abbess of Minster in Thanet; but after the succession of King Beornwulf, Wulfred compelled Cwenthryth at councils held at 'Clofesho' (825) and 'Oslafeshlau' to cede Minster and a further estate of 100 hides at Harrow, Wembley, and Yeadding, which thereafter became one of the largest archiepiscopal manors.

Wulfred's remarkable but costly victory was short-lived. Between 825 and 827 Mercian rule in Kent was ended when the kingdom was taken over by King Ecgberht of Wessex and his son, Æthelwulf, who did not recognize the archbishop as the sole lord of the Kentish minsters. They also confiscated an estate at 'Malling' on the grounds that it had been given to the church of Canterbury by the Mercian sub-king, Baldred, when in flight from the West Saxon forces. The interruption of the archbishop's minting rights for some years and the fact that his only acquisition after 827 was a grant by King Wiglaf of Mercia in 831 of land at Botwell, in what is now Middlesex (*AS chart.*, S 188), suggests that the great archbishop still preferred to operate within the Mercian political stage and had difficult relations with the West Saxon rulers. He died in 832, on 24 March, according to the Canterbury obit lists.

N. P. BROOKS

Sources *AS chart.*, S 22, 40, 90, 161, 164, 168–70, 175–8, 186–8, 1188, 1264–8, 1414, 1434, 1436, 1619 · M. Richter, ed., *Canterbury professions*, CYS, 67 (1973), nos. 7–16 · A. W. Haddan and W. Stubbs, eds., *Councils and ecclesiastical documents relating to Great Britain and Ireland*, 3 (1871) · N. Brooks, *The early history of the church of Canterbury: Christ Church from 597 to 1066* (1984), 132–42, 155–206 · C. Cubitt, *Anglo-Saxon church councils, c.650–c.850* (1995), 191–204 · M. P. Brown, 'Paris, Bibliothèque nationale lat. 10861 and the scriptorium of Christ Church, Canterbury', *Anglo-Saxon England*, 15 (1986), 119–37 · J. Crick, 'Church, land and local nobility in early ninth-century Kent: the case of Ealdorman Oswulf', *Historical Research*, 61 (1988), 251–69 · S. Keynes, 'The control of Kent in the ninth century', *Early Medieval Europe*, 2 (1993), 111–32 · W. de G. Birch, ed., *Cartularium Saxonicum*, 1 (1885), nos. 312, 332, 342 · P. Collinson and others, eds., *A history of Canterbury Cathedral, 598–1982* (1995)

Archives BL, Cotton MSS, charters · Canterbury Cathedral, Christ Church cartularies · Canterbury Cathedral, professions of faith · CCC Cam., Christ Church cartularies · LPL, Christ Church cartularies

Likenesses bust on archiepiscopal coins, repro. in Collinson and others, eds., *History of Canterbury Cathedral*, pl. 3

Wulfric of Haselbury [St Wulfric of Haselbury] (*c.*1090–1154/5), priest and hermit, spent much of his life enclosed in a cell at Haselbury Plucknett (Somerset), where he lived a life of great austerity and received many visitors, including kings and queens.

Perhaps *c.*1090, Wulfric was born to English parents of middling social rank at Compton Martin (Somerset), a village some 9 miles from Bristol, the lord of which was William FitzWalter. Having been ordained priest, Wulfric first ministered at Deverill, near Warminster (Wiltshire), where he led a worldly life and spent much time in hunting and hawking, until a chance encounter with a beggar converted him to a stricter life. William FitzWalter thereafter recalled him to be parish priest at Compton Martin. After a few years there, about 1125 William enabled him to settle as an anchorite at the parish church of Haselbury Plucknett, a village of which he was also lord, some 28 miles to the south. For the rest of his life, Wulfric occupied a cell on the north side of the chancel; he had a servant to attend to his needs. He was not the parish priest, but for the most part he co-operated amicably with the married clerk, Brictric, who had cure of souls.

Wulfric was not inducted into his cell, as would have been customary, by the bishop of Bath, then Godfrey; but he obeyed the directions of Godfrey's successor, Robert. He maintained close touch with the nearby Cluniac priory at Montacute which daily supplied him with food. Spiritually, he held the Cistercians in high regard and he especially revered the community at Ford in the east of Devon (now in Dorset); but he was not well disposed towards the Augustinian canons. His own way of life was rigorously austere. He wore a hair shirt which he soon covered with a hauberk of chain mail supplied by William FitzWalter. He undertook prolonged vigils and fasts, and he frequently immersed himself in cold water. He engaged in bookbinding and oversaw the making of church vestments.

Wulfric became famous for his miracles and gift of prophecy. Unlike Brictric, he was almost certainly bilingual in English and French. His most interesting contacts were with Anglo-Norman royalty. A courtier of Henry I, Drogo de Munci, was stricken with fits for suggesting the seizure of money from Wulfric's cell; a visit by Henry and his queen, Adeliza, led to Wulfric's healing of Drogo. Wulfric later prophesied that Henry's crossing of the English Channel in 1133 would be the last that he would make alive; upon learning in 1135 that this had come true, Wulfric declared that Henry would find mercy with the Lord, 'because in his life he had striven for peace and justice, and had built the Lord's house at Reading [Reading Abbey] with regal magnificence' (*Wulfric of Haselbury*, ed. M. Bell, 116–17). Before Stephen succeeded, he and his brother Henry, bishop of Winchester, visited Wulfric, who prophetically hailed Stephen as king. Wulfric also foretold the disturbances that would follow a divided succession, including Stephen's captivity at Lincoln in 1141. Later in his reign, Stephen visited Wulfric, who reproved him but promised that he would reign for as long as he lived. He also censured the haughtiness of Stephen's queen, Matilda, who had snubbed at court William FitzWalter's wife. Wulfric charged the future Henry II 12s. for his followers' depredations at his cell and foretold that Henry would not reign during Stephen's natural life. Another prophecy was of the failure of the second crusade.

Wulfric died on 20 February, probably in 1154 but possibly in 1155; the monks of Montacute and Ford contended for his body, but Robert, bishop of Bath, insisted upon his wish to be buried in his cell. His body was soon twice translated to places in the chancel of the church. His cult developed somewhat slowly, but throughout the latter middle ages Haselbury became a place of pilgrimage. Henry of Huntingdon was the first chronicler to refer to Wulfric, but practically all that is known about him comes from a life written c.1184 by John, prior and later abbot of Ford. Wulfric's career illustrates how, when Englishmen were largely debarred from normal ecclesiastical promotion, the eremitical life could offer a way to spiritual authority with both the French and the English. H. E. J. COWDREY

Sources Henry, archdeacon of Huntingdon, *Historia Anglorum*, ed. D. E. Greenway, OMT (1996), xxix–xxx · John, abbot of Ford, *Wulfric of Haselbury*, ed. K. Day, Corpus Christianorum · *Wulfric of Haselbury, by John, abbot of Ford*, ed. M. Bell, Somerset RS, 47 (1933) · *Rogeri de Wendover liber qui dicitur flores historiarum*, ed. H. G. Hewlett, 3 vols., Rolls Series, [84] (1886–9), vol. 1, pp. 4–9 · Paris, *Chron.*, 1.205–9 · C. Horstman, ed., *Nova legenda Anglie, as collected by John of Tynemouth, J. Capgrave, and others*, 2 (1901), 511–20 · H. Mayr-Harting, 'Functions of a twelfth-century recluse', *History*, new ser., 60 (1975), 337–52

Wulfric Spot (d. 1002×4), magnate, is described in contemporary documents as son of Wulfrun; the name of his father is unknown. The earliest evidence for his unexplained byname Spot, or Spott, is in the thirteenth-century Burton annals.

Wulfric was a member of an important Mercian family. Both he and his mother were associated, in different ways, with Tamworth, which was until the tenth century the main centre of royal power in Mercia; Wulfric apparently enjoyed exceptional privileges there. That is, at least, the implication of his bequest to his daughter of lordship of land at Tamworth that was 'not to be subject to any service nor to any man born' (AS chart., S 1536).

In the course of the tenth century several of Wulfric's kinsmen benefited greatly from royal patronage and Wulfric himself, described as *minister*, or king's thegn, attested many of King Æthelred's charters from 980 to 1002, most of which were also attested by his brother Ælfhelm, who was made ealdorman of Northumbria in 993, and Ælfhelm's son, Wulfheah. The fact that in the 990s Wulfric and his nephew were often among the first of the subscribing thegns suggests that they, like Ælfhelm, then had a leading role in meetings of the royal council.

Wulfric made his will between 1002, the date of his last subscription, and 1004, when King Æthelred confirmed the endowment and privileged status of Burton Abbey. He bequeathed land in eighty named places or districts in many parts of Mercia and southern Northumbria, most of them in Derbyshire, Staffordshire, and west Warwickshire. The size or value of most of these bequests is uncertain; some were described as small, but the Northumbrian

properties were very large, comprising the area between the rivers Ribble and Mersey (that is, south Lancashire) and the estate of Conisburgh which with its sokelands was, according to Domesday Book, in 1066 assessed at 90 carucates.

Wulfric supported Benedictine reform. The abbey, initially dedicated to St Benedict, which he founded at Burton upon Trent before making his will, received over half the estates named in it. Burton commemorated his obit on 22 October. Wulfric also left money to all the monasteries, abbots, and abbesses in England, and is among those commemorated in the *Liber vitae* (confraternity book) of the New Minster, Winchester, as a friend and benefactor. The only unreformed community to receive anything in the will was Tamworth; the absence of any bequest to his mother's foundation of Wolverhampton is remarkable.

Most other bequests were to members of Wulfric's family. He apparently had only one surviving child, an unnamed daughter, who was given a life interest in two small estates, implying that she was not expected to have an heir. The main benefactors were his brother Ælfhelm and nephew Wulfheah, who were given the Northumbrian properties and some others. His sister, Ælfthryth, apparently died before Wulfric, but he made bequests to her daughter, Ealdgyth, and to Ealdgyth's husband, Morcar, who received a compact group of estates near Chesterfield. P. H. SAWYER

Sources P. H. Sawyer, ed., *Charters of Burton Abbey*, Anglo-Saxon Charters, 2 (1979) · S. Keynes, *The diplomas of King Æthelred 'The Unready'* (978–1016): a study in their use as historical evidence, Cambridge Studies in Medieval Life and Thought, 3rd ser., 13 (1980) · P. H. Sawyer, 'The charters of Burton Abbey and the unification of England', *Northern History*, 10 (1975), 28–39 · AS chart., S 1536

Wulfsige [St Wulfsige] (d. 1002), abbot of Westminster and bishop of Sherborne, is the subject of a life written by Goscelin of St Bertin in the late eleventh century. A short description of his life was also provided by William of Malmesbury in his *Gesta pontificum*, but both Goscelin and William were writing too long after his death for their information to be necessarily reliable, and William's version in particular is open to question. Even less reliable is the account of Wulfsige's life by the fifteenth-century historian of Westminster Abbey, John Flete, who conflates Goscelin's account with details drawn from forged charters for Westminster.

According to Goscelin, Wulfsige was born in London and his parents gave him while he was still a child to the community of Westminster. This is plausible: Wulfsige had strong connections with London (one of his posthumous miracles concerned a London woman), he certainly became a member of the community at Westminster and, while Goscelin possibly might, as a Benedictine, have invented the idea of his oblation, none the less entry in childhood into non-monastic communities was just as normal as it was into monastic ones. The date of Wulfsige's birth is unknown. If William of Malmesbury's statement that he became abbot of Westminster while Dunstan was bishop of London (958–61) were to be accepted, it would have to be assumed that he was born no later than *c*.925. However, it is likely that on this point William misinterpreted Goscelin, who said that Wulfsige (who had previously risen through the clerical grades in due order and been ordained priest when of 'mature age') was made abbot of Westminster by King Edgar (*r*. 959–75, but king of Mercia from 957), who, says Goscelin, was as ever following the advice of Dunstan in all appointments of bishops and abbots. William might have wished to suggest that Wulfsige had been promoted by his diocesan rather than by a secular ruler. On the basis of Goscelin's account the date of birth might lie anywhere between the 920s and the 940s.

John Flete states that Wulfsige was put in charge of Westminster by Dunstan in 958, but that the latter retained the abbacy until 980, and that it was only at this point that Wulfsige was made abbot. Flete's dates cannot be trusted, but even so it is likely that Dunstan was abbot of Westminster during most if not all of Edgar's reign, and it is noteworthy that, apart from the narrative sources and a spurious charter of Edgar of 966 (*AS chart.*, S 741), the earliest occurrences of Wulfsige as abbot of Westminster are in charters of 988 (*AS chart.*, S 868) and 989/990 (*AS chart.*, S 877). Goscelin attributes to Wulfsige the conversion of Westminster into a Benedictine community, but a charter of Edgar for Westminster surviving in a contemporary though mutilated form (*AS chart.*, S 670) shows that Dunstan was responsible.

Goscelin states that Wulfsige retained the abbacy of Westminster for a while after his elevation to the see of Sherborne in, it has been argued, the summer of 993. He ceased to be abbot in or before 997 when his successor first appears. As bishop of Sherborne, Wulfsige was anxious to spread the ideals of the tenth-century Benedictine reform more widely. Goscelin tells that he converted his cathedral community to monastic observance, probably by 998, the date of the Sherborne foundation charter, issued by Æthelred (*AS chart.*, S 895). This charter has some unusual features but is probably genuine; it imposes the Benedictine rule, and lists the estates which were to be specifically attached to the monks. A charter purporting to have been issued by Wulfsige giving the monks permission to inherit the possessions of the clerks they had displaced is, however, a post-conquest forgery (*AS chart.*, S 1382). Wulfsige's zeal for Benedictine monasticism also found expression in his instructions to the clergy of his diocese, for whom he commissioned a letter on pastoral care from Ælfric of Eynsham. Although addressed to secular clergy, the letter advocates a model of life strongly influenced by the aims of the Benedictine reform, for Ælfric tells clerics to be chaste and to live according to a rule (perhaps the enlarged rule of Chrodegang, though this is not specified), and holds out to them monastic obedience to the rule of Benedict as an ideal. Furthermore, he provides detailed instructions about liturgical practice, perhaps the aspect of ecclesiastical life in which tenth-century reformers took most interest. The priests in the diocese of Sherborne were each expected to possess a psalter, a book of epistles, an evangeliary, a missal, antiphonals, a manual, a computus, a passional, a penitential, and a reading-book. Ælfric gave detailed instructions for prayer, at least some, if not all, of which may have come from Wulfsige, since there is reference to bishops making decisions at a synod.

A tangible sign of Wulfsige's influence in liturgical matters is the Sherborne pontifical (Paris, Bibliothèque Nationale, MS Lat. 943), written at Canterbury in the late tenth century and procured for Sherborne, probably by Wulfsige, in or by the early eleventh century. Into this manuscript were entered a letter by an anonymous archbishop to Wulfsige, exhorting him to be a good diocesan, and two letters by Wulfsige concerning penance to be performed by those who had killed close relatives. On 20 June 1001 Wulfsige presided over the translation of Edward the Martyr at Shaftesbury. He died on 8 January, his feast day, almost certainly in 1002, since his successor, Æthelric, first appears in that year. He was buried in a *porticus* in his cathedral at Sherborne and was translated twelve years later to a position at the right side of the altar.

JULIA BARROW

Sources 'The life of Saint Wulsin of Sherborne by Goscelin', ed. C. H. Talbot, *Revue Bénédictine*, 69 (1959), 68–85 • *Willelmi Malmesbiriensis monachi de gestis pontificum Anglorum libri quinque*, ed. N. E. S. A. Hamilton, Rolls Series, 52 (1870), 178–9 • J. Flete, *The history of Westminster Abbey*, ed. J. A. Robinson (1909), 78–80 • *AS chart.*, S 670, 741, 868, 876, 877, 895, 1382 • W. de G. Birch, ed., *Cartularium Saxonicum*, 3 vols. (1885–93), nos. 1048, 1178 • A. J. Robertson, ed. and trans., *Anglo-Saxon charters*, 2nd edn (1956), no. 63 • M. A. O'Donovan, ed., *Charters of Sherborne*, Anglo-Saxon Charters, 3 (1988), nos. 11–12 • D. Whitelock, M. Brett, and C. N. L. Brooke, eds., *Councils and synods with other documents relating to the English church, 871–1204*, 1 (1981), 178n, 189–232, 374 • J. Hill, 'Monastic reform and the secular church: Ælfric's pastoral letters in context', *England in the eleventh century* [Harlaxton 1990], ed. C. Hicks (1992), 103–17 • N. Brooks, 'The career of St Dunstan', *St Dunstan: his life, times and cult*, ed. N. Ramsay, M. Sparks, and T. Tatton-Brown (1992), 1–23 • S. Keynes, *The diplomas of King Æthelred 'The Unready' (978–1016): a study in their use as historical evidence*, Cambridge Studies in Medieval Life and Thought, 3rd ser., 13 (1980), 251, 258

Archives Bibliothèque Nationale, Paris, MS Lat. 943

Wulfstan (*fl.* 880), traveller, was a mariner, presumably but not certainly Anglo-Saxon in origin, who made at least one voyage in the Baltic Sea. While his motive may have been mercantile, his importance lies in the detailed, word-of-mouth report which he gave to King Alfred of Wessex, a report that constitutes the only known evidence for Wulfstan's existence. Transcribed and disseminated by Alfred, or at Alfred's command, Wulfstan's 700-word account extended the Anglo-Saxons' knowledge of geography and alien customs and culture.

The voyage described by Wulfstan began at the Danish port of Hedeby and ended seven days later at Estmere (now the Gulf of Gdańsk). After making his way up a very broad inlet Wulfstan landed at the port of Truso (now Elbląg, in the eastern half of Poland). Here, he encountered 'Este' (east Europeans), whose culture was quite unfamiliar to him. He told King Alfred that the Este always cremated their dead but that there was often an initial period during which they kept the body chilled. During this time, which might extend to several months, the body remained *inne unforbærned* ('indoors, unburnt') while family and friends who gathered in the dead man's house disported themselves in drinking and revels, thus dissipating much of his wealth. (Wulfstan referred especially to men, whose property rights and other prerogatives apparently far exceeded those of women in Este society.)

According to Wulfstan, the family and friends eventually divided such goods as remained into several lots of varying size, placing the largest about a mile from the house and successively smaller lots at intervening points. Horsemen gathered well beyond the largest lot and raced each other towards the house, each winning the lot he arrived at first, whereupon the body was borne to the pyre. Wulfstan shrewdly discerned a link between these funeral games and the high price the Este paid for fast horses, and here and elsewhere he gave complex detail clearly and vividly, but it cannot be assumed that he witnessed all that he described, and he made no claim to that effect. Indeed, a reliance on hearsay evidence can perhaps be detected in his failure to describe the method used for chilling bodies, and in the fact that he seemed unacquainted with the tribe of Este who practised this art.

Wulfstan's Este have been identified as Estonians, but the only landing he mentioned was the one at Truso, just halfway from Hedeby to modern Estonia. None the less, his stated itinerary took him much further north, and he may have reached the Gulf of Finland (possibly on another voyage, whose details he may have conflated or confused with those appertaining to his visit to Truso). His references to refrigeration may thus reflect an encounter with people who could avail themselves of natural ice. A further geographical indicator may be found in the fact that his Este drink more mead than ale.

Wulfstan's achievement did not lie in navigation or in pioneering exploration, since vikings had traversed the same waters decades earlier, often continuing eastwards up rivers. Moreover, Truso was almost certainly a well-established trading post, and Wulfstan may have gone there routinely. His achievement rests on his keen observation, anthropological interests, and lively reportage. His unexplained visit to Alfred's court enabled his account to be recorded and added to Alfred's *History of the World*, a translation, datable to the 880s, from Orosius (where it partners an account of voyages in the Norwegian Sea by another ninth-century sailor called Ohthere). As part of that *History*, Wulfstan's account reached monastic libraries throughout and possibly well beyond Wessex.

TONY D. TRIGGS

Sources *King Alfred's Orosius*, ed. H. Sweet, EETS, original series, 79 (1883) · N. Lund, *Two voyagers at the court of King Alfred* (1984) · J. M. Bately, ed., *The Old English Orosius*, EETS, supplementary ser., 6 (1980)

Wulfstan (d. 955/6), archbishop of York, of unknown family, was the first of that name to hold the see; he was archbishop from some time between 3 April and 30 June 931 until his death. Throughout his career he showed a marked readiness to support various viking ventures against the English crown. There are chronological discrepancies between accounts of his activities in various northern annals and his signatures to royal diplomas of the English kings; on the whole, the evidence of the charters is to be preferred.

Wulfstan witnessed King Æthelstan's charters regularly until 21 December 934. Later charters of Æthelstan have greatly abbreviated witness lists, in which the northern sees, including York, are unrepresented; it seems likely that he had lost effective control of the north. After Æthelstan's death in October 939, York was occupied by Óláf Guthfrithson, king of Dublin. Archbishop Wulfstan may have enthroned Óláf; certainly he became his supporter, travelling with him the following year on an expedition into the midlands. Óláf and Wulfstan were besieged by King Edmund at Leicester, but Wulfstan, together with Archbishop Oda of Canterbury, arranged a treaty by which Edmund surrendered to Óláf the territory of the Five Boroughs (Leicester, Lincoln, Nottingham, Derby, and Stamford), and Watling Street was fixed as King Edmund's new northern boundary. In the following year Óláf died, and the kingdom of York passed into the hands of his cousin, Óláf Sihtricson. In 942 King Edmund regained control of the Five Boroughs, and for a brief period Wulfstan witnessed his charters. Ragnall, Óláf Guthfrithson's brother, was then made king of York, and no surviving charter of King Edmund issued in 943 is witnessed by Wulfstan. According to Æthelweard's chronicle, however, in 944 Wulfstan drove Ragnall out of York, and King Edmund regained possession of the city. From then onwards Wulfstan's signature appears regularly on King Edmund's diplomas.

After Edmund's death, his brother Eadred became king of England and secured Wulfstan's allegiance at Tanshelf, Yorkshire, in 947; but according to the chroniclers, Wulfstan was quick to break his oath. This alleged treachery is not reflected immediately in King Eadred's charters, which Wulfstan continued to witness until 950, though Erik Bloodaxe had gained temporary control of York in 948: Wulfstan witnessed all but three of the fifteen charters of King Eadred surviving for the years 948–9, and the sole surviving charter of 950. From 951 onwards, however, Wulfstan again ceased to witness Eadred's charters, and it seems that he was out of contact with his court during most of the period in which Óláf Sihtricson, having displaced Erik from York, was reigning there for the second time.

Wulfstan's subsequent career can be followed in outline from late Northumbrian annals, originating at York and preserved in writings attributed to Symeon of Durham and the D text of the Anglo-Saxon Chronicle; but his charter subscriptions suggest that these annals have an unsatisfactory chronology for the years 951–6. Probably in 953, Wulfstan was imprisoned by King Eadred at 'Iudanbyrig'. His restoration to a bishopric, at Dorchester, should perhaps be assigned to early 955. For the rest of his life Wulfstan seems to have remained in the south. He witnessed as archbishop a number of King Eadred's charters issued in 955, but it appears unlikely that he was able to exercise jurisdiction in the northern archdiocese. According to a retrospective statement in the Anglo-Saxon Chronicle (s. a. 970, text B), Bishop Oscytel of Dorchester was given nominal charge of York late in Eadred's reign, by the king 'and all his witan'. King Eadred died on 23 November 955. Wulfstan appears as witness to two early charters of his successor, King Eadwig, but doubts have been voiced as to their authenticity. Wulfstan died and was buried at Oundle, Northamptonshire, in the diocese of Dorchester. The date of his death is disputed; the most likely date appears to be 26 December 956, but 955 cannot be completely ruled out.   CYRIL HART

Sources C. R. Hart, *The early charters of northern England and the north midlands* (1975) · D. Whitelock, *History, law and literature in 10th–11th century England* (1981) · 'Simeon of Durham's history of the kings of England', *The historical works of Simeon of Durham* (1855), vol. 3/2 of *The Church historians of England*, ed. and trans. J. Stevenson (1853–8) [repr. (1987)] · *ASC*, s. a. 943, 947, 952, 954, 957 [texts B, D, E] · AS chart., S 560, 582, 605 · A. P. Smyth, *Scandinavian York and Dublin: the history of two related Viking kingdoms*, 2 (1979) · *The chronicle of Æthelweard*, ed. and trans. A. Campbell (1962)

Wulfstan [Lupus] (d. 1023), archbishop of York and homilist, was the uncle of Brihtheah, bishop of Worcester (1033–8). Since knowledge of him has been transformed in the last hundred years, few entries in the *Oxford Dictionary of National Biography* differ so markedly from their Victorian forerunner as this on Wulfstan.

Life Wulfstan was clearly enough a product of the tenth-century monastic reform movement, though his debt to it is not so explicit as that of Ælfric, his contemporary as homilist and canonist. Unlike the earlier generation of the reform's protagonists, he was not generally regarded as a saint, so was not commemorated in a life. The only sources for his family background are a few records from Worcester and a notice of his burial at Ely in the *Liber Eliensis*. Both reveal his kinship with his successor but one at Worcester, Brihtheah. The former records a marriage agreement for an unnamed sister, as well as a lease to one Wulfgifu who may be the sister in question (the lands involved had the same tenant, elsewhere identified as Bishop Brihtheah's nephew, in 1066). Ely's notice gives a warm account of Wulfstan's stature and sanctity; his determination to be buried there (though he died as far away as York) is ascribed to a semi-miraculous event on an earlier visit and there is also a mention of *miracula* at his tomb. This implies an effort to generate a cult, even if it had only local resonance. A different story was preserved by Peterborough, where it was claimed that he had intended to be buried there, Ely acquiring him by chance; it may be significant that Wulfstan's immediate predecessor at York and Worcester was Abbot Ealdulf of Peterborough. Noble families with members named Wulfstan had featured in the tenth-century history of each abbey; the likelihood is that the archbishop belonged to one or other (or both) of them.

The first evidence of Wulfstan at work is a set of letters by or addressed to the bishop of London, Lupus (*Lat.* 'wolf'); their preservation in Wulfstan manuscript miscellanies is proof that London's Bishop Wulfstan (996–1002) was the future archbishop. Three letters are on penitential issues, while a fourth defers to Lupus's eloquence. It is an engaging possibility that the apocalyptic homilies which are usually considered among Wulfstan's earliest, and which would after all have been appropriate enough for the eve of the year 1000, first made his reputation, prompting his promotion to the sees of York and Worcester in 1002. The holding of the potentially disaffected northern archbishopric in plurality with a southern see, usually Worcester, was evidently policy in the tenth and eleventh centuries. Often, as with Wulfstan, the incumbent was someone whose Danelaw background would give him insight into northern mentalities, but whose southern landed interests would discourage support for separatist tendencies. However, Wulfstan soon became more than the government's Northumbrian lieutenant. Probably at an early stage, he drew up the so-called 'Canons of Edgar' and 'Peace of Edward and Guthrum', for the clergy and laity of his diocese respectively. By 1008 he was drafting the laws that Æthelred II issued at Enham. He played the same role for the edicts of 1009 and 1014. The first versions of his powerful 1014 'Sermon of the Wolf to the English' envisaged Swein's rampaging Danes as apocalyptic visitations of God's anger at English sins. Later drafts came to imply that the English could learn from the parallels between their recent experience and their own defeat of the Britons back in the sixth century. God would punish but could also be placated by a fresh start. Hence, Wulfstan not only dedicated the church that Cnut founded on the site of his decisive victory for the souls of those slain there (perhaps composing a homily for the occasion), he also orchestrated the reconciliation of the two peoples at the Council of Oxford in 1018. His chosen instrument was a restatement of 'Edgar's law', which in practice meant laws he had earlier issued for Æthelred. The culmination of his life's work was the great code which he drew up for promulgation by Cnut at Winchester in 1020 or 1021. In effect it codified much of the pertinent law made by English kings since Alfred, as a foundation for a regime that would now earn God's favour rather than his wrath.

Wulfstan's place at the king's right hand made him the logical choice to settle legal disputes for the churches of Hereford and Sherborne. He is also said to have refounded St Peter's Abbey at Gloucester. His administration of his own episcopal estates appears from marginalia by his hand in documents from both cathedrals. These include Worcester's first cartulary, whose compilation he probably directed and which is much the earliest such record to survive. Yet he left a bad name at Worcester. Clearly—in the circumstances, naturally—his property strategies favoured his kin. In the more reformist ecclesiastical climate of the later eleventh century, this did not seem so natural at all. Nor did pluralist tenure; and though Wulfstan ostensibly gave up Worcester in 1016, he appears to have retained a supervisory role. His reputation can only have suffered as a result, especially as Worcester had serious trouble on these scores from his successors. But at Ely his fame was secure. His obit was commemorated there on 28 May, the anniversary of his death, which took place in York in 1023. The *Liber Eliensis* notice was in fact occasioned by his translation from his original burial place at Ely to the new church's choir in 1154. He was moved again and provided with an effigy in the reign of Edward III. A drawing of this effigy survives and a bronze pin found in his tomb is preserved by the Society of Antiquaries.

As an author Wulfstan is named as author (almost always by the *nom de plume* Lupus) in only six homilies (Bethurum VI–VII, XIII, XX–XXI, Napier LIX) and the Latin version of the law-code 'VI' Æthelred. His prose style is what enables him to be identified as author of so much more. Dorothy Bethurum printed a total of thirty texts in 1957, but six of them consist of little more than preparatory matter and three are variations of the 1014 sermon. The official corpus of mainline homilies thus numbers twenty-two (Bethurum, Ib, II–VII, VIIIb, VIIIc, IX, Xc, XI–XV, XVIb, XVII–XXI). Apart from the probably early eschatological series, the heart of this collection is made up of discourses on Christian life, its prayers, beliefs, and rituals. They draw for the most part on standard authorities from the Carolingian period or earlier: Alcuin (*d.* 804), Jesse of Amiens, Theodulf of Orléans, Amalarius of Metz; also Pirmin and Defensor of Ligugé; and, for eschatological discourses, Adso of Montier-en-Der. His sources even extend to works with a much less general circulation such as Abbo of St Germain and Atto of Vercelli. The mainline corpus includes some sermons for specific occasions, among them that already mentioned for 'Dedication of a church', and one for 'Consecration of a bishop' that may have had a particular bishop in mind. Further items are a recasting of Ælfric's homily on false gods, which has been described, like its model, as 'more a piece of learning' than the sort of impassioned denunciation the archbishop built into his laws; and a pastoral letter, extant in several recensions, that does already anticipate the sort of Christian conduct (payment of church taxes, for example) demanded by the laws. Special interest, given what was to come, attaches to some sermons that meditate on the history of God's dealings with the people of Israel. The mainline homilies seem, on the whole, to predate the laws, if only because Wulfstan was well capable of incorporating his legal stipulations into sermons, and does not do so throughout this series. All of that said, it is not in fact possible to confine the canon of Wulfstan sermons to those edited by Bethurum in 1957. Her chief reason for excluding all the rest is that they are too like legal or other prescriptive works. Yet it is of vital importance that Wulfstan drew so vague a line between exhortation and decree, in that it brings out the imperative driving both modes of instruction. Assuredly genuine Wulfstan sermons printed only by Napier in 1883 are his nos. I, XXIII–XXV, XXVII, XXXV–XXXVI, XXXVIII, L–LIII, LIX–LXI. They include texts closely associated with the 1009 (and perhaps 1014 and 1018) legislation, one that seems to have been preached to an unidentifiable law-making assembly, and three, apparently from the very end of his career, where there is again a marked overlap with the laws he was by then drafting. Wulfstan's codes were those labelled by Felix Lieberman,

in his great edition of the Anglo-Saxon laws, V/VI/X Æthelred, VII Æthelred, VIII/?IX Æthelred, and I-II Cnut; along with four unofficial tracts, the 'Peace of Edward and Guthrum', *Geþyncðo*, *Hadbot*, and *Grið*; three more that he at least rewrote, *Norðleoda laga*, *Mircna laga*, and *Að*; and two in purely ecclesiastical vein, the 'Canons of Edgar' and *Episcopus*.

The relationship between Wulfstan's legislation and his homiletic work, either mainline or editorially marginalized, calls for three comments. First, the clue to the authentication of all this material is, as stressed above, Wulfstan's highly distinctive prose. One need not spend long on these works to get to know his stylistic blueprint. Among its features are a fondness for alliterative, even rhyming, verbal catalogues (usually of sins), intensitive compounds as with *woruld-*, adverbs like *georne* ('eagerly'), and phrases such as *gime se þe wille* ('let heed who will'). It is a style that depends on rhythm and repetition, not by and large on image or metaphor: a preacher's prose. Second, it is crucial that Wulfstan's preaching mode is so hard to tell apart from that of his legislation. Some of his earlier codes lack almost every penal element to be expected in laws. Æthelred's 1014 edict is more concrete, Cnut's great code more so yet; but the extant text of the 1018 agreement is again wholly devoid of sanctions. This is not to be taken as proof that English resistance to attack had crumbled into supine moralization. If God's ire was the fount of all troubles, then whatever ameliorated it made sense. Wulfstan's skills in engendering a moral crusade may in fact explain how he came to be drafting royal decrees. Third, when Wulfstan's laws are set beside his marginal, and probably in general later, homilies, it emerges that the laws look much more like enacted homilies than do the homilies like expositions of law. Wulfstan obsessively recast his work (the changes often being visible in his own hand), and the effect was nearly always to amplify, not to abridge them. Since the laws tend to contain more developed statements on church dues or clerical morals even than later homilies, they are reasonably seen as consummations of the archbishop's efforts. In other words, Wulfstan went from preaching about the standards demanded of a Christian society to organizing them by law. Such is the context of perhaps his most remarkable work, the semi-homiletic/semi-legislative programme called the *Institutes of Polity*. 'Estates literature' in a familiar sub-Carolingian mode, it is also shot through with the intensity of Wulfstan's moral purpose. It exists in evolving recensions, the trend as ever being towards a more expansive and moralistic treatment of the theme of Christian citizenship.

As a collector of manuscripts and books Wulfstan is important not only for what he wrote but also for the manuscript collections which formed a foundation for his own works and which amounted to a programme of reform for circulation in their own right. Besides those featured in Neil Ker's catalogue of 1957, they include the Latin manuscripts, Oxford, Bodleian, MS Hatton 42 and part of MS Barlow 37, and Rouen, Bibliothèque Municipale, MS 1382. Four of these books (Copenhagen, Kongelige Bibliotek,

MS Kgl. Sam. 1595; Bodl. Oxf., MS Hatton 42; and parts of BL, Cotton MS Nero A.i and MS Vespasian A.xiv) are among those containing glosses and additions in Wulfstan's hand. The others are later, in one case twelfth-century; but they are similar enough in arrangement and content to those where the archbishop perceptibly intervened for it to become highly likely that they are copies of manuscripts assembled on his initiative.

Wulfstan books fall roughly into two groups. One set consists basically of collections of his own work. In these (examples are the early parts of the Wulfstan section in BL, Cotton MS Nero A.i, the core of Cambridge, Corpus Christi College, MS 201, and Bodl. Oxf., MS Junius 121), versions of his homilies are mixed up with other prescriptive texts, his laws among them in the first two cases. It fits well with his reluctance to distinguish between the subject matter of homilies and laws that they are presented on the page in near-identical ways—as are accompanying passages from the *Institutes of Polity* or penitential formulas. The Nero manuscript is notably pocket-sized and otherwise unornamented. It may have been a book for carrying about; but if so, more probably by itinerant clergy than judges, in that legal elements are in general subordinate to pastoral.

The second and on the whole grander set comprises mainly Latin materials that often turn out to be Wulfstan's sources; this is what established their connection with him in the first place. Their content varies from the liturgical to the pastoral and canonist. In some, conceivably the earlier, little attempt is made to sort out these types of text. But liturgical works and sermons predominate in the Copenhagen manuscript; the Vespasian manuscript is an important collection of Alcuin's letters, with other early English conciliar literature (and a striking poem in the archbishop's honour which he may have composed and certainly copied out himself); while the later part of Cotton MS Nero A.i's Wulfstan section is given over to a long series of excerpts from early church councils, popes, and fathers, that was attributed through seventeenth-century codicological confusion to Archbishop Ecgberht of York (732–66). A different selection of these excerpts appears in Cambridge, Corpus Christi College, MS 265, alongside a much wider set of canonical sources. Wulfstan emerges as a close student of Carolingian models, among them the canon law collection known as the Dionysio-Hadriana, Book I of Ansegisus's edition of royal capitulary legislation, the episcopal capitularies of Radulf of Bourges and Theodulf of Orléans (his rare second capitulary as well as his widely known first), and the ninth-century canon collection *De vita sacerdotum* ascribed to Halitgar of Cambrai. He was familiar too with the insular tradition, for example as embodied in the Irish collection of canon laws, *Collectio canonum Hibernensis*. Some of what he knew was mediated by two pastoral letters that Ælfric compiled and then translated for him in 1005 or 1006.

But Wulfstan's miscellanies are ample evidence for his

eventual command of the church's law. When these collections were first isolated in 1895, they were characterized as 'a theological commonplace book specially intended for a bishop's use' (Bateson, 712). Since their connection with Wulfstan emerged, they have been known as 'Archbishop Wulfstan's commonplace book'. But they are much more substantial and systematic than what even the nineteenth century meant by commonplace books. To all intents and purposes, Corpus Christi College, MS 265, and its fellows are themselves canon collections. They are structured in the same way as the contemporary work of Abbo of Fleury (d. 1004) or Burchard of Worms (d. 1025). All that is lacking is a clear guide to what that structure was. The other difference is that Wulfstan could not draw on nearly so much of the rich Carolingian conciliar tradition. There is little or no trace of the Pseudo-Isidore decretals, which is also what mainly distinguishes his canon collection from the one that Archbishop Lanfranc brought with him. Nevertheless, Wulfstan, perhaps abetted by some of his predecessors and successors at Worcester, came closer than any other pre-conquest churchmen to giving the English church its own code of canon law.

Wulfstan's ideas Wulfstan can be viewed in a variety of lights: one of the more substantial of the eschatological moralists inspired by the millennium; archiepiscopal organizer and canonist in typical early eleventh-century vein; lieutenant and spokesman of Christian kingship. But the central idea of his writings and career, and what gives coherence to the whole, was the law of God (*Godes lage, Godes riht, lex Dei*). This was revealed above all by scripture but also by the church's councils and authorities. It meant acceptance of the full Mosaic programme, that is, justice for the socially helpless as well as prohibition of heathen cult and robbery. It meant upholding Pauline ideals of marriage: chastity was absolutely incumbent on priests and only a restrained indulgence was permitted for the laity. It meant observing all the church's festivals and (especially) fasts, adequate provision for the poor, even respect for God's handiwork in a limited recourse to capital punishment (Wulfstan did not go along with Ælfric in forbidding clergy to have anything to do with judgments of blood, but the substitution by Cnut's code of admittedly hideous mutilations for the previously decreed death penalty may have been a step in that direction). God's justice also of course involved due regard to the motives and circumstances of crime: 'if anyone acts unintentionally, he is not wholly like one who does it intentionally' (II Cnut 68.3, ed. Liebermann); this is a long way from the exclusive attention to the outcome of offences that legal historians like to detect in all primitive law. Finally, to accept God's law was to endorse the social order he had ordained, so that each class must know its station and fulfil its assigned role in society. All these divine ordinances were absolutely binding on all persons and classes. Defiance of any of them risked not only heavenly salvation but also earthly fortune; Wulfstan liked to think of law as made 'for Gode and for worulde'. Society, indeed the nation, is punished for individual transgressions. Enforcement is thus an urgent priority for the church's ministers, especially bishops, who are to teach it as much by their works as by their words. But this is also the responsibility of kings and secular officials. That is why law is almost indistinguishable from homily. It is also why the consequences of disobedience can be averted only by penance: the law-code 'VII' of Æthelred, issued at Bath in 1009, 'when the great army came', was almost wholly devoted to marshalling penitential gestures *en masse*.

Wulfstan's intellectual odyssey began with eschatological homilies, in which the imminence of the reign of Antichrist and divine judgment were God's comment on the disorders of earthly existence. He moved as he matured to a position where man is scourged by current political misfortune and social chaos. Efforts to temper God's wrath by penance and eventually by ambitious law making on behalf of a new regime then have their place. The triple climax of Wulfstan's work is therefore to be found in the 'Sermon of the Wolf', the final version of the *Institutes of Polity* and the laws of Cnut. The sermon is a fierce denunciation of sin and crime, of a deranged social order, and of treachery to kings. God's wrath is presaged by signs of the coming of Antichrist, and by the victories of a heathen people, just as God had once punished Israel with the Babylonians and the Britons with the advent of the English themselves. But the implication is that a new and better society can arise under God's auspices, as it had before. The revised *Institutes* are no longer so much a list of ranks and their proper functions, as an elaboration of the way that each should be solemnly instructed by God's servants (the bishops) in their duties to God and man. Lastly, Cnut's code draws on almost everything pertinent that the archbishop had previously written or decreed as well as on law made by earlier kings. It blends exhortation and injunction in homiletic mode with explicit penalties for breach of God's law, whether as regards the integrity of church property, loyalty to the king, and abstinence from theft, or respect for marital rights. It is as constructive a response as can be imagined to the premises that the new regime had been put in place by God's repudiation of what had gone before, and that only his favour could secure its future.

Two things about Archbishop Wulfstan are thus quite clear. On the one hand, he was a European figure: one who can be ranked with Adso and the eschatologists of the year 1000; a canonist whose work compares in ambition if not sophistication with others of the era preceding the Gregorian reform movement and who already anticipated Gregorian themes in the urgency of his assault on clerical unchastity and in his consciousness of the exalted responsibility of churchmen; finally, and perhaps above all, a Carolingian ideologue *par excellence* in his view of a holy people whose kings and bishops work together to realize the kingdom of God. On the other hand, his work was of huge importance in English history. When conquest came again, fifty years later, there is good reason to think that the new rulers paid close attention to the arrangements made for their Danish predecessors. The much-valued law of King Edward was in effect the law of Cnut, which dominated twelfth-century legal collections. Wulfstan, once

the herald of Antichrist and of the end of all things, had become the prophet and architect of transition.

Rediscovery of a reputation Wulfstan's entry in the *Dictionary of National Biography*, of some thirty-five lines, was mostly devoted to the little revealed about the archbishop by chronicle sources. It concluded by saying that he was not the bishop of London consecrated in 996 and that he perhaps did not write the Old English homilies standing in the name of Lupus. This is worth emphasis: that he was, that he did, and that he wrote a lot more besides, is one of the major discoveries of early English studies of the twentieth century; that it needed discovery is instructive in itself for Wulfstan's life and career. The first to realize that the author of the Lupus homilies was probably Wulfstan of York and Worcester was Humfrey Wanley in his 1705 catalogue of Anglo-Saxon manuscripts in England. In 1883 A. S. Napier put together a collection of the sixty homiletic pieces listed by Wanley. Next, Karl Jost in 1950 demonstrated that many of these texts drew on a common set of authorities and that it was not possible to transfer responsibility for most of them to a 'Wulfstan imitator'. Jost went on to show that Wulfstan's hallmarks were imprinted on the *Institutes of Polity*. By then, it was becoming clear that all Æthelred's later law-codes were in this increasingly familiar idiom. Dorothy Whitelock and Dorothy Bethurum in the mid-twentieth century proved just how much legislation Wulfstan had drafted, including the giant code of Cnut. They also established a close link between Wulfstan's works and a series of manuscripts of canonical, pastoral, and liturgical works that seemed to be Wulfstan's sources. Finally, Neil Ker from 1957 began to find the same distinctive handwriting throughout manuscripts with known or likely Wulfstan contents and associations, sometimes in what looked like an authorial capacity. It was a logical deduction that this was the archbishop's own hand. The result was that further books where the hand appears could be drawn into his sphere of activity. The piecing together of literary and palaeographical clues has thus transformed Wulfstan from just another doubtless worthy Anglo-Saxon prelate into one of the half dozen most significant figures even in the crowded and dramatic history of eleventh-century England.

PATRICK WORMALD

Sources *The homilies of Wulfstan*, ed. D. Bethurum (1957) · *Wulfstan Sammlung der ihm zugeschriebenen Homilien*, ed. A. S. Napier (1883) · *Sermo Lupi ad Anglos*, ed. D. Whitelock, 3rd edn (1963) [trans. in EHD, 1, no. 240, 928–34] · F. Liebermann, ed., *Die Gesetze der Angelsachsen*, 1 (Halle, 1898), 236–311, 380–85, 444–73, 477–9 · *Die 'Institutes of polity, civil and ecclesiastical': ein Werk Erzbischof Wulfstans von York*, ed. and trans. K. T. von Jost (Bern, 1959), repr. in M. Swanton, ed. and trans., *Anglo-Saxon prose*, rev. ed (1985), 125–138 · *Wulfstan's canons of Edgar*, ed. R. Fowler, EETS, 266 (1972) · N. R. Ker, ed., *Catalogue of manuscripts containing Anglo-Saxon* (1957), nos. 45, 49, 53, 99, 130, 141, 164, 190, 204, 225, 324, 331, 338, 402 · N. R. Ker, 'The handwriting of Archbishop Wulfstan', *England before the conquest: studies in primary sources presented to Dorothy Whitelock*, ed. P. Clemoes and K. Hughes (1971), 315–31 · H. R. Loyn, ed., *A Wulfstan manuscript* (1971) · J. E. Cross and J. M. Tunberg, eds., *The Copenhagen Wulfstan collection*, Early English Manuscripts in Facsimile, 25 (1993) · D. Bethurum, 'Archbishop Wulfstan's commonplace-book', *Proceedings of the Modern Languages Association of America*, 57 (1942), 916–

29 • J. E. Cross, 'Rouen Bibliothèque Municipale 1382 (U 109), fols. 173r–198v: a newly identified manuscript of Wulfstan's commonplace-book', *Journal of Medieval Latin*, 2 (1992), 63–83 • D. Whitelock, 'Archbishop Wulfstan, homilist and statesman', *TRHS*, 4th ser., 24 (1942), 25–45 • D. Whitelock, 'Wulfstan and the laws of Cnut', *EngHR*, 63 (1948), 433–52 • D. Whitelock, 'Wulfstan's authorship of Cnut's laws', *EngHR*, 70 (1955), 72–85 • K. Jost, *Wulfstanstudien* (1950) • D. Bethurum, 'Six anonymous Old English codes', *Journal of English and Germanic Philology*, 49 (1950), 449–63 • D. Bethurum, 'Wulfstan', *Continuations and beginnings*, ed. E. G. Stanley (1966), 210–46 • P. Wormald, 'Æthelred the lawmaker', *Ethelred the Unready: papers from the millenary conference* [Oxford 1978], ed. D. Hill (1978), 46–80 • A. G. Kennedy, 'Cnut's law code of 1018', *Anglo-Saxon England*, 11 (1983), 57–81 • M. Godden, 'Apocalypse and invasion in late Anglo-Saxon England', *From Anglo-Saxon to Middle English: studies presented to E. G. Stanley*, ed. M. Godden, D. Gray, and T. Hoad (1994), 143–56 • P. Wormald, *The making of English law: King Alfred to the twelfth century*, 2 vols. (1999), chap. 4, pp. 2–5; chap. 5, pp. 5, 7–8, 9; chap. 6, p. 3 • A. McIntosh, 'Wulfstan's prose', *PBA*, 35 (1949), 109–42 • D. Bethurum, '*Regnum* and *sacerdotium* in the early eleventh century', *England before the conquest: studies in primary sources presented to Dorothy Whitelock*, ed. P. Clemoes and K. Hughes (1971), 129–45 • J. Wilcox, 'The dissemination of Wulfstan homilies: the Wulfstan tradition in eleventh-century vernacular preaching', *England in the eleventh century* [Harlaxton 1990], ed. C. Hicks (1992), 199–217 • M. K. Lawson, 'Archbishop Wulfstan and the homiletic element in the laws of Æthelred II and Cnut', *EngHR*, 107 (1992), 565–86 • M. Bateson, 'A Worcester Cathedral book of ecclesiastical collections, made c.1000 AD', *EngHR*, 10 (1895), 712–31 • E. O. Blake, ed., *Liber Eliensis*, CS, 3rd ser., 92 (1962) • G. Hickes and others, *Linguarum vett. septentrionalium thesaurus grammaticocriticus et archaeologicus*, 3 vols. (1703–5)

Archives BL, Cotton MS Nero A.i, MS Vespasian A.xiv • Bodl. Oxf., MS Hatton 42 • Bodl. Oxf., MS Junius 121 • CCC Cam., MSS 201, 265 • Kongelige Bibliotek, Copenhagen, MS Kgl. Sam. 1595

Likenesses tomb effigy, 14th cent. • drawing, repro. in R. Gough, *Sepulchral monuments in Great Britain*, 1 (1786), pl. cxlvi

Wulfstan [St Wulfstan] (c.1008–1095), bishop of Worcester, was the last Anglo-Saxon bishop and played an important role in the transmission of Old English cultural and religious values to the Anglo-Norman world.

Birth and early career Wulfstan was born at Itchington in Warwickshire, an estate of Worcester Cathedral, which was appropriated by the earl of Mercia at some uncertain date. His well-born parents were named Æthelstan and Wulfgiva. Æthelstan was a priest and probably a member of the household of the bishop of Worcester. Wulfstan's brothers were Ælfstan, later a monk, and Byrcstan, a layman. They had a sister, whose name is not known, but who died shortly before Wulfstan himself. Wulfstan's schooling began at Evesham Abbey and continued at Peterborough Abbey. Afterwards (c.1024) he returned to Itchington, where a frustrating sexual encounter with an amorous girl convinced him that he was intended for a life of celibacy. His parents entered religious houses in the city of Worcester but his own career is undocumented until Bishop Brihtheah (r. 1033–8), on the recommendation of Wulfstan's kinsfolk, recruited him as an episcopal clerk. He was ordained to the priesthood and appointed to the church of Hawkesbury in Gloucestershire. Brihtheah later offered him a richer benefice on the outskirts of the city of Worcester but Wulfstan declined. He now felt drawn to the monastic life, to which he was strongly urged by his mother. He became a monk at Worcester with the approval of Brihtheah.

As a monk and prior Wulfstan was diligent in his monastic observance. His first office was that of novice master. He was promoted to the office of cantor or precentor and subsequently to that of sacrist. The hagiographers' emphasis on his prolonged austerities and lengthy prayers at this period of his life follows earlier models in this genre, particularly the lives of some of the Celtic saints whose feasts were observed at Worcester in his time. Yet these lives may have influenced not only Wulfstan's biographers but also his personal approach to the monastic life. There remains enough circumstantial detail to indicate that he went through a genuine period of crisis, praying in anguish at great length, and close to mental breakdown; but no cause of his distress is indicated. Some underlying tension between himself and his fellow monks is indicated by the fact that these marathons of prayer were not conducted in the main cathedral church, but increasingly took place by night, in other churches of the neighbourhood.

Bishop Ealdred (r. 1046–62), in his capacity as titular abbot, appointed Wulfstan to the office of prior c.1055. Hemming records that Wulfstan, together with another monk also named Wulfstan (or Wilstan), took action to recover alienated estates, a task which they had earlier begun in their capacity as the monks next in seniority after Prior Ægelwine. As prior, Wulfstan maintained strict discipline and his biographers stress the importance which he placed on chastity. He was importuned by a wealthy woman, resident in the city of Worcester: she tried to enlist him both to manage her considerable property and also to embark on a sexual relationship with her; but Wulfstan forcefully rejected her. His vulnerability to such advances by the laity resulted from his undertaking many of the pastoral duties which were within the bishop's sphere of competence, but which were left undone by Ealdred, owing to his involvement in public life. Wulfstan baptized the children of the poor (who could not afford the high fees demanded by parish priests) and also preached to the laity on the need for moral regeneration. He became prior about the same time that Harold Godwineson assumed military control in Herefordshire. Their close association probably dated from this period and Wulfstan was said to be Harold's spiritual adviser. Even Ealdred and the formidable Abbot Æthelwig were said to consult Wulfstan on spiritual matters.

Bishop of Worcester When Ealdred was elected to the archbishopric of York at Christmas 1060, Pope Nicholas II refused to allow him to retain Worcester in plurality, as several of his recent predecessors had done. Two legates accompanied Ealdred back from Rome to England, charged, among other things, with ensuring that a suitable candidate was found for Worcester. Ealdred contrived that their choice fell on its exemplary prior, envisaging that, for all practical purposes, Wulfstan would simply deputize for him there. Earl Harold and Earl Ælfgar of

Mercia energetically fostered his candidature. The election was discussed at the Easter court of 1062 and was confirmed, presumably by the legates, on 29 August, after which King Edward invested Wulfstan with the bishopric, an act ritualized by bestowing the episcopal staff and ring. The dubious credentials of Archbishop Stigand ensured that Wulfstan's consecration was performed by Archbishop Ealdred, on 8 September. According to John of Worcester, Ealdred swore, at the instigation of Stigand, and in the presence of the king and nobles, that he would not claim any ecclesiastical or secular right over Wulfstan, either by virtue of this ceremony or on the grounds that Wulfstan had been one of his monks before his consecration. Despite this, York preserved the text of a grant, in the name of King Edward, and dated 31 December 1065, granting the see of Worcester to Ealdred, in consultation with the king. It is doubtful whether the dying Edward would have made any such grant and the document probably represents York's efforts to reassert old claims over Worcester.

According to John of Worcester, Wulfstan swore canonical obedience to Stigand. Similarly, when he later swore obedience to Lanfranc, he said that although he had accepted consecration from Ealdred, he had not sworn obedience to him. Meanwhile the prognosticon (a Bible verse found at random, believed to indicate the character of the new bishop) reported at his consecration was: 'Behold an Israelite indeed—in whom there is no guile' (John 1:47). Ealdred detained Wulfstan at York, while he himself contrived to expropriate most of Worcester's episcopal (as opposed to its monastic) estates. Slowly, over a number of years, Wulfstan managed to recover the lost lands. His position at Worcester was reinforced by the promotion of his brother Ælfstan to the vacated post of dean (prior). Both the franchisal rights pertaining to the monastic estates and the bishop's share in the profits accruing from commercial activities in Worcester were strengthened by grants from King Edward.

Wulfstan proved an excellent pastor, making visitations in his diocese. His urging of moral reform included a denunciation of men who wore their hair long, arguing that they would prove incapable of defending their homeland from foreign invasion. While this preoccupation may owe much to the hagiographers' efforts to rationalize the Norman conquest, it should also be seen against a background of growing political instability. Wulfstan attended the Christmas court of 1065, at which participants witnessed the death of Edward and the accession and coronation of Harold II. The new king took Wulfstan with him when he went north to combat renewed restiveness there. Following the death of Harold in October 1066 and the ensuing devastation caused by the invading army, Wulfstan was among the magnates of church and state who took oaths of fealty to William of Normandy at Berkhamsted. They were led by Ealdred and it is likely that Wulfstan accompanied him to Westminster, where the archbishop crowned William on Christmas day 1066.

Wulfstan was summoned to attend the legatine council convened on 7 April 1070; he retained his episcopal office while many other English clerics were dismissed and was required to exercise episcopal oversight of the diocese of Lichfield between late 1070 and late 1072. When Archbishop Lanfranc eventually secured recognition of his jurisdiction over the sees of Dorchester (Lincoln from 1073 or 1074), Lichfield, and Worcester, Wulfstan was enabled to recover from Thomas of Bayeux, archbishop of York, the remainder of the vills which had been appropriated by Ealdred. Wulfstan made a written profession of obedience to Lanfranc, who nevertheless permitted him to assist Thomas in the consecration of Bishop Radulf at the request of Paul, earl of Orkney. Thomas, with the help of King William, occasionally enlisted Wulfstan to perform tasks on his behalf in the York archdiocese. He was also required by Lanfranc to assist Archbishop Thomas in consecrating William of St Calais as bishop of Durham, in Gloucester Abbey on 3 January 1081. The monastic customs introduced by Lanfranc to Canterbury were transmitted to Worcester after Wulfstan sent the monk Nicholas to learn the new ways.

Chapter and cathedral reform The chapter of Worcester Cathedral priory steadily grew in numbers. Wulfstan, towards the end of his life, is recorded as saying that whereas there were only some twelve monks at the time of his monastic profession, numbers had subsequently increased to fifty. The figures here may be formulaic; the impression of growth is none the less real. Wulfstan inaugurated the rebuilding of Worcester Cathedral in the Romanesque style in the 1080s. While he deplored the inevitable destruction of Oswald's church to clear the necessary space on the restricted site, he took great care over the construction and decoration of the new church and provided a splendid shrine for St Oswald's relics, ensuring that the translation would fall at a time of year convenient for appropriate liturgical celebration (8 October).

Wulfstan's closest colleague among the episcopate in his later years was Robert the Lotharingian, bishop of Hereford and scholar, who gave him a text of the chronicle of Marianus Scottus. Wulfstan utilized it as the basis of a locally based chronicle, continued by the monk John of Worcester.

The wide temporal powers exercised by Abbot Æthelwig in his later years prompted tenants of the church of Worcester to commend themselves to him, thereby alienating its estates. Following the abbot's death, Wulfstan was enabled to retrieve some of the service due. Wulfstan was said to be on good terms with the Norman kings, William I and William II, but inevitably lacked the influence which he was perhaps gaining before the Norman conquest. His last recorded attendance on the king was in January 1091. He took an active part in the secular administration of his diocese, while in 1075 he played a leading role in organizing its territorial defence against rebels from beyond the Severn. During the rebellion of 1088 the custody of Worcester Castle was entrusted to him. Wulfstan owed the king the service of fifty knights. The new Norman sheriff, Urse d'Abetot, was quickly established by Ealdred as a tenant on many of the lands of the bishopric, but, while his territorial encroachments were resented by the monks of Worcester, circumstantial evidence indicates that sheriff and bishop established an effective working relationship over the years. Wulfstan's great strength was as a pastor, imposing high standards of conduct on clergy and laity alike, and repeatedly preaching the need for peace and reconciliation to congregations whose tenurial interests were affected by the outcome of the Norman invasion.

In an era which witnessed a gradual change from a minster-based pastoral strategy to one based on the establishment of parish churches, Wulfstan instigated a programme of church building on his own estates and also instructed parish churches to be built elsewhere. With the permission of other diocesan bishops, he also consecrated altars for the parish churches being established further afield by English thegns who requested his services. In the absence of a surviving English aristocracy he seems gradually to have assumed a patriarch-like role for the English population. A number of lifetime miracles of healing were reported, though Wulfstan himself strongly resisted the attempts of those around him who were clearly trying to gain him a reputation in this area. He preached energetically against the export trade in slaves which operated out of Bristol and was largely successful in stopping it, though Lanfranc also played a part in this.

Promoting English values Wulfstan fostered the transmission of English spiritual and religious values to the Anglo-Norman world. His monastic confraternity league of c.1077 included not only houses which retained English heads, but also two in his diocese which by this date had 'French' abbots. Members of the league were pledged, in effect, to uphold key values of the tenth-century *Regularis concordia*, including extensive prayers for the king and queen and generous almsgiving. Throughout Wulfstan's time at Worcester, English translations continued to be made of standard works, while Latin works were frequently annotated in English. Wulfstan was a firm believer in the need for documentation as a means of securing lands and rights, and Hemming explains how Wulfstan ordered him to sort and record the Worcester muniments. Contact was maintained between Worcester and the Benedictine community in Dublin. Bishop Patrick of Dublin (1074–84) spent some time as a monk at Worcester, and Urban, bishop of Llandaff (1107–34), trained there in the last years of Wulfstan's episcopate.

Death and canonization Wulfstan died at Worcester on 20 January 1095 and was buried there on 21 or 23 January. Following his death, several miracles and visions were quickly reported and a cult tentatively began. An English life was written by the monastic chancellor, Coleman, within a few years of Wulfstan's death. This was edited, adapted, and translated into Latin, as the *Vita Wulfstani*, by William of Malmesbury, two or three decades later. Further, abridged, lives by various writers followed, from the mid-twelfth century onwards.

Wulfstan was canonized by Pope Innocent III on 21 April 1203 and was adopted by King John as his spiritual patron during his quarrel with the pope. The king understood the legend of St Wulfstan's pastoral staff, which only he could remove from the tombstone of King Edward, to denote Wulfstan's belief that kings alone were entitled to appoint to bishoprics. In 1216 John, accepting it as fact, insisted that he should be buried next to Wulfstan at Worcester.   EMMA MASON

Sources *The Vita Wulfstani of William of Malmesbury*, ed. R. R. Darlington, CS, 3rd ser., 40 (1928) · John of Worcester, *Chron.* · E. Mason, *St Wulfstan of Worcester, c.1008–1095* (1990) · *Hemingi chartularium ecclesiæ Wigorniensis*, ed. T. Hearne, 2 vols. (1723) · *Willelmi Malmesbiriensis monachi de gestis pontificum Anglorum libri quinque*, ed. N. E. S. A. Hamilton, Rolls Series, 52 (1870) · William of Malmesbury, *Gesta regum Anglorum / The history of the English kings*, ed. and trans. R. A. B. Mynors, R. M. Thomson, and M. Winterbottom, 2 vols., OMT (1998–9) · R. R. Darlington, ed., *The cartulary of Worcester Cathedral Priory (register I)*, PRSoc., 76, new ser., 38 (1968) · W. D. Macray, ed., *Chronicon abbatiae de Evesham, ad annum 1418*, Rolls Series, 29 (1863) · *The Leofric collectar*, ed. E. S. Dewick and W. H. Frere, 2 vols. (1914–21), vol. 2, pp. 589–600 · ASC, s.a.1088 (1087) [text E] · E. Mason, 'St Wulfstan's staff: a legend and its uses', *Medium Ævum*, 53 (1984), 157–79 · E. Mason, 'St Oswald and St Wulfstan', *St Oswald of Worcester: life and influence*, ed. N. Brooks and C. Cubitt (1996), 269–84
Likenesses sculpture on tomb effigy, 1230–39, Worcester Cathedral

Wulfstan Cantor [Wulfstan of Winchester] (*fl.* **996**), hagiographer and poet, was a monk, priest, and precentor at the Old Minster, Winchester. Little is known of his life, save that he was probably born *c.*960 (or slightly earlier), was given as an oblate to the Old Minster, became a pupil there of Bishop Æthelwold, and eventually became precentor (hence he is known in contemporary Winchester sources as Wulfstan Cantor). Most of his datable writings were composed at Winchester during the 990s. He may have left Winchester for Canterbury when his patron, Bishop Ælfheah, became archbishop in 1005, although the evidence for this is slight. The year of his death is unknown, but his obit is listed in a Winchester calendar against 22 July.

Wulfstan's most substantial known work is a poem called by editors the *Narratio metrica de S. Swithuno*, which at some 3300 lines is the longest surviving pre-conquest Anglo-Latin poem, and one of the most metrically accomplished. This *Narratio* reworks in hexameters the earlier *Translatio et miracula S. Swithuni* by Lantfred of Winchester. Wulfstan follows Lantfred's text closely, rarely departing from his source to add incidental details drawn from his own experience. However, Wulfstan prefaced the *Narratio* with an epistle (in elegiacs) addressed to Bishop Ælfheah; this so-called *epistola specialis* has no correlate in Lantfred, and provides a valuable account of the vast programme of reconstruction undertaken at the Old Minster by Æthelwold and Ælfheah (many details of Wulfstan's narrative were confirmed by excavation at Winchester in the 1960s and 1970s). It also describes important features of the church, now destroyed, such as the tower with its weathercock, and the noisy organ. A reference in the *epistola* to the translation of St Æthelwold implies that the poem was completed in 996 (it is preserved in a manuscript from the Old Minster, now in London, British Library, Royal MS 15

C.vii, datable to c.1000). In the same year Wulfstan completed his life of St Æthelwold, a prose account of the life and miracles of his mentor, Æthelwold, and of the events which led to the saint's translation to a shrine in the Old Minster twelve years after his death in 984. Wulfstan's poetic proficiency is revealed in a substantial poem certainly composed by him—his name VVLFSTANVS is embedded in an acrostic in the opening lines—in celebration of the feast of All Saints (the *Breviloquium de omnibus sanctis*), composed in epanaleptic verses, in which the first words of each hexameter are repeated as the last words of the following pentameter. The constraints of the form imply a poet of considerable skill, so it is likely that Wulfstan also composed the epanaleptic poems in honour of the Winchester saints Birinus, Swithun, and Æthelwold. He is similarly to be suspected as the author of mass sets and hymns (in various metres) in honour of St Æthelwold, as well as of various tropes and their melodies found in the so-called Winchester tropers, one manuscript of which (Cambridge, Corpus Christi College MS 473, datable to c.1000) may have belonged to Wulfstan himself. A work of Wulfstan described by William of Malmesbury (d. 1143) as *De tonorum harmonia* (but properly called the *Breviloquium super musicam*) has not survived, except for a few sentences preserved in fifteenth-century musical commentaries. Although his canon of writings is not fully established, there is no doubt that Wulfstan was one of the most productive and proficient of all Anglo-Latin authors, the paradigm of the tenth-century monastic writer.   MICHAEL LAPIDGE

Sources Willelmi Malmesbiriensis monachi de gestis regum Anglorum, ed. W. Stubbs, 2 vols., Rolls Series (1887–9), vol. 1, pp. 166–7 · The life of St Æthelwold / Wulfstan of Winchester, ed. M. Lapidge and M. Winterbottom, OMT (1991) · 'Le Breviloquium de omnibus sanctis: un poème inconnu de Wulfstan, chantre de Winchester', ed. F. Dolbeau, Analecta Bollandiana, 106 (1988), 35–98 · Frithegodi monachi breviloquium vitae beati Wilfredi et Wulfstani, ed. A. Campbell (Zurich, 1950), 63–177

Archives BL, Royal MS 15 C.vii · CCC Cam., MS 473

Wulfthryth [St Wulfthryth] (d. c.1000), abbess of Wilton, was queen of England, the second consort of King Edgar, for a brief period before her appointment as abbess. Details of Wulfthryth's parentage are not known, but she must have been of noble birth like her cousin *Wulfhild, with whom she was educated at Wilton. *Edgar (943/4–975) appears to have wanted to marry into their family and Wulfhild was his first choice as a bride; but when she persuaded him she would rather enter a nunnery, he married Wulfthryth. Although there has been some debate about whether Wulfthryth was a full wife or just a concubine, the late eleventh-century hagiographer Goscelin states that she and Edgar were 'bound by indissoluble vows' (Wilmart, 31) and the legitimacy of their daughter *Edith is implied by the recognition of her as the 'royal sister' of Edgar's sons Edward and Æthelred.

Wulfthryth's entrance into a religious house would have provided a pretext for the marriage to be dissolved and must have occurred by 964 when Edgar married Ælfthryth. In addition to the position as abbess of Wilton, it is likely that Wulfthryth received a substantial settlement

on her separation from Edgar and that this is represented by the six estates in Wiltshire and the Isle of Wight for which the nuns of Wilton were given confirmation of title by the king in 965 and which are described as having been granted formerly to Wulfthryth. By making the estates corporate rather than personal property, Wulfthryth was hoping to ensure that they would be retained by Wilton after her death; other grants of land from Edgar are also recorded.

Wulfthryth was also able to use her influence at the royal court to protect the interests of Wilton in other ways. According to Goscelin, who in his life of Edith provides some of the main biographical information about Wulfthryth, when Wilton's rights of sanctuary were threatened by royal servants who wanted to remove a thief from the church, she was able to intervene personally with King Æthelred (her stepson) to prevent the violation. On another occasion she was able to secure the release of two Wilton priests who had been imprisoned by the reeve of Wilton. Wulfthryth was also remembered as an *edificatrix* and is said to have enclosed the nunnery with a stone wall, which would have been in keeping with the aims of the Benedictine reform movement to achieve a stricter separation of monastic and secular life. She used her wealth to build up the relic collection of Wilton. A nail from the crucifixion of Christ was purchased from St Paulinus of Trier with the help of her chaplain Benno, who came from that foundation. She also bought the relics of the Breton saint Iwi which are included in Wilton's entry in the late Saxon list of saints' resting places. But the most important cult which Wulfthryth helped to promote was that of her own daughter Edith, who was translated between 997 and 1000.

The translation is the last datable point in Wulfthryth's life; she died at Wilton on 21 September, but the year is not known. She was buried before the main altar of the abbey church of St Mary at Wilton, where she was evidently regarded as a saint. Goscelin calls her the 'hidden treasure and light' of the community and his account reflects the affection and respect with which she seems to be remembered at Wilton (Wilmart, 278). Unlike Edith, Wulfthryth is recorded as performing miracles during her lifetime and these continued to occur after her death; however, her cult never seems to have become more widely established.   BARBARA YORKE

Sources A. Wilmart, 'La légende de Ste Édith en prose et vers par le moine Goscelin', Analecta Bollandiana, 56 (1938), 5–101, 265–307 · S. J. Ridyard, The royal saints of Anglo-Saxon England, Cambridge Studies in Medieval Life and Thought, 4th ser., 9 (1988) · AS chart., S 766, 767, 799 · S. Millinger, 'Humility and power: Anglo-Saxon nuns in Anglo-Norman hagiography', Medieval religious women, ed. J. A. Nichols and L. T. Shank, 1 (1984), 115–29 · B. A. E. Yorke, 'The legitimacy of St Edith', Haskins Society Journal, 11 (2003), 97–113

Wulfweard White (d. 1072x86), landowner, held eight estates in Buckinghamshire, amounting to 90 hides, with his wife, Eadgifu, on the eve of the Norman conquest. His name is not uncommon and only when his distinctive byname is used can he be identified with certainty, unless other indications are present, such as his connection with the queen (see below). Not all his land is listed in Domesday Book; he is named as one of the leading thegns both in Kent and in Lincolnshire, but in neither case can his estates be traced, probably because they were in the hands of tenants. Nevertheless, his recorded holding, of 150 hides scattered over eleven shires, makes him the eighth richest of the thegns below the rank of earl whose lands are recorded in Domesday Book.

Much of Wulfweard's land seems to have been the fruit of royal service, though he also held as a tenant of the Old Minster, Winchester, the bishop of Sherborne, and the abbot of Glastonbury. In Middlesex he is called 'King Edward's thegn', but in other contexts he is associated with the queen. He was probably connected with the households first of Queen Emma and then of Queen Edith, for Emma left him a life interest in land at Hayling, Hampshire, which Edith confirmed (*Domesday Book*, 1.43*v*); the land was to be held of the Old Minster, Winchester, and the agreement between the church and Wulfweard *hwita* ('white') still exists (*AS chart.*, S 1476). Wulfweard survived the conquest, for he is probably the Wulfweard who attested a royal charter of 1068, and certainly the Wulfweard *hwite* who witnessed a private sale of land in 1072, the latter in company with Queen Edith; he also attested (as Wulfweard Wita) a memorandum on the customs of Taunton, which cannot be precisely dated. It has been suggested that he was alive as late as 1084, but he was certainly dead by 1086, though his wife, Eadgifu, was then still holding two of her former tenements (*Domesday Book*, 1.87, 145). It is possible that Wulfweard predeceased Queen Edith (*d.* 1075) for it was she who arranged the marriage of his daughter with her steward, Æthelsige of Bromham; by 1086 Æthelsige had lost the land which he had held at Bromham and elsewhere in Bedfordshire, but was holding three manors of the queen's gift, two of which, the former possessions of Wulfweard White, he had received with his wife (*Domesday Book*, 1.153).

The Wulfweard Cild, son of Eadgifu, who appears among the pre-conquest landowners in Buckinghamshire, has been identified as the son of Wulfweard White and Eadgifu; but these references may be to Wulfweard White himself, for Eadgifu was a common name, and may have been borne by his mother as well as by his wife. If Wulfweard Cild was indeed Wulfweard White's son, then he probably predeceased his father, for the redistribution of Wulfweard White's lands suggests that they reverted on his death to his lords, King William and Queen Edith.

ANN WILLIAMS

Sources A. Farley, ed., *Domesday Book*, 2 vols. (1783) · P. A. Clarke, *The English nobility under Edward the Confessor* (1994) · A. Williams, *The English and the Norman conquest* (1995) · *Reg. RAN*, vol. 1 · F. E. Harmer, ed., *Anglo-Saxon writs* (1952) · A. J. Robertson, ed. and trans., *Anglo-Saxon charters*, 2nd edn (1956) · D. A. E. Pelteret, *Catalogue of English post-conquest vernacular documents* (1990) · *VCH Somerset*, vol. 1

Wulfwig (*d.* 1067), bishop of Dorchester, perhaps belonged to an Anglo-Saxon clerical dynasty. Frank Barlow has suggested that he was the brother of Alwine and Godric, who both occur as canons of St Martin's, Dover, in 1086, and he may well be the Wulfwin described as the father of Wulfstan who also occurs as canon of St Martin's in 1086; Wulfwin had preceded his son as canon, holding a prebend in 1066. If this identification is correct, Wulfwig would probably have been born in the early decades of the eleventh century and might have become a member of the community of St Martin's, Dover, before 1053.

It is likely that Wulfwig was a royal clerk by 1053, the year in which Edward the Confessor decided to appoint him as bishop of Dorchester to replace Ulf, who, although still alive and not deposed, was in exile, was branded as disreputable, and was unable to return because of the hostility of Earl Godwine and his family. It is possible that Wulfwig enjoyed the latter's support. He was, however, determined to avoid consecration by Godwine's protégé Stigand and together with two other new nominees, Cynesige, archbishop of York, and Leofwine, bishop of Lichfield, he went abroad to seek consecration. Edward further rewarded Wulfwig by giving him the well-endowed churches of Leighton Buzzard, Aylesbury, and Buckingham, which Wulfwig added to the estates of his bishopric. His diocese was one of the three largest in mid-eleventh century England, stretching from the Thames to the Humber, and formed from the old dioceses of Leicester and Lindsey. Its control of Lindsey was threatened by the archbishops of York, one of whom, Ælfric Puttoc (*d.* 1051), had claimed Lindsey as part of his own diocese. It may perhaps have been partly in an effort to ward off York's claims (though Cynesige is stated to have given his approval) that Wulfwig joined Earl Leofric and his wife, Godgifu, in richly re-endowing a large church at Stow, at some point between 1053 and 1055. This was a college of secular clerics who were expected to perform the office in the manner of the canons of St Paul's in London. On Cynesige's death in 1060 the threat posed by York increased with the appointment of Ealdred, bishop of Worcester as his successor, and Wulfwig made representations to the pope, perhaps through the newly appointed bishops Giso and Walter who travelled to Rome to seek consecration at Nicholas II's Easter Synod of 1061. Nicholas II, who in any case was shocked by Ealdred's desire to retain the see of Worcester in addition to that of York, willingly gave judgment to Wulfwig; on 3 May 1061 he issued a bull confirming that the *parochia* of Lindsey (*parochia* here meaning broad ecclesiastical jurisdiction rather than parish), with the church of Stow and the manor of Newark in Nottinghamshire, rightfully belonged to the bishop of Dorchester. It is likely that Giso, for whom Nicholas had issued a similar bull a few days earlier, acted as Wulfwig's intermediary.

There is little evidence for Wulfwig's involvement in public affairs, though Edward the Confessor entrusted to him the duty of drafting a diploma granting land at Taynton to the abbey of St Denis; clearly, however, he must have been influential, for several men are recorded as commended to him in 1066, even outside the episcopal estates of Dorchester. He died shortly after the conquest, in 1067, at Winchester, and was buried in his own cathedral church of Dorchester.

JULIA BARROW

Sources A. Farley, ed., *Domesday Book*, 2 vols. (1783), 1.1c–d, 143a, 143d, 144a, 148a, 150d, 152a, 152d, 190b, 195b, 203d, 209b, 211c, 214c, 215b, 216a, 348b, 375a, 377d · C. W. Foster and K. Major, eds., *The registrum antiquissimum of the cathedral church of Lincoln*, 1, Lincoln RS, 27 (1931), 186–8, no. 247 · F. E. Harmer, ed., *Anglo-Saxon writs* (1952), 35–6, 39, 59n., 244–5, 262–3, 579–80 · D. Whitelock, M. Brett, and C. N. L. Brooke, eds., *Councils and synods with other documents relating to the English church, 871–1204*, 1 (1981), 536n, 539–43, 548, 550–52 · F. Barlow, ed. and trans., *The life of King Edward who rests at Westminster*, 2nd edn, OMT (1992), 52n, 54n · F. Barlow, *The English church, 1000–1066: a history of the later Anglo-Saxon church*, 2nd edn (1979), 50, 76, 118n, 133, 157, 191, 215–16, 238n, 303n · *ASC*, s.a. 1053 [text C]; s.a. 1067 [text D] · John of Worcester, *Chron.*, 2.414–15

Wurm, Mary Josephine Agnes [Marie] (1860–1938), pianist and composer, was born on 18 May 1860 at 11 Windsor Terrace, Southampton, the first of the ten children of John Evangelist Wurm (c.1828–1892), formerly of Oberdorf, Bavaria, and his wife, (Marie) Sophie Niggl (c.1838–c.1883), daughter of a village schoolmaster from Denklingen. The couple, both music teachers, had emigrated to Southampton on the advice of one of Sophie's elder sisters, Josephine, herself a music teacher recently settled in the city, who was the wife of Lorenz Herkomer and mother of the artist Hubert Herkomer. The Wurms set up house next door to the Herkomers in Windsor Terrace, but soon moved to Portland Street. Besides teaching German and music peripatetically, J. E. Wurm was organist and choirmaster of St Joseph's Roman Catholic Church, Bugle Street, for more than thirty years. Sophie Wurm taught singing, the violin, the piano, and the zither. Ambitious and well organized, she took the major share in promoting her children's interests. All ten were said to be musical. In addition to Mary, Mathilde *Verne (1865–1936), Alice Barbara *Verne (1868–1958) and Adela *Verne (1877–1952) [see under Verne, Mathilde] had professional musical careers. These three changed their surname from Wurm to Verne late in 1893 and worked chiefly in England, whereas Mary, often known in English sources as Marie Wurm, lived and worked mainly in Germany.

Mary was taken by her mother to Stuttgart in 1869, becoming a pupil at the conservatory. After returning to London in 1878, she had lessons from visiting pianists including Anna Mehlig, Mary Krebs, Józef Wieniawski, and Caroline Montigny-Rémaury. In 1880 she went to Frankfurt to study with Clara Schumann and Joachim Raff; she eventually made her London début in 1882 at the Crystal Palace under August Manns, playing Robert Schumann's piano concerto. Two years later she appeared at the St James's Hall 'Popular' concerts (in a Haydn trio) and won the Mendelssohn scholarship, which provided for composition studies with Sir Arthur Sullivan, C. V. Stanford, and Frederick Bridge; in 1886 she studied with Carl Reinecke in Leipzig. From this period solo playing gave way to chamber music, at the Princes' Hall in London as well as in Vienna and Frankfurt. Mary Wurm 'assisted' at concerts of such leading performers as Sophie Löwe, Ben Davies, and Tivadar Nachez, often playing her own works. Meanwhile she established a teaching connection in Germany. Her most remarkable solo appearance was

undoubtedly that at the Queen's Hall, London, on 21 February 1895—an entirely extempore programme based on musical themes supplied by the audience and in sealed envelopes from 'music professors'. Described as clever but musically dull, the occasion was not repeated, and she returned to composition and teaching in Germany, notably in Hanover, Berlin (from 1911), Munich (from 1925), and later Berlin again. From 1898 to 1900 she conducted and toured with a women's orchestra in Germany. She died in Munich on 21 January 1938.

Wurm was a fluent composer of parlour songs and light piano works, many of them dances or duets, as well as women's part-songs and children's pieces designed for ready markets in Germany and Britain. These included a children's operetta *Prinzessin Lisa's Fee* (given in Lübeck, 1890) and two didactic works, *Das ABC der Musik* (Leipzig, n.d.) and *Praktische Vorschule zur Caland-Lehre* (Hanover, 1914). She also wrote a piano concerto, a violin sonata (op. 17), a cello sonata, a string quartet (op. 40), works for string orchestra, and a one-act opera after Goethe's *Die Mitschuldigen* (given in Leipzig, 1921).

LEANNE LANGLEY

Sources M. Verne, *Chords of remembrance* (1936) [for family background, though there's little on Mary] · E. Pauer, 'Wurm, Marie', *A dictionary of pianists and composers for the pianoforte* (1895) · 'Wurm, Mary J. A.', *Riemann Musik Lexikon*, 12th edn, ed. W. Gurlitt, 3 vols. (Mainz and London, 1961) · J. A. Fuller Maitland, 'Wurm, Marie', Grove, *Dict. mus.* (1904–10) · A. I. Cohen, 'Wurm, Mary (Marie) J. A.', *International encyclopedia of women composers*, 2nd edn, rev. and enlarged (1987) · F. Pazdírek, 'Wurm, Mary', *Universal-Handbuch der Musikliteratur*, 14 vols. (Vienna, 1904–10) · N. Burton, 'Wurm, Mary J. A.', *The new Grove dictionary of women composers*, ed. J. A. Sadie and R. Samuel (1994) · b. cert.

Archives Royal College of Music, London, concert programmes

Wyatt, Benjamin Dean (bap. 1775, d. 1855), architect, was baptized on 6 April 1775 at St Marylebone, Middlesex, the eldest son of the six children of James *Wyatt (1746–1813), architect, and his wife, Rachel Lunn (d. 1817). He was educated at Westminster School and Christ Church, Oxford, where he matriculated in 1795. As a youth he already showed signs of the financial recklessness which was to end in insolvency and poverty. He got into debt to the amount of £200 at Oxford and left early without a degree. He was originally intended for the law but showed no interest, and his father, through the influence of the royal family, was able to get him a job with the East India Company in Calcutta, which offered the opportunity of making a fortune.

In 1797 Wyatt was appointed to the secrets department of the company's office in Calcutta, while the Marquess Wellesley was governor-general. He stayed in India for six years but his hope of amassing a fortune of between £30,000 and £40,000 failed to materialize. He did, however, pay off his early debts. In 1803 he returned to England, armed with a doctor's certificate. After a time spent as an assistant in his father's office he became private secretary to Sir Arthur Wellesley, Lord Wellesley's younger brother and the future duke of Wellington. He was with Wellesley in Dublin from 1807 to 1809, but when Wellesley was appointed to command the British army in the

Peninsula, Wyatt returned to his father's office in London and decided to become an architect. His early association with Arthur Wellesley, however, was to provide him with his principal future client.

The chief architectural opportunity in London was for a design for the new Theatre Royal in Drury Lane, the previous one having burnt down. Wyatt entered, and won, the competition for the new theatre in 1811, against the wishes of his father, who wanted his younger son Philip to receive the commission. This was one of several family quarrels. Benjamin Wyatt seems to have had a disagreeable character. Contemporaries commented on his bad temper and bitterness, and his career was interrupted by a series of rows with family, friends, and clients. Nevertheless, the new theatre was a success when it opened in 1812, and made Wyatt's architectural reputation. It was greatly admired in the fashionable world. The prince regent was 'charmed with the beauty and elegance of the whole theatre' (J. MacMahon to Samuel Whitbread, 10 Nov 1812, V&A, 86.22170, Wyatt MSS).

At the time of the death of his father in 1813 Benjamin Wyatt's prospects of succeeding to his pre-eminent architectural practice must have seemed assured. He was granted the surveyorship of Westminster Abbey, previously held by his father, and in 1814 received what looked to be the most important commission of the age. Like Marlborough a century before, the victorious Wellington was offered a country seat by a grateful nation as a reward for his victories. Wyatt was appointed by Wellington to find an estate and to design the new house. He worked for six years on designs for a vast neo-classical palace but they were not to be adopted. Wellington settled on Stratfield Saye, Hampshire, and decided to keep the existing unpretentious house there with few modifications, such as a new porch, which Wyatt designed.

In London, however, Wyatt was able to remodel Apsley House for the duke. He refaced the brick eighteenth-century house in Bath stone, adding a Corinthian portico on the Piccadilly front, and enlarging the building to create the Waterloo Gallery for Wellington's paintings. Together with a lavish redecoration of the interior, these alterations involved the duke in much greater expenditure than intended, and led to an acrimonious quarrel with Wyatt, whose estimate was exceeded three times over. Mrs Arbuthnot noted that she had never seen the duke

> so vexed or so annoyed. He said the shame and ridicule of being so cheated and imposed upon and having been led on to an expenditure which must ruin his family made him quite miserable, that he c'd not bear the sight of the house … I asked him what Mr Wyatt said for himself. He told me he had abused him furiously and told him it shd be the last conversation he wd ever have with him, that he had known him for 40 years, knew all his circumstances and with his eyes open he had ruined him … (*Journal of Mrs Arbuthnot*, 355–6)

In the event the quarrel was made up, and Wellington continued to employ Wyatt for architectural work, albeit of a minor nature. By the 1830s much of the promise of Wyatt's architectural career had evaporated. His attempt to continue his father's extensive country house practice failed; most work of that type passed to his cousins Jeffry *Wyatville and Lewis *Wyatt. The enthusiasm and patronage of the duchess of Rutland and her circle, however, led to his being employed (with his brothers Philip and Matthew Cotes *Wyatt, the painter and sculptor) to complete the interior of Belvoir Castle in Leicestershire, and to undertake various works in London starting with York House, where, thanks to the duchess, he ousted Smirke as architect in 1825. This great house was to be Benjamin Wyatt's chief work and occupied him for over ten years. It was completed for the marquess of Stafford (later first duke of Sutherland), though not without contretemps. In 1838 Wyatt sued the duke of Sutherland for unpaid fees, and though he won the court case, this effectively marked the end of his architectural career.

Stafford House, as York House was renamed (now Lancaster House), is notable for its rich French and gilt interior decoration inspired by the Versailles of Louis XIV and Louis XV. The Wyatt brothers were recognized as the pioneers of this style, dubbed 'Louis Quatorze' by contemporaries; it was to be fashionable in smart London interiors for over a century. The new style first made its appearance in London at Crockford's Club in St James's Street in 1817. It led to commissions for other Louis Quatorze interiors at Londonderry House for the marquess of Londonderry (1828) and Carlton House Terrace (1831) as well as at Apsley House and Stafford House. Wyatt had a special flair for decoration, and that was his chief talent as an architect. His exteriors are unoriginal, but his interiors are well planned and richly decorated, from the rotonda at Drury Lane Theatre to the spectacular Waterloo Gallery at Apsley House and the theatrical staircases at Crockford's and Stafford House. His last important commission was the granite column (1831–4) in memory of the duke of York at the bottom end of Waterloo Place.

Wyatt's career ended in failure. He unwisely stood surety for the debts of his younger brother Philip and, when the latter went bankrupt in 1833 and was committed to debtors' prison, Benjamin Wyatt was overtaken by his brother's insolvency. At the age of sixty he had to sell his house in Foley Place and move to rented accommodation in Albany Street, Camden Town. He also had to refuse the post of architect to Dover harbour because of his temporary bankruptcy. In the event he satisfied his creditors, but he remained poor, his only means during his last years being the £1772 won in the Stafford House lawsuit. He died, unmarried, on 6 May 1855 in Stanhope Street, York Place, Regent's Park, leaving all his possessions, including a gold watch by Rundell and Bridges, to his 'good and faithful servant' Martha Turner, who had been with him for many years.   JOHN MARTIN ROBINSON

Sources J. M. Robinson, *The Wyatts: an architectural dynasty* (1979) · Colvin, *Archs.* · F. H. W. Sheppard, ed., *The Theatre Royal, Drury Lane, and the Royal Opera House, Covent Garden*, Survey of London, 35 (1970) · *The journal of Mrs Arbuthnot, 1820–1832*, ed. F. Bamford and the duke of Wellington [G. Wellesley], 2 (1950), 335–6 · *LondG* (28 May 1833), 1032 · R. Stanley-Morgan, 'Benjamin Wyatt and his noble clients', *ArchR*, 145 (1969), 101–5 · D. Linstrum, 'The Waterloo Palace', *ArchR*, 155 (1974), 217–23 · PRO, Wills, 882 · *IGI* · d. cert.

Archives RIBA, papers · Staffs. RO, papers and bills relating to Stafford House | BL, corresp. with James Wyatt and Philip Wyatt relating to Theatre Royal, Drury Lane, Add. MS 63641 · NRA, priv. coll., letters mainly relating to work for duke of Wellington · Staffs. RO, corresp. with marquess of Stafford and duke of Sutherland relating to Stafford House · V&A NAL, corresp. with duke of Wellington relating to Apsley House
Likenesses T. Blood, stipple (after S. Drummond), NPG, BM; repro. in *European Magazine* (1812) · S. Drummond, engraving, repro. in *European Magazine* (Oct 1812)
Wealth at death died in poverty: will, PRO

Wyatt, Sir Francis (1588–1644), colonial governor, was the eldest son of George *Wyatt (1553–1624) of Boxley Abbey, and Jane Finch of Eastwell, Kent. He was the grandson of Sir Thomas Wyatt the younger, leader of the rebellion under Mary Tudor. Francis Wyatt matriculated at St Mary Hall, Oxford, in 1603, and at Gray's Inn in 1604. He was knighted in 1618, and the same year married Margaret Sandys (d. 1645), the daughter of Sir Samuel Sandys of Ombersley, Worcestershire, and granddaughter of Edwin Sandys, archbishop of York. Through Margaret's uncles Sir Edwin Sandys, an influential member of the Virginia Company which had founded England's first successful colony in North America in 1607, and George Sandys, who served as the fledgeling colony's treasurer in 1619, he became acquainted with Virginia.

On 31 January 1621, acting on the recommendation of the earl of Southampton, the Virginia Company council appointed Wyatt governor of Virginia. Factional strife in the Virginia Company, between supporters of Sir Thomas Smythe and those of Sir Edwin Sandys, had plagued the colony's development. As many as 5000 English colonists had been sent to Virginia since 1607, but because of malnutrition, disease, and American Indian attacks, only about 1500 were living there when the new governor arrived at Jamestown, the colony's capital. Described as 'a worthy young Gentleman' (*Complete Works of Captain John Smith*, 2.284), he was accompanied by his wife's uncle, George Sandys, and his brother, Hawte Wyatt, a Church of England clergyman who served as chaplain at Jamestown. Wyatt brought with him the Virginia Company's new charter, with instructions to work for the conversion of the Indians, encourage the planting of corn to make the colony less dependent on the Indians for food, and to look for something to make a profit for the colony's investors, who had thus far 'only lived upon hopes' (*Complete Works of Captain John Smith*, 2.284).

Assuming the governorship on 18 November 1621, Wyatt succeeded Sir George Yeardley. In the spring of 1622 he sent an emissary to Opechancanough, the American Indian leader, to reconfirm the friendship between the English and the local Indians. But on 22 March 1622 there occurred one of the most devastating events of early Virginia's history: a surprise attack by the seemingly peaceful Indians upon the English settlements. Hoping to drive the English colonists from Virginia once and for all, they killed more than 347 'men, women, and children' (*Complete Works of Captain John Smith*, 2.294), reducing the English population to about 1200. After the attack Wyatt ordered the abandonment of outlying settlements and

sent out a number of expeditions to seek revenge upon the Indian attackers. Through all the turmoil he saw to it that the newly formed house of burgesses, created in 1619, met and held elections. Besides dealing with the Indians, he tried to encourage the English colonists to plant more corn, to forgo illicit trading aboard visiting vessels, to forbear swearing and drunkenness, and to keep 22 March, the anniversary of the Indian attack, as a 'holy day' ('Documents: Sir Francis Wyatt', 7.52).

In 1622 Nathaniel Butler, a former governor of the English colony of Bermuda, paid a visit to Virginia and then wrote a vitriolic account of conditions in that colony, 'The unmasking of Virginia'. On 24 October 1623 the privy council commissioned an investigation of the Virginia colony. Wyatt sent a petition to James I, signed by himself and all the members of the Virginia council and assembly, with a brief history of the colony, a rebuttal of Nathaniel Butler's criticism, and a plea to keep the colony from falling into the hands of the Smythe faction, who steadfastly opposed the group led by Sandys, Wyatt's kinsman by marriage. On 26 June 1624 James I ordered the Virginia Company's charter annulled, and Virginia became a royal colony. Wyatt's commission as governor was renewed, and on 26 August he became the first royal governor of Virginia. He was reappointed to that office in May 1625 by Charles I. According to a Virginia Company report, he 'carried himselfe soe worthylie in the place of Governor as appeared by the Reports of the Planters themselves … much commendinge him for his Iustice and aequanimitie towarde all men' (S. M. Kingsbury, ed., *Records of the Virginia Company*, 4 vols., 1906–1935, 2.530). In 1626, when his term as governor ended, Wyatt sailed for England to rejoin his wife and children. Lady Wyatt, who had gone to Virginia in 1622, had returned home in 1624 to await the birth of the couple's fifth child, Edwin. Four other children, Elizabeth, Henry, George, and William, had been born in England, prior to the Wyatts' time in Virginia.

Wyatt returned to Virginia to serve as governor again in 1639, succeeding John Harvey. He brought with him instructions from Charles I providing for regular meetings of the house of burgesses, thus assuring the continuance of representative government in the colony. In 1642 he was succeeded by William Berkeley. After serving for a time on the new governor's council, he left Virginia for England in 1643. On 6 August 1644 he made a will leaving his family home, Boxley Abbey, and the bulk of his estate to his wife during her lifetime, and then to his eldest son, Henry. He died in August 1644, and Lady Wyatt died the following year on 27 March. Both are buried at Boxley Abbey, Maidstone, Kent. VIRGINIA BERNHARD

Sources R. M. Glencross, 'Virginia gleanings in England', *Virginia Magazine of History and Biography*, 31 (1923), 237–44 · W. F. Craven, 'Wyatt, Sir Francis', *DAB* · *The complete works of Captain John Smith (1580–1631)*, ed. P. L. Barbour, 2 (1986), 284, 286–7, 293–4, 302 · 'Letter of Sir Francis Wyatt, governor of Virginia, 1621–1626', *William and Mary College Quarterly*, 2nd ser., 6 (1926), 114–21 · 'Documents: Sir Francis Wyatt, governor', *William and Mary College Quarterly*, 2nd ser., 7 (1927), 42–7, 125–31, 204–14, 246–54 · 'Documents: Sir Francis Wyatt, governor', *William and Mary College Quarterly*, 2nd ser., 8 (1928), 48–57, 157–67 · F. J. Fausz and J. Kukla, 'A letter of advice to the governor of Virginia, 1624', *William and Mary Quarterly*, 34 (1977), 104–29 • W. A. Shaw, *The knights of England*, 2 (1906), 169 • W. Stith, *The history of the first discovery and settlement of Virginia* (1747), 204–5, 303–4, 307–12, 323–4 • [J. J. Howard], *Miscellanea Genealogica et Heraldica*, new ser., 2 (1877), 107 • C. M. Andrews, *The colonial period of American history*, 1 (1937), 185, 188, 192, 196–7, 204 • A. Brown, *The first republic in America* (1893), 451–75, 500, 565, 568, 582 • E. S. Morgan, *American slavery, American freedom: the ordeal of colonial Virginia* (1975), 98, 124–5, 146 • L. G. Tyler, *Encyclopedia of Virginia biography*, 5 vols. (New York, 1915), vol. 1, p. 42–3

Archives BL, family MSS, Add. MSS 62135 • BL, MSS, Loan 15 • PRO, CO 1/2, 1/3, SP 16/521 | PRO, Manchester MSS, 1616–1647, Class 30/15/2

Wealth at death lands, incl. manor house Boxley Abbey, Maidstone, Kent: will, Glencross, 'Virginia gleanings in England', 238

Wyatt, George (1553–1624), landowner and writer, was born at Allington Castle, Kent, the youngest son of Sir Thomas *Wyatt the younger (*b.* in or before 1521, *d.* 1554), soldier, and his wife, Jane (*d.* in or after 1595), the daughter of Sir William Haute or Hart of Bishopbourne, Kent. The family was impoverished by Sir Thomas's attainder in 1554, and although Jane received lands and an annuity from Queen Mary in 1555 to a total value of about £200 per annum she never remarried, and her sons never obtained their father's or grandfather's place in Kentish society. The family was restored in blood in 1570, by which time George was the only surviving son. He was granted a small property at Wavering by the crown, and entered Gray's Inn in 1571. Although he left a number of writings, none of them was published, and only the skeleton of his career can be reconstructed with certainty. In 1582 he married Jane, the daughter of Sir Thomas Finch of Eastwell; they had five sons and four daughters. It can be deduced from his own words that he saw active service as a soldier, probably in the Low Countries, and was present at the siege of Bergen-op-Zoom in 1588, although in what capacity is not clear. The Mr Wiatt who was muster master there from 1588 to 1591 was always referred to (and referred to himself) as Thomas, as was the 'Capten Wiatt' who assisted Lord Cobham and Sir Thomas Wilford with the Kentish musters in the late 1590s. George Wyatt had settled down in Kent by 1593, but, as he complained to Lord Cobham, 'mine estate forceth me to retire myself' (*Papers*, 31). By 1618 he had at last inherited his mother's properties at Boxley and Southfleet, and in 1622 he recovered his family's possession of Boxley Abbey. He died there in August 1624 and was buried in the parish church. His wife survived him by twenty years, dying about 1644 at the age of over eighty.

George Wyatt was the obscure son of a famous father, and the obscure father of famous sons. Hawte, who died in 1638, was the father of Edward, the progenitor of the Virginia Wiatts, and Wyatt's son Sir Francis *Wyatt, who died in 1644, was the first royal governor of Virginia. George's main claim to fame is the papers which he wrote and collected in the latter part of his life, which provide some vivid and proximate insights into the careers of his father and grandfather, and into the military problems of late sixteenth- and early seventeenth-century England. One of the most interesting is his eulogistic treatise in defence of Anne Boleyn (*c.*1605), which contains a circumstantial

account of Sir Thomas Wyatt's journey to Rome in 1527. George was born many years after his grandfather's death, but the story may have been handed down in the family. Another is his letter to his son Sir Francis written in 1622 and containing such comments as 'I see by the map I have of the last, and by your letter, your Plantation is d[r]awen out into long, weak and skattered inhabitation with smale and unapt defences' (*Papers*, 113); it was written shortly after the destructive Indian revolt of the same year. Virtually everything which is known about George Wyatt derives from these papers, and particularly those which were put together into a commonplace book by his descendant Richard Wyatt in 1727. This commonplace book was edited for the Camden Society by David Loades in 1968.

DAVID LOADES

Sources BL, Wyatt MSS, Add. MSS 62135–62138, Add. Ch. 75893–75992, 75999–76026 • *The papers of George Wyatt, esquire, of Boxley Abbey in the county of Kent*, ed. D. M. Loades, CS, 4th ser., 5 (1968)

Archives BL

Wyatt, Sir Henry (*c.*1460–1536). *See under* Wyatt, Sir Thomas (*c.*1503–1542).

Wyatt, Henry (1794–1840), painter, was born at Thickbroom, Weeford, near Lichfield, Staffordshire, on 17 September 1794, the elder son of Joseph Wyatt (1749–1798), a surveyor, who died when Wyatt was three years old. His brother's baptismal record states that his mother's name was Jane. He was a cousin of the Wyatt family of architects. He went to live at Handsworth, near Birmingham, with his guardian, Francis *Eginton (1736/7–1805), the glass-painter, who had married his aunt, Maria Wyatt (1743?–1812). Finding that Wyatt was interested in art, Eginton sent him to London in 1811, and in the following year he was admitted to the Royal Academy Schools. Joseph Farington records in his diary that Wyatt was awarded a silver medal for the best copy in the school of painting in 1817. In 1815 he entered the studio of Sir Thomas Lawrence as a pupil, and proved so valuable an assistant that after the first twelve months Lawrence offered Wyatt £300 a year. Accounts differ about whether Wyatt declined the offer or remained in Lawrence's employ for another year. By the end of 1817 he left London and established himself as a portrait painter, practising first at Birmingham until 1819 and successively at Liverpool until 1823 and then Manchester until 1825. He returned to London, where he lived in Newman Street until 1834, when asthma caused him to move to Leamington. Early in 1829 he acted as agent for sending exhibits to the Birmingham Institution. In 1837 he went to Manchester after receiving some portrait commissions and in the following April he 'had an attack of paralysis', from which he never recovered (*GM*). Although the *Dictionary of National Biography* article on Francis Eginton states that Eginton's daughter married Henry Wyatt, no evidence has been found to support this. He died, apparently unmarried, at Prestwich, near Manchester, on 27 February 1840, and was buried in the churchyard of that village.

Both Wyatt's portraits and his subject pictures were

painted in a style similar to that of Lawrence. He was a clever artist, a skilful draughtsman, and a good colourist; both his portraits and subject pictures earned him considerable popularity. Over the course of his career he exhibited thirty-five works, most of these portraits, at the Royal Academy from 1817 to 1827, and at the British Institution twenty-eight works, mostly subject pictures, from 1826 to 1837. Two of his works, *Vigilance* (exh. RA, 1836; engraved by G. A. Periam) and *Archimedes* (also called *Galileo* and *Philosopher*; exh. RA, 1832; engraved by R. Bell), entered the National Gallery as part of the Vernon collection and are now in the Tate collection. *Fair Forester* and *Proffered Kiss*, engraved by George Thomas Doo, were popular works by Wyatt, and several of his other subject pictures, including *Juliet*, *Chapeau noir*, and *Gentle Reader*, were well known. His portrait of Thomas Harrison, architect of Chester Castle, formerly hung in Chester Castle. Wyatt was a man of refined tastes, living a quiet bachelor life but, as his sketchbooks show, always industriously working at every variety of drawing: family groups, landscapes, cattle, buildings, shipping, animals of many kinds, and flowers were alike drawn with the utmost care and with much ability. His sketchbooks (ex Christies, 22 November 1977) include studies dating from 1811 to 1833. Samuel Redgrave described him as 'a clever painter, his colour good, and his subjects pleasingly treated' (Redgrave, *Artists*, 492).

Wyatt's brother, **Thomas Wyatt** (*bap.* 1795, *d.* 1859), portrait painter and photographer, was also born at Thickbroom, where he was baptized on 20 September 1795. He studied in the Royal Academy Schools and accompanied his brother to Birmingham, Liverpool, and Manchester. At Birmingham his portraits 'were much admired, and he gained so much respect from the artists of the place that they elected him secretary to the Birmingham Society of Artists, which position he occupied for some time' (*Art Journal*). He exhibited at the Birmingham Society of Arts in 1827 and 1828, in the latter year sending eight works. He moved to Manchester in 1840 and lived in Princess Street until 1853. He exhibited several portraits and some subject pictures annually at the Royal Manchester Institution. Wyatt married Anne, daughter of George Hadfield, a manufacturer, on 15 June 1848. The couple had a son, Francis (*b.* 1851). After his brother's death Thomas Wyatt paid the pioneer photographer William Henry Fox Talbot for the sole rights to practise photography in and around Manchester. Unfortunately, he had to give up when this venture proved financially unsuccessful and he partially lost his sight. He moved to Lichfield to try again to make a living through portrait painting, but he 'was attacked by paralysis' (ibid.). For the next five years he was dependent 'upon the devoted attention of his wife and the pecuniary assistance of their friends' (ibid.). He died on 7 July 1859, survived by his wife. He was described at his death as a 'portrait painter of considerable reputation in the midland counties of England' (ibid.).

Paintings and drawings by Henry and Thomas Wyatt and engravings after their work are held in the Victoria and Albert Museum, the National Portrait Gallery, the National Maritime Museum, and the British Museum, London; the city art galleries in Birmingham and Manchester, and the Pitti Palace, Florence.

ALBERT NICHOLSON, *rev.* DIANE WAGGONER

Sources *GM*, 2nd ser., 14 (1840), 555–6 · *Art Journal*, 21 (1 Sept 1859), 288 · J. M. Robinson, *The Wyatts: an architectural dynasty* (1979) [incl. list of known works by Henry Wyatt] · D. Linstrum, *Catalogue of the drawings collection of the Royal Institute of British Architects: The Wyatt family* (1974) · *IGI* · S. C. Hall, ed., *The Vernon gallery of British art*, 2 vols. (1854) · 'The Vernon gallery', *Art Journal*, 13 (1 June 1851), 179 · Graves, *RA exhibitors* · Graves, *Brit. Inst.* · C. Holmes, 'Heirs of Lawrence, 1825–1835', *Burlington Magazine*, 69 (Nov 1936), 195–201 · 'Henry Wyatt rediscovered', *Country Life*, 163 (16 March 1978), 683 · H. Ottley, *A biographical and critical dictionary of recent and living painters and engravers* (1866) · 'A man with a hawk by Henry Wyatt', *Burlington Magazine*, 11 (June 1907), 170 · T. Fawcett, *The rise of English provincial art* (1974) · Redgrave, *Artists* · Thieme & Becker, *Allgemeines Lexikon* · Bryan, *Painters* · R. N. James, *Painters and their works*, 3 vols. (1896–7) · *Heath's gallery of British engravings*, 4 vols. (1837–8) · Farington, *Diary*, vol. 14

Archives Birm. CL, letter to Matthew Boulton, Tew MSS

Likenesses H. Wyatt, self-portrait, pencil drawing, *c.*1819, repro. in *Burlington Magazine*, 120 (April 1978), fig 59 · W. Bradley, portrait, 1839; in possession of Joseph Taylor of Ashton-on-Mersey, Cheshire, 1900

Wyatt, James (1690/91–1767), merchant and shipbuilder, was born in the Hythe area of Southampton and probably in that part of Hythe then in the parish of Dibden. Details of his parents are obscure; however, Wyatt is known to have had one elder brother, Joseph (*c.*1689–1757). Throughout his life James was to work closely with his brother, the two often involved in joint business enterprises. An early reference to Joseph appears in 1719 when he supplied boards for the gates of Beaulieu church, while in 1726 he supplied timber for a quay being built on Beaulieu River. This latter was part of the failed Montagu Town scheme in which John, second duke of Montagu, hoped to establish a major port to receive produce from plantations in the West Indies.

During the War of the Austrian Succession (1740–8) the quay was put to use by the Wyatt brothers, who jointly exported timber out of the New Forest, supplying both compass oak and treenails to the naval dockyard at Portsmouth. While Joseph continued to concentrate upon the supply of timber, acquiring rights on a number of properties throughout the New Forest, James directed his attention towards the building of ships. As the war placed considerable pressures upon existing government dockyard facilities, the Admiralty increasingly turned to private shipbuilders for the construction and repair of smaller warships. Although having no direct experience of such work, Wyatt was closely connected with the most important commodity of the shipbuilding process, that of timber. In possession, also, of certain entrepreneurial skills, he used both his knowledge of the Beaulieu area and recent experience of supplying the Admiralty to secure a shipbuilding contract and a site upon which the vessel could be built. The site chosen was Buckler's Hard, this being part of the failed Montagu Town site and secured from the duke of Montagu at a rent of £5 per annum. James Wyatt was thus the first shipbuilder to make use of this historic site which remains the property of the Montagu family and is little changed since the days of Wyatt's enterprise.

The contract secured from the Admiralty was for a 24-gun ship that was to be launched in 1745 as the *Surprise*. Overseeing construction of this vessel, the Admiralty appointed a senior naval dockyard shipwright, Henry Adams, with Wyatt having to recruit the necessary workforce. In 1746 Wyatt acquired a second Admiralty contract, the *Scorpion* (18 guns), also built at Buckler's Hard. Despite the success of the shipbuilding venture no further contracts were obtained, the Admiralty preferring to direct all new work to its own facilities now that exigencies of war had declined. In March 1748 the yard was taken over by Henry Adams. James Wyatt returned to the supply of timber, the will of Joseph Wyatt, read in 1757, noting that he possessed at least one messuage (in Fawley). Wyatt, who died in September 1767, left four children born to his first wife, Sarah (*d. c.*1729), and a further two children of his second wife, Hannah King (*d.* 1786), whom he had married in Fawley parish church on 4 February 1732. James Wyatt was buried (5 September) with his brother at Dibden; the site of the grave is marked by a magnificent tomb that depicts a ship, and declares James to have been seventy-six years of age at his death.

PHILIP MacDOUGALL

Sources A. Holland, *Buckler's Hard: maritime museum and Beaulieu River* (1993?) · A. J. Holland, *Ships of British oak. The rise and decline of wooden shipbuilding in Hampshire* (1971) · papers of Sir Stanley Wyatt, Heritage Centre, John Montagu Building, Beaulieu · parish register, Fawley, 5 Sept 1767 [burial] · will of Joseph Wyatt, PRO, PROB 11/830, sig. 143

Wyatt, James (1746–1813), architect, the sixth son of Benjamin Wyatt (1709–1772), a prosperous farmer, timber merchant, and builder, and his wife, Mary Wright (*d.* 1793), was born on 3 August 1746 at Blackbrook Farm, Weeford, Staffordshire. He was baptized at Weeford church on 30 August.

Italy and early career The building business begun by Wyatt's father was run as a family firm, and Benjamin's sons were trained to contribute different skills; for example, Samuel *Wyatt (1737–1807), the third son, became a carpenter and Joseph (1739–1785), the fourth son, a mason. James, who showed early signs of artistic talent, went to Italy to study the architecture of antiquity and the Renaissance at first hand, under the patronage of the Bagots of Blithfield, local landowners in Staffordshire. In 1762 Richard Bagot (the younger brother of Sir William Bagot, bt, of Blithfield Hall) went to Venice as secretary to the ambassador-extraordinary, Charles Compton, sixteenth earl of Northampton, taking Wyatt with him to study painting, architecture, and music. Wyatt went on to Rome from Venice, and altogether spent six years in Italy before returning to Britain about 1768. At Venice he studied architectural drawing under Antonio Visentini and admired the buildings of Andrea Palladio. In Rome he made measured drawings of various buildings, including the domes of the Pantheon and St Peter's.

Wyatt was not impressed by Roman baroque and later

James Wyatt (1746–1813), by John Charles Felix Rossi, exh. RA 1797

told Joseph Farington that 'there is no good modern architecture in Rome—the best specimens are by Raphael.—That of Michael Angelo is very bad: There is very good architecture at Venice, by Palladio' (Farington, *Diary*, 3.918). Nevertheless, his Italian sojourn provided the polish and accomplishment which enabled him to become one of the most fashionable architects of the late eighteenth century; he also made there a number of useful acquaintances, including the royal librarian Richard Dalton, who was to bring him to the notice of George III. 'His talents in architecture, painting and music were so equally developed that it was only preference for the first which decided his career', wrote an obituarist (*GM*, 83/2, 1813, 216–17). John Thorpe, the English Jesuit, wrote to Lord Arundell at Wardour Castle, Wiltshire, that Wyatt 'was esteemed to have the best talents for Architecture of any of our countrymen who for several years has been in Rome' (Wardour MSS, Wilts. & Swindon RO, 25 Jan 1775).

On his return to Britain, Wyatt divided his time between Staffordshire and London, where the second of the Wyatt brothers, John, a surgeon and fellow of the Royal Society, had a house in Great Newport Street, where both James and Samuel Wyatt stayed in London. John Wyatt was one of the shareholders in a scheme for a 'Winter Ranelagh' in

Oxford Street, London; the principal promoter and owner of the site was P. E. Turst, through whose influence James Wyatt was chosen as architect. A fashionable public building, the Pantheon which he was commissioned to design, brought James Wyatt to immediate notice. The principal domed assembly room owed much to Adam's design for the Saloon at Kedleston Hall, Derbyshire; and the team of craftsmen employed to build and decorate the Pantheon included most of those who had worked at Kedleston. Samuel Wyatt supervised the construction of the Pantheon in association with James; the brothers continued to work in close proximity until 1774, when they set up independently in London. From the moment that the Pantheon designs were exhibited at the Royal Academy in 1770, James Wyatt found himself much sought after as an architect. When the building opened in 1772 there was rapturous applause. Horace Walpole called it 'the most beautiful edifice in England' (Walpole, *Corr.*, 28, 102). The Adam brothers were disturbed by the sudden appearance of this architectural rival and accused Wyatt of plagiarism in the introduction to their *Works in Architecture*, which was published in 1773, probably as a direct counter to what they saw as the Wyatt threat.

Wyatt's patrons   In 1770, on the strength of the drawings for the Pantheon, Wyatt was elected an associate of the Royal Academy; he was elected a full academician in 1785. Important commissions were also given to him even before the Pantheon's completion. Charles Lennox, eighth duke of Richmond, for example, commissioned an unexecuted scheme for a new house at Goodwood, exhibited at the Royal Academy in 1771 as a design for a nobleman's house in Sussex. Wyatt was to work for him, on and off, until the duke's death over thirty years later.

The rumour that Catherine the Great of Russia wanted Wyatt to go to St Petersburg as her court architect was enough to encourage a group of Englishmen to club together to pay him a retainer, from *c*.1770, of £1200 to stay in London. These included the dukes of Northumberland and Devonshire; William Cavendish, fifth duke of Devonshire, paid him £50 a year from 1776 until 1790, employing him to design alterations and decorations at his various seats, including Devonshire House, Piccadilly, Chiswick House, Middlesex, and Compton Place, Eastbourne. Wyatt's involvement with the Devonshires probably came through the Northamptons: the fifth duke's younger brother George Cavendish, later fourth earl of Burlington, had married Lady Elizabeth Compton, daughter and heiress of the sixteenth earl of Northampton. Several important early Wyatt commissions seem to have been for Northampton relations and connections, including Thomas Halsey at Gaddesden Place, Hertfordshire (1768), and Sambrook Freeman at Fawley Court, Buckinghamshire (1771).

Another important group of related clients was the Assheton connection, all cousins of Lord Scarsdale of Kedleston, including Sir Thomas Egerton of Heaton Hall, Lancashire (1772), Assheton Curzon at Hagley Hall, Worcestershire (1771), and Lord Suffield at Gunton, Norfolk (1775). These formed the beginning of a country house practice which became the most extensive of the eighteenth century. For the best part of forty years Wyatt directed the major share of country house work. His houses varied from major mansions such as Heaton Hall, Heveningham Hall, Suffolk (1780–84), and Dodington Park, Gloucestershire (1798–1813), to minor additions, entrance lodges, and interior decoration. His practice extended to most parts of England and to Ireland, where he was responsible for many houses though he only visited the country once to inspect construction works at Slane Castle, co. Meath (1785). His Irish houses were all constructed under the direction of local people, including Castle Coole in co. Fermanagh for Armor Lowry-Corry, Viscount Belmore (1790), which is arguably his most perfect house design, with its finely judged proportions, exquisitely detailed execution, and rational plan.

Wyatt in practice   Much of Wyatt's time was spent in travelling the country, and his coach was fitted like a little office with a drawing-board so that he could work on his journeys, an interesting testimony to the great improvement in English roads in the late eighteenth century. In 1796 he told Farington that he travelled on average 4000 miles a year. His fees were a commission of five per cent of the cost of the building work, plus 2s. 6d. a mile travel expenses and 5 guineas for his attendance on site. For a site consultation, without any agreement being entered into, he charged 10 guineas.

In London, Wyatt maintained a large office under the direction of John Dixon, his chief draughtsman, who was with him all his working career from the time of the building of the Pantheon until Wyatt's death in 1813. Together with Dixon there was a staff of four clerks and a varying number of pupils and other assistants including, at different times, Joseph Badger (junior), William Blogg, Henry Brown, John Foster of Liverpool, John Michael Gandy, George Hadfield, Charles Humfrey, Henry Kitchen (junior), William Newham, James Parlby, John Percy, Charles and William Porden, John Rawstorne, J. W. Sanderson, James Spiller, Thomas Taylor, Thomas and John Westmacott (sons of the sculptor), M. Wynn, John Peter Gandy-Deering, Wyatt's own sons Benjamin Dean and Philip, and also his nephews Lewis and Jeffry.

Despite the size of his office and bursts of intense work, Wyatt was disorganized and a bad businessman: the sheer scale and geographical spread of his practice made it increasingly difficult for him to give proper attention to his individual clients. He took on far more work than he could manage, and lost many jobs as a result. As early as 1775 he was superseded as architect for the interior of Home House in Portman Square, London, by Robert Adam because the countess of Home was exasperated by his dilatory ways, though she did pay him his £500 fees. By the 1790s complaints were legion. The committee for rebuilding St Chad's Church in Shrewsbury were so offended by his breaking engagements that they turned to George Steuart instead. In 1804 Jeffry Wyatt told Farington that his uncle had lost many great commissions by such neglect. When first approached he would display keen enthusiasm, but when work was about to begin he would lose interest and employ himself upon trifling professional matters which others could do. In May 1809 Farington reported that after 'Wyatt's conduct in neglecting Lord Pembroke's alterations at Wilton … Lord Pembroke had given him up, his patience having been exhausted' (Farington, *Diary*, 9.3465). In 1812 William Beckford at Fonthill fulminated at the 'utter indifference to all that concerns me and his own honour, these repeated and renewed proofs are too much for me … If he goes to Bilgewater [the earl of Bridgewater at Ashridge] first I'll not receive him here' (Beckford, 129).

Disappointed clients, however, tended to forget their rage when Wyatt did appear. As Shute Barrington, the bishop of Durham, remarked: 'you forgave Wyatt disappointing you when he appeared' (Robinson, 78). Beckford's feelings, for instance, were transformed when Wyatt arrived at Fonthill: 'He works with a brio, a zeal, an energy, a faith that would move the largest mountain in the Alps' (Beckford, 129). The sculptor John Bacon (1777–1859) elaborated on this aspect of Wyatt's character: when he did eventually visit a client, 'he had such a peculiar talent in making everyone feel that he was so entirely absorbed in the wishes of his employer that his want of respect in not coming was soon forgotten' (Robinson, 78). Contemporaries commented on his charm, polished manners, and amiable character. Farington recorded that Jeffry Wyatt thought his uncle 'one of the best-tempered men living' (Farington, *Diary*, 12.4246), and others admired his 'mild and gentlemanly manners' (*European Magazine*, October 1813, 64). His attractive character, as much as his talents, must have played a part in his professional and social success.

Official architectural appointments As well as his extensive private practice, James Wyatt was also appointed to many of the most important public architectural posts in the country. In 1776 he succeeded Henry Keene as surveyor to the fabric of Westminster Abbey; in 1782 he became architect to the Board of Ordnance. In 1796 he was appointed surveyor-general and comptroller of the office of works in succession to Sir William Chambers. He was also deputy surveyor of the Office of Woods and Forests (the crown estate), surveyor to Somerset House, and honorary architect to the Middlesex Hospital. To have coped with these as well as his architectural practice would have required administrative genius combined with an unusual capacity for delegation; he possessed neither. His performance in his official posts was at best uneven. At Westminster Abbey the mason Thomas Gayfere (1755–1827) carried out a conscientious restoration of the external stonework of Henry VII's chapel under Wyatt's nominal supervision. For the Board of Ordnance Wyatt designed several substantial works, including a magnificent range of new buildings at Woolwich Arsenal, to cope with the expansion of the military establishment following the outbreak of war with France. Wyatt's grand store at Woolwich (1808–13) is a vast U-shaped layout facing the River Thames and is his most monumental public building. His time at the office of works was less happy and he ended up as a habitual absentee. Up to 1806 he attended over half the

meetings of the board, but in 1807 he was absent for fifty successive weeks. Between 1808 and 1810 he attended only 38 out of 183 meetings. Many employees did as they pleased; one went on holiday and stayed away without leave for three years. The accounts descended into confusion: bills were certified while containing substantial errors; estimates were equally slapdash and were often exceeded by up to 250 per cent. The government began serious inquiries in 1806. Wyatt's sudden death in 1813 left the affairs of the office of works in chaos; a parliamentary inquiry was necessary to disentangle matters, as a result of which the post of surveyor was abolished and the office was placed under political control. Jeffry Wyatt told Farington that his 'uncle' neglect had destroyed the office of works as it was' (Farington, *Diary*, 12.1183). The prime minister, Lord Liverpool, described Wyatt as 'certainly one of the worst public servants I recollect in any office' (Lord Liverpool to the ninth duke of Richmond, 8 Jan 1814, BL, Add. MS 38568, fol. 224).

Wyatt owed his official positions to powerful friends and patrons. His appointment to the Ordnance was at the recommendation of the eighth duke of Richmond, while Farington recorded that he owed his place of surveyor-general to Queen Charlotte and Princess Elizabeth, for whom he had remodelled Frogmore House near Windsor as a *trianon* (1793–5). He was on very good terms with George III and in 1794, two years before the death of Sir William Chambers, the king is said to have promised Wyatt the reversion of the surveyorship. The king offered it to him partly as recompense for the time and trouble taken over Frogmore and partly because he considered him 'the first Architect of the Kingdom' and therefore the most proper person for the position.

In addition to his appointment, Wyatt did much private work for the king, reconstructing the staircase at Buckingham House, beginning the Gothic reconstruction of Windsor Castle (1800–13; completed in the next reign by his nephew Jeffry), and designing a large Gothic palace at Kew (1801–11), nicknamed The Bastille, which was never fitted up and soon demolished but was nevertheless significant for the extensive use of cast iron in its construction, and as the model for Robert Smirke's castles at Eastnor, Herefordshire, and Lowther, Westmorland.

Wyatt worked for many ancient institutions as well as the crown, notably Oxford University, where he designed alterations or additions to Christ Church (1773–83), Merton (1790), Magdalen (1790–93). Worcester (1776–90), Brasenose (1779–80), New College (1778–94), Oriel (1788), and Balliol colleges (1792) as well as the new Radcliffe Observatory (1776–94). The latter is one of his most distinguished designs and architecturally the most impressive observatory in Europe. It is freely based on the Tower of the Winds in Athens and shows a neo-classical concern with geometrical composition, its design being a play on semicircles and octagons.

Wyatt's interiors The versatility, range, and easy brilliance of Wyatt's work are astonishing. He was equally adept at designing monumental classical buildings—such as the mausoleums at Brocklesby Park, Lincolnshire (1795), and

Cobham Hall, Kent (1783)—worthy of comparison with anything in Europe, or a silver candlestick of incomparable elegance for Matthew Boulton, and a painted rush-seated chair of remarkable freshness and charm for Andrew Vanneck. From the beginning of his career he adopted and improved on the Adam style of interior decoration, with dainty, filigree plaster ceilings, chaste marble chimney-pieces, scagliola columns, and small-scale painted panels, using the same team of craftsmen, including Joseph Rose, Peter van Gelder, Domenico Bartoli, and Biagio Rebecca. Like Adam, Wyatt also designed the furniture and fittings for his major interiors. These could be elaborately carved and gilded, like Adam's, but Wyatt perfected a simpler range of painted classical furniture, often using the same colours and patterns as the walls of the rooms for which it was intended, as at Heveningham Hall in Suffolk. Generally Wyatt's interiors are more chaste, elegant, and less fussy, if thinner, than Adam's; his palette of colours is also more restrained and harmonious, with a preference for light greens and lilacs. His finest surviving interiors include the dining-room at Crichel in Dorset, the hall at Heveningham in Suffolk, the vestibule at Cobham in Kent, and the staircase at Heaton in Lancashire. His little interior of the river temple at Fawley in Oxfordshire (1770–71) is the earliest example of 'Etruscan' decoration and was inspired by Wedgwood's vases and Sir William Hamilton's collection of Greek vases as engraved and published by d'Hancarville.

Wyatt as a classical architect In the 1790s Wyatt developed a more severe Graeco-Roman style which foreshadowed the Regency architecture of the following century. This was partly the result of the death of many of his old craftsmen and the emergence of a new team, notably Francis Bernasconi for plasterwork and Joseph Alcott for scagliola. His finest exercise in this vein is Dodington in Gloucestershire (1798–1813) for Christopher Codrington. The plan of Dodington is arranged round a full-height central hall with an imperial-plan staircase, an idea which Wyatt originally adopted from Carrington House, Whitehall (dem.), by Sir William Chambers and which he used whenever space permitted.

In many ways Chambers was Wyatt's architectural hero. He told a sympathetic George III that 'there had been no regular Architecture since Sir William Chambers,—that when He came from Italy He found the public taste corrupted by the Adams, and He was obliged to comply with it' (Farington, *Diary*, 6.2214). The influence of Chambers can be detected in much of Wyatt's more monumental architecture: Wyatt, however, was more eclectic and drew on a wider range of sources. He was a pioneer of the Greek revival, and used Greek Doric columns in his porticoes at Goodwood House, Sussex, the Royal Military College at Sandhurst, Berkshire, Stoke Park, Buckinghamshire, and elsewhere. His use of the classical orders, however, was rarely pure and he adapted his sources to give them a distinctive Wyatt attenuation and elegance. The Bath Lodge at Dodington uses a variant of the Delian Doric Order, while its general domed form is inspired by Claude-Nicolas Ledoux's Barrière-Monceau in Paris. The exteriors of Wyatt's buildings show the same range and versatility as the interiors. Several of the most interesting are pragmatic responses to particular problems. At Stoke Park in Buckinghamshire (1793–7) he added corner pavilions linked by colonnades round an older core to create a highly successful new composition. The final, executed, scheme for the duke of Richmond's Goodwood (1806), which takes a canted form like a three-sided belvedere, is strikingly original but perhaps less successful. The most distinctive Wyatt façades, however, are his early ones with their domed bows, tripartite windows, and extensive use of Coade stone, of which the south front of Heaton Hall, Lancashire, is the best, with Bowden Park, Wiltshire, a close runner-up.

Wyatt as Gothic architect In the latter part of his career Wyatt's classical work was increasingly overshadowed by his fame as a Gothic architect. Accomplished though his classical works always were, Gothic became his favourite style.

> His genius revived in this country the long forgotten beauties of Gothic Architecture from monastic and baronial structures … pre-eminently and indeed without a rival did he, and for the longest period of his professional life, indulge in this his favourite order. (*GM*, 1st ser., 83/2, 297)

Playing a significant role in the history of the Gothic revival in England, he bridged in his work the gap between the rococo freedom of mid-century buildings such as Strawberry Hill, Twickenham, and the more archaeological seriousness of the nineteenth century.

Like most Georgian architects, Wyatt had worked in Gothic on occasion from the beginning of his career. The Great Hall at Beaudesert in Staffordshire (dem.) was Gothic as early as 1772; it had a plaster vaulted ceiling and ogee pointed arches. But gradually more and more of his major buildings were in the Gothic style. They are remarkable for two particular qualities: their accurate detail and their picturesque massing. Unlike earlier rococo Gothic buildings, Wyatt's were modelled on well-known ecclesiastical sources, mainly English but not entirely so. James Murphy's 1795 publication on the abbey church at Batalha in Portugal, with its engravings of elaborate late Gothic detail and plan with octagonal chapels, was a potent influence on Wyatt's imagination. His Gothic compositions showed a flair for the arrangement of asymmetrical parts to form a picturesque whole. Even some of his early Gothic houses, such as Sheffield Park in Sussex (1776), have carefully arranged asymmetrical elevations, but it was at Lee Priory in Kent (dem.), built between 1785 and 1790, that he first developed an asymmetrical plan, arranged so that the various parts composed well in external views. Lee Priory had an octagonal centre, derived from Batalha, and short asymmetrical wings. Horace Walpole pronounced it 'the quintessence of Gothic taste, exquisitely executed … it has sober dignity without prelatic pomp' (Walpole to Hannah Moore, 25 July 1790, Walpole, *Corr.*, 31.342).

A whole series of buildings after 1800 developed and exploited the picturesque possibilities of Gothic as never before: Ashridge, Hertfordshire (1808–13), for John William Egerton, eighth earl of Bridgewater, Belvoir Castle, Leicestershire (1801–13), for John Henry Manners, fifth duke of Rutland, and Fonthill Abbey, Wiltshire (1796–1812), for William Beckford, gave Wyatt scope to develop the ideas sketched at Lee on a vast scale and with almost unlimited budgets. Fonthill took the Batalha-inspired scheme of Lee to its limits, with an octagonal tribune in the centre, supporting a lofty, though short-lived tower, and sublime vistas to either side down exaggeratedly long galleries in radiating wings. Of particular interest, though relatively small, were Norris Castle on the Isle of Wight (1799) and Pennsylvania Castle in Dorset (1800). These castellated houses are arranged irregularly with taller round towers to hold the composition, and they rely more on picturesque massing than historicist detailing to convey their Gothic spirit. These houses mark a significant development in the history of the English Gothic revival. Altogether, Wyatt's Gothic buildings are a key element in the development of the English picturesque aesthetic.

Wyatt's restoration work Between 1787 and 1797 Wyatt was also extensively employed in restoring several of the great cathedrals, including Lichfield, Hereford, Salisbury, and Durham. Some of this work involved essential repair, such as the partial rebuilding of the spires or the addition of buttresses to the transept at Lichfield. At Hereford the work was made necessary by the collapse of the Norman west tower and the partial destruction of the nave. But the aim of Wyatt, and the chapters who employed him, was also to 'improve' the buildings by opening up vistas, clearing away screens and other later accretions. At Salisbury this involved the removal of the Perpendicular screen and chantry chapels and two porches; the medieval tombs were arranged symmetrically in the nave like a procession of effigies while at the same time the close was raised several feet and smooth-turfed.

This 'tidying' showed a lack of respect for the historical integrity of an old building which was shocking to John Carter and later generations of antiquaries but was admired by the majority of Wyatt's contemporaries. Prince Puckler-Muskau wrote of Salisbury:

> The interior of this magnificent temple is in the highest degree inspiring and has been improved by Wyatt's genius. It was an admirable idea to remove the most remarkable old monuments from the walls and obscure corners and place them in the space between the great double avenue of pillars … Nothing can have a finer effect. (Puckler-Muskau, *Tours in England*, 1832, 2.226–7)

Wyatt in the Society of Antiquaries and the Royal Academy It was Wyatt's Gothic work, especially his cathedral improvements and his general use of such inauthentic materials as patent cement and cast iron, which aroused the ire of his bitter antiquarian critic John Carter, and led to Wyatt being blackballed when first proposed for election to the Society of Antiquaries in 1796, though he was elected at the second attempt the following year. Carter dismissed Wyatt's new House of Lords, with its plaster battlements and oriels, as an 'august pile of brickbats and stucco' (Crook, 514–19).

Though perhaps not entirely comfortable at the Antiquaries, Wyatt was very much at home at the Royal Academy, where he was actively involved in day-to-day politics and intrigues. In 1803 he was one of the members of the council which tried to assert its independence of the general assembly in an internal struggle over the governing of the academy: the resulting strife led Benjamin West to resign the presidency the following year. Wyatt was elected in his place, the first architect president of the academy. Chosen because of his good relationship with George III, he was only president for a year. Instead of resuscitating the council and starting a rotating presidency as his supporters hoped he would, he slept in committees, mumbled his speeches, and failed to attend meetings. At the Royal Academy dinner in 1806, sitting next to the prince of Wales, he 'gave the toasts in so low a voice that he could scarcely be heard. He fell below West in his manner of communicating to the Company what he had to say' (Farington, *Diary*, 7.2746).

Private life and last years James Wyatt married Rachel Lunn (*d.* 1817) in 1774. They had four sons: Benjamin Dean *Wyatt, Matthew Cotes *Wyatt, Charles Burton, Philip William, and a daughter, Jane, who died young, to the great distress of her mother. He built a house for himself in Queen Anne Street (later Foley Place), London: it was completed in 1783 and the family lived there until his death in 1813. Wyatt also had a small country house, set in 90 acres, at Hanworth in Middlesex. The last years of his life, however, were increasingly overshadowed by ill health and financial difficulties, and he died penniless. Robert Smirke reported in 1813 that

> Wyatt was in very distressed circumstances notwithstanding the vast opportunities afforded him to make a fortune … Bartolini [a plaisterer] said He himself was a Creditor for £3,000; and that he knew Wyatt's house in Foley Place was mortgaged to the utmost. He said Wyatt owed to Dixon His draughtsman, £900. (Farington, *Diary*, 12.4423–4)

Dr Thorpe told Farington the same story: James Wyatt's 'habitual neglect' and general bad management had lost him a fortune (Farington, *Diary*, 12.4246).

By 1800 Wyatt was suffering from kidney trouble and possibly cirrhosis of the liver; in 1804 Lysons reported that he was paralytic and had his mouth drawn aside. In 1807 Farington, the gossip of the Royal Academy, reported that it was not probable that he would 'ever be restored to what He was before his last illness' (Farington, *Diary*, 8.3146). He died, however, in a road accident on 4 September 1813. He was travelling back to London from Dodington, with Christopher Codrington. Near Marlborough the carriage, which was being driven at great speed, overturned. Wyatt, who was reading a newspaper, hit his head on the roof and was killed instantly. He was buried in Westminster Abbey on 28 September. He died intestate and penniless, leaving his widow dependent on a government pension of £100 per annum.

Assessment Of all the major eighteenth-century architects James Wyatt has perhaps been subjected to the greatest extremes of praise and criticism, both in his lifetime and since his death. From the beginning of his career he received, on the one hand, the enthusiastic admiration of the fashionable world and, on the other, biting criticism from disappointed clients and the sniping of jealous rivals. The latter culminated in the fierce personal attacks of John Carter, who wrote no fewer than 212 pieces in the *Gentleman's Magazine* denouncing Wyatt's work and character. These were to be responsible for the image of 'Wyatt the Destroyer', which was taken up by Pugin and has persisted to the present day. The criticism of most contemporaries was directed at his chronic professional and administrative shortcomings—his lack of punctuality and financial irresponsibility—rather than his architectural designs. Indeed, during his lifetime nearly all considered him to be an architectural genius.

The most serious charge against Wyatt was that he had no artistic principles but trimmed his work to contemporary fads and fashion. There is an element of truth in this. His early classical work, especially his interior decoration, owed more to the Adams than his own professed admiration for Palladio or Sir William Chambers. The very scale of his practice and his easy facility as a designer would also seem to substantiate accusations of superficiality and a lack of any deeply held artistic beliefs. Yet, throughout his career Wyatt showed himself a master of space, form, and composition, whether working in the classical or Gothic manners. However, it was his mastery of the Gothic style which gave Wyatt a claim to be one of the great eighteenth-century architects.

JOHN MARTIN ROBINSON

Sources A. Dale, *James Wyatt* (1956) · J. M. Robinson, *The Wyatts* (1979) · Colvin, *Archs.* · F. Fergusson, 'James Wyatt', PhD diss., Harvard U., 1972 · D. Linstrum, *Catalogue of the drawings collection of the Royal Institute of British Architects: The Wyatt family* (1974) · [W. Papworth], ed., *The dictionary of architecture*, 11 vols. (1853–92) · *GM*, 1st ser., 83/2 (1813), 296 · J. M. Crook, 'The surveyorship of James Wyatt 1796–1813', *The history of the king's works*, ed. H. M. Colvin and others, 6 (1973) · Farington, *Diary* · E. Harris and J. M. Robinson, 'New light on Wyatt at Fawley', *Architectural History*, 27 (1984), 263–7 · J. M. Frew, 'Richard Gough, James Wyatt, and late eighteenth-century preservation', *Journal of the Society of Architectural Historians*, 38 (Dec 1979), 366–74 · J. M. Frew, 'Some observations on James Wyatt's Gothic style, 1790–1797', *Journal of the Society of Architectural Historians*, 41 (Aug 1982), 144–9 · W. Beckford, *Life at Fonthill, 1807–1822*, ed. B. Alexander (1957) · parish register, Weeford, Staffordshire
Archives RIBA, office papers, WY.1 · RIBA BAL, architectural sketches and papers · V&A, office papers, 8622.170 | BL, office papers, Egerton MS 3515 · BL, corresp., mainly with Matthew Cotes Wyatt, Egerton MS 3515 · Croome Estate Trust, Severn Stoke, Worcestershire, plans, vouchers, and papers relating to Croome Court and Lord Coventry's London house · NRA, priv. coll., papers relating to Longford Castle · Royal Arch., MS Joseph Farington's diary · Wilts. & Swindon RO, notebooks, accounts, and corresp. with earl of Pembroke relating to Wilton House
Likenesses G. Dance, pencil drawing, 1795, RA · J. Singleton, stipple, 1796 (after O. Humphrey, 1796), BM, NPG · J. C. F. Rossi, bronze bust, exh. RA 1797, NPG [*see illus.*] · C. Turner, mezzotint, pubd 1809 (after M. C. Wyatt), BM, NPG · W. Beechey, oils, RA · attrib. J. Opie, oils, RIBA · J. C. F. Rossi, plaster bust, RIBA · attrib. M. C. Wyatt, oils · charcoal drawing, NPG · Wedgwood medallion, Brooklyn Museum, New York
Wealth at death more or less bankrupt: Farington, *Diary*

Wyatt, Jeffry. *See* Wyatville, Sir Jeffry (1766–1840).

Wyatt, John (1700–1766), inventor of machinery, was born in April 1700 at Thickbroom, in the parish of Weeford, near Lichfield, Staffordshire, the eldest of the eight sons of John Wyatt and his wife, Jane, *née* Jackson. His family was connected with that of Sarah Ford, Dr Johnson's mother. He was educated at Lichfield School, and after working as a carpenter, in 1730 started his career as an inventor with a plan for a file-making machine.

Wyatt's career as an inventor was dogged by poverty, which led to his imprisonment for debt on at least one occasion. His lack of funds forced him to seek partners who could supply financial help to enable him to develop his inventions, but it was unfortunate that his ingenuity as an inventor was not matched by his skills as a businessman or as a judge of partners. Initially he sought assistance in the development of his file-making machine from Richard Heeley, a Birmingham gunmaker. When Heeley was unable to keep up payments in 1732, his place was taken by the Birmingham inventor Lewis Paul. Development of the machine was soon abandoned on account of the difficulties in perfecting it.

Wyatt renewed his partnership with Paul in order to devise a machine to spin cotton. The spur to this project was the invention in 1733 of the fly-shuttle, which had greatly increased the demand for yarn. In June 1738 Paul took out a patent embodying for the first time the all-important principle of spinning by rollers revolving at different velocities. The comparative importance of the two men in the development of this invention has been a subject of controversy. The earlier contention that Wyatt was the true inventor of the spinning machine has been examined and discounted in favour of Paul, 'who originated the idea of roller spinning' (Wadsworth and Mann). A company was formed to establish a cotton mill employing the Paul–Wyatt machinery in a warehouse at Upper Priory, Birmingham. Attached to two hanks of the cotton spun at this mill, preserved in the Birmingham Museum and Art Gallery, is an inscription written by Wyatt testifying that they were spun without hands about 1741, the motive power being 'two … Ases [*sic*] walking round an Axis' under the superintendence of Wyatt himself. Although Paul–Wyatt factories were established in Northampton (1742) and Leominster (1744?), the enterprise was not a success. Wyatt's involvement with the cotton-spinning venture saw him imprisoned for debt in the Fleet between June 1742 and October 1743. The Paul–Wyatt machinery proved a commercial failure despite incorporating many of the elements that were perfected in 1769 by Richard Arkwright. Following this failure Wyatt turned for work to Matthew Boulton.

Wyatt's greatest contribution as an inventor was in the field of weighing machines. In the early 1740s he probably constructed the first true 'compound lever platform scale'. His weigh-bridge was built at the Birmingham workhouse at Snow Hill in or shortly after 1741, and others were constructed at Liverpool, Chester, Hereford, Gloucester, and Lichfield. Because of his poverty, however, he was unable to patent his invention, and his design was widely copied, denying him the fame and wealth that it merited. Before the advent of electronic weighing, the compound lever platform scale invented by Wyatt was the basis for millions of machines around the world.

Wyatt's inventive talents were employed in a wide range of schemes. In 1736 he unsuccessfully proposed a plan for a single span wooden bridge in the competition for the erection of Westminster Bridge, and in 1757 he was engaged in the use of cylindrical bearings to reduce the friction on wheels.

Wyatt died in Birmingham on 29 November 1766, and was buried there in the churchyard of St Philip's. His funeral was attended by Matthew Boulton and John Baskerville. He was married twice, and with his second wife, Marabella, *née* Craven (*d.* 1774), had four daughters and two sons—Charles, Clarrise, Cordelia, Sophia, John, and Emily. Charles served as Boulton's apprentice and took out several patents between 1790 and 1817; John was the publisher of the *Repertory of Arts*, founded in 1818.

JOHN LEON BAKER

Sources *John Wyatt, master carpenter and inventor, AD 1700–1766* (1885) • A. P. Wadsworth and J. de Lacy Mann, *The cotton trade and industrial Lancashire, 1600–1780* (1931) • archive department, Birm. CL, Wyatt MSS • L. Sanders, *A short history of weighing* (1960) • H. W. Dickinson, 'The bicentenary of the platform weighing machine', *The Engineer* (29 Dec 1944), 504–6 • Birm. CL, Matthew Boulton MSS, MBP 375
Archives Birm. CA, corresp. and technical papers • U. Birm. L., special collections department, diary fragments, corresp., and family papers

Wyatt, John (*bap.* 1825, *d.* 1874), army surgeon, was baptized in the parish church of Aldingbourne, Sussex, on 28 October 1825, the eldest son of James Wyatt of Lidsey, near Chichester, yeoman, and his wife, Caroline. He was admitted as a member of the Royal College of Surgeons of England on 26 May 1848, becoming a fellow on 13 December 1866. He entered the Army Medical Service with the rank of assistant surgeon on 17 June 1851, was gazetted surgeon on 9 April 1857, and surgeon-major on 9 January 1863, being attached throughout his life to the 1st battalion of the Coldstream Guards. He was engaged in active service in the Crimean War, and was present at the battles of Alma, Balaklava, and Inkerman, and at the siege of Sevastopol. At the close of the war he received the Crimean medal with four clasps and the Turkish medal, and was made chevalier of the Légion d'honneur. In 1870 he was selected by the war department to act as medical commissioner at the headquarters of the French army during the Franco-Prussian war. He was present in Paris during the whole of the siege. At this time he provided important services to the sick and wounded, as he was attached to an ambulance and was a member of the Société de Secours aux Blessés. For these services he was made a companion of the Bath in 1873. He wrote a *History of the First Batallion Coldstream Guards During the Eastern Campaign (1854–56)* (1858). He died at Bournemouth on 2 April 1874, and was buried at Brompton cemetery.

D'A. POWER, *rev.* TIM O'NEILL

Sources *Proceedings of the Royal Medical and Chirurgical Society*, 7 (1871–5), 320 • *Medical Times and Gazette* (11 April 1874), 414 • *Medical Times and Gazette* (15 Aug 1874), 192 • *BMJ* (15 Aug 1874), 227 • *The Lancet* (15 Aug 1874), 248 • *The Times* (8 April 1874), 5 • parish reg. (baptism), 20 Oct 1825, Aldingbourne, Sussex
Wealth at death under £12,000: resworn probate, July 1875, *CGPLA Eng. & Wales* (1874)

Wyatt, Lewis William (*bap.* 1777, *d.* 1853), architect, was baptized on 25 August 1777 in Weeford, Staffordshire, the second of the four sons of Benjamin Wyatt (1745–1818), land surveyor and occasional architect, of Weeford, later agent to the Penrhyn estate, and his wife, Sarah, daughter of William Ford, brewer, of Burton upon Trent. From 1795 to 1800 he was apprenticed to his uncle Samuel *Wyatt, during which time (in 1797) he started exhibiting at the Royal Academy. In the beginnings of his career he was indebted in different ways to both Samuel and his other architect uncle, James *Wyatt. In 1800 he became assistant to the latter, who at the same time gave him a post in the office of works as labourer in trust at Carlton House and also employed him in connection with his work as surveyor of the ordnance; his first recorded works—minor country-house commissions in Staffordshire (1803–5)—were designed in James's office for execution by the Wyatt family building business; and in 1805 he submitted designs for Downing College, Cambridge, after those by James had been severely criticized by Thomas Hope, perhaps in an attempt to salvage the commission for the family. Then, after setting up in practice on his own *c.*1806, he was employed at Heaton Hall, Lancashire, where both James and Samuel had worked previously; and on Samuel's death in 1807 he completed two of his commissions, Tatton Park, Cheshire, and Hackwood Park, Hampshire, and in effect succeeded to his practice in the Cheshire area.

Wyatt's subsequent work was primarily as a country-house architect and 'improver', although he competed unsuccessfully for a number of major public commissions and in 1816 published *A Prospectus of a Design for Various Improvements in the Metropolis*, in which he made radical proposals for replanning the West End. In 1813, however, he succeeded James Wyatt as architect to the Middlesex Hospital, a post he held until 1829, and he also made some further progress in the office of works: in 1818 he was promoted to the clerkship of the works for the eastern division, before transferring in 1829 to Hampton Court, but he then lost his position in the reorganization of the office in 1832. In 1815 he visited Paris, in 1820 he made a six months' visit to Italy, and in 1825 he was in Paris again, having been sent to supervise repairs at the British embassy.

The predominant feature of Wyatt's architecture is a marked stylistic eclecticism. A number of works, including his finest, Willey Hall, Shropshire (1813–15), are in a monumental neo-classical manner developed from the late work of his uncles Samuel and James; at Cuerden Hall, Lancashire (1815), he experimented with a 'picturesque classicist' mode reminiscent in part of the work of Sir John Vanbrugh and in part of the contemporary 'primitivist' idiom; while at Cranage Hall, Cheshire (1828–9), he used the Tudor style and at Sherborne House, Gloucestershire (1829–34), produced a convincing copy of an Elizabethan design. Similarly skilful pastiches of interior decorative styles included work at Hackwood (1807–13) and Lyme Park, Cheshire (1814–17), in an English late seventeenth-century manner, and at Hawkstone Hall, Shropshire (1832–4), and elsewhere in the Louis XIV mode particularly associated with his cousins Benjamin Dean *Wyatt and Philip Wyatt.

The death of his father in 1818 left Wyatt quite a wealthy man, able to indulge a taste for connoisseurship and collecting works of art. He married late in life, and in 1833 his wife, Louisa Wyatt, a cousin, died in childbirth (the baby also died). About two years after this tragedy and after a series of professional reverses, notably the discovery of defective work at Sherborne House, which led to a costly negligence award against him, Wyatt gave up architectural practice. He then retired to a small property near Ryde on the Isle of Wight, where he spent his later years carrying out improvements to the grounds and where he died on 14 February 1853.　　　PETER LEACH, *rev.*

Sources Colvin, *Archs.* • J. M. Crook and M. H. Port, eds., *The history of the king's works*, 6 (1973) • J. M. Robinson, *The Wyatts: an architectural dynasty* (1979) • D. Linstrum, *Catalogue of the drawings collection of the Royal Institute of British Architects: The Wyatt family* (1974)
Archives Ches. & Chester ALSS, plans and corresp. relating to work at Eaton Hall, Cheshire • Lancs. RO, letters relating to Cuerden Hall | RIBA BAL, drawings collection

Wyatt, Matthew Cotes (1777–1862), painter and sculptor, was born in London and baptized on 29 May 1778 at St Marylebone parish church, the youngest son of the architect James *Wyatt (1746–1813) and his wife, Rachel, *née* Lunn (*d.* 1817). His brother was the architect Benjamin Dean *Wyatt. He was educated at Eton College and, after some indecision over his future, he decided to be a painter and enrolled in the Royal Academy Schools in London in 1800. Through the influence of his father, he received large commissions for decorative painting, the first of which was the ceiling of the Concert Room in Hanover Square, London, in 1803. In 1805 he began work restoring and extending Antonio Verrio's ceilings in the remodelled state rooms at Windsor Castle for George III. He became a favourite of the king and queen but aroused the jealousy of other painters who, in the words of Sir Francis Bourgeois, were incensed that James Wyatt had chosen his son, 'a young inexperienced artist … to the exclusion of artists of known ability' for this well-paid job (Farington, *Diary*, 12.4246, 4252). On 29 December 1801 he married Maria McClellan (*d.* 1852), widow of Edward McClellan, a sea captain. According to Farington she was 'the *natural daugtr.* of somebody, a very pretty woman with a fortune of 1 or £2000,—& has taken a dwelling near Windsor' (ibid., 6.2198). They had four sons: Matthew, James, George, and Henry.

From 1800 to 1814 Wyatt exhibited at the Royal Academy portraits and historical subjects in oils. Proposed for associate membership in 1812, he was not elected and never became a member of the academy. At about this time he taught himself modelling and carving, and he shrewdly switched from painting to sculpture, hoping to benefit from the proposals for grandiose memorials after the battle of Waterloo. His scheme for a vast *trophaeum* at Charing Cross came to nothing. Wyatt's earliest commission for sculpture was the Nelson monument in the Exchange Flags at Liverpool, completed in 1813. He was responsible only for the design of this statue, which was cast in bronze by Richard Westmacott the younger. After the death of Princess Charlotte in 1817, Wyatt was employed to execute the marble cenotaph to her memory in St George's Chapel, Windsor, for which £15,000 had been subscribed; this was completed in 1826 and was much admired. A theatrical *tour de force*, showing the princess ascending to heaven in the manner of a baroque saint, it made his reputation, and in 1820 Lord Liverpool, the prime minister, requested him to create a national monument to George III. Wyatt prepared an ambitious design representing the king standing in a quadriga (triumphal chariot), but lack of funds necessitated its abandonment. Eventually, in 1832, a committee of the subscribers commissioned him to execute a bronze equestrian statue of the king, complete with pigtail, which now stands in Pall Mall East, London, and is considered to be his best work.

Wyatt's talents were much admired by the duke of Rutland, who employed him extensively at Belvoir Castle in Leicestershire, where he designed and decorated the Elizabeth Saloon and carved the marble monument to the duchess in the mausoleum, as well as her full-length statue and bust; he also carved a marble table, complete with cloth, in the dining-room. Much of his work was controversial; none more so than the vast bronze equestrian statue of the duke of Wellington which was placed on Decimus Burton's arch at Hyde Park Corner, London, in 1846. It was greeted with universal derision and calls for its removal but remained there until 1883, when it was removed to Aldershot in Hampshire. Perhaps his most characteristic work was a portrait of Bashaw, Lord Dudley's Newfoundland dog, sculpted in coloured marbles and precious stones. It was shown at the Great Exhibition of 1851 and is now in the Victoria and Albert Museum, London. Thanks to royal patronage and that of other influential people, Wyatt enjoyed a reputation and practice to which his practical abilities hardly entitled him. He executed very little, if any, of his own sculpture, employing others to carve the marble or cast his work in bronze. His son James Wyatt (1808–1893) was specially trained and assisted his father at Belvoir and with the statues of George III and Wellington, as well as with the marble of the dog, Bashaw. His designs represented a dramatic and full-blooded union of neo-classicism and baroque revival. He was more a theatrical designer than a sculptor in the conventional sense.

Wyatt died at his home, Dudley Grove House, Harrow Road, London, on 3 January 1862 and was buried in Highgate cemetery, leaving an estate valued at *c.*£80,000. Matthew, his eldest son, later became the standard-bearer of the queen's corps of gentlemen-at-arms, and was knighted in 1848. James followed his father's profession and designed the pediment of the Commercial Bank of

Scotland in George Street, Edinburgh. The other two, George Wyatt (d. 1880) and Henry Wyatt (d. 1899), were both architects and builders and were involved in the development of the bishop of London's estate in Paddington.

F. M. O'DONOGHUE, rev. JOHN MARTIN ROBINSON

Sources J. M. Robinson, *The Wyatts: an architectural dynasty* (1979), 173–88 · R. Gunnis, *Dictionary of British sculptors, 1660–1851* (1953), 446–8 · Farington, *Diary*, 6.2198; 10.3698; 12.4246, 4252; 13.4546; 16.5496–7 · *The exhibition of the Royal Academy* [exhibition catalogues] · Redgrave, *Artists*, 2nd edn · M. C. Wyatt, *Prospectus of a model to Lord Nelson* (1808) · H. M. Cundall, 'A mysterious bronze group', *Burlington Magazine*, 20 (1912), 289–90 · J. Harris, 'Story of the marble dog', *Country Life*, 122 (1957), 1085 · I. Eller, *History of Belvoir Castle* (1841), 207 · *Art Journal*, 24 (1862), 86 · *GM*, 1st ser., 92/1 (1822), 208 · *GM*, 2nd ser., 6 (1836), 306 · *GM*, 3rd ser., 12 (1862), 281 · *IGI* · *CGPLA Eng. & Wales* (1862)

Archives BL, family corresp., Egerton MS 3515 · priv. coll. · RIBA BAL, corresp. and papers · RIBA BAL, sketches and papers · Royal Arch. · V&A NAL, corresp.

Wealth at death under £80,000: probate, 24 April 1862, *CGPLA Eng. & Wales*

Wyatt, Sir Matthew Digby (1820–1877), architect and writer on art, was born on 28 July 1820 at Rowde, near Devizes, Wiltshire, the youngest son of Matthew Wyatt (1773–1831), a barrister and police magistrate in London and Ireland, and his wife, Anne, daughter of Brigadier-General George Hillier of Devizes. Thomas Henry *Wyatt, architect, was his eldest brother. Their branch of the Wyatts was descended from William Wyatt, uncle of James Wyatt and agent to Lord Uxbridge at Beaudesert in Staffordshire. Matthew Digby Wyatt married, on 11 January 1853, Mary (d. 1894), second daughter of Iltyd Nicholl of Ham, Glamorgan. They had no children.

Wyatt was educated at Mr Bigg's school in Devizes and then became a pupil in the office of his brother Thomas Henry. At the age of sixteen he showed his literary ability by winning the essay prize medal of the Architectural Society, the forerunner of the Institute of British Architects. In 1837 he enrolled in the Royal Academy Schools, but decided to complete his education by travel abroad. The continental tour which he undertook in 1844–6 was the occasion for making over a thousand sketches and collecting notes for a book entitled *The Geometric Mosaics of the Middle Ages* (1848), the first of a series of books on the applied arts. A lecture on mosaics at the Royal Society of Arts brought him to the attention of an influential group interested in industrial design, including Henry Cole. In 1849 Wyatt was employed by the Society of Arts to accompany Cole to Paris and report upon the French exhibition of that year. He furnished a remarkably able report, with the result that in 1851 he was selected for the post of secretary to the executive committee of the Great Exhibition in London. He was the superintendent for the execution of Paxton's glass, iron, and wood exhibition building in Hyde Park and was also responsible for arranging the exhibits, while Owen Jones did the decoration. He received a special gold medal from the prince consort and a premium of £1000 for his services to the Great Exhibition. As a result of

Sir Matthew Digby Wyatt (1820–1877), by Fradelle & Marshall

their collaboration on the exhibition building Owen Jones and Wyatt became close friends.

A paper on the construction of the exhibition building read before the Institution of Civil Engineers was awarded the Telford medal. Wyatt further contributed to the literature of the exhibition by editing *The Industrial Arts of the Nineteenth Century* (1851), a work which illustrated in colourful chromolithographs a selection of the objects exhibited. When the exhibition buildings were transferred to become the Crystal Palace at Sydenham, Wyatt acted as superintendent of the fine arts department, and, together with Owen Jones, designed the courts of architecture with plaster casts demonstrating the arts of 'the great civilizations'. A postscript to the Crystal Palace was his appointment as collaborating architect again with Owen Jones, and Isambard Kingdom Brunel, to design the decorative ironwork at Paddington Station, London, in 1852. He also designed Temple Meads station in Bristol. The year 1855 was an important one for Wyatt. He was appointed surveyor to the East India Company, following his successful design for the company's stand at the Paris Exhibition of that year. He also acted as one of the jurors, and for his services to the French government was created a chevalier of the Légion d'honneur. He designed several buildings for the company within Britain and India, including the chapel and barracks at Warley, Essex.

When, following the mutiny, the company was abolished and the Council of India was set up in its place, Wyatt became architect to the council and designed the new India Office building in Whitehall next to the Foreign Office, in collaboration with Sir George Gilbert Scott. The India Office courtyard, a *tour de force* of Italian Renaissance architecture and Minton's majolica, is his masterpiece.

From 1855 until 1859 Wyatt was honorary secretary of the Royal Institute of British Architects, and in 1866 received the gold medal of that body. On the foundation of the Slade professorship of fine arts at Cambridge in 1869 he was the first occupant of the chair, and received the honorary degree of MA. In the same year he received a knighthood. His lectures throw much light on his architectural and artistic principles. Wyatt's knowledge and use of architectural styles were catholic and comprehensive, but his best buildings were in an Italianate classical manner. His advocacy in the Slade lectures of joining the 'objective practice of Pugin and the Medievalists to the excellent subjective system transmitted to us from the Classical Ages' (Slade lecture, Cambridge, 1869) foreshadowed the free classical architecture of the later nineteenth century. To contemporaries his writings, organizational and committee work, and his crusade to improve design, seemed as important as his architecture. But his classical buildings are among the best of the mid-nineteenth century.

Wyatt's domestic works (now largely demolished) included: Alford House, in Kensington Gore, London (1871); Possingworth, Sussex (1866–8); Newells, near Horsham, Sussex (1869); The Mount, Norwood, Surrey (1862); The Ham, Glamorgan (1859–63); and the restorations of Compton Wynyates, Warwickshire (1867), and of Isfield Place, Sussex (1877). He designed the Crimean memorial arch at Chatham (1861), the Indian government stores at Lambeth (1861–4; dem.), Addenbrooke's Hospital, Cambridge (1863), and the Rothschild mausoleum at West Ham cemetery (1866). North Marston church, Buckinghamshire, was restored (1853) by Wyatt for Queen Victoria in memory of the eccentric J. C. Neild, and he was associated with his brother Thomas Henry in the design of the military chapel at Woolwich (1862–3) and the Adelphi Theatre (1848). Unexecuted competition designs include the Albert memorial, the National Gallery, the Shakespeare memorial at Stratford upon Avon, and the corn exchange in Bedford. His writings, which were numerous, include: *Metal Work and its Artistic Design* (1852); *The Art of Illuminating* (1860); *On the Foreign Artists Employed in England During the Sixteenth Century* (1868); and a paper entitled *The History of the Manufacture of Clocks* (1870). He himself designed a clock with 'M Digby Wyatt' on its dial in place of numerals, a sign of the wit and humour which also sparkle in his correspondence with friends such as Edward Lear and in his caricature sketches.

Wyatt died on 21 May 1877 at Dimlands Castle (a house which belonged to his wife's family), near Cowbridge, Glamorgan, and to which he had retired in the hope of recovering his health from the deleterious effects of excessive work. He was buried at Usk churchyard, where his tomb of pink granite was designed by Thomas Henry Wyatt. He died the most distinguished member of his family, laden with honours from home and abroad.

PAUL WATERHOUSE, *rev.* JOHN MARTIN ROBINSON

Sources *The Builder*, 35 (1877), 541, 545–7, 550 · N. Pevsner, *Matthew Digby Wyatt, the first Cambridge Slade professor of fine art: an inaugural lecture* (1950) · J. M. Robinson, *The Wyatts: an architectural dynasty* (1979), 205–18 · *The Times* (23 May 1877) · *The Times* (24 May 1877) · *PICE*, 49 (1876–7), 277–81 · *The Architect*, 17 (1877), 331, 339 · *Men of the time* (1862) · *CGPLA Eng. & Wales* (1877) · will, Mary, Lady Wyatt, 1894

Archives BL OIOC, designs for bridges · RIBA BAL, architectural sketches and papers | Canadian Centre for Architecture, Montreal, drawings made in Italy · priv. coll., corresp., caricatures, letters from Edward Lear · priv. coll., 'My memoir for Mr C. Knight's Cyclopedia', MS, 1857 · RIBA, nomination papers · RIBA BAL, biography file, photographs, MSS · V&A, drawings for Crystal Palace, Box 85

Likenesses G. B. Black, lithograph, 1863, repro. in *Dir. Brit. archs.*, 1027 · Fradelle & Marshall, photograph, priv. coll. [*see illus.*] · A. Ossani, oils, RIBA · photograph, RIBA · print (after photograph), BM; repro. in *ILN* (2 June 1977) · woodcuts, NPG

Wealth at death under £16,000: probate, 15 Aug 1877, *CGPLA Eng. & Wales*

Wyatt, Sir Myles Dermot Norris (1903–1968), air transport entrepreneur, was born on 2 July 1903, at West House, Hartford, near Northwich, Cheshire, the younger son of Arthur Norris Wyatt, master brewer, and his wife, May, *née* Reynolds.

Wyatt was educated at Radley College and New College, Oxford. In 1926 he joined the Port of Calcutta commissioners, working for the next eight years as assistant and deputy secretary. In 1934 he returned to Britain, and became general manager for Airwork Ltd. This company had been formed in 1928 by Nigel Norman and Alan Muntz to develop the airfield at Heston, in west London, as a centre for private flying. However, the number of private owners using the site grew only slowly, and Airwork diversified into aviation support services as well as opening a flying school. By the outbreak of the Second World War in 1939, Wyatt was a director of the firm.

During the war Airwork concentrated on training pilots for the Royal Air Force, and repairing combat aircraft. In 1945 Wyatt was the key figure in the company's management, and with the sale of Heston airport to the government, he and Muntz established Airwork as an independent airline. Initially this meant supplying charter services, since the Labour government had reserved scheduled flying to the new air corporations created by the 1946 Civil Aviation Act. In the following years, however, Airwork extended its range of operations, providing air trooping capacity for the government, flying colonial coach services to Commonwealth countries in Africa, and establishing a share of the new 'inclusive tour' market.

In the course of its expansion Airwork acquired other smaller airlines, including Morton Air and Freddie Laker's Air Charter Ltd in 1958. It also received substantial investment from shipping interests like Furness Withy and the Blue Star Line. In 1960, encouraged by new legislation which relaxed the air corporations' monopoly of scheduled services, Wyatt's company merged with another shipping-backed independent airline, Hunting Clan Air Transport Ltd, to form British United Airways (BUA). In 1961 BUA became a wholly owned subsidiary of Air Holdings Ltd, with Wyatt as executive chairman, and Freddie Laker as his managing director. Laker later left BUA to follow his own career as an entrepreneur.

With further acquisitions, including Silver City Airways, which had pioneered car-ferry services between England and the continent, BUA became Britain's largest independent airline. In 1966 it took over scheduled services to Brazil, Argentina, and Chile from the state-owned British Overseas Airways Corporation (BOAC), flying the new Vickers VC10 jet aircraft on the route. By the end of the decade BUA's network of services from Gatwick airport covered east and west Africa, the Canary Islands, and western Europe, as well as South America. Wyatt himself, who had been created CBE in 1954, was knighted in 1963.

Mindful of BUA's profitability, and of the large capital expenditure needed to fund the airline's investment in new aircraft, Wyatt entered into secret negotiations in 1966 to sell the company to BOAC. The proposal was vetoed by the government pending the report of the Edwards committee inquiry into British air transport. When this was released in 1969 it recommended the creation of a 'second force' in competition with the air corporations, and BUA was eventually merged with Caledonian Airways to form British Caledonian Airways.

Besides being chairman of the Air Holdings Group, Wyatt was a director of several other companies, and a long-time officer of the British Independent Air Transport Association until BUA left the organization in 1964. He was outspoken in defending the interests of Britain's independent airlines, arguing that the government should allow them a greater share of the market for scheduled passenger traffic. He was also a keen yachtsman, becoming admiral of the Royal Ocean Yacht Club, and the owner of several famous cruising yachts.

Myles Wyatt married Dorothy O'Malley in 1929, with whom he had a son and a daughter. Sir Myles died at his home, Alresford Hall, Alresford, near Colchester, on 15 April 1968.   PETER J. LYTH

Sources *The Times* (16 April 1968) · *The Times* (27 April 1968) · *IATA Bulletin* (1956–66) · M. D. N. Wyatt, 'British independent aviation: past and future', *Institute of Transport Journal*, 30 (1963), 107–15 · 'Aircraft finance: the wrong criteria?', *The Economist* (16 Feb 1963), 630, 632 · 'Air holdings', *The Aeroplane* (21 Jan 1965) [suppl.], 4–15 · R. Higham and D. J. Jeremy, 'Wyatt, Sir Myles Dermot Norris', *DBB* · b. cert. · d. cert.

Wealth at death £176,275: probate, 28 May 1968, *CGPLA Eng. & Wales*

Wyatt, Richard James (1795–1850), sculptor, was born in Oxford Street, London, on 3 May 1795, the fourth son of Edward Wyatt (1757–1833) of Oxford Street, a successful carver and gilder, and his wife, Anne Maddox. His distant cousin was the sculptor Matthew Cotes Wyatt (1777–1862). He served his apprenticeship with John Charles Felix Rossi and studied at the Royal Academy Schools where he won a silver medal in 1815. In 1818 he exhibited at the Royal Academy a *Judgment of Paris* (untraced) and in 1819 a

monument to Lady Anne Hudson; other early memorial works by him are in Esher church, Surrey, and St John's Wood Chapel, London. When Antonio Canova visited England, Wyatt was brought to his notice by Sir Thomas Lawrence and received an invitation to work with him in Rome.

Wyatt left England early in 1821 and, after studying for a few months in Paris under François-Joseph Bosio, proceeded to Rome and entered Canova's studio, where John Gibson was a fellow pupil. On Canova's death in 1822 Gibson and Wyatt transferred to the studio of the Danish sculptor Bertel Thorvaldsen. Wyatt settled permanently in Rome, in the via della Fontanella Barberini, and practised his profession there with great enthusiasm and success, and from 1831 until his death in 1850 was a frequent exhibitor at the Royal Academy in London. His first important commission was from the duke of Devonshire in 1822 for a marble version (1824) of his plaster model *Musidora* for Chatsworth, Derbyshire. Between 1830 and 1840 his art came to maturity. Among his best works are *Ino and the Infant Bacchus*, for Sir Robert Peel (marble, 1829); *Nymph Going to the Bath*, for the duke of Leuchtenburg (marble, 1831; untraced); and *Penelope with the Bow of Ulysses* (marble, c.1841–2), *Nymph of Diana Returning from the Chase*, and *Glycera* (marble, 1848), all in the Royal Collection. *Penelope* was a commission given to Wyatt by Prince Albert in 1841, at the time of Wyatt's only return visit to England. His entire life was otherwise passed in Rome, where he died, unmarried, at his home in the via dei Incurabile on 29 May 1850; he was buried in the protestant cemetery in Rome. As well as ideal statues, he also carved portrait busts, and memorial tablets which show the influence of Thorvaldsen—the best is that to Ellen Legh at Winwick, Lancashire.

Some of Wyatt's works were shown at the Great Exhibition of 1851 and were awarded silver medals for sculpture. Wyatt was a highly accomplished artist, particularly excelling in his female figures, which in purity of form and beauty of line rivalled his master Canova. His work is noted for the soft delicate finish of the marble, a technique he probably learned from Bosio in Paris. He was a sculptor of great sensitivity. His neo-classical taste, though softened by an interest in poetic and naturalistic subjects, never degenerated into sentimental naturalism.

F. M. O'DONOGHUE, rev. JOHN MARTIN ROBINSON

Sources J. M. Robinson, *The Wyatts: an architectural dynasty* (1979), 160–73 · R. Gunnis, *Dictionary of British sculptors, 1660–1851* (1953), 448 · *Art Journal*, 12 (1850), 249 · *Art Journal*, 16 (1854), 352 · *Art Journal*, 24 (1862), 23 · *GM*, 2nd ser., 22 (1844), 71 · *GM*, 2nd ser., 34 (1850), 99 · R. Martin, 'R. J. Wyatt', MA diss., U. Leeds, 1935 · Redgrave, *Artists* · Graves, *RA exhibitors* · *Art Union*, 8 (1846), 298, 304 · *ILN* (17 Aug 1850) · J. M. Robinson, 'Wyatt family', *The dictionary of art*, ed. J. Turner (1996)

Archives Biblioteca Civica, Bassano del Grappa, Canova MS 1772

Likenesses J. Partridge, pencil drawing, 1825, NPG · J. Gibson, marble medallion on tomb, c.1850, protestant cemetery, Rome · attrib. S. Pearce, oils, priv. coll. · engraving (after drawing by S. Pearce), NPG, BM; repro. in *Art Journal* (1850) · wood-engraving (after J. Partridge), NPG; repro. in *ILN* (1850)

Wealth at death work executed in lifetime computed at £20,000

Wyatt, Robert Elliott Storey (1901–1995), cricketer, was born at Milford Heath House, Witley, Surrey, on 2 May 1901, the son of John Holland Wyatt, a schoolmaster, and his wife, Edyth Elliott. He was a scion of the architectural Wyatt dynasty and a cousin of Woodrow Wyatt. He learned his cricket at his preparatory school, Milbourn Lodge, Esher, and from his father, an enthusiastic all-round sportsman. When the family moved to the midlands he went to King Henry VIII School, Coventry, and played for the Coventry and north Warwickshire club. After leaving school in 1918 he obtained a position as an engineering trainee in the repair shops of the Rover Motor Company, but in 1923 was invited to play for the Warwickshire first eleven, which marked the beginning of his county career.

As no more than a useful county cricketer, a steady, unexciting batsman and change bowler, Wyatt came well out of an exhausting MCC tour of India led by A. E. R. Gilligan in 1926–7. This proved the start of a decade wherein he toured twice each to South Africa, Australia, and the West Indies, and represented England in forty tests, in sixteen of them as captain. The first of his tours to South Africa, in 1927–8, gave an experience of matting pitches which he repeated three years later. On these tours the young man of 'rather retiring' disposition, according to *Wisden* in its article marking his selection as one of the five cricketers of the year, formed a close and lasting friendship with the more extrovert Ian Peebles.

Chosen in the fourth test against South Africa at Old Trafford in 1929, Wyatt and Frank Woolley made 245 together for the third wicket in 165 minutes. In his first home test his 113 was the first hundred by an amateur since the war. Not an aggressive batsman by nature, Wyatt could respond in kind to a free display at the other end.

It was, however, for his more sedate qualities that the England selectors astonished the cricket world by preferring Wyatt to A. P. F. Chapman as England captain for the last test against Australia at the Oval in 1930. Chapman had won back the 'Ashes' four years before on this ground, and had since retained them (4–1) in Australia. The series was level at 1–1. The change aroused deep feelings, the crowd responding to unbridled tabloid criticism of the selectors by applauding, and even cheering, the new captain all the way to the wicket when, after winning the toss, he came in to bat. Wyatt, in his autobiography (*Three Straight Sticks*, 72), quotes Sir Pelham Warner as saying he never heard its like. Wyatt played a sterling innings of 64, but Australia's answer to England's 405 was their third mammoth score of the summer, inspired as at Lord's and Headingley by Bradman. Wyatt handled his side efficiently but four missed chances by Duckworth, the wicket-keeper, were fatal and rain in the end helped Australia to an innings victory.

Wyatt went to Australia as vice-captain to D. R. Jardine in 1932–3 and played his part in holding the team together on that catastrophic tour, despite his reservations about the bodyline tactics adopted. He batted consistently in the five tests, averaging 42 with a top score of 78. He resumed the England captaincy when, after intense diplomatic activity, Australia visited England in 1934.

Wyatt was too often denied the luck which Napoleon demanded of a leader. In a test trial in May he sustained a badly broken thumb which prevented his playing in the first test and hampered him seriously—protected by an aluminium shield—in the remaining four. Again he surrendered the Ashes to Australia, but at least he led England to the only victory won against them at Lord's in the twentieth century, the match which was decided by Verity's day of triumph after rain.

Leading England the following winter (1934–5) in the West Indies, Wyatt won a lottery of a low-scoring match at Bridgetown on a rain-ruined pitch after declaring at 81 for 7, 21 behind the West Indies' first innings. Going in first against the fast attack in this series in the absence of accredited openers, Wyatt in the last test at Kingston suffered a compound fracture of the jaw, which was broken in four places. It was said that the noise of the impact of the ball was like a rifle shot.

Nothing became Wyatt's cricket life better than his reaction to this crowning misfortune. On recovering consciousness he is recorded as having called for paper and pencil to revise the batting order, and also to assure Martindale, the bowler, that he attached no blame to him. It had been a very fast one, which had got up almost from a good length. On the return voyage his diet was restricted to Ovaltine and other fluids, and his dental surgeon spoke of a bone graft and a long absence from the cricket field. Wyatt determined to disregard this prognosis, and six weeks after his accident led MCC in the first match of the season at Lord's against Surrey. Putting himself in first against Gover, the fast bowler, he saw the first ball whistle past his head, settled down, and made a hundred, batting, *Wisden* recorded, 'uncommonly well'.

Wyatt had no rivals as England's captain in the home series against South Africa. He emphasized his complete recovery by making 149 in the first test, his highest score for England. South Africa followed on, but were saved from probable defeat by the loss of the third day's play owing to rain. The series was decided by the second test at Lord's, which brought South Africa their first ever victory in England: 1935 was the year when the Lord's square was ruined by a plague of leather jackets which attacked the grass roots, so that the turf powdered. The captain made top score of 53 in England's first innings, which left England with a deficit of 30, whereupon Bruce Mitchell took out his bat for a memorable 164 not out, and a declaration left England a hopeless task on a broken pitch. The margin was 157 runs and Xenophon Balaskas, with 9 wickets in the match, had a field day. Though South Africa well deserved their success, Wyatt could justifiably say that the toss probably decided the outcome. England had the better of each of the remaining tests but on good pitches Wyatt could not force a result in three days.

There was one tour to come, this time a happy visit to Australia (1936–7) under the captaincy of Gubby Allen. The plan was for Wyatt to open the innings, and in the first match he did so and made a hundred. Thereupon misfortune struck yet again in the shape of a broken arm sustained in an up-country match on a poor pitch. He was out of action for ten weeks, available to play only in the last two tests, batting well enough in a losing cause to emphasize how much he had been missed. On this note ended his test career: in his forty tests he made 1839 runs, averaging 31, and took 18 wickets at 35 apiece.

Wyatt had led Warwickshire competently if unexcitingly since 1930, and in 1937 had his best season: 2625 runs, nine hundreds, average 53. However, disagreements with the committee and particularly with the secretary of the past forty years, R. V. Ryder, led to their supplanting him 'unanimously' in favour of the rugby union captain of England, Peter Cranmer. From the dour to the debonair, the technical to the unashamedly amateur approach: both the demotion and the manner of it hurt Wyatt greatly. Nevertheless he continued in 1938 and 1939 to play for Warwickshire, whose results were neither better nor worse than before. Leslie Duckworth, whose *The Story of Warwickshire Cricket* is the standard work, considered that 'few captains have given as much serious thought to the game and its tactics as he did' (Duckworth, 187). While giving full marks for effort, Duckworth thought that by 1938 a change of captain was justified.

Elsewhere Duckworth tabulated the injuries of this brave but brittle-boned fellow:

> In later years almost every mishap that could befall a batsman happened to Wyatt. He fractured a jaw, two toes, two ribs, had a broken bone in his foot, a broken thumb, three fractured fingers and a broken bone in his wrist. Hammond once called him 'the most fractured man in big cricket', but none of his injuries discouraged him from playing. It was not without good reason that he was also called 'one of the greatest fighting cricketers of all time'. (Duckworth, 195)

Wyatt served in the Second World War with the Royal Air Force, and it was as a pilot officer on duty that he met his wife, Mollie Wilkes (1915–1996), secretary to the manager of a Birmingham insurance company and daughter of Bernard Charles Wilkes, who ran a building business. They were married on 10 November 1942 and had one son. She identified herself wholeheartedly with the remainder of her husband's life in the cricket world; Bob, as he became, was the outwardly solemn patriarch, she the amusingly, jokingly flirtatious, inseparable spouse. The more relaxed atmosphere of Worcestershire, to whom he transferred on residential qualification, combined with his marriage to make his last six cricketing summers happy and fruitful ones. Mollie brought a ready smile to the face of the bulldog. In his last three years there the county, under his captaincy, enjoyed the most successful seasons to date, finishing third, sixth, and fourth. There was a sparkling, if rarely seen, side to his batting—as for instance in 1934, when his 104 not out in 2 hours 20 minutes enabled him to lead the Gentlemen to their first victory over the Players at Lord's since 1914—and his eve-of-retirement gesture was subsequently a source of wry amusement to him. Batting against Somerset at Taunton when five runs were needed to win off the last ball, he drove it high into the pavilion

for six: 'Not bad for a fifty-year-old!' His tally of 39,405 runs (average 40) has been exceeded by only eighteen cricketers. As an accurate change bowler, who could swing the ball dangerously on his day, he took 901 wickets (average 32). He scored 1000 runs in seventeen seasons at home and one abroad. There was never a more committed cricketer, a more dedicated trier. He combined playing and test selection in 1950 and 1951 and continued to serve as a selector until 1954. He helped choose the sides which regained the Ashes in 1953 and retained them in 1954–5.

The Wyatts retired to Cornwall in the 1960s, Bob indulging a love of sailing, Mollie's love of animals making their home on The Lizard a focus for abandoned dogs. He had a major stroke in 1991, followed by several lesser ones. Their last summers were nevertheless lightened by their friendship with J. Paul Getty, in whose box at Lord's they became co-hosts with him and his wife, Victoria, at all the big matches. When in 1993 the queen came to Lord's, Bob, confined now to a wheelchair, was as a life vice-president summoned to the committee room with Mollie in attendance. No other woman had ever been admitted to the sanctum. Bob's final and very rare honour was to be admitted as a freeman of I Zingari cricket club.

Wyatt died at Treliske, Cornwall, on 20 April 1995. Stricken by cancer, his wife survived him by little more than a year: the attendance was similarly large for their respective services of thanksgiving at St John's Wood church, London.   E. W. SWANTON

Sources R. E. S. Wyatt, *Three straight sticks* (1951) • R. E. S. Wyatt, *The ins and outs of cricket* (1936) • L. Duckworth, *The story of Warwickshire cricket* (1974) • *Wisden* (1930) • E. W. Swanton, ed., *Barclays world of cricket: the game from A–Z*, rev. edn (1986) • *The Times* (22 April 1995) • *The Independent* (22 April 1995) • *Daily Telegraph* (29 July 1996) [obituary of Mollie Wyatt] • b. cert. • m. cert. • *CGPLA Eng. & Wales* (1996)
Archives FILM BFI NFTVA, news footage
Likenesses H. J. Whitlock, photograph, repro. in Wyatt, *Three straight sticks*, frontispiece
Wealth at death £265,959: probate, 1996, *CGPLA Eng. & Wales*

Wyatt, Samuel (1737–1807), architect and engineer, was born on 8 September 1737 at Blackbrook Farm, Weeford, Staffordshire, the third of the seven sons and two daughters of Benjamin Wyatt (d. 1772), farmer and timber merchant of Weeford, who also practised as a builder and architect, and his wife, Mary Wright. Samuel began in his father's business as a carpenter, thus earning the nickname the Chip. In 1760 he was employed, first as carpenter and then as clerk of works, at the building of Kedleston Hall, Derbyshire, under Robert Adam, an experience which constituted his architectural education. In 1768 he returned to Weeford; he was first employed as an architect in 1769, on an addition to Blithfield Hall, Staffordshire. He began a close association with his younger brother James *Wyatt (1746–1813) after the latter's return from an Italian grand tour, notably at the Pantheon in Oxford Street, London (1769–71), where the domed interior put into practice on a larger scale constructional lessons learned in the saloon at Kedleston. After the death of their father in 1772, the family firm passed to their eldest brother, William; in 1774 Samuel and James each set up independent practices as architects in London.

Samuel Wyatt's career included business as a building contractor and timber merchant as well as architecture, in which he was predominantly concerned with medium-sized country houses: Doddington Hall, Cheshire (1777–98), Hooton Hall, Cheshire (1778–88; dem.), Herstmonceux Place, Sussex (1777), and Belmont Park, Kent (1787–92). He was also extensively employed in designing and building London houses, and made a speciality of the design of model farm buildings, including nearly fifty at Holkham for Thomas William Coke of Norfolk, first earl of Leicester. Other ambitious farm buildings by Wyatt can be found at Sandon, Staffordshire, Thorndon, Essex, and Somerley, Hampshire. During the 1780s he was manager and principal promoter, as well as builder and architect, of the Albion flour mill at Blackfriars. This was the most advanced industrial building of its time, designed to be steam-powered (with engines supplied by Samuel's partners in the enterprise, Matthew Boulton and James Watt). It was one of the first such buildings to incorporate a brick raft foundation, here intended to spread the downward load on the soft Thames bank. The street frontage incorporated Wyatt's own house. The mill burnt down in 1791. Wyatt was appointed surveyor of Trinity House, and clerk of works at Chelsea Hospital in 1792, and surveyor of Ramsgate harbour in 1794. In 1793 he was appointed surveyor to the Royal Mint, but was dismissed in 1794 for inattention to duty.

Wyatt's architectural work was predominantly in a chaste neo-classical manner, with the use of domed segmental projections; in his interiors he made play with geometrical plans, displaying a liking for oval and octagonal spaces which derived originally from Adam. In some of his later work, such as Trinity House at Tower Hill, London (1793–6), his finest urban building, and Hackwood Park, Hampshire (1805–7), he developed a simpler and more monumental style. He saw himself as an engineer architect, and designed a number of lighthouses, three of them—Longships, Cornwall (1792), St Agnes, Isles of Scilly (1806), and Flamborough Head, Yorkshire—as part of his lighthouse duties, one at Dungeness, Kent (1792), for a private client, Thomas Coke of Norfolk, and one (dem.) for Ramsgate harbour, where he was responsible for a series of buildings on the quayside. He experimented with cast iron, and made extensive use of Coade stone and also of slate—from the Penrhyn quarries managed by his brother Benjamin (d. 1818)—for cladding and other purposes. He invented a 'sympathetic hinge' by which both leaves of a double door opened simultaneously, and in 1787 devised a prefabricated 'movable hospital' for use in the colonies. In 1799 he was consulted about a tunnel under the Thames, and in 1800 he submitted a proposal for a cast-iron replacement for London Bridge.

An unsympathetic contemporary, Humphry Repton, described Wyatt as 'slow, plodding, heavy in carriage, dull in conceiving the ideas of others and tedious in explaining his own' (H. Repton, 'Autobiography', BL, MS 62112, fol. 198), a portrait which was something of a libel on this progressively minded architect. Wyatt became a member of the Society for the Promotion of Arts, Manufactures and Commerce, and of the Society of Civil Engineers. He was a close friend of many of the pioneer midlands industrialists, notably Matthew Boulton, whose house at Soho, Birmingham, was designed by James and Samuel Wyatt. In spite of the Albion mill disaster, he achieved his proclaimed ambition of making a fortune, largely out of his building business. In 1765 he married Ann Sherwin, daughter of the land agent at Kedleston Hall. They had no children, but on the death of his brother William in 1780 he adopted William's four-year-old daughter. Wyatt died suddenly of an 'apoplexy' at the surveyor's house, Chelsea Hospital, on 8 February 1807 and was buried in the hospital cemetery.

G. H. L. LE MAY, rev. JOHN MARTIN ROBINSON

Sources J. M. Robinson, 'Samuel Wyatt', DPhil diss., U. Oxf., 1973 · J. M. Robinson, *The Wyatts* (1979) · Colvin, *Archs.* · *The Farington diary*, ed. J. Greig, 1 (1922) · A. W. Skempton, 'Early members of the Smeatonian Society of Civil Engineers', *Transactions* [Newcomen Society], 44 (1971–2), 2, 35 · J. M. Robinson, 'A great architectural family', *Country Life* (13–20 Dec 1973), 2006–7, 2098–2101 · parish register, Weeford, Sept 1737 [birth] · parish register, Kedleston, 1765 [marriage]

Archives BL, ledger, accounts and papers relating to Dropmore and Cleveland Row, Add. MSS 69171–69173 · Cornwall RO, papers relating to building house in Cleveland Row, St James's

Likenesses L. F. Abbott, oils, 1772, Baker Furniture Museum, Holland, Michigan · G. Dupont, group portrait, oils, 1793, Trinity House, London

Wyatt, Sir Thomas (c.1503–1542), poet and ambassador, probably born at Allington Castle, Kent, was the eldest son of Sir Henry Wyatt and Anne, daughter of John Skinner of Reigate.

Sir Henry Wyatt Wyatt's father, **Sir Henry Wyatt** (c.1460–1536), politician and courtier, was a younger son of Richard Wyatt, of Yorkshire, and Margaret, the daughter and heir of William Bailif, of Reigate. His skill as a soldier and reliability as a financier made him one of the longest-serving courtiers of Henry VII and Henry VIII. His support for Henry Tudor began before 1483, and he probably participated in Buckingham's unsuccessful revolt against Richard III in that year. Family legend has it that he was imprisoned and interrogated by Richard III himself, and that during his imprisonment he was fed on pigeons brought to him by a cat. After the victory of Henry VII at Bosworth he received a number of grants and favours. In 1485 he became keeper of Norwich Castle and gaol, and before September 1486 he was made clerk of the king's jewels. He succeeded to the increasingly influential position of master of the king's jewels in June 1488, combining the office with that of clerk of the king's mint. By 1494 he was keeper of the change, assayer of the money and coinage, and comptroller of the mint.

From these grants and offices came sufficient wealth to purchase in 1492 Allington Castle in Kent. Sir Henry retained his Yorkshire links, however, and in March 1487 he became joint bailiff and constable of Conisborough Castle in Yorkshire. In June of that year he fought against the pretender Lambert Simnel in the battle of Stoke-on-Trent. He became governor of the city and castle of Carlisle in 1494, and at some point was captured and held to

Sir Thomas Wyatt (*c*.1503–1542), by Hans Holbein the younger, *c*.1535

ransom by the Scots, for which he was reimbursed by a grant on 22 August 1515. This 'two yeres and more prisonment in Scotland, in Irons and Stoks' (Muir, 40), referred to by Sir Thomas Wyatt in a letter to his son, may have occurred between 1494 and 1496. By June 1496, however, Sir Henry wrote to the king from Carlisle to discuss preparations for putting down the rebellion of Perkin Warbeck, and in June 1497 he was present at the battle of Blackheath. About 1502 he married Anne Skinner. Thomas Scott's anecdotes of the family (BL, Wyatt papers, 29) present her as a powerful overseer of the household, who caught the abbot of Boxley in a compromising position with one of her maids, and stocked him. They had two sons, Thomas and Henry (who is assumed to have died in infancy), and a daughter, Margaret, who married Sir Henry Lee. Her portrait by Holbein survives in the Metropolitan Museum of New York.

Sir Henry became a privy councillor in 1504, and was granted arms in 1507–8. He was an executor of Henry VII's will, and remained in high office in the reign of Henry VIII. Having been granted livery by virtue of his office as master of the king's jewel house at the funeral of Henry VII in May 1509, he was made knight of the Bath at the coronation of Henry VIII, and was appointed to the new privy council. He was commissioner of the peace for Middlesex and Surrey from 1509 to 1515. He established close ties with his Kentish neighbours the Boleyns of Hever Castle (Sir Henry became captain of Norwich Castle jointly with

Thomas Boleyn in 1511), and with Thomas Cromwell, who became one of his executors. His military activity also ensured his continuing favour: with a retinue of 102 he accompanied the king to Calais in 1513, and was made knight-banneret after the battle of the Spurs in August 1513. In 1519 he again attended Henry VIII to Calais. In 1520 it fell to him to transport gold and silver plate sufficient for the banquet at the Field of Cloth of Gold. He attended Henry at Canterbury during his reception of Charles V in May 1522, and was by that date sheriff of Kent.

By the later 1520s Sir Henry began to ease out of public life. He stood down as master of the jewels in 1524, and founded a chantry at Milton in Kent in that year; by 1528 he resigned as treasurer of the king's chamber and was succeeded by Sir Brian Tuke. By 1533 his retirement was complete, and his health was failing. In that year his son Thomas deputized for him as ewerer at the coronation of Anne Boleyn. From his retirement in Allington he learned of his son's imprisonment in May 1536, and wrote to thank both Cromwell and the king for his release. He died on 10 November of that year. His will provides for his burial at Milton 'nere unto dame Anee my wyfe' (PRO, PROB 11/26, fols. 49v–50r) and for the continuance of his chantry there. A portrait by Holbein survives in the Louvre, and another, showing the cat supposed to have fed him during his imprisonment, is in the possession of the earl of Romney.

Sir Thomas Wyatt: early years and marriage Sir Henry's elder son, Sir Thomas Wyatt (sometimes called the elder to distinguish him from his son), was the foremost poet of the court of Henry VIII. He is frequently represented as belonging to a new breed of young, plain-speaking, and exuberant courtiers who populated the court of the new king, and who contrasted with the bureaucrats and money men who flourished under Henry VII. Although his reputation for evangelical religious views and for loose sexual mores distinguishes him from Sir Henry, he retained and built on his father's family and regional loyalties. His fate was closely associated with those of the Boleyns and of Thomas Cromwell, and his career as an ambassador reflected the growing international ambition of his king rather than marking a temperamental difference from his father.

Thomas was born about 1503 and served as a sewer-extraordinary at the christening of Princess Mary in 1516, along with his friend and Kentish neighbour Thomas Poynings. Family legend has it that as a child he saved his father from an attack by a lion which he had raised, a tale which allegedly reached the ears of Henry VIII ('He can tame lions', he is reported to have said; Bruce, 237). Wyatt attended St John's College, Cambridge, the chief centre of humanistic learning. He did not take a degree (confusion with John Wyatt has led many authorities to suppose he did), but the foundations of his later admiration of Seneca, Epictetus, and Horace were probably laid during his time at Cambridge.

By about 1520 Wyatt had married Elizabeth (*d*. 1560), daughter of Thomas Brooke, eighth Baron Cobham, thereby consolidating his father's position among the

Kentish gentry. Thomas *Wyatt the younger was born in or before 1521. The marriage was unhappy, and, if the Spanish ambassador (writing on 27 March 1541) is to be believed, the pair were estranged by the second half of the 1520s. By 1537 Elizabeth's brother George, ninth Baron Cobham, begged Cromwell to ensure that Wyatt made provision for his wife, which he was evidently failing to do. By about that date Wyatt had as his mistress Elizabeth, daughter of Sir Edward Darrell of Littlecote, with whom he had at least one illegitimate son, Francis. He later urged his son Thomas to:

> love well and agre with your wife ... And the blissing of god for good agrement between the wife and husband is fruyt of many children, which I for the like thinge doe lacke, and the faulte is both in your mother and me, but chieflie in her. (Muir, 40–41)

It is thought the estrangement was the result of her adultery; Wyatt, however, with characteristic pith, admitted later that 'I graunte I do not professe chastite, but yet I use not abhomination' (ibid., 206).

In 1524 Wyatt became clerk of the king's jewels, which might have prepared him to succeed his father as master, and by 1525 he was an esquire of the king's body. He is mentioned in Hall's chronicle as having participated in the Christmas entertainments in 1524–5, in which an allegorical Castle of Loyalty was defended by, among others, Francis Bryan and John Pointz (to whom he later addressed epistolary satires), as well as by his brother-in-law Sir George Cobham. His first experience of diplomatic service abroad came in 1526, when he accompanied Sir Thomas Cheney (another Kentish neighbour) to France to congratulate François I on his release from imprisonment by the emperor, and to negotiate the position of England in relation to the league of Cognac. He arrived in Bordeaux in April, and on 1 May he was sent back to England, presumably to carry information to Wolsey. Cheney described him as one who 'hath as much wit to mark and remember everything he saith as any young man hath in England' (*LP Henry VIII*, 4.2135).

On 7 January 1527 Wyatt again went abroad, this time with Sir John Russell to the papal court. According to Russell the pope sent horses for them; according to George Wyatt, the poet's militantly anti-papal grandson, he sent courtesans who offered 'a plenary dispensation verbal' (*Papers of George Wyatt*, 27) for whatever the diplomats might do with them. They passed on to Venice at the end of February 1527, where Russell injured his leg. Wyatt returned via Ferrara, and was then, despite having a safe conduct from the duke, captured by imperial troops who demanded 3000 ducats for his freedom. The duke of Ferrara is said to have brought about his release by 1 April 1527. In early May Wyatt left Rome, shortly before 6 May when imperial troops sacked the city.

At new year 1528 Wyatt presented Katherine of Aragon with *Quyete of Mynde*, a translation of Plutarch from Guillaume Budé's Latin version, having baulked at the stiffer task of translating Petrarch's *De remediis utriusque fortunae*. His future mistress, Elizabeth Darrell, was a maid to Katherine, and it may be that this early association with Charles V's aunt led to Wyatt's subsequent appointment as ambassador to Spain. The work gives the first sign of his interest in Stoic retreat from the troubles of the world, which plays a significant part in his later verse.

Connection with Anne Boleyn and imprisonment From October 1529 to November 1530 Wyatt was high marshall of Calais, an office which he tried to regain in May 1536. This may have developed his interest in French verse forms, apparent in his *ballades* and *rondeaux*, although the influence of French culture was so pronounced in the English court that Calais is unlikely to have taught him anything which England could not. On 26 September 1529 he was granted a licence to import wine and woad from France. After his return to England he was appointed in 1532 a commissioner of the peace for Essex. Through this period he was becoming increasingly familiar with his father's executor Thomas Cromwell. He probably accompanied Henry VIII and Anne Boleyn (by now established as the king's mistress) to Calais to meet François I in October 1532. His *strambotto* 'Some tyme I fled the fyre that me brent' (*Poems*, ed. Muir and Thomson, poem 59) is generally taken to refer to this event, although voyages to France became a regular part of his life. On 1 June 1533 he took his father's place as sewer-extraordinary at the coronation of Anne Boleyn, whose accession can only have strengthened his family's position at court. Through the following years Wyatt consolidated both the status of his family and their connections in Kent and Yorkshire: he was granted a licence to have twenty men in his livery in June 1534. In February 1535 the king nominated him high steward of the abbey of West Malling in Kent, despite a dispute with the abbess, and in July he was granted an eighty-year lease on Arygden Park in Yorkshire. In all probability he was knighted on Easter day 1535 (the records erroneously give a date of 18 March 1536). A brief imprisonment in the Fleet in May 1534 for an affray which had resulted in the death of one of the sergeants of London did not impede his advancement.

Wyatt stated in poem 92 that in May:

> my welth and eke my liff, I say,
> Have stonde so oft in such perplexitie.

This was no exaggeration. On 5 May 1536 he was imprisoned in the Tower—very shortly after the detention of Mark Smeaton, Sir Henry Norris, William Brereton, and Sir Francis Weston, who were accused of adultery with Anne Boleyn. Contemporary witnesses associate him with Smeaton and the others, and imply that their offences were also his. John Hussee recorded in a dispatch to Lord Lisle on 12 May 1536 that Wyatt was imprisoned but not in mortal danger; by 13 May he was reporting that some believed Wyatt and Sir Richard Page were 'as like to suffer as the others' (*LP Henry VIII*, 10.865). The Spanish ambassador Chapuys recorded that Wyatt and Page had been detained on Anne's account. Wyatt himself later claimed that his imprisonment was the result of the 'undeservyd evyll will' of the duke of Suffolk (Muir, 201). Three later witnesses (Harpsfield, Sanders, and the *Spanish Chronicle*), all vigorously anti-protestant, report that the poet had been one of Anne's lovers before her accession, and that he had warned the king against marrying her. Critics have eagerly sought allusions to an affair in his verse. One poem in the Egerton manuscript (*Poems*, ed. Muir and Thomson, poem 50) asks:

> What wourde is that that chaungeth not,
> Though it be tourned and made in twain?

and is entitled 'Anna'. The title, however, is in a later hand. Another poem alludes to 'her that did set our country in a rore' (ibid., poem 97), a line carefully revised in Wyatt's hand to 'Brunet that set my welth in such a rore'. This indicates that a brunette who convulsed his heart and his nation (or perhaps simply his county, the usual sense of the word 'country' in this period) was or had been on his mind. Editors have sometimes believed that the injunction '*Noli me tangere*, for Cesars I am' (ibid., poem 7), set on the collar of the Petrarchan deer in Wyatt's version of 'una candida cerva', reflects the poet's reluctant acceptance (*c*.1526–7) that Anne Boleyn belonged to Henry VIII. That a musician, Mark Smeaton, was imprisoned and accused of intimacy with Anne in 1536 does imply that the queen had a circle of lyrists close enough to her to make a king claim that her intimacy with these men was sexual. But neither Wyatt's imprisonment nor his poetry indicates that he was a lover of Anne Boleyn.

The most probable explanation of both Wyatt's imprisonment in 1536 and his release is not romance but family loyalties and locality: his family was close to the Boleyns by geography and allegiance, and his detention, probably at the instigation of Charles Brandon, duke of Suffolk, served to indicate that all family and friends of the Boleyns were in danger. His release is likely to have resulted from his family's and his own close ties with Cromwell. On 7 May his father wrote to his son, hoping that he was 'ffounde trewe to his grace' (Muir, 30). Four days later Sir Henry wrote to thank Cromwell (who had assumed Sir Henry's former office of master of the jewels in 1532) for his efforts on his son's behalf, evidently believing that he would be released shortly, and urged Cromwell to act as a father towards him. It is probable that Wyatt witnessed the execution of Anne Boleyn's supposed lovers from the Tower on 17 May 1536:

> The bell towre showed me suche syght
> That in my hed stekys day and night.
> (*Poems*, ed. Muir and Thomson, poem 126, ll. 16–17)

By mid-June he was released.

Ambassadorial duties Wyatt grumbled vocally about his imprisonment, but after his release there was no diminution in the favours shown to him: he was made steward of Conisborough Castle (an office formerly held by his father) during the northern rising, and in October 1536 he was charged to provide 200 men to resist the rebels. He also became sheriff of Kent. The final favour bestowed on him was to prove a bitter one: on 12 March 1537 he received his instructions as ambassador to the court of the emperor Charles V, a little over a month after he had been granted livery of his father's lands. He spent most of the next two and a half years in almost constant motion abroad. He was briefed to improve relations with the emperor, which had been frosty since Henry's divorce from Katherine of Aragon (the emperor's aunt), and to negotiate a marriage between the Princess Mary and the infante of Portugal. But his main challenge was to ensure that the French king and the emperor did not form a league from which England was excluded. Cromwell also urged him to use his ability as an observer of men in order to plumb the emperor's intentions: 'fishe out the botom of his stomake' (*LP Henry VIII*, 12/2.870). Wyatt sailed in April 1537. It is likely that during this journey he composed two letters to his son, which urge him to honesty and good service to the king, and which hope that 'Senek were your studye and Epictetus, bicause it is litel to be euir in your bosome' (Muir, 43). In May–June he passed through Paris, Lyons, Avignon, Barcelona, and Saragossa, where John Briarton, his assistant, wrote to Thomas Wriothesley, 'we were extremely handeled, as though we had been Jewes' (ibid., 44). They were compelled, despite Wyatt's protestations, to pay duty on their clothing. On 22 June Wyatt had the first of several amicable audiences with the emperor, although his attempts to persuade the emperor of the invalidity of the donation of Constantine met a predictably bland response. Wyatt later experienced trouble from the Inquisition for distributing 'heretical' books. It is likely that these works touched on the temporal authority of the pope, or 'the bishop of Rome' as Wyatt and all loyal English subjects termed him by this date.

Wyatt's embassy was bound to fail. It is not clear that any parties ever wanted any of the marriages he was supposed to negotiate, and the emperor and the French king, exhausted and impoverished by war, were set on reconciliation. The birth of Prince Edward in October 1537 meant that Princess Mary, declared illegitimate and unlikely ever to succeed to the English throne, was never to become daughter-in-law to the king of Portugal. Wyatt was rebuked by Cromwell for failing to pass on to the emperor Princess Mary's letter acknowledging her illegitimacy. This he presumably withheld to increase her appeal as a dynastic partner. After the death of Jane Seymour in October 1537 a marriage was suggested between Henry VIII and the duchess of Milan, whose claim to the crown of Denmark the emperor used as an inducement to the match. While Wyatt's negotiations in Spain became increasingly complex, his debts were mounting up at home. He repeatedly pressed for an increase in his 'diet', or living expenses, and was repeatedly stalled.

The emperor and François I were set on negotiating a deal, which Wyatt attempted by increasingly desperate measures to break. They met at Nice. Here Francis Bryan, the ambassador to the French king, gambled for high stakes, and Wyatt lent him £200. The debt was repaid by Cromwell in November, but a memory of it gives a sharp bite to the start of Wyatt's epistolary satire to Bryan:

> A spending hand that always powreth owte
> Had nede to have a bringer in as fast.
> (*Poems*, ed. Muir and Thomson, poem 107, ll. 1–2)

Edmund Bonner and Simon Heynes too were in Nice. They had been dispatched in theory to assist Wyatt, but in practice to keep an eye on him. In a desperate attempt to create discord between the emperor, François, and the pope, Wyatt suggested that John Mason be sent to the papal legate Cardinal Pole (with whom Mason had an earlier association) to elicit information from him. This plan yielded no results, and about 25 May 1538, Wyatt's least happy month, he was sent home bearing an offer of marriage for both Mary and Henry on terms which his king was bound to refuse. The emperor promised Wyatt twenty-five days for his return to Nice with an answer before any peace was concluded with François. This was characteristically devious: Wyatt's absence was probably engineered to enable Charles and François to make a treaty, which they duly agreed on 20 June, just after the expiry of the twenty-five day period of grace. Henry is supposed to have thought that Wyatt was more the emperor's ambassador than his own by this point; certainly he was outmanoeuvred.

Wyatt trekked back to Barcelona in July 1538 with the imperial court, and from there went on to Toledo. In September Bonner wrote a malicious letter to Cromwell, which alleged that, while at Nice, Wyatt had treacherously sought contact with Cardinal Pole through Mason, and that he had also treasonably expressed a wish for the king's death. Cromwell detained Mason, but glossed over the accusations in his correspondence to Wyatt. He retained Bonner's letter, which was discovered and used to plague Wyatt after Cromwell's fall in 1540.

By January 1539, as the rapprochement of the emperor and François developed, and plans for the king's marriage to the duchess of Milan foundered, Wyatt declared to Cromwell, 'I ame at the wall. I ame not able to endure to March', when his recall had been promised (Muir, 86). The emperor received Cardinal Pole to his court in February 1539, and Pole detected signs of a growing coolness towards England. It is almost certain that, in desperation to break the looming alliance between the pope, François, and Charles V, Wyatt became involved in a conspiracy to assassinate Pole. Ciphered letters leave only hints of this plan, although Wyatt had discussed a quick-acting Spanish poison with Elizabeth Darrell during his return to England in June 1538, and had asked if the king wished to obtain any. That plan too came to naught, although it made Pole fear for his life: he still believed that Wyatt was on the loose and in pursuit of him in September 1539.

From June to November 1539 Wyatt was probably at Allington laying out some of the £106 which remained in his hands after paying the £3090 3s. of expenses for his embassy. But in mid-November he was once more sent to the emperor, who was at this point in Blois on his way to pacify the Low Countries. Wyatt's role was again to seek a means of creating a breach between the emperor and the French king, while congratulating both rulers on their growing amity. The measure he eventually adopted was circuitous: at Paris he seized an English traitor called Robert Brancetour, who was said to have been urging English subjects to support Cardinal Pole. Brancetour was in the entourage of the emperor, but he was under the jurisdiction of the French king, who naïvely agreed to the arrest. The emperor's fury secured the release of his follower,

and all Wyatt could do was to insinuate that the failure to yield Brancetour showed ingratitude on Charles's part towards the English king. When Wyatt called the emperor an ingrate, he exploded with rage: 'I take it so that I can not be toward hym Ingrate. The inferyour may be Ingrate to the greter, and the terme is skant sufferable bytwene like' (Muir, 135). This was relayed back to the French king as an indicator that the emperor had a 'Fantazie that he shuld be pereles' (Merriman, 2.251). Wyatt's patient fishing of the emperor's stomach eventually yielded its dram of bile; but with no marriage negotiated, Pole alive and well, and the Valois and the Habsburgs effectively reconciled, he 'trotted contynually up and downe that hell throughe heate and stinke from Councelloure to Embassator' (Muir, 181) to no avail. He was recalled in late April 1540, and shortly before his departure from Spain probably composed 'Tagus, farewell' (*Poems*, ed. Muir and Thomson, poem 99). He was not sorry to leave.

The fall of Cromwell and Wyatt's arrest May 1540 was a happy month: Wyatt was home. But by 10 June, Cromwell, his chief patron and protector, was arrested. The *Spanish Chronicle* records that Wyatt witnessed his execution on 28 July 1540, and that he was addressed from the scaffold by his patron: 'Oh, Wyatt, do not weep, for if I were no more guilty than thou wert when they took thee, I should not be in this pass' (*Chronicle of King Henry VIII*, 104). It is traditionally believed that Wyatt's imitation of Petrarch's sonnet on the death of his patron Giovanni Colonna, 'The piller pearisht is whearto I lent' (*Poems*, ed. Muir and Thomson, poem 236), reflects on Cromwell's fall. His death was indeed a disaster for a family which had developed close ties with Cromwell from the 1530s. Wyatt probably owed him his release from the Tower in 1536, and if the French ambassador is to be believed Cromwell had calmed Henry VIII's irritation with his ambassador on at least one occasion (Kaulek, 157). From July to December 1540 Wyatt probably retired to Allington, where he undertook extensive renovations of the castle. Some authorities have it that he composed his penitential psalms during this period (others favour the aftermath of the 1536 imprisonment); their preoccupation with enemies and tyrannical rulers might well grow from Wyatt's experiences in 1540.

The death and disgrace of Wyatt's protector eventually led to a revival of the accusations of Bonner and Heynes. There were two accusations which endangered Wyatt's life: Bonner's claim that he had communicated with Cardinal Pole was potentially deadly in 1540, as the king's hatred of Pole was by that date extreme; his accusation that Wyatt had said 'By goddes bludde, ye shall see the kinge our maister cast out at the carts tail, and if he soo be served, by godds body, he is well served' (Muir, 67) might mean that Wyatt had treasonably compassed the king's death by words, since Bonner claimed Wyatt meant that the king should be hanged like a thief. Wyatt was duly taken bound and under guard to the Tower on 17 January 1541. Three days later Sir Richard Southwell was instructed to confiscate plate and horses from Allington (where Elizabeth Darrell, apparently pregnant, was in residence), and to pay off Wyatt's servants. A traitor's death was almost certain to follow.

Wyatt's defence against the charges survives in BL, Harley MS 78. In it he orchestrates the full range of tones, from homely directness to ambassadorial innuendo, which run through his best poems. Similarities between the language of the defence and that of two poems to Francis Bryan, 'A Spending Hand' and 'Syghes ar my Foode' (*Poems*, ed. Muir and Thomson, poems 107 and 244), make it very likely that those works date from his period in the Tower or a time close to it. In the defence he does not deny that he had resented his imprisonment in 1536, but insists that he had not treasonably wished the king's death. In a careful mingling of outright denial and implicit confession he makes it clear both that he regarded the extension of the Treason Act in 1534 to include words as potentially a pretext for tyranny, and that he by no means considered Henry to be a tyrant. He claims he had not committed verbal treason: he had simply used the common proverb to mean that something 'is evell taken heede to, or negligently, slyppes owte of the carte and is loste' (Muir, 198); that is, he meant that Henry was likely to be left out of the league between the emperor and François. He also insists that his contact with Pole through Mason was in order to spy on him rather than to conspire with him.

It is not known whether the defence was delivered, but it confesses enough to have been regarded, with some licence, as the full confession which Wyatt is said to have made. On 19 March Katherine Howard is reported by the Spanish ambassador to have interceded on his behalf, and Wyatt was released. Henry had (for him) something approaching a sincere affection for the poet: the French ambassador Marillac reported that 'there was no one with whom the King was more private, nor to whom he gave greater demonstrations of love' (Kaulek, 263), and Henry retained in his personal possession at Hampton Court Wyatt's seal, and a set of varvels (rings attached to the jesses of a hawk, often engraved with the owner's name). Lloyd's testimony that Wyatt had prompted the English Reformation by jesting 'that a man cannot repent him of his sin but by the Pope's leave' (Lloyd, 46) can be discounted as an attempt to make the poet into a hero of protestantism; but Wyatt's combination of frankness, learning, and conversational salt appealed to the king. Wriothesley reported that Wyatt confessed his guilt and received his pardon from Henry VIII at Dover in late March. Chapuys recorded that a condition of his pardon was that he should take back his wife, 'from whom he had been separated for upwards of fifteen years' (*CSP Spain, 1538–42*, 314). It may be that Elizabeth Brooke is the 'clogg' on Wyatt's heel described in his 'Satire' to Poyntz (*Poems*, ed. Muir and Thomson, poem 105, l. 86), although some authorities date the poem to his release in June 1536.

Death and reputation Wyatt's rehabilitation after imprisonment was, once again, rapid. By April 1541 he had been appointed to command 300 horse in Calais. Grants of land and offices followed in July, and by December he had become knight of the shire and MP for Kent. In March 1542

he became steward of the manor of Maidstone, and was granted three former monastic properties, including the Carmelite priory in Aylesford, Kent. By August he was rumoured to have been appointed vice-admiral of the fleet against France. His health was not good, however. Since March 1539 he had complained of violent headaches. He made a will on 12 June 1541 (now unlocated; *LP Henry VIII*, 16.470, 18.981, 89), which made his son Thomas his chief heir, but which also provided land in Dorset and Somerset for both Elizabeth Darrell and her son Francis (or Henry as he is called in some documents).

Diplomacy was the death of him. On 3 October 1542 Wyatt was appointed by the privy council to conduct the earl of Tyrone to the king; on the same day, however, he was sent to meet the Spanish envoy Montmorency de Courrière at Falmouth. He contracted a fever on his return, and died, probably about 6 October, in the house of Sir John Horsey in Sherborne, Dorset. He was buried in the great church at Sherborne, probably in the Horsey family vault, on 11 October 1542.

Wyatt's death prompted elegies by Leland, Surrey, and Thomas Chaloner. The printing of Surrey's and Leland's elegies in 1542 was the first occasion on which a recently dead English author was publicly canonized by those who felt they were his successors. The elegies present him as a singular figure, and are right to do so. He translated and imitated sonnets (of which he is the first known English exponent) and *canzone* by Petrarch with a skill that warrants his early reputation as one of 'a new company of courtly makers' who 'having travailed into Italie … greatly polished our rude and homely manner of vulgar Poesie' (Puttenham, 60). From Serafino, Wyatt learned to craft short and pithy *ottava rima* stanzas known as *strambotti*, a form which he tended to use for verses which riddlingly appear to allude to contemporary events. Some of his stanzaic poems, such as 'My lute, awake' (*Poems*, ed. Muir and Thomson, poem 66), appear to imply musical settings, although none survives. The division between courtier poets and professional musicians in the court of Henry VIII was more or less impermeable, and Wyatt's poems, if they were sung, were probably not sung by him.

Wyatt was also the first to translate and imitate epistolary satires in *terza rima* from Horace and Alamanni. These epistles, to Sir Francis Bryan and John Poyntz, aim to appeal precisely to the experiences of their addressees, and insist that withdrawal into Horatian retirement is the only antidote to the deceptions and uncertainties of court life—of which both Wyatt and his addressees had ample experience. Wyatt's receptiveness to humanist currents of learning is matched by his willingness to experiment with the theology and vocabulary of evangelical writers. The paraphrases on the penitential psalms in *terza rima* explore evangelical vocabulary, and show signs of wide reading in Catholic, evangelical, and Lutheran sources. The psalms (one of which was at some point dedicated to Surrey) derive from so many sources and work on so many concerns—salvation, penitence, obedience and resistance to a sovereign authority—that a distinct theological position does not emerge from them. Wyatt claimed in his defence, however, that 'I thynke I shulde have more adoe with a great sorte in Inglande to purge my selffe of suspecte of a Lutherane then of a Papyst' (Muir, 195–6).

Scholars disagree over the canon of Wyatt's verse and the criteria for inclusion in it: Muir prints 268 poems as his (which is excessive), Daalder a tentative 184. The manuscript Egerton 2711 in the British Library is generally agreed to contain poems exclusively by Wyatt (a total of 108 if the psalms are counted as a single poem). Some are copied by amanuenses and revised by Wyatt, others are in Wyatt's hand throughout. Although it has been suggested that this manuscript indicates that Wyatt wished to gather his works for an audience in print, its contents probably indicate rather that he wished it to remain in his family: his verse assumes that his readers are a part of a small group who will be able to unpick the often cryptic allusions to personal and public events which it contains. The Egerton manuscript was preserved by the Harington family, as was the Arundel Harington manuscript (owned by the duke of Norfolk). This contains four additional poems ascribed to Wyatt. There are a further eleven ascriptions to him in the collection of verse in and by several hands known as the Devonshire manuscript (BL, Add. MS 17492); editors differ in their attribution of other poems in that manuscript. Six further poems are ascribed to Wyatt in the 'Blage' manuscript (TCD, MS 160). Few would now agree with Muir that the majority of unascribed poems in this manuscript are also Wyatt's work. Sixteen additional poems are printed in the section devoted to Wyatt in Tottel's miscellany (*Songes and Sonnettes*, 1557), and a number of pieces sometimes attributed to him appear in the fragmentary *Court of Venus*. There are further poems in BL, Hill MS Add. 36529, Corpus Christi College, Cambridge, Parker MS 168, and BL, Harley MS 78.

No other writer in the early Tudor period is known to have experimented in so many genres, or to have left behind such a substantial and varied body of verse. Although Wyatt is often casually referred to as the first 'Renaissance' poet, it is more accurate to regard his achievement as distinctively Henrician: he assimilated European forms of verse and a Chaucerian poetic vocabulary to the life and milieu of a Henrician courtier and diplomat, generating in the process poems which darkly allude to political events, and which testify to the habitual indirectness of expression on which the life of a courtier and diplomat in this period depended.

Colin Burrow

Sources K. Muir, *Life and letters of Sir Thomas Wyatt* (1963) · *The poems of Sir Thomas Wyatt*, ed. K. Muir and P. Thomson (1969) · P. Thomson, *Sir Thomas Wyatt and his background* (1964) · *The works of Henry Howard earl of Surrey and of Sir Thomas Wyatt the elder*, ed. G. F. Nott, 2 vols. (1815) · S. Brigden, '"The shadow that you know": Sir Thomas Wyatt and Sir Francis Bryan at court and in embassy', *HJ*, 39 (1996), 1–31 · *The papers of George Wyatt, esquire, of Boxley Abbey in the county of Kent*, ed. D. M. Loades, CS, 4th ser., 5 (1968) · W. H. Wiatt, 'On the date of Sir Thomas Wyatt's knighthood', *Journal of English and Germanic Philology*, 40 (1961), 268–72 · W. M. Tydeman, 'Biographical data on Sir Thomas Wyatt', *N&Q*, 206 (1961), 414–15 · S. C. Wyatt, *Cheneys and Wyatts: a brief history in two parts* [n.d., c.1959] · *State papers published under … Henry VIII*, 11 vols. (1830–52) · *LP Henry VIII*, 4.2135, 10.865, 12/2.870, 16.470, 18.981, 89 · *CSP Spain* · D. Starkey, 'The court: Castiglione's ideal and Tudor reality, being a discussion of Sir Thomas Wyatt's "Satire addressed to Sir Francis Bryan"', *Journal of the Warburg and Courtauld Institute*, 45 (1982), 232–9 · R. Strong, *Tudor and Jacobean portraits*, 2 vols. (1969) · R. C. Harrier, *The canon of Sir Thomas Wyatt's poetry* (1975) · J. Bruce, 'Unpublished anecdotes of Sir Thomas Wyatt the poet, and of other members of that family', *GM*, 2nd ser., 34 (1850), 235–41 · E. K. Chambers, *Sir Thomas Wyatt and some collected studies* (New York, 1965) · *The complete poems of Sir Thomas Wyatt*, ed. R. A. Rebholtz (1978) · *The collected poems of Sir Thomas Wyatt*, ed. J. Daalder (1975) · D. Lloyd, *The states-men, and favourites of England since the Reformation* (1665) · P. Beal, *English literary manuscripts*, 1 (1980) · D. Starkey, ed., *The inventory of King Henry VIII* (1998) · *Chronicle of King Henry VIII of England*, trans. M. A. S. Hume (1889) · J. Kaulek, ed., *Correspondance politique de MM. de Castillon et de Marillac, ambassadeurs de France en Angleterre (1537–1542)* (Paris, 1885) · N. Harpsfield, *A treatise on the pretended divorce between Henry VIII and Catherine of Aragon*, ed. N. Pocock (1878) · N. Sanders, *Rise and growth of the Anglican schism*, trans. D. Lewis (1877) · G. Puttenham, *The art of English poesie*, ed. G. D. Willcock and A. Walker (1970) · J. Leland, *Naeniae in mortem T. Viati, equitis incomparabilis* (1542) · H. Howard, earl of Surrey, *Songes and sonnettes, written by Henry Howard late earle of Surrey, and other* (1557) · *Life and letters of Thomas Cromwell*, ed. R. B. Merriman, 2 vols. (1902) · BL, Egerton MS 2711 · letters, BL, Harley MS 282 · Wyatt's defence, BL, Harley MS 78, fols. 5–7, 7–15 · BL, Wyatt papers, loan MS 15 · BL, Devonshire MS, Add. MS 17492

Archives BL, papers, loan MS 15 · BL, corresp. and papers as ambassador to Charles V, Harley MS 282 | BL, Devonshire MS, Add. MS 17492 · BL, defence, Harley MS 78 · TCD, 'Blage' MS, MS 160

Likenesses H. Holbein the younger, chalk drawing, c.1535, Royal Collection [*see illus.*] · attrib. H. Holbein the younger, woodcut, 1542, BL; repro. in Leland, *Naeniae* · H. Holbein the younger, oils (Henry Wyatt), Louvre, Paris · oils (after H. Holbein the younger, c.1540), NPG; version, Bodl. Oxf. · oils (Henry Wyatt), priv. coll. · oils (after H. Holbein the younger, c.1550), NPG

Wyatt, Sir Thomas (*b.* in or before **1521**, *d.* **1554**), soldier and rebel, was born in or before 1521, being of age in 1542, and was the only surviving son of Sir Thomas *Wyatt (c.1503–1542), courtier and poet, of Allington Castle, Kent, and Elizabeth (*d.* 1560), daughter of Thomas Brooke, eighth Baron Cobham, and his second wife, Dorothy. Little is known of his education. He seems to have been familiar with the classical military authorities, and his father recommended to him the study of moral philosophy. An uncorroborated family tradition records that he travelled in Italy, Germany, and France, but the dates cannot be established. In 1537 he married Jane (*d.* in or after 1595), daughter and coheir of the leading Kent gentleman, Sir William Haute of Bishopsbourne.

Early career Wyatt was closely associated with the aggressive martial values of Henry Howard, earl of Surrey, and he was first and foremost a soldier. He joined Surrey and Sir William Pickering in an episode of aristocratic hooliganism in London in 1543. They rampaged through the city in the dead of night, breaking the windows of city plutocrats and throwing stones at the Bankside whores. But the actions of these swaggering loudmouths may have been structured by a reformist agenda. Surrey later vindicated himself by taking on the role of a prophet denouncing the corruption of metropolitan society. Wyatt may

Sir Thomas Wyatt (*b.* in or before 1521, *d.* 1554), by unknown artist, *c.*1550

have shared the reformed sympathies of his noble patron: he was also in trouble at this time for eating meat on Fridays and fast days. For these various offences Wyatt was imprisoned in the Tower of London for a month. His energies were turned to the government's ends when in June 1544 he was commissioned to lead 100 men in the war against France. He acquitted himself well, being placed in charge of part of the Boulogne garrison in November 1544, and promoted to captain of Basse-Boulogne early in 1545. He was knighted between January and May 1545. There is little doubting his personal bravery. In the attack on Hardelot Castle he stormed the first gate, breaking open the door, killing one of the watchmen, and capturing another two before setting 'his hackbutters in the brage before the castle' (*Works of Howard and Wyatt*, 1.188n.). He impressed Sir William Paget, principal secretary, who commended his military discipline and skill in fortification; his only misgiving was that he might have inherited his father's weakness of 'too strong opinion' (*LP Henry VIII*, 20/2, no. 461). He was high in Surrey's confidence, earning great praise for his 'hardiness, painfulness, circumspection, and natural disposition to the war' (*Works of Howard and Wyatt*, 1.188). When the English disastrously encountered the French at St Étienne on 7 January 1546, it was to Wyatt that Surrey entrusted the task of explaining the humiliation to a hostile court. Wyatt was disappointed in his ambition of acquiring the command of the newly built fortress of Ambleteuse in 1546.

His father had died in debt, and Wyatt found it necessary to sell a portion of his estates in 1543 for £3669. His financial embarrassments perhaps explain his aggression against both tenants and neighbouring gentry. His new park at Boxley, Kent, was a target of anti-enclosure rioters in 1549, and he became embroiled in a series of lawsuits with his fellow Kent gentlemen. Nevertheless, his career prospered under the protestant regimes of Edward Seymour, duke of Somerset, and John Dudley, duke of Northumberland. He was knight of the shire for Kent in the parliament of 1547, and he served as sheriff in 1550–51. He was keenly interested in military reform, preparing a scheme for the establishment of a militia which was presented to Somerset and revised in consultation with other military men (including Sir James Croft, Pickering, Robert Rudstone, and Sir James Wilford) for consideration by parliament. These proposals came to nothing, but they were on the lines of the training of a select militia later adopted by the Elizabethan regime.

Wyatt's role in the crisis of Mary I's accession in July 1553 is obscure. Family tradition records that he opposed Northumberland's 'Device' for the succession, and that he was threatened with being sent to Ireland, but there is no independent corroboration of this story. He was involved in the proclamation of Mary at Maidstone, Kent, but it is possible that his role was more ambivalent. As he entered the Tower after his rising failed, Sir John Brydges charged him with having already borne arms against the queen. Like many others his loyalties probably wavered. He was early out of sympathy with the new regime. Again family tradition records that he obtained a licence to go overseas in the early months of the reign (perhaps into religious exile), but it was Mary's projected marriage to Philip of Spain that catapulted him to prominence.

Rebellion By the beginning of November 1553 rumours were circulating of Mary's desire to marry Philip. The marriage was widely opposed, both in the country at large and at the heart of the regime. The anomalous position of a king regnant crystallized fears about how Philip might use his powers within England; the possibility that England might become another Habsburg milch cow was very real; and there was a real risk of a succession struggle on Mary's death. Several among Mary's privy councillors, led by the lord chancellor, Stephen Gardiner, bishop of Winchester, promoted the alternative candidacy of Edward Courtenay, earl of Devon, recently released from the Tower, but Mary never seems to have seriously considered this feckless youth. On 16 November a parliamentary delegation attempted to dissuade the queen from marrying a foreigner, but it was angrily rebuffed. Wyatt was among the group of disaffected gentlemen who turned to the idea of a military coup to avert the marriage. He was present at a meeting in London on 26 November with other members of the Edwardian establishment. Sir Peter Carew, Sir Edward Rogers, Sir Edward Warner, Pickering, Sir Nicholas Throckmorton, Croft, Sir George Harper, Nicholas Arnold, William Thomas, and William Winter were recorded as being present. What these men had in common was their shared military experience in the 1540s, the enjoyment of high favour in the Edwardian regime and the prospect of thwarted careers under Mary, and probably protestantism. Wyatt was not their leader; he later claimed that he was 'but the iiijth or vth man' (Nichols, *Chronicle*, 69), and the instigator of conspiracy was more probably Croft.

By 22 December the conspirators, recently joined by Henry Grey, duke of Suffolk, decided on a plan for a fourfold rising scheduled for Palm Sunday (18 March): Carew would raise the west country, Croft Herefordshire, Suffolk the midlands, and Wyatt Kent. The impressive military expertise of the conspirators combined with the widespread popular hostility to the match appeared to give the scheme some chance of success. But there were already signs of a lack of common purpose among the rebels.

Thomas mooted the idea of assassinating Mary, but this was anathema to Wyatt and Croft. On hearing of it, Wyatt allegedly concealed a cudgel beneath his gown for four or five days, intending to beat Thomas so 'that he wolde have lefte him for dedd' (Nichols, *Chronicle*, 69). According to the later indictments of the rebels, the plotters planned to marry Courtenay to Princess Elizabeth, and to place them on the throne, but it is not clear how well developed this plan was, or even how far it commanded assent among the rebels. Would Suffolk, whose daughter, Lady Jane Grey, queen of nine days in July, was still languishing in the Tower, have been entirely at ease with this plan? Throughout his rising Wyatt maintained that he meant no harm to Mary, that his rising was only for resisting of strangers, and for the queen to appoint better privy councillors. This may well have been, as the Catholic sources suggest, a deliberate ruse to maximize his movement's appeal, but it might have reflected Wyatt's uncertainty about what he was to do when he captured the queen's person. The crown's lawyers had every interest in emphasizing the heinous nature of the purposes of conspirators, so that the indictments may not be the best guide to the objectives of the rebellion.

The conspirators undoubtedly had some contact with both Courtenay and Elizabeth. Sir Edward Rogers, a former Courtenay servant, carried communications between Wyatt and the earl, but Antoine de Noailles, the French ambassador, advised that he should not be told too much. Elizabeth, whose ties with the conspiracy the government was particularly anxious to disentangle, was careful to commit nothing to paper, but apparently sent a message of probably unspecified goodwill towards Wyatt via her servant Sir William Saintlow. The conspirators' hand was forced by the government. They had found it very difficult to keep their plans secret, and by mid-December Simon Renard, the imperial ambassador, already knew that a rebellion was in the offing. Carew was summoned to the privy council on 2 January 1554, but ignored it, and began efforts to mobilize the Devon gentry. Wyatt left London for Allington on 19 January, the day after Renard had laid all that he knew before the queen. Gardiner, fearing that he might be compromised by the involvement of his protégé Courtenay, got him to tell what he knew on 21 January, just as news broke in the capital of the rising in Devon. Wyatt had no choice but to act quickly.

At Allington, Wyatt laid plans for a co-ordinated rising in Kent. On 25 January he raised his standard in Maidstone and his supporters made simultaneous proclamations in Rochester, Tonbridge, Malling, and Milton. The government had already got wind of Wyatt's plans and loyalist forces were mobilizing under the sheriff, Sir Robert Southwell, and Henry Neville, sixth baron of Abergavenny. On 26 January the privy council ordered the immediate levy of 600 troops from the city of London and they departed two days later under the command of Thomas Howard, third duke of Norfolk, gathering reinforcements in north Kent. Although Southwell and Bergavenny may have had difficulties in recruiting (loyalists later complained bitterly about the problem of the 'neuters'), their

force of about six hundred was successful in preventing a junction between Sir Henry Isley's men at Sevenoaks and those of Wyatt, who were at Rochester on 28 January, intercepting and defeating them at Wrotham. But loyalist hopes of an early end to the rebellion were dashed on the following day. Norfolk, outnumbered by Wyatt, ignoring warnings about the likelihood of betrayal by his own troops, and making no effort to co-ordinate with Southwell and Bergavenny, moved forward on Rochester. As Norfolk advanced on the bridge, Alexander Brett, one of the Londoners' captains, urged his troops to join the rebels, claiming that they were assembled to prevent the English from becoming 'slaves and vilaynes' (Nichols, *Chronicle*, 38); the Londoners cried with enthusiasm, 'we are Englishmen' (Proctor, 231), and said they would live and die in their captains' quarrel. The defection of the whitecoats had been pre-arranged as the Londoners had been suborned by French agents, but it undoubtedly fed Wyatt's confidence that he could count on support from the city, and on this his strategy now turned. After neutralizing George Brooke, ninth Baron Cobham, at Cooling on 31 January, he marched slowly on the city, maintaining a firm military discipline, entering Southwark on 3 February and pausing there for three days.

Although the defection of the whitecoats had been a boost and there were further defections from government troops in Southwark, there are signs that Wyatt was having difficulty in keeping his forces together. These never numbered more than 3000 men and he had not succeeded in generating a large-scale popular mobilization. Most of his supporters came from within the sphere of territorial influence of his core gentry followers, especially in the Medway valley, and there was very little support from the east of the county, not even in towns like Canterbury. Some of his propaganda was wearing thin: he had claimed that the majority of the privy council was on his side; he had expected more support from the Kent gentry. John Proctor alleged that Wyatt concealed from his troops the government's promises of a pardon if they would disperse. Moreover, some of his supporters were alienated by his brusque dismissal of Mary's offer of negotiations over the marriage on 31 January; his demand that he receive custody of the queen with control of the Tower was at odds with his professed intention not to seek hurt to her. It was now evident that the risings elsewhere in the country had failed and that all turned on London. But the sojourn in Southwark was not encouraging for his prospects. London Bridge was strongly defended and all river craft confined to the north bank. There was no mass insurgency in the capital, either because the Londoners had rallied round the queen after her dramatic bid for their loyalty in her appearance at the Guildhall on 1 February, or because the aldermen had taken effective police measures against the rebels, or because the citizens feared looting. The inhabitants of the south bank became increasingly restless as the Tower artillery was trained on their homes. Proctor claimed that Wyatt considered retreat to Kent and possibly flight to France, but was forced on by pressure from Brett and the London captains.

Wyatt's forces left Southwark on 6 February, arriving at Kingston at about 4 p.m. He quickly beat off the small force of defenders but was delayed by the need to repair the damaged bridge before crossing the Thames. Wishing to maintain the advantage of surprise, he was forced to abandon his siege artillery which had become bogged down. Pausing briefly at Knightsbridge to rest, his forces left Hyde Park at 9 a.m. on 7 February. The queen's troops were commanded by William Herbert, earl of Pembroke, the foremost military commander in England, whose cavalry had been placed on Holborn, with two battalions of infantry lower down by Charing Cross. Some observers doubted the loyalty of the queen's commanders, as they apparently let Wyatt advance unmolested. There was undoubtedly some disarray among the government forces. An attack by the lord chamberlain, Sir John Gage, on Wyatt's forces at Charing Cross was repulsed, and the detachment of rebels under Cuthbert Vaughan who turned down towards Westminster caused considerable panic at court, where it was rumoured that Pembroke, a prominent Edwardian himself, had betrayed the queen. But it is unlikely that Pembroke's loyalty wavered at this stage of a disintegrating rebellion; Wyatt was being lured into a trap. The main body of the rebels moved along Fleet Street claiming loyalty to the queen, to the amazement of citizens who stood staring in their doorways. But Ludgate was barred against Wyatt by Lord William Howard, and he was forced to turn back towards Temple Bar to face Pembroke's cavalry. After some resistance, a herald appeared and asked Wyatt to surrender rather than cause further unnecessary bloodshed, and he complied, delivering himself into the custody of Sir Maurice Berkeley.

Wyatt was not arraigned until 15 March, the delay perhaps being explained by the government's efforts to gather information implicating Elizabeth. At the trial he stood firm in the claim that he had not conspired the queen's death: 'myne hole intent and styrre was agaynst the comyng in of strangers and Spanyerds and to abolyshe theym out of this realme' (Nichols, *Chronicle*, 69); and he strongly denied Elizabeth's involvement. His defence may have moved some of Mary's closest supporters, for the family tradition records that Sir Edward Hastings, master of the horse, petitioned the queen to show mercy. Wyatt went to the block on 11 April 1554. His scaffold speech showed the penitence customary on such occasions, as God had given his judgment against the rebellion, but he was determined to exculpate Courtenay and Elizabeth. He was interrupted by Dr Hugh Weston who alleged that Wyatt's previous testimony to the privy council (probably obtained under torture) contradicted this. But the government's attempt to manipulate the theatre of the scaffold backfired. Weston was widely criticized for his action; many dipped their handkerchieves in Wyatt's blood; and within a few days his head had been stolen as a martyr's relic.

Wyatt's family was threatened with poverty by his rebellion. His marriage had been fruitful. There were at least four sons and three daughters. Two of the sons were dead by 1555; another, Arthur, died before reaching his majority; Wyatt's heir was therefore George *Wyatt (1553–1624), born a few days before his father's rebellion. To George Wyatt's filial piety are owed the family recollections. Of the daughters, Mary died unmarried, Jane married Charles Scott of Egerton, Kent, and Anne married Roger Twisden. Although most of Wyatt's estate was distributed among those responsible for the suppression of the rising, Mary showed some compassion towards the widow. She received an annuity of 200 marks, and a small residue of the estate valued at £64 14s. 7d. per annum was granted to her in December 1555. The attainder was not reversed until 1570, and George Wyatt was never able to recover the family's position in county society.

Motives Wyatt's motives soon became the subject of polemics between protestants and Catholics. John Proctor, the Catholic schoolmaster of Tonbridge, published an account of the rebellion, *The Historie of Wyates Rebellion*, which stressed Wyatt's duplicity in concealing both his desire to displace Mary and his religious motives. His desire to prove the connection between heresy and sedition was strengthened by the fact that the rebellion had failed, for God had thereby shown his judgment on the religious foe. Proctor's version was repeated by later Catholic writers like Nicholas Sander in his *De origine ac progressu schismaticis Anglicani liber* (1585). For Elizabethan protestants it was essential to play down the religious motivations, because the regime was embarrassed by any association between the godly cause and rebellion. Wyatt's own son repeatedly emphasized that the rebellion had no religious motivation, and it was a version of affairs which passed on to the stage in the play by Thomas Dekker, *The Famous History of Sir Thomas Wyat* (first performed in 1602 and printed in 1607).

It is true that Wyatt's propaganda played down protestantism. When one of his supporters expressed the hope that he would restore protestantism, Wyatt is said to have replied, 'you may not so much as name religion, for that will withdraw from us the hearts of many. You must make your only quarrel for overrunning by strangers' (Proctor, 210). It is also true that many protestants refused to support the rising. Wyatt's reticence about the cause of religion was probably tactical. He was part of a co-ordinated movement which hoped to mobilize support in areas not normally regarded as being in the vanguard of protestantism. Of Wyatt's own beliefs the evidence is thin, but there is little sign of conservative sympathies, and much circumstantial evidence of his support for the evangelical cause. His father's sympathies had been with the reformers; Wyatt had married into the protestant network centred on the Hautes; and most of his fellow conspirators were decidedly evangelical in outlook. It is clear that the Kent evangelical network was mobilized in the course of the rebellion: a key recruiting agent in the Medway valley was William Tilden, a prominent protestant and jurat of Maidstone. Moreover, the actions of the rebels in Southwark are suggestive of where their sympathies lay. Wyatt sent one of his chaplains to the Marshalsea prison and, according to Thomas Mountain, offered to 'set … at libertye so manye as laye for relygyon: with the reste he wolde not medylle' (Nichols, *Narratives*, 185). It is probably unwise to try to disentangle the religious and secular motives: in the eyes of evangelicals the marriage would strengthen the forces of Catholic reaction, but they thought that they could tap a more widespread popular hostility. Doubtless John Foxe was not wide of the mark when he explained that the marriage 'was very evil taken of the people, and of many of the nobility, who for this and for religion ... made a rebellion' (*Acts and Monuments*, 6.413).   IAN W. ARCHER

Sources J. G. Nichols, ed., *The chronicle of Queen Jane, and of two years of Queen Mary*, CS, old ser., 48 (1850) · J. Proctor, 'The history of Wyatt's rebellion', *Tudor tracts, 1532–1588*, ed. A. F. Pollard (1903), 207–57; repr. (1964) · *The papers of George Wyatt, esquire, of Boxley Abbey in the county of Kent*, ed. D. M. Loades, CS, 4th ser., 5 (1968) · D. MacCulloch, 'The *Vita Mariae Angliae Reginae* of Robert Wingfield of Brantham', *Camden miscellany*, XXVIII, CS, 4th ser., 29 (1984), 181–301 · *CSP Spain*, 1553–4 · R. A. de Vertot, ed., *Ambassades de Messieurs de Noailles en Angleterre*, 5 vols. (Leiden, 1763) · *The works of Henry Howard, earl of Surrey, and of Sir Thomas Wyatt the elder*, ed. G. F. Nott, 2 vols. (1815–16) · *LP Henry VIII*, 20/2, no. 461 · *HoP, Commons, 1509–58*, 3.670–72 · D. Loades, *Two Tudor conspiracies*, 2nd edn (1992) · P. Clark, *English provincial society from the Reformation to the revolution: religion, politics and society in Kent, 1500–1640* (1977) · M. R. Thorp, 'Religion and the Wyatt rebellion of 1554', *Church History*, 47 (1978), 363–80 · S. Brigden, *London and the Reformation* (1989) · W. B. Robison, 'The national and local significance of Wyatt's rebellion in Surrey', *HJ*, 30 (1987), 769–90 · J. G. Nichols, ed., *Narratives of the days of the Reformation*, CS, old ser., 77 (1859) · *The acts and monuments of John Foxe*, ed. S. R. Cattley, 8 vols. (1837–41) · R. Strong, *Tudor and Jacobean portraits*, 2 vols. (1969) · *CPR, 1547–58* · *The dramatic works of Thomas Dekker*, ed. F. Bowers, 4 vols. (1953–61), 1.397–459

Archives BL, papers, loan MS 15 · BL, papers relating to trial of followers, Add. Ch. 76667–76670

Likenesses oils, *c.*1545–1550, priv. coll. · oils, *c.*1545–1550, priv. coll.; repro. in Strong, *Portraits*, pl. 674–5 · oils, second version, *c.*1550, NPG [*see illus.*]

Wyatt, Thomas (*bap.* **1795**, *d.* **1859**). *See under* Wyatt, Henry (1794–1840).

Wyatt, Thomas Henry (1807–1880), architect, was born on 9 May 1807 at Lough-Glin House, co. Roscommon, the eldest son of Matthew Wyatt (1773–1831), barrister and police magistrate for Lambeth and Roscommon, and his wife, Anne Hillier of Devizes, Wiltshire. Sir Matthew Digby *Wyatt was his youngest brother. In preparation for a mercantile career he was sent to Malta 'to learn the beauties of cottons, coffee and calicoes' (*The Builder*), but when he returned to Britain a preference for architecture led to his being placed in the office of Philip Charles Hardwick. While there he is reputed to have helped with the designs for the Goldsmiths' Hall, Euston Station, and the warehouses at St Katharine's docks, where Thomas Telford was the engineer. On leaving Hardwick in 1832 to begin practice on his own account he secured the appointment of district surveyor for Hackney, a post which he held until 1861. While a young man he married his first cousin Arabella Montagu Wyatt (1807–1875), the second daughter of his uncle Arthur, who was agent to the duke of Beaufort. They were among eight Wyatts in that generation who married their cousins. They had two sons, Matthew (1840–1892) and Thomas Henry junior; the former followed his father's profession, and was the last of the architect Wyatts.

In 1838, so greatly had Wyatt's practice prospered under a number of patrons, among whom were the duke of Beaufort, the earl of Denbigh, and Sidney Herbert, that he took as partner David Brandon, with whom during a connection of thirteen years he designed the assize courts at Cambridge, Brecon, and Usk, the Wiltshire and Buckinghamshire lunatic asylums, many private houses, and the railway station in Florence. He then worked independently until about 1860, when he took his son Matthew into the practice. He also had many assistants and pupils, including Stephen Salter and Henry Pope. At the time he received the RIBA gold medal in 1873, he paid tribute to his helpers: 'No-one can know as well as I do how much I am indebted to others for what there is of interest in those works—I mean to faithful and attached assistants' (*RIBA Minutes*, 1873). In forty-eight years of practice he designed over 400 buildings. His finest extant work is the church at Wilton (1840–45), an ambitious essay in the Italian basilican or Lombardic style and the largest Anglican church to have been built for a hundred years. The exterior was derived from the churches of Santa Maria and San Pietro in Toscanello, and the interior inspired by San Clemente and other early basilicas in Rome. In collaboration with his brother Sir Matthew Digby Wyatt, he designed the garrison chapel at Woolwich, also in an Italianate basilican manner, but this was largely destroyed in the Second World War.

Thomas Henry Wyatt rose to the top of the architectural profession. His efficient office was able to turn out designs for every occasion. As well as numerous private commissions he played a prominent part in public architectural affairs, and he acquired numerous official appointments. He was honorary architect to the Institution of Civil Engineers, the Athenaeum, and the Governesses' Benevolent Institution. As an acknowledged authority on hospital construction, he was appointed honorary architect to the Middlesex Hospital and consulting architect to the lunacy commissioners, and designed the Stockwell Fever Hospital and two large hospitals in Malta. He also held the post of consulting architect to the Incorporated Church Building Society and to the Salisbury diocese and was connected as designer or restorer with more than 150 churches. Although not in the absolute top rank of Victorian Gothic architects, his churches are nevertheless of consistent quality and form a microcosm of English ecclesiastical building between 1830 and 1880. The series of Wiltshire estate churches of the 1860s and 1870s—Savernake, Hindon, Fonthill Gifford, Semley, and Bemerton—are all effective designs, impressively composed and ingeniously arranged and executed, regardless of cost, in the best materials. Not only did Wyatt hold an honourable position in the Royal Institute of British Architects, of which he was president from 1870 to 1873, and gold medallist in 1873, but he was also an associate (admitted 1845) of the Institution of Civil Engineers, and served on the council in 1848. He also took an active part in the formation of the Architects' Benevolent Society.

Though failing health precluded full practice in his later years, Wyatt continued to participate actively in his profession almost to the date of his death, which occurred on 5 August 1880 at his home, 77 Great Russell Street, London. He left an estate valued at under £30,000. He was buried at the church of Weston Patrick, near Basingstoke, which he had rebuilt partly at his own expense and where he had a country house, Weston Corbett House, inherited from his godfather George Green. Although he was not an artist of great originality, most of his work is competent and scholarly and he had a good knowledge of various styles enhanced by travel in Britain and on the continent. He designed with readiness in either the classical or the Gothic manner, and was a good sketcher and able planner, clear-headed in business, and to many of his clients a valued friend. His career was that of the quintessential Victorian professional man: he played his part in the internal politics of the architectural profession, sat on all the committees, and rose to the highest posts and honours, where he presided, according to his *Builder* obituarist, 'with tact, energy and courtesy. He was conciliatory and politic; always modest and a gentleman.' The obituarist conceded, however, that he was not 'a brilliant wit'.

PAUL WATERHOUSE, *rev.* JOHN MARTIN ROBINSON

Sources The Builder, 39 (1880), 193–4 • J. M. Robinson, *The Wyatts: an architectural dynasty* (1979), 216–26 • [W. Papworth], ed., *The dictionary of architecture*, 11 vols. (1853–92) • *The Times* (12 Aug 1880) • C. L. Eastlake, *A history of the Gothic revival* (1872) • C. Olivier, *Wilton church* (1881) • *CGPLA Eng. & Wales* (1880)
Archives CUL, letters to Joseph Bonomi • NRA, priv. coll., designs and corresp. relating to 9 Chesterfield Gardens, London • RIBA BAL, corresp. and accounts relating to RIBA • Yale U. CBA, Paul Mellon collection | RIBA BAL, list of works in partnership with David Brandon
Likenesses G. Richmond, pencil drawing, exh. RA 1878, RIBA • G. Landseer, oils, NPG • attrib. G. Richmond, chalk drawing, RIBA • G. Richmond, oils, RIBA
Wealth at death under £30,000: probate, 6 Sept 1880, *CGPLA Eng. & Wales*

Wyatt, William (1622/3–1685), Church of England clergyman and schoolmaster, was born at Todenham, near Moreton in Marsh, Gloucestershire, one of at least three sons of William Wyat. He matriculated aged fifteen from St John's College, Oxford, on 16 March 1638, but did not graduate, according to Anthony Wood, because of the outbreak of the civil war. It is not known when he left Oxford. Doubtless through college connections he became acquainted with two protégés of Archbishop William Laud, William Nicholson, rector of Llandeilo Fawr, Carmarthenshire, and a noted teacher, and Jeremy Taylor, who was in Oxford in 1642 as a royal chaplain. Probably in 1645 the three men set up a school at Newton Hall, near Llanfihangel Aberbythych, also in Carmarthenshire. In collaboration with Taylor, Wyatt published *A New and Easie Institution of Grammar* (1647), with a dedication in Latin by Wyatt to Sir Christopher Hatton and in English by Taylor to Christopher Hatton, evidently a pupil at the school. Later Wyatt taught at Evesham, Worcestershire, and at William Fuller's private school at Twickenham, Middlesex.

Following the Restoration, Wyatt was created BD at Oxford on 12 September 1661. It was from St Mary Hall, Oxford, where he was perhaps acting as private tutor to an undergraduate, that he wrote on 20 September 1665 with news of the city and university to Richard *Newdigate (1644–1710), a former pupil of Fuller's. When Fuller became bishop of Lincoln in 1667 he made Wyatt his chaplain. Installed as precentor of Lincoln Cathedral on 6 November that year, Wyatt was collated to the prebend of Liddington on 22 April 1668, although not installed until 31 December. His talents as a schoolmaster were still in demand, however. From about 1680 he lived mostly at Astley Castle, near Nuneaton, Warwickshire, as tutor to the Newdigate family, whose seat was a mile away at Arbury Hall. Juliana, Lady Newdigate, left £5 to Wyatt, 'the diligent and industrious instructor of my son Newdigats children' (Warks. CRO, CR 136, C1956), in her will drafted on 6 August 1681. Having resigned his precentorship on 21 February 1682, Wyatt was often at Arbury in company with Sir Richard and by 1683 had the care of all four of his sons. He died at Arbury Hall on 9 September 1685 and was buried at Astley church. He had apparently never married: in his will, dated from Astley on 30 April 1684, he left token sums to his brother George and family, £50 each to the daughters of his deceased brother Richard, and the residue to Richard's son William of Stow on the Wold.

VIVIENNE LARMINIE

Sources Foster, *Alum. Oxon.* • Wood, *Ath. Oxon.: Fasti* (1820), 254 • *Fasti Angl., 1541–1857*, [Lincoln], 25, 88, 140 • R. E. A. Willmott, *Bishop Jeremy Taylor* (1848), 121 • H. K. Bonney, *The life of … Jeremy Taylor* (1815), 42–8 • letter to Richard Newdigate, Warks. CRO, CR136, B534 • will, PRO, PROB 11/381, sig. 144 • E. Gooder, *The squire of Arbury: Sir Richard Newdigate, second baronet, 1644–1710, and his family* (1990) • Lady Newdigate-Newdegate [A. E. Garnier], *Cavalier and puritan in the days of the Stuarts* (1901)

Wyatt, Woodrow Lyle, Baron Wyatt of Weeford (1918–1997), politician and journalist, was born on 4 July 1918 at Milbourne Lodge, Esher, Surrey, the second son and last child of Robert Harvey Lyle Wyatt, preparatory school headmaster, and his wife, Ethel, *née* Morgan, of Cardiff. He owed his first name to the fact that he was born on American independence day—indeed, his mother wrote to the then president of the United States, Woodrow Wilson, asking him to be godfather to her child (a request that was declined, if politely and at copious length). After attending his father's school, Milbourne Lodge, he was sent to Eastbourne College, where it was thought the sea air would do him good: he had suffered from glandular trouble as a young boy. From Eastbourne College, where he did not distinguish himself, he went up to Worcester College, Oxford, where he read jurisprudence and obtained a second-class degree in 1939.

After leaving Oxford he began to prepare for taking the bar finals in the spring of 1940, but the Second World War intervened and instead he volunteered for the army. Commissioned into the Suffolk regiment, by 1942 he had become a staff captain (later major) attached to 185th infantry brigade. As a staff officer with 3rd division he took part in the Normandy invasion of June 1944 (and was mentioned in dispatches) but, after launching an official complaint against his immediate superior, was posted to India. Before arriving in Bombay in January 1945 he had already used his embarkation leave to get himself selected in November 1944 as prospective Labour candidate for the Aston division of Birmingham (his only rival at the selection conference was the future Labour chancellor of the exchequer, Roy Jenkins). He duly won at Aston in the Labour landslide of 1945. At the age of twenty-seven he found himself one of the 253 new Labour MPs and almost immediately set about trying to make his own distinctive mark. His first attempt to do so was to cause him some embarrassment in his later, more right-wing days. It came in the form of a letter published in the *New Statesman and Nation* in which the second youngest Labour MP announced that 'at present the country is far to the left of Labour Ministers' and went on to pose the question: 'What is the point of having an orderly revolution if it turns out not to be a revolution at all?' (M. Sissons, *Age of Austerity*, 1986, 11).

Short, stocky, and seldom without a bow-tie and a large cigar, Wyatt started on the left wing of the Labour Party. In the spring of 1947 he was one of the fifteen back-bench MPs to sign the famous *Keep Left* pamphlet. That same year he joined the staff of the *New Statesman and Nation*, but graduated some fifteen months later to working for the then more loyalist *Tribune*. According to his own account, by the end of 1948 he had come to see that the left's 'constant carping' against the Labour government was proving unproductive (Wyatt, *Into the Dangerous World*, 173). He became a supporter of rearmament in face of the Soviet threat and his interest in defence brought him his first, and only, ministerial post as under-secretary and financial secretary at the War Office in the last months of the Attlee government, between April and October 1951.

When, after the electoral defeat of October 1951, the Bevanite split in the Labour Party widened, Wyatt strongly supported the leadership. This caused him trouble locally, and in 1955 he was beaten for the nomination in his slightly redistributed constituency. He fought instead the marginal Conservative seat of Grantham, which he did not win. This turned out to be something of a blessing in disguise. An American television network had made a documentary about that particular contest and, by chance, it was seen by a BBC television executive, Grace Wyndham Goldie. As a result, Wyatt was recruited to the BBC flagship programme *Panorama*, and over the next four years—particularly in his exposure of communist electoral malpractices in the electricians' trade union—he made a much greater impact than he had ever done in parliament. By 1959, thanks largely to the support of his mentor the new Labour leader, Hugh Gaitskell, Wyatt was back in the Commons as Labour MP for Bosworth, though even Gaitskell could not overcome his chief whip's veto against having him as a front-bench spokesman. When Gaitskell died in January 1963, it meant the end of all Wyatt's political dreams. He was offered no post in Harold Wilson's Labour government of 1964 and for his last six years in the Commons (until his defeat in the 1970 general election) he belonged unrepentantly to the Parliamentary Labour Party's 'awkward squad'.

By the early 1960s Wyatt had, however, launched a second career for himself—initially as a newspaper publisher (he introduced web-offset colour printing to Britain in a chain of local papers he owned in the midlands) and, when that pioneering enterprise failed, as a newspaper columnist of trenchant and forthright views. It was his role here—from 1973 to 1983 in the *Sunday Mirror* and then from 1983 until his death as the self-styled Voice of Reason in the *News of the World*—that enabled him still to exercise some influence in the political world. He was an early supporter of Margaret Thatcher and she, in turn, rewarded him by keeping him in office as chairman of the Horserace Totalisator Board (a post to which Roy Jenkins had appointed him in 1976), by conferring a knighthood upon him in 1983, and by creating him a life peer in 1987. In the House of Lords, Wyatt sat on the cross-benches, but that scarcely disguised his role as chief cheerleader in the press for the Conservative government, at least so long as it was headed by Mrs Thatcher.

Wyatt was a prolific author, though mainly of works of only transient interest. He wrote two volumes of autobiography, *Into the Dangerous World* (1952) and *Confessions of an Optimist* (1985). His reputation was not enhanced by the posthumous publication from 1998 of three volumes of his *Journals*. These covered merely his life on the periphery of politics from 1985 but—through their wounding references to supposed friends and their brazen breaches of even royal confidences—provoked widespread outrage.

Wyatt was four times married. In August 1939 he married an Oxford contemporary, Susan Cox (*b.* 1917). She left him in 1941, and the marriage was dissolved in 1944. In 1948 he married his secretary, Nora (Alix) Robbins, from whom he was divorced in 1956. On 22 June 1957 he married Lady Moorea Hastings (*b.* 1928), eldest daughter of the fifteenth earl of Huntingdon and his first wife, Cristina, daughter of the Marchese Casati, of Rome; they had a son. This marriage was dissolved in 1966. In December that year he married a Hungarian, Veronica (Verushka), *née* Racz, widow of Baron Dr Laszlo Banszky von Ambroz; they had a daughter. Wyatt died of cancer of the throat in a London hospital on 7 December 1997. He was survived by his wife and his two children.   ANTHONY HOWARD

Sources W. Wyatt, *Into the dangerous world* (1952) · W. Wyatt, *Confessions of an optimist* (1985) · *The journals of Woodrow Wyatt*, ed. S. Curtis, 3 vols. (1998–2000) · R. Jenkins, address at Woodrow Wyatt's memorial service, 1998, Oxford University Press, Oxford DNB archives · *The Times* (9 Dec 1997) · *The Independent* (9 Dec 1997) · *The Guardian* (9 Dec 1997) · *Daily Telegraph* (8 Dec 1997) · personal knowledge (2004) · *WWW* · Burke, *Peerage*

Archives Bodl. Oxf., corresp. and papers · Bodl. RH, corresp. on colonial issues, MS Brit. emp. s. 365 | HLRO, corresp. with Lord Beaverbrook, BBK C/332 · King's Lond., corresp. with Sir B. H. Liddell Hart

Likenesses J. Bratby, portrait, repro. in Wyatt, *Confessions*, jacket · photograph, repro. in *The Times* · photograph, repro. in *The Independent* · photograph, repro. in *The Guardian* · photograph, repro. in *Daily Telegraph*

Wealth at death £1,330,468: probate, 16 July 1998, CGPLA Eng. & Wales

Wyatville [*formerly* Wyatt], **Sir Jeffry** (1766–1840), architect, was born on 3 August 1766 at Burton upon Trent, Staffordshire, the second son of Joseph Wyatt (1739–1785) and his cousin Myrtilla Wyatt (*c*.1743–1766). His father was a member of the Wyatt dynasty of architects, surveyors, builders, sculptors, painters, and engineers, the son of Benjamin Wyatt (1709–1772), but he was one of the less distinguished, although he practised in a small way in Burton upon Trent and was employed as a stonemason on some contracts. After his first wife's death in 1766 Joseph married Mary Fortescue (*d*. 1790).

Education and early professional practice Jeffry Wyatt attended the sixteenth-century grammar school in his native town, and he intended to embark on a naval career as soon as he was old enough; but *c*.1785, the year in which his father died, he was taken into the London office of his architect uncle Samuel *Wyatt (1737–1807) at 63 Berwick Street. He served an apprenticeship of seven years, during which time, according to the *Gentleman's Magazine*, he acquired 'considerable knowledge of the ordinary business, and of practical construction', and had 'opportunities of witnessing all the processes of designing, estimating and executing buildings of various kinds' (*GM*, 545). This wide experience of both architectural design and building organization was to stand Jeffry Wyatt in good stead later; but before setting up on his own account he entered the office of his better-known uncle James *Wyatt (1746–1813) in Queen Anne Street in 1792. By this time James had become the most fashionable of London architects, with a large number of commissions, especially for country houses, which were to become a speciality of Jeffry's work. In 1795 James became a Royal Academician, and in the following year he was appointed surveyor-general and comptroller of the office of works.

In his prosperous middle age Jeffry remembered that 'When, in my younger days, I found there was a Surveyor-General of His Majesty's Works, and such a desirable thing as being a Royal Academician, I set out with a view to succeed to both, if I could' (select committee report, 1828, 99). But when he left his uncle's office in 1798 he took a step that was unlikely to lead to either by entering into partnership with John Armstrong, a prosperous London carpenter and building contractor in Avery Row, off the fashionable Lower Brook Street. Armstrong died in 1803 and Jeffry then carried on the profitable business until 1824. This provided a source of income which 'enabled him to practice architecture with great independence' (Ashton, i–ii), although it was also the reason why his ambition to be a Royal Academician was frustrated until 1824, since what had been a traditional blurring of the distinction between architectural practice and building contracting was becoming increasingly questioned. In 1809 John Soane publicly criticized those architects who chose to 'lose that high distinction and degrade themselves and the Profession by becoming contractors' (D. Watkin, *Sir John Soane: Enlightenment Thought and the Royal Academy Lectures*, 1996, 499–500). But if Jeffry Wyatt's decision was to be a disadvantage in one respect, it was to give a special character to his architectural practice.

Sir Jeffry Wyatville [Wyatt] (1766–1840), by Sir Thomas Lawrence, begun *c*.1828

Marriage and outline of career About 1800 Jeffry Wyatt married Sophia Powell (1775–1810). They had three children: George Geoffrey (1804–1833) was destined to be an architect, but he predeceased his father; Augusta Sophia (1803–1825) also died young; Emma Sophia (1801–1883) was the only survivor.

The earliest known portrait of Jeffry Wyatt, painted by a cousin, Henry Wyatt (1794–1848), about 1820, epitomizes his achievements at that time, not so much by the representation of a successful man with his family as on the reverse. Here are listed, in strict order of precedence, the names of his patrons. His greatest triumphs were to come, but half-way through his career he had arrived at a satisfying total of four dukes, one marquess, seven earls, one baron, three baronets, one general, and several distinguished but untitled gentlemen. These included great landowners, collectors, and men of taste. By the time he died he could have claimed he had worked for four sovereigns, seven dukes, three marquesses, seventeen earls, three barons, five baronets, four knights, a foreign duke, and a count, and well over thirty other distinguished gentlemen. However, an examination of the list of town and country houses on which he worked shows that only about one-fifth were for completely new buildings. The larger number were for additions, remodelling, alterations, or for estate and garden buildings. He was working at a time when the improvement of properties had become almost an obsession in order to answer new demands for comfort and convenience, or to express an advancement in the aristocratic hierarchy. Jeffry Wyatt was the ideal man to meet these requirements. He was a well-trained architect, a skilled presenter of proposed improvements which, especially in his later years, showed a sympathetic regard for the character of the house on which he was operating, and a man who was conversant with the technical practicalities of improvement schemes. 'Many of the comforts of life are heightened by the convenience of our mansions', wrote John Soane, and 'we look with pleasure on each man's improvements, and feel real satisfaction at the sight of every well-contrived and ingenious design, where beauty, elegance and convenience unite' (*Plans, Elevations and Sections of Buildings*, 1788, 5). Among the leading architects, Jeffry Wyatt was pre-eminent as an improver. Unlike his uncle James, who acquired a bad reputation on account of his lack of organization and failure to meet his clients' requirements, he was a responsible administrator with personal control of his office and site works. Every drawing was examined and signed.

Important commissions   Jeffry Wyatt was also the quintessential Regency architect in being able to work in a variety of styles, and in his first important commission he demonstrated his facility in that respect. In 1800 he was making designs for Longleat House, Wiltshire, for the second marquess of Bath. The house, according to John Britton, was 'inconvenient, incommodious, and badly arranged' behind the deceptively regular façades (*Architectural Antiquities*, 1809, 2.114). A large part of the north wing either had not been built or had been destroyed in a fire, and in reconstructing this Jeffry sympathetically followed the original design of the exterior 'in the style of the house'. Internally, however, almost all the main rooms were remodelled as comfortable Regency interiors (largely redecorated later between 1876 and 1882 by John Dibblee Crace). The most interesting aspect of the work at Longleat, however, is in the additional buildings, the stables, the lodges, and the conservatory, which were designed to complement the Elizabethan classicism of the house itself. These buildings are unusual in their confident use of late sixteenth-century form and ornament, presenting it as a very early example of an alternative to classicism and Gothic, which was to become popular later in the nineteenth century.

At the same time as he was working at Longleat, Jeffry Wyatt was carrying out similar projects on another great Elizabethan mansion, Wollaton Hall, Nottinghamshire, for the sixth Baron Middleton. In 1809 John Britton referred to 'the recent alterations which have been made and designed by Mr. Jeffry Wyatt, who has manifested much skill in converting the interior of old, ill-arranged mansions, to the present, and more comfortable modes of domestic life' (*Architectural Antiquities*, 2.116). Here, too, there was an almost complete internal remodelling although, as at Longleat, the great hall was allowed to remain; but the additional buildings, including the later Lenton Lodge (1823–5), were Elizabethan in style.

Early commissions for villas and country houses were realized in either a Gothic or a classical style, following a Wyatt family pattern. They were symmetrical, often with a central segmental bow. Hillfield Lodge, Hertfordshire (*c.*1799), for the Hon. George Villiers, was Gothic, and Woolley Park, Berkshire (*c.*1799), for the Revd Philip Wroughton, was classical; but the plans were very similar. They were comfortable Regency residences, but they also displayed a Picturesque character in the extension to one side of the house itself, which gave a degree of fashionable irregularity to the composition; it was to be a characteristic of his work, even in some unlikely commissions. It was most clearly expressed for the first time in Wyatt's design for Endsleigh, the *cottage orné* built in Devon from 1810 onwards for the sixth duke of Bedford. According to an inscription in the stable, the site had been chosen 'for the natural and picturesque beauties which surround it', and the group of rooms which form the building was designed for aspect and to suit the contours. In doing so, Jeffry Wyatt was consciously or unconsciously following the thought of Uvedale Price that the architect should 'do what has so seldom been done—accommodate his building to the scenery, not make that give way to the building' (U. Price, *Essays on the Picturesque*, 1798, 306ff.). The articulated plan of Endsleigh allowed a greater freedom than usual in adapting the building to the site, and it produced a varied massing and irregular outline.

The influence of Endsleigh and the Picturesque may be followed through most of Jeffry's later works, whatever their architectural style. Ashridge Park in Hertfordshire was designed by James Wyatt for the seventh earl of Bridgewater and building began in 1808. The house itself was symmetrical around a high staircase hall, although there was a degree of irregularity since the chapel was placed to one side and connected by a cloister. When James Wyatt died in 1813, Jeffry was appointed architect and he turned the keeplike Tudor Gothic mansion into a Picturesque composition by designing wings which broke in and out, following the contours and softening the outline of the group while adding a skyline of towers and battlements. He also showed at Ashridge how well he could detail Gothic buildings; his completion of the interior of the chapel was a serious contribution to the early Gothic revival. John Britton wrote that 'as he had studied the subject well, and was influenced by zeal, industry and knowledge, it is reasonably inferred that some of the best features of the building are to be ascribed to him' (*Graphic Illustrations of Toddington, Gloucestershire*, 1840, 18ff.). At Ashridge, Jeffry also made a major contribution to the development of the gardens following the death in 1818 of Humphry Repton.

Jeffry Wyatt made large additions and alterations, externally and internally, to such houses as Bretton Hall, Yorkshire (1811–14), for Colonel Beaumont, where he also built a camellia house, one of the group of impressive garden buildings which included those at Longleat (*c.*1814), and Belton House, Lincolnshire (1811–19). He also made designs for similar conservatories and orangeries at Thoresby House, Nottinghamshire, and at Woolley Hall, Yorkshire (1824). At Woburn Abbey, Bedfordshire, he adapted Henry Holland's greenhouse (1789) for the sixth duke of Bedford as a sculpture gallery (1816), to which at one end he added the Temple of Graces to receive Canova's famous group. He continued to design new houses in appropriate styles (as listed in Colvin, *Archs.* and Linstrum, *Sir Jeffry Wyatville*): Banner Cross, near Sheffield, Yorkshire (1817–21), for General Murray, was Tudor Gothic and irregular to suit its elevated site overlooking a valley, while Claverton Manor, near Bath, Wiltshire, for George Vivian, was symmetrical and conformed to the character of the spa town's classicism. A pair of designs, Lilleshall Hall, Shropshire (*c.*1824), for Lord Gower, and Golden Grove, Carmarthenshire (*c.*1826–1834), for the second Baron Cawdor, were Picturesque in plan and a modified, rather austere Elizabethan in character. Possibly these two houses were to some extent the work of Henry Ashton, who had entered the office *c.*1824; Jeffry Wyatt himself was occupied with the two great works of his career by the time they were being built.

Chatsworth On 16 January 1818 Jeffry Wyatt was able to write that he was on his way 'to Chatsworth to receive the Duke of Devonshire's Ideas respecting a general plan of improvement which he intends by slow degrees to proceed with, at such time as may suit him hereafter' (JRL, Bagshawe MS 6/1/361). It was a modest way of outlining the work of the next twenty years, which was described on the title-page of Jeffry's manuscript book of designs as 'formed on the Principle of adhering to the Character of the present building, of gaining all the required advantages and adding to the grandeur of the place' (Chatsworth, Devonshire collection, Wyatville drawings and MSS). It was a typical Wyatt improvement, but on a larger and more magnificent scale than any he had previously attempted. The circulation inside the house was improved, and the exterior, which consisted of four elevations designed at different times and curiously unrelated in many respects, was partly remodelled to add a uniformity of design, anticipating the later Italianate style popularized by Sir Charles Barry. But the whole appearance of the house was changed into a Picturesque composition by the addition of the long north wing ending with the massive Theatre Tower crowned by an open belvedere.

The sixth duke of Devonshire, Jeffry's munificent patron, condemned the state rooms in the house as 'this dismal ponderous range of Hampton Court like chambers' (Cavendish, 119), and commissioned a superb Regency substitute. The old long gallery was remodelled as a library, which was the beginning of the long suite which continued in an ante-library, a sophisticated domed library, a coffered dining-room, a sculpture gallery which ultimately contained seven Canovas, an orangery, and finally a theatre or ballroom, over which was built the large open belvedere that was so important visually in the new Chatsworth.

Windsor Castle The duke left a vivid description of his architect, 'a delightful man, good, simple like a child, eager, patient, easy to deal with to the highest degree' (Cavendish, 238). He was amused by Wyatt's straightforward manner of speaking his mind, and by his odd dialect, which seems to have been a cross between Staffordshire

and cockney; but he wondered, in 1823, how George IV might react to this man who refused to play the courtier even though he loved titles. The most comfort-loving of monarchs required major improvements in Windsor Castle after his accession in 1820, and the three 'attached architects' to the office of works (John Soane, John Nash, and Robert Smirke) were invited to submit designs; so was Jeffry Wyatt, thanks to the duke of Devonshire, who recommended him to the king. In 1824 Jeffry's design was selected, and he was given the Winchester Tower as his official residence; his office continued to work from his London address, 49 (now 39) Lower Brook Street. In the same year, on 9 December, the king signed a document authorizing the change of surname to Wyatville, and on 9 December 1828 he was knighted. Wyatville thought that although the historic castle was 'altogether an imposing and grand mass of building, it does not abound with picturesque parts' (Windsor, Royal Library, J. Wyatville drawings and MSS), and the programme of work, like that on so many of Wyatville's commissions, was twofold in purpose. It was intended both to improve and to add comfort to living in the castle, but equally to increase its picturesqueness. New state rooms were created, and the circulation was improved by the building of the 520 feet long gallery which also served as a background against which to display part of the Royal Collection. The new interiors followed the king's taste, and they varied in style from the Gothic St George's Hall and the dining-room, the 'Louis Quatorze' state reception room, and the opulent suite of white, crimson, and green drawing-rooms, to the Waterloo Chamber, which is difficult to describe stylistically.

The extensive work at Windsor has been described in detail by Linstrum and Colvin. Externally, picturesque views from gateways were contrived, and the stark character was romanticized by the addition of towers and bays, machicolations and crenellations, and by the raising in height of the Round Tower. Wyatville's work represented the ultimate in picturesque improvements and it was greatly admired at the time, even though later critics have been less enthusiastic. After George IV's death in 1830 William IV continued to regard the ageing architect as part of the castle circle, and when Victoria succeeded, Wyatville made his last contribution, the royal stable and riding-house.

Honours and later years When the Institute of British Architects was founded in 1834 Wyatville was immediately made an honorary fellow. In return he presented Rysbrack's model of his statue of Inigo Jones and an allegorical painting of *Architecture* by Antonio Zucchi. On 24 March 1835 it was Wyatville who presented a gold medal to Sir John Soane as 'a tribute of respect from the British architects'. By George IV's command Sir Francis Chantrey's marble bust and Sir Thomas Lawrence's portrait of the architect were placed in Windsor Castle.

Wyatville was elected ARA in 1822 and RA in 1824. He was a fellow of the Royal Society and of the Antiquarian Society, and he received the grand cross of the Saxon Ernestine order from the duke of Saxe-Meiningen, to whom he gave architectural advice on the recommendation of Queen Adelaide. Wyatville died on 18 February 1840 in his London home at 49 (now 39) Lower Brook Street and was buried in the north-east corner behind the altar in St George's Chapel, Windsor, on 25 February 1840. DEREK LINSTRUM

Sources D. Linstrum, *Sir Jeffry Wyatville: architect to the king* (1972) • D. Linstrum, *Catalogue of the drawings collection of the Royal Institute of British Architects: The Wyatt family* (1974) • *GM*, 2nd ser., 13 (1840), 545–59 • [W. Papworth], ed., *The dictionary of architecture*, 11 vols. (1853–92) • sixth duke of Devonshire [W. Cavendish], *Handbook of Chatsworth and Hardwick* (1845) • H. Ashton, *Illustrations of Windsor Castle by the late Sir Jeffry Wyatville, RA* (1841) • J. M. Crook and M. H. Port, eds., *The history of the king's works*, 6 (1973) • 'Select committee on … the office of works and public buildings', *Parl. papers* (1828), 4.315, no. 446 • 'Select committee on the expense of completing the alterations and improvements of Windsor Castle', *Parl. papers* (1830), 9.357, no. 656 • 'Select committee on expenses of Windsor Castle and Buckingham Palace', *Parl. papers* (1831), vol. 4, nos. 272, 329 • W. H. St J. Hope, *Windsor Castle, an architectural history*, 2 vols. (1913) • F. Thompson, *A history of Chatsworth* (1949) • Colvin, *Archs.* • JRL, Bagshawe MS, 6/1/361 • Wyatville drawings and MSS, Chatsworth House, Derbyshire, Devonshire collection • Wyatville drawings and MSS, Royal Library, Windsor

Archives RIBA BAL, architectural sketches and papers | Chatsworth House, Derbyshire, Devonshire collection, drawings and MSS • JRL, Banner Cross building accounts and corresp. • Northants. RO, designs for Kelmarsh rectory • NRA, priv. coll., plans and MSS relating to Cadland • priv. coll., Wyatt family MSS • PRO, letters to J. King, etc. • RIBA BAL, papers relating to the House of Commons • Royal Arch., drawings and MSS • Staffs. RO, plans for alterations to Teddesley Hall

Likenesses H. Wyatt, oils, *c.*1820, priv. coll. • T. Lawrence, oils, begun *c.*1828, Royal Collection [*see illus.*] • R. Westmacott, pencil drawing, *c.*1830, priv. coll. • M. C. Wyatt, watercolour, *c.*1830, priv. coll. • H. Robinson, stipple, pubd 1834 (after R. Evans), BM, NPG • H. Robinson, stipple prints, pubd 1834 (after T. Lawrence), BM, NPG • F. Chantrey, pencil sketches, *c.*1835, NPG • F. Chantrey, marble bust, *c.*1837, Royal Collection

Wealth at death £70,000: 1840, probate act book

Wyche, Sir Cyril (*c.*1632–1707), government official, was born in Constantinople, the second son of Sir Peter *Wyche or Wych (*d.* 1643) of London and his wife, Jane (*d.* 1660), daughter of Sir William Meredith of Stansty, Denbighshire. His elder brother was Peter *Wyche (*b.* 1628, *d.* in or after 1699). Wyche's father, a merchant, served as resident at Portugal and ambassador at Constantinople, and Cyril was named after his godfather, the patriarch of Constantinople. Educated at Westminster School, he matriculated at Christ Church, Oxford, on 27 November 1650 (BA, 1653; MA, 1655), and was created DCL in 1665. In 1657 he entered Gray's Inn, being called to the bar in 1670. He married three times: in 1663 he wed Elizabeth (*d.* 1678), daughter of Sir Thomas Jermyn of Rushbrooke, Suffolk, with whom he had at least two sons and daughters; in 1684 he married Susanna (*d.* 1690), daughter of Sir Francis Norreys of Weston on the Green, Oxford, and widow of Sir Herbert Perrot of Wellington, Herefordshire; his third wife, whom he married in 1692, with a dowry of £6300, was Mary (*d.* 1723), daughter of George Evelyn of Wotton, Surrey, and niece of the diarist John Evelyn. The last two marriages remained childless. Wyche was knighted by Charles II in The Hague in May 1660.

Considered a 'noble learned gentleman' by Evelyn, Wyche was a reliable administrator and served for many years in various government offices. Initially a six clerk in chancery (1662–75), in 1676 he was appointed secretary to the lord lieutenant of Ireland, Arthur, earl of Essex, on whose dismissal in 1677 Wyche became secretary to the new lord lieutenant, James, duke of Ormond, remaining in that post until 1685. While secretary he was appointed to the Irish privy council. Although out of office during James II's reign, Wyche continued to sit in the English House of Commons, having represented the Cornish borough of Callington from 1661 to 1679 and East Grinstead, Sussex, in 1681. In 1685 he was elected for Saltash, also a Cornish borough, and he continued to serve in the house as a court supporter. However, he had little problem accepting the revolution of 1688, which heralded a revival in his government career. Appointed gentleman of the privy chamber in 1690, a post he held until 1702, Wyche became involved once again in Irish affairs in 1692, being appointed secretary to the lord lieutenant, Henry, Lord Sidney, and reappointed to the Irish privy council. He sat as MP for Trinity College, Dublin, in the 1692 Irish parliament. However, despite his long career in government, he also found time to pursue his interest in science, and along with his elder brother, Sir Peter *Wyche, was one of the earliest fellows of the Royal Society, being included among the ninety-eight men elected by the first president and council in 1663. Sir Cyril Wyche served as president of the society in 1683–4, and in 1684 was elected a fellow of the Dublin Philosophical Society. In 1693 he played a leading role in the revival of the Dublin Society, serving as the society's president in that year. At the same time, he had become interested in the development of financial services, acting as a trustee for a mutual society which insured London houses against fire.

Following Sidney's removal as lord lieutenant in 1693 Wyche was appointed one of three lords justices to take over the chief governorship of Ireland. Despite early signs that he and his colleagues, Henry, Lord Capell, and William Duncombe, were managing to overcome the conflicts between the government and political nation which had disrupted William III's affairs during 1690–92, by 1694 they had begun to divide among themselves over the best policy to be pursued in relation to the constitutional conflict over money bills in parliament. Wyche and Duncombe advocated a more conservative policy than that advised by Capell, whose backing among the whig 'junto' in England and positive reports on the potential for a successful Irish parliamentary session won the day, despite his fellow lords justices expressing their surprise that Capell was 'sanguine enough' to believe that the Irish opposition could be brought to an accommodation (BL, Add. MS 21136, fols. 25–6). Removed from office in May 1695, Wyche and Duncombe returned to England, where, at a meeting with the English lords justices, they attacked the government's legislative programme for the forthcoming Irish parliamentary session to be held under Capell's lord deputyship. However, their action only served to convince leading members of the English government that their removal had been a wise decision. Although rumoured to be under consideration for appointment as ambassador at Constantinople that year, Wyche remained out of public affairs for the next few years, until his appointment in 1700 as a trustee for the Irish forfeitures. He returned to Ireland in June 1700, where he remained until 1703, acting as chairman of the trustees, who as a body appear to have regarded him with 'great affection and respect' (Simms, 118). He had been elected MP for Preston in 1702, but was not re-elected in 1705, when he retired to his estates in Norfolk. He died at Hockwold, Norfolk, on 29 December 1707. He was succeeded by his eldest son, Jermyn, whose inheritance was valued at over £100,000.

C. I. McGRATH

Sources HoP, *Commons, 1690–1715* [draft] · NA Ire., Wyche MSS, ser. 1 and 2 · Foster, *Alum. Oxon.* · Wood, *Ath. Oxon.*, new edn, vol. 4 · *Le Neve's Pedigrees of the knights*, ed. G. W. Marshall, Harleian Society, 8 (1873) · Evelyn, *Diary*, vols. 2, 4–5 · T. Thomson, *History of the Royal Society from its institution to the end of the eighteenth century* (1812) · BL, Add. MS 21136 · C. I. McGrath, 'Securing the protestant interest: policy, politics and parliament in Ireland in the aftermath of the Glorious Revolution, 1690–1695', MA diss., University College Dublin, 1991 · C. I. McGrath, 'The Irish revenue system: government and administration, 1689–1702', PhD diss., U. Lond., 1997 · J. G. Simms, *The Williamite confiscation in Ireland, 1690–1703* (1956) · J. R. O'Flanagan, *The lives of the lord chancellors and keepers of the great seal of Ireland*, 1 (1870) · B. M. Crook, 'Wyche, Sir Cyril', HoP, *Commons, 1660–90* · N. Luttrell, *A brief historical relation of state affairs from September 1678 to April 1714*, 2–4, 6 (1857) · R. Lascelles, ed., *Liber munerum publicorum Hiberniae … or, The establishments of Ireland*, later edn, 2 vols. in 7 pts (1852), vol. 1, pt 2 · K. T. Hoppen, *The common scientist in the seventeenth century: a study of the Dublin Philosophical Society, 1683–1708* (1970)

Archives Keele University, corresp. · NA Ire., corresp. and papers · NL Scot., accounts · Norfolk RO, letter-book and accounts · U. Reading, accounts | BL, Southwell MSS, Add. MS 21136 [contains the important letter from Wyche and Duncombe of 14 July 1694 in which they disagreed with Capell over the calling of an Irish parliament]

Likenesses oils, c.1693, NPG

Wealth at death over £100,000: HoP, *Commons*

Wyche, Sir Peter (d. 1643), diplomat, was the sixth son of Richard Wyche (1554–1621), a London merchant, and Elizabeth, daughter of Sir Richard *Saltonstall (1521?–1601). Having gained commercial experience in Spain, he moved into his diplomatic career by acting as an administrative assistant in the English embassy in Madrid. A protégé of the duke of Buckingham, he was knighted in 1626. In or before 1627 he married Jane (d. 1660), daughter of Sir William Meredith of Stansty, Denbighshire; their eldest son, Sir Peter *Wyche (b. 1628, d. in or after 1699), was baptized in London on 9 February 1628. Early in 1627 Wyche was appointed (as the crown's second choice, its first having died) to succeed Sir Thomas Roe as ambassador to the Ottoman Porte. Leaving his wife to follow him later, Wyche set sail in November and in the new year arrived in Constantinople, where he was given a thorough handover by his predecessor, who continued to correspond with him about policy throughout his journey home. He was described by Secretary Windebank as a 'prudent man' (*CSP Venice, 1632–6*, 253, no. 330).

Wyche's main responsibility was to restore the capitulations, the written consent of the Ottoman sultan for English merchants to trade in Ottoman territory which also bestowed on the English community various privileges of status and residence. He claimed that he had done so successfully in 1633, informing the secretary of state that 'no nation passeth so well, nor with so much reputation as the English doth' (PRO, SP 97/15, fol. 184). But the following year he had to fight against renewed efforts by the Ottoman authorities to curtail the privileges enjoyed by the English and other foreign communities in Constantinople. These included raids on merchant houses, and the brief imprisonment of the merchants. Wyche managed to restore most privileges although the merchants complained that weapons confiscated by the Ottoman authorities in the raids were never returned.

During his residence Wyche was preoccupied with protecting merchants in the Mediterranean and in the resident community of English traders in Constantinople. He also had to protect the community against Ottoman reprisals for naval action by the English adventurer Sir Kenelm Digby, whom the Ottoman authorities accused of piracy. Despite the great distance between Constantinople and the English merchant outpost of Aleppo, Wyche had to intervene to win the release of his consul and a number of merchants from that community in the wake of Digby's actions. He also continued his predecessor's policy of trying to encourage the Ottoman authorities to offset Habsburg influence in central Europe.

Wyche was on good terms with the Greek Orthodox church. He hosted the Oxford Arabist Edward Pococke on a research visit to the patriarchate in 1637, and made Patriarch Lukaris godfather to his son Cyril (later Sir Cyril) *Wyche (c.1632–1707). After the patriarch's assassination in 1638, probably connived at by the sultan, who saw him as a threat, Wyche provided letters enabling his Cretan secretary, Nathanial Conopius, to seek asylum in England.

Wyche used his time at the Porte to collect antiquities for King Charles I's collection. He was fiercely competitive over antiquities, noting in a letter to Endymion Porter, the king's collector, that he would send him two statues for 'there are two men in strife for them but I shall decide the differences and take them both from them both' (Townshend). The two men in question were his predecessor, Sir Thomas Roe, and William Petty.

Lady Wyche joined her husband in the autumn of 1628; they had five children during their time in Constantinople. The first of these, Thracia (named for the country in which she was born), arrived in 1630. Wyche claimed that his wife was weakened by breast-feeding 'but no persuasion can alter her minde and wee are confident that God will give a blessing upon so good a resolution' (PRO, SP 97/15, fol. 7). Unfortunately, Thracia did not survive and by the end of 1635 Wyche, whose successor, Sackville Crowe, had been appointed but who was wrangling with the company over his salary, was pleading to be recalled and replaced by a temporary agent to enable him to 'come home in safetie my wyffe and twoe children (twoe others havinge buried heere)' (PRO, SP 97/16, fol. 35). Jane remained weak although she bore two more children. By October 1637 Wyche was making yet more desperate requests to be recalled. In April 1638 he sent Jane and his surviving four children (Jane, Grace, Peter, and Cyril) on to England to petition the king to recall him.

Although Wyche's successor arrived in the autumn of 1638, Wyche was forced to remain until the return of Sultan Murad IV from campaign the following April, when Crowe could be formally accredited to the Porte, and Wyche make his formal farewell. The two men remained at the Porte together for some five months, during which time Wyche was ill. He moved out of the residence and neither negotiated on behalf of the community nor attended functions without asking Crowe's permission, although he gave advice on complex policy issues. Charles I took the unusual step of confirming a joint ambassadorship and ordering both men to share expenses, and this caused animosity between the two which was never fully resolved. When the sultan gave permission for Wyche to depart, his departure was further delayed by an absence of suitable shipping to take him home. He was forced to send express orders to Smyrna to hold all ships for England so that he could join one there.

On his return in 1641 Wyche became a comptroller of the royal household and a privy councillor. His return was marred by a long legal battle with the Levant Company. Wyche had been fighting over his right to claim consulage, the tax claimed by resident consuls from English ships when they freighted goods to Ottoman territories, since his time in Constantinople. The company had argued throughout his residence that it should be free to use the tax for commercial purposes locally. Wyche, like his predecessors, claimed that it was in the king's gift and should be used to defray the costs of maintaining a representative post. Wyche obtained a ruling stating that consulage rights were the king's and he could therefore delegate them to his ambassador, but he could not recoup the money he maintained the company owed him from his residence at the Porte. Despite this setback, he had clearly set by sufficient funds to enable him to act as a financier for the royalist cause in the civil war, although this strained his finances. He signed the king's declaration of abhorrence at the idea of making war on his parliament in 1642, but joined Charles in Oxford, where he died late the following year. He was buried on 7 December in Christ Church Cathedral. LIANE SAUNDERS

Sources PRO, SP 97/15–16 • BL, Sloane MS 856, fol. 13 • BL, Egerton MS 2541 • D. Townshend, *Life and letters of Mr Endymion Porter* (1897) • A. C. Wood, *A history of the Levant Company* (1935) • *CSP Venice, 1632–6* • Burke, *Extinct peerage* • S. Searight, 'The Turkey merchants', *History Today*, 16 (1966), 414–21 • H. R. Trevor-Roper, *Archbishop Laud, 1573–1645*, 2nd edn (1962) • D. Goffman, *Britons in the Ottoman empire, 1642–1660* (1998)
Archives PRO, SP 97/14–16 | BL, Egerton MS 2541 • BL, Sloane MS 856 • Bodl. Oxf., Tanner MS 325

Wyche, Sir Peter (*b.* **1628**, *d.* in or after **1699**), diplomat and translator, was born in 1628 and baptized at St Dunstan-in-the-East, London, on 9 February, the eldest son of Sir Peter *Wyche (*d.* 1643), ambassador to Constantinople, and his wife, Jane Meredith (*d.* 1660). Cyril *Wyche was his younger brother. He matriculated from Exeter College, Oxford, on 6 May 1643, but in October 1644 migrated first to Queens' College, Cambridge, and then to Trinity Hall, from where he graduated BA in 1645 and proceeded MA in 1648. He was admitted to the Inner Temple in November 1649, but subsequently travelled abroad. In May 1656 he was in Italy, where Edward Hyde obtained for him a passport and testimonial signed by Charles II. He was knighted by Charles at The Hague in May 1660.

At the Restoration, Wyche returned to England to find himself with no fortune, his father having substantial unpaid debts due from his service to Charles I, and his mother having bestowed substantial portions on his sister and brothers, one of whom was Sir Cyril *Wyche. Consequently he went to Portugal to serve as paymaster-general to the English forces there. He was back in England by 2 April 1662, when he became one of the early members of the Royal Society. He served on the council of the society in 1663 and 1670, and remained on the list of members until 1693. In January 1665 Wyche became chairman of the society's committee investigating means of improving the English language, a committee which met in his rooms, and received a long letter from John Evelyn at this time. On 19 February 1666 at Lincoln Cathedral he married Isabella (*b.* 1640, *d.* after 1696), daughter of Sir Robert Bolles, baronet, of Scampton, Lincolnshire; she was a dresser to Catherine of Braganza.

Wyche served as a volunteer aboard the fleet during 1666 and was sent back to Portugal by Charles II in November to congratulate King Alfonso VI on his marriage. He returned to England in February 1667, having received high praise for his conduct of the embassy. On 4 February 1669 he was appointed envoy-extraordinary to Russia, and he had an audience with the tsar on 17 June. In October he moved on briefly to Sweden, where he had an audience on 4 October, before continuing to Poland, where he had his audience on 2 January 1670. In 1673 he was secretary to the earl of Peterborough's embassy to France, the empire, and Italy, which culminated in the successful negotiation of the marriage between James, duke of York, and Mary of Modena. He was appointed resident ambassador at Hamburg on 29 October 1678, presenting his credentials there on 16 December. He undertook a special embassy to Denmark in October and November 1679, but otherwise remained at Hamburg until his recall in January 1682.

Wyche's career to this point had owed much to the patronage of Sir Joseph Williamson, who was godfather to his eldest son. He was reappointed to Hamburg on 13 April 1685, serving there until May 1689, and it may have been his overt Roman Catholicism that now commended him more to James II. In January 1686 he wrote to Sir William Trumbull of the persecution of the Huguenots:

You have almost squared my faith to the Book of Martyrs, and by your telling me what is daily acted in the reformation exceeds the reports we have of it, I am to believe the cruelty of Atreus and Medea not fabulous. (*Downshire MSS*, 1.101)

In 1685–6 Wyche was at the centre of the major crisis

that arose when Hamburg's sovereignty was threatened successively by Denmark and Celle. With both sides' troops moving against the city Wyche attempted to preserve the vital English trading interests there, and when the Danes attacked in August 1686 he and James II's ambassador to Denmark (Gabriel Sylvius) worked strenuously as mediators, earning part of the credit for the peaceful settlement that followed. Wyche was also involved in the subsequent dispute between Denmark and the duke of Holstein-Gottorp, expressing James II's support for the latter and at one point informing the duke that, if a war came about, 'the drawn sword (blind as Fortune) does not always open the path of justice' (Jones, 167).

During these crises, as on other occasions, Wyche clearly showed himself to be an efficient diplomat, reporting not only on Hamburg affairs but on those of Germany in general in extremely detailed letters. As his membership of the Royal Society suggests, he was also a man of broad intellectual interests, and an accomplished linguist. He was responsible for two translations of Portuguese works published as *The Life of Dom John de Castro, Fourth Viceroy of India* (1663), dedicated to Charles II's queen, Catherine of Braganza, and *A Short Relation of the River Nile* (1669), translated at the request of a number of members of the Royal Society. Following his return from Russia he produced *Observations on Muscovy* (1670) for the Royal Society. In 1687 he published *The World Geographically Describ'd in Fifty-Two Copper Plates*, which could either be bound or used as cards for teaching purposes.

Sir Peter's once illustrious career ended in obscurity. In the revolution of 1688 he was a vigorous supporter of King James, castigating William of Orange and his motives in his letters. As the outcome of the revolution became more and more apparent Wyche realized that this stance, and his Catholic faith, would be bound to end his diplomatic career. In his final letter from Hamburg to his friend Edmund Poley, written in March 1689, he said of his imminent dismissal that 'I hope I am prepared for the stroke, and shall find some hole where to spend the rest of my life, despairing ever to see my wife and children in England' (BL, Add. MS 45731, fol. 127). The 'hole' that he found was Lisbon, his old stamping ground. From there, on 9 June 1699, he wrote his last extant letter, congratulating an old friend on his promotion and trying to recruit him to the cause of obtaining Wyche's arrears:

> I am not so stupified by my great misfortune (having been stripped of all, and having lived these ten years only on charity, without any assistance offered me from any of my friends, or so many opulent relations) but that I sincerely rejoice when the wheel of fortune runs to my friends. (BL, Add. MS 28903, fol. 267)

Sir Peter's bitterness towards his own family was to be justified in the sequel. When, some forty years later, the 'opulent relations' contributed their family history for Thomas Wotton's survey of the baronetage, they evidently did not have the slightest idea where or when Sir Peter Wyche had died. Wyche and his wife had had at least seven children, two daughters, Mary and Isabella, and five

sons. John (*bap.* 1667, *d.* 1713), the eldest, matriculated from Trinity College, Cambridge, in 1684, was secretary to Sir William Trumbull by 1686, and eventually followed in his father's footsteps by becoming the envoy at Hamburg; his son Cyril was created a baronet in 1729. The remaining three sons who seem to have reached adulthood all became merchants. Peter and George both died unmarried, at Cambrai and Pondicherry respectively; Bernard, a merchant at Surat, was the father of Peter Wyche, high sheriff of Lincolnshire in 1741. J. D. DAVIES

Sources account of the Wyche family, 1741, BL, Add. MS 24121, fols. 353–8 · *CSP dom.*, 1660–89 · W. A. Shaw, ed., *Calendar of treasury books*, [33 vols. in 64], PRO (1904–69), esp. vol. 8 [1685–9] · G. M. Bell, *A handlist of British diplomatic representatives, 1509–1688*, Royal Historical Society Guides and Handbooks, 16 (1990) · PRO, SP 89/11–16 [state papers, Hamburg] · BL, Add. MSS 28875, 28896, 28903 [letters to J. Ellis and others]; 45731 [letters to E. Poley]; 41823–41827 [letters to Lord Middleton] · Foster, *Alum. Oxon.*, 1500–1714, 1.691 · Venn, *Alum. Cant.*, 1/4.481 · F. S. Lachs, *The diplomatic corps under Charles II and James II* (Princeton, 1965) · G. H. Jones, *Charles Middleton: the life and times of a Restoration politician* (Chicago, 1967) · *Report on the manuscripts of the marquis of Downshire*, 6 vols. in 7, HMC, 75 (1924–95), vol. 1 · M. Hunter, *The Royal Society and its fellows, 1660–1700: the morphology of an early scientific institution* (1982) · *The manuscripts of J. M. Heathcote*, HMC, 50 (1899) · *Report on the manuscripts of Allan George Finch*, 5 vols., HMC, 71 (1913–2003), vol. 2 · Evelyn, *Diary*, 3.396 · parish register, London, St Dunstan-in-the-East, LMA, 9 Feb 1628 [baptism]

Archives BL, letters to Lord Conway and William Blathwayt, Add. MS 37982 · BL, letters to John Ellis, Add. MSS 28875–28903 · BL, corresp. with Lord Middleton, Add. MSS 41823–41827 · BL, letters to E. Poley, Add. MS 45731 · BL, letters to Sir William Trumbull · PRO, state papers, Hamburg, SP 89/11–16

Wyche, Richard of [St Richard of Chichester] (*d.* 1253), bishop of Chichester, was born at Droitwich, from which the name Wyche derives, to parents of aristocratic status named Richard and Alice. A bequest in his will to a brother named Robert Chandos links him to the baronial family of Chandos, holders of the honour of Snodhill in Herefordshire. He also had a half-brother named Richard of Bagendon, who held half a knight's fee in Bagendon, Gloucestershire, and was to serve Richard when bishop as his estates steward. Master Nicholas of Wyche, a canon of Chichester, who served in his episcopal household, was also a relative. So too, possibly, was the Master John of Wyche who served with Richard in the household of Archbishop Edmund (*d.* 1240).

Early life and education The chronology of Richard's career before he entered the service of the archbishop of Canterbury is wholly conjectural. According to his confessor and biographer, Ralph *Bocking, he studied arts at a famous *studium generale*, which could be either Paris or Oxford, and then proceeded to study canon law. The other evidence points to Oxford, where he was regent first in arts, and subsequently in canon law, and where, about 1235, he was elected chancellor of the university. In this office he attracted the notice of the archbishop of Canterbury, Edmund of Abingdon, and of the bishop of Lincoln, Robert Grosseteste, who both made a bid to get him as their episcopal chancellor. In fact, he became chancellor to Archbishop Edmund. Although the earliest acts attested by him date from 1237, he probably joined the archbishop's *familia* a year or more before that.

At this period the chancellor was a close confidant and a continuous resident in the archbishop's household. To support him in this office, Richard was collated to the rectory of Charing in Kent—location of one of the archbishop's favourite palaces—and the prebend of Deal in St Martin's, Dover, both of which he held until his election to the see of Chichester. He accompanied Archbishop Edmund on his last, unfinished, journey to Rome in the autumn of 1240, witnessed his death at Soisy, and remained with the small group of clerks who escorted the body of their master back to Pontigny Abbey for burial. Deeply affected by his friendship with Edmund, Richard interrupted his career and took up the study of theology at Orléans as a pupil of the Dominican friars, whom he purposed to join. While at Orléans, he was ordained priest and he subjected himself to intensive mortifications. This period of retreat after Edmund's death is an obscure phase of his life history. In the summer of 1241 he was at Westminster attending the exchequer, probably in connection with the archbishop's estate, but his subsequent residence at Orléans is attested by a letter he wrote from there on 20 April 1242, in order to certify the archbishop's wish to be buried at Pontigny.

The struggle for Chichester Richard was catapulted back into public life by his nomination to the see of Chichester in succession to Ralph Neville, who had died on 1 February 1244. This was to involve him in a bruising conflict with Henry III. Henry had taken advantage of the vacancy of the see to push a number of his ministers into prebends in the chapter, and he intended the bishopric for Robert Passelewe, a justice of the forest and one of his most trusted administrators. The chapter duly bowed to his instructions and elected Passelewe, but their act was unexpectedly quashed by the new archbishop of Canterbury, Boniface of Savoy, to whom confirmation of the election canonically belonged. Boniface had political interests in Savoy which kept him abroad for long periods. Arriving in England in April 1244, he made a number of appointments and then returned to the continent for an absence of nearly five years. During his brief stay, however, he held a meeting with five of his suffragans at Merton Priory in June, at which he examined, and on the advice of Grosseteste quashed, the election of Passelewe and, probably at Grosseteste's suggestion, nominated Richard of Wyche in his place.

The king was still smarting from the rejection of his plans to fill the see of Winchester with one of his relatives, and the full heat of the royal displeasure was now turned on Richard. Henry refused to accept his homage or to release the temporalities. Richard therefore decided to go to the curia, then resident at Lyons, to put his case before the pope. There, despite the efforts of the king's proctors to challenge the appointment, Richard's election was confirmed by Pope Innocent IV, who consecrated him bishop on 5 March 1245. But the endgame had yet to be played out. Returning home, Richard was refused access to the royal presence, and the keepers of the temporalities were ordered to refuse him entry to the city of Chichester. Denied access to his bishopric, Richard took refuge for over a year as a guest of the parish rector of Tarring in Sussex. Eventually, in July 1246, the king relented, probably for fear of alienating the pope, and Richard was placed in possession of the temporalities and restored to grace. Thereafter he appeared periodically at court. He failed, however, to secure restitution of the income from his episcopal estates, which the crown had appropriated during the vacancy, and which he claimed to be rightly his from the date of his election.

The reforming bishop Richard now devoted himself unstintingly to the government of his diocese. The restoration of his cathedral church was a first charge on his attention. In order to encourage more of the canons to take up residence, he augmented the chapter's common fund with the income from the churches of Alciston and Lullington, which he persuaded Battle Abbey to grant him. The need to raise funds for the repair of the fabric and the completion of the building was a pressing preoccupation of his early years. In 1247 he issued an indulgence for those who made contributions, and he induced a number of his episcopal colleagues to issue similar indulgences for the Chichester fabric fund. It was evidently this concern with the state of the cathedral's finances that prompted him to revive the practice of Pentecostals, which had lapsed during the negligent regime of Ralph Neville: the clergy were instructed to bring their parishioners in procession to the mother church of the diocese at Whitsuntide; the chaplains were to collect the Pentcostal offerings from those who were unable to come.

It was as a pastoral bishop in the reforming tradition of Richard Poore and Grosseteste that Richard made his mark upon his diocese. He made it his foremost concern to ensure that parish churches and chapels were properly served and that the parish clergy were instructed in their duties and provided with an adequate income. Thus many of his surviving written acts show him ordaining vicarages for this purpose in churches which had been appropriated to monasteries, ensuring that a decent proportion of the parish endowments were allocated to the vicar, who was given security of tenure. The creation of vicarages in the diocese had begun under Bishop John Greenford (1174–80), but Richard ordained many more, usually reserving the nomination of the vicar to the bishop or, during the vacancy of the see, to the dean and chapter.

Like many English bishops of the thirteenth century, Richard used regular meetings of the diocesan synod, which was attended by the parish clergy, as his chosen instrument to enforce the disciplinary decrees of the third and fourth Lateran Councils (1179 and 1215) and to instruct the clergy in their duties. The ordinances he published in the synod are the earliest known statutes to be enacted for the Chichester diocese. They show a heavy debt to other legislators, especially to the Salisbury statutes of Richard Poore and the legatine statutes of Cardinal Otto, but Richard supplemented this material with original constitutions of his own. Here again he manifested his concern for those engaged in pastoral care at the parish level. Vicars were reminded of their obligation to receive priestly ordination so that they could administer the sacraments to their people, and detailed instructions were provided to assist them in hearing confessions. Chaplains employed in parish churches on an annual basis, provided they were adequately educated and well conducted, were to be given security of tenure and to be paid a minimum stipend of 5 marks per annum. Those serving outlying parish chapels were to attend ruridecanal chapters four times a year to hear and update the synodal statutes. Rectors and vicars were reminded of the duty of hospitality and their obligations to the poor. The legate's statutes against clergy who kept concubines were reinforced with threats of deprivation. A number of constitutions dealing with ordinations and the conduct of archdeacons and rural deans imply that a period of lax control had preceded Richard's episcopate. His statutes probably represent the first systematic effort to apply the reform programme of the councils to the diocese of Chichester.

Public life, death, and canonization No record of Richard's episcopal visitations survives. But Bocking's life of him provides a picture of a bishop constantly on the move about his diocese, visiting parishes, monastic houses, and the homes of the poor and sick. Many of the hagiographical anecdotes about him relate to his encounters with humble people, whom he met and talked to in the course of his journeyings. Like Grosseteste, he used Franciscan and Dominican friars to assist him in his visitatorial work by preaching to the laity and hearing confessions. His continuing devotion to the mendicant orders is attested by his will, in which he bequeathed to them the greater part of his personal library. Periodically, public duties took him away from his diocese. He was one of those commissioned in 1245 to conduct an inquiry into the sanctity of his old master, Edmund of Abingdon, and in the summer of 1247 he took part in the solemn translation of St Edmund's body at Pontigny. In 1250 he was given the task of collecting sums due from the redemption of crusading vows, and in 1252 he was appointed one of the collectors of the tenth levied on clerical incomes for the king's projected crusade and was commissioned to preach the crusade. In the course of his preaching tour, he travelled across southern England to Dover, where he lodged as a guest of the master and brethren of the hospital there. His last episcopal act was to consecrate a cemetery chapel for them, which he dedicated to St Edmund, on 30 March 1253. The following day he collapsed in choir, and he died on 3 April. His body was taken back to his cathedral, where it was buried before the altar of St Edmund that he had erected on the north side of the church.

Almost immediately miracles were reported at Richard's tomb. The chapter dispatched letters of postulation to Rome, and in June 1256 Pope Alexander IV set up a commission of inquiry, consisting of Walter de Cantilupe, bishop of Worcester, the Franciscan Adam Marsh, and the Dominican provincial, Simon Hinton. On 22 January 1262, Richard was canonized by Pope Urban IV in an assembly held in the church of the Friars Minor at Viterbo. The solemn translation of his remains to a costly shrine behind the high altar of Chichester Cathedral took place on 16 June 1276. The delay was caused by the temporary suspension of the bishop, Stephen Bersted, who had been compromised by supporting Montfort's party in the baronial wars. The canonization process supplied the materials on which Ralph Bocking based his life of St Richard, which he completed between 1268 and 1272, and which he dedicated to Isabella, countess of Arundel. An interpolated version of this life was, later in the century, translated into Anglo-Norman verse by Peter of Fetcham. The cult of St Richard was largely confined to southern England, but his shrine continued to attract pilgrims until the Reformation.

C. H. LAWRENCE

Sources 'Vita sancti Ricardi', *Acta sanctorum: Aprilis*, 1 (Antwerp, 1675), 277–318 · D. J. Jones, *St Richard of Chichester: the sources for his life*, Sussex RS, 79 (1995) [incl. edn of Bocking's life] · A. T. Baker, 'La vie de Saint Richard, évêque de Chichester', *Revue des Langues Romains*, 53 (1910), 245–396 [text of Anglo-Norman life] · W. H. Blaauw, 'The will of Richard of la Wych, bishop of Chichester', *Sussex Archaeological Collections*, 1 (1848), 164–92 · C. H. Lawrence, 'St Richard of Chichester', *Studies in Sussex church history*, ed. M. J. Kitch (1981), 35–55 · C. H. Lawrence, *St Edmund of Abingdon* (1960) · F. M. Powicke and C. R. Cheney, eds., *Councils and synods with other documents relating to the English church, 1205–1313*, 1 (1964) · W. D. Peckham, ed., *The chartulary of the high church of Chichester*, Sussex RS, 46 (1946) · LTR memoranda roll, PRO, E 368/13 · *Chancery records* · *Les registres d'Innocent IV*, ed. E. Berger, 4 vols. (Paris, 1884–1921) · *Paris, Chron.* · D. Jones, 'The medieval lives of St Richard of Chichester', *Analecta Bollandiana*, 105 (1987), 105–29 · *Ann. mon.* · *The historical works of Gervase of Canterbury*, ed. W. Stubbs, 2: *The minor works comprising the Gesta regum with its continuation, the Actus pontificum and the Mappa mundi*, Rolls Series, 73 (1880) · H. C. M. Lyte and others, eds., *Liber feodorum: the book of fees*, 3 vols. (1920–31) · *Statutes and constitutions of the cathedral church of Chichester*, ed. F. O. Bennett, R. H. Codrington, and C. Deeds (1904)

Wyche, Richard (*d.* 1440), Lollard heretic, was probably from the diocese of Hereford. He was presumably educated at Oxford, and at his first trial, before Bishop Skirlawe of Durham (*d.* 1406), affirmed that he had been taught by men trained in law, although he also argued cogently on theological issues, including the eucharist. Nothing is known of his background before the trial, which probably took place in the winter of 1402–3. The ecclesiastical authorities clearly sought his submission rather than his condemnation, and tried to convince him by argument. Even after being sentenced to prison and degradation (a sentence which was evidently not carried out), he wrote an account of the trial to his friends. After a later recantation, between 1404 and 1406, Wyche temporarily disappears from sight. Later, in 1419, he stated that he had been brought south by a writ of *corpus cum causa* and released in chancery. After his release he either developed or resumed contacts with Bohemia and with Jan Hus, to whom he wrote on 8 September 1410, describing him as his 'dearest brother in Christ'. He must have sent books to Bohemia, because Hus, in his reply of the following March, thanked Wyche for these. This may not have been the only letter, because Hus alluded to Wyche's troubles (not described in the surviving letter) in his reply. Before then Wyche had also become associated with Sir John Old-castle (d. 1417), who wrote on the same day to Woksa of Waldstein, one of Hus's Bohemian supporters.

Wyche, however, avoided involvement in Oldcastle's rebellion of 1414, although he was arrested in 1417 and brought to Westminster to make disclosures about money that had belonged to Oldcastle. He was brought before the Canterbury convocation in 1419, but as he was not found guilty of relapse, heresy cannot have been proved against him. After imprisonment in the Fleet, he was released under sureties in the following year, under the description of Richard Wyche alias Godwote. The authorities evidently believed that he had abandoned his heresy, for he was appointed vicar of Deptford in 1423, and rector of Leaveland in Kent in 1434. In 1437 he was appointed vicar of Harmondsworth, Middlesex, and he was still there in 1439. Shortly after, however, he was again arrested and tried by Bishop Gilbert of London. He was found guilty of heresy, degraded at St Paul's, and burnt on 17 June 1440 at Tower Hill with his servant Roger Norman. Only one chronicle mentions any of his beliefs, hostility to clerical pluralism—he declared that a layman was as entitled to have two wives as a priest two benefices.

The burning is widely recorded in the London city chronicles, which relate that Wyche was highly regarded among the common people, some of whom held that he was a saint. Chronicle and record sources (from both chancery and civic documents) relate that his followers made pilgrimages to the place of his death, and, however inappropriate it might be for Lollards to do so, some at any rate may have tried to gather together his ashes as relics. Claims were also made that miracles had taken place at the site of his death, where his followers made offerings and set up a wooden cross in his memory. In order to counter these assertions the mayor sent a number of aldermen to the place of execution to hold back the crowd, and later the civic authorities deliberately polluted the ground and turned it into a dunghill.

Wyche was probably respected by the London Lollards because he was a link with the early years of the movement; he was the last surviving academic heretic of the immediate post-Wyclif generation, and had had links with Oldcastle. The popular response to his death suggests that the Lollards still enjoyed a considerable measure of support in London.   JOHN A. F. THOMSON

Sources F. D. Matthew, 'The trial of Richard Wyche', *EngHR*, 5 (1890), 530–44 • E. F. Jacob, ed., *The register of Henry Chichele, archbishop of Canterbury, 1414–1443*, 4 vols., CYS, 42, 45–7 (1937–47), esp. vol. 3, pp. 56–7 • *The letters of John Hus*, trans. M. Spinka (1972) • 'John Benet's chronicle for the years 1400 to 1462', ed. G. L. Harriss, *Camden miscellany, XXIV*, CS, 4th ser., 9 (1972), 187 • J. Gairdner, ed., *The historical collections of a citizen of London in the fifteenth century*, CS, new ser., 17 (1876) • C. L. Kingsford, ed., *Chronicles of London* (1905) • R. Flenley, ed., *Six town chronicles of England* (1911) • CLRO, Journal 3 • J. A. F. Thomson, *The later Lollards* (1965) • A. Hudson, *The premature reformation: Wycliffite texts and Lollard history* (1988) • C. von Nolcken, 'Richard Wyche, a certain knight, and the beginning of the end', *Lollardy and the gentry in the later middle ages*, ed. M. Aston and C. Richmond (1997), 127–54

Wycherley, Sir Robert Bruce (1894–1965), building society manager, was born on 5 April 1894 at Newtown, Montgomeryshire, the son of the Revd Richard Wycherley, a Primitive Methodist minister, and his wife, Mary, née Bruce. He was educated in schools at Oakengates, Shropshire, and Scorton, Yorkshire, and first worked as a clerk in the West Riding education department. In the First World War he spent four years in the army, mostly in France; he was decorated with the Military Cross and bar and was a captain when demobilized. Following a brief return to the education department he became secretary of the West Yorkshire pensions committee and then, in 1921, of the Halifax Engineering Employers Association.

In 1929 Wycherley moved to London and joined the National Building Society, which had enjoyed very rapid growth since 1918. Its board felt that the administration had not adjusted to the size of the business and recruited Wycherley to take over the administration in due course. Starting as assistant secretary, he became secretary (1931), general manager (1933), and managing director (1937), having joined the board in 1936. He tightened and mechanized the administration, enjoying the advantage of a purpose-built head office in Moorgate opened in 1930.

The National had long been established in the heart of the City. Provided competitive interest rates were offered, there was no shortage of funds; with no branch offices, however, finding borrowers was more of a problem for the National. The solution was the employment of full-time representatives, mostly in the south-east, whose job it was to contact builders developing estates. Somewhat controversially, finance for house building was then advanced by the building society on the security of the land, and the developers were paid commission for any borrowers they introduced to the National. The builder could stimulate sales by giving, without informing the buyer, a guarantee to the building society where a loan in excess of the usual percentage of the purchase price was made. The precise details of these arrangements became the focus of increasingly intense competition between societies. The National Association of Building Societies, with Wycherley as a council member from 1934, struggled throughout the 1930s to agree and enforce a restraining code of conduct. Although the National Association was replaced in 1936 by the Building Societies Association, with support for a code a condition of membership, the forces of competition continued unchecked until restraint was imposed by the Building Societies Act 1939.

With the outbreak of war the new association appointed a committee of five to safeguard the interests of societies. This committee included Wycherley and Sir Harold Bellman of the Abbey Road Society. One consequence was the merger of their two societies in 1944 to form the Abbey National. Wycherley and Bellman were joint managing directors until 1948, after which Wycherley acted alone, although with Bellman continuing as chairman. Wycherley served as chairman of the association from 1943 to 1946—difficult years, as the prominent post-war part that societies had seen for themselves was at odds with the modest role that the government allowed. Wycherley managed to sustain reasonable co-operation between them. His condemnation of the excesses of the 1950s, with some societies making large loans to speculative property companies, made his an influential voice when new legislation to restrain these excesses was passed in 1960. Severe illness in 1962 forced Wycherley to leave the association's council in 1964 after thirty years; he was made a vice-president.

An early associate member of the Building Society Institute (the professional staff association), Wycherley became a fellow in 1939. He was a member of its council from 1935 to 1947 and chaired the superannuation and benevolent committees. He played a part in the re-establishment of the International Association of Building Societies. Other business interests were the deputy chairmanship of the Royal Insurance Company and directorships of both the Globe and the Liverpool and Lancashire insurance companies and of the South Essex Water Board. He was a fellow of the Chartered Institute of Secretaries from 1924, treasurer in 1950, and president in 1954. He received a knighthood in 1953.

Wycherley's recreations included music, as he had long been an accomplished organist, and also gardening and golf. He was a freeman of the City of London, president of the City Livery Club, and a member of the court of the Innholders' Company. A freemason, he was accorded 'grand rank' for his services, including grand deacon of England. He married twice: in 1920 Winifred (d. 1942), the daughter of Edward Land Harrison, an ironmonger of Wakefield, and in 1943 Margaret, the daughter of William L. Morton, an engineer of Forfar. He had two daughters, one from each marriage. Wycherley died from cancer on 17 March 1965 at his Kent home, High Timber, Chislehurst Road, Chislehurst, survived by his second wife. He was cremated after a funeral service at Christ Church, Chislehurst.   ESMOND J. CLEARY

Sources H. Bellman, *Bricks and mortals: a study of the building society movement and a study of the Abbey National Society* (1949) · G. Elkington, *The National Building Society, 1849–1934* (1935) · S. J. Price, *Building societies: their origin and history* [1958] · E. J. Cleary, *The building society movement* (1965) · *The Times* (18 March 1965) · *CGPLA Eng. & Wales* (1965) · E. J. Cleary, 'Wycherley, Sir Robert Bruce', *DBB*
Likenesses photograph, 1933–7, repro. in Elkington, *The National Building Society*, facing p. 64 · photograph, 1946–9, repro. in Bellman, *Bricks and mortals*, facing p. 128 · W. Stoneman, photograph, 1955, NPG · J. Gunn, oils, Abbey National head office, London
Wealth at death £41,617: probate, 28 May 1965, *CGPLA Eng. & Wales*

Wycherley, William (*bap.* 1641, *d.* 1716), playwright, was baptized on 8 April 1641 in Whitchurch, Hampshire, the son of Daniel Wycherley (1617–1697) and Bethia (*c*.1618–1700), daughter of William Shrimpton and attendant to the marquess of Winchester. The Wycherleys, a minor landowning gentry family, had been settled at Wycherley Hall, Clive, in Shropshire, since 1409. Daniel Wycherley was a royalist who exported funds to Charles I in exile and once entertained him at his house. He was very knowledgeable in the law and is said to have served a legal

William Wycherley (*bap.* 1641, *d.* 1716), by John Smith, 1703 (after Sir Peter Lely, *c*.1668)

apprenticeship in his youth. He was employed in a number of legal and financial cases for various clients, including the marquess of Winchester of Basing House, Hampshire. After Cromwell's destruction of Basing House on 14 October 1645, the marquess's title deeds and evidences were lost, and Daniel was employed to recover them, mortgaging properties and raising money to pay the marquess's debts until his lands were recovered after the Restoration. By 1647 Daniel had assumed high stewardship of his estates. A skilled, methodical, hard-nosed and ambitious administrator, Daniel acquired several estates, including some from the marquess, and a good income over a long lifetime of litigation and complex transactions. It is not clear where Daniel and Bethia were living from 1645 to 1651; at that date he took a handsome house on King's Street North in the parish of St Paul, Covent Garden, London, which he kept until 1657. Their other children were George (1651–1688), John (*d.* 1691), Henry (*b.* 1662), Elizabeth, and Frances (*d.* 1678).

Early life, education, and travel, 1641–1670 William Wycherley probably spent his earliest years at Whitchurch Farm, which his father leased until 1649. He is plausibly said to have been well educated at home by his father. This education included a good knowledge of Latin, for Seneca was one of his favourite authors, and he was especially well acquainted with the Roman satirists Juvenal and Horace. His father had high ambitions for his son and sent him, aged about fifteen, to complete his education in France. He lived on the banks of the River Charente near Angoulême, the centre for a salon presided over by the *précieuse* Julie d'Angennes, daughter of the marquise de Rambouillet, where were assembled a brilliant group of writers and nobility. Wycherley was never a *précieux*, though he acquired charming, polished manners which proved invaluable in his career. He told John Dennis he had been 'often admitted to the Conversation' of Julie d'Angennes and that he was dazzled by her intellect and beauty. Although Wycherley said she nicknamed him 'the little Huguenot', he was converted to Catholicism at this time. Wycherley was always a Francophile, and his writing is indebted to French sources. In old age he constantly reread Montaigne and Rochefoucauld, whose ideas deeply influenced his poetry and prose maxims. Wycherley took the hint for Manly in *The Plain-Dealer* from Alceste, the central character of Molière's *Le misanthrope*, whom contemporaries believed to be a portrait of d'Angennes's husband.

Wycherley may have stayed in France as long as three years, for he entered the Inner Temple aged eighteen in October 1659; his father had also enrolled there, the year before. His father may have intended him to study law seriously, as well as acquiring further social polish and connections. In 1662 Daniel Wycherley was 'controller' of the Christmas entertainments at the Inner Temple; his son gives us a glimpse of these in his description in *The Plain-Dealer* of the 'Revelling Christmas Lawyer' losing all his money in dicing, and after some 'fretting and wrangling' going 'emptily and lovingly away' with his fellows to the tavern. Wycherley's poems are late examples of inns-of-court writing, arguing positions and, as Alexander Pope said, 'studying for antitheses' (Spence, 1.39). At the Restoration in May 1660 Wycherley composed a poem, 'To King Charles II on his Return', and in that summer he became a fellow commoner of Queen's College, Oxford. Probably because of his Catholic faith, Wycherley did not matriculate. Nor did he take a degree. He lodged with the provost, Thomas Barlow, and had reading rights in the Bodleian Library as a student of philosophy in July 1660. Barlow was a fervent, dogmatic, and hard-line Calvinist. He had a formidable reputation as one of the chief theologians in the university, highly skilled in logic and casuistry. It may be that Daniel Wycherley had placed his son in Barlow's care to reclaim him from Rome; in any event Wycherley was persuaded by Barlow back to protestantism. Although he presented the college with a silver cup in 1668, Wycherley seems not to have thought much of Oxford: close friends believed he had been at no university (*Critical Works of John Dennis*, 2.409).

Wycherley left for the Inner Temple, and seems to have lodged there intermittently at least until 1671. In the summer of 1662 he was serving in Ireland with the earl of Arran's regiment of guards. In 1664 Daniel Wycherley paid for William to journey to Madrid in the service of the poet and translator Sir Richard Fanshawe during his diplomatic mission to Spain. The party began the journey by land and sea on 21 January 1664, and arrived in Spain on 23 February. The London merchant Sir Andrew King, who, with Wycherley, was described as Fanshawe's 'camarado' or personal companion, wrote to Daniel Wycherley from Madrid in October 1664 to reassure him that William, whose conversation he was enjoying, was profiting from his father's investment in him to 'improve himself for the service of his King, Church and Country' and showed no signs of backsliding from Anglicanism to Roman Catholicism (Thomas, 53–4). The ambassadorial party were entertained on their progress from Cadiz to Madrid in spring 1664 with several performances of plays, and when Wycherley left for England on 19 February 1665 he had a knowledge of Spanish which later allowed him to use plot features of two of Pedro Calderón de la Barca's plays for his first two comedies. One of Wycherley's poems describes a 'Sea Fight, which the Author was in, betwixt the English and Dutch', and it seems likely that he fought in one of the battles of the Second Anglo-Dutch War in 1665. In 1669 Wycherley published anonymously his parody *Hero and Leander in Burlesque*. This mediocre poem appeared with blanks and the omission of several lines, which seem to show the printer's censorship of obscene passages. These Wycherley filled in a copy of the poem which he presented to Anthony Henley; it is now in the Victoria and Albert Museum. He also gave him a copy of his *Miscellany Poems* in 1704.

Dramatic work, 1671–1677 Wycherley in old age told Pope 'over and over' that his four plays were all written long before their performance: '*Love in a Wood* he wrote when he was but nineteen, the *Gentleman Dancing-Master* at twenty-one, the *Plain Dealer* at twenty-five, and the *Country Wife* at one or two and thirty' (Spence, 1.34). However, Wycherley's first play, *Love in a Wood*, was entered in the Stationers' register in autumn 1671 and performed, probably in March 1671, by the King's Company. It would have been remarkable if Wycherley had written this impressively accomplished play in 1660. As it contains references to events after 1660 and shows knowledge of Calderón's *Mañanas de abril y mayo*, it seems more likely that he wrote the play after his return from Spain. However, some parts of the plays may well have been in existence much earlier. It is not clear how the play was received, but two editions of the play-text appeared in 1672 and 1694, and it was played twice in 1718. It is a fine play, with remarkable fluency of dialogue. Wycherley's second play, *The Gentleman Dancing Master*, was produced by the Duke's Company at Dorset Garden, in late December 1671 or a few weeks afterwards, and acted for six days. It was certainly acted on 6 February 1672. A competent piece, satirizing French affectation, it was then, and has remained, Wycherley's least popular play.

After the first performance of *Love in a Wood*, Wycherley gained a lover in the form of Charles II's former mistress, the beautiful and notorious Barbara Villiers [see Palmer, Barbara], countess of Castlemaine and *suo jure* duchess of Cleveland. In John Dennis's famous account, Villiers passed Wycherley's coach in Pall Mall, and leant right out of her own to shout at him, 'You, Wycherley, you are a son of a Whore', which he identified as a reference to Lady Flippant's libertine song in his play:

Great Wits, and great Braves
Have always a Punk to their Mother.

After a spirited exchange of sauciness on her part and compliment on his, she agreed to come a second night to see his play. Wycherley dedicated *Love in a Wood* to her in 1672. The dedicatory epistle refers to her seeing the play 'twice together' and demanding a copy of the play. In a minor masterpiece of innuendo, Wycherley calls himself her 'greatest' admirer, thanks her for 'favours' received from her, slyly warns her of obliging 'in excess', and says he is jealously concerned 'not to have your Grace's favours lessened, or rather my reputation'. Contemporary satires portray the duchess as visiting 'brawny Wycherley' at his Inner Temple lodgings dressed as a country girl, with straw hat, pattens, and a basket, and tell a story of his escaping muffled up in a coat, narrowly avoiding an embarrassing meeting with the king. Wycherley's handsome face, athletic physique, and supposed sexual prowess were as widely admired as his wit, charm, and manners. Pope, who saw him in old age and illness, recalled that 'Wycherley was a very genteel man and had the nobleman look' (Spence, 1.245).

Dennis claims that it was the liaison with Barbara Villiers which secured Wycherley the notice of her cousin George Villiers, second duke of Buckingham. According to Dennis, Buckingham became furious at Cleveland's persistent refusal of his sexual advances and eventually set spies to discover the identity of her lovers, which he then published through gossip, hoping to ruin her when the king got to hear of it. Wycherley approached Rochester and Sedley to intercede for him with Buckingham, fearing the ruin of his promising career at court. Their praise of Wycherley's 'shining Qualities' brought about a dinner invitation from Buckingham; he was so impressed by Wycherley's conversational performance that, Dennis reports, he loudly applauded his cousin's taste in men. The anecdote is inaccurate, as Cleveland ceased being the king's mistress in August 1670, and Buckingham probably knew Wycherley before this date: he had protected Daniel Wycherley from his creditors in the mid-1650s. However, the story, one of several of its kind, is emblematic of Wycherley's reputation as foremost comic wit of the age and of his role in the circle of courtiers and wits headed by Buckingham in the 1670s. This group included the earl of Rochester, Charles Sackville, Lord Buckhurst (later earl of Dorset), John, Lord Vaughan, Sir Charles Sedley, Sir George Etherege, Henry Savile, Thomas Shadwell, and Fleetwood Sheppard. Many of Wycherley's surviving poems, light-hearted, mediocre *vers de société* depicting him drinking, gambling, and having affairs, were produced for circulation within this group, membership of which proved decisive for Wycherley's literary career. Although many of the names of those addressed are not recorded in many of the printed texts, there are poems to Shadwell, Etherege, Buckingham, Dryden, and Sedley.

Buckingham's patronage took the form of an appointment as his equerry and on 19 June 1672 Wycherley was also made captain-lieutenant of Buckingham's own company. Dennis says Buckingham resigned his own pay to him as captain. His company embarked in July 1673 on an expedition against the Dutch, but were immediately sent to the Isle of Wight, where they were quartered all winter. There were problems obtaining money for the soldiers' pay: Wycherley had to apply to the lord treasurer for £950 owed to him, of which £480 was ordered to be paid to him on 14 October 1673. On 28 February 1674 Wycherley was promoted to captain of the company of foot, but he resigned on 6 March. In April the troops formerly under his command complained of Wycherley's 'ill usage' of them in the expedition and said they had not been fully paid. Wycherley's poems on the subject of war show little enthusiasm for it, and Horner in *The Country-Wife* says that soldiers are kept loyal by 'good pay' rather than 'Oaths'. Wycherley's loyalty to his patron was sincere: when Buckingham was in the Tower in 1677, Wycherley wrote a poem ascribing his imprisonment to 'a Court-Faction', risking the king's displeasure. Despite his connections with Buckingham, Wycherley supported the king's increasingly close links with France, and his poem on the signing of the treaty of Nijmegen praises Louis XIV. Charles Gildon claimed that Wycherley became a Jacobite because James II paid his debts, but his Catholic sympathies were deep-rooted.

The anecdotes which survive from this period depict Wycherley with friends in taverns of one sort or another. Wycherley told Major Pack of a 'House at the Bridge-Foot' to which 'Persons of Better Condition' used to resort and where canary was served. The men used to compliment their mistresses by kneeling down, taking up the bottom of their mistresses' petticoats to form a bag, pouring wine into it, and drinking their health. Wycherley's favourite eating-house was The Cock, in Bow Street, in which a scene in *The Plain-Dealer* is set. Wycherley lodged in the up-market residential street of Bow Street for much of his adult life, and visited Will's Coffee House there. Wycherley was exceptionally clubbable, with rather formal manners, keeping his real feelings in reserve. George Granville, Lord Lansdowne, insisted that Wycherley was 'gentle and inoffensive to all men', in striking contrast to his satirical literary persona (G. Granville, *Works*, 1732, 432–3), while Charles Gildon said that

> Mr. Wycherley was indeed of an affable, easie, good Temper, and perfectly inoffensive to all Company, and knew how to be Civil over a glass to Mr. Durfey as to Mr. Dryden, but this was no mark of Friendship or Intimacy. (C. Gildon, *Memoirs*, 1718, 20)

Knightley Chetwode told Jonathan Swift in 1732 that he agreed with his 'old friend Wycherley' that 'some degree of ceremony should be preserved in the strictest friendship' (*Correspondence of Jonathan Swift*, 4.13). The standard view of Wycherley was expressed by a French commentator:

> Mr. Wycherly is one of the politest Gentlemen in England, and the most civil and affable to Strangers, especially to those of our Nation, for whom he has an Esteem; he is a little shy and reserv'd in Conversation, but when a Man can be so happy as once to engage him in Discourse, he cannot but admire his profound Sense, Masculine Wit, vast Knowledge of Mankind, and noble but easie Expressions. (Boyer, 217)

Wycherley's masterpiece, the sex comedy *The Country-Wife*, was acted at the Theatre Royal, Drury Lane, on 12 January 1675, though this may not have been the première. A brilliant satire on the covert operations of selfish desire beneath the veneer of honour required by society, it reveals that society to be anarchic and incoherent. The main character is Horner, a libertine who pretends to be impotent following treatment for the pox. The play was too strong for some, and women spectators in particular were offended by the famously bawdy 'china scene', where a hypocritical club of closet she-rakes (Mrs Squeamish and Lady Fidget) cuckold their husbands under their very noses. It was successful in its day, and continued so until the early years of the eighteenth century.

Wycherley answered his women critics in his next comedy, *The Plain-Dealer*. He told Pope he wrote it in three weeks, defying Rochester's famous character, in *An Allusion to Horace*, of 'slow Wicherley' who 'spares no pains' to polish and refine his comedies. Yet he had also told Pope that the play was written ten years before performance, claiming to be both a brilliant, slapdash, spontaneous amateur and a boy genius. His contemporaries viewed it as his signature play and admired it as 'the best Comedy that ever was Compos'd in any Language. The only Fault that has been found in it, is its being too full of *Wit*; a Fault which few Authors can be guilty of' (Boyer, 217). The criticism that it was 'too witty' was widespread, and much debated by critics. The play was first performed on 11 December 1676 by the King's Company at the Theatre Royal. It was so complex, radical, and original in its use of theatrical conventions that audiences did not know what to make of it, and it had to be saved by Wycherley's powerful friends who gave it their 'loud aprobation'. These included the duke of Buckingham, the earl of Rochester, the earl of Dorset (the chief spokesman for the play, according to Matthew Prior), the earl of Mulgrave, Henry Savile, Henry Bulkeley, Sir John Denham, and Edmund Waller.

In one of many troubling reversals, the play turns Shakespeare's *Twelfth Night* into a bitter satire; its innocent heroine, Fidelia, is forced into consenting to assist her lover to rape Olivia, and Olivia herself is recast as a treacherous, scandal-mongering, mercenary, and hypocritical woman of fashion. In a brilliant imitation of Molière's *La critique de 'L'école des femmes'*, Olivia attacks 'all the hideous obscenity' to be heard at 'nasty plays', in particular *The Country-Wife*. She turns out to know the play in some detail, and considers the china scene so 'filthy' that she has smashed all in her possession. The main comic parts were played by Rebecca Marshall and Elizabeth Boutell, actresses who usually played against one another in tragedies. In a mirror image of his earlier dedication to Barbara Villiers, the play is dedicated in defiance of his feminine critics to a famous bawd, Mrs Bennet, from whom he claims not to have had the honour of a 'Favour', and signed by the Plain Dealer. The teasing, ironic, and complex interplay of author, play, character, and actor was introduced in the prologue, 'Spoken by the Plain-Dealer' in the form of Charles Hart, who played Manly.

For the rest of his life Wycherley was called Manly or the Plain-Dealer. He himself used the title of the Plain-Dealer in his correspondence with Pope, and Dryden praised Congreve for having 'the satire, wit, and strength of manly Wycherley', making no distinction between the playwright and his plays. Wycherley admired Dryden, and praised him to Pope after his death. In a poem possibly written before 1677, Wycherley tactfully praises Dryden's superior talents as a reason for turning down his proposal that they should collaborate on writing a comedy. Manly's contempt for courtly courtesy is not a portrait of Wycherley, who uses the persona to be charming, rather than to be above charm. Moreover, Manly's railing at 'Ceremony, Embraces, and Plentiful Professions' was delivered at the point when the court had most to offer Wycherley. *The Plain-Dealer* was to be his last play, and marks the highest point of his fortunes.

Illness, marriage, and debt, 1678–1695   In the spring of 1678 Wycherley went to Tunbridge Wells and there met his future wife, Letitia-Isabella Moore (d. 1685), daughter of John, Lord Robartes, earl of Radnor, and wife of Charles, second earl of Drogheda. She had been living in Bow Street, Covent Garden, in early 1678 while her husband was in Ireland. She was young and attractive, and seemed to be rich, but this last was an illusion, for she was spending far more than her precarious income. According to Dennis, Wycherley was in a bookseller's shop in Tunbridge Wells when the countess entered and asked for *The Plain-Dealer*; Wycherley's friend Robert Fairbeard of Grey's Inn pointed out the Plain-Dealer himself. Wycherley paid her a compliment as a woman whose excellence could well stand plain dealing; she replied that she loved plain dealing, especially when it told her of her faults. From then on Wycherley called on her daily at her lodgings in Tunbridge Wells, accompanied her to the public places, and continued to visit her when she returned to London.

Later that year, perhaps in late spring, Wycherley fell dangerously ill of a fever. Dryden later identified 'Wycherleys long sickness' as apoplexy (*Letters of Sir George Etherege*, ed. F. Bracher, 1974, 277); John Locke heard a rumour in Paris that summer that he had died of it. In old age Wycherley claimed that his mental and physical deterioration dated from this sickness. Dennis says that Charles II visited Wycherley in his Bow Street lodgings, an extraordinary mark of esteem, and, finding him very weakened in body and spirits, gave him £500 to take a recuperative holiday in the spa resort of Montpellier. Change of air, Wycherley later counselled a friend, is good 'after a Fever' (Dennis, *Letters*, 27–8). Wycherley claimed in a poem to have been in Holland at the signing of the treaty of Nijmegen on 31 July 1678. He was in Montpellier by September 1678, in contact with the virtuoso Walter Charleton and hoping to meet John Locke, who praised his work and described him as an 'old acquaintance'. In his absence the countess sent her maid after him with a diamond ring, and had his portrait painted. Dennis said Wycherley returned in spring 1679 when the king offered him a salary of £1500 to become governor of his son, Charles Lennox, duke of Richmond, with, according to Dennis, the promise of a substantial pension when the appointment ceased. Pope said that Charles made occasional presents to Wycherley of £100 and made him his equerry, but there is no other evidence for this (Spence, 1.35).

On 18 June 1679 the countess's husband died, and the couple agreed to marry. The countess had no surviving children, and the title passed to her brother-in-law, Henry, third earl of Drogheda; however, the second earl had drawn up a deed making over the greatest part of the inheritance to the countess, effectively disinheriting Henry. Wycherley was in Ireland for three weeks in late summer arranging legal matters, and they married secretly on 29 September 1679. Wycherley, who had his father's encouragement for the marriage, believed that he was marrying a fortune. However, the earl's finances had been in difficulties for some time and the countess, as spendthrift as her new husband, was substantially in debt. Very soon her creditors demanded payment, and the couple had to change address frequently to avoid them. They were sued by her lady's maid Sarah Barnaby, who had swindled the countess out of substantial sums of money and goods. Wycherley eventually lost his temper with Barnaby and viciously beat her up. In marrying secretly, without the king's consent, Wycherley forfeited the appointment of governor to Lennox and the king's favour and patronage. The third earl contested the will; the case dragged on expensively for years, and Gildon reports that it was not until 1697 that the countess's relations paid Wycherley £1500 for his right to the estate. The unhappy six-year marriage was blighted by litigation, mounting debt, and disappointment. Wycherley wrote a poem to 'my Lord Chancellor Boyle, at once Chancellour and Primate of Ireland: Written when the Author had a suit depending before him' (*Works*, 3.195). He says that he married for 'an Estate' and so should either be given the financial benefit of his 'Bargain' or be relieved from his wife and 'end my Law-Suit, or my Domestic Strife' (ibid., 3.196–7). Dennis blamed the countess for ruining Wycherley's career at court, and records an anecdote of her temper and jealousy, refusing to let her husband out of her sight and insisting that if he went with his friends to The Cock tavern, opposite their Bow Street lodgings, he should leave the window open so that she could see that there was no woman with him. Her cook said she was given to passionate rages in which she 'bawled and roared as if she had been stuck with a knife' (Boswell, 1001). Dennis even hints that she found her husband less virile than his reputation would have him. Wycherley describes himself in a letter of *c*.1695 as 'one sufficiently experienced in Love-disasters', saying that although love is 'for the time a pleasant Frenzy', marriage 'infallibly' proves 'a tedious Vexation' (Dennis, *Letters*, 27–8).

The countess died, according to her sister Olympia, 'in or about the month of July 1685'; Wycherley describes her as 'lately dead' in a letter written from the Fleet and dated only '9 July', with no year given. She left her whole estate to her husband, but her relatives sued Wycherley for the property, and he was unable to claim it as he was in the Fleet prison for debts of over £1590. There is considerable disagreement about the length of time he was in prison. Gildon thought it was seven years; Dennis thought it the four years from 1682 to 1686. However, he may in fact have been in prison for under a year, as he seems to have avoided arrest until 7 July 1685. He wrote a poem there, *In Praise of a Prison*, which says that:

> Love, more to my Grief, Plague, Infamy,
> Has more than Debt, caus'd my Captivity

and describes imprisonment as a welcome reprieve from marriage. However, Wycherley was in debt for the rest of his life. He was to be arrested at least twice more, and had perhaps been briefly imprisoned before this time.

When Charles II died, and James II succeeded him, the post of lord chamberlain went to the earl of Mulgrave, who had once been on easy relations with Wycherley, and to whom Wycherley still owed £500. Wycherley wrote him a formal letter on 24 October 1685 congratulating him and requesting his assistance in restoring his former favour at court. It makes a painful contrast with a relaxed, chatty letter of 1677. It got a response, for on 14 December 1685 there was a performance at Whitehall of *The Plain Dealer* engineered by Colonel Brett and Mulgrave to bring Wycherley's plight to James's attention. The king ordered that Wycherley's debts should be paid, but Wycherley foolishly claimed to be only £500 in debt. This sum the king paid him on 22 March 1686. His father and Colonel James Grahme seem to have paid some others, and many of Wycherley's debts were settled between January and April 1686, when he was released. He was paid an annuity of £200 by James until 1688. In December 1688 Wycherley's brother George died in the Fleet, and Wycherley could not afford £10 for funeral expenses.

Old age, 1695–1715 'Fortune', Wycherley observed of himself, 'leaves those in their Age, who were her Favourites in their Youth' (*Correspondence of Alexander Pope*, 1.61). In 1695 Daniel Wycherley drew up his will. He had spent his life building up the family estate, and he wanted to secure it from his son's profligacy, while relieving his debts. He forbade him to sell the estate, allowing him only a fixed annual income, and made it impossible to pay any debts contracted after his father's death nor any amounting to over £1000. He could, however, settle all the property, except the family home at Clive, on a wife or male heirs, in the event William's nephew, William Wycherley jun. It was a notorious state of affairs: Swift later described Bolingbroke as 'befathered worse than poor Wycherley' (*Correspondence of Jonathan Swift*, 4.136). At this time Wycherley was over £1000 in debt, and Daniel raised that amount by a loan secured on some of his property. Daniel died on 5 May 1697. In 1699 Wycherley mortgaged lands in Clive, Shropshire, for another £1000 to pay further debts. According to Pope, Wycherley's nephew angered him by refusing to consent to his raising funds by selling off part of the estate. In 1713 he raised £200 on further property. He spent as little time as possible at Clive, going there only to administer business and collect rents; he said that he disliked the 'Damnd Conversation' to be found there and intended only to 'rob the Country' and run away as fast as possible (*Correspondence of Alexander Pope*, 1.39, 61).

Wycherley still had a mass of unpublished literary manuscripts of poems, scraps of poems, and the like. In the late 1690s he tried to make some money by printing some of these poems, and the bookseller Samuel Briscoe issued proposals for a subscription volume in 1696. They ended up in a dispute over money, and Wycherley was again arrested for debt. It was not until 1704 that Wycherley's large folio of *Miscellany Poems* appeared. It was badly misjudged. Poems on a woman's 'Fair Back-Side' and on another's 'Fine Breasts' were entirely at odds with the new, chaster sensibility, and for its preface the work has a thirty-page torrent of abuse on those 'who were my *Critics* before they were my *Readers*'. Wycherley was a mediocre poet, and not surprisingly the volume received 'a poetical Damning' (*Correspondence of Alexander Pope*, 1.33). Several of Wycherley's presentation copies of the work are known to have existed.

The following year Wycherley met the sixteen-year-old Alexander Pope, probably at Will's Coffee House. Pope pursued the acquaintance, writing him a complimentary letter. Pope described the old playwright as his 'first poet-friend' (Spence, 1.32–3). He visited him twice a day for a whole winter, and remembered that Wycherley's usual supper was a mixture of port and sherry and 'two or three golden-pippins' (ibid., 37). Pope, like many of his contemporaries, credited Wycherley with the clearest understanding of human nature, but he said he was not 'grave enough or consistent enough' for him (*Correspondence of Jonathan Swift*, 3.364). They made an odd couple, the one old and heavily built, the other young and tiny. Pope once described himself as having followed Wycherley as faithfully in the town as his little dog followed behind him in the country. Despite some tensions they 'lived well till his death'. Wycherley also met John Dennis about this time, and they corresponded.

Wycherley did not grow old gracefully. His letter to Pope in 1706 complaining of a long coach journey to Shropshire in the company of four women who were 'useless' for the purposes of sexual molestation is an embarrassing attempt to revive his image as Restoration rake–gallant; he later described himself, more persuasively, as an 'old Gelding' trotting down to Shropshire. In 1709 he fell down the stairs of a tavern while drunk and was laid up for five weeks. In 1703 he had commissioned Smith to make an engraving of his portrait by Lely for his *Miscellany Poems*. It depicts him as a handsome man of about twenty-seven, and he accompanied it with the Virgilian motto *Quantum mutatus ab illo* ('How changed from that'). Pope said that he used to repeat this motto 'with a melancholy emphasis', and that when his portrait was drawn for Pope with 'little straggling grey hair', Wycherley could not bear it and insisted that a wig be painted on afterwards.

Wycherley still had many unpublished poems, and in February 1706 he asked for Pope's aid in selecting and revising the best poems from the *Miscellany Poems*, which he called his 'Damnd Miscellany of Madrigals', for republication with some of his unpublished poems in a second miscellany volume. This proved a great burden on Pope. By the time they met, Wycherley's memory was deteriorating. He said it was a consequence of a fever, perhaps that of 1678, but his friends took it to be old age. He repeated

himself: a quip that letters from the country are more welcome even than money sent from it is used in letters to Pope and Dennis of 1705 and 1708. Pope later commented that:

> Wycherley had this odd particularity in him from the loss of his memory: that the same chain of thought would return into his mind at the distance of two or three years, without his remembering that it had been there before. Thus perhaps he would write one year an encomium on avarice (for he loved paradoxes), and a year or two after in dispraise of liberality. In both, the words only would differ, and the thoughts be [exactly] alike. (Spence, 1.37–8)

Wycherley's works provide abundant evidence of the truth of this. One poem in Wycherley's collection is 'Against Industry: to a Laborious Poetaster, who Preferr'd Industry to Wit'. In it he says that:

> For Wit, to gain Esteem, like Beauty too,
> Must seem, an Artful Negligence, to show.
> (*Works*, 4.17)

The poem takes forty-four lines to say what could be said in a couplet.

When Pope gently suggested that revision of the better poems should take the form of pruning repetitions and imposing a logical structure, Wycherley insisted that 'the sprightliness of Wit' despises dull 'form and method'. In answer Pope suggested that Wycherley, if not prepared to undergo thorough revision, should reduce his poems to 'single thoughts in prose' like those of Rochefoucauld. This advice was followed. Wycherley continued to ask Pope's help, and Pope to give it, but no volume was published in Wycherley's lifetime, because Wycherley entirely underestimated the degree of revision and editing necessary for the task. Pope laboured hard over the poetry, and was rewarded only with the name of Wycherley's Crutch, and was rewarded only with the old man's anger at the extent of his revisions. Pope dedicated his pastoral 'Autumn' to Wycherley, describing him as one 'whose Sense instructs us, and whose Manner charms', but Wycherley's humiliation at being eclipsed by the younger poet caused a temporary estrangement in 1710.

In 1715 Wycherley visited Bath and came back dying: extremely weak, in great pain from gallstones, and unable to digest food. His memory was deteriorating severely. His hair was 'very white' and he was short-tempered. According to Pope, Spence, and Major Richardson Pack, Wycherley, ill and under pressure to repay debts, made a scandalous final marriage for money and to prevent his nephew from inheriting his entailed estate by making a jointure on that estate in favour of his wife. He died eleven days later. This is a harsh view of the facts. When the nephew sued for restoration of his inheritance, evidence was collected presenting Wycherley in his final weeks as the victim of a scheme which reads like a black parody of one of Restoration drama's most cynical plots. A cousin of his, Captain Thomas Shrimpton, came to London and discovered somehow that Wycherley had the power to make a jointure of his estate to any woman he should marry. Several witnesses testified that Shrimpton then conspired with his mistress, Elizabeth Jackson, over a number of weeks to bully, threaten, and coerce Wycherley to marry her. It was alleged that Shrimpton would call for Wycherley and take him out all day, and bring him home senseless with drink in the early hours. 'Six or seven weeks' before his death, Wycherley was allegedly arrested for a debt of £30 owed to a former servant, Thomas Barnes, and imprisoned in a bailiff's house for a week until the debt was paid. Pope said he lent him £20 a little before he died, and Shrimpton later claimed, probably falsely, to have paid the debt (Spence, 1.40).

Shrimpton persuaded Wycherley to move to a quieter lodging house in Bow Street, where Jackson was living, and then began to pressure him to marry Jackson to relieve his debts, representing her as an heiress with £1000. Wycherley refused. He had long threatened to marry for money on his deathbed to pay his debts and to 'plague his damned nephew' with whom he had quarrelled, a situation which Shrimpton worked on (*Correspondence of Alexander Pope*, 1.70). However, he was unimpressed by the size of the purported dowry, intermittently aware that he was being preyed upon, and too ill to want anything but medical attention. Wycherley granted Shrimpton power of attorney to collect rents from the Shropshire estate, but Shrimpton may have withheld some of the money. Finally Wycherley was brought, feebly protesting and begging for a physician, to sign a jointure and marry Jackson at his lodgings by special licence on 20 December 1715. Wycherley hardly knew what was happening to him. The attorney used by Shrimpton was Lewis Theobald, who thereby got his hands on Wycherley's unpublished papers, which he later published as the *Posthumous Works* (1728). Wycherley died at Mrs Armstrong's lodging house, Bow Street, about 3 a.m. on 1 January 1716, and was buried on 5 January in the vault of St Paul's Church, Covent Garden. He seems always to have had Catholic sympathies and some years before had told Pope he was a Catholic; it was in this faith that he died. Wycherley's nurse testified that he had received the sacrament some time before his marriage 'according to the Church of Rome as a Dying Man'. He complained to Pope 'on his deathbed' that it was provoking to be 'Squirted to death' by '*Potecaries Prentices*' (*Correspondence of Jonathan Swift*, 3.120). Pope uses this phrase to denote petty oppressors, and by it Wycherley may have meant not only his physicians but Shrimpton and Elizabeth, who married three months later. Wycherley's heir contested the jointure, but unsuccessfully: Elizabeth was declared to have been legally married to Wycherley, as he was judged of sound mind at the time of marriage.

Wycherley's legacy In 1728 Lewis Theobald, the Shakespeare editor, brought out a volume of Wycherley's *Posthumous Works*. The preface says that soon after Wycherley's death the 'Proprietors of the Papers' now published 'purchased them at a considerable Expense' from Captain Shrimpton. It describes the papers, implausibly, given Wycherley's care to keep them neat and the clarity of his surviving manuscripts, as 'very much interlined' and difficult to read, and offers 'but one Moiety' of Wycherley's manuscripts, promising more to follow. These were the papers on which Pope had been working for Wycherley,

and they contained much of Pope's own writing, with some of Theobald's work as editor. Pope retaliated by bringing out a 'Volume II' in 1729 to defend himself, correct Wycherley's text, and attack Theobald.

Wycherley's legacy was not only literary but also biographical. Posterity saw him as the type of the wicked, attractive, brilliant Restoration wit, rake, and gallant. Hence Samuel Richardson, whose *Clarissa* gives much space to a depiction of the bad ends made by unrepentant libertines, has Lord M. retell the well-known story of his 'old friend' Wycherley marrying in old age 'to plague his nephew' (letter 17, vol. 4). Wycherley's two greatest plays were steadily performed through the first half of the eighteenth century, but their bawdiness made them increasingly hard to stage. Benjamin Victor said that 'the severer critics say' of *The Plain-Dealer*, 'it is like reforming an old Libertine, and leaving him dull and insipid; yet, surely, it is a public Benefit to correct the Vices of an *agreeable* Libertine, although the operation in some Measure might lower his spirits' (*The History of the Theatres of London and Dublin*, 1761, 3.71–2). In 1765 Isaac Bickerstaff revised *The Plain-Dealer* after twenty-three years of non-performance. *The Country-Wife*, though still described as 'one of our most celebrated Comedies', was too obscene for eighteenth-century tastes. It was revised into a two-act play by John Lee in 1765, with Horner removed, and in 1766 Garrick recast it as the bland romantic comedy *The Country Girl*, in which Margery Pinchwife and her husband reappear as Peggy Thrift and Jack Moody. This was a great success, with fourteen performances during the season. From 1785 this play did exceptionally well thanks to the casting of Mrs Jordan as Peggy Thrift—she was widely praised for her 'innocent simplicity' and for the 'perfect symmetry' of her figure in male attire. Both plays suffered the neglect common to Restoration plays in the nineteenth century, and in 1919 Montague Summers's Phoenix Society was attacked for plans to produce 'the Restoration blackguards Wycherley and Shadwell' (J. L. Styan, *Restoration Comedy in Performance*, 1986, 2). However, their production of *The Country-Wife* in 1924 proved extremely successful. Bonamy Dobrée brilliantly characterized Wycherley as 'being all angles and unwieldy muscular lumps, shot with unexpected streaks of grace' (*Restoration Comedy*, 1924, 78). Dobrée's was an early recognition of Wycherley's complexity, a quality which has gone on to stimulate considerable debate over whether he is conservative or rebellious, satirical or farcical. Peter Holland's *The Ornament of Action* (1979) importantly traced the roots of this complexity in the relations between Wycherley's characters and the actors and actresses for whom the parts were written.

The Country-Wife has emerged as the most successful of Wycherley's plays, and was steadily performed in the twentieth century, with some particularly fine interpretations of the part of Margery. Edith Evans was praised for her performance in the Old Vic's production of *The Country-Wife* in 1936, though the reviewer for the *Catholic World* in 1937 abused Wycherley's 'dissoluteness' of life, to which she ascribed the 'incredibly vile' characteristics of the play. It was in this year that L. C. Knights published a highly influential essay in *Scrutiny* in which he insisted that all Restoration dramatists, including Wycherley, were 'dull' and had nothing to say, and claimed that they wrote for an exclusively aristocratic audience. Despite these attacks, Wycherley's plays continued to be popular; *Love in a Wood* was performed for the BBC Third Programme in 1956, and Joan Plowright played Margery in 1956 at the Royal Court. Maggie Smith's performance as Margery for the 1969 Chichester Festival was outstanding. *The Country-Wife* is now recognized as one of the period's major achievements, and is perhaps the most studied and frequently performed of all Restoration plays. Dennis's claim that Wycherley was the 'greatest of our Comick Wits' is still defensible.   KATE BENNETT

Sources *The works of William Wycherley*, ed. M. Summers, 4 vols. (1924) · *The plays of William Wycherley*, ed. A. Friedman (1979) · *The critical works of John Dennis*, ed. E. N. Hooker (Baltimore, 1939–43) · G. Thomas, 'William Wycherley in Spain: some new evidence', *N&Q*, 243 (1998), 53–4 · W. R. Chadwick, 'Wycherley: the seven lean years', *N&Q*, 216 (1971), 32–4 · *The correspondence of Alexander Pope*, ed. G. Sherburn, 5 vols. (1956) · J. Spence, *Observations, anecdotes, and characters, of books and men*, ed. J. M. Osborn, new edn, 2 vols. (1966) · H. P. Vincent, 'The death of William Wycherley', *Harvard Studies and Notes in Philology and Literature*, 15 (1933), 219–42 · E. Boswell, 'Wycherley and the countess of Drogheda', *TLS* (28 Nov 1929), 1001–2 · J. Dennis, *Letters on several occasions* (1701) · R. Gough, *The history of Myddle* (1981) · A. Boyer, ed., *Letters of wit, politicks and morality* (1701) · H. Vincent, 'William Wycherley's *Posthumous works*', *N&Q*, 185 (1943), 12–13 · *Letters of Sir George Etherege*, ed. F. Bracher (Los Angeles, 1974) · W. H. Cooke, ed., *Students admitted to the Inner Temple, 1547–1660* [1878] · *The memoirs of Anne, Lady Halkett and Ann, Lady Fanshawe*, ed. J. Loftis (1979) · R. A. Shrimpton, 'Wycherley's place of birth', *N&Q*, 11th ser., 9 (1914), 186–7 · *The correspondence of Jonathan Swift*, ed. H. Williams, 5 vols. (1963–5)

Archives V&A NAL, presentation volume, incl. MS poems | BL, Add. MSS · Cumbria AS, Kendal, Levens Hall muniments · Longleat House, Wiltshire, Portland papers, letters to Alexander Pope [transcripts] · V&A, Dyce collection

Likenesses oils, *c.*1668 (after P. Lely?), NPG · P. Lely, oils, 1669, priv. coll. · P. Cross, miniature, watercolour on vellum, *c.*1675, NPG · T. Murray, oils, *c.*1700, LUL · J. Smith, mezzotint, 1703 (after P. Lely, *c.*1668), BM, NPG [*see illus.*] · mezzotint, pubd 1704 (after P. Lely), NPG · G. Kneller?, portrait · oils, Knole, Kent

Wyck [Wijck], **Jan** [Jan van, John] (*c.*1645–1700), painter, was born in Haarlem, the son of Thomas (van) Wyck (*c.*1616–1677), also a painter. Wyck made his name in England as a specialist at painting horses in battle and hunting scenes, topographical and classical landscapes, and portraits of people, animals, and buildings. He brought the Dutch equestrian portrait genre to England. His oil studies of individual horses are perhaps his most original contribution to the history of English art.

Thomas Wyck had visited Rome in the 1630s, and his paintings and drawings show small figures in Mediterranean street or harbour scenes. He also specialized in Dutch domestic interiors and alchemists' laboratories. He had married in Haarlem on 22 May 1644, and came to England *c.*1664 where he drew and painted views of London, and night scenes of the great fire. It is assumed that Thomas, who took other pupils, taught Jan his art, but it is not known exactly when Jan arrived in England. On 17

Jan Wyck (*c.*1645–1700), by John Faber junior, 1730 (after Sir Godfrey Kneller, 1685)

June 1674 Jan promised to present his 'proofe peece', and pay his own and his father's quarterly fees to the Painter-Stainers' Company in the City of London. On 24 November 1680 he was placed upon 'The Committee of Acting Painters' of the company (City of London, Guildhall MS 5667/2, pt 1, fols. 170, 58). By then Thomas had returned to Haarlem where he died and was buried on 19 August 1677.

Jan Wyck married three times. Nothing is known about his first wife, but he was a widower aged about thirty-one and living in St Paul's, Covent Garden, when he married Ann Skynner, aged nineteen, of St Martin's-in-the-Fields, on 22 November 1676 in St Mary Savoy. Between 1678 and 1683 they had four children, but none survived and Ann died in 1687. On 9 August 1688 he married Elizabeth Holomberry, aged about twenty-two, and went to live with her in Mortlake, Surrey. They had three children: first John (*b.* 1689) and William (*b.* 1691), but then Elizabeth died giving birth to her namesake in April 1693. Wyck himself died on 26 October 1700 in Mortlake.

Wyck's oil paintings on canvas and panel show skill, vigour, and versatility. There are probably more than 150 still in existence. The battle scenes for which he was most famous owe a debt to Philips Wouwermans (1618–1688) and Jacques Courtois (Il Bourgognone; 1621–1676), and are not dissimilar to the canvases of Adam Frans van der Meulen (1632–1690). Wyck's paintings are attractively coloured and endlessly varied, depicting in the near ground horsemen and foot soldiers in violent action, flourishing swords or firing muskets, with cannon smoke and tiny fighting figures receding into an atmospheric distance. Some depict Turks with moustachios, turbans, and scimitars, reflecting contemporary interest in the Austrian-

Turkish wars. Pictures which included recognizable commanders, such as William III, often at the battle of the Boyne (numerous versions) or the siege of Namur (unfinished picture at National Army Museum, London), were much in demand. He painted one of the earliest depictions in colour of official military uniform, a portrait of Colonel Randolph Egerton seated on a fine grey horse (priv. coll.).

Wyck's hunting pieces are more repetitive, the English countryside generalized and freshly green. He painted Sir Gilbert Coventry, one of his last patrons, with his own horses and hounds in a picture still at Antony, Cornwall (priv. coll.). He also depicted imagined scenes of Mediterranean seaports and Italian *capricci*, as well as particular topographical views of England such as Windsor Castle, the city of Leicester, and Whitehaven docks. He took commissions for country house portraits such as Sprotborough Hall, Yorkshire, and made studies of animals for their owners, for instance a black bull mastiff in front of Dunham Massey Hall, Cheshire (Dunham Massey). His picture *A Gray Stallion Tethered to a Post* (ex Sothebys, 12 July 1995) is one of the earliest English horse portraits which would become so popular with country gentlemen.

Wyck's clients were illustrious. A portrait of James, duke of Monmouth, the king's eldest son, dated c.1673, is probably his earliest English portrait (priv. coll.). Monmouth commissioned four depictions of his campaigns, and paid Wyck £30 in 1676 (BL, Sloane MS 1985, fols. 95–95v). The duke and duchess of Lauderdale acquired several scenes by Thomas Wyck for Ham House, Petersham, Surrey, and a battle piece by Jan Wyck; they all remain *in situ*. Wyck drew up a valuation list of paintings for the duchess, who pawned some pictures with him in 1686 (see Laing and Strachey, 7). The duke of Grafton possesses Wyck's view of a hunt in front of Euston Hall, Suffolk (1677). The duke of Norfolk was twice painted riding a white horse by Wyck: to the artist's normal scale (priv. coll.) and life-size at Drayton House, Northamptonshire. Three scenes of cavalry engagements also hang at Drayton. There are many equestrian portraits by Wyck of William III (one, dated 1692, still hangs at Blenheim Palace, Oxfordshire).

There was only one battle scene by Wyck in the Royal Collection in 1688 (BL, Harley MS 1890, fol. 85v), but a small bronze modello of Charles II on horseback by William Larson (National Gallery of Ireland, Dublin) bears the inscription: 'Baxter taught Wyck Drew Larson Embost & Cast it tow'. Wyck kept in touch with Gerrit Uylenberg, 'Purveyor of His Maties Pictures', until the end of his life (Millar, 540). One 'Jan van Wijck' was taken to Holland in 1682 to 'help … find out horses' for the queen (PRO, warrants not relating to money, T54/9, fol. 174).

Wyck's lively designs of country pursuits appeared as engravings in Richard Blome's *The Gentleman's Recreation* (1686). Two of his preparatory drawings for Blome are in the British Museum, along with his drawing of *The Thames During the Great Frost of 1683/4*. In John Slezer's *Theatrum Scotiae* (1693) Wyck had the task of 'touching and filling up … 57 draughts with little figures at 10 shillings sterlin per piece' (Cavers, 9). Three of these draughts are in the Ashmolean Museum, Oxford. The Yale Center for British Art has a watercolour by Wyck of a stag hunt (Paul Mellon collection), and the Royal Collection a brush drawing of fishermen by a lake.

In 1685 Godfrey Kneller painted a portrait of Wyck (now lost) engraved in mezzotint in 1730 by John Faber junior. Faber also engraved Wyck's battle and hunting scenes, as did John Smith and Bernard Lens. Matthias Read and Sir Martin Beckman, an amateur artist, were both Wyck's pupils, and also John Wootton in the late 1690s. Wootton's early style is difficult to distinguish from his master's. Wyck signed his works with a monogram 'JW', or 'J. Wyck' or 'Jan van Wijck'. Examples of his work are held in the Ulster Museum, Belfast; the National Gallery of Ireland, Dublin; the National Maritime Museum, Greenwich; the Polish National Museum, Warsaw; the Royal Collection, Victoria Gallery, Bath; Temple Newsam House, Leeds; and various private collections.   KATHARINE GIBSON

Sources A. Bredius, MS archival notes, Rijksbureau voor Kunsthistorische Documentatie, The Hague · G. W. Kendall, 'John Wootton, life and a list of engravings after his pictures', *Walpole Society*, 21 (1932–3), 23–42 · O. Millar, 'Gilbert Coventry and his sporting and other paintings', *Burlington Magazine*, 133 (1991), 537–41 · W. Y. Carman, 'Major General Randolph Egerton', *Journal of the Society for Army Historical Research*, 32 (1954), 108–10 · A. Laing and N. Strachey, 'The duke and duchess of Lauderdale's pictures at Ham House', *Apollo*, 139 (1994), 3–9 · R. Blome, *The gentleman's recreation, in two parts: the first being an encyclopedy of the arts and sciences … the second part treats of horsmanship, hawking etc.* (1686) · K. Cavers, *A vision of Scotland: the nation observed by John Slezer, 1671–1717* (1993) · E. Croft-Murray and P. H. Hulton, eds., *Catalogue of British drawings*, 1 (1960), 551–5 · L. Stainton and C. White, *Drawing in England from Hilliard to Hogarth* (1987), 204–6, cat. nos. 62, 63 [exhibition catalogue, BM] · D. B. Brown, *Catalogue of the collection of drawings in the Ashmolean Museum*, 4 (1982), 136–8 · H. V. S. Ogden and M. S. Ogden, *English taste in landscape in the seventeenth century* (1955), 117, 144–5, 154 · J. L. Chester and J. Foster, eds., *London marriage licences, 1521–1869* (1887) · K. Gibson, 'Jan Wyck c.1645–1700: a painter with "a grate deal of fire"', *British Art Journal*, 2/1 (2000–01), 3–13

Likenesses J. Z. Kneller, miniature, 1684; Christies, 11 Oct 1946, lot 88 · G. Kneller, oils, 1685; now lost · attrib. A. Bannerman?, line engraving, 1700–79 · J. Faber junior, mezzotint, 1730 (after G. Kneller, 1685), BM, NPG [*see illus.*]

Wyclif [Wycliffe], **John** [*called* Doctor Evangelicus] (d. 1384), theologian, philosopher, and religious reformer, was, according to the chronicler Thomas Walsingham, a northerner.

Background and early academic career There is good reason to think that Wyclif was a member of the Richmondshire family from the North Riding village of Wycliffe; he can probably be identified with either Johannes filius Willelmi de Wyckliff or Johannes filius Simon de Wycliff, the first of whom was ordained acolyte on 18 December 1350, and both of whom were ordained subdeacon on 12 March 1351, deacon on 18 April 1351, and priest on 24 September 1351. This would suggest he was born in the mid-1320s. Since he is recorded as steward at Merton College for the week 28 May – 4 June 1356 (an outlay of £4 7s. 5d. for the entertainment of eighteen college guests on Ascension day that week), by which time as a probationary fellow he must have been a bachelor of arts, it would seem that Wyclif went to Oxford about 1350 or a little earlier. The Merton *Catalogus vetus*, a list of fellows compiled before 1422 by Thomas Robert, includes Wyclif's name under the reign of Edward III, though a side note, probably in Robert's own hand, comments that 'he was neither a fellow of this house nor did he keep his year of probation fully in it' (Oxford, Merton College, Records 3690, 4.16, fol. 64*v*). However, by December 1360 Wyclif was master of Balliol, an election which makes it likely that he had previously been fellow there, perhaps before migrating temporarily to Merton; Balliol had strong northern connections, and the influence of Archbishop John Thoresby of York (*d.* 1373) at this time on other members of the college may suggest that Wyclif could have had similar affiliations. Other Balliol documents show Wyclif's energy in pursuing arrears of rent from property of the college's living in St Lawrence Jewry, London, up to his resignation as master, when he was promoted to the college's benefice of Fillingham, Lincolnshire; he was admitted on 14 May 1361.

Wyclif held the living of Fillingham until 1368. In 1362 Oxford University sought for him preferment as canon of York, but he received only a canonry in the collegiate church of Westbury-on-Trym, Gloucestershire. On 29 August 1363 he was granted a licence of non-residence for one year from Fillingham for study at Oxford; this was belatedly renewed for a further two years in April 1368. On 28 June 1366 he was ordered to be cited, along with other canons, by Bishop William Whittlesey of Worcester (*d.* 1374) for non-residence, in his case ever since his preferment; the case seems to have been settled without penalty, and Wyclif's canonry, with the prebend of Aust, was ratified in November 1375 (although, apparently by a misapprehension that a vacancy had occurred, another man was granted both positions the same month, a grant that was revoked on the intervention of John of Gaunt, duke of Lancaster, the following month). In 1377 the accounts of the papal collector, Arnaud Garnier, record Wyclif as having paid only a small proportion of the annates on the Aust prebend, £6 13*s.* 4*d.*, with £29 5*s.* 8*d.* still outstanding.

On his return to Oxford for study Wyclif took lodgings at the Queen's College: between October 1363 and October 1364 his name appears twice in the records, once for payments to two workmen on his room, once in reference to his servant; he was later resident in the college again between September 1374 and September 1375 (payment for a latrine with walls, roof, and key for the door), and annual rent was paid for the year beginning 2 August 1380.

Advancement and disappointments On 9 December 1365 Wyclif was appointed by Archbishop Simon Islip (*d.* 1366) to be warden of his recently founded Canterbury College; Islip's original intentions for the college seem to have been for a mixed society of monks and seculars, and this appointment, which displaced a monk, Henry Wodehull, must have been designed to strengthen the role of the seculars. However, Islip's successor, Simon Langham (*d.* 1376), in the spring of 1367 moved to modify the college to

one solely for Benedictine monks, appointing first John Redyngate as warden, but then almost immediately reinstating Wodehull. The changes were resisted by Wyclif and the other secular fellows, who continued to reside and appealed to Rome. The legal case was long and bitter, but eventually was concluded on 15 May 1370 by the restoration to the monks of both occupation and revenues of the college; Wyclif later commented that the foundation of Canterbury College had been sinful, but its dissolution (as he described it) worse.

In the restoration document, which promulgated a judgment given on 23 July 1369, Wyclif is described as 'in sacra theologia bacallarius'; this implies that he must have begun studying theology at the latest by 1362–3. His further promotion to the degree of DTh is datable to 1372 or 1373 by an amplification in the renewal in December 1373 of a papal document originally of January 1371; this amplification describes Wyclif at the later date as 'soon afterwards to be licenciate in theology, and at this point master' (*CEPR letters*, 4.193), implying that Wyclif had in the meantime incepted as doctor of theology.

In November 1368 Wyclif exchanged the Fillingham living for the rectory of Ludgershall, Buckinghamshire, on the presentation of the prior of St John of Jerusalem, Clerkenwell; it is worth noticing that in May 1371 a portion of the tithes, which belonged to the prior of Bermondsey (an alien priory), was granted to him by the king, for which his guarantors were Robert Wyclif, clerk, and John Santon, mayor of York. On 28 January 1371 Wyclif by papal letter was granted expectation of a canonry and prebend of Lincoln; the confirmation of this, dated 26 December 1373, explicitly allowed that he might hold this in plurality with the position at Westbury. It seems that Wyclif did receive the canonry: in an Oxford document of January 1376 Wyclif is described as *canonicus Lincolniensis*; but his tenure of the Caistor prebend was brief, since the papal provisor, Philip Thornbury, displaced him. He appears again in the accounts of the papal collector, Arnaud Garnier, as in debt for the annates of the prebend; part was paid on his behalf by Robert Wyclif on 4 May 1377 after two warnings; the remainder was postponed to 13 January 1378 because he had been deprived by Thornbury. Wyclif regarded himself as having been ousted from his rightful position by an upstart young foreigner. Ludgershall rectory was again exchanged for the rectory of Lutterworth, Leicestershire, to which he was presented by the king on 7 April 1374. He held Lutterworth to his death on 31 December 1384. Robert Hallum, bishop of Salisbury (*d.* 1417), is reported by Thomas Netter (*d.* 1430) to have alleged that Wyclif was disappointed not to have been chosen as bishop of Worcester; the story, if it has any substance, must relate to the vacancy that ensued on the death of William Lenn in 1373, a vacancy not effectively filled until September 1375, by which time Wyclif might have hoped for some recognition of his work in the Bruges mission.

Royal service and political involvements In 1371 Wyclif was an executor of William Askeby, archdeacon of Northampton and chancellor of the exchequer, suggesting that he already may have had connections with those in high position. The point at which Wyclif first became associated with the royal service is not clear. In *De civili dominio*, book 2, chapter 1, he reports an argument in favour of the right of the secular powers to use church property in time of need which he heard in the parliament in London; this probably refers to business in the parliament of February–March 1371. The grant by the king of a portion of the Ludgershall tithes in May of that year may suggest that Wyclif had himself contributed something to urging the case. The royal presentation to the Lutterworth rectory in April 1374 likewise may indicate unspecified service on Wyclif's part. The first documented instance, however, is the appointment on 26 July 1374 of Wyclif as one of five new envoys to continue negotiations in Bruges with papal officials over clerical taxes and provisions. Unfortunately, more is known about Wyclif's finances in this embassy than about his contribution to the discussions. The negotiations in Bruges ended without conclusion, and the representatives of each side retired for further consultation; Wyclif was not reappointed for the next stage in August 1375. But some three or four years later Wyclif still spoke of himself as *peculiaris regis clericus* ('special clerk of the king').

Two years later, in September 1376, Wyclif was summoned from Oxford by John of Gaunt to appear before the king's council. Walsingham suggests both that Gaunt had identified Wyclif from the schoolman's teaching in Oxford as his tool for a campaign against the church, and that Wyclif also spread those views in public sermons in London. It is unclear what part if any Wyclif played in the parliament that ensued. On 19 February 1377, according to Walsingham, Wyclif was summoned to appear before Archbishop Simon Sudbury (*d.* 1381) and other bishops in St Paul's, charged with seditious preaching. Wyclif appeared, accompanied not only by a representative of each order of friars but also by Gaunt and Henry, Lord Percy (*d.* 1408), the last bearing his marshal's staff. Percy ordered Wyclif to be seated, a move that William Courtenay, bishop of London (*d.* 1396), forbade; angry words ensued between Gaunt and Courtenay. The tumult inflamed a riot, which worsened the following day, among the Londoners outside the church; the hostility was directed primarily against Gaunt and Percy, who fled—at which point the meeting was abandoned. Wyclif's teaching at this point seems to have offended on three matters: that the pope's excommunication was invalid, and that any priest, if he had power, could pronounce release as well as the pope; that kings and lords cannot grant anything perpetually to the church, since the lay powers can deprive erring clerics of their temporalities; that temporal lords in need could legitimately remove the wealth of possessioners. Whether the charges against Wyclif were dropped with the abandonment of the meeting is unclear: Walsingham states that the archbishop ordered him to be silent, forbidding him to allude to or argue the subject again anywhere, and ordering him to stop any others from airing it, but this follows a reference to the papal bull against Wyclif which had not been issued at the time of the meeting.

Papal censure On 22 May 1377 Gregory XI (r. 1370–78) issued five bulls condemning the views of John Wyclif, three to the archbishop of Canterbury and bishop of London, one to the king, and one to the chancellor of the University of Oxford. The first three exhort the ecclesiastical officials to inquire into Wyclif's activities and views, and, if this should prove difficult in Oxford, to cite Wyclif to appear in person before the pope within three months; the same officials should explain the problem to the king. The nineteen conclusions on which the condemnation was based are all derived, for the most part verbatim, from Wyclif's *De civili dominio*, book 1, though some of the views can be traced in earlier writings. According to one chronicle the list was reduced from a longer one of about fifty sent to the pope. The source of the pope's information seems certain to have been the Benedictine Adam Easton (*d.* 1397), at that time resident in the papal court in Avignon; Easton's prior correspondence to obtain writings by Wyclif, and his subsequent response in his *Defensorium* both confirm this.

Wyclif said that the bishop of Rochester (Thomas Brinton) in fury told him of the papal condemnation as it had been made known to him by a notary's report from the papal court during the public session of parliament; if correct, this points to a date between 13 October and 28 November 1377, indicating that the bulls were unusually slow to reach England. Before their arrival, in the autumn of 1377, according to the *Fasciculi zizaniorum*, in response to a request put to him by 'the lord king Richard II of England and his great council', Wyclif wrote a text regarding the legitimacy of withholding taxes due to the pope in time of national need; the papal collector concerned was Arnaud Garnier, against whom Wyclif had previously written, and in whose accounts he had twice appeared as a defaulter. The same source concludes the story, 'and here silence was imposed on him concerning these matters by the lord Richard and the council' (*Fasciculi zizaniorum*, 271). Given Richard's youth, it must have been the council, and presumably particularly Gaunt, that was responsible for this request and also for the suppression of Wyclif's excessive zeal.

Gregory XI's bulls were received in Oxford a few days before Christmas 1377. The continuator of *Eulogium historiarum* describes the objections of Wyclif and his associates in congregation to allowing imprisonment of an English subject as a result of a papal letter, but comments that the vice-chancellor thought that some response was needed, if only to maintain the privileges of the university; he consequently called Wyclif and ordered him to stay in the 'Black Hall'. The university's chancellor (Adam Tonworth), following scrutiny of the conclusions by the regent doctors in theology, declared that the condemned conclusions in the pope's bull 'were true, but sounded badly to those who heard them' (*Eulogium historiarum*, 3.349). Wyclif appears to have been soon released by friends. Oxford having blocked any process against Wyclif as Gregory had anticipated, Archbishop Sudbury and

Bishop Courtenay ordered the chancellor of Oxford to cite Wyclif to appear within thirty days at St Paul's to answer the charges. Some time in the early spring of 1378 (the exact date is unclear, but was before Gregory's death on 27 March, or possibly before news of that death had reached England), Wyclif duly appeared, though at Lambeth not St Paul's. Once again the investigation was disrupted. This time Sir Lewis Clifford (d. 1404), declaring himself an emissary from Joan of Kent, the king's mother, appeared to direct the prelates not to pass any decision *sententialiter* ('formally') against Wyclif. But Wyclif was questioned on the condemned conclusions, clarified his position in regard to some, and, Walsingham comments, 'fooled his investigators' (*Historia Anglicana*, 1.362). During the inquiry the Londoners burst into the chamber, but this time to express their support of Wyclif. Though no formal verdict was given, Wyclif was ordered not to discuss such matters in the schools or in sermons, for fear of scandalizing the laity. A similar prohibition at this time on John Acley, a Durham monk who had attempted to oppose Wyclif, indicates that the authorities were above all anxious to avoid any public airing of the issues.

The Westminster scandal and the peasants' revolt On 11 August 1378 Sir Alan Buxhull, keeper of the Tower of London, invaded the sanctuary of Westminster Abbey to arrest two escaped prisoners who had there taken refuge, Robert Hawley and John Shakyl; the two had been imprisoned for failing to release to Gaunt the count of Denia, a Spanish hostage for whom they were seeking ransom. Shakyl was seized, but Hawley killed while trying to avoid arrest. Three days later Archbishop Sudbury excommunicated those guilty, and Courtenay reinforced this. Gaunt was regarded by the Londoners as responsible for this blasphemy. During the session of parliament in Gloucester in October the matter was discussed; although there is no mention of Wyclif's name in the official record, it seems certain that Wyclif prepared material to defend the invasion of sanctuary, and that this material, along with rebuttals of subsequent objections, is incorporated into his *De ecclesia* from chapter 7 onwards. Wyclif comments that he writes 'at the order of the lord king … in my treatise', though later he also describes 'the decision of my lord, the lord duke [of Lancaster]' (Wyclif, *De ecclesia*, 266).

After this it is hard to trace Wyclif's direct involvement with political affairs, or the use of his powers of argument by Gaunt (though, as will be seen, contact between them was maintained). Most difficult to assess is the relation between Wyclif and the peasants' revolt of June 1381. The chroniclers almost unanimously link his ideas with the instigation of rebellion, and some attempt to portray John Ball as Wyclif's disciple, but their picture may well be distorted by the fact that the rising began within a month of the condemnation of Wyclif's eucharistic views in Oxford (Ball had been in trouble with the bishops since at the latest 1355). On 13 June 1381, Corpus Christi day, the rebels reached the outskirts of London, and forced their way into the city, where they destroyed Gaunt's palace of the Savoy and the New Temple; on 14 June, following the Mile End

conference with Richard II, Sudbury and others were killed by the rebels; on 15 June, Wat Tyler was killed at Smithfield. From chapter 13 to the end of *De blasphemia* Wyclif discusses the revolt: a dispassionate reading of that analysis reveals Wyclif as shocked, though not surprised, by the violence, deeply sympathetic to the plight of the poor laity, and fiercely critical of the policies, whether ecclesiastical or lay, that had led to that plight, but not as consciously implicated in the origins of the revolt—however much his preaching, if as provocative as Walsingham reports, and as the warning at the end of the Lambeth trial implies, may have inadvertently contributed.

Condemnation in Oxford The month before the revolt, in May 1381, a committee organized by the Oxford chancellor, William Barton, condemned the views of unnamed heretics that had been preached 'in this university and publicly outside it' (*Fasciculi zizaniorum*, 110–13). The views concerned the eucharist: that material bread and wine remain after the consecration, and that the body and blood of Christ are not present 'in substance, nor indeed physically, but figuratively or symbolically'. The condemnation was announced to Wyclif while he was lecturing in the schools of the Augustinian friars; though confused, he continued, saying that no chancellor or his allies could deter him. Though Barton asserted that the condemnation was unanimous, Wyclif claimed that the vote had gone against him by seven to five. He appealed to the king, and then to Gaunt; Gaunt appears to have come to Oxford and ordered Wyclif's silence. Not complying, Wyclif appears to have produced a declaration of his views, dated in one manuscript to 10 May 1381. In the later *Trialogus* Wyclif wrote, 'I agreed not to use in future outside the university the terms "the substance of material bread or wine"' (Wyclif, *Trialogus*, 375), an undated undertaking but one which may have been given at this stage in the hope of satisfying the committee. The ensuing outcry, however, appears to have made it plain to Wyclif that he could no longer remain in Oxford, and he withdrew in the autumn to Lutterworth; the latest evidence for his presence in the university is his deposit, along with three colleagues, of a copy of the *Decretum* (surviving as BL, Royal MS, 10 E.ii) in a loan chest on 22 October 1381.

After Sudbury's murder by the London rebels Courtenay became archbishop of Canterbury, and action against Wyclif became much more strenuous. Courtenay, realizing from the continued activities of Wyclif's disciples in Oxford through the winter of 1381–2 that action from outside the university was required, first initiated enquiries through his agent Peter Stokes (d. 1399). Subsequently he called a council (known from its venue as the Blackfriars Council, or at the time more often as the Earthquake Council from the tremor that was felt in London during its course—a portent interpreted in opposite ways by Wyclif's foes and by his friends) that assembled first on 17 May 1382. Four days later a list of twenty-four conclusions were condemned, ten as heretical, fourteen as erroneous; the first group concerned the eucharist, oral confession, the lack of powers of a priest or a pope in mortal sin, the temporalities of the church, and that no pope after Urban VI (r. 1378–89) should be accepted; the second group covered views on excommunication, unlicensed preaching, the powers of the secular rulers to deprive erring ecclesiastics, tithes, special prayers, and the religious orders including the friars. Wyclif later commented that some of the conclusions were reasonably condemned, but that no one had actually maintained them (a fair enough point, at least in regard to the seventh heresy 'quod Deus debet obedire diabolo'—'that God ought to obey the devil'). The signatories to the proceedings vary slightly in the copies, but include eight or ten bishops, representatives of the four fraternal orders, and other clerics.

On 26 May a parliamentary statute was issued, requiring sheriffs and other officials to imprison unauthorized preachers or those defending the condemned articles, and a month later the king's letters patent reinforced this statute. Through all this process none of the documents name the author of the heresies and errors, and at no point was Wyclif formally condemned. The chancellor of Oxford, by then Robert Rygge (d. 1410), on 28 May resisted the demand to publish the condemnation in Oxford, and Philip Repyndon (d. 1424) on Corpus Christi day (5 June) preached an inflammatory sermon using Wyclif's eucharistic teaching. On 30 May a London procession to proclaim the condemnation concluded with a sermon from the Carmelite John Kenningham (d. 1399). A second meeting of the Blackfriars Council on 12 June reiterated the condemnation, and this time the signatories were largely Oxford men; after dispute the condemnation was finally published in Oxford on 15 June, and Wyclif and his disciples were forbidden to preach or teach until they had purged their heresy. On 13 July the chancellor and proctors of Oxford University were ordered to inquire for supporters of Wyclif or his disciple Nicholas Hereford, to search for books or tracts by the two, and to hand them over to the archbishop.

Last years The obscurity into which Wyclif was allowed to disappear is indicative of some continued protection by John of Gaunt, though whether this was his active deflection of pursuit or the ecclesiastical authorities' unwillingness to tangle with a magnate who had once been linked with Wyclif is unclear. Certainly Wyclif in two later works wrote anxiously about a plot by the friars against Gaunt, 'because he did not wish that true priests should be punished' (Wyclif, *Polemical Works*, 1.218, 227, 332). At Lutterworth, Wyclif continued to write with increasing energy, and, to judge by the form and content of those works, continued to have channels of communication to academic and political circles. Though no formal summons has yet been traced, Wyclif himself indicates that he was cited to appear before the pope. In *De citacionibus frivolis* Wyclif writes that 'one who is paralysed and lame has been ordered to that papal court, but royal prohibition stops him going' (Wyclif, *Polemical Works*, 2.556); since the pope is in the same text described as *refuga* ('exile'), the summons was presumably to Urban VI after his flight from Rome to Naples in 1383. The rubric to another text, the letter to Urban VI, as that appears in the *Fasciculi zizaniorum*

(but not in the other thirteen copies), gives an even later date of 1384 to the citation.

Thomas Gascoigne (d. 1458), in a narrative transcribed from British Library, Cotton MS Otho A.xiv before that was burnt, reports on the authority of John Horn, a man of over eighty years who had been priest with Wyclif for the last two years of his life, that during that time Wyclif was *paralyticus*. Horn also stated that Wyclif was struck by further paralysis at the elevation while hearing mass in Lutterworth church on 28 December 1384, and that he did not speak again, and died on 31 December; the date of death is confirmed by the institution material for his successor. He was buried in the churchyard. But in the spring of 1428 on the orders of Richard Fleming, bishop of Lincoln (d. 1431), acting on the instructions of Pope Martin V (r. 1417–31) of 9 December 1427, officials exhumed the bones, burnt them, and scattered the ashes on the River Swift. Thus was completed the anathema pronounced on Wyclif, and on a list of 267 articles from his writings, at the Council of Constance on 4 May 1415.

The spread of Wyclif's ideas The anathema of 1415 reflected the inability of the ecclesiastical authorities to contain, let alone eradicate, the spread of Wyclif's ideas. Before Wyclif's departure from Oxford in late 1381 there is already evidence for the dissemination of his views and of his writings not only in England but also abroad. As early as c.1378–80 Nicholas Biceps in Prague was already debating the relevance of the view about universals that he identified as Wyclif's to the doctrine of the eucharist; a student in Paris, at the end of the somewhat abbreviated copy he made of the *De civili dominio*, recorded that on 16 January 1382 in the university a friar had been obliged to recant some views from the text that he had been defending. These contacts, and the others with Bohemia that quickly developed, began through the traditional channels of academic life. It is now clear that issues that Wyclif had raised continued to dominate Oxford academic circles up to the end of the first decade of the fifteenth century, and that defenders of Wyclif's views remained powerful in Oxford. More unconventionally Wyclif appears to have fostered the spread of his views to an audience outside the university world, an audience that had to use English rather than Latin.

Opponents observed this move, and were alarmed by it, even though, according to Wyclif, they responded in like mode. Five of his followers, Philip Repyndon, Nicholas Hereford, John Aston, Robert Alyngton, and Laurence Bedeman, had by mid-1382 undertaken expeditions to spread Wyclif's doctrine at least as far afield as Odiham, Hampshire, and Brackley, Northamptonshire; Repyndon may well have been one source of that doctrine's appearance in Leicester the same year. Whether or not Wyclif organized these expeditions, or the bands of 'poor preachers' which the chronicler Henry Knighton later recognized, Wycliffite ideas, through the medium of peripatetic priests and through the medium of the written word, spread rapidly, especially in the midlands and south of the country. Those favouring Wycliffite views came from an early stage to be known as Lollards; the first instance of the use was apparently by Henry Crump in 1382, when he was suspended from the Oxford congregation for calling the heretics 'Lollards'. Walsingham and Knighton also identify a group of 'Lollard knights', who, they allege, continued to influence the royal court against the church; research has confirmed the alliances between the men specified, though how far their activities veered towards Wyclif's own radicalism is less clear.

From 1382 onwards the ecclesiastical authorities attempted to stamp out the dissemination of Wycliffite views and materials, and to involve the secular authorities in their efforts; notable stages in the reaction against Wycliffism were the introduction in 1401 of the death penalty for heresy, and the constitutions of Archbishop Thomas Arundel (d. 1414), devised in 1407 and issued in 1409, the second of which largely ended academic involvement in Lollardy. In June 1410 a list of eighteen conclusions from named works by Wyclif was condemned by the Oxford convocation of regent and non-regent masters, and the *Opus evangelicum* and *Trialogus* were banned from further debate; in March 1411 a list of 267 propositions was added. The rising of January 1414 by Sir John Oldcastle (d. 1417), a condemned Lollard, and his supporters finally ensured the support of the royal administration for the extirpation of this heresy. Lollardy, however, persisted throughout the fifteenth century, even though the number of cases recorded between c.1435 and c.1475 is small; but the correspondence of views between suspects investigated in the early fifteenth century and in the period c.1480–c.1535, and the reappearance of the same geographical areas, such as London, the Lichfield–Coventry and Berkshire downs–Chilterns areas, and eastern Kent, make it plain that the movement, however clandestine its survival, never died out. Though there is still debate about the precise contribution of Lollardy to the sixteenth-century English Reformation, connections can be traced in numerous ways.

The influence of Wyclif was arguably greater on the continent. By means that are still largely unclear, Wyclif's writings appear to have become well known in Bohemia by 1400. Elements in his ideas fitted in closely with native preoccupations there: the realism of his philosophy proved a useful mode of opposition to the prevailing nominalism of the German majority in the University of Prague, and was eagerly seized on by the Czech minority; his outspoken criticism of the abuses in the contemporary church, and his desire for a purging of its worldliness, coalesced with the strong native reform movement of men such as Matěj of Janov and Milič of Kroměříž. In 1397 Jan Hus copied five of Wyclif's philosophical works, and in the following years was increasingly influenced also by his theological and ecclesiological writings; his own works frequently mention and quote from Wyclif's (notably Hus's *De ecclesia*, completed in 1413, which incorporates large sections from Wyclif's text of the same name). Opposition to Hus had identified the English heretic as his teacher, and, when the Council of Constance turned its attention to heresy, the ideas of the two men were closely linked. A list of 45 opinions by Wyclif was condemned on 4 May 1415, a longer list of 260 views condemned on 6 July in the presence of Hus, and the same day Hus was burnt at the stake for his heresy, a heresy that consisted, in the view of the council fathers, largely in adherence to those anathematized conclusions. The reverence for Wyclif's name and opinions, and the copying of his works, continued in Hussite Bohemia.

The transmission of Wyclif's writings The listing of Wyclif's writings has a long history, going back at least to the early years of the fifteenth century when a comprehensive catalogue, with title, incipit, and in most cases number of chapters for each work, was put together in Hussite Bohemia. Location lists of manuscripts start with John Bale in the mid-sixteenth century. Most recent and complete of the catalogues (though modifications and additions can be made) is that by W. R. Thomson (1983).

The analysis of the transmission of Wyclif's numerous writings has been complicated by the variety of audiences to which he appealed at different times of his life. His output from the time when he was still lecturing on logic in the Oxford arts faculty may appear in either English or continental manuscripts, alongside a variety of contemporary textbooks of a similar kind; recent scrutiny of these collections has turned up new manuscripts of Wyclif in Oxford, Italy, and Spain. But the transmission of his main philosophical and theological output has been largely through English, and especially Bohemian, copies; the suppression of his ideas and followers in both areas complicates any attempt to assess textual relations. There have also been less readily explicable later losses: though three copies of the *De civili dominio* are known to have survived in England until the sixteenth century, only a short extract is now found there. Many of the major texts—*De ecclesia*, *De officio regis*, *De potestate pape*, *De eucharistia*, *Trialogus*, and a multitude of the short polemical works—are now only known in manuscripts originating in Bohemia. The authenticity of the majority of texts is not in question: authorial cross-references between the major works are common, allusions to contemporary affairs frequent, along with a characteristic vocabulary; the scholarly catalogue of the writings of the Doctor Evangelicus made early in the fifteenth century by Bohemian disciples confirms most.

Chronology of writing is a much more substantial problem. Not surprisingly given the amount he wrote, Wyclif habitually reused or rearranged old material (a *De religione* criticized by William Woodford and mentioned once by Wyclif himself survives, but divided between *De civili dominio*, book 3, and *De apostasia*), and grouped together as a single whole arguments that seem to have originated as rough papers (*De ecclesia* incorporates various sets of material, and refutations of objections, produced for the Gloucester parliament of 1378). An apparently firmly dated text such as the *Confessio* on the eucharist turns out to be replicated exactly in a series of passages in *De apostasia*, with its coda (available only in Bohemian copies) in a sermon for Corpus Christi day. More troublesome is Wyclif's habit of revising early texts late in his career: a striking example is the appearance of his final eucharistic ideas at one point in the *De logica tercia* (cited in the Oxford list of 1411 as from *De arte sophistica*), deriving in origin from the 1360s. Existing editions, incomplete as they are for the *Summa de ente*, non-existent for the *Postilla* and some other works, based on only a small proportion of the manuscripts now known, are insufficient for a final view of chronology, and the following comments must be regarded as provisional.

Early writings on logic and theology Wyclif's early works mirror his academic career. Recent exploration of late medieval logical manuscripts has produced two parts of what may be one guide for students to modes of argument and terminology. The first two parts of the certainly authentic *De logica*, and probably the *De proposicionibus insolubilibus* (or *Summa insolubilium*), derive from Wyclif's period as a regent in arts, though all may have been revised later. The last named may be the first part of a largely lost collection of tracts whose outlines are traceable from references in the *De actibus anime*, itself perhaps a revised version of the fifth book; material now in the *De ente predicamentali* may have begun as the third part. This collection, the questions on Aristotle's *Physics* (still unedited), and the record of three *proposiciones Wyclif in determinacione sua* found in a Worcester student's notebook probably originated in the late 1360s. More readily discernible is the final shape intended for the *Summa de ente*, arranged in two books, the first with seven sections, the second with six, though that shape probably represents various revisions. The first four tracts of the first book and the first three of the second form two coherent sequences and were probably written consecutively about the late 1360s and 1370–73 respectively; none of them seems to have gained wide circulation, and the second book may reflect *Sentences* study. The fifth section of the first book may have been reused material; the final section of the second book, which must be later than 1368, incorporates a tract *De anichilacione*, perhaps originally independent but relevant to later views on the eucharist. The remaining four tracts are more substantial works, may be slightly later, and were far more popular: *De tempore* was added to book 1, *De trinitate* and *De ydeis* to book 2. The last, together with the *De universalibus*, the fifth and most important section of book 1 in the final arrangement, set out very clearly and influentially Wyclif's mature understanding of universals and of the relation of God and time, hence laying down the underlying thought behind his views on predestination and free will. *De logica tractatus tercius* and *De materia et forma*, both standing outside the *Summa de ente*, probably derive from about this stage.

Wyclif's transition to a study of theology is reflected in the two tracts *De composicione hominis* and *De benedicta incarnacione* (both possibly part of a commentary on the *Sentences*) but most extensively in his *Postilla in totam Bibliam*. This last, now surviving only in part, was the most comprehensive biblical commentary since Nicolas de Lyre in the early fourteenth century; it is almost entirely uncontroversial and largely derivative from standard authors. Parts of it probably represent Wyclif's notes for his required lectures on scripture, and the second prologue to the commentary on the Song of Solomon is Wyclif's inaugural lecture for the degree of DTh; these sections thus originate between 1371 and 1373, but composition was apparently not in strict biblical order. Some parts equally may have an origin other than lectures: the extended debate in the Oxford schools on biblical interpretation between Wyclif and the Carmelite John Kenningham, probably *c*.1372–3, surviving only in part, disputes understandings of specific biblical passages that are not found in the *Postilla*. Even if this is not the *Postilla privata* to which Wyclif later alludes, it certainly provided him with a resource on which he repeatedly drew until his death.

Dominion and law From about 1373 Wyclif turned his attention to the more contentious area of dominion and law. His first investigation was, to judge by the unfinished state of all three books in all surviving manuscripts of *De dominio divino*, tentative. More systematic were the next three discussions of law that later became the opening sections of the twelve-book *Summa theologie*: on divine law in *De mandatis* (which a reference to Arnaud Garnier places in 1375), on human lordship before the fall in *De statu innocencie*, and on human lordship since the fall in *De civili dominio*, book 1. This last can be fairly closely dated to 1375–6, since it was from this source that Gregory XI's bull of 22 May 1377 derived its nineteen condemned propositions. The shape that the *Summa theologie* finally took was distorted by that condemnation and the refutations produced, to which Wyclif replied in material that now forms *De civili dominio*, books 2 and 3. From this point it becomes even more difficult to fix precise dates to most works as they stand: Wyclif's involvement in political affairs, and the growing opposition from academics and other clerics, meant that he often was at work on several fronts simultaneously.

The *De ecclesia*, eventually book 7, reads as a sequence of ill-combined drafts, which, judging by internal cross-references, may have been substantially abbreviated, though the basic subject matter of many chapters, the Hawley and Shakyl sanctuary case, gives a date *post quem* of 1378 (as does a reference to Pope Urban). Equally the *De veritate sacre scripture*, finally the long sixth book, incorporates a number of sections that may have started as independent tracts; internal reference to Gregory XI's condemnation and to the outbreak of the papal schism make a date of 1377–8 feasible for parts at least of the text. The next three books of the *Summa*—*De officio regis* (with reference to the Hawley and Shakyl case, and to the papal schism), *De potestate pape* (which alludes to the conflicts between the rival popes, and is dated by an extract written by Adam Stocton as 1379), *De symonia* (this last forecast in the final words of *De veritate*)—could reasonably be assigned to the ensuing two years, though precise internal dating is not available. *De apostasia*, the eleventh, as it stands incorporates Wyclif's mature thought on the eucharist; it uses verbatim the *Confessio* of 10 May 1381, but may have been compiled two years later. The final book,

De blasphemia, is more closely datable: its first twelve chapters frequently allude to the Oxford condemnation of his eucharistic theology in the spring of 1381 and to the growing hostility of the friars, while from chapter 13 to the end the dominant concern is the peasants' revolt—it seems reasonable to date the work to May–July 1381.

Occasional writings and late compositions Along with these works whose titles provide an impression (not entirely borne out by their content) of a rational sequence, Wyclif wrote a large number of more occasional pieces; some of these were subsequently incorporated into the longer works, others remained freestanding. Thus, for instance, the opening of *De civili dominio*, book 2, provides Wyclif's answers to the objections of an unnamed Benedictine, and a large section of book 3 of the same work replies to Woodford's *Determinatio de civili dominio*; within *De veritate sacre scripture* is a reply to an attack 'by one doctor, whom I had believed to be my firm friend, and an important defender of catholic truth' (one manuscript marginally identifies this as William Barton, a credible, if not inevitable, suggestion); sections of *De officio regis* deal with arguments of the abbot of Chertsey, John Uske. Freestanding replies include answers to the objections of Uthred Boldon (*d.* 1396) and William Binham concerning Wyclif's views on endowment and the relations of the secular ruler to the church, a controversy associated with the events of 1377–8, the earlier academic answers to John Kenningham, four replies to Ralph Strode (*d.* 1387) on various topics, and a long and hostile response to a set of forty-four conclusions advanced against him by the Cistercian William Rymington written after Wyclif's retirement to Lutterworth. There is also a host of short tracts, dating mostly from the last ten years of Wyclif's career; some of these were provoked by easily identifiable events (such as the *De iuramento Arnaldi* by the activities of the papal collector Arnaud Garnier), while others are less easily datable.

Wyclif's retirement to Lutterworth in the autumn of 1381 brought a renewed outburst of new works, long and short, and of revisions of earlier texts. It was probably at this stage that a collection of early sermons was made, many of them precisely datable between 19 October 1376 and 28 August 1379 (*Sermones quadraginta*), though rearranged into a single liturgical sequence. To the Lutterworth years are also assignable three longer sets of sermons in their surviving form, on the Sunday gospels and epistles, and for the *sanctorale*; despite their date, these and the equally late *Sermones viginti* group seem incredible as a record of Wyclif's preaching to a small-town congregation, and must have been intended for a more academic readership. Equally academic is the *Trialogus*, a summary in four books of Wyclif's philosophical and theological views. Contemporary issues, involving the problems of the papal schism and of the lamentable English contribution to its process in the 'Despenser crusade' of 1383, or of the opposition to his own views, form the starting point for a number of short tracts. The final composition was the incomplete *Opus evangelicum*, to which the scribes of all four surviving manuscripts appended the note

'Auctoris vita finitur et hoc opus ita' ('The life of the author came to its end at the same time as this book'; Wyclif, *Opus evangelicum*, 2.336); this reverted to biblical commentary on Matthew 5–7 and 23–25, and John 13–17, though in peculiar and almost certainly provisional form.

English texts: the Bible It seems clear from allusions within his own works that Wyclif, in addition to his vast Latin output, also composed material in English; some allusions could be to oral teaching, but others point towards a written form. Wyclif certainly advocated the teaching of the laity in the vernacular, and those who attempted to silence him, from Gregory XI onwards, mention the dangers ensuant on the spread of his doctrines through use of the vernacular and imply that this means had already been used. Biographers from John Bale (*d.* 1563) onwards have attempted to link surviving English Wycliffite texts to Wyclif himself; the attempt has been largely unconvincing, and modern sceptics regard it as probable that nothing in English direct from Wyclif's pen now exists despite the large debt that certain vernacular works owe to his ideas and terminology.

One case deserves fuller consideration: the first complete English translation of the Bible. The claim for Wyclif's responsibility for this immense work goes back to the chronicler Henry Knighton, writing not later than 1394: the gospel, which Christ had entrusted to clerks and the doctors of the church, Wyclif 'translated from Latin into the language not of angels but of Englishmen, so that he made that common and open to the laity, and to women who were able to read, which used to be for literate and perceptive clerks' (*Knighton's Chronicle*, 242–4). Critical investigation of the processes that lie behind the final translation, itself an idiomatic revision of an earlier very literal version, as these are discernible from the account in the *General Prologue* and from a comparison of even a small proportion of the numerous surviving manuscripts, indicates that one person certainly cannot be regarded as solely responsible; a large team of academic helpers must have been involved. Whether Wyclif himself participated at an early stage seems irretrievable, though the multitude of his Latin writings from 1378 onwards can hardly have left him time. The association of biblical translation with his followers, an association which by 1407 was so close as to be an identifying mark, confirms Wyclif's inspiration as a crucial factor in the collaborative labours. The continued use of the term 'Wycliffite Bible' seems therefore justifiable, even if Wyclif's direct participation in its production seems improbable.

Authorities and influences From Wyclif's quotations and his own references it is possible to build up a picture of the influences on his thought which closer analysis of individual works shows to be largely correct. The range of his reading was enormous, even if, compared with a Paris scholar of the same period, it was restricted to relatively well-tried authors. Philosophically Aristotle was the overwhelming formative thinker—in this Wyclif was typical of medieval scholastic writers. Less familiar are Alhazen

(Ibn al-Haytham) and the thirteenth-century Polish scientist Witelo, whose works on optics Wyclif frequently cites. Theologically Augustine was, again conventionally enough, the overriding influence; while other patristic authors—Ambrose, Gregory, Pseudo-Chrysostom, Jerome—are often cited, Augustine was rightly recognized by himself and by his opponents as Wyclif's single master; Thomas Netter's description *filius Augustini* was not a misnomer. Post-patristic writers are only infrequently mentioned: Bernard of Clairvaux (whose views were not always accepted) and Hugh of St Victor make frequent appearances, but only Robert Grosseteste (*d.* 1253), *Lincolniensis*, seems to engage Wyclif's consistent enthusiasm. Despite the distaste Wyclif in his later works shows for canon law and even more for its practitioners, his mastery of its details has led to suggestions that he may at some time have intended to study in the law faculty; the *Decretum* copy deposited in October 1381 indicates a continuing interest in this area.

Two fourteenth-century writers provided crucial and acknowledged stimuli to Wyclif's thought: Thomas Bradwardine (*d.* 1349) in the area of determinism and Richard Fitzralph (*d.* 1360), whose ideas of dominion underlie Wyclif's more radical views. Aquinas is quoted with respect even if sometimes in disagreement; the commentary on the *Sentences* of William Ockham (*d.* 1349) is used in the early works, but his later political works, with large parts of which Wyclif might have found himself in sympathy, were apparently unknown; Duns Scotus is the preeminent example of the *doctores signorum* ('doctors of [superficial] signs') and as such deplored. Gregory XI in his bull of 1377 claimed that Wyclif was setting forward the repugnant views of Marsiglio da Padua and Jean de Jandun; but any claim for the similarities between Wyclif's support for the secular ruler against ecclesiastical claims and that of the *Defensor pacis* has to face the difficulties that Wyclif never mentions Marsiglio or quotes from his works, and that it is unproven that the text was known in England before Wyclif's death. Wyclif's concern with precise verbal accuracy, and with the historical status of his authorities, is frequently visible, and that concern affected some of his more perceptive opponents: his doubts about the authenticity and date of the text he quotes sometimes as Ambrose or as Fulgentius, and more often as *Auctor de divinis officiis*, are mirrored by Netter, as shown by the latter's story of the enquiry, allegedly at the instigation of Henry IV, in Oxford in the early years of the fifteenth century into the identity of this text's author.

Philosophical writings Wyclif's writings during the first decade of his academic career add up to a substantial corpus of philosophical writing. It is one that has rarely been studied for its own sake. Protestant writers have been repelled by its scholastic subtlety; Catholic writers have preferred to concentrate on scholastics who made a more orthodox end. It is not easy to make a judgement of Wyclif's philosophical originality, because this depends on a comparison with his immediate predecessors, whose works have only recently become objects of interest to scholars. Wyclif himself was in general reluctant to

acknowledge debts to his Oxford teachers and predecessors: Bradwardine, Fitzralph, and Walter Burley (*d.* 1345) stand out as exceptions. He preferred to base his system on more august and distant authors, such as Grosseteste, Anselm, and above all Augustine. But the philosophical system that he gradually developed, whatever proportion of it is original and whatever proportion derived, is of considerable interest in its own right.

Wyclif's early lecture courses on logic, it is true, make no substantial contribution to the subject, though they have their interest in the light of his later career. His *De logica* is a brisk but unadventurous treatise of elementary Aristotelian logic; it is unusual only in that most of the examples are biblical texts, and the logic itself is described as the logic of scripture. The *Logice continuacio* is more original and more discursive, and defends a novel form of atomism. Both works probably date from 1360 or shortly afterwards. The *De actibus anime* of about 1365 displays an interest in contemporary astronomy and optics; it is in part a commentary on the *Perspectiva* of Witelo.

Much more interesting is the compendium in whose composition Wyclif was engaged from about 1365 to 1371, and which was eventually given the comprehensive title of *Summa de ente*. This compendium consists of thirteen treatises grouped into two books, the first philosophical and the second largely theological and political. Wyclif's reputation as a philosopher must depend on the seven treatises of the first book of this *Summa*. However, an informed judgement of his stature has been difficult to make, since the most important of these treatises, that on universals, was not published until 1984, 600 years after his death.

Wyclif's position on universals In that treatise Wyclif presents a realist view of universals, and bitterly attacks the opposing nominalist position. Take the sentence 'Socrates is human'. By common consent, the word 'Socrates' stands for the individual Socrates. But is there anything in the real world which is related to the predicate 'human' in the way in which the man Socrates was related to the name 'Socrates'? No, says the nominalist: predicates like 'human' are simply words. Yes, says the realist: the predicate 'human' names the universal, humanity, just as 'Socrates' names the individual Socrates. Wyclif's realism is, therefore, first and foremost a theory of the nature of predication.

Wyclif's favourite examples of universals are species (such as *dog*) and genera (such as *animal*). A realist can define genus simply as what is predicated of many things which are different in species. A nominalist has to offer a complicated circumlocution: 'A genus is a term which is predicable, or whose counterpart is predicable, of many terms which signify things which are specifically distinct.' The nominalist begins his definition by trying to identify genus with a term (that is, a sound or mark on paper); but by the end of his definition he has had to abandon his pretence that species and genus are mere signs and admit that specific difference is something belonging not to the signs but to the things signified. To talk of species and genus, Wyclif insists, is not to talk of ink blots on paper; if it were, a man could be changed into a donkey by altering the significance of a term. But of course the species and genus of things cannot be altered by fiat, as the meanings of words can be altered.

Wyclif's writing includes descriptions of many different kinds of universal, of which four types may be singled out. The lowest kind are the universal terms, or grammatical universals, which even the nominalists admit. Above them are the logical universals, the concepts in created minds which are expressed in language in the grammatical universals. By means of these concepts humans grasp the metaphysical universals—the Aristotelian genera and species—which are prior to language and to human minds. Supreme above all other kinds of universal are the eternal universals, or exemplar ideas, in the mind of God: the patterns and paradigms by which he can create. Wyclif is a realist but not a Platonist: he does not believe that there are any universals outside the divine mind which are independent both of the existence of individuals and of the existence of created minds. Hence he can claim that his realism about universals is orthodox Aristotelian doctrine.

Wyclif's argument for his realism is essentially simple. Anyone who believes in objective truth, he maintains, is already committed to belief in real universals. Suppose that one individual A is perceived to resemble another individual B. There must be some respect C in which A resembles B. But seeing that A resembles B in respect of C is the same thing as seeing the C-ness of A and B; and that involves conceiving C-ness, a universal common to A and B. So anyone who can make judgements of likeness automatically knows what a universal is.

The implications of realism On his chosen ground Wyclif seems victorious against the opponents he describes, whether or not the targets he sets up are accurate representations of Ockham and the great nominalists of the previous generation. But his enthusiasm for real universals takes him far beyond the narrow ground of logic and metaphysics into that of ethics and politics. All the sin that reigns in the world, he claims, is caused by intellectual and emotional error about universals: nominalism leads to preferring the lesser good to the greater, and to the individual's valuing of self over the humanity of fellow humans. The germ of Wyclif's later communism is found in his early metaphysics.

Wyclif's theory of being is related to his theory of universals. Every creature, he maintains, can have four different kinds of being: first, ideal being in the mind of God; second, essential being in its causes; third, existence, or actuality at a given point in time; fourth, accidental being, that is to say the possession of transitory properties. Of these kinds of being it is the second, essential being, which is both the most difficult to understand and also the most characteristic of Wyclif's system. Essential being, he explains, is the kind of being that lies behind the truth of two particularly important kinds of propositions: those that identify to what species and genera things belong, and those that inform of the causal relationships between individuals at different times of the world's history.

It is the theory of essential being that lies behind the opposition to the notion of annihilation for which Wyclif later became notorious. Some theologians argued that God by his almighty power could annihilate substances. Wyclif replied that, though individuals go out of existence, they retain their essential being. Not even God could destroy the relationship to the species to which the individual belongs, or its place in the causal web of the universe. Whatever happens to the individual, that essential being could not be obliterated without the annihilation of the whole universe. Wyclif's denial of the possibility of annihilation was later to bring him into conflict with current theological accounts of the eucharist, according to which in the mass the bread and wine were annihilated when the host became the body of Christ.

A heresy for which Wyclif was condemned after his death was the doctrine that everything happens by absolute necessity. Close study of his philosophical writing shows that on this issue he was not necessarily more determinist than other scholastics whose reputations were not impeached. He introduces a battery of careful distinctions in order to reconcile God's omniscience and omnipotence with human free will. To be sure, everything that the individual thinks and does is entailed by thoughts and volitions in the mind of God; but this does not take away human freedom because the relationship between divine volition and human action is a two-way one: if God's volition causes man's act, so, in a sense, man's act causes God's volition.

Wyclif is no more successful than other theologians in providing a convincing resolution of the problem of freedom and omnipotence. But he does not go beyond other theologians in limiting human freedom in the interests of divine power; on the contrary, he safeguards human freedom by attributing to it control over God's eternal will. His posthumous reputation as an arch-determinist was unjustified.

The foundations of authority Wyclif did, of course, believe in predestination; that is to say, he believed that no one could be saved who had not been predestined to salvation by God. But in this he did not differ from orthodox Catholic theologians both before and after the Reformation. What first took him beyond the bounds of contemporary orthodoxy was the link that he made between the commonly held doctrine of predestination and his own theory of political authority.

The nineteen conclusions condemned in Gregory XI's bull of 1377 derived from *De civili dominio*, book 1, and concerned the relation of divine grace to the authority wielded by earthly institutions, and especially that of the church. Underlying the various aspects affecting fundamental issues in Christian society is Wyclif's concept of dominion, a concept that is more bluntly outlined in the list of his early heresies in that collection of anti-Wyclif materials the *Fasciculi zizaniorum*: 'no one in a state of mortal sin is a ruler, a priest or a bishop' (*Fasciculi zizaniorum*, 2). Drawing in part on Fitzralph's views, as they had been set out in *De pauperie Salvatoris*, Wyclif claimed that, since dominion only inhered by right in God, it could only be transmitted to humankind when the recipient remained in a state of grace; in such a state man was lord of the whole world. But when man was separated from God by sin, he could not properly be said to exercise dominion; in mortal sin man has no authority. Civil dominion was a result of the fall, and hence inherently imperfect; its administration was a necessity, but from that necessity the church should distance itself. Modern critics have questioned the practical significance of Wyclif's radical theory: since Wyclif stressed that only God could know whether any man was in a state of grace or, conversely, in mortal sin, how could this idea be used to question contemporary organization? This underestimates the effective removal of the locus of authority from the office to the holder of that office: if 'there is no civil dominion, unless it is based in evangelical righteousness', then it follows that 'no one has true dominion for as long as he sins mortally, or correctly true civil dominion' (Wyclif, *De civili dominio*, bk 1, 21, 37). It also underestimates the practical deductions that Wyclif drew from his theory; central to these is the unrighteousness of any perpetual grant to an institution or individual, whether of property or of moral authority.

Coupled with his view of divine foreknowledge concerning the salvation or damnation of each individual, it is a logical implication of this theory to question, as Wyclif went on to do more explicitly in later parts of the *Summa theologie*, the right of the pope to moral, let alone civil, power in Christendom. The deductions were drawn more inexorably in regard to ecclesiastical rule: in the civil domain Wyclif drew a distinction between *dominium* and *potestas*, as in the extreme case of tyrants who 'have unspecified power to rule and tyrannize, but that power is not dominion' (Wyclif, *De officio regis*, 17). The imperfection of any civil dominion implies that the clergy should not be involved in it; thus it is justifiable for the secular rulers to recall their previous abdication of wealth and of areas of rule from the church. From this it follows that the donation of Constantine, however well intended, was a grave sin; in particular it was a dire error that Pope Sylvester accepted it, and to this error the increasing corruption of the church can be attributed. The disendowment of the church was seen by Wyclif, and even more insistently by his followers, as the *sine qua non* for the restoration of the Christian community to its primal purity.

Although Wyclif explored the implications of his theory of dominion more fully in regard to the church, he did not ignore those for the secular authorities. From an early stage in his writing he emphasized the responsibility of king and lay lords towards their subjects, and their powers in regard to the church. But it is particularly in *De blasphemia*, with Wyclif's anguished reflections on the peasants' revolt, that he becomes most outspoken in his reproaches to the secular rulers: 'it is indeed an insupportable mistake for the king or any other lord of the realm to tyrannize over his people' (Wyclif, *De blasphemia*, 197); his seven petitions to the king, though they echo claims made in *De civili dominio*, book 1, now impart the urgency of current civil strife to the earlier theory.

Coupled with this theory of dominion is Wyclif's view of the true church. Underlying varying distinctions lies a threefold division: the true church of the predestined, established by Christ, living with him in heaven but incorporating those on earth foreknown by Christ to salvation even though indiscernible by humans; the physical church of wood and stone; and the institutional church on earth, encompassing both the predestinate and also those *presciti*, foreknown to damnation, the distinction between which is impossible for humans to ascertain. Only the first of these is properly the church, the 'bride of Christ', to which Christ's authority descends. Again the implication of such a view is a diminution of the authority to be given to ecclesiastical rulers: if any individual pope may not merely be sinful, but may not even be a member of the true church, why should men obey him? Contemporary and modern attempts to label Wyclif's views as Donatist seem, however, misconceived: 'the priest foreknown to damnation ministers the sacraments to the faithful even while in a state of mortal sin—damnably for himself, but usefully for his flock' (Wyclif, *De ecclesia*, 450). But the whole structure of the contemporary church, as well as its detailed procedures, comes under question.

The centrality of scripture The standard against which that contemporary church must, in Wyclif's view, be measured is that of scripture, and more particularly the gospels and the picture of the early Christian communities that emerges from the epistles and Acts. Wyclif, it is often said, acknowledged *scriptura sola* as the source for men of a model for all aspects of life; this may oversimplify, in that it ignores the complexity of Wyclif's hermeneutics, his respect for patristic writers such as Augustine, and his acceptance of certain traditions (for instance the three creeds, or in his own practice the liturgy) that cannot be traced to scripture, but it rightly identifies what for Wyclif was the sole unassailable source of law. In particular it is against that model that the practices of the contemporary church must be measured. Like others before him, Wyclif castigated at a length that often seems inordinate the malpractices of the papacy, the prelates, the monastic and fraternal orders, the abuses of indulgences, excommunication, images, pilgrimages; but in the last resort what is distinctive of Wyclif's peculiar contribution at the end of the fourteenth century is that he disputed not the malpractice but the theory of such offices because they are not to be traced to scripture—this inherently lays them open to question, and their blatant contemporary corruption merely exaggerates and reveals their misconception. The outbreak of the papal schism in 1378, he comments, is a blessing sent by God to reveal the more clearly to men the evil inherent in the institution of the papacy.

Again scripture provides the ammunition for the condemnation of clerical property: the early church, in so far as it administered wealth, held goods in common and used the laity to distribute, and hence once more the donation of Constantine with all its consequences must be regarded as damnable. From an early stage in *De civili dominio*, book 1, Wyclif castigated endowment, and hence the monastic orders; the ideal for all, but particularly for the clergy, must be *paupertas evangelica* ('evangelical poverty')—not a simple deprivation of wealth, but a separation of the mind from the affection for earthly things that wealth inculcates. But, while in the writings of his middle career Wyclif's comments often seem close to the founding ideals of St Francis, his final condemnation of the orders of friars is the logical end to his use of scripture (and not just an angry reaction to the mendicants' opposition to his eucharistic teaching). If it is easy to outline what Wyclif condemned in the church of his time, the shape of an institutional church, if any, of which he would have approved is less readily discernible. Its central function is clear: the preaching of the gospel is the single overriding duty of each priest, and indeed his only defining characteristic, though it is a duty shared by every Christian. Equally Wyclif is less than consistent in his view of the maintenance of the clergy. The mendicancy of the friars is stridently deplored, along with the endowment from which secular clergy and possessioner monks currently benefit. But support of parish priests poses problems: at times Wyclif seems content to leave in place the traditional tithes and offerings (though with the condition that these should be withheld by parishioners from those failing in their evangelical duty), but at others he seems so anxious about their potential for corrupting the recipients that he advocates a less organized charity by the laity to worthy priests, supplemented as needed by manual work from the latter.

Both of the main prerogatives of the contemporary clergy, the administration of the sacraments of confession and of the eucharist, Wyclif called in question. Just as God alone could distinguish the *predestinatus* from the *prescitus*, so God alone could know the contrition of the erring Christian; hence properly God alone could pronounce absolution, or withhold that pardon, and the priest was at best God's bedel. Oral confession, as enjoined by Pope Innocent III in 1215, had no model in scripture and should be abandoned as regular practice (even if the advisory function of private confession might occasionally be valuable); the biblical model was public, usually communal, confession, and the only proper penance was a change of life. The penalties of current excommunication were illicit and should be ignored; indulgences, and penances that involved payments or such acts as pilgrimage, were merely outrageous means of enriching the clergy. Prayers for the dead were worthless, not exemplified in scripture and improper in view of God's predestination.

Wyclif's insistence on the centrality of scripture goes back to a very early stage in his career. His *Postilla in totam Bibliam*, despite its reliance upon traditional commentators, brought him an awareness both of the variety of scriptural discourse and of the diversity of exegesis. From the surviving fragments of Wyclif's Oxford debates with the Carmelite John Kenningham it is possible to see the extent to which Wyclif was attempting to use his philosophical outlook to inform his reading of scripture; also evident in some of the understandings that Kenningham disputes is Wyclif's stress upon the literal sense of scripture.

A more extended and nuanced discussion of scripture comes in Wyclif's later *De veritate sacre scripture*. Here the apprehension of scripture's problems is much more evident: scripture is more than the volumes in which it is preserved, and that preservation may be imperfect; while the literal sense is that which is to be adopted, that literal sense is sometimes not the bare historical meaning, but rather allegorical, moral, or tropological. Scripture is the measure for the contemporary state of both church and state, and other laws are valid only in so far as they are grounded in it. Along with his views about the meaning of scripture goes a preoccupation with the need for that meaning to be known, not just to the clergy but also through preaching to the laity. Wyclif's emphasis on scripture and its modelling role is the pivot of all his mature writing.

Eucharistic ideas More central, however, to the final heretication of Wyclif was his teaching on the eucharist; this formed the first three of the views condemned by the Blackfriars Council in 1382. Those three provide an epitome of the negative aspect of Wyclif's final opinion: that the substance of bread and wine remains after the consecration, that accidents do not remain without a subject after the consecration, and that Christ is not in the sacrament of the altar 'identice, vere, et realiter in propria praesentia corporali'. Positively Wyclif, acknowledging that Christ was really present in the consecrated elements, described that presence variously as *realiter, figurative, tropice, sacramentaliter, virtualiter*. But, though the condemnation of his views came only in 1381, there is much evidence that Wyclif had been working towards such a position for a very long time and had been uneasy about the contemporary theology of the eucharist for many years. One source of his unease was plainly philosophical; the implications for the eucharist of his refusal to allow the existence of an accident without a substance were already being discussed in Prague about 1378. Scripture again indicated a difficulty with the contemporary explanations: *substancia* and *accidencia* do not occur there; the words of institution in the gospels, reiterated in 1 Corinthians, speak of bread and wine; but *est* in scripture often has the sense of *figurat* (as when the seven lean oxen or the seven thin ears are said 'to be' the seven poor years, or Christ is said 'to be' a worm and no man). Further, the stress that the Thomist or Scotist view of the eucharist placed on the nature of the change in the elements removed the sacrament as a true means of grace: it forces attention on various practical problems, such as how Christ can be physically present in a thousand simultaneous consecrated hosts, while detracting from the purpose of the sacrament—the observer of a statue does not bother whether it is made out of oak or ash, but considers whom it represents. In the *Trialogus* Wyclif stated that he undertook not to use the terms 'substantia panis materialis aut vini' ('the substance of material bread and wine'; Wyclif, *Trialogus*, 375) outside the schools, but the terms recur in his late works, including the addresses purportedly designed to be 'unpolished sermons to the people' (Hudson, 64, n. 31). Wyclif never went the further step, a step certainly taken by some of his followers, to regard the eucharist as solely a memorial of Christ's passion.

Wyclif's speculation about the eucharist began as a normal part of academic theology, a part almost inevitably confronted by the lecturer on Lombard's *Sentences*, book 4. Had he confined his discussion to the university world, and especially if he had eschewed political notoriety, it is possible that his ideas, even if not welcomed, would have been left for the normal processes of intellectual debate. Certainly by the 1380s the bounds of orthodoxy were more closely defined than they had been at the start of the century, but school debate was still possible. A concatenation of circumstances, some of them his own responsibility, removed Wyclif from that liberal world: the hostility he had already aroused because of his views of the church, the papacy, and ecclesiastical temporalities, the alliance he appeared to have made with secular rulers against the church, the destabilization caused by the schism and later in England by the peasants' revolt (for which many churchmen saw Wyclif as partially responsible), and the choice by Wyclif and by his Oxford disciples to spread the debate on the eucharist outside the university by the use of English. This last, it is clear from the authorities' reaction in the years after 1380, was by no means the least important reason for the outlawing of Wyclif's eucharistic speculation.

Posthumous influence and reputation Wyclif's repute as a philosopher and theologian was drastically curtailed, or at least diverted, by the condemnation of 1382 and its aftermath; the victory of the ecclesiastical opposition, with which the secular powers quickly aligned themselves, was complete with the banning in Arundel's constitutions of academic discussion not just of Wyclif's own arguments but also of the issues that he had raised. Whether Arundel was aware of the extent to which, even by 1409, Wyclif's ideas had been taken up by Jan Hus and his followers in Bohemia is unclear. But the perception at the Council of Constance that Wyclif was ultimately responsible for Hus's errors, and later for the division of Western Christendom wrought by the Hussite revolution, ensured that Wyclif's ideas found no dispassionate discussion in the fifteenth century and, indeed, that they largely disappeared from academic discourse. Unlike the works of even so contentious a thinker as Fitzralph, Wyclif's writings were not early put into print; the only one of his texts that was issued down to the end of the sixteenth century was the *Trialogus*, which appeared in one edition of 1525, probably from Mainz or Worms. Responsibility for that edition certainly rests in the circle of Luther. But the extent of Wyclif's influence on sixteenth-century reformers remains hard to trace; the route of that influence was certainly through Hussite channels, and Wyclif's contribution seems not to have been distinguished from that of more immediate Bohemian writers. Despite some obvious anticipations of later ideas, and despite continuing anathematization of his conclusions at the Council of Trent and in later Counter-Reformation writers, Wyclif's contribution to sixteenth-century religious thought seems constantly underestimated.

Wyclif has from his lifetime to the present remained a controversial figure, and a dispassionate evaluation is hard to reach. Along with his ready and outspoken criticism of others, Wyclif did from time to time acknowledge his own failings: he recognized his own tendency towards arrogance and anger, and acknowledged the mistakes of his younger days. While his opponents naturally concentrated on what they regarded as his mistaken ideas and his deplorable dissemination of these, they acknowledged his learning and the uprightness of his life. Woodford tells of Wyclif's willingness to exchange notes in the intervals of public debate; Winterton plainly hoped to hold back one he admired from outright heresy. Netter at the start of his *Doctrinale fidei ecclesie* wrote that he was stunned beyond measure by his enormous claims and by his wide authorities and fierce arguments. A note beside Wyclif's name in the Merton *Catalogus vetus* calls him 'doctor in theology who, as it is reported, trusted excessively in his own skill' (Oxford, Merton College, MS 4.16, fol. 64*v*). Even allowing for irony, Kenningham accords his opponent respect, and a chronicler such as Walsingham records that Wyclif was regarded as *flos Oxonie*. That Wyclif outshone all his contemporaries in the university as a lecturer seems clear from notes, observations, and the debates he engendered, though some of the qualities that must have contributed to his reputation may be hard to discern from the surviving writings.

Wyclif's dominance at Oxford, and the spread of his influence outside the university, contributed largely to the vehemence of the reaction against him once his opinions had been pronounced heretical. Adam Stocton's description *venerabilis doctor magister* of 1379–80 was altered only a year later to *execrabilis seductor*. While Wyclif in Hussite Bohemia was honoured as 'Doctor Evangelicus super omnes evangelistas', in England denunciation reached its peak in Thomas Netter's *Doctrinale fidei ecclesie* of 1421–9.

English Lollards in the fifteenth and early sixteenth centuries remained aware of their indebtedness to Wyclif, of course, and some of them apparently regarded him with a reverence that in more orthodox circles would have looked similar to that bestowed upon the saints. They did not, however, always practise exactly what their master had preached; rather Lollardy seems to have become something of a broad church in the decades after Wyclif's death, with his doctrines acquiring a penumbra of other beliefs and practices. On the issue of the reverence due to images, for instance, many Lollards took up a position of outright rejection some way removed from the cautious reservations expressed by Wyclif himself. Much in Lollard doctrine that struck an answering chord in the early protestant reformers can be traced back to Wyclif, but there was no Wycliffite canon, and no equivalent to the Lutheran doctrine of justification by faith alone.

During the sixteenth century writers such as John Bale and John Foxe attempted to reinstate Wyclif as the 'morning star of the Reformation', but, despite Bale's assiduous search for manuscripts, and the biographical endeavours of both, it is doubtful how much genuine Wyclif either they, or any of those who consulted their writings, had read. The same seems true of the host of English antiquaries and bibliographers from the next two centuries. Even Milton, with his extravagant claim that, had it not been for the persecution of the prelates, 'the glory of reforming all our neighbours had bin compleatly ours' (Milton, 552–3), shows little sign of having read Wyclif. Catholic opponents likewise seem to have derived much of their information from the list of condemned conclusions at the Council of Constance or from other second-hand detail.

Wyclif in recent times Curiosity, none the less, remained, and in some of it, as for example in the work of John Lewis (whose *History of the Life and Sufferings of … John Wicliffe* first appeared in 1720), occasional details remain valuable. Modern investigation of Wyclif began with the edition by W. W. Shirley of parts of the *Fasciculi zizaniorum* (a collection of hostile materials gathered by the Carmelite order up to about 1439) in the Rolls Series in 1858; in his preface he examined the evidence for Wyclif's life, and in an appendix listed printed books connected with him. In 1865 Shirley produced *A Catalogue of the Original Works of John Wyclif*, including both Latin and English works, and giving manuscript references. The foundation of the Wyclif Society in 1882 had the express purpose of printing the Latin works as catalogued there; between 1883 and 1921 thirty-five volumes appeared, though these did not exhaust the total, and though some erroneously attributed texts were included. Despite shortcomings, the Wyclif Society's editions remain the only available editions, supplemented more recently by a few further texts. H. B. Workman's biography published in 1926 remained the most extensive at the end of the twentieth century, though its details and some of its interpretations have been modified. In the study by K. B. Macfarlane, first published in 1952 as *John Wycliffe and the Beginnings of English Nonconformity*, the author's determination to free his subject from what he described as 'several layers of rich brown protestant varnish' resulted in a notably unsympathetic portrayal of Wyclif, who is presented as the very type of the doctrinaire intellectual—arrogant, dogmatic, and humourless. His subsequent canonization, in Macfarlane's eyes, was due entirely to 'a Reformation he did little or nothing to inspire, and in effect everything possible to delay' (Macfarlane, 10, 186). A full modern account, relating individual works to their contemporary context, and exploring Wyclif's political involvement, remains a desideratum.

Only when such an account has been written will a fair assessment of Wyclif's stature be possible. Respect for the philosopher has been increasing, as more work has been done: if Wyclif was dismissed in the 1950s as a mere schoolman, a later twentieth-century view describes him more positively as 'the last of the major scholastics … when the scholarly account can at length be cast Wyclif will be seen to rank with Scotus and Ockham as a worthy member of a great Oxford triumvirate' (Kenny, 'Wyclif', 113). Respect for Wyclif the reformer may encounter prejudice that is harder to eradicate: despite the passage of over six centuries, the issues Wyclif discussed still seem to engender distorting passions.

ANNE HUDSON and ANTHONY KENNY

Sources J. Wyclif, *Latin works*, 22 vols. in 35, Wyclif Society (1883–1922) · *Thomae Walsingham, quondam monachi S. Albani, historia Anglicana*, ed. H. T. Riley, 2 vols., pt 1 of *Chronica monasterii S. Albani*, Rolls Series, 28 (1863–4) · [T. Walsingham], *Chronicon Angliae, ab anno Domini 1328 usque ad annum 1388*, ed. E. M. Thompson, Rolls Series, 64 (1874) · [T. Netter], *Fasciculi zizaniorum magistri Johannis Wyclif cum tritico*, ed. W. W. Shirley, Rolls Series, 5 (1858) · W. R. Thomson, *The Latin writings of John Wyclyf* (1983) [incl. list of MSS] · F. S. Haydon, ed., *Eulogium historiarum sive temporis*, 3 vols., Rolls Series, 9 (1858) · Borth. Inst., Reg. 10 Zouche · episcopal registers, Lincs. Arch., VIII–IX (A–D) · episcopal registers, Lincs. Arch., X–XII · LPL, Reg. Islip; Reg. Sudbury; Reg. Courtenay · D. Wilkins, ed., *Concilia Magnae Britanniae et Hiberniae*, 4 vols. (1737) [incl. Arundel's *Constitutions*] · Merton Oxf., Records 3690, 4.16 · Balliol Oxf., archives, E.1.38b, E.7.9, E.7.12, E.7.14 · Queen's College, Oxford, archives, 2.P.12, 2.P.23, 2.P.27 · *CPR, 1374–7; 1381–5* · F. Devon, ed. and trans., *Issues of the exchequer: being payments made out of his majesty's revenue, from King Henry III to King Henry VI inclusive*, RC (1837) · *CEPR letters* · exchequer, king's remembrancer's memoranda roll, PRO, E159/147 · exchequer of receipt, issue rolls, PRO, E403/454 m.18 · lord treasurer's remembrancer, foreign accounts, PRO, E364/8 m.3 · king's remembrancer, accounts various, PRO, E101/316 no. 36 · exchequer of receipt, receipt rolls, PRO, E401/545 m.9 · *RotP* · V. H. Galbraith, ed., *The Anonimalle chronicle, 1333 to 1381* (1927) · T. Walsingham, *The St Albans chronicle, 1406–1420*, ed. V. H. Galbraith (1937) · *Knighton's chronicle, 1337–1396*, ed. and trans. G. H. Martin, OMT (1995) [Lat. orig., *Chronica de eventibus Angliae a tempore regis Edgari usque mortem regis Ricardi Secundi*, with parallel Eng. text] · T. Netter, *Doctrinale antiquitatum fidei catholicae ecclesiae*, ed. B. Blanciotti, 3 vols. (1757–9) · J. I. Catto, 'Wyclif and Wycliffism at Oxford, 1356–1430', *Hist. U. Oxf. 2: Late med. Oxf.*, 175–261 · A. Kenny, *Wyclif* (1985) · A. Kenny, 'Wyclif', *PBA*, 72 (1986), 91–113 · A. Kenny, 'The accursed memory: the Counter-Reformation reputation of John Wyclif', *Wyclif in his times*, ed. A. Kenny (1986), 147–68 · W. A. Pantin, 'A Benedictine opponent of John Wyclif', *EngHR*, 43 (1928), 73–7 · W. A. Pantin, 'The *Defensorium* of Adam Easton', *EngHR*, 51 (1936), 675–80 · W. A. Pantin, ed., *Documents illustrating the activities of the general and provincial chapters of the English black monks, 3*, CS, 3rd ser., 54 (1937) · W. A. Pantin, *Canterbury College, Oxford, 3*, OHS, new ser., 8 (1950) · J. Lewis, *The history of the life and sufferings of the reverend and learned John Wicliffe, D.D.* (1720); 2nd edn (1820) · J. H. Dahmus, *The prosecution of John Wyclyf* (1952) · B. Smalley, 'John Wyclif's *Postilla super totam Bibliam*', *Bodleian Library Record*, 4 (1953), 186–205 · B. Smalley, 'Wyclif's *Postilla* on the Old Testament and his *Principium*', *Oxford studies presented to Daniel Callus*, OHS, new ser., 16 (1964), 253–96 · B. Smalley, 'The Bible and eternity: John Wyclif's dilemma', *Journal of the Warburg and Courtauld Institutes*, 27 (1964), 73–89 · J. A. Robson, *Wyclif and the Oxford schools* (1966) · H. B. Workman, *John Wyclif: a study of the English medieval church*, 2 vols. (1926) · G. Holmes, *The Good Parliament* (1975) · A. Gwynn, *The English Austin friars in the time of Wyclif* (1940) · G. A. Benrath, *Wyclifs Bibelkommentar* (1966) · W. E. Lunt, *Financial relations of the papacy with England, 1327–1534* (1962) · W. E. Lunt and E. B. Graves, eds., *Accounts rendered by papal collectors in England, 1317–1378, 70* (1968) · A. K. McHardy, 'John Wycliffe's mission to Bruges: a financial footnote', *Journal of Theological Studies*, new ser., 24 (1973), 521–2 · Harvard U., Houghton L., MS Lat. 338 · Bodl. Oxf., MS lat. misc. e.79 · Biblioteca Capitular y Colombina, Seville, MS Cod.5-1-12 · *Guillaume Heytesbury 'Sophismata asinina': une introduction aux disputes médiévales*, ed. F. Pironet (Paris, 1994) · L. de Rijk, 'Logica Oxoniensis: an attempt to reconstruct a fifteenth-century Oxford manual of logic', *Medioevo*, 3 (1977), 121–64 · E. Doyle, 'William Woodford's *De dominio civili clericorum* against John Wyclif', *Archivum Franciscanum Historicum*, 66 (1973), 49–109 · E. Doyle, 'William Woodford

O.F.M. and John Wyclif's *De religione'*, *Speculum*, 52 (1977), 329–36 · J. Wyclif, *Tractatus de universalibus*, ed. I. J. Mueller (1985) · I. J. Mueller, 'A "lost" summa of John Wyclif', *From Ockham to Wyclif*, ed. A. Hudson and M. Wilks, SCH, Subsidia, 5 (1987), 179–83 · W. Mallard, 'Dating the *Sermones quadraginta* of John Wyclif', *Medievalia et Humanistica*, 17 (1966), 86–105 · G. Leff, 'John Wyclif: the path to dissent', *PBA*, 52 (1966), 143–80 · G. Leff, *Heresy in the later middle ages*, 2 vols. (1967) · M. Hurley, 'Scriptura sola: Wyclif and his critics', *Traditio*, 16 (1960), 275–352 · M. Aston, *Lollards and reformers* (1984) · M. Aston, *Faith and fire* (1993) · K. B. Macfarlane, *John Wycliffe and the beginnings of English nonconformity* (1952) · M. Aston, *England's iconoclasts* (1988), vol. 1 of *English iconoclasts* · J. Wyclif, 'Proposiciones Wyclif in determinacione sua', Worcester Cathedral, MS F.65, fol. 22v · A. Hudson, *The premature reformation: Wycliffite texts and Lollard history* (1988) · J. Milton, 'Areopagitica', *Complete prose works of John Milton*, ed. D. M. Wolfe, 2, ed. E. Sirluck (1959), 480–570 · W. W. Shirley, *A catalogue of the original works of John Wyclif* (1865) · J. Wyclif, *Trialogus*, ed. G. V. Lechler (1869)

Wycombe, W. of (*fl. c.*1275), music copyist and Benedictine monk, is of unknown origins. He became a monk of Reading Abbey, and inscriptions in two Reading manuscripts testify that he wrote music, but unfortunately nothing that is extant can unequivocally be ascribed to him. Wycombe describes himself, in a statement he wrote with a metal stylus at the end of Oxford, Bodleian Library, MS Bodley 125 (fols. 98v–99), as the precentor (the monk exercising overall control over the performance of services) at Leominster Priory, Herefordshire, a cell of Reading Abbey, where he stayed for four years. During this time he says he copied numerous manuscripts, musical and non-musical. He makes it clear that the work burdened him considerably, 'though it might have appeared small', and generally gives the impression that his time at Leominster—used by Reading as something of a dumping ground for troublesome monks—was spent there under sufferance. The antepenultimate paragraph mentions a *Historia* of St Margaret by Brother Hugh of Wycombe and states that *notam cantus W. ipse imposuit* ('W. himself provided the notation of the chant'). Wycombe's wording here is clearly designed to establish him firmly as the composer of what probably took the form of a rhymed office. It is noticeably different from his more common construction *scripsit eciam* ('he also wrote') by which he describes, in the paragraph which follows, his copying of two rolls containing polyphonic music. In fact, two such rolls survive: Oxford, Bodleian Library, MS Rawlinson C 400*, and the recently discovered Oxford, Bodleian, MS Lat. liturg. b. 19, both from the vicinity of Reading, though probably not the abbey. As Wycombe is not slow in establishing his status as a composer, his milder wording for the rolls suggests that he merely copied, rather than composed, this music, if indeed these be the rolls he mentions.

The name 'W. de Wic.' also occurs in the index of a book, now lost, belonging to W. of Winchester, another monk of Reading and Leominster in the years on either side of 1300. This index was copied on the last folios (160v–161) of British Library, MS Harley 978, for whose main corpus obits and other palaeographical evidence certainly indicate Reading provenance. After the first eight items of the index is written *postea responsoria W. de Wicumbe*; following

a small gap over forty Alleluia settings are listed (the Alleluia being a responsorial chant), forming a complete cycle. It is reasonable to assume that the statement 'there follow responsories of W. de Wycombe' refers either to the cycle of Alleluias subsequent to the first eight items, or else to a lacuna in the index, indicating that Wycombe's responsories are missing at this point. Several titles among the Alleluia settings come close to matching compositions in the so-called Worcester fragments. While the idea that some of Wycombe's compositions survive is seductive, the connections between Reading and Worcester have possibly been overstated and should be treated with caution.

Wycombe has also been suggested as the composer of the famous canon 'Sumer is icumen in', which occurs in the first fascicle of MS Harley 978. However, this fascicle is ruled to a size of written block different from that of the rest of the volume, and has been cut down from its original size. This raises doubts as to its original provenance, hence also to indisputable Reading origins for the 'Sumer' canon, and thus to any connection with Wycombe. In any case, there were presumably many other composers active at Reading. NICKY LOSSEFF

Sources N. Losseff, *The best concords: polyphonic music in thirteenth-century Britain* (1994) · B. Schofield, 'The provenance and date of "Sumer is icumen in"', *Music Review*, 9 (1948), 81–6 · L. Dittmer, 'An English *discantuum volumen*', *Musica Disciplina*, 8 (1954), 19–58 · E. Sanders, 'Wycombe, W. de', *New Grove* · A. Wathey, *Manuscripts of polyphonic music: the British Isles, 1100–1400* (1993)
Archives BL, MS Harley 978 · Bodl. Oxf., MS Bodley 125, fols. 98v–99; MS Lat. liturg. b.19; MS Rawl. C 400*

Wycombe [Wycumbe], **William of** (*fl. c.*1127–*c.*1148), prior of Llanthony and hagiographer, was probably, as his name suggests, a native of Buckinghamshire. From an early age he was acquainted with Robert de Béthune (*d.* 1148), whose chaplain he had become by about 1127, while Robert was still prior of the Augustinian house of Llanthony in the lordship of Monmouth, Gwent. Probably William was also a canon at Llanthony, and he certainly had become one by 1132. Even after Robert became bishop of Hereford in 1131, William remained closely associated with him, and seems to have spent periods of time in his household, since he witnesses several of his charters. William became prior of Llanthony in 1137 on the death of the previous prior, Robert de Braci, Robert de Béthune's successor; by this time the canons had been driven from Wales by the Welsh uprising of 1135, and had been provided with a new home, at Llanthony Secunda just outside Gloucester, through the assistance of Robert de Béthune and Miles of Gloucester (*d.* 1143). William's last dated occurrence as prior is 16 July 1147; soon after this he was deposed by his fellow canons, angered by his strict discipline, with the encouragement of Llanthony's patron, Roger, earl of Hereford (*d.* 1155), who had been displeased by a piece of writing by William, now lost, criticizing his father, Miles. William had been deposed before Robert de Béthune's departure for Rheims in March 1148, since he occurs without title in a charter of Robert issued between 1143 and 1148, while his successor Clement became prior in or before 1148. He moved to a cell of Llanthony at Frome where he spent the rest of his life. It was evidently here that he wrote his *Life of Robert de Béthune*, a hagiography presenting Robert as an ideal regular canon and pastor, which none the less failed to achieve Robert's canonization. One version was dedicated to Henry de Blois, bishop of Winchester (*d.* 1171), and another, only very slightly different, to Reginald, prior of Wenlock, who died in the mid-1150s. The date of William's own death is unknown.

JULIA BARROW

Sources [H. Wharton], ed., *Anglia sacra*, 2 (1691), 295–322 • B. J. Parkinson, 'The life of Robert de Béthune by William de Wycombe: translation with introduction and notes', BLitt diss., U. Oxf., 1951 • D. Knowles, C. N. L. Brooke, and V. C. M. London, eds., *The heads of religious houses, England and Wales*, 1: *940–1216* (1972), 172 • J. Barrow, ed., *Hereford, 1079–1234*, English Episcopal Acta, 7 (1993), xxvi, xxxvii, lii, 303, nos. 23, 28, 36, 38 • M. J. Franklin, ed., *Winchester, 1070–1204*, English Episcopal Acta, 8 (1993), no. 61 • W. W. Capes, ed., *Charters and records of Hereford Cathedral*, Cantilupe Society (1908), 7

Wydow, Robert (*c.*1446–1505), poet and musician, was said by informants of John Leland to have received his initial education from his stepfather, the schoolmaster of Thaxted, in Essex, where he had been born. By 1455–6 he was a chorister of the chapel of King's College, Cambridge, receiving training in music as well as in Latin. He achieved election as a scholar of Eton College in 1460, returned to King's as a scholar in 1464, and graduated, apparently MGram, in 1467–8. After a period as schoolmaster of Thaxted he progressed to tutoring the sons of nobility; presently he was brought by some patron to the notice of Edward IV, whose particular favour he earned and by whom in 1474 he was presented to a chaplaincy of the Black Prince's chantry at Canterbury Cathedral (a post he held until 1478). He then enjoyed, successively, the benefices of Monk's Eleigh, Suffolk (1479–81), Thaxted (1481–9), St Benet Paul's Wharf, London (1489–93), and Chalfont St Giles, Buckinghamshire (1493–8), though at least partly as an absentee in royal service; there is every likelihood that he is to be identified with the Mr Widdowe, priest, who occurs in 1491 as schoolmaster in Latin to the boys of Henry VII's Chapel Royal. In 1497 Wydow was collated in absence to a canonry, with the prebend of Combe Secunda, and appointed to the succentorship of Wells Cathedral, where in 1500 he entered residence and succeeded to the office of subdean (25 May), with the prebend of Holcombe. Thereafter he resided in Wells, occupying a number of offices in the cathedral administration until his death.

In his time Wydow was celebrated as both poet and musician. Survivals of writings attributable to him are exiguous, and no certain trace remains of his expertise in music. However, it is possible that he was associated in some way with Cambridge, Magdalene College, MS Pepys 1236, an important collection of liturgical polyphony believed to have been compiled at Canterbury Cathedral in the 1470s during his residence there as a chantry priest. In 1478 or 1479 he was admitted bachelor of music by Oxford University, being the earliest known recipient of this degree, which involved no resident study but was awarded to outstanding practitioners (essentially, composers). In 1501–2 his degree was incorporated by Cambridge University.

To Ralph Holinshed, Wydow was 'an excellent poet', while to Leland his importance as a Latin author, 'easily the finest' among his contemporaries, lay in his role as one of England's inaugural exponents of humanist ideals, through his adoption of the classical Latin style. Nevertheless, it may be safest to share Leland's agnosticism as to whether or not Wydow ever travelled to Italy or France for study there. He reports that Wydow's works included a verse life of the Black Prince, in terms that suggest it could be set to music, and a collection of epigrams in the contemporary style eulogizing prominent contemporaries; he is able to quote a few lines from two of them. Wydow died shortly before 4 October 1505, probably at Wells, and was buried in the south aisle of the cathedral, where an inscription was placed in his memory.

ROGER BOWERS

Sources Emden, *Cam.*, 654–5 • *Commentarii de scriptoribus Britannicis, auctore Joanne Lelando*, ed. A. Hall, 2 (1709), 484–5 • A. Hughes-Hughes, 'Wydow, Robert', Grove, *Dict. mus.* (1878–90) • H. H. Hudson, 'John Leland's list of early English humanists', *Huntington Library Quarterly*, 2 (1938–9), 301–4 • J. W. Binns, *Intellectual culture in Elizabethan and Jacobean England: the Latin writings of the age* (1990), 21–2 • R. Bowers, 'Magdalene College, MS Pepys 1236', *Cambridge music manuscripts, 900–1700*, ed. I. A. Fenlon (1982), 111–14 [exhibition catalogue, Fitzwilliam Museum, Cambridge, 1982] • mundum books and commons books, King's Cam. • *Calendar of the manuscripts of the dean and chapter of Wells*, 2, HMC, 12 (1914), 146–97 • F. W. Weaver, ed., *Somerset medieval wills*, 2, Somerset RS, 19 (1903), 88–9 • *Registrum Thomae Bourgchier … 1454–1486*, ed. F. R. H. Du Boulay, CYS, 54 (1957), 316, 333 • *Holinshed's chronicles of England, Scotland and Ireland*, ed. H. Ellis, 3 (1808), 543 • M. Williamson, 'The Eton choirbook: collegiate music-making in the reign of Henry VII', *The reign of Henry VII* [Harlaxton, 1993], ed. B. Thompson (1995), 213–28, esp. 224 • A. Ashbee, ed., *Records of English court music*, 9 vols. (1986–96), vols. 7–8
Archives Magd. Cam., MS Pepys 1236

Wyer [Wyre], **Robert** (*fl.* 1524–1556), printer and bookseller, is mainly known from his printed books as there is no record of his place of origin, date of birth, education, or family. However, possible links with the Wyers of Wendover, Buckinghamshire, with the mid-sixteenth-century printers John and Richard Wyer, and with Nicholas Wyer (possibly his son) who published books from Robert's premises from *c.*1562 have all been advanced.

Although early printers in London often co-operated with one another, no close association between Wyer and other printers can be proved. He may have started mainly as a bookseller, for he probably sold books printed by Richard Faques, Richard Pynson, and Lawrence Andrew about 1528; but the lay subsidy rolls for 1524 have Wyer enrolled as a printer with goods valued at £4. On 7 September 1527 he was summoned to appear before the vicar-general of the bishop of London for printing *Symbolum apostolicum* (of which no copy now survives). Wyer confessed he had been warned by the bishop not to print any work especially of holy writ, and was ordered to surrender all copies of the *Symbolum* to the vicar-general; he surrendered his remaining twenty-nine copies the following week. He was also ordered to appear before the bishop to receive his punishment, but no record of that meeting survives. The earliest extant dated book attributable to Wyer is *The Golden Pystle* of 1531, printed by 'Robert Wyre' at the sign of St John the Evangelist in St Martin's parish, by Charing Cross, in the bishop of Norwich's rents. One other pre-1536 book imprint has the spelling 'Wyre', but later books use 'Wyer'. The bishop of Norwich retained this property with associated rents until 1536, when it passed to the duke of Suffolk: undated books referring to the bishop's rents must therefore be dated to before 1536 and those referring to the duke to after 1536. He may well have been the Robert Wyer included in a 1538 list of members of the Salters' Company of London.

Ten major typefaces attributed to Wyer form the basis for the attribution and chronology of his publications, for fewer than thirty books are signed or dated. Some books contain his device which exists in three states, the first showing St John on Patmos against a city background, sitting or kneeling with a scroll on his right knee on which he is writing and an eagle beside him holding his inkhorn with the name ROBERT:WYRE below; the second is identical except that the name is spelt ROBERT:WYER; and the third has expunged the eagle. The first state is found first in *The Compost of Ptholomeus* (*c*.1530), and the second two in *The Golden Pystle* (1531). At least 145 books are attributed to Wyer, excluding extant fragments; but the total number of his publications probably far exceeds this figure. Both bastard (or secretary) and textura typefaces occur in the body of his books, though other types appear in his titles and running heads. He used woodcuts and initial letters regularly. A set of small woodcuts which he employed frequently was copied from blocks used by Antoine Verard of Paris in 1490. He frequently used some initials which may be identical with those used by Worde. He printed books for other publishers the most significant of which was *The Defence of Peace* printed for the translator and publisher William Marshall (1535) at a cost of over £34 and which had not sold out by December 1536. Books which record Wyer simply as the printer, such as the *School House of Women*, may have been published by others. He acted thus as printer, publisher, and bookseller. Like other printers he often notes his books are published *cum privilegio regali* or equivalent, and some add the rubric *ad imprimendum solum*.

Although his edition of Christine de Pisan's *One Hundred Histories of Troy* is both bulky and reasonably well printed, most of Wyer's output was popular, indifferently printed, and cheap, many being small octavos. The subjects were wide-ranging and included both religious and secular works; the latter consisted of poems, chronicles, and books of advice, of prognostications and astronomy, and of basic medical information. He reprinted his own books and those previously published by others and he was not averse to cutting up longer books into smaller editions and changing the titles to make them more attractive and more saleable to a wide range of people. He turned *The Kalender of Shepherdes*, which had been published several times already, into *The Compost of Ptholomeus* and divided

The Pricke of Conscience into two prints: parts I–III were published as *A Newe Treatyse* (*c*.1542) and part IV was published as *A Lytell Boke that Speketh of Purgatorye* (*c*.1550). *STC* records 1556 as the last year that Wyer is known to have been active. Although not innovative as a printer, Wyer broke new ground with his publication policy and exhibited both marketing skill and considerable energy. He appears to have been a successful businessman, and he presumably died in comfortable old age.   N. F. BLAKE

Sources H. R. Plomer, *Robert Wyer, printer and bookseller* (1897) · H. R. Plomer, *Wynkyn de Worde and his contemporaries from the death of Caxton to 1535* (1925) · *LP Henry VIII*, 11, no. 1355 · P. B. Tracy, 'Robert Wyer: a brief analysis of his types and a suggested chronology for the output of his press', *The Library*, 6th ser., 2 (1980), 293–303 · A. W. Reed, 'The regulation of the book trade before the Proclamation of 1538', *Transactions of the Bibliographical Society*, 15 (1917–19), 157–84; repr. in A. W. Reed, *Early Tudor drama* (1926), 160–86 · H. B. Lathrop, 'Some rogueries of Robert Wyer', *The Library*, 3rd ser., 5 (1914), 349–64 · J. F. Preston, '*The prick of conscience* (parts I–III) and its first appearance in print', *The Library*, 6th ser., 7 (1985), 304–14 · E. J. Devereux, 'Tyndale's *The obedyence of a Chrysten man*', *The Library*, 5th ser., 31 (1976), 251–2 · E. Salisbury, 'List of liverymen and freemen of the city companies, AD 1538', *Middlesex and Hertfordshire Notes and Queries*, 3–4 (1897–8), 39–43, 80–82, 151–4, 187–91; 17–21, 68–9 · *STC, 1475–1640*, 3.191

Wyeth, Joseph (1663–1731), religious writer, was born in the parish of St Saviour, Southwark, on 19 September 1663, the son of Henry Wyeth and his first wife, Sarah (*d.* 1669). His father remarried in 1670, his second wife being Bridgette Benson, a widow. Joseph Wyeth was a Quaker and became a successful merchant in London; he married Margaret (1672/3–1749). He wrote a number of controversial works, the most important of which was *Anguis Flagellatus, or, A Switch for the Snake* (1699), a reply to the anti-Quaker polemic *Snake in the Grass* (1697) by Charles Leslie. Wyeth sought to demonstrate Quaker consistency since the emergence of the Friends in the 1650s, and, refuting the evidence advanced by Leslie, claimed that the Friends had always professed pacifism. A supplement was added by George Whitehead, to whose *Antidote Against the Venom of the Snake in the Grass* (1697) Wyeth had written an appendix, *Primitive Christianity Continued in the Faith and Practice of the People Called Quakers* (1698). Here too he asserted that 'our principles are now no other than what they were when first a people' (p. 53).

Wyeth contributed two pamphlets to the Quaker campaign to oppose the establishment of a state church in Maryland, which Thomas Bray, commissary-general, succeeded in carrying through the English parliament in 1701. In *An Answer to a Letter from Dr Bray* (1700) and *Remarks on Dr Bray's Memorial* (1701) Wyeth objected to Bray's equation of Quakerism with atheism and to his proposal to raise tithes to fund the state church. Wyeth, who was a friend of the author for twenty years, prepared Thomas Ellwood's autobiography for the press, adding a supplement, preface, and bibliography to the first edition, printed in 1714. The supplement continued Ellwood's narrative from 1683 until his death in 1713; in preparing this work Wyeth reviewed many letters and documents that had belonged to John Milton, a number of which were later published by John Nickolls, who had been apprenticed to Wyeth. Wyeth also published *The Athenian Society unvail'd, or, Their ignorance and envious abusing of the Quakers detected and reprehended* (1692), and a defence of William Penn against the accusations of Thomas Budd.

Wyeth died, of fever, on 9 January 1731 and was buried at The Park, Worcester Street, Southwark. His widow died in Tottenham, aged seventy-six, on 13 September 1749 and was buried with him.

CHARLOTTE FELL-SMITH, *rev.* MARY K. GEITER

Sources J. Smith, ed., *A descriptive catalogue of Friends' books*, 2 vols. (1867); suppl. (1893), 965 • J. Whiting, *A catalogue of Friends' books* (1708), 215 • W. C. Braithwaite, *The second period of Quakerism*, ed. H. J. Cadbury, 2nd edn (1961), 192, 201, 489 • T. Ellwood, *The history of the life of Thomas Ellwood*, ed. J. Wyeth, 6th edn (1855) [incl. suppl.] • G. Whitehead, *The Christian progress of … G. W. [George Whitehead]* (1725), 680 • J. Nickolls, *Original letters and papers of state … found among the political collections of John Milton* (1743), preface

Wyke, Andrew (*fl.* 1645–1663), Baptist minister and Ranter, is a man of whom nothing as yet is known of his early life. His name, derived from the Old English word for dwelling or village, was spelled variously as Wyke, Wykes, Wix, and Weeks. It is found as a surname in Kent, Sussex, and Essex. It is possible that Andrew Wyke came from the Ipswich area—in 1646 he claimed to have friends living nearby. By his own account Wyke served parliament in the civil war, though in what capacity is not known. Perhaps he was a soldier; he was later to claim that he was owed over £40 in arrears of pay. At some point Wyke became associated with the soap-boiler and Baptist Thomas Lambe (d. 1673). Together with Lambe, Wyke was apprehended at an unlawful assembly, and on 1 May 1645 committed by order of the committee for plundered ministers into the custody of the city marshal of London. Lambe and Wyke were imprisoned briefly for 'anabaptisme' and then released, the prosecution failing to convict them on the newly enacted charge of lay preaching (BL, Add. MS 15669, fols. 63r, 68v, 73r, 74v). Later, Wyke was to claim that he had been ordained 'by a Reformed Church' in London, most probably Lambe's Baptist congregation meeting in Bell Alley, Coleman Street (A. Wyke?, *The Innocent in Prison Complayning*, 1646, 4). It is also likely that Wyke was rebaptized by Lambe, perhaps in 1644, before being ordained by his church in the early months of 1645.

By the autumn of 1645 Wyke had gone forth from the church to spread the gospel message. He went to live in Debach, Suffolk, and was to spend nearly nine months preaching and rebaptizing in the surrounding area. His activities came to the attention of the heresiographer Thomas Edwards, who described Wyke as 'a Mechanick' turned 'great Preacher and Dipper' (Edwards, 3.169–70). On 3 June 1646, like Lawrence Clarkson before him, Andrew Wyke was imprisoned for preaching and rebaptizing by order of the committee of Suffolk at Bury St Edmunds. Upon his release Wyke continued his Baptist evangelizing, this time in Rutland and the adjacent counties. He was joined in this endeavour by Thomas Lambe and another of Lambe's converts, the Norwich weaver

Samuel Oates (1614–1683). In December 1647 several ministers from Rutland and close by, despairing of the 'erronious & seducing spirits lately crept in amongst us', petitioned the House of Lords to apprehend Oates (Betteridge, 206). Wyke may have left the Rutland area shortly after. By 25 December 1649 he was in Essex, living in the parish of St Nicholas, Colchester.

In March 1650 Andrew Wyke, in the company of a kinswoman of his, one Mistress Wallis, made a 120 mile journey from Colchester to Coventry. He arrived in Coventry on Wednesday 6 March 1650, and was said to have lain three nights in Wallis's 'Chamber' (*A Perfect Diurnall*, 11–18 March 1650, 128). The purpose of Wyke's visit to Coventry was to visit Abiezer Coppe (1619–1672), a Baptist preacher imprisoned for blasphemy, who in January had been moved to the town gaol from Warwick. Perhaps Wyke brought with him money, collected by various Baptist churches, to pay for Coppe's prison debts. Wyke was soon joined in Coventry by a comrade of Coppe's, Joseph Salmon (*fl.* 1647–1656), who on Sunday 10 March 1650 preached in the town for an hour to the 'admiration of all honest men'. Soon after, Salmon and Wyke were believed to have said that 'the Scripture … was no more than a ballad' to them. They were also accused of denying the Devil and of swearing oaths, though they claimed that 'it was God' in them that swore. Wyke was also alleged to have called a soldier a friend of Hell and a child of the Devil, before proceeding to kiss him three times and say 'I breathe the spirit of God into thee'. Described as confident men 'of acute wits' and 'voluable tongues' they were seized by Captain Robert Beake and committed to Coventry gaol for the misdemeanour of swearing and for defying an order prohibiting the visiting of Coppe (*Leyborne-Popham MSS*, 57; *A Perfect Diurnall*, 11–18 March 1650, 128). They were bound over until the next session of the assizes while the mayor and justices of Coventry informed the council of state in London of proceedings. On 19 March 1650 Coppe was moved to Newgate prison on the instructions of the council of state. From Newgate he wrote to Salmon and Wyke, playing on the word Wick to call Wyke his 'fort and stronghold' (Smith, 117).

While imprisoned Salmon and Wyke began preaching every Sunday from the prison grate. Wyke's message was 'the Love of God in pardoning sin, finishing transgression & bringing in everlasting Righteousnesse' (A. Wyke to the mayor and aldermen of Coventry, MS Clarke 18, fol. 25v). It was reported that many stood in the streets to hear them. By the beginning of April they were prevented from preaching. News of their imprisonment began to spread, and it was during their confinement that Salmon and Wyke were visited by George Fox. In his journal, Fox was to describe them as 'Ranters' for they 'began to rant and vapour and blaspheme', saying that 'they were God', justifying their words upon the authority of the first epistle of Peter and other scriptural texts (*Journal of George Fox*, 46–7). Prison probably had a debilitating effect on Wyke. His health may have suffered in poor sanitary conditions and he may have lacked the funds necessary to secure food from his keeper, Mr Butler. To this end he wrote to the mayor and aldermen of Coventry, rebuking them for condemning 'the just' (*A Perfect Diurnall*, 18–25 March 1650, 141). His entreaties rebuffed, Wyke wrote again, this time calling himself a prophet. Adopting the mantle of Isaiah, Wyke reproduced the words of the prophet, attempting to speak with his voice to admonish his captors.

On 5 July 1650 Andrew Wyke was released from Coventry gaol on bail. He was taken to London to be questioned by the council of state. Wyke's fate is unknown. Perhaps he was imprisoned for blasphemy, though it is equally possible that he offered to recant his opinions and give an undertaking of good behaviour for one year. In August 1651, little over a year later, Wyke was dispatched to Ireland as an army preacher. After a brief stay at St Michan's, Dublin, he was moved north in October to preach the gospel at Lisburn and Belfast. Wyke was described as a man of 'meek spirit', but evidently the old fire soon returned, for in November he was being spoken of as 'a rare minister' and 'a most powerful preacher' (R. Dunlop, *Ireland under the Commonwealth*, 2 vols., 1913, 1.60–61; *CSP Ire.*, 1647–60, 383). The congregation at Lisburn swelled and Wyke came into favour. In addition to his annual salary of £120, it was ordered that he should have a house at public expense together with sufficient pasture land to provide for his wife and family. Not all, though, were as well disposed to Wyke. Dorothy Rawdon, sister of Lord Conway, disliked him; the Presbyterian minister Patrick Adair referred to him as 'an Anabaptist' and guessed at his lack of university training, describing him as 'void of human learning, never educated that way, but a tradesman, and imprudent' (Adair, 186). Wyke's preaching duties were extended in 1654 to cover Dromore, Lurgan, and Kilwarlin, but by March the following year he had become involved in a controversy with the Quaker Richard Cleaton.

George Rawdon came to despair of him, complaining of Wyke's inability to perform 'punctual duties besides preaching' (*CSP Ire.*, 1647–60, 564). In May 1658 he withheld the Lisburn tithes from Wyke, took his land from him, and petitioned for the reallocation of the tithes towards the building of a free school at Lisburn. Wyke took his case before the lord chief baron. His cause, however, did not prevail. Forced to leave Lisburn, in October 1658 Wyke was appointed on an annual salary of £100 to preach to the united parishes of Donaghcloney and Tullylish in co. Down. The following summer, Wyke's replacement at Lisburn, Philip Tandy, brought charges against Jeremy Taylor, seemingly a private chaplain to the Conway family. It has been suggested that Wyke, aggrieved by his treatment at the hands of the Rawdon and Conway families, may have encouraged Tandy to bring his action against Taylor. In September 1659 Andrew Wyke's duties were increased to include preaching the gospel to the congregation of largely English settlers at Magheralin. In 1663 the marquess of Ormond ordered the arrest of a number of nonconformist ministers. By the summer eleven, including Wyke, were incarcerated at Carrickfergus. In early August Ormond dispersed the most dangerous, Wyke among

them, to prisons in Limerick, Cork, Youghal, and Waterford. Wyke was subsequently removed to England. As yet, nothing more is known of him.   ARIEL HESSAYON

Sources BL, Add. MS 15669, fols. 63*r*, 68*v*, 73*r*, 74*v* · RS Friends, Lond., Swarthmore MS IV 62 · Worcester College, Oxford, MS Clarke 18, fols. 24*r–v*, 25*r–27r* · *CSP dom.*, 1650, 45, 133, 143, 203, 517, 550 · *CSP Ire.*, 1647–60, 383, 542, 564, 667 · *Report on the manuscripts of F. W. Leyborne-Popham*, HMC, 51 (1899), 57, 59 · *A Perfect Diurnall* (11–18 March 1650), 128 · *A Perfect Diurnall* (18–25 March 1650), 141 · *A Perfect Diurnall* (29 April–6 May 1650), 218 · *A Perfect Diurnall* (1–8 April 1650), 175 · P. Adair, *A true narrative of the rise and progress of the Presbyterian church in Ireland (1623–1670)*, ed. W. D. Killen (1866), 185–90 · T. Edwards, *Gangraena, or, A catalogue and discovery of many of the errours, heresies, blasphemies and pernicious practices of the sectaries of this time*, 3 (1646), 10, 169–70 · *The journal of George Fox*, rev. edn, ed. J. L. Nickalls (1952), 46–7 · St J. D. Seymour, *The puritans in Ireland, 1647–1661* (1912); repr. (1969), 20–22, 72–5, 170–2, 176–7, 224 · A. Betteridge, 'Early Baptists in Leicestershire and Rutland [pt 1]', *Baptist Quarterly*, 25 (1973–4), 204–11 · N. Smith, ed., *A collection of Ranter writings from the 17th century* (1983), 117 · petition of the residents of Magheralin, co. Down, 1659, PRO NIre., MS D/1759/2A/5, fol. 108 · R. Greaves, *God's other children: protestant nonconformists and the emergence of denominational churches in Ireland, 1660–1700* (Stanford, 1997), 25, 27, 86, 89, 90

Wyke, Sir Charles Lennox (1815–1897), diplomatist, born on 2 September 1815, was the son of George Wyke, of Robleston, Pembrokeshire, captain in the Grenadier Guards, and his wife, Charlotte, daughter of F. Meyrick. He was a lieutenant in the Royal Fusiliers, and afterwards a captain on the king of Hanover's staff. In 1847 he was appointed vice-consul at Port-au-Prince and in 1852 consul-general in Central America. He was appointed chargé d'affaires on 31 October 1854, and on 8 August 1859 he was nominated envoy-extraordinary; in the same year he was gazetted CB. On 23 January 1860 he was removed to Mexico as minister-plenipotentiary to the republic, and on 22 May was created KCB. On 30 June 1861 Juarez was elected president of the Mexican republic with dictatorial powers, and on 17 July the congress suspended payment of public bonds for two years. In consequence France and England broke off diplomatic relations with the republic on 27 July. Wyke left the city of Mexico in December with all his staff, but remained in the country to carry on the negotiations connected with the joint intervention of England, France, and Spain. When the design of France to subvert the Mexican government became apparent, however, England and Spain withdrew from the alliance, and Wyke returned home. On 19 January 1866 he was accredited to Hanover, but in September his mission was cut short by the Austro-Prussian War and the annexation of Hanover by Prussia. He retired on a pension but on 16 December 1867 was appointed minister at Copenhagen, where he remained for fourteen years. In August 1879 he was created GCMG, and on 22 June 1881 he was transferred to Portugal, where he remained until the close of his diplomatic career. He again retired on a pension on 21 February 1884, and was sworn of the privy council on 6 February 1886. Wyke died, unmarried, on 4 October 1897 at his residence, 23 Cheyne Walk, Chelsea, London.

E. I. CARLYLE, *rev.* H. C. G. MATTHEW

Sources *FO List* (1891) · *The Times* (5 Oct 1897)

Archives BL, letters | Bodl. Oxf., letters to Lord Clarendon · Bodl. Oxf., corresp. with Sir John Fiennes Crampton · Lpool RO, corresp. with Lord Derby · PRO, corresp. with Lord Russell, PRO 30/22
Likenesses Spy [L. Ward], caricature, watercolour study, NPG; repro. in *VF* (9 Feb 1884)
Wealth at death £84,332 18s. 7d.: probate, 10 Nov 1897, *CGPLA Eng. & Wales*

Wykeham [*formerly* Wykeham-Barnes], **Sir Peter Guy** (1915–1995), air force officer, was born at Kotra, Sandhurst, Berkshire, on 13 September 1915, the son of Captain Guy Vane Wykeham-Barnes, Army Service Corps, and his wife, Audrey Irene, *née* Rogers. Educated at Hampton grammar school, he joined the Royal Air Force as an engineering apprentice in 1932. On completing his apprenticeship at RAF Halton in 1935 he was awarded a cadetship to the RAF College, Cranwell. After graduating as a pilot in 1937, he flew Gladiator aircraft with 80(F) squadron, based in the Suez Canal zone. During the time he was detached to Ramlah in Palestine in September 1938, the young pilot officer was presented with a personal certificate of distinguished conduct by the general officer commanding British forces Palestine and Transjordan for, alone in his Gladiator aircraft, surprising and detaining a group of thirty Arab rebels in a wadi while informing the approaching ground troops by repeated message dropping. Six Arabs were captured, and Wykeham-Barnes claimed a further dozen casualties.

By June 1940 the squadron was being equipped with Hurricane fighters, and Wykeham-Barnes scored 80 squadron's first combat successes of this conflict when he shot down two Italian aircraft over north Africa. Later, flying a Gladiator, he shot down a Fiat and then destroyed another, but then had himself to bail out and walk back over the desert to his unit. He was afterwards posted as flight commander to 274 squadron, which had received the 80 squadron Hurricanes, where he shot down several more Italian aircraft and, in December 1940, was awarded the DFC. He took command of 73 squadron in April 1941, operating from within the fortress of Tobruk. Now tackling the Luftwaffe, the squadron suffered severe casualties, and Wykeham-Barnes was again shot down, but only after destroying two German aircraft. For his leadership of 73 squadron he was awarded a bar to his DFC in late 1941. With his combat experience he was sent to Washington as an air warfare instructor soon after the USA entered the war. He returned home in May 1942, and after spending a short time with another Hurricane squadron he took command of 23 squadron, based in Malta and equipped with Mosquito aircraft. For attacking Luftwaffe aircraft, axis shipping, communications, and troops, he was awarded his first DSO for operations in Italy.

Wykeham-Barnes was posted home in summer 1943 to Fighter Command but, in March 1944, and now a group captain, he was given command of 140 wing, equipped with Mosquito aircraft and tasked with intruder operations in support of the D-day landings. From RAF Thorney Island, on 12 June 1944, he gave the BBC war correspondent Richard Dimbleby a memorable but uncomfortable Mosquito reconnaissance flight over the Normandy beachhead. A recording was made and broadcast by the BBC that evening. Later that month Wykeham-Barnes took Ernest Hemingway, then an American war correspondent, on a Mosquito demonstration flight over the English Channel. Once airborne, Wykeham-Barnes sighted the red exhaust glow of a V-1 flying bomb and gave chase, but had to break off the attack once the missile entered the anti-aircraft gun and barrage-balloon belt. A second V-1 was spotted and attacked but, Wykeham-Barnes later recalled, he again 'pulled away in a confusion of searchlights and intense flak. There was a huge flash behind us and the aeroplane danced around like a leaf in a whirlwind ... Ernest seemed to love every moment' (Whiting, 68). The two remained friends and, later in recently liberated Paris, then in Brussels, Hemingway sought out the visiting Wykeham-Barnes, 'his Groupy', to join him in drinking sessions. But operational flying continued to occupy 140 wing and its commanding officer, and in October 1944 Wykeham-Barnes himself led the third of four waves of six Mosquitoes in the audacious low-level raid on the Gestapo headquarters at Århus in Denmark to liberate members of Danish resistance being held by the Gestapo and to destroy evidence against them. For this raid, which also killed the head of the Gestapo in Denmark, he was awarded a bar to his DSO, and in 1945 he was made chevalier of the order of Dannebrog by the Danish government.

In 1945 Wykeham-Barnes completed the Staff College course, and a number of staff jobs followed before he was posted in 1948 to test-flying duties at the Aeroplane and Aircraft Experimental Establishment at Boscombe Down. There he was test pilot for a number of the new experimental and demanding swept-wing jet aircraft. For his work on these new types he was appointed OBE and later awarded the AFC. On 15 January 1949 he had married the architect Barbara Elizabeth Priestley (*b.* 1923/4), the daughter of the author J. B. Priestley; they had two sons and a daughter.

When the Korean War broke out, Wykeham-Barnes's advice on night-intruder operations was requested by the American authorities, and he was loaned to the United States Air Force. He flew numerous night-bombing missions over North Korea in B-26 aircraft and was awarded the United States air medal. In 1951 he returned to the UK to command stations in Fighter Command, then spent the three years from 1953 in appointments with NATO. In 1955 he changed his name by deed poll, dropping the Barnes from the name under which he had made his reputation in the air. From 1956 he filled a number of senior appointments, including that of air officer commanding 38 group (the joint warfare group) (1960–62) and director of the joint warfare staff (1962–4). In 1960 his first book, *Fighter Command: a Study of Air Defence, 1914–60*, was well received—as was, two years later, *Santos Dumont: a Study in Obsession*, his biography (the first in English) of the pioneer Brazilian aviator. Wykeham was appointed commander of the Far East air force in 1964 during the 'confrontation' with Indonesia, when his experience of joint-service operations again came to the fore. He was appointed KCB in

1965 and promoted air marshal in 1967, when he became deputy chief of the air staff.

Elected a fellow of the Royal Aeronautical Society in 1968, Wykeham took premature retirement from the RAF a year later, at the age of fifty-four. He then became an export consultant to the civil aviation industry, living first at Kew, then at Kingston upon Thames, and finally at Stockbridge in Hampshire. He remained an expert pilot into old age and bore a painful illness with his characteristic courage. He died of non-Hodgkin's lymphoma at his home, Green Place, Winton Hill, Stockbridge, on 23 February 1995. ROBIN WOOLVEN

Sources *The Independent* (28 Feb 1995) · *The Times* (28 Feb 1995) · b. cert. · m. cert. · d. cert. · *WWW* · C. Whiting, *Hemingway goes to war* (1999), esp. 63–9 · *Air Force List* · *RAF Retired List, 1939–1995* · private information (2004) [Barbara, Lady Wykeham, widow] · PRO, AIR27/669 [operational record for no. 80 (F) squadron in Palestine]; AIR 26/204 [operational record for no. 140 wing at Thorney Island]

Likenesses photograph, repro. in *The Independent* · photograph, repro. in *The Times*

Wealth at death £243,200: probate, 4 April 1995, *CGPLA Eng. & Wales*

Wykeham, William (*c*.1324–1404), bishop of Winchester, administrator, and founder of Winchester College and New College, Oxford, was the son of John Long, a man of free condition from Wickham, Hampshire, and his wife, Sibyl, the daughter of William Bouadde (perhaps Boyatt) and Alice, the eldest daughter of Sir William Stratton. The Stratton family had rights in Selborne and elsewhere in Hampshire.

Early career to 1361 Wykeham may well have been assisted at the start of his career by two Hampshire gentry, Sir Ralph Sutton and Sir John Scures (lord of the manor of Wickham), whom he was much later to commemorate in his college foundations. Sutton was constable of Winchester Castle, and in that capacity may have been Wykeham's first employer, and perhaps helped to train him. On 12 July 1349 Wykeham secured royal presentation to the rectory of Irstead, Norfolk. He was described then as a 'chaplain', meaning an unbeneficed clerk, but not as a royal chaplain or clerk. He is first recorded as an employee of the king in the context of building works, when on 10 May 1356 he was appointed clerk of the works for the royal houses at Henley on the Heath, Surrey, and Easthampstead, Berkshire. How he attracted royal favour is unknown. It is unlikely that the duties at Henley constituted his first employment in the royal works, since within a few months of the appointment, on 30 October, he acquired another, far more important, task, as surveyor of the works in the castle and park of Windsor. Training in business speculations in government moneys came early to Wykeham: on 14 April 1355 he had been the attorney of one John Foxley, a Berkshire notable who at that time specialized in the brokerage of exchequer tallies. Foxley was the son of Wykeham's probable patron of that time, Thomas Foxley, the constable of Windsor Castle.

On 10 July 1359 Wykeham was made chief keeper and surveyor of the castles of Windsor, Leeds, Dover, and Hadleigh, and of a long list of royal manors which included

William Wykeham (*c*.1324–1404), manuscript drawing [standing, centre, with the members of New College]

Sheen, Eltham, and Langley. He was also responsible for the earlier parts of the building works at the site later known as Queenborough, in the Isle of Sheppey, Kent, which was the only wholly new royal castle to be built in England during the later middle ages. These were among the principal castles and royal residences of the kingdom, and Wykeham's appointment as chief keeper is regarded as having been a model for the later office of clerk of the king's works. The duties of the chief keeper, much like those of the later clerks, were managerial and supervisory, including those of an auditor or comptroller; there is no evidence that any of the supervising royal clerks (Wykeham included) had any technical knowledge of architecture. Their offices were connected with the royal household, and there must have been an intimate relationship between the clerks responsible for royal works and the clerks who as receivers or secretaries were responsible for the finances of the royal chamber. At this period of his life Wykeham must also have acquired the judgement and discernment regarding architecture and artefacts that were to be important for his later career as founder, patron, and benefactor.

Early political involvements From 1361 Wykeham's involvement with royal building works sharply diminished, and a new and far more political career took shape.

He was from late 1361 described as a royal secretary, a term that implied that he acted as receiver of the royal chamber. That this was so is clear from his being named as having received some of the payments of the ransom of Jean II, king of France, that were destined to go to the royal chamber. He had taken part in the negotiations to ratify the treaty of Brétigny, at Calais in 1360, and by January 1361 he had become important enough for the kings of England and France jointly to petition Pope Innocent VI to confer upon him a canonry of Lincoln. By the beginning of 1363 he was a royal councillor, and on 10 June 1363 he was given charge of the privy seal. Several letters addressed to him by Innocent VI referred to his supposed influence over the king. It was of this period of his career that the chronicler Froissart made his frequently quoted remark concerning Wykeham that 'everything was done by him, and without him nothing was done' (*Chroniques*, 7.101). At the time of Wykeham's disgrace, thirteen years later, it was claimed that he had earlier been 'chief of the privy council and governor of the great council' (Rymer, *Foedera*, 4, 4.12). In the early 1360s he began to seize eagerly the material rewards of office, both secular and church preferments. By November 1363, for example, he had been made joint warden of the royal forests south of the River Trent. When he attested the treaty with Brittany on 7 July 1362 he was described in the official document, with pardonable exaggeration, as 'noble et puissant' (Rymer, *Foedera*, 4, 3.662).

Church preferment Wykeham was, notoriously, one of the greatest church pluralists of his age. On 27 February 1357, when granted a papal indult to choose a confessor in the hour of death, he was still not described as a clerk. But in the same year, still lacking church orders (which he acquired only in 1361–2), he was granted the lucrative benefice of Pulham, in the diocese of Ely, which was in the royal gift because of the unauthorized flight of the ordinary, Bishop Thomas Lisle of Ely, to the papal court. These procedures attracted a lawsuit against him in the papal court at Avignon, and, as became customary with him in other similar cases, three or four years later he resigned the benefice as being too much trouble and expense to defend. But Pulham was the first of a large cluster of benefices and prebends held in plurality, that he exchanged or resigned according to his convenience and advantage. Wykeham was careful in matters of canon law; he secured the pope's personal attention and consent to a royal petition that he might hold two benefices with a cure of souls, one of them in a cathedral church, with the right to exchange them for others (11 December 1361).

In 1366, when Pope Urban V required a return to be made, Wykeham was the leading clerical pluralist of the southern archdiocese, holding two benefices with a cure of souls, and eleven prebends, with a total annual value of £873 6s. 8d. The next-richest pluralist held benefices for less than a third of this sum. The most valuable of Wykeham's clerical positions was the archdeaconry of Lincoln, which he had succeeded in holding against a counter-claim by a cardinal, worth £350. Wykeham's avidity as a benefice hunter and his privileged access to the

king were thought remarkable even at the curia. Robert Stratton, an English auditor of the papal rota, claimed to the pope that he went in fear and terror of Wykeham, and that he entertained no hope of ever entering the canonry and prebend in St Andrew's, Auckland, co. Durham, that was in dispute between them.

In October 1366 the king caused Wykeham to be elected to the rich and dignified see of Winchester. A royal embassy was promptly sent to Avignon to argue the case for his papal provision to the see; Urban V at first temporized. In early June of 1367 a second embassy offered bribes to the pope's brother, and to other curialists. Edward also put pressure on two French princes captured by the English at Poitiers, the dukes of Bourbon and Berri, offering them extension of their leave of absence from captivity as the price of their intercession with the pope on Wykeham's behalf. On 14 July 1367 the pope (by then in Italy) issued the bull for Wykeham's provision to the see. Wykeham was consecrated in St Paul's, London, on 10 October 1367, the temporalities were restored two days later, and he was enthroned in Winchester on 9 July 1368.

From the chancellorship to disgrace Wykeham was made royal chancellor during the late summer of 1367, when his episcopal promotion was known, and not later than 17 September. It is doubtful whether the chancellorship increased Wykeham's power, but it certainly increased his political vulnerability. The main negative element was the renewal of the war with France in 1369, a decision that lay with the king and not with his minister. Given the facts of contemporary taxation and of the nature of existing credit operations, it was impossible to keep a fully paid army in the field for very long. During Wykeham's chancellorship the king's ever-increasing physical weakness was also a factor. When the government proved incapable of exploiting what was seen as its strong position in France, and became increasingly short of money, its unpopularity was assured. Wykeham was accused of administrative laxity in his execution of the chancellor's office: more of this was heard at the time of his disgrace, five years later. In the royal court a layman, William, Lord Latimer, had replaced Wykeham in the king's favour. The anti-clericalism of the Commons contributed to weaken Wykeham's position, and he was dismissed on 24 March 1371.

After 1371 Wykeham remained a royal courtier, frequently witnessing royal charters, and being careful to maintain good relations with the royal princes, Edward Mortimer, earl of March (to whom he had earlier acted as guardian), John of Gaunt, duke of Lancaster, and Edward, the Black Prince, and also with such powerful figures as John, earl of Pembroke (*d.* 1375). He was not unmindful of his responsibilities as bishop and churchman. He initiated building and repair works on the buildings of his see and, until he clashed with the prior and monks of St Swithun's, of his cathedral church. He also began to support a number of poor scholars at Oxford University. He had no intention of retiring from the centre of political life, as became evident during the Good Parliament in 1376, when he attempted to profit politically from the fall of a group of courtiers, some of whose careers, notably that of Latimer, had been not unlike his own. After the removal of Latimer and other royal councillors Wykeham was one of four bishops appointed to the new royal council on 26 May, and sworn in parliament. He took the lead in accusing the fallen ministers of peculation of various kinds. Ironically, two of his charges, of using official powers to speculate in wool exports, and of practising brokerage of the king's debts by buying up discounted exchequer tallies and then using court influence to redeem them at a higher value, covered activities which he had himself practised while in power, and was to practise again later.

John of Gaunt felt himself under attack from Wykeham, and perhaps suspected a further hostility arising from Wykeham's connection with the earl of March. Gaunt's partisans in council mounted a counter-attack. Charges were brought against Wykeham, in some respects resembling those he had brought against Latimer. The legal procedure adopted was not called an impeachment by any contemporary, but both Wykeham himself, in his draft defence, and some chroniclers spoke of his having been denied the judgment of his peers. His pardon in the following year spoke of his restoration to the benefits of common law, suggesting that he was arraigned before the royal council, which excluded common-law procedure, perhaps at a secret meeting held on 6 November.

Wykeham was charged with mismanagement of royal policy while chancellor; there were also some specific charges of administrative abuse in the chancery and elsewhere. The fact that they included securing the release of French hostages and having unwarranted corrections made on the chancery rolls gives some idea of the range of his activities, and lends support to the claims for his omnicompetence made by Froissart and others. None of these charges was easy to prove, but he was condemned on one, and this led to the temporalities of his see being sequestrated (probably in November 1376), and to his being forbidden the court. Clerical privilege was appealed to by Wykeham in the affair, and also by his brother bishops, who refused supply to the crown until he was allowed to attend their convocation, in February 1377. Wykeham made several proffers of large sums to the crown to buy his way out, including an offer to fit out three warships. The temporalities of the see of Winchester were restored to the bishop only three days before Edward III's death on 21 June. Wykeham was pardoned by the young Richard II on 31 July 1377. No doubt Gaunt had ceased to regard him as politically dangerous, but other manoeuvres in inner court circles may have played a part.

Wykeham and the politics of Richard II's reign Wykeham's record during the difficult and dangerous rule of Richard II attests to his political skill and decision. How dangerous his career had been became clear in the Westminster parliament of 1397, when Wykeham and the duke of York, shedding tears, fell on their knees to thank the king for his favour in saying that the royal pardon that protected them from treason charges for their actions in 1386 was not withdrawn.

Wykeham resumed his regular membership of the royal council in late November of 1378, and was very probably one of the eight 'continual councillors' responsible for ordering the war and matters touching the estate of the realm, and a member of other responsible commissions. By January 1385 Wykeham had ceased to attend council meetings as a matter of routine. But from 1386 to 1394, a period of serious political conflict, he played a leading role. He participated in commissions named in the Westminster parliament of 1385, and in the following year was a member of a commission forced upon the unwilling Richard II, who later caused the judges to impute treason both to those who framed the commission and those who accepted office in it. Finally, in the confrontation between the king and the opposition in 1387–8, Wykeham's role was that of a firm, though discreet, supporter of the lords appellant. In the new year of 1388 he became one of five members of a committee 'for the day-to-day guidance of the king'—in Richard's eyes an illegal commission devised for his own constraint (*Westminster Chronicle*, 233). In March, at the end of the Merciless Parliament, he accepted membership of a new committee to exercise control over the king's person and policies. He advised against allowing sanctuary in Westminster to Sir Robert Tresilian, one of the disgraced royalist judges, and acquired lands and rights belonging to Tresilian's condemned colleague, Sir Robert Bealknap.

In effect, Wykeham had participated in a far from bloodless revolution. Wykeham was not, therefore, a political neutral, as has sometimes been implied, when he was restored to the chancellor's office from 4 May 1389 until 27 September 1391. On the other hand, while the lords appellant knew that he had on the whole acted in their interests in the crisis, Richard knew that Wykeham was an old royal servant who could be counted upon to behave with caution and prudence. It is significant that Richard stayed with Wykeham in Wolvesey Castle in July and again in September of 1393, bringing with him a train of some 180 followers, and receiving sumptuous entertainment from the bishop. It is also significant that in the charters of privileges that Richard conceded to Wykeham's two foundations at Oxford and Winchester (26 and 28 September 1395), the king remarked on his own 'affection for the bishop's person' that had helped induce him to grant them (Kirby, *Annals*, 453).

By 1399 Wykeham's main interest lay in the financial and legal security of his two educational foundations. A passing reference in one of his sermons shows that he took a keen interest in the advance of Henry Bolingbroke's forces against Richard II in the summer of 1399, but understandably he gave little away about his views or intentions. Wykeham received Henry IV in Winchester early in the new reign, but he was not among the lords who advised that the deposed king should be removed to safe custody.

Founder of colleges Wykeham accumulated great wealth in the course of his long career. The secure foundation of his wealth, especially from the time of his appointment to the very rich see of Winchester, was his revenue as a churchman. But he also at various times added to his wealth by other means, notably by dealing in property both lay and ecclesiastical, by activity in the wool market, and by speculating in the market for discounted tallies. He lent money to government and to notables, although it is uncertain whether for financial profit. By these means, without depleting the resources of his see of Winchester, he managed to live splendidly as a princely bishop, to establish two major educational foundations that have endured to the present day, to finance extensive work on his cathedral church, to set up a branch of his formerly humble family as substantial gentry, to give his Oxford college a huge cash reserve of £2000, and still to bequeath, at his death, between £6000 and £7000 in cash. He achieved this by a lifetime of tireless, shrewd business activity, and in this respect, although he was not entirely unfamiliar in his day as a churchman type, he can probably be compared as well with some modern capitalist–philanthropists as with other medieval bishops.

In 1379 (26 November; the first royal charter is dated 1 August 1379), in continuation of the provision he had earlier made for poor scholars in the university, Wykeham set up in Oxford a college (which came to be known as New College), for a warden, ten priests, three stipendiary clerks, and seventy scholars, dedicated to the Virgin. Unlike existing colleges it taught grammar, and it anticipated fifteenth-century trends by emphasizing theology in preference to canon and civil law. Wykeham referred to the deficiency in numbers of the educated clergy, due to war and pestilence, and this led him to the innovatory second foundation of another college of the Virgin near the site of his episcopal palace at Winchester, where seventy poor boys were to be educated in grammar and in the basics of the liberal arts. The papal bull of foundation for the college at Winchester was dated 1 June 1378, the royal licence to build, 6 October 1382. There is some irony in Wykeham's respectful treatment of grammar and of learned men in the foundation documents, since, although he spoke and wrote French, and certainly understood administrative Latin, he had, as far as is known, never received formal education above a humble level.

In both colleges there was an obligation to commemorate in prayers and masses King Richard and his queen, Wykeham himself, his parents, and named benefactors who included Sir Ralph Sutton, Sir John Scures, and Thomas Foxley. In elections of scholars to New College preference was to be given to Wykeham's own kin, to the poor scholars issuing from his school in Winchester, and to poor clerks originating either in the diocese of Winchester or in villages and manors owned by the college. These preferences and catchment areas were closely followed in his school. Of the idealism present in Wykeham's foundations there is no doubt: he justified the elaborate arrangements he made to ensure regular administration of the colleges, saying that if their administration was going to be lax, he would have done better to have distributed his wealth to the poor with his own hands. Wykeham's sharp business transactions were conducted more for the benefit of his foundations than for that of himself and his family, and he evidently thought that to ensure a future supply of clerks of good learning and good character, likely to undertake pastoral duties, was the best way to justify his own career.

The buildings and their finances Construction of the Oxford college began in March 1380. The buildings were erected in several campaigns, partly because of the slow progress of financial endowment, partly because in Oxford some of the land required for construction had to be acquired piecemeal. The warden (Wykeham's kinsman Nicholas Wykeham) and scholars of the Oxford college were able to occupy it on 14 April 1386, although important works still remained to be done. Work on the college at Winchester began later, in March 1387, and the main chapel and cloister there were finished in 1395. The two colleges were built on appreciably different scales, that at Oxford being the larger. Their plans were similar, although not identical, and the differences were not always attributable to the differing sites (for instance, the chapel at New College was modelled on that of Merton College, allowing a fine and spacious ante chapel). The high standard of the buildings was assured not only by Wykeham's wealth and aesthetic experience, but also by the fact that both colleges had been planned and supervised by a single distinguished architect, William Wynford. There may also have been some collaboration with a second architect who, like Wynford, had earlier been employed in the royal works, namely Henry Yevele. The works and most of the fittings at both colleges were finished a short time before the deaths of Wykeham and Wynford.

The main business opportunity that Wykeham had seized in order to help finance his colleges had been an offshoot of the Hundred Years' War. It was provided by the royal confiscation of 'alien priories', that is, estates in England belonging to French monastic houses. These were not the only estates he acquired on behalf of the new colleges: for example, Downton in Wiltshire was subtracted from the estates of the see of Winchester and given to Winchester College. The great expulsion of French monastic owners from England had resulted from a Commons petition to the parliament that met on 13 October 1377, but confiscations had begun long before this.

Wykeham, like many courtiers, became a main purchaser of alien priories. He was especially qualified to do so, not only because of his political influence, but also because his intimate knowledge of the personnel and procedures of the papal curia usually enabled him to obtain the pope's approval for his transactions, something that was just as important as English royal approval. He normally offered some compensation to the displaced foreign owners: he also struck profitable bargains with French religious houses (and on one occasion an Italian one) that found it difficult to collect their English revenues, and had these arrangements, too, approved in the curia. Wykeham made schedules for his legal representatives in Rome and England, explaining the separate legal steps to be taken in both the church and lay courts in the process of acquiring the lands of alien corporations.

Wykeham's survival to an advanced age gave protection to the colleges during the critical period of transition to Lancastrian rule. Parliament had decided in November 1402 that alien priories that had been improperly appropriated ought to be resumed by the crown. In pursuance of this decision the wardens of Winchester College and New College were required to appear before the royal council on 24 January 1403 to show all the charters and evidences for their possessions held in free alms. The two colleges might have suffered impoverishment, had Wykeham (although already infirm) not been still alive.

Patron of the arts Wykeham was among the main patrons of the arts in his day. His main achievements were the two colleges themselves, both of them consistently and intelligently planned. It has been argued that the design of the colleges was responsible for the later normal arrangement of the collegiate buildings in the two English universities, concentrating the main facilities in a single quadrangle. His contribution to the Perpendicular-style rebuilding of the nave of his cathedral, though incomplete, because not begun until 1394, is also noteworthy. His chantry chapel in his cathedral (also by Wynford) is less distinguished, although it may once have contained some accomplished sculptures. The stained glass he commissioned from Thomas Glazier of Oxford for the two college chapels was among the first and best examples of the international Gothic style in England. Most of the Winchester glass was lost in an early nineteenth-century restoration, but enough has been recovered to show the quality of the original. True to his training in the royal works, Wykeham was appreciative of the talents of individual architects and craftsmen, and he chose to have represented, in the west window of the chapel of Winchester College, figures of both Hugh Herland the carpenter and William Wynford the architect. Some artefacts associated with Wykeham are hard to assess: it is uncertain, for example, whether the crozier he bequeathed to New College was of his own commissioning, or earlier.

William Wykeham died at South Waltham in Hampshire on 27 September 1404, and was buried in his chantry in Winchester Cathedral on the south side of the nave. The painted alabaster effigy in his chantry is less likely to represent him than the contemporary bust, the dripstone on the east window of Winchester College chapel.

There was at one time a tendency among historians to divide Wykeham's career into two phases, to argue that his great period of political and administrative activity occurred under his first patron, Edward III, and that afterwards he was mostly occupied with his foundations. More recently his enduring political skills, as much in evidence under Richard II and Henry IV as under Edward, have been recognized. His skill in business and land transactions also commands some respect, even if it sometimes seems to have sat oddly with his clerical status. Although the idea that he was his own architect has been abandoned, his fine taste as a patron of the arts has been reasserted.

PETER PARTNER

Sources R. Lowth, *Life of William of Wykeham*, 2nd edn (1759) · G. H. Moberley, *Life of William of Wykeham* (1887) · T. F. Kirby, *Annals of Winchester College, from its foundation in the year 1382 to the present time* (1892), 452–523 · P. Partner, 'William of Wykeham and the historians', *Winchester College: sixth-centenary essays*, ed. R. Custance (1982), 1–36 · J. Harvey, 'The buildings of Winchester College', *Winchester College: sixth-centenary essays*, ed. R. Custance (1982), 77–127 · J. R. L. Highfield, 'The promotion of William of Wickham to the see of Winchester', *Journal of Ecclesiastical History*, 4 (1953), 37–54 · H. M. Carson, ed., *The history of the king's works*, 6 vols. (1963–73), vol. 1, pp. 166–74; vol. 2, pp. 793–4, 794n., 841, 872–80 · J. Alexander and P. Binski, eds., *Age of chivalry: art in Plantagenet England, 1200–1400* (1987), 468–75 [exhibition catalogue, RA] · J. Buxton and P. Williams, eds., *New College, Oxford, 1379–1979* (1979) · C. Given-Wilson, *The royal household and the king's affinity: service, politics and finance in England, 1360–1413* (1986), 36, 155–6, 200 · W. M. Ormrod, *The reign of Edward III* (1990), 93–4, 136 · L. C. Hector and B. F. Harvey, eds. and trans., *The Westminster chronicle, 1381–1394*, OMT (1982), 210, 324–41 · D. M. Broom, ed., 'The ransom of John II, king of France, 1360–70', in D. Broome, *Camden miscellany, XIV*, CS, 3rd ser., 37 (1926) · *Chancery records* · T. F. Kirby, ed., *Wykeham's register*, 2 vols., Hampshire RS, 11 (1896–9) · *Chroniques de J. Froissart*, ed. S. Luce and others, 7 (Paris, 1878), 101 · *VCH Berkshire*, 3.24, 101–2, 108 [John and Thomas Foxley] · W. H. Bliss, ed., *Calendar of entries in the papal registers relating to Great Britain and Ireland: petitions to the pope* (1896), 395, 470 [for Robert Stratton] · Rymer, *Foedera*, 3.662, 664 [treaty with Brittany, 1362]; 4.12

Archives Bucks. RLSS, household account roll, founders' kin, pedigrees · Hants. RO, pipe roll of the bishopric of Winchester · New College, Oxford, muniments of New College, Oxford · Winchester College, MSS 38, 47 · Winchester College, muniments of Winchester College

Likenesses J. Faber senior, mezzotint (after unknown artist), BM, NPG · alabaster tomb effigy, Winchester Cathedral · bust (William Wykeham?), Winchester College; repro. in A. F. Leach, *Winchester College* (1899), facing p. 50 · bust, Winchester College chapel; repro. in Harvey, 'The buildings of Winchester College', facing p. 168 · manuscript drawing, New College, Oxford, MS 288, fol. 3v [*see illus.*]

Wealth at death £6000–£7000 in cash; also bequests of artefacts and objects of unknown value: Lowth, *Life of William of Wykeham*, xxxii–li, 268

Wykeham, William. *See* Wickham, William (1539–1595).

Wykes, Thomas (1222–1291×3), chronicler and Augustinian canon, was born on 11 March 1222, into a family that probably came from Essex and Suffolk. Judging from information in his chronicle concerning Oxford, he may have studied there between 1238 and 1246. Three people mentioned in his chronicle may have been relatives: Robert Wykes (*d.* 1246), Edith Wyka (*d.* 1269), and John Wykes, who took vows in 1283. Denholm-Young suggests that the first of these, Robert Wykes, was his father and that a brother was the Sir Richard Wykes who held a manor at Bardwell, near Bury St Edmunds. He had another brother named Robert. In 1268–9 he bought a house, Elm Hall, and eight cottages in Oxford, and gave six cottages to Osney, the Augustinian abbey just outside Oxford, in the following year. In August 1270 the abbey granted him a pension of 1 mark and his brother Robert a pension of £1. In November 1270 he gave Elm Hall to Osney to provide a daily mass for the souls of his benefactor Philip of Eye, treasurer of England, and Philip's forebears and heirs. Wykes was permitted to live there for life, but the house would revert to Osney if he became a monk. Although he was rector of Caister St Edmunds in Norfolk by 1270, he lived in London much of the time between 1270 and 1278. When he granted his residence in London to Osney in November 1279, he had probably moved to Elm Hall. He became a canon of Osney in 1282 at the age of about sixty.

Wykes's chronicle, surviving in one manuscript, BL, Cotton MS Titus A.xiv, is related to that of Osney. The chronicles are similar from 1066 to 1256, independent of one another from 1256 to 1278, and again related from 1278 to 1289. Wykes may have had a source similar to that used by the author of the Osney chronicle up to 1256. His account of the years 1256–78 is unrelated to any chronicle, and reflects the author's own interpretation of current events; Wykes probably discontinued the use of his source at that point because, as the Osney chronicle for this period shows, it supported the barons rather than the king. His chronicle up to 1278 was probably written c.1275–82 in London and Oxford, before he became a canon. He continued it, between c.1285 and 1291, after entering Osney Abbey, and he must then have begun writing the Osney chronicle as well as his own. This would account for the similarities between the two works from 1278 to 1289, when Wykes's chronicle ends. He continued the Osney chronicle at least until near the end of 1290, when its political sentiments appear to change; it is possible, however, that he continued it until 1293.

Before becoming a canon Wykes apparently was a secular clerk who served the government through his association, possibly as chaplain, with Richard, earl of Cornwall (d. 1272), Henry III's brother. Wykes expresses more admiration for Richard than for Henry, of whom he was often critical. In fact, he attributes the successful outcome of the barons' war, not to the king, but to Prince Edward. A thirteenth-century Latin poem praising Edward I, based upon the chronicle, has been attributed to Wykes (Wright, 128–32). One of the most intelligent and reliable chroniclers of the thirteenth century, Wykes provides detailed accounts of events in London between 1256 and 1278, and his concern for financial and commercial matters affecting the government are of particular interest. Although he had contempt for citizens who sided with the barons, and had little use for rabble and troublemakers, he liked the city and its well-to-do citizens, including the Jews, who, he believed, had been treated cruelly and unjustly by greedy Londoners. He condemned the destruction of the London Jewry in 1263, and, later in the chronicle, the expulsion of the Jews in 1290, partly out of sympathy and partly because revenues collected from them were an important source of income for the government.

Wykes may have died about the summer of 1291. The evidence for this is a quit-claim, dated between Michaelmas 1290 and Michaelmas 1291, from a former owner of property that Wykes had given to Osney. The abbey's desire to re-establish its right to the property could be explained by Wykes's death. But it is also possible that he lived until 1293. Wykes's chronicle was first published in 1687 by Thomas Gale (d. 1702), as part of his *Historiae*

Anglicanae scriptores quinque. This edition was superseded in 1869 by that of H. R. Luard, published by the Rolls Series as part of the *Annales monastici*.

EDWARD DONALD KENNEDY

Sources N. Denholm-Young, 'Thomas de Wykes and his chronicle', *EngHR*, 61 (1946), 157–79 · Emden, *Oxf.*, 3.2112 · A. Gransden, *Historical writing in England*, 1 (1974), 463–70 · DNB · Ann. mon., 4.xlviii · T. Wright, ed. and trans., *The political songs of England from the reign of John to that of Edward II*, CS, 6 (1839), 128–32 · E. F. Jacob, *Studies in the period of baronial reform and rebellion, 1258–1267* (1925), 122, 134, 147, n. 2, 170, 172–3, 282–3 · H. E. Salter, ed., *Cartulary of Oseney Abbey*, 1–3, OHS, 89–90, 91 (1929–31)
Archives BL, Cotton MS Titus A.xiv | Osney chartulary

Wyld, Henry Cecil Kennedy (1870–1945), philologist and lexicographer, was born in London on 27 March 1870, the only son of Henry Wyld, a commander in the service of the East India Company, and his wife, Louise, daughter of Benjamin Kennedy, a Scottish gentleman living in the county of Fife. His paternal grandfather, James Wyld, was a Fife landowner.

After a year at Charterhouse School, Wyld was educated privately at Lausanne (1885–8) and then at the universities of Bonn and Heidelberg, and at Corpus Christi College, Oxford. In 1890 he married Grace Muriel (d. 1954), daughter of John Proctor, an Irish landowner of Ballina, co. Mayo. They had two sons and two daughters.

Wyld studied philology, phonetics, and linguistics at Oxford with Henry Sweet and took his BLitt degree in 1899. On Sweet's recommendation he was in the same year appointed independent lecturer in the English language at University College, Liverpool. In 1904 the newly chartered University of Liverpool elected him its first Baines professor of English language and philology. From 1902 to 1910 he also acted as special inspector in the teaching of phonetics in the training colleges of Scotland, for which he wrote *The Growth of English* (1907). He remained at Liverpool until 1920, active in university administration, and by his teaching, lecturing, and writing became one of the foremost philologists of his generation. Most of his books and articles were written during this period, including his excellent *Historical Study of the Mother Tongue, an Introduction to Philological Method* (1906) and *A Short History of English* (1914) which, reissued in a third edition in 1927, enlarged considerably and revised mainly in the light of the researches of himself and his pupils, long retained its value. In *A History of Modern Colloquial English* (1920; 3rd edn, with six short appendixes, 1936) he developed with obvious personal satisfaction, as well as with remarkable success, the technique, first evolved by his friend Robert Eugen Zachrisson of the University of Uppsala, Sweden, for investigating the chronological problems of the New English period. The book concentrated on phonology, leaving syntax and vocabulary, as he said, to other, later authors (preface, v).

In 1920 Wyld was elected Merton professor of English language and literature in the University of Oxford, and he held his professorial fellowship at Merton College for the rest of his life. Here he completed his short *Studies in English Rhymes* (1923), another pioneering book designed mainly for students of literature. In 1932 appeared his excellent one-volume *Universal Dictionary of the English Language*, a dictionary of contemporary usage, both literary and colloquial, which, though it imposed a 'long and laborious' task and sometimes tried his patience, stirred many of his contemporaries to think of him as a *Johnsonius redivivus*. Its size and comprehensiveness, its methodical arrangement, its unusually full treatment of etymologies, its clear and precise definitions, together with its brief and racy illustrative sentences mostly of his own coining, gave it a lasting value.

Wyld greatly enjoyed his lecturing at Oxford, and his pupils invariably found his exposition clear and intensely invigorating. Despite bad eyesight he continued his philological researches and added to the number of his learned articles. According to the *Oxford Companion to the English Language* his *Universal Dictionary* 'set a pattern followed by A. S. Hornby in the Advanced Learner's Dictionary of Current English' (Christophersen, 1135) in its use of phonetic transcriptions, detailed etymologies and illustrations of modern idiomatic use.

In 1932 Wyld was awarded the British Academy's Sir Israel Gollancz biennial prize for his contributions to the study of English philology, and the University of Uppsala conferred upon him the honorary degree of PhD. He was also an honorary member of the Modern Language Association and of the Linguistic Society of America.

Wyld was a tallish, well-built, broad-shouldered man, and in his youth was fond of outdoor pursuits, especially riding and hunting. In later years he was an enthusiastic gardener. His pleasant reverberating voice enhanced his excellent pronunciation of English. His ear was acute: one obituarist reported that 'he had an uncanny way of overhearing what others were saying at a distance, and he detected differences in pronunciation which could not be noted by every listener even after he had pointed them out' (D. N. S.). His easy flow of resounding words, his ready wit, his extensive knowledge of people, affairs, languages, and literatures, and, not least, his forceful personality made him a lively conversationalist and friend. His Johnsonian literary style reflected the man. He died at his home, Alvescot House, Alvescot, Oxfordshire, on 26 January 1945. HAROLD ORTON, *rev.* JOHN D. HAIGH

Sources *The Times* (31 Jan 1945), 7 · WWW, 1941–50 · H. C. Wyld, preface, *A history of modern colloquial English*, 3rd edn (1936), v–viii · personal knowledge (1959) · private information (1959) · P. Christophersen, 'Wyld, Henry Cecil Kennedy', *The Oxford companion to the English language*, ed. T. McArthur · D. N. S., 'Henry Cecil Kennedy Wyld', *Oxford Magazine* (15 Feb 1945), 149
Archives U. Birm. L., letters to C. T. Onions
Likenesses A. Lipczinski, group portrait, oils, 1915, U. Lpool · J. Mackie, portrait, priv. coll.
Wealth at death £7036 7s. 9d.: probate, 4 June 1945, *CGPLA Eng. & Wales*

Wyld, James, the elder (1790–1836), cartographer and geographical publisher, was the son of Joseph Woolley Wyld, cheesemonger, and his wife, Jane; his parents were both Scots, though they lived in London. James was apprenticed to the map publisher William Faden from 1804 to 1811, before entering the quartermaster-general's office,

where he remained for fourteen years. His maps of campaigns and marches of the Peninsula War were some of the earliest to be lithographed in England. In 1823 he acquired Faden's map business and reissued many of Faden's maps, often but not invariably updated and amended, over his own firm's imprint. Wyld was also accorded the title of geographer to his majesty and his royal highness the duke of York, a title previously held by Faden. This justly reflected the quality and quantity of his maps, which were second only to those of the Arrowsmiths. His 'New map of the world, exhibiting at one view the extent, religion, population, and degrees of civilisation of each country' (1815) is one of the most innovative, both in having religion as its subject matter and in using proportional letter sizes to convey an impression of the size of the phenomenon portrayed. Wyld recognized that travel and exploration gave great opportunity for the map publisher and his maps of Australia, New Zealand, and Africa established his firm's reputation for excellence. He also arranged publication of Mungo Park's *Travels in the Interior Districts of Africa* (2 vols., 1817) and compiled maps for that and for the writings of the Egyptologist Giovanni Baptista Belzoni. In 1830 Wyld was a founder fellow of the Royal Geographical Society. In or before 1812 he married Elizabeth Legg and they had at least one child, James *Wyld the younger. Wyld died on 14 October 1836.

ELIZABETH BAIGENT

Sources D. Smith, 'The Wyld family firm', *Map Collector*, 54 (1991), 32–8 · A. Robinson, *Early thematic mapping* (1982) · GM, 2nd ser., 6 (1836), 656 · IGI

Wyld, James, the younger (1812–1887), cartographer and geographical publisher, was born on 20 November 1812 in Surrey, the son of James *Wyld the elder and his wife, Elizabeth Legg. He was educated at the Royal Military Academy at Woolwich but joined his father's firm which from about 1830 traded as J. Wyld & Son. The premises were frequented by politicians and others in public life, who came for maps of areas of topical interest. These included a map of Afghanistan with notes and the routes of troops at the time of the First Anglo-Afghan War, a 'Map of the gold regions of California' (1849), 'Notes on the distribution of gold throughout the world, with a gazetteer of the gold diggings of Australia' (3rd edn, 1853), and maps of the Ottoman empire and Black Sea at the time of the Crimean War. His *Popular Atlas* contained lithographs of the maps he issued in cheap monthly numbers. Wyld profited from the railway mania of 1836–7 when he supplied the prospectus maps and plans that railway companies had to deposit to get parliamentary approval for their schemes; but when the mania collapsed he was left with heavy claims against unsuccessful companies, which he pursued in vain in the courts. The experience did not deter Wyld from further railway map publishing and he also published guide and travel books, illustrated with maps, and an extensive range of cycling maps. The timing of his map publications and their format show that he, like other cartographic publishers, was something of an opportunist and had a keen eye for publishing innovations, although, unlike many contemporaries, his maps

James Wyld the younger (1812–1887), by unknown engraver, pubd 1857 (after John Jabez Edwin Mayall)

were always of high quality, a fact acknowledged when he was accorded the title of geographer to Queen Victoria and Prince Albert.

Wyld's most spectacular enterprise was his 'great globe', exhibited in Leicester Square between 1851 and 1861 to coincide with the Great Exhibition. It was 60 feet high and 40 feet in diameter and lit by gas. On its inside painted plaster of Paris reliefs illustrated the physical features of the earth at a horizontal scale of one inch to ten miles and a vertical scale of three inches to ten miles. The object of some ridicule, it was none the less extremely popular. It was surrounded by a large spherical building entered from four loggias opening into each side of the square. In the building maps, atlases, and other globes (inevitably mostly Wyld's own) were displayed.

Wyld was Liberal MP for Bodmin for most of the period 1847–68 and used his position to castigate the surveyors of the Ordnance Survey and other official bodies for inefficiency and profligacy, an attitude shaped in large part by the threat they posed to his livelihood. He helped to found the Association of Surveyors in 1843 and the Surveyors' Institution in 1848 to unite non-government surveyors against official surveyors, but both societies failed. Despite his opposition, his firm was one of only six agencies appointed to sell Ordnance Survey maps after 1866. After retiring from parliament he represented Cornhill ward on the City's court of common council from 1871 to 1886. As a founder governor of the City and Guilds London Institute and as master in 1875–6 of the Clothworkers' Company, he helped to promote technical education, notably in Manchester, Leeds, and Bristol. His scientific reputation led to his being elected fellow of the Royal Geographical Society in 1839, and awarded membership of the Légion d'honneur and a gold medal for science from the king of Prussia.

Wyld married Ann, only daughter of John Hester, on 27 February 1838. On his death on 17 April 1887 at 29 Trebovir Road, South Kensington, he left a daughter and a son, **James John Cooper Wyld** (1845–1907), barrister and map publisher. The son was a special pleader on the western circuit and a deputy judge in the county courts. He was elected fellow of the Royal Geographical Society in 1888, but was not very much interested in geography and was reputedly arrogant and dismissive about all aspects of the map trade, which he little understood. Under him the family firm declined fatally, suffering particularly from competition from the energetic and talented Edward Stanford, from whom Wyld now had to get his Ordnance Survey maps and whose own maps were superior to Wyld's. Wyld blamed his difficulty in retaining good engravers on the Ordnance board, continuing his father's animosity towards government cartography. The stock and goodwill of the Wyld business were acquired by George Washington Bacon in October 1893. Wyld died on 30 January 1907 at his home in Ashley Road, Thames Ditton, Surrey. He was probably unmarried and childless.

ELIZABETH BAIGENT

Sources D. Smith, 'The Wyld family firm', *Map Collector*, 54 (1991), 32–8 · D. Smith, *Victorian maps of the British Isles* (1985) · *WWBMP*, vol. 1 · *CGPLA Eng. & Wales* (1907) [James John Cooper Wyld] · IGI · DNB · J. W. Sherborne, *University College, Bristol, 1876–1909* (1977) **Likenesses** etching, GL · wood-engraving (after photograph by J. J. E. Mayall), NPG; repro. in *ILN* (May 1857) [see illus.] **Wealth at death** £5846 11s. 6d.—James John Cooper Wyld: administration, 9 July 1907, *CGPLA Eng. & Wales*

Wyld, James John Cooper (1845–1907). *See under* Wyld, James, the younger (1812–1887).

Wylde, Henry (1822–1890), conductor and composer, was born in Bushey, Hertfordshire, on 22 May 1822, the son of Henry Wylde (*b.* 1795), an organist and gentleman-in-waiting to George IV. At the age of thirteen he became organist of Whitchurch, near Edgware, and then three years later received piano lessons from Ignaz Moscheles. From October 1843 to December 1846 he was a student of Cipriani Potter at the Royal Academy of Music, where he was later to become a professor of harmony. He held posts as organist of Eaton Chapel, St Anne and St Agnes, Aldersgate (1844–7), and taught the piano; J. F. Barnett was among his pupils. In 1851 he was awarded the degrees of MusB and MusD by the University of Cambridge, and that same year was a juror in the musical instrument section of the Great Exhibition, a role he repeated in 1862. In 1852 he was one of the founders of the New Philharmonic Society. With the task of introducing new or rare works, he conducted for three seasons, though Berlioz, Peter Josef von Lindpaintner, and Spohr also conducted at various times. Wylde presented some of his own works at these concerts, including the piano concerto in F minor (with Alexandre Billet) and part of his cantata *Prayer and Praise* (1852). His dealings with Berlioz, who appeared with him in the first six concerts, suggest that they had a stormy working relationship. In 1858 Wylde became the principal conductor of the society, a post he held until 1879, when Wilhelm Ganz took over. During this period he introduced to an English audience Liszt's *Die heilige Elisabeth* (1870) and Wagner's *Lohengrin* in concert (1873), as well as the concept of programme notes.

Wylde founded in 1861 the London Academy of Music and became its principal. It was first located at St James's Hall, but in 1867 it moved to a building in Langham Place erected by Wylde, and named by him St George's Hall. In 1863, on the death of Edward Taylor, Wylde was appointed professor of music at Gresham College, a position he retained until his death.

Among Wylde's works were a few piano pieces, including a couple of sonatas, songs, and the cantata *Paradise Lost* (1850), first performed in 1853. His writings include *Harmony and the Science of Music* (1865 and 1872), *Music in its Art Mysteries* (1867), *Occult Principles of Music* (1881), and *Evolution of the Beautiful in Music* (1888). He was also for many years music critic of *The Echo*. He died from bronchitis at 76 Mortimer Street, Regent Street, London, on 13 March 1890 and was buried in Kensal Green cemetery. His brother James Wylde was a harpist in London.

F. G. EDWARDS, *rev.* DAVID J. GOLBY

Sources MT, 31 (1890), 219 · J. Warrock, 'Wylde, Henry', *New Grove*
Likenesses P. N., wood-engraving, NPG; repro. in *ILN* (22 March 1890)
Wealth at death £2861 6s. 10d.: administration, 11 April 1890, *CGPLA Eng. & Wales*

Wylie, Alexander (1815–1887), missionary and Chinese scholar, was born in London on 6 April 1815, the youngest son of Alexander Wylie, an oil and colour merchant of 150 Drury Lane; his father had moved to London from Scotland about 1791. When a year old Wylie was placed in the care of a relative who lived in the Grampians. He was educated in the grammar school at Drumlithie, Kincardineshire, and after his return to London at a school in Chelsea before being apprenticed to a cabinet-maker.

Having picked up at a bookstall a copy of Joseph Premaire's *Notitia linguae Sinicae* Wylie learned sufficient Latin to read it, and this led him to study the Chinese language. He procured from the British and Foreign Bible Society a copy of the New Testament in Chinese, and as he proceeded to read it he compiled a dictionary of the characters. In December 1845 W. H. Medhurst requested that a printer and new press be sent out to the newly established printing operations of the London Missionary Society (LMS) in Shanghai. Wylie visited James Legge, who found with surprise that he had so far mastered Chinese without assistance as to be able to read the gospels with tolerable accuracy. The LMS engaged him and sent him to the offices of Charles Reed for six months to study printing, while Legge instructed him in Chinese. On 26 August 1847 Wylie arrived in Shanghai as superintendent of the mission press, his salary being paid by the Bible Society. On 22 September 1848 he married Mary Hanson, a former missionary he had met in Britain.

Wylie's work in China began unhappily. Relations with such older and autocratic colleagues as Medhurst proved difficult. In 1849 these issues came to a head, and on 7 September Wylie asked to be transferred. Since arriving in Shanghai he had not been given control of the press and he felt he was not treated as a social or professional equal by his colleagues. Medhurst and the others countered on 12 October that Wylie was incompetent and shied away from practical printing work, and that since his marriage even his interest in evangelical activities had declined. This crisis peaked during the time that Mary was dangerously ill; she gave birth to a daughter on 1 October and then died six days later. By March 1850 relations had been restored and for the next ten years Wylie seems to have worked conscientiously, and with six hours' sleep a night, at his printing. He never remarried, and at the beginning of 1853 he sent his daughter, Mary, back to Britain.

In the 1850s Wylie developed his academic interests and skills. He learned French, German, Russian, Manchu, and Mongolian, besides acquiring some knowledge of Greek, Uighur, and Sanskrit. He read deeply in the history, geography, religion, philosophy, arts, and sciences of eastern Asia, and became widely acquainted with Chinese literature. In 1852 he met the brilliant Chinese mathematician Li Shanlan (1810–1882), with whom he translated and published a series of landmark editions, including books vii–ix of Euclid, in continuation of Matteo Ricci's 1607 translation of the first six books (still, in 1987, the only translation in Chinese), and the first translation in Chinese of modern Western algebra (1859). In these works, as in his later ones, Wylie communicated the thought in the original orally, and this was then transcribed into the correct literary style by Li. Wylie's criticism of the rugged style of previous missionary translations was marked, based on his belief that educated Chinese were unlikely to take the literary efforts of self-taught missionaries at all seriously. His contribution to Chinese knowledge of Copernican theory was also noteworthy, most pointedly his translation, again with Li's help, of Herschel's *Outlines of Astronomy* (*Tan tian*, 1859). He also edited, from January 1857 to 1858, a monthly periodical in Chinese, the *Liuhe congtan*, which sought to introduce Western thought and science in translation and in short notes, mostly written by missionaries. Similarly Wylie was passionately concerned with Western knowledge of China. He was a founder member of the north China branch of the Royal Asiatic Society, and his writings on the history and achievements of Chinese mathematics, notably his 'Jottings on the science of the Chinese: arithmetic' (*North China Herald*, 1852), marked the beginning of serious Western scholarship in the field; these still make profitable reading.

Wylie remained unhappy with the LMS, however, and with the restraints of his printing job. In 1858 he asked to be transferred to a post superintending the distribution of scriptures for the Bible Society. The LMS wanted to retain him, but was unsuccessful: on 3 November 1860 Wylie left Shanghai for Britain, having sold his considerable library, the fruit of his bibliographical passion, to the Royal Asiatic Society in Shanghai. On his return to the city from leave in 1863 he became a permanent agent of the Bible Society, and thereby much more autonomous in his activities and travels. On that trip, and most unusually for the times, he journeyed through St Petersburg and Siberia to Peking (Beijing). He stayed in Shanghai until 1877.

In this period Wylie's academic researches and activities intensified. From 1868 to 1875 he was a member of the innovative translation board of the important Kiangnan (Jiangnan) arsenal in Shanghai, which was organized by John Fryer and produced Chinese texts of Western technical works. In 1874 he was, with Fryer, a founding member of the Shanghai Polytechnic Institute, whose object was to 'bring the Sciences, Arts, and Manufactures of Western Nations in the most prominent manner possible before the notice of China' (*North China Herald*, 22 Oct 1874, 399). As Henri Cordier pointed out in his memorial notice, Wylie 'never neglected his work as a missionary' ('Life and labours of Alexander Wylie'). Aside from his work for the Bible Society (to which end he made a pioneering trip into the Chinese interior with Griffith John in 1868), where he established and supervised a nationwide distribution system for the scriptures, he was editor of the *Chinese Recorder*, the most important of the missionary journals, from 1874 to 1877. The Bible Society in Shanghai greatly depended on his presence and energy, and when he visited Britain in 1869–70 its operations perceptibly lagged. In 1867 he published *Memorials of Protestant Missionaries*, an encyclopaedic bibliographical and biographical history of the protestant enterprise in China. That same year saw the publication of his *Notes on Chinese Literature*, which sealed his reputation as one of the foremost of contemporary Sinologists.

In 1877, owing to the failure of his eyesight from incessant proof-reading, he returned to London and settled with his unmarried daughter, who acted as his secretary, at 18 Christchurch Road, Hampstead, London. His health declined rapidly. In February 1883 he was taken seriously ill; his mental faculties were largely destroyed, he became totally blind, and he was bed-ridden. He died at his Hampstead home on 6 February 1887, and was buried nearby on 10 February in his father's grave in Highgate cemetery.

For Wylie there was never any contradiction between his secular and religious activities. He considered that introducing the Chinese to Western scientific facts was 'a healthful influence on the intellectual character' and led to a 'juster and more exalted' conception of God. He was also, as Cordier again pointed out, guided by the spirit of the Jesuit missionaries in Peking in the eighteenth century, who worked to establish themselves in the face of the insular arrogance of the Chinese élites by proving that Western science and philosophy were of such value that they could not be neglected.

E. I. CARLYLE, *rev.* ROBERT BICKERS

Sources letters, SOAS, Archives of the Council for World Mission, London Missionary Society MSS, Central China files · H. Cordier, 'Life and labours of Alexander Wylie', in A. Wylie, *Chinese researches*, ed. J. Thomas (1897), 7–18 · J. Edkins, 'Biographical sketch of Alexander Wylie', in A. Wylie, *Chinese researches*, ed. J. Thomas (1897), 1–6 · W. Canton, *A history of the British and Foreign Bible Society*, 2 (1904) · K. Biggerstaff, 'The Shanghai Polytechnic and reading room: an attempt to introduce Western science and technology into China', *Pacific Historical Review*, 25/2 (1956), 127–49 · A. A. Bennett, *John Fryer* (1967) · J. Needham, *Science and Civilization in China*, 3 (1959) · U. Libbrecht, *Chinese mathematics in the thirteenth century* (1993) · Li Yan and Du Shiran, *Chinese mathematics: a concise history* (1987) · *DNB*

Archives SOAS, Council for World Mission Archives, London Missionary Society MSS

Likenesses photograph, repro. in A. Wylie, *Chinese researches*, ed. J. Thownsend (1897), frontispiece

Wealth at death 2891 6s. 1d.: probate, 1 March 1887, *CGPLA Eng. & Wales*

Wylie, Charles Hotham Montagu Doughty- (1868–1915), army officer and consul, was born on 23 July 1868 at Theberton Hall, near Leiston, Suffolk, the son of Henry Montagu Doughty (1841–1916), lord of the manor of Theberton, a former naval officer who had been called to the bar in 1863, and his wife, Edith Rebecca Cameron, daughter of the chief justice of Vancouver. Charles Montagu *Doughty (1843–1926), the celebrated Arabian explorer, was his uncle. Edith Doughty died on 4 September 1870 after giving birth to another son, Henry Montagu Doughty. Charles Doughty was educated at Winchester College and the Royal Military College, Sandhurst, before being commissioned second lieutenant in the Royal Welsh Fusiliers on 21 September 1889.

The late-Victorian army offered numerous opportunities of combat experience not only in small colonial 'brush fire' wars but also in wider conflicts. Doughty took his fill. The first fifteen years of his military service involved him in one military campaign after another: the Hazara expedition (1891); Chitral (1895); Crete (1896); the Sudan (1898–9); southern Africa (1900); Tientsin (Tianjin) (1900); and Somaliland (1903–4). His military service was not only intense but also varied, involving service on the north-west frontier of India, east and southern Africa, the Mediterranean, and the Far East. At Chitral he held the key post of transport officer on the staff of Sir William Gatacre. His posting to the British garrison on Crete during the tumultuous period of civil unrest that resulted in the removal of the Turkish presence on the island (November 1898) brought him into contact for the first time with the Ottoman empire, an involvement destined to become a central part of his life and career. In the Sudan he was a brigade major. In southern Africa and China he commanded mounted infantry, in Somaliland a detachment of the Somali camel corps. He was wounded twice, in the Hazara expedition and in southern Africa.

In May 1904, while on leave in Bombay, Doughty finally found the time to marry. His bride was Lilian Oimara Adams (d. 1960), widow of Lieutenant Henry Adams (d. 1900) of the Indian Medical Service, and daughter of John Wylie, of West Cliffe Hall, Hampshire. They had no children. In December 1904 Charles Doughty added his wife's maiden name to his own by deed poll, becoming Doughty-Wylie. He was described as 'Tall and slightly though vigorously built', with a 'fair complexion and keen blue eyes' (*DNB*). 'He was an ardent sportsman, good rider and good shot … but he always retained the literary interests of a Winchester scholar. Simple, tenacious, chivalrous, and humorous, he quickly won sympathy and obedience, and was a born leader of fighting men' (ibid.).

After almost twenty years of soldiering Doughty-Wylie's career changed tack. The late-Victorian and Edwardian army also offered opportunity of political employment and in September 1906 he became British military vice-consul in the Turkish province of Konia. This appointment, in an apparent backwater, provided little respite from Doughty-Wylie's life of action. On the contrary it brought him international acclaim. The Ottoman empire was in the throes of change, during which the Armenian minority often became the victims of violence. At Adana in 1909 Doughty-Wylie displayed outstanding courage and leadership by taking command of a group of Turkish regular troops and preventing a massacre, being wounded for the third time. He was portrayed as a defender of Christianity against Islam. His actions touched a raw nerve among the Western imperialist nations, aware of the potential vulnerability of their small governing élites, surrounded by millions of 'non-believers'. Doughty-Wylie's time in Turkey also complicated his personal life. Here, in 1907, he met the archaeologist Gertrude Bell (1868–1926), with whom he began an intimate correspondence. In August 1913, following a visit to the Bell family home, Rounton Grange in the North Riding of Yorkshire, the two became lovers. Their relationship remained a secret outside the Bell family and Doughty-Wylie's letters to Gertrude did not become publicly available until after his wife's death in 1960.

Doughty-Wylie's achievements at Adana were rewarded by promotion to consul-general at Addis Ababa in Abyssinia. He served there for three years, until 1912, when he became chief director of the Red Cross on the Turkish side in the First Balkan War, a role in which he won the considerable respect and affection of the Turks. His wife, who was to develop her own distinguished career in military nursing, accompanied him to Constantinople as superintendent of nursing staff. The trust that Doughty-Wylie had established with the Turkish authorities made him an excellent choice as chairman of the commission that arbitrated the Greek–Albanian frontier in the wake of the Second Balkan War. He returned to Addis Ababa in 1913.

The outbreak of war between Great Britain and Turkey in October 1914 changed everything for Doughty-Wylie. A man of his spirit and ambition had to be involved. His experience and knowledge of the Ottoman empire were also at a premium. This was recognized by General Sir John Maxwell, commander-in-chief, Egypt, who intercepted Doughty-Wylie in Cairo *en route* for London in search of military employment. In February 1915 he was promoted lieutenant-colonel and joined the staff of General Sir Ian Hamilton, commander designate of the Mediterranean expeditionary force, shortly to be charged with launching an ambitious and risky amphibious assault on the Gallipoli peninsula. On 25 April 1915, the day of the attack, Doughty-Wylie was on the converted collier SS *River Clyde*, off V Beach where it had landed

troops under a murderous Turkish fire and with terrible loss. Aware of the desperate situation on the beach, Doughty-Wylie volunteered to go ashore after nightfall and assess the situation. The following morning he returned to the beach, together with his fellow staff officer Captain G. N. Walford, and took command. Recognizing the urgency of getting the men off the beach, he collected the remnants of three battalions, 2nd Hampshires, 1st Royal Dublin Fusiliers, and 1st Royal Munster Fusiliers, and led them in a successful attack on the old fort which commanded the approaches to the village of Sedd-el-Bahr. Doughty-Wylie personally led the charge that captured the village following the death of Walford. He then considered how best to capture hill 141, the feature that commanded the beach. He returned to the shore to arrange a naval bombardment of the position by the 15-inch guns of the *Queen Elizabeth*. The infantry assault went in immediately after the bombardment ceased, about two o'clock in the afternoon, led by Doughty-Wylie, who was armed only with a cane, not wishing to bear arms against his former friends. Hill 141 was a tough obstacle, protected by barbed wire entanglements, its summit crowned by a redoubt, surrounded by a deep moat, but the charge carried the day. On 26 April Doughty-Wylie's leadership, energy, determination, tactical awareness, and complete disregard for his own safety had succeeded in transforming the dispirited remnants of the landing force and in securing the beach. At the moment of victory, Doughty-Wylie was struck just below the eye by a bullet that blew away the side of his face. He died instantly and was buried where he lay. His grave remains the only individual one on the peninsula, flanked by trees at the summit of the hill renamed Fort Doughty-Wylie in his honour. Doughty-Wylie was posthumously awarded the Victoria Cross. He was the highest ranking officer to win the award during the Gallipoli campaign. J. M. BOURNE

Sources S. Snelling, *VCs of the First World War: Gallipoli* (1995) • *DNB* • C. F. Aspinall-Oglander, *Military operations: Gallipoli*, History of the Great War, 1 (1929) • N. Steel and P. Hart, *Defeat at Gallipoli* (1994) • H. V. Winstone, *Gertrude Bell* (1993) • W. Flynn, interview, IWM SA, interview 4103 • IWM, L. O. Doughty-Wylie papers • Royal Welch Fusiliers Regimental Museum, Caernarfon Castle, Caernarfon, Doughty-Wylie papers • *The Times* (4 May 1915) • *CGPLA Eng. & Wales* (1915)
Archives Royal Welch Fusiliers, Caernarfon, regimental museum, papers | IWM, L. O. Doughty-Wylie papers • U. Durham L., corresp. with Sir Reginald Wingate • U. Newcastle, Gertrude Bell papers | SOUND IWM SA, oral history interview
Likenesses photographs, U. Newcastle
Wealth at death £5315 14s. 0d.: probate, 17 Aug 1915, *CGPLA Eng. & Wales*

Wylie, Sir Francis James (1865–1952), university administrator, was born in Bromley, Kent, on 18 October 1865, the second son of Richard Northcote Wylie, businessman, and his wife, Charlotte Greenlaw. The Wylies had had a long connection with Russia. Wylie's father was a member of the bourse in St Petersburg, and his great-uncle, Sir James Wylie, had been physician at the court of the tsar. Wylie himself spent short periods in Russia during childhood,

Sir Francis James Wylie (1865–1952), by Lafayette, 1929

but had no special association with that country in later life.

Wylie was educated at St Edward's School, Oxford. At the suggestion of his uncle by marriage, Edward Caird (who was then professor of moral philosophy at Glasgow and was later to become master of Balliol), the promising young man went from school to pursue his classical studies at the University of Glasgow, from where he won a Snell exhibition to Balliol. He went up to Oxford in 1884 and soon showed himself a classical scholar of mark. He took a first class in honour moderations in 1886 and in *literae humaniores* in 1888. He was not, however, the 'mere bookworm' whom Cecil Rhodes deprecated; though of slight build he rowed in the Balliol eight and was elected to Vincent's Club and Leander. Throughout his long life he retained an alert and critical interest in rowing.

After taking his degree Wylie spent a few months teaching at his old school and then engaged in private tutoring until, after being made a lecturer of the college in 1891, he was elected a fellow of Brasenose in 1892. There he proved himself a successful and assiduous tutor and when he died there still survived a few of his former pupils who remembered with gratitude his lectures on Aristotle's logic. He was junior proctor in 1903–4, a year which was to prove a turning point in his lifework. He cultivated a brisk diversity of interests, not the least of them in military service. It was characteristic of his dominant sense of duty that he was a zealous member of the Oxford University Volunteers. As a company commander in that corps he took part in the official obsequies of Queen Victoria. When, in the

later chapter of his life, war broke out in 1914, he was too old for service in the field, but he threw himself with energy into the work of the Oxford University training corps and made a spirited contribution to its courses of instruction.

The will of Cecil Rhodes was made public in April 1902, and the trustees appointed by it were soon busy making plans for the inauguration of the scholarships. One of the trustees was Lord Rosebery, whom Wylie had come to know as private tutor to his two sons. George Parkin had been appointed organizing secretary to the Rhodes Trust, and in February 1903 Wylie was invited, through Rosebery, to supervise the Oxford side of the system and to assume a general tutelage of the scholars in residence. It was not an easy decision to make. He had an established position in a college to which he was much attached; he was well known in the academic sphere and was about to become a proctor; he was now invited to occupy an office with no academic standing, since the Rhodes trustees were a body outside the university organism, and to assist in launching a scheme which at that time was highly experimental. The project of the Rhodes scholarships was not universally welcomed in Oxford; the university and colleges were far more inbred in 1903 than they subsequently became, and there was considerable scepticism about an influx of colonials, Americans, and Germans, who, it was feared, might lower academic standards, especially in the classics, besides making undue demands on the limited room and resources of colleges. Wylie was under no illusions about the problems which would face him, and it was again a sense of duty which prompted him to accept the trustees' invitation. He had the opportunity, which he was amply to fulfil, of doing a notable service to imperial and Anglo-American relations, and he was never the man to shrink from responsibilities.

Wylie was soon to receive invaluable aid in his task. On 18 August 1904 he married Kathleen, daughter of Edmond Kelly, an American lawyer in Paris, where much of her girlhood was spent. Wylie had met his future wife when she was a member of Lady Margaret Hall, Oxford. For the next twenty-eight years this was to prove an ideal partnership for developing and influencing Cecil Rhodes's 'great idea' in both its administrative and its personal aspects. Four sons and two daughters were born of the marriage, the eldest son dying in childhood. The fourth son, Shaun, was elected a fellow (mathematics) of Trinity Hall, Cambridge, in 1939. One of the daughters, Vere, married an Australian Rhodes scholar, Lewis Charles Wilcher, who became in 1956 the first warden of Queen Elizabeth House, Oxford.

The story of the growing-pains and adventurous adolescence of the Rhodes scholarships has been told vividly by Wylie himself in his contribution (pp. 59–125)—which he wrote almost at the end of his life—to the volume *The First Fifty Years of the Rhodes Trust and the Rhodes Scholarships* published by the Rhodes trustees in 1955. To him, probably more than to any other individual, belongs the credit for having woven a fabric which was to become an integral part of the whole Oxford design. There were vicissitudes at first; but Wylie and his wife enjoyed the reward of seeing hundreds of young men from many far countries derive from Oxford what their benefactor had intended for them and acquit themselves with distinction in their later careers. There was none of them who did not acknowledge his debt to the Wylie influence and guidance.

Responsibilities constantly increased with the expansion of the Rhodes network by additional scholarships which the trustees established in British areas overseas, until the number of Rhodes scholars at Oxford at any one time grew to nearly two hundred, composed about equally of British and American nationals, with a small group of Germans. After twenty-eight years of arduous service, Wylie retired in 1931, but not before he had had the satisfaction of seeing the completion of a permanent memorial to the founder in Oxford, Rhodes House, of which he became the first warden. He was knighted in 1929, on the occasion of the reunion of Rhodes scholars at Oxford when Rhodes House was formally opened, and he was elected an honorary fellow of Brasenose in 1931.

Retirement, however, was by no means the end of Wylie's services to the Rhodes scholarships. For upwards of another twenty years he kept regular touch with his former charges. His world-wide correspondence with them was indefatigable and his personal memory and knowledge of them throughout the years were remarkable. Of the many Rhodes scholars who revisited Oxford from time to time few failed to make a pilgrimage to the Wylie home near Oxford, where perennial welcome awaited them, their kindred, and their friends. On Boars Hill, with a panorama of the Berkshire downlands spread before him, Wylie's tranquil life and temperament made light of the burden of years. He had always been a man of simple tastes, and he found continual refreshment in the Matthew Arnold country, which he knew intimately, in birds and flowers, in parish work, and in country walks which to the end of his life lost nothing of their zest and vigour. His faculties seemed to be quite unimpaired when, without warning, he died in his sleep at his home, Wootton Ridge, Boars Hill, on 29 October 1952.

With his wife Wylie made many journeys throughout the English-speaking world on embassies for the Rhodes trustees. Three colleges in the United States—Union College, Schenectady (1932), Swarthmore College (1933), and Bowdoin College (1933)—conferred honorary degrees upon him. In 1945 the Rhodes trustees permanently commemorated his name in Oxford by the foundation of a Wylie prize for an essay on some aspect of the relations between the American colonies or the United States and any part of the British empire or Commonwealth. Lady Wylie died in 1969.   C. K. ALLEN, *rev.*

Sources *The Times* (30 Oct 1952) · *The Times* (1 Nov 1952) · *The Times* (15 Nov 1952) · *The Times* (17 Nov 1952) · *The Times* (20 Nov 1952) · *Oxford Magazine* (29 Jan 1953) · *United Empire* (Nov 1952) · *New York Times* (3 Nov 1952) · *Bowdoin Alumnus* (Nov 1952) · Lord Elton, ed., *The first fifty years of the Rhodes Trust and the Rhodes scholarships, 1903–1953* (1955) · personal knowledge (1971) · private information (1971) · A. Kenny, ed., *The history of the Rhodes Trust, 1902–1999* (2000)
Archives Bodl. RH, corresp. relating to Rhodes Trust

Likenesses Lafayette, photograph, 1929, NPG [*see illus.*] · F. A. de Biden Footner, pencil drawing, 1935, Bodl. RH · E. I. Halliday, oils, 1952, Bodl. RH
Wealth at death £5695 1*s.* 3*d.*: probate, 12 Dec 1952, *CGPLA Eng. & Wales*

Wylie, Sir James, first baronet (1768–1854), physician, was born in Kincardine-on-Forth, Perthshire, on 13 November 1768, the second child of William Wylie (or Willie), a carrier, and Janet Meiklejohn. He studied medicine at Edinburgh for a number of years, but was awarded his MD by King's College, Aberdeen, in 1794. After leaving Edinburgh, probably through the influence of John Rogerson, physician to Empress Catherine of Russia, Wylie took up a position in St Petersburg as the medical attendant of a well-known Russian family. In December 1790 he was gazetted surgeon to the Yeletsky infantry regiment.

Wylie gained a good reputation and was promoted to staff surgeon in 1794. However, he resigned from this position in 1795 on his appointment as personal physician to Count Boris Stroganov. In 1798 he further increased his reputation by performing a life-saving lithotomy on the Danish ambassador, following which he was appointed court 'operator'. The next year he was the only surgeon with enough courage to incise a throat abscess which was threatening to choke Count A. P. Kutaysov, a favourite of Emperor Paul I. Wylie was then appointed the emperor's personal surgeon, which led to the comment that 'Dr Wylie had made his fortune by cutting Count Kutaysov's throat' (Cross, 157). Wylie was awarded a medical degree by the medical college in 1800 and was also elected an honorary member. He became president of the Medico-Surgical Academy in 1808, and director of the medical department of the war ministry in 1811.

When the mentally unstable Emperor Paul was assassinated in 1801 Wylie was the first doctor on the scene, and though the emperor had been strangled Wylie diplomatically certified the cause of death to be apoplexy. Along with two other Scottish doctors he was responsible for the embalming of the emperor's distorted features for his lying in state.

Wylie was, however, primarily a military surgeon and he saw an immense amount of active service. He was chief medical inspector of the Russian army from 1806 until his death. In 1852 he wrote to the Royal College of Physicians of Edinburgh that he had been present at twenty or more battles, had been wounded three times, had travelled 150,000 miles with the army on foot, on horseback, in a carriage, or on a sledge, and had attended or been responsible for treating 600,000 sick or wounded soldiers. At the bloody battle of Borodino in 1812 Wylie is said to have performed 200 operations, and as if these exertions were not sufficient he rode with the Cossacks on the night when, under the command of Platov, their giant leader, they drove deep into the French lines.

When the Russian commander Moreau's legs were shattered by a cannon ball at the battle of Leipzig in 1813, Wylie amputated them, though his patient died a few days later. A year before the death of Emperor Alexander I, one

Sir James Wylie, first baronet (1768–1854), by Johann Friedrich Bolt, 1816 (after Philipp Franck)

armies. To mark Wylie's fifty years in Russian service a special medal was struck in 1840.

Wylie, who lived in St Petersburg in apartments in the imperial palace, was a tall man of imposing presence, standing 6 feet 2 inches, who dined frugally like an ordinary soldier and was reckoned to be rather parsimonious. He died in St Petersburg on 2 December 1854 and was buried there. On his death he left a considerable fortune, the greater part of which was used to build a large hospital in St Petersburg, known as the Vilie Clinic. Five years after his death a large and imposing statue of him was erected in front of this building, and though it was moved to the rear of the hospital in 1950 the statue still stood fifty years later. On its base was inscribed 'to the Court Surgeon, Privy Councillor, Sir Vilie Bart. December the 9th 1859'. Below his coat of arms were carved replicas of his thirteen military and other decorations. The rest of his fortune he left, for he never married, to his relatives in Scotland. Wylie wrote *On American Yellow Fever* (1805) and *Practical Observations on the Plague* (1829), and he compiled a handbook on surgical operations. His most enduring work, however, was a Russian military pharmacopoeia, published in 1808.

After his death Wylie continued to be held in high regard in Russia. In 1946 the *Military Medical Encyclopaedic Dictionary* described him as 'A man of great gifts and talents, a good surgeon, talented administrator and organiser who enjoyed great authority in the country' (p. 718). Paradoxically, Wylie was responsible, through his efficient training of Russian military surgeons, for ending the recruitment of foreign doctors to the Russian army. Among the possessions he left was a pair of pistols, said to have come from Napoleon's carriage during his retreat from Moscow, and a chronometer, a very beautiful piece by Bréguet of Paris, which can be seen in the Royal Scottish Museum in Edinburgh.   JOHN B. WILSON

Sources A. G. Cross, *By the banks of the Neva: chapters from the lives and careers of the British in eighteenth-century Russia* (1997) · J. B. Wilson, 'Three Scots in the service of the czars [2 pts]', *The Practitioner*, 210 (1973), 569–74, 704–8 · I. G. Anderson, *Scotsmen in the service of the czars* (1990), 122–5 · C. Johnstone, *Life and times of Alexander I by C. Joinville* (1875), 3.341 · N. Shuster, 'English doctors in Russia in the early nineteenth century', *Proceedings of the Royal Society of Medicine*, 61 (1968), 185–90 · R. Hutchison, 'A medical adventurer', *Proceedings of the Royal Society of Medicine*, 21 (1927–8), 1406–8 · W. Meiklejohn, *Tulliallan: four lads o' pairts* (1990) · *Military medical encyclopaedic dictionary* (1946), 718–20 · priv. coll., Wylie family MSS · parish register (births and baptisms), Tulliallan, Perth, 13 and 20 Nov 1768

Likenesses J. F. Bolt, portrait, 1816 (after P. Franck), Royal College of Physicians of Edinburgh [*see illus.*] · oils, Royal College of Physicians of Edinburgh · photograph (after unknown portrait), priv. coll. · statue, St Petersburg, Russia

Wealth at death £100,000: Meiklejohn, *Tulliallan*

of his legs became severely infected and Wylie advised, in spite of the advice of other medical attendants, against amputation. The emperor made a full recovery and the leg was saved.

In May 1814 Wylie was made body physician to the tsar, and after Napoleon's defeat at Waterloo, Wylie accompanied Alexander to London, where he was knighted on Ascot Heath by the prince regent, using Platov's sabre. The following month at the emperor's request he was created a baronet. Thereafter Wylie travelled Europe with his strange, neurotic, and idealistic master during his twilight years, and he was present at Alexander's death at Taganrog in 1825.

Some idea of the close relationship between the emperor and his medical attendant can be gained from a letter which Wylie's nephew wrote home in 1824, after Wylie had sustained a compound fracture of his knee in a carriage accident: 'The attentions of H.I.M. to Sir James on this occasion were such as can be forgotten neither by him or me. They were really those of a brother to a brother' (Wylie MSS). After Alexander's death Wylie continued to attend his successor, Emperor Nicholas I.

Wylie's main influence in Russia was on the training of military surgeons. As director of the war ministry, a post he held from 1821 until 1836, Wylie founded academies for the training of military surgeons, wrote manuals for their instruction, and introduced the use of case notes or 'sheets of suffering'. So well known did Wylie become for this work that both the Austrian and the Prussian emperors requested him to reorganize the medical corps of their

Wylie, James Aitken (1808–1890), Free Church of Scotland minister and author, was born at Kirriemuir, Forfarshire, on 9 August 1808, son of James Wylie and his wife, Margaret Forrest. He was educated at the parish school, and at Marischal College, Aberdeen, before completing his arts course with a session at St Andrews under Thomas

Chalmers. In 1827 he entered the Divinity Hall of the Original Secession church in Edinburgh, where he came under the influence of Thomas McCrie (1772–1835). Wylie was one of a group of students, probationers, and ministers of the Original Secession church who 'renewed the covenants' in Edinburgh in 1828. He was licensed in December 1829 and ordained at Dollar, Clackmannanshire, in April 1831. In 1841 or 1842 he married Euphemia Gray (d. 1846), daughter of the Revd Thomas Gray, an Associate Presbytery minister, with whom he had two daughters.

When Wylie left Dollar, his congregation acknowledged that they had been unable fully to maintain a minister, but the new sphere to which he was called was one which gave scope to his emerging talent as a writer. In 1846 he went to work with Hugh Miller (1802–1856) as joint editor of the *Witness* newspaper in Edinburgh. In 1852, on the union of the Original Secession church with the Free Church of Scotland, he became a minister of the latter, though without a charge. He edited the *Free Church Record* from 1853 to 1860 and was honoured with an LLD from Aberdeen in 1856. In 1860, on the foundation of the Protestant Institute of Scotland by James Begg (1808–1883), Wylie was appointed to an extra-mural lectureship on popery. He retained the lectureship for the rest of his life and, although his gifts as a lecturer were not of the same order as his literary talents, he delivered a course of lectures each winter in Edinburgh and Glasgow. At the time of his ministerial jubilee in 1881 he was presented with his portrait and £300, intended to pay for a trip to Egypt and the Holy Land which, in spite of his age, he undertook the following year.

At his death Wylie was recognized as the last of a vanishing generation. In spirit he remained true to the conservative tradition in which he had been raised. His devotion to the cause of resisting what he saw as the encroachments of the Roman Catholic church was reflected in his writings on the subject, which began with his prize-winning essay *The Papacy: its History, Dogmas, Genius and Prospects* (1851). This was succeeded by numerous similar polemics, but this output was balanced by works of style and authority such as his three-volume *The History of Protestantism* (1874–7). His extensive travels on the continent also provided material for his writing, as in *Wanderings and Musings in the Valleys of the Waldenses* (1858), and he contributed the historical introduction to *Disruption Worthies* (1881).

Latterly white-haired and full-bearded, Wylie was one of the sights of Edinburgh, as he strode about on the walks with which he punctuated his literary labours. One writer described how his 'thin, agile figure and buoyant step, combined with his venerable appearance, rendered him to citizens the embodiment of a peripatetic philosopher of Modern Athens' (Scott, 566). He died at his home, 12 Archibald Place, Edinburgh, after a short illness, on 1 May 1890 and was buried in Newington cemetery, near to his friend and ally James Begg.

LIONEL ALEXANDER RITCHIE

Sources *Free Church of Scotland Monthly* (1 Aug 1890), 239–40 · D. Scott, *Annals and statistics of the Original Secession church* (1886) · The *Scotsman* (2 May 1890) · W. Ewing, ed., *Annals of the Free Church of Scotland, 1843–1900*, 1 (1914), 361–2 · R. Small, *History of the congregations of the United Presbyterian church from 1733 to 1900*, 2 (1904), 712 · T. Smith, *Memoirs of James Begg*, 2 (1888), 305–6, 362 · DNB
Likenesses portrait, repro. in *Free Church of Scotland Monthly*, 240 · stipple, NPG
Wealth at death £9527 7s. 1d.: confirmation, 19 July 1890, CCI

Wylie, William Howie (1833–1891), Baptist minister and journalist, son of William Wylie, block calico printer, of Kilmarnock, Ayrshire, and his wife, Agnes, daughter of John Howie of Lochgoin, was born at Kilmarnock on 24 February 1833. He was educated at Kilmarnock, then employed in the office of the *Kilmarnock Journal*, and became local correspondent for the Glasgow *North British Mail*. In 1847–50 he was sub-editor of the *Ayr Advertiser*. From Ayr he went to Nottingham as editor of the *Nottingham Journal* (1850–52). In 1852–3 he was sub-editor of the *Liverpool Courier*, and in 1854–5 was editor of the *Falkirk Herald* and sub-editor of the *Glasgow Commonwealth*. In 1855 Wylie moved to Edinburgh, where he became sub-editor of the *Daily Express*, at the same time contributing to the *War Telegraph*, and attending the classes at the university with a view to the ministry.

In 1859 Wylie was president of the University Dialectic Society, and soon afterwards became a student at Regent's Park College, London (the Baptist theological college which from 1927 moved to Oxford), under Joseph Angus. In 1860 he was appointed Baptist minister of Ramsey, Huntingdonshire, and in 1865 he was transferred to Accrington, Lancashire. This he had to relinquish owing to a breakdown of health. He retired to Gourock; but his health improved and he accepted a Blackpool pastorate. After a year he had to give up preaching, and resumed journalism.

From 1870 to 1877 Wylie acted as sub-editor of the *Christian World*, at the same time writing the parliamentary report for the *North British Mail* and the *Greenock Telegraph* (launched 1857), the first halfpenny evening paper in Britain, of which he was one of the original promoters, the proprietor being his brother-in-law, J. Pollock of Greenock. This paper Wylie edited more or less from the start. While in London he also contributed largely to the *Pall Mall Gazette*, *The Echo*, and the *Freeman*, the Baptist organ. For many years he also contributed to the *North British Mail* two columns of literary notes every Monday, and in 1879 a series of articles entitled 'The castles and mansions of the west'. In 1882 he founded in Glasgow the *Christian Leader*, and was its editor and proprietor until his death. He published books on Ayrshire, Nottingham, and Carlyle (the last written and published in four weeks).

Wylie invented a system of reporting verbatim speeches by turns, put to the first practical test during the 1852 Liverpool election. In politics he was a Liberal, and worked ardently for the cause.

On 11 February 1861 Wylie married Helen Young, youngest daughter of Robert Pollock of Greenock; she survived him with a daughter and a son, William Pollock Wylie, manager of the commercial department of the *Christian*

Leader. Wylie died at Troon, Ayrshire, on 5 August 1891, and was buried in St Andrew's churchyard, Kilmarnock, where a monument was erected.

GEORGE STRONACH, rev. ROGER T. STEARN

Sources *Baptist Magazine*, 83 (1891), 420–22 · *Scottish Leader* (6 Aug 1891) · *Christian Leader* (13 Aug 1891) · *The Freeman* (14 Aug 1891) · *Helensburgh Times* (12 Aug 1891) · private information (1900) · A. J. Lee, *The origins of the popular press in England, 1855–1914* (1976) · Boase, *Mod. Eng. biog.* · D. Griffiths, ed., *The encyclopedia of the British press, 1422–1992* (1992)

Likenesses portrait, repro. in *Helensburgh Times*

Wealth at death £987 2s. 2d.: confirmation, 14 March 1892, *CCI*

Wyllie, John William Shaw (1835–1870). *See under* Wyllie, Sir William (1802–1891).

Wyllie, Sir William (1802–1891), army officer, third son of John Wyllie of Holmhead House, Kilmarnock, carpet manufacturer and surveyor of taxes, and Elizabeth, daughter of William Brown of Kilmarnock, was born at Kilmarnock on 13 August 1802. His four brothers were subsequently all in the Indian army. Educated at the Kilmarnock Academy, William was commissioned ensign, Bombay native infantry, on 30 April 1819, promoted lieutenant next day, and arrived in India in August. His promotions were: captain, 24 December 1833; brevet major, 13 November 1839; major, 23 November 1841; lieutenant-colonel, 10 May 1847; brevet colonel, 1 February 1854; colonel, 14 March 1857; major-general, 28 November 1854; lieutenant-general, 24 October 1862; general, 24 February 1871.

Wyllie served in 1822 and 1823 in the Deccan, Konkan, and Gujarat. He commanded a detachment of 300 Indian infantry sent against the rebel chief Rup Sing, who in 1822 gave trouble in the south Maratha country. He became interpreter in Hindustani, and quartermaster to the 2nd battalion of the 11th Bombay native infantry on 9 May 1823, and was transferred in the same capacity to the 19th Bombay native infantry on 29 July 1824. He served throughout the operations in Cutch in 1825 and 1826. In May 1825 he received the thanks of Sir Charles Colville, commander-in-chief, for his conduct, when acting as adjutant of his regiment, in an attack on a large rebel force strongly fortified on the Jiran heights. In December 1826 he was appointed brigade major to the Malwa field force, and on 20 February 1829 was posted to Sholapur.

In 1838 Wyllie was appointed brigade major of the 1st brigade under Major-General Thomas Willshire of the Bombay column of the army of the Indus for the invasion of Afghanistan. He went with the column by sea to Vikkar on the Indus, about 50 miles east of Karachi, and then marched up the right bank of the Indus to Sukkur, following the Bengal column through the Bolan Pass to Sialkot or Quetta, and thence through the Khojak Pass, arriving at Kandahar in May 1839. After a rest of six weeks he marched with the army under John, first Baron Keane, through Afghanistan, was present at the assault and capture of Ghazni on 23 July, and at the occupation of Kabul on 7 August. He returned to Quetta with the Bombay force as assistant adjutant-general under Willshire, leaving Kabul on 18 September and marching through the Ghilzai

Sir William Wyllie (1802–1891), by unknown engraver, pubd 1891

country by Tokarak. The column arrived at Quetta on 31 October and left again to attack Kalat on 3 November. Wyllie accompanied the storming party in the successful assault and capture of the fortress on 13 November. He found in the citadel the body of Mahrab Khan, and sent it to the tent of Willshire, who was unaware the Kalat chief had fallen. Wyllie was mentioned in dispatches, was thanked by Willshire, and received brevet promotion from the date of the storming of Kalat.

Wyllie returned to his staff appointment at Poona in February 1840, and in August was appointed brigade major of the 2nd brigade of the Sind force. On 8 December he joined Major-General Richard England's column as brigade major, marching with it early in March 1842 from Dadhar to convey supplies of money, ammunition, and medicines to Major-General William Nott at Kandahar. The enemy was encountered at Haikalzai on 28 March, and the column was obliged to fall back on Quetta. It again advanced on 26 April, defeated the enemy on 28 April at Haikalzai, and, the Khojak Pass having been cleared by Colonel Wymer, sent from Kandahar by Nott, the column arrived safely at Kandahar on 10 May.

Wyllie returned in August with the Bombay column through the Khojak and Bolan passes to Sind, withdrawing the garrisons from Quetta and Kila Abdullah on the way, and was mentioned in dispatches. On 4 November 1842 he was appointed assistant adjutant-general of the forces in Sind and Baluchistan, took part in the operations under Sir Charles Napier, and was severely wounded in the early part of the battle of Miani on 17 February 1843. Napier mentioned in his dispatch of the following day that Wyllie was wounded when leading up the bank, 'gloriously animating the men to sustain the shock of numbers', and that no man had been more serviceable to him in all the previous operations (*London Gazette*, 11 April and 9 May 1843). Wyllie received for his services a brevet lieutenant-colonelcy, and was made a CB, military division (4 July 1843).

Wyllie rejoined his regiment in November 1843 and commanded the troops on the coast during the rebellion in the south Maratha country in 1844 and 1845, receiving the government's approval of his measures, and especially of the capture of rebels in the village of Kandauli on 28 March 1845. In May he went on furlough to England, and on his return was appointed deputy adjutant-general of the Bombay army on 17 January 1849. In April 1850 he was made a brigadier-general, second class, and given command of the Bombay garrison. In February 1855 he was appointed to command the brigade at Ahmednagar.

Wyllie left India in 1858. He was appointed colonel commandant of the 12th Bombay infantry on 14 March 1857, colonel of the 109th Bombay infantry on 30 September 1862, made a KCB (military division) on 28 May 1865, transferred to the colonelcy of the Royal Dublin Fusiliers on 14 February 1873, received a GCB (military division) on 2 June 1877, and retired from the service on a pension on 1 October 1877.

Wyllie married in 1831 at Sholapur, in the Bombay presidency, Amelia (1806–1891), daughter of Richards Hutt of Appley, Ryde, Isle of Wight, and sister of Sir William Hutt. Their children were John William Shaw [see below]; Francis Robert Shaw (1837–1907), under-secretary to the government of Bombay, retired in 1876, secretary to the army purchase commission from 1886 to 1891; Sir William Hutt Curzon *Wyllie (1848–1909), a lieutenant-colonel in the Indian staff corps, who, after holding the chief posts in India in the foreign department, became in 1901 political aide-de-camp to the secretary of state for India in London, and was there assassinated on 1 July 1909 by an Indian student; Emily Eliza, who married in 1856 William Patrick Adam; and Florence Amelia Julia.

Wyllie died of influenza after a few days' illness at his residence, 3 Queensborough Terrace, Kensington, London, on 26 May 1891, and was buried at Kensal Green, London, on 30 May.

John William Shaw Wyllie (1835–1870), Sir William Wyllie's eldest son, was born at Poona, Bombay presidency, on 6 October 1835. In 1841 his mother returned with the children to Britain. John Wyllie was educated by a private tutor, at Edinburgh Academy, and with his brother Frank at Cheltenham College (1849–53). His father intended him for the Indian Civil Service and obtained a nomination from Sir William Hutt, then, urged by his headmaster, agreed to his going to Oxford. He won an open scholarship at Trinity College (1854), resigning one previously gained at Lincoln (matriculating on 1 June 1853), and obtained in 1855 a first class in moderations. In 1856 he passed the new open competitive examination for the Indian Civil Service, chose the Bombay presidency, and, a 'competition-wallah', arrived in India in November 1856. On 25 January 1858 he was appointed third assistant political agent in Kathiawar. In June 1858 he went to Surat for an examination, and nearly died of Gujarat fever. It permanently impaired his health and he subsequently suffered from recurrent pain, diarrhoea, and other consequences. His services, particularly in translating Colonel Lang's *Mulk Sherista*, a Gujarati collection illustrating the common law of the 224 Indian states then in the province of Kathiawar, were favourably noticed.

After serving as an assistant commissioner in the Bara Banki and Lucknow districts, Wyllie became early in 1861 assistant secretary to Sir George Yule, then officiating as chief commissioner of the province, and in May 1862, recommended by Sir Henry Durand, was appointed to the Calcutta secretariat (the central administration of British India, of which Calcutta was the capital). On furlough (1864–5) he returned to Trinity College, passed his examinations, and took his degree (BA, 1864; MA, 1868). On his return to India he served as under-secretary to the foreign department, gained the confidence of the governor-general, Lord Lawrence, and at his request became the exponent of his foreign policy in an article, refused by the *Quarterly* but published in the *Edinburgh Review* (January 1867), 'The foreign policy of Lord Lawrence', which apparently influenced public opinion. Wyllie's phrase there, 'masterly inactivity', became widely used. He made the arrangements for the grand durbar at Agra in November 1866.

Failing health compelled Wyllie to return home in 1867, and in 1868 he was persuaded by his uncle, Sir William Hutt, to give up his Indian career for home politics. He contested the city of Hereford as a Liberal—he favoured the ballot, Irish disestablishment, and secular education—in the 1868 election. Fearing disqualification as an MP because holding an office of profit under the crown, he resigned from the Indian service (14 November) shortly before the poll. He was elected and took his seat. However, the defeated Conservatives petitioned against the result, alleging bribery and treating. The judge, Mr Justice Blackburn, ruled that a Liberal merchant who had given breakfast to Liberal electors was an agent of the sitting members, and that they had been by their agent guilty of treating. Wyllie was unseated, a bitter disappointment: 'he had forsaken the Indian service for a career that now sunk under him; he had burned his ships, and could not return' (Wyllie, xxiv). On 2 June 1869 he was made a CSI for his Indian services. His health was poor but he wrote articles of which the best-known were 'Masterly inactivity' (*Fortnightly Review*, December 1869)—again defending Lawrence's non-interventionist policy towards Afghanistan and elsewhere, and opposing occupation of Quetta—and 'Mischievous activity' (*Fortnightly Review*, March 1870), criticizing Lord Mayo's apparently more interventionist external policy: 'I pray … England may yet withdraw her hand from Central Asia' (ibid., 173). He also contributed to the *Cornhill Magazine*, and to the *Edinburgh* and *Calcutta* reviews, besides letters to *The Times* and other publications on central Asia.

In January 1870 Wyllie went to Paris to improve his French and study French politics. He suffered from a cold, then inflammation of the lungs and recurred malarial fever, and died, aged thirty-four, at the Hôtel Vouillemont, rue Boissy d'Anglas, Paris, on 15 March 1870, and was temporarily interred at Montmartre, his remains being moved to Kensal Green cemetery, London, after the Franco-Prussian war. A memorial tablet was placed in Cheltenham School chapel, and a scholarship of £70 a year, for Cheltenham boys at Trinity College, Oxford, was founded in his memory by friends and schoolfellows. His early death was lamented in the House of Commons and the London press. Some of his articles were reprinted in *Essays on the External Policy of India* (1875), edited, with a short biography, by Sir William Wilson Hunter.

R. H. VETCH, rev. ROGER T. STEARN

Sources *Black and White* (6 June 1891) · *The Times* (29 May 1891) · *Kilmarnock Standard* (30 May 1891) · BL OIOC · J. W. S. Wyllie, *Essays on the external policy of India*, ed. W. W. Hunter (1875) · V. C. P. Hodson, *List of officers of the Bengal army, 1758–1834*, 4 (1947) · Irving, *Scots.* · J. W. Kaye, *History of the war in Afghanistan*, 2 vols. (1851) · J. H. Stocqueler, *Memorials of Afghanistan: being state papers, official documents, dispatches, authentic narratives, etc.* (Calcutta, 1843) · W. F. P. Napier, *The life and opinions of General Sir Charles James Napier*, 4 vols. (1857) · W. F. P. Napier, *The conquest of Scinde: with some introductory passages in the life of Major-General Sir Charles James Napier*, 2 vols. (1845) · Boase, *Mod. Eng. biog.* · *WWBMP*, vol. 1 · private information (1900) · Foster, *Alum. Oxon.*, 1500–1714 [John William Shaw Wyllie] · *CGPLA Eng. & Wales* (1870) [John William Shaw Wyllie] · *CGPLA Eng. & Wales* (1891)

Archives NRA, priv. coll., papers relating to his military career, incl. Indian journal, corresp., commissions, etc.

Likenesses portrait, repro. in *Black and White* · wood-engraving, NPG; repro. in *ILN* (6 June 1891) [*see illus.*]

Wealth at death £3860 16s. 11d.: probate, 22 Aug 1891, *CGPLA Eng. & Wales* · under £200—John William Shaw Wyllie: administration, 21 April 1870, *CGPLA Eng. & Wales*

Wyllie, Sir William Hutt Curzon (1848–1909), army officer, born at Cheltenham on 5 October 1848, was the third and youngest son of the five children of General Sir William *Wyllie (1802–1891) and his wife, Amelia (1806–1891), daughter of Richards Hutt of Appley, Isle of Wight, and niece of Captain John Hutt RN (1746–1794). Both his brothers served in India—John William Shaw *Wyllie (1835–1870) [*see under* Wyllie, Sir William] and Francis Robert Shaw Wyllie (1837–1907). The latter, born on 4 June 1837, was educated at Cheltenham College (1849–54), the East India Company's college, Haileybury (1856–7), joined the Bombay civil service, became under-secretary to the Bombay government, and died in London in February 1907.

Educated at Marlborough College (1863–4) and the Royal Military College, Sandhurst (1865–6), Wyllie entered the army in October 1866 as ensign 106th foot (Durham light infantry). He arrived in India in February 1867, was promoted lieutenant in October 1868, joined the Indian staff corps in 1869, and was posted to the 2nd Gurkha regiment (the Sirmoor Rifles, later the 2nd King Edward's Own Gurkhas). In 1870 he was selected for civil and political employment, appointed to the Oudh commission, and served under General Barrow and Sir George Couper.

Promoted captain in October 1878, in January 1879 Wyllie was transferred to the foreign department, serving successively as cantonment magistrate of Nasirabad, assistant commissioner in Ajmer-Merwara, and assistant to the governor-general's agent in Baluchistan, Sir Robert Groves Sandeman. He went through the Afghan campaign of 1878–80, including the march on Kandahar, with Major-General Sir Robert Phayre, and was mentioned in the viceroy's dispatches. After the war he was military secretary to his brother-in-law, William Patrick Adam, governor of Madras, from December 1880 until Adam's death

in the following May, and until November 1881 he was private secretary to William Hudleston (acting governor).

Wyllie married on 29 December 1881 Katharine Georgiana, second daughter of David Fremantle Carmichael of the Indian Civil Service, then member of the council, Madras; she survived her husband.

Wyllie had charge of Malhar Rao, the former Maharaja Gaikwar of Baroda, from December 1881 to November 1882. He then became assistant resident at Hyderabad. Subsequently he was assistant commissioner, Ajmer-Merwara, 1883; first assistant in Rajputana, 1884; additional political agent, Kotah, April 1885; boundary settlement officer, Mewar–Marwar border, November 1886; political agent, Kotah, January 1889; officiating commissioner of Ajmer, July 1891; officiating political agent, Jhallawar, in addition to Kotah, 1891–2; resident, western states of Rajputana (Jodhpur), 1892–3; and resident in Mewar (Udaipur), November 1893 to February 1898, when he officiated as resident in Nepal. Later in 1898 he attained one of the highest appointments in the service, that of agent to the governor-general in central India. In May 1900 he was transferred in the same capacity to Rajputana, where he remained for the rest of his service in India. Made CIE in 1881, he was promoted major in October 1886 and lieutenant-colonel in 1892.

Throughout his long and varied service in the princely states of India, and especially in Rajputana, where seventeen of the most strenuous years of his life were spent, Wyllie gained by his courtesy, charm, and above all by his character and strength of purpose, remarkable influence over the chiefs and officials of the principalities under his administrative charge. In addition Wyllie had the reputation, so dear to Rajputs, of a keen sportsman and a skilful and daring rider, who held as a trophy the blue riband of Indian sportsmen, the Hog-hunters' Ganges cup, which he won in Oudh in April 1875.

Wyllie's example stimulated those who served under him, and it was owing to his energy and to the confidence in him of the princes and people of Rajputana that the calamity of famine during 1899–1900 was successfully overcome by the relief measures he organized.

In March 1901 Wyllie came home on being selected by Lord George Hamilton (Conservative secretary of state for India 1895–1903) as his political aide-de-camp. Wyllie's knowledge of India and the Indian princes fitted him for the important and often delicate duties, which included advising the secretary of state on political questions relating to the princely states. Arrangements for the reception of Indian magnates at the British court were in his charge, and heavy work devolved upon him at Edward VII's coronation in 1902. He was appointed KCIE and MVO in 1902 and CVO in June 1907.

Wyllie's official position brought him into close contact with Indian students in whose welfare he was deeply interested. He also devoted himself to associations and charities for the benefit of Indians.

While attending, with Lady Wyllie, an entertainment given to Indians by the National Indian Association at the Imperial Institute, South Kensington, London, on the night of Friday 1 July 1909, Wyllie was assassinated, almost under the eyes of his wife, by Madhan Lal Dhingra, a Hindu extremist student, whom Wyllie had helped, who suddenly fired at him with a revolver, killing him instantly. Dr Cawas Lalcaca, a Parsi physician of Shanghai, who bravely interposed to save Wyllie, was also mortally wounded. These crimes were precursors of terrorist crimes in India. Dhingra—a Punjabi London University engineering student and political pupil of the London-based extremist Shyamji Krishnavarma—was convicted of the double crime at the central criminal court on 23 July, and hanged at Pentonville prison on 17 August. Wyllie was buried at Richmond cemetery, Surrey, on 6 July.

Wyllie's tragic death was felt as deeply in India as at home. Flags were put at half mast, and public offices were closed throughout Rajputana and central India on reception of the news; and on the day of Wyllie's funeral (in Richmond cemetery) a salute of thirteen guns was fired from the palace fortresses of Rajputana. Viscount Morley, the secretary of state in council, recorded 'his high appreciation of Wyllie's admirable services', and his 'profound sense of the personal loss' sustained by himself and his colleagues 'by the blind, atrocious crime'. He granted a special pension of £500 to Lady Wyllie in recognition of her husband's service and death. Memorial funds were raised in Britain and India. From the British fund a marble tablet erected in the crypt of St Paul's Cathedral was unveiled by Earl Roberts on 19 October 1910, in the presence, among others, of the three successive secretaries of state (Lord George Hamilton and viscounts Midleton and Morley) whom Wyllie had served. The balance, £2551, the Curzon Wyllie memorial fund, was entrusted to the Strangers' Home for Asiatics, Limehouse, on the governing body of which he had served. At Marlborough College there was founded a Curzon Wyllie memorial medal, to be awarded annually to the most efficient member of the OTC. In India the Curzon Wyllie central memorial fund committee erected at a cost of £2000 a marble *aramgarh* (place of rest) in Ajmer, Rajputana, to provide shade, rest, and water for men and animals. Local memorials were also instituted in many of the states of Rajputana and central India.   F. H. BROWN, rev. ROGER T. STEARN

Sources *India Office List* (1909) · *Indian Magazine and Review* (Aug 1909) · *The Times* (3 July 1909) · *The Times* (4 July 1909) · *The Times* (5 July 1909) · *The Times* (7 July 1909) · *The Times* (24 July 1909) · *The Times* (18 Aug 1909) · *The Times* (20 Aug 1910) · *The Times* (13 March 1911) · Annual reports, Strangers' Home for Asiatics, 1909 · Annual reports, Strangers' Home for Asiatics, 1910 · *Homeward Mail* (3 July 1911) · personal knowledge (1912) · *WWW*, 1916–28 · Burke, *Peerage* (1907) · [A. H. Wall and D. E. Wall], eds., *Marlborough College register from 1843 to 1933*, 8th edn (1936) · *Hart's Army List* (1891) · *Annual Register* (1909), pt 1, p. 155; pt 2, pp. 22, 26 · B. R. Nanda, *Gokhale: the Indian moderates and the British raj* (1977) · L. James, *Raj: the making and unmaking of British India* (1997) · P. Spear, *The Oxford history of modern India, 1740–1947* (1965) · P. Moon, *The British conquest and dominion of India* (1989) · E. S. Skirving, ed., *Cheltenham College register, 1841–1927* (1928) · Richmond cemetery records

Likenesses H. A. Olivier, portrait, *c.*1910, priv. coll.

Wealth at death £10,073 12*s.*: resworn probate, 28 July 1909, *CGPLA Eng. & Wales*

Wyllie, William Lionel (1851–1931), artist and writer, was born at 67 Albany Street, London, on 5 July 1851, the elder son of William Morison Wyllie (1819/20–1895), artist, of London and Wimereux, France, and his wife, Katherine Smythe (*d.* 1872), singer, the daughter of John Henry Benham. Brought up in London and Boulogne, he showed early artistic promise, entering Heatherley's art school in Newman Street at a very young age. In 1866 he went on to the Royal Academy Schools, and won the Turner gold medal at the age of eighteen with *Dawn after a Storm* in 1869. He first exhibited at the Royal Academy in 1868, showing *Dover Castle and Town*. That love of the sea which was to influence his life and art so strongly soon manifested itself. From an early age, with his half-brother Lionel Percy Smythe and his younger brother Charles William Wyllie, both artists, he indulged a passion for sailing, an enthusiasm which always informed his work. The brothers freely roamed the coast of northern France where Wyllie found subjects for his earliest pictures, *Blessing the Sea* (1876) being a notable example (Walker Art Gallery, Liverpool). In 1879 Wyllie married Marian Amy (*c.*1860–1937), daughter of Captain William O'Brien Carew of the Indian marine. They had five sons, the second and fourth of whom were killed in the First World War, and two daughters, the elder of whom predeceased her father.

In the early 1870s Wyllie began working as an illustrator for the *Graphic*—a connection which lasted about twenty years—producing black and white illustrations of topical maritime subjects. In 1883 the Bond Street art dealer Robert Dunthorne showed an interest in Wyllie's work, inaugurating the artist's lifelong association with the firm. In the same year Wyllie began to make his name with more paintings of the recent bombardment of Alexandria, for which he visited Egypt. These were exhibited at the Fine Art Society where he subsequently had a series of one-man exhibitions of his watercolours, a medium in which he was particularly skilled and prolific. During the 1880s Wyllie concentrated increasingly on views of the River Thames, its estuary, and the River Medway, particularly attracted by their more industrial aspects, as exemplified by *Toil, Glitter, Grime and Wealth on a Flowing Tide*, the first of two pictures to be acquired by the Chantrey Bequest (Tate collection). At this time he began making etchings, a process that he combined with dry-point, producing numbers of technically complex plates over a period of nearly fifty years. He was elected a member of the Royal Society of Painter-Etchers and Engravers in 1904, and a member of the Royal Academy in 1907; he was also a member of the Royal Institute of Painters in Water Colours. In 1905 he published a book on J. M. W. Turner, whom he greatly admired and emulated in his work. He also wrote books on perspective and watercolour technique.

Wyllie spent much time at sea and did a good deal of work for the White Star shipping line. Following his move to a house overlooking the entrance to Portsmouth harbour in 1907 he became more closely involved with the Royal Navy, and it was with renewed energy that he depicted First World War scenes and events, sailing with the fleet by special licence in order to make drawings. In 1919 he spent a month on board HMS *Revenge* at the time of the armistice. Nevertheless he continued to paint and etch a wide range of subjects until his death, and in his later years his etchings of the busy life of the port of London brought him widespread popularity. Late in life, Wyllie became increasingly interested in British naval history and the subjects it offered. As a founder member of the Society for Nautical Research he campaigned for the restoration of HMS *Victory* at Portsmouth. He fulfilled his lifelong ambition of painting a panorama (42 ft x 12 ft) of the battle of Trafalgar in Portsmouth Dockyard; it was unveiled by George V in 1930.

A rapid and prolific worker, Wyllie could make stylish sketches even in a small boat on a choppy sea. The golden-wedding greeting which he prized most was a telegram running: 'The navy loves you—Acland.' Active, vigorous, brisk, and kindly, he worked and sailed right up to the time of his sudden death at 102 Fellows Road, Primrose Hill, London, on 6 April 1931. He was buried in the churchyard within Portchester Castle. His wife, who shared his passion for sailing, survived him until 1937 having in 1935 published a biography of him entitled *We Were One*. Their eldest son, Harold, was a marine painter, and a founder member of the Society of Marine Artists. Examples of Wyllie's works may be found in the Guildhall Art Gallery, London, the Tate collection, the National Maritime Museum, Greenwich, and the Walker Art Gallery, Liverpool.   H. B. GRIMSDITCH, rev. ROGER QUARM

Sources R. Quarm and J. Wyllie, *W. L. Wyllie: marine artist, 1851–1931* (1981) · M. A. Wyllie, *We were one* (1935) · R. M. Whitlaw and W. L. Wyllie, *Lionel P. Smythe, RA, RWS* (1923) · H. V. Barnett, 'By river and sea', *Magazine of Art*, 7 (1883–4), 309–15 · C. Bridge, 'William Lionel Wyllie', *Art Journal*, new ser., 27 (1907), 1–32 · N. J. H. Grundy, *W. L. Wyllie, RA: the Portsmouth years* (1996) · *CGPLA Eng. & Wales* (1931)
Archives Royal Naval Museum, Portsmouth, papers
Likenesses photographs, 1880–1930, priv. coll. · photograph, 1914, NPG · R. W. Robinson, photograph, NPG; repro. in *Members and associates of the Royal Academy of Arts* (1891) · L. Smythe, engraving (after unknown portrait), repro. in *ILN* (4 May 1889)
Wealth at death £11,933 7s.: resworn probate, 16 May 1931, *CGPLA Eng. & Wales*

Wyn, John, ap Maredudd (b. in or before **1494**, d. **1559**). *See under* Wynn family (*per. c.*1465–1678).

Wyn, Watcyn. *See* Williams, Watkin Hezekiah (1844–1905).

Wyndham. *See also* Windham.

Wyndham. For this title name *see* individual entries under Wyndham; *see also* Moore, Mary Charlotte [Mary Charlotte Wyndham, Lady Wyndham] (1861–1931).

Wyndham, Charles, second earl of Egremont (1710–1763), politician, was born on 19 August 1710 and baptized on the 30th at St Martin-in-the-Fields, London, the elder son of Sir William *Wyndham, third baronet (*c.*1688–1740), politician, and his first wife, Lady Catherine Seymour (*d.* 1731), the daughter of Charles *Seymour, sixth duke of Somerset. Educated at Westminster School, which he entered in 1719, and then at Christ Church,

Charles Wyndham, second earl of Egremont (1710–1763), by William Hoare, 1762

Oxford, where he matriculated on 4 May 1725, he undertook an extended grand tour in 1728–30, visiting Germany, France, and Italy. On his return he sought to enter the House of Commons, unsuccessfully contesting Launceston in 1734 but securing a seat the following year in a by-election at Bridgwater. In parliament he at first voted with the opponents of Sir Robert Walpole. This was a matter of family tradition: his father was the tory leader who had been imprisoned in the Tower for his support of the Pretender in 1715 and remained sympathetic to a Stuart restoration, being a lifelong friend of Bolingbroke and an arch-opponent of Walpole. His death on 17 June 1740 freed the younger Wyndham from the need to oppose the ministry, and during the 1740s he attached himself to Carteret, whose distant relative he was, supporting the government, and in late February 1744 seconding a loyal address to the king when a French invasion threatened. In 1741 he lost his Bridgwater seat, but in the following year he secured election for Appleby, Cumberland, which he represented until 1747; thereafter he was briefly MP for one of the family seats, that of Taunton (1747–50), a move necessitated by his decision to become a supporter of the government. More proud than able, he was allowed only the merits of a degree of good humour and common sense by his contemporaries.

On 7 February 1750 Wyndham succeeded his maternal uncle, the seventh duke of Somerset, and first earl of Egremont, under a special remainder granted the previous year, and thereby became second earl of Egremont and one of the richest peers in England. At his death it was believed he left an annual income of £18,000, together with a fortune of £170,000 in cash. His major estates were at Petworth in Sussex and the Percy lands at Cockermouth in Cumberland. In 1751 he became lord lieutenant of Cumberland, a post he retained until 1759. Petworth remained his principal residence, however, and he was lord lieutenant of Sussex in 1762–3. On 12 March 1751 he married a prominent society beauty, Alicia Maria (d. 1794), the daughter of an Irish peer, George Carpenter, second Baron Carpenter of Killaghy (c.1695–1749), politician, and Elizabeth Petty. They had four sons and three daughters. Their eldest son, George O'Brien *Wyndham, art patron, was born on 18 December 1751 and succeeded his father, becoming third earl of Egremont; he died on 11 November 1837. More decisive for Egremont's later career was the marriage of his own sister Elizabeth Wyndham to George *Grenville in 1749, which also established links with Lord Temple and, more distantly, William Pitt. Yet, at first, Wyndham's elevation to the House of Lords, where he spoke only infrequently, did not lead to an enlarged political role.

Egremont's ambitions, however, were clear. During the 1750s he assiduously pursued first the duke of Newcastle and then Henry Fox, but initially these efforts were not rewarded. His political standing clearly rose and he was involved on the fringes of the complex ministerial politics of the mid-1750s. By now his family's political rehabilitation was complete: the son of a Jacobite had moved close to the heart of the Hanoverian establishment. In 1757 he was mentioned as a likely secretary of state in a ministry which the second Earl Waldegrave unsuccessfully attempted to form. In 1761 he was named as the senior British plenipotentiary to a congress to be held at Augsburg, intended to negotiate a conclusion to the Seven Years' War, although this never in fact met, and in July he became a privy councillor. In the same year his wife became a lady of the bedchamber. On 9 October 1761 Egremont, though he totally lacked previous diplomatic or ministerial experience, was appointed by the earl of Bute, apparently at Mansfield's suggestion, to be secretary of state for the southern department, a post he was to retain until his death.

The new secretary of state was a patrician: when Egremont first entered office Horace Walpole, usually a severe critic of the earl, pronounced him 'extremely well-bred' (Letters of Horace Walpole, 21.541). Egremont's initial task was to handle the diplomacy that preceded the breach with Spain and Madrid's formal entry into the war in January 1762, on the side of its Bourbon ally, France. The campaign that followed saw a series of British successes at the expense of the Spanish monarchy, particularly the capture first of Havana and then Manila, and before long peace negotiations were under way. As southern secretary, Egremont was formally responsible for the handling of the detailed diplomacy that led to the peace of Paris, eventually signed on 10 February 1763. From the outset he was a member of the inner group that directed the peace negotiations. Within this group there were serious divisions about the terms on which a settlement should be concluded. Bute and the new king, George III, wanted to

end the costly if successful Seven Years' War, and were prepared for considerable concessions to bring this about: as was the duke of Bedford, who was sent to Paris to negotiate directly with the leading French minister, the duc de Choiseul. Egremont followed the lead of his brother-in-law Grenville in opposing the purchase of peace through unnecessary concessions, and specifically in opposing the return of Havana without Britain's receiving compensation. This firm stand resulted in Spain's cession of Florida to Britain in the final peace settlement.

Egremont was at best a competent and diligent secretary of state, although his commitment to the business of his department was not as consistent as it might have been. When Bute left office in April 1763 and George Grenville formed his own ministry, Egremont's future prospects appeared considerable, and in the political manoeuvring that characterized his brother-in-law's early months in office he played a full part. He, the earl of Halifax, and Grenville, known together as the 'triumvirate', dominated the ministry that took shape during the late spring and summer of 1763. As a secretary of state, Egremont was involved in the arrest, interrogation, and prosecution of the MP John Wilkes for publishing no. 45 of the North Briton. This affair was not without its difficulties for Egremont. One point at issue was whether an MP could be arrested. The last precedent for this was in fact his own father, Sir William Wyndham, during the 1715 rising, which the newspapers of the day did not fail to point out. Egremont himself played a notably full part in organizing the prosecution of Wilkes. In the midst of ministerial uncertainties and the Wilkes affair, on 21 August 1763 Egremont died suddenly at his home, Egremont House, Piccadilly, London, from an apoplectic stroke brought on by overeating and lack of exercise. A renowned trencherman, he had suffered milder attacks in July 1761 and March 1762, although he had recovered on both occasions. But he had ignored medical advice 'to moderate the indulgence of his palate' (Walpole, Memoirs, 1.283): Egremont allegedly remarked only a few days before his own death that he had 'but three turtle dinners to come, and if I survive them I shall be immortal' (Letters of Horace Walpole, 22.159).   H. M. SCOTT

Sources GEC, Peerage, new edn · E. Cruickshanks, 'Wyndham, Charles', HoP, Commons, 1715–54 · Walpole, Corr. · Z. E. Rashed, The peace of Paris, 1763 (1951) · H. Walpole, Memoirs of the reign of King George the Third, ed. D. Le Marchant, 4 vols. (1845) · The Devonshire diary: memoranda on state of affairs, 1759–1762, ed. P. D. Brown and K. W. Schweizer, CS, 4th ser., 27 (1982) · P. D. G. Thomas, John Wilkes: a friend to liberty (1996) · DNB

Archives NRA, priv. coll., family and estate corresp. and papers · PRO, Egremont MSS, 30/47 · PRO, political and diplomatic corresp. and papers, PRO 30/47 | BL, corresp. with George Grenville, Add. MS 57808 · BL, letters to Lord Hardwicke, Add. MSS 35596–35603 · BL, corresp. with Lord Loudon, Add. MSS 44069–44084 (mainly copies) · BL, corresp. with duke of Newcastle and others, Add. MSS 32720–33067 · BL, letters to Lord Tyrawley, Add. MSS 23635, 44070 · CKS, corresp. with Sir Jeffrey Amherst · Hunt. L., letters to Lord Loudon · NRA, letters to Alexander Malet

Likenesses W. Hoare, oils, 1762, Petworth House, West Sussex [see illus.] · attrib. W. Hoare, oils, NPG · R. Wilson, oils, Dulwich Picture Gallery, London · engraving (after E. Harding), Petworth

House, West Sussex · oils (as a child), Petworth House, West Sussex
Wealth at death annual income of £18,000; cash reserves of £170,000; landed wealth: Walpole, *Corr.*, vol. 22, p. 159

Wyndham, Sir Charles [*real name* Charles Culverwell] (1837–1919), actor and theatre manager, the second son of Major Richard Culverwell (*fl. c.*1820–1860) and his wife, Mary Ann, was born on 23 March 1837 at 19 Tithebarn Street, Liverpool, and was baptized on 18 July at St Peter's, Church Street (demolished 1922). The family moved to London when he was a boy. His brother died in infancy. He also had three sisters. His father's first name suggested military rank, but Major Culverwell had no connection with the army: he and his son claimed for him the profession of physician, but he does not appear to have possessed a British medical qualification, and in the directories he was variously described as watchmaker, hotelier, and victualler. The truth is in doubt.

Charles Culverwell's education, like much of his life, was cosmopolitan. He went to boarding-schools in England, Scotland (where he took part in amateur theatricals at St Andrews), Germany, and France. In Paris he frequented the Comédie-Française and the Palais Royal: the acting styles of each inspired his future mastery of high comedy and farce, and the Palais Royal supplied much of his repertory, 'Englished' in adaptation. His father sent him to King's College, London, to read medicine; but the student spent all available time acting at a tiny amateur house near King's Cross and theatre-going in the West End, where first he saw the light comedian Charles James Mathews, whose style of performance was to prove as strong an influence as the Parisians. None the less he became a licentiate in midwifery and MRCS (1857), and, after experience at hospitals in Ireland and Germany, a licentiate of the Society of Apothecaries and MD in the University of Giessen (1859). Uniquely, at Charing Cross Hospital in 1903, he addressed a roomful of medical students in the dual capacity of actor and doctor; but there is no public evidence of his having employed his medical skills after 1865, and by 1883 his name had disappeared from the medical registers.

The practice of Dr Charles Culverwell, which was set up at 3 Great Marlborough Street, London, failed. It was on 30 November 1860—when appearing as Captain Hawksley in an amateur performance of Tom Taylor's *Still Waters Run Deep* at the Royalty Theatre, Soho—that he first used the name Wyndham. The choice was apparently random, but was retained as his stage name ever after, and was ratified for all purposes by deed poll on 8 October 1886. As Charles Wyndham (and from 1902 Sir Charles) he worked his peculiar magic upon audiences in North America, Germany, Russia, and the West End of London, beguiling them with a rare and practised skill. He was tall, straight, and slender, with broad shoulders and long legs. In his youth his voice was harsh and inflexible, which for years he tried to conceal by speaking fast. His quickfire delivery and rugged good looks qualified him until middle age for the dashing young hero of Victorian farce. Then, in the final decade of the nineteenth century, when he switched to

Sir Charles Wyndham (1837–1919), by Langfier

the more measured elder statesmen of Henry Arthur Jones's 'society dramas', he grew more attractive still. A slightly crooked mouth and heavy eyelids lent him a quizzical or mystified look that only enhanced his appeal. As his wavy hair turned from brown to silver his charisma increased. Seldom in fifty years on the stage did he fail to capture the men's admiration or the women's hearts. With the sole exception of Ellen Terry, no British player of his era surpassed his ability to sway the audience by the power of personal charm. Appropriately, the first time he used his new name he played a seducer.

On 8 February 1862 Wyndham turned professional actor, reappearing at the Royalty in the title character of an anonymous trifle, *Christopher of Carnation Cottage*. That same year he sailed for America, enlisted in the Federal army as a medical officer, and served almost to the end of the civil war. Acting Assistant Surgeon Culverwell was close to the horrors of battle. Scarcely ever would he speak of them; their effect upon him was evident, long after, in his determined support of British disabled servicemen by means of charity performances at his own theatres during the Second South African War and the First World War.

Wyndham's American début was made on 14 April 1863 at Grover's Theatre, Washington, as Osric to the Hamlet of John Wilkes Booth, who in 1865 assassinated President

Lincoln. He landed the job by brandishing notices of his London performances without saying he had written them himself. For most of the rest of the war he alternated stage costume and uniform, and suffered in each. More than one theatre manager dismissed him for incompetence; but, undaunted, he set his sights in earnest on the English stage, and returned to London and to the wife he had left behind. Five years had passed since his marriage to Emma Silberrad (c.1837–1916) at the parish church of St Matthew, Brixton, on 27 June 1860. A merchant's child, but also a moneyed German aristocrat, she was the granddaughter of a prince of the Holy Roman empire, Baron Silberrad of Hesse. By marrying into this house of merchant princes Wyndham was spared the fear of destitution that plagued other actors.

In the autumn of 1866, having returned to the Royalty, Wyndham danced as well as acted himself into favour as Hatchett in F. C. Burnand's burlesque of Douglas Jerrold's *Black-Eyed Susan*. Other London engagements followed, most notably (in 1867–8) the inaugural season at the Queen's Theatre, Long Acre, with Ellen Terry, Henry Irving, and J. L. Toole. There he repeated the seducer Hawksley. London had been reached without hard apprenticeship in the stock companies of provincial towns, but it was not all advantageous. Wyndham lacked repertory experience, and hence versatility—as he found when attempting the part of Cyrano de Bergerac (in an adaptation of Rostand's play of that name) at Wyndham's Theatre on 19 April 1900. He was in his element, though, when acting in rattling and often *risqué* farces—such as Clement Scott's *The Great Divorce Case* (15 April 1876), James Albery's *The Pink Dominoes* (31 March 1877), and W. S. Gilbert's *Foggerty's Fairy* (15 December 1881)—especially when at the Criterion, an intimate basement theatre at Piccadilly Circus where he presided, first as co-manager, then in sole charge, from 1875 to 1899, and where he continued to have a decisive interest until his death. In 'Criterion farce', translated from French originals with names and places Anglicized, faithless husbands and suitors were seen in the most favourable light. Men in the audience smirked approvingly, and women swooned. No one was ever more able than Wyndham to commend the transgressor. He moved about the stage with perfect ease; every gesture had been rehearsed in a mirror, and to ensure a fluid use of the hands he never carried a stick. His wonderful naturalness was his greatest legacy to the next generation of actors.

Costume pieces overtook farces at the Criterion, and for six years Wyndham concentrated on showing off his legs in tight breeches. T. W. Robertson's *David Garrick* (in which he played Garrick, 13 November 1886), Boucicault's *London Assurance* (as Dazzle, 27 November 1890), and eighteenth-century comedies by Goldsmith, Sheridan, and O'Keeffe were produced. *David Garrick* became his chief piece; but many thought his finest achievement of all was the portrayal of mellow, titled men of the world, cynical but tender, in the plays that Jones moulded for him—Viscount Clivebrook in *The Bauble Shop* (26 January 1893), Sir Richard Kato QC in *The Case of Rebellious Susan* (3 October 1894), Dr

Carey in *The Physician* (25 March 1897), Colonel Sir Christopher Deering in *The Liars* (6 October 1897), all at the Criterion, and Sir Daniel Carteret in *Mrs Dane's Defence* (9 October 1900) at Wyndham's. Charles Haddon Chambers's *The Tyranny of Tears* (6 April 1899) and H. H. Davies's *The Mollusc* (7 October 1907), both at the Criterion, were among other plays that exploited his charm. Wyndham's appeal to women of all ages was immense. His voice, when excited, had a catch in it, which men thought rasping. To women it was a caress. Wyndham in his sixties, on the stage at least, was the sort of man women liked to be scolded by.

From the Criterion's profits Wyndham built Wyndham's Theatre in 1899 and the New Theatre (later renamed the Albery) in 1903, in both of which he had a managerial share to the end of his life. His was a record of continuous and simultaneous West End management that probably no actor will equal. As a manager he was indefatigable. He pioneered the 'flying matinée'—an out-of-town performance by a company playing the same evening in London. Between 1874 and 1878 he produced numerous plays for matinées at the Crystal Palace, Sydenham, using actors who were occupied in the West End. Earlier still, in 1870, he had formed the Wyndham Comedy Company and toured the American midwest for three years with a largely Robertsonian repertory; but an American farce, Bronson Howard's *Saratoga* (with Wyndham perpetually poised on the brink of matrimony with one girl or another), went down better. Having bought the British rights, he commissioned an adaptation, and on 24 May 1874 starred at London's Court Theatre in *Brighton*, the Anglicized version. It became Wyndham's standby. His Criterion company was in 1882–3 the first English troupe ever to reach America's west coast. He took them to the United States three more times between 1889 and 1910. In 1887 and 1888 he acted Garrick in German (his own translation), first in Silesia and Berlin, then at St Petersburg before Tsar Alexander III and the tsarina. For an English actor–manager of those days Wyndham's international experiences were exceptionally long and diverse.

From 1905 to 1919 Wyndham served as president of the Actors' Benevolent Fund. He excelled at after-dinner speaking, and belonged to the Garrick, Savage, Beefsteak, Eccentric, and Green Room clubs, though seldom went. He also joined the Players' Club of New York. Only on the stage, however, could he relax. Keeping fit with long walks, he got away with playing Young Marlow in Goldsmith's *She Stoops to Conquer* at the age of fifty-three and the scarcely less youthful Charles Surface in Sheridan's *The School for Scandal* at sixty-nine; but by the time of his final appearance, as Garrick at the New Theatre on 16 December 1913, he had long suffered from aphasia, which severely affected his work, and may explain the absence (unusual for an actor–manager) of an autobiography. Occasional outbursts against subordinates, including women, belied his reputation for gallantry.

Wyndham's wife, from whom he separated in 1897, died in January 1916. On 1 March of the same year, at Chertsey register office, Surrey, he married Mary Charlotte *Moore

(1861–1931), the daughter of Charles Moore, a parliamentary agent, and for a quarter of a century the widow of the dramatist James Albery. She was twenty-four years his junior. An entrancing actress of comedy, she had become his leading lady in 1885, his mistress soon after, and in 1896 his business partner. Wyndham, suffering from pneumonia and senility, died on 12 January 1919 at their home, 43 York Terrace, Regent's Park, London, survived by her and a son (Howard Wyndham, who was also a theatre manager) and daughter from his first marriage. He was buried on 16 January at Hampstead cemetery, and left a fortune of nearly £200,000.

Both Wilde and Shaw thought Wyndham the ideal comedy actor. His stage persona was the model for John Worthing in Wilde's *The Importance of Being Earnest* and the young heroes of Shaw's *The Philanderer*, *Arms and the Man*, *Candida*, and *You Never Can Tell*. He was then nearing sixty. Those plays were offered to Wyndham in preference to other managers—with the exception of *The Importance of Being Earnest*, which was dangled first before Charles Hawtrey, who could not afford it. Wyndham instantly snapped it up, but later, thinking his schedule was full, gave it to George Alexander. Had he ever produced plays of Wilde's or Shaw's, with himself in the parts conceived for him, Sir Charles Wyndham might have figured more considerably in the development of drama. As it was, he left other monuments: Wyndham's Theatre, and the establishment of English farce in a full-length form.

MICHAEL READ

Sources W. Trewin, *All on stage: Charles Wyndham and the Alberys* (1980) · Lady Wyndham [M. Moore], *Charles Wyndham and Mary Moore* (privately printed, Edinburgh, 1925) · T. E. Pemberton, *Sir Charles Wyndham* (1904) · F. T. Shore, *Sir Charles Wyndham* (1908) · W. L. Courtney, 'Sir Charles Wyndham: an appreciation', *Daily Telegraph* (15 Jan 1919) · G. Rowell, 'Wyndham of Wyndham's', *The theatrical manager in England and America: player of a perilous game*, ed. J. W. Donohue, jun. (1971), 189–213 · G. Rowell, 'Criteria for comedy: Charles Wyndham at the Criterion Theatre', *British theatre in the 1890s: essays on drama and the stage*, ed. R. Foulkes (1992), 24–37 · *Daily Telegraph* (13 Jan 1919) · *The Era* (15 Jan 1919) · *Manchester Guardian* (13 Jan 1919) · *Morning Post* (13 Jan 1919) · *The Times* (13 Jan 1919) · J. M. Bulloch, 'Sir Charles Wyndham's family, the Culverwells', *N&Q*, 168 (1935), 290–94

Archives BL, letters to George Bernard Shaw, Add. MS 50553 · U. Nott. L., letters to Lady Galway | FILM BFI NFTVA, performance footage

Likenesses Barraud, cabinet photographs, 1888, NPG · Barraud, carte-de-visite, 1888, NPG · J. Pettie, oils, exh. RA 1888 (as David Garrick), Garr. Club · H. Furniss, caricature, pen-and-ink drawing, *c*.1905, NPG · Ash, caricature, mechanical reproduction, NPG; repro. in *VF* · Barraud, photograph, NPG; repro. in *Men and Women of the Day*, 2 (1889) · M. Beerbohm, caricature, drawing, V&A · M. Beerbohm, caricature, drawing, U. Texas · L. Bertin, woodbury-type photograph, NPG · S. P. Hall, pencil sketch, NPG · Langfier, cabinet photograph, NPG [*see illus.*] · photogravure photographs, NPG

Wealth at death £197,035 14s. 11d.: probate, 4 April 1919, *CGPLA Eng. & Wales*

Wyndham, Francis (*d.* 1592), judge, was the second son of Sir Edmund Wyndham of Felbrigg, Norfolk, and his wife, Susan, daughter of Sir Roger Townshend of Raynham. The high standing of his family locally no doubt aided Wyndham in establishing his career as a magistrate and lawyer in both Norfolk and London. Having spent time in Cambridge, probably at Corpus Christi College, Wyndham appears in the records of Lincoln's Inn as a master of revels in 1554. He was called to the bar in 1560, became a bencher in 1569, and served as autumn reader in 1572. In 1570 he married Elizabeth, the daughter of Lord Keeper Nicholas *Bacon (1510–1579), solidifying a connection centred on his alliance in county politics with his brother-in-law, Nathaniel *Bacon (*d.* 1622) of Stiffkey. Wyndham was a justice of the peace in Norfolk from 1569, and during the same period served on a number of other commissions, including an arbitration between Yarmouth and the Cinque Ports (1575). He was a member for Norfolk in the parliament that sat from 1572 to 1583, making his mark primarily by serving on committees.

Maintaining a lifelong connection with Norwich, Wyndham was retained as counsel to the city in 1563, became steward in 1570, and held the position of recorder from 1575 until he resigned in 1580. In London, meanwhile, he became a serjeant-at-law in 1577, and in 1579 he was appointed a justice of the common pleas in the face of strong competition. As a judge he presided over the trials for treason of John Somerville in 1583 and William Parry in 1585, and his advice was sought on that of Mary of Scotland. He was also one of the judges appointed to hear cases in chancery during the vacancy in the lord keepership between November 1591 and May 1592.

While Wyndham evidently enjoyed the confidence of Lord Burghley, his defence of Norfolk against maladministration and his support for puritan causes brought him into bitter conflict with Lord Hunsdon, the lord chamberlain and lord lieutenant of Norfolk. Wyndham used his legal knowledge to attack informers and patentees, and in 1588 he complained to Burghley about military preparations and the way local levies of money were being spent. In 1591 he and Edward Coke gave a charge at a meeting of quarter sessions that was a notable salvo in the quarrel between the common lawyers and the ecclesiastical courts. Criticizing the use of the oath *ex officio*, they invited grand jurors to make presentments of local church court officials. Offended by the relentless affronts to his administration, Hunsdon counter-attacked at a meeting of the judges and the privy council in 1591. He suggested that the queen suspected Wyndham and other judges of sympathizing with the Martin Marprelate tracts and claimed that the criticisms of the church courts had left the bishops in doubt about how to proceed in their jurisdiction.

Wyndham died on 18 June 1592 at his house (the Committee House) in St Peter Mancroft, Norwich, and was buried a month later in the parish church there, where a monument was erected depicting him in his judicial robes. He accumulated extensive properties in Norfolk, including Pentney Priory, with the manors of Ashwood, Pentney, and West Bilney. He had no children, and appointed his countrymen Sir Francis Gawdy and Edward Coke supervisors of his will. Elizabeth Wyndham survived her husband and about 1593 married Robert Mansell of Norwich and died by 1617.

CHRISTOPHER W. BROOKS

Sources *DNB* · A. Hassell Smith, *County and court: government and politics in Norfolk, 1558–1603* (1974) · HoP, *Commons, 1558–1603*, 3.668–70 · will, PRO, PROB 11/80, fols. 109–12*v* · W. P. Baildon, ed., *The records of the Honorable Society of Lincoln's Inn: the black books*, 1–4 (1897–1902) · J. Morice, 'A just and necessarie defence of a briefe treatise made ageinst generall oathes', 1594, LPL, MS 234, fol. 99 · Baker, *Serjeants*

Likenesses effigy, St Peter Mancroft, Norwich · oils (possibly after monument), Guildhall, Norwich · watercolour on vellum, Raverringham Hall, Norfolk

Wealth at death wealthy, but not quantifiable; Committee House in Norwich valued at £400; other property in Norfolk, but no precise valuation: will, PRO, PROB 11/80, fols. 109–112*v*

George Wyndham (1863–1913), by George Charles Beresford, 1903

Wyndham, George (1863–1913), politician and author, was born in London on 29 August 1863, the eldest son in the family of two sons and three daughters of Percy Scawen Wyndham (1835–1911), politician and country gentleman, and his wife, Madeline Caroline Frances Eden (*d.* 1920), the daughter of Sir Guy *Campbell, first baronet. He was educated at Eton College, and the Royal Military College, Sandhurst, from where he was commissioned into his father's regiment, the Coldstream Guards. He served in Egypt during the Suakin campaign of 1885: he later played a prominent role as an officer of the Cheshire yeomanry. On 7 February 1887 he married Sibell Mary, Countess Grosvenor (1855–1929), daughter of Richard George Lumley, ninth earl of Scarbrough, and widow of Victor Alexander Grosvenor, Earl Grosvenor. They had one child, Percy Lyulph, born in December 1887, who followed his father into the Coldstream Guards, and who was killed in action in September 1914. Wyndham's stepson was Hugh Richard Arthur, second duke of Westminster (1879–1953).

Military and parliamentary service were engrained in the traditions of the Wyndham family, as in other tory county dynasties. Wyndham followed his father into both the army and the House of Commons, and served as MP for Dover from 1889 until his death in 1913. Ireland was also important to the family: Wyndham had connections with the Irish landed gentry (his uncle the second Lord Leconfield owned 44,000 acres in counties Clare and Limerick, while the seventh earl of Mayo, proprietor of 7500 acres in Kildare and co. Meath, was his cousin). He had a rather more distant, if much better advertised, connection with Irish insurgency (his maternal great-grandfather was Lord Edward FitzGerald, the rebel leader of 1798). Wyndham's first political employment came in 1887, as private secretary to Arthur Balfour (chief secretary for Ireland, 1887–91): later, when returned as MP for Dover, he served as Balfour's parliamentary private secretary. Wyndham was associated with the successes of Balfour's administration: he received a training in Balfourian strategy, and made personal connections that would serve him later in his ministerial career.

The Souls and literature But Wyndham possessed other social and political networks, most notably in the Souls, the aristocratic clique formed in 1887 in reaction to the philistinism and heartiness of the prince of Wales's Marlborough House set. Wyndham was central to the Souls, partly because of his family connections, and partly because of his association with Balfour, who was the guru of the group. The Souls were a carry-over from the Crabbet Club, which revolved around Wyndham's cousin Wilfrid Scawen Blunt: but Wyndham—and also his sisters Pamela and Mary [*see* Charteris, Mary Constance]—were much more central to the life of the new connection than of the old. The Souls valued intellectual dexterity, physical beauty, and (though this was less explicit) high-born connections; and Wyndham satisfied each of these requirements in full. His brightness was never much in doubt, although the diffuseness of his thought and his tireless loquacity wearied his friends. His good looks caught the notice of fellow Souls and other admiring contemporaries: Margot Asquith thought Wyndham and Lord Pembroke 'the handsomest of the Souls' (Asquith, *Autobiography*, 185). However, this handsomeness was complemented by a rather dandified and jumpy manner, which irritated even his social peers, and certainly alarmed backbench tories: Arthur Lee observed that

> the rank and file [of the party] had never cottoned to his dandified and over-polished parliamentary manners, which led one old Tory member to mutter in my hearing after one of Wyndham's Burke-conscious perorations, 'damn that fellow, he pirouettes like a dancing master'. (*Good Innings*, 128–9)

Wyndham once claimed, amid the disappointments of his later career, that he was 'an artist who has allowed himself to drift into politics' (Mackail and Wyndham, 2.656). His literary and artistic ambitions have indeed sometimes been seen as an alternative to, or diversion from, his political life. This is probably a misperception. Wyndham's literary efflorescence certainly came when the tories were out of office (1892–5) and when he had been apparently passed over for ministerial preferment (1895–8). He was an admirer of W. E. Henley, and wrote extensively for Henley's newspapers, including the imperialist weekly the *National Observer*. Wyndham also contributed to Henley's series of Tudor Translations, for which he edited North's *Plutarch* (1895). Wyndham shared some of Henley's broader artistic vision, including a passion for the work of Auguste Rodin (he commissioned a portrait bust from the sculptor). His other literary or literary–historical endeavours included an edition of *The Poems of Shakespeare* (1898), *Ronsard and La Pléiade* (1906), and an address, given as lord rector of the University of Edinburgh, *The Springs of Romance in the Literature of Europe* (1910). His *Essays in Romantic Literature* were published posthumously, in 1919.

Much of this work expressed an artistic vision which was well integrated within Wyndham's political philosophy. He was a tory romantic, who unblushingly believed that the sum of human happiness was as great in the feudal era as in his own day. He identified the governing idea of his own age as 'cosmopolitan individualism': this had suffocated the last vestiges of romance and the feudal ideal at the beginning of the nineteenth century. Cosmopolitan individualism was associated with a surfeit of democracy and with the vagaries of international finance: Wyndham was suspicious of both, and saw democracy as a precursor to 'Caesarism' and capitalism as antagonistic to his vision of Englishness. His anger at 'cosmopolitan finance' came, especially in later life, to be expressed in directly antisemitic terms. After Henley's death (in 1903) he found a receptive and stimulating audience for such speculations with Hilaire Belloc and (to a lesser extent) G. K. Chesterton.

Chief secretary for Ireland Imperialism, for Wyndham, was the only serious alternative to the rising menace of socialism. When (in 1898) he was appointed as under-secretary at the War Office, he had the opportunity to meld this imperialist vision with his extensive knowledge of the army. He had, in addition, two clear political opportunities: first, his superior, the secretary of state, was the marquess of Lansdowne, and thus in the House of Lords; and second, the outbreak of the Second South African War (in October 1899) gave his own relatively junior office an enhanced significance. The scale of the conflict, and the reverses experienced by the British in the early months of the war, made Wyndham's position at first both administratively arduous and politically vulnerable. But he defended British policy with some skill, and one speech in particular—delivered in the Commons on 1 February 1900—commanded widespread admiration.

This enhanced parliamentary standing, combined with mounting British military successes on the front, meant that Wyndham was assured of ministerial promotion. In October 1900 he was appointed chief secretary for Ireland. He was still outside the cabinet (the lord lieutenant for Ireland, Earl Cadogan, held onto this palm); but his new office was widely recognized as one of the most difficult in British politics. And his appointment—at the age of thirty-seven—identified him as one of the high-fliers among a remarkably talented younger generation of Conservative politicians.

In Ireland Wyndham followed, broadly, the strategies laid down by Balfour. Some attention was paid to the social and economic welfare of the Irish people, and determined efforts were made to advance land purchase, a central feature of Balfour's administrative programme in the late 1880s. Wyndham's tenure of the Irish Office coincided with a period of centrist political speculation, both in Britain and in Ireland: a land conference, held in 1902 and uniting landlord and tenant representatives, together with the Irish Reform Association were perhaps the most tangible expressions of this—short-lived—consensual impulse in Irish politics. The report of the land conference, which advocated an ambitious extension of the land purchase programme, formed the basis for the Land Act of 1903, known as the Wyndham Act: the measure has been seen as Wyndham's main achievement in Ireland, and it therefore marked the summit of his political career. He believed that the Land Act represented the first of a series of legislative coups by which he and his supporters would resolve many of the central dilemmas of Irish political life. The confidence was characteristic, but misplaced. Efforts to establish a Catholic university foundered in 1904. In the summer of 1904 the Irish Reform Association produced a proposal outlining a limited form of administrative devolution for Ireland. This was soon disowned by Dublin Castle. But Wyndham's senior civil servant, Sir Antony MacDonnell, had been involved in the discussions that had preceded the publication of these documents; and it came to be believed that the chief secretary himself lay behind the initiative. Denounced by Irish Unionists (who saw a betrayal of principle) and by many Irish nationalists (who feared that a relatively consensual British administration might demoralize the national cause), Wyndham resigned office in March 1905. The devolution affair hung like a pall over the remaining years of his political career.

Wyndham's fall raises wider issues concerning his administration of the Irish Office. He once declared, playfully, that Ireland 'can be governed only by conversation and arbitrary decisions' (*Letters*, 2.6). It seems clear that he could be an incurably verbal and sometimes cussed minister. The editor of his letters, J. W. Mackail, remarked that Wyndham was a good talker but a bad listener; Margot Asquith complained perceptively that Wyndham was

> never in proportion, because he cannot take in a [third] of what he gives out—and when he allows you to state your point of view you find yourself modifying your difference so as not to come out too crudely against his many long, keen, almost perorated convictions.   (Margot Asquith's diary, 28 March 1896)

Wyndham was passionate about ideas in politics and literature. He was a man with a very keen sense of honour; but this was also compatible with a sometimes cavilling or excessively legalistic approach to the truth: Margot Asquith, again, thought him 'not only nerveless but not rigidly straight' (ibid., 28 Oct 1905). There seems little doubt in fact that Wyndham debated the idea of devolution with political friends in 1903-4, even if he finally (and belatedly) grasped the political impossibility of the venture.

Wyndham had also, as a tory romantic, some bonds of

empathy with aspects of Irish nationalism: he was certainly fired by his reading of Irish history. He had a vaulting self-confidence: 'I shall pass a Land Bill, reconstruct the Agriculture Department and Congested Districts Board, stimulate Fishing and Horse-breeding; and revolutionize Education', he announced, without conscious irony, in January 1902 (Mackail and Wyndham, 2.436). In addition he had an almost Gladstonian sense of mission with regard to Ireland: the Irish, he declared in October 1903, 'do still believe in me, and tremble towards a belief in the Empire because of their belief in me' (*Letters*, 2.79). But for those Irish who already professed a belief in the empire, he and his administration had little time. Romantic Irish nationalism was closer to Wyndham's most fundamental convictions than the evangelical vulgarities, the urban grubbiness, and the commercial banalities of Ulster Unionism.

Wyndham's obsessive and passionate temperament, combined with the thinness of his political skin, meant that the last months of his time in Ireland were marred by a physical and mental breakdown: Arthur Balfour was 'seriously alarmed' by the belief that Wyndham's nerves had been 'utterly ruined', and that he was 'really hardly sane' (Balfour to Sibell Grosvenor, January 1905, Wyndham MSS). He had pursued his desperate crusade through an adrenalin-charged and oppressive routine of work: he had come to rely increasingly on drink. By the time of the devolution crisis, he had no resources upon which to draw. His racked health was the occasion, though not the reason, for his resignation from office. This very public collapse in health (regardless of the serious political questions involved) caused lasting damage to his credibility.

Disillusion and death   Wyndham survived the electoral decimation of the tories in December 1905, and was active in campaigning for his party throughout the later Edwardian period. He was increasingly attracted by tariff reform, and—while publicly loyal to Balfour—he accepted very largely the Chamberlainite prescription of protectionism and socially progressive legislation. He enjoyed a renewed prominence in 1910–11, by virtue of his significant role in the tory election campaigns in January and December 1910, and his very trenchant opposition to the Parliament Bill. He was a convinced die-hard, and was bitterly disappointed by the Lords' ultimate collapse in August 1911. Thereafter disillusionment with parliamentary politics set in. Many of his later letters betray a frustration with the fudges and compromises of political life, and an increasing thirst for action: 'Let there be murder, or even rape, rather than vague aspiration, and no end achieved. Let something be done—even to DEATH', he wrote in January 1913 (Mackail and Wyndham, 2.733). His wider cultural and temperamental affinities are illustrated by such declarations, which invite comparison (for example) with the language of advanced Irish nationalist ideologues such as Patrick Pearse. He lost faith in the future, believing that English civilization was threatened with collapse: analogies between England in 1912–13 and Constantinople in 1453 were evoked.

Wyndham once (in January 1910) defined the 'two poles of political existence' as being the frontier and the home (Mackail and Wyndham, 2.651). Having fought and lost on different political and geographical frontiers, he turned in his last months to the home. He devoted attention to the family estate (some 4000 acres in Wiltshire) and to the problems and responsibilities of the middling landowner. Public frustrations were balanced by private joys. His beloved son was married (to Diana Lister) on 17 April 1913. His last days were spent in Paris, in the company of Lady Plymouth, and among the bookshops and restaurants of that city. He died suddenly, from a blood clot, around 10 p.m. on 8 June 1913, in his rooms at the Hôtel Lotti on the rue Castiglione, Paris.

Wyndham's reputation remains entrapped within the mire of the devolution controversy. It is possible that, had another ministerial opportunity come his way, he might have combined the bitter lessons supplied by the Irish Office with his genuine political talents to good effect: there is some evidence for believing that this was his own hope. Perhaps, however, the flaws in his judgement were irredeemable. To the end his intellect blossomed with political ideas, but remained largely barren of any wider strategic sense. Margot Asquith, an admittedly unforgiving arbiter, perhaps hit the mark when, in assessing Wyndham, she decreed that 'an imagination that can work out and foresee the results of big measures is far rarer than the imagination that creates nymphs and moons and passions and patriotism' (Margot Asquith's diary, October 1904).   ALVIN JACKSON

Sources   J. W. Mackail and G. Wyndham, *The life and letters of George Wyndham*, 2 vols. (1925) • *Letters of George Wyndham, 1877–1913*, ed. G. Wyndham, 2 vols. (privately printed, Edinburgh, 1915) • M. Egremont, *The cousins: the friendship, opinions and activities of Wilfrid Scawen Blunt and George Wyndham* (1977) • J. A. Thompson, 'George Wyndham: toryism and imperialism', in J. A. Thompson and A. Mejia, *Edwardian conservatism: five studies in adaptation* (1988) • A. Jackson, *The Ulster party: Irish unionists in the House of Commons, 1884–1911* (1989) • A. Gailey, *Ireland and the death of kindness: the experience of constructive unionism, 1890–1905* (1987) • E. H. H. Green, *The crisis of conservatism: the politics, economics and ideology of the Conservative Party, 1880–1914* (1995) • C. T. Gatty, *George Wyndham: recognita* (1917) • J. Biggs-Davison, *George Wyndham: a study in toryism* (1951) • Margot Asquith's diary, priv. coll. • M. Asquith, *The autobiography of Margot Asquith*, 2 vols. (1920–22) • *A good innings: the private papers of Viscount Lee of Fareham*, ed. A. Clark (1974) • Eaton Hall, Chester, Wyndham MSS • Burke, *Peerage* (1937) [Leconfield] • WWW • CGPLA Eng. & Wales (1913)

Archives   Eaton Hall, Chester, MSS (copies in PRO NIre.) • NRA, family corresp. • NRA, priv. coll., corresp. and papers | BL, corresp. with Arthur James Balfour, Add. MSS 49803–49806 • BL, letters to G. K. Chesterton, Add. MS 73241, fols. 95–105 • BL, corresp. with Sir Charles Dilke, Add. MSS 43916–43920 • BL, corresp. with Mary Gladstone, Add. MS 46241 • Bodl. Oxf., Selborne MSS, corresp. with Lord Selborne • Glos. RO, letters to Sir Michael Hicks Beach • Herts. ALS, letters mostly to Lady Desborough • Knebworth House, letters to Lord Lytton • NA Scot., corresp. with A. J. Balfour • U. Birm., corresp. with Austen Chamberlain • U. St Andr., corresp. with Wilfrid Ward

Likenesses   B. Stone, photograph, 1902, NPG • G. C. Beresford, photographs, 1903, NPG [*see illus.*] • A. Rodin, bronze bust, 1904, Tate collection • A. Rodin, bronze bust, 1904, Hugh Lane Gallery of Modern Art, Dublin • H. Speed, oils, 1914, Dover town hall • Elliott & Fry, photograph, NPG; repro. in *Our Conservative and Unionist*

Statesmen, vol. 2 · B. Partridge, group portrait, caricature, ink drawing, NPG; repro. in *Punch* (6 May 1903) · Spy [L. Ward], caricature, lithograph, NPG; repro. in *VF* (20 Sept 1900) · photograph, NPG · plaster cast of death mask, NPG
Wealth at death £205,584 3s. 8d.: probate, 25 June 1913, *CGPLA Eng. & Wales*

Wyndham, George O'Brien, third earl of Egremont (1751–1837), art patron, agriculturalist, and philanthropist, was born on 18 December 1751 and baptized on 9 January 1752 at St Margaret's, Westminster. He was the eldest son of Charles *Wyndham, second earl of Egremont (1710–1763), statesman, patron, and collector, and his wife, Alicia Maria Carpenter (1729?–1794), a noted beauty and daughter of George, second Baron Carpenter (1695–1749). Styled Lord Cockermouth (1751–63), he was educated at Pampellone's school in Wandsworth, Westminster School, Eton College, and Christ Church, Oxford, where he matriculated on 30 June 1767. He was only eleven when his father—at that time secretary of state for the southern department—died suddenly, on 21 August 1763, whereupon he succeeded to vast ancestral property including Petworth House, Sussex, and a great collection of pictures and sculpture founded in the seventeenth century and extended by his father. He was elected fellow of the Royal Society on 7 December 1797 and fellow of the Society of Antiquaries on 3 April 1800.

In his youth Egremont's reputation was as a man of fashion; he made two grand tours of Europe between 1770 and 1772. His expensive—and by his own account—predominantly Francophile tastes embraced courtesans, one of whom, Mlle Du Thé, he imported to London. In July 1780 the 'handsome' Egremont's engagement to Lady Maria Waldegrave was broken off (Walpole, *Corr.*, 25.68, 75). The impediment was Egremont's philandering and, perhaps, the realization that he valued his freedom above a respectable alliance; his 'shy and taciturn' nature may also have been relevant (Leslie, 1.164). About 1784 Elizabeth Ilive (1769–1822) became his principal mistress and the unofficial chatelaine of Petworth, where she pursued her artistic and scientific interests. As 'Mrs Wyndham' she gave birth to seven illegitimate children, but their marriage, on 16 July 1801—which produced a legitimate daughter who died in infancy—provoked a permanent separation in 1803, due to his continued infidelities. His amours were notorious; in 1828 Thomas Creevey wrote of 'my Lord's Seraglio', noting that he had a 'very numerous Stud' (a *double entendre*, since he also had a racing stable of 300 horses; *Life and Times*, 274). His liaison with Elizabeth Milbanke, Viscountess Melbourne (1752?–1818), reputedly produced one prime minister—the second Viscount Melbourne—and the wife of another—Lady Palmerston. He is also known to have had four children with Elizabeth Fox, 'Mrs Crole' (*c.*1770–1840).

In 1794, Lord Egremont sold Egremont House, Piccadilly, and many of the pictures collected for it by his father and moved the bulk of the ancestral collection—previously displayed in London—to Petworth. In 1828 Creevey was amazed by 'the *immensity* of pictures on the ground floor of the house, and, as I was informed, all the rooms

George O'Brien Wyndham, third earl of Egremont (1751–1837), by Thomas Phillips

above are full of them. Then they are all mixed up together, good and bad … and he [the earl] is perpetually changing their places' (*Life and Times*, 277). Despite the miscellany the pictures were usually arranged symmetrically in well-balanced tiers, and Egremont was 'continually oscillating … or wandering about the enormous house in all directions' (*Greville Diary*, 1.470) 'making occasional observations upon the pictures and statues' (Maxwell, 1.164). According to Charles Greville, Egremont had a 'highly cultivated' mind and was 'remarkably acute, shrewd and observant, and in his manner blunt without rudeness, and caustic without bitterness'. His 'temper, disposition, and tastes' were unsuited to politics or high office, and he preferred to 'revel unshackled in all the enjoyments of private life, both physical and intellectual, which an enormous fortune, a vigorous constitution and literary habits placed in abundant variety before him'. His 'munificence was equal to his wealth', and Petworth was 'rarely unvisited by some painter, or sculptor, many of whom he kept in almost continual employment'. It was 'open to all his friends … provided they did not interfere with his habits or require any personal attention at his hands … [and] was consequently like a great inn. Everybody came when they thought fit, and departed without notice or leave-taking' (*Greville Memoirs*, 4.24–6).

The Petworth estate was also thrown open for the enjoyment of the local populace, who played 'bowls and cricket on the lawn before the house' (Simond, 2.250) and who were entertained to regal feasts for up to 6000 people. To his friend the painter C. R. Leslie, Egremont was 'the most munificent and at the same time least ostentatious nobleman in England' (Leslie, 1.102). He disliked 'ribbons and higher titles' (Wyndham, 223) and his official appointments, by choice, were few. He was lord lieutenant of Sussex (1819–35) and a member (from 1793) of the board of agriculture (characteristically refusing the presidency, in 1798). Hailed as 'one of the fathers of modern English agriculture' (Lower, 90), he was the friend of the famous agriculturalist Arthur Young, whose son the Revd Arthur Young continually cites Egremont's innovations in growing crops, breeding livestock, and developing machinery in his *General View of the Agriculture of the County of Sussex* (1808). Egremont was an employer on the grandest scale, encouraging the local development of roads, and especially canals, which were dug by his own labourers. The connection of Sussex with London was achieved largely by Egremont's investment in, and chairmanship of, the Wey, Rother, and Arun navigations; this was a considerable boost to the local economy, doubling the value of many estates, which were able more easily to transport their produce to the London market. Egremont was also a model landlord, planting alternative crops in times of agricultural depression, and feeding and clothing the destitute. He also financed the emigration of the poor to Canada, smallpox inoculation, and the construction of hospitals, almshouses, and schools.

Egremont lent numerous pictures to the pioneering exhibitions of the British Institution, despite being occasionally critical of its policies; 'On matters of art', wrote Leslie, 'Lord Egremont thought for himself' (Leslie, 1.105). He bought Old Masters and antique sculpture, as well as commissioning landscapes, subject pictures, and portraits (including thirty-three by Thomas Phillips). Between 1795 and 1837 he added 263 pictures by 66 painters (Walker, 12). His prime concern was to encourage inspiration rather than imitation, and the Petworth north gallery (extended twice by Egremont in 1824–7) is filled with works inspired by modern and classical literature, the Bible, mythology, and history executed by British and American painters (including Allston, Blake, Clint, Fuseli, Haydon, Leslie, Northcote, Opie, Phillips, Reynolds, Thomson, and Westall) and British and Irish sculptors (including Carew, Flaxman, Nollekens, Rossi, and Westmacott). They are top-lit and displayed among antique sculpture, Old Masters, portraits, and landscapes, as recorded in the 1835 inventory by H. W. Phillips (V&A, MS 86 FF67), which reveals that Turner's twenty paintings were confined to the north gallery and the long dining-room, or carved room. This is the famous Grinling Gibbons room, doubled in size by the third earl, who commissioned four Turner landscapes that were fixed in the panelling among elaborate carvings (partly by Egremont's own carver, Jonathan Ritson), portraits, Shakespearian

scenes by Clint and Leslie, and antique sculpture (a typically eclectic arrangement and one of only two instances in which Turner painted for a specific location). The third earl's patronage of British sculptors was even more exceptional. In 1819 Sir Francis Chantrey declared that commissions for 'an ideal subject, or anything from poetry' were not given to English artists and that 'the only sculptor among us who has been employed on anything of the kind is Flaxman, who has a commission from Lord Egremont' (Jones, 198). Flaxman's *St Michael Overcoming Satan* (c.1817–26, the subject taken from *Paradise Lost*) was sculpted for the north gallery, Egremont providing advice on its composition. From 1822 or 1823 the Irishman John Edward Carew worked almost exclusively for Egremont, and in 1831 became his in-house sculptor, creating 'colossal works' of 'heroic size' (Carew, *The Following Report*, 240, 242), for which a second sculpture gallery was constructed at the end of Egremont's life. Carew sued Egremont's executors for the astonishing sum of £50,000, despite his patron's largesse. Carew's claims were rejected by the court and he was declared bankrupt, confirming Egremont's prediction that 'you will come to the dogs' (ibid., 402). Turner, Constable, and Leslie made private sketches recording their impressions of Petworth, among them Turner's views of artists at work in the old library, still sometimes called 'Turner's Studio'. When Turner was painting in his locked studio only Egremont was allowed to enter, but Turner was once fooled by Chantrey's imitation of 'Lord Egremont's peculiar step, and the two distinct raps on the door by which his lordship was accustomed to announce himself' (Jones, 122).

Egremont's annual income was estimated at £100,000, and he owned over 110,000 acres. He was said to have 'spent in the course of sixty years in acts of charity and liberality, the enormous sum of one million two hundred thousand pounds, or about £20,000 per annum' (Lower, 90). He died, of an inflammation of the trachea, at 'about eleven on the night' of 11 November 1837 (Carew, *The Following Report*, 170) at Petworth, where 'all the inhabitants were present' at his funeral on 21 November together with the 'many artists who had enjoyed his patronage' (Leslie, 1.162). He was buried at Petworth. He was succeeded in the earldom by his nephew George Francis Wyndham (1789–1845), on whose death the title became extinct. Petworth and its estates passed to Egremont's eldest natural son, George Wyndham (1789–1869), who was created Lord Leconfield in 1859.

Petworth is the third earl's enduring monument. At his death there were (and remain) more than 600 pictures in the collection, including twenty Van Dycks. Egremont's seventy-five-year reign at Petworth has been called its golden age, and to Benjamin Robert Haydon he was 'literally like the sun' (*Diary*, ed. Pope, 3.167). Most famous as the patron of Turner and a host of British painters and sculptors, Egremont also shone as an enlightened and philanthropic landowner, an innovative farmer, an expert horticulturalist and silviculturalist, an amateur scientist, and a breeder of livestock and racehorses (he was one of the most successful owners in the history of the turf, winning both the Derby and the Oaks five times). His personal papers—apparently including most of the records of his patronage and collecting—were destroyed soon after his death, but numerous accounts of his enigmatic character and multifarious activities remain.

CHRISTOPHER ROWELL

Sources The Greville diary, ed. P. W. Wilson, 2 vols. (1927) • The Greville memoirs, ed. H. Reeve, new edn, 8 vols. (1888) • C. R. Leslie, Autobiographical recollections, ed. T. Taylor, 2 vols. (1860) • Creevey's life and times: a further selection from the correspondence of Thomas Creevey, born 1768, died 1838, ed. J. Gore (1934) • The Creevey papers, ed. H. Maxwell, 2 vols. (1903) • The diary of Benjamin Robert Haydon, ed. W. B. Pope, 5 vols. (1960–63) • J. E. Carew, Report of the trial of the cause Carew against Burrell, bt. and another, executors of the late earl of Egremont (1840) • J. E. Carew, The following report of the proceedings which have since taken place in the court for the relief of insolvent debtors (1842) • M. Egremont, 'The third earl of Egremont and his friends', Apollo, 122 (1985), 280–87 • M. Butlin, M. Luther, and I. Warrell, Turner at Petworth: painter and patron (1989) • C. Rowell, Petworth House (1997) • H. A. Wyndham, A family history, 1688–1837: the Wyndhams of Somerset, Sussex and Wiltshire (1950) • R. Walker, 'The third earl of Egremont, patron of the arts', Apollo, 58 (1953), 11–13 • A. Laing, The Oxford companion to J. M. W. Turner, ed. E. Joll, M. Butlin, and L. Herrmann (2001), 84–6 • M. A. Lower, The worthies of Sussex (1865) • L. Simond, A journal of a tour and residence in Great Britain, during the years 1810 and 1811 (1815) • G. Jones, ed., Sir Francis Chantrey RA: recollections of his life, practice and opinions (1849) • Walpole, Corr. • H. W. Phillips, 'Catalogue of the pictures in Petworth House', 1835, V&A, MS 86 FF67 • C. Rowell, I. Warrell, and D. Blayney Brown, Turner at Petworth (2002) [exhibition catalogue, Petworth House] • C. Rowell, 'Turner at Petworth: the 3rd earl of Egremont's carved room restored', Apollo, 155 (2002), 408–47 • P. McEvansoneya, 'Lord Egremont and Flaxman's St Michael overcoming Satan', Burlington Magazine, 143 (2001), 351–9

Archives NRA, priv. coll., corresp. and papers | BL, corresp. with Lord Holland, Add. MS 51725 • BL, corresp. with second earl of Liverpool, Add. MSS 38249–38295, passim • BL, letters to A. Young, Add. MSS 35127–35133, passim • CKS, corresp. with Lord Romney relating to Riddell estates and chancery suits • E. Sussex RO, corresp. with Lord Gage • NL NZ, Turnbull L., letters to Gideon Algernon Mantell • RA, corresp. with Ozias Humphry, mainly relating to purchase of a Raphael • Som. ARS, letters to J. Flaxman and others, DD/WY bx 186 • W. Sussex RO, letters to duke of Richmond • W. Yorks. AS, Leeds, estate corresp. of Lord Thomond on Egremont's behalf with Sir W. Robinson

Likenesses G. Hayter, group portrait, oils, 1820–23 (The trial of Queen Caroline, 1820), NPG • W. Ward, mezzotint, pubd 1825 (after J. J. Masquerier), BM, NPG • F. Chantrey, pencil drawing, 1829, NPG • L. Lucas, oils, 1834, Petworth House, Sussex • E. H. Baily, statue, 1840, Petworth church, Sussex • J. E. Carew, marble bust, Petworth House, Sussex • G. Clint, oils, Petworth House, Sussex • G. Clint, oils, Brighton Art Gallery • G. Garrard, bust, Petworth House, Sussex • T. Phillips, oils, Petworth House, Sussex [see illus.] • T. Phillips, oils, NPG • P. C. Wonder, group portrait, oils (study for Patrons and lovers of art, 1830), NPG

Wealth at death annual income £100,000; owned over 100,000 acres; reported to have given away £20,000 p.a.: GEC, Peerage (1982); Lower, The worthies; Wyndham, Family history

Wyndham, Henry Penruddocke

Wyndham, Henry Penruddocke (1736–1819), topographer, elder son of Henry Wyndham (1709–1780) of Compton Chamberlayne, Wiltshire, and St Edmund's College, The Close, Salisbury, and his wife, Arundel (1717–1780), daughter of Thomas Penruddocke of Compton Chamberlayne, was born at Compton Chamberlayne on 4 June 1736. There were no daughters of the marriage. Sir Wadham Wyndham was his great-grandfather. Pen, as he was called in family circles, was educated at Eton and, following family custom, at Wadham College, Oxford, from where he matriculated as gentleman commoner on 21 February 1755. On 22 March 1759 he was created MA.

With his relation Joseph Wyndham, and William Benson Earle of Salisbury, Wyndham set out on the grand tour in 1765. Theirs was not the usual party of very young men with a tutor. Pen Wyndham was by this time twenty-nine and had already demonstrated some learning as an antiquary. After leaving England in September, the party visited France, Italy, and Sicily, and returned via Geneva and the Netherlands to reach England in September 1767.

Pen Wyndham's letters to his father (now in the Wiltshire and Swindon Record Office, Trowbridge) show him very critical of much of what he saw. As well as the normal litany of complaints about the inns, food, and predations of the local people, he showed the family whig traits by complaining about the despotic rulers of the lands he passed through, and compared the poverty and ignorance of their people with the happy freedoms of the British. He enjoyed seeing John Wilkes at Dijon and was in Rome at the time of James Stuart's funeral, noting with pleasure that the pope did not accord him the dignity of a king. Wyndham's reaction to the sights of Europe was also mixed. Having found Versailles 'quite disgusting' and the cathedral of Siena 'rather gawdy' (cited in Wyndham, A Family History, 192, 198), he drew more pleasure from the Roman antiquities. He went home unmoved by much of what he had seen, and convinced that English life and manners were superior in many respects.

On 18 October 1768 Wyndham married Caroline, daughter and heir of Edward Hearst of The Close, Salisbury. They had five sons and two daughters, of whom four sons survived.

The Wyndham family had great influence in Salisbury and Pen, who lived for many years at St Edmund's College, The Close, the family home in Salisbury, was elected a freeman of the city on 15 March 1761, was mayor of Salisbury in 1770–1, and sheriff of Wiltshire in 1772. In 1794 he commanded a troop of cavalry raised in Salisbury and from 1812 he was MP for Wiltshire. He sat as a whig in the family tradition, but rarely attended the house and is thought never to have contributed to debate. His lack of interest caused disquiet in the county and he retired from politics in 1812.

Wyndham was more a topographer than a politician. In 1774 he visited Wales, and in the following year he published anonymously A Gentleman's Tour through Monmouthshire, and Wales. He revisited the area in 1777, and in 1781 published his Tour through Monmouthshire and Wales, declaring his authorship of the work. He was accompanied on his journey of 1777 by the Swiss watercolourist Samuel Hieronymus Grimm, whose works illustrated the account. Grimm was one of many artists attracted by the romantic Welsh landscape in the second half of the eighteenth century, and his views are among the most important products of the tour. The Tour is a historical and antiquarian work, intended to persuade English tourists to visit the region. There is some very sketchy information about accommodation and routes, but the bulk of the work describes the antiquities and dramatic landscapes of the region. The handsome volume shows that Wyndham had a real interest in his subject.

Wyndham was anxious to produce a county history of Wiltshire, which lagged behind other counties in having such a work. He published *Wiltshire, Extracted from the Domesday Book* (1788), which he hoped might stimulate such a work, and offered £100 towards its cost, but his attempts failed. He published some other minor works of topography and archaeology. He was elected a fellow of the Society of Antiquaries on 6 February 1777 and a fellow of the Royal Society on 9 January 1783.

Wyndham's most celebrated publication remains his *Diary of the Late George Bubb Dodington* (1784). Dodington had left his property to his cousin, Thomas Wyndham of Hammersmith, who in 1777 left it all to Henry Penruddocke Wyndham, requesting in his will that he 'not print or publish any of them, but those that ... may ... do honour to his memory' (*Diary*, vii–viii). Pen Wyndham says of the diary that 'although it may reflect a considerable degree of honour on his Lordship's abilities, yet ... it shows his political conduct ... to have been wholly directed by the base motives of avarice, vanity and selfishness' (ibid., viii). Notwithstanding this, Wyndham persuaded himself that he was justified in publishing the diaries, a decision which ensured his own fame, as the diaries went through numerous editions.

Wyndham died at Salisbury on 3 May 1819 and was buried in the family vault in St Edmund's Church.

ELIZABETH BAIGENT

Sources R. G. Thorne, 'Wyndham, Henry Penruddocke', HoP, Commons, 1790–1820 · H. A. Wyndham, *A family history, 1688–1837* (1950) · Foster, *Alum. Oxon.* · GM, 1st ser., 89/1 (1819), 484–5 · PRO, PROB 11/1617, fols. 371v–375v · H. P. Wyndham, *Diary of the late George Bubb Dodington* (1781) [preface] · H. P. Wyndham, *A tour through Monmouthshire and Wales* (1781) · P. Joyner, *Samuel Hieronymus Grimm: views in Wales* (1983) · DNB
Archives U. Cal., Los Angeles, William Andrews Clark Memorial Library, journals · Yale U., Beinecke L., description of journey from York to Rutland · Yale U., Beinecke L., journal of tour through Wales and Monmouthshire | Devizes Museum, Wiltshire, Wiltshire Archaeological and Natural History Society, letters to William Cunnington · Wilts. & Swindon RO, corresp. with his father and family bills
Wealth at death see will, PRO, PROB 11/1617, fols. 371v–375r

Wyndham, Sir Hugh

Wyndham, Sir Hugh (1602/3–1684), judge, was the eighth son of Sir John Wyndham (1558–1645) of Orchard Wyndham, Somerset, and his wife, Joan (1564/5–1633), daughter of Sir Henry Portman. Sir Wadham *Wyndham was his younger brother. He was admitted to Lincoln's Inn on 19 March 1622, being called to the bar on 16 June 1629. There is also evidence that he studied for a time at Wadham College, Oxford, for caution money was received on 10 July 1622, and repaid only on 8 December 1624. He also contributed a Latin poem, 'Camdeni insignia' (1624), and on 2 January 1643 was created MA of Oxford by royal warrant.

At some point, probably in the late 1630s or early 1640s, Wyndham married Jane (d. 1648?), daughter of Sir Thomas Wodehouse, second baronet, of Kimberley, Norfolk, and sister of Sir Philip Wodehouse, third baronet. They had two sons and three daughters. Only two daughters survived to adulthood: Blanche, who married in 1657 Sir Nathaniel Napier, second baronet; and Rachel, who married in 1663 Lord Digby, later third earl of Bristol.

Wyndham became a serjeant-at-law on the authority of parliament in February 1654. He was appointed a judge of common pleas on 30 May 1654 by Protector Oliver Cromwell, and he was appointed to the commission of oyer and terminer charged with dealing with the Penruddock rising in 1655. At the Lincoln assizes in July 1658 he gave a charge criticizing the clergy for refusing the sacrament to those requiring it: 'it being a tyranny beyond that of prelacy for a minister to deny it to such as will not pin their faith to his sleeve' (*CSP dom.*, 1658–9, 194–5). As a result several ministers were presented and subsequently petitioned Oliver Cromwell against him. Wyndham was reappointed by Richard Cromwell on 27 November 1658. He was not reappointed by parliament in May 1659, but appointed on 13 July until 20 November 1659, and reappointed on 19 January 1660. He was not reappointed a judge at the Restoration, which was not surprising given that he held that taking up arms against the supreme magistrate *de facto* was high treason under a statute of Edward III. However in June 1660 he was made a serjeant-at-law, this time by royal authority. On 20 June 1670 he was appointed a baron of the exchequer, and he was knighted on the 28th. On 22 January 1673 he was transferred to be a judge of common pleas.

As his second wife, Wyndham married Elizabeth, daughter of Sir William Minn of Woodcott, Surrey, the widow of Sir Henry Berkeley of Wimondham, Leicestershire. They had no children. Thirdly he married (licence 12 April 1675) Katherine (1637/8–1693), daughter of Thomas Fleming of North Stoneham, Hampshire, widow of Sir Edward Hooper of Beveridge, Dorset. They had no children. Wyndham died, in his eighty-second year, on 27 July 1684 while on circuit at Norwich, a published elegy referring to 'the good, the just, the learned Windham's dead' (*An Elegy*). He was buried at Silton, Dorset. His will, covering estates in Dorset and Somerset, left his lands to his two daughters.

STUART HANDLEY

Sources Sainty, *Judges* · Baker, *Serjeants* · H. A. Wyndham, *A family history*, 1: 1410–1688: the Wyndhams of Norfolk and Somerset (1939), 210–11, 252–3, 280 · Foss, *Judges*, 7.195–7 · J. Hutchins, *The history and antiquities of the county of Dorset*, 3rd edn, ed. W. Shipp and J. W. Hodson, 4 (1874), 105 · CSP dom., 1658–9, 194–5 · Fifth report, HMC, 4 (1876), 146, 154–5 · will, PRO, PROB 11/378, sig. 171 · P. M. S., *An elegy on the much lamented death of the Right Honourable Sr. Hugh Windham* (1684) · R. B. Gardiner, ed., *The registers of Wadham College, Oxford*, 1 (1889), 67 · J. L. Chester and G. J. Armytage, eds., *Allegations for marriage licences issued by the dean and chapter of Westminster, 1558 to 1699; also, for those issued by the vicar-general of the archbishop of Canterbury, 1660 to 1679*, Harleian Society, 23 (1886), 239 · W. P. Baildon, ed., *The records of the Honorable Society of Lincoln's Inn: admissions*, 1 (1896), 189 · Foster, *Alum. Oxon.*
Likenesses J. M. Wright, oils, c.1670–1674, GL · J. van Nost, statue, c.1684–1692, St Nicolas Church, Silton, Dorset
Wealth at death estates in Dorset and Somerset left to two daughters: will, PRO, PROB 11/378, sig. 171

Wyndham, Sir Hugh (1624–1671), politician, was the eldest son of Sir Edmund Wyndham MP (1600/01–1681) of Kentsford, St Decumans, Somerset, and his first wife, Christabella (d. 1658), daughter of Hugh Pyne MP of Cathanger, Somerset. His mother was governess to the infant Prince Charles, which led to later comments that Wyndham was Charles II's 'foster brother, they both sucked the same milk' (BL, Harley MS 7020, fol. 38). Wyndham was an active royalist in the civil war, receiving a knighthood at some date before 21 July 1645. He was captured at the siege of Bridgwater in 1645, and may possibly have entered Trinity College, Cambridge, on 8 October 1646. If he did enter the university, he soon abandoned his studies, for in April 1649 he was on board *The Guinea* when it was captured. Wyndham seems to have been disguised as a common sailor, and escaped to resume his royalist activities on board the *Santa Teresa*. When this ship was captured, he was sent to Pendennis Castle charged with high treason. While a captive he met his future wife, Joan (1631–1694), daughter of Sir Francis Drake, first baronet, whom he married on 4 February 1650 at Buckland. The Drakes had important parliamentarian connections and Wyndham was able to compound for his estates, selling a small parcel of land before paying off the fine in January 1652. Wyndham was not involved in royalist plotting before the Restoration.

Wyndham was elected for Minehead at the 1661 general election. He was an opponent of religious toleration and in 1664 he was noted as a court adherent. On 16 October 1667 Wyndham complained to the Commons about the conduct of Lord Chief Justice Kelyng at the Somerset assizes. Wyndham, acting as chairman of the grand jury, and his fellow jurors were confronted by a case in which they found that a man had been killed *per infortunium* (through misfortune). Kelyng refused to accept this and ordered them to consider finding a bill either *billa vera* (well founded) or *ignoramus*. When the jury refused to alter their findings Kelyng fined some of them £20 a man, and bound them to good behaviour and to appear before the king's bench. Wyndham replied that he would claim his privilege as an MP. The Commons investigated Wyndham's complaint, and on 13 December Kelyng was brought before the bar of the Commons. Upon hearing what Kelyng had to say Wyndham remarked that although the lord chief justice 'had given him some unhandsome passionate speeches, as that he was the head of a faction and that he would make [him] know he was now his servant' (*Diary of John Milward*, 169), since he had taken no notice of it in his defence he would forget it and forgive him. This no doubt helped the chief justice, for although the Commons passed resolutions affirming that the fining and imprisonment of jurors was illegal, it took no further action against the judge.

Wyndham remained a court supporter, remarking on 18 February 1668 that the new Triennial Bill was 'brought in, I had almost said with impudence' (Grey, 1.82) by Sir Richard Temple, third baronet. Following a petition of 10 December 1668 Wyndham was appointed customer of Bridgwater on 4 January 1669. Wyndham's father married for a second time in November 1669, and shortly beforehand he seems to have made over Kentsford to his son. Wyndham himself, however, was not a well man, and on 22 May 1671 his father wrote to Secretary of State Williamson informing him of his imminent journey to Somerset 'on account of the dangerous sickness of my son' (*CSP dom.*, 1671, 260). Wyndham did not recover, dying on 20 July. He was buried at St Decumans, and his epitaph complained that he had 'lost fortune, blood [and] gained nought but scars' (Wyndham, 264) during his sufferings for the crown in the civil wars. His only son, Edmund, succeeded to the estate, dying childless in 1698.

STUART HANDLEY

Sources I. Cassidy, 'Wyndham, Edmund', 'Wyndham, Sir Hugh', HoP, *Commons, 1660–90* · H. A. Wyndham, *A family history, 1410–1688* (1939), 201–2, 227–36, 263–72 · J. L. Vivian, ed., *The visitations of the county of Devon, comprising the herald's visitations of 1531, 1564, and 1620* (privately printed, Exeter, [1895]), 301 · E. F. Eliot-Drake, *The family and heirs of Sir Francis Drake*, 2 vols. (1911), vol. 1, pp. 341, 377–405; vol. 2, pp. 13–15 · *The diary of John Milward*, ed. C. Robbins (1938), 88–9, 162–9, 206 · A. Grey, ed., *Debates of the House of Commons, from the year 1667 to the year 1694*, new edn, 10 vols. (1769), vol. 1, pp. 67, 82 · M. A. E. Green, ed., *Calendar of the proceedings of the committee for compounding … 1643–1660*, 5 vols., PRO (1889–92), 964–6 · *CSP dom.*, 1649–50, 129, 235; 1668–9, 97; 1671, 260 · W. A. Shaw, ed., *Calendar of treasury books*, 3, PRO (1908), 176 · *JHC*, 9 (1667–87), 4, 20, 22, 34–6 · Venn, *Alum. Cant.* · BL, Harley MS 7020, fol. 38

Wyndham, Sir John (d. 1502). *See under* Wyndham, Thomas (d. 1554).

Wyndham, John. *See* Harris, John Wyndham Parkes Lucas Beynon (1903–1969).

Wyndham, John Edward Reginald, first Baron Egremont and sixth Baron Leconfield (1920–1972), civil servant and author, was born at Windsor, Berkshire, on 5 June 1920. He was the third child and second son in the family of three sons and one daughter of Edward Scawen Wyndham (1883–1967) and his wife, Gladys Mary, daughter of FitzRoy James Wilberforce Farquhar. His father, the fifth son of the second Baron Leconfield, was a soldier and a substantial landowner at Edmonthorpe, Leicestershire, where John Wyndham was brought up. After schooling at Eton, Wyndham went to Trinity College, Cambridge, in 1939; but his studies were interrupted by the outbreak of war. Rejected as an active serviceman because of defective eyesight, Wyndham volunteered for work in the civil service. In 1940 he was appointed private secretary to the parliamentary under-secretary in the Ministry of Supply, Harold Macmillan.

Wyndham's new boss had seemed a political misfit until the outbreak of war, but after this his ascent was rapid. The new relationship had been forged at a fortunate moment, but it would have resulted in a close friendship at any time. Like Macmillan, Wyndham was a cultured man; but he was light-spirited—even flippant at times—while Macmillan was prone to depression. The latter's biographer has described Wyndham as being something like 'a surrogate son' (Horne, 1.155); but this seems to reflect the age difference rather than the nature of the relationship. Wyndham habitually referred to Macmillan

John Edward Reginald Wyndham, first Baron Egremont and sixth Baron Leconfield (1920–1972), by Walter Bird, 1963

as his 'master' and he devoted most of his career in public life to his service. Yet if Wyndham owed his political prominence to Macmillan, the emotional dependence seems to have run if anything the other way.

In 1942 Macmillan went to the Colonial Office as parliamentary secretary, and Wyndham moved with him. In the following year the minister won the promotion which provided the launching pad for his post-war success. He was sent by Churchill to allied force headquarters in Algiers, as minister resident (with cabinet rank). Inevitably Wyndham accompanied him, and the pair went on to northern Italy and Greece as the war progressed. Macmillan's *War Diaries* (which he dedicated to Wyndham's memory) testifies to his friend's influence and efficiency. Despite a hectic travelling itinerary Wyndham ensured that the minister was always comfortably housed; and with his extensive social contacts he was a reliable source of gossip. In 1945 he was awarded the MBE for his services.

At the end of hostilities in Europe Wyndham briefly worked with Macmillan at the Air Ministry during Churchill's caretaker government. Since Wyndham was still a civil servant the fall of the Churchill government after the general election of 1945 imposed a breach in the partnership. Wyndham spent some months in Washington, as assistant secretary to the British treasury delegation headed by R. H. Brand which negotiated a loan for post-war reconstruction. When Keynes secured the deal Wyndham was offered a new post, this time in Egypt. But

evidently he was yearning for the old life, and he resigned from the civil service at the age of twenty-five. He was soon on his travels with Macmillan again, visiting the Middle East and India in 1947.

On his return Wyndham married, on 24 July 1947, a cousin, Pamela Wyndham-Quin, whom he had only recently met. She was the youngest daughter of Captain Valentine Maurice Wyndham-Quin RN, younger son of the fifth earl of Dunraven. They had two sons and one daughter. As he later confessed, he was bored by retirement, and in the same year he joined the Conservative Research Department based in Old Queen Street near the House of Commons. Although much of the routine was humdrum, this job in its own way turned out to be as interesting as his previous work. The greater part of Wyndham's day would be spent finding material for speeches in the Commons; but there was also an opportunity to float ideas of his own. The Conservative liaison committee, which provided a regular forum for discussions between the parliamentary party and Conservative central office, was originally suggested by Wyndham.

The company at Old Queen Street was also rewarding. Among his colleagues in the department were Iain Macleod, Reginald Maudling, and Enoch Powell. Typically, Wyndham seems to have got on well with this strangely assorted trio, who all found seats at the general election of 1950. Their cerebral approach to politics complemented Wyndham's early exposure to diplomacy, and with his connections he would have made an excellent parliamentary recruit for the Conservatives. But he did not follow their example, probably because he knew his future was in the House of Lords. He had to leave the Conservative Research Department in 1952 to manage the family estates following the death in that year of his uncle, the third Baron Leconfield, who had been predeceased by his only son. Wyndham's next uncle, who became fourth baron, was childless, and Wyndham's own elder brother had been killed at El Alamein so he stood eventually to succeed to the peerage after his father. In the meantime Wyndham inherited the third baron's extensive properties, mainly in Sussex and Cumberland, and the tax problems they raised.

At the research department Wyndham had found attack far more enjoyable than the defence he was called upon to conduct after the Conservatives returned to office in 1951. But in 1955 Harold Macmillan became foreign secretary, and his old friend agreed to re-enlist as his private secretary. The partnership was broken again when Macmillan became chancellor of the exchequer in the following year; Wyndham was negotiating with the treasury over death duties on his inheritance and therefore could not work in that department. By May 1957 a deal had been struck, involving the magnificent art collection at Wyndham's main residence, Petworth House in Sussex, which established for the first time the acceptance by the nation of works of art in lieu of death duties. Macmillan was now prime minister. Once again the call came, and Wyndham responded, this time staying with Macmillan until the latter's resignation in 1963.

Sir (Sidney) Harold Evans, first baronet, Macmillan's public relations adviser, recalled Wyndham as 'tall, willowy, stooping, and peering through spectacles with exceptionally thick lenses', and described his role as 'a combination of ADC, observer and commentator, contact man, cheerful but determined "fixer", good companion and court jester' (Evans, 31). In addition to Wyndham acting as 'personal friend and professional adviser' (DNB), Macmillan also enjoyed the loyal support of his principal private secretaries, Tim Bligh and Philip de Zulueta. Probably these official advisers had more influence over government policy, but Wyndham was still an essential part of the operation, helping out during Macmillan's foreign trips and, when necessary, undertaking discreet diplomatic negotiations with senior ministers. Wyndham was shrewd in his surveys of press opinion, based on his numerous Fleet Street contacts. In February 1963 Mark Chapman-Walker, general manager of the News of the World, warned Wyndham that a rival newspaper was in possession of a potentially damaging story concerning the minister at war, John Profumo. Chapman-Walker, who had worked at Conservative central office, was an old friend, and his information was reliable; but although Wyndham sent an urgent memorandum to the prime minister the scandal was allowed to fester.

Macmillan survived the Profumo affair, but his government was seriously tarnished and he resigned in October 1963. Although their professional relationship was broken Macmillan remained on close terms with Wyndham, who was created first Baron Egremont in the resignation honours (November 1963) and later succeeded his father as sixth Baron Leconfield. He devoted the rest of his life to managing his estates and to writing. He wrote a column in The Spectator, and in 1968 produced a lively memoir, Wyndham and Children First. Additional volumes were planned at the time of his death at Petworth House on 6 June 1972. Macmillan, who likened Wyndham's services to him to those of Montagu Corry to Disraeli, wrote that 'his wit, his charm, his originality and sometimes almost eccentricity, delighted all who knew him' (DNB).

MARK GARNETT

Sources DNB · The Times (7 June 1972); (9 June 1972); (19 June 1972) · Lord Egremont [J. E. R. Wyndham], Wyndham and children first (1968) · R. Lamb, The Macmillan years, 1957–1967: the emerging truth (1995) · H. Macmillan, War diaries: politics and war in the Mediterranean, January 1943 – May 1945 (1984) · A. Horne, Macmillan, 1: 1894–1956 (1988) · A. Horne, Macmillan, 2: 1957–1986 (1989) · H. Evans, Downing Street diary: the Macmillan years, 1957–1963 (1981) · Burke, Peerage (2000) · J. Ramsden, The winds of change: Macmillan to Heath, 1957–1975 (1996)
Likenesses W. Bird, photograph, 1963, NPG [see illus.] · F. de Henriques, bust, priv. coll. · A. John, drawing, priv. coll.
Wealth at death £203,519: probate, 22 June 1972, CGPLA Eng. & Wales · £1,373,000: probate, 7 July 1972, CGPLA Eng. & Wales

Wyndham, Mary. See Scott, Mary (bap. 1703, d. 1744).

Wyndham, Robert Henry Sharp (1814–1894), actor and theatre manager, was born at Dublin of 'highly respectable' parents on 8 April 1814. He made his first appearance on the stage at Salisbury in 1836, when he paid the manager of the local theatre £20 in return for being allowed to play the long-studied role of Norval in John Home's Douglas, and, as he afterwards admitted, 'make a fool of himself'. Six years later he played Romeo at Birmingham to the Juliet of Ellen Tree (later Ellen Kean), and was then seen in Paris at the Tuileries before Louis-Philippe, as Colonel Freelove in the comedietta A Day after the Wedding. During 1844 he was jeune premier at the Adelphi, Glasgow, and the following year he fulfilled his ambition of making a prominent début at Edinburgh. He went there to fill the place vacated by Leigh Murray when the latter moved to London, and appeared as Sir Thomas Clifford in The Hunchback to the Julia of Helen Faucit at the Theatre Royal, Shakespeare Square, and made a favourable impression. Among the parts allotted to him during the season were Mercutio in Romeo and Juliet, Charles Surface in The School for Scandal, and Rashleigh Osbaldistone in Rob Roy.

In 1846 Wyndham married Rose (1819–1901), the daughter of William Saker of London, an actor, and the sister of the actor Edward Saker. She was a talented actress, and developed a special aptitude for training juvenile troupes in ballet and pantomime. In May 1849 Wyndham appeared at the Adelphi Theatre, Edinburgh, as Orlando in As You Like It, and in December 1851 he opened the Adelphi as actor–manager in succession to William Henry Murray, who took his farewell of the Edinburgh stage in October 1851. The old management concluded with The Rivals, and Wyndham opened with The School for Scandal, playing Charles Surface, and followed the comedy up with Gulliver, arranged as a pantomime, for which his wife trained the children. Wyndham coped admirably with the arduous task of being leading comedian, acting manager, and stage manager in one. Later his difficulties were increased by the onset of a transitional period in the theatre when the old stock company system collapsed, theatrical stars were lured from London to Edinburgh, and touring companies received a boost from the growth of rail travel.

In 1852 Wyndham produced Macbeth with scenery that was thought to surpass any yet seen upon the Edinburgh stage; the same year he was seen as Claude Melnotte for his wife's benefit, as Robert in Robert the Bruce, as Rashleigh Osbaldistone, and, for his own benefit, as Henry, Prince of Wales, in Henry IV. When the Adelphi was destroyed by fire in May 1853, Wyndham leased the Theatre Royal, and opened in June 1853 in the part of Charles Bromley in Simpson & Co., which he followed up with Captain Absolute in The Rivals. The Adelphi, renamed the Queen's, was reconstructed during 1854–5, and Wyndham for a time managed both theatres concurrently, but the Royal remained his headquarters until it was demolished in May 1859. J. L. Toole was one of Wyndham's first stars at his new house; he appeared at the Royal in July 1853 in J. B. Buckstone's A Dead Shot. Henry Irving, fresh from his début at Sunderland, made his first appearance as a member of Wyndham's company in February 1857, as Gaston, Duke of Orleans, in Richelieu. He remained with the Wyndhams as juvenile lead until September 1859, playing often in a pantomime and two dramas in the course of a single evening. In May 1857 Wyndham revived *Macbeth*, with Rose Wyndham as Lady Macbeth and Irving as Banquo. A final performance at the Royal, doomed to destruction in order to make way for a post office, took place in May 1859, when Wyndham played Sir Charles Pomander in *Masks and Faces*; Rose Wyndham played Peg and Irving played Soaper. Wyndham then returned to the Queen's (the old Adelphi), and opened his first season there in June 1859, as Felix Featherley in *Everybody's Friend*. This was followed by *The Heart of Midlothian*, in which Montagu Williams and F. C. Burnand appeared as 'distinguished amateurs', and then *London Assurance*, with Williams as Charles Courtly, Irving as Dazzle, and Mrs Wyndham as Lady Gay Spanker. The Queen's was burnt down in January 1865 during the run of the Christmas pantomime, *Little Tom Tucker*. It was rebuilt and reopened as the Royal under Wyndham's management in December 1865, in time for the next annual pantomime, *Robin Hood*. A presentation was made by the citizens of Edinburgh to Wyndham in 1869, in recognition of his services to the theatre. In 1871 he revived a number of Waverley dramas on the occasion of Scott's centenary; but this form of entertainment showed a sadly diminished success. In February 1875, during a run of *Jack and the Beanstalk*, the Royal shared the fate of its predecessors, the Queen's and the Adelphi, when it also burnt down.

Wyndham made his last appearance on the Edinburgh stage on the opening night of the new Edinburgh Theatre, Castle Terrace, in December 1875. A year later he retired from his long and, on the whole, highly successful management. On his retirement in February 1877 he was entertained at a banquet at the Balmoral Hotel, Edinburgh, which was presided over by Sir Alexander Grant. Wyndham then left his house in Forth Street, Edinburgh, and settled at 64 Sloane Street, Chelsea, London, where he renewed a friendship with Henry Irving. He became a familiar figure at the Garrick Club. He died at his house in Sloane Street on 16 December 1894, and was buried in Brompton cemetery on 20 December 1894. He was survived by his wife, two daughters, and a son, Frederick Wyndham, who later became co-lessee of the Lyceum Theatre, Edinburgh, the Theatre Royal in Newcastle upon Tyne, and the Theatre Royal in Glasgow.

As an actor Wyndham was versatile and excelled in light comedy and the delineation of Irish characters. He was also a connoisseur of paintings and works of art and had collected in his house in Edinburgh a large number of pictures, oils and watercolours, which fetched him an unexpectedly large sum of money when sold before his departure for London. In his house in London, too, he gathered a large and valuable collection.

Rose Wyndham proved an able assistant in all her husband's ventures, and as an actress was equally at home in the roles of Peg Woffington, Helen MacGregor, and Lady Teazle as in those of Lady Macbeth and Queen Katharine in *Henry VIII*. She played many leading parts under her husband's management, enjoyed a long retirement with him, and died at the age of eighty-two, on 19 October 1901.

THOMAS SECCOMBE, *rev.* NILANJANA BANERJI

Sources *The Era* (22 Dec 1894) · *The Scotsman* (17 Dec 1894) · *The Stage* (20 Dec 1894) · *Era Almanack and Annual* (1896) · *Era Almanack and Annual* (1902) · P. Hartnoll, ed., *The concise Oxford companion to the theatre* (1972) · *The Athenaeum* (29 Dec 1894), 904 · J. C. Dibdin, *The annals of the Edinburgh stage* (1888) · P. Fitzgerald, *Sir Henry Irving: a record of twenty years at the Lyceum*, new edn (1895)
Likenesses H. Collins, oils, 1872, Scot. NPG
Wealth at death £60,861 15s. 8d.: resworn probate, July 1895, CGPLA Eng. & Wales

Wyndham, Thomas (*d.* 1554), naval officer and navigator, the only son of Sir Thomas Wyndham (*d.* 1522) of Felbrigg, Norfolk, and his second wife, Elizabeth, daughter of Sir Henry Wentworth of Nettlestead and widow of Sir Roger Darcy of Denbury, Essex, gentleman of the chamber to Henry VII.

Thomas's grandfather **Sir John Wyndham** (*d.* 1502) was knighted at the battle of Stoke on 16 June 1487. Implicated in the conspiracy of Edmund de la Pole, earl of Suffolk, he was convicted of treason on 2 May 1502 and executed on 6 May. His first wife, Thomas's grandmother, was Margaret, fourth daughter of John Howard, duke of Norfolk (*d.* 1485). Their eldest son and heir was Sir Thomas Wyndham of Felbrigg (*d.* 1522), who served in the naval war with France in 1512–13 and rose to become a vice-admiral and royal councillor. He first married, by 1505, the daughter of his father's widow. This was Eleanor, daughter and coheir of Richard Scrope of Upsall, Yorkshire, and Eleanor Wyndham, *née* Scrope (*d.* 1505/6), of Carrowe. The eldest son of Sir Thomas and Eleanor, Sir Edmond Wyndham (*d.* 1569), of Felbrigg, was in the household first of Cardinal Thomas Wolsey and then of Thomas Howard, duke of Norfolk (*d.* 1554). He was three times sheriff of Norfolk and Suffolk between 1537 and 1550, knight for the shire in the 1539 and 1559 parliaments, and the wealthiest of the Norfolk gentry. His younger brother, Sir John, established the Wyndhams of Orchard, Somerset. His only sister, Mary, married Erasmus Paston (*d.* 1540) from whom the earls of Yarmouth were descended. Their half-brother, Thomas, is the navigator.

Thomas Wyndham was well provided for at his father's death, although some seven years were required to clear the estate of the numerous legacies. In his lifetime Sir Thomas had been a notable improver of the family fortune. He redeemed the forfeited estate from Henry VII, paying £2816 13s. 4d., paid £1000 to complete the purchase of Yorkshire properties from his first wife's coheirs, and acquired additional lands in his own right. His youngest son, Thomas, was bequeathed the manor of Weighton, Yorkshire, upon reaching twenty-one, and half the manors of Bowking and Alseford, for which Sir Thomas had purchased the reversion. In addition the executors were to purchase for Thomas lands valued at £666 13s. 4d., 'to bye a marriage for him of Inheritaunce' (will, PRO, PROB 11/21, fol. 20). Finally Sir Thomas arranged his son's education. Thomas was to be sent to a northern Italian university as soon as the wars in the region permitted this, 'And in the meane tyme to the universitie of Leveyn [Louvain] and to continue his lernyng there in humanitie and cevyle [law] till he be of the age of xxi years or longer yf he

Thomas Wyndham (d. 1554), by Hans Eworth, 1550

will after that age at his owne charge' (fol. 20v). His school-master, William Chamberlayn, then resident in the Wyndham household, was contracted to attend upon his young charge overseas for a term of five years. Thomas was entrusted to the general care of his father's executors, which included 'my singuler goode lorde', Thomas Howard, earl of Surrey (d. 1554), the supervisor, Thomas Howard, duke of Norfolk (d. 1524), and 'my moost singuler good Lord' Cardinal Wolsey, 'beseching his grace to be especiall good lord to my wife and my Children ... likewise as I have always found him myn especiall good lorde in tyme of my lyfe' (fols. 20v, 21). Moreover Thomas's mother remarried, to John Bourchier, earl of Bath (d. 1539). His career appeared to be on a firm footing.

Thomas Wyndham first appeared in the public record in the years 1536–40, as a servant of Thomas Cromwell employed in Ireland. It would appear, therefore, that this is another instance where a family associated with Wolsey transferred service to the king's secretary. He was among a number of young English gentry who established outstanding military reputations in the mid-century wars. In October 1539 Wyndham was sent as a captain of one hundred soldiers to serve under James Butler, earl of Ormond, and experienced sharp fighting. Ill health brought the captain back to England in the following March, and on 20 June he was awarded the estate of the former monastery of Chicksand, Bedfordshire. In February 1541 Wyndham, described as of London, gentleman, borrowed the sum of £300 from the London merchants Christopher Campion and Robert Bower. The first notice of service at sea was in 1544, when he commanded a west country vessel in the

North Sea against Scotland. In 1545 he was placed in command of a larger ship on the Solent, but when he and William Hawkins seized the Spanish *Santa Maria de Guadeloupe* the privy council required restitution and, when that order was ignored, compensation of £380. Surety was provided by the soldier, naval commander, member of parliament, and later an executor of Wyndham's estate, John Chichester (d. 1568). New allegations of piracy appeared sporadically over the next seven years. In 1547 Wyndham was appointed master of naval ordnance and vice-admiral of the English fleet in the North Sea for Protector Somerset's invasion of Scotland. He was active at sea and on land, fortifying Dundee, burning Balmerino Abbey, and constructing Wyndham's bulwark at Haddington. In July 1548 he was one of those who attempted, in vain, to relieve Haddington. His correspondence at sea in the winter of 1547–8 revealed great sympathy for the underclothed, malnourished seamen in his squadron. By March 1550 Wyndham was in London, when ordered to carry north by post horse the three pledges required for the peace negotiations. In December of this year he was rewarded for his military services with a yearly annuity of £50 for life. Although he retained the office of master of naval ordnance until his death Wyndham's attention now turned to maritime exploration.

In 1551 Wyndham became captain and part owner of the *Lion* of London, a substantial seagoing ship of 150 tons. A syndicate of speculators, which included Wyndham's nephew, the soldier Sir John Lutterell (d. 1551) of Somerset, and Sebastian Cabot's son-in-law, Henry Ostrich, hired him in 1551 to open direct commerce with Morocco. His success on the *Lion* led in the following year to his second expedition of three ships financed by prominent London merchants. This returned from Safi and Tenerife with a cargo of dates, almonds, sugar, and molasses. These voyages established the steady routine English trade with Barbary. The next initiative, and the last of Wyndham's career, cost him his life. The captain became an investor and the commander of the first expedition to equatorial west Africa. Financed by several of the promoters of 1552, and assisted by Edward VI's government, the fleet consisted of the *Primrose*, a vessel of 300 tons leased from the crown, the *Lion*, and a royal pinnace, the *Moon*, also leased, with a total complement of approximately 160. Wyndham was assisted by a Portuguese lieutenant, Antonio Anes Pinteado, and a pilot, Francisco Rodriques. The commander began assembling the crews in April 1553. He had already secured permission to use the royal prerogatives of impressment and purveyance. The death of the king on 6 July almost spelt disaster. At this time the *Primrose* was at Portsmouth preparing for sea. It, and Wyndham, may have become briefly involved in the efforts of Northumberland's regime to prepare a naval force, for the expedition was stayed in July by order of Queen Mary and on 25 July the new privy council summoned Wyndham and other politically compromised individuals to London. Wyndham's half-brother, Sir Thomas, Lord Darcy of Chiche (d. 1558), had been one of Northumberland's closest supporters; in July 1553 Wyndham lent Darcy £600 for unspecified purposes. However, on 30 July the expedition was given permission to depart; it sailed on 12 August. The route took the fleet by way of Madeira and the Cape Verde Islands to the River Sess on the Malagueta Coast to trade for pepper, then to the Gold Coast, and finally to Benin in the quest for gold and further pepper. An unidentified fever decimated the party which had travelled upriver on the *Moon* to trade, and spread to the ships. With the death of Wyndham at the bight of Benin, and others, probably in February or early March of 1554, the expedition hastily departed for home. There were insufficient healthy sailors to bring back to England all three vessels, so the *Lion* was abandoned on the coast. The *Primrose* reached Plymouth in early August; the fate of the *Moon* is unknown. Fewer than forty individuals survived the voyage. The expedition may have made a profit for investors, but the deceased commander was blamed for mismanagement, disregarding the advice of Pinteado, and taking the fateful decision to abandon some merchants on the river.

Wyndham's last will and testament, written prior to sailing, on 14 July 1553, was eventually proved on 12 June 1555 for the estate's principal executor, Thomas, Lord Darcy. Wyndham had already broken ties with his family's customary patrons: in November 1552 he and Lord Thomas Howard were bound in recognizances of £333 6s. 8d., each to be of good behaviour to each other. His heirs were a son, Henry, and two daughters, one of whom, Margaret, later married Sir Andrew Luttrell of East Quantoxhead, Somerset. Wyndham's estate was in financial difficulty, and his residence, Marshwood Park, Somerset, was sold. His wife is not mentioned in his will and she can be presumed deceased; she has never been identified.

J. D. Alsop

Sources R. Eden, *The decades of the newe world of West India* (1955) · correspondence by Thomas Wyndham, PRO, SP 50/2–3 · will, PRO, PROB 11/37, fol. 200v [Thomas Wyndham] · will, PRO, PROB 11/21, fols. 19v–21Av [Sir Thomas Wyndham] · R. Tong, 'Captain Thomas Wyndham', *History Today*, 7 (1957) · P. E. H. Hair and J. D. Alsop, *English seamen and traders in Guinea, 1553–1565* (1992) · LP Henry VIII · APC, 1542–54 · H. A. Wyndham, *Wyndham: a family history* (1939) · R. W. Ketton-Cremer, 'Thomas Windham of Felbrigg', *Norfolk Archaeology*, 27 (1941), 417–28 · will, PRO, PROB 11/15, fols. 6v–7 [Eleanor Wyndham] · will, PRO, PROB 11/29, fols. 178–178v [George Wyndham] · will, PRO, PROB 11/34, fols. 248–248v [Sir John Lutterell] · will, PRO, PROB 11/66, fols. 59v–60v [Dame Margaret Lutterell]
Archives PRO, state papers, Scotland, SP 50/2–3
Likenesses H. Eworth, portrait, 1550, priv. coll. [*see illus.*]

Wyndham, Thomas, Baron Wyndham (1681–1745), lord chancellor of Ireland, was born at Norrington, near Salisbury, Wiltshire, on 27 December 1681; he was the fourth and youngest but the eldest surviving son of John Wyndham of Norrington, a colonel in the army and MP for Salisbury in 1681 and 1685, and his wife, Alice, daughter of Thomas Fownes. He was the grandson of Sir Wadham *Wyndham, a justice of the king's bench from 1660 to 1668. Wyndham was educated at the cathedral school, Salisbury, possibly spent some time at Eton College, and matriculated from Wadham College, Oxford, on 19 November 1698. He does not appear to have taken a degree but he was admitted of Lincoln's Inn on 11 July 1698

and called to the bar on 9 May 1705. While a law student he suffered from smallpox.

Wyndham was appointed recorder of Sarum in 1706, and in 1724 he was appointed chief justice of the court of common pleas in Ireland, in succession to Sir Richard Levinge—a very easy post, according to Hugh Boulter, archbishop of Armagh. He was elected a bencher of Lincoln's Inn, and sworn of the Irish privy council on 9 December 1724. On the death of Lord Chancellor West in November 1726 Wyndham was appointed to succeed him, having been recommended by Boulter, who actively sought to prevent native Irish being appointed to such posts. Boulter also successfully sought the appointment of his protégé the poet Ambrose Philips to be Wyndham's secretary, prompting Alexander Pope to pen the line 'Still to one bishop Philips seem[s] a wit?' (*Epistle to Dr Arbuthnot*).

On 3 February 1729 Wyndham laid the foundation stone of the Irish Parliament House in College Green. He was appointed one of the lords justices of Ireland, who exercised authority in the absence of the lord lieutenant, in 1728 and served eight times in that capacity. In 1730, in the case of Daniel Kimberly, an attorney who had been sentenced to death for abduction, petitions were presented to the lords justices, to the lord lieutenant, then in London, and to the king on a technical ground. The matter was referred to the lord lieutenant, who concurred with the lords justices that the petition should not be allowed. Wyndham convened the privy council, which then rejected the claim after taking the oral opinion of the judges and, later, the written opinion of the law officers, that is the prime serjeant, Henry Singleton, the attorney-general, Thomas Marlay, the solicitor-general, Robert Jocelyn, and serjeant John Bowes (O'Flanagan, 2.59–62). The incident established that petitions to invoke the Irish prerogative of mercy should not thereafter be sent to England.

On 18 September 1731 Wyndham was created Baron Wyndham of Finglass, co. Dublin, and was introduced to the Lords on 5 October of the same year. He presided over six sessions of the Irish parliament as speaker of the House of Lords. On 20 August 1735 Jonathan Swift dined at his table. He acted as lord high steward at the trial of Henry Barry, Baron Barry of Santry, before the Irish lords for the murder of Laughlin Murphy, a footman, whom Barry had stabbed in 'a fit of passion' (GEC, *Peerage*, 1.448). Wyndham recites in his will that this was the first trial of a peer before the Irish lords. Barry was found guilty on 27 April 1739 and Wyndham sentenced him to death. Barry was attainted and his peerage and estates forfeited, but he was pardoned, as to his life, in 1741 and later obtained a regrant of his estates but not of his peerage.

The stress of the trial affected Wyndham's health, so he relates in his will, and he resigned the chancellorship on 7 September 1739, sailing for England the following day. He died in Wiltshire on 24 November 1745, aged sixty-three, and was buried in Salisbury Cathedral, where there is a fine marble monument to him by Rysbrack on the south side of the west door. He had remained unmarried and the title became extinct on his death. He left £2500 in his will to Wadham College 'for the better appointments of the Warden', who was his cousin George Wyndham. He also left £200 to Lincoln's Inn for the decoration of the chapel or the great hall. In the summer of 1747 William Murray, then a bencher of the inn and later first earl of Mansfield, proposed that the money be used to commission a painting by William Hogarth, who produced *Paul before Felix*, which was hung in the great hall in 1750 (Uglow, 454–8).

ANDREW LYALL

Sources GEC, *Peerage*, new edn, 1.447–8; 12/2.880 · J. R. O'Flanagan, *The lives of the lord chancellors and keepers of the great seals of Ireland*, 2 (1870), 51, 59–62 · F. E. Ball, *The judges in Ireland, 1221–1921*, 2 (1926), 100–02, 106–7, 115, 126–7, 172, 186–7, 197–8 · will, dated 29 July 1745–2 September 1745, probate, 24 Dec 1745, PRO, PROB 11/743, sig. 340 · H. A. Wyndham, *A family history*, 1: *1410–1688: the Wyndhams of Norfolk and Somerset* (1939) · H. A. Wyndham, *A family history*, 2: *1688–1837: the Wyndhams of Somerset, Sussex and Wiltshire* (1950) · A. B. Lyall, 'The Irish House of Lords as a judicial body, 1783–1800', *Irish Jurist*, new ser., 28–30 (1993–5), 314–60 · 'Trial of Henry, Baron Barry of Santry, 1739', King's Inns, Dublin, archives · J. Uglow, *Hogarth: a life and a world* (1997) · Burke, *Gen. GB* · Foster, *Alum. Oxon.* · R. B. Gardiner, ed., *The registers of Wadham College, Oxford*, 2 vols. (1889–95) · *GM*, 1st ser., 15 (1745), 614 · J. Harris, *Copies of the epitaphs in Salisbury cathedral, cloisters and cemetery* (1825), 3 · *Letters written by ... Hugh Boulter ... to several ministers of state*, ed. [A. Philips and G. Faulkner], 2 vols. (1769–70); repr. (1770) · J. Barrington, *Personal sketches of his own times*, rev. T. Young, 3rd edn, 2 vols. (1869) · J. O'Brien and D. Guinness, *Dublin: a grand tour* (1994)
Archives CKS, memoranda books | TCD, corresp. with William King
Likenesses portrait, 1728, Wadham College, Oxford · I. Seeman, portrait, 1739; on loan to Maidstone county hall · Marshall, engraving (after portrait by unknown artist, 1728)
Wealth at death see will, PRO, PROB 11/743, sig. 340

Wyndham, Sir Wadham (1609–1668), judge, was born at Orchard Wyndham, Somerset, on 29 October 1609, the ninth son of Sir John Wyndham (1558–1645) of Orchard Wyndham and his wife, Joan (1564/5–1633), daughter of Sir Henry Portman. Sir Hugh *Wyndham was his elder brother. He was named after his grandmother Frances Wadham. He is recorded as providing key money at Wadham College, Oxford, in 1626 (which was returned in 1629), and entered Lincoln's Inn on 22 October 1628, being called to the bar on 17 May 1636. On 12 January 1647 Wyndham married Barbara (1627–1704), daughter of Sir George Clarke of Watford, Northamptonshire. They had eight sons (two of whom predeceased their father) and four daughters, born between 1648 and 1666.

Wyndham thrived at the bar and was one of George Cony's three counsel in May 1655 when Cony, a merchant, had refused to pay customs as they had not been authorized by parliament, and then sued the collector at common law when the tax had been taken anyway. As a result they were imprisoned in the Tower for a few days before, in Edmund Ludlow's words, 'they unworthily petitioned their fault' (*Memoirs of Edmund Ludlow*, 1.412–13), claiming that they 'never intended to provoke to sedition or discontent' (*CSP dom.*, 1655, 179), and were then released. By the late 1650s Wyndham had made sufficient money at the bar to purchase an estate for £9000 at Norrington in Wiltshire, and also purchased St Edmund's College, Salisbury.

Wyndham may have been created a serjeant-at-law on 5 July 1659 by order of parliament, but no document survives in the crown office docket book. He was made a serjeant-at-law by royal authority in October 1660, and took part in the prosecution of the regicides. On 24 November 1660 he was named a judge of king's bench, being knighted on 4 December 1660. Sir John Hawles referred to him as 'the second best judge which sat in Westminster Hall since the king's restoration' (*State trials*, 9.1003), and for North he was one of the judges 'who were and ever will be famous among the learned in the laws' (North, 1.60). Siderfin referred to his 'great discretion, especially in his calm and sedate temper upon the bench' (Foss, *Judges*). Wyndham's opinions and judgments are cited in the 1730, 1744, and 1755 editions of Sir Antoine Fitzherbert's *Natura brevium*. Wyndham died of diabetes at Norrington on 24 December 1668 and was buried in St Edmund's, Salisbury. His eldest son, John, became MP for Salisbury in 1681 and 1685, and was the father of Thomas *Wyndham, Lord Wyndham of Finglass, a lord chancellor of Ireland.

STUART HANDLEY

Sources J. J. Howard, ed., *Miscellanea genealogica et heraldica*, 2nd ser., 4 (1892) · Baker, *Serjeants* · Sainty, *Judges* · H. A. Wyndham, *A family history*, 1: *1410–1688: the Wyndhams of Norfolk and Somerset* (1939), 211, 221, 255, 267–9 · Foss, *Judges*, 7.198–9 · R. B. Gardiner, ed., *The registers of Wadham College, Oxford*, 1 (1889), 79 · *State trials*, 5.1023; 9.1003 · *The memoirs of Edmund Ludlow*, ed. C. H. Firth, 2 vols. (1894), vol. 1, pp. 412–13 · *CSP dom.*, 1655, pp. 179, 196 · R. North, *The lives of ... Francis North ... Dudley North ... and ... John North*, ed. A. Jessopp, 1 (1890), 60 · J. G. Marvin, *Legal bibliography, or, A thesaurus of American, English, Irish and Scotch law books* (1847), 311 · W. Godwin, *History of the Commonwealth of England*, 4 vols. (1828), vol. 4, pp. 174–9
Likenesses J. M. Wright, oils, *c.*1670–1674, Lincoln's Inn, London

Wyndham, Sir William, third baronet (*c.*1688–1740), politician, was born at Trentham, Staffordshire, the only son of Sir Edward Wyndham, second baronet, of Orchard Wyndham, Somerset, and his wife, Catherine, the daughter of Sir William Leveson-Gower, fourth baronet, of Trentham and Stittenham, Yorkshire. He succeeded his father as third baronet in June 1695, entered Eton College in 1698, and matriculated from Christ Church, Oxford, on 1 June 1704, when his home was said to be at Orchard Portman, near Taunton. Having left the university without taking a degree, he went on the grand tour through France and Italy before returning to marry Catherine (d. 1731), the second daughter of Charles *Seymour, sixth duke of Somerset (1662–1748), on 21 July 1708. The couple had two sons: Charles *Wyndham, later earl of Egremont, and Percy, who, adopting the surname O'Brien, became the earl of Thomond. Following Catherine's death on 9 April 1731, Wyndham married (on 1 June 1734) Maria Catherina, the daughter of Peter de Jong of Utrecht and the widow of William Godolphin, marquess of Blandford.

In April 1710 Wyndham was chosen as knight of the shire for Somerset at a by-election held just before the fall of the whig administration, and thereafter represented that county in the tory interest until his death some thirty years later. With his party now in the ascendant at court and Queen Anne apparently taking a personal interest in his education, in 1711 the young Sir William found himself appointed master of the buckhounds. In June 1712 he was promoted to the vacant post of secretary at war and in November 1713 became chancellor of the exchequer, 'at a time when', as the waspish Lord Hervey later observed, 'neither his years, his experience, his talents, his knowledge, nor his weight could give him any pretence to distinction' (Hervey, 1.19–20). This overly rapid advancement was due, it seems, to the robust patronage of Henry St John, Viscount Bolingbroke, whose struggles with Robert Harley, earl of Oxford, for control of the tory ministry overshadowed the closing years of Anne's reign. In the eyes of many contemporaries and most later commentators Wyndham was little more than Bolingbroke's creature, used principally to undermine the latter's ministerial adversaries and, through his wife, to help orchestrate his master's intrigues at court. In parliament he became an effective spokesman for the high-tory agenda, leading a personal attack on the whig polemicist Richard Steele and sponsoring Atterbury's Schism Bill in the House of Commons. On the eve of Oxford's dismissal as lord treasurer in August 1714 he was among those who dined with Bolingbroke to make arrangements for the new administration; and, had the queen's death not intervened, he would have headed a Treasury team of five commissioners. Yet if it is true that the youthful baronet owed his meteoric rise almost entirely to Bolingbroke's influence, it is equally true that the would-be first minister saw in him a fledgeling politician with aptitudes and abilities worth cultivating; for, as Speaker Onslow was later to remark, Sir William was 'the most made for a great man of any that I have known of this age' (Coxe, 2.560).

However, what blighted Wyndham's career and fatally restricted his room for manoeuvre when Bolingbroke's high-tory project collapsed was his reckless espousal of the Jacobite cause. Although he was prepared to behave in a seemly fashion upon King George's succession, and to speak in favour of paying the arrears owed to the Hanoverian troops who had fought in the War of the Spanish Succession, following Bolingbroke's flight to St Germain and the whigs' crushing victory over their opponents at the general election of February 1715 his political stance became decidedly more confrontational. He was now left as one of the *de facto* leaders of his party in the House of Commons, and he narrowly avoided being committed to the Tower for aspersions intemperately cast upon the supposed partisan bias of the king's election proclamation. Ordered by the speaker to leave the house, he withdrew, taking the bulk of his party with him, and was formally censured in his absence. He took little part in the impeachment proceedings against the former tory leaders, but did rise to oppose the vote for the king's privy purse and to defend the ministry's conduct with respect to the treaty of Utrecht. In fact, throughout the spring and summer of 1715 he appears to have been engaged in laying plans for a western rising in favour of the Stuarts, timed to coincide with Lord Mar's rebellion in Scotland, and in July sent a message to the Pretender 'not to lose a day in going over' (HoP, *Commons*). In the event, upon information received from one of the duke of Ormond's agents he was arrested at Orchard Wyndham on 21 September 1715. He escaped, but then, with a £1000 reward offered for his capture, gave himself up on the advice of his father-in-law and was sent to the Tower. According to Lord Sidney, with the ministry inclined to oblige the duke of Somerset, Wyndham might have evaded official notice altogether had not Lord Townshend insisted on his arrest, thereby precipitating the duke's departure from the cabinet. Even so, he was released on bail in the following July and never came to trial. Whether the plans for a Jacobite rising in the west country amounted to anything more than the bombast of tory squires in their cups is now impossible to determine with any certainty. What is clear is that, while the mere imputation of treasonable intent made Wyndham *persona non grata* at court, and thus with a whig party dependent on its monopoly of Hanoverian patronage, his use of family influence to escape the consequences of his actions could only damage his credibility among Jacobite stalwarts.

Wyndham was slow to share Bolingbroke's disillusionment with the reality of James's court at St Germain, and there is compelling evidence to suggest that he was at first scornful of the advice contained in his mentor's well-known letter from exile urging him to abandon the Jacobites. In August 1716 he was among those who called upon the Pretender to land in England with 5000 regular troops and arms for 20,000 volunteers and even argued for Bolingbroke's reinstatement. Indeed, as late as 1719 government agents could still report their suspicions that his attendance at hunting parties in the company of other young and disaffected tories had rather more to do with Jacobite intrigue than with his liking for the sport. Yet in 1720 Wyndham visited Bolingbroke in Paris, from where he sent his last message of support to 'King James'. While he was still identified in 1721 as a probable supporter in the event of a rising, the following year he took no part in the Atterbury plot, and from 1725 onwards, with his friend and mentor restored to his family estates, if not to his seat in the Lords, Wyndham lost no opportunity to declare his loyalty to the house of Hanover. During the early 1730s he did take part in discussions with the French ambassador in London about a possible Stuart restoration and was among the opposition leaders assured of places in a future ministry, but the talks foundered on Wyndham's insistence that James should abdicate in favour of his eldest son, who might then be raised as a protestant. When a fresh round of negotiations began in 1739 with the aim of fomenting a Jacobite rising in England backed by a French invasion, he was deliberately left out. Yet in April 1740, barely two months before his death, a Jacobite agent could observe that, though Sir William had been 'for some years very unaccountable', nevertheless he and Bolingbroke appeared 'to dread that any business of the King's [i.e. the Pretender's] should be thought of without them' (HoP, *Commons*).

The main thrust of Wyndham's later political career lay in the direction of a *rapprochement* with the Hanoverian establishment, and in particular the possibility of detaching a sufficiently large number of dissident whigs from Sir Robert Walpole's old corps to make realistic the prospect of a mixed ministry and an end to the tories' proscription from office. If the rationale for such a patriot ministry was most famously expressed by Bolingbroke, it would be an uncritical reading of contemporary whig polemic to suggest that all those who subsequently espoused the idea and worked to bring it about were acting principally as the viscount's agents. True, Wyndham was Bolingbroke's protégé and lifelong friend; but he should not simply be dismissed as his mouthpiece.

Wyndham's political fortunes began to look brighter when first Daniel and then William Pulteney broke with the ministry and declared their willingness to work in a concerted opposition with the tories. Initially hostile to such collaboration, by 1730 even the party's Jacobite faction was being encouraged by the Pretender to 'unite in the measures against the Government and even with those who oppose it for different views than theirs', and in particular to support those actions which tended 'to promote a misunderstanding between the English Government and any foreign power, but most especially France' (HoP, *Commons*). Barely a month later, Wyndham, now the nearest thing to a recognized leader of the parliamentary tory party for almost two decades, tested this new-found unity by launching into an unexpected attack on the ministry over the restoration of Dunkirk harbour contrary to the terms agreed at Utrecht.

Over the remaining years of his life Wyndham laboured to hold this uneasy coalition together. If it was clearly strengthened by the excise crisis of 1733 and the experience gained through widespread co-operation during the general election campaign of the following year, it was undoubtedly strained by such divisive issues as the princess royal's marriage portion, the proposed repeal of the Test and Septennial Acts, and the government-sponsored mortmain and Quaker tithe bills. Whenever the dissident whigs sought to accommodate their tory allies, they were taunted by Walpole for being the dupes of Jacobite policy; when they scrupled to support this or that vote proposed by Wyndham and his colleagues, they were calumnied as fair-weather friends. When the prince of Wales went into opposition Wyndham became one of his principal advisers, but when the matter of his royal highness's allowance was pressed to a vote he could not persuade enough of his party to support the measure, which failed by thirty votes, with forty-five tories abstaining. After narrowly failing to defeat the ministry in the debate on the Spanish convention, described by the bishop of Chichester as 'the greatest party struggle there has been since the Revolution' (*Buckinghamshire MSS*, 243), Wyndham led a secession of the opposition forces from the Commons. Yet though they had urged the tories to it, Pulteney's whigs quickly tired of this stratagem and returned to the house, causing their allies to look foolish and inept.

Wyndham died at Wells on 17 June 1740, leaving contemporaries to ponder his legacy. To George Lyttelton, a dissident whig, his loss was a calamity for the opposition:

> His influence with the Tories was the only means of keeping that party in any system of rational measures. Now he is gone … it is much to be feared that resentment, despair, and their inability of conducting themselves may drive the Tories back into their old prejudices, heat and extravagance. (Wyndham, 1.76)

For Arthur Onslow, Sir William had almost completed the transformation from Jacobite to whig, becoming in the process 'one of the most pleasing and able speakers of his time'. From knowing little of business and being bigoted in his opinions, he:

> wore out all the prejudices of party, grew moderate towards the dissenters, … studied and understood the nature of government and the constitution of his own country, and formed such a new set of principles with regard to the public, and from them grew to think that the religion and liberties of the nation so much depended on the support of the present family to the throne, that he lost all confidence with the Jacobites and the most rigid of the Tories, and it is thought would have left them entirely if he could have withstood the reproach of that in his county or could have maintained a prevailing interest there without them. (*Buckinghamshire MSS*, 467)

Soon after his death both of his sons, together with his friends Bathurst and Gower, went over to the whigs. Wyndham was survived by his second wife, Maria Catherina. STEPHEN W. BASKERVILLE

Sources DNB · L. Colley, *In defiance of oligarchy: the tory party, 1714–60* (1982) · H. T. Dickinson, *Bolingbroke* (1970) · E. Cruickshanks, 'Wyndham, William', HoP, *Commons, 1715–54* · Royal Arch., Stuart papers · M. Wyndham, *Chronicles of the eighteenth century*, 2 vols. (1924) · John, Lord Hervey, *Some materials towards memoirs of the reign of King George II*, ed. R. Sedgwick, 3 vols. (1931) · W. Coxe, *Memoirs of the life and administration of Sir Robert Walpole, earl of Orford*, 3 vols. (1798) · *The manuscripts of the earl of Buckinghamshire, the earl of Lindsey … and James Round*, HMC, 38 (1895), 467 · Historical Manuscripts Commission, London, Hare MSS · Foster, *Alum. Oxon.*
Archives NRA, priv. coll., corresp. and papers · Petworth House, West Sussex, mainly incoming corresp. | Devon RO, Seymour MSS, letters to the duke of Somerset
Likenesses attrib. J. Richardson, oils, c.1713–1714, NPG · G. Kneller, group portrait, c.1714 (with family), Petworth House, Sussex · G. Kneller, oils, 1714, Petworth House, Sussex · G. Kneller and J. Wootton, oils, 1715, Petworth House, Sussex · J. Faber, mezzotint, 1740 · J. Houbraken, engraving (after attrib. J. Richardson)

Wynfield, David Wilkie (1837–1887), painter and photographer, was born in India, the son of James Stainback Winfield, a captain in the 47th Bengal native infantry, and his second wife, Sophia Mary Burroughes (d. c.1899). He was named after his maternal great-uncle and godfather, the distinguished Scottish artist Sir David Wilkie. It appears that in the early 1840s Captain Winfield retired from the army, returned with his family to England, and died soon afterwards. He left his wife with, it is thought, four children: David, Amy, Martha, and Anne.

Wynfield later recalled that he was 'originally destined for the church' but that he changed his mind when a young man and 'gave myself up to art' (Wynfield to Tom Taylor, n.d. [1871], V&A NAL). In 1856 he entered the art school run by James Mathew Leigh, and three years later he had his first work accepted for exhibition at the Royal Academy of Arts. At this time his last name appeared in exhibition catalogues as Winfield, but soon afterwards it

David Wilkie Wynfield (1837–1887), self-portrait, 1860s

appeared as Wynfield. His address was given as 3 Bristol Gardens, Maida Hill, in north London.

Early in the 1860s Wynfield and his closest artist friends, William Frederick Yeames, Philip Hermogenes Calderon, George Dunlop Leslie, Henry Stacy Marks, George Adolphus Storey, and John Evan Hodgson, would meet once a week at each other's homes or studios, choose a subject (usually taken from history, mythology, or the Bible), and give themselves a set time in which each to devise a composition. They would then 'grill' one another over the success or otherwise of the results. Five of the seven had trained at Leigh's, and it was a mutual appreciation of Leigh's methods, particularly his abrasive critiques, which drew the group together. They later became known as the St John's Wood Clique (or School) of painters, after the suburb in north London in which they chose to live.

All but Leslie of the Clique specialized in what is now called 'historical genre', paintings set broadly within medieval and Renaissance times featuring historical, domestic, or romantic incident. If not always a critical success, these works were extremely popular with the reproduction-buying public and brought the Clique artists, in their late twenties or early thirties, fame and enough wealth to buy their own homes in St John's Wood. In 1867 Wynfield and his mother set up home together at 14 Grove End Road, the street to which his sister Anne had moved after her marriage in 1865 to W. F. Yeames.

Having early revealed a propensity for subjects with tragic overtones, in the late 1860s Wynfield began to alternate between solemn subjects, as in his *Oliver Cromwell on the Night before his Death* (1867; V&A), based on Thomas Carlyle's account of the protector's death, and more light-hearted ones, such as *The Rich Widow* (1869), inspired by John Forster's biography of Sir John Eliot. His most acclaimed work was *The Death of Buckingham*, which was exhibited in 1871 at the Royal Academy.

The Clique's decision to court popular success at a time when figures such as Whistler were promoting the French notion that the artist should 'épater le bourgeois' has seen their paintings identified as the foil to more significant forms of artistic production. This polarization of artistic styles and schools does not take account, however, of the then fashionable notion that all artists were brothers. This was a view actively promoted by Wynfield, who in 1867 joined the committee of the Dudley Gallery in Piccadilly, London, and encouraged artists who found their work marginalized by the establishment (such as Edouard Manet, the *enfant terrible* of the French art world) to exhibit there.

The most powerful testimony of Wynfield's commitment to promoting contemporary art and artists is the series of photographs that he made during the 1860s and 1870s. The earliest evidence of his involvement with photography dates from 1863, when—living at 3 Park Place Villas, Paddington—he registered for copyright ten bust portraits of young male artists wearing medieval and Renaissance-style costume. Early in 1864 he published through Henry Hering of Regent Street a selection of his portraits in part form under the title *The studio: a collection of photographic portraits of living artists, taken in the style of the old masters, by an amateur*. The series would seem to be a modern reworking of *The Iconography*, Van Dyck's series of graphic portraits of artists, patrons, soldiers, and statesmen. The historical costume and heightened chiaroscuro of Wynfield's photographic studies implicitly identified the contemporary artists who sat for him as the equal of their distinguished forebears.

Wynfield's use of a close-up format and a narrow depth of field created portraits startling for combining painterly *sfumato* with photographic immediacy. Julia Margaret Cameron, whose fame as a photographer has far eclipsed that of Wynfield, noted in 1866 that 'to my feeling about his beautiful photography I owed all my attempts & indeed consequently all my success' (J. M. Cameron to W. M. Rossetti, 23 Jan 1866, Gernsheim collection, University of Texas, Austin). Despite this and a handful of accolades in the popular press for his photographs, the evidence suggests that as early as 1864 Wynfield ceased to promote his works to the general public. He did, however, continue to produce studies of his contemporaries in the distinctive idiom of *The Studio*. His surviving photographs, the majority of which are albumen prints taken by the wet collodion process, present the denizens of bohemian London and the older men they admired as united by a mutual dedication to the arts. Not always wearing historical costume, Wynfield's sitters were invariably male, and include (among many others) Edward Burne-Jones, George Du Maurier, James Anthony Froude, Edouard

Manet, Henry Thoby Prinsep, Simeon Solomon (photographs all RA), William Holman Hunt and John Everett Millais (both NPG), and George Frederick Watts (V&A).

Like many of his sitters, Wynfield joined the 38th Middlesex regiment of the Artists' volunteer rifles, one of the many volunteer corps set up in 1859–60 in the face of the perceived threat of a French invasion. Unlike the majority of his friends and contemporaries, he remained dedicated to the corps, and in 1880 he became the captain of H company. When one young recruit met his captain for the first time in 1882 he was surprised by his 'big bushy beard and comfortable artistic costume' (May, 19–20). Wynfield, whose hobbies were genealogy and heraldry, was, it seems, determined to promote the idea that the *vita activa* of the military life and the *vita contemplativa* of the scholarly artist were compatible, and his photographs, which include two self-portraits (NPG and RA), look back to the medieval period in which this humanist philosophy had its origins.

Wynfield died of tuberculosis, presumably in London, on 26 May 1887, and was buried at Highgate cemetery. He was unmarried; his mother, with whom he had continued to live at 14 Grove End Road, survived him by twelve years. Although he was a well-known painter in his day, Wynfield's posthumous reputation currently owes more to the photographs he published anonymously than the paintings he exhibited publicly. An exhibition of his photographic portrait work, entitled 'Princes of Victorian Bohemia', was held at the National Portrait Gallery, London, in spring 2000.   JULIET HACKING

Sources J. Hacking, *Princes of Victorian Bohemia: photographs by David Wilkie Wynfield* (2000) [exhibition catalogue, NPG, 2000] · J. Hacking, 'Photography personified: art and identity in British photography, 1857–1869', PhD diss., U. Lond., 1998 · J. Hacking, 'David Wilkie Wynfield's photography: portraits of the artist as a young man', MA report, U. Lond., 1994 · M. Stephen Smith, *Art and anecdote: memories of William Frederick Yeames R.A., his life and friends* (1927) · T. Taylor, 'English painters of the present day: D. W. Wynfield', *Portfolio*, 1 (1871), 84–7 · E. Morris and F. Milner, *And when did you last see your father?* (1992) [exhibition catalogue, Walker Art Gallery, Liverpool, 13 Nov 1992 – 10 Jan 1993] · H. S. Marks, *Pen and pencil sketches*, 2 vols. (1894) · R. Spencer, 'Manet, Rossetti, London and "Derby day"', *Burlington Magazine*, 83 (April 1991), 228–36 · G. D. Leslie, *The inner life of the Royal Academy* (1914) · F. Moscheles, *In Bohemia with Du Maurier* (1896) · G. A. Storey, *Sketches from memory* (1899) · H. A. R. May, *Memories of the artists' rifles* (1929) · corresp., V&A NAL · *The Independent* (3 Feb 2000) [article on retrospective exhibition]
Archives V&A, corresp., etc.
Likenesses D. W. Wynfield, self-portrait, photograph, 1860–69, NPG, RA [*see illus.*] · attrib. D. W. Wynfield, self-portrait, photograph, *c*.1866 (with P. H. Calderon and W. F. Yeames), priv. coll.
Wealth at death £1246 3*s*. 0*d*.: resworn administration, June 1888, CGPLA Eng. & Wales (1887) · £236 5*s*. 7*d*.: further grant, 16 Jan 1900, CGPLA Eng. & Wales

Wynford. For this title name *see* Best, William Draper, first Baron Wynford (1767–1845).

Wynford, William (d. 1405), master mason, is first recorded in 1360, working as one of two wardens of masons at Windsor Castle under **John Sponlee** (d. 1382?), who had become master mason there in 1350. The work then in progress was the royal lodgings block in the upper ward, the chief part of the costliest building project undertaken in late medieval England. The pressures of organizing an exceptionally large workforce probably account for the departure from the usual practice of appointing only one warden, and perhaps also for Wynford's promotion to joint 'ordainer' with Sponlee in April 1361. Only in 1366 did Wynford spend the whole year at Windsor. Sponlee probably retained responsibility for the design, as he was paid at the exceptional rate of 2*s*. per day, twice the normal pay of a master mason. In 1369 Sponlee walked in Queen Philippa's funeral procession among the royal household's esquires of greater estate (whereas Wynford was ranked as an esquire of lesser estate) and he retained overall control of the works at Windsor until at least 1377. Wynford had commissions to impress masons for royal works in 1371, 1372, and 1378, the last being for Southampton Castle, where he was master mason of a great cylindrical keep hurriedly erected in response to the growing threat of invasion from France. Wynford's latest known royal work was the remodelling in 1394–5 of the aisles of the thirteenth-century great hall of Winchester Castle.

Wynford's employment at Windsor occurred while the clerk of works there was William Wykeham (d. 1404). Whether the latter's influence brought about Wynford's rapid promotion is not known, but personal links forged between the two men in 1360–61 must lie behind Wykeham's decision to entrust to his erstwhile colleague the prodigious series of works he undertook after his elevation to the see of Winchester. The 1377–8 accounts for the reconstruction of the episcopal manor house at Bishop's Waltham, Hampshire, contain a reference to Wynford as master mason for all of Wykeham's works, a position which he appears to have held continuously until the bishop's death in 1404. The earliest of Wykeham's three most important undertakings, New College, Oxford, was mostly built between 1380 and 1386. It betrays heavy influence from the upper ward at Windsor, not only in respect of the planning of its main quadrangle, which Wykeham as patron could perfectly well have stipulated, but also in terms of its detailed treatment, which is far more likely to reflect the preferences of the architect. The building accounts are lost, but the design can with confidence be attributed to Wynford, as it shows the closest stylistic kinship with Wykeham's next major project. This was Winchester College, begun in 1387, for which Wynford was certainly the master mason. Both colleges exhibit a sober elegance of treatment which is carefully modulated to underline the hierarchy of functions within a rigorously integrated ensemble. New College was to exert a strong influence on Oxford college architecture during the rest of the middle ages and beyond. Wynford built much for Wykeham at his numerous episcopal residences, but the only well-preserved survival is the manor house at East Meon, Hampshire, of *c*.1395–7.

Wykeham's and Wynford's last and greatest undertaking was the remodelling of the nave of Winchester Cathedral, begun in 1394. Alongside the nave of Canterbury Cathedral, this is the outstanding surviving work of late fourteenth-century English church architecture. Wynford hit on an ingeniously minimal method of modernizing a Romanesque fabric, namely the cutting away of the angles of the old piers to form diagonal planes. Although abnormally bulky, the resulting supports incorporate enough verticals, and possess enough variety of modelling, to give a convincing approximation to Perpendicular aesthetics. If the aim of this singular procedure was economy, it must be judged a failure, since many parts of the Romanesque facework could not be recut and had to be replaced with new masonry. The stylistic character of Wynford's design is broadly similar to that of the works of Henry Yevele (d. 1400), his leading contemporary, but it shows a less complete adherence to the formal repertory developed in the 1330s by the pioneer of Perpendicular in the south-east, William Ramsey (d. 1349). It is possible that Wynford's approach at Winchester was influenced by his experience of refashioning the Romanesque church of Abingdon Abbey, in progress c.1375–6 (destroyed).

When Wynford died in Winchester in 1405, probably on 25 July, it is likely that only that part of the cathedral nave which incorporated Wykeham's chantry chapel had been completely remodelled. Better than any other extant work, the chantry shows Wynford's skill in small-scale decorative architecture. That Wykeham regarded his architect highly is evident from the inclusion of a representation of him in the east window of Winchester College chapel. The carpenter Hugh Herland (d. 1406?) appears in the same window in a less honorific position behind Wynford, but no other fourteenth-century English architects are known to have been commemorated in this way.

In 1365 Wynford became master mason to Wells Cathedral, possibly through the influence of Wykeham, who had been a prebendary there until 1363. The upper stages of the south-west tower, built c.1385–95, are probably lower and plainer than those intended by the architect of the 150-year-old work which they surmount. Nevertheless, Wynford's design, followed in the early fifteenth-century north-west tower, provides a wholly convincing termination to this grandest of English Gothic cathedral façades. CHRISTOPHER WILSON

Sources J. Harvey and A. Oswald, *English mediaeval architects: a biographical dictionary down to 1550*, 2nd edn (1984) · H. M. Colvin and others, eds., *The history of the king's works*, 6 vols. (1963–82), vol. 1, pp. 174n., 175, 212–13, 216; vol. 2 · J. H. Harvey, *The Perpendicular style, 1330–1485* (1978), 130–6 · R. Willis, *The architectural history of Winchester Cathedral* (1846), 54–77 · E. Roberts, 'William of Wykeham's house at East Meon, Hampshire', *Archaeological Journal*, 150 (1993), 45–81 · J. N. Hare, 'Bishop's Waltham palace, Hampshire: William of Wykeham, Henry Beaufort and the transformation of a medieval episcopal palace', *Archaeological Journal*, 145 (1988), 222–54 · pipe roll of the bishops of Winchester, accounts for works at Bishop's Waltham, 1377–8, Hants. RO, 11M59/B2/11/21
Likenesses portrait, east window, 1393, Winchester College chapel; replaced by a copy in 1822 · drawing, 1822 (after unknown artist, 1393), Winchester College chapel, Hampshire · photograph, National Monuments Record, Swindon, Royal Commission on Historical Monuments

Wynman, Margaret. *See* Dixon, Ella Nora Hepworth (1857–1932).

Wynn family (*per. c.*1465–1678), landowners, can be traced to fourteenth-century minor freeholders in the townships of Pennant and Penyfed in the commote of Eifionydd, Caernarvonshire. The history of their rise to local power is described in the famous 'History of the Gwydir family' (Cardiff City Library, MS 4.101, fols. 89v–106v) by Sir John *Wynn, first baronet (1553–1627). This was compiled between about 1590 and 1614 and made use of a variety of sources, some spurious, in an attempt to establish a reputable ancestry for the family. Wynn claimed that his family was descended from Gruffudd ap Cynan (1054/5–1137), king of Gwynedd, but ambiguities in the chronicle cast doubts on the authenticity of its early sections.

The family emerged in the hundred of Nanconwy, first in the Lledr valley, from about 1489, and then in the Conwy valley, where Gwydir mansion is situated. The family founder was **Maredudd ab Ieuan ap Robert** (*c.*1465–1525), a descendant of the Eifionydd family which, judging by the 'History', had a turbulent past because of constant kindred feuds. Unlike his blood brothers Maredudd was educated at Caernarfon, the centre of government for the principality of north Wales, by his patron, reputedly a member of the Cochwillan family. Through his first marriage to Alice, daughter of William ap Gruffudd ap Robert of Cochwillan, he established important local contacts, especially with the Spicer family of Cochwillan, and moved from his home at Crug in Llanfair-is-gaer to Nanconwy. His move eastwards to Dolwyddelan, where he bought the lease of the castle, was due chiefly to his need to establish his independence from his restless kindred in Eifionydd, to extend his family influence, and to encroach on vacant royal bond townships in an inhospitable area devastated since the Black Death and subsequent economic disorder. He settled his motley group of followers in tenancies, built a home at Penamnen in Dolwyddelan, and established his authority against marauding bandits before moving to the Conwy valley about 1500 to build the earliest part of Gwydir mansion adjacent to the town of Llanrwst.

On Maredudd's death in 1525 he left a large family and was succeeded by **John Wyn ap Maredudd** (*b.* in or before 1494, *d.* 1559), his eldest legitimate son by his first marriage. John Wyn increased his status through consolidating his landed power in Nanconwy and acquiring further properties in north Merioneth and west Denbighshire, all of which was primarily a stock rearing region. In 1555 he enlarged the existing Gwydir mansion, which became the focal point of a substantial landed estate, and he improved his public image by becoming involved in local administration. In 1515 Mary Brandon, duchess of Suffolk, wrote on behalf of her husband, who was chamberlain of north Wales, to request that John Wyn give her servants any merlins taken in the region. He was supported by William Herbert, first earl of Pembroke, who appears to have been a close friend, and, besides being named to the first commission of the peace for Caernarvonshire and Merioneth when the office was introduced into Wales in 1541, he served on several other commissions, was sheriff of Caernarvonshire between 1544 and 1545, 1553 and 1554, and 1556 and 1557, MP for Caernarvonshire in 1547 (probably also in 1542), and *custos rotulorum* for Merioneth in 1543 and for Caernarvonshire from 1550 to 1559. He was elected in his brother-in-law John Puleston's place, for Caernarvonshire at a by-election in 1551. In 1530 he renewed the leases of holdings in Dolwyddelan, Gwydir, and Trefriw for the annual rent of £19 4*s*. 8*d*. He laid the foundation of the Wynn ascendancy in north Wales, extended its influence in all aspects of public affairs, and was the first member of his family to take advantage of the opportunities offered by the Acts of Union (1536–43) to broaden its interests. He married Ellen (*d*. in or after 1559), daughter of Morris ap John ap Maredudd of Clenennau, before 1520. They had five sons, including Robert Wynn (1520–1598) of Plas Mawr, Caernarvonshire, MP for Caernarfon boroughs in 1589, and Dr John Gwynne (*d*. 1574), fellow of St John's College, Cambridge, and MP for Caernarvonshire in 1572. They also had two daughters. His will was made on 14 June 1557 and he died on 9 or 17 July 1559. He was buried in Dolwyddelan parish church.

John Wyn was succeeded by his eldest son, **Morris Wynn** (*b*. in or before 1520, *d*. 1580), who was the first to assume the family surname of Wynn. Although a less assertive personality than his father he became a prominent figure in local government. He served as sheriff of Caernarvonshire between 1554 and 1555, 1569 and 1570, and 1577 and 1578, was MP for Caernarvonshire in October 1553, April 1554, and 1563, JP for Caernarvonshire and Merioneth from 1555 to 1580 and for Denbighshire from 1575 to 1580, and *custos rotulorum* for Caernarvonshire in 1562. He consolidated the Gwydir estate and supported Robert Dudley, earl of Leicester, in his efforts to discover concealed lands in the forest of Snowdon in the 1570s. He married Jane, or Siân, daughter of Sir Richard (I) Bulkeley of Beaumaris, and his wife, Catherine, by September 1551. They had three sons, including Ellis Wynn (*b*. in or before 1559, *d*. 1623), and five daughters. Ellis Wynn and his brothers were well educated, their father having set up an informal school for them at Gwydir, and were protestant. He attended Westminster School and was a member of the household of Sir Robert Cecil, principal secretary, who acquired for him the lucrative position of gentleman harbinger. He was, however, arrogant and insensitive in the execution of his office. He settled in London and at Everdon, Northamptonshire, and was returned as MP for Saltash, Cornwall, in 1597 through Cecil's influence. Morris Wynn's second wife was Anne (*d*. *c*.1570), daughter of Edward Greville of Milcote, Warwickshire. They had one daughter. After her death he married the celebrated Katherine (*d*. 1591), daughter and heir of Tudur ap Robert Fychan of Berain, Denbighshire, widow of John Salusbury of Lleweni, Denbighshire, and of Richard Clough of Bachegraig, Tremeirchion, Flintshire. They had three daughters and one son. Nothing is known of Wynn's education but he was a cultured man, a keen upholder of the native bardic tradition, an assiduous manager of his landed affairs, and a shrewd person who established important connections which enabled him to maintain his family's reputation in north Wales. However, he had difficulty supporting Leicester during the latter's dispute with other Gwynedd families, was regularly at law, and had legal wranglings over his stepson Thomas Salusbury's inheritance. He bequeathed money so that poor children from the parish of Beddgelert might be educated at Friars School, Bangor, Caernarvonshire.

On Morris Wynn's death, on 18 August 1580, the estate was inherited by Sir John *Wynn (1553–1627), his eldest son by his first marriage. He became the most illustrious member of the family and commanded a leading position in the political and administrative life of north Wales for almost half a century. He married Sidney (*c*.1560–1637), daughter of Sir William Gerard of Chester and his wife, Dorothy, about 1578. They had ten sons and two daughters. He was appointed a member of the council in the marches of Wales in 1603–4, knighted in 1606, served as deputy lieutenant of Caernarvonshire from 1586 to 1627, and was created a baronet in 1611. It was during his time that the family became firmly protestant. He died on 1 March 1627 and was buried in Llanrwst parish church.

Sir John Wynn's eldest son and namesake died in Italy in August 1614 while on the grand tour and the estate was inherited by his second son, Sir Richard *Wynn, second baronet (1588–1649), who married Anne (*d*. 1668), daughter and coheir of Sir Francis Darcy of Isleworth, Middlesex. They had no surviving children. He was knighted in 1616 and was appointed groom of the bedchamber to Charles I and Henrietta Maria and was MP for Caernarvonshire, Ilchester, Andover, and Liverpool between 1614 and 1648. Although he mainly lived in London, a lasting monument to his connections with Llanrwst is the Wynn chapel (1633) attached to the parish church, which houses the Wynn memorials. He died on 19 July 1649 and was buried in Wimbledon church on 6 August.

Wynn was succeeded by his brother **Sir Owen Wynn**, third baronet (*c*.1590–1660), who was educated at Westminster School, from 1605, at Eton College, and at St John's College, Cambridge. Close family relations with John Williams, lord keeper of the great seal, led to his marriage to Williams's niece, Grace, daughter of Hugh Williams of Y Wig, Caernarvonshire. This marriage was probably arranged because he was expected to inherit and, although neglected by his father, he had a happier youth than his elder brother. Although he lacked his father's initiative and strength of character, and revealed ambivalence in his loyalties during the 1650s and a marked lack of self-confidence, he served as JP for Caernarvonshire and Merioneth and as sheriff of Caernarvonshire from 1652 to 1653 and of Denbighshire from 1655 to 1656. Wynn showed little interest in the native bardic tradition but was a good scholar. He collected manuscripts and 'chymicke bookes' (Morris, 23–45), particularly on alchemy, the refining of metals, and other scientific subjects. He also investigated the ways in which lead mines could be worked more profitably on his lands and studied the origins of the forest of Snowdon.

Sir Owen Wynn's only son, **Sir Richard Wynn**, fourth baronet (*c*.1625–1674), succeeded him on his death on 15 August 1660. He was elected MP for Caernarvonshire on 20

January 1647, serving until 1653, and was involved in various local commissions, including the militia commission in 1648. He married Sarah (d. 1671), daughter of Sir Thomas Myddleton of Chirk Castle, Denbighshire, and his second wife, Mary, about 1654. They had one daughter, Mary (b. in or after 1654, d. 1689). Owing to his involvement in Sir George Booth's royalist insurrection in 1659 Wynn was imprisoned for a short period at Caernarfon, but subsequently became prominent in post-Restoration local politics. He served in public offices as JP for Caernarvonshire, Denbighshire, and Merioneth, sheriff of Caernarvonshire 1657–58, *custos rotulorum* from 1660, MP for Caernarvonshire again from 1661, and capital burgess (1653), alderman (1665–6), and common councilman of Denbigh from about 1665. He was addicted to drink and was frequently absent from the House of Commons, for which he was fined £20 in April 1668. His lasting memorial, however, is the small chapel which he had built in Gothic and late Renaissance styles in Gwydir Uchaf in 1673. Wynn's daughter Mary succeeded to the estate, which extended into most of the north Wales counties, on his death on 30 October 1674 and, on 30 July 1678, she married Robert Bertie, seventeenth Baron Willoughby de Eresby, fourth earl and first marquess of Lindsey and first duke of Ancaster and Kesteven. That marriage signified the demise of what had been one of the most powerful gentry families in north Wales for almost two centuries. The estate became the possession of a prominent Lincolnshire aristocratic family based at Grimsthorpe. The baronetcy fell to Sir John Wynn of Watstay (1628–1719), as fifth baronet, son of Henry Wynn, the first baronet's youngest surviving son and MP for Merioneth in 1624, 1625, 1640, and 1671, and on his death in 1719 it became extinct. At about that time the estate was valued at approximately £6000 per annum and covered well over 30,000 acres. Mary Wynn's great-granddaughter Priscilla (1761–1828) married Sir Peter Burrell (1779–1820), who became first Baron Gwydir in 1796, and their great-grandson, Gilbert Henry Heathcote, twenty-fifth Baron Willoughby de Eresby (1830–1910), who became first earl of Ancaster in 1892, began to sell the estate in the 1890s.

J. GWYNFOR JONES

Sources NL Wales, Wynn of Gwydir papers, MSS 1951E–9069E · NL Wales, Wynn of Gwydir papers, Add. MSS 464E–470E · Cardiff City Library, MS 4.101, fols. 89v–106v · *Heraldic visitations of Wales and part of the marches … by Lewys Dwnn*, ed. S. R. Meyrick, 1 (1846), 158–9 · J. E. Griffith, *Pedigrees of Anglesey and Caernarvonshire families*, 3rd edn (1997), 280–81 · Burke, *Peerage* · J. Ballinger, ed., *Calendar of Wynn (of Gwydir) papers, 1515–1690* (1926) · J. Wynn, *The history of the Gwydir family*, ed. J. Ballinger (1927) · J. Wynn, *The history of the Gwydir family and memoirs*, ed. J. G. Jones (1990) · HoP, *Commons, 1509–58* · HoP, *Commons, 1558–1603* · HoP, *Commons, 1660–90* · J. G. Jones, *The Wynn family of Gwydir: origins, growth and development, c. 1490–1674* (1995) · J. K. Gruenfelder, 'The Wynns of Gwydir and parliamentary elections in Wales, 1604–40', *Welsh History Review / Cylchgrawn Hanes Cymru*, 9/2 (1978–9), 121–41 · O. Morris, *The 'chymick bookes' of Sir Owen Wynne of Gwydir: an annotated catalogue* (1997)
Archives Cardiff Central Library, MS 4.101 · NL Wales, Add. MSS 464E–470E · NL Wales, deeds · NL Wales, deeds, various accounts, rentals, valuations; agent's corresp. etc., visitor's book · NL Wales, deeds and papers · NL Wales, MSS 9051E–9069E · NRA, priv. coll.,

family and estate papers · PRO, rent rolls, accounts, deeds, will, various counties | Gwynedd Archives, Caernarfon estate papers · Hatfield House, Hertfordshire, Salisbury MSS · PRO, state papers foreign and domestic · PRO, state papers domestic

Wynn, Charles Watkin Williams (1775–1850), politician, was born on 9 October 1775, the second son and third of the six surviving children of Sir Watkin Williams Wynn, fourth baronet (1749–1789), of Wynnstay, Denbighshire, and his second wife, Charlotte (1754–1832), the daughter of the former prime minister George *Grenville and his wife, Elizabeth (*née* Wyndham); Henry Watkin Williams *Wynn was his younger brother. His father, a well-known dilettante and member of parliament for Shropshire (1772–4) and Denbighshire (1774–89), died when Wynn was thirteen and his mother and her childless brothers Thomas and William Wyndham *Grenville (afterwards Lord Grenville) became the leading figures in his life. The estates and influence of the squires of Wynnstay ranged over seven counties in north Wales and the marches, and being assured of a parliamentary seat Wynn was encouraged to aspire to the political achievements of the Grenvilles, of his paternal grandfather, Sir Watkin Williams *Wynn (1693?–1749), who led the tory opposition to Walpole, and of his great-great-grandfather Sir William *Williams (1633/4–1700), the speaker of the House of Commons and solicitor-general.

From 1779 to 1783 Wynn and his elder brother Watkin (1772–1840) were tutored privately by Robert Nares who in 1786 also became their tutor at Westminster School, where Wynn was admitted on 12 March 1784. Wynn retained a lifelong connection with this establishment, officiating as steward at the 1799 and 1823 anniversaries and endowing an East India Company writership exclusive to Westminster boys in 1826 and again in 1829, when he was elected a Busby trustee. On 24 December 1791 he matriculated at Christ Church, Oxford, where he had rooms in Skeleton Corner. Between Westminster and Oxford he acquired a circle of lifelong friends, whose careers he helped to advance: the East India Company official George Strachey (1776–1849), the exchequer clerk Grosvenor Charles Bedford (1775–1839), and the poet Robert Southey with whom, and under the pseudonym St Pardulph, he planned *The Flagellant* in 1792 to mimic the Eton paper, *The Microcosm* (*Life and Correspondence of Robert Southey*, 1.3 n.); the classical scholar and archaeologist Peter Elmsley, churchman Bishop Reginald Heber, lawyer Joseph Phillimore, and administrator Sir Charles Sexton (1773–1835), whom his sister Harriet was to reject as a suitor in 1810. He graduated BA in 1795, MA in 1798, and was created DCL on 5 July 1810.

Wynn was admitted to Lincoln's Inn on 21 April 1795 and called to the bar on 27 November 1798. Watkin, who had succeeded to the baronetcy in 1789, appointed him recorder of Oswestry and he practised for some seven years on the Oxford and north Wales circuits. He was elected a bencher in 1835. Watkin failed to secure Wynn's election for Wenlock in 1796, but on 29 July 1797 their cousin Lord Camelford returned him for his borough of Old Sarum at Lord Grenville's request. He resigned this seat to become a candidate for Montgomeryshire, on a vacancy in March 1799. By the acquiescence of the second earl of Powis and his heirs he was elected unopposed, and retained the seat for life, defeating the whig reformer Joseph Hayes Lyon by 703 votes to 302 in the only contest in May 1831.

Wynn acted with the Grenvilles, and his maiden speech on 19 June 1798 was in justification of the Pitt ministry's decision to send the militia to Ireland. Soon afterwards he went there himself with Watkin's regiment, the ancient British fencibles. The visit confirmed his commitment to Catholic emancipation, and he did not oppose the union. A major since 1798 in the London and Westminster light horse and the Ruabon volunteer regiment in north Wales, with Watkin and their brother Henry, he featured on 21 June 1801, in military dress, in Gillray's *A Welch Tandem* (George, 8, no. 9760). He contributed regularly to the 1803 parliamentary debates on the volunteers, commanded the Montgomeryshire troop that year and the yeomanry cavalry from 1808 to 1828 and 1831 to 1844, when he retired on health grounds. He rarely missed manoeuvres and led them out against the Chartists at Llanidloes on 4 May 1839 (*The Times*, 6 May 1839).

Wynn remained with his uncles in opposition during Addington's ministry and spoke against its terms of peace with France (4 November 1801) and the treaty of Amiens (14 May 1802), but differed from his family in his support for the impeachment of Lord Melville (12 June 1805), which he helped to prepare. On 19 February 1806 he became under-secretary of state for the Home department in Lord Grenville's 'ministry of all the talents'. William Windham questioned his qualifications, and the preferment afforded to the Grenville 'cousinhood'—Buckingham, the Fortescues, Nevilles, and Wynns—induced the caricaturist James Gillray to include them among the hungry grunters sucking John Bull's old sow to death in 'More Pigs than Teats' (5 March 1806). Gillray also lampooned Watkin, whose speech was impaired by an overlarge tongue, and Wynn, who had a high-pitched voice, as 'Bubble and Squeak, a Duet' in *The Bear [C. J. Fox] and his Leader [Lord Grenville]* (19 May 1806) (George, 8, nos. 10540, 10566). Wynn was dismissed when the duke of Portland succeeded Grenville in October 1807, and considered a return to office impossible while the anti-Catholic George III reigned. He counted among his real achievements the award of a pension to Southey, and the passage in 1807 of a bill authorizing the creation of county asylums, which he improved on in 1828 and 1842.

Nothing apart from gossip and his mother's wishful speculations is known of Wynn's attachments between his unsuccessful courtship of Elizabeth Acland in 1795 and his marriage on 9 April 1806 to Mary Cunliffe (1785/6–1838), daughter of Sir Foster Cunliffe, third baronet (1755–1834), of Acton Hall, near Wrexham, Denbighshire. They settled on the Wynnstay estate at Llangedwyn near Oswestry, in a house previously occupied by Wynn's grandmother Frances, *née* Shakerley (*d.* 1803), and £300 was added to his £500 annuity, £160 of which he habitually set aside for Southey, who in 1805 dedicated *Madoc* 'Omne

solum forti patria' to him as a token of sixteen years of disinterested friendship. Wynn was not a wealthy man and experienced difficulty in supporting his career and his family of three sons and five daughters without the spoils of office.

Wynn was genuinely fond of parliamentary life. He laboured to master its procedures and drew attention to his knowledge throughout his career, intervening in debate whenever petitions, electoral corruption, and controverted elections were considered. He frequently resorted to the devices of raising points of order and precedence to harry political opponents, to mask his own policy differences with relatives and colleagues, and to advance his claim to the speakership. His advocacy of inquiry into the duke of York's alleged misconduct of army patronage and examination of General Clavering at the bar of the House of Commons in March 1809 earned him a place in the 'Westbourne Procession' (*The Satirist*, 1 April 1809), Cruickshanks's 'General Clavering' (16 June 1809), and De Wilde's 'John Bull in a Fever' (1 July 1809), and was recalled by Gillray in 'Tentanda via est qua me quoque possim tollere humo' (8 August 1810) marking Grenville's appointment as vice-chancellor of the University of Oxford, for which Wynn, who saw it as means of furthering the Catholic cause, canvassed avidly (George, 8, nos. 11297, 11339–40, 11570). Wynn's *Argument upon the jurisdiction of the House of Commons to commit in cases of breach of privilege*, published in May 1810, dealt with the arrest of Sir Francis Burdett for instigating proceedings against Speaker Abbot, Wynn being clear that the house possessed the power to do this. His speech on 8 June, when he failed by seventy-four votes to fourteen to revive the issue, and his account of Speaker Williams's case, based on documents at Wynnstay, formed an appendix to later editions. His aspirations focused firmly on the speakership, the Home Office, and Ireland, and he was loath to contemplate alternatives when overtures were made to Lord Grenville during the 1810–12 regency crisis and in 1820–21: he was included by W. H. Brooke as 'Wynny Welsh Goat called the Squeaker' in his satire 'The anti-royal menagerie' (1 December 1812) (George, 9, no. 11916).

Wynn's support for the princess of Wales and his opposition sympathies became more apparent after the 1815 peace; but he condoned the suspension of habeas corpus and the Seditious Meetings Bill in parliamentary speeches on 26 February and 3 March 1817. He was proposed to succeed Abbot as speaker on 2 June 1817, but the prime minister, Lord Liverpool, favoured his rival Charles Manners Sutton, who defeated him by 312 votes to 151. After the semi-retirement of his uncles, who still demanded consultation on all matters of policy, Wynn became leader in November 1817 of the Grenvillite squad in the House of Commons, accountable to Buckingham, who headed the group in the Lords, as they walked a tightrope between government and opposition. Though divided among themselves over the grants to royal dukes and the 1819 Bank Charter Act, the 'third party' (as they were widely known) were united in their opposition to the Aliens Bill and their support for Catholic relief, and collectively sympathized with the firm line taken by the Liverpool administration after the Peterloo massacre. Wynn had anticipated the financial and constitutional problems raised by the Queen Caroline affair, during which his opinions on procedure were valued and sought after. Despite his preference for her impeachment, he expressed full confidence in the Lords' proceedings (6 July 1820), but informed Thomas Grenville privately on 27 August that he could not approve a bill of pains and penalties, which 'without any clause for divorce', was 'subversive of every principle of our political system' (Coed-y-maen MS 183, 584–5). Its failure spared him 'the necessity of declaring my difference from my uncles and most of my political connection' (Wynn to Phillimore, 2 Nov 1820, Coed-y-maen MSS, bundle 29). Buckingham complained repeatedly and with justification in 1820 and 1821 that while he drew closer to a formal junction with the administration, Wynn followed 'his own whim' and 'half-Whig principles ... [and] everything that is told him passes immediately through the sieve of every possible uncle and aunt, and not only gets all over London, but is submitted to the question of their individual imprimatur' (Buckingham to Fremantle, 13 June 1821, Fremantle MSS).

Six months of negotiations preceded Wynn's appointment as president of the Board of Control in January 1822, which gave him a seat in the cabinet and on the council. He remained free to support Catholic relief, and did so: he appreciated the irony that passage of the measure in 1829 could only have been effected by its erstwhile opponents. Wynn's voice, and his accession to office, along with that of other Grenvillites, attracted lampoons and hostile comment and were the subject of opposition taunts and motions on 14 March, 25 April, and 15–16 May 1822. Londonderry's suicide in August 1822 deprived Wynn of support in the cabinet, and plots to oust the Grenvillites were rife, but nothing came of them or of Canning's oft-repeated suggestions that Wynn be sent out to India as governor-general or backed for the speakership. He was, however, excluded from the discussions of the inner cabinet and Wellington regularly shadowed his brief: Wynn steadfastly opposed combining the offices of governor-general and commander-in-chief, maintaining that 'Lord Hastings has done enough mischief in those capacities' (Buckingham, 2.232–3). His capacity for detail, grasp of regional and religious differences, and humane policies served him well in debate but failed to impress the India board during the First Anglo-Burmese War of 1824–6 and his indecision, particularly evident when faced with the task of recommending a successor in 1824 to Sir Thomas Munro, the governor of Madras (who eventually agreed to stay on), irritated his ministerial colleagues. Wynn's failure to secure the governorship of India for Buckingham in 1825–6, compounded by his being offered it himself, caused acrimony and their breach became complete when Buckingham's application to the newly formed Canning ministry in April 1827 also failed.

Denied the Home Office by Canning, Wynn remained at the Board of Control, which, in the guise of a fierce looking man with bull's horns, he represented in Cruikshanks's cartoon 'The wild beasts sports of the East' (9 April 1827; George, 10, no. 15370). He was glad to stay on under Goderich after Canning's death, but, after weeks of political isolation and sick with influenza and rheumatism, he was dismissed in January 1828 by Wellington, who failed to secure him a promised pension of £3000 a year. Southey, whom he assisted in editing Heber's letters, had warned him in September 'to look to another plank in the State-vessel', in the knowledge that his colleagues found him 'one of the most impracticable persons to deal with, taking crochets in his head and holding to them with invincible pertinacity' (*Life and Correspondence of Robert Southey*, 2.325, 349–53, 4.132). Wynn vented his spleen in a Commons speech on 21 February 1828, and rightly ignored reports that he would be offered the speakership. But he was not yet ready to 're-embark with the Whigs or even to join company with Lord Lansdowne' as his uncles wished (C. W. W. Wynn to Henry Wynn, 25 Jan, 1 Feb, 29 Feb, 14 March 1828, NL Wales, MS 4817 D). Forced to economize, he let his house in Whitehall Place and moved to cheaper accommodation in Clarges Street and later Jermyn Street. He continued to correspond and to contribute to debates on India, in the course of which he advocated the admission of Indians and men of mixed race to government office (4 May 1830, 10, 12, 15–19, 26 July 1833), the retention of East India College, Haileybury (29 July 1833), the removal of the East India Company monopoly of trade with China, which, as he reminded the house on 13 June 1833, he had supported since Canning suggested it in 1813.

Wynn voted against the Wellington ministry in the civil-list division on which they fell on 15 November 1830, and hoped to become home secretary or be backed for the speakership by the succeeding administration led by Lord Grey. Instead he was made secretary at war, at a salary of £2480 a year, and without a seat in the cabinet. Wynn had consistently endorsed the disfranchisement of corrupt boroughs, the transfer of their seats to large towns, and shorter polls, taken by district. But he opposed all wider plans of parliamentary reform and resigned on 5 March 1831 rather than support the government's bill. He nevertheless voted for it on 22 March and 6 July 1831, in a vain hope of quelling constituency opposition and securing concessions: he pressed for additional representation for Wales, and suggested extending its contributory boroughs system to England to avoid disfranchisements (9, 10, 13 August 1831). Unnerved by what he perceived as the political convergence of the whigs and radicals, he acted increasingly with Lord Clive and Thomas Frankland Lewis. Though he refused to join Wellington's projected administration in May 1832, he looked to the Conservatives and Peel thereafter. They endorsed his canvass for the speakership in November 1832, but he reluctantly agreed with Peel that poor health forbade his candidature when the chair became vacant in 1834. In nominating Henry Goulburn on 27 May 1839, he defined the necessary qualities as 'self possession, vigour and resolution, and at the same time, a degree of courtesy to temper all these qualities' (*Hansard 3*, 47, 1839, 1042). From December 1834 to April 1835 Wynn was chancellor of the duchy of Lancaster in Peel's ministry, serving also on the ecclesiastical duties and revenues commission from 4 February to 30 May 1835. He was not included in Peel's 1841 cabinet and declined the consolation prize of a commissionership of Greenwich Hospital.

Wynn's interest in the antiquities and language of Wales was scholarly, if at times self-serving, and included the attendance at eisteddfodau, Cymrodorion, and St David's day festivities expected of a Welsh country gentleman and MP. By 1817 he favoured the abolition of Wales's separate judicature and its assimilation into the English system, but he misjudged the strength of local opposition to the 1828–9 commission's report and the 1830 Administration of Justice Act by which this measure was effected. He admitted the case for appointing Welsh-speaking clergy (4 March 1833, 8, 12 July 1836), but was reluctant to legislate on the matter. Similarly, he spared little time for the Sabbatarians, and considered the legislation they proposed futile and impractical (16 May 1833, 30 April 1834, 18 July 1834). Convinced that religion could not be maintained without an established church, he mistrusted all measures which he perceived might weaken it, such as the abolition of church rates (21 April 1834), and the admission of dissenters to the universities (20 June 1834, 25 May 1843). Yet he condoned the use of church buildings by Wesleyans and dissenters (21 April 1824) and valued their contribution to education in Wales, which he complained was little understood outside the principality (10 March 1846).

Wynn's later life was marred by the illness and deaths of his sixteen-year-old son Henry Watkin on 9 July 1832, of his mother on 29 September 1832, and later of his uncles and of Southey. The 'one bright point amid the gloom' was the acquisition in James Milnes *Gaskell of a son-in-law 'with a passion for the House equal to his own' (F. Wynn to Henry Wynn, 15 June 1832, NL Wales, MS 2797 D). His health deteriorated markedly following the death of his wife (14 June 1838) and the waters of Wiesbaden which he visited with his unmarried daughter Charlotte Williams-*Wynn (1807–1869) failed to cure his crippling rheumatism. He could barely stand when he became father of the House of Commons in January 1847, and he made his last known intervention in debate, on insolvent MPs, on 27 July 1849. He died on 2 September 1850 at his home at 20 Grafton Street, London, and was buried on the 7th alongside his wife and son at St George's Chapel, Hanover Square. His only surviving son, Charles, succeeded to his 1600 acre Montgomeryshire estate of Coed-maen near Meifod.   MARGARET ESCOTT

Sources NL Wales, Coed-y-maen papers · NL Wales, general series, MSS 2797D, 4811–4819D, 10796C, 10796–10806D · A. W. W. Wynn, 'Charles Watkin Williams Wynn: a memoir', 1936, NL Wales, 10798C · M. Escott, 'Williams Wynn, Charles Watkin', HoP, *Commons, 1820–32* [draft] · R. G. Thorne, 'Williams Wynn, Charles Watkin', HoP, *Commons, 1790–1820* · Duke of Buckingham, *Memoir of the court of George IV*, 2 vols. (1850) · *The life and correspondence of Robert Southey*, ed. C. C. Southey, 6 vols. (1849–50) · *New letters of Robert Southey*, ed. K. Curry, 2 vols. (1965) · F. G. Stephens and M. D. George, eds., *Catalogue of political and personal satires preserved … in the British Museum*, 8–11 (1947–54) · transcripts from the Canning, Fremantle, Liverpool, Peel and Wellington MSS, HoP Archives, 15 Woburn Square, London · M. A. Whittle, 'Charles Watkin Williams Wynn (1775–1850): a political biography', MA diss., U. Wales, Aberystwyth, 1984 · G. Evans, 'Charles Watkin Williams Wynn, 1775–1850', MA diss., U. Wales, Bangor, 1934 · C. W. W. Wynn, *The Times* [parliamentary speeches] · *Hansard 1* · *Hansard 2* · *Hansard 3* · *The correspondence of Charlotte Grenville, Lady Williams Wynn, and her three sons … 1795–1832*, ed. R. Leighton (1920) · J. E. Griffith, *Pedigrees of Anglesey and Carnarvonshire families* (privately printed, Horncastle, 1914), 18–19 · *GM*, 2nd ser., 10 (1838), 107 · *GM*, 2nd ser., 34 (1850), 544–5
Archives CUL, corresp. · NL Wales, corresp. and papers · NL Wales, Williams Wynn letterbooks (and memoir), general series, MSS 4811–4818D, 10798C, 10804D, 10806D | BL, corresp. with Lord Grenville, Add. MSS 58901, 69044 · BL, letters to Thomas Grenville, Add. MSS 41857–41858 · BL, corresp. with William Huskisson, Add. MSS 38748–38752 · BL, corresp. with Lord Liverpool, Add. MSS 38290–38296, 38320–38321, 38411–38412, 38576 · BL, letters to Lord Liverpool, loan 72 · BL, corresp. with Sir Robert Peel, Add. MSS 40355–40592, *passim* · Bucks. RLSS, Fremantle MSS · Christ Church Oxf., Joseph Phillimore MSS · Hunt. L., Grenville MSS · NL Scot., letters to William Elliot · NL Wales, Henry Watkin Williams Wynn MSS, general series · NL Wales, Southey MSS, general series · U. Southampton, Wellington MSS, database
Likenesses J. Hoppner, oils, 1805, Dolben & Plas-yn-Cefn, St Asaph · M. A. Shee, oils, 1835, Christ Church Oxf. · W. J. Ward, mezzotint, pubd 1835 (after M. A. Shee), BM, NPG · G. Hayter, group portrait, oils (*The House of Commons, 1833*), NPG
Wealth at death £25,000: 1851, wills, PRO, PROB 8/243; PRO, PROB 11/2120/713; PRO, PROB 11/2128/185

Wynn, Charlotte Williams- (1807–1869), letter-writer and diarist, was born on 16 January 1807, the eldest of the five daughters and two sons of the politician and public servant Charles Watkin Williams-*Wynn (1775–1850) and his wife, Mary (d. 1838), eldest daughter of Sir Foster Cunliffe bt. Charlotte Williams-Wynn's childhood was spent at Dropmore on the Thames, the seat of her great-uncle, Lord Grenville, and at the family home at Llangedwyn; she was educated at home. Both at Dropmore and later at her parents' London home she met many distinguished people, both in politics and, because of her father's close friendship with Robert Southey, in literature. Exposed young to political society, she took a keen interest in public affairs all her life. In 1836 she travelled with her parents to Wiesbaden and on the steamer voyage up the Rhine met the Prussian statesman Baron Varnhagen von Ense. Though he was older than she, they began a friendship that continued until his death in 1858. They corresponded for twenty-two years and met during her father's annual visits to Germany. Her letters often share with the baron her views on German literature and thought, and express admiration for Kant, Hegel, Fichte, Goethe, and Luther. Others with whom she formed lasting friendships that influenced her life included Carlyle, Baron von Bunsen, M. Rio, and the Revd F. D. Maurice, the last of whom she venerated in a friendship continued from 1849 until her death. A letter from Maurice, printed with her *Memorials*,

Charlotte Williams-Wynn (1807–1869), by Henry Adlard (after Henry Tanworth Wells, 1856)

featured, strong-chinned woman with determined mouth, by H. Adlard, from a drawing by H. T. Wells RA (1856). HARRIET BLODGETT

Sources *Extracts from letters and diaries of Charlotte Williams Wynn*, ed. H. H. Lindesay (privately printed, London, 1871) • C. Williams-Wynn, *Memorials of Charlotte Williams-Wynn*, ed. H. H. Lindesay (1877) • DNB • CGPLA Eng. & Wales (1869) • d. cert.
Archives CUL, Charles Watkin Williams Wynn corresp. • NL Wales, Charles Watkin Williams Wynn MSS
Likenesses H. Adlard, engraving (after chalk drawing by H. T. Wells, 1856), NPG [*see illus.*] • attrib. H. W. Pickersgill, oils, NMG Wales
Wealth at death under £1500: probate, 5 June 1869, CGPLA Eng. & Wales

praises her devout but undogmatic Anglicanism and 'the thoroughly honest and faithful way' in which she wrestled with religious doubt (Williams-Wynn, *Memorials*, ix). She travelled in Italy and Switzerland as well as Germany, and was in Paris during the troubled days of 1851–2 which she described with an observant eye in her letters (she had similarly detailed her impressions of London during the Chartist agitation of 1848 in earlier correspondence).

Charlotte Williams-Wynn declared 'great cause for thankfulness in the never-failing enjoyment and renovation … which the employment of my intellect brings' (Williams-Wynn, *Extracts*, 38), and her personal writings reflect a woman of cultivated mind, well read in both English and foreign literature. Rich in observations of contemporary happenings, travellers' impressions, and religious speculations, they are scant in personal details and uninterested in fashion. She did not marry, but her published writings do not repine at her single state.

Charlotte Williams-Wynn lived at 43 Green Street in London from 1856 until 1866, when her health required her to live most of the year abroad. She died of cancer on 26 April 1869 at Arcachon, France, and was buried in the local cemetery.

In 1871 Charlotte Williams-Wynn's sister Mrs Harriot H. Lindesay published *Extracts* from her letters and diaries for private circulation; she added a preface to the overlapping but more inclusive *Memorials* in 1877 (reissued 1878). The two books share the same signed engraving of a well-

Wynn, Sir Henry Watkin Williams (1783–1856), diplomatist, born on 16 March 1783, was the younger brother of Charles Watkin Williams *Wynn and the son of Sir Watkin Williams Wynn, fourth baronet (d. 1789) and his wife, Charlotte, *née* Grenville (d. 1832). He entered the Foreign Office as clerk in January 1799, when his uncle, William Wyndham *Grenville, Lord Grenville, was its head, and early in 1801 was appointed Grenville's private secretary and précis writer. From April 1803 to October 1806 he was envoy-extraordinary to the elector of Saxony, and his services were rewarded with a pension of £1500 a year. For a few months (January to April 1807) he sat in parliament for the borough of Midhurst on the influence of Lord Carrington, whose daughter, Hester Frances Smith (d. 5 March 1854), he married on 30 September 1813; the couple had three sons and three daughters. Wynn's political career came to nothing, however, and, with his family in opposition to the government, his diplomatic career also foundered. His family's alliance with Lord Liverpool eventually led to Wynn's being made envoy-extraordinary and minister-plenipotentiary to Switzerland in February 1822, an appointment sharply criticized in both houses of parliament. He was transferred to a like position at the court of Württemberg in February 1823. In September 1824 he was sent in a similar capacity to Copenhagen, and remained there until early in 1853. He was sworn of the privy council on 30 September 1825, made a knight grand cross of the Royal Guelphic Order of Hanover in 1831, and created KCB on 1 March 1851. He died on 28 March 1856 at Llanroida, Shropshire.

W. P. COURTNEY, rev. H. C. G. MATTHEW

Sources GM, 2nd ser., 45 (1856), 516 • HoP, *Commons* • *Extracts from letters and diaries of Charlotte Williams Wynn* (1871) • F. Williams Wynn, *Diaries of a lady of quality from 1797 to 1844*, ed. A. Hayward, 2nd edn (1864) • Boase, *Mod. Eng. biog.*
Archives BL, letterbooks, corresp., Add. MSS 43353–43354, 43181–43182, 43237 • Bodl. Oxf., Mediterranean travel journal • NL Wales, corresp. and papers • PRO, letterbook, FO 800 | All Souls Oxf., letters to Charles Vaughan • BL, corresp. with Francis Drake, Add. MS 46837 • BL, letters to Lord Grenville, Add. MS 58900 • BL, letters to Sir Arthur Paget, Add. MS 48399 • Hunt. L., letters to Grenville family • PRO, letters to Francis Jackson, FO 353 • PRO, corresp. with Henry Manvers Pierrepont, FO 334 • Sandon Hall, Staffordshire, Harrowby Manuscript Trust, letters to first earl of Harrowby • U. Southampton L., corresp. with Lord Palmerston

Wynn, Sir John, first baronet (1553–1627), landowner and antiquary, was born at Gwydir, Llanrwst, the eldest son of

Sir John Wynn, first baronet (1553–1627), by unknown artist, 1619

a landowner, Morris *Wynn (b. in or before 1520, d. 1580) [see under Wynn family], and Jane, daughter of Sir Richard Bulkeley of Beaumaris. He claimed descent from Gruffudd ap Cynan, king of Gwynedd (d. 1137). His family sprang from modest freeholders in the township of Penyfed in the commote of Eifionydd. His great-grandfather *Maredudd ab Ieuan ap Robert [see under Wynn family], of Y Gesail Gyfarch in that township, had settled at Dolwyddelan Castle and eventually moved to a new house which he built at Cwm Penamnen. He increased his properties and settled some of his followers as tenants in the area. Before his death he moved to the Conwy valley and built a house at Gwydir, Neuadd Fredudd, to which his successors added substantially. Maredudd was followed by his son, John *Wyn ap Maredudd (b. in or before 1494, d. 1559) [see under Wynn family], and grandson Morris Wynn. On the latter's death on 18 June 1580 his eldest son, John Wynn, inherited a growing estate in Merioneth, Caernarvonshire, and parts of western Denbighshire. He was educated at Furnival's Inn (1572), the Inner Temple (1576), and All Souls College, Oxford (1578). He may have travelled abroad but settled at Gwydir on his father's death with his wife, Sidney (c.1560–1637), daughter of Sir William *Gerard, lord chancellor of Ireland, whom he had married about 1578.

For almost half a century Wynn administered his estate with an iron hand, and added substantially to it. Nothing prevented him from achieving his aims in advancing his landed interests and family fortunes. He served as MP for Caernarvonshire (1586–7), deputy lieutenant (1587–1627), custos rotulorum and sheriff (1587–8, 1602–3). He also was pricked sheriff of Merioneth (1588–9, 1600–01) and Denbighshire (1606–7), and served as JP in the three shires for most of his career. He was knighted on 14 June 1606, appointed a member of the council in the marches in 1603–4, and elevated to a baronetcy on 29 June 1611. His desire to extend his property interests and his family's reputation created for him powerful enemies such as William Williams of Cochwillan, Thomas Prys of Plas Iolyn, both of whom publicly denied him his reputed pedigree, and, in 1603–4, Bishop William Morgan of St Asaph, who quarrelled bitterly with him over church lands in Llanrwst. Wynn, however, typical of the ambitious and self-seeking squires of his age, gave his sons good education at Westminster, Bedford, and Eton, the inns of court, and the universities. His eldest son and namesake, who married the daughter of Sir Thomas Cave of Northamptonshire, died in Lucca in Tuscany on the grand tour in August 1614, and the estate was inherited by Wynn's second courtier son, Sir Richard *Wynn.

John Wynn was involved in many lawsuits, some of them, such as the conflict over tenant rights at Dolwyddelan, extending over many years. In 1615 he was fined 1000 marks by the council in the marches for acting oppressively towards his tenants in Pen-maen and Llysfaen but, after having bribed Bernard Lindsey, a groom of the bedchamber, he submitted to the court's censure and was pardoned. Despite this blemish on his career as a landed squire he continued to maintain his reputation although, by 1620, it was evident that he had lost much of his drive. On 20 December of that year Sir Richard Wynn contested and lost the Caernarvonshire election against John Griffith of Cefnamwlch, Llŷn. This was a serious blow to Gwydir domination and to Sir John Wynn's own reputation. From then on until his death the political fortunes of the Wynns wavered and declined. It can be said that Sir John Wynn was a typical homekeeping Tudor landowner who used what resources remained at his disposal to consolidate his position in the native community as well as in London circles.

Wynn was also a scholar and antiquary. He was a staunch patron of traditional poetry and granted hospitality to several itinerant bards including Siôn Tudur, Simwnt Fychan, Rhisiart Phylip, Siôn Phylip, Siôn Mawddwy, Huw Pennant, and Huw Machno, the household bard who sang lavishly to the gardens surrounding Gwydir Isaf and Gwydir Uchaf, Wynn's summer residence built in 1612. He compiled the Book of Sir John Wynn (c.1594–1615) which contained copies of bardic tributes to individual members of the family; Vita Gruffini filii Conani, a Latin version, translated by Nicholas Robinson, bishop of Bangor, of Historia Gruffud vab Kenan; and the original copy in Wynn's own hand of The History of the Gwydir Family, which traced the family's background and exploits from the twelfth century onwards. His kinsman Sir Thomas Wiliems, of Trefriw, presented Wynn with Crynodeb helaethlawn or diarebion camberaeg gorchestol (1620), his collection of Welsh proverbs, and Wynn encouraged him to publish his Latin-Welsh dictionary (Thesaurus linguae Latinae et Cambrobrytannicae). After Wiliems's death in 1622 Wynn corresponded with John Davies of Mallwyd, the leading late Renaissance scholar in Wales, which eventually led to the publication of Wiliems's work as the second part of Davies's *Antiquae linguae Britannicae dictionarium duplex* (1632).

Wynn also built up a fine library at Gwydir and was in contact with fellow scholars and antiquaries. He compiled his *Memoirs* (c.1620), which contained short biographical details of Caernarvonshire notables of his generation; wrote a *History of Penmaenmawr*; and annotated a copy of the *Record of Caernarvon*. Although there is some doubt as to whether he actually founded the free school and almshouses at Llanrwst he was closely involved with the ventures. He operated lead mines on his land in Llanrhychwyn, and proposed to develop the manufacture of Welsh friezes in the Conwy valley using Irish labour, and the Anglesey copper mines. In 1625 he approached Sir Hugh Myddelton, the London-based entrepreneur, with a proposal to reclaim land by building an embankment across Traeth Mawr in Porthmadog. Wynn lived in the years when the Welsh gentry were riding on the crest of the wave, fully established as masters of their communities and servants of the Tudors and Stuarts. He combined loyalty to the crown and the protestant church and was the chief architect of his family's prestige. His fortunes, however, were occasionally hit by economic recession and bad weather conditions which led him into debt and adversely affected his ability to maintain the estate and family commitments. Nevertheless, the Gwydir estate on his death was valued at about £3000, with properties in almost all counties in north Wales. In his efforts to increase that estate Wynn has unjustly earned the reputation of being heartless and oppressive towards his tenants, and several unfounded traditions testify to his querulous nature. A well-known brass engraving made from a likeness of him by Robert Vaughan was placed among the Wynn memorials in the Gwydir chapel in Llanrwst parish church, and portraits by anonymous artists (c.1615–1619) are in private collections. A late eighteenth-century engraving of him by William Sharp is in the British Museum. They all depict Wynn as an imperious landed squire and confirm the traditional view of him. He died at Gwydir on 1 March 1627 and was buried in Llanrwst parish church.

J. GWYNFOR JONES

Sources NL Wales, Panton MSS 9051E–1969E • *Heraldic visitations of Wales and part of the marches … by Lewys Dwnn*, ed. S. R. Meyrick, 2 (1846), 158–9 • Foster, *Alum. Oxon.* • W. H. Cooke, ed., *Students admitted to the Inner Temple, 1571–1625* (1868) • [J. Ballinger], ed., *Calendar of Wynn (of Gwydir) papers, 1515–1690, in the National Library of Wales* (1926) • J. G. Jones, *The Wynn family of Gwydir: origins, growth and development, c.1490–1674* (1995) • J. G. Jones, *Syr John Wynn* (1991) • A. Hughes, *List of sheriffs for England and Wales: from the earliest times to AD 1831*, PRO (1898); repr. (New York, 1963), 248, 251, 260 • J. R. S. Phillips, ed., *The justices of the peace in Wales and Monmouthshire, 1541 to 1689* (1975), 20–28, 38–46, 61–9 • W. R. Williams, *The parliamentary history of the principality of Wales* (privately printed, Brecknock, 1895), 59 • J. Steegman, *Houses in north Wales* (1957), vol. 1 of *A survey of portraits in Welsh houses*, 191, 200, pl. 34 (B) • E. G. Jones, 'Sir John Wynn of Gwydir', *Welsh Review*, 6 (1946), 187–91 • C. A. Gresham,

Eifionydd: a study in landownership from the medieval period to the present day (1973) • J. K. Gruenfelder, 'The Wynns of Gwydir and parliamentary elections in Wales, 1604–40', *Welsh History Review / Cylchgrawn Hanes Cymru*, 9/2 (1978–9), 121–41

Archives Cardiff Central Library, MSS • NL Wales, collections • NL Wales, personal and family papers

Likenesses oils, c.1615–1619, priv. coll. • oils, 1619, priv. coll. [*see illus.*] • W. Sharp, line engraving, BM; repro. in P. Barrington, *Miscellanies* (1781) • R. Vaughan, line engraving, BM, Gwydir Chapel, Llanrwst

Wealth at death approx. £3000: will, NL. Wales, 9062E, 1518

Wynn, Morris (*b.* in or before **1520**, *d.* **1580**). *See under* Wynn family (*per. c.*1465–1678).

Wynn, Sir Owen, third baronet (*c.***1590–1660**). *See under* Wynn family (*per. c.*1465–1678).

Wynn, Sir Richard, second baronet (**1588–1649**), courtier, was the second son of Sir John *Wynn, first baronet (1553–1627), of Gwydir, and his wife, Sydney (*fl.* 1560–1637), daughter of Sir William Gerard of Ince, Lancashire, lord chancellor of Ireland. He was educated at Lincoln's Inn (1606–8). He benefited in turn from the patronage of the Howards and the Herberts, entering the service of successive lord chamberlains, Thomas Howard, earl of Suffolk, and William Herbert, earl of Pembroke. He also enjoyed the support of his kinsman and family friend John Williams, bishop of Lincoln and lord keeper. In 1614 he was elected MP for Caernarvonshire and was knighted on 16 June 1616. He was appointed groom of the bedchamber to Charles, prince of Wales, in 1617 and in that capacity accompanied the prince to Spain in 1623 to seek the hand of the Spanish infanta. His 'Account of the journey of Prince Charles's servants into Spain in the year 1623', written for Charles, was published by Thomas Hearne in the same volume as *Historia vitae et regni Ricardi II, Angliae regis* (1729); it has been seen as demonstrating 'fairly robust Protestantism' and 'a certain insularity' (Aylmer, 363).

In 1618 Wynn married Anne (*d.* 1668), coheir of Sir Francis Darcy of Isleworth, near Brentford (or Brainford), thereby residing at Brainford House. The 1620s saw him enhance his position at court, but his failure to win the shire seat of Caernarfon in the 1621 parliament, losing to John Griffith the younger of Cefnamwlch, Llŷn, was a major blow to the public image of the Wynn family and was largely responsible for its political decline in north Wales. Instead he was elected MP for Ilchester in 1621, 1624, and 1625, probably through Pembroke's influence. In 1625 he was granted a reversion as Queen Henrietta Maria's treasurer or receiver-general and succeeded the earl of Totnes in that office in 1629, spending most of his time thereafter at the queen's palace, Wimbledon House, on the south bank of the Thames; he also had a house near the King's Head in the Strand.

On his father's death on 1 March 1627 Wynn inherited Gwydir estate and the baronetcy, his elder brother Sir John Wynn having died on 25 August 1614 at Lucca in Tuscany. He spent little time on his estate and can be described as a typical 'courtier-gentleman' whose public offices at court accounted for his absences. In 1633–4 he financed the building of Gwydir chapel, which houses the

Wynn memorials, adjoining Llanrwst parish church, as well as that of the famous bridge over the Conwy, the south stone panel on the central arch of which bears the Stuart arms and the date 1636. Although tradition has it that Inigo Jones was the architect of both works there is no firm proof that he was involved. Wynn continued bardic patronage at Gwydir and strict metre eulogies in his honour were composed by Huw Machno, Rhisiart Cynwal, and others. He also supported the incorporation of an abridged version of Sir Thomas Wiliems's *Thesaurus linguae Latinae et Cambrobrytannicae* as the Latin–Welsh section of Dr John Davies of Mallwyd's *Antiquae linguae Britannicae dictionarium duplex* (1632). That part of the work was dedicated by Davies to him in memory of the first baronet, who had been anxious to see it printed.

Wynn was appointed to local offices, and commissions, for Caernarvonshire and for Middlesex, acting as a deputy lieutenant and justice of the peace, and being named to the council for Wales (1633). In the Short Parliament elections of 1640 he was elected as a royal nominee for Andover, and also for Newton and Bodmin. He was elected to the Long Parliament for Liverpool, possibly again as a royal nominee. He voted against the attainder of Strafford and, as one with court contacts, arranged for the delegation headed by Sir Ralph Hopton to present the grand remonstrance to Charles I in December 1641. With the outbreak of civil war he did not join Charles I at Oxford or contribute actively to his campaigns, but he was suspended from parliament on 2 September 1642. His house at Brentford was turned into an advance post by parliamentary soldiers in 1642 and captured by Prince Rupert of the Rhine; in November 1645 his property at Gwydir was ransacked by royalists. By then he seems to have made his peace with parliament. From February 1645 he was repeatedly appointed an assessment commissioner for Middlesex and, from 1647, for Caernarvonshire. He was named a militia commissioner for both counties and for Surrey in December 1648 but was secluded from the Commons at Pride's Purge that same month. He died on 19 July 1649, leaving no children, and was buried in Wimbledon church on 6 August, leaving the title and estate to his next surviving brother, Owen *Wynn (c.1590–1660), who became third baronet [see under Wynn family]. His legacies amounted to about £1800, and other properties in the Strand and Middlesex were left to his younger brother Maurice Wynn. **J. GWYNFOR JONES**

Sources [J. Ballinger], ed., *Calendar of Wynn (of Gwydir) papers, 1515–1690, in the National Library of Wales* (1926) · *CSP dom.*, 1629–49 · account books, 1627–49, NL Wales, Wynnstay papers, 161–86 · *JHC*, 2 (1640–42), 330; 3 (1642–4), 256 · *Report on the manuscripts of Lord De L'Isle and Dudley*, 6, HMC, 77 (1966), 142, 234, 444, 454, 465, 587, 598 · Burke, *Peerage* · J. E. Griffith, *Pedigrees of Anglesey and Carnarvonshire families* (privately printed, Horncastle, 1914) · J. R. S. Phillips, ed., *The justices of the peace in Wales and Monmouthshire, 1541 to 1689* (1975), 28–30 · T. Pennant, *A tour in Wales*, 2 (1783); facs. edn (1991), 152–3 · J. Y. W. Lloyd, *The history of the princes, the lords marcher, and the ancient nobility of Powys Fadog*, 4 (1884), 269 · W. R. Williams, *The parliamentary history of the principality of Wales* (privately printed, Brecknock, 1895), 59 · P. Yorke, *The royal tribes of Wales* (1799), 8–9 · J. G. Jones, *The Wynn family of Gwydir: origins, growth and development, c.1490–1674* (1995) · N. Tucker, 'Sir Richard Wynn of Gwydir, 2nd baronet',

Transactions of the Caernarvonshire Historical Society, 22 (1961), 9–19 · E. G. Jones, 'County politics and electioneering, 1558–1625', *Transactions of the Caernarvonshire Historical Society*, 1 (1939), 37–46 · J. K. Gruenfelder, 'The Wynns of Gwydir and parliamentary elections in Wales, 1604–40', *Welsh History Review / Cylchgrawn Hanes Cymru*, 9/2 (1978–9), 121–41 · will, PRO, PROB 11/210, sig. 157 · T. Hearne, ed., *Historia, vitae et regni Ricardi II, Angliae regis* (1729), 297–341 · G. E. Aylmer, *The king's servants: the civil service of Charles I, 1625–1642*, rev. edn (1974), 362–3, 382, 384 · D. Brunton and D. H. Pennington, *Members of the Long Parliament* (1954), 201, 245 · C. H. Firth and R. S. Rait, eds., *Acts and ordinances of the interregnum, 1642–1660*, 1 (1911), 622, 636, 978, 1087, 1183, 1239, 1246; 2 (1911), 270 · J. Bruce, ed., *Verney papers: notes of proceedings in the Long Parliament*, CS, 31 (1845), 58 · Keeler, *Long Parliament*, 402–3 · D. Underdown, *Pride's Purge: politics in the puritan revolution* (1971), 390

Archives NL Wales, accounts · NL Wales, family and estate papers · NL Wales, Wynn of Gwydir MSS, family and estate papers

Likenesses C. J. van Ceulen, c.1630, Wynnstay Hall · F. Bartolozzi, line engraving (after C. Johnson), BM, NPG; repro. in Pennant, *A tour in Wales*, 152a

Wealth at death approx. £1800; also property in Middlesex, the Strand, London, and Gwydir: will, PRO, PROB 11/210, sig. 157

Wynn, Sir Richard, fourth baronet (c.1625–1674). *See under* Wynn family (*per.* c.1465–1678).

Wynn, Sir Watkin Williams, third baronet (1693?–1749), politician, was the grandson of Sir William *Williams and the eldest son of Sir William Williams, second baronet (c.1665–1740), of Llanforda, Shropshire, and his first wife, Jane (d. 1706), the daughter and heir of Edward Thelwall, of Plas-y-ward, Denbighshire. He was educated at Ruthin School and Jesus College, Oxford, where he had a record of idleness and extravagance. Although he did not inherit the family estate and title from his father until 20 October 1740, he had become the greatest landowner in Wales some twenty years before. His marriage to Anne Vaughan on 20 November 1715 brought him within a decade the estates of Llwydiarth, Montgomeryshire, Glan-llyn, Merioneth, and Llangedwyn, Denbighshire; and in 1719, when he took the additional surname of Wynn, he inherited from Sir John Wynn, a cousin of his mother, Rhiwgoch, Merioneth, and above all Wynnstay, Denbighshire, his main residence thenceforth. The vast Wynnstay complex of estates straddled at least five Welsh counties and extended into Shropshire, and at his death had an estimated rent roll of £20,000. That Wynn left a rumoured debt of £120,000 was due to his political zeal. Throughout his life he was a formidable electioneer, sparing neither energy nor expenditure, ruthless in his treatment of tenants and dependants, renowned for creating extra voters by making leases and admitting burgesses. Such a reputation could itself serve a purpose. 'The policy of elections is to talk great and seemingly to carry everything on with the utmost vigour and spirit and to set forth they value no expense', noted a disheartened opponent in 1741 (NL Wales, Chirk Castle MS C31). The bishop of Chester in 1739 warned the duke of Newcastle, the government's election manager, of the influence possessed by Wynn, 'whose money and unwearied application keeps up an interest in too many places' (BL, Add. MS 32692, fol. 448). Wynn's electoral activities ranged when necessary over seven

Welsh and four English counties. He himself entered the House of Commons in 1716 at a Denbighshire by-election, overthrowing the traditional hold of the Myddelton family of Chirk Castle, and held the county seat until his death, apart from foul play at the 1741 poll. Despite two Myddelton counter-attacks in 1722 and 1741, Wynn so firmly established the Wynnstay interest in Denbighshire that it dominated the county until 1885.

Wynn was an archetypal tory of the Hanoverian era. There was his incessant opposition to whig ministers. Much of his parliamentary role comprised reiteration of such 'country' principles as disapproval of a large peacetime army and complaints about government corruption, both deemed as threats to political liberty. More obviously tory than such routine opposition was his Jacobitism and his championship of the Church of England. Wynn was a man for whom Christianity was part of the fabric of life—an obituary claimed that 'every day of his life was a preparation for heaven' (GM, 1st ser., 19, 1749, 473)—and the Anglican church its embodiment in this world. In 1719 he therefore opposed attempts by the Stanhope ministry to give concessions to protestant dissenters, and in 1736, with the tacit approval of the Walpole ministry, he took a leading role in preventing repeal of the Test Act. The downside of such religious zeal was local coercion of dissenters and, in the 1740s, persecution of Methodists. There is a story, suspect in its aptness, that on the day of Wynn's accidental death a Methodist meeting uttered this prayer: 'O Arglwydd cwmpa Ddiawl mawr Wynnstay' ('O Lord, humble the great devil of Wynnstay'; Roberts, 12).

Apart from this religious dimension there was little to distinguish Wynn's electoral and parliamentary behaviour from that of other opponents of government, whig or tory; and both at Westminster and in constituencies he formed tactical alliances with opposition whigs during the 1730s and 1740s. He even secured the election of two whig cousins, both ministerial men too, for Anglesey in 1725 and Flint Boroughs in 1747, family being more important than politics even for such a committed partisan. But usually his efforts were directed to securing the return of tory MPs, the north Wales tally in the 1722 election being nine out of eleven. Wynn, apart from his own Denbighshire seat, controlled the shire and borough seats in Montgomeryshire until deprived of the latter by a notorious Commons electoral decision in 1728, and he participated in elections elsewhere as occasion demanded: for 1734 in constituencies as scattered as Anglesey, Cardigan Boroughs, Bridgnorth, Chester, and Wigan. At Westminster Wynn soon emerged as one of the Walpole ministry's most vociferous critics, and he successfully introduced an act in 1729 to curb electoral corruption, containing a 'last determinations clause' preventing the Commons changing any previous decision about a constituency franchise. By 1730 he was prominent in the parliamentary opposition, a patron of Lord Bolingbroke's political weekly The Craftsman, and a member of that inner tory council the Loyal Brotherhood. Oxford University early acknowledged Wynn's importance in tory circles by a DCL in 1732. In the 1730s, when he blossomed

into a front-line speaker, his disguised name in the scanty and unofficial reports of parliamentary debates was 'Waknits Wingal Ooynn'. In 1740 the death of the acknowledged tory leader Sir William Wyndham thrust Wynn even more into the political limelight, and the Walpole ministry in the 1741 election targeted his Denbighshire seat in one of the most notorious contests of the century. His Myddelton rival was returned by the sheriff, who disallowed 594 of Wynn's votes after he had won by 1352 to 933. It must have seemed poetic justice to Sir Watkin that Walpole's first defeat in the new parliament came over this Denbighshire election, and after the prime minister resigned early in 1742 Wynn, who had taken temporary refuge in Montgomeryshire, regained the seat and the sheriff was sent to prison. At this election Wynn brought in his two brothers, Robert Williams for Montgomeryshire and Richard Williams for Flint Boroughs.

Many tories naively expected a change of the whig political system on Walpole's fall, and on 18 February 1742 Wynn led a tory group to attend the levee of George II. Such hopes were unfounded, and Wynn was soon busy in opposition again, usually as proposer or seconder of motions critical of government. In 1744, however, the new Pelham ministry sought tory support, and at the end of the year Wynn was offered a peerage, a move reflecting both his nuisance value in the Commons and his presumed distaste for the administrative routine of office. According to Lord Hastings, Wynn's answer was that:

> as long as his Majesty's ministers acted for the good of their country, he was willing to consent to anything; that he thanked his Majesty for the earldom he had sent him, but that he was very well content with the honours he had, and was resolved to live and die Sir Watkin. (Hastings MSS, 3.49)

Early in 1745 Wynn did support the ministry in debate, but this political transformation was short-lived. Although he had accepted neither offices nor honours, he had expected that tories would now be readmitted to local government as county magistrates, and himself submitted lists for Denbighshire and Montgomeryshire. The ministerial failure to respond, and a personal attack on Wynn for deserting the cause of liberty in the pamphlet An Expostulatory Epistle to the Welch Knight caused him to revert to the more familiar and congenial role of ministerial critic before the end of the parliamentary session in the spring of 1745.

The next year was dominated by the Jacobite rising sparked off by the arrival in Scotland of the Young Pretender, Prince Charles Edward Stuart, in July 1745. That event brought out the dichotomy of Wynn's political life, that between the conventional opponent of government at Westminster and the secret Jacobite plotter. Contemporary suspicions of Wynn in the latter respect were amply justified. Wynn, who was probably converted to Jacobitism at Ruthin School by his headmaster, headed from the early 1720s one of the most famous Jacobite clubs, the Cycle of the White Rose in the Welsh border country. He never concealed his Jacobite sympathies. In 1721 he toasted the Pretender in Shrewsbury and Wrexham, and in 1722 publicly burnt a picture of George I. At the exiled Stuart court Wynn was increasingly perceived to be a key figure in any restoration attempt, and after serious plotting began in 1740 he promised to help when the Pretender arrived with a French army. That prerequisite condition was always stipulated by Wynn, who wisely refused to give any written pledge of support. He took part in London negotiations with Stuart agents in 1740, 1742, and 1743, when he also went to consult with Louis XV at Versailles. He repeated the visit in October 1744, even though Britain and France were then at war. This duplicitous behaviour does not accord with the simple, honest character customarily attributed to Wynn. When in 1745 the Young Pretender arrived without an army, Wynn made no move to assist him, and went to London for the parliamentary session instead of staying in north Wales to organize local support. There he was kept under close government surveillance, and thence he sent messages to Prince Charles Edward promising help when a French army arrived. That did not happen, and so Wynn never publicly involved himself in the rebellion. In the aftermath, incriminating evidence about Wynn's Jacobite links came from witnesses and captured papers, but legal proof was lacking, and the Pelham ministry deemed his notoriety a sufficient punishment.

Revelation of Wynn's Jacobite contacts temporarily cooled relations with opposition whigs, but at the 1747 general election mutual self-interest led to co-operation between Wynn, other tory leaders, and Frederick, prince of Wales, now at odds with his father. Wynn took little part in the election campaign apart from supporting candidates in Caernarvonshire and Staffordshire contests, and thereafter personal matters kept him out of politics. His marriage to Anne Vaughan had brought him connubial bliss, but one marred by the death of both their children. A son, born in 1716, died in infancy, and a daughter, Mary, in 1735 at the age of seventeen. Anne seemingly became ill late in 1747, and before her death on 24 May 1748 urged him to marry his goddaughter, 31-year-old Frances Shakerly (1717–1803). This he did, with what would otherwise have been unseemly haste, on 19 July. The apparent motive was a Wynnstay heir, and a son, later the second Sir Watkin, was born on 8 April 1749. A second son was born a year later, but by then Wynn had been killed in an accident, on 26 September 1749, falling off his horse when hunting. He was buried at Ruabon, Denbighshire, on 3 October, amid scenes of great mourning.

The sudden death of a prominent politician made a considerable noise. There is a story that Henry Pelham's brother the duke of Newcastle, who had found Wynn such a thorn in his flesh as both electioneer and parliamentarian, rushed exultantly to inform George II, only to meet a royal rebuff. 'I am sorry for it', answered the king, 'he was a worthy man and an open enemy' (*Bye-gones*, 1903, 140). Prime Minister Pelham took a more measured view. Writing to Wynn's Denbighshire rival Richard Myddelton on 30 September, he commented, 'I can't but be sorry that my old acquaintance met with so unhappy a fate; for set aside his party zeal, which indeed governed him almost in

everything, he was a generous, good natured man' (NL Wales, Chirk Castle MS E613).

'A simple Welsh knight of a vast estate … from whence he was called Prince of Wales' (Walpole, 17.234n): so did Horace Walpole remember the first Sir Watkin Williams Wynn. That unofficial title was bestowed on masters of Wynnstay until the nineteenth century, but the contemporary and historical reputation in Wales of Sir Watkin did not arise merely from territorial power. He was esteemed for private and public virtues, eulogized in obituary notices that conveyed a sense of the loss of a devout man of probity and equable temperament, affable and generous, without a personal enemy. Not all those who suffered from his electoral zeal and religious bigotry would have endorsed such sentiments. But the high regard with which he was held within Wales by the gentry was signified by such events as the desire of all parties that he should witness an electoral agreement of 1743 covering several south-west Wales constituencies, and an unsuccessful request that he would attend a contentious Glamorgan by-election of 1745 to keep the sheriff honest: Wynn scrupulously declined because it was outside 'his province' of north Wales. Welsh esteem for Sir Watkin is further indicated by the story that whenever he went up to London for the parliamentary session it was customary for the Welsh gentry resident in London to meet him at Finchley and form a procession to escort him into town.

At Westminster Wynn's importance stemmed from his role as one of the few spokesmen of the largely inarticulate mass of squires. Hence the significance of his customary opening phrase, 'Sir, I am one of those', mocked by the sophisticated Horace Walpole: 'Sir Watkyn's *One of Those* when rhetoric fails, gives weight to nonsense, as the Prince of Wales' (Walpole, 30.292). By the 1740s he was a leading tory, perhaps the foremost one in the Commons. To describe him as a tory leader would be misleading, for the parliamentary squirearchy was undisciplined, and their spokesmen like Wynn who temporarily joined the Pelham ministry in 1744–5 failed to carry their followers with them. Wynn's career epitomized the demise of the old tory party. Integrity of character did not compensate for lack of the oratorical and organizational skills essential for political success. If Wynn did not seek the power and responsibility of office, neither was he suited to it.

PETER D. G. THOMAS

Sources P. D. G. Thomas, *Politics in eighteenth-century Wales* (1997) · A. Roberts, *Wynnstay and the Wynns* (1876) · NL Wales, Chirk Castle papers · NL Wales, Wynnstay papers · BL, Add. MSS 32686–33072 · *GM*, 1st ser., 1–19 (1731–49) · Walpole, *Corr.*, vols. 17, 30 · *Report on the manuscripts of the late Reginald Rawdon Hastings*, 4 vols., HMC, 78 (1928–47), vol. 3 · *Bye-Gones Relating to Wales and the Border Counties*, 2nd ser., 3 (1893–4) · *Bye-Gones Relating to Wales and the Border Counties*, new ser., 8 (1903–4) · HoP, *Commons* · L. Colley, *In defiance of oligarchy: the tory party, 1714–60* (1982) · History of Parliamentary Office · *GM*, 1st ser., 73 (1803)

Archives NL Wales, Wynnstay MSS · NL Wales, corresp. · NL Wales, papers relating to Denbigh elections | BL, Newcastle MSS, Add. MSS 32686–33072 · BL, letters to F. Price, Add. MS 46400 · NL Wales, Powis Castle MSS

Likenesses attrib. T. Hudson, oils, *c.*1734–1740, Jesus College, Oxford · T. Hudson, portrait, 1740, NMG Wales · J. Aberry, etching,

1753 (after T. Hudson), NPG • J. M. Rysbrack, effigy on monument, 1754, Ruabon Church, Flintshire • J. Faber, mezzotint (after oils attrib. T. Hudson), NPG • J. Wootton, group portrait, Badminton House, Gloucestershire • oils (after M. Dahl, *c.*1729), NPG

Wealth at death £15,000–£20,000 p.a.: HoP, *Commons*, 2.544; NL Wales, Wynnstay MSS

Wynn, William (*bap.* **1709**, *d.* **1760**), Church of England clergyman and Welsh-language poet, was baptized on 19 March 1709, the son of William Wynn of Maesyneuadd, near Harlech in the parish of Llandecwyn in Merioneth, and Margaret, daughter and heir of Roger Lloyd of Ragad, near Corwen, in the same county. He matriculated from Jesus College, Oxford, on 14 March 1727, and graduated BA on 12 October 1730 and MA on 15 July 1735; his father appears to have died about 1731. Wynn was licensed on 22 September 1734 a deacon in Watlington, near Oxford, and was ordained a priest to serve that parish on 19 June 1736; he remained there until he was appointed vicar of Llanbrynmair in Montgomeryshire on 9 June 1739.

Both Wynn's father and grandfather were patrons of the Welsh poets, and it is not surprising that he himself developed an interest in the Welsh poetic tradition, his earliest poem being composed in 1733 during his Oxford years. In the following year he composed an elegy to Rhisiart Fychan, and between 1737 and 1738 he composed three poems to members of the royal family. One of them, in praise of Frederick, prince of Wales, and his wife in 1737, was printed and a copy presented to Lewis Morris on 25 June 1737 (BL, Add. MS 14929, fol. 109). In a draft letter to Edward Samuel (*d.* 1748), on 1 October 1736, Lewis Morris added a note, 'a true Coppy of Mr Wynnes Cowyddau' (BL, Add. MS 14929, fol. 54), which may indicate that Wynn and Morris were already corresponding with each other. They were certainly engaged in a correspondence before 18 November 1737 and exchanging copies of their poems. Both composed a paraphrase of Colley Cibber's 'The Blind Boy', merry verses in imitation of Edmwnd Prys's metrical psalms, as well as songs to be sung on a favourite Welsh air. Wynn, like Morris, was also a champion of the friendly poetic 'feuds' between the poets of different counties. His poetic output is limited and includes a poem to Lewis Morris in 1744, poems on the day of judgment and to William Vaughan's yacht in 1755, and a few poems in free metre including two carols to celebrate Christmas and three poems in a lighter vein. Two of his poems were printed on single sheets, nine were published in *Dewisol ganiadau* (1759), and one of his carols appeared in *Blodeugerdd Cymry* (1759). For a brief period, from 1755 to 1756, Evan Evans, the poet and scholar, served as curate to Wynn at Manafon.

It was at Oxford that William Wynn developed an interest in scholarship and antiquities, and while he was at Watlington Lewis Morris had asked him to peruse a manuscript in Jesus College on his behalf, probably the Red Book of Hergest. He had probably already inherited some Welsh manuscripts through his family, and when he died enquiries were made about them in order to secure their safe keeping. His few surviving letters suggest that he was acquainted with the works of those scholars and authors who had already contributed to Welsh scholarship and antiquities as well as with the works of his contemporaries.

On 6 August 1742 he married Martha Roberts (1715–1751) of Rhydonnen in Llandysilio parish near Denbigh. He received the rectorship of Manafon in Montgomeryshire on 15 March 1747 and resided at Aberriw, to which was added the living of Llangynhafal in Denbighshire on 28 April 1749. The couple had three children. His wife was buried on 11 June 1751. There is an elegy to her in Peniarth MS 196, fol. 107 (NL Wales).

Because of his poetic talent and his scholarship Wynn was elected a corresponding member of the Cymmrodorion Society shortly after 1751 and was an influential member of that select group, which promoted the Welsh classical revival during the first half of the eighteenth century. It might be added that, given his gifts and background, what he accomplished can only be regarded as somewhat disappointing. He died at Llangynhafal on 18 January 1760, and was interred there with his wife on 22 January.

DAFYDD WYN WILIAM

Sources R. G. Hughes, 'Bywyd a gwaith William Wynn, Llangynhafal', MS diss., 1940, vols. 1 and 2 • R. G. Hughes, 'William Wynn, Llangynhafal', *Llên Cymru*, 1 (1950–51), 22–8 • W. Wynn, letter to William Vaughan, 18 Sept 1741, U. Wales, Bangor, Mostyn papers, 9079, no. 33 • W. Wynn, letter to William Vaughan, 9 Aug 1738, U. Wales, Bangor, Nannau papers, 560 • *Additional letters of the Morrises of Anglesey (1735–1786)*, ed. H. Owen, 1–2 (1947–9) • parish register, Llandecwyn [baptism] • parish register, Llangynhafal [burial] • parish register, Llanynys [marriage]

Wynne, Arthur (**1871–1945**), crossword puzzle deviser, was born on 22 June 1871 at 2 Everton Village, Everton, Liverpool, the son of George Wynne, editor of the *Liverpool Courier*, and his wife, Delicia Eliza Ann Sheldon. He had one brother and one sister. As a young man Wynne emigrated to the United States in the mid-1890s and, according to his family tradition, he first worked for an onion farmer in Texas. He soon, however, like his father, became a newspaperman, with his first job as a society editor of a paper in east Liverpool, Ohio. He then gravitated to Pennsylvania, where he was appointed sports editor of the local newspaper at McKeesport. His versatility was demonstrated when he was appointed as the music editor and critic of the *Pittsburgh Despatch*. He even played second violin in the Pittsburgh Philharmonic Orchestra.

Wynne's two passions in life had always been music and puzzles. He was able to fulfil this latter calling when he accepted the editorship of the fun section of the Sunday newspaper *New York World*. It was on 21 December 1913, when he was pressed to fill a space on a page that printers were in a hurry to lock up, that he thought of using the space to revive the acrostic word game which dated from at least Roman times. He constructed a hollow, diamond-shaped grid of interlocking words and dubbed his creation a 'word-cross'.

It was clear from the start, from the volume of letters sent in by readers, that Wynne's word-crosses were popular. However it was not for ten years—until two young, would-be publishers, M. Lincoln Schuster and R. L. Simon, brought out the first ever crossword puzzle book—that a national fad was clearly in the making. Simon and Schuster had sought out Wynne's successor, Margaret Petheridge, and sold more than 2 million copies in the first twenty-four months.

The crossword puzzle craze spread to Britain when the London *Sunday Express* began publishing puzzles on 2 November 1924. The newspaper established that during the war years, with its long hours in air-raid shelters, barracks, and mess decks, one in twenty-five of the population did a crossword every day.

Latterly Wynne became an employee of King Features Syndicate. He did not directly benefit from the many newspapers who used the syndication service. He had never attempted to patent the concept which brought so much pleasure and frustration to so many. He was a contemplative man, with a wide circle of friends. He married twice, first Thelma Sacensen and then Lillian Webb. There was a daughter from the first marriage, and a son and a daughter by the second. He died at the Morton Plant Hospital, Clearwater, Florida, on 14 January 1945.

NORRIS MCWHIRTER

Sources 'Crossword puzzle', *The new encyclopaedia Britannica*, 15th edn (1997) · D. D. Millikin, 'Crossword puzzle', *Collier's encyclopedia*, 7 (1991), 502–3 · R. Millington, *The strange world of the crossword* (1974) · b. cert.

Wynne, Edward (*bap.* 1734, *d.* 1784), jurist, was baptized on 25 February 1734 at St Clement Danes, Strand, London, the son of William *Wynne (*bap.* 1692, *d.* 1765), serjeant-at-law, and his wife, Grace (1700–1779), daughter and coheir of William Brydges, serjeant-at-law. He was admitted to the Middle Temple on 11 February 1749 and matriculated at Jesus College, Oxford, on 11 April 1753. Wynne was called to the bar on 24 November 1758 but thanks to his large fortune did not need to pursue an active career in the law. On his father's death in 1765 he inherited the estate of Little Chelsea in Kensington. Wynne also held the manor of Polsew at St Erme, near Truro, which descended through his father from the Luttrell family, and inherited estates in Somerset on the death of his mother in 1779. In addition he owned a house in Essex Street, London, as well as an estate in Dudley and leases in Wales.

Wynne's wealth enabled him to pursue the life of a gentleman scholar. His library, which he inherited from his father, and which included the collections of Narcissus Luttrell, contained almost 2800 books. These included many scarce pamphlets and old English romances, as well as numerous works on both English and Roman law. In 1765 Wynne published *A Miscellany Containing Several Law Tracts*. The first five tracts in the collection were Wynne's own works, and included *Observations on Fitzherbert's 'Natura Brevium', with an Introduction Concerning Writs*, which grew from loose notes he made while reading the text. This work showed both Wynne's veneration of the common law and his desire to make it more accessible. His aim in publishing these tracts was to show how good sterling law could be found among the rust of antiquity. The collection also included an edition of *Observations Touching the Antiquity and Dignity of the Degree of Serjeant at Law*. This was a tract composed by his father, and had been written in response to a proposal by the chief justice of the common pleas, Sir John Willes, in 1755, to end the monopoly of the serjeants in his court.

Wynne's most important work, *Eunomus, or, Dialogues Concerning the Law and Constitution of England*, was published in 1768. Following the example of Christopher St German he chose the form of the dialogue since he wanted to show that the law was not merely a dry subject only of interest to the profession. The work sought to explain the principles of English law while at the same time refuting popular criticisms of the law, notably concerning its cost and delay, the length of conveyances, and the prolixity of pleading. Although he recognized the existence of abuses, Wynne's attitude to the law was very conservative. In a decade when the right of the jury to decide matters of law was being claimed in libel cases, he sought to demonstrate that questions of law were matters for the judge, and similarly sought to defend the criminal law from charges that it was too severe. Wynne also explained the principles of the mixed constitution, defending both the whig view of the revolution of 1688, and the unequal system of representation in parliament. The book was well received, and was praised as an 'elegant and truly Ciceronian work' (*GM*, 1st ser., 55/1, 1785, 77). However, while it reached a fifth edition in 1822, it was largely overshadowed by the publication at the same time of William Blackstone's *Commentaries*.

Wynne never married and died of cancer of the mouth on 27 December 1784 at his home in Little Chelsea. He left his estates in Somerset to his sister, Mrs Susannah Piercy, and the residue of his estate to his brother, the Revd Luttrell Wynne of All Souls College, Oxford. His library was sold by Leigh and Sotheby after his death in an auction which lasted eleven days, while his home was bought by the parish of St George's, Hanover Square, in 1787 to serve as an additional poorhouse. He was buried in the same grave as his parents in the north cloister of Westminster Abbey on 3 January 1785.

MICHAEL LOBBAN

Sources M. Lobban, *The common law and English jurisprudence, 1760–1850* (1991) · D. Lieberman, *The province of legislation determined: legal theory in eighteenth-century Britain* (1989) · *GM*, 1st ser., 55 (1785), 77 · *A catalogue of the valuable library of Edward Wynne ... which will be sold by auction, by Leigh and Sotheby* (1786) [sale catalogue, 6 March 1786] · Baker, *Serjeants*, 115 · H. A. C. Sturgess, ed., *Register of admissions to the Honourable Society of the Middle Temple, from the fifteenth century to the year 1944*, 1 (1949), 340 · Foster, *Alum. Oxon.* · J. Norris Brewer, *London and Middlesex, or, An historical, commercial and descriptive survey of the metropolis of Great Britain*, 4 (1816), 89 · F. Hitchins, *The history of Cornwall*, ed. S. Drew, 2 vols. (1824), vol. 2 · PRO, PROB 11/1126/54 · IGI · DNB

Wynne, Ellis (1671–1734), Welsh-language author, was born on 7 March 1671 at Y Lasynys, a substantial farmhouse not far from Harlech, Merioneth. He was one of two or three children of Edward Wynne of the mansion of Glyn Cywarch, not far from Y Lasynys, and the heiress of Y Lasynys, whose name is not known.

There is no knowledge as to what school Wynne attended, but the fact that he composed a poem to Beaumaris School may indicate that he went there. On 1 March

1692 he matriculated at Oxford from Jesus College. He took a BA degree and may have taken an MA degree as well. There was a tradition that he was a lawyer—and there is one reference to him as an 'Ll.B.' (M. Williams, *Cofrestr o'r holl lyfrau printjedig gan mwyaf a gyfansoddwyd yn y iaith Gymraeg neu a gyfieithwyd*, 1717, 34)—but his scurrilous attitude to lawyers makes that unlikely. In September 1698 he married Lowri Wynne of Moel-y-glo, which is not far from Harlech. On 10 July 1699 Lowri died on the birth of a baby boy, and the child died soon after. On 14 February 1702 Wynne married Lowri Lloyd of Hafod Lwyfog, a farm not far from Beddgelert in Caernarvonshire. She died in 1720. Nine children were born to them, some of whom died young. The best-known of their children were William and Edward.

In 1701 Wynne published his *Rheol buchedd sanctaidd* ('The rule of a holy life'), a translation of Jeremy Taylor's *The Rule and Exercises of Holy Living* (1650). The title of the original work, with its 'rule' and 'exercises', conveys the nature of the text. It is a devotional work which provides the reader with a set of procedures to make his life more holy. It sets forth a kind of moral and virtuous routine for spiritual fitness. In Wales in the seventeenth century such texts were common, and many of them were translations. Wynne's Welsh version is a splendid reproduction of the mighty sonority of Taylor's English prose, with an occasional adaptation of references to suit the Welsh readers (and listeners). In 1703 he published his *Gweledigaetheu y bardd cwsc* ('Visions of the Sleeping Bard'), based on two English adaptations of Quevedo's *Los sueños*, one by Sir Roger L'Estrange, *The Visions of Dom Francisco de Quevedo Villegas* (1667), and the other by John Stevens (J. S.), *The Visions of Don Francisco de Quevedo Vellegas: the Second Part* (1682). In 1710 an edition of the Welsh Book of Common Prayer prepared by Wynne appeared. In 1755 his son Edward published *Prif addysc y Cristion* ('The Christian's fundamental instruction') which contained a short explanation of the catechism and some prayers and hymns by his father.

Wynne's fame as a writer rests on his *Gweledigaetheu*, which has been acclaimed as a prose masterpiece by several generations of readers—the large number of editions of the work is evidence of its status in Welsh literature. The book consists of three visions; one of the world set out as a city of destruction, one of Death's lower kingdom, and one of hell. An angel leads the Sleeping Bard through the world and through hell, and Master Sleep leads him through Death's lower kingdom. The world's sinners are devastatingly portrayed, with panache, wit, and a satirical disgust that is worthy of Jonathan Swift. They progress from the world through the dark realm and the dark and extremely unpleasant lower court of Death into the various caverns of hell. All of this is presented from the point of view of an ardent Anglican and royalist, a puritanical (though he was no puritan) conservative who looked back with fondness and a sense of loss to his own creation of a mythical age of *noblesse oblige*, but recognized that he was in a modern world of bourgeois profiteers and self-seekers.

A letter from one Humphrey Foulkes to the eminent Welsh scholar and scientist Edward Lhuyd, dated November 1702, makes it clear that Wynne made no secret of the sources of his work:

> Mr Ellis Wynne of Harlech promises us his Bardd Cusc very shortly which is in imitation of Don Quevedo. No question but it will be very acceptable to our countrymen who have been long used to Hên Chwedlau [old tales]. Tom Browns letters from the dead etc. together with old Lucian will give him sufficient hints & he is resolved to adapt all to the Humour of the Welsh.   (R. Ellis, 'Cyfeiriadau at Fardd Cwsg', *Cymry*, 24, 1903, 14)

Visions of the 'other world' were in vogue in the seventeenth century as a literary genre in England and in France. The *Gweledigaetheu* fits into that genre. The genre harks back to Lucian and to the sixth book of Virgil's *Aeneid*, that is, classical portrayals of the other world, and medieval visions of hell. References to Dante's *Divina commedia* also occur in the genre from time to time. In Wynne's case, John Milton's *Paradise Lost* was also an influence. During the political and religious unrest of the seventeenth century in Britain, both puritans and royalists—especially royalists—made use of visions of hell as an extremely convenient convention for condemning their enemies. Wynne followed the royalist example, but he did not succumb to the mechanical operation of the less sophisticated satire.

From soon after it was first published, the style of the *Gweledigaetheu* was acknowledged to be one of its supreme excellencies. The style is very adaptable, and capable of presenting a variety of moods, emotions, and considerations. On the one hand Wynne can produce the great rhetorical sonorousness of a prose tradition that goes back, in Welsh, to the translation of the Bible into Welsh (1588) and beyond that to the cultivated style of the Welsh tradition of court poetry. The opening paragraph of the first vision is an excellent example of such a style:

> On a fine summer noontime, warm, yellow and long, I made my way to the top of one of the mountains of Wales, and took with me a telescope to help my weak eyes to see the far-off near, and little things made large; through the thin clear air and the splendid silent warmth, I could see far, far away over the Irish sea many pleasant prospects ... (Wynne, ed. Donovan and Thomas, 5)

The slow tempo, neatly balanced structure, languorous meandering of the original suggests that sleep is not far off.

On the other hand Wynne can produce vigorous, vivid descriptions and dialogues that succeed in delineating characters and caricatures in an instant. Sometimes he makes use of an earthy colloquialism that can be either properly disgusting in the service of satire, or humorous, especially in portraying pomposity or hypocrisy. Lucifer bids his minions 'roast the lawyers by their own parchment and papers until their learned entrails burst out' (Wynne, ed. Donovan and Thomas, 12).

Through this rumbustious work it may be that Wynne hoped to make his fellow Welshmen consider the spiritual quality of their lives. He certainly sought to make them realize that they ought to belong to the pure (as opposed to the degenerate) Anglican church, and that they were fortunate to live in Britain under Queen Anne rather than in any of the other places his Bard had fancied at the beginning of his *Gweledigaetheu*.

On 24 December 1704 Wynne was made a deacon in the Church of England, and on 31 December took priest's orders. In 1705 he became rector of Llandanwg and Llanbedr, near Harlech. In 1711 he exchanged his living for the rectory of Llanfair-juxta-Harlech, which he held until his death. He died at his home on 13 July 1734 and was buried on 17 July beneath the altar of the church in Llanfair. Throughout his life he lived in Y Lasynys, a house to which he made some additions. The house has now been carefully refurbished by the Friends of Ellis Wynne.

GWYN THOMAS

Sources G. Thomas, *Y Bardd Cwsg a'i gefndir* (1971) · G. Thomas, *Ellis Wynne* (1984) · G. Thomas, 'Ellis Wynne o'r Lasynys', *Llên Cymru*, 6 (1960–61), 83–96 · E. Wynne, *Gweledigaethau y bardd cwsg*, ed. P. J. Donovan and G. Thomas, new edn (1998) · E. Wynne, *Gweledigaethey y bardd cwsc*, ed. J. M. Jones (1898) · *Ellis Wynne, 1671–1734* (1934) · parish register (baptism), 13 March 1671, Llanbedr · Foster, *Alum. Oxon.* · bishop's register, Bangor diocese, NL Wales

Wynne, Greville Maynard (1919–1990), businessman and spy, was born on 19 March 1919 in Wrockwardine Wood, east of Shrewsbury, Shropshire, the only son to grow up of Ethelbert Wynne, plater, and his wife, Ada Pritchard. He had three elder sisters; an elder brother had died aged one in 1915. He was brought up at Ystradmynach, a mining village 12 miles north of Cardiff, where his father was a foreman in an engineering works. His mother died when he was fourteen. He worked in his middle teens as an electrician, and took evening courses in engineering at Nottingham University.

Called up into the army in 1939, Wynne spent the Second World War as a sergeant in the field security police, looking after elementary security in various parts of Great Britain. He acquired the vocabulary of the intelligence corps, in which he served. On being demobilized in 1946 he married, on 21 September at St Anne's, Wandsworth, Sheila Margaret, daughter of Gordon Beaton, chemist. They had a son.

Wynne already described himself, on his marriage certificate, as a consulting engineer—a trade in which he made himself useful to exporters, with whom lay the country's best hope of staying solvent. In a decade and a half he built up a profitable small business, and came to specialize in assisting exports to eastern Europe, then under rigid communist control from Moscow. He occasionally visited the USSR to forward his clients' interests. He was a short, stocky man, with a brisk, cheerful manner, a toothbrush moustache, and smooth dark hair.

As a matter of routine MI6 (the Secret Intelligence Service) briefed many British businessmen who travelled behind the iron curtain about points for which they might like to look out while there; Wynne was among them. Chance turned him into an important pawn in the 'great game'. Oleg Penkovsky, a colonel in Russian secret military intelligence, had been demoted from work he enjoyed in Turkey to run a Moscow committee that enquired into scientific matters—a cover for industrial

Greville Maynard Wynne (1919–1990), by unknown photographer, 1964 [at RAF Northolt after being exchanged for the Soviet agent Gordon Lonsdale]

espionage against the capitalist powers. Entirely disillusioned with the Soviet regime, Penkovsky sought to change sides, and through several intermediaries approached the American Central Intelligence Agency (CIA), without securing a response. He then approached Wynne, who informed MI6, which decided to take the case up, and to handle it jointly with the CIA. MI6 accepted Wynne as one of the conduits through which material could from time to time be passed to and from Penkovsky.

Some of this material was of world strategic importance, for it enabled the Americans to outface the Russians in the Cuban missile crisis of 1962. Shortly thereafter Wynne, who may have shown unprofessional enthusiasm at finding himself in Penkovsky's presence, unaware of the strictness with which Soviet citizens kept watch on each other, was abruptly arrested in Budapest on 2 November 1962. He discovered after he had been flown to Moscow that Penkovsky was already in gaol. After nine months' intermittent, fierce interrogation, the two were given a public show trial there on 7–11 May 1963.

Wynne stuck to his cover story that he was a simple businessman, admitting to having carried packets, but denying any knowledge of their contents. Penkovsky was sentenced to death, Wynne to eight years. After less than a year of hideous discomfort at Vladimir, some 120 miles east of Moscow, Wynne was, again abruptly, flown to Berlin and exchanged for a leading Soviet agent, Conon

Molody (Gordon Lonsdale), early on 22 April 1964. The exchange received a torrent of publicity in the Western news media. MI6 and the CIA paid Wynne more than $200,000 compensation.

Wynne's wife had stood by him loyally; but his marriage swiftly broke up. He went off to Majorca with his secretary, Johanna Hermania, the daughter of Dirk van Buren, a civil servant. They married on 31 July 1970 at Kensington register office; his first wife had divorced him in 1968. There were no children of the second marriage. Wynne wrote two books, to try to make money out of what had happened to him: *The Man from Moscow*, a life of Penkovsky and himself (1967), and the much more fanciful *The Man from Odessa* (1981), in which, for example, he claimed to have held an army commission, which he never did. He never went back to business, lived latterly in Spain, and died of cancer in the Cromwell Hospital, Kensington, on 27 February 1990. A memorial service was held in Chelsea Old Church, London, on 5 May 1990.

M. R. D. FOOT, *rev.*

Sources G. Wynne, *The man from Moscow* (1967) · J. L. Schechetr and P. S. Deriabin, *The spy who saved the world* (1992) · *The Times* (1 March 1990) · *The Times* (5 May 1990) · private information (1996) · *CGPLA Eng. & Wales* (1990)
Likenesses photograph, 1964, Hult. Arch. [*see illus.*] · Keystone, photograph, 1970 (with his wife), Hult. Arch. · photograph, repro. in *The Times* (1 March 1990)
Wealth at death under £100,000: probate, 4 Oct 1990, *CGPLA Eng. & Wales*

Wynne, John (1665/6–1743), bishop of Bath and Wells, was born at Maes-y-coed, Caerwys, Flintshire, one of five surviving children of Humphrey Wynne of Caerwys (*d.* 1686), and his wife, Elizabeth. He was educated at Northop and Ruthin schools, and matriculated at Jesus College, Oxford, on 31 March 1682. He graduated BA in 1685, and proceeded MA in 1688, BD in 1696, and DD in 1706. He was elected a fellow at Jesus College in January 1687 and acted as a tutor there. In this capacity he was noteworthy for his use with his pupils of John Locke's *Essay Concerning Human Understanding*, which he hoped would bring the 'Vulgar Systems' prevalent at Oxford into discredit (De Beer, 5.273). With Locke's approval he published an *Abridgment* of the *Essay* in 1696, which had been through at least eleven editions by 1774. Locke also provided him with a recommendation to the earl of Pembroke, whom Wynne accompanied as chaplain to the congress of Ryswick in 1697. In 1701 he was appointed rector of Llangelynnin, Merioneth, probably by Bishop Humphreys. He became a prebendary of Christ College, Brecon, in 1705, and in the same year he was elected Lady Margaret professor of divinity at Oxford.

Although Wynne's politics at this time are not entirely clear he was probably a moderate tory in Queen Anne's reign who became a moderate whig after the Hanoverian succession. In 1705 the Oxford high-churchman Thomas Hearne described Wynne approvingly as a 'Worthy' man, 'of good Affection to the Church of England'. But by 1713 he was denouncing his 'Whiggish, republican Principles' (*Remarks*, 1.134, 4.108). There is some evidence to link Wynne with the moderate, Harleyite tories at the time of the bitter party contest for the principalship of Jesus College in 1712, a dispute which was eventually decided in Wynne's favour by the visitor, his former patron the earl of Pembroke. If this is true it may appear surprising that he was the first bishop to be created by King George I, being consecrated as bishop of St Asaph on 6 February 1715. But contemporaries believed that Wynne's promotion owed little to the whigs, attributing it instead to the influence of Sir Roger Mostyn and his father-in-law, the earl of Nottingham, the only leading tory to be retained in high office by the new king. Once in the House of Lords, however, Wynne was generally a reliable ministerial supporter, and he even spoke against Bishop Francis Atterbury during his trial for involvement in the Jacobite plot of 1721–2. But he never became a partisan whig, and opposed both the impeachment of the earl of Oxford in 1717 and the repeal of the Occasional Conformity Act in 1718.

Between 1715 and 1720 Wynne remained principal of Jesus College and often resided in Oxford. He finally resigned this office in 1720, following his marriage to Anne Pugh (1693?–1778), who brought him considerable estates in Caernarvonshire and Merioneth. Two years later he received a prebend of Westminster, which he held until 1729, and he further added to his properties with the purchase of Soughton Hall in Flintshire for over £13,000 in 1732. The bishop and his wife had four children—John, William, Anne, and Mary. Both sons went into the law, William (1729–1815) becoming dean of the arches (1788–1809) and master of Trinity Hall, Cambridge (1803–15).

Wynne was one of the few Welshmen to be appointed to a Welsh diocese in the eighteenth century. He acquired a reputation for appointing local men to benefices in his gift and he was a notable collector and patron of Welsh books. But, apart from the *Abridgment*, he published only three single sermons. He appears to have been a diligent bishop, visiting the diocese regularly and also undertaking for his brethren confirmation tours of Canterbury and Bangor in 1720. After a storm damaged St Asaph Cathedral in 1715 Wynne organized a subscription for its repair, which raised £600, and he also did work to the episcopal palace. When Bishop Hooper of Bath and Wells died, shortly after the accession of King George II in 1727, there was a dispute about his successor. Objections were raised to Francis Hare's being appointed immediately to one of the wealthier sees. Largely on the grounds of his seniority Wynne emerged as a compromise candidate, and in September he was nominated to the bishopric, 'for which it seems he made no application himself' (Coxe, 2.240). Here he remained until his death at Soughton on 15 July 1743, and he was buried at Northop church on 20 July. The inscription on the memorial stone in the chancel is probably wrong in stating that he was 'in the 76th year of his life'.

STEPHEN TAYLOR

Sources B. Gibson, 'A Welsh bishop for a Welsh see: John Wynne of St Asaph, 1714–27', *Journal of Welsh Ecclesiastical History*, 1 (1984), 28–43 · *Remarks and collections of Thomas Hearne*, ed. C. E. Doble and others, 11 vols., OHS, 2, 7, 13, 34, 42–3, 48, 50, 65, 67, 72 (1885–1921) ·

D. R. Thomas, *Esgobaeth Llanelwy: the history of the diocese of St Asaph*, new edn (1874) • E. G. Hardy, *Jesus College* (1899) • *The correspondence of John Locke*, ed. E. S. De Beer, 5–6 (1980–81) • *DWB* • *The manuscripts of his grace the duke of Portland*, 10 vols., HMC, 29 (1891–1931), vol. 7 • Bodl. Oxf., BL Add. A. 269 • W. Coxe, *Memoirs of the life and administration of Sir Robert Walpole, earl of Orford*, 3 vols. (1798) • BL, Lansdowne MSS, 1016, 1017 • G. H. Jenkins, *Literature, religion and society in Wales, 1660–1730* (1978) • college register, 1660–1752, Jesus College, Oxford, RE 3 • *State trials*, vol. 16 • Bodl. Oxf., MS Ballard 7 • *A list of the lords spiritual and temporal, who voted for or against the repeal of the several acts made for the security of the Church of England* [1719] • BL, Add. MS 70395 • Foster, *Alum. Oxon.* • W. Gibson, 'Three Hanoverian prelates', *Somerset Archaeology and Natural History*, 128 (1984), 75–82 • Flintshire RO • will, PRO, PROB 11/728, fols. 132r–132v

Archives BL, corresp. with William Wynne, Add. MS 41843 • Flintshire RO, Hawarden, Soughton Hall MSS
Likenesses oils, *c.*1730, Jesus College, Oxford • portrait (after oils, *c.*1730), NMG Wales • portrait (after oils, *c.*1730), Soughton Hall, Flintshire • portrait (after oils, *c.*1730), dean's library, St Asaph • portrait (after oils, *c.*1730), bishop's palace, Wells
Wealth at death over £8000—and probably much higher: will, PRO, PROB 11/728, fols. 132r–132v

Wynne, John Huddlestone (*bap.* **1742**, *d.* **1788**), historian and writer, was baptized on 1 February 1742 at St Martin-in-the-Fields, Westminster, the only child of Edward Wynne (*b.* before 1719), who held a government position and resided on a small estate in Southampton, and his first wife, Elizabeth (*d.* before 1756). The boy was indulged by a superstitious mother before being sent to St Paul's School by a father with whom he did not get along. At the age of thirteen he was taken from school and apprenticed to a printer, a situation he detested. He began contributing poetry to the periodical magazines, and having served his apprenticeship obtained a lieutenancy in the East India service. According to his son's memoir of his life he served in India for less than two years and relinquished his position on account of an argument with a senior officer and disgust at the unfair proceedings he observed. Other sources report that he quarrelled on the voyage out and was left behind when the ship arrived at the Cape. Upon returning to England he settled in London, where he was coldly received by his relatives. In 1770 he married a young woman of property but was unable to obtain a legacy of £1000 left by her father, a Lambeth mason. Wynne rowed frequently with his wife and they eventually separated.

In 1770 Wynne was employed to edit John Wheeble's *Lady's Magazine*. In 1771 he published a *General History of the British Empire in America*, that celebrated the recent victories in the Seven Years' War, and *The Prostitute*, a sentimental poem that was well received. At the suggestion of Oliver Goldsmith he undertook a *General History of Ireland to the Death of William III* (1772), dedicated to the duke of Northumberland. The impoverished author waited on the duke dressed in a suit of clothes and a sword borrowed from the poet Thomas Percy, who had arranged the interview. Half of the *History* is devoted to the pre-Christian era, an emphasis that reflected contemporary interest in James Macpherson's 'translations' of Ossianic poetry. Reviewers admired Wynne's vigorous prose, though his hasty methods of composition and his tory bias drew criticism. James Dodsley offered him a hundred guineas for an

unwritten epic, *Hengist*, but the project was abandoned for lack of ready money. The poet was more successful with his *Choice Emblems … for the Instruction and Pastime of Youth* (1772; 9th edn 1799). From 1773 until the late publication of a novel, *The Child of Chance* (1787), no further volumes appeared. Wynne was reduced to living from hand to mouth, editing the *Gazetteer* and labouring as a compositor for the *General Evening Post* and the *Morning Post*. Matters took a turn for the worse when he was run over by a hackney coach about 1778. Thereafter, sustained by a leg brace and crutch, he hobbled from an attic residence in Bloomsbury to seek work from employers in Mayfair and Paternoster Row; they paid him by the inch for essays, poems, and verses for children. In his later years he frequently contributed to the *British Magazine and Review*.

Throughout his precipitous decline from gentility to indigence Wynne's pride and pugnacity were never daunted. During the American War of Independence he was a warm defender of the North administration at the Robin Hood and Coachmakers' Hall debating societies. There he was sometimes thrashed by members of the opposite party, on one occasion to the point where his tear glands were permanently damaged, and on another to the point that his life was threatened. He died of an asthmatic complaint in St Bartholomew's Hospital on 2 December 1788, leaving his estranged wife and three children unprovided for. William West's character of Wynne is one of several that remark on his furious irascibility:

> I have his form at this moment in my mind's eye: a small thin worn-out emaciated figure, worn down more by disappointment than dissipation, and with a disposition naturally honorable but irritable; rendered still more petulant from the heavy imposing daily labours of the mind to procure a daily support for the body; he was lame from accident, and always walked with a cross handled crutch cane, which he was almost as ready to raise on being thwarted on the slightest occasion, as the celebrated Worthington, of street-writing notoriety. (West, 71–2)

DAVID HILL RADCLIFFE

Sources *GM*, 1st ser., 58 (1788), 1129 • *GM*, 1st ser., 59 (1789), 555 • Nichols, *Illustrations*, 8.27–9 • 'John Huddleston Wynne', *European Magazine*, 46 (Sept 1804), 184–6 • Philomathos, *Monthly Magazine*, 21 (May 1806), 293 • C. E. Wynne, 'Account of Mr John Huddlestone Wynne', *Monthly Magazine*, 22 (Aug 1806), 16–20 • A. Chalmers, ed., *The general biographical dictionary*, new edn, 32 (1817), 368–70 • W. Mitchell, 'Anecdotes of the late J. Huddlestone Wynne', *New Monthly Magazine*, 1 (1814), 524–5 • 'Remarks on J. H. Wynne', *New Monthly Magazine*, 2 (1814–15), 329 • 'Anecdotes of the late Mr J. H. Wynne', *New Monthly Magazine*, 5 (1816), 307–10 • W. West, *Fifty years' recollections of an old bookseller* (1837), 71–6 • *Monthly Review*, 1st ser., 45 (1771), 386–94, 432–6 • *Monthly Review*, 1st ser., 48 (1773), 469–75 • *DNB* • *IGI*

Wynne, May. *See* Knowles, Mabel Winifred (1875–1949).

Wynne, Peter (*d.* **1609**), soldier and colonist in Virginia, very probably came of a Welsh family that lived near the town of Mold in Flintshire. The first evidence of his existence dates from 1586, when Sir William Stanley commissioned him to captain a company of troops that belonged to the army of Robert Dudley, earl of Leicester, that went to fight Spaniards in the Netherlands. A bit player with Leicester, a bit player he remained throughout his career.

Nevertheless he was a participant in a string of extraordinary events that ran from Stanley's desertion to the Spanish at Deventer in 1587 to the conspiracies of English Catholic expatriates, plots with Sir Francis Walsingham, the fight against the Turks in Hungary, the futile attempt of Robert Devereux, second earl of Essex, to seize power in 1601, the Anglo-Spanish war of 1588–1604, and the Jamestown venture in Virginia.

Wynne's drift to soldiery paralleled that of Captain John Smith and many other young Britons whose modest backgrounds, few prospects, but bounding ambitions suited them well to the nomadic life of a military man for hire. For officers like Smith and Wynne, who willingly hazarded their lives in combat, who could command others, who were resourceful amid adversity, and who were loyal to their patrons no matter what, turning to the sword opened an exciting world of possibilities which they gained nowhere else in late Tudor society. Such individuals possessed qualities that the founders of Virginia deemed highly appropriate, if not absolutely essential, to the success of their enterprise.

The Virginia Company recruited Captain Wynne, who had been pardoned for his desertion at Deventer, for service at Jamestown. Company investors, some of whom had soldiered on the continent too, conceived the initial settlement along military lines. That is, they recruited only men or boys, and relied upon impaled villages akin to continental military encampments or fortified towns like those that had proved effective in the conquest of northern Ireland. Settlement began in earnest in the spring of 1607. Within a matter of weeks Admiral Christopher Newport, believing all was sufficiently well in hand, weighed anchor for England.

Appearances deceived. Officers proved for the most part either incompetent or too sickly for the task at hand, and from the start Jamestown struggled. While sound from a defensive point of view the site had no source of potable water, and its marshy landscape bred huge swarms of pestilential insects. Prolonged drought diminished available stocks of indigenous edibles, while the sultry heat of a Virginia summer and skirmishes with the Indians consumed both supplies and colonists at rates faster than anyone in London or Jamestown imagined. When Newport returned with the so-called first supply of food and men in January 1608, only 37 of the original 104 colonists were still alive. Only the determined John Smith, who succeeded to the presidency of the local governing council, held things together until Newport landed the second supply the following September.

Captain Wynne was among the new colonists. Ostensibly he was named the sergeant-major of James Fort, as well as a member of the resident Virginia council, but his previous dealings in espionage may explain the underlying reason for his employment. The unmasking and execution of George Kendall eliminated that erstwhile councillor as a supposed Spanish spy and raised fears of more such conspiracies. If other traitors lurked as well, then a man of Wynne's talents might ferret them out. Whatever the reason Wynne was none too keen to accept the assignment, though once he got to Virginia he regarded his new billet as a more pleasant, plentiful place than he had ever imagined.

Wynne's relations with his fellow councillors were anything but pleasant. John Smith, for all his adeptness as a leader, irritated his colleagues, especially those who outranked him socially or who disputed his approach to the natives and salvaging the colony. As a result, strife rent the resident council into pro- and anti-Smith factions, which quickly forced Wynne to take sides. He allied himself with Smith's group. Even so Smith never entirely warmed to him. Their relationship turned ever more edgy after they disagreed over Indian policy and a boating accident drowned all of their fellow councillors. Things never reached the flashpoint because Wynne died in Virginia in 1609, some months before an accident forced Smith's return to England in that September.

Clearly Peter Wynne lived an adventurous career in an age of great adventures. He was an able man whose military experiences and personal attributes suited him to the arduous work of carving out an English toehold in North America. Just as clearly death claimed him less than a year after his arrival, and so he joined that regiment of colonists whose mark on early Virginia was negligible.

WARREN M. BILLINGS

Sources P. L. Barbour, *The three worlds of Captain John Smith* (New York, 1964) · P. L. Barbour, ed., *The Jamestown voyages under the first charter, 1606–1609*, 2 vols., Hakluyt Society, 2nd ser., 136–7 (1969) · *The complete works of Captain John Smith (1580–1631)*, ed. P. L. Barbour, 3 vols. (1986) · W. M. Billings, J. E. Selby, and T. W. Tate, *Colonial Virginia: a history* (1986) · A. Brown, ed., *The genesis of the United States*, 2 vols. (1890) · P. E. J. Hammer, 'A Welshman abroad: Captain Peter Wynne of Jamestown', *Parergon*, 16 (1988), 59–92 · S. M. Kingsbury, ed., *The records of the Virginia Company of London* (Washington, DC, 1906–35) · D. W. Stahle and others, 'The lost colony and Jamestown droughts', *Science*, 280 (1998), 564–7
Archives Hunt. L., letter · PRO

Wynne, Warren Richard Colvin (1843–1879), army officer, eldest surviving son of Captain John Wynne (1799–1884), Royal Horse Artillery, of Wynnestay, Roebuck, co. Dublin, and his wife, Anne (d. 27 Nov 1874), daughter of Admiral Sir Samuel *Warren, was born on 9 April 1843. He was descended from the Wynnes of Hazlewood, Sligo, many of whom served as army officers. After the Royal Military Academy, Woolwich, he was commissioned lieutenant in the Royal Engineers on 25 June 1862. He served at various home stations, and then for five years at Gibraltar, where he acted as adjutant of his corps. He was appointed to the Ordnance Survey in the home counties on his return to England at the end of 1871 and was promoted captain on 3 February 1875.

Wynne married first, in 1872, Eleanor (d. 1873), third daughter of J. P. Turbett of Owenstown, co. Dublin; they had one son. On 1 February 1876, he married as his second wife Lucy (d. 2 June 1946), eldest daughter of Captain Alfred Parish; they had two sons, who survived him.

On 2 December 1878 Wynne embarked in command of the 2nd field company, Royal Engineers, for Natal, and on arrival at Durban marched to join the 1st column as commanding royal engineer under Colonel Charles Knight Pearson at the mouth of the Tugela River. The river was crossed on 13 January 1879, and in the presence of hostile Zulu forces Wynne with his company of engineers, assisted by the infantry, laid out and built Fort Tenedos on the left bank of the Lower Tugela, which was completed on the 17th. He was in command of the right wing in the action on the Inyezane River on 22 January, where his company was employed as infantry, and on arrival at Eshowe, Wynne designed and began construction of the fort there.

On 28 January Lord Chelmsford's announcement that he was forced, on account of the Isandlwana disaster, to retire to the Natal frontier was received, with full discretion to Pearson to hold his position at Eshowe or retire to the Tugela. A majority of a council of war was in favour of retreat, when Wynne argued forcefully that the post should be held and succeeded, with the support of Colonel Walker and Captain H. G. MacGregor, in securing a decision to remain at Eshowe.

On 1 March Wynne was engaged in a successful sortie to destroy a Zulu kraal, and commanded the right flank of the column on its return in an engagement with the enemy, his engineers again acting as infantry. Hemmed in at Eshowe, and unable to get runners through to Lord Chelmsford, heliograph signals from the Tugela were observed on the following day, and Wynne at once constructed a large signalling screen to reply, and made a balloon to carry a message. He was indefatigable in laying out ranges, preparing mines, repairing approaches, and cutting fields of fire. Always resourceful and cheerful, providing encouragement to all and making the best of the means at hand, it was to his skill and exertions the successful defence was greatly due. Pearson, in his dispatch, expressed his high opinion of Wynne's services.

On 12 March Wynne was struck down with fever, largely the result of overwork. On the relief of Eshowe he was moved in a cart to the Tugela River, where, promoted brevet major a week before, he died at Fort Pearson on 9 April 1879, and was buried in the hillside cemetery overlooking the river and Fort Tenedos. A proficient and dedicated soldier, his name was commemorated by his corps in Rochester Cathedral.

R. H. VETCH, rev. JAMES FALKNER

Sources Army List • The Times (31 May 1879) • Hart's Army List • Royal Engineers Journal (1879) • LondG (16 May 1879) • Boase, Mod. Eng. biog. • Burke, Gen. Ire. • L. Wynne, A widow-making war: the life and death of a British officer in Zululand, 1879, ed. H. Whitehouse (1995) **Wealth at death** under £5000: probate, 28 May 1879, CGPLA Eng. & Wales

Wynne, William (bap. **1692**, d. **1765**), lawyer and author, was baptized at St Margaret's, Westminster, on 7 July 1692, the youngest of the five children, and heir, of Owen Wynne (1651–1700) and his wife, Dorothy (1659–1724), daughter of Francis Luttrell and sister of the political chronicler Narcissus Luttrell. His father was warden of the Royal Mint during the reign of James II, and under-

secretary of state to Charles II and James II. Wynne matriculated at Jesus College, Oxford, on 23 January 1709, graduated BA on 14 October 1712 and MA on 24 May 1723. He was admitted to the Middle Temple on 12 December 1712, called to the bar on 23 May 1718, and created serjeant-at-law in 1736.

Wynne benefited greatly in his legal career from his family's ecclesiastical connections. On his father's death the bishop of Bangor promised to assist his children; and he was also a relative of John Wynne, bishop of St Asaph. In 1723, only five years after being called to the bar, he was already senior enough to be retained, along with Sir Constantine Phipps, in the trial of Francis Atterbury, bishop of Rochester, for high treason. Wynne skilfully exposed the weakness of the evidence produced for the prosecution in that case.

On 30 September 1728 Wynne married Grace (1700–1779), the daughter of William Bridges, a serjeant-at-law. The couple had six sons and two daughters. Wynne's father-in-law was close to successive bishops of Hereford, and in subsequent years Wynne was 'the trusted adviser of some of the leaders of the Church while he continued to be employed generally in matters of an ecclesiastical nature' (Lemmings, 116). He appeared for the Bathurst family in a case about tithes in 1735–6 and in the 1740s he gave advice to Edmund Gibson, bishop of London, concerning the marriage articles of the latter's daughter.

In 1746 Wynne appeared with a Mr Clayton for the defence in the trial for high treason of Francis Towneley, who had commanded the Manchester regiment in the Jacobite rising of 1745. Towneley was convicted and executed, the court having rejected Wynne's argument that since Towneley held a commission from Louis XV he owed no allegiance to George II. Wynne's literary gifts were displayed in his Observations Touching the Dignity and Antiquity of the Degree of Serjeant at Law (1756). This book was written to defend the privileges of the serjeants when their exclusive rights of audience before the court of common pleas were threatened. He also wrote The Life of Sir Leoline Jenkins (1724) for which he drew upon family papers.

Wynne died on 16 May 1765 and was buried in the north cloister of Westminster Abbey on 23 May 1765. His wife survived him. Of his sons, Edward *Wynne (bap. 1734, d. 1784), was a barrister and author, and Luttrell (1738–1814), was a fellow of All Souls College, Oxford.

ROGER TURNER

Sources D. Lemmings, Gentlemen and barristers: the inns of court and the English bar, 1680–1730 (1990) • H. W. Woolrych, Lives of eminent serjeants-at-law of the English bar, 2 vols. (1869), 2.542-50 • Foster, Alum. Oxon. • Baker, Serjeants, 210, 423, 456, 546 • H. A. C. Sturgess, ed., Register of admissions to the Honourable Society of the Middle Temple, from the fifteenth century to the year 1944, 1 (1949) • Nichols, Lit. anecdotes, 8.458 • State trials, 16.516-70; 18.344-7 • J. L. Chester, ed., The marriage, baptismal, and burial registers of the collegiate church or abbey of St Peter, Westminster, Harleian Society, 10 (1876), 310, 405-6, 429, 439 • E. W. Brayley and J. P. Neale, The history and antiquities of the abbey church of St Peter, Westminster, 2 (1823), 291-2, 294 • will, proved, 1765, PRO, PROB 11/909, sig. 242
Archives Westminster Abbey, muniments, fabric fund
Likenesses Creswell, silhouette, 1819 (after sketch by R. Bockton), NPG

Wealth at death see will, PRO, PROB 11/909, sig. 242, indexed in A. J. Camp, *An index of the wills proved in the Prerogative Court of Canterbury, 1750–1800* (1992), vol. 6, p. 294

Wynne, William Watkin Edward (1801–1880), antiquary, the eldest son of William Wynne (1774–1834) of Peniarth, Merioneth, and Elizabeth (*d.* 1822), youngest daughter and coheir of Philip Puleston of Pickhill Hall, Denbighshire, was born on 23 December 1801 at Pickhill Hall. The Wynnes claimed descent from Osbwrn Wyddel ('Osborn the Irishman'), a thirteenth-century nobleman.

Wynne was admitted to Westminster School on 27 September 1814, and matriculated from Jesus College, Oxford, on 24 March 1820. On 8 May 1839 he married Mary (*d.* 1866), daughter of Robert Aglionby Slaney of Walford Manor, Shropshire; they had two sons. Wynne was Conservative MP for Merioneth from 1852 to 1865, and high sheriff in 1867. He also served as a magistrate and a deputy lieutenant and was appointed constable of Harlech Castle in 1874.

In 1859 the Hengwrt collection of manuscripts, which had been originally formed by Robert Vaughan (*d.* 1667), was bequeathed to Wynne by his distant relative Sir Robert Williames Vaughan of Nannau. Having moved the collection to Peniarth, Wynne published an excellent catalogue of its contents in the *Archaeologia Cambrensis* between 1869 and 1871. In addition to containing an early version of the *Canterbury Tales* (published in 1868 by the Chaucer Society) and some Cornish mystery plays, the collection was unequalled in its wealth of early Welsh manuscripts, which include numerous medieval romances (some of them published in Robert Williams's *Selections from Hengwrt MSS* (2 vols., 1876–92), two of the *Four Ancient Books of Wales* (edited by W. F. Skene in 1868), and no fewer than twelve versions of the laws of Howel Dda. Wynne, although a careful custodian of the manuscripts, gave to other scholars free access to examine and copy them. His own knowledge of the genealogy of north Wales families was quite unrivalled, and he was a well-informed ecclesiologist. He fixed the date of the 'extent' of Merioneth for Sir Henry Ellis's edition of the *Record of Caernarvon* in 1838 ('Introduction', xx), and himself made large collections for a history of Merioneth. He supplied genealogical notes for S. R. Meyrick's edition of Lewis Dwnn's *Heraldic Visitation of Wales* (1846), Edward Breese's *Kalendars of Gwynedd* (1873), and the *History of the Gwydir Family*, edited by Askew Roberts in 1878. Numerous contributions from his pen also appeared in the *Archaeologia Cambrensis*, starting with a 'List of the lords lieutenant of Merionethshire' in the first number of the journal in 1846 and ending with a history of his own parish of Llanegryn in 1879. He also wrote frequently for *Bye-gones*, in which his archaeological notes relating to Merioneth were published in 1895–6.

In 1872 Wynne prepared for private circulation the scholarly *Pedigree of the Family of Wynne* and, with G. T. Clark, published in 1878 a small history of Harlech Castle.

Wynne died at Peniarth on 9 June 1880, and was buried in Llanegryn church.   D. L. THOMAS, *rev.* BETI JONES

Sources G. Tibbott, 'William Watkin Edward Wynne', *Journal of the Merioneth Historical and Record Society*, 1 (1949–51), 69–76 · *DWB* · *Handlist of manuscripts in the National Library of Wales*, 1 [1940] · W. Wynne, *Pedigree of the family of Wynne* (1872) · E. Breese, *Archaeologia Cambrensis*, 4th ser., 11 (1880), 229–33 · *Bye-Gones Relating to Wales and the Border Counties*, [5] (1880–81) [June 1880] · *The Times* (11 June 1880) · Foster, *Alum. Oxon.* · Burke, *Gen. GB* (1914) · *WWBMP* · E. Poole, ed., *Old Welsh chips* (1888), 334

Archives NL Wales, corresp. and antiquarian papers · NL Wales, corresp. and papers · NL Wales, working papers and collected MSS | Bodl. Oxf., corresp. with Sir Thomas Phillipps · NL Wales, letters to Edward Breese [copies] · NL Wales, letters to D. S. Evans · NL Wales, letters to John Jones ('Myrddin Fardd') · NL Wales, Peniarth letters

Likenesses portrait, repro. in Breese, *Archaeologia Cambrensis*, 229

Wealth at death under £25,000: probate, 16 Sept 1880, *CGPLA Eng. & Wales*

Wynter, Andrew (1819–1876), physician and author, the son of Andrew Wynter, manufacturer, was born at Bristol and educated at a private school before embarking on a course of medical study that he shortly abandoned. He later returned to medicine, studying at St George's Hospital, London. He practised in London, at Curzon Street in Mayfair, and later at Coleherne Court in Old Brompton (where he maintained a large household), at Addison Road, Kensington, and finally at Chiswick. He graduated MD at St Andrews University in 1853 and was admitted MRCP (London) in 1861. Nothing is known of Wynter's first marriage except that it yielded a son, born about 1849, and ended with his wife's death. Wynter's second marriage, which took place in January 1854 at Westbury-on-Trym, Gloucestershire, was to Mary Betty Bramhall, the nineteen-year-old daughter of John Sykes Bramhall, a Sheffield manufacturer. They had two daughters and three sons.

In October 1855 Wynter was one of fourteen applicants for the editorship of the *Association Medical Journal* (*British Medical Journal* or *BMJ* from 1857), the weekly journal of the Provincial Medical and Surgical Association (from 1856 the British Medical Association). His appointment, at a salary of £250 per annum, probably owed as much to his literary as to his somewhat modest medical credentials, for he had been contributing articles to the general periodical press for years. Although he maintained the journal's editorial standards, he received, as had his predecessor, much criticism from members of the association dissatisfied with the *BMJ*'s high cost and unexceptional quality. In October 1860, following accusations that he was inaccessible to members and out of touch with recent developments in medical science, he resigned the editorship. He did not, however, resign from the association; in fact in 1867 he attended the International Medical Congress in Paris as one of its representatives. Although he may have left the *BMJ* partly in response to a hostile readership, he may also have wished to concentrate on the general literary career which he had continued to pursue throughout his editorial term.

Wynter was an extensive contributor of essays on medical, social, and entertaining subjects of a general nature to the periodical press including *Ainsworth's Magazine*, the

Cornhill Magazine, *Fraser's Magazine*, the *Edinburgh Review*, the *Quarterly Review*, the *London Review*, *Good Words*, and, from 1859, *Once a Week*. His speciality was in popularizing scientific information for general readers, but he also wrote poetry. Many of his essays were collected, often in revised form, and reissued as books. These volumes included *Odds and Ends from an Old Drawer* (1855), *Pictures of Town from my Mental Camera* (1855), *Curiosities of Civilisation* (1860), *Subtle Brains and Lissom Fingers* (1863), which, revised and enlarged by Andrew Steinmetz, was republished in 1877, *Curiosities of Toil* (1870), and *Peeps into the Human Hive* (1874).

Two of Wynter's books were published with his name rendered in reverse (as Werdna Retnyw). There was a marked similarity in the content of many of his volumes, not least because he was a master at recycling his subject matter, albeit subtly altered and retitled. Even so his work was widely and favourably reviewed, by *The Times*, the *Literary Gazette*, the *London Saturday Review*, and others. The *London Reader* praised *Subtle Brains* as 'about the pleasantest book of short collected papers of chit-chat blending information with amusement, and not overtasking the intelligence, that we have seen for a good while' (2, 1863, 307). Several of his works were reissued, and a tenth edition of *Curiosities of Civilisation* appeared in 1875. Although Wynter's post-*BMJ* literary endeavours concentrated on non-medical topics, he wrote several papers on lunacy and a well-received essay entitled 'Progress of medicine and surgery' for the *Edinburgh Review* (October 1872).

While pursuing his literary career Wynter continued to practise medicine, taking a special interest in the treatment of insanity. At his house in Chiswick he took in prosperous 'lunatics' as residential patients. In his last book, *The Borderlands of Insanity and other Allied Papers* (1875), which was his only serious and substantial treatment of a medical subject, he expressed his firm belief in the importance of treating victims of mental illness without recourse to physical restraint. This volume was reissued with five additional chapters by J. M. Granville in 1877.

Wynter died, aged fifty-six, as a result of disease of the heart and kidneys, at his home, Chestnut Lodge, 1 Bolton Road, Grove Park, Chiswick, on 12 May 1876. He was buried at Brompton cemetery on 18 May. After his death his widow, who was 'left with my four children dependent on my exertions', appealed through the pages of the *BMJ* for 'two or three invalids' in need of 'care and cheerful society' to board at her Twickenham home (*BMJ*, 15 July 1876, 84). Two of Wynter's sons from his second marriage, Walter Essex Wynter (1860–1945) and Andrew E. Wynter, pursued careers in medicine.   P. W. J. BARTRIP

Sources *Medical Times and Gazette* (20 May 1876), 565 · *The Times* (17 May 1876) · *DNB* · *BMJ* (15 July 1876), 84 · *BMJ* (20 May 1876), 637–8 · Boase, *Mod. Eng. biog.* · *GM*, 2nd ser., 41 (1854), 414 · Ward, *Men of the reign* · census returns for Coleherne Court, Old Brompton, London, 1861; for Chestnut Lodge, Bolton Road, Grove Park, Chiswick, London, 1871 · Allibone, *Dict.* · *The Times* (25 Oct 1860) · m. cert. · d. cert.

Wynter [Winter], **Thomas** (*b. c.*1510, *d.* in or after 1543), clergyman, was the illegitimate son of Thomas *Wolsey

(*d.* 1530) and a woman from his native Suffolk named Larke (later married to one Lee or Legh, of Adlington, Lancashire), possibly Joan. She was probably the daughter of Peter Larke, innkeeper, of Thetford; other Larkes rose with Wolsey, notably Thomas, briefly dean of Chichester, archdeacon of Sudbury and then of Norfolk, and (conveniently) Wolsey's confessor. Wynter seems to have been about sixteen when he was made provost of Beverley in 1526; his sister Dorothy (known as Clasey or Clansey) was born *c.*1512 and became a nun at Shaftesbury. Wynter matriculated at the University of Louvain (being, however, too young to take the oath) on 30 August 1518, with his tutor Maurice Birchynshaw, second master of St Paul's, in attendance. If Wynter was only about nine, Birchynshaw's confessions of limited progress are perhaps unsurprising.

Before or after his Louvain period Wynter spent time at 'Wilsdon' (perhaps Willesden); by 1523, he was at Padua with Thomas Lupset. He was possibly supposed to continue to Rome with John Clerk, bishop of Bath and Wells, but was prevented by illness. By September 1524 he had returned to Louvain, where Erasmus was induced to take an interest in his education, though 'Winter never impressed anyone with his brilliance' (Mayer, 48). Between 1526 and 1529 he was probably based in Paris, where in 1528 he was reported to his father to be 'spending money at a great rate', though on his own admission he found it difficult to master 'the niceties of the language' (*LP Henry VIII*, vol. 4/2, no. 4015; 4/3, no. 5642). Many efforts, including those of Lupset, Richard Pates, and probably John Bekinsau, were wasted on the 'costly and thankless' task of educating Thomas Wynter, though at least 'Wolsey was exercising an important influence on humanistic activity by maintaining ... Winter's household' (Zeeveld, 64). Wynter's own subversive reaction to exposure to distinguished humanistic teaching was to praise the supreme 'ingenious subtilty' of scholastics (*LP Henry VIII*, vol. 4/2, no. 5019).

Random rumours ascribed to Wolsey extravagant ambitions on his son's behalf: to marry the daughter of Henry Bourchier, earl of Essex (feasible, as he was not in major orders); to have François I support him for the papacy. In practice, he never became more than a surrogate for Wolsey's influence. By the end of 1526 the under-age absentee Wynter had become dean of Wells, archdeacon of York, Richmond, and Suffolk (later exchanged for Norfolk), chancellor of Salisbury, and provost of Beverley—not to mention his prebends, rectories, and the mineral rights for his father's diocese of Durham. However, the Lords' articles against Wolsey in 1529 complained that, having lavished benefices worth £2700 on Wynter, Wolsey allowed him an income of only £200 (perhaps explaining his complaints of poverty) and kept the rest. The cardinal himself, more conservatively, assured the king that if he might pass Durham on to Wynter, the latter would vacate preferments worth £2000. The burdensome implications for the English church of Wynter's existence were shown in July 1528 when John Longland, bishop of Lincoln, having informed Wolsey of the death of his dean, attempted to fend off the enforced collation of Wynter by simultaneously stating a preference for George Heneage, on the grounds that the latter was likely to be resident, while offering the archdeaconry of Oxford for Wynter and £200 for the cardinal's Ipswich college.

Longland's problem was solved when Wolsey lost control of patronage and found Wynter's existing promotions grounds for charges against him. In late 1529 Wynter returned to England to resign most of his benefices. He was archdeacon of Norfolk until the following year, when Bishop Richard Nix, seizing his opportunity, vexed him with suits until he resigned that too; he remained, however, archdeacon of York, provost of Beverley, and canon of Southwell. Otherwise Wynter weathered his father's fall fairly well. He acquired Stephen Gardiner (his successor as archdeacon of Norfolk) as his 'dearest patron' (*LP Henry VIII*, vol. 5, no. 1453), and although he quarrelled with Edmund Bonner, he felt able to assure Thomas Cromwell that 'Your friendship has been a treasure to me' (ibid., no. 1210). Wynter joined Doctors' Commons and became a royal chaplain, but concentrated on borrowing enough money to return to Italy in 1531. After another brief visit to England, he was for most of the next two to three years at Padua and in the Veneto, acting as Richard Morison's patron (rather than pupil), but then spent 1535–7 in England.

Wynter wrote to Cromwell in 1534 of the difficulties which resulted from his continuing to defer taking priest's orders—though 'devoted to letters', he thought contempt for material things could be overdone and so desired to keep his preferments (*LP Henry VIII*, vol. 7, no. 280). Cromwell, though writing off many of Wynter's bills as desperate, still lent him money against English revenues, and got him the archdeaconry of Cornwall in October 1537. Wynter soon afterwards leased the archdeaconry for thirty-five years to William Body, a layman and servant of Cromwell. This probably funded Wynter's return to Italy, but in July 1540 he was back to sign both convocations' decrees of the nullity of Henry VIII's and Anne of Cleves's marriage, as archdeacon of Cornwall and provost of Beverley (he had by now resigned the York archdeaconry). John Veysey, bishop of Exeter, cited Wynter to his diocesan court over his agreement with Body, but the king threatened Veysey's officials with *praemunire*. It was still regarded locally as sufficiently outrageous to cause disturbances when Body sought to collect archidiaconal dues and to contribute to his lynching by Cornish rebels in April 1548. Wynter finally resigned the archdeaconry in May 1543 and the Beverley provostship about the same time, obtaining for the latter a pension of £86 p.a. for five years, thereafter diminishing to £30. Possibly he returned to Italy, where his 'career as a wandering scholar' (an 'unkind parody' of that of Reginald Pole, who took over the patronage of Lupset, for instance) 'petered out ingloriously' (Dowling, 157–8). Lacking talent, it required money which he no longer had; and he presumably completed the decline into obscurity only deferred since his father's fall, and possibly accelerated by that of Cromwell.

JULIAN LOCK

Sources C. S. Knighton, 'Thomas Winter', *Contemporaries of Erasmus*, ed. P. G. Bietenholz and T. B. Deutscher, 3 vols. (1987), vol. 3, pp. 455–6 · A. F. Leach, ed., *Memorials of Beverley Minster*, 2, SurtS, 108 (1903), xcv–xcix · P. Gwyn, *The king's cardinal: the rise and fall of Thomas Wolsey* (1990) · A. F. Pollard, *Wolsey*, 2nd edn (1965) · W. G. Zeeveld, *Foundations of Tudor policy* (1948) · M. Dowling, *Humanism in the age of Henry VIII* (1987) · J. Woolfson, *Padua and the Tudors: English students in Italy, 1485–1603* (1998) · J. A. Gee, *The life and works of Thomas Lupset* (1928) · *LP Henry VIII* · *Fasti Angl., 1300–1541*, [Lincoln] · *Fasti Angl., 1300–1541*, [Salisbury] · *Fasti Angl., 1300–1541*, [Monastic cathedrals] · *Fasti Angl., 1066–1300*, [York] · *Fasti Angl., 1300–1541*, [Bath and Wells] · *Fasti Angl., 1300–1541*, [Exeter] · F. Rose-Troup, *The western rebellion of 1549* (1913), chaps. 3–4 · T. F. Mayer, *Thomas Starkey and the commonweal: humanist politics and religion in the reign of Henry VIII* (1989), 46–8 · G. Walker, *John Skelton and the politics of the 1520s* (1988), 145 · *Opus epistolarum Des. Erasmi Roterodami*, ed. P. S. Allen and others, 12 vols. (1906–58), vol. 5, p. 540; vol. 6, p. 146 · H. de Vocht, ed., *Literae virorum eruditorum ad Franciscum Craneveldum, 1522–1528* (1928), 367
Archives BL, corresp. with Thomas Cromwell, etc., Cotton MSS · PRO, corresp. with Thomas Wolsey, Stephen Gardiner, Thomas Cromwell, etc., SP 1

Wyntoun, Andrew (*c*.1350–*c*.1422), prior of St Serf's, Lochleven, and historian, says of himself that Andrew of Wyntoun was his baptismal name, but beyond this nothing is known of his family background, education, or early career. He became a canon regular of St Andrews Augustinian priory, and later claimed that it was solely due to the goodwill of his fellow monks that he was elected to the priorate of St Serf's, Lochleven, Fife, in 1393, when his probable predecessor, James Bisset, was appointed prior of St Andrews. Two years later Wyntoun's presence was recorded at a perambulation of lands pertaining to St Serf's, and between 1406 and 1411 he pursued a lengthy case in the court of the bishop of St Andrews against one William Berkely. Documentary evidence reveals that he remained in office until 1421, in which year John Cameron petitioned the pope for the vacant office. In his chronicle Wyntoun complained of old age and ill health, and it is his reference to these afflictions—surely the explanation of his resignation—which has given rise to the commonly accepted dates for his life, though these (especially his date of birth) remain speculative.

Wyntoun's metrical *Original Chronicle*, written typically in four-stress couplets, is a vernacular account of the history of the world and Scotland's place within it. The first five books, heavily indebted to the works of Peter Comestor, Orosius, and Frère Martin (Martinus Polonus), and dealing with the early—'original'—history of the world, represent a striking Scottish example of this popular genre. In book 6 of the chronicle Wyntoun turns his attention to English and Scottish 'storyis'. Here his sources clearly include several texts which no longer survive, notably John Barbour's Stewart genealogy and the great register of St Andrews Priory. Careful comparison of the manuscript witnesses reveals that Wyntoun initially envisaged a seven-book work mirroring the seven ages of the world and ending with the death of Alexander III in 1286. This plan was subsequently modified to encompass events up to the death of Robert II (1390) and, after further revision, the final redaction comprised nine books (reflecting the nine angelic orders). Book 9 covers such events as the death of the regent Robert Stewart, duke of Albany (3 September 1420), and ends, rather abruptly, with an account of the activities in England and France of Alexander Stewart, earl of Mar (*d.* 1435). In view of this, 1420 has long been accepted as the date of Wyntoun's final revision of the chronicle. According to Wyntoun, much of the later material (that dealing with the period 1325–90) was supplied by another writer. He claims the treatise was sent to him, but offers no hint as to the precise nature of the partnership and may not even have known his collaborator's identity. Internal evidence suggests that his anonymous contributor was writing some time in the early 1390s, that he was particularly well acquainted with the campaigns of the 1330s, and that he was probably from the south-east of the country. Wyntoun's failure to identify his source has led to numerous theories, including the proposal, based largely on unconvincing verbal parallels, that he was John Barbour (*d.* 1395), author of *The Bruce.* While Barbour may have written this portion of the chronicle, there is nothing to prove that he did so. Certainly the fact that Wyntoun misses the opportunity to credit a literary hero much cited elsewhere in his work seems to indicate that he, at least, was unaware of it. Future research may prove more illuminating.

In the prologue to his work Wyntoun tells us that he wrote his chronicle at the behest of Sir John Wemyss, a Fife landowner who was constable of St Andrews Castle between 1383 and 1400. The latter's connections with Albany (who as earl of Fife was his feudal superior) probably explain some of the political biases discernible in those parts of the work dealing with Scotland's recent history (though it should be remembered that this was provided, in some form, by Wyntoun's nameless contributor). Particularly notable in this respect is the extravagant eulogy of Albany and the cursory treatment accorded the death in 1402 of David Stewart, duke of Rothesay, in which Albany played a major part. Although the exact nature of Wemyss's status as literary patron remains unclear, his interest in Wyntoun's work provides important evidence for the growing literary sophistication of the fifteenth-century laity. It was this secular audience which Wyntoun explicitly addressed in his chronicle, seeking to provide moral and political instruction as well as entertainment.

The Original Chronicle is preserved in nine manuscripts, a survival rate which, second only to that of the *Scotichronicon* of Walter Bower (*d.* 1449), is testimony to the work's popularity in fifteenth- and sixteenth-century Scotland. Published first in part at the end of the eighteenth century (ed. D. Macpherson, 2 vols., 1795) and again by David Laing as one of the volumes in the Historians of Scotland series (3 vols., 1872–9), the most recent and satisfactory edition is that produced by F. J. Amours for the Scottish Text Society (6 vols., 1903–14). This gives parallel renditions of the texts found in the Wemyss and Cottonian manuscripts; the former, dating from the early sixteenth century, records the earliest version of the chronicle and the latter, a late fifteenth-century work, represents the final recension. Although few critics have found any poetic merit in Wyntoun's verse, both literary and political historians have long recognized the chronicle's worth. Not only does it shed important light on Scotland's history (containing material not found in any other source), it also tells its readers a great deal about the development of Middle Scots and Scottish historiography, and thus represents a landmark in the literary life of the nation.   C. EDINGTON

Sources The 'Original chronicle' of Andrew of Wyntoun, ed. F. J. Amours, 6 vols., STS, 1st ser., 50, 53–4, 56–7, 63 (1903–14) • T. Thomson, ed., *Liber cartarum prioratus Sancti Andree in Scotia,* Bannatyne Club, 69 (1841) • W. A. Craigie, 'Wyntoun's Original Chronicle', *The Scottish Review,* 30 (1897), 33–54 • W. A. Craigie, 'The St Andrews MS of Wyntoun's chronicle', *Anglia,* 20 (1898), 363–80 • W. Fraser, *Memorials of the family of Wemyss of Wemyss,* 3 vols. (1888) • W. Geddie, *A bibliography of Middle Scots poets, with an introduction on the history of their reputations,* STS, 61 (1912) • S. Boardman, 'Chronicle propaganda in late medieval Scotland: Robert the Steward, John of Fordun and the "Anonymous Chronicle"', *SHR,* 76 (1997), 23–43 • D. F. C. Coldwell, 'Wyntoun's anonymous contributor', *JEGP: Journal of English and Germanic Philology,* 58 (1959), 39–48

Wynyard, Diana [*real name* Dorothy Isobel Cox] (**1906–1964**), actress, was born at 96 Woolston Road, Forest Hill, London, on 16 January 1906, the daughter of Edward Thomas Cox, master printer, and his wife, Margaret Campbell Thomson. She was educated at Woodford School, Croydon. Gifted by nature with a good voice, she went in turn to two notable teachers to have it trained, and at the age of nineteen she launched herself on the professional stage. Her blonde beauty served to get her a walk-on part at the Globe in 1925 and in the same year she was taken on tour by Hamilton Deane; in just under a year she played nearly thirty parts, mainly in light comedy. Other touring engagements followed which kept her well employed until, in August 1927, she joined the much admired Liverpool repertory company under the direction of William Armstrong. There she remained for two years, playing increasingly important parts in plays of increasing weight and gaining steadily in experience and skill until, in September 1929, she was ready to make her London début and to secure a considerable success. The theatre was the St Martin's, and the play was *Sorry You've Been Troubled,* one of a series of amusing pieces written by the American dramatist Walter Hackett for his wife, Marion Lorne, a comedienne of a markedly individual personality. Diana Wynyard's part in this piece was of no great importance, but it needed to be played with assurance, charm, and distinction. So well did the young actress rise to the challenge and so exceedingly beautiful did she look while doing so that a startled London first-night audience took her to its heart upon the spot.

Wynyard was soon established as a leading lady in the West End and she was in constant demand. The plays for which she was required were still light in texture, but gradually she showed a certain ambition for more serious work. A visit to America in 1932 resulted in her first Hollywood movies, *Rasputin and the Empress* (1932) and *Cavalcade* (1933), for which she was nominated for an Academy

Diana Wynyard (1906–1964), by Dorothy Wilding, 1937

award. In 1933, returning to London, she played Charlotte Brontë in Clemence Dane's *Wild Decembers*, taking over the management for part of the run. In 1934 she scored a notable success and a long run in *Sweet Aloes*. In 1937, having succeeded the American actress Ann Harding as Candida in the play of the same name by G. B. Shaw, she went with the role to Paris, the production having been chosen to represent the British stage in the Paris Exhibition. This was followed, later in the same year, by another Shaw heroine—Eliza Doolittle in *Pygmalion* at the Old Vic. For the next ten years she maintained her high reputation with appearances in such plays as Noël Coward's *Design for Living* (1939), *No Time for Comedy* (1941), *Watch on the Rhine* (1942), and, on tour for the Entertainments National Service Association, Patrick Hamilton's *Gaslight* (1943), of which she had made a memorable film in 1940, and *Love from a Stranger* (1944).

In 1948 Wynyard took a step that was to transform her career and lift her name to a higher plane than any at which she had previously aimed. The governors of the Shakespeare Memorial Theatre, who were engaged in a campaign to raise the standard of Stratford acting, invited her to join the company. Up to that point, in a stage career of over twenty-six years, she had shown no ambition to become a classical actress, her sole appearance in a Shakespeare part having been at Liverpool as Titania. She had, however, valuable assets for the task—an excellent voice, a good sense of character, and quick intelligence. She accepted the invitation, and very soon showed that the decision was a right one. She served the company for the

seasons of 1948 and 1949 and in 1949–50 she went with them to Australia. During that time she excited admiration in a very wide range of parts; the list included Gertrude in *Hamlet*, Portia in *The Merchant of Venice*, Katherine the shrew, Hermione in *The Winter's Tale*, Desdemona, Lady Macbeth, Beatrice in *Much Ado about Nothing*, Helena in *A Midsummer Night's Dream*, and Queen Katherine in *Henry VIII*. She repeated her performances of Hermione in London in 1951 and of Beatrice in 1952. She was appointed CBE in 1953: proof of the profound impression that she had made.

Diana Wynyard was married twice: first in 1943 to film director Carol *Reed (1906–1976); second in 1951 to Tibor Csato (1906–2003), physician. Both marriages were dissolved. She died in St Paul's Hospital, Endell Street, London, on 13 May 1964.

W. A. DARLINGTON, *rev.* K. D. REYNOLDS

Sources *The Times* (14 May 1964) · b. cert. · personal knowledge (1981) · private information (1981) · D. Quinlan, *Quinlan's film stars*, 4th edn (1996) · J. Walker, ed., *Halliwell's film and video guide*, 12th edn (1997) · T. C. Kemp and J. C. Trewin, *The Stratford festival* (1953) · *CGPLA Eng. & Wales* (1964)
Likenesses photographs, c.1930–1952, Hult. Arch. · D. Wilding, photograph, 1937, NPG [*see illus.*] · E. Gabain, oils, exh. RA 1938
Wealth at death £16,921: probate, 1964

Wynyard, Edward Buckley (1788–1864). *See under* Wynyard, Robert Henry (1802–1864).

Wynyard, Robert Henry (1802–1864), army officer and colonial official, born on 24 December 1802 at Windsor Castle, was the younger son of Lieutenant-General William Wynyard (1759–1819), colonel of the 5th regiment (1812–19), equerry to George III, and deputy adjutant-general, and his wife, Jane, daughter of J. Gladwin of Hubbin in Nottinghamshire and lady-in-waiting to Queen Charlotte. After attending school at Dunmow, Essex, Wynyard received an ensigncy in the 85th foot on 25 February 1819, and was promoted lieutenant (by purchase) on 17 July 1823. In 1826 he transferred to the 58th regiment; he was promoted captain (by purchase) on 20 May 1826 and major on 25 July 1841. At Malta on 12 August 1826 he married Anne Catherine, daughter of Hugh McDonell, British consul-general at Algiers: they had four sons. From 1828 to 1841 Wynyard served in Ireland on the adjutant-general's staff. In 1842 he was recalled to England, given command of the 58th, and promoted lieutenant-colonel (by purchase, 30 December 1842).

In 1844 the 58th was sent to Sydney, New South Wales. In 1845 Wynyard was sent with part of the regiment to New Zealand, to strengthen the forces in the Bay of Islands against the Maori led by Hone Heke and Kawiti in the New Zealand War. Wynyard's force reached the Bay of Islands in late March 1845. On Sunday 11 January 1846 they took part in Lieutenant-Colonel Henry Despard's attack on Kawiti's pa (stockaded fortification) at Ruapekapeka, reportedly when most of the garrison had withdrawn to hold divine service (though this has since been denied). For his war service Wynyard was made CB (2 July 1846). In

December 1846 he returned to New South Wales, but in 1847 he was again posted to New Zealand. For the following eleven years he and his wife entertained lavishly in their residence at Official Bay, Auckland.

In January 1851 Wynyard was appointed to command the forces in New Zealand and he was lieutenant-governor of New Ulster, one of the two provinces of New Zealand, from April 1851 to March 1853, when the colony was divided into six smaller provinces. He had only limited powers, but inaugurated the first municipal corporation, in Auckland, and with others obtained Maori consent to goldmining, which had major economic consequences for Auckland province.

In 1853 the governor, Sir George Grey, introduced new provincial government under the 1852 constitution. Supported by the Auckland Constitutional Association and the votes of military pensioners and government employees, and opposed by the Progress Party—who demanded representative government and cheap land—Wynyard was elected superintendent of Auckland province. After becoming acting governor, instructed by the secretary of state for the colonies, he resigned the superintendency in January 1855. In June 1854 he was promoted colonel.

In January 1854 Grey left New Zealand, and its government devolved on Wynyard as senior military officer. The time was critical. A new Constitution Act instituting a system of parliamentary government had been received in February 1853, and Grey had already called the provincial councils into existence, but Wynyard had to deal with the new colonial assembly; he opened it on 7 May 1854 with a speech probably written for him by Edward Gibbon Wakefield. Wakefield had recently arrived in the colony, and Wynyard, realizing his need of an adviser while discharging unfamiliar duties in circumstances so unusual, largely relied on his advice. The assembly, immediately after meeting, carried an address to Wynyard, requesting him to inaugurate a system of responsible government, by ministers responsible to the electorate, for which there was no provision in the new constitution, but which had recently been introduced in Canada. Wynyard declared he had no power to do so, though members of the house argued there were no legal obstacles (a view later confirmed by the secretary of state for the colonies). The government was carried on by the executive against opposition from the newly elected members. Wynyard made several attempts to end the impasse. With the approval of William Swainson (1809–1883), the attorney-general, he compromised by adding four assembly members, including Henry Sewell and Frederick Aloysius Weld, to the executive council, but the old council members prevented them from exercising power. Not satisfied, the new nominees demanded the resignation of several council members, including the treasurer and the attorney-general. Wynyard, however, considering his temporary authority did not entitle him to replace crown officials by persons responsible to the assembly without the colonial secretary's sanction, refused. The new council members resigned. Despite an attempt to cut off supplies, and a stormy scene in the house of assembly, Wynyard maintained the original compromise until, as Wynyard requested, the colonial secretary approved the introduction of responsible government. On 15 April 1855 the royal assent was given to an act establishing the system. Politically inexperienced, Wynyard had been placed by Grey and the Colonial Office in a difficult, confused situation. He was reportedly popular in New Zealand, though some considered him well-meaning but weak and ill advised.

In September 1855 Colonel Thomas Gore Browne assumed the office of governor and Wynyard resumed his military duties. In 1858 the 58th was recalled to Britain, where on 26 October 1858 Wynyard was promoted major-general. In February 1859 he was appointed to command the troops in Cape Colony, again under Grey as governor, and between August 1859 and July 1860 he was acting governor and high commissioner during Grey's absence in Britain. This office again devolved on Wynyard, from Grey's departure for New Zealand in August 1861 until his successor's arrival in January 1862. In 1863 Wynyard returned to Britain 'in very bad health' (*GM*, 1864, 267). He received a pension for distinguished services, and on 9 October 1863 was appointed colonel of the 98th foot. Competent, practical, and apparently of average ability, Wynyard was tall, handsome, charming, and an accomplished draughtsman and watercolour painter. Retired, he resided at 6 Circus, Bath, but he died at Stanton's Hotel, Lower Berkeley Street, Portman Square, London, on 6 January 1864. His widow returned to Auckland, where she was a prominent figure until her death on 2 November 1881.

Edward Buckley Wynyard (1788–1864), army officer, was Robert Henry Wynyard's elder brother. Born at Kensington Palace, London, on 23 December 1788, he was commissioned ensign in the 1st foot guards in December 1803 and served thirty-five years in the regiment. He served in Sicily from 1808 to 1810, and was severely wounded in March 1810 during the British occupation of Santa Maura in the Ionian Islands. He was promoted captain and lieutenant-colonel in April 1814, colonel in July 1830, and major-general in November 1841. He was married and had children. He commanded the troops in Australasia from 1847 to 1852. Colonel of the 58th regiment from January 1851, he was promoted lieutenant-general in November 1851 and general in January 1860. He died at 27 Chester Street, London, on 24 November 1864.

E. I. CARLYLE, *rev.* ROGER T. STEARN

Sources *DNZB*, vol. 1 · *GM*, 1st ser., 89/1 (1819), 93 · *GM*, 3rd ser., 16 (1864), 267 · *GM*, 3rd ser., 18 (1865), 118 · Boase, *Mod. Eng. biog.* · *Hart's Army List* (1854) · J. Cowan, *The New Zealand wars: a history of the Maori campaigns and the pioneering period*, 1 (1922) · J. Belich, *The New Zealand wars and the Victorian interpretation of racial conflict*, pbk edn (1988) · P. Mennell, *The dictionary of Australasian biography* (1892) · W. L. Rees and L. Rees, *The life and times of Sir George Grey*, 2 (1892) · R. Garnett, *Edward Gibbon Wakefield: the colonisation of South Australia and New Zealand* (1898) · W. Gisborne, *New Zealand rulers and statesmen from 1840 to 1897*, rev. edn (1897) · *CGPLA Eng. & Wales* (1864)
Archives Mitchell L., NSW, letters to the New Zealand house of representatives, ML MSS62 · NL Scot., corresp. with Sir George Brown, MSS 1847–1852, 2840–2855

Wealth at death under £5000: double probate, Jan 1865, *CGPLA Eng. & Wales*

Wyon family (*per. c.*1760–1962), die-engravers and medallists, came to Britain from Germany about the middle of the eighteenth century. By 1705 the family had been established in Cologne, where in the 1730s and 1740s Peter Wyon supplied coin and medal dies to the city's ecclesiastical and civic mints, and in the 1760s Eberhart Wyon, thought to be a younger brother of Peter Wyon, signed several coin dies. The first member of the family to cross to Britain appears to have been a metalworker, Peter George Wyon (1710–1744), third son of George Wyon and Maria Sibylla Hemmerden, who had married in Cologne on 1 January 1705. It is improbable that this individual was the Peter Wyon who was working for the Cologne mints.

Peter George Wyon's son, **George Wyon** (*d.* 1797), whom he brought with him to Britain, also became a metalworker, and was apprenticed to George II's goldsmith Hemmings. George's first wife, Sarah, gave birth to a child, Ann, who was baptized in London on 13 March 1763. On 2 February 1766 George married his second wife, Ann Christy; their children Thomas and Peter were born the following year, with George and Mary following in 1771 and 1773 respectively; another son, James, was born later. In 1775 the family moved to Birmingham, where George produced designs and models for Matthew Boulton's Soho Manufactory and for the Birmingham Silver Plate Company, and where he also established the family die-engraving business, which was to remain in existence until the 1930s. All four sons learned to engrave dies, the resurgence of private tokens in the late eighteenth century accounting for a good proportion of their work. When their father died, Thomas and Peter, who had married two sisters, Ann and Elizabeth Avery, in 1790 and 1794 respectively, took over the business, which in 1800 they divided into two, with Thomas moving down to London, to open an operation in the capital.

The earliest medals of **Thomas Wyon the elder** (1767–1830) belong to 1789. Like many other members of the family, he frequently followed designs produced by other artists: for his medal of Stonehenge (1796) he engraved a design by William Blake, and his portrait of Joseph Hanson (1810), the champion of the weavers' cause, was based on a wax model by Peter Rouw. His medals range from a large piece commemorating the centenary of the Act of Union (1807) to five tiny medallets celebrating the final defeat of Napoleon (1815). He continued also to produce tokens, such as that for John Cooper's cotton mill in Staverton, Wiltshire (1811). In 1816 he was appointed chief engraver of his majesty's seals.

Thomas Wyon's eldest son, **Thomas Wyon the younger** (1792–1817), trained under his father and the gem-engraver Nathaniel Marchant, and at the Royal Academy Schools. Among his earliest medals were those commemorating the duke of Wellington's victories in Portugal (1810) and the appointment of the prince of Wales as regent (1811). He was not yet twenty when on 20 November

1811 he was appointed probationer engraver at the Royal Mint, and on 13 October 1815 he became chief engraver. He executed dies for coins for various colonies, as well as for George III's German territories and the duke of Wellington's army in France. He was involved in the production of dies for the recoinage of 1816, but his promising career was cut short by his premature death from consumption in 1817.

His brother **Benjamin Wyon** (1802–1858) was also a prolific die-engraver, who received training from his father and his elder brother and at the Royal Academy. Following his father's death in 1830, he was appointed to the post of chief engraver of seals, and took over the family firm. His seals include the great seal of William IV (1831). His medal commemorating the opening of the new London Bridge (1831) was the first of a series issued throughout the remainder of the century by the corporation of the City of London, to which the Wyons made a significant contribution. Later medals include a commemoration of the opening of London's new coal exchange (1849), and a prize medal for the Royal Scottish Academy, for which Sir Joseph Noël Paton provided the design (about 1854). He died on 21 November 1858 at his home, 14 Buckland Crescent, St John's Wood, London.

A younger brother, **Edward William Wyon** (*bap.* 1811, *d.* 1885), studied at the Royal Academy Schools from 1829, and became a celebrated sculptor, exhibiting at the Royal Academy regularly from 1831 to 1876. Among his commissions were works intended for reproduction by Wedgwood and numerous portrait busts. He executed reliefs for Drapers' Hall, London (1866), and two caryatids for the Fitzwilliam Museum, Cambridge (1874).

Benjamin Wyon married Hannah Olive Shepherd in 1835, and three of their children became die-engravers. **Joseph Shepherd Wyon** (1836–1873) and **Alfred Benjamin Wyon** (1837–1884), both of whom trained under their father and at the Royal Academy Schools, took over the firm, reconstituting it as J. S. and A. B. Wyon. Determining who was responsible for their medals can be problematical, for, although some are signed individually, others, including some made after Joseph's death, bear the firm's signature; many were exhibited jointly at the Royal Academy. Joseph Shepherd died on 12 August 1873 at Winchester, Hampshire, leaving a widow, Sarah. Alfred Benjamin died on 4 June 1884 at his home, 23 Belsize Road, Hampstead, leaving a widow, Kate. Their younger brother **Allan Wyon** (1843–1907) joined the firm in 1872. The three brothers followed their father successively as chief engraver of seals. Allan Wyon completed and brought to publication his brother Alfred's *The Great Seals of England* (1887). He died at his home, 33 Parkhill Road, Hampstead, on 25 January 1907.

Allan Gairdner Wyon (1882–1962), son of Allan and his wife, Harriet Gairdner, was primarily a sculptor, and was also the last member of the family to work as a die-engraver. He trained at the Royal Academy Schools, and worked as assistant to the sculptor William Hamo Thornycroft. His works include the *East Wind* for Charles Holden's new headquarters for London Underground at 55 Broadway (1926–9). On his father's death he took his place as head of the die-engraving firm, but under him it ceased to operate, and in 1933 the dies were transferred to John Pinches. He continued to design and model medals, however, into the 1950s. He died in 1962.

Peter Wyon (1767–1822), who had continued to run the Birmingham side of the business after Thomas the elder's departure for London, produced tokens and medals, including a large medal of Boulton after a model by Roux (1809). The Birmingham business ended with his death, by which time his son William *Wyon (1795–1851) was established at the Royal Mint in London. Following William's death, the post of modeller and engraver to the Royal Mint was created for his son Leonard Charles *Wyon (1826–1891).

The third brother, George Wyon (b. 1771), also remained in Birmingham, where on 26 August 1798 he married Elizabeth Phillips. Their son James Wyon (1804–1868) worked as assistant to his cousin William Wyon in London, and on the reorganization of the Royal Mint in 1851 became resident engraver. Two of the sons of James and his wife, Mary, Henry Wyon (1834–1856) and George Wyon (1834–1862), also became die-engravers. Another of George and Elizabeth's sons, John George (b. 1806), who remained in the west midlands and married Alice Arkinstall, was the father of Edward Wyon (1837–1906), who worked for the Birmingham mint of Heaton & Sons and, having supervised the construction of the first modern mint in China, at Canton (Guangzhou), in 1887–8, stayed on as head of the operative department.

The fourth brother, James Wyon, set up a die-engraving business in Dublin.   PHILIP ATTWOOD

Sources L. Brown, *A catalogue of British historical medals, 1760–1960*, 3 vols. (1980–95) · L. Forrer, ed., *Biographical dictionary of medallists*, 6 (1916); 8 (1930) · M. Jones, *The art of the medal* (1979) · A. Noss, *Die Münzen und Medaillen von Köln*, 4 vols. (1925–6), vols. 3–4 · Graves, *RA exhibitors* · C. Eimer, *British commemorative medals and their values* (1987) · A. Jocelyn, *Awards of honour* (1956) · P. Attwood, *Artistic circles: the medal in Britain, 1880–1918* (1992) [exhibition catalogue] · W. J. Hocking, *Catalogue of the coins, tokens, medals, dies, and seals in the museum of the royal mint*, 2 vols. (1906–10) · A. B. Wyon and A. Wyon, *The great seals of England* (1887) · A. B. Tonnochy, *Catalogue of British seal-dies in the British Museum* (1952) · C. Welch, *Numismata Londinensia* (1894) · *CGPLA Eng. & Wales* (1884) [Alfred Benjamin Wyon] · *CGPLA Eng. & Wales* (1907) [Allan Wyon] · *CGPLA Eng. & Wales* (1858) [Benjamin Wyon] · *CGPLA Eng. & Wales* (1873) [Joseph Shepherd Wyon] · *DNB* · *IGI* [Joseph Shepherd Wyon; Thomas Wyon the younger; Edward William Wyon] · R. Gunnis, *Dictionary of British sculptors, 1660–1851* (1953); new edn (1968)
Archives BL, pocket book, Egerton MS 3812 · CUL, account book · CUL, professional papers; professional and personal papers | Birm. CL, Boulton MSS · NA Scot., letters to G. W. Hope
Likenesses A. G. Wyon, medal (Allan Wyon) · W. Wyon, wax model (Peter Wyon), BM · T. Wyon junior, wax model (Thomas Wyon the elder), BM · woodcut (Joseph Shepherd Wyon), BM
Wealth at death £10,829 7s. 8d.—Alfred Benjamin Wyon: probate, 22 July 1884, *CGPLA Eng. & Wales* · £10,323 8s. 11d.—Allan Wyon: probate, 9 March 1907, *CGPLA Eng. & Wales* · under £4000—Benjamin Wyon: administration, 10 Dec 1858, *CGPLA Eng. & Wales* · under £3000—Joseph Shepherd Wyon: probate, 6 Sept 1873, *CGPLA Eng. & Wales*

Wyon, Alfred Benjamin (1837–1884). *See under* Wyon family (*per.* c.1760–1962).

Wyon, Allan (1843–1907). *See under* Wyon family (*per.* c.1760–1962).

Wyon, Allan Gairdner (1882–1962). *See under* Wyon family (*per.* c.1760–1962).

Wyon, Benjamin (1802–1858). *See under* Wyon family (*per.* c.1760–1962).

Wyon, Edward William (*bap.* 1811, *d.* 1885). *See under* Wyon family (*per.* c.1760–1962).

Wyon, George (*d.* 1797). *See under* Wyon family (*per.* c.1760–1962).

Wyon, Joseph Shepherd (1836–1873). *See under* Wyon family (*per.* c.1760–1962).

Wyon, Leonard Charles (1826–1891), die-engraver and medallist, was born on 23 November 1826 at the Royal Mint, London, the second of the five children of William *Wyon (1795–1851), a member of the famous *Wyon family of die engravers and medallists, and his wife, Catherine Sophia, *née* Keele (*d.* 1851). He was educated at the Merchant Taylors' School, London, and learned the art of die-engraving under his father, who set him to copy portraits executed by himself and Thomas Simon. He first exhibited at the Royal Academy in 1843. From 1844 he studied at the Royal Academy Schools and in the same year was appointed second or probationer engraver at the mint under his father. One of his earliest medals to be widely praised was that of the Irish temperance preacher Theobald Mathew (1846). In 1850 he was commissioned by Queen Victoria to make medallic portraits of the royal children, and in the following year he executed the reverse of the prize-medal for the Great Exhibition. Upon William Wyon's death, the reorganization of the mint then taking place was extended to include the engraving department. The post of chief engraver, which Leonard had had reason to expect would become his, was abolished, and he and his family were required to leave their house at the mint. The salaried post of modeller and engraver to the Royal Mint was created for him, enabling the mint to call on him for the production of coins and official medals as and when required; he retained this position for the rest of his life. On 22 June 1852 he married Mary Birks (1831–1902) and the couple lived in London, first in Maida Vale and from 1856 in St John's Wood; none of their numerous offspring took up their father's profession.

Leonard Wyon inherited his father's dies of medals of a wide range of institutions, and he continued to produce medals from them. He also took over from his father the production of punches for the Goldsmiths' Company. Like his father, he produced dies for coins, official and commemorative medals, and postage and other stamps. His most celebrated coin design was the so-called bun penny, named after Queen Victoria's hair-arrangement, executed for the new British bronze coinage of 1860. He also produced dies for the coinage of British colonies, including

Leonard Charles Wyon (1826–1891), by Wilhelm Kullrich, 1851

India, Australia, Canada, and other countries, sometimes from his own designs and sometimes from those by artists such as William Theed the younger and Owen Jones. His dies for the unsuccessful British jubilee coinage of 1887 followed designs by Joseph Edgar Boehm. His official medals included the South Africa medal (1853), the Arctic and Baltic medals (1855), and the Indian mutiny medal (1858); for the reverse of the Second Anglo-Asante War medal (1874) he followed a design by Edward Poynter. He also produced medals for the Society of Arts, the Royal Academy, and the Art Union of London and, for the firm of Hunt and Roskell, medals celebrating the weddings of the princess royal (1858) and the prince of Wales (1863). His medals for schools and other educational establishments included some commissioned by Queen Victoria. Among his portrait medals are those of William Wordsworth (1848), Robert Stephenson (1850), Joseph Paxton (1854), Richard Sainthill (1855), Henry Hallam (1859), and William Gladstone (1879). His style followed the combination of neo-classicism and detailed naturalism of his father's works. Although regarded as the foremost British die-engraver of his time, he lived under the shadow of the greater reputation of his father. Unsure of his own abilities as an artist, he frequently followed designs provided by others. Wyon died of Bright's disease and apoplexy at his home, 54 Hamilton Terrace, St John's Wood, London, on 20 August 1891 and was buried at Paddington old cemetery, Willesden Lane, on 25 August. The mint's abandonment in 1851 of the system whereby a chief engraver trained up his successor led to a problem in identifying a sufficiently skilled engraver to take on Wyon's duties.

PHILIP ATTWOOD

Sources L. Brown, *A catalogue of British historical medals, 1760–1960*, 2–3 (1987–95) · L. Forrer, ed., *Biographical dictionary of medallists*, 6 (1916); 8 (1930) · C. E. Challis, ed., *A new history of the royal mint* (1992) · G. P. Dyer and P. P. Gaspar, 'Richard Sainthill and the new bronze coinage', *British Numismatic Journal*, 54 (1984), 263–73 · C. W. Peck, *English copper, tin and bronze coins in the British Museum, 1558–1958*, 2nd edn (1970) · P. Attwood, 'A group of drawings by Leonard Wyon', *The Medal*, 31 (1997), 26–58 · R. Sainthill, *An olla podrida, or, Scraps numismatic, antiquarian, and literary*, 1 and 2 (1844–53) · Graves, *RA exhibitors* · M. Jones, *Designs on posterity: drawings for medals* (1994) · H. A. Grueber, 'English personal medals from 1760', *Numismatic Chronicle*, 3rd ser., 7 (1887), 247–72 · H. A. Grueber, 'English personal medals from 1760', *Numismatic Chronicle*, 3rd ser., 8 (1888), 59–94, 249–84 · H. A. Grueber, 'English personal medals from 1760', *Numismatic Chronicle*, 3rd ser., 10 (1890), 51–98 · H. A. Grueber, 'English personal medals from 1760', *Numismatic Chronicle*, 3rd ser., 11 (1891), 65–104, 377–412 · H. A. Grueber, 'English personal medals from 1760', *Numismatic Chronicle*, 3rd ser., 12 (1892), 227–46, 300–23 · E. Hawkins, *Medallic illustrations of the history of Great Britain and Ireland to the death of George II*, ed. A. W. Franks and H. A. Grueber, 2 vols. (1885) · D. J. Bryden, 'L. C. Wyon's Stephenson medal', *The Medal*, 13 (1988), 52–7 · *CGPLA Eng. & Wales* (1891) · pocket book, BL, Egerton MS 3812 · diary, BL, Add. MS 59617 · d. cert. · records, Paddington old cemetery, London

Archives BL, Add. MS 59617 · BL, pocket book, Egerton MS 3812 · BM, medals and coins · CUL, account book · V&A, medals and coins

Likenesses L. C. Wyon, self-portraits, drawings, 1841–3, repro. in Attwood, 'Group of drawings', pp. 26–58 · W. Kullrich, plaster medal, 1851, priv. coll. [*see illus.*]

Wealth at death £65,559 1s. 5d.: resworn probate, Jan 1892, *CGPLA Eng. & Wales* (1891)

Wyon, Olive (1881–1966), translator and theologian, was born on 7 March 1881 at 53 Maitland Park Road, Kentish Town, London, the eldest of the two sons and three daughters of Allan *Wyon [see under Wyon family] and his wife, Harriet Gairdner. Her father, a medallist, was her majesty's chief engraver of seals, the eighth member of his family to hold that office. She was educated at home, at Hampstead high school (briefly), and at an Anglican private school. It was only in 1899 during a year in Munich that Olive Wyon discovered that she had a natural flair for languages. For the subsequent five years, however, from the age of twenty to twenty-five, she was kept at home, her duties being housekeeping, cooking, nursing, Sunday school teaching for infants and girls, sick visiting, and being missionary secretary for Haverstock Congregational Chapel. She herself had long wished to become a missionary—ever since she had first read the life of David Livingstone in her early childhood. In the autumn of 1905, therefore, Olive Wyon went to the United Free Church Missionary Institute in Edinburgh, later St Colm's College, intending to offer herself for work with women in central Africa. After eighteen months her health collapsed and, despite successful recuperation in Switzerland where she mastered French, her application was finally rejected by the London Missionary Society on medical grounds. In 1910 she went for a course of religious study at Woodbrooke, the recently founded Quaker college in Birmingham, and she later went to work on the continent under Quaker auspices until the First World War broke out.

The first indication of Olive Wyon's radical social interpretation of Christianity was her public membership, in April 1915, of the unpopular British committee of the Women's International Congress at The Hague, whose two aims were that international disputes should in future be settled by some other means than war and that women should have a voice in the affairs of the nations. Her peace witness continued through her membership of the International Fellowship of Reconciliation in the 1920s. Her other radical stance concerned women, her most explicitly feminist work being *The Dawn Wind: a Picture of Changing Conditions among Women in Africa and the East* (1931) which is still of considerable interest and relevance today. She covered the situation of the educated minority of women in central and South Africa, India, China, Korea, Japan, and the Muslim world, in many cases her report being based not only on wide reading but on personal investigation during her travels. Olive Wyon believed that Christ 'gave to woman her charter of spiritual freedom' (Prologue to *The Dawn Wind*), but that the church had been too slow through the ages to grant her that liberty. She herself served in the mid-1920s for a short time as minister of a small Baptist church in Rushford, near Ipswich; from 1925 to 1939 she helped the minister of the Kentish Town Presbyterian Church as the director of his Sunday schools; from 1939 to 1945, at the suggestion of Canon Charles Raven, she became unofficial chaplain to women students at Cambridge; in 1947 she was appointed to head the translation department of the World Council of Churches in Geneva, and while there helped to prepare the interim report, 'The life and work of women in the church'; finally in 1948 she joined the staff of St Colm's Missionary College, Edinburgh, becoming its principal in 1951 at the age of seventy. In other words her own life demonstrated the capacity of women for spiritual ministry—as indeed did that of her sisters, one of whom was a Congregational minister and the other an Anglican deaconess.

Olive Wyon's reputation in her lifetime centred on her work as an outstanding translator of contemporary protestant theology. In 1929 she translated the massive *Social Teaching of the Christian Church* from the original by Ernst Troeltsch, and between 1934 and 1949 all Emil Brunner's primary contributions to theology. In her note to her translation *The Divine Imperative: a Study in Christian Ethics* (1936), from Brunner, she took the unusual step of guiding the reader to Brunner's important note at the back on socialism. It was an extraordinary achievement for a woman with no university degree to be acknowledged as one of the world's ablest translators, and Emil Brunner made the remarkable admission that he himself found her translations of his books more intelligible at points than his own German. In 1948 the University of Aberdeen acknowledged her feat by awarding her an honorary doctorate in divinity.

During the terrible period of Nazi tyranny and the Second World War, Olive Wyon testified to the supranationalism, supra-racialism, and anti-colonialism of the church. She was in close touch as long as that was possible with the anti-Nazi Confessing Church (Bekennende Kirche) in Germany, and her succinct summary of the revolutionary implications of applying Christianity to the socio-politics of the world in *The Church and World Peace: Principles which Should Govern a Righteous Peace Settlement*, with a foreword by Bishop George Bell (1940), based on her

reading of the report of the Oxford Conference on Church, Community, and State, *The Churches Survey their Task* (1937), testifies to her commitment to a church in the world, that struggles to remedy the injustices and cruelties of the world.

In her own personal spiritual life Olive Wyon was less a seeker than a finder. She was a pioneer of ecumenism, rejoicing to respond to the spiritual vitality and depth that she could find in religious communities as different as the Baptists, the Congregationalists, the Presbyterians, the Anglicans, the Franciscans, the Iona community, the Protestant Women's Religious Order at Grandchamp, the Catholics of Taizé, or the Orthodox monastery at Tolleshunt. Between 1943 and 1966 she published more than a dozen works on prayer and the desire for God. It was said of her that she was a practical mystic, one of the great spiritual encouragers and explorers, at home wherever Christ was Lord. At the ages of eighty-four and eighty-five she was still asked to broadcast for the BBC's religious programmes, and she helped Dame Cicely Saunders plan St Christopher's Hospice for the dying. She herself died of a pulmonary embolism and pneumonia on 21 August 1966 at Bruntsfield Hospital, Edinburgh. SYBIL OLDFIELD

Sources N. A. Oatts and J. Fraser, *Olive Wyon, D.D., 1881–1966: a chronicle* (privately printed, Edinburgh, 1971) · *The Times* (23 Aug 1966) · *The Times* (29 Aug 1966) · *Church Times* (26 Aug 1966) · *CGPLA Eng. & Wales* (1967) · b. cert. · d. cert.
Archives NL Scot., works and MSS | SOUND BL NSA(?), 'Lift up your hearts', 1964 · BL NSA(?), 'The ways of prayer', BBC, 5–10 April 1965, series of talks
Likenesses photograph, 1948, repro. in Oatts and Fraser, *Olive Wyon*, frontispiece
Wealth at death £6395: probate, 21 March 1967, *CGPLA Eng. & Wales*

Wyon, Thomas, the elder (1767–1830). *See under* Wyon family (*per. c.*1760–1962).

Wyon, Thomas, the younger (1792–1817). *See under* Wyon family (*per. c.*1760–1962).

Wyon, William (1795–1851), die-engraver and medallist, was born in Birmingham and baptized at St Philip's in the city on 23 June 1795, the eldest son of Peter Wyon (1767–1822), a member of the famous *Wyon family of die engravers and medallists, and his wife, Elizabeth Avery. He was educated in Birmingham and from 1809 was apprenticed to his father as a die-engraver. Some of his early medals bear the initials of his father. In 1812 he visited his uncle, Thomas Wyon the elder, in London and, encouraged by the gem-engraver Nathaniel Marchant, engraved a die of the head of Ceres, which in 1813 won the die-engraving competition of the Society of Arts; the die was subsequently used for the society's agricultural prize-medal (a wax model is now at the Royal Society of Arts). In 1815 he again visited London, and engraved for his uncle the new great seals for Scotland and Ireland. In May 1816 he was appointed by competition to the vacant post of second engraver at the Royal Mint under his cousin, Thomas Wyon the younger, and was employed in preparing dies for the recoinage of George III of 1816. On Thomas Wyon's

William Wyon (1795–1851), by Leonard Charles Wyon, 1854

death in 1817, however, Benedetto Pistrucci was appointed to replace him, and William Wyon remained second engraver. On 12 April 1821 he married Catherine Sophia Keele (d. 1851), third daughter of John Keele, surgeon, of Southampton; the couple subsequently had five children, one of whom, Leonard Charles *Wyon (1826–1891), took up die-engraving. In 1821 the temperamental Pistrucci refused to base his portrait for a medal of George IV on a bust by Francis Chantrey, and from this time work on the coinage was entrusted to William Wyon. The professional rivalry between the two men was accompanied by personal animosity. Their positions at the mint were regularized in 1828, when the post of chief medallist was created for Pistrucci, and Wyon became chief engraver; the salaries of the first and second engravers were divided equally between them. In 1831 Wyon produced dies for the coinage of William IV, with the portrait based on a model by Chantrey; he also executed the official coronation medal, after Pistrucci had declined to be involved. In 1838 Pistrucci engraved the official medal commemorating the coronation of Victoria, and Wyon was commissioned by the corporation of the City of London to execute a medal commemorating the queen's visit to the Guildhall. Their respective portraits of the queen rekindled the argument over their relative merits, and a heated correspondence ensued in the newspapers between their respective supporters, with the numismatists Richard Sainthill and Edward Hawkins writing in favour of Wyon (newspaper cuttings, Department of Coins and Medals, British Museum, London).

Following the introduction in 1840 of the uniform postal rate, the adhesive postage stamps indicating prepayment, including the 'penny black', bore a head of Victoria engraved from a drawing of Wyon's medal. His 'young head' of Victoria, produced for the coinage, was used on all British gold and silver coins until 1887. Besides his British coins, he executed coins for British colonies

and for other countries, including Portugal, which he visited in 1835 in order to make a portrait of Queen Maria II. He also produced official medals, including that for the First Anglo-Chinese War (1842), and the Military General Service 1793–1814 and Naval General Service medals (both 1847). His private medals were commissioned by a wide range of cultural, scientific, and philanthropic organizations. In some of his works he followed designs by others, but he also produced many compositions of his own which reveal his great admiration for the work of John Flaxman. The neo-classical ideal is evident in such works as his head of Homer for a prize-medal for the Edinburgh Academy of Literature (1824); his Cheselden medal for St Thomas's Hospital, London (1829), in which a corpse awaiting dissection is transmuted into an ancient hero; and his design of Una and the lion for a £5 pattern coin (1839). Like Chantrey, another artist whom he greatly admired, he was able to endow his portraits with a sense of nobility while at the same time retaining a likeness. In his reverses he made effective use of naturalistic detail, most notably perhaps in his representation of Bodiam Castle in Sussex on his medal for the Sea Bathing Infirmary at Hastings (1830). In his medal for the Newcastle and Carlisle Railway (1840) he successfully combined a neo-classical figure of Mercury, taken from Flaxman's relief of *Mercury Descending with Pandora*, with a view of nineteenth-century Newcastle upon Tyne, complete with factory chimneys and railway viaduct. His so-called Gothic crown (1846) had a medievalizing design; a pattern coin, it was the basis for Wyon's florin, issued for circulation in 1849. He was also responsible for the production of the punches required annually for the Goldsmiths' Company, and he engraved the punch for the embossed postal stationery that in 1841 replaced the much derided envelopes designed by William Mulready. In 1831 he was elected an ARA, and on 10 March 1838 he became a full academician, the only member of the family to do so. He was also made a member of the Accademia di Belle Arti of Parma in 1835 and the Kaiserliche Akademie der Bildenden Künste of Vienna in 1836. King Louis-Philippe of France presented him with a gold medal in 1839. On 27 September 1851 Wyon suffered a stroke in Brighton from which he did not recover, and died there on 29 October. He was buried in Norwood cemetery, Surrey.   PHILIP ATTWOOD

Sources N. Carlisle, *A memoir of the life and works of William Wyon* (1837) · L. Brown, *A catalogue of British historical medals, 1760–1960*, 3 vols. (1980–95) · L. Forrer, ed., *Biographical dictionary of medallists*, 6 (1916); 8 (1930) · M. Jones, 'The life and work of William Wyon', *La medaglia neoclassica in Italia e in Europa* [Udine 1981] (1984), 119–40 · Graves, *RA exhibitors* · R. Sainthill, *An olla podrida, or, Scraps, numismatic, antiquarian, and literary*, 1 and 2 (1844–53) · C. W. Peck, *English copper, tin and bronze coins in the British Museum, 1558–1958*, 2nd edn (1970) · D. N. Muir, *Postal reform and the penny black: a new appreciation* (1990) · M. Jones, *The art of the medal* (1979) · C. E. Challis, ed., *A new history of the royal mint* (1992) · H. A. Grueber, *Handbook of the coins of Great Britain and Ireland in the British Museum*, rev. J. P. C. Kent and others, 2nd edn (1970) · 'William Wyon and his works', *GM*, 2nd ser., 36 (1851), 609–14 · *IGI* · BM, department of coins and medals, newspaper cuttings

Archives BM, department of coins and medals · FM Cam. | NA Scot., letters to G. W. Hope

Likenesses W. Brockedon, pencil and chalk drawing, 1825, NPG · C. Vogel, drawing, 1837, Küpferstichkabinett, Staatliche Kunstsammlungen, Dresden · L. C. Wyon, drawing, 1842, repro. in Sainthill, *Olla podrida*, 88 · C. H. Lear, chalk drawing, *c.*1845, NPG · W. Kullrich, plaster medal, 1851, repro. in P. Attwood, 'A group of drawings by Leonard Wyon', *The Medal*, 31 (1997), 26–58 · L. C. Wyon, bronze medallion, 1854, BM, NPG [*see illus.*] · W. Drummond, lithograph (after E. U. Eddis), BM, NPG; repro. in *Athenaeum portraits* (1835) · J. Kirkwood, engraving (after L. C. Wyon), BM, NPG; repro. in Sainthill, *Olla podrida*, vol. 1

Wealth at death £40,000: PRO, death duty registers, IR 26/1949

Wyrley, William (1565–1618), antiquary and herald, was born, according to his own account, at Seal, Leicestershire, the son of Augustine Wyrley of Netherseal and his wife, Mary, daughter of William Charnelles of Snarestone in the same county, and the grandson of William Wyrley of Hamstead Hall in Handsworth, Staffordshire. It may have been the family's Staffordshire connections—which extended to Alrewas, where an infant sister of Wyrley was buried—that led Anthony Wood to say that he was born in Staffordshire, adding that he was 'in those parts brought up in grammar learning' (Wood, *Ath. Oxon.*, 2.217). According to Wood, he had 'from his childhood … an excellent geny for arms and armory' (ibid.) and as a result was taken into the household of Sampson Erdeswick of Sandon, the Staffordshire historian. By 1588 Wyrley was making a collection of heraldic notes for several midland counties including Staffordshire. He paid special attention to Leicestershire, and according to his friend William Burton, the Leicestershire historian, he planned to write a survey of that county. Erdeswick made only a passing reference to his assistant in his 'View of Staffordshire', but he clearly made use of Wyrley's research, although not always the best use. Whereas Erdeswick concentrated on genealogy and heraldry, Wyrley ranged more widely. Thus at Wednesbury he noted the existence of coalmining and pottery making and at Walsall the large number of lorimers making horse furniture as well as mentioning the town's borough status.

In 1592 Wyrley published *The True Use of Armorie*. Sir William Dugdale, who reprinted the main text in his *The Antient Usage in Bearing of … Arms* in 1682, quoted William Burton as saying that his friend Erdeswick had told him that he himself was the real author of the book, 'though he gave leave to Mr Wyrley (who had been bred up under him) to publish it in his own name' (Dugdale, 4). Anthony Wood, however, considered the claim one more sign that Erdeswick's mind was unbalanced.

Wyrley's research had its special dangers, especially in view of his connection with Erdeswick, a known recusant. In 1592 the Warwickshire recusancy commissioners reported that 'one Woorley, sometime servant to one Sampson Erswicke … was suspected to be a lewd and a seditious papist', resorting often 'as a wandering man, under the colour of tricking out of arms in churches' to the houses of 'gentlemen known to be ill-affected in religion' in Warwickshire and neighbouring counties. He was also suspected of secretly carrying letters between papists (Hodgetts, 7).

In 1594, at the mature age of twenty-nine, Wyrley entered Balliol College, Oxford, as a commoner. He remained there three years and took the opportunity to pursue his antiquarian interests in the area. About 1599 he went to Scotland to the court of King James. From 1603 he accompanied William Burton in a survey of churches. He was appointed Rouge Croix pursuivant at the College of Arms in 1604, and according to Anthony Wood his reputation there was that of 'a knowing and useful person in his profession' (Wood, *Ath. Oxon.*, 2.218). Wyrley died in early February 1618 at the College of Arms, London, and was buried in the college's burial-place in the nearby church of St Benet Paul's Wharf.   M. W. GREENSLADE

Sources M. W. Greenslade, *The Staffordshire historians*, Staffordshire RS, 4th ser., 11 (1982) · Wood, *Ath. Oxon.*, new edn · J. Nichols, *The history and antiquities of the county of Leicester*, 3/1 (1800), xv; 3/2 (1804), 992 · M. Hodgetts, 'A certificate of Warwickshire recusants, 1592 (cont.)', *Worcestershire Recusant*, 6 (Dec 1965), 7 · S. Shaw, *The history and antiquities of Staffordshire*, 2 (1801), 110, 115 · *VCH Warwickshire*, 7.69 · W. Dugdale, *The antient usage in bearing of … arms* (1682), 4 · Foster, *Alum. Oxon.* · parish register, Alrewas [transcript in the William Salt Library, Stafford] · yearly lists, Balliol Oxf., 2, fol. 24
Archives BL, transcripts of rolls of arms, Add. MS 51047 · Coll. Arms, Vincent 127 · Coll. Arms, church notes, Vincent 197 · Norfolk RO, armorial · S. Antiquaries, Lond., Staffordshire collection · U. Birm. L., special collections department, collections

Wyse, Andrew Reginald Nicholas Gerald Bonaparte- (1870–1940), civil servant, was born on 1 November 1870 at Cecil Street, Limerick, second of four sons of William Charles Bonaparte-*Wyse (1826–1892) [*see under* Wyse, Sir Thomas] and his wife, Ellen Linzee (d. 1925), daughter of W. G. Prout of St Mabyn, Cornwall. He was a grandson of Sir Thomas *Wyse of Waterford. The Wyse family established close ties with France and Italy throughout the nineteenth century. Sir Thomas Wyse had married a daughter of Lucien Bonaparte, his elder son wrote on Russian and French topics, and his younger son, Bonaparte-Wyse's father, published poetry in French and Provençal, and was a friend of Frédéric Mistral.

Bonaparte-Wyse shared these European affinities. Education at Downside School, Bath (1880–85), was followed by an external London University BA in French (1890) and an MA in classics (1894). On 16 September 1896 he married Mariya Dmitryevna, eldest daughter of Count Dmitry de Chripunov of Bielevetz, Oryol, Russia. Later he acquired the Château du Chêne Vert, *département* of Gard, France, and later still his son was an officer in the Free French navy during the Second World War.

Bonaparte-Wyse's working life was spent mainly in Ireland. In 1895, after a period of teaching near Chester, and at the extraordinarily early age of twenty-four, he was appointed an inspector of national schools. He served in Cork and Ballymena, but in 1897 was sent to France and Belgium to assist the Belmore commission's inquiry into the Irish primary school curriculum. He was moved to Dublin in 1903, and from 1905 served in the central office of the national commission for education. In 1915, after the smoothest of career progressions, he became junior secretary, the second highest post in the organization.

In 1921 Bonaparte-Wyse's career changed. He helped to advise Lord Londonderry on proposals for education in

Northern Ireland, and then in 1922 he transferred to the new Northern Ireland ministry of education, commuting weekly to Belfast from his home at Blackrock, co. Dublin. Northern Ireland education gained greatly from his experience and authority. In 1927 he became permanent secretary, the only Roman Catholic in that grade at Stormont. In spite of bitter political and sectarian conflicts over education he maintained the ministry's own equitable reputation. He became civil service commissioner for Northern Ireland. He was a close friend and confidant of Lord Craigavon.

Bonaparte-Wyse lived as an Irish gentleman and scholar. He inherited, and greatly valued, the family 'manor' of St John's, Waterford, largely symbolic as it was. He read daily from the classics in Greek. He was a liberal Catholic—'practically a free thinker' according to his brother (Akenson, 242). The family lived extravagantly and there were acute marital tensions. That he was ultimately an MRIA, a knight of Malta, and a CB (1939) marks his multiple distinction as a scholar, a Roman Catholic, and a public servant. He retired in 1939, and died at the Tivoli Nursing Home, Dún Laoghaire, on 1 June 1940. He was survived by his wife, his son, and two daughters.

ARTHUR GREEN

Sources WWW · Burke, *Gen. Ire.* (1958) · *Irish Times* (3 June 1940) · memoranda, letters, etc., NL Ire., P.C. 647 · private information (2004) · b. cert. · d. cert. · D. H. Akenson, *Education and enmity: the control of education in Northern Ireland, 1920–50* (1973)
Archives NL Ire.
Likenesses photographs, department of education, Northern Ireland
Wealth at death £954 6s. 8d.—in Republic of Ireland (gross): probate, 1940, *CGPLA Éire*

Wyse, Napoleon Alfred Bonaparte- (1822–1895). *See under* Wyse, Sir Thomas (1791–1862).

Wyse, Sir Thomas (1791–1862), politician and diplomatist, was born at the manor of St John, co. Waterford, on 9 December 1791, the eldest of six children of Thomas Wyse, lord of the manor of St John, and his wife, Frances Maria, heir of George Bagge of Dromore, co. Waterford. This old Anglo-Norman family descended from Andrew Wyse, who received land in co. Waterford for helping Strongbow (Richard de Clare, earl of Pembroke), who led a mercenary force to Ireland in the 1160s. Maurice Wyse became tenant of the manor of St John, the lands of a decayed monastery near Waterford, in 1495; his grandson Sir William Wyse profited from his services to King Henry VIII and from the dissolution of the monasteries by receiving absolute landlordship. Because the estate included property within the city of Waterford, the Wyse family became involved in the borough's economic, social, and political life. The family remained Roman Catholic in the seventeenth century; although it suffered economically to some extent from the penal laws, and to a greater extent from family litigation, it played a leading role in Waterford's Roman Catholic community. Thomas Wyse's father was an absentee landlord who lived near Bath and in Europe.

Sir Thomas Wyse (1791–1862), by John Partridge, 1846

Education, travels, and marriage Wyse attended the Jesuit college at Stonyhurst, Lancashire, from 1800 to 1809 and Trinity College, Dublin, from 1809 to 1812. His fellow students included his lifelong friends Richard Lalor Sheil (politician, privy councillor, and office-holder), John Talbot, sixteenth earl of Shrewsbury (the leading English Roman Catholic peer during the first half of the nineteenth century), and the future judges Nicholas Ball and Stephen Woulfe. A serious student, Wyse read widely in ancient and modern history and literature, won prizes for Greek and Latin composition, and took an active role in the Trinity College Historical Society. He spent the year 1813–14 at Lincoln's Inn. At this juncture, the end of the Napoleonic wars reopened the continent to British travellers. Wyse embarked on a grand tour in 1815, supported by an allowance of £600 p.a.; he remained abroad for most of the following decade.

Wyse wintered in 1815–16 at Rome, where he met Cardinal Consalvi, the reforming papal secretary of state, and Lucien Bonaparte, prince of Canino, a younger brother of the emperor Napoleon. Wyse and Lucien shared literary interests, and he was a frequent guest at the prince's country homes near Viterbo. He travelled through France, Switzerland, and Italy from 1816 to 1818, and ventured into the eastern Mediterranean in 1818 and 1819, touring Greece, Constantinople, Egypt, Palestine, Syria, Lebanon, and Sicily in the company of Charles Barry, the Gothic revival architect. On returning to Italy, Wyse visited Canino, where Lucien helped him convince himself that he was in love with Letitia Christine (1804–1871), Lucien's eldest daughter. Princess Letitia, accounted the most beautiful of her generation of Bonapartes, was young, unformed, and unacquainted with society; Wyse, urged on by Sheil, agreed to the enthusiastic Lucien's proposal and persuaded his reluctant parents. After eight months of negotiations over the marriage settlement, Wyse foolishly signed two: one that his father made, based on English law; the other, based on Roman law, from Lucien. The contradictory settlements (not to mention Lucien's reneging on the dowry) led to much legal wrangling in later years. The couple were married in the Great Hall of Canino on 4 March 1821.

The Wyse children Thomas and Letitia Wyse had two sons. The elder, **Napoleon Alfred Bonaparte-Wyse** (1822–1895), was born in the Palazzo Gabrielli, Rome (the residence of Letitia's sister), on 6 January 1822, and was educated at Downside Abbey, near Bath, Broadwood School, Lancashire, and Oscott College, near Birmingham. Emotionally troubled by his parents' estrangement and his father's neglect, he broke down in 1838 and was sent to a German physician and then to a French religious order. In 1839 he ran away to his mother. He lived with a paid guardian near Limoges from 1843 until his father's death in 1862. He succeeded to the family estates, but soon stepped aside for his younger brother, moved to the continent, and lived off his half-sister Studholmina-Maria. Interested in genealogy, he wrote two books, *Notes sur la Russie* (1854) and *Flores Pictavienses* (1869). He was high sheriff (1870), a justice of the peace, and a deputy lieutenant for co. Waterford and an alderman for the city of Waterford. He was awarded a knight commandership of the order of SS. Maurizio e Lazzaro. He died unmarried at Paris on 7 August 1895.

The younger son, **William Charles Bonaparte-Wyse** (1826–1892), was born at The Mall in Waterford on 20 January 1826, attended Prior Park College, near Bath, and Oscott College, and married Ellen Linzee Prout (*d.* 1925) in 1864; they had four sons. A justice of the peace and high sheriff for Waterford (1855), he was noted for his strong unionist views. His love lay in southern France, where he participated in the Félibrige, the movement to revive the Provençal literary tradition under the leadership of the poet and Nobel laureate Frédéric Mistral, whom he met in 1859. The movement's Maecenas, he translated Théodore Aubanel's *Lou pan dóu pecat* into English (1866), paid for the publication of Provençal poetry, and hosted the Fête de Fontségugne, a grand banquet, on 30 May 1867, which brought together Provençal and Catalan poets. His celebratory poem received first prize at the commemoration of the centenary of Lord Brougham's birth, held at Cannes in 1878. Mistral, who always referred to him as 'notre enthousiaste ami' (Boutière, 71), praised his volume of poetry, *Li parpaioun blu* (1868). His fellow poets honoured him by making him the only foreign 'majoral' (member of the consistory) of the Félibrige. He died at Cannes on 3 December 1892 and was buried there two days later.

Wyse provided for his sons' basic material wants, but gave them no affection, perhaps because they reminded him of his failed marriage. He was indifferent to their development and expected prompt, unquestioning obedience to his orders. The sons submitted when they had to and rebelled when they could. Both adopted the surname Bonaparte-Wyse and visited their mother, much to Wyse's fury. He tried to cut them off with annuities in his last will, but because this violated the entail on the property, it was set aside after three years of litigation and Napoleon Alfred succeeded. Both sons hated their father and loved their mother, who in turn loved them.

Break-up of marriage Thomas and Letitia Wyse had a year of happiness, but after the birth of their first child the basic incompatibility of the two became increasingly apparent. Thirteen years older than his teenaged bride, Wyse enjoyed teaching her about literature and the fine arts; he admitted that he was 'rather of a billious temperament, … of that more dull, dun, melancholic cast which … will take up with the same room, chair, and book for weeks together …' (Bonaparte-Wyse, 43). As Letitia, only sixteen years old at her marriage, matured, she came to want music, dancing, and attention, and resented that Wyse ignored her, not writing to her when he was away and keeping to his study when he was at home. Quarrels began; Letitia found like-minded friends in Viterbo, friends of whom Wyse disapproved; and after an especially violent fight in 1824 (so fierce that their carriage rocked on its springs) over charges that she had a lover, she fled to a convent and asked for a separation. Refuge became incarceration when Wyse and Lucien got a papal order of seclusion; what they were pleased to call a 'holy asylum' in fact was a prison. Letitia submitted to her husband after eight months in the convent, when Wyse threatened to leave Italy without her.

After a decade's absence, Wyse had determined to return to Ireland, largely because he wanted to join the campaign for Roman Catholic emancipation. He and his family reached Waterford in June 1825. There Wyse occupied himself with writing and political campaigning, while Letitia vegetated in provincial society. As Wyse withdrew into his library, Letitia increasingly lashed out in hostility; the two eventually agreed to a separation in May 1828. Letitia threw herself into the Serpentine and was rescued by Captain Studholm John Hodgson (1805–1890), a serving officer who later had a distinguished career in Ceylon. The two became lovers and had three children who survived to adulthood: Studholmina-Maria (1831–1902), Adeline (*b.* 1840), and Lucien (1845–1909), all of whom used the surname Bonaparte-Wyse, which led to more litigation as Wyse never missed the opportunity to deny their paternity. Both daughters married figures of the Risorgimento; the son, an engineer, persuaded the government of Colombia to grant him the concession to build a canal across the isthmus of Panama. Much of the remainder of Wyse's life was taken up by disputes over the marriage settlements, the deed of separation, the many versions of his last will and testament, and the behaviour of Letitia and her children.

Writing and politics The separation gave Wyse the freedom to devote himself fully to writing and politics. His travel diaries formed the basis for thirty unsigned articles in the *New Monthly Magazine* (1826–30) and a book, *The Continental Traveller's Oracle, or, Maxims for Foreign Locomotion* (2 vols., 1828), under the pseudonym Dr Abraham Eldon. His experiences in the Catholic Association contributed to the writing of two books on the subject (*The Political Catechism* and *Historical Sketch of the Late Catholic Association in Ireland*, both 1829). Wyse was a moderate whig, suspicious of democracy; he believed that Roman Catholic emancipation would reinforce the union between Britain and Ireland. In the 1830 general election Wyse turned to co. Tipperary for a constituency, for Waterford split its representation between the tory Beresford family and Daniel O'Connell. In parliament he supported the Reform Bill, but took little part in proceedings. Wyse contested Waterford in the 1832 election, but was defeated because he refused to pledge unqualified support for O'Connell. He represented Waterford from the 1835 general election to his defeat in 1847. He lost his seat in part because his moderate whiggish unionism was unacceptable to the Irish nationalists, in part because he was unwilling to nurse his constituency: 'I hope I can now afford to be utterly indifferent to the ignorance and malignity of the coteries at Waterford' (Auchmuty, 138).

Wyse's chief parliamentary interest lay in education. Wishing to strengthen the bonds of union between England and Ireland, between Roman Catholic and protestant, he adopted and organized the educational ideas current in progressive circles to propose common rate-aided schools for all children, separate religious indoctrination, and a national board of education. Both Wyse's scheme and that adopted by Dublin Castle in 1831 were based on the report of a parliamentary committee on Irish education chaired by Thomas Spring Rice (later first Baron Monteagle) in 1828. This provided for non-denominational state-run schools under a board of education appointed by the lord lieutenant. On his return to the house in 1835, Wyse introduced a measure to give legislative status to the Irish education commissioners, but it died for lack of parliamentary time. Later that year he chaired a select committee on Irish education; it produced impracticable recommendations in 1838 for a comprehensive centralized system of elementary, collegiate, and university schooling.

Wyse also broadcast his schemes with a book and an organization. The book, *Education Reform, or, The Necessity of a National System of Education* (1836), was his most widely read and influential work. Little in it is original; it rests on the thought of educational progressives. Wyse argued that the industrial revolution had created a new environment and transformed even the nature of society, so powerful was the impact of new technology. This transformation of society was attended by severe dislocations in the relationship of the classes, which threatened revolution unless the 'lower orders' were educated to take their place in the governing of society. English education, Wyse believed, should be modelled after the Irish system: local rate-aided schools, separate secular and religious instruction, supervision by powerful central boards. The organization the Central Society of Education was a lobbying body that published papers on current ideas in teaching methods and child psychology, on foreign educational systems, and on the state of English schools. It drew support from advanced whigs, Liberals, and philosophical radicals. On 14 June 1837 Wyse provoked a major Commons debate on the Melbourne ministry's education policy when he moved an address to the queen praying for the creation of a board of education. It failed of passage, and its failure spelt the end of the Central Society of Education as well.

Wyse was more effective as a member of committees and royal commissions than as a parliamentary debater. He was an active member of the select committee and later the royal commission on fine arts (1841), which laid down the policy for decorating the new houses of parliament and chose the artists and subjects. He chaired the select committees on art unions (1844) and on legal education (1846). Large portions of the reports of these bodies came from his pen, as did the publications of the Central Society of Education.

Wyse held office from 30 August 1839 to 8 September 1841 as a junior Treasury lord; his specific role was to be whip for the Irish supporters of Lord Melbourne's ministry. When Lord John Russell became prime minister in July 1846, he asked Wyse to return as whip, but the latter held out for something better and was made joint secretary of the Board of Control on 6 July 1846, with responsibility for Indian educational, legal, religious, and financial matters. (The family's straitened circumstances and his penchant for expensive litigation made the salary for public service welcome.) He did not have a free hand in making policy at the Board of Control. He retained the office after he was defeated in the 1847 election until a front-bencher needed it in January 1849. Russell rewarded Wyse for his services to the whig cause by making him a privy counsellor and minister-plenipotentiary to Greece, where he served from June 1849 until his death in 1862.

Minister in Greece, from 1849 Greek politics at the time of Wyse's arrival at Athens were complicated and divisive. Each of the three protecting powers that had guaranteed Greek independence—Britain, France, and Russia—wishing to advance its interests in the region, became entangled in factional politics. Some factions were liberal constitutionalists; others were less westernized. The king, Otho of Bavaria, sought to rule as well as reign. Disputes over the status of the Greek church, the pace of irredentism, and above all the control of patronage further complicated matters. Wyse's primary tasks were to obtain compensation from the Greek government for losses suffered by George Finlay, David Pacifico, and other British subjects, to encourage the government to honour its debts to the protecting powers, and to preserve the territorial integrity of the Ottoman empire from both Greek irredentism and Russian expansion. Wyse ably represented Lord Palmerston's aggressive policies in the Don Pacifico affair to the Greek government (for which he was made CB in 1851), but his habit of giving the Greeks unsolicited advice and his obstinate insistence that the Greek court receive his niece Winifrede Mary Wyse (d. 1908) (who was his hostess at the legation), in violation of diplomatic protocol, limited his effectiveness in influencing policy. It was the deployment of an Anglo-French army of occupation, not Wyse's diplomacy, that convinced the Greeks to remain neutral during the Crimean War. Nevertheless, Wyse was rewarded with a KCB and promotion to envoy-extraordinary in 1857.

Wyse continued his efforts to improve the Greeks in the years 1857–9. He chaired a commission of the protecting powers that made valuable recommendations about the reformation of Greek finances. He gave the Greek government memoranda on museums, the prison system, the legal system, education, the tax structure, the Orthodox church, and the provision of government buildings. The Greeks ignored all these suggestions.

Death and reputation Wyse's health began to decline in 1860. He prepared two books, published posthumously as *An Excursion in the Peloponnesus in the Year 1858* (1865) and *Impressions of Greece* (1871). He died of congestive heart failure early in the morning of 16 April 1862, and was buried the next day in the Roman Catholic cemetery at Athens.

Cultivated by his niece and endorsed by his biographer, Wyse's reputation as educational reformer, parliamentarian, and diplomat was somewhat exaggerated during the century after his death. The creation of both the Irish national educational system in 1831 and the education committee of the privy council in 1839 were attributed to his efforts. His biographer thought that he should have been made foreign secretary instead of Lord Palmerston in 1846 (Auchmuty, 202–3). Scholarship during the last third of the twentieth century, however, revised these views, seeing him as a source of peripheral pressure on the whig ministries of the 1830s, a conscientious participant in committees and royal commissions, and a reasonably competent diplomat. Wyse believed that systematic and rational reforms were so plainly beneficial that any detailed scheme should draw support: 'in a Reforming age, with the instruments of correction so numerous and well adapted in our own hands, to *state* an abuse ought to be to *correct* it' (T. Wyse, *Education Reform*, 1836, 19). This optimistic view, common among early Victorian progressives, failed to take into account the complexities of the institutions to be reformed, the strength of the opposition to reform, and the validity of alternative solutions. Hence despite his sobriquet 'the member for education', Wyse had little influence on the development of either the Irish or the English school systems.

Thomas Wyse was an intelligent, studious, and well-read man with a facility for languages; he was fluent in French and Italian, could speak German, and had a reading knowledge of Spanish, Portuguese, Danish, Dutch, and Flemish. He had a clear and interesting writing style; in addition to his major works discussed above, he published several speeches in pamphlet form and wrote essays for the *Dublin Review* and the *British and Foreign Review*. He was a strong-looking man, with wavy hair, a broad forehead, a distinguished nose, and a dimpled chin. His temperament was rigid; his determination to defend his dignity led him to spend much of his resources in fruitless litigation and to neglect his children; and he never doubted the righteousness of his views.   D. G. PAZ

Sources J. J. Auchmuty, *Sir Thomas Wyse, 1791–1862* (1939) • O. Bonaparte-Wyse, *The spurious brood: Princess Letitia Bonaparte and her children* (1969) • D. G. Paz, *The politics of working-class education in Britain, 1830–50* (1980) • D. Dakin, *The unification of Greece, 1770–1923* (1972) • J. Boutière, ed., *Correspondance de Frédéric Mistral avec Paul Meyer et Gaston Paris* (1978) • C. Mauron, *Frédéric Mistral* (1993) • D. H. Akenson, *The Irish education experiment: the national system of education in the nineteenth century* (1970) • J. Cosgrove, 'The educational aims and activities of Sir Thomas Wyse (1791–1862)', PhD diss., University of Manchester, 1975 • V. G. Toms, 'Secular education in England, 1800–1870', PhD diss., U. Lond., 1972 • E. Ripert, *Le Félibrige* (1924) • *DNB*

Archives NL Ire., corresp. and papers • NL Ire., diaries and notebook [microfilm] • NL Ire., papers • NRA, papers • NRA, priv. coll., political memoranda | Hants. RO, letters to Lord Malmesbury • NL Ire., William Smith O'Brien MSS • NL Scot., letters to George Combe • PRO, corresp. with Stratford Canning, FO 352 • PRO, corresp. with Lord John Russell, PRO 30/22 • U. Southampton L., corresp. with Lord Palmerston

Likenesses J. Partridge, oils, 1846, NG Ire. [*see illus.*] • photograph, c.1860, repro. in Auchmuty, *Sir Thomas Wyse* • Cossos and Brontos, marble sculpture, NG Ire. • J. Partridge, group portrait (*The fine art commissioners, 1846*), NPG • E. Scriven and B. E. Duppa, stipple, BM, NPG; repro. in J. Saunders, *Portraits and memoirs of eminent living political reformers* (1840)

Wealth at death under £8000: probate, 5 Dec 1862, *CGPLA Ire.*

Wyse, William (1860–1929), classical scholar, was born at Gurney Road, Stratford, London, on 19 March 1860, the son of William Wyse, railway contractor, and his wife, Mary Horton. He first attended school at Walthamstow until the family returned to Halford, near Shipston-on-Stour in Worcestershire, where his father owned some land. From King Edward VI Grammar School, Stratford upon Avon, he won a scholarship to King's School, Canterbury; he entered Trinity College, Cambridge, in 1878. His undergraduate career was distinguished: he was elected a scholar of Trinity (1880), won the Powis medal (1880), the Waddington scholarship (1881), and the chancellor's medal (1882), and graduated BA as fourth classic in the classical tripos (1882). Elected a fellow of his college in 1883, he was regularly in residence at Trinity, while also employed as a tutor at Walter Wren's private coaching establishment in Bayswater, which 'crammed' candidates for the civil service and other open competitive examinations. After a two-year spell in 1892–4 as professor of Greek at University College, London, he returned to Trinity as a classical tutor, but resigned for reasons of health in 1904. He retired to Halford, where he lived with his widowed mother and unmarried sister.

Apart from some contributions to the *Classical Review*, principally emendations in the newly discovered text of Aristotle's *Constitution of Athens*, Wyse's main work was a monumental edition of the speeches of the Athenian author Isaeus, who specialized in cases involving questions of family law. This edition (Cambridge, 1904) is still regarded as the standard reference book for many aspects of the subject, and justifies his friend Sir James Frazer's description of him as 'one of the finest Greek and Latin scholars of his time' (Frazer). He also contributed a chapter on Greek law to *A Companion to Greek Studies* edited by Leonard Whibley (1905). He died, unmarried, at Halford on 29 November 1929 and was cremated in Birmingham.

N. G. WILSON

Sources J. Frazer, *The Times* (9 Dec 1929) • *The Times* (5 Dec 1929) • Venn, *Alum. Cant.* • b. cert. • d. cert.

Wealth at death £23,407 1s. 7d.: resworn probate, 26 March 1930, *CGPLA Eng. & Wales*

Wyse, William Charles Bonaparte- (1826–1892). *See under* Wyse, Sir Thomas (1791–1862).

Wythe, George (1725/6–1806), lawyer and revolutionary politician in America, was born on Chesterville plantation in Elizabeth City county, Virginia, the second son of the planter Thomas Wythe (*c.*1691–1729) and Margaret Walker (*d. c.*1746), granddaughter of the Quaker George Keith. George Wythe was a lifelong member of the Church of England. He married, first, on 26 December 1747, Anne (1726/7–1748), daughter of Zachary Lewis of Spotsylvania county and Mary Waller of Williamsburg, and, second, probably in 1755, Elizabeth (*d.* 1787), daughter of Richard Taliaferro of James City county and Elizabeth Eggleston. There were no surviving children from either marriage.

According to tradition Wythe's mother was unusual for the era in her ability to teach him Latin. George may have attended a free school in Hampton and grammar school at the College of William and Mary. In the early 1740s he studied law with his mother's brother-in-law, Stephen Dewey, near Petersburg. He qualified for the bar in Elizabeth City county in June 1746 and in several other counties shortly after. He briefly practised with Zachary and John Lewis in Spotsylvania. Upon the death of his first wife Wythe relocated to Williamsburg in association with her uncle, Benjamin Waller, and secured appointment as clerk for two legislative committees, inaugurating a relationship of nearly thirty years with the house of burgesses. He also practised in association with the colony's treasurer, Robert Carter Nicholas. Wythe quickly established himself in the capital, and became alderman in 1750. Delighting in Williamsburg's intellectual atmosphere, he formed particularly close bonds with Governor Francis Fauquier, William Small, professor of natural philosophy, and Small's outstanding student, Thomas Jefferson, who read law with Wythe between 1764 and 1766.

Williamsburg elected Wythe a burgess in 1754. That year he became involved in the first of two celebrated confrontations with royal authorities. When Governor Robert Dinwiddie dismissed Peyton Randolph as attorney-general, Wythe accepted the post. By the autumn Dinwiddie had relented, and Randolph returned to office. The second episode resulted from Wythe's inheritance of Chesterville, following the death in 1755 of his elder brother without an heir. George's income significantly increased, permitting a second marriage. His propertied status led to his presiding over the Elizabeth City county court, and an involvement in the Parson's Cause. In the case of the Reverend Thomas Warrington, one of five suits on the issue, Wythe upheld Virginia's Two Penny Acts reducing the value of clerical salaries paid in tobacco when the crop failed. Wythe continued to reside in Williamsburg, where his father-in-law, a prominent builder, constructed a home for the newly-weds near the governor's palace.

In 1756 and 1758 Wythe lost bids for the legislature from Elizabeth City, but in the latter year won for William and Mary. He sat for Elizabeth City from 1761 until 1766. Committee work, rather than debate, became his forte. He helped compose the burgesses' constitutional objections to the stamp tax in December 1764, but in the following May he vehemently opposed Patrick Henry's more inflammatory resolutions. At the death of Speaker John Robinson in 1766, Wythe sought the post, and then the attorney-generalship, but failed on both occasions. The same year he provoked intense criticism by advising three general-court members that they could grant bail to an accused murderer, Colonel John Chiswell, without convening the court. To many the affair smacked of class privilege. Applauding Wythe's opposition to Henry, Governor Fauquier appointed Wythe clerk of the house of burgesses in 1767, a post he held until independence. Between 1768 and 1771 Wythe also served as Williamsburg's mayor.

For a while Wythe kept a low profile in opposing imperial policies. He did not sign the association of 1769 or of 1774 blocking British imports, but in August 1774 he supported Jefferson's argument that only the crown, not parliament, had authority over Virginia. Wythe was probably clerk for Virginia's first extralegal convention in August, and in December he served on a Williamsburg committee to enforce the association. He represented Williamsburg in August 1775 at Virginia's third convention, which elected him to the continental congress. There, too, he seldom debated, but he won praise as a committee member. Late in 1775 he engaged John Adams in discussions leading to Adams's influential pamphlet for independence, *Thoughts on Government*. Although Wythe returned from congress too late for Virginia's vote on independence, the May 1776 convention appointed him to help design a state seal. Having returned to congress in September, he signed the Declaration of Independence, then resigned before the year's end to join Jefferson and Edmund Pendleton in revising Virginia law. During the next spring and autumn Wythe was elected speaker when Pendleton could not serve. Wythe and Pendleton had long been antagonists in the courtroom, where Pendleton's eloquence favoured him. In the revisal Wythe sided with Jefferson when Pendleton opposed abolishing primogeniture and entail or disestablishing the Anglican church. In 1778 the legislature appointed both Wythe and Pendleton to the high court of chancery, and the next year put them on the court of appeals with all other superior-court judges.

As governor, Jefferson remodelled the College of William and Mary and in 1779 named Wythe the first American professor of law, a position that perfectly suited his nature. Whether at home or the college, he taught law and the classics for most of his career, and, besides Jefferson, counted among his students James Monroe, St George Tucker, Spencer Roane, John Marshall, and Henry Clay. Because war impeded implementation of the previous revisal, the legislature asked the chancellors to prepare their revisal in 1784, only to enact most of the earlier report within two years. Wythe attended the 1787 constitutional convention in Philadelphia, but his wife's fatal illness forced him to depart early. At the state ratifying convention the next year Pendleton, who presided, frequently appointed Wythe chair of the committee of the whole. Wythe introduced the resolution for ratification.

The legislature in 1789 separated the court of appeals from other courts, and transferred Pendleton to preside. Wythe remained sole chancellor. Their rivalry, formerly respectful, now became public and bitter. In over 150 appeals from Wythe's decisions, Pendleton's court reversed or modified a majority. In 1795 the chancellor rebutted his nemesis in the sometimes vituperous *Wythe's Reports.*

Wythe resigned from the college in 1789 and moved to Richmond in 1791. At first an enthusiastic federalist, as a member of the electoral college in 1800 he voted for Jefferson. He died, aged eighty, in Richmond on 8 June 1806 of arsenic poisoning by his nephew, George Wythe Sweeney, who resented not being Wythe's sole heir. A public critic of slavery, Wythe freed three slaves by will. He had earlier emancipated three others, but had divided twelve among his in-laws at his second wife's death. Wythe was buried the day after his death, in St John's churchyard, Richmond.   JOHN E. SELBY

Sources W. E. Hemphill, 'George Wythe, the colonial Briton: a biographical study of the pre-revolutionary era in Virgina', diss., University of Virgina, 1937 • R. B. Kirtland, 'George Wythe: lawyer, revolutionary judge', diss., U. Mich., 1983 • D. J. Mays, *Edmund Pendleton, 1721–1803: a biography*, 2 vols. (1952) • A. T. Dill, *George Wythe: teacher of liberty* (1979) • J. P. Boyd and W. E. Hemphill, *The murder of George Wythe: two essays* (1955) • R. Kirtland, 'Wythe, George', *ANB*
Likenesses attrib. H. Benbridge, watercolour drawing, *c.*1770, R. W. Norton Art Gallery, Shreveport, Los Angeles • J. B. Longacre, engraving, Virginia State Library, Richmond, Virginia
Wealth at death owned three slaves and a city block: Kirtland, 'George Wythe'

Wythens, Sir Francis (*c.*1635–1704), judge and politician, was born in the parish of St Mary Cray, Kent, the only son of William Wythens (*d.* in or before 1646) of Southend, Eltham, Kent, and Frances (*b.* 1606, *d.* after 1646), daughter of Robert King of St Mary Cray. He was a great-grandson of Robert Wythens, alderman of London, and grandson of Sir William Wythens, sheriff of Kent in 1610. Wythens matriculated from St John's College, Oxford, on 13 November 1650, and then entered the Middle Temple on 27 November 1654, being called to the bar on 9 February 1660, and became a bencher on 21 May 1680. On 21 May 1685 he married, in Westminster Abbey, Elizabeth (*d.* 1708), daughter of Sir Thomas Taylor, first baronet, of Park House, Maidstone, Kent. They had one daughter, Catherine, who married Sir Thomas Twisden.

About 1677 Wythens was appointed deputy to the duke of Ormond in his capacity as steward of Westminster. This gave Wythens an interest in the parliamentary constituency and he was duly returned at the general election held in September 1679, although his opponents planned to petition against his return. On 25 November 1679 he was employed as counsel to defend Thomas Knox on an indictment against him and John Lane for a conspiracy to defame Titus Oates and William Bedloe, crucial witnesses to the Popish Plot. He assisted in the prosecution on 2 July 1680 of Henry Care for a libel in publishing *The Weekly Packet of Advice from Rome.* In both these cases Wythens exhibited sympathies in keeping with the emerging tory

party in support of the crown. These became more open when he promoted and then presented an address to Charles II on 17 April 1680 from the grand jury of Westminster 'abhorring' the attempt to obtain a rival address asking for the sitting of the parliament, which had been continually prorogued by the king. Wythens was duly rewarded with a knighthood, and on 4 May was made a king's counsel.

When the parliament eventually assembled in October 1680, Wythens was attacked for his role as an 'abhorrer'. He admitted that what he had done was against the law and done only to please the king, to the evident contempt of Roger North, who believed he had been frightened into submission when he could have relied upon much support in the house: 'this sneaking come-off so disgusted even his friends, that they joined all with the country party, and with one consent, *nemine contradicente*, kicked him out of the House, as one not fit for gentleman's company' (HoP, *Commons, 1660–90*, 3.784). The speaker of the Commons, William Williams, then told Wythens that he had 'offended against your own profession; you have offended against yourself, your own right, your own liberty as an Englishman. This is not only a crime against the living but a crime against the unborn' (ibid., 3.784). Not surprisingly, on 15 November his election was declared void when the votes of the king's servants were disallowed.

Wythens's expulsion from the Commons merely enhanced his reputation at court, and the duke of Ormond refused to remove him from his office in Westminster. He also continued to work in some high profile trials, being employed by the crown in the prosecution of Edward Fitzharris, in the defence of those who had committed Shaftesbury to prison, and in Count Konigsmark's case. With the tory reaction in full swing in April 1683 he was made a serjeant-at-law, and on 25 April he was appointed a judge of king's bench. North believed Wythens to be 'of moderate capacity in the law' and of a somewhat timid disposition. However, he was a loyalist, and as such could be entrusted with implementing royal policies, particularly with reference to the *quo warranto* against the City of London, which he duly did when the case came to court. Wythens also sat in judgment of those implicated in the Rye House plot and its aftermath, including Lord William Russell and Algernon Sidney. When Sidney came into court to receive his sentence and went over the objections to the evidence against him, Burnet criticized Wythens for interrupting and 'by a strange indecency gave him the lie in open court' (*Bishop Burnet's History*, 2.408). Further, John Evelyn found it difficult to watch Jeffreys and Wythens cavorting at a wedding just over a week after they had condemned Sidney and two days before his execution: 'these great men spent the rest of the afternoon till eleven at night in drinking healths, taking tobacco, and talking much beneath the gravity of judges' (Evelyn, 4.353).

Wythens was reappointed to the bench following the accession of James II. He tried and pronounced sentence on Titus Oates for perjury on 16 May 1685, and then accompanied Jeffreys to the west country in the wake of the Monmouth rebellion. In November Wythens was made recorder of Kingston. Wythens's patent was revoked on 21 April 1687 following his refusal to allow the imposition of martial law in peacetime with respect to army deserters. He immediately returned to private practice in Westminster Hall. Following the revolution of 1688 Wythens was called before the House of Lords on 17 May 1689 to explain his judgment against Oates, which was subsequently pronounced erroneous. The House of Commons also called Wythens to account on 14 June, and on the 18th he was excepted from the Bill of Indemnity mainly on account of his role in the trial of whig plotters, such as Sir Thomas Armstrong, and his notoriety as an 'abhorrer' rather than his views on constitutional matters.

The next few years seem to have been troublesome for Wythens in a different way. His wife apparently tried to bankrupt him through her extravagance, and after a law suit he was forced to pay her bills. She was having an affair with Sir Thomas Colepeper, third baronet, of Preston Hall, Kent, and this was probably behind another suit in which Wythens prosecuted Colepeper for assault. The case was heard on 21 November 1696 when Wythens charged that he had been beaten by Sir Thomas Taylor, second baronet, deceased (his wife's brother), and that his servant had been hindered by Colepeper from coming to his assistance. Colepeper was acquitted when a group of Kentish worthies testified on his and the other defendants' behalf. Wythens died on 9 May 1704 at Southend, Eltham, and wished to be buried in St Mary Cray Church on the 12th, although his monumental inscription is at Eltham. His widow lost no time in marrying Colepeper on 23 August 1704; she died on 5 February 1708.   STUART HANDLEY

Sources HoP, *Commons, 1660–90*, 3.783–4 · Sainty, *Judges* · Baker, *Serjeants* · Sainty, *King's counsel* · Foster, *Alum. Oxon.* · H. A. C. Sturgess, ed., *Register of admissions to the Honourable Society of the Middle Temple, from the fifteenth century to the year 1944*, 1 (1949), 155 · *Archaeologia Cantiana*, 20 (1893), 38 · *Post Man* (26–8 Nov 1696) · G. W. Keeton, *Lord Chancellor Jeffreys and the Stuart cause* (1965), 141, 202, 205, 263, 272, 281, 294–5, 312 · N. Luttrell, *A brief historical relation of state affairs from September 1678 to April 1714*, 6 vols. (1857), vol. 1, pp. 41, 185, 255–6, 402, 547–8; vol. 4, p. 144 · will, PRO, PROB 11/494, sig. 128 · Cobbett, *Parl. hist.*, 5.338–9 · Foss, *Judges*, 7.284–9 · *Bishop Burnet's History* · Evelyn, *Diary* · IGI

Wyvill, Sir Christopher, third baronet (*bap.* 1614, *d.* 1681), writer and politician, was baptized on 6 December 1614 at Wycliffe in Yorkshire, the eldest of fifteen children born to Sir Marmaduke Wyvill, second baronet (*b. c.*1590, *d.* in or before 1647), of Constable Burton, and his wife, Isabell (*d. c.*1645), daughter and heir of Sir William Gascoigne of Sedbury and Barbara, *née* Anderson. Marmaduke was high sheriff of Yorkshire in 1633–4, later raising troops for the royalist cause. For this he was fined £1343 in 1646, a tenth of the value of his estates (worth £671 p.a.). Isabell was a recusant whose influence was apparent on several of her children. Wyvill's education appears to have been partly based in Epping, Essex, under the care of a Master Wroth. He matriculated as a fellow-commoner at Trinity College,

Cambridge, in 1631, and was admitted to Gray's Inn in 1633.

By license dated 12 December 1636 Wyvill married Ursula Darcy (1619–1680), daughter of Conyers, Lord Darcy and Conyers (later earl of Holdernesse), and Grace (*née* Rokeby), of Hornby Castle. They had twelve children, of whom two daughters and four sons died before them. Their surviving children were: Dorothy; William, who became the fourth baronet; Barbara; Ursula; Francis, later receiver general of land tax in the north; and Christopher, who became dean of Ripon. In 1659 Thomas Case, the well-known presbyterian, published *The Saints, Gods Precious Treasure*, the funeral sermon of Darcy Wyvill (their third son, who died at fifteen). Case pointed out that by taking six children and leaving six, God had 'divided stakes' with the Wyvills (Case, sig. A11r).

Wyvill rejected his mother's Catholic faith and in 1645 he served on the county committee. During his days at Gray's Inn he must have heard the puritan preacher Richard Sibbs (C. Wyvill, *The Pretensions of the Triple Crown Examined*, 1672, 97). He also attended the sermons of Edward Bowles (a presbyterian) in York Minster in the 1650s. In 1647 Wyvill published a volume of poetry entitled *Certain Serious Thoughts*, together with *A Chronologicall Catalogue* of rulers in neighbour states. The poetry is a mixture of devotional verse and musings on the war. Taken with the catalogue, which voices anti-papal sentiments, it expresses a protestant, royalist position. Wyvill's continuing interest in occasional poetry is evidenced by an elegy he wrote on the death of George Wandesford in 1651, recorded by Wandesford's sister Alice Thornton in her memoirs (*Autobiography*, 72–3). According to most sources, Wyvill succeeded his father in or about 1648. However, in *Thoughts* Wyvill states he has 'Two parents … in one grave' (p. 33). This would seem to place his father's death in or before 1647.

Wyvill was elected MP for Richmond in 1659, and was returned in 1660 to the Long Parliament. After this, he retired to Yorkshire, holding the offices of justice of the peace and deputy lieutenant from 1660 until his death. Wyvill's second book, published in 1672, was entitled *The Pretensions of the Triple Crown Examined*. He dedicates it first to protestant clergy, then 'To all my near Relations, and Esteemed Acquaintance of the Romish Perswasion' (sig. A3r). The first part is set out as nine letters to a Catholic, the second part deals with specific issues of doctrine in essay form. A final book, *A Discourse Prepared for the Ears of some Romanists* (1679), contains the text of a speech he delivered at a general quarter sessions for the taking of oaths. Speaking to refusers, he calls their objections 'needless scruples', saying that Charles's rule is 'an innocent kind of Supremacie' (p. 5).

Wyvill emerges as a protestant with a reputation for godliness. He used his rhetorical skills to woo his Catholic friends and relatives to the established church, apparently with some success. His wife, Ursula, reflecting on her life, praised God that she still had 'the Husband of my youth and him kind to me' (Osborn MS b 222, p. 120). She died on 30 July 1680. A manuscript poem by Wyvill, expressing his grief, begins: 'When my Deare Love sat on the flowrie side / Of the delitefull Aire'. On 8 February 1681 Wyvill was buried with her at the church of St Mary, Masham, where, as he put it, 'Yores sad murmers courts the spired Fane' (Osborn MS b 222, p. 137).

JILL SEAL MILLMAN

Sources DNB · HoP, *Commons, 1660–90* · *Dugdale's visitation of York-shire, with additions*, ed. J. W. Clay, 3 vols. (1899–1917) · J. W. Clay, ed., *Pavers marriage licences*, 40 (1909) · *The parish register of Masham, 1599–1716* (1996) · Venn, *Alum. Cant.* · H. Aveling, *Northern Catholics: the Catholic recusants of the North Riding of Yorkshire, 1558–1790* (1966) · T. Case, *The saints, Gods precious treasure* (1659) · GEC, *Baronetage*, vol. 1 · J. W. Clay, ed., *Yorkshire royalist composition papers* (1893) · W. A. Shaw, *The knights of England*, 2 (1906) · *The autobiography of Mrs Alice Thornton*, ed. [C. Jackson], SurtS, 62 (1875) · U. Wyvill, com-monplace book, Yale U., Beinecke L., Osborn Collection, Osborn MS b. 222
Archives N. Yorks. CRO | Yale U., Beinecke L., James Marshall and Marie-Louise Osborn collection, Ursula Wyvill's common-place book, Osborn MS b. 222
Likenesses double portrait (aged eleven; with his sister); for-merly at Constable Burton, Yorkshire · postcard (after unknown portrait), NPG

Wyvill, Christopher (1738–1822), political reformer, was born in Edinburgh in December 1738, the son of Edward Wyvill (1709–1791), general supervisor of the excise in Edinburgh, and Christian Catherine (1721–1740), daughter of William Clifton, solicitor to the Scottish board of excise. The Wyvill family could trace its descent from Sir Humphrey Wyvill, who came over with William the Con-queror, and for centuries it had held substantial estates in Yorkshire. Christopher Wyvill belonged to the cadet branch of the family. His father was the second son of Darcy Wyvill of Derby, an excise officer, and grandson of Sir William Wyvill (1645–1684) of Constable Burton, near Bedale in the North Riding of Yorkshire, an estate which was inherited by the senior branch of the family. His mother (who had married in December 1737) died in Janu-ary 1740, at the age of eighteen, shortly after the birth of Christopher's sister, Catherine.

Early career Christopher Wyvill was educated at Queens' College, Cambridge, where he was ordained in 1763 and where he obtained the honorary degree of LLD in 1764. While at Cambridge he seems to have imbibed the liberal religious views of the broad-minded president, Robert Plumptre, and the fellows. On leaving Cambridge he secured a good living as rector of Black Notley, in Essex, because his distant cousin Sir Marmaduke Asty Wyvill owned the advowson. From the outset he showed little interest in his clerical duties and he left them (and later the whole income) to a curate until 1806, when he finally surrendered the living. In 1771 he wrote his first tract, arguing against the utility to the state of clerical subscrip-tion to the Thirty-Nine Articles and in 1772 he acted with the small but influential group of Church of England clergy who submitted the Feathers tavern petition to par-liament seeking abolition of the obligation to subscribe to these articles. Throughout his life he regularly cam-paigned, in print and in private correspondence, for the repeal of all the laws which restricted the rights of both

Christopher Wyvill (1738–1822), by Henry Hoppner Meyer, pubd 1809 (after John Hoppner)

protestant dissenters and Roman Catholics to worship as they saw fit and to play a full role in public affairs.

On 1 October 1773 Wyvill married his cousin, Elizabeth Wyvill (1714/15–1783), a plain and much older woman, but the stepsister and heir of Sir Marmaduke Asty Wyvill, owner of Constable Burton Hall and head of the senior branch of the Wyvill family. When the unmarried Sir Mar-maduke died on 23 February 1774, Christopher Wyvill inherited his substantial estates in north Yorkshire (but not his baronetcy) and promptly moved to Constable Bur-ton to live thereafter as a prosperous country gentleman with an income reputed to be £4000 a year. His first wife died on 23 July 1783 (aged sixty-eight) without issue. On 9 August 1787 Wyvill married Sarah (d. in or after 1822), daughter of J. Codling, with whom he had six surviving children (three sons, among them Christopher *Wyvill, and three daughters). It was as a Yorkshire country gentle-man, deeply interested in the affairs of state, that Wyvill mounted the political stage as a parliamentary reformer in 1779, and he was to remain actively involved in public affairs for the next forty years.

The Yorkshire Association In 1779 there was growing public concern about the state of the nation. Britain was deeply involved in the American crisis, was fighting a very costly and unsuccessful war in North America, and was facing a possible invasion from a Franco-Spanish force in the chan-nel. Many held George III and his ministers to be directly responsible for this disastrous state of affairs. In parlia-ment the prime minister, Lord North, came under heavy pressure from the marquess of Rockingham and his polit-ical allies, though this opposition was unable to unseat him. In the country at large there were growing complaints not only against the military failures of the government but against the waste and extravagance of government and the misuse of crown patronage to secure a servile administration and a dependent parliament. Christopher Wyvill clearly shared these concerns and was determined to do something to redress the situation. He later claimed that he acted 'from a sense of duty to his country, from a detestation of corruption, that execrable principle of government; from indignation at direct and open invasions of our rights; and from an honest zeal to defend public liberty'. He declared that his aims were

> the restoration of national morals, then sinking under the debasing influence of our government; and the preservation of our constitution on its genuine principles, then nearly defaced by the wear of passing ages, and almost lost under the immense accumulation of abuses. (Wyvill, *Political Papers*, 4.52–3)

A man of high ideals, convinced of the corruption of court and government, and finding the dominant aristocratic political factions in parliament both distasteful to himself and inimical to the public interest, Wyvill believed that honest and independent men of property must rally to the defence of the constitution.

Without attachment to Whitehall or Westminster, Wyvill gave vent to the concerns and the prejudices of the independent country gentlemen who were shocked by the waste and extravagance of government and alarmed at the failures of the king's ministers. He believed that the root cause of the present crisis was the corrupting influence which the executive (and to a lesser extent the aristocratic oligarchy) exercised over the legislature. The first remedy to apply was to reduce the money and places at the disposal of ministers through crown patronage. But Wyvill soon concluded that economic or administrative reforms of this kind were not enough. A measure of parliamentary reform would also be needed in order to restore the constitution and to secure the cherished independence of parliament and the historic rights of the subject. Wyvill was never a democrat, however, and he never based his demands for political reform on natural rights or other visionary speculations. Instead, he appealed to Britain's ancient constitution and believed it could best be safeguarded by independent men of property. His moderate views shifted over the years as he continually sought an effective alliance with reformers inside and outside parliament, but he never endorsed the demands of such extreme radicals as John Jebb, John Cartwright, or Thomas Paine. At his most radical, he wished for a return to triennial parliaments, an increase in the number of MPs returned by the counties and the large boroughs, the gradual elimination of rotten boroughs, and the doubling or so of the electorate by giving the vote to copyholders and some leaseholders in the counties and to taxpaying householders in the boroughs. He always favoured a propertied franchise, never advocated manhood suffrage, believed that it was impractical to demand annual parliaments or equal-sized constituencies, and regarded the secret ballot as unmanly.

Late in November 1779 Wyvill fell to discussing public affairs with William Challenor and Lieutenant-General Hale at the home of General Cary at Leven Grove, in the North Riding of Yorkshire. They decided to call a county meeting to petition parliament for various economies in public expenditure. With the help of a few other friends, Wyvill sent out hundreds of circular letters to propertied gentlemen across the county. Over 600 of them, including Rockingham and his supporters, attended the county meeting at York assembly rooms on 30 December 1779. With firm, though not unanimous, backing, Wyvill prepared a petition to parliament demanding public economy. Late in the meeting, when many of the more conservative men had left, Wyvill went on to secure acceptance for the setting up of a committee of correspondence to support the petition and other measures which might restore the freedom of parliament. Wyvill wanted to create a political machine to keep up the pressure for his expanding reform programme and to encourage the creation of similar committees elsewhere. Determined to keep peers and MPs off this committee, he sought out the active support of independent men of property (a third of whom were Anglican clergymen) to spread the demands for moderate reform across the county and then across the nation. With deep commitment, enormous energy, and remarkable firmness of purpose, Wyvill put himself at the head of this movement in Yorkshire that set the standard for extra-parliamentary campaigning that no other county or borough ever quite matched. With the active support of about fifty members of the Yorkshire committee, Wyvill corresponded with men of property across the county, arranged county meetings, secured substantial support for the Yorkshire petitions of 1780 and 1783, and regularly publicized the activities of the Yorkshire reformers in several newspapers, most notably the *York Chronicle*. Wyvill regarded the press as a vital instrument of persuasion and propaganda, and he published more than a dozen pamphlets in the years ahead, but he also conducted a massive correspondence with leading reformers and prominent politicians over many decades.

By February 1780 Wyvill and his allies had collected about 8000 signatures for the Yorkshire petition for economic reform and they persuaded Sir George Savile, a highly respected MP for the county, to present it to parliament on the 8th. At the same time Wyvill encouraged the creation of similar committees of correspondence in other counties and boroughs. Eventually some forty-one petitions, modelled on the Yorkshire petition, with about 60,000 signatures, were presented to parliament. Meanwhile, Wyvill and his allies had set up a county association on 21 January 1780 to campaign not only for economic reform but also for shorter parliaments and a more equal representation. On 28 March the Yorkshire committee of correspondence became the guiding committee of this Yorkshire Association and Wyvill chaired its activities.

The campaign for reform Even before this Wyvill had gone to London to concert action with the leaders of other reform groups. Determined not to let the more radical metropolitan reformers dominate the movement, Wyvill persuaded the others to endorse his proposal for a meeting of deputies to consider a plan of association. He succeeded in having MPs excluded as deputies and the circular letter distributed to sympathizers was sent out over his signature on 29 February 1780. Not all local associations were prepared to follow Wyvill's lead, but on 11 March some thirty to forty deputies from twelve counties and four boroughs met in London. Over the next ten days they agreed to form a general association movement in favour of public economy, a reduction in the influence of the crown, an additional 100 county MPs, and annual parliaments. The electors were to be urged to vote for those candidates in the forthcoming general election who would pledge themselves to support these objectives. Despite this success, the deputies were far from unanimous in their discussions and the metropolitan reformers in particular supported more radical measures.

Back in Yorkshire the committee of the association voted in favour of triennial rather than annual parliaments, and by August 1780 some 5800 freeholders had agreed to support economic reform, 100 extra county seats, and triennial parliaments. This more moderate programme was accepted in several other counties, though some did not wish to go beyond economic reform. In contrast, the metropolitan reformers went very much further. Despite their efforts, the various associations had little impact on the general election of September 1780, and even Wyvill's more modest programme failed to win over Rockingham and the leading politicians in opposition to Lord North. While Wyvill was prepared to put economic reform ahead of parliamentary reform, in an effort to forge a political alliance with Rockingham, this concession only served to alienate the more radical metropolitan reformers. Despite his best efforts, Wyvill never managed to build an effective alliance with those critics of Lord North's government to the right and to the left of him.

About forty deputies from the reform associations met again in London from 3 March to 21 April 1781. Wyvill was one of the three delegates from Yorkshire and he was elected chairman at the first meeting. He gave a firm steer to discussions and helped to defeat the radical proposals for annual parliaments and universal manhood suffrage. He hoped the aristocratic leaders of the opposition in parliament might accept the more moderate proposals to increase the number of county MPs, gradually abolish the rotten boroughs, and repeal the Septennial Act, but these hopes were soon dashed. By the end of the year, he was once more circulating the more moderate Yorkshire proposals of spring 1780, but he still could not create a united front between the more moderate associations, the more conservative Rockingham opposition, and the metropolitan radicals.

When the Rockingham party finally replaced Lord North's government in March 1782, it embarked on a series of measures to secure economic reform and to reduce the political influence of the king, but it set its face against any measure of parliamentary reform that might reduce aristocratic electoral interests. Wyvill continued to move cautiously to build up support for moderate parliamentary reform inside and outside parliament, and he had high hopes that he might win over both Charles James Fox and the younger William Pitt to his Yorkshire reform programme. In December 1782 he helped to draft a Yorkshire petition to transfer parliamentary seats from the rotten boroughs to the counties and large towns, repeal the Septennial Act, enfranchise copyholders in the counties, and abolish fictitious votes in Scotland. His committee made a major effort to publicize this petition in the Yorkshire newspapers and to rally the electorate behind it. By early 1783 some 10,000 men had signed the Yorkshire petition, but few other associations matched this effort. Some associations actually collapsed, and only eleven other counties petitioned, though this time there was some support in Wales and Scotland. More boroughs petitioned this time, though less than half of these were places of great significance. Only about 20,000 signatures were appended to these petitions (half in Yorkshire alone). On 7 May 1783 William Pitt proposed creating 100 new seats for the counties and the metropolis and gradually eliminating the rotten boroughs, but his suggestion was heavily defeated by 293 to 149 votes.

Despite the lack of support in parliament and the divisions within the ranks of the reformers, Wyvill did not give up hope. He believed that a good start had been made and he was determined to stick to a moderate programme of parliamentary reform. His faith in Fox as a genuine supporter of parliamentary reform was destroyed, however, by the Fox–North coalition of 1783, and he increasingly looked to Pitt as the politician most likely to pass a reform bill. In December 1783 Wyvill secured the support of the Yorkshire committee for another petition on the same terms as before. This was adopted at a county meeting on 1 January 1784, but no attempt was made to secure mass support across the county on this occasion. Efforts to secure petitions from other counties failed, and even the radical Westminster committee ceased its active campaigning. In Yorkshire itself the association's committee was badly split between the supporters of Fox and the adherents of Pitt. Wyvill was one of those who put his faith in Pitt. He met Pitt, now prime minister, in December 1784 and pledged to rally support behind the minister's moderate reform programme. On 10 February 1785 Wyvill encouraged a county meeting in York to adopt a petition for parliamentary reform on the same moderate terms as before. He also managed to rally support in about ten other places, but he failed to rally the metropolitan radicals and only one other county, Nottinghamshire, petitioned. Wyvill helped Pitt to draw up his moderate Reform Bill, which aimed to eliminate thirty-six rotten boroughs and to transfer these seats to the counties and the metropolis, and to extend the franchise to copyholders and some leaseholders in the counties. This bill was put forward on 18 April 1785 before a packed house of over 450 MPs. It was defeated the next day by 248 to 174 votes. Wyvill did not at once lose heart, but after an extensive trip to the continent he returned to Yorkshire early in 1786 to see the Yorkshire Association wither away quite rapidly.

The French Revolution Wyvill's hopes for moderate parliamentary reform were temporarily revived by the renewed interest in political reform inspired by the French Revolution. Support for his kind of moderate reform, however, was soon destroyed by the sharp polarization of opinion between arch-conservatives and extreme radicals in the early 1790s. Wyvill once more found that the extreme demands of the urban radicals made it impossible for him to interest men of property in parliament and in the counties to support moderate parliamentary reform. He became increasingly alarmed that universal suffrage would lead the poor masses to invade the rights of property of their social superiors. While he was prepared to admit that property was divided too unequally and he did not believe that the protection of private property should be an excuse for political oppression, Wyvill did fear that universal manhood suffrage would result in anarchy and revolution. He nevertheless refused to abandon his commitment to moderate reform and he still campaigned to extend the franchise to men of modest property. Alarmed by the intransigence of Edmund Burke and others, he feared that the government's repressive measures would simply incite a popular revolt. In 1795 he supported the protests in Yorkshire against the government's legislation of that year, but he could not unite the county against these measures. By the later 1790s he was convinced that the massive scale of the war against France was once more leading to waste, extravagance, and the growth in power of the executive. Economical reform again seemed necessary and Wyvill campaigned for peace as a prelude to this. While accepting that most country gentlemen had been seduced by government propaganda to support conservative measures, Wyvill still insisted that effective parliamentary reform could not be achieved by extreme measures supported only by urban radicals. He regularly urged radical leaders such as John Cartwright to moderate their demands. In his view a popular campaign for universal suffrage would precipitate rather than prevent a revolution.

In seeking support for his moderate views, Wyvill once more put his faith in Charles James Fox, particularly after the latter had committed himself to a measure of parliamentary reform in 1797–8. In 1799 Wyvill wrote a pamphlet in defence of the whig secession from parliament and he urged reformers to rally behind Fox. He met Fox personally and corresponded with him in an effort to secure his firm commitment to parliamentary reform should he ever return to power. When Fox gained power in 1806 it was in alliance with the conservative Grenvillites, and parliamentary reform was not an option. Wyvill, however, was pleased with the ministry's abolition of the slave trade in 1807 and its support (though doomed) for Roman Catholic emancipation. With the return of successive conservative administrations from 1807, Wyvill remained largely on the sidelines while Cartwright and Francis Burdett sought to revive the movement for parliamentary reform. Most of Wyvill's writings at this time were in support of religious toleration. He remained committed to moderate parliamentary reform, but believed it could be achieved only with the support of the whigs inside parliament and the landed gentry outside it. He again argued that a campaign for parliamentary reform which had no clearly defined and limited objectives would open the way to tumult, convulsion, and revolution. Both the Burdett riots and the widespread Luddite disturbances alarmed him and he was horrified by the appeal of the radicals to what he regarded as the least informed and worst disposed men in the country, men who were already too prone to insurrection. His caution and his moderation were condemned in a series of twenty open letters which John Cartwright published in *The Statesman* between 29 October 1813 and 4 March 1814. Cartwright accused Wyvill of aristocratic leanings and of speaking of the lower orders with singular contempt. This onslaught helped persuade Wyvill to retire from active political campaigning, though he remained interested in political issues and maintained his voluminous political correspondence. He had little sympathy with the extreme and violent radicalism of the masses in the years after 1815 and he had little confidence in the reforming credentials of the parliamentary whigs.

Death and reputation Wyvill died on 8 March 1822 at his home, Constable Burton Hall, and was buried at nearby Spennithorne. His estates passed to his eldest son, Marmaduke, MP for York (1820–30). Wyvill died just when the moderate reform movement he had always advocated began to revive. County meetings came back in vogue, patronized by provincial magnates and independent country gentlemen. The younger whig politicians began to renew their commitment to moderate parliamentary reform. The Great Reform Bill which the whigs finally passed in 1832 owed much more to Wyvill's ideas than to those of Jebb, Cartwright, or Paine. Wyvill had not lived to see this success, but he had devoted nearly forty years of his life to this kind of moderate parliamentary reform. Energetic, indefatigable, sometimes tiresome, he had stuck nobly and heroically to his political principles and his pragmatic tactics. A man of great self-assurance and firmness of purpose, of integrity and vision, of ardour, caution, and sound political sense, he had tried, though in vain, to unite the more liberal political élite, independent men of property, and men of reforming sentiment behind a moderate programme of reforms that would promote what he regarded as the true interests of his country and the real welfare of its people.   H. T. DICKINSON

Sources *DNB* · N. Yorks. CRO, Wyvill papers · York City Public Library, Yorkshire Association MSS, M25, 32 · C. Wyvill, ed., *Political papers*, 6 vols. [1794–1804] · 'The Wyvill of Constable Burton family archive', *Annual Report of the North Riding of Yorkshire Record Office, Northallerton* (1967), 35–43 · H. Butterfield, *George III, Lord North, and the people, 1779–80* (1949) · H. Butterfield, 'The Yorkshire Association and the crisis of 1779–80', *TRHS*, 4th ser., 29 (1947), 69–91 · I. R. Christie, *Wilkes, Wyvill and reform: the parliamentary reform movement in British politics, 1760–1785* (1962) · I. R. Christie, 'The Yorkshire Association, 1780–4: a study in political organization', *HJ*, 3 (1960), 144–61 · I. R. Christie, 'Sir George Savile, Edmund Burke, and the

Yorkshire reform programme, February, 1780', *Yorkshire Archaeological Journal*, 40 (1959–62), 205–8 · J. R. Dinwiddy, *Christopher Wyvill and reform, 1790–1820* (1971) · N. C. Phillips, 'Country against court: Christopher Wyvill, a Yorkshire champion', *Yorkshire Archaeological Journal*, 40 (1959–62), 588–603 · N. C. Phillips, 'Edmund Burke and the county movement, 1779–80', *EngHR*, 76 (1961), 254–78 · E. C. Black, *The Association* (1963) · G. S. Veitch, *The genesis of parliamentary reform* (1913) · H. T. Dickinson, 'Radicals and reformers in the age of Wilkes and Wyvill', *British politics and society from Walpole to Pitt, 1742–1789*, ed. J. Black (1990), 123–46, 254–8 · Burke, *Gen. GB* (1865–72)

Archives N. Yorks. CRO, corresp. and papers | Beds. & Luton ARS, letters to Samuel Whitbread · Bodl. Oxf., corresp. with William Wilberforce · CKS, letters to third Earl Stanhope · Notts. Arch., corresp. with Sir George Savile and F. F. Foljambe · NRA, priv. coll., letters to Lord Lansdowne · PRO, letters to William Pitt, 30/8 · U. Durham L., letters to Charles, second Earl Grey **Likenesses** H. H. Meyer, mezzotint, pubd 1809 (after J. Hoppner), BM, NPG [*see illus.*] · J. Hoppner, oils, Constable Burton Hall, Bedale, Yorkshire

Wyvill, Christopher (1792–1863), naval officer, second son of the Revd Christopher *Wyvill (1738–1822), and his second wife, Sarah, daughter of J. Codling, was born on 6 May 1792. Educated at Eton College, he entered the navy in 1805; he served in the frigate *Tribune* in the channel and in the *Fame* in the Mediterranean. From 1810 to 1813 he was in the *Thames* with Charles Napier, and in the *Volontaire* with Captain Granville George Waldegrave. In May 1813 he was appointed lieutenant of the sloop *Kingfisher* by acting order which was confirmed on 5 July. He afterwards served on the Halifax and home stations until he was promoted commander on 29 July 1824.

In April 1827 Wyvill was appointed to the *Cameleon* (10 guns), then in the Mediterranean, and, taking a passage out in the frigate *Dartmouth*, prevented what threatened to be a terrible accident. Some of the men had got at a cask of rum, and in drawing off the spirit set it on fire. Wyvill volunteered, and, with a gunner's mate, plugged the cask and extinguished the flames. In the *Cameleon* he was employed on the coast of Greece and in the suppression of piracy. In October 1828 he was appointed to the *Asia* (84 guns), flagship of Sir Pulteney Malcolm whom he followed to the *Britannia* (120 guns) in April 1830. When she was paid off he was promoted captain on 22 February 1832.

From 1840 to 1847 Wyvill commanded the *Cleopatra* (26 guns) on the North American station, and afterwards at the Cape of Good Hope, where from 1844 she was almost continuously employed in suppressing the east-coast slave trade. From 1849 to 1853 he was again on the Cape of Good Hope station in command of the *Castor* (36 guns); and from June 1854 until 31 January 1856, when he was promoted rear-admiral, he was superintendent of Chatham Dockyard. He was naval aide-de-camp to the queen from September 1851. He died at his home, The Grange, near Bedale, Yorkshire, on 29 January 1863, aged seventy.

J. K. LAUGHTON, rev. ANDREW LAMBERT

Sources *Piracy in the Levant, 1827–8: selected from the papers of admiral Sir Edward Codrington*, ed. C. G. Pitcairn-Jones, Navy RS, 72 (1934) · Mrs F. Egerton, *Admiral of the fleet: Sir Geoffrey Phipps Hornby, a biography* (1896) · *GM*, 3rd ser., 14 (1863), 395 · Boase, *Mod. Eng. biog.* · O'Byrne, *Naval biog. dict.* · *United Service Gazette* (7 Feb 1863) · *Navy List* · *CGPLA Eng. & Wales* (1863)

Archives N. Yorks. CRO, papers **Wealth at death** under £4000: administration, 14 March 1863, *CGPLA Eng. & Wales*

Yalden, Thomas (1670–1736), poet and Church of England clergyman, was born in Oxford on 2 January 1670, the youngest son of John Yalden, esquire (c.1611–1670), an exciseman in Oxford after the restoration of Charles II, previously the king's page of the presence and groom of the chamber. Yalden was educated at Magdalen College School, where he was also a chorister (1678–89). He matriculated at Magdalen on 20 May 1685, and in 1690 he was admitted a demy of the college. At Magdalen—'Where Yalden learn'd to gain the myrtle crown' (Tickell, 7)—he was a friend and contemporary of Addison and Sacheverell. Yalden graduated BA in 1691, MA in 1694, BD in 1706, and DD in 1708. During the 1690s he began to produce translations of works by Ovid, Horace, and Homer, and publish his own verse. His 'Ode for St Cecilia's Day' (1693) was set to music by Daniel Purcell, the organist at Magdalen, and his *On the Conquest of Namur*, a Pindaric ode inscribed to William III in 1695, was well received. He was elected a probationer fellow of Magdalen College in 1698 and fellow in 1699, and, having taken holy orders, was presented by the college to the living of Willoughby, Warwickshire, on 25 September 1701, which he held until 1709.

Yalden became a high-churchman following Queen Anne's accession in 1702 (which he commemorated in verse), and was appointed chaplain to the second duke of Beaufort in 1706, thereby extending his circle of high tory friends. In 1710 he was acting as secretary to the 'Loyal Brotherhood', a convivial tory group presided over by Beaufort, and meeting regularly in London at the Queen's Arms, St Paul's Churchyard. Meanwhile, his status at Magdalen continued to rise. He was chosen Waynflete's lecturer in moral philosophy in August 1705, and became college bursar in 1707 and dean of divinity in 1709. In 1710 the duke presented him to the rectory of Sopworth, Wiltshire, but he resigned it the following year and took the rectory of Chalton with Clanfield, Hampshire, the crown having accepted Beaufort's right to present to Chalton. He was also appointed prebendary of the Deans, Lower Hayne, and Penell in the collegiate church of Chulmleigh, Devon.

Yalden relinquished his Magdalen posts in 1713 (giving the college a picture of its founder, Waynflete, as token of his gratitude) upon election on 26 June that year to the chaplaincy of Bridewell Hospital, London, which Atterbury had resigned on his promotion to the see of Rochester. The chaplaincy brought Yalden £100 p.a., 'a good House with coals, candles and some other perquisites' (*Remarks*, 4.206). Yalden had been preacher at the Bridewell as far back as 1698, and he settled into a quiet routine until caught up in the clamour surrounding the discovery of the Atterbury plot. Yalden knew the bishop, was conversant with Kelly, his secretary, and was taken into custody on suspicion of involvement. Although his papers were searched, no evidence was produced against him and he was quickly released.

Yalden did not impress Thomas Hearne as a preacher in St Mary's Church, Oxford, in 1707. He was 'a little effeminate Fantastical person' and his sermon was merely 'what might have been s'd by one who has any thing of Pts, without Divinity' (*Remarks*, 2.25). As a lyric poet, Yalden was competent in the Cowley mode, and his hymns 'To the Morning' and 'To Darkness' have an undoubted quality, sometimes a Miltonic grandeur as in the lines (from the latter):

Darkness, thou first kind Parent of us all,
Thou art our great original:
Since from thy Universal womb,
Does all thou shad'st below, thy numerous offspring come.

Many of his works originally appeared in parts 3, 4, and 5 of Tonson's *Miscellany Poems* published in London in 1693 and 1694. They are also handily available in several editions of *Works of the British Poets*, most of which exclude *The temple of fame: a poem to the memory of the most illustrious Prince William, duke of Gloucester* (1700). His *Aesop at Court, or, State Fables* (1702), a clever adaptation to circumstances at the end of William III's reign, showed that Yalden could exhibit a sardonic edge on occasion. Johnson may have included Yalden in his *Lives of the Poets* to exemplify an innocent churchman unjustly treated by overzealous prosecutors. Some minor pieces are included in the *Biographia Britannica*, and the celebrated statement of Partridge's grievances entitled 'Squire Bickerstaff Detected' is attributed by some scholars to Yalden. His interest in Jacobite politics should not be overestimated. Yalden died, unmarried, at Bridewell Hospital on 10 July 1736, and was buried in the chapel on 2 August. NIGEL ASTON

Sources Wood, *Ath. Oxon.*, new edn, 4.601 · parish register, Oxford, St John the Baptist, 16 Jan 1670 [baptism] · Foster, *Alum. Oxon.* · J. R. Bloxam, *A register of the presidents, fellows … of Saint Mary Magdalen College*, 8 vols. (1853–85), vol. 1. pp. 108; vol. 6, pp. 112, 115 · J. R. Bloxam, ed., *Magdalen College and James II, 1686–1688: a series of documents*, OHS, 6 (1886) · T. Tickell, *Oxford: a poem* (1707) · P. Smithers, *The life of Joseph Addison*, 2nd edn (1968) · archdeacon's commission to induct, Hants. RO, Winchester diocesan records, 35M48/6/285; 35M48/6/291 · *VCH Hampshire and the Isle of Wight*, 3.105, 109 · W. R. Ward, ed., *Parson and parish in eighteenth-century Hampshire*, Hampshire RS, 13 (1995), 34, 39 · Badminton Archives, FmH 4/5 · *Remarks and collections of Thomas Hearne*, ed. C. E. Doble and others, 11 vols., OHS, 2, 7, 13, 34, 42–3, 48, 50, 65, 67, 72 (1885–1921), vols. 2, 4 · *State trials*, 16.486 · Bridewell chapel burials register, GL, MS 8310/2 · *GM*, 1st ser., 6 (1736), 424 · *N&Q*, 6 (1852), 291 · *N&Q*, 4th ser., 4 (1869), 421 · R. Shiels, *The lives of the poets of Great Britain and Ireland*, ed. T. Cibber, 4 (1753), 342 · [G. Jacob], *The poetical register, or, The lives and characters of the English dramatick poets*, [2] (1720), 238 · S. Johnson, *Lives of the English poets*, ed. G. B. Hill, [new edn], 2 (1905), 297–303 · D. Griffin, 'Regulated loyalty: Jacobitism and Johnson's *Lives of the poets*', *ELH: a Journal of English Literary History*, 64 (1997), 1007–28 · parish register, Oxford, St John the Baptist [burial: John Yalden, father]

Yale, David (d. 1626). *See under* Yale, Thomas (1525/6–1577).

Yale, Elihu (1649–1721), merchant and administrator in India and benefactor, was born in Boston, Massachusetts, on 5 April 1649, the second son of David Yale (1614–1690) of Denbighshire, merchant, and Ursula Yale (b. c.1624). In 1652 Elihu's family returned to Britain. He never again saw America. After an education in London he was employed as a clerk in the East India Company offices in Leadenhall Street (1670). On 24 October 1671 he was selected to go to India as a writer on a salary of £10 per year. He sailed for India in December 1671, arriving at Madras on 23 June 1672. Between July and December 1676 he was a member of Major William Puckle's tour of inspection of the East India Company's Bengal establishment. On 31 December 1678 his promotion to factor was confirmed. He was appointed an assistant justice in the municipal court on 30 July 1679. On 4 November 1680 he married Catherine Hynmers, *née* Elford (1651–1728), the widow of his colleague Joseph Hynmers. With his marriage Yale gained access to extra capital, which he used to extremely profitable effect trading privately within the company's regulations on permitted trade for its employees, and also in the lucrative trade in precious stones, especially diamonds.

In December 1681 Yale was sent to Porto Novo, south of Madras, to secure bases from which the company could extend its trade. Against expectations, he gained permission for settlements at Porto Novo, Cuddalore, and Kunimedu, on very reasonable conditions. Between 1681 and 1684 a series of dismissals and deaths among the ranking servants at Madras saw him advance rapidly from fifth to second in council. He succeeded William Gyfford as governor of Fort St George on 25 July 1687. On 25 January 1688 Yale's only legitimate son, David, died, and a year later Catherine Yale took their three surviving daughters, Catherine, Anne, and Ursula, to England (23 February 1689). It would be ten years before the family would be reunited in London. Hieronima, the wife of one of his partners, Jaques da Paiva, a prominent diamond merchant, became Yale's mistress after the death of her husband. They had a son, Charles (1690–1712).

As governor of Fort St George, Yale demonstrated his concern for efficient administration, his fondness for ceremony and the proprieties, and his firmness towards colleagues and local Indian authorities. The general conditions he faced were difficult. The Mughals conquered the old Golconda dynasty, and struggled for supremacy over the increasingly assertive and successful Marathas, and the consequent banditry and lack of local authority in the region impeded the company's commerce. The French had to be beaten off in a naval action at Madras (15 August 1690). The war between the company and the Mughals in the north saw the evacuation of the Bengal establishment to Madras, where Yale had to preside over very difficult relationships within the personnel before Job Charnock and his agency could be returned to Bengal. He also worked to implement instructions from London to establish the mayor and corporation for Madras (29 September 1688). He developed the grants of land around Cuddalore and Teganapatnam into Fort St David. He maintained the building programmes in Madras, and increased the security of the settlement. He had to combat a severe regional famine with its attendant epidemics; one consequence of this was his effort to contain slavery, especially of children.

Throughout his administration Yale's relations with his

colleagues on council steadily deteriorated. Much of this was not caused by Yale, but as dissension worsened he certainly became more autocratic and arbitrary in his actions. There are many lurid stories about the governor's behaviour, effectively refuted in Hiram Bingham's biography. One of the serious issues was caused by his evident success as a private trader despite the conditions which interfered with the company's affairs. Yale's personal trade was spread widely, taking advantage of whatever markets he could find at any time. He acted in association with Indian merchants and other Europeans in India, as well as with his correspondents in England. His activities ranged throughout India, south-east Asia, and to China and the Philippines. He owned shares in a number of local ships from which he made money from freight charges as well as carrying his own goods. He was particularly successful in the trade in precious stones. This success created deep suspicion in London and he was superseded by Nathaniel Higginson on 23 October 1692.

Yale remained in Madras until 1699, responding to all the allegations brought against him and taking care of his private commerce. He left Madras for England on 22 February 1699 a very wealthy man. On his return to England he lived mostly in London, but maintained his father's country home, Plas Grono, near Wrexham. Although he renewed his friendships with various India merchants, he never again held an official position with the company. In 1704 he was appointed high sheriff of Denbighshire. During this period of his life he pursued his passion for collecting all manner of things, but especially art works. He also found an outlet for his lifelong Christian commitment in the Society for the Propagation of the Gospel (SPG). He put some of his wealth into supporting the missionary ideas of the Anglican bishops with whom he associated. One such idea was the desire to reclaim the American settlements for the established church. One aspect of this interest was his agreement to assist the establishment of the Connecticut collegiate school at New Haven. In 1713 he donated thirty-two books. In 1718 he presented a further 417 books, a portrait of King George by Sir Godfrey Kneller, and a quantity of textiles to be sold to benefit the college. He added a further shipment of goods for sale in 1721. The total value of these donations was some £1162. In the undated and unsigned draft of his will he bequeathed £500 to the college, but this was challenged by his family in court, with the judgment against the college. It is one of the ironies of history that the gifts Yale made to the college which took his name as Yale University were the result more of the hopes of the Anglican bishops in the SPG than of the requests of the puritans of New Haven. In his will Yale describes himself as a 'Sonn of the Church of England, As by law establish'd'.

Yale died at Queen Square, London, on 8 July 1721. His body was taken to Wrexham and buried in the yard of the church of St Giles (22 July 1721), joining his mother and father, who lie beneath the church floor.

I. B. WATSON

Sources H. Bingham, *Elihu Yale: the American nabob of Queen Square* (1939) • H. D. Love, *Vestiges of old Madras, 1640–1800*, 4 vols. (1913), vol. 1 • C. Fawcett, ed., *The English factories in India*, new ser., 4 vols. (1936–55), vols. 2–4 • *The diary of William Hedges … during his agency in Bengal; as well as on his voyage out and return overland (1681–1687)*, ed. R. Barlow and H. Yule, 2–3, Hakluyt Society, 75, 78 (1888–9) • E. L. Saxe, 'Fortune's tangled web: trading networks of English entrepreneurs in Eastern India, 1657–1717', PhD diss., Yale U., 1979 • R. Warch, *School of the prophets: Yale College, 1701–1740* (1973)

Archives Yale U., MSS | BL OIOC, signed letters, MSS, original corresp. (E/3), factory records FSG G/19; factory records G/40; home H. • PRO, CO 77/16 • PRO, Chancery Master's Exhibits, C. 108/299 • Yale U., Tibbett's collection, Yale letters

Likenesses E. Seeman, oils, Yale U. Art Gallery; repro. in Bingham, *Elihu Yale*, frontispiece • Worsdale?, portrait, repro. in Bingham, *Elihu Yale* • group portrait, repro. in Bingham, *Elihu Yale*

Wealth at death substantial property in London and Wrexham; substantial legacies in goods and money: will, Bingham, *Elihu Yale*, 265 and *passim* • stated (in 1691) that in twenty years' service in India he had accumulated by 'all honest endeavours' some £200,000 ('above five hundred thousand pagodas')

Yale, Thomas (1525/6–1577), civil lawyer, was the third son of David Lloyd ab Ellis (David Yale), a gentleman of Plas-yn-Iâl, Llanelidan, Denbighshire, and Gwenhwyfar Lloyd of Llwyn-y-Maen. Educated at Queens' College, Cambridge, he graduated BA first in the *ordo* (1544) and became a fellow of his college, proceeding MA in 1546. He was college bursar (1549–51) and a university proctor for the academic year commencing 1552, but resigned before his year in office had ended. In 1554 he was appointed commissary of the diocese of Ely under the chancellor John Fuller, and in 1555, the year in which he subscribed to the Roman Catholic articles imposed upon the whole university, he became keeper of the spiritualities of the diocese of Bangor during the vacancy caused by Bishop Arthur Bulkeley's death. He was admitted to minor orders by Bishop William Glyn on 24 September 1556 and inducted to the rectory of Llantrisant in Anglesey shortly thereafter, although he never resided there. Instead, in November of that year, he was named among the commissioners to suppress heresy in the Ely diocese and he assisted in the search for heretical books when Cardinal Pole's delegates conducted a visitation of his university. In January 1557 he was one of the number empowered by the university senate to reform the system of electing proctors and to revise the university statutes.

Having obtained the degree of LLD (1557) Yale was admitted as an advocate to the court of arches (22 April 1559) and became a member of Doctors' Commons (26 April). In the same year he and four other leading civilians signed an opinion upholding the new queen's commission issued for the consecration of Matthew Parker as archbishop of Canterbury. Parker showed his gratitude by making Yale life judge of his court of audience, official principal, chancellor, and vicar-general (28 June 1562). By this time Yale was prebendary of Ottley in Lichfield (25 March 1560) and rector of Leverington in Ely, as well as being one of the archbishop's commissioners for visiting the churches and dioceses of Canterbury, Rochester, and Peterborough. He was much used by the archbishop for such work, visiting the churches, city, and diocese of Oxford with Walter Wright (24 April 1561), All Souls and Merton colleges (May 1562), and the dioceses of Ely (1563) and Bangor (1566). He was chancellor of Bangor diocese between 1562 and 1570, and obtained the prebend of Y Faenol in St Asaph on 7 July 1564. He became a master in chancery (1566) and dean of the arches and thereby president of Doctors' Commons (5 October 1567–3 May 1573). On 12 July 1570 he was appointed joint keeper of the prerogative court of Canterbury with Parker's son.

With Parker's death in 1575 Yale, one of his executors, became vicar-general to the new archbishop, Edmund Grindal, who consulted him and William Aubrey on reform of the ecclesiastical courts and put him on a commission to repress religious malcontents. On 2 May 1576 Yale and Nicholas Robinson, bishop of Bangor, were empowered by Grindal to visit Bangor diocese on his behalf, and on 17 August a similar commission was issued to Yale and Gilbert Berkeley, bishop of Bath and Wells, to visit the church at Wells. On Grindal's sequestration (June 1577) Yale assumed the archbishop's judicial responsibilities throughout the province, but he fell ill in November and died that month or in December, when William Aubrey took over his duties; his body was buried in the church of St Gregory by Paul in London. Yale's widow, Joanna, daughter of Nicholas Waleron, survived him (until 12 September 1587).

David Yale [David Lloyd] (d. 1626), civil lawyer, was probably the illegitimate son of Thomas Yale's elder brother, John Wyn, the heir of Plas-yn-Iâl. He entered Queens' College, Cambridge, as a sizar in 1555 and graduated BA in 1564. He was presented on graduation to the rectory of Llandegla in Denbighshire, and became a fellow of his college (1565–81). He took the degree of MA in 1567 and served as proctor of the university between 1575 and 1576. He became vicar of High Ottley in Staffordshire in 1573. His legal career appears to commence with his probable uncle's death in 1577, for he succeeded him to the Faenol prebend at St Asaph and was admitted as an advocate to the court of arches on 19 October 1579, the same year that he took the degree of LLD. He became a full member of Doctors' Commons on 3 February 1582, the year in which he was appointed a prebendary of Chester. In 1583 he was named rector of Llandyrnog in Denbighshire and, with Edmund Meyrick, jointly administered Bangor diocese in 1585 when it was vacant between the episcopates of Nicholas Robinson and Hugh Bellot. He was chancellor of Chester diocese between 1587 and 1608, and in 1599 was appointed commissioner of ecclesiastical causes for York province. David Yale was only intermittently resident in London, the Denbighshire and Cheshire borders being the focus of his activities, and he was a JP for Denbigh by 1604. He purchased considerable land from the Erddigs of Erddig in 1598, retaining Plas Grono as the family seat. He also owned land in Derbyshire. He married Frances, daughter of civil lawyer John Lloyd, and their son Thomas married the daughter of George Lloyd, bishop of Chester, their grandson being Elihu *Yale, the eponymous benefactor of the American university. David Yale died in Chester in 1626, leaving chattels valued at £692, and was buried in Chester Cathedral. His wife was not mentioned in his will.   T. G. WATKIN

Sources DNB · DWB · B. P. Levack, The civil lawyers in England, 1603–1641 (1973) · Cooper, Ath. Cantab. · Venn, Alum. Cant. · will, Ches. & Chester ALSS, WS 1626
Archives BL, Cotton Cleopatra MSS · BL, Lambeth MSS · BL, Lansdowne MSS · NL Wales, Edward Owen deeds
Wealth at death £692—David Yale, chattels: will, Ches. & Chester ALSS, WS 1626, with inventory

Yallop, Edward. See Spelman, Edward (d. 1767).

Yang [née Tayler], **Gladys Margaret** (1919–1999), translator, was born on 19 January 1919 at the Peking Union Medical College Hospital, Beijing, China, the second daughter and third of the five children of John Bernard Tayler (1878–1951), professor of economics at Yenching (Yanjing) University (1917–43), a member of the Congregationalist London Missionary Society, and a pioneer of Chinese producer co-operatives, and his wife, Selina Sarah (Lena), née Peel (1881–1970), a missionary teacher. She was educated at home in Beijing until the age of seven, and to her regret did not develop a childhood fluency in Chinese. From 1927 to 1937 she was a boarder at Walthamstow Hall in Sevenoaks, Kent, a school for the daughters of nonconformist missionaries.

Gladys Tayler was admitted to read French at St Anne's College, Oxford, but succeeded in persuading the university to establish a new honours school in Chinese and became the first undergraduate to take a degree in Chinese, graduating with a second-class degree in 1940. At Oxford she met her future husband, Yang Xianyi (b. 1914), the only son of a wealthy Tianjin banker and a student at Merton College; they worked together in the university's China Society. Their relationship caused consternation to her parents, who feared the difficulties a mixed marriage might bring. A compromise was agreed: Gladys would accompany Yang Xianyi to China to see what life there was like. If she did not change her mind after arrival, her parents would consent to the marriage. The couple sailed for Hong Kong in 1940 and flew on over Japanese-occupied territory to Chongqing, China's wartime capital. Gladys's parents were present at their wedding in March 1941, a double ceremony at which Yang Xianyi's sister was also married. The brides wore Chinese silk gowns designed by Yang Xianyi's mother. Gladys was known in Chinese as Dai Naidi. Yang Xianyi and Gladys spent the rest of the war years teaching at refugee universities in south-west China, where she gave birth to a son, Yang Ye, and a daughter, Yang Ying. After the Japanese surrender, they moved first to Nanjing where their last child, a daughter, Yang Zhi, was born, and then in 1952 to Beijing, to join the Foreign Languages Press, recently established by the new communist government.

The achievements of Gladys Yang and her husband made an enormous amount of Chinese literature available in English for the first time. They translated from both classical and modern Chinese; their output included histories, novels, short stories, and poetry. Much of their best work was a team effort. Yang Xianyi would produce a rough English version on which Gladys would draw while also working from the original to produce a finished text.

Gladys Margaret Yang (1919–1999), by unknown photographer

They worked for the journal *Chinese Literature*, but also produced many book-length translations. Their first joint translation, *Mr Derelict*, a novel by the early twentieth-century writer Liu E, was published by Allen and Unwin in London in 1948. Their selection from the *Historical Records* by the historian Sima Qian (who died about 85 BC) was entertaining and readable. *The Courtesan's Jewel Box: Chinese Stories from the Xth to the XVIIth Centuries* (1957) evoked the sophisticated and lively urban culture of the Ming period. A four-volume *Selected Works of Lu Xun* (1956–7) made the major work of China's greatest twentieth-century writer available in English. Their work on the *Dream of Red Mansions*, a voluminous eighteenth-century novel still read and loved by almost all educated Chinese, was interrupted by their imprisonment, but their three-volume translation, published in 1978, was faithful, lively, and readable. Alone or with her husband, Gladys also translated works by many modern writers, among them Shen Congwen, Lao She, Cao Yu, Zhao Shuli, and Ding Ling. As a salaried translator for an official publishing house, she also had to translate much that was mediocre or worthless. She was on the whole cheerful and optimistic about China's future, despite being often, like her husband, under considerable political pressure. The Yangs' home was an oasis of learning, entertaining talk, and real engagement with politics in an intellectually repressed society. Many friends, both Chinese and foreign, benefited from their kindness, their knowledge, and their warmth.

In 1968, at the height of the 'cultural revolution', the Yangs were arrested. Gladys was held in solitary confinement without charge until 1972. In her first letter after her release she wrote: 'Till you have been held in detention for four years you never enjoy the world' (private information). She quickly resumed a life filled by reading, translation, correspondence with far-flung friends and family, and concern for her children, who had been forced to depend on themselves during the imprisonment of their parents. Her son became mentally ill and eventually committed suicide in England in 1979. Gladys never wholly recovered from this blow, though she took comfort from the way her daughters rebuilt their lives, and was immensely proud of her four grandchildren.

The 1980s brought a new burst of activity for the Yangs.

Chinese literature was allowed greater freedom to question and challenge than it had had for years. Gladys translated the work of many of the new young writers—including women such as Zhang Jie, Shen Rong, and Zhang Xinxin—befriending them and introducing them to a new generation of Western translators and scholars. She became interested in the women's movement that had developed in the West in the years when she was cut off from the world, and published some translations with Virago Press. Free to travel again, she and Xianyi visited many Asian and European universities, were honoured for their work, and renewed old friendships abroad.

In Beijing in 1989 Gladys Yang and Yang Xianyi were forthright and courageous in condemning the Tiananmen massacre. But Gladys's health was now deteriorating. She was often depressed, did less work, and wrote fewer letters. She was cared for with great devotion by her husband and her daughters. Although she had lost her great vitality, friends and family who visited her were always greeted with a smile. She died in Beijing on 18 November 1999, and was cremated there, at Babaoshan, on 25 November. She was survived by her husband and two daughters. DELIA DAVIN

Sources memoir by Yang Xianyi, priv. coll. · *The Guardian* (24 Nov 1999) · *The Times* (29 Nov 1999) · *The Independent* (1 Dec 1999) · personal knowledge (2004) · private information (2004) · *Reg. Oxf.*
Archives BL, archive
Likenesses photograph, repro. in *The Guardian* · photograph, News International Syndication, London [*see illus.*] · photograph, repro. in *The Independent*

Yaniewicz, Felix [*formerly* Feliks Janiewicz] (1762–1848), violinist, was born in Vilna, Lithuania. From 1777 for about seven years he was a violinist in the royal chapel of the last king of Poland, Stanisław August Poniatowski. He then travelled in Europe, going early in 1785 to Vienna to visit Haydn and Mozart (who, as suggested by Berwaldt, probably composed his lost *Andante* K470 for him) and spending three years in Italy, during which time he gave his first public concerts. It is possible that he was a pupil of Pietro Nardini in Florence, and he may have had contact with Gaetano Pugnani in Turin. His Paris début took place on 23 December 1787 at the Concert Spirituel, following which he was described in the *Mercure de France* (1788, 37) as a pupil of Jarnowick (also known as Giovanni Giornovichi). He was immediately recognized by the Parisians as an artist of great worth. For a short time he was a member of the chapel of the duke of Orléans, but with the outbreak of the revolution he left France for London.

Yaniewicz played at Domenico Corri's house in London in January 1792, at Growetz's concert on 9 February, and gave a benefit concert in the same month. He performed one of his violin concertos at the Salomon concerts of 17 February and 3 May (for Haydn's benefit), and subsequently decided to settle in Britain. He played in London, the provinces, and Ireland, and conducted the subscription concerts in Liverpool and Manchester for several seasons. In 1800 he married Eliza Breeze of Liverpool, with whom he had a son and two musically gifted daughters: Felicia was a pianist and singer, and Paulina, a harpist.

Yaniewicz opened a music warehouse at 25 Lord Street, Liverpool, in 1803, which flourished for some twenty-five years. His publications consisted of some of his own works and collections of modern transcriptions.

Yaniewicz was one of the founders of the Philharmonic Society in London, and in its first season (1813) was one of the leaders of the orchestra, appearing with Clementi on 14 June of that year; he played in the society's concerts for the next three years. In 1815 he appeared at the first Edinburgh festival (see Palmer), following which he decided to move to the city. He played at subsequent festivals (1819, 1824), and continued as a teacher and an active organizer of musical life. Distance prevented him from playing for the Philharmonic Society in London after 1816 (he requested 100 guineas for two concerts in 1819 just to cover his travelling expenses), but in 1822 he was recompensed for previous services with a silver plate worth £25.

Yaniewicz was not only a brilliant soloist, but an excellent leader and a conductor of great ability. His playing was considered solid, yet full of expression, and his skill in executing octave passages was widely admired. As a composer, he was essentially self-taught and conservative. His works include five violin concertos, a number of fantasias and short genre pieces for the violin, some songs, and numerous arrangements.

Yaniewicz's last public concert took place in February 1829, and he died on 21 May 1848 at 84 Great King Street, Edinburgh. He was buried in the city's Warriston cemetery.   DAVID J. GOLBY

Sources J. Berwaldt, 'Janiewicz, Feliks', *New Grove* • [J. S. Sainsbury], ed., *A dictionary of musicians*, 2 vols. (1824) • C. Ehrlich, *The music profession in Britain since the eighteenth century: a social history* (1985), 47–8 • C. Ehrlich, *First philharmonic: a history of the Royal Philharmonic Society* (1995) • F. M. Palmer, *Domenico Dragonetti in England (1794–1846): the career of a double bass virtuoso* (1997), 207–10

Yapp, Sir Arthur Keysall (1869–1936), young people's welfare organizer, was born at Orleton, near Leominster, on 12 March 1869, the son of Richard Keysall Yapp (1828/9–1873), farmer, and his wife, Jane Gammidge. For many generations his forebears had farmed in Herefordshire, and his father lived there on his own land. All his life he retained the simplicity and instincts of a countryman. His mother, youngest child of Timothy Gammidge, a Congregational minister, exercised a great influence on the lives of her three children. The father died when his elder son, Arthur, was four years old, and the family moved to Leominster. Educated at home and at the Hereford County College, Yapp entered a local firm of agricultural engineers, devoting his spare time to temperance and mission work. It was not until he was twenty-one, however, that he was first attracted to the Young Men's Christian Association (YMCA) when the local branch invited him to become its honorary secretary. To this work he gave his leisure, and two years later (1892) came a call to service as a full-time general secretary of the Derby YMCA. In 1898 he left Derby in order to undertake the extension of the YMCA work in Lancashire, where he became a pioneer in developing YMCAs in volunteer camps (1901) and, later, initiated a programme with the Territorial Force. In 1901

he married Alice Maude, second daughter of Thomas Hesketh Higson, of Southport; they had a son and a daughter.

Yapp's leadership extended throughout the north of England where in fields of widely different character he was gradually building up an experience that was to give him unique equipment for his later responsibilities. In 1907 he was invited by the Manchester YMCA to superintend its new building enterprise and to become its first general secretary. In 1912 Yapp went to London as secretary of the National Council of YMCAs, Incorporated. The movement had already gone some way towards freeing itself from its rather narrow early traditions, and at the outbreak of the First World War he inaugurated the war emergency service which was to spread throughout the world, bringing the association into a new phase of opportunity and responsibility. The red triangle sign, symbolizing spirit, mind, and body, was introduced in 1914 by Yapp. Through his inspiration, within ten days of the outbreak of war, 250 centres of rest and recreation were at the service of the forces, and before it had run its course there were more than 10,000 centres on the fighting fronts.

In 1917 Yapp was appointed KBE and was invited by Lloyd George to take charge as honorary director of the food economy campaign, and for six months a heavy programme of travel and public speaking was added to his work. In 1918 he visited the United States of America, and in the post-war years went twice to India and once round the world. After the war there was a steady development of new branches at home, and in the days of industrial depression he threw the weight of the national movement behind the work in distressed areas.

For not less than fifteen years Yapp worked eighteen hours a day and seven days a week. In 1929 he retired from active leadership owing to ill health, and became deputy president of the YMCA, which position he held until his death. He died suddenly at Chobham Road, Woking, on 5 November 1936 after visiting the YMCA there. He was buried at Orleton.

An evangelical churchman from early youth, Yapp preached in churches and chapels of all denominations, and was the first layman to speak from the pulpits of Canterbury and other cathedrals. He had a fine presence with an attractive personality and a keen sense of humour, and was a lifelong teetotaller and non-smoker. An eloquent speaker and an admirable organizer with unbounded energy and initiative, he gave his life to Christian service, with a devotion to youth in which he firmly believed.

G. L. CLAPPERTON, rev.

Sources A. K. Yapp, *In the service of youth* (1929) • A. K. Yapp, *The romance of the red triangle* (1919) • *British YMCA Review* (Dec 1936) • private information (1949) • personal knowledge (1949) • *WWW* • *The Times* (11 Nov 1936) • *CGPLA Eng. & Wales* (1936) • d. cert. [Richard Keysall Yapp] • b. cert.
Archives FILM BFI NFTVA, news footage
Wealth at death £4513 12s. 2d.: probate, 8 Dec 1936, *CGPLA Eng. & Wales*

Yard, Robert (c.1651–1705), administrator and editor of the *London Gazette*, was of obscure birth and family. Nothing is known of his parentage and only a few details of Yard's brothers and sisters are given in his will, but according to his second marriage licence he was aged about thirty in 1681. He was twice married: first to Elleanor Pearce (*d.* 1680/81) on 21 November 1680 at St Benet Fink in London. After her death he married on 22 October 1681 Jane Weston (*b. c.*1661) at St Margaret's, Westminster. She was the daughter of Henry Weston of Ockham, Surrey, and the couple had one son, Robert Yard (*d.* 1728).

Yard made his public début in government circles in 1667 as the young protégé of Sir Joseph Williamson. At that time Williamson was taking care to promote his own clients into the office structure of the secretary of state Lord Arlington. Williamson paid 115 guilders for Yard to learn languages abroad at Bruges and The Hague in 1666, and upon the young man's return to England in 1667 he gave his favourite a position as a personal clerk. Although Yard was to stray rarely from the secretariat until his retirement in 1702, in 1669 Sir Peter Wyche junior was sent on an extraordinary ambassadorship to Russia, Sweden, and Poland, and took Yard with him as a secretary. Yard had already served in this capacity earlier that year on an embassy to Spain. In May 1669 he visited Moscow, as well as Stockholm and Danzig, and claimed there to have learned of the 'necessary ceremonie of a Court to give and receive the visits of the chiefest ministers' (PRO; SP foreign, 95/ Sweden/7, fol. 150). In his role as a personal clerk Yard, like many another in the formative civil service of the period was trained in Williamson's own methods of administrative policy. That Yard was regarded, and regarded himself, as Williamson's dependent until the latter's death in 1701 is shown in the frequent correspondence between 'Robin' and his 'master', which continued even when the latter was out of office after 1679.

Having completed a suitable administrative apprenticeship Yard served under a number of secretaries as a clerk, chief clerk, and eventually under-secretary, from 1667 to 1688. Yard proved to be a worthy subordinate in the increasingly important secretariat, only occasionally distracted in his early years by his fondness for his 'young lady' (*CSP dom.*, 1673, 108). He also became a writer of newsletters and in 1670 Yard was promoted to become writer of the *London Gazette*, again under the close supervision of Williamson. The *London Gazette* (formerly *Oxford Gazette*) was often more noticeable for the news it left out than for what it actually printed, particularly in regard to domestic affairs, and with Williamson's promotion to secretary of state in 1674 James Vernon was also brought in as a 'gazetter' to work in harness with Yard. The two men's careers were from then on intertwined, and Yard in effect became Vernon's lieutenant. The inevitable personal conflicts in the office often caused Yard difficulties and he frequently got into trouble for mistakenly publishing news which the government otherwise wished to keep out of the public domain and he often bemoaned the fact that others 'endeavour all they can to run me into errors' (Christie, 1.175, 2.32). Yard survived until 1676 when he was temporarily removed as a 'gazetter' for a series of

errors in the publication. He was soon reappointed however, and held the position as editor, under a variety of masters, until 1702.

After the revolution of 1688 Yard became chief clerk in the office under Shrewsbury in February 1689. He was continued in office by Nottingham in June 1690 to March 1694. In that month Yard was finally made undersecretary, again serving under Shrewsbury. He was kept in office by Jersey in May 1699 and as his former colleague James Vernon considered Yard very capable in office affairs he retained Yard in office in November 1700. In 1698 Yard became secretary to the lords justices by using the patronage of Shrewsbury and Lord Chancellor Somers. In December 1701 Yard was elected as member of parliament for Marlborough. He held the seat in the court interest and it was paid for through the patronage of the duke of Somerset. Yard was not a very active presence in parliament, and was defeated in the election at Marlborough in the following year. He retired from the secretariat in 1702 having already been promoted to become commissioner of prizes at £500 per annum, an office he was to hold until his death in April 1705. Yard's service in government proved financially profitable. He had been a careful investor in public funds, such as the Bank of England and other public institutions, and he was able to leave a substantial financial estate to his wife, sisters, and only son in his will. Yard died at Westminster on 27 April 1705. In his will, made at his home in Westminster, he called for his body to be buried at Ockham church.

Throughout his career Yard remained a well informed, capable, and diligent civil servant and something of a fixture under a number of secretaries. He was able to maintain a wide official correspondence with many leading people both at home and abroad, although this rarely strayed into personal matters. In general Yard produced no innovations in administrative techniques, but he is notable in his career for his editorship of the *London Gazette*, as well as for being one of the administrators in the later seventeenth century who first brought a more professional outlook to the administrative work of government.

ALAN MARSHALL

Sources PRO, PROB 11/483/180–181v [will of Robert Yard, 4/1705] · G. J. Armytage, ed., *Allegations for marriage licences issued by the vicar-general of the archbishop of Canterbury, July 1679 to June 1687*, Harleian Society, 30 (1890), 76 · IGI · *CSP dom.*, 1660–1702 · W. D. Christie, ed., *Letters addressed from London to Sir Joseph Williamson*, 2 vols., CS, new ser., 8–9 (1874) · BL, Stowe MS, 549, fol. 18 · F. M. G. Evans, *The principal secretary of state: a survey of the office from 1558 to 1680* (1923) · PRO, SP foreign, 95/Sweden/7, fols. 118, 150 · PRO, SP foreign, 81/60–61/Germany 1673, fols. 138–9 · PRO, SP domestic, 291/290/fols. 169–169v. · A. Marshall, 'Sir Joseph Williamson and the conduct of administration in Restoration England', *Historical Research*, 69 (1996), 18–41 · P. M. Handover, *A history of the London Gazette, 1665–1965* (1965) · J. C. Sainty, ed., *Officials of the secretaries of state, 1660–1782* (1973) · *Daily Courant* (30 April 1705)

Archives BL, Add. MSS 46525, fols. 58–60; 28883, fol. 458; 28889, fol. 48; 34096; 37992; 40803, fol. 29 · CKS, corresp. with Alexander Stanhope · Yale U., Beinecke L., letters to William Blathway; letters to Edmund Poley

Wealth at death £4000 to son on reaching twenty-one; until then allowance of £150 p.a.; £6000 interest to wife and after her death to son; money after death to be invested in land or securities; jewels, plate, linen, household goods, and several legacies to wife: will, PRO, PROB 11/483, fols. 180–181v

Yardley, Kathleen. See Lonsdale, Dame Kathleen (1903–1971).

Yarington [Yarrington], **Robert** (*fl.* 1601), putative playwright, is known only as named author of the 1601 quarto *Two Lamentable Tragedies*, a lurid two-plot play. The first plot, concerning London innkeeper Thomas Merry's murders of chandler Robert Beech and apprentice Thomas Winchester, is based on a true crime of 23 August 1594. The second plot, the murder-for-hire of an Italian orphan, Pertillo, commissioned by his guardian uncle, Falleria, has affinities with the 'Babes in the Wood' ballad entered on the Stationers' register in 1595. The two plots are linked by a moralizing chorus of allegorical figures (Truth, Avarice, Homicide) and by the ethical dilemmas of reluctant accomplices, Rachel (Merry's sister) and Alenso (Falleria's son). The play is usually termed a domestic tragedy, although it differs from other exemplars of the type with murders motivated by avarice rather than adultery. Notable are the simulated dismemberment of Beech's body, Winchester's appearance 'in a chaire, with a hammer sticking in his head' (sig. D3v), and the onstage hangings of Merry and Rachel.

Philip Henslowe's 1599 payments to John Day and William Haughton for the lost *Tragedy of Thomas Merry* and to Henry Chettle for the unfinished *Orphan's Tragedy* once provoked speculation that *Two Lamentable Tragedies* was an inept conflation of these plays. F. G. Fleay dismissed Yarington as 'a fictitious name' (Fleay, 286) and W. W. Greg supposed him a scribe (*Henslowe's Diary*, 2.209). R. A. Law and A. C. Baugh have since argued that the play was written by 'Rob. Yarington' before 1597, then taken up for revision in 1599, and E. K. Chambers concludes that Yarington's obscurity is 'hardly sufficient reason for denying him the ascription of the title-page' (Chambers, 3.518). Greg's theory was briefly revisited with the discovery that 'Robᵗ. Yarrington junʳ' was made free of the London Scriveners' Company in 1603 (Wagner, 147), but there remain other candidates for the playwright, not all of them mutually exclusive. A 'Rob. Yarranton' was made free of the London Drapers' Company in 1592 (Boyd, 207). The parish register of St Mary Woolchurch records the 1564 wedding of 'Robart Yarington' and Alice Anthonie, the births of three daughters and five sons, the deaths of two sons and a servant, and the 1585 burial of Alice (Brooke and Hallen, 300–76). Administration of the estate of 'Robert Yarington' of St Nicholas Acon was granted to his widow Mary in 1617 (London Guildhall, MS 9168/16, fol. 288r). The will of 'Robart Yarrantonn' of St Dionis Backchurch, probated in 1625, left £80 to son Thomas and named wife, Dorothy, executor (Honigmann and Brock, 145–6).

LENA COWEN ORLIN

Sources F. G. Fleay, *A biographical chronicle of the English drama, 1559–1642*, 2 vols. (1891) • *Henslowe's diary*, ed. W. W. Greg, 2 vols. (1904–8) • R. A. Law, 'Yarington's *Two lamentable tragedies*', *Modern Language Review*, 5 (1910), 167–77 • A. C. Baugh, ed., *William Haughton's 'Englishmen for my money'* (1917) • E. K. Chambers, *The Elizabethan* stage, 4 vols. (1923) • B. M. Wagner, 'Robert Yarrington', *Modern Language Notes*, 45 (1930), 147–8 • P. Boyd, ed., *Roll of the Drapers' Company of London* (1934) • J. M. S. Brooke and A. W. C. Hallen, eds., *The transcript of the registers of … St Mary Woolnoth and St Mary Woolnoth Haw … 1538 to 1760* (1886) • E. A. J. Honigmann and S. Brock, eds., *Playhouse wills, 1558–1642: an edition of wills by Shakespeare and his contemporaries in the London theatre* (1993) • H. Jenkins, *The life and work of Henry Chettle* (1934) • A. W. Patenaude, 'A critical old-spelling edition of Robert Yarington's *Two lamentable tragedies*', PhD diss., U. Mich., 1978

Yarmouth. For this title name *see* Paston, Robert, first earl of Yarmouth (1631–1683); Wiseman, Elizabeth, Lady Wiseman [Elizabeth Paston, countess of Yarmouth] (1647–1730); Paston, William, second earl of Yarmouth (1653/4–1732) [*see under* Paston, Robert, first earl of Yarmouth (1631–1683)]; Wallmoden, Amalie Sophie Marianne von, *suo jure* countess of Yarmouth (1704–1765).

Yarranton, Andrew (1619–1684), engineer and agriculturist, was probably born at Larford in Astley, Worcestershire, the second son of Walter Yarranton (*d.* 1631), from a yeoman family long settled there, and his wife, Sara (*d.* 1641). He was baptized at Astley on 29 August 1619. About 1632 he was apprenticed to a linen draper in Worcester, but left him and 'lived a countrey-life for some years' (Yarranton, 1.193). He joined the parliamentary army, becoming a captain by 1645, serving in the garrison at Madeley, Shropshire, and perhaps later at Hartlebury Castle. In 1648 he discovered a cavalier plot by Colonel Dud Dudley and others to capture Madeley Court and Dawley Castle, Shropshire, resulting in the capture of the conspirators and their imprisonment at Hartlebury Castle, Worcestershire, for which he was awarded £500 by parliament. From 1651 to 1653 he was a commissioner for sequestrations in Worcestershire.

Earlier, in 1651, with fellow officers, Yarranton bought extensive crown woodlands in the Wyre Forest and in 1652 he 'entered upon Iron-works' (Yarranton, 1.193), setting up, with others, a furnace at Astley to smelt 'Roman' cinders from Pitchcroft, Worcester, and probably ironstone from the Forest of Dean. This business continued only for a few years, as the furnace was probably in the hands of Thomas Foley (1616–1676) in 1662. He and his partners also used Shelsley Forge at this time. In 1672, however, he had a share in another furnace, at Sudeley, near Winchcombe, Gloucestershire.

In 1655 Yarranton agreed, with Captain Wall, for £750 to connect Droitwich with the Severn by rendering the River Salwarpe navigable, thus obviating the heavy expense of carriage of salt to Worcester by land; he was to procure letters patent for doing it from the protector, the burgesses of Droitwich granting them a beneficial lease of salt vats. 'But the times being unsettled, and Yarranton and Wall not rich, the scheme, whose authors were more disinterested than projectors generally are, was never carried into execution' (Nash, 1.306). After the Restoration this scheme was taken up by Thomas, seventh Baron Windsor (later earl of Plymouth), but when five of the six locks needed were 'compleated the plan was found not to answer and the sixth lock never built' (ibid.).

At the Restoration Yarranton was imprisoned by Lord Windsor as lord lieutenant of Worcestershire 'for refusing his lordship's authority' perhaps in relation to the militia (*CSP dom., 1660–61*, 356–7). He was free in November 1661, when he was compromised by the discovery of some letters relating to an intended Presbyterian rising. On 16 November a message was sent to Sir John Packington (1620–1680) from London ordering his arrest, and in May 1662 'the escape of Andrew Yarranton, a person dangerous to the government, from the custody of the provost marshal' was reported (ibid., 383). After 'meetings with several disaffected persons', he went up to London, where he was rearrested (ibid., 385). Yarranton later published his version of the affair as *A Full Discovery of the First Presbyterian Sham Plot* (1681), when again under suspicion politically, declaring that the compromising letters were forgeries planted by Sir J— P—; this had been discovered by his wife, communicated to him, who then publicly denounced the imposture and was released; he went up to London 'and prevail [ed] with the lord of Bristol to acquaint the king of the great wrong he had received' (*A Full Discovery*, 14), was arrested, but quickly released. Less than six months later, he was arrested for having 'spoken Treasonable Words against the King and Government' (ibid., 15). At a full trial at Worcester assizes, the witnesses were not credible and he was acquitted by the jury. Yarranton's difficulties here may in part have been related to his being a trustee of a charge of £1000 imposed on the estate of Sir John Packington for the benefit of the widow and children of William Guise who had been hanged by the royalists at Worcester as a spy.

Yarranton was (after Sir Richard Weston) one of the first to appreciate the agricultural value of clover. He wrote two pamphlets recommending its use, *Yarranton's Improvement by Clover* and *The Improvement Improved by a Second Edition of the Great Improvement of Lands by Clover* (1663), though no copy of the first is known. He acted as an agent for the supply of seed, and claimed to have doubled the value of much of the land in the west midlands by this improved husbandry.

After the Restoration Yarranton's chief business was that of a river engineer, though all his schemes, except the Warwickshire Avon, were ultimately unsuccessful. The Avon had been made navigable to Stratford by William Sandys of Fladbury in the late 1630s, but had subsequently decayed. Lord Windsor acquired the navigation from the duke of York's trustees in 1664 and employed Yarranton to restore the lower navigation, and sold a share in the upper part, above Evesham, to a syndicate including Yarranton, so that they could complete it. Yarranton gave his share in the upper navigation to his son Robert in 1679.

Yarranton's principal effort was devoted to the River Stour, whose improvement below Stourbridge was authorized, with that of the Salwarpe, by statute in 1662, with Lord Windsor, Lord Bristol, and others as projectors. He was their engineer by 1666, and probably from its start. The river was supposed to be completed in two years for barges carrying 6 tons of coal down through a dozen locks to the River Severn; it was usable, though not complete, in 1665, but work on the river was still in progress over a decade later. There was a related scheme for a footrail (railway) to bring coal down to the river, and in January 1665 Yarranton became a partner in two mining enterprises, both, no doubt, intending to reap the profits of using the navigation to send coal down the River Severn. But the river improvements proved more costly than expected and further work was needed. In 1670 the river and footrail were amalgamated, and 'being a Brat of my own', says Yarranton, 'I was not willing it should be Abortive'; he therefore agreed to complete it, receiving a third share of the navigation in payment, 'upon which I fell on and made it compleately navigable from Sturbridge to Kederminster, carrying down many hundred Tuns of Coales, and laid out near one thousand pounds; and there it was obstructed for want of Money' (Yarranton, 1.65–6). In July 1674 Yarranton evolved a new scheme by which Sir Clement Clerke and others would put up more money to enable the river to be completed and an underground footrail to be made, Clerke and his partners also taking over certain ironworks, but this collapsed because most of the money was not forthcoming and little was done. In 1677 this was renegotiated, an annuity being provided for Yarranton in lieu of his own investment.

In the midst of his work on the Stour, in 1667, Yarranton was dispatched by the navigation proprietors and various persons, including Thomas Foley, concerned in the iron industry, to Saxony with an 'able fire-man', Ambrose Crowley (probably the father of Sir Ambrose Crowley), to discover how tin plate was made. As he recounted:

> Coming to the Works we were very civilly Treated; and, contrary to our Expectation, we had much liberty to … See the Works Go, with the way and manner of their Working, and Extending the Plates; as also the perfect View of such Materials as they used in Clearing the Plates to make them fit to take Tinn, with the way they use in Tinning them over, when clear'd of rust and blackness; and having (as we judged) sufficiently obtained the whole Art of Making and Tinning the Plates, we then came for *England*, where the several persons concerned in the Affair thought fit to make some Trial in making some small quantities of Plates, and Tinning them, which was done; … And all the Work-men that wrought them, agreeing, That the plates and the Mettal they were made of, was much better than those Plates which were made in *Germany*; and would work more pliable, and serve for many more Profitable uses, than the *German* plates would do. (Yarranton, 2.150–51)

Their experiments were conducted at Kings Meadow Forge, Stourbridge, and Wilden Forge, near Kidderminster, and included the use of a rolling-mill, which was not part of the German process. Two of the sponsors erected a mill at Wolverley and commenced production; in 1673, however, William Chamberlaine renewed a patent granted to him and Dud Dudley in 1661, which they had never exploited. Yarranton called the patent 'Trumpt up'; 'what with the Patent being in our way and the Richest of our Partners being not willing, or at least afraid, to offend Great men then in Power, who had their eye upon it, caused the thing to cool' (ibid., 2.151). Attempts to bring the two sides together failed, and as a result, 'neither he, that hath the patent, nor those that Countenanced him, can make one Plate fit for Use', nor because of the patent could those who knew how to (ibid., 2.151–2).

In the mid-1670s Yarranton worked as a kind of consulting engineer, visiting much of the country and advising on ironworks and river and other improvements. In 1674 he surveyed the River Dee below Chester, the Enniscorthy ironworks and nearby River Slane in Ireland, and the Avon from Salisbury to Christchurch. 'I made it my business', he wrote, 'to survey the three great rivers of England [that is, the Thames, Humber, and Severn] and some small ones; and made two navigable and a third almost compleated' (Yarranton, 1.193–4), evidently referring to the Avon, Stour, and Salwarpe. The construction of flash locks near the mouth of the Dick brook at Astley has also been attributed to Yarranton but may well belong to a later period. In 1679 he was consulted about improvements to mines at Ruperra, Monmouthshire, and to the River Rhymni there. He also drew plans of the defences of Tangier and Dunkirk.

Andrew Yarranton was married and had daughters who married Tom Coles and a Mr Osland, and two sons, Andrew and Robert. The latter assisted his father in planning improvements to the Thames navigation between London and Oxford, succeeding him as engineer on the Stour, and in 1677 contracting jointly with William Farnolls to render it navigable for vessels of at least 12 tons, but money ran out in 1680 when the river was completed only as far down as Kidderminster, and Robert Yarranton died not long after. The circumstances surrounding Andrew Yarranton's own death in 1684 remain obscure; John Aubrey noted that 'Captain Yarrington dyed at London about March last. The cause of his death was a Beating and throwne into a Tub of Water' (Brief Lives, 1949 edn, xxv–xxvi).

Andrew Yarranton is principally remembered because, besides the pamphlets mentioned, he wrote *England's Improvement by Land and Sea: how to Beat the Dutch without Fighting* (2 vols., 1677–81). In this he proposed many schemes of improvement: fire prevention, establishing linen manufacture, ironworks in Hampshire, a land bank to finance trade, and public granaries. He suggested making the Warwickshire Stour navigable up to Shipston and the Cherwell to Banbury so as to shorten the distance for carriage of goods between navigations in the Severn and Thames catchments. Another proposal concerned the River Dee up to Bangor Bridge, Flintshire. These to some extent anticipated the great changes brought about a century later by the development of still-water canals. His ideas came partly from his observations abroad in 1667, especially in Holland and Flanders. He was attacked in a pamphlet entitled *A coffee house dialogue, or, Discourse between Captain Y and a young barrister of the Middle Temple*, in which Yarranton is discovered discoursing on how to beat the Dutch by making the streets of London into navigable rivers, followed by a discussion of the Exclusion Bill, Yarranton of course being worsted. He (or his friends) refuted this with *The coffee house dialogue examined and refuted … and England's improvements justified and the author … vindicated*

from the scandals in a paper called a coffee house dialogue, defending Yarranton from the 'sulphureous fiery stink pots of calumnies and slander' directed against him; while the charges are again reinforced in *A continuation of the coffee house dialogue … wherein the first dialogue is vindicated and in it one of the improvers of England is proved to be a man of no deeper understanding than his master, Captain Y.*

ERNEST CLARKE, *rev.* P. W. KING

Sources A. Yarranton, *England's improvement by land and sea: how to beat the Dutch without fighting*, 2 vols. (1677–81) · G. H. C. Burley, 'Andrew Yarranton: a seventeenth century Worcestershire worthy', *Transactions of the Worcestershire Archaeological Society*, new ser., 38 (1961), 25–36 · J. H. Parker Oxspring, 'Andrew Yarranton, "Worcestershire worthy", 1619–84: his life and work with special reference to … River Stour', 1979, Worcester City Library, WQ B/YAR [2 vols.] · P. J. Brown, 'Andrew Yarranton and the British tinplate industry', *Historical Metallurgy*, 22 (1988), 42–8 · P. W. King, 'Wolverley Lower Mill and the beginnings of the tinplate industry', *Historical Metallurgy*, 22 (1988), 104–13 · P. J. Brown, 'The military career of Andrew Yarranton', *Transactions of the Worcestershire Archaeological Society*, 3rd ser., 13 (1992), 193–202 · C. Hadfield, 'The Avon navigation', in C. Hadfield and J. Norris, *Waterways to Stratford*, 2nd edn (1968), 15–22 · *CSP dom.*, 1648–9; 1660–62; 1680–81 · T. Nash, *Collections for the history of Worcestershire*, 1 (1781), 306 · J. M. Palmer and M. I. Berrill, 'Andrew Yarranton and the navigation works at Astley', *Journal of the Railway and Canal Historical Society* (1958), 41–6 [with comment 77–8] · P. W. King, 'Dud Dudley's contribution to metallurgy', *Historical Metallurgy*, 36 (2002), 43–53 · P. J. Brown, 'The early industrial complex at Astley, Worcestershire', *Post-Medieval Archaeology*, 16 (1982), 1–19 · PRO, E 320/V20–V21 · PRO, C 5/198/15; C 8/226/72; C 10/64/10; E 112/537/29 · PRO, SP 24/15–16 · Herefs. RO, E12/VI/KE/24, fol. 1; E12/IV/30, 26 June 1681 · T. C. Cantill and M. Wight, 'Yarranton's works at Astley', *Transactions of the Worcestershire Archaeological Society*, 2nd ser., 7 (1929), 92–115 · M. M. Hallett and G. R. Morton, 'Yarranton's furnace at Sharpley Pool, Worcs.', *Journal of the Iron and Steel Institute*, 206 (1968), 689–92 · *Aubrey's Brief lives*, ed. O. L. Dick (1949), xxv–xxvi
Archives Staffs. RO, Aqualate MSS

Yarrell, William (1784–1856), zoologist, was born in Duke Street, London, on 3 June 1784, the ninth of the twelve children of Francis Yarrell (d. 1794) and his wife, Sarah Blane of Bayford, Hertfordshire. His father was a bookseller and newsagent in partnership with his cousin William Jones (the business still survives in Bermondsey, London, under the name of Jones, Yarrell & Co.). A quiet, studious boy, Yarrell attended Dr Nicholson's school in Ealing along with Edward Jones, who was to be his business partner until 1850. Apart from a course in chemistry, which he attended at the Royal Institution in 1817, and another in anatomy, at an unknown location and date, this appears to have been the sum of his education, which makes the care and objectivity shown in his scientific work all the more remarkable. After leaving school, he spent less than a year (17 November 1802 – 30 July 1803) as a clerk with the banking firm of Heries, Farquhar & Co. He later succeeded to his father's business, of which he had sole charge after 1850.

Yarrell used his leisure to become one of the best shots of his time and an enthusiastic angler. About 1823, he began to note the occurrence and appearance of rare birds and, by 1825, was sending specimens to the artist Thomas

William Yarrell (1784–1856), by Maull & Polyblank, 1855

Bewick (1753–1828), after whom he was to name a new species of swan. He also took a great interest in the contents of poultry and fish shops and markets. Occasionally he would venture outside London to collect specimens, but he was essentially metropolitan and this had the slight disadvantage that he often relied on the observations and writings of others for his knowledge of the habits of birds. By 1825 he had assembled considerable natural history collections, notably one of birds' eggs (including the egg of a great auk). These collections included a great number of specimens collected by himself, for one of his strengths lay in careful dissection and preparation. Yarrell published his first paper, 'On the occurrence of some rare British birds', in the *Zoological Journal* in 1825, the same year that he is believed to have given up shooting. Many of his subsequent papers dealt with anatomy, such as those on the trachea and sternum of ducks, geese, and swans. He also published the results of experiments on living birds and, by this means, came close to discovering the function of the ovary in determining sexual characteristics.

In November 1825 Yarrell was elected a fellow of the Linnean Society of London. He took an active part in its meetings, later becoming a vice-president, member of its council, and serving as treasurer from 1849 until his death. Yarrell was an original member of the Zoological Society (founded 1826), serving—except for the required intervals—on its council from 1831 until his death, and briefly as secretary from 1836 to 1838. His good sense and business knowledge seem to have made him greatly in demand as an adviser to a number of organizations. In view of this, it is surprising that his short term as secretary

of the Zoological Society was not a success. It has been suggested that his own business interests distracted his attention from those of the society during this period. Yarrell also supported the Entomological Society. He seems to have considered himself too old to benefit from membership of the Royal Society.

Between 1835 and 1836 Yarrell published serially his two-volume work *A History of British Fishes*, which was very favourably reviewed. In this work he paid particular attention to species that were a source of food, and he would often eat the specimens he collected to test whether they might be added to those known to be fit for the table. John Van Voorst (who had been introduced to Yarrell by Mr Martin, the duke of Bedford's librarian) republished the work in 1836. A second edition appeared in 1841, and a third in 1859. According to the publisher, these works brought Yarrell more than £4000. In 1843 Van Voorst published Yarrell's second book, *The History of British Birds*, in three volumes (with second and third editions in 1845 and 1856 respectively). A fourth edition of *British Birds* in four volumes was published between 1871 and 1885. These two histories were the prototype of a series of books by other writers, mostly dealing with invertebrates, published by Van Voorst.

Yarrell, who never married, was of a serene and sociable disposition. At his table were to be found Thomas Bell, Edward Turner Bennett, J. E. Bicheno, John Gould, J. E. Gray, Marshall Hall, and William Thompson of Belfast. One of his most marked characteristics was a great and generous readiness to assist others in their researches. He enjoyed the theatre and sang well, occasionally diverting his companions with impromptu performances. Yarrell seems to have suffered a slight stroke on 3 August 1856, from which he recovered. At the end of the month he accompanied an invalid friend to Yarmouth, where he died suddenly on 1 September 1856. He was buried at Bayford, Hertfordshire, a week later. His library and natural history collections were auctioned after his death, the fishes going to the British Museum. 　　J. C. EDWARDS

Sources J. Van Voorst, 'Memoir', in W. Yarrell, *A history of British fishes*, 3rd edn (1859) [incl. bibliography] · *Proceedings of the Linnean Society of London* (1858–9) · L. Blomefield, *Reminiscences of William Yarrell* (privately printed, Bath, 1885) · *Zoologist*, 13 (1856) · T. R. Forbes, 'William Yarrell: British naturalist', *Proceedings of the American Philosophical Society*, 106 (1962), 505–15 · Linn. Soc. · Zoological Society, London

Archives NHM, specimens · Princeton University Library, New Jersey, fish drawings, papers, and letters received by him · S. Antiquaries, Lond., ornithological notes and papers | Bath Royal Literary and Scientific Institution, letters to Leonard Blomefield · Linn. Soc., letters to William Swainson · Marine Biological Association of the United Kingdom, Plymouth, fish drawings and press cuttings · Royal Museum of Scotland, letters to Sir William Jardine · York City Archives, letters to Thomas Allis

Likenesses Mrs Carpenter, oils, *c*.1838, Linn. Soc. · Maull & Polyblank, albumen print, 1855, NPG [*see illus.*] · photograph, *c*.1855, repro. in Lord Zuckerman [S. Zuckerman] and others, eds., *The Zoological Society of London, 1826–1976 and beyond* (1976) · F. A. Heath, stipple and line engraving, pubd 1859 (after photograph by Maull & Polyblank), NPG · N. Burnard, bas-relief memorial, St James's Church, Piccadilly, London · M. Gauci, lithograph (after E. U. Eddis), BM · T. H. Maguire, lithograph, BM, NPG; repro. in T. H.

Maguire, *Portraits of honorary members of the Ipswich Museum* (1852) · chalk drawing, U. Cam., Zoological Museum · lithograph, Zoological Society of London; repro. in T. H. Maguire, *Portraits of honorary members of the Ipswich Museum* (1852)

Wealth at death approx. £17,000: Van Voorst, 'Memoir'

Yarrow, Sir Alfred Fernandez, first baronet (1842–1932), marine engineer and shipbuilder, was born at 2 Bury Court, St Mary Axe, London, on 13 January 1842, the elder and only surviving son of the merchant Edgar Williams Yarrow (*bap.* 1805) of Barnsbury, London, and his wife, Esther Lindo (*d.* 1889), daughter of Moses Lindo, a West Indies merchant. He was of Jewish descent on his mother's side and his parents' courtship was prolonged by his mother's reluctance to upset her family by marrying a Christian. The marriage only took place, in Holborn, London, in late 1838, after her parents' death. Yarrow's relationship with his mother was one of mutual devotion and was particularly intense after his father's death and in the early stages of his business career.

Educated privately and at University College School, London, Yarrow was apprenticed to the firm of Ravenhill, Salkeld & Co., marine engine builders, at the age of fifteen. In these early years he spent much time with his friend James Hilditch, who shared his practical and inventive turn of mind. They attended Michael Faraday's lectures at the Royal Institution and installed a private telegraph line between their homes. Together they patented several inventions in 1861, including a steam carriage and a steam plough. One consequence was that Yarrow became the London representative of a firm of agricultural engineers while he continued to seek new business opportunities.

In 1865 Yarrow went into partnership with a Mr Hedley, establishing a works at Folly Wall, Isle of Dogs, Poplar, London. Initially a general engineering concern, the repair of river vessels led them to build steam launches in substantial numbers from 1868. The partnership with Hedley was dissolved in 1875 and on 24 March of that year Yarrow married Minnie Florence Franklin (1852/3–1922). They had three daughters and three sons; the youngest son was killed in action in 1915.

Yarrow rapidly developed the business after 1875. Shallow-draught river and lake boats, such as the *Ilala*, were built for use in Africa, and vessels were generally prefabricated for easy carriage and reassembly on site. The enthusiasm for torpedo boats by the world's navies was a huge boost to Yarrows and the subsequent development of destroyers was equally beneficial. The Yarrow water tube boiler, a design of classic simplicity, was another development, stemming from dissatisfaction with the performance of existing boilers. They were installed in warships from 1887 and found to be lighter and more economical.

In 1897 the business was incorporated as a limited liability company, Yarrow & Co. Ltd. Despite the success that the company enjoyed, Yarrow perceived that the Thames was in decline as a shipbuilding river and that a move was necessary in order to remain competitive. Between 1906 and 1908 the enterprise was moved to Scotstoun, on the River Clyde, a site chosen after careful deliberation. The choice may well have been influenced by the proximity of the deep-water measured mile at Skelmorlie. By 1913 Yarrow was ready to leave the business in the hands of the next generation and he retired to Hampshire until the outbreak of the First World War brought a swift return to work. In the ensuing conflict the shipyard built twenty-nine destroyers and Yarrow himself took responsibility for the development of shallow-draught gunboats for use in Mesopotamia. In 1916 he received a baronetcy for his war services. He was further honoured in 1922 when he became a fellow of the Royal Society, and in 1924 when he received the honorary degree of LLD from Glasgow University. On 2 December 1922 he married his second wife, Eleanor Cecilia Barnes (1871/2–1953), daughter of Goodwin Barnes, a coal proprietor.

A consummate businessman, and an enlightened and patriarchal employer, Yarrow was equally driven by the intellectual challenges which arose from his work. The problem of excessive vibration, caused by reciprocating ships' engines, was reduced by a method of balancing which became known—using the names of those who had collaborated on it—as the Yarrow–Schlick–Tweedy system. Yarrow was also interested in practices such as speed trials for ships and the use of new materials such as aluminium and mild steel which allowed the saving of weight in construction without the loss of strength. Another development was that of the hinged flap which, when placed across the propeller tunnel of shallow-draught vessels, closed the gap between the top of the tunnel and the water-line. This brought about a complete immersion of the propeller and generated greater power than would have been the case with a partial immersion.

A considerable benefactor, many of Yarrow's donations went to fund projects related to shipbuilding. He gave £20,000 to build a test tank for ship models at the National Physical Laboratory at Teddington, which opened in 1911, while in 1923 he gave £100,000 to the Royal Society to establish research professorships. He founded and endowed the Yarrow Home for Convalescent Children at Broadstairs, Kent, and gave generously to the London Hospital. £24,000 went to the Nurses' Training Home at Govan, in Glasgow, and towards the provision of nurses in remote areas of Scotland. Other recipients of his giving included the British Association for the Advancement of Science, the Institution of Naval Architects, and Girton College, Cambridge. Yarrow enjoyed a lively old age until his death at the Savoy Hotel, the Strand, London, on 24 January 1932; he was buried at Highgate cemetery.

Alfred Yarrow's eldest son, **Sir Harold Edgar Yarrow**, second baronet (1884–1962), shipbuilder, was born on 11 August 1884 at Ardmore House, Blackheath Park, Charlton, London. He inherited his father's business acumen and man-management skills. After attending Bedford grammar school he underwent a training which included a spell at the rival French shipyard of Augustin-Normand. He then returned to Yarrow & Co. Ltd at Poplar, London, and played a large part in the removal to Scotstoun, on the River Clyde. He was married twice. His first wife, whom he married on 27 February 1906, was Eleanor Etheldreda Aitken (1884/5–1934), daughter of W. H. M. H. Aitken, canon of Norwich; they had one son and three daughters. On 6 February 1935 Sir Harold married Rosalynde Vere (b. 1896/7), daughter of the scientist Sir Oliver Joseph Lodge; they had a daughter.

Harold Yarrow served as chairman and managing director of Yarrows for forty years; his decision to diversify into land boiler production enabled the company to survive a period in the 1920s when naval contracts all but ceased. He also maintained the family's charitable tradition, being involved in the foundation of the Princess Louise Scottish Hospital at Erskine, Renfrewshire, for disabled former servicemen, a concern that followed naturally from the contribution that the shipyard had made in the production of artificial limbs during the First World War. He died on 19 April 1962 at Overton, Kilmacolm, Renfrewshire. Continuity was maintained both in business and charitable concerns by the succession of Sir Eric Grant Yarrow, third baronet (b. 1920), to the company chairmanship on his father's death. However, though Yarrows continued until 1990 to be the main shipyard for the construction of naval frigates, it had ceased to have a separate existence, having been taken over by the General Electric Company.   LIONEL ALEXANDER RITCHIE

Sources E. C. Barnes, *Alfred Yarrow: his life and work* (1923) · A. Borthwick, *Yarrow & Company Limited, 1865–1977* (1977) · B. Baxter, 'Yarrow, Alfred Fernandez', *DSBB* · Burke, *Peerage* (1970) · *WWW* · *CGPLA Eng. & Wales* (1932) · b. cert. · m. certs. · d. cert. · *CGPLA Eng. & Wales* (1962) [H. E. Yarrow] · b. cert. [H. E. Yarrow] · m. certs. [H. E. Yarrow] · d. cert. [H. E. Yarrow]
Archives CAC Cam., letters to Lord Fisher
Likenesses H. G. Riviere, oils, 1907, Yarrow Home, Broadstairs, Kent · W. Stoneman, photograph, 1924, NPG · photographs, repro. in Barnes, *Alfred Yarrow*
Wealth at death £248,625 17s. 1d.: resworn probate, 25 Feb 1932, *CGPLA Eng. & Wales*

Yarrow, Sir Harold Edgar, second baronet (1884–1962). *See under* Yarrow, Sir Alfred Fernandez, first baronet (1842–1932).

Yate, Sir Charles Edward, baronet (1849–1940), administrator in India and politician, was born on 28 August 1849 at Holme-on-Spalding Moor, Yorkshire, the eldest of the four sons of Charles Yate (1804–1860), fellow and dean of St John's College, Cambridge, and vicar of Holme-on-Spalding Moor, and his wife, Jane Anne (d. 1900), daughter of Arthur Campbell, writer to the signet, of Catrine House, Ayrshire. In November 1867, after five years at Shrewsbury School, Yate joined the 49th Royal Berkshire regiment, then based in India, as an ensign. In 1871 he was admitted to the Bombay staff corps and subsequently transferred to the Indian political service. For some years an assistant political superintendent in Rajputana, he wrote chapters on Mewar and Partabgarh for the third volume of the *Rajputana Gazetteer* (1880).

Yate was gazetted captain in 1879 and during the Second Anglo-Afghan War, in 1879–80, returned briefly to military duty, commanding a detachment of the 29th Bombay infantry. As a member of General Roberts's staff, he was on the march from Kabul to the relief of Kandahar in August 1880 and remained as political officer in charge of the city until its evacuation in May 1881. From 1884 to 1886 he was attached to the Afghan boundary commission, a posting which supplied him with the material for a volume of descriptive letters, *Northern Afghanistan* (1888). In March 1885 Yate was British representative at Panjdeh, an oasis on Afghanistan's western frontier, when Russian troops invaded and threatened to embroil Britain in a war on Afghanistan's behalf. On 29 March, in a dramatic gesture of hospitality which typified his tendency to respond to a situation in terms of its protagonists, Yate invited the Russian officers to dine with him between the two lines of opposing soldiers. Notwithstanding the exchange of champagne toasts in no-man's-land, the Russians seized the disputed territory at dawn the following day. For his boundary work, Yate was made CSI in 1887 and CMG in 1888.

In 1889 Yate became the British consul at Muscat. From 1890 to 1892 he served as the political agent in Baluchistan, and in 1893 he was appointed British commissioner for settlement of the Kushk Canal question on the Russo-Afghan frontier. From 1893 to 1898 he was based at Mashhad in Persia as agent to the governor-general to Khorasan and Sistan. Although he later complained of having been denied the honours that a more prominent posting in Afghanistan would have afforded him, nevertheless his years in Mashhad spawned another descriptive book, *Khurasan and Sistan* (1900).

In 1898 Yate returned to India to a series of temporary postings in Rajputana. In the following year, on 18 March, he married Charlotte Heath (d. 1936), youngest daughter of Joseph Hume Burnley, chargé d'affaires at Dresden, with whom he had a son, who died in childhood, and two daughters, Lois (b. 1900) and Adelaide (b. 1904). In 1900 Lord Curzon appointed Yate chief commissioner of British Baluchistan. Yate relished the personal authority allowed to him in Baluchistan and was especially happy working under Curzon, whose vision of a stronger and more worthy empire he shared. Upon his retirement, in 1904, a clock tower and fountain were erected in his honour at Quetta by public subscription. He was gazetted colonel in 1901 and retired from the army in 1906.

Yate returned to England in 1904, hoping, as he put it to Curzon, 'to join in the fray on behalf of Imperialism as opposed to Little Englandism'. After two unsuccessful contests, at Pontefract (1906) and Melton Mowbray (January 1910), he was elected in December 1910 Conservative MP for the Melton division. In speeches renowned for their bluntness and brevity, he pilloried the advocates of political reform in India, in particular Edwin Montagu, Liberal secretary of state for India from 1917 to 1922. Yate was for many years a fellow of the Royal Geographical Society. In 1921 he was made a baronet. He retired, reluctantly, from parliament in 1924, whereupon he moved from his constituency residence, Ashfordby House, Leicestershire, to

Madeley Hall, Shropshire, home to the Yate family for several generations. He died there on 29 February 1940, aged ninety, and was survived by his daughters.

F. H. Brown, rev. Katherine Prior

Sources WWBMP, vol. 3 · BL OIOC, Curzon MSS · BL OIOC, Elgin MSS · *The Times* (2 March 1940), 1, 4 · P. M. Sykes, *The Rt Hon. Sir M. Durand: a biography* (1926) · Burke, *Peerage* (1939) · J. E. Auden, ed., *Shrewsbury School register, 1734–1908* (1909) · CGPLA Eng. & Wales (1940)
Archives BL OIOC, Curzon MSS · CUL, corresp. with Lord Hardinge
Likenesses photograph, repro. in *The Times*, 4
Wealth at death £33,465 11s. 4d.: probate, 3 July 1940, CGPLA Eng. & Wales

Yates, Dora Esther (1879–1974), bibliographer and scholar of Gypsy life, was born on 26 November 1879 in Liverpool, seventh of eight children of George Samuel Yates (1834–1887), importer of leaf tobacco, and his wife, Hannah Keyser (1840–1934). Having taught herself to read English and Hebrew before she was five, she attended Dr Lund's school, Croxteth Road. As 'a raw, unfledged girl of sixteen' (Yates, 11), she embarked on an outstanding academic career at Liverpool University College of Victoria University, Manchester. She indulged her enthusiasm for G. H. Borrow by studying Gypsy lore and language in her own time. She also scaled every pinnacle of the college building, and played hockey (with skirts decorously 10 inches off the ground), being chaired into college after scoring the winning goal against Manchester. After graduating BA she was, in 1900, the first Jewish woman to become MA of a British university, an achievement in which she took great pride.

After teaching at local private schools, Yates was tutor in English literature at Liverpool University (1906–9), then class libraries' assistant (from 1938 supervisor of class libraries) and lecturer in bibliography, being in addition curator of special collections from 1938. In the meantime she had found in Gypsy studies the ultimate outlet for her romantic imagination and scholarly aspirations, which were fostered by John Sampson, to whose hypnotic personality she succumbed, while resisting his sexual advances. She became his principal helper, the editor of his papers, and the keeper of his secrets. As his executor, she incurred the enmity of his family by organizing his funeral ceremony and handling other matters according to his wishes; it was also almost certainly she who engineered the meeting between his 25-year-old, orphaned illegitimate daughter, Mary Arnold (1906–1994), and the rest of the Sampsons.

Yates became honorary secretary of the Gypsy Lore Society in 1935, having effectively done the job since the society's revival in 1922, and officially became editor of its journal in 1955. On her retirement from Liverpool University in 1945 she was appointed curator of the Scott Macfie Gypsy Collection, which she had been instrumental in obtaining for the library.

Yates's research methods were pragmatic. She first visited a Gypsy encampment in 1903; her diary for 1973 lists the main horse fairs within a hundred miles of Liverpool, in case she was free to go. In the 1930s, under the tutelage of the legendary Ithal Lee (1860–1945), she entered more fully into 'taché Romané droma' ('true Gypsy ways'; Yates, 177) by purchasing her own Gypsy caravan, with horse, to take her around the Yorkshire dales, where, as a holiday retreat, she had bought Scott Macfie's cottage after his death in 1935. Her *Book of Gypsy Folk-Tales* (1948) included stories in Romani dialects from eleven countries, most of which she translated herself. Through her broadcasts and her unassuming but evocative autobiographical study, *My Gypsy Days* (1953), she made Gypsy ways accessible and understandable.

Yates was made DLitt of Liverpool University in 1963 in recognition of her scholarly achievements, to add to the honorific title of Rawnie ('Lady') conferred upon her by the Gypsies themselves. In her nineties she still travelled daily by taxi to her office in the university to conduct the affairs of the Gypsy Lore Society, writing letters in her own hand in English, French, German, and Romani.

Brought up in a strict, Orthodox Jewish household, Yates adhered tenaciously to her religious principles, and was an active member of the Liverpool Liberal Jewish congregation from its foundation in 1926. She was especially remembered for her twinkling eye, ringing voice, and brisk movements. She died, unmarried, at her home, Flat 2, 19 Olive Lane, Wavertree, Liverpool, on 12 January 1974, having the previous day remarked, as she briefly emerged from unconsciousness, 'This is ridiculous, Dora; pull yourself together!' She was cremated at the Liverpool crematorium on 17 January. Her collection of antiquarian books, her Borroviana, and the personal papers and two portraits of himself that Sampson had left her, she bequeathed to her friend Mary Arnold.

Antony Kamm

Sources E. Bradburn, *Dr Dora Esther Yates: an appreciation* [n.d., 1975?] · D. E. Yates, *My Gypsy days: recollections of a Romani Rawnie* (1953) · 'The Festschrift to Miss Dora Esther Yates, M. A.', *Journal of the Gypsy Love Society*, 3rd ser., 39/1 (1960) [special issue] · U. Lpool L., special collections and archive · personal knowledge (2004) · private information (2004) [family]
Archives U. Lpool, Gyspy Lore Society Archive, Gypsiologist papers, GLS D1–D11 · U. Lpool, corresp. and papers |SOUND BL NSA, performance recording · U. Lpool, recorded interview, 1973
Likenesses photographs, U. Lpool L.
Wealth at death £19,520: probate, 7 March 1974, CGPLA Eng. & Wales

Yates, Dornford. See Mercer, Cecil William (1885–1960).

Yates, Edmund Hodgson (1831–1894), journalist and novelist, was born on 3 July 1831 in Edinburgh, the only child of the well-known actors Frederick Henry *Yates (1797–1842) and Elizabeth *Yates, née Brunton (1799–1860). As a child he lived in a 'queer little private house' over the Adelphi Theatre, of which his father was manager from 1825 to 1842. From 1840 to 1846 he attended Sir Roger Cholmeley's School, Highgate; then, after nine months in Düsseldorf learning German, he started work as a clerk at the General Post Office on 11 March 1847, where he remained for twenty-five years. When appointed he was only fifteen but looked older. After his literary ambitions were fired by reading Thackeray's *Pendennis* (1850), he began contributing reviews of plays and novels, light verse, and journalistic sketches to various journals in 1852. He was helped by advice and introductions from the established writer Albert Smith. His first editorial experience was gained on two ephemeral weeklies, *Comic Times* (1855) and *The Train* (1856–8). From 1855 to the early 1860s he was theatre critic for the *Daily News*, and from 1855 to 1863 he contributed a gossip column, 'The lounger at the clubs', to the weekly *Illustrated Times*. With this he later claimed to have invented the style of personal journalism that dominated the popular press from the 1870s on, a claim modern scholars have supported. On 14 April 1853 he married Louise Katherine Wilkinson (1830?–1900), a member of the sword- and gun-making family; he was only twenty-one but added a year to his age on the marriage certificate. Four sons, including a set of twins, were born to the couple between 1855 and 1859. Yates proved a devoted but evidently not always faithful husband.

On 12 June 1858 Yates published a mildly disparaging sketch of Thackeray, his former idol, in a weekly called *Town Talk*. Thackeray complained to the committee of the Garrick Club that Yates, a fellow member, must have spied on him there. Dickens, who had stood godson to one of his sons, interceded in vain on Yates's behalf. He was expelled from the club, of which he had been a member since he was seventeen. Though probably used largely as a pawn by both parties, Yates was widely blamed for having helped to provoke the public estrangement that ensued between Dickens and Thackeray. The notoriety that the episode brought him was heightened two years later when, in June 1860, he sent the *New York Times* a story making malicious use of things his Post Office colleague Anthony Trollope had told him about the conversation at a dinner for the staff of the *Cornhill Magazine*, edited by Thackeray. Trollope never forgave him, castigating him furiously in a cancelled passage of his *Autobiography*, and helping to spread the probably spurious story that several of his novels had in fact been written, or partly written, by Frances Cashel Hoey.

Yates had nine plays produced in the West End between 1856 and 1872, all but one written in collaboration. He also established a deserved reputation as a writer of neat, sometimes witty light verse, including the anthologized epigram 'All Saints', and achieved popular, and some critical success with nineteen novels published between 1864 and 1875. The first and most original of these, *Broken to Harness* (1865), a skit on the 'pretty horse-breaker' of the period, was written to fill a gap in the monthly *Temple Bar*, of which he was assistant editor, then editor, from 1860 to 1867, his first important editorial appointment. Though lively and full of interesting topical detail, his novels became increasingly sensational and formulaic. In 1867, after leaving *Temple Bar*, he edited a new monthly, *Tinsley's Magazine*, but fell out with the proprietor who believed Yates was overpaying contributors, including himself. His official salary was by now £520 p.a. and his income from literary sources probably twice as much, but he was living beyond his means. He appeared before the court of bankruptcy in July 1868, with debts of over £7000, and his woes were compounded by the ignominious failure of his play

Tame Cats (12 December 1868), the only play he wrote on his own; his *Recollections and Experiences* (1884) mentions neither *Tame Cats* nor his bankruptcy.

Yates's fortunes began to improve in 1872. On 10 March he retired from the Post Office. On 30 August he embarked on a lecture tour of America, where he enjoyed considerable success thanks to his skills as a speaker and professional 'entertainer', his fame and notoriety as a journalist, his well-known intimacy with Dickens (who had died in 1870), and his reputation as a novelist. He arrived back in England on 23 March 1873, richer by £1500 and with an appointment as European correspondent of the *New York Herald* at £1200 p.a. The following year, in partnership with another journalist, Grenville Murray, he founded a new weekly, *The World*, advertised as 'A journal for men and women'. It began publication on 8 July 1874 and did so well that after six months he was able to buy out his partner, who made almost a tenfold profit on his investment. Its most popular feature, several columns of news and gossip entitled 'What the world says', was a more sophisticated version of Yates's youthful gossip columns, 'The lounger at the clubs' in the *Illustrated Times* and the 'Flâneur' in the *Morning Star* (1864–7). With the modest byline, 'Atlas', it was his own preserve and turned him into a celebrity and a rich man. But at the height of his prosperity his youthful notoriety caught up with him. A paragraph contributed by Lady Stradbroke to 'What the world says' on 17 January 1883 provoked a complaint from Lord Lonsdale, whose irregular love life was the subject, and Yates, accepting responsibility although he had not intended the paragraph to be published, was charged with criminal libel and sentenced to four months' imprisonment. The unexpectedly heavy sentence almost certainly owed as much to memories of his precocious insolence to Thackeray as to his relatively infrequent descents into muckraking in *The World*. He served only seven weeks of his sentence (16 January to 10 March 1885), but both his physical and mental health suffered and never fully recovered.

In 1886 Yates abandoned his lifelong allegiance to the Liberal Party and in 1889 was elected to the Carlton Club. He died at the Savoy Hotel on 20 May 1894, after suffering a seizure at the Garrick Theatre the night before. Following a funeral service in the Savoy chapel on 24 May, his body was cremated at Woking.   P. D. EDWARDS

Sources E. H. Yates, *Edmund Yates: his recollections and experiences*, 2 vols. (1884) · P. D. Edwards, *Dickens's 'young men'* (1997) · P. D. Edwards, *Edmund Yates: a bibliography* (1980) · T. H. S. Escott, *Masters of English journalism* (1911) · T. H. S. Escott, *Anthony Trollope: his public services, private friends and literary originals* (1913) · J. H. Wiener, *Papers for the millions: the new journalism in Britain, 1850s to 1914* (1988) **Archives** BL, diary, Add. MS 59871 · BL, MSS · Hunt. L., letters · Hunt. L., MSS · Princeton University Library, New Jersey, corresp. and papers · University of Queensland, Brisbane, MSS | BL, letters to T. H. S. Escott, Add. MS 58796 · BL, letters to Royal Literary Fund, loan 96 · BL, corresp. with William Archer, Add. MS 45297 · Hunt. L., E. S. Pigott MSS · NL Scot., letters to Blackwoods · U. Leeds, Brotherton L., letters, mostly to Bram Stoker **Likenesses** H. H. E.?, watercolour caricature, pubd 1884, NPG · J. Brown, stipple and line engraving (after photograph by A. Beau), NPG · Spy [L. Ward], chromolithograph, caricature, NPG; repro. in

VF (16 Nov 1878) • Walery, photograph, NPG • J. Watkins, carte-de-visite, NPG • J. & C. Watkins, carte-de-visite, NPG

Wealth at death £38,769 3*s*. 2*d*.: resworn probate, Dec 1894, *CGPLA Eng. & Wales*

Yates, Edward (1838–1907), builder, was born, probably at Ormskirk, in the second quarter of 1838, the son of Edward Yates, a gardener, and brother of John, of one of the many Lancashire working-class families of that name. He was a model example of the Victorian rags-to-riches success story. Starting as an almost penniless excavator on the barrack foundations at Aldershot in the early 1850s, this northerner established himself over the following half-century as one of the largest London suburban house-builders.

From a dozen houses at Nine Elms completed in 1867, Yates progressed in 1868–9 to build a whole street of forty-six houses, Dragon Road, Camberwell. With another builder, S. Sansom of Kennington, he formed a limited partnership in 1871 that lasted for seventeen years, initially to develop part of the ecclesiastical commissioners' Walworth estate. He also operated independently. Building primarily to let, and so in possession of a steady income, Yates progressively extended his business, little affected by the slumps in the London building industry, to reach a peak of about 150 houses a year in 1888 and 1889, when his mortgage indebtedness reached nearly a quarter of a million pounds, reduced to £1500 by 1903. North Lambeth, Newington Butts, Walworth, and Camberwell provided his field of operations, his largest and last single undertaking being the 50 acre Waverley Park estate at Nunhead, with some 700 houses, from 1884. Yates avoided the common error of building houses too expensive for a given locality, aiming at a lower middle-class market, with a prime cost usually of around £190–£350 for six- to eight-roomed houses, letting at from £26 to £38 per annum. After 1892 his output never exceeded a hundred houses per year, and there was a marked scaling down of his operations after 1896 despite the general increase in house-building in the late nineties.

Yates's significance lies in the extremely tight financial control that he exercised over his operations, so that, while sometimes operating on a profit margin as little as a half of one per cent, he was able to build up a fortune worth about a million pounds at his death. The two key aspects of this control were his raising of funds for land acquisition and building, and his developing a closely supervised system of housebuilding in quantity. The early developments on leasehold land at Nine Elms and in Camberwell were financed through a number of building societies, but he rapidly established contacts with a network of solicitors with clients ready to invest in housing speculations at 4½ or 5 per cent for a minimum of five years. Since he never sought more than about a 70 per cent loan, and frequently only 50 per cent of the property's market value, the risk was small. He was thus able to obtain money precisely when he needed it, rather than having to raise large sums in advance, so saving significantly on interest charges. By himself developing freehold land, as he preferred, he claimed that he was further able to cut costs significantly. He also reduced his need for borrowing by sales of land and property tangential (as in Blythe Road, Kensington) to his main south London interests in Lambeth, on the Walworth estates, and in Camberwell.

Yates sought also by such means as using the cheapest means of transporting materials, buying supplies in bulk (or manufacturing his own bricks) and checking deliveries, employing skilled labour at piece-rates, and establishing a site office linked to head office by telephone, to reduce building expenditure to the minimum requisite for the sort of substantial lower middle-class dwellings that were his staple. He built further down market than most of his peers, but supplied superior fittings, and charged rents lower than the norm, thereby ensuring high occupancy rates. Unlike the majority of speculative builders, he built for investment, retaining a very large stock of houses (2345 in 1905) in his own hands for renting, instead of selling them on completion to finance further work.

Conservative in outlook, Yates was active in the politics of his home parish, St George the Martyr, Southwark, conducting the successful candidacy of a tory, Colonel Marcus Beresford (a large local wharf-owner and employer of labour), in the Southwark parliamentary by-election of 1870 when the Liberal vote split between rival candidates. He tried to follow up this success by nominating a Conservative panel in the annual vestry elections, but his attempt to introduce 'party nonsense into parochial affairs' was 'tossed to the winds with scarcely a fragment of support' (*South London Press*, 14 May 1870, 9) by the £25 ratepayer electors. It was not until 1878 that he was himself elected vestryman, retiring in 1885. He was said to have shown both business ability and independence in that capacity, with an 'unflinching determination to keep down local expenditure, and to put an end to jobbery' (ibid., 12 Jan 1889). He himself paid for a local poll to prevent the Newington vestry's borrowing £20,000 to install electric street lighting in 1882. In 1889 he reluctantly stood for Walworth in the first London county council (LCC) elections, as essentially a ratepayers' candidate along with Payne, the fireworks manufacturer, against the predominant Progressives (Liberals), but finished fourth on poll.

Resolute in appearance, with high forehead and long, slightly upturned nose, at the time of his LCC candidacy Yates wore a beard without side-whiskers. He had in 1859 married Mary Ann Scarborough (*d*. 1889), a Plumstead baker's daughter. They had one son and five daughters. They appear to have lived very simply in Southwark, but the address Yates used was that of his builder's yard in Walworth Road. He acquired an early seventeenth-century farmhouse, Shore Hall, Cornish Hall End, Finchingfield, Essex, as a country home, and died there on 26 April 1907. By a will of 1895 his property was divided into unequal shares, held on trust for his children (three unmarried daughters receiving about 100 houses each), but in a codicil of June 1903 he effectively disinherited his second daughter, transferring her share to his son. Yates was buried alongside his wife in a family grave at Norwood cemetery.

M. H. PORT

Sources H. J. Dyos, *Victorian suburb* (1961) · H. J. Dyos, 'The speculative builders and developers of Victorian London', *Victorian Studies*, 11 (1967–8), 641–90 · H. J. Dyos, 'A Victorian speculative builder', *Exploring the urban past: essays in urban history*, ed. D. Cannadine and D. Reeder (1982) · 'Select committee on town holdings', *Parl. papers* (1887), 13.375–85, no. 260 [minutes of evidence] · private information (2004) · will of Edward Yates, Principal Registry of the Family Division, London · *South London Press* (1870) · *South London Press* (1889) · St George the Martyr, Southwark, vestry annual reports, 1865–95 · m. cert. · d. cert.
Likenesses F. M. Bennett, oils, 1913, Shore Hall, Cornish Hall End, Finchingfield, Essex · portrait, Geo. Yates Estate Office Ltd, 205 Walworth Road, London
Wealth at death £921,432 18s. 6d.: resworn probate, 12 Aug 1907, *CGPLA Eng. & Wales*

Yates [*née* Brunton], **Elizabeth** (1799–1860), actress, was born on 21 January 1799 at Norwich into a theatrical family. Her grandfather, John Brunton, acted at Covent Garden in 1774 and her father, also John Brunton (*b.* 1775), went on the stage in 1795 and became the manager of the Norfolk circuit. Her mother, Anna Brunton, *née* Ross (*b.* 1773), was the daughter of the actress Mrs J. Brown, formerly Mrs William Ross. Elizabeth was her second daughter. Her aunts, Anne Brunton and Louisa *Brunton, were also actresses. The latter married William Craven, first earl of Craven.

Elizabeth made her first appearance on 15 March 1815 at her father's theatre in King's Lynn, as Desdemona to the Othello of Charles Kemble, who regarded this as the most promising début he had ever seen. R. W. Elliston then engaged her for his theatre in Birmingham, where she played Letitia Hardy to his Doricourt in Hannah Cowley's *The Belle's Stratagem*. She also played in Worcester, Shrewsbury, and Leicester. Harris then took her on at Covent Garden, where on 12 September 1817 she made her first appearance in London, again as Letitia Hardy, followed by Rosalind in *As You Like It*. The *Theatrical Inquisitor* gave some praise to her Letitia but pronounced her Rosalind a failure. She played various parts during her first season, and on 29 September she was the original Rosalia in Reynolds's *The Duke of Savoy*. In 1818 she moved to Edinburgh, where she once more played Letitia Hardy. Then, back at Covent Garden for the 1818–19 season, she performed a great variety of parts, including an original role in *A Wood for the Ladies*, the first Jeanie Deans in Terry's adaptation of *The Heart of Midlothian*, and Emilia to her future husband's Iago. Next year, among other performances, she was the first Clothilde de Biron in Morton's *Henri Quatre* on 22 April 1822. When her contract at Covent Garden ended, as was usual, after three years, she toured the provinces and when her father took the West London theatre in Tottenham Street (later the Queen's and the Prince of Wales's) she joined him in 1822. After the failure of this venture she went once more into the provinces, and appeared in Bath on 23 April 1823 as Albina Mandeville in Reynolds's *The Will*. She continued there for the 1823–4 season, again in a wide repertory of roles.

On 3 November 1823 Elizabeth Brunton married, in Bath, Frederick Henry *Yates (1797–1842), of whom her family did not approve. She played with her husband at Cheltenham, where, it was said, she lost her reticule at the

races because she was so engrossed with him. On 29 October 1824 she made an appearance as Violante at Drury Lane. Her son, Edmund Hodgson *Yates, later the proprietor of *The World*, was born on 3 July 1831 during his parents' theatrical tour to Edinburgh. Further seasons at Drury Lane followed, in which Elizabeth Yates again played a variety of parts. In March 1839 she was at the Adelphi, in an adaptation of *Oliver Twist*. Her husband died suddenly in June 1842 and she at once assumed for a short time the management with Gladstane of her moiety of the Adelphi which her husband had purchased with Daniel Terry and managed with Charles Mathews and Gladstane. By the 1848–9 season she was at the Lyceum. She then retired from the stage. In 1858 Dickens wrote that it was a pleasure for him to have her attend his readings. She died after a long and painful illness, on 30 August 1860, at 2 Lower Craven Place, Kentish Town, London.

Elizabeth Yates was of middle size, graceful and attractive, with pleasant features, rather hard blue eyes, a dark complexion, beautiful teeth, and an infectious laugh. She sang with feeling though her voice was not more than adequate, and she danced delightfully.

JOSEPH KNIGHT, *rev.* J. GILLILAND

Sources Mrs C. Baron-Wilson, *Our actresses*, 2 vols. (1844) · W. C. Russell, *Representative actors* (1872) · *The Era* (9 Sept 1860) · E. H. Yates, *Edmund Yates: his recollections and experiences*, 2 vols. (1884) · ALA index · Hall, *Dramatic ports.* · d. cert. · *CGPLA Eng. & Wales* (1860)
Archives Theatre Museum, London, letter(s)
Likenesses Hopwood, engraving, repro. in *Ladies' Monthly Museum* (Nov 1817) · Kennerley, engraving, repro. in *Oxberry's Dramatic Biography*, vol. 5, p. 68 · Stump, miniature, repro. in Yates, *Edmund Yates* · T. Woolnoth, stipple (as Grace Huntley; after T. Wageman), BM; repro. in Cumberland, *British theatre* (1833) · eighteen portraits, Harvard TC · portrait, repro. in *Theatrical Magazine* (1818) · portrait, repro. in *Theatrical Times* (1846) · portrait, repro. in *La belle assemblée* (1817)
Wealth at death under £3000: probate, 19 Oct 1860, *CGPLA Eng. & Wales*

Yates, Dame Frances Amelia (1899–1981), historian, was born at Fairfax, Victoria Road North, Southsea, Hampshire, on 28 November 1899, the fourth and by ten years the youngest child of James Alfred Yates (1852–1941), of Portsmouth, naval architect, and his wife, Hannah Eliza, *née* Malpas (1856/7–1951). James Yates had entered Portsmouth Dockyard in 1866, aged fourteen; having retired in 1912 after taking an important part at Chatham (1893–5, 1902–6), Portsmouth (1895–1902), and the Clyde and Barrow districts (1906–12), in the shipbuilding programmes of Sir John Fisher, he was recalled to the Admiralty in 1916–18 for special duties.

Frances Yates had much of her early education at home, though she attended Laurel Bank School, Hillhead, Glasgow (1909–11); from 1913 to 1917 she was at Birkenhead high school, where the elder of her two sisters then taught. She never lost the impress of her observantly Anglican upbringing in an unostentatiously upright family, independent- and lively-minded, insistent on its own identity, and valuing highly industry and endeavour, Shakespeare, and France. Hopes for the youngest daughter intensified after the death in action of her only brother

(1915). Early determined to write, but disappointed in ambitions of Oxford, she took a first-class London external degree in French (1924), following it with an internal MA at University College on sixteenth-century French political drama (1926).

In 1925 the Yateses bought a newly built house in Claygate, Surrey, to which Frances Yates became much attached. It was her home and working base until death and her sisters, the first a minor novelist and second an artist and missionary, successively cared for the family and for her there. She never married. Combined family resources and a small legacy were just enough for her to pass fifteen years as a private scholar.

A chance find in the Public Record Office led to Frances Yates's first book, for which she also taught herself Italian and travelled in France, Switzerland, and Italy. *John Florio: the Life of an Italian in Shakespeare's England* (1934) won the British Academy's Rose Mary Crawshay prize and remains standard. Later, she regarded her second book, *A Study of 'Love's Labour's Lost'* (1936), as her weakest, finding its grasp of the meaning of the play inadequate. Though her response to sixteenth- and seventeenth-century French and English poetry, particularly that of Shakespeare and Spenser, was always vivid and perceptive, her preoccupations were already with the wider intellectual context, rather than the merely literary. Many of her later interests are present in these early books: religion and politics in Renaissance England and France, the influence of Italy and Italians on English life, the nature and role of a sixteenth-century academy, and more specifically the significance of the Italian philosopher Giordano Bruno, of whose *Cena delle ceneri* she then made an unpublished translation. Decisive for her development was her introduction (1936), through a fellow student of Bruno, Dorothea Waley Singer, to the staff and the collections of books and photographs in the newly arrived Warburg Institute. In 1941 she formally joined the Warburg part-time, becoming full-time lecturer and editor of publications in 1944, when the institute was incorporated in the University of London, reader in the history of the Renaissance in 1956, and, from her retirement in 1967, honorary fellow.

Behind three works published by the Warburg was Frances Yates's vision of great possibilities for universal peace in sixteenth-century Europe denied by the wars of religion. *The French Academies of the Sixteenth Century* (1947, 1988), pursuing ideas from *Love's Labour's Lost*, confirmed her standing among students of the Renaissance. It surveys in massive and recondite detail the academies' designs for a harmony of courtly, political, religious, philosophical, artistic, literary, and musical activity and for its use to eirenic ends. Her essay 'Queen Elizabeth as Astraea' (1947; republished 1975 with related papers) was a landmark in sympathetic history applied to royal ceremony and symbolism, to the celebration of the English monarch, and to manifestations of protestant imperial-messianic sentiment. The complicated narrative of *The Valois Tapestries* (1959, 1975) aimed to show how these woven records of court festivals in the 1560s and 1570s had

been ordered by William of Orange during the 1580s to influence French policy in the Netherlands.

In 1949 Frances Yates returned seriously to Giordano Bruno. Earlier articles had identified medieval elements in his religious sentiments, an unsuspected religious orientation of his Copernicanism, and influence from his philosophical poetry on English emblematic imagery. Now she approached him as system builder by way of the use in his Latin works of the medieval Majorcan philosopher Ramon Lull, whose universal combinatory 'art' linked natural and divine correspondences in order to command all knowledge. Having had to learn Catalan to work on Lull, she was past sixty-five before her revolutionary account *Giordano Bruno and the Hermetic Tradition* (1964) came out. It was the first considerable book on Bruno in English, bringing him and her to wider notice and, in its revaluation of Renaissance hermeticism, opening a new field of intellectual history. Her radically new reading, drawing attention to the role of Marsilio Ficino's translation of Hermes Trismegistus for Renaissance Neoplatonism, made of Bruno a Christian magus rather than a secular martyr to free thought. Seeing Bruno's reform of the heavens as significant in contemporary politics and the development of religious toleration, she proposed a complicated model for the relation of his cosmological beliefs to scientific thought. The so-called Yates thesis has been much disputed. Her originality was again apparent in *The Art of Memory* (1966), in some ways her most influential and her best book, demonstrating how a Roman rhetorical device to strengthen the natural memory profoundly influenced medieval and Renaissance verbal composition and was given a universal dimension by Lull and Bruno.

Among Frances Yates's ambitions was a definitive work on Shakespeare's thought. If none of her four final works, all designed ultimately to shed light on him, is completely successful, all are typically and excitingly unorthodox in discerning occult as well as classical and vernacular ideological substrata in the architectural theory, drama, religion, and politics of the day. *Theatre of the World* (1969) aimed at proving influence from the Vitruvian tradition on the building of Elizabethan public theatres. In *The Rosicrucian Enlightenment* (1972) and *Shakespeare's Last Plays: a New Approach* (1975; Northcliffe lectures, 1974) she investigated politics and drama in the reign of James I, in relation especially to the origins and diffusion of Rosicrucianism and an attempted revival of the Elizabethan imperial idea. *The Occult Philosophy in the Elizabethan Age* (1979), an impressionistic restatement of dominant themes from her later work, is the least satisfactory. Three collections of her essays and reviews (*Lull and Bruno*, for which she had made the selection; *Renaissance and Reform: the Italian Contribution*; and *Ideas and Ideals in the North European Renaissance*) were published posthumously in 1982, 1983, and 1984.

In 1965 Frances Yates was made a London University DLitt. She was awarded honorary degrees of DLitt from Edinburgh (1969), Oxford (1970), East Anglia (1971), Exeter (1971), and Warwick universities (1981). At Oxford, too, she was honorary fellow of Lady Margaret Hall and Ford lecturer (both 1970). She won the senior Wolfson history prize (1973) and the Premio Galileo Galilei (1978). Elected FBA in 1967, she was also a foreign member of the American (1975) and Royal Netherlands (1980) academies of arts and sciences. In 1972 she was appointed OBE and in 1977 DBE.

Frances Yates's unselfconsciously magisterial presence was offset by charm and a sort of grand dishevelment. By nature she was diffident, unworldly, and idealistic, but her seriousness and candour, combined with confidence in her interpretations, made her an effective and invigorating public lecturer. She wrote copiously and clearly, basing herself on the laborious, single-minded research that above all engaged and elated her. Never backward in rejecting received academic opinion, she was unperturbed by criticism from the 'Eng. lit.' or the hard-headed historical side. She achieved almost cult status in her later years and has been widely translated. Her aim was always to align herself with the thoughts and intentions of those she studied, to consider ideas, beliefs, motivations, and actions according to their contemporary relevance and effect, as a vast acquaintance with primary sources allowed her to do, rather than to assess them in modern terms. In thus reconstructing the historical moment, she owed much to Warburgian disregard for disciplinary boundaries and to the aid of her Warburg mentors, though her history was always recognizably her own, original, adventurous, and humane as well as encyclopaedic, her province concept and symbol as well as fact and event, aspiration as well as realization.

Frances Yates died on 29 September 1981 in Langley Nursing Home, Langley Avenue, Surbiton, Surrey; after cremation on 5 October at Leatherhead, Surrey, her ashes were buried in the grave of her second sister, Ruby W. Yates, in the churchyard of Holy Trinity Church, Claygate, Surrey. She left the bulk of her estate to found research scholarships at the Warburg Institute, where her books and papers are preserved.   J. B. TRAPP

Sources F. A. Yates, 'Autobiographical fragments', *Ideas and ideals in the north European Renaissance*, ed. J. N. Hillgarth and J. B. Trapp (1984), vol. 3 of *Collected essays*, 275–322 [from Yates MSS, U. Lond., Warburg Institute] · A. Barlow and J. Perkins, 'List of the writings of F. A. Y.', *Ideas and ideals in the north European Renaissance*, ed. J. N. Hillgarth and J. B. Trapp (1984), vol. 3 of *Collected Essays*, 325–36 · Yates MSS, U. Lond., Warburg Institute [MSS of writings, letters, diaries, personal papers] · U. Lond., Warburg Institute, *Frances A. Yates, 1899–1981* (1982) · personal knowledge (2004) · J. A. Yates, 'From wooden walls to Dreadnoughts in a lifetime', ed. R. W. Yates, *Mariner's Mirror*, 48 (1962), 291–303 [autobiographical notes; original in Yates MSS, U. Lond., Warburg Institute]
Archives U. Lond., Warburg Institute, corresp. and papers
Likenesses photographs, U. Lond., Warburg Institute, Yates archive · photographs, U. Lond., Warburg Institute, Yates archive; repro. in *Frances A. Yates*, Warburg Institute
Wealth at death £237,200: probate, 11 March 1982, *CGPLA Eng. & Wales*

Yates, Frank (1902–1994), statistical scientist, was born on 12 May 1902 in Didsbury, Manchester, the only son and eldest of the five children of Percy Yates (*c*.1870–*c*.1935), seed merchant, and his wife, Edith (*d*. 1958), daughter of Frank Wright, corn and seed merchant of Ashbourne, Derbyshire. An uncle's gift of a table of five-figure logarithms led to the young, precocious Yates becoming interested in mathematics. He gained a scholarship to Clifton College, which he attended from 1916 to 1920, and from where he went, with a senior mathematics scholarship, to St John's College, Cambridge. He graduated among the wranglers of 1924.

Employment opportunities for young mathematicians were few, but several years as a schoolmaster soon showed Yates's need for more practical stimuli than came from teaching differential calculus to the uninterested. In 1927 he joined the geodetic survey of the Gold Coast (now Ghana) as a research officer. Here began a deep appreciation of Gaussian least squares, and a lifelong love of the slide rule and other aids to efficient, well-organized, and accurate arithmetic. Health problems obliged Yates to return permanently to England. On 2 November 1929 in Lancaster, he married Margaret Forsythe Marsden (*b*. 1904/5), an analytical chemist and daughter of John William Marsden, a civil servant. Chance brought a meeting with Ronald Aylmer Fisher (1890–1962), whose revolutionary impact on statistical theory and practice was then at its peak. After a very informal interview Fisher engaged Yates (in August 1931) as a mathematician in his department at Rothamsted Experimental Station. Although Yates's family background had given him some insight into agricultural matters, his assimilation into agricultural research was rapid. He showed tremendous aptitude for the combinatorial aspects of experimental design. The Fisher–Yates association became both a deep personal friendship and a powerful research combination. Together they proved (in 1934) the ancient conjecture that no 6 x 6 Graeco-Latin square exists. Yates's own remarkably influential monograph on factorial design (published in 1937) contains the first instance of the subsequently overused practice of indicating levels of statistical significance by asterisks. His name is perhaps better known for the continuity correction (published in 1934) that has become standard practice in the analysis of 2 x 2 contingency tables.

In 1933, even before these seminal publications, Yates succeeded Fisher as head of Rothamsted's statistics department, a position in which he was to remain until 1968. Two important papers in 1936 typify his mastery in producing new systems of experimental design. These introduced several types of incomplete block design, well matched to the needs of comparing new crop varieties and of studying alternative crop rotations; features of these have influenced experimentation throughout biology and industrial technology. So influential was Rothamsted thought on all quantitative experimentation that in 1953 Sir Harold Jeffreys could tell the British Association: 'the standard of presentation of results in agriculture is better than in any of the so-called exact sciences' (Yates and Finney, 219).

One of the finest products of Fisher–Yates collaboration was their volume of statistical tables (1936), a model of compositor's art and a friend to all statistical scientists. A by-product of Yates's work on factorial design was an elegant algorithm that later proved important to the development of fast Fourier transforms. When invited to explain how he devised this procedure, he replied characteristically: 'Well, it's absolutely obvious isn't it?' (private information).

Yates's first marriage ended in divorce in 1933. On 14 July 1939 he married Prascovie (Pauline) Tchitchkine (d. 1976), the divorced wife of Alexis Tchitchkine and daughter of Vladimir Choubersky, a railway engineer. Shortly after the marriage, with the outbreak of the Second World War, the change in Yates's personal life was mirrored by changes in his research. He began with what would later be termed a metanalysis. He compiled all available experimental evidence on the responses of food crops to fertilizers, undertook a critical synthesis, and assessed the benefits to food supplies to be expected from wise use of fertilizer imports; this became a basis for national policy on imports in the face of the submarine menace. Friendship with Sir Solly Zuckerman led Yates to become a special consultant on allied bombing policy and assessments of its effectiveness, a type of study later to become popular in industry under the name of operational research.

After 1945 Yates's energy, determination, and earthiness made Rothamsted a world-renowned centre for research in agriculturally oriented statistical science and especially in the new field of statistical computing. Indeed, his earthiness made him, a man without formal training in agriculture or biology, a very successful deputy director of Rothamsted from 1958 to 1968. His tall, handsome figure was familiar to all as that of a colleague always prepared to help dispose of a difficulty. Though his interest in innovatory experimental design continued, it was now overshadowed by concern for the practice of sample survey. This was initially driven by a wartime need for estimation of national timber supplies, and by his own efforts to learn how farmers use fertilizers. He was one of the earliest members of the United Nations Sub-Commission on Statistical Sampling. His work with the UN led him to publish *Sampling Methods for Censuses and Surveys* (1949; 4th edn 1981), a work which did much to establish sound principles and technical terminology.

Yates's early experience in surveying led him to extend Fisher's tradition of well-planned statistical arithmetic and, ultimately, to become a pioneer of electronic computing. In 1954 he brought an early Elliott computer to the handling of Rothamsted's growing load of statistical analyses. He had to cope with programming for primitive hardware dependent upon the vagaries of thermionic valves and storage on a magnetic drum, but he saw from the start the need for the generality of structure and applicability which, by the 1990s, had become the mark of major software packages. He played a leading part in the creation and extension of the British Computer Society, of which he was president in 1960–61. He also provided much help to developing countries in respect of statistical and computing needs for agricultural research.

During his long career Yates received many honours. He was elected FRS in 1948, received the Guy medal of the Royal Statistical Society in 1960 (he was president of the society in 1967–8), and was appointed CBE in 1963. In 1966 he was awarded a royal medal of the Royal Society. In 1978 he received an honorary DSc from the University of London. He was the author of more than 150 scientific publications, ranging widely over statistical methodology and its applications. From retirement to the end he remained professionally very active, especially in producing software and as an editor of the *Journal of Agricultural Science*; for this last he did much to encourage the enlightening use of statistical procedures and clear presentation of their logic. He died on 17 June 1994 in hospital in Harpenden, and was survived by his third wife, Ruth, formerly Hunt (d. 1999), whom he had married in 1981 following the death of his second wife in 1976. DAVID J. FINNEY

Sources D. J. Finney, *Memoirs FRS*, 41 (1995), 555–73 · F. Yates and D. J. Finney, 'Statistics and computing in agricultural research', *Agricultural research, 1931–1981: a history of the Agricultural Research Council and a review of developments in agricultural science during the last fifty years* (1981), 219–36 · private information (2004) · personal knowledge (2004) · b. cert. · m. cert. [Prascovie Tchitchkine] · m. cert. [Margaret Forsythe Marsden] · d. cert.
Archives CUL, corresp. with Gordon Sutherland | SOUND BL NSA, performance recording
Likenesses photograph, repro. in Finney, *Memoirs FRS*
Wealth at death £594,930: probate, 12 Aug 1994, *CGPLA Eng. & Wales*

Yates, Frederick Dewhurst (1884–1932), chess player and journalist, was born plain Fred Yates at Huddersfield Road, Birstall, near Leeds, on 16 January 1884, the son of John Thomas Yates, a mechanical fitter, and his wife, Ada Ellen, *née* Dewhurst. On leaving Birstall Wesleyan day school in 1898 he took employment in the accounts department of the Birstall district council. In 1901 he moved to London, seeking work as a freelance journalist, with modest results. By 1905 he was back in Yorkshire, and his chess career began. He was not a born chess genius, but achieved his status by diligence. In 1906 he barely scraped into the Yorkshire team, but by 1909 he had become the county champion and made his first appearance in the British championship, held that year in Scarborough. He tied with Joseph Henry Blackburne for the fourth prize. Blackburne, near the end of his career, was the only English player to make a living solely from chess in the nineteenth century, and now Yates decided to follow the same path.

In 1910 Yates played in his first international tournament, held at Hamburg. The leading German player Dr Tarrasch objected to Yates's presence on the grounds that he was not yet strong enough. The only win Yates scored there was against Tarrasch. This is an early example of an aspect of Yates's character—a strengthening of resolve when under fire. In 1913 Yates won the first of six British championships (1913, 1914, 1921, 1926, 1928, 1931), and also his first prize in a foreign event. Perhaps because of his frail physique and nervous disposition Yates did not serve in the First World War, but in the post-war decade his career reached its peak. By then the emphasis of his play had shifted from violent tactics to subtle positional manoeuvring.

Between 1919 and 1932 Yates played in almost sixty international tournaments. Although he never quite reached the highest level, he defeated all the leading players with the exception of Capablanca and Lasker, two of the four world champions he met. A curious feature was that the better the opposition the stronger his game became. Against weaker opponents his play could be lacklustre and careless. Perhaps his best performances in grandmaster tournaments were at San Remo in 1930, when he was fifth out of sixteen, and at Carlsbad in 1923, when he won six games, drew seven, and lost four. He was awarded a special brilliancy prize there for his defeat of the future world champion Alekhine.

In many events Yates played under the serious disadvantage of also working as a journalist covering the whole competition. Some experts consider this to be equivalent to giving the odds of a pawn in each game. His reports and weekly chess columns appeared in the *Manchester Guardian*, *Daily Telegraph*, *Yorkshire Evening Post*, and *Yorkshire Weekly Post*. With his close friend William Winter, Yates wrote three books; two covered each of the world championship matches of 1927 and 1928, and the third was *Modern Master Play* (1929). Having begun an autobiographical work, *One-Hundred-and-One of my Best Games of Chess*, Yates was found dead from gas poisoning on 11 November 1932. Last seen alive at midnight on 9 November, he did not emerge from his room at 32 Coram Street, St Pancras, London, on the 10th, and his door was forced on the 11th. He was buried five days later at Birstall. The autobiography was completed by William Winter and published in 1934.

A great conversationalist over a wide range of topics, Yates enjoyed convivial company late into the night. Some disliked his bohemian lifestyle and false rumours spread, never to stop completely, that he had taken his own life. At the inquest on 15 November a gas company employee demonstrated that the tap was turned off and that a faulty fitting of an obsolete type had caused the gas leak. A verdict of accidental death was returned. As the nearest relatives, two sisters, were almost penniless, the costs of Yates's funeral and his debts to his landlady were met by the chess world. In those lean days it was not possible for a British chess professional to have a wife, family, or home.

Emanuel Lasker, world champion for a record twenty-seven years, said of Yates:

> At first he went unnoticed but very soon one awoke to the fact that he was intensely likeable and before long his great moral power became evident. He never indulged in intrigue, he never pushed himself to the fore, he never quarrelled. Cheerfully going his very straight way, ready, if need be, to undergo privations, he never did aught contrary to his self-respect. (Yates and Winter, 22–3)

KEN WHYLD

Sources F. D. Yates and W. Winter, *One-hundred-and-one of my best games of chess* (1934) · *The Times* (12 Nov 1932) · *The Times* (16 Nov 1932) · *The Times* (17 Nov 1932) · *Manchester Guardian* (12 Nov 1932) · *Yorkshire Weekly Post* (19 Nov 1932) · *British Chess Magazine* (1932) · D. Hooper and K. Whyld, *The Oxford companion to chess*, 2nd edn (1992) · b. cert. · d. cert.
Likenesses photograph, repro. in *British Chess Magazine* (1913), 36 · photograph, repro. in Yates and Winter, *One-hundred-and-one of*

my best games, frontispiece · photograph, repro. in *Yorkshire Weekly Post*, 4
Wealth at death he died in debt

Yates, Frederick Henry (1797–1842), actor and theatre manager, the youngest son of Thomas Yates, a tobacco manufacturer, of Thames Street and Russell Square, London, was born on 4 February 1797. He was educated at a preparatory school at Winchmore Hill, near Enfield, where he met John Reeve, his subsequent associate, and at Charterhouse under Drs Raine and Russell. He entered the commissariat department, and was with Wellington in the Peninsular War and possibly at Waterloo. After the peace he went to a fancy ball in the character of Somno, a part played by the elder Charles *Mathews, whom he met at that event; in the winter of 1817–18 Yates accompanied him to France.

Mathews was to have a great influence on his career. At Mathews's advice, Yates chose the stage as a profession. He made his first appearance during this trip, at Boulogne, in Richard Suett's part of Fustian in Colman's *Sylvester Daggerwood* to the Sylvester Daggerwood of his companion. On 16 February 1818, at Edinburgh, he created the part of Helgent in a tragedy called *The Appeal*. On 21 February he played Shylock, on the 26th Iago, on 13 March Richard III, on 16 March Bolingbroke to Edmund Kean's Richard II, on 6 April Jaques, and on 20 April gave for his benefit Richard III and Actor of all Work. In the summer he was seen as Buskin in *Killing No Murder*, gave imitations after the style of Mathews, and sang 'The Mail Coach'. This last was his first essay in a line in which he was later to win a reputation as an 'ingenious mimic'.

On 7 November 1818, as 'Yates from Edinburgh', Yates made his first appearance at Covent Garden, playing Iago to the Othello of Charles Young, the Cassio of Charles Kemble, the Desdemona of Eliza O'Neill, and the Emilia of Elizabeth Brunton, whom he later married. His performance was received with much favour, and he returned to continue an unfinished engagement in Edinburgh. He arrived on 4 December, and on 6 January 1819 played Falstaff in *The Merry Wives of Windsor*. Back in London before the season was over, he made his second appearance at Covent Garden on 13 April as Falstaff in *1 Henry IV*, in which he created a favourable impression. Gloster in Nicholas Rowe's *Jane Shore* followed, and on 12 May Yates was the first Berthold in Maturin's *Fredolfo*. On 23 June, for his benefit, with other entertainments he played Shylock and gave, as Dick in *The Apprentice*, imitations of Young, John Emery, Samuel Simmons, Kean, Kemble, Joseph Munden, William Blanchard, Mathews, and Master Betty.

The season of 1819–20 saw Yates as Macduff, Boniface in *The Beaux' Stratagem*, and, for his benefit, Richard III 'after his own manner'. In a revival of *The Manager in Distress* he was Gentleman 'on the stage and in the boxes', and gave further imitations. The next season, 1820–21, he was the Apothecary in *Romeo and Juliet*, Buckingham in *Richard III*, the first Peregrine Plural in *London Stars, or, 'Twas Time to Counterfeit*—a one-act piece written to suit his eccentricities—an original part in *Grand Tour, or, Stopped at Rochester*,

Moses in *The School for Scandal*, Cato the Censor in a burlesque called *State Secrets, or, Public Men in Private Life* (12 June), and Matthew Sharpset in Thomas Morton's *The Slave*. He also played an original part with W. C. Macready in *The Huguenot* (11 December 1822).

Yates remained at Covent Garden until the close of the 1824–5 season, playing a great many roles, including original creations such as Ranald of the Mist in Pocock's *Montrose, or, The Children of the Mist* (14 February 1822), Mordecai in Charles Macklin's *Love à la Mode*, and Skylark in Peake's *The Duel* (18 February 1823). He also took the principal part in *Tea and Turn out* (with imitations) on 28 May. He was announced to appear at Vauxhall on 24 July 1822 in an entertainment written for him by 'a most eminent and favourite author', to be called *Hasty Sketches, or, Vauxhall Scenery*, but he broke his leg at rehearsal on the day of performance. He subsequently gave this entertainment at Brighton. He had fallen in public estimation when his Cornet Carmine in Croly's *Pride Shall have a Fall* restored him to favour. In this piece the conduct of the 10th hussars was satirized, and the allusions to well-known proceedings on their part caught the town. Yates also appeared in a piece no longer traceable, called *The Boyhood and Old Age of Mr Yates*. He married Elizabeth Brunton [see Yates, Elizabeth (1799–1860)], the daughter of the manager of Exeter, Plymouth, and Weymouth theatres, at Bath on 30 November 1823. Their son, Edmund Hodgson *Yates, wrote several pieces which were given at London theatres.

In March 1825 the Adelphi Theatre was purchased for the sum of £25,000 by Daniel Terry and Yates. They opened it on 10 October with a drama called *Killigrew*, in which both of them appeared, together with Benjamin Wrench, John Reeve, and Fanny Elizabeth Fitzwilliam. The first season was a success, its most conspicuous feature being Fitzball's adaptation of *The Pilot* (31 October 1825), which was played for 200 nights. T. P. Cooke was Long Tom Coffin, Terry the Pilot, and Yates Barnstable. The theatre reopened with *The Pilot* and Buckstone's *Luke the Labourer*, followed in December by Fitzball's *The Flying Dutchman*, with Yates as Toby Varnish. *Thirty Years of a Gambler's Life* and *Paris and London* were also given. Terry's financial embarrassments led to his retirement from the partnership and eventual death in 1829, and the theatre opened on 29 September 1825 under the management of Charles Mathews and Yates. In *The Earthquake*, by Fitzball, Mrs Yates appeared at the Adelphi, Yates himself playing Dr Kallibos. In Fitzball's *The Red Rover*, given in 1828 and revived in 1831, he was the Red Rover, and in the revival of *The Floating Beacon*, by the same author, he was Angerstoff, captain of the beacon. Mathews and Yates also gave a joint entertainment. In Buckstone's *Wreck Ashore* (21 October 1830) Yates was Miles Bertram. In *Henriette the Forsaken* of the same author he was Ferdinand de Monval; in his *Victorine* (October 1832) Alexandre; and in his *Isabelle* (27 January 1834) Eugène le Marc. He had also been seen as Rip van Winkle, Alfred in Mathews's *Truth*, and in Holl's *Grace Huntley* and other pieces, and had given what he called 'Lenten entertainments'. At the Surrey, on 26 May 1834, he was the first Black Walter in Fitzball's *Tom Cringle*. In 1835

Yates played, at the Adelphi, Robert Macaire in a version of *L'auberge des Adrets*.

The death of Mathews, on 28 June 1835, was followed by the retirement of Yates, who for one season stage-managed Drury Lane for Alfred Bunn. In October 1836 the Adelphi opened under the sole management of Yates, who was seen in numerous roles there until in March 1842 he delivered an address at the close of the season. This was the last time he was seen in London.

Yates had in 1827 given in Edinburgh *Yates's Reminiscences*, and had been partner with William Henry Murray in 1830–31 in the management of the Caledonian Theatre, later renamed the Adelphi, in Leith Walk. Here he played Mazeppa, in which he had been seen in London, and other parts. With John Braham he managed in 1835 the Colosseum in Regent's Park, but, fortunately for himself, was bought out. Gladstane was his partner in 1841 in the management of the Adelphi, and the same two partners undertook the management of the Pavilion, from which Yates soon retired. While playing, in the winter of 1841–2, in a piece called *Agnes St Aubyn* he broke a blood vessel, having broken one previously while acting Robert Macaire. He went in 1842 to Dublin, and, while rehearsing Lord Skindeep in Jerrold's *Bubbles of the Day*, again broke a blood vessel. After a long confinement in Dublin, he reached the Euston Hotel, London, and was moved to a furnished house, 4 Mornington Crescent, Hampstead Road, where he died on 21 June 1842. He was buried on 26 June in the vaults of the church of St Martin-in-the-Fields.

In his early career Yates took a place among regular comedians, and even attempted tragic characters. The chief feature in his acting was his versatility. After he came into the management of the Adelphi he chose more eccentric parts, but would take any part that was vacant. Macready speaks of him in the disparaging tone not uncommon in dealing with associates or rivals. Yates was, however, a sound actor in a line of parts extending from Richard III and Shylock through Falstaff to Moses and Mordecai. As a manager he was full of tact and resource, but was extremely irritable.

JOSEPH KNIGHT, rev. KATHARINE COCKIN

Sources *The biography of the British stage, being correct narratives of the lives of all the principal actors and actresses* (1824) · *Oxberry's Dramatic Biography*, 5/71 (1826) · Hall, *Dramatic ports.* · E. H. Yates, *Edmund Yates: his recollections and experiences*, 2 vols. (1884) · *The Era* (26 June 1842) · *Dramatic and Musical Review*, 1 (1842), 5217.b · O. W. Hewett, *Strawberry fair: a biography of Frances, Countess Waldegrave, 1821–1879* (1956)
Archives Harvard U., Houghton L., corresp. relating to Adelphi Theatre | Som. ARS, letters to John Braham
Likenesses W. Say, mezzotint, pubd 1826 (after J. Lonsdale), BM · Ambrose, portrait; formerly in the possession of his son, Edmund Yates, 1900 · R. Cruikshank, coloured etching (as M. Grimacier in *Cozening*), BM · Deighton, watercolour sketch; formerly in the possession of his son, Edmund Yates, 1900 · J. Lonsdale, oils, Garr. Club · fifteen portraits, Harvard TC · oils, Garr. Club · portrait; formerly in the possession of J. L. Parkinson, 1900

Yates, James (*fl.* 1578–1582), poet, was the author of *The Castell of Courtesie*. No direct archival evidence survives concerning his life, but his one published volume preserves some details and permits one to work backwards from 1582. Yates was a serving man by profession, and he dedicated his book to his patrons and employers Henry and Elizabeth Reynolds, almost certainly the Henry Reynolds (d. 1587) of Belstead, Suffolk, and his wife, Elizabeth (b. 1553), daughter of Edmund Withypoll of Ipswich (Corder, 292). He had been in this couple's service at least since 1578, the year of their marriage, but there is evidence to suggest that before that date he was a family retainer to the Withypolls. Edmund Withypoll (c.1514–1582) was a wealthy merchant, educated by Thomas Lupset, who built Christchurch or Withypoll House in Ipswich. He had married, about 1535, Elizabeth Hynde, daughter of a London mercer, and they had eleven sons and eight daughters. It is likely that Yates served this family.

One of Yates's poems is an elegy on the death, in 1575, of Anne Wentworth Poley, wife of John Poley of Badley, Suffolk, identifying her further as the sister of 'my Lady Wentworth': Anne Poley is known to have had eight sisters, of whom Dorothy was the wife of Paul Withypoll, Edmund's oldest child (Corder, 168). Also interesting in this connection are the poems to 'Mr P. W.', one sent to Cambridge, referring to the father's interventions in the case of the disorderly behaviour there of 'Master B.' (Castell of Courtesie, 18): it is very tempting to read these poems in terms of the Cambridge careers of Paul and Bartholomew Withypoll, since the latter seems to have led a notably riotous life (Moore Smith, 55). Thus they would have to date to before Bartholomew's death in 1573. Another poem, 'In the Commendation of a Godly and Vertuous Matron', refers to the gentlewoman in question as 'the Hinde', and therefore seems to be referring to Elizabeth Hynde Withypoll (d. 1584). In any case, it is clear that the lyrics in Yates's production were composed over a number of years. No other Yates poems are known, nor is there any evidence as to what happened to him after 1582. He is not named in Henry Reynolds's will.

The castell of courtesie, whereunto is adjoyned The holde of humilitie: with The chariot of chastity thereunto annexed, was entered on the Stationers' register on 7 June 1582. Three copies are known to survive. J. P. Collier's cataloguing of a separate publication entitled 'The Holde of Humilitie' turns out to derive from one of these, a copy of *The Castell of Courtesie* lacking its opening sheets (Corser, 11.432).

The publication comprises three long allegorical vision-poems named in the title, which concretize the attributes of courtesy, humility, and chastity. Accompanying them are a large number of shorter pieces, dialogues, moral meditations, and occasional verse (for instance, on the 1580 earthquake). Many of them are eulogies of or addresses to members of the Withypoll family. The most interesting poems, including 'Given unto Mistresse F.W. when shee Went to Waite' and 'He Being very Sicke, and Finding Greate Courtesie at his Betters Hands, thereupon Writeth', explore aspects of the master–servant relationship.

Yates's technically unsophisticated prosody, and his tendency to restate truisms, have meant that his work has never attracted much critical attention. However, it is more interesting than it might seem: while much Elizabethan poetry explores the topic of service, Yates is unusual, indeed almost unique, in doing so explicitly from the point of view of a 'servingman'.

MATTHEW STEGGLE

Sources G. C. Moore Smith, *The family of Withypoll*, rev. P. H. Reaney (1936) · W. Hervey, *The visitation of Suffolk, 1561*, ed. J. Corder, 2 vols., Harleian Society, new ser., 2–3 (1981–4) · T. Corser, *Collectanea Anglo-poetica, or, A … catalogue of a … collection of early English poetry*, 11, Chetham Society, 111 (1883)

Yates, James (1789–1871), Unitarian minister and scholar, was born in Toxteth Park, Liverpool, on 30 April 1789, the fourth son of John *Yates (1755–1826) and his wife, Elizabeth (1749–1819), youngest daughter of John Brooks Ashton of Liverpool, and widow of John *Bostock (1744?–1774). Joseph Brooks *Yates was his brother and John *Bostock (1772–1846) was his half-brother. His father was minister (1777–1823) of the dissenting congregation in Kaye Street and later in Paradise Street, Liverpool.

After receiving his early training from William Shepherd, James Yates entered the University of Glasgow in 1805, and for his divinity course enrolled in Manchester College, York, in 1808. In 1809–10, while still a student, he acted as assistant classical tutor, pending the arrival of John Kenrick. From York in 1810 he went to the University of Edinburgh, and returned to Glasgow in 1811, graduating MA the next year. In 1811 he became the unordained minister of a Unitarian congregation in Glasgow, for which a new chapel was opened on 15 November 1812 in Union Place. He was a solid, didactic, and unimpassioned preacher, but his industry, earnestness, and forceful character helped to create a stable congregation out of previously discordant elements. On 23 July 1813, with Thomas Southwood Smith, then minister in Edinburgh, he founded the Scottish Unitarian Association.

In 1814 Ralph Wardlaw, an Independent minister in Edinburgh, delivered a series of pulpit addresses published as *Discourses on the Principal Points of the Socinian Controversy* (1814). Yates had heard the addresses as delivered, and, when they appeared in print, published his *Vindication of Unitarianism* (1815). Wardlaw replied with *Unitarianism Incapable of Vindication* (1816), to which Yates rejoined in *A Sequel* (1816). His position was one of greater breadth than was usual with theologians of his school, his aim being to take common ground on which Arians and Socinians could agree, despite their differences on the divinity or humanity of Christ. When the *Vindication* reached a fourth edition in 1850, Charles Wicksteed, a leader in the 'new school' of Unitarian thought, recognized (in the *Prospective Review* of 1851) the power of Yates's scholarship, but noted the biblical conservatism, which Yates never abandoned, as belonging to another age.

On 6 April 1817 Yates succeeded Joshua Toulmin as colleague to John Kentish at New Meeting, Birmingham. He resigned at the end of 1825, and for a time left the ministry, residing at Norton Hall, near Sheffield, the seat of the Unitarian magnates the Shores. In 1827 he spent a semester at the University of Berlin studying classical philology. In 1819 he was elected a fellow of the Geological Society, in

1822 of the Linnean Society, and in 1831 of the Royal Society. In the same year he was appointed secretary to the council of the British Association, a key post bridging provincial and metropolitan science which he resigned in 1841 when his inveterate liberalism seemed at odds with the tory and Anglican dominance of the association.

In 1832 Yates succeeded John Scott Porter as minister of Carter Lane Chapel, Doctors' Commons, London. In 1833 he issued proposals for an organization of the Unitarian congregations of Great Britain on the presbyterian model; the plan was abortive, though it was supported by some weighty names, including John Relly Beard (1800–1876), Joseph Hunter, and John James Tayler. In the long progress of the Hewley case through the courts, Sir Lancelot Shadwell had severely condemned the *Improved Version of the New Testament* issued by the Unitarians in 1808. Yates wrote *A Letter to the Vice-Chancellor* (1834) defending the version, which produced a very able reply by the influential Congregationalist minister and teacher Robert Halley. Yates's congregation was considerably enlarged by a secession in September 1834 from South Place Chapel, Finsbury, provoked by the irregular domestic arrangements of the minister, William Johnson Fox (1786–1864). Disliking this increase in responsibility, Yates resigned early in the following year. He remained a member of the presbyterian section of the general body of ministers of the three denominations, and when other Unitarians seceded in 1836 Yates retained his connection with the general body. He soon left the ministry and, being unordained, gave up using the title Reverend. His interest in denominational history and controversy was unabated. From 1831 to 1861 he served as a trustee of Dr Williams's foundations, among other great services introducing the system of competitive examinations for scholarships. A manuscript containing 186 biographies of students at Glasgow on Dr Williams's foundation, compiled by him, was presented to Dr Williams's Library by his widow.

In 1841 Yates's old Glasgow congregation appointed as minister a former Congregationalist, John Taylor (1812–1853), whose extreme views quickly divided his hearers. In refusing a demand to resign in 1844, Taylor cited not only the closeness of the vote (37 to 34 against him) but the centrality of free enquiry as Yates had set it out in his inaugural sermon; the trustees borrowed £150 to ease Taylor's departure, eventually into journalism. Yates, who had long served as a trustee and was, of course, a regular target for solicitation of funds, thought Taylor's views were 'deistical', but he was even more distressed by H. W. Crosskey, who became minister in 1852. The founders and donors, Yates said in letters of 2 August 1854 and 15 April 1859, had found authority for the religion of Jesus Christ not only in his life and doctrines but in his miracles and resurrection. Crosskey clearly belonged to those new thinkers of the past thirty years who not only departed from older believers but, as at a recent meeting in Liverpool, abused them as 'owls, bats, and moles'—certainly a sticking point with Yates, though he pleaded financial reverses as his reason for declining further contributions. It is hardly surprising, therefore, that in 1866 Yates was one of a minority of three to support the motion by Samuel Bache to limit membership in the British and Foreign Unitarian Association to those who shared the beliefs of the association's founders in 1825, beliefs that he had so brilliantly vindicated ten years earlier.

Except for Leonhard Schmitz, Yates was the largest contributor to the *Dictionary of Greek and Roman Antiquities* (1842) edited by William Smith (1813–1893); he supplied drawings for one-half of the woodcuts and wrote one-eighth of the text. His *Textrinum antiquorum* (1843), of which only the first part, with valuable appendices, was published, illustrates the minuteness and accuracy of his research. Numerous papers on archaeological subjects were contributed by him to the learned societies of London and Liverpool, and he became a strong advocate of the decimal system.

About 1820 Yates had married Dorothea (*d*. 1884), daughter of John William Crompton of Edgbaston, Birmingham; there were no children. With his inherited wealth he passed his later years in learned leisure at Lauderdale House, Highgate, Middlesex, where he had a fine library and a valuable collection of works of art. Though his own habits were simple, he was noted for his extensive hospitality, and his conversation, aided by a marvellous memory, was deeply interesting. He was small in stature with a courtly dignity in his bearing; his power of caustic remark was all the more effective, given the unvarying calmness of his measured speech. He died at Lauderdale House on 7 May 1871, and was buried at Highgate cemetery on 11 May. His will left considerable benefactions, including endowments for chairs in University College, London, but his property did not realize the estimated amount.

ALEXANDER GORDON, rev. R. K. WEBB

Sources DNB · S. A. T. Yates, *Memorials of the family of the Rev. John Yates* (privately printed, London, [1890]) · *The Inquirer* (13 May 1871) · *The Inquirer* (1 Nov 1884) · *The Inquirer* (8 Nov 1884) · minute book 1842 and trustees' minutes, Mitchell L., Glas., St Vincent's Street congregational records [esp. 2 August 1854 and 15 April 1859] · J. Morrell and A. Thackray, *Gentlemen of science: early years of the British Association for the Advancement of Science* (1981) · [C. Wicksteed], 'Vindication of Unitarianism', *Prospective Review*, 7 (1851), 50–67 · G. E. Evans, *Vestiges of protestant dissent* (1897) · register, Kaye Street/Paradise Street, Liverpool, 19 May 1789 [baptism]

Archives LUL, corresp. · RBG Kew, archives, corresp. · UCL, corresp. and papers | BL, letters to Charles Babbage, Add. MSS 37187–37201, *passim* · DWL, MS biographies of Glasgow students on Dr Williams's foundation · Linn. Soc., corresp. with Sir James Smith

Likenesses E. Ryley, bust (as young man), DWL · photograph, DWL

Wealth at death under £25,000: resworn probate, July 1875, *CGPLA Eng. & Wales* (1871)

Yates, John (*d*. 1657), Church of England clergyman and philosopher, was admitted as a sizar to Emmanuel College, Cambridge, at Easter 1604 and was subsequently elected a scholar. He graduated BA in 1608, and proceeded MA and became a fellow in 1611. In September that year he was appointed master of Dedham grammar school, but he left within a term, apparently foregoing payment. He was ordained deacon and priest on 4 and 5 September 1614. The following year he published, at Cambridge, *God's*

Arraignement of Hypocrites, a defence of Calvin and an attack on Arminius. At Emmanuel he fell under the Ramist influence of the master, Laurence Chaderton, later becoming, with William Ames, Thomas Hooker, and Charles Chauncy, one of the students boarding at Alexander Richardson's private seminary at Barking, Essex, and chaplain to Sir William Ayloffe, bt, chief justice of the liberties of Havering Bow. With Richardson and Ames he added technometria to Ramism, setting each art or discipline in the context of the entire field of knowledge.

In 1616 Yates resigned his fellowship and on 7 May married Mary Fening (d. 1650) at Saffron Walden, Essex. She had been baptized there in November 1590, the daughter of Jonas Fening, an influential glover of the town, and his wife, Agnes Meade. Also in 1616 Yates began a six-year ministry at the civic church of St Andrew the Apostle, Norwich, first as one of the corporation lecturers, then as incumbent. He quickly became the most prominent preacher in Norfolk, with a large following of influential city fathers. To the mayor and chief inhabitants of Norwich he dedicated in 1622 his Ramist treatise *A modell of divinitie, catechistically composed, wherein is delivered the matter and methode of religion according to the creed, ten commandments, Lord's prayer, and the sacraments*. Bishop Samuel Harsnett, no admirer of puritans, did his best to inhibit Yates's preaching, banning Sunday morning sermons, so Yates was glad when in October 1622 Sir Nathaniel Bacon, the most eminent puritan layman in the county, presented him to the joint rectories of St Mary with St John at Stiffkey on the north Norfolk coast. However, Bacon and his eldest daughter, Anne (who brought the property to the Townshends), died as he was moving; both were buried at Stiffkey on 7 November. Yates soon established himself with Sir Roger and Lady Townshend, presenting them with copies of his *Modell*, which, he complained in the accompanying letter, had been censored before publication and again afterwards by the archbishop's chaplain, Dr Goad, who removed two pages from copies before they were sold.

When in 1624 the king's chaplain Richard Montagu published *A New Gagg for an Old Goose*, Yates and Nathaniel Ward of Ipswich (not his brother Samuel, as often stated) were two of the petitioners to the House of Commons about Montagu's popish and Arminian opinions. James was furious, and summoned the protesters to appear before him. Yates later recalled that the king's 'words were terrible' as he threatened to 'make his kingdom too hote for [us]' (BL, Add. MS 25278). Montagu addressed the king with *Appello Caesarem* (1625), which earned him the censure of the Commons. Yates was one of several who kept the pamphlets flying, with an answer, *Ibis ad Caesarem* (1626), but Montagu was consecrated to the see of Chichester two years later, and when he was translated to Norwich in 1638 he and Yates were on friendly terms. Three later religious works, *The Saints Sufferings* (1631), *A Treatise of the Honor of God's House* (1637), and *Imago mundi, et regnum Christi* (1639), have been attributed to a contemporary namesake, although it is possible they were by John of Stiffkey. *A Treatise* represents a significantly different opinion on episcopacy from that expressed in *Ibis ad Caesarem*, but on the other hand his familiarity with Montagu brought Yates under suspicion in the early 1640s. Later Yates maintained his support for presbyterians and showed his sympathies with Congregationalists such as Jeremiah Burroughs and William Bridges. He was one of the trustees who hired the latter to preach in Norwich, and edited works by both of them for publication between 1649 and 1657.

Not much is known about Yates's local ministry, save that in 1629 he was licensed to practise medicine, giving him the cure of bodies as well as souls. His wife was buried at Stiffkey on 6 April 1650, having borne her husband ten children, four of whom were living when he wrote his will in 1656, ordering 'neither strife nor varyance after my decease'. He died and was buried with his wife at Stiffkey on 12 November 1657, leaving his eldest son, John (1617–1659) MD of Great Yarmouth, his sole executor and main beneficiary. Dr Yates's Latin epitaph laments that he who so often knew how to cure others was powerless in his own case. A daughter, Hannah, was married to Richard Briggs, incumbent of Warham St Mary, adjoining Stiffkey.

J. M. BLATCHLY

Sources K. L. Sprunger, 'John Yates of Norfolk: the radical puritan preacher as Ramist philosopher', *Journal of the History of Ideas*, 37 (1976), 697–706 • K. W. Shipps, 'The "political puritan"', *Church History*, 45 (1976), 196–205 • K. W. Shipps, 'Lay patronage of East Anglian puritan clerics in pre-revolutionary England', PhD diss., Yale U., 1971, 270–80 • J. Yates's letters, Raynham Hall, Norfolk, 'Letters to the Bacons and Townshends', nos. 414, 422, 484 [microfilm at Norfolk RO] • J. Yates's record of the 1624 parliament, c.1644, BL, Add. MS 25278, fols. 124v, 136, 138–139v • Venn, *Alum. Cant.* • original will 204, 1662, Norfolk RO, Norwich consistory court • parish registers, Norwich, St Andrew, Stiffkey, and Wells next the Sea, 12 Nov 1657, Norfolk RO [burial] • A. Milton, *Catholic and Reformed: the Roman and protestant churches in English protestant thought, 1600–1640* (1995), esp. 113–14, 194–5, 465

Archives BL, MS record of parliament, Add. MS 25278, fols. 124v, 136, 138, 138v, 139v

Wealth at death £300; plus houses and land: will, Norfolk RO, Norwich

Yates, John (1755–1826), Unitarian minister, was born in Bolton, Lancashire, the only child of John Yates, schoolmaster. He was educated at the grammar school in Bolton and entered Warrington Academy in 1772. In 1777 he became minister of Kaye Street Chapel, Liverpool; at his ordination on 1 October William Enfield delivered the charge. In 1791 the congregation moved to Paradise Street, where Yates continued to serve until 1823.

In 1777 Yates married Elizabeth Bostock (1749–1819), the youngest daughter of John Brooks Ashton (1711–1759), a Liverpool merchant, and the widow of John Bostock the elder (1740–1774), a physician in the town; her brother was said to have opposed the match because she might be pauperized, but he later relented and sent his sons to John Yates's school. The wealth that came to Yates with his marriage was expended on their house, Dingle Head, in Toxteth Park, in extensive charity, and in judicious investment in property, which increased the fortune. Five sons and three daughters were born; the eldest son was Joseph Brooks *Yates (1780–1855), merchant and antiquary, and the fourth son was James *Yates (1789–1871), Unitarian minister and antiquary.

John Yates published a few sermons and a collection of hymns; in one unpublished sermon, in 1788, he attacked the evils of the slave trade, deeply offending some of his congregation. A fluent pulpit style belied the great pains he took with composition—he reportedly never preached an old sermon—although some thought he strained for novelty: one story has it that during a sermon on the wonders of nature, he cried 'Behold the camel!', awaking a sleeping lady who exclaimed 'Where? where?' (*Memorials*, 3). He elicited great respect and affection in his congregation and the Liverpool community. Like his friend and neighbouring minister William Shepherd (1768–1847), who had for a time served as tutor to the Yates children, he was active in radical politics and, with other Liverpool worthies, belonged to a literary society that it was thought expedient to dissolve following the younger Pitt's proclamation against sedition in 1792.

In his family, although he liked jokes, read aloud to his children, and taught them to play cards, Yates was a strict disciplinarian, a possibly inherited trait since a family story tells of his mother's sending a messenger to order him home from school to close a door he had left open (*Memorials*, 1–2). Reflecting the awe in which his children held him, a daughter once said that she was certain her father never did anything but from a sense of duty, whereupon her sister-in-law asked if it was also 'from a sense of duty that he married Mrs. Bostock?' (Roberts, 330). His crustiness seems to have increased in his later years when he was lame and in pain from a badly mended leg.

Yates died on 10 November 1826 at Dingle Head. He was probably buried in the graveyard of the Park Chapel, Toxteth Park; the funeral sermon was preached on 19 November by William Shepherd.   R. K. WEBB

Sources S. A. T. Yates, *Memorials of the family of the Rev. John Yates* (privately printed, London, [1890]), 1–10 · H. D. Roberts, *Hope Street Church, Liverpool, and the allied nonconformity* (1909), 328–30 · W. Shepherd, *A sermon on occasion of the death of the Rev. John Yates … November 19th, 1826* (1826) · *Ashton family—pedigree, portraits, etc.* (1950) · *Monthly Repository*, 14 (1819), 119 · *Monthly Repository*, 21 (1826), 693
Likenesses F. Engelhart, engraving, 1826 (after H. Moses), DWL
Wealth at death under £40,000: probate record, Lancs. RO

Yates, Sir Joseph (1722–1770), judge, was born in Manchester, the younger son of Joseph Yates of Stanley House, Lancashire, barrister, and of his wife, Helen, daughter of William Maghull of Maghull, heir of her brother Edward Maghull. His father was high sheriff of the county in 1728, and his grandfather (also named Joseph Yates) was a magistrate. Baptized at the collegiate church, Manchester, on 17 July 1722, he received his early education at Appleby School in Westmorland and at Manchester grammar school.

The family's financial circumstances became distressed as a result of expenditures by the father attempting to exploit coal reserves on an estate in Little Hutton that had been inherited in 1730. Thus when Yates matriculated at Queen's College, Oxford, on 7 December 1739 he was able to continue only by means of financial assistance from his relative Mr Serjeant Bootle. Yates did not take a degree at Oxford but left to enter Staple Inn. From there he removed to the Inner Temple, where he practised as a special pleader from 1748 until he was called to the bar in July 1753. He married Elizabeth (d. 1808), daughter of Charles Baldwyn of Munslow, Shropshire.

Yates's success at the bar was rapid, despite a weak constitution, early pecuniary difficulties, and a near-foppish obsession with gentlemanly dress. He obtained general retainers from the corporation of Liverpool, Greenwich Hospital, and the East India Company. According to one character of him, his friends esteemed and admired him not only because of his abilities as a lawyer but also because of 'his intimate knowledge of the arts and sciences, a fine sense of the *Belles lettres*, joined to an uncommon philanthropy of temper' (*Lloyd's Evening Post*).

In June 1761 Yates was made king's counsel for the duchy of Lancaster. In 1763 he was employed by the crown in the proceedings against John Wilkes, and later that year, on the death of Sir Michael Foster, he was offered a judgeship on the king's bench. Although he thought himself too young for such a step and was concerned about curtailing his earnings, his friends persuaded him that the judgeship would be agreeable to his constitution and would offer opportunities for future advancement. Accordingly he was knighted on 16 December 1763 and received his patent of appointment on 23 January 1764. Soon afterwards, in February 1765, he also assumed the chancellorship of Durham.

Yates joined the king's bench during that court's ascendancy under the chief justiceship of Lord Mansfield, assisted by puisne judges Thomas Denison and John Eardley Wilmot. Yates was an able lawyer, and assumed a responsible part in the court's increasing load of business. Indeed, by the resignation of Denison in 1765 and the promotion of Wilmot in 1766 Yates rapidly became senior puisne judge, a status he retained until his transfer on 16 February 1770 to the court of common pleas. Shortly after his transfer, on 7 June 1770, he died, aged forty-eight. He was buried at Cheam, Surrey.

After Yates's death the Junius letters were published, and the first such letter to Lord Mansfield claimed that Yates, 'that great lawyer, that honest man', had fled the king's bench because he could no longer remain on 'a court whose proceedings and decisions he could neither assent to with honour nor oppose with success' (*DNB*). Some nineteenth-century biographers, including Lord Campbell, accepted this story, associating it with two famous decisions in which Yates wrote dissenting opinions, *Perrin v. Blake* (1770) and *Millar v. Taylor* (1769). The story is not credible, as more recent writers have explained. Wilmot's biographer (his son) described Yates as a man 'universally esteemed for his abilities, integrity, and learning', with whom Wilmot formed an 'indissoluble friendship' (Wilmot). There were, moreover, clear indications throughout their time on king's bench together of a mutual courtesy and respect between Yates and Mansfield. Much more plausible than Junius's charge is the suggestion that Yates transferred to common pleas because of his weak constitution, since the workload there was modest and decreasing, while the filings in king's bench were heavy and accelerating. Indeed, Yates had earlier coaxed his good friend Wilmot to accept the chief justiceship of common pleas by arguing that even the chief in that court 'might be quieter and less observed than a Puisne in the King's Bench' (Campbell, 2.289).

Yates's signal virtues—integrity, industry, ability—were widely acknowledged. He was said to have once been approached by the government to induce him to favour the crown in certain pending trials, and after one attempt failed, Yates was reportedly handed a letter from the king, which, suspecting it to be another piece of special pleading, he returned unopened. His learning is evident in his many opinions printed in *Burrow's Reports*, notably in the two famous cases in which he dissented, *Millar* v. *Taylor* and *Perrin* v. *Blake*. His judgments in both decisions were influential in their eventual reversal, even though the reversals occurred after Yates's death.

In the language of his day, Yates was a man of parts. Lord Mansfield's earliest biographer, the barrister John Holliday, recorded that Yates:

> was accustomed to declare, that whenever intense application to any legal studies became burdensome or unpleasant, he changed the scene, read a few pages of Dean Swift's Works, which ... sent him back to his dry law in perfect good humour. (Holliday, 126–7)

He accomplished much in his professional career of seventeen years after being called to the bar. He was survived by his wife and by one son and one daughter.

JAMES OLDHAM

Sources John, Lord Campbell, *The lives of the chief justices of England*, 3 vols. (1849–57) · Foss, *Judges* · *Lloyd's Evening Post* (13–15 June 1770) · W. B. Odgers, 'Sir William Blackstone', *Yale Law Journal*, 28 (1919), 542–66 · J. Haydn, *The book of dignities: containing lists of the official personages of the British empire*, ed. H. Ockerby, 3rd edn (1894) · Holdsworth, *Eng. law* · J. Burrow, *Reports of cases*, 5 vols. (1812) · J. E. Wilmot, *Memoirs of the life of the Right Honourable Sir John Eardley Wilmot* (1802) · J. Holliday, *The life of William, late earl of Mansfield* (1797) · J. C. Jeaffreson, *A book about lawyers*, 2 vols. (1867) · J. Nicholls, *Recollections and reflections, personal and political*, 2nd edn, 2 vols. (1822) · *GM*, 1st ser., 40 (1770), 279 · J. Oldham, *The Mansfield manuscripts and the growth of English law in the eighteenth century*, 2 vols. (1992)

Yates, Joseph Brooks (1780–1855), merchant and antiquary, born at Liverpool on 21 January 1780, was the eldest son of John *Yates (1755–1826), minister of the Unitarian chapel in Paradise Street, Liverpool, and his wife, Elizabeth (1749–1819), daughter of John Brooks Ashton of Woolton Hall near Liverpool and widow of John *Bostock (1744?–1774). His brothers were John Ashton Yates (1781–1863), MP for Carlow and author of pamphlets on trade and slavery; Richard Vaughan Yates (1785–1856), founder of Prince's Park, Liverpool; James *Yates (1789–1871); and Pemberton Heywood Yates (1791–1822). He was educated by the Unitarian minister William Shepherd and at Eton

College. After leaving Eton about 1796, he joined the firm of a West Indies merchant, in which he became a partner, remaining with it until shortly before he died. He was one of the leading reformers of Liverpool, and in the years after 1815 was a prominent figure in local campaigns and petitions in favour of civil liberties, adherence to constitutional rights, and democratic reform. He was also a liberal supporter of the city's literary and scientific institutions. In February 1812 he joined with Thomas Stewart Traill in founding the Liverpool Literary and Philosophical Society, of which he was president for a total of twelve years. He was president of the Liverpool Royal Institution in 1842–3, and was also one of the founders of the Southern and Toxteth Hospital at Liverpool.

Yates was elected FSA on 18 April 1852, and was also FRGS, a member of the council of the Chetham Society, and an original member of the Philological Society. He collected many fine pictures and an extensive library containing some fine manuscripts and emblem books, and was an occasional contributor to literary and other journals. He also contributed to several local journals on antiquarian subjects, and wrote a small number of pamphlets, but none of his writings has had any lasting value.

On 22 July 1813 Yates married Margaret, daughter of Thomas Taylor of Blackley, near Manchester; they had six daughters. He died at West Dingle, Toxteth, Liverpool, on 12 December 1855, and was buried in the graveyard of the Unitarian chapel, Toxteth Park.

C. W. SUTTON, rev. ALAN G. CROSBY

Sources S. A. T. Yates, *Memorials of the family of the Rev. John Yates* (privately printed, London, [1890]) · *GM*, 3rd ser., 1 (1856), 89 · J. A. Picton, *Memorials of Liverpool*, rev. edn, 2 (1875), 337, 376 · H. A. Ormerod, *The Liverpool Royal Institution* (1953) · will, proved, Lancaster, Jan 1856, Lancs. RO · H. D. Roberts, *Hope Street Church, Liverpool, and the allied nonconformity* (1909), 271

Yates [*née* Graham], **Mary Ann** (1728–1787), actress and theatre manager, was the daughter of William Graham (d. 1779), a ship's steward, and his wife, Mary (d. 1777). She may herself have encouraged the belief that she was born in London in 1737 rather than, as seems likelier, in Birmingham in 1728. Nothing of her education, beyond the discernible fact that she had some, is recorded; nor is it known how and why she came to be acting the part of Anne Bullen in *Henry VIII* with Thomas Sheridan's Dublin company in January 1753, but her début was inauspicious. Ignoring Sheridan's advice to abandon her theatrical ambitions, she sought employment with David Garrick at Drury Lane, where she made her début as Marcia in Henry Crisp's *Virginia* on 25 February 1754. Although the character offered little scope for the *grande dame* stateliness that became her hallmark, 'Mrs Graham' impressed some of the more discerning members of the Drury Lane company. Among them was the recently widowed comedian, Richard *Yates (1706?–1796), more than twenty years her senior and one of Garrick's stalwarts. When Mary Ann married him at some point in 1756, her theatrical status rose. Having not seen fit to employ her during the 1755–6

Mary Ann Yates (1728–1787), by Francis Cotes, c.1765

season, Garrick now cast her as Alcmena in John Hawkesworth's *Amphitryon* for its opening on 15 December 1756 and, for the 1757–8 season, in the coveted title role in Nicholas Rowe's *Jane Shore*, previously in the possession of his leading lady, Hannah Pritchard. 'Mrs Yates' had, by then, acquired the support of the combative playwright Arthur Murphy, who coached her privately as Mandane in his tragedy *The Orphan of China*. It was her success in this play, which opened on 21 April 1759, that confirmed her as a Drury Lane favourite.

Once established, Mary Ann Yates was never afraid to stand up for herself, overruling her more timid husband if necessary. She was one of several actresses whom Garrick found troublesome, but, above all in tragedy, he needed her as support, and eventually replacement, for Susannah Cibber and Hannah Pritchard. A regular member of his company until the end of the 1766–7 season, she was his Cleopatra in *Antony and Cleopatra*, Constance in *King John* (always a major role in the eighteenth century's refashioning of Shakespeare's play), Imogen in *Cymbeline*, Desdemona in *Othello*, Cordelia in *King Lear*, and Belvidera in Thomas Otway's *Venice Preserv'd*. There is some evidence, from her choice of plays for her own benefit nights, that she preferred to perform in comedies, but her comparative inflexibility—a monumental strength in tragedy—was a handicap, and there is more than a hint of vengefulness in some of Garrick's placing of her in comedy—as Mrs Marwood in William Congreve's *The Way of the World*, inappropriately as Sylvia in George Farquhar's *The Recruiting Officer*, above all as the Old Woman in Garrick's own

version of John Fletcher's *Rule a Wife and have a Wife*. Ambitious for control of her own life, Yates chafed under Garrick's endlessly inventive regimen. It was in conscious defiance of the great manager's wishes that in summer 1761 she led her husband into alliance with Garrick's adversary Samuel Foote and Arthur Murphy (temporarily estranged from Garrick) in a Drury Lane season during the months when the playhouse was normally closed. The original idea was that Murphy and Foote would present three of their own plays in repertory, with Richard and Mary Ann Yates featuring in most of them. In the event, Foote failed to fulfil his part of the bargain, but Mary Ann's persistent illness was the greater catastrophe for the enterprise. Unspecified illnesses (which Garrick generally considered a disguise for malevolence in his actresses) had caused her to cancel appearances in 1761, 1763, and again in April 1764. Foote and Murphy were as exasperated as Garrick had been by the preparedness of their leading lady to pronounce herself indisposed. It is not known whether their suspicions were justified, nor just how stressful the publicity surrounding actresses had become as social interest in the London theatre burgeoned.

It may well be that the death of Susannah Cibber in 1766 enhanced Mary Ann Yates's sense of her own value. It was probably the refusal of the Drury Lane management to meet her financial demands that determined her to transfer her allegiance to Covent Garden, newly under the management of George Colman the elder, in 1767. She protested against the rumours to that effect in a letter to the *Gazeteer*: 'I have offered to perform for two hundred pounds less than the late Mrs. Cibber contracted for; and Mr. Yates has demanded no more than has been often given to comedians in his walk' (quoted in Highfill, Burnim & Langhans, *BDA*, 16.327). Her first Covent Garden performance, on 16 October 1767, was a repeat of *Jane Shore*, and before the end of her engagement there after the 1771–2 season she had added to her repertory of tragic roles Lady Macbeth, Cleopatra in Dryden's *All for Love*, and Queen Gertrude in *Hamlet*, as well as two of the more stately heroines of Shakespearian comedy, Portia in *The Merchant of Venice* and Isabella in *Measure for Measure*.

The break with Covent Garden owed more to Colman's unwillingness to retain the services of Richard Yates than to his rejection of Mary Ann's demands for a seasonal salary of £600, but there is some hidden history here, too. The early 1770s witnessed a renewed clamour for a third London theatre, licensed for the performance of the legitimate drama. It was almost certainly her aspiration to leadership of the stage that, in 1773, led Mary Ann Yates to join Frances Brooke, novelist and playwright, smouldering after Garrick's rejection of her tragedy, in the management of the King's Theatre—then the home of opera in London. With Richard Yates as a generally silent partner, the two women contrived to improve the failing fortunes of opera at the same time as mounting an ultimately unsuccessful campaign to persuade the lord chamberlain to permit them to stage plays, Frances Brooke's among them. Fanny Burney's record of a visit to the opera house in 1774 suggests that Mrs Yates considered herself a hostess rather than a manager. The Burney party was ushered by Frances Brooke to 'a most magnificent apartment', where they found Mary Ann:

> seated like a stage queen, surrounded with gay courtiers and dressed with the utmost elegance and brilliancy … With an *over done* civility, as soon as our names were spoken, she rose from her seat hastily, and rather *rushed* towards, then meerly advanced to meet us; but I doubt not it was meant as the *very pink of politeness*. As to poor Mr Yates, he presumed not to take the liberty in his own house to act any other part than that of waiter, in which capacity he arranged the chairs. (*Early Journals and Letters*, 2.55–6)

Richard Yates was by then installed as manager of a newly built playhouse in Birmingham—there is no evidence that the Yateses were ever short of money—and Mary Ann played there in 1775, following a 1773 season in Edinburgh.

Despite the enmity between Garrick and Mary Ann Yates's managerial partner, Frances Brooke, she returned to Drury Lane for the 1774–5 season, and remained a member of the company after Garrick's retirement in 1776. Such was her eminence that she was chosen to deliver the elegy, written by Sheridan, at the great actor–manager's funeral in 1779. She and Frances Brooke had sold their shares in the King's Theatre to Sheridan and Thomas Harris in the previous year, and her Drury Lane salary of £750 per season was handsome. By 1779 it had risen to £800, and it is unlikely that she would, in that year, have crossed over to Covent Garden for anything less. Though never a popular idol, she was greatly admired by the theatrical public, and she always knew what she was worth. She continued to play leading roles at Covent Garden until the end of the 1782–3 season, making her last regular appearance as Hermione in *The Winter's Tale* on 11 May 1783. Despite failing health she emerged from retirement in 1785, performing in Edinburgh in March, for Tate Wilkinson in York in April, for George Anne Bellamy's benefit at Drury Lane in May (this time in one of her most celebrated roles, that of the Duchess in Robert Jephson's *Braganza*), and in Birmingham in July. There is no record of activity in 1786, however, and it may be that she was already suffering from the dropsy that caused her death between 2 and 7 May 1787 at her home in Stafford Row, Pimlico. For no known reason, she had arranged for her mother and father to be buried in Richmond, and her own body was carried to the same churchyard for burial from Stafford Row. By the terms of her will, administration of her considerable estate was granted to her husband, who died at a great age in 1796. Richard Yates had at least one daughter with his first wife, but there is no evidence that Mary Ann Yates was ever a mother, although it has been speculated that the Mary Ann Yates who first performed in 1804 was her daughter. At the time of his death, Richard Yates was still occupying the Pimlico house where his second wife had died almost exactly nine years earlier.

Mary Ann Yates was London's leading tragedienne in the years between the death of Susannah Cibber and the rise of Sarah Siddons. Her own style, finely captured in the William Dickinson engraving of Robert Pine's portrait of her as Medea (*c*.1771), was much closer to the majesty of Siddons than to the tenderness of Cibber. Fanny Burney, in the diary entry already quoted, wrote of her 'fine figure' and 'handsome face'. She added that 'the expression of her face is infinitely haughty and hard' (*Early Journals and Letters*, 2.55–6), but the diarist may well have been carrying into a private encounter impressions gleaned from a commanding stage presence. Some part, at least, of the unyielding quality possessed by the heroines she best portrayed was hers in life. She lived contentiously in an age of bitter political contention, but scandal-free among scandalmongers. Horace Walpole was among her admirers, and so was William Godwin. Indeed, Godwin's admiration, together with the friendship of Frances Brooke, legitimizes the speculation that Mary Ann Yates was as overtly a champion of the rights of women as she implicitly was through her performances. It is her historical misfortune to have been so quickly superseded in the public memory by Sarah Siddons. PETER THOMSON

Sources Highfill, Burnim & Langhans, *BDA* • T. Wilkinson, *The wandering patentee, or, A history of the Yorkshire theatres from 1770 to the present time*, 4 vols. (1795) • *The early journals and letters of Fanny Burney*, ed. L. E. Troide, 3 vols. (1988–94) • I. Woodfield, *Opera and drama in eighteenth-century London* (2001) • P. Thomson, *On actors and acting* (2000) • L. McMullen, *An odd attempt for a woman* (Vancouver, 1983) • *The letters of David Garrick*, ed. D. M. Little and G. M. Kahrl, 3 vols. (1963)

Likenesses F. Cotes, oils, *c*.1765, Garr. Club [*see illus.*] • S. Cotes, miniature on ivory, 1769, V&A • W. Dickinson, engraving, 1771 (after painting by R. E. Pine) • V. Green, mezzotint, pubd 1772 (after G. Romney), BM, NPG • J. Reynolds, oils, 1772; copy (reduced size), Boston Museum of Fine Arts • J. Collyer, line engraving, pubd 1776 (after D. Dodd), BM, Harvard TC, NPG • J. Meers, mezzotint, pubd 1776 (after T. Parkinson), BM, NPG • J. Thornthwaite, line engravings, pubd 1776 (after J. Roberts), BM, Harvard TC, NPG • J. Goldar, line engravings, pubd 1777 (after D. Dodd), BM, Harvard TC, NPG • B. Reading, line engraving, pubd 1777 (after E. Edwards), BM, Harvard TC, NPG • J. Thornthwaite, line engraving, pubd 1777 (after J. Roberts), BM, Harvard TC, NPG • line engraving, pubd 1777 (after J. Roberts), BM, Harvard TC, NPG • J. Heath, line engraving, pubd 1783 (after T. Stothard), BM, NPG • J. Thornthwaite, line engravings, pubd 1786 (after E. F. Burney), BM, Harvard TC, NPG • J. Thornthwaite, line engraving, pubd 1807 (after E. F. Burney), BM, Harvard TC, NPG • line engraving (after J. Roberts; as Lady Townley in *The provoked husband*), Harvard TC, NPG • line engraving (after unknown artist), Harvard TC, NPG • prints, BM, NPG

Yates, Richard (1706?–1796), actor and theatre manager, made his first known appearance in 1736–7 with Henry Fielding's company at the Haymarket, London, where he played Law in Fielding's *Pasquin*. The next season found him in Henry Giffard's company at Lincoln's Inn Fields, in small parts such as Roderigo in *Othello* and Ben, a 'sea dog', in William Congreve's *Love for Love*. Probably deterred by the Licensing Act of 1737, which Fielding had provoked with his Haymarket satires, Giffard did not mount a season in 1737–8, but Yates acted at Covent Garden for two seasons, 1737–9, playing such minor parts as a sailor in Thomas Shadwell's *The Fair Quaker of Deal*, Wart in *2 Henry IV*, and Sir Joseph in Congreve's *The Old Bachelor*.

In 1739 Yates moved to Drury Lane for a season. Most notable among his supporting parts there were Dapper in *The Alchemist*, by Ben Jonson, and the Ghost of Gaffer

Thumb in Fielding's *Tragedy of Tragedies*. He also played Pantaloon in a pantomime, *Harlequin Shipwrecked*. In 1740 he joined Giffard's new venture at Goodman's Fields. In two seasons he played Shakespearian clowns, including Lavache in *All's Well that Ends Well*, Autolycus in *The Winter's Tale*, and the Gravedigger in *Hamlet*. As the Usher, he supported David Garrick's first appearance as Lear, in Nahum Tate's adaptation (1742). A fine dancer, he was Harlequin in the pantomime *Harlequin Student*. Since low comedy was becoming his 'line of business', he cannot have been comfortable in some of the other parts he was assigned, such as Trueman in George Lillo's *The London Merchant*.

Again Giffard was obliged to close, and in September 1742 Yates, like Garrick, moved to Drury Lane, where he remained until 1767. In his first nine seasons he established himself as a low comedian, and he gradually achieved recognition as 'a leading man among the class of secondary players' (*Theatrical Review*, 1758, 10). From the beginning Ben, Roderigo, and the Gravedigger were exclusively his. In 1743 he added Sharp, the title role in *The Lying Valet*, which Garrick had written for himself. In the part of Peachum in John Gay's *The Beggar's Opera* (1744), Gentleman thought Yates and Macklin 'were indisputably superior to any competitors' (Gentleman, 1.37). Other repertory parts which he assumed at this period included Sir Francis Wronghead in John Vanbrugh's *The Provoked Husband* (1745), Sir Francis Gripe in Susannah Centlivre's *The Busie Body* (1748), Shylock (1749), and Sir Wilful Witwoud in Congreve's *The Way of the World* (1750). While Gentleman found Yates 'contemptible' as Shylock, Wilkes commended his 'humour, propriety, and … close adherance to nature' (Wilkes, 272) in Ben, Sharp, Wronghead, and Witwoud. Yates also made himself useful in comic parts, large and small, in plays which never entered the regular repertory, for example, Sir Paul Plyant in Congreve's *The Double Dealer* (1744), Beau Clincher in George Farquhar's *The Constant Couple* (1746), and Fribble in Garrick's *Miss in her Teens* (1749). His lively dancing won the role of Harlequin in several pantomimes.

Yates's career at Drury Lane reached its peak in 1751, when he made three major repertory parts his own. No other Malvolio was seen there while he remained with the company. Wilkes called his Brainworm in Jonson's *Every Man in his Humour* a 'masterpiece' (Wilkes, 272), and Davies commended his 'archness and varied pleasantry' in the part (Davies, 2.41). His portrait as Lovegold in Fielding's *The Miser* was painted by both T. Parkinson and S. De Wilde. Now Yates had established his position at Drury Lane, but he rose no higher: there were no more years like 1751. New roles included Touchstone (1753), Grumio in the première of Garrick's *Catharine and Petruchio* (1754), Autolycus in *Florizel and Perdita*, Garrick's adaptation of *The Winter's Tale* (1756), Trinculo in *The Tempest* (1757), Dogberry in *Much Ado about Nothing* (1758), and Scrub in Farquhar's *The Beaux' Stratagem* (1759).

During these years there were great changes in Yates's private life. His first wife, Elizabeth Mary—her maiden name is unknown—had acted with him at Goodman's Fields and Drury Lane. She died in 1753, and in 1756 he married Mary Ann Graham (1728–1787) [see Yates, Mary Ann], who first appeared at Drury Lane in 1754. She emerged as a major tragic actress, and inevitably overshadowed her low-comedian husband. In 1761 Yates played three solid new roles, Major Oakly in George Colman's *The Jealous Wife*, Sir Bashful Constant in Arthur Murphy's *The Way to Keep Him*, and Sir John Restless in Murphy's *All in the Wrong*—his wife acting with him in the latter two plays—but there was no repetition of the successes of 1751: Oakly alone became a repertory part. Yates continued to enjoy good roles such as Falstaff in *1 Henry IV*, Launce in *The Two Gentlemen of Verona* (1762), and Justice Shallow in *1 Henry IV* (1764), but only Jerry Blackacre in William Wycherley's *The Plain Dealer* (1765), Sterling in Garrick and Colman's *The Clandestine Marriage* (1766), and Freeport in Colman's *The English Merchant* (1767) remained in the repertory after their first runs. Nevertheless, it is unlikely that Yates was dissatisfied with his lot at Drury Lane. In 1767 Mary Ann asked Garrick for a higher salary (for the couple) than he was prepared to pay, and they moved to Covent Garden.

In five seasons Yates played some of his repertory parts: Oakly, Wronghead, Grumio, the Miser, Malvolio, even Shylock. New parts, however, were few, such as Cloten in *Cymbeline* (1767), Lucio in *Measure for Measure* (1771), and Sir Benjamin Done in the première of Richard Cumberland's *The Refusal* (1771). Most of his appearances were in afterpieces or small parts in the company's repertory plays. In 1772 there was another dispute about money, and the Yateses left Covent Garden. After performing in Edinburgh that autumn, Yates returned to Drury Lane in January 1773. He must have known that some of his best repertory parts were now the property of other actors and that exciting new parts for low comedians of sixty-seven were rare, but Drury Lane served him as a stable base while the Yateses went into management for themselves.

Yates was not without experience in management. In his early days he had performed at Bartholomew fair: he is first recorded there as Captain Strut in *The Modern Pimp* in 1736. In 1741 he was partner in a booth with an actor named Turbott, and by 1748 he had his own booth; he returned in 1749 and from 1757 to 1762, when the fairs were suppressed. In 1760 he tried his hand at writing his own comic material with *The Dramatic Turtle*, in 1761 he wrote *The Fair Bride* and *The British Tar's Triumph over M Soup-Maigre*, and in 1762 *Trial Scenes of the Cock Lane Ghost* and *Tars of Old England*. Long facetious playbills are extant, but the texts are not.

In September 1773 Yates signed an agreement to build a new theatre in Birmingham. In November he and his wife formed a partnership with James and Frances Brooke to manage the King's Theatre in London, licensed for the performance of opera. The Birmingham playhouse opened in June 1774 with Yates as Touchstone: as actor–manager, he could perform only in summer. In winter, while acting at Drury Lane, he actively managed the King's until it was sold in 1777. Tate Wilkinson says he was still manager of the Birmingham theatre in 1791, and that the fire that burnt it down in 1792 was deliberately set.

At Drury Lane Yates returned to some of his old repertory, including Ben—from his Goodman's Fields days—Scrub, Wronghead, Blackacre, Oakly—even Malvolio once, in 1777. Most new parts were minor, such as Burgundy in *King Lear* (1773) and Captain Otter in Jonson's *Epicene* (1776), but *The Thespian Dictionary* (1805) says he was 'much esteemed as a comedian, particularly in Fondlewife' in Sheridan's revision of Congreve's *The Old Bachelor* (1776). He also shone as the original Sir Oliver Surface in Sheridan's *The School for Scandal* (1777). By 1778 his name appeared less frequently in the playbills, although he remained with the company until 1782. In December that year he played Sir Wilful Witwoud at Covent Garden, where his last known performance in London was as Sir Edmund Travers in Cumberland's *The Mysterious Husband* (1783). In October 1783 Yates published a denial that he was over seventy years old, which was almost certainly false, but truthfully denied that his wife was over sixty and that they had retired. Nevertheless, Mary Ann's engagement at Covent Garden had ended in May, and she played in London only once more, for a benefit at Drury Lane in 1785. Richard never again appeared in London; gout obliged him to cancel an appearance as Scrub, also for a benefit, in 1786. Rather than retire, the couple retreated to the provinces. In March and April 1785 Mrs Yates starred in a short season at Edinburgh, after which she moved on to York, where Wilkinson mistakenly said she performed for the last time, and then to her husband's theatre in Birmingham in July. Richard Yates played at Edinburgh each season from 1785 to 1788, appearing in many small parts, some of them new to him. Thus he was still acting, and managing the Birmingham theatre, after his wife's death in May 1787.

Mary Ann left Richard her house in Stafford Row, Pimlico, where he lived until his own death there on 21 April 1796. It is not known whether he was buried with his wife at Richmond. There is a story of doubtful authenticity that he wished in vain to be buried under the stage of the new Drury Lane playhouse. Yates bequeathed the Pimlico house to his young housekeeper, Elizabeth Jones (*b. c.*1769), who acted once at Covent Garden in 1793. Yates's brother's son, Lieutenant Thomas Yates RN, disputed the will. Jones called in male reinforcements, one of whom shot and killed Thomas while he was attempting to enter the property through a back window. In the ensuing trial one Sellars was convicted of manslaughter, but Elizabeth Jones and the other man were acquitted. Dutton Cook incorrectly states that Yates married a third time. In fact, Sarah Yates was the wife of the murdered Thomas. She made her début at the Haymarket in 1794, as Euphrasia in Murphy's *The Grecian Daughter*. For her widow's benefit at the Haymarket in 1797 she played a part associated with Mary Ann, Margaret of Anjou in *The Earl of Warwick*, by Thomas Francklin. She later performed as Mrs Francis Hutchings Ansell, mostly in the provinces but at Drury Lane in 1807-8. A George Yates, who acted in the 1740s, may have been Richard Yates's son by his first marriage, and Mary Ann Yates, first known in 1804, a daughter by his second.

As a low comedian, Yates could not escape the established hierarchical view of art to join the first rank of actors. His face, figure, hoarse voice, and natural inclination suited him to low comedy, including Shakespeare's clowns, but the *Theatrical Review* said his imperfect judgement sometimes encouraged him to 'overtop' his parts (*Theatrical Review*, 1758, 11); Wilkes, however, said: 'His judgement and experience teach him never to overshoot the mark, but to keep nature always in view' (Wilkes, 271).

ALAN HUGHES

Sources Highfill, Burnim & Langhans, *BDA* · A. H. Scouten, ed., *The London stage, 1660–1800*, pt 3: 1729–1747 (1961) · G. W. Stone, ed., *The London stage, 1660–1800*, pt 4: 1747–1776 (1962) · C. B. Hogan, ed., *The London stage, 1660–1800*, pt 5: 1776–1800 (1968) · B. R. Schneider, *Index to 'The London stage, 1660–1800'* (1979) · *The thespian dictionary, or, Dramatic biography of the present age*, 2nd edn (1805) · T. Davies, *Dramatic miscellanies*, 3 vols. (1784) · T. Wilkes, *A general view of the stage* (1759) · F. Gentleman, *The dramatic censor, or, Critical companion*, 2 vols. (1770) · T. Wilkinson, *The wandering patentee, or, A history of the Yorkshire theatres from 1770 to the present time*, 4 vols. (1795) · [A. Hill], *The actor, or, Guide to the stage* (1821) · D. Cook, *Hours with the players*, 2 vols. (1881)
Likenesses J. Roberts, drawing, 1781, Garr. Club · G. Carter, group portrait, oils (*The apotheosis of Garrick*), Picture Gallery of Royal Shakespeare Company · S. Harding, watercolour (as Sir Oliver Surface in *School for scandal*), Harvard U., Widener College · P. J. de Loutherbourg, oils (as Launce in *Two gentlemen of Verona*), Garr. Club · theatrical prints, BM, NPG
Wealth at death left house in Stafford Row: Highfill, Burnim & Langhans, *BDA*

Yates, Richard (1769–1834), Church of England clergyman and antiquary, born in July 1769 at Bury St Edmunds, was the son of Richard Yates (1741–1803) and his wife, Jane Crisp, also of Bury. He was educated at Bury St Edmunds grammar school, but left aged fifteen to teach as usher in a school at Linton, Cambridgeshire. In 1789 he was teaching at Chelmsford grammar school, and in 1792 at a school in Hammersmith, Middlesex. Ordained deacon in September 1796, he preached his first sermon as curate at Chelsea Hospital on 2 October next; after ordination as priest in January 1797 he was in March 1798 appointed one of the chaplains there, where he became a popular preacher and maintained the connection until his death.

When on 28 April 1803 his father died at Bury, having been custodian of the abbey ruins for thirty-seven years, Yates undertook to enlarge, edit, and publish his father's extensive drawings and notes on the history of the abbey. In this work he had the assistance and encouragement of John Nichols and such able antiquaries as Richard Gough, Thomas Astle, and Thomas Martin, but the work was marred by long delays. The first part appeared soon enough in 1805 as *The Monastic History … of the Town and Abbey of St Edmund's Bury* and dealt principally with the abbey. Despite the author's assurances in the *Gentleman's Magazine* in 1819 (1st ser., 89/2.194, 386) that progress was being made, nothing further appeared until 1843, when Yates had been dead for nine years. His friend John Bowyer Nichols attempted to revive interest in the project with a 'second edition' which added little more than fourteen engravings, brief text, and transcripts of some charters. Richard's younger brother the Revd William Yates (1774–

1830), a schoolmaster of Shacklewell, Middlesex, drew the plates.

In May 1804 Yates was appointed to the rectory of Ashen in Essex. In 1805 he took the degree of BD, and in 1818 that of DD from Jesus College, Cambridge. He lived chiefly in London, often preaching at the fashionable chapels and becoming interested in the conduct and management of such charities as the asylum for the deaf and dumb, of which he was secretary. In 1805 he was elected one of the treasurers of the Literary Fund, a post in which he continued for life.

Apart from his published sermons and his history of Bury Abbey, Yates's only significant work was a pamphlet called *The church in danger: a statement of the cause, and of the probable means of averting that danger, attempted in a letter to the earl of Liverpool* (1815). This pamphlet, which pointed out the deficiency of places of public worship, was commended by Nicholas Vansittart, the chancellor of the exchequer, when advocating parliamentary grants for the erection of new churches and chapels in the metropolis and other populous places. Yates's popularity as a London preacher, and his independent means (derived from his marriage in 1810 with Ann, only daughter of Patrick Telfer of Gower Street, London, led him to decline offers of the livings of Blackburn in Lancashire and of Hilgay in Norfolk. During the last five or six years of his life he was an invalid, and he died at Penshurst in Kent on 24 August 1834. He left three children.

ERNEST CLARKE, rev. J. M. BLATCHLY

Sources J. B. Nichols, memoir, in R. Yates, *An illustration of the monastic history and antiquities of the town and abbey of St Edmund's Bury*, 2nd edn (1843) · *GM*, 2nd ser., 2 (1834), 437–9 · Yates MSS, BL, Egerton MSS · *European Magazine and London Review*, 74 (1818), 1–8 **Archives** BL, corresp. and papers incl. partly MS monastic history of Bury St Edmunds, Egerton MSS 2370–2377 | Bodl. Oxf., letters to John and John Bowyer Nichols **Likenesses** S. Drummond, portrait, repro. in *European Magazine and London Review* · H. Meyer, stipple (after S. Drummond), BM, NPG; repro. in *European Magazine and London Review* (1818) · Tannock, portrait, repro. in Yates, *Illustration of the monastic history … of St Edmund's Bury* · portrait (after Tannock), Royal Literary Fund, Adelphi Terrace, London

Yates [*née* Janau], **Rose Emma Lamartine** (1875–1954), women's activist, was born on 23 February 1875 at 33 Dalyell Road, Lambeth, London, the youngest daughter of the three children of Marie Elphege Bertoni Victor Janau (b. 1847), teacher of foreign languages, and his wife, Marie Pauline (1841–1909). Both her parents were born in France and became naturalized British subjects. Yates was schooled privately in Truro, Cornwall. Her education continued at Royal Holloway College and the University of Oxford, where she studied modern languages and philology. In 1900 she married Thomas Lamartine Yates (1849–1929), a solicitor, and eight years later gave birth to their only child, Paul. Both were passionate cyclists, touring Europe in the early years of their marriage, and were active members of the Cyclists' Touring Club. Within the club Yates was a leading figure in the reform party and in 1908 was the first woman elected to its council. She resigned her seat in 1915.

Yates's involvement with the women's suffrage campaign, in which her husband supported her, began in 1909. On 24 February she was arrested while on a deputation to the House of Commons. At her trial, where she was sentenced to one month's imprisonment in Holloway gaol, she made an impassioned defence of her actions: 'every woman must have the courage of her convictions, and not slink back when she has taken her first step' (*Votes for Women*, 5 March 1909, 407). It was a sentiment that informed Yates's life. By 1910 she was honorary secretary of the Wimbledon Women's Social and Political Union (WSPU) and under her leadership it became one of the most prosperous branches in the organization. Between 1910 and 1914 she addressed meetings across London and nationally, notably delivering a speech at the 1910 massive demonstration in Hyde Park. Throughout this period she was a contributor to the *Wimbledon Borough News*, where she made regular propaganda for the cause. Yates made little distinction between her private and public worlds. Her house—Dorset Hall in Merton—was both home and refuge: suffragettes convalesced there after periods of imprisonment. Even her enthusiasm for gardening—she was a member of the Royal Horticultural Society—was utilized for the cause. She planted a section of her garden in WSPU colours.

Yates was a committed member of the union, though not an uncritical follower. Her political sympathies lay with the left of the movement and she shared friendships with socialist suffragettes Mary Gawthorpe, Elinor Penn Gaskell, and Emily Wilding Davison—an old college friend. Her open dissent was provoked by the decision to suspend militant activity at the outbreak of the First World War. She saw no reason for campaigning to stop, and objected to the transformation of the union into a pro-war organization. In October 1915 Yates chaired a meeting protesting against using the union's name for non-suffrage activity and a year later supported the formation of 'Suffragettes of the WSPU'. Although linked with the left, it seems that Yates never joined a political party. In 1919 she contested, as an independent, the London county council seat of North Lambeth. Elected on a reform programme, she spent three years championing equal pay, increased public housing, and the provision of nursery education.

Yates was instrumental in building an archive of the suffrage campaign, and in 1939 opened the Women's Record House in Great Smith Square, London. The premises were destroyed during the Second World War. Some of its records were rescued and form part of the Suffragette Fellowship collection in the Museum of London.

Yates died of colon cancer on 5 November 1954, at her home, 11 Bede House, Manor Fields, Wandsworth, London. She was survived by her son. GAIL CAMERON

Sources G. Hawtin, *Votes for Wimbledon women* (1993) · A. Morley and L. Stanley, *The life and death of Emily Wilding Davison* (1988), 124–34 · J. Wallace, *Dorset Hall* (1991), 25 · *Votes for Women* (5 March 1909), 407 · *Votes for Women* (27 Oct 1911), 126 · *Votes for Women* (24 Nov 1911), 162 · *Calling All Women* (Feb 1955) · *Women's Bulletin* (12 Nov 1954) · *Votes for Women* (22 July 1910), 714 · 'Winning a seat on the LCC', *The Vote*, 18/490 (14 March 1919), 117 · 'London county council elections', *The Vote*, 18/488 (28 Feb 1919), 98 · A. Rosen, *Rise up, women! The militant campaign of the Women's Social and Political Union, 1903-1914* (1974), 246–55 · *CGPLA Eng. & Wales* (1955) · b. cert. · m. cert. · d. cert. · A. J. R., ed., *The suffrage annual and women's who's who* (1913) **Archives** Museum of London, Suffragette Fellowship collection · University of Warwick, Cyclists' Touring Club archive · Women's Library, London, Emily Davison collection **Likenesses** photograph, *c.*1912, Museum of London **Wealth at death** £24,389 18*s.* 11*d.*: probate, 26 Jan 1955, *CGPLA Eng. & Wales*

Yates, William (1792–1845), orientalist and missionary, was born in Loughborough, Leicestershire, on 15 December 1792, the son of a shoemaker. He was educated at Loughborough high school. It was presumed that he would follow in his father's trade, but his aptitude for preaching seemed to show that his talents lay elsewhere. He was encouraged at eighteen to study classical languages, and was taught Greek and Latin by his friends. He then became a schoolteacher and, having decided to become a minister, went to the Bristol Baptist college in 1812. At Bristol he began to study oriental languages; by 1813 he had decided to make translating the Bible into Eastern languages his life's work.

Yates's friends at Bristol thought that he should continue his studies at one of the Scottish universities, but he chose instead to join the Baptist Missionary Society, and after some obstruction from the East India Company, left for India, arriving in Calcutta on 16 April 1815. He continued to Serampore to join William Carey (1761–1834), who had been sent out by the same society in 1792, and under his direction began to study Sanskrit and Bengali. Almost immediately he began to help with the mission's publications.

In January 1816 Yates married Catherine Grant, the daughter of a missionary. In 1817, when the Serampore establishment separated from the Baptist Missionary Society, Yates remained with the latter, and moved to Calcutta, where he established a school and helped to found the Calcutta Missionary Union, besides building chapels and other religious buildings in and around Calcutta.

In the time which he could spare from preaching and travelling, Yates composed a simplified Sanskrit grammar, a Sanskrit vocabulary, and manuals of Hindustani and Arabic, as well as various handbooks on natural science, history, and evidences for the Christian instruction of Indians in Sanskrit, Hindustani, and Bengali. These were all published between 1817 and 1827. Further works during that period included, besides a translation of the Psalms into Bengali, memoirs of the lives of fellow missionaries, essays on points of Christian doctrine, and some protests against the practice of suttee, which was not declared illegal until 1831. His educational works were printed by the Calcutta Schoolbook Society (of which he was secretary from 1824) at the Baptist Mission Press, which was managed by another missionary, W. H. Pearce, who had worked for the Clarendon Press in Oxford.

Yates spent 1827 and 1828 in America and Europe. Returning to Calcutta in 1829, he was relieved of his missionary duties, and made pastor of the English church in the Circular Road which he had helped to found. He held this post until 1839, when he resigned it to devote the whole of his time to translating. Between 1829 and 1845, the year of his death, he produced a Sanskrit dictionary (abridged from Wilson's), a Hindustani dictionary, and a complete version of the Bible in Bengali which took ten years to prepare and print. He also translated considerable portions of the Bible into Sanskrit, and produced a version of the Psalms in the *sloka* metre. He composed a Bengali manual in two volumes, which was published after his death by Wenger. His educational works received considerable encouragement from the Indian government, which not only subsidized them, but offered Yates a stipend of £1000, which he declined, to devote himself entirely to such work. While most of his Sanskrit work was of a popular and synthesizing kind, his edition of the *Nalodaya* (1840) and his *Essay on Alliteration* (first published in *Asiatic Researches*, vol. 20) also represented original research. As well as an orientalist, he was a deeply read classical scholar, a Hebraist, and a student of Chinese. He published a treatise on the Hebrew verb and a manual on the Hebrew Bible. In 1831 he received the degree of AM from Brown University in the United States, followed by that of DD in 1839. After Catherine's death in 1839 he married, in 1841, Martha Pearce, the widow of his coadjutor. Yates was ordered to return to England to recover his health, but he died and was buried at sea on 3 July 1845, on his way home.   D. S. MARGOLIOUTH, *rev.* LYNN MILNE

Sources J. Hoby, *Memoir of Yates* (1847)

Yaxley, Francis (*b.* before 1528, *d.* 1565), political agent, was the eldest son of Richard Yaxley of Mellis, Suffolk, and Anne, daughter of Roger Austin of Earl Soham, Suffolk. The Yaxley family, based at Yaxley Hall, had joined the ranks of the Suffolk gentry in the fifteenth century; Francis was descended from the junior branch. At an unknown date he married Margaret, third daughter of Sir Henry Hastings of Braunstone, Leicestershire. His first patron may well have been William Cecil, whose 'godly counsels and fatherly admonitions' he later acknowledged (Ellis, 13). In 1547 he began to work for the privy council, possibly in the signet office. It was perhaps this earlier experience that secured his later appointment to the office of clerk of the signet at some point between 1555 and 1557. Although this was the only post Yaxley was given within the government he was elected to parliament on three occasions: in 1553 as MP for Dunwich, in 1555 as MP for Stamford, and finally in 1558 as MP for Saltash. In addition to the work he performed for the government at home Yaxley was also involved, albeit at a junior level, in his country's diplomatic affairs. From 1550 he joined Peter Vannes in his resident embassy to Venice, and during his return journey to England in November 1552 he visited Speyer, where he acted as cupbearer to the elector palatine. Yaxley entered Gray's Inn in 1553, but in April he returned to diplomatic service, accompanying Nicholas Wotton on his resident embassy to the French court.

However, what began as a promising career in the brief

reigns of Edward and Mary rapidly foundered in that of their sister. Yaxley's indiscretion and continuing sympathy for the Catholic cause soon led him into trouble. In January 1561 he was briefly imprisoned in the Tower of London, a punishment, according to the Spanish ambassador, Alvaro de la Quadra, for talking too openly about the possible marriage of Queen Elizabeth to Robert Dudley. The following year he was taken into custody again, the consequence of his involvement in the plans of Margaret, Lady Lennox, to marry her son Lord Darnley to Mary, queen of Scots. Although it is unclear when he was released from the Tower it was not before February 1563. No doubt owing both to his continuing adherence to the Catholic faith and to the rough treatment he had received from Elizabeth's government Yaxley's final years were devoted to the service of her rival, Mary, queen of Scots. In July 1565 he travelled to Flanders, where he may well have received messages from the Habsburg government for Mary. On 20 August he left the Low Countries for Scotland; whatever the purpose of his mission it seems to have been sufficiently interesting to the English authorities to warrant the dispatch of a man-of-war, the pursuit of which he barely eluded. Yaxley arrived in Scotland on 25 August and was immediately appointed Lord Darnley's secretary, partly in recognition of the services he had already performed, but also to lend him more credibility when Mary dispatched him as her envoy to the Spanish court less than three weeks after his arrival in Scotland.

Yaxley sailed from Dumbarton on 16 September 1565, arriving at Segovia on 20 October. In his interview with Philip he requested the use of Spanish soldiers and money to expel English sponsored rebels and heretics from Scotland. Further, he asked that the Spanish king intercede with Elizabeth both to secure the release of Darnley's mother from the Tower, and to dissuade the English queen from lending further support to Mary's opponents in Scotland. Yaxley's mission was at least partially successful. Although Philip declined to intercede with Elizabeth directly, arguing that to do so would only stiffen her opposition to Mary, he did agree to send Queen Mary 20,000 crowns which Yaxley was to collect at Brussels and transport to Scotland. The envoy left Segovia on 25 October, travelling by post to Brussels, which he reached on 9 November. There he was met by Philip's factor, Alonso del Canto, who transferred the money into his keeping and escorted him to Antwerp, from where he set sail on 28 November 1565. Although the voyage reportedly began with good weather it did not last. Off the coast of Northumberland the ship encountered a storm and foundered, Yaxley being drowned in the process. Both the envoy's body, cast up on Holy Island, and the gold he had been taking to Mary were discovered by the English. The latter was sent to Elizabeth's treasury, where it became the source of a mild diplomatic dispute; the envoy was carried to Suffolk and buried at Yaxley. If indiscretion and religious conviction denied Francis Yaxley the fruits of a successful career, they also allowed him a role in international affairs, albeit a brief one, which few of Elizabeth's servants had a chance to play. He had no children; by his will of 3 July 1561 he bequeathed his lands at Yaxley, Braiseworth, Eye, and Thornham to his father, whom he predeceased.

LUKE MACMAHON

Sources CSP for., 1547–65 • HoP, Commons, 1509–58 • W. C. Metcalfe, ed., The visitations of Suffolk (1882) • M. A. S. Hume, ed., Calendar of letters and state papers relating to English affairs, preserved principally in the archives of Simancas, 1, PRO (1892), 1558–67 • H. Ellis, ed., Original letters of eminent literary men of the sixteenth, seventeenth, and eighteenth centuries, CS, 23 (1843)

Yaxley, William. See Crathorne, William (1670–1740).

Y Cynhyrfwr. See Rees, David (1801–1869).

Y Doctor Coch. See Price, Ellis (c.1505–1594).

Yea, Lacy Walter Giles (1808–1855), army officer, born in Park Row, Bristol, on 20 May 1808, was the eldest son of Sir William Walter Yea, second baronet (d. 1862), of Pyrland, near Taunton, Somerset, and his wife, Anne Heckstetter (d. 1846), youngest daughter of Colonel David Michel of Dulish House, Dorset. Lacy Yea was educated at Eton College. Lord Malmesbury mentions a desperate fight which Yea had with a big boy of sixteen, which he won 'by sheer pluck', when he was only thirteen (Harris, 13).

Yea was commissioned as ensign in the 37th foot on 6 October 1825, obtained an unattached lieutenancy on 19 December 1826, was appointed to the 5th foot on 13 March 1827, and exchanged to the 7th (Royal Fusiliers) on 13 March 1828. He served with it in the Mediterranean and America, becoming captain on 30 December 1836, major on 3 June 1842, and lieutenant-colonel on 9 August 1850. In 1854 he went out in command of it to Turkey and the Crimea. 'A man of an onward, fiery, violent nature', he was 'so rough an enforcer of discipline that he had never been much liked in peace time by those who had to obey him' (Kinglake, 2.334, 423). He himself wrote to his sister just before the battle of the Alma: 'The Russians are before me and my own men are behind me, so I don't think you will ever see me again' (Wood, 64). At the battle of the Alma, Yea's regiment held an important position, urged on by their commander: 'his dark eyes yielded fire, and all the while from his deep-chiselled merciless lips there pealed the thunder of imprecation and command' (Kinglake, 2.424–7, 552–7). There and at the battle of Inkerman and in the severe winter of 1854–5 his care for his men belied his reputation for over-discipline.

Yea was shot dead at the assault of the Redan on 18 June 1855; his body was recovered, and buried on 20 June in the cemetery at Sevastopol (with a headstone). His eldest sister put up a marble monument to him in his parish church of Taunton St James, Somerset.

Yea was unmarried. His father survived him, dying on 20 May 1862, when the baronetcy passed to Lacy's younger brother, Sir Henry Lacy Yea, third and last baronet (d. 1864). Yea bore a strong facial likeness to Napoleon I, and he once went to a fancy-dress ball at Bath in that character, with his brother officers as his suite.

E. M. LLOYD, rev. H. C. G. MATTHEW

Sources GM, 2nd ser., 44 (1855), 203 • A. W. Kinglake, The invasion of the Crimea, 8 vols. (1863–87) • A. J. Monday, The history of the family *of Yea* (1885) • J. P. Groves, ed., *Historical records of the 7th or royal regiment of fusiliers* (1903) • E. Wood, *The Crimea in 1854 and 1894* (1895) • J. H. Harris [third earl of Malmesbury], *Memoirs of an ex-minister: an autobiography*, new edn (1885)

Yeamans [*née* Fell], **Isabel** (1637×42–1704), Quaker preacher, was born at Swarthmoor Hall, near Ulverston, Lancashire, the third of eight children (seven sisters and one brother) of Thomas *Fell (*bap.* 1599, *d.* 1658), judge and recruiter MP for Lancaster, and his wife, Margaret *Fell (1614–1702), daughter of the Lancashire gentleman John Askew of Marsh Grange near Dalton in Furness. She became deeply committed to Quakerism in 1652, when George Fox first visited Swarthmoor Hall and converted Margaret Fell and her daughters to the new sect. By 1660 Isabel became an intermittently travelling Quaker. She was known to preach throughout her adult life at the meetings she visited across England. Her signature appeared on Quaker women's meeting records from Yorkshire to Somerset between the 1670s and the 1690s, and she corresponded with other Quaker ministers such as William Penn.

In the summer of 1664 Isabel Fell married William Yeamans (1639–1674), a Quaker and merchant of Bristol. They had at least four children, three of whom died in childhood. When her mother married George Fox in Bristol in 1669 Isabel was present and signed the marriage certificate. During her married years in Bristol she helped set up the Bristol women's monthly meeting in 1671 in response to George Fox's circular letter sent out to encourage women to form separate women's meetings for business, which pronounced that men and women were 'helpmeets' for one another, and also in the wake of her mother's earlier call for women's rights in Quaker meetings in *Women's Speaking Justified* (1666). The efforts of Isabel Yeamans and the Bristol women challenged the Bristol leadership and they did meet resistance. The (all-male) Bristol two-week meeting admonished the women for exceeding the boundaries of authority in forming their own meeting without their approval. The Bristol women acquiesced.

William Yeamans died in 1674, after which Isabel returned to Swarthmoor and lived there for some time with her two surviving children, William and Rachel (an earlier William had died in 1666 and Margaret in 1674). While there she attended the women's monthly meetings. In June 1676 Rachel died at Swarthmoor, aged ten. A small note in the household account book of Isabel's sister Sarah *Fell [*see under* Fell, Margaret] of Swarthmoor, marks her passing, for 5*s.* was paid to a friend for 'her paines about Rachel Yeamans when she died' (Fell, *Household Account Book*, 285).

In the summer of 1677 Isabel Yeamans accompanied George Fox, William Penn, George Keith, and Robert Barclay to the Netherlands and then to northern Germany to visit small groups of Quakers living in the region, and in the hope of converting protestant sectaries to the Quaker 'Truth', as early Quakers termed it. The party visited Princess Elizabeth of the Palatinate, a learned woman who had shown some interest in Quaker thought in her earlier correspondence with Penn. Accompanied by Penn and Barclay, Isabel did speak during the visit with Princess Elizabeth, who was somewhat taken by her free manner of personal delivery. Fox did not attend the meeting, but rather wrote a letter which was personally delivered by Isabel to Princess Elizabeth. Fox was then fifty-three years old, and it is probable that his wife, Margaret, was concerned for his position in the Quaker leadership. Isabel Yeamans was chosen to accompany her stepfather in part for her reputation as an effective preacher, but she also acted as a support and representative for him in relation to the other influential Quaker travellers of higher social status. By the late 1670s Fox was yielding his *primus inter pares* leadership role to younger men, some of whom were of higher social rank.

Over her adult years Yeamans kept close contact with her mother and sisters. The Fell women exchanged continuous correspondence, purchased needed articles for one another when in London, and exchanged gifts and advice. The family correspondence between 1652 and 1704 resonates with affection, generosity, mutual concern, and an insatiable desire for news of one another. In 1689 Yeamans married Abraham Morrice of Lincoln, a well-to-do merchant who was an active Quaker in his monthly meeting in the south-west area of Lincolnshire. Both died in 1704, presumably at their home in Lincoln. The value of the Morrice estate is unknown.

BONNELYN YOUNG KUNZE

Sources *The journal of George Fox*, ed. N. Penney, 2 vols. (1911) • *The short journal and itinerary journals of George Fox*, ed. N. Penney (1925) • *The household account book of Sarah Fell of Swarthmoor Hall*, ed. N. Penney (1920) • *The papers of William Penn*, ed. M. M. Dunn, R. S. Dunn, and others, 5 vols. (1981–7) • W. C. Braithwaite, *The beginnings of Quakerism* (1912) • W. C. Braithwaite, *The second period of Quakerism*, ed. H. J. Cadbury, 2nd edn (1961) • B. Y. Kunze, *Margaret Fell and the rise of Quakerism* (1994) • I. Ross, *Margaret Fell: mother of Quakerism*, 2nd edn (1984) • H. L. Ingle, *First among Friends: George Fox and the creation of Quakerism* (1994) • R. Mortimer, ed., *Minute book of the men's meeting of the Society of Friends in Bristol*, Bristol RS, 26 (1971) • 'Dictionary of Quaker biography', RS Friends, Lond. [card index] **Archives** Lancs. RO, Lancashire women's quarterly meeting minutes • Lancs. RO, Swarthmoor women's monthly meeting minutes • RS Friends, Lond., Abraham MSS • RS Friends, Lond., Box Meeting MSS • RS Friends, Lond., Gibson MSS • RS Friends, Lond., Spence MSS • RS Friends, Lond., Swarthmoor MSS • RS Friends, Lond., Thirnbeck MSS

Yeamans, Sir John, first baronet (1611–1674), colonial governor, was born in February 1611 in Bristol, a younger son of John Yeamans, a brewer, and Blanche Germain. He may have served as a royalist colonel during the English civil war, though he owned land in Barbados by 1638. Acquiring more acreage there in partnership with Benjamin Berringer, he became one of the largest landholders on the island, a colonel of the militia, judge of a local court of common pleas, and, by 1660, a member of the royal council. His first marriage, to a Miss Limp, produced five sons; his second, on 11 April 1661 to Margaret Berringer, added two more sons and two daughters. Margaret was the daughter of John Foster, a clergyman, and the widow of Yeamans's former partner, who died only weeks before the wedding. Yeamans, though investigated and cleared by the council, probably had Berringer poisoned.

Yeamans's public career nevertheless reached its peak during the 1660s and early 1670s as increasingly adverse economic conditions prompted many Barbadian planters to seek better opportunities elsewhere. Yeamans headed a group that agreed with the Carolina proprietors to settle their new colony in North America. But another party, also mainly Barbadians, reached the Cape Fear River first. The proprietors named the area Clarendon county and Yeamans its governor, and the king made him a baronet on 12 January 1665. Sailing from Barbados in October 1665 with three ships, Yeamans and his men intended to join the group at Cape Fear, explore, and settle at Port Royal Sound. Two vessels were wrecked, however, and he remained at Clarendon only during November and December. Still, this was sufficient to plan the exploring expedition later commanded by Robert Sandford and his lieutenant, Joseph Woory, Yeamans's nephew. The settlers abandoned the inadequately supported outpost at Clarendon by the autumn of 1667.

Two years later, under the leadership of Sir Anthony Ashley Cooper, subsequently first earl of Shaftesbury, the proprietors tried again. This time they sent three ships with settlers from the British Isles, bound for Port Royal by way of Barbados. Instructed to name a governor for South Carolina, Yeamans chose himself and accompanied the expedition as far as Bermuda, where part of the small fleet regrouped after a storm. There he appointed an aged Bermudian, William Sayle, governor instead, and abruptly returned to Barbados, while the expedition continued on and in April 1670 founded the first permanent white settlement in South Carolina. Yeamans arrived more than a year later, and, having been named a landgrave by the proprietors on 5 April 1671, he expected to be immediately recognized as governor. But neither Joseph West, who had succeeded to the post upon Sayle's death, nor the council complied until ordered to do so by the lords proprietors. Elected to the first parliament in the interim, Yeamans became its speaker and used the position to harass West.

Yeamans took office as governor on 19 April 1672. Acting on the proprietors' orders, he initiated the survey of the present site of Charles Town. But he also established his own plantation, settled some of the first slaves in Carolina on it, and traded in scarce commodities at exorbitant prices, while he pestered the proprietors with requests for more supplies and a governor's house. Yeamans had been their second choice for governor, and his behaviour quickly undermined their confidence in him. 'If to convert all things to his present private profitt be the marke' of ability, Sir John is 'without doubt a very judicious man' (Cheves, 416), Shaftesbury observed in 1672. Accordingly, on 18 April 1674, the proprietors commissioned Joseph West as his successor. Yeamans, however, died some time between 3 and 13 August, in South Carolina, where he was probably buried.

Yeamans epitomized the enterprising Barbadians who played a large part in settling South Carolina. That some,

like him, resembled pirates ashore probably both promoted and retarded development of the colony; it certainly contributed to political factionalism endemic during the early years. ROBERT M. WEIR

Sources R. Waterhouse, 'Yeamans, Sir John', *ANB* · L. S. Butler and H. R. Paschal, 'Yeamans, Sir John', *Dictionary of North Carolina biography*, ed. W. S. Powell (1979–96) · C. H. Lesser, *South Carolina begins: the records of a proprietary colony, 1663–1721* (1995) · L. Cheves, ed., *The Shaftesbury papers and other records relating to Carolina* (1897); repr. (2000) · P. F. Campbell, ed., *Chapters in Barbados history: first series* (1986) · R. M. Weir, '"Shaftesbury's darling": The Carolinas in the seventeenth century', *The origins of empire*, ed. N. Canny (1998), vol. 1 of *The Oxford history of the British empire*, 375–97 · W. L. Saunders and W. Clark, eds., *The colonial records of North Carolina*, 30 vols. (1886–1907), vols. 1–2 · M. E. Sirmans, *Colonial South Carolina: a political history, 1663–1763* (Chapel Hill, NC, 1966) · R. Waterhouse, *A new world gentry: the making of a merchant and planter class in South Carolina, 1670–1770* (1989) · A. S. Salley, ed., *Narratives of early Carolina* (1911) · 'The Thruston family of Virginia', *William and Mary College Quarterly*, 25 (1916–17), 192–8, esp. 197 n. 5 · R. S. Dunn, 'The English sugar islands and the founding of South Carolina', *South Carolina Historical Magazine*, 72 (1971), 81–93 · *DNB* · M. A. Read, 'Notes on some colonial governors of South Carolina and their families', *South Carolina Historical and Genealogical Magazine*, 11 (1910), 107–22 · A. S. Salley, 'Where Sir John Yeamans died', *South Carolina Historical and Genealogical Magazine*, 21 (1920), 37–8
Wealth at death see Read, 'Notes on some colonial governors'

Yeamans, Robert (*d.* 1643), royalist plotter, came of a numerous Bristol family and was probably closely related to William Yeamans (1578–1632?), a graduate of Balliol College, Oxford, incumbent of St Philip's, Bristol, where he was noted as a puritan and, from 1615 until his death, prebendary of Bristol Cathedral. Robert was a Merchant Venturer and councillor of Bristol, and in 1641–2 served as sheriff.

Shortly before Bristol was garrisoned for parliament, Yeamans had received a commission from the king to raise troops there. In December 1642 the city was occupied by Colonel Essex, the command falling to Colonel Nathaniel Fiennes in February 1643. In March Yeamans acted belatedly in execution of his commission. He and his fellow Merchant Venturer George Butcher, or Bowcher, conceived a plan for betraying the city into the hands of Prince Rupert. The prince was to bring 4000 horse and 2000 foot to Durdham Down, and the royalists in Bristol, who were estimated at 2000 were to seize the Frome gate and admit Rupert's forces. The plot was to take effect on the night of 7 March 1643; but Fiennes heard of it, and on that day Yeamans and his principal confederates were arrested in his house in Wine Street. On 8 May Yeamans, Butcher, and two others were condemned to death by a court martial as traitors. King Charles made great efforts to save them and Lord Forth threatened to execute a similar number of parliamentary prisoners in his hands. The threat proved useless, and both Yeamans and Butcher were executed. Yeamans was hanged, drawn, and quartered opposite his house on 30 May, and his remains were buried on the same day in Christ Church, Bristol. When Fiennes was himself on trial before a court martial on charges of treason, cowardice, and the improper surrender of Bristol in July 1643, his execution of Yeamans was used against him by his enemies at Westminster such as William Prynne.

Administration of Yeamans's estate was granted on 7 July to his widow, Anne, said in the royalist accounts to have been a kinswoman also named Yeamans. He allegedly left eight very young children, 'the eldest not able to dresse itself … without helpe' (*Two State Martyrs*, 31), and a ninth was born posthumously. The eldest son is said to have been Sir John Yeamans and the second Sir Robert Yeamans, who, like his brother, was created a baronet on 12 January 1665 and died in South Carolina in 1674. But both affiliations are fictitious; Sir John was born in 1611, and Sir Robert was baptized on 19 April 1617, and both were apparently sons of John Yeamans, brewer, of Redcliffe, Bristol, whose will is dated 1645. Many other members of the family are mentioned as taking a prominent part in local affairs in Bristol and Barbados. The only child of the royalist whose relationship to him is established is his daughter Anne, who married Thomas Curtis, the Quaker of Reading, and interceded for George Fox's release in 1660. Other members of the Yeamans family were Quakers, and one of them married Isabel, daughter of Margaret Fell and stepdaughter of Fox.

A. F. POLLARD, *rev.* SEAN KELSEY

Sources *A briefe relation abstracted out of severall letters of a most hellish, cruell and bloudy plot against the city of Bristoll* (1643) · *An extraordinary deliverance, from a cruell plot, and bloody massacre contrived by the malignants in Bristoll* (1643) · *A full declaration … as also a relation of the late bloody conspiracy against the city of Bristoll* (1643) · *The two state martyrs, or, the murther of master Robert Yeomans, and master George Bowcher citizens of Bristoll* (1643) · J. Rushworth, *Historical collections*, new edn, 3 (1721) · *JHC*, 3 (1642–4), 97 · *CSP dom.*, 1641–3, 462–3 · Clarendon, *Hist. rebellion*, 3.37 · S. Seyer, *Memoirs historical and topographical of Bristol*, 2 (1823), 341–400 · S. R. Gardiner, *History of the great civil war*, 1642–1649, 4 vols. (1893); repr. (1987), 1.99 · P. McGrath, *Bristol and the civil war* (1981) · P. McGrath, *Records relating to the society of Merchant Venturers of the city of Bristol in the seventeenth century* (1952) · W. Hunt, *Bristol* (1887), 148–9 · J. Corry and J. Evans, *History of Bristol civil and ecclesiastical*, 2 vols. (1816), 275–8 · GEC, *Baronetage*, 4.5, 39 · J. Burke and J. B. Burke, *A genealogical and heraldic history of the extinct and dormant baronetcies of England, Ireland, and Scotland* (1838), 592–4 · PRO, PROB 6/1234, fol. 4r

Yeames, William Frederick (1835–1918), painter, was born in Taganrog, south-west Russia, on 18 December 1835, the fourth child of William Yeames (d. 1842), the British consul in Taganrog, and his wife, Eliza Mary, the daughter of John Henley. He was educated at home and, following his father's death, travelled with his family in Europe in 1842–3 attending school in Dresden, where he also studied painting. In 1848 he arrived in London to study painting and anatomy with Sir George Scharf, and he later studied drawing with the sculptor J. Sherwood Westmacott. Between 1852 and 1858 he continued his studies in art in Florence with Enrico Pollastrini and Raphael Buonajuto, then moved to Rome to study independently.

Although he was not trained at the Royal Academy, his studies in Italy enabled Yeames quickly to become assimilated into London artistic circles following his move there in 1859. With Frederic Leighton, Holman Hunt, Augustus Egg, and William Mulready he studied from the nude model at the life classes organized by John Phillip at his home in Camden Hill. He settled in St John's Wood in 1865 on his marriage on 18 August that year to Anne (d. 1934), the daughter of Major James Stainbank Winfield. She was the sister of the distinguished early photographer and painter David Wilkie Wynfield and niece of Sir David Wilkie. Yeames was a founder member of the St John's Wood Clique, an informal group which represented a new spirit in English history painting, neither Pre-Raphaelite nor traditional in affiliation but combining in their work features of several kinds of painting, including history, and genre. When the Dudley Gallery was founded in 1865 many of them served on its organizing committees and, Yeames among them, found an alternative to the Royal Academy for exhibiting drawings, watercolours, and oils. Their paintings were characterized by historical costumes and settings but were generally humorous or affecting rather than grand and morally uplifting. Yeames, however, combined such lighter subjects with a more traditional type of history painting. At the Royal Academy in 1866 he exhibited *On Bread and Water* (priv. coll.), which depicted a boy being punished by his mother for bad behaviour, and *Queen Elizabeth Receiving the French Ambassadors after the News of the Massacre of St Bartholemew*, which showed a serious political and diplomatic incident in English history. His *The Meeting of Sir Thomas More with his Daughter after his Sentence to Death* (exh. RA, 1863; priv. coll.) had already revealed Yeames's ambition to produce serious history painting. The solemnity of the scene was articulated through composition rather than size—a dramatic effect being produced from the groupings of figures rather than from magnitude.

Although Yeames rarely had the opportunity to produce large-scale public works, in the late 1860s he was invited to contribute to two decorative schemes. The first of these was the mosaic decoration for South Kensington Museum, for what was known as the Kensington Valhalla. He designed two panels, one depicting the sculptor Pietro Torrigiani (1866), the other Hans Holbein the younger (1867), the drawings for which are preserved in the Victoria and Albert Museum. The second, in 1867, was for the mosaic frieze of the Royal Albert Hall, for which Yeames designed the sections dealing with architecture.

Yeames was not a great colourist and his handling of paint is often dry, but his power as a composer of groups of figures, his ability to place figures in complex perspectives, and his feeling for narrative made his works stand out from many contemporary genre or subject paintings at the Royal Academy. *Amy Robsart* (exh. RA, 1877; Tate collection), one of the first paintings bought under the terms of the Chantrey bequest, is a striking example of his best qualities. It shows the discovery of the dead body of the wife of the earl of Leicester lying crumpled in the midst of her own white petticoats at the foot of a flight of stairs. One onlooker—her murderer—feigns horror; the other, seeing the body for the first time, expresses genuine shock. The sparseness of the composition, noted adversely by some critics in Yeames's earlier work, is here a strength. It focuses attention on the death of the friendless heroine while suggesting something of the intrigue surrounding her. Yeames's lasting fame, however, rests almost entirely upon one painting, *And when did you last see your father?* (exh. RA, 1878; Walker Art Gallery, Liverpool). The events of the civil wars are concentrated in the reactions of a little boy who is being interrogated by a parliamentary officer. Will the boy answer truthfully and betray his family or will he lie to save them? The situation is melodramatic, but the setting up of the dilemma in a frieze-like composition which allows the viewer to scrutinize all of the reactions and expressions is well handled and dramatic. While not, at the time, the most critically acclaimed of his pictures, its drama lodged in the collective consciousness of the British public, and has been much quoted and used in other works of art.

Yeames's adult life was one of ordered domesticity. He was a popular teacher at the Royal Academy Schools and a highly regarded professional. He was elected an associate of the Royal Academy in 1866 and Royal Academician in 1878. Failing eyesight led to his gradual withdrawal from exhibitions, and he retired from the Royal Academy in 1911. He held several official posts: librarian of the Royal Academy (1896–1911), curator of the painted hall at the Royal Naval Hospital, Greenwich, and examiner for the South Kensington Design Schools. Yeames died at his home, 1 Brimley House, Teignmouth, Devon, on 3 May 1918 and was buried in Teignmouth old cemetery.

COLIN CRUISE

Sources M. K. S. Smith, *Art & anecdote: recollections of W. F. Yeames RA* (1927) · E. Morris and F. Milner, *And when did you last see your father?* (1992) [exhibition catalogue, Walker Art Gallery, Liverpool, 13 Nov 1992 – 10 Jan 1993] · T. Taylor, 'W. F. Yeames', *Portfolio*, 2 (1871), 81–4 · J. Dafforne, 'The works of W. F. Yeames', *Art Journal*, 36 (1874), 97–100 · W. W. Fenn, 'William Frederick Yeames', *Magazine of Art* (1881), 196–9 · C. Austin, 'The art of Mr W. F. Yeames', *Windsor Magazine*, 26 (1907), 579–98 · J. Hacking, *Princes of Victorian Bohemia* (2000) · H. S. Marks, *Pen & pencil sketches* (1894) · m. cert. · CGPLA Eng. & Wales (1918)

Archives V&A

Likenesses W. F. Yeames, self-portrait, oils, *c*.1845, repro. in Smith, *Art & anecdote*, facing p. 76 · D. W. Wynfield, photograph, 1860–69, RA · W. F. Yeames, self-portrait, oils, 1884, Aberdeen Art Gallery · A. Bassano, photograph, *c*.1889, repro. in *Year's Art, 1889* (1890), 67 · G. Grenville Manton, group portrait, watercolour (*Conversazione at the Royal Academy, 1891*), NPG · Lock & Whitfield, woodburytype photograph, NPG; repro. in T. Cooper, *Men of mark: a gallery of contemporary portraits* (1883) · R. W. Robinson, photograph, NPG; repro. in *Members and associates of the Royal Academy of Arts, 1891* (1891) · H. T. Wells, group portrait, oils (*Friends at Yewden*), Hamburger Kunsthalle, Hamburg · group portrait, repro. in Hacking, *Princes of Victorian Bohemia* · group portrait, repro. in Marks, *Pen & pencil sketches* · wood-engraving, NPG; repro. in *ILN* (30 June 1866)

Wealth at death £5847 18s. 3d.: probate, 2 Oct 1918, CGPLA Eng. & Wales

Yeardley, Sir George (*bap.* 1588, *d.* 1627), colonial governor, was baptized in St Saviour's, Southwark, on 23 July 1588, the second son of Ralph Yeardley (1549–1603), merchant taylor, and his second wife, Rhoda Marston (*fl.* 1575–1588). About 1605 he went to the Netherlands to serve in the English army under Sir Thomas Gates. On 15 May 1609 he embarked at Woolwich for Virginia, again serving with Gates, who commanded the fleet and bore instructions to act as Virginia's lieutenant-general. Gates was shipwrecked in the Bermudas in the *Sea Adventure* in an incident that probably inspired Shakespeare's *Tempest*. The fleet's stragglers, including Yeardley and Gates, finally reached Jamestown in May 1610.

Yeardley later contrasted the actions of Virginia's early governors with the repressive, quasi-military order imposed in the colony by Marshal Sir Thomas Dale in 1611–16. However, in April 1616, just as Dale was leaving the colony, Yeardley was himself appointed deputy governor of Virginia pending the arrival of Dale's successor. He relaxed constraints on trading relations with the local Native Americans imposed by Dale, whereupon the colony briefly prospered. Samuel Argall's arrival as governor on 15 May 1617 allowed Yeardley to return that summer to England, where he married, on 18 October 1618, Temperance (1581–1630), daughter of Anthony Flowerdieu of Scatton, Norfolk, and Martha Stanley. Exactly a month later he was appointed to serve three years as governor of Virginia, and was knighted by James I during an audience at Newmarket on 24 November.

Yeardley embarked for Virginia in January 1619 with instructions to abolish martial law, address native relations, and regularize land tenure changes before summoning the first representative assembly in an English colony. He was also charged with reducing the production of tobacco, starting silk, wine, and iron production, and with preparing for large scale immigration organized under patents issued by the Virginia Company's London office. His first duty, however, was to address the alleged abuses of Argall's governorship, which ended on 10 April 1619. He then turned to Sir Thomas Smith's ambition of providing education for the natives within a university or college at Henrico; the Revd Thomas Lorkin was appointed to teach there but could not find adequate buildings within the ruinous settlement. On 30 July 1619 Yeardley summoned Virginia's first assembly but failed to win its loyalty to his reform programme, as his secretary, and the assembly's first speaker, John Pory, recorded. Meanwhile, as the London company lurched towards bankruptcy, Sir Edwin Sandys, its treasurer and a leading representative of the opposing faction within the assembly, gained such effective control of policy and partisans as to make Yeardley's programme nearly impossible to implement. John Rolfe reported that Sandys's initiatives forced Yeardley into conflicts of principle with the tobacco growers, especially after the landing of twenty negro slaves from an armed Dutch ship in 1620. Exasperated by the arrival of 1000 unskilled settlers in 1621 Yeardley resigned the governorship, but retained his responsibilities until Sir Francis Wyatt arrived on 8 November 1621 with a charter granted by James I on 24 July regularizing the assumed powers of Virginia's assembly.

This allowed Yeardley to attend to salt and tobacco production on the tidewater estates granted to him in 1618. His estate comprised Weymock, and parcels of land called Kouwan (now known as Kickotan) along the Mapsock

Creek near Charles City, and others near 'James Cittie' (Jamestown). He also acquired a land grant of 1000 acres at Stanley by the Warwick River. This site, called Hungars, was within the 80,000 acres of Northampton hundred being settled by Sandys' unskilled, hostile partisans. Here Yeardley built new corn and iron mills demonstrating the benefits of diversifying away from tobacco.

Yeardley continued to serve on the governor's council rendering valuable advice, particularly after the massacre of colonists by Native Americans in 1622. In 1625, after the revocation of the Virginia Company's charter in 1624, thereby making Virginia a royal colony, he was sent by Virginia's convention to report to the privy council in England. On 24 October the privy council accorded him immunity from any action resulting from his reports and analyses of the colony's problems of civil order and its narrow economic base, before reappointing him Virginia's royal governor on 14 March 1626. He departed in the *Ann*, with *James* as consort, on 19 April 1626, bearing instructions to list each plantation, boat, and colonist, and to make the colony diversify into fruit and corn production or regulated cattle husbandry. During 1627 the privy council sought that he regulate local shipping and open the colony's ports to ships of the Dutch West Indies Company as an extension of the Anglo-Dutch war with France and Spain. Yeardley's half-hearted response reflected the failing health mentioned in his will of 12 October 1627 and its codicil of 29 October. He died on 10 November at James City and was buried in the parish church on 13 November 1627. His will provided that Temperance, as sole executor, should realize all his estate; one third of the proceeds of sale was due to his wife and one third for his eldest son, Argall (*b.* 1619), the rest being for his younger children, Francis (*b.* 1622) and Elizabeth (*b.* 1622). However, the will's instructions were never executed because Yeardley's brother Ralph refused to account for the estate's proceeds with the executor. Temperance went on to marry Francis West, late governor of Virginia, and died in England at Stanfield, Norfolk, in 1630. Argall Yeardley remained at Hungars until 1655; Elizabeth and Francis migrated south after their marriages in 1645 and 1647 as described in Colonel Francis Yeardley's 'Narrative of Excursions into Carolina, 1653–54'.

R. C. D. BALDWIN

Sources W. F. Craven, *The southern colonies in the seventeenth century, 1607–1689* (Baton Rouge, 1949) • W. F. Craven, 'Twenty negros to Jamestown in 1619', *Virginia Quarterly Review*, 47 (1971), 416–20 • W. F. Craven, 'Yeardley, Sir George', *DAB* • E. D. Niell, *History of the Virginia Company of London*, 1 (Washington, 1869); repr. (1968) • W. L. Grant and J. F. Munro, eds., *Acts of the privy council of England: colonial series*, 1: *1613–80* (1908), 92–103, 118–19, 149–50 • *CSP col.*, 1.66–8 • S. Purchas, *Purchas his pilgrimes*, 4 (1625), 1773–5, 1792 • E. S. Morgan, 'The first American boom, Virginia 1618–1650', *William and Mary Quarterly*, 3rd ser., 28 (1971), 169–98 • *APC*, 1630–31, 38–9 • Thurloe, *State papers* • F. Yeardley, 'Narrative of excursions into Carolina, 1653–54', *Narratives of early Carolina, 1650–1708* (New York, 1911) • J. Nichols, *The progresses, processions, and magnificent festivities of King James I, his royal consort, family and court*, 3 (1828) • *IGI* • will, PRO, PROB 11/155, fols. 64–5 • H. R. McIlwaine, ed., *Journals of the house of burgesses of Virginia*, 13 vols. (1905–15)

Archives Chatsworth House, Derbyshire, Devonshire papers • Magd. Cam., Ferrar papers • Virginia State Library, Richmond, journals of the house of burgesses of Virginia

Yeardley, John (1786–1858), missionary, was the son of Joel and Frances Yeardley, small dairy farmers at Orgreave, near Rotherham, Yorkshire, where he was born on 3 January 1786. He was admitted a member of the Society of Friends in his twentieth year, entered a manufactory in Barnsley, Yorkshire, and in 1809 married Elizabeth, *née* Dunn, a convinced Quaker much his senior. He began preaching in 1815, moving from place to place in the northern counties.

In 1821 Elizabeth Yeardley died, and, led by a persistent 'call', Yeardley decided to settle in Lower Saxony, where a small body of Friends existed. To maintain himself, he arranged to represent some merchants who imported linen yarn, and later on he began bleaching on his own account. His philanthropic work included establishing schools and meetings for the young, and many notable people, including the prince and princess of Prussia, came to hear him preach. In 1824 he accompanied Martha Savory [see below], an English Quaker, on a gospel journey up the Rhine from Elberfeld in the north to Württemberg, Tübingen, and other German towns, through Switzerland to Congeniès in central France, where some Friends were settled. They visited Pastor Fliedner at Kaiserswerth, and all the principal religious and philanthropic institutions on their route. On reaching London they were married at Gracechurch Street meeting on 13 December 1826, soon resuming their missionary work in Pyrmont, Friesland, and Switzerland, and visiting asylums, reformatories, and Moravian schools.

During a short time spent in England both Yeardley and his wife studied modern Greek in preparation for a visit to the Ionian Islands, for which they started on 21 June 1833. They were warmly received by De Pressensé in Paris, and by Professor Ehrmann and Cuvier, the naturalist, at Strasbourg. In Corfu they established a girls' school, as well as a model farm, obtaining from the authorities there a grant of land on which prisoners were permitted to supply the labour.

After eight years at home, spent in studying languages, in 1842 the Yeardleys returned for the fourth time to France and Germany. In 1850, during a stay in Berlin, they became acquainted with Neander, the historian. Following Martha Yeardley's death in 1851, her husband continued his travels to Norway in 1852, and to southern Russia and Constantinople in 1853.

In his seventy-second year Yeardley began to study Turkish, and started for the East on 15 June 1858. After some work in Constantinople, and while preparing to visit the interior of Asia Minor, he was smitten with paralysis at Isnik, and was compelled to return to England, where he died on 11 August 1858 at Stamford Hill, London. He was buried nearby at Stoke Newington on the 18th.

Racy humour, with occasional lapses into his broad native Barnsley dialect, added to his uncompromising directness, did Yeardley good service as a preacher. His achievements in preaching without interpreters in various languages were remarkable, considering that his early education included no Latin. He used tracts largely as a vehicle for spreading the gospel. These, written and sometimes translated by himself, were founded upon incidents and characters met with during his travels. They are catalogued by Smith.

His second wife, **Martha Yeardley** (1781–1851), was born on 8 March 1781, the daughter of Joseph and Anna Savory. Both before and after her marriage she wrote several works in verse and prose, notably *Inspiration* (1805); *Poetical Tales Founded on Facts* (1808), reissued as *Pathetic Tales* (1813); *Poetical Sketches of Scripture Characters* (1848); and *True Tales from Foreign Lands* (n.d.). With her husband she wrote *A Brief Memoir of Mary Anne Calame, with some Account of the Institution at Locle, Switzerland* (1835) and *Eastern Customs Illustrative of Scripture* (1842). *Extracts from the Letters of J. and M. Yeardley*, from the continent, was published in 1835. She died on 8 May 1851 and was buried at Stoke Newington, Middlesex.

CHARLOTTE FELL-SMITH, rev. H. C. G. MATTHEW

Sources *Memoir and diary of John Yeardley*, ed. C. Tylor (1859) · J. Smith, ed., *A descriptive catalogue of Friends' books*, suppl. (1893) · *CGPLA Eng. & Wales* (1858) · Boase, *Mod. Eng. biog.*
Archives RS Friends, Lond., journal, memoranda, and other material · RS Friends, Lond., letters and papers
Wealth at death under £4000: probate, 7 Oct 1858, *CGPLA Eng. & Wales*

Yeardley, Martha (1781–1851). *See under* Yeardley, John (1786–1858).

Yearsley [*née* Cromartie], **Ann** (*bap.* 1753, *d.* 1806), poet and writer, was baptized on 15 July 1753 (not 1752 or 1756 as are sometimes given) at St Andrew's Church in Clifton, near Bristol, the daughter of John and Ann Cromartie (*d.* 1784). Contemporary accounts describe Ann's mother as a milkwoman who trained her daughter in the same occupation, leading to Ann's later nicknames of 'the Bristol Milkwoman' and Lactilla. Nothing is known about her father. Ann was taught reading and writing by her mother and her older brother, William, her only sibling. The mother died in March 1784, the brother at some time between 1774 and 1784.

On 8 June 1774 Ann married John Yearsley (*bap.* 1748, *d.* 1803), described as 'yeoman' in the administration document of his mother's estate in that year; between 1775 and 1790 they had five sons and two daughters. By 1784 John Yearsley had lost yeoman status and was described as 'labourer' in a deed of trust intended to protect his wife's earnings. Contemporary accounts of the family are inconsistent, but the local registers make clear that by the May of that year it comprised the parents and five children. They had fallen into destitution and were rescued from near-starvation by local charitable individuals; one of these, Hannah More, learned of Ann's local reputation as a poet. She organized, by subscription among her literary and wealthy friends, a volume of Yearsley's poetry, *Poems, on Several Occasions*, which was published to considerable acclaim in June 1785, with a 'Prefatory letter', addressed to Elizabeth Montagu, outlining More's version of Yearsley's

Ann Yearsley (*bap.* 1753, *d.* 1806), by Joseph Grozer, pubd 1787 (after Sarah Shiells)

story. Over one thousand subscribers are listed. Among members of the aristocracy and prominent churchmen are famous names such as Fanny Burney, Henry Dundas, Soame Jenyns, Sir Joshua Reynolds, Anna Seward, Lady (Eglantine) Wallace, Helen Maria Williams, and Horace Walpole. Shortly afterwards, More and Yearsley quarrelled about the profits from the book (about £600), which More, with Montagu, had put in a trust 'lest her Husband shou'd spend it' (letter to Montagu, Montagu MSS, MO 3991). Yearsley thought that there should be no restriction, at least on her use of the interest from the investment. By October 1785 More had reluctantly wound up the trust and Yearsley eventually gained access to the money. Two more editions of the book were published under More's supervision; a fourth was undertaken by a different publisher in 1786 after Yearsley had broken with More. This includes an 'Autobiographical narrative', the author's version of the quarrel, which comprehensively refutes that of More.

With encouragement and some financial help from Frederick Augustus Hervey, fourth earl of Bristol, and others Yearsley published a second volume of poetry, *Poems, on Various Subjects*, in 1787, which adds the deed of trust to the other prefaces; the subscription list to this work, though shorter, shows some continued support among prominent members of the establishment. Close associates of Hannah More dropped away, and were replaced by the earl of Bristol and members of the Irish peerage, especially the Perceval family. Lady Wallace appears again; a new literary subscriber is 'Mrs. E. Knipe' (Elizabeth). *Earl Goodwin: an Historical Play* was produced in

Bristol and Bath in November 1789 and printed in 1791. In 1795 Yearsley published a four-volume historical novel entitled *The Royal Captives: a Fragment of Secret History, Copied from an Old Manuscript*, and in 1796 *The Rural Lyre: a Volume of Poems*. Subscribers to the latter work include figures of national and international importance, such as Augustus Frederick, son of George III; Henry Dundas, now secretary of war; Georgiana Cavendish, duchess of Devonshire; members of the Esterházy family; Sir William and Lady Hamilton; Charles Jenkinson, first earl of Liverpool; and, from the literary world, Charlotte Smith. A number of occasional poems and other pieces (for instance, *A Poem on the Inhumanity of the Slave Trade* and laments for the deaths of Louis XVI and Marie Antoinette) appeared between 1788 and 1796. Some of her poems are on topics of local interest, for example, *Stanzas of woe, addressed from the heart on a bed of illness, to Levi Eames, esq., late mayor of the city of Bristol* (1790) and 'Bristol Elegy' in *The Rural Lyre*. Her poems were occasionally printed in Bristol newspapers. Twelve manuscript poems appear on the endpapers of a copy of her published poems up to 1788 held by Bristol Public Libraries. From about 1793 she ran a circulating library at the Colonnade, Hotwells. The quarrel had led to a polarization of opinion on the success of this enterprise: supporters of More tended to pronounce it a failure (Thompson, 58–9), while others refer to it as an integral part of Clifton life at the time.

Engravings of two portraits of Yearsley, both published in 1787, show a strong-featured, serious-looking woman, with dark hair and eyes; in one she is presented in becoming but unpretentious dress, perhaps indicative of her status; in the other she is wearing the characteristic broad-brimmed beaver hat of the Bristol milkwomen. Hannah More described her in a letter of 1784 as 'slender and not ill-made; her face plain, but not disagreeable, her countenance rather pensive than sad, her pronunciation vulgar and provincial' (Hannah More to Mary Hamilton, priv. coll.). In 1837 Joseph Cottle, a Bristol bookseller and literary patron, remembered her as evincing, 'even in her countenance, the unequivocal marks of genius' (Cottle, 48).

It is probable that Yearsley ceased milk-selling early in her literary career; her writing and her library appear to have furnished her with resources for a relatively comfortable life. A handwritten note on a Bath playbill now in the Harvard Theatre Collection indicates that she received at least £80 from the benefit performances of her play, and Cottle says that she was advanced an unusual £200 for her novel. In 1790 she apprenticed her eldest surviving son, William, to a famous London engraver, Anker Smith, for a premium of 100 guineas. William died in 1799, aged twenty-two; her third surviving son, Charles, also died, probably 'in battle' during the 1790s (Thompson, 61). Her remaining son, John, engaged prosperously in the cloth trade at Trowbridge, Wiltshire, becoming proprietor of the Bridge Mills, its largest steam textile mill (K. H. Rogers, *Wiltshire and Somerset Woollen Mills*, 1976). Thither Yearsley followed him with at least one of her two daughters, probably after the death of her husband in 1803, settling in nearby Melksham. She died there on 6 May 1806; she was buried on 12 May in St Andrew's churchyard at Clifton. Her death was reported in the newspapers of Bristol as that of a prominent person and local worthy. Thompson's description of her as 'outcast, desolate ... insane and destitute' at the end of her life (Thompson, 61) is without foundation.

Contemporary comment is curiously blind to the real content of Yearsley's work. She was regarded as a primitive, rural poet with a special, mysterious gift only bestowed on persons without conventional education. Her poetry is often referred to as 'wild and simple' (J. Evans, *History of Bristol*, 2 vols., 1816, 2.297). Such judgements misrepresent most of her work, which is highly sophisticated. Intense self-analysis often merges with religious and philosophical speculation. Although a number of the poems are concerned with social and political justice, she is a passionate opponent of war and revolution. Cottle is almost alone in his estimate of her as a formidable thinker, referring to her alongside Coleridge, Southey, and Humphrey Davy as one of the 'busy, the aspiring, and the intellectual spirits' who inhabited Bristol during the 1790s (Cottle, xiii).

Yearsley was also affected by the political reaction of the period which tended to categorize lower-status writers, especially women, as subversive (R. Polewhele, *The Unsex'd Females*, 1798, 20). In the nineteenth and early twentieth centuries she was remembered chiefly as the ungrateful recipient of patronage, especially in biographies of Hannah More. Southey, who in 1799 was hoping to include a poem by Yearsley in his *Annual Anthology*, later gave a rather deprecating account of her, only conceding that 'she was no mocking-bird' (R. Southey, *Attempts in Verse by John Jones, an Old Servant*, 1831, 129–30). Since the 1930s her work has been taken more seriously, though her poetry was still described as 'ungainly verse' in 1938 (Tompkins, 58). Latterly her writing has received some serious critical attention; she has also been seen by some as an early feminist and combative champion of the proletariat. Taken as a whole, her *œuvre* does not support this view; she seems rather to demonstrate a certain benevolent conservatism which influenced much of the literature of this period.

MARY WALDRON

Sources J. M. S. Tompkins, *The polite marriage: eighteenth-century essays* (1938), 50–162, 198–264 • M. Waldron, *Lactilla, milkwoman of Clifton: the life and writings of Ann Yearsley, 1753–1806* (1996) • parish register, St Andrew, Clifton, Bristol RO, 1721–1812 [baptism, marriage, burial] • W. Roberts, *Memoirs of the life and correspondence of Mrs Hannah More*, 4 vols. (1834), vol.1, pp. 361–91 • J. Cottle, *Reminiscences of Samuel Taylor Coleridge and Robert Southey* (1847), xiii, 47–52 [repr. (1970)] • A. Yearsley, 'Autobiographical narrative', in A. Yearlsey, *Poems, on several occasions*, 4th edn (1786), xviii–xxxi • A. Yearsley, 'Preface', in A. Yearsley, *Poems, on various subjects* (1787), xxvii–xxix • Hunt. L., Montagu papers MO 3986–3994 • H. Bryant, A. Hare, and K. Barker, eds., *Theatre Royal, Bath: a calendar of performances at the Orchard Street Theatre, 1750–1805* (1977), 124 • H. Thompson, *The life of Hannah More with notices of her sisters* (1838), 55–61 • D. Landry, *The muses of resistance: laboring-class women's poetry in Britain, 1739–1796* (1990), 16–22, 120–86 • R. Lonsdale, ed., *Eighteenth-century women poets: an Oxford anthology* (1989), 329–401 • M. Waldron, 'Ann Yearsley: the Bristol manuscript revisited', *Women's*

Writing, 3/1 (1996), 35–45 • M. Waldron, 'A different kind of patronage: Ann Yearsley's later friends', *Age of Johnson*, 13 (2002), 283–335
Archives Bristol Central Library, manuscript poems, endpapers of *Yearsley's poems*, letters • W. Yorks. AS, Leeds, letters | Bodl. Oxf., corresp. with R. Griffiths
Likenesses J. Grozer, mezzotint, pubd 1787 (after S. Shiells), BM, NPG [*see illus.*] • W. Lowry, line engraving, pubd 1787, BM, NPG

Yearsley, James (1805–1869), ear surgeon, was born at Cheltenham, Gloucestershire, the son of Moses Yearsley (*b.* 1776) and his wife, Jane (*d.* 1848). The family originated from the north country. In 1822 he became apprenticed to Ralph Fletcher of Gloucester, a skilled surgeon and collector of pictures. Yearsley became a student at St Bartholomew's Hospital, London, in 1824, and qualified in 1827 with the diploma of membership of the Royal College of Surgeons, London, and as a licentiate of the Society of Apothecaries. Later in life he added to these qualifications the licentiateship of the Royal College of Physicians, Edinburgh (1860), and graduated MD at St Andrews University in 1862. After practising for a short time in Cheltenham, he established himself about 1829 as a general practitioner at Ross in Herefordshire. Deciding that this was not to be his future, he studied diseases of the ear in Paris before returning to London in 1837. Here at 15 Savile Row he began to practise as an aural surgeon. In 1838 he founded the Institution for Curing Diseases of the Ear, later the Metropolitan Ear Institution, at 29 Sackville Street, Piccadilly, and in 1846 he became surgeon to the Royal Society of Musicians. The Metropolitan Ear Institution was subsequently renamed the Metropolitan Ear, Nose, and Throat Hospital, the first of its kind in the world.

James Yearsley (1805–1869), by W. E. Debenham, *c.*1855

Yearsley appreciated the influence of conditions of the nose and throat on the ear. In his book *Improved Methods of Treating Diseases of the Ear* (1840), he states: 'Almost all diseases of the ear originate in a morbid condition of the mucous membrane of the throat, nose and ear'. Yearsley also observed that he 'suspected an overlapping of the mouths of the Eustachian tubes by the loose mucous membrane', and that 'shortly after excision of a small slip of mucous membrane from underneath the arches of the palate, amendment more or less considerable (in hearing) had taken place'. He was thus close to the discovery of the adenoid, which was made by Hans Wilhelm Meyer (1824–1895) of Copenhagen in 1868. *Contributions to Aural Surgery* followed in 1841, and in the same year Yearsley published a book on stammering, in which he advocated the use of tonsillectomy, performed with a curved bistoury, as a cure. This claim produced notoriety and was subsequently found to be fallacious. Yearsley later shrewdly confined this operation to cases of deafness due to Eustachian tube obstruction, and endorsed this indication by writing *A Treatise on Enlarged Tonsils* (1842) and *On Throat Deafness* (1853).

In *The Lancet* of 1 July 1848 Yearsley published an account of his 'artificial tympanum', a small pellet of thin, wet cotton wool placed daily over a dry perforation of the ear drum. He justifiably claimed to be the originator of the artificial tympanum, as Joseph Toynbee did not publish his quite different technique, using a disc of vulcanized indiarubber attached to a fine silver wire, until 1853. There was nevertheless an unfortunate war of words, which persisted with unseemly bitterness, and was later much regretted by both of them. Yearsley returned to the ear with the publication of *Deafness Practically Illustrated* (1854). Throughout his working life he advocated the use of the Eustachian catheter.

Yearsley, with Tyler Smith and Forbes Winslow, founded in 1845 the *Medical Directory*, which, by recording the names of all recognized practitioners, was an important step towards the Medical Registration Act of 1858. Yearsley was the originator and proprietor (though not editor) of the *Medical Circular* (1852), which in 1866 was incorporated with the *Dublin Medical Press* (1839), founded by Sir William Wilde as *The Medical Press Circular*. This journal was said not to have achieved its full potential because Yearsley had not correctly judged the mood of the day and relied on a previously popular aggressive approach which was no longer in vogue. He tended to respond to criticism with impatience and intolerance.

Yearsley married Hanna Eliza (*d.* 1879), one of Ralph Fletcher's daughters, and they had three children. While not having the scientific background of Toynbee, Yearsley is remembered as perhaps the first clinician to practise as an ear, nose, and throat specialist. He died of cancer of the liver on 9 July 1869 at his home in 15 Savile Row, London, and was buried on the 14th in the churchyard at Sutton Bonington, Nottinghamshire, where his eldest son, Ralph, was rector. Yearsley's memory is perpetuated in the annual Yearsley lecture, now held at the Royal College of Surgeons of England, as part of the annual meeting of the British Association of Otorhinolaryngologists.

NEIL WEIR

Sources N. Weir, *Otolaryngology: an illustrated history* (1990) · R. Scott-Stevenson, *Goodbye Harley Street* (1954) · J. F. Clarke, *Autobiographical recollections of the medical profession* (1874) · *DNB*
Likenesses W. F. Debenham, photograph, c.1855, NPG [*see illus.*] · photograph, 1868, Wellcome L. · oils, Charing Cross Hospital, London
Wealth at death under £12,000: probate, 4 Aug 1869, *CGPLA Eng. & Wales*

Yeates, Thomas (1768–1839), orientalist and biblical scholar, born on 9 October 1768 at Snow Hill, Holborn, London, was the son of John Yeates, a wood turner, of Snow Hill, and his wife, Jane. He was at first apprenticed to his father but, showing no taste for the trade, was allowed to pursue his studies in Latin and Hebrew, his fondness for which had been noted by his schoolmaster, a Mr Kebble of Shoe Lane. In 1782 the youthful Yeates appears to have been employed as secretary to the Society for Constitutional Information, a radical association which numbered William Jones (1746–1794), another oriental scholar, among its members, but he can have held this post for only a short time. Planning to translate the New Testament into biblical Hebrew, he got into communication with the theologian and orientalist Joseph White. Shortly after his appointment as professor of Hebrew at Oxford, White obtained for Yeates a Bible clerkship at All Souls, whence he matriculated on 22 May 1802 but never graduated. Although he laboured for many years at this translation, and received encouragement from the continent as well as in England, the only portion of it ever published was a specimen which appeared in the third annual report of the London Jews' Society.

From about 1808 to 1815 Yeates was employed by Claudius Buchanan to catalogue and describe the oriental manuscripts brought by him from India; and for much of this period he lived in Cambridge, where the university press published (1812) his 'Collation of an India copy of the Pentateuch'; the copies of this work were presented by the press to Yeates. The catalogue appears to be preserved in manuscript in the Cambridge University Library. Other manuscripts and published writings of Yeates are listed in a detailed bibliography by Jean Carmignac in his introduction to the 1982 reprinting of Yeates's revision of Giovanni Battista Iona's Hebrew gospels.

Through Buchanan, Yeates obtained some employment from the Bible Society, and superintended their editions of the psalter and the Syriac New Testament. After Buchanan's death he was helped by Thomas Burgess (1756–1837), bishop of St David's, who procured for him the secretaryship of the Royal Society of Literature, and in 1823 the post of assistant in the British Museum's printed book department, where he remained until his death. In

1818 he published a work called *Indian Church History* (reprinted, 1921), compiled chiefly from Assemani and the reports of Buchanan and Kerr, and containing an account of the Christian churches in the East, with an ultra-conservative history of their origin. In the same year Yeates produced a *Variation chart of all the navigable oceans and seas between latitude 60 degrees N. and S. from documents, and delineated on a new plan*; and in 1819 a very faulty Syriac grammar, but the first to appear in English. Yeates was also employed by the publishers of Caleb Ashworth's *Hebrew Grammar* to revise the third and subsequent editions. In 1830 he published *Remarks on the Bible chronology, being an essay towards reconciling the same with the histories of the eastern nations*; in 1833 *A Dissertation on the Antiquity of the Pyramids*; and in 1835 *Remarks on the History of Ancient Egypt*. His work was judged retrograde and antiquated by the end of the nineteenth century. His astronomical publications involved him in financial difficulties, which the Literary Fund helped him to meet. He was married, but details of his wife are unknown. He died on 7 October 1839.

D. S. MARGOLIOUTH, rev. J. B. KATZ

Sources GM, 2nd ser., 12 (1839), 658–60 · *Memoirs of the life, writings and correspondence of Sir William Jones*, ed. Lord Teignmouth [J. Shore, first Baron Teignmouth] (1804), 208–12 · *European Magazine and London Review*, 73 (1818), 514 · J. Carmignac, 'Introduction', *Evangiles … traduits en Hébreu en 1668 par Giovanni Battista Iona retouchés en 1805 par Thomas Yeates* (1982), xxvii–xli · J. D. Pearson, *A guide to manuscripts and documents in the British Isles relating to south and south-east Asia*, 2 (1990), 14
Archives CUL, Add. MS 4223 · Trinity Cam., Add. MS b.133=19401 etc.

Yeatman, Robert Julian (1897–1968). *See under* Sellar, Walter Carruthers (1898–1951).

Yeats, Elizabeth Corbet (1868–1940). *See under* Yeats, Susan Mary (1866–1949).

Yeats, Grant David (1773–1836), physician, born in Florida, America, was the son of David Yeats, a physician of East Florida. His sister Jane Ellen married Admiral Charles William Paterson (1756–1841). He matriculated from Hertford College, Oxford, on 21 January 1790, and graduated BA on 15 October 1793, MA on 25 May 1796, and BM on 4 May 1797. He graduated DM from Trinity College, Oxford, on 7 June 1814. After graduating BM Yeats spent two winter sessions in Edinburgh and one in London, and then began practising at Bedford, where he helped to establish Bedford General Infirmary, and later the lunatic asylum near the town. He was nominated physician to each of these institutions. His most important work, *Observations on the Claims of the Moderns to some Discoveries in Chemistry and Physiology*, was published in 1798, soon after he had moved to Bedford. In it he called attention to the experiments of John Mayow, whose merits Thomas Beddoes had discovered two years before.

While at Bedford, Yeats became friends with Samuel Whitbread and John Russell, sixth duke of Bedford. After the duke's nomination to the lord lieutenancy of Ireland, Yeats accompanied him to Dublin, in March 1806, as his private physician. He was incorporated MB at Dublin in 1807. While at Dublin he was instrumental in establishing the Dublin Humane Society, and was made a member of Trinity College, Dublin. On the duke's return to England in 1807 Yeats resumed his position at Bedford. About 1814 he moved to London, where he was admitted a candidate of the Royal College of Physicians on 30 September 1814, and a fellow on 30 September 1815. He was Goulstonian lecturer in 1817, censor in 1818, and Croonian lecturer in 1827. He was elected a fellow of the Royal Society on 1 July 1819.

Yeats married a daughter of the magistrate and writer on political economy Patrick *Colquhoun (1745–1820), and he published *A Biographical Sketch of the Life and Writings of Patrick Colquhoun* in 1818. Yeats died at Tunbridge Wells, Kent, on 14 November 1836.

E. I. CARLYLE, *rev.* MICHAEL BEVAN

Sources Munk, *Roll* · *GM*, 2nd ser., 6 (1836), 666 · Foster, *Alum. Oxon.*

Archives Beds. & Luton ARS, letters to Samuel Whitbread

Yeats, John Butler [Jack] (1871–1957), painter, was born on 29 August 1871 in London, at 23 Fitzroy Road, north of Regent's Park, the fifth child and youngest son of the painter John Butler Yeats (1839–1922) and Susan Mary Pollexfen (1841–1900). He was the brother of William Butler *Yeats (1865–1939). He never used the name Butler, only the initial B, and in his early years was known as Johnnie. Both his parents were of Irish protestant families. The Yeatses were impoverished gentlefolk with pretensions to some landholding in Thomastown, co. Kilkenny, which was lost through John Butler Yeats's bad management; they settled in Dublin in the mid-nineteenth century. At that time the Pollexfens were a merchant family established in Sligo in the milling and shipping business.

Early years Jack Yeats spent his early years both in London and in Sligo. His father, who trained as a barrister, became an artist in London and had moved the family there after the birth of the eldest child, William Butler Yeats. He was unsuccessful as a painter, and the family, who faced shortages of money, lived in various lodgings. This persuaded his wife to spend lengthy periods of time with her parents in Sligo. Jack Yeats's early experiences were of travel, and his love of the sea, which was to inspire many of his paintings, developed during voyages in his grandfather's ships from Liverpool round the northern coast of Ireland to Sligo.

By the age of nine Jack had settled in Sligo in the care of his grandparents, an arrangement that was to last until he went to art school in 1887. He claimed that Sligo was a formative influence in his life and that he rarely painted a picture 'without a bit of Sligo in it'. He worked hard at school, was competitive and successful in most subjects (contrary to the opinion voiced by his father), and showed an early facility in drawing, particularly in caricature. He was a happy child, in marked contrast with his brother, William Butler Yeats, who was moody and introspective, and rather frightened of his grandfather. Jack, on the other hand, was particularly fond of William Pollexfen,

John Butler Yeats (1871–1957), self-portrait, *c.*1920

and seems to have exercised a youthful authority over this powerful and forbidding man of the sea. In his youth Pollexfen had commanded a coaster called the *Dasher*, and he told Jack stories about the sea and pirates that inspired his early drawings, his plays for children, and his later paintings, many of which show an outstanding grasp of seafaring life. Of his vast output of paintings, watercolours, and drawings a very substantial number draw their inspiration and subject matter directly from the Sligo life. The powerful, bearded figure of a seafaring man often features in his work.

Unlike his brother and sisters Jack Yeats was surrounded by comfort and security, lived in a large house with servants and grooms, and travelled about with his grandfather in a pony and trap. He returned to London to enrol as an art student in 1887, first at the South Kensington School of Art, under Professor Brown, and then at Chiswick School of Art, in Bedford Park, to which area the family had moved. He is recorded as being at the West London School of Art from 1890 to 1893 and also at the Westminster School of Art from 1890 to 1894. Yeats, however, found nothing strange about studying in a number of institutions, but he did find quite uncongenial the straitened circumstances at home. These included the burden of having to contribute to the family income. He escaped into the world of his own art and into the entertainment world of the Buffalo Bill Cody shows at Earls Court, near one of the houses in which the family lodged, and drew cowboy subjects obsessively. While an art student he witnessed the efforts of his brother and two sisters to earn money to keep the family together, and by 1888 he was himself contributing drawings to publications such as *The Vegetarian*. He was also privately commissioned to design menus and doilies, and he began selling drawings directly through a shop in Piccadilly. He was influenced in his early work by Randolph Caldecott and Phil May, and also greatly admired the art of Thomas Hood. He led an independent existence at Bedford Park and was the least troubled of the Yeats children. He had a great sense of fun and got on well with everyone, with the possible exception of his father, towards whom he displayed reserve on account of the blame that he placed on his father's head for the failing health of his mother, who found the family's tribulations too much to bear.

Marriage In the early 1890s Yeats determined on marriage. He had met Mary Cottenham (Cottie) White (*c*.1869–1948) in 1889; she was a fellow student at Chiswick and came from a well-to-do family with Isle of Man connections. In 1891 he announced his intentions to his father and was released from financial obligations to the family, since he was now saving for his own and Cottie's future. He was already surprisingly successful as a freelance illustrator and comic artist, and as a sporting artist recording athletics and racing scenes around the country. In the years when all the members of the Yeats family contributed to the expenses of running the home his contribution tended to outstrip that of his siblings.

Jack and Cottie were married on 23 August 1894 in Gunnersbury and went on honeymoon to Dawlish. They moved into a house in Chertsey, and Jack continued to find employment as an illustrator in both freelance and regular commissioned work: Cottie was also an accomplished painter in watercolours. Though they lived frugally they enjoyed additional income through a family settlement made on Cottie during her lifetime. Within a year they had decided to move to the west of England. The Pollexfens had originally come from Devon, and Jack discovered an old and dilapidated cottage in Strete, 4 miles south of Dartmouth. It was reconstructed, more land was acquired, and an old barn was repaired as a studio overlooking the Gara river. It took almost two years to complete the move to Strete.

Early exhibitions In their new home Yeats prepared for his first exhibition, which was held in London's Clifford Galleries late in 1897. Much of the work consisted of drawings and watercolours of life in the west of England. Scenes of racing, boxing, fairgrounds, cider-making, children, and animals made up a substantial number of works, and the critical success was resounding. In *Table Talk* P. G. Konody wrote: 'quite apart from the exquisite humour of these sketches, there is another reason which makes them quite remarkable and worthy of attention. They show an astounding capacity for grasping and retaining the impression of certain short moments' (Arnold, 68; a good example is *Waiting*, reproduced in Arnold, p. 69, fig 72). Thirty-nine individual publications noticed the show,

many of them warmly praising the talent of the drawing and the life in the subject matter. Over a quarter of the works shown were sold, and Yeats's talent was noticed by the playwright and patron of the arts Augusta, Lady Gregory. She was on the lookout for Irish artistic talent and wanted Yeats, like his brother, to become involved in the Irish artistic revival of the late nineteenth century.

Initially Yeats had no intention of returning to Ireland; his wife did not favour the idea, and he was reticent about a literary movement that was becoming dominated by his elder brother. He did return, however, to work, and travelled in the west of Ireland, painting in watercolours and filling sketchbooks with anecdotal drawings of people and places. He loved the odd and the unusual. Fights, disputes—such as *Let me See Wan Fight!* (reproduced Arnold, p. 79, fig. 84)—parades, circus giants and dwarfs, and above all scenes at race meetings and fairs repeatedly captured his imagination and provided him not only with subject matter for paintings but with illustrations that he was able to sell, for example, to the *Illustrated London News*. He held his first exhibition in Dublin in 1899 and, like his London début, it was widely mentioned and in very positive terms; the writer and painter George Russell wrote in the *Dublin Express*: 'These sketches of the West of Ireland reveal a quite extraordinary ability in depicting character and movement' (Arnold, 85). His title for both shows referred to 'Life in the West of Ireland'—the title of his book of illustrations published in 1912.

Move to Ireland In 1900 Yeats's mother died, worn out both physically and mentally by the difficult life imposed on her by her husband's ineffectual and self-indulgent behaviour. Yeats, who was greatly upset by her death, commissioned the plaque in St John's Church in Sligo, pointedly leaving out the name of his father from those listed as having placed it in the nave.

From the late 1890s until 1910, when Jack and Cottie moved to Ireland and settled in Greystones, in co. Wicklow, they regularly visited the country and spent time in the west. They stayed with Lady Gregory at Coole Park, revisited Sligo, explored Donegal, went to co. Kerry, and became marginally involved in the Irish literary revival in Dublin. With his close friend John Masefield, Yeats played games along the Gara river, constructing cardboard boats that Masefield furnished with equipment and even, at times, little engines. They bombarded and sank their own creations, Masefield writing vigorous lyrics about each vessel, Yeats producing drawings.

In 1905, through contact with the editor of the *Manchester Guardian*, Masefield obtained for Jack Yeats and John M. Synge a commission to report on the congested districts in Galway, Connemara, and Mayo. Synge wrote about their experiences, Yeats did the illustrations. The friendship flourished; they were like-minded men, contemplative, independent, reticent. Synge sought Yeats's help with certain costume aspects of his play *The Playboy of the Western World*, and Yeats was able to suggest the appearance and clothing of the hero, drawn from his experience of race meetings on Bowmore Strand, in Sligo, when he was a boy.

The two Yeats sisters, Susan Mary (Lily) *Yeats and Elizabeth Corbet (Lollie) *Yeats [see under Yeats, Susan Mary], moved to Dublin, where they were later joined by their father. There they set up the Cuala Press and the Dun Emer Guild and became engaged in fine printing, embroidery work, and other cottage-industry activities. Somewhat reluctantly both William Butler Yeats and Jack Yeats were drawn into their sisters' ventures, and Jack produced broadsheets that were coloured by hand. In 1908 their father left Dublin for New York. As with most of the movements in his life it was meant to be a temporary shift of territory, but he never returned. His son Jack was not a great traveller but he did go to New York in 1904 (he had a liking for American stories of adventure). There he met Mark Twain, whom he greatly admired, and the lawyer John Quinn, who bought some of his early watercolours and drawings.

Crisis and resolution So far Yeats's career as a painter had taken a rather limited course. His abilities as a watercolourist were not matched when he turned to oil painting, for which he had studied inadequately, in part as a result of the Yeats family's financial needs while he was at art school. His deficiencies told in the early years of the twentieth century; until 1915 his canvases lack any convincing colour sense. When engaged in the representation of human figures, as he was with the series of oil paintings used as illustrations to *Irishmen All* (1913), by George Birmingham (the pseudonym of Canon James Owen Hannay), he achieved strength of design, a clear line, and good chiaroscuro. But he was still drawing in paint, and it worked less well when he produced landscapes; early examples, such as *The Police Sergeant* (reproduced Arnold, p. 179, fig. 157), are often unsubtle and rather flat.

In 1913 Yeats was chosen for the Armory show in New York, and sent to it one of his great early paintings, *The Circus Dwarf* (1912; priv. coll.; reproduced Arnold, p. 362, colour plate 5). He had already shown the work in London, in 1912, to some critical acclaim. In an article about Yeats in 1913 the art critic for *The Star*, A. J. Finberg, wrote: 'The people Mr Yeats is interested in are a rough, hard-bitten, unshaven, and generally disreputable lot of men. His broken-down actors practising fencing, his "Circus Dwarf" … are subjects no other artist would have chosen to paint'. It is unlikely that other painters would have painted the political subjects that attracted Yeats but politics were very much part of Irish life, and he was increasingly identifying his work at this time with the events heralding the Easter Rising. Gun-running was one of these, a by-product of it his poignant study of pity, *Bachelor's Walk: in Memory* (also known as *In Memory*, 1915; priv. coll.; reproduced Arnold, p. 192, fig. 160), which shows a flower girl placing flowers on the spot in the street where a person was shot down by British soldiers who had unsuccessfully tried to prevent the Howth landing of arms. Later political works included *Communicating with Prisoners* (1924) and *The Funeral of Harry Boland* (1922; both Sligo Museum and Art Gallery).

Yeats's work in oils did not sell, and from a commercial point of view his and Cottie's decision to settle in Ireland

had not been a success. In 1915 he had a nervous breakdown, which lasted into 1917. He had been made an associate of the Royal Hibernian Academy in 1914 and a full academician in the following year. He was recognized for the originality of his vision and for his increasingly central role as a painter of Irish life at a time when nationalism demanded icon-makers, and his recovery was helped by this growing sense of a role in Dublin and in Irish society. He painted views of the city (*A Westerly Wind*, 1921; priv. coll.), its characters, its sporting events (*Singing the Dark Rosaleen, Croke Park, 1921*; priv. coll.). The country was going through the turmoil of the war of independence, the Anglo-Irish treaty, the civil war, and the grim political antagonisms that characterized the early 1920s. During this time Yeats produced a growing number of large and increasingly confident works. They show crowds attending sporting events at Croke Park; women singing in the street, in bars, or in trains; theatrical subjects; men of the streets, including newspaper-sellers and pavement artists. His early concept for exhibitions, 'Life in the west of Ireland', broadened into a succession of works that depicted the life of his country.

Yeats was fifty when Ireland became independent. Never directly involved in politics himself, he was nevertheless deeply affected by the civil war and, as a result of meeting Eamon de Valera in Paris at the Irish Race Congress in 1922, became and remained sympathetic to his political views and those of his followers. In this respect his thinking diverged from that of his brother, who had supported the treaty and become a member of the senate. At the congress Jack Yeats gave his only lecture, 'Modern aspects of Irish art' (published in Dublin in 1922). This he managed to do without naming a single painter.

Yeats sided with modernism, which in Dublin in the early 1920s had a distinctive meaning. In the absence of a strong artistic tradition based on academic art the arrival in the city of modernist principles—of abstraction, of a movement that related to European painting rather than to London—was successful. Yeats sided with the artists, led by Paul Henry, who formed the Society of Dublin Painters and became one of their number. He met Oskar Kokoschka, and they became friends. He derided the dominance of Paris and London in artistic life generally; this had been a theme of his Paris lecture, and he expressed it in respect of Picasso, suggesting that he 'would be more thrilling to his time and generation if he had jumped straight out of Spain without the use of Paris' (MS letter to Thomas MacGreevy, 8 Dec 1925; TCD). MacGreevy, who was Yeats's great champion at the time as well as a modernist, writer, and poet, crossed swords with Thomas Bodkin, a more conventional art critic, over the direction that Yeats was taking and the magnitude of his contribution to modern art and thought in Dublin. This led to public controversy. Dublin in the early 1920s was described as 'the Athens of Pericles', and it was a truthful insight into the ferment of thought and debate about the cultural life of the new state. Yeats was happy to be part of this, and his exhibitions—he showed work in New York, Rome, Pittsburgh, London, and Liverpool throughout the decade—

gave him the opportunity to represent more and more widely his chosen theme of Irish life.

Rejuvenation During the 1920s Yeats became increasingly conscious of stylistic restrictions in his work. He was still having difficulties with colour and with the reconciliation of tone and compositional balance. He sought freedom, and it was not available to him in the more conventional techniques that he was employing. He dealt with the matter summarily. He abandoned his old palette and chose a new one, using primary colours quite freely; rich inflexions of colour were achieved with a freely handled impasto, substituting the palette knife and fingers for the brush. He chose to work on large canvases, and within them quite often to present a close focus on the subject matter; large horses' heads and strong-faced Irish men and women filled large picture areas. Characteristic was his use of ultramarine and cobalt blue in generous representation of shadow and of distant horizons. Cadmium yellow and alizarin crimson, used at times direct from the tube, produced works that caused former critics of the lameness of his earlier work to marvel at this extraordinary rejuvenation. (see, for example, *Glory*, 1946, and *Freedom*, 1947; both priv. coll.; reproduced in Arnold, pp. 369, 371, colour plates 12 and 14.)

But though Dublin marvelled at Yeats's work the resources to buy it were thinly spread in Irish society, particularly among those interested in modernism, and it did not sell at all well. Yeats's output, substantial during the 1920s, fell off in the following decade, and in a mood of self-doubt he turned to writing. He produced a number of volumes—*Sligo* (1931), *The Charmed Life* (1938), *The Amaranthers* (1936), *The Careless Flower* (1947)—and had high hopes of becoming a successful writer. He had similar aspirations for the plays that he wrote during the 1930s.

In 1941, through the intervention of John Betjeman, who suggested the idea to Kenneth Clark, Yeats was invited to show at the National Gallery, in London, with William Nicholson. The exhibition, opened on new year's day 1942, was a singular success and critical acclaim raised Yeats's stature greatly in Ireland. At the end of the Second World War he was given a retrospective exhibition in Dublin, and became in his last years a revered artistic figure. His output was vast. He painted more than 1100 works in oil, over half of them in the last twenty years of his long life. He died in Portobello Nursing Home, in Dublin, on 28 March 1957, Cottie having predeceased him, in 1948. The members of the government of the day, led by Eamon de Valera, and the main opposition parties turned out for his funeral and stood on the pavement as his coffin was brought from the church. He was buried on 30 March in Dublin's Mount Jerome cemetery.

Posthumous reputation No Irish painter matched Jack B. Yeats at the end of his life, and his reputation continues to grow. In *The Painters of Ireland, 1660–1920* (1978) Anne Crookshank and the knight of Glin pronounced him 'without doubt, the greatest Irish artist of the first half of the twentieth century' (p. 285). In singling out *In Memory* (1915), they include Michael Rosenthal's comment that

this picture 'has become a symbol of the archetypal Irish woman mourning her lost men, both literally in wars and rebellions, and metaphorically through the piercing sadness of constant immigration' (ibid.). Yeats's artwork is now the focus of study by Irish cultural historians for its record of travellers, peasants, life in the west of Ireland, and larger themes of Irish cultural and national identity. Hilary Pyle's *catalogues raisonnés* of his oil paintings (1992) and of his watercolours, drawings, and pastels (1993) followed her biography, *Jack B. Yeats* (1970; 2nd edn, 1989). His cartoons and illustrations have been the subject of separate studies. Yeats's work has been exhibited separately in, for example, 'Jack B. Yeats: the Late Paintings' (Arnolfini Gallery, Bristol, and Whitechapel Art Gallery, London, 1991), 'Jack B. Yeats: a Celtic Visionary' (Manchester City Art Gallery, 1996), and jointly with other artists in 'Aspects of Irish Art' (Columbus Gallery of Fine Arts, Ohio, and elsewhere, 1974). *The Selected Writings of Jack B. Yeats*, edited by Robin Skelton, appeared in 1991. Some years after Yeats's death Thomas Kinsella celebrated his life and that of Eamon de Valera, two very different early twentieth-century Irish public figures, in his poem 'The Last'. Yet Yeats, like the figure in his painting *The Folded Heart*, remains an intensely private man.   BRUCE ARNOLD

Sources B. Arnold, *Jack Yeats* (1998) · T. Rosenthal, *The art of Jack B. Yeats* (1993) · H. Pyle, *Jack B. Yeats: a biography* (1970); 2nd edn (1989) · H. Pyle, *The different worlds of Jack B. Yeats: his cartoons and illustrations* [1994] · H. Pyle, *Jack B. Yeats: a catalogue raisonné of the oil paintings* (1992) · b. cert. · m. cert.

Archives NG Ire., archive · Stanford University Library, California, corresp. and literary papers | BL, corresp. with League of Dramatists, Add. MSS 63462–63463 · U. Leeds, Brotherton L., letters to Charles Elkin Matthews · U. Reading L., letters to Charles Elkin Matthews · University of Delaware, Newark, corresp. with Society of Authors · Yale U., Beinecke L., letters to Lawrence and Wishart Ltd, publishers | SOUND BL NSA, recorded interview

Likenesses J. B. Yeats, self-portrait, pencil drawing, 1899, NG Ire. · P. C. Smith, pen-and-ink sketches, 1901, NYPL · J. B. Yeats, self-portrait, pencil drawing, *c*.1920, NG Ire. [*see illus.*] · E. Solomons, oils, 1922, County Library and Museum, Sligo · S. O'Sullivan, charcoal drawing, 1929, NG Ire. · H. Coster, photographs, 1939, NPG · S. O'Sullivan, oils?, 1942, County Library and Museum, Sligo · J. Sleator, oils, 1942, Cork Municipal Art Gallery · S. O'Sullivan, pencil drawing, 1943, NG Ire. · L. Davidson, oils, NG Ire. · B. O'Doherty, portrait, priv. coll. · S. Purser, oils, NG Ire. · J. B. Yeats, two self-portraits, oils, NG Ire.

Wealth at death £1415 18s. 10d.—in England: probate, 9 Sept 1957, CGPLA Eng. & Wales · £34,927: probate, 25 July 1957, CGPLA Éire

Yeats, Susan Mary [Lily] (1866–1949), embroiderer, was born on 25 August 1866 at Enniscrone, co. Sligo, the second eldest of the four surviving children of John Butler Yeats (1839–1922), barrister, painter, and writer, and Susan Mary (1841–1900), eldest daughter of William Pollexfen, a merchant in Sligo, of an ancient Cornish family settled in Devon, and his wife, Elizabeth Middleton, an Irish middle-class protestant. Known as Lily, she shared the dark, good looks of her siblings, particularly the eldest, William Butler *Yeats (the poet), to whom she was particularly close, and the strong-minded, affectionate nature of her eccentric father, to whom she was both devoted and stern. Because of their father's financial problems and their mother's nervous ill health, the children led an unconventional, precocious, insecure childhood, staying with relatives in Sligo and Devon, and in a succession of rented houses in London and Dublin. What Lily and her sister, **Elizabeth Corbet** [Lollie] **Yeats** (1868–1940), printer, who was born on 11 March 1868 in Fitzroy Road, London, lacked in formal education or good health, they learned through perseverance. Eventually, through the rich artistic contacts provided by their father and brothers, W. B. Yeats and the painter and graphic illustrator Jack Butler *Yeats, and self-imposed apprenticeships in needlework and printing skills, the two women were able to provide an outlet (if not an income) for their siblings' talents from 1902 onwards.

In 1888, when the family had gone to live in a house in London's Bedford Park, Lily Yeats worked in the embroidery workshop run from nearby Kelmscott House by William Morris's daughter, May. In order to provide her family with a much-needed weekly income, she spent six years making cushion covers, firescreens, and mantelpiece covers, teaching new recruits, and sometimes running the workshop in a tedious but invaluable apprenticeship. A four-poster bed hanging she had embroidered for Kelmscott Manor (*in situ*) from May Morris's design was exhibited with the English Arts and Crafts Exhibition Society in 1893; in 1895, the year after she resigned from May Morris's workshop, an embroidered mantle border represented her work in the Arts and Crafts Society of Ireland's first exhibition.

In 1902, when Yeats and her sister, Elizabeth, were invited by Evelyn Gleeson (1855–1944), Gaelic leaguer and suffragist, to help set up a craft enterprise along the lines of Morris's utopian socialist ideals, they moved back to Dublin with their father. They took a cottage, Gurteen Dhas ('pretty little meadow'), in Churchtown, Dundrum, near the house, Dun Emer, in which Gleeson set up a printing press, carpet and needlework rooms, and other artistic ventures. While Elizabeth Yeats used her experience as a teacher, watercolourist, designer, and author of four successful books on her freehand brushwork technique, and took a short printing course in order to set up the Dun Emer Press, Lily Yeats drew on her Kelmscott experience to set up an embroidery workshop. Their brother Jack's strongly graphic designs of Irish figurative subjects, worked by local girls as banners for St Brendan's Cathedral, Loughrea, co. Galway, were among early designs adapted from the work of artists seminal to the Irish arts and crafts movement. By 1904 Lily was supervising the execution by seven girls of designs by various artists, including her sister, Elizabeth.

In 1908 disagreements with Evelyn Gleeson led to the Yeats sisters setting up their own Cuala Industries, a printing press and embroidery workshop in a nearby cottage. However successful and productive, they were continually beset with financial, emotional, and health problems. The First World War affected the luxury end of the embroidery workshop badly and in 1923 the end of the lease on Cuala forced the sisters to seek new premises. Using silk and woollen threads on linen or a distinctive blue silk poplin, their stylized floral and landscape designs were often by Elizabeth or Jack Yeats, or adapted from images by other contemporaries, even though signed 'Lily Yeats'. By 1925, when the Cuala Industries moved into Dublin, the embroidery workshop was mostly reproducing old designs, partly because of Lily Yeats's increasing ill health. The last sale of embroidery made under her direction was held in 1931, although she continued to make 'little needle pictures' from home until her death.

Elizabeth Yeats, initially guided by Emery Walker, the arts and crafts printer who had inspired William Morris, continued to handprint books, bookplates, calendars, hand-coloured prints, Christmas cards, and pamphlets featuring texts by the outstanding writers and illustrators of the Irish revival. The final catalogue of prints issued in her lifetime, *c.*1939, from Baggot Street, Dublin, offered ninety-seven different prints for sale. In total she published seventy-seven volumes, eleven of which were produced at Dun Emer, each corresponding to their earliest ideal of 14 point Caslon old style font, light ivory-toned rag, mould-made paper manufactured near Dublin, bound in a small quarto format between blue- or grey-covered boards with a linen spine. Her clearly legible, slender volumes with their distinctive paper labels may be seen as the sole survivors of the handcrafted ideal established in 1900 by Walker and T. J. Cobden-Sanderson's Doves Press. As well as exhibiting her printed and designed work throughout Britain and America, Elizabeth Yeats painted fans and furniture, and worked for the Women's National Health Association of Ireland. She died, unmarried, on 16 January 1940 in a nursing home in Dublin, and was buried on 18 January in St Nahi's Church, Dundrum, co. Dublin. Lily Yeats died, unmarried, on 5 January 1949 at her home in Churchtown following a stroke and was buried three days later at St Nahi's Church, Dundrum. A number of Yeats embroideries have been bequeathed to the National Gallery of Ireland, though many remain in private collections.

NICOLA GORDON BOWE

Sources W. M. Murphy, *Prodigal father: the life of John Butler Yeats (1839–1922)* (1978) · W. M. Murphy, *Family secrets: William Butler Yeats and his relatives* (Dublin, 1995) · G. Lewis, *The Yeats sisters and the Cuala* (1994) · N. Gordon Bowe and E. S. Cumming, *The arts and crafts movements in Dublin and Edinburgh* (1998) [incl. embroidered works by Yeats] · S. Pim, 'Dun Emer: the origins', *Irish Arts Review*, 2/2 (1985), 18–22 · L. Miller, *The Dun Emer Press, later the Cuala Press* (Dublin, 1973) · *The collected letters of W. B. Yeats*, 1, ed. J. Kelly and E. Domville (1986) · *The collected letters of W. B. Yeats*, 3, ed. J. Kelly and R. Schuchard (1994) · W. B. Yeats, *Autobiographies* (1955) · G. Lewis, 'Rediscovered embroideries by Lily Yeats', *Irish Arts Review Yearbook*, 14 (1998), 147–50 · R. F. Foster, *The apprentice mage, 1865–1914* (1997), vol. 1 of *W. B. Yeats: a life* · J. Hardwick, *The Yeats sisters: a biography of Susan and Elizabeth Yeats* (1996) · H. Pyle, *Yeats: portrait of an artistic family* (1997) [lists embroidered works] · parish records, Dundrum, St Nahi's Church, 8 Jan 1949 [burial]

Archives TCD, family collection, unpublished diary, corresp. | TCD, Cuala archives and Dun Emer archives · TCD, Dun Emer MSS, Dr Patrick Kelly collection · TCD, Michael Yeats collection, draft scrapbook · TCD, Michael Yeats collection, scrapbook

Likenesses photograph, *c.*1885 (with her sister, Elizabeth), NL Ire. · J. B. Yeats, oils, 1900–01, NG Ire. · group portrait, photograph,

1903, priv. coll. · photograph, 1903, TCD · A. Boughton, photograph, 1907 (with her father), repro. in Murphy, *Family secrets*; priv. coll. · H. M. Paget, oils, NG Ire.

Wealth at death £1165 7s.: probate, 3 June 1949, *CGPLA Éire*

Yeats, William Butler (1865–1939), poet, was born on 13 June 1865 at 1 George's Ville, 5 Sandymount Avenue, Dublin, the eldest child of John Butler Yeats (1839–1922) and Susan Mary, *née* Pollexfen (1841–1900). His father was then still a barrister; shortly he would—to the discomfiture of his wife, and still more of her family—give up the law for the uncertain life of a portrait painter in bohemian London.

Background and youth The Yeats family was, in Irish parlance 'Ascendancy', but not grand: clergymen, lawyers, Dublin Castle officials rather than landowners, married into a wide cousinage across the Irish protestant world. They were proud of their descent from the great Norman clan of the Butlers, and preserved the name in their christenings, but connections with the ducal Ormond line are tenuous at best. By the 1860s their position in the world had declined. Here as elsewhere W. B. Yeats's life is emblematic of its time, since this process reflects a wider slippage; the newly confident Irish Catholic bourgeoisie were advancing into social and professional redoubts from which they had been excluded by the privileged minority. A reaction to this conditioned the stuffy and self-conscious world of protestant Dublin, against which the young Yeats would chafe just as his father had done.

Yeats's mother's family, the Pollexfens of Sligo, were a different stock: also descended from gentry forebears, but originating in Devon. In the 1830s Yeats's maternal grandfather, William Pollexfen, had joined a branch of the family already settled in Sligo, married a cousin, and with another cousin William Middleton founded a prosperous shipping and milling business (with a profitable sideline in, among other things, wreckage rights). The Pollexfens were business people, property developers, and town councillors—ornaments of that forgotten class, the Irish Victorian bourgeoisie. They reacted with bafflement and hostility to the charming but unreliable John Butler Yeats—a brilliant talker, and eventually a first-rate painter, but cursed with a congenital inability to finish a painting or repay a debt.

W. B. Yeats and his younger surviving siblings—Susan Mary *Yeats, called Lily (1866–1949), Elizabeth Corbet *Yeats, or Lollie (1868–1940) [*see under* Yeats, Susan Mary], and John, known as Jack, Butler *Yeats (1871–1957)—grew up conscious that their father's way of life was deeply disapproved of in Sligo, where they spent much of their childhood being looked after in the Pollexfen household. They all became distinguished artists in their own fields; and, significantly, they all succeeded by employing their Pollexfen qualities of thrift, common sense, and hard concentration along with the Yeats flair and vision. Looking at his eldest son's first work, and recognizing a true poetic voice, John Butler Yeats produced what his son later claimed was the only compliment to turn his head: 'By marriage with a Pollexfen we have given a tongue to the sea-cliffs' (*Autobiographies*, 23).

William Butler Yeats (1865–1939), by Augustus John, 1907

It was not, however, an easy, nor even a particularly precocious, ascent to Olympus. When W. B. Yeats (known to his family and intimates as Willie, a name he detested) was two, the family moved to London, living at a variety of lodgings before settling in the Bedford Park area of Hammersmith, then a kind of ghetto for aesthetes and artists. However, the children continued to be shipped back to Sligo for long intervals, travelling on small vessels belonging to the family firm. W. B. Yeats's earliest education was at a dame school in Sligo, and through coaching from family friends: a slow learner in some subjects, and a spectacularly idiosyncratic speller all his life, he none the less showed remarkable if wayward intellectual capacity early on, as well as a constitutional shyness which he learned to conceal beneath a mannered public pose. Both these characteristics—intellectual and psychological—were influentially shaped by his father's stimulating but aggressive didacticism. In London Yeats attended the Godolphin School in Hammersmith from 1877 but in 1881 John Butler Yeats once more transplanted the family back to Dublin. Here, the future poet completed his education at the Erasmus Smith high school, and subsequently—like his sisters—attended the Metropolitan School of Art from 1883 to 1885. By then he was writing copious but unpublished poetry; he first appeared in print in the *Dublin University Review* of March 1885, with some brief lyrics, followed later that summer by a Shelleyan verse drama called 'The Island of Statues'.

By then Yeats was serving another apprenticeship too, in the circle of intellectuals who met at the Contemporary Club organized by the protestant nationalist C. H. Oldham, editor of the *Dublin University Review*. This actually had nothing to do with the strict unionist confines of Trinity College, Dublin, where Oldham was rather uncomfortably employed. Home rule politics were anathema in most Trinity circles, and these were the years of Parnell's growing ascendancy—and of the land war, which put paid to the few remaining rents coming to John Butler Yeats out of the small family properties in co. Kildare. He was himself a home-ruler (though he preferred Parnell's predecessor Isaac Butt—a family friend—to the icy and enigmatic Chief); both J. B. Yeats and his twenty-year-old art student son were regulars at Oldham's Club from its origins in late 1885. Through these eclectic gatherings they met the returned Fenian intellectual John O'Leary, once literary editor of the firebrand *Irish People* and still connected with nationalist journalism.

The young Yeats was already noted for his 'poetic' character, alternately vague and intense, and for the charisma lent by his dreamy good looks and passionate outbursts of eloquence. Pronouncing accurately that Willie Yeats was the only club member who possessed literary genius, O'Leary was an invaluable connection to literary outlets like *The Gael* as well as Irish–American publications run by his political friends, such as John Boyle O'Reilly's *Boston Pilot*. The nature of Yeats's very early published verse certainly owes something to the kind of journal where he knew he could get it published. None the less it seems clear that the young Yeats adopted what was called at the time 'advanced' nationalism, and may have taken the Fenian oath about 1886 before returning to London, with the rest of the family, early in 1887. This was not, however, incompatible with a belief in home rule, and—after Gladstone's adoption of the cause in 1886—a settled expectation that it was inevitable. Later in life W. B. Yeats would recall that the cultural revolution which—in his view—brought about the actual revolution of 1916–21 began after the shattering fall of Parnell in 1891. But in many ways the political and literary initiatives embraced by Yeats and his friends in the 1880s, such as the Young Ireland literary societies, should be seen as the creation of a cultural agenda in anticipation of a coming independence, achieved through the constitutional efforts of the apparently all-conquering Parnell.

Literary politics, occultism, and the 1890s None the less the appeal of Fenianism was emotionally powerful for a young Irishman moving in literary circles in London, whose background of *déclassé* protestantism and uncertain location necessitated a firm claim on Irish identity. Tutored by O'Leary in the Irish version of classical republican virtues, introduced by the same cicerone to the poetry of Samuel Ferguson, excited by the Romantic and mythic histories of Ireland's 'Heroic Age' recently published by Standish James O'Grady, and moving in literary-nationalist circles already frequented by people like Katharine Tynan and the young Douglas Hyde, Yeats was firmly convinced of the need for an Irish cultural initiative which would advance a style of writing definitively national both in form and content, and create from local traditions a sustaining 'mythology'. It would take many years to refine this ideal—years which, from one view, might be interpreted as representing a progressive process of depoliticization as well. Certainly in the late 1880s, as Yeats helped to form societies like the Irish Literary Society of London, planted out poems and reviews in an increasingly wide variety of journals, and logrolled indefatigably on behalf of his literary circle, he was developing a theory of literature which would move beyond the flyblown models of the early nineteenth century popularized by Thomas Davis and the Young Ireland movement. Significantly, the only Irish poet of the era whom Yeats continued to respect aesthetically was the maverick James Clarence Mangan (also a key influence on the young James Joyce), though in these years he also discovered a respect for the 'square-built power' of early nineteenth-century Irish fiction written by William Carleton and John and Michael Banim. By contrast, the influence on him of the great Romantics, notably Shelley, would remain as a subterranean stream, resurfacing as late as the 1920s. He also marked down William Blake as a master early on, and with Edwin Ellis produced a large-scale commentary on Blake's prophetic writings in 1893. While often erratic and idiosyncratic, it helped establish the importance of Blake's esoteric verse.

However, Yeats himself isolated as a key moment in his poetic development his famous early poem 'The Lake Isle of Innisfree'. It was initially composed in mid-December 1888, at the time he was preaching to his circle the need to 'make poems on the familiar landscapes we love not the strange and rare and glittering scenes we wonder at—these latter are the landscape of Art, the rouge of nature' (to Katharine Tynan, 21 Dec 1888, *Collected Letters*, 1.119). Published in 1890, it achieved immediate success—still pursuing him around the world, to his irritation, forty years later. His 'prentice works in Dublin, often in the form of verse drama, had been inspired by the 'strange and rare and glittering', which still affects his first collection, *The Wanderings of Oisin*, in 1889; his best writing of the 1890s would follow the form set by 'Innisfree', with its deceptively simple language and dramatic personal interventions. But the poems of this period, culminating in the consummate *symboliste* collection *The Wind among the Reeds* (1899), possessed—especially to an English ear—their own strangeness too, derived not only from Yeats's deliberate Celticism but also from his equally considered occultism.

Though this commitment had its Celtic dimension too, it serves as a useful reminder that Yeats's life was from early on divided firmly between his Irish sojourns and a London base. The Yeats family's move to London during the poet's early childhood paralleled that of many others; it also happened at a time when, as George Bernard Shaw mordantly recalled:

every Irishman who felt that his business in life was on the higher planes of the cultural professions, felt that he must have a metropolitan domicile and an international culture: that is, he felt that his first business was to get out of Ireland. (G. B. Shaw, *The Matter with Ireland*, 1902, 10)

Yeats knew this, but he also knew the uncertainty of dislocation. In London he became a central figure in the bohemian circles where literary fashion, apprentice 'decadence', and supernatural experimentalism met and often overlapped. Life in Bedford Park may have been dogged by family tensions and unpaid butchers' bills, but it was also characterized by a circle of acquaintance which included Oscar Wilde and his mother as well as William Morris (in whose workshop Lily Yeats was trained) and George Bernard Shaw. In his early twenties Yeats was already moving easily from this world to that of the young writers around W. E. Henley, or the poets who met as the Rhymers' Club in the Cheshire Cheese pub in Fleet Street (including Lionel Johnson, Ernest Dowson, and John Davidson), and on to theosophist circles around Madame Helena Petrovna Blavatsky. Though incapable of speaking French, from the 1890s Yeats was also dropping in and out of various Parisian subcultures, and experimenting with hashish and mescal. He later fixed all these worlds memorably in his *Autobiographies*, placing them in their time with a delicate sense of distancing which never quite becomes ridicule; George Yeats later remarked that she was always astonished by her husband's uncanny sense of how things would look to people afterwards. At the time these cultural underworlds served, for this most autodidactic of intellectuals, as a kind of alternative university.

This was especially true of occultism. From his time at the high school in Dublin Yeats had been interested in various exotic and mystical theories and ideas of spiritual life, from Indian philosophy to Baron Reichenbach's notions of 'Odic Force'; together with his lifelong friend George Russell (who wrote as 'AE'), he helped import theosophy to Dublin. This synthesis of spiritual enquiry, incorporating the vogue for eastern mysticism but allowing for Darwinism, briefly magnetized a surprising range of the artistic intelligentsia. Yeats later claimed that its chief charm for him was Blavatsky's entertaining personality, with her cynical Russian humour, taking the form of irreverent mockery of her most humourless and devoted disciples. But though he fell out with the theosophists, they provided an important staging post in his journey towards the kind of occult society which most closely answered his emotional and psychological requirements. He found this, more or less, in the Order of the Golden Dawn.

Despite the impression given by Yeats's autobiographical writings (and several commentaries on his life), this was not an 1890s rite of passage that petered out about the turn of the century, but an involvement that stayed with him for most of his life. The order was devoted to magical researches rather than the achievement of mystical transcendence. Built on sub-Rosicrucian and cabbalistic foundations in 1887-8, by the time Yeats was initiated on 7 March 1890, it was evolving a complex structure of hierarchies, liturgy, training processes, and examinations. The combination of secret society and intellectual obstacle race appealed to him (as to many other former theosophists); he proceeded through its grades and rituals, devoted an astonishing amount of time to it, used it to focus his wide-ranging reading in mystic and occultist writings, and through it formed some of his most important friendships and associations. It seems likely that the charisma conferred on him within the order, under his adopted name of *Demon Est Deus Inversus*, helped create the hieratic and lofty persona which would come to characterize him in the outside world as well (and correspondingly irritate his family and older friends, like Russell). It gave him the authority he always sought; it also affected his relationships with women. Sexually uncertain until a comparatively late stage of his life, and concealing a lack of confidence beneath the pose of unworldly *fin de siècle* poet, he could use his authority in occult matters to assert himself over the kind of women who appealed to him—strong-minded, unconventional, and dramatic personalities as they generally were. This was true of Olivia *Shakespear (1863–1938), the married novelist with whom he began a love affair in 1896, of the actress Florence Farr, and perhaps most of all of (Edith) Maud *Gonne (1866–1953).

The influence of Maud Gonne A year younger than Yeats, Gonne was the daughter of an English army officer stationed at the Curragh; motherless and lonely, she adopted the cause of Ireland early on, in the form of revolutionary nationalist politics. Since she was a strikingly beautiful former débutante, with the height and presence of a Valkyrie, and after her father's death possessed a large private fortune, her political extremism brought her rapid notoriety in Dublin circles. She none the less managed to keep the other side of her life, based in Paris, comparatively secret: in 1887 she began a long liaison with the right-wing French politician and journalist Lucien Millevoye, by whom she had two children (the first conceived not long after she met Yeats). Yeats first met her—or so he believed—when she arrived at his family's house on 30 January 1889, bearing an introduction from John O'Leary, and 'the troubling of my life began' (*Memoirs*, 40). She persistently stated that they had in fact met some time before, at his father's Dublin studio. But for him, that London encounter was a *coup de foudre*: his rather tepid and dutiful love interest in acquaintances like Katharine Tynan was replaced by a long-sustained passion for someone who seemed at once a heroine from a Shelleyan romance and a personification of Ireland at its most bewitching. She returned his friendship, shared his interests in the occult and mystic life, and deeply admired his poetry, but refused to give him more—without, as yet, revealing the reasons. None the less their association on the astral plane remained intense; they shared visions of previous incarnations and would in 1898 achieve through telepathic dreaming—in Yeats's view at least—a mystic marriage.

The pattern of their relationship was set early on. While

repeatedly begging her to marry him, Yeats believed that she was consecrated to 'Ireland'; though the extremism of her politics alarmed him, he followed nervously a step or two behind, and his support of her through the many vicissitudes of her life over the next thirty years or so was unfailing. In some ways the relationship—enslavement to a magically beautiful and unattainable *princesse lointaine*—was so exactly appropriate for the nature of his poetry that it is easy to assume a certain amount of contrivance in his infatuation. But his notebooks, drafts, horoscope studies, private letters all bear witness to the depth and obsessiveness of a passion continually recreated, as he himself would write, like 'the phoenix', however often he thought he had laid it to rest.

Maud Gonne supplies part—though not all—of the motivation behind Yeats's immersion in Irish political and cultural activity during the early 1890s. His efforts to commandeer the Irish Literary Society in Dublin, and to control the publication of an 'Irish Library' of canonical texts, led to intense in-fighting in 1892–3, from which he withdrew bruised; his efforts to capture Irish cultural initiatives on behalf of the neo-Fenian and Parnellite elements lost out to the more politically adept and ideologically moderate faction led by the septuagenarian Young Irelander Charles Gavan Duffy and Yeats's old companion T. W. Rolleston, who had defected to the moderates and was not forgiven for it. At the same time, the experience concentrated Yeats's enterprise to define a culture that would be definitively Irish, unmaterialistic, politically nationalist, and culturally avant-garde, and his key writings of the early 1890s demonstrate this. They also reflect the connection between folklore and occult divination which characterized Yeats's side of the movement, epitomized in his widely influential collection of prose pieces *The Celtic Twilight* (1893).

But Celtic revivalism also raised an issue just coming into prominence: the possibility of an Irish literary culture which would be un-English yet written in the English language. The Gaelic League, formed at just this time (1893), declared that this was an impossibility. Yeats made episodic efforts to learn Irish but quickly abandoned them—through a congenital inability to learn languages, rather than a considered response. His reiterated argument that a new Irish literature could be forged in English was decried by many 'advanced' nationalists in the cultural arena. His political-spiritual credo was declared through the poetic manifesto 'To Ireland in the Coming Days', published as a kind of preface to *The Countess Kathleen and Various Legends and Lyrics* (1892), and implicitly addressed to Maud Gonne as well as to his nationalist detractors. Though the next decade was to prove him right, he—and several of his literary friends and allies—would become proportionately distanced from conventional 'advanced' nationalist politics in the process.

This is exactly what seemed to be happening in the mid-1890s, when Yeats published his selected *Poems* (1895), which saw the start of his lifelong commitment to weeding and rewriting his early work into a canon. His approach, as Hugh Kenner has put it, was that of 'an architect, not a decorator; he didn't accumulate poems, he wrote books', each collection a polished and coherent whole (H. Kenner, 'The sacred book of the arts', *Gnomon: Essays on Contemporary Literature*, 1958). The mid-1890s also saw a temporary cooling in his relationship with Gonne; his close involvement in the new literary journal *The Savoy* with his friend the symbolist poet and critic Arthur Symons; and the start of his love affair (and lifelong friendship) with Olivia Shakespear, reflected in some of the haunting love poetry of *The Wind among the Reeds* ('The Shadowy Horses', 'Michael Robartes Remembers Forgotten Beauty'). Other 'answering' poems like 'Aedh Wishes his Beloved were Dead' clearly evoke his hopeless passion for Gonne. All this put London rather than Dublin at the forefront of his divided life between 1895 and 1897. But the last years of this key decade saw a dramatic intensification of his Irish activity, both political and cultural: Maud Gonne returned to the centre of his life, he became involved in the Fenian politicking around the commemoration of the 1798 rising, and he embarked on the theatrical enterprise which dominated his life for the next decade and brought him the most enduring and fruitful friendship and collaboration of his life so far.

The years 1897–8 saw a frantic round of political meetings, plotting on committees, and planning for a large-scale commemoration of the revolutionary tradition in Irish politics, all timed for the summer of 1898. Maud Gonne was a leading light (using the contacts made and publicity coups staged in the counter-jubilee demonstrations of 1897), and Yeats himself advanced to prominence as president of the '98 Centennial Association of Great Britain and France, in which guise he began to appear in police reports. Part of the reason for his excitement was a parallel burst of occultist activity. Astrological portents and prophecies had foretold great things for the Celtic revivalist movement at the end of the century, coinciding with similar revelations among the Celticist avant-garde in Scotland, Brittany, and elsewhere; with Russell and others, Yeats and Gonne had begun to plan a new Celtic Mystical Order, constructing elaborate rituals and symbolical codes, and planning a centre in the holy land of the west of Ireland. National and spiritual liberation were to coincide in a new age, which would begin late in 1898. This was reflected in the poems of vision and apocalypse which he wrote at this time ('The Unappeasable Host', 'The Valley of the Black Pig', 'The Secret Rose'), as was his private expectation that Maud Gonne would at last come to him as lover and wife. It did not fall out as foretold. The 1798 commemoration activities, though they probably put in train a long-term revival of the Irish Republican Brotherhood, seemed at the time rather a damp squib. And while Yeats did receive an apocalyptic revelation just before Christmas 1898, it took the form of Maud Gonne's telling him about her secret life—and secret family—in Paris. While it can be conjectured that she may have been clearing the way for their relationship to progress to a different level (her affair with Millevoye had recently foundered), it was put to him—and received on his part—as presenting the clinching reason why she could never marry him. His shock and disillusionment, vividly reflected in his letters of the time, were immense.

Theatrical involvements and political disillusionment, 1899–1916

Significantly, however, these letters were poured out to another woman whose very different relationship to the young poet would have an almost equal effect on his life. Yeats's friendship with Augusta *Gregory (1852–1932) had developed quickly from their meeting at Edward Martyn's Galway castle in the summer of 1896; her neighbouring house, Coole Park, became almost literally Yeats's second home from 1897, when he began the practice of spending summers there which would last thirty years. But she brought him far more than the background of 'order and labour' which he craved, and against which much of his finest work would be written. For Gregory's part, having married a much older man (Sir William Gregory, the retired politician and colonial governor) and been widowed young, the friendship with the dazzling young poet developed into a literary and theatrical collaboration, and launched her on a career of playwriting and theatrical management which put her at the centre of the developing cultural renaissance in Dublin. She was already independently interested in collecting rural folklore and superstitions, and unlike Yeats she spoke Irish. Here too they collaborated, going from cottage to cottage (where the poet's black garb meant he was sometimes mistaken for a proselytizing clergyman). Thirteen years older than Yeats (who always addressed her as Lady Gregory, though she called him Willie), she had a severe appearance and an imperious manner which concealed a passionate temperament, boundless energy, and tremendous powers of organization and perseverance; she was also capable of a racy and cynical humour. All her qualities were put to work for Yeats's benefit, and he paid poetic tributes to this most enduring of his friendships, which 'So changed me that I live, Labouring in ecstasy' ('Friends', written in January 1911).

Lady Gregory came to occupy such a central role in Yeats's life that friends and family tended to grumble at the way his natural impetuousness and enthusiasm became overlaid by a certain hauteur and arrogance, as well as a growing idealization of the eighteenth-century Ascendancy tradition which Gregory, for him, represented. It is likely, however, that these qualities were also cultivated as a defence against the derisive sniping which Yeats always attracted from Dublin's literary quidnuncs. A distant attitude may also have provided necessary armour in the enterprise of an Irish Literary Theatre, which Yeats, Martyn, and Gregory planned in 1897 and which—thanks largely to Gregory's indefatigable lobbying for support among the influential—opened on 8 May 1899 with Yeats's play *The Countess Cathleen*. This play, dealing with a saintly aristocrat who gives up her soul to the devil in order to save her people from starving, had been written ten years before, but much adapted in the interval—partly to incorporate aspects of his relationship with Gonne. The ensuing furore about its supposedly blasphemous content

set the tone for the theatre's fortunes. Run on a shoestring, and without a permanent base, the movement incorporated the talented theatrical producer Willie Fay and his actor-director brother Frank, as well as drawing on the experience of dramatic groups organized by Maud Gonne and her friends. Many of the original company were idealistic (and radical) nationalists. Gonne herself at first supported the Irish National Theatre Society, electrifying audiences with her 1902 performance in the nationalist allegory *Cathleen ni Houlihan*, jointly written by Yeats and Gregory (though it appeared under his name alone). A year later, however, Gonne left the society in protest against the plays of J. M. Synge. By then, in any case, the old Irish Literary Theatre was evolving into the Abbey Theatre company, inaugurated on 27 December 1904 and named after its permanent home, which had been provided by Yeats's wealthy fellow initiate of the Golden Dawn Annie Horniman. The reorganization also involved a triumvirate of directors, Yeats, Gregory, and Synge, wielding dictatorial power over their highly talented (and often resentful) company, and frequently finding themselves at odds with the irascible Horniman, who was romantically obsessed with Yeats. The positive result was a disciplined, innovative, and highly influential institution, which undertook tremendously successful tours in Britain and America, survived many cliffhanging crises (including the eventual departure of Horniman and her subsidy), and finally (1926) became one of the world's first state-subsidized theatres in an independent Ireland.

The effect of this involvement on Yeats's creative and personal life was immense. His first (and last) writing was in dramatic form; he was deeply stage-struck, having already seen his early play *The Land of Heart's Desire* produced in Bedford Park on 29 March 1894 as a curtain-raiser to Shaw's *Arms and the Man*. During the first decade of the twentieth century nearly all his creative effort was channelled into the theatre. His immense correspondence is dominated by questions of organization, production, and direction; he followed the Wagnerian experiment at Bayreuth from a distance, and embarked on a long-lasting preoccupation with the innovative set designs of Gordon Craig, who made a set of screens to create abstract effects for Abbey productions; and he threw himself into playwriting. The results ranged from collaborative efforts with George Moore (*Diarmuid and Grania*, 1901) and Gregory (*Cathleen ni Houlihan*, *The Pot of Broth*, both 1902) to allegorical works like *The King's Threshold* (1903) and *Where there is Nothing* (1904); he also wrote *On Baile's Strand* (1904), introducing the legendary Gaelic hero Cuchulainn, around whose life he would develop a cycle of plays, written in several forms. Dramatic form, indeed, remained a problem: the early verse plays are perhaps the least effective, but from 1915 Yeats began experimenting with elements of the Japanese Noh drama, using masks, choruses, and abstract sets, but capable of dealing with concrete themes like Irish resistance to British rule (*The Dreaming of the Bones*, 1919). There were also less successful comedies attempting to blend nihilism with farce, like *The Player Queen*, commissioned by Mrs Patrick Campbell (whom the poet-playwright approached with mingled terror and fascination) and much rewritten over a ten-year period; and a lengthy Wagnerian verse drama called *The Shadowy Waters*, never finished to his satisfaction. Yeats apprenticed himself to writing plays with all his characteristic passion and commitment, but it could be argued that real success eluded him until the short plays he wrote in his last decade—notably *The Words upon the Windowpane* (1930), where his hero Jonathan Swift speaks through a medium's mouth to riveting dramatic effect, and *Purgatory* (1938), which consummately employs Yeatsian themes of repetition, history, and violence.

It is none the less true that Yeats's theatrical involvement developed the declamatory and increasingly colloquial tone of his verse, as well as his ability as ventriloquist: the form of dramatic dialogue recurs in his verse from this period, and he continued to invent personae to express his poetic voice (Michael Robartes, Crazy Jane, Ribh the hermit, and possibly his occult 'familiar', Leo Africanus). Through the theatre he also developed one of the most influential literary friendships of his life, with the playwright John Millington Synge, whose astonishing plays formed the centre of the Abbey's avant-garde repertoire. Though there were always tensions between the two men, Yeats's admiration for the work of his enigmatic and reticent colleague was unstinting; he also recognized the shock value of Synge's uncompromising work, and its value as literature that was at once distinctively Irish and distinctively modern. Synge's work, and the angry reactions to it in Dublin, also focused Yeats's mind on his own relationship to conventional Irish nationalism. Synge's early death (1909) remained a defining point in Yeats's life, and he is an abiding theme in poems such as 'The Fisherman'. After Maud Gonne's marriage in February 1903 to an ostentatiously unmystical Irish Republican Brotherhood man of action, John MacBride, Yeats felt less trammelled by the beliefs of his youth; when Gonne left her violent husband after a short and abusive marriage, the fact that the nationalist world took his side against hers compounded Yeats's (though not Gonne's) disillusionment with Fenian pieties. His own nationalism became more and more *sui generis*, and his quarrels with the guardians of piety more and more aggressive. The stage of the Abbey provided the arena for the most celebrated of these confrontations. Plays like *The King's Threshold* and *Where there is Nothing* may be read as commentaries on the artist's relation to the politics of his day; he certainly abandoned his hopes of a revolutionary apocalypse after 1900, and avoided Fenian support groups set up in the aftermath of the Second South African War. Most of all, he opposed what he felt to be the ideals of Irish culture advanced by Arthur Griffith's Sinn Féin movement from about 1905. And if the first half of Yeats's life pivots round one great emblematic confrontation, it is the row over Synge's play *The Playboy of the Western World* in 1907, when Yeats pitted himself and the Abbey Theatre against what he saw as know-nothing pietism and intolerance. The play's opponents are often represented as the outraged Dublin bourgeoisie; but Yeats identified them specifically as Sinn Féiners, and said so.

In his essay of 1910, 'J. M. Synge and the Ireland of his Time', which is a first instalment of autobiography masquerading as an elegy for his friend, Yeats clearly constructed the arguments for a kind of nationalism which would be at once inclusive, imaginative, and realistic. Arthur Griffith (once a friend to the theatrical movement, now an enemy of the Abbey and Yeats) had described *The Playboy* as 'a vile and inhuman story told in the foulest language we have ever listened to from a public platform … the production of a moral degenerate who has dishonoured the women of Ireland before all Europe' (*Sinn Fein*, 2 February 1907). Both the play and its proponents were, in a word, un-Irish and anti-national. Yeats, in opposition, cited his own revolutionary record in Fenian organizations and accepted the directly political implications of the *Playboy* controversy, arguing (in a particularly sinewy and subtle way) that the nineteenth-century Young Ireland conventionalities no longer answered the questions of identity posed by modern Ireland. The invention of tradition, and 'images for the affections', had done their work of confidence building, and Irish national rhetoric must advance beyond chauvinism and defensiveness:

> Even if what one defends be true, an attitude of defence, a continual apology, whatever the cause, makes the mind barren because it kills intellectual innocence; that delight in what is unforeseen, and in the mere spectacle of the world, the mere drifting hither and thither that must come before all true thought and emotion. A zealous Irishman, especially if he lives much out of Ireland, spends his time in a never-ending argument about Oliver Cromwell, the Danes, the penal laws, the rebellion of 1798, the famine, the Irish peasant, and ends by substituting a traditional casuistry for a country. (*Essays and Introductions*, 1961, 314)

By 1910 Yeats had redirected into the theatre his belief in ritual, his desire to educate an Irish public away from English materialism to intellectual independence, his ability to dominate committees and set up organizations. These qualities were also displayed in his periodic efforts to exercise a decisive influence over his sisters' enterprise, the Cuala Press, not always to their pleasure. At forty-five he was determined to turn his energies back towards verse and to spend less time running the Abbey. In Dublin he sustained for some years a discreet love affair with Mabel Dickinson, an amateur actress and 'medical masseuse'; it ended in 1913, when she pressed for marriage on the basis of an unfounded pregnancy scare. But throughout he remained close to Gonne, and their relationship went through a particularly intense phase late in 1908, when they briefly became lovers at last, before reverting to the spiritualized bond which Gonne preferred: a 'mystic marriage'. Yet up to 1917, and his sudden marriage, she still haunted his poetry: 'Her Praise'. 'His Phoenix', and, 'The People' were all written in 1914–15.

In 1908, aged only forty-three, Yeats had produced an eight-volume *Collected Works*; though intended as clearing the ground in order to advance, it was a risky gesture. But by now he was a major figure in the literary firmament. Appositely for someone both preoccupied by the doctrine of the mask, and very conscious of the need for self-presentation, Yeats remained a favourite subject for artists all his life. His striking looks as a young man, with his raven hair, olive skin, and dreamy gaze, are preserved in many portraits: notably by his father (1900), William Strang (1903), Augustus John (1907), and Charles Shannon (1908). He was the subject of distinguished photographs by Alvin Langdon Coburn, Alice Broughton, and others, and was sculpted by Kathleen Bruce (1908) and Albert Power (1918). He was a favourite subject for caricature by masters such as Beerbohm and Dulac. The frontispieces to the volumes of his *Collected Works* run the gamut of images by John, Sargent, Mancini, Shannon, and J. B. Yeats: 'nobody will believe they are the same man', Yeats wrote to John Quinn, 'and I shall write an essay upon them and describe them as all the different personages that I have dreamt of being, but have never had the time for'. His omnivorous juvenile reading and the education of his father's studio had refined his critical powers and the weight and originality of his work as literary critic has never quite won its due. His contribution to the study of Blake, Spenser, Shelley, and Shakespeare is decisive, besides his reinstatement of near-forgotten Irish figures such as Carleton, Mangan, and Ferguson. Yeats was also behind the great success of Rabindranath Tagore, whose work he powerfully advocated (and subtly edited); the award of Nobel prize to Tagore in 1913 marked one of Yeats's great triumphs of literary entrepreneurship.

By 1914 Yeats, in his fiftieth year, was at a crossroads in life; old adversaries like George Moore thought he had written himself out. He had become a celebrated figure in English as well as Irish literary life. The years up to the First World War saw him become an established lion in the London social safari, sought after by hostesses like Lady Cunard, lunching at the Asquiths', an influential member of Edmund Gosse's academic committee of the Royal Society of Literature, the recipient of a civil-list pension from 1910 (for which 'advanced' Irish nationalists refused to forgive him). In 1915 he turned down a knighthood. He had achieved enormous success on the American lecture tour circuit, making extended visits in 1903–4, 1911, 1914, 1920, and 1932. He was a firm supporter of the Home Rule Bill, passed, with difficulty, by 1914, but suspended for the duration of the war, and made some eloquent speeches supporting it; but his Fenian connections had apparently lapsed. His life remained divided between Coole in the summers and his celebrated Bloomsbury rooms in Woburn Buildings, where he held court on Monday evenings, for much of the rest of the year. During the winters of 1913, 1915, and 1916 he spent much time in an Ashdown Forest cottage, accompanied by the young American poet Ezra Pound (who married Olivia Shakespear's daughter Dorothy) as secretary and amanuensis. Pound and Yeats certainly influenced each other, though the traffic was not as one-way as the American liked to suggest; from the early 1900s Yeats's verse had been striving towards the colloquial voice, as well as the ellipsis and condensation, which bewildered some critics when he published his path-breaking collection *Responsibilities* in 1914. The bitter interrogations of poems like 'To a Wealthy Man …', 'September 1913', and 'To a Shade' were also inspired by a series of public controversies in Irish life, where Yeats had opposed what he saw as the philistinism of the new Irish bourgeoisie—notably over the vexed question of municipal support for a modern art gallery to house the pictures offered by Gregory's nephew, the art dealer and connoisseur Hugh Lane—an issue left hanging when Lane went down with the *Lusitania* in 1915, leaving the disposition of the paintings legally (though not morally) uncertain.

The Irish revolution and its aftermath, 1916–1930 Yeats's distancing from conventional nationalism, his disillusionment with modern Irish life, and his apparent absorption into the English establishment, should all be borne in mind as the background to his response to the shattering Irish rising of Easter 1916. It was as much of a shock to him as to most other people, and his first reaction—as he wrote to Gregory on 11 May—was that 'all the work of years has been overturned, all the bringing together of classes, all the freeing of Irish literature and criticism from politics' (11 May 1916, *Letters*, 613). With the execution of the insurgents he began to feel an unwilling admiration for the self-sacrifice of those involved—who included John MacBride, Maud Gonne's estranged husband. Yeats's feelings (and their ambiguity) are powerfully interrogated in the key poem 'Easter 1916', composed between the execution of the insurgents in May and the end of September. It was circulated in a privately printed edition but not published for four years—partly because he feared jeopardizing the cause of reclaiming Lane's picture collection for Ireland (a campaign in which he and Gregory were lobbying English politicians), partly because his own feelings were in the process of crystallization. 'Easter 1916', in its intellectual complexity, subtle shifts of mood and form, and use of internalized dialogue, marks a new level in Yeats's 'political' poems; but it was also a last, elegiac appeal to Gonne to turn from fanatical abstractions and join him in a celebration of life. At the same time his sympathies were moving towards the revolutionary cause even before the Lloyd George government mounted its campaign against the IRA in 1920 by means of the 'black and tan' mercenary forces, which Yeats assailed in poems and speeches. By the time of the rising he was already negotiating to buy the ancient Norman tower of Ballylee in Galway, near Coole; during the Irish revolution of 1916–21 he decided to move back to his native country and, as he had put it early on, 'begin building again'.

In the same period Yeats's private life also went through dramatic upheavals: in 1916 he was a 51-year-old bachelor, by the end of 1921 he was married and the father of two children. During the summer of 1916 he visited Gonne at her seaside house in Normandy. After MacBride's death he had asked her to marry him once more, and she had once more refused. He was in any case deeply preoccupied with her daughter by Millevoye, Iseult (1894–1954) [see Stuart, Iseult], now a fascinating (and strikingly beautiful) young woman of twenty-two, who admired him deeply; by 1917 the 52-year-old poet had become entranced by her, and that summer he proposed marriage, which she refused.

He subsequently turned to another much younger woman: Bertha Georgie Hyde-Lees (1892–1968), known as George, whose mother was married to Olivia Shakespear's brother. She was a close friend of Dorothy Pound, and had collaborated on spiritualist researches with Yeats, which had become infused with romantic interest by late 1915. However, Yeats's obsession with Iseult persisted, and his marriage to George on 20 October 1917 came as a total surprise to most of their acquaintance. It also brought him very near to a total breakdown. The triangle of women in his life (Maud–Iseult–George) recurs in his poems of the time, lightly disguised, and stands behind the play *The Only Jealousy of Emer*; he was also deeply affected by the repetition of a pattern set in the 1890s, when he had been torn between his affair with Shakespear and the unattainable but disruptive image of Gonne.

Astrological calculations had played a part in Yeats's conviction that he would marry in 1917; foretold or not, it was a fortunate decision. George Yeats was highly intelligent, good-humoured (if slightly acerbic), sophisticated, and quietly unconventional. She created the first settled home the poet had known (helped by her independent means), guarded his increasingly uncertain health, and proved a heaven-sent collaborator in his work as well: preserving drafts, editing his work posthumously, and above all recharging his occult researches for nearly ten years by means of concentrated experiments in 'automatic writing', first employed as a method of assuaging his doubts and self-reproaches in the first days of their sudden marriage. She was also well aware of—as she put it—'the strange, chaotic, varied and completely unified personality that you are' (1 Jan 1935, priv. coll.).

This was just as well. Strikingly, Yeats not only remained friends with most of his past lovers, he also relied heavily on mutually supportive friendships with women. This often involved an implicitly sexual element: extraordinarily attractive all his life, he had a way of lending himself out to the fantasies of others and then withholding himself while they stayed in thrall. His marriage did not mean an end to this kind of relationship, and intense collaborative friendships, in some cases developing into love affairs, continued to be a feature of his later life—notably with Margot Ruddock, Ethel Mannin, Dorothy Wellesley, and Edith Shackleton Heald. But his marriage remained near the centre of his life, bringing him a great period of emotional and imaginative fulfilment. It is symbolically marked by the publication by Cuala of his landmark volume *The Wild Swans at Coole* a month after his wedding, but it is the extended version brought out by Macmillan in 1919 which stands as a coded autobiographical record of these eventful years. Criticized by some for uneven language and wilful obscurity, it was seen by more far-sighted commentators as his most significant advance since *The Wind among the Reeds*. The title-poem in fact revisits his 1890s themes of personal alienation and emotional deprivation, but in severely beautiful language, without a touch of ornateness. The same qualities appear in 'The Fisherman' where the poet claims not only an élite status but an ideal audience:

> All day I'd looked in the face
> What I had hoped 'twould be
> To write for my own race
> And the reality;
> The living men that I hate,
> The dead man that I loved,
> The craven man in his seat,
> The insolent unreproved

There is also a series of poems written before the upheavals of 1917 which celebrate Gonne's departed beauty and indomitable spirit, and some heartfelt lyrics inspired by his feelings for Iseult. 'In Memory of Major Robert Gregory' is the most substantial of Yeats's elegies for his friend's son, killed in the war, but it is also a sombre meditation on his own acquisition of a wife and a house, at a time of life when old friends and associations were falling away from him. Above all, 'Solomon and Sheba', 'The Phases of the Moon', and 'The Double Vision of Michael Robartes' reflect or even record the insights brought by George Yeats's mediumship. *The Wild Swans at Coole* commemorates a period of emotional turmoil as well as occult revelation.

However, politics were withheld from the volume, in the shape of the pro-rising poems written after 1916. These were cautiously published from 1920, and collected in *Michael Robartes and the Dancer*, published in 1921, embodying further fruits of this new phase in his life, while the philosophical pattern-making precipitated by George's insights were processed into *A Vision* (1926, revised 1937). But the summit of Yeats's creative achievement in these years is represented in *The Tower* (1928). This volume, decorated with one of Thomas Sturge Moore's most beautiful cover engravings, depicting Ballylee and its reflection, brought together the poems quarried out of new sources, expressed in new language. At the same time, as Richard Ellmann remarked of the breathtaking opening poem 'Sailing to Byzantium', Yeats had in a sense been writing them all his life. Thus that poem is a distillation of his well-established themes of human old age, the mutability of nature, and the eternity of art—but viewed quizzically through the prism of a millennial Byzantium created from his supercharged imagination and wide if erratic reading. As such, it has magnetized a phalanx of scholars but retains the quintessential Yeatsian combination of mystery and accessibility:

> That is no country for old men. The young
> In one another's arms, birds in the trees,
> —Those dying generations—at their song,
> The salmon-falls, the mackerel-crowded seas,
> Fish, flesh, or fowl, commend all summer long
> Whatever is begotten, born, and dies.

The Tower also contains his two great sequences about history and violence, inspired by the Bolshevik as well as the Irish revolution—'Nineteen Hundred and Nineteen' and 'Meditations in Time of Civil War'. The first interrogates 'the present state of the world' (its original title) through a complex commentary on cyclical history and personal dis-illusionment:

> We, who seven years ago
> Talked of honour and of truth,
> Shriek with pleasure if we show
> The weasel's twist, the weasel's tooth.

'Meditations' meanwhile, suggests, doubtfully enough, that the apocalyptic horses of destruction can herald a new creativity and growth, arising out of the wreckage of a superficially assured civilization. A volume that also includes 'Among School Children' and 'All Souls Night' has to be reckoned at the height of his achievement. While the personal voice is as dominant as ever, Yeats also demonstrates a new ability to raise abstruse philosophical questions in a language at once mobile, exploratory, and economical. He thought it the best book he had written, and he was right.

The Tower also contains 'Leda and the Swan', written five years before, and already notorious. That recurring theme of the birth of civilizations through acts of violence was cast into shadow by the immediacy of the erotically charged imagery when Yeats published it in *To-morrow*, a short-lived magazine edited by Iseult and her husband, Francis *Stuart (1902–2000), which had successfully outraged Irish Catholic piety. This was a deliberate strategy: Yeats also contributed an anonymous editorial, designed to provoke the self-righteous. From the early days of the new Irish Free State he set himself up as the scourge of artistic and literary censorship, not always with the approval of fellow protestants who preferred not to rock the boat.

Though the Yeatses first lived in Oxford after their marriage, George had encouraged her husband's instinct to return to Ireland and from early 1922 they divided their time between a Dublin town house and the tower at Bally-lee. The Irish civil war rumbled in the background, and its reverberations echo in 'Meditations in Time of Civil War', written at this time:

> We had fed the heart on fantasies,
> The heart's grown brutal from the fare;
> More substance in our enmities
> Than in our love; O honey-bees,
> Come build in the empty house of the stare.

The upheavals of Irish politics also brought Yeats back into public life. In 1923 he was nominated to the senate of the new Irish Free State, where he took an active role over the next five years, chairing the committee appointed to choose a new coinage for the country, and making celebrated speeches against the imposition of Catholic social teaching in Irish constitutional law. He used his public position on occasions like the Tailteann games (August 1924), as well as his platform in the senate, to further the cause. But the tide of opinion was against him, and the attitudes he struck during the 1920s and 1930s would be held against him in perpetuity. At the same time his espousal of artistic freedom and celebrated pronouncements against the prohibition of divorce (1925) conferred a special position in Irish public life. And though he saw himself as seeking, and finding, an 'Anglo-Irish solitude',

he could not stop throwing himself into public controversy when the opportunity arose.

In another key poem, 'Among School Children', Yeats described himself during his senate years as 'a smiling public man', but the smile was not always in evidence. As a politician and a poet he was always conscious that there was an audience to be addressed; this could be both a strength and a weakness. Significantly, 'Among School Children' ended by posing profoundly unanswerable Neo-platonic questions; for the centre of his imaginative life remained far from politics, a fact amply if rather mystifyingly demonstrated in *A Vision*, published in 1926. Relying on the interrogations and reflections pursued through George's automatic writing, this strange book codified human archetypes and historical cycles into a framework based on the twenty-eight phases of the moon; arcane philosophy had in some measure replaced the magical quests and rituals of the Order of the Golden Dawn, though he kept up his connection with that organization as late as 1922. In both these involvements his wife's influence was discreet but decisive: her wide reading in esoterica inform the resourceful responses which make up the vast corpus of 'Automatic Script' analysed by scholars. *A Vision* is an attempt to fashion a personal philosophy, and to codify historical change, on lines that have been described as 'Gnostic-Apocalyptic'. It might also be seen (in a private description of Oliver St John Gogarty's) as 'a geometrical rendering of the emotions, a mixture of Einstein and myth' (unpublished letter to L. A. G. Strong, 26 Jan 1926, University of Texas at Austin). Several of its preoccupations had been aired in the two essays on art and the spiritual life published as *Per amica silentia lunae* in 1918: George had seen the proofs during the first days of their marriage, and her 'instructors' had clearly taken them to heart. When writing *Per amica* Yeats had characteristically written to Craig:

> I used to think, when I was a boy, that no man should be permitted to public life till he had written first: an account of the world to come; second: a practicable scheme for the perfection of this world, and sworn to the two.
> (unpublished letter, 4 Sept 1917, Bibliothèque Nationale, Paris)

This neatly expresses his enduring belief in the interconnectedness of supernatural and everyday life, which tended to bewilder his more earthbound acquaintances, but was deeply rooted in his early devotion to Swedenborg and more especially William Blake—an admiration that never left him.

At the same time, the strength of Yeats's work—and some of his finest poetry was written in the 1920s—was also rooted in direct personal experience. It is not coincidental that he was simultaneously continuing his reflective *Autobiographies*, and still fighting hard battles over the Abbey Theatre (notably regarding the new dramatic genius Sean O'Casey, whose early plays provoked riots reminiscent of the reaction to Synge, but who broke with Yeats and Gregory when they turned down his experimental anti-war play *The Silver Tassie* in 1928).

Yeats's international status was recognized by the

award of the Nobel prize in 1923, which brought him some financial capital for the first time in his life; the lecture which he gave on the occasion, published in 'The Bounty of Sweden', stands as one of his most influential essays in autobiography. Augustus John's second portrait, of 1930, depicts Yeats in his maturity, with his disciplined mane of white hair and pugnacious lower lip. He was by now one of Dublin's great established figures, both in his own right and as the representative of the cultural renaissance which—it was generally held, and unequivocally stated by Yeats himself in his speech receiving the Nobel prize—had set in motion the Irish revolution and war of independence. Long ago, in 1913, he had emphasized to Gregory that future generations would see their era of Irish history through their own biographies, and so it was coming to be. Gregory herself died of cancer in 1932; Yeats, who had stayed with her at Coole through her last months, had lost one of the rocks of his existence, as well as the house he loved more than any other. (Taken over by the Forestry Commission, it was allowed to rot and was eventually demolished, a fate Yeats himself had proleptically dealt with in his lapidary poem to Gregory and her influence, 'Coole Park, 1929'.) He and George moved out of central Dublin in 1932 to a small country house with a large garden at Rathfarnham, beneath the Dublin mountains; he had already stopped going to Ballylee, and from 1927 was spending some of each winter in southern Europe for the sake of his health; in 1928 he had considered settling in Rapallo for good. He suffered from high blood pressure, as well as recurrent arthritis; his chest and heart gave frequent cause for alarm. He was severely ill in November–December 1929, when a haemorrhage of the lungs was followed by Malta fever, collapsed again from January to March 1935 with congestion of the lungs, and early in 1936 was threatened by acute sclerosis and kidney problems. When his doctor (and fellow poet) Oliver Gogarty read him a letter from his Spanish doctor describing him as 'an antique cardio-sclerotic of advanced years', Yeats allegedly responded that it sounded a more sonorous title than lord of Lower Egypt.

The 1930s Yeats's failing health makes the febrility and energy of his work during his last decade all the more remarkable. This energy was also reflected in surges of excitement about political issues. Though he was fully committed to the Free State, Yeats's years in the senate had not given him a high opinion of the workings of representative democracy; his naturally élitist inclinations were reinforced by the authoritarian and arcane world of occult researches, and a dislike of what he saw as the devaluation of culture in the post-war world. In Irish terms, he was still a passionate believer in the necessity of a distinctive national culture, grounded in essential Irish traditions rather than pinchbeck materialism imported from England; but he now looked for those traditions in the work of eighteenth-century luminaries of the Ascendancy like Bishop Berkeley, Edmund Burke, and perhaps most of all Jonathan Swift. Long before, in *Reveries over Childhood and Youth* (1915), he had rejoiced in 'all that joins

my life to those who had power in Ireland' (*Autobiographies*, 22); his celebration of traditional authority took a political swerve in 1933, when he became interested in the proto-fascist movement started by General O'Duffy, known as the 'blueshirts'. Yeats actually wrote some embarrassingly bad poems to be used as marching songs but rapidly distanced himself from the movement when it became clear that it stood for principles very different from those he had hoped for. Neither the fervent Catholic pietism nor the anti-intellectualism of the blueshirts and their leaders could appeal to someone who had fought so manfully against the literary censorship imposed by the Free State; the movement's real impetus came from the farming interest who felt disadvantaged by government economic policies, and from political elements antipathetic to the former revolutionary Eamon De Valera, who had just assumed power democratically, after opposing the treaty in arms only ten years before. Neither of these issues meant much to Yeats: he was nearly seventy and in some ways a man of the 1890s still and his wish had been to see the revival of a poetic and anti-modern Ireland, the 'dream of the noble and the beggar-man'.

At the same time Yeats was not immune to the currents of right-wing thought sweeping Europe; long a devoted reader of Nietzsche, he devoured Spengler's *Decline of the West*, became a member of the Eugenics Society, and from the early 1920s issued periodic denunciations of parliamentary democracy as redundant, quoting—if not necessarily endorsing—Mussolini. (Some of his intemperate pronouncements on modern politics were published in *On the Boiler* eight months after his death.) He was also a frequent visitor to Italy, where he resumed his old friendship with Pound, wintering in Rapallo in 1928 and 1929, and speaking at the fourth congress of the Alessandro Volta Foundation in Rome in October 1934. He accepted the Goethe-plakette from the city of Frankfurt in the same year, but this was purely a recognition of the first German performance of *The Countess Cathleen*. He occasionally expressed ill-advised approval of some features of the new Nazi regime, though he never visited the country. But this does not necessarily add up to fascist politics (indeed, his speech at the Roman congress stressed the necessity of artistic freedom); he was ironic about Pound's political excesses and (unlike friends such as Maud Gonne, Iseult Stuart, and Oliver Gogarty) never subscribed to any form of antisemitism. Though he refused to join his friend Ethel Mannin in her campaign to liberate Carl von Ossietzsky from Nazi Germany in 1936, it seems likely that this was because he disapproved of using a Nobel prize nomination in such a directly political way. 'Do not try to make a politician of me', he wrote to Ethel Mannin in 1936 (*Letters*, 850–51):

even in Ireland I shall never I think be that again—as my sense of reality deepens, and I think it does with age, my horror at the cruelty of governments grows greater, and if I did what you want I would seem to hold one form of governments more responsible than any other and that would betray my convictions. Communist, fascist, nationalist, clerical, anti-clerical are all responsible according to the number of their victims. I have not been silent; I have used the only vehicle I possess—verse. If you have my poems by you look up a poem called 'The Second Coming'. It was written some sixteen or seventeen years ago and foretold what is happening. I have written of the same thing again and again since … I am not callous, every nerve trembles with horror at what is happening in Europe. 'The ceremony of innocence is drowned'.

Yeats also emphasized to Mannin that he remained 'a Fenian of the school of John O'Leary'. Certainly his opposition to Britain's record in Ireland remained powerful, and was rekindled by the controversy over Roger Casement, executed for treason after the 1916 rising after agitation for a pardon was short-circuited by the release of his alleged homosexual diaries. Casement, like Parnell, recurs in Yeats's pungent late ballads, symbolizing nobility done down by 'baseness'. But his last years, like his early life, were divided between England and Ireland. In Dublin he had tried to construct a circle of sympathetic and talented literary friends, meeting regularly at his house—the kind of *cénacle* on which he had always depended. They included his oldest friend George Russell as well as the younger writers Frank O'Connor and F. R. Higgins whom he also brought into the Abbey organization, and the Irish Academy of Letters which Yeats and Shaw set up in 1932, drawing violent chauvinist abuse from the *Catholic Bulletin* and elsewhere. But in several ways the intellectual atmosphere of De Valera's Ireland was uncongenial to him—and he to it, as reflected in a series of virulent attacks on 'Pensioner Yeats' and his 'Sewage School' of poetry. And Yeats's appetite for the exotic remained undimmed: in 1934–5 he became almost as excited about the reflections of the Indian sage Shri Purohit Swami as he had been over Rabindranath Tagore twenty-five years before. He wrote the introduction to the Swami's autobiography and spent the winter of 1935–6 in Majorca with him, hoping to achieve a fruitful collaboration in spiritual and literary terms. But the episode ended disastrously: Yeats suffered his most serious illness yet, his latest admirer, Margot Ruddock, followed them to the island and produced a spectacular nervous breakdown, while an embittered female camp follower of the Swami's was only just dissuaded from precipitating a scandal.

Now seventy, Yeats continued to rage against old age—which, as he ironically pointed out to Olivia Shakespear, he had been denouncing since *The Wanderings of Oisin*, written in his early twenties. He defied it on one level by engaging in literary controversy—notably over his idiosyncratic choice for the *Oxford Book of Modern Verse* in 1936, which combined an eccentric approach to canon making with an 'Introduction' that is actually a masterly instalment of intellectual autobiography. There were also passionate friendships with younger women; much of his time from the mid-1930s was spent staying in Sussex with Wellesley or Heald. In April 1934 he underwent the celebrated Steinach operation (actually a unilateral vasectomy) with a view to prolonging (or restoring) his potency. The physiological effect was doubtful, but his powers were certainly—and miraculously—exercised at full stretch in the poetry of his last years. This is often savage, hard, and clear in the manner he had declared to be his

ideal from the turn of the century, but only intermittently embraced. Sequences like the 'Crazy Jane' poems turned back to the ballad metres and even the demotic Irish personae of his very early verse, but put them to aggressively modern use; philosophical lyrics like 'Long-legged Fly' used the cyclical ideas derived from a lifetime's speculative reading with a challenging economy and beauty. His rediscovery of themes from Indian philosophy also suggested the mystical and symbolic use of sexual desire and ecstasy. The best of his late poetry explores the myths humanity lives by, and anchors them in his own experience. At the same time he continued the interrogation of the creative process which he had been engaged in since 'Adam's Curse' (1904). Finally, in 'The Circus Animals' Desertion' he produced perhaps his most consummately expressed artistic autobiography:

> Those masterful images because complete
> Grew in pure mind, but out of what began?
> A mound of refuse or the sweepings of a street,
> Old kettles, old bottles and a broken can,
> Old iron, old bones, old rags, that raving slut
> Who keeps the till. Now that my ladder's gone,
> I must lie down where all the ladders start,
> In the foul rag-and-bone shop of the heart.

The declamatory note of his *Last Poems* is not always successful, and the lines can ring as alternately over-contrived, ragged, and jarring; nor are his ventures into demotic saltiness always happy. (F. R. Higgins, who advocated poetry that could be sung to Irish folk tunes, had a lot to answer for.) But at best this final achievement confirmed his claim to rest at the forefront of modernism, having started as an ornament of the blue-and-silver 1890s and the 'Celtic note'. The note of 'curious astringent joy' which he attributed to Nietzsche and to Blake also sounds through his late testaments, and at such junctures he makes good his sustained artistic effort to break through into the 'desolation of reality'.

When Yeats wrote 'The Circus Animals' Desertion' he had not long to live. His health necessitated a long stay in the south of France from January to March 1938. Back in Ireland, he saw the publication of *New Poems*, and the production of his play *Purgatory* which opened at the Abbey on 10 August with sets designed by his daughter Anne; it was accompanied, gratifyingly, by a theological controversy. But in December he was back on the Riviera, where he died at Roquebrune on 28 January 1939. He was writing to the end. His last play, *The Death of Cuchulain*, and his last two poems, 'Cuchulain Comforted' and 'The Black Tower', hark back to the Gaelic legendary themes of forty years before. But 'Cuchulain Comforted' is also a Dantean vision of transformation and departure into the shades, written when Yeats knew he was dying. In a sense, he choreographed the performance of his death as well as his life. *Last Poems and Two Plays* was published the following July. Shortly afterwards, the world descended into war, and the removal of Yeats's remains from Roquebrune, where they were initially interred on 30 January 1939, to his desired burial place in Sligo was postponed until nine years later, when he was interred 'under Ben Bulben', as dictated in the epitaph poem he wrote for himself. In 1939 his obituarists quarrelled about his place in Irish—or in English—letters; most expressed mystification at the tone and direction of his late poems; many harked nostalgically back to the musical clarity of his early verse, and some denounced him as from the pulpit. But in 1948 an Irish navy corvette brought his coffin back to Galway harbour, where it was conveyed to what would be rechristened 'Yeats country' and was on 17 September 1948 buried in Drumcliff, co. Sligo. The ceremony, attended by Irish government ministers who included the son of Maud Gonne and John MacBride, effectively proclaimed W. B. Yeats as pre-eminent national poet. The controversy over whether his remains had, in fact, been correctly identified in Roquebrune added a mythic flavour, suggestive of King Arthur or Charles Stewart Parnell. But it did not detract from the symbolism of the re-interment.

Posthumous reputation Yeats is now seen as one of a handful of Irish writers whose influence and example helped create twentieth-century modernist literature in the English language; but unlike that of James Joyce or Samuel Beckett (not to mention Oscar Wilde and George Bernard Shaw), his life remained intimately intertwined with the biography of his country. The period spanned by Yeats's birth and death delineates the exact period of Ireland's turbulent development towards political independence through a nationalist movement which moved between constitutional and extremist modes; as T. S. Eliot put it, Yeats was 'one of those few poets whose history is the history of their own time, who are part of the consciousness of an age which cannot be understood without them' ('The poetry of W. B. Yeats', reprinted in J. Hall and M. Steinman, eds., *The Permanence of Yeats*, 1950, 34). From the very beginning of his long literary career, his poems provided phrases which rang in the national mind and provided keys to Irish experience ('I will arise and go now, And go to Innisfree'; 'Romantic Ireland's dead and gone, It's with O'Leary in the grave', 'A terrible beauty is born', 'Things fall apart, the centre cannot hold'). Yet it is the difficulties and tensions of Yeats's relationship to Irish history and Irish identity, dramatized both directly and indirectly in some of his best writing, which give his poetry much of its dynamic tension. His huge international reputation is securely based on the mystery and grandeur of his late verse and the poignancy of his love poetry, but he first came to fame as the exotically Celtic poet of a 'new' nationalist Ireland: almost single-handed, he made Irishness culturally fashionable. Spearheading a great cultural renaissance, he moved into his maturity as the voice of his country, memorializing her heroes, sitting as a senator in her independent parliament, dying full of years and honours.

Yet throughout his career Yeats sustained an angry, quarrelsome, ambivalent relationship with his native country; and for his first fifty years he lived more in England than Ireland, a pattern recurring at the end of his life. His early poems on Celtic and faery themes became and remained canonical, but he was attacked in Ireland for the decadence, occultism, and sensuality of his verse and the arrogant iconoclasm of his public utterances—and, indeed, his personal style. His reputation was violently fought over for years after he died, and much of this quarrel revolved around the issue of whether 'England' or 'Ireland' should claim him. If this seems difficult to understand now, with pilgrims guided through co. Sligo in the footsteps of his poetry and a thriving tourist industry concentrated around every Irish resonance set up by his verses, his life and background do much to explain it.

Yeats's posthumous reputation is more monumental, and less assailable, than some of his contemporaries would have expected. During the Second World War his work went out of print, and through the 1950s Yeatsian studies were the province of a few dedicated and highly distinguished scholars—such as Cleanth Brooks, A. N. Jeffares, T. R. Henn, and most of all Richard Ellmann. However, interest in his life was sustained by Allan Wade's edition of letters and Macmillan's publication of several volumes of prose writings organized by his widow, while Peter Allt and Russel Alspach's heroic Variorum editions of poems and plays demonstrated clearly the depth of attention that needed to be paid to Yeats's endless revisions in search of a canonical text. From the 1960s his philosophical interests, and the occultist underpinnings behind much of his work, began to arouse serious interest, reflected in the work of F. A. C. Wilson, Giorgio Melchiori, James Olney, and others. His place in Irish history and political influence was examined by the new wave of Irish historians, notably Conor Cruise O'Brien and F. S. L. Lyons. By the 1970s the Yeats 'industry' was working full-scale; the massive project of a full-scale annotated *Collected Letters* was under way, two scholarly *Annuals* of Yeats studies came into existence, and the annual Yeats summer school in Sligo set a much imitated example. The deeply complex question of Yeatsian texts (complicated by the poet's own apparent authorization of different editions in the 1930s) has sparked a long controversy about the canonical version of his poetry, and has been illuminated by the publication of scholarly editions of the much revised manuscripts behind his various collections. Even a certain 1980s reaction against Yeats's work, as affected by what Seamus Deane termed 'the pathology of literary Unionism', simply added fuel to the blazing interest in his work and life. He had always been supreme among modern Irish poets and his international standing has equally been recognized as one of the great innovators of modern poetry, who developed a voice so unique as to inhibit as well as to inspire those who came after him. Early on, defending his constant poetic revisions, he had declared that he must 're-make' himself: in the process he helped re-make both his own country and world literature. R. F. FOSTER

Sources W. B. Yeats, *Autobiographies* (1955) · W. B. Yeats, *Memoirs*, ed. D. Donoghue (1972) · *The collected letters of W. B. Yeats*, ed. J. Kelly and others, [3 vols.] (1986–) · *The letters of W. B. Yeats*, ed. A. Wade (1954) · *The Gonne–Yeats letters, 1893–1938*, ed. A. MacBride White and A. N. Jeffares (1992) · E. H. Mikhail, *W. B. Yeats: interviews and recollections* (1977) · A. N. Jeffares, ed., *W. B. Yeats: the critical heritage* (1977) · A. N. Jeffares, ed., *A new commentary on the poems of W. B. Yeats* (1984) · J. V. Hone, *W. B. Yeats* (1942) · R. F. Foster, *The apprentice mage, 1865–*

1914 (1997), vol. 1 of *W. B. Yeats: a life* • R. F. Foster, *The arch-poet, 1915–1939* (2003), vol. 2 of *W. B. Yeats: a life* • W. M. Murphy, *Prodigal father: the life of John Butler Yeats, 1839–1922* (1978) • W. M. Murphy, *Family secrets: William Butler Yeats and his relatives* (1995) • R. Ellmann, *Yeats: the man and the masks*, 2nd edn (1979) • W. Gould, ed., *Yeats Annual* (1982–) • J. P. Frayne, ed., *Uncollected prose by W. B. Yeats*, 1 (1970) • J. P. Frayne and C. Johnston, eds., *Uncollected prose by W. B. Yeats*, 2 (1975) • W. B. Yeats, Lady Gregory, and J. M. Synge, *Theatre business: the correspondence of the first Abbey Theatre directors, William Butler Yeats, Lady Gregory and J. M. Synge*, ed. A. Saddlemyer (1982) • A. Gregory, *Lady Gregory's journal*, ed. J. Murphy, 2 vols. (1978–87) • *Lady Gregory's diaries, 1892–1902*, ed. J. Pethica (1996) • G. M. Harper, ed., *Yeats and the occult* (1976) • G. M. Harper, ed., *Yeats's vision papers*, 3 vols. (1992) • G. M. Harper, ed., *The making of Yeats's 'A vision': a study of the automatic script* (1987)

Archives Boston College, John J. Burns Library, family corresp. • Harvard U., Houghton L., letters and literary MSS • Hunt. L., literary and other material • Indiana University, Bloomington, Lilly Library, papers • NL Ire., corresp. and papers incl. literary and theatrical MSS • priv. coll., library • priv. coll., private papers • Ransom HRC, papers • U. Leeds, Brotherton L., corresp. • U. Reading L., corresp. and literary MSS • University of Kansas, Lawrence, theatrical and publishing corresp. | BL, letters to G. K. Chesterton, Add. MSS 73210 B fol. 138; 73232 B fol. 115; 73241 fols. 126–36 • BL, corresp. with Arthur Duff, Add. MS 55003 • BL, letters to Lady Gregory, RP1839; RP1799; RP1872; RP1789 [photocopies] • BL, corresp. with Macmillans, Add. MS 55003 • BL, corresp. with T. Sturge Moore, Add. MS 45732 • BL, letters to Ernest Rhys, Egerton MS 3248 • BL, corresp. with George Bernard Shaw, Add. MS 50553 • BL, Society of Authors file, Add. MS 56851 • Bodl. Oxf., corresp. with Robert Bridges • Bodl. Oxf., letters to H. A. L. Fisher • Bodl. Oxf., letters to Elizabeth Gorell • Bodl. Oxf., corresp. with Gilbert Murray • Bodl. Oxf., letters to Charles Ricketts • Col. U., letters to Ellen Douglas Duncan • Dublin Jesuit Community, Province Archive Access, letters to Father Matthew Russell • Harvard U., Houghton L., letters to Sir William Rothenstein • Hunt. L., letters, mainly to Katharine Tynan • JRL, letters to Katharine Tynan • Mills College Library, Oakland, California, corresp. with Albert Bender • NL Ire., letters to Augusta Gregory • NL Ire., letters to John O'Leary • NL Ire., letters to Sarah Purser • NL Ire., letters to George W. Russell • NL Ire., letters to J. M. Synge • NL Scot., letters to William Blackwood & Sons • NL Scot., letters to Sir Herbert Grierson • NYPL, Berg collection, corresp. with Augusta Gregory • NYPL, corresp. with John Quinn • PRO NIre., letters to Lady Londonderry • Queen's University, Kingston, Ontario, corresp. with W. M. Gibbon • Royal Society of Literature, London, letters • Sligo County Library, letters to Ethel Mannin • Southern Illinois University, Carbondale, Morris Library, corresp. with Katharine Tynan, Lennox Robinson, and others • TCD, corresp. with Thomas Bodkin • TCD, corresp. with J. M. Synge • U. Cal., Berkeley, Bancroft Library, letters, mainly to Mabel Dickinson • U. Leeds, Brotherton L., letters to Edmund Gosse • University of Delaware, Newark, corresp. with Shri Purohit Swami • Wellcome L., Eugenics Society papers, corresp. • Yale U., Beinecke L., letters to W. F. Stead |FILM BFI NFTVA, home footage |SOUND BL NSA, recordings of readings of own work

Likenesses H. M. Paget, oils, 1889, Ulster Museum, Belfast • J. B. Yeats, oils, *c*.1890–1899, Hugh Lane Gallery of Modern Art, Dublin • W. Rothenstein, pencil drawing, 1897, U. Texas • S. Purser, pastel drawing, 1898?, Hugh Lane Gallery of Modern Art, Dublin • W. Rothenstein, drawing, 1898, Hugh Lane Gallery of Modern Art, Dublin; related lithograph, NPG • J. B. Yeats, watercolour drawing, 1898, NG Ire. • J. B. Yeats, pencil drawing, 1899, Birmingham Museums and Art Gallery • A. Gyles, ink drawing, *c*.1900, BM • J. B. Yeats, oils, 1900, NG Ire. • pastel drawing, *c*.1900, NG Ire. • photographs, *c*.1900–*c*.1935, Hult. Arch. • AE [G. Russell], drawing, 1903, NG Ire. • W. Strang, chalk drawing, 1903, FM Cam. • W. Strang, drawing, 1903, NG Ire. • M. Beerbohm, pen and wash caricature, *c*.1904, Hugh Lane Gallery of Modern Art, Dublin • A. John, bronze bust, *c*.1907, Abbey Theatre, Dublin • A. John, etching, 1907 (after a portrait, 1907), NG Ire. • A. John, etching, 1907, NPG • A. John, oils, 1907, Man. City Gall. [*see illus.*] • A. John, oils, 1907, Tate collection; related pencil drawing, Tate collection • A. John, pencil and wash drawing, *c*.1907, NPG • Lady K. Kennet, plaster mask, 1907, NPG; bronze cast NPG • W. Orpen, pen and ink caricature, 1907, NPG • J. B. Yeats, oils, *c*.1907, Abbey Theatre, Dublin • A. L. Coburn, photogravure, 1908, NPG • J. S. Sargent, charcoal drawing, 1908?, Abbey Theatre, Dublin • C. Shannon, portrait, 1908 • E. Kapp, drawing, 1914, Barber Institute of Fine Arts, Birmingham • W. Rothenstein, chalk drawing, 1916, Hugh Lane Gallery of Modern Art, Dublin • W. Rothenstein, pencil drawing, 1916, Leeds City Art Gallery • A. Power, bronze bust, 1918, U. Texas • T. Spicer-Simson, bronze medallion, 1922, NG Ire. • W. Rothenstein, drawing, 1923, Laing Art Gallery, Newcastle upon Tyne • J. Keating, group portrait, oils, *c*.1924 (*Homage to Hugh Lane*), Hugh Lane Gallery of Modern Art, Dublin • A. John, oils, 1930, Art Gallery and Museum, Glasgow • S. O'Sullivan, drawing, 1933, NG Ire. • S. O'Sullivan, oils, 1934, Abbey Theatre, Dublin • H. Coster, photographs, 1935, NPG • I. Opffer, chalk drawing, 1935?, NPG • A. Power, bronze bust, 1939, NG Ire. • A. Power, plaster bust, 1939, NG Ire. • M. Beerbohm, caricature, drawing, AM Oxf. • M. Beerbohm, ink and watercolour caricature, NG Ire. • G. C. Beresford, photographs, NPG • E. Dulac, watercolour caricature, Abbey Theatre, Dublin • H. Kernoff, pastel and tempera drawing, U. Texas • attrib. W. Rothenstein, pen-and-ink drawing, U. Texas • G. Russell, two charcoal drawings, NG Ire. • T. Spicer-Simson, bronze medallion, NPG • photographs, Hunt. L.

Wealth at death £8329 9*s*. 11*d*.—estate in Britain and Ireland; incl. valuation of copyright fees and royalties: *The Times* (31 Aug 1939)

Yeaxlee, Basil Alfred (1883–1967), educationist, was born at 29 Oxford Street, Southampton, on 2 December 1883, the eldest son of Alfred George Yeaxlee, pastry cook and confectioner, and his wife, Lila Lavinia Read. According to an obituarist, his life was one of 'complete obscurity' until he appeared at New College, London, to prepare for the Congregational ministry (*The Times*, 24 Aug 1967). Prior to that he attended Smyth's school, Southsea, then, from 1905 to 1909, he was at Oxford University attached to Mansfield College, having matriculated as a non-collegiate. After service as an assistant Congregational minister in Bootle, Lancashire, he was appointed in 1912 educational assistant to the London Missionary Society and editor to the United Council for Missionary Education. The following year he married Annie Julie Mary Leadbeater (*d*. 1955); they had two daughters.

The First World War changed the direction of Yeaxlee's career. In the autumn of 1915 the YMCA set up a committee to organize educational facilities for the wartime army and appointed him secretary. The task was to recruit civilian lecturers, mostly people associated with the universities, to give talks, and lead classes in military locations at home and behind the fighting lines abroad. By the end of the war a far-flung structure had been created. Subsequently H. A. L. Fisher, president of the Board of Education, assigned to it 'the credit of introducing and developing the largest scheme of adult education which has ever at any time been launched from the country' (*An Educated Nation*, 1920, 58). An obituarist saw added significance in Yeaxlee's own work in France during 1917: the YMCA scheme was a calming influence in a situation where the uncertainties of world politics, and lack of information, were producing considerable unease among the troops (*The Times*, 28 Aug 1967).

By the summer of 1917 Yeaxlee was sufficiently well known to find himself part of a national inquiry into adult education, sponsored by the Ministry of Reconstruction. YMCA involvement in army education came to an end in April 1919, and he moved on to be joint secretary to the Educational Settlements Association (ESA), a body with close free-church connections. In this capacity he was recruited to the Board of Education's new advisory committee on adult education at its formation in 1921.

The eight years during which Yeaxlee was secretary to the ESA saw no remarkable progress. A successor in the office has speculated that his approach, emphasizing individual development rather than social activism, may have been inappropriate to the times (Thomas and Elsey, 664). That is debatable, but clearly his interests were recrystallizing. His doctoral thesis for London University (published as *Spiritual Values in Adult Education*, 2 vols., 1925) surveyed the place of organized religion in adult education. By 1929 his *Lifelong Education* (a very early use of what much later became a vogue term), was locating adult education in a longer process of 'growing up'. In 1930 he became principal of Westhill College, Birmingham, a centre for nonconformist teacher training; then from 1935 an increasing interest in 'modern psychology' as applied to religious development in the young (*The Approach to Religious Education*, 1931; *Religion and the Growing Mind*, 1939) brought him appointments in the department of education at Oxford University (1935–49), and a fellowship of the British Psychological Society.

There was one significant interruption to Yeaxlee's culminating Oxford career. After 1939 the Second World War forced adult education back onto the military agenda: a central advisory council for adult education in HM forces was set up, and the 'sage and experienced' Yeaxlee brought in as secretary (Kelly, 324). There was little of the improvisatory dash of twenty-five years before, but the council had an even bigger task of co-ordinating the civilian contribution. Its chief officer was later (1946) appointed CBE in recognition—a topping up, one might say, of his earlier OBE.

Retirement in 1949 did not halt Yeaxlee's involvement with Mansfield College, the British Council of Churches, and the Institute of Christian Education. In 1958, three years after his first wife's death, he married Margaret Frances Addison Tatham. He himself died at his home, Church Cottage, Islip, Oxfordshire, on 23 August 1967.

STUART MARRIOTT

Sources *WWW* · *The Times* (24 Aug 1967) · *The Times* (28 Aug 1967) · 'Second interim report of the adult education committee of the ministry of reconstruction on education in the army', *Parl. papers* (1918), 9.351, Cd 9225 · 'Final report', *Parl. papers* (1919), 28.453, Cmd 321 [from the adult education committee] · T. H. Hawkins and L. J. F. Brimble, *Adult education: the record of the British army* (1947) · T. Kelly, *A history of adult education in Great Britain*, 2nd edn (1970) · J. E. Thomas and B. Elsey, eds., *International biography of adult education* (1985) · A. Cross-Durrant, 'Basil Yeaxlee and the origins of lifelong education', *Twentieth-century thinkers in adult education*, ed. P. Jarvis (1987), 38–61 · b. cert. · Oxf. UA

Archives Bodl. Oxf., letters to Gilbert Murray
Wealth at death £8704: probate, 26 Oct 1967, *CGPLA Eng. & Wales*

Yeldard, Arthur (*c*.1526x30–1599), college head, was born in Houghton-Strother-on-Tyne, Northumberland. Nothing is known of his family background or early years, and there is no evidence for Thomas Warton's assertion that he was a chorister of Durham Cathedral and a master of Rotherham College, Yorkshire. Yeldard matriculated as a sizar of Clare College, Cambridge, in 1544. He graduated BA in 1548 and by 1550 had been elected fellow of Pembroke College, where he held office as junior treasurer the following year. Throughout his life Yeldard demonstrated a happy ability to secure the goodwill of influential patrons. He came to the attention of Princess Mary through her chaplain, Francis Mallett, dean of Lincoln, and received from her an annual exhibition. He also secured the position of tutor to Henry and Anthony, the sons of the late Sir Anthony Denny, following their matriculation in November 1552. Yeldard travelled abroad with his charges, and in December 1553 they were at Dilling in Flanders, from where he dedicated a translation of *Documenta quaedam admonitoria Agapeti Diaconi* in fulsome and grateful terms to Queen Mary.

Yeldard's most significant patron was Sir Thomas Pope, privy councillor and founder of Trinity College, Oxford. Yeldard's personable and intellectual qualities secured Pope's lasting confidence, and in 1555 Yeldard was admitted the first of the foundation fellows and philosophy lecturer of the new college. Commissions undertaken for Pope included important work on the composition of the college statutes. In July 1557 Yeldard's teaching skills were tested when Pope entrusted him with the tuition of his wayward stepson, John Basford. Yeldard persevered with his reluctant and Latin-resistant pupil and was rewarded by the friendship of the young man's mother, Elizabeth Pope, who in 1559 nominated him to succeed Thomas Slythurst as president of Trinity College. This was by no means an easy position. Pope's sudden death six months previously had left Trinity's finances precarious, while the whole college was scrutinized closely by the parliamentary commissioners of the succeeding decade. Trinity's buildings, erected for the medieval Durham College, needed constant repair. However, Yeldard proved a capable administrator. Undergraduate numbers increased and in the forty years of his presidency he did much to consolidate revenues and fabric alike. As president Yeldard could marry, and he did so, but nothing is known of his wife, except her name, Eleanor.

Warton included Yeldard among 'the capital scholars of those times', and credited his Latin prose 'with great elegance and perspicuity' (Warton, 390). Few lines survive of his fine Latin verse: eleven elegiac couplets at the end of L. Humphrey's *Vita Juelli* (1573), eight couplets prefixed to John Case's *Speculum moralium quaestionum* (1585), and twenty hexameters in Robert Wright's edition of *Funebria Henrici Unton* (1596). Yeldard proceeded to the degrees of BD in 1563 and DD in 1566. In a wider sphere he served on a number of university committees, notably for the reception of Queen Elizabeth in 1566, when he disputed before her, and on the reform of the statutes in 1576. He was elected vice-chancellor for one year in 1580. Wood relates a libellous pun on Yeldard's name, that having once left England for religious principles he later submitted to the protestant faith 'with yelding voice' (Blakiston, 82). But there is no evidence that Yeldard ever acted against his conscience; indeed, Wood also states that Ralph Kettell 'did always report him to have lived a severe and religious life' (ibid.). In his will Yeldard left six volumes of the *Centuriae Magdeburgenses* to Trinity College, and everything else to his wife. He died on 1 February 1599, and was buried in the chapel of the college he had served so faithfully.   CLARE HOPKINS

Sources T. Warton, *The life of Sir Thomas Pope, founder of Trinity College, Oxford*, 2nd edn (1780), appx, xxv · H. E. D. Blakiston, *Trinity College* (1898) · registers of Trinity College, Oxford · Wood, *Ath. Oxon.*, new edn, 1.674 · Tanner, *Bibl. Brit.-Hib.* · *DNB*
Archives BL, MS dedication, Royal MS 7 D.iv

Yeldham, Florence Annie (1877–1945), schoolteacher and historian of arithmetic, was born at School House, Brightling, Battle, Sussex, on 30 October 1877, the second daughter and second of at least seven children of Thomas Yeldham (*b. c.*1853) of Bromley, Kent, a schoolteacher who later became a school inspector, and his wife, Elizabeth Ann Chesterfield (*b.* 1854) of Leicestershire. With the family's move to London, Yeldham and three sisters had the opportunity to attend a school run by a charitable foundation, James Allen's Girls' School, Dulwich; the school awarded her an exhibition to Bedford College, University of London, where she matriculated in 1895. Meanwhile two of her brothers attended Alleyn's School, part of the same foundation, but none of the rest of her family had an extended education: one sister left school at the age of sixteen, and the other siblings even earlier. Yeldham graduated with a BSc (division two) in 1900, having chosen papers in pure mathematics, experimental physics, and zoology. She is listed as having gained honours, which one would have expected, but no details can be found.

Yeldham was appointed to her first post as a teacher by the London county council at Peckham county secondary school, London, in 1901. While there in 1913 she produced her first printed work: *Percentage Tables* (Pitman). The British Library copy comprises just one sheet (double folio size) containing the table itself, with instructions for how it should be used—not what it was for. It is clearly a very specialized type of ready reckoner, and probably provided a practical solution to some problem which had cropped up in the classroom, but its purpose today is no longer obvious.

Yeldham moved in April 1914 to the girls' county secondary school in Streatham, London, and remained there for some years, though her teaching career after 1918 is undocumented. In 1922, however, she provided evidence of the progressive educational outlook of that school, describing how it had recently introduced the Dalton plan (a scheme of work giving pupils more responsibility for

their own learning, which later became quite widely adopted): she wrote an article in the *Mathematical Gazette* (reprinted in a centenary edition of 1971) describing, with some enthusiasm, its impact on her teaching in both pure and applied mathematics and physics. Everything indicates that she was a dedicated teacher.

It can be inferred from her 1922 article that Yeldham was an early advocate of the history of mathematics as a stimulus in teaching mathematics. Despite her somewhat unremarkable classroom career, she possessed a most unusual characteristic: having deplored the lack of suitable books for her pupils (and their teachers)—as background reading or for the library—she acted positively to become an expert in order to write them herself. In 1923, at the age of forty-five, she enrolled as a PhD student of Dr Charles Singer in the history of science department of University College, London, becoming one of its earliest formal students. Her first book, *The Story of Reckoning in the Middle Ages* (1926), was submitted as part of her dissertation—which dealt with arithmetical methods up to the thirteenth century—as were four other (unpublished) papers, dealing with minor topics that had evidently intrigued her. In that book she describes Singer as 'my friend and tutor'.

Yeldham's second book, which appeared in 1936, was *The Teaching of Arithmetic through Four Hundred Years* (1535–1935). In the early twenty-first century both books were still well regarded and quite frequently cited, since she included material that was not readily available, while her critical comments, particularly on the later period, give a good sense of the unsuspected difficulties that slowed the development of arithmetic. Her treatment of the subject is generally episodic, being more factual than interpretative, but the books must certainly have met the needs of her intended readership.

In retirement Yeldham lived in Banstead, Surrey. Her last years must have been passed in some discomfort owing to chronic arthritis, probably compounded by the deprivations of wartime. She spent at least the final six months of her life in the Metropolitan Convalescent Home, Walton-on-Thames, Surrey, and died there on 10 January 1945.   A. E. L. DAVIS

Sources School Board for London, 'School Management Committee Reports', 1902–3, LMA · LMA, EO/STA/4/134, fols. 163, 193–6 · records of London University graduates, U. Lond., Senate House [calendars, etc.] · records of Bedford College, London, 1894–1900, Royal Holloway College, Egham, Surrey · admission records of James Allen's Girls' School, 1886–98 · W. A. Smeaton, 'History of science at University College, London, 1919–47', *British Journal for the History of Science*, 30 (1997) · private information (2004) · b. cert. · d. cert.
Wealth at death £1020 10s. 7d.: probate, 14 April 1945, *CGPLA Eng. & Wales*

Yelloly, John (1774–1842), physician, was born at Alnwick, Northumberland, on 30 April 1774, the youngest son and sole survivor of the seven children of John Yelloly and his wife, Jane, *née* Davison (*d.* 1799). His father died in his infancy and he was brought up by his widowed mother, whose family owned extensive property in the Vale of Whittington, near Alnwick. Yelloly was educated at

Alnwick grammar school and the University of Edinburgh, where he graduated MD in 1799. His mother died in that year, leaving him a substantial legacy and in 1800 he moved to London where he became a licentiate of the Royal College of Physicians and was physician to the General Dispensary, Aldersgate Street.

There was dissatisfaction with the Medical Society of London at the beginning of the nineteenth century and on 22 May 1805 a group of members met to discuss the establishment of a new society. The Medical and Chirurgical Society of London was founded on 28 June 1805 with William Saunders as president, Astley Cooper as treasurer, Yelloly and Arthur Aikin as secretaries, and Alexander Marcet as foreign secretary. Their aim was to exchange ideas and practical knowledge, though papers read at the meetings were not discussed. Yelloly was a zealous supporter of the new society, securing its charter and establishing its library. He also contributed articles to its journal. In 1808 he read a paper on a case of paralysis caused by a tumour of the brain. This was published in the first volume of the *Medico-Chirurgical Transactions* in 1809. With Astley Cooper's help he also investigated the distribution of the nervous influence through the spinal cord. When one of the columns of the spinal cord in a dog was divided Yelloly found that paralysis occurred on the same side of the body showing that the nervous action was direct. A second paper on anaesthesia without loss of the power of movement was published in 1812. He was elected FRS on 5 May 1814.

On 4 August 1806 Yelloly married Sarah (d. 1865), only daughter of Samuel Tyssen of Narborough Hall, Norfolk. They lived in Finsbury Square and there were ten children of the marriage. In 1807 Yelloly was appointed physician to the London Hospital, a post he held until 1818, when the poor health of his children made it desirable to live in the country. He therefore resigned from the London Hospital and moved with his family to Carrow Abbey, Norwich. In recognition of his work for the Medical and Chirurgical Society he was granted permission to receive library books from the society at his home in Norwich. In 1827 he made a tour of the Netherlands.

Yelloly became physician to the Norfolk and Norwich Hospital in 1821 and served for eleven years. Norfolk was known for an exceptionally high incidence of bladder stone and the hospital held a large collection of stones taken from patients since 1771. With the surgeon John Green Crosse, Yelloly undertook to study the epidemiology of these stones and to analyse them chemically. The results were published in the *Philosophical Transactions* of the Royal Society in 1829–30. Continuing his work on physiology and pathology Yelloly showed in 1835 that vascular fullness of the villous coat of the stomach was not necessarily a sign of disease or inflammation. His work, valuable in its own time, presaged the rapid developments in physiology, pathology, and medical chemistry which followed later in the nineteenth century. Yelloly also maintained his interest in the activities of the Medical and Chirurgical Society which was granted its royal charter in 1834. It was proposed that the name should be changed to the Royal Society of Medicine and Surgery, but Yelloly wrote at once objecting to this and his arguments prevailed with the council so that the change was not made, apart from the addition of the word Royal. Members were to become fellows, the king was to be the first patron, and Yelloly, along with Astley Cooper, were the first members of council.

Yelloly retired in 1832 and moved to Woodton Hall, near Norwich. A series of misfortunes followed. In 1836 his third son died and in 1838 he lost two daughters on successive days. He moved his family temporarily to the milder climate of Hastings and Dawlish, but in January 1840 he lost his fourth child. Then in April 1840, three days after the marriage of another daughter, he was thrown from his phaeton and received a serious injury to his forehead. Fifteen days later he became paralysed on his right side. He did not fully recover, but in July 1840 he moved to Cavendish Hall, Suffolk, where he gradually regained strength. He visited London in September 1841, but on 28 January 1842 he was seized by paralysis of the left side and was rendered speechless. Gradually losing consciousness, he died at Cavendish Hall on 31 January 1842.

N. G. COLEY

Sources Munk, *Roll*, 2.471 • *Provincial Medical and Surgical Journal*, 3 (1841–2), 422 • *The Lancet* (7 May 1842), 193 • A. Batty-Shaw, *The Norfolk and Norwich Hospital: lives of the medical staff, 1771–1971* (1971), 37–8 • A. Batty-Shaw, *Norfolk and Norwich medicine: a retrospect* (1992), 26–7 • P. Eade, *The Norfolk and Norwich Hospital, 1770–1900 with illustrations and plans* (1900) • B. B. Cooper, *The life of Sir Astley Cooper*, 2 (1843), 33, 37–41, 284–6 • N. Moore and S. Paget, *The Royal Medical and Chirurgical Society of London: centenary 1805–1905, written at the request of the president and council* (1905), 7–8, 14, 40, 69 • IGI

Archives Norfolk RO, travel journal • Royal Society of Medicine, London

Likenesses J. Jackson, oils (*First Honorary Secretary, Medical and Chirurgical Society, 1805*), Royal Society of Medicine, London • oils (after miniature by A. E. Chalon), Norfolk and Norwich University Hospital, Norwich • portrait, repro. in Batty-Shaw, *Norfolk and Norwich medicine*

Yelverton, Barry, first Viscount Avonmore (1736–1805), politician and judge, was born on 28 May 1736, the son and heir of Francis Yelverton (1705–1746) of Blackwater, co. Cork, and Elizabeth Barry (d. 1804) of Kilbrin, in the same county. Though, as he later made clear, 'of an English family by the maternal and paternal lines' (O'Connell, 121), Yelverton's family circumstances were straitened. Having been educated by the Revd Charles Egan at Charleville School he obtained a sizarship in 1753 and a scholarship two years later that allowed him to attend Trinity College, Dublin, whence he graduated BA in 1757. Obliged to embrace teaching for some years after his graduation, during which time he acted as usher to Dr Andrew Buck, who ran the well-known Hibernian Academy in North King Street, Dublin, Yelverton's object was to become a lawyer. He entered the Middle Temple in 1759 and took an LLB at Trinity College in 1761. His marriage in July of that year, to Mary Nugent (1733–1802) of Clonlost, co. Westmeath, temporarily eased his financial situation and allowed him to study for the Irish bar, to which he was called in 1764. His rise to eminence in the law was steady rather than meteoric but his knowledge and ability attracted the notice of the then lord chancellor, James Hewitt, first Viscount Lifford, who promoted his appointment as king's counsel in 1772. His emergence as one of the leading lawyers of the day was confirmed when an LLD was conferred on him in 1774.

Like many of his contemporaries who achieved 'eminence' (Hunt, 53) in the law Yelverton was possessed of political ambitions; he was provided with an opportunity to realize them when he was brought into the Irish parliament for the borough of Donegal by Arthur Saunders Gore, second earl of Arran, in 1774. At the general election two years later Arthur Chichester, fifth earl of Donegal, oversaw his return for the constituency of Carrickfergus. Despite this dependence on patrons Yelverton's political views drew him towards the patriot opposition and he quickly established himself as one of the most able and outspoken voices in the House of Commons with a series of pointed interventions that challenged the administration's policy with respect to the war in the American colonies. Yelverton's own position, as enunciated on 25 November 1775, was that 'the resistance of the Americans is not rebellion' (*Freeman's Journal*, 28 Nov 1775), and his pertinacious criticism of the policy of sending troops on the Irish army establishment to fight in America and of the imposition of an embargo on Ireland's freedom to trade as 'arbitrary, illegal and partial' (ibid., 24 Feb 1776) earned him popular applause. He consolidated his reputation as one of the foremost liberal voices of the moment by supporting, in 1778, the repeal of a substantial number of penal laws on the grounds that they were 'disgraceful to humanity' (ibid., 20 June 1778), and, in 1782, by endorsing Henry Grattan's suggestion that further concessions to Catholics would enable Ireland 'to assume the dignity of a nation, and not continue … an insignificant colony' (*Parliamentary Register*, 1.287).

Meanwhile in his capacity as founder of the influential patriot body, the Order of St Patrick (better known by its colloquial name 'the Monks of the Screw'), and as advocate of the tactic of pressurizing the British government by approving a six-month rather than a two-year money bill, Yelverton made an important contribution to the successful campaign in the winter of 1779–80 to secure the removal of the mercantilist restrictions that bound Ireland's freedom to trade. Encouraged, by the popular applause showered on him as a result, to pursue the dilution of the restrictions that bound the Irish parliament's capacity to make law, Yelverton was as active as Henry Grattan in catapulting the matter of legislative independence to the top of the political agenda in the spring of 1780. However, personal as well as strategic calculations ensured that he was not long to sustain this independent role. Though he was one of the country's leading advocates by the early 1780s, the needs of his family, combined with the calculation that constitutional reform was more likely with the support of the Irish administration, caused him to gravitate towards Dublin Castle in the winter of 1781–2. One effect of this was to expose a chasm within the ranks of the patriots between the essentially moderate

route to legislative independence identified by Yelverton and the more uncompromising way promoted by Henry Flood. Yelverton was sometimes bested in argument by Flood but he had the satisfaction of knowing that it was his proposal, commonly known as Yelverton's act, for modifying Poynings' law, that wrought one of the main legal changes that gave the Irish parliament legislative independence in 1782.

Arising out of his preparedness to work with the Irish administration Yelverton was appointed attorney-general by the lord lieutenant, William Cavendish Cavendish-Bentinck, third duke of Portland, in July 1782. This was a key position in the Irish administration, since the attorney-general was traditionally one of its leaders in the Commons. The expectation was that Yelverton would employ his acknowledged oratorical prowess and 'strong understanding' (Sayles, 236) to good effect. However, he was also possessed of 'little knowledge of the world' (ibid.), which proved a major impediment. Thus while he confidently repulsed the attempt by the volunteers to bring about the reform of the representation in November 1783, on the grounds that it was 'inconsistent with the freedom of debate' for the legislature to receive a bill originating with an armed assembly (*Parliamentary Register*, 2.226–7), his general management of men and matters left much to be desired, and he was induced to vacate the attorney-generalship for the position of chief baron of the Irish court of exchequer in December 1783.

Yelverton's elevation to the judicial bench greatly reduced his involvement in, but did not cause him to forsake, the world of politics. He remained a committed whig, and a combination of loyalty and political principle caused him, albeit with some reservations, to support whig efforts to secure an unlimited regency for George, prince of Wales. It was conjectured then that, had this ensued, he would have become lord chancellor. His most important judicial decision in this period came in 1792–3 in the case of *Maingay* v. *Gahan*, when he ruled unlawful the seizure of a cargo of brandy and wine, valued at £1600, from a ship at Bandon, co. Cork, because of the procedures employed. His ruling, however, was overturned by the court of exchequer chamber, consisting of John Fitz-Gibbon, Viscount Fitzgibbon, and later earl of Clare, lord chancellor; John Scott, earl of Clonmell, chief justice of the king's bench; and Hugh Carleton, Baron Carleton, chief justice of common pleas.

When in 1794 William Wentworth Fitzwilliam, fourth Earl Fitzwilliam, was appointed lord lieutenant of Ireland, Yelverton was again tipped for the seals but he had to make do with a belated elevation to the peerage as Baron Avonmore in June 1795. His firm stand against sedition in the late 1790s, including his role as presiding judge at the trial of William Orr at Carrickfergus in 1797, helped to dispel the shadow of suspicion that had limited his prospects until then. His support for the Act of Union dispelled this still further, for, though he was disappointing when entrusted with business in the House of Lords, he was created Viscount Avonmore in December 1800, despite the opposition of Portland, and he was an unsuccessful aspirant for the seals on the death of Clare in 1802. He died at his home, Fortfield, Rathfarnham, co. Dublin, on 19 August 1805, having served as lord chief baron for just over a quarter of a century, and was buried at Rathfarnham.

Avonmore was not regarded as a great judge, mainly because of his willingness to rush to judgment, but he did endeavour with some success to ensure that justice was imparted fairly. The preparedness of so many to speak well of him and to estimate his talents highly during his lifetime serves as ample testament to the fact that he was a man of considerable ability who did well in life both for himself and for the three sons and one daughter who survived him.   JAMES KELLY

Sources F. E. Ball, *The judges in Ireland, 1221–1921*, 2 vols. (1926) · J. Porter, P. Byrne, and W. Porter, eds., *The parliamentary register, or, History of the proceedings and debates of the House of Commons of Ireland, 1781–1797*, 17 vols. (1784–1801), vols. 1–2 · *Public Register, or, Freeman's Journal* (1775–6) · *Public Register, or, Freeman's Journal* (1778) · GEC, *Peerage* · DNB · Burtchaell & Sadleir, *Alum. Dubl.*, 2nd edn · W. Hunt, ed., *The Irish parliament, 1775* (1907) · G. O. Sayles, ed., 'Contemporary sketches of the members of the Irish parliament in 1782', *Proceedings of the Royal Irish Academy*, 56C (1953–4), 227–86, esp. 236 · M. R. O'Connell, *Irish politics and social conflict in the age of the American revolution* (1965) · H. McDougall, *Sketches of Irish political characters* (1799) · T. Bartlett, ed., *Macartney in Ireland, 1768–72* (1978) · G. O'Brien, *Anglo-Irish politics in the age of Grattan and Pitt* (1987) · J. Kelly, *Henry Flood: patriots and politics in eighteenth-century Ireland* (1998) · *Lord Shannon's letters to his son*, ed. E. Hewitt (1982) · W. Ridgway, W. Lapp, and J. Schoales, *Irish term reports* (1796) [1792–3]
Likenesses stipple, pubd 1791 (after T. Robinson, 1790), NG Ire. · T. Robinson, mezzotint and stipple, pubd 1792 (after T. Robinson, 1792), NG Ire. · T. Robinson, oils, 1792, St Louis City Art Museum, Missouri · H. D. Hamilton, oils, King's Inns, Dublin · G. F. Joseph, oils (posthumous), TCD · F. Wheatley, group portrait, oils (*The Irish House of Commons, 1780*), Lotherton Hall, West Yorkshire

Yelverton, Sir Christopher (1536/7–1612), judge, was the third of five sons of William Yelverton, of Rougham, Norfolk (*b.* in or before 1505, *d.* 1586), lawyer, and his first wife, Anne, daughter of Sir Henry Farmer of East Barsham, Norfolk, and his wife. He had four sisters. He was a member of an East Anglian legal family and was a direct descendant of William Yelverton, judge of the court of king's bench between 1443 and 1471. His father was a member of Gray's Inn and recorder of King's Lynn from 1558 to 1561. Christopher matriculated at Queens' College, Cambridge, in 1550, but is not recorded as having taken a degree. Two years later he entered Gray's Inn.

Yelverton had few advantages as a younger son and had to rely on his own abilities as a lawyer to provide himself with a living. His career was advanced greatly by marriage to Margaret (*c.*1544–1611), daughter of Thomas Catesby of Whiston, Northamptonshire, and his wife, on 4 May 1560. They had four sons, including Henry *Yelverton (1566–1630), and eight daughters. Catesby ensured his new son-in-law was elected MP for Brackley, Northamptonshire, in 1563. Yelverton was recorder of Northampton from 1568 to 1599 and JP for Northamptonshire from about 1573.

Sir Christopher Yelverton (1536/7–1612), by unknown artist, 1602

This local consequence guaranteed his election for Northampton in 1571 and 1572 and for Northamptonshire in 1593. He was an active MP and sat on many committees. He was also noted for his speeches, including one opposing the sequestration of William Strickland. His career was thriving and by the mid-1570s he was very wealthy. He purchased an estate in Oxfordshire and did not seek election to the parliaments of the 1580s. He had by his own admission enjoyed a lively youth and played an active part in the revels and masques produced at Gray's Inn. He wrote the epilogue to George Gascoigne's *Jocasta*, which was performed there in 1566. Notwithstanding his puritanism in religion, several contemporary diarists record his ribald anecdotes and conversation, and John Manningham hints that he was not averse to enjoying himself in the company of gentlewomen when he was well into his seventies. Yelverton was called to the bar, and elected treasurer of Gray's Inn in 1579 and 1585. He read twice: in 1574 and in 1584, when his subject was the statute of 1540 relating to execution for debt. He was created serjeant-at-law in 1589, served as queen's serjeant from 1598 to 1602, and was judge of the court of queen's (then king's) bench from 1602 to 1612. Yelverton was an excellent technical lawyer and was regarded as a good judge, one of the few to escape criticism by Sir Robert Cecil, principal secretary, in his memorandum on the state of the judicial bench in 1603. As queen's serjeant he led the prosecution of those involved in Essex's rebellion in 1601, and he was one of the judges ruling on the *Postnati case* in 1608. In addition, he had a broader interest in legal culture, passing on to his son a collection of legal manuscripts; and, like many other lawyers of his generation, he made his own reports of cases. These reports remained unpublished and the well-known Yelverton report is by his son Henry Yelverton. Yelverton was a conspicuously successful speaker of the House of Commons in the parliament of 1597, to which Henry Yelverton was also returned, exercising moderation and discretion to defuse tensions between it and the crown. His puritan tendencies were well known. He was an eloquent orator, though his contributions to debates show him to have been as much concerned with careful legal drafting as with rhetorical showmanship, and his conduct as speaker was marked by a lawyerly concern to establish proper procedures for the conduct of the business.

For all his finesse as speaker Yelverton was a man of considerable toughness. He was appointed second justice at Lancaster in 1598. As justice of the assize on the northern circuit and JP of many northern counties from 1599, he was in the forefront of the common lawyers' attack on the council of the north. Friction developed in 1600, when he snubbed Ralph Eure, third Lord Eure, vice-president, who was sitting with Sir John Savile as justice of gaol delivery. Matters came to a head in 1601 when he required the lord president, Sir Thomas Cecil, second Lord Burghley, to leave the court. Legal opinion was at first behind Yelverton, but in June 1602 he was summoned to the Star Chamber and publicly reprimanded for his conduct. There were more complaints about him but he weathered the criticism. Elizabeth I did not bestow a knighthood on him and it was left to James VI and I to do so. The king was more generous still, making him KB on 23 July 1603.

Yelverton, despite his complaints about poverty and the expense of providing for such a large family, was very active in the purchase of land in his adopted county of Northamptonshire, spending in excess of £5000 on properties in his lifetime, most of which descended on his death to his heir, Henry Yelverton. His wife predeceased him. He died on 31 October 1612 'of very age' at seventy-five (CSP dom., 1611–18, 154), and was buried on 3 November in the church at Easton Maudit, where a monument with his recumbent effigy in robes survives.

DAVID IBBETSON

Sources CSP dom., 1611–18, 154 • HoP, Commons, 1558–1603 • arms and genealogical data, Northants. RO, NPL 1042 • Baker, Serjeants, 546 • The reports of Sir John Spelman, ed. J. H. Baker, 1, SeldS, 93 (1977), 1.xxii • The reports of Sir John Spelman, ed. J. H. Baker, SeldS, suppl. ser., 5 (1984) • Sainty, Judges, 31 • PRO, PROB 6/8 [administration], fol. 78v • VCH Northamptonshire, 4.13–16 • R. R. Reid, The king's council in the north (1921) • Venn, Alum. Cant., 1/4.489 • monumental inscription (copy), Northants. RO, C(H)95 • Easton Maudit deeds, Northants. RO, NPL 198–202 • repertory of evidences of land purchased, Northants. RO, NPL 2937 • HoP, Commons, 1509–58 • DNB • parish register, Easton Maudit, Northamptonshire
Likenesses oils, 1602, Gray's Inn, London [see illus.] • R. Dunkarton, mezzotint, 1811 (after portrait, 1602), BM, NPG • effigy on monument, Easton Maudit church, Northamptonshire • oils, second version; in possession of family at Easton Maudit, 1866

Wealth at death lands valued above £5000: Northants. RO, NPL 2937

Yelverton [*formerly* Henry], **Sir Hastings Reginald** (1808–1878), naval officer, born in March 1808, was the son of John Joseph Henry of Straffan, co. Kildare, and his wife, Lady Emily Elizabeth Fitzgerald, daughter of the duke of Leinster. He entered the navy on 20 August 1823 as a first-class volunteer with Captain Samuel Pechell on the frigate *Sybille*, in the Mediterranean. In June 1826 he was present at a severe action with pirates off Candia, Crete. He later served as a midshipman and mate on the home station in the brig *Columbine* (Captain William Symonds), the frigate *Undaunted* (Captain Augustus Clifford), and the battleship *St Vincent* (Captain Sir Hyde Parker). On 18 December 1830 he was promoted lieutenant, and in the following year joined HMS *Asia*, flagship of Rear Admiral Sir William Parker, at Lisbon. In 1834 he joined the *Rattlesnake* (34 guns, Captain Hobson) in the East Indies, and was promoted commander on 28 June 1838. Between 1840 and 1843 he served on the home and Mediterranean stations aboard the steam vessels *Styx* and *Devastation* and as acting captain of the battleship *Queen* and the frigate *Aigle*. He achieved post rank on 23 September 1843.

On 9 April 1845 Henry married Barbara (1810–1858), widow of George Augustus Francis Rawdon Hastings, second marquess of Hastings, and only daughter of Henry Edward Gould (afterwards Yelverton), Lord Grey of Ruthin, and *suo jure* Baroness Grey of Ruthin. Henry in January 1849 by royal licence took the name Yelverton in place of Henry. In 1853 he was appointed to command the steam screw frigate *Arrogant* (46 guns) in the western squadron, and he remained in her during the Baltic campaigns of 1854 and 1855. On 19 May 1854 he led a cutting-out expedition at Eckness, several miles from the coast. The following year he was often in independent local command, destroying Russian government buildings, forts, and supplies along the Finnish coast. In July 1855 he was created CB for his services. For the 1856 campaign he moved to the 80 gun steam battleship *Brunswick* with command of a gunboat flotilla for inshore operations. The war ended before he could see any service in this capacity.

On 3 August 1859 Yelverton was appointed comptroller-general of the coastguard, a post he retained until April 1863. Promoted rear-admiral on 30 January 1863, he served as second in command on the Mediterranean station until 1866, when he became commander-in-chief of the channel squadron for one year, in recognition of his ability, to conduct sailing and steaming trials. The results convinced Yelverton that shorter, handier ironclads were required. Promoted vice-admiral on 25 May 1869, he served on the committee appointed by Hugh Childers to consider the turret ship design, later HMS *Devastation*, put forward by the chief constructor, Edward Reed. As a result of the committee's report the design was adopted. On 2 June 1869 Yelverton was created KCB (GCB 29 May 1875).

Yelverton was again temporarily commander-in-chief of the channel squadron from July to October 1870, before assuming command in the Mediterranean, where he remained until January 1874. The major episode of this period was the international effort to restrict the Cartagena revolt in 1873, where he helped to suppress the rebellion, prevented a bombardment of Valencia, and blockaded the rebel fleet.

Yelverton, by then profoundly deaf, was an unexpected choice to succeed Sir Alexander Milne as first naval lord in September 1876; the shortage of suitable flag officers left the government little choice after the post was refused by Admiral Sir Geoffrey Phipps Hornby. Yelverton, always a stopgap, served little more than a year before ill health forced him to resign in November 1877. He died in the Grand Pump Hotel, Bath, on 24 July 1878.

At the Admiralty Yelverton proved an ineffective member of an ineffective board, under George Ward-Hunt, entirely subordinate to the economic demands of the Disraeli ministry. The mid-1870s marked the nadir of the navy in the nineteenth century, and reflect no credit on those involved. Yelverton's appointment in succession to Milne, replacing the most experienced and effective naval lord of the era with a man who had never before served at the Admiralty, was indicative of the limited interest of the Disraeli ministry in naval policy. At sea Yelverton was a fine officer, as his extended periods of active service demonstrated. His opinions on ship design and tactics were highly regarded, although his predilection for short and handy ships resulted in the *Ajax* and *Agamemnon*, two of the worst battleships ever built for the navy. A conservative in all things, Yelverton made a worthy contribution to the efficiency of the seagoing navy, and his short term at the Admiralty proved a sad coda to an otherwise successful career.   ANDREW LAMBERT

Sources J. F. Beeler, *British naval policy in the Gladstone–Disraeli era, 1866–1880* (1997) • O'Byrne, *Naval biog. dict.* • A. D. Lambert, *The Crimean War: British grand strategy, 1853–56* (1990) • P. H. Colomb, *Memoirs of Admiral the Right Honble. Sir Astley Cooper Key* (1898) • W. L. Clowes, *The Royal Navy: a history from the earliest times to the present*, 7 vols. (1897–1903), vols. 6–7 • *CGPLA Eng. & Wales* (1878) • GEC, *Peerage* • Boase, *Mod. Eng. biog.*

Archives BL, letters to Sir Austen Layard, Add. MSS 39003–39005 • NMM, letters to Captain Phillimore

Wealth at death under £6000: probate, 10 Aug 1878, *CGPLA Eng. & Wales*

Yelverton, Sir Henry (1566–1630), judge and politician, was born on 29 June 1566, St Peter's day, as he noted in his will, the eldest of four sons of Sir Christopher *Yelverton (1536/7–1612) of Gray's Inn and Easton Maudit, Northamptonshire, and his wife, Margaret Catesby (c.1544–1611). Perhaps already having received some education at Oxford, in July 1581 he matriculated with his brother Thomas from a distinctly puritan college, Christ's, Cambridge; he graduated BA from Peterhouse in 1584. It is probably at this point that he began his legal studies at Gray's Inn, although there is no record of this. Thomas and another brother, Christopher, had apparently gained a special admittance on 23 January 1580. Since their father was reader at the inn in 1574 and 1584, and treasurer in 1579 and 1585, it is likely that Henry was granted similar privileges. Henry seems to have been called to the bar on 25 April 1593 and to have become an ancient on 25 May. In Michaelmas 1595 he was a reader at Staple Inn. By about

1600 he had married Mary (d. 1625), daughter of Robert *Beale (1541–1601), clerk of the council; when in London they lived in Aldersgate Street.

In 1597, following in his father's footsteps, Yelverton was elected MP for Northampton. As his father was speaker of the Commons in this parliament, he sat on committees for monopolies, the poor, draining the fens, husbandry and tillage, defence, tellers and receivers, and the better execution of judgments. Although in 1599 he succeeded his father as recorder of Northampton, Yelverton did not represent the borough in 1601, but he was returned to the first parliament of James I in 1604. An active speaker and one of the most active committee members, he gained a reputation as an independent man who spoke his mind. While his political principles supported the exercise of the royal prerogative, they also supported the ability of each house of parliament to conduct its affairs without interference. If a house did not confirm its rights, it would lose them and defraud the people. Thus when Sir Francis Goodwin's case came before the Commons on 30 March 1604, Yelverton argued for Goodwin to take his seat in the face of his rejection by the court of chancery and against the wishes of the king. He was applauded for holding that the case belonged to the Commons as a high court of parliament. On 5 April, when James had issued his decision, Yelverton said that the prince's command was like 'the roar of a lion' (Notestein, 75) but, as a working MP, he continued his independent actions. He supported granting the king a subsidy, but gradually, as grievances were handled. He supported the trial of the plotters of the Gunpowder Plot, but with 'due deliberation'. He joined the attack on the abuses of purveyors, and declared that corruption should be 'crushed' (*Diary of Robert Bowyer*, 123). When the proposed Scottish union was debated in 1606–7 Yelverton criticized the bill, assessing it as good for Scotland but not for England, and attacking George Hume, the earl of Dunbar, the king's Scottish favourite. As he said in a speech of 7 May 1607, Yelverton saw his allegiance to the law and the English crown, but not to the person of the king; there would be either a perfect union, or no union.

By this time Yelverton's legal career was well established and his puritan inclinations were visible. A keen patron of preachers, in the early years of the century he attended and took notes on the sermons of Edward Philips at St Olave's, Southwark, and subsequently published thirty-one of them, at his own expense and with a dedication to his father, as *Certaine Godly and Learned Sermons* (1605). Later he was suspected by Sir Francis Bacon of involvement in the publication of *The Argument of N. F.* (1607), an attempted vindication of fellow Gray's Inn puritan MP Nicholas Fuller, who had been charged with heresy and schism. Having been reader at the inn that Lent term, Yelverton was said by 'a professed friend and well-wisher' (Prest, 143) to have set his sights on the attorney-ship of the court of wards and to be prepared to pay its patron, Robert Cecil, earl of Salisbury, £1000 for it. On either count, he tried in the three-year hiatus between parliamentary sessions (1607–10) to repair his relations with the king. In January 1610 Lady Arabella Stuart and the earl of Dunfermline helped him gain an audience with James, in which he gave a fully detailed account of each of his positions and his best interpretation of why he advanced them. According to Bacon, Yelverton had now been 'won' to the king's cause (*Works of Francis Bacon*, 4.313), a conversion noted also by John Chamberlain on 13 January. Although unsuccessful in gaining the wards office, at some point Yelverton convinced Salisbury that he was not only learned in the law, but also blessed with elocution and sound reason.

On 23 June 1610 Yelverton brought an important defence to the claim of the crown to levy impositions without a parliamentary grant when he asserted that, since the law of England only extended to the high-water mark, on the seas the king could extract customs duties before allowing goods to land. However, he was generally in favour of commercial enterprise, supporting the enclosure of common lands for increased agrarian production. He also outlined in discussions on the royal prerogative the rights of citizens in royal leases, forfeitures, licences of alienation, fines, and wardship. Active in mediation, he began to serve the crown in legal capacities, acting as a junior member of assize commissions on the home counties circuit in 1610, and the western circuit in 1613.

Following his father's death on 31 October 1612, Yelverton succeeded to the family estates. One of the richest barristers of the Jacobean era, he came to own considerable property in London, Norfolk, Northamptonshire, and Warwickshire. He was made solicitor-general on 28 October 1613, and knighted on 8 November, according to John Chamberlain for parliamentary services to the king and his ability to survive disgrace. It was said that he attained the office through the patronage of the king's favourite, Sir Robert Carr, shortly after he became earl of Somerset. For three years from 1614 Yelverton was also counsel for the University of Cambridge. He was returned as Northampton's MP in March 1614 after drafting a new charter reincorporating the borough that was enrolled in August; the borough extended his recordership for life in 1618. In the parliament of 1614 he was not active, and abstained from speaking on the crucial question of impositions. He took an official part in the examination of Peacham under torture on 19 January 1615, as well as on 10 March, showing a toughness he was suspected of repeating during the examinations of Sir Thomas Lake in 1619 and Samuel Peacock in 1620. At the same time he joined in signing a certification in favour of the court of chancery in the conflict with Sir Edward Coke on the question of *praemunire*, and supported the king's resolution. When Somerset was indicted for the murder of Sir Thomas Overbury in 1615, Yelverton declined to appear against him and took no part in the trial.

With Bacon's appointment as lord keeper in 1617, James announced that Yelverton would succeed him as attorney-general. The warrant, however, stayed unsigned as the new favourite, the earl of Buckingham, was doubtful of his commitment to the prerogative. Yelverton refused to apply to the earl because he believed that the office concerned the king alone. When Buckingham told Yelverton that his standing would suffer if the attorney-generalship were seen to be conferred without the earl's influence, Yelverton answered that it was not the custom for favourites to meddle with legal appointments. Apparently unoffended, Buckingham took the warrant to the king and returned with it signed on 12 March. Afterwards Yelverton presented James with £4000. The favourite apparently received nothing, but on the other hand Yelverton acted as a mediator in the dispute which arose between Buckingham and members of the Coke family over the marriage of Frances Coke and John Villiers. When dissension over the fate of their daughter finally led Lady Elizabeth Coke to leave her husband, Yelverton alienated Coke by not listening to his arguments to bar his wife from her dower. Yelverton continued to use his position to support godly ministers. The same year he was responsible for the appointment of Richard Sibbes as preacher at Gray's Inn; acknowledgement of his role was made in the dedications of works by Paul Baynes, William Crashawe (preacher at the Temple), Samuel Hieron, and Thomas Gataker.

Yelverton became a commissioner of patents on 22 April 1618 and was placed on another commission, for the punishment of offenders, on 20 October. In high favour at court, he entertained it 'very bountifully' on 11 September 1619 (*Letters of John Chamberlain*, 2.263). Having previously shown some sympathy to those who infringed the patent for gold and silver thread, since they refused to give an undertaking not to repeat the offences he now sent some of them to the Fleet prison. Apparently still uncertain of the legality of such a move, he signalled that he would release them unless Bacon endorsed his ruling. Using Yelverton's initial opposition to patents, Buckingham then took the opportunity to remove him. The device was Yelverton's penning of the new charter for the City of London. Charged with introducing certain clauses not in the king's warrant, he was summoned to the privy council, which recommended on 16 June 1620 that he be suspended from office and prosecuted in the Star Chamber. Duly suspended on 27 June, a month later he acknowledged his offence in Star Chamber and, although found not guilty of corruption, was sentenced to imprisonment in the Tower during the king's pleasure on 10 November, and fined £1000. Thomas Coventry replaced him as attorney-general early in the new year.

In spite of his imprisonment Yelverton was returned for Northampton in the parliament that opened on 30 January 1621. Caught up in Bacon's bribery scandal that occupied parliament in February–March, he gained the opprobrium of Buckingham, who saw Yelverton as an agent of his destruction. This worked against Yelverton in the following debates on monopolies, where he was targeted for having imprisoned the gold and silver thread agents, whose wives and children petitioned the king for their release. On the one hand vilified in the Commons by Coke for making false arrests, on the other he was blamed for bad advice by the king, who had jurisdiction of the case transferred to the Lords on 18 April 1621. Yelverton's defence, that he had served the king by passing his patents and defusing opposition in the Commons, caused James to accuse him on 24 April of slander. Yelverton, relying on support from those who wished to use monopolies to attack Buckingham, made a powerful speech in the Lords on 30 April. In the past decade he had avoided conflict with the crown. Now he stood his ground, and blamed the arrests on the duke and his quest for profits, charging that Buckingham 'stood still att the Kinges elbowe ready to hew me downe' (*Diary of Sir Richard Hutton*, 34). This raised pandemonium in the house, and James had Yelverton seized and recommitted to the Tower. The Lords claimed that this seizure was a breach of their privileges. Petitioning the king, he was returned to the Lords, where his tumultuous trial for 'misdemeanours' ended on 14 May. The following day he was found guilty of impugning the king and slandering Buckingham, and on 16 June he was sentenced to prison with orders to submit to the king and Buckingham, and to pay them 10,000 marks and 5000 marks respectively. Once he had submitted the fines were remitted, and on 18 July Yelverton was released as part of a general pardon.

In Michaelmas term 1621 Yelverton resumed practice in the king's bench, chancery, and Star Chamber that had occupied him prior to his appointment as attorney-general in 1617. He also returned to sitting on assize circuits. Soon after Charles's accession, on 30 April 1625 he was made serjeant-at-law, and on 10 May he was promoted to judge of the court of common pleas. His wife had died four days earlier. It may have been in these later years as a judge that he prepared his and his father's law reports on the court of king's bench, 1602–12, which were later published in 1661 and 1674. He remained on the bench until his death at Aldersgate Street on 24 January 1630. Buried at Easton Maudit next to his parents, the lawyer described by Roger Wilbraham as 'the old Tribune of the people' (*Diary of Robert Bowyer*, 134), had given generously to the poor of London and Easton. In his will dated 19 July 1628, after a vividly personal expression of his faith, Yelverton left his land at Weston, Warwickshire, to his younger son, Robert, who had studied under John Preston at Queens' College, Cambridge, and who was knighted in 1631. The bulk of his estates went to the elder son, Sir Christopher (d. 1655), also a former student of Preston, who was knighted in 1623 and made a baronet in 1641, with generous provision for his three sisters, Elizabeth (the wife of Sir Lodowick Dyer), Edith, and Mary. Other beneficiaries included Yelverton's brother, now also Sir Christopher, his nephew Christopher *Sherland, and Richard Sibbes.

S. R. GARDINER, rev. LOUIS A. KNAFLA

Sources Venn, *Alum. Cant.* · Wood, *Ath. Oxon.*, new edn, 1.275 · R. J. Fletcher, ed., *The pension book of Gray's Inn*, 1 (1901), 100, 111, 138, 178, 208 · Foster, *Admissions to Gray's Inn*, 55, 74, 114 · family genealogy, BL, Add. MS 46185 · will, PRO, PROB 11/157, fols. 431v–432v · W. Notestein, *The House of Commons, 1604–1610* (1971) · D. H. Willson, *The privy councillors in the House of Commons, 1604–29* (1940) · S. R. Gardiner, *History of England from the accession of James I to the outbreak of the civil war, 1603–1642*, 10 vols. (1883–4), vol. 1, p. 169; vol. 2, pp. 80, 208; vol. 3, pp. 79–80, 93, 96; vol. 4, pp. 12, 16–17, 22, 111–15; vol. 7, p. 129 · *The parliamentary diary of Robert Bowyer, 1606–1607*, ed. D. H. Willson (1931) · *State trials*, 2.91–114, 371–533, 870–80, 1135–46 · *The letters of John Chamberlain*, ed. N. E. McClure, 2 vols. (1939) · *The letters and life of Francis Bacon*, ed. J. Spedding, R. L. Ellis, and D. D. Heath (1963), vols. 4–7, 10–14 · J. H. Baker, *Readers and readings in the inns of court and chancery*, SeldS, suppl. ser., 13 (2000) · commonplace book, BL, Add. MS 14030 · Yelverton papers, BL, Add. MSS 48000–48196 · BL, Add. MSS 33579, fols. 236–7; 61683, fols. 9–10v · BL, Harley MSS 161, fols. 32–3; 6846, fols. 131–3 · BL, Stowe MSS 159, fols. 28–37, 51–69; 423, fols. 51–69 · CUL, MS oo.VII.47, pt 4 · Inner Temple, London, MSS 537, vol. 21, fols. 272–301; 538, vol. 18, fol. 339 · notes on readings at inns of court, BL, Stowe MS 424 · *Calendar of the journals of the House of Lords*, 1 (1830), 76–125 · C. R. Kyle, ed., *Parliament, politics and elections, 1604–1648* (2001), 29, 36, 49, 113, 184 · P. E. Kopperman, *Sir Robert Heath, 1575–1649* (1989), 17, 26, 30–31, 34–7, 86–7, 142–3, 224, 278 · W. R. Prest, *The rise of the barristers: a social history of the English bar, 1590–1640* (1986), 44, 70, 142–3, 155, 219, 270, 406 · L. A. Knafla, *Law and politics in Jacobean England* (1977), 130, 132, 149, 151, 164, 203, 232, 253, 302, 305–8 · R. Zaller, *The parliament of 1621: a study in constitutional conflict* (1971), 22–3, 30, 63–4, 67, 72–3, 85, 116–24 · HoP, *Commons, 1558–1603*, 3.681–2 · *The diary of Sir Richard Hutton, 1614–1639*, ed. W. R. Prest, SeldS, suppl. ser., 9 (1991), xxx, 26, 33–6, 39, 56, 169 · F. J. C. Hearnshaw, *Southampton court leet records*, Southampton Records, 1 (1905), pt 1, p. 129; (1906), pt 2, pp. 103–5 · *Liber famelicus of Sir James Whitelocke, a judge of the court of king's bench in the reigns of James I and Charles I*, ed. J. Bruce, CS, old ser., 70 (1858), 55 · L. W. Abbott, *Law reporting in England, 1485–1585* (1973), 58, 193, 303, 310–11 · E. R. Foster, ed., *Proceedings in parliament, 1610*, 2 (1966), 28, 34–6, 225–34, 355–6 · M. Jansson, ed., *Proceedings in parliament, 1614 (House of Commons)* (1988), 41, 48, 136, 264–6 · *Notes of the debates in the House of Lords, officially taken by Henry Elsing, clerk of the parliaments, AD 1621*, ed. S. R. Gardiner, CS, 103 (1870), 43 · S. R. Gardiner, ed., *Parliamentary debates in 1610*, CS, 81 (1862), 85 · W. Dugdale, *Origines juridiciales, or, Historical memorials of the English laws* (1666), 296 · J. Bridges and P. Whalley, eds., *The history and antiquities of Northamptonshire*, rev. edn, 2 (1812), 164

Archives BL, papers, Stowe MSS 570–571, Add. MSS 48000–48196, passim

Wealth at death see will, PRO, PROB, 11/157, fols. 431v–432v

Yelverton, Sir William (d. 1477?), justice, was the son of John Yelverton of Rackheath, Norfolk, recorder of Norwich, and his second wife. She was Elizabeth, the daughter and heir of John Read of Rougham, and by 1410 was married to her second husband, Richard Clere of Stokesby. Although he was the heir to the Read property in Rougham and Bayfield, William followed his father into the legal profession. He entered Gray's Inn and appears in Segar's list of readers. By 1427 he was a JP for Norwich, and from 1433 to 1450 recorder of the city, although, curiously, he sat in the parliaments of 1435 and 1443 for Great Yarmouth. Other Norfolk employers included the duke of Norfolk. Yelverton was called to the coif in 1438, appointed to the western assize circuit in 1439, retained by the duchy of Lancaster from 1440, and by Michaelmas 1442 was a king's serjeant. On 1 July 1443 he was promoted to the court of king's bench. As a crown lawyer he was summoned to the Lords for the parliaments of 1445, and thereafter regularly until 1470–71. In May 1461 Yelverton, by then the senior puisne, had hopes of succeeding the disgraced Sir John Fortescue as chief justice, but John Markham was appointed; however, Markham used his influence to secure for Yelverton a compensating knighthood. Yelverton continued in post until 6 April 1471 when Edward IV, returning after the readeption of Henry VI, chose not to reappoint him.

Yelverton's deep involvement in East Anglian politics did not always sit easily with the substantial use the crown made of him for judicial and administrative commissions. In 1454 he even found his clerk being arrested in Westminster Hall. The judge is, however, best known for his involvement in the dispute over Sir John Fastolf's will, the central preoccupation of the Paston letters. Sir William had initially been a colleague and friend of John (I) Paston, both on the duke of Norfolk's council and as an adviser, feoffee, and executor to Sir John Fastolf. The two fell out when a will made by the dying Fastolf hugely benefited Paston, and cut out Yelverton and other former trustees and executors. William Yelverton suspected foul play—he had not, unlike Paston, reached Sir John's bedside—and he challenged the will in the Canterbury court of audience. Although in 1467 probate was awarded to the Pastons, litigation in chancery (which again Yelverton lost) only reached judgment in 1470–71. Thereafter the families were quickly reconciled, and in 1472 began negotiating a marriage between Yelverton's grandson and John Paston's younger daughter.

What Yelverton's motives were in the Fastolf affair is not obvious. William Worcester, an erstwhile ally, described him as 'the cursed Norfolk justice' (*Itineraries*, 190–91). He certainly had his fair share of acquisitiveness, and if he had been offered 'a frendelyhood' by Paston he might initially have compromised. However, it is also very probable that he felt morally obliged to protest against the subversion of Fastolf's wishes and the placing in jeopardy of the health of Sir John's soul. Sir William's genuine religious sympathy is seen elsewhere. He was especially devoted to the Virgin Mary, shown by his promoting the interests of Walsingham Priory, and he was buried before her image in the chancel of Rougham church. He was also a member of the Guild of St George in Norwich, and was promised an individual mention among the obits in recognition of his role in arbitrating between the guild and the Norwich city authorities. 'Yelverton's mediation' ended fifty years of dispute, by effectively integrating the Guild of St George and a second prominent guild, the Batchery, with the city oligarchy.

The inscription on Sir William's monumental brass is lost, but is known to have given the day and month of death as 27 March. He appears to have still been alive in November 1476 but was omitted from the Norfolk commission of the peace of 4 May 1478, which makes 1477 the most likely year of death. He bequeathed a significant East Anglian estate to John Yelverton, the son and heir of Sir William's first marriage (before 1421), to Joan, the daughter of Oliver Grose of Sloley. He apparently married twice more, first to Ela, daughter of Sir Robert Brews and thus aunt to Margery Paston, and then to Agnes Campe of Brentwood, Essex, the widow of John Rands of Barking. Agnes survived him and died in 1489. The figures of William and Agnes survive from the monumental brass in Rougham church, and depict the judge in judicial robes and a serjeant's coif, worn incongruously over full armour.   E. W. IVES

Sources E. C. Robbins, 'The cursed Norfolk justice: a defence of Sir William Yelverton', *Norfolk Archaeology*, 26 (1936–8), 1–51 · N. Davis, ed., *Paston letters and papers of the fifteenth century*, 2 vols. (1971–6) · *The Paston letters, 1422–1509 AD*, ed. J. Gairdner, new edn, 3 vols. (1872–5); repr. in 4 vols. (1910) · C. Richmond, *The Paston family in the fifteenth century: Fastolf's will* (1996) · M. Grace, ed., *Records of the Gild of St George in Norwich, 1389–1547*, Norfolk RS, 9 (1937) · E. W. Ives, *The common lawyers of pre-Reformation England* (1983) · Sainty, *Judges* · Sainty, *King's counsel* · Baker, *Serjeants* · R. J. Fletcher, ed., *The pension book of Gray's Inn*, 2 vols. (1901–10) · J. C. Wedgwood and A. D. Holt, *History of parliament ... 1439–1509*, 2 vols. (1936–8) · R. Somerville, *History of the duchy of Lancaster, 1265–1603* (1953) · *Les reports des cases* (1679), Michaelmas 33, Henry VI, fol. 55, plea 50 [year books] · *Itineraries [of] William Worcestre*, ed. J. H. Harvey, OMT (1969)
Archives Norfolk RO, Rougham MSS
Likenesses brass effigy (with wife, Agnes), Rougham church, Norfolk; rubbing, repro. in *Monumental brasses*, ed. M. W. Norris (Monumental Brass Society, 1988) no. 200

Yelverton, William Charles, fourth Viscount Avonmore

Yelverton, William Charles, fourth Viscount Avonmore (1824–1883), army officer and litigant, born on 27 September 1824, was the eldest son of Barry John Yelverton, third Viscount Avonmore (1790–1870), and his second wife, Cecilia (*d.* 1 Feb 1876), eldest daughter of Charles O'Keeffe of Hollybrooke Park, Tipperary. The third viscount's two sons with his first wife died in 1853 and 1860. Yelverton was educated for military service at Woolwich and entered the Royal Artillery. He attained the rank of major, served in the Crimean War, received a medal and clasp for Inkerman and Sevastopol, and was created a knight of the fifth class of the Mejidiye by the Turkish government.

In March 1861 Yelverton was suspended from all military duties, and on 1 April placed on half pay, as a consequence of his involvement in a scandalous legal case. Between 1859 and 1868 he was involved in litigation regarding his alleged marriage with Maria Theresa *Longworth. The couple had met in 1852, and again in 1855 when she was serving as a nurse with the French Sisters of Charity in the Crimea. In April 1857, Yelverton 'performed the ceremony' of marriage, by reading the Church of England service aloud, while in Edinburgh, and they were married by the Roman Catholic rite on 15 August 1857 at Rostrevor in Ireland. The following year, on 26 June, Yelverton married Emily Marianne (*d.* 1909), daughter of Major-General Sir Charles *Ashworth, and widow of the naturalist Edward Forbes, at Trinity Chapel, Edinburgh, according to the rites of the Church of England. In 1859, Maria Longworth unsuccessfully sued him for the restoration of conjugal rights; in 1861 a further action was brought in which the validity of the first marriage was the point at issue. The Irish court, in which this action was brought, validated the marriage, but on appeal it was annulled by the Scottish court, which judgment was confirmed by the House of Lords, and upheld through several appeals, the last in 1868.

Yelverton succeeded his father as fourth viscount on 24 October 1870, and died at Biarritz on 1 April 1883. He was succeeded by his sons, Barry Nugent, fifth viscount (1859–1885), and Algernon William, sixth viscount (1866–1910). Yelverton's marriage episode was reproduced in the novel *Gentle Blood, or, The Secret Marriage* (1861), by James Roderick

O'Flanagan, while Cyrus Redding based the plot of *A Wife and not a Wife* (1867) on the story of Yelverton's Irish marriage. E. I. CARLYLE, *rev.* K. D. REYNOLDS

Sources GEC, *Peerage* · M. T. Longworth, *The Yelverton correspondence* (1863)

Yeo, Gerald Francis (1845–1909), physiologist, was born in Dublin on 19 January 1845, the second son of Henry Yeo of Ceanchor, Howth, JP, clerk of the rules in the court of exchequer, and his wife, Jane, daughter of Captain Ferns. Yeo was educated at the Royal School, Dungannon, and at Trinity College, Dublin, where he graduated moderator in natural science in 1866, proceeding MB and MCh in 1867. In 1868 he gained the gold medal of the Dublin Pathological Society for an essay on renal disease. After studying abroad for three years, a year each in Paris, Berlin, and Vienna, he proceeded MD at Dublin in 1871, and became next year MRCP and MRCS Ireland. For two years he taught physiology in the Carmichael school of medicine in Dublin.

Yeo was appointed professor of physiology in King's College, London, in 1874, and in 1877 assistant surgeon to King's College Hospital, becoming FRCS England in 1878. However, he resigned his clinical appointment in 1880 in order to devote his time to physiology. He delivered for the College of Surgeons the Arris and Gale lectures on anatomy and physiology in 1880–82. He used the lectures to illustrate how far experimentation had advanced the cause of science in the previous thirty years. Yeo did much good work with David Ferrier, a fellow professor of neuropathology at King's College, on the cerebral localization in monkeys, work which was then entirely new, but brought them threat of prosecution for vivisection. As Ferrier had not been allowed a vivisection licence under the 1877 act it was Yeo who did the operative work.

Yeo is perhaps best known as being the first secretary of the Physiological Society, of which he was one of the founders in 1875. At first this was mainly a mutual protection society against the intrigues of antivivisectionists, but later became a learned society. Yeo conducted the society's affairs with tact and energy (although he was an indifferent minute taker) until his resignation in 1890, when he was presented with a silver tea service. In conjunction with K. H. Krönecker of Bern, Yeo inaugurated the international physiological congresses which were held triennially; the first met at Basel in 1891.

Yeo was elected FRS in 1889. He resigned his chair of physiology at King's College in 1890 and received the title of emeritus professor. He then retired to Totnes, Devon, and later to Fowey, where he devoted himself to yachting, fishing, and gardening. Yeo married first, in 1873, Charlotte, the only daughter of Isaac Kitchin of Rockferry, Cheshire (she died childless in 1884); and second, in 1886, Augusta Frances, second daughter of Edward Hunt of Thomastown, co. Kilkenny, with whom he had one son.

Yeo, who spoke several languages, was a fluent speaker with a rich brogue. He was good-natured, generous, full of common sense. His *Manual of Physiology for the Use of Students of Medicine* (1884) was a useful and popular textbook.

He contributed numerous scientific papers on bile, heart muscle, skeletal muscle, and heart sounds to the *Proceedings and Transactions of the Royal Society* and to the *Journal of Physiology*. He died at his home, Austin's Close, Harbertonford, Devon, on 1 May 1909.

D'A. POWER, *rev.* ROGER HUTCHINS

Sources *BMJ* (8 May 1909), 1158 · V. G. Plarr, *Plarr's Lives of the fellows of the Royal College of Surgeons of England*, rev. D'A. Power, 2 vols. (1930) · W. J. O'Connor, *Founders of British physiology: a biographical dictionary, 1820–1885* (1988) · WWW
Archives RS
Wealth at death £52,600 2*s.*: resworn probate, 29 May 1909, *CGPLA Eng. & Wales*

Yeo, Sir James Lucas (1782–1818), naval officer, son of James Yeo (d. 21 Jan 1825), formerly agent victualler at Minorca, and his wife (d. 13 January 1822) was born at Southampton on 7 October 1782. He was briefly at the Revd Mr Walters's academy at Bishop's Waltham, Hampshire, but when little more than ten, in March 1793, he was entered as a boy volunteer on the *Windsor Castle*, which was going to the Mediterranean as flagship of Rear-Admiral Phillips Cosby, whom he followed to the *Alcide*, returning to England with him at the end of 1794. In the spring of 1795 he joined the *Orion* with Captain John Thomas Duckworth in the channel, and was shortly afterwards taken by Duckworth to the *Leviathan*, going to Jamaica. On 20 February 1797 Yeo was promoted lieutenant of the *Albicore* until, early in 1798, after a sharp attack of yellow fever, he was sent home.

Appointed to the *Veteran* in the North Sea, and in December 1798 to the *Charon*, going to the Mediterranean, in May 1800 he was moved to the brig *El Corso* (Commander William Ricketts) and was present at the siege of Genoa. On 26 August 1800 the brig's boats, commanded by Yeo and covered by the cutter *Pigmy*, forced their way into the harbour of Cesenatico in the Adriatic, burnt or sank thirteen merchant vessels, and burnt the piers. In February 1802 Yeo was moved to the *Généreux*, in which he returned to England. In February 1805 he was appointed to the *Loire* with Captain Frederick Lewis Maitland and commanded her boats on several expeditions, notably in Muros Bay on 4 June, where, after spiking the guns of a small battery, with only 50 men he stormed a closed fort in the town (garrisoned by 250 men, whose governor Yeo killed with his sabre), spiked its guns, and made it possible for the *Loire* to seize a large privateer and some other vessels lying in the bay. The privateer, unarmed but pierced for 26 guns, was commissioned for the navy under the name of *Confiance*, and Yeo was promoted to command her; his commission was dated 21 June 1805.

After two years on the Lisbon station Yeo was sent home with dispatches in November 1807 by Sir William Sidney Smith and on 19 December was promoted captain. He was, however, continued in the *Confiance* and sent back to the Tagus, whence in the following spring he accompanied Smith to Brazil. From Rio de Janeiro he was sent in September 1808 to Para, where he suggested to the governor the practicability of taking Cayenne and French Guiana. The governor gave Yeo such Portuguese as he could add to his force, but when he landed at Cayenne on 7 January 1809 he had in all only 400 men with whom to attack a garrison of 1200 in a strongly fortified position mounting over 200 guns. When five weeks later the place surrendered Yeo found himself with upwards of 1000 prisoners on his hands and no adequate means of securing them. For more than a month, until he received reinforcements, neither Yeo nor any of his force slept out of their clothes. Most were attacked by fever, and Yeo, after being confined to bed for two months with a severe bout of malaria, was obliged to go to England to recover. At Rio the prince regent of Portugal presented him with a valuable diamond ring and nominated him knight commander of St Benedict of Aviz, an order of a semi-religious character; it was said that Yeo was the first protestant admitted. His acceptance of the order was approved by George III, and he was knighted on 17 March 1810; he received a British knighthood on 21 June.

In 1811 Yeo commanded the frigate *Southampton* on the Jamaica station, and on 3 February 1812 took the *Amethyste*, a large pirate frigate stolen from the Haitian 'emperor', Christophe, to whom it was restored. On 22 November 1812 he captured the American brig *Vixen* (14 guns), but on the 27th, returning to Jamaica via the Crooked Island passage through the Bahamas, both the *Southampton* and its prize were wrecked on an uncharted reef 4 miles off the island of Conception.

On 19 March 1813 Yeo was appointed commodore and commander-in-chief of the warships on the North American lakes and reached Kingston at the foot of Lake Ontario in the early part of May. Sending subordinate commanders to the other lakes, Yeo focused on Lake Ontario, on whose control the entire British position in Upper Canada depended. By the end of the month he had assembled an efficient squadron of two ships of 24 and 20 guns, with a 14-gun brig and some smaller vessels, and had agreed with Sir George Prevost on an attack on Sackett's Harbour, where the enemy had a couple of large vessels on the stocks. American rumour had Yeo reconnoitring their base in person, disguised as a farmer selling potatoes. On the 27th troops were embarked, but when off the harbour the cautious Prevost refused to land. Two days later he was encouraged to make another attempt. This time the men were landed, had driven out the enemy, and had set fire to the two ships when Prevost's nerve again failed him and he re-embarked, permitting the enemy to reoccupy the port and extinguish the fire. In Prevost's absence Yeo took his squadron up the lake in June, capturing or destroying enemy storeships and depots and reversing the American army's invasion.

But by the end of July 1813 the larger of the two vessels not burnt at Sackett's Harbour was ready for service. Of 850 tons, mounting twenty-eight long 24-pounders, with a crew of 400 men, she was described as nearly a match for the whole of the British squadron. The American advantage was not only in the possession of this powerful ship, but also in the heavier and more efficient armament of the rest of the squadron; and though in an engagement near Niagara on 10 August Yeo succeeded in cutting off

and capturing two of the enemy's schooners, his main ally was the caution of the American commodore. Other partial engagements took place on 11 and 28 September, in the latter of which, the so-called 'Burlington Races', Yeo was obliged to break off action and beat for Kingston. But the American refused close action, relying on his long guns alone, with which he could not obtain any marked success.

Under a more adventurous commander the American squadron on Lake Erie took full advantage of its superior force and overwhelmed the British squadron on 10 September. During the winter great exertions were made by both parties. Yeo built two large ships at Kingston, and with these added to his squadron embarked a large body of troops and attacked Oswego on 6 May 1814. After a sharp contest the place was carried, and a large quantity of ordnance stores and provisions was captured or destroyed. Yeo then blockaded Sackett's Harbour, where the enemy had also launched two large ships, which they were unable to fit out so long as the stores could be prevented from reaching them. By the end of July he was obliged to raise the blockade, and the Americans with a vastly superior force were able to drive Yeo back to Kingston and blockade him there until September. Yeo's policy was to avoid defeat and maintain his squadron in being while building the 110-gun *St Lawrence*. When he finally sailed on 15 October it was the Americans' turn to remain in harbour.

Yeo's position had all along been one of great difficulty, not only in consequence of the Americans' advantages for building and fitting out ships, but still more in consequence of the indisposition of Prevost to co-operate fully. Their differences came to a head after the catastrophe on Lake Champlain occasioned by Prevost's call on the navy for assistance and his neglect to support the squadron [*see* Walker, James Robertson-]. The case appeared so flagrant that Yeo preferred distinct charges of gross neglect of duty, and though Prevost died before he could be brought to a court martial, the court which tried Walker and the other survivors found that the disaster was 'principally caused' by Prevost's urging the squadron into battle when it was not 'in a proper state to meet the enemy', and by his not co-operating as he had promised. On 2 January 1815 Yeo was made KCB, but overwork and the marsh fever of the Kingston area played on a body debilitated by the malaria contracted in Cayenne, and he returned to Britain in May. Canadians have always regarded him as one of the heroes of the Anglo-American War of 1812–14.

On 5 June 1815 Yeo was appointed commander-in-chief on the west coast of Africa, with a broad pennant in the *Inconstant*, and special responsibility for the anti-slavery patrol. In October 1817 he moved into the *Semiramis*, in which he went to Jamaica, and sailed thence for England. On the passage, on 21 August 1818, he died 'of general debility'. His body was brought home and buried on 8 September in the garrison chapel at Portsmouth. He was not married.   J. K. LAUGHTON, *rev.* MICHAEL DUFFY

Sources *Naval Chronicle*, 24 (1810), 265–85 · *Naval Chronicle*, 40 (1818), 243–4 · *GM*, 1st ser., 88/2 (1818), 371 · *GM*, 1st ser., 89/2 (1819),

91 · *GM*, 1st ser., 92/1 (1822), 188 · *GM*, 1st ser., 95/1 (1825), 188 · H. J. Morgan, *Sketches of celebrated Canadians, and persons connected with Canada* (1902), 221-2 · J. W. Spurr, 'Yeo, Sir James Lucas', *DCB*, vol. 5 · F. C. Drake, 'Commodore Sir James Lucas Yeo and Governor General Prevost: a study in command relations, 1813-14', *New interpretations in naval history: selected papers from the eighth Naval History symposium* [Annapolis 1987], ed. W. B. Cogar (1989), 156-71 · W. James, *The naval history of Great Britain, from the declaration of war by France in 1793, to the accession of George IV*, [3rd edn], 6 vols. (1837) · T. Roosevelt, *The naval war of 1812* (1886) · PRO, ADM 9/2-17 · D. Syrett and R. L. DiNardo, *The commissioned sea officers of the Royal Navy, 1660–1815*, rev. edn, Occasional Publications of the Navy RS, 1 (1994)

Likenesses H. R. Cook, print (after A. Buck), BM, NPG; repro. in *Naval Chronicle*, 24 (1810), 265

Yeo, Richard (*d.* 1779), coin- and medal-engraver, produced silver season tickets for entry to Vauxhall Pleasure Gardens. These tickets were sold from 1737 and carried images symbolizing the arts and pleasures to be enjoyed in the gardens. Yeo's signature appears on tickets showing the muses Euterpe and Thalia. Forrer suggests that two other tickets showing the muses Calliope and Erato are by him, as is a ticket showing the sculpture of Hogarth by Roubiliac, which was erected in Vauxhall Gardens in 1738. The tickets were in an ornate rococo style with loops to enable them to be worn; the wearer's name and season number was engraved on the back.

One of the most important pieces produced by Yeo was the official Culloden medal celebrating the duke of Cumberland's victory at the battle of Culloden in 1746. The medal had an ornamental scroll border in a gently decorated style and incorporated a loop, again to enable it to be worn. Later, another Culloden medal was produced by Yeo for a collector's market. It showed the duke of Cumberland, apparently rendered from life, on the obverse, and on the reverse it carried an image of Rebellion being defied by Hercules, while Britannia stands adjusting her garments. The medal was available in gold, silver, and copper by subscription and was advertised in the *London Gazette*. In 1745 Yeo had premises in the Strand and lived in lodgings at a Mrs Sutcliff's, a druggist near Craven Street; a year later he is recorded as living in Tavistock Street, Covent Garden.

Yeo was, from 1749, employed as second engraver at the Royal Mint. In 1768 he called attention to his own great input into the production of the dies and punches for the new coinage under George III, when the chief engraver, John Sigismund Tanner, had been unable to produce very much work owing to the deterioration in his eyesight. Yeo's work was officially acknowledged and recognized by Lord Viscount Chetwynd, the mint-master, who proposed to the Treasury to make Yeo chief engraver on Tanner's death. Yeo became chief engraver of the mint in 1779.

Yeo's name appears on the establishment papers for the Society of Artists in November 1759, and he exhibited there between 1760 and 1768. He was a director of the Incorporated Society of Artists from 1765 to 1768 and was a founder member of the Royal Academy when it was established in 1768. He showed at the academy's first two exhibitions in 1769 and 1770, when his contributions to the displays included impressions on sealing wax of engraved gems (1769) and a gold proof from a die of a 5-guinea piece (1770). In 1769 the *Middlesex Journal, or, Chronicle of Liberty* accused the founder members of the Royal Academy, Yeo among them, of being self-seeking cheats who benefited from the royal prerogative for personal reasons rather than being admirable leaders in the arts.

Yeo's contribution to British coinage includes a series of pattern 5 and 2 guineas between 1768 and 1777 that were never minted for circulation. He produced pattern guineas, half-guineas, and shilling pieces, among them the Northumberland shilling issued to be distributed among the population of Dublin in 1763 when Hugh, earl of Northumberland, became lord lieutenant of Ireland. Only £100 worth of these were issued, according to Grueber. Some of the patterns are kept in the British Museum. Yeo continued to engrave medals and gems, and his 1750 medal for the Academy of Ancient Music, the 1752 Chancellor medal, and the Winchester College prize medals are in the British Museum. He probably produced other society medals, and tickets unsigned by him may still await attribution. He signed his work R. YEO; YEO:F; YEO:FECIT, or R. YEO.F. Of his gems can be mentioned *Ixion Embracing a Cloud*, a portrait bust of Cromwell in amethyst, and a bust of Shakespeare in cornelian.

After Yeo's death in London, on 3 December 1779, his tools and a small collection of medals were sold at auction. His personal belongings were distributed among his closest friends, servants, and relatives.

LORNA COLBERG GOLDSMITH

Sources *A catalogue of the collection of coins and medals, of Richard Yeo esq.* (1780) · H. Bolzenthal, *Skizzen zur Kunstgeschichte der modernen Medaillen-Arbeit (1429-1840)* (1840), 265 · R. W. Cochran-Patrick, *Catalogue of the medals of Scotland* (1884), 82 · G. F. Crowther, *A guide to English pattern coins, … from Edward I to Victoria* (1887), 36 · L. Forrer, ed., *Biographical dictionary of medallists*, 6 (1916), 701-4 · J. R. Füssli and H. H. Füssli, *Allgemeines Künstlerlexikon*, [rev. edn], 2 vols. (Zürich, 1779-1824) · Graves, *RA exhibitors* · H. A. Grueber, *Handbook of the coins of Great Britain and Ireland in the British Museum* (1899), 147-8 · E. Hawkins, *The silver coins of England* (1887), 411 · W. J. Hocking, *Catalogue of the coins, tokens, medals, dies, and seals in the museum of the royal mint*, 2 vols. (1906-10) · J. H. Mayo, *Medals and decorations of the British army and navy*, 2 vols. (1897), 1.93, 97 · C. W. King, *Antique gems and rings*, 2 vols. (1872), vol. 1 · G. K. Nagler, ed., *Neues allgemeines Künstler-Lexikon*, 22 vols. (Munich, 1835-52) · R. E. Raspe, *A descriptive catalogue of a general collection of ancient and modern engraved gems, cameos as well as intaglios* (1791) · R. Ruding, *Annals of the coinage of Great Britain and its dependencies*, 3rd edn, 1 (1840), 45 · Thieme & Becker, *Allgemeines Lexikon*, 36.354 · *GM*, 1st ser., 19 (1749), 477 · *GM*, 1st ser., 49 (1779), 616 · *Numismatic Chronicle*, 13 (1850-51), 115-19 · *Numismatic Chronicle*, new ser., 15 (1875), 90-92

Archives PRO, T 1/466/156 · PRO, T 1/466/158

Likenesses C. Grignion junior, chalk drawing, BM · J. Zoffany, group portrait, oils (*Royal Academicians*, 1772), Royal Collection · mezzotint, NPG

Yeoman, Antonia [*née* Beryl Botterill Thompson; *pseud.* Anton] (1907-1970), cartoonist and illustrator, was born on 24 July 1907 in Esk, Queensland, Australia (she took the name Antonia when she became a Roman Catholic in her early twenties, influenced by the author R. T. Regent, a family friend). She was the eldest child of Arthur Henry Thompson (1855-1911), an English sheep farmer and local agent for his father's trading company, shipping farming equipment from Liverpool to Australia. Her mother, Ida May Cooke (1882–1955), was an Australian head teacher from Brisbane, Queensland. The family visited England on holiday in 1911, staying with relatives in West Kirby in the Wirral, Cheshire, where her brother, **Harold Underwood Thompson** [*pseud.* Anton] (1911–1996), cartoonist and advertising and marketing executive, was born on 9 April of the same year, and where their father died on 5 June of a brain haemorrhage following food poisoning. The family decided to stay in Britain and eventually settled in Brighton; in the 1930s her mother married Gordon William Griffin. Beryl went briefly to a local junior school where she caught tuberculosis of the spine which confined her to bed from the age of nine until fifteen and entailed the loss of two fingers of her right hand, and a number of trips to a sanatorium in Switzerland. Taught at first by private governesses, she learned to write and draw with her left hand and attended the Royal Academy Schools (1928) and studied art under Stephen Spurrier for a year before becoming a freelance commercial and fashion artist. She also produced advertising posters and showcards jointly with her brother from about 1935. Harold himself attended the same junior school as his sister and later went to Brighton College, ran an antique shop in Hove in his late teens, and studied life drawing at Heatherley's School of Fine Art (1931–2). Here he met (and was subsequently briefly engaged to) Patricia Fell-Clark, a fellow student, later better known as the writer Patricia Angadi. He also studied lettering at St Martin's School of Art (1934), printing at Bolt Court, took private classes in illustration at Stephen Spurrier's school (1935), and spent two years drawing antique furniture in the Victoria and Albert Museum (1936–8). Self-taught as a cartoonist, he began submitting drawings (and self-illustrated short stories) under the pseudonym H. Botterill (Botterill was their paternal grandmother's maiden name) to *The Bystander* (1935–7), the *Evening News* (1936), and *Night & Day* (1937).

In 1937 Harold and Antonia formed a partnership producing cartoons as Anton (Harold suggested the name, as it sounded foreign and sophisticated), selling the first cartoons under this name to *Night & Day* (1937) and *Punch* (26 January 1938)—though the Antons in the *Evening Standard* (1939) were entirely Harold's work. 'As my line drawing was better than his and his observation and sense of form better than mine, we decided to form a partnership' (Antonia in *Illustrated*). Normally Antonia blocked out the drawing and her brother added the detail and what both of them called 'the squiggly bits', their trademark shading. However, interviewed in 1955 Antonia said: 'After all these years we have reached the point where each of us can produce an "Anton" and defy even the closest observer to say which of us drew it' (ibid.). At first they shared a flat in Earls Court, London, trading as Botterill Artists (Antonia still signing herself Beryl Botterill Thompson at this stage) and then briefly moved together to the south of France (1938–9), still drawing for London publications. During the Second World War Harold trained at St

Alfred's, Hove, Sussex, and served in the Royal Navy as a captain of minesweepers and convoy escort vessels in the Atlantic and along the British coast and was twice mentioned in dispatches. Antonia, meanwhile, worked in a canteen in Bognor Regis, Sussex, and continued to draw Anton cartoons. Here she met her husband, John Richard Harding Yeoman (1916–1988), a former teacher serving in the army, and married him three weeks later, on 29 January 1941; they had no children. Shortly after this (17 October 1942) Harold married a Wren, Mary Kateley (1918–1989), whom he had met in Plymouth; they had four children. After the war brother and sister teamed up again to produce numerous cartoons under their joint pseudonym for *Punch*, *Lilliput*, *London Opinion*, *Men Only*, and others. Harold, meanwhile, also worked in a creative capacity for Greenly's advertising agency and when this was taken over by the Lonsdale-Hands Organisation in 1954 he became creative marketing director and then senior marketing director of the company. This work left him less time for drawing—though he continued to write short stories for the *Daily Herald* and others; designed posters, showcards, and advertisements (for among others Orient Shipping Line and Northern Aluminium); and wrote a book on marketing, *Product Strategy* (1962). In consequence Antonia took over the name herself, and by 1949 the Anton cartoons were entirely hers. They often included 'elegant men-about-town, superior spivs and the middle classes' (*Daily Telegraph*, 1 July 1970) and were drawn, usually in black and white, with Gillot 290 nibs and Indian ink with a distinctive 'squiggle' technique to create half-tone effects. As well as in *Punch*, they appeared in *Tatler*, the *New Yorker*, the *Daily Telegraph* ('Way of the world' feature), and *Private Eye*. Two books of the jointly drawn cartoons were published: *Anton's Amusement Arcade* (1947) and *Low Life and High Life* (1952). Antonia also drew a series of popular Anton advertisements for Moss Bros. and others, including Simpson's Services Club, Morley Outfitters, and Saxone Shoes. In addition she illustrated seventeen books including works by Virginia Grahame and Denys Parsons. The only female member of *Punch*'s Toby Club, she was also—in 1966—the first woman to be elected to the Chelsea Arts Club (her husband—a local councillor, a governor of both the Chelsea School of Art and the Royal College of Art, and secretary of the Council for the Preservation of Rural England—was already a member). In addition she served on the council of the Artists' General Benevolent Institution for many years. Anton cartoons are held in the collections of the Victoria and Albert Museum, the Cartoon Art Trust, and the University of Kent Cartoon Centre.

Antonia was about 5 feet 2 inches tall with short dark hair and brown eyes with wide owl-like spectacles. She walked stiffly as a result of tuberculosis of the spine and later arthritis. She died at St George's Hospital, London, on 30 June 1970. Harold Underwood Thompson was about 5 feet 8 inches tall, of stocky build, and usually clean shaven. In later life he moved to Wells, Somerset. He died in Taunton Hospital, Somerset, on 21 November 1996, was cremated in Bath the following week, and interred in St Thomas's Church, Wells, Somerset, with his wife who had predeceased him. MARK BRYANT

Sources private information (2004) [family] · M. Bryant, *Dictionary of twentieth-century British cartoonists and caricaturists* (2000) · M. Bryant and S. Heneage, eds., *Dictionary of British cartoonists and caricaturists, 1730–1980* (1994) · M. Bateman, *Funny way to earn a living* (1966) · J. Yeoman, ed., *Anton* (1971) · *Illustrated* (28 May 1955), 43
Archives priv. coll., letters and photographs | SOUND "My job — being a humorous artist", BBC light programme, 14 Feb 1954
Likenesses A. Yeoman, self-portrait, caricature, repro. in Bateman, *Funny way to earn a living*, 70 · double portrait, photograph (with her brother), repro. in *Illustrated* · portraits and photographs, priv. coll.

Yeoman, Thomas (1709/10–1781), millwright and surveyor, was probably born in Somerset. Although his origins and early life are obscure, his career embraced many different aspects during a formative phase of the early industrial revolution, and he became one of the most prolific and influential civil engineers of the period and a founding father of the profession. He is first encountered as the wheelwright skilled in 'turning iron & Brass, & making machinery for grinding' (Birmingham Reference Library, Johnson MS 185602), who was recruited by Edward Cave to operate the first water-powered cotton-spinning mill at Northampton in 1741, using the system patented by Lewis Paul. At the time of his recruitment, Yeoman was probably employed at Abbey Mills in Bromley, one of several mills located on the complex of streams on the tidal reaches of the River Lea.

Moving to Northampton about 1742, Yeoman soon began to take an active role in the commercial, cultural, and religious life of the town. While working as 'Operator for Mr Cave's Cotton Engines' (*Northampton Mercury*, 5 Dec 1743), he first established himself as a millwright in St Mary's Street. From there he advertised his services, including the construction of a range of machinery such as John Wyatt's weighbridge and the ventilator invented by Stephen Hales, which provided a regular source of employment throughout the 1740s and 1750s. Yeoman corresponded frequently with Hales on this and related subjects and fitted ventilators into numerous buildings throughout the country, including the town gaol in Northampton and the infirmary, newly founded in 1743. He became president of the Northampton Philosophical Society, one of the earliest and most important provincial societies, which met in his house and numbered among its members Philip Doddridge and William Shipley, who later founded the Society of Arts. Yeoman built and sold scientific instruments from his new premises in Gold Street, and in 1746–7 he undertook a series of scientific lecture demonstrations in Northampton, Coventry, and Birmingham, with exhibits of electrical apparatus. He continued to operate an 'Experiment room' in his house and in 1748 he advertised proposals for *Uranographia Britannica*, a celestial atlas by the astronomer John Bevis, an ambitious and ultimately unsuccessful venture.

Yeoman was evidently already married when he moved to Northampton; the birth of a son, Samuel, was recorded in October 1742, but his wife, Sarah, died in 1746. On 18 August 1747 he married Anne (1707/8–1793), the sister of Joshua Remington, a wealthy grocer of the town. Two further children were born: a son, Thomas, in August 1748 and a daughter, Anne, in January 1752. In 1752 another son, James, was apprenticed to John Neale, a maker of scientific instruments in London and an occasional partner of Yeoman.

For all of his adult life, Yeoman was a Baptist and, during his time in Northampton, a prominent member of the College Lane Baptist Church. The Baptist minister, John Gill, an influential high-Calvinistic theologian, wrote to Yeoman in 1745 to promote his forthcoming *Exposition of the New Testament*. Yeoman subscribed not only to this but to all Gill's major works between 1746 and 1769. On a number of occasions he acted on behalf of the church, and he discharged his social obligations by supporting the infirmary; several times he acted as a house visitor and from 1746 to 1752 he was a member of the committee of governors. It was probably in this social context that Yeoman came to the attention of the local whig grandee Lord Halifax who, as president of the Board of Trade and later first lord of the Admiralty, was able to secure him preferment with the Admiralty.

Yeoman's interests diversified considerably while he was in Northampton and his career blossomed. Commensurate with this, his social status rose as he moved first to Gold Street and finally, in 1755, to Bridge Street. He continued to construct ventilators, for both land and sea use, and in 1751 he was commissioned to install machines in four merchantmen at Rotterdam. Work on marine ventilation was to lead to further employment by the Admiralty, first in 1756, in the naval hospitals, and later installing ventilators into vessels of the fleet itself. Yeoman's work as an engineer was reported and advertised not only locally but also nationally, through the pages of the *Gentleman's Magazine*, published by Edward Cave. During this period Yeoman also turned to surveying, both for local estate owners and for turnpike trusts. He first surveyed the River Nene in 1744 and his work in this field developed to become the major occupation of his later career. In 1756 he gave evidence to the parliamentary commission for the navigation of the River Nene, and in 1758, as the work was in progress, he was several times engaged by the commissioners to act as both surveyor and consultant engineer.

When the cotton mill declined and finally closed about 1756, Yeoman moved to London, where he established himself first in Little Peter Street, Westminster, and continued his work as a surveyor and engineer. In Thomas Mortimer's *Universal Director* (1763) Yeoman was credited with the ventilation of the Drury Lane Theatre and the houses of parliament, and for the first time he was described as a civil engineer. In 1760 he was elected to the Society of Arts, and he continued to play an active part in its proceedings until the late 1770s. He proposed numerous new members between 1760 and 1776, including a number of other surveyors and engineers. From 1763 he was chairman of the committee of mechanics and in 1768 he presented the society with a model of the Hales ventilator. In 1764 he was elected a fellow of the Royal Society, but he seems to have participated little in its activities.

During the 1760s and 1770s Yeoman's main occupation was as a surveyor and engineer of canal and river navigations and of drainage schemes. Besides the River Nene, he worked on the rivers Ivel, Stort, Chelmer, Lea, Stour, Stroud, Medway, and Thames; on the Aire and Calder Canal, and the Clyde Canal; on the draining of the level of Ancholme and of Deeping Fen; and he appeared a number of times to give evidence before parliamentary committees. He published several engineering reports, though no books; a manual for the instruction of millwrights that he was preparing in the 1740s was never completed. Probably his greatest surviving achievement is the Limehouse cut, linking the River Lea to the Thames upstream of the Isle of Dogs, which he completed, as John Smeaton's assistant, in 1770.

By about 1769 Yeoman had moved to Castle Street in Leicester Fields, Westminster, and he continued a Baptist as a member of the Grafton Street church, where he served as both deacon and secretary to the church. In 1766-7 he played a prominent part in an acrimonious dispute which ended with the congregation dismissing its minister, William Anderson, and replacing him with Benjamin Messer.

From 1770, then in his sixties, Yeoman was increasingly employed as a consulting engineer, and in recognition of his standing in the embryonic profession he was elected in 1771 the first president of the Society of Civil Engineers. His final illness was recorded in the society's minutes in April 1780; his will had been written in the previous year. In it he made provision for his widow and four surviving daughters, and listed properties in London and Trudoxhill, Somerset. Yeoman died at his home in Castle Street on 23 January 1781, and was buried on 31 January in Bunhill Fields. His wife Anne survived him until 6 November 1793, and was then buried in the same grave; the grave no longer exists, but the inscription has been preserved.

DAVID L. BATES

Sources *Northampton Mercury* (1743–62) · *GM*, 1st ser., 15–51 (1745–81) · *The report of Thomas Yeoman, engineer, concerning the drainage of the North Level of the fens and the outfal of the Wisbeach river* (1769) · *JHC*, 27–35 (1754–76) · S. Hales, *A treatise on ventilators* (1758) · T. Mortimer, *Universal director* (1763) · E. Robinson, 'The profession of civil engineer in the eighteenth century: a portrait of Thomas Yeoman', *Annals of Science*, 18 (1962), 195–215 · A. P. Wadsworth and J. de Lacy Mann, *The cotton trade and industrial Lancashire, 1600–1780* (1931) · A. W. Skempton, *British civil engineering, 1640–1840: a bibliography of contemporary printed reports, plans, and books* (1987) · A. W. Skempton and E. C. Wright, 'Early members of the Smeatonian Society of Civil Engineers', *Transactions of the Newcomen Society*, 44 (1974), 23–47 · D. L. Bates, 'All manner of natural knowledge: the Northampton Philosophical Society', *Northamptonshire Past and Present*, 8 (1993–4), 363–77 · D. L. Bates, 'Cotton-spinning in Northampton: Edward Cave's mill, 1742–1761', *Northamptonshire Past and Present*, 9 (1996–7), 237–51 · E. C. Wright, 'The early Smeatonians', *Transactions of the Newcomen Society*, 18 (1938), 101–10 · G. Watson, *The Smeatonians: the society of civil engineers* (1989) · D. G. C. Allan and R. E. Schofield, *Stephen Hales: scientist and philanthropist* (1980) · S. B. Donkin, 'The society of civil engineers (Smeatonians)', *Transactions of the Newcomen Society*, 17 (1937), 51–71 · Will of Thomas Yeoman, PRO, PROB 11/11075 · *IGI* · BL, Add MS 28516 · J. Harrison, '"The ingenious Mr Yeoman" and some associates: a practical man's contribution to the Society's formative years', *RSA Journal* (June 1997), 53–68

Archives Birm. CL, Johnson MSS · Birm. CL, Wyatt MSS · Northants. RO, records of the Nene River Board · RCP Lond., Hales MSS · RSA, minute books, Royal Society of Arts

Wealth at death see will, PRO, PROB 11/11075

Yeowell, James (*c*.1803–1875), antiquary, was born in London. Little is known about his early life, but he is said to have been employed by the vestry of Shoreditch, and to have worked at indexing and other similar tasks for London booksellers. Soon after the establishment by William John Thoms (1803–1885) of *Notes and Queries* in 1849, Yeowell became the journal's sub-editor. He held this post for more than twenty years before retiring in September 1872. During this period Yeowell supplied, after painstaking research at the British Museum, the answers which appeared each week under the heading of 'Queries with answers'. While sub-editor of *Notes and Queries* he also compiled the general indexes to the first three series and, among other indexing work, an index to Agnes Strickland's *Lives of the Queens of England* (1840–48).

Aside from compiling indexes, Yeowell wrote *Chronicles of the Ancient British Church Anterior to the Saxon Era*, which first appeared in 1839 in a monthly periodical and then in 1847 as a new edition. He also wrote *A Literary Antiquary: Memoir of William Oldys, with his Diary Notes from Adversaria and an Account of the London Libraries*, which was published in *Notes and Queries* in 1861 and 1862, and edited the poetry of Sir Thomas Wyatt and the earl of Surrey for the Aldine series (1853). In the following year he assisted Lord Braybrooke with the fourth edition of Samuel Pepys's diary, which was published in 1854.

On his retirement from *Notes and Queries* Yeowell was nominated a poor brother at the Charterhouse by the duke of Buccleuch on the suggestion of Thoms. Having lived in Pentonville, near the Sadler's Wells Theatre, and in Barnsbury, Yeowell finally moved to the Charterhouse, where he died on 10 December 1875. He was buried in Highgate cemetery on 14 December.

Yeowell's books were sold with other collections by Sotheby, Wilkinson and Hodge from 12 to 17 November 1873, and on 19 May 1876. His collections of biographical materials, including newspaper cuttings, excerpts from printed books, manuscript memoranda, and engraved portraits, are in the British Museum.

W. P. COURTNEY, rev. JOANNE POTIER

Sources *N&Q*, 5th ser., 4 (1875), 481 · Boase, *Mod. Eng. biog.* · Allibone, *Dict.* · *N&Q*, 9th ser., 4 (1899), 365 · *The Athenaeum* (18 Dec 1875), 831 · *The Athenaeum* (25 Dec 1875), 881 · private information (1900) · *CGPLA Eng. & Wales* (1876)

Archives Bodl. Oxf., notebook · U. Edin. L., corresp. | BL, collections for biography of Englishmen, 010604.p.1.

Wealth at death under £450: probate, 12 Jan 1876, *CGPLA Eng. & Wales*

Yerburgh, Robert Armstrong (1853–1916), politician, was born on 17 January 1853 at Sleaford, Lincolnshire, the third son of Richard Yerburgh (1817–1886), vicar of New Sleaford, and his first wife, Susan, daughter of John

Higgin of Greenfield, Lancaster. The Yerburgh family had been settled in Lincolnshire since before the Norman conquest. Yerburgh was educated at Rossall and Harrow schools and at University College, Oxford, where he graduated BA in 1877. He was called to the bar at the Middle Temple in 1880 and subsequently joined the northern circuit. On 8 August 1888 he married Elma Amy Thwaites at St Barnabas, Kensington. She was the only child of Daniel Thwaites of Woodfold Park, Blackburn, a former MP. There were two sons of the marriage.

Yerburgh was adopted as Unionist candidate for Chester in 1885, having been Conservative candidate for Grimsby for two years. At the general election of 1885 he lost by 300 votes to the radical candidate, Dr Walter Foster, but narrowly won the seat in 1886. He was returned again at the elections of 1892, 1895, and 1900, but narrowly lost to the industrialist Alfred Mond in 1906. He regained Chester at the general election of January 1910, retaining the seat until his retirement in 1916. In 1885–6 he was private secretary to the patronage secretary, the Rt Hon. A. Akers-Douglas, and in 1887 was assistant private secretary to W. H. Smith, then first lord of the Treasury.

A man of keen intellect, judicial temperament, and a charming manner, Yerburgh was widely respected as more than a mere party politician. He had many interests, especially imperial defence, agricultural organization, and the promotion of co-operative and co-partnership schemes. As president of the Navy League from 1900 until his death, he keenly promoted naval interests and reforms in naval administration. His strong belief in British naval supremacy was seen to be vindicated when war broke out in 1914. He was also an early advocate of national service and was a member of the Council of the National Service League which promoted universal naval or military training.

Yerburgh's deep love of rural life was reflected in his wide interest in agriculture. In 1901 he founded the Agricultural Organisation Society, of which he was president until his death. He was also a vice-president of the central chamber of agriculture and of the English Beet Sugar Pioneer Association, and a member of the Scottish chamber of agriculture. His work for the regeneration of English agriculture led a contemporary, P. J. Hannon, secretary of the Navy League, to describe him as 'the father and the founder of agricultural organisation in England' (Chester Courant).

As president of the Urban Co-operative Banks Association, Yerburgh helped to promote co-operative credit societies for the working classes. He supported many other social and philanthropic movements, including the Recreation Evening Schools Association, the National Home Reading Union, and the National League for Physical Education and Improvement. He was also a deputy lieutenant, justice of the peace, and county councillor for Lancashire, and a justice of the peace for Kirkcudbrightshire.

Yerburgh's last years were clouded by failing health, which forced his retirement from parliament in February 1916. He died from heart failure at his London home, 25 Kensington Gore, on 18 December 1916. His funeral took place on 21 December 1916 at Sleaford, where he was buried in the local cemetery. SIMON HARRISON

Sources *Chester Courant* (20 Dec 1916) • *WWW* • W. T. Pike, ed., *Contemporary biographies* (1904) • *Chester Chronicle* (23 Dec 1916) • *The Times* (19 Dec 1916) • Foster, *Alum. Oxon.* • Venn, *Alum. Cant.*
Likenesses photograph, repro. in Pike, ed., *Contemporary biographies*
Wealth at death £31,855 18s. 4d.: probate, 14 April 1917, *CGPLA Eng. & Wales*

Yerbury, Francis Rowland [Frank] (1885–1970), architectural administrator, was born on 19 November 1885 at Cricklewood, London, the youngest son of Francis William Yerbury, clerk, and his wife, Lucy Stinchcomb. His father died early, leaving his widow to bring up the family. An uncle paid for the education of Yerbury's two elder brothers, who went to good schools; Frank was not so fortunate, a circumstance which seemed to affect him throughout his life for he was rarely at ease in intellectual circles. Even among his chosen professional friends, such as architects and designers, he always regretted never having become an architect himself. In the hope that he might achieve this aim, he had accepted at the age of sixteen the post of office boy at the Architectural Association (AA) in Tufton Street, Westminster.

Yerbury did not in fact leave the AA until his retirement thirty-six years later, for when the secretary of the association died suddenly in 1911, Yerbury was appointed to succeed him and thus began his distinguished twin careers as a builder of a great school of architecture and an influential proponent and photographer of modern European building. Indeed, Yerbury became, for his architect friends in London, their prime source of information on and contact with the contemporary architecture and architects in the Netherlands, Germany, Denmark, and Sweden. His excellent photographs of modern European buildings were widely published and his many illustrated books about his travels abroad were avidly read by generations of students to whom contemporary European architecture was still an unknown quantity. Among his books were *Modern European Buildings* (1928), *Modern Dutch Buildings* (1931), and *Small Modern English Houses* (1929). While acting as the leading publicist for new continental architecture, Yerbury made a great number of friends in architectural circles abroad which were to last throughout his life and even took him on an official mission to Sweden during the Second World War to reassure his Swedish friends about the state of British morale. That he had to travel in the bomb bay of a Mosquito aircraft only reinforced his message. In recognition of his contributions to international understanding and architectural appreciation he had been made a commander of the Swedish royal order of Vasa (1929) and became a knight of the Danish royal order of the Dannebrog (1951).

As its increasingly respected secretary, Yerbury helped successive presidents and principals, especially Robert Atkinson and Howard Robertson, to build the Architectural Association into a leading centre for architectural education, discussion, thought, and controversy. Under

Francis Rowland Yerbury (1885–1970), by Francis Hodge, exh. RA 1948

his guidance the AA school even began to challenge the inter-war supremacy of the Liverpool school of architecture, where his friend C. H. Reilly was the professor. While at the AA, Yerbury encouraged a colleague, J. K. Winser, to organize a building materials samples room, which was eventually to lead to a third career for Yerbury: out of that modest collection of samples for the benefit of the AA students grew the first building centre for the architectural profession as a whole. Vincent Vincent, a director of Bovis Ltd, a well-known firm of building contractors, first saw the possibilities in Yerbury's samples room, having recently visited the Architects' Samples Bureau in New York, a commercial information service on building materials. Together Vincent and Yerbury created the Building Centre in 1931 as a non-profit-distributing educational enterprise to assist all concerned with the building industry from materials suppliers to contractors, architects, surveyors, and clients alike. By 1937 the new centre, having moved from its first home in the Conduit Street headquarters of the Royal Institute of British Architects to its own premises in Store Street, had become almost a full-time preoccupation for Yerbury. Accordingly, in that year he resigned from the AA to devote himself to directing and developing the Building Centre in London, which in due course was to become a model for other cities and indeed for other countries. At the time of Yerbury's death there were nearly 100 similar centres in operation around the globe.

Yerbury was a convivial, gregarious man, with a flair for international friendships, a great love of travel, and a real talent as a photographer. He was also reputed to be an excellent raconteur and a pillar of his favourite Arts Club in Dover Street. As one of the earliest English discoverers of modern Danish design (he wrote a short monograph on Kaare Klint's furniture in 1929), he was a staunch supporter of the British Design and Industries Association, of which he became a vice-president. He was elected an honorary associate of the Royal Institute of British Architects in 1928 and was made an OBE in 1952. He married on 28 August 1913 Winifred Constance (*b*. 1888/9), daughter of Henry Bendall; she survived him with a son and a daughter. Yerbury retired from active work in 1961 and died at Newbury on 7 July 1970.

PAUL REILLY, *rev.* CATHERINE GORDON

Sources *The Times* (9 July 1970) · *Building*, 218/29 (17 July 1970), 62 · *Arkitekten* [Denmark], 72/24 (1970), 584 · private information (2004) · m. cert. · *CGPLA Eng. & Wales* (1970)
Archives Building Centre, London
Likenesses F. Hodge, oils, exh. RA 1948, unknown collection; copyprint, NPG [*see illus.*]
Wealth at death £11,435: probate, 1970, *CGPLA Eng. & Wales*

Yerkes, Charles Tyson (1837–1905), financier of urban transport systems, was born on 28 June 1837 at Philadelphia, son of Charles Tyson Yerkes, who became president of a local bank, and his wife, Elizabeth Link, *née* Broom. A Quaker by upbringing, he left the Central High School, Philadelphia, at seventeen, and soon gained a good reputation as an investor of other people's money, due in no small part to his abilities on the local stock exchange. He made a small fortune by the age of thirty, lost it when, overextended, he was unable to meet his commitments in the panic of 1871, served a short prison sentence, and then made another quick fortune. He married Susanna Guttridge Gamble on 22 December 1862. She subsequently divorced him. He then married, on 23 September 1881, Mary Adelaide Moore.

Earlier writers have dwelt upon Yerkes's sharp financial practices and loose private morals, but more recent critics prefer to concentrate upon his achievements in developing urban transport in the rapidly growing city of Chicago, after moving there in 1881. America took the world lead in the great technical changes in urban transport in and after the later 1880s, and Yerkes, who mastered all the money-raising, cost, and other problems involved, made much money for himself, and his business associates. This, however, did not endear him to the travelling public, other residents, or the local press, who were usually hostile to the newcomer, despite his contribution to their city. He sold out very advantageously at the end of the century.

While in Chicago, Yerkes had been keeping an eye on developments in Europe. He paid visits to London and learned of plans to electrify the existing steam-operated underground and horse-drawn tramways. Electric traction also made possible the operation of railways in tubes, driven easily through the London clay. Yerkes was almost certainly the 'typical Yankee', whom Henrietta Barnett recalled meeting in 1896, who kept talking about 'a proposal … to convey all London about in tunnels'. He certainly came to inspect the steam-operated Metropolitan District Railway, part of the existing underground, in 1898. It is not known when he and Edgar *Speyer, head of the London section of an international banking concern, which also had a branch in New York, were first in touch with each other. The house of Speyer was heavily involved in railway investment in general, and the electrification of the Metropolitan District in particular. Electric traction was slow to be adopted in London because the first stretch of electric tube, the City and South London (1890), paid all the penalties of the pioneer. It was built too small, and produced poor financial results. The Central London Railway, however, opened from Shepherd's Bush under the busy road leading to the City, benefited from earlier experience, and was an instant success. It started to run in June 1900. By October of that year the world's leading expert on the financing, route planning, and day-to-day operation of urban railways had arrived in London, though whether on his own initiative, or summoned by friends, is unknown.

One of Yerkes's associates was Robert William Perks, formerly solicitor for the Metropolitan Railway (the other part of the existing steam underground), who had unrivalled knowledge of parliamentary procedure, and other relevant legal matters. Yerkes, Perks, and Speyer formed a powerful trio to bring to life various tube proposals which had gained parliamentary sanction, and another tube, partly built but abandoned because of the failure of its promoters. Yerkes lost no time in setting up a traction company, capitalized at £1 million, to electrify the Metropolitan District, and then turned his attention to the tubes. The traction company acquired the partly built Baker Street and Waterloo Railway, on which £675,000 had been spent, for £180,000. Having studied the capital's main traffic flows along routes for which tubes had been authorized, Yerkes abandoned a proposal to build the line under the Metropolitan District (intended to provide an express service into the City), and diverted it, using other franchises, from South Kensington via Piccadilly Circus to Finsbury Park. He secured additional parliamentary powers to extent a third tube, already authorized from Charing Cross to Hampstead, to a surface terminus at Golders Green, encouraging suburban growth in that area, especially in what became Henrietta Barnett's planned Hampstead Garden Suburb. He secured further powers for a branch from Camden Town to Archway. All these proposals involved greatly increasing the traction company's £1 million. Underground Electric Railways of London Ltd (UERL), capitalized at £5 million, was therefore floated in 1902 to operate the whole undertaking as a network which, as Yerkes (who became its chairman) claimed, could not but be profitable. Much more capital was needed and all Yerkes's skills in manipulating commercial paper—including the issuing of profit-sharing notes—were called for. The British were relatively unresponsive, for construction costs, as usual, exceeded

budget and traffic predictions remained uncertain. Foreign investors, and especially Americans, however, believed Yerkes's sanguine forecasts. The necessary capital, about £15 million in all, was forthcoming, some of it in the end still unallocated by Speyer Brothers. Electric trains began to run on the Metropolitan District from July 1905, and the three tubes were opened between March 1906 and June 1907. Londoners benefited enormously, but at the expense of the investors, for the forecast revenues were not forthcoming. UERL had the greatest difficulty in surviving.

Yerkes, however, did not live to see this débâcle. He died at the Waldorf-Astoria Hotel in New York (not at his own home in 5th Avenue where his wife lived) on 29 December 1905, the cause of death being said to be Bright's disease. His personal fortune suffered with the rest and his valuable art collection had subsequently to be sold by auction. 'This is one of the ordinary hazards of the modern world' commented his obituary writer, 'in which speculators make money, buy art treasures lavishly, and die in debt' (The Times, 30 Dec 1905).   THEO BARKER

Sources T. C. Barker and M. Robbins, *A history of London Transport*, 2 (1974) • H. C. Harlan, 'Charles Tyson Yerkes and the Chicago transportation system', PhD diss., University of Chicago, 1975 • R. D. Weber, 'Nationalisers and reformers: Chicago local transportation in the nineteenth century', PhD diss., University of Wisconsin, 1971 • *DAB* • T. Dreiser, *The financier: a novel* (1912) • T. Dreiser, *The Titan* (1914) • T. Dreiser, *The stoic* (1947) • *The Times* (30 Dec 1905)

Yevele, Henry (d. 1400), master mason, was the most prolific and successful master mason active in late medieval England. The son of Roger and Marion Yevele, he first appears in the documentary record on 3 December 1353, when he purchased the freedom of London; by February 1356 his standing among the city's masons was such that he was chosen as one of a commission of six cutting masons who were to inform the mayor and aldermen about the acts and articles of the craft. The starting point of Yevele's long career as an architect in royal service may have been his partial remodelling or completion of the hall of the Black Prince's manor at Kennington on the Surrey bank of the Thames. This work was carried out under contract between March 1357 and September 1359 at the high cost of £221 4s. 7d. In 1359 Yevele obtained a licence to discharge victuals at Calais, a concession which suggests strongly that he enjoyed the patronage of someone highly favoured at court. Perhaps that patron was Sir John Beauchamp (d. 1360) who figures prominently among the beneficiaries of the perpetual chantry established under Yevele's will of 1400. On 23 June 1360 Yevele became 'disposer' of the king's works of masonry in the Palace of Westminster and the Tower of London, for which he received a fee of 1s. per day, together with an annual robe like those of the sergeants of the household. This office resembled its early fourteenth-century precursors, in that it did not prevent its holder from undertaking other work. Yevele's private practice eventually grew to enormous proportions, although its full extent has undoubtedly been obscured by the low survival rate of documentary evidence outside the king's works organization.

At Westminster Palace, Yevele was responsible for two essentially utilitarian buildings, the Jewel Tower in the Privy Palace (1365–6) and the clock tower (now destroyed) which stood opposite the north door of Westminster Hall and regulated the sittings of the royal courts of justice there (1366–7). At the Tower of London several minor works, including the vaulting of the thirteenth-century watergate, were performed by Henry's brother Robert. However, the real focus of activity in the king's works at this time was Windsor Castle, and it is telling that the master mason there, John Sponlee (d. 1382?), walked in the funeral procession of Queen Philippa in 1369 as an esquire of greater estate, whereas Yevele ranked only as a lesser esquire. During Edward III's reign Yevele's strictly architectural work for the crown was, with one minor exception, confined to London, but his duties impressing masons for royal service took him further afield and he supplied materials to numerous royal building sites in Kent and Surrey as well as in London.

In March 1378 the administration of the king's works was centralized under a clerk with responsibility for (in theory) all of England. Yevele was confirmed in the position he had held since 1360, but the records relating to individual works show that the geographical scope of his work for the king had expanded in proportion to the increased threat of invasion from France—a reality reflected in the many references to him as king's chief mason with no distinction of place. He advised on repairs and new works at the castles of Southampton (1378–9), Carisbrooke (1380–85), Winchester (1390–1400), Portchester (1384–5), and on the town walls of Canterbury (1385–6), but it is uncertain to what extent this involved him in major design work. In 1381, 1389, and 1393 Yevele's advice, but almost certainly not his services as a designer, were sought by the great building bishop of Winchester, William Wykeham (d. 1404), who had been clerk of works at Windsor Castle from 1356 to 1361. On 29 August 1390 Yevele was made exempt from jury and other forms of service on account of his official duties and 'great age'.

His advancing years were probably the reason for Yevele's association with the younger architect Stephen Lote [see below] in the 1395 contract for the tomb-chest of Richard II's monument in Westminster Abbey. Similar thinking would explain why in 1394, when he took charge of Richard II's greatest architectural project, Westminster Hall, his warden was Walter Walton, an established master mason in his own right. Internally, this most splendid of medieval halls owes much less to Yevele's masonry than to the work of his carpenter colleague, Hugh Herland, but the entrance front facing the outer court is treated with a monumentality unparalleled in medieval hall design. The ecclesiastical character of the front's twin towers, 'welcoming porch', and bands of enniched imagery, is perhaps less likely to have originated with Yevele than with Richard II, for whom artistic patronage was principally a means of asserting the sacral nature of his kingship. Formally, the design typifies Yevele's work

as a whole in its great indebtedness to the version of Perpendicular Gothic pioneered by William Ramsey, his most distinguished fourteenth-century predecessor as king's chief mason.

Yevele's work for other lay patrons belonged to the 1370s and 1380s. For John of Gaunt he carried out in 1375 unspecified works at the Savoy Palace in London and, together with another mason, contracted for the duke's large and very sumptuous canopied tomb in St Paul's Cathedral. For John, third Lord Cobham he furnished the design ('devyse') for a new south aisle at the London parish church of St Dunstan-in-the-East, although he did not take charge of its building. From 1368 he served as one of the two wardens of London Bridge, the city's chief public work, and though the wardenships were purely administrative, it is highly likely that he was the designer of the two-storeyed apsidal chapel of St Thomas which projected eastwards from the middle of the bridge and which was under construction between 1384 and 1397. The chapel possessed a 'table' or handboard containing a summary history of the bridge, which was the source of the statement by the sixteenth-century antiquary John Leland that 'a mason beinge master of the bridge howse', built the chapel at his own expense (Itinerary, 5.6). This can only refer to Yevele, whose name presumably meant nothing to Leland. Minor benefactions by medieval master masons to the works on which they were engaged are occasionally recorded elsewhere, but donation of an entire building appears to be unparalleled in the European middle ages.

Assessment of Yevele's contributions to the most ambitious genres of medieval architecture, namely cathedral and monastic churches and their ancillary buildings, is hampered by the disappearance of documented works, and by the lack of written evidence for the authorship of extant buildings which can reasonably be attributed to him on the basis of stylistic and patronage evidence. The works in these categories include a large proportion of the outstanding architectural achievements of the late fourteenth century: the high altar screen of Durham Cathedral (1372–80), shipped in boxes from London to Newcastle; the east and south walks of the cloister of St Albans Abbey (probably begun c.1380), destroyed except for the east processional door leading from the nave; the south transept façade of St Paul's Cathedral (1381–8), also destroyed; and, most important of all, the nave and south cloister walk of Canterbury Cathedral (c.1382–1400). At Westminster Abbey, some parts of the existing nave undoubtedly date from Yevele's time as master mason (1387–1400), but the form of the bays had been fixed under the previous architect John Palterton. Opportunities for new design work were confined to the west front, which is notable for its 'welcoming porch' and for its towers, the latter treated as vertically continuous sheets of decorative buttressing, gablets, and tracery. The only other surviving pieces of monastic building definitely by Yevele are architecturally modest: three cell entrances at the London Charterhouse, whose construction Yevele began in 1371, and a large, plain gatehouse built at St Albans Abbey some time between 1362 and 1381.

Yevele's involvement in tomb design was undoubtedly very extensive. Apart from the two royal monuments mentioned above, his only extant and documented work of this kind is the tomb-chest of the monument to Cardinal Simon Langham (d. 1376) in Westminster Abbey, in progress in 1394. Other major tombs whose stonework may be attributed to Yevele include those of the Black Prince in Canterbury Cathedral (begun late 1370s?), Archbishop Simon Sudbury in the same church (begun mid-1380s?), and Edward III in Westminster Abbey (after 1386). Yevele's will reveals that he was the proprietor of a workshop in St Paul's Churchyard which made monumental brasses. The products of this workshop may survive in considerable numbers, but their identification has never been attempted.

Yevele owned numerous city of London properties besides his own house, which stood on Bridge Street and faced the west front of St Magnus the Martyr by London Bridge. In 1387 he acquired an extensive holding in Southwark, which probably became his main residence after his second marriage. It included two watermills and a chapel. Earlier, in 1378, he had bought a small estate in the Thames-side parishes of Aveley and Wennington in Essex, no doubt principally for recreation, but probably also in part to acquire the prestige of being a landowner. His high standing in the city community is not in doubt. From c.1373 he was a member of the Salve Regina fraternity in St Magnus; in 1383 he was a common councillor for Bridge Ward; and in 1392 he was one of twenty-four 'more substantial' citizens chosen to join the mayor, sheriffs, and aldermen to plead the city's case in its dispute with Richard II. Yevele's will, proved on 25 August 1400, makes no mention of children from either of his two marriages, to Margaret, who was dead by 1387, and to Katherine, widow of John Hadde (known as Lightfoot), who lived until 1410. Yevele died on 21 August 1400 and was buried beside his first wife in the lady chapel of St Magnus. In the late sixteenth century his monument still bore an inscription recording his service to Edward III, Richard II, and Henry IV.

Stephen Lote (d. 1417/18), master mason, had a long-standing association with Yevele which may have begun in 1381, when Lote was warden at St Paul's Cathedral. In the mid-1390s he was co-contractor with Yevele for the architectural components of the tombs of Cardinal Langham and Richard II, but a more personal bond is suggested by his witnessing a charter at Yevele's estate at Wennington in 1398 and by his participation in the execution of Yevele's will. His appearance in the list of those given esquire's livery by the prior of Canterbury Cathedral priory in 1398, which also includes Yevele, is evidence that he oversaw the completion of the latter's work on the nave and cloister there. Although employed by Anne of Bohemia and other members of the royal family in the 1390s, Lote is not known to have worked on the king's buildings until after 6 October 1400, when he succeeded Yevele as master mason at Westminster and the Tower of London. His most important royal building was the sumptuous rebuilding of Shene Manor, Surrey, from 1414 (destroyed).

Lote died during the winter of 1417–18. His will of 31 October 1417 leaves his 'patrons' (architectural designs) to Thomas Mapilton, who succeeded him as master mason both to the king and to Canterbury Cathedral. Like all other London-based architects active in the early fifteenth century, Lote and Mapilton adhered closely to the style of Henry Yevele. CHRISTOPHER WILSON

Sources J. Harvey and A. Oswald, *English mediaeval architects: a biographical dictionary down to 1550*, 2nd edn (1984), 358–66 • J. H. Harvey, 'Henry Yevele considered', *Archaeological Journal*, 108 (1951), 100–08 • J. H. Harvey, 'Some details and mouldings used by Yevele', *Antiquaries Journal*, 27 (1947), 51–60 • H. M. Colvin and others, eds., *The history of the king's works*, 6 vols. (1963–82), vol. 1, pp. 174n., 176n., 177–8, 209–13, 487–8, 529; vol. 2 • J. H. Harvey, *Henry Yevele, c. 1320 to 1400: the life of an English architect* (1944) • J. H. Harvey, *The Perpendicular style, 1330–1485* (1978), 96–135 • J. H. Harvey, 'Henry Yeveley and the nave of Canterbury Cathedral', *Canterbury Cathedral Chronicle*, 79 (1985), 20–30 • A. D. McLees, 'Henry Yevele, disposer of the king's works of masonry', *Journal of the British Archaeological Association*, 3rd ser., 36 (1973), 52–71 • C. Wilson, 'Rulers, artificers and shoppers: Richard II's remodelling of Westminster Hall, 1394–99', *The regal image of Richard II and the Wilton diptych*, ed. D. Gordon, C. Elam, and L. Monnas (1997), 33–59 • BL, Liber Benefactorum of St Alban's Abbey, late fourteenth century, Cotton MS Nero D.vii [fols. 105, 107v, 112] • will, commissary court of London, register of wills, 1374–1400, 25 May 1400, GL [fols. 453–6], MS 9171/1 [Henry Yevele] • C. Wilson, 'The Neville screen', *Medieval art and architecture of Durham Cathedral*, ed. P. Draper and N. Coldstream, British Archaeological Association Conference Transactions [1977], 3 (1980), 90–104 • *The itinerary of John Leland in or about the years 1535–1543*, ed. L. Toulmin Smith, 5 vols. (1906–10); repr. with introduction by T. Kendrick (1964)

Yevonde, Madame. *See* Middleton, Yevonde Philone (1893–1975).

Yewdall, John (1795–1856), poet, was born in Quarries, Leeds, on 29 September 1795, the second of the three children of John Youdel. Nothing further is known about Yewdall's parents, and little is known of his childhood; he received only three weeks' formal education. As a young man he undertook an apprenticeship in the cloth industry, but continued to educate himself, and was an active member of the Wesleyan community in Leeds. Yewdall married Sarah Newton on 3 March 1812 (nothing more is known about his wife, but they had three children: James, George, and Edwin). Following a decline in the woollen industry about 1820, he obtained the post of toll-keeper at Hunslet toll bar, Leeds: this experience provided the inspiration for 'The Toll Bar'.

'The Toll Bar' comprises two cantos, is written in the style of Byron's *Don Juan*, and was included within *The Toll Bar and other Poems* (1827). Canto 1 defends the conduct of toll-keepers and gives a satirical account of the means by which persons from all social ranks attempt to avoid the payment of tolls. The remaining poems within the volume touch on a variety of subjects; there are poems in praise of the Yorkshire cloth industry, two poems in praise of economy, and several poems with Wesleyan themes. Yewdall's poetry is not of great literary significance, but the unusual subject matter and the circumstances surrounding its composition lend it interest.

Yewdall became involved in local politics during the late

1820s when, as a parochial economist, he was involved in the Leeds vestry dispute. He formed an association with Edward Baines senior, and was elected to Leeds council in 1843. During this period Yewdall also established himself as a tea merchant in Briggate, and was appointed assistant overseer for Hunslet where he continued to live. He died at his home in Glasshouse Street, Hunslet, on 30 March 1856.

The autobiographical preface to *The Toll Bar and Other Poems* gives some indication of Yewdall's personality. He seems to have been pious and determined, but also to have possessed a sharp sense of humour   SIMON J. WHITE

Sources J. Yewdall, *The toll bar and other poems* (1827) • A. Bowers, 'A study of the poetry and prose descriptive of the Yorkshire dales, 1730–1830, with special reference to materials in the Brotherton Library collections', MPhil diss., U. Leeds, 1986 • D. Fraser, ed., *A history of modern Leeds* (1980) • R. J. Morris, *Class, sect, and party: the making of the British middle class, Leeds, 1820–1850* (1990) • G. D. Lumb, ed., *The registers of the chapels of the parish of Leeds, from 1764 to 1812*, Thoresby Society, 31 (1934) • *The Thoresby miscellany*, 15 (1973) • *Leeds Mercury* (1 April 1856) • d. cert.

Wealth at death left house in Glasshouse Street, Hunslet, and contents to his wife; instructed that other property in Alfred Place, Little London within the parish of Leeds, and all other real estate, plus shares in public companies, and securities be managed by his trustees for benefit of wife, so long as she remained his widow; instructed that wife continue annual payments for son's apprenticeship, and that on her death or remarriage his estate should be divided equally among his sons: will, Borth. Inst. register of wills, ref. 241/128r

Yexley, Lionel [*formerly* James Woods] (1862–1933), naval reformer, was born James Woods, on 9 July 1862 in Martin Street, Stratford, Essex, one of two children of James Woods, journeyman bootmaker, and his wife, Mary, *née* Yexley. He was educated at the Boys British School, Stratford. On 21 June 1878 he joined the navy as a boy seaman. Over the next twelve years he served in the Persian Gulf, East Indies, and Mediterranean, rising in 1890 to petty officer second class. While still an able seaman he married on 27 December 1884 Mary Ferry (1862–1943); they had two children. With family responsibilities, he opted in 1890 to complete his twenty years for pension in the coastguard.

Woods began his journalistic career while in the coastguard, submitting anonymous articles to *Hope: The Coastguard Gazette* with complaints of service conditions. After narrowly escaping a court martial for his campaigning, he applied for early discharge in October 1897 in order to edit *The Gazette*. The following year he transformed the publication into a general lower-deck magazine and renamed it *The Bluejacket*. Writing as Lionel Yexley, his aim was to expose bad lower-deck conditions, many of them unchanged for decades. His writing, which drew on firsthand experience and information from serving men, highlighted such disabilities as the inadequacy of food rations, graft and corruption in shore depots, the lack of increase in pay since 1853, the harshness of punishment, and the absence of prospects for promotion from the lower deck. Though viewed by some as a subversive, he was not 'anti-navy' but a patriotic advocate of a more modern, democratic service.

Yexley resigned from *The Bluejacket* in 1904, and in 1905 launched his own lower-deck monthly, *The Fleet*, in order to have greater editorial control. With his most productive reforming work about to begin, he settled at 8 York Road, Ilford, and remained in the district for the rest of his life.

The Fleet's initial target was the inadequacy of victualling. Yexley's trenchant criticisms soon attracted the attention of first sea lord Admiral Sir John Fisher, who invited him to his home and was won over by his arguments. Between 1906 and 1909 Fisher presided over reforms in the feeding and clothing of sailors along lines proposed by Yexley. These entailed significant financial savings for ratings, the changes in victualling constituting arguably the biggest single improvement in the quality of lower-deck life in over half a century. Yexley's association with Fisher was now firmly established and they remained close until the latter's death.

Despite ready access to first lord of the Admiralty Reginald McKenna from 1909, the major improvements that Yexley sought in pay, punishments, and promotion were blocked by the more conservative sea lords. Not until the appointment of Winston Churchill as first lord in 1911 did the climate improve. In retirement Fisher was instrumental in bringing Churchill and Yexley together, and the subsequent close collaboration between the two yielded the most significant improvements in conditions. Meeting him for the first time in December 1911, Yexley convinced Churchill of the need for change in the interest of justice and to allay growing unrest among ratings. Prodded by Yexley, Churchill introduced in 1912 far-reaching improvements in the disciplinary code, promotion prospects, and pay.

Yexley was the chief witness before the 1912 Brock committee on naval punishments, whose recommendations prepared for wholesale change. *The Fleet*'s proposals for commissions for talented young petty officers provided the basis for Churchill's mate scheme. Moreover, the first substantive increase in pay in fifty-nine years announced in 1912 was also distributed on the basis of a formula that Churchill had asked Yexley to devise.

Despite his influence with Fisher and Churchill, Yexley was loathed by many in the naval establishment. When in 1914 *The Fleet* reported on lower-deck unrest in HMS *London* caused by harsh discipline, Captain Kemp brought a libel suit against Yexley. The action became a case of ward room versus lower deck, with fellow officers supporting Kemp financially and ratings in uniform appearing as defence witnesses. Yexley lost, was ordered to pay £3000 damages (though Kemp subsequently waived these), and was bankrupted.

Amid growing agitation in the Grand Fleet in 1918, Yexley worked hard to prevent a proposed link between lower-deck benefit societies and the labour movement. In September he sent a memorandum on naval grievances to the king, the cabinet, and the Board of Admiralty arguing the case for judicious concessions to calm unrest. Despite

MI5 suspicions of Yexley, shared by many in the Admiralty, the first lord took him seriously and met him to discuss his document. Then, to avert the possibility that the lower-deck societies would back the candidature of a rating as a Labour Party candidate in Portsmouth in the December general election, Yexley stood as an independent, changing his name by deed poll so as to enter the ballot under his professional name. He polled 7063 votes against the coalition candidate's 11,427. Coinciding with the declaration of the election result, Yexley also wrote an article for *The Observer* on the urgent need for a pay increase, a call supported editorially by J. L. Garvin. The following day the Admiralty announced the setting up of the Jerram committee on naval pay, whose recommendations in 1919 led to increases of 50–80 per cent. Later, in September 1931, the abrupt withdrawal of the Jerram committee pay rises caused the Invergordon mutiny.

Yexley's influence declined in the 1920s, when his health began to fail. However, by then the most pressing reforms had been achieved. For twenty years he had been the foremost champion of the naval rating, but equally a vital safety valve for the naval establishment in times of unrest. As an advocate of lower-deck reform he was unequalled. Yexley died from kidney disease at his home, 143 Cranbrook Road, Ilford, on 18 March 1933. He was buried five days later at the City of London cemetery.

ANTHONY CAREW

Sources *The Fleet* (1905–33) · *The Bluejacket* (1898–1904) · 'Libel action', *Portsmouth Evening News* (18–22 May 1914) · 'Libel action', *Portsmouth Evening News* (25 May 1914) · H. Pursey, 'From petitions to reviews: the presentation of lower deck grievances', *Brassey's Naval Annual* (1937), 97–110 · H. Pursey, 'Lower deck to quarter deck, 1818–1937', *Brassey's Naval Annual* (1938), 1–19 · *The Times* (21 March 1933) · A. Carew, *The lower deck of the Royal Navy, 1900–39* (1981) · b. cert. · d. cert. · private information (2004) · *Ilford Recorder* (30 March 1933)
Archives NMM, Pursey Collection, papers | Broadlands, Hampshire, Prince Louis of Battenberg MSS · CAC Cam., Winston Churchill MSS · CAC Cam., corresp. with Lord Fisher · CAC Cam., Reginald McKenna MSS · NL Scot., Fisher MSS
Likenesses photograph, repro. in Carew, *Lower deck*
Wealth at death £284 10s.: probate, 6 June 1933, CGPLA Eng. & Wales

Y Ferch o Gefn Ydfa. *See* Maddocks, Ann (*bap.* 1704, *d.* 1727).

Yharom, Cecily (*d.* 1396). *See under* Women in trade and industry in York (*act. c.*1300–*c.*1500).

Ympyn, Jan (*c.*1485–1540), merchant and author of a text on double entry accounting, was born in the Low Countries (but not in Antwerp), the son of Christoffel Ympens, a merchant. He was sent to Italy to work and to learn commercial practices, spending twelve years there, mostly in Venice where he studied and practised double entry. He also travelled in Spain and Portugal. There is no record that he ever visited England. In 1519 he returned to the Low Countries, settling in Antwerp, of which he became a citizen and a member of the Mercers' Guild. He prospered as a retailer and wholesaler, importer, and exporter, of silks, woollens, and tapestries, and owned several properties. About 1525 he married Anna Swinters; there were

three children. He died in Antwerp in 1540, between 12 August and October.

Ympyn is remembered today for his posthumous treatise on double entry accounting, *Nieuwe instructie ende bewijs der looffelijcker consten des rekenboecks* (Antwerp, 1543), which was translated into French as *Nouvelle instruction et remonstration de la tresexcellente science du livre de compte* (Antwerp, 1543), and into English as *A notable and very excellente woorke, expressyng and declaryng the maner and forme how to kepe a boke of accomptes or reconynges* (London, 1547). The Dutch and French versions, which were published under the supervision of his widow, are the earliest texts on accounting in their respective languages. The English version of Ympyn, almost certainly printed by Richard Grafton, is the oldest extant text on accounting in English. Its title-page states that it has been translated 'with greate Diligence out of the Italian toung into Dutche, and out of Dutche, into French and now out of French into Englishe'. The text of Ympyn's book is in many places close to that of the first published exposition of double entry, in Luca Pacioli's *Summa di arithmetica* (1494), but is a substantial improvement on it, with rearrangements, additions, and omissions. Unlike Pacioli's text an illustrative set of account books, probably based on Ympyn's own business, is appended, although this is missing in the only known surviving copy of the English version (held in the Lenin Library, Moscow).

The title-page of the journal (account book) of Sir Thomas Gresham, begun on 26 April 1546, follows very closely the title-page of the illustrative journal of the French version of Ympyn. This strongly suggests that Gresham, who was resident in Brussels in 1543, was familiar with Ympyn's book. It has been further suggested that it was he who translated it from French into English, but this has not been proved. More certainly, Ympyn influenced James Peele's *The Maner and Fourme how to Kepe a Perfect Reconyng*, printed by Grafton in 1553, and the chapter on merchant's accounts in Gerard Malynes's *Lex Mercatoria* (1622). Peele's book in its turn was an influence on John Mellis's *A Briefe Instruction* (1588) which is mainly a revision of Hugh Oldcastle's *Profitable Treatyce* of 1543. It is because Oldcastle's book survives only through Mellis that the English translation of Ympyn is the oldest extant text in English on double entry.

R. H. PARKER

Sources O. Kojima and B. S. Yamey, eds., *A notable and very excellente woorke* (1975) · R. de Roover, 'Something new about Jan Ympyn Christoffels', *The Accountant* (13 Nov 1937), 657–8 · P. Kats, 'The *Nouvelle instruction* of Jehan Ympyn Christophle', *The Accountant* (20–27 Aug 1927), 261–9, 287–96 · R. de Roover, *Jan Ympyn: essai historique sur le premier traité flamand de comptabilité* (1928) · E. Stevelinck, 'Qui peut avoir traduit en anglais le premier livre de comptabilité paru en français?', *De Gulden Passer*, 70 (1992), 69–85

Yockney, Samuel Hansard (1813–1893), civil engineer, was born in St Martin's Lane, London, on 12 October 1813, the eldest son in the family of three sons and two daughters of Samuel Foyster Yockney, West India merchant, and his wife, Laetitia. He was educated at Mill Hill School under Dr Thorowgood and was not intended for any profession until family losses made it necessary. At the age of twenty-four he began an apprenticeship with Stothert & Co. of Bath, civil engineering contractors.

Soon afterwards, in 1838, Yockney was appointed engineer and manager on the construction of the Box Tunnel on the Great Western Railway (GWR). He acquitted himself so well that he attracted the favourable notice of Isambard K. Brunel, so that on the completion of the tunnel he joined the engineering staff of the GWR. He was first put in charge of the tunnels and other works between Bristol and Bath, as well as being responsible for the manufacture of coke at the company's Bristol works, where he initiated several important improvements.

Yockney moved in 1846 to south Wales, where he was involved in the construction of the Newport Tunnel and the Usk and Chepstow viaducts, on the railway line from Newport to Chepstow. On the completion of this he was placed in charge in 1851–2 of the heavy engineering works on the Oxford and Wolverhampton line, including high timber viaducts and the Dudley Tunnel. In late 1853 he moved to Paris, where he was engaged on bridges and embankments of the Seine, and on railways in and around the city. He then surveyed for a French company a number of railway lines in Italy and Switzerland before returning to England, where he worked on the Birmingham, Wolverhampton, and Dudley Railway and the Kennet and Avon and Stourbridge canals.

In 1858–9 Yockney was in the service of the Admiralty, before returning to south Wales, where for ten years he was engineer-in-chief and general manager of the Sirhowy tramroad, which he converted into a standard railway. During this time he introduced cast-iron brake blocks of the type which later came into general use. In 1868 he moved back to London, where he set up in practice at 46 Queen Anne's Gate as a consulting civil engineer, in association with his son Sydney William Yockney. Together they designed and supervised a large number of contracts, including the Wye Valley Railway, the Guernsey tramway, the Cardiff and Penarth tramway, the East Worcestershire waterworks, and Totland Bay pier, as well as acting as engineers to the West Bromwich sanitary commissioners. Yockney became a member of the Institution of Civil Engineers in 1860, and was also a fellow of the Geological Society (1865).

Yockney married Frances Emily, daughter of Captain Edward Holmes RN; she predeceased him. He died of diabetes at his son's home, Wye Cottage, Tidenham, Gloucestershire, on 29 December 1893.

RONALD M. BIRSE, *rev.*

Sources PICE, 116 (1893–4), 372–4 · IGI · CGPLA Eng. & Wales (1894) · d. cert.

Wealth at death £260 2s. 5d.: probate, 28 Dec 1894, CGPLA Eng. & Wales

Yolland, William (1810–1885), army officer and railway inspector, youngest surviving son of John Yolland, agent to the first earl of Morley, and his wife, Priscilla, was born at Merryfield, Plympton St Mary, Devon, on 17 March 1810. Educated at Trueman's mathematical school at Exeter, and by a Mr George Harvey of Plymouth, he passed

through the Royal Military Academy at Woolwich, and received a commission as second lieutenant in the Royal Engineers on 12 April 1828. His further commissions were dated: lieutenant, 4 September 1833; second captain, 19 December 1843; first captain, 1 March 1847; brevet major, 20 June 1854; lieutenant-colonel, 13 January 1855; brevet colonel, 13 January 1858.

After the usual course of professional instruction at Chatham and a short service at Woolwich, Yolland embarked for Canada on 2 August 1831, returning to England in October 1835. He then served at various home stations until his appointment to the Ordnance Survey in May 1838. For the next fifteen years he was employed at the Tower of London, Southampton, Dublin, and Enniskillen, superintending the publication of astronomical observations for the Board of Ordnance and on active survey work, including taking observations from the top of the cross of St Paul's Cathedral. He was also responsible for most of the 6 inch maps of Lancashire and Yorkshire then in course of publication. When the map-room of the Ordnance Survey office in the Tower of London was burnt down in 1841, Yolland moved with the headquarters to Southampton, where he was executive officer and did much valuable work under General Thomas Frederick Colby. He was an associate juror of the Great Exhibition of 1851, class eight. On his leaving Southampton for Ireland in November 1852 the mayor and corporation presented Yolland with an address in acknowledgement of the interest he had taken in the welfare of the town. His pamphlet on geodesy (1852) was used in teaching at Woolwich, and he published several works on surveying.

In July 1854 Yolland was appointed an inspector of railways under the Board of Trade. In January 1856 he was, in addition, a member of the commission appointed to consider the training of candidates for the scientific corps of the army in view of the abolition of patronage and the substitution of open competition. With his colleagues William Charles Lake and Lieutenant-Colonel William James Smythe of the Royal Artillery, he visited the principal continental countries to examine various possible systems. Yolland strongly advocated the continuance of the system of educating the candidates for the Royal Artillery and Royal Engineers together at Woolwich, while Smythe preferred that the education should be separate and distinct. Lake agreed with Yolland, and the combined system was recommended.

In 1862 Yolland was a juror of the International Exhibition in London. He retired from the military service on 2 October 1863, retaining his appointment at the Board of Trade. In 1874 he held for a few months the position of superintending engineer of the Ramsgate harbour works. On the retirement in 1877 of Sir Henry Tyler, Yolland became chief inspector of railways, holding the post until his death. It was due to him that the Metropolitan Railway was required to submerge its line between Bishop's Road and Westbourne Park stations under the Great Western main lines near Royal Oak station, instead of crossing them on the level, as they had done for some years. This was a great improvement as regards both safety and convenience, though it was strongly opposed by the Metropolitan Railway Company.

In 1880 Yolland was appointed a member of the commission which inquired into the Tay Bridge disaster of 28 December 1879, and settled the question of the amount of wind pressure which railway structures should be able to withstand. His colleagues were William Henry Barlow, president of the Institution of Civil Engineers, and Henry Cadogan Rothery, wreck commissioner. In 1881 he was made a companion in the Order of the Bath, civil division, in recognition of his services as a railway commissioner.

Yolland was elected a fellow of the Royal Astronomical Society in 1840, of the Royal Society in 1859, and a member of the Society of Arts in 1860. He belonged to other learned bodies at home and abroad. He was for many years a director of the London and St Katherine's Dock Company. His London residence was at 14 St Stephen's Square. Yolland married at Southampton, on 18 July 1843, Ellen Catherine (d. 6 Nov 1864), youngest daughter of Captain Peter Rainier, RN, aide-de-camp to William IV, and grandniece of Admiral Peter Rainier; they had five daughters and a son, William, major in the Royal Engineers. Yolland died at Baddesley vicarage, Atherstone, Warwickshire, where he was temporarily residing, on 5 September 1885, and was buried at Kensal Green cemetery on 8 September.   R. H. VETCH, rev. H. C. G. MATTHEW

Sources Army List · Hart's Army List · The Times (7 Sept 1885) · Monthly Notices of the Royal Astronomical Society, 46 (1885–6) · Bayswater Chronicle (Sept 1885) · Men of the time (1884)
Likenesses Black, engraving (after photograph by Maule), RS
Wealth at death £10,702 0s. 11d.: probate, 17 Nov 1885, CGPLA Eng. & Wales

Yong, Bartholomew (bap. 1560, d. 1612), translator, was baptized on 24 August 1560 at St Peter, Cornhill, London, the son of the Gregory (not George, as in some records) Yong (d. 1610) from Bedale, Yorkshire, a grocer, and his first wife, Margaret (d. 1563). He had three younger sisters, three half-brothers and three half-sisters. The family was Roman Catholic but conformed outwardly to the Elizabethan religious settlement. Bartholomew is first heard of going to Spain in 1578 with Richard Parker, the son of his father's second wife, Susan, and her first husband. Their return to England through France in May 1580 was reported to Walsingham by the ambassador to France, Sir Henry Cobham, who wrote that Bartholomew had 'had conference with the Duchess of Feria, being recommended by a privy token from his uncle' (Cooper, Ath. Cantab., 1.428). The authorities had ample reason to be suspicious: the uncle was Dr John *Young (1514–1581/2), a noted recusant, and the duchess was Jane Dormer, who worked tirelessly for the reversal of the Reformation in Britain. But Yong and Parker were not apprehended on their return.

Yong then entered the New Inn, London, and won a reputation for skill in French and Spanish by taking part in the plays staged there. He was admitted to the Middle Temple on 19 May 1582. There he became a close friend of Edward Banister, a well-known recusant and patron of the

arts, who later mentioned him in his will. Banister urged him to translate Jorge de Montemayor's pastoral, Diana, which had already been influential in its original Spanish. This he did in 1582–3, adding the continuations by Alonzo Perez and Gaspar del Polo. It is a competent and lively version, despite some clumsiness in the prose. His next translation was The Civile Conversation of M. Stephen Guazzo (1586), an influential manual for the educated person who sought to learn Italian manners and social skills. Yong's English version of Guazzo ranks in importance with The Courtyer and Galateo. It is supposed to have provided models for conversations in Shakespeare's Twelfth Night (Harrison, 135). Encouraged by the success of Diana, in 1587 Yong translated Boccaccio's warning on the dangers of unwisely falling in love, as Amorous Fiametta.

Yong lived in Shire Lane in Temple Bar, a street which disappeared in the mid-nineteenth century to make way for the new law courts. Because of his carelessness with money his father paid him much more 'then I have given or bestowed amongst all the rest of my children' (Harrison, 136) and left him out of the deeds of 1595 and 1597 settling the succession of his property at High Ongar, Essex, and his London house. Little else is known of Yong's circumstances. He was not married, nor did he practise law, nor had he entered his father's business, but he did speculate in land. The most important of these transactions occurred on 7 April 1595, when Bartholomew made over the manor of Chivers in Ongar to Thomas Southwell, John Darcy, Anthony Ashe, and two of Banister's cousins, Robert Awdeley and John Drury. The deed, probably a mortgage designed to raise money, could be voided by the payment of 'any peeces of golde or silver to the value of five shillings or more at or upon the Fontstone of the Temple Church' (Yong, lxiii). In 1598 Diana was finally published with a dedication dated from High Ongar to Lady Penelope Rich (Sir Philip Sidney's 'Stella'). Yong died intestate in September 1612 and was buried at St Dunstan-in-the-West, London, on 28 September. The administration of his estate was granted to Alexander Holman, the third son of Yong's sister, Jane. On 30 October 1612 Holman went to the Temple Church with 5s. 6d. to reclaim Chivers according to the 1595 agreement, but nobody came to claim the fee.   L. G. KELLY

Sources B. Yong, A critical edition of Yong's translation of George of Montemayor's 'Diana', ed. J. M. Kennedy (1968) · T. P. Harrison, 'Bartholomew Yong, translator', Modern Language Review, 21 (1926), 129–39 · J. Hutchinson, ed., A catalogue of notable Middle Templars: with brief biographical notices (1902) · Cooper, Ath. Cantab., vol. 1

Yonge, Charles Duke (1812–1891), classical scholar and historian, was born at Eton College on 30 November 1812, the eldest son of the Revd Charles Yonge (1781–1830), Eton schoolmaster, and Elizabeth (d. 1868), daughter of Joseph Lord of Pembroke; his parents had married on 4 December 1810. Yonge's father's family were Devon gentry with a seat at Puslinch, near Coombe, and their most famous ancestor was James Yonge FRS (1647–1721), the naval surgeon and medical writer. In 1746 the Revd John Yonge, his great-grandfather, had married Elizabeth Duke, a coheir to property at Otterton in Devon. Yonge was educated at

Eton College (c.1823–c.1829) and entered King's College, Cambridge, on 24 February 1831. He left the college exactly three years later, following the rejection of his case for a fellowship, and was admitted to St Mary's Hall, Oxford, on 17 May 1834. There he acquired a cricket blue and graduated BA with a first-class honours in classics in December 1835; he proceeded MA in 1874.

Until 1866, when he was appointed by the crown to the chair of English literature and history at Queen's College, Belfast, Yonge lived principally in London and worked as a private tutor and a writer. On 15 August 1837 he married Anne, daughter of J. V. Bethell of Hereford, but little is known about his personal circumstances other than that the marriage was childless, and that he was a close friend of an influential kinsman, Sir John Taylor Coleridge, the editor of Blackstone's *Commentaries* and a justice of the king's bench 1835–58. However, by the time of his appointment at Queen's, Yonge had established a reputation as a prolific classicist and historian. Between 1842 and 1855 he translated eight classical works that were published in Bohn's series of antiquarian, classical, and ecclesiastical texts and was the author of a profusion of exercises in Greek and Latin composition. The first of his principal historical works, *A History of England from the Earliest Times to the Peace of Paris*, was published in 1857 and merited a further edition in 1871. Five other major works appeared in the next ten years: *Parallel lives of ancient and modern heroes, of Epaminondas and Gustavus Adolphus, Philip of Macedon and Frederick the Great* (1858); *Life of Field Marshall, the Duke of Wellington* (2 vols., 1860), which was reissued as a single volume in 1891; *A History of the British Navy from the Earliest Period to the Present Time* (1863); an edited and revised version of *Taylor's Students' Manual of Modern History* (1866); and *History of France under the Bourbons* (1866). By the time he was appointed to Queen's he was already at work on the three-volume *Life and Administration of Robert Banks, Second Earl of Liverpool*, which was published in 1868.

Yonge's professorial duties did not lead to any significant decline in the quantity of publication. His teaching consisted principally of ten lectures each week in the first and second terms—usually six in English language and literature and the rest in history. Four notebooks of his lectures survive—one each for English language, English literature, English (and some Irish) history, and French history—and these suggest that he relied upon his first texts for the remainder of his career. He also supervised essays, one of the first that he set being entitled 'The usefulness or mischief of ambition'. Although he became one of the inner circle of professors who advised the president of the college and at one stage had pretensions to become president himself, there is no evidence that administrative ambitions on his own behalf ever detracted significantly from his teaching and writing. With an average income of about £420, he and his wife lived comfortably—at one stage in Notting Hill in the leafy suburb to the south of the college—and he continued to publish. Some of his works, such as his edition of Goldsmith's essays (1882), probably grew out of his teaching of English but the majority were historical. Apart from the life of Lord Liverpool, the most

important were a history of the English revolution of 1688 (1874), a two-volume life of Marie Antoinette (1876), which merited two further editions; and *The Constitutional History of England from 1760 to 1860* (1881), which was designed as a continuation of Hallam's *History*. It is a mark of Yonge's dedication as a scholar that he continued as professor and author until his death at his home, 12 Elmwood Avenue, Belfast, on 30 November 1891, the day of his seventy-ninth birthday. His two-volume edition of Horace Walpole's letters had been published the year before; and two further works—one on military commanders and another on Dryden—appeared in 1892. This brought his total number of separate publications to fifty. He was buried in Drumbeg churchyard, near Belfast.

Yonge probably had more lasting influence as a classicist than as either a literary or political historian. His translations and exercises appear to have been widely used in universities and schools. But his histories, although some sold well, had little impact on the historical profession. One reason for this is that his principal concern—to explore the origins and evolution of Britain's liberal constitution and her status as a great power—became increasingly outmoded. He began his enquiries along these lines in the *History of England* and most of his subsequent work was devoted to assessing the contributions of different 'commanders, or legislators, or statesmen'. In the case of politicians, for example, his thesis for the period after 1760 is that most of the leading figures had made a contribution to the evolution of a liberal constitution as a result of 'honest and patriotic' motives inspired by their education, an argument which he developed in his studies of Wellington and Liverpool. However, his books were published at a time when a younger generation of historians such as Leckey, Froude, Stubbs, and Freeman were subjecting the triumphalism of 'whig history' such as Yonge's to searching scrutiny. His work therefore received little notice from his peers in the periodicals and journals, and it is significant that he was not elected a fellow of the Royal Historical Society.

Another reason for the neglect of Yonge's historical works is that there was nothing exceptional in his research methods or his style of writing. He relied primarily on printed sources and wrote with a measured elegance that has the effect of draining the life from a subject. Although few of his books received detailed reviews, one of his life of Lord Liverpool which appeared in the *Quarterly Review* (1869) concludes with an assessment that might be applied fairly to all of his work:

> His style is not very lively; his research is not very deep; nor does he convey the impression that when undertaking the life of Lord Liverpool he could not with equal readiness have undertaken the life of Confucius. But he deserves praise for the simplicity of his language, the directness of his method, and the moderation of his opinions. (*QR*, 206)

P. J. JUPP

Sources T. W. Moody and J. C. Beckett, *Queen's, Belfast, 1845–1949: the history of a university*, 2 vols. (1959) • review, *QR*, 126 (1869), 171–206 • *DNB* • Burke, *Gen. GB* (1937) • *The Times* (2 Dec 1891) • *IGI* • *CGPLA NIre.* (1892)

Archives Queen's University, Belfast | NL Scot., letters to Black-woods
Wealth at death £232 7s. 8d.: probate, 14 March 1892, *CGPLA Eng. & Wales*

Yonge, Charlotte Mary (1823–1901), novelist, was born at Otterbourne House, near Winchester, Hampshire, on 11 August 1823, the only daughter and eldest child of William Crawley Yonge (1795–1854), magistrate, and Frances Mary Bargus (1795–1868). Both parents were from clerical families. William's marriage was conditional upon his renouncing his career as a soldier and the Devonshire attachments of his upbringing to tend the Otterbourne estate bought by Frances's mother in 1819. Charlotte was educated at home, initially by her mother, 'on the Edgeworth system'. Her father taught her classics and mathematics, and she helped to educate her brother, Julian (1830–1892). A visiting tutor instructed her in French and Spanish, but music and art were neglected. Her father's belief in higher education for women accompanied by his conviction that their talents should be employed only under the guidance of a mature Christian male authority shaped his daughter's thinking: she remained emotionally dependent upon his approval. At the age of seven she was encouraged to teach in the village Sunday school her father had started, and taught both morning and afternoon sessions until a fortnight before her death. Less formal contacts with the villagers were not encouraged.

This cloistered upbringing developed Charlotte's deep veneration and imaginative yearning for the more extended family life she glimpsed during annual visits to 'cousinland', the network of Devon relatives. The imaginary life created for her family of sixteen dolls soon took written form in the *Château de Melville* (1838), begun two years earlier as a French exercise and sold at a bazaar for the benefit of the village school: her favourite form, the family saga, could be seen in embryo here, its characters surviving and developing to reappear in subsequent novels. The successive generations of her fictional heroes and heroines are constantly evaluated by their capacity to practise the Christian values of self-sacrificial love, obedience, humility, and submission within the demanding confines of domestic relationships.

The conservatism and respect for authority learned in Charlotte's earliest years, received a boost from the induction of John Keble to the adjacent living of Hursley in 1836. Although perceived as one of the leaders of the new Tractarian party, Keble had renounced academic life in Oxford for the pastoral concerns of a country living, and represented his part in the campaign for the recognition of the spiritual authority of the Church of England as merely a continuation of his own father's teaching of the high-church tradition. *Pro ecclesia Dei* became Charlotte's motto. Keble prepared Charlotte for her confirmation in 1838, the formative experience of her spiritual life (*Musings*, 1871, iii), as her novel *The Castle Builders, or, The Deferred Confirmation* (1854), amply demonstrates. Keble, who distrusted all manifestations of self-aggrandizing cleverness or personal charisma, found an ideal pupil in the intensely reserved but precociously gifted Charlotte. The

Charlotte Mary Yonge (1823–1901), by George Richmond, 1844

Kebles also introduced her to music and drawing. Keble became both her spiritual confessor and a rigorous editor of her manuscripts. His emphasis on reserve in communicating religious knowledge was to help her avoid the crude polemics of much contemporary religious fiction and his encouragement of her writing, as an instrument to be used in God's service, legitimated the creativity of a woman whose instincts and training might otherwise have led to its suppression. The complex tensions between temperament, conscience, and authority fed into the scrupulously moral agonizing that characterizes her fiction and can also be seen in her decision to discourage any biography in her own lifetime, on the grounds that 'her mother would not have liked such a thing to be done', while leaving Christabel Coleridge with the impression that she was being fed the information necessary to enlarge a truncated autobiography into a posthumous memoir (Coleridge, viii).

Shortly after Keble's arrival, Charlotte Yonge's father embarked upon a programme of church building: St Matthew's, Otterbourne, was consecrated in 1839, a sister church at Ampfield provided in 1841, and Keble's church at Hursley replaced in 1847. The building and consecration of a new village church provided the theme for her first published novel, *Abbeychurch, or, Self Control and Self Conceit* (1844).

The family council which had acknowledged the propriety of Charlotte Yonge publishing this work simultaneously decreed that any profit should be donated to charity. She had already become an inveterate writer, recording daily incidents and discussing her work in progress with her correspondents. One friend, Marianne Dyson, twenty years her senior, elicited much of Charlotte's first educational writing for her village girls' school at Dogmersfield, near Winchester. Charlotte's contributions to Ann Mozley's *Magazine for the Young*, launched in 1842, were also directed at readers from the lower classes. The *Monthly Packet*, with Charlotte as its first editor and controlling influence, was aimed at wealthier private schoolrooms: over the years the younger relatives and friends, such as the young Mary Arnold (Mrs Humphry Ward), whose writing for privately circulated magazines she had encouraged, were invited to become contributors.

An unpublished story by Marianne Dyson provided the germ for Charlotte Yonge's greatest success: *The Heir of Redclyffe* (1853). During the tale's gestation it was discussed at length with her mother and friends and had its style honed by her father. J. W. Parker published the novel after its initial rejection by John Murray (who did not publish fiction). The work embodied Tractarian teaching through demonstrating the gradual success of religious discipline in transforming Guy Morville, a Byronic youth, into a saintly, domesticated, self-sacrificing hero. The young Pre-Raphaelites William Morris and Dante Gabriel Rossetti were inspired by this modern interpretation of knightly endeavour and Charlotte's brother Julian, who had joined the rifle brigade in 1852, found 'nearly all the young men in his regiment had a copy'. The profits were donated to Bishop Selwyn of New Zealand to finance the *Southern Cross*, a new missionary schooner, for the Melanesian Islands. Ethel May, of *The Daisy Chain* (1856), and its sequel, *The Trial* (1864), offered a pattern for middle-class Christian girls: she has to renounce her masculine intellectual aspirations and learn to channel her energies into the more appropriate feminine roles of home-maker, and educator of the poor. Charlotte's thinking on gender was based on theological conviction: 'I have no hesitation in declaring my full belief in the inferiority of women, nor that she brought it upon herself' (*Womankind*, 1877, 1–2). £2000 of the profits from *The Daisy Chain* went to the building of St Andrews College, Kohimarama.

Julian Yonge, whose army career had been cut short by ill health, brought a wife, some ten years his junior, home to Otterbourne in 1858. By 1862 his family had expanded, so Charlotte and her mother moved to a neighbouring house, Elderfield. This period also witnessed new developments in her writing: *The Dove in the Eagle's Nest* (1866), a novel set in medieval Europe, was accompanied by other historical studies such as *The Book of Golden Deeds* (1864), *Biographies of Good Women* (1865), and her most intensively researched book: *The History of Christian Names* (1863).

In the aftermath of her mother's distressing death from 'softening of the brain' Charlotte Yonge became an exterior sister of the Anglican educational order at Wantage, Berkshire, founded by the Revd William Butler, a former curate of Dogmersfield. Apart from a brief trip to Dublin in 1857, she had travelled very little, but in 1869 she went to Paris with her brother and his wife, and visited her translator, Mme de Witt, whose family lived with her father, the former prime minister Guizot, in Normandy. With her parents and Keble dead, and upon the retirement of Keble's long-serving curate, Charlotte had suddenly to confront a new authority in the village when a married clergyman, representing more recent Tractarian thinking, was appointed. These factors conspired to render *The Pillars of the House* (4 vols., 1873), the most concentrated expression of her own views: following the varied fortunes of the thirteen children of the Revd Edward Underwood, it also discusses such topical religious questions as the importance of fasting and confession.

Charlotte Yonge's interest in Tractarian missionary work made her the appropriate biographer when her cousin, John Coleridge Patteson, bishop of Melanesia, was murdered by South Sea islanders (*Life of John Coleridge Patteson*, 2 vols., 1874). Missions in South Africa also interested her: she devoted the profits of a novel, *New Ground* (1868), to the Mackenzie mission set up to commemorate Charles Mackenzie, a Keble protégé, who died in the course of his proselytizing work as bishop of central Africa. The *Monthly Packet* was used to broadcast the needs of the missionary effort abroad and her novels broke an earlier literary mould by presenting missionaries as gentlemanly Christian heroes. The attitude her characters display to the work of the mission field is a further gauge of their virtue. In old age she extended her interests to the Far East and *The Making of a Missionary* (1900) employed the Boxer uprising to produce its climax. In September 1873 her brother's youngest sister-in-law, Gertrude Walter, a chronic rheumatic, moved from the big house to Elderfield, to become 'Char's wife', or secretary-companion, until Gertrude's death in 1897 (Coleridge, 270). This tie, combined with Charlotte's heart condition, further restricted her travel and range of visitors.

Charlotte Yonge was planning a substantial endowment for St Matthew's, Otterbourne, separated from the parish of Hursley in 1875, when, in 1876, a coal-mining speculation of her brother's failed and she was required to bail him out. When writing had been her vocation she had abstained from writing fiction during Lent: now it became her profession. Despite the sale of her early copyrights, Julian was forced to sell the family estate in 1885 and move to London, but a niece remained as wife of Henry Bowles, who was to become the new incumbent of Otterbourne in 1890. The year 1885 also saw the death of her close friend Bishop George Moberly, whose family she had known since 1835, when he came to Winchester College as headmaster. By the end of the decade she was persuaded to accept Christabel Coleridge as co-editor of the *Monthly Packet*: this did not prevent its publisher, A. D. Innes, from requesting her resignation in 1893, thus lending a bittersweet flavour to the seventieth birthday celebration the magazine's readers had planned for her. She devoted their gift of £200 to a lich-gate for Otterbourne church. A further collection in 1899, the year in which the *Monthly*

Packet folded, enabled her to found a scholarship at Winchester high school to send girls to Oxford or Cambridge.

Always adept at keeping several projects running concurrently, Charlotte Yonge wrote over 200 works of fiction and non-fiction, in addition to articles for her own and other magazines, making her the Tractarian movement's most important lay voice as well as its most comprehensive chronicler. She died of pleurisy, after a short illness, at Elderfield on 24 March 1901, and was buried on the 29th at the foot of John Keble's memorial cross in Otterbourne churchyard.   ELISABETH JAY

Sources C. Coleridge, *Charlotte Mary Yonge: her life and letters* (1903) • E. Romanes, *Charlotte Mary Yonge: an appreciation* (1908) • B. Dennis, *Charlotte Yonge (1823–1901): novelist of the Oxford Movement* (1992) • J. Sturrock, *'Heaven and home': Charlotte Mary Yonge's domestic fiction and the Victorian debate over women* (1995) • G. C. Moore Smith, *The life of John Colborne, Field-Marshal Lord Seaton* (1903) • d. cert.
Archives Bodl. Oxf., letters • Girton Cam., corresp. • Hunt. L., letters • NRA, corresp. and literary papers • Plymouth and West Devon RO, Plymouth, family corresp. • Princeton University Library, New Jersey, letters and literary MSS | BL, corresp. with Macmillans, Add. MSS 54920–54921 • Bodl. Oxf., letters to J. F. W. Bullock • Bodl. Oxf., letters to John Frewen and Charles Moor • Bodl. Oxf., letters to C. K. Shorter • Hants. RO, letters to Anne Sturges Bourne; notebook • Hants. RO, letters to Helena, Caroline, and Beatrice Heathcote • JRL, letters to Edward Freeman
Likenesses G. Richmond, watercolour and chalk drawing, 1844, NPG [*see illus.*] • three photographs, before 1854, repro. in M. Mare and A. C. Percival, *Victorian best-seller: the world of Charlotte M. Yonge* (1947), facing pp. 48 and 193 • L. Carroll [C. L. Dodgson], two photographs, 1866, U. Texas, Gernsheim collection • photograph, *c.*1872, repro. in G. Battiscombe, *Charlotte Mary Yonge: the story of an uneventful life* (1943), facing p. 144 • Walker & Cockerell, photogravure (after A. Bramston), NPG • D. Yonge, photograph (age thirty-five), repro. in Coleridge, *Charlotte Mary Yonge*, frontispiece • photograph (at about thirty), repro. in Dennis, *Charlotte Yonge* • photograph, NPG • photographs, repro. in Coleridge, *Charlotte Mary Yonge*, facing pp. 204 and 280 • photographs (in old age), repro. in Romanes, *Charlotte Mary Yonge*, facing pp. 140 and 172
Wealth at death £12,913 11s. 3d.: probate, 7 June 1901, CGPLA Eng. & Wales

Yonge, Sir George, **fifth baronet** (1732–1812), politician and colonial governor, was the only surviving son of Sir William *Yonge, fourth baronet (*c.*1693–1755), of Colyton, Devon, secretary at war from 1735 to 1746, and his second wife, Anne Howard, the daughter and coheir of Thomas Howard, sixth Baron Howard of Effingham. He attended Eton College between 1742 and 1745 and the University of Leipzig from 1750 to 1752. After a brief period as secretary of the embassy at Turin in 1753, he was returned to parliament the following year as member for Honiton, which he represented continuously (except from 1761 to 1763) in successive parliaments until 1796. The Yonge family interest in Honiton was not strong enough to prevent a series of expensive contested elections in which Yonge is said to have spent enormous sums. An attempt to establish a woollen factory at Ottery St Mary reportedly also drained his finances. On 10 July 1765 he married Elizabeth (*d.* 1833), the daughter and heir of Bourchier *Cleeve (*d.* 1760), of Foot's Cray, Kent, a wealthy London pewterer.

Yonge described himself as a friend of the Grenville ministry, but in 1764 he voted against the government on general warrants and voted and spoke in favour of the repeal of the cider tax, to which he led opposition in Devon. The old corps whigs saw him as a possible friend, and although he attended the Cockpit meeting of government supporters on 9 January 1765 he was regarded favourably by the Rockingham administration. He was given office in September 1766 under the Chatham ministry as a lord of the Admiralty, and resigned from Grafton's administration in January 1770 'for the honour of Lord Chatham' (Brooke, 674). In opposition he was a prominent speaker against North's American policy, although the content of his speeches was never extraordinary. He returned to office with Rockingham in April 1782 as vice-treasurer for Ireland. Despite his doubts over Yonge's competence, Shelburne made him secretary at war in July 1782; he left office with Shelburne in April 1783 but returned to the same post under William Pitt the younger in December 1783. He remained loyal to Pitt, who nominated him KB in 1788.

In July 1794, to make room for William Windham, who had joined the administration with the Portland whigs, Yonge was moved to the mastership of the Royal Mint, on the ground that its income was equivalent to that which he had enjoyed as secretary at war. He was troubled by the possibility that this office excluded him from the Commons as a government contractor, and did not stand at the 1796 election. Yonge was now facing severe financial problems; he claimed that his income had fallen well below the £3000 he had expected as master of the mint, and he may have been living in a debtors' sanctuary at Holyrood in Edinburgh when he was offered the post of governor of the Cape in succession to George Macartney, Earl Macartney, at a salary of £4000 a year. He was refused a peerage but was returned to parliament for Old Sarum as a client of the prime minister's cousin Thomas Pitt, second Baron Camelford, to avoid prosecution for debt.

Yonge was a man of long official experience when he arrived at Cape Town on 9 December 1799, but it was an experience that had no special bearing on his new task; his motives for taking the post were not of the highest, and he was probably too old to fall readily into new lines of thought and conduct. He has been described as 'decidedly the most incompetent man who has ever been at the head of affairs in the colony, though he possessed an amazing amount of self-assurance and pertinacity' (Theal, 62) and as 'corrupt to an extent shocking even to a society well-accustomed to corruption and so gross as to procure his recall within months' (Welsh, 98). His government was incompetent. He quarrelled with General Francis Dundas, the officer in command of the troops, whose authority he attempted to usurp. He also offended the Dutch community by increased taxes—contrary, it was alleged, to the settlement following Britain's annexation of the colony—and left the administration of affairs almost entirely in the hands of Mr Blake, his private secretary, and Lieutenant-Colonel Cockburn, his principal aide-de-camp, whose influence and support were believed to be marketable commodities. Yonge was criticized for inattention to the Cape's role in protecting British interests in India; Richard, Marquess Wellesley, governor-general of India, wrote to the secretary of state for war, Henry Dundas, objecting that Yonge was more interested in 'founding theatres and masquerade rooms' (Symonds and Fisher, 665). On 12 October 1800 Dundas told George III that Yonge's conduct at the Cape:

> has in such a variety of particulars been so wild and extravagant as to render it impossible to continue him in that Government without exposing this country to the imputation of being indifferent to the concerns of that most important settlement. (*Later Correspondence of George III*, 3.428)

In January 1801 Dundas ordered Yonge home and appointed Francis Dundas acting governor. Yonge wished that the supersession should take place after a short delay, giving him time to wind up affairs; but whether in consequence of private instructions from his uncle, or from personal ill feeling, Francis Dundas insisted on the immediate transfer of authority. Yonge then applied to the commander-in-chief at the Cape, Vice-Admiral Sir Roger Curtis, for a ship of war to take him to St Helena, but this was refused; and Yonge was left, waiting at a hotel, until he could find a passage. He did not arrive in England until towards the end of the year. Meanwhile, in February 1801, he was replaced as MP for Old Sarum.

The new secretary of state for war in the Addington administration, Robert, Lord Hobart, wrote to Francis Dundas requesting a report on various abuses said to have taken place under Yonge's government. Dundas appointed a commission at Cape Town, which, after hearing evidence, charged Blake and Cockburn with many gross malpractices and Yonge with being more or less cognisant of them. Among numerous scandalous abuses were the creation of new and unnecessary civil and military offices from which Blake and Cockburn drew salaries; the imposition of monopolies in the supply of timber and other trades from which a share of the profit was drawn; and private trading in slaves and personal aggrandizement in the awarding of government contracts, agreed without the knowledge of the Colonial Office. Cockburn denied the charge, and neither he nor Blake was tried. If anything was officially done or said to Yonge, it did not abash him. In July 1802 he was received by George III at Weymouth. It was very likely this friendship which protected him from further action, for the whole matter was allowed to drop; the return of the Cape to the Dutch by the treaty of Amiens in 1802 was probably also a factor. Yonge failed to get re-elected for Honiton that year; he was spat on and his wig was set on fire when he tried to administer the bribery oath. Again in financial straits, he wrote to Hobart, claiming payment of his expenses for the journey home, and for the passage, diet, and hotel charges at Cape Town and at St Helena, which seem to have amounted to about £1000. It does not appear these were ever paid, but he was given apartments at Hampton Court and the titular governorship of Tortola in the Virgin Islands in 1806.

Yonge died at Hampton Court on 25 September 1812. He had no children, and the baronetcy became extinct. The family estates were long sold; by 1789 the estates at Coplestone and Colyton in Devon had gone, and Yonge entertained George III and Queen Charlotte at the second family seat at Escott, but that too was sold in 1794. Yonge's widow continued to reside at Hampton Court, and died there on 7 January 1833.

J. K. LAUGHTON, rev. JONATHAN SPAIN

Sources B. Burke, *A genealogical history of the dormant, abeyant, forfeited and extinct peerages of the British empire*, new edn (1866) · G. Leveson-Gower, 'The Howards of Effingham', *Surrey Archaeological Collections*, 9 (1888), 395–436 · R. A. Austen-Leigh, ed., *The Eton College register, 1753–1790* (1921) · J. Brooke, 'Yonge, George', HoP, *Commons, 1754–90* · P. A. Symonds and D. R. Fisher, 'Yonge, Sir George', HoP, *Commons, 1790–1820* · F. Welsh, *A history of South Africa* (1998) · G. M. Theal, *History of South Africa since September 1795*, 5 vols. (1908) · *European Magazine and London Review*, 62 (1812), 330 · *GM*, 1st ser., 103/1 (1833), 92 · GEC, *Baronetage* · *The later correspondence of George III*, ed. A. Aspinall, 5 vols. (1962–70)
Archives Hunt. L., corresp., mainly as secretary at war · PRO, official corresp., 30/55 | BL, letters to General Haldimand, Add. MSS 21708, 21736 · BL, letters to third Lord Hardwicke, Add. MSS 35663–35665, *passim* · CKS, letters to William Pitt · NL Wales, corresp. with Lord Clive · NRA, priv. coll., letters to Lord Shelburne · PRO, letters to Lord Cornwallis, 30/11 · PRO, letters to William Pitt, 30/8 · RBG Kew, corresp. with Sir Joseph Banks · Wilts. & Swindon RO, corresp. with George, Lord Herbert
Likenesses E. Scott, stipple, pubd 1790 (after M. Brown), BM, NPG · P. Rajon, etching (after J. Reynolds), BM

Yonge, James (*fl.* 1405–1434), translator, belonged to an English family settled in Dublin. According to deeds belonging to the parish of St John, Dublin, his family was long associated with that parish. On 16 March 1405 James Yonge, 'clerk, notary public', certified concerning a case of unlawful imprisonment, and again on 28 November 1411, concerning dower rights to a property. On 9 August 1417 he was appointed attorney in a property transaction. From January to October 1423 he was in prison in Trim Castle, Meath. Before the end of October he was moved to Dublin Castle, and was pardoned on 10 May 1425. In the will of John Lytill (probate granted 5 November 1434) he was left 20s. apparently for acting as executor. Other members of his family also appear in the parish deeds. John Yonge, possibly a brother, is cited as 'clerk, notary public' on 12 November 1411, and William Yonge, 'citizen and butcher', on 8 August 1446.

Yonge is referred to as 'James Young, or Junius, a Notar-Publick of the City of Dublin' by Sir James Ware, who (in the English version of Ware's *De scriptoribus Hiberniae* issued by Walter Harris in 1744) credits him with writing '*Monita Politica de bono Regimine*, to James, Earl of Ormond, Lord Lieutenant of Ireland (An. 1407) and a *History of the Pilgrimage of Laurence Rathold, a knight, and Baron of Hungary, to St. Patrick's Purgatory*, An. 1411' (*Whole Works*, 1.88). Yonge seems to have been working for Ormond, who was deputy lieutenant of Ireland, in some official capacity, and *Monita politica* is to be identified with the English translation, with extensive alterations and additions, which he made in 1422 at the earl's request, of the French version of the *Secreta secretorum* (a text erroneously attributed to Aristotle). The translation, which is free, is divided into seventy-two chapters, and includes additional material (mainly comprising chapters 32 and 33) on Irish history, inserted by Yonge, which discloses and affirms his prejudice in favour of the legitimacy of English rule in Ireland. Under the title *The Governaunce of Prynces, or, Pryvete of Pryveteis*, Yonge's translation was published in 1898 by Robert Steele from Bodl. Oxf., MS Rawl. B.490, one of three extant manuscripts, the other two being LPL, MS 633, and LPL, Carew MS 633. The last of these contains the note: 'This book was written in the time of King Henry V, by John Yonge, servant to James Butler, Earl of Ormond, and dedicated to his said Lord and Master'. In a prefatory note to his edition, Steele rightly describes Yonge's translation as 'perhaps the only lengthy work written in the English of the Pale early in the fifteenth century'. Yonge is also credited with an abridged translation of the *Expugnatio Hibernica* of Gerald of Wales which precedes *The Governaunce of Prynces* in the Rawlinson manuscript.

In 1411 Yonge was commissioned to write an account, in Latin, of the experiences of Laurentius Ratholdus of Paazthó in Hungary, who made the pilgrimage to the cave in Station Island on Lough Derg, Donegal, in 1411; this was edited by Delehaye in 1908, from BL, Royal MS 10 B.ix, which constitutes a copy of Yonge's original narrative, completed in 1461 by a monk named Henry Cranebrook. In this work Yonge refers to himself as 'I James Yonge, imperial notary of the citizens, and least of the scriveners, of the city of Dublin' ('Igitur ego Jacobus Yonge notarius imperialis civium et scriptorum minimus civitatis Dublinensis'; 'Pèlerinage', 58–9; J. F. Niermeyer defines *notarius imperialis* as a 'clerk in the royal chancery'). It is possible that Ratholdus's pilgrimage was a pretext for a secret diplomatic mission. Yonge's account is based on conversations which he had had with Ratholdus, and includes material of his own, containing a description of the island, as well as documents relating to the pilgrimage issued by King Sigismund of Hungary, Nicholas Fleming, archbishop of Armagh, and Matthew, prior of St Patrick's Purgatory.   T. P. DOLAN

Sources R. Steele, ed., *Three prose versions of the 'Secreta secretorum'*, EETS, extra ser., 74 (1898), pt 1 · H. Delehaye, ed., 'Le pèlerinage de Laurent de Pasztho au purgatoire de S. Patrice', *Analecta Bollandiana*, 27 (1908), 35–60 · F. J. Furnivall, ed., *The English conquest of Ireland, A.D. 1166–1185, mainly from the 'Expugnatio Hibernica' of Giraldus Cambrensis, a parallel text from 1. MS TCD 92.31. about 1425 A.D., 2. MS Rawlinson B. 490, Bodleian library, about 1440, A.D.*, EETS, ordinary ser., 107 (1896) · St J. D. Seymour, 'James Yonge: a fifteenth century Dublin writer', *Journal of the Royal Society of Antiquaries of Ireland*, 6th ser., 16 (1926), 48–50 · J. L. Robinson, 'On the ancient deeds of the parish of St John, Dublin', *Proceedings of the Royal Irish Academy*, 33C (1916–17), 175–224 · *The whole works of Sir James Ware concerning Ireland*, ed. and trans. W. Harris, rev. edn, 2 vols. in 3 (1764) · St J. D. Seymour, *Anglo–Irish literature, 1200–1582* (1929), 31–4, 135–140 · St J. D. Seymour, *St. Patrick's Purgatory* (1918) · J. Yonge, 'The gouernaunce of prynces', in T. Dolan, *The field day anthology of Irish writing*, ed. S. Deane (1991), chap. 33, 1.162–4 · E. Mullally, 'Hiberno-Norman literature and its public', *Settlement and society in medieval Ireland*, ed. J. Bradley (1988), 327–43, esp. 331–2 · E. Tresham, ed., *Rotulorum patentium et clausorum cancellariae Hiberniae calendarium*, Irish Record Commission (1828) · J. S. Brewer and W. Bullen, eds., *Calendar of the Carew manuscripts*, 5: *1603–1623*, PRO (1871) · J. T. Gilbert, ed., *Facsimiles of national manuscripts of Ireland*, 4 vols. in 5 (1874–84), vol. 3, no. 26 · J. F. Niermeyer, *Mediae latinitatis lexicon minus* (1976)

Archives Bodl. Oxf., MS Rawl. B.490 · LPL, Carew MS 633 · LPL, MS 633

Yonge, James (1647–1721), surgeon and physician, the son of John Yonge (d. 1679), surgeon, and his wife, Joanna (1618–1700), daughter of Nicholas Blackaller of Sharpham, Devon, was born at Plymouth on 27 February 1647 and was baptized at St Andrew's 'in the Presbyterian district' of Plymouth on 11 March that year. Able to read and write, at the age of nine he was sent to the Latin school where he was educated under Mr Horsman.

On 14 February 1658 Yonge was apprenticed to Silvester Richmond, surgeon of the *Constant Warwick*. He was appointed surgeon's mate to the *Montague* in 1660 and was present at the bombardment of Algiers in 1662. On his return to England, Yonge was paid off and worked for four months as assistant to an apothecary in Wapping. When Richmond retired Yonge was bound to his father and assisted him until February 1663 when he was sent on a voyage with the *Reformation* to the cod fisheries in Newfoundland. In February 1664 he joined the *Robert Bonadventure* as surgeon, visiting west Africa and the Mediterranean. On his second voyage with the ship in December 1665 he was captured by the Dutch and was held as a prisoner of war in Amsterdam until September 1666. Yonge returned to Plymouth where he practised until February 1668, at which time he made a final trip to Newfoundland.

Yonge settled in Plymouth on his return and eventually built a successful practice. On 28 March 1671 he married Jane (d. 1708), daughter of Thomas Crampporne of Buckland Monachorum, Devon; they had three sons and five daughters. Their eldest son, John (1672–1745), was great-grandfather of Charles Duke Yonge (1812–1891). James Yonge became surgeon to the naval hospital at Plymouth and in 1674 was appointed deputy surgeon-general to the navy, 'an office which brought him no inconsiderable accession of emolument' (Munk, 3). He went on to publish papers in the *Philosophical Transactions* on a bullet in the trachea, gallstones, and on an intestinal concretion. In 1678 Yonge paid a visit to London, during which he met many of the notable figures of the day. The visit led him to write *Currus triumphalis e terebintho*, two letters on the use of turpentine to control haemorrhage. In 1682 he published *Wounds of the Brain Proved Curable*.

Yonge, who was a royalist and then a tory, became an influential citizen of Plymouth: he was elected a member of the common council for the borough in 1679, churchwarden of St Andrew's in 1682, and alderman and mayor of Plymouth in 1694. From 1685 to 1689 he was surgeon to Lord Bath's regiment of militia. Yonge made a further visit to London in 1692 after his appointment as surgeon to the new dock at Hamoaze. The trip gave him the opportunity to hear Edward Tyson lecture and to be made a member of the Company of Surgeons.

In 1702 Yonge became an extra-licentiate of the Royal

College of Physicians, although he had already been licensed to practise by the bishop of Exeter. He was elected FRS on 3 November 1702. He retired from practice the next year, although he did undertake the embalming of Sir Cloudesley Shovell's body in 1707.

Yonge's journal, detailing his professional activities and family affairs, was published in 1963. He also wrote on trade with Newfoundland and on the *Eikon basilike*. Yonge died on 25 July 1721 and was buried in St Andrew's Church, Plymouth, where a monument was erected to his memory.   IAN LYLE

Sources *The journal of James Yonge (1647–1721), Plymouth surgeon*, ed. F. N. L. Poynter (1963) · Munk, *Roll* · *DNB* · Burke, *Gen. GB* (1858) **Archives** Plymouth and West Devon RO, Plymouth, papers, incl. his 'Plymouth Memoirs' and journal · Wellcome L., notebook | BL, letters to Sir Hans Sloane, Sloane MSS 3323, 4040–4048 **Likenesses** portrait, Puslinch Manor, Yealmpton, Plymouth

Yonge, James (1792–1870), physician, born in Devon, was the fourth son of Duke Yonge (1751/2–1823), vicar of Otterton, Devon, and his wife, Catherina, daughter of Thomas Crawley-Boevey of Flaxley Abbey, Gloucestershire. He was a direct descendant of James Yonge (1647–1721), a naval surgeon and medical writer. The novelist Charlotte Mary *Yonge (1823–1901) was his niece. Yonge was briefly at Eton College in 1811, the year he matriculated from Exeter College, Oxford, whence he graduated BA on 13 May 1815, MA on 22 October 1817, BM on 8 June 1819, and DM on 20 June 1821. After leaving Oxford he studied at Edinburgh University before moving to London, where he assisted John Abernethy. He was elected a fellow of the Royal College of Physicians on 30 September 1822. Yonge moved to Plymouth in 1832 and became physician to the Plymouth Dispensary. In 1840 he went on to become physician to the Devon and East Cornwall Hospital, and he was for many years one of the most prominent physicians in the west of England. He married, in 1820, his cousin Margaret, daughter of Sir Thomas Crawley-Boevey, baronet. Yonge died at his home, The Crescent, Plymouth, on 3 January 1870.

NORMAN MOORE, rev. MICHAEL BEVAN

Sources *BMJ* (15 Jan 1870), 73 · *The Lancet* (8 Jan 1870), 66 · Foster, *Alum. Oxon.* · *GM*, 1st ser., 90/1 (1820), 171 · Munk, *Roll* · Burke, *Peerage* (1857) · d. cert. **Archives** LPL, letters to Lord and Lady Selborne **Wealth at death** under £25,000: probate, 24 Jan 1870, *CGPLA Eng. & Wales*

Yonge, John (1462/3–1526), bishop and college head, was born at Newton Longville, Buckinghamshire. His father was a tenant of New College, Oxford, and it was there that John went, having attended the college's associated foundation at Winchester College, where he was admitted a scholar on 26 August 1474, aged eleven. In 1480 he went as a scholar to New College, where he graduated BA in 1484–5, MA in 1489, and DTh in 1504. He was a full fellow from 1482 to 1502, and at various times held the offices of first and second bursar and of subwarden. Ordained acolyte on 24 September 1485 and subdeacon on 14 March 1489, he is not recorded as having become a priest, but still held a

number of benefices, starting as vicar of Beckley, Oxfordshire, on 2 February 1499. Admitted rector of Birkby, Yorkshire, on 26 January 1503, he became rector of All Hallows, Honey Lane, London, but resigned the latter living on 30 October 1510. On 15 September 1509 he was nominated master of the London hospital of St Thomas of Acon, and by skilful management saved it from closure. He found the hospital over £700 in debt, but during the eight years of his mastership he paid off the debt and spent more than £1430 on repairs.

Yonge became a close associate of Bishop Richard Fitzjames of London. The two men were among those whom Edmund Dudley before his execution for treason in 1510 named as guardians of his son Jerome, and in 1513 Yonge became Fitzjames's suffragan, with the title of bishop of Gallipoli, under papal authorization issued on 15 April 1513 (at his consecration on 13 June he made his profession of obedience to the archbishop of Heraclea as his titular superior). He was licensed to remain master of St Thomas's, and subsequently secured a papal bull granting the right to appoint future masters to the Mercers' Company. He also obtained a bull (28 February 1515) empowering him to grant indulgences. On 28 March 1514 Yonge was also collated to the archdeaconry of London, and his responsibilities in London diocese grew thereafter as Fitzjames's health failed. In 1519 he was elected prior of the Augustinian house of Shulbred, Sussex, but resigned on 21 March 1521, having obtained a grant of land to the priory. About this time he became prebendary of Wightring in Chichester Cathedral.

Yonge had retained links with Oxford. In 1517 he and Fitzjames were invited by the university to assume responsibility for the codification of its statutes, and on 13 April 1521 he was elected warden of New College. This position he retained (along with his archdeaconry and Chichester prebend) for the rest of his life. In November 1524 he was admitted to the college's living of Colerne, Wiltshire. He died in Oxford on 28 March 1526 and was buried in New College chapel, where his brass survives (without its head), representing him in episcopal vestments with mitre and crozier. He gave the college a copy of St Augustine's works, published at Basel in 1506. Three Yonges from Newton Longville who were scholars and fellows of New College in the first thirty years of the sixteenth century were presumably his kinsmen.   ANDREW A. CHIBI

Sources Emden, *Oxf.*, 3.2135–6; 4.652–3 · *LP Henry VIII*, vols. 1–4 · R. Rex, *The theology of John Fisher* (1991) · Wood, *Ath. Oxon.*, new edn, 2.727–9 · *Fasti Angl., 1300–1541*, [St Paul's, London] · *Fasti Angl., 1300–1541*, [Chichester] · *Hist. U. Oxf.* 3: *Colleg. univ.* · M. Stephenson, *A list of monumental brasses in the British Isles* (1926) **Archives** BL, Lansdowne MS 979 · GL, register of Bishop Fitzjames, 1506–22, MS 9531/9 **Likenesses** brass effigy, New College chapel, Oxford

Yonge, John (1466/7–1516), civil lawyer and diplomat, was born at Heyford, Oxfordshire, a manor which belonged to New College, Oxford. Yonge later lived in Rye, Sussex. Nothing is known of his parents. When aged eleven he entered Winchester College as a scholar on 29 September 1478. He became a scholar of New College, Oxford, on 30

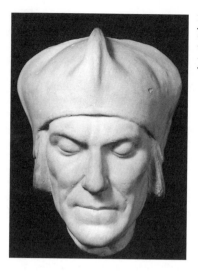

John Yonge
(1466/7–1516), by
unknown artist,
1910 (after Pietro
Torrigiano, c.1516)

January 1484; from 1486 to 1500 he held a fellowship at New College and by 1494 he had taken the BCL degree. He went to Italy for further study. After living and studying in Bologna for some years, he was admitted in 1500 to the University of Ferrara, where he took the degree of DCL.

Yonge's education in the civil law and his foreign study provided him with the background needed to enter ecclesiastical administration and royal service. For some reason his career progressed slowly. He did not gain an important office until the age of thirty-seven when on 28 January 1504 William Warham, the recently appointed archbishop of Canterbury, made him a commissary in his prerogative court. Warham and Yonge had overlapped as fellows of New College and both were civilians. Later that same year Yonge went on his first diplomatic mission which involved negotiating a mercantile treaty with Archduke Philip of Austria, the ruler of the Low Countries. During 1506 Yonge participated in another mission concerning the terms of Henry VII's engagement to Margaret of Savoy. Meanwhile Yonge began to accumulate a rich collection of sinecures. On 17 March 1503 he acquired the rectory of St Stephen Walbrook, London, which was followed by the rectory of St Mary-le-Bow, London, which he held from 19 March 1505 to May 1514. On 19 February 1506 he became the warden of St John's Hospital in South Weald, Essex, and he was dean of Chichester by August 1507. Archbishop Warham continued to support Yonge and during August 1507 made him his diocesan chancellor and auditor of causes. The culmination of Yonge's success came on 22 January 1508 when Henry VII appointed him as master of the rolls, an office Warham, now lord chancellor, had held from 1494 to 1502. More diplomatic missions quickly followed. During July 1508 he went on a mission to Emperor Maximilian and during the following October he participated with Thomas Wolsey (who reported favourably on Yonge's performance) in the negotiations leading to the treaty of Cambrai. As a final tribute to his confidence in Yonge, in his will dated 10 April 1509 Henry VII named him as one of his executors.

Apparently recognizing a valuable servant, Henry VIII reappointed Yonge as master of the rolls on 11 June 1509. The king also continued to use him as a diplomat. From early August to 2 October 1511 Yonge travelled in the company of the Spanish ambassador as a special ambassador to Louis XII of France. On this occasion Wolsey judged Yonge to have been ineffectual. Apparently Wolsey's opinion was not yet paramount, since lucrative honours still followed such service. In November 1511 Yonge became a canon of St Paul's and a prebendary of Holborn, and on 11 February 1512 he added the prebendary of Newington in St Paul's, London. From 16 May 1512 to about April 1513 he went on a long mission to the Low Countries accompanied by Sir Thomas Boleyn. They negotiated with the emperor Maximilian, King Ferdinand of Spain, and the pope concerning the activities of the Holy League, their mutual alliance against France. He crossed over to Calais with Henry VIII's invading army on 11 March 1513. The following October he went on a mission concerning a proposed marriage between Henry VIII's sister Mary and Charles of Castile, the future king of Spain and holy Roman emperor.

Yonge was obviously perceived as a person on his way up in England. On 1 January 1513 Erasmus dedicated a manuscript copy of his translation of Plutarch's *De tuenda valetudine* and presented it to him as a new year gift. The edition printed by Richard Pynson of London in August 1513 bore the same dedication. More ecclesiastical offices followed his diplomatic labours. On 4 January 1513 he became dean of Newarke Hospital and College in Leicester, an office he held until December 1515 when he vacated it in return for a pension of £20 per annum. In addition to acquiring more rectories, in 1514 Yonge became a canon of York; he quickly became dean of York and prebendary of Bugthorpe. He also acquired the archdeaconry of Barnstaple. More important, Yonge managed to gain the favourable attention of the rising Thomas Wolsey. When Wolsey became archbishop of York in mid-1514 he made Yonge his suffragan with the title of bishop of Negroponte.

Yonge appeared to have a bright future. On 4 April 1515 Henry VIII appointed him an envoy to renew the peace with Francis I of France. From there he proceeded to Tournai with a commission from the king authorizing him to organize the administration of that newly conquered city. But Yonge became seriously ill, and on 13 August 1515 Henry VIII gave him permission to return to England. Conscientiously, Yonge delayed his departure until 17 September in order to conclude his assignment. Back in London he died of the sweating sickness on 25 April 1516. Yonge was buried in the Rolls chapel, where an effigy by Pietro Torrigiano marks his tomb. It is probable that he would have climbed even higher in the government and the church if he had not died, prematurely and unmarried at the age of forty-nine.   RONALD H. FRITZE

Sources DNB · Emden, *Oxf.*, vol. 3 · R. J. Mitchell, 'English studies at Ferrara in the XV century', *Italian Studies*, 1 (1937–8), 75–82 · H. Garrod, 'Erasmus and his English patrons', *The Library*, 5th ser., 4 (1949–50), 1–13 · A. F. Pollard, *Wolsey* (1929) · P. G. Bietenholz and

T. B. Deutscher, eds., *Contemporaries of Erasmus: a biographical register*, 3 vols. (1985–7) • N. H. Nicolas, ed., *Testamenta vetusta: being illustrations from wills*, 2 vols. (1826)

Likenesses P. Torrigiano, effigy on tomb, *c*.1516, PRO; repro. in Bietenholz and Deutscher, eds., *Contemporaries of Erasmus* • sculpture, 1910 (after P. Torrigiano, *c*.1516), NPG [*see illus.*]

Yonge, Sir (Charles) Maurice (1899–1986), marine biologist, was born on 9 December 1899 at Silcoates School, near Wakefield, Yorkshire, the younger child and only son of John Arthur Yonge (1865–1946), headmaster of the school, and his wife, Sarah Edith Carr. Silcoates School was a private establishment which Maurice joined as a pupil in 1908. As the son of the headmaster he did not enjoy his schooling. Shy, sensitive, with a stammer, he became ever more self-conscious and isolated. Influenced by his mother, he found solace in reading and developed a lifelong love of history. He left school at seventeen and for a year read history at Leeds University. In 1918 he was commissioned into the Green Howards, only to be demobilized shortly afterwards. For one glorious summer he read modern history at Lincoln College, Oxford, but then, believing it important to take up a more practical subject, persuaded his father to let him study forestry at Edinburgh, a city he had loved visiting with his mother.

The forestry degree included courses in natural history, and these turned Yonge's interests to zoology. In his second year, after spending Easter at the Marine Station, Millport, 'in unspeakable weather and living conditions of the crudest', Yonge returned 'a committed marine biologist'. In 1922 he completed a degree in zoology with distinction and was awarded the Baxter natural science scholarship.

Yonge spent a further two years in Edinburgh working for his PhD on the physiology of digestion in marine invertebrates. He met Lancelot Hogben, who suggested that the clam *Mya* might be of interest. That remark led Yonge to world renown for his studies on the bivalve molluscs. During the year 1924–5 a Carnegie research scholarship took him to Naples, and on his return he joined the staff of the Marine Biological Association at Plymouth, where for two years (1925–7) he worked mainly on feeding in oysters. These remained a special interest, which was expressed in his book *Oysters* (1960). At Plymouth also he joined with Frederick Russell in writing *The Seas* (1928), a classic that inspired budding marine biologists of the 1930s and 1940s.

In 1927 Yonge was invited to Cambridge as Balfour student, with the initially hidden object of his leading the Great Barrier Reef expedition, then being planned in some confusion. The same year he married a medical student he had met in postgraduate days, Martha Jane (Mattie), daughter of Robert Torrance Lennox, of Newmilns, Ayrshire. They married on 30 June 1927, the day after Yonge was awarded his DSc degree. Mattie joined the expedition as medical officer; both the marriage and the expedition of 1928–9 were resounding successes.

From Australia, Yonge returned to Plymouth as physiologist. After three years he was disenchanted with his progress and accepted the chair of zoology at Bristol in 1933. In 1944 he became regius professor of zoology at Glasgow. By then with immense determination he had controlled his stammer and become a most effective lecturer and administrator.

Initially at Glasgow there was great sadness, for Yonge's wife, who had spent the war years away from Bristol with the children (a son and daughter), became seriously ill, required brain surgery, and died shortly afterwards in 1945. Thereafter Yonge wrote *The Sea Shore* (1949), which he dedicated to her. In 1954 he married Phyllis Greenlaw (Phyll) Fraser, helminthologist and daughter of Douglas Morrison Milne Fraser, physician, of Eastry, Kent. They had one son.

Now in demand nationally and internationally, Yonge chaired the colonial fisheries advisory committee, served on the Natural Environment Research Council, was vice-president of the Scottish Marine Biological Association, and was twice on the council of the Royal Society. He was one of a few who controlled British biological science between 1950 and 1970. In 1964 he resigned his chair at Glasgow, remaining as research fellow until 1970. In 1965 he and his wife set up house in Edinburgh and on his retirement in 1970 he became an honorary research fellow in zoology at the University of Edinburgh. The circle was complete, but his scientific output and travel continued until his Parkinson's disease became too disabling when he was eighty-three.

Although his overwhelming concern lay with molluscs, Yonge published sufficient work on corals and decapod Crustacea to have been lauded for this alone. His output of popular marine science was also immense, for he had a journalistic bent and at Oxford had considered journalism as a career. He kept up historical interests, amassed a fine library, and indulged in carpentry.

Yonge became a fellow of the Royal Society of Edinburgh in 1945 (and served as president in 1970–73), and of London in 1946 (Darwin medal, 1968). He was appointed CBE in 1954 and knighted in 1967. He was a member of the Royal Danish Academy of Sciences (1956) and had honorary degrees from the universities of Bristol (1959), Heriot-Watt (1971), Manchester (1975), and Edinburgh (1983). His last scientific paper was published three days before he died in Edinburgh, on 17 March 1986. J. A. ALLEN, *rev.*

Sources B. Morton, *Memoirs FRS*, 38 (1992), 379–412 • *The Times* (21 March 1986) • J. A. Allen, 'Sir Maurice Yonge …: an appreciation', in J. A. Allen, *The Bivalvia: proceedings of a memorial symposium in honour of Sir Charles Maurice Yonge (1899–1986)* [Edinburgh 1986] (1990), 5–7

Archives NHM, diaries, notebooks, papers, corresp. • priv. coll., items of corresp.

Likenesses photograph, repro. in Morton, *Memoirs FRS*, 378 • photograph, repro. in Allen, *The Bivalvia* (Hong Kong, 1990), 4 • photographs, U. Glas., department of zoology • photographs, repro. in J. W. Hedgpeth, 'In memoriam, Sir Maurice Yonge, FRS 1949, CBE 1954, Kt 1967', *The Veliger*, 30 (1987), 1–4

Wealth at death £75,359.12: confirmation, 1986, *CCI*

Yonge, Nicholas (*d.* 1619), music editor, may be identified with the Nicholas Yong of London who was born in Lewes, Sussex, and whose mother's name was Bray. In 1585 he applied for membership of the London waits and doubtless through the influence of his sponsor, Sir Walter Mildmay, gained a place in reversion, though there is no record of his having taken it up. He lived in the parish of St Michael Cornhill, where from 1587 onwards seven of his nine children were baptized. He was admitted lay vicar-choral of St Paul's Cathedral on 16 January 1592, and in the course of Bishop Bancroft's 1598 visitation he gave evidence concerning abuses in the choir during divine service.

Yonge is best remembered today as the editor of two anthologies of mostly Italian vocal music published, with English texts, as *Musica transalpina* in 1588 and 1597. The first volume, containing fifty-seven 'madrigals'—the first recorded English use of the term, and applied here not only to true madrigals, but also to chansons, canzonets, and other forms—was international in scope. It none the less betrayed a certain local bias: of its eighteen composers, the most liberally represented was Alfonso Ferrabosco the elder, who had lived in England from 1562 to 1578. Yonge also included William Byrd's English setting of Ariosto's 'La verginella', the first stanza of which had appeared in Italian some months earlier in the composer's own *Psalmes, Sonets & Songs*. In the dedication, addressed to Lord Gilbert Talbot, Yonge suggested that the publication grew out of the need to supply suitable material for friends to sing at daily music meetings in his home. As the repertory provided was mostly Italian, and those unfamiliar with the language either did not participate or did so 'with litle delight', he sought more music in the vernacular. Finding few suitable native compositions, he borrowed English versions of pieces translated by 'a Gentleman', and these and others like them proved so popular that he was eventually persuaded to publish a selection. A third of the pieces were drawn from madrigal anthologies issued in 1583 and 1585 by Pierre Phalèse of Antwerp. The success of Yonge's first collection led to its reprinting in 1593 or 1594. His 1597 volume, containing only twenty-four items by eleven composers, was less influential, though six of its lyrics were reset by later composers, a higher proportion than the nine reset from the first volume.

Yonge's madrigal anthologies are important because they popularized the form in England and laid the foundations for an indigenous madrigal school by providing continental models for Elizabethan composers to imitate. He made his will on 19 October 1619 and was buried at St Michael Cornhill four days later. Probate was granted to his wife, Jane, on 12 November following.

DAVID MATEER

Sources N. Yonge, *Musica transalpina: madrigales* (1588); repr. (1972) · N. Yonge, *Musica transalpina: the second booke of madrigalles* (1597); repr. (1972) · GL, MS 25,175 · GL, MS 9537/9 · will, PRO, PROB 11/134, sig. 105 · repertories of the court of aldermen, CLRO, xxi, fol. 137v · J. Kerman, *The Elizabethan madrigal: a comparative study* (1962) · E. H. Fellowes, ed., *English madrigal verse, 1588–1632*, 3rd edn, rev. F. W. Sternfeld and D. Greer (1967) · J. Kerman, 'Elizabethan anthologies of Italian madrigals', *Journal of the American Musicological Society*, 4 (1951), 122–38 · M. C. Boyd, *Elizabethan music and musical criticism*, 2nd edn (1973) · D. Scott, 'A transcription and detailed study of *Musica transalpina*', MMus diss., U. Lond., 1968 · L. Macy, 'The due decorum kept: Elizabethan translation and the madrigals Englished of Nicholas Yonge and Thomas Watson', *Journal of Musicological Research*, 17/1 (1998), 1–21 · J. L. Chester, ed., *The parish registers of St Michael, Cornhill, London*, Harleian Society, register section, 7 (1882) · *New Grove*, 2nd edn · D. Scott, 'Nicholas Yonge and his transalpine music', *MT*, 116 (1975), 875–6 · J. L. Smith, 'The hidden editions of Thomas East', *Notes*, 53/4 (June 1997), 1059–91 · A. Einstein, 'The Elizabethan madrigal and *Musica transalpina*', *Music and Letters*, 25 (1944), 66–77 · W. L. Woodfill, *Musicians in English society from Elizabeth to Charles I* (1953) · *The visitation of London, anno Domini 1633, 1634, and 1635, made by Sir Henry St George*, 1, ed. J. J. Howard and J. L. Chester, Harleian Society, 15 (1880) · H. N. Hillebrand, *The child actors*, 2 vols. (1926)

Yonge, Philip (1709–1783), bishop of Norwich, was born at Lisbon, the son of Francis Yonge, who was commissary of the ordnance during the War of the Spanish Succession, and later agent in London for South Carolina. Educated at Westminster School from 1718, Yonge was admitted a pensioner at Trinity College, Cambridge, in 1728, elected a scholar in 1729, and proceeded BA in 1732, MA in 1735, and DD in 1750. He was elected a fellow of Trinity in 1734 and ordained deacon by the bishop of Lincoln in 1735. In 1746 he became public orator at Cambridge. In 1748 the master of Trinity, Dr Smith, urged the duke of Newcastle, as chancellor of the university, to support Yonge for the regius professorship of divinity, describing Yonge as 'a very amiable man, a true friend to the government, an excellent scholar of Westminster, and esteemed by us the greatest ornament of it' (Winstanley, 182). Newcastle declined to support him, and Yonge withdrew, thereby gaining Newcastle's favour by not being importunate. In 1748 Yonge became vicar of Barrington, Cambridgeshire, in 1750 vicar of Over, Cambridgeshire, and in 1752 rector of Loughton, Buckinghamshire, all on the presentation of Trinity College, Cambridge. In 1750 he became a prebendary of Westminster Abbey but resigned in 1754 on receiving a canonry at St Paul's Cathedral, which he held until 1766. In 1757 the dean and chapter of St Paul's presented him to the rectory of Therfield, Hertfordshire, a living he resigned in 1761. On 15 December 1761 he married Anne, daughter of Calverley Bewicke, of Clapham, Surrey.

Yonge was active in Newcastle's interest in Cambridge. Probably owing to Newcastle's cordial relations with Sir Thomas Gooch, bishop of Ely, Gooch appointed Yonge to succeed Dr Ashton, a suspected Jacobite, as master of Jesus College, Cambridge, in 1752. Yonge also served as vice-chancellor of the university in 1752–5. At Newcastle's behest he took an active part in raising £3650 towards building the east front of the university library, going through college buttery books to identify anyone of distinction whom Newcastle might approach for a subscription. In 1757 Newcastle proposed Yonge as bishop of Peterborough, but was thwarted by George II. Nevertheless, in 1758 Yonge was appointed to the poorly endowed diocese of Bristol where he undertook a primary visitation in 1760. He was translated to the better-endowed diocese of Norwich in 1761.

As bishop of Norwich, Yonge continued to play an active part in university politics on Newcastle's behalf, managing the campaign in 1763 to elect Philip Yorke, second earl of Hardwicke, to succeed his father as high steward of the university. As a university politician Yonge combined great powers of detailed application with sound judgement. However, he was not servile in his support for Newcastle. He opposed Newcastle's initiative to nominate candidates for degrees granted by royal mandate, because this would endanger the independence and prestige of the university. He avoided voting in the Lords during the debate on John Wilkes's *An Essay on Woman*, which parodied *Veni Creator*. In reply to Newcastle's rebuke, Yonge pointed out that, on a matter of conscience, 'questions of friendship and attachment, of prudence, and of mere policy are … easily distinguishable from those which call upon every man to think for himself, and to consult his own heart' (Sykes, 55–6). Yonge remained on friendly terms with Newcastle after he lost political power, and conducted Newcastle's funeral.

In Yonge's primary visitation charge at Norwich he exhorted his clergy to 'dwell among their flocks … administering God's word and sacrament … diligently and frequently', and to preach 'instructive and biblical sermons' (Yonge, *The Charge*). He also criticized 'field preaching' and Methodism. Preaching in support of the Norfolk and Norwich Hospital he strongly advocated medical care for the poor, and criticized the current poor law. He was reckoned to be 'one of the best preachers in the Establishment' (*Diary of Sylas Neville*, 175). He regularly spent every summer in his diocese, and undertook improvements to the palace. Parson Woodforde found his behaviour 'exceeding handsome and free' (*Diary of a Country Parson*, 150). However, his reputation later suffered from the opinion of his successor, Lewis Bagot, who complained of 'the easiness and inactivity of his predecessor' (Nichols, *Lit. anecdotes*, 5.188). Yonge died on 23 April 1783 at Westminster, and was buried in the Grosvenor Chapel, Mayfair, on 1 May. His wife survived him. W. M. JACOB

Sources Venn, *Alum. Cant.*, 1/4.493 · D. A. Winstanley, *The University of Cambridge in the eighteenth century* (1922) · N. Sykes, *Church and state in England in the XVIII century* (1934) · A. Gray and F. Brittain, *A history of Jesus College, Cambridge*, rev. edn (1960) · Nichols, *Lit. anecdotes* · *The diary of a country parson: the Reverend James Woodforde*, ed. J. Beresford, 2 (1926) · *The diary of Sylas Neville, 1767–1788*, ed. B. Cozens-Hardy (1950) · P. Yonge, *The charge of the Rt Revd Philip, lord bishop of Norwich* (1763) · P. Yonge, *A sermon preached at the first anniversary of the Norfolk and Norwich Hospital* (1772) · *Old Westminsters*, vols. 1–2 · churchwardens' account book, St George's Church, Hanover Square, St George Street, London
Archives BL, corresp. with duke of Newcastle, etc., Add. MSS 32700–33088, *passim* · BL, letters to N. Forster, Add. MS 11275
Likenesses portrait, oils, Bishop's House, Norwich
Wealth at death see will, 30 April 1783, Venn, *Alum. Cant.*

Yonge, Sir Thomas (*c.*1405–1477), justice, was the eldest son of a Welshman, Thomas Yonge, or Mere (*d.* 1427), who was mayor of Bristol in 1411–12 and 1420–21, and represented Bristol in parliament in 1414; his mother was Joan Wotton (*d.* 1429), widow of the wealthy Bristol merchant John Canynges. William *Canynges was thus his half-brother. His younger brother, John Yonge, became a prominent London grocer, representing the city in parliament (1455–6) as well as being sheriff in 1455–6 and mayor in 1466–7. Having become a consistent Yorkist, he was knighted by Edward IV after his restoration to the throne, on 20 May 1471.

Thomas Yonge became a member of the Middle Temple, and built up a practice in Bristol and the south-west of England as well as in London. He was recorder of Bristol by 1441, serving until at least 1462, and he was one of the city's MPs in 1435, 1437, 1439–40, 1442, 1445–6, 1447, 1449, 1449–50, 1450–51, and 1455–6. It may be significant that as late as 1455 the election returns refer to him as *mercator* (merchant): for much of his career he seems to have had strong links with the commercial worlds of Bristol and London.

In June 1451 Yonge presented in parliament a petition from his constituents to the effect that the duke of York should be recognized as heir presumptive to the throne. This was part of a wider attack upon the duke of Somerset, whose position was, however, unshaken; parliament was dissolved, and Yonge was committed to the Tower of London. He was released in April 1452, on the general pardon issued after the temporary reconciliation of the two parties. Back in parliament in January 1456 he claimed redress for his arrest and imprisonment, reminding the Commons in his petition that all members:

> ought to have their freedom to speak and say in the house of their assembly as to them is thought convenient or reasonable without any manner of challenge, charge, or punition therefore to be laid to them in any wise. (*RotP*, 5.337)

The Commons sent up the bill to the Lords, and the king ordered that the lords of the council should provide a remedy; but no further proceedings in the matter are recorded.

Yonge was not elected to the strongly royalist parliament that met at Coventry in November 1459, but he was returned for Gloucestershire in 1460 to the parliament that reversed the proceedings at Coventry. It is nevertheless unclear how far he can be called a Yorkist at this time. In 1446 he was retained as legal counsel by Humphrey Stafford, duke of Buckingham, and he continued to serve the duke until at least 1457–8.

In 1442 Yonge obtained a writ exempting him from appointment as serjeant-at-law, and it was only on 7 November 1463 that he was finally appointed, the day before he was made a king's serjeant. He is described shortly after his appointment as 'arrayed yn a long blue gown ungurd, with a scarlet hode unrolled and j [one] standyng roon [round?] cap of scarlet, as the custom is of sergeantes to go' (B. R. Masters and E. Ralph, eds., *Church Book of St Ewen's, Bristol, 1454–1584*, Bristol and Gloucestershire Archaeological Society, Records Section, 5, 1967, 58). In November 1467 he was raised to the bench as justice of the common pleas. He was not, however, removed when Henry VI was restored in October 1470, but lost his position—perhaps on the grounds of age—during the rearrangement of the judiciary when Edward IV regained his throne six months later; he was, however, exempted from the operation of the Act of Resumption of 1472–3. Nevertheless, on 29 April 1475, in spite of his advanced age, Yonge was appointed a justice of the king's bench, possibly as a measure to strengthen the latter court during Edward IV's expedition to France of that year.

He was married, by 1454, to Isabel, daughter of John Burton, a prosperous Bristol merchant. He died on 3 or 4 May 1477 and was buried in the Greyfriars Church, London; his heir was his son Thomas, said to be aged thirty or more, and he also had another son and three daughters.

A. F. POLLARD, rev. NIGEL RAMSAY

Sources J. T. Driver, 'Parliamentary burgesses for Bristol and Gloucester, 1422–1437', *Transactions of the Bristol and Gloucestershire Archaeological Society*, 74 (1955), 60–127, esp. 113–21, 127 • J. C. Wedgwood and A. D. Holt, *History of parliament*, 1: *Biographies of the members of the Commons house, 1439–1509* (1936) • HoP, *Commons* • Baker, *Serjeants* • Sainty, *Judges*, 28, 70 • K. B. McFarlane, 'The Wars of the Roses', *PBA*, 50 (1964), 87–119, esp. 110 • E. W. Ives, *The common lawyers of pre-Reformation England* (1983), 480 • RotP, 5.337 • J. Maclean, 'Notes on the family of Yonge, or Young, of Bristol', *Transactions of the Bristol and Gloucestershire Archaeological Society*, 15 (1890–91), 227–45 • B. R. Masters and E. Ralph, eds., *Church book of St Ewen's, Bristol, 1454–1584*, Bristol and Gloucestershire Archaeological Society Records Section, 5 (1967), 58 • T. P. Wadley, *Notes or abstracts of the wills contained in the volume entitled the Great orphan book and Book of wills in the council house at Bristol*, Bristol and Gloucestershire Archaeological Society, 1 (1886), 134–6 • *Chancery records*

Yonge, Walter (*bap.* 1579, *d.* 1649), politician and diarist, was baptized on 16 April 1579, the second son and heir of John Yonge (*d.* 1612), of Colyton, and his wife, Alice (*d.* 1631), daughter of Richard Starre of Seaton, Devon. Yonge is thought to have descended from a junior branch of the family of the fifteenth-century judge Thomas Yonge. His immediate forebears came from Berkshire at the end of that century in the person of his great-grandfather and namesake, who bought several manors in east Devon. Yonge's grandfather John married the heir of Colyton. His father was a prominent merchant who engaged in the first trading ventures to Africa. Yonge went to Magdalen College, Oxford, matriculating in 1599, but took no degree. In 1600 he entered the Middle Temple, and was called to the bar, but it is not known how far he practised. On 6 February 1601 he married Jane (*d.* 1655), daughter and coheir of Sir John Peryam of Exeter (and niece of Sir William Peryam, chief baron of the exchequer). They had two sons and a daughter.

For the first part of his adult life Yonge lived at Upton Helions near Crediton, Devon, but because his elder brother, John, died early he succeeded to Colyton and the family's other manorial holdings on his father's death in 1612. He continued the family practice of purchasing manors, and like his father he was interested in overseas trade. In 1624 he invested in the Dorchester Company, an attempt to combine profit with consolidating godly settlements in New England. Yonge also made a notable contribution to local affairs. In 1625 he bought some land in trust under a charity which bore his name, for the benefit of the poor of Crediton; the charity was still operating 250 years later. Yonge was sheriff of Devon in 1628, and quartermaster-general to the Devon militia in 1635; he served as a JP for the county from 1622 until his death. He produced a manual listing the parliamentary statutes under which the justices worked, with the level of evidence and the penalties prescribed for each offence. In 1642 parliament ordered it to be printed for public use, as *A Justice of the Peace, his Vade-Mecum*.

This was Yonge's only published work, but for most of his life he kept a diary (now in the British Library), which is an important historical record. The volumes dating from before the civil war illustrate the growing popular criticism of the royal government. Always apprehensive of 'popish' conspiracy, Yonge became increasingly suspicious of sacramentalist tendencies in the English church. He thought religion should focus on the elucidation of scripture. He was concerned about restrictions on preaching as early as 1606, when he objected to a licensing scheme outlawing independent lecturers, though he also noted parliament's attempts to ameliorate the rules. In 1622 he was dismayed by the government's suppression of anti-Catholic sentiment, and the instructions to ministers to 'preach but once a Sabbath … and only in their own cures'. He was a stern advocate of moral discipline, believing that mixed dancing and stage plays 'tended to the high provocation of God's wrath' (*Diary*, 15, 64). He deplored the king's support for Sunday sports, and applauded parliament's opposition to them.

In the 1620s Yonge's diary was preoccupied with the Thirty Years' War. In January 1621 he cited parliament's declaration urging James I to go to war to recover the palatinate for his daughter, Elizabeth of Bohemia. But later Yonge had to record the sequence of ignominious failures of English armies in their belated interventions, followed by parliament's efforts to impeach the duke of Buckingham in 1626. Yonge is also suggested as the originator of a separate, detailed record of that controversial parliament (BL, Add. MS 22474). War accentuated the problem of finance, and Yonge disapproved of any kind of extra-parliamentary taxation. He believed that the benevolence of 1622 should have been raised 'in a legal course of Parliaments' (*Diary*, 61). He absented himself from the commission to implement the forced loan in 1626, and noted the resistance in other counties. He kept reports of the ensuing prosecutions, and indicated his belief that it was the king who was infringing the law. In the 1630s Yonge called the judges who defended ship money 'pro-rege', and those who opposed it 'pro-patria' (diary, BL, Add. MS 35331, fol. 68v).

Yonge had many reasons to stand as an MP when in December 1640 the Long Parliament approved the petition of Honiton in Devon for its electoral rights to be revived. Yonge owned a manor in Honiton parish. And he clearly had a high opinion of parliament's capacities. Puritan and 'country' sympathies may well have influenced the restoration of borough franchises in 1640. Yonge was related to one of the opposition leaders, William Strode, and must have been a welcome recruit in the house. He supported early radical demands for a parliamentary voice in ministerial appointments. On 18 December 1641 he made the 'startling suggestion' that the bill of tonnage and poundage should include a proviso that Sir Henry

Vane be retained as treasurer of the navy, against the king's wishes (*Journal*, ed. Coates, xxxi).

Yonge naturally became a parliamentarian in the civil war. He kept a parliamentary diary from September 1642 to December 1645 (BL, Add. MSS 18777–18780). It is a valuable record of the progress of the war and the state of opinion in parliament, but adds little to knowledge of Yonge's own views. He did play a significant part in the settlement of religion. In June 1643 he was one of twenty MPs named to the assembly of divines. He also sat on a subcommittee of sixteen MPs producing draft ordinances from the assembly's work for parliament to consider. In July 1643 he went to Scotland with the English commissioners. It is not clear whether he supported Scottish theocratic presbyterianism, or parliament's preference for a less restrictive, Erastian church. But his faith in the individual analysis of scripture was further revealed when the royalists in Devon captured a 'seditious lecturer' at his house in 1644 (Cliffe, 87). Yonge included detailed reports of sermons in his parliamentary notebooks. A separate collection, 'Reports of sermons in London, 1642–4', is attributed to his second son, Walter (BL, Add. MSS 18781–18782).

Yonge also specialized in committees on legal matters, and chaired the committee to turn parliament's ordinances into statutes after the war. This was an awkward proposition. But Yonge compiled a notebook of precedents suggesting that parliament held residual authority in the state. And he concluded that because parliament represented the whole kingdom, it could be regarded as the true, binding legislative power, independently of the king. Finally Yonge assisted the parliamentarian cause through his experience in naval affairs and military supply. He became a victualler of the navy after the outbreak of war, and was still acting in that capacity in October 1648.

Yonge's attitude to the army's purge of parliament in December of that year is uncertain. He had already begun to withdraw from parliamentary activities, and does not appear on the list of secluded members. He died in November 1649, and was buried at Colyton on 26 November. His widow, Jane, was buried there on 17 April 1655. His eldest son, Sir John (1603–1663), was one of the secluded MPs in 1648, and was made a baronet at the Restoration, though the family remained nonconformist in religion.

GEORGE YERBY

Sources *Diary of Walter Yonge*, ed. G. Roberts, CS, 41 (1848) · Keeler, *Long Parliament* · J. T. Cliffe, *Puritans in conflict* (1988) · M. Wolffe, *Gentry leaders in peace and war: the gentry governors of Devon in the early seventeenth century* (1997) · *The journal of Sir Simonds D'Ewes from the first recess of the Long Parliament to the withdrawal of King Charles from London*, ed. W. H. Coates (1942) · *CSP dom.*, 1644; 1648–9 · A. J. P. Skinner, ed., *The register of baptisms, marriages and burials in the parish of Colyton, Devon, 1538–1837*, 2 vols., Devon and Cornwall RS (1928) · Burke, *Extinct baronetage* · J. L. Vivian, ed., *The visitations of the county of Devon, comprising the herald's visitations of 1531, 1564, and 1620* (privately printed, Exeter, [1895]) · Devon RO, MS 3756/B/T1–2 · transcripts of wills, West Country Studies Library, vol. 32 · will, March 1645, PRO, PROB 11/211 · parish register, St Olave, Exeter, 6 Feb 1601 [marriage] · Foster, *Alum. Oxon.*

Archives BL, diaries and reports of London sermons, Add. MSS 18777–18782, 22474, 28032, 35331 · Bodl. Oxf., notebook on parliamentary precedents and privileges, MS Eng. Hist. g.19

Wealth at death £100 to wife; had already settled most of substantial estates on children: will, PRO, PROB 11/211; Keeler, *Long Parliament*

Yonge, Sir Walter, third baronet (*bap.* 1653, *d.* 1731), politician and friend of John Locke, was baptized on 8 September 1653 at Sandford, Devon, the first surviving son of Sir Walter Yonge, second baronet (*c.*1626–1670), politician, of Colyton, Devon, and his wife, Isabella (*bap.* 1631), daughter of Sir John Davie of Sandford, Devon. He matriculated at Exeter College, Oxford, in 1670, and in that year succeeded as third baronet. His background was presbyterian, his great-grandfather Walter and grandfather Sir John having been on the parliamentarian side in the civil war. Yonge's father sat in Richard Cromwell's parliament and at the Restoration was active for religious comprehension. In 1677, by a licence dated 19 April of that year, he married Gertrude (*d.* 1679), daughter of William Morice, an MP with presbyterian inclinations. They had no children.

Yonge first stood for parliament at Newport, Cornwall, in 1678, but was unsuccessful and soon turned to the family seat of Honiton, where he was the leading proprietor. He was MP for that town in eleven parliaments from 1679 to 1708, and once for Ashburton in 1689–90. He was moderately active for Anthony Ashley Cooper, first earl of Shaftesbury, in the exclusion parliaments and was a member of the Green Ribbon Club. To dissenters he was 'sober', to tories a 'fanatic' (HoP, *Commons, 1660–90*). He withstood the intrusion upon Honiton corporation by the high-churchman Sir Thomas Putt. Yonge also held a number of local offices, being commissioner of assessment for Devon in 1677–80 and 1689–90, deputy lieutenant for Devon from 1688 onwards, and colonel of militia foot from about 1697. He was also made a freeman of Lyme Regis in 1680 and of Plymouth in 1696.

In the 1680s Yonge's position was ambiguous. One historian places him with the revolutionary underground: he entertained the duke of Monmouth in 1680, was considered as a potential ally by the Rye House plotters in 1683, and was briefly arrested in 1685. But another historian calls him one of James II's 'Whig collaborators': he avoided Monmouth's rebellion, distrained on three rebel tenants, and in 1688 was appointed JP and nominated by James's electoral agents as a candidate for parliament. Yonge was sufficiently tainted that in the election to the convention of 1689 he had to fall back on the borough of his brother-in-law Richard Duke, Ashburton. However, he was soon busy in parliament demanding redress against the agents of 'popery and slavery', and sat on the committee for the Toleration Act. His first wife having died in 1679, on 18 June 1691 Yonge married Gwen, daughter of Sir Robert Williams, baronet, of Penrhyn, Cornwall. They had one son and four daughters.

John Locke called his west-country friends 'the Row', their estates running from north to south: Edward Clarke of Chipley near Taunton; Yonge, who built a new house at Escott, near Colyton, in the 1680s (he also had a London house in Bedford Row, Westminster); and Richard Duke of Otterton. In 1686 the Yonges and Dukes visited Locke in the Netherlands. Yonge received presentation copies of three of Locke's publications, and in the 1690s Yonge, with Clarke, John Freke, and John Somers, was part of Locke's 'college' of parliamentary advisers. Yonge was a reliable drafter of legislation, though no orator. He interested himself in fiscal, banking, transport, and trade policy. He supported the Triennial Act and a bill for security of tenure of judges. He and his circle were active in defending the west-country textile industry. In the early 1690s he joined the steady assault on tory ministers, which bore fruit in the whig accession to power in 1694. In this year he was appointed a customs commissioner, a post he held until 1701 and again from 1714 to 1731. He remained loyal to Somers and the junto whigs, although in 1697 he opposed the government over wine duties, preferring to defend the west-country textile trade with Portugal. He became politically less active in the new century. He remained a consistent whig, opposing the occasional conformity bills and supporting the impeachment of the high-church clergyman Dr Sacheverell. He lost his seat in the tory landslide of 1710.

Yonge died on 18 July 1731, and was buried at Colyton. His son, Sir William *Yonge, fourth baronet, was one of the most loyal and unpopular supporters of the prime minister Sir Robert Walpole. MARK GOLDIE

Sources J. P. Ferris, 'Yonge, Sir Walter', HoP, *Commons, 1660–90* · A. A. Hanham, 'Yonge, Sir Walter', HoP, *Commons, 1690–1715* · M. Goldie, 'John Locke's circle and James II', *HJ*, 35 (1992), 557–86 · *The correspondence of John Locke*, ed. E. S. De Beer, 8 vols. (1976–89) · J. L. Vivian, ed., *The visitations of the county of Devon, comprising the herald's visitations of 1531, 1564, and 1620* (privately printed, Exeter, [1895]) · *IGI*

Archives Bodl. Oxf., letters to Sir John Locke from Yonge and his sisters Elizabeth Yonge and Isabella Duke

Sir William Yonge, fourth baronet (c.1693–1755), by John Vanderbank

Yonge, Sir William, fourth baronet (c.1693–1755), politician, was born at Colyton, Devon the first son of Sir Walter *Yonge, third baronet (bap. 1653, d. 1731), and his second wife, Gwen, the daughter and coheir of Sir Robert Williams. He married Mary, the daughter of Samuel Heathcote of Hackney and the sister of Sir William Heathcote, on 30 July 1716. This marriage, which was childless, ended in an acrimonious divorce in 1724. Yonge secured evidence of his wife's adultery with Colonel Thomas Norton, won a case for damages, and was granted a divorce in the consistory court of the bishop of London and by a special act of parliament which gave him permission to remarry. His second wife, whom he married on 14 April 1729, was Anne, the daughter and coheir of Thomas Howard, sixth Baron Howard of Effingham. The couple had six daughters and two sons, including George *Yonge, fifth baronet, later governor of the Cape of Good Hope.

MP for Honiton and ally of Walpole The Yonge family, who were staunch whigs, owned estates near and in the borough of Honiton. Together with the tory Courtenay family, who were lords of the manor, they dominated the electoral interest of this notoriously venal borough. Yonge was first elected for Honiton in 1715, soon after he

came of age, and he represented the borough continuously until 1754, when he surrendered his seat to his son George and took his seat for Tiverton. As well as being elected for Honiton in every general election he was also re-elected in five by-elections required after he had taken office under the crown. Though venal, Honiton was not a pocket borough and it was quite often contested. The franchise originally belonged to all inhabitant householders who paid scot and lot (about 300–400 voters in 1715), but, after a resolution in the House of Commons in 1724, all inhabitant householders were given the vote and the number of electors doubled. Yonge favoured this decision as the leader of the more popular party in the constituency, but he retained his seat by carefully cultivating the voters and spending heavily on his elections.

A firm whig, Yonge always attached himself to the ministerial party. His first reported speech was in support of the government-sponsored Septennial Bill in 1716. During the split in the whig party in 1717 he supported the earl of Sunderland and was rewarded with a minor place in the commission for stating army debts. In a debate on the South Sea scheme, on 23 March 1720, he was one of the ministerial spokesmen who narrowly secured the rejection of Robert Walpole's motion for protecting holders of government loans by fixing the rate at which they might be converted into South Sea stock. After Sunderland's death in 1722 Yonge quickly attached himself to Walpole, becoming a commissioner of Irish revenue 1723–4 and then a lord of the Treasury in 1724. Thereafter he became one of Walpole's most dependable lieutenants in the Commons. He was particularly active in defending the armed forces raised each year by the ministry and the administration's foreign policy. In 1723 he played a major role in the impeachment of Francis Atterbury, bishop of Rochester, and on 27 May 1725 he was created one of the first knights of the Bath.

Yonge lost office in 1727, on the accession of George II. According to Lord Hervey, the new king always referred to him as 'Stinking Yonge' and had conceived such an insurmountable dislike to his person and his character that Walpole could not persuade the king to allow him to remain in office. Walpole advised him to 'be patient, not clamorous, to submit, not resent or oppose, to be subservient to the Court in attendance and give the King his assistance as constantly and as assiduously in Parliament as if he was paid for it' (Hervey, 1.35–7). Walpole's advice was heeded and his confidence justified. Yonge was made a lord of the Admiralty in 1728, advanced to a lord of the Treasury in 1730, and served as secretary at war from 1735 to 1746. This last promotion proved that he had overcome the king's aversion to him, because the post gave its holder regular access to the royal closet.

Parliamentary politician and secretary at war Yonge amply repaid Walpole's confidence in him. In the Commons he was one of the ministry's most frequent and effective speakers on a very wide range of issues. In addition to his justification of the armed forces, he played a leading role in every major debate when the parliamentary opposition proposed bills designed to reduce crown patronage and the ministry's ability to influence MPs or the electorate. He regularly accused the opposition of pursuing factious policies, of vilifying all the supporters of the ministry including the king and queen, and of undermining the existing balance of the constitution. He repeated these charges in his only pamphlet, *Sedition and Defamation Display'd* (1731). Lord Hervey added an introductory dedication to this work that subjected William Pulteney and Lord Bolingbroke to scurrilous abuse. Pulteney's printed reply, even more scurrilous and brutal, led to a famous duel between him and Hervey.

Once the country was at war from 1739, Yonge's burdens increased in weight and importance. As secretary at war he was responsible for recruitment, billeting, the supply of clothes and equipment, convoys, transport, and the care of sick and wounded troops. In parliament it was his primary duty to pilot recruiting bills and army estimates through the Commons. In regularly arguing that Britain must maintain the balance of power in Europe, which meant engaging with French forces on the continent and not merely at sea or in the colonies, he defended the need to employ German mercenaries, to keep Hanoverian troops in British pay, and to maintain a British army in Flanders in wartime.

When Walpole's long administration at last crumbled in the early 1740s, Yonge remained loyal and was determined that the opposition would not profit from the great man's fall. He worked tirelessly to ensure that the ministry safeguarded its reduced majority by persuading the committee of elections to decide disputed returns from the 1741 general election in the ministry's favour. He continued to fight every disputed election return until defeat in the case of Chippenham convinced Walpole of the need to resign.

Even then, Yonge defended the minister from every opposition attempt to inquire into abuses. When, in January 1742, Pulteney moved for a secret committee to examine whatever persons and papers the Commons pleased, Walpole rightly saw it as a malicious attack on himself and defied his critics to accuse him in an open and fair manner. In this major debate both sides brought out their best speakers and Pulteney's motion was defeated by only 253 votes to 250, one of the greatest attendances in the Commons ever recorded and the greatest number that had lost a question. Horace Walpole observed: 'When the debate was over, Mr Pultney owned that he had never heard so fine a debate on our side; and said to Sir Robert "well, no body can do what you can!" "Yes", replied Sir R[obert], "Younge did better"' (Walpole, *Corr.*, 17.299). Yonge repeated his opposition to a committee of inquiry in March 1742, after Walpole's resignation.

The duke of Newcastle and his brother, Henry Pelham, Walpole's chief lieutenants, urged the king not to give way to the opposition after Walpole's fall, but to reconstruct the ministry on much the same basis as before. The king followed this advice and Yonge remained as secretary at war under the ministry dominated by the Pelham brothers. He served this administration much as he had that of Walpole, defending the ministry's demands for troops and its conduct of war and diplomatic negotiations. He also criticized opposition motions to tax places and pensions, to repeal the Septennial Act, and to remove the right of the aldermen of the City of London to veto measures proposed by the more popular common council.

By 1745 the Pelham administration's control of the Commons was insecure and it had to consider augmenting its strength by bringing into office either Henry Fox or William Pitt, or both. There were rumours as early as December 1744 that Yonge would make way for Pitt, who was anxious to occupy his post. The king, however, deeply resented Pitt's earlier scathing comments on Hanover and so refused to have him in a post which gave him so much access to the royal closet. But by May 1746 the Pelhams were able to reconstruct the ministry. Yonge's ill health provided an excuse to transfer him to the less onerous but more lucrative post of joint vice-treasurer for Ireland. Fox replaced Yonge, and Pitt came in as paymaster-general.

Although Yonge was no longer such a prominent member of the ministry, he remained a loyal and reliable supporter of its policies. The 1745 Jacobite rising found him once more defending the settlement of 1688–9 and the Hanoverian succession. He was one of the managers of the impeachment of Lord Lovat and also led a committee of inquiry into the suspected Jacobite sympathies of the independent electors of Westminster. In the impeachment of Lovat, in December 1746, he insisted that the aged Jacobite should be denied the support of counsel, but by May 1747 Yonge himself moved a more generous bill to allow those impeached of treason the full benefit of counsel. In February 1751 he appeared in a different light, however, when he proposed that Alexander Murray, a Jacobite involved in raising a mob in the Westminster by-election of 1750, should be committed to Newgate for contempt of the Commons in refusing to receive a reprimand at the bar of the chamber in a kneeling position.

In his last years in parliament Yonge spoke up in support of Robert Nugent's Naturalization Bill in February 1751, in opposition to Hardwicke's Marriage Act in May 1753, and in support of the repeal of the Jewish Naturalization Act in November of the same year. His last reported speech in the Commons, in December 1753, found him characteristically arguing that parliamentary inquiries into crimes should be used only in the most extreme cases of the abuse of power. The last report of his activities in the house noted his vain efforts in February 1754 to repeal the Bribery Act ahead of the impending general election. In that election he surrendered his seat at Honiton and, with the support of the ministry, was returned for Tiverton.

Political talents Yonge's prime claim to fame as a politician rests on his abilities as a man of business and as one of the most effective speakers on the ministerial side in the Commons. Many contemporaries acknowledged his qualities as a speaker. One report noted that he put forward his arguments 'with great vivacity and address' (Cobbett, *Parl. hist.*, 8.409). Lord Hervey claimed that 'he had no wit in private conversation, but was remarkably quick in taking hints to harangue upon in Parliament' (Hervey, 1.36). Lord Chesterfield told his son that 'Sir William Yonge ... has, by a glibness of tongue singly, raised himself successively to the best employments of the kingdom' (*Letters*, 5.2084). Yonge himself once boasted: 'I never speak but what I dare express my meaning and speak boldly what I mean' (*Parliamentary Diary of Sir Edward Knatchbull*, 146).

The many reports of Yonge's speeches confirm that he was an effective speaker, but his parliamentary talents went beyond this. When Walpole did not care to enter early into a debate himself, he sometimes gave Yonge his notes, when the latter came into the Commons, from which Yonge would speak fluently and effectively, even though he had missed all the preceding discussion. When Walpole was reluctant to support a measure too openly, he deployed Yonge's talents instead. Thus Yonge led the ministerial side in support of the controversial Quaker Tithe Bill in 1736, while other ministers kept silent, and he spoke and voted in May 1737 against the motion to reduce the rate of interest on the national debt, while Walpole baffled the opposition by introducing the measure and then voting against it. On other occasions he deliberately proposed amendments to opposition motions in order to

make them more extreme and so ensure their defeat. He did this over the debate on the implementation of the treaty of Seville on 23 February 1731 and in the debate on reducing the rate of interest offered to some public creditors on 14 March 1737.

In two famous set-piece encounters Yonge's quick wits confounded the opposition just as they seemed to have the moral high ground. In the debate on the size of the land forces on 30 January 1730 William Shippen, a notorious Jacobite sympathizer, vehemently attacked the standing army and hoped that the ministry's proposal did not imply that the king wished to govern like a German tyrant. This reflection on George II stunned the house for several minutes. Yonge was the first to respond by accusing Shippen of an intolerable slur on his majesty and demanding that he explain himself. Shippen's confusion and the opposition's embarrassment enabled Walpole to move the question at once and to secure a handsome majority. A couple of weeks later, in the great debate on the state of the fortifications of Dunkirk, Samuel Sandys tried to embarrass the ministry by suggesting that the journal of the house should be examined to prove that the tories at the end of Anne's reign had then been vigorous in insisting that the French should destroy the fortifications of Dunkirk. Yonge, whose memory was better, promptly seconded his proposal. Unfortunately for the opposition, the journal showed that it was the tories who had tried to evade inquiries into the state of Dunkirk's fortifications: 'This silenced Mr Sands, and made Sir Robert Walpole triumph' (*Egmont Diary*, 1.43).

Assessment and reputation Yonge's recorded speeches in the Commons reveal a court whig politician whose principles were consistent and whose political ideology was coherent. He was a staunch opponent of Jacobitism, a firm supporter of the Hanoverian succession, and a regular defender of the royal prerogative and the existing balance of the constitution. In matters of religion he was hostile to Catholicism, favoured an established church subordinate to the state, and was ready to concede freedom of conscience to protestant dissenters. In foreign affairs he believed that Britain must try to maintain the balance of power in Europe and should contrive to keep up large armed forces, hire mercenary troops, subsidize European allies, and be ready to wage war in Europe in order to restrict the power of France. To achieve these ends, he was prepared to support the national debt and a substantial standing army, and the taxes necessary to finance both.

Never an idealist, Yonge consistently maintained that public virtue was in limited supply and the rewarding of friends and supporters was the necessary means to secure a parliamentary majority. He once told the Commons:

> I talk, Sir, of men as they practically are, and not as in theory we may think to make them; for while men are men, I am afraid, we shall find, that ministers will consult their safety, and members will pursue their resentment, even though their country should thereby suffer. (Cobbett, *Parl. hist.*, 13.1086)

In his opinion, virtue and vice existed among ministers

and their opponents. Those in office deserved a reasonable reward for the burdens they bore and the services they performed.

It may be that Yonge's robust defence of Walpole's political methods, his cynical attitude towards virtue and corruption, and the many lucrative government posts which he held all helped to give him the reputation for personal corruption under which he undoubtedly laboured. It is not clear, however, whether this reputation was fully deserved or not. Lord Chesterfield referred to his 'most sullied, not to say blasted character' (*Letters*, 5.2084), while Horace Walpole claimed that 'Sir Robert always said of him, that nothing but Yonge's character could keep down his parts, and nothing but his parts support his character' (Walpole, *Memoirs*, 1.15–16). Lord Hervey admitted that he could not account for Yonge's bad reputation, seeing it as an exception to the common rule that the true merits of a man usually gain their proper reputation with the public:

> for without having done anything that I know of remarkably profligate—anything out of the common trade of a ductile courtier and a parliamentary tool—his name was proverbially used to express everything pitiful, corrupt, and contemptible. It is true he was a great liar, but rather a mean than a vicious one. He had always been constant to the same party, was good-natured and good-humoured, never offensive in company, no-body's friend, no body's enemy. (Hervey, 1.35–6)

Yet, as Hervey acknowledged, even Walpole 'caressed him without loving him, and employed him without trusting him' (ibid.).

As well as being an active politician for forty years, Yonge greatly cherished his reputation as a rhyming wit, though this only served to make him the butt of genuine poets such as Alexander Pope. In 1730 he helped to convert the comedy *The Jovial Crew* by Richard Brome, first produced in 1641, into a comic opera in three acts. A considerable number of songs were added, most of them attributed to Yonge. The revised work was first performed at Drury Lane on 8 February 1731, was a considerable success, and was performed as late as 1791. In 1749 Yonge also wrote the rather coarse epilogue to Samuel Johnson's *Irene*. Elected a fellow of the Royal Society on 28 June 1748, he was awarded an honorary LLD by Cambridge University in 1749. He died following a stroke at his seat at Escott, near Honiton, on 10 August 1755 and was buried on 14 August in the family vault beneath the chancel of Colyton church.   H. T. DICKINSON

Sources Cobbett, *Parl. hist.* · *Manuscripts of the earl of Egmont: diary of Viscount Percival, afterwards first earl of Egmont*, 3 vols., HMC, 63 (1920–23) · John, Lord Hervey, *Some materials towards memoirs of the reign of King George II*, ed. R. Sedgwick, 3 vols. (1931) · H. Walpole, *Memoirs of King George II*, ed. J. Brooke, 3 vols. (1985) · Walpole, *Corr.* · *The letters of Philip Dormer Stanhope, fourth earl of Chesterfield*, ed. B. Dobrée, 6 vols. (1932) · *The parliamentary diary of Sir Edward Knatchbull, 1722–1730*, ed. A. N. Newman, CS, 3rd ser., 94 (1963) · *Tory and whig: the parliamentary papers of Edward Harley, third earl of Oxford, and William Hay, MP for Seaford, 1716–1753*, ed. S. Taylor and C. Jones (1998) · R. R. Sedgwick, 'Yonge, William', HoP, *Commons, 1715–54* · J. Brooke, 'Yonge, William', HoP, *Commons, 1754–90* · J. B. Owen, *The rise of the Pelhams* (1957) · H. T. Dickinson, *Walpole and the whig supremacy* (1973) · DNB

Archives Derbys. RO, corresp. relating to Ireland · Dorset RO, out-letter-book as secretary at war | BL, corresp. with duke of Newcastle, Add. MSS 32699–32857, *passim*
Likenesses J. Vanderbank, oils, Sudbury Hall, Derbyshire [see illus.]
Wealth at death son later deemed to have inherited £80,000

York. For this title name *see* William le Gros, count of Aumale and earl of York (*c*.1110–1179); Edmund, first duke of York (1341–1402); Edward, second duke of York (*c*.1373–1415); Joan, duchess of York (*d*. 1434) [*see under* Willoughby family (*per. c*.1300–1523)]; Richard of York, third duke of York (1411–1460); Cecily, duchess of York (1415–1495); Richard, duke of York and duke of Norfolk (1473–1483); Warbeck, Perkin, duke of York (*c*.1474–1499); Anne, duchess of York (1637–1671).

York, Cardinal. See Henry Benedict (1725–1807).

York Minster (*b. c*.1804, *d*. in or after 1851). *See under* Exotic visitors (*act. c*.1500–*c*.1855).

York, Aaron of (*d*. 1268), financier and administrator, was the son of Josce of Lincoln. Although born in Lincoln, probably before 1190, Aaron seems to have been living in York in 1210, when he was assessed for the so-called Bristol tallage. He must, therefore, have been among the early immigrants who re-established a Jewish community at York in the wake of the massacre of 1190. By 1221 his father and brothers Benedict and Samuel had also moved to York, where Aaron had become one of the leading moneylenders in the city. Working often in partnership with other lenders, Aaron lent large sums to important people, especially in the north, where he also enjoyed profitable relationships with a number of monastic houses. At York he presided over a family consortium that included Leo and Samuel l'Eveske, the father and brother of his wife, Hannah; his nephews Josce le Jovene and Isaac; and his brothers Benedict and Samuel. During the 1220s this consortium emerged as the largest supplier of credit to the rapidly expanding economy of Yorkshire. Aaron himself seems to have done a particularly brisk business in lending to Yorkshire monastic houses, who were expanding both the size of their sheep flocks and the extent of their agricultural property during this decade. By the 1230s Aaron's business connections reached into almost every shire in England. In February 1236 Henry III appointed him to sit at the Jewish exchequer, and in December of that year he became archpresbyter, the royally appointed administrative head of the English Jewish community. From this position he was able to further extend his business empire, and to increase his lending around the court. At a time of increasing royal taxation, however, his position also made him an object of hostility, both at court and in the Jewish community. In 1243 the king dismissed him from the archpresbyterate in favour of Elias l'Eveske. No grounds for his dismissal from office are known.

In 1241 Aaron's estate was valued for purposes of taxation at £40,000. Toward the Jewish tallage of 20,000 marks of that year, he paid 6000 marks (£4000). No other thirteenth-century English Jew approached this level of wealth. Between 1241 and 1255, however, royal taxation and other exactions consumed his entire fortune. Aaron told the chronicler Matthew Paris that between 1243 and 1250 he paid the king 30,000 marks, and a further 200 gold marks to the queen. The figures are credible. Despite his losses he remained, nevertheless, the dominant financial figure in the English Jewish community throughout the 1240s, and made further substantial payments to the crown in the early 1250s. By 1255, however, his business had collapsed. Unable to keep up with his tallage payments, his collectable bonds were transferred to the crown, further undermining his financial situation. He, his wife, and his children were several times imprisoned during these years, sometimes for his own debts, on other occasions because Aaron was acting as surety for the debts of the entire Jewish community. King Henry also imposed a variety of personal indignities upon him, most famously in 1251 when he ordered that Aaron's prize black palfrey be confiscated, without compensation, as a gift for Robert Passelewe (d. 1252). Charges of falsifying charters also began to be brought against Aaron, prompting further payments to the crown to avoid prosecution. Although Aaron was still able to pay part of his tallage assessment for spring 1255, when a second tallage of £1000 was imposed upon the English Jewish community in November, he was unable to pay his assessment of £100, and was exempted from the tax on grounds of poverty.

After 1255 references to Aaron of York become scarce. His nephew Isaac continued to act as his attorney as Aaron liquidated the remnants of his financial empire. In 1265 Aaron's wife, Hannah, inherited some property from her brother Samuel, but the family continued to sell assets. In 1266 Aaron sold his remaining property in London to Rabbi Elijah Menaham (d. 1284). Aaron died in 1268, before 30 August, leaving property in Oxford, Northampton, and York to his heirs. But this too was liquidated in the following decade. In 1280 Hannah and her younger son, Elias, sold their share of the family property on Coney Street in York. Samuel, Aaron's elder son, moved to London, and in 1281 he too sold his Coney Street property. No further references to Hannah, Samuel, or Elias are known. Aaron and Hannah also had a daughter, Auntera, whose first husband was her cousin Isaac, the son of Josce le Jovene. Her second husband, Lumbard, was hanged for coinage offences in 1279 or 1280.   ROBERT C. STACEY

Sources Chancery records • R. B. Dobson, 'The decline and expulsion of the medieval Jews of York', *Transactions of the Jewish Historical Society of England*, 26 (1974–8), 34–52 • M. Adler, 'Aaron of York', *Jews of medieval England* (1939) • Paris, *Chron.* • Exchequer, Treasury of receipt, Receipt rolls, PRO, E 401 • J. M. Rigg and others, *Plea rolls of the exchequer of the Jews*, 5 vols. (1905–92) • CPR, 1266–72, 255

York, Sir John (d. 1569), administrator, was the third son of John York and his wife, Katherine Patterdale. His family owed its rise to his great-grandfather **Sir Richard York** (1430–1498), administrator. Richard York became a freeman of York by purchase in 1456 and steadily worked his way into positions of increasing status and importance in the city. He was chamberlain from 1459 to 1460, sheriff from 1465 to 1466, and entered the Corpus Christi Guild in 1469. Having been installed as mayor of the staple of Calais in 1467, he was mayor of York from 1469 to 1470 and again from 1482 to 1483. In 1475 he was master of the Merchants' Guild and was made alderman of the city some time before 1487. He survived the accession of Henry VII and was knighted by the king at York in July 1487, after the victory at the battle of Stoke on 16 June, and granted a £20 annuity the following November. York acted as ambassador in France in 1486 and again in 1491. He was returned for the city of York to the parliaments of 1472–5, January 1483, October 1483, 1484, 1485–6, and 1489–90. On 2 January 1487 he treated with the embassy from Maximilian I and went with the embassy to the Hanse on 20 April 1491.

Richard York's first wife was probably Jane, daughter of Richard Mauleverer of Allerton, Lancashire. They had at least seven sons, including Richard (d. c.1508), Christopher, and Thomas, and four daughters. York's second wife, Joan (d. in or after 1498), was the widow of both John Dalton and John Whitfield (d. 1479). The couple's sons included Adam, William, and John. Sir Richard York died on 25 November 1498. His will is dated 8 April 1498, and was proved on 17 July 1499. He asked to be buried at St John the Evangelist in Ousebridge, Yorkshire. He left all his tenements in Hull to his wife. His will mentions two illegitimate sons, George and Giles York. York's executors were William Senhouse, bishop of Carlisle, Sir Reynold Bray, and his sons, Dr Christopher York, Richard, and William York. His son and heir, Sir Richard York the younger, probably died in 1508 and was buried in St John's Michaelgate in York. The glass in the east window of this building displays a kneeling effigy of Sir Richard York the younger in his surcoat and spurs. He founded a chantry there and was married twice.

Sir John York's early career, 1535–1550 John York's education and early life remain obscure. His family were merchants of the staple in York and also became involved with trading in London and Calais. It is hardly surprising therefore that he is first documented upon his arrival at Calais from Antwerp on 3 September 1535. By about 1542 he had married Anne (d. in or before 1562), daughter of Robert Smyth of London. They had eleven sons, including Peter York (c.1542–1589), of Gouthwaite in Yorkshire, and Rowland *Yorke (d. 1588), soldier and traitor. In 1544 York was appointed assay master to the first mint in the Tower of London. The following year he was transferred to Southwark, Surrey, as under-treasurer of the mint there, recently established in Henry VIII's newly acquired property Suffolk Place. He was added to the commission of the peace for Middlesex on 26 May 1547 and appointed master of the king's woods in the southern parts by August, although he did not start felling trees until autumn 1549.

The patronage of John Dudley, Viscount Lisle, was certainly a factor in York's placement at the mint. Lisle and York had long shared a mutual interest in lands belonging to the former abbeys of Byland and Fountains in Yorkshire. This close association stood Lisle in good stead. During his dispute with the lord protector, Edward Seymour, duke of Somerset, Lisle (now earl of Warwick) took up residence at York's house in the parish of St Stephen Wal- brook, London, from 6 October 1549. York's motivation for supporting Warwick is difficult to determine but was probably based on his position as a Dudley client and on apathy towards the lord protector's social policies. On 18 January 1550 Warwick himself transferred from his own house at Ely Place to

> the house of a certain sheriff [York], a personage who ranks first in the city of London after the Lord Mayor [Sir Henry Amcotes]. He lodged with the same sheriff after he conducted the intrigue against the Protector, and no doubt his purpose was the same then as now, to have the city on his side. (*CSP Spain*, 1550–52, 13)

York was sheriff of London and Middlesex from 1549 to 1550, during which time his influence was considered essential to winning the support of the mayor and com- mon council of London. On 9 October 1549 the London council or confederate lords, led by Warwick, met and dined at Walbrook, where they discussed the actions taken by Somerset to secure several of Edward VI's armouries, as well as rumours that the lord protector planned to 'convey the king out of Windsor and the realm' (*APC*, 1547–50, 337). According to Alan Bryson, 'York's role at this juncture was vital; it was he, not Sir Richard Rich, Lord Rich (as the chronicler Charles Wriothesley believed), who "opened" the request from the London council to the common council for one thousand men' (Bryson, 143). These soldiers were necessary 'for the accomplyshment of their enterprice for the spedye savegarde & conveying the kinges maiestie out of the handes of the late protector' (CLRO, Repertory 12 (1), fol. 151*v*). On 9 October the common council agreed reluc- tantly to provide the men. York and other city officials treated the London council as if it were the privy council. That the London councillors met in his home and that he acted as 'chief intermediary' between them and the com- mon council, meant that York became a permanent and prominent client of Warwick's (Bryson, 149).

York benefited from the king's gratitude. As a reward for his hospitality and loyalty, Edward dined with him at his official residence in Southwark on 17 October and there- upon knighted him. Immediately after his release from the Tower on 6 February 1550 Somerset dined at Wal- brook, where Warwick was still in residence, 'without great guard or business' and was then 'enlarged … in sort as doth appear by his recognisance' (*APC*, 1547–50, 383–4). The privy council continued to conduct its business from York's house until 8 February.

Currency speculation and restoration of the coinage, 1550–1553 The crown's desire to pay off its foreign debt and the resulting debasements of the coinage meant that York had become indispensable as a mint official by 1550. When Sir Martin Bowes was pensioned off from the Tower mint in 1550, York supervised operations there while remaining under-treasurer of the Southwark mint. When the Southwark mint was closed in September 1551, he was appointed under-treasurer of the Tower mint. Despite the end of the war with the French in March 1550 and the mint's efforts to produce very large amounts of coinage,

the king's debts continued to mount at an alarming rate. The privy council turned to York to solve the problem. He devised a plan to make a large profit on the Antwerp exchange as well as to bring home quality bullion from abroad for the production of new, finer English coin. The details of the scheme remain obscure, but it is known that in December 1550 York went to Antwerp to speculate with the king's money. Edward noted in his *Chronicle* that:

> It was agreed that [Sir John York] master of one of the mints at the Tower, should make this bargain with me, viz. to make the profit of silver rising of the bullion that he himself bought, pay all my debts, to the sum of £120,000 or above, and remain accountable for the overplus … to which I should give him £15,000 in prest-money and leave to carry £8,000 overseas to abase the exchange. (*Chronicle*, ed. Jordan, 48)

York insisted he could double the money in value each month, but by March 1551 he had suffered losses of at least £4000 of silver bullion. Edward blamed the loss on the treason of certain Englishmen who may have betrayed York's plans to the imperial government. The king hoped to recover the lost sums, but the incident proved too embarrassing, as York and his men were caught red- handed trying to smuggle £4000 in bullion out of Ant- werp, for which they were 'sorely frightened and dis- tressed … but have small sympathy from the people who say Mr York deserves it' (*CSP Spain*, 1550–52, 264).

Despite this set-back, the scheme did not fail entirely, and during his time at the mints York brought in large amounts of bullion on which he made a handsome per- sonal profit. In 1551 Sir Nicholas Throckmorton and he were charged with the task of restoring the coinage, and many of the coins issued were stamped with Y, one of York's mint marks. On 21 June 1552 York was pardoned 'for all treasons and offences concerning making and issu- ing of the king's money', on the condition that he settle his mint accounts for over £9500 'due to the king' (*CPR*, 1551–3, 301). York's fortunes were made through his ser- vice in the mint, for he was able to claim a remarkably high rate of remuneration for the bullion he supplied. He was considered valuable enough for Somerset to use him as one of his own financial officers and York disbursed £2500 of the duke's money by October 1551. York's princi- pal allegiance, however, remained with Warwick (now duke of Northumberland). This close relationship became a political liability. Already in 1550 Henry Fitzalan, twelfth earl of Arundel, and Anne Seymour, duchess of Somerset, planned to take York prisoner in order to determine whether there had been any embezzlement of royal funds. When Edward died on 6 June 1553, York firmly sup- ported Lady Jane Grey against Princess Mary, with near calamitous results. According to one witness, York was on Leadenhead Street when the proclamation of Mary's accession was read out on 19 July and 'people started run- ning in all directions and crying out'. York,

> hearing this tumult, thought it had another cause. He therefore cried out to the people that it was not true, and though he was on horse-back he escaped alive with difficulty and was taken into the house of Sheriff Garrett [William Garrard], where he was examined.

The witness reported that so many people gathered outside the sheriff's house clamouring for York, that 'he may come to a bad end' (*CSP Spain*, 1553, 108). York retreated safely to Walbrook, where his friend the lord mayor George Barne arrested him, on 23 July. On 31 July York joined Northumberland in the Tower, his property having been ordered to be inventoried and sequestrated. *The Chronicle of Queen Jane* reports that he was freed on 18 October. He had certainly been released by November, when he attended a sermon at St Stephen Walbrook, given by Dr John Feckenham, Mary I's private chaplain and confessor.

Final years, 1553–1569 During Mary's reign York conformed outwardly, but focused his energies on trading activities with Germany and the Low Countries, and his investments in Western exploration. In 1555 he was one of the twenty-four assistants of the Company of Merchant Adventurers. When Elizabeth I came to the throne he tried several means of re-entering royal service. Presumably nominated by Sir Ambrose Cave, York was returned as MP for Boroughbridge, Yorkshire, in 1559. He wrote to Sir William Cecil, principal secretary, in October 1560, asking to be restored to his office as under-treasurer, but the post was given to a former comptroller at Southwark, Thomas Fleetwood. York had made an enemy of Sir Thomas Gresham, who had been trying to monopolize the English trade in gunpowder and saltpetre in Antwerp. During Elizabeth's reign Cecil preferred to rely upon Gresham's advice about the coinage, rather than York's. Little else is known of York's last years. As a freeman of the Merchant Taylors' Company he contributed a small sum to the building of the Royal Exchange in January 1566. He may have spent the last years of his life caring for his properties in Yorkshire and Kent and enjoying his large family.

Six of York's sons were still alive when he wrote his will on 6 April 1562: Peter, William, Edmund, Rowland, Edward, and Henry York. His eldest daughter, Anne, married Sir William Hilton, one of the supervisors of his will. Another daughter, Jane, was unmarried at the making of his will and he left her £666 13s. 4d. towards her marriage portion, to be taken from his goods and his 'second cross of diamond' (PRO, PROB 11/51, sig. 4). York's widow, Anne, whom he appointed his sole executor, married Robert Paget of London. Peter York received the lion's share of the family estates, principally those concentrated in Craven and Nidderdale, Yorkshire. Sir John York's second surviving son, William York, received the manor of Pedderthrope in Yorkshire. The third son, Sir Edmund York, was granted the manor of Steddmeere, Yorkshire. Rowland and Edward York were to share the manor of Rudson or Rudston, Yorkshire, as well as many of their father's household goods and possessions. When Sir John York died in London in January or February 1569, he was a wealthy man as a result of his own expertise in financial matters. He was buried in St Stephen Walbrook.

J. G. ELZINGA

Sources A. Bryson, '"The speciall men in every shere": the Edwardian regime, 1547–1553', PhD diss., U. St Andr., 2001, 70, 138, 143–4, 149 n. 151, 163, 176, 195, 217, 254, 270 · *APC*, 1547–56 · *CSP dom.*, 1547–80; 1547–53; 1553–58 · *CSP Spain*, 1550–53 · *CPR*, 1551–3 · *Calendar of the manuscripts of the most hon. the marquis of Salisbury*, 24 vols., HMC, 9 (1883–1976) · *Calendar of the manuscripts of the marquis of Bath preserved at Longleat, Wiltshire*, 5 vols., HMC, 58 (1904–80) · *The chronicle and political papers of King Edward VI*, ed. W. K. Jordan (1966) · D. MacCulloch, 'The *Vita Mariae Angliae Reginae* of Robert Wingfield of Brantham', *Camden miscellany, XXVIII*, CS, 4th ser., 29 (1984), 181–301 · J. G. Nichols, ed., *The chronicle of Queen Jane, and of two years of Queen Mary*, CS, old ser., 48 (1850) · *The diary of Henry Machyn, citizen and merchant-taylor of London, from AD 1550 to AD 1563*, ed. J. G. Nichols, CS, 42 (1848) · C. B. Norcliffe, ed., *The visitation of Yorkshire in the years 1563 and 1564*, Harleian Society, 16 (1881) · J. C. Wedgwood and A. D. Holt, *History of parliament, 1: Biographies of the members of the Commons house, 1439–1509* (1936) · wills, PRO, PROB 11/11, sig. 36 [Sir Richard York]; PROB 11/51, sig. 4 [Sir John York] · *DNB* · W. K. Jordan, *Edward VI, 2: The threshold of power* (1970) · W. K. Jordan, *Edward VI, 1: The young king* (1968) · C. E. Challis, *The Tudor coinage* (1978) · C. E. Challis, *Currency and the economy in Tudor and early Stuart England* (1989)

Wealth at death wealthy; estates in Yorkshire, Pedderthorpe, Steddmeere, Rudston (or Rudson), Heselthorpe, Sherburn, Leigh; London mansion house in Soper Lane; lots of various gold and silver possessions: will, PRO, PROB 11/51, sig. 4

York, Richard of. *See* Richard of York (1411–1460).

York, Sir Richard (1430–1498). *See under* York, Sir John (*d.* 1569).

York, Robert [*called* Perscrutator] (*fl.* 1313–1325), natural philosopher, was a writer on alchemy and on natural philosophy more generally, especially on the implications of astrology for meteorology. He has in the past been confused with the late thirteenth-century writer on astronomy *Robert the Englishman. York's meteorology opens with mention of the year (1325) and the place (York) of its composition, and little is known about him beyond these two items of information. He has been claimed as a Dominican theologian, but the evidence for this is very weak. There is extant (in the Bodleian Library, MS Digby 208) a table of chapter headings from Isidore's *Etymologies* ascribed to one 'Robertus Anglicus, S.T.P., ordinis S. Dominici' and John Pits mentions the existence of scriptural commentaries by an English friar, Robert, in the Dominican Library in Bologna. Since Robert was a common English forename, these references are of little value. In addition to York's two chief attested works, others (on ceremonial magic and on 'secret medicine') have been ascribed to him, but the ascriptions are relatively late and might rest in part on a confusion with excerpts from the main writings. The alternative name Perscrutator seems early, although the different accounts of its origins reflect on the personalities that different writers wish to ascribe to him. Jacques Gaffarel's preface to the medical writings of Campanella (1635) hints that it stemmed from the scrutiny York gave to the hidden doctrines of secret medicine. Pits, citing John Leland, suggested that the title came from the scrutiny York gave to the inner workings of philosophy. John Ashenden, however, a later contemporary of York who knew his meteorological work, tells us that he called himself Perscrutator in that treatise; and Lynn Thorndike finds there the sentence 'Ordinem autem regularum que sunt signa 12 perscrutor' ('I scrutinize the order of the rules, which are the twelve signs'; Thorndike,

3.108), which might be the reference Ashenden had in mind. Robert York later became known simply as 'the man who called himself Perscrutator'.

One of the principal concerns of astrology, from its ancient beginnings, had been with meteorological phenomena, and it is not surprising to find that Greek and early Muslim scholars attempted to combine Aristotle's meteorological theories with astrological doctrines. Aristotle's theory of the four elements (earth, water, air, and fire) thus found its way into scholastic astrology—indeed astrology played an important part in transmitting it, and since it was of central importance to medieval alchemy, astrology found a natural place in that subject too. Robert Grosseteste and Albertus Magnus were among the more influential writers of the thirteenth century to produce amalgams of the three types of subject matter; and it was in continuation of this tradition that Robert York wrote his two chief works, the *De impressionibus aeris* (which might be freely rendered 'On forces affecting the weather') and the *Correctorium alchymiae* ('A work correcting alchemy'). These writings are known by various other titles: the first is found also as *De mutatione aeris*, or *De mutabilibus* [or *mirabilibus*] *elementorum*. The alchemical work seems to have been later redrafted by a certain Master Bernard, possibly Bernard de Treves (1406–*c*.1490), under the title *Correctio fatuorum* ('Correction of fools'), and was to be printed in due course in both versions (Nuremberg, 1541; Bern, 1545; ed. Zetzner, Strasbourg, 1659; ed. Manget, Geneva, 1702). There is a German translation dating from 1485.

York makes it clear in his meteorological work that he is proud of the fact that it is based on reason and experiment rather than mere authority. (John Ashenden was sceptical of the experiential component in York's work, however, and Pico della Mirandola was no doubt following Ashenden when he made the same point.) He discusses the forces which operate on the elements to form compounds (*mixtiones*) out of them. In this respect his work shows some originality. In the combination of any two elements he envisages one or even two motive forces (one for each element) and one or two intermediary forces. He decides that there are seven different types of force in all and that each is effected by one of the seven planets. This search for forces was not very fruitful, but it is an interesting symptom of a growing awareness of sound scientific technique, especially evident in the early fourteenth century. There are several respects in which York's work resembles the *Icocedron* of his older contemporary Walter Odington, but, of the two, York's is the more complex, and is provided with rather more theoretical applications. It is in the course of applying it to weather prediction (with results that are in the end fairly conventional) that York mentions another work of his in which the elements are held to be arranged as are the 'projections of [planetary] rays' (a technical term of astrological theory) and as harmonies in a musical scale—ideas with an important future ahead of them.

There is much more by way of astrological theory of a conventional sort, for example in the discussion of great conjunctions of Saturn and Jupiter, and of the political portents of comets. York discusses at one point a comet seen over York in 1313, and explains its consequences for a battle (presumably Bannockburn) between the English and the Scots. The sorts of conclusion he draws are not particularly new, nor are they based in a very systematic way on the twin principles of rational argument and experiment (or experience) that he had announced as his guiding lights. Much of the alchemical treatise is likewise traditional, reporting as it does a version of the sulphur–mercury theory of the formation and transmutation of the metals. For all his claims not to be beholden to authority, York is dismissive of those who perform experiments without an earlier training in philosophical theory. In particular he criticizes those who attempt to derive the philosophers' stone from common substances (dung, hair, eggs, blood, and so on) lacking in 'live sulphur', which he claims (still in a rather conventional way) to be unlike common sulphur and derivable only from either silver or gold.

There is some slight additional evidence for scientific activity in York at the time of Perscrutator's presence there, in the form of Alfonsine astronomical tables for the longitude of York, London, and Lincoln (in BL, Egerton MS 889), but there is no reason to associate him with this. Lynn Thorndike speculated that an anonymous alchemical treatise written in May 1331 at Paris might have been Perscrutator's, but on no better grounds than the author's 'self-confidence'. The character Sidonius in the dialogues written by the German humanist Johann Reuchlin (*De verbo mirifico*, 1495), alludes to a Robert of England who wrote a *De magia ceremoniali*, and who died an unpleasant death in Switzerland. There is no clear connection with Perscrutator, although several have supposed that he was meant. Robert York has occasionally been assigned the writings of others, including Robert of Chester (*fl.* 1141–1150) and Robert Cothun (*fl.* 1340), as well as Robert the Englishman. J. D. NORTH

Sources L. Thorndike, *A history of magic and experimental science*, 8 vols. (1923–58), vol. 3, pp. 103–18, 678–9 · [Bernard de Treves ?], 'Correctio fatuorum, tracta, tulus satis perutilis et artenticus foeliciter incipit', *De alchimia opuscula complura veterum philosophorum, quorum catalogus sequens pagella indicabit* (1550), 1–19

York, Rowland. *See* Yorke, Rowland (d. 1588).

York, Thomas of (*b. c.*1220, *d.* before 1269), Franciscan friar and theologian, of unknown parentage, had entered the Franciscan order in England by 1245, when Adam Marsh (*d.* 1259), a leading English Franciscan, requested the loan of a philosophy text in York's keeping. York was probably then resident at the London convent and studying arts, but must have been sent to Oxford before 1249. While studying theology at Oxford he joined for a time the household of Robert Grosseteste, bishop of Lincoln (*d.* 1253), probably through the good offices of Adam Marsh, who described York as 'active, discreet, full of goodwill and devoted to the cure of souls' (Brewer, 1.115). He was appointed lector at the Oxford Franciscan convent, but in

1253 a dispute arose at his presentation to incept as a doctor of theology, the opponents of the friars challenging his eligibility, as he had not been a master of arts. Through the firm and persuasive advocacy of Marsh he was eventually permitted to incept, but the case provoked the university to decree that in future no scholar who had not ruled in arts could proceed to a degree in theology: a statute that would engender recurrent disputes between the friars and the university. York's confrère Roger Bacon (d. 1294) was probably referring to him when he wrote scornfully of a colleague who had presumed to teach philosophy without having read it; his critics ignored his fruitful study of arts, evident in his *Sapientiale*, at the London Franciscan convent. About 1256–7 he was lector at the Cambridge convent. Bonaventure's reference in 1269 to his defence of the friars implies that York was dead by then.

York's defence of the mendicant friars' claims, *Manus quae contra omnipotentem*, was written *c*.1253–6; and his sermon, 'Christ's passion' (Cambridge, Trinity College, MS B.15.38), is probably contemporaneous with it. His major and unpublished work, the *Sapientiale* (Florence, Biblioteca Nazionale Centrale, MS Conv. sopp. A.6.437), is a digest of the principal theological issues under debate in Oxford in the early 1250s, and was probably compiled from his university lectures and disputations. He proposed independent solutions to the current problems of generation and becoming, individuation, universals, the nature of the soul, and immaterial intelligences, which were influenced but not dominated by Grosseteste's ideas. In general he attempted a series of solutions to specific questions without displaying an overall metaphysical coherence, and the work's chief contribution was to bring into consideration the ideas of recently translated Arab and Jewish philosophers, especially Averroes and Moses Maimonides. It was soon overtaken by the profounder and better known works of Bonaventure, Albert the Great (Albertus Magnus), and Aquinas.   JEREMY CATTO, rev.

Sources J. S. Brewer, ed., *Monumenta Franciscana*, 1, Rolls Series, 4 (1858) · R. Bacon, 'Opus minus', *Fr. Rogeri Bacon opera quaedam hactenus inedita*, ed. J. S. Brewer, Rolls Series, 15 (1859) [only a fragment of the 'Opus minus' is included] · Thomas of York, *Manus quae contra omnipotentem*, ed. M. Bierbaum, Franziskanische Studien, 2 (1920) · Trinity Cam., MS B.15.38 · Biblioteca Nazionale Centrale, Florence, MS Conv. sopp. A.6.437 · Emden, *Oxf.*, 3.2139–40 · E. Longpré, 'Fr Thomas d'York', *Archivum Franciscanum Historicum*, 19 (1926), 875–930 · D. E. Sharp, *Franciscan philosophy at Oxford in the thirteenth century*, British Society of Franciscan Studies, 16 (1930) · *Tractatus Fr. Thomae vulgo dicti de Eccleston de adventu Fratrum Minorum in Angliam*, ed. A. G. Little (Paris, 1909)

Archives Biblioteca Nazionale Centrale, Florence, MS Conv. sopp. A.6.437 · Trinity Cam., MS B.15.38

York, William of. *See* William of York (d. 1154).

York, William of (d. 1256), justice, and bishop of Salisbury, apparently came from the East Riding of Yorkshire, though nothing is known of his parentage or early life. He may have begun his official career as a chancery clerk, perhaps under the patronage of Ralph de Neville, since, according to Matthew Paris, Henry III said of him in 1253 that he had once been a scribbler of royal writs, and some personal letters he wrote to Neville in 1226–8, when the latter was chancellor, show Neville to have been his patron. More certainly, he served as a clerk of the bench from 1219, and probably from 1217; he may have been appointed by the chancellor for service in the bench, since he does not appear to have been the personal clerk of any of the justices. In the latter part of his period as a bench clerk one of his colleagues was his fellow East Riding man, Roger of Thirkleby, and another was William of Raleigh.

After gaining legal knowledge through his work as a clerk, York served from 1225 onwards as a commissioner of assize and special business in vacations, and in 1227–8 was three times an eyre justice in the north. Some interesting and informative letters he wrote to Ralph de Neville at that time have survived. He first sat as a justice of the bench in 1231, shortly after he had ceased to serve as a clerk, and in 1234 became the most senior justice regularly sitting there after Robert of Lexinton, remaining in that appointment until the end of 1241, when he became senior justice in the court *coram rege* upon the death of Stephen of Segrave. He served on only six eyres as a junior justice, in 1227–8 and 1232, while between 1234 and 1244 he served as chief justice on thirty-four eyres, from which six plea rolls survive which are probably his. His clerk, until 1246 and from perhaps as early as 1230, was Roger of Whitchester. During the king's absence in Gascony in 1242–3 he played an important role in government, so much so that he was incorrectly believed by the annalist of Dunstable Priory to have been one of the regents.

York held a number of church appointments, the first known being the royal living of King's Ripton in Huntingdonshire, which he held by 1220, and which he managed to pass on to two of his protégés successively. He held several livings in Yorkshire, the most senior of which was the provostship of Beverley, and others in Lancashire, Northumberland, and Cambridgeshire. He also acquired canonries at York, St Paul's, London, and Wells. By the time of his promotion to the court *coram rege* it has been estimated that he held ecclesiastical appointments to a gross value of about £800, according to valuations derived from the 1291 taxation of benefices by the pope, Nicholas IV. He eventually acquired lay interests, mostly leases or wardships, in several counties outside his native Yorkshire, including Surrey, Essex, Nottinghamshire, and Northamptonshire, as well as houses in London and York. As a cleric he had no direct heir, but before his death he conveyed his own estates in Eske, near Beverley, and Norton, near Malton, to his brother Sir Nicholas of York.

On 8 December 1246 York was elected bishop of Salisbury, and on receiving his temporalities in 1247 resigned as a justice, concentrating on his work as a bishop, although he still took part in judicial business at the greater sessions of the king's council, where he is known to have been involved in judgments against Dunstable Priory and the abbey of St Albans, and continued to witness royal charters when the king was at Winchester or in his own diocese; in 1251 he was brought out of judicial retirement to head an eyre for London. As bishop he was served as his personal official by Nicholas of York, perhaps a nephew, and was much concerned with the completion of the new cathedral at Salisbury, work which was probably assisted by his influence at court. He did not live to see its consecration. He died on 31 January 1256 and was buried in the choir of the cathedral. Matthew Paris's obituary of him was rather uncharitable, since he had given judgment against Matthew's abbey of St Albans. Nevertheless, Paris described him as 'most skilled in the laws of the kingdom' (Paris, 4.587), and his opinion was cited three times in the *De legibus* (formerly attributed to Bracton). He undoubtedly had great influence on the development of law and its administration, although all that Paris mentions is that he became unpopular through reinventing suit of court. He may well have been concerned in the extension and development of the articles of the eyre, and with the movement away from the issue of assize commissions to four, mainly local, justices to a single justice of one of the central courts, a move towards professionalization of justice in the localities. DAVID CROOK

Sources C. A. F. Meekings, *King's bench justices, 1239–58* [forthcoming] • C. A. F. Meekings, 'Martin Pateshull and William Raleigh', *BIHR*, 26 (1953), 157–80 • R. E. Latham and E. K. Timings, 'Six letters concerning the eyres of 1226–8', *EngHR*, 65 (1950), 492–504 • C. A. F. Meekings and D. Crook, eds., *The 1235 Surrey eyre*, 1, Surrey RS, 31 (1979) • Paris, *Chron.* • W. H. Rich Jones and W. Dunn Macray, eds., *Charters and documents illustrating the history of the cathedral, city, and diocese of Salisbury, in the twelfth and thirteenth centuries*, Rolls Series, 97 (1891), nos. 261, 263, 264, 266, 271 • D. Crook, *Records of the general eyre*, Public Record Office Handbooks, 20 (1982) • W. W. Shirley, ed., *Royal and other historical letters illustrative of the reign of Henry III*, 1, Rolls Series, 27 (1862) • *Ann. mon.*, vol. 3 • *Henrici de Bracton de legibus et consuetudinibus Angliae / Bracton on the laws and customs of England*, ed. G. E. Woodbine, ed. and trans. S. E. Thorne, 4 vols. (1968–77) • *Chancery records* • court of common pleas, feet of fines, PRO, CP 25/1
Wealth at death ecclesiastical appointments est. value £800

York, William [*name in religion* Laurence] (1686/7–1770), Benedictine monk and vicar apostolic of the western district, was born in London, nothing being known of his parentage. After attending the small school attached to the English Benedictine monastery of St Gregory at Douai he was professed as a monk there in 1704 or 1705. In December 1711 he was ordained priest, and for much of that decade he carried out teaching and other duties connected with the monastery school. He was cellarer at St Gregory's from 1719 to 1720 when, as a critic of the disruptive policies of the then president-general of the English Benedictine congregation, Dom Laurence Fenwick, he was ordered to join the English mission. However, after the 1721 chapter-meeting of the area, or province, concerned with the northern counties and attended by York, the general chapter elected him as prior of St Edmund's, Paris, another of the English Benedictines' continental houses. From 1725 to 1729 York served at Douai as prior of St Gregory's, after which he became secretary to President-General Southcott, an ardent and active Jacobite who was later to combine with the exiled court, and with the Old Pretender himself, in promoting the likeminded York's candidature as a bishop.

Back in England, in the Benedictines' southern province, York in 1730 was put in charge of its most important mission, that of Bath. Here the monks controlled an old-established and influential foundation, of social as well as religious significance, comprising a chapel cum lodging-house, the Bell Tree, attended by Roman Catholics from all parts of the kingdom, and described by a later incumbent as 'much sought after by visitors for lodgings … and those sometimes of the first distinction, as the Duke of Norfolk and others' (Downside Abbey, MS 252, fol. 17). In this propitious milieu Laurence York won golden opinions both for the eloquence of his preaching and for his social accomplishments: 'a man fit to appear in the best company … exceedingly agreeable to the chief of both Catholic and Protestant nobility that frequent that place' (Scott, 88)—qualities which enhanced his credentials for episcopal office.

York's mission field was the western vicariate, one of four extensive districts governed by vicars apostolic (prelates with the titles of bishoprics *in partibus infidelium*) mainly drawn from the secular clergy, though the western bishops had so far been a Benedictine chaplain and preacher to James II, Philip Michael Ellis, and a Franciscan of Jacobite sympathies, Matthew Prichard. It was to the latter that York was appointed coadjutor in 1741 in the teeth of opposition from the other vicars apostolic, who wanted the post filled by a secular priest, but with the energetic backing of Southcott and the Stuart court in order both to consolidate the regulars' hold on the western vicariate and to preserve a Jacobite presence in the Roman Catholic episcopate in England. Their manoeuvres were successful and York was consecrated bishop of Nisibis on 20 August 1741.

Until 1745 York continued to administer the Bell Tree house, after which he was offered continuing hospitality there, and Bath remained his headquarters, an arrangement which may have afforded to the south-western counties of England a greater degree of pastoral care than that hitherto provided by its Monmouthshire-based vicar apostolic, now a septuagenarian; however, the destruction of the western district archives in 1780 during Bath's Gordon riots renders most earlier episcopal activity undiscoverable. Indeed, the one confirmation traceable to York while coadjutor was in Monmouthshire itself, at Abergavenny, some months after Prichard had given up active duty. This visit occurred in the summer of 1745, when there began a period of eighteen months or so during which the bishop was away from Bath—an absence attested by himself and by a pair of informers and consistent with an account (Oliver, 55–6) of York's withdrawal from the city for his own safety at the time of the Jacobite rising, acting on the advice of the mayor, to whom had been handed a probably bogus missive thanking York for assistance given or promised to the Jacobite cause and offering him the bishopric of Carlisle in the event of a Stuart restoration. The bishop was still absent from Bath in February 1747, when he wrote to the Roman Congregatio de Propaganda Fide (responsible for missionary territories, including Britain) that for the past eighteen months he had been 'a fugitive from my ordinary residence and have as yet no fixed abode' (Brady, 293), and for part of that time he was to be found at a rural recusant enclave in the Mendips.

After York's return to Bath the papal bull *Emanivit nuper*, issued in 1745 but delayed in England owing to the 'Forty-Five and its aftermath, presented him with an unwelcome Roman rebuff to the regular clergy in their long-running losing battle against dependence on the vicars apostolic for faculties to exercise their ministry in England—a dependence strongly resisted, both before and after the bull's promulgation, by the two western bishops, of whom York, however, won commendation from a formidable opponent, Bishop Stonor of the midland district, for his 'just discernment and episcopal mind' (Berington, 420). Bishop Prichard died on 22 May 1750 and was succeeded as vicar apostolic of the western district by Laurence York, with the faculties question still not finally resolved; but three years later it was definitively settled in accordance with the wishes of the secular vicars apostolic by the bull *Apostolicum ministerium*, firmly subjecting the regular clergy to episcopal control and imposing upon them the unrealistic sexennium, requiring them, as a condition of having their faculties renewed, to undergo for three months in every six years the regime of a continental religious house, including a fifteen-day retreat. In Bishop York and his fellow regulars this obligation, reducing their mission force and involving unaffordable expense, aroused suspicion and dismay, and his fears for his district (which was not only poor, but the great majority of whose priests were regulars) were expressed in a letter to the Jesuit provincial lamenting 'our threatened ruin, which must inevitably be the case if the sexennial retreat takes place' (Foley, 5.165). In the event, however, acceptable compromises saved the situation.

York's pastoral activities are no easier to trace when vicar apostolic than earlier, but confirmation tours eastward and westward of his Bath base are perhaps reflected in register evidence (not plentiful for that period) relating to Marlborough in 1753 and Ugbrooke, Devon, in the following year. By this time the bishop was in his sixties and hoping for the appointment of a coadjutor to assist with his vast vicariate (seven English counties and the whole of Wales) and to pave the way for his own much desired retirement to monastic life, and (for the appointee must be a Benedictine) to continue that order's rule over the western district. Moves to this end had begun shortly after York's accession to the vicariate and, as in his own case, Benedictine and Jacobite backing, including that of the Pretender, still prevailed at Rome against the opposition of the secular vicars apostolic, and it was the internationally esteemed Charles Walmesley who was consecrated, with right of succession, in 1756. He it was who on 12 March 1764 delivered to the clergy of the western district a tribute prompted by his superior's retirement to his beloved St Gregory's, praising his pastoral solicitude, his piety, and his humanitarianism—qualities which, with the others already mentioned, combined to fit him well for his vocation. Six years later he died after suffering a paralytic stroke while celebrating mass at St Gregory's. A Bell Tree house document (Williams, *Post-Reformation Catholicism*, 1.176), like the *Dictionary of National Biography*, dates his death 14 April 1770, while other sources have the 20th.

He was aged about eighty-three years and was remembered as 'a holy pious prelate … ornament to his house and body' (diary of Thomas Welch).

J. ANTHONY WILLIAMS

Sources G. Scott, *Gothic rage undone: English monks in the age of Enlightenment* (1992) · P. A. Allanson, *Biographies of English Benedictines*, ed. A. Cramer, Catholic RS, Occasional Publications, 3 [forthcoming] · W. M. Brady, *Annals of the Catholic hierarchy in England and Scotland*, 3 (1877); repr. as *The episcopal succession in England, Scotland and Ireland* (1883) · Royal Arch., Stuart MSS, 225/115 · G. Oliver, *Collections illustrating the history of the Catholic religion in the counties of Cornwall, Devon, Dorset, Somerset, Wilts, and Gloucester* (1857) · J. A. Williams, 'No ordinary residence: Bishop York and the "Forty-Five"', *Recusant History*, 16 (1982–3), 217–19 · Downside Abbey, Bath, MS 252 [history of the Bath mission] · transcript of the diary of Thomas Welch OSB, Douai Abbey, Woolhampton, Berkshire · *The memoirs of Gregorio Panzani*, ed. and trans. J. Berington (1793) · B. Jarrett, ed., 'Catholic registers of Rev. James Dominic Darbyshire', *Dominicana*, Catholic RS, 25 (1925), 251–2 · J. H. Canning and E. H. Willson, eds., 'Catholic registers of Abergavenny, Mon., 1740–1838', *Miscellanea, XIV*, Catholic RS, 27 (1927), 98–235, esp. 120 · R. E. Scantlebury, ed., 'Register of Marnhull, 1772–1826', *Miscellanea*, Catholic RS, 56 (1964), 165–99, esp. 196 · J. A. Williams, ed., *Post-Reformation Catholicism in Bath*, 1, Catholic RS, 65 (1975), 50–63 · H. Foley, ed., *Records of the English province of the Society of Jesus*, 7 vols. in 8 (1875–83) · H. N. Birt, *A history of Downside School* (1902)
Archives Douai Abbey, Woolhampton, Berkshire, diary of Thomas Welch OSB · Royal Arch., Stuart MSS
Likenesses portrait, Downside Abbey, near Bath

York and Albany. For this title name *see* Ernest Augustus, Prince, duke of York and Albany (1674–1728); Edward Augustus, Prince, duke of York and Albany (1739–1767); Frederick, Prince, duke of York and Albany (1763–1827).

Yorke, Albert Edward Philip Henry, sixth earl of Hardwicke (1867–1904), politician, was born at the British embassy in Paris on 14 March 1867, the only son in the three children of Charles Philip *Yorke, fifth earl (1836–1897), and his wife, Lady Sophia Georgiana Robertina Wellesley (*d.* 1923), daughter of the first Earl Cowley. The prince of Wales, afterwards Edward VII, was his godfather. Styled Viscount Royston until 1897, he was educated at Eton College (1881–4), and served as honorary attaché at the British embassy in Vienna from 1886 to 1891. His father (Champagne Charlie) had squandered a fortune and the family's estates were put up for sale in 1891. In the following year Royston became a member of the London stock exchange, and in 1897 a partner in the stockbroking firm of Basil Montgomery & Co., succeeding to the earldom upon the death of his father in May 1897. In 1898 he was elected as a moderate (Conservative) member of the London county council, representing West Marylebone, and also acquired the largest part of the ownership of the *Saturday Review*.

Hardwicke gained significant political notoriety through a series of events played out in the House of Lords in 1899 and the following year. He was vehemently opposed to the erection of a statue of Oliver Cromwell near the entrance to the house and in August 1899 he took the opportunity, when there were only nine peers present in the house, to move a motion censuring the Salisbury government over this matter. Despite the appeals of the lord chancellor, Lord Halsbury, Hardwicke pushed the issue to a division, and the government was formally censured by five votes to four. Henry Lucy regarded this as most 'deplorable' behaviour, and when Hardwicke raised the matter again in the following session, Halsbury, 'trembling with indignation', condemned him for adding 'neither to the dignity of the House nor to respect for the decisions of Parliament' (Lucy, 367).

In November 1900 Hardwicke was appointed parliamentary under-secretary for India. The following month he again came to prominence in the Lords, this time through allegations of a conflict between his business and political interests. He had been permitted by Salisbury, upon taking his position in government, to retain his connection with the stock exchange. This unusual arrangement was immediately seized upon by Lord Rosebery as an opportunity to attack the ethics of the government, claiming that Hardwicke's case risked creating a precedent 'full of peril to the interests of the country' (*The Times*, 30 Nov 1904, 6). Hardwicke was forced to explain to the house that his 'financial embarrassments' (Searle, 50) meant that he was unable to forgo the income from his business connections.

In the office of government itself, Hardwicke was a hard-working and effective under-secretary, and he was transferred, in the same role, to the War Office in August 1902. But here again he found controversy, through his chairmanship of a committee formed to report on the establishment of a formalized intelligence division. In its recommendations the committee went 'some way beyond their original brief' (Gooch, 25) and demanded sweeping changes throughout significant parts of the office. This was 'rejected comprehensively' by senior officials (ibid., 26), and Hardwicke pursued the matter to the War Office council where, however, the matter was allowed quietly to lapse.

In 1903 Hardwicke returned to the India Office, again as under-secretary. He died suddenly of heart failure on 29 November 1904, at his home, 8 York Terrace, Regent's Park, London, and was buried at the Marylebone borough cemetery, East Finchley, Middlesex, on 3 December. He was unmarried.   MARC BRODIE

Sources DNB · *The Times* (30 Nov 1904) · *The Times* (5 Dec 1904) · *The Eton register*, 5 (privately printed, Eton, 1908) · G. R. Searle, *Corruption in British politics, 1895–1930* (1987) · H. W. Lucy, *A diary of the Unionist parliament, 1895–1900* (1901) · J. Gooch, *The plans of war: the general staff and British military strategy, c.1900–1916* (1974) · Burke, *Peerage* · GEC, *Peerage*

Likenesses Spy [L. Ward], lithograph caricature, NPG; repro. in VF (4 April 1901)

Wealth at death £7978 1s. 9d.: probate, 15 Dec 1904, CGPLA Eng. & Wales

Yorke, Charles (1722–1770), lord chancellor, was born on 30 December 1722 in Great Ormond Street, London, the second son of Philip *Yorke, first earl of Hardwicke (1690–1764), lord chancellor, and his wife, Margaret Lygon (c.1695–1761), the daughter of Charles and Mary Cocks and the widow of John Lygon. Elizabeth *Anson (1725–1760) was his sister. It was inevitable that he should be trained as a lawyer and should aim at the highest legal office. His

Charles Yorke (1722–1770), attrib. Thomas Hudson, c.1756

great-uncle Lord Somers had been lord chancellor (1697–1700) and his father held the office from 1737 to 1756. But the pressure of expectations made him irresolute, and, despite shining talents, his career ended in disappointment and tragedy.

Yorke was sent to Henry Newcome's school at Hackney before entering Corpus Christi College, Cambridge, in 1739. At university he took a major part in the private printing of *Athenian Letters*, purporting to be the comments of a Persian resident in Athens during the Peloponnesian wars. He contributed nearly fifty substantial letters and his brother Philip *Yorke, second earl of Hardwicke (1720–1790), the bulk of the remainder: they were printed for the public in 1781 and again in 1798. Having been admitted to the Middle Temple in 1735 at the age of twelve, he joined Lincoln's Inn in 1742 and was called to the bar in 1746. The following year he was given a reversionary sinecure as clerk of the crown in chancery, which he retained for the rest of his life, and was brought into parliament for Reigate, a family seat, when his elder brother, Philip, chose to sit for Cambridgeshire. His début was impressive. In 1745 he published a defence of one of his father's judgments in *Considerations of the Law of forfeiture for High Treason*, which was reprinted several times, and in his maiden speech in May 1748 he opposed to such effect a private bill sponsored by Lord Gage that, according to Dr Birch, the author abandoned it. In November 1748 he was chosen to second the vote of thanks on the address and earned more applause. By 1750 he was talked of as a possible solicitor-general. In 1751 he played an important part in the debates on the Regency Bill. His reputation at the bar also rose rapidly. He became counsel to the East India Company in 1751 and recorder of Dover and Gloucester on his father's death, and by the early years of George III's reign was earning £7500 per annum.

By then certain weaknesses had become apparent. Yorke was not in strong health and had a tendency to corpulence and to prolixity of discourse. He suffered also from what his brother Joseph *Yorke called the family weakness of 'overthinking everything'. Joseph recommended matrimony as a cure, to give him someone else to worry about, and on 19 May 1755 he married Catherine (d. 1759), the daughter and heir of William Freeman of Aspenden, Hertfordshire. They had one son, Philip *Yorke (1757–1834), who succeeded his uncle as third earl of Hardwicke. Through his wife Yorke acquired Tittenhanger Park, Hertfordshire. After she died in 1759, he married, on 30 December 1762, Agneta Johnson (1740–1820), the daughter and coheir of Henry *Johnson (1698/9–1760), a traveller, of Great Berkhamsted, Hertfordshire, and his wife, Laetitia Dowling, but did not become noticeably less irresolute. In 1754 he had been made solicitor-general to the young prince of Wales, an indication of favours to come. When his father retired from the lord chancellorship in 1756, Yorke was made solicitor-general. But his progress faltered the following year when Pitt insisted that his supporter Charles Pratt should be brought into parliament and made attorney-general. The two law officers clashed over Pratt's Habeas Corpus Bill in 1758, and Pratt was henceforth a substantial obstacle to Yorke's advance.

As solicitor-general, Yorke took part in the prosecutions of Florence Hensey in 1758 for espionage and of Lord Ferrers in 1760 for shooting his steward. His reply in the Commons on 11 December 1761 to Barré, who had attacked the previous ministers for subservience to Hanover, was greatly admired. In January 1762, when Pratt was made chief justice of common pleas, Yorke moved up to become attorney-general. But Newcastle's resignation later that year placed him in an awkward position, since the duke was anxious that his friends, including Hardwicke's sons, should resign with him. Hardwicke replied that his sons were old enough to decide for themselves, and they remained in office. In post, Yorke advised on the Wilkes issue that privilege of parliament did not extend to seditious libel, and was determined to maintain his professional opinion. But Newcastle continued to press him to resign, and on 2 November 1763, in vast agitation, he did so, bursting into tears, according to Grenville, at his audience with the king. He defended his Wilkes opinion in the debate of 24 November, and in February 1764 spoke against general warrants to great applause in the debate. But he soon began to regret his resignation. In December 1763, on a visit to Grenville, he 'spoke rather discontentedly of the exigency of the times, which had (as he called it) *whirled* him out of so eminent and advantageous a post in the law' (*Grenville Papers*, 2.239), and a little later he wrote to Newcastle: 'I do not see my way' (Yorke, 3.560). His elder brother wrote candidly that Yorke should either have resigned when Newcastle did, or not at all: 'by the part he took, neither side felt itself much obliged to him'

(Williams, 136). In May 1764 Yorke confided to James Harris that he was in danger of being isolated and hoped for some 'conciliatory scheme', and when the master of the rolls died in November he opened up negotiations with Grenville, either for that position, with a peerage and an increase in salary, or for his old office of attorney-general, now held by Sir Fletcher Norton. He was particularly anxious that it should appear that he had been summoned by the king to his service. Northington, the lord chancellor, found Yorke as usual 'very unexplicit', explaining that he would need to consult Newcastle: 'it makes one sick', added Northington tersely (*Grenville Papers*, 2.464). The negotiations broke down, and Yorke settled for a patent of precedency before the solicitor-general, promising in return 'cordial and friendly support to His Majesty's measures' (ibid., 2.469). 'We have lost a man of character', summed up the duke of Cumberland, 'but they have not gained one' (Walpole, *Memoirs of ... George III*, 2.36).

Yorke was now in the position of supporting Grenville's government while not holding office and spoke in favour of the Stamp Act and the Regency Bill. But by the summer of 1765 Grenville's ministry was in trouble, and the king turned to Lord Rockingham to form a government. Rockingham laid great weight on Yorke's inclusion and offered him his old post of attorney-general, with his elder brother, the new Lord Hardwicke, at the Board of Trade. But Hardwicke, always languid, declined, while Yorke 'made difficulties' (Bateson, 28). Rockingham found him 'not unwilling, but *timid*'. The lord chancellorship in due course was dangled before him, but still Yorke hesitated, for he 'feared too much would be expected of me in Parliament' (Cannon). A three-hour conversation with Norton left the latter nonplussed as to what Yorke had in mind. On 8 August, Whately reported to Grenville: 'Mr Yorke still hesitates. I believe that will be a paragraph in every letter I shall write this summer' (*Grenville Papers*, 3.78). Even the archbishop of Canterbury was brought in to see if he could overcome Yorke's scruples. No sooner had Yorke agreed to serve than he began to wonder if he had been wise. The new ministry was not strong and its life expectation was uncertain. Worse, it was pledged to the repeal of the Stamp Act which he had supported only the previous year. The outcome of the second difficulty was a fudge which had important consequences for the American situation. Yorke persuaded Rockingham to accompany repeal by a Declaratory Act which reasserted British sovereignty, a legalistic device which may have assisted the passage of repeal through the Commons, but went down badly in America. Yorke clashed violently with Newcastle, who objected that the Declaratory Act 'would prevent even the repeal from having its effect': Yorke accused the duke of 'insanity', on which Newcastle commented that 'he talked more like a madman than I did' (Thomas, 182). Since the government faced a number of legal issues, Yorke was one of the busiest ministers. In April 1766 he defended the administration's belief that general warrants were illegal 'and kept the field with great acclamation' (Keppel, 1.327). When Grafton resigned the following month, Hardwicke was offered a secretary-ship of state, but declined as 'prejudicial to my health', and Yorke in turn also declined, though, as usual, he was promised the lord chancellorship in the future. In any case, the ministry was turned out in July 1766 to make room for the Pitt–Grafton government, and Yorke resigned, complaining that he was 'a man sacrificed to the times' (Cannon). In November 1766 Newcastle described him as 'a very ticklish man … and seems to be much embarrassed what part to take' (ibid.). In the abortive negotiations for a return to office in the summer of 1767, Rockingham suggested that, if Camden (Pratt) retained the lord chancellorship, Yorke could be lord president of the council with a peerage, although Newcastle commented that 'the Yorkes will never be satisfied 'till Charles Yorke has the Great Seal' (Brooke, 171, 176). He was always uncomfortable in opposition and complained that Rockingham's support was too narrow, especially after the Bedford group had defected at the end of 1767 and joined the administration. A more encouraging event was his election in March 1768 as member for the University of Cambridge, where his brother Hardwicke was high steward.

Rumours during 1769 that Camden was not happy in his position held out further hope, and on 9 January 1770, after Chatham had attacked the very ministry he had himself set up and Camden had joined him, it was resolved to dismiss the lord chancellor as soon as a replacement could be found. Opposition was convinced that the government was tottering: 'the seals would go a-begging', declared Shelburne in the Lords, 'but he hoped there would not be found in the kingdom a wretch so base and mean spirited as to accept of them' (Cobbett, *Parl. hist.*, 16, 1770, 665). The crisis found Yorke, in Hardwicke's words, 'more irresolute than ever' (Williams, 144). On 12 January Grafton offered the seals to Yorke. Mansfield and the lord chief justice, Wilmot, urged him to take them, Hardwicke and Rockingham not to abandon his friends. Yorke was in violent agitation that the prize he had sought for so long could not be accepted with honour. On the 14th he declined, and he repeated his decision on the 16th. But in an audience with the king on the 17th he was pressed very hard to accept, and consented, taking a peerage as Lord Morden of Cambridgeshire. He subsequently quarrelled violently with his brother, and he died on the 20th in Great Ormond Street. He had held the lord chancellorship, the summit of his life's ambition, for three days, and his peerage had not been sealed.

The evidence of Yorke's death is confused. Rumours of suicide circulated at once. Horace Walpole, who disliked the Yorkes, insisted that Yorke had 'fallen by his own hand' (Walpole, *Memoirs of … George III*, 4.53). But he had been in poor health for some time, complaining often of the fatigue of his profession, and the week before his death he wrote to his brother that he was 'hardly fit to stir' (Cannon). The most detailed account was given in a letter from Levett Blackborne, based on a report by a young lady who was a relative of Agneta Yorke, and corroborated in most respects by Agneta Yorke's own narrative:

He ate voraciously and beyond his usual manner—which *latterly* was *generally too much*. Before the taking away of the cloth, he complained of sickness and indigestion … growing worse, he retired into a back dressing-room, where he was heard retching with vehemence. After some time the family in the parlour was alarmed, and he was carried to bed having, as supposed, broke a blood vessel in vomiting. (*Rutland MSS*, 2.313)

His body was taken to Cambridgeshire for burial in the family chapel at Wimpole. His wife and at least two of their three children, Charles Philip *Yorke and Joseph Sydney *Yorke, survived him.   JOHN CANNON

Sources P. C. Yorke, *The life and correspondence of Philip Yorke, earl of Hardwicke*, 3 vols. (1913); repr. (1977) · J. Campbell, *Lives of the lord chancellors*, 8 vols. (1845–69) · H. Walpole, *Memoirs of King George II*, ed. J. Brooke, 3 vols. (1985) · H. Walpole, *Memoirs of the reign of King George the Third*, ed. D. Le Marchant, 4 vols. (1845) · J. A. Cannon, 'Yorke, Charles', HoP, *Commons, 1754–90* · *The Grenville papers: being the correspondence of Richard Grenville … and … George Grenville*, ed. W. J. Smith, 2 (1852), 218 · G. Thomas, earl of Albemarle [G. T. Keppel], *Memoirs of the marquis of Rockingham and his contemporaries*, 2 vols. (1852) · *The correspondence of King George the Third from 1760 to December 1783*, ed. J. Fortescue, 1 (1927), 89 · *A narrative of changes in the ministry, 1765–1767*, ed. M. Bateson, CS, new ser., 59 (1898) · Walpole, *Corr.* · Cobbett, *Parl. hist.* · P. Langford, *The first Rockingham administration, 1765–1766* (1973) · J. H. Jesse, *George Selwyn and his contemporaries, with memoirs and notes*, 4 vols. (1843–4) · J. Brooke, *The Chatham administration, 1766–1768* (1956) · *Letters from George III to Lord Bute, 1756–1766*, ed. R. Sedgwick (1939) · *Autobiography and political correspondence of Augustus Henry, third duke of Grafton*, ed. W. R. Anson (1898), 35–6 · P. D. G. Thomas, *British politics and the Stamp Act crisis: the first phase of the American revolution, 1763–1767* (1975), 95 · R. Williams, 'The eclipse of the Yorkes', TRHS, 3rd ser., 2 (1908), 129–51 · GEC, *Peerage* · *The manuscripts of his grace the duke of Rutland*, 4 vols., HMC, 24 (1888–1905)

Archives BL, corresp. and papers, Add. MSS 35349–36278, 45030, 45047 · NYPL, corresp. and papers · W. Sussex RO, minutes of his speech at cabinet council | BL, letters to Thomas Birch, Add. MSS 32457–33072 · BL, Newcastle MSS · BL, corresp. with duke of Newcastle, Add. MSS 32457–33072 · Northants. RO, letters to Lord Northington · Sheff. Arch., letters to Lord Rockingham

Likenesses attrib. T. Hudson, portrait, *c*.1756, Wimpole Hall, Cambridgeshire [*see illus.*] · Bovi, print, 1796 (after wax sculpture by I. Gosset, 1766), NPG · Scheemakers, portrait, 1798, repro. in [P. C. Yorke], *Athenian letters*, new edn, 2 vols. (1798) · S. Freeman, 1803 (after print), BM; repro. in *European Magazine* (1803) · A. Ramsay, portrait, priv. coll. · print, BM

Wealth at death estates through both marriages; said to earn £7000 p.a. at bar; useful sinecure

Yorke, Sir Charles (1790–1880), army officer, born on 7 December 1790, was the son of Colonel John Yorke, deputy lieutenant of the Tower of London from 1795 until his death on 26 January 1826, and his wife, Juliana, daughter of John Dodd of Swallowfield, Berkshire.

Yorke was commissioned as ensign in the 35th foot on 22 January 1807, became lieutenant on 18 February 1808, and on the 25th exchanged to the 52nd foot. He served with that regiment throughout the Peninsular War, being present at Vimeiro, Fuentes de Oñoro, Ciudad Rodrigo, Badajoz, Salamanca, Vitoria, the battles of the Pyrenees, the Nivelle, and Nive, and at Orthez, where he was severely wounded. He was also wounded at Badajoz and the Nivelle. He afterwards received the Peninsular silver medal with ten clasps. He was promoted captain on 24 December 1813.

At Waterloo, Yorke was extra aide-de-camp to Major-General Adam, who commanded the brigade of which the 52nd formed part. He received the Waterloo medal. He was placed on half pay on 25 February 1816, but was appointed to the 13th foot on 7 August 1817, and exchanged back to the 52nd on 2 July 1818. On 9 June 1825 he was given an unattached majority, and again went on half pay. On 30 November 1826 he was made lieutenant-colonel and inspecting field officer of militia. He became colonel on 23 November 1841, and was assistant quartermaster-general, first at Cork and afterwards at Manchester from 1842 to 1851.

On 11 November 1851 Yorke was promoted major-general. He was sent to the Cape, and served in the Cape Frontier War of 1852 as second in command under General Cathcart. He was given a reward for distinguished service on 13 July 1853. In May 1854 he succeeded Colonel Airey as military secretary at headquarters in England, and consequently did not serve in the Crimea. As military secretary he was responsible for much of the paperwork at military headquarters in London.

Yorke was made colonel of the 33rd foot on 27 February 1855, and KCB on 5 February 1856. He became lieutenant-general on 13 February 1859, and was made GCB on 29 June 1860, when he ceased to be military secretary. In that office it is said that, as Lord Fitzroy Somerset had 'softened the asperity of the Iron Duke, Sir C. Yorke neutralised the exuberant kindness of the Duke of Cambridge' (Stocqueler, 250). He was made colonel-commandant of the 2nd battalion of the rifle brigade on 1 April 1863, and became general on 5 September 1865. On 5 April 1875 he was appointed constable of the Tower of London, and on 2 June 1877 he was made field marshal, a reward for competence and long service rather than distinction. He died, unmarried, at his home, 27 South Street, Grosvenor Square, on 20 November 1880, and was buried on the 24th at Kensal Green cemetery.

E. M. LLOYD, *rev.* H. C. G. MATTHEW

Sources *The Times* (22 Nov 1880) · *The Times* (25 Nov 1880) · W. S. Moorsom, ed., *Historical record of the fifty-second regiment (Oxfordshire light infantry), from the year 1755 to the year 1858* (1860) · J. H. Stocqueler, *A personal history of the Horse Guards* (1878) · *Correspondence of Lieut.-General the Hon. Sir George Cathcart* (1856) · J. Sweetman, *War and administration* (1984)
Archives NL Scot., corresp. with Sir George Brown · NRA, priv. coll., corresp. with Lord Seaton · W. Sussex RO, letters to duke of Richmond
Likenesses portrait, repro. in *ILN* (16 June 1877) · portraits, repro. in *Army and Navy Magazine*, 1 (1881), 353–8, 562
Wealth at death under £90,000: probate, 6 Dec 1880, *CGPLA Eng. & Wales*

Yorke, Charles Philip (1764–1834), politician, born on 12 March 1764, was second son of Charles *Yorke (1722–1770), lord chancellor, the first with his second wife, Agneta (1740–1820), the daughter of Henry Johnson of Great Berkhamsted, Hertfordshire. A sister, Caroline, later countess of St Germans (*d.* 1818), and Admiral Joseph Sydney *Yorke were younger siblings. Yorke was educated at Harrow School (1776–80), was admitted to Lincoln's Inn in 1780, and matriculated at St John's College, Cambridge,

in 1781 (MA, 1783). He was called to the bar at the Middle Temple in 1787 and practised unhappily on the western circuit, wintering in Italy in 1788. He was chief justice of Ely from 1789 to 1793. His elder half-brother Philip *Yorke became third earl of Hardwicke in May 1790 and vacated his seat for Cambridgeshire, which Yorke then occupied until 1810. Worth under £800 a year, he disliked undue dependence on Hardwicke's bounty. He married, on 1 July 1790, Harriet (1763–1854), daughter of Charles Manningham of Thorpe, Surrey. They had no children.

Yorke backed Pitt's ministry and partook in legal debate in the Commons, where he moved the address in 1792. He generally supported war with revolutionary France. A Cambridgeshire militia officer from 1792 to 1811 (a colonel from 1806), he persuaded Hardwicke to warn Pitt against peace negotiations. In the 1796 parliament, in which he was often a government teller, he supported wartime taxes, and as a finance committeeman specialized in the dockyards. Pitt did not promote him, but encouraged him to serve his successor, Addington, as secretary at war and privy councillor (20 February 1801). The king praised Yorke's competence. Having declined the navy treasurership and a salary rise, he launched the Royal Military College in June 1801. His army estimates proclaimed wariness of Bonaparte. In 1802 he avoided becoming chief secretary to Hardwicke, the Irish viceroy, and twice rejected the Madras government, believing that India would be won in Europe.

At the general election of 1802 Yorke survived a contest in Cambridgeshire. He proposed military enlargement, moving the address when war resumed, on 25 May 1803. In June he introduced a reserve army. Following Addington's failure to negotiate a junction with Pitt, he refused the Admiralty or Home Office, with cabinet rank. But Hardwicke dictated his accepting the latter: he did so on 17 August, but regretted switching, and in October threatened resignation, relenting only when Pitt again proved unobtainable. Saddled in debate with defence and Hardwicke's Irish problems, he shared in the ministry's collapse and surrendered his office on 11 May 1804. The king had wished him to remain and to accept the barony of Morden, which he declined for financial reasons. He eschewed hostility towards Pitt's second ministry, despite opposing his Additional Force Bill. Pitt did not appoint him chief secretary, as Hardwicke wished, believing Yorke aspired to cabinet. Disillusioned, he avoided parliament, except to amend Pitt's Enlistment Bill (28 March). He spurned office without peerage and pension. Denied the Admiralty, former colleagues warning Pitt about his irritability, he declined embassy to Russia in September 1805.

Yorke's predilection for an all-party coalition foundered in 1806. For the king's sake he disliked opposing Grenville's ministry, but criticized its military measures on 3 April. His joining a Pittite rally in July precluded Hardwicke's intercession on his behalf with the new government. In March 1807, when the Pittites parleyed with Grenville, he rejected the governorships of Madras and

Jamaica. When the ministry fell over royal opposition to Catholic relief, Hardwicke's commitment to Grenville compromised him. He stayed away in April 1807, when the Portland ministry was censured. He readily rejected Portland's offer of surveyorship of woods and forests, but annoyed Hardwicke by refusing to forswear office and by commendation of the Copenhagen expedition in the ensuing parliament. Subsequently more critical, he nevertheless privately advised the War Office, helped Perceval draft the king's speech for 1809, and defended the duke of York, whom he viewed as a victim of radical conspiracy, on 10 March. Declining the India board (Pitt's last wish for him) in April, he preferred the secretaryship at war, without cabinet rank, but Hardwicke discountenanced his re-admission to office as an isolated recruit. He opposed allegations of ministerial corruption on 5 May, whereupon Hardwicke exacted from him a renunciation of all ambitions for office. Accordingly, he requested a retirement pension on 6 June: Portland offered his, and the king's, regrets.

Hardwicke offered compensation or consideration of overtures from Portland's successor, Perceval, but Yorke declined the secretaryship at war (with cabinet) and other offices. Hardwicke torpedoed a final offer, on 24 October 1809, of the War Office. In January 1810, following Yorke's defence of the Scheldt (or Walcheren) expedition and denunciation of Sir Francis Burdett, Perceval, with royal approval, offered him the sinecure post of an exchequer tellership at £2700 a year. On 2 February Yorke obtained exclusion of 'strangers' from the Scheldt debate, a device seldom resorted to, and the opposition failed to dislodge him from the committee. These actions led the radical John Gale Jones to dub him an enemy of the people, and Yorke's charging of Jones with breach of privilege led to the latter's imprisonment. Hardwicke, who had approved Yorke's acceptance of a sinecure, dreaded an unsuccessful county contest, and so he withdrew on 16 March. Yorke's brother-in-law Lord Eliot returned him for St Germans on 27 April. Next day, with some reluctance, he accepted the office of first lord of the Admiralty.

His windows having been smashed by London rioters in April, Yorke denounced petitions against Burdett's imprisonment in June 1810. He threatened resignation when Perceval wooed Canning and Castlereagh, but defended his regency proposals of 2 January 1811. The opposition assailed him on official matters. Unhappy about Perceval's attempt to reduce navy estimates, he distrusted the prince, vowing to resign when regency restrictions expired. He was persuaded to stay but, dismayed by Baltic naval losses, resigned in March 1812, 'really a loss to the public service' according to John Wilson Croker (Jennings, 1.39). Following Perceval's assassination, he thwarted presentation to the regent of the successful motion for a stronger administration on 21 May. He declined, on health grounds, Lord Liverpool's offer of duchy of Lancaster (with cabinet), but promised support. Hardwicke distrusted his request to represent Reigate on the family interest as a non-partisan, and Yorke refused

£5000 instead. He then sat for Liskeard, another Eliot borough. His speech against admission of Catholics to parliament, to which he had always been implacably opposed, on 25 February 1813, was published. He deprecated discussion of the princess of Wales's grievances, and in April 1814 thwarted Romilly's attempt to end mutilation of traitors' carcasses, which had been upheld by Yorke's father. His defence of the corn laws and urging suppression of protest provoked another attack on his house in March 1815. Advising Castlereagh on peace-making, and Liverpool on allied military occupation of France, he backed ministers, notably on the Aliens Bill of 1816. His last speech was against Catholic relief, on 9 May 1817. A member of the secret committee on sedition, he voted for suspension of habeas corpus on 23 June.

Yorke retired from parliament in 1818. A peerage was refused him: he had been heir to Hardwicke since 1810. He declined that autumn to broker junction between Grenvillites and government; he advocated resistance to reform, solid public financing, and government economy. Outside parliament he was a fellow of the Royal Society and of the Society of Antiquaries (1801) and vice-president of the Royal Society of Literature. With William Martin Leake, he was co-author of *The Principal Egyptian Monuments in the British Museum* (1827). He died, eight months before Hardwicke, at his home, 28 Bruton Street, Berkeley Square, London, on 13 March 1834. His memorial in Wimpole church, where he was interred on 20 March, was cast from the Plymouth breakwater he had promoted at the Admiralty. ROLAND THORNE

Sources A. Aspinall and R. G. Thorne, 'Yorke, Charles Philip', HoP, *Commons, 1790–1820* · BL, Hardwick MSS, Add. MSS 35897, 35392–35394, 45033–45047 · *GM*, 2nd ser., 1 (1834), 652 · *The Times* (19 March 1834), 5 · F. G. Stephens and M. D. George, eds., *Catalogue of political and personal satires preserved ... in the British Museum*, 8 (1947) · *Parliamentary debates* (1790–1817) [Debrett and Cobbett-Hansard] · *The Croker papers: the correspondence and diaries of ... John Wilson Croker*, ed. L. J. Jennings, 1 (1884), 39 · J. Barrow, *An autobiographical memoir of Sir John Barrow* (1847), 311 · *Memoirs and correspondence of Viscount Castlereagh, second marquess of Londonderry*, ed. C. Vane, marquess of Londonderry, 12 vols. (1848–53), vol. 11, p. 56 · S. Romilly, *Memoirs of the life of Sir Samuel Romilly*, 3 (1840), 98, 132, 134 · *The later correspondence of George III*, ed. A. Aspinall, 5 vols. (1962–70) · *DNB* · W. T. J. Gun, ed., *The Harrow School register, 1571–1800* (1934), 148 · R. F. Scott, ed., *Admissions to the College of St John the Evangelist in the University of Cambridge*, 4: *July 1767 – July 1802* (1931), 577 · W. P. Baildon, ed., *The records of the Honorable Society of Lincoln's Inn: admissions*, 1 (1896), 497 · Venn, *Alum. Cant.*, 2/6.617 · monumental inscription, Wimpole church, Cambridgeshire · Burke, *Peerage* [Harwicke] · parish register, Wimpole church, Wimpole, Cambs. AS, 20 March 1834 [burial]

Archives BL, corresp. and papers, Add. MSS 35392–35394, 35897, 45033–45047 · Bodl. Oxf., corresp. · NMM, corresp. | BL, letters to Hardwicke, Add. MSS 35701–35706 · CUL, corresp. with Spencer Perceval · Devon RO, corresp. with first Viscount Sidmouth · Hants. RO, corresp. with William Wickham · HLRO, Perceval Holland MSS · NA Scot., corresp. with Thomas, Lord Cochrane · NL Scot., corresp. with Sir Alexander Cochrane · NRA, priv. coll., corresp. with Spencer Perceval · Royal Arch., letters to George III · Sandon Hall, Staffordshire, Harrowby Manuscript Trust, corresp. with Richard Ryder · Worcs. RO, letters to Lord Coventry

Likenesses G. Romney, oils, *c.*1780, Wimpole Hall, Cambridgeshire · Flaxman, relief sculpture, 1820 (with his brothers; on his mother's monument), Wimpole church, Cambridgeshire

Yorke, Charles Philip, fourth earl of Hardwicke (1799–1873), naval officer and politician, eldest son of Sir Joseph Sydney *Yorke (1768–1831), naval officer, and his first wife, Elizabeth Weake (d. 1812), daughter of James Rattray, was born at Sydney Lodge, Hamble, Hampshire, on 2 April 1799. After three years at Harrow School, he entered the Royal Naval College, Portsmouth in February 1813, and, having passed with credit, was in May 1815 appointed midshipman to the *Prince*, flagship at Spithead. From her he moved to the *Leviathan*, and from there to the *Queen Charlotte*, in which he was present at the bombardment of Algiers. He was then sent to the *Leander*, flagship of Sir David Milne, on the North American station, and on 14 August 1819 was promoted lieutenant of the *Phaëton*. On 18 May 1822 he was made commander, and in August 1823 was appointed to the *Alacrity* which he took out to the Mediterranean, where he was engaged in suppressing piracy. On 6 June 1825 he was promoted captain, and from 1828 to 1831 commanded the *Alligator* in the Mediterranean, mostly in Greek waters.

Yorke was tory MP for the family seats of Reigate (1831–2), and Cambridgeshire (1832–4).

On 4 October 1833 Yorke married Susan (1810–1886), sixth daughter of Thomas Henry Liddell, first Baron Ravensworth; among their eight children was Charles Philip *Yorke, fifth earl of Hardwicke (1836–1897), father of Albert Edward Yorke, sixth earl of Hardwicke. On the death of his uncle Philip *Yorke, third earl of Hardwicke, on 18 November 1834, Yorke succeeded to the title, and became lord lieutenant of Cambridgeshire. In the Peel administration of 1841 he was one of the lords-in-waiting, resigning in 1846 to oppose the repeal of the corn laws. He also served at sea, in command of the Admiralty steam yacht *Black Eagle*, and attended the king of Prussia and tsar of Russia, both of whom he visited in their own capitals. In 1844 Hardwicke commanded the battleship *St Vincent* for an experimental cruise. In 1848 he took command of the battleship *Vengeance*. His firm action while stationed at Genoa in April 1849 secured the city for the king of Sardinia, for which service he was decorated. Shortly afterwards he resigned his commission because of his wife's ill health.

In 1852 Hardwicke became postmaster-general in Lord Derby's brief administration. On 12 January 1854 he reached the rank of rear-admiral, and was placed on the retired list, lacking sufficient sea service as a captain for active duty. Despite this, Vice-Admiral Sir Charles Napier twice requested that he be appointed to the Baltic fleet, but the cabinet refused to restore him to active duty. From 1858 to 1859 Hardwicke served as lord privy seal, and chairman of the royal commission on manning. Although he was a close personal friend of Lord Derby, Hardwicke's ill health precluded service in the 1867 cabinet. He died at Sydney Lodge, Hamble, Hampshire, on 17 September 1873 and was buried at Wimpole, Cambridgeshire, near Royston, on 24 September.

Hardwicke was admired by all who knew him, as a seaman, a politician and a landowner. He had many virtues, but his direct and honest approach was less successful in politics than it had been at sea.

J. K. LAUGHTON, rev. ANDREW LAMBERT

Sources Lady Biddulph of Ledbury, *Charles Philip Yorke, fourth earl of Hardwicke* (1910) · *Disraeli, Derby and the conservative party: journals and memoirs of Edward Henry, Lord Stanley, 1849–1869*, ed. J. R. Vincent (1978) · BL, Hardwicke MSS · J. S. Bromley, ed., *The manning of the Royal Navy: selected public pamphlets, 1693–1873*, Navy RS, 119 (1974) · Burke, *Peerage* (1857) · *CGPLA Eng. & Wales* (1873)

Archives BL, corresp. and papers, Add. MSS 3539, 35653–35658, 35691, 35788–35813, 35900, 36248–36272 | BL, corresp. with Sir Robert Peel, Add. MSS 40404–40608 · Bodl. Oxf., letters to Benjamin Disraeli · Cambs. AS, estate journal and memorandum book · Lpool RO, letters to the fourth Earl of Derby, 920 Der 14, box 161 · W. Sussex RO, letters to duke of Richmond

Likenesses E. U. Eddis, two portraits, repro. in Biddulph, *Charles Philip Yorke*

Wealth at death under £120,000: probate, 21 Dec 1873, *CGPLA Eng. & Wales*

Yorke, Charles Philip [nicknamed Champagne Charlie], **fifth earl of Hardwicke** (1836–1897), landowner and bankrupt dandy, was born on 23 April 1836 at Wimpole Hall, Cambridgeshire, the eldest son of the five sons and three daughters of Charles Philip *Yorke, fourth earl of Hardwicke (1799–1873), and Susan Liddell (1810–1886), the sixth daughter of the first Baron Ravensworth. From 1836 until 1873, when he succeeded to the earldom, he was known by the courtesy title Lord Royston. He was educated at Harrow School and Trinity College, Cambridge, where he matriculated in 1855. He joined the army on graduating (1858), served in India in 1858–9 in the 11th hussars, and received the Indian war medal. In 1861 he left the army, and barely a year later, in March 1862, he became a figure of society scandal for a drunken quarrel and fight with Lord Hartington over an after-dinner game of billiards. In September the same year Lord Derby's diary recorded a letter from Hardwicke saying 'that Royston's marriage hangs fire; the young man's debts being so heavy as "nearly to break him down." They have been brought about mainly by gambling' (Vincent, 191). His marriage, to Sophia Georgiana Robertina Wellesley (d. 1923), the younger daughter of the first Earl Cowley, did not in the event hang fire beyond 16 February 1863, when it was celebrated in Paris, where Cowley was ambassador.

Royston had already clearly established his credentials for becoming a congenial member of the prince of Wales's Marlborough House group as soon as Albert Edward assumed the leadership of London society's fast set after his own marriage in the same year. Royston's only son, Albert Edward, was born in the Paris embassy in 1867 and the prince of Wales was one of his sponsors. Royston was amusing, cultivated, entertaining, and highly fashionable: 'speckless and faultless in dress, the one and sole professor of hats and gardenias, he is the admitted successor of D'Orsay' *Vanity Fair* proclaimed (9 May 1874, 245), and he was credited with the invention of the silk top hat. There is no documentary evidence of a link between

Royston and the popular music hall song 'Champagne Charlie was his Name', but the date when it was first performed, 1867, and the words of the second verse in particular:

> Whoever drinks at my expense
> Are treated all the same
> From Dukes and Lords, to cabmen down,
> I make them drink Champagne.

are redolent of Charlie Yorke (Davison, 17). He was also passionately fond of the turf (he had the Hardwicke Stakes at Newmarket named after him) and lost a great deal of money on the horses. Constance Rothschild, Lady Battersea, a close friend of the Yorke family, recalled that Royston was:

> an easy-going, happy-go-lucky, brilliant member of the social world in the 'sixties and 'seventies, known for a time as 'Champagne Charlie' … an entertaining talker and an agreeable companion, not devoid of talent … in faultless attire, with his carefully arranged black satin tie, his beautiful pearl pin, his lustrous hat balanced at a certain angle upon his well-brushed hair, his coat sleeves always showing precisely the same amount of white cuff, his pleased-with-himself-and-the-world expression. As a young man he was considered a success, but as an older one perhaps a disappointment.   (Battersea, 153)

This last remark was discreet to the point of deliberate falsity. Already by 1872 Lord Derby heard from Hardwicke that:

> his son Royston is in debt to the extent of £200,000 if not more, making it impossible that he should ever live on his estates, or be otherwise than very poor. All this debt has been contracted by gambling and other follies. Ld H. has during the greater part of a long life been engaged in working off the encumbrances on his estates (which he has done) … Now his work is destroyed, at least for the life of his successor. The old man takes his misfortune quietly, and says that his duty must now be to save his grandson from being involved in the ruin.   (*Diaries of E. H. Stanley*, 109)

That was a vain hope. The old man died in 1873, and Royston, become fifth earl, continued unchecked towards utter ruin. This was ascribed to self-indulgence, weakness of character, and the insidious effects of friendship with the prince of Wales. While accompanying the prince on his Indian tour in 1876 he became involved not only in the Aylesford divorce scandal but also in the competitive provision of hunting elephants for the royal tiger shoots. Back home he set increasingly lavish standards for the amusement of the prince, although when he sang bawdy songs at the request of Lady Dudley (Georgiana Moncreiffe), one of Albert Edward's early mistresses, to his own accompaniment on the guitar, no cash outlay was involved. Hardwicke was in every respect the role model for Christopher Sykes, a familiar guest at Sykes's Brantingham Thorpe parties for the Marlborough House set. Hardwicke:

> that unfortunate earl (who deserves a place in history as the inventor of the polished silk hat) had followed a similar career to Christopher's some ten years before … He also became involved in the same fatal game, first of competitive and then of commanded entertainment … The dreadful fact remained that, as a result, Lord Hardwicke lost a large part of

his fortune. He was fated to lose the home of his ancestors also.   (Sykes, 25)

The prince's patronage brought some rewards, though Hardwicke's election as MP for Cambridgeshire in 1865 was due only to the family's standing and property in the county. He was a reasonably conscientious MP, speaking at agricultural shows, showing concern for the agricultural interests of the constituency, and occasionally speaking in the Commons. But in his elevation to office, indicatively to court appointments, in the Conservative administration of 1866–8 as comptroller of the household, and that of 1874–80 as master of the buckhounds, the hand of the prince can be seen. The hand became very visible in 1875, when Disraeli noted that Hardwicke 'got the P of W to speak to me in his favor', asking unsuccessfully to be made under-secretary for war. 'Hardwicke, the least fitted for the place, will be the most dissatisfied', Disraeli continued. 'It is a curious thing, but there has not been a place, or a living of importance in my gift that HRH has not asked me for one of his friends—and always the most unqualified candidates' (*Letters*, 1.246). The prince of Wales, as befitted a true gambler, at once upped the stakes and asked Disraeli to make Hardwicke lord lieutenant of Ireland in succession to the duke of Abercorn, to be once again rebuffed with the explanation that the post required a man with 'rank, character, some degree of popular talent, particularly the gift of speech, considerable wealth, and freedom from strong religious partisanship' (Lee, 1.233), with the delicate implication that Hardwicke lacked all such qualities.

No further attempts to advance Hardwicke above his talents are recorded, and his political career ended in 1880. It appears that the prince of Wales took no further interest in him, leaving his former friend to subside into financial ruin, which was made complete and inescapable by the great fall in agricultural rents and in land values after the 1880s: the value of the 11,000 acre Wimpole estate dropped from £500,000 to little more than £250,000 by the mid-1890s. The creditors foreclosed and the estate was put on the market in 1891. It was eventually sold in 1894 to the second Lord Robartes (later sixth Viscount Clifden of Lanhydrock, Cornwall), who was a partner in the Agar Robartes Bank, the chief creditor; there was a detached 8000 acre estate also in Cambridgeshire, which seems to have been sold at the same time. The Hardwicke Papers, chiefly those of the eighteenth-century lord chancellor, were auctioned later, in February 1899. When Hardwicke died, on 18 May 1897 at 8 York Terrace, Regent's Park, London, the home was his only property, and he had to be buried in East Finchley (on 22 May) instead of in a family mausoleum. His obituary in *The Times* was brief and uninformative, suppressing all mention of both his social triumphs and his disasters. His only son, Albert Edward Philip Henry *Yorke (1867–1904), who inherited the title, being penniless, had become a stockbroker in 1892. He died in the York Terrace house, as did his mother, in 1923.

F. M. L. THOMPSON

Sources C. Battersea, *Reminiscences* (1922) · *Disraeli, Derby and the conservative party: journals and memoirs of Edward Henry, Lord Stanley,*

1849–1869, ed. J. R. Vincent (1978) • *The diaries of E. H. Stanley, 15th earl of Derby, 1869–1878*, CS, 5th series, 4 (1994) • *VF* (9 May 1874) • *Letters of Disraeli to Lady Bradford and Lady Chesterfield*, ed. marquis of Zetland, 2 vols. (1929) • S. Lee, *King Edward VII*, 2 vols. (1925–7) • C. Sykes, *Four studies in loyalty* (1946) • GEC, *Peerage* • Burke, *Peerage* • *The Times* (19 May 1897) • *Hansard 3* (1866), 182.2130–34; (1870), 201.1360–61, 1907 • *Hansard 3* (1880), 256.623–5 • P. Davison, *Songs of the British music hall* (1971)

Likenesses F. Sargent, pencil drawing, 1876, NPG • Ape [C. Pellegrini], cartoon, watercolour study, NPG; repro. in *VF*, 245

Yorke, Francis Reginald Stevens [Kay, K] (1906–1962), architect, was born at 38 West Street, Stratford upon Avon, on 3 December 1906, the only son of Francis Walter Bagnall Yorke (1879–1957) and his wife, Mary Ann Stevens. After attending Chipping Campden School, Yorke followed his father into the architectural profession and entered the Birmingham School of Architecture, where he completed his course in 1930. Among his fellow students were several other remarkable men, including Frederick Gibberd, Colin Penn, Richard Sheppard, and Robert Furneaux-Jordan, at a time when awareness of modern architecture was beginning in England. He completed some agricultural workers' cottages at Webheath, near his home town of Redditch, Worcestershire, in a simple vernacular style, in 1930. That same year, on 13 September, he married Thelma Austin Jones (*b*. 1906/7), a fashion model; they had twin daughters. Although the couple never formally separated, it was an unhappy marriage because of Yorke's tendency to have simultaneous affairs with several women, often members of his office staff, during the week, while his wife took to drink and lived in the country. Her sister Margaret married Yorke's architectural assistant (and later partner) T. Randall Evans, who came from New Zealand.

Known as Kay or K, Yorke was able to attract and often inspire people of talent, and the warmth and charm of his personality endeared him to a huge circle of friends. A great beer drinker, he looked and dressed like a gentleman farmer, which he became when after the Second World War he kept and bred his own herd of dairy cattle. He had a powerful, chunky frame, a countryman's clear, ruddy skin, and mischievous, puckered eyes, attractive to men and women alike.

After entering the profession at a time of severe economic depression, Yorke set up practice in London about 1930 but concentrated on architectural journalism as a contributor to the *Architects' Journal* on technical matters and building products, travelling abroad and establishing contacts with European modernists, particularly in Czechoslovakia and Germany. These contacts were the basis for his book *The Modern House*, published by the Architectural Press in 1934 and reprinted several times. It is a well-informed international survey, in photographs and drawings, of the flat-roofed houses which were just beginning to be built in England, although the text is almost entirely technical in content. It includes the designs for Yorke's first significant modern building, the small concrete house Torilla at Nast Hyde, Hertfordshire (1934–5). In other similar projects Yorke showed a matter-of-fact attitude to modernism. His partnership with the Hungarian-born architect Marcel Breuer, from 1935 to 1937, was formed partly to enable Breuer to practise in Britain as a refugee from Nazism. Projects were undertaken separately within the partnership, and a house in Sea Lane, Angmering, Sussex (1936), is one of several works attributable to Breuer. They worked together on a project for a 'city of the future', exhibited as a model at the Ideal Home Exhibition in 1936. Other clients included Eton College and Flower's Brewery of Stratford upon Avon, for whom Yorke, in collaboration with his father,

Francis Reginald Stevens Yorke (1906–1962), by Sam Lambert, early 1950s [centre, with Cyril Mardall (left) and Eugene Rosenberg (right)]

designed a terrace of workers' cottages in Birmingham Road. These humble buildings, with walls of brick rather than concrete, and monopitch roofs, were more significant for Yorke's future direction than Torilla (for which he is better known), and indicative of a growing maturity in English modernism. In 1937 Yorke published *The Modern House in England*, similar in style to his earlier book, and prefaced by a long quotation from the arts and crafts architect W. R. Lethaby. He collaborated with Frederick Gibberd on *The Modern Flat* (1937) and with Colin Penn on *A Key to Modern Architecture* (1939). From 1935 he used his technical and organizational knowledge to edit the annual publication *Specification*, which listed building products.

Yorke spent the early part of the war in a team of architects building factories and hostels for the Ministry of Supply. Later he became a researcher for the Ministry of Works on technical matters, and became interested in models for prefabricated housing. In 1944 he proposed an architectural partnership (initially without any formal terms of agreement) with Eugene Rosenberg, a Czech Jewish refugee whom Yorke had helped after his arrival in Britain. They invited Cyril Sjöström (later *Mardall) (1909–1994), an Anglo-Finnish architect with a specialism in prefabrication in timber, to join the practice. The Yorke, Rosenberg, and Mardall partnership was established in the years following the end of the war, and its first significant buildings were completed in 1947. Each partner tended to take charge of particular projects, but there was an intention to achieve a consistency of outlook, with emphasis on efficient production and use of new building products for industrial and transport buildings, hospitals, housing, and educational buildings, mostly in the public sector. All three partners shared an interest in contemporary art and gave commissions through their building projects to Henry Moore (the implementation of the *Family Group* at Barclay School, Stevenage, 1950), William Scott, F. E. McWilliam, Kenneth Rowntree, Michael Rothenstein, and Louis Le Brocquy. Yorke encouraged the designer and art teacher Peggy Angus to produce designs for repeating patterns on tiles, made by Carters of Poole. These he used effectively in school buildings, such as the Susan Lawrence School which formed part of the Lansbury Estate, Poplar, as a showpiece of 'live architecture' in the 1951 Festival of Britain.

Virtually all Yorke's school buildings up to 1956 used the prefabricated system developed by Hills of West Bromwich, often enlivened with blank end-walls of rough local stone. In such blends of industrial methods and good natural materials Yorke reunited his arts and crafts home background (the family home at Redditch was said to be redolent of William Morris) with his commitment to modernism. In designing the Ladyshot housing area in Harlow New Town (1951–5) Yorke virtually repeated his pre-war terrace at Stratford. His approach to design often seemed casual. He did not spend much time in the office, and delegated almost everything to office staff—recruiting some talented young designers, who before long began to rebel

against the lack of new ideas. Yorke was ready to encourage them, however, and the commission for Gatwick airport (1955–8) became an important moment of transition. David Allford and Brian Henderson were responsible, under Yorke, for designing the terminal, with its glass walling, marble floor, and crisp detailing, integrating road and rail transport links. Gatwick showed English modern architecture catching up again with international standards, now dominated by America, but the building has now been so altered that this is difficult to appreciate.

Yorke designated Allford, Henderson, and Randall Evans as partners before his early death. In his last years he was personally involved in designing new offices for the firm at 1 Greystoke Place, London, completed in 1961, a cool infill building clad in white tiles beside a historic graveyard near Chancery Lane, with a rooftop penthouse flat to house his art collection and the rosettes won by his prize cattle and as a setting for office parties, from which wives were always excluded. Shortly after being appointed CBE he died of cancer of the throat on 10 June 1962 at St Thomas's Hospital, London, which his firm largely rebuilt during the next decade.

RICHARD SHEPPARD, rev. ALAN POWERS

Sources A. Powers, *In the line of development* (1992) · *The architecture of Yorke Rosenberg Mardall, 1944–1972*, Yorke Rosenberg Mardall (1972) · *The Times* (11 June 1962) · E. M. Fry, *ArchR*, 132 (1962), 279–80 · b. cert. · m. cert. · d. cert.
Archives RIBA BAL, travel diary | University of East Anglia, Norwich, corresp. with J. C. Pritchard
Likenesses S. Lambert, group photograph, 1950–54, YRM Ltd, London [*see illus.*]
Wealth at death £85,140 2*s*. 8*d*.: probate, 12 Sept 1962, *CGPLA Eng. & Wales*

Yorke, Henry Redhead (1772–1813), political writer, seems to have been a native of the West Indies, but was brought up at Little Eaton, near Derby. In 1792, under his paternal name of Redhead, he published a pamphlet against the emancipation of slaves, but speedily changed his views on that subject, and while on a visit to Paris at the end of the same year wrote, but did not publish, a refutation of his pamphlet. In Paris he witnessed the king's appearance before the convention, and was closely connected with the brothers Robert and John Sheares and other members of the British club. He seceded from the club, however, in opposition to an address inviting the convention to liberate Britain from tyranny. This caused him to be denounced as a spy by Robert Rayment, and led to the issue of a warrant for his arrest. Assuming the surname Yorke, he left France and returned to Britain via Switzerland and the Netherlands.

Yorke's radical sympathies, however, had not diminished. Upon his return he joined the London Corresponding Society and published a letter to John Frost entitled *These are the Times that Try Men's Souls* (1793). He also joined a radical society at Derby, and in 1793 was sent by it to assist the Sheffield branch of the Society for Constitutional Information. On 7 April 1794 he addressed a large outdoor meeting at Sheffield, during which he was alleged to have exclaimed:

You behold before you, young as I am, about twenty-two years of age, a man who has been concerned in three revolutions already, who essentially contributed to serve the revolution in America, who contributed to that in Holland, who materially assisted in that of France, and who will continue to cause revolutions all over the world.

He was arrested, and at the York spring assize of 1795 true bills were found against him for conspiracy, sedition, and libel.

On 23 July 1795 Yorke was tried before Sir Giles Rooke at York for conspiracy, but his co-defendants—Joseph Gale, printer of the *Sheffield Register*, and Richard Davison, compositor—had absconded. Yorke, while continuing to advocate parliamentary reform, repudiated the boastful words imputed to him, and declared himself opposed to violence and anarchy. His speech in self-defence, however, was believed to have aided in his conviction. On 27 November 1795 he was sentenced by the king's bench to two years' imprisonment in Dorchester Castle, fined £100, and required to give sureties of good behaviour for seven years. Yorke published a report of his trial in the same year. He does not appear to have been released until March 1798. Meanwhile his opinions had undergone a complete change.

In a *Letter to the Reformers* (1798), written in prison, he justified the war with France, and on 3 August 1798, in a private letter to William Wickham, he deplored the fate and condemned the views of the brothers Henry and John Sheares (Castlereagh, 1.258). In 1802 he revisited France and documented his experience in *Letters from France* (1804), which stressed in contrast the virtues of the British constitution. He wrote letters for twelve months in *The Star* under the signature of Alfred or Galgacus (these were reprinted in a small volume), was part proprietor of the *True Briton*, and in 1806 was near having a duel with Sir Francis Burdett: both parties were bound over to keep the peace.

In the meantime Yorke became increasingly interested in the education of loyalist principles. In 1800 he published *Elements of Civil Knowledge*, a guide to the education of children in the virtues of the British state. In 1801 and again in 1810 he issued further statements of support for the constitution via synopses of lectures in London on political and historical subjects. He married, in 1800, the daughter of a man named Andrews, keeper of Dorchester Castle; they had four children. After a long illness, and having relinquished politics, he was induced by Richard Valpy to undertake a new edition and continuation of John Campbell's *Lives of British Admirals*; but before completing this work, and when about to practise as a barrister (he had been a student of the Inner Temple from 1801), he was again struck down by illness, and died at Chelsea on 28 January 1813.   J. G. ALGER, *rev.* PETER SPENCE

Sources *GM*, 1st ser., 83/1 (1813), 188, 283–4 • H. T. Blethen, 'Yorke, Henry Redhead', *BDMBR*, vol. 1 • E. Fearn, 'Henry Redhead Yorke: radical traitor', *Yorkshire Archaeological Journal*, 42 (1967–70), 187–92 • M. J. Laski, 'Recantation of Henry Redhead Yorke', *Encounter*, 41/4 (1973), 67–85 • *Annual Register* (1795), 47 • *Annual Register* (1798), 23 • *Annual Register* (1799), 160 • *Annual Register* (1806), 458 • *New Annual Register* (1795), 60 • *European Magazine and London Review*, 28 (1795), 429 • *European Magazine and London Review*, 50 (1806), 490 • *Argus, or, London Review'd in Paris* (15 Nov 1802) • *Moniteur* (26 Nov 1802) • *State trials*, vol. 24 • J. G. Alger, 'The British colony in Paris, 1792–3', *EngHR*, 13 (1898), 672–94 • T. Faulkner, *An historical and topographical description of Chelsea and its environs*, [new edn], 1 (1829), 383 • *Memoirs and correspondence of Viscount Castlereagh, second marquess of Londonderry*, ed. C. Vane, marquess of Londonderry, 12 vols. (1848–53)

Likenesses S. W. Reynolds, mezzotint, pubd 1796 (after J. R. Smith), BM • J. Ward, mezzotint, pubd 1796 (after W. Hay), BM, NPG

Yorke, Henry Vincent [*pseud.* Henry Green] (1905–1973), novelist, was born on 29 October 1905, the son of Vincent Wodehouse Yorke and his wife, Maud Evelyn, at the family home at Forthampton, near Tewkesbury in Gloucestershire. It was the kind of country house that exerted a strong pull on the imagination of Green the mature writer. He went to school at Eton College (1918–26), and to university at Magdalen College, Oxford (1926–8), leaving after two years without a degree in order to work on the factory floor of the family engineering works in Birmingham. He remained with the firm, H. Pontifex & Sons, for the rest of his working life until early retirement; but despite the demands this placed on his time, he maintained a healthy rate of literary production under the name Henry Green, particularly during the war years, publishing nine novels and one autobiography between 1926 and 1952.

Despite the regard in which his work was held by other authors, Green kept a low profile on the literary scene; he wrote unobtrusively during his lunch hour and shunned publicity, preferring to be photographed from behind (the most famous portrait, by Cecil Beaton, shows Green peering back over his shoulder, apparently eyeing the camera with suspicious distaste). The desire for privacy and inscrutability, sometimes taken to obsessive lengths, reflects an important aspect of Green's writing, which is nothing if not systematically oblique.

Green's first novel, *Blindness* (1926), written while the author was still at school, lacks the complicated syntax and generally virtuosic style of the later books, but shows his writing already in the grip of obsessional structures. The plot revolves around the aftermath of an accident in which the schoolboy John Haye is blinded and then sent to recuperate in the country, where his involvement with a local girl is paralleled by his growing devotion to the image of his dead mother. Despite the intense psychological focus of the narrative, the real centre of interest is the repetition of motifs and the duplication of character types and relationships. The book effectively lays down a template for Green's fascination with the workings of desire and with the textual expression of a compromise between concealing and revealing it.

With his second novel, *Living* (1929), Green established his credentials as an experimental modernist. The freshness and originality of his portrayal of working-class life in Birmingham was felt by the *Times Literary Supplement* to introduce 'a whole school of proletarian literature'. But *Living* anticipated neither the documentary impulses nor the socialist realist bias of some politically motivated fiction in the 1930s; it derived its most striking effects from an alertness to the patterns of working-class speech, whose idioms it put into circulation in both dialogue and narration.

Green was married in 1929 to Adelaide Mary Biddulph, with whom he was to have one son, Sebastian Yorke. She was the daughter of John Michael Gordon Biddulph, second Baron Biddulph (1869–1949), and his wife, Marjorie. Green's rate of composition slowed down during the 1930s, while he worked on the difficult project of *Party Going* (1939), an especially puzzling text that has attracted an increasing amount of attention from critics. The opening of the book describes the death of a pigeon and establishes the figure of the bird, first invoked in *Living*, as a key image in Green's writing; such recurrent motifs are never allowed the status of a symbol but are given shifting, provisional meanings in texts which work characteristically by implication and are mesmerized by thresholds, veils, and various other barriers to full understanding.

Although Green tended to distance himself from the public concerns of his time, both *Party Going* and his interim autobiography *Pack my Bag* (1940) show an awareness of psychoanalytical thought, social politics, and historical crisis. It was during the writing of *Caught* (1943) that Green conceived of the writer's role in terms of a need to capture the 'idiom of the time'. The sense of urgency behind this concern to write in a way that responds to contemporary styles of thought and feeling was sponsored by the events and conditions of wartime. The three novels *Caught* (1943), *Loving* (1945), and *Back* (1946) deal with different aspects of life on the home front; with the blitz, evacuation, and demobilization, respectively. The first two novels consider the damage wrought by class division at a time usually commemorated with a myth of social unity, while *Caught* and *Back* focus on the experience of traumatic loss and the subsequent operations of memory. All three books register shocks to the psychological and social systems, but in *Loving* in particular the sense of foreboding is offset by passages of brilliant and enlivening prose, frequently of an erotic character.

When Alan Ross challenged Green, in an interview in 1959, to define the compulsion behind his writing, the one-word rejoinder was 'Sex'. In his last three novels, *Concluding* (1948), *Nothing* (1950), and *Doting* (1952), the concerns of story and plot are sidelined in the construction of texts that circle constantly around the figures of desire and decay. *Concluding* is a mystery story, set in a future totalitarian state, whose mysteries remain unsolved and whose writing is drawn towards the breakdown of conventional forms of organization, whether textual or social. Its prose is dense with allusions and cross-references, in marked contrast to the much sparer textures of the last two books, which are restricted to dialogue and passages of description which rather mechanically recycle the imagery of Green's earlier works. The increasing repetitiveness of this late writing was followed by a twenty-year silence, during which Green was reportedly at work on a stage play but was notably prone to bouts

of depression and an accelerating reclusiveness. He died on 13 December 1973 in London, where his home latterly was 30 Wilton Place, Belgravia.   ROD MENGHAM

Sources H. Green, *Pack my bag* (1940) · H. Green, *Surviving: the uncollected writings* (1940) · J. Russell, 'There it is', *Kenyon Review*, 26 (summer 1964), 433–65 · R. Mengham, *The idiom of the time: the writings of Henry Green* (1982) · T. Southern, 'The art of fiction XXII— Henry Green', *Paris Review*, 5 (summer 1958), 61–77 · 'Henry Green', *The Oxford companion to twentieth-century literature in English*, ed. J. Stringer (1996) · D. Lygon and J. Lee-Milne, *Twentieth Century Literature*, 29/4 (winter 1983) · *DNB* · *The Times* (15 Dec 1973) · *The Times* (20 Dec 1973) · *CGPLA Eng. & Wales* (1974)
Archives BL · Eton, corresp. and literary papers | Eton, letters to Nevill Coghill
Likenesses C. Beaton, photographs, Sothebys · M. Smith, oils, repro. in *London Magazine*, 6/4 (April 1959), 32–3
Wealth at death £56,186: probate, 7 May 1974, *CGPLA Eng. & Wales*

Yorke, James (*fl.* 1640), heraldic writer, was a blacksmith in the city of Lincoln. Nothing is known of his family. He is remembered for his single folio volume, printed at London in 1640, entitled *The union of honour: containing the armes, matches and issues of the kings, dukes, marquesses and earles of England from the conquest, until … 1640*. A frontispiece, dated 1641, is inscribed to Charles I. This was probably issued with the second part of the book containing the arms of viscounts and barons, together with the gentry of Lincolnshire, which was introduced by Yorke as 'a corollary to my work before'. The book itself is prefaced by a dedicatory epistle to Henry Frederick, son and heir apparent of Thomas Howard, earl of Arundel, in which Yorke claimed he was long in 'forging and hammering it to this perfection' and that it was 'a Master-piece, not yet matched by any of my trade'. Dedicatory poems follow from eight of Yorke's friends or countrymen, including the author Richard Brathwaite and the actor and author Thomas Heywood. The text is based on Thomas Milles, John Guillim, Ralph Brooke, and Augustine Vincent, with Yorke claiming responsibility for material between 1622 and 1640. The heraldry in many surviving copies is hand-coloured. Yorke anchors his heraldic presentation of the nobility and gentry in chivalric tradition by appending a list of battles fought by the English, derived from Speed and Stow.

Yorke's work was admired by contemporaries, not least because of his humble occupation. Thomas Fuller lauded him as:

> an excellent workman in his Profession, insomuch that if Pegasus himself would wear shoes, this man alone is fit to make them. He is a servant as well of Apollo as of Vulcan, turning his stiddy into a studdy. (Fuller, *Worthies*, 2.24)

The *Union of Honour* retains some interest as a link between Vincent and William Dugdale, and as an affirmation of English social order on the eve of the civil war. Yorke's date of death is unknown.

THOMAS SECCOMBE, *rev.* PETER SHERLOCK

Sources Fuller, *Worthies* (1811), 2.24
Likenesses T. Rawlyns, line engraving, BM, NPG; repro. in J. Yorke, *The union of honour* (1640)

Yorke [*née* Campbell], **Jemima**, *suo jure* **Marchioness Grey** (1722–1797), letter writer, was born on 10 October 1722 in Copenhagen, Denmark, the second child of John *Campbell, Lord Glenorchy, later third earl of Breadalbane and Holland (*bap.* 1696, *d.* 1782), who at that time was British envoy to the Danish court, and his wife, Amabel (1698–1727), daughter of Henry *Grey, duke of Kent (*bap.* 1671, *d.* 1740), and his first wife, Jemima, *née* Crew. She spent her early childhood in Denmark, but in 1725 moved with her mother and brother Henry (1721–1728) to the Grey country seat of Wrest Park in Bedfordshire. Shortly before she died Lady Glenorchy wrote to her mother, the duchess of Kent, asking her to care for her 'poor helpless girl' (Godber, 10). Her father's diplomatic career meant that it was more convenient for her to remain in Britain with her maternal grandparents. She remained in the care of the duchess and, after her death, of the duke of Kent. Following the duchess's death in 1728, and the duke's remarriage in 1729, she and her aunt, Lady Mary Grey (only three years her senior), were settled in a house in Chelsea with a housekeeper, although they remained close to Kent and his new duchess. Probably with Kent's approval, the rector of St James's, Piccadilly, Thomas Secker, took an interest in the girls' welfare, styling himself their guardian. Through Secker, Jemima made a lifelong friend of Catherine Talbot, then becoming celebrated as a child prodigy; the two found they were reading the same books when they met, and continued to co-ordinate their reading until Catherine Talbot's death.

Following the death of Kent's son from his second marriage in 1733, Jemima became heir to Kent's barony of Lucas of Crudwell, which could be inherited by women. Consequently, the duke decided that she should become the sole heir to his estates, a position expressed in the painting *Conversation Piece at Wrest* (*c.*1735) and confirmed by Kent's will of 1736. Probably at Secker's suggestion, Jemima was betrothed early in 1740 to Philip *Yorke (1720–1790), eldest son of Philip *Yorke, baron and later first earl of Hardwicke, lord chancellor. On 19 May Kent was created Marquess Grey, with a special remainder to Jemima and the heirs male of her body. Jemima and Yorke married on 22 May 1740 in the duke of Kent's lodging in Brompton, Middlesex; Kent died there on 5 June, and Jemima succeeded to the marquessate.

Jemima's marriage had been arranged with an eye to the compatibility of her new husband's character as well as the dynastic consideration that would allow the rising Yorkes to assume the name and estates of the long-established Greys. The marriage was extremely successful, and the only prolonged period they spent apart came when Philip Yorke spent some months in Paris without his wife in 1749. The couple's mutual affection was enhanced by their shared love of scholarship and travel, and their interest in maintaining Jemima's inheritance, not only at Wrest but at other estates in Bedfordshire, Leicestershire, Wiltshire, Essex, and Herefordshire. They found that Jemima had inherited debts of £12,570, and for the first three years of their marriage Wrest was closed.

Jemima Yorke, *suo jure* **Marchioness Grey** (1722–1797), by Allan Ramsay, 1741

The duke of Kent had already arranged space in the Commons legislative timetable for a private bill that would have changed the couple's surname to Grey and entailed the estates on their descendants in the male line, but it was instead used to facilitate the sale of the Herefordshire property. After 1743 Wrest became their main residence and there Jemima was able to entertain her friends, including Catherine Talbot. Talbot's secret diary of her 1745 visit to Wrest gives an intimate picture of Jemima's life. Morning prayers were followed by a walk in the park. Tea was taken in the garden buildings or, if wet, chess or billiards were played in the house. In the evening there was an hour's reading, which could include theology, political theory, and the classics; she read French in the original but other languages, including Latin, Greek, and Italian, in translation. Jemima asserted that women could profit from a life of scholarly retirement as well as men, and once commented on Pliny's advocacy of a country life of study and exercise: 'I don't find how Mrs Pliny (for all his charming account of her and his letters to her) had any share in it' (Godber, 35). Her cultural interests in London included music and theatre, where her letters show that she followed closely strife between and within the two patent theatres, and that she was an early admirer of David Garrick.

Marriage helped widen Jemima's circle of correspondents. Catherine Talbot and Lady Mary Gregory (formerly Grey) were joined by her husband's sisters Elizabeth *Anson and Margaret Heathcote, and sister-in-law Mary Yorke, *née* Madocks, daughter of Isaac Madocks, bishop of

Worcester. Her activities were for short periods limited in the 1750s by the birth of her daughters, Amabel [see Campbell, Amabel Hume-, suo jure Countess De Grey (1751–1833)] and Mary Jemima [see below]. Amabel later transcribed her letters. These give a vivid picture of her travels, recording her impressions of architecture, estates, and (when they were present) their owners. Places visited included Warwick Castle, Holkham, Houghton, and Shugborough. Influenced by the naturalizing of Wrest Gardens in the 1730s, she criticized the gardens at Stowe: 'for such an Extent … there is the least of Management or Beauty in the Disposing of it, it affords the least variety and Surprise, and fewer pleasant Spots' (Clarke, 181). She disliked its 'stiff set plan' (ibid.).

Jemima left most matters of estate management to her husband. As head of the Grey family, she approved the marriage of her half-aunt Lady Anne Sophia Grey to John Egerton, a clergyman, who was some years her junior, over the opposition of Lady Anne Sophia's mother's family, the Bentincks. Before his death in 1764 she was subordinate in questions of Yorke family interest to her father-in-law Hardwicke, but her interventions after that date demonstrated her independence of thought. In 1770, alone among the Yorke family, she pressed Charles Yorke, through his wife Agneta, to accept the post of lord chancellor in the Grafton administration. His brothers, including Jemima's husband, felt Charles should remain outside the ministry, remain loyal to Rockingham, and expect to be included in a prospective second Rockingham administration that could succeed Grafton's; Jemima thought this unlikely and Grafton's offer Charles's best hope of attaining the great seal. In 1782, when her son-in-law Thomas Robinson, second Baron Grantham, was offered the post of foreign secretary by Shelburne, she thought his accepting the post a mistake, as 'To be hoisted up and kicked down would be unpleasant; to lose private comfort without effecting public benefit none but restless minds could wish for' (Godber, 110).

Constrained by the financial embarrassment of the estate when she inherited in 1740, and by the act of parliament that enforced her marriage settlement, Jemima made no major alterations to the house at Wrest. Change came only in 1758–60 when the gardens were altered by Lancelot 'Capability' Brown. He replaced many of the straight canals that went through the gardens with meandering streams, but in general respected the intentions of the duke of Kent and Jemima's wishes as his patron. Additional garden buildings were provided by Edward Stevens and William Chambers. In 1774 the gardens were sketched by Jemima's daughter Amabel for Catherine the Great's Wedgwood dinner service. Jemima and her husband occasionally entertained the prospect of agricultural reform, but enclosed only on the fringes of the Grey estates under pressure from neighbouring landowners. Following the death of her husband in 1790, Jemima made no changes in the running of the estate, although she did commission John Woolfe (d. 1793) to harmonize the fronts at Wrest and provide a new Chinese drawing-room. In November 1792 she was badly burnt by a fire in her bedroom, but recovered sufficiently to visit her daughter Lady Grantham at Newby Hall in Yorkshire the following August.

Jemima died at her London residence, 4 St James's Square, Westminster, on 11 January 1797, and was buried in the Grey family mausoleum at the parish church, Flitton, Bedfordshire, on 21 January. The marquessate became extinct, but another title inherited from her grandfather, the barony of Lucas of Crudwell, was inherited by her eldest daughter, Amabel.

Jemima's second daughter, Mary Jemima [**Mary Jemima Robinson** [née Yorke], Lady Grantham (1757–1830)], was born on 9 February 1757 and was educated privately at Wrest. Six years younger than her sister Amabel, she was less obviously precocious, but like her sister shared in the culturally aware ambience of her parents' household. On 17 August 1780, at her parents' town house in St James's Square, she married Thomas *Robinson, second Baron Grantham (1738–1786), until 1779 British ambassador to Spain. They had three sons, Thomas Philip [see Grey, Thomas Philip de, second Earl De Grey (1781–1859)], Philip, who died in infancy, and Frederick John *Robinson (1782–1859), prime minister from 1827 to 1828 as Viscount Goderich. The early death of her husband left Mary Jemima in charge of the boys' education and administrator of the Robinson estate at Newby Park in Yorkshire. She educated her sons herself in their early years; both Thomas and Frederick were reading at two. She once wrote, 'I shall not trouble you about politicks, foreign or domestick, as I understand neither' (Jones, 4), but both would have been among the constant topics of conversation at her homes, and helped prepare her sons for their political careers. When not at Newby she lived at Grantham House in Putney, bought by her husband before his death, or at Wrest or in St James's Square, London, with her elder sister, who had also been widowed at an early age.

Mary Jemima's judgement was said to have influenced the decisions made by her sons in their careers—for example, Frederick Robinson's refusal of office in the Portland administration in 1807. She lived long enough to see both her surviving sons attain senior office, her elder son becoming lord lieutenant of Bedfordshire in 1818, and her younger son enjoying a succession of cabinet offices. Their careers perhaps at last vindicated the decision the duke of Kent had made in 1740 to ensure that his dynasty remained prominent in public life by marrying his granddaughter Jemima to Philip Yorke. Mary Jemima died at Whitehall on 7 January 1830.   JAMES COLLETT-WHITE

Sources Beds. & Luton ARS, Wrest Park (Lucas) archives, L30/9, L30/9a [letters to and from Jemima], L30/11, L30/13 [letters to her daughters] · J. Godber, *The Marchioness Grey of Wrest Park*, Bedfordshire Historical RS, 47 (1968) · G. B. Clarke, ed., *Descriptions of Lord Cobham's gardens at Stowe* (1700–1750), Buckinghamshire RS, 26 (1990) · notes on the Grey family, Beds. & Luton ARS, CRT 190/45 · [Miss Leman], biography of Marchioness Grey, before 1966, Beds. & Luton ARS · BL, Hardwicke MSS · Nicola Smith, *Wrest Park* [n.d., 1990x99] · D. Souden, *Wimpole Hall* (1991) · W. Stokes and R. G. Thorne, 'Robinson, Hon. Frederick John', HoP, *Commons, 1790–1820* · D. R. Fisher, 'Bedfordshire', HoP, *Commons, 1790–1820*, 2.1–4 ·

W. D. Jones, 'Prosperity' Robinson: the life of Viscount Goderich (1967) · GEC, Peerage

Archives Beds. & Luton ARS, corresp. | Beds. & Luton ARS, notes on Grey family, CRT 190/45 · BL, Hardwicke MSS

Likenesses group portrait, c.1735, repro. in Godber, Marchioness Grey · A. Ramsay, portrait, 1741, Wimpole Hall, Cambridgeshire [see illus.] · J. Reynolds, group portrait, oils, c.1761, Cleveland Museum of Art, Ohio · G. Romney, oils, 1781 (Mary-Jemima, Lady Grantham), repro. in Godber, Marchioness Grey · A. Ramsay, portrait, second version, repro. in Godber, Marchioness Grey

Yorke, Joseph, **Baron Dover** (1724–1792), diplomatist, was born in London on 24 June 1724, the third son of the celebrated lawyer Philip *Yorke, first earl of Hardwicke (1690–1764), and his wife, Margaret Lygon, née Cocks (c.1695–1761). Born into the whig establishment and brought up within it, Yorke's own career became a monument to the passing of this age. In company with his four brothers, he was educated at Dr Newcombe's famous school at Hackney and by a private tutor, Dr Samuel Slater, recommended as 'a good scholar of exemplary character and Whig principles' (Life and Correspondence of Philip Yorke, 1.102). While his elder brothers Philip *Yorke (1720–1790) and Charles *Yorke (1722–1770) were destined by family strategy for the law or politics, a military career beckoned for Joe as a younger son. The political correspondent and political manager Elizabeth *Anson (1725–1760) was his sister. In April 1741 at the age of sixteen he was commissioned as an ensign in the duke of Cumberland's regiment of guards. The War of the Austrian Succession (1740–48) provided opportunities for aspiring soldiers, and Yorke's own application and abilities, together with the support of George II's favourite son, ensured that he rose rapidly. He served first with the earl of Stair's forces in the Low Countries, took part in the victory at Dettingen (June 1743), was promoted captain, and in 1745 became an aide-de-camp to Cumberland, distinguishing himself in the defeat at French hands at Fontenoy (May 1745). His bravery on this occasion secured a commission as lieutenant-colonel in the 1st regiment of foot guards. On returning with Cumberland's forces to Britain when the Jacobite rising occurred later that year, he was present on the battlefield of Culloden (April 1746), where the Young Pretender was comprehensively defeated. Back on the continent, Yorke witnessed the Maréchal de Saxe's great victory at Laufeldt (July 1747). His rising reputation was apparent in his appointment as an aide-de-camp to the king in 1749, a post he retained until 1758.

Yorke's experiences during the 1740s left him with an enduring and, before long, exaggerated fear of French military power which remained central to his political outlook. Though he had risen swiftly in the army during the war, that career did not offer a path to the political summit which was his goal. In the final stages of the fighting he had made important contacts with members of the Dutch political élite, and he now embarked upon diplomatic service as a route to high office in England. His father, then lord chancellor, and the latter's political confidant the duke of Newcastle, together secured a flying start for the young man. Having been sent to Paris as a member of the peace commission at the end of the War of

the Austrian Succession, he remained there after its conclusion and served as secretary of embassy (1749–51) to the new British ambassador, the earl of Albemarle, a post he occupied until October 1751. In December of that year Yorke was parachuted, at the tender age of twenty-seven, into the key mission to the Dutch Republic, then second only to France in the hierarchy of British diplomatic appointments. It was to be his only permanent post: he remained at The Hague until December 1780, first as minister-plenipotentiary (1751–61) and then as ambassador after August 1761, in which year he was also awarded a KB. This was the longest period of continuous service at a major post of any eighteenth-century British diplomatist.

Yorke's nomination was part of a significant reconfiguration of Anglo-Dutch relations. The two countries had been allies since the age of the stadholder-king, William III, who had ruled on both sides of the narrow seas (1689–1702) and had fought against Louis XIV's France in the wars of 1689 to 1714. The Dutch Republic had spent its power and especially its fiscal strength in that conflict, and during the 1740s the extent of its political and economic decline, under way for a generation, had finally become evident, particularly to its British ally. Though the stadholderate had been restored in 1747 in the person of William IV (1747–51), the republic could no longer play its traditional role in international relations and especially in Britain's alliance system. The solution sponsored by the leading Orangist statesman Willem Bentinck van Rhoon through his political ally Newcastle was as simple as it was ingenious. Subordinating the weakened Dutch Republic to its increasingly powerful British partner, he persuaded London to assume the twin roles of dominant force in the alliance and buttress of the house of Orange. Its fragile domestic position was further weakened shortly before Britain's new representative reached The Hague by William IV's early and unexpected death in autumn 1751. The regency for his young son, the future William V, was headed by his widow, Anna, George II's eldest daughter.

Yorke's role was to uphold the alliance and the house of Orange which protected it, and this he did throughout the next generation with exemplary diligence but rather less flexibility and intelligence. The changing balance of forces between the two countries made it an unequal partnership, and this first became evident during the Seven Years' War (1756–63). Though the republic had declined economically, it retained a substantial share of colonial and European commerce and was a natural target for France during wartime. Even worse, from a British perspective, the relevant treaties which dated from the seventeenth century gave Dutch merchants a privileged position as neutral traders during Anglo-French hostilities. In 1758 a British naval and privateering offensive against France's Caribbean trade led to the seizure of a number of Dutch ships and provoked a serious diplomatic confrontation. On this occasion a settlement was patched up, as the British government made concessions in order to support the Orangist regime, further weakened by the death of the princesse-gouvernante, Anna, at the beginning of 1759. The problems of neutral rights were already apparent, however, and they would loom even larger during the final years of Yorke's mission.

Hardwicke and Newcastle were leading figures during the 1750s and early 1760s, and their influence ensured that Yorke's star remained in the ascendant. He rejected a posting to Russia in 1754, and was sent on what became a special mission to Frederick the Great between April and June 1758: intended to replace Andrew Mitchell as Britain's representative, he was hurriedly withdrawn when both Prussian and British policy were thrown into reverse. Three years later Yorke was named as one of the three British plenipotentiaries to the abortive peace congress at Augsburg, while in 1763 and again in 1766 he was offered and rejected the post of ambassador to Madrid. Implicit in the offer of an embassy to Spain was both the reduced importance of the Dutch Republic within the wider framework of British foreign policy and Yorke's own declining connections at home.

By the 1760s an entire political generation was passing from the scene: Yorke's father, Hardwicke, died in 1764, Newcastle four years later. However, Yorke retained important connections. The new king, George III, used him secretly for private family diplomacy, most notably in 1766 in an unsuccessful attempt to substitute the king's sister, Louisa, as the stadholder's bride, thereby preventing the marriage of William V to a Hohenzollern princess. That union symbolized the Dutch Republic's transition from its traditional British orbit into a new Prussian one. Yet even the king's support could not secure the Paris embassy or a cabinet post for the ambassador, whom he famously described as Britain's 'foreign political watchman at The Hague' (*Correspondence of George III*, 4.20). Throughout his mission Yorke was an MP, successively for East Grinstead (1751–61), Dover (1761–74), and Grampound (1774–80). Unlike Horatio Walpole in an earlier generation, however, he played no discernible role in the House of Commons, where he neither spoke nor voted, valuing only the prestige conferred by membership. The ambassador's inability to take on a parliamentary role was the ostensible reason why Lord North did not appoint him to a secretaryship of state in 1778.

The decline of his political connections at home was one reason why Yorke remained marooned at The Hague throughout the 1760s and 1770s. Another was his difficult personality, which flawed his whole career. The ambassador was a man of few social graces, with a talent which bordered on genius for alienating his friends and antagonizing his opponents. James Boswell, passing through the republic shortly after the Seven Years' War, claimed that 'he seemed so anxious lest people should not know that he was an Ambassador that he held his head very high and spoke very little', styled him a 'buckram knight', and declared that he was 'rendered ridiculous by affected airs' (*Boswell on the Grand Tour*, 171). Even a more sympathetic British observer, Sir Nathaniel Wraxall, commented discreetly on Yorke's 'defects of external deportment' and declared that 'his manners and address had in them something formal and ceremonious' (Wraxall, 1.180). Dutch statesmen were considerably less charitable, finding the ambassador proud, overbearing, haughty, and prone to transact official negotiations through threats and demands rather than through the discussions and compromises which were the mainsprings of eighteenth-century diplomacy.

These shortcomings became particularly important during the final years of Yorke's mission. The outbreak of rebellion in Britain's North American colonies in 1775 once more placed the combustible issue of neutral rights at the top of the diplomatic agenda. At first the moderation exhibited by both governments kept the disputes within bounds. The outbreak of an Anglo-French war within Europe in summer 1778 sharply reduced the scope for compromise, and very soon British seizures of Dutch shipping, now on a wholly new scale, together with the decisions of English prize courts, produced Dutch complaints and reprisals. Yorke's provocative conduct exacerbated matters and further raised the political temperature as the situation deteriorated during 1779–80. He was now openly contemptuous of the Orangist regime and of William V, the unimpressive stadholder at its head. Crucially, he failed to recognize that the authorities at The Hague could not control the republic's commercial provinces, Holland and Zeeland, which had been inflamed by British seizures, and so deliver the concessions which Britain's volatile ambassador was demanding. Yorke's own political ideas had not moved beyond the 1740s and 1750s when he had grown to maturity: automatic opposition to France, support for the republic and the house of Orange. He believed that Dutch politics still revolved around the struggle of Orangists and regents: he failed to appreciate the extent to which the rise of the patriot movement, with its demand for a less oligarchical basis of Dutch political life, was changing the complexion of the republic's politics. Bad history and a worse grasp of present political reality led him to sponsor a desperate solution: a British attack on the republic, intended to revive the stadholderate exactly as the French attacks of 1672 and 1747 had done. His own influence and, more importantly, the threatened Dutch accession to Catherine II's 'armed neutrality', a league of Europe's commercial states, led to the adoption of his plan by his superiors, and on Boxing day 1780 Yorke left The Hague. The Fourth Anglo-Dutch War (1780–84) which followed had the opposite effect to that intended by the ambassador: shattering Dutch defeats further weakened the stadholderate, rather than strengthening it.

Yorke's final years in England were uneventful. On 23 June 1783 the lifelong bachelor married the Danish Baroness de Stöcken, Christiana Boetzelaer (c.1714–1793), the elderly widow of a Dutch nobleman, Baron de Boetzelaer, and the daughter of Johan Henrik, Baron de Stöcken; they had no children. Throughout his diplomatic career Yorke had received a series of military appointments and promotions, the last of which saw him rise to the rank of general (1777). During the 1780s he again seems to have played an active role in military affairs, while as late as

1787 he was consulted by the Pitt government over its foreign policy. In the following year he was created Baron Dover, a peerage which became extinct upon his death, at Hill Street, Mayfair, on 2 December 1792.

H. M. SCOTT

Sources H. M. Scott, 'Sir Joseph Yorke and the waning of the Anglo-Dutch alliance, 1747–1788', *Colonial empires compared*, ed. R. Moore (2002), 11–31 · H. M. Scott, 'Sir Joseph Yorke, Dutch politics and the origins of the Fourth Anglo-Dutch War', *HJ*, 31 (1988), 571–89 · P. C. Yorke, *The life and correspondence of Philip Yorke, earl of Hardwicke*, 3 vols. (1913) · N. W. Wraxall, *Historical memoirs of my own time*, 2nd edn, 2 vols. (1815) · *Boswell on the grand tour: Germany and Switzerland, 1764*, ed. F. A. Pottle (1953), vol. 4 of *The Yale editions of the private papers of James Boswell*, trade edn (1950–89) · R. Pares, *Colonial blockade and neutral rights, 1739–63* (1938), 242–79 · J. A. Cannon, 'Yorke, Joseph', HoP, *Commons, 1754–90* · GEC, *Peerage* · *The correspondence of King George the Third from 1760 to December 1783*, ed. J. Fortescue, 6 vols. (1927–8)
Archives BL, Add. MSS 17497, 38197–38344, 38774 · BL, Add. MSS 32026–32027, 32817, 32832–32990, 34413–34416 · BL, corresp. and papers, Add. MSS 33026–33027, 35349–36278, 45119 · PRO, official dispatches | BL, letters to S. Dayrolle, Add. MSS 15871–15875, *passim* · BL, corresp. with R. Gunning and W. Eden, Egerton MSS 2700–2703; Add. MSS 34413–34421 · BL, corresp. with Lord Holdernesse, etc., Add. MSS 6806–6820, 6831; Egerton MSS 3445–3461 · BL, corresp. with Sir James Marriott, Add. MSS 17386–17387 · BL, corresp. with duke of Newcastle, etc., Add. MSS 32686–32992, *passim* · BL, letters to Sir J. Porter, Egerton MS 2157 · BL, letters to Rainsford, Add. MS 23652 · BL, corresp. with Lord Sandwich and Richard Phelps, Stowe MSS 257–261, *passim* · BL, letters to Edward Weston, Add. MS 58213 · Bucks. RLSS, letters to George Howard and Richard Vyse · CKS, corresp. with Lord Amherst · NL Scot., letters to Hugh Elliot · NRA, priv. coll., letters to Lord Cathcart · NRA, priv. coll., corresp. with Lord Stormont · PRO, letters to Lord Amherst, WO 34 · PRO, letters to Lord Chatham, PRO 30/8 · U. Hull, Brynmor Jones L., letters to Sir Charles Hotham-Thompson
Likenesses line engraving, pubd 1780, BM, NPG · J. Alefounder, miniature on ivory, Antony, Cornwall · portrait, repro. in *Westminster Magazine* (April 1780)

Yorke, Sir Joseph Sydney

Yorke, Sir Joseph Sydney (1768–1831), naval officer, the second son of Charles *Yorke (1722–1770) and his second wife, Agneta, *née* Johnson (1740–1820), and younger brother of Charles Philip *Yorke (1764–1834), was born in London on 6 June 1768. He was educated at Harrow School (1779–80) and entered the navy in 1780. In March 1781 he joined the *Duke*, commanded by Sir Charles Douglas, whom, in December, he followed to the *Formidable*, in which he was present at the action of 12 April 1782 and continued until she was paid off in 1783. The following year he was again with Douglas, in the *Assistance*, and returned home with him in the spring of 1785. He was then in the *Salisbury*, the flagship of Commodore John Elliot, on the Newfoundland station, and in the *Adamant*, with Sir Richard Hughes, at Halifax. On 27 June 1789 he was promoted lieutenant of the *Thisbe* with Captain Samuel Hood (1762–1814), and returned to England at the end of the year. On 19 November 1790 he was promoted commander, and in February 1791 was appointed to the *Rattlesnake*, which he commanded in the channel until his promotion on 4 February 1793 to be captain of the *Circe*, in which, and afterwards in the *Stag*, the *Jason*, and the *Canada*, he served on the home station continuously until the peace of Amiens. On 22 August 1795, while in command of the *Stag*, he captured the Dutch frigate *Alliandie* off the coast of Norway. This, and other captures, earned him a significant amount of prize money, which he used to build his home, Sydney Lodge, at Southampton. On 29 March 1798 he married Elizabeth Weake (d. 1812), the daughter of James Rattray of Atherston, New Brunswick; they had six sons and a daughter. Their eldest son, Charles Philip *Yorke, became fourth earl of Hardwicke.

In August 1803 Yorke was appointed to the *Prince George* in the channel. He then commanded the *Barfleur* and the *Christian VII*, also in the channel. In June 1810 he was knighted when acting as proxy for his half-brother Philip *Yorke, the third earl of Hardwicke, on his installation as KG. On 31 July 1810 he was promoted rear-admiral, and in the following January, with his flag in the *Vengeur*, he was sent out to Lisbon with reinforcements for the army. These were landed on 4 March, leading Masséna to retreat from the lines of Torres Vedras. This was Yorke's last service afloat.

In July 1810 Yorke joined the Board of Admiralty, where he served under his elder brother Charles Philip Yorke. Although the latter resigned from the government in 1812, Yorke remained at the board, and rose to become first naval lord under Lord Melville in October 1813. He left this post, and the Admiralty borough, in 1818, at the same time that his brother retired from public life. Yorke remained an active tory member of parliament until the end of his life; he opposed Catholic emancipation, although he was prepared to support Canning's ministry. His seat at Reigate (1790–1806, 1818–31) was the family borough; St Germans (1806–10) and West Looe (1812) were nomination boroughs, while Sandwich (1812–18) was an Admiralty borough.

His first wife having died on 29 January 1812, on 22 May 1813 Yorke married Urania Annie Kington, formerly de Burgh, dowager marchioness of Clanricarde (d. 1843), widow of Colonel Peter Kington and of Henry de Burgh, marquess of Clanricarde, and daughter of George Paulet, the twelfth marquess of Winchester; they had no children. On 4 June 1814 he was made vice-admiral, on 2 January 1815 KCB, and on 22 July 1830 admiral. During his later years he lived principally at Sydney Lodge, but he devoted much time to the administration of various charities connected with the naval service. He was also chairman of the Waterloo Bridge Company, in which he took an active role. On 5 May 1831 he was drowned when the small yacht in which he was travelling from Southampton to Portsmouth was struck by lightning in Stokes' Bay. He was survived by his wife. He was interred in the family vault at Wimpole, Cambridgeshire. Yorke's career was dominated by the role of his elder brothers, the third earl of Hardwicke and Charles Philip Yorke, in the factional politics of the period, and his service at the Admiralty was always more political than administrative.

J. K. LAUGHTON, rev. ANDREW LAMBERT

Sources Lady Biddulph of Ledbury, *Charles Philip Yorke, fourth earl of Hardwicke* (1910) · D. Syrett and R. L. DiNardo, *The commissioned sea officers of the Royal Navy, 1660–1815*, rev. edn, Occasional Publications of the Navy RS, 1 (1994) • L. B. Namier, *The structure of politics at the accession of George III*, 2 vols. (1929) • J. C. Sainty, ed., *Admiralty officials, 1660–1870* (1975) • 'Yorke, C. P.', 'Yorke, J. S.', HoP, *Commons* • *GM*, 1st ser., 101/1 (1831), 477 • Burke, *Peerage* (1999)

Archives BL, corresp., letter-books and papers, Add. MSS 35201, 35395, 35651, 36261, 45042–45043, 45046 • Bodl. Oxf. • NMM | BL, Yorke MSS • Bodl. Oxf., letters to Charles Philip Yorke

Likenesses G. Romney, two portraits, repro. in Biddulph, *Charles Philip Yorke*

Wealth at death under £40,000: *GM*, 561

Yorke, Philip, first earl of Hardwicke (1690–1764),

lord chancellor, was born at Dover, Kent, on 1 December 1690, the only surviving son of Philip Yorke (*bap.* 1651, *d.* 1721), an attorney of Dover, and his wife, Elizabeth (1658/9–1727), the daughter of Richard Gibbon of Dover. He was educated at a school in Bethnal Green, Middlesex, run by a dissenter, Samuel Morland, but left at the age of sixteen to become an articled clerk to a prominent London attorney, Charles Salkend of Holborn. Mrs Salkend was said to have exploited his dependent status by sending him on grocery errands, until the young man hit upon the deterrent stratagem of charging for coach hire. Charles Salkend's perception of Yorke's talents soon launched him on the path to fame and fortune. Yorke, ambitious to be a barrister rather than a humble attorney, was entered at the Middle Temple in 1708 and about the same time became tutor to the sons of Lord Chief Justice Thomas Parker of king's bench.

These valuable connections imparted a rocket-like boost to his legal career after Yorke was called to the bar on 6 May 1715. He obtained numerous briefs from attorney friends on the western circuit and enjoyed the praise and tacit patronage of Judge Parker, first in the court of king's bench, and then, when Parker became Lord Chancellor Macclesfield in 1718, in the court of chancery. Yorke's legal connections were further enhanced by his marriage on 16 May 1719 to a widow, Margaret Lygon (*c.*1695–1761), the daughter of the Worcestershire squire and former MP Charles Cocks, for she was niece of the late Lord Somers, a former lord chancellor, and niece by marriage to Sir Joseph Jekyll, master of the rolls. They had five sons and two daughters, all well taken care of by their father, whose initial poverty was doubtless the spur to his success in securing wealth for himself and his progeny. In 1725 he bought for £24,000 the Gloucestershire estate of Hardwicke, where he never lived, and by the 1730s his avarice had won him the nickname Judge Gripus. In 1740 he was able to pay the earl of Oxford £100,000 for the estate of Wimpole in Cambridgeshire. It became the Yorke family home and the basis of an electoral interest in that county, where his local influence was signified by his appointment in 1749 as high steward of Cambridge University.

Entry into politics Yorke's ability had also attracted the attention of the wealthy duke of Newcastle, a man of his own age, who brought him into parliament at a by-election on 21 April 1719 for his borough of Lewes. At the general election of 1722 Yorke transferred to another of Newcastle's boroughs, Seaford. So began a lifelong friendship, during which, while Newcastle was secretary of state for thirty years from 1724, and then first lord of

Philip Yorke, first earl of Hardwicke (1690–1764), by William Hoare, 1763

the Treasury for nearly eight years, Yorke evolved from protégé to the duke's chief confidant. His maiden speech, on 4 March 1720 in a debate on what became the Irish Declaratory Act of that year, was his most important constitutional pronouncement in parliament. He argued that the inhabitants of Ireland were either the native Irish, a conquered people, or colonists from Britain. In either case they were subject to the British parliament. Later that month, when the post of solicitor-general fell vacant, Macclesfield secured it for Yorke, then aged twenty-nine and with less than five years at the bar, over the heads of more senior claimants. He was knighted on 11 June 1720 and promoted to attorney-general on 31 January 1724. His legal tasks soon included the successful prosecution of two notorious criminals, Jack Sheppard in 1724 and Jonathan Wild in 1725, and as attorney-general he enjoyed a profitable private practice at the bar. Yorke also did his parliamentary duty by what became the ministry of Sir Robert Walpole. Even the scanty records of the 1720s list him as speaking in every parliamentary session of the decade. He spoke on the South Sea Bubble and was prominent in pushing bills of attainder against Jacobites implicated in the 1722 plot. It was Yorke, too, who in 1723 moved for what became known as the Waltham Black Act. Embarrassment loomed in 1725 when his former patron Lord Macclesfield was accused of corruption. Yorke excused himself from the customary obligation of his office by taking no part in the impeachment proceedings, conduct which incurred criticism, and on 18 March he vainly sought mitigation of the punishment designed for the convicted and disgraced lord chancellor.

From 1727 onwards, when European war threatened, Yorke was foremost among those who supported in parliamentary debate such unpopular financial and military measures as increased army estimates and Hessian subsidy treaties. On 7 May 1728 he displayed a touch of steel when he took the opposition leader William Pulteney to task for describing as villains all MPs who supported a vote of credit, extracting an apology even before Speaker Onslow ruled the word to be unparliamentary. Attorney-General Yorke strongly backed Walpole over the unpopular Excise Bill of 1733, making a long speech when it was introduced on 14 March. He challenged the opposition propaganda claim that there was a threat to individual liberty and to the constitution, which, he commented sarcastically, did not include customs frauds.

Later that year a coincidence of vacancies led to a reshuffle of legal posts. Yorke waived precedence to allow Solicitor-General Charles Talbot, whom he had leapfrogged into office in 1720, and who was his superior in equity law, to become lord chancellor. He himself became lord chief justice of king's bench, with a salary enhanced by £2000, a peerage as Baron Hardwicke, and appointment to the privy council. His term as a common-law judge was not marked by any notable decisions, and ended unexpectedly when Lord Talbot died on 14 February 1737, at the age of fifty-one.

Lord chancellor Hardwicke, only five years younger, now claimed the honour he had seemingly forfeited. After a week of bargaining with Walpole, whereby his eldest son, Philip *Yorke (later second earl of Hardwicke), was to obtain in 1738 a lucrative life sinecure at the exchequer, Hardwicke took the woolsack on 21 February 1737; he remained lord chancellor for more than nineteen years. It was a demanding multi-function post: Hardwicke was invariably named as one of the lords justices, or regents, during George II's visits to Hanover; he was a member of the cabinet; he acted as *de facto* speaker of the House of Lords; he was the chief law lord there, hearing appeals from courts in Scotland as well as England; and he presided over the court of chancery.

Legal historians credit Hardwicke with establishing finally the freedom of his office from bribery and undue influence: it was a mere dozen years since the conviction of Macclesfield. More positively, he became renowned for immense conscientiousness in his desire to do justice. Aware that equity law, which regulated personal and property rights, was said to come from books not brains, he established precedents as the mode of procedure—often by the 1750s his own precedents. 'Certainty is the mother of repose, and therefore the law aims at certainty' was his maxim (Yorke, 2.423). To that end he mastered every aspect of law, notably learning Roman law to cope with Scottish cases. Nevertheless he was conscious that counsel might on particular points prove more erudite than himself, and he took due note of arguments advanced. 'His pen always moves at the right time', it was said. Hardwicke was never ashamed to alter his opinion, affirming 'I always thought it a much greater reproach to a Judge to continue in his error than to retract it' (Campbell,

5.46). Hardwicke was a well-mannered judge, never interrupting a legal pleading or indulging in sarcastic humour from the privilege of the bench. His rulings were so convincing in balance and erudition that even unsuccessful litigants were usually satisfied that justice had been done. 'When his Lordship pronounced his decrees', said Lord Mansfield, 'wisdom himself might be supposed to speak' (Yorke, 2.529). Hardwicke possessed the advantages of a handsome person, good looks, and a clear, sonorous voice, and his judgments became a public spectacle. 'Multitudes', Lord Camden recalled, 'would flock to hear Lord Hardwicke as to hear Garrick' (Campbell, 5.361). The quality of his decisions greatly increased chancery business, and he enjoys the reputation of being the creator of modern equity law.

Hardwicke was a more active politician, both in Lords debates and at the heart of cabinet decision making, than most other lord chancellors. In a conversation with Attorney-General Sir Dudley Ryder in 1739, Walpole apparently envisaged him as his successor: 'Lord Hardwicke was one of the greatest men this nation ever bred, and if he himself should drop or quit, the public affairs must fall into his hands, though he seemed very unwilling to accept them'. A year later Walpole sounded Hardwicke directly, and the lord chancellor made it quite clear that he had no wish 'to bear the fatigue' of being prime minister (HoP, *Commons, 1715–54*, 2.570). The political role Hardwicke chose for himself was rather that of one of the close inner circle of advisers during the ministries of Henry Pelham and his brother the duke of Newcastle. Twenty years later the courtier Lord Waldegrave wrote that, 'without affecting the name, or parade, of a Minister, Lord Hardwicke also had great weight and authority: he … was consulted on every occasion; and no important measure of government was carried into execution, without his previous consent' (*Memoirs and Speeches*, 154).

The diarist Horace Walpole sought to blacken Hardwicke's reputation for posterity in the belief that he deserted his father as his ministry fell. The parliamentary record demonstrates the contrary. The lord chancellor, unlike the Commons speaker, could take part in debate, leaving his seat on the woolsack to do so. Hardwicke was a better debater in the Lords than in the Commons, where his legalistic style had not always gone down well. Newcastle acknowledged his role in supporting the ministry's effort to avoid a Spanish war in 1739. In February 1741 Hardwicke spoke strongly against the motion by the opposition leader Carteret for Walpole's dismissal; and after Walpole's resignation in February 1742 the lord chancellor was instrumental in procuring the Lords' defeat of a bill designed to give immunity for witnesses against the fallen minister, denouncing the idea as unfair.

Walpole's reluctance to prosecute the war against Spain, and in effect France also from 1740, had nevertheless distanced him from his colleagues. When he resigned alone, it made sense for Newcastle and Hardwicke to negotiate a coalition ministry headed by Carteret as the man to run the war. Two years later, against the king's wishes, Carteret was forced to resign by the threat of parliamentary defeat, in November 1744. Hardwicke played an important role in this coup. It was he who, at the request of the Pelham brothers, drafted the memorial presented to George II on 1 November that indicted the failure of Carteret's foreign policy. Although Carteret's fall had been cleverly contrived, Hardwicke blandly disclaimed responsibility, telling George II that, by the constitution, 'your ministers, Sir, are only your instruments of government'. The king made the famous retort 'Ministers are the Kings in this country' (Yorke, 1.383). The confrontation of February 1746, when the cabinet ministers tendered their resignations to coerce George II into acceptance of their demands, served to confirm the current political reality, that there was nowhere else for the king to turn. For the decade from 1744 Hardwicke formed with Newcastle and Henry Pelham, who had taken the Treasury in 1743, a triumvirate that controlled the British political scene. Often the lord chancellor was called upon to arbitrate between the two brothers, the duke seeking his support against the power Pelham wielded as leader in the Commons. By 1747 Pelham was clearly 'the premier', as the other two both acknowledged, but he was often overruled by his colleagues, as on the continuation of the war until 1748 and Newcastle's expensive foreign policy thereafter.

Hardwicke was at the same time following his own personal agenda, to win favour with his sovereign. He did so notably by a speech in 1743 in the House of Lords defending the British hire of Hanoverian soldiers without prior parliamentary approval; he pointed out how ludicrous would have been a formal treaty of the king with himself as elector of Hanover, and lauded the value of the Hanoverian contribution to the war effort. George II doubtless also appreciated the hard line Hardwicke again, as in 1722, took against Jacobites. When invasion threatened in 1744 he insisted on strengthening a clause for forfeiture of estates as the penalty in a Treason Bill for any who corresponded with the exiled house of Stuart. After the rising of 1745 had been defeated, Hardwicke presided as lord high steward at the trial of Jacobite peers, dispensing a justice seldom tempered by mercy: some thought his severity in decreeing death sentences comparable to the 'butchery' of Cumberland on the battlefield. The evidence the trials revealed about the rising caused Hardwicke to insist on punitive and preventative legislation for Scotland. He drafted and pushed through the Hereditable Jurisdictions Act of 1747, abolishing the legal powers of the clan chiefs which had enabled them to raise their men. But the other professed object of lawyer Hardwicke was to provide for Scotland a fairer and less arbitrary system of justice. Further legislation in 1748 banned highland dress, the wearing of the kilt, and the ancient right of clansmen to bear arms, prohibitions widely resented in Scotland as breaches of national tradition.

Hardwicke's office gave him a distinctive and active role throughout the Pelham ministry. As lord chancellor he was personally involved in the negotiations in 1745 with tories about the new county commissions of the peace they were demanding as the price of their support: a few were issued, without a ban on tories for the first time since 1714, as evidence of the ministry's good faith, before that political rapprochement ended. Hardwicke's position as lord chancellor always gave weight to his advice to his sovereign and colleagues on constitutional matters and to his parliamentary opinions on legislation. When the prince of Wales died in 1751 it was Hardwicke who proposed that his widow be named prospective regent for her young son, and not the king's preferred choice, his second son, the duke of Cumberland, since the duke was highly unpopular: the Pelham brothers and even George II accepted this advice. In that same year Hardwicke gave essential support to the opposition peer Lord Chesterfield's reform of the calendar, even though Newcastle disliked the innovation. In 1753 Hardwicke strongly backed a Jewish Naturalization Act, but he accepted its repeal the following year because of the popular outcry. 'However much the people may be misled, yet in a free country I do not think an unpopular measure ought to be obstinately persisted in', he was reported to have told the House of Lords (Campbell, 5.124). 1753 also saw the passage of what became known as Lord Hardwicke's Marriage Act, designed to prevent clandestine marriages, a matter of particular concern to the propertied classes. At the time neither prior notice nor parental consent for minors was required for marriage. Hardwicke's measure remedied this situation for England and Wales by ordering banns to be read for three Sundays in the designated church; insisting on previous consent of parents or guardians in the case of minors; and directing that the ceremony be conducted by an Anglican clergyman, a ground of complaint by dissenters and Roman Catholics: Jews and Quakers were exempted. Hardwicke's immense contribution to the English legal system by his judicial decisions was complemented by important legislation.

Politician, 1754–1764 Political tranquillity ended with the sudden death of Henry Pelham on 6 March 1754. Hardwicke managed affairs during the days of Newcastle's grief, and now more than ever became the duke's prop: 'My Lord Chancellor, with whom I do everything, and without whom I do nothing'—so did Newcastle write to William Pitt on 2 April (Campbell, 5.137). The Newcastle ministry of 1754–6 was a time when the duke needed a shoulder on which to lean. He could succeed his brother at the Treasury, but management of the House of Commons was a problem not solved for long, and one rendered impossible by the disasters that marked the beginning of the Seven Years' War in 1756. Pitt's hour had arrived, to be the saviour of his country, but he would not agree to take office in partnership with Newcastle. It was at an interview with Hardwicke in October 1756 that he made this clear. On 19 November the lord chancellor followed his friend out of office, 'much to the regret of all good men, and indeed of the Nation in general', wrote Lord Waldegrave:

> He had been Chancellor near twenty years, and was inferior to few who had gone before him, having executed that high

office with Integrity, Diligence, and uncommon Abilities. The Statesman might be no wise equal to the Judge, yet even in that capacity, he had been the chief support of the Duke of Newcastle's Administration.   (*Memoirs and Speeches*, 185)

Hardwicke had warned Pitt that he would not be able to maintain a ministry without Newcastle's parliamentary strength, and so it proved. Pitt had no defence against royal antipathy, and was dismissed by George II in April 1757. The long and complicated discussions to construct a ministry in which Pitt would conduct the war and Newcastle manage parliament were finally concluded by Hardwicke, 'a proper person to negotiate', thought Lord Waldegrave, 'having great influence over the Duke of Newcastle, as well as some credit with Pitt, without being disagreeable to the King himself' (*Memoirs and Speeches*, 207). Hardwicke took care to ensure the return of his son-in-law Lord Anson to the Admiralty, but sacrificed the seniority claim of his son Charles *Yorke to be attorney-general to that of Pitt's candidate, Charles Pratt. He himself had no wish to be lord chancellor again, and that post was not filled, the work being done by Sir Robert Henley as lord keeper of the great seal. Although without office, Hardwicke attended cabinet at the request of Newcastle.

When George II died in 1760 Hardwicke thought of retiring from politics and, alone of the duke's friends, suggested to Newcastle that he should resign the Treasury and do the same—unwelcome advice for a man to whom politics was the stuff of life. The duke retained his office, only to find his influence passing to Lord Bute, favourite of the new king George III. When he complained to Hardwicke, his old friend made the unhelpful reply on 8 August 1761 that he should have retired at the change of sovereign. Hardwicke, though he refused various offers from the new king, continued to attend cabinet to support Newcastle. Both sided in the majority against Pitt when in October 1761 he made a Spanish war a resigning issue. Early in 1762 Hardwicke supported Newcastle's intention to continue a subsidy to Britain's ally Prussia. When the cabinet decided otherwise Newcastle resigned the Treasury on 7 May 1762, and Hardwicke was no longer summoned to attend cabinet.

Fearing for the careers of his sons if they were obliged to go into opposition, Hardwicke vainly renewed his pressure on the duke to retire, and was widely thought to have done so himself. By autumn 1762 Newcastle had decided to oppose the peace terms negotiated by the Bute ministry. That was contrary to the advice of Hardwicke, who nevertheless then himself attacked the peace in the Lords debate of 9 December, criticizing the restoration of Cuba and the French sugar islands. Realizing they now faced the prospect of permanent opposition, the still loyal Hardwicke made the wry comment to Newcastle that it was 'a kind of new trade to learn at a late hour' (BL, Add. MS 32948, fols. 1–2). There was not much else to oppose during that parliamentary session, but Hardwicke did make what proved to be his last speech, on 28 March 1763 against a proposed cider tax, unfairly portraying it as a second land tax on the cider counties of western England.

After George Grenville succeeded Bute as prime minister in April 1763 George III was not satisfied with his new ministry. Contrary to the advice of his cabinet, he insisted in June on Hardwicke being offered the then vacant cabinet post of lord president of the council. Hardwicke refused. The diarist Mrs Grenville noted that he said 'they would never come into office, but as a party and upon a plan concerted with Mr Pitt and the great Whig Lords, as had been practised in the late King's time' (*Grenville Papers*, 2.191). When the next month George III negotiated with Pitt for a new ministry, Pitt himself took a similar line, naming Hardwicke for the same post and Newcastle as lord privy seal. The king deemed his proposals unacceptable, and retained the Grenville ministry. The clear divide between administration and opposition that now became evident led Charles Yorke to resign the post of attorney-general he had retained under Bute and Grenville, and the younger Yorkes joined their father in opposition. But Hardwicke's political career was now over. He had always taken care of his health, by diet and exercise, and was said by his son Charles to look fifty when he was seventy. But from September 1763 what Newcastle described in December as 'a most painful and dangerous disease' (Yorke, 3.483) confined him to bed at his London home of Powis House, Great Ormond Street, until his death on 6 March 1764. He was buried at Wimpole parish church on 25 March.

Conclusion 'Men are apt to mistake, or at least seem to mistake, their own talents', wrote Lord Chesterfield. 'Thus Lord Hardwicke valued himself more on being a great minister of state, which he certainly was not, than on being a great magistrate, which he certainly was' (Campbell, 5.65). Chesterfield thought Hardwicke's 'timidity' as a politician outweighed 'his parts', and he never held responsible office. But historians have added perception of his key role in the Pelham and Newcastle ministries to appreciation of his stature as one of Britain's greatest lawyers. Doubtless as gratifying to Hardwicke as his personal success was the creation of a new wealthy and influential aristocratic dynasty. On 2 April 1754 he acquired the further titles earl of Hardwicke and Viscount Royston; the latter was enjoyed as a courtesy by his eldest son, Philip. Already possessing a lucrative exchequer tellership, Philip was married at the age of twenty to a rich heiress, Lady Jemima Campbell [see Yorke, Jemima] who within a fortnight became Marchioness Grey in her own right. The second son, Charles, guided by his father to success as a lawyer and politician, obtained a chancery sinecure in 1747. This he shared with his brother John, the fourth son, until in 1750 his father obtained another chancery sinecure for John. Hardwicke's application for this provoked the comment from George II that 'My Lord Chancellor is getting every office that falls in the law for his own children' (Yorke, 2.179). The third son, Joseph *Yorke (later Baron Dover), enjoyed rapid promotion in his chosen army career; he became a lieutenant-colonel at the age of twenty before turning to diplomacy and beginning a thirty-year spell as British minister at The Hague from 1751. All four were soon MPs, Philip for Cambridgeshire from 1747. The fifth son, James, was from 1774 successively bishop of St David's, Gloucester, and Ely. Hardwicke's elder daughter, Elizabeth [see Anson, Elizabeth, Lady Anson (1725–1760)], married in 1748 the famous Admiral Lord Anson, who as first lord of the Admiralty sat in cabinet with his father-in-law from 1751. His younger daughter, Margaret, in 1749 married Sir Gilbert Heathcote, an extremely wealthy baronet. Hardwicke would have loved Horace Walpole's comment on the Yorkes in 1757: 'The family is very powerful' (Letters, 4.91).

As a man Hardwicke commanded admiration rather than affection. There was no lighter side to his character. In later life he stated that he had been too busy in his youth to be a rake. There is no record of any recreations that he enjoyed, and unlike most lord chancellors of the age he failed to use his clerical patronage to assist men of letters. He left no legacy of anecdotes about himself, or of bons mots attributed to him. While his youthful persona was as a man of single-minded ambition, in maturity his image became one of self-importance, even pomposity. Lord Waldegrave commented on 'his usual gravity' (Memoirs and Speeches, 178). His correspondence shows that he was so conscious of his new aristocratic status that his letters to his eldest son were after 1754 addressed to 'My Dear Lord'. Of his integrity of character there can be no doubt. Despite his notorious desire for money he was never suspected of corruption, and he was a model of sobriety and connubial fidelity. Yet he was not quite a gentleman, in the opinion of Lord Waldegrave: 'He was undoubtedly an excellent Chancellor, and might have been thought a great man, had he been less avaricious, less proud, less unlike a Gentleman, and not so great a politician' (ibid., 154n.).   PETER D. G. THOMAS

Sources DNB · P. C. Yorke, The life and correspondence of Philip Yorke, earl of Hardwicke, 3 vols. (1913) · G. Harris, The life of Lord Chancellor Hardwicke, 3 vols. (1847) · J. Campbell, Lives of the lord chancellors, 8 vols. (1845–69), vol. 5 · The memoirs and speeches of James, 2nd Earl Waldegrave, 1742–1763, ed. J. C. D. Clark (1988) · R. Chandler, The history and proceedings of the House of Commons, 6–8 (1741–2) · R. R. Sedgwick, 'Yorke, Philip', HoP, Commons, 1715–54 · The letters of Horace Walpole, fourth earl of Orford, ed. P. Toynbee, 16 vols. (1903–5) · The Grenville papers: being the correspondence of Richard Grenville … and … George Grenville, ed. W. J. Smith, 4 vols. (1852–3) · J. B. Owen, The rise of the Pelhams (1957) · J. C. D. Clark, The dynamics of change: the crisis of the 1750s and English party systems (1982) · R. Browning, The duke of Newcastle (1975) · GEC, Peerage · BL, Add. MSS 32679–33201 (Newcastle MSS)
Archives BL, corresp., journals and papers, Add. MSS 35507, 35337, 35349–36278, 45224, Add. Ch 44742–44890 · NYPL, papers · Yale U., Beinecke L., corresp. | BL, letters to Lord Anson, Add. MSS 15946, 15956–15957 · BL, corresp. with Lord Holdernesse, Egerton MSS 3413–3486 · BL, corresp. with duke of Newcastle, Add. MSS 32769–33201 · Bodl. Oxf., corresp. with Thomas Edwards · Chatsworth House, Derbyshire, letters to dukes of Devonshire · CKS, letters to David Papillon · Devon RO, letters to Duke of Somerset · Glos. RO, Gloucestershire estate papers · Mount Stuart Trust Archive, corresp. with Lord Bute · NA Scot., corresp. with Lord Seafield · NL Scot., corresp. with Lord Tinwald · NMM, corresp. with Lord Sandwich · NRA, priv. coll., letters to Lord Dumfries · U. Nott., corresp. with duke of Newcastle
Likenesses A. van Straechen, oils, c.1733–1737, Middle Temple, London · studio of M. Dahl, oils, c.1735–1743, NPG · J. Faber, line engraving, 1737, BM, NPG · J. Wills, oils, 1740, Middle Temple, London · W. Hoare, oils, 1763, Antony, Cornwall [see illus.] · J. Faber, mezzotint (after T. Hudson), BM, NPG · oils (after A. Ramsay, c.1742), Lincoln's Inn, London
Wealth at death wealthy; died worth a million: Campbell, Lives of the lord chancellors, 5.167

Yorke, Philip, second earl of Hardwicke (1720–1790), politician and writer, eldest son of Philip *Yorke, first earl of Hardwicke (1690–1764), and his wife, Margaret Lygon (c.1695–1761), daughter of Charles Cocks, MP for Worcester, was born on 9 December 1720. His siblings included Joseph *Yorke, Charles *Yorke, and Elizabeth *Anson. He was educated at Newcome's school, Hackney, and afterwards by private tutors, including Samuel Salter. In 1737 he matriculated at Corpus Christi College, Cambridge, from which he received the degree of LLD in 1749. In 1738 his father provided him with the sinecure post of teller of the exchequer, which by 1782 was worth £7000 a year. On 22 May 1740 he married Lady Jemima Campbell (1722–1797) [see Yorke, Jemima, suo jure Marchioness Grey], only daughter of John *Campbell, third earl of Breadalbane (bap. 1696, d. 1782), who became Marchioness Grey upon the death of her maternal grandfather that same year. They had two daughters: Amabel [see Campbell, Amabel Hume-, suo jure Countess De Grey], who married Alexander, Viscount Polwarth, eldest son of the last earl of Marchmont, in 1772, and Mary Jemima *Robinson [see under Yorke, Jemima, suo jure Marchioness Grey], who married the second Baron Grantham in 1780.

In 1741 Yorke was elected to the House of Commons for Reigate, Surrey, which he continued to represent until 1747. His political career began promisingly, as 'he was chosen to second the address in 1743, to move it in 1744, and to be a manager of Lord Lovat's trial in 1747. He also spoke for the Government on the continuing of British troops to Flanders in January 1744 and on the Hanoverians in April 1746' (HoP, Commons, 1715–54). Beyond that, however, he was an infrequent speaker, and his main contribution to the House of Commons was a diary of debates which he kept between December 1743 and April 1745, which has been described as 'the most trustworthy and impartial authority on the parliamentary history of the period' (ibid.). In 1747 Yorke was chosen by the general meeting of the county to stand for Cambridgeshire, where his father's estate of Wimpole and near which his wife's estate of Wrest were situated. During the election, his father advised him on maintaining his health: 'If you find yourself hot and dry, drink negus, I mean wine and warm water. And be sure to take care that your bed and sheets are in all places well aired' (ibid.). In order to ensure his election, his father spent over £2000 treating the constituents, a 'monstrous sum', he later complained, 'for an election without any opposition' (ibid.).

In 1754 Yorke became Lord Royston when his father was created earl of Hardwicke. He was sworn of the privy council on the accession of George III, and he took his seat in the House of Lords as the earl of Hardwicke upon his father's death in 1764. He was a member (without office) of the first Rockingham administration, and was offered the northern seals upon Grafton's resignation in 1766, but he declined for reasons of ill health. Although his health prevented him from taking an active role in opposition during the Grafton and North administrations, he remained an important figure in whig circles. Party meetings were frequently held at his town house, and he was consulted on key matters, including the arrangements which resulted in the formation of the second Rockingham administration. He also served as lord lieutenant of Cambridgeshire from 1757 and as high steward of the University of Cambridge from 1764 until his death.

Although Hardwicke continued the family tradition in politics, he was never truly a politician. An ample income, poor health, and intellectual leanings disinclined him from an active public life. Instead, he preferred literary pursuits and collecting historical documents. In 1741 he was elected fellow of the Royal Society and in 1744 fellow of the Society of Antiquaries. While at Cambridge he contributed some English verses to the *Pietas academiae Cantabrigiensis in funere serenissimae Principis Willelminae Carolinae* (1738), and with his brother Charles wrote the greater portion of the *Athenian letters, or, The epistolary correspondence of an agent of the king of Persia, residing at Athens during the Peloponnesian War* (1741). The latter work was an academic exercise edited by Thomas Birch, and other contributors included Henry Coventry, John Green, Samuel Salter, Catherine Talbot, Daniel Wray, George Henry Rooke, John Heaston, and John Lawry. The *Athenian Letters* was printed for private circulation only, with a first edition of only ten copies and a second, which did not appear until 1781, of 100 copies. In 1792 the vogue for historic fiction created by Barthélemy's *Voyage de jeune Anacharsis en Grèce* (1788) led to a pirated edition of the *Letters* being printed in Dublin, but this was subsequently suppressed and was superseded in 1798 by a new edition that had the imprimatur of the third earl of Hardwicke and was furnished with a geographical index, maps, and engravings. A new edition by Archdeacon Coxe appeared in 1810, and another edition was printed at Basel in 1800. There were also French translations by Villeterque and Christophe, published in Paris in 1803. Hardwicke also edited *Letters from and to Sir Dudley Carleton, Knt, During his Embassy in Holland* (1757; 2nd edn, 1775; 3rd edn, 1780) and *Miscellaneous State Papers from 1501 to 1726* (1778). In 1783 he produced *Walpoliana*, a collection of anecdotes about Sir Robert Walpole, and his marginalia were used for the annotations marked 'H' in the Oxford edition of Burnet's *Own Time* (1823). Hardwicke was a prominent man in intellectual and antiquarian circles, as is evidenced by Horace Walpole's advice to Horace Mann in 1757:

> That family is very powerful; the eldest brother, Lord Royston, is historically curious and political; if, without its appearing too forced, you could at any time send him uncommon letters, papers, manifestoes, and things of that sort, it might do you good service. (HoP, *Commons, 1715–54*)

Hardwicke died on 16 May 1790, at his house in St James's Square, London. His seat at Wrest and the appendant estates of the dukes of Kent passed to his daughters. In the absence of a male heir, the title went to his nephew Philip Yorke (1757–1834), eldest son of his brother Charles. Hardwicke's wife died on 11 January 1797.

STEPHANIE L. BARCZEWSKI

Sources HoP, *Commons, 1715–54* • Burke, *Peerage* • *Collins peerage of England: genealogical, biographical and historical*, ed. E. Brydges, 9 vols. (1812) • GEC, *Peerage* • *GM*, 1st ser., 60 (1790), 479 • *GM*, 1st ser., 85/2 (1815), 405 • Nichols, *Lit. anecdotes* • Nichols, *Illustrations*
Archives Beds. & Luton ARS, corresp. • BL, corresp. and papers, Add. MSS 35337–36278, *passim* • Flintshire RO, Hawarden, family corresp. and papers • PRO NIre., corresp., D2431–2433 • Yale U., Beinecke L., letters and essays | Beds. & Luton ARS, corresp. with Lord Grantham • Beds. & Luton ARS, letters to Langton and papers • BL, letters to Thomas Birch, Add. MSS 4323, 4325, 4477 • BL, letters to T. Hutchinson, Egerton MS 2659 • BL, corresp. with Lord Liverpool, Add. MSS 38198–38214, 38307–38308, 38570, *passim* • BL, corresp. with duke of Newcastle, Add. MSS 32686–33070, *passim* • BL, corresp. with duke of Portland, Add. MS 45030 • NL Scot., letters to Lord Hailes • Sheff. Arch., letters to Lord Rockingham
Likenesses M. Bovi, stipple, pubd 1796 (after G. Romney), NPG • F. Bartolozzi, stipple (after W. Gardiner), BM, NPG; repro. in J. Adolphus, *The British cabinet*, 2 vols. (1800) • W. Ridley, stipple (after G. Romney), BM, NPG; repro. in *European Magazine* (1803)

Yorke, Philip (1743–1804), genealogist and writer, was born on 30 July 1743 at Erddig, near Wrexham, Denbighshire, the son of Simon Yorke (1696–1767), landowner, and his wife, Dorothy (1717–1787), daughter and heir of Matthew Hutton of Newnham, Hertfordshire. His grandfather, Simon Yorke, was uncle of Philip Yorke, first earl of Hardwicke. His early education was at a preparatory school in Wanstead and at Dr Henry Newcome's private academy in Hackney. After two terms at Eton College, where he met Brownlow Cust, his future brother-in-law, Philip was admitted a fellow commoner of Corpus Christi College, Cambridge, in 1762, and was created MA in 1765. He was also admitted to Lincoln's Inn on 4 November 1762 and was called to the bar on 4 July 1767. In 1768 he became a fellow of the Society of Antiquaries.

On 2 July 1770 Yorke married Elizabeth (1749–1779), the daughter of Sir John Cust, and they had two daughters and five sons. Through his wife's interest he obtained a seat in parliament for the Cornish borough of Helston, in the place of a member disqualified by order of the House of Commons (October 1774), and he retained this seat until he retired in 1781. Subsequently he sat for Grantham from 17 January 1792 until 7 January 1793, when he stood down in favour of his son Simon. Although he was something of an amateur actor and was remembered by contemporaries for his talent for conversation, he never spoke in the House of Commons, owing to a 'constitutional diffidence' (*GM*, 250). He also captained the Denbighshire regiment of militia, although he seems to have been a somewhat reluctant soldier.

Although Yorke initially had 'no great respect for the mountain Welsh, great or small' (*DWB*, 1111), his attitude began to change after his marriage in 1782 to a Welsh woman, Diana (1748–1805), daughter of Piers Wynne of Dyffryn Aled and widow of Ridgeway Owen Meyrick. The couple had two daughters and four sons. In his later years he turned his attention to Welsh history and genealogy, including his wife's descent from Marchudd, lord of Uwch Dulas. In 1795 he issued seventy copies of his *Tracts of Powys*, a genealogical history of Bleddyn ap Cynfyn, including a refutation of Polydore Virgil's critical views of the ancient Britons. The dedication, to Thomas Pennant of Downing, was dated Erddig, 20 April 1795. An appendix contained interesting letters from Lewis Morris to William Vaughan and others. In a revised and expanded form this work was reissued in 1799 as *The Royal Tribes of Wales*, a valuable brief account of the five regal tribes, with much interesting information on their distinguished descendants. The text owed much to the assistance of the Revd Walter Davies (Gwallter Mechain; 1764–1849), although the relative contribution of each is now difficult to determine. The illustrative portraits were drawn by J. Allen and engraved by W. Bond.

Yorke's genealogical works indicate that he at first largely accepted the Welsh origin myth and gave credence to the Trojan roots of the people, but that later he distanced himself from this traditionally held viewpoint. He had the intention of producing a biography of Wales, but he was unable to bring this scheme to fruition. Yorke died on 19 March 1804 at his seat of Erddig Park, Wrexham, and was buried at Marchwiel. He was succeeded by Simon Yorke (1771–1834), his eldest son from his first marriage.

Although contemporary accounts portrayed him as a rather extravagant country squire, Yorke was a prudent and meticulous landowner and did much to improve his seat of Erddig Park (which passed into the ownership of the National Trust in the twentieth century). Having made the most of his education, he became in later life a fervent Welsh patriot and, despite his English roots, made a learned contribution to the field of Welsh genealogy.

THOMAS SECCOMBE, rev. DYLAN FOSTER EVANS

Sources E. Griffiths, *Philip Yorke I (1743–1804): squire of Erthig* (1995) · A. L. Cust, *Chronicles of Erthig on the dyke*, 2 vols. (1914) · P. Yorke, *The royal tribes of Wales*, new edn, ed. R. Williams (1887) · Nimrod [C. J. Apperley], *My life & times*, ed. E. D. Cummins (1927), 57–64 · A. N. Palmer, *A history of the town and parish of Wrexham*, 5 (1903), 237–42 · J. E. Griffith, *Pedigrees of Anglesey and Carnarvonshire families* (privately printed, Horncastle, 1914), 167 · E. Rees, ed., *Libri Walliae: a catalogue of Welsh books and books printed in Wales, 1546–1820*, 2 (1987), 693–4 · M. Waterson, *The servant's hall: the domestic history of a country house* (1980) · DWB · HoP, *Commons, 1790–1820* · R. A. Austen-Leigh, ed., *The Eton College register, 1753–1790* (1921) · GM, 1st ser., 74 (1804), 280 · C. Parry, ed., *Libri Walliae: a catalogue of Welsh books and books printed in Wales, 1546–1820, supplement* (2001), 167
Archives Flintshire RO, Hawarden, corresp. and papers | BL, letters to second and third earls of Hardwicke, Add. MSS 35608–35686, *passim* · Warks. CRO, letters and verses to Thomas Pennant
Likenesses Bartolozzi, engraving (after Reynolds) · T. Gainsborough, oils, Erddig, Wrexham · E. Scriven, stipple (after T. Gainsborough), BM, NPG

Yorke, Philip, third earl of Hardwicke (1757–1834), politician, the eldest son of Charles *Yorke (1722–1770), lord chancellor, and his first wife, Catherine Freeman (d. 1759), was born in St George's parish, Bloomsbury, London, on 31 May 1757. He was educated at Harrow School (1770–71) and Queens' College, Cambridge, where he received the degree of MA in 1776 and that of LLD in 1811. From 1777 to 1779 he travelled through the Netherlands, Germany, Italy, and Switzerland and kept a journal of his grand tour. Chosen to stand for parliament for Cambridgeshire by his uncle, Philip *Yorke, second earl of Hardwicke, he was elected second county member on 14 September 1780 after a very costly election. He represented the constituency until his accession to the peerage as third earl of Hardwicke on his uncle's death, on 16 May 1790. He married, on 24 July 1782, Lady Elizabeth Lindsay (1763–1858), the third daughter of James Lindsay, fifth earl of Balcarres, and his wife, Anne Dalrymple. They had four daughters and two sons.

In politics Yorke at first followed Fox, but he grew increasingly doubtful of Fox's stance towards the king and by 1785 was giving independent support to Pitt's administration. He was appointed lord lieutenant of Ireland in March 1801, and served as the first viceroy in post-union Ireland until the formation of the 'ministry of all the talents' in February 1806. Together with his chief secretary, Charles Abbot, he did much to allay the irritation caused by the union, not least by the reforms he authorized in the Irish offices. He 'proved a very conscientious, at times indeed fussy, viceroy' (McDowell, 53), and became himself a convert to Catholic emancipation, to which cause he steadfastly adhered until its triumph in 1829. To the parliamentary Reform Bill of 1831 he gave a qualified support.

Hardwicke was a keen patron of the arts and commissioned John Soane, whom he had met in Italy on the grand tour, to make additions to his country house, Wimpole Hall in Cambridgeshire, including the celebrated neo-classical yellow drawing room. He was also FRS and FSA, and a trustee of the British Museum; from 1790 he served as lord lieutenant of Cambridgeshire and from 1806 as high steward of Cambridge University. He was elected KG on 25 November 1803 and installed by proxy, having received the insignia at Dublin on 23 April 1805. He died at Tyttenhanger, Hertfordshire, on 18 November 1834 and was buried on 21 November in the family vault at Wimpole Hall. The title devolved upon his nephew Charles Philip *Yorke (1799–1873).

J. M. RIGG, rev. HALLIE RUBENHOLD

Sources I. R. Christie, 'Yorke, Philip', HoP, *Commons, 1754–90* · M. MacDonagh, *The viceroy's post-bag* (1904) · GEC, *Peerage* · G. Harris, *The life of Lord Chancellor Hardwicke*, 3 vols. (1847) · Cobbett, *Parl. hist.*, vols. 24–36 · *Hansard 2* (1829), 20.1529 · *Hansard 3* (1831), 3.326 · *The political memoranda of Francis … duke of Leeds*, ed. O. Browning (1884) · *Memorials and correspondence of Charles James Fox*, ed. J. Russell, 4 vols. (1853–7) · J. Ingamells, ed., *A dictionary of British and Irish travellers in Italy, 1701–1800* (1997), 1035–6 · Venn, *Alum. Cant.* · GM, 2nd ser., 3 (1835), 205 · R. B. McDowell, *The Irish administration* (1964)
Archives BL, corresp. and papers, Add. MSS 35349–35350, 35377–35424, 35641–35787, 35919–35934, 36258–36260, 45031–45032 · Herts. ALS, estate corresp. and letter-books · PRO NIre., corresp. · PRO NIre., corresp. and papers | Beds. & Luton ARS, letters to Amabel, countess de Grey · Beds. & Luton ARS, letters to Samuel Whitbread · BL, corresp. with second earl of Chichester, Add. MSS 33108–33109, 33114 · BL, corresp. with Lord Grenville, Add. MS 58944 · BL, corresp. with first and second earls of Liverpool, Add. MSS 38241, 38262, 38286, 38299, 38424 · BL, letters to Arthur

Young, Add. MSS 35128, 35130, 35132 · Cambs. AS, letters to Richard Huddleston · Devon RO, corresp. with Henry Addington · Glos. RO, letters to first Baron Redesdale · Hants. RO, corresp. William Wickham · NRA, priv. coll., letters to Lord Cathcart, commander-in-chief forces Ireland · PRO, letters to William Pitt, 30/8

Likenesses W. Cuming, oils, 1802, Mansion House, Dublin · T. Lawrence, oils, exh. RA 1830, Crichel House, Dorset · W. Giller, line and stipple engraving, pubd 1836 (after T. Lawrence, 1830), NG Ire. · W. Giller, mezzotint, pubd 1836 (after T. Lawrence), BM, NPG · R. Westmacott junior, tomb effigy, 1844, St Andrew Church, Wimpole, Cambridgeshire · H. Raeburn, oils, Baltimore Museum of Arts, Maryland · J. Tannock, miniature, V&A · W. Ward, mezzotint, BM, NPG

Yorke, Philip James (1799–1874), chemist and mineralogist, was born at Ely, Cambridgeshire, on 13 October 1799, the eldest son of Philip Yorke, prebendary of Ely (1770–1817), and his wife, the Hon. Anna Maria (d. 1835), daughter of Charles Cocks, first Baron Somers. He was great-grandson on his father's side of the first earl of Hardwicke. He had two younger brothers and six sisters. Educated from about the age of nine at Dr Pearson's school at East Sheen, Surrey, he entered Harrow School in 1810. On leaving Harrow he obtained a commission in the Scots Fusilier Guards (5 May 1814), and remained in that regiment until he sold out on 5 November 1847 with the rank of lieutenant-colonel. In 1852 he was appointed colonel of the Herefordshire militia—a post which he held during the Crimean War and until 1859.

A keen amateur chemist and mineralogist, Yorke was one of the founder members of the Chemical Society of London in 1841; he was a member of council (1842–3), later became vice-president, and was president in 1853–5. He married, on 27 April 1843, Emily (b. 1814?, d. 1868), youngest daughter of William Morgan Clifford of Perrystone, Herefordshire; there were no children of the marriage. Living in London by 1834 at the latest, Yorke came into contact with many leading scientists of the time. In 1849 he was elected FRS. He was also active at the Royal Institution, of which he was a manager.

Yorke's first scientific paper, published in 1834, contained a very careful investigation of the action of lead on water. It showed him to be a skilful chemical analyst. He found among other things that, after long contact with metallic lead, water dissolves one twelve-thousandth part of its own weight of a hydrated oxide of lead (formed by the action of the water and the oxygen dissolved in it). Among the thirteen papers by Yorke listed in the Royal Society catalogue, the most important was a study of the sulphides of sodium and potassium (1849). Other chemical papers were on the brown ore of iron (hydrated ferric oxide) and the quantity of caesium in the water of the hot spring at the Wheal Clifford copper mine in Cornwall. His researches on silica and silicic acid, though inconclusive, suggested the existence of a tetrabasic silicic acid.

Yorke also made some interesting meteorological observations on the climate of Herefordshire, including a laborious comparison of barometric readings at his house near Ross with those taken at the Royal Society during the

Philip James Yorke (1799–1874), by unknown photographer

same period. He also attempted to determine the relationship between wind direction and barometric pressure. In 1853 he published a translation of *Aus meinem Leben* by the German general and military historian Baron F. C. F. von Müffling.

Yorke died at 89 Eaton Place, Pimlico, London, on 14 December 1874, and was buried in London. His death was followed, two days later at the same address, by that of his younger, unmarried sister, Juliana Caroline.

N. G. COLEY

Sources JCS, 28 (1875), 1319 · *Jubilee of the Chemical Society* (1891), 25, 180, 181, 184 · Burke, *Peerage* · Boase, *Mod. Eng. biog.* · *Catalogue of scientific papers*, Royal Society, 19 vols. (1867–1925) · election certificate, RS

Likenesses photograph, repro. in *Jubilee of the Chemical Society*, 184 · photograph, Royal Society of Chemistry, London [*see illus.*]

Wealth at death under £12,000: probate, 15 Jan 1875, CGPLA Eng. & Wales

Yorke, Roger (d. 1536), law reporter, was probably a son of the Exeter merchant Walter Yorke (d. c.1505) and his wife, Waltera. In a chancery petition which refers to his brother Walter, also a merchant, having become a prisoner of war, he is described as 'Roger Yorke of Excestre, student of Grayes Inne in Holborn' (PRO, C 1/561/23). This dates from after 1517, but 'student' here is a flexible term analogous to 'apprentice' of the law. Yorke was probably admitted to Gray's Inn soon after 1506, being Edward Montague's junior when he became a serjeant, and by 1516 he had been called to the bar long enough to become an ancient. In

1522 he was elected autumn reader, but the exercise was postponed to Lent 1523. Already he seems to have become an established practitioner, for he was assessed for the poll tax that year as having £66 a year. His name is found on over forty bills in chancery in the time of Cardinal Wolsey. Although he had a small property in St Paul's parish, Exeter, in 1522, he settled at Wellington in Somerset, probably soon after marrying Eleanor, daughter of Sir Hugh Luttrell of Dunster in that county, his stepmother's second husband, about 1520. His second wife was Margaret Erneley. From 1524 he was named in the commissions of the peace for both Devon and Somerset, and from 1531 for Wiltshire as well.

In 1531, as serjeant-elect, Yorke delivered a second reading in Gray's Inn on *Prerogativa regis*, notes from which survive. When he was created serjeant in November 1531 he was the most junior of the call, and he was still quite young when he died on 2 February 1536. His son and heir, Thomas, was then aged fifteen. Yorke's principal legacy to posterity was his series of law reports, which survive in four manuscript versions but were unidentified until the 1970s. The reports were mostly written in the 1520s and 1530s, though one or two can be dated to the first decade of Henry VIII's reign. The cases are arranged under non-alphabetical headings, and are interspersed with notes from learning exercises in Gray's Inn, including one of John Spelman's readings, several notes from the western circuit (at Exeter, Salisbury, and Yeovilchester), and, after 1531, some memoranda of discussions in Serjeants' Inn.

J. H. BAKER

Sources introduction, *The reports of Sir John Spelman*, ed. J. H. Baker, 2, SeldS, 94 (1978) · J. L. Vivian and H. H. Drake, eds., *The visitation of the county of Cornwall in the year 1620*, Harleian Society, 9 (1874), 269–70 · Baker, *Serjeants*, 168, 546 · PRO, C 1/561/23 · PRO, REQ 1/5, fol. 82 · M. M. Rowe, *Tudor Exeter* (1977), 14 · Segar's notes on Gray's Inn, BL, Harley MS 1912, fols. 34, 173, 203v · BL, Add. MS 38133, fols. 11v, 13 · BL, Hargrave MS 253, fol. 77 · F. A. Inderwick and R. A. Roberts, eds., *A calendar of the Inner Temple records*, 1 (1896), 460 [£66 in poll tax] · J. Caley and J. Hunter, eds., *Valor ecclesiasticus temp. Henrici VIII*, 6 vols., RC (1810–34), vol. 1, p. 170 · PRO, PROB 11/14, sig. 36 [Walter Yorke's will] · inquisition post mortem, PRO, C 142/58/49

Yorke [York], **Rowland** (d. 1588), soldier and traitor, was the ninth of eleven sons of Sir John *York (d. 1569), administrator, of York and St Stephen Walbrook, London, and his wife, Anne (d. in or before 1562), daughter of Robert Smyth of London. His brothers included Peter York (c.1542–1589), of Gouthwaite, Yorkshire, a landowner and MP, and he had four sisters. He was said to be 'well borne and of gentle blood' and benefited from his father's close association with John Dudley, duke of Northumberland, until the succession crisis of 1553 (Blandy, 27). The family was restored to favour at the accession of Elizabeth I. Nothing is known of Yorke's early life and education.

Yorke volunteered in 1572 for Sir Humphrey Gilbert's expedition to the island of South Beveland, important for access to Ter Goes, a major supply town used by the Spanish. Roger Williams's account describes vividly an ambush by the enemy outside Ter Goes, where most who entered with Yorke and himself were slain, leaving those who did survive to crawl through muddy ditches to escape. Yorke probably returned to England in the summer. He embarked from Gravesend, Kent, on 19 March 1573 with George Gascoigne, on a journey in which twenty men drowned; the vessel only managed to stay on course after it ran aground because Yorke and two others took control of the pumps. Having survived the seas, he joined Captain Thomas Morgan's English and Welsh force, sent unofficially to Flushing to aid the Dutch rebels against Philip II. He was initially Morgan's lieutenant but was promoted to lieutenant-colonel when his force was expanded in size.

In August 1578 Yorke was singled out by the English ambassador to the Netherlands, William Davison, in a letter to William Cecil, Lord Burghley, for his 'great value and reputacion' during the battle of Rijmenam under the command of John Norris (*CSP for.*, 1578–9, 115). Yorke lost a horse or two under him, while the Spanish retreated with heavy casualties. He, deservedly confident of his own martial abilities, was not sympathetic to captains whose methods of leadership differed from his own, writing to Davison in October 1578 that he thought some were 'indiscreet and insufficient' (ibid., 223). However, this somewhat arrogant attitude left him open to personal attack. In October 1580 he was indicted for felony, 'unjustly committed', according to William Herle, on false charges (*CSP dom.*, 1547–80, 684). Yorke's patron, Sir Francis Walsingham, principal secretary, received further reports during February 1581 that many captains had private quarrels with Yorke and 'begin to bandie against him' (*CSP for.*, January 1581 – April 1582, 44). In contrast, William Blandy tried to help Yorke's reputation by emphasizing his potential as a general and a governor, describing him as 'bolde of courage, provident in direction, industrious in labour, and quick in execution' (Blandy, 26–7).

Yorke was certainly industrious on behalf of his own men, and although professing he was 'not a good sekeritary', wrote dispatches to Walsingham about the frequent want of provisions, stressing in November 1581 from Oudenarde that he had only been paid four months out of thirteen (*CSP for.*, January 1581 – April 1582, 384–5). In June 1582 Walsingham's contacts reported the mutiny of a camp near Bruges after the captains suspected that their commander, Norris, had detained payment. Yorke was named as the 'instrument' through which the French had helped to 'blow the coals' of animosity (ibid., *May–December 1582*, 164). This recalcitrant behaviour made Yorke a potential liability, but was perhaps overlooked by his superiors because of his evident military prowess.

In March 1584 Yorke was again in difficulties, this time imprisoned in Brussels, accused of conspiring with local Catholics to betray Ghent and Dendermonde to the Spanish. He was only freed in December thanks to the efforts of his brother, Edmund York, in securing letters from Robert Dudley, earl of Leicester, and Sir Philip Sidney. However, Leicester and Sidney may only have taken action after Walsingham asked them to. The Dutch, who had dealt with their countrymen involved in the incident more ruthlessly, resented this special treatment. They remained deeply suspicious of Yorke's Catholicism. He was witnessed soon after 'frequenting the mass with his beads' (*CSP for., June 1586 – March 1587*, 87).

Yorke did not long remain out of trouble. Now owing a debt to Leicester, who was desperate for experienced officers, Yorke was appointed to the command of the Zutphen sconce, an important gain from the previous year. Leicester had fallen out with Norris and relied instead on Yorke and Sir William Stanley, who was in charge of Deventer. He granted them commissions that allowed them to serve independently of Norris. Norris wrote to Burghley in December 1586, begging that the additional powers be removed because they 'nourished factions'; the garrison of Yorke's sconce was even refusing to muster (*CSP for., June 1586 – March 1587*, 266–7). Yorke complained increasingly to the states general during December about their broken promises to supply victuals, while 'the poor miserable subjects of her majesty … now are dying of cold, yea more than two hundred since my comying' (*CSP for., June 1586 – March 1587*, 246–7). By early January 1587 it seems that he allowed his troops to extract provisions using force. Norris's grave concerns were proved correct when on 18–19 January Yorke allowed the Spanish into Zutphen, after meeting with Stanley, who had already successfully betrayed his own garrison, using a banquet to lure the council of Deventer away while his troops took the gates.

The motivation behind Yorke's actions remains the subject of debate. Contemporary opinion, such as that in the work of protestant propaganda 'The estate of English fugitives' (*State Papers and Letters of Sir Ralph Sadler*, 2.232–8), believed Yorke and Stanley were Catholic traitors. Yorke was regarded as the more dominant of the two; it was thought that he pressured Stanley to betray his garrison after secret meetings with Francisco Verdugo, the Spanish governor of the province. William Camden also believed Yorke was the one who 'drew Stanley', a soldier who had served with 'singular fidelity and valour' up until that point (Camden, 302). More recent opinion shifts the lead role to Stanley, who led Yorke astray. Charles Wilson refers to Stanley and Yorke as 'the perfect Walrus and Carpenter' (Wilson, 90). Simon Adams believes Yorke to be more personally motivated, out of fear that Norris would return him to the Dutch who were still eager to have him executed for his behaviour in 1584. As Yorke throughout his career comes across as a hothead and troublemaker, it may perhaps be that he was pushed too far by the harsh conditions within the army. Whereas another man might have been more patient, seeing the lack of provisions as unfortunate and widespread, Yorke was increasingly frustrated by the behaviour of fellow officers and his lack of reward for his years fighting for a protestant cause in which he did not really believe.

Walsingham was informed in March 1587 that Yorke had been seen in Antwerp but was determined only 'to go into Spain or Naples, there to live upon his stipend, out of the stir of these wars' (*CSP for., June 1586 – March 1587*, 392). Yorke was unable to retire quietly because the Spanish distrusted him too. It seems likely that he was poisoned at a dinner in the Netherlands in February 1588, the symptoms of which may have been mistaken for the effects of smallpox. Two fellow diners survived to relate how after Yorke's death the Spanish broke into his coffers, taking 'jewels, plate and monie', and also removed 'furniture, armes and horses' willed by him to his nephew, Edmund Yorke (*d.* 1595), who was executed at Tyburn for attempting to assassinate Elizabeth (*State Papers and Letters of Sir Ralph Sadler*, 2.238). Rowland Yorke was buried using traditional Catholic rites but the states general exhumed and hanged his remains three years later.

SARAH CLAYTON

Sources S. Adams, 'A patriot for whom? Stanley, York and Elizabeth's Catholics', *History Today*, 37 (1987), 46–50 · G. Bertie, *Five generations of a loyal house* (1845) · W. Blandy, *The castle, or, Picture of pollicy* (1581); facs. edn (1972) · *CSP dom.*, 1547–90 · *CSP for., 1577–June 1588* · W. Camden, *The history of the most renowned and victorious Princess Elizabeth*, [new edn], ed. W. T. MacCaffrey (1970) · *The state papers and letters of Sir Ralph Sadler*, ed. A. Clifford, 2 vols. (1809) · A. J. Loomie, *The Spanish Elizabethans: the English exiles at the court of Philip II* (1963) · C. R. Markham, *The fighting Veres: lives of Sir Francis Vere … and Sir Horace Vere* (1888) · E. van Meteren, *A true discourse historicall, or, The succeeding governours in the Netherlands*, trans. T. Churchyard (1602); facs. edn (1968) · J. S. Nolan, *Sir John Norreys and the Elizabethan military world* (1997) · *DNB* · R. Williams, *The actions of the Low Countries*, ed. D. W. Davies (1964) · C. Wilson, *Queen Elizabeth and the revolt of the Netherlands* (1970) · J. Foster, ed., *The visitation of Yorkshire made in the years 1584/5 … to which is added the subsequent visitation made in 1612* (privately printed, London, 1875), 382
Wealth at death possessions stolen; left by testament to brother's son (Edmund Yorke); reputedly incl. 'jewels, plate and monie … furniture, armes and horses': *State papers and letters of Sir Ralph Sadler*, ed. Clifford, vol. 2, p. 238

Yorke, Warrington (1883–1943), parasitologist, was born at Lancaster on 11 April 1883, the eldest of the six children of the Revd Henry Lefroy Yorke, a Wesleyan Methodist minister, and his wife, Margaret Warrington. He attended University School, Southport, and Epworth College, Rhyl, before studying medicine at Liverpool University. Here he was awarded the Senior Lyon Jones scholarship and the Derby exhibition in clinical medicine. He qualified MB ChB in 1905, MD in 1907, and MRCP in 1929; he was elected FRCP in 1934. In 1906 he was elected to the Holt fellowship in physiology and worked under Charles Scott Sherrington, at whose suggestion he joined the Liverpool School of Tropical Medicine in 1907. Two years later he was sent with Wakelin Barratt to Nyasaland to investigate twenty cases of blackwater fever. On his return in 1909 he was appointed research assistant to Anton Breinl at the Liverpool school's Runcorn laboratory, and he became its director a few months later.

During 1911 and 1912 Yorke was in Northern Rhodesia on the British South Africa Company's sleeping sickness commission. He showed that the tsetse fly, *Glossina morsitans*, was the transmitter of Rhodesian sleeping sickness, and that wild animals formed a reservoir of the infection. This work was carried out almost simultaneously with the researches of Sir David Bruce in Nyasaland. From 1914 until 1929 Yorke was Walter Myers professor of parasitology and from 1929 until his death he was the Alfred Jones professor of tropical medicine at Liverpool. He was honorary assistant physician for tropical diseases in the Liverpool Royal Infirmary from 1920 to 1929 and full honorary physician from 1929 to 1943. In 1916 he married Elizabeth Annie Greening; they had a son and a daughter.

Yorke's work on the trypanosomes and nematodes, and his later work on the chemotherapy of parasitic diseases, earned him an international reputation. He was very active in societies and committees, twice serving as vice-president of the Royal Society of Tropical Medicine and Hygiene. In 1927 he served on the chemotherapy committee of the Medical Research Council, and in 1935 he was on the malaria commission of the League of Nations. He was awarded the Chalmers memorial gold medal of the Royal Society of Tropical Medicine and Hygiene in 1925 for his services to tropical medicine, and he was elected FRS in 1932.

In the Second World War, Yorke served in the Royal Army Medical Corps and was stationed in Malta, where he conducted courses for service medical officers going abroad to tropical countries. Yorke was the author of a monograph on *The Nematode Parasites of Vertebrates* (1926) in collaboration with Philip Alan Maplestone, and of some 165 reports and papers, the majority of which appeared in the *Annals of Tropical Medicine and Parasitology*. His researches contributed greatly to a better understanding of tropical diseases.

Yorke was vivacious, direct, and questioning. Casual observers found him coldly analytical, but friends and colleagues knew him as kind and helpful. The *British Medical Journal* described him as the 'fountain-head and moving spirit' of the Liverpool School of Tropical Medicine (*BMJ*, 585). Yorke died at his home, 4 Bryanston Road, Prenton, Birkenhead, on 24 April 1943 and was survived by his wife.   W. J. BISHOP, *rev.* TIM O'NEILL

Sources BMJ (8 May 1943), 585 · The Lancet (8 May 1943), 601 · Munk, *Roll* · C. M. Wenyon, *Obits. FRS*, 4 (1942–4), 523–45 · *The Times* (26 April 1943) · election certificate, RS · CGPLA Eng. & Wales (1943) **Archives** U. Lpool L., special collections and archives, corresp. and papers, mainly relating to the Sierra Leone laboratory **Likenesses** photograph, Wellcome L. **Wealth at death** £22,881 3s. 0d.: probate, 31 July 1943, CGPLA Eng. & Wales

Youatt, William (1776–1847), veterinary surgeon, was the son of an Exeter surgeon. Educated for the nonconformist ministry, in 1810 he left Devon, and undertook ministerial and scholastic duties in London. In 1812 or 1813 he joined Delabere Pritchett Blaine (1768–1845) in conducting a veterinary infirmary in Wells Street, Oxford Street. This partnership continued for a little more than twelve years, when the business passed into Youatt's hands.

In the 1820s there developed a movement among practising veterinary surgeons to reform the London Veterinary College. The main complaints were that the school ignored species other than the horse, and that the governors refused to appoint veterinary surgeons to the board of external examiners, which consisted entirely of medical men with no veterinary experience whatever. Youatt was a leading reformer who devoted his life to the improvement of the profession.

In 1828 Youatt began a series of lectures and demonstrations to veterinary students at his private infirmary at Nassau Street, which were explicitly designed to include species other than the horse. His ambition was to have veterinary science recognized as a university discipline, and in 1831 he delivered his lectures at the London University (that is, University College); but his health was failing and by November 1833 he could no longer continue. The university course collapsed soon afterwards, but he continued to produce a series of monthly lectures in *The Veterinarian*, a professional monthly, started in 1828 by William Percivall, veterinary surgeon to the 1st Life Guards. Percivall was joined by Youatt as an editor soon after the journal was founded, and it was kept alive in the early years only by Youatt's dogged perseverance, at a time when even Percivall wished to abandon the venture.

Youatt's connection with *The Veterinarian* was the beginning of a notable literary career. As editor and author he was a prolific contributor to the journal. An expert on rabies he published in 1830 *On Canine Madness*, in which he expounded his firm opinion that rabies was a specific disease spread only by the bite of a rabid animal, and that it could not arise spontaneously. He gave evidence on this to the rabies committee of the House of Commons, but it conflicted with the medical opinion of the day and aroused antagonism. In 1830 he entered into an arrangement with the Society for the Diffusion of Useful Knowledge to write a series of handbooks on the various animals of the farm. Five titles appeared in this series between 1831 and 1847. The first, entitled *The Horse*, was the most successful; it included a 'Treatise on draught' by Isambard Kingdom Brunel, though the attribution does not appear in all the editions, of which there were at least a further seven, the last in 1866. Youatt had a strong sense of man's moral responsibility to animals and published these views in 1839 in *Obligation and Extent of Humanity to Brutes*. His other literary work included the editing of two editions of *The Complete Grazier* (1833, 1839) and *British Husbandry* (3 vols., 1834–40). Youatt was one of the original members of the English Agricultural Society when it was founded in 1838, and was placed on the committee of management. Here he did important work in moving and obtaining the appointment of a veterinary committee, of which he was appointed chairman. His objective was to establish a connection between the society and the London Veterinary College to promote the study of the diseases of farm animals. Two other important appointments that he held were as veterinary surgeon to the Zoological Society of London and veterinary surgeon to the Society for the Prevention of Cruelty to Animals.

Owing partly to his extensive literary work and partly to attacks of gout, Youatt's practice had devolved more and more on his assistant, Ainsley, on whose death in 1844 the establishment in Nassau Street was broken up. Youatt, though now an eminent elder of the profession, was not a registered member of it. He had attended the London Veterinary College as a mature student in 1813 or thereabouts, but his enthusiasm and his connection with Blaine led to disagreements with the college authorities and he left without a certificate of qualification. However, in 1844 the veterinary reformers achieved their ambition when Queen Victoria granted their petition for the creation of a self-governing body for the profession. In March 1844 the Royal College of Veterinary Surgeons was incorporated by royal charter and on 15 May Youatt was awarded his diploma of membership.

Youatt's missionary zeal aroused ridicule and derision among some practitioners, but the profession as a whole recognized his literary efforts and presented him with a dinner service of plate in 1839 as a mark 'of the high esteem they entertain of his literary labours in veterinary science' (*The Veterinarian*, 1839). His supreme contribution was his work on *The Veterinarian* and the influence that this had on the founding of the Royal College of Veterinary Surgeons.

Youatt was the father of four daughters. He died by suicide on 9 January 1847 in his seventy-first year and was buried in the churchyard of Old St Pancras.

ERNEST CLARKE, rev. SHERWIN A. HALL

Sources J. B. Simonds, *A biographical sketch of two distinguished promoters of veterinary science, Delabere P. Blaire, William Youatt* (1896) · F. Smith, *The early history of veterinary literature and its British development*, 3 (1930) · 'The presentation of a service of plate to Mr Youatt', *The Veterinarian*, 12 (1839), 595–619 · *The Veterinarian*, 20 (1847), 105–6 · d. cert. · *The Times* (14 Jan 1847), 8

Archives DWL, student essays | Sir John Soane's Museum, London, Soane MSS · UCL, letters to Society for the Diffusion of Useful Knowledge

Likenesses R. Ansdell, oils, Royal Agricultural Society of England

Youde, Sir Edward [Teddy] (1924–1986), diplomatist and colonial administrator, was born on 19 June 1924 at 25 Ivy Street, Penarth, Glamorgan, the son of Alfred Youde, secretary of a joinery firm, and his wife, Edith, *née* Jones. Showing an aptitude for languages at Penarth county secondary school, he won a scholarship to read Chinese at the School of Oriental and African Studies, University of London. His education there was interrupted by three years in the Royal Naval Volunteer Reserve (1943–6).

Youde (known to friends and family as Teddy) joined the foreign service in August 1947 and five months later became third secretary at the British embassy in Nanking, capital of nationalist China during the civil war. He was made MBE for crossing the front line alone on foot in April 1949 in order to try to negotiate with communist forces a safe passage for HMS *Amethyst* down the Yangtze River. After being relocated to Beijing in 1950, in 1951 he married Pamela Fitt (*b.* 1926), a foreign service typist. They had two daughters.

After a spell at the Foreign Office (1951–3) dealing with NATO issues, Youde returned to China as second secretary. Isolated in their compound, within earshot of loudspeakers denouncing them as running dogs of American imperialism, British diplomats could conduct little normal business, but Youde turned himself into an expert at divining Chinese political developments from subtle changes in the wording of official publications. In 1956 he was transferred to Washington, where, as first secretary, he helped to restore Anglo-American amity after the Suez crisis. He held the same rank when posted a third time to China (1960–62).

During a decade away from his specialization, Youde served first in the Foreign Office's northern department (monitoring northern Europe and the USSR). He then became counsellor and head of chancery at the British mission to the United Nations in New York in 1965, and private secretary (overseas affairs) to the prime minister, Harold Wilson, in 1969. After a course at the Imperial Defence College (1970–71), he spent two years as head of the personnel services department of the Foreign and Commonwealth Office (FCO) before being appointed assistant under-secretary for Asian affairs in 1973.

In August 1974 Youde succeeded Sir John Addis as ambassador to China. This was a turbulent period in Chinese politics, and the death of Mao Zedong and the deposition of the 'gang of four' in 1976 transformed relations with the West. As an acquaintance of the emergent leader Deng Xiaoping, Youde could make the most of unprecedented opportunities for trade, investment, and cultural exchanges. At last he was really dealing with China as well as studying it. The popular press in Britain seemed more exercised by his ban on gambling at embassy social nights, however, which prompted jocular references to the Chinese version of his name, Yau Tak ('abundant virtue').

Having been knighted KCMG in 1977, Youde left the embassy in the summer of 1978 to become deputy undersecretary of state (chief clerk) at the FCO, responsible for administering the diplomatic service. He continued to advise on policy towards China and urged the British government to raise the issue of the future of Hong Kong well before 1997, when 92 per cent of the colony was due to revert to Chinese sovereignty on the expiry of the British lease over the New Territories. His arguments helped to convince Margaret Thatcher that it would be futile to attempt to retain Hong Kong Island and Kowloon after that date; the fate of all Hong Kong needed to be agreed between London and Beijing.

After undergoing heart bypass surgery in 1981, Youde was named governor of Hong Kong, in succession to Sir Murray MacLehose, on 20 May 1982. Locals judged him unimpressive at first: he was small, bald, and reserved, and his fluency in Mandarin counted for little, as Hong Kong Chinese spoke Cantonese. Rumours of secret Sino-British discussions gave rise to much anxiety in the colony, which it was the task of the governor to allay. He crucially won the trust of the nine non-official members of the Hong Kong executive council (ExCo) by standing up to the FCO and insisting that they be confidentially informed of the progress of the successive rounds of negotiations in Beijing between 12 July 1983 and 26 September 1984. Youde attended these as a member of the British delegation, enduring petty diplomatic snubs intended to show that China did not recognize his right to speak for Hong

Kong. His calm and discretion meanwhile sustained cordial dialogue between ExCo and the FCO, even when he thought the latter too conciliatory to China (as in respect of the joint liaison group). The joint declaration of 1984 decreed that Hong Kong would be a special administrative region of China after 1997, with basic freedoms guaranteed for fifty years.

Aside from the sovereignty question, Youde worked to widen access to higher education in the colony and announced plans for limited democratic reforms (whereby a minority of legislative councillors might be elected). While in Beijing to attend a trade exhibition, he was found dead in his bed at the British embassy on 5 December 1986, having suffered a heart attack during the night. His body was cremated in Hong Kong after a state funeral on 9 December; the ashes were subsequently buried in the memorial garden of Canterbury Cathedral. He was survived by his wife and two daughters.

Although some of Youde's public utterances were criticized by local democrats for sounding unduly reassuring about the future, most people who understood the political constraints on him reckoned that he had fought hard for the interests of Hong Kong—and had probably shortened his life by his exertions.   JASON TOMES

Sources *The Times* (6 Dec 1986) · M. Roberti, *The fall of Hong Kong: China's triumph and Britain's betrayal*, new edn (1996) · R. Cottrell, *The end of Hong Kong: the secret diplomacy of imperial retreat* (1993) · K. Rafferty, *City on the rocks: Hong Kong's uncertain future* (1989) · P. Cradock, *Experiences of China* (1994) · P. Burgess, ed., *The annual obituary, 1986* (1989) · M. H. Murfett, *Hostage on the Yangtze: Britain, China, and the 'Amethyst' crisis of 1949* (1991) · diplomatic service list, 1972 · FO List (1952) · G. Howe, *Conflict of loyalty* (1994) · H. Trevelyan, *Worlds apart* (1971) · WWW · b. cert.

Archives PRO, FO and FCO records

Likenesses photograph, repro. in *The Times* · photographs, repro. in www.seysa.org.hk [website of Sir Edward Youde Scholars Association] · photographs, repro. in www.ust.hk [website of Hong Kong University of Science and Technology]

Wealth at death £100,282: probate, 29 July 1987, CGPLA Eng. & Wales

Youens, Bernard [*real name* Bernard Arthur Popley] (1914–1984), actor, was born on 28 December 1914 at 10 Portland Road, Hove, Sussex, the son of Leonard Arthur Popley, jeweller, and his wife, Isabel June Youens. The family moved to Newcastle upon Tyne when he was fourteen and, after finishing his education at Rutherford College two years later, he began his career in the city as an assistant stage manager at the Players' Theatre, before working in repertory theatre all over Britain. About 1933, he married the ballet dancer Edna Swallow, whom he called Teddy. They had two daughters and three sons.

Called up in 1940, Popley was a member of the 1st battalion, the loyals regiment (north Lancashire), serving in north Africa, Italy, and Palestine. In February 1944, a month after storming the beaches at Anzio, his right leg was wounded by shrapnel and he was hospitalized. He subsequently performed with an army concert-party in Italy and Palestine. On demobilization in 1946 he returned to repertory theatre, changed his professional name to Youens and starred with Sonny Burke in the Mancunian Films production *The International Circus Revue* (1948),

which also featured a circus troupe from Manchester's Belle Vue amusements in the story of the difficulties encountered by a probationary publicity manager.

Eventually work became scarce and Youens left acting to become landlord of a rundown Manchester pub with a rough bunch of regulars. He was then employed as a bread salesman and a building site labourer before trying his hand at running another pub, near Preston. When Granada Television began broadcasting as the ITV company for the north of England in 1956, he returned to show business to become one of its two continuity announcers (the other was Ray Moore, later a BBC Radio 2 presenter). The velvet-voiced southerner could not have been more removed from the character for which he was to become famous. Youens also found acting work at Granada, appearing in the early ITV drama series *Shadow Squad* and *Knight Errant*, as well as *The Disfigured Actress* story in the company's largely unscripted courtroom drama *The Verdict is Yours* (1958). Nevertheless, when *Coronation Street* began in 1960, he turned down the chance of an audition, preferring the stability of his announcer's job. But in 1964, with the programme by then a television institution, he joined the cast as Stan Ogden, henpecked husband of the Rovers Return cleaner Hilda (played by Jean Alexander). His first line in the pub was: 'A pint of mild and 20 fags, missus'.

Work-shy layabout Stan, who enjoyed propping up the Rovers bar and putting money on the horses, was a lorry driver who went through subsequent jobs as a chauffeur, waste-paper merchant, milkman, ice-cream seller, coalman, Len Fairclough's labourer, street photographer, and junk sculptor, before becoming a window cleaner, but he was more at home simply *staying* at home, doing nothing. The self-effacing, poetry-loving actor's Laurel and Hardy-style double act with actress Jean Alexander brought laughter to millions. The character played by Youens was so popular that there was even a Stan Ogden Appreciation Society, whose members dubbed their hero 'the greatest living Englishman'.

However, Youens suffered from arthritis of the neck and knees and during his later years in the serial had a series of heart attacks and a stroke that left his speech impaired, a personal tragedy for someone who had once been a television announcer. With the aid of speech therapy he battled on bravely, but he suffered more strokes and had his left leg amputated after gangrene was discovered. Shortly afterwards, on 27 August 1984, he died in his sleep at Salford Royal Hospital at the age of sixty-nine, having appeared in 1246 episodes of *Coronation Street*, the last on 7 March 1984.   ANTHONY HAYWARD

Sources A. Hayward and D. Hayward, *TV unforgettables* (1993) · *The Times* (28 Aug 1984) · *Daily Mirror* (25 March 1985) · S. I. F. T. database, BFI · CGPLA Eng. & Wales (1984) · b. cert. · d. cert.

Wealth at death £24,946: probate, 1984, CGPLA Eng. & Wales

Youl, Sir James Arndell (1811–1904), pisciculturist, born at Parramatta, New South Wales, on 28 December 1811, was the son of John Youl (1773–1827), a Church of England clergyman, and his wife, Jane Loder (d. 1877). As a child he accompanied his parents to Van Diemen's Land, his father having been appointed in 1819 military chaplain at Port Dalrymple and first incumbent of St John's, Launceston. James was sent to England to be educated at a private school near Romford, Essex. After returning to Van Diemen's Land he took up residence at Symmons Plains, which he inherited on the death of his father in March 1827. There he became a successful agriculturist and in 1837 county magistrate. On 9 July 1839, at Clarendon, he married Eliza, the daughter of William Cox, an army officer and settler in Australia. She died on 4 January 1881, leaving four sons and eight daughters.

In 1854 Youl returned to England to live permanently, at Clapham Park, London. He interested himself in Tasmanian and Australian affairs. From 1861 to 1863 he was honorary agent in London for Tasmania, and for seven years was honorary secretary and treasurer of the Australian Association. In that capacity he was instrumental in improving the mail service to Australia and getting the Australian sovereign made legal tender throughout the British dominions. He was acting agent-general for Tasmania in 1888, and was one of the founders in 1868 of the Colonial Society, later the Royal Colonial Institute, and took an active part in its management until his death.

But it is with the introduction of salmon and trout into the rivers of Tasmania and New Zealand that Youl's name is mainly associated. After many failures he at length discovered an effective method of packing the ova so that they survived a sea voyage of more than 100 days. In 1864 the first successful shipment to Tasmania was made, and for several years afterwards Youl was engaged with others in sending out shipments to Tasmania and Victoria, and, after 1868, to New Zealand. In 1866 he was awarded the gold medal of the Société d'Acclimatation and in 1868 the medal of the Acclimatization Society of Victoria. In 1874 he was made CMG and in 1891 KCMG. On 30 September 1882 he married Charlotte, the widow of William Robinson of Caldecott House, Clapham Park, and the younger daughter of Richard Williams of Philipville, Belgium. Youl died on 5 June 1904 of senile decay and bronchitis at his residence, Waratah House, King's Road, Clapham Park, London, and was buried in Norwood cemetery. He was survived by his wife.

CHEWTON ATCHLEY, rev. ELIZABETH BAIGENT

Sources P. S. Seager, *Concise history of the acclimatisation of the Salmonidae in Tasmania* (1888) · *The Times* (7 June 1904) · *The Times* (9 June 1904) · *Launceston Examiner* [Tasmania] (5 Oct 1860) · *Launceston Examiner* [Tasmania] (8 June 1904) · private information (1912) · *AusDB*, 6.449–50 · B. Burke, *A genealogical and heraldic history of the colonial gentry*, 2 (1895) · *Proceedings of the Royal Colonial Institute*, 35 (1903–4) · S. Wilson, *Salmon at the Antipodes* (1879)
Archives Tasmanian State Archives, Hobart | Wellcome L., letters to Henry Lee
Wealth at death £159,853 11s. 3d.: resworn probate, 2 July 1904, *CGPLA Eng. & Wales*

Youll, Henry (*fl.* 1608), composer, may possibly have been the son of 'Ezekiel Youel of Newark, musician' apprenticed in 1590 for seven years to 'Peter Newcombe of the same town, and song school master'. The only certain information about Youll is contained in the preface of his *Canzonets to Three Voices* (1608), dedicated to the four sons of 'Edward Bacon Esquire', now all 'in one and the same university'. These must have been Nicholas (1588/9–1658), Philip (1591/2–1635), Nathaniel (1593–1676), and Lionel (1595/6–1678), the sons of Edward Bacon of Shrubland, Suffolk, who had all matriculated from Christ's College, Cambridge, in 1606. Since Youll, in writing of his madrigals, recalled 'what a solace their company was once to you', it seems possible he had been, or still was, a household musician to the boys' parents.

Youll was a minor figure. Stylistically he remained committed to the light idioms and forms of the canzonet and ballet acclimatized into English music by Thomas Morley in the 1590s (the last six of the twenty-four compositions in Youll's volume are ballets). But by 1608 such styles had become outmoded, and Youll showed no aptitude in handling the more serious expressive issues now being increasingly favoured by composers, as his one attempt at setting such a lyric, 'Slow, Slow Fresh Fount' from the masque *Cynthia's Revels* by Ben Jonson, revealed (the suggestion that Youll's music could have been used in the masque itself is implausible). Yet despite his sometimes insecure technique Youll on occasions produced music of a modest charm. DAVID BROWN

Sources H. Youll, *Canzonets to three voices* (1608), preface · A. Smith, 'Parish church musicians in England in the reign of Elizabeth I (1558–1603): an annotated register', *Royal Musical Association Research Chronicle*, 4 (1964), 42–92 · 'Youll, Henry', *New Grove*, 2nd edn [forthcoming] · Venn, *Alum. Cant.*

Youmans [*née* Creighton], **Letitia** (1827–1896), teacher and temperance activist in Canada, was born on 3 January 1827 in Baltimore, Upper Canada, daughter of John Creighton and his wife, Annie Bishop. Her father had been born in Ireland and her mother in the United States before the couple began to clear lands for farming in Upper Canada.

Letitia Creighton was educated locally, and at the age of sixteen went to the Cobourg Ladies' Seminary and then to the Burlington Ladies' Academy in Hamilton. Upon graduation she was hired as an English teacher, but two years later she moved to the Picton Academy, and married widower Arthur Youmans (d. 1882), a farmer and mill owner, on 28 August 1850. Mrs Youmans conducted school at home for her eight step-children and taught Christian education in the Picton Methodist Church, but had no children of her own. Witnessing alcohol-related problems in the town, she organized a Band of Hope, following the practice begun in Britain in 1847, to support children from families in such situations, but objections from non-Methodists forced her to abandon the church building for a hall, where the number of children swelled to over a hundred.

Attending the summer camp in 1874 for protestant educationists at Chautauqua, New York, Letitia Youmans learned of the newly formed American Women's Christian Temperance Union, and she returned to Picton to begin the second branch established in Canada. Campaigns were mounted in the face of opposition and ridicule to abolish local liquor licences and to secure local option under a provincial statute in order to prohibit retail sales of alcoholic beverages. When the Ontario

Women's Christian Temperance Union (WCTU) was formed in 1877 Youmans became its first president, and the association adopted the white ribbon as its symbol in the following year. The Ontario WCTU adopted four approaches to achieve its ends: access to political channels to influence legislation; educational activities in provincial schools; religious techniques with prayer days and temperance revivals, as well as work through the Bands of Hope; and social and philanthropic activities.

Hired as organizer in 1880 Letitia Youmans travelled extensively in eastern Canada, where she prompted the formation of many new groups. A frequent visitor to the United States, in 1876 she provided American temperance reformer Frances Elizabeth Caroline Willard with her slogan of 'home protection'. A believer in both temperance and prohibition, Letitia Youmans forecast a new role for women in the interests of Christian service, but she opposed female enfranchisement because she thought it would weaken the argument of temperance advocates about the wrongs inflicted on women and children by men. When the Dominion Women's Temperance Union was created in Canada in 1883, Youmans was delegated as representative to the British Women's Temperance Association. Wherever she went, Youmans excelled at the podium with turgid but emotionally charged speeches.

When Arthur Youmans died in 1882, Letitia Youmans moved to Toronto, but, seeking relief from asthma, she travelled to California, British Columbia, and the prairie provinces in 1886. Painful rheumatoid arthritis curtailed her activities after 1888, but the Canadian association named her honourary president, a tribute to the woman proclaimed as 'the Deborah of the temperance reform in this Dominion'. By that time membership in Ontario had grown to 4733 women, 14,945 children in Bands of Hope, and a small organization for young women interested in the cause. Canada-wide, the number of adherents crested in the early 1890s at more than 19,000, but declined steadily thereafter. In 1893 Letitia Youmans published her autobiography, *Campaign Echoes*. Spending her last years in penury, she died in Toronto on 16 July 1896.

Letitia Youmans played a formative role in creating an association that allowed women to tackle questions beyond their immediate locality and united them internationally. Temperance unions provided skills that were readily transferred to other women's organizations as they proliferated at end of the nineteenth century, but their primary goal was not to be attained until most Canadian provinces legislated prohibition during the First World War.   TERRY CROWLEY

Sources L. Youmans, *Campaign echoes: the autobiography of Mrs Letitia Youmans, the pioneer of the white ribbon movement in Canada* [1893] · 1889–96, Archives of Ontario, Dominion WCTU annual reports · 1878–96, Archives of Ontario, Ontario WCTU minute-books · Archives of Ontario, *Woman's Journal* (1885–96) · Ontario Women's Christian Temperance Union, Toronto, Ontario Women's Christian Temperance Union Collection · T. A. Crowley, 'Creighton, Letitia (Youmans)', *DCB*, vol. 12 · S. A. Cook, *Through sunshine and shadow: the Women's Christian Temperance Union, evangelicalism, and reform in Ontario, 1874–1930* (1995) · H. G. Willies, The life of Letitia Youmans, Archives of Ontario, MU 8469, folder 5 · *The Globe* [Toronto] (20–21 July 1896) · *The Globe* [Toronto] (23 July 1896) · *The Globe* [Toronto] (25 July 1896) · G. M. Ross and H. W. Charlesworth, *A cyclopedia of Canadian biography*, 1 (1886–1919) · R. E. Spence, *Prohibition in Canada: a memorial to Francis Stephens Spence* (1919) · I. R. Tyrrell, *Woman's world, woman's empire: the Woman's Christian Temperance Union in international perspective* (1991)
Likenesses photograph (later in life), repro. in Youmans, *Campaign echoes*
Wealth at death near penury: Cook, *Through sunshine and shadow*, 153

Young. *See also* Yong, Yonge, Younge.

Young family (*per. c.*1700–1799), musicians, included two London organists and two generations of professional female singers. In August 1758 Mrs Delany wrote: 'the race of Youngs are *born* songsters and musicians' (*Autobiography … Mrs Delany*, 3.503). Anthony *Young (*bap.* 1683, *d.* 1747) [*see under* Young, William (*d.* 1662)] was a boy chorister at the Chapel Royal and became organist of St Clement Danes in 1707. He contributed songs to the *Monthly Mask of Vocal Music* between 1705 and 1709 and published *A Collection of New Songs* (1707) and *Suits of Lessons for the Harpsicord or Spinnet* (1719). Charles *Young (*bap.* 1686, *d.* 1758) [*see under* Young, William], his brother, was a music teacher, organist of All Hallows Barking from August 1713; Charles's daughters were the singers Cecilia, Isabella, and Esther [*see below*] and his son Charles (*d.* 1754), a senior clerk in the Treasury, was the father of a second generation of singers, Isabella, Elizabeth, and Mary [*see below*]. After the younger Charles's death the education of the three girls was taken over by their aunt Cecilia and her husband, the composer Thomas Augustine Arne. The family later believed that Anthony Young, the father of the organists Anthony and Charles, was the composer of the tune of Britain's national anthem.

Cecilia Young [*married name* Arne] (1712–1789), singer, daughter of the elder Charles Young and his wife, Elizabeth, was baptized at St Andrew's Church, Holborn, on 7 February 1712. At a concert for her benefit at Drury Lane Theatre on 4 March 1730 she was advertised as 'a Scholar of Signor GEMINIANI, who never yet sung in publick' (*Daily Post*, 4 March 1730). That October she appeared in concerts at Bath, where John, first Viscount Perceval, recorded in his diary that her voice was better than any Italian's he had heard 'in clearness, loudness and high compass' (*Egmont Diary*, 1.105). Her operatic début was in the title role of John Frederick Lampe's *Britannia* at the Haymarket Theatre in November 1732, and she sang the heroines in his *Amelia* on 18 December 1732 and *Dione* on 23 February 1733. She was engaged for the title role in Willem De Fesch's oratorio *Judith* at Lincoln's Inn Fields on 9 February 1733, but was replaced by Miss Chambers in a delayed première; the furious composer blamed the postponement on the 'Mis-Conduct and pretended Sickness of Cecilia Young' (*Daily Journal*, 16 Feb 1733). Handel chose her for the first performance of his *Deborah* (17 March 1733) and she later sang in the premières of his *Ariodante* and *Alcina* (both 1735), *Alexander's Feast* (1736), and *Saul* (1739).

Against her father's wishes Cecilia married the Roman Catholic Thomas Augustine *Arne (1710–1778) on 15

March 1737 and converted to Catholicism. Arne wrote delightful music for her in his *Comus* (first performed 4 March 1738), including the perennially popular 'Sweet Echo', in *Alfred*, performed before Frederick, prince of Wales, at Cliveden in 1740, and in *The Judgment of Paris* (1742), in which she was Venus. The Arnes went to Dublin in June 1742 and joined Arne's sister, the actress and singer Susanna Cibber, in benefit concerts. They were in Dublin for the 1742–4 theatre seasons; Cecilia appeared in her husband's stage works and in concerts, although she was ill in October 1742 and again in May 1743, when her physician forbade her to perform 'at the Hazard of her Life' (Greene and Clark, 352). By this time their marriage was under strain: Arne was unfaithful (an illegitimate son, Michael, was born about 1740) and James Pilkington, Arne's apprentice in Dublin, claimed that Mrs Arne was 'prodigiously fond of Gin' and that he had seen her 'toying on the Bed' with the tenor Thomas Lowe (Pilkington, 2.256–9). In his draft will of 1770 Arne denied that Cecilia had ever been unfaithful to him, but stated that her 'violent and raging passions' rendered her of no use to him or herself as a public singer. Charles Burney, Arne's apprentice from 1744 to 1746, always remembered Mrs Arne's goodness of heart and parental attention to his welfare and believed he had helped to preserve domestic harmony while he lived with them. Although Cecilia sang at Drury Lane and Vauxhall during those two years, she made very few appearances thereafter. In 1748 she went to Dublin without Arne for a season there with her sister and brother-in-law Isabella and John Frederick Lampe.

In autumn 1755 the Arnes returned to Dublin accompanied by Cecilia's young nieces Elizabeth and Mary (Polly) and Arne's pupil Charlotte Brent. Cecilia was ill at first, but then sang in several of Arne's pieces before the marriage broke down completely. Arne went back to London in 1756 with Charlotte Brent (by then almost certainly his mistress) and Elizabeth, abandoning Cecilia in Dublin with the six-year-old Mary. In 1758 Mrs Delany encountered her, 'an object of compassion', teaching singing in the household of a charitable family (*Autobiography … Mrs Delany*, 3.502). Cecilia was heard in a few concerts in Dublin, but did not resume her singing career after returning to London with Mary in 1762. The Mrs Arne who sang in London between 1766 and 1769 was Michael Arne's wife, Elizabeth. Cecilia lived with Mary and her husband, François Hippolyte Barthélémon, and performed at their benefit concert in 1774, advertised as 'the 1st Time of her singing in public these 20 Years' (*Public Advertiser*, 16 May 1774). She received an annual allowance of £40 from Arne, rather grudgingly paid. Mrs Barthélémon collected the allowance, taking her daughter Cecilia Maria with her, and it was Arne's fondness for the child which reunited him with his wife for a few months before his death in March 1778. Cecilia remained a pious Catholic until her death at the Barthélémons' home on 6 October 1789.

Cecilia's sister **Isabella Young** [*married name* Lampe] (*bap.* 1716?, *d.* 1795), singer, was probably the Isabella baptized as the daughter of John and Elizabeth Young at St Lawrence Jewry on 3 January 1716. She sang at Drury Lane in the 1733–4 season, making her stage début as Amphitrite in *The Tempest* (*Daily Journal*, 26 Nov 1733). She appeared in concerts before joining the Covent Garden company in the role of Margery, the heroine of John Frederick Lampe's burlesque opera *The Dragon of Wantley* on 26 October 1737. The opera, with its delightfully inane libretto by Henry Carey, proved hugely successful and was performed night after night, including 31 January 1738, the day of Isabella's marriage to John Frederick *Lampe (1702/3–1751). In the sequel, *Margery, or, A Worse Plague than the Dragon* (9 December 1738), the heroine falls prey to jealousy, but there is no evidence that the Lampes' marriage was other than happy. They worked together and Isabella took the female lead in all her husband's later stage pieces, among them *The Parting Lovers* (1739) and *Pyramus and Thisbe* (1745). For the two seasons 1748–50 the Lampes were engaged by Thomas Sheridan at the Smock Alley Theatre, Dublin, and they then moved to Edinburgh. Their arrival was delayed because Isabella had been seriously ill with a fever in Dublin, but it was Lampe who died from fever on 25 July 1751 in Edinburgh, where he had been 'settled very much to the satisfaction of the patrons of Music in that city, and of himself' (Burney, 4.672). Isabella returned to London and Covent Garden, and performed there every season until 1776, although her appearances grew less frequent in the later years. Her son, Charles John Frederick Lampe (*d.* 1767), succeeded his grandfather as organist at All Hallows Barking in 1758, and his wife, Ann, sang at the pleasure gardens and Sadler's Wells in the 1760s. Isabella lived with her sister Esther, whom she cared for tenderly during a long illness. She died on 5 January 1795.

Esther Young [*married name* Jones] (1717–1795), singer, was born on 14 February 1717. She joined her sisters in a benefit concert for their father at Mercers' Hall on 11 February 1736, sang with Isabella in Arne's *Grand Epithalamium* at Drury Lane that April, and made her Covent Garden début as the heroine's rival, Mauxalinda, in Lampe's *The Dragon of Wantley* in October 1737. She performed in almost every season at Covent Garden until she and her sister Isabella retired in 1776, taking numerous roles in musical afterpieces and pantomimes; she was the company's Lucy in *The Beggar's Opera* from 1746 to 1761. In Handel's oratorio season in 1744 Esther created the contralto roles of Juno and Ino in *Semele*. On 8 April 1762 she married Charles Jones, a music-seller, horn player, and flautist, who on his death on 17 March 1780 left everything to his loving wife. She had been seriously ill for some years by December 1785, when the tenor John Beard wrote to the Royal Society of Musicians in support of a pension for her, describing her blameless and amiable character. She survived her sister Isabella by a few months and was buried at St Paul's, Covent Garden, on 6 June 1795.

Isabella Young [*married name* Scott] (1740/41?–1791), singer, was the daughter of Charles Young, the Treasury clerk. A pupil of the bass Gustavus Waltz, she made her first appearance singing with him at a concert for her benefit at the Haymarket Theatre on 18 March 1751. The following year at her benefit she sang and played 'one of

Mr. Handel's Organ Concertos' (*General Advertiser*, 2 March 1752). Her father died in January 1754, and that spring she appeared in Arne's *Alfred*, described in the *Daily Advertiser* as a thirteen-year-old pupil of Arne, and in his *Rosamond* and *Eliza*. She joined the Drury Lane company to take the part of Titania in the première of John Christopher Smith's opera *The Fairies* on 3 February 1755 and the following February sang Ariel in Smith's opera *The Tempest*. She appeared at Drury Lane frequently until 1777 as an entr'acte singer, in musical afterpieces, and in singing roles, such as Ariel in Shakespeare's *The Tempest*. Handel employed her as his mezzo-soprano soloist in the last five oratorio seasons before his death in 1759 and she performed in *Messiah* at the Foundling Hospital on several occasions. She sang at Ranelagh and, being in demand at provincial festivals, at Oxford, Cambridge, Winchester, and Leicester and at the Three Choirs meetings from 1763 to 1765. The *Oxford Journal* of 12 April 1766 reported indignantly that she had not been engaged for Handel's *L'allegro* because she required 'Two and Forty Guineas, for one Night's Attendance'.

On 12 December 1757 Isabella married the Hon. John Scott, younger brother of Henry Scott, fourth earl of Deloraine. She continued to appear on stage as Miss Young until 1769, although she sang as Mrs Scott in oratorios. Her only son, John Scott (baptized on 23 November 1758), became a midshipman in the Royal Navy and was killed in action against the Americans on 9 October 1776. She retired from singing at the end of the 1776–7 season and died at her house in Kennington Lane, Vauxhall, on 17 August 1791. Her husband had died at his chambers in Gray's Inn on 31 December 1788 and in her will she left an annuity to her sister Mary Barthélémon and the bulk of her estate to Mary's daughter Cecilia Maria.

Elizabeth Young [*married name* Dorman] (1741?–1773), singer, was the daughter of Charles Young and was probably younger than her sister Isabella, who began her singing career earlier. Elizabeth was said to be over twenty-one on her marriage in 1762. She went with the Arnes and her young sister Mary to Dublin in autumn 1755 and took minor roles in the season of Arne operas at the Smock Alley Theatre. She seems to have returned to London with Arne in 1756 and that December sang in his *Eliza* as First Shepherdess. In a charity benefit performance of *The Beggar's Opera* at Drury Lane in June 1758 she played Lucy, her first speaking role, billed as 'the first Time of her appearing on any Stage' (*Public Advertiser*, 22 June 1758). She was a member of the Drury Lane company from autumn 1758, appearing as Mrs Dorman after her marriage to the violinist Ridley Dorman on 9 October 1762. In February 1764 George Rush's opera *The Royal Shepherd* was premièred with Thomas Norris, a falsetto alto, as Agenor. He was badly received and on the second night 'Mrs Dormond perform'd in his room, much applauded' (*London Stage*, pt 4, 1042). She created the old maidservant Ursula in Charles Dibdin's highly successful comic opera *The Padlock* (3 October 1768) and sang the role well over a hundred times; her last stage appearances were in June 1772. She died in the

parish of St Anne's, Soho, on 12 April 1773 and was buried on 19 April at St Paul's, Covent Garden.

Mary [Polly, Maria] **Young** [*married name* Barthélémon] (1749–1799), singer and composer, was born on 7 July 1749 and baptized at St Margaret's, Westminster, on 23 July 1749, the daughter of Charles and Mary Young. On 29 November 1755 at the Smock Alley Theatre, Dublin, 'Miss Polly Young, a Child of Six Years of Age, pleased and astonished the whole Company, having a sweet melodious Voice, accenting her Words with great Propriety, and Singing perfectly in Time and Tune' (*Dublin Journal*, 2 Dec 1755). This was in Thomas Arne's *Eliza*, and she later sang in his *Rosamond* and *Alfred*. When the Arnes parted, Polly, as Mary was known as a child, remained with her aunt Cecilia in Dublin, and her earnings then and later contributed to Cecilia's support. She sang in concerts, at the theatre, and in the pleasure gardens in Dublin for another six years, before returning with her aunt to London. On 30 September 1762 she made her début at Covent Garden, when the *Theatrical Review* commented on the agreeable innocence of her appearance and found her playing on the harpsichord equal to her excellent singing. She remained at Covent Garden as an entr'acte and chorus singer until summer 1764 and then performed with the Italian opera company at the King's Theatre for three seasons. On 10 December 1766, at the age of seventeen, she married the leader of the opera orchestra, the violinist and composer François Hippolyte *Barthélémon (1741–1808). She appeared with Barthélémon in concerts and oratorios, at Marylebone Gardens (1770, 1773), in a further Italian opera season (1770–71), and in Dublin (1771–2), where Barthélémon presided over concert seasons at the Rotunda. They made a successful tour of Germany, France, and Italy in 1776–7; Mrs Barthélémon sang in her husband's oratorio *Jefte* at Florence and Rome and in Italian opera at Leghorn. Their only child, Cecilia Maria *Barthélémon (1767–1859), who performed with her parents at the royal courts of Naples and France, later claimed that her mother refused Marie-Antoinette's offer of a court appointment because of her desire to return to England and her aunt Cecilia.

Maria Barthélémon, as she now called herself, performed in 1780–82 at the Italian Opera in London. The Barthélémons continued to give concerts together and in 1784 had another summer season at the Dublin Rotunda. On 2 November 1784 a letter from Mrs Barthélémon appeared in the *Morning Post* complaining that, despite her unblemished reputation and the honours she had received in continental courts, she was not engaged by the London managers because they were swayed by influence rather than merit. During Haydn's visits to London in the 1790s the composer became friendly with Barthélémon and visited the family at its house in Kennington Place, Vauxhall. Cecilia Maria remembered singing Handel duets with her mother to Haydn's accompaniment. Between 1776 and 1795 Maria Barthélémon published a number of her own compositions, including six sonatas for keyboard and violin, a set of English and Italian songs, and a collection of hymns and anthems for the chapels of the Asylum for Female Orphans and the Magdalen Hospital. Their friendship with Jacob Duché, the chaplain of the asylum, led to the Barthélémons' becoming Swedenborgians. Maria died at her home in Vauxhall on 20 September 1799 and was buried on 26 September 1799 at St Martin-in-the-Fields; her coffin was joined to that of her aunt Cecilia by a chain.

OLIVE BALDWIN and THELMA WILSON

Sources *The autobiography and correspondence of Mary Granville, Mrs Delany*, ed. Lady Llanover, 1st ser., 3 (1861) · [C. M. Henslowe], 'Memoir of the late F. H. Barthélémon, esq.', in F. H. Barthélémon, *Selections from the oratorio of Jefté in Masfa* (1827) · D. Dawe, *Organists of the City of London, 1666–1850* (1983) · W. H. Henslowe, *The phonarthron* (1840) · [C. Burney], 'Young', *Cyclopædia*, ed. A. Rees (1802–19) · parish register of Westminster, St Margaret's [baptism, Anthony Young, 1683] · parish register of St Martin-in-the-Fields [baptism, Charles Young, 1686] · parish register of All Hallows, Barking [burial, Charles Young, 1758] · parish register of St Clement Danes [burial, Anthony Young, 1747] · will, proved, 4 May 1747, Family Records Centre, London [copy of will of Anthony Young] · will, proved, 23 Jan 1759, Family Records Centre, London [copy of will of Charles Young] · A. Ashbee and D. Lasocki, eds., *A biographical dictionary of English court musicians, 1485–1714*, 2 vols. (1998) · L. Baillie and R. Balchin, eds., *The catalogue of printed music in the British Library to 1980*, 62 vols. (1981–7), vol. 62 · A. H. Scouten, ed., *The London stage, 1660–1800, pt 3: 1729–1747* (1961) · G. W. Stone, ed., *The London stage, 1660–1800, pt 4: 1747–1776* (1962) · C. B. Hogan, ed., *The London stage, 1660–1800, pt 5: 1776–1800* (1968) · J. Herbage, 'A page from Arne's draft will', *MT*, 112 (1971), 126–7 · W. H. Cummings, *Dr. Arne and 'Rule, Britannia'* (1912) · *Manuscripts of the earl of Egmont: diary of Viscount Percival, afterwards first earl of Egmont*, 3 vols., HMC, 63 (1920–23), vol. 1 · L. Pilkington, *Memoirs of Laetitia Pilkington*, ed. A. C. Elias, 2 vols. (1997), vol. 2 · B. Boydell, *A Dublin musical calendar, 1700–1760* (1988) · J. C. Greene and G. L. H. Clark, *The Dublin stage, 1720–45* (1993) · *Daily Post* (4 March 1731) · *Daily Journal* (9 Feb 1733) · *Daily Journal* (16 Feb 1733) · *Public Advertiser* (16 May 1774) · Burney, *Hist. mus.*, vol. 4 · H. Langley, *Doctor Arne* (1938) · will, Family Records Centre, London [copy of will of Thomas Arne] · *GM*, 1st ser., 59 (1789), 961 · parish register, Holborn, St Andrew [baptism, Cecilia Young, 1712] · parish register, Lincoln's Inn Chapel [marriage, Thomas Arne and Cecilia Young, 1737] · parish register, St Martin-in-the-Fields [burial, Cecilia Arne, 1789] · E. K. Sheldon, *Thomas Sheridan of Smock-Alley* (1967) · J. C. Dibdin, *The annals of the Edinburgh stage* (1888) · W. Wroth, *The London pleasure gardens* (1896) · records of the Royal Society of Musicians, 10 Stratford Place, London · *European Magazine*, 27 (1795), 71 · will, made, 6 Dec 1759, Family Records Centre, London [copy of will of Isabella Lampe] · parish register, Gresham Street, St Lawrence Jewry [baptism, Isabella Young, 1716] · parish register, Upper Thames Street, St Benet Paul's Wharf [marriage, John Lampe and Isabella Young, 1738] · parish register, Covent Garden, St Paul [burial, Isabella Lampe, 1795] · B. Matthews, ed., *The Royal Society of Musicians of Great Britain: list of members, 1738–1984* (1985) · will, proved, 30 March 1780, Family Records Centre, London [copy of will of Charles Jones] · parish register, Gresham Street, St Lawrence Jewry [baptism, Esther Young, 1717] · parish register, St Martin-in-the-Fields [marriage, Charles Jones and Esther Young, 1762] · parish register, Covent Garden, St Paul [burial, Esther Jones, 1795] · *General Advertiser* (18 March 1751) · *General Advertiser* (2 March 1752) · *Public Advertiser* (30 April 1753) · *Daily Advertiser* (27 March 1754) · *Oxford Journal* (12 April 1766) · O. E. Deutsch, *Dokumente zu Leben und Schaffen* (1985), vol. 4 of *Händel-Handbuch*, ed. W. Eisel and M. Eisel (1978–85) · W. Dean, *Handel's dramatic oratorios and masques* (1959) · *Music and theatre in Handel's world: the family papers of James Harris, 1732–1780*, ed. D. Burrows and R. Dunhill (2002) · D. J. Reid, 'Some festival programmes of the eighteenth and nineteenth centuries [pts 1–2]', *Royal Musical Association Research Chronicle*, 5 (1965), 51–79; 6 (1966), 3–23 · D. Lysons and others, *Origin and progress of the Meeting of the Three Choirs* (1895) ·

J. Cradock, *Literary and miscellaneous memoirs*, 1–2, 4 (1828) · W. J. Morgan, ed., *Naval documents of the American Revolution*, 6 (1972) · GEC, *Peerage*, new edn, vol. 4 · parish register, Covent Garden, St Paul [baptism, John Scott, 1758] · *GM*, 1st ser., 58 (1788), 1185 · *European Magazine*, 19 (1791), 239 · *GM*, 1st ser., 61 (1791), 782 · will, proved, 9 Jan 1789, Family Records Centre, London [copy of the will of the Hon. John Scott] · will, proved, 13 Oct 1791, Family Records Centre, London [copy of the will of Isabella Scott] · parish register, St Margaret's, Westminster [burial, Charles Young, 1754] · parish register, Eastcheap, St Clement [marriage, John Scott and Isabella Young, 1757] · parish register, Holborn, St Andrew [burial, Isabella Scott, 1791] · *Public Advertiser* (22 June 1758) · parish register, Covent Garden, St Paul [marriage, Ridley Dorman and Elizabeth Young, 1762] · parish register, Covent Garden, St Paul [burial, Elizabeth Dorman, 1773] · *The theatrical review, or, Annals of the drama*, 1 (1763) · *Dublin Journal* (29 Nov–2 Dec 1755) · *Morning Post* (3 March 1778) · *Morning Post* (2 Nov 1784) · T. J. Walsh, *Opera in Dublin, 1705–1797* (1973) · B. Boydell, *Rotunda music in eighteenth-century Dublin* (1992) · S. Sartori, *I libretti italiani* (1990–94) · M. Sands, *The eighteenth-century pleasure gardens of Marylebone* (1987) · *The thespian dictionary, or, Dramatic biography of the eighteenth century* (1802) · S. McVeigh, *The violinist in London's concert life, 1750–1784: Felice Giardini and his contemporaries* (1989) · H. C. Robbins Landon, *Haydn in England: 1791–1795* (1976), vol. 3 of *Haydn: chronicle and works* · O. Baldwin and T. Wilson, 'Barthélémon, Maria', *The new Grove dictionary of women composers*, ed. J. A. Sadie and R. Samuel (1994) · parish register, St Margaret's, Westminster [baptism, Mary Barthélémon, 1749] · parish register, Piccadilly, St James [marriage, François-Hippolyte Barthélémon and Mary Young, 1766] · parish register, Piccadilly, St James [baptism, Cecilia Maria Barthélémon, 1767] · parish register, St Martin-in-the-Fields [burial, Mary Barthélémon, 1799]

Likenesses portrait (Isabella Young) · portrait (Esther Young)

Wealth at death Isabella Young [married name Lampe] very little: will, made 6 Dec 1759, Family Records Centre, London · Esther Young [married name Jones] very little: records of the Royal Society of Musicians, 10 Stratford Place, London · Isabella Young [married name Scott]; £240 in legacies; an annuity of £100; two other annuities of £12 each; jewels, household goods, carriage horses

Young, Alfred (1873–1940), mathematician, was born at Birchfield, near Widnes, on 16 April 1873, the son of Edward Young, a Liverpool wine merchant, and his wife, Betsey, née Glynn. He was educated at Monkton Combe School, near Bath, from where he gained a scholarship to study mathematics at Clare College, Cambridge. He matriculated in 1892, graduated as tenth wrangler in 1895, and took part two of the mathematics tripos in 1896. After lecturing at Selwyn College, Cambridge, from 1901 to 1905 he was fellow, and later bursar, at Clare, and received the degree of ScD at Cambridge in 1908. In that year he was ordained, and he served as curate in Hastings from 1908 to 1910, when he was presented by Clare to the living at Birdbrook, Halstead, Essex. He married on 20 November 1907 Edith Clara Wilson, who survived him; they had no children.

Young published twenty-seven scientific papers, the first in 1899, and the last posthumously in 1952. All but one (on electromagnetism) were on algebra. His original interest lay in the algebraic theory of invariants, an important area of nineteenth-century mathematics aiming to study properties of geometric figures which remain unchanged by projection. His first paper was on the invariant theory of quartic curves, and this led him to write his only book (with J. H. Grace), *Algebra of Invariants* of 1903.

This book synthesized the English work on invariants stemming from Arthur Cayley (1821–1895) with continental work by Paul Gordan and others; Young was the algebraist and Grace the geometer of the collaboration, and the book proved to be influential in its field.

In 1901 Young began the long series of papers on quantitative substitutional analysis which became his great mathematical achievement. He published nine papers in this series (the last appeared in 1952). In modern algebraic terminology, quantitative substitutional analysis relates the theory of groups (perhaps the most important area of algebra in both the nineteenth and twentieth centuries) and their representations, a subject then undergoing intense development at the hands of William Burnside (1852–1927), Frobenius, and Schur. Young's theory forms part of the representation theory of the symmetric groups S_n (the group of permutations of n objects), where his name is commemorated in the 'Young tableaux' of which the theory makes systematic use. The significance of his work was realized after the publication in 1928 of the third paper in the series, which provided the algebraic machinery needed for important parts of the new subject of quantum mechanics. In Hermann Weyl's classic book *Theory of Groups and Quantum Mechanics* (2nd edn, 1930) Young's work is used to study quantum numbers and the Clebsch–Gordan series, important in spectroscopy and elsewhere. His ideas have also been used in pure algebra, most notably in the work by G. James and A. Kerber, *The Representation Theory of the Symmetric Group* (1981), in combinatorial theory, probability, and statistics. *The Collected Papers of Alfred Young, 1873–1940*, edited by his pupil G. de B. Robinson, was published in 1977 by the University of Toronto Press.

Young was elected fellow of the Royal Society in 1934. Unusually for a twentieth-century mathematician, he did not make mathematics his profession. He was rector of Birdbrook from 1910 to 1940. He died on 15 December 1940 at Saffron Walden General Hospital, Essex, and was buried in the churchyard at Birdbrook, where his widow was later interred.   N. H. BINGHAM

Sources H. W. Turnbull, 'Alfred Young, 1873–1940', *Journal of the London Mathematical Society*, 16 (1941), 194–208; repr. in *The Collected papers of Alfred Young, 1873–1940*, ed. G. de B. Robinson (1977), xv–xxvii · G. de B. Robinson, *The representation theory of the symmetric group* (1981) · G. E. Andrews, *Bulletin of the American Mathematical Society*, 1 (1979), 989–97 · *CGPLA Eng. & Wales* (1941) · b. cert. · m. cert. · d. cert.

Archives Clare College, Cambridge, papers · University of Toronto, Thomas Fisher Rare Book Library, mathematical papers

Wealth at death £27,262 19s. 7d.: probate, 24 March 1941, *CGPLA Eng. & Wales*

Young, Sir Allen William (1827–1915), merchant navy officer and polar explorer, was born at Twickenham on 12 December 1827, the son of Henry Young, of Riverdale, Twickenham. After being educated at home he joined the merchant service in 1842 and rose quickly. During the Crimean War he transferred from the *Marlborough*, an East Indiaman, to the command of the troopship *Adelaide*, but remained in the merchant service. In 1857, when Francis Leopold McClintock was fitting out the yacht *Fox* in order

Sir Allen William Young (1827–1915), by Stephen Pearce, 1876

to follow up the discoveries of John Rae bearing on the fate of the expedition of Sir John Franklin, he chose Young as navigating officer. Young declined any salary and contributed £500 to the cost of the expedition. During the two years spent in following Franklin's tracks, Young made notable sledge journeys, exploring about 380 miles of new coast line, including the southern and western coasts of Prince of Wales Land and both shores of Franklin Strait. He also discovered McClintock Channel, but was unable to cross its rough ice. In 1860 he had command of the *Fox* in the north Atlantic telegraph expedition, which surveyed a telegraph route between Europe and America via the Faeroes, Iceland, and Greenland. He visited the east coast of Greenland, but, believing it to be impracticable for a cable route, did not land. He sailed on for the west coast, landed with Rae (who was in charge of the land part of the expedition), and ascended to the ice cap near Julianehåb; but he returned on deciding that a telegraph line could not be carried across Greenland. He next went to China to assist Admiral Sherard Osborn in equipping the Chinese navy, and commanded the gunboat *Kwangtung* during the Taiping uprising, 1862–4. In 1871 he was commissioner to the Maritime Congress at Naples, and in 1875 he was present at Suakin, on the Red Sea, as commissioner of the National Aid Society.

With the object of assisting the government Arctic expedition which set out in May 1875 under the command of George Strong Nares, Young took his steam yacht *Pandora*, with a crew of thirty-one men, to Baffin Bay. He tried to make the north-west passage, but was stopped by heavy ice in Peel Strait. On the return journey he picked up George Nares's dispatches from the Carey Islands, bringing home the latest news of Nares's expedition. The next year he again took the *Pandora* north, continuing his efforts to pass through the north-west passage, and in spite of great difficulties landed dispatches for Nares at Cape Isabella and Littleton Island. On his return he sighted Nares's ships homeward bound off Cape Farewell. In June 1882 he commanded the whaler *Hope*, chartered with government help, in order to search for the explorer, Benjamin Leigh Smith, who had sailed for Franz Josef Land in July of the previous year. Nares and Young were instrumental in launching the relief expedition and in August 1882 the *Hope* found Leigh Smith and his party at Matochkin Shar, on the west coast of Novaya Zemlya, which they had reached in boats after the destruction of their vessel off Franz Josef Land.

Young was knighted in 1877 for his services to Nares's expedition and was created CB in 1881 and CVO in 1903. He also held orders from the crowns of Denmark, Sweden, Austria, and the Netherlands. He was a commander in the Royal Naval Reserve (1862) and a younger brother of Trinity House. A member of the wealthy brewing family Young, he was well connected. Lillie Langtry and her husband were guests on his yacht at Cowes and he introduced her to the prince of Wales, one of his close friends.

Young died at the York Hotel, 11 Albemarle Street, London, unmarried, on 20 November 1915 after a long illness. He was buried in Brookwood cemetery, near Woking, Surrey. He wrote comparatively little and had a strong dislike of publicity. He contributed to the *Cornhill Magazine* in 1860 an account of his experiences in the *Fox* expedition in search of Franklin, and was the author of *The Cruise of the Pandora* (1876) and *The Two Voyages of the Pandora* (1879). He died leaving over £35,000 and his wealth, skill, and pleasant personality all contributed to the success of his Arctic journeys.

R. N. RUDMOSE BROWN, rev. ELIZABETH BAIGENT

Sources *The Times* (23 Nov 1915) · F. L. McClintock, *The voyage of the Fox* (1859) · T. Zeilau, *Fox-expeditionen i aaret 1860 over Faeroerne, Island og Grønland* (1861) · C. R. Markham, 'Sir Allen Young', *GJ*, 47 (1916), 34–41 · A. G. E. Jones, 'Allen Young and the voyage of the "Fox"', *Fram*, 2/1 (1985), 332–43 · *CGPLA Eng. & Wales* (1916) · *WWW* · d. cert. · Burke, *Peerage*
Archives RGS, journals, logs, and papers · Scott Polar RI · Young's Brewery, Wandsworth
Likenesses S. Pearce, oils, 1876, NPG [*see illus.*]
Wealth at death £35,069 9s. 2d.: administration, 18 Jan 1916, *CGPLA Eng. & Wales*

Young, Andrew (1807–1889), hymn writer and poet, was born in Edinburgh on 23 April 1807, the second son of David Young, an Edinburgh teacher, and his wife, Margaret Merrilees. He had a brilliant career in the arts and theological classes at Edinburgh University, where he secured Professor John Wilson's (Christopher North's) prize for the best poem on the Scottish highlands. In 1830 he was appointed by the town council of Edinburgh headmaster of Niddrie Street School, where he taught for eleven years; when he started there were 80 pupils and when he left there were 600.

In 1838 Young wrote his well-known hymn 'There is a happy land', first published in James Gall's *Sacred Songs*, and afterwards copied into hymnbooks throughout the world. The words were written to an Indian air which he heard one night played on the piano by a lady. In 1840 he became head English master of Madras College, St Andrews, from which he retired in 1853 to Edinburgh, where he was until his death superintendent of the Greenside parish sabbath school, being also actively engaged in other philanthropic work.

Young was twice married. His first wife, Maria Isabella Mivart, whom he married on 20 April 1844, died in 1847. He then married on 7 August 1851 Christina Lothian Allan, niece of Sir William Allan. Many of Young's hymns and poems were contributed to periodicals. A collected edition was published in 1876 as *The Scottish Highlands and other Poems*. Young was found dead in bed at his home, 22 Elm Row, Edinburgh, on 30 November 1889, and his remains were interred in Rosebank cemetery, Edinburgh. His second wife survived him.

GEORGE STRONACH, rev. S. R. J. BAUDRY

Sources J. Julian, ed., *A dictionary of hymnology* (1892) · *The Scotsman* (2 Dec 1889) · A. Young, *The Scottish highlands and other poems* (1876), preface · private information (1900) [Miss Young] · *IGI* · m. reg. Scot. [Maria Mivart] · m. reg. Scot. [Christina Allan] · d. cert. · *CCI* (1890)
Wealth at death £1203 1s. 9d.: confirmation, 11 March 1890, *CCI*

Young, Andrew John (1885–1971), poet and clergyman, was born on 29 April 1885 at the Highland Railway Station, Elgin, Moray, the youngest of the four children of Andrew John Young (1845–1939) and Maria (1845–1925), daughter of Robert Adams, a commercial clerk in Glasgow. His father, from Perthshire, was the respected stationmaster at Elgin, but he took employment in insurance and the family moved to Edinburgh when Andrew was one and a half. Young attended James Gillespie's School and the Royal High School, where he was distinguished as an athlete rather than a scholar. He read moral philosophy at Edinburgh University from 1903 to 1907. In Edinburgh he befriended the brother artists W. W. and S. I. Peploe, and spent two summers in France learning to appreciate church architecture. While at university his older brother, a doctor, disappeared in Singapore having probably committed various criminal acts. This greatly distressed their father, a deeply religious man, and Andrew came close to a nervous breakdown. Thereafter, pressed by his father, he prepared for the ministry in the United Free Church of Scotland at New College, Edinburgh, where John Baillie, the theologian, became a lifelong friend. Throughout these early years Andrew Young was writing poetry. Some early verses, *Songs of Night*, were published by his father in 1910.

Completing his studies in 1912, Young became an assistant at Wallace Green church in Berwick upon Tweed before obtaining a charge as minister at the United Free church at Temple in Midlothian (1914–19). Andrew had earlier met Janet Green (1883–1969), a lecturer at Jordan Hill training college in Glasgow, and they married on 8 September 1914. Their son, Andrew, was born in 1915 and their daughter, Alison, in 1922. Young, inclined to be a pacifist, worked in YMCA camps in France towards the end of the First World War. Thereafter he became minister at the Presbyterian church in Hove (1920–38), a position he secured after an inspired sermon. During the 1920s and 1930s Young wrote a succession of slim volumes of short reflective verses, seven of which were published between 1920 and 1931 by a bookseller friend, J. G. Wilson. He also wrote longer religious dialogues such as *Boaz and Ruth* (1920). His reputation as a poet of the first rank was made in the thirties with *Winter Harvest* (1933), meditations on religion and nature. While in his early works he had shown influence of Swinburne and later Georgianism, in this collection he found a distinctive voice which was enhanced by his intimate knowledge of botany. He consolidated his reputation with his *Collected Poems* (1936), and the modern mystery play *Nicodemus* (1936), with incidental music by Imogen Holst.

In the late 1930s Young shared with George Bell, bishop of Chichester, his admiration for episcopalianism. He and Bell, who was very interested in modern poetry, were brought together in connection with a memorial to the poet Edward Thomas. Early in 1939 Young converted to the Church of England and in 1941 he obtained the rural parish of Stonegate, Sussex, where he remained until his retirement in 1959. He was made a canon of Chichester Cathedral (1948), and thus had a living at Yapton near Arundel until his death.

An amateur botanist, it was said that Young had seen for himself practically every British plant. He shared his highly specialized botanical knowledge in two entrancing books which illuminate both the man and his poems: *A Prospect of Flowers* (1945) and *A Retrospect of Flowers* (1950). They describe the extraordinary trouble he took to see individual species. He might plan holidays to coincide with the flowering of a particularly rare plant, or delay an appointment to see an interesting flower, as he explained in 'Spiked Rampion':

> At Uckfield; three good miles to walk
> Watch creeping close on one o'clock;
> Why did I linger in that lane?

Young's knowledge of and regard for the natural landscape of Britain formed the basis for the notable *A Prospect of Britain* (1956). Another book, *The Poet and the Landscape* (1962), and an entrancing series of prose poems, *The New Polyolbion* (1967), further these topographical themes.

Young's nature poems are remarkable: they are usually both concise and thought-provoking, yet striking in their range. They are about all kinds of flora and fauna, and about places he loved throughout the length and breadth of Britain, from *The Falls of Glomach* ('Rain drifts forever in this place') to a *Cornish Flower Farm*:

> Here where the cliff rises so high
> The sea below fills half the sky.

His poetry was also often about suffering and death, and the culmination of his religious verse was *Into Hades* (1952) and *A Traveller in Time* (1958), two longer poems, which appeared separately at first, but which were brought together later as *Out of the World and Back* (1958). Iain Crichton Smith, the poet and critic, found some of

Young's early work clumsy, but spoke of a fresh, precious 'union of precision, wit and strangeness' in his lyrics, 'essentially and idiosyncratically Young' (Crichton Smith).

Young's circle of friends included fellow poets Christopher Fry, Ted Walker, John Arlott, and Leonard Clark, his literary executor, who edited his verse and published, *Prospect of a Poet* (1957), a book of tributes to him. He was honoured with an honorary degree of LLD by the University of Edinburgh in 1951, the Royal Society of Literature conferred an honorary fellowship on him, and he received the Queen's medal for poetry in 1952.

Young, who was physically sturdy and powerful, was described as being 'mistaken for a farmer up in town for the day'. He was also 'rather a paradox, at once an uncommunicative man and a man of wit'. He was always an eloquent preacher and able to socialize as ministers must, but he was by nature both solitary and taciturn. He enjoyed being an English clergyman, yet he remained Scottish in other ways, rather Calvinistic, for example, and one who never lost his Scottish accent. His wife, who had forgone a promising career in education, faithfully supported him, but Andrew's temper, a product perhaps of self-doubt, sometimes placed a strain on family relationships. Yet before Janet Young died on 12 March 1969 after a difficult illness, Andrew faithfully looked after her. Thereafter he preferred to live alone, causing his family much anxiety. After a fall he was obliged to enter various nursing homes, and he died peacefully at Ravenna House, Bognor Regis, on 25 November 1971. His funeral service was conducted at Chichester Cathedral. He was cremated and his ashes were scattered in the cathedral grounds. Young's poetry and his essays place him in the highest class of writers about the countryside, but few such writers display affection for the qualities of such very different landscapes as Andrew Young. It is perhaps to his disadvantage that he was strictly neither a Scottish nor an English author, but he was British in a sense that few are. His daughter Alison and son-in-law Edward Lowbury wrote an affectionate and authoritative critical biography, *To Shirk No Idleness*, published in 1997. Memorial plaques were unveiled at the parish church in Stonegate and, on 1 October 1981, on the site of his birthplace in Elgin.

LOUIS STOTT

Sources E. Lowbury and A. Young, *To shirk no idleness* (1997) · I. Crichton Smith, 'The poetry of Andrew Young', *Scottish Review*, 37 (1985), 72–6 · L. Clark, *Andrew Young: prospect of a poet* (1957) · L. Clark, introduction, in A. Young, *Complete poems* (1974) · [J. Wakeman], ed., *World authors, 1950–70* (1975) · A. Young, *The new Polyolbion* (1967) [with an introductory account of the poet's early days] · *The Times* (29 Nov 1971) · b. cert. · m. cert. · d. cert.

Archives bishop's palace, Chichester, corresp. · NL Scot., notebooks and papers · priv. coll., letters | Bodl. Oxf., letters to Rowland Watson · JRL, letters to Norman Nicholson · LUL, corresp with T. S. Moore · LUL, letters to Thomas Sturge Moore and Mrs Sturge Moore · NYPL, Berg collection, letters to L. Clark [typescripts] · Ransom HRC, letters to Clifford Bax, Richard Church, Geoffrey Grigson, John Masefield, Neville Braybrooke, and Jocelyn Brooke · Royal Society of Literature, London, letters to Royal Society of Literature · U. Reading L., corresp. with Jonathan Cape Ltd ·

University of British Columbia, Vancouver, letters to John Betjeman | SOUND British Council, *Contemporary poets reading their own poems: Andrew Young*, tape 375 · *The poet speaks* [10], Argo RG 583 Mono

Likenesses photographs, repro. in Lowbury and Young, *To shirk no idleness*

Wealth at death £34,709: probate, 26 May 1972, *CGPLA Eng. & Wales*

Young, Andrew McLaren (1913–1975), art historian, was born on 19 September 1913, at the manse, Southend, Argyll, the eldest child and the only son of three children of the Revd Robert Comingo Young (1882–1946), Presbyterian minister, and his wife, Olga Parsons (1890–1939). From 1926 to 1930 McLaren Young was educated at Jamaica College, in Kingston, where his father was a missionary, and his speech always retained a distinctive Caribbean drawl. Later he attended George Watson's College, Edinburgh (1931–2), and the University of Edinburgh (1932–8). Originally intending to follow his father into the ministry, under David Talbot Rice's influence he became interested in the history of art, and although matriculating in 1933, left in 1938 without taking his degree. After a year's temporary attachment at the Tate Gallery, he was commissioned in the King's Own Yorkshire light infantry in 1939, served in Burma and north Africa, being wounded in Sicily. He was demobilized as a captain in 1945. He had married Margaret (Margie) Heath Halse (b. 1919) in 1940; they had a daughter, Caroline (b. 1944), and a son, Robert (b. 1951).

From 1946 to 1949 McLaren Young was assistant curator at the Barber Institute of Fine Arts, University of Birmingham. Then, in 1949, he was appointed senior lecturer at the University of Glasgow, with the task of establishing an art history department. He fostered high academic standards, and in 1965 the university awarded him an honorary MA on his appointment as Richmond professor of fine art. He began his life's work on James McNeill Whistler while at Glasgow, where the Birnie Philip collection—given by Whistler's sister-in-law—formed an important adjunct both to the eighteenth-century foundation collection of William Hunter and to two fine print collections. McLaren Young also planned, and fund-raised for, the new Hunterian Art Gallery, demonstrating his flair as a museum curator. The Whistler and Charles Rennie Mackintosh exhibitions which he organized in 1960 and 1968 respectively were models of scholarship and sensitive re-creations of period ambience. An inspiring leader, McLaren Young was widely read and generous towards younger scholars. Wittily caustic, he was a large man in every sense: one moment he could explode in fury, and the next, invite one to share a fine malt whisky.

On 4 February 1975 McLaren Young collapsed from a heart attack at the Royal Academy J. M. W. Turner Exhibition, and died on the way to hospital. He was buried at Keil Com Keil, Southend, Argyll. His memorials are the Whistler oil paintings *catalogue raisonné*, finished by three colleagues and published in 1980, and the new Hunterian Art Gallery, much enriched by acquisitions and benefactions secured by him.   DENNIS FARR

Sources personal knowledge (2004) · private information (2004) [archivist, U. Edin.; secretary of George Watson's College; University of Glasgow personnel services; M. H. Young] · *Who's who in art* (1968) · H. Miles, *The Times* (12 Feb 1975) · D. Farr, *Burlington Magazine*, 117 (1975), 487

Archives U. Glas., Archives and Business Records Centre

Likenesses photographs, priv. coll.

Young, Anthony (*bap.* 1683, *d.* 1747). *See under* Young, William (*d.* 1662).

Young, Sir Aretas William (1777/8–1835), army officer and colonial governor, entered the earl of Portmore's regiment as an ensign on 3 September 1795, aged seventeen. He purchased a lieutenancy in the 13th foot on 28 November 1795, and a company on 15 September 1796. He served with the 13th in Ireland during the 1798 uprising, and in Egypt in 1801. Between 1804 and 1806 he acted as aide-de-camp to General Henry Edward Fox at Gibraltar and in Sicily. On 17 December 1807 he was promoted major in the 97th, with which he served in the Peninsular campaigns of 1808–10 and 1811, and served at the battles of Vimeiro, Talavera, and Busaco, at Redinha, the taking of Olivença and the first siege of Badajoz. Whenever the 4th division moved, the light companies were entrusted to his charge, and during a part of the retreat to the lines of the Torres Vedras in 1810, those companies were embodied under his command as a light battalion.

Depleted, the 97th was ordered to England, and Young was promoted, on 25 January 1813, lieutenant-colonel in the 3rd West India regiment, stationed in Trinidad. With five companies he joined the expedition against Guadeloupe in 1815, and received one of the badges of the order of merit presented by Louis XVIII. After his return to Trinidad he was chosen by Sir James Leith to command the troops in Grenada. On his being ordered back to Trinidad in August 1816, the council of assembly of Grenada presented him with a sword. In 1820, during the absence of Sir Ralph James Woodford, he administered the government of Trinidad for four months, on the termination of which he was requested to continue as a member of the council. During a second absence of Woodford he filled the office of governor for nearly two years, and on his resignation in February 1823 received the thanks of every section of the community. In 1825 the 3rd West India regiment was disbanded, and in January 1826 Young was appointed to the newly created office of his majesty's protector of slaves in Demerara. He retired from the army by sale of his commission on 13 May, with permission to retain the local rank of lieutenant-colonel. On 25 July 1831 he was gazetted lieutenant-governor of Prince Edward Island, Canada, and on 9 July 1834 he was knighted. He married Sarah Cox of Coolcliffe, Wexford; Sir Henry Edward Fox *Young were their son. Young died at Government House, Prince Edward Island, on 1 December 1835, and was buried at the new English church.

E. I. CARLYLE, *rev.* JAMES LUNT

Sources *United Service Journal*, 1 (1836), 380–83 · L. M. Fraser, *History of Trinidad*, 2 (1896)

Young, Arthur (1693–1759), Church of England clergyman, was one of two sons of Bartholomew Young (*d.* 12

Aug 1724), landowner, of Bradfield Combust in Suffolk, and his wife, Katharine. He was admitted to Pembroke College, Cambridge, on 22 January 1711, graduating LLB in 1716 and proceeding LLD in 1728. In 1719 he was instituted to the rectories of Bradfield Combust and Bradfield St Clare. On 27 June 1746 he was installed a prebendary of Canterbury. In 1748 he was presented to the vicarage of Exning in Suffolk and received a dispensation to hold it with Bradfield St Clare. He was also chaplain to Arthur Onslow, speaker of the House of Commons. He married Anne Lucretia (1706–1785), daughter of John de Cousmaker of Weybridge in Surrey; they had two sons, John and Arthur, and a daughter, Eliza Maria, who married John Tomlinson of East Barnet in Hertfordshire. The elder son, John Young, fellow of Eton College, broke his neck in 1786 while hunting with George III. The younger son was Arthur *Young (1741–1820), the renowned agriculturist, who became secretary to the board of agriculture.

Young was the author of *An historical dissertation on idolatrous corruptions in religion from the beginning of the world, and of the methods taken by divine providence in reforming them* (2 vols., 1734). This copious text seeks to explain the rise of Judaism and Christianity as divinely instituted religions which were opposed to the error-strewn religions of idolatry. *A Dissertation on the Gospel Demoniacks* (1760) was published posthumously and had been written much earlier as a response to the reply of Richard Smalbroke, bishop of St David's, to Thomas Woolston's *Discourse on the Miracles of our Saviour* (1727–9). Young's *Dissertation* argued for a somewhat naturalistic explanation for both the condition and the cure of the gospel demoniacs, and this seems to have been the principal reason for leaving it to be published posthumously, some time after the earlier controversy to which it was a contribution had died down.

Young died on 26 June 1759 at Bradfield Combust, where he had inherited from his father an estate of about 200 acres, and where he was buried. His wife survived him.

E. I. CARLYLE, *rev.* B. W. YOUNG

Sources BL, Add. MSS 19156, fol. 336; 19166, fol. 277; 15556, fol. 201 · Venn, *Alum. Cant.* · *Fasti Angl.* (Hardy) · *GM*, 1st ser., 29 (1759), 346 · D. M. Lewis, ed., *The Blackwell dictionary of evangelical biography, 1730–1860*, 2 vols. (1995) · *IGI*
Archives BL, Davy's Suffolk Collection, Add. MSS 19156, fol. 336; 19166, fol. 277 · BL, Add. MS 15556, fol. 201

Young, Arthur (1741–1820), agricultural reformer and writer, was born at Whitehall in London on 11 September 1741. He was the younger son of Arthur Young (1693–1759), rector of Bradfield Combust, near Bury St Edmunds, Suffolk, and chaplain to Arthur Onslow, speaker of the House of Commons. His mother, Anne Lucretia (1706–1785), daughter of John de Cousmaker, brought her husband so large a dowry as to require that the manor and lands of Bradfield Hall, the small estate which the Youngs had owned since 1672, be settled on herself.

Early years and education The youngest of three children, Young was sent to a school at Lavenham which his father had attended. The son later described it as 'that wretched

Arthur Young (1741–1820), by John Russell, 1794

place' where he failed to receive a good grounding in the classics (*Autobiography*, 7). In 1758 he left school and was apprenticed to Messrs Robertson, wine merchants of King's Lynn. It was planned that subsequently he should enter the London merchants firm of Messrs Tomlinson, since his sister, Eliza Maria, had married John Tomlinson. However, her early death in childbirth put an end to the scheme. In later life Young greatly regretted not having gone to university (as his elder brother, John, had done), and since he found trade detestable, thought the £400 paid by his father for his apprenticeship wasted. Nevertheless, as an apprentice Young made the most of life in King's Lynn, patronizing its theatre and assembly rooms and cutting a figure at town balls. He had already begun to collect books while at school, and in his spare time produced his first pamphlet, *The Theatre of the Present War in North America*. It was published in 1758 when he was seventeen, and the publisher paid him in books to the value of £10. The pamphlet received favourable comment from the *Gentleman's Magazine*, but the same journal made severe criticism of his second pamphlet, *The Present State of Affairs at Home and Abroad*.

In 1761, having completed his apprenticeship, Young left King's Lynn for London, where he began at his own expense a monthly magazine, the *Universal Museum*. This he soon abandoned after Samuel Johnson, having declined to write for it, advised him to persuade the booksellers to take it on. Two years later he suffered a haemorrhage of the lung and was sent to the Hotwells, Bristol, to recuperate. There he met Major-General Sir Charles Howard, who offered him a commission in his cavalry regiment, but although Young was willing to accept, the proposal was vetoed by his mother, mainly because of his weak health.

Early career in agriculture Young was now twenty-two, and had experience only of trade, which he disliked, and of publishing, in which he had failed. His lack of a university education ruled out the church, and without other prospects he now made the key decision of his life, turning to a career in farming when his mother offered him the tenancy of a farm at Bradfield. He devoted his energies towards gaining a command of agriculture, collecting many books on the subject and reading well-known authors such as Samuel Hartlib, Jethro Tull, H. L. Duhamel du Monceau, and Walter Harte. While farming at Bradfield from 1763 to 1767 Young was again tempted to take up his pen and ventured into his new field with only one year's experience of farming. His letters to the *Museum Rusticum* were written between October 1764 and April 1765, and concerned such topics as the importance of making experiments, drainage, and the advantages of touring Europe to observe different methods of cultivation, urging the Society of Arts to support the plan. Through these letters Young became acquainted with the Revd Walter Harte, whose *Essays in Husbandry* had been published in 1764. Harte recommended Young to collect his letters and publish them with further additions as a book, and this was the origin of *The farmer's letters to the people of England ... to which are added Sylvae, or, Occasional tracts on husbandry and rural oeconomics*. Published in 1767 the book supported the bounty on the export of corn and introduced some of his enduring themes: the cultivation of waste lands, enclosure as a preliminary to improvement, and the superiority of large farms. While at Bradfield Young conducted and kept records of numerous experiments which he later incorporated in his *Elements of Agriculture*, a vast work which has never been published.

Marriage and family On 1 July 1765 Young married Martha Allen (1740–1815), daughter of a wealthy King's Lynn family. They had four children: Mary (b. 1766), Elizabeth (b. 1767), Arthur (b. 1769), and Martha Anne (b. 1783)—Young's favourite, dubbed Bobbin—but only Mary and Arthur outlived their parents. Young's marriage was happy for the first two years but subsequently his wife came to oppose his all-absorbing interest in agriculture. She accompanied him, however, on his northern tour of 1768 and joined him during his stay in Ireland in 1778. No doubt Young's frequent absences from home, his flirtations, and his expenditure on agricultural tours and experiments contributed to her hostility. She appears to have suffered mental deterioration and her surviving letters reveal confusion of mind and, at one time, an almost pathological dislike of Bradfield. Visitors described violent disputes and quarrels, and how Young treated her overbearing temper with 'calm, easy contempt' (*Early Diary of Frances Burney*, 1.114–15). According to a French visitor, François de la Rochefoucauld, who was at Bradfield in

1784, Mrs Young was 'hideously swarthy' and looked 'exactly like a devil', tormenting her children and servants and showing ill temper towards visitors (Marchand, 38). Young himself made quite a different impression as extremely good-humoured and never out of spirits, eager to show off his farm and its implements and to share his ideas. Martha Young died in 1815, and Young paid an extraordinary tribute to her memory in a plaque placed in Bradfield church, describing her only as 'the great-granddaughter of John Allen, esq., of Lyng House in the county of Norfolk, the first person, according to the Comte de Boulainvilliers, who there used marl'.

Farming and writing in Hertfordshire Late in 1767 Young and his family left Bradfield owing to friction between his wife and his mother. He advertised in the newspapers for a farm, and the journeys of inspection he made at this time formed the basis of his slim volume *A Six Weeks' Tour through the Southern Counties of England and Wales* (1768). He first took Sampford Hall, a farm of 300 acres in north-western Essex, but was obliged to relinquish it immediately when a relation failed to advance a loan for stocking it. He settled in 1768 at Bradmore Farm, North Mymms, near Hatfield in Hertfordshire. His farming failure there he ascribed to its terrible soil of 'vitriolic gravel', which he mistook on seeing it in an unusually favourable season, but his continuing financial problems also resulted from his spending money on experiments, and his frequent absences for long periods. He thought of emigrating to America but his wife opposed the idea. Instead, he resorted to his pen and based two of his most important books on tours made at this time, one to the northern counties of England, and the other to the eastern counties. In 1773 he took advantage of his proximity to London to become a parliamentary reporter for the *Morning Post*, which meant spending most of the week in London and walking home to his farm at weekends. His pamphlet *A Letter to Lord Clive*, advising his lordship to invest his Indian fortune in becoming an improving landlord, appeared in 1767 and was followed, among lesser works, by *A Six Months' Tour through the North of England* (4 vols., 1769), *The Farmer's Guide in Hiring and Stocking Farms* (2 vols., 1770), *Rural Economy, or, Essays on the Practical Parts of Husbandry* (2 vols., 1770), *A Course of Experimental Agriculture* (2 vols., 1770), *The Farmer's Tour through the East of England* (4 vols., 1771), *The Farmer's Kalendar* (1771; this book went through ten editions in Young's lifetime), *Observations on the Present State of the Waste Lands of Great Britain* (1773), and *Political arithmetic. Containing observations on the present state of Great Britain and the principles of her policy in the encouragement of agriculture* (1774). The *Course of Experimental Agriculture* Young later thought to be immature and unsound, and he bought up and destroyed all the copies he could lay hands on.

The northern and eastern tours, each covering great areas of the country, have proved valuable historical sources down to the present. Young's procedure was to announce his journey in advance in the newspapers and so meet improving landlords and leading farmers along his route, with the result that much of his material concerned the ideas and experiments they were making. In the middle 1770s Young was also active in the Society of Arts, which in 1765 and 1766 had awarded him prizes for cultivating madder. In 1769 he also won two gold medals for his papers on hogs and coleseed, and in 1773 he was elected chairman of the society's committee on agriculture. Young was also elected FRS.

While at North Mymms, Young made lifelong friends among the family of Charles Burney, the musician, whom he had first met at King's Lynn. As a widower, Burney had in 1767 married as his second wife Mrs Arthur Young's older sister, the widow Mrs Stephen Allen. Fanny, one of Burney's daughters, was in later years a frequent visitor to Bradfield and her diary recorded many glimpses of Young's life there.

Visit to Ireland By 1776 Young felt he needed a new field of interest, and he decided on a visit to Ireland, a project he had been thinking of for some time. Armed with letters of introduction, he travelled widely, returning home in October of that year 'without a shilling' (*Autobiography*, 81–2). However, by the following summer he was able to return in the capacity of resident agent to Lord Kingsborough, with responsibility for supervising a huge estate at Michelstown to the north of Cork. He now gave up Bradmore Farm, but his new career proved to be short-lived. He was at Michelstown for only a year, although in that time he set on foot ambitious improvements to the estate. The cause of his leaving the post so quickly is obscure, but he returned to Bradfield on 1 January 1779 to work on his *A Tour in Ireland* with an annuity of £72 a year in lieu of his arrears of salary. The book appeared in 1780, was well received at the time, and has since become a valuable source as one of the few accounts of conditions in Ireland at this time. Among other subjects Young had much to say on commercial policy and the activities of the Dublin Society; and in addition Young attacked the practice of subletting land to middlemen and made some interesting observations on the living conditions of the poor.

Life at Bradfield Farming again at Bradfield, Young was now famous as an agricultural expert in Britain and Europe but his financial situation was little better than before he went to Ireland and he thought again of going to America. However, he settled at Bradfield as the occupier of his mother's home farm and entered into the life of a gentleman farmer, spending each winter in London, when he met his friends and attended parliament, the Royal Society, Society of Arts, and the opera. After his great flurry of books in 1769–74, the nine years from 1775 to 1783 were, for him, remarkably unproductive, seeing only the *Tour in Ireland* and a pamphlet on building ships for the Royal Navy. Young's financial position improved substantially in the course of the 1780s. An aunt who died in 1782 left him her house, two farms, a horse and carriage, and an annuity of about £150. The aunt indicated that the annuity would have been greater had she not been offended by Young's wife. The death of his mother in 1785 and of his brother in the following year brought him the ownership

of the whole Bradfield estate. His brother, the Revd John Young, was thirteen years older than Arthur Young, and was a fellow at Eton College, chaplain to the king, and prebendary of Worcester. He suffered a broken neck in a fall while hunting on a new horse with the king.

Now well established as master of Bradfield, Young further indulged his taste for agricultural experiments, some of them of a bizarre character. After seeking advice from Joseph Priestley, he attempted to ascertain the value of 'phlogiston' as a food of plants, tried the effects of expelling air from the soil, and attempted to discover whether electricity affected plants. It seems very likely that Young devoted so much of his energy to his experiments, his correspondence, and to making tours and visiting friends, that he had little time to spare for the proper supervision of his farm. This is the impression left by the accounts of distinguished visitors who were drawn by his name to see his farming. While at North Mymms his visitors included Lord Darlington and Prince Massalsky, bishop of Vilna, who inspected his 8 acres of experimental crops, his newly introduced Suffolk swing-plough, and his collection of implements. The celebrated Northumberland breeder George Culley came to Bradfield in 1784 but in his disappointment concluded that 'people that devote their time to writing cannot act or execute; his sheep are scabbed, his cattle ill chose and worse managed, in short he exhibits a sad picture of mismanagement' (Culley MSS, ZCU 1, 18, 44). Disappointment was also expressed in the comments of other expert visitors, for example, John Boys, a large farmer from east Kent, who was at Bradfield in 1793 and was there again the following year in company with John Ellman, the pioneer breeder of the new Southdown sheep. Nevertheless, Boys found much to interest him. He took particular note of Young's novel practice of stall-feeding cattle on chicory, and his great collection of ploughing implements. He noted also Young's cultivated grasses and his sheep, which included the Spanish Merino ram presented to Young in admiration by the king, and his cross-breeding experiments with Southdowns, Norfolks, and Bakewell's New Leicesters. On the second visit to Bradfield, wrote Boys, they joined such a gathering as 'was perhaps never before collected from so great a distance, most of the party coming more than a hundred miles, and one gentleman, Mr Colhoun, to wait upon Mr Young has travelled 170 miles'. The party walked round Young's farm before dinner, and observed his Dishley rams and the 'collection of grasses in his experiment ground'. They saw how Young used only a single pair of oxen, driven by one man, to turn a stiff soil, for which a Sussex or Weald of Kent farmer would have required at least eight oxen, with perhaps a horse or two and two drivers, 'and not plough much more, in a given time, than Mr Young does with his man and a pair of oxen' (Young, *Annals of Agriculture*, 19.89–93; 21.75–7).

It appears that Young's more rational experiments were of considerable value, and this is borne out by the requests for seed and implements that he received from correspondents. By the 1780s Young's reputation had so grown that numbers of visitors, experts, and students were drawn to Bradfield from all over Europe. He was elected to numerous learned societies at home and abroad. So encouraged, in 1784 he launched his new periodical, *Annals of Agriculture*, a project which he had had in view for some years. It was intended, among other things, to put before the public the views and experience of the foremost agriculturists, but Young was bitterly disappointed in its sales. Although he managed to keep it going for thirty-two years until 1815 and included many of his own tours in it, he was constantly frustrated that it did not achieve a larger circulation than a few hundred copies. An immense amount of labour was involved in editing so large a periodical work and Young was fortunate in being able to call on the assistance of his friend the Revd John Symonds, professor of modern history at Cambridge and a keen experimental farmer, who lived close to Bury St Edmunds and thus within a few miles of Bradfield. Both Symonds and Young were involved in local society, becoming friends of the duke of Grafton, whose mansion at Euston lay to the north of Bury, while at Ickworth, a few miles to the south of the town, a select group of intellectuals, including Young and Symonds, dined regularly with Frederick Hervey, fourth earl of Bristol and bishop of Derry.

Young was an advocate of vocational forms of education, especially for the sons of landowners. He warmly supported the University of Edinburgh's proposal in 1789 to endow a chair of agriculture, asking: 'Why not a Professor of Agriculture in every University?' (Young, *Annals of Agriculture*, 11.367–8). Holding that a proper understanding of farming could be gained only by practical application, he believed that a gentleman's son should not go to university but be placed with a substantial farmer for a period of ten years—a shorter span would hardly be sufficient to learn the business properly. However, Young's own son went up to Cambridge in 1789 and was supported there for four years at a cost of £100 a year. Against Young's wishes he took holy orders, but he also showed marked agricultural interests, writing the two reports on Sussex for the board of agriculture, published in 1793 and 1808, and deputizing for his father in making a very prolonged agricultural survey in Russia from 1805 to 1814 for Tsar Alexander.

Travels in France, Catalonia, and Italy Between 1787 and 1790 Young made three lengthy visits to France, Catalonia, and northern Italy, which resulted in his very interesting and most historically valuable book, *Travels during the years 1787, 1788 and 1789, undertaken more particularly with a view of ascertaining the cultivation, wealth, resources and national prosperity of the kingdom of France*; this work was later generally known as *Travels in France*. It was published in 1793 and reprinted in various versions in 1889, 1915, and 1929, and appeared in French in 1931. The first tour, made between May and November 1787, covered a route of 2200 miles in France, together with a long excursion into Catalonia. The second journey, between August and October 1788, was the shortest but still extended to as much as 1200 miles through the western provinces of Normandy, Brittany, and Anjou. The third visit, between June 1789 and January

1790, encompassed about 2100 miles in France besides a lengthy journey through northern Italy. The interest of *Travels in France* is enhanced by the accounts of lands that were for the most part strange to Young and unknown to many of his readers. His commentaries, in consequence, were broad in scope, and in addition to farming, described aspects—the scenery, roads, inns, manners, and the signs of wealth or poverty—which in England he would have taken for granted or passed over in a very few words. His visits to France took place in a period which saw the beginnings of the revolution, and this gives his first-hand accounts an importance which is almost as vital now as it was to those who lived through these years. Indeed, historians on both sides of the channel have drawn heavily on Young for his view of France at this critical juncture.

Young's first journey arose from an invitation from his friend Maximilien de Lazowski, whom he had met at Bradfield. Lazowski was tutor to the sons of the duc de Liancourt, and he asked Young to join François de la Rochefoucauld and himself on a visit to the spa Bagnères de Luchon in the Pyrenees. Proceeding at a leisurely pace of some 30 miles a day, the party left Paris and travelled south via Orléans, Limoges, and Toulouse. Young was all admiration for the roads and he found the inns superior to English ones in food and beds if not in servants: the maids at Souillac, with his usual hyperbole, were 'walking dunghills' (Young, *Travels in France*, 1.36–7). The farming was generally backward and he noted some remarkable signs of poverty. While at Bagnères, Young and Lazowski embarked on a journey across the Pyrenees into Catalonia. Braving precipitous roads and primitive inns, they were relieved to reach the civilization of Barcelona. Their return northwards was along the coast to Perpignan. There they parted, Young to make a lengthy detour to see on his own the regions of Roussillon and Languedoc. He made his way to Bagnères via Montpellier, Nîmes, and Carcassonne, enduring heat, flies, and verminous inns. On the return to Paris, Young travelled separately for part of the way in order to see more of the country, riding through Bayonne, Auch, Bordeaux, Tours, and Blois. He spent some time in Paris, which he found more expensive than London, and he stayed also as a guest at the family estate of the duc de Liancourt. In Paris he was thrilled to meet A. L. Lavoisier, the celebrated chemist, and a number of other scientists. In discussing politics, Young found his acquaintances much in fear of the near approach of national bankruptcy and of revolutionary changes.

On his second journey in France in 1788 Young went alone and did not revisit Paris. He travelled in simple style on his own horse, with his luggage in a 'cloak-bag' slung behind him. Within a week of starting, his mare began to go blind, but he carried on and brought himself and mare safely back to Bradfield after an absence of three months. Staying at an inn the night after Charles James Fox and a female companion had lodged there, he could not help comparing his blind mare with Fox's post-chaise, waiting-woman, valet, and French courier, 'but I have been doing all my life and he has been talking' (BL, Add. MSS 35126, fol. 427). His route took him through Rouen, Le Havre, Caen, and Cherbourg, where he inspected the harbour improvements and visited a glass factory. Crossing Brittany from Rennes to Brest he was appalled by the poverty: Combourg was 'one of the most brutal filthy places that can be seen' (Young, *Travels in France*, 1.174). The contrasting luxury of Nantes was associated with such a spirit of liberty as to make him think that 'the American Revolution has laid the foundation of another in France, if the government does not take care of itself' (ibid.). He returned via Angers, Le Mans, and Rouen, with an excursion to La Roche Guyon to visit his friends the duc de la Rochefoucauld and the duchesse d'Anville.

On his third visit to France, Young arrived in Paris in June 1789, and through his friends, the Rochefoucauld–Liancourt family, he met a number of prominent figures in the rapidly changing political scene including the duc d'Orléans and the Abbé Sieyès. He attended meetings of the third estate and purchased quantities of revolutionary pamphlets (which now form one of the treasures of the Goldsmiths' Library of the University of London). Noting the violent tone of the pamphlets and the speeches he heard, he predicted the coming of a civil war and the creation of a republic. However, he did not forget the main purpose of his visit, and setting out in a purchased one-horse cabriolet, he travelled in a new direction, eastwards towards Strasbourg. As before, he discussed farming matters with acquaintances among the landowners and farmers along the way. The striking differences he found in the working people of France and England Young ascribed, as with much else, to bad government. At Strasbourg he heard the news of the fall of the Bastille, which he recognized as opening the way to either a new constitution or 'inextricable confusions and civil war' (Young, *Travels in France*, 1.293). He witnessed the sack of the city's hôtel de ville and was shocked that the troops did not restore order and even joined in the looting.

The next stage of Young's journey was south-westwards towards Toulon and was made hazardous by peasant uprisings and rumours of outrages and Parisian plots. In one town he found the inhabitants 'very menacing' (Young, *Travels in France*, 1.305), but escaped by making an impromptu speech on the steps of his inn, stating that in England it was the nobility rather than the commoners who bore the brunt of taxation. At Dijon his friends made it possible for him to obtain the passport which had become essential to a traveller, but at Thueyts, south of Clermont Ferrand, he was arrested by armed national guards. His enquiries about the farming had led to the suspicion that he was an agent of the aristocracy, sent to double the taxes. At Toulon he sold his horse and cabriolet as he was told that it would not be practicable to take them into Italy. Consequently, he walked to the border with a peasant woman whose ass he hired for his luggage.

Young was in Italy from 16 September to 25 December. He found the inns to be generally better than in France, and living far cheaper; but the roads were much poorer

while the horses and carriages offered for hire were frightful. Venice was delightfully cheap and he had his own gondolier, but the journey from Venice to Bologna took five days on a barge, the food was disgusting, and he was packed in at night with a dozen other people in a tiny cabin. However, he enjoyed two weeks in Florence with pleasant company and the hospitality of the ambassador, Lord John Augustus Hervey, as well as finding a greater interest there in scientific agriculture than in other Italian cities. By January 1790 he was back in Paris where he was again engrossed by the revolution. He saw the royal family under the watch of the national guard, and attended the national assembly to hear Mirabeau. He also found time to collect more pamphlets and copy some of the public records.

Young's experiences in France brought about a permanent change in his political views. From being a liberal and a reformer, by 1792 he had become an opponent of the revolution and a conservative in English matters. He was highly critical of the *ancien régime* but, equally, he attacked the excesses of the revolution, and now he was fearful of the consequences of reform in England, necessary though it was. In France he had seen destitute aristocrats sheltering in inns from the destruction of their châteaux, and he now received the dreadful news of the murder of his friend the duc de la Rochefoucauld, while another friend, the duc de Liancourt, had taken refuge as an *emigré* in Bury St Edmunds. What was perhaps his most influential pamphlet, *The Example of France a Warning to Britain*, appeared in 1793 and reflected his changed views.

In the recent past, however, during the intervals between his French visits, Young's former liberalism had been very evident. He took up the anti-slavery cause and wrote several articles on the subject in the *Annals*, and he also joined Sir Joseph Banks in leading the opposition to a bill intended to strengthen the prohibition on the export of wool. His journeys in England included visits to leading farmers and breeders and he published a long report on Sussex in the *Annals*. In 1790 he was involved in the agitation over a new corn law, and spent the autumn of that year recovering from a serious illness. Subsequently he was in correspondence with George Washington about farming in Pennsylvania and Virginia; the correspondence was later published as *Letters from his Excellency George Washington to Arthur Young* (1801). He also made a tour in the midlands, spending several days with Robert Bakewell, the celebrated breeder, followed by a visit to John Ellman.

The board of agriculture A new stage in Young's career began in 1793 with the establishment, with government support, of the board of agriculture. The idea for such a board had originated with William Marshall, the distinguished agricultural writer, who was a critic of Young. The board, however, was dominated by Young's friends, and aided by his shift to conservative views, he was regarded as the most suitable person to be the board's secretary, an appointment bitterly resented by Marshall. The latter's hostility became even greater when the board decided to commission a series of agricultural reports of individual counties, rather than of regions as Marshall advocated. Subsequently Marshall set out to criticize the reports at length, which he did in his *Review and Abstracts of the Reports to the Board of Agriculture* (1818).

The first editions of the county reports appeared between 1793 and 1795, followed by fuller revised versions between 1798 and 1817. The reports were uneven in quality and length but constitute nevertheless an invaluable source for farming practices at the end of the eighteenth century and the period of the Napoleonic wars. No fewer than six of the reports were written by Young himself: Suffolk (1794); Lincolnshire (1799); Hertfordshire (1804); Norfolk (1804); Essex (1807); and Oxfordshire (1809). Young's report on Lincolnshire earned him the enmity of Thomas Stone, a well-known surveyor, who had written the first version in 1794 and felt insulted not to have been asked to write the revised report. Stone had suffered a harsh review by Young of an earlier paper, and he now repaid that attack by publishing a damning review of Young's report.

Religious conversion As secretary to the board of agriculture Young now spent most of the year in London, though he still found time not only to write his county reports and produce the *Annals* but also to produce further pamphlets, particularly on his proposal for forming a voluntary yeoman cavalry for providing internal defence against a French invasion. He suffered the worst personal blow of his life in 1797 when his favourite daughter, Martha Anne (Bobbin), died from tuberculosis. His second daughter, Elizabeth, had died three years earlier from the same disease, but it was the loss of his youngest daughter that affected him more deeply, especially as he held himself partly to blame for her death. At this time he developed a close friendship with William Wilberforce, and it was under his influence that Young, never previously much interested in religion, experienced a remarkable conversion. From this time until his death, nearly twenty-three years later, his views and interests showed great changes.

In the past Young had not expressed much sympathy with poverty and suffering, although he had been much moved by the distress he saw in France. He now began to do what he could to help the poor of his neighbourhood, and some of his publications were directly concerned with the problem of rural poverty which had recently been intensified by a rapid growth of population and the high food prices of the war period. He investigated the injurious effects that had followed from many of the enclosures of open fields and commons, and he proposed measures to provide the poor with land, a remedy which he believed would restore their independence. His 1801 pamphlet *An Inquiry into the Propriety of Applying Wastes to the Maintenance and Support of the Poor* made suggestions of this kind, and his 1804 report on Norfolk included a lengthy section dealing with the effects of enclosure in that county. Similar accounts for other counties also appeared in the *Annals*. However, his *Report on Enclosures*, edited for the board of agriculture in 1808, was primarily a compilation of the statistics of enclosure and a statement of the arguments for and against it. His last important

work for the board was the publication in 1816, under the title *Agricultural State of the Kingdom*, of a digest of the replies received from landowners and farmers to a circular letter requesting information on the effects of the fall in prices and restriction of bank credit which accompanied the end of the Napoleonic wars.

Final years In 1808 when he was gathering material in Oxfordshire for his last county report, Young first noticed a deterioration in his eyesight. An operation for cataract in 1811 was unsuccessful and he became completely blind. It was in this year that he first met Marianne Francis, who was related to the Burney family. This exceptionally gifted young lady spent much time at Bradfield and kept up a correspondence with Young when not there. She became almost a granddaughter to the aged agriculturist as well as acting as an additional secretary. In her letters from Bradfield she mentioned his kindness in clothing and educating some thirty or forty poor children from the district, and his Sunday services at the hall, attended by tenants and villagers. Young, she said, had become an enthusiast for the steam engine, which he believed would play a central role in the farming of the future.

Young's last pamphlets, published between 1813 and 1817, concerned the striking changes in agricultural prices which had occurred since the outbreak of the wars, and also dealt with quite different subjects, including selections from the writings of Richard Baxter and Robert Owen. In addition, he still kept up his correspondence with many distinguished figures of the time. Though well into his seventies, he continued to spend long periods in London, continuing his work for the board and visiting friends. He died there on 12 April 1820 at Sackville Street, aged seventy-eight, after a painful illness caused by bladder calculus, and was buried at Bradfield Combust church nine days later.

Young's significance Young was not only the best-known agricultural reformer and publicist of his time, with an international reputation, but also a figure of importance in the political and social issues of the day. He had an extraordinary capacity for work, aided by an extremely strong constitution—at Bradfield he rose at five and took an early morning dip in one of the ponds. In an age of hazardous roads he travelled many thousands of miles, a high proportion of them on horseback or on foot, and he still found energy to write up his day's notes and perhaps some letters in his inn room at night. Some modern historians have criticized his agricultural work and have compared him unfavourably with his rival, William Marshall, but it is often overlooked that their approaches were different: Marshall gave an account of the farming of a region as a whole, while Young was not concerned with presenting a rounded picture of contemporary farming; his interests lay entirely in reporting on new advances and condemning old and inefficient methods. His enthusiasm often led him into hyperbole, but he was realistic in appreciating that farmers would only take up what could be shown to pay. Some of his own experiments were misconceived, but in his day the true factors in plant growth were far from understood. As a pioneering scientific spirit he was very widely respected, and his knowledge, wit, and pleasant personality made him welcome in both aristocratic mansion and modest farmhouse.

Although he always believed in the primacy of agriculture, Arthur Young also showed interest in the industrial and transport developments of the time, and his tours gave extensive descriptions, for example, of the Bridgewater Canal and Coalbrookdale ironworks. His range of correspondents was enormously broad, including not only his many friends and acquaintances in Europe, and George Washington and Lafayette, but also Joseph Priestley, William Wilberforce, Sir Humphry Davy, Thomas Malthus, James Boswell, William Pitt (1759–1806), and Edmund Burke, as well as scores of landowners and other agricultural figures. He was a man of wide culture, well read, interested in art, architecture, theatre and music, especially opera. There is no doubt that he wrote too much and too quickly, and sometimes with insufficient knowledge of the topic. Nevertheless, much of what he wrote in his vigorous, earthy style has a permanent value for the understanding of the period, most notably his three early tours in England, his books on Ireland and France, and many of his contributions to the *Annals*. This periodical he probably regarded as his greatest achievement. Less tangible, but perhaps not less significant, was the enthusiasm for improved farming that he inspired among uncounted country people whom he met on his travels.

G. E. MINGAY

Sources J. G. Gazley, *The life of Arthur Young, 1741–1820* (1973) · *The autobiography of Arthur Young*, ed. M. Beetham-Edwards (1898) · A. Young, *Travels during the years 1787, 1788 and 1789, undertaken more particularly with a view of ascertaining the cultivation, wealth, resources, and national prosperity of the kingdom of France* (1793) · C. Maxwell, ed., *Travels in France* (1950) · A. Young, *A tour in Ireland*, 2 vols. (1780) · J. Marchand, ed., *A Frenchman in England, 1933* (1784) · G. E. Mingay, ed., *Arthur Young and his times* (1975) · G. E. Fussell, 'My impressions of Arthur Young', *Agricultural History*, 17 (1943), 135–44 · R. Mitchison, 'The old board of agriculture (1793–1822)', *EngHR*, 74 (1959), 41–69 · *The early diary of Frances Burney, 1768–1778*, ed. A. R. Ellis, 2 vols. (1889) · A. Young, ed., *Annals of agriculture and other useful arts*, 46 vols. (1784–1815) · Northumbd RO, Culley papers, ZCU 1, 18, 44 · BL, Add. MS 35126, fol. 427

Archives BL, corresp. and papers, Add. MSS 34821–34864, 35126–35133 · JRL, family corresp. and papers | BL, Bentham papers, Add. MSS 33541, 35542 · BL, corresp. with Marianne Francis, etc. · BL, letters to Lord Hardwicke, Add. MSS 35643, 35652, 35697, 35700 · Essex RO, Chelmsford, letters to Thomas Ruggles · JRL, Bagshawe muniments, B3/10, 16; B22/6 · JRL, Thrale corresp., MSS 582–4 · Lincs. Arch., corresp. with John Cust · Northumbd RO, Newcastle upon Tyne, corresp. with George Culley · NRA, priv. coll., letters to Lord Egremont · NRA, priv. coll., letters to Sir John Sinclair · NYPL, H. W. and A. A. Berg collection, Burney MSS · RS, letters to RS · RSA, letters to the Royal Society of Arts · Sheff. Arch., corresp. with Edmund Burke · Spains Hall, Essex, Ruggles letters · U. Reading, Rural History Centre, corresp. and papers relating to board of agriculture · Yale U., Beinecke L., letters to Sir Joseph Banks

Likenesses G. Dance, drawing, 1794, NPG · J. Russell, pastel drawing, 1794, NPG [*see illus.*] · W. Hinten, stipple, 1795 (after J. Rising), BM, NPG; repro. in *European Magazine* (1795) · J. Barry, oils (*The Society for the Encouragement of the Arts*), RSA · G. Garrard, marble bust, Petworth House, Sussex · J. Russell, engraving, repro. in Gazley, *Life* · engravings, repro. in E. Clarke, 'History of the Board

of Agriculture', *Journal of the Royal Agricultural Society of England*, 9 (1898)

Wealth at death approx. £2000 in annuities; Bradfield Hall and estate; and personal estate: Gazley, *The life of Arthur Young*, 700

Young, Sir Arthur Edwin (1907–1979), policeman, was born at 55 Chamberlayne Road, Eastleigh, Hampshire, on 15 February 1907, one of four children of Edwin Young (1878–1936), a builder, and his wife, Gertrude Mary Brown (1880–1945). He attended Portsmouth grammar school and when aged sixteen joined the city's police against his family's wishes. For a non-Hendon graduate Young's promotion was meteoric: by 1938 he was the youngest ever chief constable (Leamington Spa). Seconded to Coventry after its blitz he introduced the good neighbour scheme for bombed out civilians later adopted by the Home Office. In 1941 he was selected as senior assistant chief constable, Birmingham, and in 1943 was chosen to establish the training school for policemen who would maintain law and order in liberated axis territory. Within ten weeks Young found himself director of public safety (Italy) in the first functioning military government. The models developed were applied across allied occupied western Europe, but his proudest achievement was the restoration of the *carabinieri*.

Appointed chief constable of Hertfordshire in 1944 (but released from the army only in 1945), Young set the pace in revitalizing long-debilitated county forces, encouraging major expenditure on officers' welfare and modern efficiency. So impressed was the home secretary that in 1947 Young was posted assistant commissioner of the Metropolitan Police. To appoint an outsider to such a rank was an unprecedented step and senior colleagues coldshouldered him. But the Met proved the stepping-stone to a post whose authority and independence allowed him to exercise a powerful influence on police affairs: as commissioner of the City of London police from 1950 to 1971. The first beat bobby made a commissioner, Young became known as the policeman's policeman. Improved pay and professional standards remained his constant preoccupations. He engineered a national recruitment revolution, running command courses and seeing through a fast-track graduate entry: Young was the first senior officer wedded to Sir Robert Peel's intention that the police be 'filled from the bottom up'. His sure-footed lobby of the 1960 royal commission overcame Home Office objections to a strengthened inspectorate (although Sir Charles Cunningham blocked his selection as inaugural chief inspector).

Young undertook three missions to remodel colonial policing: the Gold Coast (1951), Malaya (1952–3), and Kenya (1954). He set out to introduce the colonies to the common law status of English constables and the philosophy of policing as a public service. Colonial gendarmeries, he proposed, ought to be eradicated, and the police released from executive control. Young thus challenged orthodoxies in storm centres of imperial discontent, but the first two secondments proved dazzling successes. The Gold Coast embraced fundamental reform and Young's report moulded Ghana's policing after independence. To save

Sir Arthur Edwin Young (1907–1979), by Walter Bird, 1966

Malaya a new high commissioner and police commissioner were dispatched simultaneously: Gerald Templer and Arthur Young. 'No one disagreed with Templer more or got on with him better than I' Young wrote. Templer acknowledged Young's 'astounding innovations' in converting a militia into a constabulary. 'The police are the friends of the public whom they wish to serve' was the ethos of the cultural revolution which the federation police inhaled. Detention without trial ceased. Martial law was never introduced; Young talked Templer round. It was Young who was primarily responsible for Templer's success in tackling the emergency through policing, thereby conciliating local opinion. J. Edgar Hoover invited him in 1953 to brief the Federal Bureau of Investigation directorate on the methodology of defeating communist insurgency.

The cabinet sent Young to Kenya, torn by the Mau Mau uprising, to work another transformation. Everything went wrong. Nairobi resented his presence and dismissed his contention that civil disorders be resolved by civil principles. Young curtailed police use of guns and physical force. The CID was resuscitated. The first training for African constables began and, in the Church Missionary Society's opinion, he quickly improved the police's conduct towards the African population. But he could not break what he termed 'the rule of fear'. Executive interference in policing was endemic. Brutality was institutionalized in the Home Guard and condoned by district officers. Matters came to a head in November–December 1954 when the governor, (Charles) Evelyn *Baring, refused to

act on dossiers detailing official attempts to obstruct prosecutions of Home Guard personnel for murder; the governor's general amnesty of January 1955 was a subsequent device to cover the administration's tracks. When Baring simultaneously rejected his renewed plea for the structural safeguard of day-to-day policing free from the executive's control, Young resigned in December 1954, expecting to 'attract the attention of those in authority in London who had the means to put things right'. But Whitehall suppressed his resignation letter, which was packed with seismic details, while Young himself stayed silent out of a misplaced sense of duty. A sense of unfinished business led him, however, to advise Jomo Kenyatta's delegations at the pre-independence constitutional conferences.

Vetoed for Cyprus in 1956, Young's troubleshooting had ended until James Callaghan sent him to Ireland in 1969 to implement the Hunt report: his brief was to disband the B specials, demilitarize the Royal Ulster Constabulary (RUC), and create a police service. Young liberated Ulster's police from Stormont's and the army's operational control. Stormont's cabinet judged him a political liability and Unionist street graffiti declared 'Sir Arthur Young—Traitor!' Ian Paisley was a vituperative critic. But there was no way back; Young enjoyed Callaghan's confidence. With nationalists, by contrast, this imposed Englishman, an impartial and approachable policeman, was an immediate success. Falls Road residents told him 'we have waited fifty years for you'. Although he never convinced London of the need to abolish the Special Powers Act, the first steps away from aggressive policing were taken and the first moves made to heal the fateful split between Catholics and the RUC.

Autocratic and a strict disciplinarian, Young was famous for his loyalty to his men. He was married three times. On 11 March 1939 he married a nurse, Ivy Ada May Hammond (1908–1956); they had a son. His second wife was Margaret Furnival Dolphin (d. 1966), whom he married in 1957; they subsequently separated. On 16 August 1970 he married Ileen Fryer Turner, née Rayner. Although Young twice contemplated Anglican ordination, he was driven by a mission to make the police a respected profession. Young was 6 feet 4 inches tall and possessed of a formidable charm; his anti-Masonic, anti-capital punishment Christian socialist politics set him apart among post-war British police chiefs. He was appointed CMG (1953), CVO (1962), knight bachelor (1965), and KBE (1971); colleagues attempted unsuccessfully to secure him a life peerage.

Young died at St Thomas's Hospital, London, on 20 January 1979. His ashes were subsequently scattered at Beachy Head.   MARTIN D. W. JONES

Sources personal knowledge (2004) · private information (2004) · priv. coll., Young MSS · D. M. Anderson and D. Killingray, eds., *Policing and decolonisation: nationalism, politics and the police, 1917–65* (1992) · J. Cloake, *Templer, tiger of Malaya: the life of Field Marshal Sir Gerald Templer* (1985) · C. Douglas-Home, *Evelyn Baring: the last proconsul* (1978) · L. Heren, *The Times* (24 Feb 1971) · B. Castle, *Fighting all the way* (1993) · J. Callaghan, *A house divided: the dilemma of Northern Ireland* (1973) · C. Ryder, *The RUC: a force under fire* (1989) · W. D. Flackes and S. Elliott, *Northern Ireland: a political directory,*

1968–1993, rev. edn (1994) • Lord Chandos [O. Lyttleton, first Viscount Chandos], *The memoirs of Lord Chandos: an unexpected view from the summit* (1962) • N. Barber, *The war of the running dog: the Malayan emergency, 1948–1960* (1971) • N. Osborn, *The story of the Hertfordshire police* [n.d.] • P. Wright, *Spycatcher* (1987) • *WW* • *LondG* • b. cert. • baptismal cert. • b. certs. [Edwin Young; Gertrude Mary Brown] • m. cert. [Ivy Ada May Hammond] • d. cert.

Archives Bodl. RH, corresp. and papers relating to service in Gold Coast, Malaya, Kenya, MS Brit. Emp.s 486 • priv. coll., personal papers | New Scotland Yard, London, commissioner's reference library • PRO, memorandums and instructions issued by the commissioner of police, Kenya, CO 1307/40 • PRO, report of the commission of inquiry into the Kenyan police force, CO 1037/7

Likenesses W. Bird, photograph, 1966, NPG [*see illus.*] • R. Wilson, caricature, 1970, repro. in *The Observer* (23 Aug 1970) • D. Cookson, oils, 1979, City of London Police Headquarters • photographs, priv. coll.

Young, Arthur Primrose (1885–1977), electrical engineer and management adviser, was born in Shields, Ayrshire, on 2 July 1885, the seventh son and youngest of nine children of William Young, farmer, and his wife, Mary Potts, *née* Walker. The family moved to Hertfordshire when Arthur was a child. His mother died in 1890 and a decline in the family fortunes was followed by a move to London. Young was accordingly educated at London county council schools and Finsbury Technical College, which he had to leave at the age of sixteen, despite his abilities.

Chance notice of a vacancy led Young to a post as meter tester with the British Thomson-Houston Co. Ltd (BT-H) in 1901 and he remained with the company throughout his working life, including a period with the parent company, General Electric, in the United States (1906–8). During the next two decades Young took out nearly 150 patents in association with the company and developed BT-H's production of magnetos at its Coventry works in the First World War. This work was based on Simms's magneto interests, acquired by BT-H in 1914, and on research which had been carried out at General Electric's research centre in the USA. For his part in the development of the magneto to meet service requirements Young was appointed OBE in 1920.

Having declined a post with Joseph Lucas, Young was appointed acting manager of the Coventry works in 1921, and manager and engineer in the following year. Production increased fourfold in 1921–3, the range extending to radio and gramophone equipment, electric motors, timing controls, magnetos, and lighting systems for vehicles. It was at Coventry that Young developed the management principle of unified team effort with a common goal.

With some reluctance, in 1928 Young accepted the post of works manager at BT-H Rugby. Hopes he might have had of succeeding H. N. Sporborg, the senior director, were not realized, perhaps because Young acquired too high a profile in public affairs for a company man. This arose, on the one hand, from his active promotion of works management and management principles and, on the other, from his involvement in diplomacy, as a result of his semi-clandestine meetings with the conservative opponent of Hitler, Dr Carl Goerdeler, in the late 1930s.

Young's management principles may appear simplistic to later generations, but his emphasis on the human element was an important corrective to more mechanistic systems. He advised such prominent industrialists as Sir Alfred Herbert and Sir Charles John Bartlett of Vauxhall Motors and his chairmanship of the British Works Management Association, of which he was a founder member in 1931, helped the cause of industrial efficiency as Britain moved out of recession and towards preparation for war. In the war itself, Young served as a director of labour supply with the Ministry of Labour for some eighteen months (1940–41), during which time he was also seconded to the Ministry of Aircraft Production as controller of magneto production. Young found this wartime activity frustrating, as he had found his attempts to strengthen the British government's opposition to Hitler through the 'X Documents'. These recorded Young's discussions with Goerdeler (then working for Bosch, but formerly mayor of Leipzig) and called for determined and decisive action by Britain. Goerdeler was to die in February 1945 as part of Nazi reprisals for von Stauffenberg's bomb plot of 20 July 1944.

As he had long planned, Young left BT-H in 1945 at the age of sixty, to enter an active retirement in public affairs. He had already served on Coventry education committee (1928–38) and been a visiting fellow at Nuffield College, Oxford (1939–47). In retirement he was involved in more educational committee work, the South Warwickshire Hospital group management committee and the midland regional council of the United Nations Association. He was also a non-executive director of BKL Alloys from 1947 to its takeover in 1967 and continued his proselytizing work on behalf of works management. In connection with his many interests, Young travelled widely overseas, for lecture tours and to visit family members; he twice visited Goerdeler's widow. He was sustained in all his activity by his strong Christian belief. In politics he was a Liberal.

Young was twice married, in 1912 to Lily Louisa Porter of Rugby (d. 1961) and in 1962 to Winifred Rose, widow of G. H. Young. She survived him. There was one daughter of his first marriage, who predeceased him. For much of his working life and retirement Young lived in Kenilworth, a town to which he was deeply attached. Young died on 1 February 1977 at the Warneford Hospital, Leamington Spa, Warwickshire, and was buried at Sacombe, Hertfordshire, where his mother and first wife were interred.

RICHARD A. STOREY

Sources R. Storey, 'Young, Arthur Primrose', *DBB* • A. P. Young, *Across the years* (1971) • S. Aster, ed., *The X documents* (1974) • b. cert. • d. cert. • *CGPLA Eng. & Wales* (1977)

Archives Inst. EE, corresp. and papers • Institution of Industrial Managers, Luton • U. Warwick Mod. RC, corresp. and papers | JRL, letters to the *Manchester Guardian*

Wealth at death £1624: probate, 16 Aug 1977, *CGPLA Eng. & Wales*

Young, Bartholomew. See Yong, Bartholomew (*bap.* 1560, *d.* 1612).

Young, Cecilia (1712–1789). See under Young family (*per. c.*1700–1799).

Young, Charles (*bap.* **1686**, *d.* **1758**). *See under* Young, William (*d.* 1662).

Young, Sir Charles George (1795–1869), herald, was born on 6 April 1795 in the parish of St Mary, Lambeth, the eldest of three children, all sons, of Jonathan Young (1762–1826), a member of the Royal College of Surgeons, and his wife, Mary Waring (1778–1845), an illegitimate daughter of Charles Howard, eleventh duke of Norfolk and earl marshal (1746–1815). He was educated at Charterhouse School from 1807 to 1811 and was one of the esquires to Viscount Strangford at his installation as a knight of the Bath 1812. On 23 September 1813 he was appointed Rouge Dragon pursuivant on the nomination of his maternal grandfather, the earl marshal, and he was promoted to the post of York herald on 30 May 1820. He was appointed registrar of the College of Arms on 2 July 1822, an office he resigned upon his appointment on 6 August 1842 as Garter principal king of arms in succession to Sir William Woods. As became the usual custom, he was knighted (27 August) following his appointment.

Young accompanied ten missions to foreign sovereigns with the Order of the Garter, three when York herald as secretary to the missions to Denmark (1822), Portugal (1823), and France (1825), and seven as Garter and joint commissioner to Saxony (1842), Turkey (1856), Portugal (1858), Prussia (1861), Denmark (1865), Belgium (1866), and Austria (1867). He took an active part in the funerals of George III, George IV, and William IV, the coronations of George IV, William IV, and Queen Victoria, and the marriage of the prince of Wales in 1863. As Garter he was responsible under the earl marshal for the public funeral of the duke of Wellington in 1852.

Young, who was elected FSA on 21 March 1822 and was created DCL by the University of Oxford on 28 June 1854, married on 2 August 1854 Frances Susannah (*d.* 1876), sister of Sir Astley Paston Cooper, second baronet, and widow of Frederick Tyrrell, but had no children. His will (effects under £60,000) was proved by his brother Henry Young, a solicitor, and the latter's son Francis Young, a barrister-at-law who married Sir Charles's stepdaughter.

A distinguished scholar and highly competent man of business, Young rescued the finances of the Society of Antiquaries of London as chairman of its finance committee 1846–52. He had a similarly beneficial influence on the College of Arms as registrar for twenty years and Garter king of arms for twenty-seven years, and as one of the committee responsible for planning and building the new record room completed in 1844. In the gallery of the record room a special press contains most of the 922 volumes of his books and papers, which came to the College of Arms on his death in accordance with a memorandum found among his papers. Many are written in his own hand and the collection includes 250 volumes of peerage claims in which he had an extensive practice, 114 of pedigrees, 87 of will abstracts and lists, and 10 relating to precedence, on which he wrote several pamphlets and 'a subject with which no modern writer has dealt with greater scholarship' (Wagner, *Heralds*, 497).

In 1835 the committee of baronets presented two petitions to the king claiming certain privileges. These were referred to the College of Arms, and the report of October 1835 dismissing the claims was signed by Young as registrar and subsequently privately printed by him with a brief introduction. Young's other privately printed pamphlets included *The Order of Precedence with Authorities and Remarks* (1851), *Privy Councillors and their Precedence* (1860), and *The Lord Lieutenant and High Sheriff and their Precedence* (1860); he also had printed for private circulation *The Catalogue of the Arundel Manuscripts in the Library of the College of Arms* (1829), which he had employed William Henry Black to prepare.

Young died of apoplexy at his home, 9 Princes Terrace, Hyde Park Gate, London, on 31 August 1869. He had been ill for some months, and had last attended the monthly chapter meeting of the College of Arms on 1 October 1868. He was buried at Kensal Green cemetery on 6 September 1869. Writing in *The Herald and Genealogist* John Gough Nichols remarked on the 'uniform kindness and alacrity with which the late Garter had for a very long course of years encouraged and effectually aided his genealogical inquiries' and added that he was

> thoroughly devoted to the best interests of his profession as a branch of our social policy, giving that counsel and advice which on many occasions was required of him by various high Officers of the State in an enlarged and liberal spirit … Though not himself the author of any great work, he was the constant and never failing promoter of the labours of others. His services to Surtees, to Raine, to Hunter and other topographers were important and continual. More particularly he must ever be remembered as the best friend of Sir Harris Nicolas … who acknowledges his aid in nearly every preface of his numerous works.

THOMAS WOODCOCK

Sources *Herald and Genealogist*, 6 (1871), 465–71 · W. H. Godfrey, A. Wagner, and H. Stanford London, *The College of Arms, Queen Victoria Street* (1963), 67 · A. Wagner, *Heralds of England: a history of the office and College of Arms* (1967), 496–8 · A. R. Wagner, *The records and collections of the College of Arms* (1952), 44 · P. G. Begent and H. Chesshyre, *The most noble Order of the Garter: 650 years* (1999), 244–8 · *N&Q*, 4th ser., 4 (1869), 228 · *DNB* · *IGI* · *The Times* (2 Nov 1876) · *The Post Office London directory* (1855) · d. cert. · chapter minutes, Coll. Arms

Archives Coll. Arms, antiquarian and genealogical collections | BL, letters to Philip Bliss, Add. MSS 34568–34581, *passim* · BL, letters to Stacey Grimaldi, Add. MSS 34188–34189 · BL, corresp. with Sir Frederick Madden, Egerton MSS 2837–2847, *passim* · Bodl. Oxf., corresp. with Sir Thomas Phillipps · Herefs. RO, letters to R. B. Phillipps

Likenesses G. J. Black, lithograph, NPG · photograph, Coll. Arms

Wealth at death under £60,000: probate, 9 Oct 1869, *CGPLA Eng. & Wales*

Young, Charles Mayne (1777–1856), actor, the son of Thomas Young, a surgeon, and his wife, Anna, was born in Fenchurch Street, London, on 10 January 1777. He spent 1786 in Copenhagen with his father's sister Mary, who was married to Professor Müller, a court physician of Denmark, and acquired the friendly patronage subsequently maintained of the royal family of Denmark. On his return he was sent to Eton College, where he remained for three

Charles Mayne Young (1777–1856), by Henry Collen, 1824 [as Hamlet]

years, and afterwards, in 1791–2, to Merchant Taylors' School. Young's father was apparently a brutal and debauched tyrant who treated his family with great cruelty, and finally abandoned his wife for another woman. The entire family took refuge with an unmarried sister of Anna Young, by whom they were brought up with some difficulty.

Young became a clerk in a well-known city house, Loughnan & Co. After playing at one or two small theatres as an amateur he appeared under the name Green at Liverpool in 1798 as young Norval in John Home's tragedy *Douglas*. Emboldened by success, he took his own name, and accepted an engagement in Manchester to play leading business. After acting in Liverpool and Glasgow he made his first appearance in Edinburgh in January 1802 as Doricourt in Hannah Cowley's *The Belle's Stratagem*. He played during the entire season, and was taken up by Scott, whose friendship he retained, and with whom he stayed more than once. After returning to Liverpool, Young found as his leading lady Julia Ann Grimani, a descendant of the Venetian family of that name, whom he married at St Anne's Church, Liverpool, on 9 March 1805. Grimani had made her stage début at Bath on 16 April 1800, as Euphrasia in *The Grecian Daughter*. Following a season or two in Bath, she was at the Haymarket in 1803 and 1804, where she was Mrs Haller in Benjamin Thompson's *The Stranger*, Virginia in James Cobb's *Paul and Virginia*, Miss Richland in Goldsmith's *The Good-Natured Man*, and Miranda in Susannah Centlivre's *The Busybody*. She died at the reputed age of twenty-one, on 17 July 1806,

shortly after giving birth to their only son, and was buried in Prestwich churchyard.

Young, who had had some share in management in Manchester and elsewhere, after some negotiations with George Colman, went to London in June 1807, and made his first appearance there at the Haymarket, playing Hamlet. He was also seen as Hotspur, Frederick in *The Poor Gentleman*, Petruchio in *The Taming of the Shrew*, Harry Dornton in *The Road to Ruin*, and Rolla in *Pizarro*. In the two following seasons he was, among other characters, Zanga in *The Revenge*, Leon in *Rule a Wife and have a Wife*, and Falkland in *The Rivals*. Between 1807 and 1809 he was at Bath, appearing as Hamlet, and other leading characters.

In November 1808, as the original Daran in Frederick Reynolds's *The Exile*, Young appeared for the first time as a member of the Covent Garden company, then, when the theatre was burnt down, acted at the Haymarket Opera House. With the company he migrated to the other Haymarket house, where he played Othello, Macbeth, and Frederick in Elizabeth Inchbald's *Lover's Vows*. His engagement was to support John Philip Kemble, and on occasion to replace him. After the opening of the new theatre in Covent Garden and the suppression of the O. P. (Old Prices) riots (caused by an increase in the price of seats), when eventually *Julius Caesar* was produced, Young's Cassius was as good as Kemble's Brutus, and gradually, as Kemble's performances lessened in number, Young became accepted as the leading English tragedian—until his supremacy was challenged, first by Edmund Kean and then by W. C. Macready. Kean, however, did not appear at Drury Lane until 1814, and by then Young had established himself at Covent Garden in such roles as Antony in *Antony and Cleopatra*, Coriolanus, Iago, Richard III, and Macheath in *The Beggar's Opera*, as well as comic parts, notably Jacques in *As You Like It* and Prospero in *The Tempest*. Around this time Young appeared again at Bath, King Lear being his principal role this time.

In October 1822, as Hamlet, Young made his first appearance at Drury Lane, where he divided the lead with Kean, and supported him as Iago and Clytus. The following season he was back at Covent Garden, where he played Sir Pertinax Macsycophant in Charles Macklin's *The Man of the World*, one of his most successful roles. In the spring of 1826, supported by John M. Vandenhoff, he played an engagement in Edinburgh. He returned to Edinburgh in 1830 and 1831, and made his last appearance there in April 1831. In spite of tempting offers from America, he decided to retire from the stage while still young. His farewell took place on 31 January 1832 as Hamlet. Macready played the Ghost, and Charles Mathews, for that occasion only, Polonius. Young made a speech declaring that his reasons for quitting the stage were that he felt his strength declining and wished to be remembered at his best. After his retirement he lived principally in Brighton, where he died on 29 June 1856. He was buried in the churchyard at Southwick Green, near Brighton. He had one son, the Revd Julian Charles Young, who wrote his biography.

Young was fond of hunting, and had more than one accident in connection with it. He led a blameless life and was much respected. He was about 5 feet 7 inches in height, had dark eyes and a dark complexion, and was slightly plump. He had an admirable voice and a good presence and favoured the Kemble school of acting. Macready wrote with some emotion on hearing of his death, and said that he and Young disliked but respected each other. Although Young showed some promise as a comic actor, his best parts were said to have been Hamlet, Octavian, Macbeth, Prospero, Cassius, and Daran in *The Exile*. The memorialist Hester Piozzi speaks of his Lear affecting her almost to hysterics. In several of these parts Young was openly charged with imitating Kemble, but he was a good deal less self-conscious than Kemble, and he did not have the self-content which characterized the Kemble family. William Hazlitt spoke disparagingly of Young as in general a respectable actor, who seldom gratified and seldom offended. Leigh Hunt, who in many respects admired him, condemned him for being habitually incorrect in his words, except in Hamlet, which he is said to have played with 'decent' accuracy. Kean greatly admired him. He had a sort of melodious chanting in delivery, and it was said by some that he was a fine declaimer rather than a fine actor. He had many admirers and friends on the French stage.

JOSEPH KNIGHT, rev. NILANJANA BANERJI

Sources *The Era* (6 July 1856) · P. Hartnoll, ed., *The Oxford companion to the theatre*, 3rd edn (1967) · P. Hartnoll, ed., *The concise Oxford companion to the theatre* (1972) · T. Gilliland, *The dramatic mirror, containing the history of the stage from the earliest period, to the present time*, 2 vols. (1808) · *Oxberry's Dramatic Biography*, 4/49 (1826) · *The biography of the British stage, being correct narratives of the lives of all the principal actors and actresses* (1824) · J. C. Dibdin, *The annals of the Edinburgh stage* (1888) · Genest, *Eng. stage*, vol. 9 · J. C. Young, *Memoirs of Charles Young* (1871) · Hall, *Dramatic ports.* · W. C. Russell, *Representative actors* (1869)
Likenesses H. Collen, miniature, 1824 (as Hamlet), NPG [*see illus.*] · G. Clint, oils (in *Hamlet*), V&A · S. De Wilde, several watercolours (in character), Garr. Club · G. H. Harlow, oils, Garr. Club · G. H. Harlow, pencil and sanguine drawing, Garr. Club · G. Hayter, group portrait, oils (*The trial of Queen Caroline, 1820*), NPG · E. Landseer, oils (as King John), Garr. Club · J. Linnell, chalk drawing, NPG · portrait, repro. in *Monthly Mirror* (1807) · portrait, repro. in *Theatrical Inquisitor* (1813) · portrait, repro. in *British Stage* (Feb 1817) · portrait, repro. in *British Stage* (Feb 1820) · portrait, repro. in W. Oxberry, *New English drama* (1822) · portrait, repro. in *Mirror of the Stage* (1822) · portrait, repro. in *The Drama* (1822) · portrait, repro. in *Theatrical Observer* (20 March 1822) · portrait, repro. in *Theatrical Observer* (5 Feb 1822) · portrait, repro. in *Oxberry's Dramatic Biography* · portrait, repro. in *Ladies' Monthly Museum* (1828) · portrait, repro. in Cumberland, *Minor theatre* (1829) · portrait, repro. in *Memoir* · theatrical prints, BM, NPG

Young, Douglas Cuthbert Colquhoun (1913–1973), translator and Scottish nationalist, was born on 5 June 1913 at Abertay, William Street, Ferryport-on-Craig, Fife, the son of Stephen Young, a mercantile clerk, and his wife, Margaret Smart, *née* Black. He spent part of his childhood in Bengal, speaking Urdu as a second language there. He attended Merchiston Castle School in Edinburgh and graduated in classics from the University of St Andrews and New College, Oxford. His professional academic career began as an assistant in Greek at King's College, Aberdeen (1938–41), where his fellow assistant was David Murison, who was to become Scotland's leading lexicographer.

Douglas Cuthbert Colquhoun Young (1913–1973), by Lida Moser, 1949

Later Young lectured in Latin at University College, Dundee (1947–53), in Greek at St Andrews University (1953–68), and then moved across the Atlantic to a post as professor of classics at McMaster University in Hamilton, Ontario (1968–70), and finally to a professorship of Greek at the University of North Carolina at Chapel Hill (1970–73). Two of his many publications were on Greek subjects, *Chasing an Ancient Greek* (1950) and *Theognis* (1961). He also published verse translations from Aristophanes into Scots: *The Puddocks* (1957) and *The Burdies* (1959).

A very tall, striking figure, adorned with a luxuriant black beard and bright questing eyes, and an engaging personality, Young had strong political views, and was a member of both the Labour and the Scottish National (SNP) parties, serving as chair of the SNP in Aberdeen in the early 1940s. The SNP was pledged to oppose conscription, except by a Scottish government, and Young refused to register either for military service or as a conscientious objector. He served two terms in prison, reading Greek as much as possible in his cell. He contested Kirkcaldy for the SNP in 1944, winning 40 per cent of the vote, and again in 1945, when his share of the vote fell to below 20 per cent. He left the party in 1948 when the SNP banned dual membership. In 1967 he was a founder member of the 1320 Club, which sought to provide a nationalist alternative to the SNP.

Young was to be best remembered, however, for his promotional work in Scottish poetry, helping to build on the foundations laid by C. M. Grieve (Hugh MacDiarmid) and others in the years after the First World War. He contributed to periodicals such as *Poetry Scotland* in the 1940s and demonstrated that Scottish literature, especially poetry, should be seen as having strong multicultural links. He was instrumental in finding a publisher, William MacLellan, for Sorley Maclean's *Dàin do eimhir* (1943), and had a hand in translating some of these Gaelic poems, later contributing Scots versions of a good many Gaelic poems by various authors. These translations, and poems translated from Greek, French, German, Lithuanian, Russian, and Chinese, as well as poems in Greek (translations of Robert Burns's poems) and Latin and French, appeared in his two collections, *Auntran Blads* (1943) and *A Braird o Thristles* (1947). In 1952 he published an anthology of Scottish poetry, *Scottish Verse, 1851–1951*. Probably his work as a translator is the most enduring of his poetry, with highlights such as his translation of Paul Valéry's 'La cimetière marin' ('The Kirkyaird by the Sea'). His original verse has been described as 'an effort of the will and the intellect rather than as an unforced creative response to his experience' (A. A. H. Inglis, *The Penguin Companion to Literature*, 1971, 571), and somewhat caustically by Hugh MacDiarmid as 'wit-writing rather than poetry' (Kinsley, 266). For all that, there are striking lines in his original poems, for instance, his wry war-time comment:

> Instans tyrannus—But och, why fash
> for the waesome war, that doesna inspire us,
> nae me oniewey, wi onie rowth o pleasure,
> as weel warssle wi the Antinoe papyrus.
> (*Auntran Blads*, 24)

Douglas Young died suddenly in North Carolina, while perusing Homer, on 24 October 1973. He was survived by a wife, about whom no details are known.

DERICK S. THOMSON

Sources R. I. C. Lorimer, 'Young, Douglas Cuthbert Colquhoun', *A companion to Scottish culture*, ed. D. Daiches (1981), 402–3 · T. Hubbard, 'Reintegrating Scots: the post-Macdiarmid makars', *The history of Scottish literature*, 4: *Twentieth century*, ed. C. Craig (1987), 179–93 · personal knowledge (2004) · J. Kinsley, *Scottish poetry* (1955) · b. cert. · C. Harvie, *Scotland and nationalism* (1977) · private information (2004) · *The Times* (10 Nov 1973)
Archives BL, MSS and corresp. relating to Russia, Add. MSS 61844–61855 · NL Scot., corresp. and papers · NRA, corresp. and literary papers | NL Scot., letters to Neil Gunn · NL Scot., letters to R. E. Muirhead · U. Aberdeen L., letters to Alice Ivy Hay · U. St Andr. L., letters to Sir D'Arcy Wentworth Thompson
Likenesses L. Moser, photograph, 1949, NPG [*see illus.*]

Young [Younge], **Edward** (1641/2–1705), religious controversialist and Church of England clergyman, was born at Brampton, Yorkshire, the son of John Young or Younge, gentleman, of Woodhay, Berkshire. The family may have been of Yorkshire and Sussex descent, if Bodleian MS 435 is by Young's father. He had at least one sister. He was educated at Winchester College. He matriculated from New College, Oxford, on 11 September 1661, at the age of nineteen, becoming a probationary fellow in the same year. He took the degree of BCL in 1668 and may have intended an academic career teaching law, since he did not take holy orders until 1678.

Following the election of James Butler, first duke of Ormond, as chancellor of the university in 1670 Young met Ormond's son, Thomas Butler, sixth earl of Ossory, who would become an important patron. In contravention of the statutes of New College, by 1677 Young had married his wife, Judith (1645–1714), whose family name and background are unknown, and they had a child.

A surviving son, who would become the poet Edward *Young (*bap.* 1683, *d.* 1765), was not born for another six years, and a daughter, Anne, would follow in 1684. In 1677 Young was invited by Ossory, who was to be appointed general of all British forces in the Dutch service, to accompany the earl to Flanders as his chaplain. Young was reluctant to accept as he feared that his family would suffer privation should his marriage be discovered and his fellowship be taken from him during his absence. His doubts were overcome and he sailed for Flanders with Ossory in January 1678, presumably returning with him in September.

Probably with Ossory's backing Young emerged as an impressive preacher who did not lack courage on a great occasion. His sermon to the lord mayor and aldermen of the City of London on the subject of riches, and his address to Charles II on 29 December 1678 on debauchery, the Roman Catholic doctrine of purgatory, and the Roman Catholic hierarchy were subsequently published; the latter may be related to the unfolding of the Popish Plot. In 1679 he became rector of Newton Longville in Buckinghamshire, while retaining his fellowship. Ossory failed in the same year to persuade Ormond to promote Young to the bishopric of Kilkenny, as 'eminent both for preaching and good living and not being troublesome' (Shelley, 5). Instead he became rector of Upham in Wiltshire in 1680, exchanging his New College fellowship for one at Winchester College, where he would be able to make use of his good connections in Hampshire.

Ossory's death in 1680 was a setback to Young's career. He was assiduous in his duties—John Evelyn remarked favourably on his preaching in 1681—and became canon and prebend of Gillingham in 1682. Nevertheless Thomas Sprat, bishop of Rochester from 1684, expressed regret that Young had no wealthier preferment. Young preached on the apostolic succession at the consecration of Thomas Ken as bishop of Bath and Wells at Lambeth on 25 January 1685. This could have been interpreted as a defence of the claim of the Church of England to be part of the universal church. Young wished to support the kingship of James II while disagreeing with aspects of the king's policies. His sermon preached at the Winchester assizes in 1686 indicated his dilemma. He did not publish it until 1695 as it would have been 'an officious imprudence' (E. Young, *Two Assize Sermons*, 37) to have done so in the wake of the suppression of the attempt to dethrone James II by James Scott, duke of Monmouth, which had been felt particularly harshly in Winchester with the execution of Alice Lisle in September 1685. In a veiled attack on the conduct of George, Baron Jeffreys, lord chief justice, following the rising, Young considered the political end of judgement in the maintenance of laws, the securing of rights, the encouragement of industry, and the establishing of peace, cautioning the judges that the innocent would receive recompense in the hereafter. Another sermon of this period, *Amoris Christiani*, on John 13: 34–5, was preached in Latin and Greek before the metropolitan visitation of Salisbury in 1686. This moving address was later translated into English at the request of the poet Edmund Waller, who developed the theme in the poem 'Of divine love'. His sermon before the lord mayor and aldermen of London on rogation Sunday 1688, 'A friendly call to our dissenting brethren', may have been intended to discourage dissenters from aligning themselves with James's policy of inclusiveness, but may also have influenced the Toleration Act of 1689 that followed James's removal.

Young held the view that even a bad government was better for society than anarchy, an argument which he would develop in *Piety's Address to the Magistrate*, published in 1695, which shows the influence of St Paul and of Thomas Hobbes. As a result he took little part in the revolution of 1688 that overthrew James II, and was not appointed to the new ecclesiastical commission of 1689 that supervised the acceptance of the revolution settlement by the church. He had accepted the lucrative living of Combe in 1688, and afterwards became chaplain-in-ordinary to William III and Mary II. In his Winchester assize sermon of 1694 he praised the 'wonderful Providence' (*Two Assize Sermons*, 38) which had secured happiness and freedom of expression through the revolution, and declared it better for the guilty to escape by strict adherence to the forms of law than that the innocent should suffer. The sermon was a companion to his assize sermon of 1686, and was published with it as a form of atonement for Young's unwillingness to oppose James II more openly.

Young set forward his belief in a life of Christian example in his sermon *The Great Advertisement*, published in 1693. His wish to lead a religious life held him back from seeking preferment, as shown in his correspondence with John Ellis, who had been Ossory's secretary and was under-secretary of state from 1695 to 1705. In February 1702, following the accession of Queen Anne, Young reminded Ellis of his claims, and was installed as dean of Salisbury on 27 November that year. Giles Jacob asserted in the *Poetical Register*, published in 1720, that Young had held a post in Anne's household earlier in his career, and that the queen was godmother to his son; he seems to have had high-church leanings that would have complemented this relationship.

The new dean had little time to prove active in the diocese of Salisbury. He was collecting materials for a life of John Tillotson, archbishop of Canterbury, whose reissued *Wisdom of being Religious* (1693) was answered by Young's *Wisdom of Fearing God* in the same year. Young dedicated two volumes of sermons entitled *The Wisdom of Believing* (1703) to his patron, Francis Newport, first earl of Bradford. He was involved in deist controversy with the followers of John Locke concerning the relationship between human understanding and reason, and revelation through the scriptures. Young challenged the author of *Some Remarks on Mr Young's Discourses* (1701) in a reply printed at the end of the second volume of his sermons.

He answered his 'Socinian critic' by assigning reason a definite, if subsidiary, role, though his use of classical forms showed his unease.

Edward Young was unwell in March 1703, but his death at the deanery, probably from apoplexy, on 9 August 1705 was sudden, a fact noted with awe by Gilbert Burnet, bishop of Salisbury, and with regret by Martha Temple, Lady Giffard. He was buried in Salisbury Cathedral with a Latin epitaph composed by his poet son. Young's career illustrates the power of the pulpit in his time. Ultimately he contributed, by his stress on personal redemption through Christ and revelation through scripture, to the evangelical revival of John Wesley, who admired him.

V. E. CHANCELLOR

Sources E. Young, *Sermons on several occasions*, 2 vols. (1702–3); 2nd edn, 2 vols. (1706) · H. C. Shelley, *The life and letters of Edward Young* (1914) · *The correspondence of Edward Young, 1683–1765*, ed. H. Pettit (1971) · Wood, *Ath. Oxon.*, 2nd edn · Foster, *Alum. Oxon.* · F. H. [F. Hutchinson], *The life of the most reverend father in God John Tillotson ... compiled from the minutes of the Reverend Mr. Young* (1717) · [G. Jacob], *The poetical register, or, The lives and characters of the English dramatick poets*, 2 vols. (1719–20) · *The journals of John Wesley* (1735–91), ed. N. Curnock, 8 vols. (1909–16) · *The works of John Wesley*, ed. A. C. Outler, 2 (1985); 3 (1986) · J. G. Longe, *Martha, Lady Giffard, her life and correspondence, 1664–1722* (1911) · Evelyn, *Diary*, 4.239

Archives Salisbury Cathedral, dean and chapter archives · Winchester College, muniments | BL, letters to J. Ellis, Add. MSS 28883, fols. 133, 393, 395, 399, 405; 28884, fol. 43; 28888, fol. 68; 28890, fol. 138; 28894, fol. 420 · BL, Gotch MS 639 · BL, Lansdowne MS 987, fol. 278 · BL, Rawl. MS 1.93 · Kilkenny Castle, Ormond archives, IV.327

Likenesses portrait (after an engraving by Collyer), repro. in Shelley, *Life and letters*, frontispiece

Young, Edward (*bap.* 1683, *d.* 1765), writer, was baptized on 3 July 1683 at Upham near Winchester, the son of Edward *Young (1641/2–1705), rector of Upham and later dean of Salisbury, and his wife, Judith (1645–1714). Of the poet's three sisters, only Anne (1684–1714) survived infancy. She married John Harris in 1704, a month after Dean Young had resigned his Winchester fellowship for Harris and helped him become rector of Chiddingfold, Surrey. After the dean died, the poet's mother moved in with her daughter and son-in-law, and Chiddingfold became Young's second home, with Young ever remaining close to Harris and his sons. Young entered Winchester College in January 1695 and remained there until 1702. Under the headmaster William Harris until 1700, the curriculum included translating the classics into English verse. Young was a mediocre scholar, but he may have developed a love of poetry at Winchester, for many of his contemporaries became poets. Also, as Forster notes, a 'striking number' of Young's friends 'turn out to be Wykehamists' (Forster, 16).

Scoring poorly in the fellowship exam at eighteen, and superannuated at nineteen with an eighth place on the election rolls, Young failed to secure a fellowship at New College but was admitted in October 1702 as gentleman commoner by Dean Young's friend Richard Traffles, the college's warden, who provided the poet lodging to save him expense (Forster, 12–17). After Traffles died in June

Edward Young (*bap.* 1683, *d.* 1765), by Joseph Highmore, 1754

1703, Young entered Corpus Christi College as a commoner and lived with Thomas Turner, president of the college and a friend of his father. A year after the dean's death, Young was regularly absent from Corpus Christi and residing in Chiddingfold; then, in the last week of November 1708, he entered All Souls College, having been nominated for a scholarship by the archbishop of Canterbury, Thomas Tenison, and was elected a law fellow on 2 December 1709. Young graduated bachelor of civil laws (1714) and then doctor in civil laws (1719). All Souls remained his principal residence until 1730, but he spent much time in London and periodically visited his sister's family and his friends' country homes, such as George Bubb Dodington's in Eastbury, Dorset, and Walter Cary's in Sheen, Surrey. During July 1720, when Philip, duke of Wharton, went to Ireland to sell his estates, Young accompanied him, being employed that summer as a Latin tutor to the duke. It was then, while walking with Jonathan Swift, that he heard the dean speak of dying 'like that tree … at top' (ibid., 66). Wharton, having returned to the whig party in 1721, persuaded Young to stand for parliament in Cirencester against Lord Bathurst's candidate, but in the face of public hostility Young left the district without a contest (ibid., 74–7). Young never received annuities pledged by the duke in 1721 and 1722, and his suit for compensations, begun in 1723, brought none for twenty years and only then with legal entanglements until at least 1757 (ibid., 168–71, 306).

Early literary career, 1711–1730 Without any inherited wealth and with only his fellowship for subsistence into his forties, Young long supported himself through literature, writing dedications and poems aimed at preferment,

tragedies for benefit nights, and popular poems self-published with copyrights later sold for profit. By early 1711 he had composed what was later revised and published as *A Poem on the Last Day*, 100 lines of which (revised as lines 1–104 of the first edition) were published on 22 March 1711 in the Tory continuation of *The Tatler*, edited by William Harrison, Swift's protégé and Young's friend from Winchester. The letter from New College introducing the extract, signed T. L., remarks that Young had 'design'd a Tragedy for the Stage this winter … approved by Five or Six of the best Judges', but rejected by Colley Cibber. Young probably began composing before returning to Oxford, for George Bubb, later Dodington, in a prefatory poem to George Stubbes's *The Laurel and the Olive* (1710), compared Stubbes's verses for boldness to those of 'nervous Y—'. Like Harrison and Thomas Tickell, fellow Oxford poets, Young employed his poetical talents and participated in London literary circles in an effort to obtain a post.

Young's first published poem, *An Epistle to the Right Honourable the Lord Lansdown*, shared with Alexander Pope's *Windsor Forest* its occasion and dedicatee, but also reflected Young's dramatic aspirations. Appearing on 10 March 1713, the *Epistle* vilified war and praised the queen's and Bolingbroke's achievement of a peace that 'more than bids the Rage of Battle cease' and allows the cultivation of drama, that 'School of Virtue' in which Britain peacefully triumphs over France. After praising Shakespeare, Young's eulogy turns to Granville's virtues before praising Granville's nephew and lamenting the death of Young's friend Harrison. As Forster notes, Young's justifying his familiarity with 'Granvil's Name' on his acquaintance with the nephew Bevil Granville suggests that Young tutored him during a long absence from Oxford in 1711 (Forster, 28–9).

Young's first composition of note was the lengthy *A Poem on the Last Day* (1713), revised in 1715 and reprinted twenty times in the next half-century. In three books and roughly 500 couplets, Young describes the resurrection of the dead, the tortured speech of those awaiting judgment, and the final conflagration. The poem was dedicated to the queen, with mention of a personal debt, which some have supposed an allusion to Anne's being Young's godmother (Jacob, 2.241), though Forster found no support for this relationship (Forster, 5). The poem bears an imprimatur dated 19 May 1713, and was quoted and praised as forthcoming within *The Guardian* of 9 May 1713, but it did not appear until 14 July. Forster plausibly suggests that the poem was delayed to gain the queen's approval for the dedication and that Young's privately printed *Epistle to … Bolingbroke Sent with a Poem on the Last Day*, dated 'March' in the text and 1714 on the colophon, was presented in manuscript in March 1713 to gain a royal audience (ibid., 34).

A poem addressed to Bolingbroke reflects Young's acquaintance with Swift, who later claimed to have cured Young of writing triplets, two of which are in the *Tatler* version of his *Last Day* but were cut from the first edition. The familiarity of Young's first extant letter to Pope of 8 June 1715, on distributing Oxford copies of Pope's *Iliad*, suggests they had known each other for some time. By now Young had fully secured the assistance of Sir Richard Steele and Joseph Addison, as is evident from Young's prefatory poem to Addison's *Cato* (7th edn, 1713), Steele's puff of *A Poem on the Last Day* in *The Englishman* (29 Oct 1713) and its frequent advertisements therein, and the inclusion of Young's morbid epigram on Michelangelo's painting of the crucifixion in Steele's *Poetical Miscellanies* (1714), preceded by Thomas Wharton's verses on Young's *Poem on the Last Day*. Also, Addison permitted Young to inscribe to him *On the Late Queen's Death, and his Majesty's Accession to the Throne* (September 1714). Young's lines elegizing the queen (ll. 25–137) were reprinted in *The Loyal Mourner for the Best of Princes* (1716), edited by Charles Oldisworth.

In May 1714 Young tried his hand at narrative with the *Force of Religion* (1714), on the martyrdom of Lady Jane Grey, who refuses to convert to Roman Catholicism to save herself, her father, and her husband, though the two plead with her to do so. In February 1719 he published *A Paraphrase on a Part of the Book of Job*, transposing the theophany (chapters 38–41) into pentameter couplets, with special attention to sublime imagery. Always eager for help from fellow poets, Young secured revisions from Addison (the mentor he held in highest esteem) and Tickell in 1717 (*Correspondence*, 15). He revised the second and third editions (1719, 1726), and a Dublin edition appeared in 1719. Young retained copyright, enabling him to reprint it in 1748 with Nights 7–9 of *Night-Thoughts*, and, after Andrew Millar bought the copyrights to all four poems in 1749, it continued to appear in collected editions of the *Night-Thoughts*. In July 1719 Jacob Tonson, who had published Young's *Paraphrase*, brought out Young's *A Letter to Mr. Tickell* on the death of Addison, part of which presumably was written for a panegyric (1717) that Addison blocked from publication (ibid., 8). Also in 1719 Young contributed complimentary verses addressing the author Joseph Mitchell's *Lugubres cantus* (1719). Mitchell repaid Young by plagiarizing *Poem on the Last Day* in his *Jonah* (1720). Evidently a clubbable wit, Young seems to have been friends with many poets, so it is no wonder that he was one of the first London friends of Scots like David Mallet and James Thomson.

Young's ambitions in tragedy were met in March 1719 by nine performances at Drury Lane of his *Busiris, King of Egypt*. Like all his tragedies, *Busiris* was stridently melodramatic in the fashion of Jacobean drama, and contemporaries both commended and blasted its diction. Young wrote at least two acts of a play on the earl of Essex, about which he corresponded in 1719–20 with Lady Martha Giffard, sister of Sir William Temple, to whom he wrote verses on her niece's illness (*Correspondence*, 16–19). His second performed tragedy, *The Revenge*, had only a six-night run in April 1721, but its tale of the vengeful Moor Zanga, a plausible conflation of Iago and Othello and a role sought by tragedians, remained in the repertory throughout the century.

Beginning in 1724, Young sought a place in the Irish church from Lord Carteret, lord lieutenant of Ireland, making repeated entreaties to Carteret's secretary Thomas Clutterbuck and to Tickell, then secretary to the lords justices of Ireland. This campaign led Young in October 1724 to withdraw his tragedy *The Brothers* from rehearsal at Drury Lane, for a second time (in March 1724 he withdrew it as unlikely to run well), and to receive deacon's orders at the bishop of Winchester's chapel in Chelsea on 22 December. In March 1725 he became chaplain-in-ordinary to the princess of Wales, to whom he dedicated *A Vindication of Providence* in November 1727, promptly sending copies to Carteret, Clutterbuck, and Tickell (*Correspondence*, 58). Failing in this bid for preferment, perhaps in part owing to Dean Swift's opposing benefices for non-Irish clergy, Young delayed ordination to priesthood until after his appointment as chaplain-in-ordinary to the king (30 April 1728); he was privately ordained at Winchester on 9 June 1728.

Author of *The Universal Passion* The great achievement of Young's early career came in his seven satires entitled *The Universal Passion*, published in separate folios between January 1725 and February 1728 and revised and collected as *Love of Fame* with a critical preface in March 1728. These Horatian satires with occasional panegyrics and Juvenalian climaxes for variety broke new poetical ground. Epigrammatic and built of character sketches reminiscent of La Bruyère's, they were the first formal verse satires with a thematic focus to follow Dryden's prescriptions and, especially in the case of satires 5 and 6 on women, influenced Pope's satirical works, particularly his *Moral Epistles*. Satires 1 and 2 required second folio editions, and all were soon reprinted in Dublin and Edinburgh, and passed through over two dozen editions by 1765, with dedications to the duke of Dorset, Dodington, Spencer Compton, Robert Walpole, and Lady Elizabeth Germain. Their popularity fuelled new editions of Young's other works and made Young, often identified as 'The author of *The Universal Passion*', one of the four dominant poets of his age (witness Allan Ramsay's *The Quadruple Alliance* of 1728). The fifth satire in January 1726 ('the Last') concludes with fulsome praise of Walpole and the king—enough to draw fire from Swift. That panegyric—and support from Dodington and Princess Caroline—helped Young receive an annual pension of £200, awarded on 3 May 1726. Walter Chetwynd's transcript of the warrant bears the marginal gloss 'Author of the Universal Passion & such poetical Pieces' (Bodl. Oxf., MS Add. D.4, no. 96), verifying the *London Journal*'s characterization of the pension as an 'encouragement to poetry' (16 July 1726). Habitually acknowledging favours, on 5 July Young publicly owned his thanks within *The Instalment*, a celebration of Walpole's induction into the Order of the Garter on 26 May.

After the success of the first five satires, Young brought out an edition of his *Paraphrase* of Job (1726), in quarto on royal paper, as a specimen for a three-volume subscription work. The same terms appear in newspaper advertisements on 18–21 February 1727: 2 guineas down and another on delivery. Advertised as late as 22 February 1729 in Thomas Worrall's notice for Young's sermon *An Apology for Princes*, the effort was unsuccessful, but reflects Young's ambition and confidence in his literary merit. The three-volume length suggests that Young's closet held much that was never published (perhaps another tragedy) and much that was soon to be published. The latter included Young's prose discourse on the passions as impediments to human felicity, *A Vindication of Providence, or, True Estimate of Human Life*, written by October 1724 and first published in November 1727 in quarto on fine paper by Worrall. The title describes it as 'Preach'd in St. George's Church near Hanover-Square, soon after the late King's Death', but the frequently reprinted work was, at sixty-four quarto pages, too long for a sermon. Young loyally supported the king and whig commercial policies in the odes *Ocean*, published with a prefatory 'Ode to the King' and discourse on lyric poetry (1728), *Imperium pelagi, or, The Merchant*, with a preface on Pindar (1730), and *Foreign Address* (1735). No critic has thought these works successful enough to resolve the degrees to which Young's persistence in writing six-line stanzas on naval policy arose from patriotic fervour, governmental encouragement, or the aspiration to gain preferment or to domesticate Pindar. Young returned to satire with *Two Epistles to Mr. Pope: Concerning the Authors of the Age* (1730), a mixture of critical precepts and satiric characters of dunces, thrice reprinted in Dublin in 1730.

Happiness and loss, 1730–1742 In July 1730, as a benefice from All Souls, Young received the rectory of St Mary's Church, Welwyn, north of London on the York road, a living worth £300 per year. A fortnight later, on 4 August, at St Mary-at-Hill in London, he secretly married Lady Elizabeth Lee (1694–1740), daughter of Lady Charlotte Fitzroy (granddaughter of King Charles II and Lady Castlemaine) and Edward Henry Lee, raised to the earl of Litchfield on his marriage. Lady Elizabeth was the widow of Colonel Francis Henry Lee, her first cousin, who had died in March, and mother of three surviving children: Elizabeth (*b.* 1718), Charles Henry (*b. c.*1720), and Caroline (*b. c.*1727). Settling into Welwyn for life, Young leased Guessens, a large house that was the first home he had had of his own. The marriage was publicly announced in May 1731, and on 20 June 1732 the couple had a son, named Frederick after his godfather, the prince of Wales. None of Young's letters survives for 1731–8, when he was evidently preoccupied with family life. On 24 June 1735 he married his stepdaughter Elizabeth to Henry Temple, elder son of the first Viscount Palmerston.

To aid the consumptive Elizabeth, the Youngs took her and Temple to southern France, but she died on 8 October 1737 in Lyons and was buried in its protestant cemetery. Young and his wife spent the winter outside Nice, where Young wrote but later lost in transit a discourse complementing his *Vindication of Providence* (Forster, 154). Apparently ill for some time (*Works*, 3.144), Lady Elizabeth died at her brother's London home on 29 January 1740 (Forster, 158). Young had been ill in 1737 following his stepdaughter's death, and in the summer following his wife's death he came close to dying of a fever treated by Dr Richard Mead. Then came the shocking news that Temple, his beloved son-in-law and friend of two decades, had died

suddenly on 18 August 1740. Encouraged by Temple, Young had begun to court the fifty-year-old spinster Judith Reynolds of London as a helpmate and mother for Frederick; the nine-month campaign ended in February 1741, ostensibly blocked by Reynolds's brother.

Poet of the *Night-Thoughts* When Edmund Curll and other copyright holders brought out a two-volume edition of Young's *Poetical Works* in 1741, his literary career seemed over. Then, pursuing consolation for the loss of his step-daughter in 1736 and his wife and son-in-law in 1740, Young wrote *The Complaint, or, Night-Thoughts on Life, Death, and Immortality* (1742–6), arguably the century's greatest long poem. Its nine 'Nights', issued serially in quartos tending to greater length, total nearly 10,000 lines of blank verse. The first of these maintain the quasi-autobiographical fiction of a nocturnal speaker lamenting the loss of child, spouse, and friend and finding Christian consolation. Increasingly the speaker turns to theodicy, Christian apologetics, and conversion. Often addressing an apostate *adversarius* named Lorenzo, the speaker satirizes worldly infidelity and argues the sublime blessings of Christian salvation through the wonders of the gospels, the human soul, and nature (as in the cosmic voyage in Night 9). The rhetorical manner is frequently dramatic, with much use of apostrophe, question, antithesis, and paradox. With the first Nights immensely popular (Nights 1–5 all quickly required multiple editions), Young was induced to restate copiously and refine his points, overextending the work until its popularity fell off, though recent criticism has focused on these later Nights. Over 100 collected editions of the *Night-Thoughts* were published in the next five decades, including translations in most European languages, many in German. Its popularity is reflected in the court battle that Alexander Donaldson won in 1771 against London publishers attempting to prevent his editions. Illustrated by Blake and read closely by Wordsworth and Coleridge, the poem remained popular among middle-class readers well into the 1800s.

More is known about Young after 1740, when he began a correspondence lasting until 1765 with Margaret Cavendish Harley, only daughter of the second earl of Oxford; she was married to William Bentinck, second duke of Portland. Through the duchess Young met or became better acquainted with Mary Granville, then Pendarves, whom the duchess recommended to Young as a spouse (she afterwards married Dr Patrick Delany), and Elizabeth Robinson, later Mrs Montagu, who left vivid testimony to the poet's witty conversation. In her letters the duchess claims the credit for initiating and directing petitions for preferment between 1742 and 1748 and again in 1758, for which Young has been criticized. In January 1744 Young's stepson Charles Lee died of smallpox, and Young was obliged to fight a two-year legal battle against Charles's widow to preserve his son's and stepdaughter's inheritance.

In July 1748 Young had the joy and sorrow of marrying at Welwyn his beloved stepdaughter Caroline to Major William Haviland: in the autumn she joined her husband with his regiment in Scotland and then travelled with him to Ireland, where she died in November 1749. Late in 1748 Young's household was taken over by Mary Hallows, the spinster daughter of a Hertford rector. With Caroline gone and Frederick away (first at Winchester and then Balliol), and Young himself inattentive to the domestic details, he needed a domestic companion. Reserved and quiet in company, and authoritarian to judge from Frederick's response to her, Mrs Hallows remained Young's companion until his death, supplying him with eyes when he could not read and a steady hand when rheumatism prevented his writing. Between 1746 and 1753 Young was occupied with enlarging Guessens, rebuilding his church's turret, reviving Welwyn spa with new assembly rooms, and founding a charity school. He took pleasure in his daily routines about Guessens and in his visitors, including Speaker Arthur Onslow, the Swiss poet Vincenz Bernhard von Tscharner, Joseph Spence, and Mrs Montagu; many of these have recorded their pleasant visits. He travelled to spas and the homes of friends, and to London for his duties as chaplain and for visits to Samuel Richardson, often related to publications. After Richardson took over printing the quarto *Night-Thoughts* in June 1744, he sought out Young's advice on *Clarissa* (*Correspondence*, 180). Soon he became Young's most valued friend, printing and helping revise Young's first and corrected editions.

In March 1748 Young protested against Sir William Bunbury's rumoured efforts to stage *The Brothers*, whose manuscript Young had 'entrusted' to Bunbury and earlier to his uncle Sir Thomas Hanmer (*Correspondence*, 317–18). Then on 23 June 1752 Young asked Bunbury to see if Garrick would be 'willing to act [it] … early next Winter', with profits going to 'the Propagation of the Gospell in foreign Parts', whose financial distress had been recently noted by the king (ibid., 382–3). With *The Revenge* popular in the repertoire, and a cast to include Garrick and George Ann Bellamy, the revival of *The Brothers* raised high expectations. However, when performed in March 1753, the outmoded tragedy played to shrinking audiences for eight nights, with the last treated as the ninth for the author's benefit; from its profits, Henry Pettit notes, Young recouped only £400 of his £1000 donation to the Society for the Promotion of Christian Knowledge (ibid., 382n.).

In March 1755 Young published *The Centaur not Fabulous* in five letters 'addressed to a friend', that is, Richardson, who helped with its revision. Divided into six letters in the first of two revised editions that year, this prose satire and homily was directed at licentious and irreligious contemporaries who, misguided by 'infidel' philosophers like Lord Bolingbroke, resembled the fabled beasts. Here as elsewhere Young stressed human dignity as a bulwark against hedonism and atheism.

After his collected works were pirated in 1752 and 1755, Young revised for copyright holders those pieces he wished to pass on to posterity, mainly through deletions. This authorized edition (4 vols., 1757), expanded with a fifth volume in 1773 and a sixth in 1778, was often reprinted but in fewer editions than appeared unauthorized. With suggestions from Richardson, to whom it was addressed, Young wrote *Conjectures on Original Composition* (1759), an exhortative celebration of originality and an assessment of the genius of Shakespeare, Pope, Swift, Dryden, and Addison, ending with an account of Addison's pious death, thus linking literary with moral virtues. In 1761, aged seventy-eight, encouraged by Mrs Montagu, he composed and privately printed *Resignation*, a consolation addressing the widow of Admiral Edward Boscawen. Thoroughly revised and expanded to sixty quarto pages, it was published in May 1762 and reprinted in America, Germany, Ireland, and Scotland within two years. Like *Night-Thoughts* and *The Centaur, Resignation* seeks to reconcile man to God's ways, but it is marked by Young's most personal and joyous account of providence, and its attack on gloomy freethinking includes an admonition to Voltaire. The poem employs a four-line stanza rhyming *abcb*, with alternating eight- and six-syllable lines, which Samuel Johnson applauded for Young's customary 'experiment of a new mode of writing' (Johnson, *Poets*, 396).

Death and reputation After the death of George II, whom Forster convincingly argues was the 'stumbling block' to Young's preferment (Forster, 333–4), Young was appointed in January 1761 by George III as clerk of the closet to the princess dowager. In his last years Young was plagued with physical deterioration, the misadventures of a son often absent from school and prone to debt, difficulties in retaining his quarrelsome curate John Jones, and the death of dear friends like Richardson. Often accused of lacking common sense, the poet lived free of scandals and feuds and acquired a comfortable fortune, a reputation for both wit and piety, and a legion of friends, whig and tory alike. After a fortnight's illness, Young died at Guessens on Good Friday, 5 April 1765, and was buried in the chancel of St Mary's Church, Welwyn, beside his wife, on 12 April. As Young had repeatedly requested, Mrs Hallows burnt his private papers, including all correspondence and manuscripts but his account book (now lost or destroyed). His will, written on 25 April 1760 and slightly amended in 1762, left £1000 to Mrs Hallows (she had never received payment as his housekeeper), £200 to the Revd Jones, £100 for repairs to 'the Parsonage house, & the Chancell', and smaller sums to servants, his nephew the Revd Richard Harris, and All Souls library. His son Frederick inherited the remainder, estimated at £12,500 (ibid., 375–7), which he spent in ten years, well before his death in 1788.

Young's *Love of Fame*, *Night-Thoughts*, and *Conjectures on Original Composition* are still frequently anthologized. These works and his *Poem on the Last Day* were sufficiently original to inspire imitations and criticism. A copious writer given to experimentation, though sometimes lacking in judgement, Young wrote in various styles but was prone to display an imagination fertile with similitudes, epigrammatic maxims, paradoxes, and antitheses. From the beginning but particularly after years of ministry and personal losses, Young fought a rearguard action against Enlightenment criticism of Christian revelation and teleology. His later works enacted the discovery of the soul's transcendence and of divine providence, promoting an enthusiastic Christianity not unlike that of John Wesley, who twice edited versions of *Night-Thoughts*. Favourite themes included the paradoxes that humankind triumphs through loss and death and that Christ's redemption of man was too preposterous for 'human ingenuity' to have invented.

After a century, Young's religious enthusiasm and epigrammatic density cost him readers, and George Eliot's attack in 1857, that Young's place seeking undercut the artistic sincerity he had heralded, blighted his reputation. Although his works were frequently reprinted and translated, Young's place in literary history is anchored to the *Night-Thoughts* and *Conjectures*, which embodied new sensibilities and notions of literary self-consciousness and imagination. The only major literary figure spanning the reigns of Queen Anne and George III, Young has retained an importance that is also ensured by his friendships with writers as diverse as Pope, Johnson, and Richardson and his contemporaries' admiration, summed up by Johnson's judgment that Young 'was a man of genius and a poet' (Johnson, *Poets*, 399).   JAMES E. MAY

Sources H. Forster, *Edward Young: the poet of the 'Night thoughts', 1683–1765* (1986) [includes list of manuscript and printed sources] · *The correspondence of Edward Young, 1683–1765*, ed. H. Pettit (1971) · J. Spence, *Observations, anecdotes, and characters, of books and men*, ed. J. M. Osborn, new edn, 2 vols. (1966) · S. Johnson, *Lives of the English poets*, ed. G. B. Hill, [new edn], 3 (1905) · *Works of the author of the 'Night thoughts'*, 1–6 (1757–78) · H. Forster, 'Some uncollected authors: Edward Young in translation', *Book Collector*, 19 (1970), 481–500; 20 (1971), 47–67, 209–24 · H. Pettit, *A bibliography of Young's 'Night thoughts'*, 5 (1954) · J. May, 'A bibliography of secondary materials for the study of Edward Young, 1683–1765', *Bulletin of Bibliography*, 46 (1989), 230–48; [Addenda to] 57 (2000), 135–46 · A. Lindsay, 'Edward Young, 1683–1765', *Index of English literary manuscripts*, ed. P. J. Croft and others, 3/4 (1997), 573–78 · *DNB* · W. Thomas, *Le poète Edward Young: étude sur sa vie et ses œuvres* (1901) · S. Brown, 'Edward Young', *Eighteenth-century British poets: first series*, ed. J. Sitter, DLitB, 95 (1990), 353–63 · S. Brown, 'A letter from Edward Young to Caroline Lee Haviland: some biographical implications', *Philological Quarterly*, 68 (1989), 263–71 · T. C. D. Eaves and B. D. Kimpel, *Samuel Richardson: a biography* (1971) · D. F. Foxon, ed., *English verse, 1701–1750: a catalogue of separately printed poems with notes on contemporary collected editions*, 2 vols. (1975) · E. T. Collins and H. Pettit, 'The genealogy of Edward Young, 1683–1765', *University of Colorado Studies* (Series in Language and Literature), 10 (1966), 79–86 · [G. Jacob], *The poetical register, or, The lives and characters of the English dramatick poets*, 2 vols. (1719–20) · *Letters of Mrs. Elizabeth Montagu*, ed. M. Montagu, 4 vols. (1809–13) · J. May, *The Henry Pettit Edward Young collection at the University of Colorado at Boulder Library: a bibliography* (1989) · J. May, 'An unpublished letter from Edward Young to Mrs. Montague, 7 July 1761', *N&Q*, 237 (1992), 54–6 · J. May, 'Edward Young's criticism of Voltaire in *Resignation*, 1761, 1762', *Studies on Voltaire and the Eighteenth Century*, 267 (1989), 127–38 · G. Eliot, 'Worldliness and other-worldliness: the poet Young', *Westminster Magazine* (1857); repr. T. Pinney, ed., *Essays of George Eliot* (1963), 335–85 · manuscript ledger, Gosling's Bank, Barclays Group Archives, Manchester [account begins at ledger N9, fols. 16ff.] · warrants for pensions, Chetwynd papers, 1715–30, Bodl. Oxf., MS Add. D4, no. 96

Archives Barclays Group Archives, Manchester, ledger, Gosling's Bank, N9, fols. 16ff | BL, letters to George Keate, Add. MS 30992 · Bodl. Oxf., Chetwynd MS, warrants for pensions, Add. D4, no. 96 ·

Hunt. L., letters, mainly to Judith Reynolds · Longleat House, Wiltshire, letters to Lady Portland

Likenesses J. Highmore, oils, 1754, All Souls Oxf. [*see illus.*] · L. P. Boitard, line engraving (after J. Highmore), NPG; repro. in *Works of the author of the 'Night thoughts'*, 1 (1757), frontispiece

Wealth at death £1000 to housekeeper Mary Hallows; £200 to Reverend John Jones; £100 left to his successor for repairs to 'the Parsonage house, & the Chancell'; £20 divided between four housekeepers and £40 between four servants; £50 to nephew Reverend Richard Harris; £50 for books to All Souls Library; £20 to friend Henry Stevens, and various moveables to his parish church; rings to family and friends; son Frederick inherited remainder of estate (est. £12,500): Forster, *Edward Young*, 375

Young, Elizabeth (1741?–1773). *See under* Young family (*per.* c.1700–1799).

Young, Ella (1867–1956), poet and mythographer, was born on 26 December 1867, in Ballymena, co. Antrim, the eldest of the eight children of James Bristow Young, a cornbroker, and Matilda Ann, *née* Russell; her sister Elizabeth (*b.* 1876) became a successful actress as Violet Merville. The family was Presbyterian and unionist. Ella Young's parents moved to Limerick in 1871, to Portarlington, Queen's county, about 1885, and later to Rathmines, Dublin, where she completed her education, studying at Alexandra College and graduating BA in law and political science from the Royal University in 1898. She joined the Dublin Theosophical Society in the 1890s and came under the influence of George Russell, becoming part of a group of young poets whose talents he nurtured; these included Eva Gore-Booth, Patrick Colum, and Alice Milligan. Ella Young's first collection, *Poems*, was published in 1906 by the Tower Press, with which Russell was closely associated. She subsequently published two more collections in Ireland, *The Rose of Heaven* (1920) and *The Weird of Fionavar* (1922).

Visions and mystical experiences had been a part of Ella Young's life from childhood and a literal engagement with Irish mythology became the defining force in her life. W. B. Yeats respected her occult powers enough to correspond with her in 1903 on such matters as 'The hidden meaning of vegetable things' and 'The dim shapes of the blue wood' (*Collected Letters of W. B. Yeats*, 3.381), though he was later to express irritation with her claims to insight and wisdom in his 1909 journal and in his letters. Ella Young, who had learned Irish, published collections of versions of Irish mythology from 1909 onwards; these highly simplified narratives use Fiona Macleod's *The Laughter of Peterkin* (1897) as their model. Two collections were embellished with illustrations and decorations by her close friend Maud Gonne; one, *Celtic Wonder Tales* (1910), has been regularly reprinted.

Ella Young became an enthusiastic nationalist, a member of Inghnidhe na hEireann (Daughters of Ireland, a nationalist women's group) and a friend of Patrick Pearse and Constance Markiewicz; she claimed to have hidden guns and ammunition during the Howth gun-running, in the midst of the troubles and the civil war. She interpreted the 1916 rising in occult and numerological terms:

> [a] small occult society, that worked for years with the object of reaching to the power of the Stone, the Danaan Jewel with

which is bound up the Royal Sovereignty of Ireland, was told in the year 1908, that sixteen is the number of the Stone. It cannot have been a mere coincidence that the Rising took place in the year 1916, and that exactly sixteen men were executed.   (Young, *Flowering Dusk*, 130)

Her subsequent bitter disillusion with the free state government led to a quarrel with Russell and prompted her decision to move to the United States in October 1925; she became an American citizen in April 1931.

Ella Young travelled widely in the United States, spending some time in Taos, New Mexico, with Mabel Dodge Luhan investigating the rituals of the Zuñi and helping the revolutionary Ernie O'Malley to write his IRA memoir *On Another Man's Wound*. Ella Young became Phelan lecturer in Celtic mythology and Gaelic poetry at the University of California at Berkeley, a position created for her by a friend, Nöel Sullivan. She retired in 1936 and moved to Oceano, California, where she joined Halcyon, a theosophical commune with which she had an established link. During her retirement she completed her most enduring work, her autobiography, *Flowering Dusk*; she had been contemplating just such a memoir since 1920, telling her friend Estella Solomons 'If I could only think of a sufficient number of picturesque & flattering incidents in my career I'd start an autobiography. It's the only way of showing oneself as one desires to be' (TCD). This idiosyncratic memoir includes many fascinating sketches of Yeats, Maud Gonne, George Russell, Standish O'Grady, and Yeats's friend, the magician, MacGregor Mathers. It also provides a highly coloured account of Ella Young's mystical and visionary experiences and a heavily romanticized narrative of the period from the 1916 rising to the end of the Irish Civil War.

Ella Young published six collections of poetry. Her verse combines a facile Pre-Raphaelitism with a *fin de siècle* Celticism, as much influenced by Fiona Macleod (William Sharp) as by Yeats or Russell. Her earlier verse is her best and her work became increasingly mannered, saccharine, and formulaic. Her three American collections, *Marzilian and Other Poems* (1938), *Seed of the Pomegranate and Other Poems* (1949) and *Smoke of Myrrh and other Poems* (1950), were privately printed in very small editions.

Ella Young was a strikingly handsome woman and exploited her dramatic looks and vatic presence when teaching in California. Her emotional life centred on two women to whom her love poetry is addressed, 'Brysanthe' whom she had known as a child and Alys Boyd, a fellow mystic, with whom she had a close friendship in Dublin. Ella Young died in California, possibly in Oceano, in 1956.

DEIRDRE TOOMEY

Sources E. Young, *Flowering dusk: things remembered accurately and inaccurately* (1945) · W. W. Lyman, 'Ella Young: a memoir', *Éire-Ireland*, 8/3 (1973), 65-9 · E. Riehle, 'The shining land of Ella Young', *Dublin Magazine*, 33 (April-June 1958), 17-22 · *The collected letters of W. B. Yeats*, 3, ed. J. Kelly and R. Schuchard (1994) · W. B. Yeats, *Memoirs*, ed. D. Donoghue (1972) · E. Young, letters to E. Solomons, TCD · *The Gonne-Yeats letters, 1893-1938*, ed. A. MacBride White and A. N. Jeffares (1992) · R. English, *Ernie O'Malley: IRA intellectual* (1998)

Archives Hunt. L., letters, diary, literary MSS · Hunt. L., MS poetry and diaries · L. Cong., MSS · priv. coll., manuscript materials · Scripps College, Claremont, California, typed prose TS of a poem and four photographs · Simmons College, Boston, MSS · TCD, MS review · U. Cal., Berkeley, Bancroft Library, MSS | Hunt. L., letters to Charles Erskine Scott Wood · Hunt. L., letters to Sara Bard Field Wood · Mills College, California, letters to Albert Bender · NL Ire., letters to Joseph McCarrity · Scripps College, Claremont, California, corresp. with Dorothy Drake · Scripps College, Claremont, California, letters to Elsa Gidlow · TCD, letters to Joseph Campbell · TCD, letters to Seumas O'Sullivan · TCD, letters to Estella Solomons · Villanova University, Pennsylvania, letters to Joseph McCarrity
Likenesses A. E. Adams, photograph, after 1925, repro. in Young, *Flowering dusk* · R. McMahon, photograph, before 1925, repro. in Young, *Flowering dusk* · T. Handforth, drawing, repro. in Young, *Flowering dusk* · O. Maurer, photograph, repro. in Young, *Flowering dusk* · photograph, repro. in Young, *Flowering dusk* · photographs, Scripps College, Claremont, California

Young [*married name* Daniell], **Emily Hilda** (1880–1949), novelist, was born on 21 March 1880 at Whitley, Northumberland, the fourth of the seven children of William Michael Young, shipowner, and Frances Jane Young, née Venning, of Cornwall. She was educated at Gateshead high school and Penrhos College, Colwyn Bay, Wales. An accomplished rock climber, she returned on holiday to north Wales many times.

In 1902 Young married John A. H. Daniell (1874–1917), a Bristol solicitor. He was killed at Ypres in 1917. The Clifton landscape, though it was Young's home for only sixteen years, became the setting (fictionalized as Radstowe) for all but three of her eleven novels. During these years Young read classical and modern philosophy and prepared for her vocation by writing fortnightly essays. During the First World War she worked as a stables groom and then in a munitions factory; in the Second World War she was active in air raid precautions.

Through her husband Young met Ralph B. Henderson (1880–1958), headmaster of Alleyn's School in Dulwich, London. After Daniell's death, Young moved to Sydenham Hill, London, to live with Henderson as his lover, in the same house with his wife. Upon his retirement, Henderson and Young moved to Prior's Close, Bradford-on-Avon, Wiltshire, where they lived until Young's death. Henderson encouraged Young to write and watched the growth of her work 'from the first word written to the last word printed' (Henderson).

For some years Young left the house every morning to write in the drawing-room of a nearby friend. The routine included a mid-morning coffee break with her friend, but Young never discussed the progress of her work. Her antipathy to publicity seems to have been lifelong; throughout her career she maintained that her works must stand on their own merits or not at all.

Between 1910 and 1947 Young published eleven novels, several short stories, and two children's books; she published as E. H. Young. Several of her novels were later dramatized as radio plays. The beloved Clifton landscape—the placid downs leading to steep cliffs, the dramatic gorge and suspension bridge over the Avon River, and the Somerset country on the far side of the bridge—

Emily Hilda Young (1880–1949), by Howard Coster, 1932

became a favourite symbol for the duality of her characters. For example, in *The Misses Mallett* (1922) (originally
titled *The Bridge Dividing*) and in *Miss Mole* (1930), which was
awarded the James Tait Black memorial prize, the country
both reflects and complements the characters' natures,
inspiring confidence in a natural order, instilling in them
a sense of rootedness, and offering them a release from
the restrictions of societal structures.

How this natural heritage can be integrated into the
social order of the town is a question raised by many of the
novels, frequently manifested as a conflict between a
convention-bound character and one who searches for
truth independently of societal codes. Notably in *The Vicar's Daughter* (1928) and in *Miss Mole*, characters' preoccupation with female chastity and with sexual transgression
gives rise to evasion and misunderstanding, but also to
self-examination and growth. Young handles these
themes in a tone of fundamental seriousness leavened
with humour. Characteristically, her sentences embody
an ironic vision; for example, a clergyman in *The Vicar's
Daughter* is 'conscious that his calling set him apart from
other men and losing, in the consciousness, what might
have been the power of his position'.

Some contemporary reviewers compared Young to Jane
Austen. In the words of one: 'she wisely narrows her field,
and within her limits she excels all her competitors
because she does not allow her brain to override her heart'
(Mais, 148). Young's novels demonstrate that the domestic
realm can be the source of experience as significant as the
public sphere: 'here, in little, were most of the emotions,
preoccupations and duties common to mankind' (E. H.
Young, *Celia*, 1937). Young's philosophical perspective
manifests itself in the human questions her characters
address: What is beauty and how is it related to good? How
ought we to act if we cannot foresee the consequences of
our actions?

Young modernized the domestic novel by writing
frankly about marital discord in *William* (1925), the most
successful of her novels; *The Curate's Wife* (1934); *Celia*; and
Chatterton Square (1947), her patriotic final novel invoking
the domestic realm to reflect on and respond to the Munich agreement. Another mark of her modernity is her

focus on the complexity of characters' internal responses
to events.

Throughout her life, E. H. Young's remarkable qualities
commanded admiration and love. 'She was quite the most
observant person I've ever met', said a friend. Another
observed her transforming influence on those she met
even casually. She died of lung cancer on 8 August 1949 at
Prior's Close.   STELLA DEEN

Sources R. B. Henderson, undated letter to Mr Cape, U. Reading,
Jonathan Cape archive · private information (2004) · *The Times* (9
Aug 1949), 4e · *The Times* (10 Aug 1949), 7e · *The Times* (17 Nov 1958),
12c · *The Times* (20 Nov 1958), 14c · *The Times* (6 Dec 1958), 8c · S. P.
Mais, *Some modern authors* (1923), 145–8 · S. Beauman, 'Introduc-
tion', in E. H. Young, *The Misses Mallett* (1984) · *Bristol Grammar School
Chronicle*, 14 (1917)
Archives priv. coll., MSS | U. Reading, Jonathan Cape archive
Likenesses H. Coster, photograph, 1932, NPG [*see illus.*] · W. N.
Sanderson, photograph (after sculpted head), Jonathan Cape,
London
Wealth at death established school prizes for Greek history,
philosophy, drama: *The Bentleian* (Bentley Grammar School bul-
letin), 14 (summer 1950), p. 5

Young, Esther (1717–1795). *See under* Young family (*per.
c.*1700–1799).

Young, Francis Brett (1884–1954), novelist, was born on
29 June 1884 at The Laurels, Halesowen, Worcestershire,
the eldest son of Thomas Brett Young (*b.* 1855), a doctor,
and his wife, Elizabeth (Annie) Jackson (1858–1898),
daughter of John Jackson, a surgeon of Somerby, Leicestershire. From 1895 until 1901 he was educated at Epsom
College, Surrey, where he won the Sands Cox scholarship
to the University of Birmingham. In 1907 he gained a first-
class medical degree and settled in practice at Brixham,
Devon.

On 28 December 1908 Brett Young married Jessica (Jessie; *b. c.*1887), daughter of John Hankinson, a farmer; she
was a teacher of physical training who later became a concert singer. 'In between epidemics' he began to write
novels, his first, *Undergrowth*, co-authored with his
brother Eric and published in 1913. It was followed a year
later by *Deep Sea*, spoken of as 'the Fisherman's Bible', and
in 1915 by *Dark Tower*, praised for its 'almost Jamesian
subtlety of narrative method' (*The Times*, 30 March 1954).
In these early novels he drew heavily on his work as a GP
for the substance of his fiction, a trend which was to continue throughout his career, as all his novels are semi-
autobiographical. His pre-war fiction enjoyed respectable
reviews, and each book sold on average 2000 copies.

When the First World War broke out, Brett Young joined
the Royal Army Medical Corps and served with the 2nd
(Rhodesian) regiment in Jan Smuts's campaign in east
Africa. *Marching on Tanga* (1917) was inspired by his experiences and is one of the best depictions of east African life,
but the campaign took a heavy toll on his health. In 1918
he was invalided out with the rank of major, and he and
his wife moved to Capri.

While convalescing Brett Young published *The Crescent
Moon* (1918) and *Poems, 1916–1918* (1919), both influenced by

Francis Brett Young (1884–1954), by Helen Wilson, 1931

widow took his ashes to England, where they were placed in Worcester Cathedral. Despite his earlier success, 'His death passed almost unnoticed by the literary press' (Church, 13).   KATHERINE MULLIN

Sources DNB · E. G. Twitchett, *Francis Brett Young* (1935) · J. B. Young, *Francis Brett Young: a biography* (1962) · D. Cannadine, *This little world: the value of the novels of Francis Brett Young as a guide to the state of midland society, 1870–1925* (1982) · *The Times* (30 March 1954) · R. Church, 'Fashion passed him by', *Books and Bookmen*, 1/1 (1955), 13 · E. Chitham, *The Black Country* (1972), 162 · J. Leclaire, *Un témoin de l'avènement de l'Angleterre contemporaine: Francis Brett Young, l'homme et l'œuvre (1884–1954)* (1969) [trans. as *Francis Brett Young: physician, poet, novelist* (1986)] · *CGPLA Eng. & Wales* (1954)

Archives NRA, corresp. and literary papers · U. Birm. L., corresp. and papers | BL, corresp. with Society of Authors, Add. MS 63351 · Hagley Hall, Worcestershire, proofs and corresp. with George William Lyttelton · HLRO, letters to David Lloyd George · University of Cape Town Library, letters to C. J. Sibbett

Likenesses C. Mann, oils, 1922, U. Birm., school of medicine · H. Coster, photographs, 1930–39, NPG · H. Wilson, drawing, 1931, NPG [*see illus.*] · portrait, repro. in Twitchett, *Francis Brett Young*, frontispiece

Wealth at death £3408 12s. 3d. in England: South African probate sealed in England, 31 Aug 1954, *CGPLA Eng. & Wales*

his war experiences. In Capri he began to write his first essentially west midland stories, and after the publication of several unremarkable novels the appearance of *Portrait of Clare* in 1927 signalled the beginning of his career as a best-selling writer. It was his first great commercial success, won him the James Tait Black memorial prize, and was adapted for the stage in 1946 and made into a film in 1949. The *New Statesman* commented that 'We have to go back sixty years for any parallel in size and subject to this entirely English tale' (Young, 151). A year after *Portrait of Clare* the publication of *My Brother Jonathan* repeated this success, and in 1948 it was also made into a film; it was serialized on BBC television in 1985. The sales from the two novels enabled the Youngs to leave Capri and settle in the Lake District in England.

Between the wars Brett Young produced at least one novel a year, works which appealed to both the general public and the critics. John Masefield saw him as 'the most gifted, most interesting mind amongst the younger men writing English' (Young, 146). His novels, however, suffered from their great length—most were over 600 pages long—and their repetitiveness of plot and character. His belief that a medical training and a doctor's career were the best ways for a novelist to learn about humanity began to backfire; as it has been calculated that, up to and including *White Ladies* (1935), there were no fewer than thirty-three doctors of medicine in his work, an average of 3.38 per novel (Twitchett, 281). *A Man about the House* (1942; adapted for film in 1947) was his last novel to enjoy anything like the success of his writing of the late twenties; and *The Island* (1944), an ambitious verse history of England from the viking invasion to the latest Nazi attempt, was largely ignored. He was awarded the honorary degree of DLitt from the University of Birmingham in 1950.

After the Second World War Brett Young retired to South Africa on medical advice, as he was suffering from a weak heart. He and his wife settled at Santici Montagu, near Cape Town. He died of heart failure at Tamboers Kloof Nursing Home, Cape Town, on 28 March 1954. His

Young, Sir Frank George (1908–1988), biochemist and educationist, was born on 25 March 1908 at 2 Bond Street, Holford Square, Clerkenwell, London, the eldest in the family of two sons and one daughter of Frank Edgar Young, solicitor's clerk, and his wife, Jane Eleanor Pinkney. His childhood years were spent in Clerkenwell and Dulwich. He was educated at Alleyn's School, Dulwich, and at University College, London, where he graduated with first-class honours in chemistry in 1929. He rowed for both college and university.

On graduation Young decided to take up biochemistry and joined the department of physiology, pharmacology, and biochemistry at University College. He obtained his PhD in 1933, in which year he married Ruth Eleanor, daughter of Thomas Turner, a civil servant in the Home Office. She was a fellow student at University College, who qualified in medicine after a general sciences degree. They had three sons and one daughter (d. 1988). Young was a Beit memorial research fellow at University College (1932–3 and 1935–6) and at Aberdeen and Toronto in the interval. In 1936 he moved to the National Institute for Medical Research in London as a member of the scientific staff. Within a year he had discovered that a permanent form of diabetes could be induced in suitable species of animal by a short period of injection of extracts of the anterior lobe of the pituitary gland. This discovery was of major importance because it was the first time that permanent diabetes had been induced by a natural substance (later to be identified by Young as the pituitary growth hormone). His work from 1936 to 1952, on this theme and on other aspects of the regulation of growth and metabolism by hormones, gave him a substantial national and international reputation.

In 1942 Young left the institute to become professor of biochemistry at St Thomas's Hospital medical school

(1942–5) and then at University College, London (1945–9). In 1949 he was appointed to the Sir William Dunn professorship of biochemistry at Cambridge, where he stayed until his retirement in 1975. From about 1952 onwards he abandoned personal research and teaching and concentrated increasingly on educational, scientific, and medical affairs in Cambridge and at national and international level. Two major themes were the needs of postgraduate students and relations between medicine and the sciences. In Cambridge, Young was among the first to recognize the need for postgraduate colleges, and with the senior tutor of Corpus Christi College (Michael McCrum) he set out in 1956 to advocate their establishment. Their campaign bore fruit in 1963, when the founding of Darwin College, with Young as its first master, was announced; and in 1964, with the report of the council of the senate that led to the establishment of Wolfson College. Young was a highly successful first master of Darwin (1964–76). He also played a decisive part in the founding of the Cambridge University clinical school in 1975. He was a member of the royal commission on medical education (1965–8), which provided the opportunity for the creation of the school, and as chairman (1969–75) of the school planning committee he brought that opportunity to fruition. He served on the Medical Research Council, the council and other committees of the Royal Society, committees of the Department of Health, the Ciba Foundation, and the medical and scientific section of the British Diabetic Association, of which he was founding chairman. He was also president of the European Association for the Study of Diabetes and of the International Diabetes Federation. He was knighted in 1973. He had intended to resume laboratory research on retirement but a serious episode of food poisoning in 1977 impaired his mobility and made this impractical.

Young was elected a fellow of the Royal Society in 1949, and his scientific achievements were further recognized by the Croonian lectureship of the Royal Society (1962), the Banting lectureships of the British and American diabetic associations (1948 and 1950), the Upjohn award of the American Endocrine Society (1963), and honorary degrees from the Catholic University of Chile (1950) and the universities of Montpellier (1959), Aberdeen (1965), and Rhodesia (1975).

Young was a tall, broad-shouldered man, whose vitality showed in his face. His wife was a staunch supporter of his activities in Cambridge and elsewhere and her services to Darwin were recognized with an honorary fellowship in 1989. Young died on 20 September 1988 in the Evelyn Nursing Home, Cambridge.   PHILIP RANDLE, *rev.*

Sources P. Randle, *Memoirs FRS*, 36 (1990), 583–99 · *The Independent* (26 Sept 1988) · personal knowledge (1996) · *CGPLA Eng. & Wales* (1989)
Archives CUL, papers | CAC Cam., corresp. with A. V. Hill · Wellcome L., corresp. with Sir Ernst Chain | SOUND probably RCP Lond., interview taped by Sir Gordon Wolstenholme
Likenesses photograph, repro. in Randle, *Memoirs FRS*, 582
Wealth at death £29,749: probate, 3 Jan 1989, *CGPLA Eng. & Wales*

Young, Sir Frederick (1817–1913), imperial publicist, was born on 21 June 1817 at Mitre Building, Limehouse, London, the third son of the seven children of George Frederick *Young (1791–1870), London shipbuilder and politician, and his wife, Mary (c.1790–1876), youngest daughter of John Abbot, brewer of Canterbury. Young was educated first by his mother and then, from the age of ten, at Dr Burnet's school at Homerton, Middlesex, for five years. In 1833 he joined a family business, Young, Dowson & Co., copper merchants, as clerk; from 1839 he was a partner (the firm continued to make brass fittings for ships until 1911 but was latterly moribund). In the 1840s he also set up with Christopher Dowson as a baker of ships' biscuits, living on the premises in Limehouse and there entertaining Browning, Domett, and other 'colloquials'. With his father he was actively involved in promoting Victoria Park in east London (1840–45) and in the management of the London Hospital. He also helped to found Bromley cricket club, travelled to Europe and the Mediterranean, and dabbled in a few literary ventures. Above all he pursued his wish to marry his childhood sweetheart Cecilia (c.1820–1873), daughter of Thomas Drane, brewer of Torquay. In 1836 they agreed not to meet for three years, after which they were allowed to engage to marry in five years. They married in April 1845 and soon had four children.

At this time Young came under the spell of his father's close associate in the colonization of New Zealand, Edward Gibbon Wakefield. Already a shareholder in the New Zealand Company, Young became shipping manager in 1850 to the Canterbury Association, an experiment in high-Anglican colonization, and he helped to send out 1500–2000 emigrants before the venture failed in 1852. Throughout his long life Young regarded Wakefield's *Art of Colonisation* (1849) as the bible of British colonialism, inspiring his own interest in emigration (or 'transplantation' as he preferred) as well as informing his guiding principle of imperial federation. In 1857 Young left east London for Cobham, in rural Surrey, to bring up his family; he also enjoyed hunting, joined the volunteers, and helped to rebuild the parish church. He produced several 'penny readings' (see *Long Ago and now*, 1863), including an admiring biography of Garibaldi, whom he met in 1864. In 1867 the family were obliged to move back to London (to Kensington) and Young resumed an active role in the East End, promoting working-class emigration—he was chairman of the National Colonial Emigration League—and standing (unsuccessfully) for the new Tower Hamlets school board in 1870. As chairman of the Epping Forest Fund he did much to secure the act of 1878 which preserved its open spaces. In the 1880s as a trustee of the Beaumont Trust he helped to found the People's Palace in Mile End. He was also chairman of the Tower Hamlets magistrates until 1894.

Above all Young became a vigorous proponent of the ideal of closer imperial unity. He took a leading part in protests against the withdrawal of British troops from New Zealand in 1868–9, an episode which contributed to the foundation in 1868 of the Royal Colonial Institute (RCI), of which he became a fellow in 1869 and a member of council in 1871. The sudden and unexpected death of his wife in July 1873 threw Young into intense despondency. But after a recuperative European tour with his daughters, he became honorary secretary of the RCI, in 1874, and threw himself enthusiastically into its affairs, doing much to raise its public profile. He initiated a correspondence published as *Imperial Federation* in 1876, and for the rest of his life forcefully advocated the idea of an imperial parliament. He did much to keep the ideal of 'Greater Britain' in the public mind, and took an active part in the Imperial Federation League (1883–93) and in the British Empire League. Having attended, on behalf of the RCI, the first Colonial Conference in 1887, he became KCMG in January 1888.

Young kept up a regular correspondence with like-minded British and colonial politicians, including the seventh duke of Manchester. Later in life he travelled to South Africa (1889) and Canada (1901), propagating the cause he believed essential to Britain's destiny. In line with his father's earlier protectionism he supported 'fair trade' in the early 1880s and commercial union of the empire in the 1890s; in *Exit Party* (1900) he hailed Rosebery as the leader of a non-partisan Liberal Imperialism but turned to Chamberlain's tariff reform in 1903. Slim and erect in bearing, but repetitious with age, Young survived as a venerable patriarch of empire, campaigning for a monument to Wakefield in New Zealand in 1907 and active in the Royal Colonial Institute as late as 1909. By then he was living in straitened circumstances, tended by his daughter Ada, and he was eventually reconciled to his son, Brigadier-General Sir George Frederick Young (1846–1919), whose allegedly unsuitable marriage in India in 1874—to Caroline, widow of Captain W. A. Cripps—had led to their estrangement. Young died at his home, Leny, Cobham, Surrey, on 9 November 1913 and was buried with his wife at Reigate, Surrey, on 12 November.

A. C. HOWE

Sources Sir Frederick Young MSS, CUL, Royal Commonwealth Society collection · T. R. Reese, *The history of the Royal Commonwealth Society, 1868–1968* (1968) · Royal Colonial Institute MSS, CUL, Royal Commonwealth Society collection · Young papers, LMA, Metropolitan board of works archive [relating to Victoria Park] · BL, Imperial Federation League MSS, 1884–93 · F. Young, journal of South African mission, 1889, SOAS, MS 380274 · F. Young, *A pioneer of imperial federation in Canada* (1909) · *WWW*, 1897–1915 · *WWW*, 1916–28 · Burke, *Peerage* (1907) · Kelly, *Handbk* (1917)
Archives CUL, Royal Commonwealth Society Archives, corresp. and papers · LMA, papers relating to Victoria Park, MBW/OW/VP/7 · SOAS, journal of South African mission, MS 380274 | BL, letters to W. Hall Griffin, Add. MS 45564 · BL, Horace Young papers
Likenesses photograph, repro. in Reese, *History of the Royal Commonwealth Society*, facing p. 68 · photograph, repro. in Young, *Pioneer*, frontispiece
Wealth at death £4768 18s.: probate, 13 Dec 1913, *CGPLA Eng. & Wales*

Young, Frederick Archibald [Freddie] (1902–1998), cinematographer, was born on 9 October 1902 at 58 Great James Street, St Marylebone, London, the seventh of eight children of Isaac Young, otherwise Henry Young, coachman and later horse dealer, and his wife, Annie Frances Challis. He left school at fourteen, initially working in a munitions factory. He started in the film business in 1917 when he joined the Gaumont studio in Shepherd's Bush, beginning in the laboratory before moving to the camera department two years later. On 15 October 1925 he married Marjorie Elizabeth Rosa Gaffney (1896/7–1963), cinema film company's secretary and daughter of John Gaffney, theatrical manager. They adopted a son and a daughter.

Young worked as an assistant cameraman on many films, including *Rob Roy* (1922) and *Triumph of the Rat* (1926), before being given his first feature to light, in 1927. *Victory* was a film about the last weeks of the First World War and was shot on Salisbury Plain. Sound was introduced into British film production in 1929, and Young was one of the first cinematographers to gain experience with the new process, shooting inserts with synchronized dialogue for the film *White Cargo* (1929) at British International Pictures at Elstree, a week before Alfred Hitchcock shot similar sequences for *Blackmail* (1929)—the film that was to claim the honours as Britain's first 'talkie'.

It was about this time that Young joined Herbert Wilcox's company British and Dominions as senior cameraman, and over the next decade he photographed a number of important films, including many featuring the company's top star, Anna Neagle, such as *The Little Damozel* (1933), *Nell Gwyn* (1934), *Peg of Old Drury* (1935), and *Victoria the Great* (1937). The latter featured a final reel in Technicolor, one of the first times the process had been used in Britain, a feature which led to the subject being remade entirely in colour as *Sixty Glorious Years* (1938). Young was also one of the first British cinematographers to be allowed to work in Hollywood, where he shot *Nurse Edith Cavell* (1939) for Wilcox, again starring Neagle, at RKO's studios in 1939. By the end of the decade Young was by far the most high-profile English cameraman in an industry dominated by continental and American émigré technicians, and as such he was to prove a major inspiration for a younger generation of aspiring British cameramen.

During the early part of the Second World War Young worked on the propaganda feature *49th Parallel* (1941) with Michael Powell, a film made in the attempt to persuade the Americans to join the allied effort. Much of it was shot on location in Canada, achieving a dynamic new sense of realism for a fictitious subject. He followed this with the period film *Kipps* (1941), Carol Reed's version of the H. G. Wells story. Young then served with the army cinematographic service from 1942 to 1945, directing a number of training films before returning to the industry on the ill-fated epic *Caesar and Cleopatra* (1945), on which he assumed responsibility for the direction of some location sequences in Egypt after his erratic director, the Hungarian Gabriel Pascal, had fallen out with the locals.

After the war the major Hollywood companies assumed a major presence in the film industries of western Europe. MGM built a new studio at Elstree, and Young was appointed chief cameraman there, where he photographed numerous high-profile international productions featuring top Hollywood directors and stars. These included the medieval swashbucklers *Ivanhoe* (1952) and *Knights of the Round Table* (1953), the latter being the first British production in CinemaScope; *Mogambo* (1953) and *Gideon's Day* (1958), both directed by John Ford; the Indian adventure *Bhowani Junction* (1956), directed by George Cukor; the Gene Kelly musical *Invitation to the Dance* (1954); and *Lust for Life* (1956), Vincente Minnelli's biographical film of Vincent Van Gogh starring Kirk Douglas. During this period Young was also a founder member of the British Society of Cinematographers, serving as the first president from 1949 to 1951.

Young's greatest triumph came in the 1960s with a hat-trick of Oscar-winning collaborations with David Lean, on *Lawrence of Arabia* (1962), *Doctor Zhivago* (1965), and *Ryan's Daughter* (1970), a record unsurpassed by any other British cinematographer. The epic nature of these productions afforded unprecedented creative opportunities: from the breathtaking desert vistas of *Lawrence* to the exquisite winter fabrications of *Zhivago*, in which Russia was recreated in Spain, and the elemental Irish landscapes of *Ryan's Daughter*. *Zhivago* was to remain his favourite film (alongside the 1939 production *Goodbye Mr Chips*) despite the fact that he was called in to replace Lean's first-choice cinematographer, Nicolas Roeg, Young's former operator. In 1966 Young was again at the cutting edge of new film-making techniques, experimenting with the pre-exposure of film stock to create muted colour effects on *The Deadly Affair* directed by Sidney Lumet. Meanwhile, his first wife, Marjorie, having died in 1963, on 13 June 1964 he married (Nina) Joan Morduch (*b.* 1930/31), film technician and daughter of Oscar Morduch, electrical engineer. They had one son, David.

Young was appointed OBE in 1970 and continued working on top-flight productions throughout the 1970s, his films including *Nicholas and Alexandra* (1971), *Luther* (1973), from John Osborne's play, and *Permission to Kill* (1975). He also, with Paul Petzold, wrote a textbook, *The Work of the Motion Picture Cameraman* (1972). In 1985 he directed a small film for Channel 4 television, *Arthur's Hallowed Ground*, the story of an elderly cricket field groundsman. Although this was his last film, he continued to work on commercials before finally retiring in 1996. He died on 1 December 1998 at Kingston Hospital, Kingston upon Thames, of chronic obstructive airways disease. He was survived by his wife, Joan, their son, and the two adopted children of his first marriage. His autobiography, *Seventy Light Years: a Life in the Movies*, appeared posthumously, in 1999.

DUNCAN PETRIE

Sources F. Young, *Seventy light years: a life in the movies* (1999) · D. Petrie, *The British cinematographer* (1996) · K. Desmond, '70 glorious years: a profile of Freddie Young OBE', *Eyepiece* (Dec 1988), (Jan–Feb 1989), (March 1989) · K. Brownlow, *David Lean* (1996) · *The Times* (3 Dec 1998) · *Daily Telegraph* (3 Dec 1998) · *The Guardian* (3 Dec 1998) · *The Independent* (4 Dec 1998) · b. cert. · m. certs. · d. cert.
Likenesses double portrait, photograph, *c.*1961 (with David Lean), repro. in *The Independent* · double portrait, photograph, *c.*1969 (with David Lean), repro. in *The Times* · photograph, repro. in *The Guardian* (3 Dec 1998) · photograph, repro. in *Daily Telegraph*

Wealth at death £121,393—gross; £118,393—net: administration with will, 11 Feb 1999, *CGPLA Eng. & Wales*

Young, Geoffrey Winthrop (1876–1958), mountaineer and educationist, was born on 25 October 1876 in London, the second son of Sir George *Young, third baronet (1837–1930), and his wife, Alice Eacy (1840–1922), daughter of Evory Kennedy, a Dublin physician, and widow of Sir Alexander Hutchinson Lawrence, first baronet. He was the third of four children. (Edward) Hilton *Young was his brother. He was educated at Wymondley, Marlborough College (1890–95), and Trinity College, Cambridge (1895–8), where he studied classics (BA 1898, MA 1902), and was awarded the chancellor's medal for English verse in 1897 and 1898. He then studied the French and German languages in Europe, including a period in Geneva and a year at Jena University (1899–1900).

Geoffrey Young was one of the most famous British mountaineers before the First World War. He began climbing mountains as an undergraduate and popularized collegiate roof climbing with the jocular *The Roof-Climber's Guide to Trinity* (1899), and the literary *Wall and Roof Climbing* (1905). His many notable first ascents in the Alps included several ridges in the Zermatt district that became known as Younggrat. His pre-war climbing is perhaps best remembered for his description in *On High Hills* (1927) of the first ascent of the south face of the Täschhorn in 1906, with Franz Lochmatter, Josef Lochmatter, Valentine John Eustace Ryan (*d.* 1947), and Josef Knubel (1881–1961), who was frequently Young's guide. In 1907 he began organizing climbing retreats during Easter at the Pen y Pass hostel in Snowdonia, and this annual event brought together the leading British climbers for many years. Many of his companions and pupils died climbing, and he personally recovered the bodies of Donald Robertson (1879–1910) near Pen y Pass, Humphrey Owen Jones (1878–1912) in the Alps, and Hugh Rose Pope (*d.* 1912) in the Pyrenees. Another of his protégés, George Mallory, disappeared on Everest in 1924.

Young's career in education began in 1900 with brief periods teaching at various schools. In 1902 he was appointed tutor in modern languages at Eton College. There he introduced several students to climbing, including Marcus Beresford Heywood (1886–1947). In 1905 Young was dismissed from Eton for a homosexual liaison (Hankinson, 67), and became an HM inspector of secondary schools. Although he enjoyed this work, he once again resigned from it abruptly in 1913. His diaries during these years record the tension between his public probity and private pleasures in the homosexual underworlds of Berlin, Paris, and Soho (ibid., 129). During 1913–14 he retreated to an Italian villa to write about mountaineering, and lived briefly with Wilbert Spencer, a Cornish boy who was killed in action in 1915.

Young served in Belgium and France as a war correspondent for the *Daily News* during July–September 1914, and his dispatches were collected in *From the Trenches* (1914). From October 1914 to July 1915 he founded and commanded the Friends' Ambulance Unit in Flanders, and served mostly at Ypres. In August 1915 he joined his close

Geoffrey Winthrop Young (1876–1958), by unknown photographer

friend George Macaulay Trevelyan and Philip Noel-Baker to form the first British ambulance unit for Italy, which he commanded until January 1919. He was severely wounded on 31 August 1917 at the battle of Monte San Gabriele, and his left leg was amputated above the knee. He was mentioned in dispatches and received the order of Leopold from Belgium, was a member of the Légion d'honneur of France, received the order of the crown of Italy, and the British campaign medal. He married Eleanor (Len; d. 1994), an actress, the youngest daughter of William Cecil *Slingsby, on 25 April 1918 at St George's, Hanover Square. They had a son, Jocelin, in 1919, and a daughter, Marcia, in 1925, but Geoffrey continued to have homosexual affairs after their marriage (Hankinson, 210).

After the war Young also continued to write and to climb with only one leg. He published *Mountain Craft* (1920), a manual of mountaineering technique, and *On High Hills* (1927), on his pre-war ascents, both of which inspired the next generation of climbers. Most inspirational were his climbs with a custom-designed peg-leg. After ascending Monte Rosa in 1927, over the next few years he climbed Wellenkuppe, Matterhorn, Petits Charmoz, Requin, and Grépon. He resolved to give up climbing while on the summit of Zinal Rothorn in 1935, and described these ascents in *Mountains with a Difference* (1951), winner of the W. H. Heinemann prize for 1952.

Young served as consultant in the humanities for Europe to the Laura Spelman Rockefeller memorial (1925–9) and the Rockefeller Foundation (1929–33), for which he earned $10,000 a year and spent long periods in Geneva, Paris, and Berlin. In this capacity he proposed what became the Abraham Lincoln Stiftung, dispersed grants to French historians, and met Kurt Hahn, whose innovative school in Salem, Germany, included outdoor sports in the curriculum. After Hahn fled the Nazis in 1933, Young helped him start Gordonstoun School on the Moray Firth and the outward bound schools. Young was chair of the Gordonstoun board, and he recommended the school to Prince Philip of Greece (later the duke of Edinburgh), who became one of its earliest students. From 1932 to 1941 he was Thomas Wall reader in comparative education at the University of London. As president during 1941–3, he rejuvenated the Alpine Club from its Edwardian torpor and played a crucial role in founding the British Mountaineering Council, a national federation of climbing clubs. He published several volumes of poetry, including *Collected Poems* (1936), a non-climbing autobiography, *The Grace of Forgetting* (1953), and contributed to *Snowdon Biography* (1957), a history of climbing in Wales. He received an honorary DLitt from Durham University in 1950.

Later in life Young referred to himself as an 'elderly celebrity, second-class' (Hankinson, 2). Although only 5 feet 9 inches tall, he usually cut an imposing figure, with lambent eyes, bushy moustache, pipe, monocle, fedora or beret, and cascading cloak. He admired vitality above all else, and contemporaries were impressed by his forceful personality. Apart from the period when he worked for the Rockefeller Foundation, his personal finances were often precarious. In 1955 he and his wife moved into Grovehurst, Horsmonden, Kent, the first home they ever owned. He died of stomach cancer on 6 September 1958 at a nursing home, 48 Holland Park, Kensington, London. After he was cremated, his ashes were scattered on the peaks above Pen y Pass. PETER H. HANSEN

Sources A. Hankinson, *Geoffrey Winthrop Young: poet, educator, mountaineer* (1995) · *Alpine Journal*, 64 (1959), 107–14 · *The Times* (8 Sept 1958) · G. W. Young, correspondence, Alpine Club Archives, London · P. Bicknell, 'In memoriam: Eleanor Winthrop Young, 1897–1994', *Alpine Journal*, 100 (1995), 336–7, facing p. 340 · A. Zurcher, 'Joseph Knubel', trans. H. Merrick, *Alpine Journal*, 67 (1962), 269–74, esp. 271 · Venn, *Alum. Cant.* · [F. E. Thompson], ed., *Marlborough College register from 1843 to 1904 inclusive*, 5th edn (1905) · *Debrett's Peerage* · *WW* · private information (2004) · m. cert. · d. cert.

Archives Alpine Club, London · Alpine Club, London, corresp. · NRA, corresp. · Rockefeller Archive Center, Sleepy Hollow, New York · Trinity Cam., papers relating to Cambridge night-climbing | Bodl. Oxf., corresp. with Sidgwick & Jackson · CUL, Lord Kennet corresp. · Georgetown University, Washington, DC, corresp. with Sir Arnold Lunn · King's AC Cam., letters to John Maynard Keynes | FILM BFI NFTVA

Likenesses photograph, Alpine Club, London [*see illus.*]

Wealth at death £25,775 18s. 10d.: probate, 24 Nov 1958, *CGPLA Eng. & Wales*

Young, Sir George (1732–1810), naval officer, was born on 17 June 1732, eldest son of the Revd George Young of Bere Regis in Dorset (one of a family claiming descent from

John Yong of Buckhorn Weston, sheriff of Dorset in 1570), and his wife, Eleanor Knowles. He went to sea in 1746 in the *Namur* with Edward Boscawen, and saw action off the western coasts of Europe. Towards the end of 1747 Boscawen sailed to India where he participated in the siege of Pondicherry. The *Namur* sank in April 1749, but before this Young had transferred to the East India Company's marine, in which he became midshipman in 1753. Given that he later named his country seat Formosa Place, it is probable that he was then voyaging to China.

Young re-entered the Royal Navy at the beginning of the Seven Years' War, joining the *York* under Commander Hugh Pigot in December 1756; he was promoted midshipman in January 1757, participated in the campaigns against Louisbourg and Quebec, and was promoted lieutenant on 3 September 1760. In November 1761 he sailed in the *Orford* (Captain Marriot Arbuthnot) to the West Indies, where he took part in the campaign against Havana before returning to England in 1763. In the winter Young married Elizabeth Bradshaw (d. 1779); they had four children: Lucia (b. 1764), Samuel (b. 1766), George (b. 1767), and Maria (b. 1768). Between 1767 and 1772 Young commanded the small Africa squadron and made four voyages down the west coast, after the second of which he seems to have been promoted master and commander. On the fourth voyage he stopped at Tenerife, and brought off a mummy which he presented to the earl of Sandwich, who in turn presented it to Cambridge University.

In 1777 Young sailed for India in the *Cormorant*, one of the squadron under the command of Sir Edward Vernon. He was promoted post captain on arrival, becoming Vernon's flag captain, and participated in the capture of Pondicherry. Vernon then sent him home with dispatches. He arrived in London in March 1779, to find his wife had died in the previous month.

Young got married again before the end of the year, to Anne Battie (b. 1745?), daughter of the wealthy physician William Battie. This connection made him the brother-in-law of the military engineer John Call, who had married Anne's sister Philadelphia in 1772, and gave him the use of the family's London town house in Great Russell Street. He also added to his wife's land holdings at Cookham in Berkshire, where the couple built Formosa Place in the mid-1780s. He was elected fellow of the Royal Society on 15 February 1781. Later that year he was appointed commander of the royal yacht *William and Mary*; he was knighted on 24 August 1781. Command of another yacht, the *Katherine*, followed. These appointments brought him into contact with the prince of Wales, a politically dangerous association at a time when the king was much displeased with his eldest son's profligate ways. At one point his colleague Edward Thompson warned Young privately that he was in danger of losing his command. Young was treasurer to the commissioners of Thames navigation from 1786 to 1794. He became rear-admiral by seniority on 4 July 1794, vice-admiral on 14 February 1799, and admiral on 23 April 1804, but saw no further active service.

Young was by report a handsome man, socially graceful, and a keen amateur musician. He assisted Sandwich in introducing concerts to London; and he took pride in offering musical entertainments to guests at Formosa Place, where he built a music chamber. He also took an active interest in some of the important social issues of his time. He was a founding shareholder in the Sierra Leone Company, and a member of its first board; and in 1792 he testified to the House of Commons on the evils of the slave trade.

Young was clearly a person of accomplishment, and a competent naval officer. However, his principal historical significance lies in his support for the colonization of New South Wales. He sent a copy of his scheme (which exists in five versions) to William Pitt the younger. In October 1784 he joined forces with James Mario Matra, who had proposed colonization the previous year, to urge this idea on the administration; and in 1785 John Call added his support. Apart from seeing Botany Bay as a fitting place to which to send convicts and displaced American loyalists, Young thought that a settlement there would offer the East India Company ships a new and safer route to China; and 'suppose we were again involved in a war with Spain, here are ports of shelter and refreshment for our ships, should it be necessary to send any to the South Sea' (PRO, CO 201/8, fols. 152–3).

Like Matra and Call, Young was even more attracted by the idea of creating in the south-west Pacific Ocean an alternative source of hemp for the British marines, and thus diminishing Britain's dependence on Russia. He had samples of *phormium tenax* from New Zealand worked into cordage, and canvas 'which had been worn and tried in the foot or clew of a cutter's mainsail' (priv. coll.). In June 1785 he and Call asked the East India Company for permission to colonize Norfolk Island (where the fibre plant grew prolifically, and where there were as well towering pine trees) 'for the pursuit of further Discoveries—for the Cultivation of the Flax plant—& Manufacture of that valuable Material into Cordage—and for the supplying Masts from thence for Shipping with which it abounds' (BL OIOC, E/1/76, fol. 213). The pair repeated this request to the administration in May 1788 when they asked for the grant of the island in perpetuity. However, by this time Arthur Phillip had occupied it; and the dream of its becoming an emporium of naval stores was already fading. None the less Young's thinking encapsulated the Pitt administration's motives for the colonization. He died at Formosa Place on 28 June 1810.   ALAN FROST

Sources G. Young, 'Young of Formosa', priv. coll. • A. Frost, *Dreams of a Pacific empire: Sir George Young's proposal for a colonization of New South Wales, 1784–5* (1980) • PRO, CO 201/8, fols. 152–3 • BL OIOC, E/1/76, fol. 213 • BL, Thomas Rowcroft correspondence, Add. MS 42774B • BL, Edward Thompson correspondence and diary, Add. MS 46120 • *DNB*

Likenesses J. Smart, oils, 1805, V&A • O. Humphry, pastels; now lost • portrait, priv. coll.

Young, George (1777–1848), Presbyterian minister and geologist, was born on 15 July 1777 at a small farmhouse called Croxiedean in the parish of Kirknewton and East Calder, Edinburghshire, and baptized in that parish on 3

August, the son of John Young and his wife, Jean, *née* Graham. Having studied under John Playfair at the University of Edinburgh, he graduated with high honours in 1796 and commenced his training in theology with George Lawson at Selkirk. In 1801 he was licensed to preach by the presbytery of Edinburgh of the associate secession church, and in the summer of 1805 visited Whitby, with which he was to be associated for the rest of his life. In January 1806 he was ordained pastor of the Presbyterian congregation which met at the chapel there in Cliff Lane. He published some sermons, but his earliest substantial work was a defence of evangelical principles against Unitarianism, which was published in 1812, and this was followed five years later by his *History of Whitby and Streoneshalh Abbey*, a topographical and antiquarian account which was a continuation of the work of two other local antiquaries, Francis Gibson FSA and Richard Winter. In addition to providing a historical narrative, Young's account placed the town in its contemporary local context by incorporating statistical information on the demographic, economic, and geographical features of the neighbourhood. In 1819 he graduated MA at Edinburgh University, and in 1824 he produced a more popular topographical guide to his adopted town and its region, *A Picture of Whitby and its Environs*, which was reprinted in 1840, and later used by Elizabeth Gaskell as a background source for *Sylvia's Lovers*.

By this time Young had already turned his attention to geology, publishing in 1822 a comprehensive *Geological survey of the Yorkshire coast: describing the strata and fossils occurring between the Humber and the Tees, from the German ocean to the plain of York*, which was copiously illustrated by John Bird. His geological work was committed to 'honour that infinite being whose works are here examined and described' (*Geological Survey*, 12), and he accepted the biblical account of the creation and the flood, concluding that his findings did 'not contradict but confirm the sacred scripture' (ibid., 324). He returned to this theme in lectures given to the geological section of the British Association at its meeting in Newcastle upon Tyne, which were published in 1838 as *Scriptural Geology*. In this book he attacked the theories of Lyell and the pre-Adamites, claiming that the strata did not define periodic levels but were the result of natural upheavals caused by the flood. He was moved to publish a second edition in 1840 to counter the scriptural justification circulating in scientific clerical circles that the biblical flood was confined, as was man, to the Near East and central Asia, thereby allowing for older geological forms in other regions of the earth.

Young's connection to Whitby also engaged his interest in Captain Cook and the voyages of discovery, and in 1836 he published a selection from Cook's journals and other original sources, which proved popular with readers. He was an honorary member of the Hull and Yorkshire literary and philosophical societies, was active in public life in Whitby, and was a corresponding member of the Wernerian Natural History Society, Edinburgh. He had acquired a DD by 1840, but the award of that degree has not been traced. He married Margaret Hunter of Whitby on 11 April

1826 and died there on 8 May 1848, his wife having predeceased him. His will was proved in August 1848, when his goods, valued at £800, were distributed among his many nieces and nephews, among whom was William Young, the Independent minister at Beverley.

WILLIAM JOSEPH SHEILS

Sources 'Brief notice of the late Rev. George Young', *Evangelical Magazine and Missionary Chronicle*, new ser., 27 (1849), 113–17 · will, Aug 1848, Borth. Inst., Prerogative Wills · *DNB* · b. cert. · W. Gérin, *Elizabeth Gaskell: a biography* (1976), 215 · parish register (baptism), 3/8/1777, Kirknewton and East Calder
Archives U. Hull, Brynmor Jones L., shorthand sermons and lectures · Whitby Museum, Whitby Literary and Philosophical Society Library, *History of Whitby*
Likenesses E. Cockburn, portrait, Whitby Museum, Pannett Park, Whitby, North Yorkshire
Wealth at death under £800: will, Borth. Inst.

Young, George, Lord Young (1819–1907), lawyer and politician, was born on 2 July 1819 at Dumfries, the only son of Alexander Young of Rosefield, Kirkcudbrightshire, procurator fiscal of Dumfriesshire, and his wife, Marian, daughter of William Corsan of Dalwhat, Kirkcudbrightshire. He was educated at Dumfries Academy and thence proceeded to Edinburgh University. His intellectual powers were great enough to see him included in the honours list of the junior Scots law class of 1837. After a reportedly severe apprenticeship he was admitted as an advocate at the Scottish bar in December 1840. In July 1847 he married Janet (1829–1901), daughter of George Graham Bell, advocate, of Crurie, Dumfriesshire. They had four surviving sons, all in the legal profession, and six daughters. One of these daughters, Lily, married Lord Mackenzie, also a judge in the court of session.

As an advocate Young was one of the most brilliant and successful court pleaders of his day. Described as having a tall, striking figure, an unfathomable face, 'luminous, piercing eyes' and a 'resonant, incisive voice', he inspired 'the conviction that he was born to lead and not to follow' (*Juridical Review*, 209–10). This powerful character showed in his style of pleading, which was carried on with the bench as between equals and in which he apparently refused to stoop to win verdicts by flattery or wheedling. Deliberate in his method, he seems to have adopted a coercive rather than a persuasive approach. He earned a reputation as merciless cross-examiner, who excelled in difficult and desperate cases.

Whatever criticisms he attracted, Young's practice prospered and his success was paralleled by his official career. He was appointed advocate-depute in 1849 and became sheriff of Inverness in 1853. From 1860 to 1862 he was sheriff of Haddington and Berwickshire. In 1857 he acted as junior counsel to John Inglis at the celebrated trial of Madeleine Smith for murder. Their successful conduct of her defence was due partly to Young's skill in its preparation. In this trial he was, as in others in this period, on the opposite side of the case to James Moncreiff. From November 1862, when he was appointed solicitor-general for Scotland in Lord Palmerston's government, he also worked under Moncreiff as lord advocate. Linked in the public mind as a result of their contribution to the development of Scottish education, the contrast between the two men was in fact marked. Young's forceful style as an advocate was coloured by a matter-of-fact coolness that could shade into sarcasm. Moncreiff, on the other hand, was fiery and eloquent. In a working relationship which was apparently not harmonious, Young was less than loyal to a man he is said arrogantly to have regarded as his intellectual inferior.

In 1865 Young was elected unopposed to parliament as the Liberal member for Wigtown burghs. His Liberalism was of the undogmatic kind and he canvassed support as an unashamed Palmerstonian. He continued as solicitor-general after Palmerston's death until the Russell government resigned in July 1866 and was appointed to the same office by Gladstone after the Liberal election victory in December 1868. Seemingly impatient for Moncreiff to move on, his opportunity came in November 1869 when he was himself appointed lord advocate. Young's tenure in this office was certainly the high point in his career. He ruled Scottish MPs with a verbal rod of iron and, though most of his attempts to pass legislation were frustrated, his achievement in finally passing a measure to create an effective national system of education in Scotland was a lasting monument. Although there is no doubt that the ground for the Education (Scotland) Act of 1872 had been long prepared by his predecessor, the passage of this particular measure owed a lot to Young's drive and flexibility. In effect he 'solved' the religious question by leaving the management of schools to locally elected boards and therefore ensured that a system, which embodied compulsory elementary education supported by public funds and which stood the test of time, was at last put in place nearly twenty years after Moncreiff had first made the attempt.

In a parliament dominated by Irish land, English education, and army reform, Scottish business was otherwise marginalized. Although he was responsible for the Public Health Act (Scotland) in 1871, among the problems Young could not solve were the tenant farmers' grievances of hypothec and ground game, a failure which was to contribute to the poor Liberal showing in the Scottish counties at the 1874 election. Despite more than one attempt, Young was also unable to get very far with legislation to clarify and make sense of the Scottish law of entail. These difficulties do not appear to have turned Young's thoughts, as was the case in some of his Liberal parliamentary colleagues, towards a reform of the system of Scottish administration involving the appointment of a Scottish secretary. On the contrary, Young was reported to have contemplated the abolition of the court of session, for example. This would have been motivated partly by a desire to save money, but it would also have reflected his belief in the assimilation of the Scottish and English judicial systems.

Young was himself known and well regarded in English legal circles. In 1869 he was called to the English bar at the Middle Temple, London, of which he was made a bencher

two years later. What were described as his bleak, inscrutable face and his thin compressed lips were said to be familiar to students at the Middle Temple, as he dined there during term time on regular visits to London, a habit he maintained for the remainder of his life.

At the 1874 general election Young initially, and very narrowly, lost Wigtown burghs. Poor treatment of the sheriff of Lanarkshire, Henry Glassford Bell, and the opposition of local Orangemen were held up at the time as significant contributory factors in this result. In the event, after an investigation the seat was eventually awarded to Young, but he had in the meantime agreed to become a judge of the court of session, taking his seat in March 1874.

Over the succeeding thirty-one years, until his resignation in 1905, Young earned a reputation with the public for his disregard of precedent, as well as for his sardonic wit and impatience. In the eyes of the legal profession his defects almost certainly outweighed his strengths and these may help to explain why he ended his career as an ordinary member of the second division of the court's inner house. Just as he had reportedly terrorized witnesses in cross-examination as counsel and refused to soothe deputations when lord advocate, so now as a judge Young, with a mixture of equity and dispatch, bludgeoned advocates into brevity and tried to manage their cases for them. One advocate was even said to have asked him if he would like to call his next witness. He had little respect for legal precedents if he thought they were unjust, and put much emphasis on simplifying underlying principles of jurisprudence, of which he was credited with having a firm grasp. Young frequently dissented from his colleagues, could show intolerance with those he thought were litigating over trifles, and was reported to have taken his dislike for authority to the extent of trying to block the application of a House of Lords' judgment in a case involving the Free Church. By contrast he was usually lenient in judging criminal cases, and his common-sense approach to procedure was applauded as a contribution to efficiency.

Young wrote his own opinions which, lacking in terseness and finish, were seen as reflecting a spoken style, an echo of the voice of an advocate in the position of a judge. At the bar he had acted, between 1842 and 1850, as a reporter of court of session cases for *Dunlop's Reports*. The demands of his growing practice led him to give this up and in accordance with the usual custom he wrote nothing for separate publication after he became a judge. Overall, his career on the bench could be said to have reflected his frustrated ambition. He was rumoured to be ready to step down from the bench when Gladstone returned to office in 1880, because he missed life in London and the conscious exercise of power involved in holding political office.

Young, who was praised by his friends as capable of disinterested kindness and of being able to draw people out in conversation, could also snub and offend. He became famous for witty—the victim might have said sarcastic— sayings, which caught the attention of London as well as of Edinburgh society. Some may not even have originated from him, but Young was credited with them anyway. Thus, for instance, the gift of half a million pounds, given by James Baird to the Church of Scotland, was described as 'the heaviest insurance against fire on record', and a Free Churchman appearing before him in court was told he might be a good man in spite of his denominational allegiance. Young was an admirer of Tennyson and counted among his friends Sir Henry Campbell-Bannerman and above all Lord Rosebery. His summers were regularly spent at Silverknowes, near the Rosebery estate at Dalmeny. Among the honours conferred on him were his appointment as a privy councillor in 1872. He was created LLD by Edinburgh University in 1871 and by Glasgow in 1879.

Two years after Young resigned from the bench, on one of his visits to London he fainted, fell, and broke a rib, in the Middle Temple. He had been in robust good health until late in life, which he attributed to his hobby of walking. After a month's illness he died in a London nursing home on 21 May 1907. He was buried in St John's Episcopal churchyard in Edinburgh on 24 May. At the time of his death Young was praised as having been a powerful and successful advocate. As a judge he was seen, depending on the standpoint of the commentator, either as wilful and oblivious to precedent, or as forceful and humorous, and at his best when dissenting. His historical significance lies in his achievement in bringing to fruition James Moncreiff's efforts to create a compulsory national system of education in Scotland.   GORDON F. MILLAR

Sources The Scotsman (23 May 1907) · The Times (23 May 1907) · Juridical Review, 19 (1907), 209–22 · Scots Law Times (1 June 1907), 17–18 · Scots Law Times (13 May 1905), 1–2; (27 May 1905), 15–16 · G. W. T. Omond, The lord advocates of Scotland, second series, 1834–1880 (1914), 260–88 · WWW, 1897–1915 · WWBMP, 1.423 · F. J. Grant, ed., The Faculty of Advocates in Scotland, 1532–1943, Scottish RS, 145 (1944), 223 · S. P. Walker, The Faculty of Advocates, 1800–1986 (1987), 198 · DNB · Hansard 3 (1872), 209.250–76 · Galloway Gazette (13 Jan 1872) · D. K. Guthrie and C. J. Guthrie, Autobiography and memoir of Thos. Guthrie, D. D., 2 (1876), 299–307 · A. Duncan Smith, ed., Trial of Madeleine Smith (1905), 286 · Irving, Scots. · J. Foster, Members of parliament, Scotland … 1357–1882, 2nd edn (privately printed, London, 1882), 360 · A. Eddington, Edinburgh and the Lothians at the opening of the twentieth century: contemporary biographies, ed. W. T. Pike (1904); facs. edn as A dictionary of Edwardian biography: Edinburgh and the Lothians (1983), 164

Archives BL, corresp. with W. E. Gladstone, Add. MSS 44416–44471, passim · NL Scot., corresp. with Lord Rosebery

Likenesses photograph?, 1873, repro. in Juridical Review, facing p. 212 · photograph?, 1903, repro. in Juridical Review, facing p. 216 · Mrs Wallace, bust, Faculty of Advocates, Parliament House, Edinburgh · group portrait (The Lord President's breakfast at the opening of the winter session, 1865), repro. in Juridical Review, facing p. 209; priv. coll.

Wealth at death £12,133 2s. 3d.: Scottish confirmation, 21 Aug 1907, CCI

Young, Sir George, third baronet (1837–1930), civil servant, was born at Formosa Place, Cookham, Berkshire, on 15 September 1837, the eldest of the five sons of Sir George Young, second baronet (1797–1848), and his wife, Susan (1804/5–1895), daughter of William Mackworth Praed, serjeant-at-law. William Mackworth *Young was his

younger brother. The family had a strong naval tradition. His great-grandfather Sir George Young was an admiral; his grandfather Sir Samuel Young FRS, the first baronet, began his career in the navy, and his father rose to the rank of captain before his retirement from the service.

Young, who succeeded his father to the baronetcy in February 1848 at the age of ten, was educated at Eton College, where he won the Newcastle medal in 1855. In the following year he entered Trinity College, Cambridge, where he regarded the second classes which he obtained in the classical and mathematical triposes (1859) as a setback to his fellowship ambitions. After a period of intense self-analysis, he set about a course of reading in preparation for the fellowship examinations. He remained at Cambridge for a further three years, being elected president of the Cambridge Union in 1860, studying classics and philosophy. In 1861 he gained the Le Bas prize for an essay on the history of Greek literature in England, which was published in 1862, the year of his third and successful attempt at a Trinity fellowship, an outcome which illustrated his remarkable tenacity of purpose. At Eton and Cambridge, A. C. Swinburne, G. O. Trevelyan, Henry Jackson, Henry Sidgwick, Richard Jebb, Edward Bowen, and Leslie Stephen were among his friends. His enthusiasms and outlook were those of the Liberal intelligentsia of the 1860s. With the Sidgwick brothers he was one of the founders in 1864 of the Ad Eundem Club, which brought together reform-minded graduates of Oxford and Cambridge, was later a member of the Radical Club, and, in 1876, was organizer with James Bryce of the Eastern Question Association, which attacked the Disraeli government's handling of the Bulgarian crisis. He supported the campaign for repealing religious tests at the ancient universities, writing a pamphlet on the question in 1868, and contributed an article, 'The House of Commons in 1833', to the academic reformers' manifesto, Essays on Reform (1867). He shared Stephen's strenuous athleticism and was an intrepid alpinist until, in 1866, he and two of his brothers attempted to climb Mont Blanc without a guide. One of his brothers was killed and Young never climbed there again.

Young was called to the bar by Lincoln's Inn in 1864 but never practised at the law. He unsuccessfully stood for parliament as Liberal candidate for Chippenham in November 1868. Like many of his university contemporaries he was given official employment by the Gladstone administration. In April 1870 he was named, along with Charles Mitchell and W. E. Frere, one of three royal commissioners to inquire into the conditions of indentured Chinese and Indian labourers, who had been brought in to work the sugar plantations of British Guiana after the abolition of slavery. During the commission's investigations Young took part in an exploratory expedition to the recently discovered Kaieteur Falls on the Potaro River. The commission's report of February 1871 recommended changes to the system of indentured labour, and Young was given the task of drafting a new immigration ordinance, which marked the beginning of a series of reforms.

On his return to England, Young married (10 October

1871) Alice Eacy (1840–1922), 'a beautiful, witty, and most lovable woman' (*DNB*), the daughter of Evory Kennedy, a distinguished Dublin physician, and widow of Sir Alexander Hutchinson Lawrence, bt. They had three sons and a daughter, Eacy, who died in childhood. In the summer of 1871 he became one of six assistant commissioners employed by the royal commission on friendly societies, and two years later completed a survey of voluntary self-help institutions in the southern and eastern counties of England. After another unsuccessful attempt to enter parliament, standing for Plymouth in February 1874 (he was defeated twice more in that constituency, in April and June 1880), he was secretary to the royal commission on the Factory and Workshops acts (1875–6), a prelude to his major work as secretary to the Bessborough commission on the working of the 1870 Irish Land Act, set up by the second Gladstone administration in June 1880. He was responsible for drafting the commission's report, published in 1881, which made radical proposals for increasing the rights of tenants in Ireland. In 1882 Lord Frederick Cavendish, the chief secretary for Ireland, invited him to become his private secretary; Young's telegram of acceptance was in Cavendish's pocket when he and T. H. Burke were murdered in Phoenix Park, Dublin.

Later in 1882 Young was appointed by Gladstone, initially on a temporary basis, as a charity commissioner responsible for carrying out the reorganization of educational charities provided for under the Endowed Schools Acts. After careful investigation, the commissioners set about redistributing the endowments in each area of the country to provide for different grades of secondary schools. Some radicals attacked the commissioners for diverting endowments away from the education of the poor. After Joseph Chamberlain and Jesse Collings denounced the commissioners' scheme for Alderman Dauntsey's charity in West Lavington, Wiltshire, as a misappropriation of funds intended for the benefit of agricultural labourers, Young defended their policy before a parliamentary select committee in 1886. He later claimed that none of the schemes for which he had charge was ever overturned or altered on a point of law; but his belief in his own integrity and the rightness of his decisions, combined with a certain patrician confidence, 'made him a difficult colleague and an uncompromising adversary' (*DNB*). He has, however, been shown in a more favourable light for his effective work in ensuring that a portion of charitable endowments was used for the benefit of girls' schools. He was also a supporter of the movement for women's higher education in Cambridge, favouring the admission of women to degrees. From 1875 he was a member of the council of University College, London (and president, 1881–6), taking a prominent part in the Association for Promoting a Teaching University for London.

Young's position on the Charity Commission was made permanent, and in 1903 he was made chief charity commissioner for England and Wales. He retired in 1906. During his civil service career he found recreation in literature. In 1888 he published an edition of the poetry of his uncle, Winthrop Mackworth Praed. He was admired for his skill as a translator of verse; he produced *The Dramas of Sophocles Rendered in English Verse, Dramatic and Lyric* (1888) and *Poems from Victor Hugo in English Verse* (1901). He enjoyed a vigorous retirement, remaining active in local government in Berkshire, where he promoted the charter for Reading University. In his nineties he published *An English Prosody* (1928) and *Homer and the Greek Accents* (1930). A tall, bearded figure, with an impressive appearance and 'a somewhat formidable manner' (*The Times*, 5 July 1930), given to making his strong opinions known, he was the last survivor of the mid-Victorian academic Liberals. In his ninety-second year he wrote to *The Times* to correct a premature announcement of his death. Young died at Formosa Fishery, Cookham, Berkshire, on 4 July 1930. He was succeeded as baronet by his eldest son, George (1872–1952), who held diplomatic and other government positions, and was a Labour parliamentary candidate; the younger sons were Geoffrey Winthrop *Young, the educationist, and (Edward) Hilton *Young, first Baron Kennet, the Conservative politician.   M. C. CURTHOYS

Sources *DNB* · Venn, *Alum. Cant.* · *Men and women of the time* (1899) · C. Harvie, *The lights of liberalism* (1976) · W. P. Morrell, *British colonial policy in the mid-Victorian age* (1969) · S. Fletcher, *Feminists and bureaucrats* (1980) · J. Roach, *Secondary education in England, 1870–1902* (1991) · *The Times* (5 July 1930)
Archives King's AC Cam., letters to Oscar Browning · LUL, letters to Karl Pearson · NL Wales, letters to A. C. Humphreys-Owen
Likenesses J. Brett, two pencil drawings, priv. coll. · C. N. Kennedy, portrait, priv. coll.
Wealth at death £9436 5s. 8d.: probate, 22 July 1930, CGPLA Eng. & Wales

Young, George Frederick (1791–1870), shipbuilder and politician, was born at 4 Torrington Street, Ratcliffe Highway, London, the second son of thirteen children of Vice-Admiral William Young (1761–1847) and Ann, daughter of Robert Curling, shipbuilder. Young's father, after service in the American and Napoleonic wars, acted as inspecting agent for transports in the Thames (1805–30), but was also the partner of Robert Curling in the firm Curling, Young & Co. Young was mainly educated at home, and in 1814 he married Mary (*c*.1790–1876), youngest daughter of John Abbot, brewer, of Canterbury. The couple had eight children.

By the 1820s Young had become the leading partner in Curling, Young & Co., by then one of the most prominent firms in the London shipping industry. Having specialized in building East Indiamen, it went on, in the 1830s, to produce some of Britain's most notable passenger steamships, including the *Victoria* (later *British Queen*), as well as gunships during the Second South African War. Young played an important part in the master shipbuilders' conflicts with John Gast's shipwrights' union in the mid-1820s, although his paternalist strain was seen in his support for a worker's pension scheme with over 1000 members by 1830. Besides shipbuilding, Young acquired extensive interests in colonial trade and shipping, especially in whaling. He was also an enthusiastic traveller in Britain and Europe.

A zealous administrator, Young was a member of the committee at Lloyd's (Shipping Register) 1824–34, helped to amalgamate the two shipping registers in 1834, and served on Lloyd's new permanent committee, 1835–67, its longest-serving founder member. He was also a driving force in the General London Ship Owners' Society, which in 1834 he chaired for the first of an unprecedented six occasions. This was a period when, following the relaxation of the navigation laws introduced by William Huskisson, shipping questions were of growing political importance, and it was largely as a spokesman of the shipping interest that Young was elected MP for the new constituency of Tynemouth in 1832.

Young proved a vigorous defender of the shipping interest in and outside the House of Commons, for example, sternly resisting (and seeking to reverse) the liberalization of the navigation laws, but supporting the ending of impressment, and advocating marine schools. According to Dickens, he earned the reputation of 'a prodigious bore in Parliament, by speaking immediately before every division, great or small, to the anguish and horror of all parties' (*Letters of Charles Dickens*, 5.6–8). Associated at times with Joseph Hume, and in Tower Hamlets with the idiosyncratic naval reformer and novelist Captain Frederick Marryat, Young mostly took the whig whip, although he opposed the new poor law. He joined the 'Derby Dilly' in 1834–5, but subsequently supported the whigs on the appropriation of Irish church revenues. He continued to stand as a 'moderate' and 'independent' Liberal/whig at Tynemouth, drawing on cross-party support, but was not inaccurately described by one of his radical opponents as 'in heart a tory' (*Tynemouth Leaflets*, 26 June 1832, British Library). Having been unopposed in 1835, his narrow re-election in 1837 was followed by his unseating on technical grounds in 1838.

By the 1840s Young's shipping connections and his growing interest in colonial reform led him to join tory shipowners and radical Wakefieldians in the colonization of New Zealand. Young himself purchased land there, looking to New Zealand as 'a colony, better calculated than any belonging to the British Crown, to prove a blessing to our poor countrymen, and a mine of wealth and a source of power to the nation' (G. F. Young to F. Yeldham, 22 May 1846, Young MSS, BL). He was a leading working director of the New Zealand Company, chairing its shipping committee. Under its auspices, Young's son William Curling travelled to New Zealand but died soon after arrival in 1842. Ironically, he was soon to have been joined there by the poet and future prime minister of New Zealand, Alfred Domett, a close friend, and member, with Robert Browning and Christopher Dowson (1807–1848), of the 'Colloquials' who met regularly at the Young home, conscientiously managed by his wife.

A critic of Conservative colonial policy under Sir Robert Peel and Stanley, Young's domestic politics now led him away from both main parties towards advocacy of 'Young England' principles in the poorest districts of London, supporting for example, baths and washhouses as a means towards the reconciliation of classes. Unlike many of his fellow shipowners, Young lived near to his yards, and was intimately involved in the local community. He acted as chairman of the house committee of the London Hospital (1842–4), helped to create Victoria Park, and, for many years, chaired the Stepney board of guardians. Under its aegis, he was instrumental in setting up the Limehouse children's establishment (1838–73), much visited by educational reformers and philanthropists, and recommended by Dickens as a model to Angela Burdett Coutts. Young was also active as a JP (and deputy lieutenant) for Middlesex.

Young's concern for 'the producing classes' as well as for shipping and the empire as the fulcrums of national power led him, in the late 1840s, to become one of the most active, as well as the most bitter, of the opponents of free trade, especially of the repeal of the Navigation Acts. To resisting the latter he devoted indefatigable energies, giving influential evidence to the select committees of 1847, writing extensively in pamphlets and the press, and seeking to construct an alliance of the disparate opponents of free trade among shipowners, agriculturists, colonial merchants, and working men. Setting up the National Association for the Protection of British Industry and Capital in May 1849, he was ready to woo earls, dukes, farmers, seamen, and the Chartist National Association of Organised Trades. He forced Benjamin Disraeli on to the defensive (over his apparently dwindling support for protection) and became for a time a vital force in the protectionist politics of the late 1840s and early 1850s. In 1851 he was elected protectionist MP for Scarborough, and had his health not broken under the strain of his political advocacy, he would have become vice-president of the Board of Trade in Derby's administration of 1852. For some contemporaries, Young's 'absurd protectionist views' did the shipping interest 'much more harm than good' (W. S. Lindsay, journal IA, fol. 622, Lindsay MSS, NMM), but modern judgements have treated more sympathetically the protectionist ideology which Young so vigorously espoused.

Defeated in the general election of 1852, Young largely faded into obscurity, although in 1860 he characteristically opposed the Anglo-French commercial treaty as an imprudent and humiliating sacrifice of British power. With the erosion of protection in the early 1840s, he had already begun to abandon shipowning, especially since the whaling trade was now exposed to growing American competition, while his shipbuilding business found itself very much at the declining end of the industry, with the onset of iron-building and the consequent moving of this industry from the Thames to the north of England. But Young retained his links with the shipping interest through Lloyd's Register and the General London Ship Owners' Society, which he chaired for the last time in 1862.

Young had left Limehouse in the late 1840s, firstly for Walthamstow, but subsequently, in straitened circumstances, for Reigate, where he died on 23 February 1870 at Wray Park Road. He was buried in the churchyard of Reigate parish church. His wife survived him. Among his eight children, his eldest surviving son, Sir Frederick *Young (1817–1913), inherited his colonial enthusiasm, becoming a leading member of the Royal Colonial Institute and an early publicist of imperial federation, while Sidney (1821–1915), having taken over the family firm, later became merchant assessor for the Admiralty division of the royal courts, where his arbitrations included the *Alabama* claims.　　A. C. HOWE

Sources A. C. Howe, 'Free trade and the City of London, *c*.1820–1870', *History*, new ser., 77 (1992), 391–410 · S. Palmer, *Politics, shipping and the repeal of navigation laws* (1990) · S. Porter, ed., *Poplar, Blackwall and the Isle of Dogs: the parish of All Saints*, [1], Survey of London, 43 (1994) · *The letters of Charles Dickens*, ed. M. House, G. Storey, and others, 3–5 (1974–81) · BL, Tynemouth electoral ephemera · BL, National Association for Protection of British Industry, leaflets etc. · W. H. Griffin, 'Early friends of Robert Browning', *Contemporary Review*, 87 (1905), 426–46 · I. J. Prothero, *Artisans and politics in early nineteenth-century London: John Gast and his times* (1979) · *Annals of Lloyd's Register: being a sketch of the origin, constitution, and progress of Lloyd's Register of British and Foreign Shipping* (1884) · E. G. Wakefield, ed., *The founders of Canterbury* (1868); repr. (1973) · P. Burns, *Fatal success: a history of the New Zealand Company* (1989) · A. Macintyre, 'Lord George Bentinck and the protectionists: a lost cause?', *TRHS*, 5th ser., 39 (1989), 141–65 · NMM, Lindsay MSS · *CGPLA Eng. & Wales* (1870)

Archives BL, personal and family corresp., letter-book, journal of his honeymoon, Add. MSS 46712–46713, 46715 · Museum of London, corresp. with his wife | Bodl. Oxf., Disraeli MSS · CKS, Stanhope MSS · LMA, Stepney board of guardians archives · PRO, New Zealand Company MSS, CO 208 · W. Sussex RO, letters to duke of Richmond

Likenesses portrait, *c*.1948, repro. in *Lloyd's Register of Shipping* (*c*.1948)

Wealth at death under £25,000: probate, 28 April 1870, *CGPLA Eng. & Wales*

Young, George Kennedy (1911–1990), intelligence officer, was born in Dumfries on 8 April 1911, the younger son and youngest of three children of George Stuart Young, grocer, and his wife, Margaret Kennedy. He was brought up in the old covenanting traditions of the United Free Church to which his parents belonged. He was educated at Dumfries Academy and at St Andrews University, where he was an outstanding figure with his great height, red hair, outstanding intellectual ability, quick wit, and strong Independent Labour Party views. He took six years to obtain his degree, during which time he spent a year each at Giessen and at Dijon universities, and he achieved first-class honours in both French and German in 1934. He was then awarded a Commonwealth scholarship (1934–6) to Yale University, where he obtained an MA in political science.

In 1936 Young joined the staff of the *Glasgow Herald*, which he left in 1938 to join the British United Press. When war was declared in 1939 he joined the King's Own Scottish Borderers; he was commissioned in 1940 and finally achieved the rank of lieutenant-colonel. He was transferred to field security on the basis of a rather sketchy knowledge of Italian, and served with distinction in the Abyssinian campaign, during which he was mentioned in dispatches (1941). He joined MI6 in Cairo in 1943. After the war he did a stint as British United Press correspondent in Berlin in 1946. Later in the same year he was invited to rejoin MI6 and he accepted; his first job was to investigate the ramifications of German penetration of British intelligence activities in the Low Countries.

Young had the qualities to make a success in this field: a deep knowledge of and interest in politics, a first-class brain, a gift for languages, and an ability to attract the loyalty of his staff. After stints in London and Vienna he was posted to Cyprus, in 1951, as the controller of all MI6 personnel and operations in the Middle East. This task he discharged with a firm hand, and in the process he became a believer in 'covert action', encouraged in this by the success in 1952 of MI6, working with the CIA, in restoring the shah of Iran to his throne. As the Middle East drifted nearer to a major crisis and to confrontation some people in London became anxious about Young's independent plans. Sir Dick White had been appointed head of MI6, and Young was recalled to London late in 1956. He was put in charge of that part of the office concerned with the collation and distribution of intelligence. In this capacity he modernized an out-of-date system, particularly in the scientific and technological field. He was disappointed that he was unable to acquire an unmanned high-flying photo-reconnaissance plane.

After the resignation of Sir James Easton in 1958 Young was appointed vice-chief of MI6, with the rank of under-secretary in the Ministry of Defence from 1960. He became much involved in the Far East, studying the dangers of further involvement by the Americans in Vietnam. By the end of the 1950s his political views, particularly on racial matters, had moved so far to the right that he found it increasingly difficult to conform to official policies, whichever of the major parties was in power. His position as vice-chief of MI6 became difficult to sustain, and it was with some relief on both sides that he resigned in 1961.

Shortly afterwards Young joined the merchant bankers Kleinwort Benson; he worked with them more or less full-time from 1961 to 1976. The two banks had only recently amalgamated and had decided to expand their overseas business. Young's international contacts enabled him to play a quasi-ambassadorial role in this expansion, particularly in Iran, France, and Belgium. He quickly learned the broad principles of banking but was not involved in day-to-day banking operations. This happy arrangement with Kleinworts suited both parties; it gave Young space to develop his increasing interest in home politics, and time to write several books on contemporary problems. These included *Masters of Indecision* (1962), a diatribe against Whitehall in general and the Foreign Office in particular; *Merchant Banking* (1966); *Who is my Liege?* (1972); and *Subversion* (1984). He stood as Conservative parliamentary candidate at Brent East in 1974—a gesture of principle rather than of political ambition.

Young's influence on many people lay in what he was rather than in what he achieved. His ability might have taken him to the top in several fields. If he never quite succeeded it was perhaps because, while his views on policies and people were strongly held and pungently expressed, they were often unfashionable, and just occasionally his judgement was suspect. Whether politically involved with the left or the right his attraction and influence lay in his total independence of outlook. He remained at heart a militant Scottish covenanter, believing deeply in the rights of the individual against the central forces of bureaucracy. He was appointed MBE (1945), CMG (1955), and CB (1960).

In 1939 Young married Géryke, daughter of Dr Martin August Gustav Harthoorn, a distinguished Dutch lawyer who had spent most of his life in Batavia in the Dutch East Indies; there were no children of the marriage. Young and Géryke remained devoted to each other. She was a strong-minded person who forcibly expressed her views about the roles of different ethnic groups. It is hard to estimate the degree of influence she had over Young's change from a left-wing student of the 1930s to a powerful figure in the right-wing Monday Club, but it was substantial. Young died in the Charing Cross Hospital, London, on 9 May 1990.   JOHN BRUCE LOCKHART, *rev.*

Sources *The Times* (11–12 May 1990) · *The Independent* (14 May 1990) · personal knowledge (1996) · private information (1996) · *CGPLA Eng. & Wales* (1990)

Likenesses photograph, repro. in *The Times* (11 May 1990)

Wealth at death under £115,000: administration with will, 15 Aug 1990, *CGPLA Eng. & Wales*

Young, George Lewis (1922–1997), footballer, was born on 27 October 1922 at 77 Forth Street, Grangemouth, Stirlingshire, the son of John Young (1890–1959), a railway goods guard, and his wife, Martha Hunter, *née* Lewis (1891–1964). He was educated locally, played football for the district team in Falkirk, and was a Scotland international at schoolboy level. The Second World War did not mean a break in his career, because as a shipyard engineer, in Bo'ness, West Lothian, he was in a reserved occupation. In 1941 he moved from Kirkintilloch Rob Roy to Glasgow Rangers, and within eighteen months he was playing for Scotland; in one of his first matches, they lost 8–0 to England and he was dropped, but he soon found his way back into the team. He went on to captain Rangers to six Scottish League championships, two league cups, and four Scottish cups. Three of these were in succession, between 1948 and 1950, and he scored two penalties in the final of 1949. On 4 July the same year he married Thomasina (Zena) Graham (1922–1995), a housekeeper, also of Grangemouth; she was the daughter of Thomas Graham, dock labourer. They had two daughters, Irene and Muriel.

Rangers' success during this period owed much to its mean defence, known as the 'Iron Curtain', in which Young played at centre half or right back. (For eighteen minutes in the middle of the Scottish cup final against Aberdeen in 1953, however, he kept goal: the match finished 1–1 and Rangers won the replay 1–0.) Standing at 6 feet 2 inches, he dominated battles in the air, but also possessed nifty control on the ground for someone who weighed more than 15 stone, and was known for his clean tackling. He was never sent off during a match and was booked only once—which upset him for ever after—when protesting in defence of one of his team-mates. The former Scotland manager Willie Ormond, who faced Young as a forward for Hibernian, compared him to Billy Wright and Bobby Moore, claiming that 'they would work out the situation so that they were where they wanted to be before the ball was' (*The Sun*, 8 Jan 1976).

George Lewis Young (1922–1997), by unknown photographer, 1950

Young's nicknames included Gentle Giant, Rock of the North, and Corky, the last because he always carried around a champagne cork that reminded him of his first game against England, a 3–1 victory at Wembley in 1949—perhaps his fondest memory of his playing days. In 1948 he had captained Scotland for the first time, and in all he did so on forty-eight occasions, a record for the twentieth century. Between 1943 and 1957 he played in fifty-three internationals, a total eclipsed by Denis Law only when international fixtures were becoming more frequent. He also acted as something of a player-manager for the national side—possible because of the esteem in which he was held by his team-mates; he would always, for example, share a room with a new player to help him settle in. Moreover, he was respected by those from other sides; he would take the Scotland players to meet their English opponents from their train, and towards the end of his club career, which finished in 1957, he would teach the men he marked how to beat other defenders.

Young's time in the game, though successful, contained its disappointments. He never won against England at Hampden Park, and when Scotland needed a draw against their rivals to go to the world cup in 1950, his side lost 1–0. He was disappointed in 1986 when his testimonial was played not at Ibrox but at the smaller ground of Brockville in Falkirk, and when he had announced that his last appearance in all competitions would be in a world cup qualifier against Spain in Madrid in 1957, he was not selected (Scotland lost 4–1).

From 1959 until 1962 Young served as manager of Third Lanark, whom he took to third place in the first division, and he left only when the club was taken over by a property developer, William Hiddleston, whom he did not trust. (Third Lanark became defunct five years later.) But he maintained his links with the game in retirement: in 1963 Young—along with Ted Drake, Tom Finney, Tommy Lawton, and Arthur Ellis, a former referee—was one of the original 'pools panel', gathered together to forecast the results after three successive coupons had been declared void owing to the weather. He also organized tournaments and stadium tours for youngsters from abroad and wrote a column for *The People*. Away from football he worked for the Erskine Hospital for Ex-Servicemen paraplegic coach fund, regularly joining their outings. He also ran Tillietudlem Hotel, where he had lived before he was married, in Crossford, Lanarkshire, but it was said that he could not be a successful businessman because he was too kind. This was demonstrated when he travelled to Aberdeen for a testimonial dinner, at which he was due to auction his memorabilia: during the journey he gave them all away.

Young spent his final years in a nursing home in Slamannan, near Falkirk. He died on 10 January 1997 in the Royal Infirmary, Falkirk. There was a minute's silence before Rangers' game against Aberdeen at Ibrox on 12 January and five days later Young was buried in the Grand Sable cemetery, Grangemouth, where his funeral service took place in the kirk of Holy Rood. He was survived by his two daughters, his wife having predeceased him.

DANIEL CREWE

George Malcolm Young (1882–1959), by Henry Lamb, 1938

Sources *The Scotsman* (13 Jan 1997) · *The Guardian* (16 Jan 1997) · *The Independent* (13 Jan 1997) · *Daily Telegraph* (17 Jan 1997) · *The Sun* (8 Jan 1976) · *The Game* (1971) · N. Barrett, *Daily Telegraph football chronicle* (1993) · C. Nawret and S. Hutchings, *Sunday Times illustrated history of football* (1994) · private information [Muriel Stirling, daughter; Jim Hossack; Robert McElroy] · b. cert. · m. cert. · d. cert.
Archives Grangemouth Heritage Museum, international cap · priv. coll., medals
Likenesses photographs, 1949–57, Hult. Arch. [*see illus.*] · photograph, 1953, repro. in *Daily Telegraph* · photograph, 1957, repro. in *The Scotsman*

Young, George Malcolm (1882–1959), historian, was born at Charlton, Kent, on 29 April 1882, the only son of George Frederick Young, waterman, later a steamer master, of Greenhithe, and his wife, Rosetta Jane Elizabeth Ross. A scholar of St Paul's School, he became captain of the school. A scholar of Balliol College, Oxford, in the year (1900) in which William Temple was elected to an exhibition, Young gained a first in classical honour moderations (1902) and a second in *literae humaniores* (1904), having rowed in the second torpid. He was elected a fellow of All Souls in 1905 and became a tutor at St John's College (1906–8). In 1908 he joined the Board of Education, then under the sway of Sir Robert Morant, to whom he remained devoted. Young became a junior examiner in the universities branch; then, in 1911, the first secretary of what was to burgeon into the University Grants Committee. In 1916 he joined the newly formed cabinet office. Appointed CB in 1917, he was chosen as joint secretary of the new and short-lived Ministry of Reconstruction. He accompanied Arthur Henderson, then a member of the war cabinet, as secretary on his notorious visit to Russia in 1917, where Young met Francis Lindley, at that time counsellor in the British embassy. He went with Lindley to Archangel and later accompanied him to Vienna when Lindley went there as minister. In Vienna, Young was for a time a director of the newly founded Anglo-Austrian Bank: 'a curious anaemic-looking man', not mixing readily but already recognized by his younger British colleagues as 'a great scholar with a wide range of knowledge and a wonderful command of the English language'.

Abandoning the public service in the early post-war disillusion, Young decided to devote himself to writing, but nothing could remove that intense interest in education which shone throughout all his work. He was at heart a born teacher, thirsting to impart the results of his own sharp and constructive thoughts bred of a wide and deep reading in a formidable variety of subjects. Yet he was in no hurry. Although his essay 'Victorian history' had caught discerning eyes in 1931, it was not until he was fifty that he published his first book, *Gibbon* (1932), a work of *pietas* but inspired also by a desire to impress upon the new biographers that neither Freud nor Marx had yet explained why there should be great men. He noted in Gibbon that 'sense of place' which he himself displayed. He made his home in Wiltshire where at the Old Oxyard at Oare near Marlborough he fell upon the antiquities of Wessex, not forgetting 'pond barrows', with far more knowledge and no less eagerness than his favourite John

Aubrey had done. He shared house with his lifelong friend Mona *Wilson (1872–1954), the civil servant and author; there she took charge of all those details of everyday life in which Young himself was oddly helpless and dependent. Surrounded in this neighbourhood by many cronies, including a bevy of former ambassadors, Young became, alongside Miss Wilson with her short fireside pipe, the centre of intellectual gossip and a dispenser of fascinating talk drawn from the resources of an astonishing memory. Urban in origin and urbane by disposition he was no less at home with countrymen and the railway workers of Swindon. He took pleasure in finding himself a tory and 'no Tory of whatever rank or class ever thought of a merely moneyed man as his social equal'.

At the perceptive invitation of Oxford University Press, no doubt at the instigation of Humphrey Milford, Young edited the two volumes of *Early Victorian England* which appeared in 1934 and to which he himself contributed that final summary chapter which brought his especial quality to the attention of a wider and delighted public; this essay he developed into *Victorian England: Portrait of an Age* (1936), by which he will be remembered. What was important in history was, in his view, 'not what happened, but what people felt about it when it was happening'. Young had the industry, the learning, the memory, and above all the penetration to disentangle the main themes from the confused Victorian clamour. His advice to the historian was 'to go on reading until you can hear people talking'. He did not add that an interpreter of his talent, erudition, and perception—or with the gifts of his revered F. W. Maitland—might still be needed. Embedded in Young's writing was more food for thought than the common reader had been accustomed to encounter. Nor was his aim objective; even in narrative he would not forgo comment, with an epithet, an adverb, a tone of voice. His Clio was a muse with a sting.

After *Charles I and Cromwell* (1935), an essay in detection published before his developed Victorian masterpiece, came *Daylight and Champaign* (1937), a collection of essays and reviews—many of them reprinted from the literary periodicals such as the *Sunday Times*, to which Young was by now a valued contributor. There, and in other reprints, which included addresses such as his Romanes lecture on Gladstone in 1944, in his *Today and Yesterday* (1948) and in *Last Essays* (1950), he found elbow-room for good talk, addressed purposely to the middlebrow, about literature, persons, and manners. Unbuttoned, he might be colloquial, give full play to his humour, even show off a little since he was enjoying himself, yet literature remained a very serious matter for him, as were the duties of the clerisy and the continuity of civilization. He was deeply concerned with language as a means of communication; good speech he deemed 'the first political art'. A university he regarded as 'a place where young men and women educate one another by conversation, under the guidance of people a little older, and, more often than they might imagine, somewhat wiser than themselves'.

Young was a trustee of the National Portrait Gallery (from 1937) and of the British Museum (1947–57), a member of the Standing Commission on Museums and Galleries (from 1938), and of the Historical Manuscripts Commission (from 1948); all this work lay very close to his being and, until his health began to fail, he gave it much attention and thought. His was a slight figure with a scholarly stoop; he had a longish, inquisitive nose, eyes twinkling well ahead of a coming quip, an unusual manner of clearing his throat, a voice warm and vibrant. He was a shy man and, because sensitive, sometimes sharp: an intellectual who lived by his deep if hidden affections. Mona Wilson's death not long after the war, then the sale of the Oxyard, were blows from which he never recovered, but he built himself a new existence on his re-election in 1948 to All Souls, which provided him with a familiar and congenial refuge. He became a member of the royal commission on the press (1947–9) and he received honorary degrees from Durham (1950) and Cambridge (1953); and—what he valued most—an honorary fellowship at Balliol in 1953.

His last book, *Stanley Baldwin* (1952), had been undertaken reluctantly, at Baldwin's own request. As he grew closer to his subject, Young was clearly somewhat taken aback by his discoveries, and it is not a satisfying book; Young's touch had begun to fail him. In 1956 he published, in collaboration with W. D. Handcock, *English Historical Documents, 1833–74*, but Young's part in the volume, undertaken in 1947, was small. An invitation to lecture in Athens, which he had never visited, for a while renewed his flagging spirits, then a cloud descended on him and his death in the Thames Bank Nursing Home, Goring, Oxfordshire, on 18 November 1959 was a genuine release.

Young has been called a 'pantomath', a comment not displeasing to him. If he was not quite that, it was well said of him that few writers have said so many good things upon so many subjects. He lived up to his own definition of the historian as 'one for whom the past keeps something of the familiar triviality of the present, and the present has already some of the shadowy magnificence of the past'.   L. E. JONES and E. T. WILLIAMS, *rev.*

Sources *The Times* (19 Nov 1959) · *The Times* (24 Nov 1959) · W. D. Handcock, introduction, in G. M. Young, *Victorian essays* (1962) · personal knowledge (1971) · private information (1971)
Archives CUL, corresp., drafts and proofs relating to his 'Stanley Baldwin' | Bodl. Oxf., corresp. with R. W. Chapman · Bodl. Oxf., corresp. with Sybil Colefax · Bodl. Oxf., letters to Gilbert Murray · NL Scot., letters to John Dover Wilson
Likenesses H. Lamb, pencil drawing, *c*.1935, NPG · S. Botsarvis, drawing, 1938, All Souls Oxf. · H. Lamb, pencil drawing, 1938, NPG [*see illus.*]
Wealth at death £24,435 10*s*. 3*d*.: probate, 8 March 1960, *CGPLA Eng. & Wales*

Young, George Renny (1802–1853). *See under* Young, Sir William (1799–1887).

Young, Gerard Mackworth- (1884–1965), administrator in India and archaeologist, was born in London on 7 April 1884, the eldest of the four sons of Sir William Mackworth *Young (1840–1924), lieutenant-governor of the Punjab in

1897–1902, and his second wife, Frances Mary (d. 1932), eldest daughter of Sir Robert Eyles Egerton, lieutenant-governor of the Punjab in 1877–82. Major Sir Hubert Winthrop *Young and Sir Mark Aitchison *Young were his brothers. His great-uncle was the poet and tory politician Winthrop Mackworth Praed. Gerard's education and early career mirrored exactly those of his father. He was a king's scholar at Eton College, in the Newcastle select, and in 1903 went up to King's College, Cambridge, where he graduated in 1906 with a first in part one of the classics tripos (MA, 1913). In 1907 he successfully contested the Indian Civil Service examinations and, like his father and maternal grandfather before him, was assigned to the Punjab.

Steeped in the service's traditions, Young rose quickly through the ranks of district officers and was soon promoted to the inner sanctum of the secretariat: undersecretary to the government of the Punjab (1913), undersecretary to the home department of the government of India (1916–19), deputy commissioner of Delhi (1921), deputy secretary of the army department of the government of India (1924), and secretary (1926). In 1929 he was appointed CIE.

Possessor of a fine, tall, wiry physique, and capable of walking 50 miles a day, he was a natural choice for government excursions into the wilds, and in April 1912 he was dispatched on a physically taxing three-month journey to western Tibet to report on the British-Indian prospects for trade in the region and to regularize the position of the British trade agency at Gangunsa, near Gartok. In an otherwise workmanlike report Young wrote eloquently of the carved wooden temples and monasteries of Toling, crimson and white and roofed with gold, which he dated to the early seventeenth century, the time when Jesuit monks had penetrated the area and were said to have converted the king of Chaprang, Chodak Po, to Christianity.

On 9 May 1916 Young married Natalie Leila Margaret (1894–1981), daughter of the late Sir Walter Francis Hely-Hutchinson of Court Lodge at Shorne, Gravesend, who had been the Cape Colony's last governor. After the Tibetan expedition it was not surprising that the honeymoon should be spent in travel, and the pair set out from Simla on a two-month trek to Kulu and back—a journey which a wedding guest prophesied would kill the bride but which in fact she triumphantly enjoyed, for she too was a strong walker.

Good fortune in the form of a generous legacy as well as natural endowment was on the side of Gerard Young. In 1932, on completing the standard twenty-five years' duty in the civil service, he retired to pursue the diverse artistic interests which often inspired the public servant of his period and intellectual background. He had for some time been working on a verse translation of the epigrams of Callimachus: graceful, lucidly annotated, the result was published in 1934. Free now to indulge his feeling for the ancient world, in 1932 he enrolled as a student of the British School of Archaeology in Athens, lining up as a beginner with young postgraduates less than half his age.

He had, however, taken advice on finding a niche in classical archaeology and astutely mastered the technique of the still camera. In 1936 in collaboration with the then director of the school, Humfry Payne, who wrote the text, he produced a photographic catalogue, Archaic Marble Sculpture from the Acropolis. It became a standard, a second edition appearing in 1950. Meanwhile with a young archaeologist, James Brock, as partner he undertook between 1935 and 1938 excavations on the island of Sifnos, and to the publication in the school Annual contributed a carefully documented section on Roman graves of the first century AD.

In 1936 the death both of Humfry Payne and of his successor left the school without a director. Young was a comparative newcomer to archaeology, but he had the qualifications which the times demanded—sufficient scholarship, knowledge of the job, great administrative experience. And he was both well-to-do and generous; the school was to be deeply indebted for his benefactions. He remained as director until the outbreak of the Second World War in 1939, when he joined the staff of the British legation in Athens. On the German occupation of Greece he returned to India, first as joint secretary of the war department (1941–4), and afterwards as an honorary officer of the archaeological survey (1944–5).

After the war Young went back to Athens to oversee the reopening of the School of Archaeology; he finally retired in 1946, having been honoured by Greece as a commander of the order of King George I. He did not retire, however, from music which, especially singing, had been a major pleasure all his life. With a handsome bass-baritone voice and near-professional standards which at one time encouraged two years' study in Munich, he had sung in opera in Simla and given lieder recitals in Athens. A devotee of Schubert, he was practising almost to the day of his death. The value of his book What Happens in Singing (1953), a study of vocal mechanics and in particular tone and resonation, was recognized by both teacher and practitioner.

The formal and the engagingly adventurous were mingled in his character as in his life. His friendship, always kind, always generous, was enlivened by ready fun; and in his manner, suddenly and charmingly illuminated by a blazing smile, the habit of authority rarely betrayed itself. Nevertheless he had no lack of self-respect, and it was in an effort to avoid, as he put it, confusion with all the other Youngs that he first had his four children, two boys and two girls, baptized Mackworth and then himself in 1947 took by deed poll the hyphenated surname of Mackworth-Young. Prior to this he had been known as Mr Mackworth Young. He died at 12 Clarence Road, Clewer within Windsor, on 28 November 1965 and was privately cremated on 1 December after a service in St George's Chapel, Windsor Castle. The royal connection was provided by his elder son, Sir Robert Christopher Mackworth-*Young, who in 1958 had become the librarian at Windsor Castle. He was survived by his wife.

DILYS POWELL, rev. KATHERINE PRIOR

Sources *The Times* (29 Nov 1965) · *The Times* (3 Dec 1965) · Burke, *Peerage* (1959) · J. J. Withers, *A register of admissions to King's College, Cambridge, 1797–1925*, 2nd edn (1929) · *WWW*, 1961–70 · *The Eton register*, 7 (privately printed, Eton, 1922) · Bengal ecclesiastical registers, BL OIOC, N/1/413, fol. 93 · private information (1981) · personal knowledge (1981)
Archives BL, papers relating to Tibet, Add. MS 63121 | Bodl. Oxf., corresp. with J. L. Myers
Likenesses S. Mervyn, oils; in possession of Robert Christopher Young, 1981
Wealth at death £86,540: probate, 17 Jan 1966, *CGPLA Eng. & Wales*

Young [*née* Chisholm], **Grace Emily** (1868–1944), mathematician, was born in London on 15 March 1868, the youngest of four children of Henry Williams Chisholm (1809–1901) and his wife, Anna Louisa Bell (1824–1900). He was warden of the standards and chief clerk to the exchequer; the measures of length in Trafalgar Square were placed under his direction. Grace's elder brother Hugh *Chisholm (1866–1924) gained eminence as editor of the eleventh and twelfth editions of the *Encyclopaedia Britannica* and as city editor of *The Times*.

The family moved to Haslemere in 1874 upon the father's retirement. After education at home from governesses, Grace won a scholarship to Girton College, Cambridge, in 1889, and four years later passed the mathematical tripos examinations. She performed even better by gaining a first class in the final honours school examination at Oxford University, which she had been allowed to take. Disliking the British system of mathematics education, she enrolled in a newly launched programme of higher education for women conducted at Göttingen under Felix Klein, director of the mathematics faculty. Two years later she was the first to complete the programme, with a dissertation on spherical trigonometry analysed in Klein's way in terms of the group of geometrical transformations under which configurations remain unchanged. Her results have been applied to astronomy.

Grace returned home to look after her elderly parents, and once more met William Henry (Will) *Young (1863–1942), who had briefly coached her at Cambridge. She at first declined his proposal of marriage but they were married on 11 June 1896. Their first child, Frank, nicknamed Bimbo, was born in 1897. Grace drew her husband into research-level mathematics, which they pursued for the rest of their lives in continental Europe. At first they spent a year in Italy, working in geometry, but finding the topic somewhat uncongenial they returned to Göttingen in 1899 to seek Klein's advice on research topics. Klein proposed set theory, which was beginning to receive great attention from mathematicians at that time, and the couple devoted their research career to aspects of this topic. They lived in Göttingen until 1908, when they moved to Switzerland, spending seven years at Geneva, and then living near Lausanne. They existed largely on income from Young's savings as a coach, and from his salary as lecturer or professor in universities in England and India. While at Göttingen and then Geneva, Grace trained to be a medical doctor but did not take the examinations.

Two sons and three daughters were born to them at Göttingen; the eldest daughter, Rosalind Cecilia Hildegard (1900–1992), better known by her married name, Rosalind *Tanner, also achieved a notable career in mathematics and its history. Bimbo's education inspired publications from his parents. They produced *A First Book of Geometry* in 1905, based on folding paper; it was translated into several languages. Then Grace wrote two little books explaining science for children: *Bimbo* (1906), and *Bimbo and the Frogs* (1907). Frank's death in action in February 1917 as an airman in the First World War was a devastating blow.

The Youngs' research work produced about 200 papers and two books. One joint book, *The Theory of Sets of Points* (1906), was the first comprehensive introduction to several aspects of set theory in English. Their attention centred on point set topology and its application to integration, and to properties of Fourier series and sets of orthogonal functions. It is clear from the couple's correspondence that, while his research-trained wife drew the coach into creative work, he had the stronger talent of the two. Most papers appeared under his name alone, and he wrote some of them entirely; however, she wrote up the majority and checked the details, and handled the proofs. As he put it in one of his letters:

> I feel partly as if I were teaching you, and setting you problems which I could not quite do myself but could enable you to. […] The fact is that our papers ought to be published under our joint names, but if this were done neither of us get the benefit of it. No. Mine the laurels now and the knowledge. Yours the knowledge only. Everything under my name now, and later when the loaves and fishes are no more procurable in that way, everything or much under your name. (Grattan-Guinness, 'Mathematical union', 141)

From the mid-1910s Grace produced some research papers of her own, mainly applying set theory to the differential calculus. An essay on 'infinite derivatives' won a Gamble prize at Cambridge University in 1915, stimulating some later research. Later she wrote some speculative papers on aspects of Greek mathematics.

Partly because of Grace's declining health, the Youngs' research work stopped rather abruptly in the mid-1920s, but during the early 1930s she wrote a long unpublished novel entitled 'The Crown of England', on Elizabethan society. During this period she also helped Young with secretarial duties in his post as president of the International Mathematical Union.

As Paris was falling in 1940 Grace managed, at great risk, to take back to England two children of her daughter Janet, but Young refused to accompany her, fearing punishment for his many praises of German academic achievements. He died in Switzerland in 1942; she died at Janet's house, 98 Park Road, Croydon, Surrey, on 29 March 1944, aged seventy-six.   I. GRATTAN-GUINNESS

Sources I. Grattan-Guinness, 'A mathematical union', *Annals of Science*, 29 (1972), 105–86 · G. H. Hardy, *Obits. FRS*, 4 (1942–4), 307–23 [obit. of William Henry Young] · I. Grattan-Guinness, 'University mathematics at the turn of the century', *Annals of Science*, 28 (1972), 369–84 · I. Grattan-Guinness, 'Mathematical bibliography for W. H. and G. C. Young', *Historia Mathematica*, 2 (1975), 43–58 · M. L.

Cartwright, 'Grace Chisholm Young', *Journal of the London Mathematical Society*, 19 (1944), 185–92
Archives U. Lpool L., corresp. and papers
Likenesses photograph, repro. in Grattan-Guinness, 'Mathematical union'

Young, Gruffudd (*b. c.*1370, *d.* in or after **1437**), churchman and administrator, was one whose ecclesiastical career was entangled in the politics of the Glyn Dŵr rebellion and of the papal schism. Described as of illegitimate birth he was almost certainly the bastard son of Morgan Young (Morgan ab Iorwerth ap Morgan ab Iorwerth Foel), of a prominent Chirkland lineage, a landowner in the county of Flint and in the lordship of Dyffryn Clwyd, and sheriff and under-sheriff of Flint. Educated probably at the University of Oxford, he was bachelor of civil and canon laws and held several ecclesiastical preferments in Welsh dioceses, including the canonry of Abergwili (St David's), the rectory of Llanynys (Bangor), a major church in the lordship of Dyffryn Clwyd, and the church of Llanbadarn Fawr (St David's). In 1397 and 1398 he was appointed vicar-general of the diocese of St David's by its bishop, Guy Mohun, and in 1401, described as doctor of canon law, he was granted a royal pardon for accepting provision to a canonry of St David's. He is described as canon of Bangor in a letter written by Archbishop Arundel, dated 23 June 1401. A letter from Young, known only from a late source, written to the archdeacon of Anglesey and others asking them to defend the interests of a prebendary of Llanddwyn, and dated at Aberystwyth Castle, 19 January 1404 or 1405, describes him as archdeacon of Meirionydd and doctor of canon law. He is named as archdeacon of St Asaph ('archidiaconum Assavensis') in a writ of exigent dated 1405–6.

By 1404 Young, with other prominent churchmen, had attached himself to the cause of Owain Glyn Dŵr (1359–1416). His alliance with the rebel cause, in which a number of his close kinsmen were also involved, was possibly due to his thwarted ambitions for further ecclesiastical preferment under Richard II and Henry IV. His defection secured his own promotion and broadened the base of Glyn Dŵr's support. On 10 May 1404 Young, now described as Glyn Dŵr's chancellor, together with John Hanmer, was appointed ambassador to the court of Charles VI of France with powers to discuss a treaty of alliance between Glyn Dŵr, intituled prince of Wales, and the French king, and Young's seal (a lion rampant in a bordure engrailed) was appended to the treaty concluded at Paris on 14 July 1404. The formal articulation, if not the begetting, of the so-called 'Pennal policy' of 1406, by which the Welsh under Glyn Dŵr undertook to recognize the antipope and which provided for the creation of an independent ecclesiastical province in Wales with St David's as metropolitan see, may have been partly his responsibility. He remained active on Glyn Dŵr's behalf in the final stages of the revolt. Described as bishop of Bangor, he was in Paris with Philip Hanmer early in 1415, when both are referred to as ambassadors and may have been engaged in negotiations for French aid.

Although Lewis Byford, who had been provided to the see of Bangor by Boniface IX (*r.* 1389–1404) on 14 August 1404, enjoyed Glyn Dŵr's initial support, the bishop's pro-Roman sympathies may have prompted his replacement by Young, who was provided by the Avignon pope Benedict XIII (*r.* 1394–1417) to Bangor on 14 February 1407. In the same year he was provided to St David's, but it is not known whether he ever took possession. In a papal mandate of 27 August 1414 he is described as 'of the diocese of Lichfield', which may refer to an earlier connection with the diocese. He never returned to Wales after the failure of the Glyn Dŵr revolt. He was provided to the bishopric of Ross and Finlay in Scotland and appointed papal nuncio by Martin V (*r.* 1417–31) with power to receive the submissions of Benedict XIII's adherents in Scotland. It is not certain that Young took possession of Ross and in 1419 was granted benefices to hold *in commendam* in the dioceses of Nevers and le Puy 'until he obtains possession of the temporalities of Ross' (*CEPR letters*, 7.119). He was still described as bishop of Ross in 1430 but had been translated to Hippo, north Africa, by 1 February 1423. Young was alive in April 1437 when, described as 'broken with age' (*CEPR letters*, 7.647), he was granted a yearly life pension.

LLINOS SMITH

Sources *CEPR letters*, vol. 7 • Emden, *Oxf.* • T. Matthews, *Welsh records in Paris* (1910) • R. F. Isaacson, ed. and trans., *The episcopal registers of the diocese of St David's, 1397–1518*, 2 vols. in 3, Honourable Society of Cymmrodorion, Cymmrodorion Record Series (1917–20) • A. D. M. Barrell and R. R. Davies, 'Land, lineage and revolt in north-east Wales: a case study', *Cambrian Medieval Celtic Studies*, 29 (1995), 27–51 • J. R. Gabriel, 'Wales and the Avignon papacy', *Archaeologia Cambrensis*, 7th ser., 3 (1923), 70–86 • J. E. Lloyd, *Owen Glendower* (1931) • G. Williams, *The Welsh church from conquest to Reformation* (1962) • R. R. Davies, *Conquest, coexistence, and change: Wales, 1063–1415*, History of Wales, 2 (1987) • R. R. Davies, *The revolt of Owain Glyn Dŵr* (1995)

Young, Sir Henry Edward Fox (1808–1870), colonial governor, the third son of the colonial governor Sir Aretas William *Young (1777/8–1835), and his wife, Sarah, *née* Cox, of Coolcliffe, Wexford, was born on 23 April 1808 at Bradbourne, near Lee, Kent. After being educated at Deane's School, Bromley, he entered the Inner Temple in 1827 but was never called to the bar. In 1830 he went to Trinidad with his father, then to British Guiana as clerk, aide-de-camp, and acting recorder of the chamber of orphans and protector of slaves.

On 21 November 1833 Young was appointed to be treasurer of St Lucia. He arrived in January 1834 and from August acted as colonial secretary and, helped by his knowledge of French, from November also as second puisne judge. In March 1835 he was promoted to government secretary of British Guiana. On 28 January 1847, on his return to England, Young was appointed lieutenant-governor of the eastern province of the Cape Colony and was made CB and given a knighthood. In February 1848 he was offered the governorship of South Australia and returned to England, where, on 15 April 1848, he married Augusta Sophia Marryatt (*d.* 1913). They had two sons and five daughters. The couple set sail for Australia on 27 April, and Young took up his new post in August 1848.

Young's term of office as governor was marked by a vigorous but extravagant and not altogether judicious policy of development. He carried through the opening of the Murray River to steam navigation, but large sums were wasted trying to remove the bar at its mouth, and in 1854 a railway was built from Goolwa to the coast, although the port site was ill chosen. When the Victoria gold rush drained the colony of labour and money, Young's attempts to divert the stream of gold export to Adelaide and to encourage the discovery of gold in South Australia had some success; but the scarcity of currency led his advisers to fear that gold coin would disappear altogether. They persuaded Young, who was at first sceptical, to pass a measure to make gold bullion legal tender. The extraordinary measure, which was duly passed in January 1853, was short-lived.

In 1853 Young attempted to alter a bill for a constitution for responsible government. He published the resolutions framed by Sir John Morpherr when council was not sitting and withheld dispatches to have a bill passed keeping a nominated upper house. The resulting outcry saw the bill returned, and Young was censured by the secretary of state. Young was next gazetted to the government of New Zealand, but never took up his appointment, as in January 1855 he was transferred to the government of Tasmania. Here he arrived at a time of great prosperity, but again he was met by the urge for a greater degree of self-government; an act was before the queen in Great Britain, and meanwhile, on 17 July 1855, Young summoned his first council on the old footing. The council appointed a committee to review the findings of the executive council on the convict system and summoned the controller, Dr Hampton, to appear before it. Hampton denied the right of the council to summon him, while Young denied the right of the council to review the executive council's finding and prorogued the council. The Colonial Office upheld the prorogation but found fault with restrictions on the council; the supreme court and privy council found in favour of Hampton. In December 1856 Young met the first parliament under responsible government. However, he soon stood aside from politics to concentrate on the development of the country, which proceeded rapidly during his term of office. In 1857 steps were taken to improve higher education in Tasmania and gas was introduced into Hobart. The beginnings of a railway to Launceston were discussed; the first underwater telegraph cable was laid around the coast in 1858, and in 1860 the foundation of a mining industry was laid and an industrial exhibition was opened at Hobart. The new government house, a symbolic sign of the progress of colonialization, was first occupied by Young. He left the colony for England on 10 December 1861.

Young, who was a director and chairman of the Australian Mercantile Land and Finance Company from 1866 to 1868, also visited New Zealand on private business in 1866, but spent most of his time in London, where he died of kidney disease on 18 September 1870, at his home, 77 Kensington Gardens Square. A near contemporary described him as of a sanguine and enthusiastic temperament, devoted to what he believed to be his public duty, and usually generous in his judgements, if not always wise.   C. A. HARRIS, rev. LYNN MILNE

Sources H. J. Gibbney, 'Young, Sir Henry Edward Fox', *AusDB*, vol. 6 · G. W. Rusden, *History of Australia*, 3 vols. (1883)
Archives State Library of South Australia, Adelaide, letters and papers relating to South Australia | U. Durham L., corresp. with third Earl Grey
Wealth at death under £7000: probate, 8 Oct 1870, *CGPLA Eng. & Wales*

Young, (Edward) Hilton, first Baron Kennet (1879–1960), politician and writer, was born in London on 20 March 1879, the fourth child and third son of Sir George *Young, third baronet (1837–1930), and his wife, Alice Eacy, *née* Kennedy (d. 1922), widow of Sir Alexander Lawrence. His childhood was darkened by the death of a beloved sister, Eacy, and lightened by a family printing press on which his picaresque novel, *The Count*, was printed when he was nine. In 1893 he went to Eton College, where he joined the army class, then the only way to study science, and became its captain. After a short time studying chemistry under William Ramsay at University College, London, he went in 1897 to Trinity College, Cambridge, whence he emerged in 1900 as president of the Union, editor of the *Cambridge Review*, and with a first in natural sciences. His friends were G. M. Trevelyan, E. M. Forster, and the circle which later became known as Bloomsbury. It was to him that Bloomsbury turned in 1914 for evidence that their pacifism antedated the war.

Having left chemistry for law Young was called by the Inner Temple in 1904. He held a few briefs, but it did not take. After a short period studying international law at the University of Freiburg he found a truer line of progress as a writer and journalist about finance and as a Liberal Party worker. He was assistant editor of *The Economist* from 1908 to 1910, and organized free trade unions in Yorkshire and the City of London. In 1910 he became City editor of the *Morning Post* and London correspondent of the *New York Times* financial supplement. In 1912 he published *Foreign Companies and other Corporations*, and in 1915 *The System of National Finance* which, reissued in 1924 and 1936, remained the standard textbook until 1939.

Young joined the Royal Naval Volunteer Reserve in 1914. His war service was varied, including spells with the Grand Fleet, with the naval mission to the Serbian army on the Danube and its evacuation to Corfu, with light cruisers on the Harwich station, and with naval siege guns ashore on the Belgian beach at Nieuport les Bains. For this last he was awarded the DSC and the Croix de Guerre. In 1918 he volunteered for the blocking of Zeebrugge and, serving in the *Vindictive*, commanded a gun turret until his right arm was wounded; it was later amputated. From this battle he acquired a bar to his DSC, forty years of intermittent pain, and the beautiful half-uncial script he learned to write with his left hand. When he had recovered he volunteered for service in Russia, where he found himself in command of an armoured train fighting a war of head-on confrontation with Bolshevik trains coming up from

Vologda. For this he was appointed to the DSO. In 1920 he published a book of war memoirs, *By Sea and Land*, which traces his movement from a not deeply considered patriotism to the constructive internationalism which later sent him as a national delegate to the League of Nations.

Twice before the war Young had stood unsuccessfully for parliament as a Liberal; in 1915 he had been returned unopposed in his absence at a by-election in Norwich. At the 1918 general election he was returned as a 'free Liberal', but soon threw in his lot with Lloyd George. He gained the ear of the House of Commons with speeches mainly on finance, and became financial secretary to the Treasury in 1921. After the election of 1922 he became chief whip of the Lloyd George Liberals, was sworn of the privy council, and regulated the disordered finances of his party. He lost his seat in 1923 but regained it in 1924.

Socialism he would not have, and when in 1926 Lloyd George propounded a land policy which he thought socialistic, Hilton Young left the Liberals and became an independent. At the time of the general strike, believing that socialism and direct action could be effectively met only by a single party, and that this could never again be the Liberal Party, he joined the Conservatives. By agreement with his constituents he kept his seat until the general election in 1929, and was then returned for the Sevenoaks division of Kent, which he held until 1935. He was appointed GBE in 1927.

During the Labour government of 1929–31 Young attended the Conservative shadow cabinet and attained a leading position in debate in the house. He was also general editor of a group of journals, of which the *Financial News* was the chief. In 1931 he became minister of health in Ramsay MacDonald's National Government. His main job was slum clearance and rehousing. His policy was to confine subsidies to clearance, thereby encouraging local authorities to attack that vigorously, while stimulating private builders to provide new houses by releasing them from subsidized competition. The policy produced unprecedented progress with both clearing and building. But it was unpopular with the left because of its emphasis on the private builder, and alienated important interests on the right because it did not compensate slum landlords. 'You do not', he said, 'compensate the butcher for selling fly-blown meat when it is seized.' Young was responsible for the Town and Country Planning Act of 1932, the first to apply to all 'developable' land, and for a Housing Act (1935) which was the first to lay down standards of accommodation and provide for their enforcement.

When Ramsay MacDonald resigned in 1935, Hilton Young accepted a peerage as Lord Kennet of the Dene and took no further part in politics. The name Kennet was taken from the river by which he had a cottage in Wiltshire.

The unusual breadth of Kennet's early training—science, law, finance, and journalism, as well as politics—had made him a valuable negotiator and committee chairman. He was British representative at The Hague conference on credits for the Soviet Union in 1922, and a member of the British delegation to the League of Nations assemblies in 1926, 1927, 1928, and 1932: a natural fruit of his thinking about war. He headed a British mission to Poland (1923–5) which laid the foundation of a balanced budget and got the złoty through some of its early difficulties. He did much the same for Iraq in 1925 and 1930, designing the Iraqi currency and chairing the Iraq currency board in London for many years. In 1925–6 he chaired the royal commission on Indian finance, which stabilized the rupee and drew up the constitution of the Indian Reserve Bank. In 1928 he chaired a mission to east Africa which advised on the closer union of the British territories there, drawing up a plan which was partially adopted over the years.

At home Kennet chaired the 1925 departmental committee on the constitution of the University of London, and was the first lay member (for the crown) of the General Medical Council (1926–31). He refused appointments which would have entailed his leaving parliament.

During the Second World War, Kennet chaired the joint committees of the Treasury and the Ministry of Labour which administered the exemption from military service of civil servants, workers in financial institutions, and university teachers. From 1939 to 1959 he chaired the Capital Issues Committee, which administered the control of investment throughout the economy. For all this work he accepted no payment, public or private, and it was his practice to write his own reports.

At different times Kennet was also chairman and director of many commercial and financial corporations, among them English Electric, Hudson's Bay, Denny Mott and Dickson, Union Discount, British Bank of the Middle East, and Equity and Law Life Assurance. After 1935 his working life was passed mainly in the City, where he was known as a specialist in reordering the finances of companies standing in need of it. His varied presidencies included the Royal Statistical Society, the Association of Technical Institutions, the Poetry Society, the Gas Federation of Great Britain, the Association of Municipal Corporations, and the National Association of Youth Clubs.

Kennet's leisure interests were old books, which he collected—principally Venetian incunabula and first editions of the English philosophers—and birds, about which he published a book of essays, *A Bird in the Bush* (1936), illustrated by his stepson Peter Markham *Scott. He also published a book of verse, *A Muse at Sea* (1919), reprinted with additions as *Verses* in 1935. One became an anthology piece: 'A boy was born at Bethlehem'. He was an enthusiastic small-boat sailor until his sixtieth year, sailing single-handed in a stricter sense of the word than is usual, and a good swimmer and diver. He was a spirited draughtsman, usually for political or didactic purposes. All the special skills required to maintain an active physical life with one arm he carefully learned and maintained.

Kennet was of compact build and average height, handsome in youth, with curly dark hair and straight nose, alert and courteous in white-haired age. He was on affable terms with his eldest brother, Sir George Young, bt, the eccentric diplomat and historian of Turkish law, and on terms of affection with his next brother, Geoffrey Winthrop *Young, the mountaineer and writer.

Kennet was brought up in a rather rigid broad-church family but, under the influence of G. E. Moore and Bertrand Russell at Cambridge, abandoned Christianity for an aesthetically flavoured humanism. Face to face with death in 1914 he felt the need for a stricter system, and studied Spinoza among shellbursts. He remained a Spinozan pantheist until his death. Towards the end of his life he wrote essays for private circulation, tracing this philosophical development and examining the defects of democracy in general and the House of Commons in particular. He held that the chief threat to the welfare of a community comes from the excesses of extremists both left and right, and that it is the duty of rulers to counteract them by leaning right or left as the times require. Spinoza was his philosopher; 'Trimmer' Halifax his statesman.

Kennet was at home in scholarship, in administration, and in debate, but never in party politics. These he held in contempt, and it showed. A reserved manner and a certain caustic integrity prevented his achieving the highest political offices. He had a measure of the brilliant contrariety characteristic of his family, but balanced it with a genial empiricism of his own. He called himself a jack of all trades: his admirers called him an *uomo universale*.

In 1922 Young married (Edith Agnes) Kathleen *Scott (1878–1947), the sculptor. Although entered into late in life, the marriage was singularly successful, their temperaments being nicely complementary: hers passionate and intuitive; his quizzical and rather reserved. He died at his home, The Lacket, Lockeridge, in Wiltshire on 11 July 1960, and was buried at Overton parish church, near Marlborough. He was succeeded by his only child, Wayland Hilton Young (b. 1923). WAYLAND KENNET

Sources E. Hilton Young, *By sea and land* (1924) · personal knowledge (2004) · family papers, including autobiographical notes, CUL · gravestone, Overton parish church, Wiltshire

Archives CUL, papers | BL, corresp. with Sir Sydney Cockerell, Add. MS 52729 · Bodl. Oxf., letters to William Montgomery Crook · Bodl. Oxf., corresp. with Sidgwick & Jackson · Bodl. Oxf., corresp. with C. W. G. Walker · Bodl. RH, corresp. with C. W. G. Walker · CAC Cam., corresp. with Sir E. L. Spears · CUL, letters to Stanley Baldwin and others; corresp with Sir Peter Markham Scott · HLRO, corresp. with David Lloyd George · King's AC Cam., letters to Oscar Browning | FILM priv. coll., film

Likenesses W. Stoneman, three photographs, 1919–43, NPG · W. Rothenstein, chalk drawing, 1924, NPG · T. Cottrell, print, NPG · D. Low, pencil caricature, NPG · K. Scott, statuette; known to be in possession of Wayland Young, in 1971 · P. Scott, portrait; known to be in possession of Wayland Young, in 1971

Wealth at death £23,266 4s. 9d.: probate, 29 Sept 1960, CGPLA Eng. & Wales

Young, Sir Hubert Winthrop

Young, Sir Hubert Winthrop (1885–1950), army officer and administrator, born at Wrexham on 6 July 1885, was the second of the four distinguished sons of William Mackworth *Young (1840–1924) of the Indian Civil Service, and lieutenant-governor of the Punjab, and his second wife, Frances Mary (d. 8 March 1932), daughter of Sir Robert Eyles Egerton. His father and maternal grandfather were both lieutenant-governors of the Punjab. His brothers included Gerard Mackworth-*Young (1884–

Sir Hubert Winthrop Young (1885–1950), by Rose Mary Young, c.1923

1965), civil servant in India and archaeologist, and Sir Mark Aitchison *Young (1886–1974), colonial governor. Having been educated at Eton College (1898–1902), where he was a scholar, and the Royal Military Academy, Woolwich (1902–4), he was commissioned in 1904 in the Royal Garrison Artillery (lieutenant 1907). He intended to transfer to the Indian army and eventually into the Indian political service, and was advised to study Arabic to facilitate his later learning Persian or Urdu. After being posted to Aden in 1907 he studied Arabic there. He was invalided from Aden, and in England studied Arabic with a Baghdadi coach, before qualifying as an interpreter in Arabic in July 1908. In the same year he transferred to the 116th Marathas, Indian army. Returning from leave in 1913 he travelled via Syria and Iraq and at Carchemish stayed with T. E. Lawrence, there as an archaeologist. This made a deep impression on both men and had an important influence on Young's career.

When appointed adjutant of the 116th Marathas in 1913 Young was given by the colonel scope for his exceptional abilities. He transformed the battalion, increasing efficiency and morale by his energy, organizing ability, and knowledge of the men, his design of a smart *pagri*, and the composition, with the Indian officers, of marching songs celebrating the great Maratha exploits (one, *Ek sau solah mahrataja*, became very popular). When war came in 1914 Young worked at army headquarters for a while, but he returned to his regiment and served on the north-west frontier. In 1915 he was sent to Mesopotamia where he served as assistant political officer (1915–17) and was chiefly responsible for the construction of the Shaybah *bund*. He was transferred to the local resources department in 1917 as deputy director (1917–18), and was mentioned in dispatches for speeding up grain deliveries.

At Lawrence's request Young was transferred to the Hejaz operations in March 1918 as general staff officer, grade 2 (GSO2). He organized transport and supplies for the composite force which cut the railway behind the Turkish army just before Allenby's final attack. He was mentioned in dispatches, and received the DSO (1919), and order of El Nahdha, third class. After a short period as president of the local resources board in Damascus (1918), he took leave to England. In *Seven Pillars of Wisdom* (1926) Lawrence praised Young as energetic, capable, and strong-willed, 'a regular of exceptional quality … rising, as ever, to any occasion' (Lawrence, 524, 577).

Young served in the new eastern department of the Foreign Office (1919–21), where his Arab experience helped form the policy eventually adopted in Iraq. He was assistant secretary in the Middle East department, Colonial Office, from its formation in 1921 until the end of 1926. He was colonial secretary, Gibraltar (1927–9), counsellor to the high commissioner for Iraq (1929–32), and envoy-extraordinary and minister-plenipotentiary in Baghdad (October and November 1932). After this he was governor respectively of Nyasaland (1932–4), Northern Rhodesia (1934–8), and Trinidad and Tobago (1938–42). In his last post, at the most important of the Lend Lease bases, he attempted to safeguard the interests of the colony and his own authority as governor in the presence of a considerable American air, land, and naval force. In this difficult task he fell foul of an unsatisfactory and unco-operative American commanding officer, whose reports about Young led to complaints by General Marshall to Winston Churchill in Washington in 1942. In the interests of harmonious relations at this critical time, Churchill instructed the colonial secretary in February to replace him. He was given no opportunity to defend himself. His health prevented him from accepting another post, and much of his heavy wartime work in Trinidad was done despite a warning heart attack.

In the colonial service—though like other colonial officials of the period, his policy-making was much constrained by the Colonial Office—he was noted for energy and foresight in helping to develop air communications, and for his sympathy with indigenous interests, which did not, however, cause him to neglect those of the European community. At a time when the settlers were being attacked by London critics, and were pressing for amalgamation of the Rhodesias, in Northern Rhodesia Young considered the settlers beneficial, tried to encourage secondary industries, and favoured closer co-operation among the Rhodesias and Nyasaland, and the creation of a new association, British Central Africa. He negotiated with the other governors and with settler leaders, but the Colonial Office forbade any step likely to lead to amalgamation or federation of the Rhodesias. He increased the role of the settler-elected unofficial members of the legislative council, and defended against London critics his administration's policies on African employment, arguing that

these were affected by the underlying financial constraints on African education. He identified himself with provisions for the constant review of labour conditions and with the development of social services and the establishment of trust lands for Africans. In Trinidad, labour, hospitals, and housing occupied his special attention. Young was created CMG in 1923, was knighted in 1932, and appointed KCMG in 1934. After retirement he engaged in relief work, notably as European regional officer for the United Nations Relief and Rehabilitation Administration (1944–5); for this he was made a commander of the order of Orange Nassau in 1949. In 1945 he unsuccessfully contested Harrow West as a Liberal, and in 1947 Edge Hill, Liverpool. He served on the board of the Royal Free Hospital, London, from 1945 and was chairman from 1946 until his death; he was also chairman of the consultative council of the Southern Electricity area. On 7 February 1924 Young married Margaret Rose Mary, daughter of Colonel Frank Romilly Reynolds RE; they had three sons.

Young had many talents. He wrote well, as his book *The Independent Arab* (1933) showed; he talked well, was an excellent linguist, a gifted amateur pianist and organist, and keen chess-player. Intellectual and man of action, he was fertile in ideas and determined in implementing them. He appeared formidable, and was sometimes overbearing; but his moral courage made him at least as stiff with his superiors, if he thought their policy mistaken, as with anyone else. Kind-hearted, he was sympathetic to the underdog and devoted to the public service.

He died at Evora, Portugal, on 20 April 1950 and was survived by his wife.

R. W. BULLARD, *rev.* ROGER T. STEARN

Sources H. W. Young, *The independent Arab* (1933) · private information (1959, 2004) [Martin Young] · personal knowledge (1959) · *WWW* · Burke, *Peerage* (1967) · *The Eton register*, 7 (privately printed, Eton, 1922) · T. E. Lawrence, *Seven pillars of wisdom: a triumph* (1935) · L. H. Gann, *A history of Northern Rhodesia: early days to 1953* (1964) · *CGPLA Eng. & Wales* (1950)

Archives King's Lond., Liddell Hart C., letters and messages re operations in Arabia · NRA, papers · St Ant. Oxf., Middle East Centre, Middle East papers

Likenesses R. M. Young, chalk drawing, *c*.1923, unknown collection; copyprint, NPG [*see illus.*] · W. Stoneman, photograph, 1934, NPG

Wealth at death £2651 10s. 11d.: probate, 19 Aug 1950, *CGPLA Eng. & Wales*

Young, Isabella (*bap.* 1716?, *d.* 1795). *See under* Young family (*per. c.*1700–1799).

Young, Isabella (1740/41?–1791). *See under* Young family (*per. c.*1700–1799).

Young, James (*d.* 1789), naval officer, began his active naval career in the Mediterranean in 1737. He was promoted lieutenant on 9 March 1739, and became commander of the *Salamander* in 1742. On 16 May 1743 he was posted captain of the *Namur*; shortly afterwards he was in the *Kennington*. He then moved to the *Dunkirk*, and remained in the Mediterranean until the peace in 1748. In 1752 he was appointed to the *Jason* and in 1755 to the *Newark*, from which he moved in October to the *Intrepid*, which went out to the Mediterranean in spring 1756 in the squadron commanded by Admiral John Byng. At the battle of Minorca on 20 May 1756 the *Intrepid* was the last ship of the van division, and in approaching the enemy had her foretopmast shot away. Byng afterwards asserted that this event caused the disorder in the rear division of his fleet, but Young, when examined at Byng's court martial, denied such a result and was supported by other evidence.

In 1757 Young commanded the *Burford* in the expedition against Rochefort. In 1759 he was captain of the *Mars* and on 20 November he flew a commodore's broad pennant in her at the battle of Quiberon Bay. In the following years he commanded small squadrons in the channel, and on 21 October 1762 he was promoted rear-admiral. On 28 October 1770 Young was made vice-admiral, and in April 1775 he was appointed commander-in-chief on the Leeward Islands station, with his flag in the *Portland*.

Young's period of command in the West Indies covered the early years of the American War of Independence, and his small squadron had two main tasks: to cut off the supply of arms and gunpowder to the American rebels, and to protect British trade from attack by American privateers and warships. Young was more successful in the latter task than the former. His efforts to halt the supply of munitions to the Americans were hampered by a lack of fast-sailing cruisers in his squadron and the open assistance given to the Americans by the neutral islands, especially the Dutch at St Eustatius and the French at Martinique. With regard to trade protection, Young had organized a convoy system from the islands to Britain by mid-1776 and his ships had some success against American privateers and warships. In November 1776 an American warship arriving at St Eustatius received the first foreign salute to the flag of the new United States. In retaliation Young imposed a virtual blockade of the neutral Dutch island until he received orders to lift it in early 1777. During Young's command his squadron captured 205 American merchant ships and captured or destroyed seventeen American privateers and warships. Young was married twice. Details of his first wife are unknown; his second marriage (in or after 1762) was to Sophia Young.

On 29 January 1778 Young was promoted admiral and in July he returned to England. He saw no further service and lived in London, dying there on 24 January 1789. His son William followed him into the navy.

J. K. LAUGHTON, rev. ALAN G. JAMIESON

Sources A. G. Jamieson, 'War in the Leeward Islands, 1775–1783', DPhil diss., U. Oxf., 1981 • A. G. Jamieson, 'Admiral James Young and the pirateers, 1777', *Mariner's Mirror*, 65 (1979), 69–75 • A. G. Jamieson, 'American privateers in the Leeward Islands, 1776–1778', *American Neptune*, 43 (1983), 23–30 • will, PRO, PROB 11/1175, sig. 69
Archives NMM, corresp. with Lord Sandwich • PRO, admiralty MSS, dispatches, etc.

Young, James (1810–1891), railway contractor, was born on 10 February 1810 at Littlemill, near Kilmacolm, Renfrewshire, Scotland, the son of James Young, farmer and local contractor, and his wife, Margaret Glover. He had at least one brother. He was educated at the parish school, and then worked as an overseer on the building of the Glasgow and Garnkirk Railway, the first major railway contract in Scotland. He returned home to run his father's contracting business, which concentrated on road mending and dyke building. In 1836 he married Janet, daughter of Archibald Bulloch, coalmaster, of Glasgow. They had five sons and five daughters. In 1854 he won his first important contract, to build the Calderbank section of the Monklands Railway. For some years he was in partnership with Robert Ward, and their work included sections of the Caledonian, Milngavie, and Wemyss Bay railways.

In the mid-1870s Young formed two family businesses, in partnership with his brother and his eldest son: they were James Young & Sons, a coalmining and limequarrying business, which managed a mine at Baljaffray, Duntocher, and a contracting firm, James Young & Co. The latter built the western section of the Greenock and Ayrshire Railway, which ran underneath the town to the harbour. This was followed by contracts to build sections of the Glasgow, Bothwell, Hamilton, and Coatbridge Railway in 1875: Young dealt with the problem of cutting through heavy boulder clay in the Bellshill section by using a steam excavator based on an American machine, the first to be used in railway construction in the United Kingdom, thus saving on time and labour costs. Other important contracts included work on the Yoker and Clydebank Railway in 1881, and the St Andrews and Anstruther Railway. In 1882 he successfully tendered to build the western section of the first underground railway to be built in Glasgow, the Glasgow City and District Railway, running west–east across the city. Although Young's contract was for a section of only just over a mile, he had to solve the technical problem of how to tunnel through sand without disturbing the existing buildings. This contract earned the firm over £200,000.

Young retired in 1886, and moved to the sea, to Dunholme, Skelmorlie, Ayrshire. His eldest son took over the management of the business, which continued to win major railway contracts, including one for the Glasgow Central Railway, but the firm was wound up within twenty years. James Young died on 18 June 1891 at Skelmorlie, and was buried at the Glasgow necropolis.

ANNE PIMLOTT BAKER

Sources N. J. Morgan, 'Young, James', *DSBB* • B. Kettle, *The Glasgow underground* (1989) • W. A. C. Smith and P. Anderson, *Illustrated history of Glasgow's railways* (1993) • *CCI* (1891) • N. J. Morgan, 'Some brief notes on the history of James Young Ltd, and James Young and Sons Ltd, railway and public works contractors', *Scottish Industrial History*, 6/1 (1983), 2–9
Wealth at death £52,112 11s. 4d.: confirmation, 16 Sept 1891, *CCI*

Young, James (1811–1883), chemist and philanthropist, was born on 13 July 1811 at Drygate, Glasgow, the eldest son of John Young, a self-employed carpenter, and his wife, Jean Wilson (married on 9 February 1809). Young worked for his father and in 1830 began to attend the evening lectures in chemistry of Professor Thomas Graham, at Anderson's University. By the session of 1831–2 he had become Graham's laboratory assistant. He also became the friend of David Livingstone and Lyon Playfair, made the acquaintance of many sons of industrialists, and in 1834 began giving lectures for Graham to the mechanics' class. He was presented with an inscribed silver watch by this class in 1836 and, when he was about to leave on 28 June 1837 to join Graham at University College, London, he was also given a testimonial. His first scientific paper, dated 4 January 1837 and published in the *Philosophical Magazine*, described a miniature voltaic battery, a modification of Faraday's invention.

On 21 August 1838 Young married his cousin, Mary Young, and thereafter he began to seek better-paid employment outside academic life. In 1839 he became manager of James Muspratt & Sons at Newton-le-Willows, Lancashire. Muspratt's sons, Sheridan (who had been at Anderson's University) and James, were laboratory students at University College and it was through the latter that an initial offer of £140 per year and a house (Alkali Cottage, St Helens) was made to Young in October 1838. Young was involved in the layout of the plant and became its technical director; his first patent for the production of ammonia (11 November 1841) was an industrial application of his earlier work in Graham's laboratory. Young joined Tennant, Clow & Co. on 12 January 1844 as manager of their Ardwick Bridge chemical works in Manchester. Tennants paid its managerial staff well and allowed them to patent processes, to act as consultants to customers, and to undertake business ventures on their own behalf, provided there was no conflict of interest. Young made improvements to methods of production at a number of their plants. In 1844 he produced a cheaper indigo dye and in 1848 he patented a method of producing sodium and potassium stannate from tinstone.

Young, a Liberal radical, joined the Manchester branch of the Anti-Corn Law League in 1844 and was so dissatisfied with the politics of the *Manchester Guardian* that he helped to found the *Manchester Examiner* (1846) under the editorship of Thomas Ballantyne. A member of the Manchester Mechanics' Institute, he served in 1845 on a committee established by the Manchester Literary and Philosophical Society to investigate the Irish potato blight, and compiled its report. Young was elected to the society on 19 October 1847, having already organized a chemical group which became a section. His first paper to the society concerned the health of towns and the need to deodorize cesspools using chloride of manganese.

On 3 December 1847 Lyon Playfair wrote to Young, telling him of a petroleum spring yielding 300 gallons daily in the Riddings colliery near Alfreton, Derbyshire, on the estate of his brother-in-law, James Oakes. Young visited Riddings in December 1847 and conducted experiments. Thereafter he suggested to Tennants that the firm might refine this petroleum, but they decided that the likely scale of operations was too small. James Oakes then suggested that with his help Young should establish his own refinery, an arrangement to which Tennants agreed. The main customers bought lubricants, and the textile firms soon realized the products' advantages and relative cheapness. Young erroneously thought that the Riddings

petroleum had been condensed from the coal and deposited in the strata above. He therefore began to experiment with the dry distillation of coal at various temperatures and, having explored the characteristics of the main oil-bearing coals and shales, he enrolled the crucial patent for this process on 17 October 1850.

The best material was torbanite, a geological curiosity found in the coal measures near Bathgate and first mined as Boghead coal; Young and his partners, E. W. Binney, a Manchester lawyer, and Edward Meldrum, opened an oilworks in 1851 2 miles from the pithead, having secured an exclusive contract from James Russel & Son, the mineral lessees. The first products were naphtha (used as a solvent) and various lubricants, but by 1855 paraffin for lamps had become most profitable; paraffin wax was not sold until 1856 and in quantity for candles only from 1859. Any attempt to maintain secrecy about production was vitiated by the litigation (1853) brought by the owners of the Torbane Hill estate, Mr and Mrs William Gillespie, against Russels, on the grounds that torbanite was not coal and therefore not included in their lease. Profit margins were discussed in court and were so wide as to encourage patent infringements and competition. Fortunately for Young the Gillespies lost their case, but further legal actions were necessary to sustain the patent. Young was successful in winning costs and damages against Stephen White and others (1854), the Clydesdale Chemical Company (1860–61), John Miller & Co., and William Miller & Co. (1861). The greatest test, which ended in the House of Lords, was the case against Ebenezer Fernie, William Carter, and Joseph Robinson (1862–4), which resulted in costs of £10,000 and damages of £11,422 in Young's favour.

Yet Young's reluctance to grant licences and the gradual discovery of cheaper but lower-yielding oil shales stimulated the growth of competition; by the time his British patent expired in 1864, there was a Scottish oil mania, and by 1870 ninety-seven firms had been established, most of them since 1859. American petroleum and kerosene firms also used Young's process and after 1862 brought more competition to European markets. Young broke with his partners in 1864 and established a new works at Addiewell before launching Young's Paraffin Light and Mineral Oil Company with a capital of £600,000 (1866).

By 1870 'Paraffin Young', as he had become known, had retired from business and gradually reduced his shareholding in his limited company. He spent his time on science, leisure, and philanthropy. An active supporter of a channel tunnel, he conducted experiments on the velocity of light, and he was very interested in the practical development of electric light and the telephone. Elected to the Royal Society of Edinburgh (1861) and the Royal Society (1873), he had a fine collection of works on alchemy and the early history of chemistry. A trustee of Anderson's University from 1858, he became a manager and its president (1868–77), endowing the Young chair of technical chemistry and the Young Laboratory, and making many other gifts. Active in the British Association for the Advancement of Science, he was a member of the

Chemical Society and its vice-president from 1879 to 1881. The University of St Andrews conferred the degree of LLD upon him in 1879. He gave statues of David Livingstone and Thomas Graham to the city of Glasgow, and despite colour-blindness he was a keen collector of Dutch and Flemish art. He sailed far and wide on his steam yacht, *Nyanza*, and farmed three estates, Limefield (Linlithgowshire), Durris (Kincardineshire), and Kelly (Renfrewshire), where he spent most of his latter years. Young's friendship with Livingstone led to his financial support for Livingstone's second and third expeditions to Zanzibar and for the search expedition. He also brought Livingstone's servants to Britain to clarify details of the last days of the explorer, and he acted as guardian to Livingstone's children. A Presbyterian in religion, he was generally tolerant in his approach to other faiths and gave widely to a range of good causes. He died a widower at Kelly House, Wemyss Bay, Renfrewshire, on 13 May 1883, and was buried at Inverkip cemetery. He was survived by three sons and four daughters and left a gross estate of £165,000.

JOHN BUTT

Sources Strathclyde University, James Young MSS · J. Butt, *James 'Paraffin' Young*, Scottish Men of Science (1983) · *Memoirs and portraits of 100 Glasgow men*, 2 (1886) · *The Bailie* (19 Nov 1879), 1–2 · J. Butt, 'James Young, industrialist and philanthropist', PhD diss., U. Glas., 1964 · d. cert. · *CCI* (1883)
Archives University of Strathclyde, Glasgow, diaries and notebooks, patents, financial papers, newspaper cuttings, etc.
Likenesses Gilmour and Dean, portrait, repro. in *The Bailie* · J. W. Gordon, oils, University of Strathclyde, Glasgow · photographs, University of Strathclyde, Glasgow
Wealth at death £165,660 16s. 3d.: confirmation, 9 Aug 1883, *CCI*

Young, Jane Elizabeth. *See* Vezin, Jane Elizabeth (1827–1902).

Young, John (1514–1581/2), college head, was a native of Yorkshire. He was elected fellow of St John's College, Cambridge, in 1536, having graduated BA in 1535. He proceeded MA in 1539 and BTh in 1546 and was nominated a fellow of Trinity College in the same year. In June 1549 he took part on the Catholic side in the disputations before Ridley at Cambridge. In 1550 he enjoyed a prominent role in public disputations with Martin Bucer and commenced a series of lectures on the first epistle of Timothy, during which he is said to have scorned Bucer and his views. A quarrel ensued between the two men and Young expressed alarm that he was being held up as an opponent of the authorized homily on good works. In 1551 he was accused in February before the privy council of preaching against the religious proceedings of Edward VI; on 25 November and 3 December he took part in the disputations on the sacraments at the houses of William Cecil and Richard Morison, still defending the Catholic tenets. However, it is possible that Young also translated some of Cranmer's polemic into Latin for the benefit of an international audience.

With the accession of Mary I, Young's support of the Catholic faith was recognized. He was created a doctor of theology at Cambridge in 1553 and incorporated at Oxford

in the following year. He was appointed master of Pembroke College, Cambridge, on Ridley's deprivation, and instituted canon of Ely on 12 April 1554. He was vice-chancellor of Cambridge in 1553–5, and in 1555 or 1556 he became regius professor of divinity. As vice-chancellor Young delivered a series of lectures entitled 'Ennarationes Joelis prophetae', dedicated to Cardinal Pole, which are extant in the Bodleian Library. He disputed with Cranmer, Ridley, and Latimer at Oxford in 1554, and extracts from his 'socratical interrogations' are reproduced by Foxe. Young took an active role in restoring his university to the Catholic faith. At the accession of Elizabeth I he was deprived of his mastership and committed to prison in Wood Street, London, for refusing to take the oath of supremacy. Before 1574 he was transferred to the Marshalsea prison, from where on 13 June that year he was temporarily released on the surety of his brother, Gregory Young. On 28 July 1577 he was transferred to the custody of the dean of Canterbury and on 18 February 1578 he was committed to the queen's bench prison. In 1580 he was moved to Wisbech Castle, where he made his will on the 20 April 1581; it was proved on 6 June 1582. Bequests included 'a Mapp of the whole worlde' to his brother Gregory, and £10 and his books to 'his man' Henry Crosse.

Referred to by his enemies not as 'Jungus' but as 'Fungus' (Porter, 63), Young is said to have been 'litigious, vain and inconstant' (Cooper, *Ath. Cantab.*, 1.428) but there is little evidence to support this view. It has been suggested that he was not on amicable terms with the fellows of Pembroke, but this is not supported by the warm commendations he received in letters sent by the fellows to Edmund Grindal inviting Grindal to become master following Young's deprivation. His talent and scholarship have not been disputed. He translated into English John Redman's *De gratia* (published under the title of *The Complaint of Grace* in eight volumes in 1556), and his own *De schismate, sive, De ecclesiasticae unitatis divisione liber unus* was published in eight volumes in Louvain in 1573, and Douai in 1603. A portrait of Young belongs to Cambridge University.

JUDITH FORD

Sources Cooper, *Ath. Cantab.*, 1.427–8, 568 · APC, 1571–5, 253; 1577–8, 4, 168 · *The letters of Stephen Gardiner*, ed. J. A. Muller (1933), 456–7, 463–4, 469, 476 · will, 1582, PRO, PROB 11/64, sig. 40 · *The acts and monuments of John Foxe*, ed. S. R. Cattley, 8 vols. (1837–41), vol. 6, pp. 461–4 · J. Bentham, *The history and antiquities of the conventual and cathedral church of Ely*, ed. J. Bentham, 2nd edn (1812), 244 · P. Collinson, *Archbishop Grindal, 1519–1583: the struggle for a reformed church* (1979), 40 · CSP dom., 1547–80, 293, 328 · H. P. Stokes, *The chaplains and the chapel of the University of Cambridge, 1256–1568* (1906), 36 · H. C. Porter, *Reformation and reaction in Tudor Cambridge* (1958), 63 · T. D. Atkinson and J. W. Clark, *Cambridge described and illustrated, being a short history of town and university* (1897), 289 · D. MacCulloch, *Thomas Cranmer: a life* (1996), 535
Likenesses oils, 1579, Old Schools, Cambridge · portrait, Pembroke Cam.
Wealth at death see will, PRO, PROB 11/64, sig. 40

Young, John (c.1532–1605), bishop of Rochester, was born in the London parish of St Magnus the Martyr and educated at the Mercers' School. He graduated BA from Cambridge in 1552, doubtless from Pembroke College (whose admission register is lost), since he was elected fellow of Pembroke in 1553. After proceeding MA in 1555, he seems to have remained quietly in Cambridge until Elizabeth's accession.

Ordained deacon at Ely on 22 March 1562, Young proceeded BTh in 1563, and having resigned his fellowship was collated on 31 August to the city rectory of St Martin Ludgate by Edmund Grindal, bishop of London and former master of Pembroke, whose chaplain he became. On 3 May 1564 Grindal instituted him prebendary of Cadington Major in St Paul's on the presentation of Sir John Mason, ordaining him priest on 25 February 1565, when he was described as MA, born in St Magnus, and aged about thirty-three. On 7 May 1566 he received the prebend of North Muskham in Southwell Minster by letters patent. After Miles Coverdale had resigned the rectory of St Magnus at the height of the vestiarian controversy, Young was collated there (24 September 1566), resigning St Martin Ludgate.

On 12 July 1567, on Grindal's advice, Young was elected master of Pembroke in succession to John Whitgift. As vice-chancellor in 1568–9 he stoutly resisted the attempts of Archbishop Parker to impose the authority of the ecclesiastical commission on the university. Parker expressed extreme astonishment, but does not seem to have retaliated.

Young proceeded DTh in 1569, and on 19 August that year, at the petition of Sir William Cecil, received letters patent for the rectory of Little Wilbraham, Cambridgeshire, from the lord keeper, Sir Nicholas Bacon, presumably in order to allow him to support the dignity of his mastership. On 20 March 1572 he was granted letters patent for the tenth stall in Westminster Abbey, taking possession on 26 April and preaching at convocation that year.

Although he seems to have been seldom resident at Pembroke, Young's mastership has always been celebrated for the number of eminent scholars and writers active there during his tenure. Edmund Spenser matriculated in 1569. Lancelot Andrewes, Edward Kirke, Thomas Neville, and Gabriel Harvey were all elected fellows under him. Six letters from Harvey to Young survive in Harvey's letter-book. The most enduring monument to his capacity for securing his subordinates' loyalty is Spenser's portrait of Young as 'faithful Roffy' in *The Shepherd's Calendar*, the name being an affectionate abbreviation of *Roffensis*, his Latin title after 16 March 1578, when he was consecrated bishop of Rochester.

Retaining his Westminster prebend and the rectory of St Magnus *in commendam*, Young resigned his other promotions and married in 1578 Grace (*née* Cocke), widow of Thomas Watts, archdeacon of Middlesex, one of Pembroke's most notable benefactors.

Young was one of a coterie promoted to the bench— John Aylmer, John Piers, and John Whitgift were the others—at a time when Sir Christopher Hatton wielded particular influence at court following Elizabeth's suspension of Grindal, now archbishop of Canterbury, for his refusal to suppress the clerical exercises known as prophesyings. All four men were regarded as stern disciplinarians, having little or no sympathy for nonconformity, but while Piers became archbishop of York and Whitgift succeeded Grindal as primate, Young never prospered. He remained at Rochester for twenty-seven years, one of only four out of twenty-two occupants of the see between 1472 and 1629 who were not translated to a wealthier one.

In 1581, as bishop of London and *de facto* primate after Grindal's suspension, Aylmer urged Cecil, now Lord Burghley, to promote Young to Norwich for his 'quickness in government' and ability 'to bridle the innovators' (BL, Lansdowne MS 33, fol. 52r). Whitgift revived the proposal on his elevation to Canterbury in 1583 without success, but in September 1584 was authorized to offer Young Chichester instead. Young was 'very well content' to abide by Burghley's 'disposition for that matter' (SP12/173/15), but again failed to win promotion.

At the end of the decade Young was one of those charged with pursuing the authors of the Martin Marprelate tracts in which, like many of his colleagues, he was denigrated as a 'petty pope' and also castigated for presenting himself to a benefice in his gift. Although Martin did not name the benefice, it was presumably this charge that led to the erroneous statement that in 1592 he 'exposed himself to no little animadversion' by presenting himself to the rectory of Wouldham in Kent (Cooper, *Ath. Cantab.*, 2.406), a benefice he never, in fact, occupied.

In 1594, refusing the bishopric of Norwich on the grounds that Edmund Scambler had despoiled the revenues, Young was credited with the remark that 'it was not so easy a seat for an old man since the cushion was taken away' (Cooper, *Ath. Cantab.*, 2.406). His fastidiousness evidently riled Burghley, who reacted by accusing him of covetousness and of keeping poor hospitality. Young penned an icy letter in his own defence, claiming that he maintained 'as good a table as any in England, excepting that which is prodigal', but pointing out that his income from his see and his *commendams* was so small that the discharge of his obligations of hospitality left him with only £90 per annum to live on. Nevertheless, he took care to assure Burghley that he would not refuse further preferment if it was 'meet' for him to accept (BL, Lansdowne MS 79, fol. 114r). This correspondence hardly leaves room for the tradition that he 'nobly declined' to leave Rochester on the grounds that a man should not leave his wife because she is poor (White, 251–2).

Although mentioned for the bishopric of Salisbury in 1596–7, Young scarcely surfaces in the official records thereafter. In his will, dated 13 March 1605, he directed that he be buried in a simple tomb in the chancel of Bromley church, with a suitable inscription. His sole bequests were to Grace and their only child, John. Grace received household stuff and the plate which she had brought him from her marriage to Thomas Watts, but no hard cash or life interest in any property. As sole executor John received the residue, being directed to bestow what he felt he could afford on 'poor kinsmen and servants'.

The will's most arresting feature is what appears to be a

specific allusion to his quarrel with Burghley. Given the 'debility' of his 'spiritual living ..., which never amounted to above three hundred pounds a year', he observed that the provisions made for his funeral ought to be accounted a 'liberal expense' by anyone 'possessed with an equal and indifferent opinion and not foreprized with a will and conceit of mine wealth and riches, as many, yea too many hath been' (PRO, PROB 11/108, sig. 100, fol. 384v).

Young died at Bromley Palace on 10 April 1605, aged seventy-one, and was duly buried in Bromley church under a brass bearing both his own arms and those of his see, and with a conventionally phrased inscription listing his virtues. For unknown reasons probate of his will was not granted until 22 November 1606. He published a single sermon, and that only to justify himself because 'it was not well taken in part of some of the hearers, where it was spoken' (*A Sermon Preached before the Queenes Maiestie, the Second of March, An. 1575*, sig. A1v). He also contributed 'Notes upon the booke entituled *Euangelium regni*' to William Wilkinson's *Confutation of Certaine Articles Delivered unto the Familye of Love* (1579).   BRETT USHER

Sources Venn, *Alum. Cant.*, 1/4.493 · Cooper, *Ath. Cantab.*, 2.405–7 · G. Hennessy, *Novum repertorium ecclesiasticum parochiale Londinense, or, London diocesan clergy succession from the earliest time to the year 1898* (1898) · GL, MS 9535/1 [ordination] · A. L. Attwater, *Pembroke College, Cambridge: a short history*, ed. S. C. Roberts (1936), 43–50 · E. J. L. Scott, ed., *Letter book of Gabriel Harvey, AD 1573–1580*, Camden, new ser. 33 (1884) · *CPR, 1566–72; 1575–8* · F. O. White, *Lives of the Elizabethan bishops of the Anglican church* (1898) · *Calendar of the manuscripts of the most hon. the marquis of Salisbury*, 6–7, HMC, 9 (1895–9) · *CSP dom., 1581–90*, 201 · will, PRO, PROB 11/108, sig. 100 · PRO, state papers domestic, Elizabeth, SP 12/173/15 · BL, Lansdowne MS 33, fol. 52r · BL, Lansdowne MS 79, fol. 114r

Archives BL, Lansdowne MSS, letters to Burghley · CKS, Rochester diocesan records

Wealth at death modest: will, PRO, PROB 11/108, sig. 100

Young, John (1585–1654), dean of Winchester, was born in Seaton, Forfarshire, on 25 June 1585, the sixth of eight sons and the eighth of twelve children of Sir Peter *Young (1544–1628), tutor to James VI of Scotland, and his first wife, Elizabeth Gibb (d. 1593). He attended St Andrews University and took his MA by 1606, when he was incorporated at Cambridge and elected a fellow of Sidney Sussex College. He is alleged to have been one of the first Scots to take a degree at Cambridge. He was ordained priest in December 1610 by Bishop George Abbot of London, had received his BD by 1611 and his DD by 1613, and for a time was tutor to Lord Wharton's son.

As son of the king's tutor and brother of Patrick *Young, the royal librarian, Young enjoyed excellent court connections, which explains his steady preferment after 1611. He was created chancellor of Wells Cathedral in 1611 by Bishop James Montagu, and probably received a canonry at York in 1613; he became a royal chaplain, and in 1616 dean of Winchester. He and his heirs were granted free denization in 1616, and he became rector of Over Wallop in Hampshire in 1620. About 1615 Young married Sarah (d. before 1652), daughter of Andrew Bourman of Wells. They had three sons and two daughters, all of whom were to predecease him except his youngest son, John.

As dean of Winchester, Young was an active servant of James I. Between 1616 and 1621 he made repeated visits to Scotland on royal business, accompanying the king in 1617, and attending the general assembly in Perth in 1618 in support of the king's five articles of ceremonial reform. Young's Scottish background, Calvinist convictions, and diplomatic skills made him an ideal emissary, and he was praised by the archbishop of St Andrews, among others, for his persuasive performance.

During the Synod of Dort (1618–19) he was an important intermediary between Samuel Ward (d. 1643), one of the British delegates, and the king, whom he persuaded to moderate the British position on the universality of divine grace. In 1622 he was ordered to interview the archbishop of Spalato, a convert on the point of returning to Rome, and letters between the two survive. Young could reasonably have expected a bishopric, but he was repeatedly passed over and in 1626 apparently offered £15,000 for the vacant see of Winchester. In 1633 Young was tipped to become bishop of the new see of Edinburgh but the post eventually went to William Forbes; although he remained a royal chaplain until at least 1644, Young evidently did not enjoy the same regard from Charles I or Archbishop William Laud as he had from James I. His activities as dean of Winchester are recorded in his diary, preserved in Winchester Cathedral. He regularly urged the chapter to attend prayers, observe the preaching rota, and practise collegiality. In the 1630s, in particular, he presided over a fractious chapter, divided by personal and some ideological conflict.

Young took little part in the civil war, but was ejected from his deanery in 1645 and retired to Over Wallop, where he lived until he died on 20 July 1654. He was buried in Exton, Hampshire. His will, dated 2 August 1652, was proved on 18 September 1654.   KENNETH FINCHAM

Sources *The diary of John Young STP, dean of Winchester, 1616 to the Commonwealth*, ed. F. R. Goodman (1928) · State Papers, 1603–40, PRO · PRO, PROB, 11/234/88 · Venn, *Alum. Cant.*, 1/4 · R. Neile, M. Ant. de D[omi]nis, archbishop of Spalato, his shiftings in religion: a man for many masters (1624) · Wentworth Woodhouse Muniments, Strafford MSS, 13/65 · N. Tyacke, *Anti-Calvinists: the rise of English Arminianism, c.1590–1640* (1987) · GL, MS 9535/2, fol. 175r

Archives Winchester Cathedral, diary | Bodl. Oxf., Tanner MSS

Wealth at death property in Hampshire and elsewhere: will, PRO, PROB 11/234/88

Young, John (1742/3–1806), minister of the Secession church and political commentator, was born in Kinross-shire of unknown parentage. Details of his marriage are similarly obscure although he is known to have had at least two daughters. He received a university education in languages and philosophy, and then studied at the Secession theological seminary until 1766 under the Anti-Burgher professor of theology, the Revd William Moncrieff of Alloa. He was licensed to preach in 1766 by the Anti-Burgher presbytery of Sanquhar, and quickly established a reputation as a talented preacher. On 7 October 1767 he was ordained to the ministry of the General Associate Synod and inducted to the Anti-Burgher charge of Hawick after spending a trial period of several weeks with the congregation at Orrock Place, Hawick. Young was the first minister of this congregation, which had been formed about 1763 and which had erected its church building about three years later. He is credited with having built it up into one of the most numerous Anti-Burgher congregations: it already had a membership of about 400 by 1780. He is said to have been a diffident and modest man, but was held in great respect by his friends and colleagues.

The esteem of Young's colleagues in the Anti-Burgher ministry, however, was jeopardized by his political writings published at the time of the French Revolution. His most famous work, *Essays on Government, Revolution, the British Constitution, Kingly Government, etc.* (1794), was a defence of the British constitution and of the government's decision to wage war against revolutionary France, and a deliberate attempt to erase the seceders' reputation for political radicalism. It ran through several editions in the space of a few months, and earned him the first DD given by King's College, Aberdeen, to a secession clergyman and the offer of a government pension (which he declined, but from which his daughters later benefited). Lord Loughborough, the lord chancellor, said it was the best publication on the French Revolution he had seen (M'Kerrow, 375). However, it also plunged Young into controversy within his own denomination. Most Anti-Burghers were opposed to Erastianism and sympathetic to the voluntary principle, and they resented Young's identification of seceders with explicit political loyalism. A formal complaint was made at the synod of 1795, and a committee of three was appointed to examine the book for its harmony or otherwise with seceding principles. However, seven other ministers dissented from this measure, which they described as 'altogether improper and unseasonable' (M'Kerrow, 376), and no further formal action on the matter appears to have been taken. Young died before the Anti-Burghers split into New Light and Old Light branches on 28 August 1806, over the question of the relationship between church and state (as the Burghers had done seven years earlier), but it seems likely that he would have tended towards the Old Light minority who believed that church and state had some obligations towards each other.

Young also published *A history of the commencement, progress and termination of the late war between Britain and France* (1802), which again condemned the French Revolution and the supporters of political reform in Britain, three volumes of sermons, and two single sermons (1778 and 1795). He suffered from a paralytic affection or nervous disorder for several years before his death, and for the last year of his life this seriously impaired his ability to speak audibly to his congregation. Plans were made to appoint an assistant, but before one could be found Young died in Hawick on 25 March 1806.   EMMA VINCENT MACLEOD

Sources R. Small, *History of the congregations of the United Presbyterian church from 1733 to 1900*, 2 vols. (1904) · J. M'Kerrow, *History of the Secession church*, rev. edn (1841) · H. W. Meikle, *Scotland and the French Revolution* (1912) · D. Scott, *Annals and statistics of the Original Secession church till its disruption and union with the Free Church of Scotland in 1852*

(1886) · *Caledonian Mercury* (3 April 1806) · *Scots Magazine and Edinburgh Literary Miscellany*, 68 (1806), 319

Young, John (1744–1835), politician in Hawaii, was born on 17 March 1744 in Liverpool. His parentage and lineage are unknown. He received a seaman's apprentice education and journeyed to America to sail on fur trading ships bound for China from the Pacific northwest. Young sailed on vessels out of New York and Philadelphia before signing aboard the fur trading ship *Eleanora* as its boatswain in 1789. He arrived in Hawaii in the following year. Political mishaps ensued between the *Eleanora*'s crew and the local Hawaiians, resulting in the theft of a cutter from the *Eleanora* and the death of a crewman in its defence. The *Eleanora*'s captain, Simon Metcalf, retaliated by firing among unarmed native Hawaiians who sought to trade alongside his vessel, killing over 100 (the Olowalu massacre, near Honuaula). In response a local chief of Kohala, Kameeiamoku, attacked the companion vessel, *Fair American*, off the coast of Kona, Hawaii, resulting in the death of Metcalf's son, Thomas Humphrey, and all of the crew members save one, Issac Davis (1753/4–1810). Due to these circumstances Young, who was ashore on Hawaii at the time of the attack, was not permitted to rejoin the *Eleanora* by the king Kamehameha I (the Great), who feared further reprisals should news of the death of Metcalf's son reach the ship. The king protected both Young and Davis from further revenge and warfare between local chiefs, making the two Englishmen high ranking chiefs (*alii*) and granting them vast lands and wives of noble lineage. Kamehameha made each man responsible for the other; the escape of one meant certain death for the other. Their one attempt to escape together to the ship of Captain Colnett failed in April 1791 and again Kamehameha protected them against rival chiefs who sought their destruction.

Subsequently Young and Davis worked together with Kamehameha. In exchange for protection, status, and lands John Young became Kamehameha's most trusted adviser. His integrity, honesty, and character, in addition to his bilingual ability and knowledge of Hawaiian customs, made him a favourite among the local inhabitants and foreigners alike. Young also proved invaluable to Kamehameha's attempt to subdue rival local chiefs and bring all islands under his monarchy. Young's military strategy in a famed sea battle (Kepuwahaulauha or 'the red-mouth gun'), in 1791, which allowed Kamehameha to capture the channel between the islands of Maui and Hawaii, further confirmed his position.

Young's importance was recognized by Captain George Vancouver, who visited Hawaii in 1793. Vancouver noted in his logs and journal how Young oversaw trade between his vessels, the *Discovery* and *Chatam*, and the islanders. Through Young, Kamehameha sought to 'be answerable for the safety and security of every thing we might have occasion to put on shore, without having any guard there for its protection' (Vancouver, 1145). Young also negotiated all the circumstances of gift-giving and trade between Kamehameha's islanders and Vancouver. In doing so he contributed to the improvement of relations in the wake of Captain James Cook's death on the island in 1779 and established the basis for a solid friendship between Vancouver and the Hawaiian king. Writing later of their first meeting Vancouver described how: 'Tamaah-maah (Kamehameha I) came on board in a very large canoe, accompanied by John Young, an English seaman, who appeared to be not only a great favourite, but to possess no small degree of influence with his great chief' (ibid., 807).

Furthermore, Vancouver's testimonial to the good character of Young and Davis greatly aided Hawaii in developing commerce with other foreign nations, while Kamehameha's tendency to ally himself principally with Great Britain owed something to Young's influence, as 'he had no comparable [relationship] with any American' (Vancouver, 152). Originally Kamehameha had desired weapons and firearms in trade, but slowly Young and Vancouver persuaded the king of the advantages of peace and the expansion of foreign commerce. Young proved invaluable, too, in negotiating not only with foreigners but also with local rival chiefs. Vancouver had noticed that jealous chiefs sought to harbour a few rogue adventurers, but 'their machinations to the prejudice of the existing government (of Kamehameha), however, will prove ineffectual' as they fell under the 'watchful attention' of the Englishmen. Upon his sailing for England, Vancouver offered Young and Davis passage home, but both declined. Vancouver wrote in his testimonial letter on their behalf

> that through the uniformity of their conduct and unremitting good advice to Tamaah Maah and the different chiefs, that they have been materially instrumental in causing the honest, civil, and attentive behaviour, lately experienced by all visiters [sic] from the inhabitants of this Island.   (ibid., 1597)

For his virtues and wise counsel, both military and commercial, Young's *alii* status was enhanced by further grants of land near Kawaihae, and in 1795 he married Namokuelua (1780–1804), with whom he had two children; upon her death, he married Kaoanaeha (d. 1850), with whom he had four children. His son John (Keoni Ana) later served Kamehameha III as prime minister and minister of the interior. His daughter Fannie was the natural mother, and his daughter Grace the *hanai* (adoptive) mother, of the future Queen Emma, wife of Kamehameha IV. The Young family attained the highest rank and position in Hawaiian society, siring nobility. From 1802 to 1812 Young was appointed as governor of Hawaii in the king's absence and attended the king on his deathbed in 1819, committing himself to carrying out his wishes and the smooth transition of power to Kamehameha II. Young supported the claims of Kaahumanu, Kamehameha I's widow, before the council of chiefs when she proclaimed that Kamehameha had wished her to be co-ruler or *kuhina-nui*. Following the destruction of the *heiaus* (religious temples) in 1819, Young supported the new Christian faith introduced by the missionaries who arrived a year later. He also worked to uphold the first law code proclaimed by the *kuhina-nui* which forbade murder, theft, and fighting, and the proclamation for universal public education in 1824. A

year on Young and the council of chiefs also supported the proclamation of trial by jury. In May 1825, with the royal entourage, Young received the bodies of Kamehameha II and Queen Kamamalu, who had died from measles while visiting England. In 1816, in order to fortify Honolulu on Oahu, Young had supervised the building of a fort on the abandoned grounds of a Russia trading post on what became Fort Street. The Russians had been expelled, and increasingly Hawaii relied upon balancing foreign interests especially between America, France, and Britain. Young, Kaahumanu, and the ruling chiefs negotiated the first trade agreement with the American Captain Thomas ap Catesby Jones. Through such connections Hawaii became self-sufficient in commerce and trade relations, and was able to maintain her independence.

Young died at Honolulu on 17 December 1835 after forty-five years in Hawaii as a revered statesman of the court and adviser to Hawaii's kings. He had been nicknamed Olohana (Hawaiian for 'all hands'), which indicated his numerous accomplishments and contributions to Hawaii's monarchs. On his death he owned thirty pieces of property throughout the islands. He was buried with royalty in the grounds of Iolani Palace, later being reburied at the royal mausoleum in 1866.

BARBARA BENNETT PETERSON

Sources G. Vancouver, *A voyage of discovery to the north Pacific Ocean and round the world, 1791–1795*, ed. W. Kaye Lamb, 4 vols., Hakluyt Society (1984) · R. Hackler, 'Young, John', *ANB* · G. R. Carter, 'A new document of John Young', *Annual Report* [Hawaiian Historical Society] (1924), 51–3 · J. F. G. Stokes, 'Nationality of John Young', *Annual Report* [Hawaiian Historical Society] (1938) · B. B. Peterson, ed., *Notable women of Hawaii* (1984) · E. Bell, 'Journal', 1 Jan 1791–26 Feb 1794, NL NZ, Turnbull L. · T. Manby, 'Journal and log', 18 Feb 1791–22 June 1793, Yale U., William Coe collection · A. Menzies, 'Journal', 21 Feb 1794–18 March 1795, NL Aus., MS 155 · G. Daws, *Shoal of time: a history of the Hawaiian Islands* (1968) · E. Cahill, *The life and times of John Young* (1999) · State Archives of Hawaii, Honolulu, Hawaii
Likenesses portrait, State Archives of Hawaii, Honolulu
Wealth at death thirty pieces of valuable property throughout Hawaii: will, State Archives of Hawaii, Honolulu; Daws, *Shoal of time*, 46

Young, John (1746/7–1820), university teacher, was born in Glasgow, the second son of John Young, a cooper in the city. He matriculated from Glasgow University in 1764 and proceeded MA in 1769. He was installed professor of Greek at the university on 9 June 1774 and was noted as a popular teacher with a good sense of humour, and one who deeply enjoyed the Greek language and oratory. He published sparingly but was passionately interested in classical theatre, and greatly admired the acting of Edmund Kean. He was nicknamed Cocky Bung by the students on account of his father's occupation. He married, on 25 September 1780, Jean, daughter of Colin Lamont of Knockdow, in Argyll; they had seven children. His eldest son, John (1781–1852), was for a time chaplain to the East India Company and died rector of Newdigate, Surrey; his fourth son, Charles (1796–1822), was a promising classical scholar who died in Glasgow on 17 December 1822.

As a professor Young attempted to extend the rights of professors while at the same time guarding his own.

About the time of his election he argued with another professor over the house that could have come with his post, but in 1781 he gained accommodation when he was made curator of the college chambers. He objected to moves that would have spared students taking the obligatory examination in Greek before studying logic, as this would have diminished his own income, but he was one of the group of professors who sought to apply to parliament to allow them the right of electing the rector. On the whole he was fairly resistant to change, and maintained his chair even in old age, when he became feebler. He died, aged seventy-three, on 18 November 1820 at The George inn, Glasgow, while taking a bath. He was buried in Glasgow Cathedral.   T. W. BAYNE, *rev.* CAMPBELL F. LLOYD

Sources J. Coutts, *A history of the University of Glasgow* (1909) • J. D. Mackie, *The University of Glasgow, 1451–1951: a short history* (1954) • W. I. Addison, ed., *The matriculation albums of the University of Glasgow from 1728 to 1858* (1913) • W. I. Addison, *A roll of graduates of the University of Glasgow from 31st December 1727 to 31st December 1897* (1898) • *GM*, 1st ser., 93/1 (1823) • *GM*, 2nd ser., 37 (1852), 105
Archives BL, letters to Samuel Rose, Add. MS 31897 • NL Scot., letters to Charles Burney

Young, John (1755–1825), mezzotint-engraver, studied under Valentine Green, with whom he remained familiar until the latter's death in 1813. He continued to work with several of the painters who collaborated with Green, notably Benjamin West, John Hoppner, and Johann Gerhard Huck. On 16 July 1784 he married Elizabeth Gibbs, of South Mimms, Hertfordshire. He began to publish his own prints in 1785 and was trading with Pierre-François Basan in France before 1788. At this time he lived adjacent to Green at 28 Newman Street, a street that was then home to several leading artists. He moved to Store Street in 1789 and later to Charlotte Street, but remained in this area of Westminster throughout his life. Young executed some eighty portraits after various contemporaries, including several notable portraits of boxers, but was better known for his subject pieces, chiefly after West, Johann Zoffany, and especially Richard Morton Paye and Hoppner, with whom he collaborated frequently. In 1789 he was appointed mezzotint engraver to the prince of Wales, to whom Hoppner was portrait painter.

In 1813 Young succeeded Green as keeper of the British Institution, an arduous post which he filled until his death with unfailing tact and efficiency, for, as his obituarist recorded, 'he was a friend of artists, and a conciliator where many sore feelings, jealousies and angry passions are constantly generated' (*GM*, 95/1, 1825, 466). He was honorary secretary of the Artists' Benevolent Fund from 1810 to 1813, when he transferred his services to the rival body, the Artists' General Benevolent Institution. In later life he published *Portraits of the Emperors of Turkey from the Foundation of the Monarchy to the Year 1808* (1815), thirty plates printed in colours, with the lives of the emperors in English and French text. He then worked on a series of catalogues, illustrated by his own etchings, of some leading collections of paintings in Britain—the Grosvenor, Leicester, Miles, Angerstein, and Stafford galleries. He was working on a catalogue of the king's collection at Carlton Palace at the time of his death, after a long illness, at his house at 65 Upper Charlotte Street on 7 March 1825. A sale of his prints and books was held on 25 May.

TIMOTHY CLAYTON and ANITA MCCONNELL

Sources Redgrave, *Artists* • J. C. Smith, *British mezzotinto portraits*, 4 vols. in 5 (1878–84) • *GM*, 1st ser., 95/1 (1825), 466 • J. Pye, *Patronage of British art: an historical sketch* (1845); repr. (1970) • will, PRO, PROB 11/1701, sig. 353 • Farington, *Diary*, 7.2502
Archives Ches. & Chester ALSS, letters and receipts to Sir John Leicester

Young, John (1773–1837). *See under* Young, Sir William (1799–1887).

Young, John, Baron Lisgar (1807–1876), politician and colonial administrator, born at Bombay on 31 August 1807, was the eldest son of Sir William Young, first baronet (*d.* 10 March 1848) and his wife, Lucy (*d.* 8 Aug 1856), youngest daughter of Lieutenant-Colonel Charles Frederick. His father was a director and large shareholder of the East India Company. Young was educated at Eton College, and matriculated from Corpus Christi College, Oxford, on 13 June 1825, graduating BA in 1829. On 26 January 1829 he was admitted to Lincoln's Inn, and in 1834 he was called to the bar, but he never practised. On 5 April 1835 he married Adelaide Annabella, daughter of Edward Tuite Dalton and his wife, Olivia (later Lady Headfort).

On 19 May 1831 Young was elected as a tory for the county of Cavan, and held the seat until 1855. He was throughout associated with Peel. When Peel took office in 1841 Young was appointed a lord of the Treasury on 16 September, and on 21 May 1844 he became one of the secretaries of the Treasury. On the overthrow of Peel's ministry he resigned office on 7 July 1846. Between 1846 and 1852 he was one of those who favoured integration of the Peelites into a coherent group, and he sometimes represented Peel's views to his followers. He was more inclined to Liberalism than some Peelites.

Under Lord Aberdeen he became chief secretary for Ireland on 28 December 1852, and was nominated a privy councillor. On 20 March 1855 he resigned the Irish secretaryship on being appointed lord high commissioner of the Ionian Islands, and on 25 March was made a GCMG. He commenced his duties on 13 April 1855, and found himself immediately at variance with the representative assembly, which his predecessor, Sir Henry George Ward, had also found difficult to conciliate. Young was not in sympathy with the desire of the majority of the inhabitants for union with Greece; and in a dispatch to the colonial secretary, Henry Labouchere (afterwards Baron Taunton), dated 10 June 1857, he recommended that Corfu and Paxo should be converted into British colonies, with the consent of their inhabitants. The dispatch was stolen from the Colonial Office and published in the *Daily News* on 12 November 1858. This misfortune rendered Young's position impossible, and in the same year Gladstone, who had been sent out as high commissioner extraordinary, recommended Young's recall. He gave strong testimony,

John Young, Baron Lisgar (1807–1876), by unknown engraver

annexed to the dominion until 1873. He reached Canada towards the end of November, and found the rebellion of Louis Riel in progress. It was not suppressed until September 1870, when Riel fled into the United States. Young played an important role in the transfer to Canada of the Hudson's Bay territory of Rupert's Land and in Manitoba's joining the confederation. He acted, to the mutual irritation of both sides, as broker between the British and Canadian governments about terms for Canada's agreement to the treaty of Washington. His agreement to a Canadian bill for differential duties against American tea and coffee was given without consultation with London and raised the general question of colonial tariffs in British free-trade policy.

On 26 October 1870 Young was created Baron Lisgar of Lisgar and Baillieborough, co. Cavan. In poor health, he resigned in June 1872, before the end of his term, and he returned to Ireland, leaving behind him in Canada a reputation for ability and sound judgement but in the Gladstone cabinet considerable irritation. He died, childless, at Lisgar House, Baillieborough, on 6 October 1876. His widow later married Sir Francis Charles Fortescue Turville of Bosworth Hall, Leicestershire; she died in 1895. Lisgar had many opportunities and was generously handled by his colleagues. But his career was the least successful of the leading Peelites.

E. I. CARLYLE, *rev.* H. C. G. MATTHEW

Sources GEC, *Peerage* · Boase, *Mod. Eng. biog.* · Gladstone, *Diaries* · J. D. Gardner, *The Ionian islands in relation to Greece* (1859) · B. Knox, 'British policy and the Ionian Islands, 1847–1864: nationalism and imperial administration', *EngHR*, 99 (1984), 503–29 · J. B. Conacher, *The Peelites and the party system* (1972) · *DCB*, vol. 10
Archives NA Canada, letters and papers relating to Canada · NRA, priv. coll., letter-book · U. Nott. L., corresp. and papers | BL, corresp. with W. E. Gladstone, Add. MS 44237 · BL, letters to Henry Labouchere, Add. MS 62940 · BL, corresp. with Sir Robert Peel, Add. MSS 40550–40603 · Bodl. Oxf., corresp. with Lord Kimberley · W. Yorks. AS, Leeds, corresp. with Lord Canning
Likenesses D. Holmes, watercolour and gouache drawing, 1850, Royal Ontario Museum, Toronto · G. Hayter, group portrait, oils (*The House of Commons, 1833*), NPG · engraving (after unknown artist), repro. in *Eclectic Magazine of Foreign Literature* (1872) · engraving, NPG [*see illus.*]
Wealth at death under £14,000 effects in England: probate, 5 Feb 1877; Irish probate resealed in England, 15 Feb 1877, *CGPLA Eng. & Wales*

however, to the mild and conciliatory nature of Young's administration, and recommended that he should be employed elsewhere. Young left Corfu on 25 January 1859, and on 4 February was nominated KCB.

On 22 March 1861 Young was appointed governor-general and commander-in-chief of New South Wales, in succession to Sir William Thomas Denison. Immediately after his arrival he was persuaded by the premier, Charles Cowper, to endeavour, by nominating fifteen new members, to compel the upper house of New South Wales to pass a measure regulating the allotment of crown lands. Denison, before his departure, had refused to accede to this expedient. Young was reprimanded by the duke of Newcastle, the colonial secretary, but allowed to complete his term. Soon after the end of his term of office, on 24 December 1867, he returned to England, and was created GCB on 13 November 1868.

Young determined on his return to enter active political life. Inclining to Liberalism, he consulted Gladstone as to a constituency, but found himself in disagreement with the Liberal leader on the question of the ballot. In 1868 the Conservative ministry offered him the governorship of Canada, which several men of their party, including Lord Mayo, had declined, because the Canadian parliament had impaired the dignity of the office by reducing the governor's salary. Young accepted the post, and on 2 January 1869 he was appointed governor-general of Canada and governor of Prince Edward's Island, which was not

Young, John (1811–1878), entrepreneur and politician in Canada, was born at Ayr, Scotland, on 11 March 1811, the son of William Young, a cooper, and Janet Gibson. He finished his education at Ayr Academy in 1824, then taught briefly in the parish school at Colyton, near Ayr, before emigrating to Canada. Having arrived in Upper Canada in 1826 he worked for a merchant in Kingston, and in the early 1830s moved to Montreal to work for a wholesale merchant on the St Lawrence. Initially a clerk, he rose to be partner of the business (1835–40), after which he set up in partnership with Harrison Stephens as a merchant, trading especially with the mid-western United States. In 1846 the partnership broke up, and Young formed a new trading partnership with Benjamin Holmes. He was an enthusiastic advocate of waterways, particularly the construction of the Caughnawaga Canal to link the St Lawrence and Lake Champlain, which he championed ceaselessly but unsuccessfully for thirty years. He was also closely involved with projects to give ice-bound Montreal year-round rail access to the Atlantic via Portland, Maine, and to the Pacific via the American network. Young's economic interests expanded to include milling and telegraph companies.

Young's enthusiastic belief in free trade, expressed in numerous articles in the *Canadian Economist*, led to his involvement in politics as a Liberal. During the late 1840s he actively supported the Lower Canada Reformers led by Louis-Hyppolyte LaFontaine. Indeed Young was one of only a handful of leading Montreal merchants who did not sign the 1849 annexation manifesto. Rather reluctantly he joined the government as commissioner for public works on 28 October 1851. Because of his commercial experience and ability, his appointment was welcomed even by those who disagreed with his politics. He was elected to the assembly in December 1851 and kept his seat for two parliaments. In office he helped improve communications on the St Lawrence, but resigned from the executive council in 1852 when tariffs and tolls were used to penalize American goods after efforts to agree a reciprocity treaty had failed. In the election of 1854 he opposed his former colleagues and stood for the *rouge* party. He was elected to represent Montreal, but did not stand in 1857, for reasons which are unclear, and was defeated in 1863. After confederation in 1867 he became an outspoken advocate of a customs union with the United States, and he joined the *parti national*, which was associated with the Liberal Party in Quebec. In 1872 he was elected to represent Montreal, but the following year he chose not to stand.

Young was particularly influential on the Montreal harbour commission, of which he was a member from 1850 and chairman from 1853. Under him the commission expanded its scope and very substantially improved its facilities and its training of personnel. Young made personal financial gains as the harbour's fortune rose dramatically. His business interests centred chiefly on grain transport and milling, associated with which he owned substantial tracts of land, buildings, and transport facilities. He retired from active business in 1860 to devote more time to his family and to curling. In 1861 he, his wife, and their thirteen children moved to Scotland for two years to give the children a Scottish upbringing. They survived shipwreck on the return journey.

After his return Young continued active on the harbour commission and the Montreal and later the dominion board of trade: but as a result of debts incurred through speculations he lost his money and the family home was sold. His appeals for a government pension were refused, although he was given a number of patronage places. He died on 12 April 1878 of heart trouble exacerbated by sunstroke and was buried at the expense of the merchants of Montreal. He was one of the foremost Montreal businessmen of his day and left his mark in a number of lasting improvements to the city's transport links.

T. B. BROWNING, rev. ELIZABETH BAIGENT

Sources DCB, vol. 6 · F. Taylor, *Portraits of British Americans*, 3 vols. (1865) · J. C. Dent, *The Canadian portrait gallery*, 4 vols. (1881) · W. Kingsford, *The Canadian canals* (1865)
Wealth at death 'poor': DCB

Young, John Radford (1799–1885), mathematician, was born in London in April 1799. Little is known of his background. According to *Men of the time* his parents were of 'humble' status, and he was 'almost entirely self-educated'. At an early age he became acquainted with Olinthus Gilbert Gregory, who perceived his mathematical ability and assisted him in his studies. In 1823, while holding a post at a private establishment for deaf people in Walworth Road, Young published *An Elementary Treatise on Algebra*, with a dedication to Gregory. Young's prolific output of elementary books contributed to the movement, led by Robert Woodhouse, to disseminate continental methods of mathematical analysis in Britain. Young's works covered subjects which included geometry, trigonometry, calculus, mechanics, equations, mensuration, logarithms, and navigation and nautical astronomy. His *Elements of Plane and Spherical Trigonometry* (1833) contained an appendix by Thomas Stephens Davies. His *Rudimentary Treatise on Arithmetic* (1858) reached ten editions.

In 1833 Young was appointed professor of mathematics at Belfast College. In 1849, on the opening of Queen's College, the presbyterian party which controlled the professorial nominations prevented his reappointment as professor in the new establishment. From that time he devoted himself more completely to the study of mathematical analysis, and made several original discoveries. In 1844 he had discovered and published a proof of Newton's rule for determining the number of imaginary roots in an equation. In 1866 he completed his proof, publishing in the *Philosophical Magazine* a demonstration of a principle which in his earlier paper he had assumed as axiomatic. His contributions to the *Proceedings of the Royal Irish Academy* included a memoir in 1868 'On the imaginary roots of numerical equations'. In the 1860s, he wrote several theological tracts, such as *Science Elucidative of Scripture and not Antagonistic to it* (1863).

Young was married and had at least one child. He died at Peckham on 5 March 1885.

E. I. CARLYLE, rev. ALAN YOSHIOKA

Sources *Men of the time* (1884) · *The Times* (23 March 1885)

Young, John Zachary (1907–1997), zoologist, known universally as J. Z., was born at Fishponds, Bristol, on 18 March 1907, the first of three sons and two daughters of Philip Young (1878–1965), engineer, and his wife, Constance Maria, née Lloyd (1875–1955), schoolteacher. A great-great-grandfather, Richard, was brother to Thomas Young (1773–1829), physician, physicist, and hieroglyphist. Other distinguished scientific relations, from his mother's side, were Luke Howard (1772–1864), meteorologist, great-

John Zachary Young (1907–1997), by Walter Stoneman, 1950

great-grandfather to Sir Alan Hodgkin (1914–1998), neuroscientist, and father of John Eliot Howard (1807–1883), quinologist. Although on both sides many of his family were Quakers, Young's parents brought him up in an Anglo-Catholic tradition. Bishop Charles Gore was his godfather. He left religious belief during the Oxford Moral Re-Armament movement of the 1930s, but retained a lifelong interest in philosophy and ethics. Much of this thinking was expressed in the Reith lectures for 1950 and in the last of his nine books, *Philosophy and the Brain* (1987).

His mother taught Young until he was nine years old, then he was sent to board at Wells House, Malvern Wells, Worcestershire. At thirteen he entered Marlborough College. In 1925 he became a demy at Magdalen College, Oxford, whence he graduated in 1928 with first-class honours in zoology. Successive college and university appointments followed, and in 1943 he was elected vice-president of Magdalen. In 1945, having failed to succeed Edwin Stephen Goodrich in the Oxford zoology chair, he accepted that of human anatomy at University College, London. There he stayed until his retirement in 1974. For the next twenty-three years he was based at the Wellcome Foundation and, later, in the psychology department, Oxford. During this time he continued to research and lecture, and published two books on neural mechanisms.

Between 1929 and 1945 Young came to be regarded as the outstanding tutor and zoologist in Oxford. All his teaching and research had flair and enthusiasm. A dominating and charismatic personality he could sometimes be

overbearing, arrogant, and unwilling to listen to criticism. In fact he was too interested in science for this behaviour to last long and usually he responded well to valid arguments, even from juniors. His dynamism and enthusiasm inspired many to careers in biology and medicine. As Professor David Barker, a former pupil, wrote: 'It was his intense interest in all living things, his almost childlike wonder and curiosity about them, that made Young such an inspiring teacher. That, and his contempt for established dogma, his insistence on establishing everything afresh'. In tutorials 'his sharp intellect could be ruthless, his exposure of flaws and errors merciless but mixed in with the criticism there would usually be some praise and always encouragement and inspiration to move on to the next topic and improve' (Boycott, 490).

Young was without medical qualifications, and he never became a DPhil. Thus his appointment to head a department in a medical school (at University College, London) was vociferously opposed by a conservative establishment largely composed of medical anatomists and surgeons. He overcame their opposition by ignoring it, meanwhile getting his staff to use a more functional approach when teaching human anatomy and insisting they undertook significant research. He founded an intercalated BSc anatomy course, lasting 12–18 months, for those medical students who had become interested in basic biological science. These reforms triggered similar course changes in other medical schools. The department soon became a place of choice for postdoctoral workers, particularly from the USA. Opposition to his appointment evaporated.

In Oxford, Young had begun to write a textbook that expanded to become two. These were finished during his first decade at University College, London. *The Life of Vertebrates* (1950) and *The Life of Mammals* (1957) were a national and international success. Their style was enjoyable to read, an innovation for zoology texts of the time. Another innovation was Young's treatment of comparative anatomy. Until these books were published animal structures were described as assemblages of facts to provide evidence for evolution. Young was brought up in this tradition, which he thought intellectually rigorous but dull and limited. He now took those facts, organized them from a functional, as well as a comparative anatomical, viewpoint, then presented them as a study of the responses of organisms to the functional and behavioural requirements of the environment. This was refreshing and the books led several generations of students and their teachers to a clearer understanding of animal structure and its evolution, as well as many other biological problems.

Young was an effective teacher and administrator; he was also a deeply committed research worker. In his autobiographical notes he explained that he was never certain why he decided to specialize in nervous system research. However, some of the early influences on his thinking about nervous systems and on his choice of cephalopods for his main research studies are clear. He always acknowledged the special influence of Derek Denny-Brown (later professor of neurology at Harvard), who introduced him to the histological techniques he was to use throughout his career. Denny-Brown and several other friends, including John Carew Eccles, were members of Sir Charles Scott Sherrington's group in the Oxford physiology department. Sherrington always emphasized the need to search for the anatomical basis of the physiology of, and hence the behaviour generated by, central nervous systems. He sought to resolve difficulties of observation and interpretation by working on 'simpler' systems, such as the mammalian spinal cord. Modifications and amplifications of this approach became the basis for much of Young's thinking on neural mechanisms. Thus early in his career (1938) he proposed a theory of reverberating neural circuits (based on the anatomy of the vertical and superior frontal lobes of cephalopod brains) to account for the persistence in time of memories of events. This theory derived, in part, from the then current explanations of the mechanisms involved in the persistence of rhythmic scratching generated within the mammalian spinal cord after the initiating stimulus has stopped.

A second, more practical, influence on Young's development as a research worker was Enrico Sereni. In 1929 Young became the Oxford scholar at the 'Anton Dohrn' zoological station in Naples. Sereni (an anti-fascist who was later found dead in mysterious circumstances) was the resident physiologist. He introduced Young to cephalopods as experimental animals. Together they worked on the time course and nature of degeneration and regeneration when the peripheral nerves of octopods were severed. During these experiments Young noticed an epistellar body on the stellate ganglion of the lesser octopus (*Eledone*). Out of curiosity he made a comparative anatomical study of this structure and looked for it in decapods (squids and cuttlefishes). The work unexpectedly came to be of immense general importance because it led to the discovery of the giant nerve fibre systems of decapods. These systems are made up of large diameter nerve fibres, which are, therefore, fast conducting. They control the musculature involved in a squid's fast escape responses. A single nerve fibre in the common squid can be more than 0.5 mm in diameter. This size caused great excitement among physiologists who had been trying to isolate and record from much smaller single nerve fibres. Indeed the fibres are so large that, within a few years, it even proved possible regularly to insert an electrode inside one. This innovation meant that the potential difference between the inside and the outside of a nerve fibre at rest and during activity could be measured directly, then interpreted in terms of the movements of ions back and forth across the axonal membrane. The results became basic to later theories of nerve cell conduction and fundamental to understanding the ionic properties of membranes of cells in general. Sir Alan Hodgkin and Sir Andrew Huxley were awarded a Nobel prize in 1963 for this work. Hodgkin later remarked, 'it is arguable that the introduction of the squid giant nerve fibre by J. Z. Young in 1936 did more for axonology than any other single advance in technique during the last 40 years' (Boycott, 493).

The experience of studying degeneration and regeneration in octopus nerves became important during the Second World War. Young was asked by the Medical Research Council to organize a small group in Oxford to study peripheral nerve wounds and their repair. The group soon made some useful surgical improvements to aid regeneration, but a great deal of their work had to be basic. For example, there was little information on the rate of growth of nerve fibres and the details of the conditions affecting this. The dynamic relationships of the axoplasm, myelin, Schwann cells, the cell bodies of nerve cells, and the structures innervated, all had to be investigated and quantified. Looking back, the influence of Young's wartime group can be seen as a bridge between the descriptive past and current molecular biological approaches to problems of neural repair.

Young did not belong to what he called the reductionist school of biological sciences. Thus he did not follow his discovery of giant nerve fibres into the study of the biophysics of their membranes, nor did he long continue research on the mechanisms of the growth and development of nerve cells. He seems to have regarded investigating cellular mechanisms as scientifically too narrow. He saw this type of work as necessary but too limited in scope to help in study of the 'big problems', such as memory. The best science, he felt, should be the study of integrated functions of organs and systems. Thus as soon as possible after the war he initiated a programme to study memory mechanisms using octopus brains.

The practical parts of Young's octopus memory studies were carried out at the zoological station in Naples. Except for a return, when over eighty years old, to his earliest research on the autonomic nervous systems of fishes at the Marine Biology Station in Plymouth, cephalopod brain and behaviour studies were to occupy most of his personal research time from 1947 until his death. Initially the memory experiments were designed to be interpreted in terms of specified neural networks and their synapses. As time passed the emphasis shifted to a study of the interrelationship of the lobes of the octopus brain during visual and tactile learning paradigms. In short, the work became more of a cognitive study of the properties of the lobes. Perhaps this was a result of the influence of Young's reading of developments in cognitive psychology. Young had always followed this literature and expected his work on octopus brains to contribute simpler paradigms to aid the understanding of human brain mechanisms. This shift to a more cognitive study was consistent with his emphasis on the need to study organ systems as a whole. But, ironically, it seems to have made his work more limited, to understanding the brain and behaviour of cephalopods, than he had intended when he began.

Young did not produce any deep theory or unifying hypothesis of neural action. He made the important discovery of squid giant nerve fibres, and wrote major papers and a book on the structure of cephalopod brains. He emphasized the relation between structure and function through this work and his textbooks. He was a great enthusiast for, and enabler and inspirer of, the research of others. Over sixty of his former pupils and staff became professors and directors of departments around the world. One, Sir Peter Medawar, was a Nobel laureate for immunology in 1960, and at least nine were elected fellows of the Royal Society. There were many more former pupils in positions of influence and importance. A remarkable feature of Young's impact was that all those he most influenced developed their own independent lines of work. He encouraged imagination and initiative; he did not expect, or encourage, intellectual clones, as do so many dominating personalities.

Although a compulsive hard worker Young liked partying and was an accomplished ballroom dancer. He was greatly interested in art and some of his drive as a biologist was his aesthetic response to the 'sheer beauty of living things'. Both his wives were painters. He married Phyllis Heaney (b. 1905) on 17 December 1931; they had a son and a daughter. They separated in 1957; she died in March 1987. Young also had a daughter with his second partner, Raymonde May Parsons (b. 1916), whom he married on 29 August 1987.

Young was elected a fellow of the Royal Society in 1945 and was awarded its royal medal in 1967. He received eight honorary degrees and many other distinctions, including the gold medal of the Linnean Society in 1973 and honorary citizenship of Naples in 1991. He was made an honorary fellow of the British Academy in 1986. For twenty-one years he was president and vice-president of the Marine Biological Association of Great Britain. He died of heart failure at the John Radcliffe Hospital, Oxford, on 4 July 1997, and was buried at All Saints' Church, Brill, Buckinghamshire, six days later. He was survived by his second wife and his three children.   B. B. BOYCOTT

Sources B. B. Boycott, *Memoirs FRS*, 44 (1998), 487–509 • UCL, J. Z. Young MSS [incl. unpubd autobiography] • RS • L. R. Squire, ed., *The history of neuroscience in autobiography*, 1 (1996), 554–86 • WWW • *The Independent* (8 July 1997) • *The Times* (9 July 1997) • *Daily Telegraph* (11 July 1997) • *The Guardian* (14 July 1997) • personal knowledge (2004) • private information (2004) [Sir. R. Young, S. Young, D. Barker]
Archives UCL, scientific corresp. and papers | Rice University, Houston, Texas, Woodson Research Center, corresp. with Sir Julian Huxley | FILM Physiological Society of Great Britain, London, film of Young dissecting giant nerve fibres (also includes Alan Hodgkin and Andrew Huxley) | SOUND 1950 Reith lectures, BBC recordings (?)
Likenesses W. Stoneman, photograph, 1950, NPG [*see illus.*] • photograph, repro. in Boycott, *Memoirs FRS*, 486 • photograph, repro. in *The Independent* • photograph, repro. in *The Times* • photograph, repro. in *Daily Telegraph* • photograph, repro. in *The Guardian*
Wealth at death under £180,000: probate, 10 Oct 1997, *CGPLA Eng. & Wales*

Young, Kathleen, Lady Kennet. *See* Scott, (Edith Agnes) Kathleen, Lady Scott (1878–1947).

Young, Margaret Paulin (1864–1953), headmistress, was born on 4 December 1864 in Lilliesleaf, Roxburghshire, where her father, the Revd William Langlands Young (d. 1907), had been United Presbyterian minister since 1857.

Her mother was Margaret Brown Paulin. Her vivacious family circle included two sisters; J. M. Barrie was a cousin. In 1874 William Young was inducted as minister at Parkhead United Presbyterian Church and the family moved to Glasgow. In 1880 Margaret Young went to the Park School, Glasgow, enrolling on the second day of the new school. Remembered as a gay, lively schoolgirl, she was also one of the oldest pupils and soon became head girl. On finishing her schooling she went to London to attend the Training College for Teachers in Middle and Higher Schools for Girls (from 1885 the Maria Grey College), then the only institution in Britain providing such training.

In 1884 Margaret Young obtained her first teaching post, at the Oxford High School for Girls, where she taught classics for two years. In 1886 she returned to the Park School as an assistant mistress, teaching English, mathematics, and Latin. She was especially good at making dry subjects interesting, enlivening her lessons with amusing stories and racy comments. If she taught a double lesson she let the girls run round at half-time and even joined in playing 'prisoners' base'.

Miss Young was also obvious headmistress material and was groomed for such a post by the Park headmistress Miss Georgina Kinnear. In 1897 the Glasgow Girls' School Trust opened a third school at Kilmacolm (later St Columba's School) and Margaret Young was appointed the first headmistress at a salary of £200.

Three years later, having firmly established the new school at Kilmacolm, Miss Young was appointed headmistress at the Park School following the retirement of Miss Kinnear, a post she held until 1929. Her first task was to advise the school directors on modernizing the school facilities. During her headship pupil numbers continued to grow, specialized courses in science and art were established, and a domestic science department was added. Miss Young also actively supported the introduction of hockey at the Park School about 1901, attending all subsequent school matches, regardless of the weather. She approved the establishment of a school council, which resulted in the introduction of a school uniform, and she introduced the house system to the school. She encouraged the former pupils' club, the Park School Students' Association (PSSA), to undertake social projects and was herself active in the Glasgow section of the Girls' Guildry (a non-denominational organization linked to local churches), of which she was president for five years. During her last year as headmistress Miss Young initiated a London branch of the PSSA; after her retirement she remained an active member of the association and was for two years its president.

As one of the original pupils, assistant mistress for eleven years, and head for twenty-nine, Miss Young became so involved in the Park School that on her retirement she admitted finding it difficult to think of herself and the school as separate entities. The pupils presented her with a portrait by James Gunn as a leaving present and the board of directors established a fund of £500 to be used for an annual prize for the school dux.

Miss Young's lively, outgoing personality was always

combined with a sense of responsibility. As a young teacher she was tall and slim, with an encouraging smile, brown hair drawn rather severely back, and a 'delicious laugh', which bubbled up irrepressibly in the midst of the serious business of the hour. In later years she had a more motherly appeal and was remembered for her pungent wit, gracious courtesy, gaiety, and dignity. She was always beautifully dressed, with a habit of passing the long strings of beads she wore between her hands as she talked. Her leisure interests included needlework, motoring, and photography. Margaret Young died on 15 January 1953 at her home, 64 Hillhead Street, Hillhead, Glasgow, and was buried on 19 January at the Maryhill crematorium following a burial service at Claremont North, Church of Scotland.   LINDY MOORE

Sources J. Lightwood, *The Park School, 1880–1980* (1980) · *The Park School, Glasgow, 1880–1930* (1930) · *Glasgow Herald* (16 Jan 1953) · *Glasgow Herald* (20 Jan 1953) · *Scottish Educational Journal* (23 Jan 1953), 58 · *St Columba's School Magazine* (1952–3), 11–12 · b. cert.
Likenesses H. J. Gunn, oils, 1929; known to be at Park School, Glasgow, in 1995 · H. J. Gunn, oils, 1929, repro. in Lightwood, *The Park School*, facing p. 49 · group portrait, photograph, repro. in Lightwood, *The Park School*, facing p. 97
Wealth at death £14,440 9s. 4d.: confirmation, 18 March 1953, *CCI*

Young [*née* Ridgway; *other married name* Postans], **Marianne** (**1811–1897**), writer, was born in Pimlico, London, on 4 January 1811, the daughter of Richard Bowling Hunter Ridgway and his wife, Elizabeth. On 9 February 1833 she married Thomas Postans (1808–1846), an officer in the Bombay native infantry. The couple had no children.

Marianne Postans returned with her husband to India, and early in 1834 accompanied him to Cutch, a remote area in western India. There she gathered material on the region and its peoples, their customs, religion, manufactures, and literary and musical traditions, which she incorporated into *Cutch, or, Random Sketches* (1839). *Western India* (2 vols., 1839) covered a wider area: the Deccan, Surat, the Saurashtra peninsula, and Bombay, describing recent developments in the last. Her husband's transfer to Sind in 1839 provided information on an area little known to the British, which she used in *Facts and Fictions* (3 vols., 1844).

In the absence of a family, Marianne Postans's main focus of interest was travelling and investigating Indian life, enthusiasms which, in addition to drawing, she shared with her husband. But while Lieutenant Postans recorded his researches in reports to learned bodies and works of largely professional interest, his wife's aim was to popularize information about India. She sought to remedy the lack of interest in Britain about India by clothing in more alluring form the facts which she had obtained through firsthand experience, often in little-known areas; she was aided in her researches by her fluent Hindustani. Although she was scholarly in her interests, she wore her learning lightly, and her writing is marked by liveliness and the personal voice of the author.

Postans also turned to fiction to engage the attention of the reading public. The nature of Indian women's lives, which, because of their seclusion in the zenana, could

only be penetrated by other women, had always intrigued the West. Postans had unrivalled opportunities to meet Indian women, and incorporated her knowledge of them in a number of stories in *Facts and Fictions*, many of which depict strong-willed women asserting their power despite the limitations of their circumstances. Although she stressed her status as a woman in acquiring such information, she did not restrict her views to 'feminine' issues, entering into debates of general public concern. She believed that India was in urgent need of reform, and that it was Britain's moral duty (as well as being in her interest) to promote India's progress. Improved communications and commerce, up-to-date agricultural techniques, and, above all, education would help lead India forward. Postans also hoped that a changed intellectual climate would encourage Indians to accept Christianity, in which endeavour missionaries had largely failed. She nevertheless realized that such a 'Westernizing' policy might eventually challenge the British position in India. Her work was warmly received in Britain, where her 'active and lively habits of observation and research, and pleasing and racy style' were applauded (*Monthly Review*, 1, 1840, 80), and the *Asiatic Journal* complimented her on her success in popularizing Indian subjects.

Marianne Postans's life in India was cut short by the sudden death of her husband in 1846. She returned to England, where, on 8 July 1848, she married an army surgeon, William Henry Young (1787–1879); he was a widower, considerably older than herself, whom she had met while he was stationed in India. She accompanied him to the Crimea in 1854, publishing an account of her experiences, *Our Camp in Turkey and the Way to it*, in the same year; an account of the army camp at Aldershot and its environs followed in 1857. In her final work, *The Moslem Noble* (1857), she returned to her Indian experiences, calling among other things for greater sympathy between British and Indians. However, her call met a cold response in the aftermath of the Indian mutiny, and the work was poorly received. The Youngs retired to Wrington in Somerset some time before 1861. William Young's granddaughter Mary Anne lived with them for many years, and was treated by the childless Marianne as her own daughter. William Young died at Wrington on 12 August 1879; his widow survived until 1897. She died on 6 October 1897 at Wrington, and was buried there three days later.

ROSEMARY CARGILL RAZA

Sources Marianne Young's will, Probate Department of Principal Registry of Family Division, First Avenue House, London · census returns, 1861, 1871, 1881, 1891 · parish register (baptism), London, St George's, Hanover Square, 10 May 1811 · parish register (marriage), London, St George's, Hanover Square · m. cert. [to W. H. Young] · d. cert. · *CGPLA Eng. & Wales* (1879) [William Henry Young] · *CGPLA Eng. & Wales* (1897) · BL OIOC · PRO
Wealth at death £15,032 9s. 5d.: probate, 6 Nov 1897, *CGPLA Eng. & Wales*

Young, Sir Mark Aitchison (**1886–1974**), colonial governor, was born on 30 June 1886 in India, the third son of the six children of Sir William Mackworth *Young (1840–1924), lieutenant-governor of the Punjab from 1897 to

Sir Mark Aitchison Young (1886–1974), by Elliott & Fry

1902, and his wife, Frances Mary, daughter of Sir Robert Eyles Egerton and his wife, Mary Warren Hickey. He was educated at Eton College and then at King's College, Cambridge, where he graduated with a first-class degree in classics. Geoffrey Winthrop *Young (1876–1958) was his cousin and Sir Hubert Winthrop *Young (1885–1950) and Gerard Mackworth-*Young (1884–1965) were his elder brothers. Young joined the colonial service as an eastern cadet in Ceylon in 1909. His career was interrupted by service in the First World War, but he rose to the rank of principal assistant colonial secretary in 1923–8. He then served as colonial secretary in Sierra Leone in 1928–30 and Palestine in 1930–33, before being promoted governor of Barbados, where he served from 1933 to 1938. From November 1937 to February 1938 he also administered the government of Trinidad and Tobago and then served as governor of the Tanganyika Territory in 1938–41. He married Josephine Mary, daughter of Walter C. Price, and they had six children. Young was appointed CMG in 1931 and was knighted in 1934.

Sharp minded, intelligent, courageous, far-sighted, energetic, dedicated to doing his duties as well as possible, somewhat austere in character, and very able as an administrator, Young often appeared intimidating to people of lesser intellect. These personal qualities were put to test when he became governor of the Tanganyika Territory. With war looming in Europe there was considerable apprehension in the territory that it might be returned to its former German rulers as part of a deal for appeasement. To allay such concern Young quickly set about laying down plans for economic and other developments, and enlarged the legislative and the executive councils. Confidence returned. When war broke out he swiftly disarmed and interned the large German population, which removed a potential source of instability and maintained good order and morale. It was the strong leadership, resilience, and resourcefulness which he showed in Tanganyika that commended him to the British government to take charge of Hong Kong on the eve of the Pacific war.

When Young assumed the governorship on 10 September 1941 a Japanese attack on Hong Kong was a real possibility, and Britain was in no position to relieve the colony. Prime Minister Winston Churchill knew Hong Kong could not be defended and instructed Young to hold it for as long as possible in order to give the British empire time to prepare for the eventual counter-attack. With about 10,000 men at his disposal, including two newly arrived Canadian battalions which were not combat ready, Young took Churchill's instruction to heart and put up the most gallant defence in Britain's Asian empire. Repeatedly he refused the demand of the overwhelmingly superior Japanese forces to capitulate. When he did eventually become the first British governor to surrender a colony during the war, on Christmas day 1941, he was told by the senior military commander Major-General Christopher Malby that useful military resistance was no longer possible. He surrendered in order to reduce further heavy loss of life and to avoid provoking the Japanese to brutalize the civilian population. Nevertheless, following Churchill's order to resist with utmost stubbornness 'in spirit and to the letter', the Hong Kong garrison under Young earned, in Churchill's words, the 'lasting honour' (Churchill, 3.563). He was a prisoner of the Japanese, in Taiwan and Manchuria until August 1945.

Young's other major contribution was in energetically pursuing an albeit limited programme of democratic reform in post-war Hong Kong. At the end of the war, Young took about eight months to restore his health from the deprivations and sufferings as a Japanese prisoner of war. Advanced to GCMG, he was sent back to resume his interrupted governorship on 1 May 1946 so as to restore his, and above all, Britain's military honour. However, because of a recognition that a return to the *status quo ante* would be seized upon by the Chinese government to clamour for the retrocession of Hong Kong, London felt it necessary to limit his remaining tenure to one year. Upon his return, Young carefully tested public opinion and vigorously pushed for the introduction of what in effect was a 'super municipal council', with 'a degree of administrative and financial autonomy unknown in other British municipal councils' (Tsang, *Democracy Shelved*, 183–4) of the time so that it could, if the political environment should permit, gradually replace the existing colonial government and give the local Chinese greater self-government. Young advocated such an unorthodox approach because he believed the only way to keep the colony British in the face of Chinese irredentism was to persuade the local people to embrace the idea of keeping Hong Kong within the British empire-Commonwealth.

In order to achieve these objectives Young saw no better way than to involve the local people in the administration of their own affairs. He also recognized the reality that the Chinese people of Hong Kong in those days were divided in their loyalty, above all between the two warring factions in the Chinese Civil War, the ruling Kuomintang and the Chinese Communist Party, and normal democratization at the colonial legislature might lead to it being turned into a political cockpit of the two Chinese parties. Hence, his proposals for a 'super municipal council' by which the electoral elements could be introduced and gradually expanded and, if the elected members should prove politically responsible, its scope of government expanded without allowing Chinese politics to dominate its proceedings. Young advocated democratization in Hong Kong partly in response to the general British recognition that a new approach had become desirable, but mainly to pre-empt irrendentist pressure from China. Although his reform proposals were approved by London they did not survive his retirement on 17 May 1947. His successor, Sir Alexander *Grantham, deemed him misguided and reversed course, leading to the eventual abandonment of any major political reform in 1952, a position that was maintained until the onset of Sino-British negotiations over the future of Hong Kong in the early 1980s.

After he left Hong Kong, Young retired to Winchester where he devoted much time to his great love, music. In particular he enjoyed the piano and choral singing; but he also renewed his interest in the classics, and read widely. He died on 12 May 1974 at Bereweeke Nursing Home, Winchester.   STEVE TSANG

Sources S. Y. S. Tsang, *Democracy shelved: Great Britain, China, and attempts at constitutional reform in Hong Kong, 1945–1952* (1988) · O. Lindsay, *The lasting honour: the fall of Hong Kong, 1941* (1978) · battle of Hong Kong, 1942, PRO, CO129/590/25 · arrival of governor in Hong Kong, resumption of duty, 1946, PRO, CO129/595/4 · proposed new constitution, 1946, PRO, CO537/1651 · policy: proposed new constitution, 1947, PRO, CO537/2188 · W. S. Churchill, *The Second World War, 3* (1950), vol. 3 · G. B. Endacott, *Hong Kong eclipse* (1978) · T. Carew, *Fall of Hong Kong* (1960) · S. Tsang, *Hong Kong: appointment with China* (1997) · G. B. Endacott, *Government and people in Hong Kong* (1964) · *Annual Report of the Council* [King's College, Cambridge] (1974) · CGPLA Eng. & Wales (1974) · d. cert. · WWW
Archives NRA, papers | PRO, corresp. relating to Hong Kong, CO967/69–70
Likenesses Elliott & Fry, photograph, NPG [*see illus.*]
Wealth at death £48,047: probate, 8 July 1974, CGPLA Eng. & Wales

Young, Mary (c.1704–1741), pickpocket, was probably born in the north of Ireland, although she claimed to be an 'English woman' (*The Ordinary of Newgate*, 1.7). Nothing is known of her parents nor whether she had any siblings. She was also known as Mrs Murphy or Murphew, as Jane Webb, and as Diving Jenny or Jenny Diver, popular sobriquets for female pickpockets and the name of a character in John Gay's *The Beggar's Opera* (1728). She was said to have been educated in Ireland, although where and for how long are unknown. It is not known if she ever married. She does appear to have had a child, who was about three years old at her death, but the child's name, father, gender, and fate are all unknown.

Young probably left Ireland when she was fifteen, going first to Liverpool and then to London. There she lived in Long Acre with a woman, possibly Ann Murphew, who inducted her into the art of picking pockets. She became 'one of the most artfullest Pick-pockets in the World' (*The Ordinary of Newgate*, 1.7) and the leader of a gang which operated in crowded places, such as theatres and churches, using techniques that were by turns imaginative and violent. To draw a crowd and divert people's attention from their pockets, Young would place a pillow under her dress to give the appearance of being pregnant, she would then faint, and, as people rushed to her aid, the gang moved in. On other occasions this fake lump was used to conceal her hands while false arms dangled in the sleeves of her dress, and she was by this means able to steal from people in church without them suspecting her. The gang operated mainly in London because of its relative anonymity, large crowds, and rich pickings, but gang members also travelled to the large fairs held across the south of England. At least some of the goods stolen were probably sold to Roger Johnson, a pawnbroker who operated a trade in stolen goods to the Netherlands and whose boat had been fitted out for this purpose by Jonathan Wild. Young supposedly organized the gang around a rigid code, which included the establishment of a general fund to provide for any member who was arrested and the requirement that gang members give evidence as to the good character of any of their number who was prosecuted. At Young's first trial at the Old Bailey in April 1738, six people performed this function, and one of the prosecution witnesses, Mr Addy, claimed to have been offered £50 not to testify.

On that occasion Young was convicted in the name of Jane Webb of robbing Mary Rowley in Cannon Alley, Paternoster Row, London, and was sentenced to transportation. Eschewing their more imaginative methods, two gang members had held Rowley while Young stole from her. Although this seems to have been her first appearance in court, Addy claimed she was an infamous pickpocket and 'so well known, that I could have brought a Dozen People to have proved this' (*Old Bailey Sessions Paper*, April 1738). While in prison waiting for the sentence to be carried out, she allegedly dealt in stolen goods, earning enough money to ensure that she was able both to buy a more comfortable berth on the convict ship, the *Forward*, which sailed to Virginia in June 1738, and to return to England fairly quickly. Although returning before a term of transportation had expired was a capital offence, she went back to London (possibly, Little Britain), presumably because her friends were there and her income depended on renewing their acquaintance. In January 1741 Young and Elizabeth Davis (also known as Catherine Huggins) were condemned to death at the Old Bailey for robbing Judith Gardener, although Davis had her sentence reduced to transportation, probably because she was a first offender. Young claimed at her trial that she was pregnant, which, if proved, would have delayed the execution and might have led to her being transported. However, a 'jury of matrons' found that she was 'Not Quick with Child' (*Daily Post*).

On the day of her execution there seems to have been some concern that Young's gang might attempt to rescue her during the several hours that the procession took to wind its way from Newgate prison to Tyburn, and additional soldiers were stationed along the route. Young appeared at her execution 'gaily dressed … yet deeply affected with her approaching Fate' (*GM*, 161). Her relative wealth was evidenced by her clothing and by her travelling to Tyburn not in a cart, as was normal, but in a mourning coach, accompanied by Thomas Broughton, a Methodist minister who often attended such events to give succour to the condemned. She was hanged on 18 March 1741 and was buried in St Pancras Old Church cemetery, an indication that she may have been a Roman Catholic. The allegations about the gang's organization, its ability to avoid detection, and willingness to corrupt witnesses confirmed contemporary fears about the nature of crime and the inefficiency of the criminal justice system, while the ineffectuality of the sentence of transportation in Young's case and the rarity of a woman as a gang leader ensured her fame.

PHILIP RAWLINGS

Sources J. Guthrie, *The ordinary of Newgate: his account of … the malefactors, who were executed at Tyburn, on Wednesday the 18th of March, 1740* (1740/41) · Gordon, chaplain of Newgate, *The life … of … Jenny Diver: the most noted pickpocket of her time* (1745?) · P. Rawlings, *Drunks, whores and idle apprentices: criminal biographies of the eighteenth century* (1992) · *The proceedings at the sessions of the peace* (1737–8) [Old Bailey sessions papers, 12–15 April 1738]; (1740–41) [16–20 Jan 1741] · *Daily Post* [London] (21 Jan 1741) · *London Daily Post and General Advertiser* (21 Jan 1741) · *London Evening-Post* (10–12 March 1741) · *GM*, 1st ser., 11 (1741), 161–2

Young, Mary (1749–1799). *See under* Young family (*per. c.*1700–1799).

Young, Mary Helen (1883–1945), nurse and resistance worker, was born on 5 June 1883 at 24 View Terrace, Aberdeen, the youngest of the three children of Alexander Young (1855–1913), a grocer's clerk, and his wife, Elizabeth Ann Burnett (1854–1884). Her mother died while Mary was still a baby, and the family later moved to Edinburgh, where Alexander Young worked as a brewery clerk.

On leaving school Mary became a dressmaker in Jenners, the well-known Edinburgh department store, but left after several years to study nursing. Despite her sister Annie's belief that she could never be a nurse because she was too small—just 4 feet 11 inches—she secured a place at the recently opened nurse-training school at Kingston County Hospital, in Surrey. She qualified in 1908, and in September 1909 travelled to France, where she began practice as a private nurse.

When war was declared in 1914 Mary Young was one of the first nurses in Paris to volunteer for service with the allied forces. She worked in the British army zone in France, nursing wounded on the western front, at one time being based near Courtrai. Her fiancé was killed in the First World War, and she remained unmarried for the rest of her life. After the war she resumed private nursing in Paris but made regular visits to Scotland, staying for part of each visit with her aunt Mrs Farquharson, who owned the Temperance Hotel at Ballater. Most of Mary Young's savings were held in British banks or invested in British stocks and shares, and during her time in France she also sent money to her sister Annie Sutherland, to help her to keep up the house at 179 Rosemount Place, Aberdeen, as she intended to retire there.

On her last visit to Scotland, in 1937, Mary Young again spoke of returning to Aberdeen to make a home with her sister, but when the Second World War began she remained in Paris, choosing to continue her work there even after the Germans occupied the city in June 1940. In December of that year she was sent to a civilian internment camp (Front Stalag 142) near Besançon, in eastern France, but after several months was released on account of ill health and allowed to return to her Paris home, 69 rue Laugier. There, though under Gestapo surveillance, she managed to receive personnel sent from London to organize French resistance and also to provide a base for transmitting radio messages to London.

Late in 1943 Mary Young was arrested by the Gestapo on suspicion of helping British prisoners to escape, and after interrogation was sent as a political prisoner to the women's concentration camp at Ravensbrück, in Germany. She arrived there in February 1944, aged sixty and already in poor health. In one of the messages that she had sent to her sister under the auspices of the International Red Cross before her arrest she indicated that her heart was weak—a possible consequence of the gas that she had suffered in the First World War. Physically small and slight, she was too feeble to do the heavy work required of camp inmates. The poor conditions worsened her health, and she died. News of her death did not reach Scotland until September 1945; when information about her role in the French resistance movement became public British newspapers hailed her as a second Edith Cavell, dying at the hands of the Germans because she had helped British prisoners to escape.

Following investigations by the British Foreign Office, the Red Cross, the British embassy in Paris, and the United Nations War Crimes Commission it was concluded that Mary Young died in Ravensbrück at the end of February or beginning of March 1945, possibly in the gas chamber. On 30 January 1948, in a judgment in the Scottish Court of Session on an action brought by Annie Sutherland to have her sister's estate settled, the death of Mary Helen Young was judicially presumed to have occurred on 14 March 1945. Letters produced in evidence referred to her indomitable courage and cheerfulness while in the camp. A fellow inmate, Simone Saint-Clair, said: 'She always kept her chin up … and all of us liked the little Scotswoman, Mees Young' ('Nazis sent Aberdeen heroine to gas chamber').

FIONA R. WATSON

Sources court of session, unextracted process, 1948, NA Scot., CS 46/1948 Feb 55 · Edinburgh sheriff court commissary office records, 1948, NA Scot., SC 70/1/1123, pp. 552–7 · 'Gallant nurse aided underground work', *Press and Journal* (28 Sept 1945) · 'Last message: Marie Helene sends her love', *Press and Journal* (27 Sept 1945) · 'Nazis sent Aberdeen heroine to gas chamber', *Press and Journal* (27 Sept 1945) · 'Nazis murdered nurse for aiding French',

Press and Journal (31 Jan 1948) · civil register of births, marriages, and deaths, Aberdeen and Edinburgh · census returns, 1881 · 'Tribute to the brave', *Press and Journal* (27 Sept 1945) · A. Harmon, 'A "Nurse Cavell" of Scotland', *Daily Record and Mail* (27 Sept 1945) · 'They gassed the second "Cavell"', *Daily Herald* (27 Sept 1945) · 'Refused chance to flee', *Daily Herald* (28 Sept 1945)
Likenesses photograph, *c.*1908, repro. in 'Tribute to the brave'
Wealth at death £1316 17*s*. 8*d*.: Edinburgh sheriff court commissary office records, SC70/1/1123, pp. 552–7, NA Scot., 1948 [inventory of the personal and moveable estate and effects of the late Mary Helen Young, 29 April 1948]

Young, Matthew (1750–1800), university teacher and bishop of Clonfert, was born on 3 October 1750 at Castlerea, co. Roscommon, and was the fourth son of Owen Young and Olivia Maria Bell. He matriculated at Trinity College, Dublin, on 8 July 1766, obtained a scholarship in 1769, and graduated BA (1772), MA (1774), and BD (1782). Young married Anne, daughter of Captain Bennet Cuthbertson; the couple had eleven children.

Elected fellow in 1775, Young was appointed Donegal lecturer at Trinity College in 1782. Two years later he published, in Dublin and in London, *An Enquiry into the Principal phænomena of Sounds and Musical Strings*, an endeavour to vindicate Isaac Newton's work on air pulses in *Principia*. In 1786 he was awarded the degree of DD and he was elected professor of natural philosophy in Trinity College. Young enthusiastically promoted private research at the college. In 1777 he founded a society for the study of Syriac and theology, as well as a philosophical society, the forerunner of the Royal Irish Academy, of which he was a founder member. To the transactions of this body Young contributed several papers, chiefly on scientific subjects, as well as one on ancient Gaelic poetry, in which he took much interest. His *Ancient Gaelic Poems, Collected in the Highlands of Scotland* appeared in 1787. In 1790 Young published an anonymous tract, *An enquiry how far the provost of Trinity College, Dublin, is vested with a negative upon the proceedings of the senior fellows*. The question arose from the claim of the provost, John Hely Hutchinson, from which Young himself had suffered, to overrule elections of fellows even against a clear majority of the electors.

On 2 February 1798 Young was consecrated as bishop of Clonfert, Ireland's poorest diocese, on the recommendation of the lord lieutenant's principal secretary, who considered Young 'the most distinguished literary character in the kingdom'. This was also the opinion of William Bennet, bishop of Cloyne, who described Young as 'the ablest man I have seen in the country, with a keen and logical mind, united to exquisite taste. He has the playfulness and ingenuousness of a schoolboy'. Besides his scientific and theological attainments Young was an amateur landscape painter and an enthusiastic botanist. Following his appointment as bishop of Clonfert he studied Syriac with special reference to an amended version of the Psalms which he had undertaken, and which was printed, but not published, in his lifetime. Young's work remained unfinished at his death from cancer at Whitworth, Lancashire, on 28 November 1800. His remains were brought to Dublin and interred in Trinity College chapel. A more important work in preparation at the time of his death was his

Matthew Young (1750–1800), by John Comerford (after Thomas Hickey, 1796)

Method of Prime and Ultimate Ratios, Illustrated by a Comment on the Principia, in Latin; it was never published. Thomas Elrington, bishop of Ferns, published a sermon on Young's death, with biographical details, which appeared in three editions in 1800. A pension of £500 per annum was obtained for Young's widow and children. In 1803 there appeared *An Analysis of the Principles of Natural Philosophy*, a compendium of his lectures given at Trinity.

RICHARD GARNETT, *rev.* J. FALVEY

Sources B. Bradshaw and others, 'Bishops of the Church of Ireland from 1534', *A new history of Ireland*, ed. T. W. Moody and others, 9: *Maps, genealogies, lists* (1984), 392–438 · H. Cotton, *Fasti ecclesiae Hibernicae*, 6 vols. (1845–78) · R. Mant, *History of the Church of Ireland*, 2 vols. (1840) · Burtchaell & Sadleir, *Alum. Dubl.* · J. J. Falvey, 'The Church of Ireland episcopate in the eighteenth century', MA diss., University College, Cork, 1995 · R. J. Hayes, ed., *Manuscript sources for the history of Irish civilisation*, 11 vols. (1965)
Archives TCD, mathematical papers, etc., MS 949 | TCD, MS 950, N.5.2–6, MS 1203, N.5.1
Likenesses T. Kirk, marble bust, 1827, TCD · J. Comerford, miniature (after T. Hickey, 1796); Bonhams, 19 June 1996, lot 90 [*see illus.*] · oils, TCD

Young [Junius], **Patrick** (1584–1652), librarian and scholar, was born on 29 August 1584 at Seaton, Forfarshire, the fifth son of Sir Peter *Young (1544–1628), tutor to James VI of Scotland, and his first wife, Elizabeth Gibb (*d*. 1593). John *Young (1585–1654) was his younger brother. He was educated at the University of St Andrews, graduating MA in 1603.

On the accession of James I, Young accompanied his father south in the train of the king. Initially attached to Bishop George Lloyd of Chester as his librarian, he was incorporated at Oxford in 1605 with the degree of MA. On appointment as deacon he became a chaplain of All Souls College. His sojourn in Oxford not only benefited his development as a Greek scholar as he also developed an interest in history. On his return to London his patron, Richard Montague, bishop of Bath and Wells, ensured Young's welfare by obtaining for him a pension of £50 a year in return for occasional work as a secretary for the king.

Young is best known for his role in the reorganization of the Royal Library, indeed he has been credited with its virtual refoundation, and, in so doing, creating the preconditions for the eventual foundation of the British Museum. Since the petitions for the re-establishment of a royal library by John Dee in 1556, and by Robert Cotton in the reign of Queen Elizabeth I, had fallen on deaf ears, the royal library at St James's Palace at the time of Young's appointment consisted principally of the collections of Henry VII. Faced with only two surviving sixteenth-century library catalogues—the 1534 collection of Richmond and the 1542 Westminster library catalogue—not to mention other unlisted royal collections at Greenwich, Hampton Court, and Windsor, Young began a systematic cataloguing of the disparate royal collections. The initiative received an invaluable encouragement with the acquisition by Henry, prince of Wales, of the Lumley collection for his private library in 1609. In 1609 and 1610 Young undertook the construction of a new library building at St James's Palace, and on the death of Henry the prince's vast library became part of the Royal Collection. Young also played an important role in the acquisition of the library of the renowned scholar Isaac Casaubon, travelling to Paris for the purpose in 1617.

In 1622 Young was ordered 'to make search in all cathedrals for old manuscripts and ancient records, and to bring an inventory of them to His Majesty'. This initiated a programme of compiling useful library catalogues for a number of cathedral libraries, starting with Lichfield, St Paul's, Salisbury, Winchester, and Worcester, and endeavouring to ensure that the works within these libraries would be made known to scholars and that copies of some manuscripts should be placed in the Royal Library. Seven years later Young joined Dr Augustine Lindsell in drawing up an inventory of the Barocci collection of 251 manuscripts for the Bodleian Library, to which was appended a 1628 catalogue of the Greek manuscript collection of Sir Thomas Roe. Young's readiness to collate material from other libraries—such as his collation about 1619 of the Codex Bezae Cantabrigiensis at Cambridge—sometimes led to confusion among his contemporaries as to which library he was assigned to, which is evident from Jean Morin's identification of him as the librarian of the university library at Cambridge.

Young was the recipient of various ecclesiastical and secular honours. His income was augmented in 1613 when he became a prebend of Chester Cathedral and on 9 January 1618 he was made a burgess of Dundee. In 1620, shortly after marrying his wife, Elizabeth, he was allocated the salary of the rectory of Llanynys in Denbighshire, and he was also incorporated as MA at Cambridge. In 1621 he was appointed a prebend of St Paul's and a treasurer of the same cathedral. 1623 witnessed his appointment to a rectorship of Hayes, Middlesex, a position that he held until 1647. By 1624 he had been appointed to the office of Latin secretary by Bishop John Williams.

As secretary and royal librarian Young acted not only as a vital node in British scholarly networks, but his contacts and reputation extended into continental Europe where he developed long-lasting collections with individual scholars such as Lucas Holstenius (1596–1661). This was sustained by his considerable academic ability, most notably in the field of Greek studies. Young's published works are relatively few in number, but he did much to encourage contemporary authors such as Daniel Heinsius who, though interested in classical scholarship, published works chiefly concerned with biblical scholarship, with Young acting as either his editor or his translator. Young and Thomas Reid worked as translators on James I's *Serenissimi … principis Jacobi … opera*, which had been edited by Young's patron Montague, and was published in London in 1619. Young continued to translate works, particularly from Greek to Latin, as his 1637 edition of Nicetas's *Catena Graecorum patrum in beatum Job collectore Niceta* testifies. This work was followed in 1638 by his edition of a treatise by Bishop Gilbert Foliot, *Gilberti Foliot episcopi Londinensis, expositio in Canticum*. As early as 1613 he contemplated an edition of the works of Origen and Theodoret, and by 1628 he was entrusted with the task of preparing an edition of the famous Alexandrian codex of the Septuagint, which had been presented to the Royal Library. 1633 saw the publication of his *Clementis ad Corinthios epistola prior. Latinè vertit, et notis brevioribus illustravit. P. Junius, Gr.a Lat*, at Oxford, (a work by Pope Clement I). Some works appeared only after his death. An edition of his annotations on the Alexandrian manuscript was appended to a 1657 edition of a polyglot Bible: *P. Junii annotationes quas paraverat ad MS Alexandrini editionem, in quibus codicem illum antiquiss. cum textu Hebr … confert*. His comments on and abridgement of Louis Savot's work on the coins of the Roman emperors were published with Leland's *Collectanea* (vol. 5, 1770 and 1774).

Young was deprived of his position as royal librarian in 1649 and he retired to the house of his son-in-law, John Atwood, at Broomfield in Essex, where he died on 7 September 1652, leaving two daughters, Elizabeth and Sarah. The true extent of his fame among contemporaries is evident from the many eulogies of him following his death, cited in his chief biography by Thomas Smith.

ELIZABETHANNE BORAN

Sources T. Smith, 'Vita Viri Clarissimi Patricii Junii', *Vitae quor. Edrudit. et Illustr. Virorum* (1707) • S. Jayne, *Library catalogues of the English Renaissance* (1956) • N. R. Ker, 'Salisbury Cathedral manuscripts and Patrick Young's catalogue', *Wiltshire Archaeological and Natural History Magazine*, 53 (1949–50), 153–83 • N. R. Ker, 'Patrick Young's catalogue of the manuscripts of Lichfield Cathedral', *Mediaeval and Renaissance Studies*, 2 (1950), 151–68 • I. Atkins and N. R. Ker, eds., *Catalogus librorum Manuscriptorum Bibliotechae Wigorniensis* (1944) • F. J. M. Blom, 'Lucas Hostenius (1596–1661) England', *Studies in seventeenth-century English literature, history, bibliography, ed.*

G. A. M. Janssens and F. G. A. M. Aarts (1984), 25–39 · R. C. Strong, *Henry, prince of Wales, and England's lost Renaissance* (1986), 211 · G. Leyh, ed., *Handbuch der Bibliothekswissenschaft*, vol. 3 (1957) · J. C. T. Oates, *Cambridge University Library: a history from the beginnings to the Copyright Act of Queen Anne* (1986) · M. Feingold, 'The humanities', *Hist. U. Oxf. 4: 17th-cent. Oxf.*, 211–358 · *Fasti Angl., 1300–1541* · *DNB* · Wing, *STC*

Archives BL, Royal MSS, papers as royal librarian · Bodl. Oxf., corresp. and papers, MSS Smith 22, 34, 37–38, 75–76, 89, 97 | BL, Add. MS 15671, p. 185 · BL, Lansdowne MS 985, fol. 188

Sir Peter Young (1544–1628), by unknown artist

Young, Sir Peter (1544–1628), royal tutor and diplomat, was born on 15 August 1544 at Dundee, the second son of John Young (*b.* 1497), burgess of Edinburgh and Dundee, and Margaret, daughter of Walter Scrymgeour of Glasswell. John Young's third son, Alexander, was usher of the king's privy chamber to James VI, and died on 29 December 1603. Peter was educated at Dundee grammar school, and possibly matriculated at St Andrews University since he was designated *magister* when admitted a burgess of Dundee. From 1562 until 1568 he studied at Geneva under the care of his uncle Henry *Scrimgeour, who held the chair of civil law there. Young became acquainted with the theologian Theodore Beza and corresponded with him after returning to Scotland. Other correspondents included the reformer Andrew Melville and the astronomer Tycho Brahe.

In 1569 the regent of Scotland, James, earl of Moray, appointed Young co-tutor to the infant James VI along with George Buchanan. Young appears to have taken the lead in teaching the king—who lived at Stirling Castle—since Buchanan was by now elderly. The teaching day consisted of Isocrates, Plutarch, and the New Testament before breakfast; Livy, Cicero, and a modern historian after breakfast; and, in the afternoon, logic and rhetoric. Young made it his concern to build up the royal library which had been dispersed during the deposition of Queen Mary; he collected or recovered some 600 books consisting of theology, classical authors, modern history, and political theory. He himself donated a Bible and several works by Greek and Latin writers. Young carried himself as a courtier, and according to Sir James Melville of Halhill 'was laith till offend the kyng at any tym, and used him self wairly, as a man that had mynd of his awen weill be keping of his Majestie's favour' (*Memoirs of His Own Life*, 262).

In August 1570 Young was presented to a subchantory of Glasgow and the parsonage of Durisdeer in Nithsdale as 'pedagog to oure soverane lord' but was forced to demit since he was not qualified to serve as its minister (Donaldson, 6.164, 505; 7.3). However, he was compensated with revenues from the archbishopric of Glasgow, and in 1579 with the rights to rents from the king's lordship of Torphichen for his service 'in educatioun and instructioun of his hienes … and contenuall attendance and awayting on his majestie almaist ever sen his nativitie' (ibid., 7.341). On 25 October 1577 Young had been appointed maister elemosinare (master almoner) to the king with a yearly pension of £200. He was involved in several scholarly enterprises; in 1574 he served on kirk committees and in 1575 he acted as deputy for Buchanan on the committee for standardizing the teaching of Latin in schools. On 3 January 1577 he and others were granted licence to print works by classical writers and 'ane onomastik, certane select sentences, the catechisme for the young bairns' for fifteen years (ibid., 7.121). During the 1590s Tycho Brahe asked him several times to write a life of Buchanan, but Young excused himself due to a lack of source materials. In 1598 he was appointed to the commission reporting on the state of Scottish universities.

When Danish ambassadors asked for the redemption of Orkney, Young was sent to Denmark in July 1586. On this occasion he satisfied Frederick II on certain points and began negotiations for a royal marriage. On his return he was admitted to the privy council (7 November 1586); he remained a frequent attender until 1622. In May 1587 he and Sir Patrick Vans of Barnbarroch embarked on a second embassy to Denmark, and avoided the question of Orkney and Shetland by claiming they had no commission from the king to discuss the matter; they then proposed a marriage with the Princess Elizabeth. In 1588 Young returned to Denmark only to discover she had been promised to another, and so Princess Anne was offered instead. The death of Frederick in 1588 delayed negotiations but the queen regent sent Young back to Scotland with a portrait of the princess and he spoke favourably of her to King James. Early in 1589 Young went to Denmark to complete the negotiations, and he was present at the marriage of James VI in Oslo, Norway, in October.

Throughout the 1590s Young continued to serve James as an ambassador. In 1590 he was sent to the Danish court and presented a portrait of Buchanan to Tycho Brahe. In April 1594 he was ambassador to Denmark and the empire when he gave assurances regarding the quarrel between

Queen Anne and Chancellor Thirlstane over her marriage-portion lands. On his return Young brought back Duke Ulric of Mecklenburg, grandfather to Anne, and the duke of Brunswick, her brother-in-law, to attend the baptism of Prince Henry; both were offended because James had not sent a special envoy to each of them, so neither would accompany Young from Leith. In 1595 he was appointed one of the eight octavians charged with managing the king's financial affairs. The following year Young and Lord Ogilvy were sent to Denmark to ask for ships and soldiers for an expedition against the Isles, and the question of support for James's claim to the English throne was discussed. In 1598 James VI sent the bishop of Aberdeen and Young on an embassy to Denmark and the empire with secret instructions to negotiate a league of princes to persuade Elizabeth of England publicly to acknowledge James as her heir. Young and Cunningham were instructed to secure a loan from Christian IV and the German princes for hiring soldiers to press the Scottish claim to England. During this same embassy Young met David Chytraeus, who had published an attack on Queen Mary based on Buchanan's *Detectio*, but persuaded Chytraeus to retract it at the prompting of King James. Young accompanied James to England in 1603; he remained master almoner and in November 1604 was made tutor and 'chief overseer' in the household of Prince Charles. He was knighted on 19 February 1605.

Young married three times. He and his first wife, Elizabeth (*d.* 1593), daughter of John Gibb, a gentleman of the king's bedchamber, had eight sons and four daughters. The fifth son was Patrick *Young (*d.* 1652), royal librarian and editor of some of the writings of King James VI, while the sixth, John *Young (1585–1654), was for nearly thirty years dean of Winchester. Young's second wife, Joanna Murray, survived her marriage for only six months, dying in November 1596. In 1600 he married Marjory Nairne of Sandfurd; they had four daughters, and she was still living in 1642. In 1616 Young was appointed titular master of St Cross Hospital, Winchester. He had purchased the estate of Easter Seaton, near Arbroath, Angus (Forfarshire), in 1580, and died there on 7 January 1628 in his eighty-fourth year. He was buried in the vault of St Vigean's Church near Arbroath. DAVIE HORSBURGH

Sources *Memoirs of his own life by Sir James Melville of Halhill*, ed. T. Thomson, Bannatyne Club, 18 (1827) • G. F. Warner and others, eds., *Miscellany … I*, Scottish History Society, 15 (1893) • *Letters of King James VI & I*, ed. G. P. V. Akrigg (1984) • *The Warrender papers*, ed. A. I. Cameron, 2, Scottish History Society, 3rd ser., 19 (1932) • M. Livingstone, D. Hay Fleming, and others, eds., *Registrum secreti sigilli regum Scotorum / The register of the privy seal of Scotland*, 6–7 (1963–6) • *The memoirs of Sir James Melville of Halhill*, ed. G. Donaldson (1969) • I. D. McFarlane, *Buchanan* (1981) • E. C. Williams, *Anne of Denmark, wife of James VI of Scotland: James I of England* (1970) • DNB
Archives NRA, diary
Likenesses oils, Scot. NPG [*see illus.*]
Wealth at death total sum unknown; pensions in arrears

Young, Peter (1915–1988), army officer and military historian, was born at 54 Fulham Road, London, on 28 July 1915, the son of Dallas Hales Wilkie Young, clerk, and Irene Barbara Lushington Mellor, and educated at Monmouth School and Trinity College, Oxford. He was commissioned second lieutenant in the Bedfordshire and Hertfordshire regiment in 1937, and was wounded during the evacuation from Dunkirk in 1940. As soon as he was fit again he volunteered for the newly formed commandos, with whom he had a distinguished war record, taking part in the commando raids on Guernsey, Lofoten and Vaagso, Dieppe, Sicily, and Italy, Normandy, and the Arakan (Burma). He was awarded the DSO and MC in 1942, and received in 1943 two more bars to his MC. When the war ended he was commanding the 1st commando brigade with the temporary rank of brigadier, aged only 30.

In the Dieppe raid Young was the only commando officer to reach his objective and bring back all his men. He managed to take his raiding force up the cliffs on a network of barbed wire which, as he put it, an over-conscientious German officer had inadvertently provided for them to walk on. He was awarded the DSO for his part in this raid. Later, in the Arakan, a fellow officer recalls seeing Young's commandos under attack at Kangaw from hordes of Japanese, and sending a message asking Young if he would like reinforcements. 'No thanks', came back the message, 'we can see this lot off all right' (*Daily Telegraph*, 14 Sept 1988).

It is not surprising that such an outstanding battlefield leader did not find it easy to adjust to more mundane peacetime soldiering. Young found it difficult to decide whether to remain in the army, where he would undoubtedly go far, or return to his first love, which was history, and which won in the end. But before retiring in 1959 in the rank of brigadier, Young enjoyed three successful and exhilarating years (1953–6) in command of the 9th infantry regiment in the Arab Legion in Jordan. The 9th regiment was almost entirely Bedouin, and Young's somewhat swashbuckling character and obvious military ability led to a remarkable rapport between him and his *jundis* (Arab soldiers). This was notably increased when as commander of the Jerusalem garrison he successfully thwarted an Israeli attack. His prompt and effective handling of a very dangerous situation brought *sharf* (honour) to the regiment and added greatly to Young's popularity. However, it did not save Young from being included among the first of the British officers to be sent home in the wake of Glubb Pasha's dismissal in March 1956. This was owing to the fact that he and his regiment had been prominent in suppressing the anti-Baghdad pact riots that had torn Jordan apart at the end of 1955. He had married Joan Rathbone (*née* Duckworth) on 23 June 1950. They had no children.

Young retired from the army in order to become reader in military history at Sandhurst in 1959. He was there for ten years and his effect on the teaching of military history was dramatic. He recruited some of Britain's outstanding military historians—John Keegan, David Chandler, and Christopher Duffy, to name but a few—and inspired them by his own enthusiasm and erudition. He had always been particularly interested in the English civil war and in 1968 he founded the Sealed Knot Society of Cavaliers and Roundheads, in order to re-enact battles and engagements of that conflict. Dressed in period costume, which they had to provide themselves, they refought Naseby, Marston Moor, and so on, with Young as the somewhat portly 'Captain Generall' sporting a Van Dyck beard and flowing locks, mounted on a horse and directing proceedings. The society won for itself a national reputation, and people flocked to watch the battles taking place at various pageants and shows.

A prolific writer of books and articles, Young as an author might have been wiser to concentrate on the civil war, on which he became something of an authority. *The Great Civil War* (1959) was typical. He was editor-in-chief of Purnell's *History of the First World War* and Orbis's *History of World War II*. He also published an interesting account of his time in the Arab Legion, entitled *Bedouin Command* (1956). His books on the civil war are likely to outlive the others. In the field of military history his opinions were always listened to with respect, if not always without argument. As a soldier he possessed nearly all the qualities which could have taken him to the highest ranks—physical courage, robustness, common sense, personality, intelligence, and leadership—but he did not much enjoy peacetime soldiering, and would not have fitted easily into Whitehall. His decision to go for history was probably the right one.

There was about him something larger than life. He was in character essentially Elizabethan, a robust and rumbustious soldier–scholar, as ready to singe the king of Spain's beard as to enter into disputation with learned men concerning some matter of academic controversy. He also possessed a remarkably kind heart and gave much of his time to helping others, particularly budding historians. He died in Cheltenham General Hospital on 13 September 1988, and his funeral took place at St Mary's Church, Ripple, Worcestershire, on 4 October.   JAMES LUNT

Sources J. B. Glubb, *The story of the Arab legion* (1948) · *Daily Telegraph* (14 Sept 1988) · P. Young, *Bedouin command* (1956) · P. Young, *Storm from the sea* (1958) · P. Young, *The great civil war* (1959) · G. Lias, *Glubb's legion* (1956) · J. D. Lunt, *Glubb Pasha: Lieutenant-General Sir John Bagot Glubb, commander of the Arab legion, 1939–1956* (1984) · T. Royle, *Glubb Pasha* (1992) · personal knowledge (2004) · b. cert. · m. cert. · d. cert. · *CGPLA Eng. & Wales* (1989)

Archives NAM, corresp. and papers relating to his military career and historical studies | King's Lond., Liddell Hart C., corresp. with Sir B. H. Liddell Hart · S. Antiquaries, Lond., letters to A. W. G. Lowther | FILM BFI NFTVA, documentary footage

Wealth at death under £70,000: probate, 18 Jan 1989, *CGPLA Eng. & Wales*

Young, Robert (*c*.1656–1700), forger and false witness, had his criminal career to 1692, mainly as a clerical impostor, traced in unique detail through a dozen aliases by his intended victim Thomas Sprat, bishop of Rochester. Yet even Sprat could not certainly establish his origin. Young in different impostures claimed Chester and Warrington as his birthplace; the Irish bishops investigating his early frauds thought him a Scot; but a king's messenger met his father, a wandering fortune-teller and conjuror (evidently protestant), in Ireland, at Limerick. When imprisoned in 1681 Young mentioned a brother willing to stand bail. Young's spelling and dog-Latin discredit his occasional

claims to have attended Enniskillen School and Trinity College, Dublin, or Magdalen College, Oxford. His real education was in counterfeiting handwriting and forging documents. He was tall, swarthy, and long-faced, with straight black hair.

Ireland In 1677 Young tricked John Roan, bishop of Killaloe, by forging certificates of his learning and moral character, into granting him deacon's orders. He then and later forged several letters of ordination for himself from Roan and other Irish bishops. In 1679–80 he held three successive curacies, at Tallogh, co. Waterford, Castlerea, co. Roscommon, and Kildallon, co. Cavan, but soon fled from each for offences including forging bills of exchange, horse-stealing, fathering a bastard, and performing illegal marriages. He himself had in 1675 married Ann Apsly or Yeabsly, a yeoman's daughter of Ards, co. Cork; they had three children (two were dead by 1681). In 1680 (after attempts with other women) he bigamously married Mary Hutt, the daughter of a Cavan innkeeper, for her £150 dowry. By 1681 he was in Cavan gaol awaiting trial for his life for bigamy. Since he might nevertheless genuinely be one of the more demoralized Irish Restoration lower clergy, Francis Marsh, bishop of Kilmore, degraded him from his clerical orders. From gaol Young wrote to both his wives, assuring each with exaggerated protestations that he loved only her, and persuaded them not to appear against him at the assizes. Still detained for unpaid prison fees, he gained release by offering to reveal to Lord Lieutenant Ormond further permutations of the Popish Plot, implicating noblemen and bishops (presumably including his protestant diocesans), but absconded *en route* for Dublin.

Early years in England In 1683 Young fled to England with his second 'wife', Mary. (By one account they had two children, by another five who died.) Having failed to trick Archbishop Sancroft into granting him preferment, Young in mid-1684 forged a charitable recommendation from him, and the couple travelled as brother and sister collecting to ransom 'Mary Green's' husband, a cleric captured by Moorish pirates. They were arrested at Bury St Edmunds, tried as cheats on 6 October 1684, and pilloried. Young had written to Sancroft a long, florid letter containing another false autobiography, expressing hostility to 'discentors ... specially that damnable faction of Presbytery' (*State trials*, 12.1126), and blaming the forgery on Wright, a non-existent Oxford scrivener, but Sancroft did not recommend him to the judges, and Young vowed revenge. Imprisoned at Bury for a year, he again invented a plot to obtain release, petitioning James II and his parliament in May 1685 offering to discover whig conspirators including ten (unnamed) presbyterian ministers. He vindictively accused of treason a fellow prisoner against whom he and Mary unsuccessfully testified at Ipswich assizes.

In 1686 Young forged a fresh licence from Sancroft to beg, with which the couple, with new aliases and a new story, solicited successfully until the archbishop, alerted to letters which Young had forged skilfully enough (spelling excepted) to deceive three bishops intimate with him, inserted advertisements warning the charitable against 'Smith' and 'Mrs Jones' in the *London Gazette* in September–October 1687. During 1688–9 Young, having gained access to the mail at St Albans by corrupting the postmaster and his family, carried out large-scale forgeries of midland merchants' bills of exchange on London, until Mary Young was arrested there presenting one. With the proceeds Young posed at Lichfield as a refugee Irish dean, courted an heiress, and, when Mary inconveniently escaped from prison and arrived, allegedly plotted her murder. However, one of their victims had the couple arrested in December 1689. Tried in London on 15 January 1690 for two forgeries only, they were pilloried again. Young was also fined 200 marks (Mary Young only 20 marks) but, unable to pay, they were still in Newgate two years later.

Young, seeking release, yet again turned plot-forger. About Christmas 1691 he sent to Archbishop Tillotson forged treasonable letters from important men. Tillotson showed these to King William, but expressed his total disbelief, with which William concurred. Young would need a crisis to obtain a favourable hearing, and accomplices on the outside: the unexplained disgrace of John Churchill, earl of Marlborough, in January 1692 and the French invasion threat that spring inspired him.

The Flowerpot Plot Jacobite and opposition writers hinted that the government ministers sponsored Young's plot, but their surviving private correspondence shows them as genuinely duped. In the paper he left at his execution, Young claimed that a surgeon imprisoned for debt called Henry Pearson had prompted him. A discredited plot-forger, John Capel, in October 1692 warned George Savile, marquess of Halifax, then in opposition, that two allies of Young were preparing to accuse Sprat and Halifax before parliament. Yet both these and Pearson may be as imaginary as scrivener Wright. In the false plots of the 1690s the inventor often initially remained in the background while a younger disciple made the accusations, a pattern compulsory here because Young, in Newgate, could not plausibly claim to have met his 'fellow conspirators'. Young's accomplice, Stephen Blackhead, was a bankrupt tailor turned debt-collector, also tried for a forgery on 15 January 1690 and pilloried and imprisoned in Newgate for a year. He had avoided, by bribery, losing an ear as well; but his gaolbird looks made him an implausible Jacobite go-between to peers and bishops. Captain Lawe, another former fellow prisoner whom Young named as a witness (he himself and Blackhead, convicted forgers, were legally ineligible), never came forward.

Young's forgeries have disappeared, and Sprat's report is the principal source of information about them. The main one was a Jacobite association. Its promises—to raise 30,000 men to assist a French invasion, to seize Queen Mary dead or alive—were as absurd as its style, but the seven signatures were brilliantly forged. Of the victims, Sancroft had retired to his Suffolk birthplace, but Young, experienced in his handwriting, probably still wanted revenge. Giles Willcox, a nonjuring cleric already arrested for treason, might be frightened into becoming another witness. Accusations against the others might please their enemies across the political spectrum. Marlborough, Viscount Cornbury, and Sprat had offended both sides by abrupt changes of allegiance in or after 1688. The earl of Salisbury had turned Catholic to obtain James's favour. The tory London merchant Sir Basil Firebrace was notorious for extortionate avarice. Young obtained answers in their handwriting to letters written under various aliases and pretexts—ironically, he had Blackhead carry to Sprat a query whether an (imaginary) curate had forged his orders—and supplemented the association with forged letters from and between Sprat and Marlborough. Though the ease-loving bishop was an unlikely conspirator, he was made the central figure, drafting a declaration for James's invasion, because Young knew his palace at Bromley from a brief 1687 stint as curate at the local almshouses. Young sent Blackhead there again in Sprat's absence to hide the forged association in his study but, denied access there, he concealed it in a flower-pot in the servants' parlour.

Marlborough's arrest on suspicion on 3 May 1692, when the alarm of French invasion was at its height, led Young, timing his plot to a nicety, to demand a hearing from the cabinet. On 7 May he and Blackhead testified before them and, thanks to the forged Marlborough letters, were taken seriously. Both urged the messengers sent to Bromley to seize Sprat and his papers to search the flowerpots, gaining the affair the nickname the Flowerpot Plot. However, the search, restricted to Sprat's private rooms, fortunately missed the association, and for lack of solid evidence the bishop, after examination and ten days' house arrest in London, was allowed home.

Meanwhile Young got Blackhead to retrieve the paper, and renewed his accusations. Independently, the government's newest agent, Richard Kingston (later its best anti-Jacobite spy but, like Young, a loose-living clerical impostor), alleged on 1 June that Sprat was deeply implicated in Jacobite pamphleteering. The government freed the Youngs from Newgate on 25 May, a source of later embarrassment. On 10 June (when the victory of La Hogue had ended invasion fears) the privy council confronted Sprat, whose story his servants confirmed, with Blackhead, who finally broke down under interrogation. Young, arrested with him, now produced the association, and Mary Young supported his story. On 13 June, confronted before the council by Blackhead, who confessed everything, and the bishop, Young remained unabashed, accusing them of combining to stifle the plot and even denying that he had advised searching the flowerpots. However, the truth and Sprat's innocence were clear. One indirect beneficiary was Marlborough, bailed on 15 June, whose partisans then and since blamed his imprisonment merely on Young's accusations.

Aftermath That autumn Young unsuccessfully tempted yet another former fellow prisoner, Richard Holland, to confirm his story of the association, and somehow arranged for fresh Jacobite forgeries to be hidden under the duchess of Richmond's hall floorboards. As Sprat deduced, had his first accusations succeeded he would have claimed many more victims.

'Confessed: no; you shall find to your sorrow, all is not confessed yet', snarled Young when Sprat rebuked him; 'a parliament will come, and then you shall hear from me' (*State trials*, 12.1081). However, he had miscalculated politically. Marlborough had since late 1691 been intermittently allied with the largely whig parliamentary opposition, who denounced his detention. The false witnesses opposition whigs encouraged were those—the most dangerous—who accused government ministers of treason. Instead, the failure to prosecute Young at the October 1692 sessions, and Blackhead's escape from custody, encouraged genuine opposition fears that Young's perjuries might be government-inspired. Sprat began to share them. He had completed a narrative of his deliverance by 1 August, and most of a detailed biography of Young, with documents furnished by Sancroft and the Irish hierarchy, by early autumn, but heavy official pressure had restrained him from publication. Now both parts appeared successively in November. The skilful narrative and ample, damning documentation destroyed Young's credibility for good.

On 7 February 1693 Young was tried in the king's bench for the forgery. Charles Hatton wrote:

> by impudence [he] far outdid even Dr Oates. He had not a ranting impudence, but a most unparalleled sedate composed impudence, and pretends to be as great a martyr for his zeale for the present governm^t as Oates did for his for the protestant religion. The jury without stirring from the barre found him guilty. (Thompson, 2.189–90)

He was sentenced to be pilloried three times (he was heavily pelted) and fined £1000, to be imprisoned until he paid it, and meanwhile denied pen, ink, and paper.

Last years: king's bench, the Fleet, and Newgate Young remained in the king's bench prison (or, briefly, the Fleet) for nearly six years. The 1696 assassination plot inspired him, like other plot-forgers, to fresh activity, bombarding William and his ministers with miscellaneous accusations, including conspiracies by Sprat to destroy him. But his sting had been drawn: the lords justices, presented with a letter, 'would not so much as hear of such a villain as Rob. Young …, with all indignation' (*Downshire MSS*, 1.665).

In both the Fleet and king's bench prisons Young had resumed his criminal career, now also forging leases while outside accomplices collected the money. After Young had escaped from the king's bench in December 1698, he and Mary, under the aliases John Larkin and Mary Robinson, carried on small-scale swindling of tradesmen. Arrested again, they were tried at the Guildhall sessions on 19 September 1699. He was fined 200 marks and she £30, and they were committed to Newgate until they could pay.

Young still exploited his skills, getting a prisoner released by counterfeiting both the sheriffs' signatures. He now became involved with coiners, fellow prisoners,

intending 'to accuse them, and to Witness against them, in hopes to purchase his liberty' (*London Post*, no. 134), since for each conviction the informer received a £40 reward. For once Young was presumably truthful in claiming in his last paper that he had merely watched Daniel Jones coining money within Newgate, where he was arrested in the act on 14 March 1700. The calendar of prisoners for the April sessions listed Daniel and Mary Jones (the coincidence with Mary Young's frequent alias was evidently mere coincidence) to be tried for high treason for coining; 'Larkin' and 'Mary Robinson' merely had their former orders as convicts continued. However, in tackling a class of criminal accustomed to survive by unscrupulously framing colleagues, Young was again out of his depth. Probably the Joneses turned the tables by making clear to the authorities his real identity, for on 12 April he was convicted of coining, while they, as mere accessories, and another couple, the Iversons, were the witnesses. Young was executed at Tyburn on 19 April 1700, apparently penitent. He left a paper, supplementing Sprat's account of his life (since he lacked time to write, as he wanted, a full confession), admitting that the 1692 plot was forged, largely confessing his part in it, and mentioning his main swindles and accomplices since. Four months later, Mary 'Robinson' was discharged from Newgate.   PAUL HOPKINS

Sources *State trials*, 12.1055–1166 • T. Sprat, *A relation of the late wicked contrivance of Stephen Blackhead and Robert Young .. in two parts* (1692) • *Report on the manuscripts of Allan George Finch*, 5 vols., HMC, 71 (1913–2003), vol. 4 • *Report on the manuscripts of the marquis of Downshire*, 6 vols. in 7, HMC, 75 (1924–95), vol. 1 • P. A. Hopkins, 'Sham plots and real plots in the 1690s', *Ideology and conspiracy: aspects of Jacobitism, 1689–1759*, ed. E. Cruickshanks (1982), 89–111 • minute books, 1699–1700, CLRO, London sessions, SM 69–70; sessions rolls, Jan 1690, CLRO, SF 367; sessions rolls, July 1699–Aug 1700, CLRO, SF 443–5 • *London Post*, BL, Burney newspaper collection, 134, vol. 122A • *Flying Post*, BL, Burney newspaper collection, 757, 772, vol. 122A • *Post Boy*, BL, Burney newspaper collection, 770, 782, 784, vol. 122A • N. Luttrell, *A brief historical relation of state affairs from September 1678 to April 1714*, 2–4 (1857) • E. M. Thompson, ed., *Correspondence of the family of Hatton*, 2, CS, new ser., 23 (1878) • marquess of Halifax's notebook, BL, Add. MS 51511, fols. 54v, 59v • *The life and letters of Sir George Savile … first marquis of Halifax*, ed. H. C. Foxcroft, 2 (1898), 154–5 • letters, Archbishop Sancroft to Bishop William Lloyd of Norwich, 1692, LPL, MS 3894 • R. Young, letter to duke of Shrewsbury, 14 March 1696, Northants. RO, Buccleuch papers, vol. 63, no. 1 • deposition of Dr K[ingston], 1/11 June 1692, U. Nott. L., Portland MSS, PwA 2504 • [N. Hooke], *An account of the conduct of the dowager duchess of Marlborough … in a letter from herself to my lord* (1742), 60–62 • T. B. Macaulay, *The history of England from the accession of James II*, new edn, ed. C. H. Firth, 6 vols. (1913–15), vol. 5, pp. 2196–205

Archives BL, Trumbull MSS • Leics. RO, Finch MSS • Northants. RO, Buccleuch papers
Wealth at death prisoner in Newgate, unable to pay fine; executed for treason, so any possessions confiscated

Young, Robert (1822–1888), philologist and translator, son of George Young, manager of a flour mill, and Jean Dudgeon, was born in Edinburgh or in East Lothian on 10 September 1822; his father died when Robert was a child. After education at private schools, he was apprenticed to the printing trade and set up as a printer and bookseller on his own account in 1847. During his apprenticeship he used his spare time to study Hebrew and other oriental languages, and also interested himself in religious work; for three years he was connected with Thomas Chalmers's territorial church sabbath school in the deprived district of West Port, Edinburgh. He published a variety of works of oriental grammar and translation, which chiefly focused upon the study of the Old Testament in its ancient versions. His first production was an edition with translation of Maimonides's 613 precepts. In 1856 he married, and until 1861 he was literary missionary and superintendent of the mission press at Surat; during this time in India he added Gujarati to his linguistic portfolio, which already included Gaelic and Finnish, in addition to the Romance and Teutonic languages. From 1864 to 1874 he conducted the Missionary Institute in Edinburgh, and in 1867 he visited the most important cities in the United States.

The best-known of Young's works is his *Analytical Concordance to the Bible* (1st edn, 1879), which went through many editions, and more than a century later remained in print in two American editions and one British. Young said that the object of his *Concordance*, as Tyndale said of his New Testament, was that every 'ploughboy' should know more of the scriptures than the 'ancients'. He maintained that the main feature of the *Concordance* was the analytical arrangement of each English word under its original in Hebrew or Greek, with the literal meaning being given in each case. This enabled the reader to distinguish differences which were frequently obscured in the English Bible and which could not be ascertained from the *Concordance* produced by Alexander Cruden in 1737.

In 1871 Young stood unsuccessfully for the Hebrew chair at St Andrews University. Most of his life was passed in Edinburgh, where he died at The Grange, on 14 October 1888, leaving two sons and four daughters.

D. S. MARGOLIOUTH, *rev.* ROGER STEER

Sources *Banner of Ulster* (18 Dec 1855) • P. Schaff and S. M. Jackson, *Encyclopedia of living divines and Christian workers of all denominations in Europe and America: being a supplement to Schaff-Herzog encyclopedia of religious knowledge* (1887) • *IGI* • *The Times* (17 Oct 1888)

Young, Sir Robert (1872–1957), trade unionist and politician, was born at 5 Hopehill Place, Glasgow, on 26 January 1872, the son of Robert Young, journeyman shipwright, and his wife, Mary Ann Layburn. He received an elementary education at Monsbank School, Glasgow, but left school at the age of twelve and went to work in a stationer's shop. In 1888 he joined a firm of Glasgow locomotive engineers as an apprentice, and remained there until 1902. As a member of the Amalgamated Society of Engineers (ASE), he spent twenty weeks locked out during the 1897 national engineering dispute. This experience made him believe that industrial disputes were best avoided if possible. In 1903 he was one of the first students to enter Ruskin College, Oxford, sponsored by the ASE. Subsequently he lectured on the college's behalf. He became an ASE clerical officer in 1906. He was described as a widower, when, on 16 May 1910, he married, at the Wesleyan Methodist Chapel, Walton Street, Oxford, Bessie Laurina

Choldcroft (1880/81–1950), a hairdresser, daughter of Christopher James Choldcroft of Oxford, also a hairdresser; they had two sons and one daughter.

Young climbed rapidly within the ASE, becoming its assistant general secretary in 1908. In 1913 he stood for election as general secretary against the incumbent, Jenkin Jones, alleging in no uncertain terms that Jones was unfit for office. Although Young was elected, Jones sued him for defamation and won the case. However, the society's final appeal court ruled that the election result should stand. Jones and the old executive committee now barricaded themselves into the ASE's offices, and were removed only after a pitched battle with their successors. As general secretary, Young proved a moderate. During the First World War he was fully behind the war effort, co-operating in attempts to increase production and opposing unofficial strikes. It was in recognition of his services in these areas that he was appointed OBE in 1917. However, he was also keen to see that pre-war trade practices were restored after the war, and in this he was largely successful.

In 1918 Young was forced, under ASE rules, to step down as general secretary on his election as Labour MP for the Newton division of Lancashire. Although he never became part of the Labour Party leadership, he filled the role of chairman of ways and means and deputy speaker during the tenure of the first Labour government in 1924, a sign of his reliability, his growing mastery of parliamentary procedure, and his loyalty to the party leader, Ramsay MacDonald. He filled the role successfully then, and again under the second Labour government (1929–31), and was knighted in the new year's honours of 1931. When the government fell, he refused an offer to stay on under the National Government and resigned as chairman of ways and means in September 1931, at the request of the Amalgamated Engineering Union (Young to MacDonald, 8 Sept 1931, PRO 30/69/1314). He went into opposition with the rest of his party, and at the general election which followed, in October 1931, narrowly lost his seat.

Young regained the Newton parliamentary seat in 1935 and held it until his retirement in 1950. He became a temporary chairman of committees and served on a number of parliamentary bodies, including the select committees on national expenditure (1941–4) and House of Commons procedure (1945–6); he was also chairman of the standing committee for the consideration of bills. Otherwise, he remained a frequent Commons attender, and was particularly interested in issues relating to industry, housing, health, and the navy.

Young was a smoker and, in the 1930s at least, a freemason, but he was also a lifelong teetotaller. He played a leading part in the formation of the Workers' Temperance League, and was from 1935 chairman of the National Temperance Federation, becoming its president in 1950. He was also chairman of the parliamentary temperance group from 1935 to 1950. Here again, though, he was a moderate, perhaps realizing that the heyday of the movement had passed. He was also the independent chairman of the ophthalmic benefit approved committee between 1937 and 1948. He died at 213 Barry Road, East Dulwich, London, on 13 July 1957.   ANDREW THORPE

Sources *The Times* (15 July 1957) · *WWW*, 1951–60 · *WWBMP*, vol. 4 · J. B. Jefferys, *The story of the engineers, 1800–1945* [1946]; repr. (1970) · *Labour party conference report* (1957) · C. J. Wrigley, *David Lloyd George and the British labour movement: peace and war* (1976) · R. Bassett, *1931: political crisis* (1958) · *The political diary of Hugh Dalton, 1918–1940, 1945–1960*, ed. B. Pimlott (1986) · *Hansard 5C* (1927), 206.1755; (1936), 309.1741; (1939), 351.1710 · b. cert. · m. cert. · d. cert. · PRO, 30/69/1314
Wealth at death £7779 6s. 2d.: probate, 7 Oct 1957, *CGPLA Eng. & Wales*

Young, Sir Robert Arthur (1871–1959), physician, was born on 6 November 1871 in the Norfolk village of Hilborough, the only son of William Young, labourer, and his wife, Hannah Elizabeth Ann Fairs, who when registering the birth signed her name with a mark. After attending Westminster city school and King's College, London, Young became a medical student at the Middlesex Hospital. He obtained his BSc with a first class in physiology in 1891 and his MB in 1894, and he became a licentiate of the Society of Apothecaries in a period when the quill pen was still used and the doctor carried his stethoscope in his silk hat. He was elected a member of the Royal College of Physicians in 1897 and a fellow in 1905. After obtaining his MD, London, with gold medal (1895) and doing postgraduate work at Vienna, he settled in London as a consulting physician. He was appointed to the Middlesex Hospital, the Brompton Hospital, and later the King Edward VII Sanatorium at Fenhurst, near Midhurst. In 1912 Young married Fanny Caroline Phoebe (d. 1944), daughter of Robert Muirhead Kennedy, of the Indian Civil Service; they had one son.

A chest specialist at that time had to rely entirely on observation and the patient's story, aided only by the five senses. Of this personal technique Young became one of the greatest exponents medicine has ever known. He was incapable of superficiality and with extraordinary tenacity would relentlessly pursue each sign and symptom until he penetrated its meaning. Even when X-ray diagnosis became general, he never consulted the film until he had carried his personal methods as far as they would go.

In his large consulting room in Harley Street, which was over-furnished with cupboards and clocks, Young sat at an overcrowded desk and inscrutably pursued his remorseless clinical routine. Nothing was allowed to come between him and the patient, and he never gave up until he had used every available method and discovered all he needed. His remarkable clinical sense was built on memory and observation and he certainly understood that the physician's role includes giving not merely a diagnosis but some comfort and hope. His practice flourished long after he retired in 1936 from the Middlesex Hospital and even after the age of eighty he gave a sound opinion. Before George VI underwent an operation for lung cancer in 1951 Young was the leader in a group of eminent clinicians summoned to advise.

Young was chairman of innumerable societies and committees, notably the National Association for the Prevention of Tuberculosis. He was an excellent leader, governing the proceedings with suavity and an extra sense of what was being thought round the table. He was an accomplished conciliator, adept in the formula which unites. Large affairs did not attract him, and he kept clear of medical controversies over the National Health Service.

Young had a rather hieratic manner, sedulously cultivated as a young man, which mellowed greatly in later life, though his speech kept a touch of unctuous sentiment belonging to an earlier period. He made a considerable fortune from medical practice in an age when this was an accepted measure of professional success. His private passion was collecting. Over the years a prodigious accumulation of china, glass, prints, clocks, and old instruments filled his rooms. He had not much artistic sense and preferred the quaint rather than the enduring. He cherished every object and nothing was ever allowed to go.

'R. A.' (as Young was affectionately known) was of medium height with a large, impressive head, and eyes which seemed to penetrate to the depths, though they also flickered with kindly reassurance. He never missed a medical banquet and kept up his committee work, full of industrious goodwill, until a week before his death.

Young's prodigious industry and impressive personal qualities brought him wide recognition. He was Harveian orator (1939) of the Royal College of Physicians; and both the Society of Apothecaries and the Royal Society of Medicine gave him their gold medals. He was appointed CBE in 1920 and knighted in 1947. He died in London on 22 August 1959.   HARLEY WILLIAMS, *rev.* H. C. G. MATTHEW

Sources *The Times* (24 Aug 1959) · *The Times* (26 Aug 1959) · *BMJ* (29 Aug 1959), 307–9 · *The Lancet* (5 Sept 1959), 298 · private information (1971) · personal knowledge (1971)
Archives RCP Lond., case notes and papers
Wealth at death £115,322 16s. 10d.: probate, 19 Oct 1959, *CGPLA Eng. & Wales*

Young, Sir Robert Christopher [Robin] **Mackworth-** (1920–2000), librarian and courtier, was born in London on 12 February 1920, the elder son of Gerard Mackworth-*Young (1884–1965), member of the Indian Civil Service and archaeologist, of Burleigh Court, near Stroud, Gloucestershire, and his wife, Natalie Leila Margaret (1894–1981), daughter of Sir Walter Hely-Hutchinson and his wife, May. His grandfather, Sir Mackworth Young, had been lieutenant-governor of the Punjab. He was sent to boarding-school at five and was a scholar at Eton from 1933 to 1938. During the Second World War he served in the RAF, first as a signals officer in Egypt; he subsequently went to Normandy two days after D-day and was involved in planning tactical air cover. He reached the rank of squadron leader. He was an exhibitioner at King's College, Cambridge (1946–8), where he read economics, and was president of the Union Society in 1948. He joined the Foreign Office in 1948 and served in Singapore and Prague. He met (Helen Editha) Rosemarie Aue (b. 1926) through the

Foreign Office; they married on 17 December 1953 and had one son.

In 1955 Mackworth-Young was appointed deputy librarian in the Royal Library, Windsor Castle, and took over as librarian and assistant keeper of the Royal Archives from Sir Owen Morshead in 1958. His work in the Royal Archives concentrated on helping many historians and biographers of members of the royal family, such as Elizabeth Longford (Queen Victoria), Cecil Woodham-Smith (Queen Victoria), Philip Magnus (Edward VII), Georgina Battiscombe (Queen Alexandra), James Pope-Hennessy (Queen Mary), John Brooke (George III), Christopher Hibbert (George IV), Philip Ziegler (William IV and Lord Melbourne), Arthur Aspinall (the later correspondence of George III, and George IV as prince of Wales), Roger Fulford (correspondence of Queen Victoria and Princess Victoria), and Robert Rhodes-James (Prince Albert). He was appointed MVO (1961), CVO (1968), KCVO (1975), and GCVO (1985).

Mackworth-Young wrote a history and description of the Royal Archives and gave it as a lecture in 1977; it was published in the journal *Archives* in 1978. He also lectured on the subject of Prince Albert and the Victorian age at the first annual conference of the Prince Albert Society at the Ehrenburg Palace in Coburg in 1980. He established the royal photograph collection as a separate entity within the Royal Archives in 1974.

The print room of the Royal Library contains the Royal Collection of some 40,000 old master drawings and watercolours; in 1972 Mackworth-Young established a full-time paper conservation studio, which enabled the gradual restoration of the finest drawings in the Royal Collection, particularly the 600 by Leonardo da Vinci. With the queen's permission, this in turn enabled him to institute and oversee a large number of exhibitions of these drawings both in Britain and in many countries overseas (from America and Italy to Australia and Mexico). Many of the exhibitions in the Queen's Gallery at Buckingham Palace showed drawings from the Royal Library. He was instrumental in setting up the gallery in Windsor Castle which ensures that old master drawings from the Royal Collection are available for the public to see. He arranged for reproductions of many of these images to be available for purchase. He began the special exhibitions in the Royal Library which the queen shows to her 'dine and sleep' guests at Windsor Castle in April every year. He supported the continuing publication (mainly by Phaidon) of the distinguished series of *catalogues raisonnés* on the old master drawings. He lectured on the drawings and on the history of Windsor Castle. He wrote several editions of the official guidebook of the castle, and his *History and Treasures of Windsor Castle* (1982) remains a standard work.

Sir Robin was a member of the Roxburghe Club, for which he had produced in 1977 an illustrated volume on the Sobieski Book of Hours, the library's finest illuminated manuscript, dating from the 1420s. He retired in June 1985 but remained librarian emeritus to the queen. He served on the Royal Mint advisory committee (1962–84)

and on the board of the British Library (1984–90). He was a fellow of the Society of Antiquaries from 1959.

Like his parents, Mackworth-Young had a deep love of music, especially Bach, and he played the piano, harpsichord, and clavichord. This, together with his knowledge of electronics, led him to invent a tuning instrument, the pitchmeter, which became a leader in its field in the late 1970s. His own firm, Clavitune, made them; Glyndebourne had one and the duke of Edinburgh gave one to Kneller Hall. He particularly enjoyed mountain walking and was a fine skier. He was a perceptive man with an original mind. He inherited an acute but reserved personality from his father and his gentle style concealed a firm purpose and high intelligence. He studied philosophy from an early age and had an abiding interest in Jung's works and thinking. He planned to complete a series of philosophical essays on his retirement to Somerset, but this was prevented by the onset of Parkinson's disease, which gradually increased in severity up to his death at his home, Blandford House, Sutton Montis, near Yeovil, on 5 December 2000. He was buried on 13 December at the church of the Holy Trinity, Sutton Montis.

OLIVER EVERETT

Sources papers, Royal Arch. · private information (2004) [family] · *Daily Telegraph* (11 Dec 2000) · *The Times* (12 Dec 2000) · *The Independent* (14 Dec 2000)

Young, Roland Keith (1887–1953), actor, was born in Hollington, Ealing, London, on 11 November 1887, the son of Keith Downes Young (1848–1929), an architect, and his wife, Emily Cornelia Ash. He was educated at Sherborne School in Dorset and at University College School, London. He then studied architecture with a view to following his father into that profession, but he briefly attended the Tree Dramatic School and then became a student at the Academy of Dramatic Art. His professional début, in London, was in *Find the Woman* by Charles Klein (1908). He played in the provinces for a few years before scoring a big success in *Improper Peter* in London at the Garrick (1912). As a result he was offered the part of Alan Jeffcote in W. S. Houghton's play *Hindle Wakes* at the Maxine Elliott Theatre in New York.

Young decided to stay in America and quickly became an established stage name—in short plays with the Darlington Square players; in major plays such as Ibsen's *John Gabriel Borkman* (1915) and *A Doll's House* (1918), and Chekhov's *The Seagull* (1917); and especially in three comedies by Clare Kummer. These were *Good Gracious, Annabelle* (1916) (in a film version of which, *Annabelle's Affairs*, he also appeared in 1931), *A Successful Calamity* (1917), and *Rollo's Wild Oat* (1920), in which he played an incompetent actor who attempts Hamlet. Young married Marjorie Beecher Kummer (*b*. 1899), on 5 September 1921. He served briefly in the US army during the First World War (having become a US citizen in 1918), after which he resumed his successful stage career in *Luck in Pawn* and the musical *Buddies* (both 1919); as General Burgoyne in G. B. Shaw's *The Devil's Disciple* at the Garrick in London (1923); in *Beggar on Horseback* by G. S. Kaufman and M. Connelly, and Ibsen's

Hedda Gabler (both 1924); and in *The Last of Mrs Cheyney* by Frederick Lonsdale (1925), which ran for well over a year.

In 1922 Young appeared in his first film, playing Dr Watson to John Barrymore's Holmes in *Sherlock Holmes*. His only other silent film was *Grit* (1924). With the arrival of the talkies he signed a contract with the MGM studio, although many of his early films were made on loan to other studios; he began to freelance from 1932. His talkie début was as Lord Montague in *The Unholy Night* (1929), directed by Lionel Barrymore. Short and dapper, with a neatly trimmed moustache, Young was at his best in light comedy, and it was chiefly in this field that he played leading roles throughout the 1930s. He was often 'somewhat bemused, vaguely quizzical and never surprised at the madness of others [and] underplayed with skill and charm' (Shipman, 568). He appeared in *The Bishop Murder Case*, Cecil B. De Mille's *Madam Satan*, and *New Moon* with Lawrence Tibbett (all 1930), *The Guardsman* (1931), and Ernst Lubitsch's *One Hour with you* (1932). Occasionally in the 1930s he returned to Britain to film, notably in Alexander Korda's *Wedding Rehearsal* (1932), *The Man who could Work Miracles* from H. G. Wells's story (1936), *King Solomon's Mines* (1937), and *Sailing Along* (1938), with Jessie Matthews. He also returned to the New York stage, in *Her Master's Voice*, again by Kummer (1933), *The Distant Shore* and *A Touch of Brimstone* (both 1935), and *Spring Thaw* (1938). Back on the screen Young was a memorable, snivelling Uriah Heep in MGM's splendid, star-laden *David Copperfield*, and excellent as the Earl of Burnstead ('George') in *Ruggles of Red Gap* (both 1935). He became friendly with the humorous writer Thorne Smith, either when in New York or at MGM where Smith briefly worked. How they met is not certain, but both were avid collectors of walking canes and pens. In 1934, the year of Smith's death, Young wrote a brief biography of his friend, *Thorne Smith, his Life and Times*.

Young's friendship with Smith probably led to his greatest film success, *Topper* (1937), in which he played the mild, hen-pecked banker Cosmo Topper, befuddled by two squabbling ghosts (played by Cary Grant and Constance Bennett) who, to gain acceptance into the next world, have to perform a good deed, and decide to teach Topper how to live life to the full. Young was nominated for an Academy award as best supporting actor, and the film's success led to two sequels, in 1939 and 1941. Despite this, his film roles soon became smaller, often being little more than supporting parts, but he was excellent as the whimsical Uncle Willie in *The Philadelphia Story* (1941), and the support he gave was to such stars as Marlene Dietrich, in *The Flame of New Orleans*, and Greta Garbo, in *Two-Faced Woman* (both 1941), and Joan Crawford, in *They All Kissed the Bride* (1942). He was one of the many stars in *Tales of Manhattan* (1942) and *Forever and a Day* (1943), almost stealing the latter. He was on stage again in 1943, in *Ask my Friend Sandy* and *Another Love Story*. He starred in a radio series in 1945 and later became a familiar face on television as he made fewer films. Young returned to Britain in 1947, appearing at St James's theatre in *Truant in Park Lane* and playing the bride's father in the 'dreary' film *Bond Street*. Of his final films a couple, *The Great Lover* (1949) with Bob Hope and

Let's Dance (1950) with Fred Astaire, were fine, but the last two, *St Benny the Dip* (1951) and *That Man from Tangier* (1953), were not.

Young was divorced from his first wife in 1940; he later married (Dorothy) Patience May DuCroz, in 1948. There were no children from either marriage. An animal lover, he collected rare goldfish and porcelain penguins, and loved cartoons. He was also well-read and an active book collector. In his younger days he enjoyed tennis, fishing, and riding. He wrote a book of theatrical caricatures, *Actors and Others*, in 1925 and a book of pictures and verse, *Not for Children*, in 1934. He died at his New York city home on 5 June 1953, survived by his second wife.

ROBERT SHARP

Sources D. Shipman, *The great movie stars: the golden years* (1970) · *The Times* (8 June 1953) · *The Times* (11 June 1953) · *Who was who in the theatre, 1912–1976*, 4 vols. (1978) · b. cert.
Likenesses photographs, *c*.1931–1946, Hult. Arch. · photograph, repro. in Shipman, *Great movie stars*, 570

Young, Rosalind Cecilia Hildegard. *See* Tanner, Rosalind Cecilia Hildegard (1900–1992).

Young, Stuart (1934–1986), accountant and broadcasting executive, was born on 23 April 1934 at home in Stamford Hill, London, the younger child and younger son of Joseph Young, who was in the flour business, and his wife, Rebecca (Betty) Sterling. The family were religious Jews and his mother made Young very conscious of his religious and charitable duties. Indeed, he met his wife on a charity committee when he was only sixteen, and he continued to be active in Jewish and other charities until his death. His brother, David, later became Baron Young of Graffham. He was educated at Woodhouse grammar school, North Finchley, Middlesex, left school at sixteen, and qualified as a chartered accountant in 1956. In that year he married Shirley, daughter of Harry Aarons, a fashion company director; there were two daughters of the marriage.

Young was a highly successful accountant. He set up his own practice in 1958, when he was only twenty-four. From 1960 he was the senior partner of his own firm, Hacker Young. He was hard working and decisive, with a very logical financial mind. In the early 1960s, when his practice was already well established, he began to get business from the interests of Sir Isaac Wolfson, including Great Universal Stores. He became a director of many companies, including Tesco, the food store group (from 1982), and of Caledonian Airways (from 1973).

In the summer of 1981 Young was appointed a governor of the BBC. From the beginning of his term he was uneasy about what he regarded as the financial laxity and the overmanning of the corporation, though he felt great admiration for its broadcasting quality. This contrast between financial concern and admiration for the broadcast product marked his work both as a governor and as chairman of the BBC. Within a few weeks the financial concern led to a confrontation, which he won. The governors had to approve a new contract to promote BBC sales in American television. Young and another governor asked to see the contract; they were told that this would not be customary and that Alasdair Milne, the managing director of BBC television, was reluctant to agree. Young told the chairman, George Howard, that he would not approve a contract that he had not read, whereupon he was shown the contract. When Howard's term came to an end in 1983 Young was appointed chairman of the BBC governors. Margaret Thatcher, as prime minister, wanted the BBC to be put under stronger financial control. By that time Alasdair Milne had succeeded Sir Ian Trethowan as director-general. Young promoted and encouraged Michael Checkland, who was eventually to succeed Milne as director-general, as the member of the board of management who was to carry out the financial reforms he considered urgently necessary.

Within a few weeks of his appointment as chairman Young suffered the first symptoms of the lung cancer which proved fatal to him, and his whole period as chairman was conducted under this disability, which he bore with great courage. His illness allowed him to form a personal link with Alasdair Milne, whose wife suffered from recurrent cancer; Milne had a sympathetic understanding of Young's condition. Yet Young did not feel that Milne had an adequate grasp of the business aspects of running so large a corporation and he did not find in him the partner who might have welcomed necessary reforms. If he had been in better health he might have been more ruthless in dealing with the problems that he recognized. None the less the reforms and the demanning, which were later associated with the chairmanship of Marmaduke Hussey, his successor, were started in Young's time.

During Young's chairmanship, which he regarded as a high honour, there were a number of BBC crises of a characteristic kind. One was the libel action which arose out of *Maggie's Militant Tendency*, a television attack, which proved to be defamatory, on some right-wing Conservative MPs; another was the dispute in late July 1985 between the board of governors and the board of management over the *Real Lives* interviews with Irish terrorists (made contrary to BBC producer guidelines); and a third was the dismissal of Richard Francis as managing director (radio) by Alasdair Milne. In all of these matters Young took a moderate position, trying to reconcile the warring parties in the interest of the BBC as a whole. His period as chairman was circumscribed by his illness; instead of being the radical reforming chairman that he, and Margaret Thatcher, had hoped he might be, he could only start to turn the tide from the extravagant BBC triumphalism of Howard and Milne toward the neo-puritanism of Hussey and John Birt, a later director-general. Young was courteous and friendly to his colleagues and staff. His balanced judgement and diplomatic approach were matched by firmness of purpose.

Young did much charitable work, which included aid for Israel, and he was treasurer of the Joint Israel appeal; he was also involved in local charities in north London, and in heritage appeals. He was a trustee of the National Gallery from 1980. From 1977 he was a member of the finance and investment committee of Wolfson College,

Cambridge, of which he became an honorary fellow in 1983. He was 6 feet tall, good-looking, and always well dressed, and he had a calm and friendly expression. His two passions were chess and golf. Young died of lung cancer at his home in Hampstead Garden Suburb, 29 Ingram Avenue, on 29 August 1986, and was survived by his wife and daughters. A celebration of his life and work was held at Guildhall, London, on 10 December 1986.

REES-MOGG, *rev.*

Sources *The Times* (30 Aug 1986) · *The Times* (11 Dec 1986) · personal knowledge (1996) · private information (1996) · *CGPLA Eng. & Wales* (1986)
Likenesses photograph, repro. in *The Times* (30 Aug 1986)
Wealth at death £1,083,254: probate, 14 Nov 1986, *CGPLA Eng. & Wales*

Young, Sydney (1857–1937), chemist, was born at Farnworth, Lancashire, on 29 December 1857, the third and youngest son of Edward Young JP, a Liverpool merchant, and his first wife, Anne Eliza Gunnery. He was educated at Southport (privately) and at the Royal Institution, Liverpool. At Owens College, Manchester, he studied chemistry under Sir Henry Roscoe and Carl Schorlemmer, matriculating at London University in 1877 and graduating as an external student in 1880. Young then worked under Fittig at Strasbourg and obtained the London DSc in 1883. In those days he was a good swimmer and skater, did some climbing, and painted in watercolours.

In 1882 Young was appointed lecturer in chemistry under William Ramsay at University College, Bristol. He had already published some work, but he now joined Ramsay in a most fruitful partnership which lasted until 1887, when Ramsay was appointed to the chair of chemistry at University College, London, and Young succeeded him at Bristol. Their researches involved accurate measurements of the vapour pressures of solids and liquids at various temperatures, and the examination of the relevant thermodynamic equations. They published more than thirty papers arising from the work of these five years. Many of these are classics of accurate physico-chemical investigation.

From 1887 to 1904 Young, with a succession of collaborators, carried out many studies of the physical properties of pure liquids and of the behaviour of mixed liquids when distilled. Initially the emphasis was on the determination of the vapour pressures, specific volumes, and critical constants of a series of pure liquids, with the particular aim of testing the generalizations of van der Waals regarding corresponding temperatures, pressures, and volumes. Later there was interest in the relationship between physical properties and molecular structure in homologous series and with different functional groups. Young devoted particular attention to the paraffin hydrocarbons; the problems of obtaining pure samples of these led to his investigations of distillation and to the construction of improved forms of the necessary apparatus. With such apparatus he was able to separate pure samples of some of the constituents of American petroleum.

In 1893 Young was elected FRS: his youngest half-brother, the Revd Alfred Young, was elected in 1934 as a mathematician. In 1896 Young married Grace Martha, daughter of James Kimmins, of Stonehouse, Gloucestershire. They had twin sons born in 1897: Sydney Vernon was killed in action at Ypres in 1915; Charles Edgar survived the war and ultimately became headmaster of Rossall School. In 1904 Young succeeded J. E. Reynolds in the chair of chemistry at Trinity College, Dublin. This appointment involved a large increase in his administrative and teaching duties, so that his output of original work was greatly reduced, but from time to time he published articles and books. His *Fractional Distillation* had already appeared in 1903, and *Stoichiometry* followed in 1908, with a second edition in 1918. In 1922 came *Distillation, Principles and Processes*, which was written in collaboration with various experts, and included chapters on the distillation of petroleum, coal tar, alcohol, and so on. Young also wrote for the revised edition (1921–7) of *Thorpe's Dictionary of Applied Chemistry* the articles on 'Distillation', 'Sublimation', and 'Thermometers'. His publications extended from 1880 to 1928.

In 1904 Young was president of the chemical section of the British Association's meeting at Cambridge. He received the honorary degree of ScD from Trinity College, Dublin, in 1905 and that of DSc from Bristol University in 1921. He was a founder fellow of the Institute of Physics, and became a fellow of the Institute of Chemistry in 1888. He was vice-president of the Chemical Society from 1917 to 1920, and a member of the advisory council of the Department of Scientific and Industrial Research from 1920 to 1925. From 1921 to 1926 he was president of the Royal Irish Academy. In 1928 he resigned from his chair and retired to live outside Bristol. After a very brief illness Young died at the Chesterfield Nursing Home, Bristol, on 8 April 1937. His wife survived him.

W. R. G. ATKINS, rev. JOHN SHORTER

Sources W. R. G. Atkins, *Obits. FRS*, 2 (1936–8), 371–9 · F. Francis, *JCS* (1937), 1332–6 · *The Times* (9 April 1937) · *CGPLA Eng. & Wales* (1937)
Archives U. Leeds, Brotherton L., letters to Smithells
Likenesses photograph, repro. in *Obits. FRS*, following p. 371
Wealth at death £15,957 19s. 5d.: resworn probate, 12 June 1937, *CGPLA Eng. & Wales*

Young, (Stewart) Terence Herbert (1915–1994), film director, was born on 20 June 1915 in Shanghai, the son of Stewart Crommie Young, deputy commissioner of police. He came home to be educated, and read history at St Catharine's College, Cambridge. Tall, good-looking, and athletic, he was described by one obituarist as dapper, with 'vivid good looks, his short sleeved sports shirts and the perennial silk handkerchief blossoming from his top jacket pocket' (*The Times*, 8 Sept 1994).

As an undergraduate Young wrote film reviews for *Granta* and took holiday jobs in the studios. After graduation he had several scripts accepted and worked as an assistant director. He continued writing scripts intermittently during the Second World War, in which he served as a captain in the intelligence corps of the guards armoured division, and during which he was wounded. On 24 June 1942 he married Dorothea Alice (Dosia) Nissen (*b.* 1913/14),

daughter of William Bennett, medical practitioner, and divorced wife of Erik Martin Ruzt Nissen. They had a son and two daughters, and remained married for more than fifty years.

For a few years after the war Young directed films for mainstream British companies with big studios, but he got poor reviews and was savagely criticized by such serious critics as Graham Greene and the new wave of young cineastes. After this, for several years he worked on the fringes of the industry in small independent companies, often set up for a single film. From the early 1950s the government subsidized film production in Britain by the Eady levy. This attracted American finance and two experienced Hollywood executives, Albert (Cubby) Broccoli and Irving Allen, formed Warwick Pictures to produce run-of-the-mill films in Britain, bringing an American star for each. Four of these were directed by Terence Young. His connection with Broccoli was to have a profound effect on his career, and in 1961 his luck changed dramatically.

Enter James Bond, 'licensed to kill'. The first of Ian Fleming's novels featuring Bond had appeared in 1953. Harry Saltzman, a Canadian Hollywood executive now in England, went into partnership with Broccoli as Eon Productions and acquired options on the novels, but investors hung back. Eventually they raised reluctant backing from United Artists. They went into production with *Dr. No* at Pinewood in early 1961, with a modest budget and no great expectations, and Broccoli engaged Young to direct it. For 007 he appointed a little-known Scottish actor, Sean Connery. The far-fetched tale of Bond's exploits had ingredients which were to recur in further Bond films—an evil master-criminal, a vaguely cold war background, a threatened world calamity, M, 007's boss at MI5, and his secretary, Miss Moneypenny, spectacular settings and exotic locations, hilariously unlikely gadgetry to get the hero out of apparently hopeless predicaments, and gorgeous girls.

To general surprise *Dr. No* (1962) was a runaway success, and set the pattern for the many Bond films that followed, even those with different directors and Bonds. Three of the first four were directed by Young, whose input was considerable. He later claimed he had felt the need to 'heat up' and give 'pace' to the original story, which he dismissed as B-movie stuff. The result was a fast, tongue-in-cheek comic strip treatment, an enjoyable spoof spy film, with its sex and violence robbed of offensiveness by the general air of nonsense. The contribution of production designer Ken Adams, and Connery's personification of the hero (with his delightful throwaway asides) as rough, tough, and sexy—which immediately made him a star—also became part of the style which was to become known to those involved in making the films as 'Bondian'.

They made *From Russia with Love* (1963) with twice the budget and even greater success. The third film, *Goldfinger* (1964), was to have been directed by Young but he fell out with Eon over money and it was directed by Guy Hamilton. Now held to be a useful director of blockbusters, Young was engaged by a mainstream producer, Marcel Hellman, to make *The Amorous Adventures of Moll Flanders* (1965) as a successor to the recent roisterous eighteenth-century classic *Tom Jones* (1963). But this was not a success, possibly partly because of the strange miscasting of Kim Novak as the bawdy heroine. After another extremely successful Bond film by Young, *Thunderball* (1965), he resumed his disjointed and disappointing career, with only one more outstanding film, the American film *Wait until Dark* (1967). A tense and claustrophobic study of a blind woman terrorized in her own home by thugs, this brilliant film starred Audrey Hepburn, who was nominated for an Oscar.

Young continued to make films until the early 1980s, but once more on the fringes of commercial production. A fluent linguist, as before he worked frequently in France, Italy, and other countries, but hardly ever for mainstream companies. The resulting films were not always shown in Britain. He was an eclectic film-maker, often drawn to out of the way subjects such as a French film of four ballets by Roland Petit. He even strayed into the bizarre. An early film, *Corridor of Mirrors* (1948), had a hero and heroine who believed they were reincarnations of lovers in a painting. Many fine actors appeared in his films but few gave their best performances. After 1974 he at last got a foothold in Hollywood and made several films there, but none of them was successful. One, *Inchon*, made in 1979 with money provided by the Moonies religious sect, featured Laurence Olivier as General MacArthur during the Korean War, receiving divine guidance—tipped by some as possibly the worst film ever made.

The brilliant success of the three Bond films Young made for Broccoli at Pinewood and the outstanding film *Wait until Dark* for Warner Brothers suggest that his early promise might have been better served by working in a more stable production and studio set-up. He died of a heart attack in hospital in Cannes on 7 September 1994, after a long and uneven career. He was survived by his wife and three children.   RACHAEL LOW

Sources *The Times* (8 Sept 1994) · *Daily Telegraph* (10 Sept 1994) · *The Independent* (16 Sept 1994) · *Time Magazine* (19 Sept 1994) · J. Walker, ed., *Halliwell's film and video guide*, 14th edn (1999) · D. Gifford, *The British film catalogue, 1895–1985: a reference guide*, [2nd edn] (1986) · E. Katz, *The international film encyclopedia* (1980) · J. Woollacott, 'The James Bond films: conditions of production', *British cinema history*, ed. J. Curran and V. Porter (1983), 208–25 · G. Perry, *Movies from the mansion* (1976) · R. Grimes, *A critical history of British cinema* (1978), 254–7 · M. Dickinson and S. Street, *Cinema and state* (1985) · J. Brosnan, *James Bond in the cinema* (1972) · J. G. Pearson, *The life of Ian Fleming* (1966) · m. cert.
Archives FILM BFI NFTVA
Likenesses photograph, 1963, repro. in *Independent*

Young, Thomas (1507–1568), archbishop of York, was born at Hodgeston, near Lamphey, Pembrokeshire, the son of John Young and Eleanor, his wife. He was a student at Broadgates Hall, Oxford, graduating BA in 1529 and MA in 1533.

Early career in Wales and Emden According to a later report of John Philpott, Young had studied civil law for some years before taking holy orders. He was appointed principal of his hall in 1542 and resigned in 1546. By this time he had become vicar of Llanfihangel Castle, Walter, Cardiganshire (1541), and in close succession rector of Hodgeston and Nashwith-Upton (1542) and prebendary of Trallong in the collegiate church of Abergwili, near Carmarthen (1545). In 1542 he became precentor of St David's, entering into residence in 1547, though his time in the cathedral was marked by an acrimonious dispute with the new bishop and later Marian martyr, Robert Ferrar. On his appointment in 1548 Ferrar accused Young and the chancellor, Roland Meyrick, of having despoiled the see during the vacancy; the two men were alleged to have made away with crosses, chalices, and other plate to the value of 500 marks or more. Both were dismissed and promptly drew up counter-articles against their bishop. It was in pursuit of this suit that Ferrar found himself in London in 1553 at the time of Edward VI's death. The bishop was arrested and condemned; following the passage of the appropriate legislation he became one of the first of the Marian martyrs. Young is said to have visited him in prison and asked his forgiveness for the unseemly wrangle in St David's.

On Mary's accession Young was at least prepared boldly to aver his own protestantism. He was one of the six protestant divines who defended the faith at the convocation of 1553, as John Philpott records. This made him a marked man, and he soon after elected to join the exile abroad; though not apparently without attempting to secure some continuing benefit from his Welsh benefices by leasing his prebend at Lampeter to George Lee, a Calais merchant and brother to his close friend Thomas Lee. Like others leaving the country, Young attempted to obscure his intentions by antedating the lease, a common enough stratagem, but in this case unavailing. Little was previously known of this phase of his life, but documents which came to light in Germany in the 1990s confirm that he spent the entirety of Mary's reign in Emden, the most northerly of the exile congregations. Indeed he played a far more prominent role in the affairs of the church there than was formerly recognized. Also, the church had more members (about 100) and was better organized: it met for services three times a week and followed a church order and discipline modelled on John à Lasco's church order for the London stranger church, the *Forma ac Ratio*. Young served as one of the two ministers, alongside John Scory, former bishop of Rochester; he enrolled as a citizen of Emden on 5 November 1555. They were assisted in the care of the congregation by six elders and nine deacons. Both ministers were of a stubborn and disputatious temper, and this was reflected in a bitter dispute with one of their own members, John Dowley. Dowley had taken offence that the congregation had moved its services from the normal place of worship close to a house infected by the plague. When he pursued the matter, the ministers denounced him in open church. Young, who was described in the proceedings as well trained in English jurisprudence, took a particularly prominent part against him. The case was appealed by Dowley to the local town community, which, perhaps inflamed by the refusal of the English ministers to appear and answer, essentially ruled in Dowley's favour.

St David's and York On the death of Mary, Young swiftly returned to England. With a chequered and not particularly successful career behind him he was not initially marked out for high office; his gradual but inexorable rise to one of the greatest prizes of the new church hierarchy is among the most fascinating tales of the Elizabethan settlement. He was not on Cecil's early lists of those intended for episcopal positions, but refusals on the part of some of the leading candidates, together with the queen's aversion to any taint of Genevan influence, opened the path to higher things. Young certainly proved himself an able courtier. Named to both the Canterbury visitation and the western circuit (the Welsh dioceses and Hereford and Worcester), he demonstrated his zeal for the new settlement with a long, arduous summer ensuring its enforcement. By the autumn he was earmarked for a return to St David's, but now as bishop. He was elected on 6 December 1559, confirmed on 18 January following, and consecrated at Lambeth three days later. On 23 March he obtained the restitution of his temporalities. But Young did not have to content himself with the modest Welsh see for long. In the matter of the temporalities he had secured the good offices of Lord Robert Dudley, and this proved to be an enduring alliance. Archbishop Parker too became a generous patron. Already in April 1560 he had written to hint to Young that he might expect 'other places … more honourable and more profitable' than St David's (Bruce and Perowne, 114).

Meanwhile the new establishment's failure to provide for the northern province was becoming ever more scandalous and urgent. When consideration turned in the summer of 1560 to filling the vacant positions Parker was quick to nominate Young: 'if you would have a lawyer at York, the Bishop of St David's, Dr Young, is both witty, prudent, and temperate, and man-like' (Bruce and Perowne, 123). With such an endorsement and the support of the new court favourite, Dudley, Young's success was assured. He was elected archbishop on 27 January 1561 and confirmed on 5 February, and received restoration of his temporalities on 4 March. Even here he was marked by conspicuous signs of royal favour, being assessed for the first fruit due to the crown on a careful survey which set them at the modest figure of £1449 (against an assessment in the *valor ecclesiasticus* of £2036). This was at pains to point out that a figure of £130 13s. 7d. had been abated by royal warrant because of the queen's 'favourable consideration' of Young himself.

Once established in the northern province Young was notable for an absence of crusading zeal. The puritan Thomas Wood singled him out as one of the most infamous of the non-preaching bishops. A fairer assessment might regard him as pragmatic, rather than negligent. The north country was notoriously conservative, and he had few supporters for a campaign for active evangelism, even in the limited urban centres of his diocese. In the 1564 survey of religious opinions demanded by the government Young was able to return only two of York's thirteen aldermen as favourers of religion. It may have been that a more active policy might simply have provoked a more adverse reaction. Arguably, the limited popular support for the rising of the northern earls in 1569 may be considered the ultimate test of his pragmatic policies.

An archbishop's occupations In truth Young was first and foremost a royal agent and administrator. In 1564 he was named president of the council of the north, a signal mark of royal confidence, for which he received a stipend of £666 13s. 4d. per annum. In the large questions of ecclesiastical politics he offered Parker strong support, at the same time continuing assiduously to cultivate his relationship with Dudley. In the controversy over clerical dress in 1566 Young stoutly upheld Parker's *Advertisements* with none of the apparent misgivings of several of his fellow bishops, smoothly assuring the queen that her firmness would be 'a very great comfort to many good subjects that now stand amazed and discouraged' (Collinson, 73). The obligation to Dudley proved increasingly burdensome, since the royal favourite was not slow to exploit his position with former clients upon whom he had special claims. A series of disadvantageous land transactions was the result. Towards the end of his life Young was bold enough to refuse the earl a requested loan of £1000 on the grounds that he was too poor, only to be compromised by the discovery of a shipload of lead from the roof of York palace hall which he had consigned for sale in London.

The management of the archiepiscopal estates perforce absorbed a great deal of Young's attention in the northern counties. Always the supplicant in his relationship with Dudley, locally the tables were turned, and Young was the recipient of useful favours from compliant local powers. In 1565 he was given an exceptionally long lease on a city moat and rampart (useful grazing ground) by York city council, so that he should 'contynewe good and gracyouse lord to this city' (Palliser, 265). The archbishop responded by inviting a mayor of York, Robert Paycok, to act as godfather to his son George. Young was an assiduous steward of the interests of his family, having provided his elder son, Thomas, to the prebend of Barnby in 1561, when the boy was only sixteen. Local opinion would hardly have censured him for this: later in the century Archbishop Sandys was far more energetic in the pursuit of offices for a larger family. A more serious charge was that he abused his office and from motives of personal gain sometimes advanced men who were scarcely favourable to the Reformation. One protégé, Sir John Constable, was removed from the council of the north in 1567, only a year after Young had supported his appointment, on the grounds of his untrustworthy reputation in matters of religion. Venal or not, the archbishop seems to have been a more than capable manager of his lands and flocks. An inventory of his goods at the time of his death records that he had corn in stock to the value of £113 and livestock worth £324, including a flock of over 800 sheep. Indeed he seems to have been exceptionally successful in husbanding the meagre assets of his northern see. The account of his administrator reveals an inventory of goods worth £2657 and good debts of over £1000. Part of this capital was realized by the questionable practice of lending money at interest, though he was not alone among his fellow bishops in resorting to this.

There is also more than a hint that in his capacity as president of the northern council Young exploited his position as judge for private gain. His successor as president, the third earl of Sussex, made short shrift of cases that Young had unaccountably allowed to linger in the court; though the extent to which this might have been attributable to his failing powers in old age rather than to deliberate corruption is difficult to determine. Certainly in early 1567 he was provided with a suffragan (Richard Barnes, chancellor of York, who became bishop of Nottingham) because of his age.

Young died at Sheffield on 26 June 1568 and was buried in York Minster. He married twice. His first wife (forename unknown) was a daughter of George Constantine, registrar of St David's and subsequently a fellow exile with Young in Emden. Following her death he married Jane, daughter of Thomas Kynaston of Estwick, Staffordshire; she was the mother of his son George, who was later knighted.

ANDREW PETTEGREE

Sources C. H. Garrett, *The Marian exiles: a study in the origins of Elizabethan puritanism* (1938) · A. Pettegree, 'The English church at Emden', *Marian protestantism: six studies* (1996), 10–38 · B. Usher, 'William Cecil and episcopacy' [unpublished manuscript] · M. Bateson, ed., 'A collection of original letters from the bishops to the privy council, 1564', *Camden miscellany, IX*, CS, new ser., 53 (1893) · F. Heal, *Of prelates and princes: a study of the economic and social position of the Tudor episcopate* (1980) · D. M. Palliser, *Tudor York* (1979) · P. Collinson, *The Elizabethan puritan movement* (1967), 73 · *Correspondence of Matthew Parker*, ed. J. Bruce and T. T. Perowne, Parker Society, 42 (1853) · J. Philpott, *The trew report of the dysputacyon* (1554) · G. Williams, *Wales and the Reformation* (1997) · G. E. Aylmer and R. Cant, eds., *A history of York Minster* (1977) · R. R. Reid, *The king's council in the north* (1921); facs. edn (1975) · Emden, *Oxf.*, 4.652–3 · *The letters of Thomas Wood, puritan, 1566–1577*, ed. P. Collinson (1960) · E. B. Fryde and others, eds., *Handbook of British chronology*, 3rd edn, Royal Historical Society Guides and Handbooks, 2 (1986)

Likenesses effigy? on monument, York Minster

Wealth at death assets in hand or realizable totalling just over £4000: F. Heal, *Of prelates and princes: a study of the economic and social position of the Tudor episcopate* (1980), 290, 313

Young, Thomas (*c.*1587–1655), Church of England clergyman and college head, was probably born in Luncarty, Perthshire, about 1587, if the age at death recorded on his memorial at Stowmarket is accurate. He was the son of William Young (*d.* 1625), who served as minister of several parishes in Perthshire (Pitcairne, Auchtergaven, and Redgorton as well as Luncarty), and his wife, Janet Glas. He had a sister, Janet, who later married John Crookshanks, eventually William Young's successor at Luncarty. Thomas attended the grammar school at Perth before matriculating at St Leonard's College, St Andrews, in 1602. He graduated MA in July 1606, one of eighteen students designated in the college registers as being of the poorer class. That year his father, a vocal presbyterian, opposed the introduction into Scotland of a powerful episcopate backed by the crown.

During the next seven years Young may have pursued ministerial training on the continent before moving to

London. Comments in Thomas Gataker's *Londinatis cinnus, sive, Adversaria miscellanea* (1651) and Simeon Ashe's *Gray Hayres Crowned with Grace* (1655) indicate that Young lived with and worked as assistant to Gataker at Rotherhithe, Surrey, some time after the latter became rector there in 1611. But Young apparently also maintained ties with Scotland. In 1614 he was appointed to the vicarage of Resolis in Ross, a living he held until 1649, largely as a non-resident. Two other records connect him to the parish (he witnessed charters for the bishop of Ross in 1618 and 1635) and confirm that Young became a pluralist early in his ministerial career; he remained one until the last years of his life. Over the next four decades he can be found on several occasions travelling between England and Scotland, presumably to fulfil responsibilities in each location.

In either 1617 or 1618 Young became the tutor of the future poet John Milton, probably because Gataker recommended him to his good friend Richard Stock, the Milton family's rector at All Hallows, Bread Street. Details concerning the actual arrangement are ambiguous (it is unclear where the instruction took place) and further compounded by evidence linking Young during this time to Rotherhithe and parishes in Essex and Hertfordshire (Ware). Some time before April 1620 Young's instruction of Milton ended with his appointment as chaplain to the English Merchant Adventurers in Hamburg. Parish registers record his presence there from this month, together with his wife, Rebecca, whom he had married at an unknown date, and about whom little is known.

It is not clear whether Young's departure from England was for religious, economic or other reasons. However his eight-year ministry in Hamburg was successful and he referred to it in his writings with fondness. On 24 March 1621 Joseph Mead wrote to Sir Martin Stuteville that Young was invited to preach in front of Frederick V, the exiled king of Bohemia, and had received a chain of gold for his efforts. Perhaps mindful that he would eventually have to return to England, Young maintained relations with notable individuals like Mead and the royal librarian Patrick Young by writing letters and making periodic visits to London and Cambridge. Two letters and a verse epistle, *Elegia quarta*, from his former pupil testify to the affection and respect Milton and Young continued to have for each other through the 1620s. Milton praised his tutor as 'a pastor illustrious for his honor of the primitive faith and well instructed how to feed the sheep that love Christ'; this was a man under whose guidance Milton 'first visited the Aonian retreats and the sacred lawns of the twin-peaked mountains' (*Elegia quarta*, ed. M. Hughes, 1957, 26–7). Their mutual regard is also illustrated by their exchange of presents: a Hebrew Bible (now lost) to Milton; a copy of Thomas Cranmer's *Reformatio legum ecclesiasticarum* to Young.

On 27 March 1628 Young returned to England and was instituted to the living of St Peter and St Mary, Stowmarket, Suffolk. This parish was his permanent home for the rest of his life, although he lived elsewhere for extended periods of time. For the next seven years (1628–35) he remained largely in residence, as evidenced by his signature of the parish vestry accounts and his participation in the combination lecture at Mendlesham. However, from 1638 his signature ceased and the church controversies resulting from the reform policies of Archbishop William Laud increasingly took Young to London. By 1635 he had begun work on his principal work, *Dies dominica*, a sabbatarian apology and effective attack on the Book of Sports, published anonymously in 1639. By 1640 he was meeting with puritan clergy and may have joined William Spurstowe and others in the gatherings which met at the house of Edmund Calamy, minister of St Mary Aldermanbury. Following the publication by Bishop Joseph Hall of *Episcopacie by Divine Right* (1640) and *An Humble Remonstrance to the High Court of Parliament* (1641) Young, with Spurstowe, Calamy, Stephen Marshall, and Matthew Newcomen, writing under the name Smectymnuus, launched an attack on 'the prelaticall church'. In *An Answer to … an Humble Remonstrance* (1641) the group, apparently led by Young, argued for the parity of bishops and presbyters in scripture and for the antiquity of church government by ruling elders rather than bishops. When Hall defended his position, they replied with *A Vindication of the Answer* (1641). Their cause was supported by Milton who contributed five anti-prelatical tracts of his own in 1641 and 1642, the most overtly supportive entitled *An Apology for Smectymnuus*. While the exchange contained much reasoned argument, it was also characterized by some strong and abusive language which, together with the distinctive acronym, ensured that the episode remained fresh in the popular mind for some time afterwards. In 1647 the poet John Cleveland poked fun in the verse 'Smectymnuus, or, The clus divines', while *Smectymnuus redivivus*, stating the ministers' own case, was reissued as late as 1680.

The outbreak of the civil war kept Young in London. In 1643 the earl of Manchester appointed him to the parish of St James's, Duke's Place, and during the same year he was nominated to represent Suffolk in the Westminster assembly of divines. Young was among the more active members, arguing the presbyterian position from the outset, and was among those deputed to negotiate with the Scottish commissioners. He also signed the anti-Independent, anti-sectarian pamphlet *Certain Considerations* (1643). In February 1644 he delivered a fast-day sermon to parliament, published as *Hope's Encouragement* (1644). While remaining active in the assembly until its regular sessions petered out in 1648, on 12 April 1644 Young was installed as master of Jesus College, Cambridge. Here he did not hesitate to use his position to secure appointments for his sons Thomas, Roger, and Henry. He proceeded DD in 1649, but, suspected of writing a remonstrance against the engagement, and refusing to take it, he was ejected from Jesus College on 1 January 1651. He returned to Stowmarket where his wife was buried that April. His signature on the vestry accounts resumed in 1652, although his activities from that point remain unclear. He died at Stowmarket on 28 November 1655, and was buried in the parish church on 1 December; Simeon Ashe's funeral sermon was published as *Gray Hayres Crowned with Grace* (1655). In his will, drawn up on 27 September 1653 and proved on 31 January 1656, Young left to his son and executor Roger land in Suffolk, which had been placed in the hands of trustees, Francis Bacon of Ipswich, John Hale of Mildenhall, Anthony Bedingfield of London, and John Haynard of Stowmarket. Other beneficiaries included his son Henry, his grandchildren Elizabeth and John Torell, and the poor of Stowmarket.

EDWARD JONES

Sources S. Ashe, *Gray hayres crowned with grace* (1655) · D. Laing, *Biographical notices of Thomas Young, S.T.D.* (1870) · *Fasti Scot.*, new edn, 4.241, 243 · Venn, *Alum. Cant.* · will, PRO, PROB 11/252, sig. 27 · H. F. Fletcher, 'Richard Stock, rector of All Hallows Church, Bread Street, and his friend, Thomas Gataker' and 'Thomas Young', *The intellectual development of John Milton*, 1 (1956), 63–72, 136–53 · A. Barker, 'Milton's schoolmasters', *Modern Language Review*, 32 (1937), 517–36 · T. Gataker, *Londinatis cinnus, sive, Adversaria miscellanea* (1651) · A. G. H. Hollingsworth, *The history of Stowmarket* (1844) · R. S. Paul, *The assembly of the Lord: politics and religion in the Westminster assembly and the 'Grand debate'* (1985) · W. M. Hetherington, *History of the Westminster Assembly of Divines* (1843) · W. R. Parker, 'Milton and Thomas Young, 1620–28', *Modern Language Notes*, 53 (1938), 399–407 · T. Webster, *Godly clergy in early Stuart England: the Caroline puritan movement, c.1620–1643* (1997) · *Patricius Junius (Patrick Young), Bibliothekar der Könige Jacob I und Carl I. von England: Mitteilungen aus seinem Briefwechsel*, ed. J. Kemke (Leipzig, 1898) · N. Evans, ed., *The wills of the archdeaconry of Sudbury, 1630–35*, Suffolk RS, 29 (1987), 263, no. 627 · T. Birch, *The court and times of James I* (1849) · registers, U. St Andr. · parish register, Stowmarket, April 1651 [burial of Rebecca Young] · parish register, Stowmarket, 1 Dec 1651 [burial]

Archives Jesus College, Cambridge, college registers · U. St Andr., college registers, St Leonards

Likenesses photozincography copy (after portrait at Stowmarket), repro. in Laing, *Biographical notices* · portrait, Stowmarket vicarage

Young, Thomas (1773–1829), physician and natural philosopher, was born on 13 June 1773 at Milverton, Somerset, the eldest of ten children of Thomas Young, cloth merchant and banker, and his wife, Sarah, daughter of Robert Davis of Minehead, Somerset, and his wife, Hannah Brocklesby. Both parents were active and strict members of the Society of Friends who impressed Quaker values on their son.

Education Young's early years were spent at the home of his maternal grandfather, who encouraged his education and introduced him to classical literature. After a short stay at a 'miserable boarding-school' (Peacock, 4) he moved in 1782 to a school in Compton Abbas, Dorset—presumably a Friends' school—run by a Mr Thompson. There he studied Latin, Greek, mathematics, and natural philosophy, and one of the ushers also taught him various mechanical skills. Although Young's formal schooling lasted some six years it is clear that he was partially, if not largely, self-taught. Leaving the school in 1787 he joined the household of the Quaker banker David Barclay at Youngsbury, Hertfordshire. Here Young became the tutor and companion to Barclay's grandson Hudson Gurney, who was only two years his junior. They were later joined at Youngsbury by John Hodgkin, a Quaker tutor who was likewise an accomplished classical scholar.

Thomas Young (1773–1829), by Charles Turner, pubd 1830 (after Sir Thomas Lawrence, after 1820)

With the encouragement of his mother's uncle Dr Richard Brocklesby, who had tended him during an extended illness, Young decided to pursue the career of a physician. Moving to London he attended the medical school founded by William Hunter and, in 1793, entered St Bartholomew's Hospital. During this period he attended lectures delivered by many of the key men on the London medical circuit including John Hunter, William Cumberland Cruikshank, James Edward Smith, and Matthew Baillie. In 1794 he also attended chemical lectures at the home of Bryan Higgins and gained some familiarity with experimental techniques that Higgins encouraged in his students. Moreover, through Brocklesby the young Quaker was introduced to many of the leading lights of London society. With his developing interest in science and his eye on a successful medical career he was drawn towards the Royal Society of London. Before his twentieth birthday he presented his first paper to the society and was elected in June 1794, his election being supported by Brocklesby and fifteen others including several medical men of high standing.

Young has sometimes been hailed as a child prodigy who, by the age of sixteen, had not only mastered Latin and Greek but also possessed a good working knowledge of several other languages and gained a firm background in the sciences. He clearly possessed considerable mental abilities, while his Quaker upbringing encouraged the habit of hard work and proscribed frivolous activities. So effective was his training that later in life he claimed never to have wasted a single day. While his academic interests were also encouraged by his parents and teachers they would not have supported his growing enthusiasm for both music and dancing. Membership of the Quaker community also stood in the way of his career. In the heady life of London the socially ambitious Young cast off the distinctive dress and modes of address accepted by his parents. When he moved to Edinburgh in October 1794 a certificate slowly followed from the Westminster monthly meeting passing responsibility to the Edinburgh Friends, and another certificate was subsequently issued by the Edinburgh monthly meeting after he left the city. However, Young had probably forsaken many of his parents' religious principles by the time he arrived in Edinburgh. Quaker bureaucracy appears not to have been particularly efficient since it was only in February 1798 that he was formally disowned. The appropriate minute noted that Young had 'attended places of public diversion' (RS Friends, Lond., Dictionary of Quaker biography). Indeed by the time he arrived in Edinburgh, if not before, he frequented the theatre and took lessons in dancing and playing the flute. When interviewed by a deputation from the Westminster meeting-house he evinced no remorse about his conduct, but 'by his own acknowledgement [was] estranged from us in principle and practice' (ibid.). He subsequently became a member of the Church of England.

Two other events deserve notice. The death of Young's kinsman Richard Brocklesby in 1797 provided him with a comfortable living. He inherited Brocklesby's London house, his library, pictures, and a sum of £10,000. Additional income was subsequently derived from his medical practice, his various scientific, medical, and civic appointments, and from his numerous literary ventures. One further source of income was the £500 per annum he received between 1824 and 1829 from the Palladian Insurance Company as its physician and inspector of calculations. The second event was his marriage on 14 June 1804 to Eliza (1785–1859), second daughter of James Primrose Maxwell, who was related to the aristocratic Maxwells of Calderwood. Through this marriage, which was childless, Young further strengthened his position within the London establishment.

Meanwhile, between 1794 and 1799, Young's pursuit of a medical education had taken him to universities in three countries. The medical school at Edinburgh was still in its heyday and attracted large numbers of students, including many from dissenting backgrounds. Here he attended lectures spanning materia medica (Francis Home), chemistry (Joseph Black), and anatomy and surgery (Alexander Monro secundus). Although Young recognized the quality of medical education in Edinburgh his comments on his lecturers were less than generous. Yet he continued his classical studies, was a voracious reader, and improved his dancing and flute playing. After touring Scotland in the summer of 1795 he enrolled at the University of Göttingen, which he appears to have found more intellectually challenging than Edinburgh. Not only did he attend lectures on various branches of medicine but also on history and natural philosophy. He even found time for twice-weekly lessons in drawing, riding, dancing, and playing the clavichord. Before he departed from Göttingen he submitted his dissertation, entitled 'De corporis humani viribus conservatricibus', and graduated doctor of physic in July 1796.

A London practice It is not clear why Young subsequently decided to continue his education at Cambridge. Regulations relating to the admission of fellows of the Royal College of Physicians had recently changed and Young, having spent but one year at both Edinburgh and Göttingen, may not have been eligible for a fellowship. He may therefore have decided to seek a Cambridge degree. Having passed six terms in residence at Emmanuel College (1797–9), he gained his MB in 1803. However, he appears to have spent as much time as possible in London. Setting up practice in Welbeck Street as soon as he left Cambridge, Young tried to make a name for himself in affluent London circles. Despite his dedication to medicine, his practice developed slowly. In 1808 he obtained his MD from Cambridge, the earliest date under the university's regulations.

During the next few years Young's career progressed rapidly. In 1808 he also obtained the coveted fellowship of the Royal College of Physicians and delivered the Croonian lecture, entitled 'The function of the heart and arteries' at the Royal Society. In 1810–11 he delivered two courses of medical lectures at the Middlesex Hospital. Then, early in 1811, he was appointed physician at St George's Hospital, a position he held until his death. As well as his hospital practice and his private one, he spent most summers in Worthing where he tended his patients on their vacations. Young was probably reasonably effective as a physician but he did not possess a congenial bedside manner and experienced difficulty in attracting patients. By temperament he was more inclined to literary and scientific studies than to being a practising physician. It is perhaps fitting that one of his main contributions to medicine was his carefully compiled *Introduction to Medical Literature* (1813; second edition, 1823) in which he provided a detailed taxonomy of diseases. In both 1813 and 1823 he served as one of the censors of the Royal College of Physicians, where he delivered an endowed Croonian lecture in 1822–3.

Optics Although Young's medical career started slowly it enabled him to devote a considerable amount of time to studying various scientific subjects. While still a student in London he read to the Royal Society a paper postulating that the eye's ability to accommodate to objects at various distances was due to the deformation of its crystalline lens. This conclusion was subsequently supported in his more carefully argued Bakerian lecture for 1800, entitled 'The mechanism of the eye'. The propagation of sound provided another early research topic. Although he first engaged with the subject in his Göttingen dissertation, he subsequently developed it in a series of papers in which he sought to account for various acoustical phenomena in terms of the vibration of particles composing the medium of transmission. In particular, he explained 'beats' as resulting from the mechanical effect of two vibrations.

His main contribution to this topic, which was read before the Royal Society in January 1800, contained a concluding section in which he explored the analogy between sound and light. Here we find his initial attempt to articulate a wave theory of light on the assumption that light is also a vibratory motion; for Young, light was a longitudinal vibration of particles composing a ubiquitous ether.

Young's immersion in physical optics must be related to an important two-year diversion to his career. The Royal Institution, which had been founded by Count Rumford and others in 1799, appointed him to its professorship of natural philosophy in July 1801. With a salary of £300 and rooms at the institution he became superintendent of the house and editor of its journals. Yet the most challenging aspect of his appointment was the preparation of an extensive course on natural philosophy which he delivered on two occasions; fifty lectures in 1802 and sixty in 1803. His lectures were not very well received since he pitched their content far above the capabilities of his audience. However, in preparing these courses, which covered mechanics, hydrodynamics, astronomy, and physics, he was forced to analyse critically a wide range of topics and in many areas he made small but significant innovations. The lectures were subsequently published as *A Course of Lectures on Natural Philosophy and the Mechanical Arts* (2 vols., 1807; revised by P. Kelland, 2 vols., 1845), and were dedicated to Thomas Grenville. Here, for example, we find the definition of the modulus of elasticity that has become associated with Young's name. One major theme linking several of these lectures was his attempt to construct a unified natural philosophy based on a ubiquitous ether. In this he developed some of the queries added to the 1717 edition of Newton's *Opticks*. However, in contrast to Newton he suggested that ether was attracted to gross bodies so as to form atmospheres around them. Although somewhat successful in explaining thermal, electrical, magnetic, and optical phenomena by this ether density hypothesis, he soon abandoned it, and it did not appear in the published version of his lectures.

The majority of Young's contemporaries followed Newton in accepting that light consists of small particles emitted from luminous sources at high speeds and in rejecting all theories that attributed light to a vibration in the ubiquitous ether. As noted above, in his acoustical paper of 1800 Young explored the analogy between light and sound and here he followed Leonhard Euler in propounding a vibratory theory in which the perceived colour of light depends on the frequency of the vibrating ether, such that the longest wavelengths correspond to the red end of the visible spectrum. Here he also attempted to show that the standard arguments against wave theories carried little weight. In November 1801 he presented to the Royal Society a more sustained defence of wave optics. In this Bakerian lecture entitled 'On the theory of light and colours' he sought to extend the theory's explanatory power by integrating it with his ether density hypothesis. One significant innovation was the application to optics of the principle of interference which he had developed in his work on acoustics. He envisaged two nearly parallel light rays meeting so that the ether particle at that point would undertake a combination of the two vibratory motions; depending on the phase relationship, this might result in either constructive or destructive interference. In this and two subsequent publications he showed how this two-ray account of interference could explain such phenomena as the colours of thin plates and those seen when a fibre is held close to the eye. Only in the published *Lectures* of 1807 did he apply his principle of interference to the two-slit experiment which has become associated with his name.

Young's early attempts at framing a wave theory suffered from internal contradictions. Few took either his theory or his notion of interference seriously, and we have to wait a decade and a half for Augustin Fresnel's far more complete and mathematically sophisticated articulation of wave interference which helped to convince many of the superiority of a wave theory of light. In the meantime Young made several minor contributions to the explanation of polarization and double refraction that Étienne Malus, David Brewster, François Arago, and Fresnel were rapidly developing. In 1817 Young sought to extend the scope of the wave theory by suggesting that polarization might be explained on the assumption that light is a transverse vibration of the ether particles. In contrast to Fresnel's far more incisive pronouncements on this issue Young remained rather uncertain and even pointed out in 1823 the awkward implication that transverse vibrations required the luminiferous ether to be 'not only highly elastic, but [also] absolutely solid!!!' (*Works of Thomas Young*, 1855, 1.415)

In his 1801 Bakerian lecture Young also laid the basis of his theory of colour sensation. In rejecting the view, often attributed to Newton, that each ray of light corresponded to one of seven distinct spectral colours, Young conceived the visible spectrum as continuous. Moreover, a continuous spectrum seemed also to undermine the theory that required each point on the retina to contain a vast number of receptors, each tuned to a different frequency. Instead he proposed that colour vision could be explained if there were just three types of receptor, according to the three principal colours—red, yellow, and blue. He subsequently modified this theory in his published *Lectures* and in his 1817 article on 'Chromatics'. In his mature theory he postulated just three types of receptor, corresponding to the colours red, green, and violet. He claimed that this was the simplest theory and that any intermediate frequency, or colour, of light would affect more than one receptor. Thus yellow light would affect equally the green and red receptors, while white light would have an equal effect on all three. Hermann von Helmholtz subsequently rediscovered the three-colour theory, which is now generally known as the Young–Helmholtz theory.

Although Young is often remembered for advancing theories especially in optics, it should be remembered that much of his literary output was far less innovative. As a man of considerable erudition and an inveterate reader and writer, Young participated in many literary ventures, contributing at various times and on a variety of subjects, to the *Gentleman's Magazine*, the *British Magazine*, the *Imperial Magazine*, the *Journal of the Royal Institution*, the *Quarterly Review*, Brande's *Philosophical Review*, and the *Nautical Almanac* (which he edited from 1818). He also contributed over sixty anonymous articles to a supplement of the *Encyclopaedia Britannica* edited by Mcvey Napier. Many of these were biographies—including those of Richard Porson and Lagrange—but others dealt with technological and scientific subjects. Although some of these articles were highly derivative, others show Young's ability to draw out and develop his own understanding of a complex subject. Perhaps the most innovative were his articles on 'Egypt', 'Tides', and 'Chromatics'.

Royal Society activities Young played an active role in the affairs of the Royal Society, being its foreign secretary for a quarter of a century beginning in 1804 and a regular attender at council meetings. For much of this time he served under the presidency of Joseph Banks and he readily identified with Banks's vision of the society as a club for gentlemen interested in science. Satisfied with the current system of patronage he was generally viewed as a reactionary who rejected any interference by the government and manifested no sympathy for the increasingly vocal group of fellows who sought to reform the society along meritocratic lines. On several occasions he travelled on the continent, where he met such leading savants as Laplace, Arago, and Humboldt. In 1827 he was honoured by being elected one of the eight foreign members of the Paris Académie des Sciences.

Young's extensive network of connections through the Royal Society enabled him to play a significant role on several committees charged with pursuing investigations into matters of civic concern. In 1814 he became a member of a committee charged with investigating the risk of introducing gas light in London. Two years later he was appointed secretary of the commission charged with ascertaining the length of the seconds pendulum; subsequently he became secretary to a parliamentary commission on the subject. His involvement with the Admiralty was even more extensive. He examined new methods of ship construction and submitted a report to the Royal Society in 1814 which was generally deemed too theoretical to be of practical use.

Four years later Young was appointed superintendent of the *Nautical Almanac* and secretary of the board of longitude. These two positions were among the few salaried scientific posts in England, and from them he received £400 per annum. However, his work for the Admiralty also led to controversy with a number of astronomers, especially Francis Baily and James South, who considered that under Young's direction the *Almanac* was overzealous in satisfying the needs of navigators to the neglect of its traditional astronomical functions. Moreover, his critics charged that the *Almanac* contained a significant number of errors. Partly in response to such criticism the Admiralty disbanded the board of longitude in 1828 and replaced it by a scientific advisory committee to which Michael Faraday, Edward Sabine, and Young were appointed.

Egyptology Having shown an early and prodigious interest in languages Young's attention was drawn to the Rosetta stone and to the initial attempts made to decipher both the demotic and the hieroglyphic inscriptions. His first communication on this subject was presented to the Society of Antiquaries in 1814 and over the next few years he published several pieces on the subject, including an article on 'Egypt' that appeared in an 1819 supplement to the *Encyclopaedia Britannica*. Young proceeded on the assumption that the demotic, hieroglyphic, and Greek inscriptions on the Rosetta stone were rough inter-translations and that some of the demotic characters had been derived from the hieroglyphic. Further evidence was gleaned from other Egyptian texts that he was able to consult. Personal names offered a particularly fruitful line for initial investigation. He assumed that each pictorial character possessed a phonetic value such that the hieroglyphs within each cartouche contained such names as Ptolemaios and Birenike. In his article on 'Egypt' he was able to identify approximately 200 separate hieroglyphic signs and at the time of his death was completing his 'Rudiments of an Egyptian dictionary in the ancient enchorial character' which subsequently appeared as an appendix to Henry Tattam's *A Compendious Grammar of the Egyptian Language* (1830). Young's contributions to the study of ancient Egyptian languages have sometimes been compared unfavourably with those of Jean François Champollion. Although his interventions were perhaps less intense than Champollion's he made a number of original and insightful innovations, especially in the mid-1810s.

Although Young was raised in a dissenting household he subsequently sought to set aside the Quakerism of his childhood and to align himself with the religious, scientific, and medical establishment. In this he was largely successful. Given to caution he was increasingly viewed as a conservative. Living in a period when the social élite was under attack both at home and abroad, Young never wavered in his defence of the status quo and he remained mindful of his position as an English gentleman. Socially he mixed with other gentlemen of the scientific and medical élite. Although he was widely admired for his knowledge and intellectual achievements most of his acquaintances found him rather stiff and experienced difficulty in establishing close friendships. He was certainly highly intelligent but he appears to have lacked the discipline and insight necessary to pursue topics in great depth. He was most comfortable writing on subjects where he could organize the views of others in original ways.

After visiting Geneva in 1828 Young's health began to fail. Progressive heart disease slowed him considerably, as with increasing difficulty he sought to complete his Egyptian dictionary. On 10 May 1829 he died at his home in Park Square, London, and six days later he was buried in his wife's family vault at Farnborough, Kent. Subsequently his widow pressed for a more public recognition of her husband's achievements; these were celebrated on a plaque erected in Westminster Abbey, close to the spot where Newton was buried.   GEOFFREY CANTOR

Sources [H. Gurney], *Memoir of the life of Thomas Young … with a catalogue of his works and essays* (1831) · G. Peacock, *Life of Thomas Young* (1855) · A. Wood, *Thomas Young natural philospher, 1773–1829* (1954) · E. W. Morse, 'Young, Thomas', *DSB*, 14.562–72 · G. N. Cantor, 'Thomas Young's lectures at the Royal Institution', *Notes and Records of the Royal Society*, 25 (1970), 87–112 · G. Cantor, 'The changing role of Young's ether', *British Journal for the History of Science*, 5 (1970–71), 44–62 · N. H. Kipnis, *History of the principle of interference of light* (1990) · private information (2004) · election certificate, RS · 'Dictionary of Quaker biography', RS Friends, Lond. [card index]
Archives BL, Egyptological collections and corresp., Add. MSS 21026–21027, 27281–27285 · RS, corresp. · UCL, lecture notes | BL, corresp. with Macvey Napier, Add. MSS 34611–34613, *passim* · RS, corresp. with Sir John Herschel
Likenesses C. Turner, engraving, pubd 1830 (after T. Lawrence, after 1820), NPG [*see illus.*] · H. P. Briggs, oils (after T. Lawrence), RS · T. Brigstocke, portrait (after H. P. Briggs), St George's Hospital, London · F. Chantrey, medallion portrait on memorial tablet, Westminster Abbey · J. F. Skill, J. Gilbert, W. Walker, and E. Walker, group portrait, pencil and wash (*Men of science living in 1807–08*), NPG · portrait (after H. P. Briggs), Royal Institution of Great Britain, London · portrait (after H. P. Briggs), Emmanuel College, Cambridge

Young, William (*d.* 1662), composer and viol player, was among several English musicians who gained distinction while working abroad. His English origins are unknown and documentation of his employment is sparse. Anthony Wood notes him as 'a great violist, bred in Rome, spent several years there' (Bodl. Oxf., MS Wood D 19(4), fol. 138*r*), which, if true, suggests that he may have been a Roman Catholic, out of tune with the puritan regime at home. By 1652 he had found employment in the household of Archduke Ferdinand Karl of Austria, count of Innsbruck (previously a governor of the Netherlands before moving to Innsbruck in 1646). He is presumed to have married; several children were born to the couple in Innsbruck and perhaps died in infancy.

Between February and May 1652 Young was among several hundred people who travelled with the archduke at carnival time to the Italian cities of Mantua, Parma, Modena, Florence, and Ferrara; on the ship he is recorded as playing 'auf der geigen'. An unnamed English musician, evidently Young, was rewarded with 100 ducats on 28 March 1654 by Emperor Ferdinand III: the reason is not indicated, but Young certainly performed for him. On 3 April following he received expenses of 64 florins after visiting Regensburg, where a new theatre had been built for opera, with the master of the chamber music, Marc' Antonio Cesti.

Young's skill as a player was acknowledged by many, including Queen Kristina of Sweden, who heard him at Innsbruck in 1655. On 26 February 1656 the English traveller Robert Bargrave

> went to receive a most pleasing entertainment of Musique from Mr William Young, Groome of the bed-chamber and cheife Violist to the Archduke, espetially on an Octo-cordal Viall, of his own Invention, apted for the Lira way of playing, farr beyond those with six strings only … (Bodl. Oxf., MS Rawl. C.799, fol. 180)

Young was also praised by Jean Rousseau in his *Traité de la viole* (1687).

Young published two fine collections of sonatas and

suites in three, four, and five parts (Innsbruck, 1653), and three parts (Innsbruck, 1659), which mix continental (Italian and German) and English traits, both in scoring and in structure; his use of the term 'sonata' is one of the first known by an Englishman. There are many first-rate compositions by him for one and two bass or lyra viols, most of them quite demanding in technique. Young travelled to England on 26 August 1660, perhaps with a view to obtaining a place at Charles II's court, but he soon returned to Innsbruck, where he died on 23 April 1662; he was buried at the Jakobikirche there.

A whole dynasty of musical Youngs flourished in the seventeenth and eighteenth centuries. **Anthony Young** (*bap.* 1683, *d.* 1747), organist and composer, was baptized on 11 February 1683 at St Margaret's, Westminster, the son of Anthony and Elizabeth Young. He was dismissed from the Chapel Royal in 1700 when his voice broke. He is presumed to have been the organist of St Clement Danes, London, by 1707 and was still there in 1743. He subscribed to the Royal Society of Musicians at its formation on 28 August 1739. His *Suits of Lessons* for harpsichord (1719) are conservative in style. His numerous songs include *A Collection of New Songs, for One or Two Voices* (1707). He died in London, and was buried on 8 May 1747. **William Young** (*d.* 1670) is presumed to have been the son of Thomas Young of Ripon, Yorkshire, and an apprentice in the Farriers' Company from 1632 to 1640, later supervising his own apprentices. He served among the violins at court from midsummer 1660, also gaining a flautist's place from midsummer 1665. He was buried at St Margaret's, Westminster, on 5 November 1670. The compositions by 'William Young' in English manuscripts, however, seem to be by the Innsbruck musician. **Charles Young** (*bap.* 1686, *d.* 1758), composer of songs, was the brother of Anthony Young, and was baptized on 7 October 1686 at St Martin-in-the-Fields, Westminster. He was possibly the St Paul's chorister of this name in 1698. He was organist of All Hallows Barking, Byward Street, from 21 August 1713 to his death on 12 December 1758. He was buried there on 16 December 1758. Three of his daughters were famous singers: Cecilia *Young married Thomas Arne, Isabella *Young married John Frederick *Lampe, and Esther (or Hester) *Young married Charles Jones (*d.* 1780), a music seller, horn player, and flautist [*see under* Young family (*per. c.*1700–1799)]. ANDREW ASHBEE

Sources J. Rousseau, *Traité de la viole* (Paris, 1687) • W. Senn, *Musik und Theater am Hof zu Innsbruck* (Innsbruck, 1954) [documents Young at Innsbruck court] • P. Evans, 'Seventeenth-century chamber music manuscripts at Durham', *Music and Letters*, 36 (1955), 205–23 • W. S. Newman, *The sonata in the Baroque era* (1959) [on musical style of the pubd collection] • M. Tilmouth, 'Music on the travels of an English merchant, Robert Bargrave (1628–61)', *Music and Letters*, 53 (1972), 143–59 • J. D. Shute, 'Anthony A Wood and his manuscript Wood D 19(4) at the Bodleian Library, Oxford: an annotated transcription', PhD diss., International Institute for Advanced Musical Studies, Missouri, 1979 • G. Dodd, *Thematic index of music for viols* (1980–) • M. Tilmouth and P. Holman, 'Young, William', *New Grove*, 2nd edn • O. Baldwin and T. Wilson, 'Young', *New Grove*, 2nd edn • A. Ashbee, ed., *Records of English court music*, 1 (1986) [Anthony and William Young] • A. Ashbee, ed., *Records of English court music*, 2 (1987) [Anthony and William Young] • A. Ashbee, ed., *Records of English court music*, 5 (1991) [Anthony and William Young] • A. Ashbee, ed., *Records of English court music*, 8 (1995) [Anthony and William Young] • A. Ashbee and D. Lasocki, eds., *A biographical dictionary of English court musicians, 1485–1714*, 2 vols. (1998) [see also Anthony Young] • D. Dawe, *Organists of the City of London, 1666–1850* (1983) [Anthony and Charles Young] • E. B. Schnapper, ed., *The British union-catalogue of early music printed before the year 1801*, 2 (1957), 1098–9 [Anthony and Charles Young] • J. Harley, *British harpsichord music*, 2 (1994), 103, 246 [Anthony Young] • *The travel diary of Robert Bargrave, Levant merchant, 1647–1656*, ed. M. G. Brennan, Hakluyt Society, 3rd ser., 3 (1999)
Archives Landesregierungsarchiv, Innsbruck, Ferdinandeum Bibliotheca Dip. 905 [1652 trip]; Leopoldinum [box] B/63 [1652 trip]; Raitbuch der tirolischen Kammer, Jahr 1655, I.s. 788 [Regensburg trip]

Young, William (*d.* **1670**). *See under* Young, William (*d.* 1662).

Young, Sir William, second baronet (1749–1815), colonial governor and politician, born at Charlton in Kent in December 1749, was the eldest son of Sir William Young, first baronet (1724/5–1788), governor of Dominica, and his second wife, Elizabeth (1729–1801), the only child of Brook *Taylor. In 1767 he was entered at Clare College, Cambridge, but, some difference arising, he was removed and matriculated from University College, Oxford, on 26 November 1768. He later travelled in France, Italy, and Sicily and published an account of part of his travels. He gained some fame for a work he published in 1777 entitled *The spirit of Athens, being a political and philosophical investigation of the history of that republic*. On 12 August that year, at St George the Martyr, Queen's Square, London, he married Sarah (*d.* 1791), the daughter and coheir of Charles Lawrence and his wife, Mary, *née* Mihil. They had four sons and two daughters. Young married, secondly, on 22 April 1793 at St George, Hanover Square, London, Barbara (*d.* 1830), the daughter of Colonel Richard Talbot and his wife, Margaret, *née* O'Reilly, later *suo jure* Baroness Talbot of Malahide.

In 1782 Young was deputed by the proprietors of the colony of Tobago to negotiate their interests in the French court after the preliminaries of peace with France and the United States had been agreed. Two years later he was returned to parliament for St Mawes, Cornwall. He retained this seat until 1806, when he was returned for the town of Buckingham. He was a follower of William Pitt until 1801, when he joined the ranks of his patron, Lord Grenville. Young was a frequent speaker in the House of Commons on a variety of topics, including poor-law reform, income tax, military affairs, the slave trade, union with Ireland, foreign and colonial policy, and parliamentary reform. In 1786 he was elected a fellow of the Royal Society and in 1791 a fellow of the Society of Antiquaries. He was secretary to the Association for Promoting the Discovery of the Interior Parts of Africa. In 1807 he was appointed governor of Tobago, a post which he retained until his death in January 1815.

At the death of his father in 1788 Young inherited four sugar plantations—one in Antigua, two in St Vincent, and one in Tobago—and a total of 896 African slaves. He also inherited his father's debts, amounting to approximately

£110,000. On 30 October 1791 he embarked on a voyage to the West Indies which he later wrote about under the title *A tour through the several islands of Barbadoes, St Vincent, Tobago, and Grenada, in the years 1791 and 1792*. It was first published in 1801 as an appendix to the second edition of *An Historical Survey of the Island of Saint Domingo* by Bryan Edwards, the whole work being edited by Young. He undertook this tour to save his plantations from bankruptcy, which he eventually failed to do, and to gain information about slavery and the sugar industry of the West Indies which would support his agenda in parliament to gain votes for an alternative to the campaign led by William Wilberforce and his allies, who worked persistently and with widespread public support for abolition of the slave trade. On his tour of the islands Young said he was greeted wholeheartedly by his slaves, and he reciprocated by granting them extra holidays and gifts of herrings and rum, holding balls in the great house, and at Christmas feasting, drinking, dancing, and exchanging gifts. He was pleased that he discovered little evidence of harsh treatment of his and other planters' slaves. In all of the islands he visited he was observant of the methods of feeding, housing, clothing, disciplining, providing medical care, and religious instruction of the slaves.

After returning to his seat in parliament Young drew upon his recent experience in the West Indies to argue that, by ameliorating the condition of the slaves, their numbers would increase by natural propagation and, in time, the trade from Africa to the islands would die a natural death without intervention by act of parliament. However, Young's reform plans were naïve and utopian, and Wilberforce and his allies finally succeeded in getting the necessary votes to abolish the British transatlantic slave trade.

Young was the author of works on a variety of subjects, including *The rights of Englishmen, or, The British constitution of government compared with that of a democratic republic* (1793); *The West Indian Commonplace Book* (1807); *Considerations on Poorhouses and Workhouses: their Pernicious Tendency* (1796); and *Instructions for the Armed Yeomanry* (1797). He died on 10 January 1815 at Government House, Tobago.

E. I. CARLYLE, rev. RICHARD B. SHERIDAN

Sources GM, 1st ser., 81/2 (1811), 90 · GM, 1st ser., 85/1 (1815), 373 · GM, 1st ser., 86/2 (1816), 632 · Foster, *Alum. Oxon.* · Burke, *Peerage* (1953) · HoP, *Commons, 1790–1820* · V. L. Oliver, *The history of the island of Antigua*, 3 (1899), 280–84 · K. G. Laurence, 'Tobago and British imperial authority, 1793–1802', *Trade, government and society in Caribbean history, 1700–1920: essays presented to Douglas Hall* (1983) · R. B. Sheridan, 'Sir William Young (1749–1815): planter and politician, with special reference to slavery in the British West Indies', *Journal of Caribbean History* [forthcoming] · memoranda of transactions, accounts, and correspondence, March 1810, Bodl. RH, Young Collection · D. H. Porter, *The abolition of the slave trade in England* (1970), 18–29 · B. Marshall, 'Society and economy in the British Windward Islands, 1763–1823', PhD diss., University of West Indies, Mona, Jamaica, 1972 · R. B. Sheridan, 'The condition of the slaves in the settlement and economic development of the British Windward Islands, 1763–1775', *Journal of Caribbean History*, 24 (1990), 132–4 · Cobbett, *Parl. hist.*, 30.513–14 · GEC, *Baronetage*

Archives BL, papers, Stowe MSS 488, 791, 921–923, 1022 · Bodl. RH, corresp. and papers · NRA, priv. coll., letters · PRO, letter-book as agent for St Vincent, CO 261/9 · U. Lond., Institute of Commonwealth Studies, watercolours and notes

Likenesses B. West, oils, 1767, Eton · T. Holloway, line engraving, 1787, BM, NPG; repro. in *European Magazine* (1787) · J. Collyer, stipple, 1788 (after J. Brown), BM, NPG · W. Say, mezzotint, pubd 1805 (after W. Beechey), BM

Wealth at death some large debts owing: Bodl. RH, Young collection

Young, Sir William (1751–1821), naval officer, was the eldest of six children born to James Young and a Miss Vasmer. He was descended from a long-established Devon family, the Yonges of Puslinch. A quarrel between brothers in the late seventeenth century (about Charles I's execution) changed the spelling of the name of the branch of the family from which William Young was descended. He entered the navy in April 1761 as captain's servant to Mark Milbanke in the *Guernsey* (50 guns). In December 1762 he was moved to the *Wasp* (8 guns), a two-masted sloop, but in October 1764 he returned to the *Guernsey*, now under Commodore Hugh Palliser. Young passed his examination on 10 January 1769 and was promoted lieutenant, at Plymouth, into the *Nautilus* (16 guns) on 12 November 1770. On 21 May 1771 he was made fourth lieutenant in the *Trident* (64 guns), Sir Peter Denis's flagship in the Mediterranean. Nearly four years later, on 23 January 1775, he became third lieutenant in the *Portland* (50 guns), flagship of Vice-Admiral James Young at the Leeward Islands. The American War of Independence now speeded promotion and on 10 May 1777 Young was given command of the sloop *Snake*. This was confirmed on 23 September 1778 and the same day he was promoted captain of the *Hind* (24 guns). He served in her until 15 April 1782, when he moved to the *Ambuscade* (32 guns) until the peace in 1783. Peacetime employment was always uncertain but Young possessed sufficient influence and merit to command the *Perseverance* (36 guns) from October 1787, and the *Crescent* (36 guns) from 10 May until November 1790.

On 31 January 1793 Young was appointed to the *Fortitude* (74 guns) before going to the Mediterranean in Lord Hood's fleet, and taking part in the occupation of Toulon. After its evacuation, in December 1793 Hood determined to gain a base in Corsica. Based at Porto Ferrajo, in Elba, he detached a small squadron, under Commodore Linzee, of three ships of the line and two frigates, escorting troops under Major-General Dundas, to Mortella Bay in Corsica. The squadron arrived on 7 February 1794, and next day two of the ships, the *Fortitude* and *Juno* (32 guns), were part of a combined attempt to take a small tower on a promontory in Mortella Bay, immediately south of Pointe de la Mortella, on the north-west Corsican coast. This was necessary if the bay was to be safe as an anchorage. But the well-placed tower, though possessed of only one 24-pounder gun, was too strong for the ships to destroy. Instead they suffered heavy losses. After a bombardment of over two hours the *Fortitude* had been set on fire by red-hot shot and forced to retreat with six men killed and fifty-six wounded. The tower was taken only by guns from a commanding position above, on shore. This incident prompted an exaggerated belief in the strength of such towers and numbers were built on the south coast of England as an anti-invasion device, under the name 'martello towers'.

Young was in the inconclusive actions between the British and French fleets of 14 March 1794 and 13 July 1795 off Hyères and returned to England with a convoy in the autumn. He had been awarded the honorary rank of colonel of marines on 4 July 1794 and was promoted rear-admiral of the white on 1 June 1795. From 20 November of that year until 19 February 1801 he was a member of the Board of Admiralty. As such he was one of the committee of conciliation which visited Portsmouth in April 1797 during the Spithead mutiny. Although Young took an orthodox view of these events his letters to Captain Charles Morice Pole reveal some sympathy with the seamen's grievances and an attempt to try to influence seamen's views by allowing the calculated conversations of officers, contrasting the situation of British with the wretched state of French seamen, to be deliberately overheard. But Young was shocked by the 'total want of confidence the seamen have shewn in their officers, a circumstance so new that I never remember to have heard of anything like it' (Young to Pole, 8 May 1797). He thought many officers showed 'a sad want of energy and of particular attention to duty which the government of large bodies of men requires especially in these times and an absent or indifferent man can produce incalculable mischief' (Young to Pole, 22 June 1797) and while at the Admiralty he strove to improve conditions and tighten discipline. He was made vice-admiral of the blue on 14 February 1799 and vice-admiral of the white on 1 January 1801. Admiral Sir William Hotham, who had earlier served with him, thought Young, while at the Admiralty, 'diligent in application, clear in method and generally informed' (Stirling, 1.59n) and Young's letters bear this out.

On 23 April 1804 Young was promoted vice-admiral of the red and a few weeks later, on 18 May, he was appointed commander-in-chief at Plymouth, a position he held until 1807. Here he was accused by Lord Cochrane of excessive greed for prize money, but as commander-in-chief Young's claims to issue orders to warships sailing from Plymouth accorded with naval practice and the issue of prize money caused frequent bitter disputes between naval officers. Young was promoted admiral of the blue on 9 November 1805 but the ill health and tiredness he mentions in his letters in the autumn of 1806 probably explain his unemployment in the following years. In July 1809 he was the senior admiral at the board of the court martial on James, Lord Gambier. Lord Cochrane accused Young of undue bias in Gambier's favour but Cochrane himself was hardly impartial. He had already clashed with Young over prize money and when elected MP for Westminster in 1807 had accused Young of inefficiency in fitting out ships at Plymouth. During the court martial Young objected to Cochrane's discursive answers and attempted detailed explanations of his actions, but he seems to have been no more hostile than other members of the board.

Young was promoted admiral of the white on 31 July 1810 and in the spring of 1811 he was appointed to command of the North Sea Fleet, arriving at the Downs on 26 April and immediately hoisting his flag in the *Christian VII* (83 guns). So unexpected was the appointment that he told Sir Thomas Foley that he had 'everything to get as if I had never been afloat' (Young to Foley, 6 April 1811). The squadron he took over was in a high state of order though short of men. Charles Philip Yorke, first lord of the Admiralty, expressed the administration's complete confidence in Young's ability and zeal to blockade the Scheldt and the whole of the Dutch and north German coast, enforcing the orders in council against Napoleon's empire and preventing all neutral trade with the enemy. It was an arduous and unpleasant task. Young faced the problems of all commanders of blockading forces, constantly cruising, always needing more ships as bad weather took its toll, concerned about regular supplies of food and water. Moreover the Admiralty's ready granting of trading licences made for difficulties with neutrals and, though Young hoped the French could be lured out of Flushing and engaged in a battle which would destroy them, he was disappointed.

Lord Keith's appointment to command the Channel Fleet in February 1812 offended Young. He considered his position as senior admiral undermined and the hoped for command of the 'Great Fleet of England, the Fleet on which the safety, perhaps the existence of the Country might depend', an object 'worthy of any man's ambition' (Young to C. P. Yorke, 25 Feb 1812), had been lost to him. He resigned, but on Yorke's persuasion resumed his command until the end of the war. On 28 July 1814 he was nominated KB, and following the reconstruction of the Order of the Bath he became GCB on 2 January 1815. In 1819 he was appointed vice-admiral of the United Kingdom. His heath in these last years was not good; in November 1818 he was at Bath. He died, unmarried, at his house in Queen Anne Street, London, on 25 October 1821 after a short illness.

Young never took part in a major fleet action, though the difficult and important blockade in the North Sea, in the last years of the French wars, was well performed and praiseworthy. Most of his professional life was passed in administration, at the Admiralty or at Plymouth. He was a conventional upholder and representative of the existing naval social order, though aware of the need for some reform and having some sympathy with seamen's grievances. He was unsympathetic to Cochrane's radicalism and insubordinate attitude to superior officers, and admirers of Cochrane, like Captain Marryat who portrayed him as Sir Hurricane Humbug, have treated him harshly. Yet Sir William Hotham thought his manners 'tho' rather formal and cold, were those of a perfect gentleman, while he had the most punctilious sense of integrity' (Stirling, 1.58–9), and Young's personal letters reveal a more agreeable nature than his critics have allowed.

P. K. CRIMMIN

Sources DNB · W. Young, letters to Pole, 1788–1808, NMM, Pole papers, WYN/104, 105, 128 · W. Young, letters from Young to Foley, 1811–14, NMM, Foley papers, FOL/20, A, B, C, D · W. Young, letters to Yorke, 1811–12, NMM, Yorke papers, YOR/20 • PRO, ADM/6/21, 22, 23, 24, 29, 30, 31 • PRO, ADM/7/237, 238 • Burke, *Gen. GB* (1843–9), 3.319 • *GM*, 1st ser., 91/2 (1821), 477 • will, PRO, PROB 11/1650/639 [17 Jan 1815, codicils of 10 May 1820 and 11 July 1820] • *Naval Chronicle*, 22 (1809), 107–30, 215–42 • *Annual Register* (1809), 295–300 • D. Syrett and R. L. DiNardo, *The commissioned sea officers of the Royal Navy, 1660–1815*, rev. edn, Occasional Publications of the Navy RS, 1 (1994) • D. Lyon, *The sailing navy list: all the ships of the Royal Navy, built, purchased and captured, 1688–1860* (1993) • *Pages and portraits from the past: being the private papers of Sir William Hotham*, ed. A. M. W. Stirling, 2 vols. (1919)

Archives NMM, letters [copies] | BL, Althorp MSS, letters, Add. MSS 41364, 41365 • BL, letters and dispatches to Lord Nelson, Add. MSS 34904–34934, *passim* • NA Scot., letters to Lord Melville, GD51 • NMM, letters to Sir Thomas Foley, FOL/20 A, B, C, D • NMM, letters to Sir Charles Pole, WYN/104, 105 • NMM, Yorke papers, YOR/20

Likenesses W. Beechey, 1803–4 • R. Dighton, caricature etching, 1809, NPG • oils, NMM

Wealth at death approx. £30,000–£40,000; house in Queen Anne Street, Cavendish Square: will, 1815, PRO, PROB 11/1650/639

Young, Sir William (1799–1887), politician and lawyer in Nova Scotia, was born on 8 September 1799 at Falkirk, the son of John Young and his wife, Agnes Renny, the daughter of George Renny of Falkirk. His father **John Young** (1773–1837), merchant and writer on agriculture in Nova Scotia, was born near Falkirk on 1 September 1773, the son of William Young, a merchant, and his wife, Janet. He studied at Glasgow University about 1790 before sailing with his wife, Agnes, and their four children to Halifax in April 1814. The British occupation of Calais, Maine, provided him with a profitable market from September 1814 until April 1815 for goods which he had brought from Scotland. In the economic disarray which followed the war Young decided that there would be public support for agricultural reform, and between 1818 and 1821 he published sixty-four letters in the Halifax *Acadian Recorder* under the pen-name Agricola. Of these, thirty-eight were collected and published in a volume entitled *Letters of Agricola on the Principles of Vegetation and Tillage*. He advocated improvements in agriculture based on both theoretical scientific knowledge and empirically derived practice. His expectations were realized when a central board of agriculture was established in 1819. Young was named secretary and treasurer, but his desultory performance contributed to the abolition of the board in 1826. He was never an enthusiast for agriculture *per se*; rather he saw its improvement as a vehicle for his own social elevation. He managed to be elected for Sydney county in 1826 and held this seat until his death, on 6 October 1837, at his home, Willow Park Farm, Halifax.

William Young's career had an early start. He later claimed to have studied at the University of Glasgow before his family emigrated when he was fourteen. When his father was trading in Calais, William acted as his agent in Halifax; he also acted as his father's agent in New York from June until October 1815. In late 1815 he and James Cogswell became partners in an auction and commission business which probably continued until he entered into an indenture of apprenticeship with the legal firm of Charles Rufus and Samuel Prescott Fairbanks. This indenture ended acrimoniously when C. R. Fairbanks in 1823 accused William of having revealed Fairbanks's campaign strategy to John Young, who had unsuccessfully contested a Halifax by-election against him.

Having been admitted to the bar as an attorney in 1825 and as a barrister in 1826, Young established a flourishing private law practice in Halifax. In spite of a poor technical knowledge of law, he was a very effective advocate in the court room. Although he was an adherent to the Church of Scotland, on 30 August 1830 he married Anne (1803/4–1883), the daughter of Michael Tobin, a prominent Irish Roman Catholic merchant in Halifax. They had no children. In 1834 Young established a legal and insurance partnership with his brother George Renny. **George Renny Young** (1802–1853), lawyer and politician in Nova Scotia, born on 4 July 1802 in Falkirk, was active in his father's commercial business until 1821, when he began his studies at Pictou Academy. When he graduated in late 1824 he began to publish *The Novascotian, or, Colonial Herald*; however, he sold this paper to Joseph Howe in December 1827 in order to devote himself to legal studies, principally in Britain. He was admitted to the Nova Scotian bar as an attorney on 22 January 1833 and as a barrister on 22 July 1834. His legal knowledge and capacity for research was superior to that of his brother, and he published eight pamphlets on matters of contemporary public concern, the most notable being *The British North American Colonies* (1834). During an extended visit to England in 1837–8 he married Jane, the daughter of Thomas Holdsworth Brooking.

In the 1832 general election William Young was returned for Cape Breton county, only to be unseated by the legislature on the grounds that a riot during the election had been organized by his brother George. William was successful in the 1836 general election as a supporter of the Reform Party, but his reputation for being overly ambitious and engaging in sharp practice meant that he did not advance as rapidly as his talents warranted. Nevertheless, he was part of a delegation of four which held constitutional discussions with Lord Durham at Quebec, and in 1839 he was one of two representatives sent to Britain to argue the case of the assembly before the British government. In 1842 he was appointed to the executive council and in 1844 became speaker of the house.

William Young was joined in the assembly in 1843 by his brother George, who was elected for Pictou, and they subsequently became involved in promoting the Halifax to Quebec railway. Following the 1847 general election George entered the new Reform ministry. However, George's continued support of his own Quebec railway project, rather than the ministry's own scheme, contributed to his breaking with the government in 1851. A further contributing factor was his poor deteriorating physical and mental health. He did not stand for re-election in 1851 and died in Halifax on 30 June 1853.

William Young remained as speaker of the assembly until April 1854, when, partly because there were no other prominent contenders, he became attorney-general and leader of the government. His government was brought down on 18 February 1857 after having alienated Roman

Catholics, which was ironic considering that Young represented a riding that had a large Catholic population. In the 1859 general election Young was elected in the protestant county of Cumberland, and his party managed to gain a fragile majority in the assembly.

When Chief Justice Haliburton died on 16 July 1860, Young gained the office which he had long wanted. Although he served until 1881, his judgments were not particularly distinguished. Displaying a sense of civic duty, however, he became a generous benefactor to the city and Dalhousie University. In addition to numerous gifts made during his lifetime, he bequeathed $200,000 out of his total estate of $350,000 to a variety of causes. In 1869, perhaps as a reward for his support of confederation, he was awarded a KB. He died in Halifax on 8 May 1887.

Although William Young became both premier and chief justice of Nova Scotia, he did not make a particularly positive contribution to the public life of his time. Moreover, his unrelenting and calculating pursuit of self-interest throughout his public career, similar to that of his father John and his brother George, was frequently disruptive and did nothing to alleviate the highly polemical and partisan nature of politics in this period.

K. G. PRYKE

Sources 'Journal of William Young, 1839', *Report of the Public Archives of Nova Scotia* (1973), 22–74 • Agricola [J. Young], *The letters of Agricola on the principles of vegetation and tillage, written for Nova Scotia, and published first in the 'Acadian Recorder' by John Young, secretary of the provincial agricultural board* (1822) • J. M. Beck, 'Young, Sir William', *DCB*, vol. 11 • R. A. MacLean, 'Young, John', *DCB*, vol. 7 • J. M. Beck, 'Young, George Renny', *DCB*, vol. 8 • J. M. Beck, 'The Nova Scotian "disputed election" of 1859 and its aftermath', *Canadian Historical Review*, 36 (1955), 293–315 • P. B. Waite, *The lives of Dalhousie University: Lord Dalhousie's college*, 1 (1994) • D. C. Harvey, 'Pre-Agricola John Young, or a compact family in pursuit of fortune', *Collections of the Nova Scotia Historical Society*, 32 (1959), 125–59 • J. S. Martell, 'The achievement of Agricola and the agricultural societies, 1818–25', *Bulletin of the Public Archives of Nova Scotia*, 2/2 (1940) • B. Russell, 'Reminiscences of the Nova Scotia judiciary', *Dalhousie Review*, 5 (1925–6), 499–512 • R. Grant, *Life and times of George R. Young* (1886) • G. Morrison, 'The brandy election of 1830', *Collections of the Nova Scotia Historical Society*, 37 (1970), 151–83 • *Cyclopedia of Canadian biography* (1888) • *Canadian portrait gallery*, 4.43–7

Archives Public Archives of Nova Scotia, Halifax | NA Canada, Joseph Howe MSS • Public Archives of Nova Scotia, Halifax, Thomas McCullough MSS • Public Archives of Nova Scotia, Halifax, Symond Robie MSS • Public Archives of Nova Scotia, Halifax, George Rennie Young MSS • Public Archives of Nova Scotia, Halifax, John Young MSS

Likenesses W. Notman, photograph, Public Archives of Nova Scotia, Halifax

Wealth at death C$350,000—value of estate: Beck, 'Young, Sir William', 948

Young, William Henry (1863–1942), mathematician, was born in London on 20 October 1863, the eldest son of Henry Young, a grocer and a member of the Turners' and the Fishmongers' companies, and his wife, Hephzibah, daughter of John Jeal. He attended the City of London School and went up in 1881 as a scholar to Peterhouse, Cambridge. He took his degree as fourth wrangler in 1885,

William Henry Young (1863–1942), by Walter Stoneman, 1920

his friends having expected him to be higher in the list. In later years he related that he would not restrict the width of his interests (intellectual and athletic) by the intensive preparation necessary to become senior wrangler. Instead of sending in an essay for a Smith's prize as most young mathematicians did, he competed for and won a prize for theology.

Young was a fellow of Peterhouse from 1886 to 1892 but he held no permanent office in either the college or the university. He established himself as a very successful tripos coach and taught or examined in some public schools for a few years. On 11 June 1896 he married Grace Emily (1868–1944), daughter of Henry Williams Chisholm, warden of the standards; she was known thereafter as Grace Chisholm *Young. They had three sons and three daughters, two of whom, Rosalind Cecilia *Tanner and Laurence Chisholm Young, continued their parents' work in pure mathematics and received honorary degrees.

In 1897 Christian Felix Klein, under whom Grace had studied at Göttingen, travelled to Cambridge to receive an honorary degree and his visit set the seal on a resolution which he had urged at the Youngs' wedding, for them to acquire a wider outlook on mathematics. The Youngs moved to Göttingen for some months. They then lived in Italy with their first child for more than a year, and Young wrote his first papers, on multi-dimensional geometry; they developed the insights made in the book *Flatland* (1882) by Edwin Abbott, his old schoolteacher. After meeting Klein in Turin, the family returned in September 1899 to Göttingen, where they made their home until 1908.

They then moved to Geneva, and from 1915 their permanent home was in or near Lausanne. Young mastered many languages, and he twice travelled round the world.

While the family lived on various investments Young took posts for part of the academic years: some teaching and coaching at Cambridge; special lecturer at the University of Liverpool from 1906 to 1913; Hardinge professor of mathematics at the University of Calcutta from 1913 to 1919; and finally professor at the University College of Wales at Aberystwyth from 1919 to 1923. For Calcutta he wrote, but did not finish, a long comparative report on university mathematics education in many countries. He did hardly any research until he was in his late thirties, but between 1900 and 1924 his activity was intense and he wrote three books and more than 200 papers. His wife collaborated officially in two of the books and a number of the papers, prepared many others for publication, and checked proofs, while continuing her own research. As joint researchers they constituted the first significant husband-and-wife team in mathematics, and they operated at the top level for a quarter of a century. One curious feature is that after Grace drew him into research from the coaching treadmill Young then displayed the stronger creative gift.

Towards the close of the nineteenth century it was broadly true that the processes of mathematical analysis could be carried out provided that continuous functions only were encountered: artificial restrictions had to be made to handle discontinuities. The time was ripe for new ideas to transform the subject, and Georg Cantor's point set topology provided the techniques needed. A group in Paris round Emile Borel and Jacques Hadamard took this as a speciality, and Henri Lebesgue made a spectacular contribution in 1902 with a definition of the integral which was more general than those developed hitherto.

Following Klein's advice the Youngs had transferred to this topic in 1900 after the foray in geometry, and in 1904 Young found definitions of measure and integration different in form from Lebesgue's, but equivalent in essentials. The anticipation by two years was a blow but Young recognized it magnanimously—'the Lebesgue integral' is his own phrase—and set himself wholeheartedly to develop the theory of integration. He made several contributions, notably his treatment of the Stieltjes integral and his method of monotone sequences. The Youngs' book *The Theory of Sets of Points* (1906) was the first textbook in English on the subject and is recognized as a classic; an extended posthumous edition appeared in 1972.

There are two other fields in which Young's powers are shown at their highest. In the first of these, the theory of Fourier series and other orthogonal series, he proved theorems of striking simplicity and beauty. Moreover, he initiated many lines of thought which were worked out more fully by younger men, notably G. H. Hardy and J. E. Littlewood. The second field—and therein lay what was probably his most fundamental work—was the differential calculus of functions of more than one variable. This is well expounded in his Cambridge tract (1910), but perhaps the best tribute to it is that the Belgian analyst Charles de la Vallée Poussin rewrote part of his *Cours d'analyse infinitésimale* in 1912 in accordance with Young's treatment.

The immediate and abiding impression which Young gave was one of restless vitality; it was shown in his gait, his gestures, and his words. His appearance was striking: in early married life he grew a beard, red in contrast with his dark hair, and he wore it very long in later years. Many stories were current about him, all turning on his mental and physical energy. Young did not meet the recognition he deserved, due in part to his late start, and in part to a certain conservative hostility to the modern theory of real functions—a theory which few Englishmen in the early years of the twentieth century understood. Even when his profundity and originality were better appreciated, he was passed over in elections to chairs in favour of men who might be expected to be less exacting colleagues.

Young gained the ScD at Cambridge in 1903, was an honorary doctor of the universities of Calcutta, Geneva, and Strasbourg, an honorary fellow of Peterhouse (1939), fellow (1907) and Sylvester medallist (1928) of the Royal Society, De Morgan medallist (1917) and president (1922–4) of the London Mathematical Society, and president of the International Union of Mathematicians (1929–36). In this latter post he tried hard to raise the international community spirit among mathematicians, to build upon the reconciliation with Germans at the International Congress at Bologna in 1928, but he met with much apathy.

The fall of France in 1940 found Young at Lausanne, and he remained in Switzerland, unhappy and restive, until his sudden death at Château Corcelles, Chavornay, Canton de Vaud, on 7 July 1942.

J. C. BURKILL, *rev.* I. GRATTAN-GUINNESS

Sources I. Grattan-Guinness, 'A mathematical union', *Annals of Science*, 29 (1972), 105–86 • G. H. Hardy, *Obits. FRS*, 4 (1942–4), 307–23 • I. Grattan-Guinness, 'University mathematics at the turn of the century', *Annals of Science*, 28 (1972), 369–84 • I. Grattan-Guinness, 'Mathematical bibliography for W. H. and G. C. Young', *Historia Mathematica*, 2 (1975), 43–58 • G. H. Hardy, 'William Henry Young', *Journal of the London Mathematical Society*, 17 (1942), 218–37 • *Nature*, 150 (1942), 227–8 • *G. E. Young and W. H. Young, selected papers*, ed. S. D. Chatterji and H. Wetelscheid (Lausanne, 2000) • personal knowledge (1959) • private information (1959) • private information (2004)

Archives U. Lpool, corresp. and papers | CUL, corresp. with Lord Hardinge, memo relating to university education in Calcutta

Likenesses W. Stoneman, photograph, 1920, NPG [see illus.] • W. Stoneman, photograph, 1933, NPG • photograph, RS • photographs, repro. in Grattan-Guinness, 'Mathematical union'

Wealth at death nil: probate, 2 July 1943, *CGPLA Eng. & Wales*

Young, Sir William Mackworth (1840–1924), administrator in India, was born at Cookham, Berkshire, on 15 August 1840, the third son of Captain Sir George Young, second baronet (1797–1848), RN, of Formosa Place, Cookham, and his wife, Susan (1804/5–1895), daughter of William Mackworth Praed, serjeant-at-law, of Bitton Court, Devon. Sir George *Young, third baronet (1837–1930), was his eldest brother, and Winthrop Mackworth Praed (1802–1839), poet and politician, was a maternal uncle. Young, known throughout his life as Mackworth, was a scholar of

Eton College and of King's College, Cambridge, and a fellow of King's from 1863 to 1869. He joined the Indian Civil Service in 1862, and in December the following year was posted to the Punjab as an assistant commissioner. It was a felicitous assignment: the Punjab service had a history of evangelicalism and easily accommodated Young's own commitment to missionary endeavour. He became a member of the Church Missionary Society corresponding committee for the Punjab and Sind. His first marriage, on 17 August 1869, to Isabel Maria (1841/2–1870), daughter of Charles Boileau Elliott, rector of Tattingstone, Suffolk, was performed by John Barton of the Church Missionary Society. Unhappily, Isabel died in the following May, two weeks after giving birth to a daughter, Isabel Mary.

Young was quickly singled out for secretariat work. In 1875 he became settlement secretary to the Punjab financial commissioner, in 1878 acting superintendent of Kapurthala, and in 1880 chief secretary to the Punjab government, in which post he remained for seven years. On 21 April 1881 he married Frances Mary (d. 1932), daughter of his chief, Sir Robert Eyles Egerton. Egerton thought highly of his son-in-law's abilities, but although Young officiated in several important posts, including that of provincial home secretary (1888), he repeatedly missed out on the best appointments. In 1893–4 he presided over the Indian hemp drugs commission, and in September 1895 was made resident of Mysore, a princely state in southern India. Finally, in March 1897, Lord Elgin appointed him lieutenant-governor of the Punjab, the post he had coveted most, and promoted him to KCSI (he had been made a CSI in January 1890).

Young's lieutenant-governorship was dominated by two issues: the administration of the north-west frontier and the transfer of land from indebted peasants to urban trading castes. On the latter subject, Young argued that the laws of political economy should be applied regardless of societal differences, but in the face of the government of India's enthusiasm for intervention he drew up a bill which allowed for a minimum of legislative interference. In October 1900, when it came before the central legislative council, he spoke against it but did not vote on it, a compromise which in Lord Curzon's eyes had neither the merit of loyalty nor that of conviction.

Young's accommodating demeanour and thin, almost ascetic, appearance belied a tenacious and inflexible nature. In Curzon, however, he met his match, especially on the subject of the north-west frontier. Young was jealous of encroachments on his authority, but Curzon was determined to free the frontier from the Punjab's lumbering administrative machinery. In September 1900, frustrated by Young's touchy reaction to criticism, Curzon sent his proposals for a separate frontier agency direct to the secretary of state for India in London without first consulting Young. Young was furious; while he did not expect support from his own frontier specialists (each of whom, hoping to be chosen chief commissioner of the new province, had privately told Curzon to go ahead), he had expected to have sufficient warning to rally old Punjab hands in London against Curzon's plans. His ire stemmed

in part from being comprehensively outmanoeuvred by the viceroy.

Relations worsened in the summer of 1901 when Young learned that Curzon intended to shift the Punjab's summer capital from Simla. In a widely reported speech at a Masonic banquet, Young let it be known that he looked forward to 'a hill station where the full glare of the Supreme Government might be softened by distance'. He apologized almost instantly for his indiscretion, but although Curzon accepted the apology graciously, he henceforth spurned Young's social invitations because of what he insisted was the vituperative backbiting of Young's wife. Young was a courteous and scholarly man with a fine ear for music, and an evening at the gubernatorial residence, Barnes Court, was considered one of Simla's more refined social offerings. The viceroy's refusal to go there pitched Simla society into turmoil and deeply offended Young. Upon leaving India in February 1902 he rebuffed Curzon's farewell courtesies, observing bitterly that he had publicly dishonoured him and his wife.

In retirement, Young settled at St Leonards and, despite capricious health, became vice-president of the Church Missionary Society, chairman of the Church of England Zenana Missionary Society and of the Church Education Corporation, and a member of the Central Board of Missions. He died on 10 May 1924 at his home, Lerryn, Weybridge, and was buried on 13 May at Weybridge parish church. He was survived by the daughter of his first marriage, and by his second wife and four sons and a daughter from his second marriage: the eldest son, Gerard Mackworth-*Young (1884–1965) of the Indian Civil Service, was a director of the British School of Archaeology at Athens; the second, Major Sir Hubert Winthrop *Young (1885–1950), was governor of Nyasaland, Northern Rhodesia, and Trinidad and Tobago; the third, Sir Mark Aitchison *Young (1886–1974), was chief secretary of Palestine and governor of Barbados, Tanganyika, and Hong Kong; the youngest was Norman Egerton Young (1892–1964), of the Treasury and government director of the Suez Canal Company; the daughter of his second marriage, Lucia Katherine Young, married Arthur John Beamish and was an associate of the Royal College of Music and a professional singer.   KATHERINE PRIOR

Sources correspondence, BL OIOC, Elgin MSS · correspondence, BL OIOC, Curzon MSS · *The Times* (12 May 1924), 1, 16 · *The Times* (14 May 1924), 9 · *The Times* (24 June 1924), 16 · P. H. M. van den Dungen, *The Punjab tradition: influence and authority in nineteenth-century India* (1972) · Burke, *Peerage* (1959) · ecclesiastical records, BL OIOC · *India List, and India Office List* (1901) · Burke, *Gen. GB* (1937) · Venn, *Alum. Cant.* · *DNB* · H. E. C. Stapylton, *Second series of Eton school lists … 1853–1892* (1900)

Archives BL OIOC, corresp. with Lord Curzon, NO 298 · BL OIOC, Elgin MSS · King's AC Cam., letters to Henry Bradshaw · U. Birm. L., Church Missionary Society archives

Wealth at death £22,054 2s. 2d.: resworn probate, 1924, CGPLA Eng. & Wales

Younge, Elizabeth. *See* Pope, Elizabeth (1739x45–1797).

Younge, Richard (*fl.* 1636–1673), religious writer, was a member of the Young family who held land in Roxwell in

Essex; otherwise nothing more is known of his family background and parentage. He moved to London and settled first in Moorgate, then moved out east to Stratford in Essex and finally south of the river to Newington Causeway. In one work he described himself as 'gentleman' (Younge, *Englands Unthankfulness*, 1653, title page) but in 1646 George Thomason thought he was a grocer (it is not clear whether by this he meant Younge's occupation or his livery company).

Younge devoted much of his time to writing short moralistic and evangelical tracts and publishing them, often at his own expense. He was moderately well versed in the classics, and had read in the fathers as well as many current works, and was able to imitate a variety of literary genres, such as dialogues, 'characters', open letters, allegories, commonplaces, and devotional verse, as well as write short treatises and compose prayers. He sometimes called himself R. Junius, probably a play on his surname, or Florilegus, referring to his technique of picking the best flowers from 'the choicest authors ancient and modern' and arranging them in attractive 'nosegays' to catch readers' attention (*A Soveraigne Antidote Against All Griefe*, 1647, title page; *A Christian Library*, 1655, sig. 2r). He was regarded as sufficiently orthodox to receive the imprimatur of both the episcopalian authorities in the late 1630s and the 1660s, and the parliamentarian and Commonwealth authorities in the 1640s and 1650s. Some of his works also bear flattering epistles from a variety of leading clergy of the day, such as Daniel Featley, Thomas Goodwin, Edmund Calamy, and Richard Baxter. By the Restoration, Younge was hostile to the sects but loyal to Charles II, and it was for 'the common good' of all unregenerate people that he posed as the 'impartial monitor' warning of the penalties of sin and the need to repent at once (*The Cure of Misprision*, 1646, title page; *The Peoples Impartiall and Compassionate Monitor*, 1659, title page).

Younge wrote and published over fifty works between 1636 and 1673: the exact number is hard to pin down since he reworked the content or changed the titles of many of his earlier works. He admitted frankly that he published as fast as the material came from his pen, with little planning. If a work was too long he persuaded the printer to cram text onto the final page in smaller typeface, or promised to complete his argument in a later work; if it was too short he provided a filler from his own or others' work. The contents of his composite works were also rarely as promised in the contents, and vary from copy to copy.

To maximize the impact of his works, especially among those with limited literacy and funds, Younge opted for simple messages and colourful language, long print runs, and constantly referred to where his other publications could be obtained. His habit of selling works at below cost price, or lending copies (on deposit of 2d.), or even giving them away, did not endear him to regular booksellers, and to circulate his works he had to use his own house, or inns, or the premises of friendly members of the trade, such as James Crump, a bookbinder in Well Yard, St Bartholomew by the Exchange. Several works were sufficiently popular to be reprinted more than once, and of his *Serious and Pathetical Description of Heaven and Hell* (1658) Younge claimed that a hundred copies a day were being 'fetcht' (p. 37). Copies were also sent to America, and his *Short and Sure Way to Grace and Salvation* was translated into German in 1704.

About a quarter of Younge's works were indictments of drinking, swearing, keeping evil company, covetousness, and ambition, and the evil consequences these had for England. *Englands Unthankfulness Striving with Gods Goodness* was said to have reached its fourth edition by 1643; *A Hopefull Way to Cure that Horrid Sinne of Swearing* was his best-selling title between about 1643 and 1659; *The Blemish of Government*, written on behalf of 'the sober party in three nations' contained an appeal to stamp out drunkenness directed in 1655 to the protector and in 1664 to Charles II (*The Blemish of Government*, 1656, title page; *A Sovereign Antidote*, 1664, 7). He returned to similar material in *An Account of the Four Late Judgements* on England in the years 1665–7. Other works stressed the importance of hearing good sermons, the need for knowledge of God's word, and for the rich to help the poor, but a higher proportion was devoted to spiritual matters, often reflecting high Calvinist emphases. Early works on the benefits of affliction such as *The Victory of Patience* (1636) and *A Counterpoyson, or, Soverain Antidote Against All Griefe* (1641) gave way to later emphases on the need for introspective 'trying' of the heart and conversion, as in three works first published in 1658: *A Short and Sure Way to Grace and Salvation*, *An Experimental Index of the Heart*, and *Preparation to Conversion*.

In the 1660s, when the cost of paper and printing rose, Younge was forced to admit that his works could 'no longer be given or sold to loss', and he was becoming tired and disillusioned. If men did not think his books 'worth penny a sheet, I shall not think them worth my labour', and so 'farewell printing, welcome rest, and a retired life' (R. Younge, *An Account of the Four Late Judgements*, 1667, sig. D2r). But the response must have encouraged him to carry on, and by 1671 copies were again being given away 'to many that desire but will not buy' (R. Younge, *A Sparke of Divine Light*, 1671, 24). The limited number of repeat editions after 1673, and reference in a 1674 reprint to the 'late' author, suggest that by then death had finally removed Younge's drive to publish.

It is striking that new editions of three of Younge's later works were taken up and 'printed at the charge of Christs-Hospital' on at least six occasions between 1674 and 1776, presumably for distribution among its residents. Younge had successfully anticipated the tactics of the charitable societies and evangelical organizations of the eighteenth and nineteenth centuries, but a full study of his life and works is awaited.

IAN GREEN

Sources DNB · R. Younge, *Englands unthankfulness* (1653) · R. Younge, *A Christian library* (1655–6) · R. Younge, *An infallible way to farewell* (1660/61) · R. Younge, *An account of the four late judgements* (1667) · R. Younge, *A sparke of divine light* (1671) · R. Junius, *The cure of misprision* (1646) [Thomason tract E 1144(1)] · STC, 1475–1640 · Wing, STC · ESTC

Younger [*married name* Finch]**, Elizabeth** (1699–1762), actress and dancer, was born on 2 September 1699, the daughter of James Younger, a soldier, and his wife, Margaret Keith (d. 1713). Both her parents were born in Scotland. Her elder sister was the actress and dancer Margaret *Bicknell. Elizabeth Younger began her acting career as a child: she probably appeared as Princess Elizabeth in John Banks's *Vertue Betray'd, or, Anna Bullen*, to which she also spoke the epilogue, at Drury Lane on 27 March 1706. She was first cited in the bills on 29 January 1711, when she took the part of Lightning in George Villiers's *The Rehearsal*, again at Drury Lane. For the 1712 summer season she appeared with a company of child actors at the playhouse in St Martin's Lane, where her roles included Cherry in George Farquhar's *The Stratagem* and Miranda in Susannah Centlivre's *The Busy Body*.

On 30 September 1712 Elizabeth Younger joined the adult company at Drury Lane, playing Rose in Farquhar's *The Recruiting Officer*. During her first season her appearances were few, perhaps partly because of the death of her mother, who was buried at St Paul's, Covent Garden, on 11 February 1713. On 3 May 1714 she was billed as a dancer in a Saraband and a Jig, 'being the first time of her Dancing alone on the Stage'. In her early years on the stage she played a variety of supporting parts; in the 1714–15 season her roles included Philadelphia in Thomas Betterton's *The Amorous Widow* and Flora in Colley Cibber's *She Would and She Would Not*. On 23 February 1715 she created the role of Joyce in John Gay's farce *The What d'ye Call it*, and Sir Richard Steele took notice of her, for on 28 May 1715 she spoke the prologue at the opening of his *Censorium* at York Buildings. During the 1715–16 season she took over some of the roles of her sister Mrs Bicknell, including Dol Mavis in Ben Jonson's *The Silent Woman* and Lucy in Thomas Southerne's *Oroonoko*. She was absent from the stage during the early months of 1719, when her illegitimate daughter Charlotte (by an unknown father) was probably born.

It was only when her sister died in 1723 that Mrs Younger was able to take on more important roles. From Mrs Bicknell she inherited Charlotte in *Oroonoko* and Silvia in *The Recruiting Officer*. She was similarly restricted to supporting roles as a dancer for, although her repertory encompassed both serious and comic dances, she was billed irregularly in the entr'actes. Her most popular dance was *Tollet's Ground*, which she performed with her sister; a *Turkish Dance* choreographed by Anthony L'Abbé, which she performed with the French dancer Denoyer, was published in notation in the mid-1720s in *A New Collection of Dances*. She also danced supporting roles in afterpieces, appearing as Thalia in John Weaver's innovative dramatic entertainment of dancing *The Loves of Mars and Venus* in 1717 and as Ceres in John Thurmond's pantomime *Harlequin Doctor Faustus* in 1723.

After an absence during the 1724–5 season Elizabeth Younger returned to the stage at Lincoln's Inn Fields on 4 October 1725 as Margery Pinchwife in William Wycherley's *The Country Wife*. She immediately became one of John Rich's leading actresses; during her first season with his company she played such roles as Helena in Aphra Behn's *The Rover*, Desdemona in *Othello*, Cordelia in Nahum Tate's version of *King Lear*, and Miranda in *The Busy Body*. She was also able to create new roles, such as Myrtilla in Gay's revised version of *The Wife of Bath* (1730) and Hermione in Lewis Theobald's *Orestes* (1731). She played the part of Millamant in William Congreve's *The Way of the World* when Rich opened his new theatre in Covent Garden on 7 December 1732. Although she did not dance in the entr'actes at Lincoln's Inn Fields, she danced frequently in pantomimes. She appeared as the Miller's Wife in *The Necromancer* (1725), and subsequently took the role of Colombine in *Apollo and Daphne* (1726), *The Rape of Proserpine* (1727), and *Perseus and Andromeda* (1730).

A later commentator, Thomas Davies, described both her strengths and her weaknesses in his *Dramatic Miscellanies* (1784):

> Mrs Younger ... was an actress much followed in this [Belinda in Congreve's *The Old Bachelor*] and many other comic characters, especially the Country Wife. But Mrs Younger was a general actress, and sometimes appeared in tragedy, though, I think, not to advantage.

At the end of the 1733–4 season Mrs Younger retired from the stage. Following her retirement she married John Finch (1692?–1763), the third son of Daniel Finch, sixth earl of Winchilsea, although the date and place of their marriage are unknown. Their daughter Elizabeth (born before the marriage of her parents) married a John Mason of Greenwich on 2 June 1757. Elizabeth Younger died on 24 November 1762.
MOIRA GOFF

Sources E. L. Avery, ed., *The London stage, 1660–1800*, pt 2: *1700–1729* (1960) • A. H. Scouten, ed., *The London stage, 1660–1800*, pt 3: *1729–1747* (1961) • T. Betterton, [W. Oldys and others], *The history of the English stage* (1741), 162–3 • T. Davies, *Dramatic miscellanies*, 3 (1784), 368 • A. L'Abbé, *A new collection of dances* (c.1725), 84–96 • Genest, *Eng. stage* • A. Collins, *The peerage of England: containing a genealogical and historical account of all the peers of England* • Highfill, Burnim & Langhans, *BDA* • *The letters of Horace Walpole, fourth earl of Orford*, ed. P. Toynbee, 2 (1903), 269–70

Younger, George, first Viscount Younger of Leckie (1851–1929), brewer and politician, was born on 13 October 1851 at the Brewery House, Bank Street, Alloa, Clackmannanshire, the eldest of six children of James Younger (1818–1868) and his wife, Janet (d. 1912), elder daughter of John McEwan, of Alloa. Robert *Younger, Baron Blanesburgh was his younger brother. Educated at Edinburgh Academy and, briefly, at the University of Edinburgh, Younger at the age of sixteen succeeded his father as head of the family brewing business, George Younger & Son, established by his great-great-grandfather. On 10 June 1879, he married Lucy (d. 26 May 1921), daughter of Edward *Smith, MD, FRS, of Harley Street, London, and Heanor, Derbyshire; they had three sons.

Younger was a member of the Clackmannanshire county council from 1890 to 1906 (convenor, 1895–1906); a member of the royal commission on the licensing laws in 1896; vice-president of the County Councils Association of Scotland in 1902–4; and president of the National Union of Conservative Associations of Scotland in 1904. After unsuccessfully contesting Clackmannan and Kinross (1895, 1899, 1900) and Ayr burghs (1904), he was elected

George Younger, first Viscount Younger of Leckie (1851–1929), by Bassano, 1922

Unionist MP for Ayr burghs in 1906, representing it until 1922. He was recognized as a capable debater in the Commons, notably when opposing the 'people's budget' in 1909. He became a respected and popular Scottish whip, and was a candidate to succeed Lord Balcarres as Unionist chief whip in 1913. He was awarded a baronetcy in 1911. Younger achieved historical significance, however, not as a parliamentarian but as a party organizer and adviser to successive party leaders. In 1911 Arthur J. Balfour, the Unionists' leader, appointed Younger to a blue ribbon committee to reform the party organization, which created the posts of party chairman and treasurer. These officers were to take over from the chief whip management and fund-raising for the unionist central office and the party outside parliament. As Scottish whip, Younger retained considerable autonomy, managed several Unionist by-election victories, and in 1914 was one of ten Unionist leaders to sign the new year's message to party activists.

In 1917 Younger succeeded Arthur Steel-Maitland as party chairman. He whipped into shape a party machine seriously weakened by the war, appointing new constituency agents and London office staff. He prepared energetically for the general election expected to follow the 1918 Reform Act, which more than doubled the electorate. After parliament was dissolved in November 1918, he revised and edited the so-called 'coupon letter' issued by prime minister David Lloyd George and Unionist leader Andrew Bonar Law to the official Coalition Liberal and Unionist candidates. Younger looked upon the coalition as a necessary evil to keep a possible labour–socialist government from power. He regretted the issuing of the coupon to many Coalition Liberals, as it forced Unionist candidates to stand down after nursing their constituencies, with his help, for years. He was especially irritated that his subordinates had mistakenly assigned six Scottish coupons to the Coalition Liberals. However, he heatedly denied Liberal charges that he had outmanoeuvred Lloyd George and the Coalition Liberal chief whip, Frederick Guest, in a 'Scottish grab' of constituencies for the Unionists. The 1918 election campaign, resulting in the return of many unattractive 'hard-faced men', prejudiced Younger against the new parliament. He hoped for Unionist withdrawal from the coalition once the latter had implemented its pledge to reform the House of Lords into a powerful second chamber.

Between 1919 and 1921 Younger worked closely with the Unionist chief whip, Sir Robert Sanders, a tory squire who largely shared his negative view of the coalition. Although Younger asked to be relieved as party chairman after his wife's death in 1921, Austen Chamberlain, the new Unionist leader, persuaded him to stay on. Younger had been on excellent terms with Chamberlain's predecessor, Bonar Law, a fellow Scot, but the new leader treated him rather coolly. Younger was also disturbed by Chamberlain's admiration for Lloyd George and his support for Unionist–Coalition Liberal fusion into a new centre party.

Differences between Chamberlain and Younger came to a head in January 1922, when the latter strongly opposed Lloyd George's plan to seek an early new mandate for the coalition. Although Chamberlain himself criticized this strategy, he was indignant when Younger attacked the scheme in the Unionist press. To the annoyance of Lloyd George and Chamberlain, Younger also sent a circular letter to Unionist constituency chairmen warning that the prime minister's scheme would split their party from top to bottom.

Younger again clashed with Chamberlain in September 1922. The Unionist leader now supported Lloyd George's call for an election. Younger realized that Lloyd George and Chamberlain wanted to preclude a probable vote by the forthcoming Unionist annual conference to withdraw from the coalition. Infuriated by Lloyd George's abuse of royal honours and his attempt to exploit the Chanak crisis with Turkey to stay in power, and convinced that the coalition ministry would not reform the House of Lords, Younger determined to use his influence to bring down the government. During early October 1922 he worked closely with Stanley Baldwin, Sir Arthur Griffith-Boscawen, Sir Samuel Hoare, and other anti-coalitionists within the government and the Unionist parliamentary party. Younger (assisted by Sanders, now a junior minister) was the chief liaison between these Unionist rebels and Bonar Law, whom he was trying to persuade to lead the revolt.

It was Younger, more than anyone else, who induced Bonar Law to attend the decisive meeting of the Unionist parliamentary party at the Carlton Club on 19 October 1922 and to furnish the moral support needed to jettison the coalition. In the election campaign that followed, his command of the party machine was strengthened rather than weakened by Lord Birkenhead's gibe that he was the cabin boy who had taken over the ship. Younger's fear that the Unionists could obtain no more than a small majority of seats, and might even lose, was proved unduly pessimistic by the election results.

In 1923 Younger exchanged the party chairmanship for the office of treasurer, and went to the Lords as first Viscount Younger of Leckie. His power and influence within the Conservative Party (as it was again called) remained high during the next six years. To obviate another financial scandal such as had clouded the tenure of the previous treasurer, Lord Farquhar, he arranged that party funds should be safeguarded in a complicated system of trusts. He also insisted that the party chairman should be responsible for raising party funds. He argued strongly for the utmost probity in party money-raising, and its divorce from the honours list. He was pleased when his protégé, J. C. C. Davidson, assumed the chairmanship in 1926, and they worked together amicably. Although frequently critical of Stanley Baldwin's party leadership, Younger staunchly supported him as an obstacle to revival of the coalition spirit.

Younger died of a heart attack, while attending the theatre in London, on 29 April 1929, and was buried at Alloa. His successor as second viscount was his eldest son, James Younger (1880–1946). Two other sons had been killed in action, the second in the Second South African War and the third in the First World War. Younger was chairman of the family brewing firm until his death, and was also a director of the National Bank of Scotland, Lloyds Bank, the North British and Mercantile Insurance Company, and the Southern Railway. At the time of his death he was lord lieutenant of Stirlingshire and vice-lieutenant of Clackmannanshire.   D. M. CREGIER

Sources *The Times* (30 April 1929), 16, 21 • *Memoirs of a Conservative: J. C. C. Davidson's memoirs and papers, 1910–37*, ed. R. R. James (1969) • *Real old tory politics: the political diaries of Robert Sanders, Lord Bayford, 1910–35*, ed. J. Ramsden (1984) • *The Crawford papers: the journals of David Lindsay, twenty-seventh earl of Crawford … 1892–1940*, ed. J. Vincent (1984) • *The modernisation of conservative politics: the diaries and letters of William Bridgeman, 1904–1935*, ed. P. Williamson (1988) • M. Cowling, *The impact of labour, 1920–1924: the beginning of modern British politics* (1971) • K. O. Morgan, *Consensus and disunity: the Lloyd George coalition government, 1918–1922* (1979) • J. Ramsden, *The age of Balfour and Baldwin, 1902–1940* (1978) • R. Blake, *The unknown prime minister: the life and times of Andrew Bonar Law* (1955) • K. Middlemas and J. Barnes, *Baldwin: a biography* (1969) • N. R. McCrillis, 'Taming democracy?: the conservative party and House of Lords' reform, 1916–1929', *Parliamentary History*, 12 (1993), 259–80 • S. E. Koss, *The rise and fall of the political press in Britain*, 2 (1984)

Archives Bodl. Oxf., conservative party archives • Bodl. Oxf., corresp. with H. A. Gwynne • CUL, Baldwin MSS • HLRO, corresp. with Lord Beaverbrook • HLRO, corresp. with Andrew Bonar Law • HLRO, Davidson MSS • HLRO, letters to David Lloyd George • U. Birm., Austen Chamberlain MSS

Likenesses Bassano, photograph, 1922, NPG [*see illus.*] • H. C. O., caricature, Hentschel-colourtype, NPG; repro. in *VF* (6 Jan 1910) • W. Orpen, portrait; known to be at Leckie, Stirlingshire, in 1937; replica, Carlton Club, London

Wealth at death £327,642 16*s*. 9*d*.: confirmation, 16 Aug 1929, *CCI* • £3782 16*s*. 5*d*.: additional estate, 29 Dec 1930, *CCI*

Younger, Henry Johnston (1832–1913), brewer, was born on 5 October 1832 at Moffat, Dumfriesshire, Scotland, the second son of William Younger III, of Craigielands, Dumfriesshire, and his wife, the daughter of an Edinburgh surgeon. He was educated at Edinburgh Academy and the Royal College for Civil Engineers in London and first joined the family brewing firm in Edinburgh in 1852. After two years—presumably having completed an apprenticeship—he left for Australia, and spent much of the period 1855–61 at a sheep farm in the Upper Murray river valley in Victoria, where many Scots had already settled before the gold rush of 1851. Coincidentally, in 1856 the firm entered the Australian market, which, on account of the gold rush, was experiencing boom conditions, and it is likely that Younger played a role in developing the business via Adelaide and Melbourne. Younger returned to Edinburgh in 1861 and became a junior partner to his elder brother, William Younger IV, and another senior partner, Andrew Smith, whose family had been associated with the brewery since 1836.

When Henry Younger rejoined the business in 1861 William's share was estimated at £82,000 and Smith's at £46,000, while Henry's was a junior partner's modest contribution of £2000. But within four years, when the joint capital was put at £180,000, his share was nearly £20,000, a tenfold increase on his initial holding. The old-established firm of William Younger already had an extensive trade at home and overseas, with important markets south of the border, mainly on Tyneside and in London, where in 1866 Younger was put in charge of the new office. William Younger IV and Andrew Smith retired from the business in 1869, leaving control in the hands of three partners, Henry Younger, who became senior partner, his brother David, who had joined the brewery after studying at the University of St Andrews, and Alexander Smith, the son of Andrew Smith.

The firm expanded considerably in the 1870s and early 1880s, and by 1885 its home sales alone were worth more than £400,000 a year, making it the leading brewing enterprise in Scotland. Scottish markets absorbed a little over half of sales, while English and overseas outlets accounted for much of the remainder. During this period both the Abbey and the Holyrood breweries were greatly extended (including stores and bottling plant), and new maltings were built on the Water of Leith at Canonmills. Younger's attention to the London end of the business, a high proportion of which was directed to colonial markets, as well as his passionate concern for quality control, clearly enhanced the firm's reputation in this highly competitive sector.

William Younger & Co. was the first major brewery in Scotland to register with limited liability, in 1887, and three years later, during the general boom in brewery shares caused by the increasing prosperity of the industry, it was floated as a public company. With Younger (as chairman), Andrew Smith (grandson of the first Andrew Smith), and Alexander Bruce (son-in-law of the explorer and missionary David Livingstone) as leading members of the board, the company had an authorized capital of £1 million, divided equally between ordinary and preference shares—a capitalization matched only by their great Edinburgh rival, the more recently established firm of William McEwan.

This was a period when important scientific discoveries were being made in the chemistry of brewing, leading to significant improvements in quality control and a wider range of products, including bottled beers and lagers. In 1884 Younger had ordered the translation of Louis Pasteur's famous paper on fermentation and the chemistry of yeasts, and later welcomed the scientist to Edinburgh. He also donated £500 to Edinburgh University for its building extension fund in Pasteur's honour.

Although he effectively retired from active management on becoming chairman of the board, Younger continued to take a keen interest in the company and kept in constant touch with its affairs. In 1889 he bought the adjoining estates of Benmore and Kilmun at the head of Holy Loch in Argyll, part of which was maintained and developed as an arboretum and later gifted to the nation by his son Harry George Younger. The estate ultimately became an important satellite to the Royal Botanic Garden in Edinburgh. Younger was a deputy lieutenant and JP in Argyll for many years and was described as 'an all-round sportsman and an ideal host'.

Younger was twice married, firstly to Sarah Emma Lowman. The name of his second wife is unknown. He had four sons and five daughters—three of the sons ultimately becoming directors of William Younger & Co. He suffered a heart condition for some years prior to his death, at Earls Court Hotel, Tunbridge Wells, Kent, on 6 March 1913. He left a personal estate of £509,000 gross, with holdings in William Younger & Co. Ltd valued at £181,000, and other major holdings in railway and industrial enterprises. Younger's career might be compared with that of his near contemporary, the apparently more dynamic William McEwan. The latter entered politics and hence had a higher public profile, whereas Younger confined himself mainly to his business and family. Nevertheless Younger made a significant contribution to the success of a major brewing enterprise in the heyday of the industry before the First World War.   IAN DONNACHIE

Sources D. Keir, *The Younger centuries: the story of William Younger & Co. Ltd, 1749 to 1949* (1951) • I. Donnachie, *A history of the brewing industry in Scotland* (1979) • I. Donnachie, 'Younger, Henry Johnston', *DSBB* • b. cert. • d. cert.
Archives U. Glas., Scottish Brewing archive
Likenesses photograph, 1876, repro. in Keir, *The Younger centuries*, facing p. 62 • photograph, repro. in Keir, *The Younger centuries*, facing p. 63
Wealth at death £509,000: will, NA Scot. • £385,043 9s. 6d.: confirmation, 3 June 1913

Younger, John (1785–1860), writer and shoemaker, the youngest of the six children of William Younger, a shoemaker from the Scottish borders, and his wife, Jean Henderson, was born at Longnewton in the parish of Ancrum, Roxburghshire, on 5 July 1785. He had little formal schooling and from the age of nine worked at his father's trade.

The poverty of his youth drove him to excel in poaching and angling. When conditions began to improve he married (9 August 1811) Agnes Riddle (d. 1856), and settled at St Boswells, some 3 miles from Longnewton, as the village shoemaker.

Having bought a copy of Burns for 6d. at St Boswells fair, Younger determined to try his own hand at poetry, although he did not publish anything until *Thoughts as they Rise* in 1834. He also wrote on angling, publishing *River angling for salmon and trout, more particularly as practised in the Tweed and its tributaries* (1840), which was highly praised by *The Field* for its 'practical' value.

Although he was contemptuous of working-class movements, Younger despised the rich, a feeling possibly accentuated by the growing imposition by riparian owners of restrictions on who could fish their waters. He loathed the 'baronial hall'. He had little time for classical Scottish literature, and regarded Sir Walter Scott with especial abomination. He dismissed the Waverley novels as 'old piper stories', 'dwarf and witch tales', and monstrous caricatures of Scottish manners. He was as keen an observer of men as of fish, and he became known as the 'Tweedside Gnostic', as well as being courted as the most proficient Scottish angler. His essay of 1847, 'The temporal advantage of the Sabbath … in relation to the working classes' (published in 1851 as *The Light of the Week*), for which he was awarded a prize of £15, presented to him by Lord Shaftesbury at a ceremony in London, was illuminated by vivid illustrations.

About 1849 Younger was appointed village postmaster, but the routine work proved beyond his patience, and in January 1856 he threw up the post and returned to cobbling. He died at St Boswells, very poor, but honest and industrious to the last, on 18 June 1860, and was buried in St Boswells kirkyard beside his wife, Nannie, whom he had often celebrated in his writings. He left some rich materials for a memoir of himself, to which he had given the title 'Obscurities in private life developed, or, Robinson Crusoe untravelled'. These were recast into an *Autobiography of John Younger*, and published at Kelso in 1881.

THOMAS SECCOMBE, rev. WRAY VAMPLEW

Sources *Autobiography of John Younger*, ed. W. Brockie (1881) • J. Younger, *River angling for salmon and trout, with a memoir of the author* (1860) • W. Henderson, *My life as an angler* (1879) • T. Westwood and T. Satchell, *Bibliotheca piscatoria* (1883) • *The Scotsman* (20 June 1860) • *Sunderland Times* (22 June 1860) • W. E. Winks, *Lives of illustrious shoemakers* (1883) • S. J. Kunitz and H. Haycraft, eds., *British authors of the nineteenth century* (1936)
Likenesses engraving, repro. in Brockie, ed., *Autobiography of John Younger* • engraving, repro. in Younger, *River angling*

Younger, Sir Kenneth Gilmour (1908–1976), politician and reformer, was born on 15 December 1908 at Colton, Dunfermline, Fife, the second child and younger son (there were also two daughters) of James Younger (1880–1946), later second Viscount Younger of Leckie, the son of George *Younger, the first viscount, who was chairman of the Conservative Party. His mother was Maud (d. 1957), daughter of Sir John Gilmour, baronet, and sister of Sir

Sir Kenneth Gilmour Younger (1908–1976), by Bassano, 1947

John Gilmour, a Conservative secretary of state for Scotland. Such parentage did not prevent Younger from joining the Labour Party, which he did as a young man after leaving New College, Oxford, which he had entered from Winchester College. In 1930 he obtained a third-class degree in philosophy, politics, and economics. In 1932 he was called to the bar (Inner Temple) and practised up to 1939. During the war he served in the intelligence corps, finishing as a temporary major on the staff of Field Marshal Montgomery.

After the general election of 1945, at which he was returned as Labour member for Grimsby, Younger seemed set on a political career destined to take him to the highest office. Almost at once he was attached as parliamentary private secretary to the minister of state at the Foreign Office. Thus he put down the root of one of the interests he was to follow all his life: the promotion of international goodwill and the development of supra-national institutions. In December 1945 he was sent as a British alternate delegate to the United Nations, and in 1946 was appointed chairman of the European committee of the United Nations Relief and Rehabilitation Administration. In 1947 he moved to the Home Office after a brief spell in the Ministry of Civil Aviation and there put down the root of his other interests, individual rights and penal reform.

In the parliament of 1950–51 Younger was minister of state at the Foreign Office under Ernest Bevin. Owing to Bevin's ill health a great deal of the work fell to Younger in the difficult and shifting world of post-war international relations. These two—looking, as someone remarked, like an old polar bear attended by a lively cub—became a

familiar and welcome sight in the House of Commons. Younger was an outstandingly efficient departmental minister who inspired trust and affection in those with whom he dealt, and some of the acclaim which has rightly been accorded to Bevin as foreign secretary should be shared by his minister of state. In 1951 he was made a privy councillor.

Though Younger joined the shadow cabinet after 1951 when Labour went into opposition his heart was not in the often negative and wearisome battles which an opposition must wage; he was essentially constructive. Nor could he pretend to an indignation he did not feel, a faculty considered essential to the ambitious. He was in politics not for the glittering prizes, but to achieve results in his chosen fields. When he felt this could be done better by service elsewhere he felt no great compulsion to stay in parliament. So in 1959 he left the House of Commons and shortly afterwards became director of Chatham House—the Royal Institute of International Affairs. Here he was able to return to one of his main interests: foreign policy. Younger realized sooner than most people that Britain was no longer an imperial power nor a superpower but that her role lay through the United Nations and world and regional co-operation. To such co-operation Younger believed Britain could bring particular talents through her long experience and through her position on the Atlantic seaboard of Europe and in the Commonwealth.

In the meantime Younger maintained his interest in legal and penal matters. From 1966 he was chairman of the Advisory Council on the Penal System. In 1970 he was appointed chairman of the committee of inquiry into privacy. In 1972 he was a member of the committee on Northern Ireland chaired by Lord Diplock, and for thirteen years from 1960 to 1973 was chairman of the Howard League for Penal Reform. He served on many other bodies, and was a governor of St George's Hospital. In 1968 he was given an honorary doctorate by St John's University, New York, and in 1972 was appointed KBE. He published and edited various Fabian and other essays connected with his public work. *A Study in International Affairs* (ed. R. P. Morgan, 1972) was compiled in his honour.

Younger's premature death deprived the country of an able and unselfish public servant and his friends of a delightful and incisive companion. His modesty, his innocent appearance, and his courtesy could mislead casual acquaintances. They would be brought up short by his precise and often radical opinions caustically expressed. He was no tolerator of slovenliness. Indeed at Chatham House he ruthlessly weeded out those whom he felt had nothing to contribute, however venerable and respected they might be. His own contributions, whether in formal meetings or private conversation, were invariably to the point. He was in the tradition of practical reformers. He had no great interest in fashionable dogma, but to the end developed his opinions from a firm belief in the possibility of improving the human lot by firm guidance of the institutions at our command. On 23 August 1934 he had married Elizabeth Kirsteen, daughter of William Duncan Stewart JP, of Achara, Duror, Argyll, a wife who matched his abilities and his temperament. They had one son and two daughters. Younger died at his London home, 3 Clareville Grove, on 19 May 1976. He was survived by his wife.

J. GRIMOND, rev.

Sources personal knowledge (1986) · *The Times* (21 May 1976) · Burke, *Peerage* (1999) · *CGPLA Eng. & Wales* (1976)
Archives Bodl. RH, corresp. relating to colonial issues · NRA, papers | King's Lond., Liddell Hart C., corresp. with Sir B. H. Liddell Hart | FILM BFI NFTVA, party political footage
Likenesses Bassano, photograph, 1947, NPG [*see illus.*]
Wealth at death £44,320: probate, 26 Aug 1976, *CGPLA Eng. & Wales*

Younger, Robert, Baron Blanesburgh (1861–1946), judge, was born at Alloa, Clackmannanshire, on 12 September 1861, the fifth son of James Younger (1818–1868), of the well-known family of brewers, and his wife, Janet (*d.* 1912), daughter of John McEwan. His eldest brother was George *Younger, first Viscount Younger of Leckie. Educated at the Edinburgh Academy and at Balliol College, Oxford, Younger gained a third class in classical moderations in 1881 and a second in jurisprudence in 1883. In 1884 he was called to the bar by the Inner Temple in London and entered the chambers of John Gorell Barnes as a pupil. Later he transferred locally, to Lincoln's Inn, where he devilled for some years for Henry Burton Buckley.

Younger's career was helped by his successful advocacy and his legal competence. In 1900 he took silk, and as a leader he came to be well liked. In 1915 he was appointed a judge of the Chancery Division in succession to Sir Thomas Rolls Warrington and received the customary knighthood. His next move was to the Court of Appeal in 1919, in succession to Sir Henry Edward Duke. Finally, after Lord Cave became lord chancellor in 1922, Younger succeeded him in 1923 as a lord of appeal, with a life peerage as Baron Blanesburgh of Alloa. It has been said that his career was largely a tribute to his personality and the charm it radiated. He was a cultivated man with a love of books, painting, and music, something his wealth allowed him to pursue without restraint.

As a judge Younger was competent rather than distinguished. As a lord of appeal he sat from 1923 to 1937. It was a time when Atkin, Macmillan, and Wright held sway, but Blanesburgh was overshadowed by his peers. His vision of the role of an appeal judge was to look for the current law. He saw little role for any creative function in the final Court of Appeal. He was thus a dissenter in the seminal case of *Donoghue* v. *Stevenson* (1932), establishing the modern tort of negligence, and he favoured a narrow view of contract (*Bell* v. *Lever Bros*, 1932). His preferred solution was to leave any change in the law to parliament, as in *Harett* v. *Fisher* (1927). For Younger the search for the *ratio decidendi* was all: 'I agree, of course, at once, that by the *ratio decidendi* of that case—if it can be discovered—and by the decision itself—whether its *ratio decidendi* can be discovered or not—your Lordships are as much bound as is at least every English Court' (*Great Western Railway* v. *The Mostyn* (*owners*), [1928] AC 57, 99). Formalism was all. As the years passed, however, Blanesburgh's narrow views irritated his colleagues. In 1935, in a memorandum to the incoming Lord Chancellor Hailsham, his fellow law lord, Lord Dunedin, said of him: 'You will *not* as Sankey did, refuse his resignation' (Heuston, 481). Eventually poor eyesight forced him out in 1937.

Apart from the law, Younger was involved in various public service activities during the First World War. In May 1915 he was appointed a member of an advisory committee set up to deal with claims by enemy subjects in the United Kingdom for exemption from internment or deportation. In September 1915 the Home Office appointed him chairman of a committee on the treatment by the enemy of British prisoners of war. Younger was also chairman of a committee established in 1920 to advise on applications from ex-enemy nationals for release of their property. Probably his most arduous public service was rendered from 1925 to 1930 as principal British representative on the reparation commission under the treaty of peace with Germany. For his public services he was appointed GBE in 1917.

The ample means which he enjoyed enabled Younger to gratify his generous instincts by many benefactions. He was, in turn, honoured for his distinction. He became a bencher of Lincoln's Inn in 1907 and was treasurer in 1932. Balliol College, of which he was made an honorary fellow in 1916 and in 1934 visitor, had special reason for gratitude since he helped renovate the dining hall and chapel. Oxford University made him an honorary DCL (1928), and from the universities of Edinburgh (1919) and St Andrews (1929) he received the honorary degree of LLD. He was also chairman of the delegates of King's College, London (1929–44), prime warden of the Goldsmiths' Company (1931–2), and chairman of the Royal Caledonian Schools. He died, unmarried, at his Sussex home, the Grey Friars, Winchelsea, on 17 August 1946.

MACMILLAN, rev. ROBERT STEVENS

Sources *The Times* (20 Aug 1946) · *Law Times* (31 Aug 1946) · personal knowledge (1959) · R. Stevens, *Law and politics: the House of Lords as a judicial body, 1800–1976* (1978) · R. F. V. Heuston, *Lives of the lord chancellors, 1885–1940* (1964) · Burke, *Peerage* (1939)
Likenesses H. G. Riviere, oils, *c.*1933, Balliol Oxf.
Wealth at death £337,980 11s. 10d.: probate, 7 Nov 1946, *CGPLA Eng. & Wales*

Younger, Sir William McEwan, of Fountainbridge, baronet (1905–1992), brewer and political activist, was born at Ravenswood, Melrose, Roxburghshire, on 6 September 1905, the second son in a family of two sons and one daughter of William Younger (1857–1925), brewer, of Ravenswood, Melrose, and his wife, Katharine Theodora (*d.* 1961), daughter of Commander Adam Alexander Duncan Dundas, 27th chief of Dundas, naval officer. His father was the brother of George Younger, first Viscount Younger, and of Robert Younger, Baron Blanesburgh; his paternal grandmother, Janet, *née* McEwan, was the eldest sister of William McEwan, Gladstonian Liberal MP for Edinburgh and the founder of McEwan's Brewery. He was thus brought up with a background of brewing and politics, and heavily influenced by an atmosphere of free trade and competition. He was educated at Winchester College, but blossomed during his time at Balliol College, Oxford, from 1924 to 1928. While at Oxford he was introduced to mountaineering and he became an accomplished rock-climber in the Alps, the Lake District, and the Cuillins, and was on the shortlist, though not selected, for the Everest expedition of 1928. For a not overconfident young man, the acquisition of skill and daring learned in rock climbing, together with the general ethos of the pursuit of excellence inherent in a Balliol education, produced a spirit ready to challenge existing attitudes in both commerce and politics. He graduated with a second-class degree in modern history in 1928.

On leaving Oxford, Younger (known as Bill) joined the firm of Wm McEwan & Co., brewers, of which his father had been the managing director. He learned his trade from the bottom, with spells as maltman, shift brewer, and salesman. Part of his training took place in London, where he stayed in the house of the celebrated Dame Margaret *Greville, Edwardian hostess and heir and presumed daughter of William McEwan. Dame Margaret was so impressed by the young man that when she died she left him all her ordinary shares, though they were at that time unquoted.

In 1931 the Edinburgh brewing firms of Wm Younger (not a relative) and Wm McEwan amalgamated with a joint equity as Scottish Brewers Ltd but in trade continued to compete fiercely with each other. However, the older William Younger was still very much the senior partner and Younger found his radical business ideas had to be suppressed. On 24 June 1936 he married Nora Elizabeth (b. 1916), eldest daughter of Brigadier Edward William Sturgis Balfour and Lady Ruth Balfour of Balbirnie; there was one daughter, Caroline Ruth, born in 1946. In 1937 Younger joined the Royal Artillery, in the Territorial Army. When war came in 1939 he quickly rose to be a major in the 40th light anti-aircraft (LAA) battery and in November 1940 he was sent to the Middle East. While in command of the LAA battery he took part in the first siege of Tobruk, where his valiant and original air defence of the fortress earned him the DSO. He was subsequently promoted lieutenant-colonel commanding the 14th LAA regiment, took part in the remainder of the north African campaign, and, after landing at Salerno, followed the war in Italy until the armistice. Known by his men as Colonel Screwtop, the main supplier of beer to the army being McEwan Youngers, he returned from the war with greatly increased self-confidence and a determination to put his radical ideas to the test.

Younger stood twice as the tory candidate for West Lothian, a seat almost certainly unattainable for a conservative, but after defeat in the 1950 election he confined his political ambitions to work for the party and concentrated his main efforts on brewing.

In the immediate post-war years the brewing industry was dominated by family-owned companies. The relaxation of rationing allowed much increased production from existing equipment, and consumption rose rapidly. The main place of sale was the public house; lager was a minor brand and cans had only just begun. As the families of the many smaller, family-owned brewers sought to realize the value of their investments, these breweries fell into the hands of larger companies seeking to enlarge the number of their tied outlets. The process was accelerated in the late 1950s when the Canadian brewer Ed Taylor started to buy up individual companies and amalgamate them to make larger groups. The whole industry was thrown into turmoil, and many firms sought protection by running for cover to larger groups.

In Scotland the situation was somewhat different. The tenanted public house was a rarity and customers were tied to a brewery by loans, often at lower than commercial rates. A large proportion of the trade was completely free and depended on the marketing of individual brands. Younger, by now managing director of Scottish Brewers Ltd, saw this as an opportunity, concentrated on the free trade, and developed brand marketing to an extent not previously seen in the industry. He encouraged the development of the can, which was particularly suited to the growing trade in off-licences and eventually supermarkets. Under his leadership Scottish Brewers Ltd became the dominant force in Scotland and the north of England.

Although many smaller brewers came to him for protection, Younger refused to buy except for cash, taking the view that the issue of shares would cause a dilution of shareholder equity. He believed strongly in competition, and when the main rival to Scottish Brewers Ltd in Scotland was offered to him he refused the offer on the basis that the resultant combine would so dominate the Scottish brewing scene as to extinguish competition and blunt the competitive edge of his company. His business philosophy was at variance with that of the rest of the brewing industry and he took no part in the councils of the various trade associations. In 1961 Newcastle Breweries joined the group. The name was changed to Scottish and Newcastle, and Younger became the chairman and managing director.

In spite of his education and background, Younger was anything but a conventional establishment figure. His business philosophy often consisted in seeing what the opposition was up to and then doing something completely different. Within the parameters of his policy directives, he allowed his subordinates to get on with their work without interference. Under his leadership the Scottish and Newcastle group developed rapidly during the 1960s, and the shareholding left him by Dame Margaret Greville made him a rich man. By 1970 he felt he needed a change, and he retired in order to devote himself to politics and his other business interests, and to dispose of a large part of his fortune. His marriage had started to fail in the 1960s and he was divorced in 1967.

Younger was the honorary secretary of the Scottish Unionist Association from 1955 to 1964, when he was made a baronet. In 1968 he and two colleagues were asked to go to Belfast to see whether Stormont could be a pattern for a Scottish assembly. The report was accepted by a large majority of Scottish tories and Edward Heath announced in 1970 in the declaration of Perth that there would be a

Scottish assembly. Younger was chairman of the Conservative Party in Scotland from 1971 to 1974 and worked closely with Heath. He was a left-centre tory and when Margaret Thatcher disavowed the declaration of Perth he withdrew.

Younger was a director of many Scottish businesses including the Scottish Widows Fund, the British Linen Bank, and Scottish Television, and was for several years chairman of the Scottish Investment Trust. He was the moving spirit behind the successful annual international forum of the Scottish Council (Development and Industry). He was a founder, trustee, and generous supporter of the Institute of Economic Affairs. In the 1950s he had given away his house at Balerno to the Save the Children Fund. He now created the Craignish Trust, one of the chief beneficiaries being Balliol College, as a result of which he was made an honorary fellow, a distinction of which he was immensely proud.

In 1983 Younger married June Peck (b. 1933), but by now his health was starting to fail and he retired to Little Hill Cottage, Harpsden, Henley-on-Thames, where he died on 14 April 1992. He was cremated at Reading on 23 April, and was survived by his wife and the daughter of his first marriage.   P. E. G. BALFOUR

Sources b. cert. · m. cert. · college register, Balliol Oxf. · P. E. G. Balfour, *Address given at memorial service, Canongate church* (1992) · private information (2004) [Lord Stodart, Viscount Younger of Leckie, Lady Younger] · *WWW* · Burke, *Peerage* · A. Glen, 'Sir William McEwan Younger (1905–1992)', *Balliol College Annual Record* (1992), 31–3 · I. Donnachie, *A history of the brewing industry in Scotland* (1979) · *CCI* (1992) · d. cert.

Likenesses C. Sims, portrait, tempera, priv. coll. · A. Sutherland, drawing, Scottish & Newcastle plc, boardroom · photograph, repro. in *Balliol College Annual Record*, 31

Wealth at death £1,214,372.72: confirmation, 1992, *CCI*

Younghusband, Dame Eileen Louise (1902–1981), welfare worker, was born in London on 1 January 1902, the only daughter and younger child (her brother died in infancy) of Sir Francis Edward *Younghusband (1863–1942), explorer and founder of the World Congress of Faiths, and his wife, Helen Augusta, daughter of Charles Magniac MP of Colworth, Bedfordshire. She lived in India for the first seven years of her life before returning to England with her parents. Her unusual father was one of the formative influences on her life, and her mother, who was descended from an aristocratic Irish family, wrote a number of books but expected her daughter to lead the life of a débutante and to marry. After a private education Eileen Younghusband attended the London School of Economics (LSE), to her mother's dismay. There she gained an external certificate in social studies, followed by the university diploma in sociology (1926).

In 1929 Eileen Younghusband was appointed half-time tutor at LSE, but four years later she obtained a full-time post there. Her interests lay in the problems of the poor and deprived, and much of her time was spent as a voluntary social worker with such organizations as the Citizens' Advice Bureau and the London county council care committees. In 1933 she was appointed a JP in Stepney; her

Dame Eileen Louise Younghusband (1902–1981), by Kyffin Williams

work in the juvenile court meant much to her. She worked in the clubs run by the Bermondsey settlement and also became involved in courses financed by the British Council for refugee women returning to their own countries after the Second World War.

In 1941 Eileen Younghusband became principal officer for training and employment for youth leaders for the National Association of Girls' Clubs. Two years later, at the request of the National Assistance Board, she undertook a survey of the welfare needs of the recipients of benefit, which took her to all parts of England and Wales. In 1945 she undertook for the United Kingdom Carnegie Trust a survey which stressed the need for the provision of training for social workers. This was updated in 1951. In 1955 the Ministry of Health invited her to chair a working party on the role of social workers in the local authority health and welfare services. This covered elderly people, disabled persons, and people with mental illnesses. So great was the need for social workers that what became known as the Younghusband report recommended that training courses should be set up in the polytechnics and colleges of further education as well as in the universities. As a result the Council for Training in Social Work was set up and the social work certificate initiated. The health visitors formed their own council. There were those who regretted that the childcare officers in the children's departments were not included. A further outcome of the Younghusband report was the establishment of the National Institute for Social Work Training in which she was much involved, acting subsequently as its consultant (1961–7).

Eileen Younghusband was much influenced by social work practice and training in the United States, where she was a frequent visitor. On the basis of the American experience she worked for a course, to be called applied social studies, to be set up in the London School of Economics. Despite considerable disagreement among the staff she remained fiercely adamant; finally, with a Carnegie grant and encouragement from Baroness Elliot of Harwood, she pioneered in 1954 a generic course, known as the Carnegie experiment, which became the prototype for professional social work training in other universities. The considerable disagreement among the LSE staff led to her resignation in 1957; in 1961 she was awarded an honorary fellowship.

Eileen Younghusband maintained that there were basic social work principles which applied to all settings of need, but did not deny the need for specialization in particular fields such as the care of children and elderly and disabled people. She believed in the integration of theory and practice, with theory concentrating on the understanding of human growth and development and the use of personal relationships to effect change. She recommended qualified tutors able to knit together theory and practice. She insisted that good social work practice lay not only in acquiring knowledge and skill, but in the possession of personal qualities of a high order.

Eileen Younghusband was tireless in her work overseas. After the Second World War she worked for the United Nations Relief and Rehabilitation Administration, and in 1948 went to Geneva as a consultant on the social welfare fellowship programme. In 1952–3 she made a study visit of five weeks to India and Pakistan and in 1954 she took a six-month course in the USA on a Smith Mundt fellowship. She was a consultant to the School of Social Work in Greece and the social welfare department in Hong Kong, and she served as an external examiner at the universities of Hong Kong, Columbia, Nottingham, Khartoum, and at the University College of Makerere. She was president of the International Association of Schools of Social Work, and later an honorary life president; this gave her the opportunity to visit Africa and Asia. To crown her international work, in 1976 she was given the René Sand award, the highest award in the field of international social work.

Eileen Younghusband was a very private person who talked little about herself or her early life. She was humane and had a wide range of deep friendships; many friends visited her in her top-floor flat in Holland Park, London, and to them in her later years she would drop her front door key from her window. She had an intense curiosity about people. Her interests, which were not confined to social work and education, were wide-ranging and included the stock exchange. She had an abiding love for mountains, wild flowers, birds, and butterflies. There were aspects of her personality which presented paradoxes; she was on occasion domineering, yet also humble;

towards herself she was frugal, towards others she was generous. She was sophisticated and yet was almost childlike in her enjoyment of simple things—food, a journey, a flight. She was a realist, on occasions an opportunist, stubborn and manipulative, but never for herself and only for the things in which she believed. She is remembered for her contribution to the training of social workers, her belief in social justice, and her influence on social policy. She also had a depth of spirituality, derived perhaps from her father, which was not obtrusive but of which one was aware.

Eileen Younghusband was appointed MBE (1946), CBE (1955), and DBE (1964). She had honorary degrees from the universities of British Columbia, Nottingham, Bradford, York, and Hong Kong. Throughout her working life she experienced happiness and stimulation from her many friends in the USA—a country she loved. It was on her way to Raleigh airport, North Carolina, that she was killed outright in a car accident at Raleigh on 27 May 1981. She was unmarried.
LUCY FAITHFULL, *rev.*

Sources The Times (30 May 1981) · CGPLA Eng. & Wales (1981) · K. Jones, Eileen Younghusband (1984) · personal knowledge (1990) · private information (1990) [R. H. Jones]
Archives BLPES, papers · National Institute for Social Work, Tavistock Place, London, corresp. and papers
Likenesses K. Williams, oils, NPG [see illus.]
Wealth at death £414,932: probate, 3 Aug 1981, CGPLA Eng. & Wales

Younghusband, Sir Francis Edward (1863–1942), explorer, geographer, and mystic, was born on 31 May 1863 at Murree, India, the fourth of the five children of Major (later Major-General) John William Younghusband and his wife, Clara Jane, daughter of Robert Grant Shaw; he had two brothers and two sisters. He was educated at Clifton College and at the Royal Military College, Sandhurst, and was commissioned in the 1st (King's) dragoon guards in 1882, then stationed at Meerut, India.

Younghusband made his name as an exploring soldier and imperialist. His was a classic British imperialism, not shy of exercising brute power, but more typically presenting itself as a paternalistic endeavour, helping 'lower' races while furthering Britain's cause against imperial rivals. The empire exemplified his principle of 'unity in difference', in which the 'advanced' races dictated terms for all. In 1886 he accompanied a seven-month expedition to Manchuria. In Peking (Beijing) in March 1887 he met his superior Colonel Mark Sever Bell, and the two men obtained leave to return to India by separate land routes. Younghusband, alone with hired guides, spent seven months crossing the Gobi Desert to Hami, and over the Himalaya via Kashgar and the Muztagh Pass to Kashmir. The crossing of this 19,000 foot pass was a rite of passage which heightened his sense of being a lone Englishman carrying 'England's mission' into new territory. In a letter of 1901 to his friend Henry Newbolt he would write: 'The Empire must grow: we can't help it' (French, 156). On returning to London in April 1888 Younghusband lectured to the Royal Geographical Society; he was elected their

Sir Francis Edward Younghusband (1863–1942), by Sir William Quiller Orchardson, 1906

youngest fellow, and awarded the founder's medal in 1890. In 1889–91 he consolidated his role as a trekking arm of empire in the border zones of British India, Russia, China, and Afghanistan, and recorded these journeys in *The Heart of a Continent* (1896). In 1891 he was appointed CIE; in August 1892 he became political officer in Hunza; and in 1893–4 he was political agent in Chitral, overseeing British interests in the region. Replaced in 1894, he returned as the *Times* correspondent with the Chitral relief force in 1895. His long leave from 1895 to 1897 was spent as the *Times* correspondent in Rhodesia and Transvaal, recorded in *South Africa of Today* (1897). He later regretted his part in the Jameson raid on Johannesburg against the Boer government as a mercenary undertaking.

In August 1897 Younghusband married Helen Augusta, the eldest daughter of Charles Magniac MP, of Colworth, Bedfordshire; they had a son who died in infancy and a daughter, Eileen Louise *Younghusband, born in 1902. Younghusband returned to India with his wife in November 1898. After a year in administration he became political agent at Deoli, and in 1900 was awarded the kaisar-i-Hind gold medal. In 1902 Curzon appointed him resident in Indore, and in 1903 leader of a mission to Tibet to establish British political and commercial interest, and to survey the region, a focus of Anglo-Russian rivalry. Younghusband entered Tibet in December 1903. With a mainly Indian fighting force, eventually exceeding 10,000, he advanced in stages towards Lhasa. A massacre of 700 Tibetans at Chumi Shengo in April 1904 caused disquiet in Britain. After further bloodshed he rode into Lhasa in August. Crowds clapped his entry; Younghusband took as a welcome what was a Tibetan gesture to ward off an evil spirit. The government considered he had exceeded his instructions by negotiating a treaty, signed on 7 September 1904 and regarded the treaty itself as damaging to Anglo-Russian relations. A renegotiated treaty, finally agreed in 1906, drastically reduced Britain's commitment to and power over the region. In Verrier's view (1991) Younghusband was politically naïve, pursuing a chivalrous quest rather than a strategic mission, and exceeded his brief even by advancing to Lhasa. French (1994) presents the Tibet mission as the embodiment of empire at its overstretched zenith. Younghusband was in effect reprimanded in 1904 by the award of the low honour of knight commander of the Indian Empire. He recounted the mission in *India and Tibet* (1910). He was made knight commander of the Star of India in 1917.

In 1905 Younghusband received honorary degrees from Cambridge (DSc) and Edinburgh (LLD). In 1906 he returned to central Asia as resident in Kashmir, retiring to England in 1910, where he joined the Conservative general election campaign. He reflected on his imperial career in *The Light of Experience* (1927), and the autobiographical romance *But in our Lives* (1926). In 1912 he received an honorary LLD from Bristol University. In the First World War, after an unsuccessful attempt to set up a travellers' battalion, he prepared daily news telegrams for the India Office, and in 1916 founded the Fight for Right society, for whom Sir Hubert Parry set Blake's 'Jerusalem' as a rallying hymn in their campaign for the continuation of the war. Younghusband's interest in central Asia and India remained. He was a founder and later vice-president (1934–42) of the Royal Central Asian Society, and chairman of the Royal India and Pakistan Society for eighteen years. He modified his bullish imperialism, however, and, after the publication in 1930 of *Dawn in India*, became known as a progressive advocate of a managed shift towards Indian self-government.

From 1910 religion and philosophy played an increasing role in Younghusband's public life. His first predominantly spiritual text, *Within* (1912), was a vitalist mix of science and spirit written in convalescence after being hit by a car in Belgium. *Mutual Influence* followed in 1915. He drew inspiration from Eastern religions as well as Christianity, especially in his linkage of mysticism and sex. Younghusband's imperialism sought a mutual exchange of Western 'civilization' and Eastern spirituality. His was a philosophically speculative religion, and he was a member of the Aristotelian Society from 1910, and president in 1924–7 of the Patrick Geddes-inspired Sociological Society. His presidential address on 'The sense of society' appeared in the *Sociological Review* (17.1–13) for 1925. He was vice-chairman of the religion and ethics branch of the League of Nations Union, League of Nations' representative at the Parliament of Religions in Calcutta in 1937, and chairman of the Society for the Study of Religions. In 1930, inspired by seeing the Oberammergau passion play, he became chairman of the interdenominational Religious Drama Society, founded by Olive Stevenson. The society sponsored conferences, drama schools, and touring productions. Younghusband remained chairman until death; in 1930 he published a play, *The Reign of God*. The Religious Drama Society was anticipated by the Sacred Drama Society of his bizarre utopian religious fantasy, *The Coming Country* (1928), which is peopled by characters such as Percy Veerance and Golden Promyss. In 1936 Younghusband founded the World Congress of Faiths to bring together the chief world religions in a communion for peace. He presided at meetings and wrote circulars to members until his death. For Younghusband the divide was less between Christian and heathen, than between religious and faithless; the villains in *The Coming Country* are rationalism, secularism, and materialism.

A sense of religion as universal lay at the heart of Younghusband's mysticism. A member of the Church of England, he had worshipped with other Christian denominations, and engaged with other faiths on his travels. He sought a direct mystical encounter with a divine and feminized nature, and often recounted a formative moment outside Lhasa in 1904 when he felt himself 'boiling over with love for the whole world' (French, 252). He outlined his nature-mysticism in his 1920 presidential address to the Royal Geographical Society on 'Natural beauty and geographical science', *GJ*, 1920, 56.1–13, and in *The Heart of Nature* (1921), *Mother World* (1924), *The Living Universe* (1933), *Modern Mystics* (1935), and *Vital Religion* (1940). His outdoor mysticism demanded action as much as introspection, and sought the mystical through the visible world in a way both metaphorically and literally visionary. *The Coming Country* proposed a 'new faculty' of 'endsight': 'a kind of spiritual television' (p. 9). His mysticism, linking science and spirit, was presented not as misty unreason but as the clearest insight into the material world, serving evolution by anticipating future higher states. Evolution advanced through disciplined joy, a progressive ecstasy achieved by mystics alone, and by others in sexual union within marriage. *Wedding* (1942), written with his mistress, Madeline Lees, with whom he harboured thoughts of siring a new God-child, offered a guide to such married love.

Younghusband's spiritual journeys were conducted in the language of Himalayan exploring; he could describe an intensive reading course in philosophy as 'bracing' (Seaver, 277). This practical mysticism was reflected in his presidency from 1934 of Richard St Barbe Baker's practical and spiritual forestry group, the Men of the Trees. The mystic could offer socio-spiritual unity and leadership. *The Heart of Nature* foresees a 'naturalist-artist' who might lead human evolution from *Homo sapiens* to *Homo mysticus*. *Modern Mystics* presents exemplary Hindu, Muslim, Roman Catholic, and protestant mystics, male and female, recalls his enthusiasm in 1905 for the 'mass mysticism' of the Welsh revival, and looks for a future 'master mystic'. The espousal of joy, struggle, and the evolutionary leaving-behind of 'sluggards' (p. 279) prompts an admiring reference to Mussolini.

Younghusband's mysticism did not shy from speculation. *Life in the Stars* (1927) is subtitled: 'An exposition of the view that on some planets of some stars exist beings higher than ourselves, and on one a world-leader, the supreme embodiment of the eternal spirit which animates the whole'. *The Living Universe* posits a planet, Altair, on which live higher beings, who embody his ideal characteristics of family, team spirit, leadership, ecstasy, struggle. His astro-theology fits a general pattern of ascendancy in his thought. Star-gazing prompts many a spiritual reflection and advance is typically ascent. The mountains of central Asia, recalled in *Wonders of the Himalaya* (1924), were the key landscape of his life. Immanent and transcendent, the 'holy Himalaya' envelop and rise above, a mystical immensity landscaped in his image of God.

Younghusband promoted British expeditions to Everest, chairing the Mount Everest committee formed by the RGS, of which he was president in 1919–22, and the Alpine Club. Mountaineering exercised mind, body, and spirit, and through it a rising British masculinity might scale for empire and humankind the heights of nature. A founder member of the Himalayan Club in 1928, he recalled Everest attempts in *The Epic of Mount Everest* (1926), and *Everest: the Challenge* (1936). Had Everest been conquered in his lifetime, there would have been a hole in his philosophy: ascendancy depended on there being something left to scale.

Younghusband retained a late-Victorian masculine sense of himself and others. Shorter than the 5 feet 5 inches he claimed, he sported a prominent moustache throughout adult life. His biographers present a determined individual committed to the camaraderie of the couple, family, troop, nation, empire, and world—yet who found it hard to get close to others. His ideal leaders and heroes resolve the tensions between individualism and collective organization in the regiment, exploring party, and climbing team. In his Everest writings physical heroism is projected onto others; elsewhere he himself is the hero in his own landscape, with action and environment feeding off one another. Younghusband remained loyal to his ideal of England/Britain (the two were symbolically equivalent for him) throughout his life. In the Second World War he fire-watched in London, and melted his medals down for the war effort. French suggests that Younghusband's intense care for humanity as a whole coincided with an ironic neglect of individuals close to him, notably his wife and his sister Emmie. His marriage lacked emotional depth: Helen Younghusband led a quiet and melancholy home life (from 1921 to 1937 at Westerham, Kent), while her husband ranged around the country and the globe. In 1939 he met Madeline Lees, thirty-two years his junior and mother of seven children, with whom he conducted a passionately mystical affair until his death.

Younghusband was erroneously reported dead by *The Times* in 1891. On 20 July 1942, after addressing the World Congress of Faiths in Birmingham, he was taken ill and suffered a stroke a few days later. He died of cardiac failure at Madeline Lees's home at Post Green, Lytchett Minster, near Poole, Dorset, on 31 July 1942, and was buried in the village churchyard. Since his death Younghusband has attracted sporadic attention. Early works, notably Seaver's 1952 biography, are informative but hagiographic. Later work is more critical: military historians such as Verrier (1991) have presented the Tibet mission in less flattering light. French's 1994 account shows Younghusband less as a hero than as a fascinating embodiment of the contradictions and eccentricities of the imperial age. Matless (1991) and Bishop (1989), drawing on Younghusband's mystical environmental writings, similarly stress complex contradiction rather than straightforward heroism, seeing mysticism, exploration, and imperialism as connected spheres.   DAVID MATLESS

Sources P. French, *Younghusband: the last great imperial adventurer* (1994) · G. Seaver, *Francis Younghusband: explorer and mystic* (1952) · D. Matless, 'Nature, the modern and the mystic: tales from early twentieth century geography', *Transactions of the Institute of British Geographers*, new ser., 16 (1991), 272–86 · P. Bishop, *The myth of Shangri-La: Tibet, travel writing, and the Western creation of sacred landscape* (1989) · A. Verrier, *Francis Younghusband and the great game* (1991) · *DNB* · d. cert.
Archives BL · BL OIOC, corresp. and papers, MS Eur. F 197 · NRA, corresp. and literary papers · RGS, journals and letters | BL OIOC, corresp. with F. M. Bailey, MS Eur. F 157 · BL OIOC, letters to Sir James Dunlop Smith · Bodl. Oxf., letters to Gilbert Murray · Bodl. Oxf., letters to Sir Horace Rumbold · CUL, letters to Sir Martin Conway · CUL, corresp. with Lord Hardinge · JRL, letters to the *Manchester Guardian* · RGS, Asia travel journal · RGS, letters to RGS
Likenesses W. Q. Orchardson, oils, 1906, NPG [*see illus.*] · J. E. Hyett, bronze bust, *c*.1917, RGS · W. Stoneman, photograph, 1929, NPG · H. Speed, oils, *c*.1937, World Congress of Faiths, London

Youngman, Nancy Mayhew [Nan] (1906–1995), painter and art educationist, was born in Lensfield House, Maidstone, Kent, on 28 June 1906, the daughter of John Henry Youngman (1868?–*c*.1948), a partner in the corn merchants Bradley, Taylor, and Youngman, and his wife, Adelaide Edith (Bida), *née* Marshall (1871?–*c*.1950). Nan Youngman had two elder brothers, one of whom was killed in Flanders in 1916. She was educated at Wycombe Abbey School, Buckinghamshire, and at the Slade School of Fine Art (1924–7). Nan Youngman lived through one of the most formative periods in British painting during a period of social, ideological, and political change to which most artists of her time felt obliged to respond. Her painting was anchored in the craftsmanship demanded by Henry Tonks and Philip Wilson Steer at the Slade and was initially linked, broadly, with social realism. Her painting was always uncompromisingly original as was her approach to her work in education, her personal life, and the relationships in which she was involved. Nan Youngman belonged to no school. While moving on from her rather austere palette knife paintings of the 1930s she remained consciously apart from any of the modernist movements. But her sharp and humorous eye for the incongruous resulted in what are, at times, surrealist images—a ruined freestanding wall and iron gate juxtaposed with an ancient bicycle, a forlorn red sign on a deserted station, or a couple of windswept beach huts which appear to be knowingly returning the viewer's gaze. The

Nancy Mayhew Youngman (1906–1995), self-portrait, 1948

people in her paintings are acutely observed but this acuity of vision is recorded more through their signs and works than in their figures. The surrealist quality of these pictures, while less obvious, is present in the gentle irony that informs all her work, even the most serious of her industrial landscapes.

Nan Youngman saw herself as a socialist, but was offended by Soviet communism. She was a freethinker and a religious sceptic with a liking for ribald and irreverent jokes. Behind the diminutive figure with the pudding basin haircut, trousers, blue smock, and ready grin was a formidable organizer, a leader, and a teacher who inspired admiration, at times adulation, among those she led and taught.

Nan Youngman's working life was divided between painting and teaching. After leaving the Slade she took an art teacher's diploma at the London Day Training Centre under Marion Richardson and began to teach part-time at Highbury Girls' School, London. From Richardson she inherited the strong belief in the importance of art in the curriculum which underlay all her subsequent work in art education.

In the 1930s she showed at the Wertheim Gallery and with the London Group. In 1936 Youngman became involved in the left-wing Artists' International Association (AIA) after the death in action in Spain of her Slade friend Felicia Browne. Here she met the sculptor Betty *Rea, with whom she lived until Rea's death in 1965. She worked on the Paris World Fair peace pavilion in 1937 with Rea and many other AIA artists including Mary Adshead. In 1939 Youngman and Rea moved, after the evacuation of Highbury School to Huntingdon, first to a caravan in the grounds of Hinchingbrooke Castle and then to Godmanchester. In 1944 she was appointed art adviser for Cambridgeshire. She became chair of the Society for Education through Art and was on the editorial board of *Athene*. In 1947 she founded the 'Pictures for Schools' series of exhibitions showing the work of many distinguished artists, which was widely patronized by local education authorities. These exhibitions later extended to Wales and Scotland. She was a chief examiner, founder of the Cambridge Studio Workshop, later extended to the Mill

Group at Overy Staithe, Norfolk, and lectured widely in Britain and abroad. Archive material on Youngman's educational work, including writing on art teaching, is held at Reading University.

In 1954, encouraged by the writer and art critic Bryan Robertson, Nan Youngman began full-time painting, showed at the Leicester Gallery, and, in 1955, with Rea, Cecil Collins, Elisabeth Vellacott, and others founded the Cambridge Society of Painters and Sculptors. Papermills, the large and picturesque house in Cambridge she shared with Rea and her children and many visitors, was the social centre of the society. This was a productive period yielding many of her best and most important oil paintings, especially those of the south Wales mining valleys then at their peak. These were shown in many one-woman and group exhibitions and are in several permanent public collections. With Rea's death in 1965, Nan Youngman moved to The Hawks, Ely Road, Waterbeach. She continued to spend time in Cardiff with the Welsh painter Esther Grainger but her life became quieter and her paintings increasingly focused on the works of nature rather than man. Many of her later paintings are of the sands and skyscapes of the Norfolk coast, mainly in watercolour and gouache. The first Youngman retrospective was held at the Minories Gallery, Colchester, in 1974. Apart from selling exhibitions her work was shown in 'The story of the AIA' at the Oxford Gallery in 1983, at her second retrospective at Kettles Yard, Cambridge, in 1987 and in the 'Ten decades' exhibition of leading women artists of her generation in Norwich and London in 1991. She was appointed OBE in 1987 for services to art.

Nan Youngman died at home, at The Hawks, on 17 April 1995. She was cremated in Cambridge. A summary exhibition of her life and work was held at the Morley Gallery, London, in October 1997. Nan Youngman distrusted the commercial establishment surrounding artists. She never employed an agent and her work was never self-consciously promoted. Despite this there is a large body of her work in public collections including *Steelworks Ebbw Vale* (1951; Newport Gallery), *Rhondda Saturday* (1953; Newport Gallery), the Welsh Contemporary Art Society, Manchester City Galleries, the Whipple Museum, and numerous local authorities, colleges, and schools. There are a number of private collections of her work in Britain and the United States. JULIAN REA

Sources S. Malvern, *Nan Youngman, 1906–1995* (1997) [exhibition catalogue, Morley Gallery, London, Oct 1997] · P. Black, ed., *Nan Youngman: paintings, drawings, prints, 1924–1986* (1987) [exhibition catalogue, Kettles Yard Gallery, Cambridge, 24 Jan – 1 March 1987] · M. Black, ed., *Festschrift* (1986) [privately printed] · *Nan Youngman retrospective* (1974) [exhibition catalogue, Minories Gallery, Colchester] · N. Youngman, MS autobiography, priv. coll. · U. Reading, Society for Education through Art, 'Pictures for schools' archive · personal knowledge (2004) · private information (2004)
Archives Tate Collection, papers, list of paintings and drawings · U. Reading L., corresp. and papers relating to her work in promoting art through education
Likenesses N. Youngman, self-portrait, 1948, priv. coll. [*see illus.*] · B. Rea, portrait, priv. coll. · photographs, priv. coll.
Wealth at death £338,427: probate, 17 Aug 1995, *CGPLA Eng. & Wales*

Young Pretender, the. *See* Charles Edward (1720–1788).

Yoxall, Sir James Henry (1857–1925), educationist, was born on 15 July 1857 at Redditch, Worcestershire, the eldest son of Henry Houghton Yoxall, fishing tackle manufacturer, and his wife, Elizabeth Smallwood. At the age of thirteen he left what he called his small, pinched Wesleyan school in Redditch to become a pupil teacher, first at the Wesleyan school in Bridgehouses, Sheffield, then at the Pyebank School under the Sheffield school board. He won a queen's scholarship, and from 1876 to 1878 attended Westminster Training College in London, for which the examining inspector was Matthew Arnold, whose writings long influenced him.

Yoxall returned to Sheffield and was employed by the board first as an assistant master, then from 1887 as headmaster of the Sharrow Lane School, which became famous—even though 'payment by results' was still in force—for its academic, artistic, and sporting achievements. He married in 1886 Elizabeth (1858–1925), daughter of Lieutenant-Colonel William Coles RE; she had trained at the National School of Cookery, London, and taught domestic subjects at Sheffield schools. They were to have one son and two daughters. As a member of the National Union of Elementary Teachers, Yoxall established his reputation at the Cheltenham conference of 1888 when, with T. J. Macnamara, he organized the so-called 'symposium of the indefatigables' to boost membership. He became vice-president, then acting president in 1891, and president and general secretary in 1892. Retaining the latter post, he gave up teaching.

At the Leeds conference of 1892, what had now become the National Union of Teachers (NUT) resolved to advance its aims by sponsoring its leaders as members of parliament. Having unsuccessfully contested Bassetlaw as a Liberal in that year, Yoxall was returned for Nottingham West in 1895, just as he was completing his duties as a member of the Bryce commission on secondary education. Incorporated into the commission's report was his memorandum, based on NUT policy, advocating the reform of both the central and local administration of publicly provided education. The incoming Unionist government created a central ministry (the Board of Education) in 1899; replacing the school boards, set up under Forster's Act of 1870, proved more difficult. Sir John Gorst's bill of 1896 failed; it also almost split the union. Nevertheless Yoxall and his fellow NUT MPs, Ernest Gray (Unionist) and Macnamara (Liberal) persisted. They encouraged A. J. Balfour to make another attempt and gave him every assistance in refining the successful Education Bill of 1902 (which invested the administrative counties and county boroughs with educational responsibilities at both elementary and post-elementary levels), winning general approval for their effective participation in the parliamentary process.

Over the next few years Yoxall was closely concerned in monitoring the implementation of the new Education Act and its counterpart for London, passed in 1903. Against

Sir James Henry Yoxall (1857–1925), by Sir Benjamin Stone, 1901

union expectation the Board of Education, under its permanent secretary R. L. Morant, assumed a directive stance, encroaching upon the autonomy of the new local authorities. Resisting Morant's plans for selective post-elementary education, Yoxall referred to the terms in which the consultative committee's report on higher elementary schools (1906) was cast as 'snobbish and caddish to the last degree'. He sought instead to secure equal opportunities for children transferring from elementary to secondary schools. Five years later Morant's apparent approval of derogatory comments about elementary school educated local inspectors, expressed in the board's so-called Holmes circular, left, according to Yoxall, a hundred thousand teachers aggrieved that they had been unjustly condemned and held up to ridicule. A mass meeting organized by the NUT hastened the permanent secretary's resignation.

Much of the latter part of Yoxall's career as general secretary of the NUT was taken up with teachers' salaries and pensions. A salaries committee of the union, set up in 1913 to advance the adoption of a national scale, launched a campaign which won support from some 150 local authorities. Suspended as the war began, it was renewed in July 1916 in response to a general rise in wages and supported by strikes. During the second reading of H. A. L. Fisher's Education Bill, in March 1918, Yoxall urged the president of the Board of Education to secure salaries, promotions, and pensions for teachers on civil service lines. The existing pension scheme, originally set up with Yoxall's support in 1898, was reorganized on a non-contributory basis by the Teachers (Superannuation) Act of 1918. In September the following year Fisher established, under the chairmanship of Lord Burnham, the standing joint committee on a provisional minimum scale of salaries for teachers in public elementary schools, with Yoxall (who had resigned his parliamentary seat as the war ended) as joint secretary as well as NUT spokesman. National salary scales were duly agreed (except by some women teachers who now aspired to equal pay) but they were soon under attack from the government which, as the post-war boom ended, strove to amend the new superannuation scheme and to reduce salaries. Yoxall, giving evidence in 1922 to the parliamentary select committee on teachers in grant-aided schools (superannuation) pointed out that teachers had accepted low salary scales on the assumption that the pension question was settled. The government, however, was adamant. The NUT was obliged to accept new superannuation terms and a reduction of 5 per cent in teachers' salaries. Consequently 1923 was a year of strikes. At the Scarborough conference, the following April, Yoxall resigned as general secretary.

Yoxall received honorary MAs from Cambridge (1899) and Oxford (1907) during NUT annual conferences. From June 1909, the year in which he was knighted (he was the first elementary school teacher to receive this honour), until April 1924 he edited *The Schoolmaster*, the union's weekly journal. Since his student days, Yoxall had been a prolific writer. Besides magazine articles, he published school textbooks (for example, *The Pupil Teacher's Geography*, 1891) and several novels, including *The Romany Stone* (1902), *Smalilou* (1904), and *Château Royal* (1908). A keen traveller and collector, he had a developed interest in the decorative arts. In *The Schoolmaster* he wrote a regular column entitled 'Books and pictures'; *Collecting Old Miniatures* and *Collecting Old Glass, English and Irish* appeared in 1916. He and his wife settled at Kew, where she was active in local affairs and organizations, including the Social Purity Crusade and the National Suffrage Union. She was a co-opted member of the local education committee, a manager of Darell Road School, and, from 1919, Richmond's first woman magistrate.

Slightly above medium height, well built, with a beard, Yoxall remained to the end of his life an alert, sociable, and sympathetic figure. As Isabel Cleghorn, later first woman president of the NUT, said in 1903: 'they all loved Mr Yoxall. He was so tactful, so kindly, so gracious and helpful to anyone who went to him' (*The Schoolmaster*, 11 April 1903). He died of influenza at his home, Springfield, 20 Kew Gardens Road, Kew, Surrey, on 2 February 1925. Lady Yoxall died on 18 July.   ROBIN BETTS

Sources *Schoolmaster and Woman Teacher's Chronicle* (6 Feb 1925) · *Schoolmaster and Woman Teacher's Chronicle* (13 Feb 1925) · *The Times* (3 Feb 1925) · *MAP* (*Mainly About People*) (20 Aug 1898), 228–9 · A. Tropp, *The school teachers* (1957) · *CGPLA Eng. & Wales* (1925) · *WWW*

Archives King's AC Cam., letters to Oscar Browning
Likenesses B. Stone, photographs, 1898–1901, NPG [see illus.] ·
bust, National Union of Teachers headquarters, Hamilton House,
Mabledon Place, London
Wealth at death £12,559 11s. 9d.: probate, 11 March 1925, CGPLA
Eng. & Wales

Ypres. For this title name see French, John Denton Pink-
stone, first earl of Ypres (1852–1925).

Ypres, William of. See William of Ypres, styled count of
Flanders (d. 1164/5).

Y Prydydd Bychan. See Gwilym ap Phylip Brydydd (fl. 1222–
1268).

Yudenitch [Yudenich], **Flora Sandes-** (1876–1956), nurse
and soldier in the Serbian service, was born on 22 January
1876 at Nether Poppleton, near York, the youngest daughter of the Revd Samuel Dickson Sandes (1822–1914) and his
wife, Sophia Julia Besnard (d. 1911). She came from a large
family, was educated by governesses, and trained as a secretary. She also received first-aid training with the Ladies'
Nursing Yeomanry. When war broke out in August 1914
Sandes's immediate offer of service to the War Office as a
Volunteer Aid Detachment nurse was rejected. But if Britain did not want her, Serbia did. On 12 August she left London with Madame Mabel Grouitch's Red Cross nursing
unit bound for Salonika in Greece. Her first journey to Serbia was fraught with difficulties: France was still mobilizing, trains were disrupted, platforms choked with soldiers
on their way to the front, and boats were often scarce. But
the nurses arrived after a memorable thirty-six hour voyage from Piraeus to Salonika on the deck of a Greek cattle
ship in a raging thunderstorm. From there they travelled
by train through the Vardar valley to Kragujevac. A telegram was waiting when Sandes arrived, stating that her
father, with whom she had lived until her abrupt departure, had died on 23 August.

Sandes plunged into work at the First Reserve Hospital,
where seven English nurses worked with Serbian doctors
to tend more than 1000 sick and wounded soldiers. They
were casualties of the Serbs' efforts to repel the Austrian
invasion across the Danube. After exhausting hours on
duty the nurses took turns sleeping on straw mattresses,
sharing a single blanket, and eating, all in the same room.
The hospital was desperately short of medicine and other
supplies, and only the worst cases could be treated with
anaesthetic. After the first three months Sandes became
deeply committed to the Serbian cause. When she
returned to London it was to raise funds for medical supplies, and after only six weeks Sandes's country-wide tour
had yielded more than £2000. She returned to Serbia
accompanied by an American nurse, Emily Simmonds, literally sitting on packing cases containing 120 tons of cotton, gauze, and other much needed materials.

By this time, the British nurses and doctors in Serbia had
assumed political significance. Sandes visited the English
consul before leaving Nish and was handed a letter from
Sir Edward Grey, the British foreign secretary. Whatever
assistance the nurses gave Serbia, he said, was helping
Britain and the allies and was of inestimable benefit to the
common cause. The British nurses were a highly visible
sign of allied concern. The door was thus opened for
British women to set their own course of action in Serbia.
Flora Sandes became indispensable as a nurse, surgeon,
and hospital administrator in Valjevo, where the death
rate of typhus victims soared to 70 per cent and more than
200 died each day. Although qualified only as a nurse,
Sandes was soon performing minor surgery. The loss of
medical staff to typhus was enormous. At the end of the
month only one Serbian doctor, an orderly, and the nurses
remained. 'Looking back', Sandes wrote in 1927, 'I have
just naturally drifted by successive stages from nurse to
soldier' (Sandes, *Autobiography*, 12). But it was actually only
fifteen days after joining the Serbian army's 2nd regiment's ambulance unit that she was asked to stay on.
When the regiment pulled back to within a few miles of
Monastir, the regimental commander, Colonel Milic,
required Sandes to make a decision. Unequivocally, she
chose to remain with the regiment, overjoyed that 'I represented England!' (ibid., 14). From the Serbs' perspective,
it was entirely reasonable since there were other women
in the army; enlistment was often haphazard and
Sandes's ability to shoot and ride were highly prized. At
home on leave the following year she undertook major
fund-raising throughout England.

Whatever reservations were expressed about women in
the ranks at home, however, Sandes's experience and position demanded the same respect shown to any official
representative of an allied army. She had returned home
wearing the Kara George star—the highest medal
awarded to non-commissioned officers—for her bravery
during the Serbian retreat into Albania. She had lived in
the trenches with her comrades, shared their food, slept
underneath their overcoats, divided her last cigarettes
and crusts of bread with them, and was severely wounded
in November 1915 by a Bulgarian bomb. Promoted to sergeant she was wounded again in July 1917 and returned to
her unit the following October. She participated in the
final offensive against the Austrian and Bulgarian forces
and was demobilized on 31 October 1922. She also acted
for the Serbs as a fund-raiser and unofficial ambassador,
conducting speaking tours in Australia and Britain and
along the western front.

After more than six years serving in the Serbian army,
and having reached the rank of captain, Flora Sandes settled in Belgrade and found that demobilization made it
necessary to relinquish her hard-won honorary male status. On 14 May 1927 she married a fellow officer, a Russian
named Yuri Vladimovich Yudenich, and though they both
retired to civilian life, she felt a permanent incapacity to
settle down to anything. She tried her hand at driving
Belgrade's first taxi cab, wrote an autobiography, acquired
a speed-boat licence, taught English, and acted as a
matron to a dancing troupe in Paris. She was called up for
service again in 1941 but after the bombing of Belgrade,
both she and Yuri were interned by the Germans. They
were released but Yuri died in September 1941 and Flora
returned to England via South Africa.

Flora Sandes-Yudenitch died from obstructive jaundice

at the Ipswich and East Suffolk Hospital, Anglesea Road, Ipswich, on 24 November 1956. She was cremated on 27 November at the Ipswich crematorium and her ashes were placed in the garden of remembrance.

JULIE WHEELWRIGHT

Sources F. Sandes, *An Englishwoman-sergeant in the Serbian army* (1916) • F. Sandes, *The autobiography of a woman soldier: a brief adventure with the Serbian army* (1927) • J. Wheelwright, *Amazons and military maids*, new edn (1994) • private information (2004) • *CGPLA Eng. & Wales* (1957) • b. cert. • m. cert. • d. cert. • baptismal certificate
Wealth at death £480 18s. 3d.: probate, 2 Jan 1957, *CGPLA Eng. & Wales*

Yule family (*per.* 1863–1928), merchants and industrialists, came to prominence with **Andrew Yule** (1834–1902), born on 30 August 1834 at Stonehaven, Kincardineshire, the fourth son of Robert Yule, a linen and wool draper, and Elizabeth Law. Andrew and his elder brother **George Yule** (*bap.* 1829, *d.* 1892) moved to Manchester about 1858 to work for the warehousemen Andrew Collie & Co. In 1863 Andrew went to Calcutta to set up in business as an agent and merchant. His firm, Andrew Yule & Co., joined the Bengal chamber of commerce in 1866. The company acted as agents for several British firms, and also became involved on its own account in the trade in Indian jute, cotton, tea, and other commodities. Andrew Yule married Emma Porter and they had a son, Robert Andrew Alexander, and a daughter, Annie Henrietta *Yule, Lady Yule (1874/5–1950).

George Yule had set up as a warehouseman in London and Manchester by 1868. In 1870 the brothers founded George Yule & Co., East India merchants in London, to act as agents for Andrew Yule & Co. Although each firm subsequently recruited other partners, the capital remained in the hands of the two brothers. Andrew Yule & Co. expanded its activities during the 1870s, to become managing agents on a commission basis for Budge Budge Jute Mills Ltd, Bengal Mills Ltd, Jheerie Ghout Tea Ltd, and other companies in India. However, Andrew Yule was also involved in commercial enterprise on his own account. In 1873, for example, he joined with Samuel Bird and Octavius Steel to form New Beerbhoom Coal Ltd.

In 1875 George Yule and his nephew **Sir David Yule**, baronet (1858–1928), of Hooghly River, went to Calcutta to manage the Bengal Cotton Mills for the firm. David Yule was born in Edinburgh on 4 August 1858, one of the three sons and three daughters of David Yule (*b.* 1826), chief assistant keeper of the general register of the sasines, and his wife, Margaret Young. He was educated at the Royal High School, Edinburgh, and spent three years in Oldham learning the cotton trade. Andrew Yule returned to England shortly after the arrival of his nephew, to become resident partner of George Yule & Co., while George stayed in India as resident partner of Andrew Yule & Co. George was active in public life: he became sheriff of Calcutta in 1886, was president of the Bengal chamber of commerce, and in 1888 was elected the fourth president of the Indian National Congress. He retired to live in England in 1891 and died on 26 March 1892 at his home, Springfield, Kingswood Road, in Dulwich Wood Park, London.

He was survived by his wife, Frances Caroline, and their only child, Harriet. Andrew Yule died at Braeside, Fountain Road, Norwood, Surrey, on 18 July 1902. He was also survived by his wife. By that time Andrew Yule & Co. managed four jute mills, fifteen tea plantations, four coal companies, a railway company, an inland navigation company, two flour mills, a cotton mill, and a zemindary company in India.

Meanwhile David Yule, a partner in Andrew Yule & Co. since 1887, had acquired George's share in the firm and replaced him as resident partner in India. He acquired a reputation as a shy and reclusive man, who preferred to live in the mill compound than to move to the fashionable areas of Calcutta favoured by other Europeans. He did not move to the city until 1900, when he married his cousin Annie Henrietta, daughter of Andrew Yule. They had one daughter, Gladys, and mother and daughter were to spend most of their lives in England. It is said that David never took a holiday, and he did not pay a visit to Britain for eighteen years after his arrival in India. At Morgan Grenfell, Yule's merchant bank in the City of London, it was reported that his 'sole idea was Calcutta and he entirely ignored the London office' (Chapman, 225). Typically, his Calcutta home after 1907 was at 8 Clive Row, above the offices of Andrew Yule & Co.

The range of the company's business interests increased dramatically under David Yule's direction. David was largely responsible for increasing the firm's involvement in the jute industry. In 1895 he had formed the Bengal Assam Steamship Company, to re-enter the inland navigation trade in which the firm had been involved, briefly, when Andrew Yule was building the company. The success of this venture encouraged him in 1906 to form Port Shipping Ltd, Calcutta's largest lighterage company. Andrew Yule had acquired substantial interests in the Indian coal industry, and in 1908 David consolidated the firm's interest in this field when Andrew Yule & Co. became managing agents of Bengal Coal Ltd. David was also enthusiastic about the prospects for estate management in India, and in 1902 formed Midnapore Zemindary Ltd (MZC) to acquire and develop land in Bengal. The MZC estates comprised 2400 square miles, on which the company promoted agriculture, forestry, fisheries, and other rural industries. By 1928 David Yule was arguably the most important businessman in India. He was later described as 'an outstanding personality in India and especially in Bengal' (Catto, 68); and his personal friendship with Vivian Hugh Smith, a partner in Morgan Grenfell, was undoubtedly commercially advantageous. Yet his significance, as well as his retiring disposition, were shown to good effect during the visit of George V and Queen Mary to India in 1911. The king expressed a desire to meet the leading businessman of Calcutta, whom he was told was David Yule. This was brought about by the lieutenant-governor of Bengal, who had never met Yule. The meeting with the sovereign, and George V's visit to one of Yule's jute mills, went well; but at one point Yule asked who the gentleman was accompanying the king.

'Don't you know him?', replied George V, 'he is the Viceroy of India' (Catto, 73). Yule subsequently received a knighthood in the Durbar honours list of 1912 and in 1922 he was created a baronet. He was also made a knight of St John of Jerusalem, in 1915.

By 1917 Andrew Yule & Co. managed more than sixty companies and was one of the leading businesses in Calcutta. Nevertheless, Sir David decided to dispose of the firm. His brothers Andrew (1863–1916) and William Mann Yule (1866–1899), had both worked for the firm as assistants, and Andrew had become a partner: both were now dead, and Sir David had no son to inherit the business. In 1919 he sold the goodwill and business of the firms for £600,000 to a newly created company Andrew Yule & Co. Ltd, in which the major shareholders were J. P. Morgan & Co. and some of the leading partners in Morgan Grenfell & Co., including Vivian Smith. However, Yule agreed to stay on as chairman of the company, with Thomas Sivewright Catto as vice-chairman and in charge of the business in India (and a partner in the London agency, George Yule & Co., which in 1920 became Yule, Catto & Co. Ltd). Catto had a very clear idea how the firm should develop, seeing the London house as potentially 'the merchant department of J. P. M[organ] & Co. and M[organ] G[renfell] & Co. … with a splendid opportunity to develop A[ndrew] Y[ule] & Co. into a great merchant firm not only in India but in other parts of the world' (Burk, 82).

Sir David retired from active participation in the affairs of Andrew Yule & Co. Ltd in 1922 and returned to England to settle at Hanstead House, Bricket Wood, near St Albans, Hertfordshire. However, he did not withdraw from the world of business. He was a director of the Midland Bank, the Mercantile Bank of India, Royal Exchange Assurance, Electric Holdings Ltd, International Sleeping Car Share Trust, Metropolitan-Vickers Electrical Company, Malaya General Company, Vickers Ltd, and other companies. In 1926, with his friend Sir Thomas Catto and with the former viceroy of India, Lord Reading, he purchased United Newspapers (1918) Ltd from David Lloyd George, after giving undertakings that the *Daily Chronicle* and other titles published by the company would continue to support the policies of progressive Liberalism and that Reading would act as chairman of the company. The following year Sir David acquired two Calcutta newspapers, *The Statesman* and *The Englishman*.

Sir David had revealed the extent of his attachment to India when in 1921 he had instructed that his will was to be construed as if he was still domiciled in India; his executors were named as the Mercantile Bank of India, his wife, and business associates Sir Onkar Mull Jatia and N. Radhakrishna Tyer. On 3 July 1928 Sir David Yule died of heart failure at Hanstead House, near St Albans. He was survived by his wife. In his obituary in *The Times* he was described as 'one of the wealthiest men, if not the wealthiest man, in the country' (14 July 1928). He was buried at St Albans Cathedral on 16 July 1928.

The achievements of the Yule family and of Andrew Yule & Co. have been largely neglected by economic historians in Britain. Yet Andrew Yule laid the foundations of a firm, Andrew Yule & Co., which became one of the greatest trading and industrial empires in India. His brother George played a significant role in the political life of Bengal, and his nephew Sir David became one of the richest and most powerful men on the subcontinent. Both Yule, Catto & Co. plc and Andrew Yule & Co. Ltd (a public limited company largely owned by the government of India) continued to thrive in the 1990s.   IAIN F. RUSSELL

Sources *Andrew Yule & Co., Ltd, 1863–1963* (privately printed, Edinburgh, 1963) · *The Times* (24 July 1902), 10 · *The Times* (4 July 1928), 21 · Boase, *Mod. Eng. biog.* · *CGPLA Eng. & Wales* (1892) [George Yule] · *CGPLA Eng. & Wales* (1902) [Andrew Yule] · *CGPLA Eng. & Wales* (1928) [David Yule] · T. S. Catto, *A personal memoir and a biographical note* (1962) · K. Burk, *Morgan Grenfell, 1838–1988: the biography of a merchant bank* (1989) · S. D. Chapman, *Merchant enterprise in Britain: from the industrial revolution to World War I* (1992) · R. P. T. Davenport-Hines and G. Jones, eds., *British business in Asia since 1860* (1989) · A. K. Bagchi, *Private investment in India, 1900–1939* (1972) · IGI

Likenesses photographs, repro. in *Andrew Yule and Co Ltd, 1863–1963*

Wealth at death £156,442 3s. 0d.—Andrew Yule: probate, 5 Sept 1902, *CGPLA Eng. & Wales* · £71,907 5s.—George Yule: probate, 4 June 1892, *CGPLA Eng. & Wales* · £348,038 18s. 7d.—effects in England, David Yule: probate, 29 Oct 1928, *CGPLA Eng. & Wales*

Yule, Andrew (1834–1902). *See under* Yule family (*per.* 1863–1928).

Yule, Annie Henrietta, Lady Yule (1874/5–1950), film industry financier, was the only daughter in a family of two children of Andrew *Yule (1834–1902) [*see under* Yule family], merchant of Calcutta, and his wife, Emma Porter. In 1900 she married her first cousin David *Yule (1858–1928) [*see under* Yule family], who until his marriage had lived a solitary bachelor existence over his business premises in Calcutta. They lived briefly together in Calcutta until she contracted malaria. She refused thereafter to spend prolonged periods in India, and he bought for her Hanstead House at Bricket Wood near St Albans, where their only child, Gladys Meryl, was born in 1903. In 1922 her husband returned to England, latterly working from a frugally furnished office in Finsbury Circus in his shirt sleeves.

By her husband's death on 3 July 1928 Annie Yule came to command between £8 and £15 million. She was then probably the richest British widow, surpassing even Dame Fanny Houston. Aged only about fifty-three when Yule died, she was restless and easily bored. As a diversion she joined J. Arthur Rank in forming a film-making company called British National (1934). Her strong if unsystematic patriotism was indicated by the title of the company. She was an original shareholder in Pinewood Studios (1936), but exchanged her stake with Rank's interest in British National (1937). Under the management of John Corfield British National produced a series of thrillers. The eerie *Dead Men Tell No Tales* (1938), about the murder of a school matron who won a lottery, was among the most successful. Though Lady Yule's commitment to filming was spasmodic, her financing of *Contraband* (1940) by Michael Powell and Emeric Pressburger early in the Second World War was a fillip to British film production at a moment when it might have perished. British National's low-budget melo-drama *Love on the Dole* and its propagandist *One of our Air-craft is Missing* were notable successes of 1941. The chair-manship of British National and of the National Studios at Elstree was delegated by Lady Yule to Sir Henry Richard-son, a director of her husband's old firm Yule, Catto. The company closed in 1948 at a time when the British film industry was stricken by a crisis of confidence and finance as a result of ill-judged meddling by the Labour govern-ment headed by Clement Attlee.

Lady Yule owned a stud farm at Bricket Wood, where she also kept prize-winning Jersey and Aberdeen Angus herds. Her horses enjoyed every equine luxury, including mech-anical drinking-troughs. After buying a Newmarket racing stable called Balaton Lodge she ordered that her jockeys must never use their whips. She subsidized the Olympia International Horse Show, for which on one occasion she ordered forty horses to be taught to dance a quadrille to prove that English horses could be trained to do almost anything. She kept penguins and wallabies in her grounds, and formed an institution in the south of France to care for weary or ill-treated animals. Lady Yule had little obvious affection for humans other than her daughter, who having received a thousand proposals of marriage from fortune-hunters became increasingly reclusive. Although in 1946 she gave Balaton Lodge to the Veterinary Educational Trust as an equine research sta-tion, her daughter maintained the thoroughbred stud at Bricket Wood and was the leading horsewoman in Britain at her death in 1957.

Lady Yule had strong religious opinions, a sharp tongue, and imperious habits. She tried to enforce her teetotalism on the fifty-one crew of her yacht *Nahlin*, which she sold to Carol II of Romania shortly before the Second World War. A heavy cigarette smoker, she died of a coronary throm-bosis on 14 July 1950 at Hanstead House, Bricket Wood, St Albans, Hertfordshire.   RICHARD DAVENPORT-HINES

Sources *The Times* (15 July 1950) · A. Wood, *Mr Rank: a study of J. Arthur Rank and British films* (1952) · G. Macnab, *J. Arthur Rank and the British film industry* (1993) · R. Low, *The history of the British film*, 7: *1929–1939: film making in 1930s Britain* (1985) · *CGPLA Eng. & Wales* (1950) · d. cert. · K. Burk, *Morgan Grenfell, 1838–1988: the biography of a merchant bank* (1989) · T. S. Catto, *A personal memoir and a biograph-ical note* (1962) · Burke, *Peerage*
Likenesses photographs, 1930–39, Hult. Arch.
Wealth at death £523,198 16s. 7d.: probate, 17 Nov 1950, *CGPLA Eng. & Wales*

Yule, Sir David, baronet (1858–1928). *See under* Yule family (*per.* 1863–1928).

Yule, George (*bap.* 1829, *d.* 1892). *See under* Yule family (*per.* 1863–1928).

Yule, Sir George Udny (1813–1886). *See under* Yule, Sir Henry (1820–1889).

Yule, George Udny (1871–1951), statistician, was born at Morham, near Haddington, East Lothian, on 18 February 1871, the youngest of the three children surviving infancy of Sir George Udny *Yule (1813–1886) [see under Yule, Sir

George Udny Yule (1871–1951), by unknown photographer

Henry] of the Indian Civil Service, and his wife, Henrietta Peach, daughter of Captain Robert Boileau Pemberton, of the Indian army. Sir Henry Yule, the geographer of India, was his uncle.

Yule was educated at Bayswater, London, at Dunchurch near Rugby, and at Winchester College; he was intended for the Royal Engineers but objected, and instead studied civil engineering at University College, London, which he entered at the age of sixteen. As there was then no engin-eering degree he left after three years without graduating. He spent two years as an apprentice in private engineer-ing works, but in 1892 he went to study physics at Bonn University. While at University College he had become acquainted with Karl Pearson, then professor of applied mathematics, and in 1893 Pearson offered him a job as demonstrator. He was promoted to assistant professor of applied mathematics in 1896; and this marked the begin-ning of his interest in statistics.

In 1899 Yule married May Winifred, daughter of Wil-liam Hayman *Cummings, principal of the Guildhall School of Music, but the marriage was not a success and in 1912 it was annulled. There were no children. In conse-quence of his marriage he gave up his post in University College and took up more remunerative work as assistant to Sir Philip Magnus, superintendent of the department of technology of the City and Guilds Institute. Yule was, how-ever, able to keep up his statistical work in the evenings and in 1902 he was appointed Newmarch lecturer in statis-tics at University College, holding the two posts concur-rently until 1909. His new duties included lecturing in the evenings to a small class, largely of civil servants, and these lectures provided the foundation of his *Introduction to the Theory of Statistics* (1911), which became a standard textbook and by 1932 had run through ten editions and been translated into Czech in 1926. Revised in collaboration with Maurice Kendall, it achieved widespread popularity.

In 1912 Yule accepted the newly established university lectureship in statistics at Cambridge and concurrently became statistician to the school of agriculture. He was made a member of St John's College in 1913, elected a fellow in 1922, was college director of studies in natural sciences from 1923 to 1935, and lived in college for almost the whole of the rest of his life. In 1915–19 he was seconded as a statistician to the director of army contracts and later worked with the Ministry of Food; he was appointed CBE in 1918.

Yule had great influence on the early development of modern statistics, particularly on experimentation in biology and agriculture, and analysis of vital and industrial statistics. His main contributions in the theoretical field were concerned with regression and correlation, with association, particularly in 2x2 contingency tables, with time-series, with Mendelian inheritance, and with epidemiology. He was elected FRS in 1921. He played a very active part in the affairs of various scientific societies, such as the Royal Anthropological Institute and in particular the Royal Statistical Society, of which he was honorary secretary (1907–19) and president (1924–6); he was awarded the society's Guy gold medal in 1911. He was elected to honorary membership by the statistical societies of America, Czechoslovakia, and Hungary, and contributed numerous papers to the *Journal of the Royal Statistical Society*, *Biometrika*, and the *Proceedings* of the Royal Society.

Yule did not regard himself as a great mathematician, but he had a very clear idea of what could and could not be accomplished by mathematical analysis. In his early years he was a good friend of Pearson, and had Pearson been more accommodating they might have become an ideal team, for in many ways their abilities were complementary. But as Yule wrote in his obituary of Pearson, 'Those who left him and began to think for themselves were apt, as happened painfully in more instances than one, to find that after a divergence of opinion the maintenance of friendly relations became difficult, after express criticism impossible' (*Obits. FRS*, 2, 1936, 101).

Yule was a quiet and unassuming man, appreciated for his wide knowledge and interests and his kindly and gentle nature. In politics he was a strong Conservative. He was not ambitious, regarding freedom to pursue his intellectual interests as of more importance than name or fortune. He was a man of varied and surprising attainments: he had marked literary interests, and composed humorous verses in Latin and English. In his fifties he developed a keen interest in motoring, with a taste for fast driving; and on his retirement he took up flying, bought his own aeroplane, and obtained his pilot's 'certificate A' when nearly sixty-one. When nearing retirement he resumed the study of Latin with a view to reading in the original *De imitatione Christi*, St Augustine's *Confessions*, and Boethius's *De consolatione philosophiae*. The first of these led to consideration of the authorship controversy and to other works

of Thomas à Kempis. This suggested to him the idea of using statistical methods to provide evidence of authorship and in 1944 he published *The Statistical Study of Literary Vocabulary*.

After his retirement Yule continued to take an active part in college affairs, but in 1935 his heart gave serious trouble and thereafter he was compelled to be physically inactive. He died in the Evelyn Nursing Home, Cambridge, on 26 June 1951. FRANK YATES, *rev.* ALAN YOSHIOKA

Sources F. Yates, *Obits. FRS*, 8 (1952–3), 309–23 · F. L. E., 'George Udny Yule', *The Eagle*, 55 (1952–3), 89–94 · M. G. Kendall, *Journal of the Royal Statistical Society: series A*, 115 (1952), 156–61 · *The Times* (28 June 1951) · *The record of the Royal Society of London*, 4th edn (1940) · *CGPLA Eng. & Wales* (1951) · personal knowledge (1971)

Archives BL OIOC, papers of and relating to him, MS Eur. E 357 | UCL, corresp. with Karl Pearson

Likenesses Elliott & Fry, photograph, *c*.1930, repro. in F. L. E., 'George Udny Yule', 89 · H. Lamb, drawing, St John Cam. · photograph, repro. in Yates, *Obits. FRS*, facing p. 309 · photograph, RS [*see illus.*]

Wealth at death £27,288 12s. 8d.: probate, 17 Oct 1951, *CGPLA Eng. & Wales*

Yule, Sir Henry (1820–1889), geographer, born on 1 May 1820 at Inveresk, near Edinburgh, was the youngest son of Major William Yule (1764–1839) and Elizabeth Paterson (*d. c*.1827) of Braehead in Ayrshire. The Yule family had for several generations been tenant farmers at Dirleton in East Lothian. Their name was reputed to be of Scandinavian origin. Through his service in the East India Company, Major William Yule gained some knowledge of oriental literature. He retired from India in 1806, and his valuable collection of Persian and Arabic manuscripts was subsequently presented to the British Museum. In 1832 he had privately printed a lithographed edition of the *Apothegms of Ali, the Son of Abu Talib*, in Arabic, with an old Persian version and an English translation. All three of his sons were to follow him to India. The eldest son, **Sir George Udny Yule** (1813–1886), was a distinguished Indian civilian and a famous *shikari*. During the 1857 conflict, with a corps of mounted European volunteers, he was responsible throughout the division of Bhagalpur, keeping open the navigation of the Ganges, while preventing communication between the rebels in East and West Bihar. He subsequently served as chief commissioner of Oudh, as resident at Hyderabad, and finally on the governor-general's council, from which he retired in 1869. In 1862 he married Henrietta Peach, daughter of Captain Robert Boileau Pemberton. Yule was created KCSI and CB before his death in 1886. The statistician George Udny *Yule (1871–1951) was his son. Sir Henry Yule's second son, **Robert Yule** (1817–1857), published a treatise *On Cavalry Movements* (1856) as well as some minor writings in prose and verse. After much active service in Persia and Afghanistan he fell near Delhi while leading his regiment, the 9th lancers, during the Indian mutiny.

Henry Yule was educated at the high school in Edinburgh, and later became a pupil of Henry Parr Hamilton, subsequently the dean of Salisbury, and James Challis, who was afterwards appointed as the Plumian professor at Cambridge. His fellow pupils at this time included John

Sir Henry Yule (1820–1889), by Theodore Blake Wirgman, c.1890

Mason Neale and Harvey Goodwin, later bishop of Carlisle. Goodwin later recalled that Yule's intellectual development had been extraordinary for his age, noting in particular that he had 'showed much more liking for Greek plays and for German than for mathematics, though he had considerable geometrical ingenuity' (Trotter, xliv). After a brief and unrewarding spell at University College, London, Yule decided to pursue a career in the army rather than in the law, as his father had originally intended. In 1837 he joined the East India Company's Military College, at Addiscombe, and having passed out at the head of the college in 1838, he spent a year training at the headquarters of the Royal Engineers at Chatham. In 1840 he was appointed to the Bengal Engineers. His first assignment in India was in the Kasia hills, a remote region on the northeast frontier of Bengal inhabited by people of Mongolian descent. Although the official objective of this mission (to establish means of transporting local coal to the plains) was unsuccessful, Yule's fascination with the Kasia led him to publish two accounts of the region and its people.

In 1843 Yule took leave from India to marry his cousin Anna Maria (d. 1875), daughter of General Martin White of the Bengal army. She initially joined him in India, but was soon forced to return to Britain because of ill health. For six years Yule served with men such as Robert Napier, William Baker, and Richard Strachey in the restoration and development of the Mughal irrigation system in the North-Western Provinces. In addition to his role in the organization of extensive engineering works, he was also involved in an official inquiry into the relationship between irrigation and public health in the area of the proposed Ganges Canal. During this period, he also saw active service in the Anglo-Sikh wars of 1845–6 and 1848–9. He then took extended leave, returning to Edinburgh to live with his wife for three years. During this period he lectured at the Scottish Military Academy and published an authoritative volume on fortification (1851), which was translated into French in 1858. Other publications, illustrating his diverse interests at this time, included a polemical defence of the role of the navy in the suppression of the east African slave trade (1850), and an article on Tibet for *Blackwood's Magazine*.

A few weeks after the birth of his only child, Amy, in 1852, Yule returned to service in Bengal. Having fulfilled various tasks, including reports on the relatively inaccessible country between Aracan and Burma, and on the defences of Singapore, he was appointed under-secretary to the newly formed department of public works, with particular responsibility for the development of the railway system. His work on the railways was interrupted by an appointment in 1855 as secretary to Colonel Arthur Phayre's mission to Burma, which resulted in Yule's first widely acclaimed publication, *A Narrative of the Mission … to … Ava* (1858), illustrated by his own sketches. His ordinary duties were considerably augmented by the violent conflict of 1857, which led to a large influx of troops into India. While his relations with the governors-general during this period (Dalhousie and Canning) appear to have been close, Yule seems to have become increasingly disenchanted with his work in India and in 1862 he retired from the army for good. Canning's death in the same year reduced his chances of securing an official appointment in London, but through the influence of Sir Roderick Murchison he was in 1863 created CB.

After spending some time in Switzerland, Tuscany, and Savoy (where he met John Ruskin), Yule and his family eventually settled at Palermo, in Sicily. The location suited his wife, by now an invalid, and also provided ample opportunities for further study in the richly stocked public libraries. Two publications for the Hakluyt Society (*Mirabilia descripta: the Wonders of the East* (1863), a translation from the Latin of Friar Jordanus's fourteenth-century narrative, and *Cathay and the Way Thither* (1866), a substantial compendium of extracts from other travellers) established his reputation as a scholar of medieval European literature on the East. But it was his new edition of the *Travels of Marco Polo*, published in 1871 (for which he was awarded the gold medal of the Italian Geographical Society and the founder's medal of the Royal Geographical Society), which secured him lasting fame. This two-volume work, long in gestation, represented the fruit not only of his own extensive researches in Palermo, Venice, Florence, Paris, and London, but also of extensive correspondence with scholars throughout the world, including Cristoforo Negri (founder of the Italian Geographical Society) and George Perkins Marsh. It has long been considered an authoritative, if somewhat voluminous, source on Marco Polo's travels.

Yule returned to England in 1875, following the death of his first wife, and soon afterwards was appointed to the

Council of India, on which he continued to serve until shortly before his death. During the years which followed the publication of his *magnum opus*, an enlarged edition of which appeared in 1875, Yule was considered to be one of the leading authorities on the historical geography of central Asia in general and the history of medieval travel writing in particular. Some contemporaries even compared central Asia before Yule to central Africa before Livingstone. Yule's pioneering and meticulous scholarship was certainly unrivalled, perhaps extravagant. He had an encyclopaedic memory, and, as his daughter later observed, he was always restless away from his books. He was president of the Hakluyt Society (1877–89) and of the Asiatic Society (1885–7), and, late in his life, became a vice-president of the Royal Geographical Society (1887–9). He would probably have become president of this last society earlier in his career, were it not for his protest against its decision in 1878 to provide a formal welcome for Henry Morton Stanley, whose violent methods of exploration in central Africa had attracted considerable criticism. Yule's protest, in which he was joined by the young H. M. Hyndman, led to his resignation from the council. In this, and in other matters, his characteristic integrity was combined with a single-mindedness which could strain even the closest of his friendships.

Yule's edition of Marco Polo was succeeded by several other scholarly works, including a fine essay on the topography of the Upper Oxus region (for a new edition of John Wood's *Journey to the Oxus*, 1872), and introductions to Nikolay Przhevalsky's *Mongolia* (1876) and Captain William Gill's account of the vast river system originating in eastern Tibet, *The River of Golden Sand* (1880). During the last fifteen years of his life, he devoted his energies to a range of works, including a series of astute biographical notices (mainly for the *Royal Engineers' Journal*) and a number of geographical entries for the *Encyclopaedia Britannica*. His last major publication was a three-volume edition of the *Diary of Sir William Hedges* (1887) for the Hakluyt Society, a work which provides considerable insight into the working of the East India Company, and much else besides. However, Yule's reputation rests less on these scholarly writings than on his authorship (with A. C. Burnell) of an extraordinary glossary of Anglo-Indian colloquial words and phrases, published under the felicitous title *Hobson-Jobson*, in 1886. This encyclopaedic work, which has been reprinted several times since, provides modern historians with a unique view of the everyday language of British officers in colonial India. Yule was fascinated by the complex history of the incorporation of Hindustani, Bengali, and other Indian terms into English usage, and his rendering of this history in the form of an idiosyncratic yet highly engaging glossary has proved, perhaps ironically, to be his most enduring literary contribution.

Yule's second marriage in 1877 to Mary Wilhelmina Skipwith, daughter of Fulwar Skipwith of the Bengal civil service, was cut short by her death on 26 April 1881. He received the honorary degree of LLD from Edinburgh in 1884, served as a royal commissioner for the Indian and Colonial Exhibition of 1886, and was created KCSI in 1889. He died at his residence 3 Pen-y-Wern Road, Earls Court, London on 30 December 1889, and was buried on 3 January 1890 at Tunbridge Wells. Shortly before his death he received the news that he had been nominated as a corresponding member of the Institut de France. His reply, dictated through his daughter, was composed with characteristic grace and economy: 'Reddo gratias, Illustrissimi Domini, ob honores tanto nimios quanto immeritos. Mihi robora deficiunt, vita collabitur, accipiatis voluntatem pro facto. Cum corde pleno et gratissimo morituros vos, illustrissimi domini, saluto. Yule' (Yule, lxx–lxxi). While his obituarists treated these noble words as a fitting epitaph, a no less telling assessment of Yule's singular character is to be found in Clements Markham's manuscript history of the Royal Geographical Society, where it is recorded that:

> Sir Henry Yule was a linguist and an accomplished scholar. He was deeply versed in historical geography. He loved intricate research and wandering into the bye paths of history ... Tyranny and cruelty aroused his scorn and indignation, and he made a strong protest against H. M. Stanley's methods. Next to cruelty what aroused his anger most was the neglect of an author to make an index to his work. (Markham, 461)

FELIX DRIVER

Sources A. Yule, 'Memoir of Sir Henry Yule', in *The book of Ser Marco Polo, the Venetian, concerning the kingdoms and marvels of the East*, ed. and trans. H. Yule, rev. H. Cordier, 3rd edn, 1 (1903), xxvii–lxxxii · C. Trotter, *Memoir of Colonel Sir Henry Yule* (1891) · E. D. Morgan, 'Colonel Sir Henry Yule', *Scottish Geographical Magazine*, 6 (1890), 93–8 · R. Maclagan, 'Colonel Sir Henry Yule', *Proceedings* [Royal Geographical Society], new ser., 12 (1890), 108–13 · T. B. Collinson, 'Col. Sir Henry Yule', *Royal Engineers Journal* (1 Feb 1890), 41–4 · C. Markham, 'The Royal Geographical Society', RGS · F. Driver, 'Henry Morton Stanley and his critics', *Past and Present*, 133 (1991), 134–66 · R. J. Bingle, 'Henry Yule: India and Cathay', *Compassing the vast globe of the earth: studies in the history of the Hakluyt Society, 1846–1996*, ed. R. Bridges and P. Hair (1996), 143–63 · Burke, *Peerage* · DNB

Archives RGS | BL OIOC, letters to Lady Strachey, MS Eur. F 127 · NL Scot., letters to Blackwoods · RGS, corresp. with J. T. Walker · U. Aberdeen L., papers relating to family and Lord Napier of Magdala

Likenesses T. B. Wirgman, oils, 1880, Royal Engineers Headquarters, Chatham · G. Shaw, photograph, c.1880–1889, repro. in Morgan, 'Colonel Sir Henry Yule' · T. B. Wirgman, etching, c.1890, NPG [*see illus.*] · T. B. Wirgman, ink drawing, Scot. NPG

Wealth at death £29,364 17s. 9d.: probate, 8 Feb 1890, CGPLA Eng. & Wales

Yule, Robert (1817–1857). *See under* Yule, Sir Henry (1820–1889).

Yworth, William (d. 1715), distiller and chemical physician, claimed to have been born in 'Shipham', in the Netherlands (this location has not been traced). His early life and education are obscure, but by 1690 he was practising as a chemical physician from his house at the sign of the Collegium Chymicum in Rotterdam. He later suggested that he had begun his studies in chemistry and philosophy about 1680. By June 1691 he had moved to England, residing at the Academia Spagyrica Nova, at the Blue Ball and Star, in the London suburb of Shadwell, from where he sold medicines, wrote works on distillation, and offered lessons in chemical philosophy and practice. He was married, his wife's name being Elizabeth.

The changed political circumstances in England following the revolution of 1688 offered fresh opportunities to Yworth, who had a fluent command of English. In particular, he was attracted by the relatively low levels of duty payable on liquor distilled from malted corn, cider, or perry, established by statute in 1690 to encourage native alternatives to French wines, whose importation had been prohibited in 1689. His earliest publications, several of which derived from his *A New Treatise of Artificial Wines*, composed while he was still resident in the Netherlands and published in 1690, discussed distillation at length, as well as exhorting English manufacturers to exploit native resources, especially metallic ores. Yworth dedicated his *Chymicus rationalis*, registered in November 1691, to Robert Boyle. Boyle's success in 1689 in bringing about the repeal of the statute, dating from the reign of Henry IV, which prohibited the multiplication of gold and silver, may also have encouraged Yworth to pursue his career in London. However, Boyle's death in December 1691 left him without the patron he had hoped for, and there is little evidence that his business prospered in its new location. Nevertheless, he was able to employ an operator, Thomas Newton, in the laboratory of his grandly titled academy.

At first most of Yworth's contacts in London came from among the members of the Society of Friends; although there is no record that he himself was a Quaker, it is tempting to suppose that his earliest English associates may have been from the Quaker community in Rotterdam. His first publisher, Andrew Sowle, as well as his initial collaborator, Charles Marshall, and his agent, John Spire, were all members of the society. Despite the similarity of the ingredients and titles of many of Yworth's pills and tonics to those which Marshall had published several years earlier, the two men soon fell out over their application. Yworth also quarrelled with Sowle, whom he accused of stealing his recipes. Yworth began to market his medicines through a network of small salesmen across London, sealing them with his own device to protect against imitations. Shortage of money, however, prevented him from pursuing the most elaborate of his schemes, which involved publishing a succession of his alchemical and medical treatises, guiding a reader through the arts of Paracelsus, van Helmont, and their followers, to a new understanding of the causes and treatment of disease, and a new wisdom about the nature of creation. It also sought to encourage the more complete exploitation of the mineral treasures of Great Britain, leading to new wealth as well as prolonged life.

Although still living from hand to mouth, Yworth was able to move his premises to King Street, Moorfields, by 1702, and publish the first of his alchemical treatises, *Mercury's Caducean Rod*, under the pseudonym Cleidophorus Mystagogus. Together with his manuscript, 'Processus mysterii magni philosophicus', composed between 1701 and 1702, this work revealed him to be a well-trained and wide-ranging alchemist. Heavily influenced by the writings of Joan Baptista van Helmont and George Starkey, he was familiar with a remarkable variety of alchemical authors, including Michael Sendivogius, Basil Valentine, and Timothy Willis. He introduced extended considerations of the processes of creation, the origins of matter, and the beliefs of the ancient philosophers, into his accounts of the preparation and purification of metals and compounds, in particular sal ammoniac and mercury. By 1702 his skills had come to the attention of Isaac Newton, who shared Yworth's belief that Boyle had succeeded in transmuting base metal into gold. Newton, then master of the Royal Mint, received copies of Yworth's books and manuscripts, read and annotated them, and used them as the basis for some of his own alchemical work. In return, he paid Yworth an allowance for a time, which aided Yworth in supporting his wife and their children. It is unclear how long this relationship with Newton lasted; in 1705 Yworth published a second part of his alchemical work, *Trifertes sagani*, but by then he was already living away from London, and had handed his business there over to his son, Theophrastus. In 1709 Yworth applied for a licence to practise as a physician from Woodbridge, Suffolk, where it appears he and his family had been living for some while. He kept a shop there, achieving moderate prosperity, and continued to operate as both a distiller and a chemical physician. He died in 1715, and was survived by his wife. Thereafter Theophrastus Yworth made an attempt for a time to trade in London on his father's reputation.

SCOTT MANDELBROTE

Sources K. Figala and U. Petzold, 'Alchemy in the Newtonian circle: personal acquaintances and the problem of the late phase of Isaac Newton's alchemy', *Renaissance and revolution*, ed. J. V. Field and F. A. J. L. James (1993), 173–91 · probate inventory, Suffolk RO, FE1/11/67 · *The correspondence of Isaac Newton*, ed. H. W. Turnbull and others, 7 (1977), 441 · T. Yworth, *A brief, plain and candid account of the vertue, use and doses of certain experienced and highly approved medicines, faithfully prepared as in my father's days* (1715) · King's Cam., Keynes MS 65 · C. Marshall, *A plain and candid relation of the nature, use, and dose of several approved medicines* (1670) · Norwich subscription books cited by D. van Zwanenberg, 'Suffolk medical biographies', Suffolk RO

Archives Hants. RO, NC 17 · King's Cam., Keynes MSS · Yale U., Mellon MSS

Wealth at death £40 7s. 6d.: will, Suffolk RO, FE1/11/67

Zacharoff, Zacharias Basileios. *See* Zaharoff, Basil (1849–1936).

Zadkiel. *See* Morrison, Richard James (1795–1874).

Zaehner, Robert Charles (1913–1974), orientalist and intelligence officer, was born on 8 April 1913 at Oak Hill Lodge, Sevenoaks, Kent, the son of Edward Zaehner, lace merchant, and his wife, Maria Louisa (*née* Zaehner). His parents were both Swiss. He was educated at Tonbridge School where, he later recalled, religion became for him 'an incoherent farce' (Zaehner, *God*, 210). Then he won a classical scholarship at Christ Church, Oxford, where he was an undergraduate from 1933 to 1937. At the age of twenty he had what he termed a 'natural mystical experience' when reading Rimbaud's poem 'Ô saisons, ô châteaux': he felt an 'uncontrollable and inexplicable expansion of the personality', while having no religious beliefs (Zaehner, *Mysticism*, xii–xiv). Subsequently he switched from his Greek and Latin studies to Persian and Avestan (the language of ancient Iranian scripture). After obtaining first-class honours in oriental languages he remained at Christ Church as a senior scholar, doing research on the veneration of the pre-Islamic Iranian god of time, called Zurvan: the results of this were eventually published as *Zurvan: a Zoroastrian Dilemma* (1955).

In the Second World War, Zaehner was recruited by the Special Operations Executive (SOE), and in 1943 was sent to the British embassy in Tehran, where he was officially assistant press attaché and then press attaché until 1947. Apparently in 1945 a Russian intelligence officer and would-be defector, Konstantin Volkov, alleged to the British authorities that their Secret Intelligence Service (MI6) had a Soviet spy among their operatives in Iran, and Zaehner was later suspected, but exonerated, of being this agent (Wright, 238, 243–6). 1946 was an eventful year for Zaehner: he was received into the Roman Catholic church, and was greatly involved in British and Iranian efforts to counter the Soviet attempt to take over northwest Iran. As SOE was dismantled, Zaehner was kept on in the embassy for the purpose of 'bribing the Persian press' (Dorril, 535). In 1947 he returned to Britain, and continued with his research, but was also involved in operations conducted by MI6. 1949 found him in Malta, training Albanians to fight against their communist government. Here his usual 'mad professor' act contrasted with his extraordinary ability to learn languages: he mastered Albanian in just three months. Now nicknamed Doc (he was usually nicknamed Robin and Prof, while being known to some Catholic friends as Andrew, his confirmation name), he was employed in Greece in 1950, taking his Albanian trainees to their homeland (Bethell, 67, 137–9).

In 1950 Zaehner was appointed lecturer in Persian at Oxford, but he was soon required to resume his intelligence duties in Tehran. For in 1951 a new Iranian prime minister, Dr Muhammad Musaddiq, nationalized the Anglo-Iranian Oil Company, and the British Foreign Office decided to try to bring him down. Zaehner was sent back to the Tehran embassy as acting counsellor with this objective, and worked on it until 1952, using large-scale bribery, before returning, unsuccessful, to Oxford. He had now been accused of being a Soviet agent by a Welsh intelligence officer, Goronwy Rees, who had himself spied for the USSR and was regarded as an extremely unreliable source. The accusation was later investigated and found to be groundless (Dorril, 562–78; Wright, 243–6).

On returning to Oxford, Zaehner was appointed to the Spalding professorship of eastern religions and ethics at All Souls College in 1952. His inaugural lecture caused enormous offence. In it he rejected one of his chair's prescribed functions, that of bringing 'the great religious systems … together in closer understanding, harmony, and friendship'. Zaehner called this 'damnable', because such

harmony would be only 'apparent, verbal and fictitious' (Zaehner, *Discord*, 429). His views were developed in a number of books, the best-known being *Mysticism Sacred and Profane* (1957). In this Zaehner attacked Aldous Huxley's claim that mescalin had given him the highest experiences of the Christian, Hindu, and Buddhist mystics. Zaehner, drawing on his vast knowledge of world literature, argued that descriptions of mystical experiences showed these to be of very different kinds. He published a record of his own reactions to taking mescalin, which made him find all things 'equally funny' (Zaehner, *Mysticism*, 226).

With time, and changes in the outside world, Zaehner's views mellowed. The pontificate of John XXIII (1958–63), for whom he had immense admiration, led him to place his Catholicism in a more welcoming position vis-à-vis other religions, among which he numbered communism. Zaehner became a leading figure in the academic world (being elected a fellow of the British Academy in 1966 and receiving an honorary DLitt from the University of Lancaster in 1970), and gave a number of lecture series, published as yet more books. In these he hailed Alexander Dubcek's reforms in Czechoslovakia in 1968 as representing 'truly Communist faith, hope, and charity' (Zaehner, *Evolution*, 4), and extolled the ideas of the French Jesuit mystic and palaeontologist Pierre Teilhard de Chardin (1881–1955) as offering the perspective of a combination of religions and Marxism (Zaehner, *Discord*, 404–27).

There was, however, to be a final phase in Zaehner's thought. In his last years he turned against Teilhard, calling his work 'pseudo-science, pseudo-theology and pseudo-philosophy' (Zaehner, *God*, 191). Instead, Zaehner turned to Aristotle, admiring his rationalism, courage, and industry. Aristotle, he declared, was 'the father of our rational civilization and stepfather of the Catholic Church', and it was his God who was that of the Christians and the Hindus (Zaehner, *City*, 142–3). Further development of this last phase was prevented by Zaehner's death from heart disease, in Oxford, on 24 November 1974; he was buried in Wolvercote cemetery, Oxford. He never married.

In assessing Zaehner's writings one must first consider his monument of scholarship, *Zurvan*. This most remarkable study of how the pre-Islamic Iranians viewed Time as a god certainly ranks as one of the greatest academic works ever written: the mastery of a number of necessary languages is dazzling, and the philosophical and theological competence complete. Second, there are his analyses of mysticism, a subject which previously had been approached with vague platitudes and sentimental assertions that it was all the same. Zaehner was really the first person to argue effectively that one had to be rigorous in distinguishing between different types of mysticism: the ecstasy of the nature-mystic was not identical with the paroxysms of the love of God. Here he laid firm foundations for any future research. Third, there are his popularizing presentations of religions in their totalities: here again he insisted on drawing clear boundaries, now between 'solitary' and 'solidary' religions, those of individual self-fulfilment and those of social cohesion. He also insisted, against the prevailing anti-critical trend, that religions should be condemned for 'criminal and impious deeds' (Zaehner, *City*, 47). In this he showed that, as an academic, he could not tolerate falsehood and diplomatic banalities, precisely because, as an intelligence officer under diplomatic cover, he had himself lived a life of what he called 'professional lying' (Zaehner, *Discord*, 6).

JULIAN BALDICK

Sources R. Zaehner, *Mysticism sacred and profane* (1957) • R. Zaehner, *Zurvan: a Zoroastrian dilemma* (1955) • R. Zaehner, *Concordant discord* (1970) • R. Zaehner, *The city within the heart* (1980) • R. Zaehner, *Our savage God* (1974) • R. Zaehner, *Evolution in religion* (1971) • S. Dorril, *MI6* (2000) • P. Wright, *Spycatcher* (1987) • N. Bethell, *The great betrayal* (1984) • *WW* (1974) • b. cert. • d. cert. • personal knowledge (2004)
Archives Wadham College, Oxford, Persian and Arabic books • Wolfson College, Oxford, books
Likenesses photograph, All Souls Oxf.
Wealth at death £85,368: probate, 17 Feb 1975, *CGPLA Eng. & Wales*

Zaehnsdorf, Joseph (1814–1886), bookbinder, the son of Gottlieb Zaehnsdorf, a furrier, was born in Pest, Hungary, on 27 February 1814 and educated at the grammar school in that city. He was apprenticed for four years to Kupp, a bookbinder of Stuttgart, where he served a fifth year before working as a journeyman with bookbinders in Vienna, Zürich, Freiburg, Baden-Baden, and Paris. This experience broadened his knowledge of his craft and familiarized him with several languages. He moved to London in 1837 and lodged at 6 Frith Street with his brother Charles, a manufacturing jeweller, and found employment with Westley & Co. of Blackfriars. He was one of the union men who were dismissed in 1839 during the dispute between the employers and the men's trade society. He then worked for John Mackenzie, regarded as one of London's finest bookbinders, until establishing his own firm, probably in 1842 although various dates were given on the firm's later publicity material. The address of this first bindery is unknown; Zaehnsdorf moved frequently during his early years and shared many of his premises with other tradesmen, but always kept within the Covent Garden area of London.

Zaehnsdorf was living at 4 Gough Street when he married Ellen, daughter of William Donovan, a tailor, on 11 January 1845; she died in 1848 and on 10 July 1849 he married Ann, daughter of William Mahoney, an engineer. Their only son, Joseph William, was born on 1 June 1853 at 72 Drury Lane, their then home. Zaehnsdorf took British nationality on 15 September 1855. His financial stability would seem to have been assured by 1858 when he leased 30 Brydges Street from the Bedford estate, adding in 1873 a showroom and residence at 14 York Street. By 1861 he had been appointed 'bookbinder to the King of Hanover', and became a member of the Society of Arts. His fine bindings, exhibited at the major international exhibitions, gained him honourable mention at the 1862 London exhibition, and medals at the Anglo-French Working Class Exhibition at Crystal Palace and at Dublin, both in 1865, and at Paris,

1867, Vienna, 1873, and the London Universal Exhibition of 1874 where he set up a bookbinding workshop to demonstrate his craft to the visitor. His bindings were highly esteemed for their artistic taste and for their craftsmanship, and examples are to be found in major libraries and the great English collections.

Zaehnsdorf came into conflict with the unions in 1872 over his employment of numerous low-paid German workmen, and his reaction, which was to place an advertisement in the *Clerkenwell News* for non-union labour, led nineteen of his men to resign under union instructions. His son, Joseph William, was educated in England, then at St Omer in France before being apprenticed to a bookbinder in Cologne, but this apprenticeship was cut short by the Franco-Prussian War and he returned to Britain in 1870, taking full control of the firm from 1882. After a painful and protracted illness Joseph Zaehnsdorf died at his home, 14 York Street, on 7 November 1886. He was buried at Kensal Green cemetery. On that occasion one of his workmen delivered a eulogy (reported in the *British and Colonial Printer and Stationer*, 23 December 1886) praising him as:

> a businessman of high and unimpeachable character, upright and straightforward in all his transactions, … strict and particular with regard to our work, but this strictness always tempered by good humour and kind-heartedness and these … were his shining virtues. His advice, his experience, what is more, his purse, were always ready and open to assist any one of us deserving of it.

ANITA McCONNELL

Sources F. Broomhead, *The Zaehnsdorfs* (1986) • *Journal of the Society of Arts*, 35 (1886–7), 38 • m. certs. • d. cert.
Likenesses portrait, repro. in Broomhead, *The Zaehnsdorfs*
Wealth at death £3893 9s. 10d.: probate, 7 Dec 1886, *CGPLA Eng. & Wales*

Zaharoff, Basil [*formerly* Zacharias Basileios Zacharoff] (1849–1936), arms dealer, was born on 6 October 1849 at Muğla, Anatolia, the only son and eldest of the four children of Basilius Zacharoff (*d.* 1878) of Constantinople, a notary, commodity dealer, and importer of attar of roses, and his (reportedly blind) wife, Helena Antonides (*d.* 1879). Afterwards he lied promiscuously about his antecedents: sometimes he claimed a Polish father and French-Levantine mother; he bamboozled the British ambassador at Paris into believing that he was an Oxford University-educated Russo-Greek; when intriguing in Romania he persuaded the British minister at Bucharest 'that he was born at Jassy of a Roumanian mother *née* Mavrocordato, and that he has revisited Roumania since his early youth' (Sir H. Dering, dispatch 580, 31 Oct 1922, PRO, FO 371/7698). Supposedly when young he worked as a brothel-tout and as an arsonist for the Constantinople firemen, who made money on salvage.

Masquerading as a Russian officer called Prince Gortzacoff, General de Kieff, he went to London, where he married, on 14 October 1872, Emily Ann Burrows (*b.* 1845?), daughter of John Burrows, builder, of Bristol. He was the first man extradited from Belgium to Britain under a new treaty in 1872 and was prosecuted for embezzlement of

Basil Zaharoff (1849–1936), by unknown photographer

merchandise worth £1000 and securities exceeding £6000. Released on his own recognizance of £100 after offering compensation, he fled in 1873 to Cyprus, where (using sundry aliases) he set up as a storekeeper and boldly unscrupulous contractor. He settled in the USA in 1881 and became interested in ranches and railroad-building. Exposed after a bigamous marriage to an heiress, Jeannie Frances Billings, in New York in 1885, he assumed the name of Basil Zaharoff.

Known to intimates as Zedzed, Zaharoff began selling armaments for the Anglo-Swedish firm of Nordenfelt in Greece in 1877, and he developed the notorious *système Zaharoff* in which he played off one country against another to create a demand. Having sold one of the world's first submarines to Greece in 1885, he sold two to Turkey in 1886. (These prototypes proved too unsafe to use.) Quick-firing guns were, however, his chief commodity in the 1880s and 1890s. Bribery was a formal preliminary rather than a determinant of the arms trade in the markets where he concentrated. A brilliantly adaptable linguist, he had a truly cosmopolitan outlook. Having engineered Nordenfelt's merger with the rival company of Hiram Maxim in 1888, he visited Russia to sell the new Maxim machine-gun, and then Chile, Peru, and Brazil in 1888–9. When the Vickers steel company acquired the Maxim-Nordenfelt Guns and Ammunition Company, he was retained by the new combine in 1897 and for thirty years acted, in the phrase of its financial comptroller, Sir

Vincent Caillard, as 'our General Representative for business abroad' (Caillard to Sir A. Chamberlain, 23 April 1925, PRO, FO 371/10604).

Maxim-Nordenfelt had a Spanish light-armaments works called Placencia, of which Zaharoff became a director in 1896; from this starting point he 'created' Vickers' business in Spain (Zaharoff to G. Sim, 18 Feb 1929, CUL, Vickers MSS, Vickers microfilm R333). Vickers not only sold weaponry to the Spanish armed forces but in 1909 formed a new naval arsenal in collaboration with the state. Zaharoff's connection with Spain was intensified by a long-standing amour with a royal duchess, the paternity of whose three daughters was attributed to him. In Russia too he did much business. During 1902–4 Vickers, Sons, and Maxim paid him a total of £109,000; in 1905, at the time of the Russo-Japanese War, Vickers disbursed £86,000 to him in commission. He exercised limited, mercenary influence at the Spanish and Russian courts before 1914 but had no political importance in London or Paris. T. P. O'Connor described his first meeting with 'Zed' in 1913: 'there entered with brisk step a very tall thin man with the air of a great fencer, with a long thin face, a slight grey moustache, and eyes of blue grey, steely almost in their strength, their penetration, and their courage' (Fyfe, 236–7). Osbert Sitwell found him 'both evil and imposing about his figure' and likened him to a vulture:

> the beaky face, the hooded eye, the wrinkled neck, the full body, the impression of physical power and the capacity to wait, the sombre alertness. … He was in outlook merely a super-croupier. And once … I heard him introducing himself to a millionaire friend of mine with the startling phrase, 'I am Basil Zaharoff: I have sixteen millions!' (Sitwell, 267–8)

Zaharoff was a mountebank who indulged in self-mystification and encouraged fabulous rumours. He lived sumptuously in Paris (with a famous set of gold dinner plate afterwards sold to King Farouk of Egypt), took French citizenship in 1908, and became a shareholder in the Banque de France. As early as 1891 he founded the Express Bank, a bureau de change in place de l'Opéra in Paris, and in 1918 he jointly formed the Banque de la Seine, which dabbled in Mesopotamian oil diplomacy (and set up the Banque Commerciale de la Méditerranée at Constantinople in 1920) but was wound up in 1925.

Zaharoff's international mischief-making was as much egotistical in motive as commercial or political. In 1912 he instigated an offer of the Portuguese throne to Prince Christopher of Greece, to whom he confided: 'I have been lucky all my life; if I hadn't been, I should have been murdered long ago, or else serving a life sentence in some prison' (Prince Christopher, 115). Zaharoff was used by the British government to induce neutral Greece to join the allied cause in 1915, and with the cognizance of David Lloyd George he was sent to Switzerland to bribe Enver Pasha and other Turkish leaders with £10 million in gold to declare an armistice in 1917. His reports of this expedition are melodramatic if not mendacious. He was created GBE in 1918 and GCB in 1919: George V, who detested him, resented his use of titles, which, as a French citizen, were only honorary. For some years Zaharoff subsidized the

Greek politician Eleutherios Venizelos, who in turn helped him in dealings with foreign powers, but ultimately the two men quarrelled. He was believed to have financed the Greek expedition which landed at Smyrna in June 1919, and was reviled for his part in promoting the Graeco-Turkish War which ended in such bloody humiliation in 1922. Like his interventions in oil diplomacy, his influence has been exaggerated.

Zaharoff was indubitably impressive. His poses convinced so worldly an Englishman as Viscount Bertie of Thame, who wrote:

> He owns half the shares in Vickers Maxim, is the largest shareholder of the Monte Carlo Casino and has big holdings in American Railways and Steel Trust shares; I am told on excellent authority that he is worth over ten millions sterling. He is a personal friend of Walter Long, Bonar Law and Steel-Maitland and knows most of the present British Cabinet. He is said to have many of the leading French politicians in his pocket. I have known him for over ten years. I believe him to be a very just man though hard. He is anti-semitic and his numerous enemies accuse him of being a poseur and to be prone to exaggeration. ... I have a great personal regard for him. (Lord Bertie of Thame, memorandum on Zaharoff, 24 June 1917, PRO, FO 800/175)

Most of these claims were bogus or overblown: his holdings in Vickers were small; though he had apparently made financial loans to the casino, his syndicate only took control in 1923 and reduced its investment by 1926. He had some small French newspaper interests. Together with Steel-Maitland and Sir Leander Jameson he briefly had a financial stake in the *Sunday Times* before it was bought by William Berry in 1915; during 1922 he teased Sir Campbell Stuart with a plan to buy *The Times* after Lord Northcliffe's death. The ambassador to Berlin, Edgar Vincent, Viscount D'Abernon, told Stresemann in 1923 that Zaharoff 'was the modern Monte Christo, and was, or had been, fabulously rich. Everything he touched had turned to gold' (Viscount D'Abernon, 2.282). Zaharoff donated £28,000 to the Sorbonne in Paris to found a chair of aviation (1909) and endowed similar chairs at Petrograd and the Imperial College of Science and Technology, London (1919). To celebrate the armistice he endowed with £25,000 the Marshal Foch chair of French literature at Oxford University, and received an honorary DCL in 1920.

In 1924 Zaharoff finally married his mistress, Marie del Pilar Antonia-Angela-Patrocinio-Simona de Muguiro y Beruete (1868–1926), recently widowed by the death of Francisco María Isabel de Borbón y Borbón, duke of Marchena, and in that year created duchess of Villafranca de los Caballeros in her own right. After her death, which made him dangerously ill, he adopted her two surviving daughters, who inherited his fortune. Later in the 1920s gout restricted his travelling and he became very deaf.

An unauthorized biography by Richard Lewinsohn issued by Victor Gollancz in 1929 excited the interest of other investigative journalists. As part of the campaign against private manufacturers of armaments, radicals such as Fenner Brockway in *The Bloody Traffic* (1933) attacked Zaharoff and his fellow merchants of death as fomenters of war. After reading the Union of Democratic Control's pamphlet, *The Secret International*, Zaharoff wrote that '25% of the facts and 75% of the conclusions are incorrect, yet many of its allusions are correct' (Zaharoff to Sir M. W. Jenkinson, 28 July 1932, CUL, Vickers MSS, Vickers microfilm R338). His reputation became an embarrassment to Vickers, particularly during the deliberations of the royal commission on the private manufacture of and trading in arms (1935–6).

Zaharoff died of heart failure on 27 November 1936 at the Hôtel de Paris, Monte Carlo, Monaco, and was interred in a mausoleum in the grounds of his château at Balincourt, Arronville, near Pontoise (Val-d'Oise), France. There are disobliging allusions to him in Ezra Pound's *Cantos*, and he is the anti-hero of Michael Edwardes's novel *The Man from the other Shore* (1981).

RICHARD DAVENPORT-HINES

Sources CUL, Vickers MSS · HLRO, Lloyd George MSS · PRO, Foreign Office MSS · A. Allfrey, *Man of arms* (1989) · R. Lewinsohn, *The man behind the scenes: the career of Sir Basil Zaharoff 'The Mystery Man of Europe'* (1929) · D. McCormick, *Pedlar of death* (1965) · R. Neumann, *Zaharoff the armaments king* (1938) · H. Fyfe, *T. P. O'Connor* (1934) · O. Sitwell, *Great morning* (1948) · Prince Christopher of Greece, *Memoirs* (1938) · E. Vincent, Viscount D'Abernon, *An ambassador of peace*, 2: *The years of crisis: June 1922 – December 1923* (1929) · C. Trebilcock, *The Vickers brothers* (1977) · J. D. Scott, *Vickers: a history* (1962) · M. Edwardes, *The man from the other shore* (1981)
Archives CAC Cam., papers | Col. U., Rare Book and Manuscript Library, corresp. with William Shaw · CUL, Vickers MSS · HLRO, Lloyd George MSS · NA Scot., Steel-Maitland MSS · Wilts. & Swindon RO, Long MSS | FILM BFI NFTVA, documentary footage
Likenesses photograph, 1924, Société des Bains de Mer, Monaco; repro. in Allfrey, *Man of arms* · photograph, 1924?, Hult. Arch.; repro. in McCormick, *Pedlar of death* · photographs, 1924–8, repro. in Lewinsohn, *The man behind the scenes*, facing pp. 82 and 200 · photograph, c.1925, BL; repro. in Allfrey, *Man of arms* · three photographs, repro. in McCormick, *Pedlar of death*, facing pp. 97, 145, 193 [see illus.]
Wealth at death £193,103 17s. 7d.: administration with will, 15 Feb 1937, CGPLA Eng. & Wales

Zaimis [née Christides; *other married name* Chrysafis], **Eleanor** (1915–1982), pharmacologist, the daughter of Jean and Helen Christides, was born on 16 June 1915 in the Peloponnese. She spent much of her childhood in Bucharest, Romania, and was educated at the Greek *Gymnasium* and the University of Bucharest before graduating from Athens University with an MB in 1938, and then for nine years was assistant to the professor of pharmacology at the university.

Eleanor Christides obtained her MD in 1941 with a thesis entitled 'Antagonism between local anaesthetics and quinine' and a BSc in chemistry in 1947. Between 1940 and 1945 she was made responsible by the municipal department of health for all the youth centres in Athens, and from 1945 to 1947 was a member of a committee set up by the Greek government to evaluate the new antibiotics penicillin and streptomycin. Christides married twice, first in 1938 Evanghelos Chrysafis, a doctor, and then in 1943 Commander John Zaimis, a noted politician, naval officer, and diplomat. This second marriage was dissolved in 1957. Although she had no children, Zaimis had twelve godchildren throughout many parts of the world with whom she kept in constant contact.

Zaimis came to England in 1947 after being awarded a British Council scholarship. She worked briefly at Bristol University, before moving to the National Institute for Medical Research in Hampstead. Here, with William Paton, she began work on the synthesis of members of a new class of drugs—the methonium compounds, the results of which were described in two papers in *Nature* in 1948. One of these, hexamethonium, was the first drug to be used clinically to treat hypertension, and another, decamethonium, was developed as a successful and novel neuromuscular blocking drug, widely used by anaesthetists. Along with Paton, she was honoured for this work by an international award from the Gairdner Foundation, Toronto, in 1958, and by the Cameron prize from Edinburgh University in 1956. Further awards included a fellowship of the Royal College of Physicians in 1974, and an honorary fellowship of the faculty of anaesthetics of the Royal College of Surgeons of England in 1979.

Zaimis moved to the department of pharmacology at the school of pharmacy of the University of London at the end of 1948, becoming lecturer in pharmacology in 1950. She held this post until 1954 when she was appointed to head of department of pharmacology at the Royal Free Hospital school of medicine, where she was awarded a chair by the University of London in 1958, a position she held until her retirement in 1980. Despite the administrative load, Zaimis remained an active researcher until near to retirement with six papers in *Nature* and twelve in the *Journal of Physiology* spanning her career. She will be particularly remembered for the development of immuno-sympathectomy by the administration of anti-nerve growth factor antiserum. She used this as a means of destroying the sympathetic nervous system, leading to greater understanding of its function (*Nature*, 206, 1965, 1220–22). Throughout her time at the Royal Free, she participated fully in both undergraduate and postgraduate education and was also strongly involved with the social side of the medical school, serving as president of the dramatic society for ten years.

Zaimis was a lively and generous person, remembered for her determination and the high standards she set herself and expected of others. A striking woman with red hair, she had a passion for international travel and driving fast cars, often with a young admirer by her side. While in England, she remained in close contact with the country of her birth, acting as an adviser to the Greek government on university and pharmacological matters throughout her career, for which she was awarded the cross of commander of the Greek royal order of Beneficence. In later years, she was beset by ill health and depression. In 1980 she returned to Athens hoping to enjoy retirement among her friends of old. Unfortunately, she was struck by failing eyesight and her health deteriorated rapidly. She died at Laiko Hospital, Athens, on 3 October 1982, with only a few close friends by her bedside.

ANNETTE C. DOLPHIN and LUCY ABRAHAM

Sources L. Bindman, A. Brading, and T. Tansey, eds., *Women physiologists: an anniversary celebration of their contributions to British physiology* (1993) • E. J. Zaimis, L. Berk, and B. A. Callingham, 'Morphological biochemical and functional changes in the sympathetic nervous system of rats treated with nerve growth factor antiserum', *Nature*, 206 (1965), 1220–22 • *BMJ* (30 Oct 1982), 285, 1280 • *CGPLA Eng. & Wales* (1983) • WWW
Wealth at death £4331: administration with will, 9 June 1983, *CGPLA Eng. & Wales*

Zambaco, Marie Terpsithea (1843–1914). *See under* Pre-Raphaelite women artists (*act.* 1848–1870s).

Zangwill, Israel (1864–1926), writer and advocate of Jewish causes, was born on 21 January 1864 in Ebenezer Square, Houndsditch, Whitechapel, London, the second of the five children of Moses Zangwill (1836?–1908), an itinerant pedlar, glazier, and rabbinical student, and his wife, Ellen Hannah Marks, a Polish Jewish immigrant. His father, according to J. H. Udelson, 'born evidently in a small Russian Baltic town, is said to have escaped czarist conscription and arrived in Britain in 1848, at the surprising age of twelve' (Udelson, 60). Israel quickly demonstrated high ability at school in Bristol, where his parents were living after moving from Plymouth. They then settled in London, where he won awards at the Jews' Free School, Bell Lane, Spitalfields. He was articled there as a teacher, and remained until 1888 when he was twenty-four. Four years earlier, in 1884, he had received his degree with honours in French, English, and mental and moral science from London University where he had attended evening classes.

Many of the contradictions and paradoxes in Zangwill's life and work have their origin in the incompatibility between his parents. His pious, observant father was a scripture reader in the synagogue, and in the 1890s left his family to live and pray in Jerusalem where he was supported by Zangwill. His mother was less religious than her husband and was remembered by her third and youngest son, Louis Zangwill (1869–1938), 'as a Tartar', living with whom 'must have been hard for Moses Zangwill, who wanted a quiet life, prayer and study' (Leftwich, 90). She was also more freethinking and independent than her husband, was the dominant force in the home, and was ambitious for her children.

By June 1888 Zangwill had resigned from his teaching position to become a journalist on the staff of the newly founded weekly newspaper the *Jewish Standard*. He wrote a weekly column for this newspaper until 27 February 1891, four months before it folded. Another reason for leaving the Jews' Free School was his collaboration with his fellow pupil teacher Louis Cowen on the novel *The Premier and the Painter* (1888), published under the pseudonym J. Freeman Bell. It dealt with political rebellion and love and went into three editions by the end of the 1890s. Zangwill's first solo success, *The Bachelors' Club* (1891), was a sequence of short stories linked to appear as a novel, and introduced 'three central Zangwillian motifs: the irony of life, the fragility of idealism, and the utility of even delusive ideals' (Udelson, 74). Some of these stories, and of those later collected as *The Old Maids' Club* (1892), first appeared in *Ariel, or,*

Israel Zangwill (1864–1926), by Alfred Wolmark, 1925

The London Puck, a comic journal edited by Zangwill which folded in February 1892. He also wrote for Jerome K. Jerome's *The Idler*—the two had become friends at London University—and Zangwill's *The Big Bow Mystery* (1891), with its non-Jewish settings and characters, appeared serially in the *London Star* (1891) and attracted a wide audience.

Notable among the myriad of miscellaneous articles Zangwill wrote, 'English Judaism: a criticism and a classification' (*Jewish Quarterly Review*, 1, July 1899) consigned traditional Orthodox Judaism to the dustbin of history while also rejecting the new Reform Judaism:

> There is something touching and sublime in the common belief of a people in an apparent impossibility, in the ultimate return of its national hero, in the recovery of its golden glories … something pathetic in its simple faith and credulous hope, as a mother who clasps her dead child to her breast and will not let it go.

Such apparent contradictions attracted the attentions of the backers of the newly founded Jewish Publication Society of America which commissioned him to write a Jewish novel. The result, *Children of the Ghetto* (1892), with its powerful realistic depiction of ghetto life, established Zangwill as a spokesperson for Jewry within and outside the Jewish world. His *Ghetto Tragedies* (1893), *The King of Schnorrers: Grotesques and Fantasies* (1894), and *Dreamers of the Ghetto* (1898) similarly presented the realities of Jewish ghetto life. *The Master* (1895) continues to explore immigrant life and the 'conflict between the demands of the artist's life and the moral values in which he was raised to believe' (Rochelson, 371), though this time using a non-Jewish setting split between Nova Scotia and London.

The year 1895 marked a watershed in Zangwill's personal life. At a reception he met Edith Ayrton (1875–1945), the daughter of the distinguished electrical engineer and physicist William Edward *Ayrton FRS (1847–1908) and stepdaughter of Ayrton's second wife, also a distinguished physicist, Phoebe Sarah (Hertha) Marks *Ayrton (1854–1923). Edith's mother, Matilda Charlotte Chaplin *Ayrton (1846–1883), one of the first women's medical doctors in Britain, had died in 1883 and Edith was brought up by Hertha, who was Jewish. Edith attended Bedford College, London University. Author of six novels, *Barbarous Babe* (1904), *The First Mrs Mollivar* (1905), *Teresa* (1909), *The Rise of a Star* (1918), *The Call* (1924), which focused on the emancipation cause, and *The House* (1928), she married Zangwill in a civil register office ceremony on 26 November 1903. Their marriage was a happy one, and they had three children: Ayrton Israel (George; *b*. 1906), who became an engineer and worked in Mexico; Oliver Louis *Zangwill (1913–1987), who became professor of experimental psychology at the University of Cambridge (1952–81); and Margaret (1910–*c*.1990), who suffered from a mental condition and was institutionalized.

Zangwill became deeply involved with the Zionist cause, in its internal politics and infighting. He travelled widely, speaking and writing on its behalf. At the seventh Zionist conference in Basel in 1905 he made impassioned pleas to the delegates to accept the scheme to resettle Jews in east Africa: as he said, 'Palestine proper has already its inhabitants. … better Zionism without Zion than Zion without Zionism' (Udelson, 177). In the aftermath of the vicious pogroms raging in eastern Europe Zangwill, Theodor Herzl, and others were primarily concerned to rescue and resettle Jews anywhere, but these plans were rejected by various Zionist conferences. As Udelson summarizes: 'From 1901 to 1905 [Zangwill] was an advocate of official Herzlian Zionism; from 1905 to 1914 he was the driving force behind insurgent Territorialism; and from 1914 to 1919 he was the leading Western advocate of a Palestine-centred Jewish nationalism' (ibid., 164). Much of Zangwill's energy between 1905 and 1914 was devoted to the 'Galveston plan', which was supported by wealthy New York Jews of German origin and involved getting thousands of persecuted Jews out of eastern Europe and resettling them in the west and midwestern United States.

Ideological and personal rivalries caused Zangwill to break with the Balfour declaration of 2 November 1917. Initially he had supported this declaration of a homeland for the Jewish people in Palestine, but he had come to believe that the Balfour declaration did not make adequate arrangements for the Arab populations there. At the 1919 Paris peace conference he advocated resettlement of these populations in a 'new and vast Arabian kingdom' (Udelson, 188). Disillusioned with what he regarded as British establishment duplicity and by internal dissension in Zionist politics, his last years were spent railing against those who he thought had betrayed his hopes for the future of the Jewish people and for the survival of their culture. In 1920 he wrote in a letter to *The Times* of 16 January:

> What is now being concocted in Paris [that is, a League of Nations mandate] is a scheme without attraction save for

mere refugees, a scheme under which a free-born Jew returning to Palestine would find himself under British military rule, aggravated by an Arab majority in civic affairs. (Udelson, 189)

Zangwill was angular, tall, gaunt, and bespectacled, and was a witty, powerful and epigrammatic speaker who attracted large audiences on both sides of the Atlantic. In addition to his novels he translated the Hebrew liturgy into English and wrote poetry and twenty dramas—many of which were adaptations from his novels. His most famous play was *The Melting Pot*, produced in Washington, DC in 1908, in New York in 1909, and in London in 1914. A political play, it advocates the message of tolerance and the assimilation of minority groups into the wider community. In *Too Much Money* (1918) he explores another of his favourite themes—the corrupting power of wealth.

Broken in health, Zangwill spent his last years tended by his wife at their home in the Sussex countryside at Far End, East Preston. He died of pneumonia on 1 August 1926 at Oakhurst, a nursing home in Midhurst, Sussex. He was cremated at Willesden Green, London on 5 August, following a service conducted by the rabbi of the Liberal Jewish synagogue at St John's Wood, London. His ashes are at Willesden Jewish cemetery. His friend and contemporary Alfred Sutro observed that:

under a somewhat truculent exterior he was curiously unselfish and tender-hearted. … A fiery spirit, a man who all his life followed a great idea, he was fitly apostrophized by Rabbi Wise in his funeral address 'Flame thou wert, to flame thou hast returned'. *(DNB)*

WILLIAM BAKER

Sources J. H. Udelson, *Dreamer of the ghetto: the life and works of Israel Zangwill* (1990) · J. Leftwich, *Israel Zangwill* (1957) · M. Wohlgelernter, *Israel Zangwill* (1964) · *DNB* · J. Sutherland, 'Zangwill, Israel', *The Stanford companion to Victorian fiction* (1989), 687–8 · M.-J. Rochelson, 'Israel Zangwill', *British short-fiction writers, 1880–1914: the realist tradition*, ed. W. B. Thesing, DLitB, 135 (1994), 362–78 · *The Times* (2 Aug 1926), 11 · E. B. Adams, *Israel Zangwill* (1971) · C. Roth, ed., *Encyclopaedia Judaica*, 16 vols. (Jerusalem, 1971–2) · D. Walden, 'Israel Zangwill', *Modern British dramatists, 1900–1945*, ed. S. Weintraub, DLitB, 10 (1982), 238–42 · W. J. Scheick, '"Murder in my soul"; genre and ethos in Zangwill's *The big Bow mystery*', *English Literature in Transition, 1880–1920*, 40 (1997), 23–33 · *CGPLA Eng. & Wales* (1926) · I. Zangwill, *Children of the ghetto: a study of a peculiar people*, ed. M.-J. Rochelson (1998)

Archives American Jewish Archives, Cincinnati · BL · Central Zionist Archives, Jerusalem, letters, diaries, photographs, etc. · NRA, corresp. and literary papers · U. Leeds, MSS and corresp. · U. Lond., Senate House · UCL | American Jewish Historical Society, Waltham, Massachusetts, letters to Philip Cowen and papers · BL, corresp. with Marie Stopes, Add. MS 58497 · Bodl. Oxf., letters to Elizabeth, Lady Lewis · Jewish Theological Seminary of America · NYPL · Richmond Local Studies Library, London, corresp. with Douglas Sladen · U. Leeds, Brotherton L., letters to Clement Shorter · U. Southampton L., papers with those of Louis Zangwill incl. letters and album of autograph postcards

Likenesses Sic, cartoon, lithograph, 1897, NPG; repro. in *VF* (25 Feb 1897) · Elliott & Fry, photogravure photograph, 1901, NPG · W. R. Sickert, oils, 1904, Scottish National Gallery of Modern Art, Edinburgh · A. L. Coburn, photogravure photograph, 1913, NPG · E. Kapp, drawing, 1924, Barber Institute of Fine Arts, Birmingham · A. Wolmark, ink drawing, 1925, NPG [see illus.] · B. Partridge, chalk drawing, NPG · C. R. Polowetski, oils, NPG · photographs, repro. in Udelson, *Dreamer of the ghetto*

Wealth at death £3267 2s. 11d.: probate, 13 Dec 1926, *CGPLA Eng. & Wales*

Zangwill, Oliver Louis (1913–1987), a founder of neuropsychology, was born on 29 October 1913 in East Preston, Sussex, the second son and youngest of three children in the family of Israel *Zangwill (1864–1926), the Anglo-Jewish literary and political figure, and his wife, Edith Ayrton (1875–1945), who was active in the establishment of the League of Nations. A cousin was the painter and writer Michael *Ayrton, the common grandfather being the physicist William *Ayrton FRS. Zangwill was educated at University College School, London (1928–31), and at King's College, Cambridge, where he obtained a second class in part one of the natural sciences tripos (1934) and a first in part two of the moral sciences tripos (1935).

At Cambridge, Zangwill was influenced by Frederic Bartlett while carrying out experiments on recognition and memory. With his lifelong friend R. C. Oldfield he wrote a critique of the celebrated concept of mental schema put forward by Sir Henry Head and Bartlett. Another influence was J. T. McCurdy, who intrigued Zangwill with hypnosis, which he later demonstrated to great effect on his students. Zangwill studied patients with Korsakov psychosis, his paper 'Amnesia and the generic image' (*Quarterly Journal of Experimental Psychology*, 2, 1950) remaining significant for the subject of whether semantic memory remains intact in amnesia. There is a story of a Korsakov patient whom Zangwill saw each week; taking a pen from his pocket he would ask, 'Have you seen this before?' Every week the patient would say, 'No.' At the final session Zangwill asked, 'Have you seen *me* before?' The patient replied, 'Are you the man with all those pens?'

Zangwill became a research psychologist at the brain injuries unit in Edinburgh (1940–45), which was directed by Norman Dott. There he did original, influential work on the psychological effects of penetrating wounds to the brain. His studies of cases of parietal lobe injury, with Andrew Patterson, led to his interest in hemispheric specialization and the complexities of right/left-handedness. His central aim was to use clinical abnormalities, especially symptoms of localized brain damage, to suggest how the normal brain functions.

While assistant director of the Institute of Experimental Psychology at the University of Oxford (1945–52) Zangwill promoted the teaching of psychology at a time when it was not considered a major subject, in spite of its importance at Cambridge. By establishing connections with the National Institute of Neurology in Queen Square, London, and with the Radcliffe Infirmary in Oxford he introduced a generation of psychologists to the study of neurological patients. His students included George Ettlinger, John McFie, Malcolm Piercy, Maria Wyke, Elizabeth Warrington, and Brenda Milner, all of whom became distinguished neuropsychologists. Appointed to the Cambridge chair (which he held from 1952 to 1981), with a fellowship of King's College, in his inaugural lecture he defined psychology as 'the study of behaviour', though he was never a behaviourist. Zangwill brought Lawrence Weiskrantz from America to set up a primate laboratory, with far-reaching consequences, especially as a result of Weiskrantz's continuing work as professor of psychology at Oxford.

Zangwill took a major part in setting up the Experimental Psychology Group, which was very influential though it was sometimes critically described as an élitist Cambridge and Oxford club. It became the larger Experimental Psychology Society, with its quarterly journal, which Zangwill edited from 1958 to 1966, serving also on the editorial board of *Neuropsychologia* (1963–81). His *Introduction to Modern Psychology* (1950) set out pathways to be followed. He also wrote *Amnesia* (1966) and edited, with W. H. Thorpe, *Current Problems in Animal Behaviour* (1961).

Zangwill was elected a fellow of the Royal Society in 1977. He had honorary degrees from Stirling (1979) and St Andrews (1980). He held the honorary post of visiting psychologist at the National Hospital for Nervous Diseases (1947–79); he also had close connections with European clinical neurology and, in the United States, with Hans-Lukas Teuber at the Massachusetts Institute of Technology.

A tall, stooping figure, with dark hair and green-grey eyes that looked everywhere, Zangwill also had an elusive, almost haunted personality with moments of witty appreciation. He had several close friendships but was generally a very private person whose thoughts were hard to interpret and whose decisions were often unpredictable, though not lacking in shrewdness. In 1947 he married Joy Sylvia, daughter of Thomas Moult, poet; they had one son, who died in infancy. The marriage was dissolved in 1976 and in the same year Zangwill married Shirley Florence Tribe, daughter of Leonard Frank Punter, a businessman; they had one adopted son. Zangwill died in Cambridge on 12 October 1987, following a long illness in which he succumbed to the losses of memory that had so much concerned him throughout his professional life.

RICHARD L. GREGORY, rev.

Sources *The Times* (14 Oct 1987) · *The Independent* (20 Oct 1987) · *Jewish Chronicle* (23 Oct 1987) · *CGPLA Eng. & Wales* (1988) · personal knowledge (1996)
Wealth at death £110,140: probate, 23 Feb 1988, *CGPLA Eng. & Wales*

Zavaroni, Lena Hilda (1963–1999), popular singer and entertainer, was born on 4 November 1963 at the Rankin Memorial Hospital, Greenock, Renfrewshire, the first of two daughters of Victor Alfredo Zavaroni and his wife, Hilda Catherine, *née* Jordan (*d.* 1989), who owned a fish and chip shop in their home town, Rothesay, Isle of Bute. Her father's family came originally from Genoa. Both her parents were keen amateur singers in local clubs, and as a child she performed regularly with them. Encouraged to enter the ITV talent show *Opportunity Knocks* when she was only nine, she won the audience's poll for five consecutive weeks, a success which resulted in a recording contract. Early in 1974 her first single, 'Ma, he's making eyes at me', entered the top ten and made her the youngest artist to appear on the television programme *Top of the Pops*. An album, *Ma*, also reached the top ten, but a subsequent top forty single, 'Personality', was her only other record to make the charts (in the summer of 1974), although several more singles and albums were released over the next eight years.

After moving to London, where she lived with her managers, Philip and Dorothy Solomons, Zavaroni was enrolled at the Italia Conti Stage School, Clapham, to be groomed as an all-round song and dance entertainer. The transition was overwhelming at first, she said later. 'Everything changed so quickly. I had never seen lifts or escalators or traffic lights' (*Daily Telegraph*, 4 Oct 1999). Over the next few years she made several appearances on stage and television in Britain and America. She topped the bill at the London Palladium, was featured in the royal variety performance, played in summer variety shows and pantomime, and appeared on several television variety and chat shows. In the United States she was invited to sing at the White House, and shared a stage with Frank Sinatra and Lucille Ball. Between 1979 and 1981 she had three series of her own on BBC television, entitled *Lena Zavaroni and her Music*. At the height of her career she was reputed to be earning £9000 a week.

When Zavaroni was thirteen anorexia nervosa was diagnosed, and her weight dropped to 4 stone. Later she recalled:

> When they tried to fit me into these costumes … they would talk about my weight. I was a plump little girl and I was also developing into a woman. I only became fanatical about not eating when the pressure became too much. (*Daily Telegraph*, 4 Oct 1999)

From the age of sixteen she was regularly undergoing hospital treatment. Her parents' divorce was another blow, though she remained close to her father, who remarried in 1981. In the following year, after playing in pantomime at the Alexandra Theatre, Birmingham, and a summer season at White Rock Pavilion, Hastings, she temporarily retired, owing to ill health.

In 1984 Zavaroni made a few tentative, well-received television appearances, and thus encouraged returned to work full-time, guesting in a summer season show at the Opera House, Blackpool, the following year. However, by 1987 she was too ill to work regularly, and announced that she was giving up show business permanently. On 30 September 1989 she married Peter Wiltshire, a businessman and computer expert, at St Mary's Church, Finchley, and they lived in north London, but her persistent depression, ill health, and reclusive behaviour overshadowed their life together. Her mother died after an overdose of drugs and alcohol shortly after the wedding. There were no children of the marriage, which ended in divorce eighteen months later. She moved to Hoddesdon, Hertfordshire, to be nearer her father, and lived on state benefits. In 1993 she made her final television appearance, on *Summer Praise*, a religious programme. Her anorexia worsened, and she spent over two years at the Montreux Counselling Centre, Canada. Attempts to write her memoirs were frustrated by what she called her lack of happy memories: 'There's no spirit in me, that's the part of depression. I still can't eat in front of anyone else, not even my own family' (*The Independent*, 4 Oct 1999).

In 1998 all Zavaroni's show business mementoes were destroyed in a fire at her home, and in March 1999 she was arrested on a charge of shoplifting, which was dropped without her going to court. Her weight had fallen to 3 and a half stone, and in September 1999 she was admitted to University of Wales Hospital, Cardiff, for a pioneering brain-surgery operation. Shortly afterwards she contracted bronchial pneumonia and died in the hospital on 1 October. She was buried at St Augustus Roman Catholic Church, Hoddesdon, on 15 October. Once touted as Britain's answer to Shirley Temple, Zavaroni's life story came more to resemble that of Judy Garland; as one obituarist wrote, she 'epitomised the potentially traumatic effects of child stardom' (*The Guardian*, 5 Oct 1999).

JOHN VAN DER KISTE

Sources *Daily Telegraph* (4 Oct 1999) · www.caringonline.com/eatdis/misc/zavaroni2.htm, April 2001 · 'Fuller up: the dead musician directory', elvispelvis.com, April 2001 · *The Independent* (4 Oct 1999) · *The Times* (4 Oct 1999) · *The Guardian* (4 Oct 1999) · *The Scotsman* (4 Oct 1999) · private information (2004)
Archives FILM BFI NFTVA, 'The real Lena Zavaroni', Channel 4, 23 Feb 2000
Likenesses photographs, *c*.1980, Hult. Arch. · portraits, repro. in www.debrajayne9.freeserve.co.uk/index.htm

Zec, Philip (1909–1983), illustrator and cartoonist, was born on 25 December 1909 on the fringe of Bloomsbury, London, the fourth of the eleven children (nine daughters and two sons) of Simon Zec, the son of a Russian rabbi and himself a master tailor, who fled with his wife, Leah Oistrakh, to England to escape tsarist oppression. His artistic talents, which may have owed something to his maternal grandfather who studied architecture in Ukraine, were revealed early. A scholarship from the local Stanhope Street elementary school took him to St Martin's School of Art, London, where his education effectively began and where his gifts, notably in portraiture, were rapidly developed. But his vigorous draughtsmanship and flair for illustration pointed more towards commercial art, and at nineteen he set up his own studio.

Working for J. Walter Thompson and other international advertising agencies, Zec became one of the leading illustrators of his day. His sculpted heads of prominent political and literary figures of the 1930s extended his range and at the same time exposed what he saw as the superficialities of the world of advertising. His work became widely recognized. One of his early posters, a vivid impression of the *Flying Scotsman* at speed against a night landscape, is still featured in exhibitions of steam railway memorabilia. But commercial art became too constricting both for his powerful analytical style and for a political consciousness spurred by the rise of Hitlerism in Germany. As a socialist and a Jew, the notion of remaining on the sidelines drawing radio valves or coffee labels in Britain's post-Munich era became unthinkable.

Fortuitously, a colleague, Basil Nicholson (creator of the Horlicks 'night starvation' strip), faced a similar dilemma. In 1937 he was hired as features editor of the *Daily Mirror* to help transform it from a genteel picture paper for the wealthy and their servants, to an outspoken radical tabloid. Nicholson recruited Zec as the paper's political cartoonist and also a former copy-writer, William Connor, who wrote a forthright column under the name Cassandra. Britain at war, and the traumas of Dunkirk and the blitz, offered a compelling landscape for political comment, especially by an artist of Zec's passion and boldness of attack. His cartoons, drawn with a starkness and ferocity of line, captured precisely the stoicism and the humour of the British at war. Unlike David Low, who created satirical stereotypes such as Colonel Blimp, or C. R. Giles, with his preposterous 'family', Zec aimed at recognizable targets. He presented Hitler, Goering, and others in the Nazi hierarchy as strutting buffoons. Replacing ridicule with venom, he often drew them in the form of snakes, vultures, toads, or monkeys. Not surprisingly, captured German documents listed Zec's name among those to be arrested immediately England had fallen. The defiance of the population caught in the prolonged air raids, the bravery of the armed services abroad, and the civil defence at home were depicted in the daily cartoons, some sketchily outlined in air raid shelters. In 1939 he married Betty, daughter of Michael Levy, a tailor. They had no children.

Zec's reputation as 'the people's cartoonist', however, suffered a blow as a result of one particular cartoon. Drawn in March 1942, it showed a torpedoed sailor adrift on a raft in a dark, empty sea. The caption read: 'The price of petrol has been increased by one penny; *Official*'. It achieved an immediate, but scarcely merited, notoriety. Zec had intended to alert the paper's millions of readers to the fact that the petrol they were using, perhaps wasting, cost not only money but men's lives. This was not the view taken by the government. Winston Churchill was enraged and endorsed the charge by the home secretary, Herbert Morrison, that the cartoon plainly implied that seamen were risking their lives for the profit of the petrol companies. Zec angrily rebutted that interpretation, submitting a shoal of readers' letters in support, some vowing to give up petrol 'for the duration'. But Morrison warned the paper's proprietors that any further 'transgression' would lead to the paper being shut down. Ironically, the offending caption had not been Zec's but Cassandra's: the columnist considered his friend's original line 'Petrol is dearer now' not strong enough. By contrast Zec's VE-day cartoon was widely acclaimed. It depicted a wounded soldier handing over a laurel representing victory and peace in Europe. The caption read: 'Here you are. Don't lose it again!' It occupied almost entirely the *Daily Mirror*'s front page on election day in 1945. Analysts of Labour's landslide victory saw that cartoon as a key factor in the paper's election campaign.

Zec continued briefly as a cartoonist after the war but with less zeal, as he became disenchanted with what he saw as growing left extremism in the Labour Party. In 1950–52 he was editor of the *Sunday Pictorial*. He left the *Mirror* for the *Daily Herald* in 1958. In that year he won an international prize for a cartoon with the greatest political impact, submitted by cartoonists from twenty-four countries: the subject was the crushing of Hungary by the Soviet army. He left the *Daily Herald* in 1961. Zec was a director of the *Jewish Chronicle* for twenty-five years. He also, as a fervent supporter of the Common Market, became editor of *New Europe*. In the last three years of his life he was blind, but nevertheless continued to proclaim his ideals as passionately and as animatedly as ever.

A tall, genial extrovert, Zec was as fastidious in his dress as he was in his draughtsmanship. Away from the drawing-board he was one of the livelier raconteurs in Fleet Street's famous hostelry, El Vino's, during the flourishing years of British journalism. Zec died in Middlesex Hospital, London, on 14 July 1983.   DONALD ZEC, *rev.*

Sources personal knowledge (1990) · *CGPLA Eng. & Wales* (1983) · *The Times* (15 July 1983)
Wealth at death £63,026: probate, 6 Dec 1983, *CGPLA Eng. & Wales*

Zeeland. For this title name *see* Jacqueline, *suo jure* countess of Hainault, *suo jure* countess of Holland, and *suo jure* countess of Zeeland (1401–1436).

Zepler, Eric Ernest [*formerly* Erich Ernst] (1898–1980), electrical engineer and university teacher, was born on 27 January 1898 in Herford, Westphalia, Germany, the younger son of Martin Zepler (1862–1939), a country doctor, and his wife, Flora Guttfreund (1866–1943). His Jewish parents converted to Christianity in 1902, and he was baptized in the Lutheran church, Herford, on 14 December 1902. He was educated at the Realgymnasium in Altena, Westphalia, and after studying physics at the universities of Bonn (1916–19) and Berlin (1919–20) took the DPhil degree at Würzburg in 1922. His radio engineering work began with three colleagues in a small workshop in St Blasien. He joined Telefunken in Berlin in 1925 and became head of design for receivers and direction finders in 1932. By 1935 he had thirty-seven individual patents and twenty-two joint patents. On 2 October 1926 he married Eleonore Johanna Fischer (1899–1990).

To escape Nazi persecution Zepler moved to England in 1935 with his wife and young children, Carole and Matthew, and continued his work on radio design at the Marconi Wireless Telegraph Company in Chelmsford until 1940. During the Second World War airborne radio receivers and transmitters based on his designs were used by both the RAF and the Luftwaffe. Zepler's remarkable insight into radio circuits, and his analytical ability, enabled him to transform the design of radio systems from a black art of trial and error into a modern engineering discipline where the performance of equipment is determined before it is constructed. This pioneering work was encapsulated in his classic book *The Technique of Radio Design*, which was published in 1943. His analytical method of design was later applied to other electronic systems and thus made an important contribution to the flowering of electronic engineering during the next half-century.

After internment in 1940, Zepler became a lecturer in 1941 at the University College in Southampton, which became a university in 1952. He worked there for the rest

of his career, except for three years from 1943, which he spent at Cambridge University. He became a naturalized British subject in 1947. At Southampton that same year he founded the first department of electronics in Britain and launched a postgraduate diploma in electronics, which became a highly regarded qualification. He became the first professor of electronics in 1949, and introduced the first BSc course in electronics in Britain in 1959. Zepler's inspirational teaching stimulated students and conveyed to them his insight into electronic systems. With modesty and dedication he led by example the small team of staff which established the teaching and research in what became the leading university department of electronics in Britain. With some of those colleagues he published books on *Electronic Devices and Networks* (1963), *Electronic Circuit Techniques* (1963), and *Transients in Electronic Engineering* (1971). After retiring in 1963, he worked in the Institute of Sound and Vibration Research for ten years. In 1977 he was awarded the honorary degree of DSc. In 1995, in the department of electronics at Southampton University, an exhibition was set up of some of the pre-war radio receivers which he designed, including the Telefunken T9W and the Marconi B28.

Zepler was a distinguished radio engineer whose interests included music, literature, and bridge. His lifelong passion was the composition of chess problems, which led him to publish *Under the Spell of the Chess Problem* with Ado Krämer in 1951, and to be granted the title of international master of chess composition. His portrait, which was commissioned to mark his presidency of the British Institution of Radio Engineers in 1959–60, and which is kept at the Institution of Electrical Engineers in London, catches the twinkle in his eyes that his colleagues knew so well. Zepler died on 13 May 1980 at Moorgreen Hospital, Southampton, and was cremated at Southampton on 16 May.   GREVILLE BLOODWORTH

Sources *WW* (1981) · B. Bosch, 'Dr Erich Zepler: ein wechselvolles Leben für die Funktechnik', *Funkgeschichte*, no. 72 (1990), 9–15 · *The Times* (16 May 1980) · D. J. Morris, 'Telefunken T9W receiver', *Bulletin of the British Vintage Wireless Society*, 16/4 (1991), 50 · *Southern Evening Echo* (16 May 1980) · personal knowledge (2004) · private information (2004) · b. cert. [Ger.] · m. cert. [Ger.]
Likenesses D. Houston, oils, 1960, Inst. EE
Wealth at death £21,461: probate, 28 July 1980, *CGPLA Eng. & Wales*

Zerffi, George Gustavus (1821–1892), writer on art and history, was born in Hungary, where he edited the *Ungar* newspaper in Pest, and took part in the 1848 revolution, serving as a captain in the revolutionary army. In 1849 he moved to England, where he was naturalized. Some years later he was employed by the Department of Science and Art at the South Kensington Museum (Victoria and Albert Museum), and in 1868 was appointed a lecturer. He lectured on historic ornament, and published a revised version of his lectures under the title 'Historical art studies' in *Building News* (1872–6). *A manual of the historical development of art … with special reference to architecture, sculpture, painting, and ornament* appeared in 1876 and went to three editions.

Zerffi was also interested in the philosophy of history, publishing *The Science of History* (1879), a work written for Japanese scholars according to instructions prepared by K. Suyematz of Japan. He planned a general work on similar lines, entitled *Studies in the Science of General History*, two volumes of which—dealing with ancient and medieval history—came out in 1887 and 1889. He was a member of the council of the Royal Historical Society, for many years, and at one time its chairman; he was also a fellow of the Royal Society of Literature.

Zerffi was a popular lecturer, publishing many of his lectures delivered to the Sunday Lecture Society, including *Natural Phenomena and their Influence on Different Religious Systems* (1873), *Dogma and Science* (1876), and *Long and Short Chronologists, or, Egypt from a Religious, Social, and Historical Point of View* (1878). His English version of Goethe's *Faust*, with critical notes, was published in 1859. *Spiritualism and Animal Magnetism* appeared in 1871, and *Immanuel Kant in his Relation to Modern History* in 1875. Zerffi died on 28 January 1892 at his home, 2 Albert Villas, Chiswick High Road, Acton, leaving a widow, Josephine, and a son.

G. Le G. Norgate, *rev.* Anne Pimlott Baker

Sources *The Times* (30 Jan 1892) · *The Athenaeum* (6 Feb 1892), 189 · *Building News* (5 Feb 1895) · Boase, *Mod. Eng. biog.* · *CGPLA Eng. & Wales* (1892) · d. cert.
Wealth at death £578 2*s. od.*: administration, 28 March 1892, *CGPLA Eng. & Wales*

Zernov, Nicolas Mikhailovich (1898–1980), Russian Orthodox theologian and pioneer in the movement for Christian unity, was born in Moscow on 9 October 1898 os, the eldest of four children (two sons, two daughters) of Mikhail Stefanovich Zernov (1857–1938) and his wife, Sofia Aleksandrovna Kesler (1865–1942). The children were brought up in a strongly religious atmosphere. In 1917 Nicolas entered the school of medicine at Moscow University (his father was a doctor), but his studies were interrupted by the October revolution. During the civil war he served in the Caucasus as a volunteer with the White Army, and in 1921 he emigrated with his family to Yugoslavia. He studied theology at Belgrade University, graduating in 1925, but was never ordained priest.

From 1925 to 1930 Nicolas worked in Paris as one of the general secretaries of the Russian Student Christian Movement. The French capital was at this time the foremost intellectual centre of the Russian emigration, and Nicolas played a full part in its life. He was deeply influenced by one of the outstanding Russian theologians in Paris, Archpriest Sergei Bulgakov. In 1927 Nicolas married Militza Vladimirovna Lavrova (1899–1994), who possessed a medical training and later worked as a dental surgeon. A woman of strong character and high intelligence, she participated wholeheartedly in all Nicolas's projects. Especially in later years it was a close and happy marriage, but to their disappointment there were no children.

It was a visit to England in 1923 that first brought Nicolas into contact with non-Orthodox Christians, arousing his interest in what became the chief inspiration of his life: work for Christian unity. While secretary of the Russian Student Christian Movement, he organized two Anglo-Russian student conferences held at St Albans in 1927–8. These led to the foundation of the Fellowship of St Alban and St Sergius, which at the beginning of the twenty-first century still remained the leading society dedicated to Anglican–Orthodox *rapprochement*.

After less than eighteen months of postgraduate study at Oxford (1931–2), Nicolas gained the degree of DPhil. His dissertation, which has remained largely unpublished, was on church unity during the first four centuries of Christianity. The ideas developed here continued to dominate his later thinking: unity cannot be imposed by coercive measures; state intervention leads to the hardening of schisms; the distinctive characteristic of the church, when true to itself, is free unanimity. Much of this recalls the ecclesiology of *sobornost*, propounded by Khomiakov and the Slavophils. In later writings Nicolas deepened this approach by emphasizing the supreme importance of the eucharist.

After two further years in Paris (1932–4), Nicolas and Militza moved in 1934 to England, which became their home for the remainder of their lives. From 1934 to 1947 Nicolas worked, mainly in London, as secretary of the Fellowship of St Alban and St Sergius. Its membership increased fourfold during his period of office, despite the difficulties caused by the war, and in 1943 it acquired a centre in London: St Basil's House, sold in 1993. The first of his books now began to appear: *Moscow, the Third Rome* (1937), *St Sergius: Builder of Russia* (1939), *The Church of the Eastern Christians* (1942), *Three Russian Prophets: Khomiakov, Dostoevsky, Soloviev* (1944), *The Russians and their Church* (1945). These were popular works, lively and readable, which presented Orthodoxy to the British public at a time when it was very little known.

In 1947 Nicolas became the first Spalding lecturer in Eastern Orthodox culture at the University of Oxford, a post which he held until his retirement in 1966. Through his lectures, and through the tireless hospitality that he and Militza offered in their home, he introduced the Christian East to a surprisingly wide range of undergraduates and senior members. In 1952 there appeared what was his most controversial work, *The Reintegration of the Church*, advocating intercommunion as a means of promoting Christian reunion, a viewpoint which was rejected by most Orthodox. His two most ambitious books appeared in the next decade: *Eastern Christendom* (1961) and *The Russian Religious Renaissance of the Twentieth Century* (1963). This last is a ground-breaking study of the revival of Orthodox theology, first in Russia itself immediately prior to the 1917 revolution, and then in the emigration. Although unavoidably incomplete and sometimes inaccurate, it remained a valuable work of reference. Many of those about whom he wrote with such vividness were people he had known personally in Belgrade and Paris.

A visit to the Syrian Orthodox of the Malabar in 1953–4 convinced Nicolas that the members of this ancient Indian church were not to be dismissed as 'monophysite heretics'. He prepared the way for the reunion discussions undertaken from 1966 onwards between the non-

Chalcedonian 'Oriental' Orthodox and the main body of Chalcedonian Orthodox.

Undoubtedly the achievement at Oxford which brought Nicolas the greatest happiness was the foundation of the House of St Gregory and St Macrina, of which he became the first warden. This was established as a meeting place between Eastern and Western Christians, and at the same time as a centre for the Orthodox resident in Oxford. An Orthodox church was built in the garden during 1972–3. In the year of his retirement (1966), he was awarded an Oxford DD. Although suffering in later years from failing eyesight, he continued actively at work, speaking and animating discussion groups, until his death at his home, 4A Northmoor Road, Oxford, on 25 August 1980. He was buried in Wolvercote cemetery.

Although a fluent writer and an attractive speaker, Nicolas Zernov was not a systematic scholar. He was in the best sense of the word a popularizer, endowed with a gift for warm friendship, with an infectious enthusiasm, and with an exploratory mind that was constantly crossing frontiers. Profoundly loyal to the Orthodox church, he was at the same time convinced that Orthodox Christians need the stimulus of the West in order to rediscover the treasures of their own tradition.   KALLISTOS WARE

Sources K. Ware, 'In memoriam Nicholas Zernov', *Sobornost, incorporating Eastern Churches Review*, 3/1 (1981), 11–38 • N. M. Zernov and M. V. Zernov, eds., *Za rubezhom: Belgrad, Parizh, Oksford, 1921–1972* [Beyond the borders: Belgrade, Paris, Oxford, 1921–1972] (1973) • N. Zernov, *Sunset years: a Russian pilgrim in the West* (1983) • d. cert.

Archives St Theoseria Centre for Christian Spirituality, 2 Canterbury Road, Oxford

Zetland. For this title name *see* Dundas, Lawrence John Lumley, second marquess of Zetland (1876–1961).

Zia ul Haq, Mohammad (1922–1988), president of Pakistan, was born on 12 August 1922 in Jullundur in the pre-partition Punjab province of British India. He was born into a lower-middle-class Arain family. This was not the martial caste background from which the Indian army traditionally drew its Punjabi Muslim recruits. Zia was, however, able to take advantage of the widening of the army's base during the Second World War. He completed his studies at the élite St Stephen's College in Delhi and, following a short period at the College of Combat, Mhow, joined the British Indian army in 1944. He was commissioned into the 13th lancers and saw service in Burma, Malaya, and Java. After the creation of Pakistan, he was posted to the armoured corps centre at Nowshera in the North-West Frontier Province.

Zia was profoundly influenced by his family's uprooting from their native Jullundur to Peshawar. He was thereafter to share many of the attitudes of the east Punjabi refugee community in Pakistan. These included distrust of India, a fierce national pride, and commitment to the cause of Kashmiri self-determination. Zia's personal piety, arising from his attachment to the puritanical Deobandi sect of Sunni Islam, was also to touch a popular chord.

Shortly after his marriage to his cousin Shafiqa in

Mohammad Zia ul Haq (1922–1988), by Tony McGrath, *c*.1982

August 1950, Zia joined the Guides Cavalry. However, his military career really took off only after a highly successful period at the Command and Staff College in Quetta in 1955. He now rose steadily through the ranks; he was promoted brigadier in 1969 and seconded to Jordan, where he helped King Hussein's forces in their operations against the Palestine Liberation Organization. On his return home Zia commanded the 1st armoured division for three years. He was still relatively unknown, however, when in the spring of 1976 he became head of the Pakistan army. The prime minister, Zulfikar Ali Bhutto, had promoted him over the heads of half a dozen more senior generals. Ironically, the very characteristics which had appealed to Bhutto, Zia's piety, patriotism, and professionalism, turned him into a successful coup-maker in the troubled period which followed the prime minister's alleged rigging of the 1977 national elections. Zia shared the important group of corps commanders' belief that the country was slipping into chaos. He also sympathized with the opposition Pakistan National Alliance's portrayal of the Bhutto regime as morally corrupt.

Zia launched the coup against Bhutto—code-named operation Fairplay—on 5 July 1977. He served first as chief martial law administrator, and from September 1978 as president. Martial law was withdrawn on 30 December 1985, but Zia retained his post as chief of army staff and continued to wield power through the presidency. Unlike his predecessor Ayub Khan, who was hounded from office, Zia remained firmly in control until the end.

Zia's political survival rested on his skill in wrong-footing opponents, and on the favourable external environment following the December 1979 Soviet occupation of Afghanistan. This transformed him overnight from an international pariah to America's front-line ally in the fight against communism. The Reagan administration provided $3.2 billion of military and economic assistance, despite concerns over human rights abuses and Pakistan's clandestine nuclear weapons programme. The Pakistan economy also benefited from the large sums sent home by skilled migrant workers in the countries around the Persian Gulf. These amounted to about 40 per cent of total foreign exchange earnings, and enabled annual rates of economic growth in excess of 6 per cent during the Zia era.

The martial law era was punctuated by unfulfilled promises of national elections and by discussion of the relevance of democracy for an Islamic state. Zia maintained that a Western-style democracy was unsuitable for Pakistan. A 350-member nominated assembly, known as the Majlis-i-Shura, was formed at the end of 1981 to suggest plans of action for the establishment of an Islamic democracy. Zia eventually agreed to hold 'party-less' elections in February 1985, following a referendum on his Islamic policies which was linked with his re-election as president. The eleven-party Alliance Movement for the Restoration of Democracy, which had mounted a major campaign in Sind in 1983 against the Zia regime, boycotted both the polls. Sind missed out on the prosperity of the Zia era partly because it did not export labour to the gulf. The sense of alienation felt by its populace was completed by Zia's hanging of Bhutto, Pakistan's first Sindhi prime minister, on 4 April 1979.

The Islamization process became the most identifiable feature of the Zia regime, and increasingly its *raison d'être*. It encompassed the areas of personal religious observance and dress codes, judicial reform, education, and the attempt to abolish interest from banking practices. The 1981 Ramadan ordinance made eating, drinking, and smoking in public a crime during the period of fasting. Prayer wardens were introduced some three years later to persuade and inspire persons to perform their daily prayers. Zia introduced special shariat courts, with the power to strike down any law found 'repugnant' to Islam. In May 1981, for the first time in Pakistan's history, *'ulama'* (religious scholars) were appointed as judges. From 1979 theft, murder, adultery, and intoxication were subject to the Islamic penal code and laws of evidence. The enforcement of an Islamic code with respect to sexual crimes was especially controversial because of its discrimination against women. Cases arose in which female rape victims were convicted of adultery and publicly flogged, while their assailants went free. Further Islamization measures included the establishment in 1980 of an Islamic university in Islamabad and the massive expansion of mosque schools. Many of the later Taliban fighters in Afghanistan were to graduate from these schools. Provision of Islamic banking facilities through profit and loss accounts was introduced in January 1981. As a social welfare measure, the government sought to oversee the collection of zakat (alms) by compulsorily deducting this charity tax from bank accounts.

Islamization, which was stoutly opposed by women's groups and human rights activists, stirred up sectarian tensions between Sunnis and Shi'a. It thus did not provide the ideological glue for Pakistani society for which Zia had hoped. The Shi'a felt increasingly estranged from the state-sponsored Islamization process which encouraged Sunni legal practice.

Karachi experienced mounting ethnic violence from 1986 onwards. Ethnic allegiances had been encouraged by the party-less 1985 elections. Some writers have also claimed that Zia sought to undermine opposition to his regime in Sind by dividing and ruling on ethnic lines in the province. Clashes between *mohajirs* and Pushtuns, later extended to the Sindhi community. The growing lawlessness was encouraged by the ready availability of weapons and drugs as a result of the war in Afghanistan. Zia justified his dismissal of the hand-picked prime minister, Muhammad Khan Junejo, on 29 May 1988, in terms of the deteriorating security situation. Party-less elections were scheduled for November. However, Zia died on 17 August 1988, following the unexplained crash of his C-130 aircraft minutes after its take-off from Bahawalpur. Others killed in the crash included the US ambassador Arnold Raphel.

Zia's supporters viewed him as a pious Muslim who halted his country's moral decay and contributed to the collapse of the Soviet empire through support for the Afghan freedom fighters. Detractors condemn him as an intolerant and vindictive ruler who cynically manipulated Islam to remain in power. His popularity with certain sections of Punjabi society was demonstrated by the huge crowds of mourners at his burial on 20 August 1988 at the Faisal mosque in Islamabad. IAN TALBOT

Sources R. LaPorte and K. Azfar, *Pakistan under the military: eleven years of Zia ul-Haq*, ed. S. J. Burki and C. Baxter (1991) · C. Baxter, ed., *Zia's Pakistan: politics and society in a front-line state* (1985) · K. Mumtaz and F. Shaheed, eds., *Women of Pakistan: two steps forward, one step back?* (1987) · S. J. Burki, 'Pakistan under Zia, 1977–88', *Asian Survey*, 28/10 (1988), 1082–1100 · F. A. Chishti, *Betrayals of another kind: Islam, democracy and the army in Pakistan* (1989) · A. M. Weiss, ed., *Islamic reassertion in Pakistan: the application of Islamic laws in a modern state* (1986) · K. M. Arif, *Working with Zia: Pakistan's power politics, 1977–1988* (1995) · H. A. Rizvi, *The military and politics in Pakistan, 1947–86* (1988) · R. G. Wirsing, *Pakistan's security under Zia, 1977–1988: the policy imperatives of a peripheral Asian state* (1991) · E. R. Girardet, *Afghanistan: the Soviet war* (1985) · C. G. P. Rakisits, 'Centre-province relations in Pakistan under President Zia: the government's and the opposition's approaches', *Pacific Affairs*, 61/1 (1988), 78–97 · I. Talbot, *Pakistan: a modern history* (1998)
Archives George Bush Presidential Library, Texas · Ronald Reagan Presidential Library, California | FILM BFI NFTVA, current affairs footage · IWM FVA, documentary footage | SOUND BBC WAC · BL NSA, *Analysis*, 1979, T2312 WXR · BL NSA, 'Zia ul Haq', B3672101
Likenesses photographs, 1978–c.1982, Hult. Arch. · T. McGrath, photograph, c.1982, Hult. Arch. [*see illus.*]

Zilliacus, Konni (1894–1967), internationalist and politician, was born on 13 September 1894 in Kobe, Japan, the elder son of Konrad Viktor (Konni) Zilliacus sen. (1855–1924) and Lilian McLaurin Grafe (1873–1938). His mother was an American of Scottish and Alsatian extraction, and his father a Swedo-Finn who was prominent in the movement for Finnish independence. Zilliacus sen., who had trained as a lawyer and been a gentleman farmer in Finland, was living in exile in Japan when his sons Konni and Laurin were born.

Because of his father's travels Zilliacus had a peripatetic childhood: in addition to periods of private tuition he attended a primary school in Brooklyn, New York; the Lundsbergs Skola, Vaemland in Sweden; and he completed his schooling at Bedales School in England. As a boy he showed an aptitude for languages and in the course of his life he learnt to speak Czech, English, French, German, Italian, Russian, Serbo-Croat, Swedish, and Spanish. He spoke English without an accent and was equally fluent in French and Swedish.

Zilliacus graduated from Yale University in 1915, the first of his class. He studied science for his first two years, and history and social science in his third year. After graduation he returned to England with the aim of enlisting in the Royal Flying Corps, but after rejection he became a civilian medical orderly. He served for a year in a field hospital in France, until he was invalided back to England suffering from diphtheria. After recovery he took temporary posts in London: first as an assistant to G. Lowes Dickinson, editor of *The Nation*; then as an aide to the Liberal MP, Noel Buxton; and, finally, as Norman Angell's private secretary. Working for these foreign-policy dissenters brought Zilliacus into contact with the Union of Democratic Control, and he was strongly influenced by its views on the causes of war and the need for a world organization.

In October 1917 Zilliacus joined the Royal Flying Corps and was posted to flying school, but in January 1918 he was chosen by Josiah Wedgwood, the Liberal MP, to accompany him on an official fact-finding visit to Siberia. Zilliacus was promptly naturalized as a British subject (his naturalization certificate gave his nationality as Finnish) and was commissioned into the Royal Flying Corps. When Wedgwood returned to Britain, Lieutenant Zilliacus was retained in Siberia on the staff of the British Military Mission, where he witnessed the use of allied forces against the Bolsheviks. On his return to London in 1919 he joined the Labour Party, and in the following year he became a member of the information section of the League of Nations secretariat in Geneva.

In the 1920s Zilliacus worked closely with Arthur Henderson and Hugh Dalton in their efforts to persuade the Labour Party to accept a foreign policy based on support for the League of Nations, and he served as Arthur Henderson's private secretary at the world disarmament conference in 1933.

Zilliacus was a prolific writer and the author of several books written under various pseudonyms, the most widely read being his attacks on British foreign policy published under the *nom de plume* Vigilantes. He resigned from the league secretariat on the eve of the Munich agreement, in 1938, and returned to London. At the same time he separated from his wife, Eugenia Nowicka (1899–1997), a member of a Polish family who had been exiled to Siberia. They had married in 1918 and had one son and one daughter.

Zilliacus was selected as the Labour candidate for Gateshead in 1939, and on the outbreak of war he joined the Ministry of Information, where he was responsible for censoring the reports of Swedish correspondents. In 1942 Janet Harris (1912–1999), the daughter of the Hollywood film director Laurence Trimble, became his common-law wife and they had one daughter. Zilliacus became a member of J. B. Priestley's 1941 Committee but was not tempted to follow others of the committee into the Common

Wealth Party. In the general election of 1945 he was elected Labour MP for Gateshead.

In parliament Zilliacus soon emerged as the leading critic of Ernest Bevin's foreign policy, which he believed was creating two armed blocs, and he favoured a more conciliatory approach towards the Soviet Union. Zilliacus paid several visits to the Soviet Union, where he had two interviews with Stalin, and he travelled widely in eastern Europe. When Yugoslavia was expelled from the Cominform in June 1948 Zilliacus supported Tito. As a result he was vilified in the communist press and at the Slansky trial, held in Prague in December 1952, he was denounced as an agent of British intelligence.

Zilliacus was expelled from the Labour Party in 1949 for his persistent opposition to the Labour government's foreign policy, but his support for Tito opened up a gap between himself and the three other MPs who had been expelled from the Labour Party for their 'fellow travelling' activities. These three—John Platts-Mills, Leslie Solley, and Lester Hutchinson—strongly supported all aspects of Soviet policy, including the Cominform's anti-Tito campaign, and although Zilliacus initially joined them, together with the left-wing independent MP D. N. Pritt, in a Labour independent group in the Commons, he soon broke with his associates and followed his own line. He fought Gateshead as an independent Labour candidate at the general election of 1950, when he failed to retain his seat. In 1952 he was readmitted to membership of the Labour Party and returned to the Commons as MP for Manchester Gorton in 1955. He became an active member of the Victory for Socialism group and the Campaign for Nuclear Disarmament, and he helped to organize the East–West round-table conferences. He was sympathetic to the Castro regime in Cuba and opposed American intervention in Vietnam.

In 1959 Zilliacus was diagnosed as suffering from leukaemia and he died in St Bartholomew's Hospital, London, on 6 July 1967. After a private ceremony he was cremated and his ashes taken to Finland, where they were deposited in the Zilliacus family's vault at the Sandudd cemetery in Helsinki.　　ARCHIE POTTS

Sources Museum of Labour History, Manchester, Zilliacus papers · private information (2004) [Jan Zilliacus, widow; Linden Zilliacus, daughter; Dawn Harris Stanford, stepdaughter] · personal knowledge (2004) · A. Potts, *Zilliacus: a life for peace and socialism* (2002) · *CGPLA Eng. & Wales* (1967)
Archives Gateshead Borough Library, collection · People's History Museum, Manchester, papers | CAC Cam., Attlee papers, corresp. · CAC Cam., Noel-Baker papers, corresp. · JRL, letters to *Manchester Guardian* · King's AC Cam., corresp. with A. E. Felkin · U. Sussex, corresp. with *New Statesman* magazine
Wealth at death £2204: probate, 13 Sept 1967, *CGPLA Eng. & Wales*

Zimmern, Sir Alfred Eckhard (1879–1957), internationalist, was born in Surbiton, Surrey, on 26 January 1879, the only son of Adolf Zimmern, China and East India merchant, and his wife, Matilda Sophia Eckhard. His father's family were liberal-minded German Jews who had migrated to Britain in the wake of the 1848 revolution, while his mother was of Huguenot ancestry. Zimmern's family background gave him an easy and exceptional familiarity with continental Europe and its languages. Although he had an early interest in Zionism, he grew up a Christian. Educated at Winchester College and at New College, Oxford, Zimmern was an outstanding classical scholar, and obtained first classes in honour moderations (1900) and *literae humaniores* (1902). In 1902 he was awarded the Stanhope historical essay prize, and published a study of Henry Grattan. He remained at New College for a year as lecturer in ancient history, and from 1904 to 1909 as fellow and tutor. With a natural gift for teaching, Zimmern became involved, from 1907, in working-class education, and was an inspector of the Board of Education in 1912–15. Wanting more time to write, Zimmern left New College in 1909. Financed by his father, he travelled to Greece, where he wrote *The Greek Commonwealth* (1911), a study of fifth-century Athens, which quickly won a worldwide reputation. In it Zimmern presented an idealized account of Greek values, and drew parallels between the ancient and modern worlds.

Zimmern was 'a man of considerable imagination and a keen sense of the tendencies of international politics' (Miller, 160). In 1905, after hearing the news of the first major victory of Japan over Russia, he went into his ancient history class at Oxford and said that he was going to lay aside Greek history for that morning to speak about 'the most historical event which has happened ... in our lifetime, the victory of a non-white people over a white people'. Twenty years later he identified the causes of war as being threefold: relations between the white and non-white peoples; the economic issue of the 'haves' and the 'have-nots'; and the problem of nationality, 'between the peoples who consider themselves culturally superior and those whom they despise' (ibid., 161).

Zimmern believed that it was both necessary and possible to outlaw war. During the First World War he wrote on the causes of war for the American liberal journal *The New Republic*. From 1917 he worked in the Ministry of Reconstruction, and in 1918–19 in the political intelligence department of the Foreign Office. A founder, in 1920, of the Institute of International Affairs (Chatham House), he was a leading figure in those circles advocating national self-determination, the establishment of a league of nations to prevent future wars, and the federation of the British Commonwealth. In July 1917, at the first annual meeting of the League of Nations Society, he proposed a treaty making 'war a crime in any circumstances' (Markwell, 280). Zimmern was the author of a Foreign Office memorandum which was the basis of the 'Cecil draft' for the organization of the League of Nations which the British took to the Paris peace conference of 1919. Like Keynes, Zimmern severely criticized the reparations clauses of the treaty, but he approved of the political settlement.

In 1919–21 Zimmern was Wilson professor of international relations at the University College of Wales, Aberystwyth—the first such appointment anywhere in the world. His time there was cut short by his marriage on 31 March 1921 to French-born Lucie Anna Elisabeth Olympe Barbier (1875–1963), daughter of Pastor Maurice Hirsch Flotron and previously the wife of a fellow professor at Aberystwyth. She was a noted musician, and had helped popularize French music in England. Although Zimmern had learned Welsh and was a popular lecturer, 'the distinction of having acquired the language was more than outweighed by the opprobrium of having acquired the lady, and so he was prevailed upon to resign' (Markwell). In 1922–3 Zimmern and his wife visited the USA, where he taught at Cornell University and completed *Europe in Convalescence* (1922), in which he castigated the policies of Lloyd George. In the general election of October 1924 he stood unsuccessfully as a Labour candidate for Caernarfon against Lloyd George himself.

Zimmern spent the rest of the decade working mainly in Paris and Geneva. In 1926–30 he was deputy director of the League of Nations' Institute of Intellectual Co-operation (the forerunner of UNESCO) in Paris; from 1924, for many years, he and his wife conducted a summer school of international relations in Geneva. These schools were extremely popular, and allowed him the opportunity to observe closely the sessions of the league. The publication of *The Third British Empire* (1926) reflected his keen interest in the evolution of the British empire into the (British) Commonwealth, which he saw as a model for internationalism. By 1929 he had also published three collections of essays. His wife played a significant role in the development of his views.

Zimmern was a 'cautious' idealist (Rich, 79). While a believer in the chances of positive change in international affairs, and an advocate for the role of educated public opinion in bringing about those changes, he stood apart from those internationalists who placed their faith in world government. He regarded such views as naïve and as taking too little account of the realities of nationalism. In 1933 he condemned the Oxford Union's 'King and Country' motion, which he believed 'helped to intensify the reign of terrorism in Germany' (Markwell, 281).

In 1930 Zimmern was appointed the first Montague Burton professor of international relations at Oxford. In 1936 he published *The League of Nations and the Rule of Law*, and was knighted shortly afterwards. This book is Zimmern's most significant work, but is flawed through being time-bound, dominated by the events and spirit of its day. Its most striking aspect was Zimmern's belief in a continuing movement towards progress in international affairs. Although Zimmern was a pioneer in the development of international relations as an academic discipline, by the 1930s his writings 'began to bear more resemblance to idealist propaganda than serious academic concern' (Rich, 81).

Zimmern remained in his Oxford post until 1944. During the Second World War, when Chatham House moved to Oxford, he worked in its foreign research and press service, which did much work for the Foreign Office. When this service moved to London in 1943, Zimmern became its deputy director until 1945. He served as secretary-general of the constituent conference of UNESCO in 1945, was first executive secretary and later adviser to the preparatory commission for UNESCO, and remained a force on behalf of the organization during his final years in the USA.

Zimmern's replacement as secretary-general of UNESCO by Julian Huxley left him with a sense of grievance. In 1947 he left Europe for good, taking up the post of visiting professor at Trinity College, Hartford, Connecticut. He was director of the Hartford study centre for world affairs from 1948. From 1950 he also taught at the American International College, Springfield, Massachusetts. Zimmern's idealism now embraced the role of the USA in the cold war, identifying it with the rule of law in the world. He died at Avon, Connecticut, on 24 November 1957 and was survived by his wife, a daughter, and a step-daughter.

Of short stature and full-faced, Zimmern was warm and persuasive in personal contact, and remained vigorous until the end of his life. His thinking was neither especially deep nor distinctive, yet he attained extraordinary influence at the peak of his career in the 1920s, when journalists labelled him 'the ideal Prime Minister' (Markwell, 280).   D. J. MARKWELL

Alice Louisa Theodora Zimmern (1855–1939), by Kenneth Green, 1930s

Sources D. J. Markwell, 'Sir Alfred Zimmern revisited: fifty years on', *Review of International Studies*, 12 (1986), 279–92 · P. Rich, 'Alfred Zimmern's cautious idealism: the League of Nations, international education and the commonwealth', *Thinkers of the twenty years' crisis: inter-war idealism reassessed*, ed. D. Long and P. Wilson (1995) · J. D. B. Miller, 'The commonwealth and world order: the Zimmern vision and after', *Journal of Imperial and Commonwealth History*, 8 (1979–80), 159–74 · A. J. Toynbee, *Acquaintances* (1967) · *New York Times* (25 Nov 1957) · *The Times* (25 Nov 1957) · *Manchester Guardian* (25 Nov 1957) · *The Times* (31 Oct 1963) [Lady Zimmern] · DNB

Archives Bodl. Oxf., MSS | BL, letters to Albert Mansbridge, Add. MSS 65257 A, 65258 · BLPES, corresp. with Violet Markham · Bodl. Oxf., corresp. with L. G. Curtis; Round Table corresp. · Bodl. Oxf., corresp. and papers relating to League of Nations · Bodl. Oxf., letters to Francis Marvin and Edith Marvin · Bodl. Oxf., corresp. with Gilbert Murray · Bodl. Oxf., corresp. with J. L. Myres · JRL, letters to the *Manchester Guardian* · NL Wales, corresp. with Thomas Jones

Likenesses W. Stoneman, photograph, 1944, NPG · photograph, repro. in Toynbee, *Acquaintances*

Zimmern, Alice Louisa Theodora (1855–1939), educationist and suffragist, was born on 22 September 1855 at Postern Street, Nottingham, the youngest of three daughters of Hermann Theodor Zimmern, a German Jewish immigrant with scholarly interests who was in business as a lace merchant, and his wife, Antonia Marie Therese Regina, *née* Leo. Helen *Zimmern was her elder sister and they collaborated in compiling two volumes of translations (1880, 1884) from the works of European novelists designed to interest English readers in the cultures of continental Europe. Alfred Eckhard *Zimmern, the authority on international relations, was her cousin. Alice was educated at a private school, then at Bedford College, London, before being admitted to Girton College, Cambridge, in 1881. Like other Girton students of the time, Zimmern found her years at university offered an incomparable opportunity for intellectual expansion and freedom. With Janet Case she organized a society to produce classical

drama which resulted, most notably, in the 1883 college production of *Elektra*, 'breaking down', as Virginia Woolf noted, 'the tradition that only men acted in the Greek play' (*The Times*, 13 Jan 1934).

After leaving Girton in 1885, having gained honours in both parts of the Cambridge classical tripos, Zimmern held teaching posts in classics and English at girls' schools between 1886 and 1894. She was an assistant mistress at Tunbridge Wells high school from 1888 to 1891. For school use she produced an edition of the *Meditations of Marcus Aurelius* (1887) and a translation, entitled *The Home Life of the Ancient Greeks* (1893), from Hugo Bluemner's German, which she later followed with children's books on ancient Greece and Rome (1895, 1906). In 1893, with four other women educators, she was awarded a Gilchrist travelling scholarship which required her to study educational methods in the United States with particular reference to the training of girls. Her *Methods of Education in America* (1894) reflects Zimmern's interest in a less rigid system of education. She was particularly impressed with the way in which American children were more articulate in discussion and how the American methods of teaching literature inspired 'a real living love for our own English classics' which was almost unknown in English schools because of the overemphasis on exams. At the same time she deplored the low quality of American students' written work, the inanity of many of their textbooks, and the ludicrously 'over-patriotic' way of teaching American history.

In 1894 Zimmern resigned her school position, though she continued to teach classics to private pupils to supplement her small private income. In the years that followed she contributed numerous articles to journals such as *Forum* and the *Leisure Hour*, comparing different education systems she observed in her travels, and, increasingly, reflecting on the education of women. In *Women's Suffrage in Many Lands* (1909), written to coincide with the Fourth Congress of the International Women's Suffrage Alliance, Zimmern finds a number of historical precedents for women's entitlement to the franchise and makes the argument that granting women the vote would be, in some cases, merely reinstating a previously held right. More importantly she shows, through a wide range of examples from different countries, that there is an 'intimate … connexion between enfranchisement and the just treatment of women'. While most of the arguments she presents are moderate and pragmatic, she readily acknowledges the militant tactics of British suffragettes as effective in making women's suffrage 'the question of the day'.

Both Zimmern's *The Renaissance of Girls' Education* (1898) and *Women's Suffrage in Many Lands* made a major contribution to contemporary debates about the education and political rights of women. In numerous articles she also offered insight into the material conditions which defined the quality of women's lives. 'Ladies' clubs in London', published in *Forum* (1896), and 'Ladies' dwellings', which appeared in the *Contemporary Review* (1900), show all too clearly that the opportunity offered by Girton to young women 'to carry on their studies in congenial and stimulating surroundings, unhampered by cares of earning and unhindered by conflicting duties' (*The Renaissance of Girls' Education*, 104–5) was one which would never be replicated in later life.

Zimmern's ability to travel widely was increasingly limited by arthritis in the last decades of her life, though she continued to entertain many international visitors with feminist and pacifist interests in her Hampstead flat. Her last publication, a translation of Také Ionescu's work, was *The Origins of the War* (1917), published by the Council for the Study of International Relations. Alice Zimmern, who was unmarried, died at her home, 45 Clevedon Mansions, Highgate Road, London, on 22 March 1939, and was buried on 25 March at Kentish Town parish church. She was representative of a distinguished generation of Girtonians who made important contributions to the women's movement. GILLIAN THOMAS

Sources *The Times* (23 March 1939) · *Daily Telegraph* (24 March 1939) · *British Weekly* (30 March 1939) · WW · K. T. Butler and H. I. McMorran, eds., *Girton College register, 1869–1946* (1948) · b. cert. · d. cert.
Archives Girton Cam.
Likenesses Elliott & Fry, photograph, 1883?, Girton Cam. · group portrait, photograph, 1883, Girton Cam. · K. Green, oils, 1930–39, Girton Cam. [*see illus.*]
Wealth at death £5789 5s. 2d.: probate, 24 May 1939, *CGPLA Eng. & Wales*

Zimmern, Helen (1846–1934), translator and author, was born in Hamburg, Germany, on 25 March 1846. She was the daughter of Hermann Theodor Zimmern a lace merchant, and his wife, Antonia Marie Therese Regina, sister of Carl Leo, a syndic of Hamburg. Alice Louisa Theodora *Zimmern was her younger sister, and she was a cousin of Alfred Eckhard *Zimmern. As a result of the events of 1848, she emigrated to Britain with her parents in 1850. She was naturalized when she came of age. After first settling in Nottingham the family moved to London in 1856. Her formal education suffered from her designation as a 'delicate' child. Sometimes she was taught at school, and

sometimes at home by masters. Between the ages of fourteen and eighteen she attended a finishing school in Bayswater, London.

When she was eighteen Zimmern resolved to earn her living as a writer and shortly afterwards she embarked on a career of abundant, intelligent, and highly varied publication. As a translator and as an author, her work ranges across history, biography, philosophy, art, and literature. She was a frequent contributor to *The Examiner*, *Blackwood's Magazine*, and *Fraser's Magazine*. In the early 1870s she published two volumes of fiction. A biography of Arthur Schopenhauer followed in 1876, which did much to arouse British interest in its subject and in 'pessimistic literature'. It aroused interest in Zimmern too. Wagner invited her to the first performance of the Bayreuth festival on the strength of it, and Nietzsche (whom she first met in Bayreuth) was sufficiently impressed by it to suggest her as a translator of his *Twilight of the Gods*. She was seriously ill from 1876 to 1878 but recovered well enough to publish a biography of G. E. Lessing in 1878.

Zimmern's edition of *The Discourses of Joshua Reynolds* contains an introductory account of the state of art in England before Reynolds's contribution, in which she comments that it 'was reserved to Reynolds to open out to English understanding the vista of Italian art' (*The Discourses of Joshua Reynolds*, ed. H. Zimmern, 1887, x). Her own role can be similarly described. In much of her work she was a channel through which European culture, and—in her later career—Italian culture in particular, was made accessible to the British. In 1880 she collaborated with her sister Alice on an edition of translations of sections of European novels, which she intended as an introduction not only to foreign literature, but also to the geography and culture of the countries represented. She was a prolific translator of Italian fiction, drama, and history throughout her career. She lectured on Italian art in Germany and Britain. The 1880s also saw her *Tales from the Edda*, a collection of Indo-European mythology and folklore, as well as a volume on the life and work of the Dutch-born artist Lawrence Alma-Tadema and a history of *The Hansa Towns*.

By 1887 Zimmern was living in Italy, in the Palazzo Buondelmonti, Florence. In several of her later writings she displays a keen desire to present a favourable image of Italy to a British audience. In *The New Italy* (1918) she appeals for an enhanced understanding of Italy and a commercial and general alliance between Italy and Britain, against the economic and cultural expansionism of Germany. The strongly anti-German tone of this text is foreshadowed in her 1881 article for *Fraser's Magazine*, 'Jewish home life', in which she condemns the Germans for their persecution of Jews and makes the case for Jewish assimilation. In Italy she became a member of the Association de la Presse de Rome. For many years she was associated with the *Corriere della Sera* and over several years she edited the *Florence Gazette*. She was not in sympathy with the political climate that developed in Italy during her final years.

Among Zimmern's most significant contributions are

her translations into English of two volumes by Friedrich Nietzsche. She came to know Nietzsche when they were both staying in Sils Maria in the canton of Grisons, Switzerland, in the mid 1880s. He frequently walked with her beside Lake Silvaplana and discussed his current work. In letters he refers to her as 'extremely clever' and as the woman 'who introduced Schopenhauer to the English' (Kaufmann, xiii). On the strength of this good impression, Oscar Levy chose her translation of *Beyond Good and Evil* (completed around 1897 and published in 1907) for inclusion in his edition of *The Complete Works of Nietzsche*. Its unexpected success revitalized the Nietzsche movement in Britain and encouraged it to continue its project of translating Nietzsche. Accordingly, her translation of *Human, All Too Human*, appeared in 1909. Marion Faber, a subsequent translator of this text, refers to Zimmern's 'antiquated Victorian style', which makes 'Nietzsche come to sound ... like a fusty contemporary of Matthew Arnold' (Faber, xxv). Although often resourceful and generally accurate, her translation contains, according to Faber, numerous inaccuracies and a number of bowdlerizations. In Aphorism 144, for example, Zimmern has Nietzsche speaking of Jesus's 'idea' that he was the son of God, where 'fantasy' would have been a more accurate translation.

The vivacity and intelligence that had impressed Nietzsche persisted into Zimmern's final years. When she was eighty she had, according to Oscar Levy, 'a very youthful smile' and a face that was 'illuminated and translucent with intellect' (Gilman, 169). She was at this time dedicated to the beautiful rose garden that she cultivated in Florence. She became ill early in 1933. Her condition improved during the summer but she died in Florence on 11 January 1934. There is no evidence that she married.

C. A. CREFFIELD

Sources *The Times* (13 Jan 1934), 12 • *Letters of Friedrich Nietzsche*, ed. C. Middleton (1969) • W. Kaufmann, 'Translator's preface', in F. Nietzsche, *Beyond good and evil*, trans. W. Kaufmann (1966) • M. Faber, 'Introduction', in F. Nietzsche, *Human, all too human* (1984) • S. L. Gilman, *Conversations with Nietzsche* (1987) [incl. excerpts from O. Levy's unpubd 'Nietzsche's englische Freundin'] • A. de Gubernatis, *Dictionnaire international des écrivains du monde latin* (1905) • A. T. C. Pratt, ed., *People of the period: being a collection of the biographies of upwards of six thousand living celebrities*, 2 vols. (1897) • *Wellesley index* • F. Hays, *Women of the day: a biographical dictionary of notable contemporaries* (1885)

Zincke, Christian Frederick (1684?–1767), miniature painter, was born in Dresden, probably in 1684 (other accounts say 1683 or 1685). His father, Christian Zincke (*d.* 1719), and his grandfather, Paul Zincke (1608–1678), were Dresden goldsmiths. Having learned enamelling and attended the drawing-school in Dresden conducted by Heinrich Christoph Fehling, he was invited to England either in 1704 or 1706 by Charles Boit, the leading practitioner of enamel portraiture. Boit had started a very large enamel commemorating the victory of Blenheim, and Zincke worked on this uncompleted project. He soon became proficient enough to form his own practice. On 4

Christian Frederick Zincke (1684?–1767), by William Hoare, 1752

November 1718 he married Elizabeth Tanton at St Martin-in-the-Fields, London. Their son, Christian Zincke, was baptized on 27 January 1724 at St Paul's, Covent Garden, London.

The earliest known signed work by Zincke is an enamel miniature of Sarah, duchess of Marlborough, based on a painting by Sir Godfrey Kneller and dated 1711 (Royal Collection). After Boit fled to France in 1714 to avoid his creditors Zincke enjoyed a near monopoly of enamel portraiture in England. The accession of George II in 1727 consolidated his position at court. The king, who usually hated sitting to painters, enjoyed Zincke's company and admired his portraits. Zincke was also patronized by Frederick, prince of Wales, who in 1732 made him his cabinet painter. He was complaining of eye strain in 1725, and in 1742 raised his price for an enamel from 20 guineas to 30, to reduce the demand for his work. He had effectively retired by about 1746 and at that time moved from Covent Garden to South Lambeth.

Vertue recorded in 1726 that Zincke 'has had more persons of distinction daily sitting to him than any other painter living' (Vertue, *Note books*, 3.30). Although he copied other portraits he preferred to paint sitters *ad vivum*. His earlier works embody the staid qualities of Kneller and Michael Dahl, but his later miniatures have a more relaxed air. His handling at its best is exquisite. Horace Walpole owned one of his finest enamels, now in the Fitzwilliam Museum, Cambridge. Once regarded as a portrait of the poet Abraham Cowley, it is copied from a painting of an Arcadian shepherd by Sir Peter Lely. Shortly before he retired he made a remarkable portrait of Sir Robert Walpole (priv. coll.; another version in the Royal Collection). He was not always truthful in his images. George II asked him to paint Queen Caroline as if she were twenty-eight when she actually was forty-nine, and the queen urged him to make the king look twenty-four years younger. The similarity of his female portraits is satirized in a poem of 1740 describing a visit of Venus, Juno, and Minerva to Zincke's studio, during which each goddess takes a portrait of the poet's mistress Chloe to be her own.

The Royal Collection contains many enamels by Zincke of George II, Caroline of Ansbach, and Frederick, prince of Wales, and their other children. The numerous family portraits he made for Edward Harley, earl of Oxford, became part of the Portland collection at Welbeck Abbey, Nottinghamshire. There are many examples of his work in the Victoria and Albert Museum, London, the Ashmolean Museum, Oxford, and other collections.

Zincke, who was short in stature, was not made vain by his success. When Philip Mercier tried to prevent him making an *ad vivum* portrait of the prince of Wales, leading to a bitter quarrel, Zincke was clearly in the right, and he seems to have been a well-loved character. The fact that he got on well with both George II and the prince of Wales testifies to his amenable temperament. An abstemious man, he generally drank port, though when Prince Frederick prophesied that Zincke would celebrate the Peace of Vienna in 1731 by getting drunk, he agreed that he would indulge himself in claret. On 25 May 1748 he married his second wife, Elizabeth Bothmar (d. 1772), at St George's, Hanover Square, London. A double portrait of him and his first wife was engraved in mezzotint after Hans Hysing by John Faber.

The portrait of Zincke drawn in 1752 by his friend William Hoare is an exceptionally informal representation of an artist at work; it shows him in retirement painting his daughter's portrait at a standard miniaturist's desk. Zincke died on 24 March 1767 at South Lambeth, Surrey; he was survived by his second wife. One of his sons was appointed to the six clerks office, chancery. A grandson, Paul Francis Zincke (d. 1830), attained notoriety as a faker of Shakespeare portraits; one of them, the 'Bellows' portrait, belonged to the French actor François-Joseph Talma. GRAHAM REYNOLDS

Sources Vertue, *Note books*, vols. 1–5 · H. Walpole, *Anecdotes of painting*, ed. M. Berry (1798), vol. 3 of *The works of Horatio Walpole, earl of Orford*, ed. M. Berry, Lord Holland, and J. Croker (1798–1825), 475–6 · R. W. Goulding, 'The Welbeck Abbey miniatures', *Walpole Society*, 4 (1914–15), esp. 53–4 [whole issue] · B. S. Long, *British miniaturists* (1929), 471–5 · Thieme & Becker, *Allgemeines Lexikon* · GM, 1st ser., 10 (1740), 620 · GM, 1st ser., 37 (1767), 144 · J. C. Smith, *British mezzotinto portraits*, 1 (1878), 455 · D. Piper, *O sweet Mr Shakespeare, I'll have his picture* (1962) · R. Walker, *The eighteenth and early nineteenth century miniatures in the collection of her majesty the queen* (1992), xi–xiv, 18–36 · IGI

Archives Institut Néerlandais, Paris, Fondation Custodia, MS receipt for payment by duke of Rutland for three pictures by other artists, 11/6/1745

Likenesses W. Hoare, black and red chalk drawing, 1752, BM [see illus.] · J. Bretherton, engraving (after the double portrait or the Faber mezzotint after H. Hysing), repro. in Walpole, *Anecdotes of painting*, facing p. 475 · J. Faber junior, mezzotint (with his first wife Elizabeth; after H. Hysing), BM · H. Robinson, engraving

Zincke, Foster Barham (1817–1893), author, was born on 5 January 1817, at Eardley, a sugar estate in Jamaica, the third son of Frederick Burt Zincke, of Jamaica and his wife, a Miss Lawrence, a descendant of Henry Lawrence, president of Cromwell's council. He was fourth in descent from Christian Frederick Zincke, the German miniature and enamel painter. He passed most of his childhood on the sugar estate, living a free outdoor life. He returned to England with his mother to enter Bedford grammar school in 1828, where he developed a particular interest in geography. He matriculated from Wadham College, Oxford, on 5 March 1835, graduating BA on 18 May 1839. With his once wealthy family in financial difficulty after the emancipation of the slaves, his godmothers paid for him to attend university and he afterwards had to support himself. He was ordained in 1840 and became curate of Andover in 1840 and of Wherstead and Freston near Ipswich in 1841. He was appointed vicar there in 1847 and remained there for the rest of his life, despite being offered good livings and headships of schools and colleges elsewhere. He published a work on extempore preaching (1866, American edition 1867) after becoming aware of how ill his bookish sermons suited his unlettered congregation. He also began to contribute to *Fraser's Magazine* and the *Quarterly Review* and in 1852 published *Some Thoughts about the School of the Future* in which he criticized the system of education of English universities and public schools. Shortly afterwards he was appointed one of the queen's chaplains, through the influence of Prince Albert with whom he had discussed educational matters.

Zincke loved travel. In September 1853 he visited Ireland and became convinced that the distress there was due largely to English misrule, particularly by absent exploitative landlords. In 1867–8 he visited the USA and gave an appreciative view of the country in *Last Winter in the United States* (1868). A visit to Egypt was recorded in print (1871) and he published three books on travel in Switzerland (1873, 1874, and 1875).

On 30 May 1865 Zincke married at St Mary's, Bryanston Square, London, Caroline Octavia, Lady Stevenson, daughter of Joseph Seymour Biscoe and widow of Zincke's cousin, Sir William Stevenson; they had no children. In 1885 Zincke energetically supported his stepson Francis Seymour Stevenson who stood successfully for election as a Liberal MP. From then on Zincke took an active part in local politics and wrote many pamphlets expressing radical and humane views. His *The Plough and the Dollar, or, The Englishry of a Century Hence* (1883) was an interesting exercise in speculation, involving him in correspondence with Gladstone. He continued to write on various other themes, including a local history of Wherstead (1887 and 1893) and in 1891 published an autobiography, which, like all his works, whatever their ostensible theme, contained thoughtful comments on the condition of life and how it could be improved. He died at Wherstead vicarage on 23 August 1893 and was buried in the churchyard there on 26 August. ELIZABETH BAIGENT

Sources F. B. Zincke, *The days of my years* (1891) · *The Times* (25 Aug 1893) · *Suffolk Chronicle* (26 Aug 1893) · *Suffolk Chronicle* (2 Sept 1893) ·

Foster, *Alum. Oxon.* · Boase, *Mod. Eng. biog.* · Gladstone, *Diaries* · *DNB*
Likenesses autotype (aged fifty-four), repro. in Zincke, *Days of my years*, frontispiece

Zinkeisen, Anna Katrina (1901–1976), artist, was born in Kilcreggan, Dunbartonshire, on 28 August 1901, the second daughter of Victor Zinkeisen, a research chemist whose family, settled in Scotland for over a century, was of German origin, and Claire Bolton-Charles. Their youngest child was a son, Jack, and the family moved to Harrow, Middlesex, in 1909. Zinkeisen began her art studies young at a technical school, and in 1917 she entered the Royal Academy Schools. There she studied painting under Sir George Clausen, Glyn Philpot, and Charles Sims, although Sir William Orpen suggested that she should work in the sculpture school. Following this training she received her first commission, from the firm of Wedgwood, for some circular plaques. The two reliefs *Adam* and *Earth, Fire and Water* were awarded a silver medal at the Exposition des Arts Décoratifs in Paris in 1925. From about 1922 until her marriage she shared a studio in Yeoman's Row, south-west London, with her sister Doris Clare (who was best known for her portraits and designs for the stage). At eighteen Anna first exhibited in the Royal Academy, and she thereafter showed regularly there and at the Royal Institute of Oil Painters. Her self-portrait *AKZ* (oil, 1925) won a silver medal at the academy in 1925. In 1927 she exhibited *The Olympians* and *The Tilting Yard* at the Society of Women Artists.

Anna Zinkeisen designed magazine covers and book jackets, including several for Barbara Cartland and Doris Leslie, as well as painting portraits. She illustrated many books with her lively and witty line drawings, including A. P. Herbert's *She-Shanties* (1926) and *Plain Jane* (1927) (both published by T. Fisher Unwin, London). She created the well-known image of the elegant male smoker who was represented on De Reszke cigarette advertisements and packets. In 1928 she married Colonel Guy R. N. Heseltine MC (d. 1967), and they had one daughter, Julia. They lived for many years in St Andrew's Place, Regent's Park, and later also had a cottage in Suffolk.

In 1934 Anna Zinkeisen was commissioned to paint a mural, *The Four Seasons*, for the ballroom of the liner *Queen Mary*, which was destroyed after the war; she was commissioned in 1947 to execute a new work for the liner, *The Chase*, for a smaller dance room and restaurant. She executed many other murals during the 1950s and 1960s. During the Second World War, Zinkeisen worked as a volunteer from 1939 in the first aid post at St Mary's Hospital, Paddington, becoming an officer in the St John Ambulance Brigade. In her spare time she painted *First Aid Post by Candlelight* (oil, n.d.; Imperial War Museum); another oil painting of this period, *Operation in Progress* (1944), is in the collection of ICI. She also drew severe injuries suffered by victims of the bombing; *Arm and Hand Shell Wound*, *Shell Fragment Wound*, and *Internal Thigh Wound* are examples of her meticulous draughtsmanship now owned by the Royal College of Surgeons. In 1949 she and her sister Doris executed a ceiling painting in the Russell-Cotes Museum

in Bournemouth. An evocation of classical gods and goddesses frolicking in the heavens at dawn, it is a characteristically sprightly pastiche of Regency decoration. Her later portraits include those of the duke of Edinburgh (1956), Sir Robert Mark (1974), and Sister Grace Alexander of the Royal Homoeopathic Hospital (1976), the last portrait she completed. Anna Zinkeisen died in hospital in Holborn, London, after a short illness, on 22 September 1976. The funeral service was held at Burgh parish church, Woodbridge, Suffolk, and following cremation at Ipswich her ashes were interred at Burgh parish church in her husband's grave. A memorial service was held on 2 November in Chelsea Old Church. A member of the Pytchley hunt, Zinkeisen was elegant and beautiful all her life, with fair, reddish-brown hair, and green eyes.   ALAN WINDSOR

Sources J. Walpole, *Anna: a memorial tribute to Anna Zinkeisen* (1978) · *The Times* (25 Sept 1976) · P. Dunford, *A biographical dictionary of women artists in Europe and America since 1850* (1990) · *Paintings and drawings by some women war artists* (1958) [IWM, London] · J. Johnson and A. Greutzner, *The dictionary of British artists, 1880–1940* (1976), vol. 5 of *Dictionary of British art* · Thieme & Becker, *Allgemeines Lexikon* · b. cert. · *WWW, 1961–70* · G. M. Waters, *Dictionary of British artists, working 1900–1950* (1975) · *The Independent* (13 Dec 1988), 28 · *Daily Telegraph* (4 Nov 1978), 18 · *CGPLA Eng. & Wales* (1977)
Archives Tate collection
Likenesses A. K. Zinkeisen, self-portrait, oils, 1944, NPG
Wealth at death £30,129: administration with will, 1977, *Daily Telegraph* (10 March 1977), 2

Zoffany, Johan Joseph (1733–1810), portrait painter, was born on 13 March 1733 near Frankfurt am Main, Germany, and baptized on 15 March at St Bartholomew's Cathedral, Frankfurt, the son of Anton Franz Zauffaly (1699–1771), court cabinet-maker and architect to Alexander Ferdinand, prince of Thurn and Taxis, and his wife, Anna Ursula Dreiling (*bap.* 1704, *d.* 1779). The family soon moved to Regensburg with the prince and the young Johan was brought up in the circle of the court.

Education, early years, and arrival in England In 1747 with the encouragement of his mother, Zoffany was apprenticed to Martin Speer (*c.*1702–1765), a local painter who worked in the late baroque style, but becoming impatient for the wider world Zoffany followed that essential means to self-improvement for an aspiring artist and in 1750 took himself to Rome. There he studied under Agostino Masucci, a fashionable painter of the classicist tradition whose pupils had included Pompeo Batoni and Gavin Hamilton. He attended the Accademia del Nudo, founded in 1754 on the Capitoline, placing himself under the German painter Anton Raphael Mengs, who taught drawing from the life and introduced Zoffany to the circles of nascent neo-classicism.

About 1757 after a second visit to Rome, Zoffany returned again to Germany to become court painter to Johann Philipp von Walderdorf, elector of Trier, who commissioned paintings and frescoes to decorate rooms in the Residenz at Trier and a chapel in the castle of Ehrenbreitstein at Koblenz. With the possible exception of *Venus Marina* and *Venus and Adonis* (1760; Musée des Beaux-Arts, Bordeaux), which may have been painted for the bedroom of

Johan Joseph Zoffany (1733–1810), self-portrait, 1776

the Residenz, none of these works is known to have survived, but a few studies in chalk and in oils (British Museum, London, and City of Manchester Art Gallery), in which the heroic baroque is modified into rococo prettiness, perhaps indicate their style.

At the same time Zoffany painted a number of ambitious mythological and historical pictures that were overlaid by a baroque emphasis more theatrical than convincing where movement and emotion are expressed in accentuated gestures to illustrate the story: *The Sacrifice of Iphigenia* (1758; Mittelrhein Museum, Koblenz) and *Odysseus Seizing Andromache's Son Astyanax* (ex Christies, 18 November 1988) showing a greater realism enhanced by a smooth finish and a relatively dark tonality typical of the German version of the international style. A still life (1760; Museum der Stadt, Trier) is a further example of the eclecticism of style which German court painters liable to be called on to paint works of every kind were required to master.

Towards the end of the 1750s Zoffany married Anthonie Theophista Juliane Eiselein (*d. c.*1771/2), the daughter of a *Hofkammerrat* (court councillor) of Würzburg, and making use of her dowry he left the confined life of the electoral court for the greater artistic horizons of London. Arriving there towards the end of 1760 he had difficulty in establishing himself, at first painting decorative scenes on clockfaces for Stephen Rimbault, a leading clockmaker, and then working as a drapery painter to Benjamin Wilson. From Wilson's studio he was rescued by the great actor David Garrick who commissioned Zoffany to paint informal scenes of his domestic life at his villa at Hampton—*Mr and Mrs Garrick by the Shakespeare Temple at Hampton*, *A View in Hampton Garden with Mr and Mrs Garrick Taking Tea* (1762; priv. coll.).

The many portraits of himself in various roles that Garrick subsequently commissioned began with *The Farmer's Return* (1762; priv. coll.). This picture showed Zoffany's remarkable ability to paint lively figures in vivid interaction, to catch a fleeting expression, and to portray a likeness, and laid the foundation of his future reputation. It was exhibited at the Society of Artists in 1762 and was received with many accolades in the press. Setting up his own studio in Covent Garden, Zoffany painted many such pictures, which became known as theatrical conversations and were essentially publicity pictures, of Garrick, his friends, and his rivals. So pleased were the actors who were his subjects that Zoffany was commissioned to paint one or more versions of the same composition by others acting in the scene. Further publicity came for actors and artist from the large and handsome mezzotints that were immediately made from many of these theatrical conversation pieces. He painted Garrick with Mrs Cibber in *Venice Preserv'd* (1762–3; priv. coll.), in *The Provok'd Wife* (1763–5; Wolverhampton Art Gallery), in *Lethe* (1766; Birmingham City Museums and Art Gallery), with Mrs Pritchard in *Macbeth* (1768; priv. coll.), and to great acclaim as Abel Drugger in Ben Jonson's *The Alchemist* (1770; priv. coll.). Zoffany received many commissions to paint other actors in favourite roles, thus leaving vivid illustrations of one of the most brilliant periods in English theatrical history. Mrs Abington in *The Way to Keep Him* (1768; National Trust, Egremont Collection, Petworth House, Sussex), Charles Macklin as Shylock in *The Merchant of Venice* (*c.*1768; Tate collection), Samuel Foote in *The Devil upon Two Sticks* (*c.*1768–9; priv. coll.), and Thomas King and Mrs Baddeley in *The Clandestine Marriage* (1769–70; Garrick Club, London), painted by order of George III, demonstrate Zoffany's success in transporting the spectator back to the theatre.

Through Garrick, Zoffany was introduced to the notice of the earl of Bute, prime minister to the young George III, for whom he painted a portrait of his eldest son, Lord Mountstuart (1763–4; priv. coll.) wearing fashionable masquerade dress and the two companion paintings of Lord Bute's younger sons and daughters (1763–4; priv. coll.), posed with the artful naturalness of motif that marks Zoffany's early success as a painter of the family or conversation piece. Zoffany was soon taken up by the circle of Scottish politicians who surrounded Bute and quickly entered into the spirit of a new informality in group portraiture, developing the family piece—a genre which was well established but unfashionable in Germany—into a lively composition in which natural actions are intertwined into a unity of responding gestures in a tightly composed group set in a context at once decorative and evocative of the lives of the sitters. Zoffany rendered the draperies and accessories of his sitters in a suavely rococo manner with a smoothness of finish and warm tone, painting the lustrous satins and intricate lace with skilful fidelity. His imitative skill was equally to the fore in his depiction of furnishings and interior settings, of still life, paintings, and sculptures. His musical sitters hold and play their instruments using the correct fingering, reflecting his own knowledge and enthusiasm, while his genuine sympathy with children is reflected in the imaginative amusements with which he animates their poses.

Among the commissions the Scottish connection brought Zoffany were the splendid full-length portrait of *Mrs Oswald* (1764; National Gallery, London), the conversation piece of *John, 3rd Duke of Atholl and his Family* (1765–7), the duke and duchess with their seven children grouped informally beside the Tay in the grounds of their seat at Dunkeld, painted to fit the overmantel of the great drawing-room at Blair Castle. Zoffany's receipt for this picture specifies that he charged 20 guineas a figure. He also painted a powerful full-length portrait of Andrew Drummond (1766; Drummond's Bank, London), the founder of Drummond's Bank where Zoffany himself opened an account in 1765. In *Sir Lawrence Dundas with his Grandson* (1769–70; priv. coll.) Zoffany shows Dundas in the library of his London house newly remodelled by Adam; this is a documented example of how an interior which apparently reproduces an actual room is a most artful painter's composition showing Sir Lawrence as a connoisseur of the arts.

Royal patronage Probably through Bute, Zoffany obtained the patronage of George III and Queen Charlotte. His charming conversation piece of Queen Charlotte at her dressing table with her two eldest sons (1764; Royal Collection) marks the beginning of the informal royal conversation piece as a genre and is one of Zoffany's most elaborately contrived and perfectly finished works. Until he went to Florence in 1772 at Queen Charlotte's command, Zoffany continued to paint a number of conversation pieces and graciously informal portraits of the royal family capturing one of the characteristic expressions of eighteenth-century monarchy, one that he was later to employ for the family of the empress Maria Theresa.

Perhaps one reason why Zoffany made himself so acceptable at court was that he spoke German, for a number of the intimate court servants were Germans, with whom Charlotte, a German princess, evidently felt herself at ease. Zoffany seems never to have mastered English perfectly—his one surviving autograph letter is largely written in a rather incorrect and slightly Germanized Italian. His accent and his broken English—his third language after Italian—are remarked on in several English memoirs. But he came to identify himself with England and was granted denization on 3 April 1772.

Zoffany also painted charming small single portraits or groups of two sitters, such as the *Reverend Randall Burroughes and his Son Ellis* (1769; Louvre Museum, Paris) in which he invents the setting: propped on a chair which can be identified as Zoffany's sitter's chair is Zoffany's own copy of *Perspective of Architecture* (1761) by his friend and neighbour Joshua Kirby. The set properties of eighteenth-century portraiture with curtain, column, books, and pose of *Mr Gawler's Cousin* (Yale U. CBA) is redeemed by the animation of the figure—seated on the same sitter's chair—and by the lustrous finish and brilliant colour. Under the influence of Reynolds's conception of the portrait as a historical painting Zoffany composed the life-size portrait of Henry Knight of Tythegston with his three children (1770; NMG Wales) linked in an inventive and lively manner in which the eye is carefully led round the sitters.

In the later 1760s Zoffany began painting genre pictures. Some, like the *Caritas Romana* (c.1769; National Gallery of Victoria, Melbourne) and *The Beggars on the Road to Stanmore* (c.1769–70; priv. coll.), painted for his banker, Andrew Drummond, are pleasing exercises in the prevailing sensibility, while in the highly finished picture *John Cuff and an Assistant* (1772; Royal Collection), painted in the Dutch manner, the still-life details of the optician's workshop are rendered with a sympathetic precision and fidelity that was distasteful to English connoisseurs of high art.

From 1762 Zoffany had exhibited at the Society of Artists but resigned in 1769 shortly after the establishment of the Royal Academy to which George III nominated him on a footing equal to the founding members. Probably for the king he painted his famous group portrait of *The Academicians of the Royal Academy* (1771–2; Royal Collection) which made a sensation when it was exhibited at the Royal Academy in 1772.

In spite of his success at court and his prominence as an academician Zoffany felt restless and in 1771 arranged to go with Sir Joseph Banks, accompanying as an artist Captain Cook's second voyage to the South Seas, but the accommodation proving inadequate he withdrew.

Visit to Italy Mrs Zoffany later related:

> Being, however, in an unsettled state, having given up his house & business, and displeased many of his patrons by leaving their pictures in an unfinished state, He determined to revisit Italy. Upon declaring this intention to Her Majesty, she patronised Him, and procured him letters of introduction to the principal persons there, with a present of £300 for His Journey and an order to paint for Her, the Florence Gallery, which he executed & recd for it a thousand pounds. (J. Farington, MS notebooks, 4 fols., 41–3 (A), cited in Millar, *Zoffany and his Tribuna*, 37–9)

This commission from Queen Charlotte became a new turning point in Zoffany's life and in his artistic career.

The Tribuna of the Uffizi in Florence housed the finest paintings, antique sculptures, and works of art of the Medici collections and was famous throughout Europe. Neither Queen Charlotte nor George III could hope to visit Italy to see and admire its riches of ancient and modern art and Zoffany's picture was to be a painted substitute. In order to paint his picture, which was largely executed in the Tribuna itself, Zoffany needed special facilities which, since this was a royal commission, were granted without difficulty by the grand duke Pietro Leopoldo. Zoffany began work on the picture shortly after his arrival in Florence in August 1772, and continued to add to it until at least the end of 1777. The arrangement of the pictures hanging on the walls and of the statues and objects differs from their actual disposition in the Tribuna in the 1770s for he had leave to have brought into the Tribuna works from other parts of the gallery and from the Pitti Palace.

Zoffany captured the culminating artistic experience of the grand tour in his *Tribuna of the Uffizi* (Royal Collection), a technical *tour de force* with its accurate imitation of the manner of the different painters and of the textures of the works of art he copied. Following the tradition of pictures of galleries small figures as spectators were to be included, but Zoffany's portraits of English travellers on their grand tour were an innovation.

Zoffany was secretly followed to Florence by a young girl of humble origins whom he had made pregnant. Finding that his first wife, who had returned homesick to Germany, had died, about 1772/1773 he married Mary Thomas (*c.*1755–1832) in Florence after the birth there of a son. The self-portraits he painted while living in Italy (Uffizi, Florence, and Galleria di Parma), confessional and penitential in mood, reflect the conflicting drives tempting the painter from the pursuit of his art.

While living in Florence, Zoffany joined the English colony, finding a patron in Earl Cowper who had been settled there since 1759. He painted a fine and vigorous portrait of Lord Cowper, of his fiancée, Hannah Anne Gore, playing a hurdy-gurdy (both priv. coll.), and a conversation piece of Lord Cowper with the Gore family (1775; Yale U. CBA) in which he figured the cultivated life of the family and an allegory of the forthcoming marriage.

Zoffany also found favour at the grand-ducal court of Pietro Leopoldo, son of the empress Maria Theresa, from whom he received commissions for family pictures like those he had painted for George III and Queen Charlotte. The intimate charm of his English portraits was tempered with pomp and ceremony in keeping with Habsburg formality for the portrait of the young Archduke Francis (1775) and in the life-size group of the whole grand-ducal family (1776) (both Kunsthistorisches Museum, Vienna) painted against a background of the courtyard of the Pitti Palace. Zoffany took this portrait in a specially constructed carriage to Vienna where he completed it and was rewarded by the empress on 4 December 1776 with the title of baron of the Holy Roman empire. Honoured by his fellow artists during his stay in Italy, Zoffany was elected to the academies of Florence, Bologna, Cortona, and Parma.

Having moved in May 1778 to the duchy of Parma ruled by Ferdinand of Bourbon Parma whose wife was a Habsburg archduchess, he painted a group of the four grandchildren of Maria Theresa (1778; Kunsthistorisches Museum, Vienna), one of his most charming formal compositions of children with their playthings set against the trappings of their princely rank. In a vivacious composition of the celebrations at the *scartocchiata* (or maize harvest) (1778; Galleria di Parma) and a *Florentine Fruit Stall* (*c.*1777; Tate collection) Zoffany's feelings for Italian life are painted with the affectionate observation that he introduced into the landscapes, prospects, and plants in the backgrounds of his Italian portraits.

Zoffany arrived back in London late in 1779 to disappointment and long wrangles over his picture of the Tribuna with the king and queen who were displeased with the groups of Englishmen introduced into the picture; there was now no more hope of royal commissions. But in this second short period in England from 1779 to 1783 Zoffany painted two of his most important pictures, *The Sharp Family* (1779–81; NPG) and, as a gift for his friend, *Charles Townley in his Library* (1781–3; Townley Hall Art Gallery and Museums), the most neo-classical in feeling and colour of his paintings and a vivid record of a circle of collectors whose enthusiasm for the antique was important for the development of neo-classical taste. As in *The Tribuna*, Zoffany did not paint a straightforward view of the library but brought into his composition marbles displayed in other parts of the house.

Although at the height of his powers, Zoffany cannot have been too busy during these years for he painted a most accomplished life-size *Self-Portrait with his Daughter and Two Friends* (*c.*1782; Yale U. CBA). Adapting the principles of the no longer fashionable small conversation piece to a larger scale he produced a glittering double portrait, *John Wilkes and his Daughter Polly* (NPG). However his long absence had cost him his vogue as a portrait painter. He appears to have been living in too extravagant a style, buying in 1780 a house at Strand on the Green where he clothed his servants in liveries of scarlet, gold, and blue, the colours of his new arms as a baron. He now took the desperate step of resolving to restore his fortune in Bengal.

Sojourn in India Zoffany sailed for India in March 1783 and arrived at Calcutta on 15 September. He was well recommended and immediately taken up by the governor, Warren Hastings. In India, Zoffany painted both small conversation pieces of English families, some conventional, others with Indian attendants and Indianized settings such as *Colonel Blair and his Family* (1786; ex Sothebys, 18 March 1981), and life-size swagger portraits whose brilliance of colour and Indian features celebrate the exotic years of their sitters' lives, *General Norman Macleod of Macleod* and *Sarah, Wife of Norman Macleod* (1787; priv. coll.). He responded to the Indian scene with genuine delight, making drawings of the landscape, crumbling buildings, and twisted trees.

In May 1784 Hastings summoned Zoffany to Lucknow, the capital of Oudh, to paint a portrait of the nawab vizier Asaf ud-Daula (India Office Library and Records, BL). In Lucknow, where Zoffany was to reside for much of his time in Bengal, he painted his most brilliant pictures of European life in India and of Indian princes and notables. There he made friends with the Swiss colonel Anthony Polier and the Frenchman General Claude Martin, both cultivated men who had entered the nawab's service. In one of his finest Indian works Zoffany has shown himself painting with these two friends, who are engaged with pictures and oriental manuscripts (Victoria Memorial Hall, Calcutta). The other side of life in Lucknow is illustrated in *Colonel Mordaunt's Cock Fight* (1784–6; Tate collection), an unforgettable image of a moment when Indians and Europeans mingled on the easiest of terms at the court of a Muslim prince, which he painted for Warren Hastings.

As a token of his gratitude for the kindness and patronage he had received in Bengal, Zoffany presented in 1787 an altarpiece of the last supper to the new Anglican church of St John's in Calcutta. He also became a member of the newly founded Asiatic Society of Bengal. Zoffany left India in January 1789, with his fortune made. He continued to use drawings made in India for pictures painted after his return to England, such as the *Death of the Royal Tiger* (Victoria Memorial Hall, Calcutta) and *Hyderbeg's Embassy to Lord Cornwallis* (exh. RA, 1796; Victoria Memorial Hall, Calcutta).

Return to England The Europe to which he returned was the Europe of the French Revolution and Zoffany's easygoing eighteenth-century liberalism was shocked by the Parisian massacres of 1792 into horrified reaction. In *The Plundering of the King's Cellar* (exh. RA, 1794; Wadsworth Atheneum), his painting of the populace sacking the Tuileries, Zoffany depicted the scene of wanton brutality with dramatic force. In contrast to this and other similar compositions Zoffany painted two altarpieces for his local parish churches at Brentford and Chiswick, but his powers began to fail and he exhibited in 1800 for the last time at the Royal Academy.

Zoffany's later years were saddened by senile decay and on 11 November 1810 he died at Strand on the Green; he was buried on 17 November in Kew parish church, Surrey. His widow held a sale on 9–10 May 1811 of his unsold and unfinished pictures, his collections of books and prints, together with the armour and oriental curiosities he had brought back from his travels; any drawings, letters, notebooks or accounts she may have kept were burnt after she died of cholera in 1832. From the 1920s attempts have been made to increase Zoffany's *oeuvre* by adding a substantial number of controversial attributions. More recently, his work has also attracted speculative publications on the subject matter of his compositions.

MARY WEBSTER

Sources M. Webster, *Johan Zoffany, 1733–1810* (1977) [exhibition catalogue, NPG] · O. Millar, *Zoffany and his Tribuna* (1967) · M. Archer, *India and British portraiture, 1770–1825* (1979), 130–77 · J. G. Meusel, ed., *Miscellaneen*, 15 (1783), 131–5 · O. Millar, *The later Georgian pictures in the collection of her majesty the queen*, 2 vols. (1969) · W. T. Whitley, *Artists and their friends in England, 1700–1799*, 2 vols. (1928) · B. de Boysson, *Johan Zoffany: 'Vénus sur les eaux' et 'Le triomphe de Vénus'* (Bordeaux, 1990) · J. R. Füssli and H. H. Füssli, *Allgemeines Künstlerlexikon*, [rev. edn] 2 vols. (Zürich, 1779–1824), 6195–7 · V. Manners and G. C. Williamson, *John Zoffany R. A.* (1920) · *Court and private life in the time of Queen Charlotte, being the journals of Mrs Papendiek*, ed. V. D. Broughton, 1 (1887) · I. Mackintosh and G. Ashton, *The Georgian playhouse* (1975) [exhibition catalogue] · W. L. Pressly, 'Genius unveiled: the self-portraits of Johan Zoffany', *Art Bulletin*, 69 (1987), 86–100 · W. L. Pressly, *The French Revolution as blasphemy: Johan Zoffany's paintings of the massacre at Paris, August 10 1792* (1999) · W. L. Pressly, 'Johan Zoffany as "David the Anointed One"', *Apollo*, 141 (March 1995), 49 · Abschrift aus dem Taufbuch der Domgemeinde für die Jahre 1717–1753, Bischöfliches Kommissariat, Frankfurt, p. 111, no. 309 · M. Piendl, *Die fürstliche Residenz in Regensburg im 18. und beginnenden 19. Jahrhundert* (Kallmunz, 1963), 15 · inscribed altar-tomb, Kew churchyard, Surrey

Likenesses J. Zoffany, self-portrait, drawing, *c.*1775, BM · J. Zoffany, self-portrait, oils, 1776, Uffizi Gallery, Florence [*see illus.*] · J. Zoffany, self-portrait, oils, 1776, Accademia Etrusca, Cortona · J. Zoffany, self-portrait, oil on panel, 1778, Uffizi Gallery, Florence · J. Zoffany, self-portrait, drawing, 1782, AM Oxf. · J. Zoffany, self-portrait, oils, *c.*1782 (with his daughter and two friends), Yale U. CBA · J. Zoffany, group portrait, oils, 1784–6 (*Colonel Mordaunt's cock fight*), Tate collection · G. Dance, drawing, 1793, RA · J. Zoffany, group portrait (*The Tribuna of the Uffizi*), Royal Collection · J. Zoffany, group portrait, oils (*Royal Academicians, 1772*), Royal Collection · miniature, V&A

Wealth at death house at Strand on the Green; substantial sum invested: will, Manners and Williamson, *John Zoffany R.A.*, 297–8

Zouch, Henry (1725?–1795), magistrate and writer on the poor, was the eldest surviving son of Charles Zouch (d. 1754), the vicar of Sandal Magna, near Wakefield, Yorkshire, and Dorothy, *née* Norton (1695/6–1760); he was the brother of Thomas *Zouch. Henry was educated at Wakefield School and was admitted as pensioner to Trinity College, Cambridge, in 1743, where he graduated BA in 1746 and MA in 1750. In 1754 he took over his father's old parish of Sandal Magna, where he served as vicar until 1789. He was also rector for the parishes of Swillington and Tankersley and chaplain to the marchioness of Rockingham. He married Elizabeth (d. 1796), the daughter and heir of William Spinke of Wakefield, but they remained childless.

A minor poet, scholar, and keen antiquarian, Zouch is best known for his work as a social reformer. He was a long-serving active magistrate and chairman of the quarter sessions in the West Riding of Yorkshire. From this experience stemmed his interest in the reform of the poor laws, the administration of justice, and, especially, the improvement of the manners and morals of the common people. The West Riding of Yorkshire in the late eighteenth century was ill-famed for its robust and independent plebeian culture. To this Zouch reacted with concern and great reforming zeal, but rather less sympathy and understanding of the significance of the customary culture of the poor. Traditional customs of the manufacturing districts included dog-fighting, street-football, and the holding of riotous wakes and village fairs. The godly complained of disruption to the sabbath while manufacturers bemoaned lost days of work. Zouch saw all these things as breeding grounds for crime, vice, and immorality and, along with others of his generation, he sought to regenerate the old campaign for the reformation of manners. He promoted Sunday schools to instil good habits in the young, called for the suppression of village feasts, and urged magistrates and other authority figures to take a more active role in the superintendence of their subordinates. He was also concerned at what appeared to be a crime wave following a rash of poaching and nocturnal crime. Making a strong connection between crime and poverty, immorality and vice, he battled against unlicensed drinking houses, brothels, and other unofficial meeting-places. His dislike of popular entertainments and suspicion of theatrical and musical performances went even so far as proscribing the performance of oratorios in church.

In the 1780s a broad-based national movement of like-minded contemporaries emerged to combat vice among the lower orders, and Zouch was to play a leading role as an organizer and as a publicist. Next to William Wilberforce, Zouch emerged as a key figure in the Proclamation Society (the Society for the Suppression of Vice and Prophaneness), which set out to enforce royal proclamations against vice and immorality dating from the 1690s. This movement agitated outside of the church for a general reformation of conduct among the high and the low by setting worthy examples of leadership and moral seriousness. Zouch was the West Riding delegate to the national convention of magistrates that met in London in 1790 to confer with the Proclamation Society on the best means to improve police and prisons. A follower of John Howard on penal reform, Zouch reorganized the county gaol at Wakefield and sought to improve the administration of justice by example and precept. Although he was not an original thinker, his written works reached a wide audience and carried some influence. These combined an interest in the Enlightenment battle to reform and modernize criminal justice, along with respect for the ancient tradition of English law. His *Hints Respecting the Public Police* (1786) made ten recommendations ranging from the formation of private associations for the prosecution of felons to the promotion of Sunday schools. Henry Zouch died on 17 June 1795 and was buried in his garden at Sandal on 21 June, a final wish that sealed his reputation for eccentricity. His wife died in the following year.   R. D. SHELDON

Sources DNB · H. Zouch, *Remarks upon the late resolutions of the House of Commons, respecting the proposed change of the poor laws* [1776] · H. Zouch, *Hints respecting the public police* (1786) · S. Webb and B. Webb, *The parish and the county* (1906) · *Leeds Intelligencer* (21 July 1789) · *Leeds Intelligencer* (29 June 1795) · H. Zouch, 'Observations upon a bill to punish by imprisonment and hard labour certain offenders', 1779, BL, Add. MS 34416, fol. 201 · *The manuscripts of the earl of Lonsdale*, HMC, 33 (1893), 136–9 · Walpole, *Corr.* · *N&Q*, 8th ser., 3 (1893), 125, 195

Archives Cumbria AS, Carlisle, corresp. | Sheff. Arch., corresp. with second marquess of Rockingham; corresp. with Earl Fitzwilliam

Zouch, Thomas (1737–1815), biographer and Church of England clergyman, was born in the rectory at Sandal Magna, near Wakefield, Yorkshire, on 12 September 1737, the second son of Charles Zouch (d. 1754), vicar of Sandal Magna, and his wife, Dorothy (1695/6–1760), daughter of Gervase Norton of Wakefield. His early years seem to have been happy, and he remained deeply attached to Yorkshire and particularly to the country around Sandal Magna throughout his life. Zouch began his studies at home where, under his father's tutelage, he developed a solid grounding in Latin and Greek, before attending Wakefield's free grammar school, which counted Richard Bentley and John Radcliffe among its alumni. There he was taught by Benjamin Wilson and John Clarke, both masters of the school. Much later in life Zouch published a biography of Clarke, celebrating him as the model of 'the good schoolmaster', one who, though exacting in the teaching of ancient literatures, still 'accommodated himself with equal affability and kindness to all' (Zouch, *Works*, 2.14). In part, Zouch writes his own life in writing Clarke's, a life happily passed in the study of antiquity and the defence of England's ecclesiastical constitution.

It was to Clarke's college, Trinity, Cambridge, that Zouch proceeded at the relatively advanced age of eighteen, being admitted pensioner on 8 July 1756. Zouch's academic career was without a doubt brilliant, and he garnered many awards and honours in his thirteen years at Trinity. Within a year he became a scholar of the college—a welcome saving, since his father had now been dead three years. In 1760 he won one of two university-wide Craven scholarships, worth £20 per annum, and graduated BA, with the distinction of second wrangler. He was ordained a deacon and stayed at Trinity, winning two prizes of 15 guineas each in the annual members' Latin essay competition: in 1762 he came second among the middle bachelors and in 1763 first among the seniors, in the latter case for a lively satirical essay on Rousseau's account of the origins of society. Zouch showed diligence in performing the drudgery reserved for junior fellows—including, it seems, writing college verses in Greek for Michael Lort, professor of Greek, who had little taste for such tiresome exercises—and he was rewarded with considerable responsibility. He held various college appointments and offices—minor fellow (1762), major fellow (1764), *sublector primus* (1765), *lector linguae Latinae* (1768). His main income in these years was from teaching: as assistant tutor to Thomas Postlethwaite he earned £60 per annum, and he took on several private pupils. He also contributed verses in Latin and English to various university collections celebrating state occasions, and his much admired poem 'Crucifixion' won the Seatonian prize in 1765. When the master of Trinity, Robert Smith, died in 1768, Zouch was chosen to deliver the Latin funeral oration. But he was already experiencing bouts of deafness, a condition from which he suffered for the rest of his life. These attacks became so severe that he often could not hear the responses to the psalms, and once began a sermon while the organ was still playing. Deafness was not readily compatible with the largely oratorical world of Cambridge teaching and ceremony, and Zouch sought more secluded employment in a university living. In recognition of his services he was instituted in 1770 to the rectory of Wycliffe, in the North Riding of Yorkshire, where he was to live for the next twenty-three years.

After an initial contest with the local Roman Catholic landholders who had the patronage of Wycliffe and who objected to the university's nomination, Zouch settled down in his early thirties to what was promising to be a relatively quiet and undemanding clerical life. On 9 July 1772 he married Isabella (d. 1803), daughter of John Emerson, rector of Winston, co. Durham. To supplement his income he took in pupils from the local gentry, three at a time, but his duties left him ample time to study, and he devoted himself to ancient and modern literature, and to the antiquities and botany of his home county; in particular he began gathering information towards a comprehensive biographical dictionary of Yorkshire worthies, a project he never completed. This middle period of Zouch's life was uneventful, almost reclusive. In 1780 he became, at the encouragement of his more politically active elder brother Henry *Zouch, a member of the York-shire Association, and undoubtedly he sympathized with that society's protest against recent royal excesses and its call for moderate electoral reform, but he never attended a meeting and soon let his membership lapse. Similarly, although he had gained sufficient repute as a botanist to be elected fellow of the Linnean Society when it first met in 1788, he never communicated any of his discoveries or specimens to that body.

Zouch might well have lived his life in this modest retirement but for the energetic interference of two powerful friends. The first was Richard Pepper Arden (1745–1804), later Baron Alvanley, who had been one of Zouch's private pupils at Trinity. From Cambridge, Pepper Arden had gone to Lincoln's Inn, where he shared a stair-case with William Pitt, before proceeding on a brilliant legal and political career, ultimately serving Pitt as solicitor-general and attorney-general. Zouch's second well-wisher was the younger William Lowther. Zouch's sister Anne had married Sir William Lowther, rector of Swillington and third cousin to the unsavoury James Low-ther, earl of Lonsdale (1736–1802), the support of whose extensive and powerful political machine was much val-ued by Pitt. Their eldest son, William, was chosen by the childless earl as heir to his enormous wealth. William had been tutored by Zouch at Wycliffe, and the two remained close throughout Zouch's life. A more ambitious (and, pos-sibly, a healthier) cleric than Zouch might have made more of two such patrons as Pepper Arden and Lowther, but then no doubt he was sought out for his solidity rather than his brilliance as a theologian or energy as an adminis-trator of the church. In any case his first sinecures came thanks to Pepper Arden, who made Zouch his chaplain when he became master of the rolls in 1788, and who secured for him the deputy commissary of the arch-deaconry of Richmond. Then Pitt, who at the behest of the Lowthers had been seeking out a richer living for Zouch for some time, was able in the king's name to bestow the rectory of Scrayingham in the East Riding of Yorkshire in 1793. When Zouch's brother Henry died in 1795 Zouch inherited the family estate at Sandal Magna, where he went to live in 1796, establishing a curate at Scrayingham. From 1799 to 1805 Zouch was a governor of Wakefield school, and he also founded an endowed school at Sandal Magna. Pitt remained active on Zouch's behalf, proposing him in 1798 for the mastership of Trinity College (a post that went to William Mansel, bishop of Bristol) and finally securing Zouch a lucrative place as canon and prebendary of Durham Cathedral in 1805, upon which occasion Zouch took the degree of doctor of divinity.

It was during these latter years at Sandal Magna that Zouch began publishing. Apart from sermons and a few tracts on biblical prophecy, Zouch concentrated his energy on biography. He wrote and circulated privately several brief accounts of pious and eminent Yorkshire-men, but is chiefly remembered for his more substantial lives of Izaak Walton and Sir Philip Sidney. Zouch's first publication on Walton was an edition of the rare 1680 tract *Love and Truth in Two Modest and Peaceable Letters* (1795),

followed by a splendid edition, dedicated to Pepper Arden, of Walton's *Lives of Donne, Wotton, Hooker, Herbert and San-derson* (1796), fully annotated and introduced with Zouch's own life of Walton. Here Zouch casts Walton as the exem-plary Londoner, fully conversant with the world but unwavering in his attachment to church and crown, one who adopts a 'mild spirit of moderation' in a troubled age (p. xlix). If Zouch models in Walton the long-suffering protestant citizen, he finds in Sidney the perfect protest-ant knight. *The Memoirs of the Life and Writings of Sir Philip Sydney* (1808), dedicated to Zouch's nephew William Low-ther, now earl of Lonsdale, is a response in part to the unflattering character given to Sidney by Horace Walpole. Zouch depicts late sixteenth-century Europe as a Gothic world of seductive Jesuits and brutal Catholic princes, all bent upon the genocide of protestants. Sidney as diplomat and soldier stands alone amid these dangers in his 'uni-form zeal for the reformed religion' (Zouch, *Memoirs of Sir Philip Sydney*, 91). Like so many writing in the wake of the French Revolution, Zouch is most concerned with shoring up British social and religious hierarchies and promoting political order. Although he can be credited with much original archival research on both Walton and Sidney, in general he practises the same improving biographical method he found at work in Walton's *Lives*, presenting 'examples of men strictly and faithfully discharging their professional duties' with the overall aim of invigorating his reader's 'efforts to excel in moral worth' (Walton, *Lives*, ed. Zouch, ix). Zouch did not move in literary circles, but his biographies were widely read. Robert Southey, visiting his brother at Durham in the summer of 1809, made a point of dining with Zouch. And in 1805 Zouch admired (and corrected) some of Wordsworth's poetry, passed on to him in manuscript by Lonsdale; Zouch complained that 'the terms *green* and *bowers* are used too often' (*Lonsdale MSS*, 154).

In 1807 Zouch was offered the bishopric of Carlisle, but he declined on determining that Carlisle was not worth more than the livings he had in hand. His health was not good and there was little financial incentive to move. Isa-bella had died in 1803, and on 25 August 1808 Zouch mar-ried Margaret (1743–1833), second daughter of William Brooke of Dodworth, Yorkshire. Neither marriage pro-duced any children. Zouch died at Sandal Magna on 17 December 1815 and was buried there on 23 December.

PETER WALMSLEY

Sources *The works of the Rev Thomas Zouch*, ed. F. Wrangham, 2 vols. (1820) · F. Wrangham, 'A memoir of the life of the Rev Thomas Zouch', in *The works of the Rev Thomas Zouch*, ed. F. Wrangham (1820) · *The manuscripts of the earl of Lonsdale*, HMC, 33 (1893), 135, 146, 150–54, 232–4 · *N&Q*, 8th ser., 3 (1893), 125, 198, 334 · T. Zouch, letters, 1769, BL, Add. MS 35639, fols. 91, 136 · *N&Q*, 3rd ser., 6 (1864), 279

Archives Denbighshire RO, Ruthin, corresp., diaries, and papers · York Minster Library, York Minster Archives, notes on nat-ural history | BL, Hardwicke papers, Add. MS 35639 · Cumbria AS, Carlisle, corresp. with first earl of Lonsdale

Zouche. For this title name *see* individual entries under Zouche; *see also* Curzon, Robert, fourteenth Baron Zouche of Harringworth (1810–1873).

Zouche [de la Zouche] **family** (*per. c.*1254–1415), magnates, were descended from Alan de la Zouche (*d.* 1190), who arrived in England from Brittany in the reign of Henry II. The Northamptonshire branch of the family was established by **Eudo** [i] **de la Zouche** (*d.* 1279), grandson of Alan, son of Roger (*d.* 1238), and younger brother of Alan de la *Zouche (*d.* 1270), justiciar of Ireland. As a younger son Eudo sought advancement through royal service, which he had already entered before 1254 when he escorted Queen Eleanor to join Henry III in Gascony. He associated with the Lord Edward in the late 1250s when he acted as witness to the prince's charters. Furthermore, during disturbances in the Welsh marches in 1262 he was entrusted with the defence of Edward's castles in Cheshire. Eudo's continuing support for the royal cause in the barons' war is suggested by his summons in arms to the king at Windsor in 1263. Royal service notwithstanding it was Eudo's marriage in 1268 to Millicent (*d.* 1299), widow of John de Montalt and sister and coheir of Sir George de *Cantilupe (1251–1273), which established the family's landed fortune. Millicent inherited a scattered estate comprising lands in Ireland and manors in the south-west and midlands, along with the family's *caput* of Harringworth. The marriage to Millicent produced three daughters and at least two sons, including **William** [i] **Zouche**, first Lord Zouche (*c.*1277–1352).

William was the first of his family to receive a writ of summons to parliament in 1308 as Lord Zouche. His opposition to Edward II's government included involvement in the summary execution of Piers Gaveston in 1312, for which his proposed pilgrimage to Santiago de Compostela in 1317 may have been intended as an act of atonement. William's talents, however, were expressed mainly through military exploits. From 1301 he saw frequent service against the Scots. He also campaigned in Ireland and Gascony and had, too, experience in the law. In May 1330 he was justice in eyre in Derbyshire but had to be replaced before the end of the month because of ill health. Although his disease was believed to be incurable, he did recover, and continued to play a role in local administration and on the king's council (1337). After his recovery he began to make modest alienations of lands and rents in mortmain. William's marriage before February 1296 to Maud, daughter of John, Lord Lovell of Titchmarsh (*d.* 1310), was clearly designed to extend and strengthen the Zouches' estate in the midlands. Maud was heir of her maternal uncle, William du Bois (*d.* 1313?), from whom she inherited manors in Northamptonshire, Leicestershire, and Warwickshire. The marriage produced three daughters and seven sons, one of whom, John, maintained the family's court connections as purveyor in Queen Isabella's household between 1327 and 1333, while another, Edmund, was prebendary at St Paul's in London. It is sometimes claimed that William *Zouche, king's clerk and archbishop of York (1342–52), was a son of William [i]. In addition to the fact that one of William [i]'s sons was indeed called William, there is other circumstantial evidence to lend credence to such claims. For example, in 1328 William, the king's clerk, held the rectorship of

Clipsham in Rutland, a living in the gift of Lord Zouche of Harringworth. Also, again in 1328, William [i]'s daughter-in-law granted to William, king's clerk, her lands in Latchingdon in Essex. Nevertheless, it is more likely that this William was a younger brother of Roger Zouche of Lubesthorpe; in 1337 the two were jointly granted licence to alienate land and rent at Lubesthorpe to fund masses for the souls of their progenitors.

William [i]'s large family naturally made demands on his estate but his gifts to his children were life grants, with reversions to William and his heirs. He thus ensured that the long-term integrity of the estate and, therefore, the status of the family were maintained. For a time it appeared that his son and heir, **Eudo** [ii] **Zouche** (1298–1326) would continue his father's careful strategies. In or before 1317 Eudo married Joan, daughter and heir of Sir William *Inge (*d.* 1322), chief justice of the king's bench, and of Sir William's wife, Margery, herself a daughter and coheir of Henry Grapinel of Essex. In 1322 Joan and Eudo had seisin of her inheritance, spanning eight counties from Hampshire to Essex. The same year Eudo was commissioned to follow Hugh Despenser in the renewed war against the Scots. In February 1326, however, he became entangled in a confederacy of his Leicestershire cousins and their neighbours, the delinquent Folvilles, in a murderous attack on Justice Roger Beler. To escape retribution Eudo fled to Paris, where he died on 27 April 1326. He was buried there in the church of the Augustinian friars.

Eudo's son, **William** [ii] **Zouche**, second Baron Zouche (*c.*1317–1382), commonly known as 'of Totnes' in Devon, similarly entered royal service. He joined Henry Burghersh's embassy to Germany in 1337. He also performed military service in France, participating in the siege of Calais in 1347. His appointment to various commissions in Northamptonshire between 1351 and 1380 was interrupted in October 1362 when he nominated attorneys to attend to his affairs while he went on pilgrimage to the Holy Land. His last official appointment was in 1381 to the commission of inquiry into the royal household. He was already married by July 1334 to Elizabeth, daughter of William *Ros, Lord Ros of Helmsley. There were two daughters and three sons of the marriage; one of the sons, Eudo, was canon of Lincoln and chancellor at Cambridge. Before his death in April 1382 William [ii] requested burial in Biddlesden Abbey and bequeathed £60 for masses at his tomb.

William's heir, **William** [iii] **Zouche**, third Baron Zouche (*c.*1340–1396), continued the family tradition of service to the crown at a time when close association with Richard II provided doubtful security. In 1384 he was accused, but later acquitted, of having slandered John of Gaunt, duke of Lancaster. The following year he accompanied Richard II on his Scottish campaign, but was removed from court by the lords appellant in 1388 as a malign influence on the king. At the height of fears of invasion in 1383 he was ordered to repair to one of his manors in Devon to defend the coast there, but he resided mainly at Harringworth, which he had licence to crenellate and fortify in 1387. He first married, before October

1351, Agnes, daughter of Sir Henry Green and, after her death, Elizabeth, widow of John, Lord Arundel, and daughter of Edward *Despenser, Lord Despenser. After his death he was buried in the chapel at Harringworth. Despite William [iii]'s attachment to Richard II, his son and heir, **William** [iv] **Zouche**, fourth Baron Zouche (*c.*1373–1415), was a member of Henry IV's council. He negotiated with Owen Glyn Dŵr in 1402 and performed escort duties for Blanche of Lancaster and Joan of Navarre. Early in Henry V's reign he briefly held the lieutenancy of Calais but his last official act was as one of the peers commissioned to judge the rebels after the Southampton plot in 1415. He died on 3 November 1415 and was succeeded by his eldest son, William (*d.* 1462), then still a minor.

The Zouches of Harringworth reveal how a junior branch of a baronial family could establish and maintain itself through royal service and judicious marriages. The family, however, remained among the second rank of the nobility, suggesting that bureaucratic and military competence were insufficient talents to ensure further social advancement. Their arms were gules, ten bezants, a canton ermine.   ERIC ACHESON

Sources Chancery records · A. Gibbons, ed., *Early Lincoln wills* (1888) · J. Bridges, *The history and antiquities of Northamptonshire*, ed. P. Whalley, 2 vols. (1791) · N. H. Nicolas, ed., *Proceedings and ordinances of the privy council of England*, 7 vols., RC, 26 (1834–7), vols. 1–2 · W. A. Shaw, *The knights of England*, 2 vols. (1906); repr. (1971) · J. Nichols, *The history and antiquities of the county of Leicester*, 4 vols. (1795–1815) · *Thomae Walsingham, quondam monachi S. Albani, historia Anglicana*, ed. H. T. Riley, 2 vols., pt 1 of *Chronica monasterii S. Albani*, Rolls Series, 28 (1863–4) · *CEPR letters*, vol. 2, pp. 276, 292, 376, 520, 524, 547, 550 · G. F. Farnham, *Leicestershire medieval pedigrees* (1925) · *VCH Rutland* · *VCH Northamptonshire* · *VCH Leicestershire* · H. L. Gray, 'Incomes from land in England in 1436', *EngHR*, 49 (1934), 607–39

Wealth at death income of £533 p.a. in 1436 tax: Gray, 'Incomes from land', p. 617

Zouche [Zouch], **Alan de la** (*d.* 1270), administrator and soldier, was one of Henry III's trusted supporters and servants. His grandfather, also called Alan, had arrived in England from Brittany in the 1170s, and had founded the family's fortunes in England by his marriage to the heiress Alice de Belmeis, thereby securing extensive estates including Tong (Shropshire), Ashby (Leicestershire), and North Molton (Devon). A junior branch of the family was established in Northamptonshire by Eudo de la *Zouche (*d.* 1279) [*see under* Zouche family]. Alan succeeded his father, Roger, in 1238, and was soon active in the service of Henry III: in 1242 he was one of those who effected the capture of the notorious outlaw William de Marisco on Lundy island, and in 1242–3 he saw military service in Gascony. His first taste of high office came in 1250 when he was appointed justice of the county of Chester and the Four Cantrefs (the district of north Wales east of the River Conwy). He paid 1000 marks for the post, allegedly outbidding the current holder of the office. He flaunted the wealth he raised from the district, and boasted that the whole of Wales was now reduced to obedience. But his high-handed and insensitive behaviour provoked royal investigation, and fuelled the resentment in the area against the English, which led to the violent overthrow of

English rule in 1256. By then Zouche had entered the service of the Lord Edward (who had been given the royal lands in Wales, Ireland, and Chester in February 1254), and acted as his justiciar in Ireland from June 1256 to October 1258.

With the onset of civil discord in England in June 1258, Zouche was given ample opportunity to display his unflinching loyalty to the king. His closeness to Henry III during these years is indicated by the fact that he is described at various times between October 1261 and January 1263 as steward of the royal household. He was also given important posts in the country: sheriff of Northamptonshire (1261–4), justice of the forests south of the Trent (from June 1261), and constable of Rockingham Castle (1261–4) and Northampton Castle (1261–3). His Welsh experience prompted the king to dispatch him to guard the Welsh marches against Llywelyn ap Gruffudd in December 1262. Two events in December 1263 showed the measure of the king's confidence in him: on 12 December he was one of the barons chosen on the king's side to submit all points in the political dispute to the arbitration of Louis of France; and on 24 December he was given custody of the counties of Devon, Somerset, and Dorset as a military lieutenant. Taken prisoner at the battle of Lewes (14 May 1264), Zouche escaped to Lewes Priory, where he disguised himself as a monk, but he was recaptured and imprisoned. In the aftermath of the king's victory at Evesham (4 August 1265) he played an important part in the pacification of the country: he was one of the twelve arbitrators appointed to arrange the terms of the surrender of Kenilworth Castle in 1266, and was one of the justices appointed to hear the pleas of the disinherited. The reward for his loyalty included handsome gifts and appointment to the important and lucrative post of warden of London and constable of the Tower from June 1267 to April 1268.

During 1270 Zouche became involved in a dispute with John de Warenne (*d.* 1304), almost certainly over the manors of Ashby and Chadston in Northamptonshire. The manors had been forfeited by their owner, David Ashby, for his support for Simon de Montfort and granted to Zouche; but Warenne, as the guardian of Ashby's granddaughter, also had an interest in them. During an altercation in Westminster Hall on 1 July 1270 Warenne and his men assaulted Zouche and his son in the presence of the royal justice and the chancellor. Zouche suffered wounds from which he died on 10 August 1270. Warenne was forced to perform public acts of contrition for the assault and to offer a fine of 10,000 marks to the king.

Zouche was a benefactor of the knights templars and of the Cistercian abbey of Buildwas in Shropshire. He married, before 1242, Helen, one of the daughters and coheirs of Roger de Quincy, earl of Winchester, and in 1267 secured her share of the Quincy estates. He was succeeded by his son Roger la Zouche (*d.* 1285); his widow died on 20 August 1296.   T. F. TOUT, *rev.* R. R. DAVIES

Sources GEC, *Peerage* · *Chancery records* · *CIPM* · Paris, *Chron.* · A. J. Roderick, 'The Four Cantrefs', *BBCS*, 10 (1939–41), 246–56 · F. M.

Powicke, *King Henry III and the Lord Edward: the community of the realm in the thirteenth century*, 2 vols. (1947) • R. W. Eyton, *Antiquities of Shropshire*, 12 vols. (1854–60), vol. 2

Zouche, Edward la, eleventh Baron Zouche (1556–1625), landowner, was born on 6 June 1556, at Harringworth, Northamptonshire, the only son of George la Zouche, tenth Baron Zouche of Harringworth (*c*.1526–1569), landowner, and his wife, Margaret (*d*. in or after 1569), daughter and coheir of William Welby of Molton, Lincolnshire. He succeeded as eleventh Lord Zouche on the death of his father on 30 June 1569. The main estates were concentrated in Northamptonshire. As a minor, Zouche became the ward of Sir William Cecil, principal secretary, who entrusted his education to John Whitgift, master of Trinity College, Cambridge. Zouche matriculated there in Easter 1570, and gained an MA in 1571.

Zouche was summoned to parliament on 2 April 1571, but as a minor he did not take his seat for some years. Subsequently he said 'the greatest evil hath been the fond spending of my time in my youth' (PRO, SP 12/239, fol. 156*r*). In 1575 he quarrelled with Roger North, second Baron North, and on 12 February 1576 both peers were summoned before the privy council and bound over to keep the peace. He married his cousin Eleanor (*d*. 1611), daughter of Sir John Zouche of Codnor, Derbyshire, and his wife, Eleanor, about 1578. Relations with his wife were not cordial and the couple were estranged in 1582. He put her away without an allowance and was sued in the ecclesiastical court for support. Sentenced to pay £2 10*s*. per week, he refused, was excommunicated, and went abroad before returning to abide by the orders of the court. According to Sir John Holles, while Lady Zouche was 'oft dangerously sick … he [Lord Zouche] never disbursed a penny, and now dead she might have rotted in her chamber as he would have buried her' (*Portland MSS*, 9.83–4). The couple had two daughters, Elizabeth (*d*. 1617) and Mary (*d*. 1652).

While abroad, Zouche became interested in diplomatic service, perhaps when he travelled in Scotland. He was appointed one of the peers to try Mary, queen of Scots, at Fotheringhay Castle, Northamptonshire, in 1586, and in the following year he returned to the continent, partly to qualify himself for public service, and partly to advance and enrich his education. He went by sea to Hamburg in March 1587, and then to Heidelberg and Frankfurt. In April 1588 he was at Basel, and in 1590 at Altdorf he met Sir Henry Wotton, with whom he corresponded frequently. In August 1591 Zouche was living in Vienna. He then proceeded to Verona, but in 1593 returned to England.

Zouche's diplomatic career was launched on 22 December 1593, when he was sent as envoy-extraordinary to James VI of Scotland to protest against his leniency towards George Gordon, first marquess of Huntly, Francis Hay, ninth earl of Erroll, and William Douglas, tenth earl of Angus, who were known to be in league with Spain, and to inform him that Elizabeth I would resist with military force the landing of any Spanish troops in Scotland. He

Edward la Zouche, eleventh Baron Zouche (1556–1625), by unknown artist

had an audience with James on 15 January 1594, urging him to take vigorous action against the Spanish faction in Scotland. Unsuccessful, he asked to be sent home. Returning in the following April, he had no better success. In June 1598 Zouche was sent on a commercial mission to Denmark with Sir Christopher Perkins, who had served several times as envoy to the Danish court and was selected to accompany him.

These missions did nothing to restore Zouche's private fortunes, and in December 1599 he begged Sir Robert Cecil, principal secretary, for a public office. The result was an appointment in August 1600 to a place where he could 'live cheaply' (*Salisbury MSS*, 9.302), the island of Guernsey, where he acted as deputy governor. He seems to have enjoyed life there and patronized Thomas Cartwright. His tenure, however, was short-lived. In June 1602 he was appointed president of the council of Wales and the marches, probably through Cecil's influence.

Zouche arrived at Ludlow on 13 August, sorry to leave the warmer Channel Islands. The situation in the marches was disordered and he set out to resolve the defects of the council and the court. His task was made more difficult because of the entrenched interests of the officials, who 'resented the intrusion of a lay nobleman' (Williams, 304). Shocked at the state of affairs, he wrote that Wales and the border shires were 'stuffed with Papists' (*Salisbury MSS*, 15.17). Trying to take control of the region at the expense of local interests, he exercised his authority 'soe muche that his jurisdiction is allready brought in question' (Manningham, 95). Later, John Chamberlain wrote that 'Lord Zouche plays *rex* in Wales … with the council and justices, as also with the poor Welchmen' (*CSP dom., 1601–3, 249*). Zouche continued in office under James, who made him grants of land worth £80 a year in 1604, and continued to reward him in subsequent years.

Zouche was sworn of the privy council on 11 May 1603, shortly after James first arrived in London. He served on various commissions over the next twenty years. The most prominent dealt with France, in July 1610, the treasury, in June 1612, Flushing and Brill, in May 1616, abuses in the treasury, in July 1618, ecclesiastical causes, in April 1620, and defective land titles, in June 1622. He was one of the first councillors for the Virginia Company, from May 1609, and the New England Company, from November 1620, and was sworn of the Scottish privy council in June 1617. Lady Zouche died early in 1611 and was buried at Heanor, Derbyshire, on 3 April. By October of that year Zouche had married Sarah (*c.1566–1629*), daughter of Sir James Harrington of Exton, Rutland, and his wife, Lucy, and widow of Sir George Kingsmill, justice of the common pleas, and of Francis Hastings, Baron Hastings.

After the death of the earl of Salisbury (Cecil) in 1612, Zouche supported anti-Spanish interests among the English privy council against the king's favourite, Robert Carr, earl of Somerset. The distinguished botanist Mathias de L'Obel, a guest in Zouche's household, learned, through his friend Dr John Nasmith, James's chief surgeon, of attempts to poison Somerset's secretary, Sir Thomas Overbury. Zouche was caught up in the resulting court intrigue. His friendship with Thomas Egerton, Baron Ellesmere, lord chancellor, and George Abbot, archbishop of Canterbury, allowed the anti-Spanish interests at court and in the privy council to discover the plot and oust the Spanish faction from the king's favour. Appointed a commissioner in September 1615 to assist Sir Edward Coke, chief justice of the king's bench, in his investigation of the affair, it was said that Zouche was chosen because he was 'a man void of all partiality' (Molyneaux, 75).

Zouche was also engaged in these years in his new position as lord warden of the Cinque Ports. He was appointed in July 1615 at the nomination of Abbot, who promoted him to thwart Somerset's nominee on behalf of the pro-Spanish interests. The Cinque Port burgesses (or 'barons') elected to the House of Commons for the seven ports were under the patronage of the lord warden as constable of Dover Castle and sheriff for the ports. The growing economic decay of the ports increased Zouche's patronage in parliament and at court because the interests of, and therefore the ability of, the burgesses to interfere were diminishing too, which enabled him to extract greater electoral influence. Zouche became very successful in obtaining the placement of his nominees. As lord warden from 1615 to 1624, in the elections of 1621 and 1624 he placed twenty of the twenty-eight seats in the face of pressure from George Villiers, first duke of Buckingham, and the boroughs, the highest number ever obtained in the early Stuart period. His success was due in part to his strong advocacy of the independence and privileges of the

port towns. He maintained a steady correspondence, promoting their custumals, economic interests, Dover harbour, and the channel passage. When these were challenged at court in 1621, he defended them vigorously. His relationship with the port towns, however, was reciprocal: he did not interfere with their business nor demand control of their votes in the Commons. He held the wardenship of the Cinque Ports until 17 July 1624, when ill health and Buckingham's persuasions, reinforced by a grant of £1000 and a pension of £500, induced him to resign the office, which was bestowed upon the duke himself.

Zouche's major intellectual interests were history, literature, and mathematics. His literary friends included Sir Henry Wotton, Ben Jonson, and William Browne. Wotton, a lifelong friend, collected books, manuscripts, and paintings for him as well as reports on news and life on the continent. Zouche's cousin Richard *Zouche dedicated to him *The Dove, or, Passages of Cosmography* (1613). Claude Holyband dedicated *A Dictionaire French and English* (1593) to him and he was also the dedicatee of the first part of William Browne's *Britannia's Pastorals* (1613).

The reduction of Zouche's wealth and patrimony was due largely to his passion for horticulture. He spent considerable sums on gardens, cultivating a 'physic-garden' in Hackney, Middlesex, and was a friend of the herbalist John Gerard. L'Obel superintended this garden, accompanied Zouche on his embassy to Denmark in 1598, and dedicated to him his *Pharmaceuticam officinam animadversiones* (1605). Zouche spent most of his later years at Bramshill House, Hampshire, where he styled himself 'Lord Souch, Saint Maure and Cantelupe' (PRO, PROB 11/146, sig. 101). Besides designing the house, he also designed the gardens. A keen collector of shrubs and trees, he imported Scottish firs. His garden at Hackney was full of plants which he obtained on his foreign travels in the 1580s and 1590s.

It was at Bramshill that Abbot accidentally shot and killed Zouche's warden Peter Hawkins in July 1621, mistaking him for a deer. Abbot was there to consecrate the new chapel. A royal commission found Hawkins's death was the result of accidental homicide, and Abbot was granted a dispensation. Despite this, the archbishop's career was effectively over, paving the way for William Laud. The event marked the waning influence of the anti-Spanish interests on the privy council and the subsequent political decline of Zouche. None the less, he maintained his ties with Edward Russell, third earl of Bedford, William Hanley, sixth earl of Derby, William Herbert, third earl of Pembroke, and Henry Wriothesley, third earl of Southampton, because of his lineage, offices, politics, and religion. His religious zeal for the protestant faith was exhibited in his will.

Zouche's closest relation was Sir Edward Zouche, who was known as Edmund and was the son of John Zouche of Ansty, Wiltshire. He was the main benefactor of Zouche's will, and called 'the son of him I loved best in life (except the lord Grey of Wilton)' (PRO, PROB 11/146, sig. 101). Lady Zouche had to employ lawyers to secure her share of the estate. Zouche's lifelong estate steward and servant, William Randolph (father of Thomas Randolph, poet and dramatist, and half-brother of William Randolph, the Virginia colonist) benefited also.

Zouche died on 18 August 1625 at Bramshill, and was buried the next day in the family vault at Eversley, Hampshire. The fact that this vault was connected with Zouche's wine cellar provoked from Jonson the lines:

> Wherever I die, oh, here may I lie,
> Along by my good Lord Zouche,
> That when I am dry, to the tap I may hie,
> And so back again to my couch.
> (Herford, Simpson, and Simpson, 8.444)

Lady Zouche married Sir Thomas Edmondes on 11 September 1626. Since Zouche did not have any sons his baronies fell into abeyance between the heirs of his daughters.

LOUIS A. KNAFLA

Sources Burke, *Peerage* (1898) · GEC, *Peerage* · Bodl. Oxf., MS Western 5006, fol. 92 · BL, Add. MS 29995, fols. 166v–184r · will, PRO, PROB 11/146, sig. 101 · *CSP dom., 1581–1626* · PRO, SP 12 · *APC, 1600–04* · *Calendar of the manuscripts of the most hon. the marquis of Salisbury*, 24 vols., HMC, 9 (1883–1976), vols. 7–9, 12, 15 · *The letters of John Chamberlain*, ed. N. E. McClure, 2 vols. (1939) · T. Birch, *Memoirs of the reign of Queen Elizabeth*, 2 vols. (1754) · T. Birch, *The court and times of James the First*, 2 vols. (1848) · J. Manningham, *The diary of John Manningham of the Middle Temple, 1602–1603*, ed. R. P. Sorlien (1976), 82, 95, 334, 341–2 · *The manuscripts of his grace the duke of Portland*, 10 vols., HMC, 29 (1891–1931), vol. 9, pp. 83–4 · *Ben Jonson*, ed. C. H. Herford, P. Simpson, and E. M. Simpson, 11 vols. (1925–52) · *CSP col.*, vols. 1, 5, 7, 9–45 · W. M. Molyneaux, *Archaeologia* (1867), 75 · BL, Add. MSS 48126, 48152, 48156 · BL, Cotton MS, Nero B.iv · BL, Egerton MS 2812 · BL, Add. MSS 12496–12497, 12504, 12507 · BL, Lansdowne MS 161 · BL, Egerton MSS 1615, 2552, 2584 · BL, Add. MSS 33512, 35832, 37818, 42075 · BL, Harley MSS 806, fol. 12r; 807, fol. 26v; 1233, fol. 142v; 1411, fol. 10r; 1529, fol. 53v; 6601 · S. R. Gardiner, *History of England from the accession of James I to the outbreak of the civil war, 1603–1642*, 10 vols. (1883–4), 2.145, 327; 5.69, 310 · J. K. Gruenfelder, 'The lord warden and elections, 1604–1628', *Journal of British Studies*, 16 (1976), 1–23 · P. Williams, *The council in the marches of Wales under Elizabeth I* (1958) · B. White, *Cast of ravens: the strange case of Sir Thomas Overbury* (1965), 96, 105, 202–5 · P. A. Welsby, *George Abbot: the unwanted archbishop, 1562–1633* (1962), 91, 95 · R. E. Ruigh, *The parliament of 1624: politics and foreign policy* (1971), 131–7

Archives BL, corresp. as warden of the Cinque Ports, Egerton MS 2584 · BL, letter-book as deputy to governor of Guernsey, Egerton MS 2812

Likenesses attrib. D. Mytens, oils, c.1618, Royal Collection · oils, Parham Park, West Sussex [*see illus.*] · portrait (after engraving by S. De Wilde), repro. in A. Brown, *The genesis of the United States* (1890), 2.1060

Zouche, Eudo (1298–1326). *See under* Zouche family (*per. c.*1254–1415).

Zouche, Eudo de la (d. 1279). *See under* Zouche family (*per. c.*1254–1415).

Zouche, Richard (1590–1661), civil lawyer, the son of Francis Zouche, lord of the manor of Anstey, Wiltshire, and, reputedly, of Philippa, sixth daughter of George Ludlow of Hill Deverel, Wiltshire, was born at Anstey. He was the great-grandson of the eighth Baron Zouche of Harringworth.

Education and early career Zouche was elected a scholar of Winchester College in 1601 and, in 1607, a scholar of New

Richard Zouche (1590–1661), attrib. Cornelius Johnson, 1620

College, Oxford, where in 1609 he became a fellow. He graduated BCL in 1614 and in January 1618, unusually, since he had not yet taken his doctorate, was admitted to Doctors' Commons. On 8 April 1619 he took the degree of DCL and on 30 April was admitted an advocate of the court of arches. In 1620 he succeeded his teacher John Budden as regius professor of civil law at Oxford and held the chair until his death. In 1621 and again in 1624 he was elected MP for Hythe, through the patronage of his cousin Edward, eleventh Baron Zouche, lord warden of the Cinque Ports, and in a Bill on Penal Statutes, he sought a proviso for the Cinque Ports.

It was probably in 1622 that Zouche married Sarah, daughter of John Hart, a proctor in Doctors' Commons, and sister of Dr Richard Hart, a fellow civilian; they had six children. Having to resign his fellowship on marriage, Zouche became a fellow-commoner of Wadham College until in 1625 he was appointed principal of St Alban Hall. He acted as assessor, or judge, of the vice-chancellor's court, which followed the civil law, and took part in the Laudian codification of the university statutes (1629–33). In 1632 he became chancellor of the Oxford diocese and was a prebendary of Salisbury. From 1626 to 1634 he was a member of the high court of delegates. Having practised in admiralty cases for many years, he was made commissioner for piracy in London, Hampshire, and Dorset and in 1641 was appointed judge of the high court of admiralty, but was removed during the civil war.

Civil war years Since Zouche was royalist in sympathy, his practice suffered during the civil war and he spent his time mainly in Oxford. Indeed, when he left London for Oxford in 1643 without paying the parliamentary subsidy, the furniture of his chambers in Doctors' Commons was confiscated by way of distress. He negotiated on behalf of the royalist forces in Oxford on their surrender in 1646. The articles allowed him and other royalists to compound for their estates without taking the covenant, and in November he was permitted to compound for interests in land at Harefield near Uxbridge, Ascott in Oxfordshire, and at Doctors' Commons at one-tenth of their value, namely £333. In 1647 he was one of those who drafted the reasons given by the University of Oxford for rejecting the solemn league and covenant. Zouche must have made some accommodation with the Commonwealth, for in 1648 he was permitted by the parliamentary visitors to retain his academic offices and his son Richard was restored to a demyship at Magdalen College of which he had been deprived. Later Zouche became a member of the mixed commission of common lawyers and civilians set up to investigate the charge of murder against the Portuguese ambassador's brother, Don Pantaleone Sa, who was condemned and executed in 1654. Three years later Zouche published a justification of the commissioners' view that an ambassador's exemption from prosecution does not extend to a member of his suite: *Solutio quaestionis veteris et novae, sive, De legati delinquentis judice competente*, which was published at Oxford in 1657, at Cologne in 1662, at Berlin in 1669, and translated into German at Jena in 1717.

Zouche was a candidate for election as the keeper of the archives of the university in 1658 and in support of his case prepared a manuscript collection of the privileges of the University of Oxford, of which there is a transcript in St John's College Library, but he was defeated, possibly as a result of sharp practice, by Dr John Wallis.

Published works On becoming professor Zouche embarked on a systematic survey of the whole field of law in a series of short books intended for students of the civil law and published between 1629 and 1650. He explains the whole scheme in the preface to the last of the series, the famous textbook on international law.

It begins with *Elementa jurisprudentiae*, published at Oxford in 1629 and 1636, at Leiden in 1652 and 1653, and at The Hague in 1665, which is illustrated by maxims, definitions, and general rules, taken exclusively from the texts of the civil law, and divided, as were most of his writings, into substantive law (*jus*) and civil procedure (*judicium*). In the *Elementa* his purpose was to show the foundations of law and procedure for a community in general. The aim of jurisprudence is the enforcement of justice, and the principles of justice are derived from natural law, the law of nations, and civil law. They apply to the human communities that exist between private individuals, between sovereign and subject, between persons in special relationships, and between one sovereign and another. Of the means by which justice is applied to these relationships, the most important is *judicium*, legal procedure.

After mapping out the field of law Zouche came to the law of these various communities, his emphasis being on the laws applicable in England, which were of practical importance to civilians, ecclesiastical law, military law, maritime law, and international law. The largest community is that which subsists between one private person and another and between private persons and princes (*Descriptio juris et judicii temporalis, secundum consuetudines feudales et Normannicas*, 1636, reprinted in R. Moket, *Tractatus de politeia ecclesiae Anglicanae*, 1683). The sequence continued with five short monographs devoted to special communities: feudal law, based on the customs of Milan and Normandy; ecclesiastical law, essentially Anglican canon law; sacred law, which is concerned with religion and pious causes; military law, concerned with military service in war and peace and with the law of nobility; and maritime law, concerned with navigation and commerce. Finally he came to international law: *Juris et judicii fecialis, sive, Juris inter gentes et quaestionum de eodem explicatio*, printed at Oxford in 1650, at Leiden in 1651, at The Hague in 1659, at Mainz in 1661, and translated into German as *Allgemeines Völkerrecht* at Frankfurt in 1666; it was edited, with an English translation, by T. E. Holland in *The Classics of International Law* (2 vols., 1911). Because of the paucity of sources in this area of law, Zouche says that he found it necessary to consult other authors, in particular Alberico Gentili and Hugo Grotius. His method was to set out first those propositions of law as to which there was little doubt (part 1) and then, where the matter appeared to be controversial, to treat the law as a set of open questions, with arguments both ways (part 2). In this pioneering work Zouche was one of the first writers to treat international law systematically as a whole, and essentially as a law that applied in time of peace. He treated war as a means of enforcing the rights that arose from status, from ownership, from duty or from wrongdoing in time of peace. He adopted an empirical and positivist approach, not based on natural law or religion, and drew his examples both from classical antiquity and from recent European history. He argued in favour of the term *jus inter gentes* ('law between nations') rather than *jus gentium* ('law of nations') to describe the subject.

Cases and Questions Resolved According to the Civil Law (1652) is a casebook of problems taken from the texts of Justinian's *Digest*, with full references, primarily for the use of students of the civil law. It was originally intended to be published in 'the proper language of the civil law', but, he explained cautiously, it appeared exceptionally in English, 'that others also might discerne that the study of that learning conduceth to the knowledge of some things worthy of consideration'. Although the Roman fact-situations might appear 'forraigne', the doubts expressed and their resolution could be applied to more familiar topics. *Specimen quaestionum juris civilis* (1653) was published anonymously. It is a series of civil-law problems on which different views are found in the literature, arranged in ten classes and addressed to students. Each problem is accompanied merely by references to enable the student to find the different opinions in the texts. *Quaestionum juris civilis centuria, in decem classes distributa*, published at Oxford in 1660 and at London in 1682, follows the same scheme as the *Specimen*, although the problems treated in the ten classes are somewhat amplified and the arguments are set out extensively, instead of by reference only. In the preface, written from St Alban Hall in 1659, Zouche refers back to the *Specimen* and says that these 'efforts of his old age' were intended specially for the alumni of Winchester and New College, in which he himself had learned classics and civil law. In the same mode a collection of logical, rhetorical, and moral maxims, *Eruditionis ingenuae specimen, scilicet artium logicae, dialecticae et rhetoricae nec non moralis philosophiae* (1657), illustrated from definitions, maxims, and opinions taken from Cicero's writings, was published anonymously but introduced from the 'Wicchamical museum' of St Alban Hall in 1656.

Zouche's last book was *The jurisdiction of the admiralty of England asserted against Sir Edward Coke's 'Articuli admiralitatis' in chap. xxii of his 'Jurisdiction of courts'*, a polemical work, published posthumously (1663, repr. in G. Malynes's *Consuetudo, vel, Lex mercatoria*, 1686). Dr T. Baldwyn of Doctors' Commons certified in a preface that he received the manuscript from Zouche himself to be printed. Coke's attack on the admiralty jurisdiction is systematically refuted. Zouche argues that the law merchant did not derogate from the common law; admiralty law and common law coexist and litigants may choose their court; the special admiralty procedure makes it more convenient to litigants.

With the end of the Commonwealth, Zouche's fortunes improved. He was a member of the commission sent to Oxford to review the work of the parliamentary visitors and to restore those who had been deprived of their posts. In July 1660 he appears as president of Doctors' Commons. On 4 February 1661 he recovered his old position as judge of the court of Admiralty, but on 1 March 1661 he died in London at Doctors' Commons and was buried in Fulham parish church. In his will he divided his estate into three parts for his wife, Sarah, who lived on until 1683, being buried in St Peter-in-the-East, Oxford, for his son Richard and for his daughter Anne, who had married Robert Say, provost of Oriel. (Another daughter, Sarah, married Dr Lydall, warden of Merton.)

Posthumous reputation Zouche left a considerable body of published work. His earliest publication was a rather feeble poem in English called *The Dove, or, Passages of Cosmography* (1613), which described the known world after the manner of the *Periegesis* of Dionysius Periegetes. His only other literary work is possibly *The Sophister, a Comedy* (1639), an anonymous work which is attributed to Zouche in an old note in the Bodleian Library copy. In his own field, however, he made a major contribution to the pedagogic literature of the civil law, usually writing in Latin. He was descriptive rather than original, inclined to synthesis rather than analysis.

His contemporary Anthony Wood, describes Zouche as:

an exact artist, a subtile logician, expert historian, and for the knowledge in, and practice of, the civil law, the chief person of his time; as his works, much esteemed beyond the seas (where several of them are reprinted), partly testify. He was so well vers'd also in the statutes of the university, and

controversies between the members thereof and the city, that none after Twyne's death went beyond him. As his birth was noble, so was his behaviour and discourse, and as personable and handsome, so naturally sweet, pleasing and affable. The truth is that there was nothing wanting but a froward spirit for his advancement.   (Wood, *Ath. Oxon.*, 3.511)

Levack in his chapter on law in the seventeenth-century volume of the *History of the University of Oxford*, describes him as 'clearly the most distinguished civilian [lawyer] that Oxford produced in the seventeenth century. He was also the last of his kind: an English civil lawyer whose writings acquired a durable European reputation' (*Hist. U. Oxf.* 4: *17th-cent. Oxf.*, 563).   PETER STEIN

Sources T. E. Holland, *Introduction to Zouche 'Juris et judicii fecialis'*, 1 (1911) • B. P. Levack, *The civil lawyers in England, 1603–1641* (1973) • D. R. Coquillette, *The civilian writers of Doctors' Commons, London* (1988) • G. D. Squibb, *Doctors' Commons: a history of the College of Advocates and Doctors of Law* (1977) • Wood, *Ath. Oxon.*, new edn • *Hist. U. Oxf.* 4: *17th-cent. Oxf.*

Likenesses attrib. C. Johnson, oils, 1620, NPG [*see illus.*]

Zouche, William, first Lord Zouche (*c.*1277–1352). See *under* Zouche family (*per. c.*1254–1415).

Zouche, William (*d.* 1352), administrator and archbishop of York, was most likely a son of the Roger la Zouche who died in 1302 holding the manor of Lubbesthorpe in Leicestershire. If this identification is correct, William's birth would have taken place some time after 1292–3, the year in which Roger, the eldest son and heir to the Lubbesthorpe manor, was born. In 1337 the two brothers, William and Roger, founded chantries at Lubbesthorpe and at Clipsham, Rutland. The future archbishop was a kinsman (but not a younger son, as has sometimes been supposed) of William, first Lord Zouche (*d.* 1352) of Harringworth. It was the baron's mother, Millicent de Monte Alto, who had granted Lubbesthorpe to Roger la Zouche the elder in 1267–8, and it was the baron himself who presented the young William to his first ecclesiastical benefice, the rectory of Clipsham, in 1315.

By this date Zouche had been ordained acolyte. During the ensuing year he proceeded to the subdiaconate, but thereafter his progress through the orders was slow. He was still a subdeacon in 1324, and as late as 1330 he was granted letters dimissory by Bishop John Grandison of Exeter, enabling him to proceed to all orders. His long period as a subdeacon indicates that the benefice of Clipsham was intended to finance his studies at university. In accordance with the papal constitution *Cum ex eo*, he was granted four separate dispensations for study by successive bishops of Lincoln: two by John Dalderby in 1316 and 1318, and two by Henry Burghersh in 1320 and 1324. He had attained the degree of master of arts by 1320, and it seems likely that he remained at university for a total period of some twelve years, culminating in the award of the degree of bachelor of civil law, which he is known to have received before, and probably well before, 1335. The place of his studies is not known, but as the two earlier dispensations stipulated that he was to study

William Zouche
(*d*. 1352), seal

within England it is quite possible that he attended the schools at Oxford.

At the conclusion of his university career Zouche entered royal service. By April 1328 he was a king's clerk, employed within the wardrobe. His efficient work as clerk of the spicery brought him promotion in January 1329, when he was appointed keeper of the great wardrobe. The favour with which he was regarded by the administration governing England in the name of the young Edward III was underlined in July 1328 by the grant, nominally at the king's petition, of a papal provision to a canonry of Exeter with reservation of a prebend. The prebend soon followed, and to it was added in December 1329 the archdeaconry of Barnstaple. He vacated this six months later for the archdeaconry of Exeter which he exchanged in turn, in June 1331, for the valuable rectory of Yaxley, Huntingdonshire. It is unlikely that Zouche personally carried out the duties of any of these ecclesiastical offices, which are probably to be seen as the means of providing him with an income. As keeper of the great wardrobe, he was based initially at Westminster; in both 1332 and 1333 he spent some time in Flanders for the purpose of obtaining cloth. In 1333, however, the wardrobe, along with other government departments, moved to York, where it was involved in providing clothing, arms, and equipment for the Scottish campaigns of 1333–5.

Zouche's work at the great wardrobe marked him out for further promotion. On 31 July 1334 he was appointed controller of the wardrobe, and eight months later, on 1 April 1335, he was made keeper of the privy seal. In this capacity Zouche was involved in the campaign against the Scots in the summer of 1335. His more eminent role in government was reflected in two further ecclesiastical benefices, both in York Minster where he was made a prebendary in November 1335, and, twelve months later, dean. The culmination of Zouche's career as a civil servant came in March 1337 with his appointment as treasurer of the exchequer. He took office at a time when preparations

for war with France and negotiations with potential allies in the Low Countries were placing ever-increasing burdens on the nation's finances. One symptom of this strain can be seen in the frequency with which the office of treasurer changed hands. After a year in office Zouche was replaced by Robert Wodehouse (*d*. 1346), only to be recalled to the post nine months later. He was unable, however, to satisfy the king who was becoming increasingly impatient at the delays in producing adequate money and supplies for the war. Zouche's standing began to deteriorate, particularly since he was now working with Archbishop John Stratford (*d*. 1348), a man whom Edward regarded with growing disfavour.

William Melton, archbishop of York, died on 4 April 1340. Three days later the king granted custody of the temporalities to Zouche. The *congé d'élire* was issued on 13 April and Zouche, leaving the treasury in the hands of a deputy, set out for York to oversee the temporalities and, as dean, to preside at the election. On the following day the king suddenly ordered the transfer of the temporalities to the officials of the chamber. It is not clear what caused this reversal: perhaps the king had been told that Stratford favoured Zouche for the vacant archbishopric. It is certain that the king wanted the post for his closest adviser, William Kilsby (*d*. 1346). Accordingly Kilsby was sent to York, and steps were taken to secure for him a seat in the chapter. The king issued letters praising Kilsby and denying 'slanderous reports' that he had been excommunicated. On 2 May, Zouche was relieved of his office as treasurer but on the same day he found himself elected, by twelve votes to five, archbishop of York.

No doubt foreseeing a struggle, Zouche prudently had himself installed archbishop on the day of the election. Kilsby refused to abandon his claim, and both parties appealed to Avignon. The king wrote to Pope Benedict XII (*r*. 1334–42) in support of Kilsby, and attempts were made to prevent Zouche from leaving England. On 13 August the pope ordered the excommunication of all who sought to detain Zouche, who was now finally able to set out for the papal court. Travelling via the Low Countries and Germany, on account of the French war, he had just passed through Geneva when he was kidnapped by three knights and confined in a remote place on the north side of Lake Geneva. This was clearly another attempt to prevent him from reaching Avignon, and Kilsby's involvement was strongly suspected. At length Zouche was released on payment of a ransom and after swearing not to reveal the identity of his captors. On his arrival at Avignon, Zouche was released from his oath by the pope, who took vigorous measures to bring the culprits to justice. Nevertheless, the matter of the disputed election was left unresolved for more than two years until on 26 June 1342, Zouche was granted a papal provision to the see of York by Clement VI (*r*. 1342–52). He was consecrated at Avignon on 7 July, returned to England in September, and on 8 December his enthronement took place at York. Edward III must have come to accept Zouche's elevation, since the temporalities were restored on 19 September. The question of his successor as dean gave rise to another lengthy dispute,

Zouche's involvement in which led ultimately to his excommunication by Pope Clement for opposing the papal nominee. This sentence was not lifted by Clement until July 1352, three months before Zouche's death.

Although Zouche's relations with the king had cooled during the dispute over the archbishopric, Edward was not one to harbour grudges against anyone who was likely to prove useful to him. With English military resources overwhelmingly committed on the continent, the border with Scotland remained vulnerable. Zouche, who had himself been involved in the Scottish campaigns of the 1330s, was well placed as archbishop to help in consolidating the country's defence. In 1346 Edward III's victory at Crécy moved the Scots to attempt a diversionary action to relieve their French allies. In expectation of this Zouche had been appointed warden of the Scottish march and joint commissioner of array for the northern army When King David of Scotland invaded in October, Zouche, along with Henry Percy and Ralph Neville, mustered an army to oppose him. At the decisive action of Nevilles Cross on 17 October, Zouche commanded one of the three divisions. His part in the victory, erasing the unhappy memory of the defeat of his predecessor, Archbishop William Melton, at Myton in 1319, secured him considerable renown in the north of England.

Apart from this excursion into military affairs Zouche spent most of his time as archbishop residing in his diocese, occupied in routine administration. The smooth running of the diocese was severely challenged during the plague epidemic of 1349. Zouche warned of the imminent arrival of the disease in a letter dated 28 July 1348, in which he ordered the litany to be sung in procession on Wednesdays and Fridays, and special collects to be said at mass, in every church in the diocese. The black death arrived in Yorkshire in May 1349; it has been estimated that mortality among the beneficed clergy was over 40 per cent during July and August. Zouche remained in his diocese, moving between his manors of Cawood, Ripon, and Bishop Burton, where large numbers of clergy came to him, seeking institution to the numerous benefices which had fallen vacant through death. On one day two successive candidates were admitted to the same benefice, the first having presumably succumbed to the disease within a few hours of his institution. Meanwhile Zouche's suffragan Hugh, archbishop of Damascus, was commissioned to hold additional ordinations and to consecrate new burial-grounds.

During the course of the epidemic, on 28 June 1349, Zouche drew up his will. It was said that he had long been suffering with a serious illness. He made provision in his will for the foundation of a chantry chapel in York Minster, where he asked to be buried, and in April 1351 he received permission from the dean and chapter to proceed with this work; it was still in progress at the time of his death. Zouche died at his manor of Cawood on 19 July 1352, and was buried in York Minster before the altar of St Edward. His chapel was eventually completed, but his executors not only failed to found his chantry but also neglected to erect any monument to his memory, 'a proof'

according to the chronicler Thomas Stubbs 'of the ingratitude of his kindred and those to whom he had been an exceptional benefactor' (Raine, *Fasti*, 2.419).

NICHOLAS BENNETT

Sources W. H. Dixon, *Fasti Eboracenses: lives of the archbishops of York*, ed. J. Raine (1863) · Tout, *Admin. hist.* · bishops' registers, Lincs. Arch., Lincoln diocesan archives, nos. 2, 4, 5 · *CIPM*, 4.112 · *CPR, 1334–8*, 406 · *CEPR letters*, vol. 2 · F. C. Hingeston-Randolph, ed., *The register of John de Grandisson, bishop of Exeter*, 3 vols. (1894–9) · A. H. Thompson, 'The pestilences of the fourteenth century in the diocese of York', *Archaeological Journal*, 71 (1914), 97–154 · J. S. Miller, 'The building of the Zouche chapel', *Friends of York Minster Annual Report*, 63 (1992), 53–62 · Emden, *Oxf.* · J. Raine, ed., *The historians of the church of York and its archbishops*, 2, Rolls Series, 71 (1886), 418–19 **Archives** Borth. Inst., Reg. 10–10A
Likenesses seal, BL; Birch, *Seals*, 2317 [*see illus.*]

Zouche, William, second Baron Zouche (*c.*1317–1382). See *under* Zouche family (*per. c.*1254–1415).

Zouche, William, third Baron Zouche (*c.*1340–1396). See *under* Zouche family (*per. c.*1254–1415).

Zouche, William, fourth Baron Zouche (*c.*1373–1415). See *under* Zouche family (*per. c.*1254–1415).

Zuccarelli, (Giacomo) Francesco (*bap.* 1702, *d.* 1788), landscape painter and draughtsman, was born at Pitigliano, Grosseto, Italy, and baptized there on 15 August 1702, the third son of Bartolomeo Zuccarelli (1641–1706), a tradesman, and his wife, Orazia Parrini (*b.* 1675), daughter of Domenico Parrini. He went when very young to Rome, studying there under several painters and practising as figure painter before specializing in landscape. By 1728 he was in Florence, where he etched some prints after earlier Florentine artists and exhibited two religious paintings in 1729.

From approximately 1732 Zuccarelli was settled in Venice and soon became widely celebrated for his prolific output of pastoral scenes, frequently engraved. He was extensively patronized by Joseph Smith, the British consul, for whom he painted some of his more vigorous and varied compositions (Royal Collection), and for Smith he collaborated with the architect Antonio Visentini on a series of fanciful landscapes with English Palladian buildings (the majority are in the Royal Collection). He also painted small portraits for Italian patrons, notably his friend in Bergamo, Count Francesco Maria Tassi, who subsequently published useful information about him. A rare example of an altarpiece by Zuccarelli is that of St Jerome Emiliani (1748, Pinacoteca Repossi, Chiari, Brescia).

In 1752 Zuccarelli left Venice for London. In the previous year he had met in Venice Richard Wilson and been painted by him (1751, Tate collection). Along with Smith, Wilson may have encouraged his travelling to a country where his landscapes were already popular. He remained in London until 1762, when a sale of his work was held on 10 February and announced in the catalogue as 'by reason of his returning to Italy'. In 1765 he was back in London, exhibiting in that and the following year at the Free Society. In 1767 the paintings he sent to the Society of Artists

(Giacomo) **Francesco Zuccarelli** (*bap.* 1702, *d.* 1788), by Richard Wilson, 1751

included *Macbeth Encountering the Witches* (a version: Shakespeare Memorial Gallery, Stratford upon Avon). He was made a founder member of the Royal Academy in 1768. George III commissioned some paintings from him, including probably the large *Finding of Moses* (1768, Royal Collection), possibly the picture of the same subject exhibited at the Royal Academy in 1773 after Zuccarelli had returned finally to Italy. In 1774 he settled in Florence, where he died at his home in the via del Parione on 30 December 1788, being buried on the 31st in Santissima Trinita. His will refers to his wife, Giustina Agata Simonetti.

Under numerous influences, Zuccarelli created a distinctive style of decorative pastoral landscape, evolving little in his long, productive career. Some monotony is inevitable but his work at its best is agreeable and highly accomplished. MICHAEL LEVEY

Sources F. Dal Forno, *Francesco Zuccarelli, pittore paesaggista del settecento* (1994) [with bibliography and check-list of paintings] · *Francesco Zuccarelli, 1702–1788: atti delle onoranze Pitigliano 1989* (1991) · M. Levey, 'Francesco Zuccarelli in England', *Italian Studies*, 14 (1959), 1–20 · F. M. Tassi, *Le vite de' pittori, scultori e architetti bergamaschi* (1793), 2.85–8 · A. Morassi, 'Documenti, pitture e disegni inediti dello Zuccarelli', *Emporium* (Jan 1960), 7–22 · R. Bassi-Rathgeb, *Un album inedito di Francesco Zuccarelli* (1948) · P. D. Massar, 'The prints of Francesco Zuccarelli', *Print Quarterly*, 15 (1998), 247–63 · E. Martini, *La pittura del settecento Veneto* (1982), 87–8 · M. Levey, *The later Italian pictures in the collection of HM the queen*, 2nd rev. edn (1991), 163–77 · M. Levey, 'Wilson and Zuccarelli at Venice', *Burlington Magazine*, 101 (1959), 139–43 · G. Rosa, *Zuccarelli* (1945) · registro battezzati, archivio vescovile, Pitigliano · Santissima Trinita, Florence, archivio parrochiale

Archives Biblioteca Accademia Carrara, Bergamo, Italy, MS Epistolario Tassi · Cumbria AS, Carlisle, corresp. with Lonsdale family relating to Lowther Castle

Likenesses R. Wilson, oils, 1751, Tate collection [*see illus.*] · J. Zoffany, group portrait, oils (detail of *The Founder Academicians, R. A.*), Royal Collection

Zuccaro, Federico (1539/40–1609), painter, was born at Sant'Angelo in Vado in the Marche Italy, the son of the painter Ottaviano Zuccaro (*b.* 1505) and Antonia Nari. His birth date is calculated from an inscription on a festival design executed in 1565 that identifies the artist as twenty-five years old. Zuccaro has suffered historically from the comparison with his older and shorter-lived brother and frequent collaborator Taddeo Zuccaro (1529–1566), about whom far less is known although he possessed, by consensus, a far greater artistic talent. The more copious documentary evidence on Federico—including his own published writings, correspondence, and often angry marginal annotations to his personal copy of Giorgio Vasari's biography of his brother—forms the impression of a worldly and ambitious artist, sensitive to slights, who exploited the more conservative religious atmosphere following the Council of Trent to achieve success.

Federico Zuccaro went to Rome in 1550 while still a youth to live and train with his brother whom he assisted on several frescoed façade commissions between 1555 and 1560. In 1559 he received his first independent façade commission, for the Roman house of Tizio Chermandio da Spoleto, the *maestro di casa* of Cardinal Alessandro Farnese. Thereafter, in addition to continuing to work with his brother on the decorations of Farnese's country villa at Caprarola and Vatican projects for Pope Pius through the early 1560s, Federico also went to Venice in October 1563 until July 1565, where he received commissions from the Grimani family for both their palace and their family chapel in the church of San Francesco della Vigna. He also competed unsuccessfully to replace a large fourteenth-century painting in the sala del gran consiglio. His departure from Venice was prompted by the invitation to journey to Florence to contribute to the wedding decorations of Grand Duke Francesco de' Medici and Joanna of Austria, an event that took place on 26 December 1565. While in Florence he was elected to membership in the Accademia delle Arti del Disegno on 14 October 1565. Following Taddeo's death in 1566 Federico was asked to complete his brother's paintings in the Pucci chapel in the church of Trinità dei Monti and to oversee the continuing work at Caprarola, the latter involvement lasting until his resignation under duress in July 1569. Until June 1573 Federico was active on commissions in Rome and Orvieto, at which time he left Italy and arrived in Paris in September to enter the service of Cardinal Carlo di Guisa.

After the cardinal's death in December 1574 Zuccaro moved on to Antwerp and then to London, where he was introduced into the circle of Robert Dudley, earl of Leicester and, consequently, to the court of Elizabeth I, where he remained from March to August 1575. The assumed purpose of his visit was to paint the portraits of Leicester and the queen. While no such image of Elizabeth survives, it is thought that the portrait of Leicester was executed and that it was destroyed during the Second World War.

Both sitters are rendered in autograph red and black chalk studies by Zuccaro in the collection of the British Museum. Owing to a misunderstanding of how long he was actually in residence Zuccaro has traditionally been credited with stimulating the revival in full-length portraits in England. Given his brief presence there, however, and a number of full-length English portraits that predate 1575, it is doubtful that this is the case. Apart from the surviving drawings of Dudley and Elizabeth, only two drawings unquestionably from his English sojourn survive. These are chalk copies in Berlin after Hans Holbein's lost paintings for the Steelyard Guild in London. Zuccaro, however, made many sketches after works of art during his travels and some additional works with English provenance might still be identified.

From 1575 to 1579, with brief interruptions, Federico executed the remaining two-thirds of the frescoes of the last judgement in the cupola of the Florentine cathedral of Santa Maria dei Fiore left unfinished by Vasari at his death in the summer of 1574. In 1578 he married Francesca Genga. By the end of 1579 he returned to Rome and work on decorations for the Pauline chapel for Pope Gregory XIII Boncampagni of Bologna. A simultaneous commission for an altarpiece in Bologna, when rejected by its patron, provoked the sensitive artist to design a large allegorical satire against his detractors, the so-called Port Virtutis, that was set up in Rome against the façade of the church of San Luca a Monte Santa Maria Maggiore on 18 October 1581, the feast day of St Luke, patron saint of artists. This act resulted in the artist's immediate expulsion from the city by the pope. He was not pardoned until the end of 1583, by which time the ever-enterprising artist had achieved commissions in Venice and Urbino. A major commission from Philip II to participate in the painted decorations at El Escorial brought Federico to Spain in late 1585, where he remained until the end of 1588. His return to Rome was marked by an elevation of his status as artist and gentleman as he was made a citizen by senate decree in 1591, began work on an impressive palazzo on the Pincian Hill not far from Trinità dei Monti, and was named *principe* of the Accademia di San Luca in 1593. His well-preserved painted decorations at the Palazzo Zuccaro (now the German art history institute in Rome) are an inventive combination of high-minded allegory and family history. Several important public Roman fresco and altarpiece commissions were executed during this late period; most noteworthy are those in the cappella degli Angeli in the church of the Gesù in 1592 and in the cappella Ascoli of Santa Sabina in 1600.

The last decade of Federico Zuccaro's life was dedicated to some lesser paintings executed for patrons in Pavia, Turin, Bologna, and the Borromeo Islands in Lake Maggiore, but this was also the period of publication of his elaborate biographical and theoretical treatises *Lettere e principi et signori amatori del disegno, pittura, scultura et architettura* published in Mantua in 1605 and *Idea dei pittori, scultori et architetti* published in Turin in 1607. He died of a fever in Ancona while travelling from Loreto to Urbino on 20 July 1609. In August his remains were interred with those of his brother Taddeo in the Pantheon in Rome. In his memoir of Zuccaro in the *Dictionary of National Biography* Lionel Cust drew attention to the 'reckless profusion' of British portraits that had been attributed to that artist, and stated that Zuccaro was in Britain for a much shorter period than was originally believed. Subsequent research has reduced further the period of his stay in Britain and the number of works he produced there. Zuccaro was a successful pan-continental artist employed by popes, cardinals, and kings in Italy, Spain, England, and France.   JAMES MUNDY

Sources C. Acidini Luchinat, *Taddeo e Federico Zuccari fratelli pittori del cinquecento*, 2 vols. (1998–9) · *Scritti d'arte di Federico Zuccaro*, ed. D. Heikamp (1961) · B. Cleri, ed., *Per Taddeo e Federico Zuccari nelle Marche* (1993) · E. J. Mundy, *Renaissance into Baroque: Italian master drawings by the Zuccari, 1550–1600* (1989) · K. Hearn, ed., *Dynasties: painting in Tudor and Jacobean England, 1530–1630* (1995) [exhibition catalogue, Tate Gallery, London, 12 Oct 1995 – 7 Jan 1996]
Likenesses F. Galizia, oils, 1604, Uffizi Gallery, Florence · attrib. F. Pourbus, oils, Uffizi Gallery, Florence · F. Zuccaro, self-portrait, fresco (with his wife), Palazzo Zuccaro, Rome · F. Zuccaro, self-portrait, oils, Museo di Palazzo Venezia, Rome · F. Zuccaro, self-portrait, oils, Pinacoteca Nazionale, Lucca · portrait, Accademia di San Luca, Rome

Zucchi, Antonio Pietro Francesco (1726–1795), painter, was born in Venice on 1 May 1726, the son of Francesco Zucchi (1692–1764), an engraver. He was a member of a large family of artists, and studied with his father, his uncle Carlo Zucchi, a master of perspective and teacher of Piranesi, Francesco Fontebasso, and Jacopo Amigoni. His extant works in Venice include the *Via crucis* (c.1750; San Giobbe) and *The Incredulity of St Thomas* (c.1766; San Toma). His style developed from Venetian rococo to neo-classical. He was elected a member of the Accademia di Pittore e Scultore, Venice (1759). Conceivably the architect Robert Adam engaged Zucchi to make drawings from the Spalatro sketches for plates in *The Ruins of the Palace of Diocletian at Spalatro* (1764), to which Zucchi subscribed, but Zucchi did not accompany Adam and C.-L. Clérisseau to Dalmatia in 1757, as stated by Goethe and in the *Dictionary of National Biography*. Zucchi visited Pola, Istria, with James Adam and Clérisseau in 1760 and in 1761 went to live with them in Rome. They sketched in the city and the surrounding countryside and visited Naples. Goethe stated that 'he [Zucchi] drew figures for buildings and ruins which Clérisseau later published' (Goethe, 169). In 1763 James Adam noted that 'Zucchi [was] a worthy honest lad, a most singular character' (Clerk MSS, GD 18/4955).

In 1766 Zucchi and his brother Giuseppe [*see below*] arrived in London to work for Robert Adam. Zucchi became his chief decorative painter, especially known for his large capriccios (for example, those at Harewood House, Yorkshire), illustrations from Homer and Virgil (examples at Home House, London), and arabesque work (as in the Lansdowne House drawing-room, now in the Philadelphia Museum of Art); he also made a drawing for a carpet at 20 St James's Square, London. He was elected an associate of the Royal Academy in 1770. He designed the frontispiece for *The Works in Architecture of Robert and James Adam* (1773).

The diarist Joseph Farington noted that 'Zucchi … courted Angelica Kauffman, the Artist' (Farington, *Diary*, 1.74). Fifteen years her senior, he married her [*see* Kauffman, (Anna Maria) Angelica Catharina (1741–1807)] on 14 July 1781 and shortly afterwards they returned to Italy. He took charge of their household in Rome and showed great concern for her welfare. He recorded her work in his 'Memorandum of paintings of Maria Angelica Kauffmann'. A stroke and ill health led to his death on 26 December 1795 at his home, via Sistina 72, Rome, and he was buried in S. Andrea delle Frate, Rome, where his wife was later to be interred beside him. A tablet bears witness to their mutual devotion. His will nominated the major part of his fortune to his own family. Alessandro Longhi drew and engraved Zucchi's portrait for his *Compendio delle vite de' pittori Veneziani istorici* (1762).

Antonio Zucchi's brother, **Giuseppe Carlo Zucchi** (1721–1805), engraver, was born in Venice and studied there with Francesco Zugno. He assisted his father, but, according to G. A. Moschini, appears never to have signed works until his father died in 1764, hence the difficulty in identifying which Zucchi engraved plates in Robert Adam's *Spalatro*. He went with his brother to London in 1766 and engraved four plates signed J. Zucchi for Robert and James Adam's *Works in Architecture* volumes 2 and 3 (1774–5). He was included in the circle of friends of Angelica Kauffmann, many of whose etchings he strengthened with a burin. He returned to Italy (1779) and became a professor at the Accademia di Roma. In 1786 Giuseppe Carlo Zucchi wrote 'Memorie cronologiche della famiglia' (MS, untraced) and in 1788 'Memorie istoriche di Maria Angelica Kauffmann Zucchi' (Vorarlberger Landesmuseum, Bregenz). Both works were consulted by G. G. de Rossi for his *Vita di Angelica Kauffmann, pittrice* (1810). Giuseppe Carlo Zucchi died in Venice in 1805.   MALISE FORBES ADAM

Sources J. Fleming, *Robert Adam and his circle in Edinburgh and Rome* (1962), 271–315, 370 • E. Croft-Murray, *Decorative painting in England, 1537–1837*, 2 (1970), 296 • NA Scot., Clerk of Penicuik Collection, GD18/4955 • J. Turner, ed., *The dictionary of art*, 34 vols. (1996), vol. 33, p. 271 • G. A. Moschini, *Dell'incisione in Venezia* (1924), 58 • V. Moschini, 'Antonio Zucchi Veneziano', *Ateneo Veneta*, 11 (1957), 168–72 n. 6 • T. McCormick, *Charles-Louis Clérisseau and the genesis of neo-classicism* (1990), 68, 69 • G. G. de Rossi, *Vita di Angelica Kauffmann, pittrice* (Florence, 1810); trans. D. Sherwood (1991), 35 [privately printed] • J. W. Goethe, *Italian journey*, trans. W. H. Auden and E. Mayer (1962), 169 • Farington, *Diary*, 1.74 • A. Longhi, *Compendio delle vite de' pittori Veneziani istorici* (1762) • E. Harris and N. Savage, *British architectural books and writers, 1556–1785* (1990), 93–4 • V. Manners and G. C. Williamson, *Angelica Kauffmann* (1924) • F. Gerard, *Angelica Kauffmann* (1893) • DNB • G. Beard, *Craftsmen and interior decoration in England, 1660–1820* (1981), 208, 211

Archives NA Scot., Clerk of Penicuik collection • W. Yorks. AS, Leeds, corresp. with Sir Rowland Winn

Likenesses A. Kauffmann, oils, 1782, priv. coll. • A. Longhi, drawing and engraving, repro. in Longhi, *Compendio*

Wealth at death £4800 cash: Gerard, *Angelica Kauffmann*, 290, 291; Manners and Williamson, *Angelica Kauffmann*, 122

Zucchi, Giuseppe Carlo (1721–1805). *See under* Zucchi, Antonio Pietro Francesco (1726–1795).

Zuckerman, Joan Alice Violet Rufus, Lady Zuckerman (1918–2000). *See under* Zuckerman, Solly, Baron Zuckerman (1904–1993).

Zuckerman, Solly, Baron Zuckerman (1904–1993), scientist and public servant, was born on 30 May 1904 in Cape Town, Cape Colony, the eldest son and second of the five children of Moses Zuckerman, furniture and hardware merchant, and his wife, Ruth, *née* Glaser, a prominent Zionist and social worker. His grandparents on both sides emigrated from eastern Europe in the latter part of the nineteenth century. Little is known of their origins: 'Wandering Jews were not in the habit of carrying their genealogical records with them', wrote Zuckerman in his autobiography (Zuckerman, *Apes*, 2). He was educated from 1915 to 1920 at the South African College School, which he loathed, and Cape Town University (to 1924), which he loved and where he won a scholarship to study abroad. His special field of study was the baboon, an interest which he widened to include the chimpanzee soon after he started work in London in 1925. Professor Grafton Elliot Smith encouraged him to join the University College Hospital medical school where he remained until, at the unusually early age of twenty-four, he was appointed anatomical research fellow, prosector, at the Zoological Society in Regent's Park. Thus began a lifelong association with that body. This period was crowned by the publication of what many people would consider his most important scientific work, *The Social Life of Monkeys and Apes* (1932), a monograph whose appearance was followed by an invitation to work at a new ape research centre set up in Florida by Yale University. Eighteen months at Yale, interspersed with hectic and highly enjoyable interludes in the high bohemia of New York, were followed in 1934 by his appointment as demonstrator and lecturer in the anatomy department at Oxford. His particular interest was the study of hormones and reproductive rhythms; for this purpose he installed a team of apes in the grounds of the department.

On 30 October 1939 Zuckerman married Lady Joan Rufus Isaacs [*see below*], daughter of the second marquess of Reading. Lord Reading was not best pleased at the prospect of acquiring an unknown South African scientist as a son-in-law, but Zuckerman had charm and determination as well as being obviously destined to succeed. Opposition did not last long, and though Zuckerman was sometimes inconsiderate as a husband and detached as a parent, the marriage endured successfully until his death. There were two children: Paul Sebastian (*b.* 1945) and Stella Maria (*b.* 1947).

Towards the end of 1939 Zuckerman had been offered and had provisionally accepted the Sands Cox chair of anatomy at Birmingham University. The war put a temporary stop to any such move and instead he found himself researching the effects of blast on the human body. It was the start of an involvement with questions of defence and weaponry which was to occupy much of his next fifty years. So little was known about the subject that Zuckerman was soon the leading authority, and when the blitz

Solly Zuckerman, Baron Zuckerman (1904–1993), by Baron
Studios, 1962

began in the autumn of 1940 he and Professor (John) Desmond Bernal were perpetually on the move, assessing the
effects of bombs on buildings and the human beings
inside them. This experience inevitably led to Zuckerman
being enmeshed in the controversy over the proper use of
Bomber Command. On the one hand Air Chief Marshal Sir
Arthur Harris, backed by Winston Churchill's scientific
guru, Professor Frederick Alexander Lindemann, claimed
that saturation bombing of Germany's urban centres
would critically damage that country's industrial capacity
and destroy civilian morale. On the other, Air Chief Marshal Sir Arthur Tedder, backed by Patrick Blackett, Henry
Tizard, and most of the other scientists, maintained that
this strategy was expensive and wasteful, and that the
bombers would be far better employed attacking communications behind the enemy front line. Zuckerman was
emphatically in the second camp; he was right, and his
arguments were cogent and forcefully put, but his indifference to the sensibilities of others alienated some
potential allies and increased the obstinacy of his opponents.

Bernal had been recruited as scientific adviser to Lord
Louis Mountbatten's fledgeling combined operations
organization, and he introduced Zuckerman in his wake.
It proved an instant success. Mountbatten found in
Zuckerman an endless source of ideas and a dry realism
which curbed his own more extravagant flights of impetuosity. One of Zuckerman's first tasks was to establish on
how many nights a month tides, winds, and darkness

would favour landings on the French coast. He devoted
several weeks to this study and then reported proudly:
'Well, it turns out that there will never be a night suitable
for a landing' (Ziegler, 188). In time this relationship with
Mountbatten was to become highly important in
Zuckerman's career. For the rest of the war, however, it
was Tedder who made the greatest use of his skills. As
commander-in-chief, Mediterranean air command, and
deputy supreme commander under General Eisenhower,
he relied on Zuckerman's advice on a multitude of issues,
great and trivial. Perhaps the most significant related to
the attack on Pantelleria. This rugged volcanic island
between Tunisia and Sicily was heavily defended and
was deemed impregnable by its Italian occupants.
Zuckerman's task was to gauge the level of bombardment
necessary to reduce the defences to impotence. His calculations were amply corroborated; the garrison surrendered just as the assault troops were about to land. The lessons learned in this operation were applied in the invasion of Sicily and, eventually, at D-day.

When the war ended Zuckerman took up his long
deferred appointment as professor of anatomy at Birmingham. Though the buildings were magnificent, equipment was woefully deficient and the department existed
only in embryo. With characteristic ebullience, and sublime indifference to the demands of other sectors of the
medical faculty, Zuckerman built up an élite and highly
successful student body. Charles Oxnard, later professor
of anatomy at the University of Western Australia, wrote
that the department 'produced an exodus that has taken
individuals to every continent, filled many Chairs in Britain and around the world and formed a Zuckerman mafia
that has had an incredible influence in each of his areas of
biological research' (private information). Zuckerman
could sometimes be ungenerous in the credit he gave to
his collaborators and he made ferocious demands on their
time and energies, but nobody could deny that he was an
inspiring teacher and endlessly stimulating to work with.

For some years Zuckerman's energies were mainly concentrated on Birmingham, but he continued to cherish
his contacts with Whitehall. At the end of 1945 he was
invited to join Sir Alan Barlow's committee considering
how best to develop the country's scientific resources over
the next decade. One recommendation was that an advisory committee on scientific policy should be established.
The recommendation was accepted. The new council was
appointed in January 1947, and Zuckerman, according to
his autobiography, was taken aback to be asked to join it.
He would have been still more taken aback, outraged
indeed, if he had not been. Over the next thirty years he
was to serve, often as chairman, on every Whitehall committee in which issues of scientific importance were discussed: the agricultural resources council, the fuel and
power scientific advisory committee, the natural
resources (technical) committee, the committee on scientific manpower, the committee on control of research and
development—the list could be almost interminable.

In 1960 Zuckerman's career took a decisive turn when
he became chief scientific adviser to the Ministry of

Defence. He retained his chair at Birmingham but on an absentee basis, drawing no salary. His first task in Whitehall was to help implement the Zuckerman procedures, the rules (for whose drafting he himself had been largely responsible) for the control of defence projects and the strengthening of the role of the defence research policy committee. During his four years at the Ministry of Defence his influence was at its greatest. He renewed his close relationship with Mountbatten, who was now chief of defence staff, and the 'Zuk-Batten Axis', as it was nicknamed, became one of the dominant forces in Whitehall. In 1964 the incoming prime minister, Harold Wilson, urged Zuckerman to become minister of state dealing with disarmament negotiations. Zuckerman had no wish to become a politician and refused, Whereupon Wilson replied that, in that case, he must serve as chief scientific adviser to the government as a whole, not just to the Ministry of Defence. Though clearly a promotion, this meant that his influence was spread more thinly and the power that he had exercised was substantially reduced.

Zuckerman retired as chief scientific adviser in 1971, at which point he was created a life peer. He did not lose his interest in public life or defence issues, however. He was particularly active on nuclear matters. He believed that the so-called independent deterrent was neither independent nor likely to deter, and that the limited use of tactical nuclear weapons to combat Russian numerical superiority would inevitably lead to catastrophic escalation. What the West needed, he believed, was not ever larger nuclear stockpiles but more mobile, well-equipped, conventional forces capable of dealing with enemy incursions. As chief scientific adviser he had been closely involved in negotiations for a partial test ban, and he continued to urge a complete cessation of testing until his death. He was an active member of the Pugwash group.

Zuckerman had renewed his connection with the London Zoo in 1955 when he became a member of the council of the Zoological Society of London, and two years later became secretary. He claimed to have supposed that this title was largely honorific, but passivity did not come easily to him and he became in effect chief executive officer. His most controversial reform was to open the zoo to the public on Sunday mornings—thereby abolishing the privileged entry reserved for fellows. This greatly boosted the zoo's revenues but infuriated many of the fellows. It was the first of many campaigns to modernize the zoo and put it on a sound financial basis. In 1960 he installed Prince Philip as president, and in 1977 retired as secretary and took on the presidency himself. There he remained until 1984. His contribution was immense; it must also be admitted that his increasingly autocratic attitude and intolerance of those with slower minds or bureaucratic dispositions caused much discontent.

From time to time it was rumoured that Zuckerman was to become head of some Oxbridge college. He would undoubtedly have been effective, both as administrator and fund-raiser, but he might well have caused considerable disruption in the senior common room. Instead he became a founding force in the new University of East Anglia—a part of England dear to him since he had settled at the Shooting Box in Burnham Thorpe, Norfolk, in 1956. His particular responsibility was the school of biological sciences, the first at any British university, but he intervened vigorously in many other fields, invariably assertive, pugnacious, convinced that he was right, and usually justified in that conviction. He left his extensive archives to the university at his death.

Zuckerman wrote three volumes of autobiography: *From Apes to Warlords* (1978), *Monkeys, Men and Missiles* (1988), and *Six Men out of the Ordinary* (1992). He was prone to drop names and overstate his own achievements, but he had plenty of names to drop, his achievements were genuinely impressive, and his writing was always lively. The book to which he attached most importance was *Nuclear Illusion and Reality* (1982), a passionate plea for reason and restraint in a world where a single mistake could spell the end of civilization.

Zuckerman was short and stocky, with a prominent nose and rugged features; he was not conventionally good looking, but his energy, vivacity, and directness made him attractive to many women. He received numerous honorary degrees and other honours, was made a CB in 1946, was knighted in 1956, became a KCB in 1964, and was appointed to the Order of Merit in 1968. He died of a thrombosis at his home in Burnham Thorpe on 1 April 1993; his ashes were interred in his garden. He was survived by his wife and son, his daughter having predeceased him.

Zuckerman's wife, **Joan Alice Violet Rufus Zuckerman** [*née* Lady Joan Alice Violet Rufus Isaacs], Lady Zuckerman (1918–2000), hostess and painter, was born on 19 July 1918 in Sussex, the elder daughter of Gerald Rufus Isaacs, second marquess of Reading (1889–1960), barrister and Conservative politician, and his wife, the Hon. Eva Violet, *née* Mond (1895–1973), eldest daughter of Alfred Moritz Mond, first Baron Melchett (1868–1930), industrialist and politician. Both parents came from wealthy and politicized families prominent in liberal Jewry, and her mother worked for women's emancipation and for poor children. Her great-uncle Sigismund Christian Herbert Goetze (1866–1939) was an artist and painted murals for the foreign office. She trained at St John's Wood Art School (1937–8). After marriage she supported her husband's career, entertaining politicians and royalty, but also did voluntary work with poor children, and produced pastel landscapes. She was a vice-president of the King's Lynn Arts Centre and for many years chairwoman of the Friends of the Sainsbury Centre for Visual Arts at the University of East Anglia. Proud of her Jewishness, she was devoted to 'her people'. She died on 25 March 2000 at Burnham Thorpe, Norfolk, and was survived by her son, Paul.

PHILIP ZIEGLER

Sources S. Zuckerman, *From apes to warlords* (1978) · S. Zuckerman, *Monkeys, men and missiles* (1988) · S. Zuckerman, *Six men out of the ordinary* (1992) · private information (2004) [John, Lord Peyton] · P. L. Krohn, *Memoirs FRS*, 41 (1995), 577–98 · P. Ziegler, *Mountbatten* (1985) · *The Times* (2 April 1993) · *The Independent* (2 April

1993) • *WWW*, 1991–5 • Burke, *Peerage* [Lady Zuckerman] • *The Independent* (31 March 2000) [Lady Zuckerman] • *Daily Telegraph* (17 April 2000) [Lady Zuckerman]

Archives University of East Anglia, Norwich, corresp. and papers • Zoological Society, London, papers | CAC Cam., corresp. with Sir Edward Bullard • CAC Cam., corresp. with Lord Gladwyn • CUL, corresp. with Sir Peter Markham Scott; corresp. with Sir Frank Young • Nuffield Oxf., corresp. with Lord Cherwell • PRO, registered files as chief scientific adviser to the Cabinet Office, CAB 168 • Rice University, Houston, Texas, Woodson Research Centre, corresp. with Sir Julian Huxley • RS, corresp. with Lord Blackett • U. Birm. L., corresp. with L. T. Hogben [copies] • U. Sussex, letters to J. G. Crowther • Wellcome L., corresp. with Sir Ernest Chain • Wellcome L., corresp. with Sir Peter Brian Medawar | SOUND BL NSA, current affairs recording • BL NSA, performance recording • BL NSA, recorded lectures

Likenesses Baron Studios, photograph, 1962, NPG [*see illus.*] • photograph, 1978, repro. in Krohn, *Memoirs FRS*, 576 • photograph, 1980, repro. in *The Independent* (2 April 1993) • E. Frink, bronze head, 1986, NPG • N. Sinclair, bromide print, 1991, NPG • R. Buhler, oils, Zoological Society, London • D. Hill, oils, priv. coll. • H. Mee, oils, Birmingham Medical School • photograph, repro. in *The Times*

Wealth at death £1,013,604: probate, 25 Aug 1993, CGPLA Eng. & Wales

Zukertort, John Hermann (1842–1888), chess player, was born on 7 September 1842, probably at Lublin in Russian Poland, the son of a converted Jew, who had been a protestant pastor of very humble means. In 1855 he entered the *Gymnasium* at Breslau in Silesia, and in 1861 he was transferred to the university, whence (he said later) he graduated after a full course in medicine in 1866, serving with the medical corps of the German army in the campaign of that year and in 1870–71. It seems generally agreed, however, that his account of this period was exaggerated and that his interest in chess prevented completion of his degree. He learned chess at Breslau in 1861, entering for a handicap tourney in that year, and losing every game that he played, although he received the odds of the queen. He now purchased Bilguer's *Handbook* and studied the game.

Before the close of 1862 Zukertort encountered Adolf Anderssen, receiving the odds of the knight, and won a number of games. Henceforth, as Anderssen's most talented pupil, he began to meet first-class players on equal terms. By 1867 he was known as one of the strongest players in north Germany, and assumed the editorship (at first in conjunction with Anderssen and afterwards alone) of the *Neue Berliner Schachzeitung*, which had been founded by Neumann and Suhle after the retirement of P. Hirschfeld from the editorship of the Leipzig *Schachzeitung*. In this he published a number of brilliant games and new variations of the openings, representing the strategic school of that period. During the previous two years he had joined Jean Dufresne in editing the invaluable *Grosses Schach-Handbuch* (see Van der Linde, *Geschichte und Litteratur des Schachspiels*, 1874, 2.23–4). In 1871 he defeated Anderssen in a set match, and at the close of the same year the *Neue Berliner Schachzeitung* collapsed.

Early in 1872 Zukertort arrived in Britain by invitation of the St George's chess club, and in the tourney of that year he won the third prize (Wilhelm Steinitz taking the first

and J. H. Blackburne, the second). It has been disputed whether he was naturalized, but he was thereafter regarded as an English representative in all contests abroad. The rapid strides that he made as an exponent of the game between 1872 and 1878 were attributed by him to the advantage derived from his 'assimilation of English characteristics', steadying his natural nervousness somewhat.

From 1873 to 1876 Zukertort contributed to the *Westminster Papers* (the official organ of the St George's club). In 1878 he won the first prize at the Paris Exhibition tournament, after a tie-match with Winawer. In September 1879, in conjunction with Leopold Hoffer, he founded and co-edited *Chess Monthly*, which continued for seventeen years to be the leading chess magazine. In March 1881 he captained the City of London club in its match with the rival St George's club, and later in the year was second to Blackburne in the Berlin tournament. He defeated Blackburne (1881) and the brilliant Paris master Rosenthal (1880) in two matches, annotating the games with an elaboration hitherto unknown in chess periodicals. In 1882 he shared the third position in the Vienna tournament.

In 1883 Zukertort achieved one of the great objects of his ambition by triumphing over Steinitz—possibly precipitating the latter's piqued emigration to the USA—and winning the first prize of £300 in the London international chess tournament, in which Steinitz came second and Blackburne third. This tournament, which was the first important gathering of the kind held in London since 1862, took place at the Victoria Hall in the Criterion between 26 April and 21 June 1883. During the first six weeks of the tournament Zukertort achieved a record in first-class chess by winning twenty-two games to one defeat, showing in the performance a combination of brilliance, energy, and accuracy unequalled by any great master hitherto. His games against Winawer (of Warsaw) and Rosenthal (of Paris) were of the very highest order, while that against Blackburne, played on 5 May, was, in Steinitz's opinion, 'one of the most brilliant games on record'. But the master's nervous energy had been maintained only by recourse to opiates, leading to a breakdown on 7 June. On that day he made an elementary blunder in his game with Mackenzie, and on the two following days he was successively defeated by the weakest players in the tournament, fortunately only after his position as winner of the first prize had been assured. He never fully recovered the extraordinary mental vigour that he had exhibited during the early part of the London tournament.

Contrary to medical advice, Zukertort persisted in accepting the challenge of Steinitz to an 'international match'—subsequently regarded as a world championship match to which Steinitz was provoked by his tournament defeat—the conditions of which (including the innovative use of time limits) were highly unfavourable to a man of his nervous temperament. He could not afford to lose the £400 staked. Twenty games were to be played, at New York, St Louis, and New Orleans. The British chess club entertained him in London in November 1885, before his departure. He won four out of the first five games, but was crushed by ten games to five (with five draws) before the match ended at New Orleans on 29 March 1886. 'He returned from the States a broken-down man. His nerves seemed overstrained, an impediment in his speech was noticeable, and he had not the energy to rouse himself from a kind of mental torpor' (*The Field*, 71 1888, 905).

Zukertort lost a short match with Blackburne (1887); more hopefully, in the summer handicap of the British chess club (1888) he headed the list, but on 19 June, while playing at Simpson's chess divan, he had a stroke. He was moved to Charing Cross Hospital and died there on 20 June 1888. He left two young daughters, who later returned to Germany. He was buried at Brompton cemetery on 26 June, when most of the prominent British chess players were represented at his graveside. From 1878 to 1883, said *The Times* justly, in an obituary notice, 'Dr. Zukertort was considered by many to have attained a degree of excellence in chess that has never been exceeded' (21 June 1888, 9).

Zukertort was a clever conversationalist and linguist (speaking English like a native), with a marvellous memory and a large store of general information (not always strictly accurate). His memory, it was said, failed him only when he had to answer a letter or keep an appointment; consequently he was known as 'the late Dr Zukertort'. At the chess-board it was impossible to gather from his countenance whether he was winning or losing, for he presented in either case the picture of abject misery, clutching his head in his hands. His gaunt, haggard, and 'corrugated' appearance was well conveyed by a pen-and-ink caricature which appeared in the *Westminster Papers* (1 June 1876). At New York in 1886 he was described as illustrating nerves, while Steinitz illustrated solidity.

As a blindfold player Zukertort was not surpassed even by Blackburne, and as an analyst he probably had no equal. His annotations upon the Morphy–Anderssen match in the pages of the *Chess Monthly* were a revelation, entirely superseding the previous analysis by Loewenthal. His knowledge of the openings was exhaustive, and his analyses of the Evans, Muzio, and Allgaier gambits completely altered long-established opinions as to their value. Very few British players equalled Zukertort in devotion and service to the game of which he was such a brilliant exponent.   THOMAS SECCOMBE, *rev.* JULIAN LOCK

Sources D. Hooper and K. Whyld, *The Oxford companion to chess*, 2nd edn (1992), 458–60 · H. E. Bird, *Chess history and reminiscences* (1893) · P. W. Sergeant, *A century of British chess* (1934) · *The Field* (23 June 1888), 905 · *British Chess Magazine*, 8 (1888), 313–16, 325–7, 338–40, 388–90 · *The Times* (21 June 1888), 9 · *ILN* (30 June 1888), 710 · J. Adams, *Johannes Zukertort: artist of the chessboard* (1989) · Boase, *Mod. Eng. biog.* · L. Hoffer, 'The chess masters of today', *Fortnightly Review*, 46 (1886), 753–65 · J. H. Blackburne, *Mr Blackburne's games at chess*, ed. P. A. Graham (1899); facs. edn with introduction by D. Hooper (1979) · R. N. Coles, *Battles-royal of the chessboard* (1948) · K. Matthews, *British chess* (1948) · www.chessarch.com/excavations/0003_tomasz/tomasz.shtml · www.chessmail.com/zukertort/life.html

Likenesses A. Rosenbaum, group portrait, oils, 1880 (*Chess Players*), NPG · caricature, repro. in *Westminster Papers*, 9 (1876), facing p. 25 · photograph, repro. in *ILN*, 73 (1878), 236 · photograph, repro. in *ILN*, 92 (1888), 708 · photograph, repro. in *Chess Monthly* (July 1888) · photograph, repro. in *British Chess Magazine*, 104 (1984), 305 · portrait, repro. in G. A. Macdonnell, *The knights and kings of chess* (1894) · wood-engraving (after photograph by A. E. Fradelle), NPG; repro. in *ILN* (7 Sept 1878)

Zulueta, Francis [*formerly* Francisco Maria José] **de** (1878–1958), jurist, was born on 12 September 1878 in the Spanish embassy in London. His father, Don Pedro Juan de Zulueta, was a member of the Spanish diplomatic service; his mother, Laura Mary, daughter of Sir Justin Sheil, at one time British minister in Persia. Although a Spaniard by birth, and a cousin of Cardinal Merry del Val, he was only one-quarter of Spanish blood: his father was on one side Scottish, descended in the female line from Brodie M'Ghie Willcox, one of the founders of the P. & O. Steam Navigation Company. The Zuluetas, a Basque family, settled in Cadiz in the eighteenth century, had left Spain on account of their liberal opinions and later established a business in London where for much of the nineteenth century they served as the agents of the Spanish government. Don Pedro felt himself so much at home that in order to remain permanently in London he resigned from the Spanish diplomatic service. His son regarded himself as British rather than Spanish.

Zulueta was educated at Beaumont College, Berkshire, and the Oratory School, Edgbaston, and went with an open scholarship to New College, Oxford, where he was placed in the first class in classical moderations (1899), *literae humaniores* (1901), and jurisprudence (1902). He was elected to a prize fellowship at Merton in 1902, won the Vinerian law scholarship in 1903, and was called to the bar by Lincoln's Inn in 1904. In 1907 he returned to New College as a tutorial fellow and from 1912 to 1917 was All Souls reader in Roman law.

On the outbreak of war in 1914 Zulueta felt himself so closely identified with Britain that he became naturalized, obtained a commission in the Worcestershire regiment, and served in France. On his return to Oxford in 1919 he was appointed to the regius chair of civil law at All Souls, which he held until 1948. In 1915 he married Marie Louise (*d.* 1970), daughter of Henry Alexander Lyne Stephens, of Grove House, Roehampton; they had one son, Sir Philip Francis de *Zulueta.

A first-rate classical scholar, Zulueta had also the good fortune to be one of the earliest members of the seminar of Paul Vinogradoff, the first to be established on continental lines in Oxford. He always admitted his deep indebtedness to Vinogradoff and the methods of research inculcated by him. The fruit of this work was an essay, contributed in 1909 to Vinogradoff's *Oxford Studies in Social and Legal History*, 'Patronage in the later empire'. Thereafter he published much less than his contemporaries desired and expected. He became in truth too learned to see opportunities for originality in a well-tilled field; and his scepticism in matters of legal scholarship not only led him to leave questions open which others might have answered, but to entertain a radical and very un-Catholic disbelief in natural law. He was out of tune with the dominant school of

Francis de Zulueta (1878–1958), by Lafayette, 1926

Romanistic research, then devoted to the search for interpolations in the corpus juris, which he regarded as piling hypothesis upon hypothesis and encouraging anyone who practised it not to admit the unsoundness of any theory he had once adopted. He is also reported to have said to a younger friend, 'Don't read, or you won't write'. It was characteristic that much of his most valuable work is to be found in his bibliographical contributions to the *Journal of Egyptian Archaeology*. One of his colleagues once likened him to a person with a big bunch of keys: he might not be able to tell you what you wanted to know but he would certainly be able to tell you where to find it. His relative unproductiveness was perhaps partly due to an unfortunate occasion, during his period of teaching at New College, when a number of undergraduates, finding their stock of combustible materials running out, burnt the papers he had prepared for a forthcoming book. This rankled, though in the end he came to think that the enforced rewriting had resulted in a much better book. However surprising it may have been to those who knew him later, he was at that time rather unpopular, being less able than subsequently to control a naturally quick temper.

In 1927 Zulueta edited for the Selden Society Vacarius's *Liber pauperum*. But he will be best-known to ordinary students by three most useful works: his little edition of the *Digest* titles on ownership and possession (1922) for use by BCL candidates, his *Roman Law of Sale* (1945), and his edition of the *Institutes of Gaius*, of which the text and translation appeared in 1946 and the commentary in 1953. In all these he displayed a conciseness of utterance which is often disconcerting, not only to the elementary student, but which on more diligent perusal discloses the products of his profound erudition.

In lecturing Zulueta believed in systematic exposition which did not perhaps show him at his best. Temperamentally he was better fitted to the more explosive method appropriate to informal instruction or to revision lectures in which he could assume a general knowledge of the subject and needed only to draw attention to interesting points which had probably been neglected.

A devout Roman Catholic, Zulueta actively supported the Oxford University Catholic Association and the local branch of the Society of St Vincent de Paul. His religious convictions made him effective in helping Polish refugees during the Second World War although they were not so exclusive as to preclude his doing just as much for Jewish and other refugees. They prompted his intervention in Malta's constitutional controversy in the 1930s and combined with his intense conservatism to make him an ardent supporter of General Franco in the Spanish Civil War.

As a young man Zulueta had taken a prominent part in sport. Those who knew him later remember his handsome face and figure, the natural courtesy of his manners, perfect in his relations with all sorts of people and especially with children, and his great usefulness, with a knowledge of many languages, in dealing with foreign scholars. He was a loyal colleague whose sound legal instinct was displayed not only in his own special field and whose shrewdness and sagacity in discussions of policy and of ways and means were highly prized by his colleagues on the board of the faculty. His helpfulness to scholars of all ages even extended to the humble but exacting tasks of the editor and translator. He received many honours, including fellowship of the British Academy, an honorary fellowship of Merton, an honorary doctorate of Paris and of Aberdeen, and fellowship of the Accademia dei Lincei. Zulueta died at his home, 85 Cadogan Gardens, London, on 16 January 1958. A list of his publications is prefixed to *Studies in the Roman Law of Sale* (1959), dedicated to his memory and edited by David Daube.

F. H. LAWSON, *rev.*

Sources *The Times* (18 Jan 1958) · private information (1971) · *CGPLA Eng. & Wales* (1958) · *WWW* · F. H. Lawson, *The Oxford law school, 1850–1965* (1968) · personal knowledge (1971)
Archives U. Aberdeen L., papers, catalogue of his library
Likenesses Lafayette, photograph, 1926, NPG [*see illus.*] · W. Stoneman, three photographs, 1927–45, NPG
Wealth at death £8588 11s. 8d.: probate, 23 April 1958, *CGPLA Eng. & Wales*

Zulueta, Sir Philip Francis de (1925–1989), civil servant and businessman, was born in Oxford on 2 January 1925, the only child of Francis (Francisco Maria José) de *Zulueta (1878–1958), regius professor of civil law and fellow of All

Souls College, Oxford, and his wife, Marie Louise (*d.* 1970), daughter of Henry Alexander Lyne Stephens. His childhood was spent in Oxford, where his parents had a house in Norham Road. His father was of distinguished Spanish descent and a cousin of Cardinal Merry de Val, secretary of state at the Vatican, but took British nationality in order to fight in the First World War. De Zulueta was educated at the Dragon School, Oxford, and at the Roman Catholic Beaumont College, from where he won a scholarship to New College, Oxford. After taking a wartime second class in modern history in 1943 he joined the Welsh Guards in the same year and served with the regiment in north-west Europe until 1947, participating in the liberation of Brussels with the guards armoured division; he attained the rank of captain. Thus did he gain early experience of two institutions to which he was to remain loyal throughout his life: the brigade of guards and the Roman Catholic church.

Having returned to New College in 1947 de Zulueta studied jurisprudence but found it hard to settle down to study after the war, and in 1948 he left with a third-class degree. After Oxford he read for the bar with the encouragement of his father, who was a strong influence on him. However, he decided not to proceed with his legal studies and joined the foreign service in 1949, serving in Moscow from 1950 to 1952 as private secretary to the ambassador, Sir David Kelly. On his return to London he became resident clerk at the Foreign Office; then in 1955 he began his long association with three prime ministers, when Sir Anthony Eden took him to 10 Downing Street as one of his two private secretaries for foreign affairs. Also in 1955 he married Marie-Louise, daughter of James Bryan George Hennessy, second Baron Windlesham (1903–1962); they had a daughter and a son.

De Zulueta soon showed great aptitude for this work for Eden, and after Harold Macmillan became prime minister in 1957 he was the only representative of the Foreign Office among the private secretaries. He stayed on with Sir Alec Douglas-Home from October 1963 to October 1964 but of all his masters it was Macmillan with whom he built up the greatest rapport, admiring his style of government, intellect, and wit and accompanying him often on foreign tours. Macmillan came to depend upon de Zulueta's loyalty, calm in a crisis, knowledge of the main foreign-policy issues of the time, and linguistic ability, and used him as an interpreter at several of his meetings with Charles de Gaulle. 'Philip knows my mind', he observed, and he remarked teasingly on de Zulueta's gravitas, determination, and strength of personality, for with the intelligence and fundamental kindness came a tendency to be impatient with the foolish or the slow. In Macmillan's resignation honours list of 1963 de Zulueta was given a knighthood.

In 1964, having always been interested in financial affairs and feeling that a diplomatic posting might be an anticlimax after his years in 10 Downing Street, de Zulueta left the Foreign Office for the City. There he spent a six-month training period before joining Philip Hill-Higginson Erlangers. He was a director of the newly merged Hill Samuel from 1965 to 1972. In 1973 he joined Antony Gibbs Holdings, serving as chief executive from 1973 to 1976 and as chairman from 1976 to 1981. He was made chairman of Tanks Consolidated Investments in 1983 and a director of the Belgian Société Générale when that company took over Tanks in 1982. In 1984 he became a director of Abbott Laboratories of Chicago. Among his outside interests were the Franco-British Council, the Institute of Directors, and the Trilateral Commission. Increasingly he suffered from serious heart trouble.

De Zulueta was extremely hard-working and energetic, deriving much self-confidence from an exceptionally happy family life. Tall, dark-haired, thickset, always immaculately dressed, quiet of voice, and often leaning forward slightly in a rather courtly way to catch every nuance of the conversation, he also had an urbane, formidable presence and high standards; the morality and certainty of his strong religious faith never left him. Beneath this exterior, however, lay humour and sympathy, qualities particularly evident at his homes in London and later at Eastergate House in Sussex, where he was a relaxed and generous host. In 1984 he became an officer of the Légion d'honneur.

De Zulueta died on 15 April 1989 on board a British Airways flight, when returning from a business trip to the United States; he had a fatal coronary thrombosis as the aeroplane was coming in to land at London. A thanksgiving mass was celebrated at the guards' chapel, Wellington barracks, London, on 22 May 1989.

MAX EGREMONT, *rev.*

Sources *The Times* (18 April 1989) · *The Times* (23 May 1989) · *The Independent* (18–19 April 1989) · personal knowledge (1996) · private information (1996) · *CGPLA Eng. & Wales* (1989)
Archives BLPES, corresp. with Lady Rhys Williams · Bodl. Oxf., corresp. with Lord Monckton · U. Birm. L., corresp. with Lord Avon
Likenesses photograph, repro. in *The Times* (18 April 1989) · photograph, repro. in *The Independent*
Wealth at death £1,748,004: probate, 31 July 1989, *CGPLA Eng. & Wales*

Zurbriggen, Mattias (1856–1917). *See under* FitzGerald, Edward Arthur (1871–1931).

Zuylestein, William Henry. *See* Nassau van Zuylestein, William Frederick van, first earl of Rochford (1649–1708).

Zuylestein, William Henry Nassau van. *See* Nassau van Zuylestein, William Henry van, fourth earl of Rochford (1717–1781).

PICTURE CREDITS

Wolseley, Frances Garnet, Viscountess Wolseley (1872–1936)—© National Portrait Gallery, London

Wolseley, Garnet Joseph, first Viscount Wolseley (1833–1913)—© National Portrait Gallery, London

Wolseley, William (c.1640–1697)—photograph by courtesy Sotheby's Picture Library, London

Wolsey, Thomas (1470/71–1530)—© National Portrait Gallery, London

Wombwell, George (1777–1850)—© National Portrait Gallery, London

Wood, Alexander (1726–1807)—reproduced with the kind permission of the Royal College of Surgeons of Edinburgh

Wood, Anthony (1632–1695)—© National Portrait Gallery, London

Wood, (John) Christopher [Kit] (1901–1930)—Kettle's Yard, University of Cambridge / Bridgeman Art Library

Wood, Edward Frederick Lindley, first earl of Halifax (1881–1959)—Estate of the Artist / private collection. Photograph: Photographic Survey, Courtauld Institute of Art, London

Wood, Ellen [Mrs Henry Wood] (1814–1887)—courtesy of Worcester City Council

Wood, Sir (Henry) Evelyn (1838–1919)—© National Portrait Gallery, London

Wood, Henry Harvey (1903–1977)—in the collection of the Royal Scottish Academy

Wood, Sir Henry Joseph (1869–1944)—reproduced by courtesy of the Savage Club, photograph © Gerald Place

Wood, John George (1827–1889)—© National Portrait Gallery, London

Wood, John Muir (1805–1892)—Scottish National Portrait Gallery

Wood, Sir (Howard) Kingsley (1881–1943)—© National Portrait Gallery, London

Wood, Matilda Charlotte (bap. 1831, d. 1915)—© National Portrait Gallery, London

Wood, Thomas (1661–1722)—© National Portrait Gallery, London

Woodall, John (1570–1643)—© National Portrait Gallery, London

Woodcock, George (1904–1979)—© National Portrait Gallery, London

Woodfall, William (bap. 1745, d. 1803)—© National Portrait Gallery, London

Woodford, James Russell (1820–1885)—© National Portrait Gallery, London

Woodforde, James (1740–1803)—unknown collection / Christie's; photograph National Portrait Gallery, London

Woodhouse, Barbara Kathleen Vera (1910–1988)—Getty Images - Hulton Archive

Woodhouse, Violet Kate Eglinton Gordon (1871–1948)—© National Portrait Gallery, London

Woodroffe, Sir John George (1865–1936)—© National Portrait Gallery, London

Woodruff, (John) Douglas (1897–1978)—© National Portrait Gallery, London

Woods, Samuel (1846–1915)—© National Portrait Gallery, London

Woods, Sir Wilfrid John Wentworth (1906–1975)—© National Portrait Gallery, London

Woodsworth, James Shaver (1874–1942)—National Archives of Canada / C-057365

Woodville, Anthony, second Earl Rivers (c.1440–1483)—His Grace the Archbishop of Canterbury / The Church Commissioners for England

Woodville, Richard Caton (1856–1927)—© National Portrait Gallery, London

Woodward, Sir Arthur Smith (1864–1944)—© National Portrait Gallery, London

Woodward, Benjamin (1816–1861)—© National Portrait Gallery, London

Woodward, Henry (1714–1777)—The Lord Egremont. Photograph: Photographic Survey, Courtauld Institute of Art, London

Woodward, John (1665/1668–1728)—Ashmolean Museum, Oxford

Wooldridge, Sidney William (1900–1963)—© Royal Society; photograph National Portrait Gallery, London

Woolf, Leonard Sidney (1880–1969)—© National Portrait Gallery, London

Woolf, (Adeline) Virginia (1882–1941)—© National Portrait Gallery, London

Woollcombe, Dame Jocelyn May (1898–1986)—© National Portrait Gallery, London

Wooler, Wilfred (1912–1997)—© Empics

Woollett, William (1735–1785)—© Tate, London, 2004

Woolley, Frank Edward (1887–1978)—© Popperfoto

Woolley, Sir (Charles) Leonard (1880–1960)—© Science & Society Picture Library; photograph National Portrait Gallery, London

Woolner, Thomas (1825–1892)—© National Portrait Gallery, London

Wootton, Barbara Frances, Baroness Wootton of Abinger (1897–1988)—© National Portrait Gallery, London

Wootton, John (1681/2–1764)—private collection. Photograph courtesy of the Holburne Museum of Art, Bath

Wordsworth, Charles (1806–1892)—© National Portrait Gallery, London

Wordsworth, Dorothy (1771–1855)—The Wordsworth Trust, Dove Cottage, Grasmere, UK

Wordsworth, Dame Elizabeth (1840–1932)—private collection

Wordsworth, William (1770–1850)—© National Portrait Gallery, London

Worlidge, Thomas (1700–1766)—© Copyright The British Museum

Worlock, Derek John Harford (1920–1996)—© Paul Woodward; collection National Portrait Gallery, London

Worms, Henry De, first Baron Pirbright (1840–1903)—© National Portrait Gallery, London

Worrell, Sir Frank Mortimer Maglinne (1924–1967)—Getty Images

Worsley, Charles (1622–1656)—© Manchester City Art Galleries

Wortley, Lady Emmeline Charlotte Elizabeth Stuart- (1806–1855)—© National Portrait Gallery, London

Wotton, Edward, first Baron Wotton (1548–1628)—private collection in England. Photograph: Photographic Survey, Courtauld Institute of Art, London

Wotton, Sir Henry (1568–1639)—by permission of the Provost and Fellows of Eton College. Photograph: Photographic Survey, Courtauld Institute of Art, London

Wotton, Nicholas (c.1497–1567)—The Dean and Chapter of Canterbury, photograph Mike Waterman

Wrangham, Francis (1769–1842)—© National Portrait Gallery, London

Wray, Sir Christopher (1522–1592)—© National Portrait Gallery, London

Wren, Sir Christopher (1632–1723)—Ashmolean Museum, Oxford

Wren, Matthew (1585–1667)—Pembroke College, Cambridge

Wrench, Sir (John) Evelyn Leslie (1882–1966)—© National Portrait Gallery, London

Wright, Sir Almroth Edward (1861–1947)—© reserved; collection Wright Fleming Institute of Microbiology, St Mary's Hospital, London; © reserved in the photograph

Wright, Christian Edington Guthrie (1844–1907)—Queen Margaret University College, Edinburgh; photograph © National Portrait Gallery, London

Wright, Helena Rosa (1887–1982)—private collection. Photograph courtesy of the Wellcome Library, London

Wright, Sir James, first baronet (1716–1785)—unknown collection; photograph Sotheby's Picture Library, London / National Portrait Gallery, London

Wright, Joseph, of Derby (1734–1797)—© National Portrait Gallery, London

Wright, Joseph (1855–1930)—© National Portrait Gallery, London

Wright, Peter (1603–1651)—© National Portrait Gallery, London

Wright, Peter Maurice (1916–1995)—© News International Newspapers Ltd

Wright, Sir Robert (c.1634–1689)—© National Portrait Gallery, London

Wright, Robert Alderson, Baron Wright (1869–1964)—Estate of the Artist; the Masters of the Bench of the Inner Temple. Photograph: Photographic Survey, Courtauld Institute of Art, London

Wright, Thomas (1789–1875)—© National Portrait Gallery, London

Wright, Thomas (1810–1877)—© National Portrait Gallery, London

Wright, Whitaker (1845–1904)—© National Portrait Gallery, London

Wright, William Aldis (1831–1914)—© National Portrait Gallery, London

Wright, William Ambrose [Billy] (1924–1994)—Getty Images - Hulton Archive

Wriothesley, Henry, third earl of Southampton (1573–1624)—in the collection of the Duke of Buccleuch and Queensberry KT; photograph National Portrait Gallery, London

Wriothesley, Thomas, first earl of Southampton (1505–1550)—© Photo RMN

Wriothesley, Thomas, fourth earl of Southampton (1608–1667)—Christie's Images Ltd. (2004)

Wyatt, James (1746–1813)—© National Portrait Gallery, London

Wyatt, Sir Matthew Digby (1820–1877)—private collection; photograph © National Portrait Gallery, London

Wyatt, Sir Thomas (c.1503–1542)—The Royal Collection © 2004 HM Queen Elizabeth II

Wyatt, Sir Thomas (b. in or before 1521, d. 1554)—© National Portrait Gallery, London

Wyatville [Wyatt], Sir Jeffry (1766–1840)—The Royal Collection © 2004 HM Queen Elizabeth II

Wycherley, William (bap. 1641, d. 1716)—© National Portrait Gallery, London

Wyck, Jan (c.1645–1700)—© National Portrait Gallery, London

Wykeham, William (c.1324–1404)—© Bodleian Library, University of Oxford

Wyld, James, the younger (1812–1887)—© National Portrait Gallery, London

Wylie, Sir Francis James (1865–1952)—© National Portrait Gallery, London

Wylie, Sir James, first baronet (1768–1854)—Royal College of Physicians of Edinburgh

Wyllie, Sir William (1802–1891)—© National Portrait Gallery, London

Wyndham, Charles, second earl of Egremont (1710–1763)—Petworth House, The Egremont Collection (The National Trust). Photograph: Photographic Survey, Courtauld Institute of Art, London

Wyndham, Sir Charles (1837–1919)—© National Portrait Gallery, London

Wyndham, George (1863–1913)—© National Portrait Gallery, London

Wyndham, George O'Brien, third earl of Egremont (1751–1837)—National Trust Photographic Library / A. C. Cooper

Wyndham, John Edward Reginald, first Baron Egremont and sixth Baron Leconfield (1920–1972)—© National Portrait Gallery, London

Wyndham, Thomas (d. 1554)—private collection. Photograph: Photographic Survey, Courtauld Institute of Art, London